Holy Bible
English Version for the Deaf

Holy Bible
English Version for the Deaf

Translated from the original languages.

BakerBooks
a division of Baker Publishing Group
Grand Rapids, Michigan

Published by Baker Book House Company
in cooperation with copyright holder

Also published under the title
Holy Bible: Easy-to-Read Version
Copyright © 1987, 1989, 1992
World Bible Translation Center, Inc.
P.O. Box 820648
Fort Worth, Texas 76182-0648

The New Testament: Easy-to-Read Version
© 1978, 1981, 1982, 1987, 1990
by World Bible Translation Center, Inc.

ISBN: 978-0-8010-6520-0

Portions of this Bible have been previously published under the following copyrights by World Bible Translation Center, Inc.: Genesis © 1983 and Jonah © 1986.

This copyrighted material may be quoted and/or reprinted for non-commercial purposes up to and inclusive of fifty (50) verses without written permission of World Bible Translation Center, Inc., providing the following credit line appears with the material being quoted:

Taken from the HOLY BIBLE: EASY-TO-READ VERSION
© 1987, 1989, 1992 by World Bible Translation Center, Inc.
and used by permission.

Quotations and/or reprints for commercial purposes or in excess of fifty (50) verses, or other permission requests, must be directed to and approved in writing by World Bible Translation Center, Inc.

Printed in the United States of America

Books of the Old Testament

Book	Abbreviation	Page	Book	Abbreviation	Page
Genesis	*Gen.*	1	Ecclesiastes	*Ecc.*	684
Exodus	*Ex.*	55	Song of Solomon	*S. of S.*	695
Leviticus	*Lev.*	104	Isaiah	*Isa.*	703
Numbers	*Num.*	140	Jeremiah	*Jer.*	774
Deuteronomy	*Deut.*	187	Lamentations	*Lam.*	855
Joshua	*Josh.*	227	Ezekiel	*Ezek.*	863
Judges	*Judges*	252	Daniel	*Dan.*	920
Ruth	*Ruth*	282	Hosea	*Hos.*	938
1 Samuel	*1 Sam.*	287	Joel	*Joel*	949
2 Samuel	*2 Sam.*	322	Amos	*Amos*	954
1 Kings	*1 Kings*	352	Obadiah	*Obad.*	964
2 Kings	*2 Kings*	386	Jonah	*Jonah*	966
1 Chronicles	*1 Chron.*	422	Micah	*Micah*	969
2 Chronicles	*2 Chron.*	456	Nahum	*Nahum*	977
Ezra	*Ezra*	498	Habakkuk	*Hab.*	980
Nehemiah	*Neh.*	510	Zephaniah	*Zeph.*	984
Esther	*Esther*	527	Haggai	*Hag.*	987
Job	*Job*	536	Zechariah	*Zech.*	989
Psalms	*Ps.*	572	Malachi	*Mal.*	998
Proverbs	*Prov.*	660			

Books of the New Testament

Book	Abbreviation	Page	Book	Abbreviation	Page
Matthew	*Mt.*	1003	1 Timothy	*1 Tim.*	1251
Mark	*Mk.*	1045	2 Timothy	*2 Tim.*	1256
Luke	*Lk.*	1070	Titus	*Titus*	1260
John	*Jn.*	1112	Philemon	*Phm.*	1263
Acts	*Acts*	1142	Hebrews	*Heb.*	1264
Romans	*Rom.*	1183	James	*Jas.*	1279
1 Corinthians	*1 Cor.*	1201	1 Peter	*1 Pet.*	1284
2 Corinthians	*2 Cor.*	1217	2 Peter	*2 Pet.*	1289
Galatians	*Gal.*	1226	1 John	*1 Jn.*	1292
Ephesians	*Eph.*	1232	2 John	*2 Jn.*	1297
Philippians	*Phil.*	1238	3 John	*3 Jn.*	1298
Colossians	*Col.*	1242	Jude	*Jude*	1299
1 Thessalonians	*1 Th.*	1246	Revelation	*Rev.*	1301
2 Thessalonians	*2 Th.*	1249			

Preface

This version of the Bible has been prepared to meet the special needs of the deaf. Whether it is published as the English Version for the Deaf or the Easy-to-Read Version, the text is the same. People who can hear are not usually aware of the particular problems that the deaf face in reading standard English. Hearing persons learn English largely through oral conversation. The deaf do not have this advantage, so their experience with the language is severely limited. It is this limited experience with the spoken language that causes most of the problems the deaf face in learning to read. But the deaf are not the only ones with limited language experience. Children, people who learn English as a foreign language, and many others face similar difficulties in reading. This specialized English version is designed to help such people overcome or avoid the most common obstacles to reading with understanding.

One of the basic ideas that guided the work on this version of the Scriptures was that good translation is good communication. The main concern of the translators was always to communicate to the reader the message of the Biblical writers as effectively and as naturally as the original writings did to people in that time. Faithful translation is not just matching words in a dictionary. It is a process of expressing the original message in a form that will not only have the same meaning, but will sound as relevant, attract the same interest, and have the same impact today as it did thousands of years ago.

Effective communication, then, was very important to the translators of this text. This desire to communicate did not make accuracy any less important, but "accuracy" was understood to be the faithful representation of ideas, not the exact correspondence of formal linguistic features.

The writers of Scripture, especially those who produced the New Testament writings, showed by the language style they used that they were interested in good communication. The translators of this English version considered this an important example to follow. So they worked to convey to their special audience the meaning of the Biblical text in a form that would be simple and natural. They used language that, instead of working as a barrier to understanding, would provide a key to unlock the truths of the Scriptures to a large segment of the English-speaking world.

Several special features are used in this translation to aid understanding. Brief explanations or synonyms sometimes follow difficult or ambiguous words in the text. These explanatory words are italicized within parentheses. Words or phrases that need fuller explanation are followed by an asterisk (*) and explained in footnotes at the bottom of the page. In addition, Scripture quotations are identified and variant readings are frequently given in the footnotes. Occasionally, words or statements that are implied by the context are supplied in the text to make the meaning clear. Such explanatory words or phrases are marked by half-brackets ⌐ ¬.

Introduction

The word *Bible* comes from a Greek word meaning "books." The Bible is actually two collections of books, often referred to as the "Old Testament" and the "New Testament." The word translated "testament" was used to mean a "covenant" or "agreement." It refers to God's promise to bless his people. The Old Testament is the collection of writings that relate to the agreement God made with the Jewish people (Israel) in the time of Moses. The New Testament is the collection of writings that relate to the agreement God made with all people who believe in Jesus Christ.

The Old Testament writings give an account of God's great acts in dealing with the Jewish people and reveal God's plan for using those people to bring his blessings to the whole world. Those writings look forward to the coming of a Savior (or "Messiah") that God would send to accomplish his plan. The New Testament writings are a sequel to the Old Testament story. They describe the coming of that Savior (Jesus Christ) and the meaning of his coming for all mankind. The Old Testament is important for understanding the New Testament, since it provides the necessary background. And the New Testament completes the story of salvation that began in the Old Testament.

THE OLD TESTAMENT

The Old Testament writings are a collection of thirty-nine different books produced by many different authors. They were written mainly in Hebrew, the language of ancient Israel. There are a few sections in Aramaic, the official language of the Babylonian empire. Portions of the Old Testament were written over 3,500 years ago, and more than 1,000 years passed between the writing of the first book and the last. In this collection there are books of law, history, prose, songs, poetry, and teachings from wise men.

The Old Testament is often divided into three main sections: the Law, the Prophets, and the Holy Writings. The Law contains five books called "The Five Books of Moses." The first book is Genesis. It tells about the beginning of the world as we know it, the first man and woman, and their first sin against God. It tells about the Great Flood and the family God saved through that flood, and it tells about the beginnings of the nation of Israel, the people God chose to use for a special purpose.

THE STORY OF ABRAHAM

God made an agreement with Abraham, a great man of faith. In that agreement God promised to make Abraham the father of a great nation and to give him and his descendants the land of Canaan. Abraham was circumcised to show that he accepted the agreement, and circumcision became the proof of the agreement between God and his people. Abraham did not know how God would do the things he had promised, but Abraham trusted God. This pleased God very much.

God told Abraham to leave his home among the Hebrews of Mesopotamia and led him to the promised land, Canaan (also called Palestine). In his old age Abraham had a son named Isaac. Isaac had a son named Jacob. Jacob (also called Israel) had twelve sons and a daughter. This family became the nation of Israel, but it never forgot its tribal origin. It continued to refer to itself as the twelve tribes (or "family groups") of Israel—descendants of the twelve sons of Jacob: Reuben, Simeon, Levi, Judah, Dan, Naphtali, Gad, Asher, Issachar, Zebulun, Joseph, and Benjamin. The three main ancestors—Abraham, Isaac, and Jacob (Israel)—are known as the "fathers" or "patriarchs" of Israel.

Abraham was also a "father" of another kind. Many times in ancient Israel, God called certain people to be his spokesmen. These spokesmen, or prophets, were God's representatives to the people. Through the prophets God gave the people of Israel promises, warnings, laws, teachings, lessons drawn from past experiences, and lessons based on future events. Abraham "the Hebrew" is the first prophet mentioned in the Scriptures.

ISRAEL FREED FROM SLAVERY

The family of Jacob (Israel) grew to include about 70 of his direct descendants. One of his sons, Joseph, became a high official in Egypt. Times were hard, so Jacob and his family moved to Egypt, where food was plentiful and life was easier. This tribe of Hebrews grew to a small nation, and the Pharaoh (the king of Egypt) made slaves of these people. The book of Exodus tells about how finally, after 400 years, God used the prophet Moses to free the people of Israel from slavery in Egypt and take them back to Palestine. The price for freedom was high; but it was the Egyptians who had to pay. The Pharaoh and all the families of Egypt lost their firstborn sons before the Pharaoh finally agreed to let the people go free. The firstborn had to die so that the people could be freed—and the people of Israel later remembered this in many ways in their worship and sacrifices.

The people of Israel were ready for their trip to freedom. They had dressed for the escape from Egypt. Each family killed and roasted a lamb. They put the blood from the lamb on their doorposts as a special sign to God. They hurriedly baked bread without yeast and ate their meal. That night the Angel of the Lord went through the land. If the blood of the lamb was not on the doorposts, the firstborn of that family died. The people of Israel were freed. But as the slaves were about to leave Egypt, the Pharaoh changed his mind. He sent his army to catch the Israelite slaves and bring them back, but God saved his people. God split the Red Sea, led his people through to freedom on the other side, and destroyed the pursuing army of Egypt.

Then, somewhere on the Arabian peninsula, at a mountain in the Sinai desert, God made a special agreement with those people.

THE LAW OF MOSES

God's rescue of the people of Israel and his agreement with them at Sinai set this nation apart from all others. This agreement contained promises and laws for the people of Israel. A part of this agreement, known as the Ten Commandments, was written by God on two stone tablets and given to the people. These commands contain the basic principles for the kind of life God expected the people of Israel to live. They cover an Israelite's duty to his God, his family, and his fellow-man.

The Ten Commandments and the rest of the rules and teachings given at Mount Sinai became known as "the Law of Moses" or simply "the Law." Many times these terms are used to refer to the first five books of the Scriptures and often to the entire Old Testament.

Besides the Ten Commandments and other rules of conduct, the Law of Moses contains rules about priests, sacrifices, worship, and holy days. These rules are found in the book of Leviticus. According to the Law of Moses, all priests and their helpers came from the tribe of Levi. These helpers were called "Levites." The most important priest was called the High Priest.

The Law includes instructions for building the Holy Tent ("tabernacle"), or Meeting Tent, the place the people of Israel went to worship God. It also has instructions for making all the things to be used in their worship. This prepared the Israelites for the building of the temple, the holy building in Jerusalem on Mount Zion, where the people would later go to worship God. The rules about sacrifices and worship forced the people to see that they sinned against each other and against God. But they also gave the people a way to be forgiven and re-united with one another and with God. These sacrifices prepared the way for a better understanding of the sacrifice God was preparing to give for all mankind.

The Law contained instructions for celebrating a number of holy days or festivals. Each festival had its own special meaning. Some festivals were happy occasions to celebrate special times of the year, such as the harvest festivals of First Fruits, Shabuoth (Pentecost or the Festival of Weeks), and Succoth (the Festival of Shelters).

Some festivals were for remembering the wonderful things God had done for his people. Passover was such a festival. Each family relived the escape from Egypt. The people sang songs of praise to God. A lamb was slaughtered and the meal prepared. Each cup of wine and morsel of food reminded the people of the things God had done to save them from a life of pain and sadness.

Other festivals were very serious. Every year, on the Day of Atonement, the people had to remember the many bad things they had done to others and to God. This was a day of sadness, and the people did not eat. But on that day the High Priest offered special sacrifices to cover over, or atone for, their sins.

The agreement between God and Israel was very important to the writers of the Old Testament. Almost all of the books of the Prophets and Holy Writings are based on the fact that the nation of Israel, and every citizen of Israel, had made a very special agreement with their God. They called it the "Agreement of the Lord" or simply "the Agreement." Their books of history interpret events in light of the Agreement: If the individual or nation was faithful to God and the Agreement, then God rewarded them. If the people abandoned the Agreement, then God punished them. God sent his prophets to remind the people of their agreement with God. The poets of Israel sang of the wonderful things God did for his obedient people, and they mourned over the pain and punishments that came to those who disobeyed God. These writers based their concepts of right and wrong on the teaching of the Agreement. And when innocent people suffered, the poets struggled to understand why.

THE KINGDOM OF ISRAEL

The story of ancient Israel is the story of the people abandoning God, God rescuing the people, the people turning back to God and eventually abandoning God again. This cycle began immediately after the people accepted God's Agreement, and it was repeated again and again. At Mount Sinai the people of Israel agreed to follow God, and then they rebelled and were forced to wander 40 years in the desert. Finally, Moses' helper, Joshua, led the people into the promised land. There was an initial conquest and a partial settling of the land of Israel. For the first few centuries after this settlement, the people were governed by local leaders called judges.

Eventually, the people wanted a king. The first king was Saul. Saul did not obey God, so God chose a shepherd boy named David to be the new king. The prophet Samuel came and poured oil on his head, anointing him king of Israel. God promised David that the future kings of Israel would be his descendants from the tribe of Judah. David conquered the city of Jerusalem and made it his capital and the future site of the temple. He organized the priests, prophets, song writers, musicians, and singers for the temple worship. David even wrote many of the songs (or psalms) himself, but God did not let him build the temple.

When David was old and about to die, he made his son Solomon king of Israel. David warned his son to always follow God and obey the Agreement. As king, Solomon built the temple and expanded Israel's borders. At this time Israel was at the height of its glory. Solomon became famous. Israel became strong.

JUDAH AND ISRAEL–THE DIVIDED KINGDOM

At Solomon's death there was civil strife, and the nation was divided. The northern ten tribes called themselves Israel. The southern tribes called themselves Judah. (The modern term "Jew" comes from this name.) Judah remained loyal to the Agreement, and David's dynasty (family of kings) continued ruling in Jerusalem until Judah was finally conquered and its people led away into exile by the Babylonians.

In the northern kingdom (Israel) several dynasties came and went, because the people did not follow the Agreement. The kings of Israel had several capital cities at various times, the last of which was Samaria. In order to strengthen their hold on the people, the kings of Israel changed the way to worship God. They chose new priests and they built two new temples: one at Dan (on the northern border of Israel) and the other at Bethel (along Israel's border with Judah). There were many wars between Israel and Judah.

During this time of civil war and troubles, God sent many prophets to Judah and Israel. Some of the prophets were priests; others were farmers. Some were advisors to kings; others lived a much simpler life. Some of the prophets wrote their teachings or prophecies; many others did not. But all the prophets came preaching of justice, fairness, and the need to depend on God for help.

Many prophets warned that the people would be defeated and scattered if they did not turn back to God. Some of these prophets saw visions of future glories as well as future punishments. Many of them looked forward to the time when a new king would come to rule the kingdom. Some saw this king as a descendant of David who would lead the people of God into a new Golden Age. Some spoke of this king as ruling forever over an eternal kingdom. Others saw him as a servant who would suffer many things in order to bring his people back to God. But all of them saw him as the Messiah, the one anointed (chosen) by God to bring in the new age.

THE DESTRUCTION OF ISRAEL AND JUDAH

The people of Israel did not listen to God's warnings, so in 722/721 B.C. Samaria fell to the invading Assyrians. The people of Israel were taken from their homes and scattered throughout the Assyrian empire, lost forever to their brothers and sisters in Judah. The Assyrians then brought in foreigners to re-settle the land of Israel. These people were taught about the religion of Judah and Israel, and many of them tried to follow the Agreement. These people came to be known as the Samaritans. The Assyrians tried to invade Judah. Many cities fell to the invaders, but God saved Jerusalem. The defeated king of Assyria returned to his homeland, and there he was assassinated by two of his sons. So Judah was saved.

For a short time the people of Judah changed. They began to obey God for a short time, but they too were finally defeated and scattered. The nation of Babylon rose to power and invaded Judah. At first they took only a few important people away as captives. But a few years later, in 587/586 B.C., they returned to destroy Jerusalem and the temple. Some of the people escaped to Egypt, but most of them were taken as slaves to Babylon. Again God sent prophets to the people, and they began to listen. It seems that the destruction of the temple and Jerusalem and the exile in Babylon brought about a real change in the people. The prophets spoke more and more about the new king and his kingdom. One of the prophets, Jeremiah, even spoke of a New Agreement. This New Agreement would not be written on tablets of stone, but would be in the hearts of God's people.

THE JEWS RETURN TO PALESTINE

Meanwhile, Cyrus came to power over the Medo-Persian empire and conquered Babylon. Cyrus allowed people to return to their homelands. So after 70 years of exile, many of the people of Judah went back home. The people tried to rebuild their nation, but Judah remained small and weak. The people built the temple again, although it was not as beautiful as the one Solomon had built. Many of the people truly turned to God and began studying the Law, the writings of the prophets, and the other holy writings. Many men became scribes (special scholars), who made copies of the Scriptures. Eventually, these men organized schools for studying the Scriptures. The people began meeting together on the Sabbath (Saturday) to study, pray, and worship God together. In their synagogues (meetings) they studied the Scriptures, and many people began looking for the Messiah to come.

In the West, Alexander the Great gained control of Greece and soon conquered the world. He spread the Greek language and the customs and culture of Greece to many parts of the world. When he died, his kingdom was divided, and soon another empire grew and gained control of a large part of the known world, including Palestine, where the people of Judah lived.

The new rulers, the Romans, were often cruel and harsh, and the Jews were proud and defiant. In these troubled times there were many Jews who were looking for the Messiah to come in their own lifetime. The Jews wanted to be ruled only by God and the Messiah that God promised to send them. They did not understand that God planned to save the world through the Messiah. They thought that God's plan was to save the Jews from the world! Some Jews were content to wait for God to send his Messiah. But others decided to "help" God establish his new kingdom. These Jews were called "Zealots." The Zealots tried to fight against the Romans and often killed other Jews that cooperated with the Romans.

THE JEWISH RELIGIOUS GROUPS

By the first century B.C., the Law of Moses had become extremely important to the Jews. The people had studied and argued over the Law. The people understood the Law in different ways, but many Jews were ready to die for that Law. There were three major religious groups among the Jews, and there were scribes (lawyers or scholars) in each group.

The Sadducees

One of the groups was called the Sadducees. This name probably comes from the name Zadok, the High Priest in King David's time. Many of the priests and the people in authority were Sadducees. These men accepted only the Law (the five books of Moses) as their authority in religious matters. The Law taught many things about the priests and sacrifices, but it did not teach about life after death. So the Sadducees did not believe in people being raised from death.

The Pharisees

Another group was called the Pharisees. This name comes from a Hebrew word meaning "to interpret (explain)" or "to separate." These men tried to teach or interpret the Law of Moses to the common people. The Pharisees believed that there was an oral tradition going back to Moses' time. They believed that men of each generation could interpret the Law in a way that would allow it to meet the needs of that generation. This meant that the Pharisees could accept not only the Law of Moses as their authority, but also the Prophets, the Holy Writings, and even their own traditions. These men tried very hard to follow the Law and their traditions. So they were very careful about what they ate and what they touched. They were careful about washing their hands and bathing. They also believed that people would be raised from death, because they understood many of the prophets to say that would happen.

The Essenes

The third major group was the Essenes. Many of the priests in Jerusalem did not live the way God wanted them to. Also, the Romans had appointed many of the High Priests, and some of these men were not qualified according to the Law of Moses. Because of this, the Essenes did not think the worship and sacrifices were being done properly in Jerusalem. So the Essenes moved out into the Judean desert to live. They formed their own community, where only other Essenes could come and live. The Essenes fasted and prayed and waited for God to send the Messiah and purify the temple and the priesthood. Many scholars believe that the Essenes were connected in some way with the Qumran Community and the many ancient writings found at Qumran and other places in that area of the Judaean desert.

THE NEW TESTAMENT

God had begun his plan. He had chosen a special nation. He had made an Agreement with those people that would prepare them to understand his justice and his goodness. Through prophets and poets he had revealed his plan to bless the world by establishing a perfect spiritual "kingdom" based on a new and better Agreement. This plan would begin with the coming of the promised Messiah. The prophets had spoken of his coming in great detail. They had told where the Messiah would be born, the type of person he would be, and the work he would have to do. It was now time for the Messiah to come and begin the New Agreement.

The writings of the New Testament describe how God's New Agreement was revealed and put into effect by Jesus, who was the Christ (meaning "the Anointed One," the Messiah). They teach that this New Agreement was to be for all people. And they tell how people in the first century responded to God's gracious offer of love and became a part of the New Agreement. These writings give instructions to God's people about how to live in this world. They also describe the blessings that God promises his people for a full and meaningful life here and for life with him after death.

The New Testament writings include twenty-seven different "books" by at least eight different writers. All of them wrote in Greek, which was widely spoken in the first-century world. More than half of the total writing was done by four "apostles," men chosen by Jesus to be his special representatives or helpers. Three of these, Matthew, John, and Peter, were among the twelve closest followers of Jesus during his life on earth. The other writer, Paul, was chosen as an apostle later by Jesus through a miraculous appearance.

The first four books, called "Gospels," are separate accounts of the life and death of Jesus Christ. Generally, these books emphasize Jesus' teaching, the purpose of his appearance on earth, and the crucial significance of his death, rather than just the historical facts of his life. This is especially true of the fourth book, the Gospel of John. The first three Gospels are very similar in content. In fact, much of the material in one is found in one or both of the others. Each writer, however, is writing to a different audience and seems to have a slightly different goal in view.

The four Gospels are followed by Acts, a history of the events following the death of Jesus. It describes how God's offer of love to all people was announced throughout the world by Jesus' followers. It tells how the proclaiming of this "gospel" or "Good News" resulted in the widespread acceptance of Christian faith throughout Palestine and the Roman world. The book of Acts was written by Luke, an eyewitness of much that he recorded. Luke was also the author of the third Gospel. His two books make a logical unit, Acts being the natural sequel to his account of the life of Jesus.

Following Acts, there is a collection of letters written to individuals or groups of Christians. These letters were sent from Christian leaders such as Paul and Peter, two of Jesus' apostles. These letters were written to help the people of that time deal with problems they were facing. They serve to inform, correct, teach, and encourage not only those people but all Christians in regard to their faith, their life together, and their life in the world.

The final book of the New Testament, Revelation, is different from all the other books. It uses highly figurative language and tells of visions seen by the author, the apostle John. Many of the figures and images are from the Old Testament and can best be understood by comparing them to the Old Testament writings. This last book assures Christians of ultimate victory over the forces of evil through the power of God and Jesus Christ, their leader and helper.

THE BIBLE AND THE MODERN READER

Today's reader of the Bible should keep in mind that these books were written thousands of years ago for people who lived in a culture very different from our own. Generally, the writings focus on principles that are universally true, though many of the historical accounts, illustrations they use and references they make can only be understood with some knowledge of the time and culture in which they lived. For example, Jesus told a story about a man sowing grain in a field that had different types of soil conditions. Those exact conditions may be unfamiliar to a person today, but the lesson Jesus draws from the example fits people in any time or place.

The modern reader may find the world of the Bible somewhat strange. The customs, the attitudes, the way people talk may be quite unfamiliar. It is only reasonable to evaluate these things by the standards of that time and place, not by modern standards. It is also important to note that the Bible was not written as a book of science. It was written mainly to describe historical events and present the significance of those events for mankind. It's teachings involve universal truths that are beyond the realm of science. It remains relevant even in this modern age, because it deals with people's basic spiritual needs, which never change.

Any person who reads the Bible objectively can expect to gain many benefits. He will acquire knowledge about the history and culture of the ancient world. He will learn about the life and teachings of Jesus Christ and what it means to be his follower. He will gain basic spiritual insights and learn practical lessons for living a dynamic and joy-filled life. He will find answers to life's most difficult questions. There are, therefore, many good reasons for reading this book, and the person who reads it with an open and inquisitive mind will likely discover God's purpose for his life.

The Old Testament

Genesis

THE BEGINNING OF THE WORLD

The First Day—Light

1 God made the sky and earth. At first, ²the earth was completely empty; nothing was on the earth. Darkness covered the ocean, and God's Spirit moved over* the water. ³Then God said, "Let there be light!"* And light began to shine. ⁴God saw the light, and he knew it was good. Then God separated the light from the darkness. ⁵God named the light "day," and he named the darkness "night."

There was evening, and then there was morning. This was the first day.

The Second Day—Sky

⁶Then God said, "Let there be air* to separate the water into two parts!" ⁷So God made the air and separated the water. Some of the water was above the air, and some of the water was below the air. ⁸God named the air "sky."

There was evening, and then there was morning. This was the second day.

The Third Day—Dry Land and Plants

⁹Then God said, "Let the water under the sky be gathered together so the dry land will appear." And it happened. ¹⁰God named the dry land "earth." And God named the water that was gathered together "seas." God saw this was good.

¹¹Then God said, "Let the earth grow grass, plants that make grain, and fruit trees. The fruit trees will make fruit with seeds in it. And each plant will make its own kind of seed. Let these plants grow on the earth." And it happened. ¹²The earth grew grass and plants that made grain. And it grew trees that made fruit with seeds in it. Every plant made its own kind of seeds. And God saw this was good.

¹³There was evening, and then there was morning. This was the third day.

The Fourth Day—Sun, Moon, and Stars

¹⁴Then God said, "Let there be lights in the sky. These lights will separate the days from the nights. These lights will be used for special signs and to show when special meetings* begin. And they will be used to show the days and years. ¹⁵These lights will be in the sky to shine light on the earth." And it happened. ¹⁶So God made the two large lights. God made the larger light to rule during the day. He made the smaller light to rule during the night. God also made the stars. ¹⁷God put these lights in the sky to shine on the earth. ¹⁸God put these lights in the sky to rule over the day and over the night. These lights separated the light from the darkness. And God saw this was good.

¹⁹There was evening, and then there was morning. This was the fourth day.

The Fifth Day—Fish and Birds

²⁰Then God said, "Let the water be filled with many living things. And let there be birds to fly in the air over the earth." ²¹So God made the large

---

moved over The Hebrew word means "to fly over" or "to swoop down," like a bird flying over its nest to protect its babies.

God made ... light Or, "In the beginning, God made the heavens and the earth. While ²the earth had no special shape, and darkness covered the ocean, and God's Spirit hovered over the water, ³God said, 'Let there be light!'" Or, "When God began to create the sky and the earth, ²while the earth was completely empty, and darkness covered the ocean, and a powerful wind blew over the water, ³God said, 'Let there be light.'"

air The Hebrew word means "bowl," or "dome."

special meetings The Israelites used the sun and moon to decide when the months and years began. And many Jewish holidays and special meetings began at the time of the new moon or full moon.

sea animals.* God made every living thing that moves in the sea. There are many different kinds of sea animals—and God made them all! God also made every kind of bird that flies in the sky. And God saw this was good. ²²God blessed these animals. God told them to have many babies and fill the seas. And God told the birds on land to make many more birds.

²³There was evening, and then there was morning. This was the fifth day.

The Sixth Day—Land Animals and People

²⁴Then God said, "Let the earth make many kinds of living things. Let there be many different kinds of animals. Let there be large animals and small crawling animals of every kind. And let all these animals make more animals." And all these things happened. ²⁵So God made every kind of animal. God made the wild animals, the tame animals, and all the small crawling things. And God saw this was good.

²⁶Then God said, "Now let's make man.* We will make people as a copy of ourselves. People will be like us. They will rule over all the fish in the sea and the birds in the air. They will rule over all the large animals and all the little things that crawl on the earth."

²⁷So God made people in his own image. God made people as a copy of himself.* God made them male and female. ²⁸God blessed them and said to them, "Have many children. Fill the earth and take control of it. Rule over the fish in the sea and the birds in the air. Rule over every living thing that moves on the earth."

²⁹God said, "I am giving you all the grain bearing plants and all the fruit trees. Those trees make fruit with seeds in it. This grain and fruit will be your food. ³⁰And I am giving all the green plants to the animals. Those green plants will be their food. Every animal on earth, every bird in the air, and all the little things that crawl on the earth will eat that food." And all these things happened.

³¹God looked at everything he had made. And God saw that everything was very good.

There was evening, and then there was morning. This was the sixth day.

The Seventh Day—Rest

2 So the earth, the sky, and everything in them were finished. ²God finished the work he was doing. So on the seventh day God rested from his work. ³God blessed the seventh day and made it a holy day. God made that day special because on that day he rested from all the work he did while making the world.

THE BEGINNING OF MANKIND

⁴This is the history of the sky and the earth. This is the story about the things that happened at the time God made the earth and the sky. ⁵This was before there were plants on the earth. Nothing was growing in the fields. This was because the Lord had not yet made it rain on the earth. And there was no person to care for the plants. ⁶Water* came up from the earth and spread over the ground.

⁷Then the Lord God took dust from the ground and made a man.* The Lord breathed the breath of life into the man's nose, and the man became a living thing. ⁸Then the Lord God planted a garden in the East,* in a place named Eden. The Lord God put the man he made in that garden. ⁹The Lord God made every beautiful tree and every tree that was good for food to grow in the garden. In the middle of the garden, the Lord God put the tree of life and also the tree that gives knowledge about good and evil.

¹⁰A river flowed from Eden and watered the garden. That river then separated and became four smaller rivers. ¹¹The name of the first river was Pishon. This river flowed around the entire country of Havilah.* ¹²(There is gold in that country, and that gold is good. There are also Bdellium* and Onyx* in that country.) ¹³The name of the second river was Gihon. This river

---

large sea animals Or, "sea monsters."
man The Hebrew word means "man," "people," or the name "Adam." It is like the word meaning "earth," or "red clay."
God made people ... himself Compare Gen. 5:1,3.

Water Or, "A mist."
East This usually means the area between the Tigris and Euphrates rivers as far east as the Persian Gulf.
Havilah The land along the west coast of the Arabian peninsula and, possibly, the part of Africa south of Ethiopia.
Bdellium An expensive, sweet-smelling gum.
Onyx A precious stone with many layers of blue or gray.

flowed around the entire country of Ethiopia.* ¹⁴The name of the third river was Tigris.* This river flowed east of Assyria. The fourth river was the Euphrates.*

¹⁵The Lord God put the man in the garden of Eden to work the soil and take care of the garden. ¹⁶The Lord God gave the man this command. The Lord God said, "You may eat from any tree in the garden. ¹⁷But you must not eat from the tree that gives knowledge about good and evil. If you eat fruit from that tree you will die!"

The First Woman

¹⁸Then the Lord God said, "I see that it is not good for the man to be alone. I will make a person like him to help him."

¹⁹The Lord God used dust from the ground and made every animal in the fields and every bird in the air. The Lord God brought all these animals to the man, and the man gave everything a name. ²⁰The man gave names to all the tame animals, to all the birds in the air, and to all the wild animals of the forest. The man saw many, many animals and birds, but the man could not find a helper that was right for him. ²¹So the Lord God caused the man to sleep very deeply. While the man was asleep, the Lord God took one of the ribs from the man's body. Then the Lord God closed the man's skin at the place where he took the rib. ²²The Lord God used the rib from the man to make a woman. Then the Lord God brought the woman to the man. ²³And the man said,

> "Finally! ₍A person like me₎.
> Her bones are from my bones.
> Her body is from my body.
> She was taken out of man,
> so I will call her woman."

²⁴That is why a man leaves his father and mother and is joined to his wife. This way, two people become one.

²⁵The man and his wife were naked, but they were not ashamed.

The Beginning of Sin

3 The snake was the most clever of all the wild animals that the Lord God had made. ₍The snake wanted to trick the woman₎. The snake spoke to the woman and said, "Woman, did God really tell you that you must not eat from any tree in the garden?"

²The woman answered the snake, "₍No! God did not say that!₎ We can eat fruit from the trees in the garden. ³But there is one tree we must not eat from. God told us, 'You must not eat fruit from the tree that is in the middle of the garden. You must not even touch that tree or you will die.'"

⁴But the snake said to the woman, "You will not die. ⁵God knows that if you eat the fruit from that tree you will learn about good and evil. And then you will be the same as God!"

⁶The woman saw the tree was beautiful. She saw the fruit was good to eat. And it was exciting that the tree would make her wise. So the woman took fruit from the tree and ate it. Her husband was there with her, so she gave some of the fruit to him and he ate it.

⁷Then ₍both the man and the woman changed. It was like₎ their eyes opened, ₍and they saw things differently₎. They saw that they had no clothes on—they were naked. So they got some fig leaves and sewed them together and wore the fig leaves for clothes.

⁸During the cool part of the day, the Lord God was walking in the garden. The man and the woman heard him, and they hid among the trees in the garden. ⁹The Lord God called to the man and said, "Where are you?"

¹⁰The man said, "I heard you walking in the garden, and I was afraid. I was naked, so I hid."

¹¹The Lord God said to the man, "Who told you that you were naked? ₍What caused you to be ashamed?₎ Did you eat fruit from that special tree? I told you not to eat from that tree!"

¹²The man said, "The woman you made for me gave me fruit from that tree. So I ate it."

¹³Then the Lord God said to the woman, "What have you done?"

The woman said, "The snake tricked me. He fooled me and I ate the fruit."

¹⁴So the Lord God said to the snake,

> "You did this very bad thing,
> so bad things will happen to you.
> It will be worse for you
> than for any other animal.
> You must crawl on your belly
> and eat dust all the days
> of your life.
> ¹⁵ I will make you and the woman
> enemies to each other.
> Your children and her children
> will be enemies.

Ethiopia Or, "Cush," a country in Africa by the Red Sea.
Tigris, Euphrates The two largest rivers flowing through the countries of Babylonia and Assyria.

GENESIS 3:16–4:8

You will bite her child's foot,
but he will crush your head."

¹⁶Then the Lord God said to the woman,

"I will cause you to have much trouble
when you are pregnant.
And when you give birth to children,
you will have much pain.
You will want your husband very much,
but he will rule over you."*

¹⁷Then the Lord God said to the man,

"I commanded you
not to eat from that tree.
But you listened to your wife,
and you ate from that tree.
So I will curse* the ground
because of you.
You will have to work very hard
all the days of your life
for the food the ground gives.
¹⁸ The ground will grow thorns and weeds
for you.
And you will have to eat the plants
that grow wild in the fields.*
¹⁹ You will work hard for your food,
until your face is covered with sweat.
You will work hard until the day you die.
And then you will become dust again.
I used dust to make you.
And when you die
you will become dust again."

²⁰Adam* named his wife Eve.* Adam gave her this name because Eve is the mother of every person who ever lived.

²¹The Lord God used animal skins and made some clothes for the man and his wife. Then he put the clothes on them.

²²The Lord God said, "Look, the man has become like us—he knows about good and evil. And now the man might take the fruit from the tree of life. If the man eats that fruit, he will live forever."

²³So the Lord God forced the man to leave the garden of Eden. Adam* was forced to go and work the ground he was made from. ²⁴The Lord God forced the man to leave the garden. Then he put Cherub angels* at the entrance to the garden to protect it. The Lord God also put a sword of fire there. This sword flashed around and around guarding the way to the tree of life.

The First Family

4 Adam and his wife Eve had sexual relations, and Eve gave birth to a baby. The baby was named Cain.* Eve said, "With the Lord's help, I have made a man!"

²After that, Eve gave birth to another baby. This baby was Cain's brother, Abel. Abel became a shepherd. Cain became a farmer.

The First Murder

³⁻⁴At harvest time,* Cain brought a gift to the Lord. Cain brought some of the food that he grew from the ground. But Abel brought some animals from his flock. Abel brought the best parts of his best sheep.*

The Lord accepted Abel and his gift. ⁵But the Lord did not accept Cain and his offering. Cain was sad because of this, and he became very angry. ⁶The Lord asked Cain, "Why are you angry? Why does your face look sad? ⁷If you do good things, you will be right with me. Then I will accept you. But if you do wrong things, then that sin is in your life. Your sin will want to control you, but you must control that sin."*

⁸Cain said to his brother Abel, ₍"Let's go out to the field."₎ So Cain and Abel went to the field. Then Cain attacked his brother Abel and killed him.

You ... you Or, "You will want ₍to rule₎ your husband, but he will rule over you." In Hebrew this is like Gen. 4:7.
curse To ask for bad things to happen to a thing or person.
The ground ... fields See Gen. 1:28-29.
Adam This name means, "man" or "people." It is like the word meaning "earth" or "red clay."
Eve This name is like the Hebrew word meaning "life."
Cherub angels Special angels from God. Statues of these angels were on top of the Box of the Agreement.
Cain This is like the Hebrew word meaning "make" or "get."
At harvest time Literally, "at the end of days."
Abel brought ... best sheep Literally, "Abel brought some of his firstborn sheep, especially their fat."
But if you ... control that sin Or, "But if you don't do right, then sin is crouching at your door. It wants you, but you must rule over it."

⁹Later, the Lord said to Cain, "Where is your brother Abel?"

Cain answered, "I don't know. Is it my job to watch and care for my brother?"

¹⁰Then the Lord said, "What have you done? ⌊You killed your brother!⌋ His blood is like a voice shouting to me from the ground. ¹¹⌊You killed your brother,⌋ and the ground opened up to take his blood from your hands. So now, I will cause bad things to happen to that ground. ¹²In the past, ⌊you planted, and your plants grew well. But now⌋ you will plant, and the ground will not help your plants grow. You will not have a home on the earth. You will wander from place to place."

¹³Then Cain said, "This punishment is more than I can bear! ¹⁴Look, you are forcing me to leave my land. I won't be able to see you or be near you! I won't have a home! I will be forced to wander from place to place on the earth. And whoever finds me will kill me."

¹⁵Then the Lord said to Cain, "⌊I will not let that happen!⌋ If anyone kills you, Cain, then I will punish that person much, much more." Then the Lord put a mark on Cain. This mark showed that no person should kill him.

Cain's Family

¹⁶Cain went away from the Lord. Cain lived in the land of Nod.*

¹⁷Cain had sexual relations with his wife. She became pregnant and gave birth to a son named Enoch. Cain built a city and gave the city the same name as his son Enoch.

¹⁸Enoch had a son named Irad. Irad had a son named Mehujael. Mehujael had a son named Methushael. And Methushael had a son named Lamech.

¹⁹Lamech married two women. One wife was named Adah, and the other wife was named Zillah. ²⁰Adah gave birth to Jabal. Jabal was the father* of people who live in tents and earn their living by keeping cattle. ²¹Adah also had another son Jubal. (Jubal was Jabal's brother.) Jubal was the father of people who play the harp and flute. ²²Zillah gave birth to Tubal-Cain. Tubal-Cain was the father of people who work with bronze and iron. The sister of Tubal-Cain was named Naamah.

²³Lamech said to his wives:

"Adah and Zillah,
 hear my voice!
You wives of Lamech,
 listen to me.
A man hurt me,
 so I killed him.
A child hit me,
 so I killed him.
²⁴ The punishment for killing Cain
 was very great!
So the punishment for killing me
 will be much, much greater!"

Adam and Eve Have a New Son

²⁵Adam again had sexual relations with Eve. And Eve gave birth to another son. They named him Seth.* Eve said, "God has given me another son. Cain killed Abel, but now I have Seth." ²⁶Seth also had a son. He named him Enosh. At that time, the people began to trust the Lord.*

Adam's Family History

5 This is the book about the family of Adam.* God made people a copy of himself.* ²God made them male and female. And on the same day he made them, God blessed them and named them "Adam."*

³After Adam was 130 years old, he had another son. This son looked just like Adam.* Adam named his son Seth. ⁴After Seth was born, Adam lived 800 years. During that time, Adam had other sons and daughters. ⁵So Adam lived a total of 930 years; then he died.

⁶After Seth was 105 years old, he had a son named Enosh. ⁷After Enosh was born, Seth lived 807 years. During that time, Seth had other sons and daughters. ⁸So Seth lived a total of 912 years; then he died.

⁹After Enosh was 90 years old, he had a son named Kenan. ¹⁰After Kenan was born, Enosh lived 815 years. During that time, he had other sons and daughters. ¹¹So Enosh lived a total of 905 years; then he died.

Nod This name means "wandering."
father This probably means that this man invented these things, or was the first person to use them.
Seth This is like a Hebrew word meaning "to give."
people ... the Lord Literally, "people began calling on the name Yahweh."
Adam This name means "man" or "people." It is like the word meaning "earth" or "red clay."
God made people ... himself Literally, "He made him in the image of God." See Gen. 1:27; 5:3.
he had ... like Adam Or, "he fathered a son in his image and likeness." In Hebrew this is like Gen. 1:27; 5:1.

GENESIS 5:12–6:14

[12] After Kenan was 70 years old, he had a son named Mahalalel. [13] After Mahalalel was born, Kenan lived 840 years. During that time, Kenan had other sons and daughters. [14] So Kenan lived a total of 910 years; then he died.

[15] When Mahalalel was 65 years old, he had a son named Jared. [16] After Jared was born, Mahalalel lived 830 years. During that time, he had other sons and daughters. [17] So Mahalalel lived a total of 895 years; then he died.

[18] After Jared was 162 years old, he had a son named Enoch. [19] After Enoch was born, Jared lived 800 years. During that time, he had other sons and daughters. [20] So Jared lived a total of 962 years; then he died.

[21] After Enoch was 65 years old, he had a son named Methuselah. [22] After Methuselah was born, Enoch walked with God for 300 years more. During that time, he had other sons and daughters. [23] So Enoch lived a total of 365 years. [24] One day Enoch was walking with God, and Enoch disappeared. God took him.*

[25] After Methuselah was 187 years old, he had a son named Lamech. [26] After Lamech was born, Methuselah lived 782 years. During that time, he had other sons and daughters. [27] So Methuselah lived a total of 969 years; then he died.

[28] When Lamech was 182 years old, he had a son. [29] Lamech named his son Noah.* Lamech said, "We work very hard as farmers because God cursed the ground. But Noah will bring us rest."

[30] After Noah was born, Lamech lived 595 years. During that time he had other sons and daughters. [31] So Lamech lived a total of 777 years; then he died.

[32] After Noah was 500 years old, he had sons named Shem, Ham, and Japheth.

People Become Evil

[6] The number of people on earth continued to increase. There were girls born to these people. [2-4] The sons of God saw that these girls were beautiful. So the sons of God married any of the girls they chose.

These women gave birth to children. During that time and later, the Nephilim* people lived in the land. They were famous people. They were heroes from ancient times.*

Then the Lord said, "People are only human; I will not let my Spirit be troubled by them forever. I will let them live 120 years."*

[5] The Lord saw that the people on the earth were very evil. The Lord saw that people thought only about evil things all the time. [6] The Lord was sorry that he had made people on the earth. It made the Lord very sad in his heart. [7] So the Lord said, "I will destroy all the people that I made on the earth. I will destroy every man and every animal and everything that crawls on the earth. And I will destroy all the birds in the air. Why? Because I am sorry that I have made all these things."

[8] But there was one man on earth that pleased the Lord—Noah.*

Noah and the Great Flood

[9] This is story about the family of Noah. Noah was a good man all his life. Noah always followed God. [10] Noah had three sons: Shem, Ham, and Japheth.

[11-12] God looked at the earth, and he saw that people had ruined it. Violence was everywhere—ₗpeople had become evil and cruelⱼ and had ruined their life on earth.

[13] So God said to Noah, "All people have filled the earth with anger and violence. So I will destroy all living things. I will remove them from the earth. [14] Use cypress wood* and build a boat for yourself. Make rooms in the boat,* and cover the boat with tar.*

One day ... God took him Or, "Enoch pleased God. Enoch disappeared. God took him."

Noah This name means "rest."

Nephilim This name is like the Hebrew word meaning "People who have fallen." Later, the Nephilim were a famous family of large fighting men. See Num. 13:32-33.

These women ... times. Or, "The Nephilim lived in the land in those days and also later, when the sons of God married the daughters of men, and these women had given birth to children who were famous heroes from ancient times."

People ... 120 years Or, "My Spirit will not live with people forever, because they are flesh. They will live only 120 years." Or, "My Spirit will not judge people forever because they will all die in 120 years."

Noah This name is like the Hebrew word meaning "to be sorry," "to comfort," or "to rest."

cypress wood Literally, "gopher-wood." We do not know exactly what kind of wood this is. It might be a kind of tree or squared timbers.

Make rooms in the boat Or, "Make caulking for the boat," This could be small plants that were stuffed into the cracks and covered with tar.

tar Or, "pitch," a thick oil that must be heated to become liquid.

¹⁵"This is the size I want you to make the boat: 300 cubits* long, 50 cubits* wide, and 30 cubits* high. ¹⁶Make a window for the boat about 18 inches* below the roof.* Put a door in the side of the boat. Make three floors in the boat; a top deck, a middle deck, and a lower deck.

¹⁷"Understand what I am telling you. I will bring a great flood of water on the earth. I will destroy all living things that live under heaven. Everything on the earth will die. ¹⁸I will make a special agreement with you. And you, your sons, your wife, and your son's wives will all go into the boat. ¹⁹Also, you must find two of every living thing on the earth. Find male and female and bring them on the boat. Keep them alive with you. ²⁰Find two of every kind of bird on the earth. And find two of every kind of animal on the earth. And find two of every kind of thing that crawls on the ground. Male and female of every kind of animal on the earth will be with you. Keep them alive on the boat. ²¹Also bring every kind of food on earth into the boat. The food will be for you and for the animals."

²²Noah did all these things. Noah obeyed all the things that God commanded.

The Flood Begins

7 Then the Lord said to Noah, "I have seen that you are a good man, even among the evil people of this time. So gather your family and all of you go into the boat. ²Get seven pairs (seven males and seven females) of every kind of clean animal.* And get one pair (one male and one female) of every other animal on the earth. Lead all these animals into the boat with you. ³Get seven pairs (seven males and seven females) of all the birds. This will allow all these animals to continue living on the earth after the other animals are destroyed. ⁴Seven days from now I will send much rain on the earth. It will rain for 40 days and 40 nights. And I will wipe everything off the face of the earth. I will destroy everything I made." ⁵Noah did everything the Lord told him to do.

⁶Noah was 600 years old at the time the rains came. ⁷Noah and his family went into the boat to be saved from the flood. Noah's wife and his sons and their wives were on the boat with him. ⁸All the clean animals,* all the other animals on the earth, the birds, and everything that crawls on the earth ⁹went into the boat with Noah. These animals went into the boat in groups of two, male and female, just like God commanded. ¹⁰Seven days later the flood started. The rain began to fall on the earth.

¹¹⁻¹³On the 17th day of the second month, when Noah was 600 years old, all the springs under the ground split open, ₍and water began flowing from the ground₎. That same day the rains began falling hard on the earth. It was like windows in the sky were opened. The rain fell on the earth for 40 days and 40 nights. That very same day Noah and his wife, his sons—Shem, Ham, and Japheth—and their wives went into the boat. ¹⁴Those people and every kind of animal on the earth were in the boat. Every kind of cattle, every kind of animal that crawls on the earth, and every kind of bird were in the boat. ¹⁵All these animals went into the boat with Noah. They came in groups of two from every kind of animal that had the breath of life. ¹⁶All these animals went into the boat in groups of two, just like God had commanded Noah. Then the Lord closed the door behind him.

¹⁷Water flooded the earth for 40 days. The water began rising and lifted the boat off the ground. ¹⁸The water continued to rise, and the boat floated on the water high above the earth. ¹⁹The water rose so much that even the highest mountains were covered by the water. ²⁰The water continued to rise above the mountains. The water was more than 20 feet* above the highest mountain.

²¹⁻²²Every living thing on earth died—every man and woman, every bird, and every kind of animal on earth died. All the many kinds of animals and all the things that crawl on the ground died. Every living, breathing thing on dry land died. ²³In this way, God wiped the earth clean—God destroyed every living thing on the earth—every man, every animal, everything that crawls, and every bird. All these things were destroyed from the earth. The only life that was left was

---

300 cubits 442' 10 15/16" (135m.) if this was the short cubit or 516' 0" (157.5m.) if it was the long cubit.

50 cubits 73' 9 3/16" (22.5m.) if this was the short cubit or 86' 1 1/2" (26.25m.) if it was the long cubit.

30 cubits 44' 3 7/16" (13.5m.) if this was the short cubit or 51' 8 1/8" (15.75m.) if it was the long cubit.

one cubit 1' 5 11/16" (45cm) if this was the short cubit or 1' 8 5/8" (52.5cm) if it was the long cubit.

Make a window ... below the roof Or "Make an opening for the boat about 18 inches tall."

clean animal(s) Birds and animals that God said could be used for sacrifices.

20 feet Literally, "15 cubits" which would be 22' 1 11/16" (6.75m.) if this was the short cubit or 25' 10" (7.875m.) if it was the long cubit.

GENESIS 7:24–9:10

Noah and those people and animals that were with him in the boat. ²⁴The water continued to cover the earth for 150 days.

The Flood Ends

8 But God did not forget about Noah. God remembered Noah and all the animals that were with him in the boat. God made a wind blow over the earth. And all the water began to disappear. ²Rain stopped falling from the sky. And water stopped flowing from under the earth. ³⁻⁴The water that covered the earth began to go down and down. After 150 days, the water was low enough that the boat touched land again. The boat stopped on one of the mountains of Ararat.* This was the 17th day of the seventh month. ⁵The water continued to go down, and by the first day of the tenth month the tops of the mountains were above the water.

⁶Forty days later, Noah opened the window he had made in the boat. ⁷Noah sent out a raven.* The raven flew from place to place until the ground was dry and the water was gone. ⁸Noah also sent out a dove. Noah wanted the dove to find dry ground. He wanted to know if water still covered the earth.

⁹The dove could not find a place to rest because water still covered the earth, so the dove came back to the boat. Noah reached out his hand and caught the dove and brought it back into the boat. ¹⁰After seven days, Noah again sent out the dove. ¹¹And that afternoon the dove came back to Noah. The dove had a fresh olive leaf in its mouth. This was a sign to show Noah that there was dry ground on the earth. ¹²Seven days later, Noah sent the dove out again. But this time the dove never came back.

¹³After that, Noah opened the door* of the boat. Noah looked and saw that the ground was dry. This was the first day of the first month of the year. Noah was 601 years old. ¹⁴By the 27th day of the second month the ground was completely dry.

¹⁵Then God said to Noah, ¹⁶"Leave the boat. You, your wife, your sons, and your sons' wives should go out now. ¹⁷Bring every living animal out of the boat with you—all the birds, animals, and everything that crawls on the earth. Those animals will make many more animals, and they will fill the earth again."

¹⁸So Noah went out with his sons, his wife, and his sons' wives. ¹⁹All the animals, everything that crawls, and every bird left the boat. All the animals came out of the boat in family groups.

²⁰Then Noah built an altar* to the Lord. Noah took some of all the clean birds and some of all the clean animals,* and Noah burned them on the altar as a gift to God.

²¹The Lord smelled these sacrifices, and it pleased him. The Lord said to himself, "I will never again curse the ground as a way to punish people. People are evil from the time that they are young. So I will never again destroy every living thing on the earth like I have just done. ²²As long as the earth continues, there will always be a time for planting and a time for harvest. There will always be cold and hot, summer and winter, day and night on earth."

The New Beginning

9 God blessed Noah and his sons. God said to him, "Have many children. Fill the earth with your people. ²Every animal on earth, every bird in the air, every animal that crawls on the ground, and every fish in the sea will be afraid of you. All of them will be under your control. ³[In the past], I gave you the green plants to eat. Now, every animal will also be food for you. I give you everything on earth—it is yours. ⁴But I give you one command. You must not eat meat that still has its life (blood) in it. ⁵I will demand your blood for your lives. That is, I will demand the life of any animal that kills a person. And I will demand the life of any person who takes another person's life.

⁶ "God made people as a copy of himself.
So any person who kills a person
must be killed by a person.

⁷"Noah, you and your sons have many children. Fill the earth with your people."

⁸Then God said to Noah and his sons, ⁹"I now make my promise to you and to your people who will live after you. ¹⁰I make my promise to all the birds, and to all the cattle, and to all the animals that came out of the boat with you. I make my

---

Ararat Or, "Urartu," an area in Eastern Turkey.
raven A kind of bird.
opened the door Literally, "removed the covering."

altar(s) A stone table used for burning sacrifices that were offered as gifts to God.
clean birds ... animals Birds and animals that God said could be used for sacrifices.

promise to every living thing on earth. ¹¹This is my promise to you: All life on the earth was destroyed by the flood. But that will never happen again. A flood will never again destroy all the life on the earth."

¹²And God said, "And I will give you something to prove that I made this promise to you. This proof will show that I have made an agreement with you and every living thing on earth. This agreement will continue for all times to come. This is the proof: ¹³I have made a rainbow in the clouds. That rainbow is proof of the agreement between me and the earth. ¹⁴When I bring clouds over the earth, you will see the rainbow in the clouds. ¹⁵When I see this rainbow, I will remember the agreement between me and you and every living thing on the earth. That agreement says that a flood will never again destroy all life on the earth. ¹⁶When I look and see the rainbow in the clouds, I will remember the agreement that continues forever. I will remember the agreement between me and every living thing on the earth."

¹⁷So the Lord said to Noah, "That rainbow is proof of the agreement that I made with all living things on earth."

Problems Begin Again

¹⁸Noah's sons came out of the boat with him. Their names were Shem, Ham, and Japheth. (Ham was the father of Canaan.) ¹⁹Those three men were Noah's sons. And all the people on earth came from those three sons.

²⁰Noah became a farmer. He planted a field of grapes. ²¹Noah made wine and drank it. He became drunk and lay in his tent. Noah was not wearing any clothes. ²²Ham, the father of Canaan, looked at his naked father. Ham told his brothers outside the tent. ²³Then Shem and Japheth got a coat. They carried the coat on their backs into the tent. They walked backwards into the tent. In this way, they did not see their father without clothes.

²⁴Later, Noah woke up. (He was sleeping because of the wine.) Then he learned what his young son, Ham, had done to him. ²⁵So Noah said,

> "May there be a curse on Canaan*!
> May he be a slave to his brothers."

²⁶Noah also said,

> "Bless the Lord, God of Shem!
> May Canaan be Shem's slave.
> ²⁷ May God give more land to Japheth.
> May God live in Shem's tents.
> And may Canaan be their slave."

²⁸After the flood Noah lived 350 years. ²⁹Noah lived a total of 950 years; then he died.

Nations Grow and Spread

10 Noah's sons were Shem, Ham, and Japheth. After the flood, these three men became the fathers of many more sons. Here is a list of the sons that came from Shem, Ham, and Japheth.

Japheth's Descendants

²Japheth's sons were: Gomer, Magog, Madai, Javan, Tubal, Meshech, and Tiras. ³Gomer's sons were: Ashkenaz, Riphath, and Togarmah. ⁴Javan's sons were: Elishah, Tarshish, Kittim, and Dodanim.*

⁵All the people who lived in the area around the Mediterranean Sea came from these sons of Japheth. Each son had his own land. All the families grew and became different nations. Each nation had its own language.

Ham's Descendants

⁶Ham's sons were: Cush,* Mizraim,* Put, and Canaan.

⁷Cush's sons were: Seba, Havilah, Sabtah, Raamah, and Sabtecah.

Raamah's sons were: Sheba and Dedan.

⁸Cush also had a son named Nimrod. Nimrod became a very powerful man on earth. ⁹Nimrod was a great hunter before the Lord. That is why people compare other men to Nimrod and say, "That man is like Nimrod, a great hunter before the Lord."

¹⁰Nimrod's kingdom began in Babylon, Erech, and Akkad in the country of Shinar. ¹¹Nimrod also went into Assyria. In Assyria, Nimrod built the cities of Nineveh, Rehoboth Ir, Calah, and ¹²Resen. (Resen is the city between Nineveh and Calah, the big city.)

Canaan Ham's son. The people of Canaan lived along the coast of Palestine, Lebanon, and Syria. Later, God gave this land to the people of Israel.

Dodanim Or, "Rodanim," or "the people of Rhodes."
Cush This is also another name for Ethiopia.
Mizraim This is also another name for Egypt.

GENESIS 10:13–11:13

¹³Mizraim *(Egypt)* was the father of the people of Lud, Anam, Lehab, Naphtuh, ¹⁴Pathrus, Casluh, and Caphtor. (The Philistine people came from Casluh.)
¹⁵Canaan was the father of Sidon. Sidon was Canaan's first son. Canaan was also the father of ⌊Het, the father of⌋ the Hittite people. ¹⁶And Canaan was the father of the Jebusite people, the Amorite people, the Girgashite people, ¹⁷the Hivite people, the Arkite people, the Sinite people, ¹⁸the Arvadite people, the Zemarite people, and the people from Hamath. The families of Canaan spread to different parts of the world.

¹⁹The land of the people of Canaan was from Sidon in the north to Gerar in the south, from Gaza in the west to Sodom and Gomorrah in the east, from Admah and Zeboiim to Lasha.

²⁰All those people were descendants* of Ham. All those families had their own languages and their own lands. They became separate nations.

Shem's Descendants

²¹Shem was Japheth's older brother. One of Shem's descendants was Eber, the father of all the Hebrew people.*

²²Shem's sons were Elam, Asshur, Arphaxad, Lud, and Aram.

²³Aram's sons were Uz, Hul, Gether, and Mash.

²⁴Arphaxad was the father of Shelah. Shelah was the father of Eber. ²⁵Eber was the father of two sons. One son was named Peleg.* He was given this name because the earth was divided during his life. The other son was named Joktan.

²⁶Joktan was the father of Almodad, Sheleph, Hazarmaveth, Jerah, ²⁷Hadoram, Uzal, Diklah, ²⁸Obal, Abimael, Sheba, ²⁹Ophir, Havilah, and Jobab. All those people were Joktan's sons. ³⁰Those people lived in the area between Mesha and the hill country in the East.* Mesha was toward the country of Sephar.

³¹Those are the people from the family of Shem. They are arranged by families, languages, countries, and nations.

³²That is the list of the families from Noah's sons. They are arranged according to their nations. From those families came all the people who spread across the earth after the flood.

The World Divided

11 ¹⌊After the flood,⌋ the whole world spoke one language. All people used the same words. ²People moved from the East.* They found a plain in the country of Shinar. The people stayed there to live.

³The people said, "We should make bricks and put them in fire so that they will become very hard." So the people used bricks, not stones, to build their houses. And the people used tar,* not mortar.*

⁴Then the people said, "We should build a city for ourselves. And we should build a tower that will reach to the sky. We will be famous. ⌊And this will keep us together.⌋ We will not be scattered all over the earth."

⁵The Lord came down to see the city and the very tall building. The Lord saw the people building these things. ⁶The Lord said, "These people all speak the same language. And I see that they are joined together to do this work. This is only the beginning of what they can do. Soon they will be able to do anything they want. ⁷So let's go down and confuse their language. Then they will not understand each other."

⁸So the Lord caused the people to spread all over the earth. So the people did not finish building the city. ⁹That is the place where the Lord confused the language of the whole world. So that place is called Babel.* So the Lord caused the people to spread out from that place to all the other places on earth.

The Story of Shem's Family

¹⁰This is the story of Shem's family. Two years after the flood, when Shem was 100 years old, his son Arphaxad was born. ¹¹After that Shem lived 500 years. He had other sons and daughters.

¹²When Arphaxad was 35 years old, his son Shelah was born. ¹³After Shelah was born, Arphaxad lived 403 years. During that time he had other sons and daughters.

---

descendant(s) A person's children and their future families.
One ... Hebrew people Literally, "To Shem was born the father of Eber's sons."
Peleg This name means, "division."
East This usually means the area between the Tigris and Euphrates rivers as far east as the Persian Gulf.
tar Or, "pitch," a thick oil that must be heated to become liquid.
mortar Cement used when building with bricks.
Babel Or, "Babylon." This is like a word meaning "confuse."

¹⁴After Shelah was 30 years old, his son Eber was born. ¹⁵After Eber was born, Shelah lived 403 years. During that time he had other sons and daughters.
¹⁶After Eber was 34 years old, his son Peleg was born. ¹⁷After Peleg was born, Eber lived 430 years more. During that time he had other sons and daughters.
¹⁸After Peleg was 30 years old, his son Reu was born. ¹⁹After Reu was born, Peleg lived 209 years more. During that time he had other sons and daughters.
²⁰After Reu was 32 years old, his son Serug was born. ²¹After Serug was born, Reu lived 207 years more. During that time he had other sons and daughters.
²²After Serug was 30 years old, his son Nahor was born. ²³After Nahor was born, Serug lived 200 years more. During that time he had other sons and daughters.
²⁴After Nahor was 29 years old, his son Terah was born. ²⁵After Terah was born, Nahor lived 119 years more. During that time he had other sons and daughters.
²⁶After Terah was 70 years old, his sons Abram, Nahor, and Haran were born.

The Story of Terah's Family

²⁷This is the story of Terah's family. Terah was the father of Abram, Nahor, and Haran. Haran was the father of Lot. ²⁸Haran died in his home town, Ur of Babylonia,* while his father Terah was still alive. ²⁹Abram and Nahor both married. Abram's wife was named Sarai. Nahor's wife was named Milcah. Milcah was the daughter of Haran. Haran was the father of Milcah and Iscah. ³⁰Sarai did not have any children because she was not able to have children.
³¹Terah took his family and left Ur of Babylonia.* They planned to travel to Canaan. Terah took his son Abram, his grandson Lot (Haran's son), and his daughter-in-law Sarai (Abram's wife). They traveled to the city of Haran and decided to stay there. ³²Terah lived to be 205 years old. He died in Haran.

Ur of Babylonia Literally, "Ur of the Chaldeans." A city in southern Babylonia.

God Calls Abram

12 The Lord said to Abram,
"Leave your country and your people.
Leave your father's family
    and go to the country I will show you.
² I will build a great nation from you.
I will bless you
    and make your name famous.
People will use your name
    to bless other people.
³ I will bless people who bless you,
    and I will curse people who curse* you.
I will use you to bless
    all the people on earth."

Abram Goes to Canaan

⁴So Abram left Haran just like the Lord said. And Lot went with him. Abram was 75 years old when he left Haran. ⁵Abram took his wife Sarai, his nephew Lot, all the slaves and all the other things he got in Haran. Then Abram and his group moved to the land of Canaan. ⁶Abram traveled through the land of Canaan as far as the town of Shechem and then went to the big tree at Moreh. The Canaanite people lived in that place at this time.
⁷The Lord appeared* to Abram. The Lord said, "I will give this land to your descendants."
The Lord appeared to Abram at that place. So Abram built an altar* for worshiping the Lord there. ⁸Then Abram left that place and traveled to the mountains east of Bethel. Abram set up his tent there. The city of Bethel was to the west. The city of Ai was to the east. At that place Abram built another altar to the Lord. And Abram worshiped the Lord there. ⁹After this, Abram began traveling again. He traveled toward the Negev.*

curse To ask for bad things to happen to a thing or person.
The Lord appeared God often used special shapes so people could see him. Sometimes he was like a man, an angel, a fire, or a bright light.
altar(s) A stone table used for burning sacrifices that were offered as gifts to God.
Negev The desert area in the southern part of Judah.

Abram in Egypt

¹⁰During this time, the land was very dry. There was no rain, and no food was able to grow. So Abram went down to Egypt to live. ¹¹Abram saw how beautiful his wife Sarai was. So just before they arrived in Egypt, Abram told Sarai, "I know that you are a very beautiful woman. ¹²The Egyptian men will see you. They will say, 'This woman is his wife.' Then they will kill me because they want you. ¹³So tell people that you are my sister. Then they will not kill me. They will think I am your brother, and they will be kind to me. In this way, you will save my life."

¹⁴So Abram went into Egypt. The men of Egypt saw that Sarai was a very beautiful woman. ¹⁵Some of the Egyptian leaders saw her also. They told Pharaoh that she was a very beautiful woman. Those leaders took Sarai to Pharaoh's home. ¹⁶Pharaoh was kind to Abram because he thought Abram was Sarai's brother. Pharaoh gave Abram sheep, cattle, and donkeys. Abram also got men servants, women servants, and camels.

¹⁷Pharaoh took Abram's wife. So the Lord caused Pharaoh and all the people in his house to have very bad diseases. ¹⁸So Pharaoh called Abram. Pharaoh said, "You have done a bad thing to me! You didn't tell me Sarai was your wife! Why? ¹⁹You said, 'She is my sister.' Why did you say that? I took her so she could be my wife. But now I give your wife back to you. Take her and go!" ²⁰Then Pharaoh commanded his men to lead Abram out of Egypt. So Abram and his wife left that place. And they carried everything they had with them.

Abram Returns to Canaan

13 So Abram left Egypt. Abram traveled through the Negev* with his wife and everything he owned. Lot was also with them. ²At this time, Abram was very rich. He had many animals and much silver and gold.

³Abram continued traveling around. He left the Negev* and went back to Bethel. He went to the place between the city of Bethel and the city of Ai. This was the same place Abram and his family had camped before. ⁴This was the place Abram had built an altar.* So Abram worshiped the Lord at this place.

Negev The desert area in the southern part of Judah.
altar(s) A stone table used for burning sacrifices that were offered as gifts to God.

Abram and Lot Separate

⁵During this time, Lot was also traveling with Abram. Lot had many animals and tents. ⁶Abram and Lot had so many animals that the land could not support both of them together. ⁷And the Canaanite people and the Perizzite people were also living in this land at the same time. The shepherds of Abram and Lot began to argue.

⁸So Abram said to Lot, "There should be no arguing between you and me. Your people and my people should not argue. We are all brothers. ⁹We should separate. You can choose any place you want. If you go to the left, I will go to the right. If you go to the right, I will go to the left."

¹⁰Lot looked and saw the Jordan Valley. Lot saw that there was much water there. (This was before the Lord destroyed Sodom and Gomorrah. At that time the Jordan Valley all the way to Zoar was like the Lord's Garden. This was good land, like the land of Egypt.) ¹¹So Lot chose to live in the Jordan Valley. The two men separated, and Lot began traveling east. ¹²Abram stayed in the land of Canaan, and Lot lived among the cities in the valley. Lot moved far south to Sodom and made his camp there. ¹³The Lord knew that the people of Sodom were very evil sinners.

¹⁴After Lot left, the Lord said to Abram, "Look around you. Look north and south and east and west. ¹⁵All this land that you see I will give to you and your people who live after you. This will be your land forever. ¹⁶I will make your people as many as the dust of the earth. If people could count all the dust on earth, then they could count your people. ¹⁷So go. Walk through your land. I now give it to you."

¹⁸So Abram moved his tents. He went to live near Mamre's big trees. This was near the city of Hebron. At that place Abram built an altar* for worshiping the Lord.

Lot Is Captured

14 Amraphel was the king of Shinar. Arioch was the king of Ellasar. Kedorlaomer was the king of Elam. And Tidal was the king of Goiim. ²All these kings fought a war against Bera the king of Sodom, Birsha the king of Gomorrah, Shinab the king of Admah, Shemeber the king of Zeboiim, and the king of Bela. (Bela is also called Zoar.)

³All these kings joined their armies in the Valley of Siddim. (The Valley of Siddim is now the Salt Sea.) ⁴These kings had served Kedorlaomer for twelve years. But in the 13th

year they all rebelled against him. ⁵So in the 14th year, King Kedorlaomer and the kings with him came to fight against them. Kedorlaomer and the kings with him defeated the Rephaim people in Ashteroth Karnaim. They also defeated the Zuzim people in Ham. They defeated the Emim people in Shaveh Kiriathaim. ⁶And they defeated the Horite people who lived in the area from the hill country of Seir* to El Paran.* (El Paran is near the desert.) ⁷Then King Kedorlaomer turned back and went to En Mishpat (that is Kadesh) and defeated the Amalekite people. He also defeated the Amorite people living in Hazezon Tamar.

⁸At that time, the king of Sodom, the king of Gomorrah, the king of Admah, the king of Zeboiim, and the king of Bela (Zoar) joined together and went to fight against their enemies. ₆They went to fight₎ in the Valley of Siddim.* ⁹They fought against Kedorlaomer the king of Elam, Tidal the king of Goiim, Amraphel the king of Shinar, and Arioch the king of Ellasar. So there were four kings fighting against five.

¹⁰There were very many holes filled with tar* in the Valley of Siddim. The kings of Sodom and Gomorrah ₆and their armies₎ ran away. Many of the soldiers fell into those holes. But the others ran away to the mountains.

¹¹So their enemies took all the things that the people of Sodom and Gomorrah owned. They took all their food and clothing and left. ¹²Lot, the son of Abram's brother, was living in Sodom, and the enemy captured him. The enemy also took everything he owned and left. ¹³One of the men that was not captured went to Abram the Hebrew and told him what happened. Abram was camped near the trees of Mamre the Amorite. Mamre, Eshcol, and Aner had made an agreement to help each other.* And they had also signed an agreement to help Abram.

Abram Rescues Lot

¹⁴Abram learned that Lot was captured. So Abram called all of his family together. There were 318 trained soldiers. Abram led the men and chased the enemy all the way to the town of Dan. ¹⁵That night, he and his men made a surprise attack against the enemy. They defeated the enemy and chased them to Hobah, north of Damascus. ¹⁶Then Abram brought back all the things that the enemy had stolen. Abram brought back the women and servants, and also Lot and everything Lot owned.

¹⁷Then Abram went home after he defeated Kedorlaomer and the kings with Kedorlaomer. When he came home, the king of Sodom went out to meet him in the Valley of Shaveh. (This is now called King's Valley.)

Melchizedek

¹⁸Melchizedek, the king of Salem, also went to meet Abram. Melchizedek was a priest of God Most High. Melchizedek brought bread and wine. ¹⁹Melchizedek blessed Abram and said,

> "Abram, may God Most High bless you.
> God made heaven and earth.
> ²⁰ And we praise God Most High.
> God helped you to defeat your enemies."

Abram gave Melchizedek one tenth of everything he had taken during the battle. ²¹Then the king of Sodom told Abram, "You can keep all these things for yourself. Just give me my people that the enemy took away."

²²But Abram said to the king of Sodom, "I promise to the Lord, the God Most High, the One who made heaven and earth—²³I promise that I will not keep anything that is yours—not even a thread or a shoestring! I don't want you to say, 'I made Abram rich.' ²⁴The only thing I will accept is the food that my young men have eaten. But you should give the other men their share. Take the things we won in battle and give some to Aner, Eshcol, and Mamre. These men helped me in the battle."

God's Agreement With Abram

15 After all these things happened, the word of the Lord came to Abram in a vision.* God said, "Abram, don't be afraid. I will defend you. And I will give you a great reward."

Seir Or, "Edom."
El Paran Probably the town Elath, at the southern tip of Israel near the Red Sea.
Valley of Siddim The valley or plain along the eastern or southeastern side of the Dead Sea.
tar Or, "pitch," a thick oil that must be heated to become liquid.
Mamre ... other. Literally, "Mamre ... was a brother of Eshcol and a brother of Aner."

vision Like a dream. God gave messages to his special people by letting them see and hear things in visions.

²But Abram said, "Lord God, there is nothing you can give me that will make me happy. Why? Because I have no son. So my slave Eliezer from Damascus will get all the things I own after I die." ³Abram said, "You have given me no son. So a slave born in my house will get everything I have." ⁴Then the Lord spoke to Abram. God said, "That slave will not be the one to get the things you have. You will have a son. And your son will get the things you have." ⁵Then God led Abram outside. God said, "Look at the sky. See the many stars. There are so many you can't count them. In the future, your family will be like that." ⁶Abram believed God. And God decided Abram's faith was the same as living right and doing a good work. ⁷God said to Abram, "I am the Lord who led you from Ur of Babylonia.* I did this so I could give you this land—you will own this land."

⁸But Abram said, "Lord, my Master, how can I be sure that I will get this land?"

⁹God said to Abram, "₍We will make an agreement.₎ Bring me a three-year-old cow, a three-year-old goat, and a three-year-old ram. Also, bring me a dove and a young pigeon."

¹⁰Abram brought all these things to God. Abram killed these animals and cut each of them into two pieces. Then Abram laid each half across from the other half. Abram did not cut the birds into two pieces. ¹¹Later, large birds flew down to eat the animals. But Abram chased them away.

¹²Later in the day, the sun was going down. Abram became very sleepy and fell asleep. While he was asleep a very terrible darkness came. ¹³Then the Lord said to Abram, "You should know these things: Your descendants will live in a country that is not their own. They will be strangers there. And the people there will make them slaves and do bad things to them for 400 years. ¹⁴But then I will punish the nation that made them slaves. Your people will leave that land, and they will take many good things with them.

¹⁵"You yourself will live to be very old. You will die in peace. And you will be buried with your family. ¹⁶After four generations your people will come to this land again. At that time, your people will defeat the Amorite people. I will use your people to punish the Amorites living here. This will be in the future, because the Amorite people are not yet evil enough to punish."

¹⁷After the sun went down, it became very dark. The dead animals still lay on the ground— each animal cut in two pieces. At that time, a column of smoke and fire* passed between the halves of the dead animals.*

¹⁸So on that day, the Lord made a promise and an agreement with Abram. The Lord said, "I will give this land to your descendants. I will give them the land between the River of Egypt* and the great river Euphrates. ¹⁹This is the land of the Kenite people, the Kenizzite people, the Kadmonite people, ²⁰the Hittite people, the Perizzite people, the Rephaim people, ²¹the Amorite people, the Canaanite people, the Girgashite people, and the Jebusite people."

Hagar the Servant Girl

16 Sarai was Abram's wife. She and Abram had no children. Sarai had a servant from Egypt. Her name was Hagar. ²Sarai said to Abram, "The Lord has not allowed me to have children. So go with my servant Hagar. I will accept the child that is born from her like it is my own."

Abram obeyed his wife Sarai. ³This was after Abram lived ten years in the land of Canaan. And Sarai gave Hagar to her husband Abram. (Hagar was her servant from Egypt.)

⁴Hagar became pregnant from Abram. When Hagar saw this, she became very proud and began to feel that she was better than Sarai her master. ⁵But Sarai said to Abram, "My servant now hates me. And I blame you for this. I gave her to you. She became pregnant. And then she began to feel that she is better than I am. I want the Lord to judge which of us is right."

⁶But Abram said to Sarai, "Hagar is your slave. You can do anything you want to her." So Sarai was mean to her servant Hagar, and Hagar ran away.

Ur of Babylonia Literally, "Ur of the Chaldeans." A city in southern Babylonia.

column of smoke and fire A sign that God used to show that he was with his people.

passed between the halves of the dead animals This showed that God "signed" or "sealed" the agreement he made with Abraham. In those days, a person making an agreement showed he was sincere by walking between the cut animals and saying something like, "May this same thing happen to me if I don't keep the agreement."

River of Egypt That is, the stream called, "Wadi El Arish."

Hagar's Son Ishmael

⁷The Angel of the Lord found Hagar near a pool of water in the desert. The pool was by the road to Shur. ⁸The Angel said, "Hagar, you are Sarai's servant. Why are you here? Where are you going?"

Hagar said, "I am running away from Sarai."

⁹The Angel of the Lord said to Hagar, "Sarai is your master. Go home to her and obey her." ¹⁰The Angel of the Lord also said to Hagar, "From you will come many people. There will be so many people that they cannot be counted."

¹¹The Angel of the Lord also said,

"Hagar, you are now pregnant,
and you will have a son.
You will name him Ishmael,*
because the Lord has heard
that you were treated badly,
⌐and he will help you⌐.
¹² "Ishmael will be wild and free,
like a wild donkey.
He will be against everyone.
And everyone will be against him.
He will move from place to place
and camp near his brothers,
but he will be against them."

¹³The Lord talked to Hagar. Hagar began to use a new name for God. She said to him, "You are 'God Who Sees Me.'" She said this because she thought, "I see that even in this place God sees me and cares for me!" ¹⁴So that well was called Beer Lahai Roi.* That well is between Kadesh and Bered.

¹⁵Hagar gave birth to Abram's son. And Abram named the son Ishmael. ¹⁶Abram was 86 years old when Ishmael was born from Hagar.

Circumcision—Proof of the Agreement

17 When Abram was 99 years old, the Lord appeared to him. The Lord said, "I am God All-Powerful.* Do these things for me: Obey me and live the right way. ²If you do this, I will prepare an agreement between us. I will promise to make your people a great nation."

³Then Abram bowed down before God. God said to him, ⁴"This is my part of our agreement: I will make you the father of many nations. ⁵I will change your name. Your name will not be Abram*—your name will be Abraham.* I give you this name because I am making you the father of many nations. ⁶I will give you a many, many descendants. New nations and kings will come from you. ⁷And I will prepare an agreement between you and me. This agreement will also be for all your descendants.* This agreement will continue forever. I will be your God and the God of all your descendants. ⁸And I will give this land to you and to all your descendants. I will give you the land you are traveling through—the land of Canaan. I will give you this land forever. And I will be your God."

⁹And God said to Abraham, "Now, this is your part of the agreement. You and all your descendants* will obey my agreement. ¹⁰This is the agreement that you will obey. This is the agreement between you and me. This is for all your descendants: Every boy that is born must be circumcised.* ¹¹You will cut the skin to show that you follow the agreement between me and you. ¹²When the baby boy is eight days old, you will circumcise him. Every boy born among your people and every boy that is a slave of your people must be circumcised. ¹³So every baby boy in your nation will be circumcised. Every boy that is born from your family or bought as a slave will be circumcised. ¹⁴⌐Abraham, this is the agreement between you and me:⌐ Any male that is not circumcised will be cut off from his people.* Why? Because that person has broken my agreement."

Isaac—The Promised Son

¹⁵God said to Abraham, "I will give Sarai,* your wife, a new name. Her new name will be

---

Ishmael This name means "God hears."
Beer Lahai Roi This means "The well of the Living One who sees me."
God All-Powerful Literally, "El Shaddai."
Abram This means "honored father."
Abraham This means "great father" or "father of many."
descendant(s) A person's children and their future families.
circumcise(d) Cutting the foreskin from a man. In Israel this was proof that a man had made a special agreement to obey God's laws and teachings.
cut off from his people This means a person must be separated from his family and lose his share of the inheritance.
Sarai A name, probably Aramaic, meaning "princess."

Sarah.* ¹⁶I will bless her. I will give her a son, and you will be the father. She will be the mother of many new nations. Kings of nations will come from her."

¹⁷Abraham bowed his face to the ground ⌊to show he respected God⌋. But he laughed and said to himself, "I am 100 years old. I can't have a son. And Sarah is 90 years old. She can't have a child."

¹⁸Then Abraham said to God, "I hope Ishmael will live and serve you."

¹⁹God said, "No! I said that your wife Sarah will have a son. You will name him Isaac.* I will make my agreement with him. That agreement will be an agreement that continues forever with all his descendants.*

²⁰"You mentioned Ishmael, and I heard you. I will bless him. He will have many children. He will be the father of twelve great leaders. His family will become a great nation. ²¹But I will make my agreement with Isaac. Isaac will be the son that Sarah will have. This son will be born at this same time next year."

²²After God finished talking with Abraham, God went up ⌊into heaven⌋. ²³⌊God had told Abraham to circumcise* all the men and boys in his family.⌋ So Abraham gathered Ishmael and all the slaves born in his house together. Abraham also gathered together the slaves that were bought with money. Every man and boy in Abraham's house was gathered together, and they were all circumcised. Abraham circumcised them that day, just like God told him.

²⁴Abraham was 99 years old when he was circumcised. ²⁵And Ishmael, his son, was 13 years old when he was circumcised. ²⁶Abraham and his son were circumcised on that same day. ²⁷Also, on that day all the men in Abraham's house were circumcised. All the slaves born in his house and all the slaves that he had bought were circumcised.

The Three Visitors

18 Later, the Lord again appeared to Abraham. Abraham was living near the oak trees of Mamre. One day, at the hottest part of the day, Abraham was sitting at the door of his tent. ²Abraham looked up and saw three men standing in front of him. When Abraham saw the men, he ran to them and bowed before them. ³Abraham said, "Sirs,* please stay awhile with me, your servant. ⁴I will bring some water to wash your feet. You can rest under the trees. ⁵I will get some food for you, and you can eat as much as you want. Then you can continue your journey."

The three men said, "That is fine. We will do as you say."

⁶Abraham hurried to the tent. Abraham said to Sarah, "Quickly, prepare enough wheat for three loaves of bread." ⁷Then Abraham ran to his cattle. Abraham took his best young calf. Abraham gave the calf to the servant. Abraham told the servant to hurry, kill the calf, and prepare it for food. ⁸Abraham brought the meat and some milk and cheese and set them down in front of the three men. Then Abraham stood near the men ⌊ready to serve them⌋ while they sat under the tree and ate.

⁹Then the men said to Abraham, "Where is your wife Sarah?"

Abraham said, "She is there, in the tent."

¹⁰Then the Lord said, "I will come again in the spring. At that time, your wife Sarah will have a son."

Sarah was listening in the tent and heard these things. ¹¹Abraham and Sarah were very old. Sarah was past the right age for women to have children. ¹²So Sarah ⌊did not believe what she heard. She⌋ laughed to herself and said, "I am old and my husband is old. I am too old to have a baby."

¹³Then the Lord said to Abraham, "Sarah laughed and said she was too old to have a baby. ¹⁴Is anything too hard for the Lord? No! I will come again in the spring when I said I would. And your wife Sarah will have a son."

¹⁵But Sarah said, "I didn't laugh!" (She said this because she was afraid.)

But the Lord said, "No. I know that is not true. You did laugh!"

¹⁶Then the men got up to leave. They looked toward Sodom ⌊and began walking in that direction⌋. Abraham walked with them to send them on their way.

Sarah A Hebrew name meaning "princess."
Isaac This name means "he laughs."
descendant(s) A person's children and their future families.
circumcise(d) Cutting the foreskin from a man. In Israel this was proof that a man had made a special agreement to obey God's laws and teachings.

Sirs This Hebrew word can mean "sirs" or "Lord." This might show that these were not ordinary men.

Abraham's Bargain With God

¹⁷The Lord said to himself, "Should I tell Abraham the thing that I will now do? ¹⁸Abraham will become a great and powerful nation. And all the people on earth will be blessed because of him. ¹⁹I have made a special agreement with Abraham. I did this so he would command his children and his descendants* to live the way the Lord wants them to. I did this so they would live right and be fair. Then I, the Lord, can give him the things I promised."

²⁰Then the Lord said, "I have heard many times that the people of Sodom and Gomorrah are very evil. ²¹So I will go and see if things are as bad as I have heard. Then I will know for sure."

²²So the men turned and started walking toward Sodom. But Abraham stood there before the Lord. ²³Then Abraham approached the Lord and asked, "Lord, do you plan to destroy the good people while you are destroying the evil people? ²⁴What if there are 50 good people in that city? Will you still destroy the city? Surely you will save the city for the 50 good people living there. ²⁵Surely you would not destroy the city. You would not destroy 50 good people to kill the evil people. If that happened, then good people and evil people would be the same—they would both be punished. You are the judge of all the earth. I know you will do the right thing."

²⁶Then the Lord said, "If I find 50 good people in the city of Sodom, I will save the whole city."

²⁷Then Abraham said, "Compared to you, Lord, I am only dust and ashes. But let me bother you again and ask you this question: ²⁸What if five good people are missing? What if there are only 45 good people in the city? Will you destroy a whole city for just five people?"

The Lord said, "If I find 45 good people there, I will not destroy the city."

²⁹Abraham spoke again. He said, "And if you find only 40 good people there, will you destroy the city?"

The Lord said, "If I find 40 good people, I will not destroy the city."

³⁰Then Abraham said, "Lord, please don't be angry with me. Let me ask you this: If only 30 good people are in the city, will you destroy the city?"

The Lord said, "If I find 30 good people there, I will not destroy the city."

³¹Then Abraham said, "May I bother my Lord again and ask, what if there are 20 good people?"

The Lord answered, "If I find 20 good people, I will not destroy the city."

³²Then Abraham said, "Lord, please don't be angry with me, but let me bother you this one last time. If you find ten good people there, what will you do?"

The Lord said, "If I find ten good people in the city, I will not destroy it."

³³The Lord was finished speaking to Abraham, so the Lord left. And Abraham went back to his home.

Lot's Visitors

19 That evening the two angels came to the city of Sodom. Lot was sitting near the city gates and saw the angels. ₍Lot thought they were men traveling through town.₎ Lot got up and went to them and bowed down on the ground. ²Lot said, "Sirs, please come to my house, and I will serve you. There you can wash your feet and stay the night. Then tomorrow you can continue your journey."

The angels answered, "No, we will stay the night in the square.*"

³But Lot continued to ask them to come to his house. So the angels agreed to go to Lot's house. They went to Lot's house. Lot gave them something to drink. Lot cooked some bread for the angels, and they ate it.

⁴That evening, just before bedtime, men from every part of town came to Lot's house. The men from Sodom stood around the house and called to Lot. They said, ⁵"Where are the two men *(angels)* that came to you tonight? Bring them out to us. We want to have sex with them."

⁶Lot went outside, and closed the door behind him. ⁷Lot said to the men, "No! Friends, I beg you, please don't do this evil thing! ⁸Look, I have two daughters who have never slept with a man before. I will give my daughters to you. You can do anything you want with them. But please don't do anything to these men. These men have come to my house, and I must protect them.*

---

square An open area in a city near the city gates. Travelers often camped there when they came to town.

I must protect them If a person invited a traveler to stay with him, then he was also promising to protect the traveler. So Lot was trying to protect these men, even if it meant that he might lose his own daughters.

---

descendant(s) A person's children and their future families.

⁹The men surrounding the house answered, "Move out of the way!" Then the men said to themselves, "This man Lot came to our city as a visitor. Now he wants to tell us how we should live!" Then the men said to Lot, "We will do worse things to you than to them." So the men started moving closer and closer to Lot. They were about to break down the door. ¹⁰But the two men staying with Lot opened the door, pulled Lot back inside the house, and closed the door. ¹¹Then they did something to the men outside the door—they caused all those evil men, young and old, to become blind. So the men trying to get in the house could not find the door.

The Escape From Sodom

¹²The two men said to Lot, "Are there any other people from your family living in this city? Do you have any sons-in-law, sons, daughters, or any other people from your family here? If so, then you should tell them to leave now. ¹³We are going to destroy this city. The Lord heard how evil this city is, so he sent us to destroy it."

¹⁴So Lot went out and spoke to his sons-in-law, the men who had married his ₍other₎ daughters. Lot said, "Hurry and leave this city! The Lord will soon destroy it!" But those men thought Lot was joking.

¹⁵The next morning at dawn, the angels were trying to make Lot hurry. They said, "This city will be punished. So take your wife and your two daughters who are still with you and leave this place. Then you will not be destroyed with the city."

¹⁶But Lot was confused ₍and did not hurry to leave₎. So the two men (*angels*) held the hands of Lot and his wife and his two daughters. The two men led Lot and his family out of the city safely. The Lord was kind to Lot and his family. ¹⁷So the two men brought Lot and his family out of the city. After they were out, one of the men said, "Now run to save your life! Don't look back at the city. And don't stop any place in the valley. Run until you are in the mountains. If you stop, then you will be destroyed with the city!"

¹⁸But Lot said to the two men, "Sirs, please don't force me to run so far! ¹⁹You have been very kind to me, your servant. You have been very kind to save me. But I can't run all the way to the mountains. What if I am too slow and something happens? I will be killed! ²⁰Look, there is a very small town near here. Let me run to that town. I can run to that town and be safe."

²¹The angel said to Lot, "Fine. I'll let you do that. I won't destroy that town. ²²But run there fast. I can't destroy Sodom until you are safely in that town." (That town is named Zoar,* because it is a small town.)

Sodom and Gomorrah Destroyed

²³Lot was entering Zoar just as the sun was coming up. ²⁴At the same time, the Lord began to destroy Sodom and Gomorrah. The Lord caused fire and burning sulfur to fall out of the sky from the Lord. ²⁵So the Lord destroyed those cities. The Lord destroyed the whole valley—all the plants and all the people living in the cities.

²⁶While they were running away, Lot's wife looked back at the city and became a block of salt.

²⁷Early that same morning, Abraham got up and went to the place where he stood before the Lord. ²⁸Abraham looked down toward the cities of Sodom and Gomorrah. Abraham looked at all the land in the valley. Abraham saw much smoke rising from the land. It looked like smoke from a very big fire.

²⁹God destroyed the cities in the valley. But when God did this, he remembered Abraham ₍and did not destroy Abraham's nephew₎. Lot had been living among the cities in the valley. But God sent Lot away from there before he destroyed those cities.

Lot and His Daughters

³⁰Lot was afraid to stay in Zoar. So he and his two daughters went to live in the mountains. They lived in a cave there. ³¹One day the older daughter said to the younger, "Everywhere on the earth, men and women marry ₍and have a family₎. But our father is old and there are no men around here to give us children. ³²So let's get our father drunk with wine. Then we can have sexual relations with him. That way we can use our father to keep our family alive!"

³³That night the two girls went to their father and got him drunk with wine. Then the older daughter went into her father's bed and had sexual relations with him. Lot ₍was so drunk₎ that he did not even know when she came to bed or when she got up.

³⁴The next day, the older daughter said to the younger daughter, "Last night I went to bed with my father. Let's get him drunk with wine again tonight. Then you can go into his bed and have

Zoar This name means "small."

sex with him. In this way we can use our father to have children and our family will not come to an end." ³⁵So that night the two girls got their father drunk with wine. Then the younger daughter went into his bed and had sexual relations with him. Again, Lot ⌊was so drunk⌋ that he did not know when she came to bed or when she got up.

³⁶Both of Lot's daughters became pregnant. Their father was the father of their babies. ³⁷The older daughter gave birth to a son. She named him Moab.* Moab is the father of all the Moabite people living today. ³⁸The younger daughter also gave birth to a son. She named him Ben-Ammi.* Ben-Ammi is the father of all the Ammonite people living today.

Abraham Goes to Gerar

20 Abraham left that place and traveled to the Negev.* Abraham settled in the city of Gerar, between Kadesh and Shur. While in Gerar, ²Abraham told people that Sarah was his sister. Abimelech, king of Gerar, heard this. Abimelech wanted Sarah, so he sent some servants to take her. ³But one night, God spoke to Abimelech in a dream. God said, "You will die. That woman you took is married."

⁴But Abimelech had not yet slept with Sarah. So Abimelech said, "Lord, I am not guilty. Would you kill an innocent person? ⁵Abraham himself told me, 'This woman is my sister.' And the woman also said, 'This man is my brother.' I am innocent. I did not know what I was doing."

⁶Then God said to Abimelech in a dream, "Yes, I know that you are innocent. And I know that you did not know what you were doing. I saved you. I did not allow you to sin against me. I was the One who did not allow you to sleep with her. ⁷So give Abraham his wife again. Abraham is a prophet.* He will pray for you, and you will live. But if you do not give Sarah back to Abraham, then I promise that you will die. And all your family will die with you."

⁸So very early the next morning, Abimelech called all his servants and told them about the dream. The servants were scared. ⁹Then Abimelech called Abraham and said to him, "Why have you done this to us? What wrong did I do against you? Why did you lie and say that she was your sister? You brought much trouble to my kingdom. You should not have done these things to me. ¹⁰What were you afraid of? Why did you do these things to me?"

¹¹Then Abraham said, "⌊I was afraid.⌋ I thought no one in this place respected God. I thought someone would kill me to get Sarah. ¹²She is my wife, but she is also my sister. She is the daughter of my father, but not the daughter of my mother. ¹³God led me away from my father's house. God led me to wander to many different places. When that happened, I told Sarah, 'Do something for me; wherever we go, tell people you are my sister.'"

¹⁴⌊Then Abimelech understood what had happened.⌋ So Abimelech gave Sarah back to Abraham. Abimelech also gave Abraham some sheep, cattle, and slaves. ¹⁵And Abimelech said, "Look all around you. This is my land. You may live any place you want."

¹⁶Abimelech said to Sarah, "I gave your brother Abraham 1,000 pieces of silver. I did this to show that I am sorry for all these things. I want everyone to see that I did the right thing."

¹⁷⁻¹⁸The Lord made all the women in Abimelech's family not able to have children. God did this because Abimelech had taken Sarah, Abraham's wife. But Abraham prayed to God, and God healed Abimelech, his wife, and his servant girls.

Finally, a Baby for Sarah

21 The Lord kept the promise he had made to Sarah. The Lord did for Sarah what he had promised. ²Sarah became pregnant and gave birth to a son for Abraham in his old age. All these things happened exactly like God promised. ³Sarah gave birth to a son, and Abraham named him Isaac.* ⁴Abraham circumcised* Isaac when Isaac was eight days old like God had commanded.

⁵Abraham was 100 years old when his son Isaac* was born. ⁶And Sarah said, "God has made me happy. Every person who hears about this will be happy with me. ⁷No one thought that I, Sarah,

---

Moab In Hebrew, this name sounds like "From father."
Ben-Ammi In Hebrew, this name sounds like "Son of my father" or "Son of my people."
Negev The desert area in the southern part of Judah.
prophet A person God called to speak for him.

Isaac This name means "he laughs" or "he is happy."
circumcise(d) Cutting the foreskin from a man. In Israel this was proof that a man had made a special agreement to obey God's laws and teachings.

would be able to have Abraham's child. But I have given Abraham a son even though he is old."

Trouble at Home

⁸Isaac continued to grow. Soon he was old enough to begin eating solid food. So Abraham gave a big party. ⁹Hagar was the Egyptian slave woman who had had Abraham's first son. Sarah saw Hagar's son playing. ₍Sarah became upset.₎ ¹⁰Sarah said to Abraham, "Get rid of that slave woman and her son. Send them away! When we die, our son Isaac will get everything we have. I don't want that slave woman's son sharing those things with my son Isaac!"

¹¹This upset Abraham very much. He was worried about his son ₍Ishmael₎. ¹²But God said to Abraham, "Don't worry about the boy and the slave woman. Do what Sarah wants. Isaac will be your only heir.* ¹³But I will also bless the son of your slave woman. He is your son, so I will make a great nation from his family also."

¹⁴Early the next morning, Abraham got some food and some water. Abraham gave these things to Hagar. Hagar carried these things and left with her boy. Hagar left that place and wandered in the desert of Beersheba.

¹⁵After some time, all the water was gone. There was none left to drink. So Hagar put her son under a bush. ¹⁶Hagar walked a short distance away. Then she stopped and sat down. Hagar thought her son would die because there was no water. She did not want to watch him die. She sat there and began to cry.

¹⁷God heard the boy crying. And God's angel called to Hagar from heaven. He said, "What is wrong, Hagar? Don't be afraid! The Lord has heard the boy crying there. ¹⁸Go help the boy. Hold his hand and lead him. I will make him the father of many, many people."

¹⁹Then God allowed Hagar to see a well of water. So Hagar went to the well and filled her bag with water. Then she gave water to the boy to drink.

²⁰God continued to be with the boy while he grew up. Ishmael lived in the desert and became a hunter. He learned to shoot a bow very well. ²¹His mother found a wife for him in Egypt. They continued living in the Paran desert.

Abraham's Bargain With Abimelech

²²Then Abimelech and Phicol spoke with Abraham. Phicol was the commander of Abimelech's army. They said to Abraham, "God is with you in everything you do. ²³So make a promise to me here before God. Promise that you will be fair with me and with my children. Promise that you will be kind to me and the country here where you have lived. Promise you will be as kind to me as I have been to you."

²⁴And Abraham said, "I promise to treat you the same way you have treated me." ²⁵Then Abraham complained to Abimelech. Abraham complained because Abimelech's servants had captured a well of water.

²⁶But Abimelech said, "I don't know who has done this thing. You never told me about this before today!"

²⁷So Abraham and Abimelech made an agreement. Abraham gave Abimelech some sheep and cattle as proof of the agreement. ²⁸Abraham also put seven* female lambs in front of Abimelech.

²⁹Abimelech asked Abraham, "Why did you put these seven female lambs by themselves?"

³⁰Abraham answered, "When you accept these lambs from me, it will be proof that I dug this well."

³¹So after that, the well was called Beersheba.* He gave the well this name because it was the place where they made a promise to each other.

³²So Abraham and Abimelech made an agreement at Beersheba. Then Abimelech and his military commander went back to the country of the Philistines.

³³Abraham planted a special tree at Beersheba. At that place, Abraham prayed to the Lord, the God who lives forever. ³⁴And Abraham stayed a long time in the country of the Philistines.

Abraham, Kill Your Son!

22 After those things, God decided to test Abraham's faith. God said to him, "Abraham!"

And Abraham said, "Yes!"

---

heir A person who receives his parents' property when they die.

seven The Hebrew word for "seven" is like the Hebrew word for "oath" or "promise" and it is like the last part of the name Beersheba. The seven animals were proof of this promise.
Beersheba This name means "well of the oath."
sacrifice(s) A gift to God. Usually it was a special animal that was killed and burned on an altar.

²Then God said, "Take your son to the land of Moriah. At Moriah kill your son as a sacrifice* for me. This must be Isaac, your only son—the son you love. Use him as a burnt offering on one of the mountains there. I will tell you which mountain."

³In the morning Abraham got up and saddled his donkey. Abraham took Isaac and two servants with him. Abraham cut the wood for the sacrifice.* Then they went to the place God told them to go. ⁴After they traveled three days, Abraham looked up and in the distance, he saw the place they were going to. ⁵Then Abraham said to his servants, "Stay here with the donkey. I will take my son and go to that place and worship. Then we will come back to you later."

⁶Abraham took the wood for the sacrifice* and put it on his son's shoulder. Abraham took the special knife and fire. Then both Abraham and his son went together to the place for worship.

⁷Isaac said to his father Abraham, "Father!"

Abraham answered, "Yes, son."

Isaac said, "I see the wood and the fire. But where is the lamb we will burn as a sacrifice*?"

⁸Abraham answered, "God himself is providing the lamb for the sacrifice,* my son."

Isaac Is Saved

So both Abraham and his son went together to that place. ⁹They came to the place where God told them to go. There, Abraham built an altar.* Abraham laid the wood on the altar. Then Abraham tied his son Isaac. Abraham laid Isaac on the altar on the wood. ¹⁰Then Abraham took his knife and prepared to kill his son.

¹¹But then the Angel of the Lord stopped Abraham. The angel called from heaven and said, "Abraham, Abraham!"

Abraham answered, "Yes."

¹²The angel said, "Don't kill your son or hurt him in any way. Now I can see that you do respect and obey God. I see that you are ready to kill your son, your only son, for me."

¹³Then Abraham saw a ram. The ram's horns were caught in a bush. So Abraham went and got the ram and killed it. Abraham used the ram as a sacrifice* to God. Abraham's son was saved. ¹⁴So Abraham gave that place a name, "Yahweh Yireh."* Even today people say, "On this mountain, the Lord can be seen."

¹⁵The Angel of the Lord called to Abraham from heaven a second time. ¹⁶The angel said, "You were ready to kill your son for me. This was your only son. Because you did this for me, I make you this promise: I, the Lord, promise that ¹⁷I will truly bless you. I will give you many, many descendants,* as many as the stars in the sky. There will be as many people as sand on the seashore. And your people will defeat all their enemies. ¹⁸Every nation on the earth will be blessed through your descendants.* I will do this because you obeyed me."

¹⁹Then Abraham went back to his servants. They all traveled back to Beersheba and Abraham stayed there.

²⁰After all these things happened, a message was sent to Abraham. The message said, "Your brother Nahor and his wife Milcah have children now. ²¹The first son is Uz. The second son is Buz. The third son is Kemuel, the father of Aram. ²²Then there are Kesed, Hazo, Pildash, Jidlaph, and Bethuel." ²³Bethuel was the father of Rebekah. Milcah was the mother of these eight sons, and Nahor was the father. Nahor was Abraham's brother. ²⁴Also Nahor had four other sons from his woman servant* Reumah. The sons were Tebah, Gaham, Tahash, and Maacah.

Sarah Dies

23 Sarah lived to be 127 years old. ²She died in the city of Kiriath Arba (Hebron) in the land of Canaan. Abraham was very sad and cried for her there. ³Then Abraham left his dead wife and went to talk to the Hittite people. He said, ⁴"I am only a traveler staying in your country. I have no place to bury my wife. Please give me some land so I can bury my wife."

⁵The Hittite people answered Abraham, ⁶"Sir, you are one of God's great leaders among us. You can have the best place we have to bury your dead. You can have any of our burying places that

---

sacrifice(s) A gift to God. Usually it was a special animal that was killed and burned on an altar.

altar(s) A stone table used for burning sacrifices that were offered as gifts to God.

Yahweh Yireh Or, "Jehovah Jireh." This means "the Lord sees" or "the Lord gives."

descendant(s) A person's children and their future families.

descendants Or "Descendant." See Paul's discussion in Gal 3:16.

woman servant Literally, "concubine." A slave woman who was like a wife to a man.

you want. None of us will stop you from burying your wife there."

⁷Abraham got up and bowed to the people. ⁸Abraham said to them, "If you truly want to help me bury my dead wife, then speak to Ephron the son of Zohar for me. ⁹I would like to buy the cave of Machpelah. Ephron owns this. It is at the end of his field. I will pay him the full price—all that it is worth. I want all of you to be witnesses that I am buying it as a burial place."

¹⁰Ephron was sitting there among the people. Ephron answered Abraham, ¹¹"No, sir. Here, in front of all my people, I give you that land and the cave on it so you can bury your wife."

¹²Abraham bowed before the Hittite people. ¹³Abraham said to Ephron before all the people, "But I want to pay you the full price for the field. Accept my money, and I will bury my dead."

¹⁴Ephron answered Abraham, ¹⁵"Sir, listen to me. 10 pounds* of silver means nothing to you and me! Take the land, and bury your dead wife."

¹⁶Abraham understood that Ephron was telling him the price of the land.* So Abraham paid him for the land. Abraham weighed 10 pounds* of silver for Ephron and gave it to the merchant.*

¹⁷⁻¹⁸So the field of Ephron changed owners. This field was in Machpelah, east of Mamre. Abraham became the owner of the field, the cave on the field, and all the trees that were on that field. All the people in the city saw the agreement between Ephron and Abraham. ¹⁹After this, Abraham buried Sarah his wife in the cave of that field near Mamre (Hebron) in the land of Canaan. ²⁰Abraham bought the field and the cave on it from the Hittite people. This became his property, and he used it as a burying place.

A Wife for Isaac

24 Abraham lived to be a very old man. The Lord blessed Abraham and everything that he did. ²Abraham's oldest servant was in charge of everything Abraham owned. Abraham called that servant to him and said, "Put your hand under my leg.* ³Now I want you to make a promise to me. Promise to me before the Lord, the God of heaven and earth, that you will not allow my son to marry a girl from Canaan. We live among those people but don't let him marry a Canaanite girl. ⁴Go back to my country to my own people. There find a wife for my son Isaac and bring her here to him."

⁵The servant said to him, "Maybe this woman will not want to come back with me to this land. If that happens, should I take your son with me to your homeland?"

⁶Abraham said to him, "No! Don't take my son to that place. ⁷The Lord, the God of heaven, brought me from my homeland to this place. That place was the home of my father and the home of my family. But the Lord promised that this new land here would belong to my family. May the Lord send his angel before you so you can choose a wife for my son. ⁸But if the girl refuses to come with you, then you will be free from this promise. But you must not take my son back to that place."

⁹So the servant put his hand under his master's leg and made the promise.

The Search Begins

¹⁰The servant took ten of Abraham's camels and left that place. The servant carried with him many different kinds of beautiful gifts. The servant went to Mesopotamia to Nahor's city. ¹¹The servant went to the water well outside the city. It was in the evening when the women come out to get water. The servant made the camels kneel down there.

¹²The servant said, "Lord, you are the God of my master Abraham. Allow me to find a wife for his son today. Please show this kindness to my master Abraham. ¹³Here I am, standing by this well of water, and the young women from the city are coming out to get water. ¹⁴I am waiting for a special sign to know which is the right young woman for Isaac. ₍This is the special sign:₎ I will say to the girl, 'Please put your jar down so I can drink.' I will know if she is the right young woman if she says, 'Drink, and I will also give water to your camels.' If that happens, then you will have proved that she is the right young woman for Isaac. And I will know you have shown kindness to my master."

A Wife Is Found

¹⁵Then, before the servant finished praying, a young woman named Rebekah came to the well.

---

10 pounds Literally, "400 shekels."
Abraham understood ... the price of the land Literally, "Abraham heard."
merchant A person who earns his living buying and selling things. Here this is probably a person who was helping Abraham and Ephron write the contract in verses 17 and 18.
Put your hand under my leg This showed that this was a very important promise and that Abraham trusted his servant to keep it.

Rebekah was the daughter of Bethuel. Bethuel was the son of Milcah and Nahor, Abraham's brother. Rebekah came to the well with her water jar on her shoulder. ¹⁶She was very pretty. She was a virgin; she had never slept with a man. She went down to the well and filled her jar. ¹⁷Then the servant ran to her and said, "Please give me a little water to drink from your jar."

¹⁸Rebekah quickly lowered the jar from her shoulder and gave him a drink. Rebekah said, "Drink this, sir." ¹⁹As soon as she finished giving him something to drink, Rebekah said, "I will also pour some water for your camels." ²⁰So Rebekah quickly poured all the water from her jar into the drinking trough for the camels. Then she ran to the well to get more water. And she gave water to all the camels.

²¹The servant quietly watched her. He wanted to be sure that the Lord had given him an answer and had made his trip successful. ²²After the camels finished drinking, he gave Rebekah a gold ring that weighed 1/4 ounce.* He also gave her two gold arm bracelets that weighed 5 ounces* each. ²³The servant asked, "Who is your father? And is there a place in your father's house for my group to sleep?"

²⁴Rebekah answered, "My father is Bethuel, the son of Milcah and Nahor." ²⁵Then she said, "And yes, we have straw for your camels and a place for you to sleep."

²⁶The servant bowed and worshiped the Lord. ²⁷The servant said, "Blessed is the Lord, the God of my master Abraham. The Lord has been kind and loyal to my master. The Lord has led me to the right girl for my master's son."

²⁸Then Rebekah ran and told her family about all these things. ²⁹⁻³⁰Rebekah had a brother. His name was Laban. Rebekah told about the things the man had said to her. Laban was listening to her. And when Laban saw the ring and the bracelets on his sister's arms, he ran out to the well. And there the man was—standing by the camels at the well. ³¹Laban said, "Sir, you are welcome to come in!* You don't have to stand outside here. I have prepared a room for you to sleep in and a place for your camels."

³²So Abraham's servant went into the house. Laban helped him with the camels and gave him straw for the camels to eat. Then Laban gave him water so he and the other men with him could wash their feet. ³³Then Laban gave him food to eat. But the servant refused to eat. He said, "I will not eat until I have told you why I came."

So Laban said, "Then tell us."

Bargaining for Rebekah

³⁴The servant said, "I am Abraham's servant. ³⁵The Lord has greatly blessed my master in everything. My master has become a great man. The Lord has given Abraham many flocks of sheep and herds of cattle. Abraham has much silver and gold and many servants. Abraham has many camels and donkeys. ³⁶Sarah was my master's wife. When she was very old, she gave birth to a son. And my master has given everything he owns to that son. ³⁷My master forced me to make a promise to him. My master said to me, 'You must not allow my son to marry a girl from Canaan. We live among those people, but I don't want him to marry one of the Canaanite girls. ³⁸So you must promise to go to my father's country. Go to my family and choose a wife for my son.' ³⁹I said to my master, 'Maybe the woman will not come back to this place with me.' ⁴⁰But my master said to me, 'I serve the Lord, and the Lord will send his angel with you and help you. You will find a wife for my son among my people there. ⁴¹But if you go to my father's country, and they refuse to give you a wife for my son, then you will be free from this promise.'

⁴²"Today I came to this well and said, 'Lord, God of my master Abraham, please make my trip successful. ⁴³I will stand by this well and wait for a young woman to come to get water. Then I will say; Please give me water from your jar to drink. ⁴⁴The right young woman will answer in a special way. She will say; Drink this water, and I will also get water for your camels. That way I will know that she is the woman the Lord has chosen for my master's son.'

⁴⁵"Before I finished praying, Rebekah came out to the well to get water. She had her water jar on her shoulder as she went to get water from the well. I asked her to give me some water. ⁴⁶She quickly lowered the jar from her shoulder and poured me some water. Then she said, 'Drink this and I'll get some water for your camels.' So I drank the water, and she gave water to my camels. ⁴⁷Then I asked her, 'Who is your father?' She answered, 'My father is Bethuel the son of Milcah

---

1/4 ounce Literally, "one beka."
5 ounces Literally, "five measures."
Sir ,you are welcome to come in Literally, "Come in, blessed of the Lord!"

and Nahor.' Then I gave her the ring and bracelets for her arms. ⁴⁸I bowed my head and thanked the Lord. I blessed the Lord, the God of my master Abraham. I thanked him for leading me straight to the granddaughter of my master's brother. ⁴⁹Now, tell me, will you be kind and loyal to my master and give him your daughter? Or will you refuse to give him your daughter? Tell me so I will know what I should do."

⁵⁰Then Laban and Bethuel answered, "We see this is from the Lord, so there is nothing we can say to change it. ⁵¹Here is Rebekah. Take her and go. Let her marry your master's son. This is what the Lord wants."

⁵²When Abraham's servant heard this, he bowed to the ground before the Lord. ⁵³Then he gave Rebekah the gifts he brought. He gave her beautiful clothes and gold and silver jewelry. He also gave expensive gifts to her mother and brother. ⁵⁴Then he and his men had something to eat and drink and then spent the night there. Early the next morning, they got up and said, "Now we must go back to my master."

⁵⁵Rebekah's mother and her brother said, "Let Rebekah stay with us for a short time. Let her stay with us ten days. After that she can go."

⁵⁶But the servant said to them, "Do not make me wait. The Lord has made my trip successful. Now let me go back to my master."

⁵⁷Rebekah's brother and mother said, "We will call Rebekah and ask her what she wants." ⁵⁸They called Rebekah and asked her, "Do you want to go with this man now?"

Rebekah said, "Yes, I will go."

⁵⁹So they allowed Rebekah to go with Abraham's servant and his men. Rebekah's nurse also went with them. ⁶⁰While Rebekah was leaving they said to her,

> "Our sister, may you be the mother of millions of people.
> And may your descendants* defeat their enemies and take their cities."

⁶¹Then Rebekah and her nurse got on the camels and followed the servant and his men. So the servant took Rebekah and left on the trip back home.

⁶²Isaac had left Beer Lahai Roi and was now living in the Negev.* ⁶³One evening, Isaac went out to the field to think.* Isaac looked up and saw the camels coming from far away.

⁶⁴Rebekah looked and saw Isaac. Then she jumped down from the camel. ⁶⁵She said to the servant, "Who is that young man walking in the field to meet us?"

The servant said, "That is my master's son." So Rebekah covered her face with her veil.

⁶⁶The servant told Isaac about all the things that had happened. ⁶⁷Then Isaac brought the girl into his mother's tent. Rebekah became Isaac's wife that day. Isaac loved her very much. So Isaac was comforted after his mother's death.

Abraham's Family

25 Abraham married again. His new wife was named Keturah. ²Keturah gave birth to Zimran, Jokshan, Medan, Midian, Ishbak, and Shuah. ³Jokshan was the father of Sheba and Dedan. The people of Asshur,* Leum, and Letush were descendants of Dedan. ⁴The sons of Midian were Ephah, Epher, Hanoch, Abida, and Eldaah. All these sons came from the marriage of Abraham and Keturah. ⁵⁻⁶Before Abraham died, he gave some gifts to the sons of his women servants* and sent those sons to the East.* He sent them away from Isaac. Then Abraham gave everything he owned to Isaac.

⁷Abraham lived to be 175 years old. ⁸Then Abraham grew weak and died. He had lived a long and satisfying life. He died and was gathered to his people. ⁹His sons Isaac and Ishmael buried him in the cave of Machpelah. This cave is in the field of Ephron, the son of Zohar. It was east of Mamre. ¹⁰This is the same cave that Abraham bought from the Hittite people. Abraham was buried there with his wife Sarah. ¹¹After Abraham died, God blessed Isaac. And Isaac continued to live at Beer Lahai Roi.

¹²This is the list of Ishmael's family. Ishmael was Abraham and Hagar's son. (Hagar was Sarah's Egyptian maid.) ¹³These are the names of Ishmael's sons: The first son was Nebaioth, then

---

descendant(s) A person's children and their future families.
Negev The desert area in the southern part of Judah.
think Or, "to go for a stroll."
Asshur Or, "Assyria."
woman servant Or, "concubine," a slave woman who was like a wife to a man.
East This usually means the area between the Tigris and Euphrates rivers as far east as the Persian Gulf.

Kedar was born, then Adbeel, Mibsam, ¹⁴Mishma, Dumah, Massa, ¹⁵Hadad, Tema, Jetur, Naphish, and Kedemah. ¹⁶Those were the names of Ishmael's sons. Each son had his own camp that became a small town. The twelve sons were like twelve princes with their own people. ¹⁷Ishmael lived to be 137 years old. Then he died and was gathered to his ancestors.* ¹⁸Ishmael's descendants* camped throughout the desert area. This area went from Havilah to Shur, near Egypt. And it went from Shur all the way to Assyria. Ishmael's descendants often attacked his brothers' people.*

Isaac's Family

¹⁹This is the story of Isaac. Abraham had a son named Isaac. ²⁰When Isaac was 40 years old he married Rebekah. Rebekah was from Paddan Aram. She was Bethuel's daughter and the sister of Laban the Aramean. ²¹Isaac's wife could not have children. So Isaac prayed to the Lord for his wife. The Lord heard Isaac's prayer. And the Lord allowed Rebekah to become pregnant.

²²While Rebekah was pregnant, she had much trouble with the babies inside her. Rebekah prayed to the Lord and said, "Why is this happening to me?" ²³The Lord said to her, "Two nations are in your body. The rulers of two families will be born from you. And they will be divided. One son will be stronger than the other. The older son will serve the younger." ²⁴And when the right time came, Rebekah gave birth to twins. ²⁵The first baby was red. His skin was like a hairy robe. So he was named Esau.* ²⁶When the second baby was born, he was holding tightly to Esau's heel. So that baby was named Jacob.* Isaac was 60 years old when Jacob and Esau were born.

²⁷The boys grew up. Esau became a skilled hunter. He loved to be out in the fields. But Jacob was a quiet man. He stayed in his tent. ²⁸Isaac loved Esau. He liked to eat the animals Esau killed. But Rebekah loved Jacob.

²⁹One time Esau came back from hunting. He was tired and weak from hunger. Jacob was boiling a pot of beans. ³⁰So Esau said to Jacob, "I am weak with hunger. Let me have some of those red beans." (That is why people call him Edom.*) ³¹But Jacob said, "You must sell me your rights as the firstborn son* today."

³²Esau said, "I am almost dead with hunger. If I die, all of my father's wealth will not help me. So I will give you my share."

³³But Jacob said, "First, promise me that you will give it to me." So Esau made a promise to Jacob. Esau sold his part of their father's wealth to Jacob. ³⁴Then Jacob gave Esau bread and food. Esau ate and drank and then left. So Esau showed that he did not care about his rights as the firstborn son.*

Isaac Lies to Abimelech

26 Once there was a famine.* This was like the famine that happened during Abraham's life. So Isaac went to the town of Gerar, to Abimelech the king of the Philistine people. ²The Lord spoke to Isaac. The Lord said, "Don't go down to Egypt. Live in the land that I commanded you to live in. ³Stay in that land, and I will be with you. I will bless you. I will give you and your family all these lands. I will do what I promised to Abraham your father. ⁴I will make your family as many as the stars of heaven. And I will give all these lands to your family. Through your descendants,* every nation on earth will be blessed. ⁵I will do this because your father Abraham obeyed my words and did the things I said. Abraham obeyed my commands, my laws, and my rules."

⁶So Isaac stayed and lived in Gerar. ⁷Isaac's wife Rebekah was very beautiful. The men of that place asked Isaac about Rebekah. Isaac said, "She is my sister." Isaac was afraid to tell them Rebekah was his wife. Isaac was afraid the men would kill him so that they could have her.

⁸After Isaac had lived there a long time, Abimelech looked out his window and saw Isaac and his wife playing. ⁹Abimelech called for Isaac

---

gathered to his ancestors This often means a person was buried in the same tomb or grave as his ancestors.

descendant(s) A person's children and their future families.

attacked his brothers 'people See Genesis 16:12.

Esau This name is like the word meaning "hairy."

Jacob This name is like the Hebrew word meaning "heel." It also means "the one who follows" or "tricky."

Edom This name means "red."

rights as the firstborn son Usually the firstborn son got half of the father's property after the father died and then became the new head of the family.

famine A time when there is no rain and no crops can grow. People and animals often die from lack of food and water.

descendants Or "Descendant." See Gal 3:16.

and said, "This woman is your wife. Why did you tell us that she was your sister?"

Isaac said to him, "I was afraid that you would kill me so you could have her."

¹⁰Abimelech said, "You have done a bad thing to us. One of our men might have slept with your wife. Then he would be guilty of a great sin."

¹¹So Abimelech gave a warning to all the people. He said, "No person must hurt this man or this woman. If any person hurts them, then that person will be killed."

Isaac Becomes Rich

¹²Isaac planted fields in that place. And that year he gathered a great harvest. The Lord blessed him very much. ¹³Isaac became rich. He gathered more and more wealth until he became a very rich man. ¹⁴He had many flocks and herds of animals. He also had many slaves. All the Philistine people were jealous of him. ¹⁵So the Philistine people destroyed all the wells that Isaac's father Abraham and his servants had dug many years before. The Philistines filled those wells with dirt. ¹⁶And Abimelech said to Isaac, "Leave our country. You have become much more powerful than we are."

¹⁷So Isaac left that place and camped near the little river of Gerar. Isaac stayed there and lived. ¹⁸Long before this time, Abraham had dug many wells. After Abraham died, the Philistines filled the wells with dirt. So Isaac went back and dug those wells again. Isaac gave them the same names his father had given them. ¹⁹Isaac's servants also dug a well near the little river. A spring of water flowed from that well. ²⁰But the men who herded sheep in the Valley of Gerar argued with Isaac's servants. They said, "This water is ours." So Isaac named that well Esek.* He gave it that name because that was the place where those people argued with him.

²¹Then Isaac's servants dug another well. The people of that place also argued because of that well. So Isaac named that well Sitnah.*

²²Isaac moved from there and dug another well. No men came to argue about that well. So Isaac named that well Rehoboth.* Isaac said, "Now the Lord has found a place for us. We will grow and be successful in this place."

²³From that place Isaac went to Beersheba. ²⁴The Lord spoke to Isaac that night. The Lord said, "I am the God of your father Abraham. Don't be afraid. I am with you, and I will bless you. I will make your family great. I will do this because of my servant Abraham." ²⁵So Isaac built an altar and worshiped the Lord in that place. Isaac set up camp there and his servants dug a well.

²⁶Abimelech came from Gerar to see Isaac. Abimelech brought with him Ahuzzath, his adviser, and Phicol, the commander of his army. ²⁷Isaac asked, "Why have you come to see me? You were not friendly with me before. You even forced me to leave your country."

²⁸They answered, "Now we know that the Lord is with you. We think that we should make an agreement. We want you to make a promise to us. ²⁹We did not hurt you, now you should promise not to hurt us. We sent you away, but we sent you away in peace. Now it is clear that the Lord has blessed you."

³⁰So Isaac gave a party for them. They all ate and drank. ³¹Early the next morning, each man made a promise and a vow.* Then the men left in peace.

³²On that day, Isaac's servants came and told them about the well they had dug. The servants said, "We found water in that well." ³³So Isaac named that well Shibah.* And that city is still called Beersheba.*

Esau's Wives

³⁴When Esau was 40 years old, he married two Hittite women. One was Judith the daughter of Beeri. The other was Basemath the daughter of Elon. ³⁵These marriages made Isaac and Rebekah very upset.

Inheritance Problems

27 Isaac grew old, and his eyes became so weak he could not see clearly. One day he called his older son Esau to him. Isaac said, "Son!"

Esau answered, "Here I am."

²Isaac said, "I am old. Maybe I will die soon! ³So take your bow and arrows and go hunting. Kill an animal for me to eat. ⁴Prepare the food that I love. Bring it to me, and I will eat it. Then I will bless you before I die." ⁵So Esau went hunting.

Esek This means "argument" or "fight."
Sitnah This means "hatred" or "being an enemy."
Rehoboth This means "open place" or "crossroads."

vow A special promise to God.
Shibah A Hebrew word meaning "seven" or "oath."
Beersheba This name means "well of the oath."

Jacob Tricks Isaac

Rebekah was listening when Isaac told those things to his son Esau. ⁶Rebekah said to her son Jacob, "Listen, I heard your father talking to your brother Esau. ⁷Your father said, 'Kill an animal for me to eat. Prepare the food for me, and I will eat. Then I will bless you before I die.' ⁸So listen son, and do what I tell you. ⁹Go out to our goats and bring me two young goats. I will prepare them the way your father loves them. ¹⁰Then you will carry the food to your father. And he will bless you before he dies."

¹¹But Jacob told his mother Rebekah, "My brother Esau is a hairy man. I am not hairy like him. ¹²If my father touches me, he will know that I am not Esau. Then he will not bless me—he will curse* me! Why? Because I tried to trick him."

¹³So Rebekah said to him, "I will accept the blame if there is trouble. Do the things I said. Go and get the goats for me."

¹⁴So Jacob went out and got two goats and brought them to his mother. His mother cooked the goats in the special way that Isaac loved. ¹⁵Then Rebekah took the clothes that her older son Esau loved to wear. Rebekah put those clothes on the younger son Jacob. ¹⁶Rebekah took the skins of the goats and put them on Jacob's hands and on his neck. ¹⁷Then Rebekah got the food she had cooked and gave it to Jacob.

¹⁸Jacob went to his father and said, "Father."

His father said, "Yes, son. Who are you?"

¹⁹Jacob said to his father, "I am Esau, your first son. I have done the things you told me. Now sit up and eat the animals that I hunted for you. Then you can bless me."

²⁰But Isaac said to his son, "How have you hunted and killed the animals so quickly?"

Jacob answered, "Because the Lord your God allowed me to find the animals quickly."

²¹Then Isaac said to Jacob, "Come near to me so that I can feel you, my son. If I can feel you, then I will know if you are really my son Esau."

²²So Jacob went to Isaac his father. Isaac felt him and said, "Your voice sounds like Jacob's voice. But your arms are hairy like the arms of Esau." ²³Isaac did not know it was Jacob, because his arms were hairy like Esau's arms. So Isaac blessed Jacob.

²⁴Isaac said, "Are you really my son Esau?"

Jacob answered, "Yes, I am."

The Blessing for Jacob

²⁵Then Isaac said, "Bring me the food. I will eat it and bless you." So Jacob gave him the food, and he ate it. Then Jacob gave him some wine, and he drank it.

²⁶Then Isaac said to him. "Son, come near and kiss me." ²⁷So Jacob went to his father and kissed him. Isaac smelled Esau's clothes and blessed him. Isaac said,

> My son smells like the fields
>   that the Lord has blessed.
> ²⁸ May the Lord give you plenty of rain
>   so you will have good crops and wine.
> ²⁹ May all people serve you.
>   May nations bow down to you.
>   You will rule over your brothers.
>   Your mother's sons will bow down to you
>   and obey you.
>
> Whoever curses* you will be cursed.
> Whoever blesses you will be blessed."

Esau's "Blessing"

³⁰Isaac finished blessing Jacob. Then, just as Jacob left his father Isaac, Esau came in from hunting. ³¹Esau prepared the food in the special way his father loved. Esau brought it to his father. He said to his father, "Father, I am your son. Get up and eat the meat that I killed ⌊and cooked⌋ for you. Then you can bless me."

³²But Isaac said to him, "Who are you?"

He answered, "I am your son—your first son—Esau."

³³Then Isaac became very worried and said, "Then who was it that cooked and brought me food before you came? I ate it all and I blessed him. Now it is too late to take back my blessing."

³⁴Esau heard his father's words. He became very angry and bitter. He cried out. He said to his father, "Then bless me also, father!"

³⁵Isaac said, "Your brother tricked me! He came and took your blessing!"

³⁶Esau said, "His name is Jacob *('Tricky')*. That is the right name for him. He has tricked me twice. He took away my rights as the firstborn son.* And now he has taken away my blessing."

---

curse To ask for bad things to happen to a thing or person.

rights as the firstborn son Usually, after the father died, the firstborn son got half of the father's property and became the new head of the family.

---

curse To ask for bad things to happen to a thing or person.

Then Esau said, "Have you saved any blessing for me?"

³⁷Isaac answered, "No, it's too late. I gave Jacob the power to rule over you. And I said all his brothers will be his servants. And I have given him the blessing for much grain and wine. There is nothing left to give you son."

³⁸But Esau continued to beg his father. "Do you have only one blessing, father? Bless me also, father!" Esau began to cry.

³⁹Then Isaac said to him,

"You will not live on good land.
  And you will not have much rain.
⁴⁰ You will have to fight to live.
  And you will be a slave to your brother.
  But you will fight to be free.
  You will break away from his control."

⁴¹After that Esau hated Jacob because of this blessing. Esau thought to himself, "My father will soon die, and there will be a time of sadness for him. But after that I will kill Jacob."

⁴²Rebekah heard about Esau's plan to kill Jacob. She sent for Jacob and said to him, "Listen, your brother Esau is planning to kill you. ⁴³So, son, do what I say. My brother Laban is living in Haran. Go to him and hide. ⁴⁴Stay with him for a short time. Stay with him until your brother stops being angry. ⁴⁵After a short time, your brother will forget what you did to him. Then I will send a servant to bring you back. I don't want to lose both of my sons in the same day."

⁴⁶Then Rebekah said to Isaac, "Your son Esau married Hittite women. I am very upset about these women. Why? Because they are not our people. I'll just die if Jacob marries one of these women too!"

Jacob Searches for a Wife

28 ¹Isaac called Jacob and blessed him. Then Isaac gave him a command. Isaac said, "You must not marry a Canaanite woman. ²So leave this place and go to Paddan Aram. Go to the house of Bethuel, your mother's father. Laban, your mother's brother, lives there. Marry one of his daughters. ³I pray that God All-Powerful* will bless you and give you many children. I pray that you will become the father of a great nation. ⁴I pray that God will bless you and your children the same way he blessed Abraham. And I pray that you will own the land where you live. This is the land God gave to Abraham."

⁵So Isaac sent Jacob to Rebekkah's brother in Paddan Aram. So Jacob went to Laban son of Bethuel the Aramean. Laban was the brother of Rebekkah. Rebekkah was the mother of Jacob and Esau.

⁶Esau learned that his father Isaac blessed Jacob. And Esau learned that Isaac sent Jacob away to Paddan Aram to find a wife there. Esau learned that Isaac commanded Jacob not to marry a Canaanite woman. ⁷And Esau learned that Jacob obeyed his father and his mother and went to Paddan Aram. ⁸Esau saw from this that his father did not want his sons to marry Canaanite women. ⁹Esau already had two wives. But he went to Ishmael and married another woman. He married Mahalath, the daughter of Ishmael. Ishmael was Abraham's son. Mahalath was Nebaioth's sister.

God's House—Bethel

¹⁰Jacob left Beersheba and went to Haran. ¹¹While Jacob was traveling, the sun set. So Jacob went to a place to stay the night. Jacob found a rock at that place and laid his head on it to sleep. ¹²Jacob had a dream. He dreamed there was a ladder that was on the ground and reached up into heaven. Jacob saw the angels of God going up and down the ladder. ¹³And then Jacob saw the Lord standing by the ladder. The Lord said, "I am the Lord, the God of your grandfather Abraham. I am the God of Isaac. I will give you the land that you are lying on now. I will give this land to you and to your children. ¹⁴You will have many, many descendants.* They will be as many as the pieces of dust on earth. They will spread east and west, north and south. All the families on earth will be blessed because of you and your descendants.

¹⁵"I am with you, and I will protect you every place you go. And I will bring you back to this land. I will not leave you until I have done what I promised."

¹⁶Then Jacob woke from his sleep and said, "I know that the Lord is in this place. But I did not know he was here until I slept."

¹⁷Jacob was afraid. He said, "This is a very great place. This is the house of God. This is the gate to heaven."

¹⁸Jacob got up very early in the morning. Jacob took the rock he had slept on and set it up on its

---

God All-Powerful Literally, "El Shaddai."   **descendant(s)** A person's children and their future families.

edge. Then he poured oil on the rock. In this way, he made this rock a memorial to God. ¹⁹The name of that place was Luz. But Jacob named it Bethel.*

²⁰Then Jacob made a promise. He said, "If God will be with me, and if God will protect me on this trip, and if God gives me food to eat and clothes to wear, ²¹and if I return in peace to my father's house—if God does all these things—then the Lord will be my God. ²²I am setting this stone up as a memorial stone. It will show that this is a holy place for God. And I will give God one tenth of all he gives me."

Jacob Meets Rachel

29 Then Jacob continued his trip. He went to the country in the East. ²Jacob looked, and he saw a well in the field. There were three flocks of sheep lying near the well. This well was the place where these sheep drank water. There was a large rock covering the mouth of the well. ³When all the flocks gathered there, the shepherds rolled the rock away from the well. Then all the sheep could drink from the water. After the sheep were full, the shepherds put the rock back in its place.

⁴Jacob said to the shepherds there, "Brothers, where are you from?"

They answered, "We are from Haran."

⁵Then Jacob said, "Do you know Laban, the son of Nahor?"

The shepherds answered, "We know him."

⁶Then Jacob said, "How is he?"

They answered, "He is well. Everything is fine. Look, that is his daughter Rachel coming now with his sheep."

⁷Jacob said, "Look, it is still day and long before the sun sets. It is not yet time for the animals to be gathered together for the night. So give them water and let them go back into the field."

⁸But this shepherd said, "We can't do that until all the flocks are gathered together. Then we will move the rock from the well, and all the sheep will drink."

⁹While Jacob was talking with the shepherds, Rachel came with her father's sheep. (It was Rachel's job to take care of the sheep.) ¹⁰Rachel was Laban's daughter. Laban was the brother of Rebekah, Jacob's mother. When Jacob saw Rachel, he went and moved the rock and gave water to the sheep. ¹¹Then Jacob kissed Rachel and cried. ¹²Jacob told Rachel that he was from her father's family. He told Rachel that he was the son of Rebekah. So Rachel ran home and told her father.

¹³Laban heard the news about his sister's son Jacob. So Laban ran to meet him. Laban hugged him and kissed him and brought him to his house. Jacob told Laban everything that had happened.

¹⁴Then Laban said, "This is wonderful! You are from my own family." So Jacob stayed with Laban for a month.

Laban Tricks Jacob

¹⁵One day Laban said to Jacob, "It is not right for you to continue working for me without pay. You are a relative, ₍not a slave₎. What should I pay you?"

¹⁶Laban had two daughters. The older was Leah and the younger was Rachel. ¹⁷Rachel was beautiful. And Leah's eyes were gentle.* ¹⁸Jacob loved Rachel. Jacob said to Laban, "I will work seven years for you if you will allow me to marry your daughter Rachel."

¹⁹Laban said, "It would be better for her to marry you than someone else. So stay with me."

²⁰So Jacob stayed and worked for Laban for seven years. But it seemed like a very short time because he loved Rachel very much.

²¹After seven years Jacob said to Laban, "Give me Rachel so that I can marry her. My time of work for you is finished."

²²So Laban gave a party for all the people in that place. ²³That night, Laban brought his daughter Leah to Jacob. Jacob and Leah had sexual relations together. ²⁴(Laban gave his maid Zilpah to his daughter to be her maid.) ²⁵In the morning Jacob saw that it was Leah he had slept with. Jacob said to Laban, "You have tricked me. I worked hard for you so that I could marry Rachel. Why did you trick me?"

²⁶Laban said, "In our country we do not allow the younger daughter to marry before the older daughter. ²⁷But continue for the full week of the marriage ceremony, and I will also give you Rachel to marry. But you must serve me another seven years."

²⁸So Jacob did this and finished the week. Then Laban gave him his daughter Rachel as a wife. ²⁹(Laban gave his maid Bilhah to his daughter Rachel to be her maid.) ³⁰So Jacob had sexual

---

Bethel This name means "God's house."

Leah's eyes were gentle This might be a polite way of saying Leah was not very pretty.

relations with Rachel also. And Jacob loved Rachel more than Leah. Jacob worked for Laban for another seven years.

Jacob's Family Grows

³¹The Lord saw that Jacob loved Rachel more than Leah. So the Lord made it possible for Leah to have children. But Rachel did not have any children. ³²Leah gave birth to a son. She named him Reuben.* Leah named him this because she said, "The Lord has seen my troubles. My husband doesn't love me. So now maybe my husband will love me." ³³Leah became pregnant again and had another son. She named this son Simeon.* Leah said, "The Lord has heard that I am not loved, so he gave me this son." ³⁴Leah became pregnant again and had another son. She named the son Levi.* Leah said, "Now, surely my husband will love me. I have given him three sons." ³⁵Then Leah gave birth to another son. She named this son Judah.* Leah named him this because she said, "Now I will praise the Lord." Then Leah stopped having children.

30 Rachel saw that she was not giving Jacob any children. Rachel became jealous of her sister Leah. So Rachel said to Jacob, "Give me children or I will die!" ²Jacob became angry with Rachel. He said, "I am not God. God is the One who has caused you to not have children." ³Then Rachel said, "You can have my maid Bilhah. Sleep with her and she will have a child for me.* Then I can become a mother because of her." ⁴So Rachel gave Bilhah to her husband Jacob. Jacob had sexual relations with Bilhah. ⁵Bilhah became pregnant and gave Jacob a son. ⁶Rachel said, "God has listened to my prayer. He decided to give me a son." So Rachel named this son Dan.*

⁷Bilhah became pregnant again and gave Jacob a second son. ⁸Rachel said, "I have fought hard to compete with my sister. And I have won." So she named that son Naphtali.* ⁹Leah saw that she could have no more children. So she gave her slave girl Zilpah to Jacob. ¹⁰Then Zilpah had a son. ¹¹Leah said, "I am lucky." So she named the son Gad.* ¹²Zilpah gave birth to another son. ¹³Leah said, "I am very happy! Now women will call me happy." So she named that son Asher.*

¹⁴During the wheat harvest, Reuben went into the fields and found some special flowers.* Reuben brought these flowers to his mother Leah. But Rachel said to Leah, "Please give me some of your son's flowers."

¹⁵Leah answered, "You have already taken away my husband. Now you are trying to take away my son's flowers."

But Rachel answered, "If you will give me your son's flowers, then you can sleep with Jacob tonight."

¹⁶Jacob came in from the fields that night. Leah saw him and went out to meet him. She said, "You will sleep with me tonight. I have paid for you with my son's flowers." So Jacob slept with Leah that night.

¹⁷Then God allowed Leah to become pregnant again. She gave birth to a fifth son. ¹⁸Leah said, "God has given me a reward because I gave my slave to my husband." So Leah named her son Issachar.*

¹⁹Leah became pregnant again and gave birth to a sixth son. ²⁰Leah said, "God has given me a fine gift. Now surely Jacob will accept me, because I have given him six sons." So Leah named the son Zebulun.*

²¹Later Leah gave birth to a daughter. She named the daughter Dinah.

Reuben This is like the word meaning "Look, a son."
Simeon This is like the word meaning "He hears."
Levi This is like the word meaning "accompany," "be joined together," or "become close."
Judah This is like the word meaning "He is praised."
she will have a child for me Literally, "She will give birth on my knees, and I too will have a son through her."
Dan This is like the word meaning "to decide" or "to judge."

Naphtali This is like the word meaning "my struggle."
Gad This is like the word meaning "lucky," or "fortunate."
Asher This is like the word meaning "happy" or "blessed."
special flowers Or, "mandrakes." The Hebrew word means "love plant." People thought these plants could help women have babies.
Issachar This is like the word meaning "reward" or "salary."
Zebulun This is like the word meaning "praise" or "honor."

²²Then God heard Rachel's prayer. God made it possible for Rachel to have children. ²³⁻²⁴Rachel became pregnant and gave birth to a son. Rachel said, "God has taken away my shame and given me a son." So Rachel named the son Joseph.*

Jacob Tricks Laban

²⁵After the birth of Joseph, Jacob said to Laban, "Now let me go to my own home. ²⁶Give me my wives and my children. I have earned them by working for you ⌊14 years⌋. You know that I served you well."

²⁷Laban said to him, "Let me say something!* I know* that the Lord has blessed me because of you. ²⁸Tell me what I should pay you, and I will give it to you."

²⁹Jacob answered, "You know that I have worked hard for you. Your flocks have grown and been well while I cared for them. ³⁰When I came, you had little. Now you have much, much more. Every time I did something for you, the Lord blessed you. Now it is time for me to work for myself—it is time to build my own house."

³¹Laban asked, "Then what should I give you?"

Jacob answered, "I don't want you to give me anything. I only want you to ⌊pay me for the work I have done⌋. Just do this one thing: I will go back and take care of your sheep. ³²But let me go through all your flocks today and take every lamb with spots or stripes. And let me take every black young goat. And let me take every female goat with stripes or spots. That will be my pay. ³³In the future, you can easily see if I am honest. You can come to look at my flocks. If I have any goat that isn't spotted or any sheep that isn't black, then you will know that I stole it."

³⁴Laban answered, "I agree to that. We will do what you ask." ³⁵But that day Laban hid all the male goats that had spots. And Laban hid all the female goats that had spots on them. Laban also hid all the black sheep. Laban told his sons to watch these sheep. ³⁶So the sons took all the spotted animals and led them to another place. They traveled for three days. Jacob stayed and took care of all the animals that were left. ⌊But there were no animals there that were spotted or black.⌋

³⁷So Jacob cut green branches from poplar and almond trees. Jacob stripped off some of the bark so that the branches had white stripes on them. ³⁸Jacob put the branches in front of the flocks at the watering places. When the animals came to drink, they also mated in that place. ³⁹Then when the goats mated in front of the branches, the young that were born were spotted, striped, or black.

⁴⁰Jacob separated the spotted and the black animals from the other animals in the flock. Jacob kept his animals separate from Laban's. ⁴¹Any time the stronger animals in the flock were mating, Jacob put the branches before their eyes. The animals mated near those branches. ⁴²But when the weaker animals mated, Jacob did not put the branches there. So the young animals born from the weak parents were Laban's. And the young animals born from the stronger parents were Jacob's. ⁴³In this way, Jacob became very rich. He had large flocks, many servants, camels, and donkeys.

Time To Leave—Jacob Runs Away

31 One day, Jacob heard Laban's sons talking. They said, "Jacob has taken everything that our father owned. Jacob has become rich—and he has taken all this wealth from our father." ²Then Jacob noticed that Laban was not as friendly as he had been in the past. ³The Lord said to Jacob, "Go back to your own land where your ancestors* lived. I will be with you."

⁴So Jacob told Rachel and Leah to meet him in the field where he kept his flocks of sheep and goats. ⁵Jacob said to Rachel and Leah, "I have seen that your father is angry with me. He was always friendly with me in the past, but now he is not. ⁶You both know that I have worked as hard as I can for your father. ⁷But your father cheated me. Your father has changed my pay ten times. But during all this time, God protected me from all of Laban's tricks.

⁸"At one time Laban said, 'You can keep all the goats with spots. This will be your pay.' After he said this, all the animals gave birth to spotted babies. So they were all mine. But then Laban said, 'I will keep the spotted goats. You can have all the striped goats. That will be your pay.' After

---

Joseph This is like the word meaning "to add," "collect," or "gather."
Let me say something Literally, "If I find favor in your sight." This is a polite way to ask permission to speak.
know Or, "guessed," "divined," or "concluded."

ancestors Literally, "fathers." This means a person's parents, grandparents, and all the people they are descended from.

he said this, then all the animals gave birth to striped babies. ⁹So God has taken the animals away from your father and has given them to me. ¹⁰"I had a dream during the time when the animals were mating. I saw that the only male goats who were mating were the ones with stripes and spots. ¹¹The angel of God spoke to me in that dream. The angel said, 'Jacob!'

"I answered, 'Yes!'

¹²"The angel said, 'Look, only the striped and spotted goats are mating. I am causing this to happen. I have seen all the wrong things Laban is doing to you. I am doing this so that you can have all the new baby goats. ¹³I am the God who came to you at Bethel. At that place, you made an altar. You poured olive oil on the altar. And you made a promise to me. Now I want you to be ready to go back to the country where you were born.'"

¹⁴⁻¹⁵Rachel and Leah answered Jacob, "Our father has nothing to give us when he dies. He treated us like strangers. He sold us to you, and then he spent all the money that should have been ours! ¹⁶God took all this wealth from our father, and now it belongs to us and our children. So you should do whatever God told you to do!"

¹⁷So Jacob prepared for his trip. He put his sons and his wives on camels. ¹⁸Then they began traveling back to the land of Canaan where his father lived. All the flocks of animals that Jacob owned walked ahead of them. He carried everything that he had gotten while he lived in Paddan Aram.

¹⁹At this time, Laban was gone to cut the wool from his sheep. While he was gone, Rachel went into his house and stole the false gods that belonged to her father.

²⁰Jacob tricked Laban the Aramean. He did not tell Laban he was leaving. ²¹Jacob took his family and everything he owned and left quickly. They crossed the Euphrates River and traveled toward the hill country of Gilead.

²²Three days later, Laban learned that Jacob had run away. ²³So Laban gathered his men together and began to chase Jacob. After seven days, Laban found Jacob near the hill country in Gilead. ²⁴That night God went to Laban in a dream. God said, "Be careful! Be careful of every word you say to Jacob."

The Search for the Stolen Gods

²⁵The next morning Laban caught Jacob. Jacob had set his camp on the mountain. So Laban and all his men set their camp in the hill country of Gilead.

²⁶Laban said to Jacob, "Why did you trick me? Why did you take my daughters like they were women you captured during war? ²⁷Why did you run away without telling me? If you had told me, I would have given you a party. There would have been singing and dancing with music. ²⁸You didn't even let me kiss my grandchildren and my daughters goodbye. You were very foolish to do this! ²⁹I have the power to really hurt you. But last night your father's God came to me in a dream. He warned me not to hurt you in any way. ³⁰I know that you want to go back to your home. That is why you left. But why did you steal the gods from my house?"

³¹Jacob answered, "I left without telling you, because I was afraid! I thought you would take your daughters away from me. ³²But I did not steal your gods. If you find any one here with me that has taken your gods, then that person will be killed. Your men will be my witnesses. You can look for anything that belongs to you. Take anything that is yours." (Jacob did not know that Rachel had stolen Laban's gods.)

³³So Laban went and looked through Jacob's camp. He looked in Jacob's tent and then in Leah's tent. Then he looked in the tent where the two slave women stayed. But he did not find the gods from his house. Then Laban went into Rachel's tent. ³⁴Rachel had hidden the gods inside her camel's saddle, and she was sitting on them. Laban looked through the whole tent, but he did not find the gods.

³⁵And Rachel said to her father, "Father, don't be angry with me. I am not able to stand up before you. I am having my monthly time of bleeding." So Laban looked through the camp, but he did not find the gods from his house.

³⁶Then Jacob became very angry. Jacob said, "What wrong have I done? What law have I broken? Why do you have the right to chase me and stop me? ³⁷You have looked through everything I own. You have found nothing that belongs to you. If you have found anything, then show it to me. Put it here where our men can see it. Let our men decide which one of us is right. ³⁸I have worked 20 years for you. During all that time, none of the baby sheep and goats died during birth. And I have not eaten any of the rams from your flocks. ³⁹Any time a sheep was killed by wild animals, I always paid for that myself. I did not take the dead animal to you and say that it was not my fault. But I was robbed day and night. ⁴⁰In the daytime, the sun took away my strength, and at night sleep was taken from my eyes by the

cold. ⁴¹I worked 20 years like a slave for you. For the first 14 years I worked to win your two daughters. The last six years I worked to earn your animals. And during that time you changed my pay ten times. ⁴²But the God of my ancestors,* the God of Abraham and the Fear of Isaac,* was with me. If God had not been with me, then you would have sent me away with nothing. But God saw the trouble that I had. God saw the work that I did. And last night God proved that I am right."

Jacob and Laban's Treaty

⁴³Laban said to Jacob, "These women are my daughters. And these children belong to me. And these animals are mine. Everything you see here belongs to me. But I can do nothing to keep my daughters and their children. ⁴⁴So I am ready to make an agreement with you. We will set up a pile of stones to show that we have an agreement."

⁴⁵So Jacob found a large rock and put it there to show that he had made an agreement. ⁴⁶He told his men to find some more rocks and make a pile of rocks. Then they ate beside the pile of rocks. ⁴⁷Laban named that place Yegar Sahadutha.* But Jacob named that place Galeed.*

⁴⁸Laban said to Jacob, "This pile of rocks will help us both remember our agreement." That is why Jacob called the place Galeed.

⁴⁹Then Laban said, "Let the Lord watch over us while we are separated from each other." So that place was also named Mizpah.*

⁵⁰Then Laban said, "If you hurt my daughters, remember that God will punish you. If you marry other women, remember that God is watching. ⁵¹Here are the rocks that I have put between us. And here is the special rock to show that we made an agreement. ⁵²This pile of rocks and this one special rock both help us remember our agreement. I will never go past these rocks to fight against you. And you must never go on my side of these rocks to fight against me. ⁵³May the God of Abraham, the God of Nahor, and the God of their ancestors* judge us guilty if we break this agreement."

Jacob's father, Isaac, called God "Fear." So Jacob used that name to make the promise. ⁵⁴Then Jacob killed an animal and offered it as a sacrifice* on the mountain. And he invited his men to come and share a meal. After they finished eating, they spent the night on the mountain. ⁵⁵Early the next morning, Laban kissed his grandchildren and his daughters goodbye. He blessed them and went back home.

Reunion With Esau

32 Jacob also left that place. While he was traveling, he saw God's angels. ²When Jacob saw them he said, "This is God's camp!" So Jacob named that place Mahanaim.*

³Jacob's brother Esau was living in the area called Seir. This area was the hill country of Edom.* Jacob sent messengers to Esau. ⁴Jacob told the messengers, "Tell these things to my master Esau: 'Your servant Jacob says, I have lived with Laban all these years. ⁵I have many cows, donkeys, flocks, and men and women servants. Sir, I am sending you this message to ask you to accept us.'"

⁶The messengers came back to Jacob and said, "We went to your brother Esau. He is coming to meet you. He has 400 men with him."

⁷That message scared Jacob. He divided the people who were with him into two groups. He divided all the flocks and the herds and the camels into two groups. ⁸Jacob thought, "If Esau comes and destroys one group, then the other group can run away and be saved."

⁹Jacob said, "God of my father Abraham! God of my father Isaac! Lord, you told me to come back to my country and to my family. You said that you would do good to me. ¹⁰You have been very kind to me. You did many good things for me. The first time I traveled across the Jordan River, I owned nothing—only my walking stick. But now I own enough things to have two full groups. ¹¹I ask you to please save me from my brother. Save me from Esau. I am afraid of him. I am afraid that he will come and kill all of us, even the mothers with the children. ¹²Lord, you said to

---

ancestors Literally, "fathers." This means a person's parents, grandparents, and all the people they are descended from.
Fear of Isaac A name for God.
Yegar Sahadutha Aramaic words meaning "rock pile of the agreement."
Galeed Another name for Gilead. This Hebrew name means "rock pile of the agreement."
Mizpah This means "a place to watch from."

sacrifice A gift to God. Usually it was a special animal that was killed and burned on an altar.
Mahanaim This name means "two camps."
Edom A country east of Judah.

me, 'I will be good to you. I will increase your family and make your children as many as the sands of the sea. There will be too many to count.'"

¹³Jacob stayed in that place for the night. Jacob prepared some things to give to Esau as a gift. ¹⁴Jacob took 200 female goats and 20 male goats, 200 female sheep and 20 male sheep. ¹⁵Jacob took 30 camels and their colts, 40 cows and 10 bulls, 20 female donkeys and 10 male donkeys. ¹⁶Jacob gave each flock of animals to his servants. Then Jacob said to the servants, "Separate each group of animals. Go ahead of me and keep some space between each herd." ¹⁷Jacob gave them their orders. To the servant with the first group of animals Jacob said, "When Esau my brother comes to you and asks you, 'Whose animals are these? Where are you going? Whose servant are you?' ¹⁸Then you should answer, 'These animals belong to your servant Jacob. Jacob sent them as a gift to you my master, Esau. And Jacob is also coming behind us.'"

¹⁹Jacob also ordered the second servant, the third servant, and all the other servants to do the same thing. He said, "You will do the same thing to Esau when you meet him. ²⁰You will say, 'This is a gift to you, and your servant Jacob is behind us.'"

Jacob thought, "If I send these men ahead with gifts, then maybe Esau will forgive me and accept me." ²¹So Jacob sent the gifts to Esau. But Jacob stayed that night in the camp.

²²Later that night, Jacob got up and left that place. Jacob took his two wives, his two maids, and his eleven sons with him. Jacob crossed the Jabbok River at the crossing. ²³Jacob sent his family across the river. Then Jacob sent everything he had across the river.

The Fight With God

²⁴Jacob was the last person to cross the river. But before he could cross, while he was still alone, a man came and wrestled with him. The man fought with him until the sun came up. ²⁵The man saw that he could not defeat Jacob. So he touched Jacob's leg. At that time, Jacob's leg was put out of joint.

²⁶Then the man said to Jacob, "Let me go. The sun is coming up."

But Jacob said, "I will not let you go. You must bless me."

²⁷And the man said to him, "What is your name?"

And Jacob said, "My name is Jacob."

²⁸Then the man said, "Your name will not be Jacob. Your name will now be Israel.* I give you this name because you have fought with God and with men, and you have not been defeated."

²⁹Then Jacob asked him, "Please tell me your name."

But the man said, "Why must you ask my name?" At that time, the man blessed Jacob.

³⁰So Jacob named that place Peniel.* Jacob said, "At this place, I saw God face to face, but my life was spared." ³¹Then the sun came up as he passed Penuel.* Jacob was walking crippled because of his leg. ³²So even today, the people of Israel don't eat the muscle that is on the hip joint, because this is the muscle where Jacob was hurt.

Jacob Shows His Bravery

33 Jacob looked and saw Esau coming. Esau was coming and 400 men were with him. Jacob divided his family into four groups. Leah and her children were in one group, Rachel and Joseph were in one group, and the two maids and their children were in two groups. ²Jacob put the maids with their children first. Then Jacob put Leah and her children behind them. And Jacob put Rachel and Joseph in the last place.

³Jacob himself went out toward Esau. So he was the first person Esau came to. Jacob bowed on the ground seven times while he was walking toward his brother.

⁴When Esau saw Jacob, he ran to meet him. Esau put his arms around Jacob and hugged his neck and kissed him. Then they both cried. ⁵Esau looked up and saw the women and children. He said, "Who are all these people with you?"

Jacob answered, "These are the children that God gave me. God has been good to me."

⁶Then the two maids and the children with them went to Esau. They bowed down before him. ⁷Then Leah and the children with her went to Esau and bowed down. And then Rachel and Joseph went to Esau and bowed down.

⁸Esau said, "Who were all those people I saw while I was coming here? And what were all those animals for?"

Israel This name might mean "he fights for God," "he fights with God," or "God fights."
Peniel, Penuel Two forms of the same name which means "the face of God."

Jacob answered, "Those are my gifts to you so that you might accept me."
⁹But Esau said, "You don't have to give me gifts, brother. I have enough for myself."
¹⁰Jacob said, "No! I beg you! If you truly accept me, then please accept the gifts I give you. I am very happy to see your face again. It is like seeing the face of God. I am very happy to see that you accept me. ¹¹So I beg that you also accept the gifts I give you. God has been very good to me. I have more than I need." In this way Jacob begged Esau to take the gifts. So Esau accepted the gifts.
¹²Then Esau said, "Now you can continue your journey. I will go with you."
¹³But Jacob said to him, "You know that my children are weak. And I must be careful with my flocks and their young animals. If I force them to walk too far in one day, all the animals will die. ¹⁴So you go on ahead. I will follow you slowly. I will go slow enough for the cattle and other animals to be safe. And I will go slow enough so that my children will not become too tired. I will meet you in Seir."
¹⁵So Esau said, "Then I will leave some of my men with you to help you."
But Jacob said, "That is very kind of you. But there is no need to do that." ¹⁶So that day Esau started on his trip back to Seir. ¹⁷But Jacob went to Succoth. In that place he built a house for himself and small barns for his cattle. That is why the place was named Succoth.*
¹⁸Jacob safely ended his trip from Paddan Aram when he came to the town of Shechem in Canaan. Jacob made his camp in a field near the city. ¹⁹Jacob bought the field where he camped from the family of Hamor, father of Shechem. Jacob paid 100 pieces of silver. ²⁰Jacob built an altar there to worship God. Jacob named the place "El, the God of Israel."

The Rape of Dinah

34 Dinah was the daughter of Leah and Jacob. One day, Dinah went out to see the women of that place. ²Hamor was the king of that land. His son Shechem saw Dinah. Shechem kidnapped her and raped her. ³Then Shechem fell in love with Dinah and wanted to marry her. ⁴Shechem told his father, "Please get this girl for me so that I can marry her."

⁵Jacob learned that the boy had done this very bad thing to his daughter. But all Jacob's sons were out in the field with the cattle. So Jacob did nothing until they came home. ⁶At that time, Shechem's father, Hamor, went to talk with Jacob. ⁷In the fields, Jacob's sons heard the news about what happened. They were very angry when they heard this. They were mad because Shechem had brought shame to Israel by raping Jacob's daughter. The brothers came in from the fields as soon as they heard about the terrible thing Shechem had done.

⁸But Hamor talked to the brothers. He said, "My son Shechem wants Dinah very much. Please let him marry her. ⁹This marriage will show we have a special agreement. Then our men can marry your women, and your men can marry our women. ¹⁰You can live in the same land with us. You will be free to own the land and to trade here."

¹¹Shechem also talked to Jacob and the brothers. Shechem said, "Please accept me. I will do anything you ask me to do. ¹²I will give you any gift* you want if you only allow me to marry Dinah. I will give you anything you ask, but let me marry Dinah."

¹³Jacob's sons decided to lie to Shechem and his father. The brothers were still mad because Shechem had done such a bad thing to their sister Dinah. ¹⁴So the brothers said to him, "We cannot allow you to marry our sister because you are not yet circumcised.* It would be wrong for our sister to marry you. ¹⁵But we will allow you to marry her if you do this one thing: Every man in your town must become circumcised like us. ¹⁶Then your men can marry our women, and our men can marry your women. Then we will become one people. ¹⁷If you refuse to be circumcised, then we will take Dinah away."

¹⁸This agreement made Hamor and Shechem very happy. ¹⁹Shechem was very happy to do what Dinah's brothers asked.

Revenge

Shechem was the most honored man in his family. ²⁰Hamor and Shechem went to the meeting place of their city. They spoke to the men

---

Succoth A town east of the Jordan River. This name means "temporary shelters."

gift Or, "dowry." Here, the money a man paid for a wife.
circumcise(d) Cutting the foreskin from a man. In Israel this was proof that a man had made a special agreement to obey God's laws and teachings.

of the city and said, ²¹"These people of Israel want to be friends with us. We want to let them live in our land and be at peace with us. We have enough land for all of us. We are free to marry their women. And we are happy to give them our women for marriage. ²²But there is one thing that all our men must agree to do. All our men must agree to become circumcised* the same as the people of Israel. ²³If we do this, then we will become rich from all their cattle and animals. So we should make this agreement with them, and they will stay here with us." ²⁴All the men who heard this in the meeting place agreed with Hamor and Shechem. And every man was circumcised at that time.

²⁵Three days later, the men who were circumcised were still sore. Two of Jacob's sons, Simeon and Levi, knew that the men would be weak at this time. So they went to the city and killed all the men there. ²⁶Dinah's brothers, Simeon and Levi, killed Hamor and his son Shechem. Then they took Dinah out of Shechem's house and left. ²⁷Jacob's sons went to the city and stole everything that was there. They were still angry because of what Shechem did to their sister. ²⁸So the brothers took all their animals. They took all their donkeys and everything else in the city and in the fields. ²⁹The brothers took everything those people owned. The brothers even took the wives and children.

³⁰But Jacob said to Simeon and Levi, "You have given me much trouble. All the people in this place will hate me. All the Canaanite people and the Perizzite people will turn against me. There are only a few of us. If the people in this place gather together to fight against us, then I will be destroyed. And all our people will be destroyed with me."

³¹But the brothers said, "Should we let those people treat our sister like a prostitute?* No! Those people were wrong to do that to our sister!"

Jacob in Bethel

35 God said to Jacob, "Go to the town of Bethel.* Live there and make an altar* for worship. Remember El,* the God who appeared* to you there when you were running away from your brother Esau. Make your altar to worship that God there."

²So Jacob said to his family and to all his servants, "Destroy all those foreign gods made of wood and metal that you have. Make yourselves pure. Put on clean clothes. ³We will leave here and go to Bethel. In that place, I will build an altar to the God who helped me during my time of trouble. And that God has been with me everywhere I went."

⁴So the people gave Jacob all the foreign gods that they had. And they gave Jacob all the rings they were wearing in their ears. Jacob buried all these things under an oak tree near the town called Shechem.

⁵Jacob and his sons left that place. The people in that area wanted to follow and kill them. But they became very afraid and did not follow Jacob. ⁶So Jacob and his people went to Luz. Luz is now called Bethel.* It is in the land of Canaan. ⁷Jacob built an altar* there. Jacob named the place "El Bethel." Jacob chose this name because that is the place God first appeared to him when he was running from his brother.

⁸Deborah, Rebekah's nurse, died there. They buried her under the oak tree at Bethel. They named that place Allon Bacuth.*

Jacob's New Name

⁹When Jacob came back from Paddan Aram, God appeared to him again. And God blessed Jacob. ¹⁰God said to Jacob, "Your name is Jacob. But I will change that name. You will not be called Jacob now. Your new name will be Israel.*" So God named him Israel.

¹¹God said to him, "I am God All-Powerful. ⌊And I give you this blessing⌋: Have many children and grow into a great nation. Other nations and other kings will come out of you. ¹²I

---

circumcise(d) Cutting the foreskin from a man. In Israel this was proof that a man had made a special agreement to obey God's laws and teachings.
prostitute A woman paid by men for sexual sin.
Bethel This name means "God's house."
altar(s) A stone table used for burning sacrifices that were offered as gifts to God.

El A Hebrew name for God.
God who appeared God often used special shapes so people could see him. Sometimes he was like a man, an angel, a fire, or a bright light.
Allon Bacuth This name means "the oak tree of sadness."
Israel This name might mean "he fights for God" or "he fights with God."

gave Abraham and Isaac some special land. Now I give that land to you. And I also give that land to all your people who live after you." ¹³Then God left that place. ¹⁴⁻¹⁵Jacob set up a memorial stone* in this place. Jacob made the rock holy by pouring wine and oil on it. This was a special place because God spoke to Jacob there. And Jacob named the place Bethel.*

Rachel Dies Giving Birth

¹⁶Jacob and his group left Bethel. Just before they came to Ephrath *(Bethlehem)*, Rachel began giving birth to her baby. ¹⁷But Rachel was having much trouble with this birth. She was having great pain. Rachel's nurse saw this and said, "Don't be afraid Rachel. You are giving birth to another son."
¹⁸Rachel died while giving birth to the son. Before dying, Rachel named the boy Benoni.* But Jacob called him Benjamin.*
¹⁹Rachel was buried on the road to Ephrath. (Ephrath is Bethlehem.) ²⁰And Jacob put a special rock on her grave to honor Rachel. That special rock is still there today. ²¹Then Israel *(Jacob)* continued his journey. He camped just south of Eder tower.*
²²Israel stayed there for a short time. While he was there, Reuben slept with Israel's woman servant* Bilhah. Israel heard about this and was very angry.

The Family of Israel

Jacob (Israel) had twelve sons.
²³Jacob and Leah's sons were: Jacob's firstborn son Reuben, Simeon, Levi, Judah, Issachar, and Zebulun.
²⁴Jacob and Rachel's sons were Joseph and Benjamin.
²⁵Bilhah was Rachel's maid. Jacob and Bilhah's sons were Dan and Naphtali.

²⁶Zilpah was Leah's maid. Jacob and Zilpah's sons were Gad and Asher.
Those are Jacob's (Israel's) sons who were born in Paddan Aram.
²⁷Jacob went to his father Isaac at Mamre in Kiriath Arba (Hebron). This is where Abraham and Isaac had lived. ²⁸Isaac lived 180 years. ²⁹Then Isaac became weak and died. Isaac had lived a long and full life. His sons Esau and Jacob buried him in the same place as his father.

Esau's Family

36 The family history of Esau (Edom). ²Esau married women from the land of Canaan. Esau's wives were: Adah, the daughter of Elon the Hittite, Oholibamah, the daughter of Anah, the son of Zibeon the Hivite, and ³Basemath, Ishmael's daughter, the sister of Nebaioth. ⁴Esau and Adah had a son named Eliphaz. Basemath had a son named Reuel. ⁵And Oholibamah had three sons: Jeush, Jalam, and Korah. Those were Esau's sons that were born in the land of Canaan.

⁶⁻⁸Jacob and Esau's families became too big for the land in Canaan to support them all. So Esau moved away from his brother Jacob. Esau took his wives, sons, daughters, all his slaves, cows and other animals, and everything else that he got in Canaan and moved to the hill country of Seir.* (Esau is also named Edom—₁and this is another name for the country Seir₁.)

⁹Esau is the father of the people of Edom.* These are the names of Esau's family living in the hill country of Seir (Edom):
¹⁰Esau and Adah's son was Eliphaz. Esau and Basemath's son was, Reuel.
¹¹Eliphaz had five sons: Teman, Omar, Zepho, Gatam, and Kenaz. ¹²Eliphaz also had a woman servant* named Timna. Timna and Eliphaz had a son named Amalek.
¹³Reuel had four sons: Nahath, Zerah, Shammah, and Mizzah.
Those were Esau's grandsons from his wife Basemath.
¹⁴Esau's third wife was Oholibamah, the daughter of Anah. (Anah was the son of Zibeon.) Esau and Oholibamah's children were: Jeush, Jalam, Korah.

---

memorial stone A stone that was set up to help people remember something special. In ancient Israel people often set up stones as special places to worship false gods.
Bethel A town in Israel. This name means "God's house."
Benoni This name means "son of my suffering."
Benjamin This name means "right-hand (favorite) son."
Eder tower Or, "Migdal Eder."
woman servant Or, "concubine," a slave woman who was like a wife to a man.

Seir A mountain range in Edom.
Edom A country east of Judah.

¹⁵These are the family groups* that came from Esau (Edom):

Esau's first son was Eliphaz. From Eliphaz came: Teman, Omar, Zepho, Kenaz, ¹⁶Korah, Gatam, and Amalek.

All those family groups* came from Esau's wife Adah.

¹⁷Esau's son Reuel was the father of these families: Nahath, Zerah, Shammah, and Mizzah.

All those families came from Esau's wife Basemath.

¹⁸Esau's wife Oholibamah, daughter of Anah, gave birth to Jeush, Jalam, and Korah. Those three men were the fathers of their families. ¹⁹Those men were all family leaders from Esau (Edom).

²⁰Seir, a Horite man, lived in Edom* before Esau. These are the sons of Seir: Lotan, Shobal, Zibeon, Anah, ²¹Dishon, Ezer, Dishan. Those sons were all Horite family leaders from Seir in Edom.

²²Lotan was the father of Hori and Heman*. (Timna was Lotan's sister.)

²³Shobal was the father of Alvan, Manahath, Ebal, Shepho, and Onam.

²⁴Zibeon had two sons Aiah and Anah. (Anah is the man who found the hot springs in the mountains while he was caring for his father's donkeys.)

²⁵Anah was the father of Dishon and Oholibamah.

²⁶Dishon had four sons. They were Hemdan, Eshban, Ithran, and Keran.

²⁷Ezer had three sons. They were Bilhan, Zaavan, and Akan.

²⁸Dishan had two sons. They were Uz and Aran.

²⁹These are the names of the leaders of the Horite families: Lotan, Shobal, Zibeon, Anah, ³⁰Dishon, Ezer, and Dishan. Those men were the leaders of the families that lived in the country of Seir *(Edom.*)*. ³¹At that time, there were kings in Edom. Edom had kings a long time before Israel did.

³²Bela son of Beor was a king who ruled in Edom.* He ruled over the city of Dinhabah. ³³When Bela died, Jobab became king. Jobab was the son of Zerah from Bozrah. ³⁴When Jobab died, Husham ruled. Husham was from the land of the Temanite people. ³⁵When Husham died, Hadad ruled that area. Hadad was the son of Bedad. (Hadad was the man who defeated Midian in the country of Moab.) Hadad was from the city of Avith. ³⁶When Hadad died, Samlah ruled that country. Samlah was from Masrekah. ³⁷When Samlah died, Shaul ruled that area. Shaul was from Rehoboth on the Euphrates River. ³⁸When Shaul died, Baal Hanan ruled that country. Baal Hanan was the son of Acbor. ³⁹When Baal Hanan died, Hadad* ruled that country. Hadad was from the city of Pau. Hadad's wife's name was Mehetabel, the daughter of Matred. (Mezahab was Matred's father.)

⁴⁰⁻⁴³Esau was the father of the Edomite families: Timna, Alvah, Jetheth, Oholibamah, Elah, Pinon, Kenaz, Teman, Mibzar, Magdiel, and Iram. Each of these families lived in an area that was called by the same name as their family.

Joseph the Dreamer

37 Jacob stayed and lived in the land of Canaan. This is the same land where his father had lived. ²This is the story of Jacob's family.

Joseph was a young man, 17 years old. His job was to care for the sheep and the goats. Joseph did this work with his brothers, the sons of Bilhah and Zilpah. (Bilhah and Zilpah were his father's wives.) Joseph told his father about the bad things that his brothers did. ³Joseph was born at a time when his father Israel *(Jacob)* was very old. So Israel *(Jacob)* loved Joseph more than he loved his other sons. Jacob gave his son a special coat. This coat was long and was very beautiful.* ⁴Joseph's brothers saw that their father loved Joseph more than he loved them. They hated their brother because of this. They refused to say nice things to Joseph.

⁵One time Joseph had a special dream. Later, Joseph told his brothers about this dream. After this, his brothers hated him even more.

⁶Joseph said, "I had a dream. ⁷We were all working in the field. We were tying stacks of wheat together. Then my sheaf got up. It stood there while all of your sheaves made a circle around mine. Then all of your stacks of wheat bowed down to mine."

⁸His brothers said, "Do you think this means you will be a king and rule over us?" His brothers hated Joseph more now because of the dreams he had about them.

---

family groups Or, "family leaders." These families became large tribes and nations.
Edom A country east of Judah.
Heman Or "Homam."

Hadad Or, "Hadar."
beautiful The Hebrew means "striped" or possibly, "many colored."

⁹Then Joseph had another dream. Joseph told his brothers about this dream. Joseph said, "I had another dream. I saw the sun, the moon, and eleven stars bowing down to me." ¹⁰Joseph also told his father about this dream. But his father criticized him. His father said, "What kind of dream is this? Do you believe that your mother, your brothers, and I will bow down to you?" ¹¹Joseph's brothers continued to be jealous of him. But Joseph's father thought much about all these things and wondered what they could mean.

¹²One day, Joseph's brothers went to Shechem to care for their father's sheep. ¹³Jacob said to Joseph, "Go to Shechem. Your brothers are there with my sheep."

Joseph answered, "I will go."

¹⁴Joseph's father said, "Go and see if your brothers are safe. Come back and tell me if my sheep are all fine." So Joseph's father sent him from the Valley of Hebron to Shechem.

¹⁵At Shechem, Joseph became lost. A man found him wandering in the fields. The man said, "What are you looking for?"

¹⁶Joseph answered, "I am looking for my brothers. Can you tell me where they are with their sheep?"

¹⁷The man said, "They have already gone away. I heard them say that they were going to Dothan." So Joseph followed his brothers and found them in Dothan.

Joseph Sold into Slavery

¹⁸Joseph's brothers saw him coming from far away. They decided to make a plan to kill him. ¹⁹The brothers said to each other, "Here comes Joseph, the one who dreams. ²⁰We should kill him now while we can. We can throw his body into one of the empty wells. We can tell our father that a wild animal killed him. Then we will show him that his dreams are useless."

²¹But Reuben wanted to save Joseph. Reuben said, "Let's not kill him. ²²We can put him into a well without hurting him." Reuben planned to save Joseph and send him back to his father. ²³Joseph came to his brothers. They attacked him and tore off his long and beautiful coat. ²⁴Then they threw him into an empty well that was dry.

²⁵While Joseph was in the well, the brothers sat down to eat. Then they looked and saw a group of traders* traveling from Gilead to Egypt. Their camels were carrying many different spices and riches. ²⁶So Judah said to his brothers, "What profit will we get if we kill our brother and hide his death? ²⁷We will profit more if we sell him to these traders. Then we will not be guilty of killing our own brother." The other brothers agreed. ²⁸When the Midianite traders came by, the brothers took Joseph out of the well. They sold him to the traders for 20 pieces of silver. The traders took him to Egypt.

²⁹During all this time, Reuben was not there with the brothers. He did not know they had sold Joseph. When Reuben came back to the well, he saw that Joseph was not there. Reuben tore his clothes ₁to show his sadness₁. ³⁰Reuben went to the brothers and said, "The boy is not in the well! What will I do?" ³¹The brothers killed a goat and put the goat's blood on Joseph's beautiful coat. ³²Then the brothers showed the coat to their father. And the brothers said, "We found this coat. Is this Joseph's coat?"

³³The father saw the coat and knew that it was Joseph's. The father said, "Yes, that is his! Maybe some wild animal has killed him. My son Joseph has been eaten by a wild animal!" ³⁴Jacob was so sorry about his son that he tore his clothes. Then Jacob put on special clothes to show that he was sad. Jacob continued to be sad about his son for a long time. ³⁵All of Jacob's sons and daughters tried to comfort him. But Jacob was never comforted. Jacob said, "I will be sorry for my son until the day I die."* So Jacob continued to be sad for his son Joseph.

³⁶The Midianite traders later sold Joseph in Egypt. They sold him to Potiphar, the captain of the Pharaoh's guards.

Judah and Tamar

38 About that time, Judah left his brothers and went to stay with a man named Hirah. Hirah was from the town of Adullam. ²Judah met a Canaanite girl there and married her. The girl's father was named Shua. ³The Canaanite girl gave birth to a son. She named him Er. ⁴Later, she gave birth to another son. She named him Onan. ⁵Later she had another son named Shelah. Judah lived in Kezib when his third son was born.

⁶Judah chose a woman to be the wife of his first son Er. The woman's name was Tamar. ⁷But Er did many bad things. The Lord was not happy

---

I will be sorry ... die Literally, "I will go down to my son in Sheol *(the place of death)* in sadness."

traders Literally, "Ishmaelites."

with him. So the Lord killed him. ⁸Then Judah said to Er's brother Onan, "Go and sleep with your dead brother's wife.* Become like a husband to her. If children are born, then they will belong to your brother Er."

⁹Onan knew that the children from this union would not belong to him. Onan had sexual relations with Tamar, but he did not allow himself to stay inside her. ¹⁰This made the Lord angry. So the Lord killed Onan also. ¹¹Then Judah said to his daughter-in-law Tamar, "Go back to your father's house. Stay there and don't marry until my young son Shelah grows up." Judah was afraid that Shelah would also be killed like his brothers. Tamar went back to her father's home.

¹²Later, Judah's wife, the daughter of Shua, died. After Judah's time of sadness, he went to Timnah with his friend Hirah from Adullam. Judah went to Timnah to have the wool cut from his sheep. ¹³Tamar learned that Judah, her father-in-law, was going to Timnah to cut the wool from his sheep. ¹⁴Tamar always wore clothes that showed that she was a widow. So she put on some different clothes and covered her face with a veil. Then she sat down near the road going to Enaim, a town near Timnah. Tamar knew that Judah's younger son Shelah was now grown up. But Judah would not make plans for her to marry him.

¹⁵Judah traveled on that road. He saw her but thought that she was a prostitute.* (Her face was covered with a veil like a prostitute.) ¹⁶So Judah went to her and said, "Let me have sexual relations with you" (Judah did not know that she was Tamar, his daughter-in-law).

She said, "How much will you give me?"

¹⁷Judah answered, "I will send you a young goat from my flock."

She answered, "I agree to that. But first you must give me something to keep until you send me the goat."

¹⁸Judah asked, "What do you want me to give you as proof that I will send you the goat?"

Tamar answered, "Give me your seal and its string* that you use on your letters. And give me your walking stick." Judah gave these things to her. Then Judah and Tamar had sexual relations, and Tamar became pregnant. ¹⁹Tamar went home and took off the veil that covered her face. Then she again wore the special clothes that showed she was a widow.

²⁰Later, Judah sent his friend Hirah to Enaim to give the prostitute* the goat he promised. Also Judah told Hirah to get the special seal and the walking stick from her. But Hirah could not find her. ²¹Hirah asked some of the men at the town of Enaim, "Where is the prostitute that was here by the road?"

The men answered, "There has never been a prostitute here."

²²So Judah's friend went back to Judah and said, "I could not find the woman. The men that lived in that place said that there was never a prostitute there."

²³So Judah said, "Let her keep the things. I don't want people to laugh at us. I tried to give her the goat, but we could not find her. That is enough."

Tamar Is Pregnant

²⁴About three months later, someone told Judah, "Your daughter-in-law Tamar sinned like a prostitute,* and now she is pregnant."

Then Judah said, "Take her out and burn her."

²⁵The men went to Tamar to kill her. But she sent a message to her father-in-law. Tamar said, "The man who made me pregnant is the man who owns these things. Look at these things. Whose are they? Whose special seal and string* is this? Whose walking stick is this?"

²⁶Judah recognized those things and said, "She is right. I was wrong. I did not give her my son Shelah like I promised." And Judah did not sleep with her again.

²⁷The time came for Tamar to give birth. They saw she was going to have twins. ²⁸While she was giving birth, one baby put his hand out. The nurse tied a red string on the hand and said, "This baby was born first." ²⁹But that baby pulled his hand back in. Then the other baby was born first. So the nurse said, "So you were able to break out first!" So they named him Perez.* ³⁰After this, the other baby was born. This was the baby with the red string on his hand. They named him Zerah*

Go and sleep ... wife In Israel if a man died without children, one of his brothers would take the widow. If a child was born, it would be considered the dead man's child.

prostitute A woman paid by men for sexual sins.

seal ... string People wrote a contract, folded it, tied it with string, put wax or clay on the string, and pressed the seal onto it to seal it. This was like signing the agreement.

Perez This name is like the word meaning "to break out."
Zerah This name is like the word meaning "bright."

Joseph Is Sold to Potiphar in Egypt

39 The traders* who bought Joseph took him down to Egypt. They sold him to the captain of Pharaoh's guard, Potiphar. ²But the Lord helped Joseph. Joseph became a successful man. Joseph lived in the house of his master, Potiphar the Egyptian.

³Potiphar saw that the Lord was with Joseph. Potiphar saw that the Lord helped Joseph be successful in everything he did. ⁴So Potiphar was very happy for Joseph. Potiphar allowed Joseph to work for him and help him to rule the house. Joseph was the ruler over everything Potiphar owned. ⁵After Joseph was made the ruler over the house, the Lord blessed the house and everything that Potiphar owned. The Lord did this because of Joseph. And the Lord blessed everything that grew in the fields of Potiphar. ⁶So Potiphar allowed Joseph to take responsibility for everything in the house. Potiphar worried about nothing, only the food he ate.

Joseph Refuses Potiphar's Wife

Joseph was a very handsome, good-looking man. ⁷After some time, the wife of Joseph's master began to like Joseph. One day she said to him, "Sleep with me."

⁸But Joseph refused. He said, "My master trusts me with everything in his house. He has given me responsibility for everything here. ⁹My master has made me almost equal to him in his house. I must not sleep with his wife! That is wrong! It is a sin against God."

¹⁰The woman talked with Joseph every day, but Joseph refused to sleep with her. ¹¹One day Joseph went into the house to do his work. He was the only man in the house at the time. ¹²His master's wife grabbed his coat and said to him, "Come to bed with me." But Joseph ran out of the house so fast that he left his coat in her hand.

¹³The woman saw Joseph had left his coat in her hands and had run out of the house. ₁So she decided to lie about what had happened.₁ ¹⁴She called to the men outside. She said, "Look! This Hebrew slave was brought here to make fun of us. He came in and tried to attack me, but I screamed. ¹⁵My scream scared him and he ran away. But he left his coat with me." ¹⁶Then she kept his coat until her husband, Joseph's master, came home. ¹⁷And she told her husband the same story. She said, "This Hebrew slave you brought here tried to attack me! ¹⁸But when he came near me I screamed. He ran away, but he left his coat."

Joseph in Prison

¹⁹Joseph's master heard what his wife said. And he became very angry. ²⁰There was a prison where the king's enemies were put. So Potiphar put Joseph into that prison. And Joseph stayed there.

²¹But the Lord was with Joseph. The Lord continued to show his kindness to Joseph. After some time, the commander of the prison guards began to like Joseph. ²²The commander of the guards put Joseph in charge of all the prisoners. Joseph was their leader, but he still did the same work they did. ²³The commander of the guards trusted Joseph with everything that was in the prison. This happened because the Lord was with Joseph. The Lord helped Joseph be successful in everything he did.

Joseph Interprets Two Dreams

40 Later, two of Pharaoh's servants did something wrong to Pharaoh. These servants were the baker and the man who served wine to Pharaoh. ²Pharaoh became angry with his baker and wine server. ³So Pharaoh put them in the same prison as Joseph. Potiphar, the commander of Pharaoh's guards, was in charge of this prison. ⁴The commander put the two prisoners under Joseph's care. The two men continued to stay in prison for some time. ⁵One night, both of the prisoners had a dream. (The two prisoners were the servants of the king of Egypt—the baker and the wine server.) Each prisoner had his own dream. And each dream had its own meaning. ⁶Joseph went to them the next morning. Joseph saw that the two men were worried. ⁷Joseph asked them, "Why do you look so worried today?"

⁸The two men answered, "We dreamed last night, but we don't understand what we dreamed. There is no one to interpret or explain the dreams to us."

Joseph said to them, "God is the One who can understand and interpret dreams. So I beg you, tell me your dreams."

The Wine Server's Dream

⁹So the wine server told Joseph his dream. The server said, "I dreamed I saw a vine. ¹⁰On the vine there were three branches. I watched the branches grow flowers and then become grapes. ¹¹I was holding Pharaoh's cup. So I took the grapes and

---

traders Literally, "Ishmaelites."

squeezed the juice into the cup. Then I gave the cup to Pharaoh."

¹²Then Joseph said, "I will explain the dream to you. The three branches mean three days. ¹³Before the end of three days, Pharaoh will forgive you and allow you to go back to your work. You will do the same work for Pharaoh as you did before. ¹⁴But when you are free, remember me. Be good to me and help me. Tell Pharaoh about me so that I can get out of this prison. ¹⁵I was taken from my own home, the land of my people, the Hebrews. I have done nothing wrong. So I should not be in prison."

The Baker's Dream

¹⁶The baker saw that the other servant's dream was good. So the baker said to Joseph, "I also had a dream. I dreamed there were three bread baskets on my head. ¹⁷In the top basket there were all kinds of baked food. This food was for the king. But birds were eating this food."

¹⁸Joseph answered, "I will tell you what the dream means. The three baskets mean three days. ¹⁹Before the end of three days, the king will take you out of this prison. Then the king will cut your head off! He will hang your body on a pole. And birds will eat your body."

Joseph Is Forgotten

²⁰Three days later, it was Pharaoh's birthday. Pharaoh gave a party for all his servants. At the party, Pharaoh allowed the wine server and the baker to leave the prison. ²¹Pharaoh freed the wine server. Pharaoh gave him his job back. And the wine server put a cup of wine in Pharaoh's hand. ²²But Pharaoh hanged the baker and everything happened the way Joseph said it would. ²³But the wine server did not remember to help Joseph. He said nothing about Joseph to Pharaoh. The wine server forgot about Joseph.

Pharaoh's Dreams

41 Two years later, Pharaoh had a dream. He dreamed that he was standing by the Nile River. ²In the dream, seven cows came out of the river and stood there eating grass. They were healthy, good-looking cows. ³Then seven more cows came out of the river and stood on the bank of the river by the healthy cows. But these cows were thin and sick looking. ⁴The seven sick cows ate the seven healthy cows. Then Pharaoh woke up.

⁵Pharaoh went back to sleep and began dreaming again. This time, he dreamed that he saw seven heads of grain growing on one plant. They were healthy and full of grain. ⁶And then he saw seven more heads of grain sprouting. But they were thin and scorched by the hot wind. ⁷The thin heads of grain ate the seven good heads of grain. Then Pharaoh woke up again and realized it was only a dream. ⁸The next morning Pharaoh was worried about these dreams. So he sent for all the magicians and wise men of Egypt. Pharaoh told these men the dreams, but none of them could interpret the dreams.

The Servant Tells Pharaoh About Joseph

⁹Then the wine servant remembered Joseph. The servant said to Pharaoh, "I remember something that happened to me. ¹⁰You were angry with me and the baker, and you put us in prison. ¹¹Then one night he and I had a dream. Each dream had a different meaning. ¹²There was a young Hebrew man in prison with us. He was a servant of the commander of the guards. We told him our dreams, and he explained them to us. He told us the meaning of each dream. ¹³And what he said came true. He said I would be free and have my old job back. And that happened. He also said the baker would die, and that happened!"

Joseph Is Called to Interpret the Dreams

¹⁴So Pharaoh called Joseph from the prison. The guards quickly got Joseph out of prison. Joseph shaved and put on some clean clothes. Then he went to see Pharaoh. ¹⁵Pharaoh said to Joseph, "I had a dream. But no one can interpret the dream for me. I heard that you can interpret dreams when someone tells you about them."

¹⁶Joseph answered, "I can't! But maybe God will explain them for you, Pharaoh."

¹⁷Then Pharaoh said to Joseph, "In my dream, I was standing by the Nile River. ¹⁸Then seven cows came up out of the river and stood there eating the grass. They were healthy, good-looking cows. ¹⁹Then I saw seven more cows come out of the river after them. But these cows were thin and sick looking. They were the worst cows I had ever seen anywhere in Egypt! ²⁰Then the thin, sick cows ate the first healthy cows! ²¹But they still looked thin and sick. You couldn't even tell they had eaten the healthy cows. They looked as thin and sick as they did in the beginning. Then I woke up.

22"In my next dream I saw seven heads of grain growing on one plant. They were healthy and full of grain. 23And then seven more heads of grain grew after them. But they were thin and scorched by the hot wind. 24Then the thin heads of grain ate the seven good heads of grain.

"I told these dreams to my magicians. But no one could explain the dreams to me. What do they mean?"

Joseph Explains the Dream

25Then Joseph said to Pharaoh, "These two dreams are about the same thing. God is telling you what will happen soon. 26Both dreams really mean the same thing. The seven good cows and the seven good heads of grain are seven ⌊good⌋ years. 27And the seven thin, sick-looking cows and the seven thin heads of grain mean that there will be seven years of hunger in this area. These seven bad years will come after the seven good years. 28God has shown you what will happen soon. And God will make these things happen just like I told you. 29For seven years there will be plenty of food in Egypt. 30But then there will be seven years of hunger. People in Egypt will forget how much food there had been in the past. This famine* will ruin the country. 31People will forget what it was like to have plenty of food.

32"Pharaoh, you had two dreams about the same thing. Why? God wanted to show you that he really will make this happen. And he will make it happen soon! 33So Pharaoh, you should choose a wise, intelligent man and put him in charge of Egypt. 34Then you should choose other men to collect food from the people. During the seven good years, the people must give them one fifth of all the food they grow. 35In this way, these men will collect lots of food during the seven good years and store it in the cities until it is needed. In this way, Pharaoh, this food will be under your control. 36Then during the seven years of hunger, there will be food for the country of Egypt. And Egypt will not be destroyed by the famine."

37This seemed like a very good idea to Pharaoh, and all his officials agreed. 38Then Pharaoh told them, "I don't think we can find anyone better than Joseph to take this job! God's Spirit is in him making him very wise!"

39So Pharaoh said to Joseph, "God showed these things to you, so you must be the wisest man. 40I will put you in charge of my country, and the people will obey all your commands. I will be the only person more powerful than you."

41⌊There was a special ceremony and parade when Pharaoh made Joseph the governor.⌋ Pharaoh said to Joseph, "I now make you governor over all of Egypt." 42Then Pharaoh gave his special ring to Joseph. The royal seal was on this ring. Pharaoh also gave Joseph a fine linen robe and put a gold chain around his neck. 43Pharaoh told Joseph to ride in the second chariot ⌊in the parade⌋. Special guards walked ahead of Joseph's chariot and told the people, "Bow down to Joseph."

So Joseph became the governor over all of Egypt. 44Pharaoh said to him, "I am Pharaoh, the king, ⌊so I will do what I want to do⌋. But no other person in Egypt can lift a hand or move a foot unless you say he can."

45Pharaoh gave Joseph another name, Zaphenath Paneah.* Pharaoh also gave Joseph a wife named Asenath. She was the daughter of Potiphera, a priest in the city of On. So Joseph became the governor over the whole country of Egypt.

46Joseph was 30 years old when he began serving the king of Egypt. Joseph traveled throughout the country of Egypt. 47During the seven good years, the crops in Egypt grew very well. 48And Joseph saved the food in Egypt during those seven years. Joseph stored the food in the cities. In every city, Joseph stored grain that grew in the fields around the city. 49Joseph stored very much grain. It was like the sands of the sea. He stored so much grain that it could not be measured.

50Joseph's wife was Asenath. She was the daughter of Potiphera, the priest in the city of On. Before the first year of hunger came, Joseph and Asenath had two sons. 51The first son was named Manasseh.* Joseph named him this because Joseph said, "God made me forget all of the troubles I have had, and everything about my home." 52Joseph named the second son Ephraim.* Joseph gave him this name because Joseph said, "I had great troubles, but God has made me successful in everything."

---

famine A time when there is no rain and no crops can grow. People and animals often die from lack of food and water.

Zaphenath Paneah This Egyptian name probably means "sustainer of life," but it is like Hebrew words meaning "a person who explains secret things."

Manasseh This is like the Hebrew word meaning "to forget."

Ephraim This is like the Hebrew word meaning "twice fruitful."

GENESIS 41:53–42:24

The Time of Hunger Begins

⁵³For seven years, people had all the food they needed. But then those years ended. ⁵⁴And the seven years of hunger began, just like Joseph had said. No food grew anywhere in any of the countries in that area. But in Egypt, people had plenty to eat! Why? Because Joseph had stored the grain. ⁵⁵The time of hunger began, and the people cried to Pharaoh for food. Pharaoh said to the Egyptian people, "Go ask Joseph what to do."

⁵⁶There was famine* everywhere, so Joseph gave the people grain from the warehouses. Joseph sold the stored grain to the people of Egypt. The famine was bad in Egypt. ⁵⁷But the famine was bad everywhere! So people from the countries around Egypt had to come to Egypt to buy grain.

The Dreams Come True

42 ⌊The famine* was also bad in Canaan.⌋ But Jacob learned that there was grain in Egypt. So Jacob said to his sons, "Why are we sitting here doing nothing? ²I heard there is grain in Egypt for sale. So let's go there to buy grain. Then we can live instead of just letting ourselves die!"

³So ten of Joseph's brothers went to Egypt to buy grain. ⁴Jacob did not send Benjamin. (Benjamin was Joseph's only full brother.*) Jacob was afraid that something bad might happen to Benjamin.

⁵The famine was very bad in Canaan, so there were many people from Canaan who went to Egypt to buy grain. Among them were the sons of Israel.

⁶Joseph was the governor of Egypt at the time. And Joseph was the man who checked the sale of grain to people who came to Egypt. So, Joseph's brothers came to him and bowed before him. ⁷Joseph saw his brothers. Joseph recognized them, but he acted like he didn't know them. He was rude when he spoke to them. He said, "Where do you come from?"

The brothers answered, "We come from the land of Canaan. We have come here to buy food."

⁸Joseph knew that these men were his brothers. But they did not know who he was. ⁹And Joseph remembered the dreams that he had dreamed about his brothers.

Joseph Calls His Brothers Spies

Joseph said to his brothers, "You have not come to buy food! You are spies. You came to learn where we are weak."

¹⁰But the brothers said to him, "No, sir! We come as your servants. We have come only to buy food. ¹¹We are all brothers—we all have the same father. We are honest men. We have come only to buy food."

¹²Then Joseph said to them, "No! You have come to learn where we are weak."

¹³And the brothers said, "No! We are all brothers. There are twelve brothers in our family. We all have the same father. Our youngest brother is still at home with our father. And the other brother died a long time ago. We are like servants before you. We are from the land of Canaan."

¹⁴But Joseph said to them, "No! I can see I am right. You are spies. ¹⁵But I will let you prove that you are telling the truth. In the name of Pharaoh, I swear that I won't let you go until your youngest brother comes here. ¹⁶I'll let one of you go back and bring your youngest brother here to me while the others will stay here in prison. We will see if you are telling the truth. But I believe you are spies." ¹⁷Then Joseph put them all in prison for three days.

Simeon Kept as a Hostage

¹⁸After three days, Joseph said to them, "I am a God-fearing man! Do this, and I will let you live. ¹⁹If you are really honest men, then one of your brothers can stay here in prison. And the others can go and carry grain back to your people. ²⁰But then you must bring your youngest brother back here to me. Then I will know that you are telling the truth and you won't have to die."

The brothers agreed to this. ²¹They said to each other, "We are being punished for the bad thing we did to our younger brother Joseph. We saw the trouble he was in. He begged us to save him. But we refused to listen. So now we are in trouble."

²²Then Reuben said to them, "I told you not to do anything bad to that boy. But you refused to listen to me. So now we are being punished for his death."

²³Joseph was using an interpreter to talk to his brothers. So the brothers did not know that Joseph understood their language. But Joseph heard and understood everything they said. ²⁴⌊Their words

---

famine A time when there is no rain and no crops can grow. People and animals often die from lack of food and water.

full brother Literally, "brother." Joseph and Benjamin had the same mother.

made Joseph very sad. So Joseph left them and cried. After a short time, Joseph went back to them. He took Simeon, one of the brothers, and tied him while the other brothers watched. ²⁵Joseph told some servants to fill their bags with grain. The brothers gave Joseph the money for this grain. But Joseph didn't keep the money. He put the money in their bags of grain. Then Joseph gave them things they would need for their trip back home.

²⁶So the brothers put the grain on their donkeys and left. ²⁷That night the brothers stopped at a place to spend the night. One of the brothers opened his sack to get some grain for his donkey. And there in the sack, he saw his money! ²⁸He said to the other brothers, "Look! Here is the money I paid for the grain. Someone put the money back in my sack!" The brothers were very scared. They said to one another, "What is God doing to us?"

The Brothers Report to Jacob

²⁹The brothers went back to their father Jacob in the land of Canaan. They told Jacob about everything that had happened. ³⁰They said, "The governor of that country spoke rudely to us. He thought that we were spies! ³¹But we told him that we weren't spies, we were honest men! ³²We told him that we were twelve brothers. We told him about our father, and we told him about our youngest brother who was still at home in Canaan.

³³"Then the governor of that country said this to us, 'Here is a way to prove that you are honest men: Leave one of your brothers here with me. Take your grain back to your families. ³⁴Then bring your youngest brother to me. Then I will know if you are honest men, or if you were sent from an army to destroy us. If you are telling the truth, I will give your brother back to you. I will give him to you, and you will be free to buy grain in our country.'"

³⁵Then the brothers started taking the grain out of their sacks. And every brother found his bag of money in his sack of grain. The brothers and their father saw the money and they were scared.

³⁶Jacob said to them, "Do you want me to lose all of my children? Joseph is gone. Simeon is gone. And now you want to take Benjamin away too!"

³⁷But Reuben said to his father, "Father, you may kill my two sons if I don't bring Benjamin back to you. Trust me. I will bring Benjamin back to you."

³⁸But Jacob said, "I will not let Benjamin go with you. His brother is dead, and he is the only son left from my wife Rachel. It would kill me if anything happened to him during the trip to Egypt. You would send me to the grave* a very sad, old man."

Jacob Agrees for Benjamin to go to Egypt

43 The time of hunger was very bad in that country. ²The people ate all the grain they had brought from Egypt. When that grain was gone, Jacob said to his sons, "Go to Egypt and buy some more grain for us to eat."

³But Judah said to Jacob, "But the governor of that country warned us. He said, 'If you don't bring your brother back to me, then I will refuse to talk to you.' ⁴If you will send Benjamin with us, then we can go down and buy grain. ⁵But if you refuse to send Benjamin, then we will not go. That man warned us to not come back without him."

⁶Israel *(Jacob)* said, "Why did you tell him you had another brother? Why did you do such a bad thing to me?"

⁷The brothers answered, "That man asked lots of questions. He wanted to know all about us and about our family. He asked us, 'Is your father still alive? Do you have another brother at home?' We only answered his questions. We didn't know he would ask us to bring our brother to him!"

⁸Then Judah said to his father Israel, "Let Benjamin go with me. I will take care of him. We have to go to Egypt to get food. If we don't go, then we will all die, including our children. ⁹I will make sure he is safe. I will be responsible for him. If I don't bring him back to you, then you can blame me forever. ¹⁰If you had let us go before, we could already have made two trips for food."

¹¹Then their father Israel said, "If it is really true, then take Benjamin with you. But take some gifts to the governor. Take some of the things we have been able to gather in our land. Take him some honey, pistachio nuts, almonds, gum, and myrrh.* ¹²Take twice as much money with you this time. Take the money that was given back to you after you paid last time. Maybe the governor made a mistake. ¹³Take Benjamin, and go back to the man. ¹⁴I pray that God All-Powerful will help you when you stand before the governor. I pray that he will let Benjamin, and also Simeon, come

---

grave Literally, "Sheol," the place for people after death.
gum ,and myrrh The sap from certain plants. This was used to make expensive perfumes and incense.

back safely. If not, I will again be sad from losing my son."

¹⁵So the brothers took the gifts to give to the governor. And the brothers took twice as much money with them as they took the first time. This time, Benjamin went with the brothers to Egypt.

The Brothers Are Invited to Joseph's House

¹⁶In Egypt, Joseph saw Benjamin with them. Joseph said to his servant, "Bring those men into my house. Kill an animal and cook it. Those men will eat with me at noon today." ¹⁷The servant did as he was told. He brought the men into Joseph's house.

¹⁸The brothers were scared when they were taken to Joseph's house. They said, "We have been brought here because of the money that was put back in our sacks the last time. They will use that as proof against us. And they will steal our donkeys and make us slaves."

¹⁹So the brothers went to the servant in charge of Joseph's house. ²⁰They said, "Sir, I promise this is the truth: The last time we came, we came to buy food. ²¹⁻²²On the way home, we opened our sacks and found our money in every sack. We don't know how it got there. But we brought that money with us to give it back to you. And we have brought more money to pay for the food that we want to buy this time."

²³But the servant answered, "Don't be afraid; believe me. Your God, the God of your father, must have put the money in your sack as a gift. I remember that you paid me for the grain the last time."

Then the servant brought Simeon out of the prison. ²⁴The servant led the men into Joseph's house. He gave them water. And they washed their feet. Then he gave their donkeys food to eat.

²⁵The brothers heard that they were going to eat with Joseph. So they worked until noon preparing their gifts for him.

²⁶Joseph came home, and the brothers gave him the gifts that they had brought with them. Then they bowed down on the ground in front of him.

²⁷Joseph asked them how they were doing. Joseph said, "How is your elderly father you told me about. Is he still alive and well?"

²⁸The brothers answered, "Yes sir, our father is still alive." And they again bowed before Joseph.

Joseph Sees His Brother Benjamin

²⁹Then Joseph saw his brother, Benjamin. (Benjamin and Joseph had the same mother.) Joseph said, "Is this your youngest brother that you told me about?" Then Joseph said to Benjamin, "God bless you, my son!"

³⁰Then Joseph ran from the room. Joseph wanted very much to show his brother Benjamin that he loved him. He felt like crying, ₍but he didn't want his brothers to see him crying₎. So Joseph ran to his room and cried there. ³¹Then Joseph washed his face and came out. He took control of himself and said, "Now it is time to eat."

³²The servants seated Joseph at a table by himself. His brothers were at another table by themselves. And the Egyptians were at table by themselves. The Egyptians believed that it was wrong for them to eat with Hebrews. ³³Joseph's brothers sat at a table in front of him. The brothers were sitting in order, from the oldest brother to the youngest. All the brothers kept looking at each other, wondering what was happening. ³⁴Servants were taking food from Joseph's table and bringing it to them. But the servants gave Benjamin five times more than the others. The brothers continued to eat and drink there with Joseph until they were almost drunk.

Joseph Sets a Trap

44 Then Joseph gave a command to his servant. Joseph said, "Fill the men's sacks with as much grain as they can carry. And put each man's money into his sack with the grain. ²Put the the youngest brother's money in his sack too. But also put my special silver cup in his sack." So the servant obeyed Joseph.

³Early the next morning, the brothers and their donkeys were sent back to their country. ⁴After they had left the city, Joseph said to his servant, "Go and follow the men. Stop them and say to them, 'We were good to you! So why have you been bad to us? Why did you steal my master's silver cup? ⁵My master drinks from that cup and he uses it to learn secret things. What you did was wrong!'"

⁶So the servant obeyed. He rode out to the brothers and stopped them. The servant said the things to them that Joseph told him to say.

⁷But the brothers said to the servant, "Why does the governor say these things? We wouldn't do anything like that! ⁸We brought back the money that we found in our sacks before. So surely we wouldn't steal silver or gold from your

master's house. ⁹If you find that silver cup in any of our sacks, then let that man die. You can kill him, and we will be your slaves."

¹⁰The servant said, "We will do as you say. But I will not kill the man. If I find the silver cup, then that man will be my slave. The others will be free."

The Trap Is Sprung; Benjamin Is Caught

¹¹Then every brother quickly opened his sack on the ground. ¹²The servant started looking in the sacks. He started with the oldest brother and ended with the youngest. He found the cup in Benjamin's sack. ¹³The brothers were very sad. They tore their clothes to show their sadness. They put their sacks back on the donkeys and went back to the city.

¹⁴Judah and his brothers went back to Joseph's house. Joseph was still there. The brothers fell to the ground and bowed down before him. ¹⁵Joseph said to them, "Why have you done this? Didn't you know that I have a special way of learning secrets. No person can do this better than me!"

¹⁶Judah said, "Sir, there is nothing we can say! There is no way to explain. There is no way to show that we are not guilty. God has judged us guilty for something else we did. So all of us, even Benjamin, will be your slaves."

¹⁷But Joseph said, "I will not make you all slaves! Only the man who stole the cup will be my slave. You others can go in peace to your father."

Judah Pleads for Benjamin

¹⁸Then Judah went to Joseph and said, "Sir, please let me speak plainly with you. Please don't be angry with me. I know that you are like Pharaoh himself. ¹⁹When we were here before, you asked us, 'Do you have a father or a brother?' ²⁰And we answered you, 'We have a father—he is an old man. And we have a young brother. Our father loves that son because he was born while our father was old. And that young son's brother is dead. So this is the only son that is left born from that mother. Our father loves him very much.' ²¹Then you said to us, 'Then bring that brother to me. I want to see him.' ²²And we said to you, 'That young boy can't come. He can't leave his father. If his father loses him, then his father would be so sad that he would die.' ²³But you said to us, 'You must bring your youngest brother or I will not sell you grain again.' ²⁴So we went back to our father and told him what you said.

²⁵"Later, our father said, 'Go back and buy us some more food.' ²⁶And we said to our father, 'We can't go without our youngest brother. The governor said he will not sell us grain again until he sees our youngest brother.' ²⁷Then my father said to us, 'You know that my wife Rachel gave me two sons. ²⁸I let one son go away, and he was killed by a wild animal. And I haven't seen him since. ²⁹If you take my other son away from me, and something happens to him, then I will be sad enough to die.' ³⁰Now, imagine what will happen when we go home without our youngest brother— That boy is the most important thing in our father's life! ³¹Our father will die if he sees that the boy isn't with us—and it will be our fault! We will send our father to his grave a very sad man!

³²"I took responsibility for the young boy. I told my father, 'If I don't bring him back to you, then you can blame me all my life.' ³³So now I beg you, please let the boy go back with his brothers. And I will stay and be your slave. ³⁴I can't go back to my father if the boy is not with me. I am very afraid of what would happen to my father."

Joseph Tells Who He Is

45 Joseph could not control himself any longer. He cried in front of all the people who were there. Joseph said, "Tell everyone to leave here." So all the people left. Only the brothers were left with Joseph. Then Joseph told them who he was. ²Joseph continued to cry, and all the Egyptian people in Pharaoh's house heard it. ³Joseph said to his brothers, "I am your brother Joseph. Is my father doing well?" But the brothers did not answer him. They were confused and scared.

⁴So Joseph said to his brothers again, "Come here to me. I beg you, come here." So the brothers went close to Joseph. And Joseph said to them, "I am your brother Joseph. I am the one you sold as a slave to Egypt. ⁵Now, don't be worried. Don't be angry with yourselves for what you did. It was God's plan for me to come here. I am here to save your life. ⁶This terrible time of hunger has continued for two years now. And there will be five more years without planting or harvest. ⁷So God sent me here ahead of you so that I can save your people in this country. ⁸It wasn't your fault that I was sent here. It was God's plan. God made me like a father to Pharaoh. I am the governor over all his house and over all of Egypt."

Israel Invited to Egypt

⁹Joseph said, "Hurry up and go to my father. Tell him his son Joseph sent this message." God made me the governor of Egypt. So come here to me. Don't wait. Come now. ¹⁰You can live near me in the land of Goshen. You, your children, your grandchildren, and all of your animals are welcome here. ¹¹I will take care of you during the next five years of hunger. So you and your family will not lose everything you own.

¹²Joseph told his brothers, "Surely you can see that I really am Joseph. Even my brother Benjamin knows it is me, your brother, talking to you. ¹³So tell my father about the honor I have received here in Egypt. Tell him about everything you have seen here. Now hurry, go bring my father back to me." ¹⁴Then Joseph hugged his brother Benjamin, and they both began crying. ¹⁵Then Joseph kissed all his brothers and cried on them. After this, the brothers began talking with him.

¹⁶Pharaoh learned that Joseph's brothers had come to him. This news spread all through Pharaoh's house. Pharaoh and his servants were very excited! ¹⁷Pharaoh told Joseph, "Tell your brothers to take all the food they need and go back to the land of Canaan. ¹⁸Tell them to bring your father and their families back here to me. I will give you the best land in Egypt to live on. And your family can eat the best food we have here." ¹⁹Then the Pharaoh said, "Also give your brothers some of our best wagons. Tell them to go to Canaan and bring your father and all the women and children back in the wagons. ²⁰Don't worry about bringing all of their belongings. We can give them the best of Egypt."

²¹So the sons of Israel did this. Joseph gave them good wagons like the Pharaoh had promised. And Joseph gave them enough food for their trip. ²²Joseph gave each brother a suit of beautiful clothes. But Joseph gave Benjamin five suits of beautiful clothes. And Joseph also gave Benjamin 300 pieces of silver. ²³Joseph also sent gifts to his father. He sent ten donkeys with bags full of many good things from Egypt. And he sent ten female donkeys full of grain, bread, and other food for his father on his trip back. ²⁴Then Joseph told his brothers to go. And while they were leaving, Joseph said to them, "Go straight home. And don't fight on the way."

²⁵So the brothers left Egypt and went to their father in the land of Canaan. ²⁶The brothers told him, "Father, Joseph is still alive! And he is the governor over the whole country of Egypt."

Their father did not know what to think. At first he didn't believe them. ²⁷But then they told him everything Joseph had said. And Jacob saw the wagons Joseph had sent for him to bring him back to Egypt. Then Jacob became excited and very, very happy. ²⁸Israel said, "Now I believe you. My son Joseph is still alive! I am going to see him before I die!"

God Assures Israel

46 So Israel began his trip to Egypt. First Israel went to Beersheba. There, Israel worshiped God, the God of his father Isaac. He offered sacrifices.* ²During the night, God spoke to Israel in a dream. God said, "Jacob, Jacob."

And Israel answered, "Here I am."

³Then God said, "I am God, the God of your father. Don't be afraid to go to Egypt. In Egypt I will make you a great nation. ⁴I will go to Egypt with you. And I will bring you out of Egypt again. You will die in Egypt, but Joseph will be with you. His own hands will close your eyes when you die."

Israel Goes to Egypt

⁵Then Jacob left Beersheba and traveled to Egypt. His sons, the sons of Israel, brought their father, their wives, and all their children to Egypt. They traveled in the wagons the Pharaoh had sent. ⁶They also had their cattle and all the things that they owned in the land of Canaan. So Israel went to Egypt with all his children and his family. ⁷With him were his sons and his grandsons, his daughters and his granddaughters. All of his family went with him into Egypt.

Jacob's Family

⁸Here are the names of Israel's* sons and family that went into Egypt with him:

Reuben was Jacob's first son. ⁹Reuben's sons were Hanoch, Pallu, Hezron, and Carmi.

¹⁰Simeon's sons were Jemuel, Jamin, Ohad, Jakin, and Zohar. There was also Shaul. (Shaul was born from a Canaanite woman.)

¹¹Levi's sons were Gershon, Kohath, and Merari.

---

sacrifice(s) A gift to God. Usually it was a special animal that was killed and burned on an altar.

Israel Another name for Jacob. This name means "he fights for God" or "he fights with God."

¹²Judah's sons were Er, Onan, Shelah, Perez, and Zerah. (Er and Onan died while still in Canaan.) Perez's sons were Hezron and Hamul.
¹³Issachar's sons were Tola, Puah, Job, and Shimron.
¹⁴Zebulun's sons were Sered, Elon, and Jahleel.
¹⁵Reuben, Simeon, Levi, Judah, Issachar, and Zebulun were Jacob's sons from his wife Leah. Leah had those sons in Paddan Aram. She also had a daughter named, Dinah. There were 33 people in this family.
¹⁶Gad's sons were Zephon, Haggi, Shuni, Ezbon, Eri, Arodi, and Areli.
¹⁷Asher's sons were Imnah, Ishvah, Isvi, Beriah, and their sister, Serah. Also there were Beriah's sons, Heber and Malkiel.
¹⁸All those were Jacob's sons from his wife's servant, Zilpah. (Zilpah was the maid that Laban had given to his daughter Leah.) There were 16 people in this family.
¹⁹Benjamin was also with Jacob. Benjamin was Jacob and Rachel's son. (Joseph was also Rachel's son, but Joseph was already in Egypt.)
²⁰In Egypt, Joseph had two sons, Manasseh and Ephraim. (Joseph's wife was Asenath, the daughter of Potiphera, the priest in the city of On.)
²¹Benjamin's sons were Bela, Beker, Ashbel, Gera, Naaman, Ehi, Rosh, Muppim, Huppim, and Ard.
²²Those were the sons of Jacob from his wife Rachel. There were 14 people in this family.
²³Dan's son was Hushim.
²⁴Naphtali's sons were Jahziel, Guni, Jezer, and Shillem.
²⁵Those were the sons of Jacob and Bilhah. (Bilhah was the maid that Laban had given to his daughter Rachel.) There were seven people in this family.
²⁶The total number of Jacob's direct descendants* that went with him to Egypt was 66 people. (The wives of Jacob's sons were not counted in this number.) ²⁷Also, there were the two sons of Joseph. They had been born in Egypt. So there was a total of 70 people in Jacob's family in Egypt.

Israel Arrives in Egypt

²⁸Jacob sent Judah ahead to speak to Joseph first. Judah went to Joseph in the land of Goshen. Then Jacob and his people followed into that land. ²⁹Joseph learned that his father was coming. So Joseph prepared his chariot and went out to meet Israel, his father, in Goshen. When Joseph saw his father, he hugged his neck and cried for a long time.
³⁰Then Israel said to Joseph, "Now I can die in peace. I have seen your face and I know that you are still alive."
³¹Joseph said to his brothers and to the rest of his father's family, "I will go and tell Pharaoh that you are here. I will say to Pharaoh, 'My brothers and the rest of my father's family have left the land of Canaan and have come here to me. ³²They are a family of shepherds. They have always kept sheep and cattle. They have brought all their animals and everything they own with them.' ³³When Pharaoh calls you, he will ask, 'What work do you do?' ³⁴You tell him, 'We are shepherds. All our lives we have been shepherds. And our ancestors* were shepherds before us.' Then Pharaoh will allow you to live in the land of Goshen. Egyptian people don't like shepherds, so it is better that you stay in Goshen."

Israel Settles in Goshen

47 ¹Joseph went in to Pharaoh and said, "My father and my brothers and all their families are here. They have all their animals and everything they own from the land of Canaan with them. They are now in the land of Goshen." ²Joseph chose five of his brothers to be with him before the Pharaoh.
³Pharaoh said to the brothers, "What work do you do?"
The brothers said to Pharaoh, "Sir, we are shepherds. And our ancestors* were shepherds before us." ⁴They said to Pharaoh, "The time of hunger is very bad in Canaan. There are no fields left with grass for our animals. So we have come to live in this land. We ask you to please let us live in Goshen."
⁵Then Pharaoh said to Joseph, "Your father and your brothers have come to you. ⁶You can choose any place in Egypt for them to live. Give your father and your brothers the best land. Let them live in the land of Goshen. And if they are skilled shepherds, then they can also care for my cattle."
⁷Then Joseph called his father Jacob to come in to meet Pharaoh. Jacob blessed Pharaoh. ⁸And Pharaoh said to him, "How old are you?"

---

descendant(s) A person's children and future family.

ancestors Literally, "fathers." This means a person's parents, grandparents, and all the people they are descended from.

⁹Jacob said to Pharaoh, "I have had a short life with many troubles. I have lived only 130 years. My father and his ancestors* lived to be much older than I am."
¹⁰Jacob blessed Pharaoh. Then Jacob left from his meeting with Pharaoh.
¹¹Joseph did what Pharaoh said and gave his father and brothers land in Egypt. It was the best land in Egypt, near the city of Rameses. ¹²And Joseph gave his father, his brothers, and all their people the food that they needed.

Joseph Buys Land for Pharaoh

¹³The time of hunger became worse. There was no food anywhere in the land. Egypt and Canaan became very poor because of this bad time. ¹⁴People in the land bought more and more grain. Joseph saved the money and brought it to Pharaoh's house. ¹⁵After some time, the people in Egypt and Canaan had no money left. They had spent all their money to buy grain. So the people of Egypt went to Joseph and said, "Please give us food. Our money is gone. If we don't eat, we will die while you are watching."
¹⁶But Joseph answered, "Give me your cattle, and I will give you food." ¹⁷So the people used their cattle and horses and all their other animals to buy food. And that year, Joseph gave them food and took their animals.
¹⁸But the next year, people had no animals and nothing to buy food with. So the people went to Joseph and said, "You know that we have no money left. And all our animals belong to you. So we have nothing left—only what you see—our bodies and our land. ¹⁹Surely we will die while you are watching. But if you give us food, then we will give Pharaoh our land, and we will be his slaves. Give us seed so that we can plant. Then we will live and not die. And the land will grow food for us again."
²⁰So Joseph bought all the land in Egypt for Pharaoh. All the people in Egypt sold Joseph their fields. They did this because they were very hungry. ²¹And all the people became slaves of Pharaoh. Everywhere in Egypt, people were Pharaoh's slaves. ²²The only land Joseph didn't buy was the land that the priests owned. The priests didn't need to sell their land because Pharaoh paid them for their work. So they used this money to buy food to eat.
²³Joseph said to the people, "Now I have bought you and your land for Pharaoh. So I will give you seed, and you can plant your fields. ²⁴At harvest time, you must give one fifth of your crops to Pharaoh. You can keep four-fifths for yourselves. You can use the seed you keep for food and planting the next year. Now you can feed your families and your children."
²⁵The people said, "You have saved our lives. We are happy to be slaves to Pharaoh."
²⁶So Joseph made a law at that time in the land. And that law still continues today. The law says that one fifth of everything from the land belongs to the Pharaoh. The Pharaoh owns all the land. The only land he doesn't own is the land of the priests.

"Don't Bury Me in Egypt"

²⁷Israel *(Jacob)* stayed in Egypt. He lived in the land of Goshen. His family grew and became very large. They got that land in Egypt and did very well.
²⁸Jacob lived in Egypt 17 years. So Jacob was 147 years old. ²⁹The time came when Israel *(Jacob)* knew he would soon die, so he called his son Joseph to him. He said, "If you love me, then put your hand under my leg and make a promise.* Promise that you will do what I say and that you will be truthful with me. When I die, don't bury me in Egypt. ³⁰Bury me in the place where my ancestors* are buried. Carry me out of Egypt and bury me in our family grave."
Joseph answered, "I promise that I will do what you say."
³¹Then Jacob said, "Make a vow to me." And Joseph vowed to him that he would do this. Then Israel *(Jacob)* laid his head back down on the bed.*

Blessings for Manasseh and Ephraim

48 Some time later, Joseph learned that his father was very sick. So Joseph took his two sons Manasseh and Ephraim and went to his

---

ancestors Literally, "fathers." This means a person's parents, grandparents, and all the people they are descended from.

put you hand ... make a promise This showed that this was a very important promise and that Jacob trusted Joseph to keep his promise.

Then Israel ... on the bed Or, "Then Israel worshiped on the head of this staff." The Hebrew word for "staff" is like the word for "bed." And the word for "worship" also means to "bow down" or "lie down."

father. ²When Joseph arrived, someone told Israel, "Your son Joseph has come to see you." Israel was very weak, but he tried hard and sat up in his bed. ³Then Israel said to Joseph, "God All-Powerful appeared to me at Luz in the land of Canaan. God blessed me there. ⁴God said to me, 'I will make you a great family. I will give you many children and you will be a great people. Your family will own this land forever.' ⁵And now you have two sons. These two sons were born here in the country of Egypt before I came. Your two sons Ephraim and Manasseh will be like my own sons. They will be the same as Reuben and Simeon to me. ⁶So these two boys will be my sons. They will share in everything I own. But if you have other sons, they will be your sons. But they will also be like sons to Ephraim and Manasseh—that is, in the future, they will share in everything that Ephraim and Manasseh own. ⁷On the trip from Paddan Aram, Rachel died. This made me very sad. She died in the land of Canaan. We were still traveling toward Ephrath. I buried her there on the road to Ephrath. (Ephrath is Bethlehem.)"

⁸Then Israel saw Joseph's sons. Israel said, "Who are these boys?"

⁹Joseph said to his father, "These are my sons. These are the boys God gave me."

Israel said, "Bring your sons to me. I will bless them."

¹⁰Israel was old and his eyes were not good. So Joseph brought the boys close to his father. Israel kissed and hugged the boys. ¹¹Then Israel said to Joseph, "I never thought I would see your face again. But look! God has let me see you and your children."

¹²Then Joseph took the boys off of Israel's lap and they bowed down in front of his father. ¹³Joseph put Ephraim on his right side and Manasseh on his left side. (So Ephraim was on Israel's left side, and Manasseh was on Israel's right side.) ¹⁴But Israel crossed his hands and put his right hand on the head of the younger boy Ephraim. Then Israel put his left hand on the head of the older boy Manasseh. He had his left hand on Manasseh, even though Manasseh was firstborn. ¹⁵And Israel blessed Joseph and said,

"My ancestors,* Abraham and Isaac,
   worshiped our God.
And that God has led me all of my life.
¹⁶ He was the Angel who saved me
   from all my troubles.
And I pray that he will bless these boys.
Now these boys will have my name
   and the name of our ancestors,
      Abraham and Isaac.
I pray that they will grow to become
   great families and nations on earth."

¹⁷Joseph saw that his father put his right hand on Ephraim's head. This didn't make Joseph happy. Joseph took his father's hand. He wanted to move it from Ephraim's head and put it on Manasseh's head. ¹⁸Joseph said to his father, "You have your right hand on the wrong boy. Manasseh is the firstborn. Put your right hand on him!"

¹⁹But his father argued and said, "I know, son. I know. Manasseh is the firstborn. And he will be great. He will also be the father of many people. But the younger brother will be greater than the older brother. And the younger brother's family will be much larger."

²⁰So Israel blessed them that day. He said,

"The people of Israel will use your names
   whenever they bless someone.
They will say,
  "May God make you like
     Ephraim and Manasseh.""

In this way, Israel made Ephraim greater than Manasseh.

²¹Then Israel said to Joseph, "Look, my time to die is almost here. But God will still be with you. He will lead you back to the land of your ancestors*. ²²I have given you something that I did not give your brothers. I give you the mountain that I won from the Amorite people. I used my sword and bow to fight for that mountain. And I won."

Jacob Blesses His Sons

49 Then Jacob called all his sons to him. He said, "All my sons, come here to me. I will tell you what will happen in the future.

---

ancestors Literally, "fathers." This means a person's parents, grandparents, and all the people they are descended from.

GENESIS 49:2–19

² "Come together and listen, sons of Jacob.
Listen to Israel, your father."

Reuben

³ "Reuben, my first son,
  you are my first child,
    the first proof of my power as a man.
  You were the most honored and powerful
    of all my sons.
⁴ But your passion was like a flood
  you couldn't control.
  So you will not remain my most honored son.
  You climbed into your father's bed
    ₁and slept with one of his wives₁.
  You brought shame to my bed
    to the bed you lay on."

Simeon and Levi

⁵ "Simeon and Levi are brothers.
    They love to fight with their swords.
⁶   They planned evil things in secret.
  My soul wants no part in their plans.
  I will not accept their secret meetings.
  They killed men when they were angry.
  And they hurt animals only for fun.
⁷ Their anger is a curse.
  It is too strong.
  They are too cruel when they are mad.
  They will not get their own land
    in the land of Jacob.
  They will be spread throughout Israel."

Judah

⁸ "Judah, your brothers will praise you.
  You will defeat your enemies.
    Your brothers will bow down to you.
⁹ Judah is like a lion.
  My son, you are like a lion
    standing over the animal it killed.
  Judah is like a lion.
  He lies down to rest,
    and no one is brave enough
      to disturb him.
¹⁰ Men from Judah's family will be kings.
  The sign that his family rules
    will not leave his family,
    before the real king comes.*
  Then many people will obey and serve him.

before the real king comes Or, "until Shiloh comes" or "until the man it belongs to comes."

¹¹ He ties his donkey to a grapevine.
  He ties his young donkey to the best
    grapevines.
  He uses the best wine to wash his clothes.
¹² His eyes are red from drinking wine.
  His teeth are white from drinking milk.*"

Zebulun

¹³ "Zebulun will live near the sea.
    His seacoast will be a safe place
      for ships.
    His land will continue as far as the city
      of Sidon."

Issachar

¹⁴ "Issachar is like a donkey who has worked
    too hard.
  He will lie down after carrying a heavy load.
¹⁵ He will see his resting place is good.
  He will see his land is pleasant.
  Then he will agree to carry heavy loads.
  He will agree to work as a slave."

Dan

¹⁶ "Dan* will judge his own people,
    like the other families of Israel.
¹⁷ Dan will be like a snake
    at the side of the road.
  He will be like a dangerous snake
    lying near the path.
  That snake bites a horse's foot,
    and the rider falls to the ground.

¹⁸ "Lord, I am waiting for your salvation."

Gad

¹⁹ "A group of robbers will attack* Gad.
    But Gad will chase them away."

He ties his donkey ... milk Or, "¹¹His donkey will be tied to the grapevine, his young donkey to the best grapevines. He will wash his clothes in wine, his best clothes in the blood of the grapes. ¹²His eyes will be redder than wine, his teeth whiter than milk."

Dan This is like the Hebrew word meaning "judge."

A group of robbers will attack The Hebrew words for "group of robbers" and "attack" sound like the name Gad.

Asher

20 "Asher's land will grow much good food.
He will have food fit for a king!"

Naphtali

21 "Naphtali is like a deer running free,
and his words like their beautiful babies."

Joseph

22 "Joseph is very successful.
Joseph is like a vine covered with fruit,
like a vine growing by a spring,
like a vine growing along a fence.

23 Many people turned and fought against him.
People with arrows became his enemies.
24 But he won the fight
with his mighty bow
and his skillful arms.
He gets power
from the Mighty One of Jacob,
from the Shepherd,
the Rock of Israel,
25 from the God of your father.
God blesses you.

May God All-Powerful bless you
and give you blessings from the sky above,
and blessings from the deep below.
May he give you blessings
from breast and womb.
26 My parents had many, many good things
happen to them.
And I, your father,
was blessed even more.
Your brothers left you with nothing.
But now I pile all my blessings on you,
as high as a mountain."

Benjamin

27 "Benjamin is like a hungry wolf.
In the morning he kills and eats.
In the evening he shares what is left."

28 Those are the twelve families of Israel. And those are the things their father said to them. He gave each son a blessing that was right for him. 29 Then Israel gave them a command. He said, "When I die, I want to be with my people. I want to be buried with my ancestors* in the cave in the field of Ephron the Hittite. 30 That cave is in the field of Machpelah near Mamre. It is in the land of Canaan. Abraham bought that field from Ephron so that he could have a burying place. 31 Abraham and his wife Sarah are buried in that cave. Isaac and his wife Rebekah are buried in that cave. I buried my wife Leah in that cave. 32 That cave is in the field that was bought from the Hittite people." 33 After Jacob finished talking to his sons, he lay down, put his feet back on the bed and died.

Jacob's Funeral

50 When Israel died, Joseph was very sad. He hugged his father and cried on him and kissed him. 2 Joseph commanded his servants to prepare his father's body. (These servants were doctors.) The doctors prepared Jacob's body to be buried. They prepared the body in the special way of the Egyptians. 3 When the Egyptians prepared the body in this special way, they waited 40 days before they buried the body. Then the Egyptians had a special time of sadness for Jacob. This time was 70 days.

4 After 70 days, the time of sadness was finished. So Joseph spoke to the Pharaoh's officers. Joseph said, "Please tell this to Pharaoh: 5 'When my father was near death, I made a promise to him. I promised that I would bury him in a cave in the land of Canaan. This is the cave that he prepared for himself. So please let me go and bury my father. Then I will come back here to you.'"

6 Pharaoh answered, "Keep your promise. Go and bury your father."

7 So Joseph went to bury his father. All of Pharaoh's officials, Pharaoh's elders *(leaders)* and all the elders of Egypt went with Joseph. 8 All the people in Joseph's family, his brothers, and all the people in his father's family went with him. Only the children and the animals stayed in the land of Goshen. 9 It was a very large group of people. There was even a group of soldiers riding chariots and horses.

10 They went to Goren Atad,* east of the Jordan River. At this place they had a long funeral service for Israel. This funeral service continued for seven days. 11 The people who lived in Canaan saw the funeral service at Goren Atad. They said,

---

ancestors Literally, "fathers." This means a person's parents, grandparents, and all the people they are descended from.
Goren Atad Or, "Atad's threshing floor."

"Those Egyptians are having a very sad service!" So now that place across the Jordan River is named Abel Mizraim.*

¹²So Jacob's sons did what their father told them. ¹³They carried his body to Canaan and buried it in the cave at Machpelah. This was the cave near Mamre in the field that Abraham bought from Ephron the Hittite. Abraham bought that cave to use as a burial place. ¹⁴After Joseph buried his father, he and everyone in the group with him went back to Egypt.

The Brothers Are Still Afraid of Joseph

¹⁵After Jacob died, Joseph's brothers became worried. They were afraid that Joseph would still be mad at them for what they had done years before. They said, "Maybe Joseph still hates us for what we did." ¹⁶So the brothers sent this message to Joseph:

Before your father died, he told us to give you a message. ¹⁷He said, 'Tell Joseph that I beg him to please forgive his brothers for the bad things they did to him.' So now Joseph, we beg you, please forgive us for the bad things we did to you. We are the servants of God, the God of your father.

That message made Joseph very sad, and he cried. ¹⁸His brothers went to him and bowed down in front of him. They said, "We will be your servants."

¹⁹Then Joseph said to them, "Don't be afraid. I am not God! ⌊I have no right to punish you.⌋ ²⁰It is true that you planned to do something bad to me. But really, God was planning good things. God's plan was to use me to save the lives of many people. And that is what happened! ²¹So don't be afraid. I will take care of you and your children." In this way, Joseph said nice things to his brothers. This made his brothers feel good.

²²Joseph continued to live in Egypt with his father's family. Joseph died when he was 110 years old. ²³During Joseph's life, Ephraim had children and grandchildren. And his son Manasseh had a son named Makir. Joseph lived to see Makir's children.

The Death of Joseph

²⁴When Joseph was near death, he said to his brothers, "My time to die is almost here. But I know that God will take care of you and lead you out of this country. God will lead you to the land he promised to give Abraham, Isaac, and Jacob."

²⁵Then Joseph asked his people to make a promise. Joseph said, "Promise me that you will carry my bones with you when God leads you to that new land."

²⁶Joseph died in Egypt when he was 110 years old. Doctors prepared his body for burial and put the body in a coffin in Egypt.

Abel Mizraim This means "Egyptian time of sadness."

Exodus

Jacob's Family in Egypt

1 Jacob *(Israel)* traveled to Egypt with his sons. Each son had his own family with him. These are the sons of Israel: ²Reuben, Simeon, Levi, Judah, ³Issachar, Zebulun, Benjamin, ⁴Dan, Naphtali, Gad, Asher. ⁵There was a total of 70 people who were direct descendants* of Jacob. (Joseph was one of the twelve sons, but he was already in Egypt.)

⁶Later, Joseph, his brothers, and all the people of that generation died. ⁷But the people of Israel had many children, and their number grew and grew. The people of Israel became strong, and the country of Egypt was filled with the Israelites.

Trouble for the People of Israel

⁸Then a new king began to rule Egypt. This king did not know Joseph. ⁹This king said to his people, "Look at the people of Israel. There are too many of them! And they are stronger than we are! ¹⁰We must make plans to stop the Israelites from growing stronger. If there is a war, the people of Israel might join our enemies. Then they might defeat us and escape from us."

¹¹The Egyptian people decided to make life hard for the people of Israel. So the Egyptians put slave masters over the people. These masters forced the Israelites to build the cities of Pithom and Rameses for the king. The king used these cities to store grain and other things.

¹²The Egyptians forced the Israelites to work harder and harder. But the more the people of Israel were forced to work, the more they grew and spread. And the Egyptian people became more and more afraid of the people of Israel. ¹³So the Egyptians forced the people of Israel to work even harder.

¹⁴The Egyptians made life hard for the Israelites. They forced the Israelites to work very hard making bricks and mortar. They also forced them to work hard in the fields. They forced them to work very hard in everything they did.

The Nurses Who Followed God

¹⁵There were two nurses who helped the Israelite women give birth to children. They were named Shiphrah and Puah. The king of Egypt talked to the nurses. ¹⁶The king said, "You will continue to help the Hebrew* women give birth to their children. If a girl baby is born, then let the baby live. But if the baby is a boy, then you must kill him!"

¹⁷But the nurses trusted* God. So they did not obey the king's command. They let all the boy babies live.

¹⁸The king of Egypt called for the nurses and told them, "Why did you do this? Why did you let the boy babies live?"

¹⁹The nurses said to the king, "The Hebrew* women are much stronger than the Egyptian women. They give birth to their babies before we can go to help them." (²⁰⁻²¹God was happy with the nurses. So God was good to them and allowed them to have their own families. And the Hebrew people continued to have more children, and they became very strong.)

²²So Pharaoh* gave this command to all of his own people: "Let all the girl babies live. But every time a boy baby is born, you must throw him into the Nile River."

Baby Moses

2 There was a man from the family of Levi. He married a woman who was also from the family of Levi. ²The woman became pregnant and

---

descendants A person's children and their future families.

Hebrew Or, "Israelite." This name might also mean, "descendants of Eber (Gen.10:25-31) or "people from west of the Euphrates River."

trusted Literally, "feared" or "respected."

Pharaoh A title people used for the king of Egypt. This word means "the Great House."

gave birth to a baby boy. The mother saw how beautiful the baby was, and she hid him for three months. ³The mother was afraid that the baby would be found and killed because he was a boy. After three months, she made a basket and covered it with tar* so that it would float. She put the baby in the basket. Then she put the basket in the river in the tall grass. ⁴The baby's sister stayed and watched. She wanted to see what would happen to the baby.

⁵Just then, Pharaoh's daughter went to the river to bathe. She saw the basket in the tall grass. Her servants were walking beside the river. So she told one of them to go get the basket. ⁶The king's daughter opened the basket and saw a baby boy. The baby was crying and she felt sorry for it. Then she noticed that it was one of the Hebrew* babies.

⁷The baby's sister ⌊was still hiding. She stood and⌋ asked the king's daughter, "Do you want me to go find a Hebrew* woman who can nurse the baby and help you care for it?"

⁸The king's daughter said, "Yes, please."

So the girl went and brought the baby's own mother.

⁹The king's daughter said to the mother, "Take this baby and feed him for me. I'll pay you to take care of him."

So the woman took her baby and cared for him. ¹⁰The baby grew, and after some time, the woman gave the baby to the king's daughter. The king's daughter accepted the baby as her own son. She named him Moses* because she had pulled him from the water.

Moses Helps His People

¹¹Moses grew and became a man. He saw that his own people, the Hebrews,* were forced to work very hard. One day Moses saw an Egyptian man beating a Hebrew* man. ¹²Moses looked around and saw that no one was watching. Then Moses killed the Egyptian and buried him in the sand.

¹³The next day Moses saw two Hebrew* men fighting each other. Moses saw that one man was wrong. Moses said to that man, "Why are you hurting your neighbor?"

¹⁴The man answered, "Did anyone say you could be our ruler and judge? No! Tell me, will you kill me like you killed the Egyptian yesterday*?"

Then Moses was afraid. Moses thought to himself, "Now everyone knows what I did."

¹⁵Pharaoh heard about what Moses did, so he decided to kill Moses. But Moses ran away from Pharaoh. Moses went to the land of Midian.

Moses in Midian

Moses stopped near a well in Midian. ¹⁶There was a priest in Midian who had seven daughters. Those girls came to that well to get water for their father's sheep. They were trying to fill the water trough with water. ¹⁷But there were some shepherds there who chased the girls away and would not let them get water. So Moses helped the girls and gave water to their animals.

¹⁸Then they went back to their father, Reuel.* Their father said to them, "You have come home early today!"

¹⁹The girls answered, "Yes, sir. The shepherds tried to chase us away, but an Egyptian man helped us. He got water for us and gave it to our animals."

²⁰So Reuel said to his daughters, "Where is this man? Why did you leave him? Call him here and let him eat with us."

²¹Moses was happy to stay with that man. Reuel let Moses marry his daughter, Zipporah. ²²Zipporah became pregnant and had a son. And Moses named him Gershom.* Moses gave his son this name because Moses was a stranger in a land that was not his own.

God Decides to Help Israel

²³A long time passed and that king of Egypt died. But the people of Israel were still forced to work very hard. They cried for help, and God heard them. ²⁴God heard their prayers, and he remembered the agreement he made with Abraham, Isaac, and Jacob. ²⁵God saw the troubles of the people of Israel, and he knew ⌊that he would soon help them⌋.

---

tar Or, "pitch," a thick oil that must be heated to become liquid.
Hebrew Or, "Israelite."
Moses This name is like a Hebrew word meaning "to pull or draw out."

yesterday This word is in the ancient Greek translation, but not in the Hebrew text.
Reuel He is also called Jethro.
Gershom This is like the Hebrew words meaning "a stranger there."

The Burning Bush

3 Moses' father-in-law was named Jethro.* (Jethro was a priest of Midian). Moses took care of Jethro's sheep. One day, Moses led the sheep to the west side of the desert. Moses went to a mountain called Horeb *(Sinai)*, the mountain of God. ²On that mountain, Moses saw the Angel of the Lord in a burning bush. ₁This is how it happened.₁ Moses saw a bush that was burning without being destroyed. ³So Moses decided to go closer to the bush and see how a bush could continue burning without being destroyed.

⁴The Lord saw Moses was coming to look at the bush. So God called to Moses from the bush. God said, "Moses, Moses!"

And Moses said, "Yes, Lord."

⁵Then the Lord said, "Don't come any closer. Take off your sandals. You are standing on holy ground. ⁶I am the God of your ancestors.* I am the God of Abraham, the God of Isaac, and the God of Jacob."

Moses covered his face because he was afraid to look at God.

⁷Then the Lord said, "I have seen the troubles my people have suffered in Egypt. And I have heard their cries when the Egyptians hurt them. I know about their pain. ⁸Now I will go down and save my people from the Egyptians. I will take them from that land. And I will lead them to a good land where they can be free from troubles.* It is a land filled with many good things.* Many different people live in that land: the Canaanites, the Hittites, the Amorites, the Perizzites, the Hivites, and the Jebusites. ⁹I have heard the cries of the people of Israel. I have seen the way the Egyptians have made life hard for them. ¹⁰So now I am sending you to Pharaoh. Go! Lead my people, the people of Israel, out of Egypt!"

¹¹But Moses said to God, "I am not a great man! How can I be the person to go to Pharaoh and lead the people of Israel out of Egypt?"

¹²God said, "You can do it because I will be with you! This will be the proof that I am sending you: After you lead the people out of Egypt, you will come and worship me on this mountain!"

¹³Then Moses said to God, "But if I go to the people of Israel and say to them, 'The God of your ancestors* sent me,' then the people will ask, 'What is his name?' What should I tell them?"

¹⁴Then God said to Moses, "₁Tell them,₁ 'I AM WHO I AM.'* When you go to the people of Israel, tell them, 'I AM' sent me to you.'"

¹⁵God also said to Moses, "This is what you should tell the people: 'YAHWEH* is the God of your ancestors,* the God of Abraham, the God of Isaac, and the God of Jacob. My name will always be YAHWEH. That is how the people will know me for generations and generations to come.' ₁Tell the people,₁ 'YAHWEH has sent me to you!'"

¹⁶₁The Lord also said,₁ "Go and gather together the elders ₁(leaders)₁ of the people and tell them, 'YAHWEH,* the God of your ancestors,* has appeared to me. The God of Abraham, Isaac, and Jacob spoke to me. The Lord says: I have thought about you and the things that have happened to you in Egypt. ¹⁷And I have decided that I will take you from the troubles you are suffering in Egypt. I will lead you to the land that now belongs to many different people: the Canaanites, the Hittites, the Amorites, the Perizzites, the Hivites, and the Jebusites. I will lead you to a land filled with many good things.*

¹⁸"The elders *(leaders)* will listen to you. And then you and the elders *(leaders)* will go to the king of Egypt. You will tell him that 'YAHWEH! is the God of the Hebrew* people. Our God came to us and told us to travel three days into the desert. There we must offer sacrifices* to YAHWEH our God.'

¹⁹"But I know that the king of Egypt will not let you go. Only a great power will force him to let you go. ²⁰So I will use my great power against Egypt. I will cause amazing things to happen in that land. After I do this, he will let you go. ²¹And I will cause the Egyptian people to be kind to the

---

Jethro He is also called Reuel.
ancestors Literally, "fathers," meaning a person's parents, grandparents, and all the people they are descended from.
land ... troubles Literally, "a spacious land."
land filled with many good things Literally, "a land flowing with milk and honey."

I AM WHO I AM The Hebrew words are like the name YAHWEH ("Lord").
YAHWEH This name, usually translated "Lord," is like the Hebrew word meaning, "He is" or "He makes things exist."
filled with many good things Literally, "flowing with milk and honey."
Hebrew Or, "Israelite."
sacrifice(s) A gift to God. Usually it was a special animal that was killed and burned on an altar.

people of Israel. The Egyptians will give many gifts to your people when they leave Egypt.

²²"All of the Hebrew* women must ask their Egyptian neighbors and the Egyptian women living in their houses for gifts. And those Egyptian women will give them gifts. Your people will get gifts of silver, gold, and fine clothing. Then, when you leave Egypt, you will put those gifts on your children. In this way, you will take away the wealth of the Egyptians."

Proof for Moses

4 Then Moses said to God, "But the people of Israel will not believe me when I tell them that you sent me. They will say, 'The Lord* did not appear to you.'"

²But God said to Moses, "What is that you have in your hand?"

Moses answered, "It is my walking stick."

³Then God said, "Throw your walking stick on the ground."

So Moses threw his walking stick on the ground. And the stick became a snake. Moses was afraid and ran from it. ⁴But the Lord said to Moses, "Reach out and grab the snake by its tail."

So Moses reached out and caught the snake's tail. When Moses did this, the snake became a walking stick again. ⁵Then God said, "Use your stick in this way and the people will believe that you saw the Lord, the God of your ancestors,* the God of Abraham, the God of Isaac, and the God of Jacob."

⁶Then the Lord said to Moses, "I will give you another proof. Put your hand under your robe."

So Moses opened his robe and put his hand inside. Then Moses brought his hand out of the robe and it was changed. His hand was covered with spots that were white like snow.

⁷Then God said, "Now put your hand into your robe again." So Moses put his hand into his robe again. Then Moses brought his hand out, and his hand was changed. Now his hand was good again, like it was before.

⁸Then God said, "If the people don't believe you when you use your walking stick, then they will believe you when you show them this sign. ⁹If they still refuse to believe after you show them both of these things, then take some water from the Nile River. Pour the water on the ground, and as soon as it touches the ground, it will become blood."

¹⁰But Moses said to the Lord, "But Lord, I am telling you the truth, I am not a skilled speaker. I have never been able to speak well. And now, even after talking to you, I am still not a good speaker. You know that I talk slowly and don't use the best words."*

¹¹Then the Lord said to him, "Who made man's mouth? And who can make a man deaf or not able to speak? Who can make a man blind? Who can make a man able to see? ₁I am the One who can do all these things—₁I am YAHWEH.* ¹²So go. I will be with you when you speak. I will give you the words to say."

¹³But Moses said, "My Lord, I beg you to send another person—not me."

¹⁴Then the Lord became angry with Moses and said, "Fine! I'll give you someone to help you. I will use your brother Aaron, from the family of Levi. He is a skilled speaker. Aaron is already coming to see you. He will be happy to see you. ¹⁵He will go with you to Pharaoh. I will tell you what to say. Then you will tell Aaron. And Aaron will choose the right words to speak to Pharaoh. ¹⁶Aaron will also speak to the people for you. You will be like a great king, and he will be your official speaker.* ¹⁷So go. And carry your walking stick with you. Use your stick and the other miracles to show the people that I am with you."

Moses Returns to Egypt

¹⁸Then Moses went back to Jethro, his father-in-law. Moses said to Jethro, "Please let me go back to Egypt. I want to see if my people are still alive."

Jethro said to Moses, "Sure! And may you go in peace."

¹⁹Then, while Moses was still in Midian, God said to him, "It is safe for you to go back to Egypt now. The men who wanted to kill you are now dead."

²⁰So Moses put his wife and children on the donkey and returned to Egypt. Moses carried his walking stick with him—the walking stick with the power of God.

Hebrew Or, "Israelite."
Lord Or, "YAHWEH."
ancestors Literally, "fathers." This means a person's parents, grandparents, and all the people they are descended from.

I talk ... words Or, "I stutter and don't speak clearly."
I am YAHWEH Or, "I am the Lord."
You will be ... speaker Literally, "He will be your mouth, and you will be his God."

EXODUS 4:21–5:14

²¹While Moses was traveling back to Egypt, God spoke to him. God said, "When you talk to Pharaoh remember to show him all the miracles that I have given you the power to do. But I will cause Pharaoh to be very stubborn. He will not let the people go. ²²Then you should say to Pharaoh: ²³The Lord says, 'Israel is my firstborn* son. And I am telling you to let my son go and worship me! If you refuse to let Israel go, then I will kill your firstborn son.'"

Moses' Son Circumcised

²⁴On the way to Egypt, Moses stopped at a place to spend the night. The Lord met Moses at that place and tried to kill him.* ²⁵But Zipporah took a flint knife* and circumcised* her son. She took the skin and touched his feet. Then she said ⌊to Moses⌋, "You are a bridegroom of blood to me." ²⁶Zipporah said this because she had to circumcise her son. So God forgave Moses ⌊and did not kill him⌋.*

Moses and Aaron before God

²⁷The Lord had spoken to Aaron. The Lord had told him, "Go out into the desert and meet Moses." So Aaron went and met Moses at the Mountain of God.* Aaron saw Moses and kissed him. ²⁸Moses told Aaron why the Lord had sent him. And Moses told Aaron about all the miracles and things he must do to prove that God had sent him. Moses told Aaron everything the Lord had said. ²⁹So Moses and Aaron went and gathered together all the elders *(leaders)* of the people of Israel. ³⁰Then Aaron spoke to the people. He told them all the things that the Lord had told Moses. Then Moses did the proofs for all the people to see. ³¹The people believed that God had sent Moses. The people of Israel knew that God had seen their troubles, and that he had come to help them. So they bowed down and worshiped God.

Moses And Aaron Before Pharaoh

5After Moses and Aaron talked to the people, they went to Pharaoh. They said, "The Lord* God of Israel says, 'Let my people go into the desert so they can have a feast to honor me.'"

²But Pharaoh said, "Who is the Lord? Why should I obey him? Why should I let Israel go? I don't even know who this Lord is, so I refuse to let Israel go."

³Then Aaron and Moses said, "The God of the Hebrew* people has talked with us. So we beg you to let us travel three days into the desert. There we will offer a sacrifice* to the Lord our God. If we don't do this, he might become angry and destroy us. He might make us die from sickness or war."

⁴But Pharaoh said to them, "Moses and Aaron, you are bothering the workers. Let them do their work! Go mind your own business! ⁵There are very many workers, and you are keeping them from doing their jobs."

Pharaoh Punishes the People

⁶That same day, Pharaoh gave a command to make work harder for the people of Israel. Pharaoh said to the slave masters and Hebrew foremen, ⁷"You have always given the people straw and they use it to make bricks. But now, tell them they have to go and find their own straw to make bricks. ⁸But they must still make the same number of bricks as they did before. They have become lazy. That is why they are asking me to let them go. They don't have enough work to do. That is why they asked me to let them make sacrifices* to their God. ⁹So make these people work harder. Keep them busy. Then they will not have enough time to listen to the lies of Moses."

¹⁰So the Egyptian slave masters and the Hebrew* foremen went to the people of Israel and said, "Pharaoh has decided that he will not give you straw for your bricks. ¹¹You must go and get the straw for yourselves. So go and find straw. But you must still make as many bricks as you made before."

¹²So the people went everywhere in Egypt looking for straw. ¹³The slave masters forced the people to work even harder. They forced the people to make as many bricks as before. ¹⁴The

---

firstborn The first child born into a family. The firstborn son was very important in ancient times.
tried to kill him Or possibly, "wanted to circumcise him."
flint knife A sharp knife made from flint rock.
circumcise(d) Cutting off the foreskin. In Israel this was proof that a man had made a special agreement to obey God's laws and teachings.
Verse 26 Or, "And he was healed. She said, 'You are a bridegroom of blood' because of the circumcision."
Mountain of God That is, Mount Horeb (Sinai).

Lord Or, "YAHWEH."
Hebrew Or, "Israelite."
sacrifice(s) A gift to God. Usually it was a special animal that was killed and burned on an altar.

EXODUS 5:15–6:22

Egyptian slave masters had chosen the Hebrew* foremen and had made them responsible for the work the people did. The Egyptian slave masters beat these foremen and said to them, "Why aren't you making as many bricks as you made in the past? If you could do it then, you can do it now!"

¹⁵Then the Hebrew* foremen went to Pharaoh. They complained and said, "We are your servants. Why are you treating us like this? ¹⁶You won't give us any straw, but you tell us to make as many bricks as before. And now our masters are beating us. Your people are wrong for doing this."

¹⁷Pharaoh answered, "You are lazy. You don't want to work. That is why you ask me to let you go. And that is why you want to leave here and make sacrifices* to the Lord. ¹⁸Now, go back to work! We will not give you any straw! And you must still make as many bricks as you did before!"

¹⁹The Hebrew* foremen knew they were in trouble. The foremen knew they could not make as many bricks as they made in the past.

²⁰When they were leaving the meeting with Pharaoh, they passed Moses and Aaron. Moses and Aaron were waiting for them. ²¹So they said to Moses and Aaron, "You really made a mistake when you told Pharaoh to let us go. May the Lord punish you because you caused Pharaoh and his rulers to hate us. You have given them an excuse to kill us."

Moses Complains to God

²²Then Moses prayed to the Lord and said, "Master, why have you done this terrible thing to your people? Why did you send me here? ²³I went to Pharaoh and said the things you told me to say. But since that time he has been mean to the people. And you have done nothing to help them!"

6 Then the Lord said to Moses, "Now you will see what I will do to Pharaoh. I will use my great power against him, and he will let my people go. He will be so ready for them to leave that he will force them to go."

²Then God said to Moses, ³"I am the Lord. I appeared to Abraham, Isaac, and Jacob. They called me El Shaddai *(God All-Powerful)*. They did not know my name, YAHWEH *(Lord)*. ⁴I made an agreement with them. I promised to give them the land of Canaan. They lived in that land, but it was not their own land. ⁵Now, I know about the troubles of the people of Israel. I know that they are the slaves of Egypt. And I remember my agreement. ⁶So tell the people of Israel that I say to them, 'I am the Lord. I will save you. I will make you free. You will not be slaves of the Egyptians. I will use my great power and bring terrible punishment to the Egyptians. Then I will save you. ⁷You will be my people and I will be your God. I am the Lord your God, and you will know that I made you free from Egypt. ⁸I made a great promise to Abraham, Isaac, and Jacob. I promised to give them a special land. So I will lead you to that land. I will give you that land. It will be yours. I am the Lord.'"

⁹So Moses told this to the people of Israel. But the people would not listen to him. They were working so hard that they were not patient with Moses.

¹⁰Then the Lord said to Moses, ¹¹"Go tell Pharaoh that he must let the people of Israel leave his land."

¹²But Moses answered, "The people of Israel refuse to listen to me! So surely Pharaoh will also refuse to listen. I am a very bad speaker!*"

¹³But the Lord talked with Moses and Aaron. God commanded them to go and talk to the people of Israel. He also commanded them to go and talk to Pharaoh. God commanded them to lead the people of Israel out of the land of Egypt.

Some of the Families of Israel

¹⁴Here are the names of the leaders of the families of Israel: Israel's first son, Reuben, had four sons. They were Hanoch, Pallu, Hezron, and Carmi. ¹⁵Simeon's sons were Jemuel, Jamin, Ohad, Jakin, Zohar, and Shaul. (Shaul was the son from a Canaanite woman). ¹⁶Levi lived 137 years. Levi's sons were Gershon, Kohath, and Merari. ¹⁷Gershon had two sons, Libni and Shimei. ¹⁸Kohath lived 133 years. Kohath's sons were Amram, Izhar, Hebron, and Uzziel. ¹⁹Merari's sons were Mahli and Mushi. All these families were from Israel's son Levi.

²⁰Amram lived 137 years. Amram married his father's sister, Jochebed. Amram and Jochebed gave birth to Aaron and Moses. ²¹Izhar's sons were Korah, Nepheg, and Zicri. ²²Uzziel's sons were Mishael, Elzaphan, and Sithri.

Hebrew Or, "Israelite."
sacrifice(s) A gift to God. Usually it was a special animal that was killed and burned on an altar.

I am a very bad speaker Or, "I sound like a foreigner." Literally, "I have uncircumcised lips."

²³Aaron married Elisheba. (Elisheba was the daughter of Amminadab, and the sister of Nahshon). Aaron and Elisheba gave birth to Nadab, Abihu, Eleazar, and Ithamar. ²⁴The sons of Korah, ₍the ancestors of₎ the Korahites, were Assir, Elkanah, and Abiasaph. ²⁵Aaron's son, Eleazar, married a daughter of Putiel. And she gave birth to Phinehas. All these people were from Israel's son, Levi.

²⁶Aaron and Moses were from this family group. And they are the men that God spoke to and said, "Lead my people out of Israel in groups.*" ²⁷Aaron and Moses are the men that talked to Pharaoh, the king of Egypt. They told Pharaoh to let the people of Israel leave Egypt.

God Repeats His Call to Moses

²⁸In the land of Egypt God spoke to Moses. ²⁹He said, "I am the Lord. Tell the king of Egypt everything that I tell you."

³⁰But Moses answered, "I am a very bad speaker. The king will not listen to me."

7 The Lord said to Moses, "I will be with you. You will be like a great king* to Pharaoh. And Aaron will be your official speaker.* ²Tell Aaron everything that I command you. Then he will tell the king the things I say. And Pharaoh will let the people of Israel leave this country. ³But I will make Pharaoh stubborn. ₍He will not obey the things you tell him.₎ Then I will do many miracles in Egypt to prove who I am. But he will still refuse to listen. ⁴So then I will punish Egypt very much. And I will lead my people out of that land. ⁵Then the people of Egypt will know that I am the Lord. I will be against them, and they will know that I am the Lord. Then I will lead my people out of their country."

⁶Moses and Aaron obeyed these things the Lord told them. ⁷Moses was 80 years old at the time, and Aaron was 83.

Moses' Walking Stick Becomes a Snake

⁸The Lord said to Moses and Aaron, ⁹"Pharaoh will ask you to prove your power. He will ask you to do a miracle. Tell Aaron to throw his walking stick on the ground. While Pharaoh is watching, the stick will become a snake."

¹⁰So Moses and Aaron went to Pharaoh and obeyed the Lord. Aaron threw his walking stick down. While Pharaoh and his officers watched, the stick became a snake. ¹¹So the king called for his wise men and magicians. These men used their tricks and they were able to do the same thing as Aaron. ¹²They threw their walking sticks on the ground, and their sticks became snakes. But then Aaron's walking stick ate theirs. ¹³Pharaoh still refused to let the people go. This happened just like the Lord said it would. The king refused to listen to Moses and Aaron.

The Water Becomes Blood

¹⁴Then the Lord said to Moses, "Pharaoh is being stubborn. Pharaoh refuses to let the people go. ¹⁵In the morning, Pharaoh will go out to the river. Go to him by the edge of the Nile River. Take the walking stick that became a snake. ¹⁶Tell him this: 'The Lord, the God of the Hebrew people, sent me to you. The Lord told me to tell you to let his people go worship him in the desert. Until now you have not listened to the Lord. ¹⁷So the Lord says that he will do something to show you that he is the Lord. I will hit the water of the Nile River with this walking stick in my hand, and the river will change into blood. ¹⁸The fish in the river will die, and the river will begin to stink. Then the Egyptians will not be able to drink the water from the river.'"

¹⁹The Lord said to Moses: "Tell Aaron to hold the walking stick in his hand over the rivers, canals, lakes and every place where they store water. When he does this, all the water will change into blood. All of the water, even the water stored in wood and stone jars, will change into blood."

²⁰So Moses and Aaron did what the Lord commanded. Aaron raised the walking stick and hit the water in the Nile River. He did this in front of Pharaoh and his officials. So all the water in the river changed into blood. ²¹The fish in the river died, and the river began to stink. So the Egyptians could not drink water from the river. The blood was everywhere in Egypt.

²²The magicians used their tricks and did the same thing. So Pharaoh refused to listen to Moses and Aaron. This happened just like the Lord said. ²³Pharaoh ignored what Moses and Aaron had done. Pharaoh just turned and went into his house.

²⁴The Egyptians could not drink the water from the river. So they dug wells around the river for water to drink.

---

groups Or, "divisions." This is a military term that shows Israel was organized like an army.
a great king Or, "God."
official speaker Or, "prophet."

The Frogs

²⁵Seven days passed after the Lord changed the Nile River.

8 Then the Lord told Moses, "Go to Pharaoh and tell him that the Lord says, 'Let my people go to worship me! ²If you refuse to let my people go, then I will fill Egypt with frogs. ³The Nile River will be filled with frogs. They will come from the river and enter your houses. They will be in your bedrooms, and in your beds. The frogs will be in the houses of your officials and in your ovens and in your jars of water. ⁴The frogs will be all over you, your people, and your officials.'"

⁵Then the Lord said to Moses, "Tell Aaron to hold the walking stick in his hand over the canals, rivers, and lakes. Then the frogs will come out onto the land of Egypt."

⁶So Aaron raised his hand over the waters of Egypt, and the frogs began coming out of the water and covered the land of Egypt.

⁷The magicians used their tricks to do the same thing—so even more frogs came out onto the land in Egypt!

⁸Pharaoh called for Moses and Aaron. Pharaoh said, "Ask the Lord to remove the frogs from me and my people. I will let the people go to offer sacrifices to the Lord."

⁹Moses said to Pharaoh, "Tell me when you want the frogs to go away. I will pray for you, your people, and your officials. Then the frogs will leave you and your houses. The frogs will remain only in the river. ₍When do you want the frogs to leave?₎"

¹⁰Pharaoh said, "Tomorrow."

Moses said, "It will happen as you say. In this way, you will know that there is no god like the Lord our God. ¹¹The frogs will leave you, your house, your officials, and your people. The frogs will remain only in the river."

¹²Moses and Aaron left Pharaoh. Moses prayed to the Lord about the frogs he had sent against Pharaoh. ¹³And the Lord did what Moses asked. The frogs died in the houses, in the yards, and in the fields. ¹⁴They began to rot, and the whole country began to stink. ¹⁵Pharaoh saw that they were free of the frogs, and he again became stubborn. Pharaoh did not do what Moses and Aaron had asked him to do. This happened just like the Lord had said.

The Lice

¹⁶Then the Lord said to Moses, "Tell Aaron to raise his stick and hit the dust on the ground, and everywhere in Egypt dust will become lice."

¹⁷They did this. Aaron raised the stick in his hand and hit the dust on the ground, and everywhere in Egypt the dust became lice. The lice got on the animals and the people.

¹⁸The magicians used their tricks and tried to do the same thing. But the magicians could not make lice come from the dust. The lice remained on the animals and the people. ¹⁹So the magicians told Pharaoh that the power of God did this. But Pharaoh refused to listen to them. This happened just like the Lord had said.

The Flies

²⁰The Lord said to Moses, "Get up in the morning and go to Pharaoh. Pharaoh will go out to the river. Tell him that the Lord says, 'Let my people go and worship me! ²¹If you don't let my people go, then flies will come into your houses. The flies will be on you and your officials. The houses of Egypt will be full of flies. The flies will be all over the ground too! ²²But I will not treat the people of Israel the same as the Egyptian people. There will not be any flies in Goshen, where my people live. In this way you will know that I, the Lord, am in this land. ²³So tomorrow I will treat my people differently from your people. That will be my proof."

²⁴So the Lord did just what he said. Many, many flies came into Egypt. The flies were in Pharaoh's house, and they were in all his officials' houses. The flies were all over Egypt. The flies were ruining the country. ²⁵So Pharaoh called for Moses and Aaron. Pharaoh told them, "Offer sacrifices* to your God here in this country."

²⁶But Moses said, "It would not be right to do that. The Egyptians think that it is a terrible thing to ₍kill animals as₎ sacrifices* for the Lord our God. If we do this here, then the Egyptians will see us, and they will throw stones at us and kill us. ²⁷Let us go three days into the desert and offer sacrifices* to the Lord our God. This is what the Lord told us to do."

²⁸So Pharaoh said, "I will let you go and offer sacrifices* to the Lord your God in the desert. But, you must not go very far! Now, go and pray for me."

---

sacrifice(s) A gift to God. Usually it was a special animal that was killed and burned on an altar.

²⁹Moses said, "Look, I will leave and ask the Lord to remove the flies from you, your people, and your officials tomorrow. But you must not stop the people from offering sacrifices* to the Lord." ³⁰So Moses left Pharaoh and prayed to the Lord. ³¹And the Lord did what Moses asked. The Lord removed the flies from Pharaoh, his officials, and his people. None of the flies remained. ³²But Pharaoh again became stubborn and did not let the people go.

The Disease of the Farm Animals

9 Then the Lord told Moses to go to Pharaoh and tell him: "The Lord, the God of the Hebrew people, says, 'Let my people go to worship me!' ²If you continue to hold them and refuse to let them go, ³then the Lord will use his power against your animals in the fields. The Lord will cause all of your horses, donkeys, camels, cattle, and sheep to become sick with a terrible disease. ⁴The Lord will treat Israel's animals differently from the animals of Egypt. None of the animals that belong to the people of Israel will die. ⁵The Lord has set the time for this to happen. Tomorrow the Lord will cause this to happen in this country.'"

⁶The next morning, all the farm animals in Egypt died. But none of the animals that belonged to the people of Israel died. ⁷Pharaoh sent people to see if any of the animals of Israel died. And not one of the animals of Israel died. Pharaoh remained stubborn. He did not let the people go.

The Boils

⁸The Lord said to Moses and Aaron, "Fill your hands with the ashes from an oven. Moses, throw the ashes into the air in front of Pharaoh. ⁹This will become dust that will go throughout the land of Egypt. Whenever the dust touches a person or an animal in Egypt, boils *(sores)* will break out on the skin."

¹⁰So Moses and Aaron took ashes from a furnace. Then they went and stood before Pharaoh. They threw the ashes into the air, and boils began breaking out on people and animals. ¹¹The magicians could not stop Moses from doing this, because even the magicians had the boils. This happened everywhere in Egypt. ¹²But the Lord made Pharaoh stubborn. So Pharaoh refused to listen to Moses and Aaron. This happened just like the Lord had said.

---

sacrifice(s) A gift to God. Usually it was a special animal that was killed and burned on an altar.

The Hail

¹³Then the Lord said to Moses, "Get up in the morning and go to Pharaoh. Tell him that the Lord, the God of the Hebrew people says, 'Let my people go to worship me! ¹⁴If you don't do this, then I will use my full power against you, your officials, and your people. Then you will know that there is no god in the world like me. ¹⁵I could use my power and cause a disease that would wipe you and your people off the earth. ¹⁶But I have put you here for a reason. I have put you here so that I could show you my power. Then people all over the world will learn about me! ¹⁷You are still against my people. You are not letting them go free. ¹⁸So, at this time tomorrow, I will cause a very bad hailstorm. There has never been a hailstorm like this in Egypt, not since Egypt became a nation. ¹⁹Now, you must put your animals in a safe place. Everything you own that is now in the fields must be put in a safe place. Why? Because any person or animal that remains in the fields will be killed. The hail will fall on everything that is not gathered into your houses.'"

²⁰Some of Pharaoh's officials paid attention to the Lord's message. Those men quickly put all of their animals and slaves into houses. ²¹But other people ignored the Lord's message. Those people lost all their slaves and animals that were in the fields.

²²The Lord told Moses, "Raise your arms into the air and the hail will start falling all over Egypt. The hail will fall on all the people, animals, and plants in all the fields of Egypt."

²³So Moses raised his walking stick into the air, and the Lord caused thunder, lightning, and hail to fall to earth. The hail fell all over Egypt. ²⁴The hail was falling. And there was lightning flashing all through it. It was the worst hailstorm that had ever hit Egypt since it had been a nation. ²⁵The storm destroyed everything in the fields in Egypt. The hail destroyed people, animals, and plants. The hail also broke all the trees in the fields. ²⁶The only place that did not get hail was the land of Goshen, where the people of Israel lived.

²⁷Pharaoh sent for Moses and Aaron. Pharaoh told them, "This time I have sinned. The Lord is right, and I and my people are wrong. ²⁸The hail and thunder from God are too much! Ask God to stop the storm and I will let you go. You don't have to stay here."

²⁹Moses told Pharaoh, "When I leave the city, I will lift my arms in prayer to the Lord. And the thunder and hail will stop. Then you will know that the Lord is in this land. ³⁰But I know that you

and your officials don't really fear and respect the Lord yet."

³¹The flax had already developed its seeds. And the barley was already blooming. So these plants were destroyed. ³²But the wheat and spelt ripen later than the other grains, so these plants were not destroyed.

³³Moses left Pharaoh and went outside the city. He lifted his arms in prayer to the Lord. And the thunder and hail stopped, and then even the rain stopped. ³⁴When Pharaoh saw that the rain, hail, and thunder had stopped, he again did wrong. He and his officials became stubborn again. ³⁵Pharaoh refused to let the people of Israel go free. This happened just like the Lord had said through Moses.

The Locusts

10 The Lord said to Moses, "Go to Pharaoh. I have made him and his officials stubborn. I did this so I could show them my powerful miracles. ²I also did this so you could tell your children and your grandchildren about the miracles and other wonderful things that I have done in Egypt. Then all of you will know that I am the Lord."

³So Moses and Aaron went to Pharaoh. They told him, "The Lord, the God of the Hebrew people, says, 'How long will you refuse to obey me? Let my people go to worship me! ⁴If you refuse to let my people go, then tomorrow I will bring locusts into your country. ⁵The locusts will cover the land. There will be so many locusts that you won't be able to see the ground. Anything that was left from the hailstorm will be eaten by the locusts. The locusts will eat all the leaves from every tree in the field. ⁶The locusts will fill all your houses, and all your officials' houses, and all the houses in Egypt. There will be more locusts than your fathers or your grandfathers ever saw. There will be more locusts than there have ever been since people began living in Egypt.'" Then Moses turned and left Pharaoh.

⁷Then the officials asked Pharaoh, "How long will we be trapped by these people. Let the men go to worship the Lord their God. If you don't let them go, then before you know it, Egypt will be destroyed!"

⁸So Pharaoh told his officials to bring Moses and Aaron back to him. Pharaoh said to them, "Go and worship the Lord your God. But tell me, exactly who is going?"

⁹Moses answered, "All of our people, young and old, will go. And we will take our sons and daughters, and our sheep and cattle with us. We will all go because the Lord's feast is for all of us."

¹⁰Pharaoh said to them, "The Lord really will have to be with you before I let you and all of your children leave Egypt. Look, you are planning something bad. ¹¹The men can go worship the Lord. That is what you asked for in the beginning. But all of your people can't go." Then Pharaoh sent Moses and Aaron away.

¹²The Lord told Moses, "Raise your arm over the land of Egypt and the locusts will come! The locusts will spread all over the land of Egypt. The locusts will eat all the plants that the hail did not destroy."

¹³So Moses raised his walking stick over the land of Egypt, and the Lord caused a strong wind to blow from the east. The wind blew all that day and night. When morning came, the wind had brought the locusts to the land of Egypt. ¹⁴The locusts flew into the country of Egypt and landed on the ground. There were more locusts than there had ever been in Egypt. And there will never again be that many locusts there. ¹⁵The locusts covered the ground, and the whole country became dark. The locusts ate every plant on the ground and all of the fruit in the trees that the hail had not destroyed. There weren't any leaves left on any of the trees or plants anywhere in Egypt.

¹⁶Pharaoh quickly called for Moses and Aaron. Pharaoh said, "I have sinned against the Lord your God and against you. ¹⁷Now, forgive me for my sins this time. Ask the Lord to remove this 'death' *(locusts)* from me."

¹⁸Moses left Pharaoh and prayed to the Lord. ¹⁹So the Lord changed the wind. The Lord made a very strong wind blow from the west, and it blew the locusts out of Egypt and into the Red Sea. Not one locust was left in Egypt! ²⁰But the Lord caused Pharaoh to be stubborn again. And Pharaoh did not let the people of Israel go.

The Darkness

²¹Then the Lord told Moses, "Raise your arm into the air and darkness will cover Egypt. It will be so dark you can feel it!"

²²So Moses raised his arm into the air and a cloud of darkness covered Egypt. The darkness stayed in Egypt for three days. ²³None of the people could see each other. And no one got up to go any place for three days. But there was light in all the places where the people of Israel lived.

²⁴Again Pharaoh called for Moses. Pharaoh said, "Go and worship the Lord! You can take your children with you. But you must leave your sheep and cattle here." ²⁵Moses said, "₍Not only will we take our sheep and cattle with us, but when we leave,₎ even you will give us offerings and sacrifices* for us to use in worshiping the Lord our God! ²⁶Yes, we will take our animals with us to worship the Lord. Not one hoof* will be left behind. We don't know yet exactly what we will need to worship the Lord. We will learn that only when we get to the place we are going to. So we must take all of these things with us."

²⁷The Lord made Pharaoh stubborn again. So Pharaoh refused to let them go. ²⁸Then Pharaoh told Moses, "Get out of here! I don't want you to come here again! The next time you come to see me, you will die!"

²⁹Then Moses told Pharaoh, "You are right about one thing. I won't come to see you again!"

The Death of the Firstborn

11 Then the Lord told Moses, "I have one more disaster to bring against Pharaoh and Egypt. After this, he will send you out of Egypt. In fact, he will force you to leave this country. ²You must give this message to the people of Israel: 'Men and women, you must ask your neighbors to give you things made of silver and gold. ³The Lord will cause the Egyptians to be kind to you. The Egyptian people, even Pharaoh's own officials, already consider Moses to be a great man.'"

⁴Moses said to the people, "The Lord says, 'At midnight tonight, I will go through Egypt, ⁵and every firstborn* son in Egypt will die, from the firstborn son of Pharaoh, the ruler of Egypt, to the firstborn son of the slave girl grinding grain. Even the firstborn animals will die. ⁶The crying in Egypt will be worse than at any time in the past. And it will be worse than it will ever be in the future. ⁷But none of the people of Israel will be hurt—not even a dog will bark at them. None of the people of Israel or any of their animals will be hurt. In this way, you will know that I have treated Israel differently from Egypt. ⁸Then all of these slaves of yours *(the Egyptians)* will bow down and worship me. They will say, "Leave and take all your people with you." Then in anger, I will leave Pharaoh.'"

⁹Then the Lord told Moses, "Pharaoh has not listened to you. Why? So that I could show my great power in Egypt." ¹⁰That is why Moses and Aaron did all these great miracles in front of Pharaoh. And that is why the Lord made Pharaoh so stubborn that he would not let the people of Israel leave his country.

Passover

12 While Moses and Aaron were still in Egypt, the Lord spoke to them. The Lord said, ²"This month* will be the first month of the year for you. ³This command is for the whole community of Israel: On the tenth day of this month each person must get one lamb for the people in his house. ⁴If there are not enough people in his house to eat a whole lamb, then he should invite some of his neighbors to share the meal. There must be enough lamb for everyone to eat. ⁵The lamb must be a one-year-old male, and it must be completely healthy. This animal can be either a young sheep or a young goat. ⁶You should watch over the animal until the 14th day of the month. On that day, all the people of the community of Israel must kill these animals at twilight.* ⁷You must collect the blood from these animals. Put the blood on the top and sides of the door frames of the houses where the people eat this meal.

⁸"On this night, you must roast the lamb and eat all of the meat. You must also eat bitter herbs and bread made without yeast. ⁹You must not boil the lamb in water. You must roast the whole lamb over a fire. The lamb must still have its head, legs, and inner parts. ¹⁰You must eat all of the meat that night. If any of the meat is left until morning, then you must burn that meat in the fire.

¹¹"When you eat the meal, you must be fully dressed like you are going on a journey. You must have your shoes on, and your walking stick in your hand. You must eat in a hurry. Why? Because this is the Lord's Passover*—₍the time when the Lord protected his people and led them quickly out of Egypt₎.

---

sacrifice(s) A gift to God. Usually it was a special animal that was killed and burned on an altar.
hoof The hard part of the foot of certain animals.
firstborn The first child born into a family. The firstborn son was very important in ancient times.
month That is, the month of Abib (Nisan). This was about the middle of March to the middle of April.
twilight The time after the sun goes down, but before dark.
Passover The Hebrew word means "to skip, pass over" or "to protect."

¹²"Tonight I will go through Egypt and kill every firstborn* man and animal in Egypt. In this way, I will judge all the gods of Egypt. I will show that I am the Lord. ¹³But the blood on your houses will be a special sign. When I see the blood, I will pass over* your house. I will cause bad things to happen to the people of Egypt. But none of those bad diseases will hurt you.

¹⁴"So you will always remember tonight—it will be a special holiday for you. Your descendants* will honor the Lord with this holiday forever. ¹⁵On this holiday, you will eat bread made without yeast for seven days. On the first day of this holiday, you will remove all the yeast from your houses. No one should eat any yeast for the full seven days of this holiday. If anyone eats yeast, then you must separate that person from the rest of Israel. ¹⁶There will be holy assemblies on the first and last days of the holiday. You must not do any work on these days. The only work you can do on these days is prepare the food for your meals. ¹⁷You must remember the Festival of Unleavened Bread.* Why? Because on this day I took all of your people out of Egypt in groups.* So, all of your descendants* must remember this day. This is a law that will last forever. ¹⁸So, on the evening of the 14th day of the first month *(Nisan)* you will begin eating bread without yeast. You will eat this bread until the evening of the 21st day of the same month. ¹⁹For seven days there must not be any yeast in your houses. Any person, either a citizen of Israel or a foreigner, who eats yeast at this time must be separated from the rest of Israel. ²⁰On this holiday, you must not eat yeast. You must eat bread without yeast wherever you live."

²¹So Moses called all the elders *(leaders)* together. Moses told them, "Get the lambs for your families. Kill the lambs for the Passover. ²²Take bunches of hyssop* and dip them in the bowls filled with blood. Paint the blood on the sides and tops of the door frames. No one must leave his house until morning. ²³At the time the Lord goes through Egypt to kill the firstborn, the Lord will see the blood on the sides and tops of the door frames. Then the Lord will protect* that house. The Lord will not let the Destroyer come into your houses and hurt you. ²⁴You must remember this command. This law is for you and your descendants* forever. ²⁵You must remember to do this even when you go to the land the Lord is giving you. ²⁶When your children ask you, 'Why are we doing this ceremony?' ²⁷you will say, 'This Passover is to honor the Lord. Why? Because when we were in Egypt, the Lord passed over* the houses of Israel. The Lord killed the Egyptians, but he saved the people in our houses. So now the people bow down and worship the Lord.'"

²⁸The Lord had given this command to Moses and Aaron. So the people of Israel did what the Lord commanded.

²⁹At midnight, the Lord killed all the firstborn sons in Egypt, from the firstborn son of Pharaoh (who ruled Egypt) to the firstborn son of the prisoner sitting in jail. Also all the firstborn animals died. ³⁰That night someone died in every house in Egypt. Pharaoh, his officials, and all the people of Egypt began crying very loudly.

Israel Leaves Egypt

³¹So that night, Pharaoh called for Moses and Aaron. Pharaoh said to them, "Get up and leave my people. You and your people can do as you say. Go and worship the Lord! ³²And you can take all of your sheep and cattle with you, just like you said you would. Go! And bless me too!" ³³The people of Egypt also asked them to hurry and leave. Why? Because they said, "If you don't leave, we will all die!"

³⁴The people of Israel did not have time to put the yeast in their bread. They just wrapped the bowls of dough with cloth and carried them on their shoulders. ³⁵Then the people of Israel did what Moses asked them to do. They went to their Egyptian neighbors and asked for clothing and things made from silver and gold. ³⁶The Lord caused the Egyptians to be kind to the people of Israel. So the Egyptians gave their riches to the people of Israel.

³⁷The people of Israel traveled from Rameses to Succoth. There were about 600,000 men. This does not include the children. ³⁸There were many, many sheep, cattle and other things. There were also many different kinds of people traveling with

---

firstborn The first child born into a family. The firstborn son was very important in ancient times.
pass over Or, "protect."
descendants A person's children and their future families.
Unleavened Bread Bread made without yeast.
group(s) Or, "divisions." This is a military term that shows Israel was organized like an army.
hyssop A plant with stems about 3 feet long. The leaves and branches are like hair, so they could be used like a brush.

protect Or, "pass over."
passed over Or, "protected."

them. These people were not Israelites, but they left Egypt with the people of Israel. ³⁹The people did not have time to put yeast in their bread. And they did not make any special food for their journey. So they had to bake their bread without yeast.

⁴⁰The people of Israel had lived in Egypt* for 430 years. ⁴¹After 430 years, to the very day, all the armies of the Lord* left Egypt. ⁴²So that is a very special night when the people remember what the Lord did. All the people of Israel will remember that night forever.

⁴³The Lord told Moses and Aaron, "Here are the rules for Passover: No foreigner is to eat the Passover. ⁴⁴But if a person buys a slave, and if he circumcises* him, then the slave can eat the Passover. ⁴⁵But if a person just lives in your country, or if a person is only hired to work for you, then that person must not eat the Passover. ⌊Passover is for the people of Israel.⌋

⁴⁶"⌊Each family must⌋ eat the meal in one house. None of the food is to be taken outside the house. Don't break any of the lamb's bones. ⁴⁷The whole community of Israel must do this ceremony. ⁴⁸If a non-Israelite lives with you, and if he wants to share in the Lord's Passover, then he must be circumcised.* Then he will be the same as any other citizen of Israel, so he can share in the meal. But if a man is not circumcised, then he cannot eat the Passover meal. ⁴⁹The same rules are for everyone. It does not matter if a person is a citizen or a non-Israelite living in your country—the same rules are for everyone."

⁵⁰So all the people of Israel obeyed the commands that the Lord gave to Moses and Aaron. ⁵¹So on that same day, the Lord led all the people of Israel out of the country of Egypt. The people left in groups.*

13 Then the Lord said to Moses, ²"Every Israelite woman's first baby boy will belong to me. Every firstborn baby and every firstborn animal will be mine."

³Moses said to the people, "Remember this day. You were slaves in Egypt. But on this day the Lord used his great power and made you free. You must not eat bread with yeast. ⁴Today, in the month of Abib,* you are leaving ⌊Egypt⌋. ⁵The Lord made a special promise to your ancestors.* The Lord promised to give you the land of the Canaanite people, the Hittite people, the Amorite people, the Hivite people, and the Jebusite people. After the Lord leads you to the land filled with many good things,* then you must remember this day. You must have a special day of worship on this day during the first month of every year.

⁶"For seven days you must eat only bread that has no yeast. On the seventh day there will be a great feast. This feast will show honor to the Lord. ⁷So for seven days you must not eat any bread made with yeast. There must be no bread with yeast any place in your land. ⁸On this day, you should tell your children, 'We are having this feast because the Lord took me out of Egypt.'

⁹"This holiday will help you remember—it will be like a string tied on your hand. It will be like a sign before your eyes.* This holiday will help you remember the Lord's teachings. It will help you remember that the Lord used his great power to take you out of Egypt. ¹⁰So remember this holiday every year at the right time.

¹¹"The Lord will lead you into the land he promised to give you. The Canaanite people now live there. But God promised your ancestors* that he would give you this land. After God gives you this land, ¹²you must remember to give him every firstborn boy. And every male animal that is the firstborn must be given to the Lord. ¹³Every firstborn donkey can be bought back from the Lord. You can offer a lamb and keep the donkey. If you don't want to buy the donkey from the Lord, then kill it. It will be a sacrifice*—you must break its neck. Every firstborn baby boy* must be bought back from the Lord.

Egypt The ancient Greek and Samaritan translations say, "Egypt and Canaan." This would mean they counted the years from about Abraham's time, not from Joseph's. See Gen. 15:12-16 and Gal. 3:17.
armies of the Lord The people of Israel.
circumcise(d) To have the foreskin cut off. This was done to every Jewish male to show he shared in the agreement God made with Israel. See Gen. 17:9-14.
groups Or, "divisions." This is a military term, and it shows the people were organized as the "army of the Lord."
Abib Or, "spring." This is Nisan, the first month of the ancient Jewish year.
ancestors Literally, "fathers." This means a person's parents, grandparents, and all the people they are descended from.
filled with many good things Literally, "flowing with milk and honey."
string ... eyes Literally, "a mark on your hands and a reminder between your eyes." This might refer to the special things a Jewish man ties to his arm and forehead to help him remember God's laws for him.
sacrifice(s) A gift to God. Usually it was a special animal that was killed and burned on an altar.
baby boy Or, "baby."

EXODUS 13:14–14:14

¹⁴"In the future, your children will ask why you do this. They will say, 'What does all this mean?' And you will answer, 'The Lord used his great power to save us from Egypt. We were slaves in that place. But the Lord led us out and brought us here. ¹⁵In Egypt, Pharaoh was stubborn. He refused to let us leave. But the Lord killed every firstborn* in all the land. (The Lord killed the firstborn animals and the firstborn sons.*) So that is why I give every firstborn male animal to the Lord. And that is why I buy back each of my firstborn sons* from the Lord.' ¹⁶This is like a string tied on your hand. And it is like a sign in front of your eyes.* It helps you remember that the Lord brought us out of Egypt with his great power."

The Trip out of Egypt

¹⁷Pharaoh made the people leave Egypt. The Lord did not let the people take the road leading to the land of the Philistines. That road ₍by the sea₎ is the shortest way, but the Lord said, "₍If the people go that way₎ they will have to fight. Then they might change their minds and go back to Egypt." ¹⁸So the Lord led them another way. He led them through the desert by the Red Sea.* The people of Israel were dressed for war when they left Egypt.

Joseph Goes Home

¹⁹Moses carried the bones of Joseph with him. (Before Joseph died, he made the sons of Israel promise to do this for him. Joseph said, "When God saves you, remember to carry my bones with you out of Egypt.")

The Lord Leads His People

²⁰The people of Israel left Succoth and camped at Etham. Etham was near the desert. ²¹The Lord led the way. During the day, the Lord used a tall cloud to lead the people. And during the night, the Lord used a tall column of fire to lead the way. This fire gave them light so they could also travel at night. ²²The tall cloud was always with them during the day, and the column of fire was always with them at night.

14 Then the Lord said to Moses, ²"Tell the people to go back to Pi Hahiroth. Tell them to spend the night between Migdol and the ₍Red₎ Sea, near Baal Zephon. ³Pharaoh will think that the people of Israel are lost in the desert. And he will think that the people will have no place to go. ⁴I will make Pharaoh brave, and he will chase you. But I will defeat Pharaoh and his army. This will bring honor to me. Then the people of Egypt will know that I am the Lord." The people of Israel obeyed God—they did what he told them.

Pharaoh Chases the Israelites

⁵Pharaoh received a report that the people of Israel had escaped. When he heard this, he and his officials changed their minds about what they had done. Pharaoh said, "Why did we let the people of Israel leave? Why did we let them run away? Now we have lost our slaves!"

⁶So Pharaoh prepared his chariot* and took his men with him. ⁷Pharaoh took 600 of his best men and all of his chariots. There was an officer in each chariot. ⁸The people of Israel were leaving with their arms raised in victory. But the Lord caused Pharaoh, the king of Egypt, to become brave. And Pharaoh chased the people of Israel.

⁹The Egyptian army had many horse soldiers and chariots. They chased the people of Israel and caught up with them while they were camped near the Red Sea* at Pi Hahiroth, east of Baal Zephon.

¹⁰The people of Israel saw Pharaoh and his army coming toward them. The people were very scared. They cried to the Lord for help. ¹¹They said to Moses, "Why did you bring us out of Egypt? Why did you bring us out here in the desert to die? We could have died peacefully in Egypt—there were plenty of graves in Egypt. ¹²We told you this would happen! In Egypt we said, 'Please don't bother us. Let us stay and serve the Egyptians.' It would have been better for us to stay and be slaves than to come out here and die in the desert."

¹³But Moses answered, "Don't be afraid! Don't run away! Just stand still and watch the Lord save you today. You will never see these Egyptians again! ¹⁴And you won't have to do anything but stay calm. The Lord will do the fighting for you."

---

firstborn The first child born into a family. The firstborn son was very important in ancient times.
sons Or, "children."
string ... eyes Literally, "a mark on your hands, a symbol on your forehead." This might refer to the special things a Jewish man tied to his arm and forehead to help him remember God's laws.
Red Sea Or, "Reed Sea." But see 1 Kings 9:26.

chariot(s) A small wagon used in war.

¹⁵Then the Lord said to Moses, "Why are you still crying to me! Tell the people of Israel to start moving. ¹⁶Raise the walking stick in your hand over the Red Sea,* and the sea will split. Then the people can go across on dry land. ¹⁷I have made the Egyptians brave, so they will chase you. But I will show you that I am more powerful than Pharaoh and all of his horses and chariots. ¹⁸Then Egypt will know that I am the Lord. They will honor me when I defeat Pharaoh and his horse soldiers and chariots."

The Lord Defeats the Egyptian Army

¹⁹Then the angel of the Lord moved to the back of the people. (The angel of the Lord was usually at the front of the people, leading them.) So the tall cloud moved from in front of the people and went to the back of the people. ²⁰In this way the cloud stood between the Egyptians and the people of Israel. There was light for the people of Israel. But there was darkness for the Egyptians. So the Egyptians did not come any closer to the people of Israel that night.

²¹Moses raised his arm over the Red Sea,* and the Lord caused a strong wind to blow from the east. The wind blew all night long. The sea split, and the wind made the ground dry. ²²The people of Israel went through the sea on dry land. The water was like a wall on their right and on their left. ²³Then all of Pharaoh's chariots and horse soldiers followed them into the sea. ²⁴Early that morning, the Lord looked down from the tall cloud and column of fire at the Egyptian army. Then the Lord attacked and defeated them all.

²⁵The wheels of the chariots became stuck. It was very hard to control the chariots. The Egyptians shouted, "Let's get out of here! The Lord is fighting against us. The Lord is fighting for the people of Israel."

²⁶Then the Lord told Moses, "Raise your hand over the sea, and the water will fall and cover the Egyptian chariots and horse soldiers."

²⁷So, just before daylight, Moses raised his hand over the sea. And the water rushed back to its proper level. The Egyptians were running as fast as they could from the water, but the Lord swept them away with the sea. ²⁸The water returned to its proper level and covered the chariots and horse soldiers. Pharaoh's army had been chasing the people of Israel, but that army was destroyed. None of them survived!

Red Sea Or, "Reed Sea." But see 1 Kings 9:26.

²⁹And the people of Israel crossed the sea on dry land. The water was like a wall on their right and on their left. ³⁰So that day, the Lord saved the people of Israel from the Egyptians. And later the people of Israel saw the dead bodies of the Egyptians on the shore of the Red Sea.* ³¹The people of Israel saw the great power of the Lord when he defeated the Egyptians. So the people feared and respected the Lord. They began to trust the Lord and his servant Moses.

The Song of Moses

15 Then Moses and the people of Israel began singing this song to the Lord:

"I will sing to the Lord!
    He has done great things.
    He threw horse and rider into the sea.
² The Lord is my strength.
    He saves me,
    and I sing songs of praise to him.*
    The Lord is my God,
    and I praise him.
    The Lord is the God of my ancestors,*
    and I honor him.
³ The Lord is a great soldier.
    The Lord is his name.
⁴ He threw Pharaoh's chariots and
    soldiers
    into the sea.
    Pharaoh's very best soldiers
    drowned in the Red Sea.*
⁵ The deep water covered them.
    And they sank to the bottom like
    rocks.

⁶ "Your right arm is amazingly strong.
    Lord, your right arm shattered the
    enemy.
⁷ In your great majesty you destroyed
    the men who stood against you.
    Your anger destroyed them,
    like fire burning straw.
⁸ The wind you sent in anger
    piled the water high.
    The flowing water became a solid wall.
    The sea became solid to its deepest parts.

The Lord ... him Literally, "Yah is my strength and praise. And he becomes my salvation."

ancestors Literally, "fathers," meaning a person's parents, grandparents, and all the people they are descended from.

⁹ "The enemy said,
   'I'll chase them and catch them.
   I'll take all their riches.
   I'll take it all with my sword.
   I'll take everything for myself.'
¹⁰ But you blew on them
   and covered them with the sea.
   They sank like lead into the deep sea.

¹¹ "Are there any gods like the Lord?
   No! There are no gods like you—
   You are wonderfully holy!
   You are amazingly powerful!
   You do great miracles!
¹² You could raise your right hand
   and destroy the world!
¹³ But with your kindness
   you lead the people you saved.
   And with your strength
   you lead them to your holy,
   pleasant land.

¹⁴ "The other nations will hear this story,
   and they will be frightened.
   The people Philistia will shake with
   fear.
¹⁵ The leaders of Edom will shake with
   fear.
   The leaders of Moab will shake with
   fear.
   The people of Canaan will lose courage.
¹⁶ Those people will be filled with fear
   when they see your strength.
   They will be as still as a rock
   until the Lord's people pass by,
   until the people you have made pass by.
¹⁷ Lord, you will lead your people
   to your mountain.
   You will let them live near the place
   you prepared for your throne.
   Master, you will build your temple!

¹⁸ The Lord will rule forever and ever!"

¹⁹Yes, it really happened! Pharaoh's horses and riders and chariots went into the sea. And the Lord brought all the water of the sea down on top of them. But the people of Israel walked through that sea on dry land.

²⁰Then Aaron's sister, the woman prophet Miriam, took a tambourine. Miriam and the women began singing and dancing. Miriam repeated the words,

²¹ "Sing to the Lord!
   He has done great things.
   He threw horse and rider into the
   sea..."

²²Moses led the people of Israel away from the Red Sea* and into the Shur desert. They traveled for three days in the desert. The people could not find any water. ²³After three days, the people came to Marah. There was water at Marah, but it was too bitter to drink. (That is why the place was named Marah.*) ²⁴The people began complaining to Moses. The people said, "Now what will we drink?" ²⁵Moses called to the Lord. So the Lord showed him a tree. Moses put the tree in the water. When he did this, the water became good to drink.

In that place, the Lord judged the people and gave them a law. The Lord also tested the faith of the people. ²⁶The Lord said, "You must obey the Lord, your God. You must do the things he says are right. If you obey all the Lord's commands and laws, then you will not be sick like the Egyptians. I, the Lord, will not give you any of the sicknesses I gave the Egyptians. I am the Lord. I am the one who makes you well."

²⁷Then the people traveled to Elim. At Elim there were twelve springs of water and 70 palm trees. So the people made their camp there near that water.

16 Then the people left Elim and came to the Sinai desert, between Elim and Sinai. They arrived at that place on the 15th day of the second month* after leaving Egypt. ²Then the people of Israel began complaining again. They complained to Moses and Aaron in the desert. ³The people said, "It would have been better if the Lord had just killed us in the land of Egypt. At least there we had plenty to eat. We had all the food we needed. But now you have brought us out here into this desert. And we will all die of hunger here."

⁴Then the Lord said to Moses, "I will cause food to fall from the sky. This food will be for you to eat. Every day the people should go out and gather the food they need to eat that day. I will do this to see if the people will do what I tell them. ⁵Every day the people will gather only enough food for one day. But on Friday, when the

Red Sea Or, "Reed Sea." But see 1 Kings 9:26.
Marah This name means "bitter."
15th day of the second month That is, the 15th of Iyyar. The people of Israel had been traveling for a month.

people prepare their food, they will see that they have enough food for two days.*

⁶So Moses and Aaron said to the people of Israel, "Tonight you will see the power of the Lord. You will know that he is the One who brought you out of Egypt. ⁷You complained to the Lord, and he heard you. So tomorrow morning you will see the Glory of the Lord.* You have been complaining and complaining to us. Maybe now we can have a little rest."

⁸And Moses said, "You have been complaining, and the Lord has heard your complaints. So tonight the Lord will give you meat. And in the morning you will have all the bread you need. You have been complaining to Aaron and me. But now, maybe we will have a little rest. Remember, you are not complaining against Aaron and me. You are complaining against the Lord."

⁹Then Moses said to Aaron, "Speak to all the people of Israel. Say to them, 'Come together before the Lord, because he has heard your complaints.'"

¹⁰Aaron spoke to all the people of Israel. They were all gathered together in one place. While Aaron was talking, all the people turned and looked into the desert. And they saw the Glory of the Lord* appear in a cloud.

¹¹The Lord said to Moses, ¹²"I have heard the complaints of the people of Israel. So tell them, 'Tonight you will eat meat. And in the morning you will eat all the bread you want. Then you will know you can trust the Lord, your God.'"

¹³That night, quails *(birds)* came all around the camp. ⌊The people caught these birds for meat.⌋ And in the morning dew lay on the ground near the camp. ¹⁴After the dew was gone, something like thin flakes of frost was on the ground. ¹⁵The people of Israel saw it and asked each other, "What is that?"* They asked this question because they did not know what it was. So Moses told them, "This is the food the Lord is giving you to eat. ¹⁶The Lord says, 'Each person should gather what he needs. Each of you should gather about 2 quarts* for every person in your family.'"

¹⁷So the people of Israel did this. Each person gathered this food. Some people gathered more than others. ¹⁸The people gave the food to everyone in their family. After the food was measured, there was always enough for every person, but there was never too much. Each person gathered just enough for himself and his family to eat.

¹⁹Moses told them, "Don't save that food to eat the next day." ²⁰But some of the people did not obey Moses. Those people saved their food for the next day. But worms got into the food and it began to stink. Moses was angry with the people who did this.

²¹Every morning the people gathered the food. Each person gathered as much as he could eat. But by noon* the food melted and was gone.

²²On Friday, the people gathered twice as much food. They gathered 16 cups* for every person. So all the leaders of the people came and told this to Moses.

²³Moses told them, "This is what the Lord said would happen. It happened because tomorrow is the Sabbath, the special day of rest to honor the Lord. You can cook all the food you need to cook for today. But save the rest of this food for tomorrow morning."

²⁴So the people saved the rest of the food for the next day. And none of the food spoiled. And worms did not get into any of it.

²⁵On Saturday, Moses told the people, "Today is the Sabbath, the special day of rest to honor the Lord. So none of you should be out in the fields. Eat the food you gathered yesterday. ²⁶You should gather the food for six days. But the seventh day ⌊of the week⌋ is a day of rest—so there will not be any of the special food on the ground."

²⁷On Saturday, some of the people went out to gather some of the food, but they could not find any. ²⁸Then the Lord said to Moses, "How long will you people refuse to obey my commands and teachings? ²⁹Look, the Lord has made the Sabbath a day of rest for you. So, on Friday the Lord will give you enough food for two days. Then, on the Sabbath, each of you should sit down and relax! Stay where you are." ³⁰So the people rested on the Sabbath.

³¹The people began calling the special food "manna.*" The manna was like small white coriander seeds, and it tasted like thin cakes made

---

Friday .. two days This happened so that the people would not have to work on the Sabbath (Saturday), the day of rest.
Glory of the Lord One of the forms God used when he appeared to people. It was like a bright shining light.
What is that? In Hebrew this is like the word "manna."
2 quarts Literally, "1 omer."

noon Literally, "the heat of the day."
16 cups Literally, "2 omers."
manna This is like the Hebrew words meaning "What is that?"

with honey. ³²Moses said, "The Lord said: 'Save 8 cups* of this food for your descendants.* Then they can see the food that I gave to you in the desert when I took you out of Egypt.'"

³³So Moses told Aaron, "Take a jar and fill it with 8 cups* of manna. Save this manna to put before the Lord. Save it for our descendants.*" ³⁴(Aaron ⌊later⌋ did what the Lord had commanded Moses. Aaron put the jar of manna in front of the Agreement.*) ³⁵The people ate the manna for 40 years. They ate the manna until they came to the land of rest, that is until they came to the edge of the land of Canaan. (⌊³⁶The measure they used for the manna was an omer.⌋ An omer was about 8 cups.*)

17 All the people of Israel traveled together from the desert of Sin. They traveled from place to place as the Lord commanded. The people traveled to Rephidim and camped there. There was no water there for the people to drink. ²So the people turned against Moses and started arguing with him. The people said, "Give us water to drink."

Moses said to them, "Why have you turned against me? Why are you testing the Lord? ⌊Do you think the Lord is not with us?⌋"

³But the people were very thirsty for water. So they continued complaining to Moses. The people said, "Why did you bring us out of Egypt? Did you bring us out here so that we, our children, and our cattle will all die without water?"

⁴So Moses cried to the Lord, "What can I do with these people? They are ready to kill me."

⁵The Lord said to Moses, "Go before the people of Israel. Take some of the elders *(leaders)* of the people with you. Carry your walking stick with you. This is the stick that you used when you hit the Nile River. ⁶I will stand before you on a rock at Horeb *(Mount Sinai)*. Hit that rock with the walking stick and water will come out of it. Then the people can drink."

Moses did these things and the elders *(leaders)* of Israel saw it. ⁷Moses named that place Meribah* and Massah,* because this was the place that the people of Israel turned against him

and tested the Lord. The people wanted to know if the Lord was with them or not.

⁸At Rephidim the Amalekite people came and fought against the people of Israel. ⁹So Moses said to Joshua, "Choose some men and go and fight the Amalekites tomorrow. I will stand on the top of the hill and watch you. I will be holding the walking stick God gave me."

¹⁰Joshua obeyed Moses and went to fight the Amalekite people the next day. At the same time, Moses, Aaron, and Hur went to the top of the hill. ¹¹Any time Moses held his hands in the air, the men of Israel would win the fight. But when Moses put his hands down, the men of Israel began to lose the fight.

¹²After some time, Moses' arms became tired. ⌊The men with Moses wanted to find a way to keep Moses' hands in the air.⌋ So they put a large rock under Moses for him to sit on. Then Aaron and Hur held Moses' hands in the air. Aaron was on one side of Moses and Hur was on the other side. They held his hands up like this until the sun went down. ¹³So Joshua ⌊and his men⌋ defeated the Amalekites in this battle.

¹⁴Then the Lord said to Moses, "Write about this battle. Write these things in a book so people will remember what happened here. And be sure to tell Joshua that I will completely destroy the Amalekite people from the earth."

¹⁵Then Moses built an altar.* Moses named the altar, "The Lord is my flag." ¹⁶Moses said, "I lifted my hands toward the Lord's throne. So the Lord fought against the Amalekites, like he always has."

Advice from Moses' Father-in-Law

18 Jethro, Moses' father-in-law, was a priest in Midian. Jethro heard about the many ways that God helped Moses and the people of Israel. Jethro heard about the Lord leading the people of Israel out of Egypt. ²So Jethro went to Moses while Moses was camped near the mountain of God.* Jethro brought Moses' wife, Zipporah, with him. (Zipporah was not with Moses, because Moses had sent her home.) ³Jethro also brought Moses' two sons with him. The first son was named Gershom,* because when he was born, Moses said, "I am a stranger in a foreign country."

---

8 cups Literally, "1 omer."
descendants A person's children and their future families.
Agreement Literally, "Proof." The two stone tablets with the Ten Commandments written on them were proof of the Agreement between God and Israel.
about 8 cups Literally, "1/10 of an Ephah."
Meribah This name means "rebellion."
Massah This name means "trial," "temptation," or "test."

altar A table or raised area used for offering sacrifices.
mountain of God That is, "Mount Horeb," also called "Mount Sinai."
Gershom This name is like the Hebrew words meaning "a stranger there."

⁴The other son was named Eliezer,* because when he was born, Moses said, "The God of my father helped me and saved me from the king of Egypt." ⁵So Jethro went to Moses while Moses was camped in the desert near the mountain of God *(Mount Sinai)*. Moses' wife and his two sons were with Jethro.

⁶Jethro sent a message to Moses. ⌐Jethro said, "This is your father-in-law Jethro. I am bringing your wife and her two sons to you."

⁷So Moses went out to meet his father-in-law. Moses bowed down before him and kissed him. The two men asked about each other's health. Then they went into Moses' tent to talk more. ⁸Moses told Jethro everything the Lord had done for the people of Israel. Moses told about the things the Lord did to Pharaoh and the people of Egypt. Moses told about all the problems they had along the way. And Moses told his father-in-law how the Lord saved the people of Israel every time there was trouble.

⁹Jethro was happy when he heard all the good things the Lord had done for Israel. He was glad that the Lord had freed the people of Israel from the Egyptians. ¹⁰Jethro said,

"Praise the Lord!
   He freed you from the power of
     Egypt.
   The Lord saved you from Pharaoh.
¹¹ Now I know the Lord
   is greater than all the gods.
   They thought they were in control,
   but look what God did!"

¹²Jethro got some sacrifices* and offerings to honor God. Then Aaron and all the elders *(leaders)* of Israel came to eat with Moses' father-in-law Jethro. They all ate together there with God.

¹³The next day, Moses had the special job of judging the people. ⌐There were very many people,⌐ so the people had to stand before Moses all day.

¹⁴Jethro saw Moses judging the people. He asked, "Why are you doing this? Why are you the only judge? And why do people come to you all day?"

¹⁵Then Moses said to his father-in-law, "The people come to me and ask me to ask for God's decision to their problem. ¹⁶If people have an argument, they come to me. I decide which person is right. In this way, I teach the people God's laws and teachings."

¹⁷But Moses' father-in-law said to him, "This isn't the right way to do this. ¹⁸It is too much work for you to do alone. You can't do this job by yourself. It wears you out. And it makes the people tired too! ¹⁹Now, listen to me. Let me give you some advice. And I pray God will be with you. You should continue listening to the problems of the people. And you should continue to speak to God about these things. ²⁰You should teach God's laws and teachings to the people. Warn them not to break the laws. Tell them the right way to live. Tell them what they should do. ²¹But you should also choose some of the people to be judges and leaders.

"Choose good men you can trust—men who respect God. Choose men who will not change their decisions for money. And make these men rulers over the people. There should be rulers over 1,000 people, 100 people, 50 people, and even over ten people. ²²Let these rulers judge the people. If there is a very important case, then they can come to you and let you decide what to do. But they can decide the other cases themselves. In this way, these men will share your work with you and it will be easier for you to lead the people. ²³If you do these things, Lord willing, then you will be still able to do your job. And at the same time, the people can go home with their problems solved."

²⁴So Moses did what Jethro told him. ²⁵Moses chose good men from among the people of Israel. Moses made them leaders over the people. There were rulers over 1,000 people, 100 people, 50 people, and ten people. ²⁶These rulers were judges for the people. The people could always bring their arguments to these rulers. And Moses had to decide only the most important cases.

²⁷After a short time, Moses said goodbye to his father-in-law Jethro. And Jethro went back to his own home.

God's Agreement with Israel

19 The people of Israel reached the Sinai desert in the third month of their trip from Egypt. ²They had traveled from Rephidim to the Sinai desert. The people of Israel camped in the desert near the mountain *(Mount Horeb)*. ³Then Moses climbed up the mountain to meet with God. God spoke to him on the mountain and said, "Tell these things to the people of Israel, the great family of Jacob: ⁴'You people have seen what I can do to my enemies. You saw what I did to the

---

Eliezer This name means "My God helps."
sacrifice(s) A gift to God. Usually, it was a special animal that was killed and burned on an altar.

people of Egypt. You saw that I carried you out of Egypt like an eagle and brought you here to me. [5]So now I tell you to obey my commands. Keep my Agreement. If you do this, then you will be my own special people. The whole world belongs to me. But I am choosing you to be my own special people. [6]You will be a special nation—a kingdom of priests.' Moses, you must tell the people of Israel what I have said."

[7]So Moses climbed down the mountain and called the elders *(rulers)* of the people together. Moses told the elders everything the Lord had commanded him to tell them. [8]All the people spoke at the same time and said, "We will obey everything the Lord says."

Then Moses went back to God on the mountain. Moses told God that the people would obey him. [9]And the Lord said to Moses, "I will come to you in the thick cloud. I will speak to you. All of the people will hear me talking to you. I will do this so that the people will always believe the things you tell them."

Then Moses told God all the things the people had said.

[10]And the Lord said to Moses, "Today and tomorrow you must prepare the people for a special meeting. The people must wash their clothes [11]and be ready for me on the third day. On the third day the Lord will come down to Mount Sinai. And all the people will see me. [12-13]But you must tell the people to stay away from the mountain. Make a line and don't let the people cross that line. Any person or animal that touches the mountain must be killed. He must be killed with rocks or shot with arrows. But don't let anyone touch him. The people must wait until the trumpet blows. Only then can they go up the mountain."

[14]So Moses climbed down the mountain and went to the people. Moses got them ready for the special meeting and they washed their clothes.

[15]Then Moses said to the people, "Be ready for the meeting with God in three days. Until that time, the men must not touch the women."

[16]On the morning of the third day, a thick cloud came down onto the mountain. There was thunder and lightning and a very loud sound from a trumpet. All the people in the camp were frightened. [17]Then Moses led the people out of the camp to a place near the mountain to meet God. [18]Mount Sinai was covered with smoke. Smoke rose off the mountain like smoke from a furnace. This happened because the Lord came down to the mountain in fire. Also, the whole mountain began to shake. [19]The noise from the trumpet became louder and louder. Every time Moses spoke to God, God answered him with a voice like thunder.

[20]So the Lord came down to Mount Sinai. The Lord came from heaven to the top of the mountain. Then the Lord called Moses to come up to the top of the mountain with him. So Moses went up the mountain.

[21]The Lord said to Moses, "Go down and warn the people not to come near me and look at me. If they do this, then many people will die. [22]Also tell the priests who will come near me that they must prepare themselves for this special meeting. If they don't do this, then I will punish them."

[23]Moses told the Lord, "But the people cannot come up the mountain. You yourself told us to make a line and not allow the people to cross the line to holy ground."

[24]The Lord said to him, "Go down to the people. Get Aaron and bring him back with you. But don't let the priests or the people come near me. I will punish them if they come too close."

[25]So Moses went down to the people and told them these things.

The Ten Commandments

20 Then God said, [2]"I am the Lord* your God. I led you out of the land of Egypt where you were slaves. So you must obey these commands:

[3]"You must not worship any other gods except me.

[4]"You must not make any idols.* Don't make any statues or pictures of anything up in the sky or of anything on the earth or of anything down in the water. [5]Don't worship or serve idols of any kind. Why? Because I, the Lord, am your God. I hate my people worshiping other gods.* People who sin against me become my enemies. And I will punish those people. And I will punish their children, their grandchildren, and even their great-grandchildren. [6]But I will be very kind to people who love me and obey my commands. I will be kind to their families for thousands of generations!*

[7]"You must not use the name of the Lord your God in a wrong way. If a person uses the Lord's name in a wrong way, then that

Lord Or, "YAHWEH."
idols Statues of false gods that people worshiped.
I hate ... gods Or, "I am El Kanah—the Jealous God."
But I will be ... generations Or, "But I will show mercy to thousands of people that love me and obey my commands."

person is guilty. And the Lord will not make him innocent. ⁸"You must remember to keep the Sabbath* a special day. ⁹Work at your job six days a week. ¹⁰But the seventh day is a day of rest in honor of the Lord your God. So on that day no person should work—not you, your sons and daughters, or your men and women slaves. Even your animals and the foreigners living in your cities must not work! ¹¹Why? Because the Lord worked six days and made the sky, the earth, the sea, and everything in them. And on the seventh day, God rested. In this way, the Lord blessed the Sabbath—the day of rest. The Lord made that a very special day.

¹²"You must honor *(respect)* your father and your mother. Do this so you will have a full life in the land that the Lord your God gives you.

¹³"You must not murder anyone.

¹⁴"You must not do the sin of adultery.*

¹⁵"You must not steal anything.

¹⁶"You must not tell lies about other people.*

¹⁷"You must not want to take your neighbor's house. You must not want his wife. And you must not want his men and women servants, or his cattle, or his donkeys. You must not want to take anything that belongs to another person!"

The People Are Afraid of God

¹⁸During all this time, the people in the valley heard the thundering and saw the lightning on the mountain. They saw smoke rising from the mountain. The people were afraid, and they shook with fear. They stood away from the mountain and watched. ¹⁹Then the people said to Moses, "If you want to speak to us, then we will listen. But please don't let God speak to us. If this happens, we will die."

²⁰Then Moses said to the people, "Don't be afraid! The Lord has come to prove that he loves you. He wants you to respect him so that you will not sin."

²¹The people stood away from the mountain while Moses went to the dark cloud where God was. ²²Then the Lord told Moses to say these things to the people of Israel: "You people have seen that I talked with you from heaven. ²³So you must not make idols using gold or silver to compete with me. You must not make these false gods.

²⁴"Make a special altar* for me. Use dirt to make this altar. Offer burnt offerings and fellowship offerings on this altar as a sacrifice* to me. Use your sheep and your cattle to do this. Do this in every place where I tell you to remember me. Then I will come and bless you. ²⁵If you use stones to make an altar, then don't use stones that were cut with an iron tool.* If you do that, it will make the altar not acceptable. ²⁶And you must not make steps leading up to the altar. If there are steps, then when people look up to the altar, they will be able to see under your clothes."

Other Laws and Commands

21 ₍Then God said to Moses,₎ "These are the other laws that you will give to the people:

²"If you buy a Hebrew* slave, then that slave will serve for only six years. After six years he will become free. He will have to pay nothing. ³If the person is not married when he becomes your slave, then when he becomes free, he will leave without a wife. But if the man is married when he becomes your slave, then he will keep his wife at the time he is made free. ⁴If the slave is not married, the master can give him a wife. If that wife gives birth to sons or daughters, then she and her children will belong to the master. After the slave is finished with his years of service, then he will be made free.

⁵"But maybe the slave will decide that he wants to stay with the master. Then he must say, 'I love my master. I love my wife and my children. I will not become free—I will stay.' ⁶If this happens, then the master will bring the slave before God. The master will take the slave to a door or the wooden frame around the door. And the master will make a hole through the slave's ear using a sharp tool. Then the slave will serve that master for all his life.

⁷"A man might decide to sell his daughter as a slave. If this happens, the rules for making her free are not the same as the rules for making the men slaves free. ⁸If the master is not pleased with

---

Sabbath Saturday, a special day of rest and worship for Jews.
adultery Breaking the marriage promise by doing sexual sin.
You must not tell lies about other people Or, "You must not be a false witness against your neighbor."
altar A table or raised area used for offering sacrifices.
sacrifice A gift to God. Usually, it was a special animal that was killed and burned on an altar.
iron tool Literally, "sword."
Hebrew Or, "Israelite."

the woman, then he can sell the woman back to her father. If the master promised ₍to marry the woman₎, then he loses the right to sell the woman to other people. ⁹If the master promised to let the slave woman marry his son, then she must not be treated like a slave. She must be treated like a daughter.

¹⁰"If the master marries another woman, then he must not give less food or clothing to the first wife. And he must continue to give her the things she has a right to have in marriage. ¹¹The man must do these three things for her. If he does not, then the woman is made free, and it will cost her nothing. She owes no money to the man.

¹²"If a person hits someone and kills him, then that person must be killed too. ¹³But if an accident happens, and a person kills someone without planning it, then God allowed that thing to happen. I will choose some special places where people can run for safety. So that person can run to one of those places. ¹⁴But if a person planned to kill another person because he is angry or hates him, then that killer must be punished. Take him away from my altar* and kill him.

¹⁵"Any person who hits his father or his mother must be killed.

¹⁶"If a person steals someone to sell him as a slave or to keep him for his own slave, then that person must be killed.

¹⁷"Any person who curses* his father or his mother must be killed.

¹⁸"Two men might argue and one might hit the other with a rock or with his fist. ₍How should you punish that man?₎ If the man who was hurt is not killed, then the man who hurt him should not be killed. ¹⁹If the man was hurt and must stay in bed for some time, then the man who hurt him must support him. The man who hurt him must pay for the loss of his time. The man must support him until he is completely healed.

²⁰"Sometimes people beat their men or women slaves. If the slave dies after he is beaten, then the killer must be punished. ²¹But if the slave does not die and after a few days the slave becomes well, then that person will not be punished.* Why? Because the master paid his money for the slave, and the slave belongs to him.

²²"Two men might be fighting and they might hurt a pregnant woman. This might make the woman give birth to her baby ₍before its time₎. If the woman was not hurt badly, then the man who hurt her must pay a fine. The woman's husband will decide how much the man must pay. The judges will help the man decide how much the fine will be. ²³But if the woman was hurt badly, then the man who hurt her must be punished. ₍If a person is killed, then the person who caused it must be killed.₎ You must trade one life for another life. ²⁴You must trade an eye for an eye, a tooth for a tooth, a hand for a hand, a foot for a foot, ²⁵a burn for a burn, a bruise for a bruise, a cut for a cut.

²⁶"If a man hits a slave in the eye, and the slave is blinded in that eye, then the slave will be allowed to go free. His eye is the payment for his freedom. This is the same for a man or a woman slave. ²⁷If a master hits his slave in the mouth, and the slave loses a tooth, then the slave will be allowed to go free. The slave's tooth is payment for the slave's freedom. This is the same for a man or a woman slave.

²⁸"If a man's bull kills a man or woman, then you should use rocks and kill that bull. You should not eat the bull. But the owner of the bull is not guilty. ²⁹But if the bull had hurt people in the past, and if the owner was warned, then the owner is guilty. Why? Because he did not keep the bull tied or locked in its place. So if the bull is allowed to be free and kills someone, then that owner is guilty. You should kill the bull with rocks and also kill the owner. ³⁰But the family of the dead man may accept money. If they accept money, then the man who owned the bull should not be killed. But he must pay as much money as the judge decides.

³¹"This same law must be followed if the bull kills a person's son or daughter. ³²But if the bull kills a slave, then the owner of the animal must pay the master 30 pieces of silver.* And the bull must also be killed with rocks. This law will be the same for men and women slaves.

³³"A man might take a cover off a well or he might dig a hole and not cover it. If another man's animal comes and falls into that hole, then the man who owns the hole is guilty. ³⁴The man who owns the hole must pay for the animal. But after he pays for the animal, then he will be allowed to keep the body of that animal.

altar A table or raised area used for offering sacrifices. It was one of the special places an innocent person could run for safety.
curse To ask for bad things to happen to someone.
punished Or, "punished for murder."

30 pieces of silver The price for a new slave.

³⁵"If one man's bull kills another man's bull, then they should sell the bull that is alive. Both men will get half of the money that comes from selling the bull, and both men will also get half of the bull that was killed. ³⁶But if a man's bull has hurt other animals in the past, then that owner is responsible for his bull. If his bull kills another bull, then he is guilty because he allowed the bull to be free. That man must pay bull for bull. He must trade his bull for the bull that was killed.

22 "How should you punish a man who steals a bull or a sheep? If the man kills the animal or sells it, then he can't give it back. So he must pay five bulls for the one he stole. Or, he must pay four sheep for the one he stole. He must pay for stealing. ²⁻⁴If he owns nothing, then he will be sold as a slave. But if the man still has the animal and you find it, then that man must give the owner two animals for every animal he stole. It doesn't matter if the animal was a bull or a donkey or a sheep.

"If a thief is killed while trying to break into a house ⌊at night⌋, then no one will be guilty for killing him. But if this happens during the day, then the person who killed him will be guilty ⌊of murder⌋.

⁵"A man might start a fire in his field or vineyard. If he lets the fire spread and it burns his neighbor's field or vineyard, then he must use his best crops to pay his neighbor for his loss.*

⁶"A man might start a fire to burn thorn bushes on his field. But if the fire grows and burns his neighbor's crops or the grain growing on the neighbor's field, then the man that started the fire must pay for the things he burned.

⁷"A man might ask a neighbor to keep some money or other things for him in his neighbor's house. What should you do if that money or those things are stolen from the neighbor's house? You should try to find the thief. If you find the thief, then he must pay twice as much as the things are worth. ⁸But if you can't find the thief, then God will judge if the owner of the house is guilty. The owner of the house must go before God, and God will decide if the person stole something.

⁹"What should you do if two men disagree about a bull or a donkey or sheep or clothing or something that is lost. One man says, 'This is mine,' and the other says, 'No, it is mine.' Both men should go before God. God will decide who is guilty. The person who was wrong must pay the other man twice as much as the thing is worth.

¹⁰"A person might ask his neighbor to take care of an animal for a short time. It might be a donkey or a bull or a sheep. But what should you do if that animal is hurt or dies or someone takes the animal while no one is looking? ¹¹That neighbor must explain that he did not steal the animal. If this is true, then the neighbor will promise to the Lord that he did not steal it. The owner of the animal must accept this promise. The neighbor does not have to pay the owner for the animal. ¹²But if the neighbor stole the animal, then he must pay the owner for the animal. ¹³If wild animals killed the animal, then the neighbor should bring the body as proof. The neighbor will not have to pay the owner for the animal that was killed.

¹⁴"If a man borrows anything from his neighbor, he is responsible for that thing. If an animal is hurt, or if the animal dies, then the neighbor must pay the owner for the animal. The neighbor is responsible, because the owner was not there himself. ¹⁵But if the owner was there with the animal, then the neighbor does not have to pay. Or, if the neighbor was paying money to use the animal for work, then he will not have to pay if the animal dies or is hurt. The money he paid to use the animal will be enough payment.

¹⁶"If a man has sexual relations with a pure young woman who is not married,* then he must marry her. And he must pay her father the full dowry.* ¹⁷If the father refuses to allow his daughter to marry him, then the man must still pay the money. He must pay the full amount for her.

¹⁸"You must not allow any woman to do evil magic. If she does magic, then you must not let her live.

¹⁹"You must not allow any person to have sexual relations with an animal. If this happens, then that person must be killed.

²⁰"If any person makes a sacrifice* to a false god, then that person should be destroyed. The Lord God is the only one you should make sacrifices to.

A man ... loss Or, "⁵A man might let his animal graze in his field or vineyard. If the animal wanders into another person's field or vineyard, then the owner must pay. The payment must come from the best of his crop."

married Or, "engaged." In ancient Israel, many of the rules concerning an engaged woman were the same as the rules for a married woman.

dowry The money a man gave the father of the bride so the man could marry the woman.

sacrifice(s) A gift to God. Usually, it was a special animal that

²¹"Remember, in the past you were foreigners in the land of Egypt. So you should not cheat or hurt any person who is a foreigner in your land. ²²"You must never do anything bad to women whose husbands are dead or to children without parents. ²³If you do anything wrong to those widows or orphans, then I will know it. I will hear about their suffering. ²⁴And I will be very angry. I will kill you with a sword. Then your wives will become widows. And your children will become orphans.

²⁵"If one of my people is poor, and you lend him money, then you must not charge him for that money. And you must not force him to pay you quickly. ²⁶Someone might give you his coat as a promise that he will pay you the money he owes you. But you must give that coat back to him before the sun goes down. ²⁷If that person doesn't have his coat, then he will have nothing to cover his body. He will get cold in his sleep. And if he cries to me, I will hear him. I will listen, because I am kind.

²⁸"You must not curse* God or the leaders of your people.

²⁹"At harvest time you should give me the first grain and the first juice from your fruit. Don't wait until late in the year.

"Give me your firstborn* sons. ³⁰Also, give me your firstborn cattle and sheep. Let the firstborn stay with its mother for seven days. Then on the eighth day, give him to me.

³¹"You are my special people. So don't eat the meat from something that was killed by wild animals. Let the dogs eat that dead animal.

23 "Don't tell lies against other people. If you are a witness in court, then don't agree to help a bad person tell lies.

²"Don't do something just because everyone else is doing it. If a group of people are doing wrong, don't join them. You must not let those people persuade you to do wrong things—you must do what is right and fair.

³"If a poor man is being judged, sometimes people will support him because they feel sorry for him. You must not do that. ⌈Support him only if he is right.⌉

⁴"If you see a lost bull or donkey, then you must return it to its owner. You must do this even if the owner is your enemy.

⁵"If you see an animal that can't walk because it has too much to carry, you must stop and help that animal. You must help that animal even if it belongs to one of your enemies.

⁶"You must not let people be unfair to a poor man. He must be judged the same as any other person.

⁷"Be very careful if you say that a person is guilty of something. Don't make false charges against a person. Never allow an innocent person to be killed as punishment for something he did not do. Any person who kills an innocent man is evil, and I will not pardon *(forgive)* that person.

⁸"If a person tries to pay you to agree with him when he is wrong, don't accept that payment. A payment like that can blind judges so that they can't see the truth. And a payment like that can make good people tell lies.

⁹"You must never do wrong things to a foreigner. Remember, at one time you were also foreigners when you lived in the land of Egypt.

The Special Holidays

¹⁰"Plant seeds, harvest your crops, and work the ground for six years. ¹¹But the seventh year, don't use your land. ⌈The seventh year must be a special time of rest for the land.⌉ Don't plant anything in your fields. If any crops grow there, then allow the poor people to have it. And allow the wild animals to eat the food that is left. You should do the same with your vineyards and with your fields of olive trees.

¹²"Work for six days. Then on the seventh day, rest! This will allow your slaves and other workers a time for rest and relaxation. And your bulls and donkeys will also have a time of rest.

¹³"Be sure that you obey all these laws. Don't worship false gods. You should not even speak their names!

¹⁴"You will have three special holidays each year. On these holidays, you will come to my special place to worship me. ¹⁵The first holiday will be the Festival of Unleavened Bread. This is like I commanded you. At this time you will eat bread that is made without yeast. This will continue for seven days. You will do this during the month of Abib,* because this is the time when you came out of Egypt. Every person must bring a sacrifice to me at that time.

---

curse To say bad things about someone or to ask for bad things to him.

firstborn The first child born in a family. The firstborn son was very important in ancient times.

month of Abib Or, "the spring month," that is, Nisan. This is about March-April.

¹⁶"The second holiday will be the Festival of Pentecost. This holiday will be ₍during the early summer time₎ when you begin harvesting the crops you planted in your fields.

"The third holiday will be the Festival of Shelters.* This will be in the fall* when you gather all the crops from your fields.

¹⁷"So three times each year all the men will come ₍to the special place₎ to be with the Lord your Master.

¹⁸"When you kill an animal and offer its blood as a sacrifice,* you must not offer bread that has yeast in it. ₍And when you eat the meat from this sacrifice, you must eat all of the meat in one day.₎ Don't save any of the meat for the next day.

¹⁹"When you gather your crops at harvest time, you should bring the first of everything you harvest to the house* of the Lord your God.

"You must not eat the meat from a young goat that is boiled in its mother's milk.

God Will Help Israel Take Their Land

²⁰₍God said,₎ "I am sending an angel before you. This angel will lead you to the place that I have prepared for you. The angel will protect you. ²¹Obey the angel and follow him. Don't rebel against him. The angel will not forgive the wrong things you do to him. He has my power in him. ²²You must obey everything he says. You must do everything that I tell you. If you do this, then I will be with you. I will be against all of your enemies. And I will be an enemy to every person who is against you."

²³₍God said,₎ "My angel will lead you through the land. He will lead you against many different people—the Amorites, the Hittites, the Perizzites, the Canaanites, the Hivites, and the Jebusites. But I will defeat all of those people.

²⁴"Don't worship the gods of those people. Don't ever bow down to those gods. You must never live the way those people live. You must destroy their idols.* And you must break the stones that help them remember their gods.* ²⁵You must serve the Lord your God. If you do this, I will bless you with plenty of bread and water. I will take away all sickness from you. ²⁶Your women will all be able to have babies. None of their babies will die at birth. And I will allow you to live long lives.

²⁷"When you fight against your enemies, I will send my great power before you.* I will help you defeat all your enemies. The people that are against you will become confused in battle and run away. ²⁸I will send the hornet* in front of you. He will force your enemies to leave. The Hivite people, the Canaanite people, and the Hittite people will leave your country. ²⁹But I will not force all those people out of your land quickly. I will not do this in only one year. The land will be empty if I force the people out too fast. Then all the wild animals would increase and control the land. And they would be much trouble for you. ³⁰So I will force those people out of your land very slowly. You will continue to move across the land. And wherever you go I will force the other people to leave.

³¹"I will give you all the land from the Red Sea to the Euphrates River. The western border will be the Philistine Sea *(Mediterranean Sea)*, and the eastern border will be the Arabian Desert. I will let you defeat the people living there. And you will force all those people to leave.

³²"You must not make any agreements with any of those people or their gods. ³³Don't let them stay in your country. If you let them stay, they will be like a trap to you—they will cause you to sin against me. And you will begin worshiping their gods."

God and Israel Make Their Agreement

24 ₍God₎ told Moses, "You, Aaron, Nadab, Abihu, and the 70 elders *(leaders)* of Israel must come up the mountain and worship me from a distance. ²Then Moses will come close to the Lord by himself. The other men must not come close to the Lord, and the rest of the people must not even come up the mountain."

Festival of Shelters Also called "Succoth" and "Feast of Tabernacles." At this time, the people lived in tents or shelters for seven days to help them remember the time in the Sinai desert.

in the fall Literally, "at the end of the year." This means the end of the growing season.

sacrifice(s) A gift to God. Usually, it was a special animal that was killed and burned on an altar.

house The "Holy Tent" where the people went to meet with God. See Ex. 25:8,9.

idols Statues of false gods that people worshiped.

stones that help them remember their gods Or, "memorials." Here, these were stone markers that people used in worshiping their gods.

When you fight ... you Or, "News of my power will go before you, and your enemies will be frightened."

hornet A stinging insect like a wasp or bee. This might be a real hornet or it might mean God's angel or his great power.

EXODUS 24:3–25:9

³Moses told the people all the rules and commands from the Lord. Then all the people said, "We will obey all the commands that the Lord has spoken."

⁴So Moses wrote all of the commands of the Lord ₍on a scroll₎. The next morning, Moses got up and built an altar* near the bottom of the mountain. And he set up twelve stones—one for each of the twelve family groups of Israel. ⁵Then Moses sent young men of Israel to offer sacrifices.* These men offered bulls to the Lord as burnt offerings and fellowship offerings.

⁶Moses saved the blood from these animals. Moses put half of the blood in bowls. And he poured the other half of the blood on the altar.*

⁷Moses read the scroll with the special Agreement written on it. Moses read the Agreement so all the people could hear him. And the people said, "We have heard ₍the laws that the Lord has given us₎. And we agree to obey them."

⁸Then Moses held the bowls full of the blood from the sacrifices.* Moses threw that blood on the people. He said, "This blood shows that the Lord has made a special Agreement with you. The laws God gave you explain the Agreement."

⁹Then Moses, Aaron, Nadab, Abihu, and the 70 elders *(leaders)* of Israel went up the mountain. ¹⁰On the mountain, these men saw the God of Israel. God was standing on something that looked like blue sapphires, as clear as the sky! ¹¹All the leaders of Israel saw God, but God did not destroy them.* They all ate and drank together.

Moses Goes to Get God's Law

¹²The Lord said to Moses, "Come to me on the mountain. I have written my teachings and laws on two flat stones. These teachings and laws are for the people. I will give these flat stones to you."

¹³So Moses and his helper, Joshua, went up the mountain of God. ¹⁴Moses said to the elders *(leaders)*, "Wait here for us, we will come back to you. While I am gone, Aaron and Hur will rule over you. Go to those men if anyone has a problem."

Moses Meets with God

¹⁵Then Moses went up the mountain. And the cloud covered the mountain. ¹⁶The Glory of the Lord* came down on Mount Sinai. The cloud covered the mountain for six days. On the seventh day, the Lord spoke to Moses from the cloud. ¹⁷The people of Israel could see the Glory of the Lord. It was like a fire burning on top of the mountain.

¹⁸Then Moses went higher up the mountain into the cloud. Moses was on the mountain for 40 days and 40 nights."

Gifts for the Holy Things

25 The Lord said to Moses, ²"Tell the people of Israel to bring me gifts. Each person must decide in his heart what he wants to give me. Accept these gifts for me. ³Here is the list of the things that you should accept from the people: gold, silver, and bronze*; ⁴blue, purple, and red yarn and fine linen; goat hair, ⁵ram skins dyed red, and fine leather*; acacia wood; ⁶oil for the lamps; spices for the anointing oil* and spices for the sweet-smelling incense* ⁷Also accept onyx stones and other jewels to be put on the Ephod* and the Judgment Pouch.*"

The Holy Tent

⁸₍God also said,₎ "The people will build a holy place for me. Then I can live among them. ⁹I will show you what the Holy Tent* and everything in it should look like. Build everything exactly like I show you.

---

altar A table or raised area used for offering sacrifices.

sacrifice(s) A gift to God. Usually it was a special animal that was killed and burned on an altar.

Moses saved the blood ... altar The blood was used to seal the Agreement between God and the people. It was poured on the altar to show that God shared in the Agreement.

saw God ... destroy them The Bible says that people cannot see God. But God wanted these leaders to know what he was like, so he let them see him in some special way.

Glory of the Lord One of the forms God used when he appeared to people. It was like a bright, shining light.

bronze A metal. The Hebrew word can mean "copper," "bronze," or "brass."

fine leather A special kind of leather made from the skin of an animal like a seal or sea cow.

anointing oil Fine olive oil that was poured on people or things to show they were chosen for a special work or purpose.

incense Special dried tree sap. Burned to make a sweet-smelling smoke, it was offered as a gift to God.

Ephod A special coat worn by the priests. See Ex. 28:6-14.

Judgment Pouch A piece of clothing like a bib or an apron that covered the priest's chest.

Holy Tent Or, "tabernacle," the tent where God came to live among his people. It was often called the "Meeting Tent."

The Box of the Agreement

10"Use acacia wood and build a special box. This Holy Box must be 2 1/2 cubits* long, 1 1/2 cubits* wide, and 1 1/2 cubits.* 11Use pure gold to cover the Box inside and out. Put gold trim around the edges of the Box. 12Make four gold rings for carrying the Box. Put the gold rings on the four corners, two rings on each side. 13Then make poles for carrying the Box. These poles should be made from acacia wood and covered with gold. 14Put the poles through the rings on the corners of the Box. Use these poles to carry the Box. 15These poles should always stay in the rings of the Box. Don't take the poles out. 16[God said,] "I will give you the Agreement.* Put the Agreement into this Box. 17Then make a cover.* Make it from pure gold. Make it 2 1/2 cubits* long and 1 1/2 cubits* wide. 18"Then make two Cherub angels* and put them on each end of the cover. Hammer gold to make these angels. 19Put one angel on one end of the cover, and put the other angel on the other end. Join the angels together with the cover to make one piece. 20The wings of these angels should spread up toward the sky. The angels should cover the Box with their wings. The angels should face each other, looking toward the cover.

21"I will give you the Agreement.* Put that Agreement in the Box, and put the cover* on the Box. 22When I meet with you, I will speak from between the Cherub angels* on the cover that is on the Box of the Agreement.* From that place I will give all my commands to the people of Israel.

The Table

23"Make a table from acacia wood. The table must be 2 cubits* long, 1 cubit* wide, and 1 1/2

2 1/2 cubits 4' 3 5/8" (1.31m.)
1 1/2 cubits 2' 7" (78.75cm)
Agreement Literally, "Proof." The flat stones with the Ten Commandments written on them were proof of the Agreement between God and the people of Israel.
cover Also called "mercy seat." The Hebrew word can mean "lid," "cover," or "the place where sins are forgiven."
Cherub angels Special angels from God. Statues of these angels were on top of the Box of the Agreement.
Agreement Literally, "Proof." The flat stones with the Ten Commandments written on them were proof of the Agreement between God and the people of Israel.
Box of the Agreement Or, "ark of the Covenant." The box containing the flat stones with the Ten Commandments written on them and other things that proved God was with the people of Israel during their time in the Sinai desert.
2 cubits 3' 5 5/16" (105cm.)
1 cubit 1' 8 5/8" (52.5cm).

cubits* high. 24Cover the table with pure gold and put gold trim around it. 25Then make a frame 1 handbreadth* wide around the table. And put gold trim on the frame. 26Then make four gold rings and put them on the four corners of the table, where the four legs are. 27Put the rings close to the frame [around the top of the table]. These rings will hold the poles used to carry the table. 28Use acacia wood to make the poles, and cover them with gold. The poles are for carrying the table. 29Make the plates, the spoons, the pitchers, and the bowls from pure gold. The pitchers and bowls will be used for pouring [the drink offerings]. 30Put the special bread* before me on the table. It must always be there in front of me.

The Lampstand

31"Then you must make a lampstand. Use pure gold and hammer it to make the base and the shaft.* Make flowers, buds, and petals from pure gold. Join all these things together into one piece. 32"The lampstand must have six branches—three branches on one side, and three branches on the other. 33Each branch must have three flowers. Make these flowers like almond flowers with buds and petals. 34Make four more flowers for the lampstand. These flowers must be made like almond flowers with buds and petals. 35There will be six branches on the lampstand—three branches coming out from each side of the shaft. Make a flower with buds and petals below each of the three places where the branches join the shaft. 36The whole lampstand with the flowers and branches must be made from pure gold. All this gold must be hammered and joined together into one piece. 37Then make seven lamps* to go on the lampstand. These lamps will give light to the area in front of the lampstand. 38Use pure gold to make the wick trimmers* and the trays. 39Use 75 pounds* of pure gold to make the lampstand and the things to be used with it. 40Be very careful to make everything exactly the way I showed you on the mountain."

1 handbreadth The width of 4 fingers, about 3" (7.7cm).
special bread Also called "bread of the Presence." Every day this bread was put before God on the special table in the Holy Place.
base and the shaft Or, "flared base."
lamps These lamps were small bowls filled with oil. A wick was put in the bowl and lit to produce light.
wick trimmers Tools used to extinguish the lamps.
75 pounds Literally, "a kikar."

EXODUS 26:1–32

The Holy Tent

26 ⌊The Lord said to Moses,⌋ "The Holy Tent* should be made from ten curtains. These curtains must be made from fine linen* and blue, purple, and red yarn. A skilled worker should sew pictures of Cherub angels* with wings into the curtains. ²Make each curtain the same size. Each curtain should be 28 cubits* long and 4 cubits* wide. ³Join the curtains together into two groups. Join five curtains together to make one group, and join five curtains together to make the other group. ⁴Use blue cloth to make loops along the edge of the end curtain in one group. Do the same on the end curtain in the other group. ⁵There must be 50 loops on the end curtain of the first group. And there must be 50 loops on the end curtain of the other group. ⁶Then make 50 gold rings to join the curtains together. This will join the Holy Tent together into one piece.

⁷"Make another tent that will cover the Holy Tent.* Use eleven curtains to make this tent. Make these curtains from goat hair. ⁸All these curtains must be the same size. They must be 30 cubits* long and 4 cubits* wide. ⁹Join five of the curtains together into one group. Then join the other six curtains together into another group. Fold back half of the sixth curtain at the front of the Tent. ¹⁰Make 50 loops down the edge of the end curtain of one group. Do the same for the end curtain of the other group. ¹¹Then make 50 bronze* rings to join the curtains together. This will join the tent together into one piece. ¹²Half of the end curtain of this tent will hang down below the back edge of the Holy Tent. ¹³On the sides, the curtains of this tent will hang down 1 cubit* below the bottom edges of the Holy Tent. So this tent will completely cover the Holy Tent. ¹⁴Make two coverings to go over the outer tent. One covering should be made from ram skins dyed red. The other covering should be made from fine leather.*

¹⁵"Use acacia wood to make frames to support the Holy Tent.* ¹⁶The frames should be 10 cubits* high and 1 1/2 cubits* wide. ¹⁷Two side poles should be joined together with cross pieces to make each frame. All the frames for the Holy Tent must be the same. ¹⁸Make 20 frames for the south side of the Holy Tent. ¹⁹And make 40 silver bases for the frames. Each frame should have two silver bases to go under it—one base for each side pole. ²⁰Make 20 more frames for the other side *(the north side)* of the Holy Tent. ²¹And make 40 silver bases for these frames—two bases under each frame. ²²Make six more frames for the back *(the west side)* of the Holy Tent. ²³Make two frames for the corners at the back of the Holy Tent. ²⁴The frames at the corners should be joined together at the bottom. At the top, a ring will hold the frames together. Do the same for both corners. ²⁵There will be a total of eight frames ⌊for the west end of the Tent⌋. And there will be 16 silver bases—two bases under each frame.

²⁶"Use acacia wood and make braces for the frames of the Holy Tent.* There should be five braces for the first side of the Holy Tent. ²⁷And there should be five braces for the frames on the other side of the Holy Tent. And there should be five braces for the frames at the back *(the west side)* of the Holy Tent. ²⁸The middle brace should pass through the frames from one end to the other. ²⁹"Cover the frames with gold. And make rings for the frames to hold the braces. Make these rings from gold. Also, cover the braces with gold. ³⁰Build the Holy Tent* the way I showed you on the mountain.

Inside the Holy Tent

³¹"Use fine linen* and make a special curtain ⌊to divide the inside of the Holy Tent⌋. Use blue, purple, and red yarn and sew pictures of Cherub angels into the curtain. ³²Make four posts from acacia wood, and cover the posts with gold. Put hooks made from gold on the four posts. Put four

---

Holy Tent Or, "tabernacle," the tent where God came to live among his people.
linen Thread or cloth made from the fibers of the flax plant.
Cherub angels Special angels from God. Statues of these angels were on top of the Box of the Agreement.
28 cubits 48' 2 3/4" (14.7m).
4 cubits 6' 10 13/16" (2.1m).
30 cubits 51' 8 1/16" (15.75m).
bronze A metal. The Hebrew word can mean "copper," "bronze," or "brass."
1 cubit 1' 8 5/8" (52.5cm).

fine leather Leather made from the skin of an animal like a seal or a sea cow.
10 cubits 17' 2 11/16" (5.25m).
1 1/2 cubits 2' 7" (78.75cm).

silver bases under the posts. Then hang the curtain on the gold hooks. ³³Put the curtain under the gold rings.* Then put the Box of the Agreement* behind the curtain. This curtain will separate the Holy Place from the Most Holy Place. ³⁴Put the cover* on the Box of the Agreement in the Most Holy Place.

³⁵⌊In the Holy Place⌋ on the other side of the curtain put the special table you made. The table should be on the north side of the Holy Tent.* Then put the lampstand on the south side. This will be across from the table.

The Door of the Holy Tent

³⁶"Then make a curtain to cover the entrance to the ⌊Holy⌋ Tent.* Use blue, purple, and red yarn and fine linen to make this curtain. And weave pictures into it. ³⁷Make gold hooks for this curtain. And make five posts using acacia wood covered with gold. And make five bronze* bases for the five posts."

The Altar for Burning Offerings

27 ⌊The Lord said to Moses,⌋ "Use acacia wood and build an altar.* The altar should be square. It must be 5 cubits* long, 5 cubits* wide, and 3 cubits* high. ²Make a horn for each of the four corners of the altar. Join each horn to its corner so that everything is one piece. Then cover the altar with bronze.*

³"Use bronze* to make all the tools and dishes that will be used on the altar.* Make pots, shovels, bowls, forks, and pans. These will be used for cleaning ashes from the altar. ⁴Make a grating for the altar. This grating will be shaped like a net. And make a bronze ring at each of the four corners of the grating. ⁵Put the grating under the ledge at the bottom of the altar. The grating will go halfway up into the altar from below.

⁶"Use acacia wood to make poles for the altar,* and cover them with bronze.* ⁷Put the poles through the rings on both sides of the altar. Use these poles for carrying the altar. ⁸Make the altar like an empty box with the sides made from boards. Make the altar just like I showed you on the mountain.

The Courtyard Around the Holy Tent

⁹"Make a courtyard for the Holy Tent.* The south side should have a wall of curtains 100 cubits* long. These curtains must be made from fine linen.* ¹⁰Use 20 posts and 20 bronze* bases under the posts. The hooks for the posts and the curtain rods* should be made from silver. ¹¹The north side must also have a wall of curtains 100 cubits* long. It must have 20 posts, and 20 bronze bases. The hooks for the posts and the curtain rods must be made from silver.

¹²"On the west side of the courtyard there must be a wall of curtains 50 cubits* long. There must be ten posts and ten bases. ¹³The east side of the courtyard must also be 50 cubits* long. ¹⁴⌊This east side is the entrance to the courtyard.⌋ One side of the entrance must have curtains 15 cubits* long. There must be three posts and three bases on this side. ¹⁵The other side must also have curtains 15 cubits* long. There must be three posts and three bases on that side.

¹⁶Make a curtain 20 cubits* long to cover the entrance to the courtyard. Make that curtain from fine linen* and blue, purple, and red yarn. Weave designs into that curtain. There must be four posts and four bases for that curtain. ¹⁷All the posts around the courtyard must be joined with silver ⌊curtain rods⌋. The hooks on the posts must be made from silver, and the bases for the posts must be bronze.* ¹⁸The courtyard should be 100 cubits* long and 50 cubits* wide. The wall of curtains around the courtyard should be 5 cubits* high. The curtains must be made from fine linen. The bases under the posts must be bronze. ¹⁹All the tools, tent pegs, and other things used in the Holy Tent* must be made from bronze. And all the pegs ⌊for the curtains around the courtyard⌋ must be made from bronze.

---

under the gold rings The 50 gold rings that joined together the two parts of the Holy Tent. See Ex. 26:6.
Box of the Agreement Or, "ark of the Covenant." The box containing the flat stones with the Ten Commandments written on them and the other things that proved God was with the people of Israel during their time in the Sinai desert.
cover Also called "mercy seat." The Hebrew word can mean "lid," "cover" or "the place where sins are forgiven."
Holy Tent Or, "tabernacle," the tent where God came to live among his people.
bronze A metal. The Hebrew word can mean "copper," "bronze," or "brass."
altar A table or raised area used for offering sacrifices.
5 cubits 8' 7 5/16" (2.625m).
3 cubits 5' 2" (1.575m).

100 cubits 172' 3" (52.5m).
linen Thread or cloth made from the fibers of the flax plant.
curtain rods These were either rods that joined the posts together or grommets (rings) sewn into the curtains.
50 cubits 86' 1 1/2" (26.25m).
15 cubits 25' 10" (7.875m).
20 cubits 34' 5 3/8" (10.5m).

EXODUS 27:20–28:24

Oil for the Lamp

²⁰"Command the people of Israel to bring the best olive oil. Use this oil for the lamp that must be lit each evening. ²¹Aaron and his sons will have the job of caring for the lamp. They will go into ⌊the first room of⌋ the Meeting Tent.* This is outside ⌊the room with⌋ the Agreement* that is behind the curtain ⌊that separates the two rooms⌋. In this place they will make sure the lamp continues burning before the Lord from evening till morning. The people of Israel and their descendants* must obey this law forever."

Clothes for the Priests

28 ⌊The Lord said to Moses,⌋ "Tell your brother Aaron and his sons, Nadab, Abihu, Eleazar, and Ithamar, to come to you from the people of Israel. These men will serve me as priests.

²"Make special clothes for your brother Aaron. These clothes will give him honor and respect. ³There are skilled men among the people who can make these clothes. I have given these men special wisdom. Tell those men to make the clothes for Aaron. These clothes will show that he serves me in a special way. Then he can serve me as a priest. ⁴These are the clothes the men should make: the Judgment Pouch,* the Ephod,* a blue robe, a white woven robe, a turban* and a sash (belt). The men must make these special clothes for your brother Aaron and his sons. Then Aaron and his sons can serve me as priests. ⁵Tell the men to use gold threads, fine linen,* and blue, purple and red yarn.

The Ephod and the Sash

⁶"Use gold threads, fine linen,* and blue, purple, and red yarn to make the Ephod.* This must be the work of a very skilled person. ⁷At each shoulder of the Ephod there should be a shoulder piece. These shoulder pieces should be tied to the two corners of the Ephod.

⁸"The men will very carefully weave a sash (belt) for the Ephod. This sash must be made the same way as the Ephod—use gold threads, fine linen,* and blue, purple, and red yarn.

⁹"Take two onyx stones. Write the names of the twelve sons of Israel *(Jacob)* on these jewels. ¹⁰Write six names on one jewel and six names on the other jewel. Write the names in order, from the oldest son to the youngest. ¹¹Cut the names of the sons of Israel on these stones. Do this the way a worker makes a seal.* Put the jewels in gold settings. ¹²Then put these two jewels on the shoulder pieces of the Ephod. Aaron will wear this special coat when he stands before the Lord. And the two stones with the names of the sons of Israel will be on the Ephod. These jewels will cause God to remember the people of Israel. ¹³Use fine gold to hold the stones on the Ephod. ¹⁴Twist chains of pure gold together like a rope. Make two of these gold chains and fasten them to the gold settings.

The Judgment Pouch

¹⁵"Make the Judgment Pouch* for the high priest. Skilled workers should make this pouch like they made the Ephod.* They must use gold threads, fine linen,* and blue, purple, and red yarn. ¹⁶The Judgment Pouch should be folded double to make a square ⌊pocket⌋. It should be 1 span* long and 1 span* wide. ¹⁷Put four rows of beautiful jewels on the Judgment Pouch. The first row of jewels should have a ruby, a topaz, and a beryl. ¹⁸The second row should have a turquoise, a sapphire, and an emerald. ¹⁹The third row should have a jacinth, an agate, and an amethyst. ²⁰The fourth row should have a chrysolite, an onyx, and a jasper. Set all these jewels in gold. ²¹There will be twelve jewels on the Judgment Pouch—one jewel for each of the sons of Israel *(Jacob)*. Write the name of one of the sons of Israel on each of the stones. Cut these names into each stone like a worker makes a seal.*

²²"Make chains of pure gold for Judgment Pouch.* These chains must be braided like a rope. ²³Make two gold rings and put them on two corners of the Judgment Pouch. ²⁴Put the two golden chains through the two rings at the corners

---

Meeting Tent The Holy Tent (tabernacle), where the people of Israel went to meet with God.
Agreement Literally, "Proof." The flat stones with the Ten Commandments written on them. These were proof of the Agreement between God and the people of Israel.
descendants A person's children and their future families.
Judgment Pouch A piece of clothing like a bib or an apron that covered the high priest's chest.
Zepho A special coat worn by the priests.
turban Head covering made by wrapping a long piece of cloth around the head or around a cap worn on the head.
linen Thread or cloth made from the fibers of the flax plant.
seal Small stones with designs cut into them. Pressed into wet clay or hot wax, they made a special mark.
1 span About 9" (23cm). This is the distance from the tip of the thumb to the tip of the little finger.

of the Judgment Pouch. ²⁵Fasten the other ends of the gold chains to the two settings. This will fasten them to the two shoulder pieces of the Ephod* on the front. ²⁶Make two more gold rings and put them on the other two corners of the Judgment Pouch. This will be on the inside edge of the Judgment Pouch next to the Ephod. ²⁷Make two more gold rings and put them on the bottom of the shoulder pieces on the front of the Ephod. Put the gold rings above the sash *(belt)* of the Ephod. ²⁸Use blue ribbon to tie the rings of the Judgment Pouch to the rings of the Ephod. In this way the Judgment Pouch will rest close to the sash and will be held against the Ephod.

²⁹"When Aaron enters the Holy Place,* he must wear the Judgment Pouch.* In this way he will wear the names of the twelve sons of Israel over his heart. And the Lord will always be reminded of them. ³⁰Put the Urim and Thummim* inside the Judgment Pouch. They will be over Aaron's heart when he goes before the Lord. So Aaron will always carry with him a way of judging the people of Israel when he is before the Lord.

Other Clothes for the Priests

³¹"Make a blue robe for the Ephod.* ³²Make a hole in the center for the head. And sew a piece of cloth around the edge of this hole. This cloth will be like a collar that keeps the hole from tearing. ³³Use blue, purple, and red yarn to make cloth pomegranates.* Hang these pomegranates around the bottom edge of the robe. And hang gold bells between the pomegranates. ³⁴So around the bottom edge of the robe there should be bells and pomegranates. There should be a bell between each pomegranate. ³⁵Aaron will wear this robe when he serves as a priest. The bells will ring as Aaron goes into the Holy Place* to stand before the Lord. And the bells will ring as he leaves the Holy Place. This way Aaron will not die.

³⁶"Make a strip of pure gold and carve words into the gold the way people make a seal.* Write these words: HOLY TO THE LORD. ³⁷Fasten the gold strip to a blue ribbon. Tie the blue ribbon around the turban.* The gold strip should be on the front of the turban. ³⁸Aaron will wear this on his head. This will show that Aaron is carrying the guilt represented by all the holy offerings that the people of Israel have given to the Lord.* Aaron will always wear this on his head so that the Lord will accept the gifts of the people.

³⁹"Use fine linen to make the white woven robe. And use fine linen to make the turban.* The sash *(belt)* should have designs sewn into it. ⁴⁰Also make coats, belts, and turbans for Aaron's sons. This will give them honor and respect. ⁴¹Put the clothes on your brother Aaron and his sons. Then pour the special oil on them to make them priests. This will make them holy, and they will serve me as priests.

⁴²"Use linen* to make underclothes for the priests. These underclothes will cover them from the waist to the thighs. ⁴³Aaron and his sons must wear these clothes anytime they enter the Meeting Tent.* They must wear these clothes when they come near to the altar to serve as priests in the Holy Place. If they don't wear these clothes, then they will be guilty of wrong, and they will have to die. All this should be a law that continues forever for Aaron and all his family after him."

The Ceremony for Appointing the Priests

29 ₁Then the Lord said to Moses,₁ "Now I will tell you what you must do to show that Aaron and his sons serve me in a special way as priests. Find one young bull and two rams that have nothing wrong with them. ²Then use fine wheat flour without yeast to make three kinds of bread: unleavened bread, unleavened bread mixed with oil, and thin cakes spread with oil. ³Put this bread and the cakes in a basket. Then give the basket to Aaron and his sons. At the same time give them the bull and the two rams.

⁴"Then bring Aaron and his sons to the entrance of the Meeting Tent.* Wash them with

---

Ephod A special coat worn by the priests.
Holy Place One of the two rooms in the Holy Tent.
Judgment Pouch A piece of clothing like a bib or an apron that covered the high priest's chest.
Urim and Thummim Used by the priest to learn God's answer to questions. They were probably like lots—stones, sticks, or bones that were thrown like dice.
Ephod A special coat worn by the priests.
pomegranates A red fruit about the size of an orange.
seal Small stones with designs cut into them. Pressed into wet clay or hot wax, they made a special mark.

turban Head covering made by wrapping a long piece of cloth around the head or around a cap worn on the head.
Aaron ... Lord. Or, "This will be on Aaron's head so he may take away any sin caused by the holy offerings and gifts that the people of Israel give to the Lord."
linen Thread or cloth made from the fibers of the flax plant.
Meeting Tent The Holy Tent (tabernacle) where the people of Israel went to meet with God.

water. ⁵Put the special clothes on Aaron. Put on him the white woven robe and the blue robe that is worn with the Ephod.* Put the Ephod and the Judgment Pouch* on him. Then tie the beautiful sash *(belt)* on him. ⁶Put the turban* on his head. And put the special crown around the turban. ⁷Take the anointing oil* and pour it on Aaron's head. This will show that Aaron is chosen for this work.

⁸"Then bring Aaron's sons to that place. Put the white woven robes on them. ⁹Then tie sashes *(belts)* around their waists. Give them the special hats to wear. At that time they will begin to be priests. They will be priests because of the special law that will continue forever. This is the way you will make Aaron and his sons priests.

¹⁰"Then bring the bull to that place at the front of the Meeting Tent.* Aaron and his sons must put their hands on the bull's head. ¹¹Then kill that bull there at the entrance to the Meeting Tent. The Lord will see this. ¹²Then take some of the bull's blood and go to the altar.* Use your finger to put some blood on the horns of the altar. Pour all the blood that is left at the bottom of the altar. ¹³Then take all the fat from inside the bull, the fatty part of the liver, both kidneys, and the fat around them. Burn this fat on the altar. ¹⁴Then take the bull's meat, his skin, and his other parts and go outside your camp. Burn these things there outside the camp. This is an offering to take away the sins of the priests.

¹⁵"Then tell Aaron and his sons to put their hands on the head of one of the rams. ¹⁶Kill that ram and save the blood. Throw the blood against the altar* on all four sides. ¹⁷Then cut the ram into several pieces. Wash all the parts from inside the ram and the legs. Put these things with the head and the other pieces of the ram. ¹⁸Then burn everything on the altar. It is a burnt offering, an offering made by fire to the Lord. Its smell will please the Lord.

¹⁹"Tell Aaron and his sons to put their hands on the other ram. ²⁰Kill that ram and save some of its blood. Put that blood on the right earlobes of Aaron and his sons. Also put some of the blood on the thumbs of their right hands. And put some of the blood on the big toes of their right feet. Then throw blood against all four sides of the altar. ²¹Then take some of the blood from the altar. Mix it with the special oil and sprinkle it on Aaron and his clothes. And sprinkle it on their sons and their clothes. This will show that Aaron and his sons serve me in a special way. And it will show that their clothes are used only at special times.

²²"Then take the fat from the ram. (This is the ram that will be used in the ceremony to make Aaron the high priest.) Take the fat from around the tail and the fat that covers the organs inside the body. Then take the fat that covers the liver, both kidneys and the fat on them, and the right leg. ²³Then take the basket of bread that you made without yeast. This is the basket you put before the Lord. Take these things out of the basket: one loaf of bread, one cake made with oil, and one small thin cake. ²⁴Give these things to Aaron and his sons. Tell them to hold these things in their hands before the Lord. This will be a special offering to the Lord. ²⁵Then take these things from Aaron and his sons and put them on the altar* with the ram. Then burn everything on the altar. It is a burnt offering, an offering made by fire to the Lord. Its smell will please the Lord.

²⁶"Then take the breast from the ram.* (This is the ram that will be used in the ceremony to make Aaron the high priest.) Hold the breast of the ram before the Lord as a special offering. Then take it back and keep it. This part of the animal will be for you. ²⁷Take the breast and the leg of the ram that was used to make Aaron the high priest and make those parts holy *(special).* Then give those special parts to Aaron and his sons. ²⁸The people of Israel will always give Aaron and his sons these parts. Those parts will always belong to the priests when the people of Israel make an offering

---

Meeting Tent The Holy Tent (tabernacle), where the people of Israel went to meet with God.

Ephod A special coat worn by the priests.

Judgment Pouch A piece of clothing like a bib or an apron that covered the high priest's chest.

turban Head covering made by wrapping a long piece of cloth around the head or around a cap worn on the head.

anointing oil Fine olive oil that was poured on things or people to show they were chosen for a special work or purpose.

altar A table or raised area used for offering sacrifices.

ram(s) A male sheep.

to the Lord. When they give these parts to the priest, it will be the same as giving them to the Lord.

²⁹"Save those special clothes that were made for Aaron. Those clothes will belong to all his people who live after him. They will wear those clothes when they are chosen to be priests. ³⁰Aaron's son will become the next high priest after him. That son will wear those clothes seven days when he comes to the Meeting Tent* to serve in the Holy Place.*

³¹"Cook the meat from the ram* that was used to make Aaron the high priest. Cook that meat in a holy place. ³²Then Aaron and his sons must eat the meat at the front door of the Meeting Tent.* And they must also eat the bread that is in the basket. ³³These offerings were used to take away their sins when they were made priests. Now they should eat those offerings. ³⁴If any of the meat from that ram or any of the bread is left the next morning, then it must be burned. You must not eat that bread or the meat because it should be eaten only in a special way at a special time.

³⁵"You must do all these things for Aaron and his sons. You must do them exactly as I told you. The ceremony for appointing them to be priests must continue for seven days. ³⁶You must kill one bull every day for seven days. This will be an offering for the sins of Aaron and his sons. You will use these sacrifices* to make the altar* pure. And pour olive oil on the altar to make it holy. ³⁷You will make the altar pure and holy for seven days. At that time the altar will become most holy. Anything that touches the altar will also be holy.

³⁸"Every day you must make an offering on the altar.* You must kill two lambs that are one year old. ³⁹Offer one lamb in the morning and the other in the evening. ⁴⁰⁻⁴¹When you kill the first lamb, also offer 8 cups* of fine wheat flour. Mix that flour with 1 quart* of wine as an offering. When you kill the second lamb in the evening, also offer the 8 cups* of fine flour. And offer 1 quart* of wine. This is the same as you did in the morning. This will be a food offering for the Lord. When you burn this offering, the Lord will smell it, and it will please him.

⁴²"You must burn these things as an offering to the Lord every day. Do this at the entrance of the Meeting Tent* before the Lord. Continue to do this for all time. When you make the offering, I the Lord will meet you there and speak to you. ⁴³I will meet with the people of Israel at that place. And my Glory* will make that place holy.

⁴⁴"So I will make the Meeting Tent* holy. And I will make the altar* holy. And I will make Aaron and his sons holy so that they can serve me as priests. ⁴⁵I will live with the people of Israel. I will be their God. ⁴⁶The people will know that I am the Lord, their God. They will know that I am the One who led them out of Egypt so I could live with them. I am the Lord, their God."

The Altar for Burning Incense

30 God said to Moses, "Make an altar* from acacia wood. You will use this altar for burning incense.* ²You must make the altar square—1 cubit* long and 1 cubit* wide. It must be 2 cubits* high. There will be horns at the four corners. These horns must be made as one piece with the altar. ³Cover the top and all the sides of the altar with pure gold. And put gold trim all around the altar. ⁴Below this trim there should be two gold rings. There should be two gold rings on opposite sides of the altar. These gold rings will be used with poles to carry the altar. ⁵Make the poles from acacia wood also. Cover the poles with gold. ⁶Put the altar in front of the special curtain. The Box of the Agreement* is behind that curtain.

Meeting Tent The Holy Tent (tabernacle), where the people of Israel went to meet with God.
Holy Place One of the rooms in the Holy Tent.
ram(s) A male sheep.
sacrifice(s) A gift to God. Usually it was a special animal that was killed and burned on an altar.
altar A table or raised area used for offering sacrifices.
8 cups Literally, "1/10 of a measure."
1 quart Literally, "1/4 hin."

Glory The Glory of the Lord. One of the forms God used when he appeared to people. It was like a bright shining light.
incense Special dried tree sap. Burned to make a sweet-smelling smoke, it was offered as a gift to God.
1 cubit 1' 8 5/8" (52.5cm).
2 cubits 3' 5 5/16" (105cm).
Box of the Agreement Or, "ark of the Covenant." The box containing the flat stones with the Ten Commandments written on them and other things that proved God was with the people of Israel during their time in the Sinai desert.

The altar will be in front of the cover* that is above the Agreement.* This is the place where I will meet with you.

⁷"Aaron must burn sweet smelling incense* on the altar* every morning. He will do this when he comes to care for the lamps. ⁸He must burn incense again in the evening. This is the time when he checks the lamps in the evenings. So that incense will be burned before the Lord every day forever. ⁹Don't use this altar for offering any other kind of incense or burnt offering. Don't use this altar to offer any kind of grain offering or drink offering.

¹⁰"Once a year Aaron must make a special sacrifice* to the Lord. Aaron will use the blood of the sin offering to erase the sins of the people. Aaron will do this at the horns of this altar.* This day will be called the Day of Atonement. This will be a very special day for the Lord."

The Temple Tax

¹¹The Lord said to Moses, ¹²"Count the people of Israel so that you will know how many people there are. Every time this is done, every person must make a payment for himself to the Lord. If each person does this, then no terrible thing will happen to the people. ¹³Every person who is counted must pay ½ shekel. (That is ½ shekel by the official measure.* This shekel weighs 20 gerahs.*) This half shekel is an offering to the Lord. ¹⁴Every person who is at least 20 years old will be counted. And every person counted must give the Lord this offering. ¹⁵Rich people must not give more than ½ shekel. And poor people must not give less than ½ shekel. All people will make the same offering to the Lord. This will be a payment for your life. ¹⁶Gather this money from the people of Israel. Use the money for the service in the Meeting Tent.* This payment will be a way for the Lord to remember his people. They will be paying for their own lives."

The Washing Bowl

¹⁷The Lord said to Moses, ¹⁸"Make a bronze* bowl and put it on a bronze base. You will use this for washing. Put the bowl between the Meeting Tent* and the altar.* Fill the bowl with water. ¹⁹Aaron and his sons must wash their hands and feet with the water from this bowl. ²⁰Every time they enter the Meeting Tent or come near the altar they must wash with water. This way they will not die. ²¹And they must wash their hands and their feet so they won't die. This will be a law that continues forever for Aaron and his people. This law will continue for all Aaron's people who will live in the future."

The Anointing Oil

²²Then the Lord said to Moses, ²³"Find the finest spices. Get 12 pounds* of liquid myrrh, half that amount (that is, 6 pounds*) of sweet smelling cinnamon, and 12 pounds* of sweet smelling cane, ²⁴and 12 pounds* of cassia. Use the official measure* to measure all these things. Also get 1 gallon* of olive oil.

²⁵"Mix all these things to make a special sweet-smelling anointing oil.* ²⁶Pour this oil on the Meeting Tent* and on the Box of the Agreement.*

---

cover Also called "mercy seat." The Hebrew word can mean "lid," "cover" or "the place where sins are forgiven."
Agreement Literally, "Proof." The flat stones with the Ten Commandments written on them. These were proof of the Agreement between God and the people of Israel.
incense Special dried tree sap. Burned to make a sweet-smelling smoke, it was offered as a gift to God.
altar A table or raised area used for offering sacrifices.
sacrifice(s) A gift to God. Usually, it was a special animal that was killed and burned on an altar.
official measure Literally, "holy shekel," the standard of measure used by the priests in the tabernacle or temple.
gerah(s) 1/50 of an ounce.

Meeting Tent The Holy Tent (tabernacle), where the people of Israel went to meet with God.
bronze A metal. The Hebrew word can mean "copper," "bronze," or "brass."
12 pounds Literally, "500 measures."
6 pounds Literally, "250 measures."
1 gallon Literally, "a hin."
anointing oil Olive oil that was poured on things or people to show that they were chosen for a special work or purpose.
Box of the Agreement Or, "ark of the Covenant." The box containing the flat stones with the Ten Commandments written on them and other things that proved God was with the people of Israel during their time in the Sinai desert.

This will show that these things have a special purpose. ²⁷Pour the oil on the table and on all the dishes on the table. And pour this oil on the lamp and on all its tools. Pour the oil on the incense* altar. ²⁸Also, pour the oil on the altar for burning offerings to God. Pour this oil on everything on that altar. Pour this oil on the bowl and on the base under it. ²⁹You will make all these things holy. They will be very special to the Lord. Anything that touches these things will also become holy.

³⁰"Pour the oil on Aaron and his sons. This will show that they serve me in a special way. Then they can serve me as priests. ³¹Tell the people of Israel that the anointing oil* is holy—it must always be used only for me. ³²No one should use this oil like an ordinary perfume. Don't make perfume the same way you make this special oil. This oil is holy, and it should be very special to you. ³³If anyone makes a perfume like this holy oil, and if he gives it to a foreigner, then that person must be separated from his people."

The Incense

³⁴Then the Lord said to Moses, "Get these sweet-smelling spices: resin, onycha, galbanum, and pure frankincense. Be sure that you have equal amounts of these spices. ³⁵Mix the spices together to make a sweet-smelling incense.* Do this the same as a perfume maker would do it. Also mix salt with this incense. This will make it pure and special. ³⁶Grind some of the incense until it becomes a fine powder. Put this incense in front of the Agreement* in the Meeting Tent.* This is the place where I meet with you. You must use this incense powder only for its very special purpose. ³⁷You must use this incense only in this special way for the Lord. You will make this incense in a special way. Don't make any other incense in this special way. ³⁸A person might want to make some of this incense for himself, so he can enjoy the smell. But if he does this, then he must be separated from his people."

Bezalel and Oholiab

31 Then the Lord said to Moses, ²"I have chosen a man from the family group of Judah to do some special work for me. His name is Bezalel son of Uri son of Hur. ³I have filled Bezalel with the Spirit of God—I have given him the skill and knowledge to do all kinds of things. ⁴Bezalel is a very good designer. And he can make things from gold, silver, and bronze. ⁵Bezalel can cut and set beautiful jewels. And he can work with wood. Bezalel can do all kinds of work. ⁶I have also chosen Oholiab to work with him. Oholiab is the son of Ahisamach from the family group of Dan. And I have given skills to all the other workers so they can make all the things that I have commanded you:

⁷ the Meeting Tent,*
the Box of the Agreement,*
the cover* for the Box,
⁸ the table and everything on it,
the altar* for burning incense,*
⁹ the altar for burning offerings
and the things used at the altar,
the bronze bowl and the base under it,
¹⁰ the special clothes for Aaron the priest,
the special clothes for Aaron's sons
when they serve as priests,
¹¹ the sweet-smelling anointing oil,*
the sweet-smelling incense for
the Holy Place.*

Meeting Tent The Holy Tent (tabernacle), where the people of Israel went to meet with God.
Box of the Agreement Or, "ark of the Covenant." The box containing the flat stones with the Ten Commandments written on them and other things that proved God was with the people of Israel during their time in the Sinai desert.
incense Special dried tree sap. Burned to make a sweet-smelling smoke, it was offered as a gift to God.
anointing oil Fine olive oil that was poured on things or people to show they were chosen for a special work or purpose.
Agreement Literally, "Proof." The flat stones with the Ten Commandments written on them. These were proof of the Agreement between God and the people of Israel.

cover Also called "mercy seat." The Hebrew word can mean "lid," "cover" or "the place where sins are forgiven."
altar A table or raised area used for offering sacrifices.
incense Special dried tree sap. Burned to make a sweet-smelling smoke, it was offered as a gift to God.

These workers must make all these things the way that I have commanded you."

The Sabbath

¹²Then the Lord said to Moses, ¹³"Tell the people of Israel this: 'You must follow the rules about my special days of rest. You must do this because they will be a sign between you and me for all generations. This will show you that I, the Lord, have made you my special people.
¹⁴"'Make the Sabbath* a special day. If a person treats the Sabbath like any other day, then that person must be killed. Any person who works on the Sabbath day must be cut off *(separated)* from his people. ¹⁵There are six other days in the week for working. But the seventh day is a very special day of rest. That is the special day to honor the Lord. Any person who works during the Sabbath must be killed. ¹⁶The people of Israel must remember the Sabbath and make it a special day. They must continue to do this forever. It is an agreement between them and me that will continue forever. ¹⁷The Sabbath will be a sign between me and the people of Israel forever. The Lord worked six days and made heaven and earth. And on the seventh day he rested and relaxed.'"

¹⁸So the Lord finished speaking to Moses on Mount Sinai. Then the Lord gave him the two flat stones with the Agreement* on them. God used his finger and wrote on the stones.

The Golden Calf

32 The people saw that a long time had passed and Moses had not come down from the mountain. So the people gathered around Aaron. They said to him, "Look, Moses led us out of the land of Egypt. But we don't know what has happened to him. So make us some gods to go before us and lead us."

²Aaron said to the people, "Bring me the gold earrings that belong to your wives, sons, and daughters."

³So all the people gathered their gold earrings and brought them to Aaron. ⁴Aaron took the gold from the people. Then he used it to make a statue of a calf. Aaron used a chisel to carve the statue, ₍and then he covered it with gold₎. Then the people said, "Israel, these are the gods that led you out of Egypt."

Then the people said, "People of Israel, here are your gods! These are the gods who brought you out of the land of Egypt!"

⁵Aaron saw all these things. So he built an altar* in front of the calf. Then Aaron made an announcement. He said, "Tomorrow will be a special feast to honor the Lord."

⁶The people woke up very early the next morning. They killed animals and offered them as burnt offerings and fellowship offerings. The people sat down to eat and drink. Then they got up and had a wild party.

⁷At the same time, the Lord said to Moses, "Go down from this mountain. Your people, the people you brought out of the land of Egypt, have done a terrible sin. ⁸They have very quickly turned away from the things I commanded them to do. They made a calf from melted gold for themselves. They are worshiping that calf and making sacrifices* to it. The people have said, 'Israel, these are the gods that led you out of Egypt.'"

⁹The Lord said to Moses, "I have seen these people. I know that they are very stubborn people. They will always turn against me. ¹⁰So now let me destroy them in anger. Then I will make a great nation from you."

¹¹But Moses begged the Lord his God, "Lord, don't let your anger destroy your people. You brought these people out of Egypt with your great power and strength. ¹²₍But if you destroy your people,₎ then the Egyptians can say, 'The Lord planned to do bad things to his people. That is why he led them out of Egypt. He wanted to kill them in the mountains. He wanted to wipe them

---

anointing oil Fine olive oil that was poured on things or people to show they were chosen by God for a special work or purpose.
Holy Place One of the rooms in the Holy Tent.
Sabbath Saturday, a special day of rest and worship for Jews.
Agreement Literally, "Proof." The two flat stones with the Ten Commandments written on them. These were proof of the Agreement between God and the people of Israel.

altar A table or raised area used for offering sacrifices.
sacrifice(s) A gift to God. Usually, it was a special animal that was killed and burned on an altar.

off the earth.' So don't be angry at your people. Please change your mind! Don't destroy your people. ¹³Remember Abraham, Isaac, and Israel (Jacob). Those men served you. And you used your name to make a promise to them. You said: 'I will make your people as many as the stars in the sky. I will give your people all this land like I promised. This land will be theirs forever.'"

¹⁴So the Lord felt sorry ₍for the people₎. The Lord did not do the thing that he said he might do—he did not destroy the people.

¹⁵Then Moses went down the mountain. Moses had the two flat stones with the Agreement* on them. Those commandments were written on both sides of the stone, front and back. ¹⁶God himself had made those stones. And God himself wrote the commandments on those stones.

¹⁷₍While going down the mountain, Joshua heard the noise from the party in camp. Joshua said to Moses, "It sounds like war down in the camp!"

¹⁸Moses answered, "It is not the noise of an army shouting for victory. And it is not the noise of an army crying from defeat. The noise I hear is the sound of music.*"

¹⁹Moses came near the camp. He saw the golden calf, and he saw the people dancing. Moses became very angry, and he threw the flat stones on the ground. The stones broke into several pieces at the bottom of the mountain. ²⁰Then Moses destroyed the calf that the people had made. He melted it in the fire. Then he ground the gold until it became dust. And he threw the dust in the water. He forced the people of Israel to drink that water.

²¹Moses said to Aaron, "What did these people do to you? Why did you lead them to do such a bad sin?"

²²Aaron answered, "Don't be angry, sir. You know that these people are always ready to do wrong. ²³The people said to me, 'Moses led us out of Egypt. But we don't know what has happened to him. So make us some gods to lead us.' ²⁴So I told the people, 'If you have any gold rings, then give them to me.' The people gave me their gold. I threw the gold into the fire, and out of the fire came this calf!"

²⁵Moses saw that Aaron had let the people lose control. The people were being wild, and all their enemies could see them acting like fools. ²⁶So Moses stood at the entrance to the camp. Moses said, "Any person who wants to follow the Lord should come to me." And all the people from the family of Levi ran to Moses.

²⁷Then Moses said to them, "I will tell you what the Lord, the God of Israel, says: 'Every man must get his sword and go from one end of the camp to the other. ₍You must punish these people, even if₎ each man must kill his brother, friends, and neighbors.'"

²⁸The people from the family of Levi obeyed Moses. That day about 3,000 of the people of Israel died. ²⁹Then Moses said, "The Lord has chosen you today to be the people who will bless your sons and brothers."

³⁰The next morning Moses told the people, "You have done a terrible sin! But now I will go up to the Lord, and maybe I can do something so he will forgive you for your sin." ³¹So Moses went back to the Lord and said, "Please listen! These people did a very bad sin and made a god from gold. ³²Now, forgive them of this sin! If you will not forgive them, then erase my name from the book* you have written."

³³But the Lord said to Moses, "The only people that I erase from my book are the people who sin against me. ³⁴So now, go down and lead the people where I tell you. My angel will go before you and lead you. When the time comes to punish the people who sinned, then they will be punished." ³⁵So the Lord caused a terrible sickness to come to the people. He did this because they told Aaron to make the golden calf.

"I Will Not Go with You"

33 Then the Lord said to Moses, "You and the people you brought out of Egypt must leave this place. Go to the land that I promised to give to Abraham, Isaac, and Jacob. I promised them

---

Agreement Literally, "Proof." The flat stones with the Ten Commandments written on them. These were proof of the Agreement between God and the people of Israel.

music Or, "singing."

the book This is the "Book of Life," a book with all the names of God's people written in it.

that I would give that land to their descendants. ²So I will send an angel to go before you. And I will defeat the Canaanites, the Amorites, the Hittites, the Perizzites the Hivites, and the Jebusites. I will force those people to leave your land. ³So go to the land filled with many good things.* But I will not go with you. You people are very stubborn, ₍and you make me very angry₎. If I go with you, I might destroy you along the way."

⁴The people heard this bad news and became very sad. And the people stopped wearing jewelry. ⁵Why? Because the Lord said to Moses, "Tell the people of Israel, 'You are a stubborn people. I might destroy you even if I travel with you only a short time. So take off all your jewelry while I decide* what to do with you.'" ⁶So the people of Israel stopped wearing their jewelry at Mount Horeb *(Sinai)*.

The Temporary Meeting Tent

⁷Moses used to take a tent a short way outside the camp. Moses called it "the meeting tent.*" Any person who wanted to ask something from the Lord would go to the meeting tent outside the camp. ⁸Any time Moses went out to the tent, all the people watched him. The people stood at the entrance of their tents and watched Moses until he entered the meeting tent. ⁹Whenever Moses went into the tent, the tall cloud would come down and stay at the entrance to the tent. And the Lord would speak with Moses. ¹⁰So when the people saw the cloud at the entrance of the tent, they would go to the entrance of their own tents and bow down ₍to worship God₎.

¹¹In this way the Lord spoke to Moses face to face. The Lord spoke to Moses like a man speaks with his friend. After speaking with the Lord, Moses would go back to the camp. But his helper always stayed in the tent. This helper was Joshua son of Nun.

Moses Sees the Glory of the Lord

¹²Moses said to the Lord, "You told me to lead these people. But you did not say who you would send with me. You said to me, 'I know you very well, and I am pleased with you.' ¹³If I have truly pleased you, then teach me your ways. I want to know you. Then I can continue to please you. Remember that all these are your people."

¹⁴The Lord answered, "I myself will go with you. I will lead you.*"

¹⁵Then Moses said to the Lord, "If you don't go with us, then don't send us away from this place. ¹⁶Also, how will we know if you are pleased with me and these people? If you go with us, then we will know for sure! If you don't go with us, then I and these people will be no different than any other people on the earth."

¹⁷Then the Lord said to Moses, "I will do what you ask. I will do this because I am pleased with you and because I know you very well."*

¹⁸Then Moses said, "Now, please show me your Glory."*

¹⁹Then the Lord answered, "I will cause my perfect Goodness to go before you. I am the Lord and I will announce my name so that you can hear it. Why? Because I can show my kindness and love to any person I choose. ²⁰But you can't see my face. No person can see me and continue to live.

²¹"There is a rock at a place near me. You can stand on that rock. ²²My Glory* will pass by that place. I will put you in a large crack in that rock, and I will cover you with my hand while I pass. ²³Then I will take away my hand, and you will see my back. But you will not see my face."

The New Stone Tablets

34 Then the Lord said to Moses, "Make two more flat stones like the first two that were broken. I will write the same words on these stones that were written on the first two stones. ²Be ready tomorrow morning and come up on Mount Sinai. Stand before me there on the top of

---

filled ... good things Literally, "flowing with milk and honey."

jewelry ... decide This is a word play in Hebrew, but people often wore jewelry to remind them of their false gods.

meeting tent This is probably a tent that Moses used only until the real Meeting Tent was built.

lead you Or, "give you rest."

I know you very well Literally, "I know you by name."

Glory The Glory of the Lord. One of the forms God used when he appeared to people. It was like a bright shining light.

the mountain. ³No person will be allowed to come with you. No person should even be seen any place on the mountain. Even your herds of animals or flocks of sheep will not be allowed to eat grass at the bottom of the mountain."

⁴So Moses made two more flat stones like the first ones. Then early the next morning he went up Mount Sinai. Moses did everything like the Lord had commanded him. Moses carried the two flat stones with him. ⁵After Moses was on the mountain, the Lord came down to him in a cloud. The Lord stood there with Moses, and Moses called the Lord's name.*

⁶The Lord passed in front of Moses and said, "YAHWEH,* the Lord, is the kind and merciful God. The Lord is slow to become angry. The Lord is full of great love. The Lord can be trusted. ⁷The Lord shows his kindness to thousands ₍of generations₎. The Lord forgives* people for the wrong things they do. But the Lord does not forget to punish guilty people. The Lord will punish not only the guilty people, but their children, their grandchildren, and their great-grandchildren will suffer for the bad things those people do.*"

⁸Then Moses quickly bowed to the ground and worshiped ₍the Lord₎. Moses said, ⁹"Lord, if you are pleased with me, then please go with us. I know that these are stubborn people. But forgive us for the bad things we did! Accept us as your people."

¹⁰Then the Lord said, "I am making this agreement with all of your people. I will do amazing things that have never before been done for any other nation on earth. The people with you will see that I, the Lord, am very great. The people will see the wonderful things that I will do for you. ¹¹Obey the things I command you today, and I will force your enemies to leave your land. I will force out the Amorites, the Canaanites, the Hittites, the Perizzites, the Hivites, and the Jebusites. ¹²Be careful! Don't make any agreement with the people who live in the land where you are going. If you make an agreement with those people, then it will bring you trouble. ¹³So destroy their altars.* Break the stones they worship. Cut down their idols.* ¹⁴Don't worship any other god. I am Yahweh Kanah—the jealous Lord. That is my name. I am El Kanah—the jealous God.

¹⁵"Be careful not to make any agreements with the people who live in that land. If you do this, then you might join them when they worship their gods. Those people will invite you to join them, and you will eat their sacrifices.* ¹⁶You might choose some of their daughters as wives for your sons. Those daughters serve false gods. They might lead your sons to do the same thing.

¹⁷"Don't make idols.*

¹⁸"Celebrate the Festival of Unleavened Bread. For seven days eat that bread made without yeast like I commanded you before. Do this during the month I have chosen, the month of Abib.* Why? Because that is the month you came out of Egypt.

¹⁹"A woman's first baby always belongs to me. Even the first animals that are born from your cattle or sheep belong to me. ²⁰If you want to keep a donkey that is the first born, then you can buy it with a lamb. But if you don't buy that donkey with a lamb, then you must break the donkey's neck. You must buy back all of your firstborn* sons from me. No person should come before me without a gift.

²¹"You will work for six days. But on the seventh day you must rest. You must rest even during the times of planting and harvesting.

altar A table or raised area used for offering sacrifices.
stones ... idols Literally, "memorials ... Asherah poles." These were stone markers and wood poles that the people set up to help them remember and honor false gods.
sacrifice(s) A gift to God. Usually, it was a special animal that was killed and burned on an altar.
idols Statues of false gods that people worshiped.
Ai Or, "spring." This is Nisan, the first month of the ancient Jewish year.
firstborn The first child born into a family. The firstborn son was very important in ancient times.
Festival of Weeks Also called "Pentecost" or "Shavuoth."
fall Literally, "at the changing of the year."
Festival of Harvest Also called "Feast of Ingathering" or "Succoth."

Moses called the Lord's name Literally, "He called on the name of the Lord." This might mean Moses worshiped the Lord, or it might mean the Lord spoke his name to Moses.
YAHWEH This name, usually translated "Lord," is like the Hebrew word meaning, "He is" or "He makes things exist."
forgives Or, "spares."
The Lord ... people do Or, "The Lord credits the guilt of the fathers to their children and grandchildren, to the third and fourth generation."

²²"Celebrate the Festival of Weeks.* Use the first grain from the wheat harvest for this festival. And in the fall* celebrate the Festival of Harvest.*

²³"Three times each year all your men must go to be with the Master, the Lord, the God of Israel.

²⁴"When you go into your land, I will force your enemies out of that land. I will expand your borders—you will get more and more land. You will go before the Lord your God three times each year. At that time, no one will try to take your land from you.

²⁵"Whenever you offer blood from a sacrifice* to me, don't offer yeast at the same time.

"Don't leave any of the meat from the Passover* meal until the next morning.

²⁶"Give the Lord the very first crops that you harvest. Bring those things to the house* of the Lord your God.

"Never cook a young goat in its mother's milk."

²⁷Then the Lord said to Moses, "Write all the things that I have told you. Those things are the Agreement that I made with you and the people of Israel."

²⁸Moses stayed there with the Lord for 40 days and 40 nights. Moses did not eat any food or drink any water. And Moses wrote the words of the Agreement (the Ten Commandments) on the two flat stones.

Moses' Shining Face

²⁹Then Moses came down from Mount Sinai. He carried the two flat stones with the Agreement* on them. Moses' face was shining because he had talked with the Lord. But Moses did not know this. ³⁰Aaron and all the people of Israel saw that Moses' face was shining bright. So they were afraid to go near him. ³¹But Moses called to them. So Aaron and all the leaders of the people went to Moses. Moses talked with them. ³²After that, all the people of Israel came near Moses. And Moses gave them the commands that the Lord had given him on Mount Sinai.

³³When Moses finished speaking to the people, he put a covering over his face. ³⁴Any time Moses went before the Lord to speak with him, Moses took off the covering. Then Moses would come out and tell the people of Israel the things the Lord commanded. ³⁵The people would see that Moses' face was shining bright, so Moses would cover his face again. Moses kept his face covered until the next time he went in to speak with the Lord.

Rules About the Sabbath

35 Moses gathered all the people of Israel together. Moses said to them, "I will tell you the things the Lord has commanded you to do:

²"There are six days for working. But the seventh day will be a very special day of rest for you. You will honor the Lord by resting on that special day. Any person who works on the seventh day must be killed. ³On the Sabbath* you should not even light a fire in any of the places where you live."

Things for the Holy Tent

⁴Moses said to all the people of Israel, "This is what the Lord commanded: ⁵Gather special gifts for the Lord. Each of you should decide in your heart what you will give. And then you should bring that gift to the Lord. Bring gold, silver, and bronze*; ⁶blue, purple, and red yarn and fine linen*; goat hair; ⁷ram skins dyed red and fine leather*; acacia wood; ⁸oil for the lamps; spices for the anointing oil* and spices for the sweet-

---

Festival of Weeks Also called "Pentecost" or "Shavuoth."
fall Literally, "at the changing of the year."
Festival of Harvest Also called "Feast of Ingathering" or "Succoth."
sacrifice(s) A gift to God. Usually, it was a special animal that was killed and burned on an altar.
Passover An important Jewish holy day. They ate a special meal on this day every spring to remember that God freed them from slavery in Egypt.
house The Holy Tent (tabernacle) or temple, where God came to live among his people.
Agreement Literally, "Proof." The flat stones with the Ten Commandments written on them. These were proof of the Agreement between God and the people of Israel.

Sabbath Saturday, a special day of rest and worship for Jews.
bronze A metal. The Hebrew word can mean "copper," "bronze," or "brass."
linen Thread or cloth made from the fibers of the flax plant.
fine leather A special kind of leather made from the skin of an animal like a seal or sea cow.
anointing oil Fine olive oil that was poured on things or people to show they were chosen for a special work or purpose.

smelling incense.* ⁹Also, bring onyx stones and other jewels to be put on the Ephod* and the Judgment Pouch.*

¹⁰All of you people who are skilled workers should make all of the things the Lord commanded: ¹¹the Holy Tent,* its outer tent, and its covering; the hooks, boards, braces, posts, and bases; ¹²the Holy Box,* its poles, the cover,* and the curtain that covers the area where the Box stays; ¹³the table and its poles, all the things on the table, and the special bread on the table; ¹⁴the lampstand that is used for light and the things used with the lampstand, the lamps, and oil for the light; ¹⁵the altar* for burning incense* and its poles; the anointing oil* and the sweet-smelling incense; the curtain that covers the door at the entrance to the Holy Tent; ¹⁶the altar for burning offerings and its bronze* grating, the poles, and all the things used at the altar; the bronze bowl and its base; ¹⁷the curtains around the yard, their posts and bases, and the curtain that covers the entrance to the yard; ¹⁸the pegs used to support the Tent and ⌊the wall of curtains around⌋ the courtyard, and the ropes that tie to the pegs; ¹⁹and the special woven clothes for the priest to wear in the Holy Place.* These are the special clothes for Aaron the priest and his sons to wear. They will wear these clothes when they serve as priests."

The Great Offering from the People

²⁰Then all the people of Israel went away from Moses. ²¹All the people who wanted to give came and brought a gift to the Lord. These gifts were used for making the Meeting Tent,* all the things in the Tent, and the special clothes. ²²All the men and women who wanted to give brought gold jewelry of all kinds. They brought pins,* earrings, rings, and other jewelry. They all gave their jewelry to the Lord. This was a special offering to the Lord.

²³Every person who had fine linen* and blue, purple, and red yarn brought it to the Lord. Any person who had goat hair or ram skins dyed red or fine leather* brought it to the Lord. ²⁴Every person who wanted to give silver or bronze* brought that as a gift to the Lord. Every person who had acacia wood came and gave it to the Lord. ²⁵Every skilled woman made fine linen and blue, purple, and red yarn. ²⁶And all the women who were skilled and wanted to help made cloth from the goat hair.

²⁷The leaders brought onyx stones and other jewels. These stones and jewels were put on the Ephod* and Judgment Pouch* of the priest. ²⁸The people also brought spices and olive oil. These things were used for the sweet-smelling incense,* the anointing oil,* and the oil for the lamps.

²⁹All the people of Israel that wanted to help brought gifts to the Lord. The people gave these gifts freely, because they wanted to. These gifts were used to make all the things the Lord had commanded Moses and the people to make.

Bezalel and Oholiab

³⁰Then Moses said to the people of Israel, "Look, the Lord has chosen Bezalel son of Uri, from the family group of Judah. (Uri was the son of Hur.) ³¹The Lord filled Bezalel with the Spirit of God—he gave Bezalel special skill and knowledge to do all kinds of things. ³²He can design and make things with gold, silver, and bronze*. ³³He can cut and set stones and jewels.

---

incense Special dried tree sap. Burned to make a sweet-smelling smoke, it was offered as a gift to God.

Ephod A special coat worn by the priests.

Judgment Pouch A piece of clothing like a bib or an apron that covered the high priest's chest. See Ex. 28:15-30.

Holy Tent Or, "tabernacle," the tent where God came to live among his people.

Holy Box The Box of the Agreement, the box containing the flat stones with the Ten Commandments written on them and other things that proved God was with the people of Israel during their time in the Sinai desert.

cover Also called "mercy seat." The Hebrew word can mean "lid," "cover" or "the place where sins are forgiven."

altar A table or raised area used for offering sacrifices.

anointing oil Fine olive oil that was poured on things or people to show they were chosen for a special work or purpose.

bronze A metal. The Hebrew word can mean "copper," "bronze," or "brass."

Holy Place One of the rooms in the Holy Tent.

Meeting Tent The Holy Tent (tabernacle), where the people of Israel went to meet with God.

pins Or, "hooks." These were like safety pins and were used like buttons to fasten their robes.

linen Thread or cloth made from the fibers of the flax plant.

fine leather A special kind of leather made from the skin of an animal like a seal or sea cow.

Bezalel can work with wood and make all kinds of things. ³⁴The Lord has given Bezalel and Oholiab special skills to teach other people. (Oholiab was the son of Ahisamach from the family group of Dan.) ³⁵The Lord has given both of these men special skill to do all kinds of work. They are able to do the work of carpenters and metal workers. They can weave cloth with designs in it from the blue, purple, and red yarn and fine linen.* And they are able to weave things with wool."

36 "So, Bezalel, Oholiab and all the other skilled men must do the work the Lord has commanded. The Lord has given these men the wisdom and understanding to do all the skilled work needed to build this holy place."

²Then Moses called Bezalel and Oholiab and all the other skilled people that the Lord had given special skills to. And these people came because they wanted to help with the work. ³Moses gave these people all the things the people of Israel had brought as gifts. And they used these things to build [God's] holy place. The people continued to bring gifts each morning. ⁴Finally, all the skilled workers left the work they were doing on the holy place, and they went to speak to Moses. They said, ⁵"The people have brought too much! We have more than we need to finish the work on the Tent!"

⁶Then Moses sent this message throughout the camp: "No man or woman should make anything else as a gift for the holy place." So the people were forced to stop giving more. ⁷The people had brought more than enough things to finish the work [of building God's holy place].

The Holy Tent

⁸Then the skilled workers began making the Holy Tent.* They made the ten curtains from fine linen and blue, purple, and red yarn. And they sewed pictures of Cherub angels* with wings into the curtains. ⁹Each curtain was the same size—28 cubits* long and 4 cubits* wide. ¹⁰The workers joined the curtains together into two groups of curtains. They joined five curtains together to make one group and five curtains together to make the other group. ¹¹Then they used blue cloth to make loops along the edge of the end curtain of one group. And they did the same on the end curtain in the other group. ¹²There were 50 loops on the end curtain in one group, and 50 loops on the end curtain in the other group. The loops were opposite each other. ¹³Then they made 50 gold rings to join the two curtains together. So the Holy Tent was joined together into one piece.

¹⁴Then the workers made another tent to cover the Holy Tent.* They used goat hair to make eleven curtains. ¹⁵All the curtains were the same size—30 cubits* long and 4 cubits* wide. ¹⁶The workers joined five curtains together into one group and six curtains together into another group. ¹⁷They put 50 loops along the edge of the end curtain of one group. And they did the same on the end curtain of the other group. ¹⁸The workers made 50 bronze* rings to join the two groups of curtains together to form one tent. ¹⁹Then they made two more coverings for the Holy Tent. One covering was made from ram skins dyed red. The other covering was made from fine leather.*

²⁰Then the workers made frames from acacia wood to support the Holy Tent.* ²¹Each frame was 10 cubits* long and 1 1/2 cubits* wide. ²²There were two side poles joined together with cross pieces to make each frame. Every frame for the Holy Tent was made the same. ²³They made 20 frames for the south side of the Holy Tent. ²⁴Then they made 40 silver bases for the frames. There were two bases for each frame—one base for each side pole. ²⁵They also made 20 frames for

---

28 cubits 48' 2 3/4" (14.7m).
4 cubits 6' 10 13/16" (2.1m).
30 cubits 51' 8 1/16" (15.75m).
bronze A metal. The Hebrew word can mean "copper," "bronze," or "brass."
fine leather A special kind of leather made from the skin of an animal like a seal or a sea cow.
10 cubits 17' 2 11/16" (5.25m).
1 1/2 cubits 2' 7" (78.75cm).

---

linen Thread or cloth made from the fibers of the flax plant.
Holy Tent Or, "tabernacle." the tent where God came to live among his people.
Cherub angels Special angels from God. Statues of these angels were on top of the Box of the Agreement.

the other side (the north side) of the Holy Tent. ²⁶They made 40 silver bases for the frames—two bases for each frame. ²⁷They made six more frames for the back (the west side) of the Holy Tent. ²⁸They also made two frames for the corners at the back of the Holy Tent. ²⁹These frames were joined together at the bottom. And at the top a ring held the corner frames together. They did the same for both corners. ³⁰There was a total of eight frames for the west side of the Holy Tent. And there were 16 silver bases—two bases for each frame.

³¹Then the workers used Acacia wood to make the braces for the frames—five braces for the first side of the Holy Tent,* ³²five braces for the other side, and five braces for the back of the Holy Tent (that is, the west side). ³³They made the middle brace so that it passed through the frames from one end to the other. ³⁴They covered these frames with gold. Then they used gold to make the rings to hold the braces. And they covered the braces with gold.

³⁵They used fine linen and blue, purple, and red yarn to make the special curtain ⌊for the entrance to the Most Holy Place⌋. And they sewed pictures of Cherub angels into the curtain. ³⁶They made four posts using acacia wood, and they covered the posts with gold. Then they made gold hooks for the posts. And they made four silver bases for the posts. ³⁷Then they made the curtain to cover the entrance to the Tent. They used blue, purple, and red yarn and fine linen to make this curtain. And they wove pictures into it. ³⁸Then they made the five posts and the hooks ⌊for this curtain over the entrance⌋. They covered the tops of the posts and the curtain rods* with gold. And they made the five bronze* bases for the posts.

The Box of the Agreement

37¹Bezalel made the Holy Box* from acacia wood. The Box was 2 1/2 cubits* long, 1 1/2 cubits* wide, and 1 1/2 cubits* high. ²He covered the inside and outside of the Box with pure gold. Then he put gold trim around the Box. ³He made four rings of gold and put them on the four corners. These rings were used for carrying the Box. There were two rings on each side. ⁴Then he made the poles for carrying the Box. He used acacia wood and covered the poles with pure gold. ⁵He put the poles through the rings on each side of the Box. ⁶Then he made the cover* from pure gold. It was 2 1/2 cubits* long and 1 1/2 cubits* wide. ⁷Then Bezalel hammered gold to make two Cherub angels. He put the Cherub angels on each end of the cover. ⁸He put one angel on one end of the cover, and he put the other angel on the other end. The angels were joined together with the cover to make one piece. ⁹The wings of the angels were spread up toward the sky. The angels covered the Box with their wings. The angels faced each other, looking toward the cover.

The Table

¹⁰Then he made the table from acacia wood. The table was 2 cubits* long, 1 cubit* wide, and 1 1/2 cubits* high. ¹¹He covered the table with pure gold. He put gold trim around the table. ¹²Then he made a frame 1 handbreadth* wide around the table. He put gold trim on the frame. ¹³Then he made four gold rings and put them at the four corners of the table, where the four legs were. ¹⁴He put the rings close to the frame ⌊around the table⌋. The rings were to hold the poles used to carry the table. ¹⁵Then he used acacia wood to make the poles for carrying the table. He covered the poles with pure gold. ¹⁶Then he made all the things that were used on the table. He made the plates, the spoons, the bowls, and the pitchers

---

Holy Tent Or, "tabernacle," the tent where God came to live among his people.
curtain rods Or, "fasteners."
bronze A metal. The Hebrew word can mean, "copper," "bronze," or "brass."
1 1/2 cubits 2' 7" (78.75cm).
cover Also called, "mercy seat." The Hebrew word can mean "lid," "cover" or "the place where sins are forgiven."
2 cubits 3' 5 5/16" (105cm).
1 cubit 1' 8 5/8" (52.5cm).
1 handbreadth The width of 4 fingers, about 3" (7.7cm).

The Lampstand

¹⁷Then he made the lampstand. He used pure gold and hammered it to make the base and the shaft.* Then he made flowers, buds, and petals. He joined all these things together into one piece. ¹⁸The lampstand had six branches—three branches on one side and three branches on the other side. ¹⁹Each branch had three flowers on it. These flowers were made like almond flowers with buds and petals. ²⁰The shaft of the lampstand had four more flowers. They were also made like almond flowers with buds and petals. ²¹There were six branches—three branches coming out from each side of the shaft. And there was a flower with buds and petals below each of the three places where the branches joined the shaft. ²²The whole lampstand, with the flowers and branches, was made from pure gold. All this gold was hammered and joined together into one piece. ²³He made seven lamps for this lampstand. Then he made wick trimmers and trays from pure gold. ²⁴He used 75 pounds* of pure gold to make the lampstand and the things used with it.

The Altar for Burning Incense

²⁵He made the altar* for burning incense.* He made this from acacia wood. The altar was square. It was 1 cubit* long, 1 cubit* wide, and 2 cubits* high. There were four horns on the altar. There was one horn on each corner. These horns were joined together with the altar to make one piece. ²⁶He covered the top and all the sides and the horns with pure gold. Then he put gold trim around the altar. ²⁷He made two gold rings for the altar. He put the gold rings below the trim on each side of the altar. These gold rings held the poles for carrying the altar. ²⁸He made the poles from acacia wood and covered them with gold. ²⁹Then he made the holy anointing oil.* He also made the pure, sweet-smelling incense.* These things were made the same way that a perfume maker would make them.

The Altar for Burning Offerings

38 Then Bezalel used acacia wood to build the altar. This was the altar used for burning offerings. The altar was square. It was 5 cubits* long, 5 cubits* wide, and 3 cubits* high. ²He made a horn for each of the four corners of the altar. He joined each horn to its corner so that everything was one piece. He covered the altar with bronze.* ³Then he used bronze to make all the tools to be used on the altar. He made the pots, shovels, bowls, forks, and pans. ⁴Then he made a bronze grating for the altar. This grating was shaped like a net. The grating was put under the ledge at the bottom of the altar. It went halfway up into the altar from below. ⁵Then he made bronze rings. These rings were used to hold the poles for carrying the altar. He put the rings at the four corners of the grating. ⁶Then he used acacia wood to make the poles and covered them with bronze. ⁷He put the poles through the rings on the sides of the altar. The poles were used for carrying the altar. He used boards to make the sides of the altar. It was hollow, ₍like an empty box₎.

⁸The women that served at the entrance to the Meeting Tent* gave their bronze* mirrors. Bezalel used the bronze from these mirrors to make the bowl and its base.

The Courtyard Around the Holy Tent

⁹Then he made ₍a wall of curtains around₎ the courtyard. On the south side he made a wall of curtains 100 cubits* long. The curtains were made from fine linen.* ¹⁰The curtains on the south side were supported by 20 posts. The posts were on 20

---

base and the shaft Or, "flared base."
75 pounds Literally, "1 kikar."
altar A table or raised area used for offering sacrifices.
incense Special dried tree sap. Burned to make a sweet-smelling smoke, it was offered as a gift to God.
1 cubit 1' 8 5/8" (52.5cm).
2 cubits 3' 5 5/16" (105cm).
5 cubits 8' 7 5/16" (2.625m).
3 cubits 5' 2" (1.575m).
bronze A metal. The Hebrew word can mean "copper," "bronze," or "brass."
Meeting Tent The Holy Tent (tabernacle), where the people of Israel went to meet with God.
100 cubits 172' 3" (52.5m).
linen Thread or cloth made from the fibers of the flax plant.

bronze* bases. The hooks for the posts and the curtain rods* were made from silver. ¹¹The north side of the courtyard also had a wall of curtains 100 cubits* long. There were 20 posts with 20 bronze bases. The hooks for the posts and the curtain rods were made from silver.

¹²On the west side of the courtyard the wall of curtains was 50 cubits* long. There were 10 posts and 10 bases. The hooks for the posts and the curtain rods* were made from silver.

¹³The east side of the courtyard was 50 cubits* wide. ⌊The entrance to the courtyard was on this side.⌋ ¹⁴On one side of the entrance the wall of curtains was 15 cubits* long. There were also three posts and three bases on this side. ¹⁵The wall of curtains on the other side of the entrance was also 15 cubits* long. There were three posts and three bases on that side. ¹⁶All the curtains around the courtyard were made from fine linen.* ¹⁷The bases for the posts were made from bronze*. The hooks and the curtain rods* were made from silver. The tops of the posts were covered with silver also. All the posts in the courtyard had silver curtain rods.

¹⁸The curtain for the entrance of the courtyard was made from fine linen* and blue, purple, and red yarn. Designs were woven into that curtain. The curtain was 20 cubits* long and 5 cubits* high. It was the same height as the curtains around the courtyard. ¹⁹The curtain was supported by four posts and four bronze* bases. The hooks on the posts were made from silver. The tops on the posts were covered with silver, and the curtain rods* were also made from silver. ²⁰All the tent pegs for the Holy Tent* and for the curtains around the courtyard were made from bronze.

²¹Moses commanded the Levite people to write down all the things that were used to make the Holy Tent,* that is, the Tent of the Agreement.* Ithamar son of Aaron, was in charge of keeping the list.

²²Bezalel son of Uri, the son of Hur, from the family group of Judah, made everything the Lord commanded Moses. ²³Also Oholiab son of Ahisamach, from the family group of Dan, helped him. Oholiab was a skilled worker and designer. He was skilled at weaving fine linen* and blue, purple, and red yarn.

²⁴More than 2 tons* of gold was given as an offering to the Lord for his holy place. (This was weighed using the official measure.*)

²⁵The total number of men that were counted gave more than 3 ¾ tons* of silver. (This was weighed using the official measure.*) ²⁶All the men 20 years old or older were counted. There were 603,550 men, and each man had to pay a tax of 1 beqa* of silver. (Using the official measure, a beqa is ½ shekel.*) ²⁷They used 3 ¾ tons* of that silver to make the 100 bases for the ⌊Lord's⌋ holy place and for the curtain. They used 75 pounds* of silver for each base. ²⁸The other 50 pounds* of silver was used to make the hooks, the curtain rods,* and the silver covering at the top of the posts.

²⁹More than 26 ½ tons* of bronze* was given to the Lord. ³⁰That bronze was used to make the bases at the entrance of the Meeting Tent.* They also used the bronze to make the altar* and the bronze grating. And the bronze was used to make all the tools and dishes for the altar. ³¹It was also used to make the bases for the curtains around the courtyard and the bases for the curtains at the entrance. And the bronze was used to make the

---

bronze A metal. The Hebrew word can mean "copper," "bronze," or "brass."
curtain rods Or, "fasteners."
100 cubits 172' 3" (52.5m).
50 cubits 86' 1 1/2" (26.25m).
15 cubits 25' 10" (7.875m).
linen Thread or cloth made from the fibers of the flax plant.
20 cubits 34' 5 3/8" (10.5m)
5 cubits 8' 7 5/16" (2.625m).
Holy Tent Or, "tabernacle," the tent where God came to live among his people.

2 tons Literally, "29 kikars and 730 shekels."
official measure Literally, "holy shekel," the official standard of measure used in the tabernacle or temple.
3 3/4 tons Literally, "100 kikars and 1,775 shekels."
1 beqa Or, "1/5 of an ounce."
shekel Or, "2/5 of an ounce."
75 pounds Literally, "1 kikar."
50 pounds Literally, "1,775 shekels."
26 1/2 tons Literally, "70 kikars and 2,400 shekels."
Meeting Tent The Holy Tent (tabernacle), where the people of Israel went to meet with God.
altar A table or raised area used for offering sacrifices.

EXODUS 39:1-25

tent pegs for the Holy Tent* and for the curtains around the courtyard.

The Priests' Special Clothes

39 The workers used the blue, purple, and red yarn to make special clothes for the priest to wear when they served in the ₍Lord's₎ holy place. They also made the special clothes for Aaron like the Lord had commanded Moses.

The Ephod

²They made the Ephod* from gold thread, fine linen,* and blue, purple, and red yarn. ³(They hammered the gold into thin strips. Then they cut the gold into long threads. And they wove the gold into the blue, purple, and red yarn and fine linen. This was the work of a very skilled person.) ⁴They made the shoulder pieces for the Ephod. They fastened these shoulder pieces to the two corners of the Ephod. ⁵They wove the sash *(belt)* and fastened it to the Ephod. It was made the same way as the Ephod—they used gold thread, fine linen and blue, purple, and red yarn, just like the Lord commanded Moses.

⁶The workers put the onyx stones ₍for the Ephod₎ in gold settings. They wrote the names of the sons of Israel on these stones. ⁷Then they put these jewels on the shoulder pieces of the Ephod.* These jewels were to help God to remember the people of Israel. This was done like the Lord commanded Moses.

The Judgment Pouch

⁸Then they made the Judgment Pouch.* It was the work of a skilled person, just like the Ephod.* It was made from gold threads, fine linen,* and blue, purple, and red yarn. ⁹The Judgment Pouch was folded in half to make a square ₍pocket₎. It was 1 span* long and 1 span* wide. ¹⁰Then the workers put four rows of beautiful jewels on the Judgment Pouch. The first row had a ruby, a topaz, and a beryl. ¹¹The second row had a turquoise, a sapphire, and an emerald. ¹²The third row had a jacinth, an agate, and an amethyst. ¹³The fourth row had a chrysolite, an onyx, and a jasper. All these jewels were set in gold. ¹⁴There were twelve jewels on the Judgment Pouch—one jewel for each of the sons of Israel *(Jacob)*. Each stone had the name of one of the sons of Israel carved onto it, like a seal.*

¹⁵The workers made two chains from pure gold for the Judgment Pouch.* The chains were braided like a rope. ¹⁶The workers made two gold rings and fastened them to two corners of the Judgment Pouch. And they made two gold settings ₍for the shoulder pieces₎. ¹⁷They fastened the gold chains to the rings at the corners of the Judgment Pouch. ¹⁸They fastened the other ends of the gold chains to the settings on the shoulder pieces. They fastened these to the front of the Ephod.* ¹⁹Then they made two more gold rings and put them on the other two corners of the Judgment Pouch. This was on the inside edge of the Judgment Pouch next to the Ephod. ²⁰They also put two gold rings on the bottom of the shoulder pieces on the front of the Ephod. These rings were near the fastener, just above the sash *(belt)*. ²¹Then they used a blue ribbon and tied the rings of the Judgment Pouch to the rings of the Ephod. In this way the Judgment Pouch would rest close to the sash and would be held tight against the Ephod. They did everything just like the Lord commanded.

Other Clothes for the Priests

²²Then they made the robe for the Ephod.* They made it from blue cloth. It was woven by a skilled worker. ²³They made a hole in the center of the robe and sewed a piece of cloth around the edge of this hole. This cloth kept the hole from tearing.

²⁴Then they used fine linen* and blue, purple, and red yarn to make the ₍cloth₎ pomegranates.* They hung these pomegranates around the bottom edge of the robe. ²⁵Then they made bells from

---

Holy Tent Or, "tabernacle," the tent where God came to live among his people.
Ephod A special coat worn by the priests.
linen Thread or cloth made from the fibers of the flax plant.
Judgment Pouch A piece of clothing like a bib or an apron that covered the high priest's chest. See Ex. 28:15-30.
1 span About 9" (23cm). This is the distance from the tip of the thumb to the tip of the little finger.
seal(s) Small stones with designs cut into them. Pressed into wet clay or hot wax, they made a special mark.
pomegranates A red fruit about the size of an orange.

pure gold. They hung these bells around the bottom edge of the robe between the pomegranates. ²⁶Around the bottom edge of the robe there were bells and pomegranates. There was a bell between each pomegranate. This robe was for the priest to wear when he served the Lord, just like the Lord commanded Moses.

²⁷Skilled workers wove robes for Aaron and his sons. These robes were made from fine linen.* ²⁸And the workers made a turban* from fine linen. They also used fine linen to make decorated turbans and underclothes. ²⁹Then they made the sash *(belt)* from fine linen and blue, purple, and red yarn. Designs were sewn into the cloth. These things were made like the Lord had commanded Moses.

³⁰Then they made the strip of gold for the holy crown. They made it from pure gold. They wrote words into the gold. They wrote these words: HOLY TO THE LORD. ³¹They fastened the gold strip to a blue ribbon. Then they tied the blue ribbon around the turban* like the Lord had commanded Moses.

Moses Inspects the Holy Tent

³²So all the work on the Holy Tent,* that is, the Meeting Tent was finished. The people of Israel did everything exactly like the Lord had commanded Moses. ³³Then they showed the Holy Tent to Moses. They showed him the Tent and all the things in it. They showed him the rings, the frames, the braces, the posts, and the bases. ³⁴They showed him the covering of the Tent that was made from ram skins dyed red. And they showed him the covering that was made from fine leather.* And they showed him the curtain that covered ₗthe entrance to the Most Holy Placeⱼ.

³⁵They showed Moses the Box of the Agreement.* They showed him the poles used for carrying the Box and they showed him the cover* for the Box. ³⁶They showed him the table with everything on it and the special bread.* ³⁷They showed him the pure gold lampstand and the lamps on it. And they showed him the oil and all the other things that were used with the lamps. ³⁸They showed Moses the gold altar,* the anointing oil,* the sweet-smelling incense,* and the curtain that covered the entrance to the Tent. ³⁹They showed him the bronze* altar and the bronze screen. They showed him the poles used for carrying the altar. And they showed him all the things that were used on the altar. They showed him the bronze bowl and its base.

⁴⁰They showed Moses the wall of curtains around the courtyard with the posts and bases. They showed him the curtain that covered the entrance to the courtyard. They showed him the ropes and the tent pegs. They showed him all the things in the Holy Tent,* that is, the Meeting Tent.

⁴¹Then they showed Moses the clothes that were made for the priests serving in the holy area. They showed him the special clothes for Aaron the priest and his sons. These were clothes for them to wear when they served as priests.

⁴²The people of Israel did all this work exactly like the Lord had commanded Moses. ⁴³Moses looked closely at all the work. Moses saw that the work was done exactly like the Lord had commanded. So Moses blessed them.

Moses Sets Up the Holy Tent

40 Then the Lord said to Moses, ²"On the first day of the first month, set up the Holy Tent,* that is, the Meeting Tent. ³Put the Box of the Agreement* in the Holy Tent. Cover the Box with the curtain. ⁴Then bring in the table. Put the

---

linen Thread or cloth made from the fibers of the flax plant.
turban Head covering made by wrapping a long piece of cloth around the head or around a cap worn on the head.
Holy Tent Or, "tabernacle," the tent where God came to live among his people.
fine leather A special kind of leather made from the skin of an animal like a seal or sea cow.
Box of the Agreement Or, "ark of the Covenant." The box containing the flat stones with the Ten Commandments written on them and other things that proved God was with the people of Israel during their time in the Sinai desert.

special bread Also called "Bread of the Presence." Every day this this bread was put before God on the special table in the Holy Place.
altar A table or raised area used for offering sacrifices.
anointing oil Fine olive oil that was poured on things or people to show that they were chosen for a special work or purpose.
incense Special dried tree sap. Burned to make a sweet-smelling smoke, it was offered as a gift to God.
bronze A metal. The Hebrew word can mean "copper," "bronze," or "brass."

things on the table that should be there. Then put the lampstand in the Tent. Put the lamps on the lampstand in the right places. ⁵Put the gold altar* for offering incense* in the Tent. Put the altar in front of the Box of the Agreement. Then put the curtain at the entrance to the Holy Tent.

⁶"Put the altar* for burning offerings in front of the entrance of the Holy Tent,* that is, the Meeting Tent. ⁷Put the bronze bowl between the Meeting Tent and the altar. Put water in the bowl. ⁸Set up ⌊the wall of curtains around⌋ the courtyard. Then put the curtain at the entrance to the courtyard.

⁹"Use the anointing oil and anoint* the Holy Tent* and everything in it. When you put the oil on these things, you will make them holy.* ¹⁰Anoint the altar for burning offerings. Anoint everything on the altar. You will make the altar holy. It will be very holy. ¹¹Then anoint the bronze bowl and its base. Do this to make those things holy.

¹²"Bring Aaron and his sons to the entrance of the Meeting Tent.* Wash them with water. ¹³Then put the special clothes on Aaron. Anoint* him with the oil and make him holy.* Then he can serve me as a priest. ¹⁴Then put the clothes on his sons. ¹⁵Anoint the sons in the same way that you anointed their father. Then they can also serve me as priests. When you anoint them, they will become priests. That family will continue to be priests for all time to come." ¹⁶Moses obeyed the Lord. He did everything that the Lord commanded him.

¹⁷So the Holy Tent* was set up on the first day of the first month during the second year ⌊from the time they left Egypt⌋. ¹⁸Moses set up the Holy Tent like the Lord had said. He put the bases down first. Then he put the frames on the bases. Then he put the braces on and set up the posts. ¹⁹After that, Moses put the outer tent over the Holy Tent. Then he put the covering over the outer tent. He did these things like the Lord had commanded.

²⁰Moses took the Agreement* and put it in the Holy Box. Moses put the poles ⌊through the rings⌋ on the Box. Then he put the cover* on the Box. ²¹Then Moses put the Holy Box into the Holy Tent.* He hung the curtain in the right place to protect it. In this way, he protected the Box of the Agreement* ⌊behind the curtain⌋ like the Lord had commanded him. ²²Then Moses put the table in the Meeting Tent. He put it on the north side of the Holy Tent. He put it ⌊in the Holy Place,⌋ in front of the curtain. ²³Then he put the bread on the table before the Lord. He did this like the Lord had commanded him. ²⁴Then Moses put the lampstand in the Meeting Tent. He put the lampstand on the south side of the Tent, across from the table. ²⁵Then Moses put the lamps on the lampstand before the Lord. He did this like the Lord had commanded him.

²⁶Then Moses put the gold altar in the Meeting Tent.* He put the altar in front of the curtain. ²⁷Then he burned sweet-smelling incense on the altar. He did this like the Lord had commanded him. ²⁸Then Moses put the curtain at the entrance to the Holy Tent.*

²⁹Moses put the altar for burning offerings at the entrance to the Holy Tent,* that is, the Meeting Tent. Then Moses offered a burnt offering on that altar. He also offered grain offerings to the Lord. He did these things like the Lord had commanded him.

³⁰Then Moses put the bronze bowl between the Meeting Tent* and the altar. Moses put water in the bowl for washing. ³¹Moses, Aaron, and Aaron's sons used this bowl to wash their hands and feet. ³²They washed themselves every time they entered the Meeting Tent. They also washed

---

altar A table or raised area used for offering sacrifices.
incense Special dried tree sap. Burned to make a sweet-smelling smoke, it was offered as a gift to God.
Holy Tent Or, "tabernacle," the tent where God came to live among his people. It is often called the "Meeting Tent."
anoint To pour olive oil on things or people to show they are chosen by God for a special work or purpose.
holy Set aside or chosen for a special purpose.
Meeting Tent The Holy Tent (tabernacle), where the people of Israel went to meet with God.

Agreement Literally, "Proof." The two flat stones with the Ten Commandments written on them. These were proof of the Agreement between God and the people of Israel.
cover Also called "mercy seat." The Hebrew word can mean "lid," "cover" or "the place where sins are forgiven."
Box of the Agreement Or, "ark of the Covenant." The box containing the flat stones with the Ten Commandments written on them and other things that proved God was with the people of Israel during their time in the Sinai desert.

themselves every time they went near the altar. They did these things like the Lord commanded Moses.

³³Then Moses set up ⌊the curtains around⌋ the courtyard of the Holy Tent.* Moses put the altar in the courtyard. Then he put the curtain at the entrance to the courtyard. So Moses finished all the work that the Lord had given him to do.

The Glory of the Lord

³⁴Then the cloud covered the Meeting Tent* and the Glory of the Lord* filled the Holy Tent.* ³⁵Moses could not go into the Meeting Tent because the cloud had settled on it, and the Glory of the Lord had filled the Holy Tent.

³⁶⌊This was the cloud that showed the people when to move.⌋ When the cloud rose from the Holy Tent, the people of Israel would begin to travel. ³⁷But when the cloud stayed on the Holy Tent, the people did not try to move. They stayed in that place until the cloud rose. ³⁸So the cloud of the Lord was over the Holy Tent during the day. And at night, there was a fire in the cloud. So all the people of Israel could see the cloud while they traveled.

Holy Tent Or, "tabernacle," the tent where God came to live among his people. It is often called the "Meeting Tent."

Meeting Tent The Holy Tent (tabernacle), where the people of Israel went to meet with God.

Glory of the Lord One of the forms God used when he appeared to people. It was like a bright shining light.

Leviticus

Sacrifices and Offerings

1 The Lord God called to Moses and spoke to him from the Meeting Tent.* The Lord said, ²"Tell the people of Israel: When you bring an offering to the Lord, the offering must be one of your tame animals—it can be a cow, a sheep, or a goat.

³"When a person offers one of his cows as a burnt offering, then that animal must be a bull that has nothing wrong with it. The person must take the animal to the entrance of the Meeting Tent.* Then the Lord will accept the offering. ⁴The person must put his hand on the animal's head ⌊while it is being killed⌋. The Lord will accept that burnt offering as payment to make that person pure.*

⁵"The person must kill the young bull in front of the Lord. Then Aaron's sons, the priests, must bring the blood to the altar* near the entrance of the Meeting Tent* and sprinkle the blood on the altar, all around it. ⁶The priest must cut the skin from that animal and then cut the animal into pieces. ⁷Aaron's sons, the priests, must put fire on the altar and then stack wood on the fire. ⁸Aaron's sons, the priests, must lay the pieces (the head and the fat) on the wood that is on the fire on the altar. ⁹The priest must wash the legs and inside parts of the animal with water. Then the priest must burn all the animal's parts on the altar. It is a burnt offering, an offering made by fire. Its smell pleases the Lord.

¹⁰"When a person offers a sheep or a goat as a burnt offering, then that animal must be a male animal that has nothing wrong with it. ¹¹The person must kill the animal on the north side of the altar* in front of the Lord. Then Aaron's sons, the priests, must sprinkle the animal's blood on the altar, all around it. ¹²Then the priest must cut the animal into pieces. The priest must lay the pieces (the head and the fat) on the wood that is on the fire on the altar. ¹³The priest must wash the legs and inside parts of the animal with water. Then the priest must offer all the animal's parts. He must burn the animal on the altar. It is a burnt offering, an offering made by fire. Its smell pleases the Lord.

¹⁴"When a person offers a bird as a burnt offering to the Lord, then that bird must be a dove or a young pigeon. ¹⁵The priest must bring the offering to the altar.* The priest must pull off the bird's head and burn the bird on the altar. The bird's blood must be drained out on the side of the altar. ¹⁶The priest must remove the bird's crop* and feathers and throw them on the east side of the altar. This is the place where they put the ashes from the altar. ¹⁷Then the priest must tear the bird by its wings, but he must not divide the bird ⌊into two parts⌋. The priest must burn the bird on the altar, on the wood that is on the fire. It is a burnt offering, an offering made by fire. Its smell pleases the Lord.

Grain Offerings

2 "When a person gives a grain offering to the Lord God, his offering must be made from fine flour. The person must pour oil on this flour and put frankincense* on it. ²Then he must bring it to Aaron's sons, the priests. He must take a handful of the fine flour with the oil and frankincense in it. Then the priest must burn this memorial offering on the altar.* It is an offering made by fire. Its smell pleases the Lord. ³The grain offering that is

---

Meeting Tent The Holy Tent (tabernacle) where the people of Israel went to meet with God.
make ... pure Or, "make atonement." The Hebrew word means "to cover," "to hide," or "to erase sins."
altar A table or raised area used for offering sacrifices.
crop A small bag inside a bird's throat. When a bird eats, its food goes into this bag first to be made soft.
frankincense Very special dried tree sap. Burned to make a sweet-smelling smoke, it was offered as a gift to God.

left will belong to Aaron and his sons. This offering made by fire to the Lord is very holy.

Baked Grain Offerings

⁴"When a person gives a grain offering that was baked in the oven, then it must be unleavened bread* made from fine flour mixed with oil or wafers* with oil poured over them. ⁵If you bring a grain offering cooked in a baking pan, then it must be made from fine flour mixed with oil but without yeast. ⁶You must break it into pieces and pour oil over it. It is a grain offering. ⁷If you bring a grain offering cooked in a frying pan, then it must be made from fine flour mixed with oil.

⁸"You must bring grain offerings made from these things to the Lord. You must take those things to the priest, and he will put them on the altar.* ⁹Then the priest will take ₍part of the grain offering₎ and burn this memorial offering on the altar. It is an offering made by fire. Its smell pleases the Lord. ¹⁰The grain offering that is left will belong to Aaron and his sons. This offering made by fire to the Lord is very holy.

¹¹"You must not give any grain offering to the Lord that has yeast in it. You must not burn yeast or honey as an offering made by fire to the Lord. ¹²You may bring yeast and honey to the Lord as an offering from the first harvest. But yeast and honey must not be burned to go up as a sweet smell on the altar.* ¹³You must also put salt on every grain offering you bring. You must not let the salt of God's Agreement be missing from your grain offering. You must bring salt with all your offerings.

Grain Offerings from First Harvest

¹⁴"When you bring a grain offering from the first harvest to the Lord, you must bring roasted heads of grain. They must be crushed heads of fresh grain. This will be your grain offering from the first harvest. ¹⁵You must put oil and frankincense* on it. It is a grain offering. ¹⁶The priest must burn part of the crushed grain, the oil, and all the frankincense on it as the memorial offering. It is an offering by fire to the Lord.

---

unleavened bread Bread made without yeast.
wafers A thin bread, like crackers, made without yeast.
altar A table or raised area used for offering sacrifices.
frankincense A very special tree sap. Burned to make a sweet-smelling smoke, it was offered as a gift to God.

Fellowship Offerings

3"When a person gives a sacrifice as a fellowship offering, the animal can be a cow and the animal can be a male or a female. But the animal must have nothing wrong with it. ²The person must put his hand on the animal's head and kill the animal at the entrance of the Meeting Tent.* Then Aaron's sons, the priests, must sprinkle the blood on the altar,* all around it. ³The fellowship offering is an offering made by fire to the Lord. The priest must offer the fat that is in and around the animal's inside parts. ⁴The person must offer the two kidneys and the fat covering them near the lower back muscle. He must also offer the fat part of the liver. He must remove it with the kidneys. ⁵Then Aaron's sons will burn the fat on the altar. They will put it on the burnt offering that is on the wood on the fire. It is an offering by fire. Its smell pleases the Lord.

⁶"When a person gives a sheep or a goat as a fellowship offering to the Lord, the animal can be a male or a female animal. But it must have nothing wrong with it. ⁷If he brings a lamb as his offering, then he must bring it before the Lord. ⁸He must put his hand on the animal's head and kill the animal in front of the Meeting Tent.* Then Aaron's sons must sprinkle the animal's blood on the altar,* all around it. ⁹The person must give part of the fellowship offering as an offering made by fire to the Lord. The person must offer the fat, the whole fat tail, and the fat that is on and around the animal's inside parts. (He must cut off the tail close to the backbone.) ¹⁰The person must offer the two kidneys and the fat covering them near the lower back muscles. He must also offer the fat part of the liver. He must remove it with the kidneys. ¹¹Then the priest must burn them on the altar. The fellowship offering is an offering made by fire to the Lord. But it will also be food ₍for the people₎.

A Goat as a Fellowship Offering

¹²"If the offering is a goat, then the person must bring it before the Lord. ¹³The person must put his hand on the goat's head and kill it in front of the Meeting Tent.* Then Aaron's son must sprinkle the goat's blood on the altar,* all around it. ¹⁴The person must give part of the fellowship offering as an offering made by fire to the Lord. The person must offer the fat that is on and around the

---

Meeting Tent The Holy Tent (tabernacle) where the people of Israel went to meet with God.

animal's inside parts. ¹⁵The person must offer the two kidneys and the fat covering them near the lower back muscle. He must also offer the fat part of the liver. He must remove it with the kidneys. ¹⁶Then the priest must burn them on the altar. The fellowship offering is an offering made by fire. Its smell pleases the Lord. It is also food ₍for the people₎—but the best parts* belong to the Lord. ¹⁷This rule will continue forever through all your generations. Wherever you live, you must never eat fat or blood."

Offerings for Accidental Sins

4 The Lord spoke to Moses. The Lord said, ²"Tell the people of Israel: If any person sins by accident and does any of the things the Lord said must not be done, then that person must do these things:

³If the anointed priest* makes a mistake in a way that leaves the people guilty for their sin, then the priest must make an offering to the Lord for his sin. The priest must offer a young bull that has nothing wrong with it. He must offer the young bull to the Lord as a sin offering. ⁴The anointed priest must bring the bull to the entrance of the Meeting Tent* in front of the Lord. He must put his hand on the bull's head and kill the bull in front of the Lord. ⁵Then the anointed priest* must get some of the blood from the bull and take it into the Meeting Tent. ⁶The priest must put his finger in the blood and sprinkle the blood seven times before the Lord in front of the curtain of the ₍Most₎ Holy Place.* ⁷The priest must put some of the blood on the corners of the incense* altar.* (This altar is in the Meeting Tent, in front of the Lord.) The priest must pour out all of the bull's blood at the base of the altar of burnt offering. (This altar is at the entrance of the Meeting Tent.) ⁸And he must take all the fat from the bull of the sin offering. He must take the fat that is on and around the inside parts. ⁹He must take the two kidneys and the fat covering them near the lower back muscle. He must also take the fat part of the the liver. He must remove it with the kidneys. ¹⁰The priest must offer these parts just like they are offered from the bull of the fellowship offering.* The priest must burn the animal parts on the altar of burnt offering. ¹¹⁻¹²But the priest must carry out the bull's skin, inside parts and body waste, and all the meat on its head and legs. The priest must carry those parts outside the camp to the special place where the ashes are poured out. The priest must put those parts there on the wood and burn them. The bull must be burned where the ashes are poured out.

¹³"It may happen that the whole nation of Israel sins without knowing it. They might have done any of the things that the Lord has commanded them not to do. If this happens, they will become guilty. ¹⁴If they learn about that sin, then they must offer a young bull as a sin offering for the whole nation. They must bring the bull to the Meeting Tent.* ¹⁵The elders *(leaders)* of the people must put their hands on the bull's head in front of the Lord, and then a person must kill the bull in front of the Lord. ¹⁶Then the anointed priest* must get some of the bull's blood and take it into the Meeting Tent. ¹⁷The priest must put his finger in the blood and sprinkle it seven times in front of the curtain before the Lord. ¹⁸Then the priest must put some of the blood on the corners of the altar.* (This altar is in the Meeting Tent, in front of the Lord.) The priest must pour out all the blood at the base of the altar of burnt offering. (This altar is at the entrance of the Meeting Tent.) ¹⁹Then the priest must take all the fat from the animal and burn it on the altar. ²⁰The priest must offer these parts just like he offered the bull of the sin offering.* In this way, the priest will make the people pure.* And God will forgive the people of Israel. ²¹The priest must carry this bull outside the camp and burn it, just like he burned the other bull. This is the sin offering for the whole community.

²²"A ruler might sin by accident and do one of the things the Lord his God said must not be done.

---

best parts Literally, "fat."
anointed priest The priest chosen to serve at a particular time. The priests took turns. Special oil was poured on the one chosen to show that God chose him to serve.
Meeting Tent The Holy Tent (tabernacle) where the people of Israel went to meet with God.
Most Holy Place Most important room in the Holy Tent. The Holy Box with the Cherub Angels on it was in this room. It was like God's throne.
incense Special dried tree sap. Burned to make a sweet-smelling smoke, it was offered as a gift to God.
altar A table or raised area used for offering sacrifices.

just like ... fellowship offering See Lev. 3:1-5.
like ... sin offering See Lev. 4:3-12.
make ... pure Or, "make atonement." The Hebrew word means "to cover," "to hide," or "to erase sins."

The ruler will be guilty ⌊of doing wrong⌋. ²³If the ruler learns about his sin, then he must bring a male goat that has nothing wrong with it. That will be his offering. ²⁴The ruler must put his hand on the goat's head and kill the goat at the place where they kill the burnt offering before the Lord. The goat is a sin offering. ²⁵The priest must take some of the blood of the sin offering on his finger and put it on the corners of the altar* of burnt offering. The priest must pour the rest of the blood at the base of the altar. ²⁶And the priest must burn it like he burns the fat of the sacrifice of fellowship offerings. In this way, the priest will make the ruler pure.* And God will forgive the ruler.

²⁷"One of the common people might sin by accident and do one of the things that the Lord said must not be done. ²⁸If that person learns about his sin, then he must bring a female goat that has nothing wrong with it. That will be the person's sin offering. He must bring this goat for the sin that he has done. ²⁹He must put his hand on the animal's head and kill it at the place for the burnt offering. ³⁰Then the priest must take some of the goat's blood on his finger and put it on the corners of the altar* of burnt offering. Then the priest must pour out the rest of the goat's blood at the base of the altar. ³¹The priest must offer all the goat's fat, just like the fat is offered from the fellowship offerings. The priest must burn it on the altar as a sweet smell to the Lord. In this way, the priest will make that person pure.* And God will forgive that person.

³²"If that person brings a lamb as his sin offering, then he must bring a female lamb that has nothing wrong with it. ³³The person must put his hand on the animal's head and kill it as a sin offering in the place where they kill the burnt offering. ³⁴The priest must take some of the blood from the sin offering on his finger and put it on the corners of the altar* of burnt offering. Then the priest must pour out all the lamb's blood at the base of the altar. ³⁵The priest must offer all the lamb's fat, just like the fat of the lamb is offered from the fellowship offerings. The priest must burn it on the altar, just like any offering made by fire to the Lord. In this way, the priest will make that person pure* from the sin he did. And God will forgive that person.

Different Accidental Sins

5 "A person might hear a warning. Or a person might see or hear something that he should tell to other people. If that person does not tell what he saw or heard, then that person is guilty of doing wrong. ²Or a person might touch something unclean.* It might be the dead body of a tame animal, or it might be the dead body of an unclean animal. That person might not know that he touched those things, but he will still be guilty of doing wrong. ³There are many things that come from a person that make a person unclean. A person might touch any of these things from another person, but not know about it. When that person learns that he has touched something unclean, he will be guilty. ⁴Or a person might make a quick promise to do something—it makes no difference if it is bad or good. People make many kinds of quick promises. A person might make such a promise and forget it.* When he remembers* his promise, then he will be guilty, because he didn't keep his promise. ⁵So, if a person is guilty of any of these things, then he must confess (admit) the thing he did wrong. ⁶He must bring his guilt offering to the Lord for the sin he did. He must bring a female lamb or a female goat as a sin offering. Then the priest will ⌊do the things that will⌋ make that person pure* from the sin that person did.

⁷"If the person can't afford a lamb, he must bring two doves or two young pigeons to the Lord. These will be the guilt offering for his sin. One bird must be for a sin offering, and the other must be for a burnt offering. ⁸The person must bring them to the priest. First, the priest will offer one bird for the sin offering. The priest will pull off the bird's head from its neck. But the priest will not divide the bird ⌊into two parts⌋. ⁹The priest must sprinkle the blood from the sin offering on the side of the altar.* Then the priest must pour out the rest of the blood at the base of the altar. It is a sin offering. ¹⁰Then the priest must offer the second bird according to the rules for a burnt offering. In this way, the priest will make that

---

altar A table or raised area used for offering sacrifices.
make ... pure Or, "make atonement." The Hebrew word means "to cover," "to hide," or "to erase sins."
unclean Not pure or not acceptable to God for worship.
forget it Literally, "it is hid from him."
remembers Literally, "knows of."

person pure* from the sin that person did. And God will forgive that person.

¹¹"If the person can't afford two doves or two pigeons, then he must bring 8 cups* of fine flour. This will be his sin offering. The person must not put oil on the flour. He must not put frankincense* on it, because it is a sin offering. ¹²The person must bring the flour to the priest. The priest will take a handful of the flour. It will be a memorial offering. The priest will burn the flour on the altar.* It will be an offering made by fire to the Lord. It is a sin offering. ¹³In this way, the priest will make that person pure.* And God will forgive that person. The part that is left will belong to the priest, just like the grain offering."

¹⁴The Lord said to Moses, ¹⁵"A person might accidentally do something wrong with the holy things of the Lord.* Then that person must bring a ram that has nothing wrong with it. This will be his guilt offering to the Lord. You must use the official measure* and set the price of the ram. ¹⁶That person must pay for the sin he did with the holy things. He must give the things he promised, add one-fifth to the value, and give this money to the priest. In this way, the priest will make that person pure* with the ram of the guilt offering. And God will forgive that person.

¹⁷"If a person sins and does any of the things that the Lord has commanded not to be done, it does not matter if that person did not know. That person is guilty. That person must accept the responsibility for his sin. ¹⁸That person must bring a ram that has nothing wrong with it to the priest. The ram will be a guilt offering. In this way, the priest will make that person pure* from the sin that person did without knowing. And God will forgive that person. ¹⁹The person is guilty, ₍even if he did not know he was sinning₎. So he must give the guilt offering to the Lord."

Guilt Offerings for Other Sins

6 The Lord said to Moses, ²"A person might do wrong against the Lord by doing one of these sins: A person might lie about ₍what happened₎ to something he was taking care of for someone else. Or a person might lie about a deposit* he received. Or a person might steal something. Or a person might cheat someone. ³Or a person might find something that was lost and then lie about it. Or a person might promise to do something and then not do what he promised. Or a person might do some other bad thing. ⁴If a person does any of those things, then that person is guilty of sin. That person must bring back whatever he stole, or whatever he took by cheating, or whatever he took that ₍the other person asked him to hold for him₎, or whatever he found and lied about, or ⁵whatever he made a false promise about. He must pay the full price. And then he must pay an extra fifth of ₍the value of₎ the thing. He must give the money to the true owner. He must do this on the day he ₍brings₎ his guilt offering.

⁶"That person must bring a guilt offering to the priest. It must be a ram from the flock. The ram must not have anything wrong with it. It must be worth the amount that the priest says. It will be a guilt offering to the Lord. ⁷Then the priest will go to the Lord and ₍do the things that will₎ make that person pure *. And God will forgive that person for all the things that made him guilty."

Burnt Offerings

⁸The Lord said to Moses, ⁹"Give this command to Aaron and his sons: This is the law of the burnt offering. The burnt offering must ₍stay₎ on the hearth* of the altar* all night until morning. The altar's fire must be kept burning on the altar. ¹⁰The priest must put on his linen robe. He must put on his linen underwear next to his body. Then the priest must pick up the ashes left by the fire when it burned the burnt offering on the altar. The priest must put these ashes beside the altar. ¹¹Then the priest must take off his clothes and put on other clothes. Then he must carry the ashes outside the camp to a special place. ¹²But the altar's fire must be kept burning on the altar. It must not ₍be allowed to₎ stop burning. The priest must burn wood on the altar every morning. He must put the

---

make ... pure Or, "make atonement." The Hebrew word means "to cover," "to hide," or "to erase sins."

8 cups Literally, "1/10 of an ephah."

frankincense Very special dried tree sap. Burned to make a sweet-smelling smoke, it was offered as a gift to God.

altar A table or raised area used for offering sacrifices.

holy things ... Lord These are probably special gifts that a person promised but forgot to give to the Lord.

official measure Literally, "holy shekel," the official standard of measure used in the tabernacle or temple.

deposit Literally, "pledge" or "security." This is something like a down payment given as proof that something more important will be done.

hearth The place where a sacrifice is burned.

wood on the altar. He must burn the fat of the fellowship offerings. ¹³Fire must be kept burning on the altar without stopping. It must not go out.

Grain Offerings

¹⁴"This is the law of the grain offering: The sons of Aaron must bring it to the Lord in front of the altar.* ¹⁵The priest must take a handful of the fine flour from the grain offering. The oil and the frankincense* must be on the grain offering. The priest must burn the grain offering on the altar. It will be a memorial ₍offering₎ to the Lord. Its smell will please the Lord.

¹⁶"Aaron and his sons must eat the grain offering that is left. The grain offering is a kind of bread made without yeast. The priests must eat this bread in a holy place. They must eat it in the courtyard around the Meeting Tent.* ¹⁷The grain offering must not be cooked with yeast. I have given it as the priests' share of the offerings made to me by fire. It is most holy, like the sin offering and the guilt offering. ¹⁸Every male among the children of Aaron may eat from the offerings made to the Lord by fire. This is a rule forever through your generations. Touching these offerings makes those men holy."

The Priests' Grain Offering

¹⁹The Lord said to Moses, ²⁰"This is the offering that Aaron and his sons must bring to the Lord. They must do this on the day they anoint* Aaron ₍to be high priest₎. They must bring 8 cups* of fine flour for a grain offering. (This will be offered at the times of the daily offering.) They must bring half of it in the morning and half of it in the evening. ²¹The fine flour must be mixed with oil and made on a baking pan. When it is cooked, then you must bring it in. You must break the offering into pieces. Its smell will please the Lord.

²²"The priest from among Aaron's descendants* that is chosen to take Aaron's place must make this grain offering to the Lord. This rule will continue forever. The grain offering must be completely burned for the Lord. ²³Every grain offering of the priest must be completely burned. It must not be eaten."

The Law of the Sin Offering

²⁴The Lord said to Moses, ²⁵"Tell Aaron and his sons: This is the law of the sin offering. The sin offering must be killed in the place where the burnt offering is killed before the Lord. It is most holy. ²⁶The priest that offers the sin offering must eat it. But he must eat it in a holy place, in the courtyard around the Meeting Tent.* ²⁷Touching the meat ₍of the sin offering₎ makes a person or a thing holy.

"If any of the sprinkled blood falls on a person's clothes, then you must wash the clothes in a holy place. ²⁸If the sin offering was boiled in a clay pot, then the pot must be broken. If the sin offering was boiled in a bronze* pot, then the pot must be washed and rinsed in water.

²⁹"Any man in a priest's family may eat the sin offering. It is very holy. ³⁰But if the blood of the sin offering was taken into the Meeting Tent* and used in the Holy Place to make ₍people₎ pure,* then that sin offering must not be eaten. It must be burned in the fire.

Guilt Offerings

7 "These are the rules for the guilt offering. It is very holy. ²A priest must kill the guilt offering in the same place where they kill the burnt offerings. Then the priest must sprinkle the blood from the guilt offering around the altar.*

³"The priest must offer all the fat from the guilt offering. He must offer the fat tail and the fat that covers the inside parts. ⁴The priest must offer the two kidneys and the fat covering them at the lower back muscle. He must also offer the fat part of the liver. He must remove it with the kidneys. ⁵The priest must burn all those things on the altar.* This will be an offering made by fire to the Lord. It is a guilt offering.

⁶"Any male in a priest's family may eat the guilt offering. It is very holy, so it must be eaten

---

altar A table or raised area used for offering sacrifices.
frankincense Very special dried tree sap. Burned to make a sweet-smelling smoke, it was offered as a gift to God.
Meeting Tent The Holy Tent (tabernacle) where the people of Israel went to meet with God.
anoint To pour olive oil on things or people to show they were chosen for a special work or purpose.
8 cups Literally, "1/10 of an ephah."

bronze A metal. The Hebrew word can mean "copper," "bronze," or "brass."
make ... pure Or, "make atonement." The Hebrew word means "to cover," "to hide," or "to erase sins."

in a holy place. ⁷The guilt offering is like the sin offering. The same rules are for both offerings. The priest that does the sacrificing will get the meat for food. ⁸The priest that does the sacrificing can also have the skin* from the burnt offering. ⁹Every grain offering belongs to the priest that offers it. That priest will get the grain offerings that were baked in an oven, or cooked on a frying pan or a baking dish. ¹⁰The grain offerings will belong to Aaron's sons. It does not make any difference if they are dry or mixed with oil. The sons of Aaron *(priests)* will all share this food.

Fellowship Offerings

¹¹"This is the law of the sacrifice* of fellowship offerings that a person offers to the Lord: ¹²The person may bring the fellowship offering to show his thanks. If he brings his sacrifice to give thanks, he should ₍also₎ bring unleavened bread* mixed with oil, wafers* with oil poured over them, and loaves of fine flour mixed with oil. ¹³The fellowship offerings is the offering that a person brings to show thanks to God. With that offering the person must bring another offering with loaves of bread made with yeast. ¹⁴One of these loaves of bread will belong to the priest that sprinkles the blood of the fellowship offerings. ¹⁵The meat of the fellowship offering must be eaten on the same day it is offered. A person offers this gift as a way of showing thanks to God. But none of the meat should remain the next morning.

¹⁶"A person might bring a fellowship offering just because he wants to give a gift to God. Or maybe a person made a special promise to God. If this is true, then the sacrifice* must be eaten the same day he offers it. If there is any left, then it must be eaten that next day. ¹⁷But if any meat from this sacrifice is still left over on the third day, it must be burned in the fire. ¹⁸If a person eats any of the meat from his fellowship offering on the third day, then the Lord will not be happy with that person. The Lord will not count the sacrifice for him. The sacrifice will become unclean.* And if a person eats any of that meat, then that person will be responsible for his own sin.

¹⁹"Also, people must not eat the meat that touches anything that is unclean.* They must burn this meat in the fire. Every person who is clean* may eat the meat ₍from the fellowship offering₎. ²⁰But if a person is unclean and eats the meat from the fellowship offerings that belongs to the Lord, then that person must be separated from his people. ²¹"A person might touch something that is unclean.* That thing may have been made unclean by people, by an unclean animal, or by any unclean hated thing. ₍That person will become unclean, and₎ if he eats any of the meat from the fellowship offerings that belong to the Lord, then that person must be separated from his people."

²²The Lord said to Moses, ²³"Tell the people of Israel: You must not eat any fat from cows, sheep, or goats. ²⁴You may use the fat from any animal that has died by itself, or was torn by ₍other₎ animals. But you must never eat it. ²⁵If any person eats the fat from an animal that was offered by fire to the Lord, then that person must be separated from his people.

²⁶"No matter where you live, you must never eat blood from any bird or any animal. ²⁷If a person eats any blood, then that person must be separated from his people."

Rules for the Wave Offering

²⁸The Lord said to Moses, ²⁹"Tell the people of Israel: If a person brings a fellowship offering to the Lord, then that person must give a part of that gift to the Lord. ³⁰That part of the gift will be burnt in the fire. He must carry that part of the gift in his own hands. He must bring the fat and the breast ₍of the animal to the priest₎. The breast will be lifted up in front of the Lord. This will be the wave offering. ³¹Then the priest must burn the fat on the altar.* But the breast ₍of the animal₎ will belong to Aaron and his sons. ³²You must also give the right thigh from the fellowship offering to the priest. ³³The right thigh from the fellowship offerings will belong to the priest* that offers the blood and fat of the fellowship offering. ³⁴I *(the Lord)* am taking the breast of the wave offerings

---

skin This was used for making leather.
sacrifice A gift to God. Usually, it was a special animal that was killed and burned on an altar.
unleavened bread Bread made without yeast.
wafers A thin bread, like crackers, made without yeast.
sacrifice ... unclean Or, "offensive, bad, rotten." This means the meat is not good to eat as part of a sacrifice.

unclean Not pure or not acceptable to God for worship.
clean Pure or acceptable to God for worship.
altar A table or raised area used for offering sacrifices.
the priest Literally, "him of the sons of Aaron."

and the right thigh of the fellowship offerings from the people of Israel. And I am giving those things to Aaron and his sons. The people of Israel must obey this rule forever."

³⁵Those are the parts from the offerings made by fire to the Lord that were given to Aaron and his sons. Whenever Aaron and his sons serve as the Lord's priests, they get that share of the sacrifices. ³⁶At the time the Lord chose the priests, he commanded the people of Israel to give those parts to the priests. The people must give that share to the priests forever.

³⁷Those are the laws about burnt offerings, grain offerings, sin offerings, guilt offerings, fellowship offerings, and about the choosing of priests. ³⁸The Lord gave those laws to Moses on Mount Sinai. The Lord gave those laws on the day that he commanded the people of Israel to bring their offerings to the Lord in the Sinai desert.

Moses Makes the Priests Ready

8 The Lord said to Moses, ²"Take Aaron and his sons with him and the clothes, the anointing oil,* the bull of the sin offering, the two rams, and the basket of unleavened bread.* ³Then bring the people together at the entrance of the Meeting Tent.*"

⁴Moses did what the Lord commanded him. The people met together at the entrance of the Meeting Tent. ⁵Then Moses said to the people, "This is the thing that the Lord has commanded must be done."

⁶Then Moses brought Aaron and his sons. He washed them with water. ⁷Then Moses put the woven shirt on Aaron and tied the sash (belt) around him. Then Moses put the robe on Aaron. Moses next put the Ephod* on Aaron. Then Moses tied the beautiful sash (belt) on Aaron. In that way, Moses put the Ephod on Aaron. ⁸Moses put the Judgment Pouch* on Aaron. Then he put the Urim and Thummim* in ⌊the pocket of⌋ the Judgment Pouch. ⁹Moses also put the turban* on Aaron's head. Moses put the strip of gold on the front of the turban. This strip of gold is the holy crown. ⌊Moses did⌋ this just like the Lord had commanded.

¹⁰Then Moses took the anointing oil* and sprinkled it on the Holy Tent* and on all the things in it. In this way, Moses made them holy.* ¹¹Moses sprinkled some of the anointing oil on the altar* seven times. Moses sprinkled the oil on the altar and on all its tools and dishes. Moses also sprinkled the oil on the bowl and its base. In this way, Moses made them holy. ¹²Then Moses poured some of the anointing oil on Aaron's head. In this way, he made Aaron holy. ¹³Then Moses brought Aaron's sons and put the woven shirts on them. He tied sashes (belts) on them. Then he wrapped headbands on their heads. ⌊Moses did these things⌋ just like the Lord had commanded.

¹⁴Then Moses brought the bull of the sin offering. Aaron and his sons put their hands on the head of the bull of the sin offering. ¹⁵Then Moses killed the bull and collected its blood. Moses used his finger and put some of the blood on all the corners of the altar.* In this way, Moses made the altar ready for sacrifices. Then Moses poured out the blood at the base of the altar. In this way, Moses made the altar ready for sacrifices to make the people pure.* ¹⁶Moses took all the fat from the inside parts ⌊of the bull⌋. Moses took the fat part of the liver with the two kidneys and the fat on them. Then he burned them on the altar. ¹⁷But Moses ⌊took⌋ the bull's skin, its meat, and its body waste outside the camp. Moses burned those things in a fire outside the camp. Moses did those things like the Lord commanded him.

¹⁸Then Moses brought the ram of the burnt offering. Aaron and his sons put their hands on the ram's head. ¹⁹Then Moses killed the ram. He sprinkled the blood around on the altar.* ²⁰⁻²¹Moses cut the ram into pieces. Moses washed the inside parts and legs with water. Then Moses

---

anointing oil Olive oil that was poured on things or people to show that they were chosen for a special work or purpose.
unleavened bread Bread made without yeast.
Meeting Tent The Holy Tent (tabernacle) where the people of Israel came to meet with God.
Ephod A special coat worn by the high priest.
Judgment Pouch A piece of clothing like a bib or an apron that covered the high priest's chest.
turban Head covering made by wrapping a long piece of cloth around the head or around a cap worn on the head.
Holy Tent Or, "tabernacle." The place God came to live among his people.
holy Set aside or chosen for a special purpose.
altar A table or raised area used for offering sacrifices.
make ... pure Or, "make atonement." The Hebrew word means "to cover," "to hide," or "to erase sins."

burned the whole ram on the altar. Moses burned the head, the pieces, and the fat. It was a burnt offering made by fire. Its smell pleased the Lord. Moses did those things like the Lord commanded.

²²Then Moses brought the other ram. This ram was used for appointing Aaron and his sons to become priests. Aaron and his sons put their hands on the ram's head. ²³Then Moses killed the ram. He put some of its blood on the tip of Aaron's ear, on the thumb of his right hand, and on the big toe of Aaron's right foot. ²⁴Then Moses brought Aaron's sons close ₍to the altar₎. Moses put some of the blood on the tip of their right ears, on the thumb of their right hands, and on the big toe of their right feet. Then Moses sprinkled the blood around on the altar.* ²⁵Moses took the fat, the fat tail, all the fat on the inside parts, the fat covering of the liver, the two kidneys and their fat, and the right thigh. ²⁶A basket of unleavened bread* is put before the Lord each day. Moses took one of those loaves of bread, and one loaf of bread mixed with oil, and one unleavened wafer.* Moses put those pieces of bread on the fat and on the right thigh of the ram. ²⁷Then Moses put all ₍those things₎ in the hands of Aaron and his sons. Moses waved the pieces as a wave offering before the Lord. ²⁸Then Moses took these things from the hands of Aaron and his sons. Moses burned them on the altar on top of the burnt offering. So that was the offering for appointing Aaron and his sons as priests. It was an offering made by fire. Its smell pleased the Lord. ²⁹Moses took the breast, and waved it for a wave offering in front of the Lord. It was Moses' share of the ram for appointing the priests. This was like the Lord had commanded Moses.

³⁰Moses took some of the anointing oil* and some of the blood that was on the altar.* Moses sprinkled some on Aaron and on Aaron's clothes. Moses sprinkled some on Aaron's sons that were with Aaron and on their clothes. In this way, Moses made Aaron, his clothes, his sons, and his sons' clothes holy.*

³¹Then Moses said to Aaron and his sons, "₍Do you remember my command?₎ I said, 'Aaron and his sons must eat these things.' So take the basket of bread and meat from the ceremony for choosing the priests. Boil that meat at the entrance of the Meeting Tent.* Eat the meat and bread at that place. Do this like I told you. ³²If any of the meat or bread is left, then burn it. ³³The ceremony for choosing the priests will last for seven days. You must not leave the entrance of the Meeting Tent until that time is finished. ³⁴The Lord has commanded to do the things that were done today. He commanded these things to make you pure.* ³⁵You must stay at the entrance of the Meeting Tent day and night for seven days. If you don't obey the Lord's commands, then you will die! The Lord gave me those commands."

³⁶So Aaron and his sons did all the things that the Lord had commanded Moses.

God Accepts the Priests

9 On the eighth day, Moses called Aaron and his sons. He also called the elders (*leaders*) of Israel. ²Moses said to Aaron, "Take a bull and a ram. There must be nothing wrong with those animals. The bull will be a sin offering, and the ram will be a burnt offering. Offer those animals to the Lord. ³Tell the people of Israel, 'Take a male goat for a sin offering. And take a calf and a lamb for a burnt offering. The calf and the lamb must each be one year old. There must be nothing wrong with those animals. ⁴Take a bull and a ram for fellowship offerings. Take those animals and a grain offering mixed with oil, and offer those things to the Lord. Why? Because today the Lord will appear to you.'"

⁵So all the people came to the Meeting Tent.* They all brought the things that Moses had commanded. All the people stood before the Lord. ⁶Moses said, "You must do those things the Lord commanded. Then the Glory of the Lord.* will appear to you."

⁷Then Moses told Aaron these things: "Go do the things the Lord commanded. Go to the altar* and offer sin offerings and burnt offerings. Do

---

altar A table or raised area used for offering sacrifices.
unleavened bread Bread made without yeast.
wafer A thin bread, like crackers, made without yeast.
anointing oil Olive oil that was poured on things or people to show that they were chosen for a special work or purpose.
holy Set aside or chosen for a special purpose.

Meeting Tent The Holy Tent (tabernacle) where the people of Israel came to meet with God.
make ... pure Or, "make atonement." The Hebrew word means "to cover," "to hide," or "to erase sins."
Glory of the Lord One of the forms God used when he appeared to people. It was like a bright, shining light.

those things that will make you and the people pure.* Take the people's sacrifices and do the things that will make them pure."

⁸So Aaron went to the altar.* He killed the bull for the sin offering. This sin offering was for himself. ⁹Then the sons of Aaron brought the blood to Aaron. Aaron put his finger in the blood and put it on the corners of the altar. Then Aaron poured out the blood at the base of the altar. ¹⁰Aaron took the fat, the kidneys, and the fat part of the liver from the sin offering. He burned those things on the altar just like the Lord had commanded Moses. ¹¹Then Aaron burned the meat and skin on a fire outside the camp.

¹²Next, Aaron killed the ₍animal for the₎ burnt offering. ₍The animal was cut into pieces.₎ Aaron's sons brought the blood to Aaron. And Aaron sprinkled the blood around on the altar.* ¹³Aaron's sons gave the pieces and head of the burnt offering to Aaron. Then Aaron burned ₍them₎ on the altar. ¹⁴Aaron also washed the inside parts and the legs of the burnt offering. And he burned them on the altar.

¹⁵Then Aaron brought the people's offering. He killed the goat of the sin offering that was for the people. He offered the goat for sin, like the first. ¹⁶Aaron brought the burnt offering and offered it, like the Lord had commanded. ¹⁷Aaron brought the grain offering to the altar.* He took a handful of the grain and put it on the altar beside that morning's daily sacrifice.

¹⁸Aaron also killed the bull and the ram, the sacrifice of fellowship offerings for the people. Aaron's sons brought the blood to Aaron. Aaron sprinkled this blood around on the altar.* ¹⁹Aaron's sons also brought to Aaron the fat of the bull and the ram. They brought the fat tail, the ₍fat₎ covering the inside parts, the kidneys and the fat part of the liver. ²⁰Aaron's sons put these fat parts on the breasts ₍of the bull and the ram₎. Aaron burned the fat parts on the altar. ²¹Aaron waved the breasts and the right thigh for a wave offering before the Lord, like Moses had commanded.

²²Then Aaron lifted up his hands toward the people and blessed them. After Aaron finished offering the sin offering, the burnt offering, and the fellowship offerings, he came down ₍from the altar₎.

²³Moses and Aaron went into the Meeting Tent.* They came out and blessed the people. Then the Glory of the Lord* appeared to all the people. ²⁴Fire came out from the Lord and burned the burnt offering and fat on the altar.* When all the people saw this, they shouted and bowed their faces low to the ground.

God Destroys Nadab and Abihu

10 Then Aaron's sons Nadab and Abihu ₍sinned₎. Each son took a dish for burning incense.* They used a different fire and lit the incense. They did not use the fire that Moses had commanded them to use. ²So fire came from the Lord and destroyed Nadab and Abihu. They died in front of the Lord.

³Then Moses said to Aaron, "The Lord says, 'The priests that come near me must respect me! I must be holy to them and to all the people.'" So Aaron did not say anything ₍about his sons dying₎.

⁴Aaron's uncle Uzziel had two sons. They were Mishael and Elzaphan. Moses said to those sons, "Go to the front part of the Holy Place. Take your cousins' bodies and carry them outside the camp." ⁵So Mishael and Elzaphan obeyed Moses. They carried the bodies of Nadab and Abihu outside the camp. Nadab and Abihu were still wearing their special woven shirts.

⁶Then Moses spoke to Aaron and his other sons Eleazar and Ithamar. Moses told them, "₍Don't show any sadness!₎ Don't tear your clothes or mess up your hair!* Don't show your sadness and you will not be killed. And the Lord will not be angry against all the people. All the people of Israel are your relatives—they can cry about the Lord burning Nadab and Abihu. ⁷But you must not even leave the entrance of the Meeting Tent. If you leave, then you will die! Why? Because the Lord's anointing oil* is on you." So Aaron, Eleazar, and Ithamar obeyed Moses.

---

make ... pure Or, "make atonement." The Hebrew word means "to cover," "to hide," or "to erase sins."
altar A table or raised area used for offering sacrifices.
Meeting Tent The Holy Tent (tabernacle) where the people of Israel came to meet with God.
Glory of the Lord One of the forms God used when he appeared to people. It was like a bright, shining light.
incense Special dried tree sap. Burned to make a sweet-smelling smoke, it was offered as a gift to God.
tear ... hair Torn clothes and messed up hair showed a person was mourning (sad) for a dead person.
anointing oil Olive oil that was poured on things or people to show that they had been chosen for a special work or purpose.

LEVITICUS 10:8–11:17

⁸Then the Lord said to Aaron, ⁹"You and your sons must not drink wine or beer when you come into the Meeting Tent. ⌊If you drink those things,⌋ then you will die! This law continues forever through your generations. ¹⁰You must make a clear distinction *(difference)* between things that are holy and things that are not holy. You must make a clear distinction between things that are clean* and things that are unclean.* ¹¹The Lord gave his laws to Moses, and Moses gave those laws to the people. Aaron, you must teach the people about all of those laws."

¹²Aaron had two sons that were still alive, Eleazar and Ithamar. Moses talked to Aaron and his two sons. Moses said, "Some of the grain offering is left from the sacrifices that were burned on the fire. You will eat that part of the grain offering. But you must eat it without adding yeast. Eat it near the altar.* Why? Because that offering is very holy.* ¹³That is part of the offerings that were burned on the fire for the Lord. And the law I gave you teaches that a part belongs to you and your sons. But you must eat it in a holy place.

¹⁴Also you, your sons, and your daughters will be able to eat the breast from the wave offerings. ⌊You don't have to eat these in a holy place,⌋ but you must eat them in a clean* place. Why? Because they come from the fellowship offerings. The people of Israel give those gifts to God. ⌊The people eat part of those animals,⌋ but the breast is your share. ¹⁵The people must bring the fat from their animals as part of the sacrifice that is burned on the fire. They must also bring the thigh of the fellowship offering and the breast of the wave offering. That will be waved in front of the Lord, and then it will be your share of the offering. It will belong to you and your children. That part of the sacrifices will be your share forever, just like the Lord said."

¹⁶Moses looked for the goat of the sin offering. But it was already burned up. Moses became very angry at Aaron's other sons Eleazar and Ithamar. Moses said, ¹⁷"You were supposed to eat that goat in the holy area! It is very holy! Why did you not eat it in front of the Lord? The Lord gave it to you to carry away the guilt of the people—to make the people pure.* ¹⁸That goat's blood was not brought into the Holy Place.* So, you should have eaten the meat in the holy area, like I commanded!"

¹⁹But Aaron said to Moses, "Look, today they brought their sin offering and burnt offering before the Lord. But you know what happened to me today! Do you think the Lord would be happy if I ate the sin offering today? No!"

²⁰When Moses heard this, he agreed.

Rules about Eating Meat

11 The Lord said to Moses and Aaron, ²"Tell the people of Israel: These are the animals you can eat: ³If an animal has hooves* that are split into two parts, and if that animal also chews the cud,* then you can eat the meat from that animal.

⁴⁻⁶"Some animals chew the cud,* but they don't have split hooves.* Don't eat those animals. Camels, rock badgers, and rabbits are like that, so they are unclean* for you. ⁷Other animals have hooves* that are split into two parts, but they don't chew the cud. Don't eat those animals. Pigs are like that, so they are unclean* for you. ⁸Don't eat the meat from those animals! Don't even touch their dead bodies! They are unclean for you!

Rules about Sea Food

⁹"If an animal lives in the sea or in a river and if the animal has fins and scales, then you can eat that animal. ¹⁰⁻¹¹But if an animal lives in the sea or in a river and does not have fins and scales, then you must not eat that animal. It is one of the animals the Lord says is bad to eat. Don't eat the meat from that animal. Don't even touch its dead body! ¹²You must treat any animal in the water that does not have fins and scales as one of the animals that God says are bad to eat.

Birds That Must Not Be Eaten

¹³"You must also treat these birds as animals God says are bad to eat. Don't eat any of these birds: eagles, vultures, buzzards, ¹⁴kites,* all kinds of falcons, ¹⁵all kinds of black birds, ¹⁶ostriches, nighthawks, sea gulls, all kinds of hawks, ¹⁷owls,

---

clean Pure or acceptable to God for worship.
unclean Not pure or not acceptable to God for worship.
altar A table or raised area used for offering sacrifices.
holy Set aside or chosen for a special purpose.

make ... pure Or, "make atonement." The Hebrew word means "to cover, "to hide," or "to erase sins."
Holy Place One of the rooms in the Holy Tent.
hooves The hard part of the foot of certain animals.
cud The food that is brought up from the stomach of some animals (like cows) and chewed again.
kite(s) A bird like a hawk.

cormorants, great owls, ¹⁸water hens, pelicans, carrion-vultures, ¹⁹storks, all kinds of herons, hoopoes, and bats.

Rules about Eating Insects

²⁰"If insects have wings and crawl,* then you should treat them as things the Lord says you must not eat. Don't eat those insects! ²¹But you can eat those insects if they have legs with joints above their feet so they can jump. ²²You can also eat all kinds of locusts, all kinds of winged locusts, all kinds of crickets, and all kinds of grasshoppers.

²³"But all the other insects that have wings and crawl* are things the Lord says you must not eat. ²⁴Those insects will make you unclean.* Any person who touches the dead bodies of these insects will become unclean until evening. ²⁵If a person picks up one of those dead insects, then that person must wash his clothes. That person will be unclean until evening.

More Rules about Animals

²⁶⁻²⁷"Some animals have split hooves,* but the hooves don't make exactly two parts. Some animals don't chew the cud.* Some animals ⌊don't have hooves—they⌋ walk on their paws.* All of those animals are unclean* for you. Any person who touches them will become unclean. That person will be unclean until evening. ²⁸If any person picks up their dead bodies, that person must wash his clothes. That person will be unclean until evening. Those animals are unclean to you.

Rules about Crawling Animals

²⁹"These crawling animals are unclean* for you: moles, mice, all kinds of great lizards, ³⁰geckos, crocodiles, lizards, sand reptiles, and chameleons. ³¹Those crawling animals are unclean for you. Any person who touches their dead bodies will be unclean until evening.

Rules about Unclean Animals

³²"If any of those unclean* animals dies and falls on something, then that thing will become unclean. It might be something made from wood, cloth, leather, a cloth of sadness or some work tool. Whatever it is, it must be washed with water. It will be unclean until evening. Then it will become clean again. ³³If any of those unclean animals dies and falls into a clay dish, then anything in the dish will become unclean. And you must break the dish. ³⁴If water ⌊from the unclean clay dish⌋ comes on any food, then that food will become unclean. Any drink in the unclean dish will become unclean. ³⁵If any part of a dead unclean animal falls on something, then that thing is unclean. It may be a ⌊clay⌋ oven or a ⌊clay⌋ baking pan. It must be broken into pieces. Those things will not be clean ⌊any more⌋. They will always be unclean for you.

³⁶"A spring or a well that collects water will ⌊stay⌋ clean.* But any person who touches the dead bodies of any unclean animal will become unclean. ³⁷If any part of those dead unclean* animals falls on any seed that is to be planted, then that seed is ⌊still⌋ clean. ³⁸But if you put water on some seeds and then if any part of those dead unclean animals falls on those seeds, then those seeds are unclean for you.

³⁹"Also, if an animal ⌊that you use for food⌋ dies, then the person who touches its dead body will be unclean* until evening. ⁴⁰And the person who eats meat from this animal's body must wash his clothes. This person will be unclean until evening. The person who picks up the dead body of the animal must wash his clothes. This person will be unclean until evening.

⁴¹"Every animal that crawls on the ground is one of the animals the Lord says you must not eat. You must not eat it. ⁴²You must not eat any of the reptiles that crawl on their stomachs or that walk on all four feet, or any of the animals that have many feet. Don't eat those animals! ⁴³Don't let those animals make you filthy.* You must not become unclean! ⁴⁴Why? Because I am the Lord your God! I am holy, so you should keep yourselves holy! Don't make yourselves unclean with those crawling things! ⁴⁵I brought you people from Egypt. I did this so you could be my special people and I could be your God. I am holy, so you must be holy too!"

⁴⁶Those are the rules about all of the tame animals, birds, and other animals on earth. Those are the rules about all of the animals in the sea and

---

crawl Literally, "walk on four feet."
unclean Not pure or not acceptable to God for worship.
hooves The hard part of the foot of certain animals.
cud The food that is brought up from the stomach of some animals (like cows) and chewed again.
paws The soft feet with claws on certain animals.

clean Pure or acceptable to God for worship.
filthy Or, "hated." Not pure or not acceptable to God for worship.

all of the animals that crawl on the ground. ⁴⁷Those teachings are so people can know unclean* animals from clean* animals. So people will know which animals they can eat and which animals they must not eat.

Rules for New Mothers

12 The Lord said to Moses, ²"Tell the people of Israel: If a woman gives birth to a baby boy, then that woman will be unclean* for seven days. This will be like her being unclean during her monthly time of bleeding. ³On the eighth day, the baby boy must be circumcised.* ⁴Then it will be 33 days before she becomes clean* from her loss of blood. She must not touch anything that is holy. She must not enter the Holy Place until the time of her being made clean is finished. ⁵But if the woman gives birth to a girl, then the mother will be unclean for two weeks, the same as for her monthly time of bleeding. It will be 66 days before she becomes clean from her loss of blood.

⁶"After the time for being made clean* is finished, the new mother of a baby girl or boy must bring special sacrifices to the Meeting Tent.* She must give those sacrifices to the priest at the entrance of the Meeting Tent. She must bring a one-year-old lamb for a burnt offering and a dove or young pigeon for a sin offering. ⁷⁻⁸If the woman can't afford a lamb, she may bring two doves or two young pigeons. One bird will be for a burnt offering and one for a sin offering. The priest will offer those things before the Lord. In this way, the priest will make her pure.* Then she will be clean from her loss of blood. Those are the rules for a woman who gives birth to a baby boy or a baby girl."

Rules about Skin Diseases

13 The Lord said to Moses and Aaron, ²"A person might have a swelling on his skin, or it may be a scab or a bright spot. If the sore looks like the disease of leprosy,* then the person must be brought to Aaron the priest or to one of his sons the priests. ³The priest must look at the sore on the person's skin. If the hair in the sore has become white, and if the sore seems deeper than the person's skin, then it is a leprosy disease. When the priest has finished looking at the person, the priest must announce that the person is unclean.*

⁴"Sometimes there is a white spot on a person's skin. But the spot does not seem deeper than the skin. If that is true, then the priest must separate that person from other people for seven days. ⁵On the seventh day, the priest must look at the person. If the priest sees that the sore has not changed and has not spread on the skin, then the priest must separate the person for seven more days. ⁶Seven days later the priest must look at the person again. If the sore has faded, and has not spread on the skin, then the priest must announce that the person is clean.* The sore is only a scab. The person must wash his clothes and become clean again.

⁷"But if, after the person has shown himself to the priest to be made clean ₍again,₎ the scab spreads more over the skin, then the person must come again to the priest. ⁸The priest must look. If the scab has spread on the skin, then the priest must announce that the person is unclean.* That is a leprosy* disease.

⁹"If a person has leprosy,* he must be brought to the priest. ¹⁰The priest must look at that person. If there is a white swelling in the skin, and if the hair has become white, and if the skin looks raw in the swelling, ¹¹then it is a leprosy that has continued for a long time on that person's skin. The priest must announce that the person is unclean.* The priest does not have to separate that person from other people for a short time. Why? Because ₍the priest already knows₎ that the person is unclean.

¹²"Sometimes a skin disease* will spread all over a person's body. The skin disease will cover that person's skin from his head to his feet. The priest must look at that person's whole body. ¹³If the priest sees that the skin disease covers the whole body and that it has turned all of that person's skin white, then the priest must announce that the person is clean.* ¹⁴But if the person has raw skin, then he is not clean. ¹⁵When the priest

---

unclean Not pure or not acceptable to God for worship.
clean Pure or acceptable to God for worship.
circumcised To have the foreskin cut off. This was done to every Jewish male to show he shared in the Agreement God made with Israel. See Gen. 17:4-14.
Meeting Tent The Holy Tent (tabernacle) where the people of Israel came to meet with God.
make ... pure Or, "make atonement." The Hebrew word means "to cover," "to hide," or "to erase sins."
leprosy The Hebrew word includes mildew, fungus, and bad skin diseases, not just the disease we call leprosy.
skin disease Literally, "leprosy." The Hebrew word can mean many kinds of skin disease.

sees the raw skin, he must announce that the person is unclean.* The raw skin is not clean. It is a leprosy* disease. ¹⁶"If the raw skin changes and becomes white, then the person must come to the priest. ¹⁷The priest must look at the person. If the infection has become white, then the priest must announce that the person who has the infection is clean.* That person is clean.

¹⁸"A person might get a boil on his skin that heals over. ¹⁹Then that boil might become a white swelling or a bright, white spot with red streaks in it. If this happens, the person must show that spot to a priest. ²⁰The priest must look at it. If the swelling is deeper than the skin and the hair on it has become white, then the priest must announce that the person is unclean.* The spot is the infection of leprosy.* The leprosy has broken out from inside the boil. ²¹But if the priest looks at the spot, and there are no white hairs in it, and the spot is not deeper than the skin, but is faded, then the priest must separate the person for seven days. ²²If more of the spot spreads on the skin, then the priest must announce that the person is unclean. It is an infection. ²³But if the bright spot stays in its place, and does not spread, then it is only the scar from the old boil. The priest must announce that the person is clean.

²⁴⁻²⁵"A person might get a burn on his skin. If the raw skin becomes a white spot or white spot with red streaks in it, the priest must look at it. If that white spot seems to be deeper than the skin, and the hair at that spot has become white, then it is a leprosy* disease. The leprosy has broken out in the burn. The priest must announce that the person is unclean.* It is a leprosy disease. ²⁶But if the priest looks at the spot, and there is no white hair in the bright spot, and the spot is not deeper than the skin, but is faded, then the priest must separate the person for seven days. ²⁷On the seventh day the priest must look at the person again. If the spot spread on the skin, then the priest must announce that the person is unclean. It is a leprosy disease. ²⁸But if the bright spot did not spread on the skin, but is faded, it is the swelling from the burn. The priest must announce the person clean. It is only the scar from the burn.

²⁹"A person might get an infection on his scalp* or beard. ³⁰A priest must look at the infection. If the infection seems to be deeper than the skin, and if the hair around it is thin and yellow, then the priest must announce that the person is unclean.* It is a bad skin disease.* ³¹If the disease does not seem deeper than the skin, but there is no dark hair in it, then the priest must separate that person for seven days. ³²On the seventh day the priest must look at the infection. If the disease has not spread, and there are no yellow hairs growing in it, and the disease does not seem deeper than the skin, ³³then the person must shave himself. But he must not shave the disease. The priest must separate that person for seven more days. ³⁴On the seventh day, the priest must look at the disease. If the disease has not spread through the skin, and it does not seem deeper than the skin, then the priest must announce that the person is clean.* The person must wash his clothes and become clean. ³⁵But if the disease spreads on the skin after the person has become clean, ³⁶then the priest must look at the person again. If the disease has spread in the skin, the priest does not need to look for the yellowish hair. The person is unclean.* ³⁷But if the priest thinks that the disease has stopped, and black hair is growing in it, the disease has healed. The person is clean. The priest must announce that the person is clean.

³⁸"If a person has white spots on his skin, ³⁹then a priest must look at those spots. If the spots on that person's skin are only dull white, then the disease is only a harmless rash. That person is clean.*

⁴⁰"A man might lose hair from his head. He is clean. It is only baldness. ⁴¹A man might lose hair from the sides of his head. He is clean. It is only another kind of baldness. ⁴²But if there is a red and white infection on his scalp,* then it is a skin disease.* ⁴³A priest must look at that person. If the swelling of the infection is red and white and looks like the leprosy* on other parts of the body, ⁴⁴then that person has a leprosy disease on his scalp. The person is unclean.* The priest must announce that the person is unclean.

⁴⁵"If a person has a leprosy* disease, ₁then that person must warn other people₁. That person must shout, 'Unclean, unclean!' That person's clothes

---

unclean Not pure or not acceptable to God for worship.
leprosy The Hebrew word includes mildew, fungus, and bad skin diseases, not just the disease we call leprosy.
clean Pure or acceptable to God for worship.
scalp The skin on a person's head.
skin disease Literally, "leprosy." The Hebrew word can mean many different kinds of skin disease.

must be torn at the seams. That person must let his hair grow wild.* And that person must cover his mouth. ⁴⁶That person will be unclean* the whole time he has the infection. That person is unclean. He must live alone. His home must be outside the camp.

⁴⁷⁻⁴⁸"Some clothing might have mildew* on it. The cloth might be linen* or wool. The cloth might be woven or knitted. Or the mildew might be on a piece of leather or on something made from leather. ⁴⁹If that mildew is green or red, then it must be shown to a priest. ⁵⁰The priest must look at the mildew. He must put that thing in a separate place for seven days. ⁵¹⁻⁵²On the seventh day, the priest must look at the mildew. It does not matter if the mildew is on leather or cloth. It does not matter if the cloth is woven or knitted. It does not matter what the leather was used for. If the mildew spread, then that cloth or leather is unclean.* The infection is unclean. The priest must burn that cloth or leather.

⁵³"If the priest sees that the mildew* did not spread, then that cloth or leather must be washed. It does not matter if it is leather or cloth, or if the cloth is knitted or woven, it must be washed. ⁵⁴The priest must order the people to wash that piece of leather or cloth. Then the priest must separate the clothing for seven more days. ⁵⁵After that time, the priest must look again. If the mildew still looks the same, then that thing is unclean.* It does not matter if the infection has not spread. You must burn that cloth or piece of leather.

⁵⁶"But if the priest looks at that piece of leather or cloth, and the mildew has faded, then the priest must tear the infection out of the piece of leather or cloth. It does not matter if the cloth is woven or knitted. ⁵⁷But the mildew* might come back to that piece of leather or cloth. If that happens, then the mildew is spreading. That piece of leather or cloth must be burned. ⁵⁸But if the mildew did not come back after washing, then that piece of leather or cloth is clean.* It does not matter if the cloth was woven or knitted. That cloth is clean."

⁵⁹Those are the rules for mildew* on pieces of leather or cloth. It does not matter if the cloth is woven or knitted.

Rules for the Leper Made Clean

14 The Lord said to Moses, ²"These are the rules for people who had a skin disease* and became well. These rules are for making that person clean.*

"A priest must look at the person who had the skin disease.* ³The priest must go to that person outside the camp. The priest must look to see if the skin disease is healed. ⁴If the person is healthy, then the priest will tell him to do these things: That person must get two living clean* birds. He must also get a piece of cedar wood, a piece of red cloth, and a hyssop* plant. ⁵Then the priest must order one bird to be killed in a clay bowl over running water. ⁶The priest must take the other bird that is still alive and the piece of cedar wood, the piece of red cloth, and the hyssop plant. He must dip the living bird and the other things in the blood of the bird that was killed over the running water. ⁷The priest must sprinkle the blood seven times on the person who had the skin disease. Then the priest must announce that the person is clean. After that, the priest must go to an open field and let the living bird go free.

⁸"Then that person must wash his clothes. He must shave off all his hair. And he must wash with water. Then he will be clean.* Then that person may go into the camp. But he must stay outside his tent for seven days. ⁹On the seventh day, he must shave off all his hair. He must shave his head, his beard, and his eyebrows—yes, all his hair. Then he must wash his clothes and bathe his body in water. Then he will be clean.

¹⁰"On the eighth day, the person who had a skin disease* must take two male lambs that have nothing wrong with them. He must also take a one-year-old female lamb that has nothing wrong with it. He must take 24 cups* of fine flour mixed with oil. This fine flour is for a grain offering. The person must take 2/3 of a pint* of olive oil. ¹¹The

---

That person's clothes ... wild These things also showed a person was very sad about something.
unclean Not pure or not acceptable to God for worship.
mildew A kind of fungus that often grows on cloth, leather, or wood that is in a warm, damp place. The Hebrew word also means, "leprosy," or "skin disease."
linen Thread or cloth made from the fibers of the flax plant.
clean Pure or acceptable to God for worship.

skin disease Literally, "leprosy." The Hebrew word can mean many different kinds of skin disease.
hyssop A plant with fine branches and leaves used for sprinkling blood or water in cleansing ceremonies.
24 cups Literally, "3/10," probably meaning 3/10 of an ephah.
2/3 of a pint Literally, "1 log."

LEVITICUS 14:12–32

priest must bring that person and his sacrifices before the Lord at the entrance of the Meeting Tent.* (This must be the same priest who announces that the person is clean*) ¹²The priest will offer one of the male lambs as a guilt offering. He will offer that lamb and some of the oil as a wave offering before the Lord. ¹³Then the priest will kill the male lamb in the holy place where they kill the sin offering and the burnt offering. The guilt offering is like the sin offering. It belongs to the priest. It is very holy.

¹⁴"The priest will take some of the blood of the guilt offering. The priest will put some of this blood on the tip of the right ear of the person to be made clean.* The priest will put some of this blood on the thumb of the right hand and on the big toe of the right foot of that person. ¹⁵The priest will also take some of the oil and pour it into his left palm. ¹⁶Then the priest will dip the finger of his right hand into the oil that is in his left palm. He will use his finger to sprinkle some of the oil seven times before the Lord. ¹⁷Then the priest will put some of the oil that is in his palm on the person to be made clean. He will put that oil on ⌊the same places he put⌋ the blood of the guilt offering. The priest will put some of the oil on the tip of the person's right ear. He will put some of the oil on the thumb of the right hand. And he will put some of the oil on the big toe of the person's right foot. ¹⁸The priest will put the oil that is left in his palm on the head of the person to be made clean. In this way, the priest will make that person pure* before the Lord.

¹⁹"Then the priest must offer the sin offering for the person to be made clean.* The priest will offer the sin offering and make that person pure.* After that, the priest will kill the animal for the burnt offering. ²⁰Then the priest will offer up the burnt offering and the grain offering on the altar.* In this way, the priest will make that person pure. And the person will be clean.

²¹"But if the person is poor, and he can't afford ⌊those offerings⌋, then he must take one male lamb for a guilt offering. That will be a wave offering ⌊so that the priest can⌋ make that person pure.* He must take 8 cups* of fine flour mixed with oil. This flour will be used for a grain offering. The person must take 2/3 of a pint* of olive oil ²²and two doves or two young pigeons. Even poor people can afford those things. One bird will be a sin offering, and the other will be a burnt offering.

²³"On the eighth day, the person will bring those things to the priest at the entrance of the Meeting Tent. Those things will be offered before the Lord so that person can become clean.* ²⁴The priest will take the lamb for the guilt offering and the oil, and the priest will offer them as a wave offering before the Lord. ²⁵Then the priest will kill the lamb of the guilt offering. The priest will take some of the blood of the guilt offering. The priest will put some of this blood on the tip of the right ear of the person to be made clean. The priest will put some of this blood on the thumb of the right hand and on the big toe of the right foot of this person. ²⁶The priest will also pour some of this oil into his left palm. ²⁷The priest will use the finger of his right hand to sprinkle some of the oil that is in his left palm seven times before the Lord. ²⁸Then the priest will put some of the oil that is in his palm on the same places he put the blood from the guilt offering. He will put some of the oil on the tip of the right ear of the person to be made clean. The priest will put some of the oil on the thumb of the right hand. And he will put some of the oil on the big toe of the person's right foot. ²⁹The priest will put the oil that is left in his palm on the head of the person to be made clean. In this way, the priest will make that person pure* before the Lord.

³⁰"Then the priest must offer one of the doves or young pigeons. (He must offer whatever the person can afford.) ³¹He must offer one of these birds as a sin offering and the other bird as a burnt offering. He must offer the birds with the grain offering. In this way, the priest will make that person pure* before the Lord. And that person will become clean.*"

³²Those are the rules for making a person clean after he becomes well from a skin disease.* Those

---

Meeting Tent The Holy Tent (tabernacle) where the people of Israel went to meet with God.
clean Pure or acceptable to God for worship.
make ... pure Literally, "make atonement." The Hebrew word means "to cover," "to hide," or "to erase sins."
make ... pure Literally, "make atonement." The Hebrew word means "to cover," "to hide," or "to erase sins."
altar A table or raised area used for offering sacrifices.

8 cups Literally, "1/10 of an ephah."
2/3 of a pint Literally, "1 log."
skin disease Literally, "leprosy." The Hebrew word can mean many different kinds of skin disease.

are the rules for people who cannot afford the regular sacrifices for becoming clean.

Rules for Mildew in a House

33 The Lord also said to Moses and Aaron, 34 "I am giving the land of Canaan to your people. Your people will enter that land. At that time, I might cause mildew* to grow in some person's house. 35 The person who owns that house must come and tell the priest, 'I see something like mildew in my house.'

36 "Then the priest must order the people to take everything out of the house. The people must do this before the priest goes in to look at the mildew.* Then the priest will not have to say everything in the house is unclean.* After the people have taken everything out of the house, the priest will go in to look at the house. 37 The priest will look at the mildew. If the mildew on the walls of the house has holes that are a green color or red color, and if the mildew goes into the wall's surface, 38 then the priest must go out of the house and lock the house for seven days.

39 "On the seventh day, the priest must come back and check the house. If the mildew* has spread on the walls of the house, 40 then the priest must order the people to tear out the stones with the mildew on them and throw them away. They must put those stones at a special unclean* place outside the city. 41 Then the priest must have all the house scraped inside. The people must throw away the plaster* that they scrape off. They must put that plaster at a special unclean place outside the city. 42 Then that person must put new stones in the walls. And he must cover those walls with new plaster.

43 "Maybe a person took away the old stones and plaster and put in new stones and plaster. And maybe mildew* again appears in that house. 44 Then the priest must come in and check the house. If the infection has spread in the house, then it is a disease that spreads quickly to other places. So the house is unclean.* 45 That person must tear down the house. They must take all of the stones, plaster, and pieces of wood to the special unclean place outside the city. 46 And any person who goes into that house will be unclean until evening. 47 If any person eats in that house or lies down in there, then that person must wash his clothes.

48 "After new stones and plaster are put in a house, the priest must check the house. If the mildew* has not spread through the house, then the priest will announce that the house is clean.* Why? Because the mildew is gone!

49 "Then, to make the house clean,* the priest must take two birds, a piece of cedar wood, a piece of red cloth, and a hyssop* plant. 50 The priest will kill one bird in a clay bowl over running water. 51 Then the priest will take the cedar wood, the hyssop, the piece of red cloth, and the living bird. The priest will dip those things in the blood of the bird that was killed over running water. Then the priest will sprinkle ⌊that blood⌋ on the house seven times. 52 The priest will use those things in that way to make the house clean.* 53 The priest will go to an open field outside the city and let the living bird go free. In this way, the priest will make the house pure.* The house will be clean.*"

54 Those are the rules for any infection of leprosy,* 55 for mildew* on pieces of cloth or in a house. 56 Those are the rules for swellings, rashes, or bright spots on the skin. 57 Those rules teach when things are clean* and when things are unclean.* Those are the rules about those kinds of disease.

Rules for Discharges from the Body

15 The Lord also said to Moses and Aaron, 2 "Say to the people of Israel: When any person has a discharge* from his body, then that person is unclean.* 3 It does not matter if the discharge flows freely from his body or if his body stops it from flowing.

4 "If the person who has a discharge* lies on any bed, that bed becomes unclean.* Everything that person sits on becomes unclean. 5 If any

---

mildew   A kind of fungus that often grows on cloth, leather, or wood that is in a warm, damp place.
unclean   Not pure or not acceptable to God for worship.
plaster   A type of mud or cement that people used to cover a wall and make it smooth.

clean   Pure or acceptable to God for worship.
hyssop   A plant with fine branches and leaves used for sprinkling blood or water in cleansing ceremonies.
make ... pure   Literally, "make atonement." The Hebrew word means "to cover," "to hide," or "to erase sins."
leprosy   The Hebrew word includes mildew, fungus, and bad skin diseases, not just the disease we call leprosy.
discharge   Fluid from a person's body, including pus from sores, a man's semen, or a woman's period flow.

person touches that person's bed, then he must wash his clothes and bathe in water. He will be unclean until evening. ⁶If any person sits on anything that the person with the discharge sat on, then he must wash his clothes and bathe in water. He will be unclean until evening. ⁷Also, if any person touches the person who has the discharge, then he must wash his clothes and bathe in water. He will be unclean until evening.

⁸"If the person with a discharge* spits on a clean person, then the clean person must wash his clothes and bathe in water. This person will be unclean* until evening. ⁹Any saddle the person with the discharge sits on will become unclean. ¹⁰So any person who touches any of the things that were under the person with the discharge will be unclean until evening. The person who carries these things ₁that were under the person with the discharge₁ must wash his clothes and bathe in water. He will be unclean until evening.

¹¹"It may happen that the person with a discharge* has not washed his hands in water and touches another person. Then that other person must wash his clothes and bathe in water. He will be unclean* until evening.

¹²"But if the person with a discharge* touches a clay bowl, then that bowl must be broken. If the person with the discharge touches a wooden bowl, then that bowl must be washed in water.

¹³"When the person with a discharge* is ready to be made clean, he must wait seven days before he will be made clean. Then he must wash his clothes and bathe his body in running water. Then he will become clean.* ¹⁴On the eighth day, that person must take for himself two doves or two young pigeons. He must come before the Lord at the entrance of the Meeting Tent.* That person will give the two birds to the priest. ¹⁵The priest will offer the birds, one for a sin offering, and the other for a burnt offering. In this way, the priest will make that person pure* before the Lord.

Rules for Men

¹⁶"If a man has a flow of semen,* he must bathe his whole body in water. He will be unclean until evening. ¹⁷If the semen is on any clothing or leather, then that clothing or leather must be washed with water. It will be unclean* until evening. ¹⁸If a man sleeps with a woman and has a flow of semen, then both the man and the woman must bathe in water. They will be unclean until evening.

Rules for Women

¹⁹"If a woman has a discharge* from her monthly time of bleeding, she will be unclean* for seven days. If any person touches her, that person will be unclean until evening. ²⁰Also, everything the woman lies on during her monthly time of bleeding will be unclean. And everything she sits on during that time will be unclean. ²¹If any person touches the woman's bed, that person must wash his clothes and bathe in water. He will be unclean until evening. ²²If any person touches anything the woman has sat on, that person must wash his clothes and bathe in water. He will be unclean until evening. ²³It does not matter if the person touched the woman's bed or if he touched something she sat on, that person will be unclean until evening.

²⁴"And if a man has sexual relations with a woman during her monthly time of bleeding, then the man will be unclean* seven days. Every bed that man lies on will be unclean.

²⁵"If a woman has a discharge* of blood many days, not during her monthly time of bleeding, or if she has a discharge after that time, then she will be unclean,* like the time of monthly bleeding. She will be unclean for as long as she has a discharge. ²⁶Any bed the woman lies on during all the time of her discharge will be like her bed during her time of monthly bleeding. Everything the woman sits on will be unclean, like during the time she is unclean from her monthly time of bleeding. ²⁷If any person touches those things, that person will be unclean. That person must wash his clothes and bathe in water. He will be unclean until evening. ²⁸After the woman's discharge stops, she must wait seven days. After that, she will be clean. ²⁹Then on the eighth day, the woman must take two doves or two young pigeons. She must bring them to the priest at the entrance of the Meeting Tent.* ³⁰Then

---

discharge Fluid from a person's body, including pus from sores, a man's semen, or a woman's period flow.
unclean Not pure or not acceptable to God for worship.
clean Pure or acceptable to God for worship.
Meeting Tent The Holy Tent (tabernacle) where the people of Israel went to meet with God.
make ... pure Literally, "make atonement." The Hebrew word means "to cover," "to hide," or "to erase sins."

semen The fluid produced by a man's sexual organs.

the priest must offer one bird for a sin offering and the other bird for a burnt offering. In this way, the priest will make her pure* before the Lord.

³¹"So you must warn the people of Israel about being unclean.* ⌊If you don't warn the people, then⌋ they might make my Holy Tent* unclean. And then they would have to die!"

³²Those are the rules for people with a discharge.* Those rules are for men who become unclean* from a flow of semen.* ³³And those rules are for women who become unclean from their monthly time of bleeding. And those are the rules for any person that becomes unclean by sleeping with another person who is unclean.

The Day of Atonement

16 Two of Aaron's sons died while offering incense* to the Lord.* After that time, the Lord spoke to Moses. ²The Lord said, "Talk to your brother Aaron. Tell him that he cannot go behind the curtain into the Most Holy Place* anytime he wants to. The Holy Box* is in the room behind that curtain. The special cover* is on top of that Holy Box. And I appear in a cloud over that special cover. If Aaron goes into that room, he might die!

³"Before Aaron enters the ⌊Most⌋ Holy Place ⌊on the Day of Atonement⌋, he must offer a bull for a sin offering and a ram for a burnt offering. ⁴Aaron must wash his ⌊whole⌋ body with water.

Then he must put these clothes on: Aaron must put on the holy* linen shirt. The linen underclothes will be next to his body. He must tie the linen sash (belt) around him. And he must put on the linen turban.* These are holy clothes.

⁵"Aaron must take from the people of Israel two male goats for a sin offering, and one ram for a burnt offering. ⁶Then Aaron must offer the bull for the sin offering. This sin offering is for himself. Aaron must do this to make him and his family pure.*

⁷"Then Aaron must take the two goats and bring them before the Lord at the doorway of the Meeting Tent. ⁸Aaron will throw lots* for the two goats. One lot will be for the Lord. The other lot will be for Azazel.*

⁹"Then Aaron will offer the goat chosen by the lot* for the Lord. Aaron must make this goat a sin offering. ¹⁰But the goat chosen by the lot for Azazel* must be brought alive before the Lord. And then this goat will be sent out to Azazel in the desert. This is to make the people pure.*

¹¹"Then Aaron will offer the bull as a sin offering for himself. Aaron will make himself and his family pure.* Aaron will kill the bull for the sin offering for himself. ¹²Then he must take a firepan* full of coals of fire from the altar* before the Lord. Aaron will take two handfuls of sweet incense* that has been ground into powder. Aaron must bring that incense into the room behind the curtain. ¹³Aaron must put the incense on the fire before the Lord. Then the cloud of incense will cover the special cover* that is over the Agreement.* This way Aaron will not die. ¹⁴Also, Aaron must take some of the blood from the bull and sprinkle it with his finger toward the east, onto the special cover. He will sprinkle the blood

---

make ... pure Literally, "make atonement." The Hebrew word means "to cover," "to hide," or "to erase sins."
unclean Not pure or not acceptable to God for worship.
Holy Tent Or, "tabernacle." The place God came to live among his people.
discharge Fluid from a person's body, including pus from sores, a man's semen, or a woman's period flow.
semen The fluid produced by a man's sexual organs.
incense Special dried tree sap. Burned to make a sweet-smelling smoke, it was offered as a gift to God.
Two of Aaron's sons ... Lord See Lev. 10:1-2.
Most Holy Place The room in the Holy Tent where the Holy Box was.
Holy Box The Box of the Agreement—the box containing the flat stones with the Ten Commandments written on them and other things that proved God was with the people of Israel during their time in the Sinai desert.
cover Also called "mercy seat." The Hebrew word can mean "lid," "cover," or "the place where sins are forgiven."

holy Set aside or chosen for a special purpose.
turban Head covering made by wrapping a piece of cloth around the head or around a cap worn on the head.
lot(s) Sticks, stones, or pieces of bone used like dice for making decisions. See Proverbs 16:33.
Azazel Or, "scapegoat." The meaning of this word or name is not known. The main idea seems to be that the goat "carried away" the sins of the people.
firepan A small shovel for taking the ashes from the altar.
altar A table or raised area used for offering sacrifices.
Agreement Literally, "Proof." The flat stones with the Ten Commandments written on them. These were proof of the Agreement between God and the people of Israel.

seven times with his finger in front of the special cover. ¹⁵"Then Aaron must kill the goat of the sin offering for the people. Aaron must bring this goat's blood into the room behind the curtain. Aaron must do with the goat's blood as he did with the bull's blood. Aaron must sprinkle the goat's blood on the special cover* and in front of the cover. ¹⁶In this way, Aaron will do the things to make the Most Holy Place* pure.* Aaron must do these things because the people of Israel are unclean.* They do wrong and have many sins. Aaron must also do these things for the Meeting Tent* because it stays in the middle of unclean people! ¹⁷At the time that Aaron goes into the Most Holy Place to make ⌊it and the people⌋ pure,* no person must be in the Meeting Tent. No person must go in there until Aaron comes out. So, Aaron will make himself and his family pure. And he will make all the people of Israel pure. ¹⁸Then Aaron will go out to the altar* that is before the Lord. Aaron will make the altar pure. Aaron will take some of the bull's blood and some of the goat's blood and put it on the corners of the altar on all sides. ¹⁹Then Aaron will sprinkle some of the blood with his finger on the altar seven times. In this way, Aaron will make the altar holy* and clean* from all the sins of the people of Israel.

²⁰"So Aaron will make the Most Holy Place,* the Meeting Tent,* and the altar* pure.* After that, Aaron will bring the live goat ⌊to the Lord⌋. ²¹Aaron will put both his hands on the head of the living goat. Then Aaron will confess *(admit)* the sins and crimes of the people of Israel over the goat. In this way, Aaron will lay the people's sins on the goat's head. Then he will send the goat away to the desert. A man will be standing by, ready to lead this goat away. ²²So the goat will carry all the people's sins on itself to the empty desert. The man who leads the goat will let it loose in the desert.

²³"Then Aaron will enter the Meeting Tent.* He will take off the linen clothes that he put on when he went into the Holy Place. He must leave these clothes there. ²⁴He will wash his ⌊whole⌋ body with water in a holy place. Then he will put on his ⌊other special⌋ clothes. He will come out and offer his burnt offering and the people's burnt offering. He will make himself and the people pure.* ²⁵Then he will burn the fat of the sin offering on the altar.*

²⁶"The person that led the goat to Azazel* must wash his clothes and his whole body with water. After that, he can come into the camp.

²⁷"The bull and the goat for the sin offerings must be taken outside the camp. (The blood from those animals was brought into the Holy Place to make ⌊the holy things⌋ pure.) ⌊The priests⌋ must burn the skins, bodies, and body waste of those animals in the fire. ²⁸Then the person who burns them must wash his clothes and wash his ⌊whole⌋ body with water. After that, he can come into the camp.

²⁹"This law will always continue for you: On the tenth ⌊day⌋ of the seventh month, you must not eat food.* You must not do any work. None of the travelers or foreigners living in your land can do any work either. ³⁰Why? Because on this day, the priest will make you pure* and wash away your sins. Then you will be clean* to the Lord. ³¹This day is a very important day of rest for you. You must not eat food.* This law will continue forever.

³²"So the man chosen to be the high priest will do the ceremony to make things pure.* This is the man appointed to serve as high priest after his father. That priest must put on the holy linen clothes. ³³He must make the Most Holy Place,* the Meeting Tent,* and the altar* pure. And he must make the priests and all the people ⌊of Israel⌋ pure. ³⁴That law for making the people of Israel pure will continue forever. You will do those things one time every year. Why? Because of the sins of the people of Israel."

---

cover Also called "mercy seat." The Hebrew word can mean "lid," "cover," or "the place where sins are forgiven."

Most Holy Place The room in the Holy Tent where the Holy Box was.

make ... pure Literally, "make atonement." The Hebrew word means "to cover," "to hide," or "to erase sins."

unclean Not pure or not acceptable to God for worship.

Meeting Tent The Holy Tent (tabernacle) where the people of Israel went to meet with God.

altar A table or raised area used for offering sacrifices.

holy Set aside or chosen for a special purpose.

clean Pure or acceptable to God for worship.

to Azazel Or, "as a scapegoat." The meaning of this word or name is not known. The main idea is that the goat "carried away" the sins of the people.

not eat food Literally, "humble yourselves."

So they did the things that the Lord had commanded Moses.

Rules about Killing and Eating Animals

17 The Lord said to Moses, ²"Speak to Aaron and to his sons, and to all the people of Israel. Tell them, this is what the Lord has commanded: ³An Israelite person might kill a bull, or a lamb, or a goat in the camp or outside the camp. ⁴That person must bring that animal to the entrance of the Meeting Tent.* He must give ⌊a part of⌋ that animal as a gift to the Lord. That person has spilled blood *(killed)*, so he must take his gift to the Lord's Holy Tent.* If he does not take ⌊part of the animal as a gift to the Lord⌋, then that person must be separated from his people! ⁵This rule is so people will bring their fellowship offering to the Lord. The people of Israel must bring the animals they kill in the fields. They must bring those animals to the Lord at the entrance of the Meeting Tent. They must bring those animals to the priest. ⁶Then the priest will throw the blood from those animals onto the Lord's altar* near the entrance of the Meeting Tent. And the priest will burn the fat from those animals ⌊on the altar⌋. Its smell will please the Lord. ⁷They must not offer any more sacrifices to their 'goat idols'! They have chased after those other gods. In that way, they have acted like prostitutes.* These rules will continue forever!

⁸"Tell the people: Some citizen of Israel or some traveler or foreigner living among you might offer a burnt offering or a sacrifice. ⁹That person must take his sacrifice to the entrance of the Meeting Tent and offer it to the Lord. If that person does not do this, then that person must be separated from his people.

¹⁰"I *(God)* will be against any person who eats blood. It does not matter if that person is a citizen of Israel or if that person is a foreigner living among you! I will separate that person from his people. ¹¹Why? Because the life of the body is in the blood. I have given you rules for pouring that blood on the altar.* You must do this to make yourselves pure.* You must give that blood ⌊to me⌋ as payment for the life ⌊that you took⌋. ¹²So I tell the people of Israel: None of you people may eat blood. And no foreigner living among you may eat blood.

¹³"If any person catches a wild animal or a bird that can be eaten, then that person must pour the blood on the ground and cover it with dirt. It does not matter if that person is a citizen of Israel or a foreigner living among you! ¹⁴Why must you do this? Because, if blood is still in the meat, that animal's life is still in the meat. So I give this command to the people of Israel: Don't eat meat that still has blood in it! Any person who eats blood must be separated ⌊from his people⌋.

¹⁵"Also, if any person eats an animal that died by itself, or if any person eats an animal that was killed by some other animal, then that person will be unclean* until evening. That person must wash his clothes and wash his ⌊whole⌋ body with water. It does not matter if that person is a citizen of Israel or if he is a foreigner living among you! ¹⁶If that person does not wash ⌊his clothes⌋ or bathe his body, then he will be guilty ⌊of sin⌋."

Rules about Sexual Relations

18 The Lord said to Moses, ²"Tell the people of Israel: I am the Lord your God. ³In the past, you lived in Egypt. You must not do the things that were done in that country! I am leading you to Canaan. You must not do the things that are done in that country! Don't follow their customs. ⁴You must obey my rules and follow my laws! Be sure to follow those rules! Why? Because I am the Lord your God. ⁵So you must obey my laws and rules. If a person obeys my laws and rules, he will live! I am the Lord!

⁶"You must never have sexual relations with* your close relatives! I am the Lord.

⁷"You must never have sexual relations with* your father or mother. This woman is your mother. So you must not have sexual relations with her. ⁸You must not have sexual relations with

---

Meeting Tent The Holy Tent (tabernacle) where the people of Israel went to meet with God.
Holy Tent Or, "tabernacle." The place God came to live among his people.
altar A table or raised area used for offering sacrifices.
prostitute(s) A woman who sells her body for sex. Sometimes this also means a person who is not faithful to God and starts worshiping other gods.

make ... pure Literally, "make atonement." The Hebrew word means "to cover," "to hide," or "to erase sins."
unclean Not pure or not acceptable to God for worship.
have sexual relations with Literally, "uncover the nakedness of."

your father's wife ⌊even if she is not your mother⌋. Why? Because that is like having sexual relations with your father.*

⁹"You must not have sexual relations with* your sister. It doesn't matter if she is the daughter of your father or your mother. And it does not matter if your sister was born in ⌊your⌋ house* or at another place.

¹⁰"You must not have sexual relations with* your granddaughter. They are a part of you!

¹¹"If your father and his wife* have a daughter, then she is your sister. You must not have sexual relations with* her.

¹²"You must not have sexual relations with* your father's sister. She is your father's close relative. ¹³You must not have sexual relations with your mother's sister. She is your mother's close relative. ¹⁴You must not have sexual relations with your father's brother. You must not go near your uncle's wife ⌊for sexual relations⌋. She is your aunt.

¹⁵"You must not have sexual relations with* your daughter-in-law. She is your son's wife. You must not have sexual relations with her.

¹⁶"You must not have sexual relations with* your brother's wife. That would be like having sexual relations with your brother.*

¹⁷"You must not have sexual relations with* a mother and her daughter. And you must not have sexual relations with this woman's granddaughter. It does not matter if this granddaughter is the daughter of this woman's son or daughter. Her granddaughters are her close relatives. It is wrong ⌊to have sexual relations with them⌋.

¹⁸"While your wife is still living, you must not take her sister as ⌊another⌋ wife. This will make the sisters become enemies. You must not have sexual relations with* your wife's sister.

¹⁹"Also you must not go near a woman to have sexual relations with* her during her monthly time of bleeding. She is unclean* during this time.

²⁰"And you must not have sexual relations with your neighbor's wife. This will only make you filthy*!

²¹"You must not give any of your children through ⌊the fire⌋ to Molech.* If you do this, you will show that you don't respect the name of your God! I am the Lord.

²²"You must not have sexual relations with a man as with a woman. That is a terrible sin!

²³"You must not have sexual relations with any animal. This will only make you filthy*! Also, a woman must not have sexual relations with an animal. It is against nature!

²⁴"Don't make yourself unclean* with any of those wrong things! I am throwing nations out of their countries and giving their land to you! Why? Because those people did those terrible sins! ²⁵They made the land filthy*! Now the land ⌊is sick of those things⌋! And the land is vomiting out the people who lived there!

²⁶"So you must obey my laws and rules. You must not do any of those terrible sins. Those rules are for the citizens of Israel, and they are for the people living among you! ²⁷The people who lived in the land before you did all those terrible things. So the land became filthy*! ²⁸⌊If you do these things⌋, then you will make the land filthy. And it will vomit you out like it vomited out the nations that were ⌊there⌋ before you. ²⁹If any person does any of those terrible sins, then that person must be separated from his people! ³⁰Other people have done those terrible sins. But you must obey my laws! You must not do any of those terrible sins! Don't make yourself filthy with those terrible sins! I am the Lord your God."

Israel Belongs to God

19 The Lord said to Moses, ²"Tell all the people of Israel: I am the Lord your God! I am holy, so you must be holy!

---

sexual relations ... father Literally, "She is the nakedness of your father." Husband and wife are like one person. See Gen 2:24.

have sexual relations with Literally, "uncover the nakedness of."

sister was born in ⌊your⌋ house Or, "household." If a man had many wives, each wife and her children had their own tent or part of the house. They were like a small family group within the family. So this probably means a person was not supposed to have sexual relations with any of his father's daughters, whether sister or half-sister.

his wife This probably means "your stepmother."

sexual relations ... brother Literally, "She is the nakedness of your brother."

unclean Not pure or not acceptable to God for worship.
filthy Or, "polluted" or "unclean."
Molech A false God. People often killed their children as part of their worship to Molech.
unclean Or, "unacceptable." Not pure or not able to be used in worshiping God. See Lev. 11-15 for the rules about clean and unclean things.

³"Each person among you must honor his mother and father and keep my special days of rest.* I am the Lord your God!

⁴"Don't worship idols.* Don't make melted statues of gods for yourselves. I am the Lord your God!

⁵"When you offer a sacrifice* of fellowship offerings to the Lord, you must offer it in the right way so you will be accepted. ⁶You may eat it the same day you offer it, and also on the next day. But if any of that sacrifice is left on the third day, then you must burn it in the fire. ⁷You must not eat any of that sacrifice on the third day. It will be unclean.* It will not be accepted. ⁸A person will be guilty of sin if he does that! Why? Because he did not respect the holy things that belong to the Lord. That person must be separated from his people.

⁹"When you cut your crops at harvest time, don't cut all the way to the corners of your fields. And if grain falls on the ground, you must not gather up that grain. ¹⁰Don't pick all the grapes in your vineyards and don't pick up the grapes that fall to the ground. Why? Because you must leave those things for poor people and for people traveling through your country. I am the Lord your God!

¹¹"You must not steal. You must not cheat people. You must not lie to each other. ¹²You must not use my name to make false promises. If you do that, then you will show that you don't respect the name of your God. I am the Lord!

¹³"You must not do bad things to your neighbor. You must not rob ₍him₎. You must not hold a hired worker's salary all night until morning.*

¹⁴"You must not curse a deaf man. You must not put something in front of a blind person to make him fall. But you must respect your God. I am the Lord!

¹⁵"You must be fair in judgment. You must not show special favor to poor people. And you must not show special favor to important people. You must be fair when you judge your neighbor. ¹⁶You must not go around spreading false stories against other people. Don't do anything that would put your neighbor's life in danger. I am the Lord!

¹⁷"You must not hate your brother in your heart. If your neighbor does something wrong, then talk to him about it. But forgive him! ¹⁸Forget about the wrong things people do ₍to you₎. Don't try to get even. Love your neighbor as yourself. I am the Lord!

¹⁹"You must obey my laws. You must not breed together two kinds of animals. You must not sow your field with two kinds of seed. You must not wear clothing made from two kinds of material mixed together.

²⁰"It may happen that a man has sexual relations with a woman who is the slave of ₍another₎ man. But this slave woman has not been bought or given her freedom. If this happens, then there must be punishment. But they will not be put to death. Why? Because the woman was not free. ²¹The man must bring his guilt offering to the Lord at the entrance of the Meeting Tent.* The man must bring a ram for a guilt offering. ²²The priest will do the things that will make the man pure.* The priest will offer the ram as a guilt offering before the Lord. It will be for the sins the man did. Then the man will be forgiven for the sins he did.

²³"In the future, you will enter your country. At that time, you will plant many kinds of trees for food. After planting a tree, you must wait three years before you can use any of the fruit from that tree. You must not use that fruit. ²⁴In the fourth year, the fruit from that tree will be the Lord's. It will be a holy offering of praise to the Lord. ²⁵Then, in the fifth year, you can eat the fruit from that tree. And the tree will produce more and more fruit for you. I am the Lord your God!

²⁶"You must not eat any meat with blood still in it.

"You must not try to use magic and other things to predict the future.

---

special days of rest Or, "Sabbaths." This might mean Saturday, or it might mean all of the special days when the people were not supposed to work.

idols Statues of false gods that people worshiped.

sacrifice(s) A gift to God. Usually, it was a special animal that was killed and burned on an altar.

sacrifice ... unclean Or "offensive, bad, rotten." This means the meat is not good to eat as part of a sacrifice.

You must not hold ... until morning Workers were paid at the end of each day for the work they did that day. See Mt. 20:1-16.

Meeting Tent The Holy Tent (tabernacle) where the people of Israel went to meet with God.

make ... pure Literally, "make atonement." The Hebrew word means "to cover," "to hide," or "to erase sins."

²⁷"You must not round off the hair that grows on the side of your face. You must not cut your beard that grows on the side of your face. ²⁸You must not cut your body as a way to remember dead people. You must not make any tattoo marks on yourselves. I am the Lord!

²⁹"Don't make your daughter become a prostitute.* That only shows you don't respect her! Don't let people be prostitutes in your country. Don't let your country be filled with that kind of sin.

³⁰"You must not work on my special days of rest.* You must honor my holy place. I am the Lord!

³¹"Don't go to mediums* or wizards* for advice. Don't go to them; they will only make you unclean.* I am the Lord your God!

³²"Show honor to old people. Stand up when they come into the room. Show respect to your God. I am the Lord!

³³"Don't do bad things to foreigners living in your country! ³⁴You must treat foreigners the same as you treat your own citizens. Love foreigners like you love yourselves. Why? Because you were foreigners one time—in Egypt. I am the Lord your God!

³⁵"You must be fair when you judge people. And you must be fair when you measure and weigh things. ³⁶Your baskets should be the right size. Your jars should hold the right amount of liquids. Your weights and balances should weigh things correctly. I am the Lord your God! I brought you out from the land of Egypt!

³⁷"You must remember all my laws and rules. And you must obey them. I am the Lord!"

Warning Against Worshiping Idols

20 The Lord said to Moses, ²"You must also tell the people of Israel these things: A person in your country might give one of his children to the false god Molech.* That person must be killed! It does not matter if that person is a citizen of Israel or a foreigner living in Israel, you must throw stones at that person and kill him. ³I will be against that person! I will separate him from his people. Why? Because he gave his children to Molech. He showed that he did not respect my holy name. And he made my holy place unclean.* ⁴Maybe the common people will ignore that person. Maybe they will not kill that person who gave his children to Molech. ⁵But I will be against that person and his family! I will separate him from his people. I will separate any person who is unfaithful to me and chases after Molech.

⁶"I will be against any person who goes to mediums* and wizards* for advice. That person is being unfaithful to me. So I will separate that person from his people.

⁷"Be special. Make yourselves holy*. Why? Because ⌊I am holy⌋! I am the Lord your God. ⁸Remember and obey my laws. I am the Lord. And I have made you ⌊my⌋ special ⌊people⌋.

⁹"If any person curses* his father or mother, that person must be put to death. He cursed his father or mother, so he is responsible for his own death!*

Punishments for Sexual Sins

¹⁰"If a man has sexual relations with his neighbor's wife, then both the man and the woman are guilty of adultery. So both the man and the woman must be put to death! ¹¹If a man has sexual relations with his father's wife, then both the man and the woman must be put to death. They are responsible for their own death.* It is as if that man had had sexual relations with his father!*

¹²"If a man has sexual relations with his daughter-in-law, both of them must be put to death. They have done a very bad sexual sin! They are responsible for their own death.*

¹³"If a man has sexual relations with another man as with a woman, then these two men have done a terrible sin. They must be put to death. They are responsible for their own death.*

---

prostitute(s) A woman who sells her body for sex.
special days of rest Or, "Sabbaths." This might mean Saturday, or it might mean all of the special days when the people were not supposed to work.
medium(s) A person who tries to communicate with the spirits of dead people.
wizard(s) A person who tries to use evil spirits to do magic.
unclean Not pure or not acceptable to God for worship.
Molech A false god. People often killed their children as part of their worship to Molech.

holy Set aside or chosen for a special purpose.
curse To ask for bad things to happen to someone.
he ... death Literally, "his blood is on him."
They ... death Literally, "Their blood is on them."
man ... father Literally, "He uncovered his father's nakedness."

¹⁴"It is a sexual sin if a man has sexual relations with a woman and her mother. The people must burn that man and the two women in fire! Don't let this sexual sin happen among your people!
¹⁵"If a man has sexual relations with an animal, that man must be put to death. And you must also kill the animal. ¹⁶If a woman has sexual relations with an animal, then you must kill the woman and the animal. They must be put to death. They are responsible for their own death.*
¹⁷"If a brother and his sister or half sister marry each other and have sexual relations with each other,* it is a shameful thing! They must be punished in public! They must be separated from their people! The man who has sexual relations with his sister must be punished for his sin!*
¹⁸"If a man has sexual relations with a woman during her monthly time of bleeding, then both the woman and the man must be separated from their people. They sinned because they exposed her source of blood.
¹⁹"You must not have sexual relations with* your mother's sister or your father's sister. That is a sin of incest.* You must be punished for your sins.*
²⁰"A man must not have sexual relations with his uncle's wife. It would be like having sexual relations with his uncle. That man and his uncle's wife will be punished for their sins. They will die without children.*
²¹It is wrong for a man to take his brother's wife. It would be like having sexual relations with* his brother! They will have no children.
²²"You must remember all my laws and rules. And you must obey them. I am leading you to your land. You will live in that country. If you obey my laws and rules, then that land will not vomit you out. ²³I am forcing other people to leave that country. Why? Because those people did all of those sins! I hate those ⌊sins⌋! So don't live the way those people lived!
²⁴"I have told you that you will get their land. I will give their land to you. It will be your land! It is a land filled with many good things.* I am the Lord your God!
"⌊I have made you my special people.⌋ I have treated you differently from other people. ²⁵So you must treat clean* animals differently from unclean* animals. You must treat clean birds differently from unclean birds. Don't eat any of those unclean birds, and animals, and things that crawl on the ground. I have made those things unclean. ²⁶I have made you my special people. So you must be holy for me! Why? Because I am the Lord, and I am holy!
²⁷"A man or a woman who is a medium* or a wizard,* must be put to death. The people must kill them with stones. They must be killed.*"

Rules for Priests

21 The Lord said to Moses, "Tell these things to Aaron's sons, the priests: A priest must not make himself unclean* by touching a dead person. ²But if the dead person was one of his close relatives, ⌊then he can touch the dead body⌋. The priest can make himself unclean if the dead person is his mother or father, his son or daughter, his brother or ³his unmarried* sister. (This sister is close to him because she has no husband. So the priest may make himself unclean for her ⌊if she dies⌋.) ⁴But a priest must not make himself unclean if the dead person was only one of his slaves.*
⁵"Priests must not shave their heads bald. Priests must not shave off the edges of their beards. Priests must not make any cuts in their bodies. ⁶Priests must be holy for their God. They

---

They ... death Literally, "Their blood is on them."
sexual relations with each other Literally, "he sees her nakedness, and she sees his nakedness."
The man ... sin Literally, "he will carry his guilt."
have sexual relations with Literally, "uncover the nakedness of."
incest Having sexual relations with a close relative.
you ... sins Literally, "You will carry your guilt."
That man ... children Literally, "They must bear their childlessness. They will die."
have sexual relations with Literally, "uncover the nakedness of."

filled ... things Literally, "flowing with milk and honey."
clean Pure or acceptable to God for worship.
unclean Not pure or not acceptable to God for worship.
medium(s) A person who tries to communicate with the spirits of dead people.
wizard(s) A person who tries to use evil spirits to do magic.
They must be killed Literally, "Their blood is on them."
unmarried Literally, "virgin," a girl that was never married and never had sexual relations with anyone.
But a priest ... slaves Or, "A master must not become unclean for his people."

must show respect for God's name. Why? Because they carry the bread and the offerings by fire to the Lord. So they must be holy.*

⁷"A priest serves God in a special way. So a priest must not marry a woman who had sexual relations with some other man. A priest must not marry a prostitute* or a divorced woman. ⁸A priest serves God in a special way. So you must treat him in a special way. Why? Because he carries holy things! He brings the holy bread to God, and I am holy! I am the Lord, and I make you holy!

⁹"If a priest's daughter becomes a prostitute,* then she ruins her reputation, and she brings shame to her father! So she must be burned.

¹⁰"The high priest was chosen from among his brothers. The anointing oil* was poured on his head. In this way, he was chosen for the special job of being high priest. He was chosen to wear the special clothes. ⌊So he must not do things to show his sadness in public.⌋ He must not let his hair grow wild. He must not tear his clothes. ¹¹He must not make himself unclean* ⌊by touching a dead body⌋. He must not go near a dead body, even if it is his own father or mother. ¹²The high priest must not go out of God's holy place. ⌊Then he might become unclean,⌋ and ⌊then he might⌋ make God's holy place unclean.* The anointing oil was poured on the high priest's head. This separated him ⌊from the rest of the people⌋. I am the Lord!

¹³"The high priest must marry a woman who is a virgin.* ¹⁴The high priest must not marry a woman who has had sexual relations with another man. The high priest must not marry a prostitute,* a divorced woman, or a widow. The high priest must marry a virgin from his own people. ¹⁵In this way, people will show respect for his children.* I, the Lord, have separated the high priest for his special work."

¹⁶The Lord said to Moses, ¹⁷"Tell Aaron: If any of your descendants'* children have something wrong with them, then they must not carry the special bread to God. ¹⁸Any man who has something wrong with him must not ⌊serve as priest and⌋ bring sacrifices to me. These men cannot serve as priests:

> blind men,
> crippled men,
> men with bad scars on their faces,
> men with arms or legs that are too long,
> ¹⁹ men with broken feet or hands,
> ²⁰ men with bent backs,
> men who are dwarfs,*
> men who are cross-eyed,
> men with rashes or a bad skin diseases,
> men with crushed testicles.

²¹If one of Aaron's descendants has something wrong with him, then he cannot offer sacrifices by fire to the Lord. And that person cannot carry the special bread to God. ²²⌊That person is from the family of priests,⌋ so he can eat the holy bread. He can also eat the very holy bread. ²³But he cannot go through the curtain ⌊into the Most Holy Place⌋ and he cannot go near the altar.* Why? Because he has something wrong with him. He must not make my holy places not holy. I, the Lord, make those places holy!"

²⁴So Moses told these things to Aaron, Aaron's sons, and all the people of Israel.

22 The Lord God said to Moses, ²"Tell Aaron and his sons: The people of Israel will give things to me. Those things will become holy. They are mine. So you priests must not take those things. If you use those holy things ⌊for yourselves⌋, then you will show that you don't respect my holy name. I am the Lord! ³If any person from among all your descendants* touches those things, then that person will become unclean.* That person must be separated from me!

---

holy   Chosen or set aside for a special purpose.
prostitute   A woman who sells her body for sex.
anointing oil   Olive oil that was poured on people or things to show they were chosen for a special work or purpose.
unclean   Not pure or not acceptable to God for worship.
virgin   A pure woman who has never been married.
people ... children   Or, "his children will not become unclean from the people."
descendant(s)   A person's children and their future families.

dwarf(s)   A small person whose body stopped growing properly.
altar   A table or raised area used for offering sacrifices.
bad skin diseases   This could be leprosy, or it could be some other serious skin disease.
discharge   Fluid from a person's body, including pus from sores, a man's semen, or a woman's period flow.

The people of Israel gave those things to me. I am the Lord!

⁴"If any of Aaron's descendants* has one of the bad skin diseases* or a discharge* he can't eat the holy food until he becomes clean.* That rule is for any priest that becomes unclean.* That priest can become unclean from a dead body or from his own semen.* ⁵He can become unclean if he touches any unclean crawling animals. And he can become unclean if he touches an unclean person. It does not matter what made that person unclean. ⁶If a person touches any of those things, he will become unclean until evening. That person must not eat any of the holy food. Even if he washes with water, he can't eat the holy food. ⁷He will be clean only after the sun goes down. Then he can eat the holy food. Why? Because ₍after sunset he is clean and₎ that food belongs to him.

⁸"If a priest finds an animal that died by itself or that was killed by wild animals, he must not eat that dead animal. If that person eats that animal, he will become unclean.* I am the Lord!

⁹"The priests will have special times to serve me. They must be careful at those times. They must be careful not to make the holy things not holy. If they are careful, then they will not die. I, the Lord, have separated them for this special job. ¹⁰Only people from a priest's family can eat the holy food. A visitor staying with the priest or a hired worker must not eat any of the holy food. ¹¹But if the priest buys a person as a slave with his own money, then that person may eat some of the holy things. ₍Slaves₎ that were born in the priest's house may also eat some of the priest's food. ¹²A priest's daughter might marry a person who is not a priest. If she does that, then she can't eat any of the holy offerings. ¹³A priest's daughter might become a widow,* or she might become divorced. If she does not have any children ₍to support her₎ and she goes back to her father's house ₍where she lived₎ as a child, then she can eat some of her father's food. But only people from a priest's family can eat this food.

¹⁴"A person might eat some of the holy food by mistake. That person must give the same amount to the priest, and he must give another fifth of the price of that food.

¹⁵"The people of Israel will give gifts to the Lord. Those gifts become holy. So the priest must not make those holy things not holy. ¹⁶If the priests treat those things as not holy, then they will add to their sin when they eat the holy food. I, the Lord, make them holy!"

¹⁷The Lord God said to Moses, ¹⁸"Tell Aaron and his sons and all the people of Israel: Maybe a citizen of Israel or a foreigner will want to bring an offering. Maybe it is for some special promise that person made. Or maybe it is some special sacrifice that person wanted to bring. ¹⁹⁻²⁰Those are gifts that the people bring because they really want to give a gift to God. You must not accept any offering that has anything wrong with it. I will not be happy with that gift! If the gift is a bull, or a sheep, or a goat, then that animal must be a male. And it must not have anything wrong with it!

²¹"A person might bring a fellowship offering to the Lord. That fellowship offering might be payment for a special promise that person made. Or maybe it is a special gift that person wanted to give to the Lord. It might be a bull or a sheep. But it must be healthy. There must be nothing wrong with that animal! ²²You must not offer to the Lord any animal that is blind, or has broken bones, or is crippled, or has a discharge,* or a bad skin disease. You must not offer sick animals on the fire of the Lord's altar.*

²³"Sometimes a bull or lamb will have a leg that is too long, or a foot that did not grow right. If a person wants to give that animal as a special gift to the Lord, then it will be accepted. But it will not be accepted as payment for a special promise that person made.

²⁴"If an animal has bruised, crushed, or torn testicles, then you must not offer that animal to the Lord.

²⁵"You must not take animals from foreigners as sacrifices to the Lord. Why? Because the animals might have been hurt in some way. They might have something wrong with them. They will not be accepted!"

²⁶The Lord said to Moses, ²⁷"When a calf, or a sheep, or a goat is born, it must stay seven days with its mother. Then on the eighth day and after,

---

clean Pure or acceptable to God for worship.
unclean Not pure or not acceptable to God for worship.
semen The fluid produced by a man's sexual organs.
widow(s) Women whose husbands have died. Often these women had no one to care for them.

discharge Fluid from a person's body, including pus from sores, a man's semen, or a woman's period flow.
altar A table or raised area used for offering sacrifices.

this animal will be accepted as a sacrifice offered by fire to the Lord. ²⁸But you must not kill the animal and its mother on the same day! This rule is the same for cows and sheep.

²⁹"If you want to offer some special offering of thanks to the Lord, then you are free to offer that gift. ₍But you must do it in a way that pleases God.₎ ³⁰You must eat the whole animal that day. You must not leave any of the meat for the next morning. I am the Lord!

³¹"Remember my commands, and obey them. I am the Lord! ³²Show respect for my holy name! I must be very special to the people of Israel. I, the Lord, have made you my special people. ³³I brought you from Egypt. I became your God. I am the Lord!"

Special Holidays

23 The Lord said to Moses, ²"Tell the people of Israel: You will announce the Lord's chosen festivals as holy meetings. These are my special holidays:

Sabbath

³"Work for six days. But the seventh day, the Sabbath, will be a special day of rest, a holy meeting. You must not do any work. It is a Sabbath to the Lord in all your homes.

Passover

⁴"These are the Lord's chosen holidays. You will announce the holy meetings at the times chosen for them. ⁵The Lord's Passover is on the 14th day of the first month* at twilight.*

Festival of Unleavened Bread

⁶"The Festival of Unleavened Bread* is on the 15th day of the same month *(Nisan)*. You will eat unleavened bread for seven days. ⁷On the first day of this holiday you will have a special meeting. You must not do any work ₍on that day₎. ⁸For seven days, you will bring sacrifices offered by fire to the Lord. Then there will be another special meeting on the seventh day. You must not do any work ₍on that day₎."

Festival of the First Harvests

⁹The Lord said to Moses, ¹⁰"Tell the people of Israel: You will enter the land that I will give you. You will reap its harvest. At that time, you must bring in the first sheaf* of your harvest to the priest. ¹¹The priest will wave the sheaf before the Lord. Then you will be accepted. The priest will wave the sheaf on Sunday morning.*

¹²"On the day when you wave the sheaf,* you will offer a one-year-old male lamb. There must be nothing wrong with that lamb. That lamb will be a burnt offering to the Lord. ¹³You must also offer a grain offering of 16 cups* of fine flour mixed with olive oil. You must also offer 1 quart* of wine. The smell of that offering will please the Lord. ¹⁴You must not eat any of the new grain, or fruit, or bread made from the new grain, until you bring that offering to your God. This law will always continue through your generations wherever you live.

Festival of Pentecost

¹⁵"From that Sunday morning,* (the day you bring the sheaf* for the wave offering) count seven weeks. ¹⁶On the Sunday following the seventh week, (that is 50 days later) you will bring a new grain offering to the Lord. ¹⁷On that day, bring two loaves of bread from your homes. That bread will be for a wave offering. Use yeast and 16 cups* of flour to make those loaves of bread. That will be your gift to the Lord from your first harvest.

¹⁸"One bull, one ram, and seven one-year-old male lambs will be offered with the grain offerings from the people. There must be nothing wrong with those animals. They will be a burnt offering to the Lord. They will be an offering by fire. Its smell will please the Lord. ¹⁹You will also offer one male goat for a sin offering and two one-year-old male lambs as a fellowship offering.

²⁰"The priest will wave them with the bread from the first harvest for a wave offering with two lambs before the Lord. They are holy to the Lord. They will belong to the priest. ²¹On that same day, you will call a holy meeting. You must not do any work. This law continues forever in all your homes.

---

first month Nisan, the first month of the Jewish calendar. It was during March-April.
twilight The time after the sun goes down, but before dark.
Unleavened Bread Bread made without yeast.
sheaf A stack of grain.
Sunday morning Literally, "the morning after the Sabbath."
16 cups Literally, "2/10 of an ephah."
1 quart Literally, "1/4 of a hin."

²²"Also, when you harvest the crops on your land, don't cut all the way to the corners of your field. Don't pick up the grain that falls on the ground. Leave those things for poor people and for foreigners traveling through your country. I am the Lord your God!"

Festival of Trumpets

²³Again the Lord said to Moses, ²⁴"Tell the people of Israel: On the first day of the seventh month, you must have a special day of rest. Blow the trumpet to remind the people that this is a holy meeting. ²⁵You must not do any work. You will bring an offering by fire to the Lord."

Day of Atonement

²⁶The Lord said to Moses, ²⁷"The Day of Atonement* will be on the tenth day of the seventh month. There will be a holy meeting. You must not eat food* and you must bring an offering by fire to the Lord. ²⁸You must not do any work on that day. Why? Because it is the Day of Atonement. On that day, ⌊the priests will go⌋ before the Lord and do the ceremony that makes you pure.*

²⁹"If any person refuses to fast* on this day, he must be separated from his people. ³⁰If a person does any work on this day, I *(God)* will destroy that person from among his people. ³¹You must not do any work at all. This is a law that continues forever for you, wherever you live. ³²It will be a special day of rest for you. You must not eat food.* You will start this special day of rest on the evening following the ninth day of the month.* This special day of rest continues from that evening until the next evening."

Festival of Shelters

³³Again the Lord said to Moses, ³⁴"Tell the people of Israel: On the 15th day of the seventh month is the Festival of Shelters. This holiday to the Lord will continue for seven days. ³⁵There will be a holy meeting on the first day. You must not do any work. ³⁶You will bring an offering by fire to the Lord for seven days. On the eighth day you will have another holy meeting. You will bring an offering by fire to the Lord. This will be a holy meeting. You must not do any work.

³⁷"Those are the Lord's special holidays. There will be holy meetings on those holidays. You will bring offerings by fire to the Lord—burnt offerings, grain offerings, sacrifices, and drink offerings. You will bring those gifts at the right time. ³⁸You will celebrate those holidays in addition to remembering the Lord's Sabbath* days. You will offer those gifts in addition to your other gifts to the Lord. You will offer those things in addition to any offerings you give as payment for your special promises. They will be in addition to any special offerings you want to give to the Lord.

³⁹"On the 15th day of the seventh month, when you have gathered in the crops of the land, you will celebrate the Lord's festival for seven days. The first day will be a special day of rest, and then the eighth day will be a special day of rest. ⁴⁰On the first day you will take good fruit from fruit trees. And you will take branches from palm trees, poplar trees and willow trees by the brook. You will celebrate before the Lord your God for seven days. ⁴¹You will celebrate this holiday to the Lord for seven days each year. This law will continue forever. You will celebrate this holiday in the seventh month. ⁴²You will live in temporary shelters for seven days. All the people born in Israel will live in those shelters. ⁴³Why? So all of your descendants* will know that I made the people of Israel live in temporary shelters during the time I brought them from Egypt. I am the Lord your God!"

⁴⁴So Moses told the people of Israel about all of the special meetings ⌊to honor⌋ the Lord.

Day of Atonement Also called "Yom Kippur"—the most important Jewish holy day. On this day the high priest went into the Most Holy Place and did the ceremony that atoned (covered or erased) the sins of the people.
not eat food Literally, "humble yourselves."
make ... pure Literally, "make atonement." The Hebrew word means "to cover," "to hide," or "to erase sins."
fast To live without food for a time of prayer and worship.
You must not eat food Literally, "You must humble yourselves."
evening following ... month According to Jewish time, the day starts at sunset.

Sabbath Saturday, a special day of rest and worship for Jews.
descendant(s) A person's children and their future families.

The Lampstand and the Holy Bread

24 The Lord said to Moses, ²"Command the people of Israel to bring to you pure oil from crushed olives. That oil is for the lamps. Those lamps must burn without stopping. ³Aaron will keep the light burning in the Meeting Tent* before the Lord from evening until morning. The light will be outside the curtain ₍that hangs₎ in front of the ₍Box of the₎ Agreement.* This law will continue forever. ⁴Aaron must always keep the lamps burning on the lampstand of pure gold before the Lord.

⁵"Take fine flour and bake twelve loaves with it. Use 16 cups* of flour for each loaf. ⁶Put them in two rows on the golden table before the Lord. Six loaves will be in each row. ⁷Put pure frankincense* on each row. This will help the Lord remember the offering by fire to the Lord. ⁸Every Sabbath* day Aaron will put the bread in order before the Lord. This must be done forever. This Agreement with the people of Israel will continue forever. ⁹That bread will belong to Aaron and his sons. They will eat the bread in a holy place. Why? Because that bread is one of the offerings made by fire to the Lord. That bread is Aaron's share forever."

The Man Who Cursed God

¹⁰There was a son of an Israelite woman. His father was an Egyptian. This Israelite woman's son was an Israelite. He was walking among the people of Israel, and he started fighting in camp. ¹¹The Israelite woman's son began cursing and saying bad things about the Lord's name. So the people brought this man to Moses. (The name of the man's mother was Shelomith, the daughter of Dibri, from the family group of Dan.) ¹²The people held the man as a prisoner and waited for the Lord's command to be made clear to them.

¹³Then the Lord said to Moses, ¹⁴"Bring the man who cursed to a place outside the camp. Then bring together all the people who heard him curse. Those people will put their hands on his head.* And then all the people must throw stones at him and kill him. ¹⁵You must tell the people of Israel: If a person curses his God, then he must be punished.* ¹⁶Any person who speaks against the name of the Lord must be put to death. All the people must stone him. Foreigners must be punished just like the person who was born in Israel. If a person curses the ₍Lord's₎ name, then he must be put to death.

¹⁷"And if one person kills another person, he must be put to death. ¹⁸The person who kills an animal ₍that belongs to another person₎ must give another animal to take its place.*

¹⁹"And if a person causes an injury to his neighbor, then the same kind of injury must be given that person. ²⁰A broken bone for a broken bone; an eye for an eye; and a tooth for a tooth. The same kind of injury a person gives another person must be given that person. ²¹So if a person kills an animal, then that person must pay for the animal. But if a person kills another person, then he must be put to death.

²²"The law will be ₍fair₎—it will be the same for foreigners and for people from your own country. Why? Because I am the Lord your God."

²³Then Moses spoke to the people of Israel, and they brought the man who cursed to a place outside the camp. Then they killed him with stones. So the people of Israel did just what the Lord had commanded Moses.

A Time of Rest for the Land

25 The Lord spoke to Moses at Mount Sinai. The Lord said, ²"Tell the people of Israel: You will enter the land that I am giving to you. At that time, you must let the land have a special time of rest. This will be a special time of rest to honor the Lord. ³You will plant ₍seed₎ in your field for six years. You will trim the plants in your grape fields for six years and bring in its fruits. ⁴But during the seventh year, you will let the land rest. This will be a special time of rest to honor the Lord. You must not plant seed in your field or trim the plants in your grape fields. ⁵You must not

---

Meeting Tent The Holy Tent (tabernacle) where the people of Israel went to meet with God.

Agreement Literally, "Proof." The flat stones with the Ten Commandments written on them. These were proof of the Agreement between God and the people of Israel.

16 cups Literally, "2/10 of an ephah."

frankincense Very special dried tree sap. Burned to make a sweet-smelling smoke, it was offered as a gift to God.

Sabbath Saturday, a special day of rest and worship for Jews.

put their hands on his head This shows that all those people were sharing in punishing the man.

he must be punished Literally, "he must bear his sin."

give another animal to take its place Literally, "pay for it; life for life."

cut the crops that grow by themselves after your harvest. You must not gather the grapes from your vines that are not trimmed. The land will have a year of rest.

⁶"₍The land will have a year of rest,₎ but you will still have enough food. There will be enough food for your men and women servants. There will be food for your hired workers and for the foreigners living in your country. ⁷And there will be enough food for your cows and other animals to eat.

Jubilee — The Year of Release

⁸"You will also count seven groups of seven years. This will be 49 years. During that time, there will be seven years of rest for the land. ⁹On the Day of Atonement,* you must blow a ram's horn. That will be on the tenth day of the seventh month. You must blow the ram's horn through the whole country. ¹⁰You will make the 50th year a special year. You will announce freedom for all the people living in your country. This time will be called "Jubilee."* Each of you will go back to his own property.* And each of you will go back to his family. ¹¹The 50th year will be a special celebration* for you. Don't plant seeds. Don't harvest the crops that grow by themselves. Don't gather grapes from the vines that are not trimmed. ¹²That year is Jubilee. It will be a holy time for you. You will eat the crops that come from the field. ¹³In the year of Jubilee, each person will go back to his own property."

¹⁴"Don't cheat your neighbor when you sell your land to him. And don't let him cheat you when you buy land from him. ¹⁵If you want to buy your neighbor's land, then count the number of years since the last Jubilee, ₍and use that number to decide the right price₎. Why? Because he is really only selling you the rights for harvesting crops ₍until the next Jubilee₎. ¹⁶If there are many years ₍before the next Jubilee₎, then the price will be high. If the years are few, then the price will be lower. Why? Because your neighbor is really only selling a number of crops to you. ₍At the next Jubilee the land will again belong to his family.₎ ¹⁷You must not cheat each other. You must honor your God! I am the Lord your God!

¹⁸"Remember my laws and rules. Obey them! Then you will live safely in your country. ¹⁹And the land will produce good crops for you. Then you will have plenty of food and you will live safely on the land.

²⁰"But maybe you will say, 'If we don't plant seeds or gather our crops, we will not have anything to eat during the seventh year.' ²¹₍Don't worry!₎ I will order my blessing to come to you during the sixth year. The land will continue growing crops for three years. ²²When you plant in the eighth year, you will still be eating things from the old crop. You will eat the old crop until the ninth year, when the crop ₍you planted in the eighth year₎ comes in.

Property Laws

²³"The land really belongs to me. So you can't really sell it permanently. You are only foreigners and travelers living ₍on my land₎ with me. ²⁴People might sell their land, but the family will always get their land back. ²⁵A person in your country might become very poor. He might be so poor that he must sell his property. So his close relative must come and buy back the property for his relative. ²⁶A person might not have a close relative to buy back his land for him. But he might get enough money to buy back the land for himself. ²⁷Then he must count the years since the land was sold. ₍He must use that number to decide how much to pay for the land.₎ Then he must buy back the land. Then the land will be his property again. ²⁸But if this person can't find enough money to get the land back for himself, then what he has sold will stay in the hands of the person who bought it until the year of Jubilee.* Then during that special celebration, the land will go back ₍to the first owner's family₎. So the property will again belong to the right family.

²⁹"If a person sells a home in a walled city, then he still has the right to get it back until a full year after he sold the house. His right to get the house back will continue one year. ³⁰But if ₍the owner does not₎ buy back the house before a full

---

Day of Atonement Also called "Yom Kippur"—the most important Jewish holy day. On this day the high priest went into the Most Holy Place and did the ceremony that atoned (covered or erased) the sins of the people.

Jubilee The word comes from the Hebrew word for the horn that was blown at this time.

own property In Israel, the land belonged to the family or family group. A person might sell his land, but at Jubilee that land again belonged to the family and family group that it was originally given to.

special celebration Literally, "Jubilee."

descendant(s) A person's children and their future families.

year is finished, then the house that is in the walled city will belong to the person who bought it, and to his descendants.* The house will not go back ₍to the first owner₎ at the time of Jubilee.* ³¹Towns without walls around them will be treated like open fields. So houses built in those small towns will go back to the first owners at the time of Jubilee.*

³²"But about the cities of the Levites: The Levites can buy back their houses at any time in the cities that belong to them. ³³If a person buys a house from a Levite, that house in the Levites' city will again belong to the Levites at the time of Jubilee.* Why? Because houses in Levite cities belong to people from the family group of Levi. The people of Israel gave those cities to the Levite people. ³⁴Also, the fields and pastures around the Levite cities can't be sold. Those fields belong to the Levites forever.

Rules for Slave Owners

³⁵"Maybe a person from your own country* will become too poor to support himself. You must let him live with you like a visitor. ³⁶Don't charge him any interest ₍on money you might loan to him₎. Respect your God, and let your brother* live with you. ³⁷Don't charge him interest on any money you lend him. And don't try to make a profit from the food you sell him. ³⁸I am the Lord your God. I brought you out of the land of Egypt to give the land of Canaan to you and to become your God.

³⁹"Maybe a person from your own country* will become so poor that he sells himself as a slave to you. You must not make him work like a slave. ⁴⁰He will be like a hired worker and a visitor with you until the year of Jubilee.* ⁴¹Then he can leave you. He can take his children and go back to his family. He can go back to the property of his ancestors.* ⁴²Why? Because they are my servants! I brought them out ₍of slavery₎ in Egypt. They must not become slaves ₍again₎. ⁴³You must not be a cruel master to this person. You must respect your God.

⁴⁴"About your men and women slaves: You may get men and women slaves from the other nations around you. ⁴⁵Also, you may get children as slaves if they come from the families of the foreigners living in your land. Those children slaves will belong to you. ⁴⁶You may even pass these foreign slaves on to your children after you die so that they will belong to your children. They will be your slaves forever. You may make slaves of these foreigners. But you must not be a cruel master over your own brothers, the people of Israel.

⁴⁷"Maybe a foreigner or visitor among you will become rich. Maybe a person from your own country* will become poor, so that he sells himself as a slave to a foreigner living among you or to a member of a foreigner's family. ⁴⁸That person will have the right to be bought back ₍and become free₎. One of his brothers* can buy him back. ⁴⁹Or his uncle or his cousin can buy him back. Or one of his close relatives from his family can buy him back. Or if the person gets enough money, he can pay the money himself ₍and become free again₎.

⁵⁰"How do you decide the price? You must count the years from the time he sold himself to the foreigner up to the next year of Jubilee.* Use that number to decide the price. Why? Because really the person only 'hired' him for a few years! ⁵¹If there are still many years ₍before the year of Jubilee₎, then the person must give back a large part of the price. It all depends on the numbers of years. ⁵²If only a few years are left until the year of Jubilee, then the person must pay a small part of the original price. ⁵³But that person will live like a hired man with the foreigner every year. Don't let the foreigner be a cruel master over that person.

⁵⁴"That person will become free, even if no one buys him back. At the year of Jubilee* he and his children will become free. ⁵⁵Why? Because the people of Israel are my servants. They are the servants that I brought out of ₍slavery in₎ Egypt. I am the Lord your God."

Jubilee The word comes from the Hebrew word for the horn that was blown at this time. See Leviticus 25:9.
a person ... country Literally, "one of your brothers."
your brother Or, "the person from your own country."
ancestors Literally, "fathers," meaning a person's parents, grandparents, and all the people they are descended from.

person ... country Literally, "one of your brothers."
One ... brothers Or, "A person from his own country."
memorial A stone marker to help people remember something special. In ancient Israel, people often set up stone markers as places to worship false gods.

Rewards for Obeying God

26 "Don't make idols for yourselves. Don't set up statues or memorials* in your land to bow down to. Why? Because I am the Lord your God!

²"Remember my special days of rest* and honor my holy place. I am the Lord!

³"Remember my laws and commands, and obey them! ⁴If you do those things, then I will give you rains at the time they should come. The land will grow crops and the trees of the field will grow their fruit. ⁵Your threshing* will continue until it is time to gather grapes. And your grape gathering will continue until it is time to plant. Then you will have plenty to eat. And you will live safely in your land. ⁶I will give peace to your country. You will lie down in peace. No person will come to make you afraid. I will keep harmful animals out of your country. And armies will not come through your country.

⁷"You will chase your enemies, and defeat them. You will kill them with your sword. ⁸Five of you will chase 100 men, and 100 of you will chase 10,000 men. You will defeat your enemies and kill them with your sword.

⁹"Then I will turn to you. I will let you have many children. I will keep my Agreement with you. ¹⁰You will have enough crops to last for more than a year. You will harvest the new crops. But then you will have to throw out the old crops to make room for the new crops! ¹¹Also, I will place my Holy Tent* among you. I will not turn away from you! ¹²I will walk with you and be your God. And you will be my people. ¹³I am the Lord your God. You were slaves in Egypt. But I brought you out of Egypt. You were bent low from the heavy weights you carried as slaves. But I broke the poles that were on your shoulders. I let you walk tall again!

Punishment for Not Obeying God

¹⁴"But if you don't obey me and all my commands, then these bad things will happen. ¹⁵If you refuse to obey my laws and commands, then you have broken my Agreement. ¹⁶If you do that, then I will cause terrible things to happen to you. I will cause you to have disease and fever. They will destroy your eyes and take away your life. You will not have success when you plant your seed. And your enemies will eat your crops! ¹⁷I will be against you, so your enemies will defeat you. Those enemies hate you, and they will rule over you. You will run away even when no one is chasing you.

¹⁸"After these things, if you still don't obey me, I will punish you seven times more for your sins. ¹⁹And I will also destroy the ⌊great cities that⌋ make you proud. The skies will not give rain, and the earth will not produce crops.* ²⁰You will work hard, but it will not help. Your land will not give any crops, and your trees will not grow their fruit.

²¹"If you still turn against me and refuse to obey me, then I will beat you seven times harder! The more you sin, the more you will be punished! ²²I will send wild animals against you. They will take your children away from you. They will destroy your animals. They will kill many of your people. ⌊People will be afraid to travel—⌋the roads will be empty!

²³"If you don't learn your lesson after all those things, and if you still turn against me, ²⁴then I will also turn against you. I—yes, I *(the Lord)*—will punish you seven times for your sins. ²⁵You will have broken my Agreement, so I will punish you. I will bring armies against you. You will go into your cities for safety. But I will cause diseases to spread among you. And your enemies will defeat you. ²⁶I will give you a share of the grain ⌊left in that city⌋. ⌊But there will be very little food to eat.⌋ Ten women will be able to cook all their bread in one oven. They will measure each piece of bread. You will eat, but you will still be hungry!

²⁷"If you still refuse to listen to me, and if you still turn against me, ²⁸then I will really show my anger! I—yes, I *(the Lord)*—will punish you seven times for your sins! ²⁹⌊You will become so hungry that⌋ you will eat the bodies of your sons and daughters. ³⁰I will destroy your high places.* I will cut down your incense* altars.* I will put

---

special days of rest Or, "Sabbaths."
threshing Beating grain to remove its hulls.
Holy Tent Or, "tabernacle." The place God came to live among his people.
The skies ... crops Literally, "Your skies will be like iron, your land like bronze."
high places Places for worshiping God or false gods. These places were usually on the hills and mountains.
incense Special dried tree sap. Burned to make a sweet-smelling smoke, it was offered as a gift to God.
altars A table or raised area used for offering sacrifices.
idols Statues of false gods that people worshiped.

your dead bodies on the dead bodies of your idols.* You will be very disgusting to me. ³¹I will destroy your cities. I will make your holy places empty. I will stop smelling your offerings. ³²I will make your land empty. And your enemies that come to live there will be shocked at it. ³³I will scatter you among the nations. I will pull out my sword and destroy you. Your land will become empty and your cities will be destroyed.

³⁴"You will be taken to your enemy's country. Your country will be empty. So your land will finally get its rest. The land will enjoy its time of rest. ³⁵⌊The law says the land should have a year of rest every seven years.⌋ During the time that the land is empty, it will get the time of rest that you did not give it while you lived there. ³⁶The survivors* will lose their courage in the land of their enemies. They will be scared of everything. They will run around like a leaf being blown by the wind. They will run like someone is chasing them with a sword. They will fall even when no one is chasing them! ³⁷They will run like someone is chasing them with a sword. They will fall over each other— even when no person is chasing them.

"You will not be strong enough to stand up against your enemies. ³⁸You will be lost in other nations. You will disappear in the land of your enemies. ³⁹So the survivors* will rot away in their sin in their enemies' countries. They will rot away in their sins just like their ancestors* did.

There Is Always Hope

⁴⁰"But maybe the people will confess (admit) their sins. And maybe they will confess the sins of their ancestors.* Maybe they will admit that they turned against me. Maybe they will admit that they sinned against me. ⁴¹Maybe they will admit that I turned against them and brought them into the land of their enemies. Those people will be like strangers to me. But maybe they will become humble* and accept the punishment for their sin. ⁴²If they do, then I will remember my Agreement with Jacob. I will remember my Agreement with Isaac. I will remember my Agreement with Abraham. And I will remember the land.

⁴³"The land will be empty. The land will enjoy its time of rest. Then the survivors* will accept the punishment for their sins. They will learn that they were punished because they hated my laws and refused to obey my rules. ⁴⁴They truly sinned. ⌊But if they come to me for help,⌋ I will not turn away from them. I will listen to them, even if they are in the land of their enemies. I will not completely destroy them. I will not break my Agreement with them. Why? Because I am the Lord their God! ⁴⁵For them, I will remember the Agreement with their ancestors.* I brought their ancestors out of the land of Egypt so I could become their God. The other nations saw those things. I am the Lord!"

⁴⁶Those are the laws, rules and teachings that the Lord gave to the people of Israel. ⌊Those laws are the Agreement⌋ between the Lord and the people of Israel. The Lord gave those laws to Moses at Mount Sinai ⌊and Moses gave them to the people⌋.

Promises Are Important

27 The Lord said to Moses, ²"Tell the people of Israel: A person might make a special promise to the Lord. That person might promise to give a person to the Lord. ⌊That person will then serve the Lord in a special way.⌋ The priest must set a price for that person. ⌊People will have to pay that price if they want to buy the person back from the Lord.⌋ ³The price for a man from 20 to 60 years old is 50 shekels* of silver. (You must use the official measure* for the silver.) ⁴The price for a woman ⌊that is 20 to 60 years old⌋ is 30 shekels. ⁵The price for a man from 5 to 20 years old is 20 shekels. The price for a woman ⌊from 5 to 20 years old⌋ is 10 shekels. ⁶The price for a baby boy from one month to five years old is 5 shekels. For a baby girl, the price is 3 shekels. ⁷The price for a man who is 60 years old or older is 15 shekels. The price for a woman is 10 shekels.

⁸"If a person is too poor to pay the price, then bring that person to the priest. The priest will decide how much money the person can afford to pay.

---

survivor(s) people who escaped some disaster. Here, this means the Jewish people who survived the destruction of Judah and Israel by its enemy's armies.
ancestors Literally, "fathers," meaning a person's parents, grandparents, and all the people they are descended from.
Those people ... humble Literally, "If they humble their uncircumcised heart."
shekels A shekel is 2/5 of an ounce.
official measure Literally, "holy shekel," the official standard of measure used in the tabernacle or temple.

Gifts to the Lord

⁹"Some animals can be used as sacrifices to the Lord. If a person brings one of those animals, then that animal will become holy. ¹⁰That person promises to give that animal to the Lord, so that person must not try to put another animal in its place. He must not try to change it for something else. He must not try to change a good animal for a bad animal. He must not change a bad animal for a good animal. If that person does try to change animals, then both animals will become holy—both animals will belong to the Lord.

¹¹"Some animals can't be offered as sacrifices to the Lord. If a person brings one of those unclean* animals to the Lord, then that animal must be brought to the priest. ¹²The priest will decide a price for that animal. It does not make any difference if the animal is good or bad. If the priest decides on a price, then that is the price for the animal. ¹³If the person wants to buy back the animal,* then he must add a fifth to the price.

The Value of a House

¹⁴"Now if a person dedicates his house as holy to the Lord, then the priest must decide its price. It does not make any difference if the house is good or bad. If the priest decides on a price, then that is the price for the house. ¹⁵But if the person who gave the house wants to get it back, then he must add a fifth to the price. Then the house will belong to that person.

Value of Property

¹⁶"If a person dedicates part of his fields to the Lord, the value of those fields will depend on how much seed is needed to plant it. It will be 50 shekels* of silver for each homer* of barley seed. ¹⁷If the person gives his field to God during the year of Jubilee,* then its value will be whatever the priest decides. ¹⁸But if the person gives his field after the Jubilee, then the priest must calculate its exact price. He must count the number of years to the next year of Jubilee. Then he must use that number to decide the price. ¹⁹If the person who gave the field wants to buy back the field, then he must add a fifth to that price. Then the field will again belong to that person. ²⁰If the person does not buy back the field, then the field will always belong to the priests. If the land is sold to someone else, then that first person can't buy back the land. ²¹If the person did not buy back the land, then at the year of Jubilee,* the field will remain holy to the Lord—it will belong to the priest forever! It will be like land that was given completely to the Lord.

²²"If a person dedicates to the Lord a field that he has bought, and it is not a part of his family's property,* ²³then the priest must count the years to the year of Jubilee* and decide the price for the land. Then that land will belong to the Lord. ²⁴At the year of Jubilee, the land will go to the original owner. It will go back to the family that owns the land.

²⁵"You must use the official measure* in paying those prices. The shekel by that measure weighs 20 gerahs.*

Value of Animals

²⁶"People can give cows and sheep as special gifts to the Lord. But if the animal is the firstborn, then that animal already belongs to the Lord. So people can't give those animals as special gifts. ²⁷People must give firstborn animals to the Lord. But if the firstborn animal is an unclean* animal, then the person must buy back that animal. The priest will decide the price of the animal, and the person must add a fifth to that price. If the person does not buy back that animal, then the priest must sell the animal for the price he decided.

Special Gifts

²⁸"There is a special kind of gift* that people give to the Lord. That gift belongs only to the Lord. That gift cannot be bought back or sold. That gift belongs to the Lord. That type of gift

---

unclean Not pure or not acceptable to God for worship.
buy back the animal See Exodus 13:1-16 for the laws about giving to God or "buying back" firstborn children or animals.
shekels A shekel was 2/5 of an ounce.
homer A dry measure equal to about 6 bushels.
Jubilee The word comes from the Hebrew word for the horn that was blown at this time. See Leviticus 25:9.
family's property That is, land that was owned originally by his family and family group.
official measure Literally, "holy shekel," the official standard of measure used in the tabernacle or temple.
gerahs A gerah is 1/50 of an ounce.
special kind of gift This usually means things taken in war. Those things (gifts) belonged only to the Lord, so they could not be used for anything else.

includes people, animals, and fields from the family property.

²⁹"If that special kind of gift* to the Lord is a person, then that person cannot be bought back. That person must be killed.

³⁰"A tenth of all crops belong to the Lord. This means the crops from fields and the fruit from trees—a tenth belongs to the Lord. ³¹So if a person wants to get back his tenth, he must add a fifth to its price ⌊and then buy it back⌋.

³²"⌊The priests will⌋ take every tenth animal from a person's cows or sheep. Every tenth animal will belong to the Lord. ³³The owner should not worry if the chosen animal is good or bad. He should not change the animal for another animal. If he decides to change it for another animal, then both animals will belong to the Lord. That animal can't be bought back."

³⁴Those are the commands that the Lord gave Moses at Mount Sinai for the people of Israel.

Numbers

Moses Counts the People of Israel

1 The Lord spoke to Moses in the Meeting Tent.* This was in the Sinai Desert. It was on the first day of the second month of the second year after the people of Israel left Egypt. The Lord said to Moses: ²"Count all the people of Israel. List the name of each man with his family and his family group. ³You and Aaron must count all the men of Israel who are 20 years old or older. (These are the men who serve in the army of Israel.) List them by their group.* ⁴One man from each and every family group ₍will help you₎. This man will be the leader of his family group. ⁵These are the names of the men who will stand with you ₍and help you₎:

> from Reuben's family group—Elizur son of Shedeur;
> ⁶ from Simeon's family group—Shelumiel son of Zurishaddai;
> ⁷ from Judah's family group—Nahshon son of Amminadab;
> ⁸ from Issachar's family group—Nethanel son of Zuar;
> ⁹ from Zebulun's family group—Eliab son of Helon;
> ¹⁰ from the descendants of Joseph
> from Ephraim's family group—Elishama son of Ammihud;
> from Manasseh's family group—Gamaliel son of Pedahzur;
> ¹¹ from Benjamin's family group—Abidan son of Gideoni;
> ¹² from Dan's family group—Ahiezer son of Ammishaddai;
> ¹³ from Asher's family group—Pagiel son of Ocran;
> ¹⁴ from Gad's family group—Eliasaph son of Deuel;*
> ¹⁵ from Naphtali's family group—Ahira son of Enan."

¹⁶All those men are the leaders of their families. The people also chose them to be leaders of their family groups. ¹⁷Moses and Aaron took these men who had been chosen to be leaders. ¹⁸And Moses and Aaron called all the people of Israel together. Then the people were listed by their families and their family groups. All the men who were 20 years old or older were listed. ¹⁹Moses did exactly what the Lord commanded—Moses counted the people while they were in the Sinai desert.

²⁰They counted Reuben's family group. (Reuben was the firstborn* son of Israel.) The names of all the men who were 20 years old or older and able to serve in the army were listed. They were listed with their families and family groups. ²¹The total number of men counted from Reuben's family group was 46,500.

²²They counted Simeon's family group. The names of all the men who were 20 years old or older and able to serve in the army were listed. They were listed with their families and family groups. ²³The total number of men counted from Simeon's family group was 59,300.

²⁴They counted Gad's family group. The names of all the men who were 20 years old or older and able to serve in the army were listed. They were listed with their families and family groups. ²⁵The total number of men counted from Gad's family group was 45,650.

²⁶They counted Judah's family group. The names of all the men who were 20 years old or older and able to serve in the army were listed.

Meeting Tent The Holy Tent (tabernacle) where the people of Israel went to meet with God.
group Or, "division." This is a military term that shows Israel was organized like an army.
Deuel Or, "Reuel."
firstborn The first child born into a family. The firstborn son was very important.

They were listed with their families and family groups. ²⁷The total number of men counted from Judah's family group was 74,600.

²⁸They counted Issachar's family group. The names of all the men who were 20 years old or older and able to serve in the army were listed. They were listed with their families and family groups. ²⁹The total number of men counted from Issachar's family group was 54,400.

³⁰They counted Zebulun's family group. The names of all the men who were 20 years old or older and able to serve in the army were listed. They were listed with their families and family groups. ³¹The total number of men counted from Zebulun's family group was 57,400.

³²They counted Ephraim's family group. (Ephraim was Joseph's son.) The names of all the men who were 20 years old or older and able to serve in the army were listed. They were listed with their families and family groups. ³³The total number of men counted from Ephraim's family group was 40,500.

³⁴They counted Manasseh's family group. (Manasseh was also Joseph's son.) The names of all the men who were 20 years old or older and able to serve in the army were listed. They were listed with their families and family groups. ³⁵The total number of men counted from Manasseh's family group was 32,200.

³⁶They counted Benjamin's family group. The names of all the men who were 20 years old or older and able to serve in the army were listed. They were listed with their families and family groups. ³⁷The total number of men counted from Benjamin's family group was 35,400.

³⁸They counted Dan's family group. The names of all the men who were 20 years old or older and able to serve in the army were listed. They were listed with their families and family groups. ³⁹The total number of men counted from Dan's family group was 62,700.

⁴⁰They counted Asher's family group. The names of all the men who were 20 years old or older and able to serve in the army were listed. They were listed with their families and family groups. ⁴¹The total number of men counted from Asher's family group was 41,500.

⁴²They counted Naphtali's family group. The names of all the men who were 20 years old or older and able to serve in the army were listed. They were listed by name with their families and family groups. ⁴³The total number of men counted from Naphtali's family group was 53,400.

⁴⁴Moses, Aaron, and the twelve leaders of Israel counted these men. (There was one leader from each family group.) ⁴⁵They counted every man who was 20 years old or older and able to serve in the army. Each man was listed with his family. ⁴⁶The total number of men counted was 603,550 men.

⁴⁷The families from the Levi family group were not counted with the other people of Israel. ⁴⁸The Lord had told Moses: ⁴⁹"Don't count the men from Levi's family group or include them with the other people of Israel. ⁵⁰Tell the people of Levi that they are responsible for the Holy Tent* of the Agreement. They must take care of that tent and all the things that are with it. They must carry the Holy Tent and everything in it. They must make their camp around it and take care of it. ⁵¹Whenever the Holy Tent is moved, the people of Levi must do it. Whenever the Holy Tent is set up, the people of Levi must do it. They are the people who will take care of the Holy Tent. If any person who is not from Levi's family group tries to take care of the tent, he must be killed. ⁵²The people of Israel will make their camps in separate groups.* Each person should camp near his family flag. ⁵³But the people of Levi must make their camp around the Holy Tent. The people of Levi will guard the Holy Tent of the Agreement. ₍They will protect the Holy Tent₎ so that nothing bad will happen to the people of Israel."

⁵⁴So the people of Israel obeyed all the things that the Lord commanded Moses.

The Camp Arrangement

2 The Lord said to Moses and Aaron: ²"The people of Israel should make their camps around the Meeting Tent.* Each group* will have its own special flag, and each person will camp near his group's flag."

³The flag of the camp of Judah will be on the east side, where the sun rises. The people of Judah will camp near its flag. The leader of the people of Judah is Nahshon son of Amminadab. ⁴There are 74,600 men in his group.*

⁵Issachar's family group will camp next to Judah's family group. The leader of the people of

---

Holy Tent Or, "tabernacle," the tent where God came to live among his people.

group(s) Or, "division(s)." This is a military term that shows Israel was organized like an army.

Meeting Tent The Holy Tent (tabernacle) where the people of Israel went to meet with God.

Issachar is Nethanel son of Zuar. ⁶There are 54,400 men in his group.*

⁷Zebulun's family group will also camp next to Judah's family group. The leader of the people of Zebulun is Eliab son of Helon. ⁸There are 57,400 men in his group.*

⁹There is a total of 186,400 men in Judah's camp. All these men are divided into their different family groups. Judah will be the first group to move when the people travel from one place to another.

¹⁰The flag of Reuben's camp will be south of the Holy Tent.* Each group will camp near its flag. The leader of the people of Reuben is Elizur son of Shedeur. ¹¹There are 46,500 people in this group.*

¹²Simeon's family group will camp next to Reuben's family group. The leader of the people of Simeon is Shelumiel son of Zurishaddai. ¹³There are 59,300 people in this group.*

¹⁴Gad's family group will also camp next to the people of Reuben. The leader of the people of Gad is Eliasaph son of Deuel.* ¹⁵There are 45,650 people in this group.*

¹⁶There are 151,450 men in all the groups* in Reuben's camp. Reuben's camp will be the second group to move when the people travel from place to place.

¹⁷When the people travel, Levi's camp will move next. The Meeting Tent* will be with them between the other camps. The people will make their camps in the same order that they move. Each person will be with his family flag.

¹⁸The flag of the Camp of Ephraim will be on the west side. The family groups* of Ephraim will camp there. The leader of the people of Ephraim is Elishama son of Ammihud. ¹⁹There are 40,500 people in this group.*

²⁰Manasseh's family group will camp next to Ephraim's family. The leader of the people of Manasseh is Gamaliel son of Pedahzur. ²¹There are 32,200 people in this group.*

²²Benjamin's family group will also camp next to Ephraim's family. The leader of the people of Benjamin is Abidan son of Gideoni. ²³There are 35,400 people in this group.*

²⁴There are 108,100 men in Ephraim's camp. They will be the third family to move when the people travel from one place to another.

²⁵The flag of Dan's camp will be on the north side. The family groups* of Dan will camp there. The leader of the people of Dan is Ahiezer son of Ammishaddai. ²⁶There are 62,700 people in this group.*

²⁷The people from Asher's family group will camp next to Dan's family group. The leader of the people of Asher is Pagiel son of Ocran. ²⁸There are 41,500 people in this group.*

²⁹Naphtali's family group will also camp next to Dan's family group. The leader of the people of Naphtali is Ahira son of Enan. ³⁰There are 53,400 people in this group.*

³¹There are 157,600 men in Dan's camp. They will be the last family to move when the people travel from place to place. Each person will be with his family's flag.

³²So those were the people of Israel. They were counted by families. The total number of Israelites in the camps, counted by groups,* is 603,550. ³³Moses obeyed the Lord and did not count the Levites with the other people of Israel.

³⁴So the people of Israel did everything the Lord told Moses. Each group camped under its own flag. And each person stayed with his own family and family group.

Aaron's Family, the Priests

3 This is the family history of Aaron and Moses at the time the Lord talked to Moses on Mount Sinai.

²Aaron had four sons. Nadab was the firstborn* son. Then there were Abihu, Eleazar, and Ithamar. ³These sons were the chosen* priests.

These sons were given the special work of serving the Lord as priests. ⁴But Nadab and Abihu died ₍because they sinned₎ while serving the Lord. They used fire that the Lord did not allow when they made an offering to the Lord. So Nadab and Abihu died there, in the Sinai desert. They had no sons, so Eleazar and Ithamar took their place and served the Lord as priests. This happened while their father Aaron was still alive.

---

group(s) Or, "division(s)." This is a military term that shows Israel was organized like an army.
Holy Tent Or, "tabernacle," the tent where God came to live among his people.
Deuel Or, "Reuel."
Meeting Tent The Holy Tent (tabernacle) where the people of Israel went to meet with God.

firstborn The first child born into a family. The firstborn son was very important in ancient times.
chosen Or, "anointed." A special oil was poured on their heads to show they were chosen by God.

Levites—the Priests' Helpers

⁵The Lord said to Moses, ⁶"Bring all the people from Levi's family group. Bring them to Aaron the priest. Those people will be Aaron's helpers. ⁷The Levites will help Aaron when he serves at the Meeting Tent.* And the Levites will help all the people ₍of Israel₎ when they come to worship at the Holy Tent.* ⁸The people of Israel should protect all the things in the Meeting Tent; it is their duty. But the Levites will serve the people of Israel by caring for these things. This will be their way of worshiping at the Holy Tent.

⁹"Give the Levites to Aaron and his sons. The Levites were chosen from all the people of Israel to help Aaron and his sons.

¹⁰"Appoint Aaron and his sons to be priests. They must do their duty and serve as priests. Any other person who tries to come near the holy things* must be killed."

¹¹The Lord also said to Moses, ¹²"I told you that every family of Israel must give their firstborn* son to me₎—but now I am choosing the Levites to serve me. They will be mine. So all the other people of Israel will not have to give their firstborn sons to me.

¹³"When you were in Egypt, I killed all the firstborn* children of the Egyptian people. At that time, I took all of the firstborn children of Israel to be mine. All of the firstborn children and all the firstborn animals are mine. ₍But now I am giving your firstborn children back to you, and I am making the Levites mine.₎ I am the Lord."

¹⁴The Lord again talked to Moses in the Sinai desert. The Lord said, ¹⁵"Count all the families and family groups in Levi's family group. Count every man or boy that is a month old or older." ¹⁶So Moses obeyed the Lord. He counted them all.

¹⁷Levi had three sons. Their names were: Gershon, Kohath, and Merari. ¹⁸Each son was the leader of several family groups.

The Gershon family groups were: Libni and Shimei.

¹⁹The Kohath family groups were: Amram, Izhar, Hebron, and Uzziel.

²⁰The Merari family groups were: Mahli and Mushi.

Those are the families that belonged to Levi's family group.

²¹The families of Libni and Shimei belonged to the family of Gershon. They were the Gershonite family groups. ²²There were 7,500 men and boys over one month old in these two family groups. ²³The Gershonite family groups were told to camp in the west. They made their camp behind the Holy Tent.* ²⁴The leader of the family groups of the Gershonite people was Eliasaph son of Lael. ²⁵In the Meeting Tent,* the Gershonite people had the job of taking care of the Holy Tent, the outer tent, and the covering. They also took care of the curtain at the entrance of the Meeting Tent. ²⁶They cared for the curtain in the courtyard. And they cared for the curtain at the entrance of the courtyard. This courtyard was around the Holy Tent and the altar.* And they cared for the ropes and for everything that was used with the curtains.

²⁷The families of Amram, Izhar, Hebron, and Uzziel, belonged to the family of Kohath. They were the Kohathite family groups. ²⁸In this family group there were 8,300* men and boys a month old or over. The Kohathite people were given the job of taking care of ₍the things in₎ the holy place. ²⁹The Kohathite family groups were given the area to the south of the Holy Tent.* This was the area where they camped. ³⁰The leader of the Kohathite family groups was Elizaphan son of Uzziel. ³¹Their job was to take care of the Holy Box,* the table, the lampstand, the altars, and the dishes of the Holy Place.* They also cared for the curtain and all the things that were used with the curtain.

³²The leader over the leaders of the Levite people was Eleazar son of Aaron the priest. Eleazar was in charge of all the people that took care of the holy things.

³³⁻³⁴The family groups of Mahli and Mushi belonged to the Merari family. There were 6,200 men and boys that were one month old or older in the Mahli family group. ³⁵The leader of the Merari family group was Zuriel son of Abihail. This

---

Meeting Tent The Holy Tent (tabernacle) where the people of Israel went to meet with God.
Holy Tent Or, "tabernacle," the tent where God came to live among his people.
tries ... holy things Or, "tries to serve as a priest."
firstborn The first child born into a family. The firstborn son was very important in ancient times.
altar A table or raised area used for offering sacrifices.
8,300 Some copies of the ancient Greek version have "8,300." The Hebrew copies have "8,600." See Num. 3:22, 28, 34, 39.
Holy Box Or, "ark of the Covenant," the box containing the flat stones with the Ten Commandments written on them and other things that proved God was with the people of Israel during their time in the Sinai desert.
Holy Place One of the rooms in the Holy Tent.

family group was given the area to the north of the Holy Tent.* This is the area where they camped. ³⁶The people from the Merari family were given the job of caring for the frames of the Holy Tent. They cared for all the braces, posts, bases, and everything that was used with the frames of the Holy Tent. ³⁷They also cared for all the posts in the courtyard around the Holy Tent. This included all the bases, tent pegs, and ropes.

³⁸Moses, Aaron, and his sons camped east of the Holy Tent,* in front of the Meeting Tent. They were given the work of caring for the Holy Place. They did this for all the people of Israel. Any other person who came near the Holy Place was to be killed.

³⁹The Lord commanded Moses and Aaron to count all the men and boys one month old or older in Levi's family group. The total number was 22,000.

Levites Take the Place of the Firstborn Sons

⁴⁰The Lord said to Moses, "Count all the firstborn* men and boys in Israel who are at least one month old. Write their names on a list. ⁴¹⌊In the past I said that⌋ I would take all the firstborn* men and boys of Israel. But now I, the Lord, will take the Levites. I will also take the firstborn animals from the Levites instead of taking all the firstborn animals from the other people in Israel."

⁴²So Moses did what the Lord commanded. Moses counted all the firstborn* children of the people of Israel. ⁴³Moses listed all the firstborn men and boys that were one month old or older. There were 22,273 names on that list.

⁴⁴The Lord also said to Moses, ⁴⁵"I, the Lord, give this command: 'Take the Levites instead of all the firstborn* men from the other families of Israel. And I will take the animals of the Levites instead of the animals of the other people. The Levites are mine. ⁴⁶There are 22,000 Levites, but there are 22,273 firstborn sons from the other families. This leaves 273 more firstborn sons than Levites. ⁴⁷Using the official measure,* collect five shekels* of silver for each of the 273 people. (The shekel by the official measure weighs 20 gerahs.*) Collect that silver from the people of Israel. ⁴⁸Give that silver to Aaron and his sons. It is the payment for the 273 people of Israel.'"

⁴⁹There were not enough Levites to take the place of 273 men from the other family groups. So Moses gathered the money for those 273 men. ⁵⁰Moses collected the silver from the firstborn* men of the people of Israel. He collected 1,365 shekels* of silver, using the official measure.* ⁵¹Moses obeyed the Lord. Moses gave the silver to Aaron and his sons just like the Lord commanded.

The Jobs of the Kohath Family

4 The Lord said to Moses and Aaron, ²"Count the men in the families of the Kohath family group. (The Kohath family group is a part of Levi's family group.) ³Count all the men from 30 to 50 years old that served in the army. These men will work in the Meeting Tent.* ⁴Their job is to take care of the most holy things in the Meeting Tent.

⁵"When the people of Israel travel to a new place, then Aaron and his sons must go into the Meeting Tent* and take down the curtain and cover the Holy Box of the Agreement* with it. ⁶Then they must cover all of this with covering made from fine leather.* Then they must spread the solid blue cloth over the leather and put the poles ⌊in the rings on the Holy Box⌋.

⁷"Then they must spread a blue cloth over the holy table. Then they must put the plates, spoons, bowls, and the jars for drink offerings on the table. Also, put the special bread on the table. ⁸Then you must put a red cloth over all of these things. Then cover everything with fine leather.* Then put the poles ⌊in the rings of the table⌋.

⁹"Then they must cover the lampstand and its lamps with a blue cloth. They must also cover all the things used to keep the lamps burning and all the jars of oil that are used in the lamps. ¹⁰Then wrap everything in fine leather.* Then they must

---

Holy Tent Or, "tabernacle," the tent where God came to live among his people.
firstborn The first child born into a family. The firstborn son was very important in ancient times.
official measure Literally, "holy shekel," the standard of measure used in the tabernacle and the temple.
five shekels Or, "2 ounces."
1,365 shekels Or, "35 pounds."
Meeting Tent The Holy Tent (tabernacle) where the people of Israel went to meet with God.
Holy Box of the Agreement Also called "ark of the Covenant," the box containing the flat stones with the Ten Commandments written on them. These were proof of the Agreement between God and the people of Israel.
fine leather A special kind of leather made from the skin of an animal like the seal or sea cow.

put all these things on poles used for carrying them. ¹¹"They must spread a blue cloth over the golden altar. They must cover that with fine leather.* Then they must put the poles for carrying it ⌊in the rings on the altar⌋.

¹²"Then they must gather together all the special things that are used for worship in the Holy Place.* They must gather them together and wrap them in a blue cloth. Then they must cover that with fine leather.* They must put these things on a frame for carrying them.

¹³"They must clean the ashes out of the ⌊bronze⌋ altar and spread a purple cloth over it. ¹⁴Then they must gather together all the things that are used for worship at the altar. These are the fire pans, forks, shovels, and the bowls. They must put these things on the ⌊bronze⌋ altar. Then they must spread a covering of fine leather* over the altar. They must put the poles for carrying it in ⌊the rings on the altar⌋.

¹⁵"Aaron and his sons must finish covering all the holy things in the Holy Place.* Then the men from the Kohath family can go in and begin carrying those things. In this way, they will not touch the Holy Place and die.

¹⁶"Eleazar son of Aaron the priest will be responsible for the Holy Tent.* He will be responsible for the Holy Place* and for everything in it. He will be responsible for the oil for the lamp, the sweet-smelling incense,* the daily offering,* and the anointing oil."*

¹⁷The Lord said to Moses and Aaron, ¹⁸"Be careful! Don't let these Kohathite men be destroyed. ¹⁹You must do these things so that the Kohathite men can go near the Most Holy Place* and not die. Aaron and his sons must go in and show each Kohathite man what to do. They must give each man the things he needs to carry. ²⁰If you do not do this, then the Kohathite men might go in and look at the holy things. If they look at those things, even for a moment, then they must die."

The Jobs of the Gershon Family

²¹The Lord said to Moses, ²²"Count all the people of the Gershon family. List them by family and family group. ²³Count all the men who are from 30 to 50 years old that served in the army. These men will have the job of caring for the Meeting Tent.*

²⁴"This is what the Gershonite family must do and the things they must carry: ²⁵They must carry the curtains of the Holy Tent,* the Meeting Tent, its covering, and the covering made from fine leather.* They must also carry the curtain at the entrance of the Meeting Tent. ²⁶They must carry the curtains of the courtyard that are around the Holy Tent and the altar. And they must carry the curtain for the entrance of the courtyard. They must also carry all of the ropes and all the things that are used with the curtains. The Gershonite men will be responsible for anything that needs to be done with these things. ²⁷Aaron and his sons will watch all the work that is done. Everything the Gershonite people carry and the other work they do will be watched by Aaron and his sons. You must tell them all the things that they are responsible for carrying. ²⁸This is the work that the men of the Gershonite family group must do for the Meeting Tent. Ithamar son of Aaron the priest will be responsible for their work."

The Jobs of the Merari Family

²⁹"Count all of the men in the families and family groups in the Merari family group. ³⁰Count all the men who are from 30 to 50 years old and served in the army. These men will do a special work for the Meeting Tent.* ³¹When you travel, it is their job to carry the frames of the Meeting Tent. They must carry the braces, the posts, and the bases. They must also carry the posts that are around the courtyard. They must carry the bases, the tent pegs, the ropes, and everything that is used for the poles around the courtyard. List the names and tell each man exactly what he must carry. ³³These are the things that the people from the Merari family will do to serve in the work for

---

fine leather A special kind of leather made from the skin of an animal like the seal or sea cow.
Holy Place One of the rooms in the Holy Tent.
Holy Tent Or, "tabernacle," the tent where God came to live among his people.
incense Special dried tree sap. Burned to make a sweet-smelling smoke, it was offered as a gift to God.
daily offering Offerings that were placed twice each day in the Holy Place as a gift to God.
anointing oil Olive oil that was poured on people or things to show they were chosen for a special work or purpose.
Most Holy Place The room inside the Holy Tent where the Holy Box was kept.

Meeting Tent The Holy Tent (tabernacle) where the people of Israel went to meet with God.

the Meeting Tent. Ithamar son of Aaron the priest will be responsible for their work."

The Levite Families

³⁴Moses, Aaron, and the leaders of the people of Israel counted the Kohathite people. They counted them by families and family groups. ³⁵They counted all the men from 30 to 50 years old that served in the army. These men were given special work to do for the Meeting Tent.*

³⁶There were 2,750 men in the Kohath family group that were qualified to do this work. ³⁷So these men from the Kohath family group were given their special work to do for the Meeting Tent.* Moses and Aaron did this the way the Lord had told Moses to do.

³⁸Also, the Gershonite family group was counted. ³⁹All the men from 30 to 50 years old that served in the army were counted. These men were given their special work to do for the Meeting Tent.* ⁴⁰There were 2,630 men in the families of the Gershon family group that were qualified. ⁴¹So these men from the Gershon family group were given their special work to do for the Meeting Tent. Moses and Aaron did this the way the Lord had told Moses to do.

⁴²Also, the men in the families and family groups of the Merari family were counted. ⁴³All the men from 30 to 50 years old that had served in the army were counted. These men were given their special work to do for the Meeting Tent.* ⁴⁴There were 3,200 men in the families of the Merari family group that were qualified. ⁴⁵So these men from the Merari family group were given their special work. Moses and Aaron did this the way the Lord told Moses to do.

⁴⁶So Moses, Aaron, and the leaders of the people of Israel counted all the people in Levi's family group. They had counted each family and each family group. ⁴⁷All the men between the ages of 30 and 50 that served in the army were counted. These men were given a special work to do for the Meeting Tent.* They did the work of carrying the Meeting Tent when they traveled. ⁴⁸The total number was 8,580.

⁴⁹So, each man was counted like the Lord commanded Moses. Each man was given his own work and told what he must carry. This was done just like the Lord commanded.

Rules About Cleanliness

5 The Lord said to Moses, ²"I command the people of Israel to keep their camp free from sickness and disease. Tell the people to send away from the camp any person who has a bad skin disease.* Tell them to send away from the camp any person who has a discharge.* And tell them to send away from their camp any person who has touched a dead body. ³It doesn't matter if that person is a man or a woman, send them away from your camp. Send them away so that they will not cause any more sickness and disease. I am living among you in your camp."

⁴So the people of Israel obeyed God's command. They sent those people outside the camp. They did what the Lord had commanded to Moses.

Paying for Doing Wrong

⁵The Lord said to Moses, ⁶"Tell this to the people of Israel: A person might do something bad to another person. (When someone does bad things to other people, he is really sinning against God.) That person is guilty. ⁷So that person must tell the people about the sin he has done. Then that person must fully pay for that wrong thing he did. He must add and add one-fifth to the payment and give it all to the person he had done wrong to. ⁸But maybe the person he did wrong to is dead. And maybe that dead person doesn't have any close relatives to take the payment. In that case, the person who did wrong will give the payment to the Lord. That person will give the full payment to the priest. The priest must sacrifice the ram that makes people pure. This ram must be sacrificed to cover over the sins of the person who did wrong. But the priest can keep the rest of the payment.

⁹"If one of the people of Israel gives a special gift to God, then the priest that accepts that gift can keep it. It is his. ¹⁰A person doesn't have to give these special gifts. But if he gives them, then the gifts belong to the priest."

Suspicious Husbands

¹¹Then the Lord said to Moses, ¹²"Tell these things to the people of Israel: A man's wife might

---

Meeting Tent The Holy Tent (tabernacle) where the people of Israel went to meet with God.

bad skin disease Or, "leprosy." The Hebrew word includes many kinds of skin diseases.

discharge Fluid from a person's body, including pus from sores, a man's semen, or a woman's period flow.

be unfaithful to him. ¹³She might have sexual relations with another man and hide this from her husband. And there might not be anyone to tell him that she did this sin. Her husband might never know about the wrong thing she did. And the woman might not tell her husband about her sin. ¹⁴But the husband might begin to suspect that his wife sinned against him. He might become jealous. He might begin to believe that she is not pure and true to him. ¹⁵If that happens, then he must take his wife to the priest. The husband must also take an offering of 8 cups* of barley flour. He must not pour oil or incense* on the barley flour. This barley flour is a grain offering to the Lord. It is given because the husband is jealous. This offering will show that he believes that his wife has been unfaithful to him.

¹⁶"The priest will take the woman before the Lord and make her stand there. ¹⁷Then the priest will take some special water and put it in a clay jar. The priest will put some dirt from the floor of the Holy Tent into the water. ¹⁸The priest will force the woman to stand before the Lord. Then he will loosen her hair and put the grain offering in her hand. This is the barley flour that her husband gave because he was jealous. At the same time, he will hold the clay jar of special water. This is the special water that brings trouble to the woman.

¹⁹"Then the priest will tell the woman that she must not lie. She must promise to tell the truth. The priest will say to her: 'If you have not slept with another man, and if you have not sinned against your husband while you were married to him, then this water that causes trouble will not hurt you. ²⁰But if you have sinned against your husband—if you had sexual relations with a man who is not your husband—then you are not pure. ²¹If that is true, then you will have much trouble when you drink this special water. You will not be able to have any children. And if you are pregnant now, your baby will die.* Then your people will leave you and say bad things about you.'

"Then the priest must tell the woman to make a special promise to the Lord. The woman must agree that these bad things will happen to her if she lies. ²²The priest must say, 'You must drink this water that causes trouble. If you have sinned, you will not be able to have children and any baby you have will die before it is born.' And the woman should say: 'I agree to do as you say.'

²³"The priest should write those warnings on a scroll.* Then he should wash the words off into the water. ²⁴Then the woman must drink the water that brings trouble. This water will enter her and, ⌊if she is guilty,⌋ it will cause her much suffering.

²⁵"Then the priest will take the grain offering from her (the offering for jealousy) and raise it before the Lord. Then he will carry it to the altar.* ²⁶The priest will fill his hands with some of the grain and put it on the altar and let it burn there. After that, he will tell the woman to drink the water. ²⁷If the woman has sinned against her husband, then the water will bring her trouble. The water will go into her body and cause her much suffering. Any baby that is in her will die before it is born, and she will never be able to have children. All the people will turn against her.* ²⁸But if the woman has not sinned against her husband and she is pure, then the priest will say that she is not guilty. Then she will be normal, and able to have children.

²⁹"So that is the law about jealousy. That is what you should do when a woman sins against her husband while she is married to him. ³⁰Or if the man becomes jealous and suspects his wife has sinned against him, then that is what the man should do. The priest must tell the woman to stand before the Lord. Then the priest will do all those things. This is the law. ³¹The husband will not be guilty of doing anything wrong. But the woman will suffer if she has sinned."

Nazirites

6 The Lord said to Moses, ²"Tell these things to the people of Israel: A man or a woman might want to separate from other people for a time. This special time of separation allows a person to give himself totally to the Lord for a time. That person will be called a Nazirite.* ³During that time, that person must not drink any wine or other

---

8 cups Literally, "1/10 of an ephah."
incense Special dried tree sap. Burned to make a sweet-smelling smoke, it was offered as a gift to God.
You will ... die Literally, "Your loins will fall and your belly will swell."
scroll A long roll of leather or papyrus (paper) used for writing books, letters, and legal documents.
altar A table or raised area used for offering sacrifices.
All ... turn against her Literally, "She will be like a curse among the people."
Nazirite A person who has made a special promise to God. The name is from a Hebrew word meaning, "to separate from."

strong drink. The person must not drink vinegar that is made from wine or from other strong drink. That person must not drink grape juice or eat grapes or raisins. ⁴That person must not eat anything that comes from grapes during that special time of separation. That person must not even eat the seeds or the skins from grapes.

⁵"That person must not cut his hair during that special time of separation. He must be holy until the time that his separation is ended. He must let his hair grow long. That person's hair is a special part of his promise to God. ₍He will give that hair as a gift to God.₎ So, that person must let his hair grow long until the time of separation is ended.

⁶"A Nazirite* must not go near a dead body during that special time of separation,. Why? Because that person has given himself fully to the Lord. ⁷Even if his own father or mother or brother or sister dies, he must not touch them. This would make him unclean. He must show that he is separated and has given himself fully to God. ⁸During the whole time of his separation, he is giving himself fully to the Lord.

⁹"It might happen that the Nazirite* is with another person who dies suddenly. ₍If the Nazirite touches this dead man, the Nazirite will become unclean.*₎ If that happens, then the Nazirite must shave the hair from his head. (That hair was part of his special promise.) He must cut his hair on the seventh day, because on that day he is made clean.* ¹⁰Then on the eighth day, that Nazirite must bring two doves and two young pigeons to the priest. He must give them to the priest at the entrance of the Meeting Tent.* ¹¹Then the priest will offer one as a sin offering. He will offer the other as a burnt offering. The burnt offering will be a payment for the Nazirite's sin. (He sinned because he was near a dead body.) At that time, the person will again promise to give the hair on his head as a gift to God. ¹²This means that person must again give himself to the Lord for another time of separation. That person must bring a one-year-old male lamb. He must give this lamb as a guilt offering. All of the days that he was separated are forgotten. The man must start over with a new time of separation. This must be done because he touched a dead body during his first time of separation.

¹³"After his time of separation is ended, a Nazirite must go to the entrance of the Meeting Tent* ¹⁴and give his offering to the Lord. His offering must be:

> A one-year-old male lamb with nothing wrong with it for a burnt offering;
> A one-year-old female lamb with nothing wrong with it for a sin offering;
> One ram with nothing wrong with it for a fellowship offering;
15 A basket of bread made without yeast (cakes made with fine flour mixed with oil).
> Oil must be spread on these cakes.
> The grain offerings and drink offerings that are a part of these gifts.

¹⁶"The priest will give these things to the Lord. And then the priest will make the sin offering and the burnt offering. ¹⁷The priest will give the basket of bread without yeast to the Lord. Then he will kill the ram as a fellowship offering to the Lord. He will give it to the Lord with the grain offering and the drink offering.

¹⁸"The Nazirite* must go to the entrance of the Meeting Tent.* There he must shave off his hair that he grew for the Lord. That hair will be put in the fire that is burning under the sacrifice of the fellowship offering.

¹⁹"After the Nazirite* has cut off his hair, then the priest will give him a boiled shoulder from the ram and a large and a small cake from the basket. Both of these cakes are made without yeast. ²⁰Then the priest will wave these things before the Lord. This is a wave offering. These things are holy and belong to the priest. Also, the breast and the thigh from the ram are waved before the Lord. These things also belong to the priest. After that, the Nazirite man can drink wine.

²¹"Those are the rules for a person who decides to make the Nazirite* promise. That person must give all of those gifts to the Lord. But a person might be able to give much more to the Lord. If a person promises to do more, then he must keep his promise. But he must give at least all the things listed in these rules for the Nazirite promise.

Nazirite A person who has made a special promise to God. The name is from a Hebrew word meaning, "to separate from."
unclean Not pure or not acceptable to God for worship.
clean Pure or acceptable to God for worship.
Meeting Tent The Holy Tent (tabernacle) where the people of Israel went to meet with God.

The Priests' Blessings

²²The Lord said to Moses, ²³"Tell Aaron and his sons that this is the way they should bless the people of Israel. They should say:

²⁴ May the Lord bless you and keep you.
²⁵ May the Lord be good to you*
   and show you his kindness.
²⁶ May the Lord answer your prayers*
   and give you peace."

²⁷Then the Lord said, "In that way, Aaron and his sons will use my name to give a blessing to the people of Israel. And I will bless them."

Dedicating the Holy Tent

7 Moses finished setting up the Holy Tent.* On that day, he dedicated it to the Lord. Moses anointed* the Tent and all the things in it. Moses also anointed the altar* and all the things used with it. This showed that these things should be used only for worshiping the Lord.

²Then the leaders of Israel gave offerings to the Lord. These men were the heads of their families and leaders of their family groups. These were the same men who were in charge of counting the people. ³These leaders brought gifts to the Lord. They brought six covered wagons and twelve cows for pulling the wagons. (One cow was given by each leader. Each leader joined with another leader to give one wagon.) The leaders gave these things to the Lord at the Holy Tent.

⁴The Lord said to Moses, ⁵"Accept these gifts from the leaders. These gifts can be used in the work of the Meeting Tent.* Give these things to the Levite men. This will help them do their work."

⁶So Moses accepted the wagons and the cows. He gave these things to the Levite men. ⁷He gave two carts and four cows to the men in Gershon's group. They needed the wagons and the cows for their work. ⁸Then Moses gave four wagons and eight cows to the men in Merari's group. They needed the wagons and cows for their work. Ithamar son of Aaron the priest was responsible for the work of all these men. ⁹Moses did not give any cows or wagons to the men in Kohath's group. Why? Because their job was to carry the holy things on their shoulders.

¹⁰Moses anointed* the altar.* That same day, the leaders brought their offerings for dedicating the altar. They gave their offerings to the Lord at the altar. ¹¹The Lord told Moses, "Each day one leader must bring his gift for dedicating the altar."

¹²⁻⁸³*⌊Each of the twelve leaders brought his gifts. These are the gifts:⌋

Each leader brought one silver plate that weighed 3 1/4 pounds.* Each leader brought one silver bowl that weighed 1 3/4 pounds.* Both of these gifts were weighed by the official measure.* The bowl and the plate were each filled with fine flour mixed with oil. This was to be used as a grain offering. Each leader also brought a large gold spoon that weighed about 4 ounces.* The spoon was filled with incense.*

Each leader also brought 1 young bull, 1 ram, and 1 male lamb a year old. These animals were for a burnt offering. Each leader also brought 1 male goat to be used as a sin offering. Each leader brought 2 cows, 5 rams, 5 male goats, and 5 male lambs a year old. All of these things were sacrificed for a fellowship offering.

On the first day, the leader of Judah's family group, Nahshon son of Amminadab brought his gifts.

On the second day, the leader of Issachar, Nethanel son of Zuar brought his gifts.

On the third day, the leader of the people of Zebulun, Eliab son of Helon brought his gifts.

On the fourth day, the leader of the people of Reuben, Elizur son of Shedeur brought his gifts.

May the Lord be good to you Literally, "May the Lord make his face shine on you."

May the Lord answer your prayers Literally, "May the Lord lift his face to you."

Holy Tent Or, "tabernacle," the tent where God came to live among his people.

anoint To pour olive oil on people or things to show they are chosen for a special work or purpose.

altar A table or raised area used for offering sacrifices.

Meeting Tent The Holy Tent (tabernacle) where the people of Israel went to meet with God.

Verses 12-83 In the Hebrew text each leader's gift is listed separately. But the text is the same for each gift, so it has been merged for easier reading.

3 1/4 pounds Or, "130 shekels."

1 3/4 pounds Or, "70 shekels."

official measure Literally, "holy shekel," the standard of measure used in the tabernacle and the temple.

4 ounces Or, "10 shekels."

incense Special dried tree sap. Burned to make a sweet-smelling smoke, it was offered as a gift to God.

On the fifth day, the leader of the people of Simeon, Shelumiel son of Zurishaddai brought his gifts.

On the sixth day, the leader of the people of Gad, Eliasaph son of Deuel* brought his gifts.

On the seventh day, the leader of the people of Ephraim, Elishama son of Ammihud brought his gifts.

On the eighth day, the leader of the people of Manasseh, Gamaliel son of Pedahzur brought his gifts.

On the ninth day, the leader of the people of Benjamin, Abidan son of Gideoni brought his gifts.

On the tenth day, the leader of the people of Dan, Ahiezer son of Ammishaddai brought his gifts.

On the eleventh day, the leader of the people of Asher, Pagiel son of Ocran brought his gifts.

On the twelfth day, the leader of the people of Naphtali, Ahira son of Enan brought his gifts.

⁸⁴So all those things were the gifts from the leaders of the people of Israel. They brought those things during the time that Moses dedicated the altar* by anointing* it. They brought 12 silver plates, 12 silver bowls, and 12 gold spoons. ⁸⁵Each silver plate weighed about 3 1/4 pounds.* And each bowl weighed about 1 3/4 pounds.* The silver plates and the silver bowls together all weighed about 60 pounds,* using the official measure* ⁸⁶The 12 gold spoons filled with incense* weighed 4 ounces* each, using the official measure. The 12 gold spoons all together weighed about 3 pounds.*

⁸⁷The total number of animals for the burnt offering was 12 bulls, 12 rams, and 12 one-year-old male lambs. There were also the grain offerings that must be given with those offerings. And there were 12 male goats that were used for a sin offering to the Lord. ⁸⁸The leaders also gave animals to be killed and used as a fellowship offering. The total number of these animals was 24 bulls, 60 rams, 60 male goats, and 60 one-year-old male lambs. In this way, they dedicated the altar after Moses anointed* it.

⁸⁹Moses went into the Meeting Tent* to speak to the Lord. At that time, he heard the Lord's voice speaking to him. The voice was coming from the area between the two Cherub angels on the special cover* on top of the Box of the Agreement.* ₍This was the way₎ God spoke to Moses.

The Lampstand

8 The Lord said to Moses, ²"Tell Aaron to put the seven lamps in the place I showed you. Those lamps will light the area in front of the lampstand."

³Aaron did this. Aaron put the lamps in the right place and faced them so that they lighted the area in front of the lampstand. He obeyed the command that the Lord gave Moses. ⁴This is how the lampstand was made: It was made from hammered gold, all the way from the gold base ₍at the bottom₎ to the gold flowers ₍at the top₎. It looked just like the pattern that the Lord had shown to Moses.

Dedicating the Levites

⁵The Lord said to Moses, ⁶"Separate the Levites from the other people of Israel. Make those Levites clean.* ⁷This is what you should do to make them pure. Sprinkle the special water from the sin offering* on them. This water will make them pure. Then they must shave their bodies and wash their clothes. This will make their bodies clean.

Deuel Or, "Reuel."
altar A table or raised area used for offering sacrifices.
anoint To pour olive oil on people or things to show they are chosen for a special work or purpose.
3 1/4 pounds Or, "130 shekels."
1 3/4 pounds Or, "70 shekels."
60 pounds Or, "2,400 shekels."
official measure Literally, "holy shekel," the standard of measure used in the tabernacle and the temple.
incense Special dried tree sap. Burned to make a sweet-smelling smoke, it was offered as a gift to God.
4 ounces Or, "10 shekels."
3 pounds Or, "120 shekels."

Meeting Tent The Holy Tent (tabernacle) where the people of Israel went to meet with God.
cover Also called "mercy seat." The Hebrew word can mean "lid," "cover," or "place where sins are forgiven."
Box of the Agreement Or, "ark of the Covenant," the box containing the flat stones with the Ten Commandments written on them and other things that proved God was with the people of Israel during their time in the Sinai Desert.
clean Pure or acceptable to God for worship.
water from the sin offering In this water were the ashes from the red cow that had been burnt on the altar as a sin offering.

⁸"The Levite men must take a young bull and the grain offering that must be offered with it. This grain offering will be flour mixed with oil. Then take another young bull for a sin offering. ⁹Bring the Levite people to the area in front of the Meeting Tent.* Then bring all the people of Israel together at that place. ¹⁰Bring the Levite people before the Lord. The people of Israel will put their hands on them.* ¹¹Then Aaron will give the Levite people to the Lord—they will be like an offering to God. In this way, the Levite people will be ready to do their special work for the Lord.
¹²"Tell the Levite people to put their hands on the heads of the bulls. One bull will be a sin offering to the Lord. The other bull will be used as a burnt offering to the Lord. These offerings will make the Levite people pure.* ¹³Tell the Levite people to stand in front of Aaron and his sons. Then give the Levite men to the Lord. They will be like a wave offering. ¹⁴This will make the Levite people holy—it will show that they will be used in a special way for God₁. They will be different from the other people of Israel. The Levite people will belong to me.
¹⁵"So make the Levite people pure.* And give them to the Lord. They will be like a wave offering. After you do this they can come and do their work at the Meeting Tent.* ¹⁶The Israelite people will give me the Levites. They will belong to me. In the past, I told every Israelite family to give me their firstborn* son. But now I am taking the Levite people in place of those firstborn sons from the other families in Israel. ¹⁷Every firstborn male in Israel is mine. It doesn't matter if it is a man or animal, it is still mine. Why? Because I killed all the firstborn children and animals in Egypt. And I chose to take the firstborn sons to belong to me. ¹⁸But now I will take the Levite people in their place. I will take the Levite people in place of all the firstborn sons from the other families in Israel. ¹⁹I chose the Levite people from among all the people of Israel. And I give them as gifts to Aaron and his sons. I want them to do the work at the Meeting Tent. They will serve for all the people of Israel. They will help make the sacrifices that make the people of Israel pure. Then no great sickness or trouble will come to the people of Israel when they come near the holy place."

²⁰So Moses, Aaron, and all the people of Israel obeyed the Lord. They did with the Levite people everything that the Lord commanded Moses. ²¹The Levites washed themselves and their clothes. Then Aaron gave them to the Lord like wave offerings. Aaron gave the offerings that covered their sins and made them pure. ²²After that, the Levite people came to the Meeting Tent* to do their work. Aaron and his sons watched them. They were responsible for the work of the Levite people. Aaron and his sons did the things that the Lord told Moses.

²³Then the Lord said to Moses, ²⁴"This is a special command for the Levite people: Every Levite man who is 25 years old or older must come and share in the work at the Meeting Tent.* ²⁵But when a man is 50 years old, he must retire from this work. He will not need to work again. ²⁶Those men 50 years old or older can help their brothers with their work at the Meeting Tent. But those men must not do the work themselves. You must do these things when you choose Levite men to do their work."

Passover

9 The Lord spoke to Moses in the Sinai desert. This was during the first month of the second year after the people of Israel came out of Egypt. The Lord said to Moses, ²"Tell the people of Israel to celebrate Passover at the chosen time— ³they must eat the Passover* meal at twilight* on the 14th day of this month. They must do this at the chosen time, and they must follow all the rules about Passover."

⁴So Moses told the people of Israel to celebrate Passover.* ⁵The people did this in the Sinai desert at twilight* on the 14th day of the first month. The Israelites did everything just like the Lord commanded Moses.

Meeting Tent The Holy Tent (tabernacle) where the people of Israel went to meet with God.
put their hands on them This showed the people shared in appointing the Levite people to their special work.
make ... pure Literally, "make atonement." The Hebrew word means "to cover," "to hide," or "to erase sins."
firstborn The first child born into a family. In ancient times, the firstborn son was very important.

Passover Important Jewish holy day. They ate a special meal on this day every spring to remember that God freed them from slavery in Egypt.
twilight The time after the sun goes down, but before dark.

⁶But some of the people could not celebrate Passover* that day. They were unclean* because they had touched a dead body. So they went to Moses and Aaron that day. ⁷Those people said to Moses, "We touched a person's dead body and became unclean. The priests stopped us from giving gifts to the Lord at the chosen time. So we can't ₁celebrate Passover₁ with the other people of Israel! ₁What should we do?₁"

⁸Moses said to them, "I will ask the Lord what he says about this."

⁹Then the Lord said to Moses, ¹⁰"Tell these things to the people of Israel: This rule will be for you and your descendants.* Maybe a person is not able to celebrate Passover* at the right time. Maybe that person is unclean* because he touched a dead body. Or maybe that person was away on a trip. ¹¹That person will still be able to celebrate Passover ₁at another time₁. That person must celebrate Passover at twilight* on the 14th day of the second month. At that time, he must eat the lamb, the bread made without yeast, and the bitter herbs. ¹²That person must not leave any of that food until the next morning. And that person must not break any of the bones of the lamb. That person must follow all the rules about Passover. ¹³But any person who is able must celebrate Passover at the right time. If he is clean* and he is not away on a trip, then he has no excuse. If that person does not celebrate Passover at the right time, then he must be separated from his people. He is guilty and must be punished! Why? Because he did not give the Lord his gift at the right time.

¹⁴"A foreigner living among you might want to share in the Lord's Passover* with you. This is allowed, but that person must follow all the rules about Passover. The same rules are for everyone."

The Cloud and the Fire

¹⁵On the day the Holy Tent,* the Tent of the Agreement, was set up, the Lord's cloud covered it. At night, the cloud over the Holy Tent looked like fire. ¹⁶The cloud stayed over the Holy Tent all the time. And at night the cloud looked like fire. ¹⁷When the cloud moved from its place over the Holy Tent, the Israelites followed it. When the cloud stopped, that is the place where the people of Israel camped. ¹⁸This was the way the Lord showed the people of Israel when to move and when to stop and set up camp. While the cloud stayed over the Holy Tent, the people continued to camp in that same place. ¹⁹Sometimes the cloud would stay over the Holy Tent for a long time. The Israelites obeyed the Lord and did not move. ²⁰Sometimes the cloud was over the Holy Tent for only a few days. So the people obeyed the Lord's command—they followed the cloud when it moved. ²¹Sometimes the cloud stayed only during the night—the next morning the cloud moved. So the people gathered their things and followed it. If the cloud moved, during the day or during the night, then the people followed it. ²²If the cloud stayed over the Holy Tent for two days, or a month, or a year, the people continued to obey the Lord. They stayed at that place and did not leave until the cloud moved. Then when the cloud rose from its place and moved, the people also moved. ²³So the people obeyed the Lord's commands. They camped when the Lord told them to. And they moved when the Lord told them to. The people watched carefully and obeyed the Lord's commands to Moses.

The Silver Trumpets

10 The Lord said to Moses: ²"Make two trumpets. Use silver and hammer it to make the trumpets. These trumpets will be for calling the people together and for telling them when it is time to move the camp. ³If you blow long blasts on both trumpets, then all the people must meet together at the entrance of the Meeting Tent.* ⁴But if you blow long blasts on only one trumpet, then only the leaders will come to meet with you. (These are the leaders of the twelve family groups of Israel.)

⁵"Short blasts on the trumpets will be the way to tell the people to move the camp. The first time you blow a short blast on the trumpets, the family groups camping on the east ₁side of the Meeting Tent₁ must begin to move. ⁶The second time you blow a short blast on the trumpets, the family

---

Passover Important Jewish holy day. They ate a special meal on this day every spring to remember that God freed them from slavery in Egypt.
unclean Not pure or not acceptable to God for worship.
descendants A person's children and their future families.
twilight The time after the sun goes down, but before dark.
clean Pure or acceptable to God for worship.
Holy Tent Or, "tabernacle," the tent where God came to live among his people.

Meeting Tent The Holy Tent (tabernacle) where the people of Israel went to meet with God.

groups camping on the south side of the Meeting Tent will begin to move. ⁷But if you want to gather the people together for a special meeting, then blow the trumpets in a different way—blow a long steady blast on the trumpets. ⁸Only Aaron's sons, the priests, should blow the trumpets. This is a law for you that will continue forever, for generations to come.

⁹"If you are fighting an enemy in your own land, then blow loudly on the trumpets before you go to fight them. The Lord your God will hear you, and he will save you from your enemies. ¹⁰Also you should blow these trumpets for your special meetings, new moon days, and all your happy times together. Blow the trumpets when you give your burnt offerings and fellowship offerings. This will be a special way for the Lord your God to remember you. I command you to do this; I am the Lord your God."

The People of Israel Move Their Camp

¹¹On the 20th day of the second month of the second year after the people of Israel left Egypt, the cloud rose from above the Tent of the Agreement.* ¹²So the people of Israel began their journeys. They left the Sinai desert and traveled until the cloud stopped in the desert of Paran. ¹³This was the first time the people moved their camp. They moved it the way the Lord commanded Moses.

¹⁴The three groups* from Judah's camp went first. They traveled under their flag. The first group was Judah's family group. Nahshon son of Amminadab was the commander of that group. ¹⁵Next came Issachar's family group. Nethanel son of Zuar was the commander of that group. ¹⁶And then came Zebulun's family group. Eliab son of Helon was the commander of that group.

¹⁷Then the Holy Tent* was taken down. And the men from the Gershon and the Merari families carried the Holy Tent. So the people from these families were next in line.

¹⁸Then came the three groups* from Reuben's camp. They traveled under their flag. The first group was Reuben's family group. Elizur son of Shedeur was the commander of that group. ¹⁹Next came Simeon's family group. Shelumiel son of Zurishaddai was the commander of that group. ²⁰And then came Gad's family group. Eliasaph son of Deuel* was the commander of that group. ²¹Then came the people from the Kohath family. They carried the holy things from inside the Holy Place. These people came at this time so that the other people could set up the Holy Tent* and make it ready at the new camp before these people arrived.

²²Next came the three groups from Ephraim's camp. They traveled under their flag. The first group was Ephraim's family group. Elishama son of Ammihud was the commander of that group. ²³Next came Manasseh's family group. Gamaliel son of Pedahzur was the commander of that group. ²⁴Then came Benjamin's family group. Abidan son of Gideoni was the commander of that group.

²⁵The last three family groups in the line were the rear guard for all the other family groups. These were the groups from Dan's camp. They traveled under their flag. The first group was Dan's family group. Ahiezer son of Ammishaddai was their commander. ²⁶Next came Asher's family group. Pagiel son of Ocran was the commander of that group. ²⁷Then came Naphtali's family group. Ahira son of Enan was the commander of that group. ²⁸That was the way the people of Israel marched when they moved from place to place.

²⁹Hobab was the son of Reuel, the Midianite. (Reuel was Moses' father-in-law.) Moses said to Hobab, "We are traveling to the land that God promised to give to us. Come with us and we will be good to you. The Lord has promised good things to the people of Israel."

³⁰But Hobab answered, "No, I will not go with you. I will go back to my homeland and to my own people."

³¹Then Moses said, "Please don't leave us. You know more about the desert than we do. You can be our guide. ³²If you come with us, then we will share with you all the good things that the Lord gives us."

³³So Hobab agreed, and they began traveling from the mountain of the Lord. The priests took the Box of the Lord's Agreement* and walked in

---

Tent of the Agreement The Holy Tent (tabernacle) where the Box of the Agreement was kept.

groups Or, "divisions." This is a military term that shows Israel was organized like an army.

Holy Tent Or, "tabernacle," the tent where God came to live among his people.

Deuel Or, "Reuel."

Box of the Lord's Agreement Or, "ark of the Covenant," the Holy Box containing the flat stones with the Ten Commandments written on them. These were proof of the Agreement between God and the people of Israel.

front of the people. They carried the Holy Box for three days, looking for a place to camp. ³⁴The Lord's cloud was over them every day. And when they left their camp every morning, the cloud was there to lead them.

³⁵When the people lifted the Holy Box to move the camp, Moses always said,

> "Get up, Lord!
> May your enemies be scattered.
> May your enemies run away from
>   you."

³⁶And when the Holy Box was put in its place, Moses always said,

> "Come back, Lord,
> to the millions of people of Israel."

The People Complain Again

11 The people started complaining about their troubles. The Lord heard their complaints. The Lord heard these things and became angry. Fire from the Lord burned among the people. The fire burned some of the areas at the edge of the camp. ²So the people cried to Moses for help. Moses prayed to the Lord and the fire stopped burning. ³So that place was called Taberah.* The people gave the place that name because the Lord caused a fire to burn in their camp.

The 70 Older Leaders

⁴The foreigners that had joined the people of Israel began wanting other things to eat. Soon all the people of Israel began complaining again. The people said, "We want to eat meat! ⁵We remember the fish we ate in Egypt. That fish cost us nothing. We also had good vegetables like cucumbers, melons, chives, onions, and garlic. ⁶But now we have lost our strength. We never eat anything—only this manna!" ⁷(The manna was like small coriander seeds, and it looked like gum from a tree. ⁸The people gathered the manna. Then they used rocks to crush it and cooked it in a pot. Or they ground it into a flour and made thin cakes with it. The cakes tasted like sweet cakes cooked with olive oil. ⁹The manna fell on the ground each night when the ground became wet with dew.)

¹⁰Moses heard the people complaining. People from every family were sitting by their tents and complaining. The Lord became very angry, and this made Moses very upset. ¹¹Moses asked the Lord, "Lord, why did you bring this trouble on me? I am your servant. What did I do wrong? What did I do to upset you? Why did you give me responsibility over all these people? ¹²You know that I am not the father of all these people. You know that I did not give birth to them. But I must take care of them, like a nurse carrying a baby in her arms. Why do you force me to do this? Why do you force me to carry them to the land that you promised to our fathers? ¹³I don't have enough meat for all these people! And they continue complaining to me. They say, 'Give us meat to eat!' ¹⁴I cannot take care of all these people alone. The burden is too heavy for me. ¹⁵If you plan to continue giving me their troubles, then kill me now. If you accept me as your servant, then let me die now. Then I will be finished with all my troubles!"

¹⁶The Lord said to Moses, "Bring to me 70 of the elders of Israel. These men are the leaders among the people. Bring them to the Meeting Tent.* Let them stand there with you. ¹⁷Then I will come down and speak with you there. The Spirit* is on you now. But I will also give some of that Spirit* to them. Then they will help you take care of the people. In this way, you will not have to be responsible for these people alone.

¹⁸"Tell these things to the people: Make yourselves ready for tomorrow. Tomorrow you will eat meat. The Lord heard you when you cried. The Lord heard your words when you said, 'We need meat to eat! It was better for us in Egypt!' So now the Lord will give you meat. And you will eat it. ¹⁹You will eat it for more than one, or two, or five, or ten, or even twenty days! ²⁰You will eat that meat for a whole month. You will eat the meat until you are sick of it. This will happen to you because you complained against the Lord. The Lord lives among you and knows what you need. But you cried and complained to him! You said, 'Why did we ever leave Egypt?'"

²¹Moses said, "Lord, there are 600,000 men walking around here. And you say, 'I will give them enough meat to eat for a whole month!' ²²If we were to kill all of the sheep and cattle, then that would still not be enough to feed this many

---

Taberah This name means "burning."
Meeting Tent The Holy Tent (tabernacle) where the people of Israel came to meet with God.
Spirit Or, "spirit."

people for a month. And if we caught all the fish in the sea, it would not be enough for them!" ²³But the Lord said to Moses, "Don't limit the power of the Lord! You will see that I can do the things I say I can do." ²⁴So Moses went out to speak with the people. Moses told them what the Lord said. Then Moses gathered 70 of the elders *(leaders)* together. Moses told them to stand around the Tent. ²⁵Then the Lord came down in the cloud and spoke to Moses. The Spirit* was on Moses. The Lord put that same Spirit on the 70 elders *(leaders)*. After the Spirit came down on them, they began to prophesy.* But that was the only time these men ever did this.

²⁶Two of the elders, Eldad and Medad, did not go out to the Tent. Their names were on the list of elders *(leaders)*, but they stayed in camp. But the Spirit also came on them, and they began prophesying* in camp. ²⁷A young man ran and told Moses. The man said, "Eldad and Medad are prophesying in camp."

²⁸Joshua son of Nun said to Moses, "Moses, sir, you must stop them!" (Joshua had been Moses' helper since Joshua was a young boy.)

²⁹But Moses answered, "Are you afraid the people will think that I am not the leader now? I wish that all the Lord's people were able to prophesy. I wish that the Lord would put his Spirit* on all of them!" ³⁰Then Moses and the leaders of Israel went back to the camp.

The Quails Come

³¹Then the Lord made a powerful wind to blow in from the sea. The wind blew quail* into that area. The quail flew all around the camp. There were so many quail that the ground was covered. The quail were about three feet deep on the ground. There were quail in every direction as far as a man can walk in one day. ³²⌊The people went crazy!⌋ They went out and gathered quail all that day and all that night. And they gathered quail all the next day too! The smallest amount any person gathered was 60 bushels. Then the people spread the quail meat all around the camp ⌊to dry in the sun⌋.

³³People began to eat the meat, but the Lord became very angry. While the meat was still in their mouth, before the people could finish eating it, the Lord caused the people to become very sick. ⌊Many people died and were buried in that place.⌋ ³⁴So the people named that place Kibroth Hattaavah.* They gave the place that name because that is the place they buried the people who had the strong desire for meat.

³⁵From Kibroth Hattaavah the people traveled to Hazeroth and stayed there.

Miriam and Aaron Complain About Moses

12 Miriam and Aaron began to talk against Moses. They criticized him because he married an Ethiopian* woman. They thought that it was not right for Moses to marry an Ethiopian woman. ²They said to themselves, "The Lord used Moses to speak to the people. But Moses is not the only one. The Lord also spoke through us!"

The Lord heard this. ³(Moses was a very humble man. He did not boast or brag. He was more humble than any other person on earth.) ⁴So, suddenly, the Lord came and spoke to Moses, Aaron, and Miriam. The Lord said, "You three, come to the Meeting Tent,* now!"

So Moses, Aaron, and Miriam went to the Tent. ⁵The Lord came down in the tall cloud and stood at the entrance to the Tent. The Lord called out, "Aaron and Miriam!" Aaron and Miriam went to him. ⁶God said, "Listen to me! You will have prophets.* I, the Lord, will show myself to them in visions.* I will speak to them in dreams. ⁷But Moses is not like that. Moses is my faithful servant—I trust him with my whole house *(family)*! ⁸When I speak to him, I talk face to face with him. I don't use stories with hidden meanings—I show him clearly the things I want him to know. And Moses can look at the very image of the Lord. So why were you brave enough to speak against my servant Moses?"

⁹The Lord was very angry at them. The Lord left them. ¹⁰The cloud rose from the Tent. Aaron

---

Spirit Or, "spirit."
prophesy Usually this means "to speak for God." But here it might mean that God's Spirit took control of these men in some special way.
quail A kind of bird.

Kibroth Hattaavah This name means "Graves of Strong Desire."
Ethiopian Or, "Cushite," a person from Ethiopia, in Africa.
Meeting Tent The Holy Tent (tabernacle) where the people of Israel came to meet with God.
prophet(s) A person called by God to be a special servant. God gave them messages to tell the people.
vision(s) Something like a dream that God used to speak to people.

turned and looked at Miriam. Her skin was white like snow—she had a terrible skin disease! ¹¹Then Aaron said to Moses, "Please, sir, forgive us for the foolish sin that we did. ¹²Don't let her lose her skin like a baby that is born dead." (Sometimes a baby will be born like that, with half of its skin eaten away.) ¹³So Moses prayed to the Lord, "God, please heal her from this sickness!" ¹⁴The Lord answered Moses, "If her father spit in her face, then she would be shamed for seven days. So put her outside the camp for seven days. After that time, she ₁will become well₁. Then she can come back into the camp."

¹⁵So they took Miriam outside the camp for seven days. And the people did not move from that place until she was brought in again. ¹⁶After that, the people left Hazeroth and traveled to the desert of Paran. The people camped in that desert.

The Spies Go to Canaan

13 The Lord said to Moses, ²"Send some men to explore the land of Canaan. This is the land that I will give to the people of Israel. Send one leader from each of the twelve family groups." ³So Moses obeyed the Lord's command. Moses sent out these leaders while the people were camped in the desert of Paran. ⁴These are the names of those leaders:

    from Reuben's family group—
        Shammua son of Zaccur;
⁵ from Simeon's family group—Shaphat son of Hori;
⁶ from Judah's family group—Caleb son of Jephunneh;
⁷ from Issachar's family group—Igal son of Joseph;
⁸ from Ephraim's family group—Hoshea* son of Nun;
⁹ from Benjamin's family group—Palti son of Raphu;
¹⁰ from Zebulun's family group—Gaddiel son of Sodi;
¹¹ from Joseph's family group (Manasseh)—Gaddi son of Susi;
¹² from Dan's family group—Ammiel son of Gemalli;
¹³ from Asher's family group—Sethur son of Michael;
¹⁴ from Naphtali's family group—Nahbi son of Vophsi;
¹⁵ from Gad's family group—Geuel son of Maki.

¹⁶Those are the names of the men that Moses sent to look at and study the land. (Moses called Hoshea son of Nun by another name. Moses called him Joshua.) ¹⁷When Moses was sending them out to explore Canaan, he said, "Go through the Negev* and then into the hill country. ¹⁸See what the land looks like. Learn about the people who live there. Are they strong or are they weak? Are they few or are they many? ¹⁹Learn about the land that they live in. Is it good land or bad land? What kind of towns do they live in? Do the towns have walls protecting them? Are the towns strongly defended? ²⁰And learn other things about the land. Is the dirt good for growing things, or is it poor soil? Are there trees on the land? Also, try to bring back some of the fruit from that land." (This was during the time when the first grapes should be ripe.)

²¹So they went to explore the country. They explored the area from the Zin desert to Rehob and Lebo Hamath. ²²They entered the country through the Negev* and went to Hebron. (The town of Hebron was built seven years before the town of Zoan in Egypt.) Ahiman, Sheshai, and Talmai lived there. These men were descendants* of Anak. ²³Then the men went to Eshcol Valley. There, the men cut off a branch from a grapevine. The branch had a bunch of grapes on it. They put that branch on a pole. And two men carried it between them. They also carried some pomegranates,* and figs. ²⁴That place is called the Eshcol* Valley, because that is the place where the men of Israel cut off the bunch of grapes.

²⁵The men explored that country for 40 days. Then they went back to the camp. ²⁶The people of Israel were camped near Kadesh, in the desert of Paran. The men went to Moses and Aaron and all the Israelite people. The men told Moses, Aaron, and all the people about the things they saw. And

---

Negev The desert area south of Judah.
descendants A person's children and their future families.
pomegranates A red fruit with many small seeds inside it. Each seed is covered with the soft, juicy part of the fruit.
Eshcol This name is like the Hebrew word meaning "a bunch of grapes."

Hoshea Or, "Joshua."

they showed them the fruit from the land. ²⁷The men told Moses, "We went to the land where you sent us. It is a land filled with many good things*! Here is some of the fruit that grows there. ²⁸But the people living there are very powerful. The cities are very large. The cities are strongly defended. We even saw some Anakite* people there. ²⁹The Amalekite people live in the Negev.* The Hittites, the Jebusites, and the Amorites live in the hill country. The Canaanites live near the sea and by the Jordan River."

³⁰Caleb told the people near Moses to be quiet. Then Caleb said, "We should go up and take that land for ourselves. We can easily take that land."

³¹But the men that had gone with him said, "We can't fight those people! They are much stronger than we are." ³²And those men told all the people of Israel that they were not strong enough to defeat the people in that land. They said, "The land we saw is full of strong people. Those people are strong enough to easily defeat any person who goes there. ³³We saw the giant Nephilim* people there! (The descendants* of Anak come from the Nephilim people.) They looked at us like we were little grasshoppers. Yes, we were like grasshoppers to them!"

The People Complain Again

14 That night all the people in the camp began yelling loudly. ²The people of Israel complained against Moses and Aaron. All the people came together and said to Moses and Aaron, "We should have died in Egypt or in the desert. ₍That would have been better than being killed in this new land.₎ ³Did the Lord bring us to this new land to be killed in war? The enemy will kill us and take our wives and children! It would be better for us to go back to Egypt."

⁴Then the people said to each other, "Let's choose another leader and go back to Egypt."

⁵Moses and Aaron bowed low to the ground in front of all the people gathered there. ⁶Joshua and Caleb became very upset. (Joshua son of Nun and Caleb son of Jephunneh were two of the men who explored the land.) ⁷These two men said to all of the people of Israel gathered there, "The land that we saw is very good. ⁸It is a land filled with many good things.* And if the Lord is pleased with us, then he will lead us into that land. And the Lord will give that land to us! ⁹So don't turn against the Lord! Don't be afraid of the people in that land. We can defeat them. They have no protection, nothing to keep them safe. But we have the Lord with us. So don't be afraid!"

¹⁰All of the people began talking about killing Joshua and Caleb with stones. But the Glory of the Lord* appeared over the Meeting Tent* where all the people could see it. ¹¹The Lord spoke to Moses. He said, "How long will these people continue to turn against me? They show that they don't trust me. They show that they don't believe in my power. They refuse to believe me, even after I have shown them many powerful signs. I have done many great things among them. ¹²I will kill them all with a terrible sickness. I will destroy them, and I will use you to make another nation. And your nation will be greater and stronger than these people."

¹³Then Moses said to the Lord, "If you do that, the Egyptians will hear about it! They know that you used your great power to bring your people out of Egypt. ¹⁴And the people of Egypt told the people in Canaan about it. They already know you are the Lord. They know that you are with your people. They know that the people saw you. Those people know about the special cloud. They know you use the cloud to lead your people during the day. And they know the cloud becomes a fire to lead your people at night. ¹⁵So you must not kill these people now. If you kill them, then all the nations that have heard about your power will say, ¹⁶'The Lord was not able to bring these people into the land he promised them. So the Lord killed them in the desert.'

¹⁷"So now, Master, show your strength! Show it the way you said you would! ¹⁸You said, 'The Lord is slow to become angry. The Lord is full of great love. The Lord forgives* people who are

---

filled with many good things Literally, "flowing with milk and honey."

Anakite These people were famous for being big, powerful fighters.

Negev The desert area south of Judah.

Nephilim A famous family of tall and powerful fighting men. See Gen. 6:2-4.

descendants A person's children and their future families.

Glory of the Lord One of the forms God used when he appeared to people. Here this might be a bright shining light, or it might be the tall cloud.

Meeting Tent The Holy Tent (tabernacle) where the people of Israel came to meet with God.

forgives Or, "spares."

guilty and break the law. But the Lord always punishes people who are guilty. The Lord punishes those people, and he also punishes their children, their grandchildren, and even their great-grandchildren for those bad things!'* ¹⁹Now, show your great love to these people. Forgive their sin. Forgive them the same way you have been forgiving them since the time they left Egypt until now."

²⁰The Lord answered, "Yes, I will forgive the people like you asked. ²¹But, I tell you the truth. As surely as I live and as surely as my power fills the whole earth, I make you this promise! ²²None of the people I led out of Egypt will ever see the land of Canaan. Those people saw my glory and the great signs that I did in Egypt. And they saw the great things that I did in the desert. But they disobeyed me and tested me ten times. ²³I made a promise to their ancestors.* I promised that I would give them that land. But none of these people who turned against me will ever enter that land! ²⁴But my servant Caleb was different. He follows me completely. So I will bring him into the land that he has already seen. And his people will get that land. ²⁵The Amalekite and the Canaanite people are living in the valley. So tomorrow you must leave this place. Go back to the desert on the road to the Red Sea."

The Lord Punishes the People

²⁶The Lord said to Moses and Aaron, ²⁷"How long will these bad people continue to complain against me? I have heard their complaints and their griping. ²⁸So tell them, 'The Lord says that he will surely do all those things to you that you complained about. This is what will happen to you: ²⁹You will die in this desert. Every person who is 20 years old or older and was counted as one of my people will die. You complained against me, the Lord. ³⁰So none of you will ever enter and live in the land that I promised to give you. Only Caleb son of Jephunneh and Joshua son of Nun will enter that land. ³¹You were afraid and complained that your enemies in that new land would take your children away from you. But I tell you that I will bring those children into the land. They will enjoy the things that you refused to accept. ³²As for you people, you will die in this desert.

³³"Your children will be shepherds here in the desert for 40 years. They will suffer because you were not faithful to me. They must suffer until all of you lie dead in the desert. ³⁴For 40 years you will suffer for your sins. (That is one year for each of the 40 days that the men explored the land.) You will know that it is a terrible thing for me to be against you.

³⁵"I am the Lord, and I have spoken. And I promise that I will do these things to all of these evil people. These people have come together against me. So they will all die here in this desert."

³⁶Those men that Moses sent to explore the new land were the ones that came back and spread complaining among all the Israelite people. Those men said that the people were not strong enough to enter that land. ³⁷Those men were responsible for spreading the trouble among the Israelite people. So the Lord caused a sickness to kill all of those men. ³⁸But Joshua son of Nun and Caleb son of Jephunneh were among the men that were sent out to explore the land. And the Lord saved those two men. They did not get the sickness that caused the other ten men to die.

The People Try to Go into Canaan

³⁹Moses told all these things to the Israelite people. The people were very, very sad. ⁴⁰Early the next morning the people started to go up to the high hill country. The people said, "We have sinned. We are sorry that we did not trust the Lord. We will go to the place that the Lord promised."

⁴¹But Moses said, "Why are you not obeying the Lord's command? You will not be successful! ⁴²Don't go into that land. The Lord is not with you so your enemies will easily defeat you. ⁴³The Amalekite people and Canaanite people will fight against you there. You have turned away from the Lord. So he will not be with you when you fight them. And you will all be killed in battle."

⁴⁴But the people did not believe Moses. They went toward the high hill country. But Moses and the Box of the Lord's Agreement* did not go with

---

But the Lord ... bad things Or, "The Lord credits the guilt of the fathers to their children and grandchildren, to the third and fourth generation."

ancestors Literally, "fathers," meaning a person's parents, grandparents, and all the people they are descended from.

Box of the Lord's Agreement Or, "ark of the Covenant," the box containing the flat stones with the Ten Commandments written on them. These were proof of the Agreement between God and the people of Israel.

the people. ⁴⁵The Amalekite people and the Canaanite people living in the hill country came down and attacked the people of Israel. The Amalekites and the Canaanites easily defeated them and chased them all the way to Hormah.

Rules About Sacrifices

15 The Lord said to Moses, ²"Speak to the people of Israel and say to them: I am giving you a land to be your home. When you enter that land, ³you must give special offerings made by fire to the Lord. Their smell will please the Lord. You will use your cows, sheep, and goats for burnt offerings, sacrifices, special promises, special gifts, fellowship offerings, or special holidays.

⁴"At the time a person brings his offering, he must also give a grain offering to the Lord. The grain offering will be 8 cups* of fine flour mixed with 1 quart* of olive oil. ⁵Each time you offer a lamb as a burnt offering, you must also prepare a quart of wine as a drink offering.

⁶"If you are giving a ram, then you must also prepare a grain offering. This grain offering should be 16 cups* of fine flour mixed with 1 1/4 quarts* of olive oil. ⁷And you must prepare 1 1/4 quarts* of wine as a drink offering. Its smell will please the Lord.

⁸"You might prepare a young bull as a burnt offering, a sacrifice, a fellowship offering, or to keep a special promise to the Lord. ⁹At that time, you must also bring a grain offering with the bull. That grain offering should be 24 cups* of fine flour mixed with 2 quarts* of olive oil. ¹⁰Also bring 2 quarts* of wine as a drink offering. This will be an offering made by fire. Its smell will please the Lord. ¹¹Each bull or ram, or lamb or young goat that you give to the Lord must be prepared in this way. ¹²Do this for every one of these animals that you give.

¹³"That is the way every citizen of Israel must give the offerings made by fire to please the Lord. ¹⁴Foreigners will live among you. If those people give offerings made by fire to please the Lord, then they must offer them the same way you do. ¹⁵The same rules will be for everyone—the people of Israel and the foreigners living in your country. This law will continue forever. You and the people living among you will be the same before the Lord. ¹⁶This means that you must follow the same laws and the same rules. Those laws and rules are for you people of Israel and for the other people who are living among you."

¹⁷The Lord said to Moses, ¹⁸"Tell the people of Israel these things: I am taking you to another land. ¹⁹When you eat the food that grows in that land, you must give part of that food as an offering to the Lord. ²⁰You will gather grain and grind it into flour to make dough for bread. You must give the first of that dough as a gift to the Lord. It will be like the grain offering that comes from the threshing floor.* ²¹This rule will continue forever, you must give the first of that dough as a gift to the Lord.

²²"Now what should you do if you make a mistake and forget to obey one of the commands that the Lord gave Moses? ²³The Lord gave these commands to you through Moses. These commands started the day that the Lord gave them to you. And the commands continue forever. ²⁴So, what do you do if you make a mistake and forget to obey all of these commands. If all the people of Israel made that mistake, then together the people must offer one young bull as a burnt offering to the Lord. Its smell will please the Lord. Also remember to give the grain offering and the drink offering that must be offered with the bull. You must also give a male goat as a sin offering.

²⁵"So the priest must do the things that will make the people pure.* He must do this for all of the people of Israel. The people did not know they were sinning. But when they learned about it, they brought a gift to the Lord. They brought the offering made by fire and the sin offering. So the people will be forgiven. ²⁶All of the people of Israel and all the other people living among them will be forgiven. They will be forgiven because they did not know they were doing wrong.

²⁷"But if only one person makes a mistake and sins, then he must bring a female goat that is one year old. That goat will be the sin offering. ²⁸The priest must do the things that will make the person pure.* That person made a mistake and sinned before the Lord. But the priest made that person pure, and he will be forgiven. ²⁹That law is for

---

8 cups Literally, "1/10 of an ephah."
1 quart Literally, "1/4 hin."
16 cups Literally, "2/10 of an ephah."
1 1/4 quarts Literally, "1/3 hin."
24 cups Literally, "3/10 of an ephah."
2 quarts Literally, "1/2 hin."

threshing floor A place where grain is beaten or walked on to remove the hulls from the grain.
make ... pure Or, "make atonement." The Hebrew word means "to cover," "to hide," or "to erase sins."

every person who makes a mistake and sins. The same law is for the people born in the family of Israel and for the foreigners living among you. ³⁰"But if a person sins and knows that he is doing wrong, then that person is against the Lord. That person must be separated from his people. It is the same for a person born into the family of Israel or for a foreigner living among you. ³¹That person did not think the Lord's word was important. He broke the Lord's commands. That person must surely be separated from your group. That person is guilty and must be punished!*"

A Man Works on the Day of Rest

³²At this time, the people of Israel were still in the desert. It happened that a man found some wood to burn. So the man was gathering the wood, but it was the Sabbath * day. Some other people saw him doing this. ³³The people who saw him gathering the wood brought him to Moses and Aaron. And all the people gathered around. ³⁴They kept the man there because they did not know how they should punish him.
³⁵Then the Lord said to Moses, "The man must die. All the people must throw stones at him outside the camp." ³⁶So the people took him outside the camp and killed him with stones. They did this the way that the Lord commanded Moses.

God Helps His People Remember the Rules

³⁷The Lord said to Moses, ³⁸"Speak to the people of Israel. Tell them these things: ₍I will give you something to remember my commands.₎ Tie several pieces of thread together and tie them in the corner of your clothes. Put a piece of blue thread in each one of these tassels. You must wear these things now and forever. ³⁹You will be able to look at these tassels and remember all the commands that the Lord has given you. Then you will obey the commands. You will not do wrong by forgetting about the commands and doing the things that your own bodies and eyes want. ⁴⁰You will remember to obey all my commands. Then you will be God's special people. ⁴¹I am the Lord your God. I am the One who brought you out of Egypt. I did this to be your God. I am the Lord your God."

Some Leaders Turn Against Moses

16 Korah, Dathan, Abiram, and On turned against Moses. (Korah was the son of Izhar. Izhar was the son of Kohath, and Kohath was the son of Levi. Dathan and Abiram were brothers, the sons of Eliab. And On was the son of Peleth. Dathan, Abiram, and On were descendants* of Reuben.) ²Those four men gathered 250 other men from Israel together and came against Moses. They were leaders that had been chosen by the people. All the people knew them. ³They came as a group to speak against Moses and Aaron. These men said to Moses and Aaron, "You have gone too far—you are wrong! All the people of Israel are holy—the Lord still lives among them! You are making yourself more important than the rest of the Lord's people."

⁴When Moses heard these things, he bowed his face to the ground ₍to show he was not being proud₎. ⁵Then Moses said to Korah and all his followers, "Tomorrow morning the Lord will show which person truly belongs to him. The Lord will show which person is truly holy. And the Lord will bring that person near to him. The Lord will choose that man, and the Lord will bring that man near to him. ⁶So Korah, you and all your followers should do this: ⁷Tomorrow put fire and incense* in some special pans. Then bring those pans before the Lord. The Lord will choose the person who is truly holy. You Levites have gone too far—you are wrong!"

⁸Moses also said to Korah, "You Levites, listen to me. ⁹You should be happy that the God of Israel chose you and made you special. You are different from the rest of the Israelite people. The Lord brought you near to him to do the special work in the Lord's Holy Tent* to help the people of Israel worship him. Isn't that enough? ¹⁰The Lord brought you Levite people near to him ₍to help the priests₎. But now you are trying to become priests also. ¹¹You and your followers have joined together and turned against the Lord! Did Aaron do anything wrong? No! So why are you complaining against Aaron?"

¹²Then Moses called Dathan and Abiram, the sons of Eliab. But the two men said, "We will not

---

That person is guilty and must be punished Literally, "His guilt is on him."
Sabbath Saturday, a day of rest and worship for the Jews.
descendants A person's children and their future families.
incense Special dried tree sap. Burned to make a sweet-smelling smoke, it was offered as a gift to God.
Holy Tent Or, "tabernacle," the tent where God came to live among his people.

come! ¹³You have brought us out of a land filled with many good things.* You brought us to the desert to kill us. And now you want to show that you have even more power over us. ¹⁴Why should we follow you? You did not bring us into the new land filled with many good things.* You did not give us the land God promised. You did not give us the fields or the vineyards. Will you make these men your slaves? No! We will not come."

¹⁵So Moses became very angry. He said to the Lord, "I never did anything wrong to these people. I never took anything from them—not even a donkey! Lord, don't accept their gifts!"

¹⁶Then Moses said to Korah, "You and all your followers will stand before the Lord tomorrow. There will be Aaron and you and your followers. ¹⁷Each of you must bring a pan, put incense* on it, and present it to the Lord. There will be 250 pans ⌊for the leaders⌋ and one pan for you and one pan for Aaron."

¹⁸So each man got a pan and put burning incense* on it. Then they stood at the entrance of the Meeting Tent.* Moses and Aaron also stood there. ¹⁹Korah also gathered all the people together at the entrance of the Meeting Tent. Then the Glory of the Lord* appeared to every person there.

²⁰The Lord said to Moses and Aaron, ²¹"Move away from these men! I want to destroy them now!"

²²But Moses and Aaron bowed to the ground and cried out, "God, you know what people are thinking.* Please don't be angry at all these people. Only one man really sinned."

²³Then the Lord said to Moses, ²⁴"Tell the people to move away from the tents of Korah, Dathan, and Abiram."

²⁵Moses stood and went to Dathan and Abiram. All the elders (leaders) of Israel followed him. ²⁶Moses warned the people, "Move away from the tents of these evil men. Don't touch anything that belongs to them! If you do, then you will be destroyed because of their sins."

²⁷So the men moved away from the tents of Korah, Dathan, and Abiram. Dathan and Abiram went to their tents. They stood outside of their tents with their wives, children, and little babies.

²⁸Then Moses said, "I will show you proof that the Lord sent me to do all the things I told you. I will show you that all those things were not my own idea. ²⁹These men here will die. But if they die in a normal way—the way men always die—then that will show that the Lord did not really send me. ³⁰But if the Lord causes these men to die in a different way—something new—then you will know that these men have truly sinned against the Lord. ⌊This is the proof:⌋ the earth will open and swallow these men. They will go down to their grave still alive. And everything that belongs to these men will go down with them."

³¹When Moses finished saying these things, the ground under the men opened. ³²It was like the earth opened its mouth and swallowed them. All of Korah's men, their families, and everything they owned went down into the earth. ³³Those people went down into their grave alive. Everything they owned went with them. Then the earth closed over them. They were finished—gone from the camp!

³⁴The people of Israel heard the cries of the men being destroyed. So they all ran in different directions and said, "The earth will kill us, too!"

³⁵Then a fire came from the Lord and destroyed the 250 men who were offering the incense.*

³⁶The Lord said to Moses, ³⁷⁻³⁸"Tell Eleazar son of Aaron the priest to get all the incense* pans from the fire. Tell him to scatter the coals and ashes. Those men sinned against me, and their sin cost them their lives. But the incense pans are still holy.* The pans are holy because they gave them to the Lord. Hammer the pans into flat sheets. Use the metal sheets to cover the altar.* This will be a warning to all of the people of Israel."

³⁹So Eleazar the priest gathered together all the bronze* pans that the men had brought. Those men were all burned up, but the pans were still there. Then Eleazar told some men to hammer the pans into flat metal. Then he put the metal sheets on the altar.* ⁴⁰He did this the way the Lord

---

filled with many good things Literally, "flowing with milk and honey."
incense Special dried tree sap. Burned to make a sweet-smelling smoke, it was offered as a gift to God.
Meeting Tent The Holy Tent (tabernacle) where the people of Israel came to meet with God.
Glory of the Lord One of the forms God used when he appeared to people. This was like a bright shining light.
God ,you know what people are thinking Literally, "God, God of the spirits of all people."

holy Set aside or chosen for a special purpose.
altar A table or raised area used for offering sacrifices.
bronze A metal. The Hebrew word can mean "copper," "bronze," or "brass."

commanded him through Moses. This was a sign to help the people of Israel remember that only a person from the family of Aaron should burn incense* before the Lord. Any other person who burns incense before the Lord will die like Korah and his followers.

Aaron Saves the People

⁴¹The next day all the people of Israel complained against Moses and Aaron. They said, "You killed the Lord's people."

⁴²Moses and Aaron were standing at the entrance of the Meeting Tent.* The people gathered together at that place to complain against Moses and Aaron. But when they looked toward the Meeting Tent, the cloud covered it and the Glory of the Lord* appeared there. ⁴³Then Moses and Aaron went to the front of the Meeting Tent.

⁴⁴The Lord said to Moses, ⁴⁵"Move away from those people so that I can destroy them now." So Moses and Aaron bowed with their faces to the ground.

⁴⁶Then Moses said to Aaron, "Get your bronze* pan and some fire from the altar.* Then put incense* on it. Hurry to the group of people and do the things that will make the people pure.* The Lord is angry at them. The trouble has already started."

⁴⁷⁻⁴⁸So Aaron did what Moses said. Aaron got the incense* and the fire, and he ran to the middle of the people. But the sickness had already started among the people. So Aaron stood between the dead people and the people who were still alive. Aaron did the things to make the people pure.* And the sickness stopped there. ⁴⁹But 14,700 people died from that sickness—and that is not counting the people who died because of Korah. ⁵⁰So, the terrible sickness was stopped and Aaron went back to Moses at the entrance of the Meeting Tent.*

God Proves Aaron Is the High Priest

17 The Lord said to Moses, ²"Speak to the people of Israel. Get twelve wooden walking sticks from them. Get one from the leader of each of the twelve family groups. Write the name of each man on his walking stick. ³On the stick from Levi, write Aaron's name. There must be one stick for the head of each of the twelve family groups. ⁴Put these walking sticks in the Meeting Tent* in front of the Box of the Agreement.* This is the place where I meet with you. ⁵I will choose one man to be the true priest. You will know which man I choose because his walking stick will begin to grow new leaves. In this way, I will stop the people from always complaining against you and me."

⁶So Moses spoke to the people of Israel. Each of the leaders gave him a walking stick. There were twelve walking sticks. There was one stick from each leader of each family group. One of the walking sticks belonged to Aaron. ⁷Moses put the walking sticks before the Lord in the Tent of the Agreement.*

⁸The next day Moses entered the Tent. He saw that Aaron's walking stick, the stick from the family of Levi, was the one that had grown new leaves. That walking stick had even grown branches and made almonds. ⁹So Moses brought out all the sticks from the Lord's place. Moses showed the walking sticks to the people of Israel. They all looked at the sticks, and each man took his own stick back.

¹⁰Then the Lord said to Moses, "Put Aaron's walking stick back into the Tent in front of the Agreement.* This will be a warning for these people who are always turning against me. This will stop their complaining against me, so that I won't destroy them." ¹¹So Moses did what the Lord commanded him.

---

incense Special dried tree sap. Burned to make a sweet-smelling smoke, it was offered as a gift to God.

Meeting Tent The Holy Tent (tabernacle) where the people of Israel came to meet with God.

Glory of the Lord One of the forms God used when he appeared to people. This was like a bright shining light.

bronze A metal. The Hebrew word can mean "copper," "bronze," or "brass."

altar A table or raised area used for offering sacrifices.

make ... pure Or, "make atonement." The Hebrew word means "to cover," "to hide," or "to erase sins."

Box of the Agreement Or, "ark of the Covenant," the box containing the flat stones with the Ten Commandments written on them. These were proof of the Agreement between God and the people of Israel.

Tent of the Agreement The Holy Tent where the Box of the Agreement was kept.

Agreement Literally, "Proof." The flat stones with the Ten Commandments written on them. These were proof of the Agreement between God and the people of Israel.

¹²The people of Israel said to Moses, "We know that we will die! We are lost! We will all be destroyed! ¹³Any person who even comes near the Lord's holy place will die. Is it true that we will all die?"

The Work of the Priests and Levites

18 The Lord said to Aaron, "You, your sons, and all the people in your father's family are now responsible for any wrong things that are done against the holy place. You and your sons are responsible for wrong things that are done against the priests. ²Bring the other Levite men from your family group to join you. They will help you and your sons do your work in the Tent of the Agreement.* ³Those people from the family of Levi are under your control. They will do all the work that needs to be done in the Tent. But they must not go near the things in the Holy Place* or the altar.* If they do, then they will die—and you will die also. ⁴They will join you and work with you. They will be responsible for caring for the Meeting Tent.* All the work that must be done in the Tent will be done by them. No one else may come near the place where you are.

⁵"You are responsible for caring for the holy place and the altar.* I don't want to become angry with the people of Israel again. ⁶I myself chose the Levite people from among all the people of Israel. They are like a gift to you. I gave them to you to serve the Lord and work in the Meeting Tent.* ⁷But, Aaron, only you and your sons may serve as priests. You are the only ones that can go near the altar. You are the only ones that can go inside the curtain ⌊into the Most Holy Place⌋. I am giving you a gift—your service as a priest. Anyone else that comes near ⌊my⌋ holy place must be killed."

⁸Then the Lord said to Aaron, "I myself gave you responsibility over all the special gifts people give to me. All the holy* gifts that the people of Israel give to me, I give to you. You and your sons can share in these gifts. They will always belong to you. ⁹The people will bring sacrifices, grain offerings, sin offerings, and guilt offerings. Those offerings are most holy. Your share in the most holy offerings will come from the parts that are not burned. All those things will be for you and your sons. ¹⁰Eat those things only in the very holy place. Every male in your family may eat them, but you must remember that those offerings are holy.

¹¹"And all the gifts that the Israelite people give as wave offerings will also be yours. I give this to you and your sons and your daughters. This is your share. Every person in your family that is clean* will be able to eat it.

¹²"And I give you all the best olive oil and all the best new wine and grain. These are the things that the people of Israel give to me, the Lord. These are the first things that they gather in their harvest. ¹³When the people gather a harvest, they bring all the first things to the Lord. So these things I will give to you. And every person in your family that is clean* may eat it.

¹⁴"Everything in Israel that is given to the Lord* is yours.

¹⁵"A woman's first baby and an animal's first baby must be given to the Lord. That baby will belong to you. If the firstborn animal is unclean,* then it must be bought back. If the baby is a child, that child must be bought back. ⌊That child will again belong to its family.⌋ ¹⁶They must make the payment when the baby is one month old. The cost will be 2 ounces* of silver. You must use the official measure* to weigh this silver. A shekel by the official measure is 20 gerahs.*

¹⁷"But you must not make a payment for the firstborn cow, sheep, or goat. Those animals are holy.* Sprinkle their blood on the altar* and burn their fat. This is an offering made by fire. Its smell pleases the Lord. ¹⁸But the meat from those animals will be yours. And also the breast from a wave offering will be yours. And the right thigh from other offerings will be yours. ¹⁹Anything that the people offer as holy gifts, I, the Lord, give to you. This is your share. I give it to you and your sons and your daughters. This law will continue forever. It is an agreement with the Lord that can't

---

Tent of the Agreement The Holy Tent where the Box of the Agreement was kept.
Holy Place One of the rooms in the Holy Tent.
altar A table of raised area used for offering sacrifices.
Meeting Tent The Holy Tent (tabernacle) where the people of Israel came to meet with God.
holy Chosen or set aside for God.
clean Pure or acceptable to God for worship.
given to the Lord Things that were given to God and could not be bought back. See Lev. 27:28-29.
unclean Not pure or not acceptable to God for worship.
2 ounces Literally, "5 shekels."
official measure The standard measure used in the tabernacle or temple.
gerah(s) Or, "2/5 of an ounce."

be broken.* I make this promise to you and to your descendants.*"

²⁰The Lord also said to Aaron, "You will not get any of the land. And you will not own anything that the other people own. I, the Lord, will be yours. The Israelite people will get the land that I promised. But I am my gift to you. ²¹"The people of Israel will give one tenth of everything they have. So I give that one tenth to all the descendants* of Levi. This is their payment for the work that they do while they serve at the Meeting Tent.* ²²But the other people of Israel must never go near that Meeting Tent. If they do, then they must be put to death! ²³The Levite people who are working in the Meeting Tent are responsible for any sins against it. This is a law that will continue forever. The Levite people will not get any of the land that I promised to the other people of Israel. ²⁴But the people of Israel will give one tenth of everything they have to me. And I will give that one tenth to the Levite people. That is why I said these words about the Levite people: Those people will not get the land that I promised the people of Israel."

²⁵The Lord said to Moses, ²⁶"Speak to the Levite people and tell them: The people of Israel will give one tenth of everything they own to the Lord. That one tenth will belong to the Levite people. But you must give one tenth of that to the Lord as his offering. ²⁷You will be given grain after it is harvested and juice from the winepress. Then that will also be your offering to the Lord. ²⁸In this way, you will also give an offering to the Lord in the same way that the other people of Israel do. You will get the one tenth that the people of Israel give to the Lord. And then you will give one tenth of that to Aaron the priest. ²⁹When the people of Israel give you one tenth of everything that they own, then you should choose the best and the holiest part of those things. That is the one tenth that you must give to the Lord.

³⁰"Moses, tell the Levite people: The people of Israel will give you one tenth of their harvest and of their wine. Then you will give the best part of that to the Lord. ³¹You and your families can eat all that is left. This is your payment for the work you do in the Meeting Tent.* ³²And if you always give the best part of it to the Lord, then you will never be guilty. You will always remember that those gifts are the holy* offerings from the people of Israel. And you will not die."

The Ashes of the Red Cow

19 The Lord spoke to Moses and Aaron. He said, ²"These are the laws from the teachings that the Lord gave to the people of Israel. Get a red cow that has nothing wrong with it. That cow must not have any bruises. And that cow must never have worn a yoke.* ³Give that cow to Eleazar the priest. Eleazar will take the cow outside the camp and kill it there. ⁴Then Eleazar the priest must put some of its blood on his finger and sprinkle some of the blood towards the Holy Tent. He must do this seven times. ⁵Then the whole cow must be burned in front of him. The skin, the meat, the blood, and the intestines must all be burned. ⁶Then the priest must take a cedar stick, a hyssop* branch, and some red string. The priest must throw those things into the fire where the cow is burning. ⁷Then the priest must wash himself and his clothes with water. Then he must come back into the camp. The priest will be unclean* until evening. ⁸The person who burns that cow must wash himself and his clothes in water. He will be unclean until evening.

⁹"Then a person who is clean* will collect the ashes from the cow. He will put those ashes in a clean place outside the camp. These ashes will be used when people must keep a special ceremony to become clean. These ashes will also be used to remove a person's sins.

¹⁰"The person who collected the cow's ashes must wash his clothes. He will be unclean* until evening.

"This rule will continue forever. This rule is for the citizens of Israel. And this rule is for the foreigners living with you. ¹¹If someone touches a dead person's body, then he will be unclean* for seven days. ¹²He must wash himself with the special water on the third day and again on the seventh day. If he does not do this, then he will remain unclean. ¹³If a person touches a dead body,

---

It is an agreement ... broken Literally, "It is an eternal, salt agreement before the Lord."
descendants A person's children and their future families.
Meeting Tent The Holy Tent (tabernacle) where the people of Israel came to meet with God.

holy Chosen or set aside for God.
yoke A piece of wood that joins two work animals together for pulling a wagon or plow.
hyssop A plant with fine branches and leaves used for sprinkling water or blood in cleansing ceremonies.
unclean Not pure or not acceptable to God for worship.
clean Pure or acceptable to God for worship.

then that person is unclean. If that person stays unclean and then goes to the Holy Tent,* then the Holy Tent becomes unclean. So that person must be separated from the people of Israel. If the special water is not thrown on an unclean person, then that person will stay unclean.

[14]"This is the rule about people who die in their tents. If a person dies in his tent, then everyone in the tent will be unclean.* They will be unclean for seven days. [15]And every jar or pot without a lid becomes unclean. [16]If anyone touches a dead body, then that person will be unclean for seven days. This is true if the dead body is out in the field or if the person was killed in war. Also, if anyone touches the bones from a dead person then that person is unclean.

[17]"So you must use the ashes from the burnt cow to make that person clean* again. Pour fresh water* over the ashes into a jar. [18]A clean person must take a hyssop* branch and dip it into the water. Then he must sprinkle it over the tent, the dishes, and the people who were in the tent. You must do this to anyone that touches a dead person's body. You must do this to anyone that touches the body of someone killed in war and to anyone that touches a grave or the bones from a dead person.

[19]"Then a clean* person must sprinkle this water on the unclean* person on the third day and again on the seventh day. On the seventh day, that person becomes clean. He must wash his clothes in water. He will become clean in the evening.

[20]"If a person becomes unclean* and does not become clean,* that person must be separated from the people of Israel. That person was not sprinkled with the special water. He did not become clean. So he might make the Holy Tent* unclean. [21]This rule will be for you forever. If a person is sprinkled with the special water, then he must also wash his clothes. Any person who touches the special water will be unclean until evening. [22]If an unclean person touches someone else, then that other person also becomes unclean. That person will be unclean until evening."

Miriam Dies

20 The people of Israel arrived at the Zin desert on the first month. The people stayed at Kadesh. Miriam died, and she was buried there.

Moses Makes a Mistake

[2]There was not enough water for the people at that place. So the people met together to complain to Moses and Aaron. [3]The people argued with Moses. They said, "Maybe we should have died in front of the Lord like our brothers did. [4]Why did you bring the Lord's people into this desert? Do you want us and our animals to die here? [5]Why did you bring us from Egypt? Why did you bring us to this bad place? There is no grain. There are no figs, grapes, or pomegranates.* And there is no water to drink. [6]So Moses and Aaron left the crowd of people and went to the entrance of the Meeting Tent.* They bowed down to the ground. And the Glory of the Lord* appeared to them.

[7]The Lord spoke to Moses. He said, [8]"Get the ₁special₁ walking stick. Take your brother Aaron and the crowd of people and go to that rock. Speak to the rock in front of the people. Then water will flow from the rock. And you can give that water to the people and to their animals."

[9]The walking stick was ₁in the Holy Tent,₁ in front of the Lord. Moses took the walking stick like the Lord said. [10]Moses and Aaron told the people to meet together in front of the rock. Then Moses said, "You people are always complaining. Now listen to me. I will cause water to flow from this rock." [11]Moses lifted his arm and hit the rock twice. Water began flowing from the rock. And the people and their animals drank that water.

[12]But the Lord said to Moses and Aaron, "All the people of Israel were gathered around. But you did not show me honor. You did not show the people of Israel that the power to make the water came from me. You did not show the people that you trusted in me. I will give those people the land that I promised them. But you will not lead them into that land!"

Holy Tent Or, "tabernacle," the tent where God came to live among his people.
unclean Not pure or not acceptable to God for worship.
clean Pure or acceptable to God for worship.
fresh water Literally, "living water." This means fresh, flowing water.
hyssop A plant with fine branches and leaves used for sprinkling water or blood in cleansing ceremonies.
pomegranate A red fruit with many small seeds inside it. Each seed is covered with the soft, juicy part of the fruit.
Meeting Tent The Holy Tent (tabernacle) where the people of Israel came to meet with God.
Glory of the Lord One of the forms God used when he appeared to people. This was like a bright, shining light.

NUMBERS 20:13–21:5

¹³This place was called the waters of Meribah.* This was the place where the Israelite people argued with the Lord. And this was the place that the Lord showed them that he was holy.

Edom Won't Let Israel Pass

¹⁴While Moses was at Kadesh, he sent some men with a message to the king of Edom. The message said: "Your brothers, the people of Israel, say to you: You know about all the troubles that we have had. ¹⁵Many, many years ago our ancestors* went down into Egypt. And we lived there for many years. The people of Egypt were cruel to us. ¹⁶But we asked the Lord for help. The Lord heard us and sent an angel to help us. The Lord has brought us out of Egypt.

"Now we are here at Kadesh, where your land begins. ¹⁷Please let us travel through your country. We will not travel through any fields or vineyards. We will not drink water from any of your wells. We will travel only along the King's Road. We will not leave that road to the right or to the left. We will stay on the road until we have traveled through your country."

¹⁸But ₍the king of₎ Edom answered, "You may not travel through our land. If you try to travel through our land, then we will come and fight you with swords."

¹⁹The people of Israel answered, "We will travel along the main road. If our animals drink any of your water, we will pay you for it. We only want to walk through your country. We don't want to take it for ourselves."

²⁰But again Edom answered, "We won't allow you to come through our country."

Then ₍the king of₎ Edom gathered a large and powerful army and went out to fight against the people of Israel. ²¹₍The king of₎ Edom refused to let the people of Israel travel through his country. And the people of Israel turned around and went another way.

Aaron Dies

²²All the people of Israel traveled from Kadesh to Mount Hor. ²³Mount Hor was near the border of Edom. The Lord said to Moses and Aaron, ²⁴"It is time for Aaron to die and₎ go to be with his ancestors.* Aaron will not enter the land that I promised to the people of Israel. Moses, I say this to you because both you and Aaron did not fully obey the command I gave you at the waters of Meribah.

²⁵"Now, bring Aaron and his son Eleazar up to Mount Hor. ²⁶Take Aaron's special clothes from him and put those clothes on his son Eleazar. Aaron will die there on the mountain. And he will go to be with his ancestors.*"

²⁷Moses obeyed the Lord's command. Moses, Aaron, and Eleazar went up on Mount Hor. All the people of Israel watched them go. ²⁸Moses removed Aaron's special clothes and put those clothes on Aaron's son Eleazar. Then Aaron died there on top of the mountain. Moses and Eleazar came back down the mountain. ²⁹All the people of Israel learned that Aaron was dead. So every person in Israel mourned* for 30 days.

War with the Canaanites

21 The Canaanite king of Arad lived in the Negev.* He heard that the people of Israel were coming on the road to Atharim. So the king went out and attacked the people of Israel. Arad captured some of the people and made them prisoners. ²Then the people of Israel made a special promise to the Lord: "Lord, please help us defeat these people. If you do this, then we will give their cities to you. We will totally destroy them."

³The Lord listened to the people of Israel. And the Lord helped the people of Israel to defeat the Canaanite people. The people of Israel completely destroyed the Canaanite people and their cities. So that place was named Hormah.*

The Bronze Snake

⁴The people of Israel left Mount Hor and traveled on the road that goes to the Red Sea. They did this to go around the country of Edom. But the people became impatient. ⁵They began complaining against God and Moses. The people said, "Why did you bring us out of Egypt? We will die here in the desert! There is no bread!

Meribah This name means "argument," or "rebellion."
ancestors Literally, "fathers," meaning a person's parents, grandparents, and all the people they are descended from.
mourn To show sadness for a person who died. In ancient Israel people often cried very loudly, wore special clothes, and put ashes on their head to show their sadness.
Negev The desert area south of Judah.
Hormah This name means "completely destroyed," or "a gift given totally to God." See Lev. 27:28-29.

There is no water! And we hate this terrible food!" ⁶So the Lord sent poisonous snakes among the people. The snakes bit the people, and many of the people of Israel died. ⁷The people came to Moses and said, "We know that we sinned when we spoke against the Lord and against you. Pray to the Lord. Ask him to take away these snakes." So Moses prayed for the people.

⁸The Lord said to Moses, "Make a bronze* snake and put it on a pole. If any person is bitten by a snake, then that person should look at the bronze snake on the pole. Then that person will not die." ⁹So Moses obeyed the Lord. He made a bronze snake and put it on a pole. Then when a snake bit any person, that person looked at the bronze snake on the pole and lived.

The Trip to Moab

¹⁰The people of Israel left that place and camped at Oboth. ¹¹Then they left Oboth and camped at Iye Abarim in the desert east of Moab. ¹²They left that place and camped in Zered Valley. ¹³Then they moved and camped across from the Arnon River in the desert. This river started at the Ammonite border. The valley was the border between Moab and the Amorites. ¹⁴That is why these words are written in the Book of the Wars of the Lord:

"... and Waheb in Suphah, and the Valleys
of the Arnon, ¹⁵and the hills by the valleys
that lead to the town of Ar. These places are
at the border of Moab."

¹⁶The people of Israel left that place and traveled to Beer.* This was the place with the well. This was the place where the Lord said to Moses, "Bring the people together here and I will give them water." ¹⁷Then the people of Israel sang this song:

"Well, flow with water!
  Sing about it!
¹⁸ Great men dug this well.
  Important leaders dug this well.
  They dug this well with their staffs
  and walking sticks.
  It is a gift in the desert.*"

So the people called that well "Mattanah." ¹⁹The people traveled from Mattanah to Nahaliel. Then they traveled from Nahaliel to Bamoth. ²⁰The people traveled from Bamoth to the Valley of Moab. In this place the top of the Pisgah Mountain looks over the desert.

Sihon and Og

²¹The people of Israel sent some men to Sihon, the king of the Amorite people. The men said to the king, ²²"Allow us to travel through your country. We will not go through any field or vineyard. We will not drink water from any of your wells. We will travel only along King's Road. We will stay on that road until we have traveled through your country."

²³But King Sihon would not allow the people of Israel to travel through his country. The king gathered together his army and marched out to the desert. He was marching to fight against the people of Israel. At Jahaz, the king's army fought against the people of Israel.

²⁴But the people of Israel killed the king. Then they took his land from the Arnon River to the Jabbok River. The people of Israel took the land as far as the Ammonite border. They stopped at that border because it was strongly defended by the Ammonite people. ²⁵Israel took all the Amorite cities and began living in them. They even defeated the city of Heshbon and all the small towns around it. ²⁶Heshbon was the city where Sihon, the Amorite king, lived. In the past, Sihon had fought with the king of Moab. Sihon had taken the land as far as the Arnon River. ²⁷That is why the singers sing this song:

"Heshbon, you should be built again.
  Let Sihon's city be built again.
²⁸ A fire began in Heshbon.
  That fire began in Sihon's city.
  The fire destroyed the city of Ar in
    Moab.
  It burned the hills above the Arnon
    River.
²⁹ It is bad for you, Moab.
  Chemosh's* people have been
    destroyed.
  His sons ran away.
  His daughters were taken prisoners
    by Sihon, king of the Amorites.

---

bronze A metal. The Hebrew word can mean "copper," "bronze," or "brass."
Beer This Hebrew name means "Well."
gift in the desert In Hebrew this is the name "Mattanah."

Chemosh The god of the Moabite people.

³⁰ But we defeated those Amorites.
We destroyed their towns
 from Heshbon to Dibon,
 from Nashim to Nophah, near
  Medeba."

³¹So the people of Israel made their camp in the land of the Amorite people. ³²Moses sent some men to look at the town of Jazer. After Moses did this, the people of Israel captured that town. They captured the small towns that were around it. The people of Israel forced the Amorite people who were living there to leave.

³³Then the people of Israel traveled on the road toward Bashan. Og, the king of Bashan, got his army and marched out to meet the people of Israel. He fought against them at Edrei. ³⁴But the Lord said to Moses, "Don't be afraid of that king. I will allow you to defeat him. You will take his whole army and all his land. Do the same to him as you did to Sihon, the Amorite king that lived in Heshbon." ³⁵So the people of Israel defeated Og and his army. They killed him and his sons and all his army. Then the people of Israel took all his land.

Balaam and the King of Moab

22 Then the people of Israel traveled to the Jordan Valley in Moab. They camped near the Jordan River across from Jericho.

²⁻³Balak son of Zippor saw all the things that the people of Israel had done to the Amorite people. ⌊The king of⌋ Moab was very afraid, because there were so many people of Israel. Moab was really scared of them.

⁴The ⌊king of⌋ Moab said to the leaders of Midian, "This large group of people will destroy everything around us, the way a cow eats all the grass in a field."

Balak son of Zippor was the king of Moab at this time. ⁵He sent some men to call Balaam son of Beor. Balaam was at Pethor, near the Euphrates River. This was where Balaam's people lived.* This was Balak's message: "A new nation of people has come out of Egypt. There are so many people that they cover all the land. They have camped next to me. ⁶Come and help me. These people are too powerful for me. I know that you have great power. If you bless a person, then good things happen to him. And if you speak against a person, then bad things happen to him. So come and speak against these people. Maybe then I will be able to defeat them. Then I can force them to leave my country."

⁷The leaders of Moab and Midian left. They went to talk to Balaam. They carried with them money to pay him for his service.* Then they told him what Balak had said.

⁸Balaam said to them, "Stay here for the night. I will talk to the Lord and tell you the answer he gives me." So the leaders of Moab stayed there with Balaam that night.

⁹God came to Balaam and asked, "Who are these men with you?"

¹⁰Balaam said to God, "The king of Moab, Balak son of Zippor, sent them to give me a message. ¹¹This is the message: A new nation of people has come out of Egypt. There are so many people that they cover the land. So, come and speak against these people. Then maybe I will be able to fight them and force them to leave my land."

¹²But God said to Balaam, "Don't go with them. You must not speak against those people. They are my people."

¹³The next morning Balaam got up and said to leaders from Balak, "Go back to your own country. The Lord will not let me go with you."

¹⁴So the leaders of Moab went back to Balak and told him this. They said, "Balaam refused to come with us."

¹⁵So Balak sent other leaders to Balaam. This time he sent many more than the first time. And these leaders were much more important than the first ones he sent. ¹⁶They went to Balaam and said: "Balak son of Zippor says this to you: Please don't let anything stop you from coming. ¹⁷I will pay you very much if you will do what I ask.* Come and speak against these people for me."

¹⁸Balaam gave Balak's officials his answer. He said, "I must obey the Lord my God. I cannot do anything against his command. I cannot do anything, great or small, unless the Lord says that I can. I will not do anything against the Lord's

---

This was where Balaam's people lived Or, "This was the land of the Ammonites."

for his service Or, "for the things he needed to make curses." In ancient times, when people asked bad things to happen to other people, they often wrote the curses on special bowls and used them in ceremonies. They did this to try to force those bad things to happen. See Deut. 18:10.

I will pay you very much if you will do what I ask Or, "I will honor you very much."

command, even if King Balak gives me his beautiful home filled with silver and gold. ¹⁹But you can stay here tonight like the other men did. And during the night I will learn what the Lord wants to tell me."

²⁰That night, God came to Balaam. God said, "These men have come again to ask you to go with them. So you can go with them. But do only the things that I tell you to do."

Balaam and His Donkey

²¹The next morning, Balaam got up and put a saddle on his donkey. Then he went with the leaders of Moab. ²²Balaam was riding on his donkey. Two of his servants were with him. While Balaam was traveling, God became angry. So the Lord's angel stood in the road in front of Balaam. The angel was going to stop* Balaam.

²³Balaam's donkey saw the Lord's angel standing in the road. The angel was holding a sword in his hand. So the donkey turned from the road and went into the field. Balaam could not see the angel. So he was very angry with the donkey. He hit the donkey and forced it to go back on the road.

²⁴Later, the Lord's angel stood at a place where the road became narrow. This was between two vineyards. There were walls on both sides of the road. ²⁵Again the donkey saw the Lord's angel. So the donkey walked very close to one wall. This crushed Balaam's foot against the wall. So Balaam hit his donkey again.

²⁶Later the Lord's angel stood at another place. This was another place where the road became narrow. There was no place where the donkey could go around him. The donkey could not turn to the left or to the right. ²⁷The donkey saw the the Lord's angel. So the donkey lay down with Balaam sitting on top of it. Balaam was very angry at the donkey. So he hit it with his walking stick.

²⁸Then the Lord caused the donkey to speak. The donkey said to Balaam, "Why are you angry at me? What have I done to you? You have hit me three times!"

²⁹Balaam answered the donkey, "You have made me look foolish. If I had a sword in my hand, I would kill you right now!"

³⁰But the donkey said to Balaam, "Look, I am your own donkey! You have ridden me for many, many years. And you know that I have never done this to you before!"

"That is true," Balaam said.

³¹Then the Lord allowed Balaam to see the angel. The Lord's angel was standing in the road, holding a sword in his hand. Balaam bowed low to the ground.

³²Then the Lord's angel asked Balaam, "Why did you hit your donkey three times? I am the one that came to stop* you. But just in time,* ³³your donkey saw me and turned away from me. That happened three times. If the donkey had not turned away, I probably would have killed you already. And I would have let your donkey live."

³⁴Then Balaam said to the Lord's angel, "I have sinned. I did not know that you were standing in the road. If I am doing wrong, then I will go back home."

³⁵Then the Lord's angel said to Balaam, "No! You can go with these men. But be careful. Speak only the words that I will tell you to say." So Balaam went with the leaders that Balak had sent.

³⁶Balak heard that Balaam was coming. So Balak went out to meet him at the Moabite town* near the Arnon River. This was at the northern border of his country. ³⁷When Balak saw Balaam, he said to him, "I asked you before to come. I told you it was very, very important. Why didn't you come to me? I might not be able to pay you now."

³⁸Balaam answered, "But I am here now. I came, but I might not be able to do the thing you asked. I can only say the words that the Lord God tells me to say."

³⁹Then Balaam went with Balak to Kiriath Huzoth. ⁴⁰Balak killed some cattle and some sheep as his sacrifice. He gave some of the meat to Balaam and some to the leaders that were with him.

⁴¹The next morning Balak took Balaam to the town of Bamoth Baal. From there, they could see part of the Israelite camp.

Balaam's First Message

23 Balaam said, "Build seven altars* here. And prepare seven bulls and seven rams for me." ²Balak did the thing that Balaam asked. Then

---

But just in time Literally, "Just as the path in front of me dropped away,... " or, "Because you are not doing right,.... " The Hebrew is very hard to understand.

Moabite town Or possibly, "Ar Moab."

altar A table or raised area used for offering sacrifices.

stop Or, "oppose" or "accuse."

Balak and Balaam killed a ram and a bull on each of the altars.

³Then Balaam said to Balak, "Stay here near this altar.* I will go to another place. Then the Lord will come to me, and he will tell me what I must say." Then Balaam went away to a higher place.

⁴God came to Balaam at that place. And Balaam said, "I have prepared seven altars.* And I have killed a bull and a ram as a sacrifice on each altar."

⁵Then the Lord told Balaam what he should say. Then the Lord said, "Go back to Balak and say these things that I have given you to say."

⁶So Balaam went back to Balak. Balak was still standing near the altar.* And all the leaders of Moab were standing there with them. ⁷Then Balaam said these things:

> Balak king of Moab brought me here
>   from the eastern mountains of Aram.
> Balak said to me,
>   "Come, speak against Jacob* for me.
>   Come, speak against the people of
>   Israel."
>
> ⁸ But God is not against those people,
>   So I can't speak against them either!
> The Lord has not asked for bad things to
>   happen to those people.
>   So I can't do that either.
> ⁹ I see those people from the mountain.
>   I see them from the high hills.
> Those people live alone.
>   They are not part of another nation.
> ¹⁰ Who can count Jacob's people? They
>   are as many as the grains of dust.
> No one can count even a fourth of
>   the people of Israel.
> Let me die like a good man.
>   Let my life end as happy as theirs!

¹¹Balak said to Balaam, "What have you done to me? I brought you here to speak against my enemies. But you have only blessed them!"

¹²But Balaam answered, "I must say the things that the Lord tells me to say."

¹³Then Balak said to him, "So come with me to another place. At that place you can see more of those people. You can't see all of them—you can only see part of them. Maybe from that place you can speak against them for me." ¹⁴So Balak led Balaam to Watchmen Hills.* This was on top of Mount Pisgah. At that place, Balak built seven altars.* And then Balak killed a bull and a ram on each altar as a sacrifice.

¹⁵So Balaam said to Balak, "Stay here by this altar.* I will go meet with God over at that place."

¹⁶So the Lord came to Balaam and told Balaam what to say. Then the Lord told Balaam to go back to Balak and say those things. ¹⁷So Balaam went to Balak. Balak was still standing near the altar.* The leaders of Moab were there with him. Balak saw Balaam coming and said, "What did the Lord say?"

Balaam's Second Message

¹⁸Then Balaam said these things:

> "Stand up, Balak, and listen to me.
>   Hear me, Balak son of Zippor.
> ¹⁹ God is not a man;
>   he will not lie.
> God is not a human being;
>   his decisions will not change.
> If the Lord says he will do something,
>   then he will do it.
> If the Lord makes a promise,
>   then he will do the thing he promised.
> ²⁰ The Lord told me to bless those people.
>   The Lord blessed them,
>   so I cannot change that.
> ²¹ God saw no wrong in Jacob's people.
>   God saw no sin in the people of Israel.
> The Lord is their God,
>   and he is with them.
> The Great King is with them!
> ²² God brought those people out of Egypt.
>   They are as strong as a wild ox.
> ²³ There is no power that can defeat
>   the people of Jacob.*
> There is no magic that can stop
>   the people of Israel.
> People will say this about Jacob
>   and about the people of Israel:
>   "Look at the great things God did!"
> ²⁴ The people are as strong as a lion.
>   They fight like a lion.
> And that lion will not rest,
>   until he has eaten his enemy.
> And that lion will not rest,
>   until he drinks the blood
>   of the people who are against him."

---

altar(s) A table or raised area used for offering sacrifices.
Jacob This is another name for Israel.
Watchmen Hills Or, "the fields of Zophim."

²⁵Then Balak said to Balaam, "You didn't ask for good things to happen to those people. But you didn't ask for bad things to happen to them either!" ²⁶Balaam answered, "I told you before that I can only say the things that the Lord tells me to say." ²⁷Then Balak said to Balaam, "So come with me to another place. Maybe God will be pleased and will allow you to curse them from that place." ²⁸So Balak led Balaam to the top of Mount Peor. This mountain looks out over the desert. ²⁹Balaam said, "Build seven altars* here. Then prepare seven bulls and seven rams for the altars." ³⁰Balak did the thing that Balaam asked. Balak offered the bulls and rams on the altars.

Balaam's Third Message

24 Balaam saw that the Lord wanted to bless Israel. So Balaam did not try to change that by using any kind of magic. But Balaam turned and looked toward the desert. ²Balaam looked out across the desert and saw all the people of Israel. They were camped with the family groups in their different areas. Then the Spirit of God came to Balaam. ³And Balaam said these words:

"This message is from
   Balaam son of Beor.
I am speaking about things I see clearly.
⁴ I heard this message from God.
I saw what God All-Powerful*
   showed me.
I humbly tell what I clearly see.

⁵ "People of Jacob, your tents are beautiful!
People of Israel, your homes are beautiful!
⁶ You are like gardens
   planted by the streams.
You are like gardens
   growing by the rivers.
You are like sweet-smelling bushes
   planted by the Lord.
You are like beautiful trees
   growing by the water.
⁷ You will always have enough water,
   enough water for your seeds to grow.
Your king will be greater than king Agag.
Your kingdom will be very great.

⁸ "God brought those people out of Egypt.
They are as strong as a wild ox.
They will defeat all their enemies.
They will break their bones
   and shatter their arrows.
⁹ "Israel is like a lion,
   curled up and lying down.
Yes, they are like a young lion,
   and no one wants to wake him!
Any person who blesses you will be
   blessed.
And any person who speaks against
   you will have great troubles."

¹⁰Balak became very angry at Balaam. Balak said to Balaam, "I called you to come and speak against my enemies. But you have blessed them. You have blessed them three times. ¹¹Now leave and go home! I told you that I would give you a very good payment. But the Lord has caused you to lose your reward."

¹²Balaam said to Balak, "You sent men to me. Those men asked me to come. But I told them, ¹³'Balak can give me his most beautiful house filled with silver and gold. But I can still say only the things that the Lord commands me to say. I cannot do anything myself, good or bad. I must say what the Lord commands.' Surely you remember that I told your men these things. ¹⁴Now I am going back to my own people. But I will give you this warning. I will tell you what these people of Israel will do to you and your people in the future."

Balaam's Last Message

¹⁵Then Balaam said these things:

"This message is from
   Balaam son of Beor.
I am speaking about things I see clearly.
¹⁶ I heard this message from God.
I learned what God Most-High taught me.
I saw what God All-Powerful*
   showed me.
I humbly tell what I clearly see.

¹⁷ "I see the Lord coming, but not now.
I see him coming, but not soon.
A star will come from the family
   of Jacob.*

---

altar(s) A table or raised area used for offering sacrifices.
God All-Powerful Literally, "El Shaddai."

Jacob This is another name for Israel.

> A new ruler will come from the people of Israel.
> That ruler will crush the heads of the Moabite people.
> That ruler will crush the heads of all the sons of Sheth.*
>
> ¹⁸ Israel will grow strong!
> He will get the land of Edom.
> He will get the land of Seir,* his enemy.
>
> ¹⁹ "A new ruler will come from the family of Jacob.*
> That ruler will destroy the people left alive in that city."

²⁰Then Balaam saw the Amalekite people and said these words:

> "Amalek is the strongest of all nations.
> But even Amalek will be destroyed!"

²¹Then Balaam saw the Kenite people and he said these words:

> "You believe that your country is safe, like a bird's nest* high on a mountain.
> ²² But you Kenite* people will be destroyed, just like the Lord destroyed Cain.*
> Assyria will make you prisoners."

²³Then Balaam said these words:

> "No person can live when God does this.
> ²⁴ Ships will come from Cyprus.*
> They will defeat Assyria and Eber.*
> But those ships will also be destroyed."

²⁵Then Balaam got up and went back home. And Balak went his own way.

Israel at Peor

25 The people of Israel were camped near Acacia. At that time, the men began doing sexual sins* with Moabite women. ²⁻³The Moabite women invited the men to come and join in their sacrifices to their false gods. So the Israelites joined in worshiping those false gods—they ate the sacrifices and worshiped those gods. At that place, the people of Israel began worshiping the false god, Baal of Peor. And the Lord became very angry at them.

⁴The Lord said to Moses, "Get all the leaders of these people. Then kill them so that all the people can see.* Lay their bodies before the Lord. Then the Lord will not show his anger against all the people of Israel."

⁵So Moses said to Israel's judges, "Each of you must find the men in your family group that have led people to worship the false god, Baal of Peor. Then you must kill those men."

⁶At the time, Moses and all the elders *(leaders)* of Israel were gathered together at the entrance to the Meeting Tent.* An Israelite man brought a Midianite woman home to his brothers.* He did this where Moses and all the leaders could see. Moses and the leaders were very sad. ⁷Phinehas was the son of Eleazar and the grandson of Aaron the priest. Phinehas saw this man bring the woman into camp. So Phinehas left the meeting and got his spear. ⁸He followed the Israelite man into the tent. Then he used the spear to kill the Israelite man and the Midianite woman in her tent.* He push the spear through both of their bodies. At that time, there was a great sickness among the Israelite people. But when Phinehas killed these two people, the sickness stopped. ⁹A total of 24,000 people died from that sickness.

¹⁰The Lord said to Moses, ¹¹"I have strong feelings for my people—I want them to belong only to me! Phinehas son of Eleazar, son of Aaron the priest, saved the people of Israel from my

---

sons of Sheth Or, "Seth." Seth was Adam's third son. This might be like the phrases "son of Man (Adam)" and "son of Enosh" and mean simply "all those people."
Seir Another name for Edom.
Jacob This is another name for Israel.
nest, Kenite, Cain A play on words. The names "Cain" and "Kenite" are like the Hebrew word meaning "nest."
Cyprus Literally, "Kittim." This might be Cyprus, Crete, or other places west of Israel in the Mediterranean Sea.
Eber This might mean the people living west of the Euphrates River, or it might mean the "Hebrews," the descendants of Eber. See Gen. 10:21.

sexual sins Sexual sin was often part of the worship of false gods. So this can mean that the men were unfaithful to their wives and also that they were unfaithful to God by worshiping false gods.
so that all the people can see Literally, "before the sun."
Meeting Tent The Holy Tent (tabernacle) where the people of Israel came to meet with God.
brothers Or, "family."

anger. He did this by showing those feelings for my people. So I will not kill the people like I wanted to. ¹²Tell Phinehas that I am making a peace agreement with him. ¹³This is the agreement: He and all of his family that live after him will always be priests. Why? Because he had strong feelings for his God. And he did the things that made the people of Israel pure.*"

¹⁴The Israelite man who was killed with the Midianite woman was named Zimri son of Salu. He was the leader of a family in Simeon's family group. ¹⁵And the name of the Midianite woman who was killed was Cozbi.* She was the daughter of Zur. Zur was the head of a family and leader of a Midianite family group.

¹⁶The Lord said to Moses, ¹⁷"The Midianite people are your enemies. You must kill them. ¹⁸They have already made you their enemies. They tricked you at Peor. And they tricked you with the woman named Cozbi.* She was the daughter of a Midianite leader. But she was killed when the sickness came to the Israelite people. That sickness was caused because the people were tricked into worshiping the false god Baal of Peor."

The People Are Counted

26 After the great sickness, the Lord spoke to Moses and Eleazar son of Aaron the priest. ²He said, "Count the people of Israel. Count all the men who are 20 years old or older and list them by families. These are the men who are able to serve in the army of Israel."

³At this time the people were camped in the Jordan Valley in Moab. This was near the Jordan River, across from Jericho. So Moses and Eleazar the priest spoke to the people. They said, ⁴"You must count every man who is 20 years old or older. The Lord gave Moses this command." Here is the list of the people of Israel that came out of Egypt:

⁵These are the people from Reuben's family. (Reuben was the firstborn* son of Israel *(Jacob)*.) The families were:

6
Hanoch—the Hanochite family.
Pallu—the Palluite family.
Hezron—the Hezronite family.
Carmi—the Carmite family.

⁷Those were the families in Reuben's family group. There was a total of 43,730 men.

⁸Pallu's son was Eliab. ⁹Eliab had three sons—Nemuel, Dathan, and Abiram. Remember, Dathan and Abiram were the two leaders that turned against Moses and Aaron. They followed Korah when Korah turned against the Lord. ¹⁰That was the time when the earth opened and swallowed Korah and all of his followers. And 250 men died! That was a warning to all the people of Israel. ¹¹But the other people who were from the family of Korah did not die.

¹²These are the families from Simeon's family group:

13
Nemuel—the Nemuelite family.
Jamin—the Jaminite family.
Jakin—the Jakinite family.
Zerah—the Zerahite family.
Shaul—the Shaulite family.

¹⁴Those were the families in Simeon's family group. There was a total of 22,200 men.

¹⁵These are the families in Gad's family group:

16
17
Zephon—the Zephonite family.
Haggi—the Haggite family.
Shuni—the Shunite family.
Ozni—the Oznite family.
Eri—the Erite family.
Arodi—the Arodite family.
Areli—the Arelite family.

¹⁸Those were the families in Gad's family group. There was a total of 40,500 men.

¹⁹⁻²⁰These are the families in Judah's family group:

Shelah—the Shelanite family.
Perez—the Perezite family.
Zerah—the Zerahite family.
(Two of Judah's sons, Er and Onan, died in Canaan.)

---

her tent This was probably a special tent that showed this woman was a prostitute serving the false god Baal of Peor.
made ... pure Or, "atoned." The Hebrew word means "to cover," "to hide," or "to erase sins."
Cozbi This name is like the Hebrew word meaning "my lie."

firstborn The first child born into a family. The firstborn son was very important in ancient times.

²¹ These are the families from Perez:

> Hezron—the Hezronite family.
> Hamul—the Hamulite family.

²²Those were the families from Judah's family group. The total number of men was 76,500.
²³The families in Issachar's family group were:

> Tola—the Tolaite family.
> Puah—the Puite family.
> ²⁴ Jashub—the Jashubite family.
> Shimron—the Shimronite family.

²⁵Those were the families from Issachar's family group. The total number of men was 64,300.
²⁶The families in Zebulun's family group were:

> Sered—the Seredite family.
> Elon—the Elonite family.
> Jahleel—the Jahleelite family.

²⁷Those were the families from Zebulun's family group. The total number of men was 60,500.
²⁸Joseph's two sons were Manasseh and Ephraim. Each son became a family group with its own families. ²⁹Manasseh's families were:

> Makir—the Makirite family. (Makir was the father of Gilead.)
> Gilead—the Gileadite family.

³⁰ The families from Gilead were:

> Iezer—the Iezerite family.
> Helek—the Helekite family.
> ³¹ Asriel—the Asrielite family.
> Shechem—the Shechemite family.
> ³² Shemida—the Shemidaite family.
> Hepher—the Hepherite family.

³³Zelophehad was the son of Hepher. But he had no sons—only daughters. His daughters names were Mahlah, Noah, Hoglah, Milcah, and Tirzah.
³⁴Those are all the families in Manasseh's family group. The total number of men was 52,700.
³⁵The families in Ephraim's family group were:

> Shuthelah—the Shuthelahite family.
> Beker—the Bekerite family.
> Tahan—the Tahanite family.

³⁶ Eran was from Shuthelah's family. Eran's family was the Eranite family.

³⁷Those were the families in Ephraim's family group. The total number of men was 32,500. Those are all the people who came from Joseph's family groups.
³⁸The families in Benjamin's family group were:

> Bela—the Belaite family.
> Ashbel—the Ashbelite family.
> Ahiram—the Ahiramite family.
> ³⁹ Shupham—the Shuphamite family.
> Hupham—the Huphamite family.

⁴⁰ The families from Bela were:

> Ard—the Ardite family.
> Naaman—the Naamanite family.

⁴¹Those were all the families in Benjamin's family group. The total number of men was 45,600.
⁴²The families in Dan's family group were:

> Shuham—the Shuhamite family group.

That was the family group from Dan's family group. ⁴³There were many families in the Shuhamite family group. The total number of men was 64,400.
⁴⁴The families in Asher's family group were:

> Imnah—the Imnite family.
> Ishvi—the Ishvite family.
> Beriah—the Beriite family.

⁴⁵ The families from Beriah were:

> Heber—the Heberite family.
> Malkiel—the Malkielite family.

⁴⁶(Asher also had a daughter named Serah.) ⁴⁷Those were the families in Asher's family group. The total number of men was 53,400.
⁴⁸The families from Naphtali's family group were:

> Jahzeel—the Jahzeelite family.
> Guni—the Gunite family.
> ⁴⁹ Jezer—the Jezerite family.
> Shillem—the Shillemite family.

⁵⁰Those were the families from Naphtali's family group. The total number of men was 45,400.

⁵¹So the total number of men of Israel was 601,730.

⁵²The Lord said to Moses, ⁵³"The land will be divided and given to these people. Each family group will get enough land for all of the people who were counted. ⁵⁴A large family will get much land, and a small family will get less land. The land that they get will be equal to the number of people who were counted. ⁵⁵But you must use lots* to decide which family gets which part of the land. Each family group will get its share of the land. And that land will be given the name of that family group. ⁵⁶Land will be given to each family—large and small. And you will throw lots to make the decisions."

⁵⁷They also counted Levi's family group. These are the families from Levi's family group:

> Gershon—the Gershonite family.
> Kohath—the Kohathite family.
> Merari—the Merarite family.

⁵⁸These are also families from Levi's family group:

> The Libnite family.
> The Hebronite family.
> The Mahlite family.
> The Mushite family.
> The Korahite family.

Amram was from the Kohath family group. ⁵⁹Amram's wife was named Jochebed. She was also from Levi's family group. She was born in Egypt. Amram and Jochebed has two sons, Aaron and Moses. They also had a daughter, Miriam.

⁶⁰Aaron was the father of Nadab, Abihu, Eleazar, and Ithamar. ⁶¹But Nadab and Abihu died. They died because they made an offering to the Lord with fire that was not allowed.

⁶²The total number of men from Levi's family group was 23,000. But these men were not counted with the other people of Israel. They did not get a share of the land that the Lord gave to the other people.

⁶³Moses and Eleazar the priest counted all these people. They counted the people of Israel while they were in the Jordan Valley in Moab. This was near the Jordan River across from Jericho. ⁶⁴Many years before, in the Sinai desert, Moses and Aaron the priest counted the people of Israel. But all those people were dead. None of those people were still alive. ⁶⁵Why? Because the Lord told those people of Israel that they would all die in the desert. The only two men who were left alive were Caleb son of Jephunneh and Joshua son of Nun.

Zelophehad's Daughters

27 Zelophehad was the son of Hepher. Hepher was the son of Gilead. Gilead was the son of Makir. Makir was the son of Manasseh. Manasseh was the son of Joseph. Zelophehad had five daughters. Their names were Mahlah, Noah, Hoglah, Milcah, and Tirzah. ²These five women went to the Meeting Tent* and stood before Moses, Eleazar the priest, the leaders, and all the people of Israel.

The five daughters said, ³"Our father died while we were traveling through the desert. Our father died a natural death. He was not one of the men that joined Korah's group. (Korah was the man who turned against the Lord.) But our father had no sons. ⁴This means that our father's name will not continue. It is not fair that our father's name will not continue. His name will end because he had no sons. So we ask you to give us some of the land that our father's brothers will get."

⁵So Moses asked the Lord what he should do. ⁶The Lord said to him, ⁷"The daughters of Zelophehad are right. They should share the land with their father's brothers. So give them the land that you would have given to their father.

⁸"So make this law to the people of Israel, 'If a man has no son, and he dies, then everything he owns should be given to his daughter. ⁹If he has no daughter, then everything he owns should be given to his brothers. ¹⁰If he has no brothers, then everything he owns should be given to his father's brothers. ¹¹If his father had no brothers, then everything he owns should be given to the closest relative in his family. This should be a law among the people of Israel. The Lord gives this command to Moses.'"

---

lots Sticks, stones, or pieces of bone used like dice for making decisions. See Proverbs 16:33.

Meeting Tent The Holy Tent (tabernacle) where the people of Israel came to meet with God.

Joshua Is the New Leader

[12] Then the Lord said to Moses, "Go up on one of mountains in the desert east of the Jordan River. There you will see the land that I am giving to the people of Israel. [13] After you have seen this land, then you will die like your brother Aaron. [14] Remember when the people became angry at the water in the desert of Zin. Both you and Aaron refused to obey my command. You did not honor me and show the people that I am holy." (This was at the water of Meribah near Kadesh in the desert of Zin.)

[15] Moses said to the Lord, [16] "The Lord is the God who knows what people are thinking. Lord, I pray that you will choose a leader for these people.* [17] I pray that the Lord will choose a leader that will lead them out of this land and bring them into the new land. Then the Lord's people will not be like sheep without a shepherd."

[18] So the Lord said to Moses, "Joshua son of Nun will be the new leader. He is very wise.* Make him the new leader. [19] Tell him to stand before Eleazar the priest and all the people. Then make him the new leader.

[20] "Show the people that you are making him leader,* then all the people will obey him. [21] If Joshua needs to make a decision, then he will go to Eleazar the priest. Eleazar will use the Urim* to learn the Lord's answer. Then Joshua and all the people of Israel will do the things God says. If he says, 'go to war,' then they will go to war. And if he says, 'go home,' then they will go home."

[22] Moses obeyed the Lord. Moses told Joshua to stand before Eleazar the priest, and all the people of Israel. [23] Then Moses put his hands on him to show that he was the new leader. He did this the way the Lord had told him.

Daily Offerings

28 Then the Lord spoke to Moses. He said, [2] "Give this command to the people of Israel. Tell them to be sure to give the grain offerings and sacrifices to me at the right time. Those are the offerings made by fire. Their smell will please the Lord. [3] These are the offerings made by fire that they must give to the Lord. Every day they must give 2 lambs that are one year old. There must be nothing wrong with them. [4] Offer one of the lambs in the morning, and offer the other lamb at twilight.* [5] Also give a grain offering of 8 cups* of fine flour mixed with 1 quart* of olive oil." [6] (They started giving the daily offerings at Mount Sinai. They were offerings made by fire. Their smell pleased the Lord.) [7] The people must also give the drink offerings that go with the offerings made by fire. They must give 1 quart* of wine with every lamb. Pour that drink offering ₁on the altar₁ in the Holy Place. This is a gift to the Lord. [8] Offer the second lamb at twilight.* Offer it just like the morning offering. Also give the drink offering that goes with it. This will be an offering made by fire. Its smell will please the Lord."

Sabbath Offerings

[9] "On the Sabbath,* you must give 2 lambs that are one year old. There must be nothing wrong with them. You must also give a grain offering of 16 cups* of fine flour mixed with olive oil, and a drink offering. [10] This is a special offering for the day of rest. This offering is in addition to the regular daily offering and drink offering."

Monthly Meetings

[11] "On the first day of each month you will offer a special burnt offering to the Lord. This offering will be 2 male bulls, 1 ram, and 7 lambs that are one year old. There must be nothing wrong with them. [12] With each bull, you must give a grain offering of 24 cups* of fine flour mixed with olive oil. And with the ram, you must give a grain offering of 16 cups* of fine flour mixed with olive

---

The Lord ... these people Literally, "May the Lord, the God of the spirits of all people, appoint a man for this community."
Joshua ... wise Literally, "Take Joshua son of Nun. He is a man with a spirit in him." This might mean that Joshua was very wise, or it might mean that God's Spirit was with him.
Show ... leader Literally, "Give him some of your glory."
Urim Used together with the Thummim to learn God's answer to questions. They were probably like lots—stones, sticks, or bones that were thrown like dice to make decisions.

twilight The time after the sun goes down, but before dark.
8 cups Literally, "1/10 of an ephah."
1 quart Literally, "1/4 hin."
Sabbath Saturday, a day of rest and worship for the Jews.
16 cups Literally, "2/10 of an ephah."
24 cups Literally, "3/10 of an ephah."

oil. ¹³Also give a grain offering of 8 cups* of fine flour mixed with olive oil with each lamb. This will be an offering made by fire. Its smell will please the Lord. ¹⁴The drink offering will be 2 quarts* of wine with each bull, 1 1/4 quarts* of wine with the ram, and 1 quart* of wine with each lamb. That is the burnt offering that must be offered each and every month of the year. ¹⁵In addition to the regular daily burnt offering and drink offering, you must also give 1 male goat to the Lord. That goat will be a sin offering.

Passover

¹⁶"The Lord's Passover will be on the 14th day of the first month. ¹⁷The Festival of Unleavened Bread begins on the 15th day of that month. This holiday lasts for seven days. The only bread you can eat is bread made without yeast. ¹⁸You must have a special meeting on the first day of this holiday. You will not do any work on that day. ¹⁹You will give burnt offerings to the Lord. The burnt offerings will be 2 bulls, 1 ram, and 7 lambs that are one year old. There must be nothing wrong with them. ²⁰⁻²¹You must also give a grain offering of 24 cups* of fine flour mixed with olive oil with each bull, and 16 cups* of fine flour mixed with oil with the ram, and 8 cups* of fine flour mixed with oil for each lamb. ²²You must also give 1 male goat. That goat will be a sin offering to make you pure.* ²³You must give those offerings in addition to the morning burnt offerings that you give every day.

²⁴In the same way, each day for seven days, you must give the offerings made by fire to the Lord and the drink offerings that go with them. The smell of these offerings will please the Lord. The offerings will be food ₍for the people₎. You must give these offerings in addition to the burnt offerings that you give every day.

²⁵Then, on the seventh day ₍of this holiday₎, you will have another special meeting. You will not do any work on that day.

Festival of Weeks (Pentecost)

²⁶"At the Festival of Firstfruits* (the Festival of Weeks) use the new crops to give a grain offering to the Lord. At that time, you must also call a special meeting. You must not do any work on that day. ²⁷You must offer a burnt offering. It will be an offering made by fire. Its smell will please the Lord. You must offer 2 bulls, 1 ram, and 7 lambs that are one year old. There must be nothing wrong with them. ²⁸You must also give 24 cups* of fine flour mixed with oil with each bull and 16 cups* with each ram, ²⁹and 8 cups* with each lamb. ³⁰You must also sacrifice 1 male goat to make you pure.* ³¹You must give those offerings in addition to the daily burnt offerings and the grain offering you give with them. Be sure there is nothing wrong with the animals or the drink offerings that you give with them.

Festival of Trumpets

29 "There will be a special meeting on the first day of the seventh month. You will not do any work on that day. That is the day for blowing the trumpet.* ²You will offer burnt offerings. Their smell will please the Lord. You will offer 1 bull, 1 ram, and 7 lambs that are one year old. There must be nothing wrong with them. ³You will also offer 24 cups* of fine flour mixed with oil with the bull, 16 cups* with the ram, ⁴and 8 cups* with each of the 7 lambs. ⁵Also, offer 1 male goat for a sin offering to make you pure.* ⁶Those offerings are in addition to the New Moon* sacrifice and its grain offering. And they are in addition to the daily sacrifice and its grain offerings and drink offerings. Those must be done according to the rules. They must be offerings made by fire. Their smell will please the Lord.

The Day of Atonement

⁷"There will be a special meeting on the tenth day of the seventh month. During that day you must not eat any food.* And you must not do any work. ⁸You will offer burnt offerings. Their smell

---

8 cups Literally, "1/10 of an ephah."
2 quarts Literally, "1/2 hin."
1 1/4 quarts Literally, "1/3 hin."
1 quart Literally, "1/4 hin."
24 cups Literally, "3/10 of an ephah."
16 cups Literally, "2/10 of an ephah."
make ... pure Or, "make atonement." The Hebrew word means "to cover," "to hide," or "to erase sins."
Firstfruits Grain, such as wheat, and other crops that began to ripen around May and June. The first crops harvested were given to God.
blowing the trumpet Or, "shouting." This might mean that this is a day for shouting and being happy.
New Moon The first day of the Jewish month. This was a special day of worship.
you must not eat any food Literally, "You will humble your souls."

will please the Lord. You must offer 1 bull, 1 ram, and 7 lambs that are one year old. There must be nothing wrong with them. ⁹You must also offer 24 cups* of fine flour mixed with olive oil with the bull, 16 cups* with the ram, ¹⁰and 8 cups* with each of the 7 lambs. ¹¹You will also offer 1 male goat as a sin offering. This will be in addition to the sin offering for the Day of Atonement.* This will also be in addition to the daily sacrifice and its grain offerings and drink offerings.

Festival of Shelters

¹²"There will be a special meeting on the 15th day of the seventh month. ₍This will be the Festival of Shelters.₎* You must not do any work on that day. You must celebrate a special holiday for the Lord for seven days. ¹³You will offer burnt offerings. They will be offerings made by fire. Their smell will please the Lord. You will offer 13 bulls, 2 rams, and 14 lambs that are one year old. There must be nothing wrong with them. ¹⁴You must also offer 24 cups* of fine flour mixed with oil with each of the 13 bulls, 16 cups* with each of the 2 rams, ¹⁵and 8 cups* with each of the 14 lambs. ¹⁶You must also offer 1 male goat. This must be in addition to the daily sacrifice and its grain offerings and drink offerings.

¹⁷"On the second day ₍of this holiday₎, you must offer 12 bulls, 2 rams, and 14 lambs that are one year old. There must be nothing wrong with them. ¹⁸You must also give the right amount of grain and drink offerings with the bulls, rams, and lambs. ¹⁹You must also offer 1 male goat as a sin offering. This must be in addition to the daily sacrifice and its grain offerings and drink offerings.

²⁰"On the third day ₍of this holiday₎, you must offer 11 bulls, 2 rams, and 14 lambs that are one year old. There must be nothing wrong with them. ²¹You must also give the right amount of grain and drink offerings with the bulls, rams, and lambs. ²²You must also give 1 goat as a sin offering. This must be in addition to the daily sacrifice and its grain offerings and drink offerings.

²³"On the fourth day ₍of this holiday₎, you must offer 10 bulls, 2 rams, and 14 lambs that are one year old. There must be nothing wrong with them. ²⁴You must also give the right amount of grain and drink offerings with the bulls, rams, and lambs. ²⁵You must also give 1 male goat as a sin offering. This must be in addition to the daily sacrifice and its grain offerings and drink offerings.

²⁶"On the fifth day ₍of this holiday₎, you must offer 9 bulls, 2 rams, and 14 lambs that are one year old. There must be nothing wrong with them. ²⁷You must also give the right amount of grain and drink offerings with the bulls, rams, and lambs. ²⁸You must also give 1 male goat as a sin offering. This must be in addition to the daily sacrifice and its grain offerings and drink offerings.

²⁹"On the sixth day ₍of this holiday₎, you must offer 8 bulls, 2 rams, and 14 lambs that are one year old. There must be nothing wrong with them. ³⁰You must also give the right amount of grain and drink offerings for the bulls, rams, and lambs. ³¹You must also give 1 male goat as a sin offering. This must be in addition to the daily sacrifice and its grain offerings and drink offerings.

³²"On the seventh day ₍of this holiday₎, you must offer 7 bulls, 2 rams, and 14 lambs that are one year old. There must be nothing wrong with them. ³³You must also give the right amount of grain and drink offerings with the bulls, rams, and lambs. ³⁴You must also give 1 male goat as a sin offering. This must be in addition to the daily sacrifice and its grain offerings and drink offerings.

³⁵"The eighth day ₍of this holiday₎ is a very special meeting for you. You must not do any work on that day. ³⁶You must offer a burnt offering. It will an offering made by fire. Its smell will please the Lord. You must offer 1 bull, 1 ram, and 7 lambs that are one year old. There must be nothing wrong with them. ³⁷You must also give the right amount of grain and drink offerings with the bull, ram, and lambs. ³⁸You must also give 1 male goat as a sin offering. This must be in addition to the daily sacrifice and its grain offerings and drink offerings.

³⁹"At the special holidays you must bring your burnt offerings, grain offerings, drink offerings,

---

24 cups Literally, "3/10 of an ephah."
16 cups Literally, "2/10 of an ephah."
8 cups Literally, "1/10 of an ephah."
Day of Atonement Also called "Yom Kippur"—a very important holiday for the Jews. On this day, the high priest went into the Most Holy Place and did the ceremony that atoned (*covered or erased*) the sins of the people.
Festival of Shelters Also called "Succoth" or "Feast of Tabernacles." At this time in ancient Israel, Jewish people traveled to Jerusalem and camped out in tents and temporary shelters to help them remember their time in the Sinai desert.

and fellowship offerings. You must give those offerings to the Lord. Those offerings are in addition to any special gift you might want to give to the Lord and any offering that is part of any special promise you make."

⁴⁰Moses told the people of Israel about all of the things that the Lord had commanded him.

Special Promises

30 Moses spoke with all the leaders of the Israelite family groups. Moses told them about these commands from the Lord:

²If a person wants to make a special promise to God, or if that person promises to give something special to God, then let him do that thing. But that person must do exactly what he promises!

³A young woman might still be living in her father's house. And that young woman might make a special promise to give something to the Lord. ⁴If her father hears about the promise and agrees, then the young woman must do the thing she promised. ⁵But if her father hears about the promise and does not agree, then she is free from her promise. She does not have to do the thing she promised. Her father stopped her, so the Lord will forgive her.

⁶A woman might make a special promise to give something to the Lord and then get married. ⁷If the husband hears about the promise and doesn't object, then the woman must do the thing she promised. ⁸But if the husband hears about the promise and refuses to let her keep her promise, then the wife does not have to do the thing she promised. Her husband broke the promise—he did not let her do the thing she said. So the Lord will forgive her.

⁹A widow* or a divorced woman might make a special promise. If she does, then she must do exactly what she promised. ¹⁰A married woman might make a promise to give something to the Lord. ¹¹If her husband hears about the promise and lets her keep her promise, then she must do exactly what she promised. She must give everything she promised. ¹²But if her husband hears about the promise and refuses to let her keep the promise, then she does not have to do what she promised. It does not matter what she promised, her husband can break the promise. If her husband breaks the promise, then the Lord will forgive her. ¹³A married woman might promise to give something to the Lord, or she might promise to do without something,* or she might make some other special promise to God. The husband can stop any of those promises, and the husband can let her keep any of those promises. ¹⁴How does the husband let his wife keep her promises? If he hears about the promises and does not stop them, then the woman must do exactly what she promised. ¹⁵But if the husband hears about the promises and stops them, then he is responsible for breaking her promises.*

¹⁶Those are the commands that the Lord gave to Moses. Those are the commands about a man and his wife, and about a father and his daughter that is still young and living at home in her father's house.

Israel Fights Back Against the Midianites

31 The Lord spoke to Moses. He said, ²"I will help the people of Israel get even with the Midianites. After that, Moses, you will die.*

³So Moses spoke to the people. He said, "Choose some of your men to be soldiers. The Lord will use those men to get even with the Midianites. ⁴Choose 1,000 men from each of the family groups of Israel. ⁵There will be a total of 12,000 soldiers from the family groups of Israel."

⁶Moses sent those 12,000 men to war. He sent Eleazar the priest with them. Eleazar took the holy things and the horns and trumpets with him. ⁷The people of Israel fought the Midianites like the Lord had commanded. They killed all of the Midianite men. ⁸Among the people that they killed were Evi, Rekem, Zur, Hur, and Reba—the five kings of Midian. They also killed Balaam son of Beor with a sword.

⁹The people of Israel took the Midianite women and children as prisoners. They also took all their sheep, cows, and other things. ¹⁰Then they burned all their towns and villages. ¹¹They took all the people and animals ¹²and brought them to Moses, Eleazar the priest, and all the other people of Israel. They brought all of the things they took in war to the camp of Israel. The people of Israel were camped in the Jordan Valley in Moab. This was on the east side of the Jordan

---

widow(s) Women whose husbands have died. Often these women had no one to take care of them.

do without something Literally, "humble her soul." Usually this means to make the body suffer in some way, such as by not eating food.

he ... promises Literally, "he carries her guilt."

you will die Literally, "you will be gathered to your people."

River across from Jericho. ¹³Then Moses, Eleazar the priest, and the leaders of the people went out of the camp to meet with the soldiers.

¹⁴Moses was very angry against the leaders of the army. He was angry against the commanders of 1,000 men and against the commanders of 100 men that came back from the war. ¹⁵Moses said to them, "Why did you let the women live? ¹⁶These women will be bad for the men of Israel. The people will turn away from the Lord. It will be like the time of Balaam. It will be like at Peor. The disease will again come to the Lord's people. ¹⁷Now, kill all the Midianite boys. And kill all the Midianite women who had lived with a man. Kill all the Midianite women who had sexual relations with any man. ¹⁸You can let all the young girls live—but only if they never had sexual relations with any man. ¹⁹And then, all of you men who killed other people must stay outside the camp for seven days. You must stay outside the camp even if you just touched a dead body. On the third day, you and your prisoners must make yourselves pure. You must do the same thing again on the seventh day. ²⁰You must wash all of your clothes. You must wash anything made with leather, wool, or wood. You must become pure."

²¹Then Eleazar the priest spoke to the soldiers. He said, "Those are the rules that the Lord gave to Moses. Those rules are about soldiers coming back from war. ²²⁻²³But the rules for things that can be put in the fire are different. You must put gold, silver, bronze, iron, tin, or lead into the fire. And then wash those things with water and they will be pure. If things cannot be put in fire, then you must still wash them with water. ²⁴On the seventh day you must wash all of your clothes. Then you will become pure. After that you can come into camp."

²⁵Then the Lord said to Moses, ²⁶"You, Eleazar the priest, and all the leaders should count all of the prisoners, animals, and all of the things that the soldiers took in war. ²⁷Then divide those things between the soldiers that went to war and the rest of the people of Israel. ²⁸Take part of those things from the soldiers that went to war. That part will belong to the Lord. The Lord's share is one thing for every 500 things. This includes people, cows, donkeys, and sheep. ²⁹Take those things from the soldiers' half of the things they took in war. Then give those things to Eleazar the priest. That part will belong to the Lord. ³⁰And then, from the people's half, take one thing for every 50 things. This includes people, cows, donkeys, sheep, or any other animal. Give that share to the Levites. Why? Because the Levites take care of the Lord's Holy Tent."

³¹So Moses and Eleazar did what the Lord commanded Moses. ³²The soldiers had taken 675,000 sheep, ³³72,000 cows, ³⁴61,000 donkeys, ³⁵and 32,000 women. (Those are only the women who had not had sexual relations with any man.) ³⁶The soldiers that went to war got 337,500 sheep. ³⁷They gave 675 sheep to the Lord. ³⁸The soldiers got 36,000 cows. They gave 72 cows to the Lord. ³⁹The soldiers got 30,500 donkeys. They gave 61 donkeys to the Lord. ⁴⁰The soldiers got 16,000 women. They gave 32 women to the Lord. ⁴¹Moses gave all of those gifts for the Lord to Eleazar the priest, like the Lord had commanded him.

⁴²Then ⌊Moses counted⌋ the people's half. This was their share that Moses had taken from the soldiers that had gone to war. ⁴³The people got 337,500 sheep, ⁴⁴36,000 cows, ⁴⁵30,500 donkeys, ⁴⁶and 16,000 women. ⁴⁷For every 50 things, Moses took one thing for the Lord. This included the animals and the people. Then he gave those things to the Levites. Why? Because they took care of the Lord's Holy Tent. Moses did this like the Lord commanded.

⁴⁸Then the leaders of the army (the leaders over 1,000 men and the leaders over 100 men) came to Moses. ⁴⁹They told Moses, "We, your servants, have counted our soldiers. We have not missed any of them. ⁵⁰So we are bringing the Lord's gift from every soldier. We are bringing things that are made of gold—arm bands, bracelets, rings, earrings, and necklaces. This gift to the Lord is to make us pure.*

⁵¹So Moses took all of those things made from gold and gave them to Eleazar the priest. ⁵²The gold that the leaders of 1,000 men and the leaders of 100 men gave to the Lord weighed about 420 pounds.* ⁵³The soldiers kept the rest of their share of the things they took in war. ⁵⁴Moses and Eleazar the priest took the gold from the leaders of 1,000 men and the leaders of 100 men. Then they put that gold in the Meeting Tent.* This present was a memorial* before the Lord for the people of Israel.

make ... pure Or, "make atonement." The Hebrew word means "to cover," "to hide," or "to erase sins."
420 pounds Literally, "16,750 shekels."
Meeting Tent The Holy Tent (tabernacle) where the people of Israel came to meet with God.
memorial Something that helps people remember things that happened in the past.

The Family Groups East of the Jordan River

32 The family groups of Reuben and Gad had many, many cows. Those people looked at the land near Jazer and Gilead. They saw that this land was good for their cows. ²So the people from the family groups of Reuben and Gad came to Moses. They spoke to Moses, Eleazar the priest, and the leaders of the people. ³⁻⁴They said, "We, your servants, have many, many cows. And the land that we have fought against is a good land for cows. This land includes the area around Ataroth, Dibon, Jazer, Nimrah, Heshbon, Elealeh, Sibmah,* Nebo, and Beon. ⁵If it pleases you, we would like this land to be given to us. Don't take us to the other side of the Jordan River."

⁶Moses told the people from the family groups of Reuben and Gad, "Will you let your brothers go and fight while you settle here? ⁷Why are you trying to discourage the people of Israel? You will make them not want to cross the river and take the land that the Lord has given to them! ⁸Your fathers did the same thing to me. In Kadesh Barnea I sent spies to look at the land. ⁹Those men went as far as Eshcol Valley. They saw the land. And those men discouraged the people of Israel. Those men made the people of Israel not want to go into the land that the Lord had given to them. ¹⁰The Lord became very angry at the people. The Lord made this promise: ¹¹'None of the people who came from Egypt and are 20 years old or older will be allowed to see this land. I made a promise to Abraham, Isaac, and Jacob. I promised to give this land to these people. But they have not truly followed me. ₍So they will not get this land₎. ¹²Only Caleb son of Jephunneh the Kenizzite and Joshua son of Nun truly followed the Lord!'

¹³"The Lord was very angry against the people of Israel. So the Lord made the people stay in the desert for 40 years. The Lord made them stay there until all the people who had sinned against the Lord were dead. ¹⁴And now you are doing the same thing that your fathers did. You sinful people, do you want the Lord to be even more angry against his people? ¹⁵If you quit following the Lord, then the Lord will make Israel stay even longer in the desert. Then you will destroy all of these people!"

¹⁶But the people ₍from Reuben's and Gad's family groups₎ went to Moses. They said, "We will build cities for our children and barns for our animals here. ¹⁷Then our children can be safe from the other people that live in this land. But we will gladly come and help the other people of Israel. We will bring them to their land. ¹⁸We will not come back home until everyone in Israel has taken his part of the land. ¹⁹We won't take any of the land west of the Jordan River. No! Our part of the land is east of the Jordan River."

²⁰So Moses told them, "If you do all of these things, then this land will belong to you. But your soldiers must go before the Lord into battle. ²¹Your soldiers must cross the Jordan River and force the enemy to leave the country. ²²After the Lord helps us all take the land, then you can go back home. Then the Lord and Israel will not think that you are guilty. Then the Lord will let you have this land. ²³But if you don't do these things, then you will be sinning against the Lord. And know for sure that you will be punished for your sin. ²⁴Build cities for your children and barns for your animals. But then, you must do what you promised."

²⁵Then the people from the family groups of Gad and Reuben said to Moses, "We are your servants. You are our master. So we will do what you say. ²⁶Our wives, children, and all our animals will stay in the Gilead cities. ²⁷But we, your servants, will cross ₍the Jordan River₎. We will march before the Lord into battle, like our master says."

²⁸So Moses, Eleazar the priest, Joshua son of Nun, and all the leaders of the family groups of Israel heard them make that promise. ²⁹Moses said to them, "The people of Gad and Reuben will cross ₍the Jordan River₎. They will march before the Lord into battle. They will help you take the land. And you will give the land of Gilead as their part of the country. ³⁰They promise to help you take the land of Canaan."

³¹The people of Gad and Reuben answered, "We promise to do what the Lord commanded. ³²We will cross ₍the Jordan River₎ and march before the Lord into the land of Canaan. And our part of the country is the land east of the Jordan River."

³³So Moses gave that land to the people of Gad, to the people of Reuben, and to half of Manasseh's family group. (Manasseh was Joseph's son.) That land included the kingdom of Sihon the Amorite and the kingdom of Og, king of Bashan. That land included all the cities around that area.

³⁴The people of Gad built the cities of Dibon, Ataroth, Aroer, ³⁵Atroth Shophan, Jazer,

---

Sibmah Or, "Sebam."

Jogbehah, ³⁶Beth Nimrah, and Beth Haran. They built cities with strong walls, and they built barns for their animals.

³⁷The people of Reuben built Heshbon, Elealeh, Kiriathaim, ³⁸Nebo, Baal Meon, and Sibmah. They used the names of the cities that they built again. But they changed the names of Nebo and Baal Meon.

³⁹People from Makir's family group, went to Gilead. (Makir was Manasseh's son.) They defeated the city. They defeated the Amorites that lived there. ⁴⁰So Moses gave Gilead to Makir from Manasseh's family group. So his family settled there. ⁴¹Jair, from the family of Manasseh, defeated the small towns there. Then he called them Towns of Jair. ⁴²Nobah defeated Kenath and the small towns near it. Then he called that place by his own name.

Israel's Journey from Egypt

33 Moses and Aaron led the people of Israel out of Egypt in groups.* Here are the places they traveled. ²Moses wrote about the places they traveled. Moses wrote the things that the Lord wanted. Here are the places they traveled and when they left:

³On the 15th day of the first month, they left Rameses. That morning after Passover, the people of Israel marched out of Egypt with their arms raised ₍in victory₎. All the people of Egypt saw them. ⁴The Egyptians were burying all of the people that the Lord killed. They were burying all of their firstborn* ₍sons₎. The Lord had shown his judgment against the gods* of Egypt.

⁵The people of Israel left Rameses and traveled to Succoth. ⁶From Succoth they traveled to Etham. The people camped there at the edge of the desert. ⁷They left Etham and went to Pi Hahiroth. This was near Baal Zephon. The people camped near Migdol.

⁸The people left Pi Hahiroth and walked through the middle of the sea. They went toward the desert. Then they traveled for three days through the Etham desert. The people camped at Marah.

⁹The people left Marah and went to Elim and camped there. There were 12 springs of water and 70 palm trees there.

¹⁰The people left Elim and camped near the Red Sea.*

¹¹The people left the Red Sea* and camped in the Zin desert.

¹²The people left the Zin desert and camped at Dophkah.

¹³The people left Dophkah and camped at Alush.

¹⁴The people left Alush and camped at Rephidim. At that place, there was no water for the people to drink.

¹⁵The people left Rephidim and camped in the Sinai desert.

¹⁶The people left the Sinai desert and camped at Kibroth Hattaavah.

¹⁷The people left Kibroth Hattaavah and camped at Hazeroth.

¹⁸The people left Hazeroth and camped at Rithmah.

¹⁹The people left Rithmah and camped at Rimmon Perez.

²⁰The people left Rimmon Perez and camped at Libnah.

²¹The people left Libnah and camped at Rissah.

²²The people left Rissah and camped at Kehelathah.

²³The people left Kehelathah and camped at Mount Shepher.

²⁴The people left Mount Shepher and camped at Haradah.

²⁵The people left Haradah and camped at Makheloth.

²⁶The people left Makheloth and camped at Tahath.

²⁷The people left Tahath and camped at Terah.

²⁸The people left Terah and camped at Mithcah.

²⁹The people left Mithcah and camped at Hashmonah.

³⁰The people left Hashmonah and camped at Moseroth.

³¹The people left Moseroth and camped at Bene Jaakan.

³²The people left Bene Jaakan and camped at Hor Haggidgad.

³³The people left Hor Haggidgad and camped at Jotbathah.

---

groups Or, "divisions." This is a military term that shows Israel was organized like an army.

firstborn The first child born into a family. The firstborn son was very important in ancient times.

gods This might be the false gods of Egypt or here it might mean the king and other powerful leaders in Egypt.

Red Sea Or, "Reed Sea." See 1 Kings 9:26.

³⁴The people left Jotbathah and camped at Abronah. ³⁵The people left Abronah and camped at Ezion Geber. ³⁶The people left Ezion Geber and camped at Kadesh, in the Zin desert. ³⁷The people left Kadesh and camped at Hor. This was the mountain at the border of the country Edom. ³⁸Aaron the priest obeyed the Lord and went up Mount Hor. Aaron died at that place. Aaron died on the first day of the fifth month. That was the 40th year after the people of Israel had left Egypt. ³⁹Aaron was 123 years old when he died on Mount Hor.

⁴⁰Arad was a town in the Negev,* in the land of Canaan. The Canaanite king in that place heard that the people of Israel were coming. ⁴¹The people left Mount Hor and camped at Zalmonah. ⁴²The people left Zalmonah and camped at Punon. ⁴³The people left Punon and camped at Oboth. ⁴⁴The people left Oboth and camped at Iye Abarim. This was at the border of the country Moab. ⁴⁵The people left Iyim *(Iye Abarim)* and camped at Dibon Gad. ⁴⁶The people left Dibon Gad and camped at Almon Diblathaim. ⁴⁷The people left Almon Diblathaim and camped on the mountains of Abarim near Nebo. ⁴⁸The people left the mountains of Abarim and camped in the Jordan Valley in Moab. This was near the Jordan River across from Jericho. ⁴⁹They camped by the Jordan River in the Jordan Valley in Moab. Their camp went from Beth Jeshimoth to Acacia Field.

⁵⁰At that place, the Lord spoke to Moses. He said, ⁵¹"Speak to the people of Israel. Tell them these things: You will cross the Jordan River. You will go into the land of Canaan. ⁵²You will take the land from the people you find there. You must destroy all of their carved statues and idols. You must destroy all of their high places.* ⁵³You will take the land and you will settle there. Why? Because I am giving this land to you. It will belong to your families. ⁵⁴Each of your families will get part of the land. You will throw lots* to decide which family gets each part of the country. Large families will get large parts of the land. Small families will get small parts of the land. The lots will show which family gets which part of the land. Each family group will get its part of the land. ⁵⁵You must force those other people to leave the country. If you let those people stay in your country, then they will bring many troubles to you. They will be like stickers in your eyes and they will be like thorns in your side. They will bring many troubles to the country where you will be living. ⁵⁶I showed you what I would do—and I will do that to you ⌊if you let those people stay in your country⌋.

The Borders of Canaan

34 The Lord spoke to Moses. He said, ²"Give this command to the people of Israel: You are coming to the land of Canaan. You will defeat this country. You will take the whole land of Canaan. ³On the south, you will get part of the Zin desert near Edom. Your southern border will start at the southern end of the Dead Sea. ⁴It will cross south of Scorpion Pass. It will go through the Zin desert to Kadesh Barnea, and then to Hazar Addar and then it will pass through Azmon. ⁵From Azmon, the border will go to the River of Egypt,* and it will end at the Mediterranean Sea. ⁶Your western border will be the Mediterranean Sea. ⁷Your northern border will begin at the Mediterranean Sea and go to Mount Hor *(in Lebanon)*. ⁸From Mount Hor, it will go to Lebo Hamath, and then to Zedad. ⁹Then that border will go to Ziphron and it will end at Hazar Enan. So that will be your northern border. ¹⁰Your eastern border will begin at Enan and it will go to Shepham. ¹¹From Shepham, the border will go east of Ain to Riblah. The border will continue along the hills by Lake Galilee.* ¹²Then the border will continue along the Jordan River. It will end at the Dead Sea. Those are the borders around your country."

¹³So Moses gave this command to the people of Israel: That is the land that you will get. You will throw lots* to divide the land among the nine family groups and half of Manasseh's family group. ¹⁴Reuben's and Gad's family groups, and half of Manasseh's family group have already

---

Negev The desert area south of Judah.
high places Places for worshiping God or false gods. These places were usually on the hills and mountains.
lot(s) Sticks, stones, or pieces of bone used like dice for making decisions. See Proverbs 16:33.

River of Egypt That is, the stream called, "Wadi El-Arish."
Lake Galilee Literally, "Kinnereth Lake."

taken their land. ¹⁵Those two and a half family groups took the land near Jericho—they took the land east of the Jordan River."

¹⁶Then the Lord spoke to Moses. He said, ¹⁷"These are the men who will help you divide the land: Eleazar the priest, Joshua son of Nun, ¹⁸and the leaders of all the family groups. There will be one leader from each family group. Those men will divide the land. ¹⁹These are the names of the leaders:

> from Judah's family group—Caleb son of Jephunneh;
> 20 from Simeon's family group—Shemuel son of Ammihud;
> 21 from Benjamin's family group—Elidad son of Kislon;
> 22 from Dan's family group—Bukki son of Jogli;
> 23 from Joseph's descendants
> from Manasseh's family group—Hanniel son of Ephod;
> 24 from Ephraim's family group—Kemuel son of Shiphtan;
> 25 from Zebulun's family group—Elizaphan son of Parnach;
> 26 from Issachar's family group—Paltiel son of Azzan;
> 27 from Asher's family group—Ahihud son of Shelomi;
> 28 from Naphtali's family group—Pedahel son of Ammihud."

²⁹The Lord chose those men to divide the land of Canaan among the people of Israel.

The Levites' Towns

35 The Lord spoke to Moses. This was in the Jordan Valley in Moab, near the Jordan River, across from Jericho. The Lord said, ²"Tell the people of Israel that they should give some of the cities in their part of the land to the Levites. The people of Israel should give those cities and the pastures around them to the Levites. ³The Levites will be able to live in those cities. And all the cows and other animals that belong to the Levites will be able to eat from the pastures around those cities. ⁴ₗHow much of your land should you give to the Levites?ⱼ From the walls of the cities, go out 1,500 feet*—all of that land will belong to the Levites. ⁵ₗAlsoⱼ all of the land 3,000 feet* east of the city, and 3,000 feet south of the city, and 3,000 feet west of the city, and 3,000 feet north of the city will belong to the Levites. (The city will be in the middle of all that land.) ⁶Six of those cities will be cities of safety. If a person ₗaccidentallyⱼ kills someone, then that person can run to those towns for safety. In addition to those six cities, you will also give 42 more cities to the Levites. ⁷So you will give a total of 48 cities to the Levites. You will also give them the land around those cities. ⁸The large families of Israel ₗwill get large pieces of landⱼ. The small families of Israel ₗwill get small pieces of landⱼ. So the large family groups will give more cities and the small family groups will give fewer cities to the Levites."

⁹Then the Lord spoke to Moses. He said, ¹⁰"Tell the people these things: You people will cross the Jordan River and go into the land of Canaan. ¹¹You must choose towns to be cities of safety. If a person accidentally kills another person, then that person can run to one of those cities for safety. ¹²That person will be safe from anyone from the dead man's family that wants to get even. That person will be safe until he is judged in court. ¹³There will be six cities of safety. ¹⁴Three of those cities will be east of the Jordan River. And three of those cities will be in the land of Canaan, ₗwest of the Jordan Riverⱼ. ¹⁵Those cities will be places of safety for citizens of Israel, and for foreigners and travelers. Any of those people will be able to run to one of those cities if he accidentally kills someone.

¹⁶"If a person uses an iron weapon* to kill someone, then that person must die. ¹⁷And if a person takes a rock and kills someone, then that person must die. (But the rock must be the size of rock that would normally be used for killing people.) ¹⁸And if a person uses a piece of wood to kills someone, then that person must die. (The piece of wood must be a weapon that people normally use for killing people.) ¹⁹A member of the dead man's family* can chase that murderer and kill him.

3,000 feet Literally, "2,000 cubits." The Levites probably used this land for gardens and vineyards.

iron weapon This shows the murderer chose a weapon he knew could kill the other person.

member of the dead man's family Literally, "the blood avenger." Usually, this was a friend or family member that would chase a dead man's murderer and kill him.

1,500 feet Literally, "1,000 cubits." The people probably let their sheep and cows use this land.

20-21"A person might hit someone with his hand and kill him. Or a person might push someone and kill him. Or a person might throw something at someone and kill him. If the killer did that from hate, then he is a murderer. That person must be killed. A member of the dead man's family* can chase that murderer and kill him.

22"But a person might accidentally kill someone. That person didn't hate the person he killed—it was only an accident. Or a person might throw something and accidentally kill someone—he didn't plan to kill anyone. 23Or a person might throw a rock. And that rock might fall on someone that person didn't see and the rock might kill that person. That person didn't plan to kill anyone. That person didn't hate the person he killed—it was only an accident. 24If that happens, then the community must decide what to do. The community's court must decide if a member of the dead man's family* can kill that person. 25If the community decides to protect the killer from the dead man's family, then the community must take him back to his city of safety. And the killer must stay there until the official high priest* dies.

26-27"That man must never go outside the limits of his city of safety. If he goes outside those limits, and if a member of the dead man's family* catches him and kills him, then that member won't be guilty of murder. 28The person who accidentally killed someone must stay in his city of safety until the high priest dies. After the high priest dies, that person can go back to his own land. 29Those rules will be the law forever in all of the towns of your people.

30"A killer should be put to death as a murderer only if there are witnesses. No person can be put to death if there is only one witness.

31"If a person is a murderer, then he must be put to death. Don't take money and change his punishment. That murderer must be killed.

32"If a person killed someone and then ran to one of the cities of safety, then don't take money to let him go home. That person must stay in that city until the high priest dies.

33"Don't let your land be ruined with innocent blood. If a person murders someone, then the only payment for that crime is that the murderer must be killed! There is no other payment that will free the land from that crime. 34I am the Lord! I will be living in your country with the people of Israel. I will be living there, so don't make it unclean* ₁with the blood of innocent people₁."

The Land of Zelophehad's Daughters

36 Manasseh was Joseph's son. Makir was Manasseh's son. Gilead was Makir's son. The leaders of Gilead's family went to talk to Moses and the leaders of Israel's family groups. 2They said, "Sir, the Lord commanded us to get our land by throwing lots.* And sir, the Lord commanded Zelophehad's land to be given to his daughters. Zelophehad was our brother. 3Maybe a man from one of the other family groups will marry one of Zelophehad's daughters. Will that land leave our family? Will the people of that other family group get that land? Will we lose the land that we got by throwing lots? 4₁People might sell their land. But₁ in the Jubilee year,* all of the land is returned to the family group that really owns it. At that time, who will get the land that belongs to Zelophehad's daughters? Will our family lose that land forever?"

5Moses gave this command to the people of Israel. This command was from the Lord. "These men from Joseph's family group are right! 6This is the Lord's command to Zelophehad's daughters: If you want to marry someone, then you must marry someone from your own family group. 7In this way, land will not be passed from family group to family group among the people of Israel. Each Israelite will keep the land that belonged to his own ancestors.* 8And if some woman gets her father's land, then she must marry someone from her own family group. In this way, each person will keep the land that belonged to his ancestors. 9So, the land must not be passed from family group to family group among the people of Israel. Each Israelite will keep the land that belonged to his own ancestors."

10Zelophehad's daughters obeyed the Lord's command to Moses. 11So Zelophehad's

---

member of the dead man's family Literally, "the blood avenger." Usually, this was a friend or family member that would chase a dead man's murderer and kill him.

official high priest Literally, "the high priest who was anointed with the holy oil."

unclean Not pure or not acceptable to God for worship.

lot(s) Sticks, stones, or pieces of bone used like dice for making decisions. See Proverbs 16:33.

Jubilee year See Lev. 25 for the rules the Jews were to follow during this special time.

ancestors Literally, "fathers," meaning a person's parents, grandparents, and all the people they are descended from.

daughters—Mahlah, Tirzah, Hoglah, Milcah, and Noah—married their cousins on their father's side of the family. ¹²Their husbands were from Manasseh's family group, so their land continued to belong to their father's family and family group.

¹³So those are the laws and commands that the Lord gave to Moses in the Jordan Valley in Moab by the Jordan River, across from Jericho.

Deuteronomy

Moses Talks to the People of Israel

1 This is the message that Moses gave the people of Israel. He told them these things while they were in the Jordan Valley, in the desert east of the Jordan River. This was across from Suph, between the desert of Paran and the cities Tophel, Laban, Hazeroth, and Dizahab. ²The trip from Mount Horeb *(Sinai)* through the Seir mountains to Kadesh Barnea takes only eleven days. ³But it was 40 years from the time the people of Israel left Egypt until the time they came to this place. On the first day of the eleventh month of the 40th year, Moses spoke to the people. Moses told them all the things the Lord commanded. ⁴This was after the Lord defeated Sihon and Og. (Sihon was the king of the Amorite people. Sihon lived in Heshbon. Og was the king of Bashan. Og lived in Ashtaroth and Edrei.) ⁵The people of Israel were on the east side of the Jordan River in the land of Moab, and Moses began to explain the things that God commanded. Moses said:

⁶"At Mount Horeb *(Sinai)* the Lord our God spoke to us. He said, 'You have stayed at this mountain long enough. ⁷Go to the hill country where the Amorite people live. Go to all the places around there. Go to the Jordan Valley, the hill country, the western slopes, the Negev,* and the seacoast. Go through the land of Canaan and Lebanon as far as the great river, the Euphrates. ⁸Look, I am giving you that land. Go and take it. I promised to give that land to your ancestors*— Abraham, Isaac, and Jacob. I promised to give that land to them and to their descendants.*'"

Moses Chooses Leaders

⁹Moses said, "At that time I told you I couldn't take care of you by myself. ¹⁰And now, there are even more of you! The Lord your God has added more and more people, so that today you are as many as the stars in the sky! ¹¹May the Lord, the God of your ancestors,* make you 1,000 times more than you are now! May he bless you like he promised! ¹²But I couldn't take care of you and solve all your arguments by myself. ¹³So I told you: 'Choose some men from each family group, and I will make them leaders over you. Choose wise men that have understanding and experience.'

¹⁴"And you said, 'That is a good thing to do.'

¹⁵"So I took the wise and experienced men you chose from your family groups, and I made them your leaders. In this way, I gave you leaders over 1,000 people, leaders over 100 people, leaders over 50 people, leaders over 10 people. I also gave you officers for each of your family groups. ¹⁶"At that time, I told those judges, 'Listen to the arguments between your people. Be fair when you judge each case. It does not matter if the problem is between two Israelite people or between an Israelite and a foreigner. You must judge each case fairly. ¹⁷When you judge, you must not think that one person is more important than another person. You must judge every person the same. Don't be afraid of anyone, because your decision is from God. But if there is a case too hard for you to judge, then bring it to me and I will judge it.' ¹⁸At that same time, I also told you all the other things you must do.

The Spies Go to Canaan

¹⁹"Then we obeyed the Lord our God. We left Mount Horeb *(Sinai)* and traveled toward the hill country of the Amorite people. We went through that big and terrible desert that you saw. We came to Kadesh Barnea. ²⁰Then I said to you, 'You have now come to the hill country of the Amorites. The Lord our God will give us this country. ²¹Look,

---

Negev The desert area south of Judah.
ancestors Literally, "fathers," meaning a person's parents, grandparents, and all the people they are descended from.
descendant(s) A person's children and their future families.

there it is! Go up and take the land for your own! The Lord, the God of your ancestors,* told you to do this. So don't be afraid. Don't worry about anything!'

²²"But you all came to me and said, 'Let's send some men to look at the land first. They can look for all the strong and weak places there. Then they can come back and tell us the way we should go. They can also tell us about the cities we will come to.'

²³"I thought that was a good idea. So I chose twelve men from among you, one man from each family group. ²⁴Then those men left and went up to the hill country. They came to the Valley of Eshcol and explored it. ²⁵They took some of the fruit from that land and brought it back to us. They told us about the land. They said, 'The Lord our God is giving us a good land!'

²⁶"But you refused to go into the land. You refused to obey the Lord your God. ²⁷You went to your tents and began to complain. You said, 'The Lord hates us! He brought us out of the land of Egypt just to let the Amorite people destroy us! ²⁸Where can we go now? Our brothers *(the twelve spies)* have made us afraid with their report. They said: The people there are bigger and taller than we are! The cities are big and have walls as high as the sky! And we saw giants* there!'

²⁹"So I said to you, 'Don't be upset! Don't be afraid of those people! ³⁰The Lord your God will go before you and fight for you. He will do this the same as he did in Egypt. You saw him go before you there ³¹and in the desert. You saw how the Lord your God carried you, like a man carries his son. The Lord brought you safely all the way to this place.'

³²"But you still did not trust the Lord your God! ³³When you were traveling, he went before you to find a place for you to put your camp. He went before you in a fire by night and in a cloud by day to show you which way you should go.

People Not Allowed to Enter Canaan

³⁴"The Lord heard what you said, and he became angry. He made a strong promise. He said, ³⁵'None of you evil people who are living now will go into the good land that I promised to your ancestors.* ³⁶Only Caleb son of Jephunneh will see that land. I will give Caleb the land he walked on. And I will give that land to Caleb's descendants.* Why? Because Caleb did all that I commanded.'

³⁷"The Lord was also angry with me because of you. He said to me, 'Moses, you can't enter the land, either. ³⁸But your helper, Joshua son of Nun will go into the land. Encourage Joshua, because he will lead the people of Israel to take the land for their own.'

³⁹"And the Lord said to us, 'You said your little children would be taken by your enemies. But those children will go into the land. ⌊I don't blame your children for your mistake, because⌋ they are still too young to know if something is right or wrong. So I will give the land to them. Your children will take the land for their own. ⁴⁰But you—you must turn around and go back to the desert on the road that leads to the Red Sea.'

⁴¹"Then you said, 'Moses, we have sinned against the Lord. But now we will go and fight, like the Lord our God commanded us before.' Then each of you put on your weapons. You thought it would be easy to go and take the hill country.

⁴²"But the Lord said to me, 'Tell the people not to go up there and fight. Why? Because I will not be with them, and their enemies will defeat them!'

⁴³"I spoke to you, but you did not listen. You refused to obey the Lord's command. You thought you could use your own power. So you went up into the hill country. ⁴⁴But the Amorite people living there came out to fight against you. They were like a swarm of bees chasing you. They chased you all the way from Seir to Hormah. ⁴⁵Then you came back and cried to the Lord for help. But the Lord refused to listen to you. ⁴⁶So you stayed at Kadesh a long time.

Israel Wanders through the Desert

2 "Then we did what the Lord told me to do. We went back into the desert on the road that leads to the Red Sea. We traveled for many days to go around the Seir* mountains. ²Then the Lord said to me, ³'You have traveled around these mountains long enough. Turn north. ⁴Tell these things to the people: You will pass through the land of Seir. This land belongs to your relatives,

---

ancestors Literally, "fathers," meaning a person's parents, grandparents, and all the people they are descended from.
giants Literally, "Anakites," descendants of Anak, a family famous for tall and powerful fighting men. See Num. 13:33.

descendant(s) A person's children and their future families.
Seir Another name for Edom.

the descendants* of Esau. They will be afraid of you. Be very careful. ⁵Don't fight them. I will not give you any of their land—not even a foot of it. Why? Because I gave the hill country of Seir to Esau to keep as his own. ⁶You must pay the people of Esau for any food you eat or water you drink there. ⁷Remember that the Lord your God has blessed you in everything you have done. He knows about your walking through this great desert. The Lord your God has been with you these 40 years. You have always had everything you needed.'

⁸"So we passed by our relatives, the people of Esau living there in Seir. We left the road that leads from the Jordan Valley to the towns of Elath and Ezion Geber. We turned onto the road that goes to the desert in Moab.

Israel at Ar

⁹"The Lord said to me, 'Don't bother the people of Moab. Don't start a war against them. I will not give you any of their land. They are the descendants of Lot,* and I gave them the city of Ar.'"

(¹⁰In the past, the Emite people lived in Ar. They were strong people, and there were many of them. They were very tall, like the Anakite* people. ¹¹The Anakites were part of the Rephaite people. People thought the Emites were also Rephaites. But the people of Moab called them Emites. ¹²The Horite people also lived in Seir before, but Esau's people took their land. Esau's people destroyed the Horites and settled on their land. That is the same thing the people of Israel did to the people in the land that the Lord gave them for their own.)

¹³"The Lord told me, 'Now, go to the other side of Zered Valley.' So we crossed Zered Valley. ¹⁴It was 38 years from the time we left Kadesh Barnea until the time we crossed Zered Valley. All the fighting men of that generation in our camp had died. The Lord had sworn that that would happened. ¹⁵The Lord was against those men until they were all dead and gone from our camp.

¹⁶"After all the fighting men were dead and gone, ¹⁷the Lord said to me, ¹⁸'Today you must cross the border at Ar and go into Moab. ¹⁹You will go near the Ammonite people. Don't bother them. Don't fight with them, because I will not give you their land. Why? Because they are descendants* of Lot, and I have given that land to them.'"

²⁰(That country is also known as the Land of Rephaim. The Rephaite people lived there in the past. The people of Ammon called them the Zamzummites. ²¹There were many Zamzummites, and they were very strong. They were tall, like the Anakite* people. But the Lord helped the Ammonite people destroy the Zamzummites. The Ammonite people took that land and live there now. ²²God did the same thing for Esau's people. In the past, the Horite people lived in Seir *(Edom)*. But Esau's people destroyed the Horites, and Esau's descendants still live there today. ²³God did the same thing for some people from Crete. The Avvite people lived in the towns around Gaza. But some people came from Crete and destroyed the Avvites. Those people from Crete took that land and live there now.)

Fighting the Amorite People

²⁴"The Lord told me, 'Get ready to go across Arnon Valley. I will let you defeat Sihon the Amorite, the king of Heshbon. I will let you take his country. So fight against him and take his land. ²⁵Today I will make all people everywhere afraid of you. They will hear the news about you, and they will be afraid and shake with fear.'

²⁶"While we were in the desert of Kedemoth, I sent messengers to Sihon, the king of Heshbon. The messengers offered peace to Sihon. They said, ²⁷'Let us go through your land. We will stay on the road. We will not turn off the road to the right or to the left. ²⁸We will pay you in silver for any food we eat or any water we drink. We only want to march through your country. ²⁹Let us go through your land until we go across the Jordan River into the land that the Lord our God is giving us. Other people have let us go through their land—the people of Esau living in Seir and the Moabite people living in Ar.'

³⁰"But Sihon, the king of Heshbon, would not let us pass through his country. The Lord your God had made him very stubborn. The Lord did this so he could let you defeat King Sihon. And today, we know that really happened!

³¹"The Lord said to me, 'I am giving King Sihon and his country to you. Now, go take his land!'

³²"Then King Sihon and all his people came out to fight against us at Jahaz. ³³But the Lord our

---

descendant(s) A person's children and their future families.
descendants of Lot Lot's sons were Moab and Ammon. See Gen. 19:30-38.
Anakite(s) Descendants of Anak, a family famous for tall and powerful fighting men. See Num. 13:33.

God gave him to us. We defeated King Sihon, his sons, and all his people. ³⁴We captured all the cities that belonged to King Sihon at that time. We completely destroyed the people in every city—the men, women, and children. We did not leave anyone alive! ³⁵We took only the cattle and the valuable things from those cities. ³⁶We defeated the town of Aroer on the edge of the Arnon Valley and the other town in the middle of that valley. The Lord let us defeat all the cities between the Arnon Valley and Gilead. No city was too strong for us. ³⁷But you did not go near the land that belongs to the people of Ammon. You did not go near the shores of the Jabbok River or the cities of the hill country. You did not go near any place that the Lord our God would not let us have.

Fighting the People of Bashan

3 "We turned and went on the road to Bashan. Og, the king of Bashan, and all his men came out to fight against us at Edrei. ²The Lord said to me, 'Don't be afraid of Og. I have decided to give him to you. I will give you all his men and his land. You will defeat him just like you defeated Sihon, the Amorite king who ruled in Heshbon.'

³"So the Lord our God let us defeat Og, the king of Bashan. We destroyed him and all his men. None of them were left. ⁴Then we took all the cities that belonged to Og at that time. We took all the cities from Og's people—60 cities in the area of Argob, Og's kingdom in Bashan. ⁵All these cities were very strong. They had high walls, gates, and strong bars on the gates. There were also many towns that did not have walls. ⁶We destroyed them just like we destroyed the cities of Sihon king of Heshbon. We completely destroyed every city and all the people in them, even the women and the babies. ⁷But we kept all the cows and the valuable things from the cities for ourselves.

⁸"In that way, we took the land from the two Amorite kings. We took that land on the east side of the Jordan River, from Arnon Valley to Mount Hermon. ⁹(The people from Sidon call Mount Hermon, Sirion. But the Amorites called it Senir.) ¹⁰We took all the cities in the high plain and all of Gilead. We took all of Bashan, all the way to Salecah and Edrei. Salecah and Edrei were cities of Og's kingdom of Bashan."

(¹¹Og was the king of Bashan. Og was one of the few Rephaite people still alive. Og's bed was made from iron. It was over 13 feet long and 6 feet wide.* The bed is still in the city of Rabbah, where the Ammonite people live.)

The Land East of the Jordan River

¹²"So we took that land to be ours. I gave part of this land to the families groups of Reuben and Gad. I gave them the land from Aroer in the Arnon Valley to the hill country of Gilead with the cities in it. They got half of the hill country of Gilead. ¹³I gave the other half of Gilead and the whole area of Bashan to half of the family group of Manasseh."

(Bashan was Og's kingdom. Part of Bashan was called Argob. It was also called the Land of Rephaim. ¹⁴Jair, from the family group of Manasseh, took the whole area of Argob (Bashan). That area went all the way to the border of the Geshurite people and the Maacathite people. That area was named for Jair. So even today, people call Bashan the Towns of Jair.)

¹⁵"I gave Gilead to Makir. ¹⁶And to the Reuben family group and the Gad family group, I gave the land that begins at Gilead. This land goes from the Arnon Valley to the Jabbok River. The middle of the valley is one border. The Jabbok River is the border for the Ammonite people. ¹⁷The Jordan River near the desert is their western border. Lake Galilee* is north of this area and the Dead Sea* (the Salt Sea) is to the south. It is at the bottom of the cliffs of Pisgah. They are to the east.

¹⁸"At that time, I gave those family groups this command: 'The Lord your God has given you the land on this side of the Jordan River to live in. But now your fighting men must take their weapons and lead the other Israelite family groups across the river. ¹⁹Your wives, your little children, and your cows (I know you have many cows) will stay here in the cities I have given you. ²⁰But you must help your Israelite relatives until they take the land that the Lord is giving them on the other side of the Jordan River. Help them until the Lord gives them peace there, just as he did for you here. Then you may come back to this land that I have given you.'

²¹"Then I told Joshua, 'You have seen all the things the Lord your God has done to these two kings. The Lord will do the same thing to all the kingdoms you will enter. ²²Don't fear the kings of

---

13 feet long and 6 feet wide Literally, "9 cubits long and 4 cubits wide, following the measure of a man's cubit."
Lake Galilee Literally, "Kinnereth Lake."
Dead Sea Literally, "Arabah Sea."

these lands, because the Lord your God will fight for you.'

Moses Not Allowed In Canaan

²³"Then I begged the Lord to do something special for me. I said, ²⁴'Lord my Master, I am your servant. I know that you have shown me only a small part of the wonderful and powerful things you will do. There is no god in heaven or earth that can do the great and powerful things you have done! ²⁵Please let me go across the Jordan River and see the good land on the other side. Let me see the beautiful hill country and Lebanon.' ²⁶"But the Lord was angry at me because of you. He refused to listen to me. The Lord said to me, 'That's enough! Don't say another word about this. ²⁷Go up to the top of Mount Pisgah. Look to the west, to the north, to the south, and to the east. You may see these things with your eyes, but you can never go across the Jordan River. ²⁸You must give instructions to Joshua. Encourage him. Make him strong! Why? Because Joshua must lead the people across the Jordan River. You can see the land, but Joshua will lead them into that land. He will help them take the land and live in it. '

²⁹"So we stayed in the valley across from Beth Peor."

Moses Tells the People to Obey God's Laws

4 "Now, Israel, listen to the laws and to the commands that I teach you. Obey them and you will live. Then you can go in and take the land that the Lord, the God of your ancestors, is giving you. ²You must not add to the things that I command you. And you must not take anything away. You must obey the commands of the Lord your God that I have given you.

³"You have seen what the Lord did at Baal Peor. The Lord your God destroyed all your people who followed the false god Baal* at that place. ⁴But all of you who stayed with the Lord your God are alive today.

⁵"I taught you the laws and rules that the Lord my God commanded me. I taught you these laws so that you could obey them in the land you are ready to enter and take for your own. ⁶Obey these laws carefully. This will show the people of the other nations that you are wise and understanding. The people of those nations will hear about these laws. Then they will say, 'Truly, the people of this great nation *(Israel)* are wise and understanding.'

⁷"The Lord our God is near when we ask him to help us. No other nation has a god like that! ⁸And no other nation is great enough to have laws and rules as good as the teachings I give you today. ⁹But you must be careful! Be sure that as long as you live you never forget the things you have seen. You must teach those things to your children and grandchildren. ¹⁰Remember the day you stood before the Lord your God at Mount Horeb *(Sinai)*. The Lord said to me, 'Gather the people together to listen to the things I say. Then they will learn to respect me as long as they live on earth. And they will teach these things to their children.' ¹¹You came near and stood at the bottom of the mountain. The mountain burned with fire that reached up to the sky. There were thick black clouds and darkness. ¹²Then the Lord spoke to you from the fire. You heard the sound of someone speaking, but you did not see any form. There was only a voice. ¹³The Lord told you his Agreement. He told you the Ten Commandments and commanded you to follow them. The Lord wrote those laws of the Agreement on two stone tablets. ¹⁴At that time, the Lord also commanded me to teach you the other laws and rules that you must follow in the land you are going to take and live in.

¹⁵"On the day the Lord spoke to you from the fire at Mount Horeb *(Sinai)*, you did not see him—there was no shape for God. ¹⁶So be careful! Don't sin and destroy yourselves by making false gods or statues in the shape of any living thing. Don't make an idol that looks like a man or a woman. ¹⁷Don't make an idol that looks like an animal on the earth or like a bird that flies in the sky. ¹⁸And don't make an idol that looks like anything that crawls on the ground or like a fish in the sea. ¹⁹And be careful when you look up to the sky and see the sun, the moon, and the stars—all the many things in the sky. Be careful that you are not tempted to worship and serve those things. The Lord your God lets the other people in the world do those things. ²⁰But the Lord brought you out of Egypt and made you his own special people. It was as if the Lord reached into a hot furnace for melting iron and pulled you out of that fire. And now you are his people!

²¹"The Lord became angry at me because of you. The Lord swore *(promised)* that I could not go across the Jordan River. He told me that I

Baal A false god that the Canaanite people worshiped.

could not go into the good land that the Lord your God is giving you. ²²So I must die here in this land. I can't go across the Jordan River, but you will soon go across and take that good land and live there. ²³In that new land, you must be careful not to forget the Agreement that the Lord your God made with you. You must obey the Lord's command. Don't make any idols in any form! ²⁴Why? Because the Lord your God hates for his people to worship other gods. And the Lord can be like a fire that destroys!

²⁵"You will live in the country a long time. You will have children and grandchildren there. You will grow old there. And then you will ruin your lives—you will make all kinds of idols! When you do that, you will make God very angry! ²⁶So, I am warning you now. Heaven and earth are my witnesses! If you do that evil thing, then you will quickly be destroyed! You are crossing the Jordan River now to take that land. But if you make any idols, then you will not live there very long. No, you will be completely destroyed! ²⁷The Lord will scatter you among the nations. And only a few of you will be left alive to go to the countries where the Lord will send you. ²⁸There you will serve gods made by men—things made of wood and stone that can't see or hear or eat or smell! ²⁹But there in these other lands you will look for the Lord your God. And if you look for him with all your heart and soul, you will find him. ³⁰When you are in trouble—when all those things happen to you—then you will come back to the Lord your God and obey him. ³¹The Lord your God is a merciful God! He will not leave you there. He will not destroy you completely. He will not forget the Agreement that he made with your ancestors.*

Think About the Great Things God Did

³²"Has anything this great ever happened before? Never! Look at the past. Think about all the things that happened before you were born. Go all the way back to the time when God made people on the earth. Look at all the things that have happened anywhere in the world. Has anyone ever heard about anything as great as this? No! ³³You people heard God speaking to you from a fire, and you are still alive! Has that ever happened to anyone else? No! ³⁴And has any other god ever tried to go and take a people for himself from inside another nation? No! But you yourselves have seen the Lord your God do all these wonderful things! He showed you his power and strength. You saw the troubles that tested the people. You saw miracles and wonders. You saw war and the terrible things that happened. ³⁵The Lord showed you these things so that you would know that he is God. There is no other god like him! ³⁶The Lord let you hear his voice from heaven so he could teach you a lesson. On earth he let you see his great fire, and he spoke to you from it.

³⁷"The Lord loved your ancestors.* That is why he chose you, their descendants.* And that is why the Lord brought you out of Egypt. He was with you and brought you out with his great power. ³⁸When you moved forward, the Lord forced out nations that were greater and more powerful than you. And the Lord led you into their land. He gave you their land to live in. And is still doing that today.

³⁹"So today you must remember and accept that the Lord is God. He is God in heaven above and on the earth below. There is no other God! ⁴⁰And you must obey his laws and commands that I give you today. Then everything will go well with you and your children who live after you. And you will live a long time in the land the Lord your God is giving you—it will be yours forever!"

Moses Chooses the Cities of Safety

⁴¹Then Moses chose three cities on the east side of the Jordan River. ⁴²If a person accidentally killed another person, he could run away to one of those three cities and not be put to death. But he could be safe only if he did not hate the other person and did not mean to kill him. ⁴³The three cities that Moses chose were: Bezer in the high plains for Reuben's family group; Ramoth in Gilead for Gad's family group; and Golan in Bashan for Manasseh's family group.

Introduction to the Law of Moses

⁴⁴Moses gave God's law to the people of Israel. ⁴⁵Moses gave these teachings, laws, and rules to the people after they came out of Egypt. ⁴⁶Moses gave them these laws while they were on the east side of the Jordan River, in the valley across from Beth Peor. They were in the land of Sihon, the

---

ancestors Literally, "fathers," meaning a person's parents, grandparents, and all the people they are descended from.

descendant(s) A person's children and their future families.

Amorite king that lived at Heshbon. (Moses and the people of Israel had defeated Sihon when they came out of Egypt. ⁴⁷They took Sihon's land to keep. They also took the land of Og, the king of Bashan. These two Amorite kings lived on the east side of the Jordan River. ⁴⁸This land goes from Aroer on the edge of the Arnon Valley all the way to Mount Sirion* (Mount Hermon). ⁴⁹This land also included the whole Jordan Valley on the east side of the Jordan River. To the south, this land reached to the Dead Sea.* To the east, it reached to the foot of Mount Pisgah.)

The Ten Commandments

5 Moses called together all the people of Israel and said to them, "People of Israel, listen to the laws and rules that I tell you today. Learn these laws and be sure to obey them. ²The Lord our God made an agreement with us at Mount Horeb (Sinai). ³The Lord did not make this agreement with our ancestors,* but with us—yes, with all of us who are alive here today. ⁴The Lord spoke with you face to face at that mountain. He spoke to you from the fire. ⁵But you were afraid of the fire. And you did not go up the mountain. So I stood between the Lord and you to tell you what the Lord said. The Lord said: ⁶I am the Lord your God. I led you out of Egypt where you were slaves. So you must obey these commands:

⁷"You must not worship any other gods except me.

⁸"You must not make any idols.* Don't make any statues or pictures of anything up in the sky or of anything on the earth or of anything down in the water. ⁹Don't worship or serve idols of any kind. Why? Because I am the Lord your God. I hate for my people to worship other gods.* People who sin against me become my enemies. And I will punish those people. And I will punish their children, their grandchildren, and even their great-grandchildren. ¹⁰But I will be very kind to people who love me and obey my commands. I will be kind to their families for thousands of generations!*

¹¹"You must not use the name of the Lord your God in a wrong way. If a person uses the Lord's name in a wrong way, then that person is guilty. And the Lord will not make him innocent.

¹²"You must keep the Sabbath* a special day like the Lord your God commanded. ¹³Work at your job six days a week. ¹⁴But the seventh day is a day of rest in honor of the Lord your God. So on that day no person should work—not you, your sons and daughters, foreigners living in your cities or your men and women slaves. Not even your cows, donkeys, and other animals should do any work! Your slaves should be able to rest just like you. ¹⁵Don't forget that you were slaves in the land of Egypt. The Lord your God brought you out of Egypt with his great power. He made you free. That is why the Lord your God commands you to always make the Sabbath* a special day.

¹⁶"You must honor (respect) your father and your mother. The Lord your God has commanded you to do this. If you follow this command, then you will live a long time, and everything will go well for you in the land that the Lord your God gives you.

¹⁷"You must not murder anyone.

¹⁸"You must not do the sin of adultery.*

¹⁹"You must not steal anything.

²⁰"You must not tell lies about other people.*

²¹"You must not want another man's wife. You must not want his house, his fields, his men and women servants, his cows or his donkeys. You must not want to take anything that belongs to another person!"

Sirion Or "Siyon."
Dead Sea Literally, "Arabah Sea."
ancestors Literally, "fathers," meaning a person's parents, grandparents, and all the people they are descended from.
idols Statues of false gods that people worshiped.
I hate ... gods Or, "I am El Kanah—the Jealous God."
But I ... generations Or, "I will show mercy to thousands of people who love me and obey my commandments."
Sabbath Saturday, a day of rest and worship for the Jews.
adultery Breaking the marriage promise by doing sexual sin.
You must not tell lies about other people Or, "You must not be a false witness against your neighbor."

The People Were Afraid of God

22 ₍Moses said,₎ "The Lord gave these commands to all of you when you were together there at the mountain. The Lord spoke with a loud voice that came from the fire, the cloud, and the thick darkness. After he gave us these commands, he didn't say any more. He wrote his words on two stone tablets and gave them to me.

23 "You heard the voice from the darkness while the mountain was burning with fire. Then all the elders* and the other leaders of your family groups came to me. **24** They said, 'The Lord our God has shown us his Glory and his greatness! We heard him speak from the fire! We have seen today that it is possible for a person to continue living even after God speaks to him. **25** But if we hear the Lord our God speak to us again, surely we will die! That terrible fire will destroy us! We don't want to die! **26** No person has ever heard the living God speak from the fire like we have and still lived! **27** Moses, you go near and hear all the things the Lord our God says. Then tell us all the things the Lord tells you. We will listen to you, and we will do everything you say.'

The Lord Speaks to Moses

28 "The Lord heard what you said. And the Lord said to me, 'I heard what the people said. And that is fine. **29** I only wanted to change their way of thinking—I wanted them to respect me and obey all my commands from the heart! Then everything would be fine with them and with their descendants* forever.

30 "'Go and tell the people to go back to their tents. **31** But you, Moses, stand here near me. I will tell you all the commands, laws, and rules that you must teach them. They must do these things in the land that I am giving them to live in.'

32 "So, you people must be careful to do all the things the Lord commanded you. Don't stop following God! **33** You must live the way the Lord your God commanded you. Then you will continue to live, and everything will be fine with you. You will live a long life in the land that will belong to you.

Always Love and Obey God!

6 "These are the commands, the laws, and the rules that the Lord your God told me to teach you. Obey these laws in the land that you are entering to live in. **2** You and your descendants* must respect the Lord your God as long as you live. You must obey all his laws and commands that I give you. If you do this, then you will have a long life in that new land. **3** People of Israel, listen carefully and obey these laws. Then everything will be fine with you. You will have many children, and you will get the land filled with many good things*—just like the Lord, the God of your ancestors,* promised.

4 "Listen, people of Israel! The Lord is our God. The Lord is one! **5** You must love the Lord your God with all your heart, with all your soul, and with all your strength. **6** Always remember these commands that I give you today. **7** Be sure to teach them to your children. Talk about these commands when you sit in your house and when you walk on the road. Talk about them when you lie down and when you get up. **8** ₍Write these commands and₎ tie them on your hands and wear them on your foreheads to help you remember ₍my teachings₎. **9** Write them on the doorposts of your houses and on your gates.

10 "The Lord your God made a promise to your ancestors,* Abraham, Isaac, and Jacob. The Lord promised to give you this land. The Lord will give you that land! And he will give you great and rich cities that you did not build. **11** The Lord will give you houses full of good things that you did not put there. The Lord will give you wells that you did not dig. The Lord will give you fields of grapes and olive trees that you did not plant. And you will have plenty to eat.

12 "But be careful! Don't forget the Lord. You were slaves in Egypt, but the Lord brought you out of the land of Egypt. **13** Respect the Lord your God and serve only him. And you must use only his name to make promises. ₍Don't use the names of false gods!₎ **14** You must not follow other gods. You must not follow the gods of the people who live around you. **15** The Lord your God is always with you. And the Lord hates his people worshiping other gods! So if you follow those

---

elders Older men that were city leaders; they helped make decisions for the people.
descendant(s) A person's children and their future families.
filled with many good things Literally, "flowing with milk and honey."
ancestors Literally, "fathers," meaning a person's parents, grandparents, and all the people they are descended from.

other gods, the Lord will become very angry at you. He will destroy you from the face of the earth. ⁱ⁶"You must not test the Lord your God like you tested him at Massah. ¹⁷You must be sure to obey the commands of the Lord your God. You must follow all the teachings and laws he has given you. ¹⁸You must do the things that are right and good—things that please the Lord. Then everything will go well for you, and you can go in and take the good land that the Lord promised your ancestors.* ¹⁹And you will force out all your enemies, just like the Lord said.

Teach Your Children the Things God Did

²⁰"In the future, your son might ask you, 'The Lord our God gave you teachings, laws, and rules. What do they mean?' ²¹Then you will say to your son, 'We were Pharaoh's slaves in Egypt, but the Lord brought us out of Egypt with his great power. ²²The Lord did great and amazing things. We saw him do these things to the Egyptian people, to Pharaoh, and to the people in Pharaoh's house. ²³And the Lord brought us out of Egypt so that he could give us the land that he promised our ancestors.* ²⁴The Lord commanded us to follow all these teachings. We must respect the Lord our God. Then the Lord will always keep us alive and doing well, as we are today. ²⁵If we carefully obey the whole law, exactly like the Lord our God told us to, then God will say that we have done a very good thing.'*

Israel, God's Special People

7 "The Lord your God will lead you into the land that you are entering to take for your own. The Lord will force out many nations for you—the Hittites, the Girgashites, the Amorites, the Canaanites, the Perizzites, the Hivites, and the Jebusites—seven nations greater and more powerful than you. ²The Lord your God will put these nations under your power. And you will defeat them. You must destroy them completely. Don't make an agreement with them. Don't show them mercy. ³Don't marry any of those people, and don't let your sons or daughters marry any of the people from those other nations. ⁴Why? Because those people will turn your children away from following me. Then your children will serve other gods. And the Lord will become very angry at you. He will quickly destroy you.

Destroy False Gods

⁵"This is what you must do to those nations: You must smash their altars* and break their memorial stones* into pieces. Cut down their Asherah poles* and burn their statues! ⁶Why? Because you are the Lord's own people. From all the people on earth, the Lord your God chose you to be his special people—people that belong only to him. ⁷Why did the Lord love and choose you? It was not because you are such a large nation. You had the fewest of all people! ⁸But the Lord brought you out of Egypt with great power. He made you free from slavery. He freed you from the control of Pharaoh, the king of Egypt. Why? Because the Lord loves you and because he wanted to keep the promise he made to your ancestors.*

⁹"So remember that the Lord your God is the only God, and you can trust him! He keeps his Agreement. He shows his love and kindness to all people who love him and obey his commands. He continues to show his love and kindness through a thousand generations. ¹⁰But the Lord punishes people who hate him. He will destroy them. He will not be slow to punish people who hate him. ¹¹So you must be careful to obey the commands, laws, and rules that I give you today.

¹²"If you listen to these laws, and if you are careful to obey them, then the Lord your God will keep his Agreement of love with you. He promised this to your ancestors.* ¹³He will love you and bless you. He will make your nation grow. He will bless your children. He will bless your fields with good crops. He will give you grain, new wine, and oil. He will bless your cows with baby calves and your sheep with lambs. You will have all these blessings in the land that he promised your ancestors* to give you.

---

ancestors Literally, "fathers," meaning a person's parents, grandparents, and all the people they are descended from.

If we ... good thing Or, "The Lord our God will credit us with righteousness (goodness) if we carefully obey the whole law, exactly as he commanded us."

altar(s) A table or raised area used for offering sacrifices.

memorial stones Stones that were set up to help people remember the false gods they worshiped.

Asherah poles Poles used to honor the goddess Asherah. People thought she could help them have many children.

¹⁴"You will be blessed more than all people. Every husband and wife will be able to have children. Your cows will be able to have calves. ¹⁵And the Lord will take away all sickness from you. The Lord will not let you catch any of the terrible diseases that you had in Egypt. But the Lord will make your enemies catch those diseases. ¹⁶You must destroy all the people that the Lord your God helps you defeat. Don't feel sorry for them. Don't worship their gods! Why? Because they are a trap—they will ruin your life.

The Lord Promises to Help His People

¹⁷"Don't say in your heart, 'These nations are stronger than we are. How can we force them out?' ¹⁸You must not be afraid of them. You must remember what the Lord your God did to Pharaoh and to all the people of Egypt. ¹⁹You saw the great troubles he gave them. You saw the amazing things he did. You saw the Lord use his great power and strength to bring you out of Egypt. The Lord your God will use that same power against all the people you fear.

²⁰"The Lord your God will even send the hornet* to find all the people that escape from you and hide themselves. He will destroy all those people. ²¹Don't be afraid of those people. Why? Because the Lord your God is with you. He is a great and awesome God. ²²The Lord your God will force those nations to leave your country little by little. You will not destroy them all at once. If you did, then the wild animals would grow to be too many for you. ²³But the Lord your God will let you defeat those nations. The Lord will confuse them in battle, until they are destroyed. ²⁴The Lord will help you defeat their kings. You will kill them, and the world will forget they ever lived. No man will be able to stop you. You will destroy them all!

²⁵"You must throw the statues of their gods into the fire and burn them. You must not want to keep the silver or the gold that is on those statues. You must not take that silver or gold for yourselves. It will be like a trap to you—it will ruin your life. Why? Because the Lord your God hates those idols. ²⁶And you must not bring any of those terrible idols into your homes. You must hate those terrible things! You must destroy those idols!

Remember the Lord

8 "You must obey all the commands that I give you today. Why? Because then you will live and grow to become a great nation. You will get the land that the Lord promised to your ancestors.* ²And you must remember the whole trip that the Lord your God has led you through these 40 years in the desert. The Lord was testing you. He wanted to make you humble. He wanted to know the things in your heart. He wanted to know if you would obey his commands. ³The Lord humbled you and let you be hungry. Then he fed you with manna*—something you did not know about before, something your ancestors* had never seen. Why did the Lord do these things? Because he wanted you to know that it is not just bread that keeps people alive. People's lives depend on what the Lord says. ⁴These past 40 years, your clothes did not wear out, and your feet did not swell. Why? Because the Lord protected you! ⁵You must remember that the Lord your God did all those things for you. God was like a father teaching and correcting his son.

⁶"You must obey the commands of the Lord your God. Follow him and respect him. ⁷The Lord your God is bringing you into a good land—a land with rivers and pools of water. Water flows out of the ground in the valleys and hills. ⁸It is a land with wheat and barley, grape vines, fig trees, and pomegranates.* It is a land with olive oil and honey. ⁹There you will have plenty of food. You will have everything you need. It is a land where the rocks are iron. You can dig copper out of the hills. ¹⁰You will have all you want to eat. Then you will praise the Lord your God for the good land he has given you.

Don't Forget What the Lord Did

¹¹"Be careful. Don't forget the Lord your God! Be careful to obey the commands, laws, and rules that I give you today. ¹²Then you will have plenty to eat, and you will build good houses and live in them. ¹³Your cows, sheep, and goats will grow large. You will get plenty of gold and silver. You

---

ancestors Literally, "fathers," meaning a person's parents, grandparents, and all the people they are descended from.

manna The special food God sent to the people of Israel while they wandered through the desert for 40 years.

hornet A stinging insect, like a large wasp or bee. Here, it might mean God's angel or his great power.

pomegranate A red fruit with many small seeds inside it. Each seed is covered with the soft, juicy part of the fruit.

will have plenty of everything! ¹⁴When that happens, you must be careful not to become proud. You must not forget the Lord your God. You were slaves in Egypt. But the Lord made you free and brought you out of that land. ¹⁵The Lord led you through that great and terrible desert. Poisonous snakes and scorpions* were in that desert! The ground was dry, and there was no water anywhere. But the Lord gave you water out of the rock. ¹⁶In the desert, the Lord fed you manna*—something your ancestors* had never seen. The Lord tested you. Why? Because the Lord made you humble so that things would go well for you in the end. ¹⁷Don't ever say to yourself, 'I got all this wealth by my own power and ability.' ¹⁸Remember the Lord your God. Remember that he is the One who gives you power to do those things! Why does the Lord do this? Because he wants to keep the Agreement that he made with your ancestors*—just like he is doing today!

¹⁹"Don't ever forget the Lord your God. Don't ever follow other gods! Don't worship and serve them. If you do that, then I warn you today: You will surely be destroyed! ²⁰The Lord is destroying other nations for you. But if you follow those other gods, then you will be destroyed just like them! Why? Because you stopped listening to the Lord your God!

The Lord Will Be with Israel

9 "Listen, you people of Israel! You will go across the Jordan River today. You will go into that land to force out nations greater and stronger than you. Their cities are big and have walls as high as the sky! ²The people there are tall and strong. They are the Anakites.* You know about those people. You heard our spies say, 'No person can win against the Anakites.' ³But you can be sure that it is the Lord your God who goes across the river before you—and God is like a fire that destroys! The Lord will destroy those nations. He will make them fall before you. You will force those nations out. You will quickly destroy them. The Lord has promised you that this will happen.

⁴"The Lord your God will force those nations out for you. But don't say to yourselves, 'The Lord brought us to live in this land because we are such good people!' ⌊That is not the reason!⌋ The Lord forced those nations out because they were evil—⌊not because you were good⌋. ⁵You are going in to take their land, but not because you are good and live right. You are going in, and the Lord your God is forcing those people out because of the evil way they lived. And the Lord wants to keep the promise he made to your ancestors*—Abraham, Isaac, and Jacob. ⁶The Lord your God is giving you that good land to live in, but you should know that it is not because you are good. The truth is that you are very stubborn people!

Remember the Lord's Anger

⁷"Don't forget that you made the Lord your God angry in the desert! You have refused to obey the Lord from the day you left the land of Egypt to the day you came to this place. ⁸You made the Lord angry at Mount Horeb *(Sinai)*. The Lord was angry enough to destroy you! ⁹I went up the mountain to get the flat stones. The Agreement that the Lord made with you was written on those stones. I stayed on the mountain 40 days and 40 nights. I did not eat any food or drink any water. ¹⁰The Lord gave me the flat stones. God wrote his commands on the stones with his finger. God wrote everything he said to you from the fire when you were gathered together at the mountain.

¹¹"So, at the end of 40 days and 40 nights, the Lord gave me two flat stones—the stones of the Agreement. ¹²Then the Lord said to me, 'Get up and quickly go down from here. The people you brought out of Egypt have ruined themselves. They stopped obeying my commands so quickly! They melted gold and made an idol for themselves.'

¹³"The Lord also said to me, 'I have watched these people. They are very stubborn! ¹⁴Let me destroy these people completely, so no one will even remember their names! Then I will make another nation from you that is stronger and greater than these people.'

The Golden Calf

¹⁵"Then I turned and came down from the mountain. The mountain was burning with fire. And the two flat stones of the Agreement were in my hands. ¹⁶I looked and I saw you had sinned

---

scorpions Insects with stingers in their tails that cause pain.
manna The special food God sent to the people of Israel while they wandered through the desert for 40 years.
ancestors Literally, "fathers," meaning a person's parents, grandparents, and all the people they are descended from.
Anakites Descendants of Anak, a family famous for tall and powerful fighting men. See Num. 13:33.

against the Lord your God. I saw the calf you made from melted gold! You stopped obeying the Lord so quickly! ¹⁷So I took the two flat stones and threw them down. There before your eyes I broke the stones to pieces. ¹⁸Then I bowed down before the Lord with my face to the ground for 40 days and 40 nights, like I did before. I did not eat any food or drink any water. I did this because you had sinned so badly. You did the thing that is evil to the Lord, and you made him angry. ¹⁹I was afraid of the Lord's terrible anger. He was angry enough to destroy you. But the Lord listened to me again. ²⁰The Lord was very angry with Aaron—enough to destroy him! So I also prayed for Aaron at that time. ²¹I took that terrible thing—the calf you made—and burned it in the fire. I broke it into small pieces. And I crushed the pieces until they were dust. Then I threw the dust into the river that came down from the mountain.

Moses Asks God to Forgive Israel

²²"Also, at Taberah, Massah, and Kibroth Hattaavah you made the Lord angry. ²³And you did not obey when the Lord told you to leave Kadesh Barnea. He said, 'Go up and take the land I am giving you.' But you refused to obey the Lord your God. You did not trust him. You did not listen to his command. ²⁴All the time that I have known you, you have refused to obey the Lord.

²⁵"So I bowed down before the Lord 40 days and 40 nights. Why? Because the Lord said he would destroy you. ²⁶I prayed to the Lord. I said: Lord my Master, don't destroy your people. They belong to you. You freed them and brought them out of Egypt with your great power and strength. ²⁷Remember ⌊your promise to⌋ your servants Abraham, Isaac, and Jacob. Forget how stubborn these people are. Don't look at their evil ways or their sins. ²⁸If you punish your people, the Egyptians might say, 'The Lord was not able to take his people into the land he promised them. And he hated them. So he took them into the desert to kill them.' ²⁹But they are your people, Lord. They belong to you. You brought them out of Egypt with your great power and strength.

New Stone Tablets

10"At that time, the Lord said to me, 'You must cut out two flat stones like the first two stones. Then you must come up to me on the mountain. Also make a wooden box. ²I will write on the flat stones the same words that were on the first stones—the stones you broke. Then you must put these new stones in the Box.'

³"So I made a box from acacia wood. I cut two flat stones like the first two stones. Then I went up on the mountain. I had the two flat stones in my hand. ⁴And the Lord wrote on the stones the same words he had written before—the Ten Commandments he spoke to you from the fire, when you were gathered together at the mountain. Then the Lord gave the two flat stones to me. ⁵I came back down from the mountain. I put the stones in the Box I had made. The Lord commanded me to put them there. And the stones are still there in that Box."

(⁶The people of Israel traveled from the wells of the people of Jaakan to Moserah. There Aaron died and was buried. Aaron's son Eleazar served in Aaron's place as priest. ⁷Then the people of Israel went from Moserah to Gudgodah. And they went from Gudgodah to Jotbathah, a land of rivers. ⁸At that time the Lord separated the family group of Levi from the other family groups for his special work. They had the work of carrying the Lord's Box of the Agreement.* They also served as priests before the Lord. And they had the work of blessing people in the Lord's name. They still do this special work today. ⁹That is why the Levites* did not get any share of land like the other family groups did. The Levites have the Lord for their share. That is what the Lord your God promised them.)

¹⁰"I stayed on the mountain 40 days and 40 nights, like the first time. The Lord also listened to me at that time. The Lord decided not to destroy you. ¹¹The Lord said to me, 'Go and lead the people on their trip. They will go in and live in the land that I promised their ancestors* to give them.'

What the Lord Really Wants

¹²"Now, people of Israel, listen! What does the Lord your God really want from you? The Lord wants you to respect him and do what he says.

Box of the Agreement Or, "ark of the Covenant, the box containing the flat stones with the Ten Commandments written on them and other things that proved God was with the people of Israel during their time in the Sinai desert.

Levite(s) People from the tribe of Levi. They helped the priests in the temple and worked for the civil government.

ancestors Literally, "fathers," meaning a person's parents, grandparents, and all the people they are descended from.

God wants you to love him and to serve the Lord your God with all your heart and with all your soul. ¹³So obey the laws and commands of the Lord that I am giving you today. These laws and commands are for your own good.

¹⁴"Everything belongs to the Lord your God. The heavens, even the highest heavens, belong to the Lord. The earth and everything on it belong to the Lord your God. ¹⁵The Lord loved your ancestors* very much. He loved them so much that he chose you, their descendants,* to be his people. He chose you instead of any other nation. And you are still his chosen people today.

¹⁶"Stop being stubborn. Give your hearts to the Lord. ¹⁷Why? Because the Lord is your God. He is the God of gods and the Lord of lords. He is the great God. He is the amazing and powerful fighter. To the Lord every person is the same. The Lord does not accept money to change his mind. ¹⁸He helps children that have no parents. He helps widows.* He loves even the strangers in our country. He gives them food and clothes. ¹⁹So you must also love those strangers. Why? Because you yourselves were strangers in the land of Egypt.

²⁰"You must respect the Lord your God and worship only him. Never leave him. When you make promises, you must use only his name. ²¹The Lord is the one you should praise. He is your God. He has done great and amazing things for you. You have seen those things with your own eyes. ²²When your ancestors* went down into Egypt, there were only 70 people. Now the Lord your God has made you many, many people—as many as the stars in the sky.

Remember the Lord

11 "So you must love the Lord your God. You must do the things he tells you to do. You must always obey his laws, rules, and commands. ²Remember today all the great things the Lord your God has done to teach you. It was you, not your children, that saw those things happen and lived through them. You saw how great the Lord is. You saw how strong he is, and you saw the powerful things he does. ³You, not your children, saw the miracles he did. You saw the things he did in Egypt to Pharaoh, the king of Egypt, and to his whole country. ⁴You, not your children, saw the things the Lord did to the Egyptian army—to their horses and chariots.* They were chasing you, but you saw the Lord cover them with the water from the Red Sea. You saw the Lord completely destroy them. ⁵It was you, not your children, that saw all the things the Lord your God did for you in the desert until you came to this place. ⁶You saw what the Lord did to Dathan and Abiram, the sons of Eliab from Reuben's family. All the people of Israel watched as the ground opened up like a mouth and swallowed those men. It swallowed their families, their tents, and all of their servants and animals. ⁷It was you, not your children, that saw all those great things the Lord did.

⁸"So you must obey every command I tell you today. Then you will be strong. And you will be able to go across the Jordan River and take the land that you are ready to enter. ⁹Then you will live a long life in that country. The Lord promised to give that land to your ancestors* and all their descendants.* It is a land filled with many good things.* ¹⁰The land that you will get is not like the land of Egypt that you came from. In Egypt, you planted your seeds, and then you used your feet ⌊to pump water from the canals⌋ to water your plants. ⌊You watered your fields⌋ the same way you water a vegetable garden. ¹¹But the land that you will soon get is not like that. In Israel there are mountains and valleys. And the land gets its water from the rain that falls from the sky. ¹²The Lord your God cares for that land! The Lord your God watches over that land, from the beginning to the end of the year.

¹³⌊The Lord says,⌋ 'You must listen carefully to the commands I give you today: You must love the Lord your God, and serve him with all your heart and all your soul. If you do that, then ¹⁴I will send rain for your land at the right time. I will send the autumn rain and the spring rain. Then you can gather your grain, your new wine, and your oil. ¹⁵And I will make grass grow in your fields for your cows. You will have plenty to eat.'

¹⁶"But be careful! Don't be fooled. Don't turn away to serve and worship other gods. ¹⁷If you do that, then the Lord will become very angry at you. He will shut the skies, and there will be no rain. The land will not make a harvest. And you will

---

ancestors Literally, "fathers," meaning a person's parents, grandparents, and all the people they are descended from.
descendant(s) A person's children and their future families.
widows Women whose husbands have died.
chariot(s) A small wagon used in war.
filled with many good things Literally, "flowing with milk and honey."

soon die in the good land that the Lord is giving you. ¹⁸"Remember these commands I give you. Keep them in your hearts. ₍Write these commands and₎ tie them on your hands and wear them on your foreheads for a way to help you remember ₍my laws₎. ¹⁹Teach these laws to your children. Talk about these things when you sit in your houses, when you walk on the road, when you lie down, and when you get up. ²⁰Write these commands on the doorposts of your houses and on your gates. ²¹Then both you and your children will live a long time in the land that the Lord promised to give to your ancestors.* You will live there as long as the skies are above the earth.

²²"Be careful to obey every command I have told you to follow: Love the Lord your God, follow all his ways, and be faithful to him. ²³Then, when you go into the land, the Lord will force all those other nations out. You will take the land from nations that are larger and more powerful than you. ²⁴All the land you walk on will be yours. Your land will go from the desert ₍in the south₎ all the way to Lebanon ₍in the north₎. It will go from the Euphrates River ₍in the east₎ all the way to the Mediterranean Sea. ²⁵No person will be able to stand against you. The Lord your God will make the people fear you wherever you go in that land. That is what the Lord promised you before.

Israel's Choice: Blessings or Curses

²⁶"Today I am giving you a choice. You may choose the blessing or the curse. ²⁷You will get the blessing if you listen and obey the commands of the Lord your God that I have told you today. ²⁸But you will get the curse if you refuse to listen and obey the commands of the Lord your God. So don't stop living the way I command you today. And don't follow other gods. ₍You know me, but₎ you don't know those gods.

²⁹"The Lord your God will lead you to your land. You will soon go in and take that land. At that time, you must go to the top of Mount Gerizim and read the blessings to the people from there. And then, you must go to the top of Mount Ebal and read the curses to the people from there. ³⁰These mountains are on the other side of the Jordan River in the land of the Canaanite people living in the Jordan Valley. These mountains are toward the west, not far from the oak trees of Moreh near the town of Gilgal. ³¹You will go across the Jordan River. You will take the land that the Lord your God is giving you. This land will belong to you. When you are living in this land, ³²you must carefully obey all the laws and rules I give you today.

The Place for Worshiping God

12 "These are the laws and rules that you must obey in your new land. You must carefully obey these laws as long as you live in this land. The Lord is the God of your ancestors.* And the Lord is giving this land to you. ²You will take that land from the nations that live there now. You must completely destroy all the places where the people of these nations worship their gods. These places are on high mountains, on hills, and under green trees. ³You must smash their altars* and break their stone memorials* into pieces. You must burn their Asherah poles* and cut down the statues of their gods.

⁴"You must not worship the Lord your God in the same way that those people worship their gods. ⁵The Lord your God will choose a special place among your family groups. The Lord will put his name there. That will be his special house. You must go to that place to worship him. ⁶There you must bring your burnt offerings, your sacrifices, one tenth of your crops and animals,* your special gifts, any gifts you promised to the Lord, any special gift you want to give, and the first animals born in your herds and flocks. ⁷You and your families will eat together at that place, and the Lord your God will be there with you. At that place, you will enjoy sharing the things you worked for. You will remember that the Lord your God blessed you and gave you those good things.

⁸"You must not continue to worship the way we have been worshiping. Until now, each of us has been worshiping God any way we wanted. ⁹Why? Because we have not yet entered the peaceful land that the Lord your God is giving you. ¹⁰But you will go across the Jordan River and

---

ancestors Literally, "fathers," meaning a person's parents, grandparents, and all the people they are descended from.

altar(s) A table or raised area used for offering sacrifices.
memorial(s) Stones that were set up to help people remember the false gods they worshiped.
Asherah poles Poles used to honor the goddess Asherah. People thought she could help them have many children.
one tenth ... animals Or, "tithes." See Deut. 14:22-29.

live in that land. The Lord is giving that land to you. And the Lord will give you rest from all your enemies. You will be safe. [11]Then the Lord will choose a place to be his special house. The Lord will put his name there. And you must bring all the things I command you to that place. Bring your burnt offerings, your sacrifices, one tenth of your crops and animals,* your special gifts, any gifts you promised to the Lord, and the first animals born in your herd and flock. [12]Come to that place with all your people—your children, all your servants, and the Levites* living in your towns. (These Levites will not have a share of the land for their own.) Enjoy yourselves together there with the Lord your God. [13]Be sure you don't offer your burnt offerings in just any place you see. [14]The Lord will choose his special place among your family groups. Offer your burnt offerings and do all the other things I told you only in that place.

[15]"Wherever you live you may kill and eat any good animals, like gazelles and deer. You may eat as much of the meat as you want, as much as the Lord your God gives to you. Any person may eat this meat—people who are clean* and people who are unclean.* [16]But you must not eat the blood. You must pour the blood on the ground like water.

[17]"There are some things you must not eat in the places where you live. These things are: the part of your grain that belongs to God, the part of your new wine and oil that belongs to God, the first animals born in your herd or flock, any gift that you promised to God, any special gifts you want to give or any other gifts for God. [18]You must eat those offerings only at the place where the Lord your God will be together with you—the special place that the Lord your God will choose. You must go there and eat together with your sons, your daughters, all your servants, and the Levites* living in your towns. Enjoy yourselves there with the Lord your God. Enjoy the things you have worked for. [19]But be sure that you always share these meals with the Levites. Do this as long as you live in your land.

[20-21]"The Lord your God promised to make your country larger. When the Lord does this, you might live too far from the place he chooses to be his special house. If it is too far, and you are hungry for meat, then you may eat any meat you have. You may kill any animal from the herd or flock that the Lord has given you. Do this the way I have commanded you. You may eat this meat there where you live any time you want. [22]You may eat this meat the same as you would eat gazelle or deer meat. Any person can do this—people who are clean* and people who are unclean.* [23]But be sure not to eat the blood. Why? Because the life is in the blood. And you must not eat meat that still has life in it. [24]Don't eat the blood. You must pour the blood onto the ground like water. [25]So don't eat blood. You must do everything that the Lord says is right. Then good things will happen to you and to your descendants.*

[26]"If you decide to give something special to God, then you must go to the special place that the Lord your God will choose. And if you make a special promise, then you must go to that place to give that gift to God. [27]You must offer your burnt offerings in that place. Offer the meat and the blood of your burnt offerings on the altar* of the Lord your God. For your other sacrifices, you must pour the blood on the altar of the Lord your God. Then you may eat the meat. [28]Be careful to obey all the commands that I give you. When you do the things that are good and right—the things that please the Lord your God—then everything will go well for you and for your descendants* forever.

[29]"You are going to take your land from other people. The Lord your God will destroy those people for you. You will force those people out of that land, and you will live there. [30]After that happens, be careful! You will destroy those people. So don't fall into the trap of worshiping their false gods. Be careful! Don't go to those false gods for help. Don't say, 'Those people worshiped these gods, so I will worship that way too!' [31]Don't do that to the Lord your God! ₁Don't worship God like that! Why?₁ Because those people do all kinds of bad things that the Lord

---

one tenth ... animals Or, "tithes." See Deut. 14:22-29.
Levite(s) People from the tribe of Levi. They helped the priests in the temple and worked for the civil government.
clean Pure or acceptable to God for worship.
unclean Not pure or not acceptable to God for worship.

descendant(s) A person's children and their future families.
altar(s) A table or raised area used for offering sacrifices.

hates. They even burn their children as sacrifices to their gods!

³²"You must be careful to do everything I command you. Don't add anything to the things I tell you, and don't take anything away.

False Prophets

13 "A prophet or a person that explains dreams might come to you. He might tell you that he will show you a sign or a miracle. ²And the sign or miracle he told you about might come true. Then he might ask you to follow other gods (gods you don't know). He might say to you, 'Let's serve those gods!' ³Don't listen to that person. Why? Because the Lord your God is testing you. The Lord wants to know if you love him with all your heart and all your soul. ⁴You must follow the Lord your God! Respect him. Obey the Lord's commands, and do what he tells you. Serve the Lord, and never leave him! ⁵Also, you must kill that prophet or person that explains dreams. Why? Because he told you to turn against the Lord your God. And it was the Lord who brought you out of the land of Egypt, where you were slaves. That person tried to pull you away from the life the Lord your God commanded you to live. So you must kill that person to remove that evil from your people.

⁶"Someone close to you might secretly persuade you to worship other gods. It might be your own brother, your son, your daughter, the wife you love or your closest friend. That person might say, 'Let's go and serve other gods.' (These are gods that you and your ancestors never knew. ⁷They are the gods of the people that live in the other lands around you, some near and some far away.) ⁸You must not agree with that person. Don't listen to him. Don't feel sorry for him. Don't let him go free. And don't protect him. ⁹⁻¹⁰No! You must kill that person! You must kill him with stones. You be the first person to pick up stones and throw at him. Then all the people must throw stones to kill him. Why? Because that person tried to pull you away from the Lord your God. And it was the Lord who brought you out of the land of Egypt, where you were slaves. ¹¹Then all the people of Israel will hear and be afraid. And they will not do those evil things any more.

Cities that Must Be Destroyed

¹²"The Lord your God has given you cities to live in. Sometimes you might hear some bad news about one of these cities. You might hear that ¹³some bad people in your own nation are persuading the people of their city to do bad things. They might say to the people of their city, 'Let's go and serve other gods.' (These gods would be gods that you never knew before.) ¹⁴If you hear this kind of news, you must do all you can to learn if it is true. If you learn that it is true—if you prove that such a terrible thing really did happen—¹⁵then you must punish the people of that city. You must kill them all. And kill all their animals, too. You must destroy that city completely. ¹⁶Then you must gather all the valuable things and take them to the center of the city and burn the city and everything in it. It will be a burnt offering to the Lord your God. The city must become an empty pile of rocks forever. That city must never be built again. ¹⁷Everything in that city must be given to God to be destroyed. So you must not keep any of the things for yourselves. If you follow this command, then the Lord will stop being so angry at you. The Lord will be kind to you. He will feel sorry for you. He will let your nation grow larger, like he promised your ancestors.* ¹⁸This will happen if you listen to the Lord your God—if you obey all his commands that I give you today. You must do the things that the Lord your God says are right.

Israel, God's Special People

14 "You are the children of the Lord your God. When someone dies, you must not cut yourselves or shave your heads to show your sadness. ²Why? Because you are different from other people. You are the Lord's special people. From all the people in the world, the Lord your God chose you to be his own special people.

Food the Israelites Are Allowed to Eat

³"Don't eat anything that the Lord hates. ⁴You may eat these animals: cows, sheep, goats, ⁵deer, gazelles, roe deer, wild sheep, wild goats, antelopes, and mountain sheep. ⁶You may eat any animal that has hooves* divided into two parts and that chews the cud.* ⁷But don't eat camels, rabbits or rock badgers. These animals chew the cud, but they don't have split hooves. So those

---

ancestors Literally, "fathers," meaning a person's parents, grandparents, and all the people they are descended from.

hooves The hard part of the foot of certain animals.

cud The food that is brought up from the stomach of some animals (like cows) and chewed again.

clean Pure or acceptable for eating or for worship.

animals are not a clean* food for you. ⁸And you must not eat pigs. Their hooves are divided, but they don't chew the cud. So pigs are not a clean food for you. Don't eat any meat from pigs. Don't even touch a pig's dead body.

⁹You may eat any kind of fish that has fins and scales. ¹⁰But don't eat anything living in the water that does not have fins and scales. It is not a clean* food for you.

¹¹"You may eat any clean* bird. ¹²But don't eat any of these birds: eagles, vultures, buzzards, ¹³red kites, falcons, any kind of kite, ¹⁴any kind of raven, ¹⁵horned owls, screech owls, sea gulls, any kind of hawk, ¹⁶little owls, great owls, white owls, ¹⁷desert owls, ospreys, cormorants, ¹⁸storks, any kind of heron, hoopoes or bats.

¹⁹"All insects with wings are unclean.* So don't eat them. ²⁰But you may eat any clean* bird.

²¹"Don't eat any animal that has died by itself. You may give the dead animal to the foreigner in your town, and he can eat it. Or you may sell the dead animal to a foreigner. But you yourselves must not eat the dead animal. Why? Because you belong to the Lord your God. You are his special people.

"Don't cook a baby goat in its mother's milk.

Giving One Tenth

²²"Every year you must be sure to save one tenth of all the crops that grow in your fields. ²³Then you must go to the place the Lord chooses to be his special house. You will go there to be with the Lord your God. At that place you will eat the tenth of your crops—one tenth of your grain, your new wine, your oil, and the first animals born in your herds and flocks. In this way, you will always remember to respect the Lord your God. ²⁴But that place might be too far for you to travel to. Maybe you will not be able to carry one tenth of all the crops that the Lord has blessed you with. If that happens, then ²⁵sell that part of your crops. Take the money with you and go to the special place that the Lord has chosen. ²⁶Use the money to buy anything you want—cows, sheep, wine or beer or any other food. Then you and your family should eat and enjoy yourselves there in that place with the Lord your God. ²⁷But don't forget the Levites* living in your town. ₍Share your food with them₎ because they don't have a share of the land like you have.

²⁸"At the end of every three years, you must gather one tenth of your harvest for that year. Store this food in your towns ₍where other people can use it₎. ²⁹This food is for the Levites,* because they don't have any land of their own. This food is also for other people in your towns that need it. That food is for foreigners, widows, and children that have no parents. If you do this, then the Lord your God will bless you in everything you do.

The Special Year of Canceling Debts

15 "At the end of every seven years, you must cancel debts. ²This is the way you must do this: Every person that has lent money to another Israelite must cancel that debt. He should not ask a brother (an Israelite) to pay back that debt. Why? Because the Lord said to cancel debts during that year. ³You may require a foreigner to pay you back. But you must cancel any debt another Israelite owes you. ⁴There should not be any poor people in your country. Why? Because the Lord is giving you this land. And the Lord will greatly bless you. ⁵But this will happen only if you obey the Lord your God. You must be careful to obey every command that I have told you today. ⁶Then the Lord your God will bless you, like he promised. And you will have enough money to make loans to many nations. But you will not need to borrow from anyone. You will rule over many nations. But none of those nations will rule over you.

⁷"When you are living in the land the Lord your God is giving you, there might be a poor person among your people. You must not be selfish. You must not refuse to give help to that poor person. ⁸You must be willing to share with him. You must lend that person whatever he needs.

⁹"Don't ever refuse to help someone simply because the seventh year, the year for canceling debts, is near. Don't let an evil thought like that enter your mind. You must never have bad thoughts about a person that needs help. You must not refuse to help him. If you don't help that poor person, then he will complain to the Lord against you. And the Lord will find you guilty of sin.

¹⁰"Give the poor person all that you can. Don't feel bad about giving to him. Why? Because the Lord your God will bless you for doing this good thing. He will bless you in all your work and in

---

clean Pure or acceptable for eating or for worship.
unclean Not pure or not acceptable for eating or for worship.
Levite(s) People from the tribe of Levi. They helped the priests in the temple and worked for the civil government.

everything you do. ¹¹There will always be poor people in the land. That is why I command you to be ready to help your brother. Give to the poor people in your land that need help.

Letting Slaves Go Free

¹²"You might buy a Hebrew man or woman to serve you as a slave. You may keep that person as a slave for six years. But in the seventh year, you must let that person go free. ¹³But when you let your slave go free, don't send him away with nothing. ¹⁴You must give that person some of your animals, grain, and wine. The Lord your God blessed you and gave you plenty of good things. In the same way, you must give plenty of good things to your slave. ¹⁵Remember, you were slaves in Egypt. And the Lord your God set you free. So that is why I am giving you this command today.

¹⁶"But one of your slaves might say to you, 'I will not leave you.' He might say this because he loves you and your family and because he has a good life with you. ¹⁷Make this servant put his ear against your door, and use a sharp tool to make a hole in his ear. This will show that he is your slave forever. You must do this even to the women slaves that want to stay with you.

¹⁸"Don't feel bad about letting your slave go free. Remember, he served you six years at only half the money you would have paid a hired person. The Lord your God will bless you in everything you do.

Rules About Firstborn Animals

¹⁹"All the first male animals born in your herd and flock are special. You must give them to the Lord. Don't use any of those animals for your work. And don't cut wool from any of those sheep. ²⁰Every year you must take those animals to the place the Lord your God will choose. There with the Lord, you and your family will eat those animals.

²¹"But if an animal has something wrong with it—if it is crippled or blind or has something else wrong with it—then you must not sacrifice that animal to the Lord your God. ²²But you may eat the meat from that animal at home. Any person may eat it—people who are clean* and people who are unclean.* The rules for eating this meat is the same as the rules for eating gazelles and deer.

²³But you must not eat the blood from the animal. You must pour the blood out on the ground like water.

Passover

16"Remember the month of Abib.* At that time, you must celebrate Passover* to honor the Lord your God. Why? Because in that month the Lord your God brought you out from Egypt by night. ²You must go to the place the Lord will choose to be his special house. There you must offer the Passover sacrifice to honor the Lord. You must offer the cows and goats. ³Don't eat bread that has yeast in it with this sacrifice. You must eat unleavened bread* for seven days. This bread is called "Bread of Trouble." It will help you remember the troubles you had in Egypt. Remember how quickly you had to leave that country! You must remember that day as long as you live. ⁴There must be no yeast in anyone's house anywhere in the country for seven days. Also, all the meat you sacrifice on the evening of the first day must be eaten before morning.

⁵"You must not sacrifice the Passover animal in any of the towns that the Lord your God gives you. ⁶You must sacrifice the Passover animal only at the place that the Lord your God will choose to be his special house. There you must sacrifice the Passover animal in the evening when the sun goes down. This is the holiday when you remember that God brought you out of Egypt. ⁷You must cook the Passover meat and eat it at the place the Lord your God will choose. Then, in the morning, you may go back home. ⁸You must eat unleavened bread* six days. On the seventh day you must not do any work. On this day, the people will come together for a special meeting to honor the Lord your God.

Festival of Weeks (Pentecost)

⁹"You must count seven weeks from the time you began to harvest the grain. ¹⁰Then celebrate the Festival of Weeks for the Lord your God. Do this by bringing him some special gift you want to

---

Abib This name means "young heads of grain." This is the first month of the Jewish calendar, also called Nisan. It was about the same time as March and April.

Passover Important Jewish holy day. They ate a special meal on this day every spring to remember that God freed them from slavery in Egypt.

unleavened bread Bread made without yeast.

clean Pure or acceptable to God for worship.
unclean Not pure or not acceptable to God for worship.

bring. Decide how much to give by thinking about how much the Lord your God has blessed you. ¹¹Go to the place the Lord will choose to be his special house. You and your people should enjoy yourselves together there with the Lord your God. Take all your people with you—your sons, your daughters, and all your servants. Also, take the Levites,* foreigners, orphans,* and widows* living in your towns. ¹²Remember, you were slaves in Egypt. So be sure to obey these laws.

Festival of Shelters

¹³"Seven days after you have gathered your harvest in from your threshing floor* and from your winepress,* you should celebrate the Festival of Shelters. ¹⁴Enjoy yourselves at this festival—you, your sons, your daughters, all your servants, and the Levites,* foreigners, orphans,* and widows* living in your towns. ¹⁵Celebrate this festival for seven days at the special place the Lord will choose. Do this to honor the Lord your God. The Lord your God blessed your harvest and all the work you did. So be very happy!

¹⁶"Three times a year all your men must come to meet with the Lord your God at the special place he will choose. They must come for the Festival of Unleavened Bread, the Festival of Weeks, and the Festival of Shelters. Every person that comes to meet with the Lord must bring a gift. ¹⁷Each man should give as much as he can. He should decide how much to give by thinking about how much the Lord has given him.

Judges and Officers for the People

¹⁸"Choose men to be judges and officers in every town that the Lord your God gives you. Every family group must do this. And these men must be fair in judging the people. ¹⁹You must always be fair. You must not favor some people over other people. You must not take money to change your mind in judgment. Money blinds the eyes of wise people and changes what a good person will say. ²⁰Goodness and Fairness! You must try very hard to be good and fair all the time! Then you will live and keep the land that the Lord your God is giving you.

God Hates Idols

²¹"When you set up an altar* for the Lord your God, you must not place beside the altar any of the wooden poles that honor the goddess Asherah.* ²²And you must not set up special stones for worshiping false gods. The Lord your God hates those things.

Use Only Good Animals for Sacrifices

17 "You must not sacrifice to the Lord your God a cow or sheep if there is anything wrong with it. Why? Because the Lord your God hates it!

Punishment for Worshiping Idols

²"You might hear about an evil thing that happens in one of the cities that the Lord your God is giving you. You might hear that a man or woman in your group has sinned against the Lord. You might hear that they have broken the Agreement of the Lord—³that they have worshiped other gods. Or maybe that they have worshiped the sun, the moon or the stars. That is against the Lord's command that I gave you. ⁴If you hear bad news like this, then you must check it carefully. You must learn if it is true that this terrible thing has really happened in Israel. If you prove that it is true, ⁵then you must punish the person that did that evil thing. You must take that man or woman out to a public place near the city gates and kill them with stones. ⁶But a person should not be punished with death if only one witness says that person did the evil thing. But if two or three witnesses say it is true, then the person must be killed. ⁷The witnesses must throw the first stones to kill that person. Then the other people should throw stones to finish killing him. In this way, you will remove that evil from your group.

Levite(s) People from the tribe of Levi. They helped the priests in the temple and worked for the civil government.
orphans Children whose parents have died.
widows Women whose husbands have died. Often these women had no one to care for them.
threshing floor A place where grain is beaten or walked on to remove the hulls from the grain.
winepress A place where people pressed grapes to make wine. This was often a shallow hole carved in rock.

altar(s) A table or raised area used for offering sacrifices.
Asherah A goddess that the Assyrians and Canaanites worshiped. They thought she could help them have children.

Difficult Court Decisions

⁸"There might be some problems that are too hard for your courts to judge. It might be a murder case or an argument between two people. Or it might be a fight in which someone was hurt. When these cases are argued in your towns, your judges there might not be able to decide what is right. Then you must go to the special place that the Lord your God will choose. ⁹The priests are from the Levi family group. You must go to those priests and to the judge on duty at that time. Those men will decide what to do about that problem. ¹⁰There at the Lord's special place they will tell you their decision. You must do whatever they say. Be sure to do all the things they tell you to do. ¹¹You must accept their decision and follow their instructions exactly. You must do exactly what they tell you to do —don't change anything!

¹²"You must punish any person that refuses to obey the judge or the priest that is there at that time serving the Lord your God. That person must die. You must remove that evil person from Israel. ¹³All the people will hear about this punishment and be afraid. And they will not be stubborn any more.

How to Choose a King

¹⁴"You will enter the land that the Lord your God is giving you. You will take that land and live in it. Then you will say, 'We will put a king over us, like all the nations around us.' ¹⁵When that happens, then you must be sure to choose the king that the Lord chooses. The king over you must be one of your own people. You must not make a foreigner your king. ¹⁶The king must not get more and more horses for himself. And he must not send people to Egypt to get more horses. Why? Because the Lord has told you, 'You must never go back that way.' ¹⁷Also, the king must not have too many wives. Why? Because that will make him turn away from the Lord. And the king must not make himself rich with silver and gold.

¹⁸"And when the king begins to rule, he must write a copy of the law for himself in a book. He must make that copy from the books that the priests and Levites* keep. ¹⁹The king must keep that book with him. He must read from that book all his life. Why? Because the king must learn to respect the Lord his God. And the king must learn to completely obey everything the law commands. ²⁰Then the king will not think that he is better than any of his own people. And he will not turn away from the law, but he will follow it exactly. Then that king and his descendants* will rule the kingdom of Israel a long time.

Supporting the Priests and Levites

18"The family group of Levi will not get any share of land in Israel. Those people will serve as priests. They will live by eating the sacrifices that are cooked on the fire and offered to the Lord. That is the share for the people from the Levi family group. ²Those Levites* will not get any share of land like the other family groups. The Levites' share is the Lord himself, just like the Lord said to them.

³"When you kill a cow or a sheep for a sacrifice, you must give the priests these parts: the shoulder, both cheeks, and the stomach. ⁴You must give the priests the first part of your harvest. You must give them the first part of your grain, your new wine, and your oil. You must give the Levites* the first wool cut from your sheep. ⁵Why? Because the Lord your God looked at all your family groups and chose Levi and his descendants* to serve him as priests forever.

⁶"⌊Every Levite* man has a special time to work at the temple. But if he wants to work there some other time too, then he may work anytime he wants.⌋ Any Levite living in any town anywhere in Israel may leave his home and come to the Lord's special place. He may do this any time he wants. ⁷And this Levite may serve in the name of the Lord his God, the same as all his brother Levites that are on duty before the Lord. ⁸And that Levite will get an equal share with the other Levites, in addition to the share his family normally gets.

Israel Must Not Live Like Other Nations

⁹"When you come into the land that the Lord your God is giving you, don't learn to do the terrible things the people of the other nations there do. ¹⁰Don't sacrifice your sons or daughters in the fires on your altars.* Don't try to learn what will

---

Levite(s) People from the tribe of Levi. They helped the priests in the temple and worked for the civil government.

descendant(s) A person's children and their future families.
altar(s) A table or raised area used for offering sacrifices.

happen in the future by talking to a fortune teller or by going to a magician, a witch or a sorcerer. ¹¹Don't let anyone try to put magic spells on other people. Don't let any of your people become a medium* or a wizard.* And no person should try to talk with someone that has died. ¹²The Lord your God hates people doing those things. That is why he is forcing those other nations out of this country for you. ¹³You must be faithful to the Lord your God.

The Lord's Special Prophet

¹⁴"You must force those other nations out of your land. The people of those nations listen to people who use magic and try to tell the future. But the Lord your God will not let you do those things. ¹⁵The Lord your God will send to you a prophet.* This prophet will come from among your own people. He will be like me. You must listen to this prophet. ¹⁶God will send you this prophet because that is what you asked him to do. When you were gathered together at Mount Horeb (Sinai), ⌊you were afraid of God's voice and the great fire you saw on the mountain. So⌋ you said, 'Don't let us hear the voice of the Lord our God again! Don't let us see that great fire or we will die!'

¹⁷"The Lord said to me, 'The thing they ask for is good. ¹⁸I will send them a prophet* like you. This prophet will be one of their own people. I will tell him the things he must say. And he will tell the people everything I command. ¹⁹This prophet will speak for me. And when he speaks, if any person refuses to listen to my commands, then I will punish that person.'

How to Know False Prophets

²⁰"But a prophet* might say something that I did not tell him to say. And he might tell people that he is speaking for me. If this happens, then that prophet must be killed. Also, a prophet might come that speaks for other gods. That prophet must also be killed. ²¹You might be thinking, 'How can we know if something a prophet says is not from the Lord?' ²²If a prophet says he is speaking for the Lord, but the thing does not happen, then you will know that the Lord did not say it. You will know that this prophet was speaking his own ideas. You don't need to be afraid of him.

Cities of Safety

19 "The Lord your God is giving you land that belongs to other nations. The Lord will destroy those nations. You will live where those people lived. You will take their cities and their houses. When that happens, ²⁻³you must divide the land into three parts. Then in each part you must choose a city close to everyone in that area. And you must prepare roads to those cities. Then any person that kills another person may run to that city for safety.

⁴"This is the rule for the person that kills someone and runs away to one of those three cities to be safe: It must be a person that killed the other person accidentally. It must be a person that did not hate the person he killed. ⁵Here is an example: A man goes into the forest with another person to cut wood. The man swings his axe to cut down a tree, but the head of the axe separates from the handle. The axe head hits the other person and kills him. The man who swung the axe may then run to one of those three cities and be safe. ⁶But if the city is too far away, he might not be able to run there fast enough. A close relative* of the person he killed might run after him and catch him before he reaches the city. The close relative might be very angry and kill the man. But the man did not deserve death. He did not hate the person he killed. ⁷⌊The cities must be close to everyone.⌋ That is why I command you to choose three special cities.

⁸"The Lord your God promised your fathers that he would make your land larger. He will give you all the land that he promised to give to your ancestors.* ⁹He will do this if you completely obey his commands that I give you today—if you love the Lord your God and always live the way he wants. Then, when the Lord makes your land larger, you should choose three more cities for safety. They should be added to the first three cities. ¹⁰Then innocent people will not be killed in

---

medium A person that tries to talk with the spirits of dead people.
wizard A person that tries to use evil spirits to do magic.
prophet A person called by God to be a special servant. God used dreams and visions to show them things to teach to the people.

close relative Literally, "avenger of blood." When a person was killed, his relative had to be sure the killer was punished.
ancestors Literally, "fathers," meaning a person's parents, grandparents, and all the people they are descended from.

the land that the Lord your God is giving you. And you will not be guilty for any deaths.

¹¹"But a man might hate another person. That man might hide, waiting to kill the person he hates. He might kill that person and run away into one of those cities of safety. ¹²If that happens, then the elders *(leaders)* in that man's home town must send someone to get him and take him away from the city of safety. Those leaders must give that man to the close relative.* The murderer must die. ¹³You must not feel sorry for him. He was guilty of killing an innocent person. You must remove that guilt from Israel. Then everything will go well for you.

Property Lines

¹⁴"You must not move the stones that mark your neighbor's property. People put those stones there in the past to mark each person's property. Those stones mark the land that the Lord your God gave you.

Witnesses

¹⁵"If a person is accused of doing something against the law, one witness is not enough to prove that the person is guilty. There must be two or three witnesses to prove that the person really did wrong.

¹⁶"A witness might try to hurt another person by lying and saying that this person did wrong. ¹⁷If that happens, then both of those people must go to the Lord's special house and be judged by the priests and judges that are on duty at that time. ¹⁸The judges must ask careful questions. They might find that the witness lied against the other person. If the witness lied, ¹⁹then you must punish him. You must do to him the same thing he wanted to do to the other person. In this way, you will remove that evil from your group. ²⁰Other people will hear about this and be afraid. And those people will not do evil things like that again.

²¹ ⌈"Punishment must be as severe as the crime.⌋ Don't feel sorry about punishing a person that does wrong. If a person takes a life, then he must pay with his own life. The rule is: an eye for an eye, a tooth for a tooth, a hand for a hand, a foot for a foot.

Rules for War

20"When you go out to battle against your enemies, and you see horses, chariots,* and many more people than you have, you must not be afraid of them. Why? Because the Lord your God is with you—and the Lord brought you out of Egypt.

²"When you go to the battle, the priest must go to the soldiers and speak to them. ³The priest will say, 'Men of Israel, listen to me! Today you are going against your enemies in battle. Don't lose your courage! Don't be troubled or upset! Don't be afraid of the enemy! ⁴Why? Because the Lord your God is going with you. He will help you fight against your enemies. The Lord your God will help you win!'

⁵"Those ⌈Levite⌋ officers will say to the soldiers, 'Is there any man here that has built a new house, but has not yet dedicated it? That man should go back home. He might be killed in the battle. And then another person will dedicate that man's house. ⁶Is there any man here that has planted a field of grapes, but has not yet gathered any of the grapes? That man should go back home. If that man dies in the battle, then another person will enjoy the fruit from his field. ⁷Is there any man here that is engaged to be married? That man should go back home. If he dies in the battle, then another man will marry the woman he is engaged to.'

⁸"Those ⌈Levite⌋ officers must also say to the people, 'Is there any man here that has lost his courage and is afraid? He should go back home. Then he will not cause the other soldiers to lose their courage too.' ⁹Then, after the officers have finished speaking to the army, they must choose captains to lead the soldiers.

¹⁰"When you go to attack a city, you must first offer peace to the people there. ¹¹If they accept your offer and open their gates, then all the people in that city will become your slaves and be forced to work for you. ¹²But if the city refuses to make peace with you and fights against you, then you should surround the city. ¹³And when the Lord your God lets you take the city, you must kill all the men in it. ¹⁴But you may take for yourselves the women, the children, the cows, and everything else in the city. You may use all these things. The Lord your God has given these things to you. ¹⁵That is what you must do to all the cities that are very far from you—the cities that are not in the land where you will live.

¹⁶"But when you take cities in the land that the Lord your God is giving you, you must kill

---

close relative Literally, "avenger of blood." When a person was killed, his relative had to be sure the killer was punished.
chariot(s) A small wagon used in war.

everyone. ¹⁷You must completely destroy all the people—the Hittites, the Amorites, the Canaanites, the Perizzites, the Hivites, and the Jebusites. The Lord your God has commanded you to do this. ¹⁸Why? Because then they won't be able teach you to sin against the Lord your God. They will not be able to teach you to do any of the terrible things they do when they worship their gods.

¹⁹"When you are making war against a city, you might surround that city for a long time. You must not cut down the fruit trees around that city. You may eat the fruit from these trees, but you must not cut them down. These trees are not the enemy, so don't make war against them! ²⁰But you may cut down the trees that you know are not fruit trees. You may use these trees to build weapons for making war against that city. You may use them until the city falls.

If a Person Is Found Murdered

21 "In the land that the Lord your God is giving you, a man might be found murdered in a field. But no one knows who killed him. ²Then your leaders and judges must come out and measure the distance to the towns around the person that was killed. ³When you learn which town is nearest to the dead man, the leaders of that town must take a cow from their herds. It must be a cow that never had a calf. And it must be a cow that has never been used for work. ⁴The leaders of that town must then bring the cow down to a valley with running water. It must be a valley that has never been plowed or had anything planted in it. Then the leaders must break the cow's neck there in that valley. ⁵The priests, the descendants* of Levi, must also go there. (The Lord your God has chosen these priests to serve him and to bless people in his name. The priests will decide who is right in every argument where a person is hurt.) ⁶All the leaders of the town nearest the murdered man must wash their hands over the cow that had its neck broken in the valley. ⁷These leaders must say, 'We did not kill this man. And we did not see it happen. ⁸Lord, you saved Israel. We are your people. Now make us pure.* Don't blame us for killing an innocent man.' In this way, those men will not be blamed for killing an innocent man. ⁹In this way, you will do the right thing. And you will remove that guilt from your group.

Women Captured in War

¹⁰"You might fight against your enemies, and the Lord your God might let you defeat them. You might carry your enemies away as captives. ¹¹You might see a beautiful woman among the captives that you want to be your wife. ¹²You must then bring her into your house. She must shave her head and cut her nails. ¹³She must take off the clothes she was wearing that showed she was taken in war. She must stay in your house and be sad about losing her father and her mother for a full month. After that, you may go to her and become her husband. She will be your wife. ¹⁴If you are not pleased with her, then you must divorce her and let her go free. You cannot sell her. You must not treat her like a slave. Why? Because you had sexual relations with her.

The Oldest Son

¹⁵"A man might have two wives. And he might love one wife more than the other. Both wives might have children for him. And the first child might be the child of the wife he does not love. ¹⁶When the man divides his property among his children, he can't give the son of the wife he loves the things that belong to the firstborn* child. ¹⁷The man must accept the first child, the son of the wife he doesn't love. The man must give the first son a double share of all his things. Why? Because that child is his first child. The right of the firstborn* child belongs to that child.

Children Who Refuse to Obey

¹⁸"A man might have a son who is stubborn and refuses to obey. This son doesn't obey his father or mother. They punish the son, but he still refuses to listen to them. ¹⁹His father and mother must then take him to the leaders of the town at the town meeting place. ²⁰They must say to the leaders of the town: 'Our son is stubborn and refuses to obey. He doesn't do anything we tell him to do. He eats and he drinks too much.' ²¹Then the men in the town must kill the son with stones. By doing this you will remove this evil from yourselves. All the people of Israel will hear about this and be afraid.

---

descendant(s) A person's children and their future families.
make ... pure Or, "make atonement." The Hebrew word means "to cover," "to hide," or "to erase sins."

firstborn The first born child. The firstborn son was very important in ancient times.

Criminals Killed and Hung on a Tree

²²"A person might be guilty of a sin that must be punished by death. After he is killed, people might hang his body on a tree. ²³You must not let that body stay on the tree all night. You must be sure to bury this man on the same day. Why? Because the person that hangs on a tree is cursed by God. You must not ruin the land that the Lord your God is giving you.

Other Laws

22 "If you see that your neighbor's cow or sheep is loose, you must not ignore it. You must be sure to take it back to its owner. ²If the owner does not live near you or if you don't know who it belongs to, then you may take the cow or sheep to your house. And you may keep it with you until the owner comes looking for it. Then you must give it back to him. ³You must do the same thing when you find your neighbor's donkey, your neighbor's clothes or anything else your neighbor loses. You must help your neighbor.

⁴"If your neighbor's donkey or cow has fallen down on the road, you must not ignore it. You must help him lift it up again.

⁵"A woman must not wear men's clothes. And a man must not wear women's cloths. That is very disgusting to the Lord your God.

⁶"You might be walking along a path and find a bird's nest in a tree or on the ground. If the mother bird is sitting with her baby birds or on the eggs, then you must not take the mother bird with the babies. ⁷You may take the babies for yourself. But you must let the mother go. If you obey these laws, then things will go well for you, and you will live a long time.

⁸"When you build a new house, you must build a wall around your roof.* Then you will not be guilty for the death of a person that falls from the house.

Things That Must Not Be Put Together

⁹"You must not plant seeds of grain in the same fields as your grapevines. Why? Because then they become useless,* and you can't use either the grapes or the grain that grows from the seeds you planted.

¹⁰"You must not plow with a cow and a donkey together.

¹¹"You must not wear cloth made by weaving together wool and linen.

¹²"Tie several pieces of thread together. Then put these tassels* on the four corners of the robes you wear.

Marriage Laws

¹³"A man might marry a girl and have sexual relations with her. Then he might decide that he does not like her. ¹⁴He might lie and say, 'I married this woman, but when we had sexual relations, I found she was not a virgin.*' By saying this against her, people might think bad things about her. ¹⁵If this happens, the girl's father and mother must bring the proof that the girl was a virgin to the town elders *(leaders)* at the meeting place of the town. ¹⁶The girl's father must say to the leaders, 'I gave my daughter to this man to be his wife, but now he does not want her. ¹⁷This man has told lies against my daughter. He said, 'I did not find the proof that your daughter is a virgin.' But here is the proof that my daughter was a virgin.' Then they should show the cloth* to the town leaders. ¹⁸Then the leaders of that town must take that man and punish him. ¹⁹They must fine him 40 ounces of silver.* They must give the money to the girl's father because her husband brought shame to an Israelite girl. And the girl must continue to be the man's wife. He can't divorce her all his life.

²⁰"But the things that the husband said about his wife might be true. The wife's parents might not have the proof that she was a virgin.* If this happens, ²¹then the town leaders must bring the girl to the door of her father's house. Then the men of the town must kill her with stones. Why?

---

wall around your roof In ancient Israel the roofs of houses were flat, and people used them like an extra room. This law made the roof a safer place.

they become useless Literally, "they become holy." This means these things belonged only to God, so they couldn't be used by the people."

tassels These pieces of string were made from different materials, so they became holy. This helped the people remember God and his commands.

virgin A woman who has not had sexual relations with anyone.

cloth The blood-stained bed cover that the bride kept from her wedding night to prove she was a virgin when she married.

40 ounces of silver This is probably twice the amount of money that a man usually paid the father of the bride to seal the marriage agreement. See Deut. 22:29.

Because she has done a shameful thing in Israel. She has acted like a prostitute* in her father's house. You must remove that evil from your people.

Sexual Sins

²²"If a man is found having sexual relations with another man's wife, then both of them must die—the woman and the man that had sexual relations with her. You must remove that evil from Israel.

²³"A man might meet a virgin* girl engaged to another man. He might have sexual relations with her. If this happens in the city, ²⁴then you must bring them both out to the public place near the gate of that city, and you must kill them with stones. You must kill the man, because he used another man's wife for sexual sin. And you must kill the girl, because she was in the city but did not call for help. You must remove that evil from your people.

²⁵"But if a man finds an engaged girl out in the field and forces her to have sexual relations with him, then only the man must die. ²⁶You must do nothing to the girl. She did nothing that deserves the punishment of death. This is like a person attacking his neighbor and killing him. ²⁷The man found the engaged girl out in the field. He attacked her. And maybe she called for help, but there was no one to help her. ⌊So she must not be punished.⌋

²⁸"A man might find a virgin* girl that is not engaged and force her to have sexual relations with him. If other people see this happen, ²⁹then he must pay the girl's father 20 ounces of silver.* And the girl will become the man's wife. Why? Because he used her for sexual sin. He can't divorce her all his life.

³⁰"A man must not bring shame to his father by having sexual relations with his father's wife.

People Who Can Join in Worship

23 "A man with crushed testicles or part of his sex organs cut off may not join with the men of Israel to worship the Lord. ²If a man's parents were not legally married, then that man may not join with the men of Israel to worship the Lord. And none of his descendants*—to the tenth generation—may join in that group!

³"An Ammonite or Moabite may not join with the men of Israel to worship the Lord. And none of their descendants*—to the tenth generation—may join in that group. ⁴Why? Because the Ammonites and Moabites refused to give you bread and water on your trip at the time you came from Egypt. They also tried to hire Balaam to curse you. (Balaam was the son of Beor from the city of Pethor in Mesopotamia.) ⁵But the Lord your God refused to listen to Balaam. The Lord changed the curse into a blessing for you. Why? Because the Lord your God loves you. ⁶You must never try to make peace with the Ammonite or Moabite people. As long as you live, don't be friendly to them.

People the Israelites Must Accept

⁷"You must not hate an Edomite. Why? Because he is your relative. You must not hate an Egyptian. Why? Because you were a stranger in his land. ⁸The children of the third generation born to the Edomites and Egyptians may join with the men of Israel to worship the Lord.

Keeping the Army Camp Clean

⁹"When your army goes to fight against your enemies, stay away from everything that would make you unclean.* ¹⁰If there is any man who is unclean because he had a wet dream during the night, then he must go out of the camp. He must stay away from the camp. ¹¹Then, when evening comes, the man must bathe himself in water. And when the sun goes down, he may come into the camp again.

¹²"You also must have a place outside the camp where you can go to have a bowel movement. ¹³With your weapons, you must also carry a stick to dig with. Then, when you have a bowel movement, you must dig a hole and cover it up. ¹⁴Why? Because the Lord your God is there with you in your camp to save you and to help you defeat your enemies. So the camp must be holy. Then the Lord will not see something disgusting and leave you.

---

prostitute A woman paid by men for sexual sin.
virgin A woman who has not had sexual relations with anyone.
20 ounces of silver This money became the dowry, the money a man paid to a woman's father to seal the marriage agreement. Often the father saved this money to take care of the woman if something happened to her husband.

unclean Not pure or not acceptable to God for worship.

Other Laws

¹⁵"If a slave runs away from his master to you, you must not give this slave back to his master. ¹⁶This slave may live with you wherever he likes. He may live in whatever city he chooses. You must not trouble him.

¹⁷"An Israelite man or woman must never become a temple prostitute.* ¹⁸The money earned by a man* or woman prostitute must not be brought to the special house of the Lord your God. A person can't use that money to pay for the things he promised to give to God. Why? Because the Lord your God hates for people to sell their bodies for sexual sin.

¹⁹"When you loan something to another Israelite, you must not charge interest. Don't charge interest on money, on food or on anything that may earn interest. ²⁰You may charge interest to a foreigner. But you must not charge interest to another Israelite. If you follow these rules, then the Lord your God will bless you in everything you do in the land where you are going to live.

²¹"When you make a promise to the Lord your God, don't be slow to pay all that you promised. Why? Because the Lord your God will demand that you pay it. You will sin if you don't pay the things you promised. ²²If you don't make a promise, then you are not sinning. ²³But you must do the things you say you will do. If you make a special promise to God, then you chose to make that promise. God did not force you to make that promise. So you must do the thing you promised!

²⁴"When you go through another person's field of grapes, you may eat as many grapes as you want. But you can't put any of the grapes in your basket ₍and take them with you₎. ²⁵When you go through another person's field of grain, you may eat all the grain you can pick with your hands. But you can't use a sickle to cut that person's grain and take it with you.

24 "A man might marry a woman, and then find some secret thing about her that he does not like. If that man is not pleased with her, he must write the divorce papers and give them to her. Then he must send her from his house. ²When she has left his house, she may go and become another man's wife. ³⁻⁴But suppose the new husband also does not like her and sends her away. If that man divorces her, then the first husband may not take her again to be his wife. Or if the new husband dies, then her first husband may not take her again to be his wife. She has become unclean to him. If he married her again, he would be doing something the Lord hates. You must not sin like this in the land that the Lord your God is giving you.

⁵"When a man is newly married, he must not be sent into the army. And he must not be given any other special work. For one year he must be free to stay home and make his new wife happy.

⁶"When you lend a person something, you must not take any part of the stones he uses to grind flour as security.* Why? Because that would be the same as taking away his food.

⁷"A person might kidnap another Israelite—one of his own people. And that kidnapper might sell that person as a slave. If that happens, then that kidnapper must be killed. You must remove that evil from your group.

⁸"When you have a very bad skin disease* be very careful to follow all the things the Levite priests teach you. You must follow carefully the things I told the priests to do. ⁹Remember what the Lord your God did to Miriam* on your trip out of Egypt.

¹⁰"When you give a person any kind of loan, you must not go into his house to get security.* ¹¹You must stand outside. Then the person that you gave the loan to will bring out the security to you. ¹²If he is a poor man, ₍then he might give the clothes that keep him warm₎. You must not keep that security overnight. ¹³You must give his security back to him every evening. Then he will have clothes to sleep in. He will bless you, and the Lord your God will accept this as living right and doing good.

¹⁴"You must not cheat a hired servant that is poor and needy. It does not matter if he is an Israelite or if he is a foreigner living in one of your cities. ¹⁵Give him his pay every day before sunset. Why? Because he is poor and depends on the money. If you don't pay him, he will complain

---

temple prostitute The people who worshiped false gods in the land of Canaan had both men and women serving as priests by giving their bodies in sexual sin.

man Literally, "dog." This probably means a man paid by other men that use him for sexual sin.

security Anything a person gives to show he will pay his loan. If the person does not pay back his loan, then the lender can keep that thing.

a very bad skin disease Or, "leprosy."

Miriam See Num. 12:1-15.

against you to the Lord. And you will be guilty of sin.

¹⁶"Parents must not be put to death for something their children did. And children must not be put to death for something their parents did. A person should be put to death only for a bad thing that he himself did.

¹⁷"You must make sure that foreigners and orphans* are treated fairly. And you must never take clothes from a widow* for security.* ¹⁸Remember, you were poor slaves in Egypt. And the Lord your God took you from that place and set you free. That is why I tell you to do these things for poor people.

¹⁹"You might be gathering your harvest in the field, and you might forget and leave some grain there. You must not go back to get it. It will be for the foreigners, the orphans,* and the widows.* If you leave some grain for them, then the Lord your God will bless you in everything you do. ²⁰When you beat your olive trees, you must not go back to check the branches. The olives you leave will be for the foreigners, the orphans, and the widows. ²¹When you gather the grapes from your vineyard, you must not go back to gather the grapes you left. Those grapes will be for the foreigners, the orphans, and the widows. ²²Remember you were poor slaves in Egypt. That is why I tell you to do these things for poor people.

25 "When two people have an argument, they should go to the court. The judges will decide which person is right and which person is wrong. ²If the judge decides a person must be beaten with a whip, then the judge must make that person lie face down. Someone will beat the guilty person while the judge watches. The number of times he must be hit depends on the crime. ³You must never hit a person more than 40 times. If you beat a person more than 40 times, then that shows that person's life is not important to you.

⁴"When an animal is being used to separate grain, you must not cover its mouth to stop it from eating.

⁵"If two brothers live together, and one of them dies and has no son, then the wife of the dead brother must not be married to a stranger outside the family. Her husband's brother must take her as a wife and have sexual relations with her. Her husband's brother must do the duty of a husband's brother for her. ⁶Then the first child that she gives birth to will take the place of the man's dead brother. Then the dead brother's name will not be taken out of Israel. ⁷If the man does not want to take his brother's wife, then the brother's wife must go to the leaders at the town meeting place. His brother's wife must say to the leaders, 'My husband's brother refuses to keep his brother's name alive in Israel. He will not do the duty of a husband's brother to me.' ⁸Then the leaders of the city must call the man and talk to him. If the man is stubborn and says, 'I don't want to take her,' ⁹then his brother's wife must come to him in front of the leaders. She must take his shoe off his foot. Then she must spit in his face. She must say, 'This is being done to the man who will not build up his brother's family!' ¹⁰Then that brother's family will be known in Israel as 'the family of the man who had his shoe taken off.'

¹¹"Two men might be fighting against each other. One man's wife might come to help her husband. But she must not grab the other man's private parts. ¹²If she does that, then cut off her hand. Don't feel sorry for her.

¹³"⌊Don't carry trick weights for cheating people.⌋ Don't use weights that are too heavy or too light. ¹⁴Don't keep measures in your house that are too large or too small. ¹⁵You must use weights and measures that are correct and accurate. Then you will live a long time in the land that the Lord your God is giving you. ¹⁶The Lord your God hates people that cheat with false weights and measures. Yes, he hates all people who do wrong.

The Amalekites Must Be Destroyed

¹⁷"Remember what the people of Amalek did to you when you were coming from Egypt. ¹⁸The Amalekites did not respect God. They attacked you when you were weak and tired. They killed all your people who were slow and walking behind everyone else. ¹⁹That is why you must destroy the memory of the Amalekites from the world. You will do this when you enter the land that the Lord your God is giving you. There he will give you rest from all the enemies around you. But don't forget to destroy the Amalekites!

The First Harvest

26 "You will soon enter the land that the Lord your God is giving you. You will take that

---

orphans Children whose parents have died.

widow(s) Women whose husbands have died. Often these women had no one to care for them.

security Anything a person gives to show he will pay his loan. If the person does not pay back his loan, then the lender can keep that thing.

DEUTERONOMY 26:2–27:3

land and live there. ²You will gather the crops that grow in the land the Lord is giving you. You must take the first crops and put them in baskets. Then take that first part of your harvest to the place the Lord your God chooses to be his special house. ³Go to the priest that is serving at that time. Tell him, 'The Lord promised our ancestors that he would give us some land. Today I come to announce to the Lord your God that I have come to that land!'

⁴"Then the priest will take the basket from you. He will put it down in front of the altar* of the Lord your God. ⁵Then there before the Lord your God you will say: 'My ancestor was a wandering Aramean.* He went down into Egypt and stayed there. When he went there, he had only a few people in his family. But in Egypt he became a great nation—a powerful nation with many people. ⁶The Egyptians treated us badly. They made us slaves. They hurt us and forced us to work very hard. ⁷Then we prayed to the Lord, the God of our ancestors,* and complained about them. And the Lord heard us. He saw our trouble, our hard work, and our suffering. ⁸Then the Lord brought us out of Egypt with his great power and strength. He used great miracles and wonders. He did amazing things. ⁹So he brought us to this place. He gave us this land—a land filled with many good things.* ¹⁰Now, Lord, I bring you the first harvest from the land that you gave me.'

"Then you must put the harvest down before the Lord your God and bow down to worship him. ¹¹Then you must ₁have a meal together and₁ enjoy all the good things that the Lord your God has given to you and your family. You must share those things with the Levites* and the foreigners living among you.

¹²"Every third year is the Year of Tithes. In that year, you must give one tenth of your harvest to the Levites,* to the foreigners living in your country, and to the widows* and orphans.* Then those people will have plenty to eat in every city. ¹³You must say to the Lord your God, 'I have taken out of my house the holy part of my harvest. I have given it to the Levites,* to the foreigners, and to the orphans and widows. I have followed all the commands you gave me. I have not refused to obey any of your commands. I have not forgotten them. ¹⁴I have not eaten this food when I was sad.* I was not unclean when I collected this food.* I have not offered any of this food for dead people. I have obeyed you, Lord my God. I have done all the things you commanded me. ¹⁵Look down from your holy home, from heaven, and bless your people Israel. And bless the land that you gave us. You promised our ancestors* to give us this land—a land filled with many good things.*'

Obey the Lord's Commands

¹⁶"Today the Lord your God commands you to obey all these laws and rules. Be careful to follow them with all your heart and soul. ¹⁷Today you have said that the Lord is your God. You have promised to live the way he wants. You promised to follow his teachings, and to obey his laws and commands. You said you will do everything he tells you to do. ¹⁸And today the Lord has accepted you to be his own people. He has promised you this. The Lord also said that you must obey all his commands. ¹⁹The Lord will make you greater than all the nations he made. He will give you praise, fame, and honor. And you will be his own special people—just like he promised."

Stones Memorials for the People

27 Moses and the elders *(leaders)* of Israel spoke to the people. Moses said, "Obey all the commands that I give you today. ²You will soon go across the Jordan River into the land that the Lord your God is giving you. On that day, you must put up large stones. Cover those stones with plaster.* ³Then write on those stones all these

---

altar(s) A table or raised area used for offering sacrifices.
Aramean A person from ancient Syria. Here this might be Abraham, Isaac or probably Jacob (Israel).
ancestors Literally, "fathers," meaning a person's parents, grandparents, and all the people they are descended from.
filled with many good things Literally, "flowing with milk and honey."
Levite(s) People from the tribe of Levi. They helped the priests in the temple and worked for the civil government.

orphans Children whose parents have died.
I have ... sad People ate this food to be happy about the many things God gave them, so it could not be from food used during a time of sadness.
I was ... food This would mean other people could not eat this food during the celebration to honor the Lord.
plaster A type of mud or cement that people used to cover a wall and make it smooth.

commands and teachings. You must do this when you go across the Jordan River. Then you may go into the land that the Lord your God is giving you—a land filled with many good things.* The Lord, the God of your ancestors,* promised to give you this land.

⁴"After you go across the Jordan River, you must do the things I command you today. You must set up the stones on Mount Ebal. You must cover these stones with plaster.* ⁵Also, use some stones there to build an altar* to the Lord your God. Don't use iron tools to cut the stones. ⁶You must not use cut stones to build the altar for the Lord your God. Offer burnt offerings on this altar to the Lord your God. ⁷And you must sacrifice and eat fellowship offerings there. Eat and enjoy yourselves there together with the Lord your God. ⁸You must write all of these teachings on the stones that you set up. Write clearly so they are easy to read."

The People Agree to the Curses of the Law

⁹Moses and the priests spoke to all the people of Israel. Moses said, "Be quiet and listen, Israel! Today you have become the people of the Lord your God. ¹⁰So you must do everything that the Lord your God tells you. You must obey his commands and his laws that I am giving you today."

¹¹The same day, Moses also told the people, ¹²"After you have gone across the Jordan River, these family groups will stand on Mount Gerizim to read the blessings to the people: Simeon, Levi, Judah, Issachar, Joseph, and Benjamin. ¹³And these family groups will stand on Mount Ebal to read the curses: Reuben, Gad, Asher, Zebulun, Dan, and Naphtali.

¹⁴"And the Levites* will say to all the people of Israel with a loud voice: ¹⁵Cursed is the person that makes a false god and puts it in its secret place. Those false gods are only statues that some worker makes from wood, stone or metal. The Lord hates those things!'

"Then all the people will answer, 'Amen!'*

¹⁶"[The Levites will say,] 'Cursed is the person that does things that show he does not respect his father or his mother!'

"Then all the people will answer, 'Amen!'

¹⁷"[The Levites will say,] 'Cursed is the person that moves his neighbor's landmark*!'

"Then all the people will say, 'Amen!'

¹⁸"[The Levites will say,] 'Cursed is the person that is mean to a blind man and tricks him into walking off the road!'

"Then all the people will say, 'Amen!'

¹⁹"[The Levites will say,] 'Cursed is the person that does not give fair judgment for the foreigners, orphans,* and widows*!'

"Then all the people will say, 'Amen!'

²⁰"[The Levites will say,] 'Cursed is the person that has sexual relations with his father's wife.* Why? Because he brings shame to his father*!'

"Then all the people will say, 'Amen!'

²¹"[The Levites will say,] 'Cursed is the person that has sexual relations with any kind of animal!'

"Then all the people will say, 'Amen!'

²²"[The Levites will say,] 'Cursed is the person that has sexual relations with his sister or half sister!'

"Then all the people will say, 'Amen!'

²³"[The Levites will say,] 'Cursed is the person that has sexual relations with his mother-in-law!'

"Then all the people will say, 'Amen!'

²⁴"[The Levites will say,] 'Cursed is the person that kills another person, even if he is not caught!'

"Then all the people will say, 'Amen!'

²⁵"[The Levites will say,] 'Cursed is the person that takes money to kill an innocent person!'

"Then all the people will say, 'Amen!'

²⁶"[The Levites will say,] 'Cursed is the person that does not support this law and agree to obey it.'

"Then all the people will say, 'Amen!'"

---

filled with many good things Literally, "flowing with milk and honey."

ancestors Literally, "fathers," meaning a person's parents, grandparents, and all the people they are descended from.

plaster A type of mud or cement that people used to cover a wall and make it smooth.

altar(s) A table or raised area used for offering sacrifices.

Levite(s) People from the tribe of Levi. They helped the priests in the temple and worked for the civil government.

Amen This Hebrew word means "This is true," or "I agree."

landmark A stone or sign that showed where the limits of a person's property were.

orphans Children whose parents have died.

widows Women whose husbands have died. Often these women had no one to care for them.

father's wife Here this means the father's wife, even if she is not the mother of the son.

brings shame to his father Literally, "uncovers his father's nakedness."

Blessings for Obeying the Law

28 "Now, if you will be careful to obey the Lord your God and follow all his commands that I tell you today, then the Lord your God will put you high above all the nations on earth. ²If you will obey the Lord your God, then all these blessings will come to you and be yours:

3 "The Lord will bless you
   in the city and in the field.
4 The Lord will bless you
   and give you many children.
   He will bless your land
   and give you good crops.
   He will bless your animals
   and let them have many babies.
   He will bless all your calves and lambs.
5 The Lord will bless your baskets and pans
   and fill them with food⌐.
6 The Lord will bless you at all times
   in everything you do.

⁷"The Lord will help you defeat your enemies that come to fight against you. Your enemies will come against you one way, but they will run away from you seven different ways!
⁸"The Lord will bless you and fill your barns. He will bless everything you do. The Lord your God will bless you in the land that he is giving you. ⁹The Lord will make you his own special people, like he promised. The Lord will do this if you follow the Lord your God and obey his commands. ¹⁰Then all the people in that land will see that you are called by the name of the Lord. And they will be afraid of you.
¹¹"And the Lord will give you many good things. He will give you many children. He will give your cows many calves. He will give you a good harvest in the land that the Lord promised your ancestors* to give you. ¹²The Lord will open his storehouse where he keeps his rich blessings. The Lord will send rain at the right time for your land. The Lord will bless everything you do. You will have money to lend to many nations. And you will not need to borrow anything from them. ¹³The Lord will make you be like the head, not the tail. You will be on top, not on the bottom. This will happen if you listen to the commands of the Lord your God that I tell you today. You must carefully obey these commands. ¹⁴You must not turn away from any of the teachings that I give you today. You must not turn away to the right or to the left. You must not follow other gods to serve them.

Curses for Not Obeying the Law

¹⁵"But if you don't listen to things the Lord your God tells you—if you don't obey all his commands and laws that I tell you today—then all these bad things will happen to you:

16 "The Lord will curse you
   in the city and in the field.
17 The Lord will curse your baskets and pans
   and they will have no food in them⌐.
18 The Lord will curse you,
   and you will not have many children.
   He will curse your land
   and you will not get good crops.
   He will curse your animals
   and they will not have many babies.
   He will curse all your calves and lambs.
19 The Lord will curse you at all times
   in everything you do.

²⁰"If you do evil and turn away from the Lord, then he will make bad things happen to you. You will have frustration and trouble in everything you do. He will continue to do this until you are quickly and completely destroyed. He will do this because you turned away from him and left him. ²¹The Lord will cause you to have terrible diseases until you are finished —destroyed from the land you are going to take. ²²The Lord will punish you with diseases, fever, and swelling. The Lord will send you terrible heat and you will have no rain. Your crops will die from the heat and disease.* All these bad things will happen until you are destroyed! ²³⌐There will be no clouds in the sky⌐— the sky will look like polished brass. And the ground under you will be hard like iron. ²⁴The Lord will not send rain—only sand and dust will fall from the sky. It will come down on you until you are destroyed.
²⁵"The Lord will let your enemies defeat you. You will go to fight against your enemies one way, but you will run away from them seven different ways. The bad things that happen to you will make all the people on earth afraid. ²⁶Your dead bodies will be food for the wild birds and

---

ancestors Literally, "fathers," meaning a person's parents, grandparents, and all the people they are descended from.

disease This might be mildew, a disease that turns the heads of grain yellow and stops them from growing seeds.

animals. There will be no one to scare them away from your dead bodies. ²⁷"The Lord will punish you with boils, like those he sent on the Egyptians. He will punish you with tumors, sores that run, and an itch that can't be cured. ²⁸The Lord will punish you by making you crazy. He will make you blind and confused. ²⁹In daylight, you will have to feel your way like a blind man. You will fail in everything you do. Again and again people will hurt you and steal things from you. And there will not be anyone to save you.

³⁰"You will be engaged to a woman, but another man will have sexual relations with her. You will build a house, but you will not live in it. You will plant a field of grapes, but you will not gather anything from it. ³¹People will kill your cows in front of you. But you will not eat any of the meat. People will take your donkeys. And they will not give them back to you. Your enemies will get your sheep. And there will not be anyone to save you.

³²"Other people will be allowed to take your sons and your daughters. Day after day, you will look for your children. You will look for them until your eyes become weak and blind—but you will not find them. And God will not help you.

³³"A nation that you don't know will take all your crops and all the things you worked for. People will treat you badly and abuse you. ³⁴The things you see will make you go crazy! ³⁵The Lord will punish you with sore boils that can't be healed. These boils will be on your knees and legs. The boils will be on every part of your body—from the bottom of your feet to the top of your head.

³⁶"The Lord will send you and your king away to a nation you don't know. You and your ancestors* have never seen that nation. There you will serve false gods made of wood and stone. ³⁷In the countries where the Lord will send you, the people will be shocked at the bad things that happen to you. They will laugh at you and say bad things about you.

The Curse of Failure

³⁸"Your fields will produce plenty of grain. But your harvest will be small. Why? Because the locusts* will eat your harvest. ³⁹You will plant fields of grapes and work hard in them. But you will not gather the grapes or drink the wine from them. Why? Because the worms will eat them. ⁴⁰You will have olive trees everywhere on your land. But you will not have any of the oil to use. Why? Because the olives will drop to the ground and rot. ⁴¹You will have sons and daughters. But you will not be able to keep them. Why? Because they will be captured and taken away. ⁴²Locusts will destroy all your trees and the crops in your fields. ⁴³The foreigners living among you will get more and more power. And you will lose the power you had. ⁴⁴The foreigners will have money to loan you. But you will not have any money to loan them. They will control you like the head ₍controls the body₎. You will be like the tail.

⁴⁵"All these curses will come on you. They will keep chasing you and catching you, until you are destroyed. Why? Because you did not listen to the things the Lord your God told you. You did not obey the commands and laws that he gave you. ⁴⁶These curses will show people that God judged you and your descendants* forever. People will be amazed at the terrible things that happen to you.

⁴⁷"The Lord your God gave you many blessings. But you did not serve him with joy and a glad heart. ⁴⁸So you will serve the enemies that the Lord will send against you. You will be hungry, thirsty, naked, and poor. The Lord will put a load on you that can't be removed. You will carry that load until he destroys you.*

The Curse of an Enemy Nation

⁴⁹"The Lord will bring a nation from far away to fight you. You will not understand their language. They will come quickly, like an eagle coming down from the sky. ⁵⁰Those people will be cruel. They will not care about old people. They will not show mercy to young children. ⁵¹They will take your animals and the food you grow. They will take everything until they destroy you. They will not leave you any grain, wine, oil, cows, sheep or goats. They will take everything, until they destroy you.

---

ancestors Literally, "fathers," meaning a person's parents, grandparents, and all the people they are descended from.

locusts Insects like grasshoppers. Locusts can destroy a large crop very quickly.

descendant(s) A person's children and their future families.

The Lord ... until he destroys you Literally, "The Lord will put an iron yoke on your neck until he destroys you."

⁵²"That nation will surround and attack your cities. You think that the tall, strong walls around your cities will protect you. But those walls will fall down. The enemy will surround all your cities everywhere in the land the Lord your God is giving you. ⁵³You will suffer very much. The enemy will surround your cities. They will not let you have any food. You will become very hungry. You will be so hungry that you will eat your own sons and daughters—you will eat the bodies of the children that the Lord your God gave you.

⁵⁴"Even the most gentle and kind man among you will become cruel. He will be cruel to other people. He will be cruel to his wife that he loves so much. And he will be cruel to his children that are still alive. ⁵⁵He will have nothing left to eat, so he will eat his own children. And he will not share that meat with anyone—not even the other people in his own family! All those bad things will happen when your enemy comes to surround your cities and make you suffer.

⁵⁶"Even the most gentle and kind woman among you will become cruel. She might be a lady so gentle and delicate that she never put her feet on the ground to walk anywhere. But she will become cruel to her husband that she loves so much. And she will be cruel to her own son and daughter. ⁵⁷She will hide and give birth to a baby. And she will eat the baby and everything that comes out of her body with it. All those bad things will happen when your enemy comes to surround your cities and make you suffer.

⁵⁸"You must obey all the commands and teachings that are written in this book. And you must respect the wonderful and awesome name of the Lord your God. If you don't obey, then ⁵⁹the Lord will give you and your descendants* many troubles. Your troubles and diseases will be terrible! ⁶⁰You saw many troubles and diseases in Egypt, and they made you afraid. The Lord will bring all those bad things against you! ⁶¹The Lord will even bring troubles and diseases that are not written in this Book of Teachings. He will continue to do this until you are destroyed. ⁶²You might have as many people as the stars in the sky. But only a few of you will be left. Why? Because you did not listen to the Lord your God.

⁶³"The Lord was happy to be good to you and to make your nation grow. In the same way, the Lord will be happy to ruin and destroy you. You are going to take that land to be yours. But people will take you out of that land! ⁶⁴The Lord will scatter you among all the people in the world. The Lord will scatter you from one end of the earth to the other. There you will serve false gods made of wood and stone. They are false gods that you or your ancestors* never worshiped.

⁶⁵"You will not have any peace among these nations. You will have no place to rest. The Lord will fill your mind with worry. Your eyes will feel tired. You will be very upset. ⁶⁶You will live with danger and always be afraid. You will be afraid night and day. You will never feel sure about your life. ⁶⁷In the morning you will say, 'I wish it were evening!' In the evening you will say, 'I wish it were morning!' Why? Because of the fear that will be in your heart, and because of the bad things you will see. ⁶⁸The Lord will send you back to Egypt in ships. I said you would never have to go to that place again, but the Lord will send you there. In Egypt, you will try to sell yourselves as slaves to your enemies. But no person will buy you."

The Agreement in Moab

29 The Lord made an agreement with the people of Israel at Mount Horeb *(Sinai)*. In addition to that agreement, the Lord also commanded Moses to make another agreement with them while they were in Moab. This is that agreement.

²Moses called together all the Israelite people. He said to them, "You saw all the things the Lord did in the land of Egypt. You saw the things he did to Pharaoh, to Pharaoh's officers, and to his whole country. ³You saw the great troubles he gave them. You saw the miracles and amazing things he did. ⁴But even today you still don't understand what happened. The Lord has not let you really understand what you saw and heard. ⁵The Lord led you through the desert for 40 years. And during all that time your clothes and your shoes did not wear out. ⁶You did not have any food with you. You did not have any wine or anything else to drink. ⌊But the Lord took care of you.⌋ He did this so that you would understand that he is the Lord your God.

⁷"You came to this place, and King Sihon from Heshbon and King Og from Bashan came out to

---

descendant(s) A person's children and their future families.

ancestors Literally, "fathers," meaning a person's parents, grandparents, and all the people they are descended from.

fight against us. But we defeated them. ⁸Then we took their land and gave it to the people in the family groups of Reuben and Gad, and to half the family group of Manasseh. ⁹If you obey all the commands in this agreement, then you will continue to succeed in everything you do.

¹⁰"Today all of you are standing here before the Lord your God. Your leaders, your officials, your elders *(leaders)*, and all the other men are here. ¹¹Your wives and children are here and also the foreigners living among you—the people who cut your wood and bring you water. ¹²You are all here to enter into an agreement with the Lord your God. The Lord is making this agreement with you today. ¹³With this agreement, the Lord is making you his own special people. And he himself will become your God. He told you this. He promised this to your ancestors*—Abraham, Isaac, and Jacob. ¹⁴The Lord is making this agreement with its promises not only with you people. ¹⁵He is making this agreement with all of us that stand here today before the Lord our God. But this agreement is also for our descendants* that are not here with us today. ¹⁶You remember how we lived in the land of Egypt. And you remember how we traveled through the countries that were on our way here. ¹⁷You saw their hated things—the idols* they had made from wood, stone, silver, and gold. ¹⁸Be sure that there is no man, woman, family or family group here today that turns away from the Lord our God. No person should go and serve the gods of the other nations. People who do that are like a plant that grows bitter and poisonous fruit.

¹⁹"A person might hear these curses, but he might comfort himself and say, 'I will continue doing what I want. Nothing bad will happen to me.' That person might cause bad things to happen not only to himself but to everyone—even to the good people.* ²⁰⁻²¹The Lord will not forgive that person. No, the Lord will be angry and upset at that person. The Lord will punish that person. The Lord will separate that person from all the family groups of Israel. The Lord will completely destroy him. All the bad things that are written in this book will happen to him. Those things are a part of the Agreement that is written in this Book of Teachings.

²²"In the future, your descendants* and foreigners from faraway countries will see how the land has been ruined. They will see the diseases that the Lord has brought to it. ²³All the land will be useless—destroyed by burning sulfur and covered with salt. The land will have nothing planted in it. Nothing will be growing—not even weeds. The land will be destroyed like Sodom, Gomorrah, Admah, and Zeboiim, the cities the Lord destroyed when he was very angry.

²⁴"All the other nations will ask, 'Why did the Lord do this to this land? Why was he so angry?' ²⁵The answer will be: 'The Lord is angry because the people of Israel left the Agreement of the Lord, the God of their ancestors.* They stopped following the Agreement that the Lord made with them when he brought them out of Egypt. ²⁶The people of Israel started serving other gods—gods they never worshiped before. The Lord told his people not to worship those gods. ²⁷That is why the Lord became very angry against the people of this land. So he brought to them all the curses that are written in this book. ²⁸The Lord became very angry and upset at them. So he took them out of their land. He put them in another land, where they are today.'

²⁹"There are some things that the Lord our God has kept secret. Only he knows those things. But the Lord told us about these things! The Lord gave his teachings to us and our descendants.* He told us to obey them forever!

The Israelites Will Return to Their Land

30 "All these things I have said will happen to you. You will have good things from the blessings, and you will have bad things from the curses. The Lord your God will send you away to other nations. Then you will think about these things. ²At that time, you and your descendants* will return to the Lord your God. You will follow him with all your heart and completely obey all his commands that I have given you today. ³Then the Lord your God will be kind to you. The Lord will make you free again! He will bring you back from those nations where he sent you. ⁴Even if you were sent to the farthest parts of the earth, the Lord your God will gather you and bring you back from there. ⁵The Lord will bring you into the land your ancestors* had, and the land will become

---

ancestors Literally, "fathers," meaning a person's parents, grandparents, and all the people they are descended from.
descendant(s) A person's children and their future families.
idols Statues of false gods that people worshiped.
That person ... good people Literally, "thereby bringing to an end the soaked and the thirsty."

yours. The Lord will do good to you, and you will have more than your ancestors had. You will have more people in your nation than they ever had. ⁶The Lord your God will make you and your descendants want to obey him.* Then you will love the Lord with all your heart. And you will live!

⁷"Then the Lord your God will make all those bad things happen to your enemies. Why? Because those people hate you and give you trouble. ⁸And you will again obey the Lord. You will obey all his commands that I give you today. ⁹The Lord your God will make you successful in everything you do. He will bless you with many children. He will bless your cows—they will have many baby calves. He will bless your fields—they will grow many good crops. The Lord will be good to you. The Lord will again enjoy doing good for you, the same as he enjoyed doing good for your ancestors.* ¹⁰But you must do the things that the Lord your God tells you to do. You must obey his commands and follow the rules that are written in this Book of Teachings. You must obey the Lord your God with all your heart and with all your soul. Then these good things will happen to you.

Life or Death

¹¹"This command that I give you today is not too hard for you. It is not far off. ¹²This command is not in heaven so that you should say, 'Who will go up to heaven for us and bring it to us, so that we can hear and do it?' ¹³This command is not on the other side of the sea so that you should say, 'Who will go across the sea for us and bring it to us, so that we can hear it and do it?' ¹⁴No, the word is very near to you! It is in your mouth and in your heart. So you can obey it!

¹⁵"Today I have given you a choice between life and death, good and evil. ¹⁶I command you today to love the Lord your God. I command you to follow him and to obey his commands, laws, and rules. Then you will live, and your nation will grow larger. And the Lord your God will bless you in the land that you are entering to take for your own. ¹⁷But if you turn away from the Lord and refuse to listen—if you are led away to worship and serve other gods, ¹⁸then you will be destroyed. I am warning you! If you turn away from the Lord, you will not live long in that land across the Jordan River that you are ready to enter and take for your own.

¹⁹"Today I am giving you a choice of two ways. And I ask heaven and earth to be witnesses of your choice. You can choose life or death. The first choice will bring a blessing. The other choice will bring a curse. So choose life! Then you and your children will live. ²⁰You must love the Lord your God and obey him. Never leave him! Why? Because the Lord is your life. And the Lord will give you a long life in the land that he promised to give to your ancestors*—Abraham, Isaac, and Jacob."

Joshua Will Be the New Leader

31 Then Moses went and spoke these words to all the people of Israel. ²Moses said to them, "I am now 120 years old. I can't lead you any more. The Lord said to me: 'You will not go across the Jordan River.' ³But, the Lord your God will lead you people into that land! The Lord will destroy these nations for you. You will take their land away from them. But the Lord said that Joshua must lead you.

⁴"The Lord destroyed Sihon and Og. The Lord destroyed those Amorite kings. And the Lord will do the same thing for you again! ⁵The Lord will help you defeat these nations. But you must do to them everything I told you to do. ⁶Be strong and be brave. Don't be afraid of those people! Why? Because the Lord your God is with you. He will not fail you or leave you."

⁷Then Moses called Joshua. All the people of Israel watched while Moses said to Joshua, "Be strong and brave. You will lead these people into the land that the Lord promised to give to their ancestors.* You will help the people of Israel take this land to be their own. ⁸The Lord will lead you. He himself is with you. He will not fail you or leave you. Don't worry. Don't be afraid!"

Moses Writes the Teachings

⁹Then Moses wrote the Teachings and gave them to the priests. The priests are from the family group of Levi. They have the work of carrying the Lord's Box of the Agreement.* Moses also gave

---

make you ... obey him Literally, "circumcise the hearts of you and your seed."

ancestors Literally, "fathers," meaning a person's parents, grandparents, and all the people they are descended from.

Box of the Agreement Or, "ark of the Covenant," the box containing the flat stones with the Ten Commandments written on them and other things that proved God was with the people of Israel during their time in the Sinai desert.

the Teachings to all the elders *(leaders)* of Israel. ¹⁰Then Moses spoke to the leaders. He said, "At the end of every seven years, in the Year of Freedom, read these Teachings at the Festival of Shelters. ¹¹At that time, all the people of Israel must come to meet with the Lord your God at the special place he will choose. Then you must read the Teachings to the people so that they can hear them. ¹²Bring together all the people—the men, the women, the little children, and the foreigners living in your cities. They will hear the Teachings, and they will learn to respect the Lord your God. Then they will be able to do all the things in the Teachings. ¹³If their descendants* don't know the Teachings, then they will hear them. And they will learn to respect the Lord your God. They will respect him as long as you live in your country. You will soon go across the Jordan River and take that land to be your own."

The Lord Calls Moses and Joshua

¹⁴The Lord said to Moses, "Now the time is near for you to die. Get Joshua and come to the Meeting Tent.* I will tell Joshua the things he must do." So Moses and Joshua went to the Meeting Tent. ¹⁵The Lord appeared at the Tent in a tall cloud. The tall cloud stood over the entrance of the Tent. ¹⁶The Lord said to Moses, "You will die soon. And after you have gone to be with your ancestors,* these people will not continue to be faithful to me. They will break the Agreement I made with them. They will leave me and begin worshiping other gods—the false gods of the land where they are going. ¹⁷At that time, I will become very angry at them, and I will leave them. I will refuse to help them, and they will be destroyed. Terrible things will happen to them, and they will have many troubles. Then they will say, 'These bad things happened to us because our God is not with us.' ¹⁸And I will refuse to help them, because they have done evil and worshiped other gods.

¹⁹"So write down this song, and teach it to the people of Israel. Teach them to sing this song. Then this song will be a witness for me against the people of Israel. ²⁰I will take them into the land that I promised to give to their ancestors* — a land filled with many good things.* And they will have all they want to eat. They will have a rich life. But then they will turn to other gods and serve them. They will turn away from me and break my Agreement. ²¹Then many terrible things will happen to them. They will have many troubles. At that time, their people will still know this song, and it will show them how wrong they are. I have not yet taken them into the land I promised to give them. But I already know what they are planning to do there."

²²So that same day Moses wrote down the song. And he taught the song to the people of Israel.

²³Then the Lord spoke to Joshua son of Nun. The Lord said, "Be strong and brave. You will lead the people of Israel into the land I promised them. And I will be with you."

Moses Warns the People of Israel

²⁴Moses carefully wrote all these teachings in a book. When he finished, ²⁵he gave a command to the Levites.* (These men carry the Lord's Box of the Agreement.*) Moses said, ²⁶"Take this Book of Teachings and put it by the side of the Box of the Agreement of the Lord your God. Then it will be a witness against you. ²⁷I know you are very stubborn. I know you want to live your own way. Look, you refused to obey the Lord while I was with you. So I know you will refuse to obey him after I die. ²⁸Bring together all the officers and leaders of your family groups. I will tell them these things. And I will call heaven and earth to be witnesses against them. ²⁹I know that after my death you will become evil. You will turn from the way I commanded you to follow. Bad things will happen to you in the future. Why? Because you want to do the things that the Lord says are evil. You will make him angry because of the bad things you do."

The Song of Moses

³⁰All the people of Israel were gathered together. And Moses sang this song for them. Moses sang the whole song:

---

descendant(s) A person's children and their future families.

Meeting Tent The Holy Tent (tabernacle) where the people of Israel went to meet with God.

ancestors Literally, "fathers," meaning a person's parents, grandparents, and all the people they are descended from.

filled with many good things Literally, "flowing with milk and honey."

Levite(s) People from the tribe of Levi. They helped the priests in the temple and worked for the civil government.

32 ¹"Skies, listen and I will speak.
Earth, hear the words of my mouth.
² My teachings will come like the rain,
like a mist falling ⌊to the ground⌋,
like a gentle rain on the soft grass,
like rain on the green plants.
³ Praise God* as I speak the Lord's name!

⁴ "The Rock *(the Lord)*—his work is perfect!
Why? Because all his ways are right!
God is true and faithful.
He is good and honest.
⁵ And you are not really his children.
Your sins would make him dirty.
You are crooked liars.
⁶ Is that the way you should pay back the
Lord ⌊for all that he did for you? No!⌋
You are stupid, foolish people.
The Lord is your Father.
He made you.
He is your Creator.
He supports you.

⁷ "Remember what happened long ago.
Think about the things that happened
many, many years ago.
Ask your father;
he will tell you.
Ask your leaders;
they will tell you.
⁸ God Most-High separated the people
on earth.
He gave each nation its own land.
God set up borders for those people.
There are as many nations
as there are people in Israel.
⁹ The Lord's share is his people;
Jacob *(Israel)* belongs to the Lord.

¹⁰ "The Lord found Jacob *(Israel)* in
a desert land,
an empty, windy land.
The Lord surrounded Jacob
to watch over him.
He protected him,
like the pupil of his eye.
¹¹ The Lord was like an eagle to Israel.
An eagle pushes her babies from the nest
⌊to teach them to fly⌋.
She flies with her babies to protect them.
She spreads her wings to catch them
⌊when they fall⌋.
And she carries them on her wings
⌊to a safe place⌋.
The Lord is like that.

¹² "The Lord alone led Jacob *(Israel)*.
No foreign gods helped him.
¹³ The Lord led Jacob to take control of
the hill country.
Jacob took the harvest in the fields.
The Lord gave Jacob honey from the rock;
he made olive oil flow from the hard rock.
¹⁴ ⌊The Lord gave Israel⌋ butter from the herd
and milk from the flock.
He gave ⌊Israel⌋ fat lambs and goats,
the best rams from Bashan,
and the finest wheat.
You ⌊people of Israel⌋ drank wine
from the red juice of the grape.

¹⁵ "But Jeshurun* became fat
and kicked ⌊like a bull⌋.
(Yes, you were fed well!
You became full and fat!)
Then he left the God who made him!
He ran away from the Rock who saved him.
¹⁶ The Lord's people made him jealous—
They worshiped other gods!
They worshiped those horrible idols.
And that made God angry.
¹⁷ They offered sacrifices to demons
that were not real gods.
Those were new gods
that they did not know.
Those were new gods
that your ancestors did not know.
¹⁸ You left the Rock *(God)* who made you;
you forgot the God who gave you life.

¹⁹ The Lord saw this and became upset.
His sons and daughters made him angry!
²⁰ So the Lord said,
'I will turn away from them,
then let's see what happens!
²⁰ They are a rebellious people.
They are like children who won't learn
their lessons!
They made me jealous with ⌊demons⌋
that aren't gods.
They made me angry with those
worthless idols.

Praise God Or "Give honor to God" or "Speak of the greatness of God."

Jeshurun This is another name for Israel. This name means "good" or "honest."

So I will make them jealous with people
   that are not a real nation.
I will make them angry with people
   that are a foolish* nation.
22 My anger will burn like a fire,
   burning down to the deepest grave,*
   burning the earth and all it produces,
   burning deep down below the mountains!
23 "'I will bring troubles to the Israelites.
   I will shoot all my arrows at them.
24 They will become thin from hunger.
   Terrible diseases will destroy them.
   I will send wild animals against them.
   Poisonous snakes and lizards will bite them.
25 In the streets, soldiers will kill them.
   In their houses, terrible things will happen.
   Soldiers will kill young men and women.
   They will kill babies and old people.
26 I thought about destroying the Israelites
   so people would forget them completely!
27 But I know what their enemies would say.
   The enemy would not understand.
   They would brag and say,
   "The Lord did not destroy Israel.
   We won by our own power!"'
28 "The people ⌊of Israel⌋ are foolish.
   They don't understand.
29 If they were wise,
   they would understand,
   they would know what
      would happen to them!
30 Can one person chase away 1,000 men?
   Can two men cause 10,000 men to run away?
   That will happen only if the Lord
      gives them to their enemy!
   That will happen only if their Rock* *(God)*
      sells them like slaves!
31 The 'rock' of our enemies is not strong
   like our Rock *(the Lord)*.
   Even our enemies know that!
32 Their vines and fields will be destroyed,
   like Sodom and Gomorrah.*
   Their grapes are like bitter poison.
33   Their wine is like poison from snakes.
34 "⌊The Lord says,⌋
   'I am saving that punishment.
   I have it locked up in my storehouse!
35 I will punish them
   for the bad things they did.
   But I am saving that punishment
   for when they slip and do bad things.
   Their time of trouble is near.
   Their punishment will come quickly.'
36 "The Lord will judge his people.
   They are his servants,
   and he will show them mercy.
   He will see that their power is gone.
   He will see that they are all helpless—
   the slaves and free people, too.
37 Then the Lord will say,
   'Where are the false gods?
   Where is the 'rock' that you ran to
      for protection?
38 Those false gods ate the fat of your sacrifices.
   And they drank the wine of your offerings.
   So let those gods get up and help you!
   Let them protect you!
39 "'Now, see that I and only I am God!
   There is no other God!
   I put people to death
      and I let people live.
   I can hurt people,
      and I can make them well.
   No one can save another person
      from my power!
40 I raise my hand toward heaven
      and make this promise.
   As surely as I live forever,
      these things will happen!
41 I swear, *(promise)*
   I will sharpen my flashing sword.
   I will use it to punish my enemies.
   I will give them the punishment
      they deserve.
42 My enemies will be killed and taken
      as prisoners.
   My arrows will be covered with
      their blood.
   My sword will cut off the heads of
      their soldiers.'

Sodom and Gomorrah Two cities God destroyed because the people were so evil. See Gen. 19.
foolish This is a word play. The Hebrew word meaning "foolish" is like the word meaning "worthless."
grave Or, "Sheol," the place of death.
Rock A name for God. It shows he is like a fortress or a strong place of safety.

⁴³ "The whole world should be happy for
    God's people!
  ₍Why? Because he helps them₎—
    he punishes people who kill his servants.
  He gives his enemies
    the punishment they deserve.
  And he makes his land and people pure.*"

Moses Teaches the People His Song

⁴⁴Moses came and spoke all the words of this song for the people of Israel to hear. Joshua son of Nun was with Moses. ⁴⁵When Moses finished giving these teachings to the people, ⁴⁶he said to them, "You must be sure to pay attention to all the commands I tell you today. And you must tell your children to completely obey the commands in this Law. ⁴⁷Don't think these teachings are not important! They are your life! Through these teachings you will live a long time in the land across the Jordan River that you are ready to take."

Moses on Mount Nebo

⁴⁸The Lord spoke to Moses that same day. The Lord said, ⁴⁹"Go to the Abarim Mountains. Go up on Mount Nebo in the land of Moab across from the city of Jericho. Then you can look at the land of Canaan that I am giving to the people of Israel to live in. ⁵⁰You will die on that mountain. You will go to be with your people, the same as your brother Aaron died on Mount Hor. ⁵¹Why? Because you both sinned against me. You were at the waters of Meribah near Kadesh. That was in the desert of Zin. There, in front of the people of Israel, you did not honor me and show that I am holy. ⁵²So now you may see the land that I am giving to the people of Israel. But you can't go into that land."

Moses Blesses the People

33 This is the blessing that Moses, the man of God, gave the people of Israel before he died. ²Moses said:

  "The Lord came from Sinai,
    like a light shining at dawn over Seir.
    like a light shining from Mount Paran.
  The Lord came with 10,000 holy ones.
    God's mighty soldiers were by his side.*
³ Yes, the Lord loves his people.
    All his holy people are in his hand.
  They sit at his feet
    and learn his teachings!
⁴ Moses gave us the Law.
    Those teaching are for Jacob's people.
⁵ At that time, the people of Israel
    and their leaders met together,
    and the Lord became Jeshurun's* king!

Reuben's Blessing

⁶ "Let Reuben live, and not die!
    But let there be only a few people
    in his family group!"

Judah's Blessing

⁷Moses said these things about Judah:

  "Lord, listen to the leader from Judah
    when he calls for help.
  Bring him to his people.
  Make him strong,
    and help him defeat his enemies!"

Levi's Blessing

⁸Moses said these things about Levi:

  "Levi is your true follower.
    He keeps the Urim and Thummim.*
  At Massah you tested the people of Levi.
  At the waters of Meribah* you proved
    that they are yours.
⁹ ₍They cared more for you, Lord,
    than for their own families.₎
  They ignored their fathers and mothers.
  They did not recognize their brothers.
  They did not pay attention to their children.
  But they obeyed your commands.
    They kept your Agreement.

---

make ... pure Or, "make atonement for ...." The Hebrew word means "to cover," "to hide," or "to erase sins."

The Lord came ... side. Or, "The Lord came from 10,000 holy ₍angels₎ where his troops were by his right side."

Jeshurun This is another name for Israel. This name means "good" or "honest."

Urim and Thummim Used by the priest to learn God's answer to questions. They were probably like lots—stones, sticks or bones that were thrown like dice to make decisions.

Massah ... Meribah See Num. 20:1-13 for the story.

¹⁰ They will teach your rules to Jacob*
They will teach your Law to Israel.
They will burn incense* before you.
They will offer burnt offerings
   on your altar.*

¹¹ Lord, bless the things that belong to Levi.
Accept the things he does.
Destroy the men who attack him!
Defeat his enemies,
   so that they will never attack again."

Benjamin's Blessing

¹²Moses said this about Benjamin:

"The Lord loves Benjamin.
Benjamin will live safely near him.
The Lord protects him all the time.
And the Lord will live in his land.*"

Joseph's Blessing

¹³Moses said this about Joseph:

"May the Lord bless Joseph's land.
Lord, send them rain from the skies above
   and water from the ground below.
¹⁴ Let the sun give them good fruit.
Let each month bring its best fruit.
¹⁵ Let the hills and ancient mountains
   produce their best fruit.
¹⁶ Let the earth gives its best to Joseph.
Joseph was separated from his brothers.
So may the Lord in the ₍burning₎ bush
   give his best to Joseph.
¹⁷ Joseph is like a powerful bull.
His two sons are like bull's horns.
They will attack other people
   and push them to the ends of the earth!
Yes, Manasseh has thousands of people,
and Ephraim has ten thousands."

Zebulun's and Issachar's Blessing

¹⁸Moses said this about Zebulun:

"Zebulun, be happy, when you go out.
Issachar, ₍be happy₎, in your tents at home.
¹⁹ They will call the people to their mountain.
There they will offer good sacrifices.
They will take riches from the sea
and treasures from the shore."

Gad's Blessing

²⁰Moses said this Gad:

"Praise ₍God₎ who gave Gad more land!
Gad is like a lion.
He lies down and waits.
Then he attacks
   and tears the animal in pieces.
²¹ He chooses the best part for himself.
He takes the king's share.
The leaders of the people come to him.
He does what the Lord says is good.
He does what is right
   for the people of Israel."

Dan's Blessing

²²Moses said this about Dan:

"Dan is a lion's cub
   that jumps out from Bashan."

Naphtali's Blessing

²³Moses said this about Naphtali:

"Naphtali, you will get plenty of good things.
The Lord will truly bless you.
You will get the land by Lake Galilee."

Asher's Blessing

²⁴Moses said this about Asher:

"Asher* is the most blessed of the sons.
Let him be the favorite of his brothers.
And let him wash his feet in oil.
²⁵ Your gates will have locks
   made from iron and bronze.
You will be strong all your life."

Jacob Another name for Israel.
incense Special dried tree sap. Burned to make a sweet-smelling smoke, it was offered as a sacrifice to God.
altar A table or raised area used for offering sacrifices.
And the Lord will live in his land Literally, "And he will dwell between his shoulders." This probably means that the Lord's temple will be in Jerusalem, at the border between Benjamin and Judah's land.

Asher This name means, "blessed" or "happy."

Moses Gives Praise to God

26 "There is no one like God, Jeshurun*!
   God rides on the clouds in his glory
      through the skies to help you.
27 God lives forever.
      He is your place of safety.
   God's power continues forever!
      He is protecting you.
   God will force your enemies
      to leave your land.
   He will say,
      'Destroy the enemy!'
28 So Israel will live in safety,
      Jacob's well belongs to them.
   They will get a land of grain and wine.
      And that land will get plenty of rain.
29 Israel, you are blessed.
      No other nation is like you.
         The Lord saved you.
   The Lord is like a strong shield
      protecting you.
   The Lord is like a powerful sword.
      Your enemies will be afraid of you.
      And you will trample their holy places!"

Moses Dies

34 Moses climbed Mount Nebo. Moses went from the Jordan Valley in Moab to the top of Mount Pisgah. This was across the Jordan River from Jericho. The Lord showed Moses all the land from Gilead to Dan. ²The Lord showed him all the land of Naphtali, Ephraim, and Manasseh. He showed him all the land of Judah as far as the Mediterranean Sea. ³The Lord showed Moses the Negev* and the valley that goes from Zoar to Jericho, the city of palm trees. ⁴The Lord said to Moses, "This is the land I promised to Abraham, Isaac, and Jacob. I said to them, 'I will give this land to your descendants.* I have let you see the land, but you cannot go there."

⁵Then Moses, the Lord's servant, died there in the land of Moab. The Lord had told Moses this would happen. ⁶The Lord buried Moses in Moab. This was in the valley across from Beth Peor. But even today no person knows exactly where Moses' grave is. ⁷Moses was 120 years old when he died. He was as strong as ever, and his eyes were still good. ⁸The people of Israel cried for Moses for 30 days. They stayed in the Jordan Valley in Moab until the time of sadness was finished.

Joshua Becomes the New Leader

⁹Moses had put his hands on Joshua [and appointed him to be the new leader]. Then Joshua son of Nun was filled with the spirit of wisdom. So the people of Israel began to obey Joshua. They did the things that the Lord had commanded Moses.

¹⁰Israel never had another prophet* like Moses: The Lord knew Moses face to face. ¹¹The Lord sent Moses to do powerful miracles in the land of Egypt. Pharaoh, all his officers, and all the people in Egypt saw those miracles. ¹²No other prophet ever did all the powerful and amazing things that Moses did. All the people of Israel saw the things he did.

Jeshurun This is another name for Israel. This name means "good" or "honest."

Negev The desert area south of Judah.

prophet A person chosen by God to be a special servant.

Joshua

God Chooses Joshua to Lead Israel

1 Moses was the Lord's servant. Joshua son of Nun was Moses' helper. After Moses died, the Lord spoke to Joshua. The Lord said, ²"My servant Moses is dead. Now you and these people must go across the Jordan River. You must go into the land I am giving to you, the people of Israel. ³I promised Moses that I would give you this land. So, I will give you that land wherever you go. ⁴All the land of the Hittite people, from the desert and Lebanon all the way to the Great River (that is, the Euphrates River) will be yours. And all the land from here to the Mediterranean Sea in the west (that is, the place where the sun sets) will be within your borders. ⁵I will be with you the same as I was with Moses. No person will be able to stop you all your life. I will not abandon you. I will never leave you.

⁶Joshua, you must be strong and brave! You must lead these people so they can take their land. I promised their fathers that I would give them this land. ⁷But you must also be strong and brave about another thing. You must be sure to obey the commands my servant Moses gave you. If you follow his teachings exactly, then you will be successful in everything you do. ⁸Always remember the things written in that book of law. Study that book day and night. Then you can be sure to obey the things that are written there. If you do this, then you will be wise and successful in everything you do. ⁹Remember, I commanded you to be strong and brave. So don't be scared, because the Lord your God will be with you wherever you go."

Joshua Takes Command

¹⁰So Joshua gave orders to the leaders of the people. He said, ¹¹"Go through the camp and tell the people to get ready. Say to the people, 'Get some food ready. Three days from now we will go across the Jordan River. We will go and take the land that the Lord your God is giving you.'"

¹²Then Joshua spoke to the family groups of Reuben, Gad, and half of the family group of Manasseh. Joshua said, ¹³"Remember what the Lord's servant Moses told you. He said that the Lord your God would give you a place to rest. The Lord will give you that land! ¹⁴In fact, the Lord has already given you this land east of the Jordan River. Your wives and children can stay in this land with your animals. But your fighting men must cross the Jordan River with your brothers. You must be ready for war and help them ₁take their land₎. ¹⁵The Lord gave you a place to rest, and he will do the same for your brothers. But you must help them until they get the land that the Lord their God is giving them. Then you can come back to your own land, the land east of the Jordan River. The Lord's servant Moses gave you that land."

¹⁶Then the people answered Joshua, "We will do whatever you command us to do! We will go wherever you tell us to go! ¹⁷We will obey whatever you say, the same as we obeyed Moses. We only ask one thing from the Lord. We ask that the Lord your God will be with you the same as he was with Moses. ¹⁸Then, if any person refuses to obey your commands or if any person turns against you, that person will be killed. Just be strong and brave!"

Spies in Jericho

2 Joshua son of Nun and all the people were camped at Acacia.* Joshua sent out two spies. No one knew that Joshua sent out these men. Joshua said to the men, "Go and look at the land, especially the city of Jericho."

So the men went to the city of Jericho. They went to the house of a prostitute and stayed there. This woman's name was Rahab.

Acacia Or, "Shittim," a town east of the Jordan River.

² Someone told the king of Jericho, "Last night some men from Israel came to look for weaknesses in our country."

³ So the king of Jericho sent this message to Rahab: "Don't hide those men that came and stayed in your house. Bring them out. They have come to spy on our country."

⁴ The woman had hidden the two men. But the woman said, "Those two men did come here, but I didn't know where they came from. ⁵ In the evening, when it was time to close the city gate, the men left. I don't know where they went. But if you go quickly, maybe you can catch them." ⁶ (Rahab said those things, but really, she had taken the men up to the roof,* and she was hiding them in the hay* she had piled up there.)

⁷ So the king's men went out of the city, and the people closed the city gates. The king's men went to look for the two men from Israel. They went to the Jordan River and looked at all the places where people cross the river.

⁸ The two men were ready to sleep for the night. But Rahab went to the roof and talked to them. ⁹ Rahab said, "I know that the Lord has given this land to your people. You frighten us. All the people living in this country are afraid of you. ¹⁰ We are afraid because we have heard about the ways that the Lord helped you. We heard that he dried the water at the Red Sea when you came out of Egypt. We also heard what you did to the two Amorite kings, Sihon and Og. We heard how you destroyed those kings living east of the Jordan River. ¹¹ We heard about those things and we became very afraid. And now, none of our men are brave enough to fight you. Why? Because the Lord your God rules the heavens above and the earth below! ¹² So now, I want you to make a promise to me. I was kind to you and helped you. So promise before the Lord that you will be kind to my family. Please tell me that you will do this. ¹³ Tell me that you will allow my family to live—my father, mother, brothers, sisters, and all of their families. Promise that you will save us from death."

¹⁴ The men agreed. They said, "We will trade our lives for yours. Don't tell anyone what we are doing. Then, when the Lord gives us our land, we will be kind to you. You can trust us."

¹⁵ The woman's house was built into the city wall. It was part of the wall. So the woman used a rope to let the men down through a window. ¹⁶ Then the woman said to them, "Go ₍west₎ into the hills so the king's men will not accidentally find you. Hide there for three days. After the king's men come back you can go on your way."

¹⁷ The men said to her, "We made a promise to you. But you must do one thing or we will not be responsible for our promise. ¹⁸ You are using this red rope to help us escape. We will come back to this land. At that time, you must tie this red rope in your window. You must bring your father, your mother, your brothers, and all your family into your house with you. ¹⁹ We will protect every person who stays in this house. If anyone in your house is hurt, then we will be responsible. But if any person goes out of your house, then that person might be killed. We will not be responsible for that person. It will be his own fault. ²⁰ We are making this agreement with you. But if you tell anyone about what we are doing then we are free from this agreement."

²¹ The woman answered, "I will do exactly what you said." The woman said goodbye, and the men left her house. Then the woman tied the red rope in the window.

²² The men left her house and went into the hills. They stayed there for three days. The king's men looked all along the road. After three days, the king's men gave up and went back to the city. ²³ Then the two men went back to Joshua. The men left the hills and crossed the river. They went to Joshua son of Nun. They told Joshua everything that they had learned. ²⁴ They said to Joshua, "The Lord really has given us all of the land. All of the people in that country are afraid of us."

Miracle at the Jordan River

3 Early the next morning, Joshua and all the people of Israel got up and left Acacia.* They traveled to the Jordan River and camped there before they went across. ² After three days, the leaders went through the camp. ³ The leaders gave orders to the people. They said, "You will see the

---

roof In Israel, the roofs were flat and people used them like an extra room for storing things.
hay Literally, "flax," a plant used to make linen.

Acacia Or, "Shittim," a town east of the Jordan River.

priests and Levites* carrying the Box of the Agreement* of the Lord your God. At that time, you must follow them. ⁴But do not follow too closely. Stay about 1,000 yards* behind them. You have not been here before. But if you follow them, then you will know where to go."

⁵Then Joshua told the people, "Make yourselves pure. Tomorrow the Lord will use you to do amazing things."

⁶Then Joshua said to the priests, "Take the Box of the Agreement and go across the river in front of the people." So the priests lifted the Box and carried it in front of the people.

⁷Then the Lord said to Joshua, "Today I will begin to make you a great man for all the people of Israel to see. Then the people will know that I am with you the same as I was with Moses. ⁸The priests will carry the Box of the Agreement.* Tell the priests this, 'Walk to the shore of the Jordan River and stop just before you step into the water.'"

⁹Then Joshua said to the people of Israel, "Come and listen to the words of the Lord your God. ¹⁰Here is proof that the living God is truly with you. Here is proof that he will truly defeat your enemies. He will defeat the Canaanite people, the Hittite people, the Hivite people, the Perizzite people, the Girgashite people, the Amorite people, and the Jebusite people, he will force them to leave that land. ¹¹Here is the proof. The Box of the Agreement* of the Master of the whole world will go before you as you cross the Jordan River. ¹²Now, choose twelve men. Choose one man from each of the twelve family groups of Israel. ¹³The priests will carry the Box of the Lord.* The Lord is the Master of the whole world. They will carry that Box in front of you into the Jordan River. When they enter the water, the water of the Jordan River will stop flowing. The water will stop and fill behind that place like a dam."

¹⁴The priests carried the Box of the Agreement* and the people left the place they had camped. The people started going across the Jordan River. ¹⁵(During harvest time the Jordan River overflows its banks. So the river was at its fullest.) The priests who were carrying the Box came to the shore of the river. They stepped into the water. ¹⁶And immediately, the water stopped flowing. ⌊The water filled behind that place like a dam.⌋ The water piled high a long way up the river—all the way to Adam (a town near Zarethan). The people crossed the river near Jericho. ¹⁷The ground at that place became dry, and the priests carried the Box of the Agreement* of the Lord to the middle of the river and stopped. The priests waited there while all the people of Israel walked across the Jordan River on dry land.

Rocks to Remind the People

4 After all the people had crossed the Jordan River the Lord said to Joshua, ²"Choose twelve men. Choose one man from each family group. ³Tell them to look in the river where the priests were standing. Tell them to find twelve rocks in that place. Carry those twelve rocks with you. Put the twelve rocks in the place where you stay tonight."

⁴So Joshua chose one man from each family group. Then he called the twelve men together. ⁵Joshua said to the men, "Go out into the river where the Holy Box* of the Lord your God is. Each of you must find one rock. There will be one rock for each of the twelve family groups of Israel. Carry that rock on your shoulder. ⁶These rocks will be a sign for you. In the future, your children will ask you, 'What do these rocks mean?' ⁷You will tell the children that the Lord stopped the water from flowing in the Jordan River. When the Holy Box of the Lord's Agreement crossed the river, the water stopped flowing. Those rocks will help the people of Israel remember this thing forever."

⁸So the people of Israel obeyed Joshua. They carried twelve rocks from the middle of the Jordan River. There was one rock for each of the twelve family groups of Israel. They did this the way the Lord commanded Joshua. The men carried the rocks with them. Then they put the rocks at the place where they made their camp. ⁹(Joshua also put twelve rocks in the middle of the Jordan River. He put them at the place where the priests

---

Levites People from the tribe of Levi. The Levites helped the priests in the temple and also worked for the civil government.

Box of the Agreement Or, "ark of the Covenant," the box containing the flat stones with the Ten Commandments written on them and other things that proved God was with the people of Israel during their time in the Sinai desert.

1,000 yards Literally, "2,000 cubits."

Box of the Lord Also called the Box of the Agreement.

Holy Box Also called the Box of the Agreement.

stood while carrying the Lord's Holy Box.* Those rocks are still at that place today.)

¹⁰The Lord had commanded Joshua to tell the people what to do. Those were the things Moses had said Joshua must do. So the priests carrying the Holy Box continued standing in the middle of the river until all those things were done. The people hurried across the river. ¹¹The people finished crossing the river. After that, the priests carried the Box of the Lord to the front of the people.

¹²The men from the family groups of Reuben, Gad, and half of the family group of Manasseh obeyed Moses. These men crossed the river in front of the other people. These men were prepared for war. They were going to help the rest of the people of Israel take the land God had promised to give them. ¹³About 40,000 soldiers, prepared for war, passed before the Lord. They were marching toward the plains of Jericho.

¹⁴That day the Lord made Joshua a great man to all the people of Israel. The people respected Joshua from that time on. They respected Joshua all his life, the same as they respected Moses.

¹⁵While the priests carrying the Box were still standing in the river, the Lord said to Joshua, ¹⁶"Command the priests to come out of the river."

¹⁷So Joshua commanded the priests. He said, "Come out of the Jordan River."

¹⁸The priests obeyed Joshua. They carried the Box with them and came out of the river. When the priests' feet touched the land on the other side of the river, the water in the river began flowing again. The water again overflowed its banks as it had before the people crossed.

¹⁹The people crossed the Jordan River on the tenth day of the first month. The people camped at Gilgal, east of Jericho. ²⁰The people carried with them the twelve rocks that they had taken from the Jordan River. And Joshua set up those rocks at Gilgal. ²¹Then Joshua told the people, "In the future, your children will ask their parents, 'What do these rocks mean?' ²²You will tell the children, 'Those rocks help us remember the way the people of Israel crossed the Jordan River on dry land. ²³The Lord your God caused the water in the Jordan River to stop flowing. The river was dry until the people finished crossing it, the same as at the Red Sea. Remember, the Lord stopped the water at the Red Sea so that the people could cross. ²⁴The Lord did this so that all the people in this country would know that the Lord is very powerful. Then those people will always be afraid of the Lord your God.'"

5 So the Lord dried up the Jordan River until the people of Israel finished crossing it. The kings of the Amorites living west of the Jordan River and the Canaanites living by the Mediterranean Sea heard about this and became very scared. After that they were not brave enough to stand and fight against the people of Israel.

The Israelites Are Circumcised

²At that time, the Lord said to Joshua, "Make knives from flint rocks and circumcise* the men of Israel."

³So Joshua made knives from flint rocks. Then he circumcised* the people of Israel at Gibeath Haaraloth.*

⁴⁻⁷This is why Joshua circumcised* the men: After the people of Israel left Egypt, all the men that were able to be in the army were circumcised. While in the desert, many of the fighting men did not listen to the Lord. So the Lord promised that those men would not see the "land where much food grows." The Lord promised our ancestors* to give us that land, but, because of those men, God forced the people to wander in the desert for 40 years—that way all those fighting men would die. All those fighting men died, and their sons took their place. But none of the boys that were born in the desert on the trip from Egypt had been circumcised. So Joshua circumcised them.

⁸Joshua finished circumcising all the men. The people camped at that place until all the men were healed.

First Passover in Canaan

⁹At that time, the Lord said to Joshua, "You were slaves in Egypt. And this made you ashamed. But today I have taken away that shame." So Joshua named that place Gilgal.* And that place is still named Gilgal today.

---

circumcise(d) To cut off the foreskin. This was done to every Jewish male to show he shared in the Agreement God made with Israel. See Gen. 17:9-14.
Gibeath Haaraloth This name means "Circumcision Hill."
ancestors Literally, "fathers," meaning a person's parents, grandparents, and all the people they are descended from.
Gilgal This name is like the Hebrew word meaning, "to roll away."

Holy Box Also called the Box of the Agreement.

¹⁰The people of Israel celebrated Passover while they were camped at Gilgal on the plains of Jericho. This was on the evening of the 14th day of the month. ¹¹The day after Passover, the people ate food that grew in that land. They ate bread made without yeast and roasted grain. ¹²The next morning, the special food from heaven stopped coming. This happened the day after the people ate the food that grew in the land of Canaan. From that time on, the people of Israel did not get the special food from heaven.

¹³When Joshua was near Jericho he looked up and saw a man standing in front of him. The man had a sword in his hand. Joshua went to the man and asked, "Are you a friend to our people, or are you one of our enemies?"

¹⁴The man answered, "I am not an enemy. I am the commander of the Lord's army. I have just now come to you."

Then Joshua bowed his face to the ground. ₍He did this to show respect.₎ He asked, "I am your servant. Does my master have a command for me?"

¹⁵The commander of the Lord's army answered, "Take off your shoes. The place where you are standing now is holy." So Joshua obeyed him.

Jericho Captured

6 The city of Jericho was closed. The people in the city were afraid because the people of Israel were near. No one went in the city and no one came out of the city.

²Then the Lord said to Joshua, "Look, I will let you defeat the city of Jericho. You will defeat the king and all the fighting men in the city. ³March around the city with your army one time every day. Do this for six days. ⁴Tell seven priests to carry trumpets made from the horns of male sheep. ₍Carry the Holy Box.*₎ Tell the priests to march in front of the Holy Box. On the seventh day, march around the city seven times. On the seventh day, tell the priest to blow the trumpets when they march. ⁵The priest will make one loud noise from the trumpets. When you hear that noise, tell all the people to begin shouting. When you do this, the walls of the city will fall down and your people will go straight into the city."

⁶So Joshua son of Nun called the priests together. Joshua said to them, "Carry the Holy Box* of the Lord. And tell seven priests to carry the trumpets and march in front of the Box."

⁷Then Joshua ordered the people, "Now go! March around the city. The soldiers with weapons will march in front of the Holy Box* of the Lord."

⁸After Joshua finished speaking to the people, the seven priests began marching before the Lord. They carried the seven trumpets and blew them while they marched. The priests carrying the Lord's Holy Box followed them. ⁹The soldiers with weapons marched in front of the priests. And the men walking behind the Holy Box marched and blew their trumpets. ¹⁰Joshua had told the people not to give a war cry. He said, "Don't shout. Don't say a word until the day I tell you. Then you can shout!"

¹¹So Joshua made the priests carry the Holy Box of the Lord around the city one time. Then they went back to the camp and spent the night there.

¹²Early the next morning, Joshua got up. The priests carried the Lord's Holy Box again. ¹³And the seven priests carried the seven trumpets. They walked in front of the Lord's Holy Box, marching and blowing their trumpets. The soldiers with weapons marched in front of them. The priests walking behind the Lord's Holy Box were marching and blowing their trumpets.

¹⁴So on the second day, they all marched around the city one time. And then they went back to the camp. They continued to do this every day for six days.

¹⁵On the seventh day they got up at dawn. And they marched around the city seven times. They marched in the same way they had marched on the days before, but on that day they marched around the city seven times. ¹⁶The seventh time they marched around the city, the priests blew their trumpets. At that time, Joshua gave the command: "Now, shout! The Lord is giving you this city! ¹⁷The city and everything in it belongs to the Lord.* Only Rahab the prostitute and all the people in her house will remain alive. These people must not be killed because Rahab helped the two spies. ¹⁸Also remember that we must

---

Holy Box The Box of the Agreement—the box containing the flat stones with the Ten Commandments written on them and other things that proved God was with the people of Israel during their time in the Sinai desert.

belongs to the Lord This usually meant that these things were saved in the temple treasury or they were destroyed so that other people would not use them.

destroy everything else. Don't take those things. If you take those things and bring them into our camp then you yourselves will be destroyed. And you will also bring trouble to all the people of Israel. ¹⁹All the silver and gold and the things made from bronze and iron belong to the Lord. Those things must be put in the Lord's treasury."

²⁰The priests blew the trumpets. The people heard trumpets and began shouting. The walls fell down and the people ran straight into the city. So the people of Israel defeated that city. ²¹The people destroyed everything in the city. They destroyed everything that was living there. They killed the young men and old men, young women and old women, cattle, sheep, and donkeys.

²²Joshua talked to the two spies. Joshua said, "Go into the prostitute's house. Bring her out. And bring all the people who are with her. Do this because of the promise you made to her."

²³So the two men went into the house and brought out Rahab. They also brought out her father, mother, brothers, all her family, and all the other people that were with her. They put all the people in a safe place outside the camp of Israel.

²⁴Then the people of Israel burned the whole city. They burned everything in the city except the things made from silver, gold, bronze, and iron. They put those things in the Lord's treasury. ²⁵Joshua saved Rahab the prostitute, her family, and all the other people that were with her. Joshua let them live because Rahab helped the spies that Joshua had sent out to Jericho. Rahab still lives among the people of Israel today.

²⁶At that time, Joshua made this important promise. He said:

"Whoever builds Jericho again
    will be in danger from the Lord.
The man who lays the foundation of this city,
    will lose his oldest son.
The man who sets up the gates
    will lose his youngest son."*

²⁷So the Lord was with Joshua. And Joshua became famous all throughout the whole country.

Achan's Sin

7 But the people of Israel did not obey God. There was a man from the family group of Judah named Achan son of Carmi, grandson of Zimri. Achan kept some of the things that should have been destroyed. So the Lord became very angry at the people of Israel.

²After they defeated Jericho, Joshua sent some men to Ai.* Ai was near Beth Aven, east of Bethel. Joshua told them, "Go to Ai and look for weaknesses in that area." So the men went to spy on that land.

³Later the men came back to Joshua. They said, "Ai is a weak area. We will not need all of our people to defeat that place. Send 2,000 or 3,000 men to fight there. There is no need to use the whole army. There are only a few men there to fight against us."

⁴⁻⁵So about 3,000 men went to Ai. But the people of Ai killed about 36 men of Israel. And the people of Israel ran away. The people of Ai chased them from the city gates all the way to the quarries.* The people of Ai beat them badly.

When the people from Israel saw this, they became very frightened and lost their courage. ⁶When Joshua heard about this, he tore his clothes ₍to show his sadness₎. He bowed down on the ground before the Holy Box. Joshua stayed there until evening. The leaders of Israel did the same thing. They also threw dirt on their heads ₍to show their sadness₎.

⁷Joshua said, "Lord my Master! You brought our people across the Jordan River. Why did you bring us this far and then allow the Amorite people to destroy us? We should have been satisfied and stayed on the other side of the Jordan River! ⁸I promise by my life, Lord! There is nothing I can say now. Israel has surrendered to the enemy. ⁹The Canaanite people and all the other people in this country will hear about what happened. Then they will attack us and kill all of us! Then what will you do to protect your great name?"

¹⁰The Lord said to Joshua, "Why are you down there with your face on the ground? Stand up! ¹¹The people of Israel sinned against me. They broke the Agreement that I commanded them to obey. They took some of the things that I commanded them to destroy. They have stolen from me. They have lied. They have taken those things for themselves. ¹²That is why the army of Israel turned and ran away from the fight. They did that because they have done wrong. They should be destroyed. I will not continue to help

---

The man ... son See 1 Kings 16:34.

Ai This name means, "the ruins."
quarries A place where people cut stones from the solid rock.

you. I will not continue to be with you unless you destroy everything I commanded you to destroy.

¹³"Now go and make the people pure. Tell the people, 'Make yourselves pure. Prepare for tomorrow. The Lord God of Israel says that some people are keeping things that he commanded to be destroyed. You will never be able to defeat your enemies until you throw away those things.

¹⁴"'Tomorrow morning you must all stand before the Lord. All of the family groups will stand before the Lord. The Lord will choose one family group. Then only that family group will stand before the Lord. Then the Lord will choose one clan* from that family group. Then only that clan must stand before the Lord. Then the Lord will look at each family in that clan. Then the Lord will choose one family. Then the Lord will look at each man in that family. ¹⁵The man who is keeping those things that we should have destroyed will be caught. Then that man will be destroyed by fire. And everything that he owns will be destroyed with him. That man broke the Agreement with the Lord. He has done a very bad thing to the people of Israel!'"

¹⁶Early the next morning, Joshua led all the people of Israel before the Lord. All of the family groups stood before the Lord. The Lord chose the family group of Judah. ¹⁷So all the clans* of Judah stood before the Lord. The Lord chose the Zerah clan. Then all the families of the Zerah clan stood before the Lord. The family of Zimri was chosen. ¹⁸Then Joshua told all the men in that family to come before the Lord. The Lord chose Achan the son of Carmi. (Carmi was the son of Zimri. And Zimri was the son of Zerah.)

¹⁹Then Joshua said to Achan, "Son, ₍say your prayers₎. You should honor the Lord God of Israel and confess your sins to him. Tell me what you did, and don't try to hide anything from me!"

²⁰Achan answered, "It is true! I sinned against the Lord God of Israel. This is what I did: ²¹₍We captured the city of Jericho and all the things in it.₎ I saw a beautiful coat from Babylon, about 5 pounds* of silver; and about a pound* of gold. I wanted these things for myself. So I took them. You will find those things buried in the ground under my tent. The silver is under the coat."

²²So Joshua sent some men to the tent. They ran to the tent and found those things hidden there in the tent. The silver was under the coat. ²³The men brought the things out of the tent. They took those things to Joshua and all the people of Israel. They threw them on the ground before the Lord.

²⁴Then Joshua and all the people led Achan son of Zerah to the valley of Achor. They also took the silver, the coat, the gold, Achan's sons and daughters, his cattle, his donkeys, his sheep, his tent, and everything he owned. They took all these things to the Valley of Achor with Achan. ²⁵Then Joshua said, "You caused much trouble for us! But now the Lord will bring trouble to you!" Then all the people threw stones at Achan and his family until they died. Then the people burned them and everything he owned. ²⁶After they burned Achan, they put many rocks over his body. Those rocks are still there today. ₍So God brought trouble to Achan.₎ That is why that place is called the Valley of Achor.* After this the Lord was not angry with the people.

Ai Destroyed

8 Then the Lord said to Joshua, "Don't be afraid. Don't give up. Lead all your fighting men to Ai.* I will help you defeat the king of Ai. I am giving you his people, his city, and his land. ²You will do to Ai and its king the same thing you did to Jericho and its king. Only this time you can take all the wealth and animals and keep it for yourselves. You will share the wealth with your people. Now, tell some of your soldiers to hide behind the city."

³So Joshua led his whole army toward Ai.* Then Joshua chose 30,000 of his best fighting men. He sent these men out at night. ⁴Joshua gave them this command: "Listen carefully to what I tell you. You must hide in the area behind the city. Wait for the time to attack. Don't go far from the city. Continue to watch and be ready. ⁵I will lead the men with me to march toward the city. The men in the city will come out to fight against us. We will turn and run away from them, like we did before. ⁶Those men will chase us away from the city. They will think that we are running away from them like we did before. So we will run away. ⁷Then you should come out of your hiding place and take control of the city. The Lord your God will give you the power to win.

---

clan A group of families.
5 pounds Literally, "200 shekels."
a pound Literally, "50 shekels."

Achor This name means "trouble."
Ai See Josh. 7:2. The name of this town means "the ruins."

⁸You must do what the Lord says. Watch me and I will give you the command to attack the city. Take control of the city, and then burn it."

⁹Then Joshua sent those men to their hiding place and waited. They went to a place between Bethel and Ai. This was to the west of Ai. And Joshua stayed the night with his people. ¹⁰Early the next morning Joshua gathered the men together. Then Joshua and the leaders of Israel led the men to Ai. ¹¹All of the soldiers that were with Joshua marched to Ai. They stopped in front of the city. The army made its camp north of the city. There was a valley between the army and Ai.

¹²Then Joshua chose about 5,000 men. Joshua sent these men to hide in the area west of the city, between Bethel and Ai. ¹³So Joshua had prepared his men for the fight. The main camp was north of the city. The other men were hiding to the west. That night Joshua went down into the valley.

¹⁴Later, the king of Ai saw the army of Israel. The king and his people hurried out to fight the army of Israel. The king of Ai went out the east side of the city toward the Jordan Valley, so he did not see the soldiers hiding behind the city.

¹⁵Joshua and all the men of Israel let the army of Ai push them back. Joshua and his men began running east toward the desert. ¹⁶The people in the city began shouting and started chasing Joshua and his men. All the people left the city. ¹⁷All the people of Ai and Bethel chased the army of Israel. The city was left open—no one stayed to protect the city.

¹⁸Then the Lord said to Joshua, "Hold your spear toward the city of Ai. I will give you that city." So Joshua held his spear toward the city of Ai. ¹⁹The men of Israel that were hiding saw this. They quickly came out from their hiding place and hurried toward the city. They entered the city and took control of it. Then the soldiers started fires to burn the city.

²⁰The men from Ai looked back and saw their city burning. They saw the smoke rising into the sky. So they lost their strength and courage. They quit chasing the men of Israel. The men from Israel stopped running away. They turned and went to fight the men from Ai. There was no safe place for the men from Ai to run to. ²¹Joshua and his men saw that his army had taken control of the city. They saw the smoke rising from the city. This was when they stopped running away, turned and ran toward the men of Ai to fight them. ²²Then the men that had hid themselves came out of the city to help with the fight. The army of Israel was on both sides of the men of Ai—the men of Ai were trapped. Israel defeated them. They fought until none of the men from Ai were left alive—none of the enemy escaped. ²³But the king of Ai was left alive. Joshua's men brought him to Joshua.

A Review of the Fighting

²⁴During the fighting, the army of Israel chased the men from Ai into the fields and into the desert. So the army of Israel finished killing all the men from Ai in the fields and in the desert. Then the men of Israel went back to Ai and killed all the people that were still alive in the city. ²⁵All the people of Ai died that day. There were 12,000 men and women. ²⁶Joshua had held his spear toward Ai as a sign to his people to destroy the city. And Joshua did not stop until all the people of Ai were destroyed. ²⁷The people of Israel kept the animals and other things from the city for themselves. This is what the Lord said they could do when he gave Joshua the commands.

²⁸Then Joshua burned the city of Ai.* That city became an empty pile of rocks. It is still like that today. ²⁹Joshua hanged the king of Ai on a tree. He left him hanging on the tree until evening. At sunset, Joshua told his men to take the king's body down from the tree. They threw his body down at the city gate. Then they covered the body with many rocks. That pile of rocks is still there today.

Reading the Blessings and Curses

³⁰Then Joshua built an altar for the Lord, the God of Israel. He built the altar on Mount Ebal. ³¹The Lord's servant Moses told the people of Israel how to build altars. So Joshua built the altar the way it was explained in the book of the Law of Moses. The altar was made from stones that were not cut. No tool had ever been used on those stones. They offered burnt offerings to the Lord on that altar. They also gave fellowship offerings.

³²In that place Joshua wrote the law of Moses on stones. He did this for all the people of Israel to see. ³³The elders *(leaders)*, officers, judges, and all the people of Israel were standing around the Holy Box. They were standing in front of the Levite priests who carried the Holy Box for the Lord's Agreement. The people of Israel and the other people with them were all standing there. Half of the people stood in front of Mount Ebal

---

Ai The name of this town means "the ruins".

and the other half of the people stood in front of Mount Gerizim. The Lord's servant Moses had told the people to do this. Moses told them to do this for this blessing.

³⁴Then Joshua read all the words from the law. Joshua read the blessings and the curses. He read everything the way it was written in the Book of the Law. ³⁵All the people of Israel were gathered together there. All the women and children and all the foreigners that lived with the people of Israel were there. And Joshua read every command that Moses had given.

Gibeonites Trick Joshua

9 All the kings west of the Jordan River heard about these things. These were the kings of the Hittite people, the Amorite people, the Canaanite people, the Perizzite people, the Hivite people, and the Jebusite people. They lived in the hill country and in the plains. They also lived along the sea coast of the Mediterranean Sea as far as Lebanon. ²All these kings came together. They made plans to fight against Joshua and the people of Israel.

³The people from the city of Gibeon heard about the way Joshua had defeated Jericho and Ai. ⁴So those people decided to try to fool the people of Israel. This was their plan: They gathered together old wineskins* that were cracked and broken. They put these old wine skins on the backs of their animals. They put old pieces of cloth on their animals to look like they had traveled from far away. ⁵The men put old shoes on their feet. The men wore old clothes. The men found some old bread that was dry and moldy. So the men looked like they had traveled from a faraway place. ⁶Then the men went to the camp of the people of Israel. This camp was near Gilgal.

The men went to Joshua and said to him, "We have traveled from a faraway country. We want to make a peace agreement with you."

⁷The men of Israel said to these Hivite men, "Maybe you are trying to trick us. Maybe you live near us. We can't make a peace agreement with you until we know where you are from."

⁸The Hivite men said to Joshua, "We are your servants."

But Joshua asked, "Who are you? Where do you come from?"

⁹The men answered, "We are your servants. We have come from a faraway country. We came because we heard of the great power of the Lord your God. We heard about the things he did. We heard about everything he did in Egypt. ¹⁰And we heard that he defeated the two kings of the Amorite people east of the Jordan River. This was Sihon, king of Heshbon, and Og, the king of Bashan, in the land of Ashtaroth. ¹¹So our elders *(leaders)* and our people said to us, 'Take enough food for your journey. Go and meet with the people of Israel. Tell them, "We are your servants. Make a peace agreement with us."'

¹²"See our bread! When we left home it was warm and fresh. But now you can see that it is dry and old. ¹³See our wineskins! When we left home they were new and filled with wine. Now you can see that they are cracked and old. See our clothes and sandals! You can see that the long journey has almost destroyed the things we wear."

¹⁴The men of Israel wanted to know if these men were telling the truth. So they tasted the bread—but they did not ask the Lord what they should do. ¹⁵Joshua agreed to make peace with them. He agreed to let them live. The leaders of Israel agreed with this promise of Joshua.

¹⁶Three days later, the people of Israel learned that those men lived very near their camp. ¹⁷So the people of Israel went to the place where those men lived. On the third day the people of Israel came to the cities of Gibeon, Kephirah, Beeroth, and Kiriath Jearim. ¹⁸But the army of Israel did not try to fight against those cities. They had made a peace agreement with those people. They had made a promise to the people before the Lord, the God of Israel.

All the people complained against the leaders that made the agreement. ¹⁹But the leaders answered, "We have given our promise. We promised before the Lord, the God of Israel. We cannot fight against them now. ²⁰This is what we must do. We must let them live. We cannot hurt them or God will be angry at us because we broke the promise we made to them. ²¹So let them live. But they will be our servants. They will cut wood for us and carry water for all of our people." So the leaders did not break their promise of peace to those people.

---

wineskin(s) A bottle made from the skin of an animal and used for storing wine.

22 Joshua called the Gibeonite people. He said, "Why did you lie to us? Your land was near our camp. But you told us you were from a faraway country. 23 Now, your people will have many troubles. All of your people will be slaves—they will have to cut wood and carry water for the house of God.*"
24 The Gibeonite people answered, "We lied to you because we were afraid you would kill us. We heard that God commanded his servant Moses to give you all of this land. And God told you to kill all the people that lived in this land. That is why we lied to you. 25 Now we are your servants. You can do whatever you think is right."
26 So the people of Gibeon became slaves. But Joshua let them live. Joshua did not allow the people of Israel to kill them. 27 Joshua made the people of Gibeon become slaves of the people of Israel. They cut wood and carried water for the people of Israel and for the altar of the Lord—wherever the Lord chose it to be. Those people are still slaves today.

The Day the Sun Stood Still

10 At this time Adoni Zedek was the king of Jerusalem. This king heard that Joshua had defeated Ai and completely destroyed it. The king learned that Joshua had done the same thing to Jericho and its king. The king also learned that the people of Gibeon had made a peace agreement with Israel. And those people lived very near Jerusalem. 2 So Adoni Zedek and his people were very scared. Gibeon was not a little town like Ai. Gibeon was a very big city—it was as big as any royal city.* And all the men in that city were good fighters. So the king was afraid. 3 Adoni Zedek, the king of Jerusalem, talked with Hoham, king of Hebron. He also talked with Piram, king of Jarmuth, Japhia, king of Lachish, and Debir, king of Eglon. The king of Jerusalem begged these men, 4 "Come with me and help me to attack Gibeon. Gibeon has made a peace agreement with Joshua and the people of Israel."
5 So these five Amorite kings joined armies. (The five kings were the king of Jerusalem, the king of Hebron, the king of Jarmuth, the king of Lachish, and the king of Eglon.) Those armies went to Gibeon. The armies surrounded the city and began fighting against it.

house of God This might mean the "family of God" (Israel), the "Holy Tent" or the "temple."
royal city Strong well-protected cities that controlled smaller towns nearby.

6 The people in the city of Gibeon sent a message to Joshua at his camp at Gilgal. The message said: "We are your servants! Don't leave us alone. Come and help us! Hurry! Save us! All the Amorite kings from the hill country have brought their armies together to fight against us."
7 So Joshua marched out of Gilgal with his whole army. Joshua's best fighting men were with him. 8 The Lord said to Joshua, "Don't be afraid of those armies. I will allow you to defeat them. None of those armies will be able to defeat you."
9 Joshua and his army marched all night to Gibeon. [The enemy did not know that Joshua was coming.] So it was a complete surprise when he attacked them.
10 The Lord caused those armies to be very confused when Israel attacked. So Israel defeated them and won a great victory. Israel chased the enemy from Gibeon on the road going to Beth Horon. The army of Israel killed men all the way to Azekah and Makkedah. 11 Then the army of Israel chased the enemy down the road from Beth Horon to Azekah. While they were chasing the enemy, the Lord caused large hailstones to fall from the sky. Many of the enemy were killed by these large hailstones. More men were killed by the hailstones than by the swords of the soldiers of Israel.
12 That day the Lord allowed Israel to defeat the Amorite people. And that day Joshua stood before all the people of Israel and said to the Lord:

"Sun, stop over Gibeon.
Moon, stand still over
the Valley of Aijalon."

13 So the sun did not move, and the moon stopped until the people defeated their enemies. This story is written in the Book of Jashar. The sun stopped in the middle of the sky. It did not move for a full day. 14 That had never happened before. And it has never happened again! That was the day the Lord obeyed a man. The Lord really was fighting for Israel!
15 After this, Joshua and his army went back to the camp at Gilgal. 16 But during the fight, the five kings ran away. They hid in a cave near Makkedah. 17 But someone found them hiding in that cave. Joshua learned about this. 18 Joshua said, "Cover the entrance to the cave with large rocks. Put some men there to guard the cave. 19 But don't stay there yourselves. Continue chasing the enemy. Continue to attack them from behind. Don't let the enemy get back to their cities. The

Lord your God has given you the victory over them."

²⁰So Joshua and the people of Israel killed the enemy. But some of the enemy were able to go to their cities that had tall walls around them and hide. These men were not killed. ²¹After the fighting, Joshua's men came back to him at Makkedah. None of the people in that country were brave enough to say anything against the people of Israel.

²²Joshua said, "Move the rocks that are covering the entrance to the cave. Bring those five kings to me." ²³So Joshua's men brought the five kings out of the cave. They were the kings of Jerusalem, Hebron, Jarmuth, Lachish, and Eglon. ²⁴They brought the five kings to Joshua. Joshua called all his men to come to that place. Joshua said to the officers of his army, "Come here! Put your feet on the necks of these kings." So the officers of Joshua's army came close. They put their feet on the necks of the kings.

²⁵Then Joshua said to his men, "Be strong and brave! Don't be afraid. I will show you what the Lord will do to all of the enemies that you will fight in the future."

²⁶Then Joshua killed the five kings. He hanged their bodies on five trees. Joshua left them hanging in the trees until evening. ²⁷At sunset Joshua told his men to take the bodies down from the trees. So they threw the bodies into the cave where the kings had been hiding and covered the entrance of the cave with large rocks. Those bodies are still in that cave today.

²⁸That day Joshua defeated Makkedah. Joshua killed the king and the people in that city. There were no people left living. Joshua did the same thing to the king of Makkedah as he had done to the king of Jericho.

Taking the Southern Cities

²⁹Then Joshua and all the people of Israel traveled from Makkedah. They went to Libnah and attacked that city. ³⁰The Lord allowed the people of Israel to defeat that city and its king. The people of Israel killed every person in that city. No people were left alive. And the people did the same thing to that king as they had done to the king of Jericho.

³¹Then Joshua and all the people of Israel left Libnah and went to Lachish. Joshua and his army camped around that city and attacked it. ³²The Lord allowed them to defeat the city of Lachish. They defeated that city on the second day. The people of Israel killed every person in that city, just like they did in Libnah. ³³Horam king of Gezer came to help Lachish, but Joshua also defeated him and his army. Not one of them was left alive.

³⁴Then Joshua and all the people of Israel traveled from Lachish to Eglon. They camped around Eglon and attacked it. ³⁵That day they captured the city and killed all the people in the city. This was the same thing they had done to Lachish.

³⁶Then Joshua and all the people of Israel traveled from Eglon to Hebron. Then they attacked Hebron. ³⁷They captured the city and all the little towns near Hebron. The people of Israel killed every person in the city. No one was left alive there. This was the same thing they did to Eglon. They destroyed the city and killed all the people in it.

³⁸Then Joshua and all the people of Israel went back to Debir and attacked that city. ³⁹They captured that city, its king, and all the little towns near Debir. They killed every person in that city. No one was left alive there. The people of Israel did to Debir and its king the same thing they did to Hebron and its king. This was the same thing they had done to Libnah and its king.

⁴⁰So Joshua defeated all the kings of the cities of the hill country, the Negev,* the western foothills, and the eastern foothills. The Lord God of Israel had told Joshua to kill all the people. So Joshua did not leave anyone alive in those places.

⁴¹Joshua captured all the cities from Kadesh Barnea to Gaza. He captured all the cities from the land of Goshen *(in Egypt)* to Gibeon. ⁴²Joshua captured all those cities and their kings on one trip. Joshua did this because the Lord God of Israel was fighting for Israel. ⁴³Then Joshua and all the people of Israel returned to their camp at Gilgal.

Defeating the Northern Cities

11 Jabin, king of Hazor, heard about all these things that happened. So he decided to call together the armies of several kings. Jabin sent a message to Jobab, king of Madon, to the king of Shimron, the king of Acshaph, ²and to the kings of the north, in the hill country and in the desert. Jabin sent the message to the kings of the Kinnereth,* the Negev,* and the western foothills. Jabin also sent the message to the king of Naphoth Dor in the west. ³Jabin sent that message to the

---

Negev The desert area south of Judah.
Kinnereth The area near the Sea of Galilee.

kings of the Canaanite people in the east and in the west. He sent the message to the Amorite people, the Hittite people, the Perizzite people, and the Jebusite people living in the hill country. He also sent the message to the Hivite people living below Mount Hermon near Mizpah. ⁴So the armies of all these kings came together. There were many fighting men and many horses and chariots. It was a very, very large army—it looked like there were as many men as grains of sand on the sea shore.

⁵All of these kings met together at the small river of Merom. They joined their armies together into one camp and made plans for the battle against Israel.

⁶Then the Lord said to Joshua, "Don't be afraid of that army. I will allow you to defeat them. By this time tomorrow, you will have killed them all. You will cut the legs of the horses and burn all their chariots."

⁷Joshua and his whole army surprised the enemy. They attacked the enemy at the river of Merom. ⁸The Lord allowed Israel to defeat them. The army of Israel defeated them and chased them to Greater Sidon, Misrephoth Maim, and the Valley of Mizpah in the east. The army of Israel fought until none of the enemy was left alive. ⁹Joshua did what the Lord said he would do—Joshua cut the legs of their horses and burned their chariots.

¹⁰Then Joshua went back and captured the city of Hazor. Joshua killed the king of Hazor. (Hazor was the leader of all the kingdoms that fought against Israel.) ¹¹The army of Israel killed every person in that city. They completely destroyed all the people. There was nothing left alive. Then they burned the city.

¹²Joshua captured all of these cities. He killed all of their kings. Joshua completely destroyed everything in these cities. He did this the way Moses, the Lord's servant, had commanded. ¹³But the army of Israel did not burn any cities that were built on hills. The only city built on a hill that they burned was Hazor. This is the city Joshua burned. ¹⁴The people of Israel kept for themselves all the things they found in the cities. They kept all the animals that they found in the city. But they killed all the people there. They did not allow any people to be left alive. ¹⁵Long ago the Lord commanded his servant Moses to do this. Then Moses commanded Joshua to do this. So Joshua obeyed God. Joshua did everything that the Lord had commanded Moses.

¹⁶So Joshua defeated all the people in that whole country. He had control over the hill country, the Negev, all the area of Goshen, the area of the western foothills, Jordan Valley, and the mountains of Israel and all the hills near them. ¹⁷Joshua had control of all the land from Mount Halak near Seir to Baal Gad in the Valley of Lebanon below Mount Hermon. Joshua captured all the kings in that land and killed them. ¹⁸Joshua fought against those kings many years. ¹⁹Only one city in all the land made a peace agreement with Israel. That was the Hivite city of Gibeon. All the other cities were defeated in war. ²⁰The Lord wanted those people to think they were strong. Then they would fight against Israel. This way he could destroy them without mercy. He could destroy them the way the Lord had commanded Moses to do.

²¹The Anakite people* lived in the hill country in the area of Hebron, Debir, Anab, and Judah. Joshua fought and completely destroyed all those people and their towns. ²²There were no Anakite people left living in the land of Israel. The only Anakite people that were left alive were in Gaza, Gath, and Ashdod. ²³Joshua took control of the whole land of Israel, just as the Lord had told Moses long ago. The Lord gave that land to Israel just like he promised. And Joshua divided the land among the family groups of Israel. Finally, the fighting ended and there was peace in the land.

Kings Defeated by Israel

12 The people of Israel had taken control of the land east of the Jordan River. They had all the land from Arnon Ravine to Mount Hermon and all the land along the eastern side of the Jordan Valley. Here are all of the kings the people of Israel defeated to take this land:

²⌊They defeated⌋ Sihon, the king of the Amorite people living in the city of Heshbon. He ruled the land from Aroer at the Arnon Ravine to the Jabbok River. His land started in the center of that ravine. This was their border with the Ammonite people. Sihon ruled over half of the land of Gilead. ³He also ruled over the eastern side of Jordan Valley from Lake Galilee to the Dead Sea (Salt Sea). And he ruled from Beth Jeshimoth to the south to the hills of Pisgah.

⁴⌊They also defeated⌋ Og, king of Bashan. Og was from the Rephaite people. He ruled the land

---

Anakite people Descendants of Anak. They were a family famous for tall and powerful fighting men. See Num. 13:33.

in Ashtaroth and Edrei. ⁵Og ruled over Mount Hermon, Salecah, and all of the area of Bashan. His land ended where the people of Geshur and Maacah lived. Og also ruled half of the land of Gilead. This land stopped at the land of Sihon, the king of Heshbon.

⁶The Lord's servant Moses and the people of Israel defeated all these kings. And Moses gave that land to the family group of Reuben, the family group of Gad, and half the family group of Manasseh. Moses gave them this land to be their own.

⁷The people of Israel also defeated kings in the land that was west of the Jordan River. Joshua led the people in this land. Joshua gave the people this land and divided it among the twelve family groups. This was the land that God promised to give to them. This land was between Baal Gad in the Valley of Lebanon and Mount Halak near Seir. ⁸This included the hill country, the western foothills, the Jordan Valley, the eastern mountains, the desert, and the Negev.* This was the land where the Hittite people, the Amorite people, the Canaanite people, the Perizzite people, the Hivite people, and the Jebusite people lived. Here is a list of the kings the people of Israel defeated:

⁹	the king of Jericho	1
	the king of Ai near Bethel	1
¹⁰	the king of Jerusalem	1
	the king of Hebron	1
¹¹	the king of Jarmuth	1
	the king of Lachish	1
¹²	the king of Eglon	1
	the king of Gezer	1
¹³	the king of Debir	1
	the king of Geder	1
¹⁴	the king of Hormah	1
	the king of Arad	1
¹⁵	the king of Libnah	1
	the king of Adullam	1
¹⁶	the king of Makkedah	1
	the king of Bethel	1
¹⁷	the king of Tappuah	1
	the king of Hepher	1
¹⁸	the king of Aphek	1
	the king of Sharon	1
¹⁹	the king of Madon	1
	the king of Hazor	1
²⁰	the king of Shimron Meron	1
	the king of Acshaph	1
²¹	the king of Taanach	1
	the king of Megiddo	1
²²	the king of Kedesh	1
	the king of Jokneam in Carmel	1
²³	the king of Dor at Mount Dor	1
	the king of Goyim in Gilgal	1
²⁴	the king of Tirzah	1
	Total number of kings	31

Land Not Yet Taken

13 When Joshua was very old, the Lord said to him, "Joshua you have grown old, but there is still much land for you to take control of. ²You have not yet taken the land of Geshur or the land of the Philistines. ³You have not yet taken the area from the Shihor River* at Egypt to the border of Ekron and the land further north. That land still belongs to the Canaanite people. You must still defeat the five Philistine leaders at Gaza, Ashdod, Ashkelon, Gath, and Ekron. You must also defeat the Avvite people ⁴who live south of the Canaanite land. ⁵You have not yet defeated the area of the Gebalites. And also there is the area of Lebanon east of Baal Gad below Mount Hermon to Lebo Hamath.

⁶"People of Sidon are living in the hill country from Lebanon to Misrephoth Maim. But I will force out all of these people for the people of Israel. Be sure to remember this land when you divide the land among the people of Israel. Do this like I told you. ⁷Now, divide the land among the nine family groups and half of the family group of Manasseh."

Dividing the Land

⁸The family groups of Reuben, Gad, and the other half of Manasseh have already taken all of their land. The Lord's servant, Moses gave them the land east of the Jordan River. ⁹Their land started at Aroer by the Arnon Ravine and continued to the town in the middle of the ravine. And it included the whole plain from Medeba to Dibon. ¹⁰All the towns that Sihon the king of the Amorite people ruled were in that land. That king ruled in the city of Heshbon. The land continued to the area where the Amorite people lived. ¹¹Also the town of Gilead was in that land. And the area where the people of Geshur and Maacah lived was in that land. All of Mount Hermon and all of Bashan as far as Salecah was in that land. ¹²All

---

Negev The desert area south of Judah.

Shihor River Probably one of the eastern branches of the Nile River.

the kingdom of King Og was in that land. King Og ruled in Bashan. In the past he ruled in Ashtaroth and Edrei. Og was from the Rephaite people. In the past Moses had defeated those people and had taken their land. ¹³The people of Israel did not force out the people of Geshur and Maacah. Those people still live among the people of Israel today.

¹⁴The family group of Levi is the only family group that did not get any land. Instead, the people of Levi get all the animals that are offered as burnt offerings to the Lord God of Israel. That is what the Lord promised them.

¹⁵Moses had given each family group from the family group of Reuben some land. This is the land they received: ¹⁶It was the land from Aroer near the Arnon Ravine to the town of Medeba. This included the whole plain and the town in the middle of the ravine. ¹⁷The land continued to Heshbon. It included all the towns on the plain. Those towns were Dibon, Bamoth Baal, Beth Baal Meon, ¹⁸Jahaz, Kedemoth, Mephaath, ¹⁹Kiriathaim, Sibmah, Zereth Shahar on the hill in the valley, ²⁰Beth Peor, the hills of Pisgah, and Beth Jeshimoth. ²¹So that land included all the towns on the plain and all the area that Sihon the king of the Amorite people had ruled. That king ruled at the town of Heshbon. But Moses had defeated him and the leaders of the Midianite people. Those leaders were Evi, Rekem, Zur, Hur, and Reba. (All these leaders fought together with Sihon.) All these leaders lived in that country. ²²The people of Israel defeated Balaam son of Beor. (Balaam tried to use magic to tell the future.) The people of Israel killed many people during the fighting. ²³The land that was given to Reuben stopped at the shore of the Jordan River. So the land that was given to the family groups of Reuben included all these towns and their fields that were listed.

²⁴This is the land Moses gave to the family group of Gad. Moses gave this land to each family group:

²⁵The land of Jazer and all the towns of Gilead. Moses also gave them half of the land of the Ammonite people as far as Aroer near Rabbah. ²⁶That land included the area from Heshbon to Ramath Mizpah and Betonim. That land included the area from Mahanaim to the land of Debir. ²⁷That land included the valley of Beth Haram, Beth Nimrah, Succoth and Zaphon. All the other land that Sihon, the king of Heshbon, had ruled was included in this land. This is the land on the east side of the Jordan River. The land continued to the end of Lake Galilee. ²⁸All this land is the land Moses gave the family group of Gad. That land included all the towns that were listed. Moses gave that land to each family group.

²⁹This is the land Moses gave to half of the family group of Manasseh. Half of all the families in the family group of Manasseh got this land:

³⁰The land started at Mahanaim. The land included all of Bashan, all the land ruled by Og, king of Bashan, all the towns of Jair in Bashan. (In all, there were 60 cities.) ³¹The land also included half of Gilead, Ashtaroth, and Edrei. (Gilead, Ashtaroth, and Edrei were the cities where king Og had lived.) All this land was given to the family of Makir son of Manasseh. Half of all those sons got this land.

³²Moses gave all this land to these family groups. Moses did this while the people were camped on the plains of Moab. This was across the Jordan River, east of Jericho. ³³Moses did not give any land to the family group of Levi. The Lord, God of Israel, promised that he himself would be the gift for the family group of Levi.

14 Eleazar the priest, Joshua son of Nun, and the leaders of all the family groups of Israel decided what land to give to the people. ²The Lord had commanded Moses long ago the way he wanted the people to choose their land. The people of the nine and a half family groups threw lots* to decide which land they would get. ³Moses had already given the two and a half family groups their land east of the Jordan River. But the family group of Levi was not given any land like the other people. ⁴₍The twelve family groups were given their own land.₎ The sons of Joseph had divided into two family groups—Manasseh and Ephraim. ₍And each family group received some land. But₎ the people from the family group of Levi were not given any land. They were given only some towns to live in. ₍And these towns were in every family group's land.₎ They were also given fields for their animals. ⁵The Lord had told Moses how to divide the land among the family groups of Israel. The people of Israel divided the land the way the Lord had commanded.

Caleb Gets His Land

⁶One day some people from the family group of Judah went to Joshua at Gilgal. One of those

---

lot(s) Sticks, stones, or pieces of bone used like dice for making decisions. See Proverbs 16:33.

his servant Literally, "the man of God."

people was Caleb, the son of Jephunneh the Kenizzite. Caleb said to Joshua, "You remember the things the Lord said at Kadesh Barnea. The Lord was speaking to Moses, his servant.* The Lord was talking about you and me. ⁷Moses, the Lord's servant, sent me to look at the land where we were going. I was 40 years old at that time. When I came back I told Moses what I thought about the land. ⁸The other men that went with me told the people things that made them afraid. But I truly believed that the Lord would allow us to take that land. ⁹So that day Moses made a promise to me. He said, 'That land where you went will become your land. Your children will own that land forever. I will give you that land because you truly believed in the Lord, my God.'

¹⁰"Now, the Lord has kept me alive 45 years—like he said he would do. During that time we all wandered in the desert. Now, here I am, 85 years old. ¹¹I am still as strong today as I was the day Moses sent me out. I am as ready to fight as I was then. ¹²So now, give me the hill country that the Lord promised me that day long ago. At that time, you heard that the strong Anakite people* lived there. And the cities were very big and well protected. But now, maybe the Lord will be with me, and I will take that land like the Lord said."

¹³Joshua blessed Caleb son of Jephunneh. Joshua gave him the city of Hebron as his own. ¹⁴And that city still belongs to the family of Caleb son of Jephunneh, the Kenizzite. That land still belongs to his people because he trusted and obeyed the Lord, God of Israel. ¹⁵In the past that city was called Kiriath Arba. That city was named for the greatest man among the Anakite people—a man named Arba.

After this, there was peace in that land.

Land for Judah

15 The land that was given to Judah was divided among the families of that family group. That land went to the border of Edom and south all the way to the desert of Zin at the edge of Teman. ²The southern border of Judah's land started at the south end of the Dead Sea. ³The border went south to Scorpion Pass and continued on to Zin. Then the border continued south to Kadesh Barnea. The border continued past Hezron to Addar. From Addar the border turned and continued to Karka. ⁴The border continued to Azmon, the brook of Egypt, and then to the Mediterranean Sea. All that land was on their southern border.

⁵Their eastern border was the shore of the Dead Sea to the area where the Jordan River flowed into the sea.

Their northern border started at the area where the Jordan River flowed into the Dead Sea. ⁶Then the northern border went to Beth Hoglah and continued north of Beth Arabah. The border continued to the stone of Bohan. (Bohan was the son of Reuben). ⁷Then the northern border went through the Valley of Achor to Debir. There the border turned to the north and went to Gilgal. Gilgal is across from the road that goes through the mountain of Adummim. That is on the south side of the brook. The border continued along the waters of En Shemesh. The border stopped at En Rogel. ⁸Then the border went through the Valley of Ben Hinnom beside the southern side of the Jebusite city. (That Jebusite city was called Jerusalem.) At that place the border went to the top of the hill on the west side of Hinnom Valley. This was at the northern end of Rephaim Valley. ⁹From that place the border went to the spring of water of Nephtoah. Then the border went to the cities near Mount Ephron. At that place the border turned and went to Baalah. (Baalah is also called Kiriath Jearim.) ¹⁰At Baalah the border turned west and went to the hill country of Seir. The border continued along the north side of Mount Jearim (Kesalon) and continued down to Beth Shemesh. From there the border went past Timnah. ¹¹Then the border went to the hill north of Ekron. From that place the border turned to Shikkeron and went past Mount Baalah. The border continued on to Jabneel and ended at the Mediterranean Sea. ¹²The Mediterranean Sea was the western border of the land of Judah. So the land of Judah was inside these four borders. The families of Judah lived in this area.

¹³The Lord had commanded Joshua to give Caleb son of Jephunneh part of the land in Judah. So Joshua gave Caleb the land God commanded. Joshua gave him the town of Kiriath Arba (Hebron). (Arba was the father of Anak.) ¹⁴Caleb forced the three Anakite families living in Hebron to leave there. Those families were Sheshai, Ahiman, and Talmai. They were from the family of Anak. ¹⁵Then Caleb fought against the people living in Debir. (In the past, Debir was also called Kiriath Sepher.) ¹⁶Caleb said, "I want to attack Kiriath Sepher. I will give my daughter Acsah to

---

Anakite people Descendants of Anak. They were a family famous for tall and powerful fighting men. See Num. 13:33.

the man that attacks and defeats that city. I will let that man marry my daughter."

¹⁷Othniel was the son of Caleb's brother Kenaz. Othniel defeated that city, so Caleb gave his daughter Acsah to Othniel to be his wife. ¹⁸Acsah went to live with Othniel. Othniel told Acsah* to ask her father Caleb for some more land. ₍Acsah went to her father.₎ When she got off her donkey, Caleb asked her, "What do you want?"

¹⁹Acsah answered, "Give me a blessing.* You gave me dry desert land in the Negev.* Please give me some land with water on it." So Caleb gave her what she wanted. He gave her the upper and lower pools of water in that land.

²⁰The family group of Judah got the land that God promised them. Each family group got part of the land. ²¹The family group of Judah got all the towns in the southern part of the Negev.* These towns were near the border of Edom. Here is a list of those towns: Kabzeel, Eder, Jagur, ²²Kinah, Dimonah, Adadah, ²³Kedesh, Hazor, Ithnan, ²⁴Ziph, Telem, Bealoth, ²⁵Hazor Hadattah, Kerioth Hezron (Hazor), ²⁶Amam, Shema, Moladah, ²⁷Hazar Gaddah, Heshmon, Beth Pelet, ²⁸Hazar Shual, Beersheba, Biziothiah, ²⁹Baalah, Iim, Ezem, ³⁰Eltolad, Kesil, Hormah, ³¹Ziklag, Madmannah, Sansannah, ³²Lebaoth, Shilhim, Ain, and Rimmon. In all, there were 29 towns and all their fields.

³³The family group of Judah also got towns in the western foothills. Here is a list of those towns: Eshtaol, Zorah, Ashnah, ³⁴Zanoah, En Gannim, Tappuah, Enam, ³⁵Jarmuth, Adullam, Socoh, Azekah, ³⁶Shaaraim, Adithaim, and Gederah (Gederothaim). In all, there were 14 towns and all their fields.

³⁷The family group of Judah was also given these towns: Zenan, Hadashah, Migdal Gad, ³⁸Dilean, Mizpah, Joktheel, ³⁹Lachish, Bozkath, Eglon, ⁴⁰Cabbon, Lahmas, Kitlish, ⁴¹Gederoth, Beth Dagon, Naamah, and Makkedah. In all, there were 16 towns and all the fields around them.

⁴²The people of Judah also got these towns: Libnah, Ether, Ashan, ⁴³Iphtah, Ashnah, Nezib, ⁴⁴Keilah, Aczib, and Mareshah. In all, there were nine towns and all the fields around them.

⁴⁵The people of Judah also got the town of Ekron and all the small towns and fields near it. ⁴⁶They also got the area west of Ekron and all the fields and towns near Ashdod. ⁴⁷All the area around Ashdod and the small towns there were part of the land of Judah. The people of Judah also got the area around Gaza and fields and the towns that were near it. Their land continued to the River of Egypt. And their land continued along the coast of the Mediterranean Sea.

⁴⁸The people of Judah were also given towns in the hill country. Here is a list of those towns: Shamir, Jattir, Socoh, ⁴⁹Dannah, Kiriath Sannah, (Debir), ⁵⁰Anab, Eshtemoh, Anim, ⁵¹Goshen, Holon, and Giloh. In all, there were eleven towns and all the fields around them.

⁵²The people of Judah were also given these towns: Arab, Dumah, Eshan, ⁵³Janim, Beth Tappuah, Aphekah, ⁵⁴Humtah, Kiriath Arba (Hebron), and Zior. There were nine towns and all the fields around them.

⁵⁵The people of Judah were also given these towns: Maon, Carmel, Ziph, Juttah, ⁵⁶Jezreel, Jokdeam, Zanoah, ⁵⁷Kain, Gibeah, and Timnah. In all, there were ten towns and all the fields around them.

⁵⁸The people of Judah were also given these towns: Halhul, Beth Zur, Gedor, ⁵⁹Maarath, Beth Anoth, and Eltekon. In all, there were six towns and all the fields around them.

⁶⁰The people of Judah were also given the two towns of Rabbah and Kiriath Beth (Kiriath Jearim).

⁶¹The people of Judah were also given towns in the desert. Here is a list of those towns: Beth Arabah, Middin, Secacah, ⁶²Nibshan, Salt City, and En Gedi. In all, there were six towns and all the fields around them.

⁶³The army of Judah was not able to force out the Jebusite people living in Jerusalem. So today there are still Jebusite people living among the people of Judah in Jerusalem.

Land for Ephraim and Manasseh

16 This is the land that the family of Joseph got. This land started at the Jordan River near Jericho and continued to the waters of Jericho. (This was just east of Jericho.) The border went up from Jericho to the hill country of Bethel. ²Then the border continued from Bethel (Luz) to the Arkite border at Ataroth. ³Then the border went west to the border of the Japhletite people. The border continued to Lower Beth Horon. Then the border went to Gezer and continued to the Mediterranean Sea.

Give me a blessing Or, "Please welcome me." Or, "Give me a stream of water."
Negev The desert area south of Judah.

⁴So the people of Manasseh and Ephraim got their land. (Manasseh and Ephraim were sons of Joseph.)

⁵This is the land that was given to the people of Ephraim: Their eastern border started at Ataroth Addar near Upper Beth Horon. ⁶And the western border started at Micmethath. The border turned to the east to Taanath Shiloh and continued east to Janoah. ⁷Then the border went from Janoah down to Ataroth and to Naarah. The border continued until it touched Jericho and stopped at the Jordan River. ⁸The border went from Tappuah west to Kanah Ravine and ended at the sea. This is all the land that was given to the Ephraim people. Each family in that family group got a part of this land. ⁹Many of the border towns of Ephraim were actually in Manasseh's borders, but the people of Ephraim got those towns and the fields around them. ¹⁰But the Ephraimite people were not able to force the Canaanite people to leave the town of Gezer. So the Canaanite people still live among the Ephraimite people today. But the Canaanite people became slaves of the Ephraimite people.

17 Then land was given to the family group of Manasseh. Manasseh was Joseph's first son. Manasseh's first son was Makir, the father of Gilead.* Makir was a great soldier, so the areas of Gilead and Bashan were given to the Makir family. ²Land was also given to the other families in the family group of Manasseh. Those families were Abiezer, Helek, Asriel, Shechem, Hepher, and Shemida. All these men were the other sons of Manasseh, the son of Joseph. The families of these men got their share of the land.

³Zelophehad was the son of Hepher. Hepher was the son of Gilead. Gilead was the son of Makir, and Makir was the son of Manasseh. Zelophehad did not have any sons, but he had five daughters. The daughters were named Mahlah, Noah, Hoglah, Milcah, and Tirzah. ⁴The daughters went to Eleazar the priest, Joshua son of Nun, and all the leaders. The daughters said, "The Lord told Moses to give us land the same as our male relatives." So he obeyed the Lord and gave the daughters some land. So these daughters got land the same as their uncles.

⁵So the family group of Manasseh had ten areas of land west of the Jordan River and two more areas of land, Gilead and Bashan, on the other side of the Jordan River. ⁶So these women from the family group of Manasseh got land the same as the men. The land of Gilead was given to the rest of the families of Manasseh.

⁷The lands of Manasseh were in the area between Asher and Micmethath. This is near Shechem. The border went south to the En Tappuah area. ⁸The land around Tappuah belonged to Manasseh, but the town itself did not. The town of Tappuah was at the border of Manasseh's land and it belonged to the people of Ephraim. ⁹The border of Manasseh continued south to Kanah Ravine. This area belonged to Manasseh's family group, but the cities belonged to the people of Ephraim. Manasseh's border was on the north side of the river and it continued west to the Mediterranean Sea. ¹⁰The land to the south belonged to Ephraim. And the land to the north belonged to Manasseh. The Mediterranean Sea was the western border. The border touched Asher's land in the north and Issachar's land in the east.

¹¹The people of Manasseh also had towns in the area of Issachar and Asher. Beth Shean, Ibleam and the small towns around them belonged to the people of Manasseh. People of Manasseh also lived in Dor, Endor, Taanach, Megiddo, and the small towns around those cities. They also lived in the three towns of Naphoth. ¹²The people of Manasseh were not able to defeat those cities. So the Canaanite people continued to live there. ¹³But the people of Israel grew strong. When this happened, they forced the people of Canaan to work for them. But they did not force the Canaanite people to leave that land.

¹⁴The family group of Joseph spoke to Joshua and said, "You gave us only one area of land. But we are many people. Why did you only give us one part of all the land that the Lord gave his people?"

¹⁵Joshua answered them, "If you have too many people, then go up to wooded area in the hill country and clear that land and make it useable. That land now belongs to the Perizzite people and the Rephaite people. But if the hill country of Ephraim is too small for you, then go take that land."

¹⁶The people of Joseph said, "It is true that the hill country of Ephraim is not large enough for us. But the Canaanite people living there have powerful weapons—they have iron chariots!*

---

father of Gilead Or, "the leader of the area of Gilead."

chariots Small wagons used in war. They were much faster and could carry more weapons than soldiers on foot.

And those people control Jezreel Valley, Beth Shean and all the small towns in that area."

[17] Then Joshua said to the people of Joseph, to Ephraim, and to Manasseh, "But there are many, many of you. And you are very powerful. You should get more than one share of the land. [18] You will take the hill country. It is a forest, but you can cut down the trees and make it a good place to live. And you will own all of it. You will force the Canaanite people to leave that land. You will defeat them even if they are strong and have powerful weapons."

Dividing the Rest of the Land

18 All of the Israelite people gathered together at Shiloh. At that place they set up the Meeting Tent.* The people of Israel controlled that country. They had defeated all the enemies in that land. [2] But at this time there were still seven family groups of Israel that had not yet gotten the land God had promised them.

[3] So Joshua said to the people of Israel, "Why do you wait so long to take your land? The Lord, the God of your fathers, has given this land to you. [4] So each of your family groups should choose three men. I will send those men out to study the land. They will describe that land, and then they will come back to me. [5] They will divide the land into seven parts. The people of Judah will keep their land in the south. The people of Joseph will keep their land in the north. [6] But you should describe the land and divide it into seven parts. Bring the map to me, and we will let the Lord our God decide which family group will get which land.* [7] The Levite people do not get a share of the land. Their share is to serve the Lord as priests. Gad, Reuben, and half the family group of Manasseh have already received the land that was promised to them. They are on the east side of the Jordan River. Moses, the Lord's servant, already gave them that land."

[8] So the men that were chosen went to look at the land and write a description of it. Joshua told them, "Go all through the land and write a description of it. Then come back to me at Shiloh. Then I will throw lots* and let the Lord divide the land for you."

[9] So the men went into the land. The men went all through the and and wrote a description of if for Joshua. They listed all the cities and divided the land into seven parts. Then they went back to Joshua at Shiloh. [10] Joshua threw lots* for them in front of the Lord at Shiloh. In this way, Joshua divided the land and gave each family group its part of the land."

Land for Benjamin

[11] The family group of Benjamin was given the land that was between the areas of Judah and Joseph. Each family in the family group of Benjamin got their land. This is the land that was chosen for Benjamin: [12] The northern border started at the Jordan River. The border went along the northern edge of Jericho. Then the border went west into the hill country. The border continued until it was just east of Beth Aven. [13] Then the border went south to Luz (Bethel). Then the border went down to Ataroth Addar. Ataroth Addar is on the hill south of Lower Beth Horon. [14] At the hill south of Beth Horon, the border turned south and went along the west side of the hill. The border went to Kiriath Baal (also called Kiriath Jearim). This town belonged to the people of Judah. This was the western border.

[15] The southern border started near Kiriath Jearim and went to the River of Nephtoah. [16] Then the border went down to the bottom of the hill near the valley of Ben Hinnom, north of Rephaim Valley. The border continued down Hinnom Valley just south of the Jebusite city. Then the border went on to En Rogel. [17] There, the border turned north and went to En Shemesh. The border continued to Geliloth. (Geliloth is near the Adummim Pass in the mountains.) The border went down to the Great Stone that was named for Bohan, the son of Reuben. [18] The border continued to the northern part of Beth Arabah. Then the border went down into the Jordan Valley. [19] Then the border went to the northern part of Beth Hoglah and ended at the north shore of the Dead Sea. This is where the Jordan River flows into that sea. That was the southern border.

[20] The Jordan River was the eastern border. So this was the land that was given to the family group of Benjamin. Those were the borders on all sides. [21] Each family got its land. These are their cities: Jericho, Beth Hoglah, Emek Keziz, [22] Beth Arabah, Zemaraim, Bethel, [23] Avvim, Parah, Ophrah, [24] Kephar Ammoni, Ophni, and Geba. There were twelve cities and their fields around them.

Meeting Tent The Holy Tent (tabernacle) where the people of Israel went to meet with God.

we ... land Literally, "I will throw lots here before the Lord our God."

lot(s) Sticks, stones, or pieces of bone used like dice for making decisions. See Proverbs 16:33.

²⁵The family group of Benjamin also got Gibeon, Ramah, Beeroth, ²⁶Mizpah, Kephirah, Mozah, ²⁷Rekem, Irpeel, Taralah, ²⁸Zelah, Haeleph, the Jebusite city *(Jerusalem)*, Gibeah, and Kiriath. There were 14 cities and the fields around them. The family group of Benjamin got all these areas.

Land for Simeon

19Then Joshua gave all the families in the family group of Simeon their share of the land. The land they got was inside the area that belonged to Judah. ²This is what they got: Beersheba (also called Sheba), Moladah, ³Hazar Shual, Balah, Ezem, ⁴Eltolad, Bethul, Hormah, ⁵Ziklag, Beth Marcaboth, Hazar Susah, ⁶Beth Lebaoth, and Sharuhen. There were 13 towns and all the fields around them.

⁷They also got the towns of Ain, Rimmon, Ether, and Ashan. There were four towns and all the fields around them. ⁸They also got all the fields around the cities as far as Baalath Beer (Ramah in the Negev). So that was the area that was given to the family group of Simeon. Each family got its land. ⁹Simeon's share of land was within the area that Judah got. The people of Judah had more land than they needed, so the people of Simeon got part of their land.

Land for Zebulun

¹⁰The next family group that got their land was Zebulun. Each family in Zebulun got the land that was promised to them. The border of Zebulun went as far as Sarid. ¹¹Then the border went west to Maralah and just touched Dabbesheth. Then the border went along the ravine near Jokneam. ¹²Then the border turned to the east. It went from Sarid to Kisloth Tabor. Then the border went on to Daberath and to Japhia. ¹³Then the border continued to the east to Gath Hepher and Eth Kazin. The border ended at Rimmon. Then the border turned and went to Neah. ¹⁴At Neah the border turned again and went north to Hannathon and then continued to the Valley of Iphtah El. ¹⁵Inside this border were the cities of Kattath, Nahalal, Shimron, Idalah, and Bethlehem. In all, there were twelve towns and all the fields around them.

¹⁶So these are the towns and fields around them that were given to Zebulun. Each family in Zebulun got its part of the land.

Land for Issachar

¹⁷The fourth part of the land was given to the family group of Issachar. Each family in that family group got its part of the land. ¹⁸This is the land that was given to that family group: Jezreel, Kesulloth, Shunem, ¹⁹Hapharaim, Shion, Anaharath, ²⁰Rabbith, Kishion, Ebez, ²¹Remeth, En Gannim, En Haddah, and Beth Pazzez. ²²The border of their land touched Tabor, Shahazumah, and Beth Shemesh. The border stopped at the Jordan River. In all, there were 16 towns and the fields around them. ²³These cities and towns were part of the land that was given to the family group of Issachar. Each family got its part of the land.

Land for Asher

²⁴The fifth part of land was given to the family group of Asher. Each family in that family group got its part of the land. ²⁵This is the land that was given to that family group: Helkath, Hali, Beten, Acshaph, ²⁶Allammelech, Amad, and Mishal.

The western border continued to Mount Carmel and Shihor Libnath. ²⁷Then the border turned to the east. The border went to Beth Dagon. The border touched Zebulun and the Valley of Iphtah El. Then the border went north of Beth Emek and Neiel. The border passed north of Cabul. ²⁸Then the border went to Abdon,* Rehob, Hammon, and Kanah. The border continued to the Greater Sidon area. ²⁹Then the border went back south to Ramah. The border continued to the strong city of Tyre. Then the border turned and went to Hosah. The border ended at the sea, near Aczib, ³⁰Ummah, Aphek, and Rehob.

In all there were 22 towns and the fields around them. ³¹These cities and the fields around them were given to the family group of Asher. Each family in that family group got its share of the land.

Land for Naphtali

³²The sixth part of land was given to the family group of Naphtali. Each family in that family group got its share of the land. ³³The border of their land started at the large tree near Zaanannim. This is near Heleph. Then the border went through Adami Nekeb and Jabneel. The border continued to Lakkum and ended at the Jordan River. ³⁴Then the border went to the west through Aznoth Tabor. The border stopped at Hukkok. The

Abdon Or, "Ebron."

southern border touched Zebulun and the western border touched Asher. The border went to Judah, at the Jordan River to the east. ³⁵There were some very strong cities inside these borders. Those cities were Ziddim, Zer, Hammath, Rakkath, Kinnereth, ³⁶Adamah, Ramah, Hazor, ³⁷Kedesh, Edrei, En Hazor, ³⁸Iron, Migdal El, Horem, Beth Anath, and Beth Shemesh. In all, there were 19 towns and all the fields around them.

³⁹These cities and the fields around them were given to the family group of Naphtali. Each family in that family group got its land.

Land for Dan

⁴⁰Then land was given to the family group of Dan. Each family in that family group got its land. ⁴¹This is the land that was given to them: Zorah, Eshtaol, Ir Shemesh, ⁴²Shaalabbin, Aijalon, Ithlah, ⁴³Elon, Timnah, Ekron, ⁴⁴Eltekeh, Gibbethon, Baalath, ⁴⁵Jehud, Bene Berak, Gath Rimmon, ⁴⁶Me Jarkon, Rakkon, and the area near Joppa. ⁴⁷But the people of Dan had trouble taking their land. There were strong enemies there and the people of Dan could not easily defeat them. So the people of Dan went ₍to the north part of Israel₎ and fought against Laish.* They defeated Laish and killed the people who lived there. So the people of Dan lived in the town of Laish. They changed the name to Dan because that was the name of the father of their family group. ⁴⁸All of these cities and fields around them were given to the family group of Dan. Each family got its share of the land.

Land for Joshua

⁴⁹So the leaders finished dividing the land and giving it to the different family groups. After they finished, all the people of Israel decided to give Joshua son of Nun some land too. This was land that was promised to him. ⁵⁰The Lord had commanded that he get this land. So they gave Joshua the town of Timnath Serah* in the hill country of Ephraim. This was the town that Joshua told them he wanted. So Joshua built the town stronger and lived there.

⁵¹So all of these lands were given to the different family groups of Israel. Eleazar the priest, Joshua son of Nun, and the leaders of each family group met together at Shiloh to divide the land. They met before the Lord at the entrance of the Meeting Tent.* So they finished dividing the land.

Cities of Safety

20 Then the Lord said to Joshua: ²"I used Moses to give you a command. Moses told you to choose cities to be special cities of safety. ³If any person kills another person, but it is an accident and he did not mean to kill that person, then he can go to a city of safety to hide from the relatives who want to kill him.

⁴"This is what that person must do. When he runs away and goes to one of those cities, he must stop at the entrance of the city. He must stand at the gate and tell the leaders of the people what happened. Then the leaders can allow him to enter the city. They will give him a place to live among them. ⁵But the man who is chasing that person might follow him to that city. If this happens, the leaders of the city must not give him up. They must protect the person who came to them for safety because he killed a person by accident. He was not angry and did not plan to kill the person. It was something that just happened. ⁶That person should stay in the city until he has been judged by the court in that city. And he should stay in that city until the time that the high priest dies. Then he can go back to his own home in the town he ran away from."

⁷So the people of Israel chose some cities to be called "Cities of Safety." These cities were:

> Kedesh in Galilee in the hill country
>   of Naphtali;
> Shechem in the hill country of Ephraim;
> Kiriath Arba (Hebron) in the hill
>   country of Judah.
> ⁸ Bezer on the east side of the Jordan
>   River near Jericho in the desert in
>   the land of Reuben;
> Ramoth in Gilead in the land of Gad;
> Golan in Bashan in the land of Manasseh.

⁹Any Israelite or any foreigner living among them who killed someone accidentally was allowed to run away to one of those cities of safety. Then the person could be safe there and would not be killed by anyone who was chasing him. The person would be judged by the court in that city.

Laish Or, "Leshem."
Timnath Serah Or, "Timnath Heres."
Meeting Tent The Holy Tent (tabernacle) where the people of Israel went to meet with God.

Meeting Tent The Holy Tent (tabernacle) where the people of Israel went to meet with God.

Towns for Priests and Levites

21 ¹The family rulers of the Levite family group went to talk to Eleazar the priest, to Joshua son of Nun, and the rulers of the other family groups of Israel. ²This happened at the town of Shiloh in the land of Canaan. The Levite rulers said to them, "The Lord gave Moses a command. He commanded that you give us towns to live in. And he commanded that you give us fields where our animals can eat." ³So the people of Israel obeyed this command from the Lord. They gave the Levite people these towns and the land around them for their animals:

⁴The Kohath family were descendants of Aaron the priest from the family group of Levi. Part of the Kohath family was given 13 towns in the areas that belonged to Judah, Simeon, and Benjamin.

⁵The other Kohath families were given ten towns in the areas that belonged to Ephraim, Dan, and half of Manasseh.

⁶The people from the Gershon family were given 13 towns. These towns were in the areas that belonged to Issachar, Asher, Naphtali, and the half of Manasseh that was in Bashan.

⁷The people from the Merari family were given twelve towns. These twelve towns came from the areas that belonged to Reuben, Gad, and Zebulun.

⁸So the people of Israel gave the Levite people these towns and the fields around them, just like the Lord had told Moses.

⁹These are the names of the towns that were in the areas that belonged to Judah and Simeon. ¹⁰The first choice of towns was given to Levites from the Kohath family. ¹¹They gave them Kiriath Arba (This is Hebron. It was named for a man named Arba. Arba was the father of Anak.) They also gave them some land near the town for their animals. ¹²But the fields and the small towns around the city of Kiriath Arba belonged to Caleb son of Jephunneh. ¹³So they gave the city of Hebron to Aaron's descendants. (Hebron was a city of safety.) They also gave Aaron's descendants the towns of Libnah, ¹⁴Jattir, Eshtemoa, ¹⁵Holon, Debir, ¹⁶Ain, Juttah, and Beth Shemesh. They also gave them some of the land near these towns for their animals. They gave nine towns to these two groups.

¹⁷They also gave Aaron's descendants cities that belonged to the family group of Benjamin. These cities were Gibeon, Geba, ¹⁸Anathoth, and Almon. They gave them these four towns and some of the land near the towns for their animals. ¹⁹In all, they gave 13 towns to the priests. (All priests were descendants of Aaron.) They also gave them some land near each town for their animals.

²⁰The other people from the Kohathite family were given towns that were in the areas that belonged to the family group of Ephraim. They got these towns: ²¹The city of Shechem from the hill country of Ephraim. (Shechem was a city of safety.) They also got Gezer, ²²Kibzaim, and Beth Horon. In all, Ephraim gave them four towns and some land around each town for their animals.

²³The family group of Dan gave them Eltekeh, Gibbethon, ²⁴Aijalon, and Gath Rimmon. In all, Dan gave them four towns and some land around each town for their animals.

²⁵Half of the family group of Manasseh gave them Taanach and Gath Rimmon. In all, this half of Manasseh gave them two towns and some land around each town for their animals.

²⁶In all, the rest of the people from the Kohath family got ten towns and some land around each town for their animals.

²⁷The Gershon family was also from the family group of Levi. They got these towns:

Half of the family group of Manasseh gave them Golan in Bashan. (Golan was a city of safety.) Manasseh also gave them Be Eshtarah. In all, this half of Manasseh gave them two towns and some land around each town for their animals.

²⁸The family group of Issachar gave them Kishion, Daberath, ²⁹Jarmuth, and En Gannim. In all, Issachar gave them four towns and some land around each town for their animals.

³⁰The family group of Asher gave them Mishal, Abdon, ³¹Helkath, and Rehob. In all, Asher gave them four towns and some land around each town for their animals.

³²The family group of Naphtali gave them Kedesh in Galilee. (Kedesh was a city of safety.) Naphtali also gave them Hammoth Dor and Kartan. In all, Naphtali gave them three towns and some land around each town for their animals.

³³In all, the Gershon family got 13 towns and some land around each town for their animals.

³⁴The other Levite group was the Merari family. The Merari family got these towns:

The family group of Zebulun gave them Jokneam, Kartah, ³⁵Dimnah, and Nahalal. In all, Zebulun gave them four towns and some land around each town for their animals.

³⁶The family group of Reuben gave them Bezer, Jahaz, ³⁷Kedemoth, and Mephaath. In all, Reuben gave them four towns and some land around each town for their animals.

³⁸The family group of Gad gave them Ramoth in Gilead. (Ramoth was a city of safety.) They also gave them Mahanaim, ³⁹Heshbon, and Jazer. In all, Gad gave them four towns and some land around each town for their animals.

⁴⁰In all, the last family of Levites, the Merari family, got twelve towns.

⁴¹So the Levites got a total of 48 towns and some land around each town for their animals. All these towns were in areas that belonged to the other family groups. ⁴²Each of these towns had some land in it for their animals. That was true for every town.

⁴³So the Lord kept the promise that he had made to the people of Israel. He gave the people all the land that he had promised. The people took the land and lived there. ⁴⁴And the Lord allowed them to have peace on all sides of their land, just like he had promised their ancestors.* None of their enemies defeated them. The Lord allowed the people of Israel to defeat every enemy. ⁴⁵The Lord kept every promise that he made to the people of Israel. There were no promises that he failed to keep. Every promise came true.

Three Family Groups Go Home

22 Then Joshua called a meeting of all the people from the family groups of Reuben, Gad, and Manasseh. ²Joshua said to them, "Moses was the Lord's servant. You obeyed all things that Moses told you to do. And also, you obeyed all of my commands. ³And all this time you have supported all the other people of Israel. You carefully obeyed all the commands that the Lord your God gave you. ⁴The Lord your God promised to give the people of Israel peace. And now, the Lord has kept his promise. So now you can go home. The Lord's servant Moses gave you the land on the east side of the Jordan River. Now you can go home to that land. ⁵But remember—continue to obey the law that Moses gave you. You must love the Lord your God and obey his commands. You must continue to follow him and serve him the very best that you can."

⁶Then Joshua said goodbye to them and they left. They went home. ⁷Moses had given the land of Bashan to half of the Manasseh family group. Joshua gave land on the west side of the Jordan River to the other half of the Manasseh family group. Joshua blessed them and sent them home.

⁸He said, "You have become very rich. You have many animals. You have gold and silver and expensive jewelry. You have many beautiful clothes. You have taken many things from your enemies. Divide these things among yourselves and go home."

⁹So the people from the family groups of Reuben, Gad, and Manasseh left the other people of Israel. They were at Shiloh in Canaan. They left that place and went back to Gilead. They went home to their own land—the land that Moses gave them. The Lord had commanded Moses to give them this land.

¹⁰The people of Reuben, Gad, and Manasseh went to the place called Geliloth. This was near the Jordan River in the land of Canaan. At that place the people built a beautiful altar. ¹¹But the other people of Israel that were still at Shiloh heard about the altar that these three family groups built. They heard that the altar was at the border of Canaan at the place called Geliloth. It was near the Jordan River on Israel's side. ¹²All the people of Israel became very angry at these three family groups. They met together and decided to fight against them.

¹³So the people of Israel sent some men to talk to the people of Reuben, Gad, and Manasseh. The leader of these men was Phinehas, son of Eleazar the priest. ¹⁴They also sent ten of the leaders of the family groups there. There was one man from each family group of Israel that was at Shiloh.

¹⁵So these eleven men went to Gilead. They went to talk to the people of Reuben, Gad, and Manasseh. The eleven men said to them, ¹⁶"All the people of Israel ask you: Why did you do this thing against the God of Israel? Why did you turn against the Lord? Why did you build an altar for yourselves? You know that this is against God's teachings! ¹⁷Remember what happened at Peor? We are still suffering because of that sin. Because of that great sin, God caused many of the people of Israel to become very sick. And we are still suffering because of that sickness today. ¹⁸And now you are doing the same thing! You are turning against the Lord! Will you refuse to follow the Lord? If you don't stop what you are doing, the Lord will be angry with every person in Israel.

¹⁹"If your land is not a good enough place to worship, then come over into our land. The Lord's Tent is in our land. You can have some of our land and live there. But don't turn against the Lord. Don't build another altar. We already have the altar of the Lord our God at the Meeting Tent.

---

ancestors Literally, "fathers," meaning a person's parents, grandparents, and all the people they are descended from.

⁂⁰"Remember the man named Achan son of Zerah. He refused to obey the command about things that must be destroyed. That one man broke God's law, but all the people of Israel were punished. Achan died because of his sin. But also many other people died."

²¹The people from the family groups of Reuben, Gad, and Manasseh answered the eleven men. They said, ²²"The Lord is our God! Again we say that the Lord is our God!* And God knows why we did this thing. We want you to know also. You can judge what we did. If you believe that we have done something wrong, then you can kill us. ²³If we broke God's law, then we ask the Lord himself to punish us. ²⁴Do you think we built this altar for burnt offerings, grain offerings and fellowship offerings? No! We did not build it for that reason. Why did we build this altar? We were afraid that in the future your people would not accept us as part of your nation. Then your people would say that we can't worship the Lord God of Israel. ²⁵God gave us land on the other side of the Jordan River. This means that the Jordan River separates us. We were afraid that when your children grew up and ruled your land, they would not remember that we were also your people. They would say to us, 'You people of Reuben and Gad aren't part of Israel!' Then your children would make our children stop worshiping the Lord.

²⁶"So we decided to build this altar. But we did not plan to use it for burning offerings and sacrifices. ²⁷The real reason we wanted our altar was to show our people that we worship the same God as you. This altar will be the proof to you and to us and to all our future children that we worship the Lord. We give our sacrifices, grain offerings and fellowship offerings to the Lord. We wanted your children to grow up and know that we are also people of Israel like yourselves. ²⁸In the future, if it happens that your children say that we do not belong to Israel, then our children can say, 'Look! Our fathers who lived before us made an altar. That altar is exactly like the Lord's altar [at the Holy Tent]. We do not use this altar for sacrifices—this altar is proof that we are part of Israel.'

²⁹"Truly, we do not want to be against the Lord. We don't want to stop following him now.

We know that the only true altar is the one that is in front of the Holy Tent. That altar belongs to the Lord our God."

³⁰Phinehas the priest and the leaders with him heard these things the people from Reuben, Gad, and Manasseh said. They were satisfied that these people were telling the truth. ³¹So Phinehas the priest said, "Now we know that the Lord is with us. And we know that you did not turn against him. We are happy that the people of Israel will not be punished by the Lord."

³²Then Phinehas and the leaders left that place and went home. They left the people of Reuben and Gad in the land of Gilead and went back to Canaan. They went back to the people of Israel and told them what happened. ³³The people of Israel were also satisfied. They were happy and thanked God. They decided not to go and fight against the people of Reuben, Gad, and Manasseh. They decided not to destroy the land where those people live.

³⁴The people of Reuben, and Gad gave the altar a name. They called it, "Proof That We Believe the Lord is God."

Joshua Encourages the People

23 The Lord gave Israel peace from their enemies around them. The Lord made Israel safe. Many years passed, and Joshua became very old. ²At this time, Joshua called a meeting of all the older leaders, heads of families, judges, and officers of the people of Israel. Joshua said, "I have grown very old. ³You have seen the things that the Lord did to our enemies. He did this to help us. The Lord your God fought for you. ⁴Remember that I told you your people could have that land between the Jordan River and the Mediterranean Sea in the west. I promised to give you that land, but you don't control it yet. ⁵But the Lord your God will force the people living there to leave. You will take that land. The Lord will force the people living there to leave! The Lord your God promised to do this for you.

⁶"You must be careful to obey all the things the Lord has commanded us. Obey everything that is written in the book of the Law of Moses. Don't turn away from that law. ⁷There are still some people living among us that are not people of Israel. Those people worship their own gods. Don't become friends with those people. Don't serve or worship their gods. ⁸You must continue to follow the Lord your God. You have done this in the past, and you must continue to do it.

The Lord is ... our God Or, "Yahweh is the true God! Yahweh is the true God!" Literally, "El Elohim Yahweh! El Elohim Yahweh."

⁹"The Lord helped you to defeat many great and powerful nations. The Lord forced those people to leave. No nation has been able to defeat you. ¹⁰With the Lord's help, one man from Israel could defeat 1,000 enemy soldiers. Why? Because the Lord your God fights for you. The Lord promised to do this. ¹¹So you must continue to love the Lord your God.

¹²"Don't stop following the Lord. Don't become friends with these other people that are not part of Israel. Don't marry any of their people. But if you do become friends with these people, ¹³then the Lord your God will not help you to defeat your enemies. These people will become like a trap for you. They will cause you pain—like smoke and dust in your eyes. And you will be forced to leave this good land. The Lord your God gave you this land. But you can lose it if you don't obey this command.

¹⁴"It is almost time for me to die. You know and truly believe that the Lord has done many great things for you. You know that he has not failed in any of his promises. The Lord has kept every promise that he has made to us. ¹⁵Every good promise that the Lord your God made to us has come true. But in the same way, the Lord will make his other promise come true. He promised that if you do wrong, then bad things will happen to you. He promised that he will force you to leave this good land that he gave you. ¹⁶This will happen if you refuse to keep your agreement with the Lord your God. You will lose this land if you go and serve other gods. You must not worship those other gods. If you do, the Lord will become very angry at you. Then you will quickly be forced to leave this good land that he gave you."

Joshua Says Goodbye

24 Joshua called all the family groups of Israel to meet together at Shechem. Then Joshua called the older leaders, the heads of the families, the judges, and the officers and the rulers and the judges of Israel. These men stood before God.

²Then Joshua spoke to all the people. He said, "I am telling you what the Lord, the God of Israel, says to you:

A long time ago, your ancestors lived on the other side of the Euphrates River. I am talking about men like Terah, the father of Abraham and Nahor. At that time, those men worshiped other gods. ³But I, the Lord, took your father Abraham out of the land on the other side of the River. I led him through the land of Canaan and gave him many, many children. I gave Abraham his son named Isaac. ⁴And I gave Isaac two sons named Jacob and Esau. To Esau, I gave the land around the mountains of Seir. Jacob and his sons did not live there. They went to live in the land of Egypt.

⁵Then I sent Moses and Aaron to Egypt. I wanted them to bring my people out of Egypt. I caused many terrible things to happen to the people of Egypt. Then I brought your people out of Egypt. ⁶So I brought your ancestors out of Egypt. They came to the Red Sea, and the men of Egypt were chasing them. There were chariots and men on horses. ⁷So the people asked me, the Lord, for help. And I caused great trouble to come to the men of Egypt. I, the Lord, caused the sea to cover them. You yourselves saw what I did to the army of Egypt.

After that, you lived in the desert for a long time. ⁸Then I brought you to the land of the Amorite people. This was east of the Jordan River. Those people fought against you, but I allowed you to defeat them. I gave you the power to destroy those people. Then you took control of that land.

⁹Then Balak, the son of Zippor, the king of Moab, prepared to fight against the people of Israel. The king sent for Balaam the son of Beor. He asked Balaam to curse* you. ¹⁰But I, the Lord, refused to listen to Balaam. So Balaam asked for good things to happen to you! He blessed you many times. I saved you and brought you out of trouble.

¹¹Then you went across the Jordan River to the city of Jericho. The people in Jericho fought against you. Also, the Amorite people, the Perizzite people, the Canaanite people, the Hittite people, the Girgashite people, the Hivite people, and the Jebusite people fought against you. But I allowed you to defeat all of them. ¹²While your army traveled forward, I sent hornet* ahead of them. These hornets made the people leave. So you took the land without using your swords and bows.

¹³I, the Lord, gave that land to you! You didn't work for that land—I gave it to you! You did not build those cities—I gave them

---

curse To ask for bad things to happen to someone.
hornet A stinging insect, like a large wasp or bee. Here, it might mean God's angel or his great power.

to you! And now you live in that land and in those cities. You have gardens of grapevines and olive trees, but you did not have to plant those gardens. ¹⁴Then Joshua said to the people, "Now you have heard the Lord's words. So you must respect the Lord and truly serve him. Throw away the false gods that your ancestors worshiped. That was something that happened a long time ago on the other side of the Euphrates River and in Egypt. Now you must serve only the Lord.

¹⁵"But maybe you don't want to serve the Lord. You must choose for yourselves today. Today you must decide who you will serve. Will you serve the gods that your ancestors worshiped when they lived on the other side of the Euphrates River? Or will you serve the gods of the Amorite people that lived in this land? You must choose for yourselves. But as for me and my family, we will serve the Lord!"

¹⁶Then the people answered, "We will never stop following the Lord. We will never serve other gods! ¹⁷We know that it was the Lord God who brought our people out of Egypt. We were slaves in that land. But the Lord did great things for us there. He brought us out of that land and protected us while we traveled through other lands. ¹⁸The Lord helped us to defeat the people living in these lands. The Lord helped us to defeat the Amorite people who lived in this land where we are now. So we will continue to serve the Lord. Why? Because he is our God."

¹⁹Then Joshua said, "[That is not true.] You will not be able to continue serving the Lord. The Lord God is holy. And God hates his people worshiping other gods. God will not forgive you if you turn against him like that. ²⁰But you will leave the Lord and serve other gods. And the Lord will cause terrible things to happen to you. The Lord will destroy you. The Lord God has been good to you, but if you turn against him he will destroy you."

²¹But the people said to Joshua, "No! We will serve the Lord."

²²Then Joshua said, "Look around at yourselves and the people with you here. Do you all know and agree that you have chosen to serve the Lord? Are you all witnesses to this?"

The people answered, "Yes, it is true! We all see that we have chosen to serve the Lord."

²³Then Joshua said, "So throw away the false gods that you have among you. Love the Lord the God of Israel with all your heart."

²⁴Then the people said to Joshua, "We will serve the Lord our God. We will obey him."

²⁵So that day Joshua made an agreement for the people. Joshua made this agreement at the town called Shechem. It became a law for them to follow. ²⁶Joshua wrote these things in the book of the Law of God. Then Joshua found a large stone. [This stone was proof of this agreement.] He put the stone under the oak tree near the Lord's Holy Tent.

²⁷Then Joshua said to all the people, "This stone will help you remember the things we said today. This stone was here when the Lord was speaking to us today. So this stone will be something that helps you remember what happened today. The stone will be a witness against you. It will stop you from turning against the Lord your God."

²⁸Then Joshua told the people to go home. So every person went back to his own land.

Joshua Dies

²⁹After that Joshua son of Nun died. Joshua was 110 years old. ³⁰Joshua was buried on his own land at Timnath Serah. This was in the hill country of Ephraim north of Mount Gaash.

³¹The people of Israel had served the Lord during the time Joshua was living. And after Joshua died, the people continued to serve the Lord. The people continued to serve the Lord while their leaders were alive. These were the leaders that had seen the things that the Lord had done for Israel.

Joseph Comes Home

³²When the people of Israel left Egypt, they carried the bones from the body of Joseph with them. So the people buried the bones of Joseph at Shechem. They buried the bones on the land that Jacob had bought from the sons of Hamor, the father of the man named Shechem. Jacob had bought that land for 100 pieces of pure silver. This land belonged to Joseph's children.

³³Aaron's son, Eleazar, died and was buried at Gibeah in the hill country of Ephraim. Gibeah had been given to Eleazar's son Phinehas.

Judges

Judah Fights the Canaanites

1 Joshua died. Then the people of Israel prayed to the Lord. They said, "Which of our family groups should be the first to go and fight for us against the Canaanite people?"

² The Lord said to the Israelite people, "The family group of Judah will go. I will let them take this land."

³ The men of Judah asked for help from their brothers from the family group of Simeon. The men of Judah said, "Brothers, the Lord promised to give each of us some land. If you will come and help us fight for our land, then we will go and help you fight for your land." The men of Simeon agreed to help their brothers from Judah fight.

⁴ The Lord helped the men of Judah defeat the Canaanites and the Perizzites. The men of Judah killed 10,000 men at the city of Bezek. ⁵ In the city of Bezek the men of Judah found the ruler of Bezek* and fought him. The men of Judah defeated the Canaanites and the Perizzites.

⁶ The ruler of Bezek* tried to escape. But the men of Judah chased him and caught him. When they caught him, they cut off his thumbs and big toes. ⁷Then the ruler of Bezek said, "I cut the thumbs and big toes off of 70 kings. And those kings had to eat pieces of food that fell from my table. Now God has paid me back for the things I did to those kings." The men of Judah took the ruler of Bezek to Jerusalem and he died there.

⁸The men of Judah fought against Jerusalem and captured it. The men of Judah used their swords to kill the people of Jerusalem. Then they burned the city. ⁹Later, the men of Judah went down to fight against some more Canaanites. Those Canaanites lived in the hill country, in the Negev,* and in the western foothills.

¹⁰Then the men of Judah went to fight against the Canaanite people that lived in the city of Hebron. (Hebron used to be called Kiriath Arba.) The men of Judah defeated the men named Sheshai, Ahiman, and Talmai.*

Caleb and His Daughter

¹¹The men of Judah left that place. They went to the city of Debir to fight against the people there. (In the past, Debir was called Kiriath Sepher.) ¹²Before the men of Judah started to fight, Caleb made a promise to the men. Caleb said, "I want to attack Kiriath Sepher. I will give my daughter Acsah to the man that attacks and captures that city. I will let that man marry my daughter."

¹³Caleb had a younger brother named Kenaz. Kenaz had a son named Othniel. Othniel captured the city of Kiriath Sepher. So Caleb gave his daughter Acsah to Othniel to be his wife.

¹⁴Acsah went to live with Othniel. Othniel told Acsah* to ask her father for some land. [Acsah went to her father.] When she got off her donkey, Caleb asked her, "What is wrong?"

¹⁵Acsah answered Caleb, "Give me a blessing.* You gave me dry desert land in the Negev.* Please give me some land with water on it." So Caleb gave her what she wanted. He gave her the upper and lower pools of water in that land.

¹⁶The Kenite people left the City of Palm Trees (Jericho) and went with the men of Judah. Those people went to the Desert of Judah to live with the people there. This was in the Negev* near the city Arad. (The Kenite people were from the family of Moses' father-in-law.)

¹⁷Some Canaanite people lived in the city of Zephath. So the men of Judah and men from the family group of Simeon attacked those Canaanite

---

Sheshai, Ahiman, Talmai Three sons of a man named Anak. They were giants. See Num. 13:22.
Othniel told Acsah Or, "Acsah told Othniel."
Give me a blessing Or, "Please welcome me." Or, "Give me a stream of water."

ruler of Bezek Or, "Adoni Bezek."
Negev The desert area south of Judah.

people. They completely destroyed the city. So they named the city Hormah.*

¹⁸The men of Judah also captured the city of Gaza and the small towns around it. The men of Judah also captured the cities of Ashkelon and Ekron and all the small towns around them.

¹⁹The Lord was on the side of the men of Judah when they fought. They took the land in the hill country. But the men of Judah failed to take the land in the valleys, because the people living there had iron chariots.*

²⁰Moses had promised to give the land near Hebron to Caleb. So that land was given to Caleb's family. The men of Caleb forced the three sons of Anak* to leave that place.

The Men of Benjamin Settle in Jerusalem

²¹The family group of Benjamin could not force the Jebusite people to leave Jerusalem. So even today, the Jebusite people live with the people of Benjamin in Jerusalem.

The Men of Joseph Capture Bethel

²²⁻²³Men from the family group of Joseph went to fight against the city of Bethel. (In the past, Bethel was named Luz.) The Lord was on the side of the men from the family group of Joseph. The men from the family group of Joseph sent some spies to the city of Bethel. ₍These men looked for ways to defeat the city of Bethel.₎ ²⁴While the spies were watching the city of Bethel, they saw a man come out of the city. The spies said to the man, "Show us a secret way into the city. We will attack the city. But if you help us, we will not hurt you."

²⁵The man showed the spies the secret way into the city. The men of Joseph used their swords to kill the people of Bethel. But they did not hurt the man that helped them. And they did not hurt the people in his family. That man and his family were allowed to go free. ²⁶That man then went to the land where the Hittite people lived and built a city. He named the city Luz. And that city is still called Luz today.

The Other Family Groups Fight the Canaanites

²⁷There were Canaanite people living in the cities of Beth Shean, Taanach, Dor, Ibleam, Megiddo, and the small towns around those cities. The people from the family group of Manasseh could not force those people to leave those towns. So the Canaanite people stayed. They refused to leave their homes. ²⁸Later the people of Israel grew stronger and forced the Canaanite people to work as slaves for them. But the people of Israel could not force all of the Canaanite people to leave their land.

²⁹₍The same thing happened with the people from the family group of Ephraim.₎ There were Canaanite people living in Gezer. And the people of Ephraim did not make all of those Canaanite people leave their land. So the Canaanite people continued to live in Gezer with the people of Ephraim.

³⁰₍The same thing happened with the people from the family group of Zebulun.₎ Some Canaanite people lived in the cities of Kitron and Nahalol. The people of Zebulun did not force those people to leave their land. Those Canaanite people stayed and lived with the people of Zebulun. But the people of Zebulun made those people work for them as slaves.

³¹₍The same thing happened with the people from the family group of Asher.₎ The people of Asher did not force the other people to leave the cities of Acco, Sidon, Ahlab, Aczib, Helbah, Aphek, and Rehob. ³²The people of Asher did not force those Canaanite people to leave their land. So the Canaanite people continued to live with the people of Asher.

³³₍The same thing happened with the people from the family group of Naphtali.₎ The people of Naphtali did not force the people to leave the cities of Beth Shemesh and Beth Anath. So the people of Naphtali continued to live with the people in those cities. Those Canaanite people worked as slaves for the people of Naphtali.

³⁴The Amorite people forced the people of the family group of Dan to live in the hill country. They had to stay in the hills because the Amorite people would not let them come down to live in the valleys. ³⁵The Amorite people decided to stay in Mount Heres, Aijalon, and Shaalbim. Later, the family group of Joseph grew stronger. Then they made the Amorite people work as slaves for them. ³⁶The land of the Amorite people was from Scorpion Pass to Sela and up into the hill country past Sela.

Hormah This name means "completely destroyed."
iron chariots Small wagons used in war. They were faster and could carry more weapons than soldiers on foot.
three sons of Anak Sheshai, Ahiman, and Talmai, mentioned above in verse 10.

The Angel of the Lord at Bokim

2 The Angel of the Lord went up to the city of Bokim from the city of Gilgal. The angel spoke a message from the Lord to the people of Israel. This was the message: "I brought you out of Egypt. I led you to the land that I promised to give to your ancestors.* I told you I would never break my agreement with you. ²But in return, you must never make any agreement with the people living in that land. You must destroy their altars.* I told you that. But you didn't obey me!

³"Now I will tell you this, 'I will not force the other people to leave this land any longer. These people will become a problem for you. They will be like a trap to you. Their false gods will become like a net to trap you.'"

⁴After the angel gave the people of Israel this message from the Lord, the people cried loudly. ⁵So the people of Israel named the place where they cried, Bokim.* At Bokim the people of Israel offered sacrifices to the Lord.

Disobedience and Defeat

⁶Then Joshua told the people to go home. So each family group went to take their area of land to live in it. ⁷The people of Israel served the Lord as long as Joshua was alive. They continued serving the Lord during the lifetimes of the elders (leaders) that lived after Joshua had died. These old men had seen all the great things the Lord had done for the people of Israel. ⁸Joshua son of Nun, the servant of the Lord, died at the age of 110 years. ⁹The people of Israel buried Joshua. They buried Joshua on the land that he had been given. That was at Timnath Heres, in the hill country of Ephraim, north of Mount Gaash.

¹⁰After that whole generation died, the next generation grew up. This new generation did not know about the Lord and what the Lord had done for the people of Israel. ¹¹So the people of Israel did evil and served the false god Baal.* The Lord saw the people doing this evil thing. ¹²The Lord had brought the people of Israel out of Egypt. And the ancestors* of these people had worshiped the Lord. But the people of Israel quit following the Lord. The people of Israel began to worship the false gods of the people living around them. That made the Lord angry. ¹³The people of Israel quit following the Lord and began worshiping Baal and Ashtoreth.*

¹⁴The Lord was angry with the people of Israel. So the Lord let enemies attack the people of Israel and take their possessions. The Lord let their enemies that lived around them defeat them. The people of Israel could not protect themselves from their enemies. ¹⁵When the people of Israel went out to fight, they always lost. They lost because the Lord was not on their side. The Lord had already warned the people of Israel that they would lose if they served the gods of the people living around them. The people of Israel suffered very much.

¹⁶Then the Lord chose leaders called judges. These leaders saved the people of Israel from the enemies that took their possessions. ¹⁷But the people of Israel did not listen to their judges. The people of Israel were not faithful to God—they followed other gods.* In the past, the ancestors* of the people of Israel obeyed the Lord's commands. But now the people of Israel changed and stopped obeying the Lord.

¹⁸Many times the enemies of Israel did bad things to the people. So the people of Israel would cry for help. And each time, the Lord felt sorry for the people. Each time he sent a judge to save the people from their enemies. The Lord was always with those judges. So each time, the people of Israel were saved from their enemies. ¹⁹But when each judge died, the people of Israel again sinned and started worshiping the false gods. The people of Israel were very stubborn—they refused to change their evil ways.

²⁰So the Lord became angry with the people of Israel, and he said, "This nation has broken the Agreement that I made with their ancestors.* They have not listened to me. ²¹So I will no longer defeat the nations and clear the way for the people of Israel. Those nations were still in this land when Joshua died. And I will let those nations stay in this land. ²²I will use those nations to test the people of Israel. I will see if the people of Israel can keep the Lord's commands like their

---

ancestors Literally, "fathers," meaning a person's parents, grandparents, and all the people they are descended from.

altar(s) A stone table used for burning sacrifices that were offered as gifts to God.

Bokim This name means "People crying."

Baal The Canaanite people believed that this false god brought the rain and storms. They also thought that he made the land produce good crops.

Ashtoreth The Canaanite people thought that this false goddess could make people able to have babies. She was their goddess of love and war.

were not faithful ... other gods Literally, "acted like a prostitute to other gods."

ancestors did." ²³The Lord allowed those nations to stay in the land. The Lord did not force those nations to quickly leave the country. He did not help Joshua's army defeat them.

3 ¹⁻²The Lord did not force all the people of those other nations to leave Israel's land. The Lord wanted to test the people of Israel. None of the people of Israel living at this time had fought in the wars to take the land of Canaan. So the Lord let those other nations stay in their country. (The Lord did this to teach the people of Israel that had not fought in those wars.) Here are the names of the nations the Lord left in the land: ³the five rulers of the Philistine people, all of the Canaanite people, the people of Sidon, and the Hivite people that lived in the Lebanon mountains from Mount Baal Hermon to Lebo Hamath. ⁴The Lord left those nations in the land to test the people of Israel. He wanted to see if the people of Israel would obey the Lord's commands that he had given to their ancestors* through Moses.

⁵The people of Israel lived with the Canaanite people, the Hittite people, the Amorite people, the Perizzite people, the Hivite people, and the Jebusite people. ⁶The people of Israel began to marry the daughters of those people. The people of Israel allowed their own daughters to marry the sons of those people. And the people of Israel began to worship the gods of those people.

Othniel, the First Judge

⁷The Lord saw that the people of Israel did evil things. The people of Israel forgot about the Lord their God and served the false gods Baal* and Asherah.* ⁸The Lord was angry with the people of Israel. The Lord allowed Cushan Rishathaim, the king of Aram Naharaim* to defeat the people of Israel and to rule over them. The people of Israel were under that king's rule for eight years. ⁹But the people of Israel cried to the Lord for help. The Lord sent a man to save them. That man's name was Othniel. He was the son of a man named Kenaz. Kenaz was Caleb's younger brother. Othniel saved the people of Israel. ¹⁰The Spirit of the Lord came on Othniel and he became a judge for the people of Israel. Othniel led the people of Israel to war. The Lord helped Othniel defeat Cushan Rishathaim, the king of Aram. ¹¹So the land was at peace for 40 years, until Othniel son of Kenaz died.

Ehud, the Judge

¹²Again the Lord saw the people of Israel do evil things. So the Lord gave Eglon king of Moab power to defeat the people of Israel. ¹³Eglon got help from the Ammonite people and the Amalekite people. They joined him and attacked the people of Israel. Eglon and his army defeated the people of Israel and forced them to leave the City of Palm Trees *(Jericho)*. ¹⁴Eglon king of Moab ruled over the people of Israel for 18 years.

¹⁵The people cried to the Lord. The Lord sent a man to save the people of Israel. This man's name was Ehud. Ehud was the son of a man named Gera from the family group of Benjamin. Ehud was left-handed. The people of Israel sent Ehud with a gift to Eglon king of Moab. ¹⁶Ehud made a sword for himself. That sword had two sharp edges and was about 18 inches* long. Ehud tied the sword to his right thigh and hid it under his clothes.

¹⁷So Ehud brought the gift to Eglon king of Moab. (Eglon was a very fat man.) ¹⁸After offering the gift, he sent away the men that had carried the gift. ¹⁹When ₁Eglon₁ returned from the statues of the gods of Gilgal, Ehud said to Eglon, "King, I have a secret message for you."

The king told him to be quiet and then sent all of the servants out of the room. ²⁰Ehud went to King Eglon. Eglon was now sitting all alone in the room on the top of his summer palace.*

Then Ehud said, "I have a message from God for you." The king stood up from his throne, he was very close to Ehud. ²¹As the king stood up from his throne,* Ehud reached with his left hand and took out the sword that was tied to his right thigh. Then Ehud pushed the sword into the king's belly. ²²The sword went into Eglon's belly so far that even the handle sank in. The king's fat

---

ancestors Literally, "fathers." This means a person's parents, grandparents, and all the people they are descended from.
Baal The Canaanite people believed that this false god brought the rain and storms. They also thought that he made the land produce good crops.
Asherah An important Canaanite goddess. The people thought she was the wife of El or the lover of Baal.
Aram Naharaim The area in Northern Syria between the Tigris and Euphrates rivers.

18 inches Literally, "1 cubit."
palace A large house for the king and his family.
he ... throne This section of the text is found in the ancient Greek translation, but it is not in the Hebrew text.

covered the whole sword. So Ehud left the sword in Eglon. ²³Ehud went out of the room and closed and locked the doors behind him.

²⁴The servants came back just after Ehud left. The servants found the doors to the room locked. So the servants said, "The king must be relieving himself in his restroom." ²⁵So the servants waited for a long time. Finally they became worried. They got the key and unlocked the doors. When the servants entered, they saw their king lying on the floor dead.

²⁶While the servants were waiting for the king, Ehud had time to escape. Ehud passed by the idols and went toward the place named Seirah. ²⁷Ehud arrived at the place named Seirah. Then he blew a trumpet there in the hill country of Ephraim. The people of Israel heard the trumpet and went down from the hills, with Ehud leading them. ²⁸Ehud said to the people of Israel, "Follow me! The Lord has helped us to defeat our enemies, the people of Moab."

So the people of Israel followed Ehud. They followed Ehud down to take control of the places where the Jordan River could easily be crossed. Those places led to the land of Moab. The people of Israel did not allow any one to go across the Jordan River. ²⁹The people of Israel killed about 10,000 strong and brave men from Moab. Not one Moabite man escaped. ³⁰So on that day the people of Israel began to rule over the people of Moab. And there was peace in the land for 80 years.

Shamgar, the Judge

³¹After Ehud saved the people of Israel, another man saved Israel. That man's name was Shamgar son of Anath.* Shamgar used an oxgoad* to kill 600 Philistine men.

Deborah, the Woman Judge

4 After Ehud died, the people again did the things the Lord said are evil. ²So the Lord allowed Jabin king of Canaan to defeat the people of Israel. Jabin ruled in a city named Hazor. A man named Sisera was the commander of King Jabin's army. Sisera lived in a town called Harosheth Haggoyim. ³Sisera had 900 iron chariots, and he was very cruel to the people of Israel for 20 years. So they cried to the Lord for help.

⁴There was a woman prophet named Deborah. She was the wife of a man named Lappidoth. She was judge of Israel at that time. ⁵One day, Deborah was sitting under the Palm Tree of Deborah. And the people of Israel came up to her to ask her what to do about Sisera. The Palm Tree of Deborah is between the cities of Ramah and Bethel, in the hill country of Ephraim. ⁶Deborah sent a message to a man named Barak. She asked him to come to meet with her. Barak was the son of a man named Abinoam. Barak lived in the city of Kedesh, which is in the area of Naphtali. Deborah said to Barak, "The Lord God of Israel commands you: 'Go and gather 10,000 men from the family groups of Naphtali and Zebulun. Lead those men to Mount Tabor. ⁷I will make Sisera, the commander of King Jabin's army, come to you. I will make Sisera, his chariots and his army come to the Kishon River.* I will help you to defeat Sisera there.'"

⁸Then Barak said to Deborah, "I will go and do this if you will go with me. But if you will not go with me, then I won't go."

⁹"Of course I will go with you," Deborah answered. "But because of your attitude, you will not be honored when Sisera is defeated. The Lord will allow a woman to defeat Sisera."

So Deborah went with Barak to the city of Kedesh. ¹⁰At the city of Kedesh, Barak called the family groups of Zebulun and Naphtali together. Barak gathered 10,000 men to follow him from those family groups. Deborah also went with Barak.

¹¹Now there was a man named Heber, that was from the Kenite people. Heber had left the other Kenite people. (The Kenite people were descendants* of Hobab. Hobab was Moses' father-in-law.*) Heber had made his home by the oak tree in a place named Zaanannim. Zaanannim is near the city of Kedesh.

¹²Someone told Sisera that Barak son of Abinoam was at Mount Tabor. ¹³So Sisera got together his 900 iron chariots. Sisera also got together all the men with him. They marched from

---

Anath The Canaanite goddess of war. Here this might be Shamgar's father or mother or it might mean, "Shamgar the great soldier" or "Shamgar from the town of Anath."
oxgoad A sharp stick used to make cattle go the right way.

Kishon River A river about ten miles from Mount Tabor.
descendant(s) A person's children and their future families.
father-in-law Or possibly, "son-in-law."

the city of Harosheth Haggoyim to the Kishon River. ¹⁴Then Deborah said to Barak, "Today the Lord will help you defeat Sisera. Surely you know that the Lord has already cleared the way for you." So Barak led the 10,000 men down from Mount Tabor. ¹⁵Barak and his men attacked Sisera. During the battle, the Lord confused Sisera and his army and chariots. They did not know what to do. So Barak and his men defeated Sisera's army. But Sisera left his chariot and ran away on foot. ¹⁶Barak continued fighting Sisera's army. Barak and his men chased Sisera's chariots and army all the way to Harosheth Haggoyim. Barak and his men used their swords to kill all of Sisera's men. Not one of Sisera's men was left alive.

¹⁷But Sisera ran away. He came to the tent where a woman named Jael lived. Jael was the wife of a man named Heber. He was one of the Kenite people. Heber's family was at peace with Jabin king of Hazor. So Sisera ran to Jael's tent. ¹⁸Jael saw Sisera coming, so she went out to meet him. Jael said to Sisera, "Sir, come into my tent. Come in. Don't be afraid." So Sisera went into Jael's tent, and she covered him with a carpet.

¹⁹Sisera said to Jael, "I am thirsty. Please give me a little water to drink." Jael had a bottle made from animal skin. She kept milk in that bottle. Jael gave Sisera a drink of that milk. Then she covered Sisera up.

²⁰Then Sisera said to Jael, "Go stand at the entrance to the tent. If someone comes by and asks you, 'Is anyone in there?', tell him, 'No.'"

²¹But Jael found a tent peg and a hammer. Jael quietly went to Sisera. Sisera was very tired, so he was sleeping. Jael put the tent peg to the side of Sisera's head and hit it with a hammer. The tent peg went through the side of Sisera's head and into the ground! Sisera died.

²²Just then Barak came by Jael's tent, looking for Sisera. Jael went out to meet Barak and said, "Come in here, and I will show you the man that you are looking for." So Barak entered the tent with Jael. There Barak found Sisera lying dead on the ground, with the tent peg through the side of his head.

²³On that day God defeated Jabin king of Canaan for the people of Israel. ²⁴So the people of Israel became stronger and stronger until they defeated Jabin king of Canaan. The people of Israel finally destroyed Jabin king of Canaan.

The Song of Deborah

5 On the day that the people of Israel defeated Sisera, Deborah and Barak son of Abinoam sang this song:*

2 The men of Israel prepared for battle.*
   They volunteered to go to war!
   Bless the Lord!

3 Listen, kings.
   Pay attention, rulers.
   I will sing.
   I myself will sing to the Lord.
   I will make music to the Lord,
   to the God of the people of Israel.

4 Lord, in the past you came from Seir.*
   You marched from the land of Edom.*
   You marched and the earth shook.
   The skies rained.
   The clouds dropped water.

5 The mountains shook
   before the Lord, the God of
   Mount Sinai,
   before the Lord, the God of Israel!

6 In the days of Shamgar son of Anath,*
   and in the days of Jael,
   the main roads were empty.
   Caravans* and travelers
   traveled on the back roads.

7 There were no soldiers.
   There were no soldiers in Israel
   until you came, Deborah,
   until you came to be a mother to Israel.*

Chapter 5 This is a very old song and many of the lines are hard to understand in the original language.

prepared ... battle This might also mean "When leaders led in Israel," or "When men wore long hair in Israel." Soldiers often dedicated their hair as a special gift to God.

Seir Another name for the land of Edom.

Edom This land was south and east of Israel.

Shamgar son of Anath A judge of Israel. See Judges 3:31.

Caravans Groups of traders. Usually many traders traveled together with their things packed on donkeys or camels.

until you came ... to Israel Or, "until I came, Deborah, until I came, mother of Israel." Or, "until I established you, Deborah, until I established you, mother of Israel."

⁸ God chose new ₗleadersⱼ
   to fight at the city gates.*
   No one could find a shield or a spear
   among the 40,000 soldiers of Israel.

⁹ My heart is with the commanders of Israel
   who volunteered to go to war!
   Bless the Lord!

¹⁰ Pay attention you people
   riding on white donkeys,
   sitting on saddle blankets,*
   and walking along the road!

¹¹ At the watering holes for the animals,
   we hear the music of cymbals.
   People sing about
   the victories of the Lord,
   the victories of his soldiers in Israel
   when the Lord's people fought
   at the city gates ₗand wonⱼ!

¹² Wake up, wake up, Deborah!
   Wake up, wake up, sing the song!
   Get up, Barak!
   Go capture your enemies, son of Abinoam!

¹³ Now, survivors, go to the leaders.
   People of the Lord, come with me and
   the soldiers.

¹⁴ The men of Ephraim came
   from the hill country of Amalek.*
   Benjamin, those men followed you
   and your people.
   And there were commanders
   from the family of Makir.*
   Leaders from the family group of Zebulun
   came with their bronze clubs.

¹⁵ The leaders of Issachar were with Deborah.
   The family of Issachar was true to Barak.
   Those men marched to the valley on foot.

   Reuben, there are many brave soldiers
   in your army groups.
¹⁶ So why did you sit there
   against the walls of your sheep pens.*?

   The brave soldiers of Reuben
   thought hard about war.
   But they stayed home
   listening to the music
   they played for their sheep.

¹⁷ The people of Gilead* stayed in their camps
   on the other side of the Jordan River.
   As for you, people of Dan,
   why did you stay by your ships?
   The people of Asher stayed by the seashore.
   They camped by their safe harbors.

¹⁸ But the men of Zebulun and Naphtali
   risked their lives fighting on those hills.

¹⁹ The kings of Canaan came to fight,
   but they didn't carry any treasures home!
   They fought
   at the city of Taanach,
   by the waters of Megiddo.

²⁰ The stars fought ₗagainst themⱼ from heaven.
   From their paths ₗacross the skyⱼ,
   they fought against Sisera.

²¹ The Kishon River, that ancient river,
   swept Sisera's men away.
   My soul, march on with strength!*

²² The horses' hooves hammered the ground.
   Sisera's mighty horses ran and ran.

²³ The Angel of the Lord said,
   "Curse the city of Meroz.
      Curse its people!
   They did not come with soldiers
   to help the Lord."

²⁴ Jael was the wife of Heber the Kenite.
   She will be blessed above all women.

²⁵ Sisera asked for water.
   Jael gave him milk.
   In a bowl fit for a ruler,
   she brought him cream.

²⁶ Then Jael reached out
   and took the tent peg.
   Her right hand reached for the hammer
   that a worker would use.
   Then she used the hammer on Sisera!
   She hit him on the head
   and made a hole through his temple!

God chose ... city gates Or, "They chose to follow new gods. So they had to fight at their city gates." The Hebrew here is hard to understand."

saddle blankets We are not sure of the meaning of this Hebrew word.

hill country of Amalek The area settled by the family group of Ephraim. See Judges 12:15.

Makir This family was part of the family group of Manasseh that settled in the area east of the Jordan River.

walls of the sheep pen Or, "campfires" or "saddlebags."

Gilead These people lived in the area east of the Jordan River.

My soul, march on with strength Or, with some changes it could be, "His mighty charging horses marched forward."

27 He sank between Jael's feet.
   He fell.
   And there he lay.
   He sank between her feet.
   He fell.
   Where Sisera sank,
      there he fell.
   And there he lay, dead!

28 There is Sisera's mother,
      looking out the window,
      looking through the curtains
      and cying.
   "Why is Sisera's chariot so late?
   Why can't I hear his wagons yet?"

29 Her wisest servant girl answers her,
   Yes, the servant gives her an answer:
30 "I'm sure they won the war
   and they are now taking things
      from the people they defeated!
   They are dividing those things
      among themselves!
   Each soldier is taking a girl or two.
   Maybe Sisera found a piece of dyed cloth.
   That's it!Sisera found a piece of fancy cloth
      —or maybe two—
      for Sisera the Conqueror to wear."

31 May all of your enemies die this way, Lord!
   And may all the people who love you
      be strong like the rising sun!

So there was peace in the land for 40 years.

The Midianites Fight Israel

6 Again the people of Israel did things the Lord said were evil. So for seven years the Lord allowed the people of Midian to defeat the people of Israel.

²The people of Midian were very powerful and were cruel to the people of Israel. So the people of Israel made many hiding places in the mountains. They hid their food in caves and places that were hard to find. ³They did that because the Midianite and Amalekite people from the east always came and destroyed their crops. ⁴Those people camped in the land and destroyed the crops that the people of Israel had planted. Those people ruined the crops of the people of Israel as far as the land near the city of Gaza. Those people did not leave anything for the people of Israel to eat. They did not even leave them any sheep, or cattle, or donkeys. ⁵The people of Midian came up and camped in the land. They brought their families and their animals with them. They were as many as swarms of locusts! There were so many of those people and their camels that it was not possible to count them. All of these people came into the land and ruined it. ⁶The people of Israel became very poor because of the people of Midian. So the people of Israel cried to the Lord for help.

⁷The people* of Midian did all those bad things. So the people of Israel cried to the Lord for help. ⁸So the Lord sent a prophet to them. The prophet said to the people of Israel, "This is what the Lord, the God of Israel, says: 'You were slaves in the land of Egypt. I made you free and brought you out of that land. ⁹I saved you from the powerful people of Egypt. Then the people of the land of Canaan hurt you. So I again saved you. I made those people leave their land. And I gave their land to you.' ¹⁰Then I said to you, 'I am the Lord your God. You will live in the land of the Amorite people, but you must not worship their false gods.' But you did not obey me."

The Angel of the Lord Visits Gideon

¹¹At that time, the Angel of the Lord came to a man named Gideon. The Angel of the Lord came and sat down under an oak tree at a place called Ophrah. This oak tree belonged to a man named Joash. Joash was from the Abiezer family. Joash was the father of Gideon. Gideon was beating some wheat* in a winepress.* The Angel of the Lord sat down near Gideon. Gideon was hiding so the Midianites could not see the wheat. ¹²The Angel of the Lord appeared to Gideon and said to him, "The Lord be with you, great soldier!"

¹³Then Gideon said, "I promise sir, if the Lord is with us, then why are we having so many troubles? We heard that he did wonderful things for our ancestors.* Our ancestors told us that the Lord took them out of Egypt. But the Lord left us. The Lord has allowed the people of Midian to defeat us."

¹⁴The Lord turned toward Gideon and said, "Use your power. Go save the people of Israel from the people of Midian. I am sending you to save them!"

¹⁵But Gideon answered and said, "Pardon me, sir. How can I save Israel? My family is the

---

The people Verses 7-10 do not appear in the oldest Hebrew copy of the book of Judges, the Dead Sea Scroll fragment, 4QJudgesA.

weakest in the family group of Manasseh. And I am the youngest one in my family."

¹⁶The Lord answered Gideon and said, "I am with you! So you can defeat the people of Midian! It will seem like you are fighting against only one man."

¹⁷Then Gideon said to the Lord, "If you are pleased with me, give me proof that you really are the Lord. ¹⁸Please wait here. Don't go away until I come back to you. Let me bring my offering and set it down in front of you."

And the Lord said, "I will wait until you come back."

¹⁹So Gideon went in and cooked a young goat in boiling water. Gideon also took about 20 pounds* of flour and made bread without yeast. Then Gideon put the meat into a basket and the water from the boiled meat into a pot. Gideon brought out the meat, the water from the boiled meat, and the bread without yeast. Gideon gave that food to the Lord under the oak tree.

²⁰The angel of God said to Gideon, "Put the meat and the bread without yeast on that rock over there. Then pour the water out." Gideon did as he was told.

²¹The Angel of the Lord had a walking stick in his hand. The Angel of the Lord touched the meat and the bread with the end of the stick. Then fire jumped up from the rock! The meat and the bread were completely burned up! Then the Angel of the Lord disappeared.

²²Then Gideon realized that he had been talking to the Angel of the Lord. So Gideon shouted, "Lord All-Powerful! I have seen the Angel of the Lord face to face!"

²³But the Lord said to Gideon, "Calm down!* Don't be afraid! You will not die!"*

²⁴So Gideon built an altar* in that place to worship the Lord. Gideon named that altar, "The Lord is Peace." That altar still stands in the city of Ophrah. Ophrah is where the Abiezer family lives.

Gideon Tears Down the Altar of Baal.

²⁵That same night the Lord spoke to Gideon. The Lord said, "Take the full-grown bull that belongs to your father, the one that is seven years old. Your father has an altar* to the false god Baal.* There is also a wooden pole beside the altar. That pole was made to honor the false god Asherah.* Use the bull to pull down the Baal altar, and cut down the Asherah pole. ²⁶Then build the right kind of altar for the Lord your God. Build that altar on this high ground. Then kill and burn the full-grown bull on this altar. Use the wood from the Asherah pole to burn your offering."

²⁷So Gideon got ten of his servants and did what the Lord had told him to do. But Gideon was afraid that his family and the men of the city might see what he was doing. Gideon did what the Lord told him to do. But he did it at night, and not in the daytime.

²⁸The men of the city got up the next morning. And they saw that the altar for Baal* had been destroyed! They also saw that the Asherah* pole had been cut down. The Asherah pole had been sitting next to the altar for Baal. Those men also saw the altar that Gideon had built. And they saw the bull that had been sacrificed on that altar.

²⁹The men of the city looked at each other and asked, "Who pulled down our altar? Who cut down our Asherah* pole? Who sacrificed this bull on this new altar?" They asked many questions and tried to learn who did those things.

Someone told them, "Gideon son of Joash did this."

³⁰So the men of the city came to Joash. They said to Joash, "You must bring your son out. He pulled down the altar* for Baal.* And he cut down the Asherah* pole that was by that altar. So your son must die."

³¹Then Joash spoke to the crowd that was standing around him. Joash said, "Are you going to take Baal's side? Are you going to rescue Baal?

Calm down Literally, "Peace."
You will not die! Gideon thought he would die because he had seen the Lord face to face.
altar(s) A stone table used for burning sacrifices that were offered as gifts to God.
Baal The Canaanite people believed that this false god brought the rain and storms. They also thought that he made the land produce good crops.
Asherah An important Canaanite goddess. The people thought she was the wife of El or the lover of Baal.

beating some wheat This was the way people separated the grains of wheat from the other parts of the plants.
winepress A place for squeezing juice from grapes, often it was only a shallow hole in a large rock in the ground.
ancestors Literally, "fathers," meaning a person's parents, grandparents, and all the people they are descended from.
20 pounds Literally, "1 ephah."

If anyone takes Baal's side, let him be put to death by morning. If Baal really is a god, let him defend himself when someone pulls down his altar." ³²Joash said, "If Gideon pulled Baal's altar down, then let Baal argue with him." So on that day Joash gave Gideon a new name. He called him Jerub Baal.*

Gideon Defeats the People of Midian

³³The people of Midian, Amalek, and other people from the east joined together ₍to fight against the people of Israel₎. Those people went across the Jordan River and camped in Jezreel Valley. ³⁴The Spirit of the Lord came to Gideon ₍and gave him great power₎. Gideon blew a trumpet to call the Abiezer family to follow him. ³⁵Gideon sent messengers to all the people of the family group of Manasseh. Those messengers told the people of Manasseh to get their weapons and prepare for battle. Gideon also sent messengers to the family groups of Asher, Zebulun, and Naphtali. The messengers took the same message. So those family groups also went up to meet Gideon and his men.

³⁶Then Gideon said to God, "You said that you would help me save the people of Israel. Give me proof! ³⁷I will put a sheepskin on the threshing floor.* If there is dew only on the sheepskin, while all of the ground is dry, then I will know that you will use me to save Israel, like you said."

³⁸And that is exactly what happened. Gideon got up early the next morning and squeezed the sheepskin. He was able to drain a bowl full of water from the sheepskin.

³⁹Then Gideon said to God, "Don't be angry with me. Let me ask just one more thing. Let me test you one more time with the sheepskin. This time let the sheepskin be dry, while the ground around it gets wet with dew."

⁴⁰That night God did that very thing. Just the sheepskin was dry, but the ground around it was wet with dew.

7Early in the morning Jerub Baal *(Gideon)* and all his men set up their camp at the spring of Harod. The people of Midian were camped in the valley at the bottom of the hill called Moreh. This was north of Gideon and his men.

²Then the Lord said to Gideon, "I am going to help your men to defeat the people of Midian. But you have too many men for the job. I don't want the people of Israel to forget me and brag that they saved themselves. ³So now, make an announcement to your men. Tell them, 'Anyone that is afraid may leave Mount Gilead. He may go back home.'"

At that time, 22,000 men left Gideon and went back home. But 10,000 still remained.

⁴Then the Lord said to Gideon, "There are still too many men. Take the men down to the water, and I will test them for you there. If I say, 'This man will go with you,' he will go. But if I say, 'That one will not go with you,' then he will not go."

⁵So Gideon led the men down to the water. At the water the Lord said to Gideon, "Separate the men like this: The men who drink the water by using their tongue to lap it up like a dog will be in one group. And the men who bend down to drink will be in the other group."

⁶There were 300 men that used their hands to bring water to their mouth and lapped it like a dog does. All the other people bent down and drank the water. ⁷The Lord said to Gideon, "I will use the 300 men who lapped the water like a dog. I will use those men to save you, and I will allow you to defeat the people of Midian. Let the other men go to their homes."

⁸So Gideon sent the other men of Israel home. Gideon kept the 300 men with him. Those 300 men kept the supplies and the trumpets of the other men who went home.

The people of Midian were camped in the valley below Gideon's camp. ⁹During the night the Lord spoke to Gideon. The Lord said to him, "Get up. I will let you defeat the Midianite army. Go down to their camp. ¹⁰If you are afraid to go alone, then take Purah your servant with you. ¹¹Go into the camp of the people of Midian. Listen to the things those people are saying. After that, you will not be afraid to attack them."

Baal The Canaanite people believed that this false god brought the rain and storms. They also thought that he made the land produce good crops.

Asherah An important Canaanite goddess. The people thought she was the wife of El or the lover of Baal.

altar(s) A stone table used for burning sacrifices that were offered as gifts to God.

Jerub Baal This is like the Hebrew words meaning, "Let Baal argue." The same verb is translated "take one's side" and "defend" in verse 31.

threshing floor The place where people beat wheat to separate the grain from the other parts of the plants.

So Gideon and Purah his servant went down to the edge of the enemy camp. ¹²The people of Midian, the people of Amalek, and all the other people from the east were camped in that valley. There were so many people that they seemed like a swarm of locusts.* It seemed like those people had as many camels as there are grains of sand on the seashore.

¹³Gideon came to the enemy camp, and he heard a man talking. That man was telling his friend about a dream that he had. The man was saying, "I dreamed that a round loaf of bread came rolling into the camp of the people of Midian. That loaf of bread hit the tent so hard that the tent turned over and fell flat."

¹⁴The man's friend knew the meaning of the dream. He said, "Your dream can only have one meaning. Your dream is about that man from Israel. It is about Gideon son of Joash. It means that God will let Gideon defeat the whole army of Midian."

¹⁵After he heard the men talking about the dream and what it meant, Gideon bowed down to God. Then Gideon went back to the camp of the people of Israel. Gideon called out to the people, "Get up! The Lord will help us defeat the people of Midian." ¹⁶Then Gideon divided the 300 men into three groups. Gideon gave each man a trumpet and an empty jar. A burning torch was inside each jar. ¹⁷Then Gideon told the men, "Watch me and do what I do. Follow me to the edge of the enemy camp. When I get to the edge of the camp, do exactly what I do. ¹⁸You men surround the enemy camp. I and all the men with me will blow our trumpets. When we blow our trumpets, you blow your trumpets, too. Then shout these words: 'For the Lord and for Gideon!'"

¹⁹So Gideon and the 100 men with him went to the edge of the enemy camp. They came there just after the enemy changed guards. It was during the middle watch of the night. Gideon and his men blew their trumpets and smashed their jars. ²⁰Then all three groups of Gideon's men blew their trumpets and smashed their jars. The men held the torches in their left hands and the trumpets in their right hands. As those men blew their trumpets, they shouted, "A sword for the Lord, and a sword for Gideon!"

²¹Gideon's men stayed where they were. But inside the camp, the men of Midian began shouting and running away. ²²When Gideon's 300 men blew their trumpets, the Lord caused the men of Midian to kill each other with their swords. The enemy army ran away to the city of Beth Shittah, which is toward the city of Zererah. Those men ran as far as the border of the city of Abel Meholah, which is near the city of Tabbath.

²³Then soldiers from the family groups of Naphtali, Asher, and all of Manasseh were told to chase the people of Midian. ²⁴Gideon sent messengers through all the hill country of Ephraim. The messengers said, "Come down and attack the people of Midian. Take control of the river as far as Beth Barah and the Jordan River. Do this before the people of Midian get there."

So they called all men from the family group of Ephraim. They took control of the river as far as Beth Barah. ²⁵The men of Ephraim caught two of the Midianite leaders. These two leaders were named Oreb and Zeeb. The men of Ephraim killed Oreb at a place named the Rock of Oreb. They killed Zeeb at a place named the Winepress of Zeeb. The men of Ephraim continued chasing the people of Midian. But they first cut off the heads of Oreb and Zeeb and took the heads to Gideon. Gideon was at the place where people cross the Jordan River.

8 The men of Ephraim were angry at Gideon. When the men of Ephraim found Gideon, they asked Gideon, "Why did you treat us this way? Why didn't you call us when you went to fight against the people of Midian?"

²But Gideon answered the men of Ephraim, "I have not done as well as you men have done. You people of Ephraim have a much better harvest than my family, the Abiezers. At harvest time, you leave more grapes in the field than my family gathers! Isn't that true? ³ɪIn the same way, you have a better harvest now.ɹ God allowed you to capture Oreb and Zeeb, the leaders of Midian! How can I compare my success with what you did?" When the men of Ephraim heard Gideon's answer, they were not as angry as they had been.

Gideon Captures Two Kings of Midian

⁴Then Gideon and his 300 men came to the Jordan River and went across to the other side.

---

locusts Insects like grasshoppers. Locusts can destroy a large crop very quickly.

But they were tired and hungry.* ⁵Gideon said to the men of the city of Succoth, "Give my soldiers something to eat. My soldiers are very tired. We are still chasing Zebah and Zalmunna, kings of Midian."

⁶But the leaders of the city of Succoth said to Gideon, "Why should we give your soldiers something to eat? You haven't caught Zebah and Zalmunna yet."

⁷Then Gideon said, "You won't give us food. The Lord will help me capture Zebah and Zalmunna. After that, I will come back here. And I will beat your skin with thorns and briers from the desert."

⁸Gideon left the city of Succoth and went to the city of Penuel. Gideon asked the men of Penuel for food, just as he had asked the men of Succoth. But the men of Penuel gave Gideon the same answer that the men of Succoth had given. ⁹So Gideon said to the men of Penuel, "After I win the victory, I will come back here and pull this tower down."

¹⁰Zebah and Zalmunna and their army were in the city of Karkor. Their army had 15,000 soldiers in it. These soldiers were all that were left of the army of the people of the east. 120,000 strong soldiers of that army had already been killed. ¹¹Gideon and his men used Tent Dwellers' Road. That road is east of the cities of Nobah and Jogbehah. Gideon came to the city of Karkor and attacked the enemy. The enemy army did not expect the attack. ¹²Zebah and Zalmunna, kings of the people of Midian, ran away. But Gideon chased and caught those kings. Gideon and his men defeated the enemy army.

¹³Then Gideon son of Joash returned from the battle. Gideon and his men returned by going through a mountain pass called the Pass of Heres. ¹⁴Gideon captured a young man from the city of Succoth. Gideon asked the young man some questions. The young man wrote down some names for Gideon. The young man wrote down the names of the leaders and elders of the city of Succoth. He gave the names of 77 men.

¹⁵Then Gideon came to the city of Succoth. He said to the men of that city, "Here are Zebah and Zalmunna. You made fun of me by saying, 'Why should we give food to your tired soldiers? You have not caught Zebah and Zalmunna yet.'" ¹⁶Gideon took the elders of the city of Succoth, and he beat them with thorns and briers from the desert to punish them. ¹⁷Gideon also pulled down the tower in the city of Penuel. Then he killed the men living in that city.

¹⁸Then Gideon said to Zebah and Zalmunna, "You killed some men on Mount Tabor. What were those men like?"

Zebah and Zalmunna answered, "Those men were like you. Each one of them seemed like a prince."

¹⁹Gideon said, "Those men were my brothers! My mother's sons! As the Lord lives, if you had not killed them, then I wouldn't kill you now."

²⁰Then Gideon turned to Jether. Jether was Gideon's oldest son. Gideon said to him, "Kill these kings." But Jether was only a boy and was afraid. So he would not take out his sword.

²¹Then Zebah and Zalmunna said to Gideon, "Come on, kill us yourself. You are a man and strong enough to do the job." So Gideon got up and killed Zebah and Zalmunna. Then Gideon took the decorations shaped like the moon off their camels' necks.

Gideon Makes an Ephod

²²The people of Israel said to Gideon, "You saved us from the people of Midian. So now, rule over us. We want you, your son and your grandson to rule over us."

²³But Gideon told the people of Israel, "The Lord will be your ruler. I will not rule over you. And my son will not rule over you."

²⁴Some of the people that the men of Israel defeated were Ishmaelites. And the Ishmaelite men wore gold earrings. So Gideon said to the people of Israel, "I want you to do this one thing for me. I want each of you to give me a gold earring from the things you took in the fighting."

²⁵So the people of Israel said to Gideon, "We will gladly give you what you want." So they put a coat down on the ground. Each man threw an earring onto the coat. ²⁶When those earrings were gathered up, they weighed about 43 pounds.* This did not include the other gifts the people of Israel gave to Gideon. They also gave him jewelry shaped like the moon and jewelry shaped like teardrops. And they gave him purple robes. These were things that the kings of the people of Midian had worn. They also gave him the chains from the camels of the Midianite kings.

---

hungry This if from the ancient Greek translation. The Hebrew has, "chasing."

43 pounds Literally, "1,700 [shekels]."

²⁷Gideon used the gold to make an ephod.* He put the ephod in his home town, the town called Ophrah. All the people of Israel worshiped the ephod. In this way, the people of Israel were not faithful to God—they worshiped the Ephod.* The ephod became a trap that caused Gideon and his family to sin.

The Death of Gideon

²⁸The people of Midian were forced to be under the rule of the people of Israel. The people of Midian did not cause trouble any more. And the land was at peace for 40 years, as long as Gideon was alive. ²⁹Jerub Baal *(Gideon)* son of Joash went home. ³⁰Gideon had 70 sons of his own. He had so many sons because he had many wives. ³¹Gideon had a concubine* that lived in the city of Shechem. He had a son with that concubine. He named that son Abimelech.

³²So Gideon son of Joash died at a good old age. Gideon was buried in the tomb that Joash, his father, owned. That tomb is in the city of Ophrah, where the Abiezer family lives. ³³As soon as Gideon died, the people of Israel again were not faithful to God—they followed Baal.* They made Baal Berith* their god. ³⁴The people of Israel did not remember the Lord their God, even though the Lord had saved them from all their enemies that were living all around the people of Israel. ³⁵The people of Israel were not loyal to the family of Jerub Baal *(Gideon)*, even though he had done many good things for them.

Abimelech Becomes King

9 Abimelech was the son of Jerub Baal *(Gideon)*. Abimelech went to his uncles that lived in the city of Shechem. He said to his uncles and all of his mother's family, ²"Ask the leaders of the city of Shechem this question: 'Is it better for you to be ruled by the 70 sons of Jerub Baal, or to be ruled by only one man? Remember, I am your relative.'"

³Abimelech's uncles spoke to the leaders of Shechem and asked them that question. The leaders of Shechem decided to follow Abimelech. The leaders said, "After all, he is our brother." ⁴So the leaders of Shechem gave Abimelech 70 pieces of silver. That silver was from the temple of the god Baal Berith.* Abimelech used the silver to hire some men. These men were worthless, reckless men. They followed Abimelech wherever he went.

⁵Abimelech went to his father's house at Ophrah. Abimelech murdered his brothers. Abimelech killed the 70 sons of his father, Jerub Baal *(Gideon)*. He killed them all at the same time.* But Jerub Baal's youngest son hid from Abimelech and escaped. The youngest son's name was Jotham.

⁶Then all of the leaders in Shechem and the house of Millo* came together. All those people gathered beside the big tree of the pillar in Shechem and made Abimelech their king.

Jotham's Story

⁷Jotham heard that the leaders of the city of Shechem had made Abimelech king. When he heard this, he went and stood on the top of Mount Gerizim.* Jotham shouted out this story to the people,

Listen to me you leaders of the city of Shechem. Then let God listen to you.
⁸One day the trees decided to choose a king to rule over them. The trees said to the olive tree, "You be king over us."
⁹But the olive tree said, "Men and gods praise me for my oil. Should I stop making my oil just to go and sway over the other trees?"
¹⁰Then the trees said to the fig tree, "Come and be our king."
¹¹But the fig tree answered, "Should I stop making my good, sweet fruit just to go and sway over the other trees?"
¹²Then the trees said to the vine, "Come and be our king."

---

ephod We do not know exactly what this was. It may have been a special vest or coat, like the High Priest of Israel wore (see Exodus 28). Or it may have been an idol.
were not faithful ... Ephod Literally, "acted like a prostitute to it."
concubine A slave woman that was like a wife to a man.
were not faithful ... Baal Literally, "they acted like a prostitute to Baal."
Baal Berith The name of this god means "Lord of the Agreement."
all at the same time Literally, "on one stone."
Millo This was probably a well protected part of the city. It might have been in the city itself, or somewhere near the city.
Mount Gerizim This mountain is right beside the city of Shechem.

¹³But the vine answered, "My wine makes men and kings happy. Should I stop making my wine just to go and sway over the trees?"
¹⁴Finally all the trees said to the thornbush, "Come and be our king."
¹⁵But the thorn bush said to the trees, "If you really want to make me king over you, come and find shelter in my shade. But if you do not want to do this, then let fire come out of the thorn bush. Let the fire burn even the cedar trees of Lebanon."
¹⁶Now if you were completely honest when you made Abimelech king, then may you be happy with him. And if you have been fair to Jerub Baal and his family, fine. And if you have treated Jerub Baal as you should, fine. ¹⁷But think what my father did for you. My father fought for you. He risked his life when he saved you from the people of Midian. ¹⁸But now you have turned against my father's family. You have killed 70 of my father's sons all at the same time.* You made Abimelech the new king over the city of Shechem. He is only the son of my father's slave girl. But you made him king because he is your relative. ¹⁹So, if you have been completely honest to Jerub Baal and his family today, then I hope you are happy with Abimelech as your king. And I hope he will be happy with you. ²⁰But leaders of Shechem and house of Millo,* if you have not acted right, then I hope that Abimelech destroys you. And I hope that Abimelech is destroyed too!"
²¹After Jotham had said all of this, he ran away. He escaped to the city named Beer. Jotham stayed in that city because he was afraid of his brother Abimelech.

Abimelech Fights Against Shechem

²²Abimelech ruled the people of Israel for three years. ²³⁻²⁴Abimelech had killed Jerub Baal's 70 sons—and they were Abimelech's own brothers! The leaders of Shechem had supported him in doing this bad thing. So God caused trouble between Abimelech and the leaders of Shechem. And the leaders of Shechem began planning ways to hurt Abimelech. ²⁵The leaders of the city of Shechem did not like Abimelech anymore. Those people put men on the hilltops to attack and rob everyone that went by. Abimelech found out about those attacks.

²⁶A man named Gaal son of Ebed and his brothers moved to the city of Shechem. The leaders of the city of Shechem decided to trust and follow Gaal.

²⁷One day the people of Shechem went out to the fields to pick grapes. The people squeezed the grapes to make wine. And then they had a party at the temple of their god. The people ate and drank and said bad things about Abimelech.

²⁸Then Gaal son of Ebed said, "We are the men of Shechem. Why should we obey Abimelech? Who does he think he is? Abimelech is one of Jerub Baal's sons, right? And Abimelech made Zebul his officer, right? We should not obey Abimelech! We should follow our own people, men from Hamor.* (Hamor was the father of Shechem.) ²⁹If you make me the commander of these people, then I will destroy Abimelech. I will say to him, 'Get your army ready and come out to battle.'"

³⁰Zebul was the governor of the city of Shechem. Zebul heard what Gaal son of Ebed said, and Zebul became very angry. ³¹Zebul sent messengers to Abimelech in the city of Arumah.* This is the message:

Gaal son of Ebed and Gaal's brothers have come to the city of Shechem. They are making trouble for you. Gaal is turning the whole city against you. ³²So now you and your men should come tonight and hide in the fields outside the city. ³³Then, when the sun comes up in the morning, attack the city. Gaal and his men will come out of the city to fight you. When those men come out to fight, do what you can to them.

³⁴So Abimelech and all his soldiers got up during the night and went to the city. Those soldiers separated into four groups. They hid near the city of Shechem. ³⁵Gaal son of Ebed went out and was standing at the entrance to the gate of the city of Shechem. While Gaal was standing there, Abimelech and his soldiers came out of their hiding places.

---

all at the same time Literally, "on one stone."
house of Millo Or, "Royal Family of Millo." The Millo was probably a well protected part of the city, perhaps even the palace area.
men from Hamor This refers to native born citizens of Shechem. Hamor was the father of Shechem in a story in Genesis 34. The city of Shechem is said to have been named after Hamor's son.
in the city of Arumah Or, "secretly" or "in Tormah," the town where Abimelech lived as king. It was probably about eight miles south of Shechem.

[36] Gaal saw the soldiers. Gaal said to Zebul, "Look, there are people coming down from the mountains."

But Zebul said, "You are only seeing the shadows of the mountains. The shadows just look like people."

[37] But again Gaal said, "Look, there are some people coming down from that place over there, by Land's Navel. And there! I saw someone's head over by Magician's Tree.*" [38] Zebul said to Gaal, "Why aren't you bragging now? You said, 'Who is Abimelech? Why should we obey him?' You made fun of these men. Now go out and fight them."

[39] So Gaal led the leaders of Shechem out to fight Abimelech. [40] Abimelech and his men chased Gaal and his men. Gaal's men ran back toward the gate of the city of Shechem. Many of Gaal's men were killed before they could get back to the gate.

[41] Then Abimelech returned to the city of Arumah. Zebul forced Gaal and his brothers to leave the city of Shechem.

[42] The next day the people of Shechem went out to the fields to work. Abimelech found out about that. [43] So Abimelech separated his men into three groups. He wanted to attack the people of Shechem by surprise. So he hid his men in the fields. When he saw the people coming out of the city he jumped up and attacked them. [44] Abimelech and his group ran to a place near the gate to Shechem. The other two groups ran out to the people in the fields and killed them. [45] Abimelech and his men fought against the city of Shechem all that day. Abimelech and his men captured the city of Shechem and killed the people of that city. Then Abimelech tore down the city and threw salt over the ruins.

[46] There were some people that lived at the Tower of Shechem.* When the people of that place heard what had happened to Shechem, they gathered together in the safest room* of the temple of the god El Berith.*

[47] Abimelech heard that all the leaders of the Tower of Shechem had gathered together. [48] So Abimelech and all his men went up to Mount Zalmon.* Abimelech took an axe and cut off some branches. He carried those branches on his shoulders. Then Abimelech said to the men with him, "Hurry! Do the same thing that I have done." [49] So all those men cut branches and followed Abimelech. They piled the branches against the safest room* of the temple of the god El Berith.* Then they set the branches on fire and burned the people in the room. So about 1,000 men and women living near the Tower of Shechem died.

Abimelech's Death

[50] Then Abimelech and his men went to the city of Thebez. Abimelech and his men captured that city. [51] But inside the city there was a strong tower. All the leaders and other men and women of that city ran to the tower. When the people were inside the tower, they locked the door behind them. Then they climbed up to the roof of the tower. [52] Abimelech and his men came to the tower to attack it. Abimelech went up to the door of the tower. He wanted to burn the tower. [53] But, while Abimelech was standing at the door of the tower, a woman on the roof dropped a grinding stone on his head. The grinding stone crushed Abimelech's skull. [54] Abimelech quickly said to the servant that carried his weapons, "Take out your sword and kill me. I want you to kill me so that people won't say, 'A woman killed Abimelech.'" So the servant stabbed Abimelech with his sword, and Abimelech died. [55] The people of Israel saw that Abimelech was dead. So they all went back home.

[56] In that way, God punished Abimelech for all the bad things he did. Abimelech sinned against his own father by killing his 70 brothers. [57] God also punished the men of the city of Shechem for the bad things they did. So the things Jotham said came true. (Jotham was Jerub Baal's youngest son. Jerub Baal was Gideon.)

Tola the Judge

10 After Abimelech died, God sent another judge to save the people of Israel. That man's name was Tola. Tola was the son of a man named Puah. Puah was the son of a man named Dodo. Tola was from the family group of Issachar. Tola lived in the city of Shamir. The city of Shamir was in the hill country of Ephraim.

Land's Navel ... Magician's Tree Two places in the hills near Shechem.

Tower of Shechem This was probably a place near Shechem, but not actually part of the city.

safest room We are not sure of the meaning of this Hebrew word.

El Berith The name of this god means "God of the Agreement."

Mount Zalmon This is probably another name for Mount Ebal, a mountain near Shechem.

safest room We are not sure of the exact meaning of the Hebrew word here.

²Tola was a judge for the people of Israel for 23 years. Then Tola died and was buried in the city of Shamir.

Jair the Judge

³After Tola died, another judge was sent by God. That man's name was Jair. Jair lived in the area of Gilead. Jair was a judge for the people of Israel for 22 years. ⁴Jair had 30 sons. Those 30 sons rode 30 donkeys.* Those 30 sons controlled 30 towns in the area of Gilead. Those towns are called the Towns of Jair to this very day. ⁵Jair died and was buried in the city of Kamon.

The Ammonites Fight Against Israel

⁶Again the people of Israel did things the Lord said are evil. They began worshiping the false gods Baal* and the Ashtoreth.* They also worshiped the gods of the people of Aram, the gods of the people of Sidon, the gods of the people of Moab, the gods of the people of Ammon, and the gods of the Philistine people. The people of Israel left the Lord and stopped serving him.

⁷So the Lord became angry with the people of Israel. The Lord allowed the Philistine people and the Ammonite people to defeat them. ⁸In that same year those people destroyed the people of Israel that lived on the east side of the Jordan River, in the area of Gilead. That is the land where the Amorite people had lived. Those people of Israel suffered for 18 years. ⁹The Ammonite people then went across the Jordan River. They went to fight against the people of Judah, Benjamin, and Ephraim. The Ammonite people brought many troubles to the people of Israel.

¹⁰So the people of Israel cried to the Lord for help. They said, "God, we have sinned against you. We left our God and worshiped the false god Baal.*"

¹¹The Lord answered the people of Israel, "You cried to me when the people of Egypt, the Amorite people, the Ammonite people, and the Philistine people hurt you. I saved you from these people. ¹²You cried to me when the people of Sidon, the Amalekite people, and the Midianite* people hurt you. I also saved you from those people. ¹³But you left me and started worshiping other gods. So I refuse to save you again. ¹⁴You like worshiping those gods, so go call to them for help. Let those gods save you when you are in trouble."

¹⁵But the people of Israel said to the Lord, "We have sinned. Do whatever you want to do to us. But please save us today." ¹⁶Then the people of Israel threw away the foreign gods. They started worshiping the Lord again. So the Lord felt sorry for them when he saw them suffering.

Jephthah Is Chosen as a Leader

¹⁷The Ammonite people gathered together for war. Their camp was in the area of Gilead. The people of Israel gathered together. Their camp was at the city of Mizpah. ¹⁸The leaders of the people living in the area of Gilead said, "Whoever leads us in the attack against the people of Ammon will become the head of all the people living in Gilead."

11 Jephthah was from the family group of Gilead. He was a strong soldier. But Jephthah was the son of a prostitute. His father was a man named Gilead. ²Gilead's wife had several sons. When those sons grew up, they did not like Jephthah. Those sons forced Jephthah to leave his home town. They said to him, "You will not get any of our father's property. You are the son of another woman." ³So Jephthah went away because of his brothers. He lived in the land of Tob. In the land of Tob, some rough men began to follow Jephthah.

⁴After a time the Ammonite people fought with the people of Israel. ⁵The Ammonite people were fighting against Israel, so the elders *(leaders)* in Gilead went to Jephthah. They wanted Jephthah to leave the land of Tob and come back to Gilead.

⁶The elders said to Jephthah, "Come and be our leader so that we can fight the Ammonite people."

⁷But Jephthah said to the elders *(leaders)* of the land of Gilead, "You forced me to leave my father's house. You hate me! So why are you coming to me now that you are having trouble?"

---

30 sons rode 30 donkeys This showed these men were important leaders, possibly the mayors of the 30 towns in Gilead.

Baal The Canaanite people believed that this false god brought the rain and storms. They also thought that he made the land produce good crops.

Ashtoreth The Canaanite people thought that this false goddess could make people able to have babies. She was their goddess of love and war.

Midianite This is the ancient Greek translation. The Hebrew has, "The Maonite people."

⁸The elders *(leaders)* from Gilead said to Jephthah, "That is the reason that we have come to you now. Please come with us and fight against the Ammonite people. You will be the commander over all the people living in Gilead."

⁹Then Jephthah said to the elders *(leaders)* from Gilead, "If you want me to come back to Gilead and fight the Ammonite people, fine. But if the Lord helps me win, then I will be your new leader."

¹⁰The elders *(leaders)* from Gilead said to Jephthah, "The Lord is listening to everything we are saying. And we promise to do all that you tell us to do."

¹¹So Jephthah went with the elders *(leaders)* from Gilead. Those people made Jephthah their leader and their commander. Jephthah repeated all of his words in front of the Lord at the city of Mizpah.

Jephthah's Message to the Ammonite King

¹²Jephthah sent messengers to the king of the Ammonite people. The messengers gave the king this message: "What is the problem between the Ammonite people and the people of Israel? Why have you come to fight in our land?"

¹³The king of the Ammonite people said to the messengers of Jephthah, "We are fighting Israel because the people of Israel took our land when they came up from Egypt. They took our land from the Arnon River to the Jabbok River to the Jordan River. Now tell the people of Israel to give our land back to us in peace."

¹⁴So the messengers of Jephthah took this message back to Jephthah.* Then Jephthah sent the messengers to the king of the Ammonite people again. ¹⁵They took this message:

This is what Jephthah says: Israel did not take the land of the people of Moab or the land of the people of Ammon. ¹⁶When the people of Israel came out of the land of Egypt, the people of Israel went into the desert. The people of Israel went to the Red Sea. Then they went to Kadesh. ¹⁷The people of Israel sent messengers to the king of Edom. The messengers asked for a favor. They said, "Let the people of Israel cross through your land." But the king of Edom didn't let us go through their land. We also sent the same message to the king of Moab. But the king of Moab would not let us go through his land either. So the people of Israel stayed at Kadesh.

¹⁸Then the people of Israel went through the desert and around the edges of the land of Edom and the land of Moab. The people of Israel traveled east of the land of Moab. They made their camp on the other side of the Arnon River. They did not cross the border of the land of Moab. (The Arnon River was the border of the land of Moab.)

¹⁹Then the people of Israel sent messengers to Sihon the king of the Amorite people. Sihon was the king of the city of Heshbon. The messengers asked Sihon, 'Let the people of Israel pass through your land. We want to go to our land.' ²⁰But Sihon, the king of the Amorite people would not let the people of Israel cross his borders. Sihon gathered all of his people and made a camp at Jahaz. Then the Amorite people fought with the people of Israel. ²¹But the Lord, the God of Israel, helped the people of Israel to defeat Sihon and his army. So the land of the Amorite people became the property of the people of Israel. ²²So the people of Israel got all of the land of the Amorite people. That land went from the Arnon River to the Jabbok River. That land also went from the desert to the Jordan River.

²³It was the Lord, the God of Israel, who forced the Amorite people to leave their land. And the Lord gave the land to the people of Israel. Do you think you can make the people of Israel leave this land? ²⁴Surely you can live in the land which Chemosh* your god has given to you. So we will live in the land that the Lord our God has given to us! ²⁵Are you any better than Balak son of Zippor?* He was the king of the land of Moab. Did he argue with the people of Israel? Did he actually fight with the people of Israel? ²⁶The people of Israel have lived in the city of Heshbon and the towns around it for 300 years. The people of Israel have lived in the city of Aroer and the towns around it for 300 years. The people of Israel

---

So the messengers ... Jephthah This is from the ancient Greek translation. The Hebrew text does not have this sentence.

Chemosh The national god of the land of Moab, even though Milcom was the god of the Ammonite people.

Balak son of Zippor See Num. 22-24 for his story.

have lived in all of the cities along the side of the Arnon River for 300 years. Why have you not tried to take these cities in all that time? ²⁷The people of Israel have not sinned against you. But you are doing a very bad thing against the people of Israel. May the Lord, the true Judge, decide whether the people of Israel are right or the Ammonite people!" ²⁸The king of the Ammonite people refused to listen to this message from Jephthah.

Jephthah's Promise

²⁹Then the Spirit of the Lord came on Jephthah. Jephthah passed through the area of Gilead and Manasseh. He went to the city of Mizpah in Gilead. From the city of Mizpah in Gilead, Jephthah passed through to the land of the Ammonite people. ³⁰Jephthah made a promise to the Lord. He said, "If you will let me defeat the Ammonite people, ³¹I will give you the first thing that comes out of my house when I come back from the victory. I will give it to the Lord as a burnt offering."

³²Then Jephthah went to the land of the Ammonite people. Jephthah fought the Ammonite people. The Lord helped him defeat them. ³³He defeated them from the city of Aroer to the city of Minnith. Jephthah captured 20 cities. Then he fought the Ammonite people to the city of Abel Keramim. The people of Israel defeated the Ammonite people. It was a very great defeat for the Ammonite people.

³⁴Jephthah went back to Mizpah. Jephthah went to his house and his daughter came out of the house to meet him. She was playing a tambourine and dancing. She was his only daughter. Jephthah loved her very much. Jephthah did not have any other sons or daughters. ³⁵When Jephthah saw that his daughter was the first thing to come out of his house, he tore his clothes to show his sadness. Then he said, "Oh, my daughter! You have ruined me! You have made me very, very sad! I made a promise to the Lord, and I cannot change it!"

³⁶Then his daughter said to Jephthah, "Father, you have made a promise to the Lord. So keep your promise. Do what you said you would do. After all, the Lord did help you defeat your enemies, the Ammonite people."

³⁷Then Jephthah's daughter said to her father, "But do this one thing for me first. Let me be alone for two months. Let me go to the mountains. I will not marry and have children, so let me and my friends go and cry together."

³⁸Jephthah said, "Go and do that." Jephthah sent her away for two months. Jephthah's daughter and her friends stayed in the mountains. They cried for her because she would not marry and have children.

³⁹At the end of two months, Jephthah's daughter returned to her father. Jephthah did what he promised to the Lord. Jephthah's daughter never had sexual relations with anyone. So this became a custom in Israel. ⁴⁰Every year the women of Israel remembered the daughter of Jephthah from Gilead. The women of Israel cried four days every year for Jephthah's daughter.

Jephthah and Ephraim

12 The men from the family group of Ephraim called all their soldiers together. Then they went across the river to the city of Zaphon. They said to Jephthah, "Why didn't you call us to help you fight the Ammonite people? We will burn your house down with you in it."

²Jephthah answered them, "The Ammonite people have been giving us many problems. So I and my people fought against them. I called you, but you didn't come to help us. ³I saw that you would not help us. So I risked my own life. I went across the river to fight against the Ammonite people. The Lord helped me to defeat them. Now why have you come to fight against me today?"

⁴Then Jephthah called the men of Gilead together. They fought against the men from the family group of Ephraim. They fought against the men of Ephraim because those men had insulted the men of Gilead. They had said, "You men of Gilead are nothing but survivors of the men of Ephraim. ⌊You don't even have your own land!⌋ Part of you belong to Ephraim, and part of you belong to Manasseh." The men of Gilead defeated the men of Ephraim.

⁵The men of Gilead captured the places where people cross the Jordan River. Those places led to the country of Ephraim. Any time a survivor from Ephraim came to the river and said, "Let me cross," the men of Gilead would ask him, "Are you from Ephraim?" If he said, "No," ⁶they would say, "Say the word 'Shibboleth.'" The men of Ephraim could not say that word correctly. They pronounced the word "Sibboleth." So if the person said, "Sibboleth," then the men of Gilead knew he was from Ephraim. So they would kill him at the crossing place. They killed 42,000 men from Ephraim.

⁷Jephthah was a judge for the people of Israel for six years. Then Jephthah from Gilead died. They buried him in his town in Gilead.

Ibzan, the Judge

⁸After Jephthah, a man named Ibzan was a judge for the people of Israel. Ibzan was from the city of Bethlehem. ⁹Ibzan had 30 sons and 30 daughters. He told his 30 daughters to marry men that were not his relatives. And he found 30 women that were not his relatives, and his sons married these women. Ibzan was a judge for the people of Israel for seven years. ¹⁰Then Ibzan died. He was buried in the city of Bethlehem.

Elon, the Judge

¹¹After Ibzan, a man named Elon was a judge for the people of Israel. Elon was from the family group of Zebulun. He was a judge for the people of Israel for ten years. ¹²Then Elon from the family group of Zebulun died. He was buried in the city of Aijalon, Zebulun.

Abdon, the Judge

¹³After Elon died, a man named Abdon son of Hillel was a judge for the people of Israel. Abdon was from the city of Pirathon. ¹⁴Abdon had 40 sons and 30 grandsons. They rode on 70 donkeys.* Abdon was a judge for the people of Israel for eight years. ¹⁵Then Abdon son of Hillel died. He was buried in the city of Pirathon. Pirathon is in the land of Ephraim. This is in the hill country where the Amalekite people lived.

The Birth of Samson

13 Again the Lord saw the people of Israel doing evil things. So the Lord allowed the Philistine people to rule over them for 40 years.

²There was a man from the city of Zorah. The man's name was Manoah. He was from the family group of Dan. Manoah had a wife. But she was not able to have any children. ³The Angel of the Lord appeared to Manoah's wife. He said, "You have not been able to have children. But you will become pregnant and have a son. ⁴Don't drink any wine or any other strong drink. Don't eat any food that is unclean.* ⁵Why? Because you are pregnant, and you will have a son. He will be dedicated to God in a special way: He will be a Nazirite.* So you must never cut his hair. He will be God's special person from before he is born. He will save the people of Israel from the power of the Philistine people."

⁶Then the woman went to her husband and told him what had happened. She said, "A man from God came to me. He looked like an angel from God. He made me afraid. I didn't ask him where he was from. He didn't tell me his name. ⁷But he said to me, 'You are pregnant and will have a son. Don't drink any wine or other strong drink. Don't eat any food that is unclean.* Why? Because the boy will be dedicated to God in a special way. The boy will be God's special person from before he is born until the day he dies.'"

⁸Then Manoah prayed to the Lord. He said, "Lord, I beg you to send the man of God to us again. We want him to teach us what we should do for the boy that will soon be born."

⁹God heard Manoah's prayer. The angel of God came to the woman again. She was sitting in a field and her husband Manoah was not with her. ¹⁰So the woman ran to tell her husband, "The man is back! The man that came to me the other day is here!"

¹¹Manoah got up and followed his wife. When he came to the man, he said, "Are you the same man that spoke to my wife before?"

The angel said, "I am."

¹²So Manoah said, "I hope that what you say will happen. Tell me what kind of life will the boy live? What will he do?"

¹³The Angel of the Lord said to Manoah, "Your wife must do everything I told her. ¹⁴She must not eat anything that grows on a grapevine. She must not drink any wine or strong drink. She must not eat any food that is unclean.* She must do everything that I have commanded her to do."

¹⁵Then Manoah said to the Angel of the Lord, "We would like for you to stay a while. We want to cook a young goat for you to eat."

¹⁶The Angel of the Lord said to Manoah, "Even if you keep me from leaving, I will not eat your food. But if you want to prepare something, then offer a burnt offering to the Lord." (Manoah did not understand that the man was really the Angel of the Lord.)

They rode on 70 donkeys This showed they were important leaders, possibly mayors of their towns.

Nazirite A person that made a special promise to God. See Num. 6:1-21 for the rules about the Nazirite promise.

¹⁷Then Manoah asked the Angel of the Lord, "What is your name? We want to know so that we can honor you when what you have said really happens."
¹⁸The Angel of the Lord said, "Why do you ask my name? It is too amazing ₍for you to believe₎.*"
¹⁹Then Manoah sacrificed a young goat on a rock. He offered the goat and a grain offering as a gift to the Lord and to the Person Who Does Amazing Things.* ²⁰Manoah and his wife were watching what happened. As the flames went up to the sky from the altar,* the Angel of the Lord went up to heaven in the fire!

When Manoah and his wife saw that, they bowed down with their faces to the ground. ²¹Manoah finally understood that the man was really the Angel of the Lord. The Angel of the Lord did not appear to Manoah again. ²²Manoah said to his wife, "We have seen God! Surely we will die because of this!"

²³But his wife said to him, "The Lord does not want to kill us. If the Lord wanted to kill us, he would not have accepted our burnt offering and grain offering. He would not have shown us all these things. And he would not have told us these things."

²⁴So the woman had a boy. She named him Samson. Samson grew and the Lord blessed him. ²⁵The Spirit of the Lord began to work in Samson while he was in the city of Mahaneh Dan. That city is between the cities of Zorah and Eshtaol.

Samson's Marriage

14 Samson went down to the city of Timnah. He saw a young Philistine woman there. ²When he got back home he said to his father and mother, "I saw a Philistine woman in Timnah. I want you to get her for me. I want to marry her."

³His father and his mother answered, "But surely there is a woman from the people of Israel that you can marry. Do you have to marry a woman from the Philistine people? Those people are not even circumcised."*

But Samson said, "Get that woman for me! She is the one I want!" ⁴(Samson's parents did not know that the Lord wanted this to happen. The Lord was looking for a way to do something against the Philistine people. The Philistine people were ruling over the people of Israel at that time.)

⁵Samson went down with his father and mother to the city of Timnah. They went as far as the grape fields near that city. At that place, a young lion suddenly roared and jumped at Samson! ⁶The Spirit of the Lord came on Samson with great power. He tore the lion apart with his bare hands. It seemed easy to him. It was as easy as tearing apart a young goat. But Samson did not tell his father or mother what he had done.

⁷So Samson went down to the city and talked to the Philistine woman. She pleased him. ⁸Several days later, Samson came back to marry the Philistine woman. On his way, he went over to look at the dead lion. He found a swarm of bees in the dead lion's body. They had made some honey. ⁹Samson got some of the honey with his hands. He walked along eating the honey. When he came to his parents, he gave them some of the honey. They ate it too. But Samson did not tell his parents that he had taken the honey from the body of the dead lion.

¹⁰Samson's father went down to see the Philistine woman. The custom was for the bridegroom to give a party. So Samson gave a party. ¹¹When the ₍Philistine₎ people saw that he was having a party, they sent 30 men to be with him.

¹²Then Samson said to the 30 men, "I want to tell you a story. This party will last for seven days. Try to find the answer during that time. If you can answer the riddle in that time, I will give you 30 linen shirts and 30 changes of clothes. ¹³But if you can't find the answer, then you must give me 30 linen shirts and 30 changes of clothes." So the 30 men said, "Tell us your riddle, we want to hear it."

¹⁴Samson told them this riddle:

> Out of the eater came something to eat.
> Out of the strong came something sweet.

The 30 men tried for three days to find the answer, but they couldn't.

It is too amazing ... to believe Or, "It is Pelei." This means "amazing," "wonderful." This is like the name, "Wonderful Counselor" in Isaiah 9:6.

Lord ... Amazing Things Or, "The Lord Who Does Amazing Things." Both of these are names for God, but Manoah didn't know the man was really the Angel of the Lord.

altar(s) A stone table used for burning sacrifices that were offered as gifts to God.

circumcise(d) Cutting the foreskin from a man. In Israel this was proof that a man had made a special agreement to obey God's laws and teachings.

¹⁵On the fourth day,* the men came to Samson's wife. They said, "Did you invite us here just to make us poor? You must trick your husband into telling us the answer to the riddle. If you don't get the answer for us, we will burn you and all the people in your father's house to death."

¹⁶So Samson's wife went to him and began crying. She said, "You just hate me! You don't really love me! You told my people a riddle, and you won't tell me the answer."

¹⁷Samson's wife cried for the rest of the seven days of the party. So he finally gave her the answer to the riddle on the seventh day. He told her because she kept bothering him. Then she went to her people and told them the answer to the riddle.

¹⁸So before the sun went down on the seventh day of the party, the Philistine men had the answer. They came to Samson and said,

"What is sweeter than honey?
What is stronger than a lion?"

Then Samson said to them,

"If you had not plowed with my cow,
you would not have solved my riddle!"

¹⁹Samson was very angry. The Spirit of the Lord came on Samson with great power. He went down to the city of Ashkelon. In that city he killed 30 ⌊Philistine⌋ men. Then he took all of the clothes and property from the dead bodies. He brought those clothes back and gave them to the men that had answered his riddle. Then he went to his father's house. ²⁰Samson did not take his wife. The best man at the wedding kept her.

Samson Makes Trouble for the Philistines

15 At the time of the wheat harvest, Samson went to visit his wife. He took a young goat with him as a gift. He said, "I am going to my wife's room."

But her father would not let Samson go in. ²Her father said to Samson, "I thought you hated her. So I let her marry the best man at the wedding. Her younger sister is more beautiful. Take her younger sister."

³But Samson said to him, "Now I have a good reason to hurt you Philistine people. No one will blame me now."

⁴So Samson went out and caught 300 foxes. He took two foxes at a time and tied their tails together to make pairs. Then he tied a torch between the tails of each pair of foxes. ⁵Samson lit the torches that were between the foxes' tails. Then he let the foxes run through the grain fields of the Philistine people. In this way, he burned up the plants growing in their fields and the stacks of grain they had cut. He also burned up their fields of grapes and their olive trees.

⁶The Philistine people asked, "Who did this?"

Someone told them, "Samson, the son-in-law of the man from Timnah, did this. He did this because his father-in-law gave Samson's wife to the best man at his wedding." So the Philistine people burned Samson's wife and her father to death.

⁷Then Samson said to the Philistine people, "You did this bad thing to me. So now I will do bad things to you. Then I will be finished with you!"

⁸Then Samson attacked the Philistine people. He killed many of them. Then he went and stayed in a cave. The cave was in a place named the Rock of Etam.

⁹Then the Philistine people went to the land of Judah. They stopped near a place named Lehi. Their army camped there ⌊and prepared for war⌋. ¹⁰The men of the family group of Judah asked them, "Why have you Philistine people come here to fight us?"

They answered, "We have come to get Samson. We want to make him our prisoner. We want to punish him for the things he did to our people."

¹¹Then 3000 men from the family group of Judah went to Samson. They went to the cave near the Rock of Etam. They said to him, "What have you done to us? Don't you know that the Philistine people rule over us?"

Samson answered, "I only punished them for the things they did to me."

¹²Then they said to Samson, "We have come to tie you up. We will give you to the Philistine people."

Samson said to the men from Judah, "Promise me that you yourselves will not hurt me."

¹³The men from Judah said, "We agree. We will just tie you up and give you to the Philistine people. We promise that we will not kill you." So they tied Samson with two new ropes. They led him up from the cave in the rock.

¹⁴When Samson came to the place called Lehi, the Philistine people came to meet him. They were shouting from joy. Then the Spirit of the

---

fourth day This is from the ancient Greek translation. The Hebrew has, "seventh day."

Lord came on Samson with great power. ⌊Samson broke the ropes.⌋ The ropes seemed weak like burnt strings. The ropes fell off his arms as if they had melted. ¹⁵Samson found a jawbone of a donkey that had died. He took the jawbone and killed 1,000 Philistine men with it.

¹⁶Then Samson said,

> With a donkey's jawbone
> I killed 1,000 men!
> With a donkey's jawbone
> I piled* them into a tall pile.

¹⁷When Samson finished speaking, he threw the jawbone down. So that place was named Ramath Lehi.*

¹⁸Samson was very thirsty. So he cried to the Lord. He said, "I am your servant. You gave me this great victory. Please don't let me die from thirst now? Please don't let me be captured by men who are not even circumcised?"

¹⁹There is a hole in the ground at Lehi. God made that hole crack open, and water came out. Samson drank that water and felt better. He felt strong again. So he named that water spring En Hakkore.* It is still there in the city of Lehi today.

²⁰So Samson was a judge for the people of Israel for 20 years. That was during the time of the Philistine people.

Samson Goes to the City of Gaza

16 One day Samson went to the city of Gaza. He saw a prostitute there. He went in to stay the night with her. ²Someone told the people of Gaza, "Samson has come here." They wanted to kill Samson, so they surrounded the city. They hid near the city gate and waited all night for Samson. They were very quiet all night long. They had said to each other, "When morning comes, we will kill Samson."

³But Samson only stayed with the prostitute until midnight. Samson got up at midnight. Samson grabbed the doors of the city gate and pulled them loose from the wall. Samson pulled down the doors, the two posts, and the bars that lock the door shut. Samson put those things on his shoulders and carried them to the top of the hill near the city of Hebron.

Samson and Delilah

⁴Later, Samson fell in love with a woman named Delilah. She was from Sorek Valley.

⁵The rulers of the Philistine people went to Delilah. They said, "We want to know what makes Samson so strong. Try to trick him into telling you his secret. Then we will know how to capture him and tie him up. Then we will be able to control him. If you do this, each one of us will give you 28 pounds* of silver."

⁶So Delilah said to Samson, "Tell me why you are so strong. How could someone tie you up and make you helpless?"

⁷Samson answered, "Someone would have to tie me up with seven bowstrings that have not been dried yet. If someone did that, I would be weak like any other man."

⁸Then the rulers of the Philistine people brought seven new bowstrings to Delilah. Those bowstrings had not been dried. Delilah tied up Samson with the bowstrings. ⁹Some men were hiding in the next room. Delilah said to Samson, "Samson, the Philistine men are going to capture you!" But Samson easily broke the bowstrings. They broke like ashes from a piece of string burned in a lamp. So the Philistine people did not find out the secret of Samson's strength.

¹⁰Then Delilah said to Samson, "You lied to me! You made me look foolish. Please tell me the truth, how could someone tie you up?"

¹¹Samson said, "Someone would have to tie me up with new ropes. They would have to tie me with ropes that have not been used before. If someone did that, I would become as weak as any other man."

¹²So Delilah took some new ropes and tied up Samson. Some men were hiding in the next room. Then Delilah called out to him, "Samson, the Philistine men are going to capture you!" But he broke the ropes easily. He broke them like they were threads.

¹³Then Delilah said to Samson, "You lied to me again! You made me look foolish. Now, tell me how someone could tie you up."

Samson said, "If you use the loom* to weave the seven braids* of hair on my head and tighten it with a pin, I will become as weak as any other man."

---

piled In Hebrew, the word "pile" is like the word, "donkey."
Ramath Lehi This name means "Jawbone Heights."
En Hakkore This means "The spring of the one that calls."

28 pounds Literally, "1,100 ⌊shekels⌋."

Later, Samson went to sleep. So Delilah used the loom to weave the seven braids of hair on his head.* ¹⁴Then Delilah fastened the loom to the ground with a tent peg. Again she called out to him, "Samson, the Philistine men are going to capture you!" Samson pulled up the tent peg, the loom,* and the shuttle!*

¹⁵Then Delilah said to Samson, "How can you say, 'I love you,' when you don't even trust me? You refuse to tell me your secret. This is the third time you made me look foolish. You haven't told me the secret of your great strength." ¹⁶She kept bothering Samson day after day. He got so tired of her asking him about his secret that he felt like he was going to die. ¹⁷Finally, Samson told Delilah everything. He said, "I have never had my hair cut. I was dedicated to God before I was born. If someone shaved my head, then I would lose my strength. I would become as weak as any other man."

¹⁸Delilah saw that Samson had told her his secret. She sent a message to the rulers of the Philistine people. She said, "Come back again. Samson has told me everything." So the rulers of the Philistine people came back to Delilah. They brought the money that they had promised to give her. ¹⁹Delilah got Samson to go to sleep while he was lying in her lap. Then she called in a man to shave off the seven braids* of Samson's hair. In this way she made Samson weak. Samson's strength left him. ²⁰Then Delilah called out to him, "Samson, the Philistine men are going to capture you!" He woke up and thought, "I will escape like I did before and free myself." But Samson did not know that the Lord had left him.

²¹The Philistine men captured Samson. They tore out his eyes, and took him down to the city of Gaza. Then they put chains on him to keep him from running away. They put Samson in prison and made him work grinding grain. ²²But Samson's hair began to grow again.

²³The rulers of the Philistine people came together to celebrate. They were going to offer a great sacrifice to their god Dagon.* They said, "Our god helped us defeat Samson our enemy."

²⁴When the Philistine people saw Samson, they praised their god. They said,

"This man destroyed our people!
This man killed many of our people!
But our god helped us take our enemy!"

²⁵The people were having a good time at the celebration. So they said, "Bring Samson out. We want to make fun of him." So they brought Samson from the prison and made fun of him. They made Samson stand between the columns in the temple of the god Dagon. ²⁶A servant was holding Samson's hand. Samson said to him, "Put me where I can feel the columns that hold this temple up. I want to lean against them."

²⁷The temple was crowded with men and women. All the rulers of the Philistine people were there. There were about 3,000 men and women on the roof* of the temple. They were laughing and making fun of Samson. ²⁸Then Samson said a prayer to the Lord. He said, "Lord All-Powerful, remember me. God, please give me strength one more time. Let me do this one thing to punish these Philistines for tearing out my two eyes!" ²⁹Then Samson held the two columns in the center of the temple. These two columns supported the whole temple. He braced himself between the two columns. One column was at his right side and the other at his left side. ³⁰Samson said, "Let me die with these Philistines!" Then he pushed as hard as he could. And the temple fell on the rulers and all the people in it. In this way, Samson killed many more Philistine people when he died than when he was alive.

³¹Samson's brothers and all the people in his father's family went down to get his body. They brought him back and buried him in his father's tomb. That tomb is between the cities of Zorah and Eshtaol. Samson was a judge for the people of Israel for 20 years.

Micah's Idols

17 There was a man named Micah that lived in the hill country of Ephraim. ²Micah said to his mother, "Do you remember that someone stole

---

loom A machine for making cloth from thread.
braids Hair that has been twisted together like a rope.
So Delilah ... head This is found in the ancient Greek translation. It is not in the Hebrew text.
shuttle The tool used to pull the threads back and forth on a loom to make cloth.

Dagon The Canaanite people worshiped this false god hoping he would give them a good harvest of grain. This was probably the most important god for the Philistine people.
roof In ancient Israel, a roof was often flat and used as an exra room.

28 pounds* of silver from you. I heard you say a curse about that. Well, I have the silver. I took it."

His mother said, "The Lord bless you, my son." ³Micah gave the 28 pounds* of silver back to his mother. Then she said, "I will give this silver as a special gift to the Lord. I will give it to my son so he can make a statue and cover it with the silver. So now, son, I give the silver back to you."

⁴But Micah gave the silver back to his mother. So she took about 5 pounds* of the silver and gave them to a silversmith.* The silversmith used the silver to make a statue covered with silver. The statue was put in Micah's house. ⁵Micah had a temple for worshiping idols. He made an ephod* and some house idols. Then Micah chose one of his sons to be his priest. (⁶At that time, the people of Israel did not have a king. So each person did what he himself thought was right.)

⁷There was a young man that was a Levite.* He was from the city of Bethlehem, Judah. He had been living among the family group of Judah. ⁸That young man left Bethlehem, Judah. He was looking for another place to live. As he was traveling, he came to Micah's house. Micah's house was in the hill country of the land of Ephraim. ⁹Micah asked him, "Where have you come from?"

The young man answered, "I am a Levite* from the city of Bethlehem, Judah. I am looking for a place to live."

¹⁰Then Micah said to him, "Live with me. Be my father and my priest. I will give you 4 ounces* of silver each year. I will also give you clothes and food."

The Levite* did what Micah asked. ¹¹The young Levite agreed to live with Micah. The young man became like one of Micah's own sons. ¹²Micah chose him to be his priest. So the young man became a priest and lived in Micah's house. ¹³And Micah said, "Now I know that the Lord will be good to me. I know this because I have a man from the family group of Levi to be my priest."

28 pounds Literally, "1,100 ₁shekels₁."
5 pounds Literally, "200 ₁shekels₁."
silversmith A person that makes things from silver.
ephod We do not know exactly what this was. It may have been a special vest or coat, like the High Priest of Israel wore (see Exodus 28). Or it may have been an idol.
Levite A person from the tribe of Levi. The Levites helped the priests in the temple and also worked for the civil government.
4 ounces Literally, "10 ₁shekels₁."

Dan Captures the City of Laish

18 At that time, the people of Israel did not have a king. And at that time, the family group of Dan was still looking for a place to live. They did not have their own land yet. The other family groups of Israel already had their land. But the family group of Dan had not taken their land yet.

²So the family group of Dan sent five soldiers to look for some land. They went to search for a good place to live. Those five men were from the cities of Zorah and Eshtaol. They were chosen because they were from all the families of Dan. They were told, "Go, look for some land."

The five men came to the hill country of Ephraim. They came to Micah's house and spent the night there. ³When the five men came close to Micah's house, they heard the voice of the young Levite man. They recognized his voice, so they stopped at Micah's house. They asked the young man, "Who brought you to this place? What are you doing here? What is your business here?"

⁴The young man told them about the things Micah had done for him. "Micah hired me," the young man said. "I am his priest."

⁵So they said to him, "Please ask God something for us. We want to know something: Will our search for a place to live be successful?"

⁶The priest said to the five men, "Yes. Go in peace. The Lord will lead you on your way."

⁷So the five men left. They came to the city of Laish. They saw that the people of that city lived in safety. They were ruled by the people of Sidon. Everything was peaceful and quiet. The people had plenty of everything. And they didn't have any enemies nearby to hurt them. Also, they lived a long way from the city of Sidon and they did not have any agreements with the people of Aram.*

⁸The five men went back to the cities of Zorah and Eshtaol. Their relatives asked them, "What did you learn?"

⁹The five men answered, "We have found some land, and it is very good. We should attack them. Don't wait! Let's go and take that land! ¹⁰When you come to that place, you will see that there is plenty of land. There is plenty of everything there. You will also see that the people are not expecting an attack. Surely God has given that land to us."

¹¹So 600 men from the family group of Dan left the cities of Zorah and Eshtaol. They were ready

they did not have ... Aram Or, "they did not have any dealings with people."

for war. ¹²On their way to the city of Laish, they stopped near the city of Kiriath Jearim in the land of Judah. They set up a camp there. That is why the place west of Kiriath Jearim is named Mahaneh Dan* to this very day. ¹³From that place, the 600 men traveled on to the hill country of Ephraim. Then they came to Micah's house.

¹⁴So the five men that had explored the land around Laish spoke. They said to their relatives, "There is an ephod* in one of these houses. And there are also household gods, a carved statue, and a silver idol. You know what to do—go get them↓." ¹⁵So they stopped at Micah's house, where the young Levite man lived. They asked the young man how he was. ¹⁶The 600 men from the family group of Dan stood at the entrance of the gate. They all had their weapons and were ready for war. ¹⁷⁻¹⁸The five spies went into the house. The priest stood just outside by the gate with the 600 men that were ready for war. The men took the carved idol, the ephod,* the house idols, and the silver idol. The young Levite priest said, "What are you doing?"

¹⁹The five men answered, "Be quiet! Don't say a word. Come with us. Be our father and our priest. You must choose. Is it better for you to be a priest for just one man? Or is it better for you to be a priest for a whole family group of Israelite people?"

²⁰This made the Levite man happy. So he took the ephod*, the house idols, and the idol. He went with those men from the family group of Dan.

²¹Then the 600 men from the family group of Dan, with the Levite priest, turned and left Micah's house. They put their little children, their animals, and all their things in front of them.

²²The men from the family group of Dan went a long way from that place. But the people living near Micah met together. Then they began chasing the men of Dan and caught up with them. ²³The men with Micah were shouting at the men of Dan. The men of Dan turned around. They said to Micah, "What's the problem? Why are you shouting?"

²⁴Micah answered, "You men from Dan took my idols. I made those idols for myself. You have also taken my priest. What do I have left now? How can you ask me, 'What's the problem?'"

²⁵The men from the family group of Dan answered, "You had better not argue with us. Some of our men have hot tempers. If you shout at us, those men might attack you. You and your families might get killed."

²⁶Then the men of Dan turned around and went on their way. Micah knew that those men were too strong for him. So he went back home.

²⁷So the men of Dan took the idols that Micah made. They also took the priest that had been with Micah. Then they came to Laish. They attacked the people living in Laish. Those people were at peace. They were not expecting an attack. The men of Dan killed those people with their swords. Then they burned the city. ²⁸The people living in Laish did not have anyone to rescue them. They lived too far from the city of Sidon for those people to help. And the people of Laish did not have any agreements with the people of Aram— so those people did not help them. The city of Laish was in a valley which belonged to the town of Beth Rehob. The people from Dan built a new city in that place. And that city became their home. ²⁹The people of Dan gave that city a new name. That city had been called Laish, but they changed the name to Dan. They named the city after their ancestor* Dan, one of the sons of Israel.

³⁰The people of the family group of Dan set up the idols in the city of Dan. They made Jonathan son of Gershom their priest. Gershom was the son of Moses.* Jonathan and his sons were priests for the family group of Dan until the time when the Israelite people were taken as prisoners ↓to Babylon↓. ³¹The people of Dan worshiped the idols that Micah had made. They worshiped those idols the whole time that the house of God was in Shiloh.

A Levite Man and His Woman Servant

19 At that time, the people of Israel did not have a king.

There was a Levite* man that lived far back in the hill country of Ephraim. That man had a woman as a servant that was like a wife to him. That woman servant* was from the city of Bethlehem in the country of Judah. ²But his woman servant had an argument with the Levite

---

Mahaneh Dan This name means "The Camp of Dan."

ephod We do not know exactly what this was. It may have been a special vest or coat, like the High Priest of Israel wore (see Exodus 28). Or it may have been an idol.

ancestor Literally, "father." This means a person that people are descended from.

Moses Or, "Manasseh."

man. She left him and went back to her father's house in Bethlehem, Judah. She stayed there for four months. ³Then her husband went after her. He wanted to speak kindly to her so that she would come back to him. He took with him his servant and two donkeys. The Levite man came to her father's house. Her father saw the Levite man and came out to greet him. The father was very happy. ⁴The woman's father led the Levite man into his house. The Levite's father-in-law invited him to stay. So the Levite man stayed for three days. He ate, drank, and slept in his father-in-law's house.

⁵On the fourth day, they got up early in the morning. The Levite* man was getting ready to leave. But the young woman's father said to his son-in-law, "Eat something first. After you eat, then you can go." ⁶So the Levite man and his father-in-law sat down to eat and drink together. After that, the young woman's father said to the Levite man, "Please stay tonight. Relax and enjoy yourself. Wait until this afternoon to leave." So the two men ate together. ⁷The Levite got up to leave, but his father-in-law persuaded him to stay the night again.

⁸Then, on the fifth day, the Levite man got up early in the morning. He was ready to leave. But the woman's father said to his son-in-law, "Eat something first. Relax and stay until this afternoon." So they both ate together again.

⁹Then the Levite man, his woman servant,* and his servant got up to leave. But the young woman's father said, "It is almost dark. The day is almost gone. So stay the night here and enjoy yourself. Tomorrow morning you can get up early and go on your way."

¹⁰But the Levite man did not want to stay another night. He took his two donkeys and his woman servant.* He traveled as far as the city of Jebus. (Jebus is another name for Jerusalem.) ¹¹The day was almost over. They were near the city of Jebus. So the servant said to his master, the Levite* man, "Let's stop at this Jebusite city. Let's stay the night here."

¹²But his master, the Levite man, said, "No. We won't go inside a strange city. Those people are not Israelite people. We will go to the city of Gibeah."* ¹³The Levite man said, "Come on. Let's try to make it to Gibeah or Ramah. We can stay the night in one of those cities."

¹⁴So the Levite* man and the people with him traveled on. The sun was going down just as they entered the city of Gibeah. Gibeah is in the area that belongs to the family group of Benjamin. ¹⁵So they stopped at Gibeah. They planned to stay the night in that city. They came to the city square* in the city and sat down there. But no one invited them home to stay the night.

¹⁶That evening an old man came into the city from the fields. His home was in the hill country of Ephraim. But now he was living in the city of Gibeah. (The men of Gibeah were from the family group of Benjamin.) ¹⁷The old man saw the traveler, (the Levite man) in the public square. The old man asked, "Where are you going? Where did you come from?"

¹⁸The Levite* man answered, "We are traveling from the city Bethlehem, Judah. We are going home. I am from far back in the hill country of Ephraim. I have been to Bethlehem, Judah. And now, I am going to my house.* ¹⁹We already have straw and food for our donkeys. There is also bread and wine for me, the young woman and my servant. We don't need anything."

²⁰The old man said, "You are welcome to stay at my house. I will give you anything you need. Only, don't stay the night in the public square!" ²¹Then the old man took the Levite* man and the people with him to his house. He fed their donkeys. They washed their feet. Then they had something to eat and drink.

²²While the Levite* man and those that were with him were enjoying themselves, some of the men from that city surrounded the house. They were very bad men. They began beating on the door. They shouted at the old man that owned the house. They said, "Bring out the man that came to your house. We want to have sex with him."

²³The old man went outside and spoke to those bad men. He said, "No, my friends, don't do such bad things! That man is a guest in my house.* Don't do this terrible sin. ²⁴Look, here is my daughter. She has never had sex before. I will bring her out to you now. You can use her any

---

Levite A person from the tribe of Levi. The Levites helped the priests in the temple and also worked for the civil government.

woman servant Or, "concubine," a slave woman who was like a wife to a man.

Gibeah Gibeah was a few miles north of Jebus.

square A public place near the city gates. The people of the city had meetings there, and visitors often camped there.

my house This is from the ancient Greek translation. The Hebrew has, "the Lord's house."

way you want. But don't do such a terrible sin against this man."

²⁵But those bad men would not listen to the old man. So the Levite* man took his woman servant* and put her outside with those evil men. Those evil men hurt her and raped her all night long. Then, at dawn, they let her go. ²⁶At dawn, the woman came back to the house where her master was staying. She fell down at the front door. She lay there until it was daylight.

²⁷The Levite* man got up early the next morning. He wanted to go home. He opened the door to go outside. And a hand fell across the threshold of the door. There was his woman servant.* She had fallen down against the door. ²⁸The Levite man said to her, "Get up, let's go!" But she did not answer—she was dead.

The Levite man put his woman servant* on his donkey and went home. ²⁹When he arrived at his house, he took a knife and cut his woman servant* into 12 parts. Then he sent those 12 parts of the woman to all the areas where the people of Israel lived. ³⁰Everyone that saw this said, "Nothing like this has ever happened in Israel before. We haven't seen anything like this from the time we came out of Egypt. Discuss this and tell us what to do."

The War Between Israel and Benjamin

20 So all the people of Israel joined together. They all came together to stand before the Lord in the city of Mizpah. People came from everywhere in Israel.* Even the Israelite people from Gilead* were there. ²The leaders of all the family groups of Israel were there. They took their places in the public meeting of God's people. There were 400,000 soldiers with swords in that place. ³The people from the family group of Benjamin heard that the people of Israel were meeting together in Mizpah. The people of Israel said, "Tell us how this terrible thing happened."

⁴So the husband of the woman that had been murdered told them the story. He said, "My woman servant* and I came to the city of Gibeah in the area of Benjamin. We spent the night there. ⁵But during the night the leaders of the city of Gibeah came to the house where I was staying. They surrounded the house, and they wanted to kill me. They raped my woman servant,* and she died. ⁶So I took my woman servant* and cut her into pieces. Then I sent one piece to each of the family groups of Israel. I sent the 12 pieces to the lands we have received. I did that because the people of Benjamin have done this terrible thing in Israel. ⁷Now, all you men of Israel, speak up. Give your decision about what we should do."

⁸Then all the people stood up at the same time. They said together, "None of us will go home. No, not one of us will go back to his house. ⁹Now this is what we will do to the city of Gibeah: We will throw lots* to let God show us what to do to those people. ¹⁰We will choose ten men from every 100 from all the family groups of Israel. And we will choose 100 men from every 1,000. We will choose 1,000 men from every 10,000. Those men we have chosen will get supplies for the army. Then the army will go to the city of Gibeah in the area of Benjamin. The army will punish those people for the terrible thing they did among the people of Israel."

¹¹So all the men of Israel gathered together at the city of Gibeah. They were all agreed to what they were doing. ¹²The family groups of Israel sent men to the family group of Benjamin with a message. The message was: "What about this terrible thing that some of your men have done? ¹³Send those bad men from the city of Gibeah to us. Give us those men so that we can put them to death. We must remove the evil from among the people of Israel."

But the people from the family group of Benjamin would not listen to the messengers from their relatives, the other people of Israel. ¹⁴The people from the family group of Benjamin left their cities and went to the city of Gibeah. They went to Gibeah to fight against the other family groups of Israel. ¹⁵The people from the family group of Benjamin got 26,000 soldiers together. All those soldiers were trained for war. They also had 700 trained soldiers from the city of Gibeah. ¹⁶There were also 700 trained soldiers that were

---

That man ... my house At this time, it was a custom that if you invited people to be your guests, then you had to protect and care for those people.

Levite A person from the tribe of Levi. The Levites helped the priests in the temple and also worked for the civil government.

woman servant Or, "concubine," a slave woman who was like a wife to a man.

from everywhere in Israel Literally, "from Dan to Beersheba."

Gilead This area was east of the Jordan River.

lot(s) Sticks, stones, or pieces of bone used like dice for making decisions. See Proverbs 16:33.

left-handed. Each one of them could use a sling* with great skill. They all could use a sling to throw a stone at a hair and not miss! ¹⁷All the family groups of Israel, except Benjamin, gathered together 400,000 fighting men. Those 400,000 men had swords. Each one was a trained soldier. ¹⁸The people of Israel went up to the city of Bethel. At Bethel they asked God, "Which family group will be first to attack the family group of Benjamin?"

The Lord answered, "The family group of Judah will go first."

¹⁹The next morning the people of Israel got up. They made a camp near the city of Gibeah. ²⁰Then the army of Israel went out to fight the army of Benjamin. The army of Israel got ready for a battle against the army of Benjamin at the city of Gibeah. ²¹Then the army of Benjamin came out of the city of Gibeah. The army of Benjamin killed 22,000 men in the army of Israel during the battle that day. ²²⁻²³The people of Israel went to the Lord. They cried until evening. They asked the Lord, "Should we go to fight the people of Benjamin again? Those people are our relatives."

The Lord answered, "Go fight against them." The men of Israel encouraged each other. Then they again went out to fight, like they did the first day. ²⁴Then the army of Israel came near the army of Benjamin. This was the second day of the war. ²⁵The army of Benjamin came out of the city of Gibeah to attack the army of Israel on the second day. This time, the army of Benjamin killed another 18,000 men from the army of Israel. All of those men in the army of Israel were trained soldiers.

²⁶Then all the people of Israel went up to the city of Bethel. At that place they sat down and cried to the Lord. They did not eat anything all day, until evening. They also offered burnt offerings and fellowship offerings to the Lord. ²⁷The men of Israel asked the Lord a question. (In those days God's Box of the Agreement* was there at Bethel. ²⁸Phinehas was the priest that served God there. Phinehas was the son of Eleazar. Eleazar was the son of Aaron.) The people of Israel asked, "The people of Benjamin are our relatives. Should we again go to fight against them? Or should we stop fighting?"

The Lord answered, "Go. Tomorrow I will help you to defeat them."

²⁹Then the army of Israel hid some men all around the city of Gibeah. ³⁰The army of Israel went to fight against the city of Gibeah on the third day. They got ready for battle, like they did before. ³¹The army of Benjamin came out of the city of Gibeah to fight the army of Israel. The army of Israel backed up and let the army of Benjamin chase them. In this way, the army of Benjamin was tricked into leaving the city far behind them.

The army of Benjamin began to kill some of the men in the army of Israel, like they did before. They killed about 30 men from Israel. They killed some of those men in the fields, and they killed some of those men on the roads. One road led to the city of Bethel. The other road led to the city of Gibeah. ³²The men of Benjamin said, "We are winning like before!"

The men of Israel were running away, but it was a trick. They wanted to lead the men of Benjamin away from their city and onto the roads. ³³So all the men ran away. They stopped at a place named Baal Tamar. Some of the men of Israel were hiding west of Gibeah. They ran from their hiding places ₁and attacked Gibeah₁. ³⁴10,000 of Israel's best trained soldiers attacked the city of Gibeah. The fighting was very heavy. But the army of Benjamin did not know what terrible thing was going to happen to them.

³⁵The Lord used the army of Israel and defeated the army of Benjamin. On that day, the army of Israel killed 25,100 soldiers from Benjamin. All those soldiers had been trained for war. ³⁶So the people of Benjamin saw that they were defeated.

The army of Israel had moved back. They moved back because they were depending on the surprise attack. They had men hiding near Gibeah. ³⁷The men that were hiding rushed into the city of Gibeah. They spread out and killed everyone in the city with their swords. ³⁸Now the men of Israel had made a plan with the men that were hiding. The men that were hiding were supposed to send a special signal. The men were supposed to make a big cloud of smoke.

³⁹⁻⁴¹The army of Benjamin had killed about 30 Israelite soldiers. So the men of Benjamin were saying, "We are winning, like before." But then a big cloud of smoke began to rise from the city.

---

sling A strip of leather for throwing rocks.

The men of Benjamin turned around and saw the smoke. The whole city was on fire. Then the army of Israel stopped running away. They turned around and began to fight. The men of Benjamin were afraid. Now they knew what terrible thing had happened to them.

⁴²So the army of Benjamin ran away from the army of Israel. They ran toward the desert. But they could not escape the fighting. And the men of Israel came out of the cities and killed them. ⁴³The men of Israel surrounded the men of Benjamin and began chasing them. They did not let them rest. They defeated them in the area east of Gibeah. ⁴⁴So 18,000 brave and strong fighters from the army of Benjamin were killed.

⁴⁵The army of Benjamin turned around and ran toward the desert. They ran to a place called the Rock of Rimmon. But the army of Israel killed 5,000 soldiers from Benjamin along the roads. They kept chasing the men of Benjamin. They chased them as far as a place named Gidom. The army of Israel killed 2,000 more men from Benjamin in that place.

⁴⁶On that day, 25,000 men of the army of Benjamin were killed. All those men fought bravely with their swords. ⁴⁷But 600 men from Benjamin ran into the desert. They went to the place called the Rock of Rimmon and stayed there for four months. ⁴⁸The men of Israel went back to the land of Benjamin. They killed the people in every city they came to. They also killed all the animals. They destroyed everything they could find. They burned every city they came to.

Getting Wives for the Men of Benjamin

21 At Mizpah, the men of Israel made a promise. This was their promise: "Not one of us will let his daughter marry a man from the family group of Benjamin."

²The people of Israel went to the city of Bethel. There they sat before God until evening. They cried loudly as they sat there. ³They said to God, "Lord, you are the God of the people of Israel. Why has this terrible thing happened to us? Why has one family group of the people of Israel been taken away?"

⁴Early the next day, the people of Israel built an altar.* They put burnt offerings and fellowship offerings to God on that altar. ⁵Then the people of Israel said, "Are there any family groups of Israel that did not come here to meet with us before the Lord?" They asked this question because they had made a serious promise. They had promised that anyone that did not come together with the other family groups at the city of Mizpah would be killed.

⁶Then the people of Israel felt sorry for their relatives, the people of Benjamin. They said, "Today, one family group has been separated from Israel. ⁷We made a promise before the Lord. We promised not to allow our daughters to marry a man from Benjamin. How can we make sure that the men of Benjamin will have wives?"

⁸Then the people of Israel asked, "Which one of the family groups of Israel did not come here to Mizpah? We have come together before the Lord. Surely one family was not here!" Then they found that no one from the city of Jabesh Gilead had met together with the other people of Israel. ⁹The people of Israel counted everyone to see who was there and who was not. They found that no one from Jabesh Gilead was there. ¹⁰So the people of Israel sent 12,000 soldiers to the city of Jabesh Gilead. They told those soldiers, "Go to Jabesh Gilead, and use your swords to kill every person that lives there, even the women and children. ¹¹You must do this! You must kill every man in Jabesh Gilead. Also kill every woman that has had sexual relations with a man. But do not kill any woman that has never had sex with a man." So the soldiers did those things.* ¹²Those 12,000 soldiers found 400 young women in the city of Jabesh Gilead, that had never had sex with a man. The soldiers brought those women to the camp at Shiloh. Shiloh is in the land of Canaan.

¹³Then the people of Israel sent a message to the men of Benjamin. They offered to make peace with the men of Benjamin. The men of Benjamin were at the place named the Rock of Rimmon. ¹⁴So the men of Benjamin came back to Israel. The people of Israel gave them the women from Jabesh Gilead that they had not killed. But there were not enough women for all the men of Benjamin.

¹⁵The people of Israel felt sorry for the men of Benjamin. They felt sorry for them because the Lord had separated them from the other family groups of Israel. ¹⁶The elders *(leaders)* of the people of Israel said, "The women of the family group of Benjamin have been killed. Where can we get wives for the men of Benjamin that are still alive? ¹⁷The men of Benjamin that are still alive must have children to continue their families. This must be done so that a family group in Israel will

---

But do not kill ... those things This is in the ancient Greek translation, but not in the Hebrew.

not die out! ¹⁸But we cannot allow our daughters to marry the men of Benjamin. We have made this promise: 'Bad things will happen to anyone that gives a wife to a man of Benjamin.' ¹⁹We have an idea! This is the time for the festival of the Lord at the city of Shiloh. This festival is celebrated every year there." (The city of Shiloh is north of the city of Bethel, and east of the road that goes from Bethel to Shechem. And it is also to the south of the city of Lebonah.)

²⁰So the elders *(leaders)* told the men of Benjamin about their idea. They said, "Go and hide in the vineyards. ²¹Watch for the time during the festival when the young women from Shiloh come out to join the dancing. Then run out from where you are hiding in the vineyards. Each of you should take one of the young women from the city of Shiloh. Take those young women to the land of Benjamin and marry them. ²²The fathers or brothers of those young women will come and complain to us. But we will say, 'Be kind to the men of Benjamin. Let them marry those women. They took women from you, but they did not make war against you. They took the women, so you didn't break your promise to God. You promised that you would not give them women to marry—you did not give the women to the men of Benjamin, they took the women from you! So you did not break your promise.'"

²³So that is what the men of the family group of Benjamin did. While the young women were dancing, each man caught one of them. They took those young women away and married them. They went back to their land. The men of Benjamin built cities again in that land, and they lived in those cities. ²⁴Then the people of Israel went home. They went to their own land and family group.

²⁵In those days the people of Israel did not have a king. So everyone did whatever he thought was right.

Ruth

Famine in Judah

1 Long ago, during the time the judges* ruled, there was a bad time when there was not enough food to eat. A man named Elimelech left Bethlehem, Judah. He, his wife and his two sons moved to the hill country of Moab.* ²The man's wife was named Naomi and his two sons were named Mahlon and Kilion. These people were from the Ephrathah family of Bethlehem, Judah. The family traveled to the hill country of Moab and stayed there.

³Later, Naomi's husband, Elimelech, died. So only Naomi and her two sons were left. ⁴Her sons married women from the country of Moab. One wife's name was Orpah, and the other wife's name was Ruth. They lived in Moab about ten years, ⁵and Mahlon and Kilion also died. So Naomi was left alone without her husband or her two sons.

Naomi Goes Home

⁶While Naomi was in the hill country of Moab, she heard that the Lord had helped his people. He had given food to his people ₍in Judah₎. So Naomi decided to leave the hill country of Moab and go back home. Her daughters-in-law also decided to go with her. ⁷They left the place where they had been living and started walking back to the land of Judah.

⁸Then Naomi told her daughters-in-law, "Each of you should go back home to your mother. You have been very kind to me and my dead sons. So I pray the Lord will be just as kind to you. ⁹I pray that he helps each of you to find a husband and a nice home." Naomi kissed her daughters-in-law, and they all started crying.

¹⁰Then the daughters said, "But we want to come with you and go to your family."

¹¹But Naomi said, "No, daughters, go back to your own homes. Why should you go with me? ₍I cannot help you.₎ I don't have any more sons in me to be your husbands. ¹²Go back home! I am too old to have a new husband. Even if I thought I could be married again, I could not help you. If I became pregnant tonight and had two sons, ₍it would not help₎. ¹³You would have to wait until they grew to become men before you could marry them. I can't make you wait that long for husbands. That would make me very sad! ₍And I am already sad enough₎—the Lord has done many things to me!"

¹⁴So the women cried very much again. Then Orpah kissed Naomi ₍and left₎. But Ruth hugged her ₍and stayed₎.

¹⁵Naomi said, "Look, your sister-in-law has gone back to her own people and her own gods. So you should do the same thing."

¹⁶But Ruth said, "Don't force me to leave you! Don't force me to go back to my own people. Let me go with you. Wherever you go, I will go. Wherever you sleep, I will sleep. Your people will be my people. Your God will be my God. ¹⁷Where you die, I will die. And that is where I will be buried. I ask the Lord to punish me if I do not keep this promise: Only death will separate us."*

The Homecoming

¹⁸Naomi saw that Ruth wanted very much to go with her. So Naomi stopped arguing with her. ¹⁹Naomi and Ruth traveled until they came to the town of Bethlehem. When the two women entered Bethlehem, all the people were very excited. They said, "Is this Naomi?"

---

judges Special leaders that God sent to help and protect the people of Israel. This was before there were kings in Israel.
Moab A country east of Israel.

I ask the Lord ... separate us Literally, "May the Lord do this to me, and even more, unless death separates us!"

²⁰But Naomi told the people, "Don't call me Naomi,* call me Marah.* Use this name because ₍God₎ All-Powerful has made my life very sad. ²¹I had everything I wanted when I left. But now, the Lord brings me home with nothing. The Lord has made me sad, so why should you call me 'Happy'?* ₍God₎ All-Powerful has given much trouble to me."

²²So Naomi and her daughter-in-law Ruth (the woman from Moab) came back from the hill country of Moab. These two women came to Bethlehem, Judah at the beginning of the barley harvest.

Ruth Meets Boaz

2 There was a rich man living in Bethlehem. His name was Boaz. Boaz was one of Naomi's close relatives* from Elimelech's family.

²One day Ruth (the woman from Moab) said to Naomi, "I think I will go to the fields. Maybe I can find someone that would be kind to me and let me gather the grain he leaves in his field."

³Naomi said, "Fine, daughter, go ahead."

So Ruth went to the fields. She followed the workers that were cutting the grain, and she gathered the grain that was left.* It happened that part of the field belonged to Boaz, the man from Elimelech's family.

⁴Later, Boaz came to the field from Bethlehem. Boaz greeted his workers. He said, "The Lord be with you!"

And the workers answered, "And may the Lord bless you!"

⁵Then Boaz spoke to his servant that was in charge of the workers. He asked, "Whose girl is that?"

⁶The servant answered, "She is that Moabite woman who came with Naomi from the hill country of Moab. ⁷She came early this morning and asked me if she could follow the workers and gather the grain that was left on the ground. And she has been working ever since. That is her house over there."*

⁸Then Boaz said to Ruth, "Listen, child. Stay here in my field to gather grain for yourself. There is no need for you to go to any other person's field. Continue following behind my women workers. ⁹Watch to see which fields they go to, and follow them. I have warned the young men not to bother you. When you are thirsty, go and drink from the same water jug my men drink from."

¹⁰Then Ruth bowed very low to the ground. She said to Boaz, "I am surprised you even noticed me! I am a stranger, ₍but you have been very kind to me₎."

¹¹Boaz answered her, "I know about all the help you have given to Naomi, your mother-in-law. I know you helped her even after your husband died. And I know that you left your father and mother and your own country and came here to this country. You did not know any people from this country, but you came here with Naomi. ¹²The Lord will reward you for all the good things you have done. You will be paid in full by the Lord, the God of Israel. You have come to him for safety,* ₍and he will protect you₎."

¹³Then Ruth said, "You are very kind to me, sir. I am only a servant. I am not even equal to one of your servants. But you have said kind words to me and comforted me."

¹⁴At lunch time, Boaz told Ruth, "Come here! Eat some of our bread. Here, dip your bread in our vinegar."

So Ruth sat down with the workers. Boaz gave her some roasted grain. Ruth ate until she was full, and there was some food left. ¹⁵Then Ruth got up and went back to work.

Then Boaz told his servants, "Let Ruth gather even around the piles of grain. Don't stop her. ¹⁶And make her work easier by dropping some full heads of grain for her. Let her gather that grain. Don't tell her to stop."

Naomi This name means "Happy" or "Pleasant."
Marah This name means "Bitter" or "Sad."
Happy This is the name Naomi.
close relative(s) In ancient Israel, if a man died without children, one of his close relatives would take the dead man's wife so she could have children. He would care for this family, but this family and their property would not belong to him. It would all be in the dead man's name.
gathered the grain that was left There was a law that a farmer must leave some grain in his field during harvest. This grain was left so the poor people could find something to eat. See Lev. 19:9; 23:22.
That is her house over there Or, "She only rested a short time in that shelter."
You have come to him for safety Literally, "You have come under his wings for safety."

Naomi Hears About Boaz

¹⁷Ruth worked in the fields until evening. Then she separated the grain from the chaff.* There was about 1/2 bushel* of barley. ¹⁸Ruth carried the grain into town to show her mother-in-law what she had gathered. She also gave her the food that was left from lunch.

¹⁹Her mother-in-law asked her, "Where did you gather all this grain? Where did you work? Bless the man who noticed you."

Then Ruth told her who she had worked with. She said, "The man I worked with today is a man named Boaz."

Naomi told her daughter-in-law, "Lord bless him! He has continued showing his kindness to the living as well as the dead." ²⁰Then Naomi told her daughter-in-law, "Boaz is one of our relatives. Boaz is one of our protectors."*

²¹Then Ruth said, "Boaz also told me to come back and continue working. Boaz said that I should work closely with his servants until the harvest is finished."

²²Then Naomi said to her daughter-in-law Ruth, "It is good for you to continue working with his women servants. If you work in another field, some man might hurt you." ²³So Ruth continued working closely with the women servants of Boaz. She gathered grain until the barley harvest was finished. She also worked there through the end of the wheat harvest. Ruth continued living with Naomi, her mother-in-law.

The Threshing Floor

3 Then Naomi, Ruth's mother-in-law, said to her, "My daughter, maybe I should find ₍a husband and₎ a nice home for you. That would be good for you. ²₍Maybe Boaz is the right man.₎ Boaz is our close relative.* You worked with his women servants. Tonight he will be working at the threshing floor.* ³Go wash and get dressed. Put on a nice dress, and go down to the threshing floor. But don't let Boaz see you until he has finished eating supper. ⁴After he eats, he will lie down to rest. Watch him so that you will know where he lies down. Go there and lift the cover off his feet.* Then lie down there with Boaz. He will tell you what you should do ₍about marriage₎."

⁵Then Ruth answered, "I will do the thing you say."

⁶So Ruth went down to the threshing floor.* Ruth did everything that her mother-in-law told her to do. ⁷After eating and drinking, Boaz was very satisfied. Boaz went to lie down near the pile of grain. Then Ruth went to him very quietly and lifted the cover from his feet. Ruth lay down by his feet.

⁸About midnight, Boaz rolled over ₍in his sleep and woke up₎. He was very surprised. There was a woman lying near his feet. ⁹Boaz said, "Who are you?"

She said, "I am Ruth, your servant girl. Spread your cover over me.* You are my protector.*

¹⁰Then Boaz said, "May the Lord bless you, young woman. You have been very kind to me. Your kindness to me is greater than the kindness you showed to Naomi in the beginning. You could have looked for a young man to marry, rich or poor. But you did not. ¹¹Now, young woman, don't be afraid. I will do the things you ask. All the people in our town know that you are a very good woman. ¹²And it is true, I am a close relative.* But there is a man that is a closer relative to you than I. ¹³Stay here tonight. In the morning we will see if he will help* you. If he decides to help you, then that is fine. If he refuses to help, then I promise, as the Lord lives, I will

---

chaff Parts of grain a farmer throws away. Farmers cracked the hulls from seeds and let the wind blow these hulls (chaff) away.

1/2 bushel Literally, "One Ephah."

Protector(s) Or, "Redeemer," a person who cared for and protected the family of a dead relative. Often this person bought back (redeemed) the poor relatives from slavery, making them free again.

close relative This is a close relative that could marry Ruth, so she could have children. This man would care for this family, but this family and their property would not belong to him. They would belong to Ruth's dead husband.

lift the cover off his feet Literally, "uncover his legs." This showed Ruth was asking Boaz to be her Protector.

Spread your cover over me Or, "Spread your wing over me." This showed Ruth was asking for help and protection. See Ruth 2:12.

protector, close relative This is a close relative that could marry Ruth, so she could have children. This man would care for this family, but this family and their property would not belong to him. They would belong to Ruth's dead husband.

help Or, "redeem." This meant the close relative would care for and protect the dead man's family and property, but that property would not be his.

marry you and buy back Elimelech's land for you.* So lie here until morning."

¹⁴So Ruth lay near Boaz's feet until morning. She got up while it was still dark, before it was light enough for people to recognize each other.

Boaz said to her, "We will keep it a secret that you came here to me last night." ¹⁵Then Boaz said, "Bring me your coat. Now, hold it open."

So Ruth held her coat open, and Boaz measured about a bushel of barley* as a gift to Naomi, her mother-in-law. Boaz then wrapped it in Ruth's coat, and put it on her back. Then he went to the city.

¹⁶Ruth went to the home of her mother-in-law, Naomi. Naomi ₍went to the door and₎ asked, "Who's there?"

₍Ruth went in the house₎ telling Naomi everything that Boaz did for her. ¹⁷She said, "Boaz gave me this barley as a gift for you. Boaz said that I must not go home without bringing a gift for you."

¹⁸Naomi said, "Daughter, be patient until we hear what happens. Boaz will not rest until he has finished doing what he should do. We will know what will happen before the day is ended."

Boaz and the Other Relative

4 Boaz went to the place where people gather near the city gates. Boaz sat there until the close relative* Boaz had mentioned passed by. Boaz called to him, "Come here, friend! Sit here!"

²₍Then Boaz gathered some witnesses.₎ Boaz gathered ten of the elders* of the city. He told them, "Sit here!" So they sat down.

³Then Boaz spoke to the close relative.* He said, "Naomi came back from the hill country of Moab. She is selling the land* that belonged to our relative Elimelech. ⁴I decided to tell you about this in front of the people living here and in front of the elders* of my people. If you want to buy back the land, then buy it! If you don't want to redeem the land, then tell me. I know that I am the next person after you that can redeem the land. If you don't buy the land back, then I will."

⁵Then Boaz said, "If you buy the land from Naomi, you also get the dead man's wife, Ruth the Moabite woman. ₍When Ruth has a child, the child will get the land.₎ That way, the land will stay in the dead man's family."

⁶The close relative* answered, "I cannot buy back the land. That land should belong to me. But I cannot buy it. If I do, I might lose my own land. So you can buy the land." ⁷(Long ago in Israel, when people bought or redeemed property, one person took off his shoe and gave it to the other person. This was their proof of purchase.) ⁸So the close relative* said, "Buy the land." And then the close relative took off his shoe ₍and gave it to Boaz₎.

⁹Then Boaz said to the elders* and all the people, "You are witnesses today that I am buying from Naomi everything that belonged to Elimelech, Kilion, and Mahlon. ¹⁰I am also buying Ruth to be my wife. I am doing this so the dead man's property will stay with his family. This way, the dead man's name will not be separated from his family and his land. You are witnesses this day."

¹¹So all the people and elders* that were near the city gates were witnesses. They said,

> May the Lord make this woman
> who is coming into your home
> like Rachel and Leah
> who built the house of Israel.*
> Become powerful in Ephrathah!*
> Be famous in Bethlehem!

> 12 Tamar gave birth to Judah's son Perez.*
> And his family became great.
> In the same way, may the Lord give you
> many children through Ruth.
> And may your family be great like his.

¹³So Boaz married Ruth. The Lord allowed Ruth to become pregnant, and she had a son. ¹⁴The women ₍of the town₎ told Naomi,

---

I will marry ... you Literally, "I will redeem you."
bushel of barley Literally, "six ₍measures₎ of barley."
protector, close relative This is a close relative that could marry Ruth, so she could have children. This man would care for this family, but this family and their property would not belong to him. They would belong to Ruth's dead husband.
elders Older men who were city leaders; they helped make decisions for the people.
She is selling the land Or, "She has sold the land."

built the house of Israel The Hebrew word "built" is like the word meaning "gave birth to sons."
Ephrathah Another name for Bethlehem.
Perez One of Boaz's ancestors.

Bless the Lord who gave you this child.*
He will become famous in Israel.
¹⁵ He will make you alive again!
And he will care for you in your old age.
Your daughter-in-law made it happen.
She bore this child for you.
She loves you.
And she is better for you
than seven sons."

¹⁶Naomi took the boy, held him in her arms, and cared for him. ¹⁷The neighbors gave the boy his name. These women said, "Naomi has a son now!"* And they named him Obed. Obed was Jesse's father. And Jesse was the father of ⌊King⌋ David.

Ruth and Boaz's Family

¹⁸This is the family history of Perez:

Perez was the father of Hezron.
¹⁹ Hezron was the father of Ram.
Ram was the father of Amminadab.
²⁰ Amminadab was the father of Nahshon.
Nahshon was the father of Salmon.
²¹ Salmon was the father of Boaz.
Boaz was the father of Obed.
²² Obed was the father of Jesse.
Jesse was the father of David.

---

child Literally, "Protector" or "Redeemer." The women used this name for the baby because he will be the one to care for Naomi and her family and to carry on the name of Elimelech.
Naomi ... now Literally, "A son was born for Naomi."

1 Samuel

Elkanah and His Family Worship at Shiloh

1 There was a man named Elkanah from Ramah in the hill country of Ephraim. Elkanah was from the Zuph* family. Elkanah was the son of Jeroham.* Jeroham was Elihu's son. Elihu was Tohu's son. Tohu was the son of Zuph, from the family group of Ephraim. ²Elkanah had two wives. One wife was named Hannah and the other wife was named Peninnah. Peninnah had children, but Hannah did not.

3Every year Elkanah left his town Ramah and went up to Shiloh. Elkanah worshiped the Lord All-Powerful at Shiloh and offered sacrifices* to the Lord there. Shiloh was where Hophni and Phinehas served as priests of the Lord. Hophni and Phinehas were the sons of Eli. ⁴Every time Elkanah offered his sacrifices, he always gave one share of the food to his wife Peninnah. Elkanah also gave shares of the food to Peninnah's children. ⁵Elkanah always gave an equal share* of the food to Hannah. Elkanah did this even though the Lord had not let Hannah have any children. Elkanah did this because Hannah was the wife he really loved.

Peninnah Upsets Hannah

⁶Peninnah always upset Hannah and made her feel bad. Peninnah did this because Hannah was not able to have children. ⁷The same thing happened every year. Every time their family went to the Lord's house at Shiloh, Peninnah made Hannah upset. One day Elkanah was giving sacrifices.* Hannah became upset and began to cry. Hannah would not eat anything. ⁸Her husband, Elkanah, said to her, "Hannah, why are you crying? Why won't you eat? Why are you sad? You have me—I am your husband. You should think I am better than ten sons."

Hannah's Prayer

⁹After eating and drinking, Hannah quietly got up and went to pray to the Lord. Eli the priest was sitting on a chair near the door of the Lord's Holy Building.* ¹⁰Hannah was very sad. She cried very much while she prayed to the Lord. ¹¹She made a special promise to God. She said, "Lord All-Powerful, see how very sad I am. Remember me! Don't forget me. If you will give me a son, then I will give him to you. He will be a Nazirite: He will not drink wine or strong drink.* And no one will ever cut his hair.*"

¹²Hannah prayed to the Lord a long time. Eli was watching Hannah's mouth while she was praying. ¹³Hannah was praying in her heart. Her lips were moving, but she did not say the words out loud. So Eli thought Hannah was drunk. ¹⁴Eli said to Hannah, "You have had too much to drink! It is time to put away the wine."

¹⁵Hannah answered, "Sir, I have not drunk any wine or beer. I am deeply troubled. I was telling the Lord about all my problems. ¹⁶Don't think I am a bad woman. I have been praying so long because I have so many troubles and I am very sad."

¹⁷Eli answered, "Go in peace. May the God of Israel give you the things you asked."

Holy Building This could mean the Holy Tent at Shiloh where people went to worship the Lord or a larger area where they put the Holy Tent.
He will ... not drink This is in the ancient Greek translation and one of the ancient Hebrew scrolls from Qumran, but not in the standard Hebrew text.
No one ... hair Nazirites were people who made a promise to serve God in a special way. They did not cut their hair and they did not eat grapes or drink wine. See Num. 6:5.

Zuph A family of Levites. See 1 Chron. 6:33-38.
Jeroham, Elihu, Tohu Or, "Jerahmeel, Eliel, Toah."
sacrifice(s) A gift to God. Usually it was a special animal that was killed and burned on an altar.
equal share Or, "double share."

1 SAMUEL 1:18–2:7

¹⁸Hannah said, "I hope you are happy with me." Then Hannah left and ate something. She was not sad any more.

¹⁹Early the next morning Elkanah's family got up. They worshiped the Lord and then went back home to Ramah.

Samuel's Birth

Elkanah had sexual relations with his wife Hannah, and the Lord remembered Hannah. ²⁰By that time the following year, Hannah had become pregnant and had a son. Hannah named her son Samuel.* She said, "His name is Samuel because I asked the Lord for him."

²¹That year Elkanah went ⌊to Shiloh⌋ to offer sacrifices and to keep the promises he made to God. He took his family with him. ²²But Hannah did not go. She told Elkanah, "When the boy is old enough to eat solid food, I will take him to Shiloh. Then I will give him to the Lord. He will become a Nazirite.** He will stay there at Shiloh."

²³Hannah's husband Elkanah said to her, "Do what you think is best. You may stay home until the boy is old enough to eat solid food. May the Lord do what you have said." So Hannah stayed at home to nurse her son until he was old enough to eat solid food.

Hannah Takes Samuel to Eli at Shiloh

²⁴When the boy was old enough to eat solid food, Hannah took him to the Lord's house at Shiloh. Hannah also took a bull that was three years old, 20 pounds* of flour, and a bottle of wine.

²⁵They went before the Lord. Elkanah killed the bull as a sacrifice to the Lord like he usually did.* Then Hannah gave the boy to Eli. ²⁶Hannah said to Eli, "Pardon me, sir. I am the same woman that stood near you praying to the Lord. I promise that I am telling the truth. ²⁷I prayed for this child, and the Lord answered my prayer. The Lord gave me this child. ²⁸And now I give this child to the Lord. He will serve* the Lord all his life."

Then Hannah left the boy there* and worshiped the Lord.

Hannah Gives Thanks

2 Hannah said:

"My heart is happy in the Lord!
I feel very strong* in my God!
I laugh at my enemies.*
I am very happy in my victory!

2 "There is no Holy God like the Lord.
There is no God but you!
There is no Rock* like our God.

3 Don't continue bragging!
Don't speak proud words!
Why? Because the Lord God knows everything,
God leads and judges people.

4 The bows of strong soldiers break!
And weak people become strong!

5 People who had plenty of food in the past,
must now work to get food.
But people who were hungry in the past,
now grow fat on food!
The woman who was not able to have children
now has seven children!
But the woman who had many children
is sad because her children are gone.

6 The Lord causes people to die,
and he causes them to live.
The Lord sends people down to the grave,*
and he can raise them up ⌊to live again⌋.

7 The Lord makes some people poor,
and he makes other people rich.

Samuel This name means "His name is El (God)." But in Hebrew it is like the word "ask" or the name "Saul." There are many places in 1 Samuel where there are word plays with the names Saul and Samuel and the word "ask."

Nazirite A person who has made a special promise to God. This name is from the Hebrew word meaning "to separate from."

He will become a Nazirite This is not in the standard Hebrew text, but it is in the ancient Greek translation and in one of the Hebrew scrolls from Qumran.

20 pounds Literally, "an Ephah."

They went ... he usually did This is from the ancient Greek translation and one of the ancient Hebrew scrolls from Qumran. It is not in the standard Hebrew text.

serve Or, "belong to."

left the boy there This is from one of the ancient Hebrew scrolls from Qumran. It is not in the standard Hebrew text.

I feel very strong Literally, "In the Lord my horn is lifted high." The horn is a symbol of strength.

I laugh at my enemies Literally, "My mouth is wide open over my enemies."

Rock A name for God. It shows he is like a fortress or a strong place of safety.

grave Or, "Sheol," the place of death.

The Lord humbles some people,
   and he honors other people.
⁸ The Lord raises poor people from the dust.
   He takes away their sadness*
The Lord makes poor people important.
   He seats them with princes
      and at the places for honored guests.
The Lord made the whole world!
And the whole world belongs to him!*
⁹ The Lord protects his holy people.
   He keeps them from stumbling.
But bad people will be destroyed.
   They will fall in the darkness.
   Their power will not help them win.
¹⁰ The Lord destroys his enemies.
      God Most-High will thunder in heaven
         against people.
   The Lord will judge even the faraway
      lands.
   He will give power to his king.
   He will make his special king strong."

¹¹Elkanah ⌊and his family⌋ went home to Ramah. The boy stayed in Shiloh and served the Lord under Eli the priest.

Eli's Evil Sons

¹²Eli's sons were bad men. They did not care about the Lord. ¹³They did not care about how priests were supposed to treat people. This is what priests should do for people: Each time a person brings a sacrifice, the priests should put the meat in a pot of boiling water. Then the priest's servant should get the special fork that has three points. ¹⁴The priest's servant should use that fork to get some meat out of the pot or kettle. The priest should get only whatever meat the servant removes from the pot with the fork. That is what the priests should have done for all the Israelites who came ⌊to offer sacrifices⌋ at Shiloh.
¹⁵⌊But Eli's sons did not do that⌋. Even before the fat was burned on the altar, their servant would go to the people offering sacrifices. The priest's servant would say, "Give the priest some meat to roast. The priest won't accept boiled meat from you."
¹⁶Maybe the man offering the sacrifice would say, "Burn the fat* first, and then you can take anything you want." Then the priest's servant would answer: "No, give me the meat now. If you don't give it to me, I'll take it from you!"
¹⁷In this way, Hophni and Phinehas showed that they did not respect the offerings made to the Lord. This was a very bad sin against the Lord!
¹⁸But Samuel served the Lord. Samuel was a helper who wore the linen ephod.* ¹⁹Every year Samuel's mother made a little robe for Samuel. She took the little robe to Samuel when she went up ⌊to Shiloh⌋ with her husband for the sacrifice every year.
²⁰Eli would bless Elkanah and his wife. Eli would say, "May the Lord give you more children through Hannah. These children will take the place of the boy Hannah prayed for and gave to the Lord."
Elkanah and Hannah went home and ²¹the Lord was kind to Hannah. She had three sons and two daughters. And the boy Samuel grew up ⌊at the holy place⌋ near the Lord.

Eli Fails to Control His Evil Sons

²²Eli was very old. He heard again and again about the things his sons were doing to all the Israelites at Shiloh. Eli also heard about his sons sleeping with the women who served at the door of the Meeting Tent.
²³Eli said to his sons, "The people here told me about the bad things you have done. Why do you do these bad things? ²⁴Sons, don't do these bad things. The Lord's people are saying bad things about you. ²⁵If a person sins against another person, God may help him. But if a person sins against the Lord, then who can help that person?"
But Eli's sons refused to listen to Eli. So the Lord decided to kill Eli's sons.
²⁶The boy Samuel kept growing. He was pleasing to God and to the people.

---

takes away their sadness Literally, "He picks up poor people from the ashes."
The Lord made ... belongs to him Literally, "The whole world, even to its foundations, belongs to the Lord. The Lord set the world on those pillars."
Burn the fat The fat was the part of the animal that belonged only to God. The priests were supposed to burn the fat on the altar as a gift to God.

ephod A special coat a man wore to show that he was a priest or a priest's helper.
man of God A prophet, a person that God sent to speak to the people.
ancestors Literally, "father's house." This means the people that a person is descended from.

The Terrible Prophecy about Eli's Family

²⁷A man of God* came to Eli and said, "The Lord says these things, 'Your ancestors* were slaves of Pharaoh's family. But I appeared to your ancestors* at that time. ²⁸I chose your family group from all the family groups of Israel. I chose your family group to be my priests. I chose them to offer sacrifices on my altar. I chose them to burn incense* and wear the ephod.* I also let your family group have the meat from the sacrifices that the people of Israel give to me. ²⁹So why don't you respect those sacrifices and gifts. You honor your sons more than me. You become fat on the best parts of the meat—and the people of Israel bring that meat to me.'

³⁰"The Lord God of Israel promised that your father's family would serve him forever. But now the Lord says this, 'That will never be! I will honor people who honor me. But bad things will happen to people who refuse to respect me. ³¹The time is coming when I will destroy all your descendants.* No one in your family will live to be an old man. ³²Good things will happen to Israel, but you will see bad things happening at home.* No one in your family will live to be an old man. ³³There is one man that I will save to serve ⌊as priest⌋ at my altar. ⌊He will live to be very old.⌋ He will live until his eyes wear out and his strength is gone. All of your descendants* will die by the sword. ³⁴I will give you a sign ⌊to show these things will come true⌋. Your two sons, Hophni and Phinehas, will die on the same day. ³⁵I will choose a faithful priest for myself. This priest will listen to me and do what I want. I will make this priest's family strong. He will always serve before my chosen king.* ³⁶Then all the people who are left in your family will come and bow down before this priest. They will beg for a little money or a piece of bread. They will say,

"Please give me a job as priest so I can have some food to eat."'"

God Calls Samuel

3 The boy Samuel served the Lord under Eli. At that time, the Lord did not speak directly to people very often. There were very few visions.* ²Eli's eyes were so weak he was almost blind. One night he lay down in bed. ³Samuel lay in bed in the Lord's Holy Building.* God's Holy Box* was in that Holy Building. The Lord's lamp was still burning. ⁴The Lord called Samuel. Samuel answered, "Here I am." ⁵⌊Samuel thought Eli was calling him. So⌋ Samuel ran to Eli. Samuel said to Eli, "Here I am. You called me."

But Eli said, "I didn't call you. Go back to bed."

Samuel went back to bed. ⁶Again the Lord called, "Samuel!" Again Samuel ran to Eli and said, "Here I am. You called me."

Eli said, "I didn't call you. Go back to bed."

⁷Samuel did not yet know the Lord. The Lord had not spoken directly to him yet.*

⁸The Lord called Samuel the third time. Again Samuel got up and went to Eli. Samuel said, "Here I am. You called me."

Then Eli understood that the Lord was calling the boy. ⁹Eli told Samuel, "Go to bed. If he calls you again, say, 'Speak, Lord. I am your servant, and I am listening.'"

So Samuel went back to bed. ¹⁰The Lord came and stood there. He called as he did before. He said, "Samuel, Samuel!"

Samuel said, "Speak. I am your servant, and I am listening."

¹¹The Lord said to Samuel, "I will soon do something in Israel. People who hear about it will be shocked. ¹²I will do everything I said I would do against Eli and his family. I will do everything from the beginning to the end. ¹³I told Eli I would punish his family forever. I will do that because

---

incense A kind of spice that smells good when it is burned. It was burned as a gift to God.
ephod A special coat a man wore to show that he was a priest or a priest's helper.
descendant(s) A person's children and their future families.
but you will see bad things happening at home This phrase is not in the ancient Greek translation or the Hebrew scrolls from Qumran.
chosen king Literally, "anointed one."
visions Like dreams. God gave messages to his special people by letting them see and hear things in visions.

Holy Building This could mean the Holy Tent at Shiloh where people went to worship the Lord, or a larger area where they put the Holy Tent.
God's Holy Box The Box of the Agreement. In this box were many things from the time Israel was in the Sinai desert.
The Lord had not spoken directly to him yet Literally, "The word of the Lord had not yet been revealed to him."

Eli knew that his sons were saying and doing bad things against God. And Eli failed to control them. ¹⁴That is why I swore *(promised)* that sacrifices and grain offerings will never take away the sins of the people in Eli's family."

¹⁵Samuel lay down in bed until the morning came. He got up early and opened the doors of the Lord's house. Samuel was afraid to tell Eli about the vision.*

¹⁶But Eli said to Samuel, "Samuel, my son!" Samuel answered, "Yes, sir."

¹⁷Eli asked, "What did the Lord say to you? Don't hide it from me. God will punish you if you hide anything from the message God spoke to you."

¹⁸So Samuel told Eli everything. Samuel did not hide anything from Eli.

Eli said, "He is the Lord. Let him do whatever he thinks is right."

¹⁹The Lord was with Samuel while he grew up. The Lord did not let any of Samuel's messages prove false. ²⁰Then all Israel, from Dan to Beersheba, knew that Samuel was a true prophet of the Lord. ²¹And the Lord continued to appear to Samuel at Shiloh. The Lord revealed himself to Samuel as the word of the Lord.*

4 News about Samuel spread through all of Israel. Eli was very old. His sons kept doing bad things before the Lord.*

The Philistines Defeat the Israelites

At that time, the Israelites went out to fight against the Philistines. The Israelites made their camp at Ebenezer. The Philistines made their camp at Aphek. ²The Philistines prepared to attack Israel. The battle began.

The Philistines defeated the Israelites. The Philistines killed about 4,000 soldiers from Israel's army. ³The Israelite soldiers came back to their camp. The elders *(leaders)* of Israel asked, "Why did the Lord let the Philistines defeat us? Let's bring the Lord's Box of the Agreement* from Shiloh. ₁In this way, God will go with us into battle.ⱼ He will save us from our enemies."

⁴So the people sent men to Shiloh. The men brought back the Lord All-Powerful's Box of the Agreement.* On top of the Box are the Cherub angels. And they are like the throne that the Lord sits on. Eli's two sons, Hophni and Phinehas, came with the Box.

⁵When the Lord's Box of the Agreement* came into the camp, all the Israelites gave a great shout. That shout made the ground shake. ⁶The Philistines heard Israel's shout. They asked, "Why are the people so excited in the Hebrew* camp?"

Then the Philistines learned that the Lord's Holy Box* had been brought into Israel's camp. ⁷The Philistines became afraid. The Philistines said, "Gods have come to their camp! We're in trouble. This has never happened before! ⁸We are worried. Who can save us from these powerful gods? These gods are the same gods that gave the Egyptians those diseases and terrible sicknesses. ⁹Be brave, Philistines! Fight like men! In the past, the Hebrew people were our slaves. So fight like men or you will become their slaves!"

¹⁰So the Philistines fought very hard and defeated the Israelites. Every Israelite soldier ran away to his tent. It was a terrible defeat for Israel. 30,000 Israelite soldiers were killed. ¹¹The Philistines took God's Holy Box* and killed Eli's two sons, Hophni and Phinehas.

¹²That day a man from the family group of Benjamin ran from the battle. He tore his clothes and put dust on his head ₁to show his great sadnessⱼ. ¹³Eli was sitting on a chair near the city gates when this man came to Shiloh. Eli was worried about God's Holy Box,* so he was sitting there waiting and watching. Then the Benjamite man came into Shiloh and told the bad news. All the people in town began to cry out loud. ¹⁴⁻¹⁵Eli was 98 years old. Eli was blind, ₁so he could not see what was happeningⱼ. But he could hear the loud noise of the people crying. Eli asked, "Why are the people making this loud noise?"

The Benjamite man ran to Eli and told him what happened. ¹⁶The Benjamite man told Eli, "I

---

vision Like a dream. God gave messages to his special people by letting them see and hear things in visions.

word of the Lord Sometimes this means simply, "a message from God." But sometimes it seems that this was a special way or form that God used when he spoke with his prophets.

Eli ... Lord This phrase is in the ancient Greek translation, but not in the Hebrew.

Box of the Agreement Also called the "Ark of the Covenant." This box contained the Ten Commandments written on stone tablets and the other things that proved God was with the people of Israel during their time in the Sinai Desert.

Hebrew Or, "Israelite."
Holy Box The Box of the Agreement.

am the man who just came from the battle. I ran away from the battle today!"

Eli asked, "What happened, son?"

¹⁷The Benjamite man answered, "Israel ran away from the Philistines. The Israelite army has lost many soldiers. Your two sons are both dead. And the Philistines took God's Holy Box.*"

¹⁸When the Benjamite man mentioned God's Holy Box,* Eli fell backward off his chair near the gate and broke his neck. Eli was old and fat, so he died. Eli had led Israel for 20 years.*

The Glory Is Gone

¹⁹Eli's daughter-in-law, the wife of Phinehas, was pregnant. It was nearly time for her baby to be born. She heard the news that God's Holy Box* was taken. She also heard that her father-in-law Eli and her husband Phinehas were both dead. As soon as she heard the news, her pain started and she began giving birth to her baby. ²⁰She was about to die when the women who were helping her said, "Don't worry! You have given birth to a son."

But Eli's daughter-in-law did not answer or pay attention. ²¹Eli's daughter-in-law named the baby Ichabod,* that is to say, "Israel's glory has been taken away!"* She did this because God's Holy Box* was taken away and because both her father-in-law and husband were dead. ²²She said, "Israel's glory has been taken away" because the Philistines had taken God's Holy Box.

The Holy Box Troubles the Philistines

5 The Philistines carried God's Holy Box,* from Ebenezer to Ashdod. ²The Philistines carried God's Holy Box into the temple of Dagon* and put it next to the statue of Dagon. ³The next morning, the people of Ashdod got up and found Dagon lying face down on the ground. Dagon had fallen down before the Lord's Box.

The people of Ashdod put the statue of Dagon* back in its place. ⁴But the next morning when the people of Ashdod got up, they found Dagon on the ground again! Dagon had fallen down before the Lord's Holy Box.* This time, Dagon's head and hands were broken off and lying on the threshold.* Only Dagon's body was still in one piece. ⁵That is why, even today, Dagon's priests or any other people who enter Dagon's Temple at Ashdod refuse to step on the threshold.

⁶The Lord made life hard for the people of Ashdod and their neighbors. The Lord gave them many troubles. He caused them to get tumors.* The Lord also sent mice to them. The mice ran all over their ships and then onto their land. The people in the city were very afraid.* ⁷The people of Ashdod saw what was happening. They said, "The Holy Box* of the God of Israel can't stay here! God is punishing us and Dagon* our god."

⁸The people of Ashdod called the five Philistine rulers together. The people of Ashdod asked the rulers, "What must we do with the Holy Box* of the God of Israel?"

The rulers answered, "Move the Holy Box* of the God of Israel ₜto Gath₁." So the Philistines moved God's Holy Box.

⁹But after the Philistines had moved God's Holy Box* to Gath, the Lord punished that city. The people became very scared. God caused many troubles for all the people—young and old. God caused the people in Gath to have tumors.* ¹⁰So the Philistines sent God's Holy Box to Ekron.

But when God's Holy Box* came into Ekron, the people of Ekron complained. They said, "Why are you bringing the Box of the God of Israel to our city Ekron? Do you want to kill us and our people?" ¹¹The people of Ekron called all the Philistine rulers together. The people of Ekron said to the rulers, "Send the Box of the God of Israel back to its place before it kills us and our people!"

Holy Box The Box of the Agreement, the box that contained the stone tablets with the Ten Commandments written on them and the other things that proved God was with the people of Israel during their time in the Sinai Desert.
20 years This is from the ancient Greek translation and Josephus. The standard Hebrew text has "40 years."
Ichabod This name means "No glory!" The Greek has "Ouai Barchaboth"
Eli's daughter-in-law ... taken away This is not in the Greek translation.
Dagon The Canaanite people worshiped this false god hoping he would give them a good harvest of grain. This was probably the most important god for the Philistine people.

threshold The bottom part of a door opening.
tumors Bad growths on the skin.
verse 6 This is from the ancient Greek translation.

The people of Ekron were very scared! God made life very hard for them in that place. ¹²₍Many people died.₎ And the people who did not die, had tumors.* The people of Ekron cried loudly to heaven.

God's Holy Box Is Sent Back Home

6 The Philistines kept the Holy Box* in their land seven months. ²The Philistines called their priests and magicians. The Philistines said, "What must we do with the Lord's Box? Tell us how to send the Box back home!"

³The priests and magicians answered, "If you send back the Holy Box* of the God of Israel, don't send it away empty. You must offer gifts so the God of Israel will take away your sins. Then you will be healed. You will be made pure. You should do these things so God will stop punishing you."*

⁴The Philistines asked, "What kind of gifts should we send for Israel's God to forgive us?"

The priests and magicians answered, "There are five Philistine leaders. ₍One leader for each city.₎ All of you people and your leaders had the same problems. So you must make five gold models to look like five tumors. And you must make five gold models to look like five mice. ⁵So, make models of the tumors and models of the mice that are ruining the country. Give these gold models to the God of Israel as payment. Then maybe the God of Israel will stop punishing you, your gods, and your land. ⁶Don't be stubborn like Pharaoh and the Egyptians. God punished the Egyptians. That is why the Egyptians let the Israelites leave Egypt.

⁷"You must build a new wagon and get two cows that just had calves. These must be cows that have never worked in the fields. Tie the cows to the wagon so they can pull it. Then take the calves back home and put them in their pen. Don't let them follow their mothers.* ⁸Put the Lord's Holy Box* on the wagon. You must put the golden models in the bag beside the Box. The golden models are your gifts for God to forgive your sins. Send the wagon straight on its way. ⁹Watch the wagon. If the wagon goes toward Beth Shemesh in Israel's own land, then the Lord has given us this great sickness. But if the cows do not go straight to Beth Shemesh, then we will know that Israel's God has not punished us. We will know that our sickness just happened."

¹⁰The Philistines did what the priests and magicians said. The Philistines found two cows that had just had calves. The Philistines tied the cows to the wagon and put the calves in their pens at home. ¹¹Then the Philistines put the Lord's Holy Box* on the wagon. They also put the bag with the golden models of the tumors and mice on the wagon. ¹²The cows went straight to Beth Shemesh. The cows stayed on the road, mooing all the way. The cows did not turn right or left. The Philistine rulers followed the cows as far as the city limits of Beth Shemesh.

¹³The people of Beth Shemesh were harvesting their wheat in the valley. They looked up and saw the Holy Box.* They were very happy to see the Box again. They ran to get it. ¹⁴⁻¹⁵The wagon came to the field that belonged to Joshua of Beth Shemesh. In this field the wagon stopped near a large rock. The people of Beth Shemesh cut up the wagon. Then they killed the cows. They sacrificed the cows to the Lord.

The Levites* took down the Lord's Holy Box.* They also took down the bag that had the golden models. The Levites put the Lord's Box and the bag on the large rock. That day the people of Beth Shemesh offered burnt offerings to the Lord.

¹⁶The five Philistine rulers watched the people of Beth Shemesh do all these things. Then the five Philistine rulers went back to Ekron that same day.

¹⁷In this way, the Philistines sent golden models of tumors as gifts for their sins to the Lord. They sent one golden model of a tumor for each Philistine town. These Philistine towns were Ashdod, Gaza, Ashkelon, Gath, and Ekron. ¹⁸And the Philistines also sent golden models of mice. The number of these golden mice was the same

---

Holy Box The Box of the Agreement, the box that contained the stone tablets with the Ten Commandments written on them and the other things that proved God was with the people of Israel during their time in the Sinai Desert.

You should do ... punishing you This is from the ancient Greek translation and one of the ancient Hebrew scrolls from Qumran. The standard Hebrew has "Then you will know why God did not stop punishing you."

Don't ... follow their mothers The Philistines thought that if the cows did not try to find their calves it would prove that God was leading them and that he had accepted their gifts.

Levites People from the family group of Levi who helped the priests.

number as the towns that belonged to the five Philistine rulers. These towns had walls around them. And each town had villages around it.

The people of Beth Shemesh put the Lord's Holy Box* on a rock. That rock is still in the field of Joshua from Beth Shemesh. ¹⁹But there were no priests* there when the men of Beth Shemesh saw the Holy Box of the Lord. So God killed 70 men from Beth Shemesh. The people of Beth Shemesh cried because the Lord punished them so severely. ²⁰So the people of Beth Shemesh said, "Where is a priest that can care for this Holy Box? Where should the Box go from here?"

²¹⌊There was a priest at Kiriath Jearim.⌋ The people of Beth Shemesh sent messengers to the people of Kiriath Jearim. The messengers said, "The Philistines have brought back the Lord's Holy Box.* Come down and take it to your city."

7 The men of Kiriath Jearim came and took the Lord's Holy Box.* They took the Lord's Box to Abinadab's house on the hill. They did a special ceremony to prepare Abinadab's son, Eleazar, to guard the Lord's Box. ²The Box stayed at Kiriath Jearim a long time. It stayed there 20 years.

The Lord Saves the Israelites

The people of Israel began to follow the Lord again. ³Samuel told the people of Israel, "If you are really coming back to the Lord—with all your heart—then you must throw away your foreign gods. You must throw away your idols of Ashtoreth.* And you must give yourselves fully to the Lord. You must serve only the Lord! Then the Lord will save you from the Philistines."

⁴So the Israelites threw away their statues of Baal* and Ashtoreth.* The Israelites served only the Lord.

⁵Samuel said, "All Israel must meet at Mizpah. I will pray to the Lord for you."

⁶The Israelites met together at Mizpah. They got water and poured it out before the Lord. ⌊In this way, they began a time of fasting.⌋ They did not eat any food that day and they confessed their sins. They said, "We have sinned against the Lord." So Samuel served as a judge* of Israel at Mizpah.

⁷The Philistines heard that the Israelites were meeting at Mizpah. The Philistine rulers went to fight against the Israelites. The Israelites heard the Philistines were coming, and they became afraid. ⁸The Israelites said to Samuel, "Don't stop praying to the Lord our God for us! Ask the Lord to save us from the Philistines!"

⁹Samuel took a baby lamb. He burned the lamb as a whole burnt offering to the Lord. Samuel prayed to the Lord for Israel. The Lord answered Samuel's prayer. ¹⁰While Samuel was burning the sacrifice, the Philistines came to fight Israel. But the Lord caused loud thunder near the Philistines. This confused the Philistines. The thunder scared the Philistines, and they became confused. ⌊Their leaders were not able to control them.⌋ So the Israelites defeated the Philistines in battle. ¹¹The men of Israel ran out of Mizpah and chased the Philistines. They chased them all the way to Beth Car. They killed Philistine soldiers all along the way.

Peace Comes to Israel

¹²After this, Samuel set up a special stone. ⌊He did this to help people remember the things God did.⌋ Samuel put the stone between Mizpah and Shen.* Samuel named the stone "Stone of Help."* Samuel said, "The Lord helped us all the way to this place!"

¹³The Philistines were defeated. They did not enter the land of Israel again. The Lord was against the Philistines during the rest of Samuel's life. ¹⁴The Philistines had taken towns from Israel. The Philistines took the towns in the area from Ekron to Gath. But the Israelites won back those towns. And Israel also took back the land around these towns.

There was also peace between Israel and the Amorites.

---

no priests Only priests were allowed to carry the Box of the Agreement.
Holy Box The Box of the Agreement, the box that contained the stone tablets with the Ten Commandments written on them and the other things that proved God was with the people of Israel during their time in the Sinai Desert.
Ashtoreth The Canaanite people thought that this false goddess could make people able to have babies. She was their goddess of love and war.
Baal The Canaanite people believed that this false god brought the rain and storms. They also thought that he made the land produce good crops.

judge(s) Special leaders who had the work of leading, judging, and protecting the people of Israel before there were kings in Israel.
Shen Or, "Jeshanah," a town about 17 miles north of Jerusalem.
Stone of Help Or, "Ebenezer."

¹⁵Samuel led Israel all his life. ¹⁶Samuel went from place to place judging the people of Israel. Every year he traveled around the country. He went to Bethel, Gilgal, and Mizpah. So he judged and ruled the people of Israel in all these places. ¹⁷But Samuel's home was in Ramah. So Samuel always went back to Ramah. Samuel judged and ruled Israel from that town. And Samuel built an altar to the Lord in Ramah.

Israel Asks For A King

8 When Samuel became old, he made his sons judges* for Israel. ²Samuel's first son was named Joel. His second son was named Abijah. Joel and Abijah were judges in Beersheba. ³But Samuel's sons did not live the same way he did. Joel and Abijah accepted bribes. They took money secretly and changed their decisions in court. They cheated people in court. ⁴So all the elders *(leaders)* of Israel met together. They went to Ramah to meet with Samuel. ⁵The elders *(leaders)* said to Samuel, "You're old, and your sons don't live right. They are not like you. Now, give us a king to rule us like all the other nations." ⁶So, the elders *(leaders)* asked for a king to lead them. Samuel thought this was a bad idea. So Samuel prayed to the Lord. ⁷The Lord told Samuel, "Do what the people tell you. They have not rejected you. They have rejected me! They don't want me to be their king! ⁸They are doing the same thing they have always done. I took them out of Egypt. But they left me and served other gods. They are doing the same to you. ⁹So listen to the people [and do what they say]. But give them a warning. Tell the people what a king will do to them! Tell them how a king rules people."

¹⁰Those people asked for a king. So Samuel told those people everything the Lord said. ¹¹Samuel said, "If you have a king ruling over you, this is what he will do: He will take away your sons. He will force your sons to serve him. He will force them to be soldiers—they must fight from his chariots and become horse soldiers in his army. Your sons will become guards running in front of the king's chariot. ¹²A king will force your sons to become soldiers. Some of them will be officers over 1,000 men. And others will be officers over 50 men. A king will force some of your sons to plow his fields and gather his harvest. He will force some of your sons to make weapons for war. He will force them to make things for his chariots! ¹³"A king will take your daughters. He will force some of your daughters to make perfume for him. And he will force some of your daughters to cook and bake for him.

¹⁴"A king will take your best fields, vineyards, and olive groves. He will take those things from you and give them to his officers. ¹⁵He will take one tenth of your grain and grapes. He will give these things to his officers and servants. ¹⁶This king will take your men and women servants. He will take your best cattle* and your donkeys. He will use them all for his own work. ¹⁷And he will take one tenth of your flocks.

"And you yourselves will become slaves of this king. ¹⁸When that time comes, you will cry because of the king you chose. But the Lord will not answer you at that time."

¹⁹But the people would not listen to Samuel. They said, "No! We want a king to rule over us. ²⁰Then we will be the same as all the other nations. Our king will lead us. He will go with us and fight our battles."

²¹Samuel listened to the people and then repeated their words to the Lord. ²²The Lord answered, "You must listen to them! Give them a king."

Then Samuel told the people of Israel, "[Fine! You will have a new king.] Now, all of you people go back home."

Saul Looks for His Father's Donkeys

9 Kish was an important man from the family group of Benjamin. Kish was the son of Abiel. Abiel was the son of Zeror. Zeror was the son of Becorath. Becorath was the son of Aphiah, a man from Benjamin. ²Kish had a son named Saul. Saul was a handsome young man. There was no one more handsome than Saul. Saul stood a head taller than any other man in Israel.

³One day, Kish's donkeys became lost. So Kish said to his son Saul, "Take one of the servants and go look for the donkeys." ⁴Saul went to look for the donkeys. Saul walked through the hills of Ephraim. Then Saul walked through the area around Shalisha. But Saul and the servant could not find Kish's donkeys. So Saul and the servant

---

judge(s) Special leaders who had the work of leading, judging, and protecting the people of Israel before there were kings in Israel.

cattle This is from the ancient Greek translation. The Hebrew has, "young men."

went to the area around Shaalim. But the donkeys were not there either. So Saul traveled through the land of Benjamin. But he and the servant still could not find the donkeys.

⁵Finally, Saul and the servant came to the town named Zuph. Saul said to his servant, "Let's go back. My father will stop thinking about the donkeys and start worrying about us."

⁶But the servant answered, "A man of God* is in this town. People respect him. Everything he says comes true. So let's go into town. Maybe the man of God will tell us where we should go next."

⁷Saul said to his servant, "Sure, we can go into town. But what can we give to him? We have no gift to give the man of God. Even the food in our bags is gone. What can we give him?"

⁸Again the servant answered Saul. "Look, I have a little bit of money.* Let's give it to the man of God.* Then he will tell us where we should go."

⁹⁻¹¹Saul said to his servant, "That is a good idea! Let's go!" So they went to the town where the man of God was.

Saul and the servant were walking up the hill toward town. They met some young women on the road. The young women were coming out to get water. Saul and the servant asked the young women, "Is the seer here?" (In the past, people in Israel called a prophet a "seer." So if they wanted to ask something from God, they would say, "Let's go to the seer.")

¹²The young women answered, "Yes, the seer* is here. He is just up the road. He came to town today. Some people are meeting together today to share in a fellowship offering at the place for worship.* ¹³So, go into town and you will find him. If you hurry, you can catch him before he goes up to eat at the place for worship. The seer* blesses the sacrifice. So the people won't start eating until he gets there. If you hurry, you can find the seer."

¹⁴Saul and the servant started walking up the hill to town. Just as they came into town, they saw Samuel walking toward them. Samuel was just coming out of town on his way to the place for worship.*

¹⁵The day before, the Lord had told Samuel, ¹⁶"At this time tomorrow I will send a man to you. He will be from the family group of Benjamin. You must anoint* him and make him the new leader over my people Israel. This man will save my people from the Philistines. I have seen my people suffering. I have listened to the cries from my people."

¹⁷Samuel saw Saul and the Lord said to him, "This is the man I told you about. He will rule my people."

¹⁸Saul came to Samuel near the gate. Saul asked Samuel, "Please tell me, where is the seer's* house?"

¹⁹Samuel answered, "I am the seer.* Go ahead of me to the place for worship.* You and your servant will eat with me today. I will let you go home tomorrow morning. I will answer all your questions. ²⁰And don't worry about the donkeys that you lost three days ago. They have been found. Now, all of Israel wants you. They want you and all of the people in your father's family."

²¹Saul answered, "But I am a member of the family group of Benjamin. It is the smallest family group in Israel. And my family is the smallest in the family group of Benjamin. Why do you say Israel wants me?"

²²Then Samuel took Saul and his servant to the eating area. About 30 people had been invited to eat together ₍and share the sacrifice₎. Samuel gave Saul and his servant the most important place at the table. ²³Samuel said to the cook, "Bring the meat I gave you. It is the share I told you to save."

²⁴The cook brought out the thigh* and put it on the table in front of Saul. Samuel said, "Eat the meat that was put in front of you. It was saved for you for this special time when I called the people together." So Saul ate with Samuel that day.

---

man of God A prophet, a person that God sent to speak to the people.
a little bit of money Literally, "1/4 shekel of silver." This was about 1/10 ounce of silver.
seer Another name for a prophet. This shows that prophets often saw their message from God in some special way.
place for worship Literally, "high place."

thigh This was probably the left thigh that was reserved for important guests. The right thigh was reserved for the priest that sacrificed the animal. This priest helped kill the animal and put the fat from the animal on the altar as a gift to God.
Samuel made a bed for Saul on the roof This is from the Greek translation. The Hebrew has, "Samuel spoke with Saul on the roof." In Israel the roofs were flat, and people used them like an extra room and for storing things.

²⁵After they finished eating, they came down from the place for worship* and went back to town. Samuel made a bed for Saul on the roof* and Saul went to sleep. ²⁶Early the next morning, Samuel shouted to Saul on the roof. Samuel said, "Get up. I will send you on your way." Saul got up and went out of the house with Samuel. ²⁷Saul, his servant, and Samuel were walking together near the edge of town. Samuel said to Saul, "Tell your servant to go on ahead of us. I have a message for you from God." So the servant walked ahead of them.

Samuel Anoints Saul

10 Samuel took a jar of the special oil. Samuel poured the oil on Saul's head. Samuel kissed Saul and said, "The Lord has anointed (chosen) you to be the leader over the people who belong to him. You will control the Lord's people. You will save them from the enemies that are all around them. The Lord has anointed you to be ruler over his people. Here is a sign that will prove this is true:* ²After you leave me today, you will meet two men near Rachel's tomb on the border of Benjamin at Zelzah. The two men will say to you, 'Someone found the donkeys you were looking for. Your father stopped worrying about his donkeys. Now he is worrying about you. He is saying: What will I do about my son?'"

³[Samuel said,] "Then you will go until you come to the large oak tree at Tabor. Three men will meet you there. Those three men will be on their way to worship God at Bethel. One man will be carrying three young goats. The second man will be carrying three loaves of bread. And the third man will have a bottle of wine. ⁴These three men will say hello to you. They will offer you two loaves of bread. And you will accept those two loaves of bread from them. ⁵Then you will go to Gibeath Elohim. There is a Philistine fort in that place. When you come to this town, a group of prophets will come out. These prophets will come down from the place for worship.* They will be prophesying.* They will be playing harps, tambourines, flutes, and lyres. ⁶Then the Lord's Spirit will come on you with great power. You will be changed. You will be like a different man. You will begin to prophesy with these prophets. ⁷After that happens, you can do whatever you choose to do. Why? Because God will be with you.

⁸"Go to Gilgal before me. Then I will come there to you. And I will offer burnt offerings and fellowship offerings. But you must wait seven days. Then I will come and tell you what to do."

Saul Becomes Like the Prophets

⁹Just as Saul turned to leave Samuel, God turned Saul's life around. All those things happened that day. ¹⁰Saul and his servant went to Gibeath Elohim. At that place, Saul met a group of prophets. God's Spirit came on Saul with great power, and Saul prophesied with the prophets. ¹¹Some of the people who had known Saul before saw him prophesying* with the prophets. So they asked each other, "What has happened to Kish's son? Is Saul also one the prophets?"

¹²A man living in Gibeath Elohim said, "Yes! And it seems that he is their leader."* That is why this became a famous saying: "Is Saul also one of the prophets?"

Saul Arrives Home

¹³After Saul finished prophesying,* he went to the place for worship [near his home]. ¹⁴Saul's uncle asked Saul and his servant, "Where have you been?"

Saul said, "We were looking for the donkeys. When we couldn't find them, we went to see Samuel."

¹⁵Saul's uncle said, "Please tell me, what did Samuel say to you?"

¹⁶Saul answered, "Samuel told us the donkeys were already found." Saul did not tell his uncle everything. Saul did not tell him the things Samuel said about the kingdom.

Samuel Announces Saul as King

¹⁷Samuel told all the people of Israel to meet together with the Lord at Mizpah. ¹⁸Samuel told the people of Israel, "The Lord, the God of Israel says, 'I led Israel out of Egypt. I saved you from Egypt's control and from the other kingdoms that

---

You will control ... true These lines are from the ancient Greek translation. They are not in the Hebrew text.

place for worship Literally, "high place."

prophesying Usually, this means "speaking for God." But here this also means that the Spirit of God took control of the person and caused him to sing and dance.

Yes ... leader. Literally, "And who is their father?" Often the man who taught and led other prophets was called "father."

1 SAMUEL 10:19–11:13

tried to hurt you.' ¹⁹But today you have rejected your God. Your God saves you from all your troubles and problems. But you said, 'No, we want a king to rule us.' Now come, stand before the Lord in your families and family groups."

²⁰Samuel brought all the family groups of Israel near. ₍Then Samuel began to choose the new king.₎ First, the family group of Benjamin was chosen. ²¹Samuel told each family in the family group of Benjamin to pass by. Matri's family was chosen. Then Samuel told each man in Matri's family to walk by. Saul son of Kish was chosen. But when the people looked for Saul, they could not find him. ²²Then they asked the Lord, "Has Saul come here yet?"

The Lord said, "Saul is hiding behind the supplies."

²³The people ran and took Saul out from behind the supplies. Saul stood up among the people. Saul was a head taller than any other person.

²⁴Samuel said to all the people, "See the man the Lord has chosen. There is no person like Saul among the people."

Then the people shouted, "Long live the king!"

²⁵Samuel explained the rules of the kingdom to the people. He wrote the rules in a book. He put the book before the Lord. Then Samuel told the people to go home.

²⁶Saul also went to his home in Gibeah. God touched the hearts of brave men, and these brave men began to follow Saul. ²⁷But some troublemakers said, "How can this man save us?" They said bad things about Saul and refused to bring gifts to him. But Saul said nothing.

Nahash, King of the Ammonites

Nahash, the king of the Ammonites, had been hurting the family groups of Gad and Reuben. Nahash poked out the right eye of each of the men. Nahash did not allow anyone to help them. Nahash king of the Ammonites poked out the right eye of every Israelite man living in the area east of the Jordan River. But 7,000 Israelite men ran away from the Ammonites and came to Jabesh Gilead.*

11 About a month later, Nahash the Ammonite and his army surrounded Jabesh Gilead. All the people of Jabesh said to Nahash, "If you will make a treaty with us, we will serve you."

²But Nahash the Ammonite answered, "I will make a treaty with you people only if I can poke out the right eye of each person. Then all Israel will be ashamed!"

³The leaders of Jabesh said to Nahash, "Let us have seven days. We will send messengers through all Israel. If no one comes to help us, we will come up to you ₍and surrender to you₎."

Saul Saves Jabesh Gilead

⁴The messengers came to Gibeah where Saul lived. They told the news to the people. The people cried loudly. ⁵Saul had been out in the field with his cows. Saul came in from the field and heard the people crying. Saul asked, "What's wrong with the people? Why are they crying?"

Then the people told Saul what the messengers from Jabesh said. ⁶Saul listened to their story. Then God's Spirit came on Saul with great power. Saul became very angry. ⁷Saul took a pair of cows and cut them in pieces. Then he gave the pieces of those cows to messengers. He ordered the messengers to carry the pieces throughout the land of Israel. He told them to give this message to the people of Israel: "Come follow Saul and Samuel. If any person does not come and help them, then this same thing will happen to his cows!"

A great fear from the Lord came on the people. They all came together like one person. ⁸Saul gathered the men together at Bezek. There were 300,000 men from Israel and 30,000 men from Judah.

⁹Saul and his army told the messengers from Jabesh, "Tell the people at Jabesh in Gilead that by noon tomorrow, you will be saved."

The messengers told Saul's message to the people at Jabesh. The people at Jabesh were very happy. ¹⁰Then the people of Jabesh said to Nahash the Ammonite, "Tomorrow we will come to you. Then you can do anything you want to us."

¹¹The next morning Saul separated his soldiers into three groups. At sunrise, Saul and his soldiers entered the Ammonite camp. Saul attacked while they were changing guards that morning. Saul and his soldiers defeated the Ammonites before noon. The Ammonite soldiers all ran away in different directions—no two soldiers stayed together.

¹²Then the people said to Samuel, "Where are the people who said they didn't want Saul to rule as king? Bring those people here, and we will kill them!"

¹³But Saul said, "No! Don't kill anyone today! The Lord saved Israel today!"

Nahash ... came to Jabesh Gilead This part is not in the standard Hebrew text, but is found in some ancient translations and in one of the ancient Hebrew scrolls from Qumran.

[14]Then Samuel said to the people, "Come, let's go to Gilgal. At Gilgal we will again make Saul the king."

[15]All the people went to Gilgal. There, in front of the Lord, the people made Saul king. They offered fellowship offerings to the Lord. Saul and all the Israelites had a great celebration.

Samuel Talks to the Israelites About the King

12 Samuel said to all Israel: "I have done everything you wanted me to do. I have put a king over you. [2]Now you have a king to lead you. I am old and gray, but my sons are here with you. I have been your leader since I was a young boy. [3]Here I am. If I have done anything wrong, you must tell those things to the Lord and his chosen king. Did I steal anyone's cow or donkey? Did I hurt or cheat anyone? Did I ever take money, or even a pair of shoes, to do something wrong? If I did any of these things, then I will make it right."

[4]The Israelites answered, "No! You never did anything bad to us. You never cheated us or took things from us!"

[5]Samuel said to the Israelites, "The Lord and his chosen king are witnesses today. They heard what you said. They know that you could find nothing wrong with me." The people answered, "Yes! The Lord is witness!"

[6]Then Samuel said to the people, "The Lord has seen what happened. The Lord is the One who chose Moses and Aaron. And he is the one who brought your ancestors* out of Egypt. [7]Now, stand there and I will tell you about the good things the Lord did for you and your ancestors. [8]Jacob went to Egypt. Later, the Egyptians made life hard for his descendants.* So they cried to the Lord for help. The Lord sent Moses and Aaron. Moses and Aaron took your ancestors out of Egypt and led them to live in this place.

[9]"But your ancestors* forgot the Lord their God. So the Lord let them become the slaves of Sisera. Sisera was the commander of the army at Hazor. Then the Lord let them become the slaves of the Philistines and the king of Moab. They all fought against your ancestors. [10]But your ancestors cried to the Lord for help. They said, 'We have sinned. We left the Lord, and we served the false gods Baal* and Ashtoreth.* But now save us from our enemies, and we will serve you.'

[11]"So the Lord sent Jerub Baal *(Gideon)*, Barak, Jephthah, and Samuel. The Lord saved you from your enemies around you. And you lived in safety. [12]But then you saw Nahash king of the Ammonites coming to fight against you. You said, 'No! We want a king to rule over us!' You said that, even though the Lord your God was already your king! [13]Now, here is the king you chose. The Lord put this king over you. [14]You must fear and respect the Lord. You must serve him and obey his commands. You must not turn against him. You and the king ruling over you must follow the Lord your God. If you do those things, then God will save you.* [15]But if you don't obey the Lord and if you turn against him, then he will be against you. The Lord will destroy you and your king!

[16]"Now stand still and see the great thing the Lord will do before your eyes. [17]Now is the time of the wheat harvest.* I will pray to the Lord. I will ask him to send thunder and rain. Then you will know you did a very bad thing against the Lord when you asked for a king."

[18]So Samuel prayed to the Lord. That same day the Lord sent thunder and rain. And the people became very afraid of the Lord and Samuel. [19]All the people said to Samuel, "Pray to the Lord your God for us, your servants. Don't let us die! We have sinned many times. And now we have added to those sins—we have asked for a king."

[20]Samuel answered, "Don't be afraid. It is true! You did all those bad things. But don't stop following the Lord. Serve the Lord with all your heart. [21]Idols are only statues—they can't help you! So don't worship them. Idols can't help you or save you. They are nothing!

[22]"But the Lord won't leave his people. No, the Lord was pleased to make you his own people. So, for his own good name, he won't leave you.

Baal The Canaanite people believed that this false god brought the rain and storms. They also thought that he made the land produce good crops.

Ashtoreth The Canaanite people thought that this false goddess could make people able to have babies. She was their goddess of love and war.

then God will save you This is from the ancient Greek translation.

time of ... harvest This was the dry time of year when no rains fell.

---

ancestors Literally, "fathers." This means a person's parents, grandparents, and all the people they are descended from.

descendant(s) A person's children and their future families.

²³And as for me, I would never stop praying for you. If I stopped praying for you, then I would be sinning against the Lord. I will continue to teach you the right way to live a good life. ²⁴But you must honor the Lord. You must truly serve the Lord with all your heart. Remember the wonderful things he did for you! ²⁵But if you are stubborn and do evil, then God will throw you away and your king away—like sweeping dirt out with a broom."

Saul Makes His First Mistake

13 At that time, Saul had been king one year. After Saul had ruled over Israel two years,* ²he chose 3,000 men from Israel. There were 2,000 men who stayed with him at Micmash in the hill country of Bethel. There were 1,000 men who stayed with Jonathan at Gibeah in Benjamin. Saul sent the other men in the army back home.

³Jonathan defeated the Philistines at their camp in Geba. The Philistines heard about this. They said, "The Hebrews have rebelled."

Saul said, "Let the Hebrew people hear what happened." So Saul told the men to blow trumpets through all the land of Israel. ⁴All the Israelites heard the news. They said, "Saul has killed the Philistine leader. Now the Philistines really hate the Israelites!"

The people of Israel were called to join Saul at Gilgal. ⁵The Philistines gathered to fight Israel. The Philistines had 3,000* chariots and 6,000 horse soldiers. There were as many Philistine soldiers as sand on the shore. The Philistines camped at Micmash. (Micmash is east of Beth Aven.)

⁶The Israelites saw that they were in trouble. They felt trapped. They ran away to hide in caves and cracks in the rock. They hid among the rocks, in wells, and in other holes in the ground. ⁷Some Hebrews even went across the Jordan River to the land of Gad and Gilead. Saul was still at Gilgal. All the men in his army were shaking with fear.

⁸Samuel said he would meet Saul at Gilgal. Saul waited there seven days. But Samuel had not yet come to Gilgal, and the soldiers began to leave Saul. ⁹So Saul said, "Bring me the burnt offerings and the fellowship offerings." Then Saul offered the burnt offering. ¹⁰As soon as Saul finished offering that sacrifice, Samuel arrived. Saul went out to meet him.

¹¹Samuel asked, "What have you done?"

Saul answered, "I saw the soldiers leaving me. You were not here on time, and the Philistines were gathering at Micmash. ¹²I thought to myself, 'The Philistines will come here and attack me at Gilgal. And I haven't asked the Lord to help us yet! So I forced myself to offer the burnt offering."

¹³Samuel said, "You did a foolish thing! You did not obey the Lord your God! If you had obeyed God's command, then he would have let your family rule Israel forever. ¹⁴But now your kingdom will not continue. The Lord was looking for a man who wants to obey him! The Lord has found that man—and the Lord is choosing him to be the new leader of his people. You didn't obey the Lord's command, so the Lord is choosing a new leader." ¹⁵Then Samuel got up and left Gilgal.

The Battle at Micmash

Saul and the rest of his army left Gilgal. They went to Gibeah in Benjamin. Saul counted the men who were still with him. There were about 600 men. ¹⁶Saul, his son Jonathan, and the soldiers went to Geba in Benjamin.

The Philistines were camped at Micmash. ¹⁷⌊The Philistines decided to punish the Israelites living in that area.⌋ So their best soldiers began the attack. The Philistine army split into three groups. One group went ⌊north⌋ on the road to Ophrah, near Shual. ¹⁸The second group went ⌊southeast⌋ on the road to Beth Horon. And the third group went ⌊east⌋ on the road to the border. That road looks over the Valley of Zeboim toward the desert.

¹⁹None of the people of Israel could make things from iron. There weren't any blacksmiths* in Israel. The Philistines did not teach the Israelites how to make things from iron because the Philistines were afraid the Israelites would make iron swords and spears. ²⁰Only the Philistines could sharpen iron tools. So if the Israelites needed to sharpen their plows, hoes, axes or sickles, they had to go to the Philistines. ²¹The Philistine blacksmiths charged 1/3 ounce* ⌊of silver⌋ for sharpening plows and hoes. And

---

verse 1 Or, "Saul was ___ 1 year(s) old when he became king. He ruled ___ 2 years." This verse is very hard to understand in Hebrew. Part of the numbers may be missing. This verse is not in the ancient Greek translation.
3,000 The Hebrew has, "30,000."

blacksmiths Workers that make things from iron.
1/3 ounce Literally, "1 pim."

they charged 1/6 ounce* ₎of silver₎ for sharpening picks, axes and the iron tip on oxgoads.* ²²So, on the day of battle, none of the Israelite soldiers with Saul had ₎iron₎ swords or spears. Only Saul and his son Jonathan had ₎iron₎ weapons.

²³A group of Philistine soldiers guarded the mountain pass at Micmash.

Jonathan Attacks the Philistines

14 That day, Saul's son Jonathan was talking with the young man who carried his weapons. Jonathan said, "Let's go to the Philistine camp on the other side ₎of the valley₎." But Jonathan did not tell his father.

²Saul was sitting under a pomegranate* tree in Migron at the edge of the hill.* This was near the threshing floor* at that place. Saul had about 600 men with him. ³One man was named Ahijah. Eli had been the Lord's priest at Shiloh. Now Ahijah was the priest—Ahijah now wore the ephod.* Ahijah was a son of Ichabod's brother Ahitub. Ichabod was the son of Phinehas. Phinehas was the son of Eli. The people did not know that Jonathan had left.

⁴There was a large rock on each side of the pass. Jonathan planned to go through that pass and go to the Philistine camp. The large rock on one side was named Bozez. The large rock on the other side was named Seneh. ⁵One large rock stood looking north toward Micmash. The other large rock stood looking south toward Geba.

⁶Jonathan said to his young helper who carried his weapons, "Come on, let's go to the camp of those foreigners.* Maybe the Lord will use us to defeat these people! Nothing can stop the Lord—it doesn't matter if we have many soldiers or just a few soldiers."

⁷The young man who carried Jonathan's weapons said to him, "Do what you think is best. I am with you all the way."

⁸Jonathan said, "Let's go! We'll cross ₎the valley₎ and go to those Philistine guards. We'll let them see us. ⁹If they say to us, 'Stay there until we come to you,' we will stay where we are. We won't go up to them. ¹⁰But if the Philistine men say, 'Come up here,' we will climb up to them. Why? Because that will be a sign from God. That will mean that the Lord will allow us to defeat them."

¹¹So Jonathan and his helper let the Philistines see them. The Philistine guards said, "Look! The Hebrews are coming out of the holes they were hiding in!" ¹²The Philistines in the fort shouted to Jonathan and his helper, "Come up here. We'll teach you a lesson!"

Jonathan said to his helper, "Follow me up the hill. The Lord is letting Israel defeat the Philistines!"

¹³⁻¹⁴So Jonathan climbed up the hill with his hands and feet. And his helper was right behind him. Jonathan and his helper attacked those Philistines. In the first attack, they killed 20 Philistines in an area about one-half acre in size. Jonathan fought the men who attacked from the front. And Jonathan's helper came behind him and killed the men who were only wounded.

¹⁵All of the Philistine soldiers became scared—the soldiers in the field, the soldiers in the camp, and the soldiers at the fort. Even the bravest soldiers were scared. The ground began to shake and that really scared the Philistine soldiers!

¹⁶Saul's guards at Gibeah in the land of Benjamin saw the Philistine soldiers running away in different ways. ¹⁷Saul said to the army with him, "Count the men. I want to know who left camp."

They counted the men. Jonathan and his helper were gone.

¹⁸Saul said to Ahijah, "Bring God's Holy Box!*" (At that time God's Holy Box was there with the Israelites.) ¹⁹Saul was talking to Ahijah the priest. ₎Saul was waiting for advice from God.₎ But the noise and confusion in the Philistine camp was growing and growing. ₎Saul was becoming

---

1/6 ounce Literally, "1/3 ₎shekel₎."

oxgoad(s) A sharp stick that a person used to make animals go the right way.

pomegranate A red fruit with many tiny seeds inside it. Each seed is covered with a soft, tasty part of the fruit.

edge of the hill Or, "the edge of Gibeah."

threshing floor A place where grain is beaten or walked on to remove the hulls from the grain.

ephod A special coat a man wore to show that he was a priest or a priest's helper.

foreigners Literally, "uncircumcised." This showed these people were not Israelites and had not shared in their special agreement with God.

Holy Box The Box of the Agreement, the box that contained the stone tablets with the Ten Commandments written on them and the other things that proved God was with the people of Israel during their time in the Sinai Desert.

impatient. Finally, Saul said to Ahijah the priest, "That's enough! Put your hand down [and stop praying]!" ²⁰Saul gathered his army together and went to the battle. The Philistine soldiers were really confused! They were even fighting each other with their swords! ²¹There were Hebrews who served the Philistines in the past and who stayed in the Philistine camp. But now these Hebrews joined the Israelites with Saul and Jonathan. ²²All the Israelites who had hidden in the hill country of Ephraim heard the Philistine soldiers were running away. So these Israelites also joined in the battle and began chasing the Philistines.

²³So the Lord saved the Israelites that day. The battle moved on past Beth Aven. The whole army was with Saul—he had about 10,000 men. The battle spread to every city in the hill country of Ephraim.*

Saul Makes Another Mistake

²⁴But Saul made a big mistake that day.* The Israelites were tired and hungry. This was because Saul forced the people to make this promise: Saul said, "If any man eats food before evening comes and before I finish defeating my enemies, then that man will be punished!" So none of the Israelite soldiers ate any food.

²⁵⁻²⁶Because of the fighting, the people went into some woods. Then they saw a honeycomb on the ground. The Israelites went up to the honeycomb, but they didn't eat any it. They were afraid to break the promise. ²⁷But Jonathan didn't know about that promise. Jonathan didn't hear his father force the people to make that promise. Jonathan had a stick in his hand. He dipped the end of the stick into the honeycomb and pulled out some honey. He ate the honey and began to feel much better.

²⁸One of the soldiers told Jonathan, "Your father forced the soldiers to make a special promise. Your father said that any man who eats today will be punished! [So the men have not eaten anything.] That is why the men are weak."

²⁹Jonathan said, "My father has brought a lot of trouble to the land! See how much better I feel after just tasting a little of this honey! ³⁰It would have been much better for the men to eat the food that they took from their enemies today. We could have killed many more Philistines!"

³¹That day the Israelites defeated the Philistines. They fought them all the way from Micmash to Aijalon. So the people were very tired and hungry. ³²They had taken sheep, cows, and calves from the Philistines. Now the people of Israel were so hungry they killed the animals on the ground and ate them. And the blood was still in the animals!

³³A person said to Saul, "Look! The men are sinning against the Lord. They're eating meat that still has blood in it!"

Saul said, "You have sinned! Roll a large stone over here. Now!" ³⁴Then Saul said, "Go to the men and tell them each person must bring his bull and sheep to me. Then the men must kill their bulls and sheep here. Don't sin against the Lord! Don't eat meat that still has blood in it."

That night every person brought his animals and killed them there. ³⁵Then Saul built an altar for the Lord. Saul himself began building that altar for the Lord!

³⁶Saul said, "Let's go after the Philistines tonight. We will take everything from them! We will kill them all!"

The army answered, "Do whatever you think is best."

But the priest said, "Let's ask God."

³⁷So Saul asked God, "Should I go chase the Philistines? Will you let us defeat the Philistines?" But God did not answer Saul that day.

³⁸So Saul said, "Bring all the leaders to me! Let's find who did the sin today. ³⁹I swear *(promise)* by the Lord who saves Israel, even if my own son Jonathan did the sin, he must die." None of the people said a word.

⁴⁰Then Saul said to all the Israelites, "You stand on this side. I and my son Jonathan will stand on the other side."

The soldiers answered, "As you wish, sir!"

⁴¹Then Saul prayed, "Lord, God of Israel, why haven't you answered your servant today? If I or my son Jonathan have sinned, Lord God of Israel, give Urim. If your people Israel have sinned, give Thummim.*

Saul and Jonathan were chosen, and the people went free. ⁴²Saul said, "Throw them again to show

---

The whole army ... Ephraim These words are in the ancient Greek translation, but not in the Hebrew.

But Saul ... that day These words are in the ancient Greek translation, but not in the Hebrew.

Urim ... Thummim The priest used Urim and Thummim to learn God's answer to questions. We don't know exactly what they were, but they were used like lots—stones, sticks, or bones that were thrown like dice to help people make decisions.

who is guilty—me or my son Jonathan." Jonathan was chosen.

⁴³Saul said to Jonathan, "Tell me what you have done."

Jonathan told Saul, "I only tasted a little honey from the end of my stick. Should I die for doing that?"

⁴⁴Saul said, "I made a promise and asked God to punish me if I didn't keep my promise! Jonathan must die!"

⁴⁵But the soldiers said to Saul, "Jonathan led Israel to a great victory today. Must Jonathan die? Never! We swear *(promise)* by the living God that ⌊no one will hurt Jonathan⌋—not one hair of Jonathan's head will fall to the ground! God helped Jonathan fight against the Philistines today!" So the people saved Jonathan. He was not put to death.

⁴⁶Saul did not chase the Philistines. The Philistines went back to their place.

Saul Fights Israel's Enemies

⁴⁷Saul took full control of Israel. Saul fought all the enemies that lived around Israel. Saul fought Moab, the Ammonites, Edom, the king of Zobah, and the Philistines. Saul defeated Israel's enemies wherever he went. ⁴⁸Saul was very brave. Saul saved Israel from all the enemies who tried to take things from the people of Israel. Saul defeated even the Amalekites!

⁴⁹Saul's sons were Jonathan, Ishvi and Malki Shua. Saul's older daughter was named Merab. Saul's younger daughter was named Michal. ⁵⁰Saul's wife was named Ahinoam. Ahinoam was the daughter of Ahimaaz.

The commander of Saul's army was named Abner son of Ner. Ner was Saul's uncle. ⁵¹Saul's father Kish and Abner's father Ner were sons of Abiel.

⁵²Saul was brave all his life. He fought hard against the Philistines. Any time Saul saw a man who was strong or brave, he took that man and put him into the group of soldiers that stayed near the king and protected him.

Saul Destroys the Amalekites

15 ⌊One day⌋ Samuel said to Saul, "The Lord sent me to anoint* you king over his people Israel. Now listen to the Lord's message. ²The Lord All-Powerful says: 'When the Israelites came out of Egypt, the Amalekites tried to stop them from going to Canaan. I saw what the Amalekites did. ³Now, go fight against the Amalekites. You must completely destroy the Amalekites and everything that belongs to them. Don't let anything live; you must kill all the men and women and all of their children and little babies. You must kill all of their cows and sheep and all of their camels and donkeys.'"

⁴Saul gathered the army together at Telaim. There were 200,000 foot soldiers and 10,000 other men. That includes the men from Judah. ⁵Then Saul went to the city of Amalek and waited in the valley. ⁶Saul said to the Kenite people, "Go away, leave the Amalekites. Then I won't destroy you with the Amalekites. You showed kindness to the Israelites when they came out of Egypt." So the Kenite people left the Amalekites.

⁷Saul defeated the Amalekites. He fought them and chased them all the way from Havilah to Shur, at the border of Egypt. ⁸Agag was the king of the Amalekites. Saul captured Agag alive. Saul let Agag live, but he killed all the men in Agag's army. ⁹Saul and the Israelite soldiers felt bad about destroying everything. So they let Agag live. They also kept the fat cows, the best sheep, and the lambs. They kept everything that was worth keeping. They didn't want to destroy those things. They destroyed only the things that were not worth keeping.

Samuel Tells Saul About His Sin

¹⁰Then Samuel received a message from the Lord. ¹¹The Lord said, "Saul has stopped following me. So I am sorry that I made Saul king. He is not doing what I tell him." Samuel became angry and cried to the Lord all night.

¹²Samuel got up early the next morning and went to meet Saul. But the people told Samuel, "Saul went to ⌊the town in Judah named⌋ Carmel. Saul went there to set up a stone monument to honor himself. Saul is traveling around to several places and will finally go down to Gilgal."

So Samuel went to the place where Saul was. Saul had just offered the first part of the things he took from the Amalekites. Saul was offering them as a burnt offering to the Lord.* ¹³Samuel went to

---

anoint To pour olive oil on a person's head to show he was chosen by God to be a king, priest, or prophet.

Saul had just offered ... Lord This is from the ancient Greek Translation. It is not in the standard Hebrew text.

Saul and Saul said hello. Saul said, "Lord bless you! I obeyed the Lord's commands."

¹⁴But Samuel said, "Then what is that sound I hear? Why do I hear sheep and cattle?"

¹⁵Saul said, "The soldiers took them from the Amalekites. The soldiers saved the best sheep and cattle to burn as sacrifices* to the Lord your God. But we destroyed everything else."

¹⁶Samuel said to Saul, "Stop! Let me tell you what the Lord said to me last night."

Saul answered, "Fine, tell me what he said."

¹⁷Samuel said, "In the past, you thought you were not important. But then you became the leader of the family groups of Israel. The Lord chose you to be king over Israel. ¹⁸The Lord sent you on a special mission. The Lord said, 'Go and destroy all of the Amalekites. They are evil people. Destroy them all! Fight them until they are completely finished!' ¹⁹But you didn't listen to the Lord! Why? You wanted to keep those things, so you did what the Lord said is bad!"

²⁰Saul said, "But I did obey the Lord! I went where the Lord sent me. I destroyed all the Amalekites! I brought back only one person—their king Agag. ²¹And the soldiers took the best sheep and cattle to sacrifice* to the Lord your God at Gilgal!"

²²But Samuel answered, "Which pleases the Lord more: burnt offerings and sacrifices* or obeying the Lord's command? It is better to obey God than to offer sacrifices to him. It is better to listen to God than to offer the fat from rams. ²³Refusing to obey is as bad as the sin of sorcery.* Being stubborn and doing what you want is like the sin of worshiping idols. You refused to obey the Lord's command. For this reason, the Lord now refuses to accept you as king."

²⁴Then Saul said to Samuel, "I have sinned. I did not obey the Lord's commands, and I did not do what you told me. I was afraid of the people, and I did what they said. ²⁵Now I beg you, forgive me for doing this sin. Come back with me, so I may worship the Lord."

²⁶But Samuel said to Saul, "I won't go back with you. You refused the Lord's command, and now the Lord refuses you as king of Israel."

²⁷When Samuel turned to leave, Saul caught Samuel's robe. The robe tore. ²⁸Samuel said to Saul, "⌊You tore my robe. In the same way,⌋ the Lord has torn the kingdom of Israel from you today. The Lord has given the kingdom to one of your friends. This man is a better person than you. ²⁹The Lord is the God of Israel. The Lord lives forever. The Lord does not lie or change his mind. The Lord is not like a man who changes his mind."

³⁰Saul answered, "Alright, I sinned! But please come back with me. Show me some respect in front of the leaders and the people of Israel. Come back with me so I may worship the Lord your God." ³¹Samuel went back with Saul, and Saul worshiped the Lord.

³²Samuel said, "Bring Agag, the king of the Amalekites, to me."

Agag came to Samuel. Agag was tied with chains. Agag thought, "Surely he won't kill me."*

³³But Samuel said to Agag, "Your sword took babies from their mothers. So now, your mother will have no children." And Samuel cut Agag to pieces before the Lord at Gilgal.

³⁴Then Samuel left and went to Ramah. And Saul went up to his home in Gibeah. ³⁵After that Samuel never saw Saul again all his life. Samuel was very sad for Saul. And the Lord was very sorry that he had made Saul king of Israel.

Samuel Goes to Bethlehem

16 The Lord said to Samuel, "How long will you feel sorry for Saul? You are feeling sorry for him, even after I told you that I refuse to let Saul be the king of Israel! Fill your horn* with oil and go to Bethlehem. I am sending you to a man named Jesse. Jesse lives in Bethlehem. I have chosen one of his sons to be the new king."

²But Samuel said, "If I go, Saul will hear the news. Then he will try to kill me."

The Lord said, "Go to Bethlehem. Take a young calf with you. Say, 'I have come to make a sacrifice* to the Lord.' ³Invite Jesse to the sacrifice. Then I will show you what to do. You must anoint* the person I show you."

⁴Samuel did what the Lord told him to do. Samuel went to Bethlehem. The elders *(leaders)* of Bethlehem shook with fear. They met Samuel and asked, "Do you come in peace?"

---

sacrifice(s) A gift to God. Usually it was a special animal that was killed and burned on an altar.
sorcery When a person tries to use the power of demons and bad spirits to do magic.
"Surely ... kill me" Or, "This treatment is worse than death."
horn An animal's horn is hollow and was often used like a bottle.
anoint To pour olive oil on a person's head to show he was chosen by God to be a king, priest, or prophet.

⁵Samuel answered, "Yes, I come in peace. I come to make a sacrifice* to the Lord. Prepare yourselves and come to the sacrifice with me." Samuel prepared Jesse and his sons. Then Samuel invited them to come and share the sacrifice.

⁶When Jesse and his sons arrived, Samuel saw Eliab. Samuel thought, "Surely this is the man that the Lord has chosen!"

⁷But the Lord said to Samuel, "Eliab is tall and handsome. But don't think about things like that. God does not look at the things people see. People look only at the outside of a person, but the Lord looks at his heart. Eliab is not the right man."

⁸Then Jesse called his second son, Abinadab. Abinadab walked by Samuel. But Samuel said, "No, this is not the man that the Lord chose."

⁹Then Jesse told Shammah to walk by Samuel. But Samuel said, "No, the Lord did not choose this man, either."

¹⁰Jesse showed seven of his sons to Samuel. But Samuel said to Jesse, "The Lord has not chosen any of these men."

¹¹Then Samuel asked Jesse, "Are these all the sons you have?"

Jesse answered, "No, I have another son—my youngest, but he is out taking care of the sheep."

Samuel said, "Send for him. Bring him here. We will not sit down to eat until he arrives."

¹²Jesse sent someone to get his youngest son. This son was a good-looking, red-faced* young man. He was very handsome.

The Lord said to Samuel, "Get up and anoint* him. He is the one."

¹³Samuel took the horn* with the oil in it, and poured the special oil on Jesse's youngest son in front of his brothers. The Lord's Spirit came on David with great power from that day on. Then Samuel went back home to Ramah.

A Bad Spirit Bothers Saul

¹⁴The Lord's Spirit left Saul. Then the Lord sent a bad spirit to Saul. It caused him much trouble. ¹⁵Saul's servants said to him, "A bad spirit from God is bothering you. ¹⁶Give us the command and we will look for someone who can play the harp. If the bad spirit from the Lord comes on you, this person will play music for you. Then you will feel better."

¹⁷So Saul said to his servants, "Find a person who plays music well and bring him to me."

¹⁸One of the servants said, "There is a man named Jesse living in Bethlehem. I saw Jesse's son. He knows how to play the harp. He is also a brave man and fights well. He is smart and handsome. And the Lord is with him."

¹⁹So Saul sent messengers to Jesse. They told Jesse, "You have a son named David. He takes care of your sheep. Send him to me."

²⁰So Jesse got some things as a gift for Saul. Jesse got a donkey, some bread and a bottle of wine, and a young goat. Jesse gave those things to David and sent him to Saul. ²¹So David went to Saul and stood in front of him. Saul loved David very much. David became the helper who carried Saul's weapons. ²²Saul sent a message to Jesse. "Let David stay and serve me. I like him very much."

²³Any time the bad spirit from God came on Saul, David would take his harp and play it. The bad spirit would leave Saul and he would begin to feel better.

Goliath Challenges Israel

17 The Philistines gathered their armies together for war. They met at Socoh in Judah. Their camp was between Socoh and Azekah, at a town called Ephes Dammim.

²Saul and the Israelite soldiers also gathered together. Their camp was in the Valley of Elah. Saul's soldiers were lined up and ready to fight the Philistines. ³The Philistines were on one hill. The Israelites were on the other hill. And the valley was between them.

⁴The Philistines had a champion fighter named Goliath. Goliath was from Gath. Goliath was over 9 feet* tall. Goliath came out of the Philistine camp. ⁵He had a bronze helmet on his head. He wore a coat of armor that was made like the scales on a fish. This armor was made of bronze and weighed about 125 pounds.* ⁶Goliath wore bronze protectors on his legs. He had a bronze

---

sacrifice(s) A gift to God. Usually it was a special animal that was killed and burned on an altar.

red-faced Or "tanned" or possibly, "red-haired." The Hebrew word means "red" or "ruddy."

anoint To pour olive oil on a person's head to show he was chosen by God to be a king, priest, or prophet.

horn An animal's horn is hollow and often used like a bottle.

over 9 feet Literally, "6 cubits and 1 span." Josephus, the ancient Greek translation, and one of the ancient Hebrew scrolls from Qumran all have "4 cubits and 1 span," or about 6 feet 9 inches.

125 pounds Literally, "5,000 shekels."

javelin* tied on his back. ⁷The wooden part of Goliath's spear was as big as a weaver's rod. The spear's blade weighed 15 pounds.* Goliath's helper walked in front of him, carrying Goliath's shield.

⁸Each day Goliath would come out and shout a challenge to the Israelite soldiers. He would say, "Why are all of your soldiers lined up ready for battle? You are Saul's servants. I am a Philistine. So choose one man and send him to fight me. ⁹If that man kills me, then we Philistines will become your slaves. But if I kill your man, then I win, and you will become our slaves. You will have to serve us!"

¹⁰The Philistine also said, "Today I stand and make fun of the army of Israel! I dare you to send me one of your men and let us fight!"

¹¹Saul and the Israelite soldiers heard the things Goliath said. And they were very afraid.

David Goes to the Battle Front

¹²David was the son of Jesse. Jesse was from the Ephrathah family in Bethlehem, Judah. Jesse had eight sons. In Saul's time Jesse was an old man. ¹³Jesse's three oldest sons went with Saul to the war. The first son was Eliab. The second son was Abinadab. And the third son was Shammah. ¹⁴David was the youngest son. The three oldest sons were in Saul's army. ¹⁵But David left Saul from time to time to take care of his father's sheep at Bethlehem.

¹⁶The Philistine (Goliath) came out every morning and evening and stood before the Israelite army. Goliath made fun of Israel like this for 40 days.

¹⁷One day, Jesse said to his son David, "Take this basket* of cooked grain and these ten loaves of bread to your brothers in the camp. ¹⁸Also take these ten pieces of cheese for the officer who commands your brothers' group of 1,000 soldiers. See how your brothers are doing. Bring back something to show me your brothers are all right. ¹⁹Your brothers are with Saul and all the Israelite soldiers in the Valley of Elah. They are there to fight against the Philistines."

²⁰Early in the morning, David let another shepherd take care of the sheep. David took the food and left as Jesse had told him to. David drove their wagon to the camp. The soldiers were going out to their battle positions just as David arrived. The soldiers began shouting their war cry. ²¹The Israelites and Philistines were lined up and ready for battle.

²²David left the food and things with the man who kept supplies. David ran to the place where the Israelite soldiers were. David asked about his brothers. ²³David began talking with his brothers. Then Goliath, the Philistine champion fighter from Gath, came out from the Philistine army. Goliath shouted things against Israel as usual. David heard what he said. ²⁴The Israelite soldiers saw Goliath and ran away. They were all afraid of Goliath.

²⁵One of the Israelite men said, "Did you see that guy! Look at him! Goliath comes out and makes fun of Israel again and again. Whoever kills that guy will get rich! King Saul will give him a lot of money. Saul will also let his daughter marry the man who kills Goliath. And Saul will also make that man's family free in Israel."

²⁶David asked the men standing near him, "⌊What did he say?⌋ What is the reward for killing this Philistine and taking away this shame from Israel? Who is this Goliath anyway? He is only some foreigner.* Goliath is nothing but a Philistine. Why does he think he can speak against the army of the living God?"

²⁷So the Israelite told David about the reward for killing Goliath. ²⁸David's oldest brother Eliab heard David talking with the soldiers. Eliab became angry at David. Eliab asked David, "Why did you come here? Who did you leave those few sheep with in the desert? I know why you came down here! You didn't want to do what you were told to do. You just wanted to come down here to watch the battle!"

²⁹David said, "What did I do now? I didn't do anything wrong! I was only talking." ³⁰David turned to some other people and asked them the same questions. They gave David the same answers as before.

³¹Some men heard David talking. They took David to Saul and told him what David had said. ³²David said to Saul, "People shouldn't let Goliath discourage them. I am your servant. I will go fight this Philistine!"

---

javelin A small spear.
15 pounds Literally, "600 shekels."
basket Literally, "ephah."

foreigner Literally, "uncircumcised." This shows Goliath was a foreigner and did not share in the agreement God made with the people of Israel.

[33]Saul answered, "You can't go out and fight against this Philistine (Goliath). You're not even a soldier!* And Goliath has been fighting in wars since he was a boy." [34]But David said to Saul, "I, your servant, was taking care of my father's sheep. A lion and a bear came and took a sheep from the flock. [35]I chased that wild animal. I attacked it and took the sheep from its mouth. That wild animal jumped on me, but I caught it by the fur under its mouth. And I hit it and killed it. [36]I killed a lion and a bear! And I will kill that foreigner,* Goliath, just like them! Goliath will die because he made fun of the army of the living God. [37]The Lord saved me from the lion and the bear. The Lord will also save me from this Philistine."

Saul said to David, "Go and may the Lord be with you." [38]Saul put his own clothes on David. Saul put a bronze helmet on David's head and armor* on David's body. [39]David put on the sword and tried to walk around. David tried to wear Saul's uniform, but David was not used to all those heavy things.

David said to Saul, "I can't fight in these things. I'm not used to them." So David took them all off. [40]David took his walking stick in his hand and went to find five smooth stones from the stream. He put the five stones in his shepherd's bag and held his sling* in his hand. And then he went to meet the Philistine (Goliath).

David Kills Goliath

[41]The Philistine (Goliath) slowly walked closer and closer to David. Goliath's helper walked in front of him, carrying the shield. [42]Goliath looked at David ₍and laughed₎. Goliath saw that David was only a handsome, red-faced* boy* [43]Goliath said to David, "What is that stick for? Did you come to chase me away like a dog?" Then Goliath used the names of his gods to say curses against David. [44]Goliath said to David, "Come here, and I'll feed your body to the birds and wild animals!" [45]David said to the Philistine (Goliath), "You come to me using sword, spear, and javelin.* But I come to you in the name of the Lord All-Powerful, the God of the armies of Israel! You have said bad things about him. [46]Today the Lord will let me defeat you! I will kill you. Today I will cut off your head and feed your body to the birds and wild animals. We will do that to all the other Philistines too! Then all the world will know there is a God in Israel! [47]All the people gathered here will know that the Lord does not need swords or spears to save people. The battle belongs to the Lord! And the Lord will help us defeat all of you Philistines."

[48]Goliath the Philistine got up to attack David. Goliath slowly came closer and closer. Then David ran to meet Goliath. [49]David took out a stone from his bag. He put it in his sling* and swung the sling. The stone flew from the sling and hit Goliath right between the eyes. The stone sank deep into his head, and Goliath fell to the ground—face down.

[50]So David defeated the Philistine with only a sling* and one stone! He hit the Philistine and killed him. David didn't have a sword, [51]so he ran and stood beside the Philistine. Then David took Goliath's own sword out of its sheath* and used it to cut off Goliath's head. And that is how David killed the Philistine.

When the other Philistines saw their hero was dead, they turned and ran. [52]The soldiers of Israel and Judah shouted and started chasing the Philistines. The Israelites chased the Philistines all the way to the city limits of Gath and to the gates of Ekron. They killed many of the Philistines. Their bodies were scattered along the Shaaraim road all the way to Gath and Ekron. [53]After chasing the Philistines, the Israelites came back to the Philistine camp and took many things from that camp.

[54]David took the Philistine's head to Jerusalem. David kept the Philistine's weapons and put them in his own tent.

Saul Begins to Fear David

[55]Saul watched David go out to fight Goliath. Saul spoke to Abner, commander of the army. "Abner, who is that young man's father?"

You're not even a soldier! Or, "You are only a boy!" The Hebrew word for "boy" often means "servant" or "the helper that carries a soldier's weapons."

foreigner Literally, "uncircumcised." This shows Goliath was a foreigner and did not share in the agreement God made with the people of Israel.

armor The heavy clothes made from leather and metal that a soldier wore to protect himself.

sling A strip of leather for throwing rocks.

red-faced Or, "tanned" or possibly "red-haired." The Hebrew word means "red" or "ruddy."

boy Or, "teenager" or "soldier's helper."

javelin A small spear.

sheath A case for carrying a sword.

Abner answered, "I swear I don't know, sir."
⁵⁶King Saul said, "Find out who that young man's father is."
⁵⁷When David came back after killing Goliath, Abner brought him to Saul. David was still holding the Philistine's head.
⁵⁸Saul asked him, "Young man, who is your father?"
David answered, "I am the son of your servant Jesse, from Bethlehem."

David and Jonathan Become Close Friends

18 After David finished talking with Saul, Jonathan became very close to David. Jonathan loved David as much as he loved himself.

²Saul kept David with him from that day on. Saul did not let David go back home to his father.

³Jonathan loved David very much. Jonathan made an agreement with David. ⁴Jonathan took off the coat he was wearing and gave it to David. Jonathan also gave David his uniform. Jonathan even gave David his bow, his sword, and his belt.

Saul Notices David's Success

⁵Saul sent David to fight in many different battles. And David was very successful. Then Saul put David in charge of the soldiers. This pleased everyone, even Saul's officers! ⁶David would go out to fight against the Philistines. On the way home after the battles, women in every town in Israel would come out to meet David. They laughed and danced and played drums and lutes.* They did this right in front of Saul! ⁷The women sang,

> "Saul has killed thousands of enemies.
> But David has killed tens of thousands!"

⁸The women's song upset Saul and he became very angry. Saul thought, "The women say David killed tens of thousands ₍of enemies₎. And they say I killed only thousands ₍of enemies₎." ⁹So from that time on, Saul watched David very closely.

Saul Is Afraid of David

¹⁰The next day, a bad spirit from God took control of Saul. Saul became wild* in his house. David played the harp like he usually did. ¹¹But Saul had a spear in his hand. Saul thought, "I'll pin David to the wall." Saul threw the spear two times. But David escaped both times.

¹²The Lord was with David. And the Lord had left Saul. So Saul was afraid of David. ¹³Saul sent David away from him. Saul made David a commander over 1,000 soldiers. David led the soldiers in battle. ¹⁴The Lord was with David. So David was successful in everything. ¹⁵Saul saw that David was very successful. And Saul became more and more afraid of David.

¹⁶But all the people of Israel and Judah loved David. They loved him because he led them into battle ₍and fought for them₎.

Saul Wants His Daughter to Marry David

¹⁷₍But Saul wanted to kill David. Saul thought of a way to trick David.₎ Saul said to David, "Here is my oldest daughter, Merab. I will let you marry her. Then you can become a powerful soldier. You will be like a son to me! Then you will go and fight the Lord's battles!" ₍This was a trick.₎ Saul was really thinking, "Now I won't have to kill David. I will let the Philistines kill him for me!"

¹⁸But David said, "I am not from an important family! And I am not an important man! I can't marry the king's daughter."

¹⁹So when the time came for Saul's daughter Merab to marry David, Saul let her marry Adriel from Meholah.

²⁰Saul's other daughter Michal loved David. The people told Saul that Michal loved David. This made Saul happy. ²¹Saul thought, "I will use Michal to trap David. I will let Michal marry David. And then I will let the Philistines kill him." So Saul said to David a second time, "You can marry my daughter today."

²²Saul gave an order to his officers. Saul told them, "Speak to David in private. Tell him, 'Look, the king likes you. His officers like you. You should marry his daughter.'"

---

lutes A musical instrument with strings like a harp.

Saul became wild Or, "Saul prophesied." The Hebrew word means that the person lost control of the things he said and did. Usually this meant that God was using the person to give a special message to other people.

²³Saul's officers said those things to David. But David answered, "Do you think it is easy to become the king's son-in-law? ⌊I don't have the money to pay for the king's daughter!⌋ I am just a poor, ordinary guy."
²⁴Saul's officers told Saul what David said. ²⁵Saul told them, "Say this to David, 'David, the king doesn't want you to pay money for his daughter!* Saul wants to get even with his enemy. So the price for marrying his daughter is 100 Philistine foreskins.'" That was Saul's secret plan. Saul thought the Philistines would kill David.
²⁶Saul's officers told those things to David. David was happy that he had a chance to become the king's son-in-law, so he did something immediately. ²⁷David and his men went out to fight the Philistines. They killed 200* Philistines. David took these Philistine foreskins and gave them to Saul. David did this because he wanted to become the king's son-in-law.

Saul let David marry his daughter Michal. ²⁸Saul saw that the Lord was with David. Saul also saw that his daughter, Michal, loved David. ²⁹So Saul became even more afraid of David. Saul was against David all that time.

³⁰The Philistine commanders continued to go out to fight the Israelites. But every time, David defeated them. David was Saul's best officer! David became famous.

Jonathan Helps David

19 Saul told his son Jonathan and his officers to kill David. But Jonathan liked David very much. ²⁻³Jonathan warned David. "Be careful! Saul is looking for a chance to kill you. In the morning, go into the field and hide. I will go out into the field with my father. We will stand in the field where you are hiding. I will talk to my father about you. Then I will tell you what I learn."

⁴Jonathan talked to his father Saul. Jonathan said good things about David. Jonathan said, "You are the king. David is your servant. David hasn't done anything wrong to you. So don't do anything wrong to him. David has always been good to you. ⁵David risked his life when he killed the Philistine *(Goliath)*. The Lord won a great victory for all Israel. You saw it, and you were happy. Why do you want to hurt David? He's innocent. There is no reason to kill him!"

⁶Saul listened to Jonathan. Saul made a promise. Saul said, "As surely as the Lord lives, David won't be put to death."

⁷So Jonathan called David and told him everything that was said. Then Jonathan brought David to Saul. So David was with Saul like before.

Saul Again Tries to Kill David

⁸War started again and David went out to fight the Philistines. David defeated the Philistines, and they ran away from him. ⁹But a bad spirit from the Lord came on Saul. Saul was sitting in his house. Saul had his spear in his hand. David was playing the harp. ¹⁰Saul tried to throw his spear into David's body and pin him to the wall. But David jumped out of the way. The spear missed David and stuck in the wall. That night, David ran away.

¹¹Saul sent men to David's house. The men watched David's house. They stayed there all night. They were waiting to kill David in the morning. But David's wife Michal warned him. She said, "You must run away tonight and save your life. If you don't, then you will be killed tomorrow." ¹²Then Michal let David down out of a window. David escaped and ran away. ¹³Michal took the household god and put clothes on it. Then she put that statue in the bed. She also put goats' hair on its head.

¹⁴Saul sent messengers to take David prisoner. But Michal said, "David is sick."

¹⁵The men went and told Saul, but he sent the messengers back to see David. Saul told these men, "Bring David to me. Bring him lying on his bed if you must! And I will kill him."

¹⁶The messengers went to David's house. They went inside to get David, but they saw it was only a statue on the bed. And they saw its hair was only goat's hair.

¹⁷Saul said to Michal, "Why did you trick me like this? You let my enemy escape! David has run away!"

Michal answered Saul, "David told me he would kill me if I didn't help him escape!"

David Goes to the Camps at Ramah

¹⁸David escaped and ran away to Samuel at Ramah. David told Samuel everything that Saul had done to him. Then David and Samuel went to the camps ⌊where the prophets stayed⌋. David stayed there.

---

money for his daughter In Bible times a man usually had to give money to a woman's father before he could marry her.
200 The ancient Greek translation has "100."

¹⁹Saul heard that David was there in the camps near Ramah. ²⁰Saul sent men to arrest David. But when those men came to the camps, there was a group of prophets prophesying.* Samuel was standing there leading the group. God's Spirit came on Saul's messengers and they began prophesying.
²¹Saul heard about this, so he sent other messengers. But they also began prophesying. So Saul sent messengers a third time. And they also began prophesying. ²²Finally, Saul himself went to Ramah. Saul came to the big well by the threshing floor* at Secu. Saul asked, "Where are Samuel and David?"

The people answered, "In the camps near Ramah."

²³Then Saul went out to the camps near Ramah. God's Spirit also came on Saul, and Saul began prophesying.* Saul prophesied more and more all the way to the camps at Ramah. ²⁴Then Saul took off his clothes. So even Saul was prophesying there in front of Samuel. Saul lay there naked all day and all night.

That is why people say, "Is Saul also one of the prophets?"

David and Jonathan Make an Agreement

20 David ran away from the camps near Ramah. David went to Jonathan and asked him, "What have I done wrong? What is my crime? Why is your father trying to kill me?"

²Jonathan answered, "That can't be true! My father isn't trying to kill you! My father doesn't do anything without first telling me. It doesn't matter if it is very important or just a small thing, my father always tells me. Why would my father refuse to tell me that he wants to kill you? No, it is not true!"

³But David answered, "Your father knows very well that I am your friend. Your father said to himself, 'Jonathan must not know about it. If he knows, he will tell David.' But as sure as you and the Lord are alive, I am very close to death!"

⁴Jonathan said to David, "I will do anything you want me to do."

⁵Then David said, "Look, tomorrow is the New Moon Feast.* I am supposed to eat with the king. But let me hide in the field until the evening. ⁶If your father notices I am gone, tell him, 'David wanted to go home to Bethlehem. His family is having its own feast for this monthly sacrifice. David asked me to let him run down to Bethlehem and join his family.' ⁷If your father says, 'Fine,' then I am safe. But if your father becomes angry, then you will know that he wants to hurt me. ⁸Jonathan, be kind to me. I am your servant. You have made an agreement with me before the Lord. If I am guilty, then you may kill me yourself! But don't take me to your father."

⁹Jonathan answered, "No, never! If I learn that my father plans to hurt you, then I will warn you."

¹⁰David said, "Who will warn me if your father says bad things to you?"

¹¹Then Jonathan said, "Come, let's go out into the field." So Jonathan and David went together into the field.

¹²Jonathan said to David, "I make this promise before the Lord, the God of Israel. I promise that I will learn how my father feels about you. I will learn if he feels good about you or not. Then, in three days, I will send a message to you in the field. ¹³If my father wants to hurt you, I will let you know. I will let you leave in safety. May the Lord punish me if I don't do this. May the Lord be with you as he has been with my father. ¹⁴Be kind to me as long as I live. And after I die, ¹⁵don't ever stop showing your kindness to my family. The Lord will destroy all your enemies from the earth. ¹⁶If at that time Jonathan's family must be separated from David, then let it happen. May the Lord punish David's enemies."

¹⁷Then Jonathan asked David to repeat his promise of love for him. Jonathan did this because he loved David as much as he loved himself.

¹⁸Jonathan said to David, "Tomorrow is the New Moon Feast.* Your seat will be empty, so my father will see that you are gone. ¹⁹On the third day, go to the same place you hid when this trouble began. Wait by that hill. ²⁰On the third day, I will go to that hill and act like I am shooting at a target. I will shoot some arrows. ²¹Then I will tell the boy to go find the arrows. If everything is fine, then I will tell the boy, 'You

---

prophesying Usually, this means "speaking for God." But here this also means that the Spirit of God took control of the person and caused him to sing and dance.

threshing floor A place where grain is beaten or walked on to remove the hulls from the grain.

New Moon Feast The first day of the Jewish month. This was a special day of rest and worship. The people met together and shared in the fellowship offerings like those described in Lev. 7:16-21.

went too far! The arrows are closer to me. Come back and get them.' If I say that, then you can come out of hiding. I promise, as surely as the Lord lives, you are safe. There is no danger. ²²But if there is trouble, then I will say to the boy, 'The arrows are farther away. Go get them.' If I say that, then you must leave. The Lord is sending you away. ²³Remember this agreement between you and me. The Lord is our witness forever!"
²⁴Then David hid in the field.

Saul's Attitude at the Feast

The time for the New Moon Feast* came, and the king sat down to eat. ²⁵The king sat next to the wall where he usually sat. Jonathan sat across from Saul. Abner sat next to Saul. But David's place was empty. ²⁶That day Saul said nothing. He thought, "Maybe something happened to David so that he is not clean.*"
²⁷On the next day, the second day of the month, David's place was empty again. Then Saul said to his son Jonathan, "Why didn't Jesse's son come to the New Moon Feast* yesterday or today?"
²⁸Jonathan answered, "David asked me to let him go to Bethlehem. ²⁹He said, 'Let me go. Our family is having a sacrifice* in Bethlehem. My brother ordered me to be there. Now if I am your friend, please let me go and see my brothers.' That is why David has not come to the king's table."
³⁰Saul was very angry with Jonathan. He said to Jonathan, "You are the son of a slave woman who refuses to obey. ⌊And you are just like her.⌋ I know you are on David's side! You bring shame to yourself and to your mother. ³¹As long as Jesse's son lives, you'll never be king and have a kingdom. Now, bring David to me! He is a dead man!"
³²Jonathan asked his father, "Why should David be killed? What did he do wrong?"
³³But Saul threw his spear at Jonathan and tried to kill him. So Jonathan knew that his father wanted very much to kill David. ³⁴Jonathan became angry and left the table. Jonathan was so upset and angry at his father that Jonathan refused to eat any food on the second day of the feast. Jonathan was angry because Saul humiliated him and because Saul wanted to kill David.

David and Jonathan Say Goodbye

³⁵The next morning Jonathan went out to the field. He went to meet David just like they agreed to do. Jonathan brought a little boy with him. ³⁶Jonathan said to the boy, "Run. Go find the arrows I shoot." The boy began to run, and Jonathan shot the arrows over his head. ³⁷The boy ran to the place where the arrows fell. But Jonathan called, "The arrows are farther away!" ³⁸Then Jonathan shouted, "Hurry! Go get them! Don't just stand there!" The boy picked up the arrows and brought them back to his master. ³⁹The boy knew nothing about what went on. Only Jonathan and David knew. ⁴⁰Jonathan gave his bow and arrows to the boy. Then Jonathan told the boy, "Go back to town."
⁴¹The boy left, and David came out from the place he was hiding on the other side of the hill. David bowed with his face to the ground in front of Jonathan. David bowed three times. Then David and Jonathan kissed each other. They both cried together, but David cried more than Jonathan.
⁴²Jonathan said to David, "Go in peace. We used the Lord's name and promised to be friends. We said that the Lord will be the witness between us and our descendants* forever."

David Goes to See Ahimelech the Priest

21 Then David went away, and Jonathan went back to the town. ²David went to the town named Nob to see Ahimelech the priest.
Ahimelech went out to meet David. Ahimelech was shaking with fear. Ahimelech asked David, "Why are you alone? Why isn't anyone with you?"
³David answered Ahimelech, "The king gave me a special order. He told me, 'Don't let anyone know about this mission. No person must know what I told you to do.' I told my men where to meet me. ⁴Now, what food do you have with you? Give me five loaves of bread or whatever you have to eat."
⁵The priest said to David, "I don't have any ordinary bread here, but I do have some of the

---

New Moon Feast The first day of the Jewish month. This was a special day of rest and worship. The people met together and shared in the fellowship offerings like those described in Lev. 7:16-21.

clean Or, "acceptable." Pure or able to be used in worshiping God. See Lev. 11-15 for the Old Testament rules about clean and unclean things.

sacrifice(s) A gift to God. Usually it was a special animal that was killed and burned on an altar.

descendant(s) A person's children and their future families.

Holy Bread.* Your officers can eat it if they have not had sexual relations with any women."*

⁶David answered the priest, "We have not been with any women. My men keep their bodies holy every time we go out to fight, even on ordinary missions.* And this is especially true today, when our work is so special."

⁷There was no bread except the Holy Bread.* So the priest gave David that bread. This was the bread that the priests put on the holy table before the Lord. Each day they took this bread away and put fresh bread in its place.

⁸One of Saul's officers was there that day. He was Doeg the Edomite. Doeg was the leader of Saul's shepherds.* Doeg had been kept there before the Lord.*

⁹David asked Ahimelech, "Do you have a spear or sword here? The king's business is very important. I had to leave quickly, and I didn't bring my sword or any other weapon."

¹⁰The priest answered, "The only sword here is the sword of Goliath the Philistine. It is the sword you took from him when you killed him in the Valley of Elah. That sword is behind the ephod,* wrapped in a cloth. You may take it if you want to."

David said, "Give it to me. There is no sword like Goliath's sword!"

David Runs Away to the Enemy at Gath

¹¹That day David ran away from Saul. David went to Achish king of Gath. ¹²Achish's officers ₍did not like this. They₎ said, "This is David, the king of the land ₍of Israel₎. He is the person the Israelites sing about. They dance and sing this song about him:

"Saul has killed thousands of enemies.
But David has killed tens of thousands!"

¹³David paid close attention to what they said. David was afraid of Achish, king of Gath. ¹⁴So David pretended to be crazy in front of Achish and his officers. While David was with them he acted like a crazy man. He spat on the doors of the gate. He let spit fall down his beard.

¹⁵Achish said to his officers, "Look at the man! He is crazy! Why did you bring him to me? ¹⁶I have enough crazy men. I don't need you to bring this man to my house to act crazy in front of me! Don't let this man come into my house again!"

David Goes to Different Places

22 David left Gath. David ran away to the cave* of Adullam. David's brothers and relatives heard that David was at Adullam. They went to see David there. ²Many people joined David. There were men who were in some kind of trouble. And there were men who owed someone a lot of money. And there were men who were just not satisfied with life. All those kind of people joined David, and David became their leader. David had about 400 men with him.

³David left Adullam and went to Mizpah in Moab. David said to the king of Moab, "Please let my father and mother come and stay with you until I learn what God is going to do to me." ⁴So David left his parents with the king of Moab. David's parents stayed with the king of Moab as long as David was at the fort.

⁵But the prophet Gad said to David, "Don't stay in the fort. Go to the land of Judah." So David left and went to Hereth Forest.

Saul Destroys Ahimelech's Family

⁶Saul heard that the people had learned about David and his men. Saul was sitting under the tree on the hill at Gibeah. Saul had his spear in his hand. All of his officers were standing around him. ⁷Saul said to his officers that were standing around him, "Listen, men of Benjamin! Do you think the son of Jesse *(David)* will give you fields and vineyards? Do you think David will promote you and make you officers over 1,000 men and officers over 100 men? ⁸You men are plotting against me! You made secret plans. Not one of you told me about my son Jonathan. Not one of you told me that he made an agreement with the

---

Holy Bread This was the special bread that was put in the Holy Tent. It is also called "shewbread" or "the bread of the Presence." Normally, only the priests should eat this bread. See Lev. 24:5-9.

Your officers ... women This would make the men unclean and not able to eat any food that had been made holy by offering it to God. See Lev. 7:21,15:1-33.

My men ... missions See 2 Sam. 11:11 and the rules in Deut. 23:9-14.

shepherds Or, "messengers."

kept there before the Lord This might mean that Doeg was there as part of a special promise to God or some other religious reason. Or it might mean he was being held there because of some crime, such as accidentally killing a man.

ephod A special coat a man wore to show that he was a priest or a priest's helper.

cave Or possibly, "fortress."

son of Jesse! Not one of you cares about me! Not one of you told me that my son Jonathan encouraged David. Jonathan told my servant David to hide and attack me! And that is what David is doing now!"

⁹Doeg the Edomite was standing there with Saul's officers. Doeg said, "I saw Jesse's son (David) at Nob. David came to see Ahimelech son of Ahitub. ¹⁰Ahimelech prayed to the Lord for David. Ahimelech also gave David food. And Ahimelech gave David the sword of Goliath the Philistine."

¹¹Then king Saul ordered some men to bring the priest to him. Saul told them to bring Ahimelech son of Ahitub and all his relatives. Ahimelech's relatives were priests at Nob. All of them came to the king. ¹²Saul said to Ahimelech, "Listen now, son of Ahitub."

Ahimelech answered, "Yes, sir."

¹³Saul said to Ahimelech, "Why did you and Jesse's son (David) make secret plans against me? You gave David bread and a sword! You prayed to God for him. And right now, David is waiting to attack me!"

¹⁴Ahimelech answered, "David is very faithful to you. Not one of your other officers is as faithful as David. David is your own son-in-law. And David is the captain of your bodyguards. Your own family respects David. ¹⁵That was not the first time I prayed to God for David. Not at all. Don't blame me or any of my relatives. We are your servants. I know nothing about what is happening."

¹⁶But the king said, "Ahimelech, you and all your relatives must die!" ¹⁷Then the king told the guards at his side, "Go and kill the priests of the Lord. Do this because they are on David's side also. They knew David was running away, but they didn't tell me!"

But the king's officers refused to hurt the priests of the Lord.

¹⁸So the king gave the order to Doeg. Saul said, "Doeg, you go kill the priests." So Doeg the Edomite went and killed the priests. That day Doeg killed 85 men priests.* ¹⁹Nob was the city of the priests. Doeg killed all the people of Nob. Doeg used his sword and killed men, women, children and small babies. And Doeg killed their cows, donkeys, and sheep.

²⁰But Abiathar escaped. Abiathar was the son of Ahimelech. Ahimelech was the son of Ahitub. Abiathar ran away and joined David. ²¹Abiathar told David that Saul had killed the Lord's priests. ²²Then David told Abiathar, "I saw Doeg the Edomite at Nob that day. And I knew he would tell Saul! I am responsible for the death of your father's family. ²³The man (Saul) who wants to kill you also wants to kill me. Stay with me. Don't be afraid. You will be safe with me."

David at Keilah

23 People told David, "Look, the Philistines are fighting against Keilah. They are robbing grain from the threshing floors.*

²David asked the Lord, "Should I go and fight these Philistines?"

The Lord answered David, "Yes, go attack the Philistines. Save Keilah."

³But David's men said to him, "Look, we are here in Judah and we are scared. Just think how scared we will be if we go to where the Philistine army is."

⁴David again asked the Lord. And the Lord answered David, "Go down to Keilah. I will help you defeat the Philistines." ⁵So David and his men went to Keilah. David's men fought the Philistines. David's men defeated the Philistines and took their cattle. In this way, David saved the people of Keilah. ⁶(When Abiathar ran away to David, Abiathar took an ephod* with him.)

⁷People told Saul that David was now at Keilah. Saul said, "God has given David to me! David has trapped himself. He went into a town that has gates and bars to lock the gates." ⁸Saul called all his army together for battle. They prepared to go down to Keilah to attack David and his men.

⁹David learned Saul was making plans against him. David then said to Abiathar the priest, "Bring the ephod."*

¹⁰David prayed, "Lord God of Israel, I have heard that Saul plans to come to Keilah and destroy the town because of me. ¹¹Will Saul come to Keilah? Will the people of Keilah give me to Saul? Lord God of Israel, I am your servant! Please tell me!"

The Lord answered, "Saul will come."

---

priests Literally, "men who wore the linen ephod."

threshing floors Places where grain is beaten or walked on to remove the hulls from the grain.

ephod A special coat a man wore to show that he was a priest or a priest's helper. The priest wore an ephod when he went to ask the Lord for advice.

¹²Again David asked, "Will the people of Keilah give me and my men to Saul?"
The Lord answered, "They will."
¹³So David and his men left Keilah. There were about 600 men who went with David. David and his men kept moving from place to place. Saul learned that David escaped from Keilah. So Saul did not go to that city.

Saul Chases David

¹⁴David went to the desert and stayed in the fortresses* there. David also went to the hill country in the Desert of Ziph. Every day Saul looked for David, but the Lord didn't let Saul take David. ¹⁵David was at Horesh in the Desert of Ziph. He was afraid because Saul was coming to kill him. ¹⁶But Saul's son Jonathan went to see David at Horesh. Jonathan helped David to have a stronger faith in God. ¹⁷Jonathan told David, "Don't be afraid. My father Saul won't hurt you. You will become the king of Israel. And I will be second to you. Even my father knows this."
¹⁸Jonathan and David both made an agreement before the Lord. Then Jonathan went home. And David stayed at Horesh.

The People of Ziph Tell Saul About David

¹⁹The people from Ziph came to Saul at Gibeah. They told Saul, "David is hiding in our area. He is at the fortresses* of Horesh on Hakilah Hill, south of Jeshimon. ²⁰Now, King, come down any time you want. It is our duty to give David to you."
²¹Saul answered, "The Lord bless you for helping me. ²²Go and learn more about him. Learn where David is staying. And learn who has seen David there. Saul thought 'David is smart. He is trying to trick me.' ²³Find all the hiding places that David uses. Then come back to me and tell me everything. Then I'll go with you. If David is in the area, I will find him. I will find him even if I must look through all the families in Judah."
²⁴Then the people from Ziph went back to Ziph. Saul went there later.
David and his men were in the Desert of Maon. They were in the desert area south of Jeshimon. ²⁵Saul and his men went to look for David. But people warned David. They told him that Saul was looking for him. David then went down to "The Rock" in the Desert of Maon. Saul heard that David had gone to the Desert of Maon. So Saul went to that place to find David.
²⁶Saul was on one side of the mountain. David and his men were on the other side of the same mountain. David was hurrying to get away from Saul. Saul and his soldiers were going around the mountain to capture David and his men.
²⁷Then a messenger came to Saul. The messenger said, "Come quickly! The Philistines are attacking us!"
²⁸So Saul stopped chasing David and went to fight the Philistines. That is why people call this place "Slippery Rock."* ²⁹David left the Desert of Maon and went to the fortresses* near En Gedi.

David Shames Saul

24 After Saul had chased the Philistines away, people told Saul, "David is in the desert area near En Gedi." ²So Saul chose 3,000 men from all over Israel. Saul took these men and began looking for David and his men. They looked near Wild Goat Rocks. ³Saul came to the sheep pens beside the road. There was a cave near there. Saul went into the cave to relieve himself. David and his men were hiding far back in the cave. ⁴The men said to David, "Today is the day the Lord talked about! The Lord told you, 'I will give your enemy to you, then you can do anything you want with your enemy.'"
Then David crawled closer and closer to Saul. Then David cut off a corner of Saul's robe. Saul did not see David. ⁵Later, David felt bad about cutting off a corner of Saul's robe. ⁶David said to his men, "I hope the Lord stops me from doing anything like that to my master again! Saul is the Lord's chosen king. I should not do anything against Saul— he is the Lord's chosen king!" ⁷David said these things to stop his men. David would not let his men hurt Saul.
Saul left the cave and went his way. ⁸David came out of the cave. David shouted to Saul, "My lord the king!"
Saul looked back. David bowed with his face to the ground. ⁹David said to Saul, "Why do you listen when people say, 'David plans to hurt you'? ¹⁰I don't want to hurt you! You can see that with your own eyes! The Lord let me have you today in the cave. But I refused to kill you. I was merciful to you. I said, 'I won't hurt my master.

---

fortress(es) A building or city with tall, strong walls for protection.

Slippery Rock Or "Sela Hammahlekoth."

Saul is the Lord's chosen king!' ¹¹Look at this piece of cloth in my hand. I cut off the corner of your robe. I could have killed you, but I didn't! Now, I want you to understand this. I want you to know that I am not planning anything against you! I did nothing wrong to you! But you are hunting me and trying to kill me. ¹²Let the Lord be the judge! The Lord might punish you for the wrong you did me. But I myself won't fight you. ¹³There is an old saying:

'Bad things come from bad people.'

₍I haven't done anything bad! I am not a bad person!₎ I won't hurt you. ¹⁴Who are you chasing? Who is the king of Israel coming to fight against? You are not chasing someone who will hurt you! It is like you are chasing a dead dog or a flea. ¹⁵Let the Lord be the judge. Let him decide between you and me. The Lord will support me and show that I am right. The Lord will save me from you."

¹⁶David finished speaking, and Saul asked, "Is that your voice, David my son?" Then Saul began to cry. Saul cried very much. ¹⁷Saul said, "You are right, and I am wrong. You have been good to me. But I have been bad to you. ¹⁸You told me about the good things you did. The Lord brought me to you, but you did not kill me. ¹⁹₍This shows I am not your enemy.₎ A man doesn't catch his enemy, and then just let him go! He doesn't do good things for his enemy. I hope the Lord rewards you for being good to me today. ²⁰I know that you will become the new king. You will rule the kingdom of Israel. ²¹Now make a promise to me. Use the Lord's name and promise that you will not kill my descendants.* Promise me that you will not destroy my name from my father's family."

²²So David made a promise to Saul. David promised that he would not kill Saul's family. Then Saul went back home. David and his men went up to the fort.

David and Nabal the Fool

25 Samuel died. All the Israelites met together and showed their sadness about Samuel's death. They buried Samuel at his home in Ramah. Then David moved to the Desert of Paran.

²There was a very rich man living in Maon. He had 3,000 sheep and 1,000 goats. That man was in Carmel taking care of some business. He went there to cut the wool from his sheep. ³This man's name was Nabal. He was from Caleb's family. Nabal's wife was named Abigail. She was a wise and beautiful woman. But Nabal* was a mean and cruel man.

⁴David was in the desert when he heard that Nabal was cutting the wool from his sheep. ⁵David sent ten young men to talk to Nabal. David told them, "Go to Carmel. Find Nabal and tell him 'Hello' for me." ⁶David gave them this message for Nabal, "I hope you and your family are fine. I hope that everything you own is fine. ⁷I heard that you are cutting wool from your sheep. Your shepherds were with us for a while. And we did nothing wrong to them. We never took anything from your shepherds while they were at Carmel. ⁸Ask your servants and they will tell you this is true. Please be kind to my young men. We come to you now, at this happy time. Please give these young men anything you can. Please do this for me, your friend* David."

⁹David's men went to Nabal. They gave David's message to Nabal. ¹⁰But Nabal ₍was mean to them₎. Nabal said, "Who is David? Who is this son of Jesse? There are many slaves that have run away from their masters these days! ¹¹I have bread and water. And I have the meat I killed for my servants who cut the wool from my sheep. But I won't give them to men I don't even know!"

¹²David's men went back and told David everything that Nabal said. ¹³Then David said to his men, "Put on your swords!" So David and his men put on their swords. About 400 men went with David. And 200 men stayed with the supplies.

Abigail Prevents Trouble

¹⁴One of Nabal's servants spoke to Nabal's wife Abigail. The servant said, "David sent messengers from the desert to meet our master (Nabal). But Nabal was mean to David's messengers. ¹⁵These men were very good to us. We were out in the fields with the sheep. David's men were with us the whole time. And they never did anything wrong to us! They did not steal anything from us the whole time! ¹⁶David's men protected us night and day! They were like a wall around us—they protected us while we were with them caring for the sheep. ¹⁷Now think about it

---

descendant(s) A person's children and their future families.
Nabal This name means "foolish."
friend Literally, "son."

1 SAMUEL 25:18–26:1

and decide what you can do. Nabal was foolish to say the things he did! Terrible trouble is coming to our master *(Nabal)* and all his family."

¹⁸Abigail hurried and took 200 loaves of bread, two full winebags, five cooked sheep, about a bushel* of cooked grain, about 2 quarts* of raisins, and 200 cakes of pressed figs. She put them on donkeys. ¹⁹Then Abigail told her servants, "Go on. I'll follow you." But she did not tell her husband.

²⁰Abigail rode her donkey and came down to the other side of the mountain. She met David and his men coming from the other direction.

²¹⌊Before David met Abigail,⌋ David was saying, "I protected Nabal's property in the desert. I made sure none of his sheep were missing. I did all that for nothing! I did good things to him, but he has been bad to me. ²²I hope God punishes me if I let even one man in Nabal's family live till tomorrow morning."

²³Just then Abigail arrived. When Abigail saw David, she quickly got off her donkey. She bowed down with her face to the ground in front of David. ²⁴Abigail lay at David's feet and said, "Sir, please let me talk to you. Listen to what I say. Blame me for what happened. ²⁵I didn't see the men you sent. Sir, don't pay any attention to that worthless man *(Nabal)*. He is the same as his name. His name means 'Foolish,' and he really is foolish. ²⁶The Lord has kept you from killing innocent people. Surely as the Lord lives, and surely as you live, I hope your enemies and all the people who want to harm you become like Nabal. ²⁷Now, I am bringing this gift to you. Please give these things to your men. ²⁸Please forgive me for doing wrong. I know the Lord will make your family strong ⌊many kings will come from your family⌋! The Lord will do this because you fight his battles. People will never find anything bad about you as long as you live! ²⁹If a person chases you to kill you, the Lord your God will save your life! But the Lord will throw away your enemies' lives like a stone from a sling!* ³⁰The Lord promised to do many good things for you. And the Lord will keep all his promises! God will make you leader over Israel. ³¹And you won't be guilty of killing innocent people. You won't fall into that trap. Please remember me when the Lord brings you success."

³²David answered Abigail, "Praise the Lord, the God of Israel. Praise God for sending you to meet me. ³³God bless you for your good judgment. You kept me from killing innocent people today. ³⁴Surely as the Lord, the God of Israel lives, if you hadn't come quickly to meet me, then not one man in Nabal's family would have lived until tomorrow morning."

³⁵Then David accepted Abigail's gifts. David told her, "Go home in peace. I have listened to your request, and I will do what you asked."

Nabal's Death

³⁶Abigail went back to Nabal. Nabal was in the house. Nabal had been eating like a king. Nabal was drunk and feeling good. So Abigail told Nabal nothing until the next morning. ³⁷The next morning, Nabal was sober. So his wife told him everything. Nabal had a heart attack and became as stiff as a rock! ³⁸About ten days later, the Lord caused Nabal to die.

³⁹David heard that Nabal was dead. David said, "Praise the Lord! Nabal said bad things about me, but the Lord supported me. The Lord kept me from doing wrong. And the Lord caused Nabal to die because he did wrong."

Then David sent a message to Abigail. David asked her to become his wife. ⁴⁰David's servants went to Carmel and said to Abigail, "David sent us to get you. David wants you to become his wife."

⁴¹Abigail bowed her face to the ground. She said, "I am your woman servant. I am ready to serve you. I am ready to wash the feet of my master's *(David's)* servants."*

⁴²Abigail quickly got on a donkey and went with David's messengers. Abigail brought five maids with her. She became David's wife.

⁴³David had also married Ahinoam of Jezreel. Both Abinoam and Abigail were David's wives. ⁴⁴David was also married to Saul's daughter Michal. But Saul had taken her away from him and had given her to a man named Palti son of Laish. Palti was from the town named Gallim.

David and Abishai Enter Saul's Camp

26 The people of Ziph went to see Saul at Gibeah. They said to Saul, "David is hiding on the hill of Hakilah. This hill is across from Jeshimon."

---

about a bushel Literally, "5 seahs."
2 quarts Literally, "1 omer."
sling A strip of leather for throwing rocks.

wash the feet ...servants This showed Abigail was humble and willing to be like a servant.

²Saul went down to the desert of Ziph. Saul took the 3,000 soldiers he had chosen from all over Israel. Saul and these men looked for David in the desert of Ziph. ³Saul set up his camp on the hill of Hakilah. The camp was beside the road across from Jeshimon.

David was staying in the desert. David learned that Saul had followed him there. ⁴So David sent out spies.* David learned that Saul had come to Hakilah. ⁵Then David went to the place where Saul had set up his camp. David saw where Saul and Abner were sleeping. (Abner son of Ner was the commander of Saul's army.) Saul was sleeping in the middle of the camp. The army was all around Saul.

⁶David talked to Ahimelech the Hittite and Abishai son of Zeruiah. (Abishai was Joab's brother.) He asked them, "Who will go down into the camp with me to Saul?"

Abishai answered, "I'll go with you."

⁷Night came. David and Abishai went into Saul's camp. Saul was asleep in the middle of the camp. His spear was stuck in the ground near his head. Abner and the other soldiers were asleep around Saul. ⁸Abishai said to David, "Today God has let you defeat your enemy. Let me pin Saul to the ground with his spear. I'll only do it once!"

⁹But David said to Abishai, "Don't kill Saul! Any person who hurts the Lord's chosen king must be punished! ¹⁰Surely as the Lord lives, the Lord himself will punish Saul. Maybe Saul will die naturally, or maybe Saul will be killed in battle. ¹¹But I pray that the Lord never lets me hurt the Lord's chosen king! Now pick up the spear and water jug by Saul's head. Then let's go."

¹²So David took the spear and water jug that were near Saul's head. Then David and Abishai left Saul's camp. No one knew what had happened! No one saw it. No one even woke up! Saul and all of his soldiers slept because the Lord had put them into a deep sleep.

David Shames Saul Again

¹³David crossed over to the other side of the valley. David stood on top of the mountain across the valley from Saul's camp. David and Saul's camp were far apart. ¹⁴David shouted to the army and to Abner son of Ner, "Answer me, Abner!"

Abner answered, "Who are you? Why are you calling the king?"

¹⁵David said, "You are a man, aren't you? And you are better than any other man in Israel. Is that right? Then why didn't you guard your master, the king? An ordinary man came into your camp to kill your master, the king. ¹⁶You made a big mistake! As sure as the Lord is alive, you and your men should die. Why? Because you didn't protect your master, the Lord's chosen king. Look for the king's spear and the water jug that was near Saul's head? Where are they?"

¹⁷Saul knew David's voice. Saul said, "Is that your voice, David my son?"

David answered, "Yes, it is my voice, my master and king." ¹⁸David also said, "Sir, why are you chasing me? What wrong have I done? What am I guilty of? ¹⁹My master and king, listen to me! If the Lord caused you to be angry at me, then let him accept an offering. But if men caused you to be angry at me, then let the Lord cause bad things to happen to them. Men have forced me to leave the land the Lord gave me. Men have told me, 'ₗGo live with the foreigners.ⱼ Go and serve other gods.' ²⁰Now don't make me die far away from the Lord's presence. The king of Israel has come out looking for a flea. You are like a man hunting partridges in the mountains!"*

²¹Then Saul said, "I have sinned. Come back, David my son. Today you showed me that my life is important to you. So I will not try to hurt you. I have acted foolishly. I have made a big mistake."

²²David answered, "Here is the king's spear. Let one of your young men come here and get it. ²³The Lord pays every man for the things he does—he rewards him if he does right, and he punishes him if he does wrong. The Lord let me defeat you today, but I wouldn't hurt the Lord's chosen king. ²⁴Today I showed you that your life is important to me! In the same way, the Lord will show that my life is important to him! The Lord will save me from every trouble."

²⁵Then Saul said to David, "God bless you, David my son. You will do great things and you will succeed."

David went on his way, and Saul went back home.

---

hunting partridges in the mountains People hunted these birds until the birds became too tired to go on. Then they killed the birds. Saul was chasing David the same way. This is also a word play. The Hebrew word for "partridge" is like the word for "calling" in verse 14.

---

spies People who secretly go to learn about the enemy's strengths and weaknesses.

David Lives with the Philistines

27 But David thought to himself, "Saul will catch me someday. The best thing I can do is to escape to the land of the Philistines. Then Saul will give up looking for me in Israel. That way I will escape from Saul." ²So David and his 600 men left Israel. They went to Achish son of Maoch. Achish was king of Gath. ³David, his men, and their families lived in Gath with Achish. David had his two wives with him. They were Ahinoam of Jezreel and Abigail of Carmel. Abigail was the widow* of Nabal. ⁴People told Saul that David had run away to Gath. So Saul stopped looking for him.

⁵David said to Achish, "If you are pleased with me, then give me a place in one of the country towns. I am only your servant. I should live there, not here with you in this royal city."

⁶That day Achish gave David the town of Ziklag. And Ziklag has belonged to the kings of Judah ever since. ⁷David lived with the Philistines one year and four months.

David Fools King Achish

⁸David and his men went to fight the Amalekites and Geshurites who lived in the area from Telem near Shur all the way to Egypt. David's men defeated them and took their wealth. ⁹David defeated the people in that area. David took all their sheep, cattle, donkeys, camels and clothes and brought them back to Achish. But David didn't let any of those people live.

¹⁰David did this many times. Each time Achish asked David where he fought and took those things. David said, "I fought against the southern part of Judah," or "I fought against the southern part of Jerahmeel," or "I fought against the southern part of the Kenizzites."* ¹¹David never brought a man or woman alive to Gath. David thought, "₁If we let any person live,₁ that person might tell ₁Achish₁ what I really did!"

David did this all the time he lived in the Philistine land. ¹²Achish began to trust David. Achish said to himself, "Now David's own people hate him. The Israelites hate David very much. Now David will serve me forever."

The Philistines Prepare for War

28 Later the Philistines gathered their armies to fight against Israel. Achish said to David, "Do you understand that you and your men must go with me to fight ₁against Israel₁?"

²David answered, "Certainly! Then you can see for yourself what I can do!"

Achish said, "Fine, I'll make you my bodyguard. You will protect me forever."

Saul and the Woman at Endor

³Samuel died. All the Israelites showed their sadness about Samuel's death. They buried Samuel in Ramah, his home town. Earlier, Saul had forced the mediums* and fortune tellers to leave Israel.

⁴The Philistines prepared for war. They came to Shunem and made their camp at that place. Saul gathered all the Israelites and made his camp at Gilboa. ⁵Saul saw the Philistine army, and he was scared. His heart pounded with fear. ⁶Saul prayed to the Lord, but the Lord did not answer him. God did not talk to Saul in dreams. God did not use the Urim* to give him an answer. And God did not use prophets to speak to Saul. ⁷Finally, Saul said to his officers, "Find me a woman who is a medium.* Then I can go ask her what will happen ₁in this war₁."

His officers answered, "There is a medium* at Endor."

⁸Saul put on different clothes so no one would know who he was. That night Saul and two of his men went to see the woman. Saul said ₁to the woman,₁ "I want you to bring up a ghost who can tell me what will happen in the future. You must call for the ghost of the person I name."

⁹But the woman said to Saul, "You know what Saul did! He has forced all of the mediums* and fortune tellers to leave the land of Israel. You are trying to trap me and kill me."

¹⁰Saul used the Lord's name to make a promise to the woman. He said, "As surely as the Lord lives, you will not be punished for doing this."

¹¹The woman asked, "Who do you want me to bring up for you?"

Saul answered, "Bring up Samuel."

---

widow A woman whose husband has died.
I fought ... Judah, Jerahmeel, Kenizzites All these places belonged to Israel. David made Achish think he had fought against his own people, the Israelites.

medium(s) A person who tries to communicate with the spirits of dead people.
Urim Priests used these stones to get answers from God. See Num. 27:20-22.
medium(s) A person who tries to communicate with the spirits of dead people.

¹²⌊And it happened!⌋ The woman saw Samuel and screamed loudly. She said to Saul, "You tricked me! You are Saul."
¹³The king said to the woman, "Don't be afraid! What do you see?"
The woman said, "I see a spirit coming up out of the ground.*"
¹⁴Saul asked, "What does he look like?"
The woman answered, "He looks like an old man wearing a special robe."
Then Saul knew it was Samuel. Saul bowed down. His face touched the ground. ¹⁵Samuel said to Saul, "Why did you bother me? Why did you bring me up?"
Saul answered, "I am in trouble! The Philistines have come to fight against me, and God left me. God won't answer me any more. He won't use prophets or dreams to answer me. That's why I called you. I want you to tell me what to do!"
¹⁶Samuel said, "The Lord left you. Now he is with your neighbor *(David)*. So why are you bothering me? ¹⁷The Lord used me to tell you what he would do. And now the Lord is doing what he said he would do! The Lord is pulling the kingdom from your hands. And he is giving the kingdom to one of your neighbors. That neighbor is David. ¹⁸You did not obey the Lord. You did not destroy the Amalekites and show them how angry the Lord was at them. That is why the Lord is doing this to you today. ¹⁹The Lord will let the Philistines defeat you and the army of Israel today. And tomorrow, you and your sons will be here with me!"
²⁰Saul quickly fell to the ground and lay there. Saul was afraid because of the things Samuel said. Saul was also very weak because he did not eat any food all that day and night.
²¹The woman came to Saul. She saw Saul was really scared. She said, "Look, I am your servant. I have obeyed you. I risked my life and did what you told me to do. ²²Now please listen to me. Let me give you some food. You must eat. Then you will have enough strength to go on your way."
²³But Saul refused. He said, "I won't eat."
Saul's officers joined the woman and begged him to eat. Finally, Saul listened to them. He got up from the ground and sat on the bed. ²⁴The woman had a fat calf at the house. She quickly killed the calf. She took some flour and pressed it with her hands. Then she baked some bread without yeast. ²⁵The woman put the food before Saul and his officers. Saul and his officers ate. Then that same night they got up and left.

"David Can't Come With Us!"

29 The Philistines gathered all their soldiers at Aphek. The Israelites camped by the spring at Jezreel. ²The Philistine rulers were marching with their groups of 100 men and 1,000 men. David and his men were marching at the back with Achish.
³The Philistine captains asked, "What are these Hebrews doing here?"
Achish told the Philistine captains, "This is David. David was one of Saul's officers. David has been with me for a long time. I found nothing wrong in David since the time he left Saul and came to me."
⁴But the Philistine captains were angry with Achish. They said, "Send David back! David must go back to the city you gave him. He can't go with us into battle. ⌊If he is here,⌋ then we will have an enemy in our own camp. He would please his king *(Saul)* by killing our own men. ⁵David is the same person the Israelites sing and dance about in this song:

> "Saul has killed thousands of enemies.
> But David has killed tens of thousands!"

⁶So Achish called David and said, "As sure as the Lord lives, you are loyal to me. I would be pleased to have you serve in my army. Since the day you came to me, I have found nothing wrong in you. Also the ⌊Philistine⌋ rulers think you are a good man.* ⁷Go back in peace. Don't do anything against the Philistine rulers."
⁸David asked, "What have I done wrong? Have you found anything wrong with me since the day I came to you? ⌊No!⌋ Why won't you let me go to fight the enemies of my lord the king?"
⁹Achish answered, "I believe that you are a good man. You are like an angel from God. But the Philistine captains still say, 'David can't go with us into battle.' ¹⁰Early in the morning, you and your men should go back to the city I gave you. Don't pay attention to the bad things the captains say about you. You are a good man. So leave as soon as the sun comes up."

---

ground Or, "Sheol, the place of death."

the Philistine rulers ... man The Philistine rulers are pleased with David. It is the Philistine commanders of the army who are against him.

¹¹So David and his men got up early in the morning and went back to the country of the Philistines. And the Philistines went up to Jezreel.

The Amalekites Attack Ziklag

30 On the third day, David and his men arrived at Ziklag. They saw that the Amalekites had attacked Ziklag. The Amalekites invaded the Negev area. They attacked Ziklag and burned the city. ²They took the women in Ziklag as prisoners. They took all the people, both young and old. They did not kill any of the people. They only took them away.

³When David and his men came to Ziklag, they found the city burning. Their wives, sons, and daughters were all gone. The Amalekites had taken them. ⁴David and the other men in his army cried loudly until they were too weak to cry any more. ⁵The Amalekites had taken David's two wives, Ahinoam of Jezreel and Abigail, the widow* of Nabal from Carmel.

⁶All the men in the army were sad and angry because their sons and daughters were taken as prisoners. The men were talking about killing David with stones. This made David very upset. But David found strength in the Lord his God. ⁷David said to Abiathar the priest, "Bring the ephod."*

⁸Then David prayed to the Lord. "Should I chase the people who took our families? Will I catch them?"

The Lord answered, "Chase them. You will catch them. You will save your families."

David and His Men Find the Egyptian Slave

⁹⁻¹⁰David took the 600 men with him and went to Besor Ravine. About 200 of his men stayed at this place. They stayed there because they were too weak and tired to continue. So David and 400 men continued to chase the Amalekites.

¹¹David's men found an Egyptian in a field. They took the Egyptian to David. They gave the Egyptian some water to drink and some food to eat. ¹²They gave the Egyptian a piece of fig cake and two clusters of raisins. He felt better after eating. He had not had any food or water for three days and nights.

¹³David asked the Egyptian, "Who is your master? Where do you come from?"

The Egyptian answered, "I am an Egyptian. I am the slave of an Amalekite. Three days ago I became sick and my master left me. ¹⁴We had attacked the Negev area where the Kerethites* live. We attacked the land of Judah, and in the Negev area where Caleb's people live. We also burned Ziklag."

¹⁵David asked the Egyptian, "Will you lead me to the people who took our families?"

The Egyptian answered, "If you make a special promise before God, then I will help you find them. But you must promise that you won't kill me or give me back to my master."

David Defeats The Amalekites

¹⁶The Egyptian led David to the Amalekites. They were lying around on the ground, eating and drinking. They were celebrating with the many things they had taken from the land of the Philistines and from Judah. ¹⁷David attacked them and killed them. They fought from sunrise until the evening of the next day. None of the Amalekites escaped, except 400 young men who jumped onto their camels and rode away.

¹⁸David got back everything the Amalekites had taken, including his two wives. ¹⁹Nothing was missing. They found all the children and old people. They found all their sons and daughters. And they found all their valuable things. They got back everything the Amalekites had taken. David brought everything back. ²⁰David took all the sheep and cattle. David's men made these animals go in front. David's men said, "They are David's prize."

All Men Will Share Equally

²¹David came to the 200 men who had stayed at Besor Ravine. These were the men who were too weak and tired to follow David. These men came out to meet David and the soldiers that went with him. The men at the Besor Ravine greeted David and his army as they came near. ²²There were some bad men who were trouble-makers in the group that went with David. Those trouble-makers said, "These 200 men didn't go with us. So we won't give them any of the things we took. These men get only their own wives and children."

---

widow A woman whose husband has died.
ephod A special coat a man wore to show that he was a priest or a priest's helper. The priest wore an ephod when he went to ask the Lord for advice.

Kerethites Or "people from Crete." This is probably the Philistines, but some of David's best soldiers were Kerethites.

²³David answered, "No, my brothers. Don't do that! Think about what the Lord gave us! The Lord let us defeat the enemy that attacked us. ²⁴No one will listen to what you say! The share will be the same for the man who stayed with the supplies and for the man who went into battle. Everyone will share alike." ²⁵David made this an order and rule for Israel. This rule continues even today.

²⁶David arrived in Ziklag. Then he sent some of the things he took ₍from the Amalekites₎ to his friends, the leaders of Judah. David said, "Here is a present for you from the things ₍we took from₎ the Lord's enemies."

²⁷David sent some of those things from the Amalekites to the leaders in Bethel, Ramoth in the Negev, Jattir, ²⁸Aroer, Siphmoth, Eshtemoa, ²⁹Racal, the cities of the Jerahmeelites and the cities of the Kenites, ³⁰Hormah, Bor Ashan, Athach, ³¹and Hebron. David sent some of those things to the leaders in all the other places where David and his men had been.

The Death of Saul

31 The Philistines fought against Israel, and the Israelites ran away from the Philistines. Many Israelites were killed at Mount Gilboa. ²The Philistines fought hard against Saul and his sons. The Philistines killed Saul's sons Jonathan, Abinadab, and Malki Shua.

³The battle became worse and worse against Saul. The archers* shot arrows at Saul, and Saul was hurt very badly. ⁴Saul said to the servant that carried his armor, "Take your sword and kill me. Then those foreigners can't hurt me and make fun of me." But Saul's helper was scared and refused to kill him.

So Saul took his own sword and killed himself. ⁵The helper saw that Saul was dead., so he used his own sword and killed himself. He died there with Saul. ⁶So Saul, his three sons, and the boy who carried his armor all died together that day.

The Philistines are Happy About Saul's Death

⁷The Israelites ₍that lived₎ on the other side of the valley saw the Israelite army running away. They saw that Saul and his sons were dead. So those Israelites left their cities and ran away. Then the Philistines came and lived in those cities.

⁸The next day, the Philistines went back to take things from the dead bodies. They found Saul and his three sons dead on Mount Gilboa. ⁹The Philistines cut off Saul's head and took his armor. They carried the news to the Philistine people and to the temple of their idols.* ¹⁰They put Saul's armor in the temple of Ashtoreth.* The Philistines also hung Saul's body on the wall of Beth Shan.*

¹¹The people living in Jabesh Gilead heard about the things that the Philistines did to Saul. ¹²So all the soldiers of Jabesh went to Beth Shan.* They marched all night! Then they took Saul's body off the wall at Beth Shan. They also took down the bodies of Saul's sons. Then they took those bodies to Jabesh. There the people of Jabesh burned the bodies of Saul and his three sons. ¹³Then these people took the bones of Saul and his three sons and buried them under the big tree in Jabesh. Then the people of Jabesh showed their sadness—they did not eat for seven days.

---

archers Soldiers that used bows and arrows.

idols Statues of false gods.
Ashtoreth The Canaanite people thought that this false goddess could make people able to have babies. She was their goddess of love and war.
Beth Shan Or possibly, "Beth Shean".

2 Samuel

David Learns About Saul's Death

1 David went back to Ziklag after defeating the Amalekites. This was just after Saul had been killed. David had been there two days. ²Then, on the third day, a young soldier came to Ziklag. This man was from Saul's camp. The man's clothes were torn, and he had dirt on his head.* The man came to David and bowed with his face to the ground.

³David asked the man, "Where have you come from?"

The man answered David, "I just came from the Israelite camp."

⁴David said to the man, "Please tell me, who won the battle?"

The man answered, "Our people ran away from the battle. Many of the people were killed in the battle. Even Saul and his son Jonathan are dead."

⁵David said to the young soldier, "How do you know Saul and his son Jonathan are dead?"

⁶The young soldier said, "I happened to be on Mount Gilboa. I saw Saul leaning on his spear. The Philistine chariots and horse soldiers were coming closer and closer to Saul. ⁷Saul looked back and saw me. He called to me and I answered him. ⁸Then Saul asked me who I was. I told him that I was an Amalekite. ⁹Then Saul said, 'Please kill me. I am hurt badly. And I am about to die anyway.' ¹⁰He was hurt so bad that I knew he wouldn't live. So I stopped and killed him. Then I took the crown from his head and the bracelet from his arm. And I brought them here to you, my lord."

¹¹Then David tore his clothes to show he was very sad. All the men with David did the same thing. ¹²They were very sad and cried. They did not eat until evening. They cried because Saul and his son Jonathan were dead. David and his men cried for the Lord's people ₍that had been killed₎, and they cried for Israel. They cried because Saul, his son Jonathan, and many Israelites had been killed in battle.

David Orders the Amalekite Killed

¹³Then David talked with the young soldier who had told him about Saul's death. David asked, "Where are you from?"

The young soldier answered, "I am the son of a foreigner. I am an Amalekite."

¹⁴David said to the young soldier, "Why were you not afraid to kill the Lord's chosen king?"

¹⁵⁻¹⁶Then David told the Amalekite, "You are responsible for your own death. You said you killed the Lord's chosen king, so your own words prove you are guilty." Then David called one of his young servants and told him to kill the Amalekite. So the young Israelite killed the Amalekite.

David's Sad Song About Saul and Jonathan

¹⁷David sang a sad song about Saul and his son Jonathan. ¹⁸David told ₍his men₎ to teach the song to the people of Judah. ₍This song is called₎ "The Bow." It is written in the *Book of Jashar*.*

19 "Israel, your beauty was ruined
 on your hills.
 Oh, how those heroes fell!
20 Don't tell the news in Gath,*
 Don't announce it in the streets of Ashkelon.*
 Those Philistine cities would be happy!
 Those foreigners* would be glad.

---

clothes ... head This showed the man was very sad.

Book of Jashar An ancient book about the wars of Israel.
Gath The Philistine capital city.
Ashkelon One of the five Philistine cities.
foreigners Literally, "uncircumcised." This shows the Philistines had not shared in Israel's Agreement with God.

²¹ I hope no rain or dew falls
   on the mountains of Gilboa.
   I hope there will be no offerings
   coming from those fields.
   The shields of the heroes rusted there.
   No, Saul's shield was not rubbed with oil.
²² Jonathan's bow killed its share of enemies.
   And Saul's sword killed its share!
   They have spilled the blood
   of men now dead.
   They cut into the fat of strong men.
²³ Saul and Jonathan.
   They loved and enjoyed each other in life.
   And even death did not separate them!
   They were faster than eagles.
   They were stronger than lions.
²⁴ Daughters of Israel, cry for Saul!
   Saul gave you beautiful red dresses
   and covered them with gold jewelry!
²⁵ Strong men have fallen in the battle.
   Jonathan is dead on Gilboa's hills.
²⁶ Jonathan, my brother,
   I miss you so much!
   I enjoyed being with you so much.
   Your love for me was more wonderful
   than the love of women.
²⁷ Strong men have fallen in battle.
   The weapons of war are gone."

David and His Men Move to Hebron

2 Later David asked the Lord for advice. David said, "Should I take control* of any of the cities of Judah?"

The Lord said to David, "Yes."

David asked, "Where should I go?"

The Lord answered, "To Hebron."

²So David and his two wives moved to Hebron. (His wives were Ahinoam from Jezreel and Abigail, the widow* of Nabal from Carmel.) ³David also brought his men and their families. All of them made their homes in Hebron and the towns nearby.

David Thanks the People of Jabesh

⁴The men of Judah came to Hebron and anointed* David to be the king of Judah. Then they told David, "The men of Jabesh Gilead buried Saul."

⁵David sent messengers to the men of Jabesh Gilead. These messengers told the men in Jabesh: "The Lord bless you, because you have shown kindness to your lord Saul by burying ⌊his ashes⌋.* ⁶The Lord will be kind and true to you. And I will also be kind to you. ⁷Now be strong and brave. Your lord, Saul, is dead. But the family group of Judah has anointed* me to be their king."

Ish Bosheth Becomes King

⁸Abner son of Ner was the captain of Saul's army. Abner took Saul's son Ish Bosheth to Mahanaim ⁹and made him king of Gilead, Asher, Jezreel, Ephraim, Benjamin, and all of Israel.*

¹⁰Ish Bosheth was Saul's son. Ish Bosheth was 40 years old when he began to rule over Israel. He ruled two years. But the family group of Judah followed David. ¹¹David was king in Hebron. David ruled over the family group of Judah for seven years and six months.

The Deadly Contest

¹²Abner son of Ner and the officers of Saul's son Ish Bosheth left Mahanaim and went to Gibeon. ¹³Joab, Zeruiah's son, and the officers of David also went to Gibeon. They met Abner and Ish Bosheth's officers at the pool of Gibeon. Abner's group sat on one side of the pool. Joab's group sat on the other side of the pool.

¹⁴Abner said to Joab, "Let's have the young soldiers get up and have a contest here."

Joab said, "Yes, let's have a contest."

¹⁵So the young soldiers got up. The two groups counted their men for the contest. They chose twelve men from the family group of Benjamin to fight for Saul's son Ish Bosheth. And they chose twelve men from David's officers. ¹⁶Each of the men grabbed his opponent's head and stabbed him in the side with his sword, and then they fell down together. That is why the place is called "The Field of the Sharp Knives."* The place is in Gibeon.

---

his ashes The bodies of both Saul and Jonathan were burned. See 1 Sam. 31:12.
Israel Sometimes this means the whole country, Judah and Israel. Here it means only the family groups that were not united with Judah.
The Field of the Sharp Knives Or, "Helkath Hazzurim."

---

take control Literally, "go up against."
widow A woman whose husband has died.
anoint(ed) To pour olive oil on a person's head to show he was chosen by God to be a king, priest, or prophet.

Abner Kills Asahel

17That contest became a terrible battle and David's officers defeated Abner and the Israelites that day. 18Zeruiah had three sons, Joab, Abishai, and Asahel. Asahel was a fast runner. He was as fast as a wild deer. 19Asahel ran straight toward Abner and began chasing him. 20Abner looked back and asked, "Is that you, Asahel?"

Asahel said, "Yes, it's me."

21⌊Abner didn't want to hurt Asahel.⌋ So Abner said to Asahel, "Stop chasing me— go after one of the young soldiers. You could easily take his armor* for yourself." But Asahel refused to stop chasing Abner.

22Abner again said to Asahel, "Stop chasing me or I will have to kill you. Then I won't be able to look your brother Joab in the face again."

23But Asahel refused to stop chasing Abner. So Abner used the back end of his spear and pushed it into Asahel's stomach. The spear went ⌊deep into Asahel's stomach and came⌋ out of his back. Asahel died right there.

Joab and Abishai Chase Abner

Asahel's body lay on the ground. All of the men that ran that way stopped ⌊to look at Asahel⌋. 24But Joab and Abishai* continued chasing Abner. The sun was just going down when they came to Ammah Hill. (Ammah Hill is in front of Giah on the way to Gibeon Desert.) 25The men from the family group of Benjamin gathered around Abner at the top of the hill.

26Abner shouted to Joab and said, "Must we fight and kill each other forever? Surely you know that this will only end in sadness. Tell the people to stop chasing their own brothers."

27Then Joab said, "It is a good thing you said that. As sure as God is alive, if you had not said something, then people would still be chasing their brothers in the morning." 28So Joab blew a trumpet, and his people stopped chasing the Israelites. They did not try to fight the Israelites any more.

29Abner and his men marched all night through the Jordan Valley. They crossed the Jordan River and marched all day until they came to Mahanaim.

30Joab stopped chasing Abner and went back. Joab had gathered his men and learned that 19 of David's officers were missing, including Asahel. 31But David's officers had killed 350 of Abner's men from the family group of Benjamin. 32David's officers took Asahel and buried him in the tomb of his father at Bethlehem.

Joab and his men marched all night. The sun came up just as they reached Hebron.

War Between Israel and Judah

3 There was war for a long time between Saul's family and David's family. David became stronger and stronger. And Saul's family became weaker and weaker.

David's Six Sons Born at Hebron

2David had these sons that were born at Hebron. The first son was Ammon. Ammon's mother was Ahinoam from Jezreel. 3The second son was Kileab. Kileab's mother was Abigail, the widow* of Nabal from Carmel. The third son was Absalom. Absalom's mother was Maacah daughter of Talmai, king of Geshur. 4The fourth son was Adonijah. Adonijah's mother was Haggith. The fifth son was Shephatiah. Shephatiah's mother was Abital. 5The sixth son was Ithream. Ithream's mother was David's wife Eglah. David had these ⌊six sons⌋ born at Hebron.

Abner Decides to Join David

6Abner became more and more powerful in Saul's army while the families of Saul and David fought each other. 7Saul had a woman servant* named Rizpah daughter of Aiah. Ish Bosheth said to Abner, "Why did you have sexual relations with my father's servant woman?"

8Abner was very angry because of what Ish Bosheth said. Abner said, "I have been loyal to Saul and his family. I did not give you to David— ⌊I did not let him defeat you⌋. I am not a traitor working for Judah.* But now you are saying that I did this bad thing. 9-10I make this promise—I will now make sure that the things God said will happen. The Lord said he would take the kingdom away from Saul's family and give it to David. The Lord will make David king of Judah and Israel.

---

armor Clothing that had metal or hard things in it to protect the person wearing it in war.

Joab and Abishai Brothers of Asahel, the man that Abner killed. See verse 18.

widow A woman whose husband has died.

woman servant Or, "concubine," a slave woman who was like a wife to a man.

I am not a traitor working for Judah Literally, "Am I a dog's head of Judah?"

He will rule from Dan to Beersheba.* And I hope God does bad things to me if I don't make that happen!"

¹¹Ish Bosheth could not say anything to Abner. Ish Bosheth was too afraid of him.

¹²Abner sent messengers to David. Abner said, "Who do you think should rule this country? Make an agreement with me, and I will help you become the ruler of all the people of Israel."

¹³David answered, "Good! I will make an agreement with you. But I ask you only one thing: I will not meet with you until you bring Saul's daughter Michal to me."

David Gets His Wife Michal Back

¹⁴David sent messengers to Saul's son Ish Bosheth. David said, "Give me my wife Michal. She was promised to me. I killed 100 Philistines to get her."*

¹⁵Then Ish Bosheth told the men to go and take Michal from a man named Paltiel son of Laish. ¹⁶Michal's husband ₍Paltiel₎ went with Michal. Paltiel was crying while he followed Michal to Bahurim. But Abner said to Paltiel, "Go back home." So Paltiel went back home.

Abner Promises to Help David

¹⁷Abner sent this message to the leaders of Israel. He said, "You have been wanting to make David your king. ¹⁸Now do it! The Lord was talking about David when he said, 'I will save my people the Israelites from the Philistines and all their other enemies. I will do this through my servant David.'"

¹⁹Abner said these things to David in Hebron. And he said these things to the people of the Benjamin family group. The things Abner said sounded good to the Benjamin family group and to all the people of Israel.

²⁰Then Abner came up to David at Hebron. Abner brought 20 men with him. David gave a party for Abner and for all the men who came with him.

²¹Abner said to David, "My lord and king, let me go bring all the Israelites to you. Then they will make an agreement with you. And you will rule over all Israel, like you wanted."

So David let Abner leave. And Abner left in peace.

Abner's Death

²²Joab and David's officers came back from battle. They had many valuable things that they had taken from the enemy. David had just let Abner leave in peace. So Abner was not there in Hebron with David. ²³Joab and all his army arrived ₍at Hebron₎. The army said to Joab, "Abner son of Ner came to King David, and David let Abner leave in peace."

²⁴Joab came to the king and said, "What have you done? Abner came to you, but you sent him away without hurting him! Why? ²⁵You know Abner son of Ner. He came to trick you. He came to learn all about the things you are doing."

²⁶Joab left David and sent messengers to Abner at the well of Sirah. The messengers brought Abner back, but David did not know this. ²⁷When Abner arrived at Hebron, Joab took him to one side in the middle of the gateway to talk with him in private. And then Joab stabbed Abner in the stomach, and Abner died. Abner had killed Joab's brother Asahel. So now Joab killed Abner.

David Cries for Abner

²⁸Later David heard the news. David said, "My kingdom and I are innocent of the death of Abner son of Ner. The Lord knows this. ²⁹Joab and his family are responsible for this, and all his family are to be blamed. I hope many troubles will come to Joab's family. I hope the people in his family will be sick with leprosy, and crippled, and killed in war, and not have enough food to eat!"

³⁰Joab and his brother Abishai killed Abner because Abner had killed their brother Asahel in the battle at Gibeon.

³¹⁻³²David said to Joab and to all the people with Joab, "Tear your clothes and put on clothes of sadness. Cry for Abner." They buried Abner in Hebron. David went to the funeral. King David and all the people cried at Abner's grave.

³³King David sang this sad song at Abner's funeral:

34   "Did Abner die like some foolish criminal?
    Abner, your hands were not tied.
    Your feet were not put in chains.
    No Abner, evil men killed you!"

Dan to Beersheba This means the whole nation of Israel, north and south. Dan was a town in the northern part of Israel and Beersheba was in the southern part of Judah.

I killed ... to get her Literally, "I paid for her with 100 Philistine foreskins." See 1 Sam. 18:20-30 and 1 Sam. 25:44.

Then all the people cried again for Abner. ³⁵All day long people came to encourage David to eat food. But David had made a special promise. He said, "May God punish me and give me many troubles if I eat bread or any other food before the sun goes down." ³⁶All the people saw what happened, and they were pleased with what King David had done. ³⁷All the people of Judah and Israel understood that King David had not killed Abner son of Ner.

³⁸King David said to his officers, "You know that a very important leader died today in Israel. ³⁹And it was on the very same day that I was anointed* to be the king. These sons of Zeruiah have caused me a lot of trouble. I hope the Lord gives these men the punishment they deserve."

Troubles Come to Saul's Family

4 Saul's son *(Ish Bosheth)* heard that Abner had died at Hebron. Ish Bosheth and all his people became very scared. ²Two men went to see to Saul's son *(Ish Bosheth)*. These two men were captains in the army. They were Recab and Baanah, the sons of Rimmon from Beeroth. (They were Benjamites because the town Beeroth belonged to the family group of Benjamin. ³But all the people in Beeroth ran away to Gittaim. And they are still living there today.)

⁴Saul's son Jonathan had a son named Mephibosheth. Mephibosheth was five years old when the news came from Jezreel that Saul and Jonathan had been killed. The woman who cared for Mephibosheth ₍was scared that the enemy was coming, so she₎ picked him up and ran away. But while running away, she dropped the boy. And he became crippled in both feet.

⁵Recab and Baanah, sons of Rimmon from Beeroth, went to Ish Bosheth's house at noon. Ish Bosheth was resting because it was hot. ⁶⁻⁷Recab and Baanah came into the house like they were going to get some wheat. Ish Bosheth was lying on his bed in his bedroom. Recab and Baanah stabbed and killed Ish Bosheth. Then they cut off his head and took it with them. They traveled all night by the way leading through the Jordan Valley. ⁸They arrived at Hebron. And they gave Ish Bosheth's head to David.

Recab and Baanah said to the King David, "Here is the head of your enemy, Ish Bosheth son of Saul. He tried to kill you. The Lord has punished Saul and his family for you today."

⁹But David told Recab and his brother Baanah, "As sure as the Lord is alive, he has saved me from all trouble. ¹⁰But once before a person thought he would bring me good news. He told me, 'Look! Saul is dead.' He thought I would reward him for bringing me the news. But I grabbed this man and killed him at Ziklag. ¹¹So I must kill you and remove you from this land. Why? Because you evil men killed a good man sleeping on his own bed, in his own house."

¹²So David commanded the young soldiers to kill Recab and Baanah. The young soldiers cut off the hands and feet of Recab and Baanah and hanged them by the pool of Hebron. Then they took the head of Ish Bosheth and buried it in the same place where Abner was buried at Hebron.

The Israelites Make David King

5 Then all the family groups of Israel came to David at Hebron. They said to David, "Look, we are one family!* ²Even when Saul was our king, you were the one who led us into battle. And you were the one who brought Israel back home from war. And the Lord himself said to you, 'You will be the shepherd of my people, the Israelites. You will be the ruler over Israel.'"

³So all the leaders of Israel came to meet with King David at Hebron. King David made an agreement with these leaders in Hebron in front of the Lord. Then the leaders anointed* David to be the king of Israel.

⁴David was 30 years old when he began to rule. He was king for 40 years. ⁵In Hebron, he ruled over Judah for 7 years and 6 months. And in Jerusalem, he ruled over all of Israel and Judah for 33 years.

David Wins the Town of Jerusalem

⁶The king and his men went to fight against the Jebusites living in Jerusalem. The Jebusites said to David, "You can't come into ₍our city₎.* Even our blind and crippled people can stop you."

---

one family Literally, "Your flesh and blood."

anoint(ed) To pour olive oil on a person's head to show he was chosen by God to be a king, priest, or prophet.

You can't come ... city The city of Jerusalem was built on a hill. And the city had high walls around it. So it was very hard to capture.

---

anoint(ed) To pour olive oil on a person's head to show he was chosen by God to be a king, priest, or prophet.

(They said this because they thought that David would not be able to enter into their city. ⁷But David did take the fort of Zion. This fort became the City of David.*)

⁸That day David said to his men, "If you want to defeat the Jebusites, go up through the water shaft* and reach those 'crippled and blind' enemies."

This is why people say, "The blind and the crippled can't come into the house.*

⁹David lived in the fort and called it "The City of David."* David built the area called the Millo.* He also built more buildings inside the city. ¹⁰David became stronger and stronger because the Lord All-Powerful was with him.

¹¹Hiram king of Tyre sent messengers to David. Hiram also sent cedar trees, carpenters and stonemasons. They built a house for David. ¹²Then David knew that the Lord had really made him king of Israel. And David knew that the Lord had made his kingdom very important to God's people, the people of Israel.

¹³David moved from Hebron to Jerusalem. In Jerusalem, David got more women servants* and wives. Some more of David's children were born in Jerusalem. ¹⁴These are the names of David's sons that were born in Jerusalem: Shammua, Shobab, Nathan, Solomon, ¹⁵Ibhar, Elishua, Nepheg, Japhia, ¹⁶Elishama, Eliada, and Eliphelet.

David Fights Against the Philistines

¹⁷The Philistines heard that the Israelites had anointed* David to be the king of Israel. So the Philistines went to look for David ⌊to kill him⌋. But David heard about this and went into the fort ⌊at Jerusalem⌋. ¹⁸The Philistines came and camped in the Rephaim Valley.

¹⁹David asked the Lord, saying, "Should I go to war against the Philistines? Will you help me defeat the Philistines?"

The Lord said to David, "Yes. I will certainly help you defeat the Philistines."

²⁰Then David went to Baal Perazim and defeated the Philistines in that place. David said, "The Lord broke through my enemies like water breaking through a broken dam." That is why David named that place "Baal Perazim."* ²¹The Philistines left the statues of their gods behind at Baal Perazim. David and his men took those statues away.

²²Again the Philistines came and camped in Rephaim Valley.

²³David prayed to the Lord. This time the Lord told David, "Don't go there. Go around them to the back of their army. Attack them near the balsam trees. ²⁴⌊Climb up into the trees.⌋ From the top of the balsam trees, you will hear the Philistines marching into battle. Then you must act quickly, because at that time the Lord will go ahead of you and defeat the Philistines for you."

²⁵David did what the Lord commanded him to do. And he defeated the Philistines. He chased them and killed them all the way from Geba to Gezer.

God's Holy Box Is Moved to Jerusalem

6David again gathered all of the best soldiers in Israel. There were 30,000 men. ²Then David and all his men went to Baalah in Judah.* They took God's Holy Box* from Baalah in Judah ⌊and moved it to Jerusalem⌋. People go to the Holy Box to worship the Lord. ⌊The Holy Box is like the Lord's throne.⌋ There are statues of Cherub angels* on top of the Holy Box. And the Lord sits as king on these angels. ³David's men brought the Holy Box out of Abinadab's house on the hill. Then they put God's Holy Box on a new wagon.

City of David A southeast and oldest part of the city of Jerusalem.
water tunnel There was a tunnel with water in it that went under the wall of the ancient city of Jerusalem, and then a narrow shaft (tunnel) went straight up into the city. People in the city used it as a well. One of David's men probably climbed up the shaft to get into the city.
house This probably means the kings palace or possibly the temple.
Millo Probably one of the strong places that made up the ancient fort of Zion.
woman servants Or, "concubines," slave woman who were like wives to a man.
anoint To pour olive oil on a person's head to show he was chosen by God to be a king, priest, or prophet.

Baal Perazim This name means "The Lord breaks through."
Holy Box The Box of the Agreement. Also called "The Ark of the Covenant," the box containing the stone tablets with the Ten Commandments written on them and the other things that proved God was with the people of Israel during their time in the Sinai Desert.
Baalah in Judah Another name for Kiriath Jearim. See 1 Chron. 13:6.
Cherub angels Special angels from God. Statues of these angels were on top of the Box of the Agreement.

Uzzah and Ahio, sons of Abinadab, were driving the new wagon.

⁴So they carried the Holy Box out of Abinadab's house on the hill. ₍Uzzah was on the wagon₎ with God's Holy Box.* And Ahio was walking in front of the Holy Box. ⁵David and all the Israelites were dancing in front of the Lord and playing all kinds of musical instruments. There were lyres,* harps, drums, rattles, instruments made from cypress wood, and cymbals.* ⁶When David's men came to the threshing floor* of Nacon, the cows stumbled, and God's Holy Box began to fall off the wagon. Uzzah caught the Holy Box. ⁷But the Lord was angry at Uzzah and killed him.* Uzzah showed he did not honor God when he touched the Holy Box. Uzzah died there by God's Holy Box. ⁸David was upset because the Lord had killed Uzzah. David called that place "Perez Uzzah."* That place is still called Perez Uzzah today.

⁹David became afraid of the Lord that day. David said, "How can I bring God's Holy Box* here now?" ¹⁰So David would not move the Lord's Holy Box into the City of David.* David put the Holy Box at the house of Obed Edom from Gath. David carried the Holy Box off the road to the house of Obed Edom of Gath.* ¹¹The Lord's Holy Box stayed in Obed Edom's house for three months. The Lord blessed Obed Edom and all his family.

¹²Later, people told David, "The Lord has blessed the family of Obed Edom and everything he owns, because God's Holy Box* is there." So David went and brought God's Holy Box from Obed Edom's house. David was very happy and excited. ¹³When the ₍men₎ that carried the Lord's Holy Box had walked six steps, ₍they stopped and₎ David sacrificed a bull and a fat calf. ¹⁴David was dancing in front of the Lord. David was wearing a linen ephod.*

¹⁵David and all the Israelites were excited—they shouted and blew the trumpet as they brought the Lord's Holy Box* into the city. ¹⁶Saul's daughter Michal was looking out the window. While the Lord's Holy Box was being carried into the city, David was jumping and dancing before the Lord. Michal saw this, and she was upset at David. ₍She thought he was making a fool of himself.₎

¹⁷David put up a tent for the Holy Box.* The Israelites put the Lord's Holy Box in its place under the tent. Then David offered burnt offerings and fellowship offerings before the Lord. ¹⁸After David had finished offering the burnt offerings and the fellowship offerings, he blessed the people in the name of the Lord All-Powerful. ¹⁹David also gave a share of bread, a raisin cake and some date bread, to every man and woman of Israel. Then all the people went home.

Michal Scolds David

²⁰David went back to bless his house. But Saul's daughter Michal came out to meet him. Michal said, "The king of Israel did not honor himself today! You took off your clothes in front of your servants' girls.* You were like a fool who takes off his clothes without shame!"

²¹Then David said to Michal, "The Lord chose me, not your father or any person from his family. The Lord chose me to be leader of his people, the Israelites. So I will continue dancing and celebrating in front of the Lord. ²²I might do things that are even more embarrassing! Maybe you won't respect me, but the girls you are talking about are proud of me!"

²³Saul's daughter Michal never had a child. She died without having any children.

David Wants to Build a Temple

7 After King David moved into his new house the Lord gave him peace from all of his enemies around him. ²King David said to Nathan the prophet, "Look, I am living in a fancy house

---

Holy Box The Box of the Agreement. Also called "The Ark of the Covenant," the box containing the stone tablets with the Ten Commandments written on them and the other things that proved God was with the people of Israel during their time in the Sinai Desert.
lyres Musical instruments that are like small harps.
cymbals Brass plates that were hit together to make a loud noise.
threshing floor A place where grain is beaten or walked on to remove the hulls from the grain.
the Lord ... killed him Only the Levites could carry God's Holy Box or any other furniture from the Holy Tent. Uzzah was not a Levite. See Num. 1:50.
Perez Uzzah This name means "The Punishment of Uzzah."
City of David A part of the city of Jerusalem.
Obed Edom of Gath A person from the family group of Levi that lived near Jerusalem.

ephod A vest usually worn by priests.
You took off ... girls David had on only a holy coat (ephod). We don't know how much of his body was covered.

made of cedar wood, but God's Holy Box* is still kept in a tent! ₁We should build a nice building for the Holy Box.₁" ³Nathan said to King David, "Do whatever you want to do. The Lord will be with you."

⁴But that night, the Lord's word came to Nathan. The Lord said, ⁵"Go and tell my servant David, 'This is what the Lord says: You are not the person to build a house for me to live in. ⁶I did not live in a house at the time I took the Israelites out of Egypt. No, I traveled around in a tent. I used the tent for my home. ⁷I never told any of the family groups of Israel to build me a fancy house made from cedar wood.'

⁸"You must say this to my servant David: 'This is what the Lord All-Powerful says: I chose you while you were out in the pasture following the sheep. I took you from that job and made you the leader of my people, the Israelites. ⁹I have been with you every place you went. I have defeated your enemies for you. I will make you one of the most famous people on earth. ¹⁰⁻¹¹And I chose a place for my people, the Israelites. I planted the Israelites—I gave them their own place to live. I did that so they will not have to move from place to place any more. In the past, I sent judges to lead my people of Israel. But evil people gave them many troubles. That will not happen now. I am giving you peace from all of your enemies. I promise that I will make your family a family of kings.*

¹²"When your life is finished, you will die and be buried with your ancestors. But then I will make one of your own children become the king. ¹³He will build a house *(temple)* for my name. And I will make his kingdom strong forever. ¹⁴I will be his father, and he will be my son.* When he sins, I will use other people to punish him. They will be my whips. ¹⁵But I will never stop loving him. I will continue to be loyal to him. I took away my love and kindness from Saul. I pushed Saul away when I turned to you. ₁I will not do that to your family.₁ ¹⁶Your family of kings will continue—you can depend on that! For you, your kingdom will continue forever! Your throne *(kingdom)* will stand forever!"

¹⁷Nathan told David about that vision.* He told David everything God had said.

David Prays to God

¹⁸Then King David went in and sat in front of the Lord. David said, "Lord, my Master, why am I so important to you? Why is my family important? Why have you made me so important? ¹⁹I am nothing but a servant. ₁And you have been so kind to me.₁ But you have also said these kind things about my future family. Lord, my Master, you don't always talk like this to people, do you? ²⁰How can I continue talking to you? Lord, my Master, you know that I am only a servant. ²¹You will do all these wonderful things because you said you would do them and because you want to do them. And you decided to let me know about all these things. ²²Lord, my Master, that is why you are so great! There is no one like you. There is no god except you! ₁We know that₁ because of what we ourselves have heard ₁about the things you did₁.

²³"And there is no nation on earth like your people, the people of Israel. They are a special people. ₁They were slaves,₁ but you took them out of Egypt and made them free. You made them your people. You did great and wonderful things for the Israelites. You did wonderful things for your land. ²⁴You made the people of Israel your very own people forever. And Lord, you became their God.

²⁵"Now, Lord God, you promised to do things for me, your servant, and for my family. Now please do the things you promised—make my family a family of kings forever! ²⁶Then your name will be honored forever. People will say, 'The Lord God All-Powerful rules Israel! And may the family of your servant David continue to be strong in serving you.'

²⁷"You, Lord All-Powerful, the God of Israel, have shown things to me. You said, 'I will make your family great.' That is why I, your servant, decided to pray this prayer to you. ²⁸Lord my Master, you are God. And I can trust the things you say. And you said that these good things will happen to me, your servant. ²⁹Now, please, bless my family. Let them stand before you ₁and serve

---

Holy Box The Box of the Agreement. Also called "The Ark of the Covenant," the box containing the stone tablets with the Ten Commandments written on them and the other things that proved God was with the people of Israel during their time in the Sinai Desert.

make ... family of kings Literally, "make a house for you."

father ,and he will be my son God "adopted" the kings from David's family, and they became his "sons". See Ps. 2:7.

vision Like a dream. God gave messages to his special people by letting them see and hear things in visions.

you, forever. Lord my Master, you yourself said these things. You yourself blessed my family with a blessing that will continue forever."

David Wins Many Wars

8 Later, David defeated the Philistines. The Philistine capital city had controlled a large area of land. David took control of that land. ²David also defeated the people of Moab. At that time he forced them to lie on the ground. Then he used a rope to separate them into rows. Two rows of men were killed, but the whole third row was allowed to live. In that way, the people of Moab became servants of David. They paid tribute* to him.
³Hadadezer son of Rehob was king of Zobah. David defeated Hadadezer when David went to take control* of the area near the Euphrates River. ⁴David took 1,700 horse soldiers and 20,000 foot soldiers from Hadadezer. David crippled all but 100 of the chariot horses. He saved those 100 horses.*
⁵Arameans from Damascus came to help Hadadezer king of Zobah. But David defeated those 22,000 Arameans. ⁶Then David put groups of soldiers in Damascus, Aram. The Arameans became David's servants and brought tribute.* The Lord gave victory to David in every place he went.
⁷David took the gold shields that had belonged to Hadadezer's servants. David took those shields and brought them to Jerusalem. ⁸David also took many, many things made of bronze from Tebah* and Berothai. (Tebah and Berothai were cities that had belonged to Hadadezer.)
⁹Toi king of Hamath heard that David had defeated Hadadezer's whole army. ¹⁰So Toi sent his son Joram to King David. Joram greeted David and blessed him because David had fought against Hadadezer and defeated him. (Hadadezer had fought wars against Toi before.) Joram brought things made of silver, gold, and bronze. ¹¹David took these things and dedicated* them to the Lord. He put them with the other things that he dedicated to the Lord. David had taken those things from the nations that he had defeated. ¹²David defeated Aram, Moab, Ammon, Philistia, and Amalek. David also defeated Hadadezer son of Rehob, king of Zobah. ¹³David defeated 18,000 Arameans in Salt Valley. He was famous when he came home. ¹⁴David put groups of soldiers in Edom. He put these groups of soldiers through all the land of Edom. All the people of Edom became servants for David. The Lord gave victory to David every place he went.

David's Rule

¹⁵David ruled over all of Israel. And David made good and fair decisions for all of his people. ¹⁶Joab son of Zeruiah was the captain over the army. Jehoshaphat son of Ahilud was the historian. ¹⁷Zadok son of Ahitub and Ahimelech son of Abiathar were priests. Seraiah was secretary. ¹⁸Benaiah son of Jehoiada was in charge of the Kerethites and Pelethites.* And David's sons were important leaders.*

David Is Kind to Saul's Family

9 David asked, "Is there any person still left in Saul's family? I want to show kindness to this person. I want to do it for Jonathan."
²There was a servant named Ziba from Saul's family. David's servants called Ziba to David. King David said to Ziba, "Are you Ziba?"
Ziba said, "Yes, I am your servant Ziba."
³The king said, "Is there any person left in Saul's family? I want to show God's kindness to this person."
Ziba said to King David, "Jonathan has a son still living. He is crippled in both feet."
⁴The king said to Ziba, "Where is this son?"
Ziba said to the king, "He is at the house of Makir son of Ammiel in Lo Debar."
⁵Then King David sent some of his officers to Lo Debar to bring Jonathan's son from the house of Makir son of Ammiel. ⁶Jonathan's son Mephibosheth came to David, and bowed with his face low to the floor.
David said, "Mephibosheth?"
Mephibosheth said, "Yes sir, it is I, your servant Mephibosheth."

---

tribute Money that a people gave to a king that defeated them.
take control Literally, "set up his marker." Kings often set up stone markers to show they had won a war or conquered a certain place.
David crippled ... horses Or, "David destroyed all but 100 chariots."
Tebah The Hebrew has, "Betah." See 1 Chron. 18:8.
dedicated To give for a special use.

Kerethites and Pelethites These were David's special bodyguards. An ancient Aramaic translation has "the archers and stonethrowers." This would mean these men were specially trained in using bows and arrows and slings.
important leaders Literally, "priests."

⁷David said to Mephibosheth, "Don't be afraid. I will be kind to you. I will do this because of father Jonathan. I will give back to you all of the land of your grandfather Saul. And you will always be able to eat at my table." ⁸Mephibosheth bowed to David again. Mephibosheth said, "I am no better than a dead dog, but you are being very kind to me."

⁹Then King David called Saul's servant Ziba. David said to Ziba, "I have given Saul's family and everything he owns to your master's grandson *(Mephibosheth)*. ¹⁰You will farm the land for Mephibosheth. Your sons and servants will do this for Mephibosheth. You will harvest the crops. Then your master's grandson *(Mephibosheth)* will have plenty of food to eat. But Mephibosheth, your master's grandson, will always be able to eat at my table."

Ziba had 15 sons and 20 servants. ¹¹Ziba said to King David, "I am your servant. I will do everything that my lord the king commands."

So Mephibosheth ate at David's table like one of the king's sons. ¹²Mephibosheth had a young son named Mica. All the people in Ziba's family became Mephibosheth's servants. ¹³Mephibosheth was crippled in both feet. Mephibosheth lived in Jerusalem. Every day Mephibosheth ate at the king's table.

Hanun Shames David's Men

10 Later ⌊Nahash⌋ king of the Ammonites died. His son Hanun became the new king after him. ²David said, "Nahash was kind to me. So I will be kind to his son Hanun." So David sent his officers to comfort Hanun about his father's death.

So David's officers went to the land of the Ammonites. ³But the Ammonite leaders said to Hanun, their lord, "Do you think that David is trying to honor your father by sending some men to comfort you? No! David sent these men to secretly study and learn things about your city. They plan to make war against you."

⁴So Hanun took David's officers and shaved off one half of their beards. He cut their clothes in the middle down to their hips. Then he sent them away.

⁵When the people told David, he sent ⌊messengers⌋ to meet his officers. He did this because these men were very ashamed. King David said, "Wait at Jericho until your beards grow again. Then come back ⌊to Jerusalem⌋."

War Against the Ammonites

⁶The Ammonites saw that they had become David's enemies. So the Ammonites hired Arameans from Beth Rehob and Zobah. There were 20,000 Aramean foot soldiers. The Ammonites also hired the king of Maacah with 1,000 men and 12,000 men from Tob.

⁷David heard about this. So he sent Joab and the whole army of powerful men. ⁸The Ammonites came out and got ready for the battle. They stood at the city gate. The Arameans from Zobah and Rehob, and the men from Tob and Maacah did not stand together with the Ammonites in the field.

⁹Joab saw that there were enemies in front of him and behind him. So Job chose some of the best Israelite soldiers and lined them up for battle against the Arameans. ¹⁰Then Joab gave the other men to his brother Abishai to lead against the Ammonites. ¹¹Joab said ⌊to Abishai⌋, "If the Arameans are too strong for me, you will help me. If the Ammonites are too strong for you, I will come and help you. ¹²Be strong, and let us fight bravely for our people and for the cities of our God. The Lord will do what he decides is right."

¹³Then Joab and his men attacked the Arameans. The Arameans ran away from Joab and his men. ¹⁴The Ammonites saw that the Arameans were running away, so they ran away from Abishai and went back to ⌊their⌋ city.

So Joab came back from ⌊the battle with⌋ the Ammonites and went back to Jerusalem.

The Arameans Decide to Fight Again

¹⁵The Arameans saw that the Israelites had defeated them. So they came together ⌊into one big army⌋. ¹⁶Hadadezer* sent messengers to bring the Arameans that lived on the other side of the Euphrates River. These Arameans came to Helam. Their leader was Shobach, the captain of Hadadezer's army.

¹⁷David heard about this. So he gathered all of the Israelites together. They crossed over the Jordan River and went to Helam.

There the Arameans prepared for battle and attacked. ¹⁸But ⌊David defeated the Arameans, and⌋ the Arameans ran away from the Israelites. David killed 700 chariot drivers and 40,000 horse soldiers. David also killed Shobach the captain of the Aramean army.

¹⁹The kings that served Hadadezer* saw that the Israelites had defeated them. So they made

Hadadezer The ancient Greek has Hadarezer.

David Meets Bathsheba

11 ¹In the spring, at the time when kings go out to war, David sent Joab, his officers, and all of the Israelites out to destroy the Ammonites. Joab's army also attacked ₍their capital city₎ Rabbah.

But David stayed in Jerusalem. ²In the evening, he got up from his bed. He walked around on the roof of the king's house. While David was on the roof, he saw a woman bathing. The woman was very beautiful. ³So David sent for his officers and asked them who the woman was. An officer answered, "That woman is Bathsheba daughter of Eliam. She is the wife of Uriah the Hittite."

⁴David sent messengers to go and bring Bathsheba to him. When she came to David, he had sexual relations with her. She washed herself, and then went back to her house. ⁵But Bathsheba became pregnant. She sent word to David. She told him, "I am pregnant."

David Tries to Hide His Sin

⁶David sent a message to Joab. "Send Uriah the Hittite to me."

So Joab sent Uriah to David. ⁷Uriah came to David. David talked with Uriah. David asked Uriah how Joab was, how the soldiers were, and how the war was. ⁸Then David said to Uriah, "Go home and rest.*

Uriah left the king's house. The king also sent a gift to Uriah. ⁹But Uriah did not go home. Uriah slept outside the door of the king's house. He slept there like all the king's servants did. ¹⁰The servants told David, "Uriah did not go home."

Then David said to Uriah, "You came from a long trip. Why did you not go home?"

¹¹Uriah said to David, "The Holy Box* and the soldiers of Israel and Judah are staying in tents. My lord Joab, and my lord's *(King David's)* officers are camping out in the field. So it is not right for me to go home to drink, and sleep with my wife."

¹²David said to Uriah, "Stay here today. Tomorrow I will send you back ₍to the battle₎."

Uriah stayed in Jerusalem that day. He stayed until the next morning. ¹³Then David called Uriah ₍to come and see him₎. Uriah ate and drank with David. David made Uriah drunk. But Uriah still did not go home. That evening, Uriah went to sleep with the king's servants ₍outside the king's door₎.

David Plans Uriah's Death

¹⁴The next morning, David wrote a letter to Joab. David made Uriah carry the letter. ¹⁵In the letter, David wrote: "Put Uriah on the front lines where the fighting is the hardest. Then leave him there alone, and let him be killed in battle."

¹⁶Joab watched the city and saw where the bravest Ammonites were. He chose Uriah to go to that place. ¹⁷The men of the city *(Rabbah)* came out to fight against Joab. Some of David's men were killed. Uriah the Hittite was one of those men.

¹⁸Then Joab sent a report to David about what happened in the battle. ¹⁹Joab told the messenger to tell King David what had happened in the battle. ²⁰"Maybe the king will become upset. Maybe the king will ask, 'Why did Joab's army go that close the city to fight? Surely he knows that there are men on the city walls who can shoot arrows down at his men? ²¹Surely he remembers that a woman killed Abimelech son of Jerub Besheth? It was at Thebez. The woman was on the city wall and threw the top part of a grinding stone down on Abimelech. So why did he go that close to the wall?' ₍If King David says something like that₎, then you must tell him this message: 'Your officer Uriah the Hittite also died.'"

²²The messenger went in and told David everything Joab told him to say. ²³The messenger told David, "The men ₍of Ammon₎ attacked us in the field. We fought them and chased them all the way to the city gate. ²⁴Then the men on the city wall shot arrows at your officers. Some of your officers were killed. Your officer Uriah the Hittite also died."

²⁵David said to the messenger, "Give this message to Joab: 'Don't be too upset about this. A sword can kill one person as well as the next. Make a stronger attack against Rabbah and you will win.' Encourage Joab with these words."

---

rest Literally, "wash your feet."
Holy Box The Box of the Agreement. Also called "The Ark of the Covenant," the box containing the stone tablets with the Ten Commandments written on them and the other things that proved God was with the people of Israel during their time in the Sinai Desert.

David Marries Bathsheba

²⁶Bathsheba heard that her husband Uriah was dead. Then she cried for her husband. ²⁷After she had finished her time of sadness, David sent servants to take her to his house. She became David's wife and gave birth to a son for David. But the Lord did not like the bad thing David had done.

Nathan Speaks to David

12 The Lord sent Nathan to David. Nathan went to David. Nathan said, "There were two men in a city. One man was rich. But the other man was poor. ²The rich man had very many sheep and cattle. ³But the poor man had nothing, except one little female lamb that he bought. The poor man fed the lamb. The lamb grew up with this poor man and his children. The lamb ate from the poor man's food and drank from the poor man's cup. The lamb slept on the poor man's chest. The lamb was like a daughter to the poor man.

⁴"Then a traveler stopped to visit the rich man. ⌊The rich man wanted to give food to the traveler.⌋ But the rich man did not want to take anything from his own sheep or cattle to feed the traveler. No, the rich man took the lamb from the poor man. The rich man ⌊killed the lamb⌋ and cooked it for his visitor."

⁵David became very angry against the rich man. He said to Nathan, "As the Lord lives, surely the man who did this should die! ⁶He must pay four times the price of the lamb because he did this terrible thing and because he had no mercy."

Nathan Tells David About His Sin

⁷Then Nathan said to David, "You are that ⌊rich⌋ man! This is what the Lord God of Israel says: 'I chose* you to be the king of Israel. I saved you from Saul. ⁸I let you take his family and his wives. And I made you king of Israel and Judah. As if that were not enough, I gave you more and more. ⁹So why did you ignore the Lord's command? Why did you do the thing which he says is wrong? You let the Ammonites kill Uriah the Hittite, and you took his wife. In this way, you killed Uriah with a sword. ¹⁰So the sword will never leave your family. You took Uriah the Hittite's wife. In this way, you showed that you did not care for me.'

¹¹"This is what the Lord says: 'I am bringing trouble against you. This trouble will come from your own family. I will take your wives from you and give them to a person who is very close to you. This person will sleep with your wives, and everyone will know it!* ¹²You ⌊slept with Bathsheba⌋ in secret. But I will punish you so all the people of Israel can see it.'"*

¹³Then David said to Nathan, "I have sinned against the Lord."

Nathan said to David, "The Lord will forgive you, even for this sin. You will not die. ¹⁴But you did things that made the Lord's enemies lose their respect for him! So your new baby son will die."

David and Bathsheba's Baby Dies

¹⁵Then Nathan went home. And the Lord caused the baby boy that was born to David and Uriah's wife to become very sick. ¹⁶David prayed to God for the baby. David refused to eat or drink. He went into his house and stayed there. He lay on the ground all night.

¹⁷The leaders of David's family came and tried to pull David up from the ground. But David refused to get up. He refused to eat food with these leaders. ¹⁸On the seventh day, the baby died. David's servants were afraid to tell him that the baby was dead. They said, "Look, we tried to talk to David while the baby was alive. But he refused to listen to us. If we tell David that the baby is dead, maybe he will do something bad to himself."

¹⁹But David saw his servants whispering. Then David understood that the baby was dead. So David asked his servants, "Is the baby dead?"

The servants answered, "Yes, he is dead."

²⁰Then David got up from the floor. He washed himself. He changed his clothes and got dressed. Then he went into the Lord's house to worship. Then he went home and asked for something to eat. His servants gave him some food, and he ate.

²¹David's servants said to him, "Why are you doing this thing? When the baby was still living you refused to eat. You cried. But when the baby died you got up and ate food."

---

chose Literally, "anointed," to pour a special oil on a person's head to show that he was chosen by God to be a king, priest, or prophet.

and everyone will know it Literally, "in the sight of the sun."

so all ... can see it Literally, "before all of Israel and before the sun."

²²David said, "While the baby was still living, I refused to eat and I cried because I thought, 'Who knows? Maybe the Lord will feel sorry for me and let the baby live.' ²³But now the baby is dead. So why should I refuse to eat? Can I bring the baby back to life? No! Some day I will go to him, but he can't come back to me."

Solomon Is Born

²⁴Then David comforted Bathsheba his wife. He slept with her and had sexual relations with her. Bathsheba became pregnant again. She had another son. David named the boy Solomon. The Lord loved Solomon. ²⁵The Lord sent word through Nathan the prophet. Nathan gave Solomon the name, Jedidiah.* Nathan did this for the Lord.

David Captures Rabbah

²⁶Rabbah was the capital city of the Ammonites. Joab fought against Rabbah and captured it. ²⁷Joab sent messengers to David and said, "I have fought against Rabbah. I have captured the City of Waters. ²⁸Now bring the other people together and attack this city (Rabbah). Capture this city before I capture it. If I capture this city, it will be called by my name."

²⁹So David gathered all of the people and went to Rabbah. He fought against Rabbah and captured the city. ³⁰David took the crown off their king's head.* The crown was gold and weighed about 75 pounds.* This crown had precious stones in it. They put the crown on David's head. David took many valuable things out of the city.

³¹David also brought out the people of the city Rabbah and made them work with saws, iron picks, and axes. He also forced them to build things with bricks. David did the same thing to all of the Ammonite cities. Then David and all of his army went back to Jerusalem.

Amnon And Tamar

13 David had a son named Absalom. Absalom's sister was named Tamar. Tamar was very beautiful. Another one of David's sons, Amnon,* ²was in love with Tamar. Tamar was a virgin.* Amnon did not think he should do anything bad to her. But Amnon wanted her very much. Amnon thought about her so much that he made himself sick.*

³Amnon had a friend named Jonadab son of Shimeah. (Shimeah was David's brother.) Jonadab was a very clever man. ⁴Jonadab said to Amnon, "Every day you look thinner and thinner! You are the king's son! ⌊You have plenty to eat, so why are you losing weight?⌋ Tell me!"

Amnon told Jonadab, "I love Tamar. But she is the sister of my half-brother Absalom."

⁵Jonadab said to Amnon, "Go to bed. Act like you are sick. Then your father will come to see you. Tell him, 'Please let my sister Tamar come in and give me food to eat. Let her make the food in front of me. Then I will see it, and eat it from her hand.'"

⁶So Amnon lay down in bed and acted like he was sick. King David came in to see Amnon. Amnon said to King David, "Please let my sister Tamar come in. Let her make two cakes for me while I watch. Then I can eat from her hands."

⁷David sent messengers to Tamar's house. The messengers told Tamar, "Go to your brother Amnon's house and make some food for him."

Tamar Makes Food for Amnon

⁸So Tamar went to the house of her brother Amnon. Amnon was in bed. Tamar took some dough, pressed it together with her hands, and cooked the cakes. She did this while Amnon watched. ⁹Then Tamar took the cakes out of the pan and set them out for Amnon. But Amnon refused to eat. Amnon said to his servants, "Get out of here. Leave me alone!" So all of his servants left the room.

Amnon Rapes Tamar

¹⁰Then Amnon said to Tamar, "Bring the food into the bed room and feed me by hand."

So Tamar took the cakes she had made and went into her brother's bed room. ¹¹She started to feed Amnon, but he grabbed her hand. He said to her, "Sister, come and sleep with me."

¹²Tamar said to Amnon, "No, brother! Don't force me to do this! Don't do this shameful thing!

Jedidiah This name means "loved by the Lord."
their king's head Or, "Milcom's head." Milcom was a false god that the Ammonite people worshiped.
75 pounds Literally, "one talent."

virgin A woman who has not had sexual relations with anyone.
Amnon ... sick Or, "Amnon pretended he was sick."

Terrible things like this should never be done in Israel! [13]I would never get rid of my shame. And people would think that you are just a common criminal. Please, talk with the king. He will let you marry me." [14]But Amnon refused to listen to Tamar. He was stronger than Tamar. He forced her to have sexual relations with him. [15]Then Amnon began to hate Tamar. Amnon hated her much more than he had loved her before. Amnon said to Tamar, "Get up and get out of here!" [16]Tamar said to Amnon, "No! Don't send me away like this. That would be even worse than what you did before!"

But Amnon refused to listen to Tamar. [17]Amnon called his servant and said, "Get this girl out of this room, now! And lock the door after her." [18]So Amnon's servant led Tamar out of the room and locked the door after her.

Tamar was wearing a long robe with many colors.* The king's virgin daughters wore robes like this. [19]Tamar tore her robe of many colors and put ashes on her head. Then she put her hand on her head and began crying.* [20]Then, Tamar's brother Absalom said to her, "Have you been with your brother Amnon? Did he hurt you? Now, calm down sister. Amnon is your brother, so we will take care of this. Don't let it upset you too much." So Tamar did not say anything. She quietly went to live at Absalom's house.*

[21]King David heard the news and became very angry. [22]Absalom began to hate Amnon. Absalom did not say one word, good or bad, to Amnon. Absalom hated Amnon because Amnon had raped his sister Tamar.

Absalom's Revenge

[23]Two years later, Absalom had some men come to Baal Hazor to cut the wool from his sheep. Absalom invited all of the king's sons to come and watch. [24]Absalom went to the king and said, "I have some men coming to cut the wool from my sheep. Please come with your servants and watch."

[25]King David said to Absalom, "No, son. We will not all go. It will be too much trouble for you."

Absalom begged David to go. David did not go, but he did give his blessing. [26]Absalom said, "If you don't want to go, then please let my brother Amnon go with me."

King David asked Absalom, "Why should he go with you?"

[27]Absalom kept begging David. Finally, David let Amnon and all of the king's other sons go with Absalom.

Amnon Is Murdered

[28]Then Absalom gave this command to his servants, "Watch Amnon. When he is drunk and feeling good from the wine, I will give you the command. You must attack Amnon and kill him. Don't be afraid of being punished. After all, you will only be obeying my command. Now, be strong and brave."

[29]So Absalom's young soldiers did what he said. They killed Amnon. But all of David's other sons escaped. Each son got on his mule and escaped.

David Hears About Amnon's Death

[30]The king's sons were still on their way into town. But King David got a message about what happened. But the message was, "Absalom has killed all of the king's sons! Not one of the sons was left alive."

[31]King David tore his clothes and lay on the ground.* All of David's officers standing near him also tore their clothes.

[32]But then David's brother, Jonadab son of Shimeah, said, "Don't think that all of the king's sons were killed! Only Amnon is dead. Absalom has been planning this from the day that Amnon raped his sister Tamar. [33]My lord and king, don't think that all of your sons are dead. Only Amnon is dead."

[34]Absalom ran away.

There was a guard standing on the city wall. He saw many people coming from the other side of the hill. [35]So Jonadab said to King David, "Look, I was right! The king's sons are coming."

[36]The kings sons came in just after Jonadab said that. They were crying loudly. David and all

---

many colors Or, "stripes."
Tamar tore ... crying This was the way people showed how very sad and upset they were.
Tamar ... Absalom's house Or, "Tamar lived in her brother Absalom's house, a ruined woman."
tore his clothes ... ground This showed that he was very sad and upset.

of his officers began crying. They all cried very hard. ³⁷David cried for his son (Amnon) every day.

Absalom Escapes to Geshur

Absalom ran away to Talmai son of Ammihud, king of Geshur.* ³⁸After Absalom had run away to Geshur, he stayed there for three years. ³⁹King David was comforted after Amnon died, but he missed Absalom very much.

Joab Sends a Wise Woman to David

14 Joab son of Zeruiah knew that King David missed Absalom very much. ²So Joab sent ₍messengers₎ to Tekoa to bring a wise woman from there. Joab said to this wise woman, "Please pretend to be very sad. Put on clothes of sadness. Don't dress up. Act like a woman who has been crying many days for someone that died. ³Go to the king and talk to him using these words ₍that I tell you₎." Then Joab told the wise woman what to say.

⁴Then the woman from Tekoa talked to the king. She bowed with her face to the ground. Then she said, "King, please help me!"

⁵King David said to her, "What's your problem?"

The woman said, "I am a widow. My husband is dead. ⁶I had two sons. They were out in the field fighting. There was no one to stop them. One son killed the other son. ⁷Now the whole family is against me. They said to me, 'Bring us the son who killed his brother and we will kill him. Why? Because he killed his brother.' My son is like the last spark of a fire. If they kill my son, then that fire will burn out and be finished. He is the only son left alive to get his father's property. So my ₍dead₎ husband's property will go to someone else and his name will be removed from the land."

⁸Then the king said to the woman, "Go home. I will take care of things for you."

⁹The woman of Tekoa said to the king, "Let the blame be on me, my lord and king! You and your kingdom are innocent."

¹⁰King David said, "If someone is saying bad things to you, then bring that person to me. He won't bother you again."

¹¹The woman said, "Please, use the name of the Lord your God and swear (promise) that you will stop those people. They want to punish my son for murdering his brother. Swear that you won't let them destroy my son."

David said, "As the Lord lives, ₍no one will hurt your son₎. Not even one hair from your son's head will fall to the ground."

¹²The woman said, "My lord and king, please let me say something else to you."

The king said, "Speak."

¹³Then the woman said, "Why have you planned these things against the people of God? Yes, when you say these things, you show you are guilty. Why? Because you have not brought back the son that you forced to leave home. ¹⁴We will all die some day. We will be like water that is spilled on the ground. No person can gather this water back from the ground. You know God forgives people. God made plans for people who are forced to run away for safety—God doesn't force them to run away from him! ¹⁵My lord and king, I came to say these words to you. Why? Because the people made me afraid. I said to myself, 'I will talk to the king. Maybe the king will help me. ¹⁶The king will listen to me and save me from the man who wants to kill me and my son. That man just wants to keep us from getting the things God gave us.' ¹⁷I know that the words of my lord the king will give me rest, because you are like an angel from God. You know what is good and what is bad. And the Lord your God is with you."

¹⁸King David answered the woman, "You must answer the question I will ask you."

The woman said, "My lord and king, please ask your question."

¹⁹The king said, "Did Joab tell you to say all these things?"

The woman answered, "As you live, my lord and king, you are right! Your officer Joab did tell me to say these things. ²⁰₍Joab did these things₎ so that you would see things differently. My lord, you are as wise as God's angel. You know everything that happens on earth."

Absalom Returns to Jerusalem

²¹The king said to Joab, "Look, I will do what I promised. Now please bring back the young man Absalom."

²²Joab bowed with his face on the ground. He blessed King David, and said, "Today I know that you are pleased with me. I know because you have done what I asked."

²³Then Joab got up and went to Geshur and brought Absalom to Jerusalem. ²⁴But King David said, "Absalom can go back to his own house. He

---

Talmai ... king of Geshur Talmai was Absalom's grandfather. See 2 Sam. 3:3.

can't come to see me." So Absalom went back to his own house. Absalom could not go to see the king. ²⁵People really bragged about how good-looking Absalom was. No man in Israel was as handsome as Absalom. There was not a blemish on Absalom—from his head to his feet. ²⁶At the end of every year, Absalom cut the hair from his head and weighed it. The hair weighed about five pounds.* ²⁷Absalom had three sons and one daughter. This daughter's name was Tamar. Tamar was a beautiful woman.

Absalom Forces Joab to Come See Him

²⁸Absalom lived in Jerusalem for two full years without being allowed to visit King David. ²⁹Absalom sent ⌊messengers⌋ to Joab. ⌊These messengers asked Joab to⌋ send Absalom to the king. But Joab would not come to Absalom. Absalom sent ⌊a message⌋ a second time. But Joab still refused to come.

³⁰Then Absalom said to his servants, "Look, Joab's field is next to my field. He has barley growing in that field. Go burn the barley."

So Absalom's servants went and started a fire in Joab's field. ³¹Joab got up and came to Absalom's house. Joab said to Absalom, "Why did your servants burn my field?"

³²Absalom said to Joab, "I sent a message to you. I asked you to come here. I wanted to send you to the king. I wanted you to ask him why he asked me to come home from Geshur. ⌊I can't see him, so⌋ it would have been better for me to stay in Geshur. Now let me see the king. If I have sinned, then he can kill me!"

Absalom Visits King David

³³Then Joab came to the king and told him ⌊Absalom's words⌋. The king called for Absalom. Then Absalom came to the king. Absalom bowed low on the ground before the king. And the king kissed Absalom.

Absalom Makes Many Friends

15 After this, Absalom got a chariot* and horses for himself. He had 50 men run in front of him ⌊while he drove the chariot⌋. ²Absalom got up early and stood near the gate.* Absalom watched for any person with problems who was going to King David for judgment. Then Absalom would talk to that person. Absalom would say, "What city are you from?" The man would answer, "I am from such and such family group in Israel." ³Then Absalom would say to this man, "Look, you are right, but King David won't listen to you."

⁴Absalom would also say, "Oh, I wish someone would make me a judge in this country! Then I could help every man who comes to me with a problem. I would help him get a fair solution to his problem."

⁵And if a person came to Absalom and started to bow down to him, Absalom would ⌊treat him like a close friend⌋—Absalom would reach out and touch that person and kiss him. ⁶Absalom did that to all the Israelites who came to King David for judgment. In this way, Absalom won the hearts of all the people of Israel.

Absalom Plans to Take David's Kingdom

⁷After four years,* Absalom said to King David, "Please let me go to complete my special promise that I made to the Lord at Hebron. ⁸I made that promise while I was still living in Geshur, Aram. I said, 'If the Lord brings me back to Jerusalem, then I will serve the Lord.'"

⁹King David said, "Go in peace."

Absalom went to Hebron. ¹⁰But Absalom sent spies through all the family groups of Israel. These spies told the people, "When you hear the trumpet, then say, 'Absalom has become the king at Hebron!'"

¹¹Absalom invited 200 men to go with him. Those men left Jerusalem with him, but they did not know what he was planning. ¹²Ahithophel was one of David's advisers. Ahithophel was from the town of Giloh. While Absalom was offering sacrifices,* he called Ahithophel to come from his city (Giloh). Absalom's plans were working very well and more and more people began to support him.

---

five pounds Literally, "200 shekels by the king's weight."
chariot(s) A small wagon used in war.
four years Some ancient writings say "40 years."
sacrifice(s) A gift to God. Usually it was a special animal that was killed and burned on an altar.

David Learns About Absalom's Plans

¹³A man came in to tell the news to David. The man said, "The people of Israel are beginning to follow Absalom."

¹⁴Then David said to all of his officers who were with him in Jerusalem, "We must escape! ₍If we don't escape₎, then Absalom will not let us get away. Let's hurry before Absalom catches us. He will destroy us all. And he will kill the people of Jerusalem."

¹⁵The king's officers told him, "We will do anything you tell us."

David and His People Escape

¹⁶King David went out with all of the people in his house. The king left ten of his wives* to take care of the house. ¹⁷The king went out with all of his people following him. They stopped at the last house. ¹⁸All of his officers passed by the king. And all of the Kerethites, all of the Pelethites, and the Gittites (600 men from Gath) passed by the king.

¹⁹The king said to Ittai from Gath, "Why are you also going with us? Turn back and stay with the new king *(Absalom)*. You are a foreigner. This is not your home land. ²⁰Only yesterday you came to join me. Must you now wander from place to place with me? No! Take your brothers and go back. May kindness and loyalty be shown to you."

²¹But Ittai answered the king, "As the Lord lives, and as long as you live, I will stay with you. ₍I will be with you₎ in life or death!"

²²David said to Ittai, "Come, let's go cross Kidron Brook."

So Ittai from Gath and all of his people and their children crossed over ₍Kidron Brook₎. ²³All the people* were crying loudly. King David crossed over Kidron Brook. Then all of the people went out to the desert. ²⁴Zadok and all of the Levites with him were carrying the Box of God's Agreement.* They set down God's Holy Box. And Abiathar said prayers* until all of the people had left Jerusalem.

²⁵King David said to Zadok, "Take God's Holy Box* back to Jerusalem. If the Lord is pleased with me, then he will bring me back and let me see Jerusalem and his temple. ²⁶But if the Lord says that he is not pleased with me, then he can do anything he wants to me."

²⁷The king said to Zadok the priest, "You are a seer.* Go back to the city in peace. Take your son Ahimaaz and Jonathan the son of Abiathar. ²⁸I will be waiting near the places where people go across the river into the desert. I will wait there until I hear from you."

²⁹So Zadok and Abiathar took God's Holy Box* back to Jerusalem and stayed there.

David's Prayer Against Ahithophel

³⁰David went up the Mount of Olives. He was crying. He covered his head and he went without shoes on his feet. All of the people with David also covered their heads. They went with David, crying.

³¹A person told David, "Ahithophel is one of the people who made plans with Absalom." Then David prayed, "Lord, I ask you to make Ahithophel's advice useless." ³²David came to the top of the mountain. This was where he often worshiped God. At that time, Hushai the Arkite came to him. Hushai's coat was torn, and there was dust on his head.*

³³David said to Hushai, "If you go with me, then you will be just one more person to care for. ³⁴But if you go back to Jerusalem, you can make Ahithophel's advice become useless. Tell Absalom, 'King, I am your servant. I served your father, but now I will serve you.' ³⁵The priests Zadok and Abiathar will be with you. You must tell them everything you hear in the king's house. ³⁶Zadok's son Ahimaaz and Abiathar's son Jonathan will be with them. You will send them to tell me everything you hear."

³⁷Then David's friend Hushai went into the city. And Absalom arrived at Jerusalem.

---

wives Literally, "concubines," women servants that were like wives.
people Literally, "country."
Box of God's Agreement, God's Holy Box Also called "The Ark of the Covenant," the box containing the stone tablets with the Ten Commandments written on them and the other things that proved God was with the people of Israel during their time in the Sinai Desert.
said prayers Literally, "went up." This could mean, "burn incense," "offer sacrifices," or it might simply mean that Abiathar stood to one side, by the Holy Box, until all of the people passed by.
seer Another name for a prophet.
coat was torn ... head This showed he was very sad.

Ziba Meets David

16 David passed a short way over the top ⌊of the Mount of Olives⌋. There Ziba, Mephibosheth's servant, met David. Ziba had two donkeys with saddles on them. The donkeys also carried 200 loaves of bread, 100 bunches of raisins, 100 summer fruits, and a wineskin full of wine. ²King David said to Ziba, "What are these things for?"

Ziba answered, "The donkeys are for the king's family to ride on. The bread and the summer fruit are for the officers to eat. And when any person feels weak in the desert, he can drink the wine."

³The king asked, "Where is Mephibosheth?"*

Ziba answered the king, "Mephibosheth is staying in Jerusalem. He thinks, 'Today the Israelites will give my grandfather's* kingdom back to me.'"

⁴Then the king said to Ziba, "⌊Because of that,⌋ I now give you everything that belonged to Mephibosheth."

Ziba said, "I bow ⌊to you⌋. I hope I will always be able to please you."

Shimei Curses David

⁵David came to Bahurim. A man from Saul's family came out from Bahurim. This man's name was Shimei son of Gera. Shimei came out saying bad things to David. And he kept saying bad things again and again.

⁶Shimei began throwing stones at David and his officers. But the people and the soldiers gathered around David—they were all around him. ⁷Shimei cursed David. He said, "Get out, get out, you no-good murderer!* ⁸The Lord is punishing you. Why? Because you killed people in Saul's family. You stole Saul's place as king. But now the same bad things are happening to you. The Lord has given the kingdom to your son Absalom. Why? Because you are a murderer."*

⁹Abishai son of Zeruiah said to the king, "Why should this dead dog curse you, my lord the king? Let me go over and cut off Shimei's head."

¹⁰But the king answered, "What can I do, sons of Zeruiah? Sure, Shimei is cursing me. But the Lord told him to curse me."

¹¹David also said to Abishai and all his servants, "Look, my very own son *(Absalom)* is trying to kill me. This man *(Shimei)* from the family group of Benjamin has more right to kill me. Let him alone. Let him keep on saying bad things to me. The Lord told him to do this. ¹²Maybe the Lord will see the wrong things that are happening to me. Then maybe the Lord will give me something good for every bad thing that Shimei says today."

¹³So David and his men went on ⌊their way⌋ down the road. But Shimei kept following David. Shimei walked on the other side of the road by the side of the hill. Shimei kept saying bad things to David on his way. Shimei also threw stones and dirt at David.

¹⁴King David and all his people came to ⌊Bahurim⌋. The king and his people were tired. But they rested at Bahurim.

¹⁵Absalom, Ahithophel, and all the people of Israel came to Jerusalem. ¹⁶David's friend, Hushai the Arkite, came to Absalom. Hushai said to Absalom, "Long live the king! Long live the king!"

¹⁷Absalom answered, "Why are you not loyal to your friend ⌊David⌋? Why did you not leave ⌊Jerusalem⌋ with your friend?"

¹⁸Hushai said, "I belong to the person that the Lord chooses. These people and the people of Israel chose you. I will stay with you. ¹⁹In the past, I served your father. So, now I should serve David's son. I will serve you."

Absalom Asks Ahithophel for Advice

²⁰Absalom said to Ahithophel, "Please tell us what we should do."

²¹Ahithophel said to Absalom, "Your father left some of his wives* here to take care of the house. Go and have sexual relations with them. Then all the Israelites will hear that your father hates you. And all of your people will be encouraged to give you more support."

²²Then they put up a tent for Absalom on the roof of the house.* And Absalom had sexual relations with his father's wives.* All the Israelites saw it. ²³At that time, the advice of Ahithophel was very ⌊important⌋ to both David and Absalom. It was as ⌊important as⌋ God's word to a man.

Mephibosheth Literally, "your master's grandson."
grandfather's Literally, "father's."
murderer Literally, "man of blood."

wives Literally, "concubines," women servants that were like wives.
roof of the house The houses had flat roofs which were often used as an extra room.

Ahithophel's Advice About David

17 Ahithophel also said to Absalom, "Let me now choose 12,000 men. Then I will chase David tonight. ²I will catch him while he is tired and weak. I will scare him. And all his people will run away. But I will kill only King David. ³Then I will bring all the people back to you. If David is dead, then all the people will come back in peace."

⁴This plan seemed good to Absalom and all the leaders of Israel. ⁵But Absalom said, "Now call Hushai the Arkite. I also want to hear what he says."

Hushai Ruins Ahithophel's Advice

⁶Hushai came to Absalom. Absalom said to Hushai, "This is the plan Ahithophel gave. Should we follow it? If not, tell us."

⁷Hushai said to Absalom, "Ahithophel's advice is not good this time." ⁸Hushai added, "You know that your father and his men are strong men. They are as dangerous as a wild bear when something has taken its babies. Your father is a skilled fighter. He will not stay [all night] with the people. ⁹He is probably already hiding in a cave or some other place. If your father attacks your men first, then people will hear the news. And they will think, 'Absalom's followers are losing!' ¹⁰Then even the people who are as brave as a lion will become scared. Why? Because all the Israelites know that your father is a strong fighter and that his men are brave.

¹¹"This is what I suggest: You must gather all the Israelites together from Dan to Beersheba.* Then there will be many people, like the sand by the sea. Then you yourself must go into the battle. ¹²We will catch David in the place where he is hiding. We will attack David with many soldiers—We will be like the many drops of dew that cover the ground. We will kill David and all of his men. No man will be left alive. ¹³But if David escapes into a city, then all the Israelites will bring ropes to that city. We will pull down the walls of that city. We will pull them down into the valley. There won't be even a small stone left [in that city]."

¹⁴Absalom and all the Israelites said, "The advice of Hushai the Arkite is better than Ahithophel's advice." [They said this] because it was the Lord's plan. The Lord had planned to make Ahithophel's good advice useless. That is how the Lord would punish Absalom.

Hushai Sends a Warning to David

¹⁵Hushai told those things to the priests, Zadok and Abiathar. Hushai told them about the things that Ahithophel suggested to Absalom and the leaders of Israel. Hushai also told Zadok and Abiathar about the things that he himself had suggested. [Hushai said], ¹⁶"Quickly! Send [a message] to David. Tell him not to stay tonight at the places where people cross into the desert. Tell him to go across the Jordan River at once. If he crosses the river, then the king and all his people will not be caught."

¹⁷[The priests' sons], Jonathan and Ahimaaz, waited at En Rogel. They did not want to be seen going into the town, so a servant girl came out to them. She gave them the message. Then Jonathan and Ahimaaz went and told those things to King David.

¹⁸But a boy saw Jonathan and Ahimaaz. The boy ran to tell Absalom. Jonathan and Ahimaaz ran away quickly. They arrived at a man's house in Bahurim. The man had a well in his courtyard.* Jonathan and Ahimaaz went down into this well. ¹⁹The man's wife spread a sheet over the well. Then she covered the well with grain. [The well looked like a pile of grain], so no person could know [that Jonathan and Ahimaaz were hiding there]. ²⁰Absalom's servants came to the woman at the house. They asked, "Where are Ahimaaz and Jonathan?"

The woman said to Absalom's servants, "They have already crossed over the brook."

Absalom's servants then went to look for Jonathan and Ahimaaz. But they could not find them. So Absalom's servants went back to Jerusalem.

²¹After Absalom's servants left, Jonathan and Ahimaaz came up out of the well. They went and told King David. They said to David, "Hurry, go across the river. Ahithophel is planning to do these things against you."

²²Then David and all his people crossed over the Jordan River. Before the sun came up, all of David's people had already crossed the Jordan River.

Dan to Beersheba This means all the people of Israel. Dan was the town farthest north, and Beersheba was in the south.

courtyard An open area outside the house. Many houses were built around courtyards so people could work, cook, or eat outside.

Ahithophel Kills Himself

²³Ahithophel saw that the Israelites did not accept his advice. Ahithophel put a saddle on his donkey and went back to his home town. He made plans for his family and then he hanged himself. After Ahithophel died, the people buried him in his father's tomb.*

Absalom Crosses the Jordan River

²⁴David arrived at Mahanaim. Absalom and the Israelites that were with him went across the Jordan River. ²⁵Absalom had made Amasa the new captain of the army. Amasa took Joab's place.* Amasa was the son of Ithra the Ishmaelite.* Amasa's mother was Abigail, the daughter of Nahash sister of Zeruiah.* (Zeruiah was Joab's mother.)

²⁶Absalom and the Israelites made their camp in the land of Gilead.

Shobi, Makir, and Barzillai

²⁷David arrived at Mahanaim. Shobi, Makir, and Barzillai were at that place. (Shobi son of Nahash was from the Ammonite town of Rabbah. Makir son of Ammiel was from Lo Debar. Barzillai was from Rogelim in Gilead.) ²⁸⁻²⁹Those three men said, "The people in the desert are tired, hungry and thirsty." So they brought many things to David and the people that were with him. They brought them beds, bowls, and other kinds of dishes. They also brought wheat, barley, flour, roasted grain, beans, lentils, dried seeds, honey, butter, sheep, and cheese made from cow's milk.

David Gets the Battle Ready

18 David counted his people. He chose captains over 1,000 and captains over 100 to lead these people. ²⌊David separated the people into three groups.⌋ And then David sent the people out. Joab led one third of the people. Joab's brother, Abishai son of Zeruiah led another third of the people. And Ittai from Gath led the last third of the people.

King David said to the people, "I will also go with you."

³But the people said, "No! You must not go with us. Why? Because if we run away in the battle, Absalom's men will not care. Even if half of us are killed, Absalom's men will not care. But you are worth 10,000 of us! It is better for you to stay in the city. Then, if we need help, you can help us."

⁴The king said to his people, "I will do what you think is best."

Then the king stood at the side of the gate. The army went out. They went out in groups of 100 and 1,000.

"Be Gentle With Young Absalom!"

⁵The king gave a command to Joab, Abishai, and Ittai. He said, "Do this for me: Be gentle with young Absalom!"

All the people heard the king's orders about Absalom to the captains.

David's Army Defeats Absalom's Army

⁶David's army went out into the field against Absalom's Israelites. They fought in the forest of Ephraim. ⁷David's army defeated the Israelites. There were 20,000 men killed that day. ⁸The battle spread through all the country. But that day more men died in the forest than by the sword.

⁹It happened that Absalom met David's officers. Absalom jumped on his mule and tried to escape. The mule went under the branches of a large oak tree. The branches were thick, and Absalom's head got caught in the tree. His mule ran out from under him, so Absalom was hanging above the ground.*

¹⁰A man saw this happen. He told Joab, "I saw Absalom hanging in an oak tree."

¹¹Joab said to the man, "Why did you not kill him and let him fall to the ground? I would have given you a belt and ten pieces of silver!"

¹²The man said to Joab, "I would not try to hurt the king's son even if you gave me 1,000 ⌊pieces of⌋ silver. Why? Because we heard the king's command to you, Abishai, and Ittai. The king said, 'Be careful not to hurt young Absalom.' ¹³If I had killed Absalom, the king himself would find out. And you would punish me."

---

tomb A cave or a building where dead people are buried.

Amasa took Joab's place Joab still supported David. Joab was one of the three captains in David's army when David was running away from Absalom. See 2 Sam. 18:2.

Ishmaelite The Hebrew has "Israelite," but see 1 Chron 2:17 and the ancient Greek translation.

Amasa's mother ... Zeruiah Literally, "Ithra had sexual relations with Abigail, the daughter of Nahash sister of Zeruiah."

above the ground Literally, "between heaven and earth."

¹⁴Joab said, "I will not waste my time here with you!"

Absalom was still alive and hanging in the oak tree. Joab took three spears and threw them at Absalom. The spears went through Absalom's heart. ¹⁵Joab had ten young soldiers who helped him in battle. These ten men gathered around Absalom and killed him.

¹⁶Joab blew the trumpet ⌊and called⌋ the people to stop chasing ⌊Absalom's⌋ Israelites. ¹⁷Then Joab's men took Absalom's body and threw it into a large hole in the forest. They filled the large hole with many stones.

All the Israelites ⌊that followed Absalom⌋ ran away and went home.

¹⁸While Absalom was alive he put up a pillar in King's Valley. Absalom said, "I have no son to keep my name alive." So he named the pillar after himself. That pillar is called "Absalom's Monument" even today.

Joab Sends the News to David

¹⁹Ahimaaz the son of Zadok said ⌊to Joab⌋, "Let me now run and bring the news to King David. I'll tell him the Lord has destroyed the enemy for him."

²⁰Joab answered Ahimaaz, "No, you will not bring the news ⌊to David⌋ today. You can bring the news another time, but not today. Why? Because the king's son is dead."

²¹Then Joab said to a man from Ethiopia, "Go, tell the king about the things you have seen."

So the Ethiopian bowed to Joab and ran ⌊to tell David⌋.

²²But Ahimaaz son of Zadok begged Joab again, "No matter what happens, please let me also run after the Ethiopian!"

Joab said, "Son, why do you want to carry the news? You will not get any reward for the news you bring."

²³Ahimaaz answered, "No matter what happens, I will run ⌊to David⌋."

Joab said to Ahimaaz, "Fine, run ⌊to David⌋!"

Then Ahimaaz ran through Jordan Valley and passed the Ethiopian.

David Hears the News

²⁴David was sitting between the two gates ⌊of the city⌋. The watchman went up to the roof over the gate walls. The watchman looked up and saw a man running alone. ²⁵The watchman shouted to tell King David.

King David said, "If the man is alone, he is bringing news."

The man came closer and closer to the city. ²⁶The watchman saw another man running. The watchman called to the gatekeeper, "Look! Another man is running alone."

The king said, "He is also bringing news."

²⁷The watchman said, "I think the first man runs like Ahimaaz son of Zadok."

The king said, "Ahimaaz is a good man. He must be bringing good news."

²⁸Ahimaaz called to the king, "All is fine!" Ahimaaz bowed with his face to the ground in front of the king. Ahimaaz said, "Praise the Lord your God! The Lord has defeated the men who were against you, my lord and king."

²⁹The king asked, "Is young Absalom all right?"

Ahimaaz answered, "When Joab sent me, I saw some great excitement. But I don't know what it was."

³⁰Then the king said, "Step over here and wait." Ahimaaz went there and stood there waiting.

³¹The Ethiopian arrived. He said, "News for my lord and king. Today the Lord has punished the people who were against you!"

³²The king asked the Ethiopian, "Is young Absalom all right?"

The Ethiopian answered, "I hope your enemies and all people who come against you to hurt you will be ⌊punished⌋ like this young man (Absalom)."

³³⌊Then the king knew Absalom was dead⌋. The king was very upset. He went to the room over the city gate. He cried there. He went to his room. And on his way there, he said, "O my son Absalom, my son Absalom! I wish I had died for you. O Absalom, my son, my son!"

Joab Scolds David

19 People told the news to Joab. They told Joab, "Look, the king is crying and very sad for Absalom."

²⌊David's army⌋ had won the battle that day. But it became a very sad day for all the people. It was a very sad day, because the people heard, "The king is very sad for his son."

³The people came into the city quietly. They were like people who had been defeated in battle and had run away. ⁴The king had covered his face. He was crying loudly, "O my son Absalom, O Absalom, my son, my son!"

⁵Joab came into the king's house. Joab said to the king, "You are humiliating every one of your officers! Look, those officers saved your life today. And they saved the lives of your sons and daughters and your wives and women servants.* ⁶You love the people who hate you, and you hate the people who love you. Today you have made it clear that your officers and men mean nothing to you. I can see that you would be perfectly happy if Absalom had lived and all of us had been killed today! ⁷Now get up and go speak to your officers. Encourage them! I swear by the Lord that if you don't go out and do that right now, you won't have one man with you tonight. And that will be worse than all the trouble you have had since you were a child."

⁸Then the king went to the city gate.* The news spread that the king was at the gate. So all the people came to see the king.

David Is King Again

All the Israelites ⌊that followed Absalom⌋ had run away and went home. ⁹All the people in all the family groups of Israel began to argue. They said, "King David saved us from the Philistines and our other enemies. David ran away from Absalom. ¹⁰So we chose Absalom to rule us. But now Absalom is dead. He was killed in battle. So we should make David the king again."

¹¹King David sent ⌊a message⌋ to Zadok and Abiathar the priests. David said, "Speak to the leaders of Judah. Say, 'Why are you the last family group to bring King David back to his house? See, all the Israelites are talking about bringing the king back to his house. ¹²You are my brothers, you are my family. Then why are you the last family group to bring back the king?' ¹³And say to Amasa, 'You are part of my family. May God punish me if I don't make you captain of the army in Joab's place.'"

¹⁴David touched the hearts of all the people of Judah, so that they agreed like one man. The people of Judah sent ⌊a message⌋ to the king. They said, "You and all your officers come back!"

¹⁵Then King David came to the Jordan River. The people of Judah came to Gilgal to meet the king and take him across the Jordan River.

Shimei Asks David to Forgive Him

¹⁶Shimei son of Gera was from the family group of Benjamin. He lived in Bahurim. Shimei hurried down to meet King David. Shimei came with the people of Judah. ¹⁷About 1,000 people from the family group of Benjamin came with Shimei. Ziba the servant from Saul's family also came. Ziba brought his 15 sons and 20 servants with him. All these people hurried to the Jordan River to meet King David.

¹⁸The people went across the Jordan River to help bring the king's family back to Judah. The people did anything the king wanted. While the king was crossing the river, Shimei son of Gera came to meet him. Shimei bowed down on the ground in front of the king. ¹⁹Shimei said to the king, "My lord, don't think about the wrong things I did. My lord and king, don't remember the bad things I did when you left Jerusalem. ²⁰You know that I sinned. That is why today I am the first person from Joseph's family* to come down and meet you, my lord and king."

²¹But Abishai son of Zeruiah said, "We must kill Shimei because he asked for bad things to happen to the Lord's chosen king."

²²David said, "What should I to do with you, sons of Zeruiah? Today you are against me. No person will be put to death in Israel. Today I know I am king over Israel."

²³Then the king said to Shimei, "You will not die." The king made a promise to Shimei that he himself would not kill Shimei.*

Mephibosheth Goes to See David

²⁴Mephibosheth, Saul's grandson* came down to meet King David. Mephibosheth had not cared for his feet, cut his beard or washed his clothes all the time the king had left Jerusalem until he came back in peace. ²⁵Mephibosheth came from Jerusalem to meet the king. The king said to Mephibosheth, "Mephibosheth, why did you not go with me ⌊when I ran away from Jerusalem⌋?"

²⁶Mephibosheth answered, "My lord and king, my servant *(Ziba)* tricked me. I said to Ziba, 'I am

---

woman servant Or, "concubine," a slave woman who was like a wife to a man.

city gate This was where the public meetings were held.

Joseph's family This probably means the Israelites that followed Absalom. Many times the name Ephraim (a son of Joseph) is used for all of the family groups in northern Israel.

The king ... not kill Shimei David did not kill Shimei. But a few years later, David's son Solomon ordered Shimei to be put to death. See 1 Kings 2:44-46.

grandson Literally, "son."

crippled. So put a saddle on a donkey. Then I will ride on the donkey and go with the king.* ²⁷But my servant tricked me. He said bad things about me to you. But my lord and king is like an angel from God. Do whatever you think is right. ²⁸You could have killed all my grandfather's* family. But you did not do this. You put me with the people who eat at your own table. So I don't have a right to complain to the king about anything."

²⁹The king said to Mephibosheth, "Don't say anything more about your problems. This is what I decide: You and Ziba will divide the land."

³⁰Mephibosheth said to the king, "My lord and king, it is enough that you have come home in peace. Let Ziba have the land!"

David Asks Barzillai to Come with Him

³¹Barzillai of Gilead came down from Rogelim. He came to the Jordan River with King David. He went with the king to lead him across ₍the river₎. ³²Barzillai was a very old man. He was 80 years old. He had given the king food and other things when David was staying at Mahanaim. Barzillai ₍could do this because₎ he was a very rich man. ³³David said to Barzillai, "Come across ₍the river₎ with me. I will take care of you if you will live in Jerusalem with me."

³⁴But Barzillai said to the king, "Do you know how old I am? Do you think I can go with you to Jerusalem? ³⁵I am 80 years old! I am too old to tell which is bad and which is good. I am too old to taste the things I eat or drink. I am too old to hear any more the voices of men and women that sing. Why should you want to be bothered with me? ³⁶I don't need any of the things that you want to give me. I will go across the Jordan River with you. ³⁷But please, let me go back home. Then I can die in my own town and be buried in the grave of my father and mother. But here, Kimham can be your servant; let him go back with you, my lord and king. Do whatever you want with him."

³⁸The king answered, "Kimham will go back with me. I will be kind to him for you. I will do anything for you."

David Goes Back Home

³⁹The king kissed Barzillai and blessed him. Barzillai went back home. And the king and all the people went across the river. ⁴⁰The king crossed the Jordan River to Gilgal. Kimham went with him. All the people of Judah and half the people of Israel led David across the river.

The Israelites Argue with the People of Judah

⁴¹All the Israelites came to the king. They said to the king, "Our brothers, the people of Judah, stole you away and brought you and your family across the Jordan River with your men. Why?"

⁴²All the people of Judah answered the Israelites, "Because the king is our close relative. Why are you angry with us about this thing? We have not eaten food at the king's expense. The king did not give us any gifts."

⁴³The Israelites answered, "We have ten shares in David.* So we have more right to David than you do. But you ignored us. Why? We were the ones that first talked about bringing our king back."

₍But the people of Judah made a very ugly answer to the Israelites₎. The words of the people of Judah were more ugly than the words of the Israelites.

Sheba Leads Israel Away From David

20 At that place, there was a man named Sheba son of Bicri. Sheba was a good-for-nothing troublemaker from the family group of Benjamin. Sheba blew a trumpet ₍to gather the people together₎. Then he said,

"We have no share in David.
We have no part in the son of Jesse.
Israel, let's all go home to our own tents."

²So all the Israelites* left David and followed Sheba son of Bicri. But the people of Judah stayed with their king all the way from the Jordan River to Jerusalem.

I said ... king Possibly Mephibosheth was saying that his servant Ziba had taken the donkey and left Mephibosheth. Read 2 Sam. 16:1-4.
grandfather's Literally, "father's."
ten shares in David Judah and Benjamin were two of the family groups that later became the kingdom of Judah after the kingdom split. The other ten family groups were in the kingdom of Israel.
Israelites Here this means the family groups not united with Judah.

³David went back to his house in Jerusalem. David had left ten of his wives* to take care of the house. David had put these women in a special house.* He put guards around this house. The women stayed in this house until they died. David took care of the women and gave them food, but he did not have sexual relations with them. They lived like widows until they died. ⁴The king said to Amasa, "Tell the people of Judah to meet with me in three days. And you must also be here." ⁵Then Amasa went to call the people of Judah together. But he took longer than the time that the king had told him.

David Tells Abishai to Kill Sheba

⁶David said to Abishai, "Sheba son of Bicri is more dangerous to us than Absalom was. So take my officers and chase Sheba. Hurry before Sheba gets into cities with walls. If Sheba gets into the well protected cities, we won't be able to get him." ⁷So Joab left Jerusalem to chase after Sheba son of Bicri. Joab brought his own men and the Kerethites and Pelethites* and the other soldiers with him.

Joab Kills Amasa

⁸When Joab and the army came to Big Rock at Gibeon, Amasa came out to meet them. Joab was wearing his uniform. Joab had on a belt, and his sword was in its sheath.* As Joab was walking ⌊to meet Amasa⌋, Joab's sword fell out of its sheath. ⌊Joab picked up the sword and was holding it in his hand.⌋ ⁹Joab asked Amasa, "How are you doing, brother?"

Then Joab reached out with his right hand and grabbed Amasa by the beard to kiss him hello. ¹⁰Amasa didn't pay any attention to the sword that was in Joab's ⌊left⌋ hand. But then Joab stabbed Amasa in the belly with his sword. Amasa's inside parts spilled out on the ground. Joab didn't have to stab Amasa again—he was already dead.

---

wives Or, "concubines," women servants who were like wives.
David ... special house David's son Absalom had ruined David's concubines by having sexual relations with them. See 2 Sam. 16:21-22.
Kerethites and Pelethites David's special group of fighting men.
sheath A leather or metal case for carrying a sword or knife.

David's Men Continue to Look for Sheba

Then Joab and his brother Abishai again started to chase after Sheba son of Bicri. ¹¹One of Joab's young soldiers stood by Amasa's body. This young soldier said, "All of you men who support Joab and David, let's follow Joab." ¹²Amasa was there in the middle of road, lying in his own blood. The young soldier noticed that all the people kept stopping to look at the body. So the young soldier rolled the body off the road and into the field. Then he covered the body with a cloth. ¹³After Amasa's body was taken off the road, the people just passed it by and followed Joab. They joined Joab and chased after Sheba son of Bicri.

Sheba Escapes to Abel Beth Maacah

¹⁴Sheba son of Bicri passed through all the family groups of Israel on his way to Abel Beth Maacah. All the Berites also came together and followed Sheba.

¹⁵Joab and his men came to Abel Beth Maacah. Joab's army surrounded the town. They piled dirt up against the city wall. They did this so they could climb over the wall. Then Joab's men also began breaking stones out of the wall to make it fall down.

¹⁶But there was a very wise woman in that city. She shouted out from the city. She said, "Listen to me! Tell Joab to come here. I want to talk with him."

¹⁷Joab went to talk with the woman. The woman asked him, "Are you Joab?"

Joab answered, "Yes, I am."

Then the woman said, "Listen to me."

Joab said, "I am listening."

¹⁸Then the woman said, "In the past people would say, 'Ask for help in Abel and you will get what you need.' ¹⁹I am one of many peaceful, loyal people in this town. You are trying to destroy an important city of Israel. Why do you want destroy something that belongs to the Lord?"

²⁰Joab answered, "Hey, I don't want to destroy anything! I don't want to ruin your town. ²¹But there is a man in your city from the hill country of Ephraim. He is named Sheba son of Bicri. He has rebelled against King David. Bring him to me, and I will leave the city alone."

The woman said to Joab, "All right. His head will be thrown over the wall to you."

²²Then the woman spoke very wisely to all the people of the city. The people cut off the head of Sheba son of Bicri. Then the people threw Sheba's head over the city wall to Joab.

So Joab blew the trumpet and the army left the city. The soldiers went home, and Joab went back to the king in Jerusalem.

The People on David's Staff

²³Joab was captain of all the army of Israel. Benaiah son of Jehoiada led the Kerethites and Pelethites. ²⁴Adoniram led the men who were forced to do hard work. Jehoshaphat son of Ahilud was the historian. ²⁵Sheva was the secretary. Zadok and Abiathar were the priests. ²⁶And Ira the Jairite was David's chief servant.*

Saul's Family Punished

21 There was a famine while David was king. This time of hunger continued for three years. David prayed to the Lord, and the Lord answered. The Lord said, "Saul and his family of murderers* are the reason for this time of hunger. This famine came because Saul killed the Gibeonites." (²The Gibeonites were not Israelites. They were a group of Amorites. The Israelites had promised them ₍that they would not hurt the Gibeonites₎.* But Saul tried to kill the Gibeonites. He did this because of his strong feelings for the people of Israel and Judah.)

King David called the Gibeonites together and talked to them. ³David said to the Gibeonites, "What can I do for you? What can I do to take away Israel's sin, so you can bless the Lord's people?"

⁴The Gibeonites said to David, "There isn't enough gold and silver for Saul's family to pay for what they did. But we don't have the right to kill any person in Israel."

David said, "Well, what can I do for you?"

⁵The Gibeonites said to King David, "Saul made plans against us. He tried to destroy all our people living in the land of Israel. ⁶Give us seven of Saul's sons. Saul was the Lord's chosen king. So we will hang his sons in front of the Lord on Mount Gibeah of Saul."

King David said, "Fine, I will give them to you." ⁷But the king protected Jonathan's son, Mephibosheth. Jonathan was Saul's son, but David had made a promise in the Lord's name to Jonathan.* So the king did not let them hurt Mephibosheth. ⁸David gave them Armoni and Mephibosheth.* These were the sons of Saul and his wife Rizpah. Saul also had a daughter named Merab. She was married to a man named Adriel son of Barzillai from Meholah. So David took the five sons of Merab and Adriel. ⁹David gave these seven men to the Gibeonites. The Gibeonites brought them to Mount Gibeah and hanged them in front of the Lord. Those seven men died together. They were put to death during the first days of harvest. This was ₍in the spring₎ at the beginning of the barley harvest.

David and Rizpah

¹⁰Rizpah the daughter of Aiah took the cloth of sadness and put it on the rock.* That cloth stayed on the rock from the time the harvest began until the rains came. Rizpah watched the bodies day and night. She did not let the wild birds get the bodies during the day. And she did not let the wild animals get them at night.

¹¹People told David what Saul's woman servant* Rizpah was doing. ¹²Then David took the bones of Saul and Jonathan from the men of Jabesh Gilead. (The men of Jabesh Gilead got these bones after Saul and Jonathan were killed at Gilboa. The Philistines had hanged the bodies of Saul and Jonathan on a wall in Beth Shan.* But the men of Beth Shan went there and stole the bodies out of that public area.)

¹³David brought the bones of Saul and his son Jonathan from Jabesh Gilead. They also got the bodies of the seven men who were hanged. ¹⁴They buried the bones of Saul and his son Jonathan in the area of Benjamin. They buried them in one of the tunnels in the grave of Saul's father Kish. The people did everything the king commanded. So

---

chief servant Literally, "priest."
family of murderers Literally, "house of blood."
The Israelites ... Gibeonites This happened in Joshua's time when the Gibeonites tricked the Israelites. Read Joshua 9:3-15.
David had made ... to Jonathan David and Jonathan promised each other that they would not harm each other's families. Read 1 Sam. 20:12-23,42.
Mephibosheth This is another man named Mephibosheth, not Jonathan's son.
rock This might be the Big Rock at Gibeon (2 Sam. 20:8), the rock that the bodies were lying on, or a rock that marked the place where her sons were buried.
woman servant Or, "concubine," a slave woman who was like a wife to a man.
Beth Shan Or, "Beth Shean."

War with the Philistines

¹⁵The Philistines started another war with Israel. David and his men went out to fight the Philistines. But David became very tired and weak. ¹⁶Ishbi Benob was one of the giants.* Ishbi Benob's spear weighed about 7 1/2 pounds.* Ishbi Benob had a new sword. He tried to kill David. ¹⁷But Abishai son of Zeruiah killed the Philistine and saved David's life.

Then David's men made a special promise to David. They said to him, "You can't go out with us to battle any more. If you do, Israel might lose its greatest leader."

¹⁸Later, there was another war with the Philistines at Gob. Sibbecai the Hushathite killed Saph, another one of the giants.*

¹⁹Later, there was another war at Gob against the Philistines. Elhanan the son of Jaare Oregim from the family group of Benjamin killed Goliath the Gittite.* His spear was as large as a weaver's rod.

²⁰There was another war at Gath. There was a very large man. This man had six fingers on each hand and six toes on each foot. He had 24 fingers and toes in all. This man was also one of the giants.* ²¹This man challenged Israel and made fun of them. But Jonathan killed this man. (This was Jonathan, the son of David's brother Shimei.)

²²All four of these men were giants* from Gath. They were killed by David and his men.

David's Song of Praise to the Lord

22* David sang this song at the time the Lord saved him from Saul and all his other enemies.

² The Lord is my Rock,*
 my Fortress,*
 my Place of Safety.

³ He is my God,
 the Rock I run to for protection.
 God is my shield.
 His power saves me.*
 The Lord is my hiding place,
 my place of safety,
 high in the hills.
 He saves me from the cruel enemy.
⁴ They made fun of me.
 But I called to the Lord for help,
 and I was saved from my enemies!

⁵ ⌊My enemies were trying to kill me!⌋
 Waves of death were crashing around me.
 I was caught in a flood
 carrying me to that place of death.*
⁶ Ropes of the grave were all around me.
 Traps of death lay before me.
⁷ Trapped, I called to the Lord for help.
 Yes, I called to my God.

 God was in his temple.
 He heard my voice.
 He heard my cry for help.
⁸ Then the earth shook. It trembled.
 The foundations of heaven shook.
 Why? Because the Lord was angry!
⁹ Smoke came from God's nose.
 Burning flames came from his mouth,
 Burning sparks flew from him.
¹⁰ The Lord tore open the sky
 and came down!
 He stood on a thick, dark cloud!
¹¹ He was flying,
 riding on the flying Cherub angels,
 riding on the wind.
¹² The Lord wrapped the dark clouds
 around him like a tent.
 He gathered the water
 into the thick thunder clouds.
¹³ Sparks like burning coal ⌊flew⌋
 from the bright light around him!
¹⁴ The Lord thundered from the sky!
 God Most High let his voice be heard.
¹⁵ The Lord shot his arrows*
 and scattered the enemy.
 The Lord sent out lightning,
 and the people scattered in confusion.

---

one of the giants Or, "a son of Rapha (Rephaim)."
7 1/2 pounds Literally, "300 shekels of bronze."
one of the giants Or, "a son of Rapha (Rephaim)."
Goliath the Gittite In 1 Chron. 20:5 this Philistine is called Lahmi the brother of Goliath.
giants Or, "sons of Rapha (Rephaim)."
Chapter 22 This song is also found in Ps. 18.
Rock A name for God. It shows he is like a fortress or a strong place of safety.
Fortress A building or city with tall, strong walls for protection.

His power saves me Literally, "He is the horn of my salvation."
place of death Or, "the place of no return, the grave."
arrows That is, "lightning."

2 SAMUEL 22:16–46

16 Lord, you spoke strongly,
   a powerful wind blew from your mouth*
   ⌊and the water was pushed back⌋.
   We could see the bottom of the sea.
   We could see the earth's foundations.
17 ⌊The Lord helped me like that too!⌋
   The Lord reached down from above.
   The Lord grabbed me and pulled me
   out of the deep water *(trouble)*.
18 My enemies were stronger than me.
   Those people hated me.
   My enemies were too strong for me,
   so God saved me.
19 I was in trouble
   and my enemies attacked me.
   But the Lord was there to support me!
20 The Lord loves me,
   so he rescued me.
   He took me to a safe place.
21 The Lord will give me my reward
   Because I did what is right,
   I did nothing wrong,
   so he will do good things for me.
22 Why? Because I obeyed the Lord!
   I did not sin against my God.
23 I always remember the Lord's decisions.
   I obey his laws!
24 I keep myself pure and innocent before him.
25 So the Lord will give me my reward!
   Why? Because I did what is right!
   The way he sees it,
   I did nothing wrong,
   so he will do good things for me.
26 If a person really loves you,
   then you will show your true love to him.
   If a person is true to you,
   then you will be true to him.
27 Lord, you are good and pure
   to people who are good and pure.
   But, you can outsmart
   the smartest, sneakiest crook.
28 Lord, you help humble people.
   But you bring shame to proud people.
29 Lord, you are my lamp.
   The Lord lights up the darkness around me!
30 With your help, Lord,
   I can run with the soldiers.
   With God's help,
   I can climb over enemy walls.
31 God's power is complete.*
   The Lord's word has been tested.
   He protects people who trust him.
32 There is no God except the Lord.
   There is no Rock* except our God.
33 God is my strong fort.
   He helps pure people live right.*
34 God helps me run fast like a deer!
   He keeps me steady in high places.
35 God trains me for war,
   so my arms can shoot a powerful bow.
36 God, you protected me
   and helped me win.
   You helped me defeat my enemy.
37 Make my legs and ankles strong
   so I can walk fast without stumbling.
38 I want to chase my enemies,
   until I destroy them!
   I won't come back
   until they are destroyed!
39 I destroyed my enemies.
   I defeated them!
   They won't get up again.
   Yes, my enemies fell under my feet.
40 God, you made me strong in battle.
   You made my enemies fall before me.
41 You gave me a chance at my enemy's neck,
   and I cut my opponent down!
42 My enemies looked for help,
   but there was no one to save them.
   They even looked to the Lord,
   but he did not answer them.
43 I beat my enemies into pieces.
   They were like dust on the ground.
   I crushed my enemies.
   I walked on them
   like mud in the streets.
44 You saved me from the people
   who fought against me.
   You kept me as ruler of those nations.
   People I didn't know now serve me!
45 People from other lands obey me!
   When they hear about me,
   they quickly obey me.
   Those foreigners are afraid of me!
46 Those foreigners wilt with fear.
   They come out of their hiding places
   shaking with fear.

God's power ... complete Or, "God's way is perfect," or "God is true (loyal)." See verse 26
Rock A name for God. It shows he is like a fortress or a strong place of safety.
live right Literally, "walk in his ways."

mouth Or, "nostrils."

⁴⁷ The Lord is alive.
   I praise my Rock!*
   God is great!
   He is the Rock who saves me.
⁴⁸ He is the God who punished my enemies
      for me.
   He put people under my rule.
⁴⁹ God, you saved me from my enemies!
   You helped me defeat the people
      who stood against me.
   You save me from cruel men!
⁵⁰ Lord, that is why I praise you to the nations.
   This is why I sing songs about your name.
⁵¹ The Lord helps his king win many battles!
   The Lord shows his true love
      for his chosen king.
   He will be loyal to David
      and to his descendants forever!

David's Last Words

23 These are the last words
   of David:

   This message is from
      David son of Jesse.
   This message is from
      the man that God made great,
      the king chosen by the God of Jacob,
      the sweet singer of Israel.
² The Lord's Spirit spoke through me.
   His word was on my tongue.
³ The God of Israel spoke.
   The Rock of Israel said to me,
   "The person who rules people fairly,
   the person who rules with respect for God,
⁴ that person will be
      like the morning light at dawn;
      like a morning without clouds;
      like sunshine after a rain—
         the rain that makes tender grass
         grow from the ground."

⁵ God made my family strong and secure.
   He made an agreement with me forever!
   God made sure this agreement was
      good and secure in every way.
   So surely he will give me every victory.
   He will give me everything I want!

⁶ But bad people are like thorns.
   People don't hold thorns.
   They throw them away.
⁷ If a person touches them,
   it hurts like a spear
      made of wood and bronze.
   ⌊Yes, those people are like thorns.⌋
   They will be thrown in the fire,
   and they will be completely burned!

The Three Heroes

⁸These are the names of David's soldiers:
Josheb Basshebeth the Tahkemonite.* Josheb Basshebeth was captain of the chariot officers. He was ⌊also called⌋ Adino the Eznite. Josheb Basshebeth killed 800 men at one time.

⁹Next, there was Eleazar son of Dodai* from Ahoah. Eleazar was one of the Three Heroes that were with David at the time they challenged the Philistines. They had gathered for a battle, but the Israelite soldiers had run away. ¹⁰Eleazar fought the Philistines until he was very tired. But he kept holding on to the sword tightly ⌊and continued fighting⌋. The Lord gave Israel a great victory that day. The people came back after Eleazar had won the battle, but they only came to take things from the dead enemy soldiers.

¹¹Next, there was Shammah son of Agee from Harar. The Philistines came together to fight. They fought in a field of lentils.* The people ran away from the Philistines. ¹²But Shammah stood in the middle of the field and defended it. He defeated the Philistines. The Lord gave Israel a great victory that day.

¹³Once, David was at the cave of Adullam and the Philistine army was down in Rephaim Valley. Three of the Thirty Heroes* crawled flat on the ground all the way to that cave to join David.*

¹⁴Another time, David was in the fortress,* and a group of Philistines soldiers was in Bethlehem. ¹⁵David was thirsty ⌊for some water from his home town⌋. David said, "I wish someone could give me some water from the well near the city gate in Bethlehem!" ⌊David did not really want this, he was only talking.⌋

Josheb Basshebeth the Tahkemonite Or, "Jashobeam the Hacmonite." See 1 Chron. 11:11.
Eleazar son of Dodai Or, "Eleazar his cousin."
lentils Small round beans.
Thirty Heroes These men were David's famous group of very brave soldiers.
Three ... David The Hebrew is hard to understand here, but compare 1 Chron. 11:15.

Rock A name for God. It shows he is like a fortress or a strong place of safety.

¹⁶But the Three Heroes* fought their way through the Philistines army. These three men got some water from the well near the city gate in Bethlehem. Then the Three Heroes brought the water to David. But David refused to drink the water. He poured it on the ground as an offering to the Lord. ¹⁷David said, "Lord, I can't drink this water. It would be like drinking the blood of the men who risked their lives for me." This is why David refused to drink the water. The Three Heroes did many brave things like that.

Other Brave Soldiers

¹⁸Abishai was the brother of Joab son of Zeruiah. Abishai was the leader of the Three Heroes.* Abishai used his spear against 300 ₍enemies₎ and killed them. He became as famous as the Three. ¹⁹Abishai was as famous as the Three Heroes. He became their leader, even though he was not one of them.

²⁰Then there was Benaiah son of Jehoiada. He was the son of a powerful man. He was from Kabzeel. Benaiah did many brave things. Benaiah killed the two sons of Ariel from Moab. One day when it was snowing, Benaiah went down into a hole in the ground and killed a lion. ²¹Benaiah also killed a big Egyptian soldier. The Egyptian had a spear in his hand. But Benaiah only had a club in his hand. Benaiah grabbed the spear in the Egyptian's hand and took it away from him. Then Benaiah killed the Egyptian with his own spear. ²²Benaiah son of Jehoiada did many brave things like that. Benaiah was as famous as the Three Heroes.* ²³Benaiah was even more famous than the Thirty Heroes,* but he did not become a member of the Three Heroes. David made Benaiah leader of his bodyguards.

The Thirty Heroes

²⁴Asahel, the brother of Joab, was one of the Thirty Heroes.* ₍Other men in the group of Thirty Heroes were₎: Elhanan son of Dodo from Bethlehem; ²⁵Shammah the Harodite; Elika the Harodite; ²⁶Helez the Paltite; Ira son of Ikkesh from Tekoa; ²⁷Abiezer from Anathoth; Mebunnai the Hushathite; ²⁸Zalmon the Ahohite; Maharai from Netophah; ²⁹Heled son of Baanah from Netophah; Ithai son of Ribai from Gibeah of Benjamin; ³⁰Benaiah the Pirathonite; Hiddai from the Brooks of Gaash; ³¹Abi Albon the Arbathite; Azmaveth the Barhumite; ³²Eliahba the Shaalbonite; the sons of Jashen; Jonathan ³³the son of Shammah from Harar; Ahiam son of Sharar from Harar; ³⁴Eliphelet son of Ahasbai the Maacathite; Eliam son of Ahithophel the Gilonite; ³⁵Hezro the Carmelite; Paarai the Arbite; ³⁶Igal son of Nathan of Zobah; Bani the Gadite; ³⁷Zelek the Ammonite; Naharai from Beeroth (Naharai carried the armor for Joab son of Zeruiah); ³⁸Ira the Ithrite; Gareb the Ithrite; ³⁹and Uriah the Hittite. There were 37 in all.

David Decides to Count His Army

24 The Lord was angry against Israel again. The Lord caused David to turn against the Israelites. ₍David₎ said, "Go count the people of Israel and Judah."

²King David said to Joab, the captain of the army, "Go through all the family groups of Israel from Dan to Beersheba,* and count the people. Then I will know how many people there are."

³But Joab said to the king, "May the Lord your God give you 100 times as many people, no matter how many there are! And may your eyes see this thing happen. But why do you want to do this?"

⁴King David very strongly commanded Joab and the captains of the army to count the people. So Joab and the captains of the army went out from the king to count the people of Israel. ⁵They crossed over the Jordan River. They made their camp in Aroer. Their camp was on the right side of the city. (The city is in the middle of the valley of Gad, on the way to Jazer.)

⁶Then they went ₍east₎ to Gilead, all the way to Tahtim Hodshi. Then they went ₍north₎ to Dan Jaan and around to Sidon. ⁷They went to the fort of Tyre. They went to all the cities of the Hivites and of the Canaanites. Then they went south to Beersheba in the southern part of Judah. ⁸It took them nine months and 20 days for them to go through the country. After nine months and 20 days they came back to Jerusalem.

Three Heroes These were David's three bravest soldiers.
Thirty Heroes These men were David's famous group of very brave soldiers.
Three ... David The Hebrew is hard to understand here, but compare 1 Chron. 11:15.
fortress A building or city with tall, strong walls for protection.

Dan to Beersheba This means all the people of Israel. Dan was the town farthest north, and Beersheba was in the south.

⁹Joab gave the list of the people to the king. There were 800,000 men in Israel that could use the sword. And there were 500,000 men in Judah.

The Lord Punishes David

¹⁰Then David felt ashamed after he had counted the people. David said to the Lord, "I have sinned greatly in what I did! Lord, I beg you, forgive me for my sin. I have been very foolish."

¹¹When David got up in the morning, the Lord's word came to Gad, David's seer*. ¹²The Lord told Gad, "Go and tell David, 'This is what the Lord says: I offer you three things. Choose the one that I will do to you.'"

¹³Gad went to David and told him. Gad said to David, "Choose one of these three things:

1. Seven years of famine for you and your country.
2. Your enemies will chase you for three months.
3. Three days of disease in your country.

Think about it, and choose one of these things. And I will tell the Lord about your choice. The Lord sent me to you."

¹⁴David said to Gad, "I am really in trouble! But the Lord is very merciful. So let the Lord punish us. Don't let my punishment come from people."

¹⁵So the Lord sent a disease against Israel. It began in the morning and continued until the chosen time to stop. From Dan to Beersheba* 70,000 people died. ¹⁶The angel raised his arm over Jerusalem to destroy it. But the Lord felt very sorry about the bad things that had happened. The Lord said to the angel that destroyed the people, "That's enough! Put down your arm." The Lord's angel was by the threshing floor* of Araunah* the Jebusite.

David Buys Araunah's Threshing Floor

¹⁷David saw the angel that killed the people. David spoke to the Lord. David said, "I sinned! I did wrong! And these people only did what I told them—they only followed me like sheep. They did nothing wrong. Please let your punishment be against me and my father's family."

¹⁸That day Gad came to David. Gad told David, "Go and build an altar* to the Lord on the threshing floor* of Araunah* the Jebusite." ¹⁹So David did what Gad told him to. David did what the Lord wanted. David went to see Araunah. ²⁰Araunah looked and saw King David and his officers coming to him. Araunah went out and bowed his face to the ground. ²¹Araunah said, "Why has my lord and king come to me?"

David answered, "I came to buy the threshing floor* from you. Then I can build an altar* to the Lord. Then the disease will stop."

²²Araunah said to David, "My lord and king, you can take anything you want for a sacrifice.* Here are some cows for the burnt offering, and the threshing boards* and the yokes* for the wood. ²³O King, I give everything to you!" Araunah also said to the king, "May the Lord your God be pleased with you."

²⁴But the king said to Araunah, "No! I tell you the truth, I will pay you for the land. I will not offer burnt offerings to the Lord my God that cost me nothing."

So David bought the threshing floor* and the cows for 50 shekels of silver. ²⁵Then David built an altar* to the Lord there. David offered burnt offerings and peace offerings.

The Lord answered his prayer for the country. The Lord stopped the disease in Israel.

---

threshing floor A place where grain is beaten or walked on to remove the hulls from the grain.

Araunah Also spelled "Ornan."

altar(s) A stone table used for burning sacrifices offered as gifts to God.

sacrifice(s) A gift to God. Usually it was a special animal that was killed and burned on an altar.

threshing boards A place where grain is beaten or walked on to remove the hulls from the grain.

yoke(s) A pole that was put on the shoulders of men or animals to help them carry or pull things. This often showed that a person was a slave.

seer Another name for a prophet.

Dan to Beersheba This means all the people of Israel. Dan was the town farthest north, and Beersheba was in the south.

1 Kings

1 ¹King David was very old. He could not keep warm. His servants covered him with blankets, but he was still cold. ²So his servants said to him, "We will find a young woman to care for you. She will lie close to you and keep you warm." ³So the king's servants began looking everywhere in the country of Israel for a beautiful young woman to keep the king warm. They found a girl named Abishag. She was from the city Shunem. They brought the young woman to the king. ⁴The girl was very beautiful. She cared for the king and served him. But King David did not have sexual relations with her.

⁵⁻⁶Adonijah was the son of King David and his wife Haggith. Adonijah was a very handsome man. King David never corrected his son Adonijah. David never asked him, "Why are you doing these things?" Adonijah was born after his brother Absalom, but Adonijah became very proud and decided that he would be the next king. Adonijah wanted very much to be the king, so he got himself a chariot, horses, and 50 men to run ahead of him.

⁷Adonijah talked with Joab son of Zeruiah and with Abiathar the priest. They decided to help make him the new king. ⁸But several men did not agree with what Adonijah was doing. These men remained loyal to David. They were Zadok the priest, Benaiah son of Jehoiada, Nathan the prophet, Shimei, Rei, and King David's special guard.* So these men did not join with Adonijah.

⁹One day, at Zoheleth Rock near En Rogel,* Adonijah sacrificed some sheep, cows, and fat calves as a ₍fellowship offering₎. Adonijah invited his brothers (the other sons of King David) and all of the officers from Judah. ¹⁰But Adonijah did not invite the men in his father's special guard, his brother Solomon, Benaiah, or Nathan the prophet.

¹¹But Nathan heard about this and went to Solomon's mother Bathsheba. Nathan asked her, "Have you heard what Haggith's son, Adonijah, is doing? He is making himself king. And our master, King David, knows nothing about it. ¹²Your life and the life of your son Solomon may be in danger. But I will tell you what you should do to save yourself. ¹³Go to King David and say to him, 'My lord and king, you made a promise to me. You promised that my son Solomon would be the next king after you. So why is Adonijah becoming the new king?' ¹⁴Then while you are still talking with him, I will come in. After you leave I will tell the king what has happened. And that will show that what you said is true."

¹⁵So Bathsheba went in to see the king in his bedroom. The king was very old. Abishag, the girl from Shunem, was caring for him there. ¹⁶Bathsheba bowed down before the king. The king asked, "What can I do for you?"

¹⁷Bathsheba answered, "Sir, you used the name of the Lord your God and made a promise to me. You said, 'Your son Solomon will be the next king after me. Solomon will sit on my throne.' ¹⁸Now, you don't know this, but Adonijah is making himself the king. ¹⁹Adonijah ₍is giving a big fellowship meal. He₎ has killed many cows and the best sheep ₍for a fellowship offering₎. Adonijah invited all of your sons. And he invited Abiathar the priest, and Joab the commander of your army. But he did not invite your faithful son Solomon. ²⁰Now, my lord and king, all the people of Israel are watching you. They are waiting for you to decide who will be the next king after you. ²¹₍You must do something before you die.₎ If you don't, then after you are buried with your fathers, those men will say that Solomon and I are criminals."

²²While Bathsheba was still talking with the king, Nathan the prophet came to see him. ²³The servants told the king, "Nathan the prophet is here." Nathan went in to speak to the king. Nathan bowed down before the king ²⁴and said,

---

Shimei, Rei ... guard Or, "Shimei and his friends, the Heroes."

En Rogel, A spring of water in the valley southeast of Jerusalem, about 1/4 mile from Gihon Spring.

"My lord and king, did you announce that Adonijah will be the new king after you? Have you decided that Adonijah will rule the people now? ²⁵Because today he went down ₍into the valley₎ to offer many cows and the best sheep as ₍fellowship₎ offerings. And he invited all your other sons, the commanders of the army, and Abiathar the priest. They are now eating and drinking with him. And they are saying, 'Long live King Adonijah!' ²⁶But he did not invite me, or Zadok the priest, or Benaiah son of Jehoiada, or your son Solomon. ²⁷My lord and king, did you do this without telling us? Please tell us, who will be the next king after you?"

²⁸Then King David said, "Tell Bathsheba to come in!" So Bathsheba came in before the king. ²⁹Then the king made a promise: "The Lord God has saved me from every danger. As sure as the Lord is alive, I make this promise to you. ³⁰Today I will do what I promised you in the past. I made that promise by the power of the Lord God of Israel. I promised that your son Solomon would be the next king after me. And I promised that he would take my place on my throne. I will keep my promise!"

³¹Then Bathsheba bowed down on the ground before the king. She said, "Long live King David!"

³²Then King David said, "Tell Zadok the priest, Nathan the prophet, and Benaiah son of Jehoiada to come in here." So the three men came in to meet with the king. ³³Then the king said to them, "Take my officers with you. Put my son Solomon on my own mule. Take him to Gihon Spring.* ³⁴At that place, Zadok the priest and Nathan the prophet will anoint* him to be the new king of Israel. Blow the trumpet and announce, 'This is the new king, Solomon!' ³⁵Then come back here with him. Solomon will sit on my throne and be the new king in my place. I have chosen Solomon to be the ruler of Israel and Judah."

³⁶Benaiah son of Jehoiada answered the king, "Amen! The Lord God himself said it, my lord and king! ³⁷My lord and king, the Lord has been with you. And now I hope the Lord will be with Solomon! And I hope King Solomon's kingdom will grow and become even more powerful than yours, my lord and king."

³⁸So Zadok, Nathan, Benaiah, and the king's officers obeyed King David. They put Solomon on King David's mule and went with him to Gihon. ³⁹Zadok the priest carried the oil from the Holy Tent. Zadok poured the oil on Solomon's head to show that he was the king. They blew the trumpet and all the people shouted, "Long live King Solomon!" ⁴⁰Then all of the people followed Solomon into the city. The people were very happy and excited. They were playing flutes and making so much noise that the ground shook.

⁴¹Meanwhile, Adonijah and his guests with him were just finishing their meal. They heard the sound from the trumpet. Joab asked, "What is that noise? What is happening in the city?"

⁴²While Joab was still speaking, Jonathan, the son of Abiathar the priest, came there. Adonijah said, "Come here! You are a good man.* So you must be bringing good news to me."

⁴³But Jonathan answered, "No! It is not good news for you! King David has made Solomon the new king. ⁴⁴King David sent Zadok the priest, Nathan the prophet, Benaiah son of Jehoiada, and all the king's officers with him. They put Solomon on the king's own mule. ⁴⁵Then Zadok the priest and Nathan the prophet anointed* Solomon at Gihon Spring. And then they went into the city. People followed them and now the people in the city are very happy. That is the noise that you hear. ⁴⁶Solomon is now sitting on the king's throne. ⁴⁷All the king's officers are congratulating King David. They are saying, 'King David, you are a great king! And now we pray that your God will make Solomon a great king too. We hope your God will make Solomon even more famous than you. And we hope that Solomon's kingdom will be an even greater kingdom than yours is!' Even King David was there— He was bowing down, there on his bed. ⁴⁸King David said, 'Praise the Lord God of Israel. The Lord put one of my own sons on my throne. And he let me live to see it.'"

⁴⁹All of Adonijah's guests were scared and left very quickly. ⁵⁰Adonijah was also afraid of Solomon. So he went to the altar and held the

---

Gihon Spring A spring of water just outside the city walls in the valley east of Jerusalem. It was the main source of water for the city of Jerusalem.

anoint(ed) To pour olive oil on a person's head to show he was chosen by God to be a king, priest, or prophet.

good man Or "important man." This Hebrew word means a person from an important family.

horns of the altar.* ⁵¹Then someone told Solomon, "Adonijah is scared of you, King Solomon. Adonijah is ₍at the Holy Tent₎ holding onto the horns of the altar. And he refuses to leave. Adonijah says, 'Tell King Solomon to promise me that he will not kill me.'"

⁵²So Solomon answered, "If Adonijah shows that he is a good man, then I promise that not even a hair on his head will be hurt. But if he does anything wrong, then he will die." ⁵³Then King Solomon sent some men to get Adonijah. The men brought Adonijah to King Solomon. Adonijah came to King Solomon and bowed down. Then Solomon said, "Go home."

2 The time came when David was about to die. So David talked to Solomon and told him, ²"I am about to die, like all men must. But you are growing stronger and becoming a man. ³Now, carefully obey all the commands of the Lord your God. Carefully obey all his laws and commands and decisions and agreements. Obey everything that is written in the Law of Moses. If you do this, then you will be successful in everything you do and every place you go. ⁴And if you obey the Lord, then the Lord will keep his promise about me. The Lord said, 'If your sons carefully live the way I tell them, sincerely, with all their heart, then the king of Israel will always be a man from your family.'"

⁵David also said, "You remember what Joab son of Zeruiah did to me. He killed two of the commanders of Israel's army. He killed Abner son of Ner and Amasa son of Jether. Remember, he killed them during a time of peace! The blood from these men splashed on the sword belt and army boots he was wearing. I should have punished him. ⁶But you are the king now. So you should punish him in the way you think is the most wise. ₍But you must be sure that he is killed.₎ Don't let him die peacefully of old age!"

⁷"Be kind to the children of Barzillai of Gilead. Let them be your friends and eat at your table. They helped me when I ran away from your brother Absalom.

⁸"And remember, Shimei son of Gera, is still around here. He is from the family group of Benjamin in Bahurim. Remember that he said very bad things against me on the day that I ran away to Mahanaim. Then he came down to meet me at the Jordan River. I made a promise to him. I promised before the Lord that I would not kill Shimei. ⁹Now, don't leave him unpunished. You are a wise man. You will know what you must do to him. But don't let him die peacefully of old age."

¹⁰Then David died. He was buried in the City of David. ¹¹David ruled Israel 40 years. He ruled seven years in Hebron and 33 years in Jerusalem. ¹²Now Solomon was king. He sat on the throne of his father David. And there was no doubt that he was the king.

¹³Then Adonijah son of Haggith went to Bathsheba, Solomon's mother. Bathsheba asked him, "Do you come in peace?"

Adonijah answered, "Yes. This is a peaceful visit. ¹⁴I have something to say to you."

Bathsheba said, "Then speak."

¹⁵Adonijah said, "You remember that at one time the kingdom was mine. All the people of Israel thought I was their king. But things changed. Now my brother is the king. The Lord chose him to be king. ¹⁶So now I have one thing to ask you. Please do not refuse me."

Bathsheba answered, "What do you want?"

¹⁷Adonijah said, "I know that King Solomon will do anything you ask him. So please ask him to let me marry Abishag, the woman from Shunem."

¹⁸Then Bathsheba said, "Fine. I will speak to the king for you."

¹⁹So Bathsheba went to King Solomon to talk with him. King Solomon saw her and he stood to meet her. Then he bowed down to her and sat on the throne. He told some servants to bring another throne for his mother. Then she sat down at his right side.

²⁰Bathsheba said to him, "I have one small thing to ask you. Please do not refuse me."

The king answered, "You can ask anything you want, mother. I will not refuse you."

²¹So Bathsheba said, "Let your brother Adonijah marry Abishag, the woman from Shunem."

²²King Solomon answered his mother, "Why are you asking me to give Abishag to Adonijah? Why don't you just ask me to let him to be king too! After all, he is my older brother. Abiathar the priest and Joab will support him!"

²³Then Solomon made a promise with the Lord. He said, "I swear *(promise)* that I will make Adonijah pay for this. And it will cost him his

---

held the horns of the altar This showed he was asking for mercy. The law said that if a person ran into the holy place and held onto the corners of the altar he should not be punished.

life! ²⁴The Lord made me the king of Israel. He has given me the throne that belonged to my father David. The Lord kept his promise and gave the kingdom to me and my family. Now, as sure as the Lord is alive, I swear *(promise)* that Adonijah will die today!"

²⁵King Solomon gave the command to Benaiah. And Benaiah went out and killed Adonijah.

²⁶Then King Solomon said to Abiathar the priest, "I should kill you, but I will let you go back to your home in Anathoth. I will not kill you now because you helped to carry the Holy Box* of the Lord while marching with my father David. And I know that you shared in the hard times, just like my father." ²⁷Solomon told Abiathar that he could not continue to serve as a priest of the Lord. This happened the way the Lord said it would. God said this about Eli the priest and his family at Shiloh. ⌊And Abiathar was from Eli's family.⌋

²⁸Joab heard about this and became afraid. He had supported Adonijah, but not Absalom. Joab ran to the tent of the Lord and held the horns of the altar.* ²⁹Someone told King Solomon that Joab was at the altar in the Lord's Tent. So Solomon ordered Benaiah to go and kill him.

³⁰Benaiah went into the Lord's Tent and said to Joab, "The king says, 'Come out!'"

But Joab answered, "No, I will die here."

So Benaiah went back to the king and told him what Joab had said. ³¹Then the king commanded Benaiah, "Do as he says! Kill him there. Then bury him. Then my family and I will be free of the guilt of Joab. This guilt was caused because Joab killed innocent people. ³²Joab killed two men who were much better than himself. They were Abner son of Ner and Amasa son of Jether. Abner was the commander of Israel's army and Amasa was the commander of Judah's army. My father David did not know at that time that Joab had killed them. So the Lord will punish Joab for those men he killed. ³³He will be guilty for their deaths. And his family will also be guilty forever. But God will bring peace for David, his descendants,* his family of kings, and his kingdom forever."

³⁴So Benaiah son of Jehoiada killed Joab. Joab was buried near his home in the desert. ³⁵Solomon then made Benaiah, son of Jehoiada, commander of the army in Joab's place. Solomon also made Zadok the new high priest in Abiathar's place. ³⁶Next, the king sent to get Shimei. The king said to him, "Build a house for yourself here in Jerusalem. Live in that house and don't leave the city. ³⁷If you leave the city and go any further than Kidron Brook, then you will be killed. And it will be your own fault."

³⁸So Shimei answered, "That is fine, my king. I will obey you." So Shimei lived in Jerusalem for a long time. ³⁹But three years later, two of Shimei's slaves ran away. They went to Achish son of Maacah, the king of Gath. Shimei heard that his slaves were in Gath. ⁴⁰So Shimei put his saddle on his donkey and went to King Achish at Gath. He went to find his slaves. He found them there and brought them back home.

⁴¹But someone told Solomon that Shimei had gone from Jerusalem to Gath and returned. ⁴²So Solomon sent for him. Solomon said, "I used the Lord's name and swore *(promised)* that you would die if you left Jerusalem. I warned you that if you went anywhere, your death would be your own fault. And you agreed to what I said. You said that you would obey me. ⁴³Why did you break your promise? Why did you not obey my command? ⁴⁴You know the many wrong things you did against my father David. Now the Lord will punish you for those wrong things. ⁴⁵But the Lord will bless me. He will make David's kingdom safe forever."

⁴⁶Then the king ordered Benaiah to kill Shimei, and he did. Now Solomon had full control of his kingdom.

Solomon the King

3 Solomon made an agreement with Pharaoh, the king of Egypt, by marrying his daughter. Solomon brought her to the City of David.* At this time, Solomon was still building his palace and the temple of the Lord. Solomon was also building a wall around Jerusalem. ²The temple had not yet been finished. So people were still

---

Holy Box The Box of the Agreement. Also called "The Ark of the Covenant," the box containing the stone tablets with the Ten Commandments written on them and the other things that proved God was with the people of Israel during their time in the Sinai Desert.

held the horns of the altar This showed he was asking for mercy. The law said that if a person ran into the holy place and held onto the corners of the altar he should not be punished.

descendants A person's children and all of their future families.

the City of David The southeast and oldest part of the city of Jerusalem.

making animal sacrifices* on altars at the high places.* ³Solomon showed that he loved the Lord. He did this by obeying all the things his father David had told him to do. ₍But Solomon did something David did not tell him to do.₎ Solomon still used the high places to offer sacrifices and to burn incense.*

⁴King Solomon went to Gibeon to offer a sacrifice. He went there because that was the most important high place.* Solomon offered 1,000 offerings on that altar. ⁵While Solomon was at Gibeon, the Lord came to him during the night in a dream. God said, "Ask for anything you want. I will give it to you."

⁶Solomon answered, "You were very kind to your servant, my father David. He followed you. He was good and lived right. And you showed the greatest kindness to him when you allowed his son to rule on his throne ₍after him₎. ⁷Lord my God, you have allowed me to be the king in my father's place. But I am like a little child. I do not have the wisdom I need to do the things I must do. ⁸I, your servant, am here among your chosen people. There are many, many people. There are too many to count. ₍So a ruler must make many decisions among them.₎ ⁹So I ask that you give me wisdom so that I can rule and judge the people in the right way. This will allow me to know the difference between right and wrong. Without this great wisdom, it is impossible to rule these great people."

¹⁰The Lord was happy that Solomon asked him for this. ¹¹So God said to him, "You did not ask for long life for yourself. And you did not ask for riches for yourself. You did not ask for the death of your enemies. You asked for the wisdom to listen and make the right decisions. ¹²So, I will give you the thing you asked. I will make you wise and intelligent. I will make your wisdom so great, that there has never in the past been anyone like you. And in the future, there will never be anyone like you. ¹³Also, to reward you, I will give you those things that you did not ask for. All your life, you will have riches and honor. There will be no other king in the world as great as you. ¹⁴I ask you to follow me and obey my laws and commands. Do this the way your father David did. If you do this, then I will also give you a long life."

¹⁵Solomon woke up. He knew that God had talked to him in the dream. Then Solomon went to Jerusalem and stood before the Box of the Lord's Agreement.* Solomon offered a burnt offering for the Lord. And he made fellowship offerings to the Lord. After that, he gave a party for all of the leaders and officials that helped him rule.

¹⁶One day two women that were prostitutes* came to Solomon. They stood before the king. ¹⁷One of the women said, "Sir, this woman and I live in the same house. We were both pregnant and almost ready to give birth to our babies. I gave birth to my baby while she was there with me. ¹⁸Three days later, this woman also gave birth to her baby. There was no other person in the house with us. There were only the two of us. ¹⁹One night, while this woman was asleep with her baby, the baby died. ²⁰So, during the night, she took my son from my bed while I was asleep. She carried him to her bed. Then she put the dead baby in my bed. ²¹The next morning, I woke up and was ready to feed my baby. But I saw that the baby was dead. Then I looked at it more closely. I saw that it was not my baby."

²²But the other woman said, "No! The living baby is mine. The dead baby is yours!"

But the first woman said, "No! You are wrong! The dead baby is yours and the living baby is mine!" So the two women argued in front of the king.

²³Then King Solomon said, "Each of you says that the living baby is your own. And each of you says that the dead baby belongs to the other woman."

²⁴Then King Solomon sent his servant to get a sword. ²⁵And King Solomon said, "This is what we will do. Cut the living baby in two pieces. Give each woman half of the baby."

---

sacrifice(s) A gift to God. Usually it was a special animal that was killed and burned on an altar.

high place(s) Places for worshiping God or false gods. These places were often on the hills and mountains.

incense Special dried tree sap. Burned to make a sweet-smelling smoke, it was offered as a gift to God.

Box of the Lord's Agreement Also called "The Ark of the Covenant," the box containing the stone tablets with the Ten Commandments written on them and the other things that proved God was with the people of Israel during their time in the Sinai Desert.

prostitute(s) A woman paid by men for sexual sin. Sometimes this also means a person that is not faithful to God and stops following him.

²⁶The second woman said, "That is fine. Cut the baby into two pieces. Then neither of us will have him."

But the first woman, the real mother, was full of love for her son. She said to the king, "Please, Sir, don't kill the baby! Give it to her."

²⁷Then King Solomon said, "Don't kill the baby! Give it to the first woman. She is the real mother."

²⁸The people of Israel heard about King Solomon's decision. They respected and honored him very much because he was wise. They saw that he had the wisdom of God* in making the right decisions.

4 King Solomon ruled all the people of Israel. ²These are the names of his leading officials that helped him rule:

Azariah son of Zadok. Azariah was the priest.

³Elihoreph and Ahijah, sons of Shisha. Elihoreph and Ahijah had the jobs of writing notes about the things that happened in the courts.

Jehoshaphat son of Ahilud. Jehoshaphat wrote notes about the history of the people. ⁴Benaiah son of Jehoiada. Benaiah was the commander of the army.

Zadok and Abiathar. Zadok and Abiathar were priests.

⁵Azariah son of Nathan. Azariah was in charge of the district governors.

Zabud son of Nathan. Zabud was a priest and an adviser to King Solomon.

⁶Ahishar. Ahishar was responsible for everything in the king's home.

Adoniram son of Abda. Adoniram was in charge of the slaves.

⁷Israel was divided into twelve areas called districts. Solomon chose governors to rule over each district. These governors were ordered to gather food from their districts and give the food to the king and his family. Each of the twelve governors was responsible for giving food to the king one month of each year. ⁸These are the names of the twelve governors:

Ben Hur was governor of the hill country of Ephraim.

⁹Ben Deker was governor of Makaz, Shaalbim, Beth Shemesh, and Elon Bethhanan.

¹⁰Ben Hesed was governor of Arubboth, Socoh, and Hepher.

¹¹Ben Abinadab was governor of Naphoth Dor. He was married to Taphath, daughter of Solomon.

¹²Baana son of Ahilud was governor of Taanach and Megiddo and all of Beth Shan next to Zarethan. This was below Jezreel, from Beth Shan to Abel Meholah across from Jokmeam.

¹³Ben Geber was governor of Ramoth Gilead. He was governor of all the towns and villages of Jair son of Manasseh in Gilead. He was also governor of the district of Argob in Bashan. In this area there were 60 cities with big walls around them. These cities also had bronze bars on the gates.

¹⁴Ahinadab son of Iddo was governor of Mahanaim.

¹⁵Ahimaaz was governor of Naphtali. He was married to Basemath the daughter of Solomon.

¹⁶Baana son of Hushai was governor of Asher and Aloth.

¹⁷Jehoshaphat son of Paruah was governor of Issachar.

¹⁸Shimei son of Ela was governor of Benjamin.

¹⁹Geber son of Uri was governor of Gilead. Gilead was the country where Sihon the king of the Amorite people lived and the country where Og the king of Bashan lived. But Geber was the only governor of that district.

²⁰There were many, many people in Judah and Israel. The number of people was like sands on the seashore. The people lived happy lives: They ate, drank, and enjoyed themselves.

²¹Solomon ruled over all the kingdoms from the Euphrates River to the land of the Philistine people. His kingdom went as far as the border of Egypt. These countries sent gifts to Solomon and they obeyed him all of his life.*

²²⁻²³This is the amount of food that Solomon needed each day for himself and for all of the people that ate at his table:

---

the wisdom of God Or, "very great wisdom."

sent gifts ... life This showed that these countries had made peace agreements with Solomon because of his great power.

150 bushels* of fine flour,
300 bushels* of flour,
10 cows that were fed good grain,
20 cows that were raised in the fields,
100 sheep,
wild animals such as deer, gazelles, roebucks,* and game birds.

²⁴Solomon ruled over all the countries west of the Euphrates River. This was the land from Tiphsah to Gaza. And Solomon had peace on all sides of his kingdom. ²⁵During Solomon's life all of the people in Judah and Israel, all the way from Dan to Beersheba, lived in peace and security. The people were at peace sitting under their own fig trees and grape vines.
²⁶Solomon had places to keep 4,000* horses for his chariots and he had 12,000 horse soldiers. ²⁷And each month one of the twelve district governors gave King Solomon all those things that he needed. This was enough for every person that ate at the king's table. ²⁸The district governors also gave the king enough straw and barley for the chariot horses and the riding horses. Each person brought this grain to required places.
²⁹God made Solomon very wise. Solomon could understand many, many things. His wisdom was too great to imagine. ³⁰Solomon's wisdom was greater than the wisdom of all the men in the East. And his wisdom was greater than all the men in Egypt. ³¹He was wiser than any of the men on earth. He was even wiser than Ethan the Ezrahite. He was wiser than Heman, Calcol, and Darda, the sons of Mahol. King Solomon became famous in all of the countries around Israel and Judah. ³²During his life, King Solomon wrote* 3,000 wise teachings and 1,500 songs.
³³Solomon also knew very much about nature. Solomon taught about many different kinds of plants—everything from the great cedar trees of Lebanon to the vines that grow out of the walls. King Solomon also taught about animals, birds, and snakes.* ³⁴People from all nations came to listen to King Solomon's wisdom. The kings of all nations sent their wise men to listen to King Solomon.

Solomon Builds the Temple

5 Hiram was the king of Tyre. Hiram had always been David's friend. So when Hiram heard that Solomon had become the new king after David, he sent his servants to Solomon. ²This is what Solomon said to king Hiram: ³"You remember that my father, King David, had to fight many wars all around him. So he was never able to build a temple to honor the Lord his God. King David was waiting until the Lord allowed him to defeat all his enemies. ⁴But now the Lord my God has given me peace on all sides of my country. Now I have no enemies. My people are in no danger.
⁵"The Lord made a promise to my father David. The Lord said, 'I will make your son king after you. And your son will build a temple to honor me.' Now, I plan to build that temple to honor the Lord my God. ⁶And so I ask you to help me. Send your men to Lebanon. There, they should cut down cedar trees for me. My servants will work with yours. I will pay you any price that you decide as your servants' wages. But I need your help. Our carpenters* are not as good as the carpenters of Sidon."
⁷When Hiram heard what Solomon asked, he was very happy. King Hiram said, "I thank the Lord today for giving David a wise son to rule this great nation!" ⁸Then Hiram sent a message to Solomon. The message said, "I heard the thing that you asked. I will give you all the cedar trees and the fir trees you want. ⁹My servants will bring them down from Lebanon to the sea. Then I will tie them together and float them down the shore to the place you choose. There I will separate the logs, and you can take the trees."
¹⁰⁻¹¹Solomon gave Hiram about 120,000 bushels* of wheat and about 120,000 gallons* of pure olive oil every year for his family.
¹²The Lord gave wisdom to Solomon as he had promised. And there was peace between Hiram and Solomon. These two kings made a treaty between themselves.
¹³King Solomon forced 30,000 men of Israel to help in this work. ¹⁴King Solomon chose a man named Adoniram to be the boss. Solomon divided the men into three groups. There were 10,000 men in each group. Each group worked one month in Lebanon and then went home for two months.

---

150 bushels Or, "6,600 l." Literally, "30 kors."
300 bushels Or, "13,200 l." Literally, "60 kors."
deer ,gazelles ,roebucks Different kinds of wild deer.
4,000 Hebrew and Latin have 40,000, but see 2 Chron. 9:25.
wrote Literally, "spoke."
snakes Literally, "creeping things." These can be anything from insects, to lizards or snakes, and fish.

carpenters People who work with wood. In ancient times, this also meant that they cut the trees.
120,000 bushels Or, "4,400,000 l." Literally, "20,000 kors."
120,000 gallons Or, "440,000 l." Literally, "20,000 baths."

¹⁵Solomon also forced 80,000 men to work in the hill country. These men had the job of cutting rocks. And there were 70,000 men to carry the rocks. ¹⁶There were also 3,300 men who were the bosses over the people who did the work. ¹⁷King Solomon commanded them to cut out big, expensive stones to be the foundation for the temple. These stones were carefully cut. ¹⁸Then Solomon's and Hiram's builders and the men from Byblos* carved the stones. They prepared the stones and the logs for building the temple.

Solomon Builds the Temple

6 So Solomon began to build the temple. This was 480 years* after the people of Israel left Egypt. This was during Solomon's fourth year as king of Israel. It was in the month of Ziv, the second month of the year. ²The temple was 60 cubits* long, 20 cubits* wide, and 30 cubits* high. ³The porch of the temple was 20 cubits* long and 10 cubits* wide. The porch ran along the front of the main part of the temple itself. Its length was equal to the width of the temple. ⁴There were narrow windows in the temple. These windows were narrow on the outside and larger on the inside.* ⁵Then Solomon built a row of rooms around the main part of the temple. These rooms were built on top of each other. ₍This row of rooms was three stories tall.₎ ⁶The rooms touched the temple wall, but their beams were not built into that wall. ₍That temple wall became thinner at the top.₎ So the wall which made one side of those rooms was thinner than the wall below it. The rooms on the bottom floor were 5 cubits* wide. The rooms on the middle floor were 6 cubits* wide. The rooms above that were 7 cubits* wide. ⁷The workers used large stones to build the walls. The workers cut the stones at the place where they got them out of the ground. So there was no noise of hammers, axes, or any other iron tools in the temple.

⁸The entrance to the bottom rooms was on the south side of the temple. Inside, there were stairs that went up to the second floor rooms and from there to the third floor rooms.

⁹So, Solomon finished building the temple. Every part in the temple was covered with cedar boards. ¹⁰Solomon also finished building the rooms around the temple. Each story was 5 cubits* tall. The cedar beams in those rooms touched the temple.

¹¹The Lord said to Solomon, ¹²"If you obey all my laws and commands, I will do the thing for you that I promised your father David. ¹³And I will live among the children of Israel in this temple that you are building. I will never leave the people of Israel."

Details About the Temple

¹⁴So Solomon finished building the temple.

¹⁵The stone walls inside the temple were covered with cedar boards. The cedar boards went from the floor to the ceiling. The stone floor was covered with pine boards. ¹⁶They built a room 20 cubits* long deep inside the back part of the temple. They covered the walls in this room with cedar boards. The cedar boards went from the floor to the ceiling. This room was called the Most Holy Place. ¹⁷In front of the Most Holy Place, was the main part of the temple. This room was 40 cubits* long. ¹⁸They covered the walls in this room with cedar boards—none of the stones in the walls could be seen. They carved pictures of flowers and gourds* into the cedar.

¹⁹Solomon prepared the room deep inside the back part of the temple. This room was for the Lord's Box of the Agreement.* ²⁰This room was 20 cubits* long, 20 cubits* wide, and 20 cubits* high. ²¹Solomon covered this room with pure gold. He built an ₍incense₎ altar in front of this room. He covered the altar with gold, and wrapped gold chains around it. There were two statues of Cherub angels* in that room. Those

---

Byblos Or, "Gebal."
480 years This was about 960 B.C.
60 cubits 103' 4 3/16" or 31.5m.
20 cubits 29' 3 3/8" or 10.5m.
30 cubits 51' 8 1/16" or 15.75m. The ancient Greek translation has "25 cubits."
10 cubits 17' 2 11/16" or 5.25m.
These windows ... inside This might also mean, "These were windows with lattice work over them."
5 cubits 8' 7 5/16" or 2.625m.
6 cubits 10' 4" or 3.15m.
7 cubits 12' 11/16" or 3.675m.

40 cubits 68' 10 3/4" or 21m.
gourds A plant with long vines. Its fruit grows in the shape of a jar and becomes hard like wood.
Box of the Agreement Also called "The Ark of the Covenant," the box containing the stone tablets with the Ten Commandments written on them and the other things that proved God was with the people of Israel during their time in the Sinai Desert.
Cherub angels Special angels from God. Statues of these angels were on top of the Box of the Agreement.

statues were covered with gold. ²²All of the temple was covered with gold. Also, the altar in front of the Most Holy Place was covered with gold. ²³The workers made two statues of Cherub angels* with wings. The workers made the statues from olive wood. These Cherub angels were put in the Most Holy Place. Each angel was 10 cubits* tall. ²⁴⁻²⁶Both Cherub angels were the same size and built the same way. Each Cherub angel had two wings. Each wing was 5 cubits* long. From the end of one wing to the end of the other wing was 10 cubits.* And each Cherub angel was 10 cubits* tall. ²⁷These Cherub angels were put in the Most Holy Place. They stood beside each other. Their wings touched each other in the middle of the room. The other two wings touched each side wall. ²⁸The two Cherub angels were covered with gold.

²⁹The walls around the main room and the inner room were carved with pictures of Cherub angels,* palm trees, and flowers. ³⁰The floor of both rooms was covered with gold.

³¹The workers made two doors from olive wood. They put those doors at the entrance of the Most Holy Place. The frame around the doors was made with five sides.* ³²They made the two doors from olive wood. The workers carved pictures of Cherub angels,* palm trees, and flowers on the doors. Then they covered the doors with gold.

³³They also made doors for the entrance to the main room. They used olive wood to make a square door frame. ³⁴Then they used fir* to make the doors. ³⁵There were two doors. Each door had two parts, so the two doors folded. They carved pictures of Cherub angels,* ₍palm₎ trees, and flowers on the doors. Then they covered them with gold.

³⁶Then they built the inner yard. They built walls around this yard. Each wall was made from three rows of cut stones and one row of cedar timbers.

³⁷They started working on the temple in the month of Ziv, the second month of the year. This was during Solomon's fourth year as king of Israel. ³⁸The temple was finished in the month of Bul, the eighth month of the year. This was during the eleventh year that Solomon ruled over the people. It took seven years to build the temple. The temple was built exactly the way it was planned.

Solomon's Palace

7 King Solomon also built a palace* for himself. It took 13 years to finish building Solomon's palace. ²He also built the building called "the Forest of Lebanon." It was 100 cubits* long, 50 cubits* wide, and 30 cubits* high. It had four rows of cedar columns. On top of each column was a cedar capital.* ³There were cedar beams going across the rows of columns. They put cedar boards on top of these beams for the ceiling. There were 15 beams for each section of columns. There was a total of 45 beams. ⁴There were three rows of windows ₍on each of the side walls₎. The windows were across from each other. ⁵There were three doors at each end. All the door openings and frames were square.

⁶Solomon also built the "Porch of Columns." It was 50 cubits* long and 30 cubits* wide. Along the front of the porch, there was a covering supported by columns.

⁷Solomon also built a throne room where he judged people. He called this the "Hall of Judging." The room was covered with cedar from the floor to the ceiling.

⁸The house where Solomon lived was inside of the Hall of Judging. This house was built the same as the Hall of Judging. He also built the same kind of house for his wife, the daughter of the king of Egypt.

⁹All of these buildings were made with expensive blocks of stone. These stones were cut to the right size with a saw. They were cut in the front and in the back. These expensive stones went from the foundation up to the top layer of the wall. Even the wall around the yard was made with expensive blocks of stone. ¹⁰The foundations were made with large, expensive stones. Some of the stones were 10 cubits* long and others were 8 cubits* long. ¹¹On top of those stones there were

---

Cherub angels Special angels from God. Statues of these angels were on top of the Box of the Agreement.
10 cubits 17' 2 11/16" or 5.25m.
5 cubits 8' 7 5/16" or 2.625m.
The frame ... sides We are not sure of the meaning here.
fir A type of tree, like a pine tree.

palace A large house for the king and his family.
100 cubits 172' 3" or 52.5m.
50 cubits 86'1 1/2" or 26.25m.
30 cubits 51' 8 1/16" or 15.75m.
capital(s) Decorated caps of stone or wood on top of columns.
8 cubits 13' 9 5/16" or 4.2m.

other expensive stones and cedar beams. ¹²There were walls around the palace yard, the temple yard, and the porch of the temple. Those walls were built with three rows of stone and one row of cedar timbers.

¹³King Solomon sent a message to a man named Huram* in Tyre. Solomon brought Huram ₍to Jerusalem₎. ¹⁴Huram's mother was an Israelite from the family group of Naphtali. His dead father was from Tyre. Huram made things from bronze.* He was a very skilled and experienced worker. So King Solomon asked him to come, and Huram accepted. So King Solomon put Huram in charge of all the bronze work. Huram built all the things made from bronze.

¹⁵Huram* made two bronze* columns. Each column was 18 cubits* tall and 12 cubits* around. The columns were hollow and the metal was 3 inches* thick. ¹⁶Huram also made two bronze capitals* that were 5 cubits* tall. Huram put these capitals on top of the columns. ¹⁷Then he made two nets of chains to cover the capitals on top of the two columns. ¹⁸Then he made two rows of bronze* that looked like pomegranates.* They put these bronze pomegranates on the nets of each column in order to cover the capitals at the top of the columns. ¹⁹The capitals on top of the 5 cubits* tall columns were shaped like flowers. ²⁰The capitals were on top of the columns. They were above the bowl shaped net. At that place, there were 20 pomegranates in rows all around the capitals. ²¹Huram put these two bronze columns at the porch of the temple. One column was put on the south side and one was put on the north side ₍of the entrance₎. The column on the south was named Jakin. The column on the north was named Boaz. ²²They put the flower-shaped capitals on top of the columns. So the work on the two columns was finished.

²³Then Huram* made a round tank from bronze.* ₍They called this tank "The Sea."₎ The tank was about 30 cubits* around. It was 10 cubits* across and 5 cubits* deep. ²⁴There was a rim around the outer edge of the tank. Under this rim there were two rows of bronze gourds* surrounding the tank. The bronze gourds were made in one piece as part of the tank. ²⁵The tank rested on the backs of 12 bronze bulls. All 12 of these bulls were looking out, away from the tank. Three were looking north, three east, three south, and three west. ²⁶The sides of the tank were 3 inches* thick. The rim around the tank was like the rim of a cup or like the petals on a flower. The tank held about 11,000 gallons.*

²⁷Then Huram* made ten bronze* carts. Each one was 4 cubits* long, 4 cubits* wide, and 3 cubits* high. ²⁸The carts were made from square panels set in frames. ²⁹On the panels and frames were bronze lions, bulls, and Cherub angels.* Above and below the lions and bulls there were designs of flowers hammered into the bronze. ³⁰Each cart had four bronze wheels with bronze axles. At the corners there were bronze supports for a large bowl. The supports had designs of flowers hammered into the bronze. ³¹There was a frame on top for the bowl. It was 1 cubit* tall above the bowls. The opening for the bowl was round, 1 1/2 cubits* in diameter. There were designs carved into the bronze on the frame. The frame was square, not round. ³²There were four wheels under the frame. The wheels were 1 1/2 cubits* in diameter. The axles between the wheels were made as one piece with the cart. ³³The wheels were like the wheels on a chariot.* Everything on the wheels—the axles, the rims, the spokes, and the hubs were made from bronze.

³⁴The four supports were on the four corners of each cart. They were made as one piece with the cart. ³⁵There was a strip of bronze around the top of each cart. It was made as one piece with the cart. ³⁶The sides of the cart and the frames had

---

8 cubits 13' 9 5/16" or 4.2m.
Huram Or, "Hiram."
bronze A metal. The Hebrew word can mean "copper," "bronze," or "brass."
18 cubits 31' or 9.45m.
12 cubits 20' 8" or 6.3m.
3 inches Or, "8cm." Literally, "1 handbreadth."
capital(s) Decorated caps of stone or wood on top of columns.
5 cubits 8' 7 5/16" or 2.625m.
pomegranate A red fruit with many tiny seeds inside it. Each seed is covered with a soft, tasty part of the fruit.

30 cubits 51' 8 1/16" or 15.75m.
10 cubits 17' 2 11/16" or 5.25m.
gourds A plant with long vines. Its fruit grows in the shape of a jar and becomes hard like wood.
11,000 gallons Or, "44,000 l." Literally, "2,000 baths."
4 cubits 6' 10 5/8" or 2.1m.
3 cubits 5' 2" or 1.575m.
Cherub angels Special angels from God. Statues of these angels were on top of the Box of the Agreement.
1 cubit 1' 8 5/8" or 52.5cm.
1 1/2 cubits 2' 7" or 78.75cm.
chariot(s) A small wagon used in war.

pictures of Cherub angels,* lions, and palm trees carved into the bronze. These pictures were carved all over the carts— wherever there was room. And there were flowers carved on the frame around the cart. ³⁷Huram made ten carts. And they were all the same. Each cart was made from bronze. The bronze was melted and poured into a mold. So all of the carts were the same size and shape. ³⁸Huram* also made ten bowls. There was one bowl for each of the ten carts. Each bowl was 4 cubits* across. And each bowl could hold about 230 gallons.* ³⁹Huram put five of the carts on the south side of the temple and the other five carts on the north side. He put the large tank in the southeast corner of the temple. ⁴⁰⁻⁴⁵Huram also made pots, small shovels, and small bowls. Huram finished making all of the things King Solomon wanted him to make. This is a list of the things that Huram made for the Temple of the Lord:

2 columns

2 capitals* shaped like bowls for the top of the columns

2 nets to go around the capitals

400 pomegranates for the two nets. There were two rows of pomegranates for each net to cover the two bowls for the capitals on top of the columns.

10 carts with a bowl on each cart

the large tank with 12 bulls under it

the pots, small shovels, small bowls, and all the dishes for the Lord's temple.

Huram* made all the things that King Solomon wanted. They were all made from polished bronze. ⁴⁶⁻⁴⁷Solomon never weighed the bronze that was used to make these things. There was too much to weigh. So the total weight of all the bronze was never known. The king ordered these things to be made near the Jordan River between Succoth and Zarethan. They made these things by melting the bronze and pouring it into molds in the ground.

⁴⁸⁻⁵⁰Solomon also commanded that many things be made from gold for the temple. These are the things that Solomon made from gold for the temple:

the golden altar

the golden table. (The special bread offered to God was on this table.)

the lampstands of pure gold. (There were five on the south side and five on the north side in front of the Most Holy Place.)

the gold flowers, lamps, and tongs

the cups

the tools used to keep the lamps bright

the bowls

the pans

the dishes of pure gold for carrying ashes

the doors at the entrance to the temple.

⁵¹So King Solomon finished the work he wanted to do for the Lord's temple. Then King Solomon got all the things that his father David had saved for this special purpose. He brought these things into the temple. He put the silver and gold in the treasuries in the Lord's Temple.

The Box of the Agreement in the Temple

8 Then King Solomon called together all the elders of Israel, the heads of the family groups, and the leaders of the families of Israel. He asked them to come to him in Jerusalem. Solomon wanted them to join in bringing the Box of the Agreement* from the City of David* into the temple. ²So all the men of Israel came together with King Solomon. This was during the time of the special holiday *(the Festival of Shelters)* during the month of Ethanim (the seventh month of the year).

³All of the elders of Israel arrived at that place. Then the priests took the Holy Box.* ⁴They carried the Holy Box* of the Lord along with the Meeting Tent* and the holy things that were in the

---

Box of the Agreement Also called "The Ark of the Covenant," the box containing the stone tablets with the Ten Commandments written on them and the other things that proved God was with the people of Israel during their time in the Sinai Desert.

City of David The southeast and oldest part of the city of Jerusalem.

Holy Box The Box of the Agreement. Also called "The Ark of the Covenant," the box containing the stone tablets with the Ten Commandments written on them and the other things that proved God was with the people of Israel during their time in the Sinai Desert.

Meeting Tent The Holy Tent *(Tabernacle)* where the people of Israel met to worship God.

Cherub angels Special angels from God. Statues of these angels were on top of the Box of the Agreement.

Huram Or, "Hiram."

4 cubits 6' 10 5/8" or 2.1m.

230 gallons Or, "880 l." Literally, "40 baths."

capital(s) Decorated caps of stone or wood on top of columns.

tent. The Levites* helped the priests carry these things. ⁵King Solomon and all the people of Israel met together before the Box of the Agreement.* ⌊They offered many sacrifices.⌋ They killed so many sheep and cattle that no person was able to count them all. ⁶Then the priests put the Box of the Agreement of the Lord in its right place. This was inside the Most Holy Place in the temple. The Box of the Agreement was put under the wings of the Cherub angels.* ⁷The wings of the Cherub angels were spread out over the Holy Box. They covered the Holy Box and its carrying poles. ⁸These carrying poles were very long. Any person that stood in the Holy Place in front of the Most Holy Place could see the ends of the poles. But no one outside could see them. The poles are still in there today. ⁹The only thing inside the Holy Box were the two tablets. These were the two tablets that Moses put in the Holy Box at the place called Horeb. Horeb was the place that the Lord made his Agreement with the people of Israel after they came out of Egypt.

¹⁰⌊The priests put the Holy Box in the Most Holy Place.⌋ When the priests came out of the Holy Place, the Cloud* filled the Lord's Temple. ¹¹The priests could not continue their work because the temple was filled with the Glory of the Lord.* ¹²Then Solomon said:

"The Lord made the sun to shine in the sky,
  but he chose to live in the dark cloud.
¹³ I have built a wonderful temple for you,
  a place for you to live forever."

¹⁴All of the people of Israel were standing there. So King Solomon turned to them and asked God to bless them.

¹⁵Then King Solomon prayed a long prayer to the Lord. This is what he said:

"The Lord, the God of Israel, is great.
  The Lord himself has done the things that
    he promised to my father David.
  The Lord told my father,
¹⁶ 'I brought my people, Israel, out of
    Egypt.
  But I had not yet chosen a city from
    among the family groups of Israel
    for a temple to honor me.
  And I had not chosen a man to be leader
    over my people, Israel.
  But now I have chosen Jerusalem where I
    will be honored.
  And I have chosen David to rule over
    my people, Israel.'

¹⁷"My father David wanted very much to build a temple to honor the Lord, the God of Israel. ¹⁸But the Lord said to my father David, 'I know that you want very much to build a temple to honor me. And this is good that you want to build my temple. ¹⁹But you are not the one that I have chosen to build the temple. Your son will build my temple!'

²⁰"So the Lord has kept the promise that he gave. I am the king now in place of David my father. Now I rule the people of Israel like the Lord promised. And I built the temple for the Lord, the God of Israel. ²¹I have made a place in the temple for the Holy Box.* Inside that Holy Box is the Agreement that the Lord made with our ancestors. The Lord made that Agreement when he brought our ancestors out of Egypt."

²²Then Solomon stood in front of the Lord's altar.* All of the people were standing in front of him. King Solomon spread his hands and looked toward the sky. ²³He said:

"Lord, God of Israel, there is no other god like you in the skies or on the earth. You made the Agreements with your people because you love them. And you keep your Agreement. You are kind and loyal to people that follow you. ²⁴You made a promise to your servant David, my father. And you have kept that promise. You made that promise with your own mouth. And with your

---

Levites People from the family group of Levi. The Levites helped the priests in the temple and also worked for the civil government.

Box of the Agreement Also called "The Ark of the Covenant," the box containing the stone tablets with the Ten Commandments written on them and the other things that proved God was with the people of Israel during their time in the Sinai Desert.

Cherub angels Special angels from God. Statues of these angels were on top of the Box of the Agreement.

Cloud The special sign that showed that God was with the people of Israel.

Glory of the Lord One of the forms God used when he appeared to people. This was like a bright, shining light.

Holy Box The Box of the Agreement. Also called "The Ark of the Covenant," the box containing the stone tablets with the Ten Commandments written on them and the other things that proved God was with the people of Israel during their time in the Sinai Desert.

altar(s) A stone table used for burning sacrifices offered as gifts to God.

great power you have made that promise come true today. ²⁵Now, Lord, God of Israel, keep the other promises you made to your servant David, my father. You said, 'David, your sons must carefully obey me, just like you did. If they do this, then you will always have someone from your family ruling the people of Israel.' ²⁶And again, Lord, God of Israel, I ask you to please continue to keep that promise to my father.

²⁷"But, God, will you really live here with us on the earth? All the sky and the highest place in heaven cannot contain you. Certainly this house which I have built cannot contain you either. ²⁸But please listen to my prayer and my request. I am your servant, and you are the Lord my God. Hear this prayer that I am praying to you today. ²⁹In the past you said, 'I will be honored there.' So please watch this temple night and day. Please listen to the prayer that I pray to you at this temple. ³⁰Lord, I and your people Israel will turn to this place and pray to you. Please hear those prayers! We know that you live in heaven. We ask you to hear our prayer there and forgive us.

³¹"If a person does something wrong against another person, he will be brought here to the altar. If that person is not guilty, then he will make an oath. He will promise that he is innocent. ³²Then listen in heaven and judge the man. If the person is guilty, then please show us that he is guilty. And if the person is innocent, then please show us that he is not guilty.

³³"Sometimes your people Israel will sin against you, and their enemies will defeat them. Then the people will come back to you and praise you. The people will pray to you in this temple. ³⁴Please hear them in heaven. Then forgive the sins of your people Israel, and allow them to have their land again. You gave this land to their ancestors.

³⁵"Sometimes they will sin against you, and you will stop the rain from falling on their land. Then they will pray toward this place and praise your name. You make them suffer, and they will be sorry for their sins. ³⁶So please listen in heaven to their prayer. Then forgive us for our sins. Teach the people to live right. Then, Lord, please send rain to the land you gave them.

³⁷"The land might become very dry and no food will grow on it. Or maybe a great sickness will spread among the people. Maybe all of the food that is growing will be destroyed by insects. Or your people might be attacked in some of their cities by their enemies. Or many of your people might become sick. ³⁸When any of these things happen, if even one man is sorry ₍for his sins₎ and spreads his hands in prayer toward this temple, ³⁹please listen to his prayer. Listen to it while you are in your home in heaven. Then forgive the people and help them. Only you know the things that people are really thinking. So judge each person and be fair to him. ⁴⁰Do this so that your people will fear and respect you all the time that they live in this land that you gave to our ancestors.

⁴¹⁻⁴²"People from other places will hear about your greatness and your power. They will come from far away to pray at this temple. ⁴³From your home in heaven please listen to their prayers. Please do all that those people from other places ask you. Then those people will fear and respect you the same as your people in Israel. Then all people everywhere will know that I built this temple to honor you.

⁴⁴"Sometimes you will command your people to go and fight against their enemies. Then your people will turn toward this city which you have chosen and the temple that I have built for your honor. And they will pray to you. ⁴⁵At that time, listen to their prayers from your home in heaven, and help them.

⁴⁶"Your people will sin against you. I know this because every person sins. And you will be angry with your people. You will let their enemies defeat them. Their enemies will make them prisoners and carry them to some faraway land. ⁴⁷In that faraway land, your people will think about what happened. They will be sorry for their sins, and they will pray to you. They will say, 'We have sinned and done wrong.' ⁴⁸They will be in that faraway land. But if they turn toward this land that you gave to their ancestors,* and toward this city you chose, and toward this temple I built to honor you, ⁴⁹then please listen from your home in heaven. ⁵⁰Forgive your people of all their sins. And forgive them for turning against you. Make their enemies be kind to them. ⁵¹Remember that they are your people. Remember that you brought them out of Egypt. It was like you saved them by pulling them out of a hot oven!

⁵²"Lord God, please listen to my prayers and to the prayers of your people Israel. Listen to their prayers any time that they ask you for help. ⁵³You have chosen them from all the peoples of the earth

---

ancestors Literally, "fathers." This means a person's parents, grandparents, and all the people they are descended from.

to be your own special people. Lord, you promised to do that for us. You used your servant Moses at the time you brought our ancestors* out of Egypt."

⁵⁴Solomon prayed that prayer to God. He was on his knees in front of the altar.* Solomon prayed with his arms raised toward heaven. Then Solomon finished praying and stood. ⁵⁵Then, in a loud voice, he asked God to bless all the people of Israel. Solomon said:

⁵⁶"Praise the Lord! He promised to give rest to his people, Israel. And he has given us rest! The Lord used his servant Moses and made many good promises to the people of Israel. And the Lord has kept every one of those promises! ⁵⁷I pray that the Lord our God will be with us, just like he was with our ancestors.* I pray that the Lord will never leave us. ⁵⁸I pray that we will turn to him and follow him. Then we will obey all the laws, decisions, and commands that he gave our ancestors. ⁵⁹I hope that the Lord our God will always remember this prayer and the things I have asked. I pray that the Lord will do these things for his servant, the king, and for his people, Israel. I pray that he will do this every day. ⁶⁰If the Lord will do these things,ⱼ then all the people of the world will know that the Lord is the only true God. ⁶¹You people must be loyal and true to the Lord our God. You must always follow and obey all of his laws and commands. You must continue to obey in the future like you do now."

⁶²Then King Solomon and all the people of Israel with him offered sacrifices to the Lord. ⁶³Solomon killed 22,000 cattle and 120,000 sheep. These were for the fellowship offerings. This is the way the king and the Israelites dedicated the temple— they showed that they had given the temple to the Lord.

⁶⁴Also, that day King Solomon dedicated the yard in front of the temple. He offered burnt offerings, grain offerings, and the fat from the animals that were used as fellowship offerings. King Solomon made these offerings there in the yard. He did this because the bronze altar in front of the Lord was too small to hold them all.

⁶⁵So there at the temple, King Solomon and all the people of Israel celebrated the holiday.* All Israel was there, from as far away as Hamath Pass in the north, to the border of Egypt in the south. Many, many people were there. They ate, drank, and enjoyed themselves together with the Lord for seven days. Then they stayed for another seven days. They celebrated for a total of 14 days!* ⁶⁶The next day, Solomon told the people to go home. All the people thanked the king, said goodbye, and went home. They were happy because of all the good things that the Lord had done for David his servant and for his people Israel.

God Comes to Solomon Again

9 So Solomon finished building the Lord's temple and his own palace. Solomon built all the things that he wanted to build. ²Then the Lord appeared to Solomon again, just as he had done before in the town of Gibeon. ³The Lord said to him: "I heard your prayer. I heard the things that you asked me to do. You built this temple. And I have made it a holy place. So I will be honored there forever. I will watch over it and think of it always. ⁴You must serve me the same way your father David did. He was fair and sincere. And you must obey my laws and do all the things that I commanded you.

⁵"If you do all these things, then I will make sure that the king of Israel is always someone from your family. This is the promise I made to your father David. I told him that Israel would always be ruled by one of his descendants.*

⁶⁻⁷"But if you or your children stop following me, and don't obey the laws and commands I have given you, and if you serve and worship other gods, then I will force Israel to leave the land I have given to them. Israel will be an example to other people. Other people will make jokes about Israel. I made the temple holy. It is the place where people honor me. But ₗif you don't obey me,ⱼ then I will tear it down. ⁸This temple will be destroyed. Every person who sees it will be amazed. They will ask, 'Why did the Lord do this terrible thing to this land and to this temple?' ⁹Other people will answer, 'This happened because they left the Lord their God. He brought their ancestors out of Egypt. But they decided to follow other gods. They began to

---

ancestors Literally, "fathers." This means a person's parents, grandparents, and all the people they are descended from.

altar(s) A stone table used for burning sacrifices offered as gifts to God.

holiday This was probably Passover.

Then they stayed ... 14 days This is not in the ancient Greek translation.

descendants A person's children and all of their future families.

worship and serve those gods. That is why the Lord caused all these bad things to happen to them.'"

¹⁰It took 20 years for King Solomon to build the Lord's temple and the king's palace.* ¹¹And after 20 years King Solomon gave 20 towns in Galilee to Hiram the king of Tyre. Solomon gave King Hiram these towns because Hiram helped Solomon build the temple and the palace. Hiram gave Solomon all the cedar and pine and gold that Solomon wanted. ¹²So Hiram traveled from Tyre to see the towns that Solomon gave him. When Hiram saw those towns, he was not pleased. ¹³King Hiram said, "What are these towns that you have given me, my brother?" King Hiram named that land the Land of Cabul.* And that area is still called Cabul today. ¹⁴Hiram had sent to King Solomon about 9,000 pounds* of gold ₍to use in building the temple₎.

¹⁵King Solomon forced slaves to work for him to build the temple and the palace. Then King Solomon used these slaves to build many other things. He built the Millo.* He also built the city wall around Jerusalem. Then he built again the cities of Hazor, Megiddo, and Gezer.

¹⁶In the past, the king of Egypt fought against the city of Gezer and burned it. He killed the Canaanite people who lived there. Solomon married Pharaoh's daughter. So Pharaoh gave that city to Solomon as a wedding present. ¹⁷Solomon built that city again. Solomon also built the city of Lower Beth Horon. ¹⁸King Solomon also built the cities of Baalath and Tamar in the Judean desert. ¹⁹King Solomon also built cities where he could store grain and things. And he built places for his chariots and his horses. King Solomon also built many things that he wanted in Jerusalem and in Lebanon and in all the places he ruled.

²⁰There were people in the land that were not Israelites. Those people were the Amorites, the Hittites, the Perizzites, the Hivites, and the Jebusites. ²¹The Israelites had not been able to destroy those people. But Solomon forced them to work for him as slaves. They are still slaves today. ²²Solomon did not force any Israelites to be his slaves. The people of Israel were soldiers, government officials, officers, captains, and chariot commanders and drivers.

²³There were 550 supervisors over Solomon's projects. They were bosses over the men who did the work. ²⁴Pharaoh's daughter moved from the City of David to the big house that Solomon built for her. Then Solomon built the Millo.*

²⁵Three times each year Solomon offered burned sacrifices and fellowship offerings on the altar. This is the altar that Solomon built for the Lord. King Solomon also burned incense before the Lord. So he supplied the things needed for the temple.

²⁶King Solomon also built ships at Ezion Geber. This town is near Elath on the shore of the Red Sea, in the land of Edom. ²⁷King Hiram had some men who knew much about the sea. Those men often traveled in ships. King Hiram sent those men to serve in Solomon's navy and work with Solomon's men. ²⁸Solomon's ships went to Ophir. The ships brought about 31,500 pounds* of gold back from Ophir to King Solomon.

The Queen of Sheba Visits Solomon

10 The queen of Sheba heard about Solomon. So she came to test him with hard questions. ²She traveled to Jerusalem with a very large group of servants. There were many camels carrying spices, jewels, and much gold. She met Solomon and asked him all the questions that she could think of. ³Solomon answered all the questions. None of her questions were too hard for him to explain. ⁴The queen of Sheba saw that Solomon was very wise. She also saw the beautiful palace* he had built. ⁵The queen saw the food at the king's table. She saw his officials meeting together. She saw the servants in the palace and the good clothes that they wore. She saw his parties and the sacrifices that he offered in the temple. All these things really amazed her—they just 'took her breath away'!

⁶So the queen said to the king, "I heard many things in my own country about your wisdom and all the things you have done. And everything is true! ⁷I did not believe it until I came and saw it with my own eyes. Now I see that it is even greater than what I heard. Your wealth and wisdom is much greater than people told me. ⁸Your wives* and officers are very fortunate!

---

palace A large house for the king and his family.
Cabul This name is like the Hebrew word meaning "worthless."
9,000 pounds Or "4080kg." Literally, "120 talents."
Millo The Millo was probably a raised platform of land

Millo The Millo was probably a raised platform of land southeast of the temple area in Jerusalem.
31,500 pounds Or, "14,280kg." Literally, "420 talents."
wives This comes from the ancient Greek translation. The Hebrew has "men."

They can serve you and hear your wisdom every day! ⁹Praise the Lord your God! He was pleased to make you king of Israel. The Lord God loves Israel. So he made you the king. You follow the law and treat people fairly."
¹⁰Then the queen of Sheba gave the king about 9,000 pounds* of gold. She also gave him many spices and jewels. The queen of Sheba gave to Solomon more spices than anyone has ever brought into Israel.
¹¹Hiram's ships brought gold from Ophir. Those ships also brought very much wood* and jewels. ¹²Solomon used the wood to build supports in the temple and the palace. He also used the wood to make harps* and lyres* for the singers. No other person has ever brought that kind of wood ₍to Israel₎ and no person has seen that kind of wood since that time.
¹³Then King Solomon gave the queen of Sheba gifts that a king usually gives to a ruler from another country. Then he gave her anything else she asked for. After this, the queen and her servants went back to her own country.
¹⁴Every year King Solomon got about 79,920 pounds* of gold. ¹⁵Besides the gold from the cargo ships,* he also got gold from the traders and merchants,* and from the kings of Arabia and governors of the land.
¹⁶King Solomon made 200 large shields of hammered gold. Each shield contained about 15 pounds* of gold. ¹⁷He also made 300 smaller shields of hammered gold. Each shield contained about 4 pounds* of gold. The king put them in the building called the "Forest of Lebanon."
¹⁸King Solomon also built a large ivory throne. He covered it with pure gold. ¹⁹There were six steps leading up to the throne. The back of the throne was round at the top. There were armrests on both sides of the chair. And in the sides of the chair under the two armrests there were pictures of lions. ²⁰There were also two lions on each of the six steps. There was one lion at each end. There was nothing like this in any other kingdom.
²¹All of Solomon's cups and glasses were made of gold. And all of the weapons* in the building called the "Forest of Lebanon" were made from pure gold. Nothing in the palace was made from silver. ₍There was so much gold that₎ in Solomon's time people did not think silver was important!
²²The king also had many cargo ships* that he sent out to trade things with other countries. These were Hiram's ships. Every three years the ships would come back with a new load of gold, silver, ivory, and animals.
²³Solomon was the greatest king on earth. He had the most riches and wisdom of all kings. ²⁴People everywhere wanted to see King Solomon. They wanted to hear the great wisdom that God had given him. ²⁵Every year people came to see the king. And every person brought a gift. They brought things made from gold and silver, clothes, weapons, spices, horses, and mules.
²⁶So Solomon had many, many chariots and horses. He had 1,400 chariots* and 12,000 horses. Solomon built special cities for these chariots. So the chariots were kept in those cities. King Solomon also kept some of the chariots with him in Jerusalem. ²⁷The king made Israel very rich. In the city of Jerusalem, silver was as common as rocks and cedar wood was as common as the many, many fig trees growing on the hills. ²⁸Solomon brought horses from Egypt and Kue. His traders brought them in Kue and brought them to Israel. ²⁹A chariot* from Egypt cost about 15 pounds* of silver, and a horse cost about 3 3/4 pounds* of silver. Solomon sold horses and chariots to the kings of the Hittites and the Arameans.

Solomon's and His Many Wives

11 King Solomon loved women! He loved many women that were not from the nation of Israel. These included the daughter of Pharaoh, Hittite women and women from Moab, Ammon, Edom, and Sidon. ²In the past, the Lord had said to the people of Israel, "You must not marry people from other nations. If you do, then those

---

9,000 pounds Or, "4,080kg." Literally, "120 talents."
wood This is a special kind of wood called "Almug." No one knows exactly what type of wood this was.
harps Musical instruments with several strings.
lyres Musical instruments that are like small harps.
79,920 pounds Or, "22,644kg." Literally, "666 talents."
cargo ships Literally, "ships of Tarshish."
traders and merchants Businessmen who make their living buying and selling things.
15 pounds Or, "6.9kg." Literally, "600 shekels."
4 pounds Or, "1.8kg." Literally, "3 minas."

weapons The Hebrew word can mean, "dishes, tools, or weapons."
cargo ships Literally, "ships of Tarshish."
chariot(s) Small wagons used in war.
15 pounds Or, "6.9kg." Literally, "600 shekels."
3 3/4 pounds Or, "1.725kg." Literally, "150 shekels."

people will cause you to follow their gods." But Solomon fell in love with these women. ³Solomon had 700 wives. (These women were all daughters of leaders from other nations.) He also had 300 slave women that were like wives to him. His wives caused him to turn away from God. ⁴When Solomon was old, his wives caused him to follow other gods. Solomon did not follow the Lord completely the way that his father David had done. ⁵Solomon worshiped Ashtoreth.* This was the god of the people of Sidon. And Solomon worshiped Milcom.* This was that horrible idol of the Ammonite people. ⁶So Solomon did wrong before the Lord. Solomon did not follow the Lord completely the way his father David had done.

⁷Solomon built a place for worshiping Chemosh. Chemosh was that horrible idol of the Moabite people. Solomon built that worship place on a hill next to Jerusalem. On that same hill, Solomon built a worship place for Molech. Molech was that horrible idol of the Ammonite people. ⁸Then Solomon did the same thing for all of his wives from other countries. His wives burned incense* and gave sacrifices to their gods.

⁹Solomon turned away from following the Lord, the God of Israel. So the Lord became angry at Solomon. The Lord had come to Solomon twice. ¹⁰The Lord told Solomon that he must not follow other gods. But Solomon did not obey the Lord's command. ¹¹So the Lord said to Solomon, "You have chosen to break your agreement with me. You have not obeyed my commands. So I promise that I will tear your kingdom away from you. I will give it to one of your servants. ¹²But I loved your father David. So I will not take your kingdom away from you while you are living. I will wait until your son becomes king. Then I will take it from him. ¹³Still, I will not tear away all of the kingdom from your son. I will leave him one family group to rule. I will do this for David. He was a good servant. And I will also do this for Jerusalem. I chose that city!"

Solomon's Enemies

¹⁴At that time, the Lord caused Hadad the Edomite to become Solomon's enemy. Hadad was from the family of the king of Edom. ¹⁵This is how it happened: Earlier David defeated Edom. Joab was the commander of David's army. Joab went into Edom to bury dead people. Joab killed all the men still living there. ¹⁶Joab and all Israel stayed in Edom for six months. During that time they killed all the men of Edom. ¹⁷But at that time Hadad was only a young boy. So Hadad ran away to Egypt. Some of his father's servants went with him. ¹⁸They left Midian and went to Paran. In Paran some other people joined them. Then the whole group went to Egypt. They went to Pharaoh the king of Egypt and asked for help. Pharaoh gave Hadad a house and some land. Pharaoh also supported him and gave him food to eat.

¹⁹Pharaoh liked Hadad very much. Pharaoh gave Hadad a wife. The woman was Pharaoh's sister-in-law. (Pharaoh's wife was queen Tahpenes.) ²⁰So the sister of Tahpenes married Hadad. They had a son named Genubath. Queen Tahpenes allowed Genubath to grow up in Pharaoh's house with his children.

²¹In Egypt, Hadad heard that David had died. He also heard that Joab, the commander of the army was dead. So Hadad said to Pharaoh, "Let me go home to my own country."

²²But Pharaoh answered, "I have given you everything you need here! Why do you want to go back to your own country?"

Hadad answered, "Please, just let me go home."

²³God also caused another man to be an enemy against Solomon. This man was Rezon, son of Eliada. Rezon ran away from his master. His master was Hadadezer, king of Zobah. ²⁴After David defeated the army of Zobah, Rezon gathered some men and became the leader of a small army. Rezon went to Damascus and stayed there. Rezon became king of Damascus. ²⁵Rezon ruled Aram. Rezon hated Israel, so he continued to be an enemy of Israel all of the time that Solomon lived. Rezon and Hadad caused much trouble for Israel.

²⁶Jeroboam son of Nebat was one of Solomon's servants. Jeroboam was from the family group of Ephraim. He was from the town of Zeredah. Jeroboam's mother was named Zeruah. His father was dead. He turned against the king.

²⁷This is the story of why Jeroboam turned against the king. Solomon was building the Millo* and fixing the wall of the city of David his father. ²⁸Jeroboam was a strong man. Solomon saw that this young man was a good worker. So Solomon made him the boss over all of the

---

Ashtoreth The Canaanite people thought that this false goddess could make people able to have babies. She was their goddess of love and war.

Milcom The god of the Ammonite people.

incense Special dried tree sap. Burned to make a sweet-smelling smoke, it was offered as a gift to God.

workers from the family group of Joseph.* ²⁹One day Jeroboam was traveling out of Jerusalem. Ahijah the prophet from Shiloh met him on the road. Ahijah was wearing a new coat. These two men were alone in the country. ³⁰Ahijah took his new coat and tore it into twelve pieces.

³¹Then Ahijah said to Jeroboam, "Take ten pieces of this coat for yourself. The Lord the God of Israel says: 'I will tear the kingdom away from Solomon, and I will give you ten of the family groups. ³²And I will allow David's family to control only one family group. I will let them keep this group. I will do this for my servant David and for Jerusalem. Jerusalem is the city which I chose from all the family groups of Israel. ³³I will take the kingdom from Solomon because he stopped following me. He worships Ashtoreth the false goddess of Sidon. He worships Chemosh, the false god of Moab And he worships Milcom, the false god of the Ammonites. Solomon stopped doing the things that are right and good. He does not obey my laws and my commands. He is not living the way that his father David lived. ³⁴So I will take the kingdom away from Solomon's family. But I will let Solomon be their ruler for the rest of his life. I will do this for my servant David. I chose David because he obeyed all my commands and laws. ³⁵But I will take the kingdom away from his son. And Jeroboam, I will allow you to rule over the ten family groups. ³⁶I will allow Solomon's son to continue to rule over one family group. I will do this so that my servant David will always have a descendant to rule before me in Jerusalem, the city that I chose to be my own. ³⁷But I will make you rule over everything you want. You will rule over all of Israel. ³⁸I will do these things for you if you will live right and obey all my commands. If you obey the laws and commands like David, then I will be with you. I will make your family a family of kings, like I did for David. I will give Israel to you. ³⁹I will punish David's children because of ₍the things Solomon did₎. But I will not punish them forever.'"

Solomon's Death

⁴⁰Solomon tried to kill Jeroboam. But Jeroboam ran away to Egypt. He went to Shishak the king of Egypt. Jeroboam stayed there until Solomon died.

⁴¹Solomon did many great and wise things while he ruled. All of these things are written in the book *The History of Solomon*. ⁴²Solomon ruled in Jerusalem over all Israel for 40 years. ⁴³Then Solomon died and was buried with his ancestors.* He was buried in the city of David, his father. Then Solomon's son, Rehoboam, became the next king after him.

Civil War

12 ¹⁻²Jeroboam son of Nebat was still in Egypt where he had run away from Solomon. When he heard about Solomon's death, he returned to his city, Zeredah, in the hills of Ephraim.

King Solomon died and was buried with his ancestors.* After that, his son Rehoboam became the new king. ³All of the people of Israel went to Shechem. They went to make Rehoboam the king. Rehoboam also went to Shechem to become king. The people said to Rehoboam, ⁴"Your father forced us to work very hard. Now, make it easier for us. Stop the heavy work that your father forced us to do. Then we will serve you."

⁵Rehoboam answered, "Come back to me in three days and I will answer you." So the people left.

⁶There were some older men who had helped Solomon make decisions when he was alive. So King Rehoboam asked these men what he should do. He said, "How do you think I should answer these people?"

⁷The elders answered, "If you are like a servant to them today, then they will truly serve you. If you speak kindly to them, then they will work for you always."

⁸But Rehoboam did not listen to this advice. He asked the young men that were his friends. ⁹Rehoboam said, "The people said, 'Give us easier work than your father gave us.' How do you think I should answer these people? What should I tell them?"

¹⁰The king's young friends said, "Those people came to you and said, 'Your father forced us to work very hard. Now make our work easier.' So you should ₍brag and₎ tell them, 'My little finger is stronger than my father's whole body. ¹¹My father forced you to work hard. But I will make you work much harder! My father used whips to force you to work. I will beat you so hard that you will think scorpions* have stung you!'"

---

family group of Joseph The people from the family groups of Ephraim and Manasseh, Joseph's sons.

died and was buried with his ancestors Literally, "slept with his ancestors."

¹²Rehoboam had told the people, "Come back to me in three days." So after three days all the people of Israel came back to Rehoboam. ¹³At that time, King Rehoboam spoke hard words to them. He did not listen to the advice from the elders. ¹⁴He did what his friends told him to do. Rehoboam said, "My father forced you to work hard. So I will give you even more work. My father beat you with whips. But I will beat you so hard that you will think scorpions* have stung you!" ¹⁵So the king did not do what the people wanted. The Lord caused this to happen. The Lord did this in order to keep the promise he made to Jeroboam son of Nebat. The Lord used Ahijah the prophet to make this promise. Ahijah was from Shiloh.

¹⁶All the people of Israel saw that the new king refused to listen to them. So the people said to the king: "Are we part of David's family? No! Do we get any of Jesse's land? No! So Israel, let's go to our own homes. Let David's son rule his own people!" So the people of Israel went home. ¹⁷But Rehoboam still ruled over the Israelites who lived in the cities of Judah.

¹⁸A man named Adoniram was the boss over all the workers. King Rehoboam sent Adoniram ⌊to talk to the people⌋. But the people of Israel threw stones at him until he died. Then King Rehoboam ran to his chariot* and escaped to Jerusalem. ¹⁹So Israel rebelled *(turned against)* the family of David. And they are still against David's family today.

²⁰All the people of Israel heard that Jeroboam had come back. So they called him to a meeting and made him king over all of Israel. The family group of Judah was the only family group that continued to follow the family of David.

²¹Rehoboam went back to Jerusalem. He gathered together the families of Judah and the family group of Benjamin. This was an army of 180,000 men. Rehoboam wanted to fight against the people of Israel. He wanted to take his kingdom back.

²²But the Lord spoke to a man of God.* His name was Shemaiah. The Lord said, ²³"Talk to Rehoboam, the son of Solomon, king of Judah, and also to all the people of Judah and Benjamin. ²⁴Say to them, 'The Lord says that you must not go to war against your brothers. Every one of you should go home. I made all these things happen!'" So the men in Rehoboam's army obeyed the Lord's command. They all went home.

²⁵Shechem was a city in the hill country of Ephraim. Jeroboam made Shechem a very strong city and lived there. Later he went to the city of Penuel* and made it stronger.

²⁶⁻²⁷Jeroboam said to himself, "If the people continue going to the Lord's temple in Jerusalem, then they will want to be ruled by David's family. The people will follow Rehoboam, king of Judah again. Then they will kill me. ²⁸So the king asked his advisers what he should do. ⌊They gave him their advice.⌋ So Jeroboam made two golden calves. King Jeroboam said to the people, "You should not go to Jerusalem to worship. Israel, these are the gods that brought you out of Egypt."* ²⁹King Jeroboam put one golden calf in Bethel.* He put the other golden calf in the city of Dan.* ³⁰But this was a very great sin. The people of Israel traveled to the cities of Bethel and Dan to worship the calves. But this was a very great sin.

³¹Jeroboam also built temples at the high places.* He also chose priests from among the different family groups of Israel. (He did not choose priests only from the family group of Levi.) ³²And King Jeroboam started a new holiday. This holiday was like the ⌊Passover⌋ Festival in Judah. But this holiday was on the 15th day of the eighth month ⌊not the 15th day of the first month⌋. During that time the king offered sacrifices on the altar in the city of Bethel. And he made the sacrifices to the calves that he had made. King Jeroboam also chose priests in Bethel to serve at the high places* that he made. ³³So King Jeroboam chose his own time for a holiday for the Israelites. It was the 15th day of the eighth month. During that time he offered sacrifices and burned incense* on the altar that he built. This was in the city of Bethel.

---

man of God Another name for a prophet.
Penuel Or "Peniel."
Israel, these are the gods that brought you out of Egypt This is exactly the same thing that Aaron said at the time he made the golden calf in the desert. See Ex. 32:4.
Bethel, Dan Bethel was a city in the south part of Israel, near Judah. Dan was in the north part of Israel.
high places Places for worshiping God or false gods. These places were often on the hills and mountains.

---

scorpion(s) An insect with a stinger in its tail. A scorpion sting hurts very much.
chariot(s) A small wagon used in war.

God Speaks Against Bethel

13 The Lord commanded a man of God* from Judah to go to the city of Bethel. King Jeroboam was standing at the altar offering incense when the man of God arrived. ²The Lord had commanded the man of God to speak against the altar. He said,

"Altar, the Lord says to you: 'David's family will have a son named Josiah. These priests are now worshiping at the high places.* But altar, Josiah will put those priests on you and he will kill them. Now those priests burn incense upon you. But Josiah will burn human bones on you. Then you can't be used again!'"

³The man of God gave proof to the people that these things would happen. He said, "This is proof that the Lord told me about. The Lord said, 'This altar will break apart. And the ashes on it will fall onto the ground.'"

⁴King Jeroboam heard the message from the man of God* about the altar in Bethel. He took his hand off of the altar and pointed at the man. He said, "Arrest that man!" But when the king said this, his arm became paralyzed. He could not move it. ⁵Also, the altar broke into pieces. All its ashes fell onto the ground. This was the proof that the things the man of God said were from God. ⁶Then King Jeroboam said to the man of God, "Please pray to the Lord your God for me. Ask the Lord to heal my arm."

So the man of God* prayed to the Lord. And the king's arm was healed. It became like it was before. ⁷Then the king said to the man of God, "Please come home with me. Come and eat with me. I will give you a gift."

⁸But the man of God* said to the king, "I will not go home with you, even if you give me half of your kingdom! I will not eat or drink anything in this place. ⁹The Lord commanded me not to eat or drink anything. The Lord also commanded me not to travel on the same road that I used when I came here." ¹⁰So he traveled on a different road. He did not travel on the same road that he used when he came to Bethel.

¹¹There was an old prophet* living in the city of Bethel. His sons came and told him about what the man of God* did in Bethel. They told their father what the man of God had said to King Jeroboam. ¹²The old prophet said, "Which road did he use when he left?" So the sons showed their father which way the man of God from Judah had taken. ¹³The old prophet told his sons to put a saddle on his donkey. So they put the saddle on the donkey. Then the prophet left on his donkey.

¹⁴The old prophet went after the man of God.* The old prophet found the man of God sitting under an oak tree. The old prophet asked, "Are you the man of God who came from Judah?"

The man of God answered, "Yes, I am."

¹⁵So the old prophet said, "Please come home and eat with me."

¹⁶But the man of God* answered, "I can't go home with you. I can't eat or drink with you in this place. ¹⁷The Lord said to me, 'You must not eat or drink anything in that place. And you must not go back on the same road you came on.'"

¹⁸Then the old prophet said, "But I am also a prophet like you." Then the old prophet told a lie. He said, "An angel from the Lord came to me. The angel told me to bring you to my home and allow you to eat and drink with me."

¹⁹So the man of God* went to the old prophet's house and ate and drank with him. ²⁰While they were sitting at the table, the Lord spoke to the old prophet. ²¹And the old prophet spoke to the man of God from Judah. He said, "The Lord said that you did not obey him! You did not do the thing the Lord commanded. ²²The Lord commanded you not to eat or drink anything in this place. But you came back and ate and drank. So your body will not be buried in your family grave."

²³The man of God* finished eating and drinking. Then the old prophet put the saddle on the donkey for him and the man left. ²⁴On the road traveling home, a lion attacked and killed the man of God. The prophet's body was lying on the road. The donkey and the lion stood near the body. ²⁵Some other men were traveling on that road. They saw the body and the lion standing near the body. The men came to the city where the old prophet lived and told about what they had seen on the road.

²⁶The old prophet had ⌊tricked the man and⌋ brought him back. He heard about what happened and he said, "That is the man of God* who did not obey the Lord's command. So the Lord sent a lion

---

high places Places for worshiping God or false gods. These places were often on the hills and mountains.
incense Special dried tree sap. Burned to make a sweet-smelling smoke, it was offered as a gift to God.
man of God Another name for a prophet.

prophet A person called by God to be a special servant. God used dreams and visions to show them things to teach to the people.

to kill him. The Lord said that he would do this." ²⁷Then the prophet said to his sons, "Put a saddle on my donkey." So his sons put a saddle on his donkey. ²⁸The old prophet went and found the body lying on the road. The donkey and the lion were still standing near it. The lion had not eaten the body, and it did not hurt the donkey.

²⁹The old prophet put the body on his donkey. He carried the body back to the city to cry for him and bury him. ³⁰The old prophet buried the man in his own family grave. The old prophet cried for him. The old prophet said, "Oh, my brother, I am sorry for you." ³¹So the old prophet buried the body. Then he said to his sons, "When I die, bury me in this same grave. Put my bones next to his. ³²The things which the Lord spoke through him will certainly come true. The Lord used him to speak against the altar at Bethel and against the high places* in the other towns in Samaria."

³³King Jeroboam did not change. He continued doing evil things. He continued to choose people from different family groups to become priests.* Those priests served at the high places.* Any person who wanted to be a priest was allowed to become a priest. ³⁴That was the sin that caused the destruction and ruin of his kingdom.

Jeroboam's Son Dies

14 At that time, Jeroboam's son, Abijah, became very sick. ²Jeroboam said to his wife, "Go to Shiloh. Go see the prophet Ahijah. Ahijah is the man that said that I would become king of Israel. Dress yourself so people won't know that you are my wife. ³Give the prophet ten loaves of bread, some cakes, and a jar of honey. Then ask him what will happen to our son. The prophet Ahijah will tell you."

⁴So the king's wife did what he said. She went to Shiloh. She went to the home of Ahijah the prophet. Ahijah was very old and had become blind. ⁵But the Lord said to him, "Jeroboam's wife is coming to ask you about her son. He is sick." The Lord told Ahijah what he should say.

Jeroboam's wife came to Ahijah's house. She was trying to not let people know who she was. ⁶Ahijah heard her coming to the door. So Ahijah said, "Come in, Jeroboam's wife. Why are you trying to make people think you are someone else? I have some bad news for you. ⁷Go back and tell Jeroboam that this is what the Lord, the God of Israel, says. The Lord says, 'Jeroboam, I chose you from among all the people of Israel. I made you the ruler of my people. ⁸David's family was ruling the kingdom of Israel. But I took the kingdom away from them and I gave it to you. But you are not like my servant David. He always obeyed my commands. He followed me with his whole heart. He did only the things that I accepted. ⁹But you have done many great sins. Your sins are much worse than the sins of any person that ruled before you. You have quit following me. You made idols and other gods. This has made me very angry. ¹⁰So, Jeroboam, I will bring troubles to your family. I will kill all of the men in your family. I will destroy your family completely, like fire completely destroys dung. ¹¹Any person from your family that dies in the city will be eaten by dogs. And any person from your family that dies in the fields will be eaten by birds. The Lord has spoken.'"

¹²Then the prophet Ahijah continued talking to Jeroboam's wife. He said, "Now go home. As soon as you enter your city, your son will die. ¹³All Israel will cry for him and bury him. Your son will be the only person in Jeroboam's family that will be buried. This is because he is the only one in Jeroboam's family that pleased the Lord God of Israel. ¹⁴The Lord will put a new king over Israel. That new king will destroy Jeroboam's family. This will happen very soon. ¹⁵Then the Lord will hit Israel. The people of Israel will be very scared—they will shake like tall grass in the water. The Lord will pull up Israel from this good land. This is the land that he gave their ancestors. He will scatter them on the other side of the Euphrates River. This will happen because the Lord is angry with the people. The people made him angry when they made special poles to worship Asherah.* ¹⁶Jeroboam sinned. And then Jeroboam made the people of Israel sin. So the Lord will let the people of Israel be defeated."

¹⁷Jeroboam's wife went back to Tirzah. As soon as she walked into the house, the boy died. ¹⁸All Israel buried him and cried for him. This happened exactly the way the Lord said it would. The Lord used his servant, the prophet Ahijah, to say these things.

---

man of God Another name for a prophet.
high places Places for worshiping God or false gods. These places were often on the hills and mountains.
people ... become priests The Law taught that only people from the family group of Levi could become priests.

Asherah An important Canaanite goddess. At this time, the people thought she was the wife of Baal.

¹⁹King Jeroboam did many other things. He fought wars and continued to rule the people. All the things he did are written in the book *The History of the Kings of Israel*. ²⁰Jeroboam ruled as king for 22 years. Then he died and was buried with his ancestors.* His son Nadab became the new king after him.

²¹At the time that Solomon's son, Rehoboam, became king of Judah, he was 41 years old. Rehoboam ruled in the city of Jerusalem for 17 years. This is the city in which the Lord chose to be honored. He chose this city from all the other cities of Israel. Rehoboam's mother was Naamah. She was an Ammonite. ²²The people of Judah also sinned ₍and did₎ things that the Lord said were wrong. The people did more things to make the Lord angry at them. These people were worse than their fathers that lived before them. ²³The people built high places, stone memorials, and sacred poles.* They built them on every high hill and under every green tree. ²⁴There were men who served other gods by selling their bodies for sex.* So the people of Judah did many bad things. The people that had lived in the land before them did those same evil things. And God took the land away from those people and gave it to the people of Israel.

²⁵During the fifth year that Rehoboam was king, King Shishak of Egypt fought against Jerusalem. ²⁶Shishak took the treasures from the Lord's temple and from the king's palace. He even took the gold shields that David had taken from the officers of Hadadezer, king of Aram. David had taken these shields to Jerusalem. But Shishak took all the gold shields. ²⁷So king Rehoboam made more shields to put in their places. But these shields were made from bronze, ₍not gold₎. He gave the shields to the men who were guarding the palace gates. ²⁸Every time the king went to the Lord's temple, the guards went with him. They carried the shields. After they were finished, they put the shields back on the wall in the guard room.

²⁹All the things that king Rehoboam did are written in the book *The History of the Kings of Judah*. ³⁰Rehoboam and Jeroboam were always fighting a war against each other.

³¹Rehoboam died and was buried with his ancestors.* He was buried with his ancestors in the City of David.* (His mother was Naamah. She was an Ammonite.) Rehoboam's son, Abijah became the next king after him.

Abijah, King of Judah

15 Abijah became the new king of Judah. This was during the 18th year that Jeroboam son of Nebat ruled Israel. ²Abijah ruled in Jerusalem for three years. His mother's name was Maacah. She was Absalom's daughter.

³He did all the same sins that his father before him had done. Abijah was not faithful to the Lord his God. In this way, he was not like his grandfather, David. ⁴₍The Lord loved David.₎ So for him, the Lord gave Abijah a kingdom in Jerusalem. And the Lord allowed him to have a son. The Lord also allowed Jerusalem to be safe. He did this for David. ⁵David had always done the right things that the Lord wanted. He had always obeyed the Lord's commands. The only time David did not obey the Lord was the time David sinned against Uriah the Hittite.

⁶Rehoboam and Jeroboam were always fighting a war against each other.* ⁷Everything else that Abijah did are written in the book *The History of the Kings of Judah*.

There was war between Abijah and Jeroboam during the whole time that Abijah was king. ⁸When Abijah died he was buried in the City of David.* Abijah's son Asa became the new king after him.

Asa, King of Judah

⁹During Jeroboam's 20th year as king over Israel, Asa became king of Judah. ¹⁰Asa ruled in Jerusalem for 41 years. His grandmother's name was Maacah. And Maacah was the daughter of Absalom.

¹¹Asa did the good things that the Lord said are right, like his ancestor* David did. ¹²During that time there were men who served other gods by selling their bodies for sex. Asa forced those men to leave the country. Asa also took away the idols

---

died ... ancestors Literally, "slept with his ancestors."
high places, stone memorials, sacred poles People used these things to worship false gods.
men who served other gods by selling their bodies for sex Sexual sins like this were a part of the way people worshiped the Canaanite gods.

City of David The southeast and oldest part of the city of Jerusalem.
Rehoboam and Jeroboam were always fighting a war against each other This verse is not in the ancient Greek translation.

that his ancestors had made. ¹³Asa also removed his grandmother, Maacah, from being queen. Maacah had made one of those terrible images of the goddess Asherah. Asa cut down this terrible image. He burned it in Kidron Valley. ¹⁴Asa did not destroy the high places,* but he was faithful to the Lord all his life. ¹⁵Asa and his father had given some things to God. They gave gifts of gold, silver, and other things. Asa put all those things in the temple.

¹⁶During the time that king Asa was king of Judah, he was always fighting against Baasha, the king of Israel. ¹⁷Baasha fought against Judah. Baasha wanted to stop people from going into or coming out of Asa's country of Judah. So He made the city Ramah very strong. ¹⁸So Asa took silver and gold from the treasuries of the Lord's temple and the king's palace. He gave the silver and gold to his servants and sent them to Ben Hadad, the king of Aram. Ben Hadad was the son of Tabrimmon. Tabrimmon was the son of Hezion. Damascus was Ben Hadad's capital city. ¹⁹Asa sent this message, "My father and your father had a peace agreement. Now I want to make a peace agreement with you. I am sending you this gift of gold and silver. Please break your treaty with Baasah the king of Israel so he will get out of my country and leave us alone."

²⁰King Ben Hadad made that agreement with king Asa and sent his army to fight against the Israelite towns of Ijon, Dan, Abel Beth Maacah, the towns near Lake Galilee, and the area of Naphtali. ²¹Baasha heard about these attacks. So he stopped building Ramah stronger. He left that town and moved back to Tirzah. ²²Then king Asa gave an order to all of the people of Judah. Every person had to help. They went to Ramah and took all the stones and wood that Baasha was using to make that city strong. They carried those things to Geba in the land of Benjamin and to Mizpah. Then King Asa built those two towns much stronger.

²³All the other things about Asa, the great things he did, and the cities he built are written in the book *The History of the Kings of Judah*. When Asa became old, he had a disease on his feet. ²⁴Asa died and he was buried in the City of David,* his ancestor. Then Jehoshaphat, Asa's son, became the new king after him.

Nadab, King of Israel

²⁵During Asa's second year as king of Judah, Nadab, son of Jeroboam, became king of Israel. Nadab ruled over Israel for two years. ²⁶Nadab did bad things against the Lord. He sinned the same way his father Jeroboam had sinned. And Jeroboam also caused the people of Israel to sin. ²⁷Baasha was the son of Ahijah. They were from the family group of Issachar. Baasha made a plan to kill King Nadab. This was during the time that Nadab and all Israel were fighting against the town of Gibbethon. This was a Philistine town. At that place Baasha killed Nadab. ²⁸This happened during the third year that Asa was the king of Judah. And Baasha became the next king of Israel.

Baasha, King of Israel

²⁹At the time Baasha became the new king, he killed everyone in Jeroboam's family. Baasha left no person in Jeroboam's family alive. This happened the way the Lord said it would. The Lord spoke through his servant Ahijah from Shiloh. ³⁰This happened because King Jeroboam had done many sins. And Jeroboam had caused the people of Israel to do many sins. Jeroboam made the Lord, the God of Israel, very angry.

³¹The other things that Nadab did are written in the book *The History of the Kings of Israel*. ³²All during the time that Baasha ruled over Israel, he was fighting wars against Asa, king of Judah.

³³Baasha, son of Ahijah, became king Israel during the third year that Asa ruled over Judah. Baasha ruled in Tirzah for 24 years. ³⁴But Baasha did the things that the Lord said were wrong. He did the same sins that his father Jeroboam had done. Jeroboam caused the people of Israel to sin.

16 Then the Lord spoke to Jehu son of Hanani. The Lord was speaking against King Baasha. ²"I made you an important person. I made you a prince over my people Israel. But you have followed the ways of Jeroboam. You have caused my people Israel to sin. They have made me angry with their sins. ³So I will destroy you, Baasha, and your family. I will do the same to you that I did to the family of Jeroboam son of Nebat. ⁴The people in your family will die in the streets of the city. And dogs will eat their bodies. Some of the

---

ancestor Literally, "fathers." This means a person's parents, grandparents, and all the people they are descended from.

high places Places for worshiping God or false gods. These places were often on the hills and mountains.

City of David The southeast and oldest part of the city of Jerusalem.

people in your family will die in the fields. And the birds will eat their bodies."

⁵All the other things about Baasha and the great things he did are written in the book *The History of the Kings of Israel*. ⁶Baasha died and was buried in Tirzah. His son Elah became the new king after him.

⁷So the Lord gave a message to Jehu the prophet. This message was against Baasha and his family. Baasha had done much evil against the Lord. This made the Lord very angry. Baasha did the same things that Jeroboam's family had done before him. The Lord was also angry because Baasha killed all of Jeroboam's family.

Elah, King of Israel

⁸Elah became king during the 26th year that Asa was the king of Judah. Elah was the son of Baasha. He ruled in Tirzah for two years.

⁹Zimri was one of King Elah's officers. Zimri commanded half of Elah's chariots.* But Zimri made plans against Elah.

King Elah was in Tirzah. He was drinking and getting drunk at Arza's home. Arza was the man in charge of the palace* at Tirzah. ¹⁰Zimri went into that house and killed King Elah. This was during the 27th year that Asa was king in Judah. Then Zimri became the new king of Israel after Elah.

Zimri, King of Israel

¹¹After Zimri became the new king, he killed all of Baasha's family. He did not let any of the men in Baasha's family live. Zimri also killed Baasha's friends. ¹²So Zimri destroyed Baasha's family. This happened the way the Lord said it would when the Lord used the prophet Jehu to speak against Baasha. ¹³This happened because of all the sins of Baasha and his son, Elah. They sinned and caused the people of Israel to sin. The Lord was angry because they had many idols.

¹⁴The other things that Elah did are written in the book *The History of the Kings of Israel*.

¹⁵Zimri became king of Israel during the 27th year that Asa was king of Judah. Zimri ruled in Tirzah seven days. This is what happened: The army of Israel was camped near the Philistines from Gibbethon. ₍They were prepared for war.₎ ¹⁶The men in the camp heard that Zimri had made secret plans against the king. They heard that he killed the king. So all Israel made Omri king over Israel that day in the camp. Omri was the commander of the army. ¹⁷So Omri and all Israel left Gibbethon and attacked Tirzah. ¹⁸Zimri saw that the city had been captured. So he went into the palace* and started a fire. He burned the palace and himself. ¹⁹So Zimri died because he had sinned. Zimri did the things the Lord said were wrong. He sinned in the same way that Jeroboam had sinned. And Jeroboam caused the people of Israel to sin.

²⁰The story about Zimri's secret plans and the other things that Zimri did are written in the book *The History of the Kings of Israel*. And the things that happened when Zimri turned against King Elah are also written in that book.

Omri, King of Israel

²¹The people of Israel were divided into two groups. Half of the people followed Tibni the son of Ginath and wanted to make him king. The other half of the people followed Omri. ²²But Omri's followers were stronger than the followers of Tibni son of Ginath. So Tibni was killed and Omri became king.

²³During the 31st year that Asa was the king of Judah, Omri became king of Israel. Omri ruled over Israel for 12 years. Six of those years he ruled in the town of Tirzah. ²⁴But Omri bought the hill of Samaria. He bought it from Shemer for about 150 pounds* of silver. Omri built a city on that hill. He called the city Samaria after the name of its owner, Shemer.

²⁵Omri did the things that the Lord said were wrong. Omri was worse than all the kings that were before him. ²⁶He did all the same sins that Jeroboam son of Nebat did. Jeroboam caused the people of Israel to sin. So they made the Lord, the God of Israel, very angry. The Lord was angry because they worshiped worthless idols.

²⁷The other things about Omri and the great things he did are written in the book *The History of the Kings of Israel*. ²⁸Omri died and was buried in Samaria. His son Ahab became the new king after him.

Ahab, King of Israel

²⁹Ahab son of Omri became king of Israel during the 38th year that Asa was king of Judah. Ahab ruled Israel in the town of Samaria for 22 years. ³⁰Ahab did the things that the Lord said

---

chariot(s) A small wagon used in war.
palace A large house for the king and his family.

150 pounds Or, "68kg." Literally, "2 talents."

were wrong. And Ahab was worse than all the kings that were before him. ³¹It was not enough for Ahab to do the same sins that Jeroboam son of Nebat had done. So Ahab also married Jezebel daughter of Ethbaal. Ethbaal was the king of the people of Sidon. Then Ahab began to serve and worship Baal.* ³²Ahab built a temple in Samaria for worshiping Baal. He put an altar in that temple. ³³Ahab also set up a special pole for worshiping Asherah.* Ahab did more things to make the Lord the God of Israel angry than all the other kings who were before him.

³⁴During the time of Ahab, Hiel from Bethel built the town of Jericho again. At the time Hiel started work on the city, his oldest son, Abiram died. And when Hiel built the gates of the city, his youngest son, Segub, died. This happened the way that the Lord said it would happen when he spoke through Joshua son of Nun.*

Elijah and The Time Without Rain

17 Elijah was a prophet from the town of Tishbe in Gilead. Elijah said to King Ahab, "I serve the Lord God of Israel. By his power, I promise that no dew or rain will fall during the next few years. The rain will fall only if I command it to fall."

²Then the Lord said to Elijah, ³"Leave this place and go east. Hide near Kerith Ravine. This ravine is east of the Jordan River. ⁴You can drink from that stream. I have commanded ravens* to bring food to you in that place." ⁵So Elijah did what the Lord told him to do. He went to live near Kerith Ravine, east of the Jordan River. ⁶Ravens brought Elijah food every morning and every evening. Elijah drank water from that stream.

⁷There was no rain, so after a time the stream became dry. ⁸Then the Lord said to Elijah, ⁹"Go to Zarephath in Sidon. Live there. There is a woman whose husband is dead that lives in that place. I have commanded her to give you food."

¹⁰So Elijah went to Zarephath. He went to the town gate and saw a woman there. Her husband was dead. The woman was gathering wood for a fire. Elijah said to her, "Will you bring me a little water in a cup so I can drink?" ¹¹The woman was going to get his water, and Elijah said, "Bring me a piece of bread too, please."

¹²The woman answered, "I promise you before the Lord your God that I have no bread. I have only a little flour in a jar. And I have only a little olive oil in a jug. I came to this place to gather a couple of pieces of wood for a fire. I will take it back home and cook our last meal. My son and I will eat it and then die from hunger."

¹³Elijah said to the woman, "Don't worry. Go home and cook your food as you said. But first make a small loaf of bread from the flour that you have. Bring that bread to me. Then cook for yourself and your son. ¹⁴The Lord God of Israel says, 'That jar of flour will never become empty. The jug will always have oil in it. This will continue until the day the Lord sends rain to the land.'"

¹⁵So the woman went to her home. She did what Elijah told her to do. Elijah, the woman, and her son had enough food for many days. ¹⁶The jar of flour and the jug of oil were never empty. This happened just like the Lord said it would. The Lord spoke through Elijah.

¹⁷Some time later the woman's son became sick. He became more and more sick. Finally the boy stopped breathing. ¹⁸And the woman said to Elijah, "You are a man of God.* Can you help me? Or did you come here only to cause me to remember all of my sins? Did you come here only to cause my son to die?"

¹⁹Elijah said to her, "Give your son to me." Elijah took the boy from her and carried him upstairs. He laid him on the bed in the room where he was staying. ²⁰Then Elijah prayed, "Lord my God. This widow* is letting me stay in her house. Will you do this bad thing to her? Will you cause her son to die?" ²¹Then Elijah lay on top of the boy three times. Elijah prayed, "Lord my God. Allow this boy to live again!"

²²The Lord answered Elijah's prayer. The boy began breathing again. He was alive! ²³Elijah carried the boy downstairs. Elijah gave the boy to his mother and said, "Look, your son is alive!"

²⁴The woman answered, "Now I know that you really are a man from God. I know that the Lord truly speaks through you!"

Baal Baal was the main god of Sidon. People thought he could make people have many children and good crops.
Asherah An important Canaanite goddess. At this time, the people thought she was the wife of Baal.
This happened ... Joshua son of Nun See Joshua 6:26.
ravens Black birds.

man of God Another name for a prophet.
widow A woman whose husband has died.

Elijah and the Prophets of Baal

18 During the third year that no rain fell, the Lord said to Elijah, "Go and meet with King Ahab. I will soon send rain." ²So Elijah went to meet Ahab.

At that time, there was no food in Samaria. ³So King Ahab told Obadiah to come to him. Obadiah was the man in charge of the king's palace.* (Obadiah was a true follower of the Lord. ⁴One time Jezebel was killing all the Lord's prophets. So Obadiah took 100 prophets and hid them in two caves. Obadiah put 50 prophets in one cave and 50 prophets in another cave. Then Obadiah brought them food and water.) ⁵King Ahab said to Obadiah, "Come with me. We will look at every spring and every stream in the land. We will see if we can find enough grass to keep our horses and mules alive. Then we will not have to kill our animals." ⁶Each person chose the part of the country where they would go look for water. Then the two men went through the whole country. Ahab went in one direction by himself. Obadiah went in another direction by himself. ⁷While Obadiah was traveling, he met Elijah. Obadiah knew Elijah when he saw him. Obadiah bowed down before Elijah. He said, "Elijah? Is it really you, master?"

⁸Elijah answered, "Yes, it is me. Go and tell your master the king that I am here."

⁹Then Obadiah said, "If I tell Ahab that I know where you are, he will kill me! I have done nothing wrong to you! Why do you want me to die? ¹⁰As sure as the Lord your God lives, the king has been looking for you everywhere! He has sent people to every country to find you. If the ruler of a country said that you were not in his country, then Ahab forced the ruler to promise that you were not in his country. ¹¹Now you want me to go and tell him that you are here? ¹²If I go tell King Ahab that you are here, then the Lord might carry you to some other place. King Ahab will come here, and he will not be able to find you. Then he will kill me! I have followed the Lord since I was a boy. ¹³You heard what I did! Jezebel was killing the Lord's prophets, and I hid 100 prophets in caves. I put 50 prophets in one cave and 50 prophets in another cave. I brought them food and water. ¹⁴Now you want me to go and tell the king that you are here. The king will kill me!"

¹⁵Elijah answered, "As sure as the Lord All-Powerful lives, I promise that I will stand before the king today."

¹⁶So Obadiah went to King Ahab. He told him where Elijah was. King Ahab went to meet Elijah. ¹⁷When Ahab saw Elijah he said, "Is it you? You are the man that causes trouble in Israel!"

¹⁸Elijah answered, "I have not caused Israel trouble. You and your father's family caused all this trouble. You caused the trouble when you stopped obeying the Lord's commands and began following the false gods. ¹⁹Now, tell all Israel to meet me at Mount Carmel. Also bring to that place the 450 prophets of Baal.* And bring the 400 prophets of the false goddess Asherah.* Queen Jezebel supports those prophets."*

²⁰So Ahab called all the Israelites and those prophets to Mount Carmel. ²¹Elijah came to all the people. He said, "When will you people decide who to follow? If the Lord is the true God, then you should follow him. But if Baal is the true God, then you should follow him!"

The people said nothing. ²²So EliJah said, "I am the only prophet of the Lord here. I am alone. But there are 450 prophets of Baal.* ²³So bring two bulls. Let the prophets of Baal take one bull. Let them kill it and cut it into pieces. Then let them put the meat on the wood. But don't start the fire burning. Then I will do the same with the other bull. And I will not start the fire burning. ²⁴You prophets of Baal will pray to your god. And I will pray to the Lord. The god that answers the prayer and starts his wood burning is the true God."

All the people agreed that this was a good idea. ²⁵Then Elijah said to the prophets of Baal,* "There are many of you. So you go first. Choose a bull and prepare it. But don't start your fire."

²⁶So the prophets took the bull that was given to them. They prepared it. They prayed to Baal* until noon. They prayed, "Baal, please answer us!" But there was no sound. No one answered. The prophets danced around the altar that they had built. ⌊But the fire never started.⌋

²⁷At noon Elijah began to make fun of them. Elijah said, "If Baal is really a god, then maybe

---

palace A large house for the king and his family.

Baal The Canaanite people believed that this false god brought the rain and storms. They also thought that he made the land produce good crops.

Asherah An important Canaanite goddess. At this time, the people thought she was the wife of Baal.

Queen Jezebel supports those prophets Literally, "Those prophets eat at Jezebel's table."

you should pray louder! Maybe he is thinking! Or maybe he is busy! Or maybe he is traveling! He could be sleeping! Maybe you should pray louder and wake him!" ²⁸So the prophets prayed louder. They cut themselves with swords and spears. (This was the way they worshiped.) They cut themselves until the blood flowed over them. ²⁹The afternoon passed but the fire still had not started. The prophets continued to act wild* until the time came for the evening sacrifice. But nothing happened— there was no answer from Baal.* There was no voice. There was no one listening!

³⁰Then Elijah said to all the people, "Now, come to me." So all the people gathered around Elijah. The Lord's altar had been torn down. So Elijah fixed it. ³¹Elijah found twelve stones. There was one stone for each of the twelve family groups. These twelve family groups were named for the twelve sons of Jacob. Jacob was the man that the Lord had called Israel. ³²Elijah used these stones to fix the altar to honor the Lord. Elijah dug a small ditch around the altar. It was wide enough and deep enough to hold about 7 gallons* of water. ³³Then Elijah put the wood on the altar. He cut the bull into pieces. He laid the pieces on the wood. ³⁴Then Elijah said, "Fill four jars with water. Pour the water on the pieces of meat and on the wood." Then Elijah said, "Do it again." Then he said, "Do it a third time." ³⁵The water flowed off of the altar and filled the ditch.

³⁶It was time for the afternoon sacrifice. So the prophet Elijah went near the altar and prayed, "Lord, the God of Abraham, Isaac, and Jacob. I ask you now to prove that you are the God of Israel. And prove that I am your servant. Show these people that you commanded me to do all these things. ³⁷Lord, answer my prayer. Show these people that you, Lord, are God. Then the people will know that you are bringing them back to you."

³⁸So the Lord sent down fire. The fire burned the sacrifice, the wood, the stones, and the ground around the altar. The fire also dried up all the water in the ditch. ³⁹All the people saw this happen. The people bowed down on the ground and began saying, "The Lord is God! The Lord is God!"

⁴⁰Then Elijah said, "Get the prophets of Baal! Don't let any of them escape!" So the people captured all the prophets. Then Elijah led them down to Kishon Creek. At that place he killed all the prophets.

The Rain Comes Again

⁴¹Then Elijah said to King Ahab, "Now, go eat and drink. A heavy rain is coming. ⁴²So King Ahab went to eat. At the same time, Elijah climbed to the top of Mount Carmel. At the top of the mountain Elijah bent down. He put his head between his knees. ⁴³Then Elijah said to his servant, "Look toward the sea."

The servant went to the place where he could see the sea. Then the servant came back and said, "I saw nothing." Elijah told him to go and look again. This happened seven times. ⁴⁴The seventh time, the servant came back and said, "I saw a small cloud the size of a man's fist.* The cloud was coming from the sea."

Elijah told the servant, "Go to King Ahab and tell him to get his chariot* ready and go home now. If he doesn't leave now, the rain will stop him."

⁴⁵After a short time, the sky was covered with dark clouds. The wind began to blow, and a heavy rain began to fall. Ahab got in his chariot and started traveling back to Jezreel. ⁴⁶The power of the Lord came to Elijah. Elijah tightened his clothes around him ₍so he could run₎. Then Elijah ran ahead of King Ahab all the way to Jezreel.

Elijah at Mount Sinai

19 King Ahab told Jezebel all the things that Elijah did. Ahab told her how Elijah had killed all the prophets with a sword. ²So Jezebel sent a messenger to Elijah. Jezebel said, "I promise that before this same time tomorrow, I will kill you like you killed those prophets. If I don't succeed, then may the gods kill me."

³When Elijah heard this, he was afraid. So he ran away to save his life. He took his servant with him. They went to Beersheba, Judah. Elijah left his servant in Beersheba. ⁴Then Elijah walked for a whole day into the desert. Elijah sat down under a bush. He asked to die. Elijah said, "I have had

---

act wild Or, "prophesy." This form of the Hebrew word sometimes mean to "act wild," or "to lose control of yourself."

Baal The Canaanite people believed that this false god brought the rain and storms. They also thought that he made the land produce good crops.

7 gallons Or, "14.6 l." Literally, "2 seahs of seed."

fist A closed hand.

chariot(s) A small wagon used in war.

enough, Lord! Let me die. I am no better than my ancestors.*"

⁵Then Elijah lay down under the tree and slept. An angel came to Elijah and touched him. The angel said, "Get up! Eat!" ⁶Elijah saw very near him a cake baked over coals and a jar of water. Elijah ate and drank. Then he went back to sleep.

⁷Later the Lord's angel came to him again. The angel said, "Get up! Eat! If you don't, you will not be strong enough to make the long trip." ⁸So Elijah got up. He ate and drank. The food made Elijah strong enough to walk for 40 days and nights. He walked to Mount Horeb, the mountain of God. ⁹There Elijah went into a cave and stayed all night.

Then the Lord spoke to Elijah. The Lord said, "Elijah, why are you here?"

¹⁰Elijah answered, "Lord God All-Powerful, I have always served you. I have always served you the best that I can. But the people of Israel have broken their agreement with you. They destroyed your altars. They killed your prophets. I am the only prophet that is still living. And now they are trying to kill me!"

¹¹Then the Lord said to Elijah, "Go, stand in front of me on the mountain. I will pass by you."* Then a very strong wind blew. The wind caused the mountains to break apart. It broke large rocks in front of the Lord. But that wind was not the Lord! After that wind, there was an earthquake. But that earthquake was not the Lord. ¹²After the earthquake, there was a fire. But that fire was not the Lord. After the fire, there was a quiet, gentle voice.*

¹³When Elijah heard the voice* he used his coat to cover his face. Then he went and stood at the entrance to the cave. Then a voice said to him, "Elijah, why are you here?"

¹⁴Elijah said, "Lord God All-Powerful, I have always served you the best that I can. But the people of Israel broke their agreement with you. They destroyed your altars. They killed your prophets. I am the only prophet that is still living. And now they are trying to kill me."

¹⁵The Lord said, "Go back on the road that leads to the desert around Damascus. Go into Damascus, and anoint* Hazael as king over Aram.

¹⁶Then anoint Jehu son of Nimshi as king over Israel. Next, anoint Elisha son of Shaphat from Abel Meholah. He will be the prophet that takes your place. ¹⁷Hazael will kill many bad people. Jehu will kill anyone that escapes from Hazael's sword. And Elisha will kill anyone that escapes from Jehu's sword. ¹⁸Elijah, you are not the only faithful person in Israel. Those men will kill many people. But, even after that, there will still be 7,000 people living in Israel that never bowed down to Baal! I will let those 7,000 people live—and none of those people ever kissed a Baal idol.

Elisha Becomes a Prophet

¹⁹So Elijah left that place and went to find Elisha son of Shaphat. Elisha was plowing 12 acres of land. Elisha was working on the last acre when Elijah came. Elijah went to Elisha. Then Elijah put his coat* on Elisha. ²⁰Elisha immediately left his cows and ran after Elijah. Elisha said, "Let me kiss my mother and father goodbye. Then I will follow you."

Elijah answered, "That is fine. Go. I won't stop you.*"

²¹Then Elisha had a special meal with his family. Elisha went and killed his cows. He used the yoke* for firewood. Then he boiled the meat. Then he gave it to the people and they ate the meat. Then Elisha began following Elijah. Elisha became Elijah's helper.

Ben Hadad and Ahab Go To War

20 Ben Hadad was king of Aram. He gathered together all of his army. There were 32 kings with him. They had horses and chariots.* They attacked Samaria and fought against it. ²The king sent messengers into the city to King Ahab of Israel. ³This was the message, "Ben Hadad says, 'You must give me your silver and gold. You must also give me your wives and children.'"

⁴The king of Israel answered, "King, my master. I agree that I belong to you now. And everything I have belongs to you."

---

anoint(ed) To pour olive oil on a person's head to show he was chosen by God to be a king, priest, or prophet.

coat This was a special robe that showed that Elijah was a prophet. Giving this coat to Elisha showed that Elisha was taking Elijah's place as a prophet.

I won't stop you Literally, "What have I done to you?" or "What will I do to you?"

yoke A piece of wood that was put over an animal's neck so it could pull a plow or wagon.

---

ancestors Literally, "fathers." This means a person's parents, grandparents, and all the people they are descended from.

Go, stand ... you This is like the time God appeared to Moses. See Ex. 33:12-23.

voice Or, "sound."

⁵Then the messengers came back to Ahab. They said, "Ben Hadad says, 'I told you before that you must give me all of your silver and gold and your wives and children. ⁶Tomorrow I am sending my men to search through your house and through the houses of your officials. You should give my men all of your valuables, and they will bring those things back to me.'"

⁷So King Ahab called a meeting of all the elders (leaders) of his country. Ahab said, "Look, Ben Hadad is looking for trouble. First he told me that I must give him my wives, my children, my silver and my gold. I agreed to give those things to him. [And now he wants to take everything.]"

⁸But the elders (leaders) and all the people said, "Don't obey him. Don't do what he says."

⁹So Ahab sent a message to Ben Hadad. Ahab said, "I will do what you said at first. But I cannot obey your second command."

King Ben Hadad's men carried the message to the king. ¹⁰Then they came back with another message from Ben Hadad. The message said, "I will completely destroy Samaria. I promise that there won't be enough of that city left for my men to find any souvenirs* to take home. May God destroy me if I don't do this!"

¹¹King Ahab answered, "Tell Ben Hadad that the man who puts on his armor should not boast as much as the man who [lives long enough to] take it off."

¹²King Ben Hadad was drinking in his tent with the other rulers. At that time the messengers came and gave him the message from King Ahab. King Ben Hadad commanded his men to prepare to attack the city. So the men moved into their places for the battle.

¹³At the same time, a prophet went to King Ahab. The prophet said, "King Ahab, the Lord says to you, 'Do you see that big army! I, the Lord, will allow you to defeat that army today. Then you will know that I am the Lord.'"

¹⁴Ahab said, "Who will you use to defeat them?"

The prophet answered, "The Lord says, 'The young helpers of the government officials.'"

Then the king asked, "Who should command the main army?"

The prophet answered, "You will."

¹⁵So Ahab gathered the young helpers of the government officials. There were 232 of these young men. Then the king called together the army of Israel. The total number was 7,000.

¹⁶At noon, King Ben Hadad and the 32 kings helping him were drinking and becoming drunk in their tents. At this time, King Ahab's attack began. ¹⁷The young helpers attacked first. King Ben Hadad's men told him that soldiers had come out of Samaria. ¹⁸So Ben Hadad said, "They might be coming to fight. Or they might be coming to ask for peace. Capture them alive."

¹⁹The young men of King Ahab were leading the attack. The army of Israel was following them. ²⁰But each man of Israel killed the man that came against him. So the men from Aram began to run away. The army of Israel chased them. King Ben Hadad escaped on a horse from one of the chariots.* ²¹King Ahab led the army and took all horses and chariots from the army of Aram. So King Ahab caused a great defeat of the Aramean army.

²²Then the prophet went to King Ahab and said, "The king of Aram, Ben Hadad, will come to fight against you again next spring. So you should go home now and make your army stronger. And make careful plans to defend against him."

Ben Hadad Attacks Again

²³King Ben Hadad's officers said to him, "The gods of Israel are mountain gods. We fought in a mountain area. So the people of Israel won. So let's fight them on the flat land. Then we will win. ²⁴This is what you should do. Don't allow the 32 kings to command the armies. Let the commanders lead their armies.

²⁵"Now you gather an army like the army that was destroyed. Gather horses and chariots like that army. Then let's fight the Israelites on flat land. Then we will win." Ben Hadad followed their advice. He did what they said.

²⁶So in the spring, Ben Hadad gathered the people of Aram. He went to Aphek to fight against Israel.

²⁷The Israelites also prepared for war. The people of Israel went to fight the army of Aram. They made their camp opposite the camp of Aram. Compared to the enemy, Israel looked like two small flocks of goats, but the Aramean soldiers covered the whole area.

²⁸A man of God* came to the king of Israel with this message: "The Lord said, '[The people of] Aram said that I, the Lord, am God of the

---

chariot(s) A small wagon used in war.
souvenirs Things that help people remember places they have been. Literally, the Hebrew has, "handfuls of dust."

mountains. They think that I am not also the God of the valleys. So I will allow you to defeat this big army. Then you will know that I am the Lord in every place!'"

²⁹The armies were camped across from each other for seven days. On the seventh day the battle began. The Israelites killed 100,000 soldiers of Aram in one day. ³⁰The survivors ran away to the city of Aphek. The wall of the city fell on 27,000 of those soldiers. Ben Hadad also ran away to the city. He hid in a room. ³¹His servants said to him, "We heard that the kings of Israel are merciful. Let's dress in rough cloth with ropes on our heads.* Then let's go to the king of Israel. Maybe he will let us live."

³²They dressed in rough cloth with ropes on their heads.* They came to the king of Israel. They said, "Your servant, Ben Hadad, says, 'Please let me live.'"

Ahab said, "Is he still alive? He is my brother."*

³³Ben Hadad's men wanted King Ahab to say something to show that he would not kill King Ben Hadad. When Ahab called Ben Hadad his brother, the advisers quickly said, "Yes! Ben Hadad is your brother."

Ahab said, "Bring him to me." So Ben Hadad came to King Ahab. King Ahab asked him to get in the chariot with him.

³⁴Ben Hadad said to him, "Ahab, I will give you the towns that my father took from your father. And you can put shops in Damascus, like my father did in Samaria."

Ahab answered, "If you agree to this, then I will allow you to go free." So the two kings made a peace agreement. Then King Ahab let King Ben Hadad go free.

A Prophet Speaks Against Ahab

³⁵One of the prophets told another prophet, "Hit me!" He said that because the Lord had commanded it. But the other prophet refused to hit him. ³⁶So the first prophet said, "You did not obey the Lord's command. So a lion will kill you when you leave this place." The second prophet left that place and a lion killed him.

³⁷The first prophet went to another man and said, "Hit me!"

This man hit him and hurt the prophet. ³⁸So the prophet wrapped his face with a cloth. This way, no person could see who he was. The prophet went and waited for the king by the road. ³⁹The king came by and the prophet said to him, "I went to fight in the battle. One of our men brought an enemy soldier to me. The man said, 'Guard this man. If he runs away, then you will have to give your life in his place. Or you will have to pay a fine of 75 pounds* of silver.' ⁴⁰But I became busy doing other things. So the man ran away."

The king of Israel answered, "You have said that you are guilty of letting the soldier escape. So you know the answer. You must do what the man said."

⁴¹Then the prophet took the cloth from his face. The king of Israel saw him and knew that he was one of the prophets. ⁴²Then the prophet said to the king, "The Lord says to you, 'You set free the man that I said should die. So you will take his place—you will die! And your people will take the enemies' place—your people will die!'"

⁴³Then the king went back home to Samaria. He was worried and upset.

Naboth's Field of Grapes

21 King Ahab's palace* was in the city of Samaria. Near the palace there was a field of grapes. A man named Naboth owned this field. ²One day Ahab said to Naboth, "Give me your field. I want to make it a vegetable garden. Your field is near my palace.* I will give you a better grape field in its place. Or, if you prefer, I will pay you its value in money."

³Naboth answered, "I will never give my land to you. This land belongs to my family."

⁴So Ahab went home. He was angry and upset at Naboth. He did not like the things that man from Jezreel said. (Naboth had said, "I will not give you my family's land." Ahab lay down on his bed. He turned his face away and refused to eat.

⁵Ahab's wife, Jezebel, went to him. Jezebel said to him, "Why are you upset? Why do you refuse to eat?"

⁶Ahab answered, "I asked Naboth, the man from Jezreel, to give me his field. I told him that I would pay him the full price. Or if he preferred, I would give him another field. But Naboth refused to give his field to me."

---

rough cloth ... heads This showed they were being humble and that they wanted to surrender.
brother People that signed peace agreements often called each other "brother." It was like they became one family.

75 pounds Or "34kg." Literally, "a talent."
palace A large house for the king and his family.

⁷Jezebel answered, "But you are the king over Israel! Get out of your bed. Eat something and you will feel better. I will get Naboth's field for you." ⁸Then Jezebel wrote some letters. She signed Ahab's name to the letters. She used Ahab's own seal to seal the letters. Then she sent them to the elders *(leaders)* and important men who lived in the same town as Naboth. ⁹This is what the letter said:

Announce that there will be a day of fasting when the people will eat nothing. Then call all the people of the town together for a meeting. At the meeting, we will talk about Naboth. ¹⁰Find some men that will tell lies about Naboth. Those people should say that they heard Naboth speak against the king and against God. Then take Naboth out of the city and kill him with rocks.

¹¹So the elders *(leaders)* and important men of Jezreel obeyed that command. ¹²The leaders announced that there would be a day when all the people would eat nothing. On that day they called all the people together for a meeting. They put Naboth in a special place before the people. ¹³Then two men told the people that they heard Naboth speak against God and against the king. So the people carried Naboth out of the city. Then they killed him with rocks. ¹⁴Then the leaders sent a message to Jezebel. The message said: "Naboth has been killed."

¹⁵When Jezebel heard this, she said to Ahab, "Naboth is dead. Now you can go and take the field that you wanted." ¹⁶So Ahab went to the field of grapes and took it for his own.

¹⁷At this time the Lord spoke to Elijah. (Elijah was the prophet from Tishbe.) ⌊The Lord said,⌋ ¹⁸"Go to King Ahab in Samaria. Ahab will be at Naboth's field of grapes. He is there to take the field as his own. ¹⁹Tell Ahab that I, the Lord, say to him, 'Ahab! You killed the man Naboth. Now you are taking his land. So I tell you this! In the same place that Naboth died, you will also die. The dogs that licked Naboth's blood will lick your blood in the same place!'"

²⁰So Elijah went to Ahab. Ahab saw Elijah and said, "You have found me again. You are always against me."

Elijah answered, "Yes, I found you again. You have always used your life for sinning against the Lord. ²¹So the Lord says to you, 'I will destroy you. I will kill you and every male in your family. ²²Your family will be the same as the family of King Jeroboam son of Nebat. And your family will become like the family of King Baasha. Both of these families were completely destroyed. I will do this to you because you have made me angry. You have caused the people of Israel to sin.' ²³And the Lord also says, 'Dogs will eat the body of your wife Jezebel in the city of Jezreel. ²⁴Any person in your family that dies in the city will be eaten by dogs. Any person that dies in the fields, will be eaten by birds.'"

²⁵There is no other person that has done so many wrong things or sinned so much as Ahab. His wife Jezebel caused him to do those things. ²⁶Ahab did a very bad sin and worshiped those blocks of wood *(idols)*. This was the same thing that the Amorite people did. And the Lord took the land from them and gave it to the people of Israel.

²⁷After Elijah finished speaking, Ahab was very sad. He tore his clothes to show that he was sad. Then he put on special clothes of sadness. Ahab refused to eat. He slept in those special clothes. Ahab was very sad and upset.

²⁸The Lord said to Elijah the prophet, ²⁹"I see that Ahab has become humble before me. So, I will not cause the trouble to come to him during his life. I will wait until his son is king. Then I will cause the trouble to come to Ahab's family."

Micaiah Gives a Warning to Ahab

22 During the next two years, there was peace between Israel and Aram. ²Then, during the third year, King Jehoshaphat of Judah went to visit King Ahab of Israel.

³At this same time, Ahab asked his officials, "Remember that the king of Aram took Ramoth in Gilead from us? Why have we done nothing to get Ramoth back? It should be our town." ⁴So Ahab asked King Jehoshaphat, "Will you join with us and fight against the army of Aram at Ramoth?"

Jehoshaphat answered, "Yes, I will join you. My soldiers and my horses are ready to join with your army. ⁵But first we should ask the Lord for advice."

⁶So Ahab called a meeting of the prophets. There were about 400 prophets at that time. Ahab asked the prophets, "Should I go and fight against the army of Aram at Ramoth? Or should I wait for another time?"

The prophets answered, "You should go and fight now. The Lord will allow you to win."

⁷But Jehoshaphat said, "Are there any other of the Lord's prophets here? If there are, we should ask him what God says."

⁸King Ahab answered, "There is one other prophet. His name is Micaiah son of Imlah. But I hate him. When he speaks for the Lord, he never says anything good for me. He always says things that I don't like."

Jehoshaphat said, "King Ahab, you should not say those things!"

⁹So King Ahab told one of his officers to go and find Micaiah.

¹⁰At that time, the two kings were wearing their royal robes. They were sitting on the thrones. This was at the judging place near the gate of Samaria. All the prophets were standing before them. The prophets were prophesying.* ¹¹One of the prophets was named Zedekiah. He was the son of Kenaanah. Zedekiah made some iron horns.* Then he said to Ahab, "The Lord says, 'You will use these iron horns to fight against the army of Aram. You will defeat them and destroy them.'"

¹²All the other prophets agreed with what Zedekiah said. The prophet said, "Your army should march now. They should fight against the army of Aram at Ramoth. You will win the fight. The Lord will allow you to win."

¹³While this was happening, the officer went to find Micaiah. The officer found Micaiah and said to him, "All the other prophets have said that the king will succeed. So I tell you that the safest thing that you can do is to say the same thing."

¹⁴But Micaiah answered, "No! I promised that by the power of the Lord I will say the things that the Lord tells me to say!"

¹⁵Then Micaiah stood before King Ahab. The king asked him, "Micaiah, should King Jehoshaphat and I join armies? And should we go now to fight against the army of Aram at Ramoth?"

Micaiah answered, "Yes! You should go and fight them now. The Lord will let you win."

¹⁶But Ahab answered, "You are not speaking by the power of the Lord. You are saying your own words. So tell me the truth! How many times do I have to tell you? Tell me what the Lord says!"

¹⁷So Micaiah answered, "I can see what will happen. The army of Israel will be scattered over the hills. They will be like sheep without anyone to lead them. This is what the Lord says, 'These men have no leader. They should go home and not fight.'"

¹⁸Then Ahab said to Jehoshaphat, "See! I told you! This prophet never says anything good about me. He always says things that I don't want to hear."

¹⁹But Micaiah continued to speak for the Lord. Micaiah said, "Listen! These are the words that the Lord says! I saw the Lord sitting on his throne in heaven. His angels were standing near him. ²⁰The Lord said, 'Will any of you trick King Ahab? I want him to go and fight against the army of Aram at Ramoth. Then he will be killed.' The angels did not agree about what they should do. ²¹Then one angel went to the Lord and said, 'I will trick him!' ²²The Lord answered, 'How will you trick King Ahab?' The angel answered, 'I will confuse all of Ahab's prophets. I will tell the prophets to speak lies to King Ahab. The messages from the prophets will be lies.' So the Lord said, 'Good! Go and trick King Ahab. You will succeed.'"

²³Micaiah finished his story. Then he said, "So this is what has happened here. The Lord has caused your prophets to lie to you. The Lord himself has decided that great trouble should come to you."

²⁴Then the prophet Zedekiah went to Micaiah. Zedekiah hit Micaiah on the face. Zedekiah said, "Do you really believe that the Lord's power has left me and is now speaking through you?"

²⁵Micaiah answered, "Soon trouble will come. At that time, you will go and hide in a small room. And you will know that I am speaking the truth!"

²⁶Then King Ahab ordered one of his officers to arrest Micaiah. King Ahab said, "Arrest him and take him to Amon the governor of the city and prince Joash. ²⁷Tell them to put Micaiah in prison. Give him only bread and water to eat. Keep him there until I come home from the fight."

²⁸Micaiah said loudly, "All you people listen to what I say! King Ahab, if you come home alive from that fight, then the Lord has not spoken through me."

²⁹Then King Ahab and King Jehoshaphat went to fight against the army of Aram at Ramoth. This was in the area called Gilead. ³⁰Ahab said to Jehoshaphat, "We will prepare for the fight. I will wear clothes that make me look like I am not the king. But you wear your special clothes that show you are a king." So the king of Israel began the battle dressed like a person that was not a king.

³¹The king of Aram had 32 chariot commanders. That king ordered these 32 chariot commanders to find the king of Israel. The king of Aram told the commanders that they must kill the

prophesying Speaking for God.
iron horns These were a symbol of great strength.

king. ³²So during the battle, these commanders saw King Jehoshaphat. The commanders thought that he was the king of Israel. So they went to kill him. Jehoshaphat began shouting. ³³The commanders saw that he was not King Ahab, so they did not kill him. ³⁴But a soldier shot an arrow into the air—he was not aiming at any special person. But his arrow hit ⌊Ahab,⌋ the king of Israel. The arrow hit the king in a small place where his armor did not cover his body. So King Ahab said to his chariot driver, "An arrow has hit me! Drive the chariot out of this area. We must go away from the fighting."

³⁵The armies continued to fight. King Ahab stayed in his chariot. He was leaning against the sides of the chariot. He was looking at the army of Aram. His blood flowed down and covered the bottom of the chariot. Later in the evening, the king died. ³⁶Near sunset, all men in the army of Israel were commanded to go back to their own city and land.

³⁷So that is the way King Ahab died. Some men carried his body to Samaria. They buried him there. ³⁸The men cleaned Ahab's chariot at the pool of water in Samaria. The dogs licked King Ahab's blood from the chariot. And the prostitutes* used the water to wash themselves. These things happened the way the Lord said they would happen.

³⁹All the things that King Ahab did during the time he ruled are written in the book *The History of the Kings of Israel*. And that book also tells about the ivory that the king used to make his palace* more beautiful. And the book tells about the city that the king built. ⁴⁰Ahab died and his son, Ahaziah, became the next king after him.

Jehoshaphat, King of Judah

⁴¹During the fourth year that Ahab was king of Israel, Jehoshaphat became king of Judah. Jehoshaphat was the son of Asa. ⁴²Jehoshaphat was 35 years old when he became king. Jehoshaphat ruled in Jerusalem for 25 years. Jehoshaphat's mother was named Azubah. Azubah was the daughter of Shilhi. ⁴³Jehoshaphat was good. He did like his father before him. He obeyed all the things that the Lord wanted. But Jehoshaphat did not destroy the high places.* The people continued offering sacrifices* and burning incense* at those places.

⁴⁴Jehoshaphat made a peace agreement with the king of Israel. ⁴⁵Jehoshaphat was very brave and fought many wars. All the things he did are written in the book *The History of the Kings of Judah*. ⁴⁶Jehoshaphat forced all the men and women that sold their bodies for sex to leave the places of worship. Those people had served in those places of worship during the time his father Asa was king.

⁴⁷During this time, the land of Edom had no king. The land was ruled by a governor. The governor was chosen by the king of Judah.

Jehoshaphat's Navy

⁴⁸King Jehoshaphat built some cargo ships. He wanted the ships to sail to Ophir to get gold from that place. But the ships never went there—they were destroyed in their home port at Ezion Geber. ⁴⁹King Ahaziah of Israel offered to help Jehoshaphat. Ahaziah offered to put some of his own sailors with Jehoshaphat's men on those ships.* But Jehoshaphat refused to accept Ahaziah's men.

⁵⁰Jehoshaphat died and was buried with his ancestors. He was buried with his ancestors in the City of David.* Then his son, Jehoram became king.

Ahaziah, King of Israel

⁵¹Ahaziah was the son of Ahab. He became king of Israel during the 17th year that King Jehoshaphat ruled Judah. Ahaziah ruled in Samaria for two years. ⁵²Ahaziah sinned against the Lord. He did the same things as his father,

---

prostitute(s) A woman paid by men for sexual sin. Sometimes this also means a person that is not faithful to God and stops following him.

palace A large house for the king and his family.

high places Places for worshiping God or false gods. These places were often on the hills and mountains.

sacrifice(s) A gift to God. Usually it was a special animal that was killed and burned on an altar.

incense Special dried tree sap. Burned to make a sweet-smelling smoke, it was offered as a gift to God.

Ahaziah, Jehoshaphat, ships Jehoshaphat controlled the port of Ezion Geber which was Israel's only access to the Red Sea and the coasts of Africa, the Arabian Peninsula, and the coasts leading to the Persian Gulf and India. Ahaziah thought he could get control of that area by "helping" Jehoshaphat.

City of David The southeast and oldest part of the city of Jerusalem.

Ahab, his mother Jezebel, and Jeroboam, son of Nebat had done. All these rulers led the people of Israel into more sin. ⁵³Ahaziah worshiped and served the false god Baal, like his father did before him. So Ahaziah caused the Lord God of Israel to be very angry. The Lord was angry at Ahaziah like he had been angry at his father before him.

2 Kings

A Message for Ahaziah

1 After Ahab died, Moab broke away from Israel's rule. ²One day, Ahaziah was on the roof* of his house in Samaria. Ahaziah fell down through the wooden bars on top of his house. He was hurt very badly. Ahaziah called messengers and told them, "Go to ₍the priests of₎ Baal Zebub, the god of Ekron. Ask them if I will get well from my injuries."

³But the Lord's angel said to Elijah the Tishbite, "King Ahaziah has sent some messengers from Samaria. Go meet those men. Say to them, 'There is a God in Israel! So why are you men going to ask questions from Baal Zebub, the god of Ekron? ⁴₍Tell King Ahaziah these things: You sent messengers to ask questions from Baal Zebub.₎ Since you did this thing, the Lord says: You will not get up from your bed. You will die!'" Then Elijah left ₍and told these words to Ahaziah's servants₎.

⁵The messengers came back to Ahaziah. Ahaziah said to the messengers, "Why did you come back ₍so soon₎?"

⁶The messengers said to Ahaziah, "A man came up to meet us. He told us to go back to the king who sent us, and tell him what the Lord says. The Lord says, 'There is a God in Israel! So why did you send messengers to ask questions from Baal Zebub, the god of Ekron? Since you did this thing, you will not get up from your bed. You will die!'"

⁷Ahaziah said to the messengers, "What did the man look like who met you and told you these things?"

⁸The messengers answered Ahaziah, "This man was wearing a hairy coat* with a leather belt around his waist."

Then Ahaziah said, "That was Elijah the Tishbite!"

Fire Destroys the Captains Sent From Ahaziah

⁹₍Ahaziah₎ sent a captain and 50 men to Elijah. The captain went to Elijah. At that time, Elijah was sitting on top of a hill. The captain said to Elijah, "Man of God,* the king says, 'Come down.'"

¹⁰Elijah answered the captain of 50, "If I am a man of God,* let fire come down from heaven and destroy you and your 50 men!"

So fire came down from heaven and destroyed the captain and his 50 men.

¹¹Ahaziah sent another captain with 50 men to Elijah. The captain said to Elijah, "Man of God,* the king says, 'Come down quickly!'"

¹²Elijah told the captain and his 50 men, "If I am a man of God,* let fire come down from heaven and destroy you and your 50 men!"

Then God's fire came down from heaven and destroyed the captain and his 50 men.

¹³Ahaziah sent a third captain with 50 men. The third captain came to Elijah. The captain fell down on his knees. The captain begged Elijah, saying to him, "Man of God,* I ask you, please let my life and the lives of your 50 servants be valuable to you! ¹⁴Fire came down from heaven and destroyed the first two captains and their 50 men. But now, have mercy and let us live!"

¹⁵The Lord's angel said to Elijah, "Go with the captain. Don't be afraid of him."

So Elijah went with the captain to see King Ahaziah.

---

roof In ancient Israel, houses had flat roofs that were used like an extra room.
This man wore a hairy coat Or, "This man was a hairy man."
This man wore a hairy coat Or, "This man was a hairy man."
man of God Another name for a prophet.

¹⁶Elijah told Ahaziah, "There is a God in Israel. So why did you send messengers to ask questions from Baal Zebub, the god of Ekron. Since you did this thing, you will not get up from your bed. You will die!"

Jehoram Takes Ahaziah's Place

¹⁷Ahaziah died, just like the Lord said through Elijah. Ahaziah did not have a son. So Jehoram became the new king after Ahaziah. Jehoram began to rule during the second year that Jehoram son of Jehoshaphat was the king of Judah. ¹⁸The other things that Ahaziah did are written in the book *The History of the Kings of Israel*.

The Lord Makes Plans to Take Elijah

2 It was near the time for the Lord to take Elijah by a whirlwind up into heaven. Elijah went with Elisha to Gilgal. ²Elijah said to Elisha, "Please stay here, because the Lord told me to go to Bethel."

But Elisha said, "I promise, as the Lord lives and as you live, I won't leave you." So the two men went down to Bethel. ³The group of prophets* at Bethel came to Elisha and said to him, "Do you know that the Lord will take your master away from you today?"

Elisha said, "Yes, I know it. Don't talk about it."

⁴Elijah said to Elisha, "Please stay here, because the Lord told me to go to Jericho."

But Elisha said, "I promise, as the Lord lives and as you live, I won't leave you!" So the two men went to Jericho. ⁵The group of prophets* at Jericho came to Elisha and said to him, "Do you know that the Lord will take your master away from you today?"

Elisha answered, "Yes, I know it. Don't talk about it."

⁶Elijah said to Elisha, "Please stay here, because the Lord told me to go to the Jordan River."

Elisha answered, "I promise, as the Lord lives and as you live, I won't leave you!" So the two men went on.

⁷There were 50 men from the group of prophets* that followed them. Elijah and Elisha stopped at the Jordan River. The 50 men stood far away from Elijah and Elisha. ⁸Elijah took off his coat, folded it, and hit the water with it. The water separated to the right and to the left. Then Elijah and Elisha crossed the river on dry ground.

⁹After they crossed the river, Elijah said to Elisha, "What do you want me to do for you before God takes me away from you?"

Elisha said, "I ask you for a double share of your spirit on me."

¹⁰Elijah said, "You have asked a hard thing. If you see me when I am taken from you, then that will happen. But if ₗyou don't see me when I am taken from youₗ, then it won't happen."

God Takes Elijah into Heaven

¹¹Elijah and Elisha were walking and talking together. Suddenly, some horses and a chariot* came and separated Elijah from Elisha. The horses and the chariot were like fire! Then Elijah was carried up into heaven in a whirlwind.

¹²Elisha saw it, and shouted, "My father! My father! The Chariot of Israel and his horse soldiers!*"

Elisha never saw Elijah again. Elisha grabbed his own clothes and tore them ₗto show his sadnessₗ. ¹³Elijah's coat had fallen to the ground, so Elisha picked it up. Elisha hit the water and said, "Where is the Lord, the God of Elijah?"

¹⁴Just as Elisha hit the water, the water separated to the right and to the left! And Elisha crossed the river.

The Prophets Ask for Elijah

¹⁵When the group of prophets* at Jericho saw Elisha, they said, "Elijah's spirit is now on Elisha!" They came to meet Elisha. They bowed very low to the ground before Elisha. ¹⁶They said to him, "Look, we have 50 good men. Please let them go and look for your master. Maybe the Lord's Spirit has taken Elijah up and dropped him on some mountain or in some valley."

But Elisha answered, "No, don't send men ₗto look for Elijahₗ!"

¹⁷The group of prophets* begged Elisha until he was embarrassed. Then Elisha said, "Fine, send the men ₗto look for Elijahₗ."

---

group of prophets Literally, "sons of the prophets." These people were prophets and people studying to become prophets.

chariot(s) A small wagon used in war.
Chariot of Israel and his horse soldiers This probably means, "God and his heavenly army {(angels)}."

The group of prophets* sent the 50 men to look for Elijah. They looked three days, but they could not find Elijah. ¹⁸So the men went to Jericho where Elisha was staying. ₍They told him that they could not find Elijah.₎ Elisha said to them, "I told you not to go."

Elisha Makes the Water Good

¹⁹The men of the city said to Elisha, "Sir, you can see this city is in a nice place. But the water is bad. That is why the land cannot grow crops." ²⁰Elisha said, "Bring me a new bowl and put salt in it."

The people brought the bowl to Elisha. ²¹Then Elisha went out to the place where the water began flowing ₍from the ground₎. Elisha threw the salt into the water. He said, "The Lord said, 'I am making this water pure! From now on this water will not cause any more death or keep the land from growing crops.'"

²²The water became pure. And the water is still good today. It happened just like Elisha said.

Some Boys Make Fun of Elisha

²³Elisha went from that city to Bethel. Elisha was walking up the hill to the city, and some boys were coming down out of the city. They began making fun of Elisha. They said to him, "Go up, you bald headed man! Go up, you bald headed man!"

²⁴Elisha looked back and saw them. He asked the Lord to cause bad things to happen to them. Then two bears came out of the forest and attacked the boys. There were 42 boys ripped apart by the bears.

²⁵Elisha left Bethel and went to Mount Carmel. And from there, Elisha went back to Samaria.

Jehoram Becomes King of Israel

3 Jehoram son of Ahab became king over Israel at Samaria. He began to rule during Jehoshaphat's 18th year as king of Judah. Jehoram ruled 12 years. ²Jehoram did the things that the Lord said were wrong. But Jehoram was not like his father and mother, because he removed the pillar that his father had made for worshiping Baal.* ³But he continued to do the sins of Jeroboam son of Nebat. Jeroboam caused the Israelites to sin. Jehoram did not stop the sins of Jeroboam.

Moab Breaks Away from Israel

⁴Mesha was the king of Moab. Mesha owned many sheep. Mesha gave the wool of 100,000 lambs and 100,000 rams* to the king of Israel. ⁵But when Ahab died, the king of Moab broke away from the rule of the king of Israel.

⁶Then King Jehoram went out of Samaria and gathered all the men of Israel. ⁷Jehoram sent ₍messengers₎ to Jehoshaphat, the king of Judah. Jehoram said, "The king of Moab has broken away from my rule. Will you go with me to fight against Moab?"

Jehoshaphat said, "Yes, I will go with you. We will join together as one army. My people will be like your people. And my horses will be like your horses."

The Three Kings Ask Elisha for Advice

⁸Jehoshaphat asked Jehoram, "Which way should we go?"

Jehoram answered, "We should go through the Desert of Edom."

⁹So the king of Israel went with the king of Judah and the king of Edom. They traveled around for seven days. There was not enough water for the army or for their animals. ¹⁰Finally, the king of Israel *(Jehoram)* said, "Oh, I think the Lord really brought us three kings together only to let the Moabites defeat us!"

¹¹But Jehoshaphat said, "Surely one of the Lord's prophets is here. Let's ask the prophet what the Lord says we should do."

One of the servants of the king of Israel said, "Elisha son of Shaphat is here. Elisha was Elijah's servant."*

¹²Jehoshaphat said, "The Lord's word is with Elisha!"

So the king of Israel *(Jehoram)*, Jehoshaphat, and the king of Edom went down to see Elisha.

¹³Elisha said to the king of Israel *(Jehoram)*, "What do you want from me? Go to the prophets of your father and mother!"

The king of Israel said to Elisha, "No, ₍we have come to see you₎ because the Lord called us three

---

group of prophets Literally, "sons of the prophets." These people were prophets and people studying to become prophets.

rams Male sheep.

Elisha was Elijah's servant Literally, "Elisha poured water over Elijah's hands."

kings together to let the Moabites defeat us. ₍We need your help₎."

¹⁴Elisha said, "I respect Jehoshaphat the king of Judah and I serve the Lord All-Powerful. And as sure as he lives, I came here only because of Jehoshaphat. I tell you the truth, if Jehoshaphat was not here, I would not pay any attention to you. I would ignore you completely! ¹⁵But now bring me a person who plays the harp."

When the person played the harp, the Lord's power* came on Elisha. ¹⁶Then Elisha said, "This is what the Lord says: Dig holes in the valley. ¹⁷This is what the Lord says: You won't see wind, you won't see rain. But that valley will be filled with water. Then you and your cows and other animals will have water to drink. ¹⁸It is easy for the Lord to do. He will also let you defeat the Moabites. ¹⁹You will attack every strong city and every good city. You will cut down every good tree. You will stop up all the springs of water. You will ruin every good field with the stones ₍that you throw at it₎."

²⁰In the morning, at the time for the morning sacrifice, water began flowing from the direction of Edom and filled the valley.

²¹The people in Moab heard that the kings had come up to fight against them. So the people in Moab gathered together all the men old enough to wear armor.* They waited at the border, ₍ready for the battle₎. ²²The people of Moab got up early that morning. The rising sun was shining on the water in the valley, and it looked like blood to the people of Moab. ²³The people of Moab said, "Look at the blood! The kings must have fought against each other. They must have destroyed each other. Let's go take the valuable things from the dead bodies!"

²⁴The Moabite people came to the Israelite camp. But the Israelites came out and attacked the Moabite army. The Moabite people ran away from the Israelites. The Israelites followed them into Moab to fight the Moabites. ²⁵The Israelites destroyed the cities. They threw their stones* at every good field in Moab. They stopped up all the springs of water. And they cut down all the good trees. The Israelites fought all the way to Kir Hareseth. The soldiers surrounded Kir Hareseth and attacked it, too!

²⁶The king of Moab saw that the battle was too strong for him. So he took 700 men with swords to break through ₍the army and kill₎ the king of Edom. But they could not break through to the king of Edom. ²⁷Then the king of Moab took his oldest son. This was the son who would become the next king after him. On the wall around the city, the king of Moab offered his son as a burnt offering. This upset the people of Israel very much. So the people of Israel left the king of Moab and went back to their own land.

A Prophet's Widow Asks Elisha for Help

4 A man from the group of prophets* had a wife. ₍This man died.₎ His wife cried out to Elisha, "My husband was like a servant to you. Now my husband is dead! You know he honored the Lord. But he owed money to a man. And now that man is coming to take my boys and make them his slaves!"

²Elisha answered, "How can I help you? Tell me, what do you have in your house?"

The woman said, "I don't have anything in the house. I have only a jar of olive oil."

³Then Elisha said, "Go and borrow bowls from all your neighbors. They must be empty. Borrow plenty of bowls. ⁴Then go to your house and close the doors. Only you and your sons will be in the house. Then pour the oil into all those bowls. Fill those bowls, and put them in a separate place."

⁵So the woman left Elisha, ₍went into her house,₎ and shut the door. Only she and her sons were in the house. Her sons brought the bowls to her and she poured oil. ⁶She filled many bowls. Finally, she said to her son, "Bring me another bowl."

But all of the bowls were full. One of the sons said to the woman, "There aren't any more bowls." At that time, the oil in the jar was finished!

⁷Then the woman told the man of God* (Elisha) what happened. Elisha told her, "Go, sell the oil and pay your debt. After you sell the oil ₍and pay your debt₎, you and your sons can live on the money that is left."

---

power Literally, "hand."
armor The special clothes soldiers wore to protect themselves in war.
threw their stones These were probably the stones soldiers threw with slings in war.

group of prophets Literally, "sons of the prophets." These people were prophets and people studying to become prophets.
man of God Another name for a prophet.

A Woman in Shunem Gives Elisha a Room

⁸One day Elisha went to Shunem. An important woman lived in Shunem. This woman asked Elisha ₍to and₎ eat at her house. So every time Elisha went through that place, he stopped there to eat. ⁹The woman said to her husband, "Look, I can see that Elisha is a holy man of God. He passes by our house all the time. ¹⁰Please, let's make a little room on the roof* for Elisha. Let's put a bed in this room. Let's put a table, a chair, and a lampstand in there. Then when he comes to our house, he can have this room for himself."

¹¹One day Elisha came to the woman's house. He went to this room and rested there. ¹²Elisha said to his servant Gehazi, "Call this Shunammite woman."

The servant called the Shunammite woman, and she stood in front of Elisha. ¹³Elisha told his servant, "Now say to this woman, 'Look, you have done your best to take care of us. What can we do for you? Do you want us to speak to the king for you, or to the captain of the army?'"

The woman answered, "I am fine living here among my own people."

¹⁴Elisha said ₍to Gehazi₎, "What can we do for her?"

Gehazi answered, "I know! She doesn't have a son, and her husband is old."

¹⁵Then Elisha said, "Call her."

So Gehazi called the woman. She came and stood at his door. ¹⁶Elisha said ₍to the woman₎, "About this time next spring, you will be hugging your own baby boy."

The woman said, "No sir! Man of God,* don't lie to me!"

The Woman in Shunem Has a Son

¹⁷But the woman did become pregnant. She gave birth to a son that next spring, just like Elisha said.

¹⁸The boy grew. One day, the boy went out into the fields to see his father and the men cutting the grain. ¹⁹The boy said to his father, "Oh, my head! My head hurts!"

The father said to his servant, "Carry him to his mother!"

²⁰The servant took the boy to his mother. The boy sat on his mother's lap until noon. Then he died.

The Woman Goes to See Elisha

²¹The woman lay the boy on the bed of the man of God* *(Elisha)*. She shut the door to that room and went outside. ²²She called to her husband and said, "Please send me one of the servants and a donkey. Then I will go quickly to get the man of God *(Elisha)* and come back."

²³The woman's husband said, "Why do you want to go to the man of God *(Elisha)* today? It isn't the New Moon.* or Sabbath day*"

She said, "₍Don't worry.₎ Everything will be all right."

²⁴Then she put a saddle on a donkey and said to her servant, "Let's go, and hurry! Go slow only when I tell you!"

²⁵The woman went to Mount Carmel to get the man of God* *(Elisha)*.

The man of God* *(Elisha)* saw the Shunammite woman coming from far away. Elisha said to his servant Gehazi, "Look, there's the Shunammite woman! ²⁶Please run now to meet her! Say to her, '₍What's wrong?₎ Are you all right? Is your husband all right? Is the child all right?'"

₍Gehazi asked the Shunammite woman these things.₎ She answered, "Everything is fine."

²⁷But the Shunammite woman went up the hill to the man of God* *(Elisha)*. She ₍bowed down and₎ touched Elisha's feet. Gehazi came near to pull the Shunammite woman away. But the man of God *(Elisha)* said to Gehazi, "Let her alone! She's very upset, and the Lord didn't tell me about it. The Lord hid this news from me."

²⁸Then the Shunammite woman said, "Sir, I never asked for a son. I told you, 'Don't trick me'!"

²⁹Then Elisha said to Gehazi, "Get ready to go. Take my walking stick and go! ₍Don't stop to talk to anyone!₎ If you meet any person, don't even say hello to him. If any person says hello to you, don't answer him. Put my walking stick on the child's face."

³⁰But the child's mother said, "I promise, as the Lord lives and as you live, I won't leave without you!"

---

room on the roof In ancient Israel, houses had flat roofs that were used like an extra room.
man of God Another name for a prophet.
New Moon The first day of the Hebrew month. There were special meetings on these days to worship God.
Sabbath day Saturday. A special day of rest and worship for the Jews.

So Elisha got up and followed the Shunammite woman. ³¹Gehazi arrived ₍at the Shunammite woman's house₎ before Elisha and the Shunammite woman. Gehazi laid the walking stick on the child's face. But the child did not talk or show any sign that he heard anything. Then Gehazi came back to meet Elisha. Gehazi told Elisha, "The child won't wake up!"

The Shunammite Woman's Son Lives Again

³²Elisha went into the house. And there was the child, lying dead on his bed. ³³Elisha went into the room and shut the door. Elisha and the child were alone in the room now. Then Elisha prayed to the Lord. ³⁴Elisha went ₍to the bed₎ and lay on the child. Elisha put his mouth on the child's mouth. Elisha put his eyes on the child's eyes. Elisha put his hands on the child's hands. Elisha lay there on top of the child until the child's body became warm. ³⁵Then Elisha turned away and walked around the room. He went back and lay on the child until the child sneezed seven times and opened his eyes. ³⁶Elisha called Gehazi and said, "Call the Shunammite woman!"

Gehazi called the Shunammite woman, and she came to Elisha. Elisha said, "Pick up your son."

³⁷Then the Shunammite woman went into ₍the room₎ and bowed down at Elisha's feet. Then she picked up her son and went out.

Elisha and the Poisoned Soup

³⁸Elisha went to Gilgal again. There was a time of hunger in the land. The group of prophets* was sitting in front of Elisha. Elisha said to his servant, "Put the large pot on the fire, and make some soup for the group of prophets."

³⁹One man went out into the field to gather herbs. He found a wild vine and picked the fruit from it. He put that fruit in his robe and brought it back. He cut up the wild fruit and put it into the pot. But the group of prophets* did not know what kind of fruit it was.

⁴⁰Then they poured some of the soup for the men to eat. But when they began to eat the soup, they shouted out ₍to Elisha₎, "Man of God*! There's poison in the pot!" ₍The food tasted like poison₎ so they could not eat that food.

⁴¹But Elisha said, "Bring some flour." ₍They brought flour to Elisha₎, and he threw it into the pot. Then Elisha said, "Pour the soup for the people so they can eat."

And there was nothing wrong with the soup!

Elisha Feeds the Group of Prophets

⁴²A man from Baal Shalishah came and brought bread from the first harvest to the man of God* *(Elisha)*. This man brought 20 loaves of barley bread and fresh grain in his sack. Then Elisha said, "Give this food to the people, so that they can eat."

⁴³Elisha's servant said, "What? There are 100 men here. How can I give this food to all those men?"

But Elisha said, "Give the food to the people to eat. The Lord says, 'They will eat and there will still be food left over.'"

⁴⁴Then Elisha's servant put the food in front of the group of prophets.* The group of prophets had enough to eat, and they even had food left over! This happened just like the Lord said.

Naaman's Problem

5 Naaman was the captain of the army of the king of Aram. Naaman was very important to his king.* Naaman was very important because the Lord used him to lead Aram to victory. Naaman was a great and powerful man, but he was also sick with leprosy.*

²The Aramean army sent many groups of soldiers to fight in Israel. ₍The soldiers took people to be their slaves.₎ One time they took a little girl from the land of Israel. This little girl became a servant of Naaman's wife. ³This girl said to Naaman's wife, "I wish that my master *(Naaman)* would meet the prophet *(Elisha)* who lives in Samaria. That prophet could heal Naaman of his leprosy.*"

⁴Naaman went to his master *(the king of Aram)*. Naaman told ₍the king of Aram₎ the things that the Israelite girl said.

⁵Then the king of Aram said, "Go now, and I will send a letter to the king of Israel."

---

group of prophets Literally, "sons of the prophets." These people were prophets and people studying to become prophets.

king Literally, "master."
leprosy A very bad skin disease.

So Naaman went to Israel. ⌊Naaman took some gifts with him.⌋ Naaman took 750 pounds* of silver, 6,000 pieces of gold and ten changes of clothes. ⁶Naaman took the letter from the king of Aram to the king of Israel. The letter said: " ... Now, this letter is to show that I am sending my servant Naaman to you. Cure his leprosy.*"

⁷When the king of Israel had read the letter, he tore his clothes ⌊to show he was sad and upset⌋. The king of Israel said, "Am I God? No! I don't have the power over life and death. So why did the king of Aram send a man sick with leprosy* for me to heal? Think about it, and you will see ⌊that it is a trick⌋. The king of Aram is trying to start a fight!"

⁸Elisha, the man of God,* heard that the king of Israel had torn his clothes ⌊to show that he was upset⌋. So Elisha sent this message to the king: "Why did you tear your clothes? Let Naaman come to me. Then he will know there is a prophet in Israel!"

⁹So Naaman came with his horses and chariots* to Elisha's house and stood outside the door. ¹⁰Elisha sent a messenger to Naaman. ⌊The messenger⌋ said, "Go, and wash in the Jordan River seven times. Then your skin will be healed, and you will be pure and clean."

¹¹Naaman became angry and left. He said, "I thought Elisha would at least come out and stand in front of me and call on the name of the Lord his God. I thought he would wave his hand over my body and heal the leprosy*! ¹²Abana and Pharpar, the rivers of Damascus, are better than all the water in Israel! Why can't I wash in those rivers in Damascus and become clean?" Naaman was very angry and turned to leave.

¹³But Naaman's servants went to him and talked to him. They said, "Father,* if the prophet told you to do some great thing, you would do it! Right? ⌊So you should obey him even if he tells you something easy.⌋ And he said, 'Wash, and you will be pure and clean.'"

¹⁴So Naaman did what the man of God* *(Elisha)* said. Naaman went down and dipped himself in the Jordan River seven times. And Naaman became pure and clean! Naaman's skin became soft like the skin of a baby.

¹⁵Naaman and all his group came back to the man of God* *(Elisha)*. He stood before Elisha and said, "Look, I now know there is no God in all the earth except in Israel! Now please accept a gift from me!"

¹⁶But Elisha said, "I serve the Lord. And I promise, as the Lord lives, I will not accept any gift."

Naaman tried hard to make Elisha take the gift, but Elisha refused. ¹⁷Then Naaman said, "If you won't accept this gift, then at least do this for me. Let me have enough dirt from Israel to fill the baskets on two of my mules.* Why? Because I will never again offer any burnt offering or sacrifice to any other gods. I will offer sacrifices only to the Lord! ¹⁸And I now pray the Lord will forgive me for this thing: In the future, my master *(the king of Aram)* will go into the temple of Rimmon to worship ⌊that false god⌋. The king will want to lean on me for support, so I must bow down in the temple of Rimmon. I now ask the Lord to forgive me when that happens."

¹⁹Then Elisha said to Naaman, "Go in peace."

So Naaman left Elisha and went a short way. ²⁰But Gehazi, the servant of Elisha the man of God,* said, "Look, my master *(Elisha)* has let Naaman the Aramean go without accepting the gift that he brought! As the Lord lives, I will run after Naaman and get something from him!" ²¹So Gehazi ran to Naaman.

Naaman saw someone running after him. He stepped down from the chariot* to meet Gehazi. Naaman said, "Is everything all right?"

²²Gehazi said, "Yes, everything is all right. My master *(Elisha)* has sent me. He said, 'Look, two young men came to me. They were from the group of prophets* in the hill country of Ephraim. Please give them 75 pounds* of silver and two changes of clothes!'"

²³Naaman said, "Please, take 150 pounds*!" Naaman persuaded Gehazi ⌊to take the silver⌋. Naaman put 150 pounds* of silver in two bags and took two changes of clothes. Then Naaman

---

750 pounds Or, 340kg. Literally, "10 talents (kikars)."
leprosy A very bad skin disease.
man of God Another name for a prophet.
chariot(s) A small wagon used in war.
Father Slaves often called their masters "father," and the masters often called their slaves "children."
Let me have ... my mules Naaman probably thought that the ground in Israel was holy, so he wanted take some with him to help him to worship the Lord in his own country.
group of prophets Literally, "sons of the prophets." These people were prophets and people studying to become prophets.
75 pounds Or, 34kg. Literally, "1 talent."
150 pounds Or, 68kg. Literally, "2 talents."

gave these things to two of his servants. The servants carried these things for Gehazi. ²⁴When Gehazi came to the hill, he took these things from the servants. Gehazi sent the servants away, and they left. Then Gehazi hid those things in the house.

²⁵Gehazi came in and stood before his master ₍Elisha₎. Elisha said to Gehazi, "Where have you been Gehazi?"

Gehazi said, "I didn't go anywhere."

²⁶Elisha said to Gehazi, "That is not true! My heart was with you when the man ₍Naaman₎ turned from his chariot* to meet you. This is not the time to take money, clothes, olives, grapes, sheep, cows, or men and women servants. ²⁷Now, you and your children will catch Naaman's disease. You will have leprosy* forever!"

When Gehazi left Elisha, Gehazi's skin was as white as snow! Gehazi was sick with leprosy.*

Elisha and the Axhead

6 The group of prophets* said to Elisha, "We are staying in that place over there. But it is too small for us. ²Let's go to the Jordan River ₍and cut some wood₎. Each of us will get a log and we will build us a place to live there."

Elisha answered, "Fine, go and do it."

³One person said, "Please go with us."

Elisha said, "Fine, I will go with you."

⁴So Elisha went with the group of prophets.* When they arrived at the Jordan River, they began to cut down some trees. ⁵But when one man was cutting down a tree, the iron axhead slipped from the handle and fell into the water. The man shouted, "Oh, master! I borrowed that axe!"

⁶The man of God* *(Elisha)* said, "Where did it fall?"

The man showed Elisha the place ₍where the axhead fell₎. Then Elisha cut a stick and threw the stick into the water. The stick made the iron axhead float. ⁷Elisha said, "Pick up the axhead." Then the man reached out and took the axhead.

Aram Tries to Trap Israel

⁸The king of Aram was making war against Israel. He had a council meeting with his army officers. He said, "Hide in this place ₍and attack the Israelites when they come by₎."

⁹But the man of God* *(Elisha)* sent a message to the king of Israel. Elisha said, "Be careful! Don't go by that place! The Aramean soldiers are hiding there!"

¹⁰The king of Israel sent ₍a message to his men at₎ the place that the man of God* *(Elisha)* warned him about. And the king of Israel saved quite a few men.*

¹¹The king of Aram was very upset about this. The king of Aram called his army officers and said to them, "Tell me who is ₍spying₎ for the king of Israel."

¹²One of the officers of the king of Aram said, "My lord and king, not one of us is a spy! Elisha, the prophet from Israel, can tell the king of Israel ₍many secret things— even₎ the words that you speak in your bedroom!"

¹³The king of Aram said, "Find Elisha and I will send men to catch him!"

The servants told the king of Aram, "Elisha is in Dothan!"

¹⁴Then the king of Aram sent horses, chariots,* and a large army to Dothan. They arrived at night and surrounded the city. ¹⁵Elisha's servant got up early that morning. The servant went outside, and he saw an army with horses and chariots all around the city!

Elisha's servant said to Elisha, "Oh, my master, what can we do?"

¹⁶Elisha said, "Don't be afraid! The army that fights for us is larger than the army ₍that fights for Aram₎!"

¹⁷Then Elisha prayed and said, "Lord, I ask you, open my servant's eyes so he can see."

The Lord opened the eyes of the young man, and the servant saw the mountain was full of horses and chariots* of fire. They were all around Elisha!

¹⁸These horses and chariots* of fire came down to Elisha. Elisha prayed to the Lord and said, "I pray that you will cause these people to become blind."

Then the Lord did what Elisha asked. The Lord caused the Aramean army to become blind. ¹⁹Elisha said to the Aramean army, "This is not the right way. This is not the right city. Follow me. I will lead you to the man you are looking for." Then Elisha led the Aramean army to Samaria.

---

chariot(s) A small wagon used in war.
leprosy A very bad skin disease.
group of prophets Literally, "sons of the prophets." These people were prophets and people studying to become prophets.
man of God Another name for a prophet.

quite a few men Literally, "not one or two."

[20] When they arrived at Samaria,* Elisha said, "Lord, open the eyes of these men so they can see."

Then the Lord opened their eyes, and the Aramean army saw they were in the city of Samaria! [21] The king of Israel saw the Aramean army. The king of Israel said to Elisha, "My father, should I kill them? Should I kill them?"

[22] Elisha answered, "No, don't kill them. You would not kill people that you captured in war with your sword and with your bow ₍and arrows₎. Give the Aramean army some bread and water. Let them eat and drink. Then let them go home to their master."

[23] The king of Israel prepared much food for the Aramean army. The Aramean army ate and drank. Then the king of Israel sent the Aramean army back home. The Aramean army went home to their master. The Arameans did not send any more soldiers into the land of Israel to make raids.

A Terrible Time of Hunger Hits Samaria

[24] After this happened, Ben Hadad king of Aram gathered all his army and went to surround and attack the city Samaria. [25] ₍The soldiers would not let people bring food into the city.₎ So there was a time of terrible hunger in Samaria. It was so bad in Samaria that a donkey's head was sold for 80 pieces of silver. And one pint* of dove's dung sold for five pieces of silver.

[26] The king of Israel was walking on the wall around the city. A woman shouted out to him. The woman said, "My lord and king, please help me!"

[27] The king of Israel said, "If the Lord does not help you, how can I help you? ₍I have nothing to give to you—there is no grain₎ from the threshing floor* or ₍wine₎ from the winepress." [28] Then the king of Israel said to the woman, "What is your trouble?"

The woman answered, "This woman said to me, 'Give me your son so that we can ₍kill him and₎ eat him today. Then we will eat my son tomorrow.' [29] So we boiled my son and ate him. Then the next day, I said to this woman, 'Give me your son so we can ₍kill him and₎ eat him.' But she has hidden her son!"

[30] When the king heard the woman's words, he tore his clothes ₍to show he was upset₎. As the king passed by on the wall, the people saw the king was wearing under his clothes the rough cloth ₍that showed he was sad and upset₎.

[31] The king said, "May God punish me if the head of Elisha son of Shaphat is still on his body at the end of this day!"

[32] The king sent a messenger to Elisha. Elisha was sitting in his house, and the elders *(leaders)* were sitting with him. Before the messenger arrived, Elisha said to the elders, "Look, that son of a murderer *(the king of Israel)* is sending men to cut off my head! When the messenger arrives, shut the door! Hold the door and don't let him in! I hear the sound of his master's feet coming behind him!"

[33] While Elisha was still talking with the elders *(leaders)*, the messenger* came to him. This was the message: "This trouble has come from the Lord! Why should I wait for the Lord any longer?"

7 Elisha said, "Listen to the message from the Lord! The Lord says: 'About this time tomorrow, ₍there will be plenty of food, and it will be cheap again₎. A person will be able to buy a basket* of fine flour or two baskets* of barley for only one shekel* in the market place by the city gates of Samaria."

[2] Then the officer that was close to the king* answered the man of God* *(Elisha)*. The officer said, "Even if the Lord made windows in heaven, this could not happen!"

Elisha said, "You will see it with your own eyes. But you will not eat any of that food."

Lepers Find the Aramean Camp Is Empty

[3] There were four men sick with leprosy* near the city gate. They said to each other, "Why are we sitting here waiting to die? [4] There is no food in the Samaria. If we go into the city, we will die there. If we stay here, we will also die. So let's go to the Aramean camp. If they let us live, then we will live. If they kill us, then we will just die.

Samaria This was the capital city of Israel—the enemy of Aram.
one pint About 0.3 l. Literally, "1/4 cab."
threshing floor A place where grain is beaten or walked on to remove the hulls from the grain.

messenger Or possibly, "king."
basket(s) Literally, "seah(s)."
shekel Or, "2/5 of an ounce."
that was close to the king Literally, "on whose arm the king leaned."
man of God Another name for a prophet.
leprosy A very bad skin disease.

⁵So that evening the four lepers* went to the Aramean camp. They came to the edge of the Aramean camp. No people were there! ⁶The Lord had caused the Aramean army to hear the sound of chariots,* horses, and a large army. So the Aramean soldiers said to each other, "The king of Israel has hired the kings of the Hittites and Egyptians to come against us!" ⁷The Arameans ran away early that evening. They left everything behind. They left their tents, horses, and donkeys, and they ran for their lives.

The Lepers in the Enemy Camp

⁸When these lepers* came to where the camp began, they went into one tent. They ate and drank. Then the four lepers* carried silver, gold, and clothes out of the camp. They hid the silver, gold, and clothes. Then they came back and entered another tent. They carried things out from this tent. They went out and hid these things. ⁹Then these lepers* said to each other, "We are doing wrong! Today we have good news. But we are silent. If we wait until the sun comes up, we will be punished. Now let's go and tell the people who live in the king's house."

The Lepers Tell the Good News

¹⁰So these lepers* came and called to the gatekeepers of the city. The lepers told the gatekeepers, "We went to the Aramean camp. But we did not hear any people. No people were there. The horses and donkeys were still tied up, and the tents were still standing. ⌊But the people were all gone!⌋"
¹¹Then the gatekeepers of the city shouted out and told the people in the king's house. ¹²It was night, but the king got up from bed. The king said to his officers, "I will tell you what the Aramean soldiers are doing to us. They know we are hungry. They left the camp to hide in the field. They are thinking, 'When the Israelites come out of the city, we will capture them alive. And then we will enter the city.'"
¹³One of the king's officers said, "Let some men take five of the horses that are still left in the city. The horses will soon die anyway, just like all the people of Israel that are still left in the city.* Let's send these men to see what happened."

¹⁴So the men took two chariots* with horses. The king sent these men after the Aramean army. The king told them, "Go and see what happened."
¹⁵The men went after the Aramean army as far as the Jordan River. All along the road there were clothes and weapons. The Arameans had thrown these things down when they hurried away. The messengers went back to Samaria and told the king.
¹⁶Then the people ran out to the Aramean camp and took valuable things from there. ⌊There was plenty of things for everyone.⌋ So it happened just like the Lord said. A person could buy a basket* of fine flour or two baskets* of barley for only one shekel.*
¹⁷The king chose his officer that was close to him to guard the gate. ⌊But the people ran to get food from the enemy camp.⌋ The people knocked the officer down and walked on him, and he died. So all those things happened just like the man of God* *(Elisha)* said when the king came to Elisha's house. ¹⁸Elisha had said, "A person will be able to buy a basket* of fine flour or two baskets* of barley for only one shekel* in the market place by the city gates of Samaria." ¹⁹But that officer had answered the man of God, "Even if the Lord made windows in heaven, this could not happen!" And Elisha had told ⌊the officer,⌋ "You will see it with your own eyes. But you will not eat any of that food." ²⁰It happened to the officer just that way. The people knocked him down at the gate and walked on him, and he died.

The King and the Shunammite Woman

8 Elisha talked to the woman whose son he had brought back to life. Elisha said, "You and your family should move to another country. Why? Because the Lord has decided that there will be a time of hunger here. This time of hunger will be in this country for seven years."
²So the woman did what the man of God* said. She went with her family to stay in the land of the Philistines for seven years. ³After the seven years were finished, the woman came back from the land of the Philistines.

The woman went to speak with the king. She wanted to ask him to help her get back her house and land.

---

lepers   People sick with leprosy.
chariot(s)   A small wagon used in war.
The horses ... city   The Hebrew is hard to understand here.
basket(s)   Literally, "seah(s)."
shekel   Or, "2/5 of an ounce."
man of God   Another name for a prophet.

2 KINGS 8:4–23

⁴The king was talking with Gehazi, the servant of the man of God* *(Elisha)*. The king said to Gehazi, "Please tell me all the great things Elisha has done."

⁵Gehazi was telling the king about Elisha bringing a dead person back to life. At that time, the woman whose son Elisha brought back to life went to the king. She wanted to ask him to help her get back her house and land. Gehazi said, "My lord and king, this is the woman! And this is the son that Elisha brought back to life!"

⁶The king asked the woman what she wanted. And the woman told him.

Then the king chose an officer to help the woman. The king said, "Give to the woman all that belongs to her. And give her all the harvest of her land from the day she left the country until now."

Ben Hadad Sends Hazael to Elisha

⁷Elisha went to Damascus. Ben Hadad king of Aram was sick. A person told Ben Hadad, "The man of God* has come here."

⁸Then the King Ben Hadad said to Hazael, "Take a gift, and go to meet the man of God.* Ask him to ask the Lord if I will get well from my sickness."

⁹So Hazael went to meet Elisha. Hazael brought a gift with him. He brought all kinds of good things from Damascus. It took 40 camels to carry everything. Hazael went to Elisha. Hazael said, "Your follower* Ben Hadad king of Aram sent me to you. He asks if he will get well from his sickness."

¹⁰Then Elisha said to Hazael, "Go and tell Ben Hadad, 'You will live.'* But really the Lord told me, 'He will die.'"

Elisha Makes a Prophecy About Hazael

¹¹Elisha began to stare. He stared until ₍Hazael₎ felt embarrassed. Then the man of God* began to cry. ¹²Hazael said, "Sir, why are you crying?"

Elisha answered, "I am crying because I know the bad things you will do to the Israelites. You will burn their strong cities. You will kill their young men with swords. You will kill their babies. You will split open their pregnant women."

¹³Hazael said, I am not a powerful man!* I can't do these great things!"

Elisha answered, "The Lord showed me that you will be king over Aram."

¹⁴Then Hazael left Elisha, and went to his king.* Ben Hadad said to Hazael, "What did Elisha say to you?"

Hazael answered, "Elisha told me that you will live."

Hazael Murders Ben Hadad

¹⁵But the next day, Hazael took a thick cloth and dipped it in water. Then he put the cover on Ben Hadad's face ₍and smothered him₎. Ben Hadad died and Hazael became the new king.

Jehoram Begins His Rule

¹⁶Jehoram son of Jehoshaphat was the king of Judah. Jehoram began to rule in the fifth year that Joram son of Ahab was king of Israel. ¹⁷Jehoram was 32 years old when he began to rule. He ruled eight years in Jerusalem. ¹⁸But Jehoram lived like the kings of Israel and did the things that the Lord said were wrong. Jehoram lived like the people from Ahab's family. Jehoram lived like this because his wife was Ahab's daughter. ¹⁹But the Lord would not destroy Judah because of ₍the promise to₎ his servant David. The Lord had promised David that someone from his family would always be king.

²⁰In Jehoram's time Edom broke away from Judah's rule. The people of Edom chose a king for themselves. ²¹Then Jehoram and all his chariots* went to Zair. The Edomite army surrounded them. Jehoram and his officers attacked them and escaped. Jehoram's soldiers all ran away and went home. ²²So the Edomites broke away from the rule of Judah. And they have been free from the rule of Judah until today.

At the same time, Libnah also broke away from Judah's rule.

²³All the things Jehoram did are written in the book, *The History of the Kings of Judah.*

---

man of God Another name for a prophet.
follower Literally, "son."
You will live Or possibly, "You will not live."

I ... powerful man Literally, "Your servant is only a dog!"
king Literally, "master."
chariot(s) A small wagon used in war.

⁲⁴Jehoram ₍died and₎ was buried with his ancestors* in the City of David.* Jehoram's son Ahaziah became the new king.

Ahaziah Begins His Rule

²⁵Ahaziah son of Jehoram became the king of Judah in the 12th year that Joram son of Ahab was king of Israel. ²⁶Ahaziah was 22 years old when he began to rule. He ruled one year in Jerusalem. His mother's name was Athaliah. She was the daughter of Omri, the king of Israel. ²⁷Ahaziah did the things the Lord said were wrong. Ahaziah did many bad things like the people from Ahab's family. Ahaziah lived like this because his wife was from Ahab's family.

Joram Is Hurt in the War Against Hazael

²⁸Joram was from Ahab's family. Ahaziah went with Joram to fight against Hazael king of Aram at Ramoth Gilead. The Arameans wounded Joram. King Joram went back to Israel so he could get well from those wounds. Joram went to the area of Jezreel. Ahaziah son of Jehoram was the king of Judah. Ahaziah went to Jezreel to see Joram.

Elisha Tells a Young Prophet to Anoint Jehu

9 Elisha the prophet called one of the group of prophets.* Elisha said to this man, "Get ready and take this small bottle of oil in your hand. Go to Ramoth Gilead. ²When you arrive there, find Jehu son of Jehoshaphat, the son of Nimshi. Then go in and make him get up from among his brothers. Take him to an inner room. ³Take the small bottle of oil and pour the oil on Jehu's head. Say, 'This is what the Lord says: I have anointed* you to be the new king over Israel.' Then open the door and run away. Don't wait!"

⁴So this young man, the prophet, went to Ramoth Gilead. ⁵When the young man arrived, ₍he saw₎ the captains of the army sitting. The young man said, "Captain, I have a message for you."

Jehu said, "We all ₍are here.₎ Which one of us is the message for?"

The young man said, "₍The message is for₎ you, captain."

⁶Jehu got up and went into the house. Then the young prophet poured the oil on Jehu's head. The young prophet said to Jehu, "The Lord God of Israel says, 'I am anointing* you to be the new king over the Lord's people, Israel. ⁷You must destroy the family of Ahab your king. In this way I will punish Jezebel for the deaths of my servants, the prophets, and the deaths of all the Lord's servants that were murdered. ⁸So all Ahab's family will die. I will not let any male child in Ahab's family live. It doesn't matter if that male child is a slave or a free person in Israel. ⁹I will make Ahab's family like the family of Jeroboam son of Nebat, and like the family of Baasha son of Ahijah. ¹⁰The dogs will eat Jezebel in the area of Jezreel. Jezebel will not be buried.'"

Then the young prophet opened the door and ran away.

The Servants Announce Jehu as King

¹¹Jehu went back to his king's officers. One of the officers said to Jehu, "Is everything all right? Why did this crazy man come to you?"

Jehu answered the servants, "You know the man and the crazy things he says."

¹²The officers said, "No! Tell us the truth. What did he say?" Jehu told the officers the things that the young prophet said. Jehu said, "He said, 'This is what the Lord says: I have anointed you to be the new king over Israel.'"

¹³Then each officer quickly took his robe off and put it on the steps in front of Jehu. Then they blew the trumpet and made the announcement, "Jehu is king!"

Jehu Goes to Jezreel

¹⁴So Jehu son of Jehoshaphat, son of Nimshi, made plans against Joram.

At that time, Joram and the Israelites had been trying to defend Ramoth Gilead from Hazael king of Aram. ¹⁵King Joram had fought against Hazael, king of Aram. But the Arameans wounded King Joram, and he went to Jezreel to get well from those injuries.

So Jehu told ₍the officers₎, "If you agree ₍that I am the new king₎, then don't let any person escape from the city to tell the news in Jezreel."

---

ancestors Literally, "fathers." This means a person's parents, grandparents, and all the people they are descended from.
City of David A part of the city of Jerusalem.
group of prophets Literally, "sons of the prophets." These people were prophets and people studying to become prophets.
anoint(ed) To pour olive oil on a person's head to show he was chosen by God to be a king, priest, or prophet.

¹⁶Joram was resting in Jezreel. So Jehu got in his chariot* and drove to Jezreel. Ahaziah king of Judah had also come to Jezreel to see Joram. ¹⁷A guard was standing on the tower in Jezreel. He saw Jehu's large group coming. He said, "I see a large group of people!"

Joram said, "Send someone on a horse to meet them. Tell this messenger to ask if those people come in peace." ¹⁸So the messenger rode on a horse to meet Jehu. The messenger said, "King Joram says, 'Do you come in peace?'"

Jehu said, "You have nothing to do with peace! Come and follow me."

The guard told Joram, "The messenger went to the group, but he has not come back yet." ¹⁹Then Joram sent out a second messenger on a horse. This man came to Jehu's group and said, "King Joram says, 'Peace.*'"

Jehu answered, "You have nothing to do with peace! Come and follow me."

²⁰The guard told Joram, "The second messenger went to the group, but he has not come back yet. There is a man driving his chariot* like a mad man. He is driving like Jehu son of Nimshi."

²¹Joram said, "Get me my chariot!"*

So the servant got Joram's chariot. Both Joram king of Israel and Ahaziah king of Judah got their chariots* and drove out to meet Jehu. They met Jehu at the property of Naboth from Jezreel. ²²Joram saw Jehu and asked, "Do you come in peace, Jehu?"

Jehu answered, "There is no peace as long as your mother Jezebel does many acts of prostitution and witchcraft.*"

²³Joram turned the horses to run away. Joram said to Ahaziah, "It is a trick, Ahaziah!"

²⁴But Jehu pulled his bow with all his strength and shot Joram in his back.* The arrow went through Joram's heart. Joram fell dead in his chariot.* ²⁵Jehu said to his chariot driver Bidkar, "Take Joram's body up and throw it into the field of Naboth from Jezreel. Remember when you and I rode together with Joram's father Ahab, the Lord said this would happen to him. ²⁶The Lord said,

'Yesterday I saw the blood of Naboth and his sons. So I will punish Ahab in this field.' The Lord said that. So take Joram's body and throw it into the field, just like the Lord said!"

²⁷Ahaziah king of Judah saw this, so he ran away. He went by the garden house. Jehu followed after him. Jehu said, "Shoot Ahaziah in his chariot,* too!"

[So Jehu's men shot Ahaziah] on the road to Gur near Ibleam. Ahaziah ran away to Megiddo, but he died there. ²⁸Ahaziah's servants carried Ahaziah's body in a chariot to Jerusalem. They buried Ahaziah in his tomb with his ancestors* in the City of David.*

²⁹Ahaziah became king over Judah during Joram's* eleventh year as king of Israel.

The Terrible Death of Jezebel

³⁰Jehu went to Jezreel, and Jezebel heard the news. She put her makeup on and fixed her hair. Then she stood by the window and looked out. ³¹Jehu entered the city. Jezebel said, "Hello, you Zimri*! Just like him, you killed your master!"

³²Jehu looked up at the window. He said, "Who is on my side? Who?"

Two or three eunuchs* looked out [from the window] at Jehu. ³³Jehu said [to them], "Throw Jezebel down!"

Then the eunuchs* threw Jezebel down. Some of Jezebel's blood splashed on the wall and on the horses. The horses walked on Jezebel's body. ³⁴Jehu went into the house and ate and drank. Then he said, "Now see about this cursed woman. Bury her, because she is a king's daughter."

³⁵The men went to bury Jezebel. But they could not find her body. They could only find her skull, her feet, and the palms of her hands. ³⁶So the men came back and told Jehu. Then Jehu said, "The Lord told his servant Elijah the Tishbite to give this message. Elijah said: 'Dogs will eat the body of Jezebel in the area of Jezreel. ³⁷Jezebel's body will be like dung on the field in the area of Jezreel.'"

---

ancestors Literally, "fathers." This means a person's parents, grandparents, and all the people they are descended from.
City of David A part of the city of Jerusalem.
Joram's Literally, "Joram son of Ahab."
Zimri Zimri was the man that killed Elah and the family of Baasha in Israel many years before. Read 1 Kings 16:8-12.
eunuchs Men that had their sexual organs removed. Often important officials of the king were eunuchs.

chariot(s) A small wagon used in war.
Peace A way of saying "hello."
witchcraft Using magic or the power of Satan to do things.
in his back Literally, "between his arms."

People won't be able to recognize Jezebel's body!'"

Jehu Writes the Leaders of Samaria

10 Ahab had 70 sons in Samaria. Jehu wrote letters and sent them to Samaria to the rulers and leaders of Jezreel. He also sent the letters to the people that raised Ahab's sons. ₍In the letters Jehu₎ said, ²⁻³"As soon as you get this letter, choose the person that is the best and most worthy among your father's sons. You have chariots* and horses. And you are living in a strong city. You also have weapons. Put the son you choose on his father's throne. Then fight for your father's family."

⁴But the rulers and leaders of Jezreel were very much afraid. They said, "The two kings *(Joram and Ahaziah)* could not stop Jehu. So we can't stop him either!"

⁵The man that took care of Ahab's house, the man that controlled the city, the elders, and the people who raised ₍Ahab's children₎ sent a message to Jehu. "We are your servants. We will do anything you tell us. We will not make any man king. Do what you think is good."

The Leaders of Samaria Kill Ahab's Children

⁶Then Jehu wrote a second letter to these leaders. Jehu said, "If you support me and obey me, then cut off the heads of Ahab's sons. And bring them to me at Jezreel about this time tomorrow."

Ahab had 70 sons. They were with the leaders of the city that raised them. ⁷When the leaders of the city received the letter, they took the king's sons and killed all 70 of them. Then the leaders put the heads of the king's sons in baskets. They sent the baskets to Jehu at Jezreel. ⁸The messenger came to Jehu and told him, "They have brought the heads of the king's sons!"

Then Jehu said, "Lay the heads in two piles at the city gate until morning."

⁹In the morning, Jehu went out and stood before the people. He said to the people, "You are innocent. Look, I made plans against my master. I killed him. But who killed all these sons of Ahab? You killed them! ¹⁰You should know that everything the Lord says will happen. And the Lord used Elijah to say these things about Ahab's family. Now the Lord has done the things he said he would do."

¹¹So Jehu killed all the people in Ahab's family living in Jezreel. Jehu killed all the important men, close friends, and priests. None of Ahab's people were left alive.

Jehu Kills Ahaziah's Relatives

¹²Jehu left Jezreel and went to Samaria. On the way, Jehu stopped at a place called Shepherd's Camp. He went to the house on the road to Beth Eked, where the shepherds cut wool from their sheep. ¹³Jehu met with the relatives of Ahaziah king of Judah. Jehu said ₍to them₎, "Who are you?"

They answered, "We are the relatives of Ahaziah, king of Judah. We have come down to visit the king's children and the queen mother's* children."

¹⁴Then Jehu said ₍to his men₎, "Take them alive!"

Jehu's men captured Ahaziah's relatives alive. There were 42 people. Jehu killed them at the well near Beth Eked. Jehu did not leave any person alive.

Jehu Meets Jehonadab

¹⁵After Jehu left there, he met Jehonadab son of Recab. Jehonadab was on his way to meet Jehu. Jehu greeted Jehonadab and said to him, "Are you a faithful friend to me, as I am to you?*"

Jehonadab answered, "Yes, I am a faithful friend to you."

Jehu said, "If you are, then give me your hand."

Then Jehu reached out and pulled Jehonadab up into the chariot.*

¹⁶Jehu said, "Come with me. You can see how strong my feelings are for the Lord."

So Jehonadab rode in Jehu's chariot.* ¹⁷Jehu came to Samaria and killed all Ahab's family that were still alive in Samaria. Jehu killed them all. Jehu did the things that the Lord had told Elijah.

Jehu Calls the Worshipers of Baal

¹⁸Then Jehu gathered all the people together. Jehu said to them, "Ahab served Baal a little. But Jehu will serve Baal much! ¹⁹Now call together all the priests and prophets of Baal. And call together

---

queen mother The mother of the king.
Are you a faithful friend ... you? Literally, "Is your heart true to me? My heart is true to your heart."

chariot(s) A small wagon used in war.

all the people that worship Baal. Don't let any person miss this meeting. I have a great sacrifice to give to Baal. I will kill any person that doesn't come to this meeting!"

But Jehu was tricking them. Jehu wanted to destroy the worshipers of Baal. [20]Jehu said, "Prepare a holy meeting for Baal." And the priests announced the meeting. [21]Then Jehu sent a message through all the land of Israel. All the worshipers of Baal came. There was not a person that stayed home. The Baal worshipers came into the temple* of Baal. The temple was filled with people.

[22]Jehu said to the man that kept the robes, "Bring out the robes for all the worshipers of Baal." So that man brought out the robes for the Baal worshipers.

[23]Then Jehu and Jehonadab son of Recab went into the temple* of Baal. Jehu said to the worshipers of Baal, "Look around and be sure that there are no servants of the Lord with you. Be sure there are only people that worship Baal." [24]The worshipers of Baal went into the temple of Baal to offer sacrifices and burnt offerings.

But outside, Jehu had 80 men waiting. Jehu told them, "Don't let any of the people escape. If any man lets one person escape, then that man must pay with his own life."

[25]Quickly after Jehu had finished offering the burnt offering, he said to the guards and to the captains, "Go in and kill the worshipers of Baal! Don't let any person come out of the temple alive!"

So the captains used thin swords and killed the worshipers of Baal. The guards and the captains threw the bodies of the worshipers of Baal out. Then the guards and the captains went to the inner room* of the temple* of Baal. [26]They brought out the memorial stones* that were in the temple of Baal and burned the temple. [27]Then they smashed the memorial stones of Baal. They also smashed the temple of Baal. They made the temple of Baal into a restroom. People still use that place as a toilet.

[28]So Jehu destroyed Baal worship in Israel. [29]But Jehu did not completely turn away from the sins of Jeroboam son of Nebat that caused Israel to sin. Jehu did not destroy the golden calves in Bethel and in Dan.

Jehu's Rule Over Israel

[30]The Lord said to Jehu, "You have done well. You have done the things that I say are good. You destroyed Ahab's family the way I wanted you to. So your descendants* will rule Israel for four generations."

[31]But Jehu was not careful to live in the law of the Lord with all his heart. Jehu did not stop doing the sins of Jeroboam that caused Israel to sin.

Hazael Defeats Israel

[32]At that time, the Lord began to cut parts from Israel. Hazael king of Aram defeated the Israelites on every border of Israel. [33]Hazael won the land east of the Jordan River—all the land of Gilead, including the land that belonged to the family groups of Gad, Reuben, and Manasseh. Hazael won all the land from Aroer by the Arnon Valley to Gilead and Bashan.

The Death of Jehu

[34]All the other great things that Jehu did are written in the book *The History of the Kings of Israel*. [35]Jehu died and was buried with his ancestors.* The people buried Jehu in Samaria. Jehu's son Jehoahaz became the new king of Israel after him. [36]Jehu ruled over Israel in Samaria for 28 years.

Athaliah Kills All the King's Sons in Judah

11 Athaliah was Ahaziah's mother. She saw that her son was dead, so she got up and killed all the king's family.

[2]Jehosheba was King Joram's daughter and Ahaziah's sister. Joash was one of the king's sons. Jehosheba took Joash while the other children were being killed. Jehosheba hid Joash. She put Joash and his nurse in her bedroom. So Jehosheba

---

temple Here this means the building where people went to worship Baal.
inner room Literally, "The city of the temple of Baal."
memorial stones Stones that were set up to help people remember something special. In ancient Israel, people often set up stones as special places to worship false gods.

descendants A person's children and all of their future families.
ancestors Literally, "fathers." This means a person's parents, grandparents, and all the people they are descended from.

and the nurse hid Joash from Athaliah. That way Joash was not killed. ³Then Joash and Jehosheba hid in the Lord's temple.* Joash hid there for six years. And Athaliah ruled over the land of Judah.

⁴In the seventh year, Jehoiada ₍the high priest₎ sent and got the captains of the Carites* and guards.* Jehoiada brought them together in the Lord's temple.* Then Jehoiada made an agreement with them. In the temple Jehoiada forced them to make a promise. Then he showed the king's son *(Joash)* to them.

⁵Then Jehoiada gave them a command. He said, "This is the thing you must do. One-third of you must come in at the start of each Sabbath day. You men will protect the king at his house. ⁶Another third of you will be at the Sur Gate. And another third will be at the gate behind the guard. This way you will be like a wall protecting Joash. ⁷At the end of each Sabbath day, two-thirds of you will guard the Lord's temple and protect King Joash. ⁸You must stay with King Joash any time he goes any place. The whole group must surround the king. Each guard must have his weapon in his hand. And you must kill any person that comes too close to you."

⁹The captains obeyed all the things that Jehoiada the priest commanded. Each captain took his men. One group was to guard the king on Saturday. And the other groups were to guard the king during the rest of the week. All those men went to Jehoiada the priest. ¹⁰And the priest gave spears and shields to the captains. These were the spears and shields David put in the Lord's temple.* ¹¹These guards stood with their weapons in their hands from the right corner of the temple to the left corner of the temple. They stood around the altar* and the temple and around the king when he went to the temple. ¹²These men brought out Joash. They put the crown on Joash and give him the agreement between the king and God.* Then they anointed* him and made him the new king. They clapped their hands and shouted, "Long live the king!"

¹³Queen Athaliah heard the noise from the guards and the people. So she went to the people at the Lord's temple. ¹⁴Athaliah saw the king by the column where the king usually stood. She also saw the leaders and men playing the trumpets for the king. She saw that all the people were very happy. She heard the trumpets, and she tore her clothes ₍to show she was upset₎. Then Athaliah shouted, "Treason! Treason!"

¹⁵Jehoiada the priest gave a command to the captains that were in charge of the soldiers. Jehoiada told them, "Take Athaliah outside of the temple area. Kill any of her followers. But don't kill them in the Lord's temple."

¹⁶So the soldiers grabbed Athaliah. They killed her as soon as she went through the horse's entrance to the palace.

¹⁷Then Jehoiada made the agreement between the Lord and the king and the people. This agreement showed that the king and the people belonged to the Lord. Jehoiada also made the agreement between the king and the people. ₍This agreement showed what the king would do for the people. And it showed that the people would obey and follow the king.₎

¹⁸Then all the people went to the temple of ₍the false god₎ Baal. The people destroyed the statue of Baal, and they destroyed his altars.* They broke them into many, many pieces. The people also killed Baal's priest, Mattan, in front of the altars.

So ₍Jehoiada₎ the priest put men in charge of the Lord's temple. ¹⁹The priest led all the people. They went from the Lord's temple to the king's house. The king's special guards and the captains went with the king. And all the other people followed them. They went to the entrance to the king's house. Then King Joash sat on the throne. ²⁰All the people were happy. The city was peaceful. And Queen Athaliah was killed with a sword near the king's house.

²¹Joash was seven years old when he became the king.

---

temple A special building for worshiping God. God commanded the Jews to worship him at the temple in Jerusalem.

Carites Or, "Kerethites," special soldiers hired to serve the king.

guards Literally, "runners" or "messengers."

altar(s) A stone table used for burning sacrifices offered as gifts to God.

agreement between the king and God This was probably the promise the king made to serve God. See verse 17 and 1 Sam. 10:25.

Joash Begins His Rule

12 Joash began to rule during Jehu's seventh year as king of Israel. Joash ruled 40 years in Jerusalem. Joash's mother was named Zibiah of Beersheba. ²Joash did the things that the Lord said were right. Joash obeyed the Lord all his life. He did the things that Jehoiada the priest taught him. ³But he did not destroy the high places.* The people still made sacrifices and burned incense at those places of worship.

Joash Orders the Temple Repaired

⁴⁻⁵Joash said to the priests, "There is much money in the Lord's temple. People have given things to the temple. People have paid the temple tax when they were counted. And people have given money simply because they wanted to. You priests should take that money and repair the Lord's temple. Each priest should use the money he gets from the people he serves. He should use that money to repair the damages to the Lord's temple."

⁶⌊But the priests did not do the repairs.⌋ In the 23rd year that Joash was king, the priests ⌊still⌋ had not repaired the temple. ⁷So king Joash called for Jehoiada the priest and the ⌊other⌋ priests. Joash said to Jehoiada and the other priests, "Why haven't you repaired the temple? Stop taking money from the people you serve. Stop using that money. That money must be used to repair the temple."

⁸The priests agreed to stop taking money from the people. But they also decided not to repair the temple. ⁹So Jehoiada the priest took a box and made a hole in the top of it. Then Jehoiada put the box on the south side of the altar. This box was by the door where people came into the Lord's temple. Some of the priests guarded the doorway* of the temple. Those priests took the money people had given to the Lord, and they put that money into that box.

¹⁰⌊Then the people began putting money into that box when they went to the temple.⌋ Whenever the king's secretary and the high priest saw there was a lot of money in the box, they came and took the money from the box. They put the money in bags and counted it. ¹¹Then they paid the workers that worked on the Lord's temple. They paid the carpenters and other builders that worked on the Lord's temple. ¹²They used that money to pay the stoneworkers and stonecutters. And they used that money to buy timber, cut stone, and everything else to repair the Lord's temple.

¹³⁻¹⁴People gave money for the Lord's temple. But the priests could not use that money to make silver cups, snuffers,* basins, trumpets, or any gold and silver dishes. That money was used to pay the workers. And those workers repaired the Lord's temple. ¹⁵No one counted all the money or forced the workers to tell what happened to the money. Why? Because those workers could be trusted!

¹⁶People gave money at the times they offered guilt offerings and sin offerings. But that money was not used to pay the workers. That money belonged to the priests.

Joash Saves Jerusalem from Hazael

¹⁷Hazael was the king of Aram. Hazael went to fight against the city of Gath. Hazael defeated Gath. Then he made plans to go fight against Jerusalem.

¹⁸Jehoshaphat, Jehoram, and Ahaziah had been kings of Judah. They were Joash's* ancestors.* They had given many things to the Lord. Those things were kept in the temple. Joash also had given many things to the Lord. Joash took all those and all the gold that was in the temple and in his house. Then Joash sent all those expensive things to Hazael king of Aram. So they met at Jerusalem. ⌊Hazael did not fight against the city.⌋

The Death of Joash

¹⁹All the great things that Joash did are written in the book *The History of the Kings of Judah*.

²⁰Joash's officers made plans against him. They killed Joash at the house of Millo on the road that goes down to Silla. ²¹Jozabad son of Shimeath and Jehozabad son of Shomer were Joash's officers. Those men killed Joash.

The people buried Joash with his ancestors* in the City of David.* Joash's son Amaziah became the new king after him.

---

high places Places for worshiping God or false gods. These places were often on the hills and mountains.
doorway Literally, "threshold."
snuffers They were like small cups used to put out lamps.
Joash Or, "Jehoash," the long form of the name "Joash."
ancestors Literally, "fathers." This means a person's parents, grandparents, and all the people they are descended from.
City of David A part of the city of Jerusalem.

Jehoahaz Begins His Rule

13 Jehoahaz son of Jehu became king over Israel in Samaria. This was during the 23rd year that Joash son of Ahaziah was king in Judah. Jehoahaz ruled 17 years. ²Jehoahaz did those things the Lord said were wrong. Jehoahaz followed the sins of Jeroboam son of Nebat that caused Israel to sin. Jehoahaz did not stop doing those things. ³Then the Lord was angry against Israel. The Lord gave Israel into the power of Hazael king of Aram and Hazael's son Ben Hadad.

The Lord Has Mercy on the People of Israel

⁴Then Jehoahaz begged the Lord to help them. And the Lord listened to him. The Lord had seen the troubles of Israel and how the king of Aram troubled the Israelites. ⁵So the Lord sent a man to save Israel. The Israelites were free from the Arameans. So the Israelites went to their own homes, like they did before. ⁶But the Israelites still did not stop doing the sins of the family of Jeroboam that caused Israel to sin. The Israelites continued doing the sins of Jeroboam. They also kept the Asherah poles* in Samaria.

⁷The king of Aram defeated Jehoahaz's army. The king of Aram destroyed most of the men in the army. He left only 50 horse soldiers, 10 chariots,* and 10,000 foot soldiers. Jehoahaz's soldiers were like chaff* blown away by the wind at the time of threshing.*

⁸All the great things that Jehoahaz did are written in the book *The History of the Kings of Israel*. ⁹Jehoahaz ⌊died⌋ and was buried with his ancestors.* The people buried Jehoahaz in Samaria. Jehoahaz's son Jehoash became the new king after him.

Jehoash's Rule Over Israel

¹⁰Jehoash son of Jehoahaz became king over Israel in Samaria. This was during the 37th year that Joash was king of Judah. Jehoash ruled Israel for 16 years. ¹¹Jehoash king of Israel did the things the Lord said were wrong. He did not stop doing the sins of Jeroboam son of Nebat that caused Israel to sin. Jehoash continued to do those sins. ¹²All the great things that Jehoash did and his wars against Amaziah king of Judah are written in the book *The History of the Kings of Israel*. ¹³Jehoash ⌊died and⌋ was buried with his ancestors.* Jeroboam ⌊became the new king and⌋ sat on Jehoash's throne. Jehoash was buried at Samaria with the kings of Israel.

Jehoash Visits Elisha

¹⁴Elisha became sick. Later, Elisha died from this sickness. Jehoash, king of Israel, went to visit Elisha. Jehoash cried for Elisha. Jehoash said, "My father, my father! Is it time for the chariots of Israel and its horses*?"

¹⁵Elisha said to Jehoash, "Take a bow and some arrows."

Jehoash took a bow and some arrows. ¹⁶Then Elisha said to the king of Israel, "Put your hand on the bow." Jehoash put his hand on the bow. Then Elisha put his hands on the king's hands. ¹⁷Elisha said, "Open the east window." Jehoash opened the window. Then Elisha said, "Shoot."

Jehoash shot. Then Elisha said, "That is the Lord's arrow of victory! The arrow of victory over Aram! You will defeat the Arameans at Aphek. And you will destroy them."

¹⁸Elisha said, "Take the arrows." Jehoash took the arrows. Then Elisha said to the king of Israel, "Hit on the ground."

Jehoash hit the ground three times. Then he stopped. ¹⁹The man of God* *(Elisha)* was angry at Jehoash. Elisha said, "You should have hit five or six times! Then you would have defeated Aram until you destroyed it! But now, you will defeat Aram only three times!"

An Amazing Thing at Elisha's Grave

²⁰Elisha died, and the people buried him.

One time in the spring, a group of Moabite soldiers came to Israel. ⌊They came to take things in war.⌋ ²¹Some Israelites were burying a dead man, and they saw that group of soldiers. The Israelites quickly threw the dead man into Elisha's grave ⌊and ran away⌋. As soon as the dead man touched the bones of Elisha, the dead man came back to life and stood up on his feet!

---

ancestors Literally, "fathers." This means a person's parents, grandparents, and all the people they are descended from.
chariots of Israel and its horses This means, "Is it time for God to come and take you? See 1 Kings 2:12.
man of God Another name for a prophet.

Jehoash Wins Back Cities of Israel

²²During all the days that Jehoahaz ruled, Hazael king of Aram caused trouble to Israel. ²³But the Lord was kind to the Israelites. The Lord had mercy and turned to the Israelites. Why? Because of his Agreement with Abraham, Isaac, and Jacob. The Lord would not destroy the Israelites. He did not throw them away yet. ²⁴Hazael king of Aram died, and Ben Hadad became the new king after him. ²⁵ [Before he died,] Hazael had taken some cities in war from Jehoahaz, Jehoash's father. But now Jehoash took back these cities from Hazael's son Ben Hadad. Jehoash defeated Ben Hadad three times and took back the cities of Israel.

Amaziah Begins His Rule in Judah

14 Amaziah son of Joash king of Judah became king in the second year that Joash son of Jehoahaz was king of Israel. ²Amaziah was 25 years old when he began to rule. Amaziah ruled 29 years in Jerusalem. Amaziah's mother was Jehoaddin from Jerusalem. ³Amaziah did the things the Lord said were right. But he did not follow God completely like David his ancestor.* Amaziah did all the things that Joash his father had done. ⁴He did not destroy the high places.* The people still sacrificed and burned incense* in those places of worship.

⁵At the time that Amaziah had strong control of the kingdom, he killed the officers that had killed his father. ⁶But he did not kill the children of the murderers because of the rules written in the book *The Law of Moses*. The Lord gave this command [in the Law of Moses]: "Parents must not be put to death for something their children did. And children must not be put to death for something their parents did. A person should be put to death only for a bad thing that he himself did."*

⁷Amaziah killed 10,000 Edomites in the Valley of Salt. In war Amaziah took Sela and called it "Joktheel." That place is still called "Joktheel" today.

Amaziah Wants War Against Jehoash

⁸Amaziah sent messengers to Jehoash son of Jehoahaz, son of Jehu king of Israel. Amaziah's message said, "Come on, let's meet together face to face [and fight]."

⁹Jehoash king of Israel sent an answer to Amaziah king of Judah. Jehoash said, "The thorn bush in Lebanon sent a message to the cedar tree in Lebanon. It said, 'Give your daughter for my son to marry.' But a wild animal from Lebanon passed by and walked on the thorn bush. ¹⁰True, you have defeated Edom. But you have become proud because of your victory over Edom. But stay at home and brag! Don't make trouble for yourself. If you do this, you will fall, and Judah will fall with you!"

¹¹But Amaziah would not listen to Jehoash's warning. So Jehoash king of Israel went to fight against Amaziah king of Judah at Beth Shemesh in Judah.* ¹²Israel defeated Judah. Every man of Judah ran home. ¹³At Beth Shemesh, Jehoash king of Israel captured Amaziah king of Judah, the son of Joash, the son of Ahaziah. Jehoash took Amaziah to Jerusalem. Jehoash broke down the wall of Jerusalem from the Gate of Ephraim to the corner gate, about 600 feet.* ¹⁴Then Jehoash took all the gold and silver and all the dishes in the Lord's temple and in the treasures of the king's house. Jehoash also took people to be his prisoners. Then he went back to Samaria.

¹⁵All the great things that Jehoash did, including how he fought against Amaziah king of Judah, are written in the book *The History of the Kings of Israel*. ¹⁶Jehoash [died and] was buried with his ancestors.* Jehoash was buried in Samaria with the kings of Israel. Jehoash's son Jeroboam became the new king after him.

The Death of Amaziah

¹⁷Amaziah son of Joash king of Judah lived 15 years after the death of Jehoash son of Jehoahaz king of Israel. ¹⁸All the great things that Amaziah did are written in the book *The History of the Kings of Judah*. ¹⁹The people made a plan against Amaziah in Jerusalem. Amaziah ran away to

---

ancestor Literally, "father." This means a person that people are descended from.
high places Places for worshiping God or false gods. These places were often on the hills and mountains.
incense A kind of spice that smells good when it is burned. It was burned as a gift to God.
Parents ... did See Deut. 24:16.

Jehoash ... Judah Literally, "He and Amaziah king of Judah looked at each other in the face at Beth Shemesh in Judah."
about 600 feet Literally, "400 cubits."
ancestors Literally, "fathers." This means a person's parents, grandparents, and all the people they are descended from.

Lachish. But the people sent men after Amaziah to Lachish. And those men killed Amaziah in Lachish. ²⁰The people brought Amaziah's body back on horses. Amaziah was buried at Jerusalem with his ancestors* in the City of David.*

Azariah Begins His Rule Over Judah

²¹Then all the people of Judah made Azariah the new king. Azariah was 16 years old. ²²So King Amaziah died and was buried with his ancestors.* Then Azariah built Elath again and gave it back to Judah.

Jeroboam II Begins His Rule Over Israel

²³Jeroboam son of Jehoash king of Israel began to rule in Samaria during the 15th year that Amaziah son of Joash was king of Judah. Jeroboam ruled 41 years. ²⁴Jeroboam did the things the Lord said were wrong. Jeroboam did not stop doing the sins of Jeroboam son of Nebat that caused Israel to sin. ²⁵Jeroboam took back Israel's land which ran from the Lebo Hamath to the Arabah Sea.* This happened like the Lord of Israel had told his servant Jonah son of Amittai, the prophet from Gath Hepher. ²⁶The Lord saw that all the Israelites had many troubles, slaves and free men. No person was left that could help Israel. ²⁷The Lord did not say that he would take away the name of Israel from the world. So the Lord used Jeroboam son of Jehoash to save the people of Israel.

²⁸All the great things that Jeroboam did are written in the book *The History of the Kings of Israel*. This includes the story about Jeroboam winning back Damascus and Hamath for Israel. (These cities had belonged to Judah.) ²⁹Jeroboam ⌊died and⌋ was buried with his ancestors*, the kings of Israel. Jeroboam's son Zechariah became the new king after him.

Azariah's Rule Over Judah

15 Azariah son of Amaziah king of Judah became king in the 27th year of Jeroboam king of Israel. ²Azariah was 16 years old when he began to rule. He ruled 52 years in Jerusalem. Azariah's mother was named Jecoliah of Jerusalem. ³Azariah did the things that the Lord said were right, just like his father Amaziah. Azariah followed all the things his father Amaziah did. ⁴He did not destroy the high places.* People still made sacrifices and burned incense* in these places of worship.

⁵The Lord caused King Azariah to become sick with leprosy.* He was a leper until the day he died. Azariah lived in a separate house. Jotham, the king's son, took care of the king's house and judged the people.

⁶All the great things that Azariah did are written in the book *The History of the Kings of Judah*. ⁷Azariah ⌊died and⌋ was buried with his ancestors* in the City of David.* Azariah's son Jotham became the new king after him.

Zechariah's Short Rule Over Israel

⁸Zechariah son of Jeroboam ruled over Samaria in Israel for six months. This was during the 38th year that Azariah was king of Judah. ⁹Zechariah did the things the Lord said were wrong. He did the same things his ancestors* did. He did not stop doing the sins of Jeroboam son of Nebat that caused Israel to sin.

¹⁰Shallum son of Jabesh made plans against Zechariah. Shallum killed Zechariah in Ibleam. Shallum became the new king after him. ¹¹All the other things that Zechariah did are written in the book *The History of the Kings of Israel.* ¹²In this way the Lord's word came true. The Lord had told Jehu that four generations of his descendants* would be kings of Israel.

Shallum's Short Rule Over Israel

¹³Shallum son of Jabesh became king ⌊of Israel⌋ during the 39th year that Uzziah was king of Judah. Shallum ruled for one month in Samaria. ¹⁴Menahem son of Gadi came up from Tirzah to Samaria. Menahem killed Shallum son of Jabesh. Then Menahem became the new king after him.

¹⁵All the things Shallum did, including his plans against Zechariah, are written in the book *The History of the Kings of Israel*.

---

high places Places for worshiping God or false gods. These places were often on the hills and mountains.
incense A kind of spice that smells good when it is burned. It was burned as a gift to God.
leprosy A very bad skin disease.
descendants A person's children and all of their future families.

---

ancestors Literally, "fathers." This means a person's parents, grandparents, and all the people they are descended from.
City of David A part of the city of Jerusalem.
Arabah Sea The Dead Sea.

Menahem's Rule Over Israel

[16] ₍After Shallum died,₎ Menahem defeated Tiphsah and the area around it. The people refused to open ₍the city gate₎ for him. So Menahem defeated them and ripped open all the pregnant women in that city. [17] Menahem son of Gadi became king over Israel during the 39th year that Azariah was king of Judah. Menahem ruled ten years in Samaria. [18] Menahem did the things the Lord said were wrong. Menahem did not stop doing the sins of Jeroboam son of Nebat that caused Israel to sin. [19] Pul king of Assyria came to fight against Israel. Menahem gave Pul 75,000 pounds* of silver. He did this so Pul would support Menahem and make Menahem's kingdom stronger. [20] Menahem raised the money by making all the rich and powerful men pay taxes. Menahem taxed each man 20 ounces* of silver. Then Menahem gave the money to the king of Assyria. So the king of Assyria left, and did not stay there in Israel. [21] All the great things that Menahem did are written in the book *The History of the Kings of Israel*. [22] Menahem ₍died and₎ was buried with his ancestors.* Menahem's son Pekahiah became the new king after him.

Pekahiah's Rule Over Israel

[23] Pekahiah son of Menahem became king over Israel in Samaria during the 50th year that Azariah was king of Judah. Pekahiah ruled two years. [24] Pekahiah did the things that the Lord said were wrong. Pekahiah did not stop doing the sins of Jeroboam son of Nebat that caused Israel to sin. [25] The commander of Pekahiah's army was Pekah son of Remaliah. Pekah killed Pekahiah. He killed him in Samaria at the king's palace.* Pekah had 50 men from Gilead with him when he killed Pekahiah. Then Pekah became the new king after him. [26] All the great things Pekahiah did are written in the book *The History of the Kings of Israel*.

Pekah's Rule Over Israel

[27] Pekah son of Remaliah began to rule over Israel in Samaria during the 52nd year that Azariah was king of Judah. Pekah ruled 20 years. [28] Pekah did the things that the Lord said were wrong. Pekah did not stop doing the sins of Jeroboam son of Nebat that caused Israel to sin. [29] Tiglath Pileser king of Assyria came to fight against Israel. This was during the time that Pekah was king of Israel. Tiglath Pileser captured Ijon, Abel Bethmaacah, Janoah, Kedesh, Hazor, Gilead, Galilee, and all the area of Naphtali. Tiglath Pileser took the people from these places as prisoners to Assyria. [30] Hoshea son of Elah made plans against Pekah son of Remaliah. Hoshea killed Pekah. Then Hoshea became the new king after Pekah. This was during the 20th year that Jotham son of Uzziah ₍was king of Judah₎. [31] All the great things that Pekah did are written in the book *The History of the Kings of Israel*.

Jotham Rules Over Judah

[32] Jotham son of Uzziah became king of Judah. This was during the second year that Pekah son of Remaliah was king of Israel. [33] Jotham was 25 years old when he became king. Jotham ruled 16 years in Jerusalem. Jotham's mother was named Jerusha, the daughter of Zadok. [34] Jotham did the things the Lord said were right, just like his father Uzziah. [35] But he did not destroy the high places.* The people still made sacrifices and burned incense* at those places of worship. Jotham built the upper gate of the Lord's temple.* [36] All the great things that Jotham did are written in the book *The History of the Kings of Judah*. [37] At that time, the Lord sent Rezin king of Aram and Pekah son of Remaliah to fight against Judah. [38] Jotham ₍died and₎ was buried with his ancestors.* Jotham was buried in the City of David* his ancestor.* Jotham's son Ahaz became the new king after him.

75,000 pounds Or, 34,000kg. Literally, "1,000 talents (kikar)."
20 ounces Or, 575g. Literally, "50 shekels."
ancestors Literally, "fathers." This means a person's parents, grandparents, and all the people they are descended from.
palace A large house for the king and his family.
high places Places for worshiping God or false gods. These places were often on the hills and mountains.
incense A kind of spice that smells good when it is burned. It was burned as a gift to God.
temple A special building for worshiping God. God commanded the Jews to worship him at the temple in Jerusalem.
City of David A part of the city of Jerusalem.
ancestor Literally, "father." This means a person that people are descended from.

Ahaz Becomes King Over Judah

16 Ahaz son of Jotham became king of Judah during the 17th year that Pekah son of Remaliah was king of Israel. ²Ahaz was 20 years old when he became king. Ahaz ruled 16 years in Jerusalem. Ahaz did not do the things the Lord said were right. He did not obey God like his ancestor* David. ³Ahaz lived like the kings of Israel. He even sacrificed his son in fire.* He copied the terrible sins of the nations that the Lord forced to leave the country at the time the Israelites came. ⁴Ahaz made sacrifices and burned incense* at the high places* and on the hills and under every green tree.

⁵Rezin, king of Aram, and Pekah son of Remaliah, king of Israel, came to fight against Jerusalem. Rezin and Pekah surrounded Ahaz, but could not defeat him. ⁶At that time, Rezin king of Aram took back Elath for Aram. Rezin took all the people of Judah that were living in Elath. The Arameans settled in Elath, and they still live there today.

⁷Ahaz sent messengers to Tiglath Pileser, the king of Assyria. The message was: "I am your servant. I am like a son to you. Come and save me from the king of Aram and the king of Israel. They have come to fight me!" ⁸Ahaz also took the silver and gold that was in the temple* of the Lord and in the treasuries of the king's house. Then Ahaz sent a gift to the king of Assyria. ⁹The king of Assyria listened to Ahaz. The king of Assyria went to fight against Damascus. The king captured that city and took the people from Damascus as prisoners to Kir. He also killed Rezin.

¹⁰King Ahaz went to Damascus to meet Tiglath Pileser king of Assyria. Ahaz saw the altar* at Damascus. King Ahaz sent a model and pattern of this altar to Uriah the priest. ¹¹Then Uriah the priest built an altar just like the model King Ahaz had sent him from Damascus. Uriah the priest built the altar this way before King Ahaz came back from Damascus.

¹²When the King arrived from Damascus, he saw the altar.* He offered sacrifices on the altar. ¹³On the altar, Ahaz burned his burnt offerings and grain offerings. He poured his drink offering and sprinkled the blood of his fellowship offerings on this altar.

¹⁴Ahaz took the bronze altar that was before the Lord from the front of the temple. This bronze altar was between Ahaz's altar and the temple of the Lord. Ahaz put the bronze altar on the north side of his own altar. ¹⁵Ahaz gave a command to Uriah the priest. He said, "Use the large altar to burn the morning burnt offerings, the evening grain offerings, and the drink offerings from all the people of this country. Sprinkle all the blood from the burnt offering and other sacrifices on the large altar. But I will use the bronze altar to ask questions from God." ¹⁶Uriah the priest did everything that King Ahaz commanded him to do.

¹⁷There were carts with bronze panels and basins for the priests to wash their hands. King Ahaz removed the panels and basins and cut up the carts. He also took the large tank off the bronze bulls that stood under it. He put the large tank on a stone pavement. ¹⁸Workers had built a covered place inside the temple area for the Sabbath* ⌊meetings⌋. But Ahaz took away that covered place. Ahaz also took away the outside entrance for the king. Ahaz took all of these from the Lord's temple. Ahaz did this because of the king of Assyria.

¹⁹All the great things that Ahaz did are written in the book *The History of the Kings of Judah*. ²⁰Ahaz ⌊died and⌋ was buried with his ancestors* in the City of David.* Ahaz's son Hezekiah became the new king after him.

Hoshea Begins His Rule Over Israel

17 Hoshea son of Elah began to rule in Samaria over Israel. This was during the 12th year that Ahaz was king of Judah. Hoshea ruled nine years. ²Hoshea did the things the Lord said were wrong. But Hoshea was not as bad as the kings of Israel that ruled before him.

---

ancestor Literally, "father." This means a person that people are descended from.
sacrificed his son in fire Literally, "made his son to pass through the fire."
incense A kind of spice that smells good when it is burned. It was burned as a gift to God.
high places Places for worshiping God or false gods. These places were often on the hills and mountains.
temple A special building for worshiping God. God commanded the Jews to worship him at the temple in Jerusalem.
altar(s) A stone table used for burning sacrifices offered as gifts to God.

Sabbath Saturday, a special day of worship for Jews.
ancestors Literally, "fathers." This means a person's parents, grandparents, and all the people they are descended from.
City of David A part of the city of Jerusalem.

2 KINGS 17:3–21

³Shalmaneser king of Assyria came to fight against Hoshea. ₍Shalmaneser defeated Hoshea₎ and Hoshea became his servant. So Hoshea paid tribute* to Shalmaneser.

⁴Later, Hoshea sent messengers to the king of Egypt ₍to ask for help₎. That king's name was So. That year, Hoshea did not pay tribute* to the king of Assyria like he did every other year. The king of Assyria learned that Hoshea had made plans against him. So the king of Assyria arrested Hoshea and put him in jail.

⁵The king of Assyria attacked many places in Israel. Then he came to Samaria. He fought against Samaria for three years. ⁶The king of Assyria took Samaria during the ninth year that Hoshea was king of Israel. The king of Assyria captured many Israelites and took them as prisoners to Assyria. He made them live in Halah by the Habor River at Gozan and in other cities of the Medes.

⁷These things happened because the Israelites had sinned against the Lord their God. And it was the Lord that brought the Israelites out of the land of Egypt! The Lord saved them from the power of Pharaoh, the king of Egypt. But the Israelites began worshiping other gods. ⁸They began doing the same things that other people did. And the Lord had forced those people to leave their land when the Israelites came. The Israelites also chose to be ruled by kings, ₍not by God₎. ⁹The Israelites secretly did things against the Lord their God. And those things were wrong!

The Israelites built high places* in all their cities—from the smallest town to the largest city. ¹⁰The Israelites put up memorial stones* and Asherah poles* on every high hill and under every green tree. ¹¹The Israelites burned incense* there in all those places of worship. They did these things like the nations that the Lord forced out of the land before them. The Israelites did evil things that made the Lord angry. ¹²They served idols.* And the Lord had said to the Israelites, "You must not do this thing."

¹³The Lord used every prophet and every seer* to warn Israel and Judah. The Lord said, "Turn away from the evil things you do! Obey my commands and laws. Follow all the Law that I gave to your ancestors.* I used my servants the prophets to give this law to you."

¹⁴But the people would not listen. They were very stubborn like their ancestors.* Their ancestors did not believe the Lord their God. ¹⁵The people refused the Lord's laws and his Agreement that he made with their ancestors. They refused to listen to the Lord's warnings. They worshiped idols that were worth nothing and they themselves became worth nothing. They lived like the people in the nations around them. They did those bad things. And the Lord had warned the people of Israel. The Lord told them not to do those bad things.

¹⁶The people stopped following the commands of the Lord their God. They made two gold statues of calves. They made Asherah poles.* They worshiped all the stars of heaven and served Baal.* ¹⁷They sacrificed their sons and daughters in the fire. They used magic and witchcraft* to try to learn the future. They sold themselves to do what the Lord said was evil. They did this to make the Lord angry. ¹⁸So the Lord became very angry at Israel and took them out of his sight. There were no Israelites left, except the family group of Judah!

The People of Judah Are Also Guilty

¹⁹But even the people of Judah did not obey the commands of the Lord their God. The people of Judah lived just like the people of Israel.

²⁰The Lord rejected all the people of Israel. He brought them many troubles. He let people destroy them. And, finally, he threw them away and put them out of his sight. ²¹The Lord tore

---

tribute Money paid to a foreign king or nation to pay for being protected.
high places Places for worshiping God or false gods. These places were often on the hills and mountains.
memorial stones Stones that were set up to help people remember something special. In ancient Israel, people often set up stones as special places to worship false gods.
Asherah poles These poles were used to honor the female god Asherah that the Canaanite people worshiped.
incense A kind of spice that smells good when it is burned. It was burned as a gift to God.

idols Statues of false gods that people worshiped.
seer A kind of prophet, a person that spoke for God. This word shows the prophet saw things in visions.
ancestors Literally, "fathers." This means a person's parents, grandparents, and all the people they are descended from.
Baal The Canaanite people believed that this false god brought the rain and storms. They also thought that he made the land produce good crops.
witchcraft Using magic or the power of Satan to do things.

Israel from the family of David, and the Israelites made Jeroboam son of Nebat their king. Jeroboam pulled the Israelites away from following the Lord. Jeroboam caused the Israelites to do a great sin. ²²So the Israelites followed all the sins that Jeroboam did. They did not stop doing these sins ²³until the Lord took Israel away from his sight. And the Lord said this would happen! He sent his prophets to tell the people this would happen. So the Israelites were taken out of their country into Assyria. And they have been there to this day.

The Beginning of the Samaritan People

²⁴⌊The king of Assyria took the Israelites out of Samaria.⌋ Then the king of Assyria brought people from Babylon, Cuthah, Avva, Hamath, and Sepharvaim. He put those people in Samaria. Those people took over Samaria and lived in the cities around it. ²⁵When these people began to live in Samaria, they did not honor the Lord. So the Lord sent lions to attack them. These lions killed some of those people. ²⁶Some people said to the king of Assyria, "Those people that you took away and put in the cities of Samaria do not know the law of the god of that country. So that god sent lions to attack those people. The lions killed those people because those people don't know the law of the god of that country."

²⁷So the king of Assyria gave this command: "You took some priests from Samaria. Send one of those priests that I captured back to Samaria. Let that priest go and live there. Then that priest can teach the people the law of the god of that country."

²⁸So one of the priests that the Assyrians had carried away from Samaria came to live in Bethel. This priest taught the people how they should honor the Lord.

²⁹But all those people made gods of their own and put them in the temples at the high places* the Samarians had made. Those people did this wherever they lived. ³⁰The people of Babylon made ⌊the false God⌋ Succoth Benoth. The people of Cuthah made ⌊the false god⌋ Nergal. The people of Hamath made ⌊the false god⌋ Ashima. ³¹The people of Avva made ⌊the false gods⌋ Nibhaz and Tartak. And the people from Sepharvaim burned their children in the fire to honor their false gods, Adrammelech and Anammelech.

³²But those people also worshiped the Lord. They chose priests for the high places* from among the people. These priests made sacrifices for the people in the temples at those places of worship. ³³They respected the Lord, but they also served their own gods. Those people served their gods the same as they did in the countries they were taken from.

³⁴Even today those people live like they did in the past. They do not honor the Lord. They do not obey the rules and commands of the Israelites. They do not obey the Law or the commands that the Lord gave to the children of Jacob (Israel). ³⁵The Lord made an Agreement with the people of Israel. The Lord commanded them, "You must not honor other gods. You must not worship them, or serve them, or offer sacrifices to them. ³⁶But you must follow the Lord. The Lord is the God that brought you out of Egypt. The Lord used his great power to save you. You must worship the Lord and make sacrifices to him. ³⁷You must obey the rules, laws, teachings, and commands that he wrote for you. You must obey these things all the time. You must not respect other gods. ³⁸You must not forget the Agreement that I made with you. You must not respect other gods. ³⁹No! You respect only the Lord your God! Then he will save you from all your enemies."

⁴⁰But the Israelites did not listen. They kept on doing the same things they did before. ⁴¹So now those other nations respect the Lord, but they also serve their own idols. Their children and grandchildren do the same thing their ancestors* did. They still do those things to this day.

Hezekiah Begins His Rule Over Judah

18 Hezekiah son of Ahaz was king of Judah. Hezekiah began to rule during the third year that Hoshea son of Elah was king of Israel. ²Hezekiah was 25 years old when he began to rule. Hezekiah ruled 29 years in Jerusalem. His mother's name was Abi,* the daughter of Zechariah.

³Hezekiah did the things the Lord said were right, just like David his ancestor.*

---

high places Places for worshiping God or false gods. These places were often on the hills and mountains.

ancestor(s) Literally, "father(s)." This means a person's parents, grandparents, and all the people they are descended from.

Abi Or "Abijah."

2 KINGS 18:4–20

⁴Hezekiah destroyed the high places.* He broke the memorial stones* and cut down the Asherah poles.* At that time, the people of Israel burned incense* to the bronze snake made by Moses. This bronze snake was called "Nehushtan."* Hezekiah broke this bronze snake into pieces ₍because the people were worshiping that snake₎.

⁵Hezekiah trusted in the Lord God of Israel. There was no person like Hezekiah among all the kings of Judah before him or after him. ⁶Hezekiah was very faithful to the Lord. He did not stop following the Lord. He obeyed the commands that the Lord had given to Moses. ⁷The Lord was with Hezekiah. Hezekiah was successful in everything he did.

Hezekiah broke away from the king of Assyria. Hezekiah stopped serving the king of Assyria. ⁸Hezekiah defeated the Philistines all the way to Gaza and the area around it. He defeated all the Philistine cities—from the smallest town to the largest city.

The Assyrians Capture Samaria

⁹Shalmaneser king of Assyria went to fight against Samaria. His army surrounded the city. ₍This happened during₎ the fourth year that Hezekiah was king of Judah. (This was also the seventh year that Hoshea son of Elah was king of Israel.) ¹⁰At the end of the third year, Shalmaneser captured Samaria. He took Samaria during the sixth year that Hezekiah was king of Judah. (This was also the ninth year that Hoshea was king of Israel). ¹¹The king of Assyria took the Israelites as prisoners to Assyria. He made them live in Halah, on the Habor (the river of Gozan), and in the cities of the Medes. ¹²This happened because the Israelites did not obey the Lord their God. They broke the Lord's Agreement. They did not obey all the things that Moses the Lord's servant commanded. The people of Israel would not listen to the Lord's Agreement, or do the things it taught them to do.

Assyria Gets Ready to Take Judah

¹³During the 14th year that Hezekiah was king, Sennacherib king of Assyria went to fight against all the strong cities of Judah. Sennacherib defeated all those cities. ¹⁴Then Hezekiah king of Judah sent a message to the king of Assyria at Lachish. Hezekiah said, "I have done wrong. Leave me ₍alone₎. Then I will pay anything you want.

Then the king of Assyria told Hezekiah king of Judah to pay over 11 tons* of silver and over 1 ton* of gold. ¹⁵Hezekiah gave all the silver that was in the Lord's temple* and in the king's treasuries. ¹⁶At this time, Hezekiah cut off the gold that covered the doors of the Lord's temple and the doorposts. King Hezekiah had put gold on these doors and doorposts. Hezekiah gave this gold to the king of Assyria.

The King of Assyria Sends Men to Jerusalem

¹⁷The king of Assyria sent his three most important commanders with a large army to King Hezekiah in Jerusalem. Those men left Lachish and went to Jerusalem. They stood near the aqueduct* by the Upper Pool. (The Upper Pool is on the road to the Washers' Field.) ¹⁸These men called for the king. Eliakim son of Hilkiah (Eliakim was in charge of the king's house), Shebna (the secretary), and Joah son of Asaph (the record keeper) came out to meet them.

¹⁹One of the commanders said to them, "Tell Hezekiah this is what the great king, the king of Assyria says:

What do you trust in? ²⁰Your words are worth nothing.* You say, "I have enough advice and power to help me in war." But who do you trust since you have broken

---

high places Places for worshiping God or false gods. These places were often on the hills and mountains.

memorial stones Stones that were set up to help people remember something special. In ancient Israel, people often set up stones as special places to worship false gods.

Asherah poles These poles were used to honor the female god Asherah that the Canaanite people worshiped.

incense Special dried tree sap. Burned to make a sweet-smelling smoke, it was offered as a gift to God.

Nehushtan This Hebrew name is like the words meaning "bronze" and "snake."

11 tons Or, 10,200kg. Literally, "300 talents."

1 ton Or, 1,020kg. Literally, "30 talents."

temple A special building for worshiping God. God commanded the Jews to worship him at the temple in Jerusalem.

aqueduct A ditch or pipe that carries water from one place to another.

Your words ... nothing Literally, "a word of the lips."

away from my rule? ²¹You are leaning on a walking stick made of broken reed! This walking stick is Egypt. If a man leans on this walking stick, ₗit will break andⱼ go through his hand and hurt him! The king of Egypt is like that to all people that trust in him. ²²Maybe you will say, "We trust the Lord our God." But I know that Hezekiah took away the high places* and altars* where people worshiped the Lord. And Hezekiah told the people of Judah and Jerusalem, "You must worship only in front of the altar here in Jerusalem."
²³Now make this agreement with my master, the king of Assyria. I promise that I will give you 2,000 horses if you can find men to ride them. ²⁴You can't defeat one officer of the lowest of my master's officers! You depend on Egypt to give you chariots* and horse soldiers! ²⁵I have not come against Jerusalem to destroy it without the Lord! The Lord said to me, "Go up against this country and destroy it!"
²⁶Then Eliakim son of Hilkiah, Shebna, and Joah said to the commander, "Please speak to us in Aramaic. We understand that language. Do not speak with us in the language of Judah because the people on the wall can hear us!*"
²⁷But Rabshakeh said to them, "My lord did not send me to speak only to you and your king.* I also speak to the other people that sit on the wall! They will eat their own dung and drink their own urine with you!*"
²⁸Then the commander shouted loudly in the Jewish language, "Hear this message from the great king, the king of Assyria! ²⁹The king says, 'Don't let Hezekiah fool you! He can't save you from my power!' ³⁰Don't let Hezekiah make you trust in the Lord! Hezekiah says, 'The Lord will save us! The king of Assyria will not defeat this city!' ³¹But don't listen to Hezekiah!

"The king of Assyria says this: 'Make peace with me and come out to me. Then each of you can eat from his own grapes, his own fig tree, and drink water from his own well. ³²You can do this until I come and take you away to a land like your own land. It is a land of grain and new wine, a land of bread and fields full of grapes, a land of olives and honey. Then you can live, and not die. But don't listen to Hezekiah! He is trying to change your mind. He is saying, 'The Lord will save us.' ³³Did any of the gods of the other nations save his land from the king of Assyria? No! ³⁴Where are the gods of Hamath and Arpad? Where are the gods of Sepharvaim, Hena, and Ivvah? Did they save Samaria from me? No! ³⁵Did any of the gods in the other countries save their land from me? No! Can the Lord save Jerusalem from me? No!"

³⁶But the people were silent. They did not say a word to the commander because King Hezekiah had given them a command. He said, "Don't say anything to him."

³⁷Eliakim son of Hilkiah (Eliakim was in charge of the king's house), Shebna (the secretary), and Joah son of Asaph (the record keeper) came to Hezekiah. Their clothes were torn ₗto show they were upsetⱼ. They told Hezekiah the things that the Assyrian commander had said.

Hezekiah Talks with Isaiah the Prophet

19 King Hezekiah heard those things, and he tore his clothes and put on the rough cloth ₗthat showed he was sad and upsetⱼ. Then he went into the Lord's temple.* ²Hezekiah sent Eliakim (Eliakim was in charge of the king's house), Shebna (the secretary), and the elders of the priests to the prophet Isaiah son of Amoz. They wore the rough cloth ₗthat showed they were sad and upsetⱼ. ³They said to Isaiah, "Hezekiah says, 'This is a day of trouble, a day to show we are wrong. It is like the time for babies to be born, but there is no strength to give birth to them. ⁴The commander's master, the king of Assyria, has sent him to say bad things about the living God. Maybe the Lord your God will hear all those things. Maybe the Lord will prove the

---

high places Places for worshiping God or false gods. These places were often on the hills and mountains.
altar(s) A stone table used for burning sacrifices offered as gifts to God.
chariot(s) A small wagon used in war.
because the people ... hear us They did not want the people of Jerusalem that sat on the city wall to understand the terrible things that the commander was saying.
king Literally, "master."
eat ... with you The Assyrian army planned to surround Jerusalem and not let people bring any food or water into the city. He thought the people would become hungry enough to eat their own waste.

temple A special building for worshiping God. God commanded the Jews to worship him at the temple in Jerusalem.

enemy is wrong! So pray for the people that are still left alive.'"

⁵King Hezekiah's officers went to Isaiah. ⁶Isaiah said to them, "Give your master Hezekiah this message: 'The Lord says: Don't be afraid of the things that the officers of the king of Assyria have said to make fun of me. ⁷I am putting a spirit in him. He will hear a rumor. Then he will run back to his own country. And I will cause him to be killed by a sword in his own country.'"

The King of Assyria Warns Hezekiah Again

⁸The commander heard that the king of Assyria had left Lachish. So the commander found his king fighting against Libnah.* ⁹The king of Assyria heard a rumor about Tirhakah king of Ethiopia. The rumor said, "Tirhakah has come to fight against you!" So the king of Assyria sent messengers to Hezekiah again. The king of Assyria gave a message to these messengers. He said these things: ¹⁰Say this to Hezekiah king of Judah: "Don't let the God that you trust fool you. He says, 'The king of Assyria will not defeat Jerusalem!' ¹¹You have heard the things the kings of Assyria have done to all the other countries. We destroyed them completely! Will you be saved? No! ¹²The gods of those nations did not save their people. My ancestors* destroyed them all. They destroyed Gozan, Haran, Rezeph, and the people of Eden in Tel Assar! ¹³Where is the king of Hamath? The king of Arpad? The king of the city of Sepharvaim? The kings of Hena and Ivvah? ⌊They are all finished!⌋"

Hezekiah Prays to the Lord

¹⁴Hezekiah received the letters from the messengers and read them. Then Hezekiah went up to the Lord's temple* and laid the letters out in front of the Lord. ¹⁵Hezekiah prayed before the Lord and said, "Lord, the God of Israel who sits as King between the Cherub angels.* You are the God—you alone—of all the kingdoms of the earth. You made the heavens and the earth! ¹⁶Lord, please listen to me. Lord, open your eyes, and see ⌊this letter⌋. Hear the words that Sennacherib sent to insult the living God! ¹⁷It is true, Lord. The kings of Assyria did destroy all those nations! ¹⁸They did throw the gods of the nations into the fire. But those were not real gods. They were only wood and stone—statues that men made. That is why the kings of Assyria could destroy them. ¹⁹So now, Lord our God, save us from the king of Assyria. Then all the kingdoms on earth will know that you, Lord, are the only God."

²⁰Isaiah son of Amoz sent this message to Hezekiah. He said, "The Lord God of Israel says this, 'You have prayed to me against Sennacherib king of Assyria. I have heard you.' ²¹"This is the Lord's message about Sennacherib:

> The virgin daughter of Zion *(Jerusalem)*
> doesn't thinks you are important.
> She makes fun of you!
> Daughter Jerusalem shakes her head at you
> behind your back.
> 22 But who did you insult and make fun of?
> Who did you speak against?
> You were against the Holy One of Israel!
> You acted like you were better than him!
> 23 You sent your messengers to insult the Lord.
> You said,
> "I came with my many chariots*
> to the high mountains.
> I came deep inside Lebanon.
> I cut down the tallest cedar trees
> and the best fir trees of Lebanon.
> I went up to the highest part of Lebanon,
> up to its lush forest.
> 24 I dug wells, and drank water
> from new places.
> I dried up the rivers of Egypt
> and walked on that country."
> 25 ⌊That is what you said.⌋
> But haven't you heard ⌊what God said⌋?
>
> "I *(God)* planned it long ago,
> from ancient times I planned it.
> And now, I have made it happen.
> I let you tear down the strong cities
> and change them into piles of rocks.
> 26 The people in the cities had no power.

Libnah A town in Judah.
ancestors Literally, "fathers." This means a person's parents, grandparents, and all the people they are descended from.
temple A special building for worshiping God. God commanded the Jews to worship him at the temple in Jerusalem.
Cherub angels Special angels from God. Statues of these angels were on top of the Box of the Agreement.
chariot(s) A small wagon used in war.

Those people were scared and confused.
They were about to be cut down
like grass and plants in the field.
They were like grass growing
on the housetops,
dying before it grows tall.
²⁷ I know when you sit down.
I know when you go to war.
and when you come home.
And I know when you get upset at me.
²⁸ Yes, you were upset at me.
I heard your proud insults.
So I will put my hook in your nose.
And I will put my bit* in your mouth.
Then I will turn you around
and lead you back the way you came."

The Lord's Message for Hezekiah

²⁹"This will be the sign to prove I will help you: This year you will eat ⌊the grain⌋ that grows by itself. Next year you will eat the grain that comes up from that seed. But in the third year you will gather the grain from the seeds that you planted. You will plant fields of grapes and eat the grapes from them. ³⁰The people that have escaped and are left in the family of Judah will again begin to grow. ³¹Why? Because a few people will remain alive. They will go out from Jerusalem. People that have escaped will go out from Mount Zion. The Lord's strong feelings* will do this.

³²So the Lord says this about the king of Assyria:

He will not come into this city.
He will not shoot an arrow in this city.
He will not bring his shields to this city.
He will not build up a hill of dirt
to attack the walls of this city.
³³ He will go back the same way he came.
He will not come into this city.
The Lord says this!
³⁴ I will protect this city and save it.
I will do this for myself and for
my servant David.

---

bit A piece of metal people put in a horse's mouth to control the horse.
strong feelings Or, "zeal." The Hebrew word means strong feelings like zeal, jealousy, and love.

The Assyrian Army Is Destroyed

³⁵That night, the angel of the Lord went out and killed 185,000 people in the Assyrian camp. When the people got up in the morning, they saw all the dead bodies. ³⁶So Sennacherib king of Assyria left and went back to Nineveh where he stayed. ³⁷One day Sennacherib was worshiping in the temple* of Nisroch, his god. His sons Adrammelech and Sharezer killed him with a sword. Then Adrammelech and Sharezer escaped into the land of Ararat.* And Sennacherib's son Esarhaddon became the new king after him.

Hezekiah Is Sick and Near Death

20 At that time, Hezekiah became sick and almost died. The prophet Isaiah son of Amoz went to Hezekiah. Isaiah said to Hezekiah, "The Lord says, 'Put your house in order, because you will die. You will not live!'" ²Hezekiah turned his face to the wall.* He prayed to the Lord and said, ³"Lord, remember that I have truly served you with all my heart. I have done the things that you say are good." Then Hezekiah cried very hard.

⁴Before Isaiah had left the middle courtyard, the word of the Lord came to him. The Lord said, ⁵"Go back and speak to Hezekiah, the leader of my people. Tell him, 'The Lord, the God of your ancestor* David says, "I have heard your prayer and I have seen your tears. So I will heal you. On the third day, you will go up to the temple of the Lord. ⁶And I will add 15 years to your life. I will save you and this city from the power of the king of Assyria. I will protect this city. I will do this for myself and because of ⌊the promise I made to⌋ my servant David."'"

⁷Then Isaiah said, "Make a mixture of figs* ⌊and put it on the sore place⌋."

So they took the mixture of figs and put it on ⌊Hezekiah's⌋ sore place. Then Hezekiah got well.

---

temple A special building for worshiping God. God commanded the Jews to worship him at the temple in Jerusalem.
Ararat The ancient country of Urartu, an area in Eastern Turkey.
face to the wall This wall probably faced the temple.
ancestor Literally, "father." This means a person that people are descended from.
mixture of figs This was used like medicine.

A Sign for Hezekiah

⁸Hezekiah said to Isaiah, "What will be the sign that the Lord will heal me, and that I will go up to the temple of the Lord on the third day?" ⁹Isaiah said, "₍Which do you want?₎ Should the shadow go forward ten steps, or go back ten steps?* This is the sign for you from the Lord to show that the Lord will do the thing he said he would do."

¹⁰Hezekiah answered, "It is an easy thing for the shadow to go down ten steps. No, make the shadow go back ten steps."

¹¹Then Isaiah prayed to the Lord, and the Lord made the shadow move back ten steps. It went back on the steps that it had already been on.

Hezekiah and the Men from Babylon

¹²At that time, Merodach Baladan son of Baladan was king of Babylon. He sent letters and a gift to Hezekiah. Merodach Baladan did this because he heard Hezekiah had been sick. ¹³Hezekiah welcomed the men from Babylon, and showed them all the valuable things in his house. He showed him the silver, the gold, the spices, the expensive perfume, the weapons, and everything in his treasuries. There was nothing in all Hezekiah's house and kingdom that he did not show them.

¹⁴Then Isaiah the prophet came to king Hezekiah and asked him, "What did these men say? Where did they come from?"

Hezekiah said, "They came from a faraway country, from Babylon."

¹⁵Isaiah said, "What have they seen in your house?"

Hezekiah answered, "They have seen everything in my house. There is nothing in all my treasuries that I did not show them."

¹⁶Then Isaiah said to Hezekiah, "Listen to this message from the Lord. ¹⁷The time is coming when all the things in your house and all the things your ancestors* have saved until today will be carried away to Babylon. Nothing will be left! The Lord says this. ¹⁸The Babylonians will take your sons. And your sons will become eunuchs* in the palace of the king of Babylon."

¹⁹Then Hezekiah said to Isaiah, "This message from the Lord is good."

Hezekiah also said, "That is fine if there will be real peace during my lifetime."

²⁰All the great things that Hezekiah did, including his work on the pool and the aqueduct* to bring water into the city, are written in the book *The History of the Kings of Judah.* ²¹Hezekiah died and was buried with his ancestors.* And Hezekiah's son Manasseh became the new king after him.

Manasseh Begins His Evil Rule Over Judah

21 Manasseh was twelve years old when he began to rule. He ruled 55 years in Jerusalem. His mother's name was Hephzibah. ²Manasseh did the things that the Lord said were wrong. Manasseh did the terrible things the other nations did. (And the Lord forced those nations to leave their country when the Israelites came.) ³Manasseh built again the high places* that his father Hezekiah had destroyed. Manasseh also built altars* for Baal* and made an Asherah pole,* just like Ahab king of Israel. Manasseh worshiped and served the stars of heaven. ⁴Manasseh built altars ₍to honor false gods₎ in the Lord's temple. (This is the place the Lord was talking about when he said, "I will put my name in Jerusalem.") ⁵Manasseh built altars for the stars of heaven in the two courtyards of the Lord's

---

the shadow ... steps This may mean the steps of a special building outside that Hezekiah used like a clock. When the sun shone on the steps, the shadows showed what time of the day it was.

ancestors Literally, "fathers." This means a person's parents, grandparents, and all the people they are descended from.

eunuchs Men who have had their sexual organs removed. Often important officials of the king were eunuchs.

aqueduct A ditch or pipe that carries water from one place to another.

high places Places for worshiping God or false gods. These places were often on the hills and mountains.

altar(s) A stone table used for burning sacrifices offered as gifts to God.

Baal The Canaanite people believed that this false god brought the rain and storms. They also thought that he made the land produce good crops.

Asherah pole These poles were used to honor the female god Asherah that the Canaanite people worshiped.

temple. ⁶Manasseh sacrificed his son and burned him on the altar.* Manasseh used different ways of trying to know the future. He visited mediums* and wizards.*

Manasseh did more and more things that the Lord said were wrong. This caused the Lord to be angry. ⁷Manasseh made a carved statue of Asherah.* He put this statue in the temple. The Lord had said to David and to David's son Solomon about this temple: "I have chosen Jerusalem from all the cities in Israel. I will put my name in the temple in Jerusalem forever. ⁸I will not cause the people of Israel to leave the land that I gave to their ancestors.* I will let the people stay in their land if they obey all the things I commanded them and all the teachings that my servant Moses gave them." ⁹But the people did not listen to God. Manasseh did more evil things than all the nations ⌊that lived in Canaan before Israel came⌋. And the Lord destroyed those nations when the people of Israel ⌊came to take their land⌋.

¹⁰The Lord used his servants the prophets to say these things: ¹¹"Manasseh king of Judah has done these hated things and has done more evil than the Amorites before him. Manasseh also has caused Judah to sin because of his idols.* ¹²So the Lord of Israel says, 'Look! I will bring so much trouble against Jerusalem and Judah that any person who hears about it will be shocked.* ¹³I will stretch the measuring line of Samaria* and the plumb bob* of Ahab's family over Jerusalem. A man wipes a dish, and then he turns it upside down. I will do that to Jerusalem. ¹⁴There will still be a few of my people left. But I will leave those people. I will give them to their enemies. Their enemies will take them prisoners—they will be like the valuable things soldiers take in war. ¹⁵Why? Because my people did the things that I said were wrong. They have made me angry with them since the day their ancestors* came up out of Egypt. ¹⁶And Manasseh killed many innocent people. He filled Jerusalem from one end to another with blood. And all those sins are in addition to the sins that caused Judah to sin. Manasseh caused Judah to do the things that the Lord said were wrong.'"

¹⁷All the things that Manasseh did, including the sins that he did, are written in the book *The History of the Kings of Judah*. ¹⁸Manasseh ⌊died and⌋ was buried with his ancestors.* Manasseh was buried in the garden at his house. The garden was named, the Garden of Uzza. Manasseh's son Amon became the new king after him.

Amon's Short Rule

¹⁹Amon was 22 years old when he began to rule. He ruled two years in Jerusalem. His mother's name was Meshullemeth daughter of Haruz from Jotbah. ²⁰Amon did the things the Lord said were wrong, just like his father Manasseh. ²¹Amon lived just like his father. Amon worshiped and served the same idols* his father did. ²²Amon left the Lord, the God of his ancestors*, and did not live the way the Lord wanted.

²³Amon's servants made plans against him and killed him in his own house. ²⁴The common people killed all the officers that made plans against King Amon. Then the people made Amon's son Josiah the new king after him. ²⁵The other things that Amon did are written in the book *The History of the Kings of Judah*. ²⁶Amon was buried in his grave at the Garden of Uzza. Amon's son Josiah became the new king.

Josiah Begins His Rule Over Judah

22 Josiah was eight years old when he began to rule. He ruled 31 years in Jerusalem. His mother's name was Jedidah the daughter of Adaiah of Bozkath. ²Josiah did the things that the

---

sacrificed his son and burned him on the altar Literally, "Made his son pass through the fire.

medium(s) A person that tries to communicate with the spirits of dead people.

wizard(s) A person that tries to use evil spirits to do magic.

Asherah An important Canaanite goddess. At this time, the people thought she was the wife of Baal.

ancestors Literally, "fathers." This means a person's parents, grandparents, and all the people they are descended from.

idols Statues of false gods that people worshiped.

will be shocked Literally, "both his ears will tingle."

measuring line of Samaria Workers used a string with a weight to mark a straight line at the end of a stone wall. The pieces of stone that were outside the line were chipped off and thrown away. This shows that God was "throwing away" Samaria and Ahab's family of kings.

plumb bob A weight tied to a string and used to prove that something straight up and down (vertical).

plumb bob A weight tied to a string and used to prove that something straight up and down (vertical).

Lord said were right. Josiah followed God like his ancestor* David. Josiah obeyed God's teachings—he didn't change any of them.*

Josiah Orders the Temple Repaired

³During the 18th year that Josiah was king, he sent Shaphan son of Azaliah son of Meshullam, the secretary, to the Lord's temple.* Josiah said, ⁴"Go up to Hilkiah the high priest. Tell him that he must get the money that people brought to the Lord's temple. The gatekeepers collected that money from the people. ⁵The priests must use that money to pay the workers to repair the Lord's temple. The priests must give that money to the men that supervise the work on the Lord's temple. ⁶Use that money for the carpenters, stone masons, and stonecutters. And use that money to buy the timber and cut stones that are needed to fix the temple. ⁷Don't count the money that you give to the workers. Those workers can be trusted."

The Book of the Law Found in the Temple

⁸Hilkiah the high priest said to Shaphan the secretary, "Look, I found the *Book of the Law** in the Lord's temple!*" Hilkiah gave the book to Shaphan, and Shaphan read it.

⁹Shaphan the secretary went to King Josiah and told him what happened. Shaphan said, "Your servants have gathered all the money that was in the temple. They gave it to the men that supervise the work on the Lord's temple." ¹⁰Then Shaphan the secretary told the king, "And Hilkiah the priest also gave this book to me." Then Shaphan read the book to the king.

¹¹When the king heard the words of the *Book of the Law*, he tore his clothes ₁to show he was sad and upset₁. ¹²Then the king gave a command to Hilkiah the priest, Ahikam son of Shaphan, Acbor son of Micaiah, Shaphan the secretary, and Asaiah the king's servant. ¹³King Josiah said, "Go and ask the Lord what we should do. Ask the Lord for me, for the people, and for all Judah. Ask about the words of this book that was found. The Lord is angry at us. Why? Because our ancestors* did not listen to the words of this book. They did not obey all the commands that were written for us!"

Josiah and Huldah the Prophetess

¹⁴So Hilkiah the priest, Ahikam, Acbor, Shaphan, and Asaiah went to Huldah the woman prophet.* Huldah was the wife of Shallum son of Tikvah, son of Harhas. He took care of the ₁priests'₁ clothes. Huldah was living in the second quarter in Jerusalem. They went and talked with Huldah.

¹⁵Then Huldah said to them, "The Lord God of Israel says: Tell the man that sent you to me: ¹⁶'The Lord says this: I am bringing trouble on this place and on the people that live here. These are the troubles that are mentioned in the book that the king of Judah read. ¹⁷The people of Judah left me and have burned incense* to other gods. They made me very angry. They made many idols.* That is why I will show my anger against this place. My anger will be like a fire that can't be stopped!'

¹⁸⁻¹⁹"Josiah the king of Judah sent you to ask advice from the Lord. Tell Josiah these things: 'The Lord God of Israel said the words that you heard. You heard the things I said about this place and the people that live here. Your heart was soft, and you felt sorry when you heard those things. I said that terrible things would happen to this place *(Jerusalem)*. You tore your clothes ₁to show your sadness₁ and you began to cry. That is why I heard you.' The Lord says this. ²⁰'I will bring you to be with your ancestors.* You will die and go to your grave in peace. So your eyes will not see all the trouble that I am bringing on this place *(Jerusalem).*'"

Then Hilkiah the priest, Ahikam, Acbor, Shaphan, and Asaiah told that message to the king.

The People Hear the Law

23 King Josiah told all the leaders of Judah and Jerusalem to come and meet with him. ²Then the king went up to the Lord's temple. All

---

ancestor Literally, "father." This means a person that people are descended from.

Josiah obeyed ... them Literally, "Josiah did not turn to the right or to the left."

temple A special building for worshiping God. God commanded the Jews to worship him at the temple in Jerusalem.

Book of the Law This is probably the book of Deuteronomy.

prophet A person called by God to be a special servant. God used dreams and visions to show them things to teach to the people.

incense A kind of spice that smells good when it is burned. It was burned as a gift to God.

idols Statues of false gods that people worshiped.

the people of Judah and the people that lived in Jerusalem went with him. The priests, the prophets, and all the people—from the least important to the most important—went with him. Then he read the *Book of the Agreement*. This was the *Book of the Law* that was found in the Lord's temple. Josiah read the book so all the people could hear it.

³The king stood by the column and made an agreement with the Lord. He agreed to follow the Lord and to obey his commands, the Agreement, and his rules. He agreed to do this with all his heart and soul. He agreed to obey the Agreement written in this book. All the people stood to ₗshow they supportedₗ the ₗking'sₗ agreement.

⁴Then the king commanded Hilkiah the high priest, the other priests, and the gatekeepers, to bring out of the Lord's temple* all the dishes and things that were made to honor Baal,* Asherah,* and the stars of heaven. Then Josiah burned those things outside Jerusalem in the fields in Kidron Valley. Then they carried the ashes to Bethel.

⁵The kings of Judah had chosen some ordinary men to serve as priests. ₗThese men were not from the family of Aaron!ₗ Those false priests were burning incense* at the high places* in every city of Judah and all the towns around Jerusalem. They burned incense to honor Baal,* the sun, the moon, the constellations *(groups of stars)*, and all the stars in the sky. But Hezekiah stopped those false priests.

⁶Josiah removed the Asherah Pole* from the Lord's temple.* He took the Asherah pole outside the city to the Kidron Valley and burned it there. Then he beat the burnt pieces into dust and scattered the dust over the graves of the common people.*

⁷Then King Josiah broke down the houses of the male prostitutes* that were in the Lord's temple. Women also used those houses and made little tent covers to honor the false goddess Asherah.

⁸⁻⁹At that time, the priests did not bring the sacrifices to Jerusalem and offer them on the altar in the temple. The priests lived in cities all over Judah. And they burned incense* and offered sacrifices at the high places* in those cities. Those high places were everywhere, from Geba to Beersheba. And the priests ate their unleavened bread in those towns with the ordinary people—ₗnot at the special place for priests in the temple in Jerusalemₗ. But King Josiah defiled *(ruined)* those high places and brought the priests to Jerusalem. Hezekiah also destroyed the high places that were on the left, by Joshua Gate. (Joshua was the ruler of the city.)

¹⁰Topheth was a place in the Valley of Hinnom's Son where people killed their children and burned them on an altar to honor the false god Molech.* Josiah defiled *(ruined)* that place so people could not use that place again. ¹¹In the past, the kings of Judah had put some horses and a chariot* near the entrance to the Lord's temple. This was near the room of an important official named Nathan Melech. The horses and chariot were to honor the sun god.* Josiah removed the horses and burned the chariot.

¹²In the past, the kings of Judah had built altars on the roof of Ahab's building. King Manasseh had also built altars in the two courtyards of the Lord's temple. Josiah destroyed all those altars and threw the broken pieces into Kidron Valley.

¹³In the past, King Solomon built some high places* on Destroyer Hill near Jerusalem. The high places were on the south side of that hill. King Solomon built one of those places of worship to honor Ashtoreth, that horrible thing the

---

temple A special building for worshiping God. God commanded the Jews to worship him at the temple in Jerusalem.

Baal The Canaanite people believed that this false god brought the rain and storms. They also thought that he made the land produce good crops.

Asherah An important Canaanite goddess. At this time, the people thought she was the wife of Baal.

incense A kind of spice that smells good when it is burned. It was burned as a gift to God.

high place(s) Places for worshiping God or false gods. These places were often on the hills and mountains.

Asherah Pole These poles were used to honor the female god Asherah that the Canaanite people worshiped.

scattered ... common people This was a strong way of showing that the Asherah pole could never be used again.

male prostitutes Men who used their bodies for sexual sin.

people ... Molech Literally, "people made their son or daughter pass through fire to Molech."

chariot(s) A small wagon used in war.

horses ... sun god The people thought the sun was a god that drove his chariot *(the sun)* across the sky each day.

people of Sidon worship. King Solomon also built one to honor Chemosh, that horrible thing the people of Moab worship. And King Solomon built one high place to honor Milcom, that horrible thing the Ammonite people worship. But King Josiah defiled *(ruined)* all those places of worship. ¹⁴King Josiah broke all the memorial stones* and Asherah poles.* Then he scattered dead men's bones over that place.*

¹⁵Josiah also broke down the altar and high place* at Bethel. Jeroboam son of Nebat had made this altar. Jeroboam caused Israel to sin.* Josiah broke down both that altar and the high place. Josiah broke the stones of the altar to pieces. Then he beat it into dust. And he burned the Asherah pole. ¹⁶Josiah looked around and saw graves on the mountain. He sent men, and they took the bones from those graves. Then he burned the bones on the altar. In this way, Josiah defiled *(ruined)* the altar. This happened according to the message from the Lord that the man of God* announced.* The man of God announced these things when Jeroboam stood beside the altar.

Then Josiah looked around and saw the grave of the man of God.* ¹⁷Josiah said, "What is that monument I see?"

The people of the city told him, "It is the grave of the man of God* that came from Judah. This man of God told about the things you have done to the altar at Bethel. He said those things a long time ago."

¹⁸Josiah said, "Leave the man of God* alone. Don't move his bones."

¹⁹Josiah also destroyed all the temples at the high places* in the cities of Samaria. The kings of Israel had built those temples. And that made the Lord very angry. Josiah destroyed those temples, just like he destroyed the place of worship at Bethel. ²⁰Josiah killed all the priests of the high places that were in Samaria. He killed the priests on those altars. He burned men's bones on the altars. ⌞In this way he ruined those places of worship.⌟ Then he went back to Jerusalem.

The People of Judah Celebrate Passover

²¹Then King Josiah gave a command to all the people. He said, "Celebrate Passover for the Lord your God. Do this just like it is written in the *Book of the Agreement*."

²²The people had not celebrated a Passover like this since the days that the judges ruled Israel. None of the kings of Israel or the Kings of Judah ever had such a big celebration for Passover. ²³They celebrated this Passover for the Lord in Jerusalem during Josiah's 18th year as king.

²⁴Josiah destroyed the mediums,* wizards,* the house gods, the idols,* and all the horrible things people worshiped in Judah and Jerusalem. Josiah did this to obey the Law written in the book that Hilkiah the priest found in the Lord's temple.*

²⁵There had never been a king like Josiah before. Josiah turned to the Lord with all his heart, with all his soul, and with all his strength.* No king had followed all the Law of Moses like Josiah. And there has never been another king like Josiah since that time.

²⁶But the Lord did not stop being angry at the people of Judah. The Lord was still angry at them for all the things that Manasseh had done. ²⁷The Lord said, "I forced the people of Israel to leave their land. I will do the same to Judah. I will take Judah out of my sight. I will not accept Jerusalem. Yes, I chose that city. I was talking about Jerusalem when I said, 'My name will be there.' But I will destroy the temple* that is in that place."

²⁸All the other things that Josiah did are written in the book *The History of the Kings of Judah*.

---

memorial stones Stones that were set up to help people remember something special. In ancient Israel, people often set up stones as special places to worship false gods.
Asherah poles These poles were used to honor the female god Asherah that the Canaanite people worshiped.
scattered ... place This was the way he defiled {(ruined)} those places so they could not be used for places of worship.
high place(s) Places for worshiping God or false gods. These places were often on the hills and mountains.
Jeroboam ... sin See 1 Kings 12:26-30.
man of God Another name for a prophet.
announced See 1 Kings 13:1-3.

medium(s) A person that tries to communicate with the spirits of dead people.
wizard(s) A person that tries to use evil spirits to do magic.
idols Statues of false gods that people worshiped.
temple A special building for worshiping God. God commanded the Jews to worship him at the temple in Jerusalem.
with all his heart ... strength See Deut. 6:4,5.

The Death of Josiah

²⁹During Josiah's time, Pharaoh Neco, the king of Egypt went to fight against the king of Assyria at the Euphrates River. Josiah went out to meet Neco at Megiddo. Pharaoh saw Josiah and killed him. ³⁰Josiah's officers put his body in a chariot* and carried him from Megiddo to Jerusalem. They buried Josiah in his own grave.

Then the common people took Josiah's son Jehoahaz and anointed* him. They made Jehoahaz the new king.

Jehoahaz Becomes King of Judah

³¹Jehoahaz was 23 years old when he became king. He ruled three months in Jerusalem. His mother's name was Hamutal daughter of Jeremiah from Libnah. ³²Jehoahaz did the things that the Lord said were wrong. Jehoahaz did all the same things that his ancestors* had done.

³³Pharaoh Neco put Jehoahaz in prison at Riblah in the land of Hamath. So Jehoahaz could not rule in Jerusalem. Pharaoh Neco forced Judah to pay 7,500 pounds* of silver and 75 pounds* of gold.

³⁴Pharaoh Neco made Josiah's son Eliakim the new king. Eliakim took the place of Josiah his father. Pharaoh Neco changed Eliakim's name to Jehoiakim. And Pharaoh Neco took Jehoahaz away to Egypt. Jehoahaz died in Egypt. ³⁵Jehoiakim gave the silver and the gold to Pharaoh. But Jehoiakim made the common people pay taxes and used that money to give to Pharaoh Neco. So each person paid his share of silver and gold. And King Jehoiakim gave the money to Pharaoh Neco.

³⁶Jehoiakim was 25 years old when he became king. He ruled eleven years in Jerusalem. His mother's name was Zebidah daughter of Pedaiah from Rumah. ³⁷Jehoiakim did the things that the Lord said were wrong. Jehoiakim did all the same things his ancestors* had done.

King Nebuchadnezzar Comes to Judah

24 In the time of Jehoiakim, Nebuchadnezzar king of Babylon came to the country of Judah. Jehoiakim served Nebuchadnezzar for three years. Then Jehoiakim turned against Nebuchadnezzar and broke away from his rule. ²The Lord sent groups of Babylonians, Arameans, Moabites, and Ammonites to fight against Jehoiakim. The Lord sent those groups to destroy Judah. This happened just like the Lord said. The Lord used his servants the prophets to say those things.

³The Lord commanded those things to happen to Judah. In this way, he would take them out of his sight. He did this because of all the sins that Manasseh did. ⁴The Lord did this because Manasseh killed many innocent people. Manasseh had filled Jerusalem with their blood. And the Lord would not forgive ⌊those sins.⌋

⁵The other things that Jehoiakim did are written in the book *The History of the Kings of Judah*. ⁶Jehoiakim ⌊died and⌋ was buried with his ancestors.* Jehoiakim's son Jehoiachin became the new king after him.

⁷The king of Babylon captured all the land between the Brook of Egypt and the Euphrates River. So the king of Egypt did not leave Egypt any more.

Nebuchadnezzar Captures Jerusalem

⁸Jehoiachin was 18 years old when he began to rule. He ruled three months in Jerusalem. His mother's name was Nehushta daughter of Elnathan from Jerusalem. ⁹Jehoiachin did the things that the Lord said were wrong. He did all the same things that his father had done.

¹⁰At that time, the officers of Nebuchadnezzar king of Babylon came to Jerusalem and surrounded it. ¹¹Then Nebuchadnezzar king of Babylon came to the city. ¹²Jehoiachin king of Judah went out to meet the king of Babylon. Jehoiachin's mother, his officers, leaders, and officials also went with him. Then the king of Babylon captured Jehoiachin. This was during the eighth year of Nebuchadnezzar's rule.

¹³Nebuchadnezzar took from Jerusalem all the treasures in the Lord's temple* and all the treasures in the king's house. Nebuchadnezzar cut up all the golden dishes that Solomon king of

---

chariot(s) A small wagon used in war.
anoint(ed) To pour olive oil on a person's head to show he was chosen by God to be a king, priest, or prophet.
ancestors Literally, "fathers." This means a person's parents, grandparents, and all the people they are descended from.
7,500 pounds Or, 3,400kg. Literally, "100 talents (kikars)."
75 pounds Or, 34kg. Literally, "1 talent."

temple A special building for worshiping God. God commanded the Jews to worship him at the temple in Jerusalem.

Israel had put in the Lord's temple. This happened just like the Lord said. ¹⁴Nebuchadnezzar captured all the people of Jerusalem. He captured all the leaders and other wealthy people. He took 10,000 people and made them prisoners. Nebuchadnezzar took all the skilled workers and craftsmen. No person was left, except the poorest of the common people. ¹⁵Nebuchadnezzar took Jehoiachin to Babylon as a prisoner. Nebuchadnezzar also took the king's mother, his wives, officers, and the leading men of the land. Nebuchadnezzar took them from Jerusalem to Babylon as prisoners. ¹⁶There were 7,000 soldiers. Nebuchadnezzar took all of the soldiers and 1,000 of the skilled workers and craftsmen. All of these men were trained soldiers, ready for war. The king of Babylon took them to Babylon as prisoners.

King Zedekiah

¹⁷The king of Babylon made Mattaniah the new king. Mattaniah was Jehoiachin's uncle. He changed his name to Zedekiah. ¹⁸Zedekiah was 21 years old when he began to rule. He ruled 11 years in Jerusalem. His mother's name was Hamutal daughter of Jeremiah from Libnah. ¹⁹Zedekiah did the things the Lord said were wrong. Zedekiah did all the same things that Jehoiachin did. ²⁰The Lord became so angry at Jerusalem and Judah that he threw them away.

Nebuchadnezzar Ends Zedekiah's Rule

Zedekiah rebelled and refused to obey the king of Babylon.

25 So Nebuchadnezzar, the king of Babylon, and all his army came to fight against Jerusalem. This happened on the 10th day of the tenth month of Zedekiah's ninth year as king. Nebuchadnezzar put his army around Jerusalem ₍to stop people from going in and out of the city₎. Then he built a wall of dirt around the city. ²Nebuchadnezzar's army stayed around Jerusalem until Zedekiah's eleventh year as king of Judah. ³The famine was getting worse and worse in the city. By the 9th day of the fourth month there was no more food for the common people in the city.

⁴Nebuchadnezzar's army finally broke through the city wall. That night King Zedekiah and all his soldiers ran away. They used the ₍secret₎ gate that went through the double walls. It was by the king's garden. The enemy soldiers were all around the city, but Zedekiah and his men escaped on the road to the desert. ⁵The Babylonian army chased King Zedekiah and caught him near Jericho. All of Zedekiah's soldiers left him and ran away. ⁶The Babylonians took King Zedekiah to the king of Babylon at Riblah. The Babylonians decided to punish Zedekiah. ⁷They killed Zedekiah's sons in front of him. Then they put out Zedekiah's eyes. They put chains on him and took him to Babylon.

Jerusalem Is Destroyed

⁸Nebuchadnezzar came to Jerusalem on the 7th day of the fifth month of Nebuchadnezzar's nineteenth year as king of Babylon. Nebuzaradan was the captain of Nebuchadnezzar's best soldiers. ⁹Nebuzaradan burned the Lord's temple,* the king's house, and all the houses in Jerusalem. He destroyed even the largest houses. ¹⁰Then the Babylonian army that was with Nebuzaradan pulled down the walls around Jerusalem. ¹¹Nebuzaradan captured all the people that were still left in the city. Nebuzaradan took all the people as prisoners, even the people who had tried to surrender. ¹²Nebuzaradan let only the poorest of the common people stay there. He let them stay so they could take care of the grapes and other crops.

¹³The Babylonian soldiers broke to pieces all the bronze things in the Lord's temple. They broke the bronze columns, the bronze carts, and the large bronze tank. Then they took all of that bronze to Babylon. ¹⁴The Babylonians also took the pots, the shovels, the tools for trimming the lamps, the spoons, and all the bronze dishes that were used in the Lord's temple. ¹⁵Nebuzaradan took all the firepans and bowls. He took all the things made of gold for the gold. And he took all the things made of silver for the silver. ¹⁶⁻¹⁷So, Nebuzaradan took:

the 2 bronze columns (Each column was about 27 feet* tall. The capitals* on the columns were 4 1/2 feet* tall. They were made from bronze and had a design like a net and pomegranates. Both columns had the same kind of design.)

the large bronze tank*

---

temple A special building for worshiping God. God commanded the Jews to worship him at the temple in Jerusalem.
27 feet Literally, "18 cubits."
capital(s) Decorated caps of stone or wood on top of columns.
4 1/2 feet Literally, "3 cubits."
tank A very large basin for water.

the carts that Solomon made for the Lord's temple.
The bronze from these things was too heavy to be weighed.

The People of Judah Taken as Prisoners

[18] ⌊From the temple,⌋ Nebuzaradan took
Seraiah the high priest,
Zephaniah the second priest,
the three men who guarded the entrance.
[19] And from the city, Nebuzaradan took
1 official who was in charge of the army
5 of the king's advisers* who were still in the city,
1 secretary of the commander of the army. He was in charge of counting the common people and choosing some of them to be soldiers.
60 people who just happened to be in the city.
[20-21] Then Nebuzaradan took all these people to the king of Babylon at Riblah in the area of Hamath The king of Babylon killed them there at Riblah. And the people of Judah were led away as prisoners from their land.

Gedaliah Governor of Judah

[22] Nebuchadnezzar king of Babylon left some people in the land of Judah. There was a man named Gedaliah son of Ahikam son of Shaphan. Nebuchadnezzar made Gedaliah governor over those people in Judah.

[23] The army captains were Ishmael son of Nethaniah, Johanan son of Kareah, Seraiah son of Tanhumeth from Netophah, and Jaazaniah son of the Maachathite. These army captains and their men heard that the king of Babylon had made Gedaliah governor. So they went to Mizpah to meet with Gedaliah. [24] Gedaliah made promises to these officers and their men. Gedaliah said to them, "Don't be afraid of the Babylonian officers. Stay here and serve the king of Babylon. Then everything will be all right with you."

[25] Ishmael son of Nethaniah son of Elishama was from the king's family. In the seventh month Ishmael and ten of his men attacked Gedaliah and killed all the Jews and Babylonians that were with Gedaliah at Mizpah. [26] Then the army officers and all the people ran away to Egypt. Everyone, from the least important to the most important, ran away because they were afraid of the Babylonians.

[27] Later, Evil Merodach became the king of Babylon. He let Jehoiachin king of Judah out of prison. This happened in the 37th year after Jehoiachin was captured. This was on the 27th day of the twelfth month from the time that Evil Merodach began to rule. [28] Evil Merodach was kind to Jehoiachin. He gave Jehoiachin a more important place to sit than the other kings that were with him in Babylon. [29] Evil Merodach let Jehoiachin stop wearing prison clothes. And Jehoiachin ate at the same table with Evil Merodach, every day for the rest of his life. [30] So King Evil Merodach gave Jehoiachin every meal, every day, for the rest of his life.

---

king's advisers Literally, "men that saw the king's face."

1 Chronicles

Family History from Adam to Noah

1 ¹⁻³Adam, Seth, Enosh, Kenan, Mahalalel, Jared, Enoch, Methuselah, Lamech, Noah.*

⁴The sons of Noah were Shem, Ham, and Japheth.

Japheth's Descendants

⁵The sons of Japheth were Gomer, Magog, Madai, Javan, Tubal, Meshech, and Tiras.

⁶The sons of Gomer were Ashkenaz, Riphath,* and Togarmah.

⁷The sons of Javan were Elishah, Tarshish, Kittim, and Rodanim.

Ham's Descendants

⁸The sons of Ham were Cush *(Ethiopia)*, Mizraim *(Egypt)*, Put, and Canaan.

⁹The sons of Cush were Seba, Havilah, Sabtah, Raamah, and Sabtecah. The sons of Raamah were Sheba and Dedan.

¹⁰Nimrod, a descendant* of Cush, grew up to become the strongest and bravest soldier in the world.

¹¹Mizraim *(Egypt)* was the father of the people of Lud, Anam, Lehab, Naphtuh, ¹²Pathrus, Casluh, and Caphtor. (The Philistines came from Casluh.)

¹³Canaan was the father of Sidon. Sidon was his first child. Canaan was also the father of the Hittites, ¹⁴the Jebusite people, the Amorite people, the Girgashite people, ¹⁵the Hivite people, the Arkite people. the Sinite people, ¹⁶the Arvadite people, the Zemarite people, and the people from Hamath.

Shem's Descendants

¹⁷Shem's sons were Elam, Asshur, Arphaxad, Lud, and Aram. Aram's sons were Uz, Hul, Gether, and Meshech.*

¹⁸Arphaxad was the father of Shelah. Shelah was the father of Eber.

¹⁹Eber had two sons. One son was named Peleg,* because the people on the earth were divided into different languages during his lifetime. Peleg's brother was named Joktan.

²⁰Joktan was the father of Almodad, Sheleph, Hazarmaveth, Jerah, ²¹Hadoram, Uzal, Diklah, ²²Ebal,* Abimael, Sheba ²³Ophir, Havilah, and Jobab. All these men were Joktan's sons: ²⁴Shem, Arphaxad, Shelah, ²⁵Eber, Peleg, Reu, ²⁶Serug, Nahor, Terah, ²⁷and Abram. (Abram is also called Abraham.)

Abraham's Family

²⁸Abraham's sons were Isaac and Ishmael. ²⁹These are their descendants*:

Hagar's Descendants

Ishmael's first son was Nebaioth. Ishmael's other sons were Kedar, Adbeel, Mibsam, ³⁰Mishma, Dumah, Massa, Hadad, Tema, ³¹Jetur, Naphish, and Kedemah. Those were Ishmael's sons.

Keturah's Sons

³²Keturah was Abraham's woman servant.* She gave birth to Zimran, Jokshan, Medan, Midian, Ishbak, and Shuah.

Jokshan's sons were Sheba and Dedan.

³³Midian's sons were Ephah, Epher, Hanoch, Abida, and Eldaah.

Adam ... Noah This list of names gives the name of a man, followed by his descendants.
Riphath Or, "Diphath."
descendant(s) A person's children and their future families.

Meshech Or, "Mash." See Gen 10:23
Peleg This name means "division."
Ebal Or, "Obal." See Gen. 10:28.
woman servant Or, "concubine." A woman who was like a wife to a man.

These men were the descendants of Keturah.

Sarah's Sons

³⁴Abraham was the father of Isaac. Isaac's sons were Esau and Israel.*
³⁵Esau's sons were Eliphaz, Reuel, Jeush, Jalam, and Korah.
³⁶Eliphaz's sons were Teman, Omar, Zepho,* Gatam, and Kenaz. Also Eliphaz and Timna had a son named Amalek.
³⁷Reuel's sons were Nahath, Zerah, Shammah, and Mizzah.

The Edomites from Seir

³⁸Seir's sons were Lotan, Shobal, Zibeon, Anah, Dishon, Ezer, and Dishan.
³⁹Lotan's sons were Hori and Homam.* Lotan had a sister named Timna.
⁴⁰Shobal's sons were Alvan, Manahath, Ebal, Shepho, and Onam.
Zibeon's sons were Aiah and Anah.
⁴¹Anah's son was Dishon.
Dishon's sons were Hemdan, Eshban, Ithran, and Keran.
⁴²Ezer's sons were Bilhan, Zaavan, and Akan.
Dishan's sons were Uz and Aran.

The Kings of Edom

⁴³There were kings in Edom long before there were kings in Israel. These are the names of the kings of Edom:
The first king was Bela son of Beor. The name of Bela's city was Dinhabah.
⁴⁴When Bela died, Jobab son of Zerah became the new king. Jobab came from Bozrah.
⁴⁵When Jobab died, Husham became the new king. Husham was from the country of the Temanite people.
⁴⁶When Husham died, Hadad son of Bedad became the new king. Hadad defeated Midian in the country of Moab. Hadad's city was named Avith.
⁴⁷When Hadad died, Samlah became the new king. Samlah was from Masrekah.
⁴⁸When Samlah died, Shaul became the new king. Shaul was from Rehoboth by the Euphrates River.
⁴⁹When Shaul died, Baal Hanan son of Acbor became the new king.

⁵⁰When Baal Hanan died, Hadad became the new king. Hadad's city was named Pau.* Hadad's wife was named Mehetabel. Mehetabel was Matred's daughter. Matred was Mezahab's daughter. ⁵¹Then Hadad died.
The leaders of Edom were Timna, Alvah, Jetheth, ⁵²Oholibamah, Elah, Pinon, ⁵³Kenaz, Teman, Mibzar, ⁵⁴Magdiel, and Iram. This is a list of the leaders of Edom.

Israel's Sons

2 Israel's* sons were Reuben, Simeon, Levi, Judah, Issachar, Zebulun, ²Dan, Joseph, Benjamin, Naphtali, Gad, and Asher.

Judah's Sons

³Judah's sons were Er, Onan, and Shelah. Bathshua* was their mother. Bathshua was a woman from Canaan. The Lord saw that Judah's first son, Er, was evil. That is why the Lord killed Er. ⁴Judah's daughter-in-law Tamar gave birth to Perez and Zerah.* So Judah had five sons.
⁵Perez's sons were Hezron and Hamul.
⁶Zerah had five sons. They were: Zimri, Ethan, Heman, Calcol, and Darda.
⁷Zimri's son was Carmi. Carmi's son was Achar.* Achar was the man that brought many troubles to Israel. Achar kept the things he took in battle. But he was supposed to give all those things to God.
⁸Ethan's son was Azariah.
⁹Hezron's sons were Jerahmeel, Ram, and Caleb.*

Ram's Descendants

¹⁰Ram was Amminadab's father. And Amminadab was Nahshon's father. Nahshon was the leader of the people of Judah.* ¹¹Nahshon was Salmon's father. Salmon was Boaz's father.

Israel Another name for Jacob. See Gen. 32:28.
Zepho Or, "Zephi."
Homam Or, "Heman." See Gen. 36:22.

Pau Or, "Pai."
Israel Another name for Jacob. See Gen. 32:28.
Bathshua This name means, "the daughter of Shua." See Gen. 38:2.
Judah's daughter-in-law ... Perez and Zerah Judah had sexual relations with his own daughter-in-law Tamar and caused her to be pregnant. See Gen. 38:12-30.
Achar Or, "Achan." See Joshua 7:11.
Caleb Literally, "Kelubai."
Nahshon ... Judah Nahshon was leader of the family group of Judah at the time the people of Israel came out of Egypt. See Num. 1:7; 2:3; 7:12.

¹²Boaz was Obed's father. Obed was Jesse's father. ¹³Jesse was Eliab's father. Eliab was Jesse's first son. Jesse's second son was Abinadab. His third son was Shimea. ¹⁴Nethanel was Jesse's fourth son. Jesse's fifth son was Raddai. ¹⁵Ozem was Jesse's sixth son, and David was his seventh son. ¹⁶Their sisters were Zeruiah and Abigail. Zeruiah's three sons were Abishai, Joab, and Asahel. ¹⁷Abigail was Amasa's mother. Amasa's father was Jether. Jether was from the Ishmaelite people.

Caleb's Descendants

¹⁸Caleb was Hezron's son. Caleb had children with his wife Azubah. Azubah was the daughter of Jerioth.* Azubah's sons were Jesher, Shobab, and Ardon. ¹⁹When Azubah died, Caleb married Ephrath. Caleb and Ephrath had a son. They named him Hur. ²⁰Hur was Uri's father. Uri was Bezalel's father.

²¹Later, when Hezron was 60 years old, he married Makir's daughter. Makir's was the father of Gilead. Hezron had sexual relations with Makir's daughter and she gave birth to Segub. ²²Segub was Jair's father. Jair had 23 cities in the country of Gilead. ²³But Geshur and Aram took Jair's villages. Among them was Kenath and the small towns around it. There were 60 small towns in all. All of these towns belonged to the sons of Makir, the father of Gilead.

²⁴Hezron died in the town Caleb, Ephrathah. After he died, his wife Abijah had his son. That son was named Ashhur. Ashhur was the father of Tekoa.

Jerahmeel's Descendants

²⁵Jerahmeel was Hezron's first son. Jerahmeel's sons were Ram, Bunah, Oren, Ozem, and Ahijah. Ram was Jerahmeel's first son. ²⁶Jerahmeel had another wife named Atarah. Onam's mother was Atarah.

²⁷Jerahmeel's first son, Ram, had sons. They were Maaz, Jamin, and Eker.

²⁸Onam's sons were Shammai and Jada. Shammai's sons were Nadab and Abishur.

²⁹Abishur's wife was named Abihail. They had two sons. Their names were Ahban and Molid.

³⁰Nadab's sons were Seled and Appaim. Seled died without having children.

³¹Appaim's son was Ishi. Ishi's son was Sheshan. Sheshan's son was Ahlai.

³²Jada was Shammai's brother. Jada's sons were Jether and Jonathan. Jether died without having children.

³³Jonathan's sons were Peleth and Zaza. This was the list of Jerahmeel's children.

³⁴Sheshan did not have sons. He only had daughters. Sheshan had a servant from Egypt named Jarha. ³⁵Sheshan let his daughter marry Jarha. They had a son. His name was Attai.

³⁶Attai was Nathan's father. Nathan was Zabad's father. ³⁷Zabad was Ephlal's father. Ephlal was Obed's father. ³⁸Obed was Jehu's father. Jehu was Azariah's father. ³⁹Azariah was Helez's father. Helez was Eleasah's father. ⁴⁰Eleasah was Sismai's father. Sismai was Shallum's father. ⁴¹Shallum was Jekamiah's father. And Jekamiah was Elishama's father.

Caleb's Family

⁴²Caleb was Jerahmeel's brother. Caleb had some sons. His first son was Mesha. Mesha was Ziph's father. ₎There was also Caleb's₎ son Mareshah. Mareshah was the father of Hebron.

⁴³Hebron's sons were Korah, Tappuah, Rekem, and Shema. ⁴⁴Shema was Raham's father. Raham was Jorkeam's father. Rekem was Shammai's father. ⁴⁵Shammai's son was Maon. Maon was Beth Zur's father.

⁴⁶Caleb's woman servant* was named Ephah. Ephah was the mother of Haran, Moza, and Gazez. Haran was Gazez's father.

⁴⁷Jahdai's sons were Regem, Jotham, Geshan, Pelet, Ephah, and Shaaph.

⁴⁸Maacah was another woman servant* of Caleb. Maacah was the mother of Sheber and Tirhana. ⁴⁹Maacah was also the mother of Shaaph and Sheva. Shaaph was Madmannah's father. Sheva was the father of Macbenah and Gibea. Caleb's daughter was Acsah.

⁵⁰This is a list of Caleb's descendants:* Hur was Caleb's first son. He was born to Ephrathah. Hur's sons were Shobal, the founder* of Kiriath Jearim, ⁵¹Salma, the founder of Bethlehem, and Hareph, the founder of Beth Gader.

Caleb ... Jerioth Or "Caleb had children with Azubah his wife and with Jerioth."

woman servant Or, "concubine," a slave woman who was like a wife to a man.

descendant(s) A person's children and their future families.

founder Literally, "father," the person that started the city.

⁵²Shobal was the founder* of Kiriath Jearim. This is a list of Shobal's descendants:* Haroeh, half the people in Manahti; ⁵³and the family groups from Kiriath Jearim. These are the Ithrite people, the Puthite people, the Shumathite people, and the Mishraite people. The Zorathite people and the Eshtaolite people came from the Mishraite people.

⁵⁴This is a list of Salma's descendants:* The people from Bethlehem, Netophah, Atroth Beth Joab, half the people from Manahti, the Zorite people, ⁵⁵and the families of scribes* that lived at Jabez, Tirath, Shimeath, and Sucah. These scribes are the Kenite people that came from Hammath. Hammath was the founder* of Beth Recab.

David's Sons

3 Some of David's sons were born in the town of Hebron. This is a list of David's sons:

David's first son was Amnon. Amnon's mother was Ahinoam. She was from the town of Jezreel.

The second son was Daniel. His mother was Abigail from Carmel ₗJudahₗ.

²The third son was Absalom. His mother was Maacah, daughter of Talmai. Talmai was the king of Geshur.

The fourth son was Adonijah. His mother was Haggith.

³The fifth son was Shephatiah. His mother was Abital.

The sixth son was Ithream. His mother was Eglah, David's wife. ⁴These six sons were born to David in Hebron. David ruled there seven years and six months.

David was king in Jerusalem 33 years. ⁵These are the children born to David in Jerusalem:

There were four children from Bathsheba. Bathsheba was Ammiel's daughter: Shimea, Shobab, Nathan, and Solomon. ⁶⁻⁸Nine other children were: Ibhar, Elishua, Eliphelet, Nogah, Nepheg, Japhia, Elishama, Eliada, and Eliphelet. ⁹They were all David's sons. David had other sons by women servants.* Tamar was David's daughter.*

Kings of Judah after David's Time

¹⁰Solomon's son was Rehoboam. And Rehoboam's son was Abijah. Abijah's son was Asa. Asa's son was Jehoshaphat. ¹¹Jehoshaphat's son was Jehoram. Jehoram's son was Ahaziah. Ahaziah's son was Joash. ¹²Joash's son was Amaziah. Amaziah's son was Azariah. Azariah's son was Jotham. ¹³Jotham's son was Ahaz. Ahaz's son was Hezekiah. Hezekiah's son was Manasseh. ¹⁴Manasseh's son was Amon. Amon's son was Josiah.

¹⁵This is a list of Josiah's sons: The first son was Johanan. The second son was Jehoiakim. The third son was Zedekiah. The fourth son was Shallum.

¹⁶Jehoiakim's sons were Jehoiachin, his son, and Zedekiah, his son.*

David's Family Line After Babylon Defeats Judah

¹⁷This is a list of Jehoiachin's children after Jehoiachin became a prisoner in Babylon. His children were: Shealtiel, ¹⁸Malkiram, Pedaiah, Shenazzar, Jekamiah, Hoshama, and Nedabiah.

¹⁹Pedaiah's sons were Zerubbabel and Shimei. Zerubbabel's sons were Meshullam and Hananiah. Shelomith was their sister. ²⁰Zerubbabel had five other sons also. Their names were Hashubah, Ohel, Berekiah, Hasadiah, and Jushab Hesed.

²¹Hananiah's son was Pelatiah. And his son was Jeshaiah.* And his son was Rephaiah. And his son was Arnan. And his son was Obadiah. And his son was Shecaniah.*

²²This is a list of Shecaniah's descendants*: Shemaiah. Shemaiah had six sons: Shemaiah, Hattush, Igal, Bariah, Neariah, and Shaphat.

²³Neariah had three sons. They were Elioenai, Hizkiah, and Azrikam.

²⁴Elioenai had seven sons. They were Hodaviah, Eliashib, Pelaiah, Akkub, Johanan, Delaiah, and Anani.

---

founder Literally, "father." The person that started the city.
descendant(s) A person's children and their future families.
scribes Men that wrote down and copied books and letters. These men spent so much time with those writings that they often became experts at knowing what those scriptures (writings) meant.
woman servant Or, "concubine," a slave woman who was like a wife to a man.

David's daughter Literally, "their sister."
Jehoiakim's sons ... son This can be interpreted in two ways: (1) "This Zedekiah was the son of Jehoiakim and the brother of Jehoiachin," (2) "This Zedekiah is the son of Jehoiachin and the grandson of Jehoiakim."
Jeshaiah Or, "Isaiah."
Verse 21 The Hebrew is hard to understand here.

1 CHRONICLES 4:1-27

Other Family Groups of Judah

4 This is a list of Judah's sons. They were Perez, Hezron, Carmi, Hur, and Shobal. ²Shobal's son was Reaiah. Reaiah was Jahath's father. Jahath was the father of Ahumai and Lahad. The Zorathite people are descendants* of Ahumai and Lahad. ³Etam's sons were Jezreel, Ishma, and Idbash. And they had a sister named Hazzelelponi. ⁴Penuel was Gedor's father. And Ezer was Hushah's father.

These were Hur's sons. Hur was Ephrathah's first son. And Ephrathah was the founder* of Bethlehem.

⁵Tekoa's father was Ashhur. Tekoa had two wives. Their names were Helah and Naarah. ⁶Naarah had Ahuzzam, Hepher, Temeni, and Haahashtari. These were the sons Naarah had with Ashhur. ⁷The sons of Helah were Zereth, Zohar, Ethnan, and Koz. ⁸Koz was the father of Anub and Hazzobebah. Koz also was the father of the family groups of Aharhel. Aharhel was Harum's son.

⁹Jabez was a very good man. He was better than his brothers. His mother said, "I have named him Jabez* because I was in much pain when I had him." ¹⁰Jabez prayed to the God of Israel. Jabez said, "I wish you would truly bless me. I wish you would give me more land. Be near me and don't let anyone hurt me. Then I won't have any pain." And God gave Jabez what he asked for.

¹¹Kelub was Shuhah's brother. Kelub was Mehir's father. Mehir was Eshton's father. ¹²Eshton was the father of Beth Rapha, Paseah, and Tehinnah. Tehinnah was the father of Ir Nahash.* Those men were from Recah.

¹³The sons of Kenaz were Othniel and Seraiah. Othniel's sons were Hathath and Meonothai. ¹⁴Meonothai was Ophrah's father.

And Seraiah was Joab's father. Joab was the founder* of the Ge Harashim.* Those people used that name because they were skilled workers.

¹⁵Caleb was Jephunneh's son. Caleb's sons were Iru, Elah, and Naam. Elah's son was Kenaz. ¹⁶Jehallelel's sons were Ziph, Ziphah, Tiria, and Asarel.

¹⁷⁻¹⁸Ezrah's sons were Jether, Mered, Epher, and Jalon. Mered was the father of Miriam, Shammai, and Ishbah. Ishbah was the father of Eshtemoa. Mered had a wife from Egypt. She had Jered, Heber, and Jekuthiel. Jered was Gedor's father. Heber was Soco's father. And Jekuthiel was Zanoah's father. These were the sons of Bithiah. Bithiah was Pharaoh's daughter. She was Mered's wife from Egypt.

¹⁹Mered's wife was Naham's sister. Mered's wife was from Judah.* The sons of Mered's wife were the father of Keilah and Eshtemoa. Keilah was from the Garmite people. And Eshtemoa was from the Maacathite people. ²⁰Shimon's sons were Amnon, Rinnah, Ben Hanan, and Tilon.

Ishi's sons were Zoheth and Ben Zoheth.

²¹⁻²²Shelah was Judah's son. Shelah had Er, Laadah, Jokim, the men from Cozeba, Joash, and Saraph. Er was the father of Lecah. Laadah was the father of Mareshah and the family groups of linen* workers at Beth Ashbea. Joash and Saraph married Moabite women. Then they went back to Bethlehem.* The writings about this family are very old. ²³Those sons of Shelah were workers that made things from clay. They lived in Netaim and Gederah. They lived in those towns and worked for the king.

Simeon's Children

²⁴Simeon's sons were Nemuel, Jamin, Jarib, Zerah, and Shaul. ²⁵Shaul's son was Shallum. Shallum's son was Mibsam. Mibsam's son was Mishma.

²⁶Mishma's son was Hammuel. Hammuel's son was Zaccur. Zaccur's son was Shimei. ²⁷Shimei had sixteen sons and six daughters. But Shimei's brothers did not have many children. Shimei's brothers did not have large families. Their families were not large like the other family groups in Judah.

---

descendant(s) A person's children and their future families.
founder Literally, "father," the person that started the city.
Jabez This name is like the Hebrew word meaning "pain."
Tehinnah ... Ir Nahash Or, "Tehinnah was the founder of the city of Nahash." Ir means "city."
Ge Harashim This name also means, "Valley of the Skilled Workers."

Mered's wife ... was from Judah This is from the ancient Greek translation.
linen A type of cloth.
married ... Bethlehem Or, "They ruled in Moab and Jashubi Lehem."

[28] Shimei's children lived in Beersheba, Moladah, Hazar Shual, [29] Bilhah, Ezem, Tolad, [30] Bethuel, Hormah, Ziklag, [31] Beth Marcaboth, Hazar Susim, Beth Biri, and Shaaraim. They lived in those towns until David became king. [32] The five villages near these towns were Etam, Ain, Rimmon, Token, and Ashan. [33] There were also other villages as far away as Baalath. This is where they lived. And they also wrote the history about their family.

[34-38] This is the list of men who were leaders of their family groups. They were Meshobab, Jamlech, Joshah (Amaziah's son), Joel, Jehu son of Joshibiah, Joshibiah son of Seraiah, Seraiah son of Asiel, Elioenai, Jaakobah, Jeshohaiah, Asaiah, Adiel, Jesimiel, Benaiah, and Ziza (Shiphi's son). Shiphi was Allon's son, and Allon was Jedaiah's son. Jedaiah was Shimri's son, and Shimri was Shemaiah's son.

These men's families grew to be very large. [39] They went to the area outside the town of Gedor to the east side of the valley. They went to that place to look for fields for their sheep and cattle. [40] They found good fields with plenty of grass. They found plenty of good land there. The land was peaceful and quiet. Ham's descendants* lived there in the past. [41] This happened during the time that Hezekiah was king of Judah. Those men came to Gedor and fought against the Hamite people. They destroyed the Hamite peoples' tents. Those men also fought against the Meunite people that lived there. These men destroyed all the Meunite people. There are no Meunite people in this place even today. So those men began to live there. They lived there because the land had grass for their sheep.

[42] Five hundred people from Simeon's family group went to the hill country of Seir. Ishi's sons led those men. Those sons were, Pelatiah, Neariah, Rephaiah, and Uzziel. The Simeonite men fought against the people living in that place. [43] There were only a few Amalekite people still living. And these Simeonite people killed them. Since that time until now those Simeonite people have lived in Seir.

Reuben's Descendants

5 [1-3] Reuben was Israel's first son. Reuben should have received the special privileges of the oldest son. But Reuben had sexual relations with his father's wife. So those privileges were given to Joseph's sons. In the family history, Reuben's name is not listed as the first son. Judah became stronger than his brothers, so the leaders came from his family. But Joseph's family got the other privileges that belong to the oldest son. Reuben's sons were Hanoch, Pallu, Hezron, and Carmi.

[4] These are the names of Joel's descendants:* Shemaiah was Joel's son. Gog was Shemaiah's son. Shimei was Gog's son. [5] Micah was Shimei's son. Reaiah was Micah's son. Baal was Reaiah's son. [6] Beerah was Baal's son. Tiglath Pileser, the king of Assyria, forced Beerah to leave his home. So Beerah became the king's prisoner. Beerah was a leader of the family group of Reuben.

[7] Joel's brothers and all his family groups are listed just as they are written in the family histories: Jeiel was the first son, then Zechariah, [8] and Bela. Bela was Azaz's son. Azaz was Shema's son. Shema was Joel's son. They lived in the area of Aroer all the way to Nebo and Baal Meon. [9] Bela's people lived to the east as far as the edge of the desert, near the Euphrates River. They lived in that place because they had many cattle in the land of Gilead. [10] When Saul was king, Bela's people fought a war against the Hagrite people. They defeated the Hagrite people. Bela's people lived in the tents that had belonged to the Hagrite people. They lived in those tents and traveled throughout the area east of Gilead.

Gad's Descendants

[11] The people from the family group of Gad lived near the people from the family group of Reuben. The Gadite people lived in the area of Bashan, all the way to the town of Salecah. [12] Joel was the first leader in Bashan. Shapham was the second leader. Then Janai became the leader.* [13] The seven brothers in their families were Michael, Meshullam, Sheba, Jorai, Jacan, Zia, and Eber. [14] Those men were the descendants* of Abihail. Abihail was Huri's son. Huri was Jaroah's son. Jaroah was Gilead's son. Gilead was Michael's son. Michael was Jeshishai's son. Jeshishai was Jahdo's son. Jahdo was Buz's son. [15] Ahi was Abdiel's son. Abdiel was Guni's son. Ahi was the leader of their family.

[16] The people in the family group of Gad lived in the area of Gilead. They lived in the area of Bashan, in the small towns around Bashan, and in

---

descendant(s) A person's children and their future families.

Then Janai became the leader Or, "Then there was Janai. And then Shaphat was in Bashan."

all the fields in the area of Sharon all the way to the borders.

¹⁷During the time of Jotham and Jeroboam, all these people's names were written in the family history of Gad. Jotham was the king of Judah and Jeroboam was the king of Israel.

Some Soldiers Skilled in War

¹⁸From half of Manasseh's family group and from the family groups of Reuben and Gad there were 44,760 brave men ready for war. They were skilled in war. They carried shields and swords. And they were also good with bows and arrows. ¹⁹They started a war against the Hagrite people and the people of Jetur, Naphish, and Nodab. ²⁰Those men from the family groups of Manasseh, Reuben, and Gad prayed to God in the war. They asked God to help them because they trusted him. So God helped them. God allowed them to defeat the Hagrite people. And they also defeated those other people who were with the Hagrite people. ²¹They took the animals that belonged to the Hagrite people. They took 50,000 camels, 250,000 sheep, 2,000 donkeys, and 100,000 people. ²²Many Hagrite people were killed because God helped the people of Reuben win the war. Then those people from the family groups of Manasseh, Reuben, and Gad lived in the land of the Hagrite people. They lived there until the time when the army of Babylon took the people of Israel and made them prisoners in Babylon.

²³Half of Manasseh's family group lived in the area of Bashan all the way to Baal Hermon, Senir, and Mount Hermon. They became a very large group of people.

²⁴These were the family leaders from half of Manasseh's family group: Epher, Ishi, Eliel, Azriel, Jeremiah, Hodaviah, and Jahdiel. They were all strong and brave men. They were famous men. And they were leaders in their families. ²⁵But those leaders sinned against the God that their ancestors* worshiped. They began worshiping the false gods of the people living there—and those were the people God destroyed. ²⁶The God of Israel made Pul want to go to war. Pul was the king of Assyria. He was also called Tiglath Pileser. He fought against the people from the family groups of Manasseh, Reuben, and Gad. He forced them to leave their homes and made them prisoners. Pul brought them to Halah, Habor, Hara, and near the Gozan River. Those family groups from Israel have lived in those places since that time until today.

The Descendants of Levi

6 Levi's sons were Gershon, Kohath, and Merari.

²Kohath's sons were Amram, Izhar, Hebron, and Uzziel.

³Amram's children were Aaron, Moses, and Miriam.

Aaron's sons were Nadab, Abihu, Eleazar, and Ithamar. ⁴Eleazar was Phinehas's father. Phinehas was Abishua's father. ⁵Abishua was Bukki's father. Bukki was Uzzi's father. ⁶Uzzi was Zerahiah's father. Zerahiah was Meraioth's father. ⁷Meraioth was Amariah's father. Amariah was Ahitub's father. ⁸Ahitub was Zadok's father. Zadok was Ahimaaz's father. ⁹Ahimaaz was Azariah's father. Azariah was Johanan's father. ¹⁰Johanan was Azariah's father. (Azariah is the person that served as priest in the temple that Solomon built in Jerusalem.) ¹¹Azariah was Amariah's father. Amariah was Ahitub's father. ¹²Ahitub was Zadok's father. Zadok was Shallum's father. ¹³Shallum was Hilkiah's father. Hilkiah was Azariah's father. ¹⁴Azariah was Seraiah's father. Seraiah was Jehozadak's father.

¹⁵Jehozadak was forced to leave his home when the Lord sent Judah and Jerusalem away. Those people were made prisoners in another country. The Lord used Nebuchadnezzar to take the people of Judah and Jerusalem prisoners.

Other Descendants of Levi

¹⁶Levi's sons were Gershon, Kohath, and Merari.

¹⁷The names of Gershon's sons were Libni and Shimei.

¹⁸Kohath's sons were Amram, Izhar, Hebron, and Uzziel.

¹⁹Merari's sons were Mahli and Mushi.

This is a list of the families in the family group of Levi. They are listed with their fathers' names first:

²⁰These were Gershon's descendants* Libni was Gershon's son. Jahath was Libni's son. Zimmah was Jahath's son. ²¹Joah was Zimmah's

---

ancestors Literally, "fathers." This means a person's parents, grandparents, and all the people they are descended from.

descendant(s) A person's children and their future families.

son. Iddo was Joah's son. Zerah was Iddo's son. Jeatherai was Zerah's son.

²²These were Kohath's descendants:* Amminadab was Kohath's son. Korah was Amminadab's son. Assir was Korah's son. ²³Elkanah was Assir's son. Ebiasaph was Elkanah's son. Assir was Ebiasaph's son. ²⁴Tahath was Assir's son. Uriel was Tahath's son. Uzziah was Uriel's son. Shaul was Uzziah's son. ²⁵Elkanah's sons were Amasai and Ahimoth. ²⁶Zophai was Elkanah's son. Nahath was Zophai's son. ²⁷Eliab was Nahath's son. Jeroham was Eliab's son. Elkanah was Jeroham's son. ⌊Samuel was Elkanah's son.⌋ ²⁸Samuel's sons were: his oldest son Joel, and Abijah. ²⁹These are Merari's sons: Mahli was Merari's son, Libni was Mahli's son, Shimei was Libni's son. Uzzah was Shimei's son. ³⁰Shimea was Uzzah's son. Haggiah was Shimea's son. Asaiah was Haggiah's son.

The Temple Musicians

³¹These are the men that David chose to take care of the music at the tent of the Lord's house after the Box of the Agreement* was put there. ³²These men served by singing at the Holy Tent.* The Holy Tent is also called the Meeting Tent. And these men served until Solomon built the Lord's temple* in Jerusalem. They served by following the rules given to them for their work.

³³These are the names of the men and their sons that served with music:

The descendants* from the Kohath family were: Heman the singer. Heman was Joel's son. Joel was Samuel's son. ³⁴Samuel was Elkanah's son. Elkanah was Jeroham's son. Jeroham was Eliel's son. Eliel was Toah's son. ³⁵Toah was Zuph's son. Zuph was Elkanah's son. Elkanah was Mahath's son. Mahath was Amasai's son. ³⁶Amasai was Elkanah's son. Elkanah was Joel's son. Joel was Azariah's son. Azariah was Zephaniah's son. ³⁷Zephaniah was Tahath's son. Tahath was Assir's son. Assir was Ebiasaph's son. Ebiasaph was Korah's son. ³⁸Korah was Izhar's son. Izhar was Kohath's son. Kohath was Levi's son. Levi was Israel's* son.

³⁹Heman's relative was Asaph. Asaph served by Heman's right side. Asaph was Berekiah's son. Berekiah's was Shimea's son. ⁴⁰Shimea was Michael's son. Michael was Baaseiah's son. Baaseiah was Malkijah's son. ⁴¹Malkijah was Ethni's son. Ethni was Zerah's son. Zerah was Adaiah's son. ⁴²Adaiah was Ethan's son. Ethan was Zimmah's son. Zimmah was Shimei's son. ⁴³Shimei was Jahath's son. Jahath was Gershon's son. Gershon was Levi's son.

⁴⁴Merari's descendants* were the relatives of Heman and Asaph. They were the singing group on Heman's left side. Ethan was Kishi's son. Kishi was Abdi's son. Abdi was Malluch's son. ⁴⁵Malluch was Hashabiah's son. Hashabiah was Amaziah's son. Amaziah was Hilkiah's son. ⁴⁶Hilkiah was Amzi's son. Amzi was Bani's son. Bani was Shemer's son. ⁴⁷Shemer was Mahli's son. Mahli was Mushi's son. Mushi was Merari's son. Merari was Levi's son.

⁴⁸Heman's and Asaph's brothers were from the family group of Levi. The family group of Levi were also called Levites. The Levites were chosen to do the work in the Holy Tent.* The Holy Tent was God's house. ⁴⁹But only Aaron's descendants* were permitted to burn incense* on the altar of burnt offering and on the altar of incense. Aaron's descendants did all the work in the Most Holy Place* in God's house. They also did the ceremonies to make the people of Israel pure.* They followed all the rules and laws that Moses commanded. Moses was God's servant.

---

descendant(s) A person's children and their future families.

Box of the Agreement Also called "The Ark of the Covenant," the box containing the stone tablets with the Ten Commandments written on them and the other things that proved God was with the people of Israel during their time in the Sinai Desert.

Holy Tent Also called the "tabernacle." The people would go to this tent to meet with God. The people used this tent until Solomon built the temple in Jerusalem.

temple The special building in Jerusalem for Jewish worship.

Israel Another name for Jacob. See Gen. 32:28.

incense A kind of spice that smells good when it is burned. It was burned as a gift to God.

Most Holy Place The most important room in the temple. The Box of the Agreement with the Cherub Angels on it was in this room. This was like God's throne. Once each year, on the Day of Atonement, the high priest went into this room to do the ceremony that atoned (covered or erased) the sins of the people of Israel.

make ... pure Or, "make atonement." The Hebrew word means "to cover or erase a person's sins."

Aaron's Descendants

⁵⁰These were Aaron's sons: Eleazar was Aaron's son. Phinehas was Eleazar's son. Abishua was Phinehas' son. ⁵¹Bukki was Abishua's son. Uzzi was Bukki's son. Zerahiah was Uzzi's son. ⁵²Meraioth was Zerahiah's son. Amaraiah was Meraioth's son. Ahitub was Amariah's son. ⁵³Zadok was Ahitub's son. Ahimaaz was Zadok's son.

Homes for the Levite Families.

⁵⁴These are the places where Aaron's descendants* lived. They lived in their camps in the land that was given to them. The Kohath families got the first share of the land that was given to the Levite people. ⁵⁵They were given the town of Hebron and the fields around it. This was in the area of Judah. ⁵⁶But the fields farther from town and the villages near the town of Hebron were given to Caleb son of Jephunneh. ⁵⁷The descendants of Aaron were given the city of Hebron. Hebron was a city of safety.* They were also given the cities of Libnah, Jattir, Eshtemoa, ⁵⁸Hilen, Debir, ⁵⁹Ashan, Juttah, and Beth Shemesh. They got all those cities and the fields around them. ⁶⁰From the family group of Benjamin they got the cities of Gibeon, Geba, Alemeth, and Anathoth. They got all those cities and the fields around them.

Thirteen cities were given to the Kohath families.

⁶¹The rest of Kohath's descendants* got ten towns from half of Manasseh's family group.

⁶²The family groups that were the descendants* of Gershon got 13 cities. They got those cities from the family groups of Issachar, Asher, Naphtali, and the part of Manasseh living in the area of Bashan.

⁶³The family groups that were the descendants* of Merari got 12 cities. They got those cities from the family groups of Reuben, Gad, and Zebulun. They got those cities by throwing lots.*

⁶⁴So the Israelite people gave those towns and fields to the Levite people. ⁶⁵All those cities came from the family groups of Judah, Simeon, and Benjamin. They decided which Levite family got which city by throwing lots.*

⁶⁶The family group of Ephraim gave some of the Kohath families some towns. Those towns were chosen by throwing lots.* ⁶⁷They were given the city of Shechem. Shechem is a city of safety.* They were also given the towns of Gezer, ⁶⁸Jokmeam, Beth Horon, ⁶⁹Aijalon, and Gath Rimmon. They also got fields with those towns. Those towns were in the hill country of Ephraim. ⁷⁰And from half of Manasseh's family group the Israelite people gave the towns of Aner and Bileam to the Kohath families. Those Kohath families also got fields with those towns.

Other Levite Families Get Homes

⁷¹The Gershon families got the towns of Golan in the area of Bashan and Ashtaroth from half of Manasseh's family group. They also got the fields near those towns.

⁷²⁻⁷³The Gershon families also got the towns of Kedesh, Daberath, Ramoth, and Gannim from the family group of Issachar. They also got the fields near those towns.

⁷⁴⁻⁷⁵The Gershon families also got the towns of Mashal, Abdon, Hukok, and Rehob from the family group of Asher. They also got the fields near those towns.

⁷⁶The Gershon families also got the towns of Kedesh in Galilee, Hammon, and Kiriathaim from the family group of Naphtali. They also got the fields near those towns.

⁷⁷The rest of the Levite people are the Merari families. They got the towns of Jokneam, Kartah, Rimmono, and Tabor from the family group of Zebulun. They also got the fields near those towns.

⁷⁸⁻⁷⁹The Merari families also got the towns of Bezer in the desert, Jahzah, Kedemoth, and Mephaath from the family group of Reuben. The family group of Reuben lived on the east side of the Jordan River, east of the city of Jericho. These Merari families also got the fields near those towns.

⁸⁰⁻⁸¹And the Merari families got the towns of Ramoth in Gilead, Mahanaim, Heshbon, and Jazer from the family group of Gad. They also got the fields near those towns.

Issachar's Descendants

7 Issachar had four sons. Their names were Tola, Puah, Jashub, and Shimron.

---

descendant(s) A person's children and their future families.
city of safety Any city where an Israelite could run and be safe from angry relatives if he accidentally killed someone. See Josh. 20:1-9.
lot(s) Sticks, stones, or pieces of bone used like dice for making decisions. See Proverbs 16:33.

²Tola's sons were Uzzi, Rephaiah, Jeriel, Jahmai, Ibsam, and Samuel. They were all leaders of their families. Those men and their descendants* were strong soldiers. Their families grew until by the time David was king, there were 22,600 men ₍ready for war₎. ³Uzzi's son was Izrahiah. Izrahiah's sons were Michael, Obadiah, Joel, and Isshiah. All five of them were leaders of their families. ⁴Their family history shows they had 36,000 soldiers ready for war. They had a large family because they had many wives and children. ⁵The family history shows there were 87,000 strong soldiers in all the family groups of Issachar.

Benjamin's Descendants

⁶Benjamin had three sons. Their names were Bela, Beker, and Jediael. ⁷Bela had five sons. Their names were Ezbon, Uzzi, Uzziel, Jerimoth, and Iri. They were leaders of their families. Their family history shows they had 22,034 soldiers. ⁸Beker's sons were Zemirah, Joash, Eliezer, Elioenai, Omri, Jeremoth, Abijah, Anathoth, and Alemeth. They all were Beker's children. ⁹Their family history shows who the family leaders were. And their family history also shows they had 20,200 soldiers. ¹⁰Jediael's son was Bilhan. Bilhan's sons were Jeush, Benjamin, Ehud, Kenaanah, Zethan, Tarshish, and Ahishahar. ¹¹All of Jediael's sons were leaders of their families. They had 17,200 soldiers ready for war. ¹²The Shuppites and Huppites were the descendants of Ir. Hushim was the son of Aher.

Naphtali's Descendants

¹³Naphtali's sons were Jahziel, Guni, Jezer, and Shallum.
And these are the descendants of Bilhah.*
¹⁴These are Manasseh's descendants:
Manasseh and his Aramean woman servant* had a son named Asriel. They also had Makir. Makir was Gilead's father. ¹⁵Makir married a woman from the Huppite and Shuppite people. Maacah's second ₍wife₎ was named Zelophehad. Zelophehad had only daughters. Makir's sister was named Maacah.
¹⁶Makir's wife Maacah had a son. Maacah named this son Peresh. Peresh's brother was named Sheresh. Sheresh's sons were Ulam and Rakem.
¹⁷Ulam's son was Bedan.
These were the descendants of Gilead. Gilead was Makir's son. Makir was Manasseh's son. ¹⁸Makir's sister Hammoleketh* had Ishhod, Abiezer, and Mahlah.
¹⁹Shemida's sons were Ahian, Shechem, Likhi, and Aniam.

Ephraim's Descendants

²⁰These were the names of Ephraim's descendants.* Ephraim's son was Shuthelah. Shuthelah's son was Bered. Bered's son was Tahath. Tahath's son was Eleadah. ²¹Eleadah's son was Tahath. Tahath's son was Zabad. Zabad's son was Shuthelah.
Some men that grew up in the city of Gath killed Ezer and Elead. This happened because Ezer and Elead went there to steal cattle and sheep from those men in Gath. ²²Ephraim was the father of Ezer and Elead. He cried for many days because Ezer and Elead were dead. Ephraim's family came to comfort him. ²³Then Ephraim had sexual relations with his wife. Ephraim's wife became pregnant and had a son. Ephraim named this new son Beriah* because something bad had happened to his family. ²⁴Ephraim's daughter was Sheerah. Sheerah built Lower Beth Horon and Upper Beth Horon and Lower Uzzen Sheerah and Upper Uzzen Sheerah.
²⁵Rephah was Ephraim's son. Resheph was Rephah's son. Telah was Resheph's son. Tahan was Telah's son. ²⁶Ladan was Tahan's son. Ammihud was Ladan's son. Elishama was Ammihud's son. ²⁷Nun was Elishama's son. Joshua was Nun's son.
²⁸These are the cities and lands where Ephraim's descendants* lived: Bethel and the villages near it, Naaran to the east, Gezer and the villages near it on the west, and Shechem and the villages near it all the way to Ayyah and the villages near it. ²⁹Along the borders of Manasseh's land were the towns of Beth Shan,

---

descendant(s) A person's children and their future families.
Bilhah Jacob's woman servant and the mother of Dan and Naphtali. See Gen. 30:4-8.

Hammoleketh Or, "The woman that ruled," or "queen."
Beriah This is like the Hebrew word meaning, "bad," or "trouble."

Asher's Descendants

³⁰Asher's sons were Imnah, Ishvah, Ishvi, and Beriah. Their sister was named Serah. ³¹Beriah's sons were Heber and Malkiel. Malkiel was Birzaith's father. ³²Heber was the father of Japhlet, Shomer, Hotham, and of their sister Shua. ³³Japhlet's sons were Pasach, Bimhal, and Ashvath. These were Japhlet's children. ³⁴Shomer's sons were Ahi, Rohgah, Jehubbah,* and Aram. ³⁵Shomer's brother's name was Helem. Helem's sons were Zophah, Imna, Shelesh, and Amal. ³⁶Zophah's sons were Suah, Harnepher, Shual, Beri, Imrah, ³⁷Bezer, Hod, Shamma, Shilshah, Ithran, and Beera. ³⁸Jether's sons were Jephunneh, Pispah, and Ara. ³⁹Ulla's sons were Arah, Hanniel, and Rizia. ⁴⁰All these men were descendants* of Asher. They were leaders of their families. They were the best men. They were soldiers and great leaders. Their family history shows 26,000 soldiers ready for war.

The Family History of King Saul

8 Benjamin was Bela's father. Bela was Benjamin's first son. Ashbel was Benjamin's second son. Aharah was Benjamin's third son. ²Nohah was Benjamin's fourth son. And Rapha was Benjamin's fifth son. ³⁻⁵Bela's sons were Addar, Gera, Abihud, Abishua, Naaman, Ahoah, Gera, Shephuphan, and Huram. ⁶⁻⁷These were the descendants* of Ehud. They were leaders of their families in Geba. They were forced to leave their homes and move to Manahath. Ehud's descendants were Naaman, Ahijah, and Gera. Gera forced them to leave their homes. Gera was the father of Uzza and Ahihud. ⁸Shaharaim divorced his wives Hushim and Baara in Moab. After he did this he had some children with another wife. ⁹⁻¹⁰Shaharaim had Jobab, Zibia, Mesha, Malcam, Jeuz, Sakia, and Mirmah with his wife Hodesh. They were leaders of their families. ¹¹Shaharaim and Hushim had two sons named Abitub and Elpaal. ¹²⁻¹³Elpaal's sons were Eber, Misham, Shemed, Beriah, and Shema. Shemed built the towns of Ono and Lod and the small towns around Lod. Beriah and Shema were the leaders of the families living in Aijalon. Those sons forced the people that lived in Gath to leave. ¹⁴Beriah's sons were Shashak and Jeremoth, ¹⁵Zebadiah, Arad, Eder, ¹⁶Michael, Ishpah, and Joha. ¹⁷Elpaal's sons were Zebadiah, Meshullam, Hizki, Heber, ¹⁸Ishmerai, Izliah, and Jobab. ¹⁹Shimei's sons were Jakim, Zicri, Zabdi, ²⁰Elienai, Zillethai, Eliel, ²¹Adaiah, Beraiah, and Shimrath. ²²Shashak's sons were Ishpan, Eber, Eliel, ²³Abdon, Zicri, Hanan, ²⁴Hananiah, Elam, Anthothijah, ²⁵Iphdeiah, and Penuel. ²⁶Jeroham's sons were Shamsherai, Shehariah, Athaliah, ²⁷Jaareshiah, Elijah, and Zicri. ²⁸All these men were leaders of their families. They were listed in their family histories as leaders. They lived in Jerusalem.

²⁹⌊Jeiel was Gibeon's father.⌋ He lived in the town of Gibeon. Jeiel's wife was named Maacah. ³⁰Jeiel's oldest son was Abdon. Other sons were Zur, Kish, Baal, Ner, Nadab, ³¹Gedor, Ahio, Zeker, and Mikloth. ³²Mikloth was the father of Shimeah. These sons also lived near their relatives in Jerusalem.

³³Ner was Kish's father. Kish was Saul's father. And Saul was the father of Jonathan, Malki Shua, Abinadab, and Esh Baal. ³⁴Jonathan's son was Merib Baal. Merib Baal was Micah's father. ³⁵Micah's sons were Pithon, Melech, Tarea, and Ahaz. ³⁶Ahaz was Jehoaddah's father. Jehoaddah was the father of Alemeth, Azmaveth, and Zimri. Zimri was Moza's father. ³⁷Moza was Binea's father. Raphah was Binea's son. Eleasah was Raphah's son. And Azel was Eleasah's son. ³⁸Azel had six sons. Their names were Azrikam, Bokeru, Ishmael, Sheariah, Obadiah, and Hanan. All these sons were Azel's children.

³⁹Azel's brother was Eshek. Eshek had some sons. These were Eshek's sons: Ulam was Azel's oldest son. Jeush was Eshek's second son. Eliphelet was Eshek's third son. ⁴⁰Ulam's sons were strong soldiers that were very good with bows and arrows. They had many sons and

---

Israel Another name for Jacob. See Gen. 32:28.
Jehubbah Or, "Hubbah."
descendant(s) A person's children and their future families.

grandsons. In all, there were 150 sons and grandsons.

All these men were descendants* of Benjamin.

9 The names of all the people of Israel were listed in their family histories. Those family histories were put in the book *The History of the Kings of Israel.*

The People in Jerusalem

The people of Judah were made prisoners and forced to go to Babylon. They were taken to that place because they were not faithful to God. ²The first people to come back and live in their own lands and towns were some Israelites, priests, Levites, and servants that work in the temple.* ³These are the people from the family groups of Judah, Benjamin, Ephraim, and Manasseh that lived in Jerusalem:

⁴Uthai was Ammihud's son. Ammihud was Omri's son. Omri was Imri's son. Imri was Bani's son. Bani was a descendant* of Perez. Perez was Judah's son.

⁵The Shilonite people that lived in Jerusalem were: Asaiah was the oldest son and Asaiah had sons.

⁶The Zerahite people that lived in Jerusalem were: Jeuel and their relatives. There were 690 of them in all.

⁷These are the people from the family group of Benjamin that lived in Jerusalem: Sallu was Meshullam's son. Meshullam was Hodaviah's son. Hodaviah was Hassenuah's son. ⁸Ibneiah was Jeroham's son. Elah was Uzzi's son. Uzzi was Micri's son. And Meshullam was Shephatiah's son. Shephatiah was Reuel's son. Reuel was Ibnijah's son. ⁹The family history of Benjamin shows there were 956 of them living in Jerusalem. All these men were leaders in their families.

¹⁰These are the priests that lived in Jerusalem: Jedaiah, Jehoiarib, Jakin, and ¹¹Azariah. Azariah was Hilkiah's son. Hilkiah was Meshullam's son. Meshullam was Zadok's son. Zadok was Meraioth's son. Meraioth was Ahitub's son. Ahitub was the important official responsible for God's temple.* ¹²Also there was Jeroham's son, Adaiah. Jeroham was Pashhur's son. Pashhur was Malkijah's son. And there was Adiel's son, Maasai. Adiel was Jahzerah's son. Jahzerah was Meshullam's son. Meshullam was Meshillemith's son. Meshillemith was Immer's son.

¹³There were 1,760 priests. They were leaders of their families. They were responsible for the work of serving in God's temple.*

¹⁴These are the people from the family group of Levi that lived in Jerusalem: Hasshub's son, Shemaiah. Hasshub was Azrikam's son. Azrikam was Hashabiah's son. Hashabiah's was a descendant* of Merari. ¹⁵Also living in Jerusalem were Bakbakkar, Heresh, Galal, and Mattaniah. Mattaniah was Mica's son. Mica was Zicri's son. Zicri was Asaph's son. ¹⁶Obadiah was Shemaiah's son. Shemaiah was Galal's son. Galal was Jeduthun's son. And Asa's son, Berekiah lived in Jerusalem. Asa was Elkanah's son. Elkanah lived in the small towns near the people of Netophah.

¹⁷These are the gatekeepers that lived in Jerusalem: Shallum, Akkub, Talmon, Ahiman, and their relatives. Shallum was their leader. ¹⁸Now these men stand next to the King's Gate on the east side. They were the gatekeepers from the family group of Levi. ¹⁹Shallum was Kore's son. Kore was Ebiasaph's son. Ebiasaph was Korah's son. Shallum and his brothers were gatekeepers. They were from the family of Korah. They had the job of guarding the gates to the Holy Tent.* They did this just like their ancestors* had done before them. Their ancestors had the job of guarding the entrance to the Holy Tent. ²⁰In the past, Phinehas was in charge of the gatekeepers. Phinehas was Eleazar's son. The Lord was with Phinehas. ²¹Zechariah was the gatekeeper at the entrance to the Holy Tent.

²²In all there were 212 men that were chosen to guard the gates of the Holy Tent.* Their names were written in their family histories in their small towns. David and Samuel the seer* chose those men because they could be trusted. ²³The gatekeepers and their descendants* had the responsibility of guarding the gates of the Lord's house, the Holy Tent. ²⁴There were gates on the four sides: east, west, north, and south. ²⁵The gatekeepers' relatives that lived in the small towns

---

Holy Tent Also called the "tabernacle." The people would go to this tent to meet with God. The people used this tent until Solomon built the temple in Jerusalem.

ancestors Literally, "fathers." This means a person's parents, grandparents, and all the people they are descended from.

seer This is another name for a prophet. See 1 Sam. 9:9-11.

---

descendant(s) A person's children and their future families.
temple The special building in Jerusalem for Jewish worship.

had to come and help them at certain times. They came and helped the gatekeepers for seven days each time.

²⁶There were four gatekeepers that were the leaders of all the gatekeepers. They were Levite men. They had the job of caring for the rooms and treasures in God's temple.* ²⁷They stayed up all night guarding God's temple. And they had the job of opening God's temple every morning.

²⁸Some of the gatekeepers had the job of caring for the dishes used in the temple* services. They counted these dishes when they were brought in. They also counted these dishes when they were taken out. ²⁹Other gatekeepers were chosen to care for the furniture and those special dishes. They also took care of the flour, wine, oil, incense,* and special oil.* ³⁰But it was the priests that had the job of mixing the special oil.

³¹There was a Levite named Mattithiah that had the job of baking the bread used for the offerings. Mattithiah was Shallum's oldest son. Shallum was from the Korah family. ³²Some of the gatekeepers that were in the Korah family had the job of preparing the bread put on the table every Sabbath.*

³³The Levites that were singers and leaders of their families stayed in the rooms at the temple.* They did not have to do other work because they were responsible for the work in the temple day and night.

³⁴All these Levites were leaders of their families. They were listed as leaders in their family histories. They lived in Jerusalem.

King Saul's Family History

³⁵Jeiel was Gibeon's father. Jeiel lived in the town of Gibeon. Jeiel's wife was named Maacah. ³⁶Jeiel's oldest son was Abdon. Other sons were Zur, Kish, Baal, Ner, Nadab, ³⁷Gedor, Ahio, Zechariah, and Mikloth. ³⁸Mikloth was Shimeam's father. Jeiel's family lived near their relatives in Jerusalem.

³⁹Ner was Kish's father. Kish was Saul's father. And Saul was the father of Jonathan, Malki Shua, Abinadab, and Esh Baal.

⁴⁰Jonathan's son was Merib Baal. Merib Baal was Micah's father.

⁴¹Micah's sons were Pithon, Melech, Tahrea, and Ahaz. ⁴²Ahaz was Jadah's father. Jadah was Jarah's father.* Jarah was the father of Alemeth, Azmaveth and Zimri. Zimri was Moza's father. ⁴³Moza was the father of Binea. Rephaiah was Binea's son. Eleasah was Rephaiah's son. And Azel was Eleasah's son.

⁴⁴Azel had six sons. Their names were: Azrikam, Bokeru, Ishmael, Sheariah, Obadiah, and Hanan. Those were Azel's children.

The Death of King Saul

10 The Philistine people fought against the people of Israel. The people of Israel ran away from the Philistines. Many Israelite people were killed on Mount Gilboa. ²The Philistines continued chasing Saul and his sons. They caught them and killed them. The Philistines killed Saul's sons Jonathan, Abinadab, and Malki Shua. ³The fighting became heavy around Saul. The archers* shot Saul with their arrows and wounded him.

⁴Then Saul said to his armorbearer,* "Pull out your sword and use it to kill me. Then those foreigners* will not hurt me and make fun of me when they come."

But Saul's armorbearer* was afraid. He refused to kill Saul. Then Saul used his own sword to kill himself. He fell on the point of his sword. ⁵The armorbearer saw that Saul was dead. Then he also killed himself. He fell on the point of his own sword and died. ⁶So Saul and three of his sons died. All of Saul's family died together.

⁷All the people of Israel living in the valley saw that their own army had run away. They saw that Saul and his sons were dead. So they left their towns and ran away. Then the Philistine people came into the towns the people of Israel had left. And the Philistine people lived in those towns.

⁸The next day, the Philistine people came to take valuable things from the dead bodies. They

---

temple The special building in Jerusalem for Jewish worship.
incense A kind of spice that smells good when it is burned. It was burned as a gift to God.
special oil Or "perfume." This might be the oil used to anoint priests, prophets, and kings. See Ex. 30:22-38.
Sabbath Saturday. A special day of rest and worship for the Jews.

Ahaz ... Jarah's father Hebrew has only, "Ahaz was the father of Jarah."
archers Soldiers that use bows and arrows in war.
armorbearer A young man that carried a soldier's weapons.
foreigners Men from other countries that are not circumcised. This showed that those men did not share in the special agreement with God.

found Saul's body and the bodies of his sons on Mount Gilboa. ⁹The Philistines took things from Saul's body. They took Saul's head and armor. They sent messengers through all their country to tell the news to their false gods and to their people. ¹⁰The Philistines put Saul's armor in the temple of their false gods. They hung Saul's head in the temple of Dagon.*

¹¹All the people living in the town of Jabesh Gilead heard everything the Philistine people had done to Saul. ¹²All the brave men from Jabesh Gilead went to get the bodies of Saul and his sons. They brought them back to Jabesh Gilead. Those brave men buried the bones of Saul and his sons under the large tree in Jabesh. Then they fasted for seven days.

¹³Saul died because he was not faithful to the Lord. Saul did not obey the Lord's word. Saul also went to a medium* and asked her for advice ¹⁴instead of asking the Lord. That is why the Lord killed Saul and gave the kingdom to Jesse's son David.

David Becomes King Over Israel

11 All the people of Israel came to David at the town of Hebron. They said, to David, "We are your own flesh and blood.* ²In the past, you led us in war. You led us even though Saul was the king. The Lord said to you 'David, you will be the shepherd of my people, the people of Israel. You will become the leader over my people.'"

³All the leaders of Israel came to King David at the town of Hebron. David made an agreement with those leaders in Hebron before the Lord. The leaders anointed* David. That made him king over Israel. The Lord promised this would happen. The Lord had used Samuel to make that promise.

David Captures Jerusalem

⁴David and all the people of Israel went to the city of Jerusalem. Jerusalem was called Jebus at that time. The people living in that city were named Jebusites. The people that lived in the city ⁵said to David, "You can't get inside our city." But David did defeat those people. David took over the fortress* of Zion.* This place became the City of David.

⁶David said, "The person that leads the attack on the Jebusite people will become the commander over all my army." So Joab led the attack. Joab was Zeruiah's son. Joab became the commander of the army.

⁷Then David made his home in the fortress.* That is why it is named the City of David. ⁸David built the city around the fort. He built it from the Millo* to the wall around the city. Joab repaired the other parts of the city. ⁹David continued to grow greater. And the Lord All-Powerful was with him.

The Three Heroes

¹⁰This is a list of the leaders over David's special soldiers. These heroes became very powerful with David in his kingdom. They and all the people of Israel supported David and made him king. It happened just like God had promised.

¹¹This is a list of David's special soldiers:

Jashobeam the Hacmonite.* Jashobeam was the leader of the chariot officers.* Jashobeam used his spear to kill 300 men at one time.

¹²Next, there was Eleazar son of Dodai* from Ahoah. Eleazar was one of The Three Heroes. ¹³Eleazar was with David at Pasdammim. The Philistines had come to that place to fight a war. There was a field full of barley at that place. The people of Israel ran away from the Philistines. ¹⁴But the ₍Three Heroes₎ stood there in that field and defended it. They defeated the Philistines. The Lord gave the people of Israel a great victory.

Dagon The national god of the Philistine people. Its head, arms, and body looked like a person, and its lower body was like the tail of a fish.

medium A person that lets a spirit take control of him and let him tell things that would happen in the future. See 1 Sam. 28:7-19.

We are ... blood A way of saying they were David's relatives.

anoint(ed) To pour olive oil on a person's head to show he was chosen by God to be a king, priest, or prophet.

fortress A building or city with tall, strong walls for protection.

Zion The southeast part of the mountain Jerusalem is built on. Sometimes it means the people of God living in Jerusalem.

Millo The Millo was probably a raised platform of land southeast of the temple area in Jerusalem.

Jashobeam the Hacmonite This is "Josheb Basshebeth the Tahkemonite" in 2 Sam. 23:8.

chariot officers Or, "The Thirty" or "The Three." See 2 Sam. 23:8.

Eleazar son of Dodai Or, "Eleazar his cousin."

1 CHRONICLES 11:15–12:3

[15] Once, David was at the cave of Adullam and the Philistine army was down in the Valley of Rephaim. Three of the Thirty Heroes* crawled flat on the ground all the way to that cave to join David. [16] Another time, David was in the fortress,* and a group of Philistine soldiers was in Bethlehem. [17] David was thirsty ₍for some water from his home town₎. So he said, "I wish someone could give me some water from that well near the city gate in Bethlehem." ₍David did not really want this, he was only talking.₎ [18] But the Three* fought their way through the Philistine army. These three men got some water from the well near the city gate in Bethlehem. Then the Three Heroes brought the water to David. But David refused to drink the water. He poured it out on the ground as an offering to the Lord. [19] David said, "God, I can't drink this water. It would be like drinking the blood of the men who risked their lives to get this water for me." That is why David refused to drink the water. The Three Heroes did many brave things like that.

Other Brave Soldiers

[20] Joab's brother, Abishai, was the leader of the Three Heroes. He fought 300 men with his spear and killed them. Abishai was as famous as the Three Heroes. [21] Abishai was twice as famous as the Three Heroes. He became their leader, even though he was not one of them.

[22] Benaiah son of Jehoiada was the son of a powerful man. He was from Kabzeel. Benaiah did brave things. Benaiah killed two of the best men from the country of Moab. One day when it was snowing, Benaiah went down into a hole in the ground and killed a lion. [23] And Benaiah killed a big Egyptian soldier. That man was about 7 1/2 feet* tall. The Egyptian had a spear that was very large and heavy. It was as big as the pole on a weaver's loom.* Benaiah had only a club. Benaiah grabbed the spear in the Egyptian's hands and took it away from him. Then Benaiah killed the Egyptian with his own spear. [24] Benaiah son of Jehoiada did many brave things like that. Benaiah was as famous as the Three Heroes.* [25] Benaiah was more famous than the Thirty Heroes,* but he was not one of the Three Heroes. David chose Benaiah to be the leader of his bodyguards.

The Thirty Heroes

[26] The Heroic Soldiers *(The Thirty Heroes)* were: Asahel, the brother of Joab; Elhanan, son of Dodai from Bethlehem; [27] Shammoth the Harodite; Helez the Pelonite; [28] Ira son of Ikkesh from Tekoa; Abiezer from Anathoth; [29] Sibbecai the Hushathite; Ilai from Ahohite; [30] Maharai from Netophah; Heled son of Baanah from Netophah; [31] Ithai son of Ribai from Gibeah in Benjamin; Benaiah, the Pirathonite; [32] Hurai from the Brooks of Gaash; Abiel the Arbathite; [33] Azmaveth the Baharumite; Eliahba the Shaalbonite; [34] the sons of Hashem the Gizonite; Jonathan son of Shagee the Hararite; [35] Ahiam son of Sacar the Hararite; Eliphal son of Ur; [36] Hepher the Mekerathite; Ahijah the Pelonite; [37] Hezro the Carmelite; Naarai son of Ezbai; [38] Joel, Nathan's brother; Mibhar son of Hagri; [39] Zelek the Ammonite; Naharai from Beeroth (Naharai carried the armor for Joab son of Zeruaiah.); [40] Ira the Ithrite; Gareb the Ithrite; [41] Uriah the Hittite; Zabad son of Ahlai; [42] Adina son of Shiza from the family group of Reuben. (Adina was the leader of the family group of Reuben, but he was also one of the Thirty Heroes.); [43] Hanan son of Maacah; Joshaphat the Mithnite; [44] Uzzia the Ashterathite; Shama and Jeiel sons of Hotham Aroerite; [45] Jediael son of Shimri; Joha the Tizite and his brother Joha; [46] Eliel the Mahavite; Jeribai and Joshaviah the sons of Elnaam; Ithmah the Moabite; [47] Eliel; Obed; and Jaasiel the Mezobaite.

The Brave Men Who Joined David

12 This is a list of the men who came to David while he was at Ziklag. This was when David was hiding from Saul son of Kish. These men helped David in battle. [2] These men could shoot arrows from their bows with their right or left hand. They could also throw stones from their slings* with their right or left hand. They were Saul's relatives from the family group of Benjamin. Their names were:

[3] Ahiezer, their leader, and Joash (Ahiezer and Joash were sons of Shemaah the Gibeathite.);

Thirty Heroes These men were David's famous group of very brave soldiers.
fortress A building or city with tall, strong walls for protection.
Three The Three Heroes, David's three bravest soldiers.
7 1/2 feet Or, "2.25m." Literally, "5 ₍short₎ cubits."
loom A machine used for making cloth.
Three Heroes These were David's three bravest soldiers.

sling(s) A strip of leather for throwing rocks.

Jeziel and Pelet (Jeziel and Pelet were Azmaveth's sons); Beracah and Jehu from the town of Anathoth. ⁴Ishmaiah from the town of Gibeon (Ishmaiah was a hero with the Three Heroes and he was also a leader of the Three Heroes); Jeremiah, Jahaziel, Johanan, and Jozabad from the Gederathite people; ⁵Eluzai, Jerimoth, Bealiah, and Shemariah; Shephatiah from Haripha; ⁶Elkanah, Isshiah, Azarel, Joezer, and Jashobeam, all from the family group of Korah; ⁷Joelah and Zebadiah, the sons of Jeroham from the town of Gedor.

The Gadites

⁸Part of the family group of Gad joined David at his fortress* in the desert. They were brave soldiers trained for war. They were skilled with the shield and spear. They looked as fierce as lions. And they could run as fast as gazelles* in the mountains.
⁹Ezer was the leader of the army from the family group of Gad. Obadiah was the second in command. Eliab was the third in command. ¹⁰Mishmannah was the fourth in command. Jeremiah was the fifth in command. ¹¹Attai was the sixth in command. Eliel was the seventh in command. ¹²Johanan was the eighth in command. Elzabad was the ninth in command. ¹³Jeremiah was the tenth in command. Macbannai was the eleventh in command.
¹⁴Those men were leaders of the Gadite army. The weakest from that group could fight 100 enemy soldiers. The strongest from that group could fight 1,000 enemy soldiers. ¹⁵The people from the family group of Gad were the soldiers that went across the Jordan River in the first month of the year. That was a time of year when the Jordan River was flooding. They chased away all the people living in the valleys. They chased those people to the east and to the west.

Other Soldiers Join David

¹⁶Other men from the family groups of Benjamin and Judah also came to David at the fortress.* ¹⁷David went out to meet them. David said to them, "If you have come in peace to help me, I welcome you. Join me. But if you have come to spy on me when I have done nothing wrong, then may the God of our ancestors see what you did and punish you."
¹⁸Amasai was the leader of the Thirty Heroes.* Then the Spirit came over Amasai ₍and he said₎,

"We are yours, David!
We are with you, son of Jesse!
Peace, peace to you!
Peace to the people who help you.
Why? Because your God helps you!"

So David welcomed these men into his group and put them in charge of the troops.
¹⁹Some of the men from the family group of Manasseh also joined David. They joined David when he went with the Philistines to fight Saul. But David and his men did not really help the Philistines. The Philistine leaders talked about David helping them, but then they decided to send him away. Those rulers said, "If David goes back to his master Saul, then our heads will be cut off!" ²⁰These were the men from Manasseh that joined David when he went to the town of Ziklag: Adnah, Jozabad, Jediael, Michael, Jozabad, Elihu, and Zillethai. All of them were generals* from the family group of Manasseh. ²¹They helped David fight against bad men. Those bad men were going around the country and stealing things from people. All these men of Manasseh were brave soldiers. They became leaders in David's army.
²²More and more men came every day to help David. So David had a large and powerful army.

Other Men Join David at Hebron

²³These are the numbers of the men that came to David at the town of Hebron. These men were ready for war. They came to give Saul's kingdom to David. That is what the Lord said would happen. This is their number:
²⁴From the family group of Judah there were 6,800 men ready for war. They carried shields and spears.
²⁵From the family group of Simeon there were 7,100 men. They were brave soldiers ready for war.
²⁶From the family group of Levi there were 4,600 men. ²⁷Jehoiada was in that group. He was a leader from Aaron's family. There were 3,700 men with Jehoiada. ²⁸Zadok was also in that

---

fortress A building or city with tall, strong walls for protection.
gazelles Animals like deer.

Thirty Heroes Or, "The Three" or "the chariot officers."
generals Literally, "leaders over 1,000 men."

group. He was a brave young soldier. He came with 22 officers from his family.

²⁹From the family group of Benjamin there were 3,000 men. They were Saul's relatives. Most of those men stayed faithful to Saul's family until that time.

³⁰From the family group of Ephraim there were 20,800 men. They were brave soldiers. They were famous men in their own families.

³¹From half of Manasseh's family group there were 18,000 men. They were called by name to come and make David king.

³²From the family of Issachar there were 200 wise leaders. Those men understood the right thing for Israel to do at the right time. Their relatives were with them and under their command.

³³From the family group of Zebulun there were 50,000 trained soldiers. They were trained to use all kinds of weapons. They were very loyal to David.

³⁴From the family group of Naphtali there were 1,000 officers. They had 37,000 men with them. Those men carried shields and spears.

³⁵From the family group of Dan there were 28,600 men ready for war.

³⁶From the family group of Asher there were 40,000 trained soldiers ready for war.

³⁷From the east side of the Jordan River, there were 120,000 men from the family groups of Reuben, Gad, and half of Manasseh. Those men had all kinds of weapons.

³⁸All those men were brave fighters. They came to the town of Hebron fully agreed to make David king of all Israel. All the other people of Israel also agreed that David should be king. ³⁹The men spent three days at Hebron with David. They ate and drank, because their relatives had prepared food for them. ⁴⁰Also, their neighbors from the areas where the family groups of Issachar, Zebulun, and Naphtali live brought food on donkeys, camels, mules, and cattle. They brought much flour, fig cakes, raisins, wine, oil, cattle, and sheep. The people in Israel were very happy.

Bringing Back The Box of the Agreement

13 David talked with all the officers of his army. ²Then David called the people of Israel together. He said to them: "If you think it is a good idea, and if it is what the Lord wants, let us send a message to our brothers in all the areas of Israel. Let's also send the message to the priests and Levites that live with our brothers in their towns and the fields near those towns. Let the message tell them to come and join us. ³Let's bring the Box of the Agreement* back to us in Jerusalem. We did not take care of the Box of the Agreement while Saul was king." ⁴So all the people of Israel agreed with David. They all thought it was the right thing to do.

⁵So David gathered all the people of Israel from the Shihor River in Egypt to the town of Lebo Hamath. They came together to bring the Box of the Agreement* back from the town of Kiriath Jearim. ⁶David and all the people of Israel with him went to Baalah of Judah. (Baalah is another name for Kiriath Jearim.) They went there to bring out the Box of the Agreement. That Box of the Agreement is the Box of God the Lord. He sits above the Cherub angels.* It is the Box that is called by the Lord's Name.

⁷The people moved the Box of the Agreement* from Abinadab's house. They put it on a new wagon. Uzzah and Ahio were driving the wagon.

⁸David and all the people of Israel were celebrating before God. They were praising God and singing songs. They were playing harps,* lyres,* drums, cymbals,* and trumpets.

⁹They came to Kidon's threshing floor.* The bulls pulling the wagon stumbled. And the Box of the Agreement* almost fell. Uzzah reached out with his hand to catch the Box. ¹⁰The Lord became very angry at Uzzah. The Lord killed Uzzah because he touched the Box. So Uzzah died there in front of God. ¹¹God showed his anger at Uzzah. And this made David angry. Since that time until now that place has been called "Perez Uzzah."*

¹²David was afraid of God that day. David said, "I can't bring the Box of the Agreement* here to me!" ¹³So David did not take the Box of the

---

Box of the Agreement Also called "The Ark of the Covenant," the box containing the stone tablets with the Ten Commandments written on them and the other things that proved God was with the people of Israel during their time in the Sinai Desert.

Cherub angels Special angels from God. Statues of these angels were on top of the Box of the Agreement.

harps Musical instruments with several strings.

lyres An instrument with several strings, like a harp.

cymbals Brass plates that were hit together to make a ringing noise.

threshing floor A place where grain is beaten or walked on to remove the hulls from the grain.

Perez Uzzah This means "the outburst at Uzzah."

Agreement with him to the City of David.* He left the Box of the Agreement at Obed Edom's house. Obed Edom was from the city of Gath. ¹⁴The Box of the Agreement stayed with Obed Edom's family in his house for three months. The Lord blessed Obed Edom's family and everything Obed Edom owned.

David's Kingdom Grows

14 Hiram was king of the city of Tyre. Hiram sent messengers to David. Hiram also sent logs from cedar trees, stonecutters,* and carpenters* to David. Hiram sent them to build a house for David. ²Then David could see that the Lord had really made him king of Israel. The Lord made David's kingdom very large and powerful. God did this because he loved David and the people of Israel.

³David married more women in the city of Jerusalem. And he had more sons and daughters. ⁴These are the names of David's children born in Jerusalem: Shammua, Shobab, Nathan, Solomon, ⁵Ibhar, Elishua, Elpelet, ⁶Nogah, Nepheg, Japhia, ⁷Elishama, Beeliada, and Eliphelet.

David Defeats the Philistines

⁸The Philistine people heard David had been chosen to be the king of Israel. So, all the Philistine people went to look for David. David heard about it. Then he went out to fight the Philistine people. ⁹The Philistines attacked the people living in the Valley of Rephaim and stole their things. ¹⁰David asked God, "Should I go and fight the Philistine people? Will you let me defeat them?"

The Lord answered David, "Go. I will let you defeat the Philistine people."

¹¹Then David and his men went up to the town of Baal Perazim. There David and his men defeated the Philistine people. David said, "Waters break out from a broken dam. In the same way, God has broken through my enemies! God has done this through me." That is why that place is named Baal Perazim.* ¹²The Philistine people had left their idols at Baal Perazim. David ordered his men to burn those idols.

Another Victory Over the Philistine people

¹³The Philistines attacked the people living in the Valley of Rephaim again. ¹⁴David prayed to God again. God answered David's prayer. God said, "David, don't go in front of the Philistine people when you attack. Instead, go around them. Hide in the place where the balsam trees are. ¹⁵⌊Climb the trees.⌋ From the top of the trees you will hear the sounds of marching. At that time, attack the Philistines. I *(God)* will go out in front of you and defeat the Philistine army!" ¹⁶David did what God told him to do. So David and his men defeated the Philistine army. They killed Philistine soldiers all the way from the town of Gibeon to the town of Gezer. ¹⁷So David became famous in all the countries. The Lord made all nations afraid of David.

The Box of the Agreement in Jerusalem

15 David built houses for himself in the City of David.* Then he built a place to put the Box of the Agreement.* He set up a tent for it. ²Then David said, "Only the Levites are permitted to carry the Box of the Agreement. The Lord chose them to carry the Box of the Agreement and to serve him forever."

³David got all the people of Jerusalem together to bring the Box of the Agreement* to the place he had made for it. ⁴David called together the descendants* of Aaron and the Levites. ⁵There were 120 people from Kohath's family group. Uriel was their leader. ⁶There were 220 people from Merari's family group. Asaiah was their leader. ⁷There were 130 people from Gershon's family group. Joel was their leader. ⁸There were 200 people from Elizaphan's family group. Shemaiah was their leader. ⁹There were 80 people from Hebron's family group. Eliel was their leader. ¹⁰There were 112 people from Uzziel's family group. Amminadab was their leader.

David Talks to the Priests and Levites

¹¹Then David asked the priests Zadok and Abiathar to come to him. David also asked these

---

City of David The southeastern and oldest part of the city of Jerusalem.
stonecutters Men that cut stones and build things with them.
carpenters Men that build things with wood.
Baal Perazim This name means, "the Lord breaks through."
Box of the Agreement Also called "The Ark of the Covenant," the box containing the stone tablets with the Ten Commandments written on them and the other things that proved God was with the people of Israel during their time in the Sinai Desert.
descendant(s) A person's children and their future families.

Levites to come to him: Uriel, Asaiah, Joel, Shemaiah, Eliel, and Amminadab. ¹²David said to them, "You are the leaders from the family group of Levi. You and the other Levites must make yourselves holy.* Then bring the Box of the Agreement* to the place I have made for it. ¹³The last time we did not ask the Lord how to carry the Box of the Agreement. You Levites did not carry it, and that is why the Lord punished us."

¹⁴Then the priests and Levites made themselves holy* so they could carry the Box of the Agreement* of the Lord God of Israel. ¹⁵The Levites used the special poles to carry the Box of the Agreement on their shoulders, the way Moses commanded. They carried the Box just like the Lord said.

The Singers

¹⁶David told the Levite leaders to get their brothers, the singers. The singers were to take their lyres,* harps, and cymbals* and sing happy songs. ¹⁷Then the Levites got Heman and his brothers, Asaph and Ethan. Heman was Joel's son. Asaph was Berekiah's son. Ethan was Kushaiah's son. These men were from the Merari family group. ¹⁸There was also a second group of Levites. They were Zechariah, Jaaziel, Shemiramoth, Jehiel, Unni, Eliab, Benaiah, Maaseiah, Mattithiah, Eliphelehu, Mikneiah, Obed Edom, and Jeiel. These men were the Levite guards.

¹⁹The singers Heman, Asaph, and Ethan played bronze cymbals.* ²⁰Zechariah, Jaaziel, Shemiramoth, Jehiel, Unni, Eliab, Maaseiah, and Benaiah played the alamoth* lyres.* ²¹Mattithiah, Eliphelehu, Mikneiah, Obed Edom, Jeiel, and Azaziah played the sheminith* harps. This was their job forever. ²²The Levite leader Kenaniah was in charge of the singing. Kenaniah had this job because he was very skilled at singing.

²³Berekiah and Elkanah were two of the guards for the Box of the Agreement.* ²⁴The priests Shebaniah, Joshaphat, Nethanel, Amasai, Zechariah, Benaiah, and Eliezer had the job of blowing trumpets ⌈as they walked⌉ in front of the Box of the Agreement. Obed Edom and Jehiah were the other guards for the Box of the Agreement.

²⁵David, the elders *(leaders)* of Israel, and the generals went to get the Box of the Agreement.* They brought it out from Obed Edom's house. Everyone was very happy! ²⁶God helped the Levites that carried the Box of the Agreement. They sacrificed* seven bulls and seven rams. ²⁷All the Levites that carried the Box of the Agreement wore robes made from fine linen.* Kenaniah, the man in charge of the singing, and all the singers had robes made from fine linen. David also wore a robe made from fine linen. And David also wore an ephod* made of fine linen.

²⁸So all the people of Israel brought up the Box of the Agreement.* They shouted, they blew rams' horns and trumpets, and they played cymbals,* lyres,* and harps.

²⁹When the Box of the Agreement* arrived at the City of David,* Michal looked through a window. Michal was Saul's daughter. She saw King David dancing and playing around. And she lost her respect for David—⌈she thought he was being foolish⌉.

16 The Levites brought the Box of the Agreement* and put it inside the tent David had set up for it. Then they offered burnt offerings and fellowship offerings to God. ²After David had finished giving the burnt offerings and fellowship offerings, he used the Lord's name to bless the people. ³Then he gave a loaf of bread, some dates, and raisins to every Israelite man and woman.

⁴Then David chose some of the Levites to serve before the Box of the Agreement.* Those Levites had the job of celebrating and giving thanks and praise to the Lord, the God of Israel. ⁵Asaph was the leader ⌈of the first group⌉. Asaph's group played the cymbals.* Zechariah was the ⌈leader of

---

holy This means "prepared to serve the Lord.
Box of the Agreement Also called "The Ark of the Covenant," the box containing the stone tablets with the Ten Commandments written on them and the other things that proved God was with the people of Israel during their time in the Sinai Desert.
lyre(s) An instrument with several strings, like a harp.
cymbals Brass plates that were hit together to make a ringing noise.
alamoth We don't know the exact meaning of this word, but it probably means "high pitched."
sheminith We don't know the exact meaning of this word, but it probably means "low pitched."

sacrifice(d) To offer a gift to God. Usually it was a special animal that was killed and burned on an altar.
linen A type of cloth.
ephod We do not know exactly what this was. It may have been a special vest or coat, like the High Priest of Israel wore (see Exodus 28). Or it may have been an idol.
City of David The southeastern and oldest part of the city of Jerusalem.

the₁ second ₁group₁. The other Levites were: Uzziel, Shemiramoth, Jehiel, Mattithiah, Eliab, Benaiah, Obed Edom, and Jeiel. These men played the lyres* and harps. ⁶Benaiah and Jahaziel were the priests that always blew the trumpets before the Box of the Agreement. ⁷This was when David first gave Asaph and his brothers the job of singing praises to the Lord.

David's Song of Thanks

8 Praise the Lord.
  Call on his name.
  Tell people about the great things
    the Lord has done.
9 Sing to the Lord.
  Sing praises to the Lord.
  Tell about all his wonderful works.
10 Be proud of the Lord's holy name.
   All you people coming to the Lord,
     be happy!
11 Look to the Lord and his strength.
   Always go to him for help.
12 Remember the wonderful things
     that the Lord has done.
   Remember his decisions
     and the powerful things he has done.
13 The people of Israel are the Lord's servants
   The descendants of Jacob,
   are the Lord's chosen people.
14 The Lord is our God,
   His power is everywhere.
15 Remember his Agreement forever.
   He gave those commandments
     for a thousand generations.
16 Remember the Agreement
     that the Lord made with Abraham.
   Remember his promise to Isaac.
17 The Lord made it a law for Jacob.
   It is the Agreement with Israel
     that continues forever.
18 The Lord said to Israel:
   "I will give the land of Canaan to you.
   The promised land will be yours."
19 There were only a few people.
   A few strangers in a foreign land.
20 They went from one nation to another.
   They went from one kingdom to
     another.
21 But the Lord did not let anyone hurt them.
   The Lord warned kings not to hurt them.
22 The Lord told those kings,
   "Don't hurt my chosen people.
   Don't hurt my prophets."
23 Sing to the Lord, all the earth.
   Each day you must tell the good news
     about the Lord saving us.
24 Tell all nations about the Lord's glory.
   Tell everyone how wonderful he is.
25 The Lord is great,
     and he should be praised.
   The Lord is more awesome
     than all the other gods.
26 Why? Because all the gods of the world
     are only worthless statues.
   But the Lord made the skies.!
27 The Lord has glory and honor.
   The Lord is like a bright and shining
     light.
28 Families and people,
     praise the Lord's glory and power!
29 Praise the Lord's glory.
   Show honor to his name.
   Bring your offering to the Lord.
   Worship the Lord and his holy beauty.
30 The whole earth should shake with fear in
     front of the Lord!
   But he made the earth strong,
     the world won't move.
31 Let the earth and skies be happy.
   Let people everywhere say,
   "The Lord rules!"
32 Let the sea and everything in it shout!
   Let the fields and everything in them
     show their joy!
33 The trees of the forest will sing with joy in
     front of the Lord!
   Why? Because the Lord is coming.
   He is coming to judge the world.
34 Oh, thank the Lord—he is good.
   The Lord's love continues forever.
35 Say to the Lord,
   "Save us, God our Savior.
   Gather us together,
     and save us from the other nations.
   Then we can praise your holy name.
   Then we can praise you with our songs."
36 The Lord God of Israel has always been
     praised.
   Let him be praised forever.

All the people praised the Lord and said "Amen!"

---

lyre(s) An instrument with several strings, like a harp.

³⁷Then David left Asaph and his brothers there in front of the Box of the Agreement. David left them there to serve in front of it every day. ³⁸David also left Obed Edom and 68 other Levites to serve with Asaph and his brothers. Obed Edom and Hosah were guards. Obed Edom was Jeduthun's son.

³⁹David left Zadok the priest and the other priests that served with him in front of the Lord's tent* at the high place* in Gibeon. ⁴⁰Every morning and evening Zadok and the other priests offered burnt offerings on the altar of burnt offerings. They did this to follow the rules written in the Law of the Lord which the Lord had given Israel. ⁴¹Heman and Jeduthun and all the other Levites were chosen by name to sing praises to the Lord, because the Lord's love continues forever! ⁴²Heman and Jeduthun were with them. They had the job of blowing the trumpets and playing cymbals.* They also had the job of playing other musical instruments when songs were sung to God. Jeduthun's sons guarded the gates.

⁴³⌊After the celebration,⌋ all the people left. Each person went to his own home. And David also went home to bless his family.

God's Promise to David

17 After David had moved into his house, he said to Nathan the prophet, "Look, I am living in a house made of cedar wood, but the Box of the Agreement* sits under a tent. ⌊I want to build a temple* for God.⌋"

²Nathan answered David, "You may do what you want to do. God is with you."

³But that night the word of God came to Nathan. ⁴God said, "Go and tell these things to my servant David: The Lord says, 'David, you are not the person to build a house for me to live in. ⁵⁻⁶Since the time I brought Israel out of Egypt until now, I have not lived in a house. I have moved around in a tent. I chose people to be special leaders for the people of Israel. Those leaders were like shepherds for my people. While I was going around in Israel to different places, I never said to any of those leaders: Why haven't you built a house of cedar wood for me?'

⁷"Now, tell these things to my servant David: The Lord All-Powerful says, 'I took you from the fields and from taking care of the sheep. I made you king of my people Israel. ⁸I have been with you everywhere you went. I went ahead of you and I killed your enemies. Now I will make you one of the most famous men on earth. ⁹I am giving this place to my people Israel. They will plant their trees, and they will sit in peace under those trees. They won't be bothered anymore. Evil people won't hurt them like they did at first. ¹⁰Those bad things happened, but I chose leaders to care for my people Israel. And I will also defeat all your enemies.

"'I tell you that the Lord will build a house for you.* ¹¹When you die, and you join your ancestors,* then I will let your own son be the new king. The new king will be one of your sons. And I will make his kingdom strong. ¹²Your son will build a house for me. I will make your son's family rule forever. ¹³I will be his Father, and he will be my son. Saul was the king before you. And I took away my support from Saul. But I will never stop loving your son. ¹⁴I will put him in charge of my house and kingdom forever. His rule will continue forever!'"

¹⁵Nathan told David about the vision* and about all of the things that God had said.

David's Prayer

¹⁶Then King David went ⌊to the Holy Tent⌋ and sat before the Lord. David said, "Lord God, you have done so much for me and my family. And I don't understand why. ¹⁷Besides all those things,

---

Lord's tent Or, "tabernacle." Also called the "meeting tent." The people would go to this tent to meet with God. The people used this tent until Solomon built the temple in Jerusalem.

high place A place for worshiping God or false gods. These places were often on the hills and mountains.

cymbals Brass plates that were hit together to make a ringing noise.

Box of the Agreement Also called "The Ark of the Covenant," the box containing the stone tablets with the Ten Commandments written on them and the other things that proved God was with the people of Israel during their time in the Sinai Desert.

temple The special building in Jerusalem for Jewish worship.

I ... a house for you This does not mean a real house. It means the Lord would make men from David's family kings for many, many years.

ancestors Literally, "fathers." This means a person's parents, grandparents, and all the people they are descended from.

vision Like a dream. God gave messages to his special people by letting them see and hear things in visions.

you let me know what will happen to my family in the future. You have treated me like a very important man. ¹⁸What more can I say? You have done so much for me. And I am only your servant. You know that. ¹⁹Lord, you have done this wonderful thing for me. And you did it because you wanted to. ²⁰There is no one like you, Lord. There is no God except you. We have never heard of any god doing wonderful things like those! ²¹Is there any other nation like Israel? No! Israel is the only nation on earth that you have done these wonderful things for. You took us out of Egypt and you made us free. You made yourself famous! You went in front of your people, and forced other people to leave their land for us! ²²You took Israel to be your people forever. And Lord, you became their God!

²³"Lord, you made this promise to me and my family. Now, keep your promise forever. Do what you said you would! ²⁴Show that you can be trusted! And I hope people honor your name forever. Then people will say, 'The Lord All-Powerful is Israel's God!' I am your servant! Please let my family be strong and continue to serve you.

²⁵"My God, you spoke to me, your servant. You made it clear that you would make my family a family of kings. That is why I am being so bold—that is why I am asking you to do these things. ²⁶Lord, you are God. And God, you yourself promised to do these good thing for me. ²⁷Lord, you have been kind enough to bless my family. You were kind enough to promise that my family will serve you forever. Lord, you yourself blessed my family, so my family really will be blessed forever!"

David Wins Over Different Nations

18 Later David attacked the Philistine people. He defeated them. He took the town of Gath and the other small towns around it from the Philistine people.

²Then David defeated the country of Moab. The Moabite people became David's servants. They brought tribute* to David.

³David also fought against Hadadezer's army. Hadadezer was the king of Zobah. David fought against that army all the way to the town of Hamath. David did this because Hadadezer tried to spread his kingdom all the way to the Euphrates River. ⁴David took from Hadadezer 1,000 chariots, 7,000 chariot drivers, and 20,000 soldiers. David also crippled most of Hadadezer's horses that were used for pulling chariots. But David saved enough horses to pull 100 chariots.

⁵The Aramean people from the city of Damascus came to help Hadadezer. Hadadezer was the king of Zobah. But David defeated and killed 22,000 Aramean soldiers. ⁶Then David put fortresses* in the city of Damascus in Aram. The Aramean people became David's servants and brought tribute* to him. So the Lord gave victory to David everywhere he went.

⁷David took the gold shields from Hadadezer's army leaders and brought them to Jerusalem. ⁸David also took much bronze from the towns of Tebah and Cun. Those towns belonged to Hadadezer. Later, Solomon used this bronze to make the bronze tank, the bronze columns, and other things made from bronze for the temple.*

⁹Tou was king of the city of Hamath. Hadadezer was the king of Zobah. Tou heard that David had defeated all of Hadadezer's army. ¹⁰So Tou sent his son Hadoram to King David to ask for peace and to bless him. He did this because David had fought against Hadadezer and defeated him. Hadadezer had been at war with Tou before. Hadoram gave David all kinds of things made of gold, silver, and bronze. ¹¹King David made those things holy and gave them to the Lord. David did the same thing with all the silver and gold he had gotten from Edom, Moab, the Ammonite people, the Philistine people, and Amalekite people.

¹²Abishai son of Zeruiah killed 18,000 Edomite people in the Valley of Salt. ¹³Abishai also put fortresses* in Edom and all the Edomite people became David's servants. The Lord gave David victory everywhere he went.

David's Important Officials

¹⁴David was king over all of Israel. He did what was right and fair for everyone. ¹⁵Joab son of Zeruiah was the commander of David's army. Jehoshaphat son of Ahilud wrote about the things David did. ¹⁶Zadok and Abimelech were the priests. Zadok was Ahitub's son, and Abimelech

---

tribute Money and gifts paid by one king to the king that defeated him.

fortresses A building or city with tall, strong walls for protection.

temple The special building in Jerusalem for Jewish worship.

fortress(es) A building or city with tall, strong walls for protection.

was Abiathar's son. Shavsha was the scribe.* ¹⁷Benaiah was responsible for leading the Kerethite and Pelethite people.* Benaiah was Jehoiada's son. And David's sons were important officials. They served at King David's side.

The Ammonites Shame David's Men

19 Nahash was king of the Ammonite people. Nahash died, and his son became the new king. ²Then David said, "Nahash was kind to me, so I will be kind to Hanun, Nahash's son." So David sent messengers to comfort Hanun about the death of his father. David's messengers went to the country of Ammon to comfort Hanun.

³But the Ammonite leaders said to Hanun, "Don't be fooled. David didn't really send these men to comfort you or to honor your dead father! No, David sent his servants to spy on you and your land. David really wants to destroy your country!" ⁴So Hanun arrested David's servants and cut off their beards.* Hanun also cut their clothes off at the hip. Then he sent them away.

⁵David's men were too embarrassed to go home. Some people went to David and told him what happened to his men. So King David sent this message to his men: "Stay in the town of Jericho until your beards grow again. Then you can come back home."

⁶The Ammonite people saw they had caused themselves to become hated enemies of David. Then Hanun and the Ammonite people used 75,000 pounds* of silver to buy chariots and chariot drivers from Mesopotamia.* They also got chariots and chariot drivers from the towns of Maacah and Zobah in Aram. ⁷The Ammonite people bought 32,000 chariots. They also paid the king of Maacah and his army to come and help them. The king of Maacah and his people came and set up a camp near the town of Medeba. The Ammonite people themselves came out of their towns and got ready for battle.

⁸David heard that the Ammonite people were getting ready for war. So he sent Joab and the whole army of Israel to fight the Ammonite people. ⁹The Ammonites came out and got ready for battle. They were near the city gate. The kings that had come to help stayed out in the fields by themselves.

¹⁰Joab saw that there were two army groups ready to fight against him. One group was in front of him and the other group was behind him. So Joab chose some of the best soldiers of Israel. He sent them out to fight against the army of Aram. ¹¹Joab put the rest of the army of Israel under Abishai's command. Abishai was Joab's brother. Those soldiers went out to fight against the Ammonite army. ¹²Joab said to Abishai, "If the army from Aram is too strong for me, then you must help me. But if the Ammonite army is too strong for you, then I will help you. ¹³Let's be brave and strong while we fight for our people and for the cities of our God! May the Lord do what he thinks is right."

¹⁴Joab and the army with him attacked the army from Aram. The army from Aram ran away from Joab and his army. ¹⁵The Ammonite army saw that the army from Aram was running away, so they also ran away. They ran away from Abishai and his army. The Ammonites went back to their city, and Joab went back to Jerusalem.

¹⁶The Aramean leaders saw that Israel had defeated them. So they sent messengers to get help from the Aramean people living east of the Euphrates River. Shophach was the commander of Hadadezer's army from Aram. Shophach also led those other Aramean soldiers.

¹⁷David heard the news that the people of Aram were gathering for battle. So David gathered all the people of Israel. David led them across the Jordan River. They came face to face with the Arameans. David got his army ready for battle and they attacked the Arameans. ¹⁸The Arameans ran away from the Israelites. David and his army killed 7,000 Aramean chariot drivers and 40,000 Aramean soldiers. David and his army also killed Shophach the commander of the Aramean army.

¹⁹When Hadadezer's officers saw that Israel had defeated them, they made peace with David. They became David's servants. So the Arameans refused to help the Ammonites again.

Joab Destroys the Ammonites

20 In the spring,* Joab led the army of Israel out to battle. That was the time of year

---

scribe A man that wrote down and copied books and letters. He often became an expert at knowing the meaning of those writings *(scriptures)*.

Kerethite and Pelethite people These were the king's bodyguards.

cut off their beards It was against the Law of Moses for an Israelite man to cut off his beard.

75,000 pounds Or, "34,000kg." Literally, "1,000 kikars."

Mesopotamia Literally, "Aram Naharaim."

In the spring Literally, "At the return of the year."

when kings went out to battle, but David stayed in Jerusalem. The army of Israel went to the country of Ammon and destroyed it. Then they went to the city of Rabbah. The army camped around the city—they stayed there to keep people from going in or out of the city. Joab and the army of Israel fought against the city of Rabbah until they destroyed it. ²David took the crown from their king's* head. That gold crown weighed about 75 pounds.* There were valuable stones in the crown. The crown was put on David's head. Then David had a great many valuable things brought out of the city of Rabbah. ³David brought out the people in Rabbah and forced them to work with saws, iron picks, and axes. David did the same thing to all the cities of the Ammonite people. Then David and all the army went back to Jerusalem.

Philistine Giants Are Killed

⁴Later the people of Israel had war with the Philistine people at the town of Gezer. At that time, Sibbecai from Hushah killed Sippai. Sippai was one of the sons of the giants. So those Philistine people became like slaves to the Israelites.

⁵Another time, the people of Israel again had war against the Philistine people. Elhanan son of Jair killed Lahmi. Lahmi was Goliath's brother. Goliath was from the town of Gath. Lahmi's spear was very big and heavy. It was like the large pole on a loom.*

⁶Later, the Israelites fought another war with the Philistine people at the town of Gath. In this town there was a very large man. He had 24 fingers and toes. That man had six fingers on each hand and six toes on each foot. He also was a son of the giants. ⁷So when that man made fun of Israel, Jonathan killed him. Jonathan was Shimea's son. Shimea was David's brother.

⁸Those Philistine men were sons of the giants from the town of Gath. David and his servants killed those giants.

David Sins By Counting Israel

21 Satan was against the people of Israel. He encouraged David to count the people of Israel. ²So David said to Joab and the leaders of the people, "Go and count all the people of Israel. Count everyone in the country—from the town of Beersheba all the way to the town of Dan. Then tell me, so I will know how many people there are."

³But Joab answered, "May the Lord make his nation 100 times as large! Sir, all the people of Israel are your servants. Why do you want to do this thing, my lord and king? You will make all the people of Israel guilty of sin!"

⁴But King David was stubborn. Joab had to do what the king said. So Joab left and went through all the country of Israel counting the people. Then Joab came back to Jerusalem ⁵and told David how many people there were. In Israel there were 1,100,000 men who could use a sword. And there were 470,000 men in Judah who could use a sword. ⁶Joab did not count the family groups of Levi and Benjamin. Joab did not count those family groups because he did not like King David's order. ⁷David had done a bad thing in God's sight. So God punished Israel.

God Punishes Israel

⁸Then David said to God, "I have done something very foolish. I have done a very bad sin by counting the people of Israel. Now, I beg you to take the sin away from me, your servant."

⁹⁻¹⁰Gad was David's seer.* The Lord said to Gad, "Go and tell David: 'This is what the Lord says: I am going to give you three choices. You must choose one of them. Then I will punish you the way you choose.'"

¹¹⁻¹²Then Gad went to David. Gad said to David, "The Lord says, 'David, choose which punishment you want: three years without enough food, or three months of running away from your enemies while they use their swords to chase you, or three days of punishment from the Lord. Terrible sicknesses will spread through the country, and the Lord's angel will go through Israel destroying the people.' David, God sent me. Now, you must decide which answer I will give to him."

¹³David said to Gad, "I am in trouble! I don't want some man to decide my punishment. The Lord is very merciful, so let the Lord decide how to punish me."

¹⁴So the Lord sent terrible sicknesses to Israel, and 70,000 people died. ¹⁵God sent an angel to

---

their king's Or, "Milcom," the god of the Ammonite people.
75 pounds Literally, "1 kikar."
loom A machine for making cloth from thread.

seer This is another name for a prophet. See 1 Sam. 9:9-11.

1 CHRONICLES 21:16–22:4

destroy Jerusalem. But when the angel started to destroy Jerusalem, the Lord saw it and felt sorry. So the Lord decided not to destroy Jerusalem. The Lord said to the angel who was destroying, "Stop! That is enough!" The angel of the Lord was standing at the threshing floor* of Araunah the Jebusite.*

16 David looked up and saw the Lord's angel in the sky. The angel was holding his sword over the city of Jerusalem. Then David and the elders *(leaders)* bowed with their faces touching the ground. David and the elders *(leaders)* were wearing the special clothes to show their sadness. 17 David said to God, "I am the one that sinned! I gave the order for the people to be counted! I was wrong! The people of Israel did not do anything wrong! Lord my God, punish me and my family! But stop the terrible sicknesses that is killing your people!"

18 Then the angel of the Lord spoke to Gad. He said, "Tell David to build an altar* to worship the Lord. David must build that altar near the threshing floor* of Araunah the Jebusite.*" 19 Gad told those things to David, and David went to Araunah's threshing floor.

20 Araunah was threshing* the wheat. Araunah turned around and saw King David. Araunah's four sons ran away to hide. 21 David went to Araunah. Araunah left the threshing floor. He walked to David bowed with his face to the ground in front of him.

22 David said to Araunah, "Sell me your threshing floor.* I will pay you the full price. Then I can use the area to build an altar* to worship the Lord. Then the terrible sicknesses will be stopped."

23 Araunah said to David, "Take this threshing floor*! You are my lord and king. Do anything you want. Look, I will also give you cattle for the burnt offering.* I will give the wooden floor boards so you can burn them for the fire on the altar.* And I will give the wheat for the grain offering. I will give all this to you!"

24 But King David answered Araunah, "No, I will pay you the full price. I won't take anything that is yours and give it to the Lord. I won't give offerings that cost me nothing."

25 So David gave Araunah about 15 pounds* of gold for the place. 26 David built an altar* for worshiping the Lord there. David offered burnt offerings and fellowship offerings. David prayed to the Lord. The Lord answered David by sending fire down from heaven. The fire came down on the altar of burnt offering. 27 Then the Lord commanded the angel to put his sword back into its sheath.*

28 David saw that the Lord had answered him on the threshing floor* of Araunah, so David offered sacrifices to the Lord. 29 (The Holy Tent* and the altar of burnt offerings were at the high place* in the town of Gibeon. Moses had made the Holy Tent while the people of Israel were in the desert. 30 David could not go to the Holy Tent to speak with God because he was afraid. David was afraid of the angel of the Lord and his sword.)

22 David said, "The temple* of the Lord God and the altar for burning offerings for the people of Israel will be built here."

David Makes Plans for the Temple

2 David gave an order for all foreigners living in Israel to be gathered together. David chose stonecutters* from that group of foreigners. Their job was to cut stones ready to be used for building God's temple.* 3 David got iron for making nails and hinges for the gate doors. David also got more bronze than could be weighed. 4 And David got more cedar logs than could be counted. The people from the cities of Sidon and Tyre brought many cedar logs to David.

---

threshing floor A place where grain is beaten or walked on to remove the hulls from the grain.
Jebusite A person that lived in Jerusalem before the Israelites took the city. "Jebus" was the old name for Jerusalem.
altar A stone table used for burning sacrifices offered as gifts to God.
threshing Beating or walking on grain to remove the hulls from the grain.
burnt offering(s) Gifts to God. Usually these were animals that were killed and completely burned on the altar.

15 pounds Literally, "600 shekels."
sheath A case for carrying swords.
Holy Tent Also called the "tabernacle." The people would go to this tent to meet with God. The people used this tent until Solomon built the temple in Jerusalem.
high place(s) Places for worshiping God or false gods. These places were often on the hills and mountains.
temple The special building in Jerusalem for worshiping God.
stonecutters Men that cut stones and build things with them.

⁵David said, "We should build a very great temple* for the Lord. But my son Solomon is young and he hasn't learned the things he needs to know. The Lord's temple should be very great. It should be famous in all the nations because of its greatness and beauty. That is why I will make plans for building the Lord's temple." So David made many plans ₍for building the temple₎ before he died.

⁶Then David called for his son Solomon. David told Solomon to build the temple* for the Lord God of Israel. ⁷David said to Solomon, "My son, I wanted to build a temple for the name of the Lord my God. ⁸But the Lord said to me, 'David, you have fought many wars and you have killed many people. So you can't build a temple for my name. ⁹But you have a son that is a man of peace. I will give your son a time of peace. His enemies around him will not bother him. His name is Solomon.* And I will give Israel peace and quiet during the time that Solomon is king. ¹⁰Solomon will build a temple for my name. Solomon will be my son, and I will be his Father. And I will make Solomon's kingdom strong. And someone from his family will rule Israel forever!'"

¹¹David also said, "Now, son, may the Lord be with you. May you be successful and build the temple* for the Lord your God, like he said you would. ¹²The Lord will make you the king of Israel. May the Lord give you wisdom and understanding so you can lead the people and obey the law of the Lord your God. ¹³And you will have success, if you are careful to obey the rules and laws that the Lord gave Moses for Israel. Be strong and brave. Don't be afraid.

¹⁴"Solomon, I have worked hard making plans for building the Lord's temple.* I have given 3,750 tons* of gold. And I have given about 37,500 tons* of silver. I have given so much bronze and iron that it can't be weighed. And I have given wood and stone. Solomon, you can add to them. ¹⁵You have many stonecutters* and carpenters.* You have men skilled in every kind of work. ¹⁶They are skilled in working with gold, silver, bronze, and iron. You have more skilled workers than can be counted. Now begin the work. And may the Lord be with you."

¹⁷Then David ordered all the leaders of Israel to help his son Solomon. ¹⁸David said to these leaders, "The Lord your God is with you. He has given you a time of peace. The Lord helped me to defeat the people living around us. The Lord and his people are now in control of this land. ¹⁹Now give your heart and soul to the Lord your God, and do the things he says. Build the holy place of the Lord God. Build the temple* for the Lord's name. Then bring the Box of the Agreement* and all the other holy things into the temple."

Plans for the Levites to Serve in the Temple

23 David became an old man, so he made his son Solomon the new king of Israel. ²David gathered all the leaders of Israel. He also gathered the priests and Levites. ³David counted the Levites that were 30 years old and older. All together there were 38,000 Levites. ⁴David said, "24,000 Levites will supervise the work of building the Lord's temple.* 6,000 Levites will be policemen and judges. ⁵4,000 Levites will be gatekeepers. And 4,000 Levites will be musicians. I made special musical instruments for them. They will use those instruments to praise the Lord."

⁶David separated the Levites into three groups. They were the family groups of Levi's three sons, Gershon, Kohath, and Merari.

The Gershon Family Group

⁷From the family group of Gershon there were Ladan and Shimei. ⁸Ladan had three sons. His oldest son was Jehiel. His other sons were Zethan and Joel. ⁹Shimei's sons were Shelomoth, Haziel, and Haran. These three sons were leaders in Ladan's families.

¹⁰Shimei had four sons. They were Jahath, Ziza, Jeush, and Beriah. ¹¹Jahath was the oldest son and Ziza was the second son. But Jeush and Beriah did not have many children. So Jeush and Beriah were counted like one family.

---

temple The special building in Jerusalem for Jewish worship.
Solomon This name is like the Hebrew word meaning, "peace."
3,750 tons Literally, "100,000 kikars."
37,500 tons Literally, "1,000,000 kikars."
stonecutters Men that cut stones and build things with them.
carpenters Men that build things with wood.

Box of the Agreement Also called "The Ark of the Covenant," the box containing the stone tablets with the Ten Commandments written on them and the other things that proved God was with the people of Israel during their time in the Sinai Desert.

The Kohath Family Group

¹²Kohath had four sons. They were Amram, Izhar, Hebron, and Uzziel. ¹³Amram's sons were Aaron and Moses. Aaron was chosen to be very special. Aaron and his descendants* were chosen to be special forever and ever. They were chosen to prepare the holy things for the Lord's service. Aaron and his descendants were chosen to burn the incense* before the Lord. They were chosen to serve the Lord as priests. They were chosen to use the Lord's name and give blessings to the people forever.

¹⁴Moses was the man of God.* Moses's sons were part of the family group of Levi. ¹⁵Moses' sons were Gershom and Eliezer. ¹⁶Gershom's oldest son was Shubael. ¹⁷Eliezer's oldest son was Rehabiah. Eliezer had no other sons. But Rehabiah had very many sons.

¹⁸Izhar's oldest son was Shelomith.

¹⁹Hebron's oldest son was Jeriah. Hebron's second son was Amariah. Jahaziel was the third son, and Jekameam was the fourth son.

²⁰Uzziel's oldest son was Micah, and Isshiah was his second son.

The Merari Family Group

²¹Merari's sons were Mahli and Mushi. Mahli's sons were Eleazar and Kish. ²²Eleazar died without having sons. He only had daughters. Eleazar's daughters married their own relatives. Their relatives were Kish's sons. ²³Mushi's sons were Mahli, Eder, and Jeremoth. There were three sons in all.

The Levites' Work

²⁴These were Levi's descendants.* They were listed by their families. They were the leaders of families. Each person's name was listed. The people that were listed were 20 years old or older. They served in the Lord's temple.*

²⁵David had said, "The Lord God of Israel has given peace to his people. The Lord has come to Jerusalem to live there forever. ²⁶So the Levites don't need to carry the Holy Tent* or any of the things used in its services any more."

²⁷David's last instructions for the people of Israel was to count the descendants* from the family group of Levi. They counted the Levite men that were 20 years old and older.

²⁸The Levites had the job of helping Aaron's descendants* in the service of the Lord's temple.* The Levites also cared for the temple yard and the side rooms in the temple. They had the job of making all holy things pure. It was their job to serve in God's temple. ²⁹They were responsible for putting the special bread on the table in the temple. They also were responsible for the flour, the grain offerings, and the bread made without yeast. They were also responsible for the baking pans and the mixed offerings. They did all the measuring. ³⁰The Levites stood every morning and gave thanks and praise to the Lord. They also did this every evening. ³¹The Levites prepared all the burnt offerings* to the Lord on the special days of rest, at the New Moon* celebrations, and at all the special holidays. They served before the Lord every day. There were special rules for how many Levites should serve each time. ³²So the Levites did all the things they were supposed to do. They took care of the Holy Tent.* They took care of the Holy Place.* And they helped their relatives, ₍the priests,₎ Aaron's descendants. The Levites helped the priests with the services at the Lord's temple.

The Groups of the Priests

24 These were the groups of Aaron's sons: Aaron's sons were Nadab, Abihu, Eleazar, and Ithamar. ²But Nadab and Abihu died before their father did. And Nadab and Abihu had no sons. So Eleazar and Ithamar served as the priests. ³David separated the family groups of Eleazar and Ithamar into two different groups. David did that so those groups could do the duties of work they were given to do. David did this with the help of Zadok and Ahimelech. Zadok was a descendant*

---

descendant(s) A person's children and their future families.
incense A kind of spice that smells good when it is burned. It was burned as a gift to God.
man of God Another name for a prophet.
temple Here this means the Holy Tent at Shiloh where people went to worship the Lord.

burnt offering(s) Gifts to God. Usually these were animals that were killed and completely burned on the altar.
New Moon This was the first day of the Hebrew month. There were special meetings on these days to worship God.
Holy Place The room in the Holy Tent and in the temple that was used by the priests to do their daily service to God.

of Eleazar, and Ahimelech was a descendant of Ithamar. ⁴There were more leaders from Eleazar's family than from Ithamar's. There were 16 leaders from Eleazar's family and there were eight leaders from Ithamar's family. ⁵Men were chosen from each family. They were chosen by throwing lots.* Some of the men were chosen to be in charge of the Holy Place.* And other men were chosen to serve as priests. All of these men were from the families of Eleazar and Ithamar.

⁶Shemaiah was the secretary.* He was Nethanel's son. Shemaiah was from the family group of Levi. Shemaiah wrote the names of those descendants.* He wrote those names in front of King David and these leaders: Zadok the priest, Ahimelech, and the leaders from the families of the priests and of the Levites. Ahimelech was Abiathar's son. Each time they threw the lots* a man was chosen, and Shemaiah wrote down that man's name. So they divided the work among the men from families of Eleazar and Ithamar.

⁷ The first group was Jehoiarib's group.
  The second group was Jedaiah's group.
⁸ The third group was Harim's group.
  The fourth group was Seorim's group.
⁹ The fifth group was Malkijah's group.
  The sixth group was Mijamin's group.
¹⁰ The seventh group was Hakkoz's group.
  The eighth group was Abijah's group.
¹¹ The ninth group was Jeshua's group.
  The tenth group was Shecaniah's group.
¹² The eleventh group was Eliashib's group.
  The twelfth group was Jakim's group.
¹³ The thirteenth group was Huppah's group.
  The fourteenth group was Jeshebeab's group.
¹⁴ The fifteenth group was Bilgah's group.
  The sixteenth group was Immer's group.
¹⁵ The seventeenth group was Hezir's group.
  The eighteenth group was Happizzez's group.
¹⁶ The nineteenth group was Pethahiah's group.
  The twentieth group was Jehezkel's group.
¹⁷ The twenty-first group was Jakin's group.
  The twenty-second group was Gamul's group.
¹⁸ The twenty-third group was Delaiah's group.
  The twenty-fourth group was Maaziah's group.

¹⁹These were the groups chosen to serve in the Lord's temple.* They obeyed Aaron's rules for serving in the temple. The Lord God of Israel had given those rules to Aaron.

The Other Levites

²⁰These are the names of the rest of Levi's descendants:

  From Amram's descendants: Shubael.
  From Shubael's descendants: Jehdeiah.
²¹ From Rehabiah: Isshiah. (Isshiah was the oldest son.)
²² From Izhar family group: Shelomoth.
  From Shelomoth's family: Jahath.
²³ Hebron's oldest son was Jeriah.
  Amariah was Hebron's second son.
  Jahaziel was his third son,
  and Jekameam was his fourth son.
²⁴ Uzziel's son was Micah.
  Micah's son was Shamir.
²⁵ Isshiah was Micah's brother. Isshiah's son was Zechariah.
²⁶ Merari's* descendants were Mahli, Mushi, and Jaaziah his son.
²⁷ Jaaziah son of Merari had sons named Shoham and Zaccur.
²⁸ Mahli's son was Eleazar. But Eleazar did not have sons.
²⁹ Kish's son was Jerahmeel.
³⁰ Mushi's sons were Mahli, Eder, and Jerimoth.

Those are the leaders of Levite families. They are listed by their families. ³¹They ₗwere chosen for special jobs₎. They threw lots* like their relatives, the priests. The priests were Aaron's descendants.* They threw lots in front of David the king, Zadok, Ahimelech, and the leaders of the priests' and Levite families. The older families

---

lot(s) Sticks, stones, or pieces of bone used like dice for making decisions. See Proverbs 16:33.
Holy Place The room in the Holy Tent and in the temple that was used by the priests to do their daily service to God.
secretary A man that wrote down and copied books and letters.
descendant(s) A person's children and their future families.
temple The special building in Jerusalem for Jewish worship.
Merari The Hebrew in verses 26 and 27 is hard to understand.

and the younger families were treated the same when their jobs were chosen.

The Music Groups

25 David and the leaders of the army separated Asaph's sons for special service. Asaph's sons were Heman and Jeduthun. Their special service was to prophesy* God's message by using harps, lyres,* and cymbals.* Here is a list of the men that served this way:
²From Asaph's family: Zaccur, Joseph, Nethaniah, and Asarelah. King David chose Asaph to prophesy.* And Asaph led his sons.
³From Jeduthun's family: Gedaliah, Zeri, Jeshaiah, Shimei, Hashabiah, and Mattithiah. There were six of them. Jeduthun led his sons. Jeduthun used harps* to prophesy* and give thanks and praise to the Lord.
⁴Heman's sons that served were Bukkiah, Mattaniah, Uzziel, Shubael, and Jerimoth; Hananiah, Hanani, Eliathah, Giddalti, and Romamti Ezer; Joshbekashah, Mallothi, Hothir, and Mahazioth. ⁵All these men were Heman's sons. Heman was David's seer.* God promised to make Heman strong. So Heman had many sons. God gave Heman fourteen sons and three daughters. ⁶Heman led all his sons in singing in the Lord's temple.* Those sons used cymbals,* lyres,* and harps. That was their way of serving in God's temple. King David chose those men.
⁷Those men and their relatives from the family group of Levi were trained to sing. There were 288 men that learned to sing praises to the Lord.
⁸They threw lots* to choose the different kinds of work each person was to do. Every person was treated the same. Young and old were treated the same. And the teacher was treated the same as the student.
⁹First, there were 12 men chosen from Asaph's (Joseph) ₍sons and relatives₎.

Second, there were 12 men chosen from Gedaliah's sons and relatives.
¹⁰Third, there were 12 men chosen from Zaccur's sons and relatives.
¹¹Fourth, there were 12 men chosen from Izri's sons and relatives.
¹²Fifth, there were 12 men chosen from Nethaniah's sons and relatives.
¹³Sixth, there were 12 men chosen from Bukkiah's sons and relatives.
¹⁴Seventh, there were 12 men chosen from Asarelah's sons and relatives.
¹⁵Eighth, there were 12 men chosen from Jeshaiah's sons and relatives.
¹⁶Ninth, there were 12 men chosen from Mattaniah's sons and relatives.
¹⁷Tenth, there were 12 men chosen from Shimei's sons and relatives.
¹⁸Eleventh, there were 12 men chosen from Azarel's sons and relatives.
¹⁹Twelfth, there were 12 men chosen from Hashabiah's sons and relatives.
²⁰Thirteenth, there were 12 men chosen from Shubael's sons and relatives.
²¹Fourteenth, there were 12 men chosen from Mattithiah's sons and relatives.
²²Fifteenth, there were 12 men chosen from Jeremoth's sons and relatives.
²³Sixteenth, there were 12 men chosen from Hananiah's sons and relatives.
²⁴Seventeenth, there were 12 men chosen from Joshbakashah's sons and relatives.
²⁵Eighteenth, there were 12 men chosen from Hanani's sons and relatives.
²⁶Nineteenth, there were 12 men chosen from Mallothi's sons and relatives.
²⁷Twentieth, there were 12 men chosen from Eliathah's sons and relatives.
²⁸Twenty-first, there were 12 men chosen from Hothir's sons and relatives.
²⁹Twenty-second, there were 12 men chosen from Giddalti's sons and relatives.
³⁰Twenty-third, there were 12 men chosen from Mahazioth's sons and relatives.
³¹Twenty-fourth, there were 12 men chosen from Romamti Ezer's sons and relatives.

The Gate Keepers

26 The Groups of the Gatekeepers:

These are the gatekeepers from the Korah family. Meshelemiah ₍and his sons₎. (Meshelemiah was Kore's son. He was from Asaph's family group.) ²Meshelemiah had sons.

---

prophesy To announce God's message.
lyre(s) An instrument with several strings, like a harp.
cymbals A pair of metal platters that are hit against each other to make a loud sound.
prophesy To announce God's message.
harps Musical instruments with several strings.
seer This is another name for a prophet. See 1 Sam. 9:9-11.
temple Here this means the Holy Tent at Shiloh where people went to worship the Lord.
lot(s) Sticks, stones, or pieces of bone used like dice for making decisions. See Proverbs 16:33.

Zechariah was the oldest son. Jediael was the second son. Zebadiah was the third son. Jathniel was the fourth son. ³Elam was the fifth son. Jehohanan was the sixth son. And Eliehoenai was the seventh son.

⁴Obed Edom and his sons. Obed Edom's oldest son was Shemaiah. Jehozabad was his second son. Joah was his third son. Sacar was his fourth son. Nethanel was his fifth son. ⁵Ammiel was his sixth son. Issachar was his seventh son. And Peullethai was his eighth son. God truly blessed Obed Edom.* ⁶Obed Edom's son was Shemaiah. Shemaiah also had sons. Shemaiah's sons were leaders in their father's family because they were brave soldiers. ⁷Shemaiah's sons were Othni, Rephael, Obed, Elzabad, Elihu, and Semakiah. Elzabad's relatives were skilled workers. ⁸All those men were Obed Edom's descendants.* Those men and their sons and relatives were powerful men. They were good guards. Obed Edom had 62 descendants.

⁹Meshelemiah had sons and relatives that were powerful men. In all there were 18 sons and relatives.

¹⁰These are the gatekeepers from the Merari family. There was Hosah. Shimri was chosen to be the first son. Shimri was not really the oldest, but his father chose him to be the firstborn* son. ¹¹Hilkiah was his second son. Tebaliah was his third son. And Zechariah was his fourth son. In all Hosah had 13 sons and relatives.

¹²These were the leaders of the groups of the gatekeepers. The gatekeepers had a special way to serve in the Lord's temple,* just like their relatives did. ¹³Each family was given a gate to guard. Lots* where thrown to choose a gate for a family. Young and old were treated the same.

¹⁴Meshelemiah was chosen to guard the East Gate. Then lots* were thrown for Meshelemiah's son Zechariah. Zechariah was a wise counselor. Zechariah was chosen for the North Gate. ¹⁵Obed Edom was chosen for the South Gate. And Obed Edom's sons were chosen to guard the house where the valuable things were kept. ¹⁶Shuppim and Hosah were chosen for the West Gate and the Shalleketh Gate on the upper road.

Guards stood side by side. ¹⁷Six Levites stood guard every day at the East Gate. Four Levites stood guard every day at the North Gate. Four Levites stood guard at the South Gate. And two Levites guarded the house where the valuable things were kept. ¹⁸There were four guards at the western court.* And there were two guards on the road to the court.

¹⁹These were the groups of the gatekeepers. Those gatekeepers were from the families of Korah and Merari.

The Treasurers and Other Officials

²⁰Ahijah was from the family group of Levi. Ahijah was responsible for taking care of the valuable things in God's temple.* Ahijah also was responsible for the places where the holy things were kept.

²¹Ladan was from Gershon's family. Jehieli was one of the leaders of Ladan's family group. ²²Jehieli's sons were Zetham and Zetham's brother Joel. They were responsible for the valuable things in the Lord's temple.*

²³₁Other leaders were chosen₁ from the family groups of Amram, Izhar, Hebron, and Uzziel. ²⁴Shubael was the leader responsible for the valuable things in the Lord's temple.* Shubael was Gershom's son. Gershom was Moses' son. ²⁵These were Shubael's relatives: His relatives from Eliezer were: Rehabiah, Eliezer's son. Jeshaiah, Rehabiah's son. Joram, Jeshaiah's son. Zicri, Joram's son. And Shelomith, Zicri's son. ²⁶Shelomith and his relatives were responsible for all the things David had collected for the temple.

The officers of the army also gave things for the temple.* ²⁷They gave some of the things taken in wars. They gave those things to be used in building the Lord's temple. ²⁸Shelomith and his relatives also took care of all the holy things given by Samuel the seer;* Saul son of Kish; Abner son of Ner; and Joab son of Zeruiah. Shelomith and his relatives took care of all the holy things that people gave to the Lord.

Obed Edom God blessed Obed Edom when the Box of the Agreement stayed at his house. See 1 Chron. 21.

descendant(s) A person's children and their future families.

firstborn The first born child. The firstborn son was very important in ancient times.

temple The special building in Jerusalem for worshiping God.

lot(s) Sticks, stones, or pieces of bone used like dice for making decisions. See Proverbs 16:33.

court We do not know the exact meaning of this word.

seer This is another name for a prophet. See 1 Sam. 9:9-11.

²⁹Kenaniah was from the Izhar family. Kenaniah and his sons had work outside the temple. They worked as policemen and judges in different places in Israel. ³⁰Hashabiah was from the Hebron family. Hashabiah and his relatives were responsible for all the Lord's work and for the king's business in Israel west of the Jordan River. There were 1,700 powerful men in Hashabiah's group. ³¹The family history of the Hebron family shows that Jeriah was their leader. When David had been king for 40 years, he ordered his people to search through the family histories for strong and skilled men. Some of those men were found among the Hebron family living in the town of Jazer in Gilead. ³²Jeriah had 2,700 relatives that were powerful men and leaders of families. King David gave those 2,700 relatives the responsibility of leading the family groups of Reuben, Gad, and half of Manasseh in taking care of the Lord's work and the king's business.

Army Groups

27 This is the list of the Israelite people that served the king in the army. Each group was on duty one month each year. There were rulers of families, captains, generals, and the policemen that served the king. Each army group had 24,000 men.
²Jashobeam was in charge of the first group for the first month. Jashobeam was Zabdiel's son. There were 24,000 men in Jashobeam's group. ³Jashobeam was one of Perez's descendants.* Jashobeam was leader of all the army officers for the first month.
⁴Dodai was in charge of the army group for the second month. He was from Ahoah. There were 24,000 men in Dodai's group.
⁵The third commander was Benaiah. Benaiah was the commander for the third month. Benaiah was Jehoiada's son. Jehoiada was the leading priest. There were 24,000 men in Benaiah's group. ⁶He was the same Benaiah that was a brave soldier from the Thirty Heroes. Benaiah led those men. Benaiah's son Ammizabad was in charge of Banaiah's group.
⁷The fourth commander was Asahel. Asahel was the commander for the fourth month. Asahel was Joab's brother. Later, Asahel's son Zebadiah took his place as commander. There were 24,000 men in Asahel's group.
⁸The fifth commander was Shamhuth. Shamhuth was the commander for the fifth month. Shamhuth was from Zerah's family. There were 24,000 men in Shamhuth's group.
⁹The sixth commander was Ira. Ira was the commander for the sixth month. Ira was Ikkesh's son. Ikkesh was from the town of Tekoa. There were 24,000 men in Ira's group.
¹⁰The seventh commander was Helez. Helez was the commander for the seventh month. He was from the Pelonite people, and a descendant* of Ephraim. There were 24,000 men in Helez' group.
¹¹The eighth commander was Sibbecai. Sibbecai was the commander for the eighth month. Sibbecai was from Hushah. Sibbecai was from Zerah's family. There were 24,000 men in Sibbecai's group.
¹²The ninth commander was Abiezer. Abiezer was the commander for the ninth month. Abiezer was from the town of Anathoth. Abiezer was from the family group of Benjamin. There were 24,000 men in Abiezer's group.
¹³The tenth commander was Maharai. Maharai was the commander for the tenth month. Maharai was from Netophah. He was from Zerah's family. There were 24,000 men in Maharai's group.
¹⁴The eleventh commander was Benaiah. Benaiah was the commander for the eleventh month. Benaiah was from Pirathon. Benaiah was from the Ephraim family group. There were 24,000 men in Benaiah's group.
¹⁵The twelfth commander was Heldai. Heldai was the commander for the twelfth month. Heldai was from Netophah. Heldai was from Othniel's family. There were 24,000 men in Heldai's group.

Leaders of the Family Groups

¹⁶The leaders of the family groups of Israel were:

Reuben: Eliezer son of Zicri.
Simeon: Shephatiah son of Maacah.
¹⁷ Levi: Hashabiah son of Kemuel.
Aaron: Zadok.
¹⁸ Judah: Elihu. (Elihu was one of David's brothers.)
Issachar: Omri son of Michael.
¹⁹ Zebulun: Ishmaiah son of Obadiah.
Naphtali: Jeremoth son of Azriel.
²⁰ Ephraim: Hoshea son of Azaziah.
West Manasseh: Joel son of Pedaiah.

---

descendant(s) A person's children and their future families.

21 East Manasseh: Iddo son of Zechariah.
Benjamin: Jaasiel son of Abner.
22 Dan: Azarel son of Jeroham.

Those were the leaders of the family groups of Israel.

David Counts the Israelites

23 ⌊David decided to count the men in Israel.⌋ There were very many people because God promised to make the people of Israel as many as the stars in the sky. So David only counted the men that were 20 years old and older. 24 Joab son of Zeruiah began to count the people, but he did not finish.* God became angry with the people of Israel. That is why the number of the people was not put in the book *The History of King David.*

The King's Administrators

25 This is the list of men that were responsible for the king's property:

Azmaveth son of Adiel was in charge of the king's storerooms.
Jonathan son of Uzziah was in charge of the storerooms in the small towns, villages, fields, and towers.
26 Ezri son of Kelub was in charge of the field workers.
27 Shimei from Ramah was in charge of the fields of grapes.
Zabdi from Shepham was in charge of the storage and care of the wine that came from the fields of grapes.
28 Baal Hanan from Geder was in charge of the olive trees and sycamore trees in the western hill country.
Joash was in charge of storing the olive oil.
29 Shitrai from Sharon was in charge of the cattle around Sharon.
Shaphat son of Adlai was in charge of the cattle in the valleys.
30 Obil the Ishmaelite was in charge of the camels.
Jehdeiah the Meronothite was in charge of the donkeys.
31 Jaziz the Hagrite was in charge of the sheep.

All these men were the leaders that took care of King David's property.
32 Jonathan was a wise counselor and a scribe.* Jonathan was David's uncle. Jehiel son of Hacmoni took care of the king's sons. 33 Ahithophel was the king's counselor. Hushai was the king's friend. Hushai was from the Arkite people. 34 Jehoiada and Abiathar later took Ahithophel's place as the king's counselor. Jehoiada was Benaiah's son. Joab was the commander of the king's army.

David's Plans for the Temple

28 David gathered all the leaders of the people of Israel. He commanded all those leaders to come to Jerusalem. David called all the leaders of the family groups, the commanders of the army groups serving the king, the captains, the generals, the officials taking care of the property and animals that belonged to the king and his sons, the king's important officials, the powerful heroes, and all the brave soldiers.

2 King David stood up and said, "Listen to me, my brothers and my people. In my heart I wanted to build a place to keep the Box of the Lord's Agreement.* I wanted to build a place that would be God's footstool.* And I made the plans for building that house for God. 3 But God said to me, 'No David, you must not build a house for my name. You must not do that because you are a soldier, and you have killed many men.'

4 "The Lord God of Israel chose the family group of Judah to lead the twelve family groups of Israel. And then from that family group, the Lord chose my father's family. And from that family, God chose me to be the king of Israel forever! God wanted to make me king of Israel! 5 The Lord has given me many sons. And from all those sons, the Lord chose Solomon to be the new king of Israel. But really, Israel is the Lord's kingdom. 6 The Lord said to me, 'David, your son Solomon

---

Joab ... did not finish God stopped him. See 1 Chron. 21:1-30.

scribe A man that wrote down and copied books and letters. He often become an expert at the meaning of those writings (*scriptures*).

Box of the Agreement Also called "The Ark of the Covenant," the box containing the stone tablets with the Ten Commandments written on them and the other things that proved God was with the people of Israel during their time in the Sinai Desert.

footstool Usually this was a small stool in front of a chair, but here it means the temple. It is like God is the king sitting in his chair and resting his feet on the building David wanted to build.

will build my temple* and the area around it. Why? Because I have chosen Solomon to be my son, and I will be his father.* ⁷Solomon is obeying my laws and commands now. If he continues to obey my laws, then I will make Solomon's kingdom strong forever!'

⁸₍David said,₎ "Now, in front of all Israel and God, I tell you these things: Be careful to obey all the commands of the Lord your God! Then you can keep this good land. And you can pass it on to your descendants* forever.

⁹"And you, my son Solomon, know the God of your father. Serve God with a pure heart. Be happy in your heart *(mind)* to serve God. Why? Because the Lord knows what is in every person's heart *(mind)*. The Lord understands everything you think. If you go to the Lord for help, you will get an answer. But if you turn away from the Lord, he will leave you forever. ¹⁰Solomon, you must understand that the Lord has chosen you to build his holy place—the temple.* Be strong and finish the job."

¹¹Then David gave his son Solomon the plans for building the temple.* Those plans were also for the porch around the temple, and for its buildings, its storerooms, its upper rooms, its inside rooms, and for the place for the mercy seat.* ¹²David had made plans for all parts of the temple. David gave those plans to Solomon. David gave him all the plans for the yard around the Lord's temple, and for all the rooms around it. David gave him the plans for the temple storerooms and for the storerooms where they kept the holy things used in the temple. ¹³David told Solomon about the groups of the priests and Levites. David told Solomon about all the work of serving in the Lord's temple and about all the things to be used in the temple service. ¹⁴David told Solomon how much gold and silver should be used to make all the things to be used in the temple. ¹⁵There were plans for gold lamps and lampstands, and there were plans for silver lamps and lampstands. David told Solomon how much gold or silver to use for each lampstand and its lamps. The different lampstands were to be used where needed. ¹⁶David told how much gold should be for each table used for holy bread. David told how much silver should be used for the silver tables. ¹⁷David told how much pure gold should be used to make the forks, sprinkling bowls, and pitchers. David told how much gold should be used to make each gold dish, and how much silver should be used to make each silver dish. ¹⁸David told how much pure gold should be used for the altar of incense.* David also gave Solomon the plans for ₍God's₎ chariot—the mercy seat* with the Cherub angels* spreading their wings over the Box of the Lord's Agreement.* The Cherub angels were made of gold.

¹⁹David said, "All these plans were written with the Lord guiding me. The Lord helped me understand everything in the plans."

²⁰David also said to his son Solomon, "Be strong and brave and finish this work. Don't be afraid, because the Lord God, my God, is with you. He will help you until all the work is finished. He will not leave you. You will build the Lord's temple.* ²¹The groups of the priests and Levites are ready for all the work on God's temple. Every skilled worker is ready to help you with all the work. The officials and all the people will obey every command you give."

Gifts for Building the Temple

29 King David said to all the people of Israel that were gathered together, "God chose my son Solomon. Solomon is young and does not know all that he needs to do this work. But the work is very important. This house isn't for people, this house is for the Lord God. ²I have done my best to make plans to build my God's

---

temple The special building in Jerusalem for worshiping God.
I ... father This showed God was making Solomon the king. See Psalm 2:7.
descendant(s) A person's children and their future families.
mercy seat Part of the Box of the Agreement. The Hebrew word can mean "lid," "cover," or "the place where sins are atoned *(covered, erased, or forgiven)."*
incense A kind of spice that smells good when it is burned. It was burned as a gift to God.
Cherub angels Special angels from God. Statues of these angels were on top of the Box of the Agreement.
Box of the Agreement Also called "The Ark of the Covenant," the box containing the stone tablets with the Ten Commandments written on them and the other things that proved God was with the people of Israel during their time in the Sinai Desert.

temple.* I have given gold for the things made of gold. I have given silver for the things made of silver. I have given bronze for the things made of bronze. I have given iron for the things made of iron. I have given wood for the things made of wood. I have also given onyx* stones for the settings,* mosaic tiles,* all kinds of valuable stones in many different colors, and white marble stones. I have given many, many of these things for the building of the Lord's temple. ³I am making a special gift of gold and silver things for my God's temple. I am doing this because I really want the temple of my God to be built. I am giving all these things to build this holy temple. ⁴I have given 110 tons* of pure gold from Ophir. I have given 260 tons* of pure silver. The silver is for covering the walls of the buildings in the temple. ⁵I have given gold and silver for all the things made of gold and silver. I have given gold and silver so skilled men can make all different kinds of things for the temple. Now, how many of you people of Israel are ready to give yourselves to the Lord today?"

⁶The family leaders, the leaders of the family groups of Israel, the generals, the captains, and the officials responsible for the king's work, were all ready and gave their valuable things. ⁷These are the things they gave for God's house: 190 tons* of gold; 375 tons* of silver; 675 tons* of bronze; and 3,750 tons* of iron. ⁸People that had valuable stones gave them to the Lord's temple.* Jehiel took care of the valuable stones. Jehiel was from the Gershon family. ⁹The people were very happy because their leaders were happy to give so much. The leaders were happy to give freely from good hearts. King David was also very happy.

David's Beautiful Prayer

¹⁰Then David praised the Lord in front of all of the people who gathered together. David said:

"Lord God of Israel, our Father,
may you be praised forever and ever!
¹¹ Greatness, power, glory, victory, and honor
belong to you!
Why? Because everything in heaven and
on earth
belong to you;
The kingdom belongs to you, Lord!
You are the Head, the Ruler over
everything.
¹² Riches and honor come from you.
You rule everything.
You have the power and strength in your
hand!
And in your hand is the power
to make anyone great and powerful!
¹³ Now, our God, we thank you,
And we praise your glorious name!
¹⁴ All these things didn't come
from me and my people!
All these things come from you,
We are only giving back to you
things that came from you.
¹⁵ We are only strangers traveling through
this world like our ancestors.*
Our time on earth is like a passing shadow.
And we can't stop it.
¹⁶ Lord our God, we gathered all these things
to build your temple.
We build this temple to honor your
name.
But all these things have come from you.
Everything belongs to you.
¹⁷ My God, I know that you test people,
and that you are happy
when people do good.
I gladly give you all these things
with a pure, honest heart.
I see your people gathered here.
And I see that they are happy
about giving these things to you.
¹⁸ Lord, you are the God of our ancestors,
Abraham, Isaac, and Israel.*
Please help your people plan the right
things.
Help them be loyal and true to you!
¹⁹ And help my son Solomon be true to you.
Help him always obey your commands,
laws, and rules.

---

temple The special building in Jerusalem for worshiping God.
onyx A semi-precious stone with many layers of blue or gray.
settings The frames that stones are mounted in.
mosaic tiles Literally, "stones set in mortar."
110 tons Literally, "3,000 kikars."
260 tons Literally, "7,000 kikars."
190 tons Literally, "5,000 kikars and 10,000 darics."
375 tons Literally, "10,000 kikars."
675 tons Literally, "18,000 kikars."
3,750 tons Literally, "100,000 kikars."

ancestors Literally, "fathers." This means a person's parents, grandparents, and all the people they are descended from.

Help Solomon to do these things. and help him build this capital city that I have planned."

²⁰Then David said to all the group of people gathered together, "Now give praise to the Lord your God." So all the people gave praise to the Lord God, the God their ancestors* worshiped. They bowed to the ground to give honor to the Lord and to the king.

Solomon Becomes King

²¹The next day the people made sacrifices* to the Lord. They offered burnt offerings to the Lord. They offered 1,000 bulls, 1,000 rams,* 1,000 lambs, and the drink offerings that go with them. They offered many, many sacrifices for all the people of Israel. ²²That day the people were very happy as they ate and drank there together with the Lord.

And they made David's son Solomon king the second time.* They anointed* Solomon to be king, and they anointed Zadok to be priest. They did this in the place where the Lord was.

²³Then Solomon sat on the Lord's throne as king. Solomon took his father's place. Solomon was very successful. All the people of Israel obeyed Solomon. ²⁴All the leaders, soldiers, and all of King David's sons accepted Solomon as king and obeyed him. ²⁵The Lord made Solomon very great. All the people of Israel knew that the Lord was making Solomon great. The Lord gave Solomon the honor that a king should have. No king in Israel before Solomon had such honor.

David's Death

²⁶⁻²⁷David son of Jesse was king over all Israel for 40 years. David was king in the city of Hebron for seven years. Then David was king in the city of Jerusalem for 33 years. ²⁸David died when he was old. David had lived a good, long life. David had many riches and honors. And David's son Solomon became the new king after him.

²⁹The things that King David did, from beginning to end, are in the books written by Samuel the seer,* Nathan the prophet, and Gad the seer. ³⁰Those writings tell all about the things that David did as king of Israel. They tell about David's power and all that happened to him. And they tell about what happened to Israel and to all the kingdoms around them.

Israel Another name for Jacob. See Gen. 35:19.
ancestors Literally, "fathers." This means a person's parents, grandparents, and all the people they are descended from.
sacrifice(s) A gift to God. Usually it was a special animal that was killed and burned on an altar.
ram(s) A male sheep.
And they made ... time Solomon was chosen to be king the first time when his half-brother Adonijah tried to make himself king. See 1 Kings 1:5-39.
anoint(ed) To pour olive oil on a person's head to show he was chosen by God to be a king, priest, or prophet.

seer This is another name for a prophet. See 1 Sam. 9:9-11.

2 Chronicles

Solomon Asks for Wisdom

1 ¹Solomon became a very strong king because the Lord his God was with him. The Lord made Solomon very great. ²Solomon spoke to the people of Israel. He spoke to the captains, generals, judges, to every leader in all Israel, and to the leaders of the families. ³Then Solomon and all the people gathered together with him went to the high place* at Gibeon. God's Meeting Tent* was there. The Lord's servant Moses made that tent when he and the people of Israel were in the desert. ⁴David had carried God's Box of the Agreement* from Kiriath Jearim to Jerusalem. David had made a place to put it in Jerusalem. David had set up a tent for God's Box of the Agreement in Jerusalem. ⁵Bezalel son of Uri had made a bronze altar. That bronze altar was in Gibeon in front of the Holy Tent. So Solomon and the people went to Gibeon to ask the Lord for advice. ⁶Solomon went up to the bronze altar in front of the Lord at the Meeting Tent. Solomon offered 1,000 burnt offerings* on the altar.

⁷That night God came to Solomon. God said, "Solomon, ask me what you want me to give you."

⁸Solomon said to God, "You were very kind to my father David. You chose me to be the new king in my father's place. ⁹Now, Lord God, keep your promise to my father David. You have chosen me to be king of a very large nation. There are so many people—they are like the dust of the earth! ¹⁰Now give me wisdom and knowledge so I can lead these people in the right way. No one can rule these people without your help!"

¹¹God said to Solomon, "You have the right attitude. You didn't ask for wealth, riches or honor. You didn't ask for your enemies to be killed. And you didn't ask for a long life. No, you did not ask for those things. You asked for wisdom and knowledge so you could make wise decisions for my people—the people I chose you to rule over. ¹²So I will give you wisdom and knowledge. But I will also give you wealth, riches, and honor. No king who lived before you has ever had so much wealth and honor. And no king in the future will have as much wealth and honor."

¹³So, Solomon went to the place of worship at Gibeon. Then Solomon left the Meeting Tent* and went back to Jerusalem to rule as king of Israel.

Solomon Builds His Army and Wealth

¹⁴Solomon started gathering horses and chariots for his army. Solomon got 1,400 chariots and 12,000 horse soldiers. Solomon put them in the chariot cities.* Solomon also put some of them in Jerusalem where the king's home was. ¹⁵In Jerusalem, Solomon gathered a lot of gold and silver. There was so much gold and silver that it was as common as rocks. Solomon gathered a lot of cedar wood. There was so much cedar that it was as common as sycamore trees in the western hill country. ¹⁶Solomon brought in horses from Egypt and Kue.* The king's business men bought the horses in Kue. ¹⁷Solomon's business men

---

high place(s) Places for worshiping God or false gods. These places were often on the hills and mountains.
Meeting Tent The Holy Tent (Tabernacle) where the people of Israel went to meet with God.
Box of the Agreement The box containing the stone tablets with the Ten Commandments written on them and the other things that proved God was with the people of Israel during their time in the Sinai Desert. Also called "The Ark of the Covenant."
burnt offering(s) Gifts to God. Usually these were animals that were killed and completely burned on the altar.

chariot cities Cities with special places to keep the horses and chariots.
Kue Or Cilicia, a country in what is now southern Turkey.

bought a chariot from Egypt for 600 shekels* of silver, and a horse for 150 shekels* of silver. The business men then sold the horses and chariots to all the kings of the Hittite people and to the kings of Aram.

Solomon Makes Plans to Build the Temple

2 Solomon planned to build a temple* to give honor to the Lord's name. Solomon also planned to build a king's house for himself. ²Solomon got 70,000 laborers and 80,000 stonemasons to cut stones in the mountains. Solomon chose 3,600 foremen to supervise the workers.

³Then Solomon sent a message to Hiram. Hiram was the king of the city of Tyre. Solomon said, "Help me like you helped my father David. You sent wood to him from cedar trees so he could build a house for himself to live in. ⁴I will build a temple* to honor the name of the Lord my God. At the temple we will burn incense* in front of the Lord, and we will always put the holy bread* on the special table. We will offer burnt offerings every morning and evening, every Sabbath day, every New Moon,* and on the other feast days that the Lord our God has commanded us to celebrate. This is a rule for the people of Israel to obey forever.

⁵"Our God is greater than all the other gods. So I will build a great temple for him. ⁶No person can really build a house to put our God in. Not even heaven can hold God—no not even the universe can hold our God! So I cannot build a temple for God. I can only build a place to burn incense* to honor him.

⁷"Now, I would like you to send me a man who is skilled in working with gold, silver, bronze, and iron. That man must know how to work with purple, red, and blue cloth. That man will work here in Judah and Jerusalem with the craftsmen my father chose. ⁸Also send me wood from cedar trees, pine trees, and algum trees from the country of Lebanon. I know your servants are experienced at cutting down trees from Lebanon. My servants will help your servants. ⁹I will need lots of wood because the temple I am building will be very large and beautiful. ¹⁰This is what I will pay for your servants to cut down the trees for wood. I will give them 125,000 bushels* of wheat for food, 125,000 bushels* of barley, 115,000 gallons* of wine, and 115,000 gallons* of oil."

¹¹Then Hiram answered Solomon. Hiram sent a message to Solomon. This is what that message said: "Solomon, the Lord loves his people. That is why he chose you to be their king." ¹²Hiram also said, "Praise the Lord God of Israel! He made heaven and earth. He gave a wise son to King David. Solomon, you have wisdom and understanding. You are building a temple* for the Lord. You are also building a king's house for yourself. ¹³I will send you a skilled craftsman named Huram Abi.* ¹⁴His mother was from the family group of Dan. And his father was from the city of Tyre. Huram Abi has skill in working with gold, silver, bronze, iron, stone, and wood. Huram Abi also has skill in working with purple, blue, and red cloth and expensive linen.* Huram Abi can design and build anything you tell him. He will work with your craftsmen and with the craftsmen of your father King David.

¹⁵Now, Sir, you offered to give us wheat, barley, oil, and wine. Give those things to my servants. ¹⁶And we will cut wood from the country of Lebanon. We will cut as much wood as you need. We will tie the logs together and float them by sea to the town of Joppa. Then you can carry the wood to Jerusalem."

¹⁷Then Solomon counted all the strangers living in the country of Israel. This was after the time when David counted the people. David was Solomon's father. They found 153,600 strangers in the country. ¹⁸Solomon chose 70,000 strangers to carry things. Solomon chose 80,000 strangers to be cutters of stone in the mountains. And Solomon chose 3,600 strangers to be the supervisors to keep the people working.

---

600 shekels   15 pounds or 6.9kg.
150 shekels   3 3/4 pounds or 1.725kg.
temple   The special building in Jerusalem for Jewish worship.
incense   Special dried tree sap. Burned to make a sweet-smelling smoke, it was offered as a gift to God.
holy bread   This was the special bread that was put in the Holy Tent. It is also called, "shewbread" or "the bread of the Presence." See Lev. 24:5-9.
New Moon   This was the first day of the Hebrew month. There were special meetings on these days to worship God.

125,000 bushels   Or, "4,400,000 l." Literally, "20,000 cors."
115,000 gallons   Literally, "20,000 baths."
I will send ... Huram Abi   Or, "I will send one of the craftsmen of my father Hiram."
linen   A type of cloth.

Solomon Builds the Temple

3 Solomon began building the Lord's temple* at Jerusalem on Mount Moriah. Mount Moriah is the place where the Lord came to David, Solomon's father. Solomon built the temple on the place that David had made ready. This place was at the threshing floor* that had belonged to Araunah* the Jebusite. ²Solomon started the work in the second month of his fourth year as king of Israel.

³These are the measurements Solomon used for building the foundation of God's temple.* The foundation was 60 cubits* long and 20 cubits* wide. Solomon used the old cubit measure when he measured the temple. ⁴The porch in front of the temple was 20 cubits* long and 20 cubits high.* Solomon covered the inside of the porch with pure gold. ⁵Solomon put panels made of cypress wood on the walls of the larger room. Then he put pure gold over the cypress panels. And he put pictures of palm trees and chains on the pure gold. ⁶Solomon put valuable stones in the temple for beauty. The gold Solomon used was gold from Parvaim.* ⁷Solomon covered the inside of the temple with the gold. Solomon put the gold on the ceiling beams, doorposts, walls, and doors. Solomon carved cherub angels on the walls.

⁸Then Solomon made the Most Holy Place.* The Most Holy Place was 20 cubits* long and 20 cubits* wide. It was as wide as the temple* was. Solomon put pure gold on the walls of the Most Holy Place. The gold weighed about 23 tons.* ⁹The gold nails weighed 1 1/4 pounds.* Solomon covered the upper rooms with gold. ¹⁰Solomon made two cherub angels* to put in the Most Holy Place. The workers covered the cherub angels with gold. ¹¹Each wing of the cherub angels was 5 cubits* long. The total length of the wings was 20 cubits.* One wing of the first cherub angel touched the wall on one side of the room. The other wing touched one wing of the second cherub angel. ¹²And the other wing of the second cherub angel touched the other wall on the other side of the room. ¹³The cherub angels' wings covered a total of 20 cubits.* The cherub angels stood looking inside toward the Holy Place.*

¹⁴Solomon made the curtain* by using blue, purple, and red materials and expensive linen.* Solomon made cherub angels on the curtain.

¹⁵Solomon put two columns in front of the temple.* The columns were 35 cubits* tall. The top part of the two columns was 5 cubits* long. ¹⁶Solomon made chains in a necklace. He put the chains on the tops of the columns. Solomon made 100 pomegranates* and put them on the chains. ¹⁷Then Solomon put the columns up in front of the temple. One column stood on the right side. The other column stood on the left side. Solomon named the column on the right side "Jakin."* And Solomon named the column on the left side "Boaz."*

Furniture for the Temple

4 Solomon used bronze to make an altar.* That bronze altar was 20 cubits* long, 20 cubits* wide, and 10 cubits* tall. ²Then Solomon used

---

temple The special building in Jerusalem for Jewish worship.
threshing floor A place where grain is beaten or walked on to remove the hulls from the grain.
Araunah Or, "Ornan."
60 cubits 103' 4 3/16" or 31.5m.
20 cubits 34' 5 3/8" or 10.5m.
20 cubits high 34' 5 3/8" or 10.5m. Some of the Hebrew texts have "120 cubits high."
Parvaim This was a place where there was much gold. It was probably in the country of Ophir.
Most Holy Place The inside room where the Box of the Lord's Agreement sat. It is also named the "Holy of Holies." It is the spiritual place where God lives and is worshiped.
23 tons Or, "20,400kg." Literally, "600 talents (kikars)."
1 1/4 pounds Or, "575g." Literally, "50 shekels."
cherub angels Special angels from God. Statues of these angels were on top of the Box of the Agreement.
5 cubits 8' 7 5/16" or 2.625m.
Holy Place The room in the Holy Tent and in the temple that was used by the priests to do their daily service to God.
curtain This curtain was a large piece of cloth that hung between the Holy Place and the Most Holy Place so that no one could see the Lord's Box of the Agreement and cherub angels that were in there.
linen A type of cloth.
35 cubits 60' 3 7/16" or 18.375m.
pomegranates A fruit found in Israel and the area around. It looks like an apple. These were not real pomegranates, but were shaped like pomegranates.
Jakin In Hebrew, Jakin seems to mean "He establishes."
Boaz In Hebrew, Boaz seems to mean "In him is strength."
altar(s) A stone table or a stand for offering sacrifices.
10 cubits 17' 2 11/16" or 5.25m.
large tank Literally, "Sea."

melted bronze to make a large tank.* The large tank was round and it measured 10 cubits* across from edge to edge. And it measured 5 cubits* tall and 30 cubits* all around it. ³There were carvings of bulls all the way around and under the edge of the large bronze tank* for 10 cubits.* The bulls were put in two rows on the tank when the tank was shaped. ⁴The large bronze tank was on top of twelve large statues of bulls. Three bulls looked toward the north. Three bulls looked toward the west. Three bulls looked toward the south. Three bulls looked toward the east. The large bronze tank was on top of these bulls. All the bulls stood with their rear ends to each other and to the center. ⁵The large bronze tank was 3 inches* thick. The edge of the large tank was like the edge of a cup. The edge looked like a lily blossom. It could hold about 17,500 gallons.*

⁶Solomon made ten basins. He put five basins on the right side of the large bronze tank. And Solomon put five basins on the left side of the large bronze tank. These ten basins were to be used to wash the things offered for the burnt offerings.* But the large bronze tank was to be used by the priests for washing before they offered sacrifices.*

⁷Solomon made ten lampstands of gold. He followed the plans made for these lampstands. He put the lampstands in the temple.* There were five lampstands on the right side and five lampstands on the left side. ⁸Solomon made ten tables and put them in the temple.* Five tables were on the right side and five tables were put on the left side in the temple. And Solomon used gold to make 100 basins. ⁹Solomon also made the Priests' yard,* the Great yard, and the doors for the yards. He used bronze to cover the doors that opened to the yard. ¹⁰Then he put the large bronze tank* on the right side of the temple on the southeast side.

¹¹Huram made the pots, shovels, and basins. Then Huram finished his work for King Solomon on God's temple.* ¹²Huram had made the two columns and the large bowls on the top parts of the two columns. Huram also made the two net decorations to cover the two large bowls on the top parts of the two columns. ¹³Huram made 400 pomegranates* for the two net decorations. There were two rows of pomegranates for each net. The nets covered the large bowls on the top parts on the two columns. ¹⁴Huram also made the stands and the bowls on the stands. ¹⁵Huram made the one large bronze tank* and twelve bulls under the tank. ¹⁶Huram made the pots, shovels, forks, and all the things for King Solomon for the Lord's temple. These things were made of polished bronze. ¹⁷King Solomon first poured these things in clay molds. The molds were made in the Jordan Valley between the towns of Succoth and Zeredah. ¹⁸Solomon made so many of these things that no person tried to weigh the bronze used.

¹⁹Solomon also made the things for God's temple.* Solomon made the golden altar.* He made the tables where the bread of the Presence was put. ²⁰Solomon made the lampstands and their lamps of pure gold. The lamps were to burn in the way planned for them in front of the Holy Place* inside. ²¹Solomon used pure gold to make the flowers, lamps, and tongs.* ²²Solomon used pure gold to make the trimmers, bowls, pans, and the censers.* Solomon used pure gold to make the doors for the temple, the inside doors for the Most Holy Place* and the doors for the main hall.

5 Then all the work Solomon had done for the Lord's temple* was finished. Solomon brought in all the things that his father David had given for the temple. Solomon brought all the things in that were made of silver and gold and all the furniture.

---

10 cubits 17' 2 11/16" or 5.25m.
5 cubits 8' 7 5/16" or 2.625m.
30 cubits 51' 8 1/16" or 15.75m.
large bronze tank Literally, "Sea."
3 inches Or, "8cm." Literally, "1 handbreadth."
17,500 gallons Or, "66,000 l." Literally, "3,000 baths."
burnt offering(s) Gifts to God. Usually these were animals that were killed and completely burned on the altar.
sacrifice(s) A gift to God. Usually, it was a special animal that was killed and burned on an altar.
temple The special building in Jerusalem for Jewish worship.
yard A special area outside the temple.
pomegranates They were a fruit found in Israel and the area around. It looks like an apple. These were not real pomegranates but were shaped like pomegranates.
altar(s) A stone table or a stand for offering sacrifices.
Holy Place The room in the Holy Tent and in the temple that was used by the priests to do their daily service to God.
tongs Something looking like scissors, used to hold hot coals.
censers Bowls used to carry fire.
Most Holy Place The inside room where the Box of the Lord's Agreement sat. It is also named the "Holy of Holies." It is the spiritual place where God lives and is worshiped.

Solomon put all those things in the treasury rooms of God's temple.

The Holy Box Carried Into the Temple

²Solomon gathered the elders of Israel, all the leaders of the family groups, and family leaders in Israel. He gathered them all in Jerusalem. Solomon did this so they could bring the Box of the Lord's Agreement* up from David's city. David's city is Zion. ³All men of Israel met together with King Solomon at the feast. This feast was held in the seventh month. ⁴When all the elders of Israel arrived, the Levites picked up the Box of the Agreement.* ⁵Then the priests and the Levites carried the Box of the Agreement to Jerusalem. The priests and Levites also brought the Meeting Tent* and all the holy things that were in it to Jerusalem. ⁶King Solomon and all the people of Israel met in front of the Box of the Agreement. King Solomon and all the people of Israel sacrificed* sheep and bulls. There were so many sheep and bulls no person could count them. ⁷Then the priests brought the Box of the Lord's Agreement to the place that was made ready for it. That place was the Most Holy Place* inside the temple.* The Box of the Agreement was put under the wings of the cherub angels.* ⁸The cherub angels spread their wings over the place where the Box of the Agreement was. The cherub angels stood over the Box of the Agreement and the poles used to carry the Box. ⁹The poles were long enough that their ends could be seen from the front of the Most Holy Place. But no person could see the poles from the outside of the temple. The poles are still there even today. ¹⁰There was nothing in the Box of the Agreement except the two tablets.* Moses had put those two tablets in the Box of the Agreement at Mount Horeb. Horeb was the place where the Lord made an Agreement with the people of Israel. That happened after the people of Israel came out of Egypt.

¹¹Then all the priests who went into the Holy Place* came out. They had made themselves holy. It was not important at that time which group of priests they were from. They all made themselves holy after coming out of the Holy Place. ¹²And all the Levite singers stood at the east side of the altar.* All of Asaph's, Heman's, and Jeduthun's singing groups were there. And their sons and relatives were there also. Those Levite singers were dressed in white linen.* They had cymbals,* lyres,* and harps. There were 120 priests there with those Levite singers. Those 120 priests blew trumpets. ¹³The people who blew the trumpets and the people who sang were like one person. They made one sound when they praised and thanked the Lord. They made a loud noise with the trumpets, cymbals,* and instruments of music. They sang the song* *Praise the Lord Because He is Good. His True Love Continues Forever.*

Then the Lord's temple* was filled with a cloud. ¹⁴The priests could not continue to serve because of the cloud. This was because the Glory of the Lord* filled God's temple.

6 Then Solomon said, "The Lord said he would live in the dark cloud. ²I have built a house for you to live in, Lord. It is a high house, a place for you to live in forever!"

Box of the Agreement The box containing the stone tablets with the Ten Commandments written on them and the other things that proved God was with the people of Israel during their time in the Sinai Desert. Also called "The Ark of the Covenant."

Meeting Tent The Holy Tent (Tabernacle) where the people of Israel went to meet with God.

sacrifice(d) To kill a special animal and burn it on an altar as a gift to God.

Most Holy Place The inside room where the Box of the Lord's Agreement sat. It is also named the "Holy of Holies." It is the spiritual place where God lives and is worshiped.

temple The special building in Jerusalem for Jewish worship.

cherub angels Special angels from God. Statues of these angels were on top of the Box of the Agreement.

two tablets They were the two tablets on which God wrote the Ten Commandments.

Holy Place The room in the Holy Tent and in the temple that was used by the priests to do their daily service to God.

altar(s) A stone table or a stand for offering sacrifices.

linen A type of cloth.

cymbals A pair of metal platters that are hit against each other to make a loud sound.

lyre(s) An instrument with several strings, like a harp.

They sang ... song Or, "They sang the Hallel and ..." This would be Psalms 111- 118 and Psalm 136.

Glory of the Lord One of the forms God used when he appeared to people. It was like a bright shining light.

Solomon's Speech

³King Solomon turned around and blessed all the people of Israel gathered in front of him. ⁴Solomon said, "Give praise to the Lord God of Israel! The Lord has done what he promised to do when he talked to David my father. This is what the Lord God said: ⁵'Since the time I brought my people out from the country of Egypt, I have not chosen a city from any family group of Israel for a place to build a house for my name. I have not chosen a man to lead my people, the people of Israel. ⁶But now I have chosen Jerusalem as a place for my name. And I have chosen David to lead my people Israel.'

⁷"My father David wanted to build a temple* for the name of the Lord God of Israel. ⁸But the Lord said to my father, 'David, when you wanted to build a temple for my name, you did well. ⁹But, you cannot build the temple. But your own son will build the temple for my name.' ¹⁰Now, the Lord has done what he said he would do. I am the new king in my father's place. David was my father. Now I am Israel's king. That is what the Lord promised. And I have built the temple for the name of the Lord God of Israel. ¹¹I have put the Box of the Agreement* in the temple. The Box of the Agreement is where the Lord's Agreement is kept. The Lord made this Agreement with the people of Israel."

Solomon's Prayer

¹²Solomon stood in front of the Lord's altar.* He was standing in front of all the people of Israel who were gathered together. Then Solomon spread his hands and arms out. ¹³Solomon had made a bronze platform* 5 cubits* long, 5 cubits* wide and 3 cubits* and placed it in the middle of the outside yard.* Then he stood on the platform and kneeled in front of all the people of Israel who were gathered together. Solomon spread his hands out toward the sky. ¹⁴Solomon said:

"Lord God of Israel, there is no god like you in heaven or on earth. You keep your agreement of love and kindness. You keep your agreement with your servants if they live right with all their hearts and obey you. ¹⁵You kept your promise to your servant David. David was my father. You made a promise with your mouth. And today you have made that promise come true with your hands. ¹⁶Now, Lord God of Israel, keep your promise to your servant David. This is what you promised: You said, 'David, you will not fail to have a man from your family sit on Israel's throne in front of me. This will happen only if your sons are careful in what they do. They must obey my law the same as you have obeyed my law.' ¹⁷Now, Lord God of Israel, let your promise come true. You gave this promise to your servant David.

¹⁸"But we know that you, God, will not really live on the earth with people. Heaven and the highest of heavens cannot hold you! And we know that this temple* I built cannot hold you! ¹⁹But pay attention to my prayer and the times I beg for mercy. Lord my God, listen to me calling out to you! Listen to the prayer that I am praying to you. I am your servant. ²⁰I pray that your eyes will be open to look at this temple day and night. You said you would put your name in this place. May you hear my prayers when I pray while I look at this temple. ²¹Hear my prayers, and the prayers your people Israel pray. Hear our prayers while we pray looking at this temple. Hear from where you live in heaven. And when you hear our prayers, forgive us.

²²"A person might be accused of doing something wrong against another person. When that happens, the accused person will have to use your name to promise ₁that he is innocent₁. When he comes to make the promise in front of your altar* in the temple, ²³then hear from heaven. Act, and judge your servants. Punish the bad person and make him suffer the same things he made other people suffer. Prove that the person that has done right is innocent.

²⁴"An enemy might defeat your people Israel because your people have sinned against you. And then if the people of Israel come back to you and confess your name and pray and beg to you in this temple,* ²⁵then hear from heaven and forgive the

---

temple The special building in Jerusalem for Jewish worship.
Box of the Agreement The box containing the stone tablets with the Ten Commandments written on them and the other things that proved God was with the people of Israel during their time in the Sinai Desert. Also called "The Ark of the Covenant."
altar(s) A stone table or a stand for offering sacrifices.
platform Something like a table where a person stood so all the people could see the person speaking.
5 cubits 8' 7 5/16" or 2.625m.
3 cubits 5' 2" or 1.575m.
yard A special area outside the temple.

ancestors Literally, "fathers," meaning a person's parents, grandparents, and all the people they are descended from.

sin of your people Israel. Bring them back into the land you gave to them and to their ancestors.*

²⁶"The sky might close up so that there is no rain. This will happen if the people of Israel sin against you. And if the people of Israel are sorry and pray as they look at this temple,* and confess your name, and stop doing their sin because you are punishing them, ²⁷then hear from heaven. Hear and forgive their sins. The people of Israel are your servants. Then teach them the right way that they should live. And send rain on your land. That is the land you gave to your people.

²⁸"There might be a famine* in the land, or terrible sicknesses, or disease in the crops, or mildew, or locusts, or grasshoppers. Or if enemies attack the people of Israel in their cities, or if there is any kind of sickness in Israel, ²⁹and then a prayer or begging is made by any of your people of Israel—each person knowing his own trouble and pain—and if that person spreads his hands and arms out while looking at this temple,* ³⁰then hear from heaven. Heaven is where you live. Hear and forgive. Give to each person what he should get, because you know what is in each person's heart. Only you know what is in a person's heart. ³¹Then the people will fear and obey you as long as they live in the land you gave our ancestors.*

³²"There might be a stranger who is not one of your people of Israel, but who comes here from a country far away. And that stranger comes because of your great name and because of your strong hand and your arm reaching out. When this person comes and prays while looking at this temple,* ³³then hear from heaven. Heaven is where you live. And do what the stranger asks you to do. Then all the peoples of the earth will know your name and respect you, the same as your people Israel respects you. And all the people of the earth will know that this temple I built is called by your name.

³⁴"You will send your people to some place to fight against their enemies. They will pray to you as they look toward this city you chose and toward the temple* I built for your name. ³⁵Please hear their prayer in heaven. Hear them when they beg for help. And help them.

³⁶"People will sin against you—there is not a person that does not sin—and you will become angry with them. You will let an enemy defeat them, and be captured and forced to go to a land far away or near. ³⁷But then they will change their minds and beg you while they are in the land where they are prisoners. They will say, 'We have sinned, we have done wrong and we have acted wickedly.' ³⁸And then they will come back to you with all their heart and all their soul in the land where they are prisoners. And they will pray as they look toward their land, the land you gave their ancestors,* and toward the city that you chose. And they will pray as they look toward the temple* I built for your name. ³⁹When this happens, hear in heaven. Heaven is your home. Accept their prayers when they beg for help. And help them. Forgive your people who have sinned against you. ⁴⁰Now, my God, I ask you, open your eyes and your ears. Listen and pay attention to the prayers we are praying in this place.

⁴¹ "Now, Lord God, get up,
and come to your special place,
the Box of the Agreement*
that shows your strength.
May your priests be dressed with salvation.
May your true followers be happy
about these good things.
⁴² Lord God, accept your anointed* king.
Remember your loyal servant David!"

The Temple Dedicated to the Lord

7 When Solomon finished praying, fire came down from the sky and burned up the burnt

---

temple The special building in Jerusalem for Jewish worship.
famine A time when there is not enough rain for crops to grow. People and animals die without enough food or water.
ancestors Literally, "fathers," meaning a person's parents, grandparents, and all the people they are descended from.

Box of the Agreement The box containing the stone tablets with the Ten Commandments written on them and the other things that proved God was with the people of Israel during their time in the Sinai Desert. Also called "The Ark of the Covenant."
anoint(ed) To pour olive oil on things or people to show that they were chosen by God for a special work or purpose.
burnt offering(s) Gifts to God. Usually these were animals that were killed and completely burned on the altar.
sacrifice(s) A gift to God. Usually, it was a special animal that was killed and burned on an altar.
Glory of the Lord One of the forms God used when he appeared to people. It was like a bright shining light.

2 CHRONICLES 7:2–22

offering* and the sacrifices.* The Glory of the Lord* filled the temple.* ²The priests could not enter the Lord's temple because the Glory of the Lord filled it. ³All the people of Israel saw the fire come down from heaven. The people of Israel also saw the Glory of the Lord on the temple. They bowed their faces down low to the ground on the pavement. They worshiped and thanked the Lord. And they were saying,

> "The Lord is good,
> And his kindness continues forever."

⁴Then King Solomon and all the people of Israel offered sacrifices* in front of the Lord. ⁵King Solomon offered 22,000 bulls and 120,000 sheep. The king and all the people made the temple* of God holy. It was to be used only for worshiping God. ⁶The priests stood ready to do their work. The Levites also stood with the instruments of the Lord's music. These instruments were made by King David to give thanks to the Lord. The priests and Levites were saying, "The Lord's love continues forever!" The priests blew their trumpets as they stood across from the Levites. And all the people of Israel were standing.

⁷Solomon made the middle part of the yard holy. That yard is in front of the Lord's temple.* That is the place where Solomon offered burnt offerings* and the fat of the fellowship offerings. Solomon used the middle of the yard because the bronze altar* he made could not hold all the burnt offerings, grain offerings, and fat. There were many of those offerings.

⁸Solomon and all the people of Israel celebrated the feast for seven days. There was a very large group of people with Solomon. Those people came from the entrance of the town of Hamath and all the way to the Brook of Egypt. ⁹On the eighth day they had a holy meeting because they had celebrated for seven days. They made the altar* holy and it was to be used only for worshiping the Lord. And they celebrated the feast for seven days. ¹⁰On the 23rd day of the seventh month Solomon sent the people back to their homes. The people were very happy and their hearts were full of joy, because the Lord was so good to David, to Solomon, and to his people Israel.

The Lord Comes to Solomon

¹¹Solomon finished the Lord's temple* and the king's house. Solomon had success in finishing all the things he planned in the Lord's temple and in his own house. ¹²Then the Lord came to Solomon at night. The Lord said to him, "Solomon, I have heard your prayer, and I have chosen this place for myself to be a house for sacrifices.* ¹³When I close the sky so there is no rain, or I command the locusts to destroy the land, or I send sicknesses to my people, ¹⁴and if my people who are called by my name become humble and pray, and look for me, and turn away from their evil ways, then I will hear them from heaven. And I will forgive their sin and I will heal their land. ¹⁵Now, my eyes are open, and my ears will pay attention to the prayers prayed in this place. ¹⁶I have chosen this temple, and I have made it holy so that my name will be here forever. Yes, my eyes and heart will always be here in this temple.

¹⁷"Now you, Solomon, if you live in front of me the same way your father David lived, and if you obey all I have commanded, and if you obey my laws and rules, ¹⁸then I will make you a strong king and your kingdom will be great. That is the agreement I made with David your father. I told him, 'David, you will always have a man in your family that will be a king in Israel.'

¹⁹"But if you do not obey my laws and commands that I gave you, and if you worship other gods and serve them, ²⁰then I will take the people of Israel out from my land that I gave them. And I will leave this temple* that I have made holy for my name. I will make this temple something that all the nations will speak evil about. ²¹Every person who passes by this temple that was so highly honored will be surprised. They will say, 'Why has the Lord done this terrible thing to the land and to this temple?' ²²Then people will answer, 'Because the people of Israel refused to obey the Lord, the God their ancestors* obeyed. He is the God that led them out of the

---

sacrifice(s) A gift to God. Usually, it was a special animal that was killed and burned on an altar.
temple The special building in Jerusalem for Jewish worship.
burnt offering(s) Gifts to God. Usually these were animals that were killed and completely burned on the altar.
altar A stone table or a stand for offering sacrifices.

ancestors Literally, "fathers," meaning a person's parents, grandparents, and all the people they are descended from.

country of Egypt. But the people of Israel accepted other gods. They worshiped and served idol gods. That is the reason the Lord made all these terrible things happen to the people of Israel."

The Cities Solomon Built

8 The time it took Solomon to build the Lord's temple* and his own house was 20 years. ²Then Solomon built again the towns that Hiram gave him. And Solomon allowed some of the people of Israel to live in those towns. ³After this Solomon went to Hamath of Zobah and captured it. ⁴Solomon also built the town of Tadmor in the desert. He built all the towns in Hamath to store things in. ⁵Solomon built again the towns of Upper Beth Horon and Lower Beth Horon. He made those towns into strong forts. Those towns had strong walls, gates, and bars in the gates. ⁶Solomon also built again the town of Baalath and all the other towns where he stored things. He built all the cities where the chariots* were kept and all the cities where the horse riders lived. Solomon built all he wanted in Jerusalem, Lebanon, and in all the country where he was king.

⁷⁻⁸There were many strangers left in the country where the people of Israel were living. There were the Hittites, the Amorites, the Perizzites, the Hivites, and the Jebusites. Solomon forced all those foreigners to be slave workers. Those people were not from the people of Israel. Those people were the descendants* of the people that were left in the land and not yet destroyed by the people of Israel. This still continues today. ⁹Solomon did not force any of the people of Israel to be slave workers. The people of Israel were Solomon's fighting men. They were the commanders of Solomon's army officers. They were commanders of Solomon's chariots* and commanders of Solomon's chariot drivers. ¹⁰And some of the men of Israel were leaders of Solomon's important officials. There were 250 of those leaders to supervise the people.

¹¹Solomon brought Pharaoh's daughter up from the City of David to the house he built for her. Solomon said, "My wife must not live in King David's house because the places where the Box of the Agreement* has been are holy places."

¹²Then Solomon offered burnt offerings* to the Lord on the Lord's altar.* Solomon built that altar in front of the temple* porch. ¹³Solomon offered sacrifices* every day the way Moses commanded. Sacrifices were to be offered on Sabbath days,* on the New Moon* celebrations, and on the three yearly holidays. The three yearly holidays were the Festival of Unleavened Bread, the Festival of Weeks, and the Festival of Shelters. ¹⁴Solomon followed his father David's instructions. Solomon chose the groups of priests for their service. Solomon also chose the Levites for their duties. The Levites were to lead the praise and help the priests from day to day to do the things that needed to be done in the temple service. And Solomon chose the gatekeepers by their groups to serve at each gate. This is the way David, the man of God, instructed. ¹⁵The people of Israel did not change or disobey any of Solomon's instructions to the priests and Levites. They did not change any of the instructions, even in the way they should keep the valuable things.

¹⁶All Solomon's work was done. It was well planned from the day the Lord's temple* was begun until the day it was finished. So the Lord's temple was finished.

¹⁷Then Solomon went to the towns of Ezion Geber and Elath. Those towns were near the Red Sea in the country of Edom. ¹⁸Hiram sent ships to Solomon. Hiram's own men sailed the ships. Hiram's men were skilled at sailing on the sea. Hiram's men went with Solomon's servants to

burnt offering(s) Gifts to God. Usually these were animals that were killed and completely burned on the altar.
altar(s) A stone table or a stand for offering sacrifices.
sacrifice(s) A gift to God. Usually, it was a special animal that was killed and burned on an altar.
Sabbath day(s) Saturday. A special day of rest and worship for the Jews.
New Moon This was the first day of the Hebrew month. There were special meetings on these days to worship God.
Ophir A place where there was much gold. Today no person knows where Ophir really was.
17 tons of gold Or "15,300kg." Literally, "450 talents (kikars)." In today's money that would be more than $13,000,000.

temple The special building in Jerusalem for Jewish worship.
chariot(s) A small wagon used in war.
descendants A person's children and their future families.
Box of the Agreement The box containing the stone tablets with the Ten Commandments written on them and the other things that proved God was with the people of Israel during their time in the Sinai Desert. Also called "The Ark of the Covenant."

Ophir* and brought back 17 tons of gold* to King Solomon.

The Queen of Sheba Visits Solomon

9 The Queen of Sheba heard about Solomon's fame. She came to Jerusalem to test Solomon with hard questions. The Queen of Sheba had a very large group with her. She had camels that carried spices, much gold, and valuable stones. She came to Solomon and talked with him. She had many questions to ask Solomon. ²Solomon gave answers to all her questions. There was nothing too hard for Solomon to explain or answer. ³The Queen of Sheba saw Solomon's wisdom, and the house he built. ⁴She saw the food on Solomon's table, and his many important officials. She saw the way his servants worked and the clothes they wore. She saw Solomon's wine servers and the clothes they wore. She saw the burnt offerings* Solomon made in the temple* of the Lord. When the Queen of Sheba saw all these things she was amazed! ⁵Then she said to King Solomon, "The stories I heard in my country about your great works and your wisdom are true. ⁶I didn't believe those stories until I came here and saw with my own eyes. Oh, not even half of your great wisdom has been told me! You are greater than the stories I heard! ⁷Your wives* and officers are very fortunate! They can hear your wisdom while they are serving you! ⁸Praise be to the Lord your God! He is happy with you and has put you on his throne to be king for the Lord your God. Your God loves Israel, and supports Israel forever. This is why the Lord has made you king of Israel to do what is fair and what is right."

⁹Then the Queen of Sheba gave King Solomon 4 1/2 tons* of gold, a great many spices, and valuable stones. No person gave such fine spices to King Solomon as the Queen of Sheba did.

¹⁰Hiram's servants and Solomon's servants brought in gold from Ophir.* They also brought in algum wood and valuable stones. ¹¹King Solomon used the algum wood to make steps for the Lord's temple,* and for the king's house. Solomon also used the algum wood to make lyres* and harps for the singers. No person ever saw such beautiful things like those things made from the algum wood in the country of Judah.

¹²King Solomon gave to the Queen of Sheba everything she wanted and asked for. He gave her more than she brought to give him. Then the Queen of Sheba and her servants left. They went back to their own country.

Solomon's Great Wealth

¹³The amount of gold that Solomon got in one year weighed 25 tons.* ¹⁴The traveling merchants* and traders brought more gold to Solomon. All the kings of Arabia and the rulers of the land also brought gold and silver to Solomon. ¹⁵King Solomon made 200 large shields from hammered gold. About 7 1/2 pounds* of hammered gold was used to make each shield. ¹⁶Solomon also made 300 small shields of hammered gold. About 3 3/4 pounds* of gold was used to make each shield. King Solomon put the gold shields in the Forest Palace of Lebanon.

¹⁷King Solomon used ivory to make a large throne. He covered the throne with pure gold. ¹⁸The throne had six steps on it. And it had a footstool* that was made of gold. There were armrests on both sides of the throne's seat. A statue of a lion stood next to each armrest. ¹⁹There were statues of 12 lions that stood by the six steps. One lion on each side of each step. There was no throne like this made in any other kingdom. ²⁰All King Solomon's drinking cups were made of gold. All the household things in the House of the Forest of Lebanon were made of pure gold. Silver was not thought valuable in the time of Solomon. ²¹King Solomon had ships that went to Tarshish.* Hiram's men sailed Solomon's ships. Every three years the ships came back from Tarshish bringing gold, silver, ivory, apes, and peacocks to Solomon.

²²King Solomon became greater in riches and wisdom than any other king on earth. ²³All the

---

burnt offering(s) Gifts to God. Usually these were animals that were killed and completely burned on the altar.
temple The special building in Jerusalem for Jewish worship.
wives Or, "men." See 1 Kings 10:3.
4 1/2 tons Or, "4,080kg." Literally, "120 talents (kikars)."
Ophir A place where there was much gold. Today no person knows where Ophir really was.
lyre(s) An instrument with several strings, like a harp.

25 tons Or, "22,644kg." Literally, "666 talents (kikars)."
traveling merchants A person who earns his living by buying and selling things.
7 1/2 pounds Or, "3.3kg." Literally, "600 bekas."
3 3/4 pounds Or, "1.65kg." Literally, "300 bekas."
footstool A little stool that a king could use to rest his feet when sitting on his throne.
Tarshish A city far away from Israel, probably in Spain. Tarshish was famous for its large ships that sailed the Mediterranean Sea.

kings of the earth came to visit Solomon to hear wise decisions. God gave that wisdom to Solomon. ²⁴Every year those kings brought gifts to Solomon. They brought silver and gold things, clothes, armor, spices, horses, and mules. ²⁵Solomon had 4,000 stalls to keep horses and chariots. He had 12,000 chariot drivers. Solomon kept them in the special cities for the chariots and in Jerusalem with him. ²⁶Solomon was the king over all the kings from the Euphrates River all the way to the land of the Philistine people, and to the border of Egypt. ²⁷King Solomon had so much silver that it was as common as rocks in Jerusalem. And he had so much cedar wood that it was as common as sycamore trees in the hill country. ²⁸The people brought horses to Solomon from Egypt and from all the other countries.

Solomon's Death

²⁹The other things Solomon did, from the beginning to the end, are written in the writings of Nathan the Prophet, in The Prophecy of Ahijah from Shiloh and in The Visions of Iddo the Seer. Iddo was a seer.* who wrote about Jeroboam son of Nebat. ³⁰Solomon was king in Jerusalem over all Israel for 40 years. ³¹Then Solomon rested with his ancestors.* The people buried him in the City of David his father. Solomon's son Rehoboam became the new king in Solomon's place.

Rehoboam Acts Foolishly

10 Rehoboam went to the town of Shechem because all the people of Israel went there to make him king. ²Jeroboam was in Egypt because he ran away from King Solomon. Jeroboam was Nebat's son. Jeroboam heard that Rehoboam was going to be the new king. So Jeroboam came back from Egypt. ³The people of Israel called Jeroboam to come with them. Then Jeroboam and all the people of Israel went to Rehoboam. They said to him, "Rehoboam, ⁴your father made life hard for us. It was like carrying a heavy weight. Make that weight lighter, then we will serve you."

⁵Rehoboam said to them, "Come back to me after three days." So the people went away.

⁶Then King Rehoboam talked with the older men who had served his father Solomon in the past. Rehoboam said to them, "What do you advise me to say to those people?"

⁷The older men said to Rehoboam, "If you are kind to those people and please them and say good words to them, then they will serve you forever."

⁸But Rehoboam did not accept the advice the older men gave him. Rehoboam talked with the young men that had grown up with him and were serving him. ⁹Rehoboam said to them, "What advice do you give me? How should we answer those people? They asked me to make their work easier. And they want me to make the weight lighter that my father put on them."

¹⁰Then the young men that grew up with Rehoboam said to him, "This is what you should say to the people who talked with you. The people said to you, 'Your father made life hard for us. It was like carrying a heavy weight. But we want you to make that weight lighter.' But Rehoboam, this is what you should say to those people: Say to them, 'My little finger will be thicker than my father's waist! ¹¹My father loaded you with a heavy burden. But I will make that burden heavier. My father punished you with whips. But I will punish you with whips that have sharp metal tips.'"

¹²Three days later, Jeroboam and all the people came to Rehoboam. That is what King Rehoboam told them to do when he said, "Come back to me in three days." ¹³Then King Rehoboam talked to them in a mean way. King Rehoboam did not accept the advice of the older men. ¹⁴King Rehoboam talked to the people the way the young men advised him. He said, "My father made your burden heavy, but I will make it heavier. My father punished you with whips, but I will punish you with whips that have sharp metal tips." ¹⁵So King Rehoboam did not listen to the people. He did not listen to the people because this change of things came from God. God caused this to happen. This happened so that the Lord could make his word come true that he spoke through Ahijah to Jeroboam. Ahijah was from the Shilonite people, and Jeroboam was Nebat's son.

¹⁶The people of Israel saw that King Rehoboam did not listen to them. Then they said to the king, "Are we part of David's family? No! Do we get any of Jesse's land? No! So Israel, let's go to our own homes. Let David's son rule his own people!" Then all the people of Israel went to their homes. ¹⁷But there were some of the people of Israel who were living in the towns of Judah. And Rehoboam was king over those people.

---

seer This is another name for a prophet. See 1 Sam. 9:9-11.
ancestors Literally, "fathers," meaning a person's parents, grandparents, and all the people they are descended from.

18 Adoniram was in charge of the people who were forced to work. Rehoboam sent him to the people of Israel. But the people of Israel threw rocks at Adoniram and killed him. Then Rehoboam ran and jumped into his chariot* and escaped. He ran away to Jerusalem. 19 Since that time and up until now Israel has turned against David's family.*

11 When Rehoboam came to Jerusalem, he gathered 180,000 of the best soldiers. He gathered these soldiers from the family groups of Judah and Benjamin. He gathered them to fight against Israel so he could bring the kingdom back to Rehoboam. 2 But the message from the Lord came to Shemaiah. Shemaiah was a man of God. The Lord said, 3 "Shemaiah, talk to Rehoboam, Solomon's son, and the king of Judah. And talk to all the people of Israel living in Judah and Benjamin. Tell them: 4 This is what the Lord says: 'You must not fight against your brothers! Let every man go back home. I have caused this thing to happen.' So King Rehoboam and his army obeyed the Lord's message and turned back. They did not attack Jeroboam.

Rehoboam Makes Judah Strong

5 Rehoboam lived in Jerusalem. He built strong cities in Judah to defend against attacks. 6 He repaired the cities of Bethlehem, Etam, Tekoa, 7 Beth Zur, Soco, Adullam, 8 Gath, Mareshah, Ziph, 9 Adoraim, Lachish, Azekah, 10 Zorah, Aijalon, and Hebron. These cities in Judah and Benjamin were made strong. 11 When Rehoboam made those cities strong, he put commanders in them. He also put supplies of food, oil, and wine in those cities. 12 Also, Rehoboam put shields and spears in every city and made the cities very strong. Rehoboam kept the peoples and cities of Judah and Benjamin under his control.

13 The priests and the Levites from all over Israel agreed with Rehoboam and joined him. 14 The Levites left their grasslands and their own fields and came to Judah and Jerusalem. The Levites did this because Jeroboam and his sons refused to let them serve as priests to the Lord. 15 Jeroboam chose his own priests to serve in the high places,* where he set up the goat and calf idols he had made. 16 When the Levites left Israel, those people in all the family groups of Israel who were faithful to the Lord God of Israel came to Jerusalem to sacrifice to the Lord God of their fathers. 17 Those people made the kingdom of Judah strong. And they supported Solomon's son Rehoboam for three years. They did this because during that time they lived the way David and Solomon had lived.

Rehoboam's Family

18 Rehoboam married Mahalath. Her father was Jerimoth. Her mother was Abihail. Jerimoth was David's son. Abihail was Eliab's daughter, and Eliab was Jesse's son. 19 Mahalath gave Rehoboam these sons: Jeush, Shemariah and Zaham. 20 Then Rehoboam married Maacah. Maacah was Absalom's granddaughter.* And Maacah gave Rehoboam these children: Abijah, Attai, Ziza, and Shelomith. 21 Rehoboam loved Maacah more that he loved all his other wives and women servants.* Maacah was Absalom's granddaughter. Rehoboam had 18 wives and 60 woman servants. Rehoboam was the father of 28 sons and 60 daughters.

22 Rehoboam chose Abijah to be the leader among his own brothers. Rehoboam did this because he planned to make Abijah king. 23 Rehoboam acted wisely and spread all his sons through all the areas of Judah and Benjamin to every strong city. And Rehoboam gave plenty of supplies to his sons. He also looked for wives for his sons.

Shishak King of Egypt Attacks Jerusalem

12 Rehoboam became a strong king. He also made his kingdom strong. Then Rehoboam and the family group of Judah* refused to obey the law of the Lord. 2 Shishak attacked the city of Jerusalem in the fifth year that Rehoboam was king. Shishak was the king of Egypt. This happened because Rehoboam and the people of Judah were not faithful to the Lord. 3 Shishak had 12,000 chariots, 60,000 horse riders, and an army that no person could count. In Shishak's large army there were Libyan soldiers, Sukkite soldiers, and Ethiopian soldiers. 4 Shishak defeated the

---

chariot(s) A small wagon used in war.
David's family This probably means the family group of Judah. David's family was in the family group of Judah.
high places Places of worship.
granddaughter Literally, "daughter."
women servants Or, "concubines," slave women who were like wives to a man.
Judah Literally, Israel.

strong cities of Judah. Then Shishak brought his army to Jerusalem.

⁵Then Shemaiah the prophet came to Rehoboam and the leaders of Judah. Those leaders of Judah had gathered together in Jerusalem because they all were afraid of Shishak. Shemaiah said to Rehoboam and the leaders of Judah, "This is what the Lord says: 'Rehoboam, you and the people of Judah have left me and refused to obey my law. So now I will leave you to face Shishak without my help.'"

⁶Then the leaders of Judah and King Rehoboam were sorry and humbled themselves. They said, "The Lord is right."

⁷The Lord saw that the king and the leaders of Judah had humbled themselves. Then the message from the Lord came to Shemaiah. The Lord said to Shemaiah, "The king and the leaders humbled themselves. So I will not destroy them, but I will save them soon. I will not use Shishak to pour out my anger on Jerusalem. ⁸But the people of Jerusalem will become Shishak's servants. This will happen so that they may learn that serving me is different from serving the kings of other nations."

⁹Shishak attacked Jerusalem and took the treasures that were in the Lord's temple.* Shishak was the king of Egypt. And he also took the treasures that were in the king's house. Shishak took everything and carried those treasures away. He also took the gold shields that Solomon had made. ¹⁰King Rehoboam made bronze shields to take the place of the gold shields. Rehoboam gave the bronze shields to the commanders who were responsible for guarding the entrance to the king's house. ¹¹When the king entered the Lord's temple, the guards would bring the bronze shields out. Later they would put the bronze shields back into the guard room.

¹²When Rehoboam humbled himself, the Lord turned his anger away from Rehoboam. So the Lord did not fully destroy Rehoboam. There was some good in Judah.

¹³King Rehoboam made himself a strong king in Jerusalem. He was 41 years old when he became king. Rehoboam was king in Jerusalem for 17 years. Jerusalem is the city that the Lord chose from all the family groups of Israel. The Lord chose to put his name there in Jerusalem. Rehoboam's mother was Naamah. Naamah was from the country of Ammon. ¹⁴Rehoboam did evil things because he didn't decide in his heart to obey the Lord.

¹⁵The things Rehoboam did when he was king, from the beginning to the end of his rule, are written in the writings of Shemaiah the prophet and in the writings of Iddo the seer.* Those men wrote family histories. And there were wars between Rehoboam and Jeroboam all the time both kings ruled. ¹⁶Rehoboam rested with his ancestors.* Rehoboam was buried in David's city. Then Rehoboam's son Abijah became the new king.

Abijah King of Judah

13 When King Jeroboam was in his 18th year as king of Israel,* Abijah became the new king of Judah. ²Abijah was king in Jerusalem for three years. Abijah's mother was Maacah. Maacah was Uriel's daughter. Uriel was from the town of Gibeah. And there was war between Abijah and Jeroboam. ³Abijah's army had 400,000 brave soldiers. Abijah led that army into battle. Jeroboam's army had 800,000 brave soldiers. Jeroboam got ready to have a war with Abijah.

⁴Then Abijah stood on Mount Zemaraim in the hill country of Ephraim. Abijah said, "Jeroboam and all Israel, listen to me! ⁵You should know that the Lord God of Israel gave David and his sons the right to be king over Israel forever. God gave this right to David with an agreement of salt.* ⁶But Jeroboam turned against his Master! Jeroboam son of Nebat was one of the servants of David's son Solomon. ⁷Then worthless, evil men became friends with Jeroboam. Then Jeroboam and those bad men turned against Rehoboam, Solomon's son. Rehoboam was young and did not

---

seer This is another name for a prophet. See 1 Sam. 9:9-11.
ancestors Literally, "fathers," meaning a person's parents, grandparents, and all the people they are descended from.
King Jeroboam ... Israel This was about the year 923 B.C. King Jeroboam was the man who turned against King Rehoboam and began his own kingdom with ten of the family groups of Israel. See 1 Kings 12:20.
agreement of salt When people ate salt together, it meant that their agreement of friendship would never be broken. Abijah was saying here that God had made an agreement with David that would never be broken.

temple The special building in Jerusalem for Jewish worship.

have experience. So Rehoboam could not stop Jeroboam and his bad friends.

⁸"Now, you people have decided to defeat the Lord's kingdom—the kingdom that is ruled by David's sons. You have very many people with you and you have those golden calves—those 'gods' that Jeroboam made for you! ⁹You threw out the Lord's priests, the descendants of Aaron. And you threw out the Levites. Then you chose your own priests, just like every other nation on earth. And now, any person that will bring a young bull and seven rams can become a priest! A priest to serve those 'No-gods'.

¹⁰"But as for us, the Lord is our God. We people of Judah have not refused to obey God! We have not left him! The priests who serve the Lord are Aaron's sons. And the Levites help the priests serve the Lord. ¹¹They offer burnt offerings* and burn incense* of spices to the Lord every morning and every evening. They put the bread in rows on the special table in the temple.* And they take care of the lamps on the golden lampstand so it shines bright each and every evening. We very carefully serve the Lord our God. But you people have abandoned him! ¹²God himself is with us. He is our ruler, and his priests are with us. God's priests blow his trumpets to wake you up and make you excited about coming to him! Men of Israel, don't fight against the Lord God of your ancestors!* You will not succeed!"

¹³But Jeroboam sent a group of soldiers to sneak behind Abijah's army. Jeroboam's army was in front of Abijah's army. The hidden soldiers from Jeroboam's army were behind Abijah's army. ¹⁴When the soldiers in Abijah's army from Judah looked around, they saw Jeroboam's army attacking both in front and in back.* The men of Judah shouted out to the Lord and the priests blew the trumpets. ¹⁵Then the men in Abijah's army shouted. When the men of Judah shouted, God defeated Jeroboam's army. All of Jeroboam's army from Israel were defeated by Abijah's army from Judah. ¹⁶The men of Israel ran away from the men of Judah. God let the army from Judah defeat the army from Israel. ¹⁷Abijah's army greatly defeated the army of Israel, and 500,000 of the best men of Israel were killed. ¹⁸So at that time the people of Israel were defeated, and the people of Judah won. The army from Judah won because they depended on the Lord the God of their ancestors.*

¹⁹Abijah's army chased Jeroboam's army. Abijah's army captured the towns of Bethel, Jeshanah, and Ephron from Jeroboam. They captured those towns and the small villages near those towns.

²⁰Jeroboam never became strong again while Abijah lived. The Lord killed Jeroboam. ²¹But Abijah became strong. He married 14 women and was the father of 22 sons and 16 daughters. ²²All the other things that Abijah did are written in the books of the prophet Iddo.

14 Abijah rested with his ancestors.* The people buried him in David's City. Then Abijah's son, Asa, was the new king in Abijah's place. There was peace in the country for ten years in Asa's time.

Asa King of Judah

²Asa did good and right things before the Lord his God. ³Asa took away the strange altars that were used to worship idols. Asa took away the high places,* and smashed the holy stones.* And Asa broke down the Asherah poles.* ⁴Asa commanded the people of Judah to follow the Lord God. He is the God their ancestors* followed. And Asa commanded them to obey the Lord's laws and commandments. ⁵Asa also took away the high places and the incense* altars from all the towns in Judah. So the kingdom had peace when Asa was king. ⁶Asa built strong cities in Judah during the time when there was peace in Judah. Asa had no war in these years because the Lord gave him peace.

---

burnt offering(s) Gifts to God. Usually these were animals that were killed and completely burned on the altar.
incense Special dried tree sap. Burned to make a sweet-smelling smoke, it was offered as a gift to God.
temple The special building in Jerusalem for Jewish worship.
ancestors Literally, "fathers," meaning a person's parents, grandparents, and all the people they are descended from.
When the soldiers ... in back The Hebrew reads, "The battle was in front and in the back."

high places Places for worshiping God or false gods. These places were often on the hills and mountains.
holy stones The Canaanite people used these stones to worship their false gods.
Asherah poles Poles used to honor the goddess Asherah. People thought she could help them have many children.

⁷Asa said to the people of Judah, "Let's build these towns and make walls around them. Let's make towers, gates, and bars in the gates. Let's do this while we still live in this country. This country is ours because we have followed the Lord our God. He has given us peace all around us." So they built and had success.

⁸Asa had an army of 300,000 men from the family group of Judah and 280,000 men from the family group of Benjamin. The men from Judah carried large shields and spears. The men from Benjamin carried small shields and shot arrows from bows. All those men were strong and brave soldiers.

⁹Then Zerah came out against Asa's army. Zerah was from Ethiopia. Zerah had 1,000,000 men and 300 chariots* in his army. Zerah's army went as far as the town of Mareshah. ¹⁰Asa went out to fight against Zerah. Asa's army got ready for battle in the Valley of Zephathah at Mareshah.

¹¹Asa called out to the Lord his God and said, "Lord, only you can help weak people against strong people! Help us, Lord our God! We depend on you. We fight against this large army in your name. Lord, you are our God! Don't let anyone win against you!"

¹²Then the Lord used Asa's army from Judah to defeat the Ethiopian army. And the Ethiopian army ran away. ¹³Asa's army chased the Ethiopian army all the way to the town of Gerar. So many Ethiopians were killed that they could not get together as an army to fight again. They were crushed by the Lord and his army. Asa and his army carried many valuable things away from the enemy. ¹⁴Asa and his army defeated all the towns near Gerar. The people living in those towns were afraid of the Lord. Those towns had very many valuable things. Asa's army took those valuable things away from those towns. ¹⁵Asa's army also attacked the camps where the shepherds lived. They took many sheep and camels. Then Asa's army went back to Jerusalem.

Asa's Changes

15 The Spirit of God came on Azariah. Azariah was Obed's son. ²Azariah went to meet Asa. Azariah said, "Listen to me Asa, and all you people of Judah and Benjamin! The Lord is with you when you are with him. If you look for the Lord, you will find him. But if you leave him, he will leave you. ³For a long time Israel was without the true God. And they were without a teaching priest, and without the law. ⁴But when the people of Israel had trouble, they turned to the Lord God again. He is the God of Israel. They looked for the Lord and they found him. ⁵In those times of trouble, no person could travel safely. There was much trouble in all the nations. ⁶One nation would destroy another nation and one city would destroy another city. This was happening because God troubled them with all kinds of trouble. ⁷But Asa, you and the people of Judah and Benjamin, be strong. Don't be weak, don't give up because you will get a reward for your good work!"

⁸Asa felt encouraged when he heard these words and the message from Obed the prophet. Then he removed the hated idols from the whole area of Judah and Benjamin. Asa also removed those hated idols from the towns he had captured in the hill country of Ephraim. And he repaired the Lord's altar* that was in front of the porch of the Lord's temple.*

⁹Then Asa gathered all the people from Judah and Benjamin. He also gathered the people from the family groups of Ephraim, Manasseh, and Simeon who had moved from the country of Israel to live in the country of Judah. A great many of those people came to Judah because they saw that the Lord, Asa's God, was with Asa.

¹⁰Asa and those people gathered together in Jerusalem on the third month in the 15th year of Asa's rule. ¹¹At that time they sacrificed* 700 bulls and 7,000 sheep and goats to the Lord. Asa's army had taken those animals and other valuable things from their enemies. ¹²Then they made an agreement to serve the Lord God with all their heart and with all their soul. He is the God their ancestors* served. ¹³Any person that refused to serve the Lord God was to be killed. It did not matter if that person was important or not important or if that person was a man or woman. ¹⁴Then Asa and the people made an oath* to the Lord. They shouted out with a loud voice. They also blew on trumpets and rams' horns. ¹⁵All the

---

altar(s) A stone table or a stand for offering sacrifices.
temple The special building in Jerusalem for Jewish worship.
sacrifice(d) To kill a special animal and offer it on an altar as a gift to God.
ancestors Literally, "fathers," meaning a person's parents, grandparents, and all the people they are descended from.
oath A very strong promise.

chariot(s) A small wagon used in war.

people of Judah were happy about the oath, because they had promised with all their heart. They followed God with all their heart. They looked for God and found him. So the Lord gave them peace in all the country.

¹⁶King Asa also removed Maacah, his mother, from being queen mother. Asa did this because Maacah had made a terrible Asherah pole.* Asa cut down that Asherah pole and smashed it into small pieces. Then he burned the pieces in the Kidron Valley. ¹⁷The high places* were not removed from Judah, but Asa's heart was faithful to the Lord all of Asa's life.

¹⁸And Asa put the holy gifts that he and his father had given into the temple* of God. Those things were made of silver and gold. ¹⁹There was no more war until the 35th year of Asa's rule.*

Asa's Last Years

16 In Asa's 36th year as king,* Baasha attacked the country of Judah. Baasha was the king of Israel. He went to the town of Ramah and made it into a fortress.* Baasha used the town of Ramah as a place to stop people from going in or coming out to King Asa of Judah.

²Asa took silver and gold out of the storehouses in the Lord's temple.* And he took silver and gold out of the king's house. Then Asa sent messengers to Ben Hadad. Ben Hadad was the king of Aram and he was living in the town of Damascus. Asa's message said: ³"Ben Hadad let there be an agreement between you and me. Let's make it like the agreement your father and my father had. See, I am sending you silver and gold. Now, break your agreement with Baasha, king of Israel, so he will leave me alone and stop bothering me."

⁴Ben Hadad agreed with King Asa. Ben Hadad sent the commanders of his armies to attack the towns of Israel. Those commanders attacked the towns of Ijon, Dan, and Abel Maim. They also attacked all the towns in the area of Naphtali where treasures were stored. ⁵Baasha heard about the attacks on the towns of Israel. So he stopped building the town of Ramah into a fortress,* and he left his work. ⁶Then King Asa called all the men of Judah together. They went to the town of Ramah and took away the rocks and wood that Baasha used to make the fortress. Asa and the men of Judah used the rocks and wood to make the towns of Geba and Mizpah stronger.

⁷At that time Hanani the seer* came to Asa, king of Judah. Hanani said to him, "Asa, you depended on the king of Aram to help you and not the Lord your God. You should have depended on the Lord. But, because you did not depend on the Lord for help, the king of Aram's army escaped from you. ⁸The Ethiopians and the Libyans had a very large and powerful army. They had many chariots* and chariot drivers. But Asa, you depended on the Lord to help you defeat that large powerful army, and the Lord let you defeat them. ⁹The eyes of the Lord go around looking in all the earth for people who are faithful to him so he can make those people strong. Asa, you did a foolish thing. So from now on you will have wars."

¹⁰Asa was angry with Hanani because of what he said. Asa was so mad that he put Hanani in prison. Asa was very mean and rough with some of the people at that same time.

¹¹The things that Asa did, from the beginning to the end, are written in the book *The History of the Kings of Judah and Israel*. ¹²Asa's feet became diseased in his 39th year as king.* His disease was very bad, but he did not look for help from the Lord. Asa looked for help from the doctors. ¹³Asa died in the 41st year as king.* And so Asa rested with his ancestors.* ¹⁴The people buried Asa in his own tomb that he made for himself in David's City. The people laid him in a bed that was filled with spices and different kinds of mixed perfumes. The people made a large fire to honor Asa.*

Asherah Pole(s) Poles used to honor the goddess Asherah. People thought she could help them have many children.
high places Places for worshiping God or false gods. These places were often on the hills and mountains.
temple The special building in Jerusalem for Jewish worship.
35th year of Asa's rule About the year 880 B.C.
36th year as king About the year 879 B.C.
fortress A building or city with tall, strong walls for protection.
seer This is another name for a prophet. See 1 Sam. 9:9-11.
chariot(s) A small wagon used in war.
39th year as king About the year 875 B.C.
41st year as king About the year 873 B.C.
ancestors Literally, "fathers," meaning a person's parents, grandparents, and all the people they are descended from.
The people ... Asa This probably means the people burned spices in honor of Asa, but it could also mean they burned his body.

Jehoshaphat King of Judah

17 Jehoshaphat was the new king of Judah in Asa's place. Jehoshaphat was Asa's son. Jehoshaphat made Judah strong so they could fight against Israel. ²He put groups of soldiers in all the towns of Judah that were made into fortresses.* Jehoshaphat built fortresses* in Judah and in the towns of Ephraim that his father Asa captured.

³The Lord was with Jehoshaphat because in Jehoshaphat's young life he did the good things his ancestor* David did. Jehoshaphat did not follow the Baal idols. ⁴Jehoshaphat looked for the God his ancestors* followed. He followed God's commands. He did not live the same way the people of Israel lived. ⁵The Lord made Jehoshaphat a strong king over Judah. All the people of Judah brought gifts to Jehoshaphat. So Jehoshaphat had much wealth and honor. ⁶Jehoshaphat's heart found pleasure in the ways of the Lord. He took away the high places,* and the Asherah poles* out of the country of Judah.

⁷Jehoshaphat sent his leaders to teach in the towns of Judah. That happened in the third year of Jehoshaphat's rule.* Those leaders were Ben Hail, Obadiah, Zechariah, Nethanel, and Micaiah. ⁸Jehoshaphat also sent Levites with these leaders. These Levites were Shemaiah, Nethaniah, Zebadiah, Asahel, Shemiramoth, Jehonathan, Adonijah, and Tobijah. Jehoshaphat also sent the priests Elishama and Jehoram. ⁹Those leaders and Levites and priests taught the people in Judah. They had the *Book of the Law of the Lord* with them. They went through all the towns of Judah and taught the people.

¹⁰The nations near Judah were afraid of the Lord. That is why they did not start a war against Jehoshaphat. ¹¹Some of the Philistine people brought gifts to Jehoshaphat. They also brought silver to Jehoshaphat because they knew he was a very powerful king. Some Arabian people brought flocks to Jehoshaphat. They brought 7,700 rams and 7,700 goats to him.

¹²Jehoshaphat became more and more powerful. He built fortresses* and storage towns in the country of Judah. ¹³He kept many supplies in the storage towns. And Jehoshaphat kept trained soldiers in Jerusalem. ¹⁴Those soldiers were listed in their family groups. This is the list of those soldiers in Jerusalem:

From the family group of Judah, these were the generals: Adnah was the general of 300,000 soldiers. ¹⁵Jehohanan was the general of 280,000 soldiers. ¹⁶Amasiah was the general of 200,000 soldiers. Amasiah was Zicri's son. Amasiah was happy to give himself to serve the Lord.

¹⁷From the family group of Benjamin these were the generals: Eliada had 200,000 soldiers who used bows, arrows, and shields. Eliada was a very brave soldier. ¹⁸Jehozabad had 180,000 men ready for war. ¹⁹All those soldiers served King Jehoshaphat. The king also had other men in the fortresses* in all the country of Judah.

Micaiah Warns King Ahab

18 Jehoshaphat had much wealth and honor. He made an agreement with King Ahab through marriage.* ²A few years later, Jehoshaphat visited Ahab in the town of Samaria. Ahab sacrificed* many sheep and cows for Jehoshaphat and the people with him. Ahab encouraged Jehoshaphat to attack the town of Ramoth Gilead. ³Ahab said to Jehoshaphat, "Will you go with me to attack Ramoth Gilead?" Ahab was the king of Israel and Jehoshaphat was the king of Judah. Jehoshaphat answered Ahab, "I am like you, and my people are like your people. We will join you in the battle." ⁴Jehoshaphat also said to Ahab, "But first, let's look for a message from the Lord."

⁵So King Ahab gathered the prophets together, 400 men. Ahab said to them, "Should we go to war against the town of Ramoth Gilead, or not?" The prophets answered Ahab, "Go, because God will let you defeat Ramoth Gilead."

---

fortress(es) A building or city with tall, strong walls for protection.
ancestor Literally, "father," meaning a person that people are descended from.
ancestors Literally, "fathers," meaning a person's parents, grandparents, and all the people they are descended from.
high places Places of worship.
Asherah poles Poles used to honor the goddess Asherah. People thought she could help them have many children.
third year of Jehoshaphat's rule About the year 871 B.C.

Jehoshaphat ... marriage Jehoshaphat's son, Jehoram married Athaliah, Ahab's daughter. See 2 Chron. 21:6.
sacrifice(d) To kill a special animal and offer it on an altar as a gift to God.

⁶But Jehoshaphat said, "Is one of the Lord's prophets here? We need to ask the Lord through one of his prophets." ⁷Then King Ahab said to Jehoshaphat, "There is still one man here. We can ask the Lord through him. But I hate this man, because he never has a good message from the Lord about me. He always has bad messages for me. That man's name is Micaiah. He is Imlah's son." But Jehoshaphat said, "Ahab, you should not say that!" ⁸Then King Ahab called one of his officials and said, "Hurry, bring Micaiah the son of Imlah here!"

⁹Ahab the king of Israel and Jehoshaphat the king of Judah had their kings' robes on. They were sitting on their thrones at the threshing floor* near the front gate of the city of Samaria. Those 400 prophets were speaking their messages in front of the two kings. ¹⁰Zedekiah was the son of a man named Kenaanah. Zedekiah made some horns from iron. Zedekiah said, "This is what the Lord says: You will use these iron horns to stab the Aramean people until they are destroyed."

¹¹All the prophets said the same thing. They said, "Go to the town of Ramoth Gilead. You will have success and win. The Lord will let the king defeat the Aramean people."

¹²The messenger that went to get Micaiah said to him, "Micaiah, listen, all the prophets say the same thing. They are saying the king will have success. So say the same things they are saying. You also say good things."

¹³But Micaiah answered, "As sure as the Lord lives, I can only say what my God says."

¹⁴Then Micaiah came to King Ahab. The king said to him, "Micaiah, should we go to the town of Ramoth Gilead to fight or not?" Micaiah answered, "Go and attack. God will let you defeat those people."

¹⁵King Ahab said to Micaiah, "Many times I made you promise to tell me only the truth in the name of the Lord!"

¹⁶Then Micaiah said, "I saw all the people of Israel scattered on the mountains. They were like sheep without a shepherd. The Lord said, 'They have no leader. Let each person go home safely.'"

¹⁷Ahab, King of Israel said to Jehoshaphat, "I told you that Micaiah would not have a good message from the Lord about me! He only has bad messages about me!"

¹⁸Micaiah said, "Hear the message from the Lord: I saw the Lord sitting on his throne. All of heaven's army was standing around him, some on his left side and some on his right side. ¹⁹The Lord said, 'Who will trick Ahab, king of Israel, to attack the town of Ramoth Gilead so he may be killed there?' Different ones who stood around the Lord said different things. ²⁰Then a spirit came and stood before the Lord. That spirit said, 'I will trick Ahab.' The Lord asked that spirit, 'How?' ²¹That spirit answered, 'I will go out and become a lying spirit in Ahab's prophets' mouths.' And the Lord said, 'You will succeed in tricking Ahab. So go out and do it.'

²²"Now look Ahab, the Lord has put a lying spirit in your prophets' mouths. The Lord has said bad things will happen to you."

²³Then Zedekiah went over to Micaiah and hit him in the face. Zedekiah's father's name was Kenaanah. Zedekiah said, "Micaiah, which way did the spirit from the Lord go when he went from me to speak to you?" ²⁴Micaiah answered, "Zedekiah, you will find out on the day you go to hide in an inside room!"

²⁵Then King Ahab said, "Take Micaiah and send him to Amon the governor of the city and to Joash the king's son. ²⁶Say to Amon and Joash, 'This is what the king says: Put Micaiah in prison. Don't give him anything to eat except bread and water until I come back from the battle.'"

²⁷Micaiah answered, "Ahab, if you come back from battle safely, then the Lord has not spoken through me. Hear and remember my words, all you people!"

Ahab Is Killed at Ramoth Gilead

²⁸So Ahab king of Israel and Jehoshaphat king of Judah attacked the town of Ramoth Gilead. ²⁹King Ahab said to Jehoshaphat, "I will change my appearance before I go into battle. But you wear your own robes." So Ahab, king of Israel changed his appearance, and the two kings went into battle.

³⁰The king of Aram gave an order to his chariot* commanders. He told them, "Don't fight with any person, no matter how great or how humble. But fight only with Ahab, the king of Israel." ³¹When the chariot commanders saw Jehoshaphat, they thought, "There is Ahab, the king of Israel!" They turned toward Jehoshaphat to attack him. But Jehoshaphat shouted out, and

---

threshing floor A place where grain is beaten or walked on to remove the hulls from the grain.

chariot(s) A small wagon used in war.

the Lord helped him. God made the chariot commanders turn away from Jehoshaphat. ³²When they saw that Jehoshaphat was not the king of Israel, they stopped chasing him.

³³But a soldier happened to shoot an arrow from his bow without aiming at anything. That arrow hit Ahab king of Israel. It hit Ahab in an open part of his armor. Ahab said to the man driving his chariot,* "Turn around and take me out of the battle. I am hurt!" ³⁴The battle became worse that day. Ahab propped himself up in his chariot facing the Arameans until the evening. Then Ahab died at sunset.

19 Jehoshaphat the king of Judah came back safely to his house in Jerusalem. ²Jehu the seer* went out to meet Jehoshaphat. Jehu's father's name was Hanani. Jehu said to King Jehoshaphat, "Why did you help evil people? Why do you love those people that hate the Lord? That is the reason the Lord is angry with you. ³But there are some good things in your life. You removed the Asherah poles* from this country, and you decided in your heart to follow God."

Jehoshaphat Chooses Judges

⁴Jehoshaphat lived in Jerusalem. He went out again to be with the people from the town of Beersheba to the hill country of Ephraim. Jehoshaphat brought those people back to the Lord God their ancestors* followed. ⁵Jehoshaphat chose judges in Judah. He chose judges to be in each of the fortresses* of Judah. ⁶Jehoshaphat said to those judges, "Be careful in what you are doing, because you are not judging for people, but for the Lord. The Lord will be with you when you make a decision. ⁷Now each one of you must fear the Lord. Be careful in what you do because the Lord our God is fair. The Lord doesn't treat some people more important than others. And he doesn't accept money to change his judgments."

⁸And in Jerusalem, Jehoshaphat chose some of the Levites, priests, and leaders of Israelite families to be judges. Those people were to use the law of the Lord to settle problems for the people living in Jerusalem. ⁹Jehoshaphat gave them commands. Jehoshaphat said, "You must serve faithfully with all your heart. You must fear the Lord. ¹⁰You will have cases about killing, about a law, command, rule, or some other law. All these cases will come to you from your brothers living in the cities. In all of these cases you must warn the people not to sin against the Lord. If you don't serve faithfully you will cause the Lord's anger to come against you and your brothers. Do this, then you won't be guilty. ¹¹Amariah is the leading priest. He will be over you in all things about the Lord. And Zebadiah will be over you in all things about the king. Zebadiah's father's name is Ishmael. Zebadiah is a leader in the family group of Judah. Also, the Levites will serve as scribes* for you. Have courage in all you do. May the Lord be with those people who do what is right."

Jehoshaphat Faces War

20 Later the Moabite people, the Ammonite people, and some Meunite* people came to start a war with Jehoshaphat. ²Some men came and told Jehoshaphat, "There is a large army coming against you from Edom. They are coming from the other side of the ₍Dead₎ Sea. They are already in Hazazon Tamar! (Hazazon Tamar is also called En Gedi.) ³Jehoshaphat became afraid, and he decided to ask the Lord what to do. He announced a time of fasting* for everyone in Judah. ⁴The people of Judah came together to ask for help from the Lord. They came from out of all the towns of Judah to ask for the Lord's help.

⁵Jehoshaphat was in the Lord's temple* in front of the new yard. He stood up in the meeting of the people from Judah and Jerusalem. ⁶He said,

"Lord God of our ancestors,* you are the God in heaven! You rule over all the kingdoms in all the nations! You have power and strength! No

---

chariot(s) A small wagon used in war.
seer This is another name for a prophet. See 1 Sam. 9:9-11.
Asherah poles Poles used to honor the goddess Asherah. People thought she could help them have many children.
ancestors Literally, "fathers," meaning a person's parents, grandparents, and all the people they are descended from.
fortress(es) A building or city with tall, strong walls for protection.
scribes Men that wrote down and copied books and letters. They often became experts at knowing the meaning of those writings ("scriptures").
Meunite Some ancient Greek translations have "Meunite." The Hebrew has "Ammonite."
a time of fasting A time when no food was eaten.
temple The special building in Jerusalem for Jewish worship.
descendants A person's children and their future families.

person can stand against you! ⁷You are our God! You forced the people living in this land to leave. You did this in front of your people Israel. You gave this land to the descendants* of Abraham forever. Abraham was your friend. ⁸Abraham's descendants lived in this land, and built a temple* for your name. ⁹They said, "If trouble comes to us—the sword, punishment, sicknesses, or famine, we will stand in front of this temple and in front of you. Your name is on this temple. We will shout to you when we are in trouble. Then you will hear and save us.

¹⁰"But now, here are men from Ammon, Moab, and Mount Seir! You would not let the people of Israel enter their lands when the people of Israel came out of Egypt.* So the people of Israel turned away and didn't destroy those people. ¹¹But see the kind of reward those people give us for not destroying them. They have come to force us out of your land. You gave this land to us. ¹²Our God, punish those people! We have no power against this large army that is coming against us! We don't know what to do! That is why we look to you for help!"*

¹³All the men of Judah stood before the Lord with their babies, wives, and children. ¹⁴Then the Lord's Spirit came on Jahaziel. Jahaziel was Zechariah's son. Zechariah was Benaiah's son. Benaiah was Jeiel's son. And Jeiel was Mattaniah's son. Jahaziel was a Levite and a descendant* of Asaph. In the middle of the meeting, ¹⁵Jahaziel said, "Listen to me King Jehoshaphat, all you people living in Judah and Jerusalem! The Lord says this to you: 'Don't be afraid or worry about this large army, because the battle is not your battle. It is God's battle! ¹⁶Tomorrow, go down there and fight those people. They will come up through the Pass of Ziz. You will find them at the end of the valley on the other side of the Desert of Jeruel. ¹⁷You won't need to fight in this battle. Stand strong in your places. You will see the Lord save you. Judah and Jerusalem, don't be afraid! Don't worry! The Lord is with you, so go out against those people tomorrow.'"

¹⁸Jehoshaphat bowed down low. His face touched the ground. And all the people of Judah and the people living in Jerusalem fell down in front of the Lord. And they all worshiped the Lord. ¹⁹The Levites from the Kohath family groups and the Korah family stood up to praise the Lord God of Israel. Their voices were very loud as they gave praise to the Lord.

²⁰Jehoshaphat's army went out into the Desert of Tekoa early in the morning. As they were starting out, Jehoshaphat stood and said, "Listen to me people of Judah and you people from Jerusalem. Have faith in the Lord your God, and then you will stand strong. Have faith in the Lord's prophets. You will succeed!" ²¹Jehoshaphat listened to advice from the people. Then he chose men to be singers to the Lord. Those singers were chosen to give praise to the Lord because he is holy and wonderful. They marched in front of the army and praised the Lord. These singers said, "Give thanks to the Lord, because his love continues forever!" ²²As those men began to sing and to praise God, the Lord set an ambush* for the people of Ammon, Moab, and Mount Seir. Those were the people that came to attack Judah. Those people were beaten. ²³The Ammonites and the Moabites started to fight against the men from Mount Seir. The Ammonites and the Moabites killed and destroyed the men from Mount Seir. After they had killed the men from Seir, they killed each other.

²⁴The men from Judah arrived at the lookout point in the desert. They looked for the enemy's large army. But they only saw dead bodies lying on the ground. No person had survived. ²⁵Jehoshaphat and his army came to take valuable things from the bodies. They found many animals, riches, clothes, and valuable things. Jehoshaphat and his army took those things for themselves. The things were more than Jehoshaphat and his people could carry away. They spent three days taking away the valuable things from the dead bodies, because there was so much. ²⁶On the fourth day Jehoshaphat and his army met in the Valley of Beracah.* They gave praise to the Lord in that place. That is why the name of that place has been called "The Valley of Beracah" till now.

---

temple The special building in Jerusalem for Jewish worship.
You would not let ... Egypt See Deut. 2:4-9, 19 for the full story.
That is why ... help The Hebrew says, "But our eyes are on you!"
descendant(s) A person's children and their future families.

ambush A surprise attack by hidden enemies.
Beracah This word means "blessing" or "praise."
lyre(s) An instrument with several strings, like a harp.

⁲⁷Then Jehoshaphat led all the men from Judah and Jerusalem back home to Jerusalem. The Lord made them very happy because their enemies were defeated. ²⁸They came to Jerusalem with lyres,* harps, and trumpets and went to the Lord's temple.*
²⁹All the kingdoms in all the countries feared the Lord because they heard that the Lord fought against Israel's enemies. ³⁰That is why Jehoshaphat's kingdom had peace. Jehoshaphat's God gave him peace all around him.

The End of Jehoshaphat's Rule

³¹Jehoshaphat ruled over the country of Judah. Jehoshaphat was 35 years old when he began to rule. He ruled 25 years in Jerusalem. His mother's name was Azubah. Azubah was Shilhi's daughter. ³²Jehoshaphat lived the right way like Asa his father lived. Jehoshaphat didn't turn from following Asa's way. Jehoshaphat did right in the Lord's sight. ³³But the high places* were not taken away. And the people didn't turn their hearts to follow the God their ancestors* followed.

³⁴The other things Jehoshaphat did, from beginning to end, are written in The Official Records of Jehu son of Hanani. These things were copied and included in the book *The History of the Kings of Israel*.

³⁵Later on, Jehoshaphat king of Judah made an agreement with Ahaziah, king of Israel. Ahaziah did evil. ³⁶Jehoshaphat joined with Ahaziah to make ships to go to the town of Tarshish.* They made the ships in the town of Ezion Geber. ³⁷Then Eliezer spoke against Jehoshaphat. Eliezer's father's name was Dodavahu. Eliezer was from the town of Mareshah. He said, "Jehoshaphat, you joined with Ahaziah, that is why the Lord will destroy your works." The ships were wrecked, so Jehoshaphat and Ahaziah were not able to send them to Tarshish.*

21 Then Jehoshaphat died and was buried with his ancestors.* He was buried in David's City. Jehoram was the new king in Jehoshaphat's place. Jehoram was Jehoshaphat's son. ²Jehoram's brothers were Azariah, Jehiel, Zechariah, Azariah, Michael, and Shephatiah. Those men were Jehoshaphat's sons. Jehoshaphat was the king of Judah.* ³Jehoshaphat gave his sons many gifts of silver, gold, and precious things. He also gave them strong fortresses* in Judah. But Jehoshaphat gave the kingdom to Jehoram because Jehoram was his oldest son.

Jehoram King of Judah

⁴Jehoram took over his father's kingdom and made himself strong. Then he used a sword to kill all his brothers. He also killed some of the leaders of Israel. ⁵Jehoram was 32 years old when he began to rule. He ruled eight years in Jerusalem. ⁶He lived the same way the kings of Israel lived. He lived the same way Ahab's family lived. This was because Jehoram married Ahab's daughter. And Jehoram did evil in the Lord's sight. ⁷But the Lord would not destroy David's family because of the agreement the Lord made with David. The Lord had promised to keep a lamp burning for David and his children forever.*

⁸In Jehoram's time, Edom broke away from under Judah's authority. The people of Edom chose their own king. ⁹So Jehoram went to Edom with all his commanders and chariots.* The Edomite army surrounded Jehoram and his chariot* commanders. But Jehoram fought his way out at night. ¹⁰Since that time and until now the country of Edom has been rebellious against Judah. The people from the town of Libnah also turned against Jehoram. This happened because Jehoram left the Lord God. He is the God Jehoram's ancestors* followed. ¹¹Jehoram also built high places* on the hills in Judah. Jehoram caused the people of Jerusalem to stop doing what God wanted. He led the people of Judah away from the Lord.

¹²Jehoram got a message from Elijah the prophet. This is what the message said: "This is

---

lyre(s) An instrument with several strings, like a harp.
temple The special building in Jerusalem for Jewish worship.
high places Places for worshiping God or false gods. These places were often on the hills and mountains.
ancestors Literally, "fathers," meaning a person's parents, grandparents, and all the people they are descended from.
Tarshish A city far away from Israel, probably in Spain. Tarshish was famous for its large ships that sailed the Mediterranean Sea.

Judah Literally, "Israel."
fortress(es) A building or city with tall, strong walls for protection.
The Lord ... his children forever Here the writer means that one of David's descendants would always rule.
chariot(s) A small wagon used in war.

what the Lord God says. He is the God your father David followed. The Lord says, 'Jehoram, you have not lived the way your father Jehoshaphat lived. You have not lived the way Asa king of Judah lived. [13]But you have lived the way the kings of Israel lived. You have caused the people of Judah and Jerusalem to stop doing what God wants. That is what Ahab and his family did. They were unfaithful to God. You have killed your brothers. Your brothers were better than you. [14]So now, the Lord will soon punish your people with much punishment. The Lord will punish your children, wives, and all your property. [15]You will have a terrible sickness in your bowels. It will become worse every day. Then your bowels will come out because of your terrible sickness.'"

[16]The Lord caused the Philistine people and the Arab people living near the Ethiopian people to be angry at Jehoram. [17]Those people attacked the country of Judah. They took away all the wealth that belonged to the king's house and took away Jehoram's sons and wives. Only Jehoram's youngest son was left. Jehoram's youngest son was named Jehoahaz.*

[18]After those things happened, the Lord made Jehoram sick in his bowels with a sickness that could not be cured. [19]Then Jehoram's bowels fell out two years later because of his sickness. He died in very bad pain. The people did not make a large fire to honor Jehoram like they did for his father. [20]Jehoram was 32 years old when he became king. He ruled eight years in Jerusalem. No person was sad when Jehoram died. The people buried Jehoram in David's city, but not in the graves where the kings are buried.

Ahaziah King of Judah

22 The people of Jerusalem chose Ahaziah* to be the new king in Jehoram's place. Ahaziah was Jehoram's youngest son. The people that came with the Arab people to attack Jehoram's camp killed all of Jehoram's older sons. So Ahaziah began to rule in Judah. [2]Ahaziah was 22 years old when he began to rule.* Ahaziah ruled one year in Jerusalem. His mother's name was Athaliah. Athaliah's father's name was Omri. [3]Ahaziah also lived the way Ahab's family lived. He lived that way because his mother encouraged him to do wrong things. [4]Ahaziah did evil things in the Lord's sight. That is what Ahab's family did. Ahab's family gave advice to Ahaziah after Ahaziah's father died. They gave Ahaziah bad advice. That bad advice led to his death. [5]Ahaziah followed the advice Ahab's family gave him. Ahaziah went with King Joram to fight against King Hazael from Aram at the town of Ramoth Gilead. Joram's father's name was Ahab, the king of Israel. But the Arameans wounded Joram in the battle. [6]Joram went back to the town of Jezreel to get well. He was wounded at Ramoth when he fought against Hazael, king of Aram.

Then Ahaziah* went to the town of Jezreel to visit Joram. Ahaziah's father's name was Jehoram, the king of Judah. Joram's father's name was Ahab. Joram was in the town of Jezreel because he was wounded.

[7]God caused Ahaziah's* death when he went to visit Joram. Ahaziah arrived and went out with Joram to meet Jehu. Jehu's father's name was Nimshi. The Lord chose Jehu to destroy Ahab's family. [8]Jehu was punishing Ahab's family. Jehu found the leaders of Judah and Ahaziah's relatives that served Ahaziah. Jehu killed those leaders of Judah and Ahaziah's relatives. [9]Then Jehu looked for Ahaziah. Jehu's men caught him when he tried to hide in the town of Samaria. They brought Ahaziah to Jehu. They killed Ahaziah and buried him. They said, "Ahaziah is the descendant* of Jehoshaphat. Jehoshaphat followed the Lord with all his heart." Ahaziah's family had no power to hold the kingdom of Judah together.

Queen Athaliah

[10]Athaliah was Ahaziah's* mother. When she saw that her son was dead, she killed all the king's children in Judah. [11]But Jehosheba took Ahaziah's son Joash and hid him. Jehosheba put Joash and his nurse in the inside bedroom. Jehosheba was King Jehoram's daughter. She was also Jehoiada's wife. Jehoiada was a priest. And Jehosheba was Ahaziah's sister. Athaliah did not kill Joash, because Jehosheba hid him. [12]Joash was hidden with the priests in God's temple* for six years. During that time, Athaliah ruled over the land as queen.

Jehoahaz Also spelled "Ahaziah".
Ahaziah Also spelled "Jehoahaz".
Ahaziah was ... rule Some old copies say "42 years old." 2 Kings 8:26 says Ahaziah was 22 years old when he began to rule.

descendant(s) A person's children and their future families.
temple The special building in Jerusalem for Jewish worship.

Priest Jehoiada and King Joash

23 After six years, Jehoiada showed his strength. He made an agreement with the captains. Those captains were: Azariah son of Jeroham, Ishmael son of Jehohanan, Azariah son of Obed, Maaseiah son of Adaiah, and Elishaphat son of Zicri. ²They went around in Judah and gathered the Levites from all the towns of Judah. They also gathered the leaders of the families of Israel. Then they went to Jerusalem. ³All the people meeting together made an agreement with the king in God's temple.*

Jehoiada said to those people, "The king's son will rule. That is what the Lord promised about David's descendants.* ⁴Now, this is what you must do: One-third of you priests and Levites who go on duty on the Sabbath will guard the doors. ⁵And one-third of you will be at the king's house. And one-third of you will be at the Foundation Gate. But all the other people will stay in the yards of the Lord's temple.* ⁶Don't let any person come into the Lord's temple. Only the priest and Levites who serve are permitted to come into the Lord's temple because they are holy. But all the other men must do the job the Lord has given them. ⁷The Levites must stay near the king. Every man must have his sword with him. If any person tries to enter the temple, kill that person. You must stay with the king everywhere he goes."

⁸The Levites and all the people of Judah obeyed all that Jehoiada the priest commanded. Jehoiada the priest did not excuse any person from the groups of the priests. So each captain and all his men came in on the Sabbath with those who went out on the Sabbath. ⁹Jehoiada the priest gave the spears and the large and small shields that belonged to King David to the officers. Those weapons were kept in God's temple.* ¹⁰Then Jehoiada told the men where to stand. Every man had his weapon in his hand. The men stood all the way from the right side of the temple to the left side of the temple. They stood near the altar* and the temple, and near the king. ¹¹They brought the king's son out and put the crown on him. They gave him a copy of the Law.* Then they made Joash king. Jehoiada and his sons anointed* Joash. They said, "Let the king live a long time!"

¹²Athaliah heard the noise of the people running to the temple* and praising the king. She came into the Lord's temple to the people. ¹³She looked and saw the king. The king was standing by the king's column at the front entrance. The officers and the men who blew trumpets were near the king. The people of the land were happy and blowing trumpets. The singers were playing on instruments of music. The singers led the people in singing praises. Then Athaliah tore her clothes* and said, "Treason! Treason!"*

¹⁴Jehoiada the priest brought out the army captains. He said to them, "Take Athaliah outside among the army. Use your swords to kill any person that follows her." Then the priest warned the soldiers, "Don't kill Athaliah in the Lord's temple.*" ¹⁵Then those men grabbed Athaliah when she came to the entrance of the Horse Gate at the king's house. Then they killed her there at that place.

¹⁶Then Jehoiada made an agreement with all the people, and the king. They all agreed that they all would be the Lord's people. ¹⁷All the people went into the temple of the idol Baal and tore it down. They also broke the altars and idols that were in Baal's temple. They killed Mattan the priest of Baal in front of the altars of Baal.

¹⁸Then Jehoiada chose the priests to be responsible for the Lord's temple.* Those priests were Levites, and David had given them the job of being responsible for the Lord's temple. Those priests were to offer the burnt offerings* to the Lord the way the Law of Moses commanded. They offered the sacrifices* with much joy and singing the way David commanded. ¹⁹Jehoiada put guards at the gates of the Lord's temple so

---

temple The special building in Jerusalem for Jewish worship.
descendant(s) A person's children and their future families.
altar(s) A stone table or a stand for offering sacrifices.
They gave him ... Law The Hebrew reads, "They gave him testimony." Here the word means a copy of the Law that the king had to obey. See Deut. 17:18.
anoint(ed) To pour olive oil on things or people to show that they were chosen by God for a special work or purpose.
tore her clothes A way to show she was very upset.
Treason Rebelling against the government. Here Athaliah was blaming the people for turning against her government.
burnt offering(s) Gifts to God. Usually these were animals that were killed and completely burned on the altar.
sacrifice(s) A gift to God. Usually, it was a special animal that was killed and burned on an altar.

that a person who was not clean in anything could not enter the temple.

²⁰Jehoiada took the army captains, the leaders, the rulers of the people, and all the people of the land with him. Then Jehoiada took the king out of the Lord's temple,* and they went through the Upper Gate to the king's house. In that place they put the king on the throne. ²¹All the people of Judah were very happy and the city Jerusalem had peace because Athaliah was killed with a sword.

Joash Builds Again the Temple

24 ¹Joash was seven years old when he became king. He ruled 40 years in Jerusalem. His mother's name was Zibiah. Zibiah was from the town of Beersheba. ²Joash did right in front of the Lord as long as Jehoiada the priest was living. ³Jehoiada chose two wives for Joash. Joash had sons and daughters.

⁴Then later on, Joash decided to build again the Lord's temple.* ⁵Joash called the priests and the Levites together. He said to them, "Go out to the towns of Judah and gather the money all the people of Israel pay every year. Use that money to build again your God's temple. Hurry and do this." But the Levites didn't hurry.

⁶So King Joash called Jehoiada the leading priest. The king said, "Jehoiada, why haven't you made the Levites bring in the tax money from Judah and Jerusalem? Moses the Lord's servant and the people of Israel used that tax money for the Holy Tent.*"

⁷In the past, Athaliah's sons broke into God's temple.* They used the holy things in the Lord's temple for their worship of the Baal gods. Athaliah was a very wicked woman.

⁸King Joash gave a command for a box to be made and put outside the gate at the Lord's temple.* ⁹Then the Levites made an announcement in Judah and Jerusalem. They told the people to bring in the tax money for the Lord. That tax money is what Moses the servant of God had required the people of Israel to give while they were in the desert. ¹⁰All the leaders and the people were happy. They brought their money and put it in the box. They continued giving until the box was full. ¹¹Then the Levites would take the box to the king's officials. They saw that the box was full of money. The king's secretary and the leading priest's officer came and took the money out of the box. Then they took the box back to its place again. They did this often and gathered much money. ¹²Then King Joash and Jehoiada gave the money to the people that worked on the Lord's temple. And the people that worked on the Lord's temple hired skilled woodcarvers and carpenters to build again the Lord's temple. They also hired workers that knew how to work with iron and bronze to build again the Lord's temple.

¹³The men that supervised the work were very faithful. The work to build again the Lord's temple* was successful. They built God's temple the way it was before and they made it stronger. ¹⁴When the workers finished, they brought the money that was left to King Joash and Jehoiada. They used that money to make things for the Lord's temple. Those things were used for the service in the temple and for offering burnt offerings.* They also made bowls and other things from gold and silver. The priests offered burnt offerings in the Lord's temple every day while Jehoiada was alive.

¹⁵Jehoiada became old. He had a very long life, then he died. Jehoiada was 130 years old when he died. ¹⁶The people buried Jehoiada in David's City where the kings are buried. The people buried Jehoiada there because in his life he did much good in Israel for God and for God's temple.*

¹⁷After Jehoiada died, the leaders of Judah came and bowed to King Joash. The king listened to those leaders. ¹⁸The king and those leaders rejected the temple* of the Lord God. Their ancestors* followed the Lord God. They worshiped the Asherah poles* and other idols. God was angry with the people of Judah and Jerusalem because the king and those leaders were guilty. ¹⁹God sent prophets to the people to bring them back to the Lord. The prophets warned the people. But the people refused to listen.

---

temple The special building in Jerusalem for Jewish worship.
Holy Tent Or, "tabernacle." Also called the "meeting tent." The people would go to this tent to meet with God.

burnt offering(s) Gifts to God. Usually these were animals that were killed and completely burned on the altar.
ancestors Literally, "fathers," meaning a person's parents, grandparents, and all the people they are descended from.
Asherah poles Poles used to honor the goddess Asherah. People thought she could help them have many children.

²⁰God's Spirit came on Zechariah. Zechariah's father was Jehoiada the priest. Zechariah stood in front of the people and said, "This is what God says: 'Why do you people refuse to obey the Lord's commands? You will not be successful. You have left the Lord. So the Lord has also left you!'" ²¹But the people made plans against Zechariah. The king commanded the people to kill Zechariah, so they threw rocks at him until he died. The people did this in the temple* yard. ²²Joash the king didn't remember Jehoiada's kindness to him. Jehoiada was Zechariah's father. But Joash killed Zechariah, Jehoiada's son. Before Zechariah died, he said, "May the Lord see what you are doing and punish you!"

²³At the end of the year, The Aramean army came against Joash. They attacked Judah and Jerusalem and killed all the leaders of the people. They sent all the valuable things to the king of Damascus. ²⁴The Aramean army came with a small group of men, but the Lord let them defeat a very large army from Judah. The Lord did this because the people of Judah left the Lord God their ancestors* followed. So Joash was punished. ²⁵When the Arameans left Joash, he was badly wounded. Joash's own servants made plans against him. They did this because Joash killed Zechariah the son of Jehoiada the priest. The servants killed Joash on his own bed. After Joash died, the people buried him in David's City. But they didn't bury him in the place where the kings are buried.

²⁶These are the servants that made plans against Joash: Zabad and Jehozabad. Zabad's mother's name was Shimeath. Shimeath was from Ammon. And Jehozabad's mother's name was Shimrith. Shimrith was from Moab. ²⁷The story about Joash's sons, the great prophecies against him, and how he built again God's temple* are written in the book *About the Kings*. Amaziah became the new king after him. Amaziah was Joash's son.

Amaziah King of Judah

25 Amaziah was 25 years old when he became king. He ruled for 29 years in Jerusalem. His mother's name was Jehoaddin. Jehoaddin was from Jerusalem. ²Amaziah did the things the Lord wanted him to do. But he didn't do them with all his heart. ³Amaziah became a strong king. Then he killed the officials that killed his father the king. ⁴But Amaziah didn't kill those officials' children. Why? He obeyed the law written in the book of Moses. The Lord commanded, "Parents must not be put to death for something their children did. And children must not be put to death for something their parents did. A person should be put to death only for a bad thing that he himself did."*

⁵Amaziah gathered the people of Judah together. He grouped them by families and he put generals and captains in charge of those groups. Those leaders were in charge of all the soldiers from Judah and Benjamin. All the men that were chosen to be soldiers were 20 years old and older. In all there were 300,000 skilled soldiers ready to fight with spears and shields. ⁶Amaziah also hired 100,000 soldiers from Israel. He paid 3 3/4 tons* of silver to hire those soldiers. ⁷But a man of God* came to Amaziah. The man of God said, "King, don't let the army of Israel go with you. The Lord is not with Israel. The Lord is not with the people of Ephraim.* ⁸Maybe you will make yourself strong and ready for war, but God can help you win or help you lose. ⁹Amaziah said to the man of God, "But what about the money I already paid to the Israelite army?" The man of God answered, "The Lord has plenty. He can give you much more than that!"

¹⁰So Amaziah sent the Israelite army back home to Ephraim.* Those men were very angry against the king and the people of Judah. They went back home very angry.

¹¹Then Amaziah became very brave and led his army to the Salt Valley in the country of Edom. In that place, Amaziah's army killed 10,000 men from Seir.* ¹²The army of Judah also captured 10,000 men from Seir. They took those men from

---

Parents ... did See Deut. 24:16.
3 3/4 tons Literally, "100 talents (kikars)."
man of God This is another name for a prophet.
Ephraim Ephraim was Joseph's youngest son. Ephraim's family group joined Israel. Ephraim was another name for Israel.
Seir Or, "Edom."

---

temple The special building in Jerusalem for Jewish worship.
ancestors Literally, "fathers," meaning a person's parents, grandparents, and all the people they are descended from.

Seir to the top of a cliff. Those men were still alive. Then the army of Judah threw down those men from the top of the cliff and their bodies were broken on the rocks below.

¹³But at the same time, the Israelite army was attacking some towns in Judah. They attacked the towns from Beth Horon all the way to Samaria. They killed 3,000 people and took many valuable things. ₍The people of that army were angry because₎ Amaziah didn't let them join him in the war.

¹⁴Amaziah came home after he defeated the Edomite* people. He brought the idol gods the people of Seir* worshiped. Amaziah started to worship those idol gods. He bowed down in front of those gods, and he burned incense* to them. ¹⁵The Lord was very angry with Amaziah. The Lord sent a prophet to Amaziah. The prophet said, "Amaziah, why have you worshiped the gods those people worship? Those gods could not even save their own people from you!"

¹⁶When the prophet spoke, Amaziah said to the prophet, "We never made you an adviser to the king! Be quiet! If you don't be quiet, you will be killed." The prophet became quiet, but then said, "God really has decided to destroy you. Why? Because you did those bad things and didn't listen to my advice."

¹⁷Amaziah king of Judah, talked with his advisers. Then he sent a message to Jehoash. Amaziah said to Jehoash, "Let's meet face to face." Jehoash was Jehoahaz's son. Jehoahaz was Jehu's son. Jehu was the king of Israel.

¹⁸Then Jehoash sent his answer to Amaziah. Jehoash was the king of Israel and Amaziah was the king of Judah. Jehoash told this story: "A little thorn bush of Lebanon sent a message to a big cedar tree of Lebanon. The little thorn bush said, 'Let your daughter marry my son.' But a wild animal came and walked over the thorn bush and destroyed it. ¹⁹You say to yourself, 'I have defeated Edom!' You are proud and you brag. But you should stay at home. There is no need for you to get into trouble. If you fight me, you and Judah will be destroyed."

²⁰But Amaziah refused to listen. This came from God. God planned to let Israel defeat Judah, because the people of Judah followed the gods the people of Edom followed. ²¹So Jehoash king of Israel met Amaziah king of Judah face to face at the town of Beth Shemesh. Beth Shemesh is in Judah. ²²Israel defeated Judah. Every man of Judah ran away to his home. ²³Jehoash captured Amaziah at Beth Shemesh and took him to Jerusalem. Amaziah's father's name was Joash. Joash's father's name was Jehoahaz. Jehoash tore down a 600-foot section* of the wall of Jerusalem from the Ephraim Gate to the Corner Gate. ²⁴There was gold and silver and many other things in God's temple. Obed Edom was responsible for those things. But Jehoash took all of those things. Jehoash also took the treasures from the king's palace. Then Jehoash took some people as prisoners and went back to Samaria.

²⁵Amaziah lived 15 years after Jehoash died. Amaziah's father was Joash, the king of Judah. ²⁶The other things Amaziah did, from beginning to end, are written in the book *The History of the Kings of Judah and Israel*. ²⁷When Amaziah stopped obeying the Lord, the people in Jerusalem made plans against Amaziah. He ran away to the town of Lachish. But the people sent men to Lachish and they killed Amaziah there. ²⁸Then they carried Amaziah's body on horses and buried him with his ancestors* in the City of Judah.

Uzziah King of Judah

26 Then the people of Judah chose Uzziah to be the new king in place of Amaziah. Amaziah was Uzziah's father. Uzziah was 16 years old when this happened. ²Uzziah built again the town of Elath and gave it back to Judah. Uzziah did this after Amaziah died and was buried with his ancestors.*

³Uzziah was 16 years old when he became king. He ruled 52 years in Jerusalem. His mother's name was Jecoliah. Jecoliah was from Jerusalem. ⁴Uzziah did the things the Lord wanted him to do. He obeyed God the same as his father Amaziah had done. ⁵Uzziah followed God in the time of Zechariah's life. Zechariah taught Uzziah how to respect and obey God. When Uzziah was obeying the Lord, God gave him success.

⁶Uzziah fought a war against the Philistine people. He tore down the walls around the towns of Gath, Jabneh, and Ashdod. Uzziah built towns near the town of Ashdod and in other places

---

Edomite The people of Seir.
Seir Or, "Edom," a country east of Judah.
incense Special dried tree sap. Burned to make a sweet-smelling smoke, it was offered as a gift to God.
Edom A country east of Judah.

600-foot section Or, "400-cubit section."
ancestors Literally, "fathers," meaning a person's parents, grandparents, and all the people they are descended from.

among the Philistine people. ⁷God helped Uzziah fight the Philistines, the Arabs living in the town of Gur Baal, and the Meunites. ⁸The Ammonites paid tribute* to Uzziah. Uzziah's name became famous all the way to the border of Egypt. He was famous because he was very powerful.

⁹Uzziah built towers in Jerusalem at the Corner Gate, at the Valley Gate, and at the place where the wall turned. Uzziah made those towers strong. ¹⁰Uzziah built towers in the desert. He also dug many wells. He had much cattle in the hill country and in the flat lands. Uzziah had farmers in the mountains and in the lands where growth was good. He also had men that took care of fields where grapes grew. He loved farming.

¹¹Uzziah had an army of trained soldiers. Those soldiers were put in groups by Jeiel the secretary and Maaseiah the officer. Hananiah was their leader. Jeiel and Maaseiah counted those soldiers and put them into groups. Hananiah was one of the king's officers. ¹²There were 2,600 leaders over the soldiers. ¹³Those family leaders were in charge of an army of 307,500 men that fought with great power. Those soldiers helped the king against the enemy. ¹⁴Uzziah gave the army shields, spears, helmets, armor, bows, and stones for the slings.* ¹⁵In Jerusalem Uzziah made machines that were invented by clever men. Those machines were put on the towers and corner walls. These machines shot arrows and large rocks. Uzziah became famous. People knew his name in far away places. He had much help and became a powerful king.

¹⁶But when Uzziah became strong, his pride caused him to be destroyed. He was not faithful to the Lord his God. He went into the Lord's temple* to burn incense* on the altar* for burning incense. ¹⁷Azariah the priest and 80 brave priests that served the Lord followed Uzziah into the temple. ¹⁸They told Uzziah he was wrong. They said to him, "Uzziah, it is not your job to burn incense to the Lord. It is not good for you to do this. The priests and Aaron's descendants* are the ones that burn incense to the Lord. These priests were trained for holy service to burn incense. Go out of the Most Holy Place.* You have not been faithful. The Lord God will not honor you for this!"

¹⁹But Uzziah was angry. He had a bowl in his hand for burning incense.* While Uzziah was very angry at the priests, leprosy* came up on his forehead. This happened in front of the priests in the Lord's temple* by the altar* for burning incense. ²⁰Azariah the leading priest and all the priests looked at Uzziah. They could see the leprosy on his forehead. The priests quickly forced Uzziah out from the temple. Uzziah himself hurried out because the Lord had punished him. ²¹Uzziah the king was a leper.* He could not enter the Lord's temple. Uzziah's son Jotham controlled the king's house and became governor for the people.

²²The other things that Uzziah did, from beginning to the end, were written by the prophet Isaiah son of Amoz. ²³Uzziah died and was buried near his ancestors.* Uzziah was buried in the field near the king's burial places. Why? Because the people said, "Uzziah has leprosy.*" And Jotham became the new king in Uzziah's place. Jotham was Uzziah's son.

Jotham King of Judah

27 Jotham was 25 years old when he became king. He ruled 16 years in Jerusalem. His mother's name was Jerusha. Jerusha was Zadok's daughter. ²Jotham did the things the Lord wanted him to do. He obeyed God just like his father Uzziah had done. But Jotham did not enter the Lord's temple* to burn incense* like his father did. But the people continued doing wrong. ³Jotham built again the Upper Gate of the Lord's temple. He did much building on the wall at the place named Ophel. ⁴Jotham also built towns in the hill country of Judah. Jotham built fortresses* and towers in the forests. ⁵Jotham also fought against the king of the Ammonite people and his army and defeated them. So each year for three

---

tribute Money paid to a more powerful king by a weaker king to have peace.

slings Something to throw rocks in, like David used against Goliath.

temple The special building in Jerusalem for Jewish worship.

incense Special dried tree sap. Burned to make a sweet-smelling smoke, it was offered as a gift to God.

altar(s) A stone table or a stand for offering sacrifices.

descendants A person's children and their future families.

Most Holy Place The inside room where the Box of the Lord's Agreement sat. It is also named the "Holy of Holies." It is the spiritual place where God lives and is worshiped.

leprosy A very bad skin disease. The Hebrew word means any of several diseases that cause rashes or sores on the skin.

leper A person who was sick with leprosy.

ancestors Literally, "fathers," meaning a person's parents, grandparents, and all the people they are descended from.

fortress(es) A building or city with tall, strong walls for protection.

years the Ammonites gave Jotham 3 3/4 tons* of silver, 62,000 bushels* of wheat, and 62,000 bushels* of barley. ⁶Jotham became powerful because he faithfully obeyed the Lord his God. ⁷The other things Jotham did and all his wars are written in the book *The History of the Kings of Israel and Judah.* ⁸Jotham was 25 years old when he became king. He ruled 16 years in Jerusalem. ⁹Then Jotham died and was buried with his ancestors.* The people buried him in David's City.* Ahaz became the king in Jotham's place. Ahaz was Jotham's son.

Ahaz King of Judah

28 Ahaz was 20 years old when he became king. He ruled 16 years in Jerusalem. Ahaz didn't live right like David his ancestor.* Ahaz didn't do the things the Lord wanted him to do. ²Ahaz followed the bad example of the kings of Israel. He used molds to make idols to worship the Baal gods. ³Ahaz burned incense* in the Valley of Ben Hinnom.* He sacrificed* his own sons by burning them in the fire. He did the same terrible sins that the peoples living in that land did. The Lord had forced those people out when the people of Israel entered that land. ⁴Ahaz offered sacrifices* and burned incense in the high places,* on the hills, and under every green tree.

⁵⁻⁶Ahaz sinned, so the Lord his God let the king of Aram defeat Ahaz. The king of Aram and his army defeated Ahaz and made many people of Judah prisoners. The king of Aram took those prisoners to the city of Damascus. The Lord also let Pekah the king of Israel defeat Ahaz. Pekah's father's name was Remaliah. Pekah and his army killed 120,000 brave soldiers from Judah in one day. Pekah defeated those men from Judah because they stopped obeying the Lord God their ancestors obeyed. ⁷Zicri was a brave soldier from Ephraim.* Zicri killed Maaseiah, King Ahaz's son, Azrikam the officer in charge of the king's house, and Elkanah. Elkanah was second in command to the king.

⁸The Israelite army captured 200,000 of their own relatives living in Judah. They took women, children, and many valuable things from Judah. The Israelites brought those captives and those things to the city of Samaria. ⁹But one of the Lord's prophets was there. This prophet was named Oded. Oded met the Israelite army that came back to Samaria. Oded said to the Israelite army, "The Lord God your ancestors* obeyed let you defeat the people of Judah because he was angry at them. You killed and punished the people of Judah in a very mean way. Now God is angry at you. ¹⁰You plan to keep the people of Judah and Jerusalem as slaves. You also have sinned against the Lord your God. ¹¹Now listen to me. Send back your brothers and sisters that you captured. Do this because the Lord's terrible anger is against you."

¹²Then some of the leaders in Ephraim* saw the Israelite soldiers coming home from war. Those leaders met the Israelite soldiers and warned them. Those leaders were Azariah son of Jehohanan, Berekiah son of Meshillemoth, Jehizkiah son of Shallum, and Amasa son of Hadlai. ¹³Those leaders said to the Israelite soldiers, "Don't bring the prisoners from Judah here. If you do that, it will make us sin worse against the Lord. That will make our sin and guilt worse and the Lord will be very angry against Israel!" ¹⁴So the soldiers gave the prisoners and valuable things to those leaders and to the people of Israel. ¹⁵The leaders named before (Azariah, Berekiah, Jehizkiah, and Amasa) stood up and helped the prisoners. These four men got the clothes that the Israelite army took and gave them to those people that were naked. Those leaders also gave shoes to those people. They gave the prisoners from Judah something to eat and drink. They rubbed oil on those people.* Then those leaders from Ephraim put the weak prisoners on

---

3 3/4 tons Or, "3,400kg." Literally, "100 talents (kikars)."
62,000 bushels Or, "2,200,000 l." Literally, "10,000 cors."
ancestors Literally, "fathers," meaning a person's parents, grandparents, and all the people they are descended from.
David's City Another name for Jerusalem.
ancestor Literally, "father," meaning a person that people are descended from.
incense Special dried tree sap. Burned to make a sweet-smelling smoke, it was offered as a gift to God.
Valley of Ben Hinnom The Valley of Hinnom is south and west of Jerusalem. Many babies and young children were sacrificed to false gods in this valley.
sacrifice(d) To kill a special animal and offer it on an altar as a gift to God.
high places Places for worshiping God or false gods. These places were often on the hills and mountains.

Ephraim Ephraim was Joseph's youngest son. Ephraim's family group joined Israel. Ephraim was another name for Israel.
rubbed oil on those people They did this as a medicine for the people.

donkeys and took them back home to their families in Jericho. Jericho was named the city of palm trees. Then those four leaders went back home to Samaria.

¹⁶⁻¹⁷At that same time, the people from Edom came again and defeated the people of Judah. The Edomites captured people and took them away as prisoners. So King Ahaz asked the king of Assyria to help him. ¹⁸The Philistine people also attacked the towns in the hills and in south Judah. The Philistines captured the towns of Beth Shemesh, Aijalon, Gederoth, Soco, Timnah, and Gimzo. They also captured the villages near those towns. Then the Philistines lived in those towns. ¹⁹The Lord gave troubles to Judah because King Ahaz of Judah encouraged the people of Judah to sin. He was very unfaithful to the Lord. ²⁰Tiglath Pileser king of Assyria came and gave Ahaz trouble instead of helping him. ²¹Ahaz took some valuable things from the Lord's temple* and from the king's house and from the prince's house. Ahaz gave those things to the king of Assyria. But that didn't help Ahaz.

²²In Ahaz's troubles, he sinned worse and became more unfaithful to the Lord. ²³He offered sacrifices* to the gods the people of Damascus worshiped. The people of Damascus had defeated Ahaz. So he thought to himself, "The gods the people of Aram worship helped them. So if I offer sacrifices to those gods, maybe they will help me also." Ahaz worshiped those gods. In this way he sinned, and he made the people of Israel sin.

²⁴Ahaz gathered the things from God's temple* and broke them to pieces. Then he closed the doors of the Lord's temple. He made altars* and put them on every street corner in Jerusalem. ²⁵In every town in Judah Ahaz made high places* for burning incense* to worship other gods. Ahaz made the Lord God that his ancestors* obeyed very angry.

²⁶The other things that Ahaz did, from the beginning to the end, are written in the book *The History of the Kings of Judah and Israel*. ²⁷Ahaz died and was buried with his ancestors.* The people buried Ahaz in the city of Jerusalem. But they didn't bury Ahaz in the same burial place where the kings of Israel were buried. Hezekiah became the new king in Ahaz's place. Hezekiah was Ahaz's son.

Hezekiah King of Judah

29 Hezekiah became king when he was 25 years old. He ruled 29 years in Jerusalem. His mother's name was Abijah. Abijah was Zechariah's daughter. ²Hezekiah did the things the Lord wanted him to do. He did what was right just like David his ancestor* had done.

³Hezekiah fixed the doors of the Lord's temple* and made them strong. Hezekiah opened the temple again. He did this in the first month of the first year after he became king. ⁴⁻⁵Hezekiah got the priests and Levites together in one assembly. He had a meeting with them in the open yard on the east side of the temple. Hezekiah said to them, "Listen to me, Levites! Make yourselves ready for holy service. Make the temple of the Lord God ready for holy service. He is the God your ancestors obeyed. Take away the things from the temple that do not belong in there. Those things make the temple not pure. ⁶Our ancestors left the Lord and turned their faces away from the Lord's house.* ⁷They shut the doors of the porch of the temple and let the fire go out in the lamps. They stopped burning incense* and offering burnt offerings* in the Holy Place* to the God of Israel. ⁸So, the Lord became very angry at the people of Judah and Jerusalem. The Lord punished them. Other peoples became afraid and were shocked when they saw what the Lord did to the people of Judah and Jerusalem. Those other people shook their heads with hate and shame for the people of Judah. You know these things are true. You can see with your own eyes. ⁹And that is why our ancestors were killed in battle. Our sons and daughters and wives were made prisoners. ¹⁰So now I, Hezekiah, have decided to make an agreement with the Lord God of Israel. Then he

---

temple The special building in Jerusalem for Jewish worship.

sacrifice(s) A gift to God. Usually, it was a special animal that was killed and burned on an altar.

altar(s) A stone table used for burning sacrifices offered as gifts to God.

high places Places of worship.

incense Special dried tree sap. Burned to make a sweet-smelling smoke, it was offered as a gift to God.

ancestors Literally, "fathers," meaning a person's parents, grandparents, and all the people they are descended from.

ancestor Literally, "father," meaning a person that people are descended from.

Lord's house Another name for the temple in Jerusalem.

burnt offering(s) Gifts to God. Usually these were animals that were killed and completely burned on the altar.

Holy Place The room in the Holy Tent and in the temple that was used by the priests to do their daily service to God.

will not be angry at us any more. ¹¹So my sons,* don't be lazy or waste any more time. The Lord chose you to serve him. ⌊He chose you⌋ to serve him ⌊in the temple⌋ and to burn incense."

¹²⁻¹⁴This is a list of the Levites that were there that started to work: From the Kohath family there was Mahath son of Amasai and Joel son of Azariah. From the Merari family there was Kish son of Abdi and Azariah son of Jehallelel. From the Gershon family there was Joah son of Zimmah and Eden son of Joab. From Elizaphan's descendants* there was Shimri and Jeiel. From Asaph's descendants there was Zechariah and Mattaniah. From Heman's descendants there was Jehiel and Shimei. From Jeduthun's descendants there was Shemaiah and Uzziel. ¹⁵Then these Levites gathered their brothers together and make themselves ready for holy service in the temple.* They obeyed the king's command that came from the Lord. They went into the Lord's temple to clean it. ¹⁶The priests went into the inside part of the Lord's temple to clean it. They took out all the unclean* things they found in the Lord's temple. They brought the unclean things to the yard of the Lord's temple. Then the Levites took the unclean things out to the Kidron Valley. ¹⁷On the first day of the first month, the Levites began to make themselves ready for holy service. On the eighth day of the month, the Levites came to the porch of the Lord's temple. For eight more days they cleaned the Lord's temple to make it ready for holy use. They finished on the 16th day of the first month.

¹⁸Then they went to King Hezekiah. They said to him, "King Hezekiah, we cleaned all the Lord's temple* and the altar* for burning offerings and all the things in the temple. We cleaned the table for the rows of bread with all the things used for that table. ¹⁹During the time that Ahaz was king, he rebelled against God. He threw away many of the things that were in the temple. But we fixed all of those things and made them ready for their special use. They are now in front of the Lord's altar."

²⁰King Hezekiah gathered the city officials and went up to the temple* of the Lord early the next morning. ²¹They brought seven bulls, seven rams, seven lambs, and seven young male goats. These animals were for a sin offering for the kingdom of Judah, for the Holy Place* to make it clean, and for the people of Judah. King Hezekiah commanded the priests that were descendants* of Aaron to offer those animals on the Lord's altar.* ²²So the priests killed the bulls and kept the blood. Then they sprinkled the bulls' blood on the altar. Then the priests killed the rams and sprinkled the rams' blood on the altar. Then the priests killed the lambs and sprinkled the lambs' blood on the altar. ²³⁻²⁴Then the priests brought the male goats in front of the king and the people assembled together. The goats were the sin offering. The priests put their hands on the goats and killed the goats. The priests made a sin offering with the goats' blood on the altar. They did this so God would forgive the sins of the people of Israel. The king said that the burnt offering* and the sin offering should be made for all the people of Israel.

²⁵King Hezekiah put the Levites in the Lord's temple* with cymbals,* harps, and lyres* the way David, Gad the king's seer,* and Nathan the prophet had commanded. This command came from the Lord through his prophets. ²⁶So the Levites stood ready with David's instruments of music, and the priests stood ready with their trumpets. ²⁷Then Hezekiah gave the order to sacrifice* the burnt offering* on the altar.* When the burnt offering began, singing to the Lord began also. The trumpets were blown and the instruments of David king of Israel played. ²⁸All the assembly bowed down, the musicians sang, and the trumpet players blew their trumpets until the burnt offering was finished.

²⁹After the sacrifices* were finished, King Hezekiah and all the people with him bowed down and worshiped. ³⁰King Hezekiah and his officials ordered the Levites to give praise to the Lord. They sang songs that David and Asaph the seer* had written. They praised God and became

---

my sons Here Hezekiah is speaking to the priests like a father to his sons. They are not really his children.
descendants A person's children and their future families.
temple The special building in Jerusalem for Jewish worship.
unclean Or, "unacceptable." Not pure or not able to be used in worshiping God. See Lev. 11-15 for the Old Testament rules about clean and unclean things.
altar(s) A stone table or a stand for offering sacrifices.

Holy Place The room in the Holy Tent and in the temple that was used by the priests to do their daily service to God.
burnt offering(s) Gifts to God. Usually these were animals that were killed and completely burned on the altar.
cymbals A pair of metal platters that are hit against each other to make a loud sound.
lyre(s) An instrument with several strings, like a harp.
seer This is another name for a prophet. See 1 Sam. 9:9-11.
sacrifice(s) A gift to God. Usually, it was a special animal that was killed and burned on an altar.

happy. They all bowed and worshiped God. ³¹Hezekiah said, "Now you people of Judah have given yourselves to the Lord. Come near and bring sacrifices and thank offerings to the Lord's temple.*" Then the people brought sacrifices and thank offerings. Any person who wanted to, also brought burnt offerings. ³²This is how many burnt offerings the assembly brought to the temple: 70 bulls, 100 rams, and 200 lambs. All these animals were sacrificed as burnt offerings to the Lord. ³³The holy offerings for the Lord were 600 bulls and 3,000 sheep and goats. ³⁴But there were not enough priests to skin and cut up all the animals for the burnt offerings. So their relatives, the Levites, helped them until the work was finished and until other priests could make themselves ready for holy service. The Levites were more serious about making themselves ready to serve the Lord. They were more serious than the priests. ³⁵There were many burnt offerings, and the fat of fellowship offerings, and drink offerings. So the service in the Lord's temple began again. ³⁶Hezekiah and the people were very happy about the things God prepared for his people. And they were happy he did it so quickly!

Hezekiah Celebrates the Passover

30 King Hezekiah sent messages to all the people of Israel and Judah. He wrote letters to the people of Ephraim and Manasseh* also. Hezekiah invited all those people to come to the Lord's temple* in Jerusalem so they all could celebrate the Passover* for the Lord God of Israel. ²King Hezekiah agreed with all his officials and all the assembly in Jerusalem to have the Passover in the second month. ³They could not celebrate the Passover Festival at the regular time. Why? Because not enough priests had made themselves ready for holy service. And another reason is the people had not gathered in Jerusalem. ⁴The agreement satisfied King Hezekiah and all the assembly. ⁵So they made an announcement everywhere in Israel, from the town of Beersheba all the way to the town of Dan. They told the people to come to Jerusalem to celebrate the Passover for the Lord God of Israel. A large group of the people of Israel had not celebrated the Passover since a long time ago the way the law of Moses said to celebrate it. ⁶So the messengers took the king's letters all through Israel and Judah. This is what those letters said:

Children of Israel, turn back to the Lord God that Abraham, Isaac, and Israel (Jacob) obeyed. Then God will come back to you people that are still alive and have escaped from the kings of Assyria. ⁷Don't be like your fathers or your brothers. The Lord was their God, but they turned against him. So the Lord made people hate them and speak evil about them. You can see with your own eyes that this is true. ⁸Don't be stubborn like your ancestors* were. But obey the Lord with a willing heart. Come to the Most Holy Place.* The Lord has made the Most Holy Place to be holy forever. Serve the Lord your God. Then the Lord's fearful anger will turn away from you. ⁹If you come back and obey the Lord, then your relatives and your children will find mercy from the people that captured them. And your relatives and your children will come back to this land. The Lord your God is kind and merciful. He will not turn away from you if you come back to him.

¹⁰The messengers went to every town in the area of Ephraim and Manasseh. They went all the way to the area of Zebulun. But the people laughed at the messengers and made fun of them. ¹¹But, some men from the areas of Asher, Manasseh, and Zebulun humbled themselves and went to Jerusalem. ¹²Also, in Judah God's power united the people so that they would obey the king and his officials. In this way they obeyed the word of the Lord.

¹³Many people came together at Jerusalem to celebrate the Festival of Unleavened Bread* in the second month. It was a very large crowd. ¹⁴Those people took away the altars in Jerusalem that were for false gods. They also took away all the incense

---

ancestors Literally, "fathers," meaning a person's parents, grandparents, and all the people they are descended from.

Most Holy Place The inside room where the Box of the Lord's Agreement sat. It was also named the "Holy of Holies." It was the spiritual place where God lived and was worshiped.

Festival of Unleavened Bread Passover and the week following it. The people ate unleavened bread (bread made without yeast) to help them remember the time that God led the Israelites out of Egypt. The poeple did not have time to wait for the bread to rise because they were in such a hurry.

---

temple The special building in Jerusalem for Jewish worship.
Ephraim and Manasseh Joseph's sons. Since these were the largest family groups, Ephraim and Manasseh sometimes means the whole northern kingdom of Israel.
Passover An important holiday for Jews. They eat a special meal on this day every year to remember that God freed them from slavery in Egypt in the time of Moses.

altars that were for false gods. They threw those altars into the Kidron Valley. ¹⁵Then they killed the Passover lamb on the 14th day of the second month. The priests and the Levites felt ashamed. They made themselves ready for holy service. The priests and the Levites brought burnt offerings* into the Lord's temple.* ¹⁶They took their regular places in the temple the way the law of Moses, the man of God,* said. The Levites gave the blood to the priests. Then the priests sprinkled the blood on the altar.* ¹⁷There were many people in the group that had not made themselves ready for holy service, so they were not permitted to kill the Passover lambs. That is why the Levites were responsible for killing the Passover lambs for every person who was not clean. The Levites made each lamb holy for the Lord.

¹⁸⁻¹⁹Many people from Ephraim, Manasseh, Issachar, and Zebulun had not prepared themselves in the right way for the Passover* Festival. They did not celebrate the Passover the right way, like the law of Moses says. But Hezekiah prayed for those people. So Hezekiah said this prayer, "Lord God, you are good. These people truly wanted to worship you in the right way, but they did not make themselves clean like the law says. Please forgive those people. You are the God that our ancestors* obeyed. Forgive, even if someone did not make himself clean like the rules of the Most Holy Place* say." ²⁰The Lord listened to King Hezekiah's prayer. The Lord forgave the people. ²¹The children of Israel at Jerusalem celebrated the Festival of Unleavened Bread for seven days. They were very happy. The Levites and the priests gave praise to the Lord every day with all their strength. ²²King Hezekiah encouraged all the Levites that understood very well how to do the service of the Lord. The people celebrated the Festival for seven days and offered fellowship offerings. They gave thanks and praise to the Lord God of their ancestors.*

²³All the people agreed to stay seven more days. They were joyful as they celebrated the Passover* for seven more days. ²⁴Hezekiah king of Judah gave 1,000 bulls and 7,000 sheep to the assembly to kill and eat. The leaders gave 1,000 bulls and 10,000 sheep to the assembly. Many priests prepared themselves for holy service. ²⁵All the assembly of Judah, the priests, the Levites, all the assembly that came from Israel, and the travelers that came from Israel and moved to Judah—all those people were very happy. ²⁶So there was much joy in Jerusalem. There was not anything like this celebration since the time of Solomon son of David king of Israel. ²⁷The priests and the Levites stood up and asked the Lord to bless the people. God heard them. Their prayer came up to the Lord's holy home in heaven.

King Hezekiah Makes Improvements

31 The Passover* celebration was finished. The people of Israel that were in Jerusalem for Passover went out to the towns of Judah. Then they smashed the stone idols that were in those towns. Those stone idols were used to worship false gods. Those people also cut down the Asherah Poles.* And they destroyed the high places* and the altars* all through the areas of Judah and Benjamin. The people did the same things in the area of Ephraim and Manasseh. The people did these things until they destroyed all the things used for worshiping the false gods. Then all the Israelites went back home to their own towns.

²The priests and Levites had been divided into groups and each group had its own special job to do. So King Hezekiah told these groups to begin doing their jobs again. So the priests and Levites again had the job of offering the burnt offerings* and the fellowship offerings. And they had the job of serving in the temple and singing and praising God by the doors to the Lord's house.* ³Hezekiah gave some of his own animals to be offered as the burnt offerings. These animals were used for the daily burnt offerings that were given each morning and each evening. These animals were offered on the Sabbath days,* during the New

burnt offering(s) Gifts to God. Usually these were animals that were killed and completely burned on the altar.
temple The special building in Jerusalem for Jewish worship.
man of God Another name for a prophet.
altar(s) A stone table or a stand for offering sacrifices.
Passover An important holiday for Jews. They eat a special meal on this day every year to remember that God freed them from slavery in Egypt in the time of Moses.
ancestors Literally, "fathers," meaning a person's parents, grandparents, and all the people they are descended from.
Most Holy Place The inside room where the Box of the Lord's Agreement sat. It is also named the "Holy of Holies." It is the spiritual place where God lives and is worshiped.

Asherah Poles Poles used to honor the goddess Asherah. People thought she could help them have many children.
high places Places for worshiping God or false gods. These places were often on the hills and mountains.
Lord's house Or "Lord's Camp," that is, the courtyard of the temple in Jerusalem.
Sabbath days Special days of rest and worship for the Jews. Usually this means Saturday.

Moon* Festivals and the other Special Meetings.* This was done as it is written in the Lord's law. ⁴The people were supposed to give a part of their crops and things to the priests and Levites. So Hezekiah commanded the people living in Jerusalem to give them their share. In that way, the priests and Levites could spend all of their time doing what the Law told them to do. ⁵People all around the country heard about this command. So the people of Israel gave the first part of their harvest of grain, grapes, oil, honey, and all the things they grew in their fields. They brought one tenth of all these many things. ⁶The men of Israel and Judah living in the towns of Judah also brought one tenth of their cattle and sheep. They also brought one tenth of the things that were put in a special place that was only for the Lord. All these things they brought to the Lord their God. They put all these things in piles.

⁷The people began to bring those things in the third month *(May/June)* and they finished bringing the collection in the seventh month *(September/October)* ⁸When Hezekiah and the leaders came, they saw the piles of things that were collected. They praised the Lord and his people, the people of Israel.

⁹Then Hezekiah asked the priests and the Levites about the piles of things. ¹⁰Azariah the high priest from Zadok's family said to Hezekiah, "From the time that the people started bringing the offerings into the Lord's house, we have had plenty to eat. We have eaten until we are full and there is still plenty left over! The Lord has really blessed his people. That is why we have so much left over."

¹¹Then Hezekiah commanded the priests to make storerooms ready in the Lord's temple.* So this was done. ¹²Then the priests brought the offerings, tithes,* and other things that were to be given only to the Lord. All those things collected were put in the storerooms in the temple. Conaniah the Levite was in charge of all those things that were collected. Shimei was second in charge of those things. Shimei was Conaniah's brother. ¹³Conaniah and his brother Shimei were supervisors of these men: Jehiel, Azaziah, Nahath, Asahel, Jerimoth, Jozabad, Eliel, Ismakiah, Mahath, and Benaiah. Hezekiah the king and Azariah the official in charge of God's temple chose those men. ¹⁴Kore was in charge of the offerings that the people freely gave to God. He was responsible for giving out the collections that were given to the Lord. And he was responsible for giving out the gifts that were made holy for the Lord. Kore was the gatekeeper at the East Gate. His father's name was Imnah the Levite. ¹⁵Eden, Miniamin, Jeshua, Shemaiah, Amariah, and Shecaniah helped Kore. Those men served faithfully in the towns where the priests were living. They gave the collection of things to their relatives in each group of priests. They gave the same things to the more important people and to the less important. ¹⁶These men also gave the collection of things to the males three years old and older that had their names in the Levite family histories. All these males were to enter the Lord's temple for daily service to do the things they were responsible to do. Each group of Levites had their own responsibility. ¹⁷The priests were given their part of the collection. This was done by families, in the way they were listed in the family histories. The Levites 20 years old and older were given their part of the collection. This was done by their responsibilities and by their groups. ¹⁸The Levites' babies, wives, sons and daughters also got part of the collection. This was done for all the Levites who were listed in the family histories. This was because the Levites were faithful to always keep themselves holy and ready for service. ¹⁹Some of Aaron's descendants,* the priests, had some farm fields near the towns where the Levites were living. And some of Aaron's descendants were also living in the towns. Men were chosen by name in each of those towns to give part of the collection to these descendants of Aaron. Males and all those named in the family histories of the Levites got part of the collection.

²⁰So King Hezekiah did those good things in all Judah. He did what was good and right and faithful before the Lord his God. ²¹He had success in every work he began—the service of God's temple* and in obeying the law and commands, and in following his God. Hezekiah did all these things with all his heart.

New Moon The first day of the Hebrew month. There were special meetings on these days when the people shared fellowship offerings as part of their worship to God.
Special Meetings Holidays such as Passover. Many of these holidays were at the time of the full moon.
temple The special building in Jerusalem for Jewish worship.
tithes One tenth of a person's crops or animals.

descendants A person's children and their future families.

The King of Assyria Troubles Hezekiah

32 After all these things that Hezekiah had faithfully done happened, Sennacherib king of Assyria came to attack the country of Judah. Sennacherib and his army camped outside the fortresses.* He did this so he could make plans to defeat those towns. Sennacherib wanted to win those towns for himself. ²Hezekiah knew that Sennacherib came to Jerusalem to attack it. ³Then Hezekiah talked to his officials and army officers. They all agreed to stop the waters of the water springs outside the city. Those officials and army officers helped Hezekiah. ⁴Many people came together and stopped all the springs and the stream that flowed through the middle of the country. They said, "The king of Assyria will not find much water when he comes here!" ⁵Hezekiah made Jerusalem stronger. This is how he did it: He built again all the parts of the wall that were broken down. He built towers on the wall. He also built another wall outside the first wall. He built again the strong places on the east side of the old part of Jerusalem. He made many weapons and shields. ⁶⁻⁷Hezekiah chose officers of war to be in charge of the people. He met with these officers at the open place near the city gate. Hezekiah talked to those officers and encouraged them. He said, "Be strong and brave. Don't be afraid or worry about the king of Assyria or the large army with him. There is a greater power with us than the king of Assyria has with him! ⁸The king of Assyria only has men. But we have the Lord our God with us! Our God will help us. He will fight our battles!" So Hezekiah king of Judah encouraged the people and made them feel stronger.

⁹Sennacherib king of Assyria and all his army were camped near the town of Lachish so they could defeat it. Then Sennacherib sent his servants to Hezekiah king of Judah and to all the people of Judah in Jerusalem. Sennacherib's servants had a message for Hezekiah and all the people in Jerusalem. ¹⁰They said, "Sennacherib king of Assyria says this: 'What do you trust in that makes you stay under attack in Jerusalem? ¹¹Hezekiah is fooling you. You are being tricked into staying in Jerusalem so you will die from hunger and thirst. Hezekiah says to you, "The Lord our God will save us from the king of Assyria." ¹²Hezekiah himself took away the Lord's high places* and altars.* He told you people of Judah and Jerusalem that you must worship and burn incense* on only one altar. ¹³Of course, you know what my ancestors* and I have done to all the peoples in other countries. The gods of the other countries could not save their people. Those gods could not stop me from destroying their people. ¹⁴My ancestors destroyed those countries. There is no god that can stop me from destroying his people. So you think your god can save you from me? ¹⁵Do not let Hezekiah fool you or trick you. Don't believe him because no god of any nation or kingdom has ever been able to keep his people safe from me or my ancestors. So don't think your god can stop me from destroying you.'"

¹⁶The king of Assyria's servants said worse things against the Lord God and against Hezekiah, God's servant. ¹⁷The king of Assyria also wrote letters that insulted the Lord God of Israel. This is what the king of Assyria said in those letters: "The gods of the other nations could not stop me from destroying their people. In the same way Hezekiah's god won't be able to stop me from destroying his people." ¹⁸Then the king of Assyria's servants shouted loudly to the people of Jerusalem that were on the city wall. Those servants used the Hebrew language when they shouted to the people on the wall. Those servants of the king of Assyria did this to make the people of Jerusalem afraid. They said those things so they could capture the city of Jerusalem. ¹⁹Those servants said bad things against the gods people of the world worshiped. Those gods are only things people made with their hands. In the same way, those servants said the same bad things against the God of Jerusalem.

²⁰Hezekiah the king and the prophet Isaiah son of Amoz prayed about this problem. They prayed very loudly to heaven. ²¹Then the Lord sent an angel to the king of Assyria's camp. That angel killed all the soldiers and the leaders and the officers in the Assyrian army. So the king of Assyria went back home to his own country, and his people were ashamed of him. He went into the temple of his god and some of his own sons killed

---

fortress(es) A building or city with tall, strong walls for protection.

high places Places for worshiping God or false gods. These places were often on the hills and mountains.

altar(s) A stone table used for burning sacrifices offered as gifts to God.

incense Special dried tree sap. Burned to make a sweet-smelling smoke, it was offered as a gift to God.

ancestors Literally, "fathers," meaning a person's parents, grandparents, and all the people they are descended from.

him there with a sword. ²²So the Lord saved Hezekiah and the people in Jerusalem from Sennacherib the king of Assyria and from all other people. The Lord cared for Hezekiah and the people of Jerusalem. ²³Many people brought gifts for the Lord to Jerusalem. They brought valuable things to Hezekiah king of Judah. From that time on, all the nations respected Hezekiah.

²⁴It was in those days that Hezekiah became very sick and near death. He prayed to the Lord. The Lord spoke to Hezekiah and gave him a sign.* ²⁵But Hezekiah's heart was proud, so he did not give God thanks for God's kindness. This is why God was angry at Hezekiah and at the people of Judah and Jerusalem. ²⁶But Hezekiah and those people living in Jerusalem changed their hearts and lives. They became humble and stopped being proud. So the Lord's anger didn't come on them while Hezekiah was alive.

²⁷Hezekiah had very much riches and honor. He made places to keep silver, gold, valuable jewels, spices, shields, and all kinds of things. ²⁸Hezekiah had storage buildings for the grain, new wine, and oil that people sent to him. He had stalls for all the cattle and stalls for the sheep. ²⁹Hezekiah also built many towns, and he got many flocks of sheep and cattle. God gave Hezekiah very much wealth. ³⁰It was Hezekiah that stopped up the upper source of the waters of the Gihon spring in Jerusalem and made those waters flow straight down on the west side of David's city. And Hezekiah was successful in everything he did.

³¹One time the leaders of Babylon sent messengers to Hezekiah. Those messengers asked about a strange sign that had happened in the nations.* When they came God left Hezekiah alone to test him and to know everything that was in Hezekiah's heart.*

³²The others things that Hezekiah did and how he loved the Lord are written in the book *The Vision of the Isaiah Son of Amoz* and in the book *The History of the Kings of Judah and Israel*. ³³Hezekiah died and was buried with his ancestors.* The people buried Hezekiah on the hill where the graves of David's ancestors are. All the people of Judah and those living in Jerusalem gave honor to Hezekiah when he died. Manasseh became the new king in Hezekiah's place. Manasseh was Hezekiah's son.

Manasseh King of Judah

33 Manasseh was twelve years old when he became king of Judah. He was king for 55 years in Jerusalem. ²Manasseh did the things that the Lord said were wrong. He followed the terrible and sinful ways of the nations that the Lord had forced out of the land before the people of Israel. ³Manasseh built again the high places* that Manasseh his father had broken down. Manasseh built altars for the Baal gods and made Asherah Poles.* He bowed down to the constellations* and worshiped those groups of stars. ⁴Manasseh built altars for false gods in the Lord's temple.* The Lord said about the temple, "My name will be in Jerusalem forever." ⁵Manasseh built altars for all the groups of stars in the two yards of the Lord's temple. ⁶Manasseh also burned his own children for a sacrifice* in the Valley of Ben Hinnom.* Manasseh also used magic by doing soothsaying, divination, and sorcery.* He talked with mediums* and wizards.* Manasseh did many things that the Lord said was wrong, and this made the Lord angry. ⁷Manasseh also made a statue of an idol and put it in God's temple—the very same temple that God had talked about to David and his son Solomon. God had said, "I will put my name in this house and in Jerusalem—the city that I chose from ₍all the cities in₎ all the family groups—₍and my name will be there₎ forever! ⁸I will not continue to keep the Israelites off the land that I chose to give to

---

The Lord spoke ... sign See Isaiah 38:1-8 for the story about Hezekiah and how the Lord gave Hezekiah 15 more years to live.

a strange sign ... nations See Isaiah 38:1-8.

in Hezekiah's heart See 2 Kings 20:12-19.

ancestors Literally, "fathers," meaning a person's parents, grandparents, and all the people they are descended from.

high places Places for worshiping God or false gods. These places were often on the hills and mountains.

Asherah Poles Poles used to honor the goddess Asherah. People thought she could help them have many children.

constellations Groups of stars. These are probably the twelve "signs of the Zodiac." Some people thought the stars, not God, control their life.

temple The special building in Jerusalem for Jewish worship.

sacrifice(s) A gift to God. Usually, it was a special animal that was killed and burned on an altar.

Valley of Ben Hinnom Later called "Gehenna," this valley was west and south of Jerusalem. Many babies and young children were sacrificed to false gods in this valley.

soothsaying, divination, sorcery Different ways people try to do magic or tell what will happen in the future.

medium(s) A person who tries to communicate with the spirits of dead people.

wizard(s) A person who tries to use evil spirits to do magic.

their ancestors.* But they must obey all the things I commanded them. The people of Israel must obey all the laws, rules, and commands that I gave Moses to give to them."

⁹Manasseh encouraged the people of Judah and the people living in Jerusalem to do wrong. They were worse than the nations that were in the land before the Israelites—and the Lord destroyed those people! ¹⁰The Lord spoke to Manasseh and to his people, but they refused to listen. ¹¹So the Lord brought commanders from the king of Assyria's army to attack Judah. Those commanders captured Manasseh and made him their prisoner. They put hooks in him and brass chains on his hands and took him to the country of Babylon. ¹²When these troubles came to him, Manasseh begged for help from the Lord his God. Manasseh humbled himself before the God of his ancestors.* ¹³Manasseh prayed to God and begged God to help him. The Lord heard Manasseh's begging and felt sorry for him. The Lord let him return to Jerusalem and to his throne. Then Manasseh knew that the Lord was the true God.

¹⁴After that happened, Manasseh built an outer wall for the City of David.* This wall went to the west of Gihon Spring in ⌊Kidron⌋ Valley, to the entrance of the Fish Gate, and around the hill of Ophel.* He made the wall very tall. Then he put officers in all the fortresses* in Judah. ¹⁵Manasseh took away the strange idol gods. He took the idol out from the Lord's temple. He took away all the altars he had built on the temple hill, and in Jerusalem. Manasseh threw all those altars out of the city of Jerusalem. ¹⁶Then he set up the Lord's altar and offered fellowship offerings and thank offerings on it. Manasseh gave a command for all the people of Judah to serve the Lord God of Israel. ¹⁷The people continued to offer sacrifices* at the high places,* but their sacrifices were only to the Lord their God.

¹⁸The other things Manasseh did, and his prayer to his God, and the words of the seers* that spoke to him in the name of the Lord God of Israel, are all written in the book *The Official Records of the Kings of Israel*. ¹⁹Manasseh's prayer and how God listened and felt sorry for him is written in *The Book of the Seers*. Also all of Manasseh's sins and wrongs before he humbled himself, and the places where he built high places* and set up the Asherah Poles* are written in *The Book of the Seers*. ²⁰So Manasseh died and was buried with his ancestors.* The people buried Manasseh in his own king's house. Amon became the new king in Manasseh's place. Amon was Manasseh's son.

Amon King of Judah

²¹Amon was 22 years old when he became king of Judah. He was king for two years in Jerusalem. ²²Amon did evil things before the Lord. He did not do the things the Lord wanted him to do just like Manasseh his father. Amon offered sacrifices* for all the carved idols and statues that Manasseh his father made. Amon worshiped those idols. ²³Amon did not humble himself in front of the Lord like Manasseh his father humbled himself. But Amon sinned more and more. ²⁴Amon's servants made plans against him. They killed Amon in his own house. ²⁵But the people of Judah killed all those servants that planned against King Amon. Then the people chose Josiah to be the new king. Josiah was Amon's son.

Josiah King of Judah

34 Josiah was eight years old when he became king. He was king for 31 years in Jerusalem. ²Josiah did what was right. He did the things the Lord wanted him to do. He did good things like David his ancestor.* Josiah did not turn from doing right things. ³When Josiah was in his eighth year as king, he began to follow the God that David his ancestor followed. Josiah was still young when he began to obey God. When Josiah was in his twelfth year as king he began to destroy the high places*, the Asherah Poles,* and idols that were carved and idols that were made from molds from Judah and Jerusalem. ⁴The people broke down the altars for the Baal gods. They did

---

ancestors Literally, "fathers," meaning a person's parents, grandparents, and all the people they are descended from.
City of David The southeastern and oldest part of the city of Jerusalem.
Ophel The upper part of the City of David, just south of the temple area.
fortress(es) A building or city with tall, strong walls for protection.
sacrifice(s) A gift to God. Usually, it was a special animal that was killed and burned on an altar.
high places Places for worshiping God or false gods. These places were often on the hills and mountains.

seer(s) This is another name for a prophet. See 1 Sam. 9:9-11.
Asherah Poles Poles used to honor the goddess Asherah. People thought she could help them have many children.
ancestor Literally, "father," meaning a person that people are descended from.

this in front of Josiah. Then Josiah cut down the incense* altars that stood high above the people. He broke the idols that were carved and the idols that were made from molds. He beat those idols into powder. Then Josiah sprinkled the powder on the graves of the people that had offered sacrifices* to the Baal gods. ⁵Josiah even burned the bones of the priests that had served the Baal gods on their own altars. This is how Josiah destroyed idols and idol worship from Judah and Jerusalem. ⁶Josiah did the same for the towns in the areas of Manasseh, Ephraim, Simeon, and all the way to Naphtali. He did the same for the ruins near all those towns.* ⁷Josiah broke down the altars and the Asherah Poles. He beat the idols into powder. He cut down all the incense altars used for Baal worship in all the country of Israel. Then Josiah went back to Jerusalem.

⁸When Josiah was in his 18th year as king of Judah he sent Shaphan, Maaseiah, and Joah to build again and fix the temple* of the Lord his God. Shaphan's father's name was Azaliah. Maaseiah was the city leader, and Joah's father's name was Jehoahaz. Joah was the man that wrote about the things that happened. (He was the recorder.) So Josiah commanded the temple to be fixed so he could make Judah and the temple clean. ⁹Those men came to Hilkiah the High Priest. They gave him the money that people gave for God's temple. The Levite doorkeepers had collected this money from the people of Manasseh, Ephraim, and from all the Israelites that were left. They also collected this money from all Judah, Benjamin, and all the people living in Jerusalem. ¹⁰Then the Levites paid the men that supervised the work on the Lord's temple. And the supervisors paid the workers that fixed the Lord's temple. ¹¹They gave the money to carpenters and builders to buy large rocks that were already cut, and to buy wood. The wood was used to build again the buildings and to make beams for the buildings. In the past, the kings of Judah did not take care of the temple buildings. Those buildings had become old and ruined. ¹²⁻¹³The men worked faithfully. Their supervisors were Jahath and Obadiah. Jahath and Obadiah were Levites, and they were descendants* of Merari. Other supervisors were Zechariah and Meshullam. They were descendants of Kohath. The Levites that were skilled in playing instruments of music also supervised the laborers and all the other workers. Some Levites worked as secretaries, officials, and doorkeepers.

The Book of the Law Found

¹⁴The Levites brought out the money that was in the Lord's temple.* At that time Hilkiah the priest found the book of *The Law of the Lord* that was given through Moses. ¹⁵Hilkiah said to Shaphan the secretary, "I found the book of the Law in the Lord's house*!" Hilkiah gave the book to Shaphan. ¹⁶Shaphan brought the book to King Josiah. Shaphan reported to the king, "Your servants are doing everything you told them to do. ¹⁷They got the money that was in the Lord's temple and are paying the supervisors and the workers." ¹⁸Then Shaphan said to King Josiah, "Hilkiah the priest gave a book to me." Then Shaphan read from the book. He was in front of the king as he was reading. ¹⁹When King Josiah heard the words of the law being read, he tore his clothes.* ²⁰Then the king gave a command to Hilkiah, Ahikam son of Shaphan, Abdon son of Micah, Shaphan the secretary, and Asaiah the servant. ²¹The king said, "Go, ask the Lord for me, and for the people that are left in Israel and in Judah. Ask about the words in the book that was found. The Lord is very angry with us because our ancestors* did not obey the Lord's word. They did not do all the things this book says to do!"

²²Hilkiah and the king's servants* went to Huldah the prophetess.* Huldah was Shallum's wife. Shallum was Tokhath's son, Tokhath was Hasrah's son. Hasrah took care of the king's clothes. Huldah lived in the newer part of Jerusalem. Hilkiah and the king's servants told Huldah what had happened. ²³Huldah said to them, "This is what the Lord God of Israel says: Tell King Josiah: ²⁴This is what the Lord says, 'I

---

incense Special dried tree sap. Burned to make a sweet-smelling smoke, it was offered as a gift to God.

sacrifice(s) A gift to God. Usually, it was a special animal that was killed and burned on an altar.

ruins near all those towns The Hebrew is not clear here.

temple The special building in Jerusalem for Jewish worship.

Lord's house Another name for the temple in Jerusalem.

tore ... clothes In Josiah's time, tearing clothes showed that a person was very upset. Josiah was upset because his people had not obeyed the Lord's laws.

ancestors Literally, "fathers," meaning a person's parents, grandparents, and all the people they are descended from.

king's servants "The king's servants" is missing in the Hebrew.

prophetess A woman prophet, someone who spoke messages from God to his people.

will bring trouble to this place and to the people living here! I will bring all the terrible things that are written in the book that was read in front of the king of Judah. ²⁵I will do this because the people left me and burned incense* to other gods. Those people made me angry because of all the bad things they have done. So I will pour out my anger on this place. Like a hot burning fire, my anger will not be put out!'

²⁶"But tell this to King Josiah of Judah. He sent you to ask the Lord: This is what the Lord God of Israel says about the words you heard a little while ago: ²⁷'Josiah, you repented and you humbled yourself, and tore your clothes.* You cried before me. So, because your heart was tender, ²⁸I will take you to be with your ancestors.** You will go to your grave in peace. You won't have to see any of the trouble that I will bring on this place and on the people living here.'" Hilkiah and the king's servants brought back this message to King Josiah.

²⁹Then King Josiah called for all the elders of Judah and Jerusalem to come and meet with him. ³⁰The king went up to the Lord's temple.* All the people from Judah, the people living in Jerusalem, the priests, the Levites, and all the people, both important and not important, were with Josiah. Josiah read to them all the words in the book of the Agreement.* That book was found in the Lord's temple. ³¹Then the king stood up in his place. He made an agreement with the Lord. He agreed to follow the Lord, and to obey the Lord's commands, laws, and rules. Josiah agreed to obey with all his heart and soul. He agreed to obey the words of the Agreement written in this book. ³²Then Josiah made all the people in Jerusalem and Benjamin promise to accept the Agreement. The people of Jerusalem obeyed the Agreement of God, the God their ancestors* obeyed. ³³The people of Israel had idols from many different countries. But Josiah destroyed all of those terrible idols. Josiah made all the people in Israel serve the Lord their God. And as long as Josiah was alive, the people continued to serve the Lord, the God of their ancestors.

Josiah Celebrates Passover

35 King Josiah celebrated the Passover* to the Lord in Jerusalem. The Passover lamb was killed on the 14th day of the first month. ²Josiah chose the priests to do their duties. He encouraged the priests while they were serving in the Lord's temple.* ³Josiah spoke to the Levites who taught the people of Israel and who were made holy for service to the Lord. He said to those Levites: "Put the Holy Box* in the temple that Solomon built. Solomon was David's son. David was king of Israel. Do not carry the Holy Box from place to place on your shoulders again. Now serve the Lord your God. Serve God's people, the people of Israel. ⁴Make yourselves ready for service in the temple by your family groups. Do the jobs that King David and his son King Solomon gave you to do. ⁵Stand in the Holy Place* with a group of Levites. Do this for each different family group of the people so you can help them. ⁶Kill the Passover lambs, make yourselves holy to the Lord. Make the lambs ready for your brothers, the people of Israel. Do all the things the Lord commanded us to do. The Lord gave us all those commands through Moses."

⁷Josiah gave the people of Israel 30,000 sheep and goats to kill for the Passover* sacrifices. He also gave 3,000 cattle to the people. All these animals were from King Josiah's own animals. ⁸Josiah's officials also freely gave animals and things to the people, to the priests, and Levites to use for the Passover. Hilkiah the high priest, Zechariah, and Jehiel were the officials in charge of the temple. They gave the priests 2,600 lambs and goats and 300 bulls for Passover sacrifices. ⁹Also Conaniah with Shemaiah and Nethanel, his brothers, and Hashabiah, Jeiel and Jozabad gave 500 sheep and goats and 500 bulls for Passover

---

incense Special dried tree sap. Burned to make a sweet-smelling smoke, it was offered as a gift to God.

tore ... clothes In Josiah's time, tearing clothes showed that a person was very upset. Josiah was upset because his people had not obeyed the Lord's laws.

ancestors Literally, "fathers," meaning a person's parents, grandparents, and all the people they are descended from.

take you to be with your ancestors This means that Josiah would die.

temple The special building in Jerusalem for Jewish worship.

Agreement Literally, "Proof." The flat stones with the Ten Commandments written on them were proof of the Agreement between God and Israel.

Passover An important holiday for Jews. They eat a special meal on this day every year to remember that God freed them from slavery in Egypt in the time of Moses.

Holy Box The Box of the Agreement. The box containing the stone tablets with the Ten Commandments written on them and the other things that proved God was with the people of Israel during their time in the Sinai Desert. Also called "The Ark of the Covenant."

Holy Place The room in the Holy Tent and in the temple that was used by the priests to do their daily service to God.

sacrifices to the Levites. Those men were leaders of the Levites.

¹⁰When everything was ready for the Passover* service to begin, the priests and Levites went to their places. This is what the king commanded. ¹¹The Passover lambs were killed. Then the Levites skinned the animals and gave the blood to the priests. The priests sprinkled the blood on the altar. ¹²Then they gave the animals to be used for burnt offerings to the different family groups. This was done so the burnt offerings could be offered the way the Law of Moses taught. ¹³The Levites roasted the Passover sacrifices over the fire in the way they were commanded. And they boiled the holy offerings in pots, kettles, and pans. Then they quickly gave the meat to the people. ¹⁴After this was finished, the Levites got meat for themselves and for the priests that were descendants of Aaron. Those priests were kept very busy, working until it got dark. They worked hard burning the burnt offerings and the fat of the sacrifices. ¹⁵The Levite singers from Asaph's family got in the places that King David had chosen for them to stand. They were: Asaph, Heman, and Jeduthun the king's prophet. The gatekeepers at each gate did not have to leave their places because their brother Levites made everything ready for them for the Passover.

¹⁶So everything was done that day for the worship of the Lord as King Josiah commanded. The Passover* was celebrated and the burnt offerings* were offered on the Lord's altar.* ¹⁷The people of Israel that were there celebrated Passover and the Festival of Unleavened Bread* for seven days. ¹⁸Passover hadn't been celebrated like this since the time of Samuel the prophet! None of the kings of Israel had ever celebrated a Passover like this. King Josiah, the priests, the Levites, and the people of Judah and Israel that were there with all the people in Jerusalem celebrated the Passover in a very special way.

¹⁹They celebrated this Passover in Josiah's 18th year as king.

The Death of Josiah

²⁰Josiah did all those good things for the temple. Later, Neco, the king of Egypt, led an army to fight against the town of Carchemish on the Euphrates River. King Josiah went out to fight against Neco. ²¹But Neco sent messengers to Josiah. They said, "King Josiah, this war is not your problem. I didn't come to fight against you. I came to fight my enemies. God told me to hurry. God is on my side, so don't bother me. If you fight against me, God will destroy you!" ²²But Josiah didn't go away. He decided to fight Neco, so he changed his appearance and went to fight the battle. Josiah refused to listen to what Neco said about God's command. Josiah went to fight on the plain of Megiddo. ²³Then King Josiah was shot by arrows while he was in the battle. He told his servants, "Take me away, I am wounded badly!"

²⁴So the servants took Josiah out of his chariot and put him in another chariot he had brought with him to the battle. Then they took Josiah to Jerusalem. King Josiah died in Jerusalem. Josiah was buried in the graves where his ancestors were buried. All the people of Judah and Jerusalem were very sad because Josiah was dead. ²⁵Jeremiah wrote and sang some funeral songs for Josiah. And the men and women singers still sing those sad songs today. It became something the people of Israel always do—they sing a sad song for Josiah. Those songs are written in the book *Funeral Songs.*

²⁶⁻²⁷All the other things that Josiah did while he was king, from beginning to the end of his rule, are written in the book *The History of the Kings of Israel and Judah.* That book tells about his loyalty to the Lord and how he obeyed the Lord's law.

Jehoahaz King of Judah

36 The people of Judah chose Jehoahaz to be the new king in Jerusalem. Jehoahaz was Josiah's son. ²Jehoahaz was 23 years old when he became king of Judah. He was king in Jerusalem for three months. ³Then King Neco from Egypt made Jehoahaz a prisoner. Neco made the people of Judah pay 3 3/4 tons* of silver and 75 pounds* of gold for a fine. ⁴Neco chose Jehoahaz's brother

---

Passover An important holiday for Jews. They eat a special meal on this day every year to remember that God freed them from slavery in Egypt in the time of Moses.
burnt offering(s) Gifts to God. Usually these were animals that were killed and completely burned on the altar.
altar(s) A stone table or a stand for offering sacrifices.
Festival of Unleavened Bread The week after Passover. At Passover, Jewish people throw out all the yeast and eat only bread without yeast for seven days. This helps them remember the time they were leaving Egypt in a hurry and did not have time to make leavened bread.

3 3/4 tons Or, "3,400kg." Literally, "100 talents (kikars)."
75 pounds Or, "34kg." Literally, "1 talent."

to be the new king of Judah and Jerusalem. Jehoahaz's brother's name was Eliakim. Then Neco gave Eliakim a new name. He named him Jehoiakim. But Neco took Jehoahaz to Egypt.

Jehoiakim King of Judah

⁵Jehoiakim was 25 years old when he became the new king of Judah. He was king in Jerusalem for eleven years. Jehoiakim didn't do the things the Lord wanted him to do. He sinned against the Lord his God. ⁶King Nebuchadnezzar from Babylon attacked Judah. He made Jehoiakim a prisoner and put bronze chains on him. Then Nebuchadnezzar took King Jehoiakim to Babylon. ⁷Nebuchadnezzar took some of the things from the Lord's temple. He carried those things to Babylon and put them in his own house. ⁸The other things that Jehoiakim did, the terrible sins he did and everything he was guilty of doing, are written in the book *The History of the Kings of Israel and Judah*. Jehoiachin became the new king in Jehoiakim's place. Jehoiachin was Jehoiakim's son.

Jehoiachin King of Judah

⁹Jehoiachin was 18 years old when he became king of Judah. He was king in Jerusalem for three months and ten days. He didn't do the things the Lord wanted him to do. Jehoiachin sinned against the Lord. ¹⁰In the spring, King Nebuchadnezzar sent some servants to get Jehoiachin. They brought Jehoiachin and some valuable treasures from the Lord's temple* to Babylon. Nebuchadnezzar chose Zedekiah to be the new king of Judah and Jerusalem. Zedekiah was of of Jehoiachin's relatives.

Zedekiah King of Judah

¹¹Zedekiah was 21 years old when he became king of Judah. He was king in Jerusalem for eleven years. ¹²Zedekiah didn't do the things the Lord wanted him to do. Zedekiah sinned against the Lord. Jeremiah the prophet spoke messages from the Lord. But Zedekiah didn't humble himself and obey the things Jeremiah said.

Jerusalem Is Destroyed

¹³Zedekiah turned against King Nebuchadnezzar. In the past Nebuchadnezzar forced Zedekiah to make a promise to be faithful to Nebuchadnezzar. Zedekiah used God's name and promised to be faithful to Nebuchadnezzar. But Zedekiah was very stubborn and refused to change his life and come back and obey the Lord God of Israel. ¹⁴Also, all the leaders of the priests and the leaders of the people of Judah sinned worse and became more unfaithful to the Lord. They followed the evil example of the other nations. Those leaders ruined the Lord's temple.* The Lord had made the temple holy in Jerusalem. ¹⁵The Lord, the God of their ancestors,* sent prophets again and again to warn his people. The Lord did this because he felt sorry for them and for his temple. The Lord didn't want to destroy them or his temple. ¹⁶But God's people made fun of God's prophets. They refused to listen to God's prophets. They hated God's messages. Finally God could not hold his anger any longer. God became angry at his people and there was nothing that could be done to stop it. ¹⁷So God brought the King of Babylon to attack the people of Judah and Jerusalem.* The king of Babylon killed the young men even when they were in the temple. He didn't have mercy on the people of Judah and Jerusalem. The king of Babylon killed young and old people. He killed men and women. He killed sick and healthy people. God permitted Nebuchadnezzar to punish the people of Judah and Jerusalem. ¹⁸Nebuchadnezzar carried all the things in God's temple away to Babylon. He took all the valuable things from the temple, from the king, and from the king's officials. ¹⁹Nebuchadnezzar and his army burned the temple. They broke down Jerusalem's wall and burned all the houses that belonged to the king and his officials. They took or destroyed every valuable thing in Jerusalem. ²⁰Nebuchadnezzar took the people that were still alive back to Babylon and forced them to be slaves. Those people stayed in Babylon as slaves until the Persian kingdom defeated the kingdom of Babylon. ²¹And so the things the Lord told the people of Israel through the prophet Jeremiah really happened. The Lord had said through Jeremiah: "This place will be an empty wasteland for 70 years.* This will happen to make up for the Sabbath rests* that the people didn't do."

---

ancestors Literally, "fathers," meaning a person's parents, grandparents, and all the people they are descended from.
brought the King of Babylon ... Jerusalem This happened in the year 586 B.C., when Jerusalem was finally destroyed by King Nebuchadnezzar from Babylon.
This place ... for 70 years See Jer. 25:11; 29:10.
Sabbath rests The Law said that every seventh year the land was not to be farmed, see Lev. 25:1- 7.

---

temple The special building in Jerusalem for Jewish worship.

²²During the first year that Cyrus* was king of Persia, the Lord caused Cyrus to make a special announcement. He did this so that the things the Lord promised through Jeremiah the prophet would really happen. Cyrus sent messengers to every place in his kingdom. They carried this message:

²³Cyrus, King of Persia says: The Lord, the God of heaven, made me king over the whole earth. He gave me the responsibility of building a temple* for him in Jerusalem. Now, all of you who are God's people are free to go to Jerusalem. And may the Lord your God be with you.

---

first year ... Cyrus That is, 539-538 B.C.

temple The special building in Jerusalem for Jewish worship.

Ezra

Cyrus Helps the Prisoners Return

1 During the first year* that Cyrus was king of Persia, the Lord encouraged Cyrus to make an announcement. Cyrus put that announcement in writing and had it read every place in his kingdom. This happened so that the Lord's message that was spoken through Jeremiah* would truly happen. This is the announcement:

²"From Cyrus king of Persia:

The Lord, the God of heaven, gave all the kingdoms on earth to me. And the Lord chose me to build a temple for him at Jerusalem in the country of Judah. ³The Lord is the God of Israel, the God that is in Jerusalem. If any of God's people are living among you, then I pray God will bless them. You must let them go to Jerusalem in the country of Judah. You must let them go build the Lord's temple. ⁴And so in any place where there might be survivors* of Israel, the men in that place must support those survivors. Give those people silver, gold, cows, and other things. Give them gifts for God's temple in Jerusalem."

⁵So the family leaders from the family groups of Judah and Benjamin prepared to go up to Jerusalem. They were going to Jerusalem to build the Lord's temple. Also, every person that God had encouraged got ready to go to Jerusalem. ⁶All their neighbors gave them many gifts. They gave them silver, gold, cows, and other expensive things. Their neighbors freely gave them all those things. ⁷Also, King Cyrus brought out the things that belonged in the Lord's temple. Nebuchadnezzar had taken those things away from Jerusalem. Nebuchadnezzar had put those things in his temple where he kept his false gods. ⁸Cyrus king of Persia told the man that keeps his money to bring those things out. That man's name was Mithredath. So Mithredath brought those things out to Sheshbazzar,* the leader of Judah.

⁹Those things from the Lord's temple that Mithredath brought out:

	gold dishes	30
	silver dishes	1,000
	knives and pans	29
10	gold bowls	30
	silver bowls like the gold bowls	410
	other dishes	1,000

¹¹All together, there were 5,400 things made from gold and silver. Sheshbazzar* brought all these things with him when the prisoners left Babylon and went back to Jerusalem.

The List of the Prisoners That Returned

2 These are the people of the province that came back from captivity. In the past, Nebuchadnezzar king of Babylon took these people as prisoners to Babylon. These people came back to Jerusalem and Judah. Each person went back to his own town. ²These are the people who returned with Zerubbabel:* Jeshua, Nehemiah, Seraiah, Reelaiah, Mordecai, Bilshan, Mispar, Bigvai, Rehum, and Baanah. This is the list of names and numbers of men from Israel that came back:

3	The descendants of Parosh	2,172
4	the descendants of Shephatiah	372

---

first year That is, 538 B.C.
Lord's message ... Jeremiah See Jer. 25:12-14.
survivor(s) People who escaped some disaster. Here this means the Jewish people who survived the destruction of Judah and Israel by its enemy armies.

Sheshbazzar This is probably the man named Zerubbabel, a name that means "Stranger in Babylon," or "He left Babylon." Sheshbazzar is probably his Aramaic name.
Zerubbabel He is also called Sheshbazzar.

5	the descendants of Arah	775
6	the descendants of Pahath Moab of the family of Jeshua and Joab	2,812
7	the descendants of Elam	1,254
8	the descendants of Zattu	945
9	the descendants of Zaccai	760
10	the descendants of Bani	642
11	the descendants of Bebai	623
12	the descendants of Azgad	1,222
13	the descendants of Adonikam	666
14	the descendants of Bigvai	2,056
15	the descendants of Adin	454
16	the descendants of Ater through the family of Hezekiah	98
17	the descendants of Bezai	323
18	the descendants of Jorah	112
19	the descendants of Hashum	223
20	the descendants of Gibbar	95
21	from the town of Bethlehem	123
22	from the town of Netophah	56
23	from the town of Anathoth	128
24	from the town of Azmaveth	42
25	from the towns of Kiriath Jearim, Kephirah, and Beeroth	743
26	from the towns of Ramah and Geba	621
27	from the town of Micmash	122
28	from the towns of Bethel and Ai	223
29	from the town of Nebo	52
30	from the town of Magbish	156
31	from the other town named Elam	1,254
32	from the town of Harim	320
33	from the towns of Lod, Hadid, and Ono	725
34	from the town of Jericho	345
35	from the town of Senaah	3,630

³⁶These are the priests:

	The descendants of Jedaiah through the family of Jeshua	973
37	the descendants of Immer	1,052
38	the descendants of Pashhur	1,247
39	the descendants of Harim	1,017

⁴⁰These are the people from the family group of Levi:

The descendants of Jeshua and Kadmiel through the family of Hodaviah	74

⁴¹These are the singers:

The descendants of Asaph	128

⁴²These are the descendants of the temple gatekeepers:

The descendants of Shallum, Ater, Talmon, Akkub, Hatita, and Shobai	139

⁴³These are the descendants of the special temple servants:

Ziha, Hasupha, Tabbaoth,
⁴⁴ Keros, Siaha, Padon,
⁴⁵ Lebanah, Hagabah, Akkub,
⁴⁶ Hagab, Shalmai, Hanan,
⁴⁷ Giddel, Gahar, Reaiah,
⁴⁸ Rezin, Nekoda, Gazzam,
⁴⁹ Uzza, Paseah, Besai,
⁵⁰ Asnah, Meunim, Nephussim,
⁵¹ Bakbuk, Hakupha, Harhur,
⁵² Bazluth, Mehida, Harsha,
⁵³ Barkos, Sisera, Temah,
⁵⁴ Neziah, and Hatipha.

⁵⁵These are the descendants of Solomon's servants:

Sotai, Hassophereth, Peruda,
⁵⁶ Jaala, Darkon, Giddel,
⁵⁷ Shephatiah, Hattil, Pokereth Hazzebaim, and Ami
⁵⁸ The temple servants and the descendants of Solomon's servants 392

⁵⁹Some people came to Jerusalem from these towns of Tel Melah, Tel Harsha, Kerub, Addon, and Immer. But these people could not prove that their families were from the family of Israel:

⁶⁰ The descendants of Delaiah, Tobiah, and Nekoda	652

⁶¹From the family of priests there were the descendants of:

Hobaiah, Hakkoz, and Barzillai (If a man married a daughter of Barzillai from Gilead, that man was counted as a descendant of Barzillai.)

⁶²These people searched for their family histories, but they could not find them. Their names were not included in the list of priests. They could not prove that their ancestors were priests, so they could not serve as priests. ⁶³The governor ordered these people not to eat any of

the holy food. They could not eat any of this food until there was a priest who could use Urim and Thummim* to ask God what to do. ⁶⁴⁻⁶⁵All together, there were 42,360 people in the group that came back. This is not counting their 7,337 men and women servants. They also had 200 men and women singers with them. ⁶⁶⁻⁶⁷They had 736 horses, 245 mules, 435 camels, and 6,720 donkeys.

⁶⁸That group arrived at the Lord's temple in Jerusalem. Then the family leaders gave their gifts for building the Lord's temple. They would build the new temple in the same place as the temple that was destroyed. ⁶⁹Those people gave as much as they were able. These are the things those people gave for building the temple: 1,100 pounds* of gold, 3 tons* of silver, and 100 coats that priests wear.

⁷⁰So the priests, Levites, and some of the other people moved to Jerusalem and the area around it. This group included the ₍tempie₎ singers, gatekeepers, and the temple servants. The other people of Israel settled in their own home towns.

Rebuilding the Altar

3 So, by the seventh month,* the people of Israel had moved back to their own home towns. At that time, all the people met together in Jerusalem. They were all united as one people. ²Then Jeshua son of Jozadak and the priests with him, along with Zerubbabel son of Shealtiel, and the people with him, built the altar of the God of Israel. Those people built the altar of the God of Israel so they could offer sacrifices on it. They built it just like it says in the Law of Moses. Moses was God's special servant.

³Those people were afraid of the other people living near them. But that didn't stop them. They built the altar on its old foundation and offered burnt offerings on it to the Lord. They offered those sacrifices in the morning and in the evening. ⁴Then they celebrated the Festival of Shelters* just like the Law ₍of Moses₎ said. They offered the right number of burnt offerings for each day of the festival. ⁵After that, they began offering the continual burnt offerings each day, the offerings for the New Moon, and for all the other festivals and holidays that were commanded by the Lord. The people also began giving any other gifts they wanted to give to the Lord. ⁶So, on the first day of the seventh month,* these people of Israel again began offering sacrifices to the Lord. This was done even though the temple had not been built again.

Rebuilding the Temple

⁷Then those people who had come back from captivity gave money to the stonecutters and carpenters. And those people gave food, wine, and olive oil. They used these things to pay the people of Tyre and Sidon to bring cedar logs from Lebanon. Those people wanted to bring the logs in ships to the sea coast town of Joppa like ₍Solomon did when he built the₎ first temple. Cyrus king of Persia gave permission for them to do these things.

⁸So, in the second month* of the second year after their arrival at the temple in Jerusalem, Zerubbabel son of Shealtiel and Jeshua son of Jozadak began the work. Their brothers, the priests, Levites, and every person that came back to Jerusalem from captivity, began working with them. They chose Levites that were 20 years old and older to be the leaders in the building of the Lord's temple. ⁹These were the men who supervised the work of building the Lord's temple: Jeshua and his sons, Kadmiel and his sons (the descendants of Judah), the sons of Henadad and their brothers, the Levites. ¹⁰The builders finished laying the foundation for the Lord's temple. When the foundation was finished, the priests put on their priests' clothing. Then they got their trumpets. And the sons of Asaph got their cymbals. They all took their places to praise the Lord. This was done the way David, king of Israel, ordered in the past. ¹¹They sang the response songs* *Songs of Praise* and *Praise the Lord Because He is Good. His True Love Continues Forever.* And then all the people

---

Urim and Thummim Probably special stones that the High Priest wore in the judgement pouch. They were used to get decisions from God. See Ex. 28:30.
1,100 pounds Or, about 500kg. Literally, "61,000 drachmas."
3 tons Or, 3,000kg. Literally, "5,000 minas."
seventh month This was September-October, 538 B.C.
Festival of Shelters A festival in the seventh month to give thanks for the harvest. It continued for seven

seventh month That is, September-October, 538 B.C.
second month That is, April-May, 536 B.C.
response songs Songs where one group (Levites) sang one part and the other group (the people) responded with another part. Here these are probably Psalms 111-118 and Psalm 136.

cheered—they gave a loud shout and praised the Lord. They did this because the foundation of the Lord's temple had been laid. ¹²But many of the older priests, Levites, and family leaders cried. Why? Because those older people had seen the first temple—ₗand they remembered how beautiful it wasⱼ. They cried out loud when they saw the new temple. They cried while many of the other people were happy and shouting. ¹³The sound could be heard far away. All those people made so much noise that no person could tell the difference between the shouts of joy and the crying.

Enemies Against Rebuilding the Temple

4 ¹⁻²Many people living in the area were against the people of Judah and Benjamin. Those enemies heard that the people that had come from captivity were building a temple for the Lord God of Israel. So those enemies came to Zerubbabel and to the family leaders and said, "Let us help you build. We are the same as you, we ask your God for help. We have offered sacrifices to your God since the time Esarhaddon king of Assyria brought us here."

³But Zerubbabel, Jeshua, and the other family leaders of Israel answered, "No, you people can't help us build a temple for our God. Only we can build the temple for the Lord. He is the God of Israel. This is what King Cyrus, the king of Persia, commanded us to do."

⁴ₗThis made those people angryⱼ. So those people started bothering the Jews. They tried to discourage them and stop them from building the temple. ⁵Those enemies hired government officials to work against the people of Judah. Those officials constantly did things to stop the Jews' plans to build the temple. This continued the whole time that Cyrus was the king of Persia until Darius became the king of Persia.

⁶Those enemies even wrote letters to the king of Persia trying to stop the Jews. They wrote a letter the year that Xerxes* became the king of Persia.

Enemies Against Rebuilding Jerusalem

⁷And later, at the time Artaxerxes* became the new king of Persia, some of those men wrote another letter complaining about the Jews. The men who wrote the letter were: Bishlam, Mithredath, Tabeel, and the other people in their group. They wrote the letter to King Artaxerxes in Aramaic* using the Aramaic way of writing.

⁸* Then Rehum the commanding officer and Shimshai the secretary wrote a letter against the people of Jerusalem. They wrote the letter to Artaxerxes* the king. This is what they wrote:

⁹From Rehum the commanding officer and Shimshai the secretary, and from the judges and important officials over the men from Tripolis, Persia, Erech, and Babylon, and from the Elamite people from Susa, ¹⁰and from the other people that the great and powerful Ashurbanipal moved to the city of Samaria and other places in the country west of the Euphrates River.

To King Artaxerxes,*
From your servants living in the area west of the Euphrates River.

¹²King Artaxerxes, we wish to inform you that the Jews you sent away from you have come here. Those Jews are now trying to build that city again. Jerusalem is a bad city. The people in that city have always rebelled against other kings. Now those Jews are fixing the foundations and building the walls.*

¹³Also, King Artaxerxes, you should know that if Jerusalem and its walls are built again, the people of Jerusalem will stop paying their taxes. They will stop sending money to honor you. They also will stop paying duty taxes. And the king will lose all that money.

¹⁴We have a responsibility to the king. We don't want to see those things happen. So we are sending this letter to inform the king.

¹⁵King Artaxerxes, we suggest that you search the writings of the kings that ruled before you. You will see in those writings

---

Xerxes King of Persia about 485-465 B.C.
Artaxerxes King of Persia about 465-424 B.C. He was the son of Xerxes.
Aramaic The official language of the Babylonian empire.
Verse 8 Here the original language changes from Hebrew to Aramaic.
King Artaxerxes 11King of Persia about 465-424 B.C. He was the son of Xerxes.
building the walls This was a way of protecting a city, but these men wanted the king to think that the Jews were preparing to rebel against the king.

that Jerusalem always rebelled against other kings. It has caused much trouble for other kings and nations. Many rebellions have started in this city since ancient times! That is why Jerusalem was destroyed!

¹⁶King Artaxerxes, we wish to inform you that if this city and its walls are built again, you will lose control of the area west of the Euphrates River.

¹⁷Then King Artaxerxes* sent this answer:

To Rehum the commanding officer, Shimshai the secretary, and all the people with them living in Samaria and other places west of the Euphrates River.
Greetings.

¹⁸The letter you sent us has been translated and read to me. ¹⁹I gave an order for the writings of the kings before me to be searched. The writings were read, and we found out that Jerusalem has a long history of rebellion against kings. Jerusalem has been a place where rebellion and revolt has happened often. ²⁰Jerusalem has had powerful kings ruling over it and over the whole area west of the Euphrates River. Taxes and money to honor kings, and duty taxes have been paid to those kings.

²¹Now, you must give an order for those men to stop work. That order must be given to keep Jerusalem from being built again until I say so. ²²Be careful not to overlook this business. We should not let the building of Jerusalem continue. If that work continues, I will not get any more money from Jerusalem.

²³So a copy of the letter that King Artaxerxes sent was read to Rehum, Shimshai the secretary, and the people with them. Then those people went very quickly to the Jews in Jerusalem. They forced the Jews to stop building.

The Work on the Temple Stopped

²⁴So the work stopped on God's temple* in Jerusalem. The work did not continue until Darius' second year* as king of Persia.

5 At that time, the prophets Haggai* and Zechariah son of Iddo* began to prophesy* in the name of God. They encouraged the Jews in Judah and Jerusalem. ²So Zerubbabel son of Shealtiel and Jeshua son of Jozadak again started working on the temple in Jerusalem. All of God's prophets were with them and were supporting the work. ³At that time Tattenai was the governor of the area west of the Euphrates River. Tattenai, Shethar Bozenai, and the men with them went to Zerubbabel, Jeshua, and the others that were building. Tattenai and the people with him asked Zerubbabel and the people with him, "Who gave you permission to build this temple again and fix it like new?" ⁴They also asked Zerubbabel, "What are the names of the men who are working on this building?"

⁵But God was watching over the Jewish leaders. The builders didn't have to stop working until a report could be sent to King Darius. They continued working until the king sent his answer back.

⁶Tattenai the governor of the area west of the Euphrates River, Shethar Bozenai, and the important people with them sent a letter to King Darius. ⁷This is a copy of that letter:

To King Darius, greetings

⁸King Darius, you should know that we went to the province of Judah. We went to the temple of the great God. The people in Judah are building that temple with large stones. They are putting big wooden timbers in the walls. The work is being done with much care and the people of Judah are working very hard. They are building very fast, it will soon be done.

⁹We asked their leaders some questions about the work they are doing. We asked them, "Who gave you permission to build this temple again and fix it like new?" ¹⁰We

---

Artaxerxes King of Persia about 465-424 B.C. He was the son of Xerxes.
worked stopped ... temple Here this refers to the time of Xerxes, when work on the temple was stopped, not to the time of Artaxerxes, when work on the walls around Jerusalem was stopped.
worked stopped ... temple Here this refers to the time of Xerxes, when work on the temple was stopped, not to the time of Artaxerxes, when work on the walls around Jerusalem was stopped.
Darius' second year That is, 520 B.C.
Haggai See Haggai 1:1.
Zechariah son of Iddo See Zechariah 1:1.
prophesy To speak for God.

also asked for their names. We wanted to write down the names of their leaders so you would know who they are. ¹¹This is the answer they gave us:

"We are the servants of the God of heaven and earth. We are building again the temple that a great king of Israel built and finished many years ago. ¹²But our ancestors made the God of heaven angry. So God gave our ancestors to Nebuchadnezzar the king of Babylon. Nebuchadnezzar destroyed this temple, and he forced the people to go to Babylon as prisoners. ¹³But, in the first year that Cyrus was king of Babylon, King Cyrus gave a special order for God's temple to be built again. ¹⁴And Cyrus brought out from his false god's temple in Babylon the gold and silver things that were taken from God's temple in the past. Nebuchadnezzar took those things from the temple in Jerusalem and brought them to his false god's temple in Babylon. Then King Cyrus gave those gold and silver things to Sheshbazzar *(Zerubbabel)*. Cyrus chose Sheshbazzar to be governor.
¹⁵Then Cyrus said to Sheshbazzar *(Zerubbabel)*, "Take these gold and silver things and put them back in the temple in Jerusalem. Build again God's temple in the same place it was in the past." ¹⁶So Sheshbazzar *(Zerubbabel)* came and built the foundations of God's temple in Jerusalem. From that day until now the work has continued. But it is not yet finished.
¹⁷Now, if the king wants, please search the official records of the king. See if it is true that King Cyrus gave an order to build again God's temple in Jerusalem. And then, sir, please send us a letter to let us know what you have decided to do about this.

The Order of Darius

6 So King Darius gave an order to search the writings of the kings before him. Those writings were kept in Babylon in the same place the money was kept. ²A scroll* was found in the fortress* of Ecbatana. Ecbatana is in the province of Media. This is what was written on that scroll:

Official Note: ³During Cyrus' first year as king Cyrus gave an order about the temple of God in Jerusalem. The order said:
Let the temple of God be built again. It will be a place to offer sacrifices. Let its foundations be built. The temple must be 90 feet* high and 90 feet* wide. ⁴₍The wall around it₎ must have three rows of large stones and one row of big wood timbers. The cost of building the temple must be paid for from the king's treasury. ⁵Also, the gold and silver things from God's temple must be put back in their places. Nebuchadnezzar took those things from the temple in Jerusalem and brought them to Babylon. They must be put back in God's temple.
⁶Now then, I, Darius, order you Tattenai, governor of the area west of the Euphrates River, and Shethar Bozenai, and all the officials living in that province, to stay away from Jerusalem. ⁷Don't bother the workers. Don't try to stop the work on this temple of God. Let the Jewish governor and the Jewish leaders build it again. Let them build God's temple again in the same place it was in the past.
⁸Now I give this order. You must do these things for the Jewish leaders building God's temple: The cost of the building must be fully paid from the king's treasury. That money will come from the taxes collected from the provinces in the area west of the Euphrates River. Do these things quickly, so the work will not stop. ⁹Give those people anything they need. If they need young bulls, rams, or male lambs for sacrifices to the God of Heaven, give those things to them. If the priests of Jerusalem ask for wheat, salt, wine, and oil, then give those things to them every day without fail. ¹⁰Give those things to the Jewish priests so that they may offer sacrifices that please the God of Heaven. Give those things so that the priests may pray for me and my sons.
¹¹Also, I give this order: If any person changes this order, a wood beam must be pulled from that person's house. Then the wooden beam will be pushed through that

---

scroll(s) A long roll of leather or papyrus *(paper)* used for writing books, letters, and legal documents.
fortress A building or city with tall, strong walls for protection.

90 feet Or, 27m. Literally, "60 ₍short₎ cubits."

person's body. And his house will be destroyed until it is only a pile of rocks. ¹²God put his name there in Jerusalem. And I hope that God will defeat any king or other person that tries to change this order. If any person tries to destroy this temple in Jerusalem, I hope God will destroy that person.

I, Darius, have ordered it. This order must be obeyed quickly and completely!

Completion and Dedication of the Temple

¹³So, Tattenai the governor of the area west of the Euphrates River, Shethar Bozenai, and the men with them obeyed King Darius' order. Those men obeyed the order quickly and completely. ¹⁴So the Jewish elders *(leaders)* continued to build. And they were successful as Haggai the prophet and Zechariah son of Iddo encouraged them. Those people finished building the temple. This was done to obey the command of the God of Israel. It was also done to obey the orders that Cyrus, Darius, and Artaxerxes, the kings of Persia, gave. ¹⁵The temple was finished on the third day of the month of Adar.* That was in the sixth year of the rule of King Darius.*

¹⁶Then the people of Israel celebrated the dedication* of God's temple with much happiness. The priests, the Levites, and all the other people that came back from captivity joined in the celebration.

¹⁷This is the way they dedicated* God's temple: They offered 100 bulls, 200 rams, and 400 male lambs. And they offered twelve male goats for all Israel for a sin offering. That is one goat for each of the twelve family groups of Israel. ¹⁸Then they chose the priests in their groups and the Levites in their groups to serve in God's temple in Jerusalem. They did these things just like it says in the Book of Moses.

The Passover

¹⁹* On the fourteenth day of the first month,* those Jews that came back from captivity celebrated the Passover.* ²⁰The priests and Levites made themselves pure. They all made themselves clean and ready to celebrate the Passover. The Levites killed the Passover lamb for all the Jews that came back from captivity. They did that for their brothers the priests, and for themselves. ²¹So all the people of Israel that came back from captivity ate the Passover meal. Other people washed themselves and made themselves pure from the unclean* things of the people living in that country. Those pure people also shared in the Passover meal. Those people did this so they could go to the Lord, the God of Israel, for help. ²²They celebrated the Festival of Unleavened Bread* with much joy for seven days. The Lord made them very happy because he had changed the attitude of the king of Assyria.* So the king of Assyria had helped them do the work on God's temple.

Ezra Comes to Jerusalem

7 After these things,* during the rule of Artaxerxes* king of Persia, Ezra came to Jerusalem from Babylon. Ezra was the son of Seraiah. Seraiah was the son of Azariah. Azariah was the son of Hilkiah. ²Hilkiah was the son of Shallum. Shallum was the son of Zadok. Zadok was the son of Ahitub. ³Ahitub was the son of Amariah. Amariah was the son of Azariah. Azariah was the son of Meraioth. ⁴Meraioth was the son of Zerahiah. Zerahiah was the son of Uzzi.

Verse 19 Here, the original language changes from Aramaic back to Hebrew.
first month That is, March-April, 515 B.C.
Passover Important holy day for Jews. They ate a special meal on this day every year to remember that God freed them from slavery in Egypt in the time of Moses.
unclean Not pure or not acceptable for worship. See Lev. 11-15 for the laws about uncleanness.
Festival of Unleavened Bread Same as Passover Festival, the most important holy day for Jews. On this day they ate a special meal with bread that was made without yeast.
king of Assyria This probably means Darius, the king of Persia.
After these things There is a time period of 58 years between Ezra 6 and Ezra 7. The story of Esther takes place at this time.
Artaxerxes King of Persia about 465-424 B.C. He was the son of Xerxes.

third ... Adar That is, February-March. Some ancient writers have "23rd of Adar."
sixth ... Darius That is, 515 B.C.
dedication To give something for a special use, or to honor it for a special reason.
dedicate(d) To give something for a special use, or to honor it for a special reason.

Uzzi was the son of Bukki. ⁵Bukki was the son of Abishua. Abishua was the son of Phinehas. Phinehas was the son of Eleazar. Eleazar was the son of Aaron the high priest. ⁶Ezra came to Jerusalem from Babylon. Ezra was a teacher.* He knew the Law of Moses very well. The Law of Moses was given by the Lord, the God of Israel. King Artaxerxes gave Ezra everything he asked for because the Lord was with Ezra. ⁷⌊Many people of Israel came with Ezra.⌋ Those were priests, Levites, singers, gatekeepers, and temple servants. Those people of Israel arrived in Jerusalem during the seventh year of King Artaxerxes. ⁸Ezra arrived in Jerusalem in the fifth month* of the seventh year that Artaxerxes was king. ⁹Ezra ⌊and the group with him⌋ left Babylon on the first day of the first month. He arrived in Jerusalem on the first day of the fifth month. The Lord God was with Ezra. ¹⁰Ezra gave all his time and attention to studying and obeying the Law of the Lord. Ezra wanted to teach the rules and commandments of the Lord to the people of Israel. And he also wanted to help the people follow those laws in Israel.

King Artaxerxes' Letter to Ezra

¹¹Ezra was a priest and teacher. He knew much about the commands and laws the Lord gave Israel. This is a copy of the letter King Artaxerxes* gave to Ezra the teacher:

¹²* From King Artaxerxes,
To Ezra the priest, a teacher of the Law of the God of Heaven:

Greetings! ¹³I give this order: Any person, priest, or Levite from Israel living in my kingdom that wants to go with Ezra to Jerusalem, may go.

¹⁴Ezra, I and my seven advisers send you. You must go to Judah and Jerusalem. See how your people are doing in obeying the Law of your God. You have that Law with you.

¹⁵I and my advisers are giving gold and silver to the God of Israel. God lives in Jerusalem. You must take this gold and silver with you. ¹⁶You must also go through all the provinces of Babylonia. Collect the gifts from your people, from the priests, and from the Levites. Those gifts are for their God's temple in Jerusalem.

¹⁷Use this money to buy bulls, rams, and male lambs. Buy the grain offerings and drink offerings that go with those sacrifices. Then sacrifice them on the altar in the temple of your God in Jerusalem. ¹⁸Then you and the other Jews may spend the silver and gold left over any way you want to. Use it in a way that is pleasing to your God. ¹⁹Take all those things to the God of Jerusalem. Those things are for the worship in the temple of your God. ²⁰And you may get any other things that you need for the temple of your God. Use the money in the king's treasury to buy anything you need.

²¹Now I, King Artaxerxes, give this order: I order all the men who keep the king's money in the area west of the Euphrates River to give Ezra anything he wants. Ezra is a priest and a teacher of the Law of the God of Heaven. Do this quickly and completely. ²²Give this much to Ezra: 3 3/4 tons* of silver, 600 bushels* of wheat, 600 gallons* of wine, 600 gallons* of olive oil, and as much salt as Ezra wants. ²³Anything that the God of Heaven has ordered for Ezra to get, you must give to Ezra quickly and completely. Do those things for the temple of the God of Heaven. We don't want God to be angry against my kingdom or against my sons.

²⁴⌊I want⌋ you men to know that it is against the law to make the priests, Levites, singers, gatekeepers, temple servants, and other workers in God's temple pay taxes. Those people don't have to pay taxes, money to honor the king, or any duty taxes. ²⁵Ezra, I give you the authority to use the wisdom you have from your God and choose civil and religious judges. These men will be judges for all the people living in the area west of the Euphrates River. They will judge all the people who know the laws of your God. And if someone doesn't know those laws, those judges must teach him

---

teacher Literally, "scribe." This was a person that made copies of books. These men studied those books and became teachers.
fifth month This was July-August, 458 B.C.
Artaxerxes King of Persia about 465-424 B.C. He was the son of Xerxes.
Verse 12 The text changes from Hebrew to Aramaic here.

3 3/4 tons Or, 3,400 kg. Literally, "100 talents."
600 bushels Or, 22,000 l. Literally, "100 cors."
600 gallons Or, 2,200 l. Literally, "100 baths."

about those laws. ²⁶Any person that doesn't obey the law of your God, or the law of the king, must be punished. Depending on the crime, they must be punished with death, or sent away to another country, or their property taken away, or put into prison.

Ezra Praises God

²⁷* Blessed is the Lord, the God of our ancestors.
God put the idea into the king's heart
to honor the Lord's temple in Jerusalem.
²⁸ The Lord showed his true love to me
in front of the king, his advisers
and the king's important officials.
The Lord God was with me,
so I was brave.
I gathered together the leaders of Israel
to go with me to Jerusalem.

List of Leaders Returning With Ezra

8 These are the names of the family leaders and the other people that came with me *(Ezra)* to Jerusalem from Babylon. We came to Jerusalem during the rule of King Artaxerxes. Here is the list of names: ²From the descendants of Phinehas, was Gershom; from the descendants of Ithamar, was Daniel; from the descendants of David, was Hattush; ³from the descendants of Shecaniah, were the descendants of Parosh, Zechariah, and 150 other men; ⁴from the descendants of Pahath Moab, were Eliehoenai son of Zerahiah, and 200 other men; ⁵from the descendants of Zattu, were Shecaniah son of Jahaziel, and 300 other men; ⁶from the descendants of Adin, were Ebed son of Jonathan, and 50 other men; ⁷from the descendants of Elam, were Jeshaiah son of Athaliah, and 70 other men; ⁸from the descendants of Shephatiah, were Zebadiah son of Michael, and 80 other men; ⁹from the descendants of Joab, were Obadiah son of Jehiel, and 218 other men; ¹⁰from the descendants of Bani, were Shelomith son of Josiphiah, and 160 other men; ¹¹from the descendants of Bebai, were Zechariah son of Bebai, and 28 other men; ¹²from the descendants of Azgad, were Johanan son of Hakkatan, and 110 other men; ¹³from the last of the descendants of Adonikam were Eliphelet, Jeuel, Shemaiah, and 60 other men; ¹⁴from the descendants of Bigvai, were Uthai, Zaccur, and 70 other men.

The Return to Jerusalem

¹⁵I, *(Ezra)* called all those people to meet together at the river that flows toward Ahava. We camped at that place for three days. I learned there were priests in that group, but there were no Levites. ¹⁶So I called these leaders: Eliezer, Ariel, Shemaiah, Elnathan, Jarib, Elnathan, Nathan, Zechariah, and Meshullam. And I called Joiarib and Elnathan. (These men were teachers.) ¹⁷I sent those men to Iddo. Iddo is the leader at the town of Casiphia. I told those men what to say to Iddo and his relatives. His relatives are the temple workers in Casiphia. I sent those men to Iddo so that Iddo might send us workers to serve in God's temple. ¹⁸Because God was with us, Iddo's relatives sent these men to us: Sherebiah, a wise man from the descendants of Mahli. Mahli was one of Levi's sons. Levi was one of Israel's sons. And they sent us Sherebiah's sons and brothers. In all there were 18 men from that family. ¹⁹And they also sent to us Hashabiah and Jeshaiah from the descendants of Merari. They also sent their brothers and nephews. In all there were 20 men from that family. ²⁰They also sent 220 of the temple workers. Their ancestors were the people David and the important officials had chosen to help the Levites. The names of all those men were written on the list.

²¹There near the Ahava River, I *(Ezra)* announced that we all should fast.* We should fast to make ourselves humble before our God. We wanted to ask God for a safe trip for ourselves, our children, and for all the things we owned. ²²I was embarrassed to ask King Artaxerxes for soldiers and horsemen to protect us as we traveled. There were enemies on the road. The reason I was embarrassed to ask for protection was because of what we had told the king. We had said to King Artaxerxes, "Our God is with every person that trusts him. But God is very angry with every person that turns away from him." ²³So we fasted and prayed to our God about our trip. He answered our prayers.

²⁴Then I chose twelve of the priests that were leaders. I chose Sherebiah, Hashabiah, and ten of their brothers. ²⁵I weighed the silver, gold, and the other things that were given for God's temple. I

Verse 27   The text changes from Aramaic to Hebrew here.

fast   To live without food for a special time of prayer and worship to God.

gave those things to the twelve priests I had chosen. King Artaxerxes, his advisers, his important officials, and all the people of Israel in Babylon gave those things for God's temple. ²⁶I weighed all these things. There were 25 tons* of silver. There were also 3 3/4 tons* of silver dishes and things. There were 3 3/4 tons* of gold. ²⁷And I gave them 20 gold bowls. The bowls weighed about 19 pounds.* And I gave them two beautiful dishes made from polished bronze that were as valuable as gold. ²⁸Then I said to those twelve priests: "You and these things are holy to the Lord. People gave this silver and gold to the Lord, the God of your ancestors. ²⁹So guard these things carefully. You are responsible for them until you give them to the temple leaders in Jerusalem. You will give them to the leading Levites and the family leaders of Israel. They will weigh those things and put them in the rooms of the Lord's temple in Jerusalem.

³⁰So the priests and Levites accepted the silver, gold, and special things that Ezra had weighed and given to them. They were told to take those things to God's temple in Jerusalem.

³¹On the twelfth day of the first month* we left the Ahava River and started toward Jerusalem. God was with us, and he protected us from enemies and robbers along the way. ³²Then we arrived in Jerusalem. We rested there for three days. ³³On the fourth day, we went to the temple and weighed the silver, gold, and special things. We gave those things to Meremoth son of Uriah the priest. Eleazar son of Phinehas was with Meremoth. And the Levites, Jozabad son of Jeshua and Noadiah son of Binnui, were with them also. ³⁴We counted and weighed everything. Then we wrote down the total weight at that time.

³⁵Then the Jewish people that came back from captivity offered burnt offerings to the God of Israel. They offered twelve bulls for all Israel, 96 rams, 77 male lambs, and twelve male goats for a sin offering. All this was a burnt offering to the Lord.

³⁶Then those people gave the letter from King Artaxerxes to the royal satraps (*leaders*) and to the governors of the area west of the Euphrates River. Then those leaders gave their support to the people of Israel and to the temple.

25 tons Or, 22,100 l. Literally, "650 talents."
3 3/4 tons Or, 3,400 kg. Literally, "100 talents."
19 pounds Or, about 8.5 kg. Literally, "1,000 darics."
first month That is, March-April, 458 B.C.

Marriages to Non-Jewish People

9 After we finished all these things, the leaders of the people of Israel came to me. They said, "Ezra, the people of Israel have not kept themselves separate from the other people living around us. And the priests and the Levites have not kept themselves separate. The people of Israel are being influenced by the very bad things done by the Canaanite people, the Hittite people, the Perizzite people, the Jebusite people, the Ammonite people, the Moabite people, the people from Egypt, and the Amorite people. ²The people of Israel have married the people living around us. The people of Israel are supposed to be special. But now they are mixed with the other people living around them. The leaders and important officials of the people of Israel have set a bad example in this thing." ³When I heard about this, I tore my robe and my coat ₁to show I was upset₁. I pulled hair from my head and beard. I sat down, shocked and upset. ⁴Then every person that respected God's Law shook with fear. They were afraid because the people of Israel that came back from captivity were not faithful to God. I was shocked and upset. I sat there until the evening sacrifice. And those people gathered around me.

⁵Then, when it was time for the evening sacrifice, I got up. I had made myself look shameful while I was sitting there. My robe and coat were torn, and I fell on my knees with my hands spread out to the Lord my God. ⁶Then I prayed this prayer:

My God, I am too ashamed and embarrassed to look at you. I am ashamed because our sins are higher than our heads. Our guilt has reached all the way up to the heavens. ⁷We have been guilty of many, many sins from the days of our ancestors until now. We sinned so our kings and priests were punished. Foreign kings attacked us and took our people away. Those kings took away our wealth and made us ashamed. It is the same even today.

⁸But now, finally, you have been kind to us. You have let a few of us escape captivity and come to live in this holy place. Lord, you gave us new life and relief from our slavery. ⁹Yes, we were slaves, but you would not let us be slaves forever. You were kind to us. You made the kings of Persia be kind to us. Your temple was ruined. But you gave us new life so we can build your temple again and fix it like new. God, you helped us build a wall to protect Judah and Jerusalem.

¹⁰Now, God, what can we say to you? We have stopped obeying you again! ¹¹God, you used your

servants, the prophets, and gave those commands to us. You said: "The land you are going to live in and own is a ruined land. It has been ruined by the very bad things the people living there have done. Those people have done very bad things in every place in this land. They have made this land dirty with their sins. ¹²So, people of Israel, don't let your children marry their children. Don't join those people! Don't want the things they have! Obey my commands so you will be strong and enjoy the good things of the land. And then you can keep this land and give it to your children."

¹³The bad things that happened to us are our own fault. We have done evil things, and we have much guilt. But you, our God, have punished us much less than we should have been. We have done many terrible sins, and we should have been punished worse. And you have even let some of our people escape captivity. ¹⁴So we know that we must not break your commands. We must not marry those people. Those people do very bad things. God, if we continue to marry those bad people, we know you will destroy us! Then there would be no person from the people of Israel left alive.

¹⁵Lord, God of Israel, you are good! And you still have let some of us live. Yes, we are guilty! And because of our guilt, not one of us should be allowed to stand in front of you.

The People Confess Their Sin

10 Ezra was praying and confessing. He was crying and bowing down in front of God's temple. While Ezra was doing that, a large group of the people of Israel—men, women, and children—gathered around him. Those people were also crying very hard. ²Then Shecaniah son of Jehiel, one of the descendants of Elam, spoke to Ezra. Shecaniah said, "We have not been faithful to our God. We have married the people living around us. But, even though we have done this, there is still hope for Israel. ³Now let us make an agreement before our God to send away all those women and their children. We will do that to follow the advice of Ezra and the people who respect the laws of our God. We will obey God's law. ⁴Get up Ezra, this is your responsibility, but we will support you. So be brave and do it."

⁵So Ezra got up. He made the leading priests, the Levites, and all the people of Israel promise to do what he said. ⁶Then Ezra went away from the front of God's house. Ezra went to the room of Jehohanan son of Eliashib. While Ezra was there, he didn't eat food, and he didn't drink water. He did that because he was still very sad. He was very sad about the people of Israel that came back to Jerusalem. ⁷Then he sent a message to every place in Judah and Jerusalem. The message told all the Jewish people that had come back from captivity to meet together in Jerusalem. ⁸Any person that didn't come to Jerusalem in three days would have to give up all his property. The important officials and the elders *(leaders)* made that decision. And that person could no longer be a member of the group of people where he was living.

⁹So, in three days all the men from the families of Judah and Benjamin gathered in Jerusalem. And on the twentieth day of the ninth month,* all the people met together in the temple yard. They were very upset because of the reason for the meeting and because of the heavy rain. ¹⁰Then Ezra the priest stood and said to those people, "You people have not been faithful to God. You have married foreign women. You have made Israel more guilty by doing that. ¹¹Now, you people must confess to the Lord that you have sinned. The Lord is the God of your ancestors. You must obey the Lord's command. Separate yourselves from the people living around you and from your foreign wives."

¹²Then the whole group that met together answered Ezra. They said with a loud voice: "Ezra, you are right! We must do the things you say. ¹³But there are many people here. And it is the rainy time of year, so we can't stay outside. This problem can't be solved in a day or two because we have sinned in a very bad way. ¹⁴Let our leaders decide for the whole group meeting here. Then let every person in our towns that married a foreign woman come here to Jerusalem at a planned time. Let them come here with the elders *(leaders)* and judges of their towns. Then God will stop being angry at us."

¹⁵Only a few men were against this plan. They were Jonathan son of Asahel and Jahzeiah son of Tikvah. Meshullam and Shabbethai the Levite also were against that plan.

¹⁶So the people of Israel that came back to Jerusalem agreed to accept that plan. Ezra the priest chose men that were family leaders. He chose one man from each family group. Each man was chosen by name. On the first day of the tenth month* those men that were chosen sat down to

---

ninth month That is, November-December.
tenth month That is, December-January.

study each of the cases. ¹⁷And by the first day of the first month,* they finished discussing all the men who had married foreign women.

The List of Men Who Married Foreign Women

¹⁸These are the names of the descendants of the priests that married foreign women:

From the descendants of Jeshua son of Jozadak, and Jeshua's brothers, these men: Maaseiah, Eliezer, Jarib, and Gedaliah. ¹⁹All those promised to divorce their wives. And then each one of them offered a ram from the flock for a guilt offering. They did that because of their guilt.

²⁰From the descendants of Immer, these men: Hanani and Zebadiah.

²¹From the descendants of Harim, these men: Maaseiah, Elijah, Shemaiah, Jehiel, and Uzziah.

²²From the descendants of Pashhur, these men: Elioenai, Maaseiah, Ishmael, Nethanel, Jozabad, and Elasah.

²³Among the Levites, these are the men who married foreign women: Jozabad, Shimei, Kelaiah (he is also called Kelita), Pethahiah, Judah, and Eliezer.

²⁴Among the singers, this is the man who had married a foreign woman: Eliashib.

Among the gatekeepers, these are the men who had married foreign women: Shallum, Telem, and Uri.

²⁵Among the people of Israel, these men married foreign women:

From the descendants of Parosh, these men: Ramiah, Izziah, Malkijah, Mijamin, Eleazar, Malkijah, and Benaiah.

²⁶From the descendants of Elam, these men: Mattaniah, Zechariah, Jehiel, Abdi, Jeremoth, and Elijah.

²⁷From the descendants of Zattu, these men: Elioenai, Eliashib, Mattaniah, Jeremoth, Zabad, and Aziza.

²⁸From the descendants of Bebai, these men: Jehohanan, Hananiah, Zabbai, and Athlai.

²⁹From the descendants of Bani, these men: Meshullam, Malluch, Adaiah, Jashub, Sheal, and Jeremoth.

³⁰From the descendants of Pahath Moab, these men: Adna, Kelal, Benaiah, Maaseiah, Mattaniah, Bezalel, Binnui, and Manasseh.

³¹From the descendants of Harim, these men: Eliezer, Ishijah, Malkijah, Shemaiah, Shimeon, ³²Benjamin, Malluch, and Shemariah.

³³From the descendants of Hashum, these men: Mattenai, Mattattah, Zabad, Eliphelet, Jeremai, Manasseh, and Shimei.

³⁴From the descendants of Bani, these men: Maadai, Amram, Uel, ³⁵Benaiah, Bedeiah, Keluhi, ³⁶Vaniah, Meremoth, Eliashib, ³⁷Mattaniah, Mattenai, and Jaasu.

³⁸From the descendants of Binnui, these men: Shimei, ³⁹Shelemiah, Nathan, Adaiah, ⁴⁰Macnadebai, Shashai, Sharai, ⁴¹Azarel, Shelemiah, Shemariah, ⁴²Shallum, Amariah, and Joseph.

⁴³From the descendants of Nebo, these men: Jeiel, Mattithiah, Zabad, Zebina, Jaddai, Joel, and Benaiah.

⁴⁴All of those men had married foreign women. And some of them had children with those wives.

---

first month That is, March-April.

Nehemiah

Nehemiah's Prayer

1 These are the words of Nehemiah. Nehemiah was the son of Hacaliah: I, Nehemiah, was in the capital city of Susa in the month of Kislev. This was in the 20th year* that Artaxerxes was king. ²While I was in Susa, one of my brothers named Hanani and some other men came from Judah. I asked them about the Jews living there. These were the Jews that had escaped captivity and still lived in Judah. And I also asked them about the city of Jerusalem.

³Hanani and the men with him said, "Nehemiah, those Jews that escaped captivity and are in the land of Judah are in much trouble. Those people are having many problems and are full of shame. Why? Because the wall of Jerusalem is broken down, and its gates have been burned with fire."

⁴When I heard those things about the people of Jerusalem and about the wall, I was very upset. I sat down and cried. I was very sad. I fasted* and prayed to the God of Heaven for several days. ⁵Then I prayed this prayer:

Lord, God of Heaven, you are the great and powerful God. You are the God who keeps his agreement of love with people that love you and obey your commands.

⁶Please open your eyes and ears and listen to the prayer your servant is praying before you day and night. I am praying for your servants, the people of Israel. I confess the sins we people of Israel have done against you. I am confessing that I have sinned against you and that the other people in my father's family have sinned against you. ⁷We people of Israel have been very bad to you. We have not obeyed the commands, teachings, and laws you gave your servant Moses.

⁸Please remember the teaching you gave your servant Moses. You said to him, "If you people of Israel are not faithful, I will force you to be scattered among the other nations. ⁹But if you people of Israel come back to me and obey my commands, then this is what I will do: Even if your people have been forced to leave their homes and go to the ends of the earth, I will gather them from there. And I will bring them back to the place I have chosen to put my name."

¹⁰The people of Israel are your servants and your people. You used your great power and rescued those people. ¹¹So Lord, please listen to my prayer. I am your servant. And please listen to the prayers of your servants that want to show respect for your name. Lord, you know I am the king's wine servant.* So please help me today. Help me as I ask the king for help. Give me success and help me to be pleasing to the king.

Artaxerxes Sends Nehemiah to Jerusalem

2 In the month of Nisan in the 20th year* of King Artaxerxes, some wine was brought to the king. I took the wine and gave it to the king. I had never been sad when I was with the king, but now I was sad. ²So the king asked me, "Are you sick? Why do you look sad? I think your heart is full of sadness."

Kislev ... 20th year This was about December, 444 B.C.
fast(ed) To live without food for a special time of prayer and worship to God.
wine servant A very important job. This official was always close to the king and tasted the king's wine to make sure no one was trying to poison the king.
Nisan ... 20th year This was March-April, 443 B.C.

Then I was very much afraid. ³But even though I was afraid, I said to the king, "May the king live forever! I am sad because the city where my ancestors* are buried lies in ruins. And the gates of that city have been destroyed by fire."

⁴Then the king said to me, "What do you want me to do?"

Before I answered, I prayed to the God of Heaven. ⁵Then I answered the king, "If it would please the king, and if I have been good to you, please send me to ⌊Jerusalem,⌋ the city in Judah where my ancestors* are buried. I want to go there and build that city again."

⁶The queen was sitting next to the king. The king and queen asked me, "How long will your trip take? When will you get back here?"

The king was happy to send me, so I gave him a certain time. ⁷I also said to the king, "If it would please the king to do something else for me, let me ask. Please give me some letters to show the governors of the area west of the Euphrates River. I need these letters so those governors will give me permission to pass safely through their lands on my way to Judah. ⁸I also need lumber for the heavy wooden beams for the gates, the walls, the walls around the temple,* and my house. So I need a letter from you to Asaph. Asaph is in charge of your forests."

The king gave me the letters and everything I asked for. The king did that because God was kind to me.

⁹So I went to the governors of the area west of the Euphrates River. I gave those governors the letters from the king. The king had also sent army officers and soldiers on horses with me. ¹⁰Sanballat and Tobiah were two men that heard about what I was doing. They were very upset and angry that someone had come to help the people of Israel. Sanballat was from Horon and Tobiah is an Ammonite official.

Nehemiah Inspects the Walls of Jerusalem

¹¹⁻¹²I went to Jerusalem and stayed there three days. Then at night I started out with a few men. I had not said anything to anyone about what God had put into my heart to do for Jerusalem. There were no horses with me except the horse I was riding. ¹³While it was dark I went out through the Valley Gate. I rode toward the Dragon Well and the Gate of the Ash Piles. I was inspecting the walls of Jerusalem that had been broken down. And the gates in the wall that had been burned with fire. ¹⁴Then I rode on toward the Fountain Gate and the King's Pool. But as I got close, I could see there was not enough room for my horse to get through. ¹⁵So I went up the valley in the dark, inspecting the wall. Finally, I turned back and went back in through the Valley Gate. ¹⁶The officials and important people of Israel didn't know where I had gone. They didn't know what I was doing. I had not yet said anything to the Jews, the priests, the king's family, the officials, or any of the other people that would be doing the work.

¹⁷Then I said to all those people, "You can see the trouble we have here: Jerusalem is a pile of ruins, and its gates have been burned with fire. Come, let's build the wall of Jerusalem again. Then we won't be ashamed any more."

¹⁸I also told those people that God had been kind to me. I told them the things the king had said to me. Then those people answered, "Let's start to work, now!" So we began this good work. ¹⁹But Sanballat from Horon, Tobiah the Ammonite official, and Geshem the Arab heard that we were building again. They made fun of us in a very ugly way. They said, "What are you doing? Are you turning against the king?"

²⁰But this is what I said to those men: "The God of Heaven will help us succeed. We are God's servants and we will build this city again. And you can't help us in this work. None of your family lived here in Jerusalem. You don't own any of this land. You have no right to be in this place!"

Builders of the Wall

3 The name of the high priest was Eliashib. Eliashib and his brothers the priests went to work and built the Sheep Gate. They prayed and made that gate holy to the Lord. They set its doors in place in the wall. Those priests worked on the wall of Jerusalem as far as the Tower of the Hundred and the Tower of Hananel. They prayed and made their work holy to the Lord.

²The men from Jericho built the wall next to the priests. And Zaccur son of a man named Imri built the wall next to the men of Jericho.

³The sons of a man named Hassenaah built the Fish Gate. They set the beams in place. They put doors on the building. Then they put the locks and bolts on the doors.

---

ancestors Literally, "fathers," meaning a person's parents, grandparents, and all the people they are descended from.

temple The special building in Jerusalem for Jewish worship.

⁴Meremoth son of Uriah fixed the next section of the wall. (Uriah was the son of Hakkoz.) Meshullam son of Berekiah fixed the next section of the wall. (Berekiah was the son of Meshezabel.) Zadok son of Baana fixed the next section of the wall. ⁵The men from Tekoa fixed the next section of the wall. But the leaders from Tekoa refused to work for ⌊Nehemiah⌋ their governor.

⁶Joiada and Meshullam fixed the Old Gate. Joiada is the son of Paseah and Meshullam is the son of Besodeiah. They set the beams in place. They put the doors on the hinges. Then they put the locks and bolts on the doors.

⁷The men from Gibeon and Mizpah fixed the next section of the wall. A man named Melatiah from Gibeon and a man named Jadon from Meronoth did the work. Gibeon and Meronoth are places that are controlled by the governors of the area west of the Euphrates River.

⁸Uzziel son of Harhaiah fixed the next section of the wall. Uzziel was a goldsmith.* Hananiah was one of the perfume makers. Those men built and fixed Jerusalem as far as the Broad Wall.

⁹Rephaiah son of Hur fixed the next section of the wall. Rephaiah was the governor of half of Jerusalem.

¹⁰Jedaiah son of Harumaph fixed the next section of the wall. Jedaiah fixed the wall next to his own house. Hattush son of Hashabneiah fixed the next section. ¹¹Malkijah son of Harim and Hasshub son of Pahath-Moab fixed the next section. Those men also fixed Oven Tower.

¹²Shallum son of Hallohesh fixed the next section of the wall. His daughters helped him. Shallum was the governor of the other half of Jerusalem.

¹³The Valley Gate was fixed by a man named Hanun and the people that live in the town of Zanoah. Those people built the Valley Gate. They put the doors on their hinges. Then they put the locks and bolts on the doors. They also fixed 500 yards* of the wall. They worked on the wall all the way to the Gate of Ash Piles.

¹⁴Malkijah son of Recab fixed the Gate of Ash Piles. Malkijah was the governor of the district of Beth Hakkerem. He fixed that gate. He put the doors on the hinges. Then he put the locks and bolts on the doors.

¹⁵Shallun son of Col-Hozeh fixed the Fountain Gate. Shallun was the governor of the district of Mizpah. He fixed that gate and put a roof over it. He put the doors on the hinges. Then he put the locks and bolts on the doors. Shallun also fixed the wall of the Pool of Siloam that is next to the King's Garden. He fixed the wall all the way to the steps that go down from the City of David.*

¹⁶Nehemiah son of Azbuk fixed the next section. This Nehemiah was the governor of half the district of Beth Zur. He made repairs up to a place that is across from the tombs of David. And he worked as far as the man-made pool and the House of Heroes.

¹⁷The men from the family group of Levi fixed the next section. Those men from Levi worked under Rehum son of Bani. Hashabiah fixed the next section. Hashabiah was governor of half the district of Keilah. He made repairs for his own district.

¹⁸Their brothers fixed the next section. They worked under Binnui son of Henadad. Binnui was the governor of the other half of the district of Keilah.

¹⁹Ezer son of Jeshua fixed the next section. Ezer was governor of Mizpah. He fixed the section of wall from the room for weapons to the corner of the wall. ²⁰Baruch son of Zabbai fixed the next section. Baruch worked very hard and fixed the section of wall from the corner to the entrance to the house of Eliashib the high priest. ²¹Meremoth son of Uriah, the son of Hakkoz, fixed the next section of wall from the entrance to Eliashib's house to the end of that house. ²²The next section of walls was fixed by the priests that lived in that area.*

²³Benjamin and Hasshub fixed the wall in front of their own house. And Azariah son of Maaseiah, the son of Ananiah, fixed the wall next to his house.

²⁴Binnui son of Henadad fixed the section of wall from Azariah's house to the bend in the wall and then to the corner.

²⁵Palal son of Uzai worked across from the bend in the wall near the tower. This is the tower at the king's upper house. That is near the courtyard of the king's guard. Pedaiah son of Parosh worked next to Palal.

goldsmith A person that makes things from gold.
500 yards Literally, "1,000 cubits."
City of David The southeast and oldest part of the city of Jerusalem.
that area Or possibly, "the Jordan Valley."

²⁶The temple servants lived on Ophel Hill. They fixed the next section all the way to the east side of the Water Gate and the tower near it.

²⁷The men from Tekoa fixed the rest of that section from the big tower all the way to the Ophel wall.

²⁸The priests fixed the section over the Horse Gate. Each priest fixed the wall in front of his own house. ²⁹Zadok son of Immer fixed the section in front of his house. Shemaiah son of Shecaniah fixed the next section. Shemaiah was the guard of the East Gate.

³⁰Hananiah son of Shelemiah and Hanun son of Zalaph fixed the rest of that section of wall. (Hanun was Zalaph's sixth son.)

Meshullam son of Berekiah fixed the section in front of his house. ³¹Malkijah fixed the next section of wall all the way to the houses of the temple servants and the businessmen. That is across from the Inspection Gate. Malkijah fixed the section all the way to the room over the corner of the wall. Malkijah was a goldsmith.* ³²The goldsmiths and the businessmen fixed the section of wall between the room over the corner to the Sheep Gate.

Sanballat and Tobiah

4 Sanballat heard that we were building the wall of Jerusalem. He became very angry and upset. He started making fun of the Jews. ²Sanballat talked with his friends and the army at Samaria. He said, "What are these weak Jews doing? Do they think we will leave them alone? Do they think they will offer sacrifices?* Maybe they think they can finish building in only one day. They can't bring stones back to life from these piles of trash and dirt. These are just piles of ashes and dirt!"

³Tobiah the Ammonite was with Sanballat. Tobiah said, "What do these Jews think they are building? If even a small fox climbed up on it, he would break down their wall of stones!"

⁴[Nehemiah prayed to God. He said,] "Our God, listen to our prayer. Those men hate us. Sanballat and Tobiah are insulting us. Make those bad things happen to them. Make them ashamed, like people taken away as prisoners. ⁵Don't take away their guilt or forgive the sins they have done in your sight. They have insulted and discouraged the builders."

⁶We built the wall of Jerusalem. We built the wall all the way around the city. But it was only half as tall as it should be. We did this much because the people worked with all their heart.

⁷But Sanballat, Tobiah, the Arabs, the Ammonites, and the men from Ashdod were very angry. They heard that the people continued working on the walls of Jerusalem. They heard the people were fixing the holes in the wall. ⁸So all those men got together and made plans against Jerusalem. They planned to stir up trouble against Jerusalem. They planned to come and fight against the city. ⁹But we prayed to our God. And we put guards on the walls to watch day and night so we could be ready to meet those men.

¹⁰And so at that time, the people of Judah said, "The workers are becoming tired. There is too much dirt and trash in the way. We can't continue to build the wall. ¹¹And our enemies are saying, 'Before the Jews know it or see us, we will be right there among them. We will kill them and that will stop the work.'"

¹²Then the Jews living among our enemies came and said this to us ten times, 'Our enemies are all around us. They are everywhere we turn.'"

¹³So I put some of the people behind the lowest places along the wall. And I put them by the holes in the wall. I put families together, with their swords, spears, and bows. ¹⁴I looked the whole situation over. Then I stood up and spoke to the important families, the officials, and the rest of the people. I said, "Don't be afraid of our enemies. Remember our Master. The Lord is great and powerful! You must fight for your brothers, your sons, and your daughters! You must fight for your wives and your homes!"

¹⁵Then our enemies heard that we knew about their plans. They knew that God ruined their plans. So we all went back to work on the wall. Each person went back to his own place and did his part. ¹⁶From that day on, half of my men worked on the wall. The other half of my men were on guard, ready with spears, shields, bows, and armor. The army officers stood behind all the people of Judah that were building the wall. ¹⁷The builders and their helpers had their tools in one hand and a weapon in the other hand. ¹⁸Each of the builders wore his sword at his side as he worked. The man that blew the trumpet to warn the people stayed next to me. ¹⁹Then I spoke to the leading families, the officials, and the rest of the people. I said, "This is a very big job and we

---

goldsmith A person that makes things from gold.
sacrifice(s) A gift to God. Usually, it was a special animal that was killed and burned on an altar.

are spread out along the wall. We are far from one another. ²⁰So, if you hear the trumpet, run to that place. We will all meet together there, and God will fight for us!"

²¹So we continued to work on the wall of Jerusalem, and half the men held spears. We worked from the first light of the morning till the stars came out at night.

²²At that time I also said this to the people: "Every builder and his helper must stay inside Jerusalem at night. Then they can be guards at night and workers during the day." ²³So none of us took off our clothes—not me, not my brothers, not my men, and not the guards. Each of us had our weapon ready at all times, even when we went to get water.

Nehemiah Helps the Poor People

5 Many of the ₁poor₁ people began to complain against their Jewish brothers. ²Some of them were saying, "We have many children. We must get some grain if we are going to eat and stay alive!"

³Other people were saying, "This is a time of famine.* We are having to mortgage* our fields, vineyards, and homes to get grain."

⁴And still other people were saying, "We have to pay the king's tax on our fields and vineyards. But we can't afford to pay, so we are having to borrow money to pay the tax. ⁵₁Look at those rich people!₁ We are as good as they are. Our sons are as good as their sons. But we will have to sell our sons and daughters as slaves. Some of us have already had to sell our daughters as slaves! There is nothing we can do! We already lost our fields and vineyards! Other people own them now!"

⁶When I heard their complaints, I became very angry. ⁷I calmed myself down and then I went to the rich families and the officials. I told them, "You are forcing your own people to pay interest on the money you loan them! ₁You must stop doing that!₁ Then I called for all the people to meet together. ⁸And I said to those people, "Our Jewish brothers were sold as slaves to people in other countries. We did our best to buy them back and make them free. And now, you are selling them like slaves again!"

Those rich people and officials kept quiet. They could not find anything to say. ⁹So I continued speaking. I said, "What you people are doing is not right! You know that you should fear and respect God. You should not do the shameful things other people do! ¹⁰My men, my brothers, and I are also lending money and grain to the people. But let's stop forcing them to pay interest on those loans! ¹¹You must give their fields, vineyards, olive fields, and houses back to them, right now! And you must give back the interest you charged them! You charged them one per cent for the money, grain, new wine, and oil that you loaned them. ₁You must give that back to them!₁

¹²Then the rich people and the officials said, "We will give it back. And we won't demand anything more from them. Nehemiah, we will do as you say."

Then I called the priests. I made the rich people and the officials promise to God that they would do what they said. ¹³Then I shook out the folds of my clothes. I said, "God will do the same thing to every person that doesn't keep his promise. God will shake them out of their houses and they will lose everything they worked for! That person will lose everything!"

I finished saying these things and all those people agreed. They all said, "Amen!" And they praised the Lord. And so the people did as they had promised.

¹⁴And also, during the whole time that I was appointed to be governor in the land of Judah, neither I nor my brothers ate the food that was allowed for the governor. ₁I never forced the people to pay those taxes to buy my food.₁ I was governor from the 20th year until the 32nd year that Artaxerxes was king.* I was governor of Judah for twelve years. ¹⁵But the governors that ruled before me made life hard for the people. Those governors forced every person to pay 1 pound* of silver. They also made those people give them food and wine. The leaders under those governors also ruled over the people ₁and made life even harder₁. But I respected and feared God, so I didn't do things like that. ¹⁶I worked hard at building the wall of Jerusalem. All my men gathered there to work on the wall. We didn't take any land from anyone!

---

famine A time when there is not enough rain for crops to grow. People and animals die without enough food or water.
mortgage A way to borrow money. People use things, land, or houses as a promise to pay their loan. If they fail to pay the loan, then the lender can take their property.

20th year ... king This was from 444-432 B.C.
1 pound Literally, "40 shekels."

¹⁷Also, I regularly fed 150 Jews that were always welcome at my table. And I fed the people that came to us from the nations around us. ¹⁸Every day I fixed this much food for the people that ate at my table: one cow, six good sheep, and different kinds of birds. And every ten days all kinds of wine were brought to my table. Yet, I never demanded the food that was allowed for the governor. ₍I never forced the people to pay those taxes to pay for my food.₎ I knew that the work the people were doing was very hard. ¹⁹God, remember all the good I have done for these people.

More Problems

6 Then Sanballat, Tobiah, Geshem the Arab, and our other enemies heard that I had built the wall. We fixed all the holes in the wall. But we had not yet put the doors in the gates. ²So Sanballat and Geshem sent me this message: "Come Nehemiah, let's meet together. We can meet in the town of Kephirim on the plain of Ono." But they were planning to hurt me.

³So I sent messengers to them with this answer: "I am doing important work, so I can't come down. I don't want the work to stop just so I can come down and meet with you."

⁴Sanballat and Geshem sent the same message to me four times. And I sent back the same answer to them each time. ⁵Then, the fifth time, Sanballat sent his helper to me with the same message. And he had a letter in his hand that was not sealed. ⁶This is what that letter said: "There is a rumor going around. People are talking about it everywhere. And, by the way, Geshem says it is true. People are saying that you and the Jews are planning to turn against the king. That is why you are building the wall of Jerusalem. People are also saying that you will be the new king of the Jews.

⁷"And the rumor is that you have chosen prophets to announce this about you in Jerusalem: 'There is a king in Judah!'

Now I warn you, Nehemiah, King Artaxerxes will hear about this. So come, let's meet and talk about this together."

⁸So I sent this answer back to Sanballat: "Nothing that you are saying is happening. You are just making all that up in your own head."

⁹Our enemies were only trying to make us afraid. They are thinking to themselves, "The Jews will be afraid, and will become too weak to keep on working. Then the wall won't be finished."

But I prayed, "God, make me strong."

¹⁰One day I went to the house of a man named Shemaiah son of Delaiah. Delaiah was the son of Mehetabel. Shemaiah had to stay in his house. Shemaiah said,

"Nehemiah, let's meet in God's temple.*
Let's go inside and close the doors.
Why? Because men are coming to kill you.
Tonight they are coming to kill you."

¹¹But I said to Shemaiah, "Should a man like me run away? You know that a man like me should not run into the temple to save his life. I won't go!"

¹²I knew that God had not sent Shemaiah. I knew that he had preached against me because Tobiah and Sanballat had paid him to do that. ¹³Shemaiah had been hired to bother me and make me afraid. They wanted me to sin by being afraid and running to the temple to hide. Then my enemies would have a reason to embarrass me and give me a bad name.

¹⁴God, please remember Tobiah and Sanballat. Remember the bad things they have done. Also remember the woman prophet Noadiah and the other prophets that have been trying to make me afraid.

The Wall Is Finished

¹⁵So the wall of Jerusalem was finished on the 25th day of the month of Elul.* It had taken 52 days to finish building the wall. ¹⁶Then all our enemies heard that we had completed the wall. And all the nations around us saw that it was finished. So they lost their courage. Why? Because they understood that this work had been done with the help of our God.

¹⁷Also, in those days after the wall had been completed, the rich people of Judah were sending many letters to Tobiah. And Tobiah was answering their letters. ¹⁸They sent those letters because many people in Judah had promised to be loyal to him. The reason for this is because Tobiah was son-in-law to Shecaniah son of Arah. And Tobiah's son Jehohanan had married the daughter of Meshullam. Meshullam is the son of Berekiah. ¹⁹And in the past, those people had made a special promise to Tobiah. So those people kept telling me how good Tobiah was. And

---

temple The special building in Jerusalem for Jewish worship.
Elul This was August-September, 443 B.C.

they kept telling Tobiah about the things I was doing. Tobiah kept sending me letters to make me afraid.

7 So, we finished building the wall. Then we put the doors in the gates. Then we chose the men that would guard the gates. And we chose the men to sing in the temple* and help the priests. ²Next, I put my brother Hanani in charge of Jerusalem. I chose another man named Hananiah to be the commander of the fort. I picked Hanani because he was a very honest man and he feared God more than most men do. ³Then I said to Hanani and Hananiah, "Each day you must wait until the sun has been up for several hours before you open the gates of Jerusalem. And you must shut and lock the gates before the sun goes down. Also choose people that live in Jerusalem as guards. Put some of those people at special places to guard the city. And put the other people near their own houses."

The List of Captives That Returned

⁴Now the city was large and there was plenty of room. But there were few people in it and the houses had not yet been built again. ⁵So my God put it in my heart to have all the people meet together. I called together all the important people, the officials, and the common people. I did this so I could make a list of all the families. I found the family lists* of the people that had been the first to return from captivity. This is what I found written there:

⁶These are the people of the province that came back from captivity. In the past, Nebuchadnezzar king of Babylon took these people as prisoners to Babylon. These people came back to Jerusalem and Judah. Each person went to his own town. ⁷These people returned with Zerubbabel:* Jeshua, Nehemiah, Azariah, Raamiah, Nahamani, Mordecai, Bilshan, Mispereth, Bigvai, Nehum, and Baanah. This is the list of names and numbers of men from Israel that came back:

⁸	The descendants of Parosh	2,172
⁹	the descendants of Shephatiah	372
¹⁰	the descendants of Arah	652
¹¹	the descendants of Pahath Moab of the family line of Jeshua and Joab	2,818
¹²	the descendants of Elam	1,254
¹³	the descendants of Zattu	845
¹⁴	the descendants of Zaccai	760
¹⁵	the descendants of Binnui	648
¹⁶	the descendants of Bebai	628
¹⁷	the descendants of Azgad	2,322
¹⁸	the descendants of Adonikam	667
¹⁹	the descendants of Bigvai	2,067
²⁰	the descendants of Adin	655
²¹	the descendants of Ater through the family of Hezekiah	98
²²	the descendants of Hashum	328
²³	the descendants of Bezai	324
²⁴	the descendants of Hariph	112
²⁵	the descendants of Gibeon	95
²⁶	from the towns of Bethlehem and Netophah	188
²⁷	from the town of Anathoth	128
²⁸	from the town of Beth Azmaveth	42
²⁹	from the towns of Kiriath Jearim, Kephirah, and Beeroth	743
³⁰	from the towns of Ramah and Geba	621
³¹	from the town of Micmash	122
³²	from the towns of Bethel and Ai	123
³³	from the other town of Nebo	52
³⁴	from the other town of Elam	1,254
³⁵	from the town of Harim	320
³⁶	from the town of Jericho	345
³⁷	from the towns of Lod, Hadid, and Ono	721
³⁸	from the town of Senaah	3,930

³⁹These are the priests:

The descendants of Jedaiah through the family of Jeshua	973
⁴⁰the descendants of Immer	1,052
⁴¹the descendants of Pashhur	1,247
⁴²the descendants of Harim	1,017

⁴³These are the people from the family group of Levi:

The descendants of Jeshua through Kadmiel through the family of Hodeiah*	74

⁴⁴These are the singers:

The descendants of Asaph	148

---

temple The special building in Jerusalem for Jewish worship.
family lists See Ezra 2.
Zerubbabel He is also called Sheshbazzar.
Hodeiah Or, "Hodaviah."

⁴⁵These are the gatekeepers:

The descendants of Shallum, Ater, Talmon, Akkub, Hatita, and Shobai   138

⁴⁶These are the special temple servants:

The descendants of Ziha, Hasupha, Tabbaoth,
⁴⁷ Keros, Sia, Padon,
⁴⁸ Lebana, Hagaba, Shalmai,
⁴⁹ Hanan, Giddel, Gaher,
⁵⁰ Reaiah, Rezin, Nekoda,
⁵¹ Gazzam, Uzza, Paseah,
⁵² Besai, Meunim, Nephussim,
⁵³ Bakbuk, Hakupha, Harhur,
⁵⁴ Bazluth, Mehida, Harsha,
⁵⁵ Barkos, Sisera, Temah,
⁵⁶ Neziah and Hatipha.

⁵⁷These are the descendants of the servants of Solomon:

Sotai, Sophereth, Perida,
⁵⁸ Jaala, Darkon, Giddel,
⁵⁹ Shephatiah, Hattil, Pokereth Hazzebaim, and Amon.

⁶⁰ The temple servants and the descendants of Solomon's servants   392

⁶¹Some people came to Jerusalem from these towns of Tel Melah, Tel Harsha, Kerub, Addon, and Immer. But these people could not prove that their families really came from the people of Israel:

⁶² The descendants of Delaiah, Tobiah and Nekoda   642

⁶³From the family of priests there were the descendants of:

Hobaiah, Hakkoz, and Barzillai
(If a man married a daughter of Barzillai from Gilead, that man was counted as a descendant of Barzillai.)

⁶⁴These people searched for their family histories, but they could not find them. They could not prove that their ancestors were priests, so they could serve as priests. Their names were not included in the list of priests. ⁶⁵The governor ordered these people not eat any of the most holy food. They could not eat any of this food until the ₍high₎ priest could use the Urim and Thummim* to ask God what to do.

⁶⁶⁻⁶⁷All together, there were 42,360 people in the group that came back. This is not counting their 7,337 men and women servants. They also had 245 men and women singers with them. ⁶⁸⁻⁶⁹They had 736 horses, 245 mules, 435 camels, and 6,720 donkeys.

⁷⁰Some of the family leaders gave money to support the work. The governor gave 19 pounds* of gold to the treasury. He also gave 50 bowls and 530 pieces of clothing for the priests. ⁷¹The family leaders gave 375 pounds* of gold to the treasury to support the work. And they also gave 1 1/3 tons* of silver. ⁷²And all together the other people gave 375 pounds* of gold, 1 1/3 tons* of silver, and 67 pieces of clothing for the priests.

⁷³So, the priests, the people from the family group of Levi, the gatekeepers, the singers, and the temple servants settled down in their own towns. And all the other people of Israel settled down in their own towns. And by the seventh month* of the year all the people of Israel had settled down in their own towns.

Ezra Reads the Law

8 So all the people of Israel met together in the seventh month* of the year. They were together and in agreement just as if they were one man. They all met together in the open place in front of the Water Gate. All those people asked Ezra the teacher to bring out the Book of the Law of Moses. That is the Law that the Lord had given to the people of Israel. ²So Ezra the priest brought the Law before those people that had met together. This was on the first day of the month.* It was the seventh month of the year. At that meeting were men and women, and anyone old enough to listen and understand. ³Ezra read in a

Urim and Thummim Used by the priest to learn God's answer to questions. They were something like lots—stones, sticks, or bones that were thrown like dice to make decisions.
19 pounds Literally, "1,000 drachmas."
375 pounds Literally, "20,000 drachmas."
1 1/3 tons Literally, "2,200 minas."
375 pounds Literally, "20,000 drachmas."
1 1/3 tons Literally, "2,200 minas."
seventh month That is, September-October.
seventh month That is, September-October.
first day of the month This was a special day of worship. The people met together and shared a fellowship meal.

loud voice from the Book of the Law from early morning until noon. Ezra was facing the open place that was in front of the Water Gate. He read to all the men and women, and to everyone old enough to listen and understand. All the people listened carefully and paid attention to the Book of the Law. ⁴Ezra stood on a high wooden stage. It had been built just for this special time. On Ezra's right side stood Mattithiah, Shema, Ananiah, Uriah, Hilkiah, and Maaseiah. And on Ezra's left side stood Pedaiah, Mishael, Malkijah, Hashum, Hashbaddanah, Zechariah, and Meshullam. ⁵So Ezra opened the book. All the people could see Ezra because he was standing above them on the high stage. And as Ezra opened the Book of the Law, all the people stood up. ⁶Ezra praised the Lord, the great God. And all the people held up their hands and said, "Amen! Amen!" Then all the people bowed down and put their faces low to the ground and they worshiped the Lord.

⁷These men from the family group of Levi taught the people about the Law as they were all standing there. Those Levites were: Jeshua, Bani, Sherebiah, Jamin, Akkub, Shabbethai, Hodiah, Maaseiah, Kelita, Azariah, Jozabad, Hanan, and Pelaiah. ⁸Those Levites read the Book of the Law of God. They made it easy to understand, and explained what it meant. They did this so the people could understand what was being read.

⁹Then Nehemiah the governor, Ezra the priest and teacher, and the men from the Levites that were teaching the people spoke. They said, "Today is a special day* to the Lord your God. Don't be sad and cry." They said that because all the people had begun to cry as they were listening to the messages of God in the Law.

¹⁰Nehemiah said, "Go and enjoy the good food and sweet drinks. And give some food and drinks to those people that didn't prepare any food. Today is a special day to the Lord. Don't be sad! Why? Because the joy of the Lord will make you strong."

¹¹The men from the family group of Levi helped the people to calm down. They said, "Be quiet, calm down, this is a special day. Don't be sad."

¹²Then all the people went to eat the special meal. They shared their food and drinks. They were very happy and celebrated that special day.

They finally understood the lessons from the Lord that the teachers had been trying to teach them.

¹³Then on the second day of the month,* the leaders of all the families went to meet with Ezra, the priests, and the Levites. They all gathered around Ezra the teacher to study the words of the Law.

¹⁴⁻¹⁵They studied and found these commands in the Law. The Lord give this command to the people through Moses: In the seventh month* of the year, the people of Israel must ₍go to Jerusalem₎ to celebrate a special holiday. They must live in temporary shelters. And the people are supposed to go through all of their towns and Jerusalem and say these things: "Go out into the hill country and get branches from different kinds of olive trees. Get branches from myrtle trees, palm trees, and shade trees. Use those branches to make temporary shelters. Do what the Law says."

¹⁶So the people went out and got those tree branches. Then they built temporary shelters for themselves. They built shelters on their own roofs and in their own yards. And they built shelters in the temple* yard, in the open place near the Water Gate, and near Ephraim Gate. ¹⁷The whole group of the people of Israel that had come back from captivity built shelters. They lived in the shelters they had built. Since the days of Joshua son of Nun up until that day, the people of Israel had not celebrated the Festival of Shelters like this. Everyone was very happy!

¹⁸Ezra read to them from the Book of the Law every day of the festival. Ezra read the Law to them from the first day of the festival to the last day. The people of Israel celebrated the festival for seven days. Then on the eighth day the people met together for a special meeting, like the Law says.

The People of Israel Confess Their Sins

9 Then on the 24th day of that same month, the people of Israel gathered together for a day of fasting.* They wore clothes of sadness and put ashes on their heads ₍to show they were sad and upset₎. ²Those people that were true Israelites

---

special day The first and second days of each month were special days of worship. The people met together and shared a fellowship meal.

second day of the month The first and second days of each month were special days of worship. The people met together and shared a fellowship meal.

seventh month That is, September-October.

temple The special building in Jerusalem for Jewish worship.

fast(ing) To live without food for a special time of prayer and worship to God.

separated themselves from foreigners. The Israelites stood ⌊in the temple⌋ and confessed their sins and the sins of their ancestors.* ³They stood there for about three hours, and the people read the Book of the Law of the Lord their God. Then for three more hours they confessed their sins and bowed down to worship the Lord their God.

⁴Then these Levites stood on the stairs: Jeshua, Bani, Kadmiel, Shebaniah, Bunni, Sherebiah, Bani, and Kenani. They called out to the Lord their God with loud voices. ⁵Then these Levites spoke again: Jeshua, Bani, Kadmiel, Bani, Hashabneiah, Sherebiah, Hodiah, Shebaniah, and Pethahiah. They said: "Stand up and praise the Lord your God!"

> God has always lived!
> And God will live forever!
> People should praise your glorious name!
> May your name be lifted above all
>   blessing and praise!
> 6 You are God!
> Lord, only you are God!
> You made the sky!
> You made the highest heavens,
>   and everything in them!
> You made the earth,
>   and everything on it!
> You made the seas,
>   and everything in them!
> You give life to everything!
> And all the heavenly angels
>   bow down and worship you!
> 7 You are the Lord God.
> You chose Abram.
> You led him from Ur in Babylonia.
> You changed his name to Abraham.
> 8 You saw he was true and loyal to you.
> And you made an agreement with him.
> You promised to give him the land of
>   the Canaanites, Hittites, and Amorites,
>   the Perizzites, Jebusites, and
>   Girgashites.
> But you promised to give that land to
>   Abraham's descendants.
> And you kept your promise!
> Why? Because you are good!
> 9 You saw our ancestors suffering in Egypt.
> And you heard them call for help
>   by the Red Sea.

ancestors Literally, "fathers," meaning a person's parents, grandparents, and all the people they are descended from.

> 10 You showed the miracles to Pharaoh.
> You did amazing things to his officials
>   and his people.
> You knew that the Egyptians thought
>   they were better than our ancestors.
> But you proved how great you are!
> And they remember that even today!
> 11 You split the Red Sea in front of them.
> And they walked through on dry land!
> The Egyptian soldiers were chasing them.
> But you threw that enemy into the sea.
> And they sank like a rock into the sea.
> 12 You used the tall cloud to lead them by day.
> And at night you used the column of fire.
> That is the way you lit their path,
>   and showed them where to go.
> 13 Then you came down to Mount Sinai.
> You spoke to them from heaven.
> You gave them good laws.
> You gave them true teachings.
> You gave them laws and commands that
>   were very good!
> 14 You told them about your special day of
>   rest—the Sabbath.
> You used your servant Moses to give them
>   commands, laws, and teachings.
> 15 They were hungry,
>   so you gave them food from heaven.
> They were thirsty,
>   so you gave them water from a rock.
> And you told them,
>   'Come, take this land.'
> You used your power,
>   and took the land for them!
> 16 But those people, our ancestors,
>   became proud.
> They became stubborn.
> They refused to obey your commands.
> 17 They refused to listen.
> They forgot the amazing things you did
>   with them!
> They became stubborn.
> They followed Miriam,
>   and became slaves again!
> But you are a forgiving God!
> You are kind and full of mercy.
> You are patient and full of love.
> So you didn't leave them!
> 18 You didn't leave them even when
>   they made golden calves and said,
>   'These are the gods
>   that led us out of Egypt!'

19 You are very kind!
  So you didn't leave them in the desert.
  You didn't take the tall cloud
    away from them by day.
  You continued to lead them.
  You didn't take the column of fire
    away from them at night.
  You continued to light their path
    and show them which way to go.
20 You gave them your good Spirit
    to make them wise.
  You gave them manna for food.
  You gave them water for their thirst.
21 You took care of them for 40 years!
  They had all they needed in the desert.
  Their clothes didn't wear out.
  And their feet didn't swell and hurt.
22 Lord, you gave them kingdoms and nations.
  And you gave them faraway places
    where few people live.
  They got the land of Sihon, king of
    Heshbon.
  They got the land of Og, king of Bashan.
23 You made their descendants
    as many as the stars in the sky.
  You brought them to the land
    you promised to give their ancestors.
  They went in and took that land.
24 Those children took the land.
  They defeated the Canaanites living there.
  You let them defeat those people!
  You let them do whatever they wanted
    to those nations, people, and kings!
25 They defeated powerful cities.
  They took the fertile land.
  They got houses filled with good things.
  They got wells that were already dug.
  They got vineyards, olive trees, and plenty
    of fruit trees!
  They ate until they were full and fat.
  They enjoyed all the wonderful things
    you gave them.
26 And then they turned against you!
  They threw away your teachings!
  They killed your prophets.
  Those prophets warned the people.
  They tried to get them to come back to you.
  But our ancestors did terrible things to you!
27 So you let their enemies have them.
  The enemy caused them much trouble.
  When trouble came,
    our ancestors called to you for help.
  And in heaven, you heard them.
  You are very kind.
  So you sent people to save them.
  And those people rescued them from
    their enemies.
28 Then, as soon as our ancestors were rested,
    they started doing terrible things again!
  So you let the enemy defeat them
    and punish them.
  They called to you for help,
    and in heaven you heard them
    and helped them.
  You are so kind!
  That happened so many times!
29 You warned them.
  You told them to come back.
  But they were too proud.
  They refused to listen to your commands.
  If people obey your laws,
    then they will truly live!
  But our ancestors broke your laws.
  They were stubborn.
  They turned their backs on you.
  They refused to listen.
30 You were very patient with our ancestors.
  You let them mistreat you for many years.
  You warned them with your Spirit.
  You sent the prophets to warn them.
  But our ancestors didn't listen.
  So you gave them to people in other
    countries.
31 But you are so kind!
  You didn't destroy them completely.
  You didn't leave them.
  You are such a kind and merciful God!
32 Our God, you are the great God,
    the awesome, powerful soldier!
  And you are kind and loyal!
  You keep your agreement!
  We have had many troubles.
  And our troubles are important to you!
  Bad things happened to all our people,
    and to our kings and leaders,
    and to our priests and prophets.
  Those terrible things have happened
    from the days of the king of Assyria
    until today!
33 But God, you were right
    about everything that happens to us.
  You were right.
  And we were wrong.
34 Our kings, leaders, priests, and ancestors
    did not obey your law.
  They didn't listen to your commands.
  They ignored your warnings.

35 Our ancestors didn't serve you
even when they were living
in their own kingdom,
They didn't stop doing evil things.
They enjoyed all the wonderful things
you gave them.
They enjoyed the rich land
and they had plenty of room,
but they didn't stop their evil ways.
36 And now, we are slaves.
We are slaves in this land,
the land you gave our ancestors
so they could enjoy its fruit
and all the good things that grow here.
37 The harvest is big in this land.
But we sinned, so that harvest
goes to the kings you put over us.
Those kings control us and our cattle.
They do anything they want.
We are in a lot of trouble.

38 Because of all of these things,
we are making an agreement
that can't be changed.
We are putting this agreement in writing.
Our leaders, and Levites, and priests
are signing their names on this
agreement
and sealing it with a seal.*

10 These are the names on the sealed agreement: Nehemiah the governor. Nehemiah was the son of Hacaliah. Zedekiah, ²Seraiah, Azariah, Jeremiah, ³Pashhur, Amariah, Malkijah, ⁴Hattush, Shebaniah, Malluch, ⁵Harim, Meremoth, Obadiah, ⁶Daniel, Ginnethon, Baruch, ⁷Meshullam, Abijah, Mijamin, ⁸Maaziah, Bilgai, and Shemaiah. These were the names of the priests that put their names on the sealed agreement.

⁹And these are the Levites that put their names on the sealed agreement: Jeshua son of Azaniah, Binnui from the family of Henadad, Kadmiel, ¹⁰and their brothers: Shebaniah, Hodiah, Kelita, Pelaiah, Hanan, ¹¹Mica, Rehob, Hashabiah, ¹²Zaccur, Sherebiah, Shebaniah, ¹³Hodiah, Bani, and Beninu.

¹⁴And these are the names of the leaders that put their names on the sealed agreement: Parosh, Pahath-Moab, Elam, Zattu, Bani, ¹⁵Bunni, Azgad, Bebai, ¹⁶Adonijah, Bigvai, Adin, ¹⁷Ater, Hezekiah, Azzur, ¹⁸Hodiah, Hashum, Bezai, ¹⁹Hariph, Anathoth, Nebai, ²⁰Magpiash, Meshullam, Hezir, ²¹Meshezabel, Zadok, Jaddua, ²²Pelatiah, Hanan, Anaiah, ²³Hoshea, Hananiah, Hasshub, ²⁴Hallohesh, Pilha, Shobek, ²⁵Rehum, Hashabnah, Maaseiah, ²⁶Ahiah, Hanan, Anan, ²⁷Malluch, Harim, and Baanah.

²⁸⁻²⁹So, all these people now make this special promise to God. And they all ask for bad things to happen if they don't keep their promise. All these people promise to follow the Law of God. That Law of God was given to us through Moses his servant. These people promise to carefully obey all the commands, rules, and teachings of the Lord our God. Now, these are the people that are making this promise: The rest of the people—the priests, Levites, gatekeepers, singers, temple servants, and all the people of Israel that separated themselves from the people living around them. They have separated themselves to obey God's law. And also all their wives and all their sons and daughters that are able to listen and understand. All these people joined their brothers and the important people to accept for themselves the promise to obey God's Law. And they accepted the curse that asks for bad things to happen to them if they don't obey God's Law.

³⁰"We promise not to let our daughters marry the people living around us. And we promise not to let our sons marry their daughters.

³¹"We promise not to work on the Sabbath day. If the people living around us bring grain or other things to sell on the Sabbath, we won't buy those things on that special day or on any other holiday. Every seventh year,* we won't plant or work the land. And every seventh year, we will cancel every debt that other people owe to us.

³²"We will accept the responsibility for obeying the commands to take care of God's temple.* We will give 1/3 shekel* ₍of silver₎ each year to support the temple service to honor our God. ³³This money will pay for the special bread that the priests put on the table in the temple. It will pay for the daily grain offerings and burnt

---

seal(s) Small stones or rings with special shapes that could be used like a rubber stamp. When pressed into wet clay or hot wax, they left a special mark that was like a signature.

seventh year See Ex. 23:10, 11.
temple The special building in Jerusalem for Jewish worship.
1/3 shekel This was probably a coin at this time, but 1 shekel is about 2/5 ounce (11.5 g.).

offerings. It will pay for the offerings on the Sabbaths, New Moon* festivals, and other special meetings. It will pay for the holy offerings and for the sin offerings that make the people of Israel pure.* It will pay for any work needed on the temple of our God.

³⁴"We—the priests, the Levites, and the people—have thrown lots.* Why? To decide when each of our families is to bring a gift of wood to the temple of our God at certain times each year. The wood is to burn on the altar of the Lord our God. We must do that just as it is written in the Law.

³⁵"We also accept the responsibility of bringing the firstfruits from our crops and from every fruit tree. We will bring that fruit to the Lord's temple* each year.

³⁶"Just as it is also written in the Law, this is what we will do: We will bring our firstborn sons, and the firstborn cows, sheep, and goats. We will bring those firstborn to the temple of our God. We will bring them to the priests that are serving there.

³⁷"And we will also bring to the storage rooms of the Lord's temple,* to the priests, these things: The first of our ground meal, the first of our grain offerings, the firstfruit from all our trees, and first part from our new wine and oil. And we will bring a tenth of our crops to the Levites. Why? Because the Levites collect these things in all the towns where we work. ³⁸A priest from the family of Aaron must be with the Levites when they receive those crops. And then the Levites must bring those crops to the temple of our God. Then they will put them in the storerooms of the temple treasury. ³⁹The people of Israel and the Levites must bring their gifts to the storerooms. They are to bring their gifts of grain, new wine, and oil. All the things for the temple are kept in those storerooms. And that is where the priests that are on duty stay. And also the singers and gatekeepers stay there.

"We all promise that we will take care of the temple of our God!"

New Moon This was the first day of the Hebrew month. There were special meetings on these days to worship God.
make ... pure Or, "make atonement." The Hebrew word means "to cover or erase a person's sins."
lot(s) Sticks, stones, or pieces of bone used like dice for making decisions. See Prov. 16:33.
temple The special building in Jerusalem for Jewish worship.

New People Move into Jerusalem

11 Now the leaders of the people of Israel moved into the city of Jerusalem. The other people of Israel had to decide who else would move into the city. So they threw lots,* and one out of every ten people had to live in Jerusalem, the holy city. The other nine people could live in their own home towns. ²Some people volunteered to live in Jerusalem. The other people thanked and blessed them for volunteering.

³Here are the leaders of the provinces that lived in Jerusalem. (Some of the people of Israel, priests, Levites, temple servants, and descendants of Solomon's servants lived in the towns of Judah. Each person lived on his own land in the different towns. ⁴And other people from the families of Judah and Benjamin lived in the city of Jerusalem.)

These are the descendants of Judah that moved into Jerusalem: Athaiah son of Uzziah (Uzziah was the son of Zechariah, who was the son of Amariah, who was the son of Shephatiah, who was the son of Mahalalel, who was a descendant of Perez) ⁵and Maaseiah son of Baruch, (Baruch was the son of Col-Hozeh, who was the son of Hazaiah, who was the son of Adaiah, who was the son of Joiarib, who was the son of Zechariah, who was a descendant of Shelah). ⁶The number of Perez's descendants living in Jerusalem was 468. All of them were brave men.

⁷These are the descendants of Benjamin that moved into Jerusalem: Sallu son of Meshullam (Meshullam was the son of Joed, who was the son of Pedaiah, who was the son of Kolaiah, who was the son of Maaseiah, who was the son of Ithiel, who was the son of Jeshaiah), ⁸and those that followed Jeshaiah were Gabbai and Sallai. All together there were 928 men. ⁹Joel son of Zicri was in charge of them. And Judah son of Hassenuah was in charge of the Second District of the city of Jerusalem.

¹⁰These are the priests that moved into Jerusalem: Jedaiah son of Joiarib, Jakin, ¹¹and Seraiah son of Hilkiah (Hilkiah was the son of Meshullam, who was the son of Zadok, who was the son of Meraioth, who was the son of Ahitub, who was the supervisor in the temple of God), ¹² 822 men of their brothers that did the work for the temple, and Adaiah son of Jeroham (Jeroham was the son of Pelaliah, who was the son of Amzi, who was the son of Zechariah, who was the son of Pashhur, who was the son of Malkijah), ¹³ 242 men that were Malkijah's brothers (These men were leaders of their families), Amashsai son of

Azarel (Azarel was the son of Ahzai, who was the son of Meshillemoth, who was the son of Immer), ¹⁴and 128 of Immer's brothers. (These men were brave soldiers. The officer over them was Zabdiel son of Haggedolim.)

¹⁵These are the Levites that moved into Jerusalem: Shemaiah son of Hasshub (Hasshub was the son of Azrikam, who was the son of Hashabiah, who was the son of Bunni), ¹⁶Shabbethai and Jozabad (These two men were leaders of the Levites. They were in charge of the outside work of God's temple), ¹⁷Mattaniah (Mattaniah was the son of Mica, who was the son of Zabdi, who was the son of Asaph, who was the choir director. Asaph led the people in singing songs of praise and prayer), Bakbukiah (Bakbukiah was the second in charge over his brothers), and Abda son of Shammua, (Shammua was the son of Galal, who was the son of Jeduthun). ¹⁸So, there were 284 Levites that moved into Jerusalem, the holy city.

¹⁹These are the gatekeepers that moved into Jerusalem: Akkub, Talmon, and 172 of their brothers. They watched and guarded the gates of the city.

²⁰The other people of Israel, and the other priests and Levites, lived in all the towns of Judah. Each person lived on the land that his ancestors had owned. ²¹The temple servants lived on the hill of Ophel. Ziha and Gishpa were in charge of those temple servants.

²²The officer over the Levites in Jerusalem was Uzzi. Uzzi was the son of Bani (Bani was the son of Hashabiah, who was the son of Mattaniah, who was the son of Mica). Uzzi was a descendant of Asaph. Asaph's descendants were the singers that were responsible for the service in God's temple. ²³The singers obeyed orders from the king. Those orders from the king told the singers what to do from day to day. ²⁴The man that told the people what the king wanted done was named Pethahiah. (Pethahiah was the son of Meshezabel, who was one of the descendants of Zerah. Zerah was Judah's son.)

²⁵The people of Judah lived in these towns: In Kiriath Arba and the small towns around it, in Dibon and the small towns around it, in Jekabzeel and the small towns around it, ²⁶and in Jeshua, in Moladah, in Beth Pelet, ²⁷in Hazar Shual, in Beersheba and the small towns around it, ²⁸and in Ziklag, in Meconah and the small towns around it, ²⁹and in En Rimmon, in Zorah, in Jarmuth, ³⁰and in Zanoah and Adullam and the small towns around them, in Lachish and the fields around it, and in Azekah and the small towns around it. So the people of Judah were living all the way from Beersheba to the Valley of Hinnom.

³¹The descendants of the family of Benjamin from Geba lived in Micmash, Aija, Bethel and the small towns around it, ³²in Anathoth, Nob and Ananiah, ³³in Hazor, Ramah and Gittaim, ³⁴in Hadid, Zeboim, and Neballat, ³⁵in Lod and Ono, and in the Valley of the Craftsmen. ³⁶Some of the groups of the people from the family of Levi moved to the land of Benjamin.

Priests and Levites

12 These are the priests and Levites that came back to the land of Judah. They came back with Zerubbabel son of Shealtiel and Jeshua. This is a list of their names: Seraiah, Jeremiah, Ezra, ²Amariah, Malluch, Hattush, ³Shecaniah, Rehum, Meremoth, ⁴Iddo, Ginnethon, Abijah, ⁵Mijamin, Maadiah, Bilgah, ⁶Shemaiah, Joiarib, Jedaiah, ⁷Sallu, Amok, Hilkiah, and Jedaiah. These men were the leaders of the priests and their relatives. They were leaders in the days of Jeshua.

⁸The Levites were: Jeshua, Binnui, Kadmiel, Sherebiah, Judah, and also Mattaniah. These men, with Mattaniah's relatives, were in charge of the songs of praise to God. ⁹Bakbukiah and Unni were the relatives of those Levites. These two men stood across from them in the services. ¹⁰Jeshua was the father of Joiakim. Joiakim was the father of Eliashib. Eliashib was the father of Joiada. ¹¹Joiada was the father of Jonathan, and Jonathan was the father of Jaddua.

¹²In the days of Joiakim, these men were the leaders of the families of priests:

	The leader of Seraiah's family was Meraiah.
13	The leader of Jeremiah's family was Hananiah.
	The leader of Ezra's family was Meshullam.
14	The leader of Amariah's family was Jehohanan.
	The leader of Malluch's family was Jonathan.
15	The leader of Shecaniah's family was Joseph.
	The leader of Harim's family was Adna.
16	The leader of Meremoth's family was Helkai.
	The leader of Iddo's family was Zechariah.
17	The leader of Ginnethon's family was Meshullam.
	The leader of Abijah's family was Zicri.
18	The leader of Miniamin's and Maadiah's families was Piltai.
	The leader of Bilgah's family was Shammua.

The leader of Shemaiah's family was Jehonathan.
19 The leader of Joiarib's family was Mattenai. The leader of Jedaiah's family was Uzzi.
20 The leader of Sallu's family was Kallai. The leader of Amok's family was Eber.
21 The leader of Hilkiah's family was Hashabiah. The leader of Jedaiah's family was Nethanel.

22 The names of the leaders of the families of the Levites and the priests in the days of Eliashib, Joiada, Johanan, and Jaddua were written down during the rule of Darius the Persian king. 23 The family leaders among the descendants* of the family of Levi and up to the time of Johanan son of Eliashib were written in the history book. 24 And these were the leaders of the Levites: Hashabiah, Sherebiah, Jeshua the son of Kadmiel, and their brothers. Their brothers stood across from them to sing praise and honor to God. One group answered the other group. That is what was commanded by David the man of God.

25 The gatekeepers that guarded the storerooms next to the gates were: Mattaniah, Bakbukiah, Obadiah, Meshullam, Talmon, and Akkub. 26 Those gatekeepers served in the days of Joiakim. Joiakim was the son of Jeshua, who was the son of Jozadak. And those gatekeepers also served in the days of Nehemiah the governor and in the days of Ezra the priest and teacher.

Dedication of the Wall of Jerusalem

27 The people dedicated the wall of Jerusalem. They brought all the Levites to Jerusalem. The Levites came from the towns they lived in. They came to Jerusalem to celebrate the dedication of the wall of Jerusalem. The Levites came to sing songs of praise and thanks to God. They played their cymbals,* harps, and lyres.*

28-29 And all the singers also came to Jerusalem. Those singers came from the towns all around Jerusalem. They came from the town of Netophah, from Beth Gilgal, Geba, and Azmaveth. The singers had built small towns for themselves in the area around Jerusalem.

30 So, the priests and Levites made themselves pure in a ceremony. Then they also made the people, the gates, and the wall of Jerusalem pure in a ceremony.

31 I told the leaders of Judah to go up and stand on top of the wall. I also chose two large singing groups to give thanks to God. One group was to start going up on top of the wall on the right side, toward the Ash Pile Gate. 32 Hoshaiah and half of the leaders of Judah followed those singers. 33 Also following them were Azariah, Ezra, Meshullam, 34 Judah, Benjamin, Shemaiah, and Jeremiah. 35 And some of the priests with trumpets also followed them up to the wall. Also Zechariah followed them. (Zechariah was the son of Jonathan, who was the son of Shemaiah, who was the son of Mattaniah, who was the son of Micaiah, who was the son of Zaccur, who was the son of Asaph.) 36 There were also Asaph's brothers, who were Shemaiah, Azarel, Milalai, Gilalai, Maai, Nethanel, Judah, and Hanani. They had the musical instruments that David, man of God, had made. Ezra the teacher led the group of people that were there to dedicate the wall. 37 They went to the Fountain Gate. They walked up the stairs all the way to the City of David.* They were on top of the city wall. They walked over the house of David and went toward the Water Gate.

38 The second group of singers started out in the other direction, to the left. I followed them as they went up to the top of the wall. Half of the people also followed them. They went past the Tower of Ovens to the Broad Wall. 39 Then they went over these gates: the Gate of Ephraim, the Old Gate, and the Fish Gate. And they went over the Tower of Hananel and the Tower of the Hundred. They went as far as the Sheep Gate. They stopped at the Guard Gate. 40 Then the two singing groups went to their places in God's temple.* And I stood in my place. And half the officials stood in their places in the temple. 41 Then these priests stood in their places: Eliakim, Maaseiah, Mijamin, Micaiah, Elioenai, Zechariah, and Hananiah. Those priests had their trumpets with them. 42 Then these priests stood in their places in the temple: Maaseiah, Shemaiah, Eleazar, Uzzi, Jehohanan, Malkijah, Elam, and Ezer.

Then two singing groups began singing with Jezrahiah leading them. 43 So, on that special day, the priests offered many sacrifices.* Everyone

City of David The southeastern and oldest part of the city of Jerusalem.
temple The special building in Jerusalem for Jewish worship.
sacrifice(s) A gift to God. Usually, it was a special animal that was killed and burned on an altar.

descendants A person's children and all of their future families.
cymbals A pair of metal platters that are hit against each other to make a loud sound.
lyre(s) An instrument with several strings, like a harp.

was very happy. God had made everyone happy. Even the women and children were excited and happy. People far away could hear the happy sounds coming from Jerusalem.

⁴⁴Men were chosen to be in charge of the storerooms on that day. People brought their firstfruits and a tenth of their crops. So the men in charge put those things in the storerooms. The Jewish people were very happy about the priests and Levites on duty. So they brought many things to be put in the storerooms. ⁴⁵The priests and Levites did their work for their God. They did the ceremonies that made people pure. And the singers and gatekeepers did their part. They did everything that David and Solomon had commanded. ⁴⁶(Long ago, in the days of David, Asaph had been the director. And he had many songs of praise and thanks to God.)

⁴⁷So in the days of Zerubbabel and of Nehemiah, all the people of Israel gave every day to support the singers and gatekeepers. The people also set aside the money for the other Levites. And the Levites set aside the money for the descendants of Aaron *(the priests).*

Nehemiah's Last Commands

13 On that day, the Book of Moses was read out loud so all the people could hear. They found this law written in the Book of Moses: No Ammonite person and no Moabite person would be permitted to join in the meetings with God. ²That law was written because those people didn't give the people of Israel food and water. And those people had paid Balaam to say a curse* against the people of Israel. But our God changed that curse and made it a blessing for us. ³So when the people of Israel heard that law, they obeyed it. They separated themselves from the people that were descendants* of foreigners.

⁴⁻⁵But, before that happened, Eliashib had given a room in the temple* to Tobiah. Eliashib was the priest in charge of the storerooms in God's temple. And Eliashib was a close friend of Tobiah. That room had been used for storing the grain offerings, incense, and the temple dishes and things. They also kept the tenth of grain, new wine, and oil for the Levites, singers, and gatekeepers in that room. And they also kept the gifts for the priests in that room. But Eliashib gave that room to Tobiah.

⁶I was not in Jerusalem while all of this was happening. I had gone back to the king of Babylon. I went back to Babylon in the 32nd year that Artaxerxes was king of Babylon.* Later, I asked the king for permission to go back to Jerusalem. ⁷So I came back to Jerusalem. In Jerusalem I heard about the sad thing that Eliashib had done. Eliashib had given Tobiah a room in the temple* of our God! ⁸I was very angry about what Eliashib had done. So I threw all of Tobiah's things out of the room. ⁹I gave commands for those rooms to be made pure and clean. Then I put the temple dishes and things, the grain offerings, and the incense back into those rooms.

¹⁰I also heard that the people had not given the Levites their share. So the Levites and singers had gone back to work in their own fields. ¹¹So I told the officials that they were wrong. I asked them, "Why didn't you take care of God's temple*?" Then I called all Levites together. I told them to go back to their places and duties in the temple. ¹²Then, everyone in Judah brought their tenth of grain, new wine, and oil to the temple. Those things were put into the storerooms.

¹³I put these men in charge of the storerooms: Shelemiah the priest, Zadok the teacher, and a Levite named Pedaiah. And I made Hanan son of Zaccur, son of Mattaniah, their helper. I knew I could trust these men. They were responsible for giving the supplies to their relatives.

¹⁴God, please remember me for these things I have done. And don't forget all I have faithfully done for the temple of my God and for its services.

¹⁵In those days in Judah, I saw people working on the Sabbath* day. I saw people pressing grapes to make wine. I saw people bringing in grain and loading it on donkeys. I saw people carrying grapes, figs, and all kinds of things in the city. They were bringing all these things into Jerusalem on the Sabbath day. So I warned them about this. I told them they must not sell food on the Sabbath day.

¹⁶There were some men from the city of Tyre living in Jerusalem. Those men were bringing fish and all kinds of things into Jerusalem and selling them on the Sabbath* day. And the Jews were buying those things. ¹⁷I told the important people

---

curse To ask for bad things to happen to someone.
descendants A person's children and all of their future families.
temple The special building in Jerusalem for Jewish worship.

32nd year ... Babylon That is, 432 B.C.
Sabbath Saturday, a special day of rest and worship for Jews.

of Judah that they were wrong. I said to those important people, "You are doing a very bad thing. You are ruining the Sabbath. You are making the Sabbath day like it was any other day. ¹⁸You know that your ancestors* did the same things. That is why our God brought all the troubles and disaster to us and to this city. Now you people are making it so more of these bad things will happen to Israel. Why? Because you are ruining the Sabbath day and making it like it is not an important day."

¹⁹So, this is what I did: Every Friday evening, just before dark, I commanded the gatekeepers to shut and lock the gates to Jerusalem. They were not to be opened until the Sabbath* day was over. I put some of my own men at the gates. Those men were commanded to make sure that no load was brought into Jerusalem on the Sabbath day.

²⁰One or two times businessmen and merchants* had to stay the night outside Jerusalem. ²¹But I warned those businessmen and merchants. I said to them, "Don't stay the night in front of the wall. If you do that again, I will arrest you." So from that time on they didn't come on the Sabbath* day to sell their things.

²²Then I commanded the Levites to make themselves pure. After they did that, they were to go and guard the gates. This was done to make sure the Sabbath* day was kept a holy day.

God, please remember me for doing these things. Be kind to me and show me your great love!

²³In those days I also noticed that some Jewish men had married women from the countries of Ashdod, Ammon, and Moab. ²⁴And half of the children from those marriages didn't know how to speak the Jewish language. Those children spoke the language of Ashdod, Ammon, or Moab. ²⁵So I told those men that they were wrong. I said bad things to them. I hit some of those men, and I pulled out their hair. I forced them to make a promise in God's name. I said to them, "You must not marry the daughters of those people. Don't let the daughters of those foreign people marry your sons. And don't let your daughters marry the sons of those foreign people. ²⁶You know that marriages like this caused Solomon to sin. In all the many nations, there was not a king as great as Solomon. God loved Solomon. And God made Solomon king over the whole nation of Israel. But even Solomon was made to sin because of foreign women. ²⁷And now, we hear that you also are doing this terrible sin. You are not being true to God. You are marrying foreign women."

²⁸Joiada was the son of Eliashib the high priest. One of Joiada's sons was a son-in-law of Sanballat from Horon. I forced that man to leave this place. I forced him to run away.

²⁹My God, punish those people. They made the priesthood unclean. They treated it like it was not important. They did not obey the agreement that you made with the priests and Levites. ³⁰So I made the priests and Levites clean and pure. I took away all the foreigners and the strange things they taught. And I gave the Levites and priests their own duties and responsibilities. ³¹And I made sure that people will bring gifts of wood and firstfruits at the right times.

My God, remember me for doing these good things.

---

ancestors Literally, "fathers," meaning a person's parents, grandparents, and all the people they are descended from.

Sabbath Saturday, a special day of rest and worship for Jews.

merchant(s) A person who earns his living by buying and selling things.

Esther

Queen Vashti Disobeys the King

1 This is what happened during the time that Xerxes was king. Xerxes ruled over the 127 provinces from India to Ethiopia. ²King Xerxes ruled from his throne* in the capital city of Susa. ³In the third year of Xerxes' rule, he gave a party for his officers and leaders. The army leaders and important leaders from all of Persia and Media were there. ⁴The party continued for 180 days. All during that time, King Xerxes was showing the great wealth of his kingdom. And he was showing everyone the majestic beauty and wealth of his palace.* ⁵And when those 180 days were over, King Xerxes gave another party that continued for seven days. That party was held in the inside garden of the palace. All the people that were in the capital city of Susa were invited, from the most important to the least important person. ⁶That inside garden had white and blue linen* hangings around the room. Those hangings were held in place with cords of white linen and purple material on silver rings and marble pillars. There were couches made of gold and silver. Those couches were setting on mosaic pavement of porphyry, marble, mother-of-pearl, and other expensive stones. ⁷Wine was served in golden cups. And every cup was different! And there was plenty of the king's wine, because the king was very generous. ⁸The king had given a command to his servants. He told them that each guest must be given as much wine as he wanted. And the wine server obeyed the king.

⁹Queen Vashti also gave a party for the women in the king's palace.

¹⁰⁻¹¹On the seventh day of the party, King Xerxes was in high spirits from drinking the wine. He gave a command to the seven eunuchs* that served him. Those eunuchs were: Mehuman, Biztha, Harbona, Bigtha, Abagtha, Zethar, and Carcas. He commanded those seven eunuchs to bring Queen Vashti to him wearing her royal crown. She was to come so she could show her beauty to the leaders and important people. She was very beautiful.

¹²But when those servants told Queen Vashti about the king's command, she refused to come. Then the king became very angry. ¹³⁻¹⁴It was the custom for the king to ask the advice of the experts about the law and punishments. So King Xerxes spoke with the wise men that understood the laws. Those wise men were very close to the king. Their names were: Carshena, Shethar, Admatha, Tarshish, Meres, Marsena, and Memucan. They were the seven most important officials of Persia and Media. They had special privileges to see the king. They were the highest officials in the kingdom. ¹⁵The king asked those men, "What does the law say must be done to Queen Vashti? She has not obeyed the command of King Xerxes that the eunuchs have taken to her."

¹⁶Then Memucan answered the king with the other officials listening, "Queen Vashti has done wrong. She has done wrong against the king and also against all the leaders and people of all the provinces of King Xerxes. ¹⁷I say that, because all the other women will hear about what Queen Vashti did. And then other women will stop obeying their husbands. They will say to their husbands, 'King Xerxes commanded Queen Vashti to be brought to him, but she refused to come.'

¹⁸"Today the wives of the Persian and Median leaders have heard what the queen did. And those women will be influenced by the thing she did. Those women will do the same thing to the king's important leaders. And there will be plenty of disrespect and anger.

---

throne The chair of a king or queen.
palace A large house for the king and his family.
linen Thread or cloth made from the fibers of the flax plant.

¹⁹"So, if it pleased the king, here is a suggestion: Let the king give a royal command and let it be written in the laws of Persia and Media. The laws of Persia and Media can't be changed. The royal command should be that Vashti is never again to enter the presence of King Xerxes. Also let the king give her royal position to someone else that is better than she. ²⁰Then when the king's command is announced in all parts of his large kingdom, all the women will respect their husbands. From the most important to the least important, all the women will respect their husbands."

²¹The king and his important officials were happy with this advice. So King Xerxes did as Memucan suggested. ²²King Xerxes sent letters to all parts of the kingdom. He sent those letters to each province, written in its own language. He sent those letters to each nation in its own language. Those letters announced in every person's language that every man was to be ruler over his own family.

Esther Made Queen

2 Later, King Xerxes stopped being angry. Then he remembered Vashti and what she had done. He remembered his commands about her. ²Then the king's personal servants had a suggestion. They said, "Search for beautiful young virgins* for the king. ³Let the king choose leaders in every province of his kingdom. Then let those leaders bring every beautiful young virgin to the capital city of Susa. Those girls will be put with the group of the king's women. And they will be under the care of Hegai, the king's eunuch, that is in charge of the women. Then give beauty treatments to all of them. ⁴Then let the girl that is pleasing to the king become the new queen in Vashti's place." The king liked this suggestion, so he accepted it.

⁵Now there was a Jew from the family group of Benjamin named Mordecai. Mordecai was the son of Jair, and Jair was the son of Kish. Mordecai was in the capital city, Susa. ⁶Mordecai had been carried into captivity from Jerusalem by Nebuchadnezzar, king of Babylon. He was with the group that was taken into captivity with Jehoiachin, king of Judah. ⁷Mordecai had a girl cousin named Hadassah. She didn't have a father or a mother, so Mordecai took care of her. Mordecai had adopted her as his own daughter when her father and mother died. Hadassah was also called Esther. Esther had a very pretty face and a good figure.

⁸When the king's command had been heard, many girls were brought to the capital city of Susa. Those girls were put under the care of Hegai. Esther was one of these women. Esther was taken to the king's palace* and put into Hegai's care. Hegai was in charge of the king's women. ⁹Hegai liked Esther. She became his favorite. So Hegai quickly gave Esther beauty treatments and special food. Hegai chose seven women servants from the king's palace and gave them to Esther. Then Hegai moved Esther and her seven girl servants into the best place where the king's women lived. ¹⁰Esther didn't tell anyone that she was a Jew. She didn't tell anyone about her family background, because Mordecai had told her not to. ¹¹Every day Mordecai walked back and forth near the area where the king's women lived. He did that because he wanted to find out how Esther was, and what was happening to her.

¹²Before a girl could take her turn to go in before King Xerxes, this is what she had to do: She had to complete twelve months of beauty treatments. That was six months with oil of myrrh and six months with perfumes and different kinds of makeup. ¹³And this is the way a girl would go to the king: They gave her anything she wanted from the house of the king's women. ¹⁴In the evening, the girl would go to the king's palace.* And in the morning, she would return to another area where the king's women lived. Then she would be placed under the care of a man named Shaashgaz. Shaashgaz was the king's eunuch* in charge of the concubines.* The girl would not go back to the king again unless he was pleased with her. Then he would call her by name to come back to him.

¹⁵When the time came for Esther to go to the king, she didn't ask for anything. She only wanted Hegai, the king's eunuch* that was in charge of the king's women, to suggest what she should take. (Esther is the girl Mordecai had adopted, the daughter of his uncle Abihail.) Everyone that looked at Esther liked her. ¹⁶So Esther was taken to King Xerxes in the palace.* This happened in

---

virgin(s) A pure woman that has not had sexual relations with anyone.

palace A large house for the king and his family.
eunuch A man whose testicles have been removed. Rulers often gave such men important positions.
concubines Women that were like wives to a man.

the tenth month, the month of Tebeth, in the seventh year of his rule. ¹⁷The king loved Esther more than any of the other girls. And she became his favorite. He approved of her more than any of the other girls. So King Xerxes put a crown on Esther's head and made her the new queen in Vashti's place. ¹⁸And the king gave a big party for Esther. It was for all his important people and leaders. He announced a holiday in all the provinces. And he sent out gifts to people, because he was a generous king.

Mordecai Learns about an Evil Plan

¹⁹Mordecai was sitting next to the king's gate at the time the girls were gathered together the second time. ²⁰Esther had still kept it a secret that she was a Jew. She had not told anyone about her family background. That is what Mordecai had told her to do. She still obeyed Mordecai just as she had done when he was taking care of her.

²¹During the time Mordecai was sitting next to the king's gate, this happened: Bigthana and Teresh, two of the king's officers that guarded the doorway, became angry at the king. They began to make plans to kill King Xerxes. ²²But Mordecai learned about those plans and told Queen Esther. Then Queen Esther told the king. She also told the king that Mordecai was the one that had learned about that evil plan. ²³Then the report was checked out. It was learned that Mordecai's report was true. The two guards that had planned to kill the king were hanged on a post. All these things were written down in a book of the king's histories in front of the king.

Haman's Plan to Destroy the Jews

3 After these things happened, King Xerxes honored Haman. Haman was the son of a man named Hammedatha, the Agagite. The king promoted Haman and gave him a place of honor more important than any of the other leaders. ²All of the king's leaders at the king's gate would bow down and give honor to Haman. That is what the king commanded those men to do. But Mordecai refused to bow down or give honor to Haman. ³Then the king's leaders at the gate asked Mordecai, "Why don't you obey the king's command to bow down to Haman?"

⁴Day after day, those king's leaders spoke to Mordecai. But he refused to obey the command to bow down to Haman. So those leaders told Haman about it. They wanted to see what Haman would do about Mordecai. Mordecai had told those leaders that he was a Jew. ⁵When Haman saw that Mordecai refused to bow down to him or give him honor, he was very angry. ⁶Haman had learned that Mordecai was a Jew. But he was not satisfied with killing only Mordecai. Haman also wanted to find a way to destroy all of Mordecai's people, the Jews, in all of Xerxes' kingdom.

⁷In the twelfth year of King Xerxes' rule, in the first month, the month of Nisan, Haman threw lots* to choose a special day and month. And the twelfth month, the month of Adar was chosen. (At that time, the lot was called "pur.") ⁸Then Haman came to King Xerxes. He said, "King Xerxes, there is a certain group of people scattered among the people in all the provinces of your kingdom. Those people keep themselves separate from other people. Their customs are different from those of all other people. And those people don't obey the king's laws. It is not best for the king to allow those people to continue to live in your kingdom. ⁹"If it pleases the king, I have a suggestion: Give a command to destroy those people. And I will put 10,000 silver coins into the king's treasury. That money could be used to pay the men that do these things."

¹⁰So the king took the official ring off his finger and gave it to Haman. Haman was the son of Hammedatha, the Agagite. Haman was the enemy of the Jews. ¹¹Then the king said to Haman, "Keep the money. Do what you want with those people."

¹²Then on the 13th day of the first month the king's secretaries were called. They wrote out all of Haman's commands in the language of each province. And they wrote them in the language of each group of people. They wrote to the king's satraps *(leaders)*, the governors of the different provinces, and the leaders of the different groups of people. They wrote with the authority of King Xerxes himself, and sealed the commands with the king's own ring.

¹³Messengers carried the letters to all the king's provinces. The letters were the king's command to ruin, kill, and completely destroy all the Jews. That meant young people and old people, women, and little children, too. The command was to kill all the Jews on a single day. That day was to be the 13th day of the twelfth month, the month of Adar. And the command was to take all of the things that belonged to the Jews.

---

lot(s) Sticks, stones, or pieces of bone used like dice for making decisions. See Proverbs 16:33.

¹⁴A copy of the letters with that command was to be given as a law. It was to be a law in every province and announced to the people of every nation living in the kingdom. Then all those people would be ready for that day. ¹⁵At the king's command the messengers hurried off. The command was given in the capital city of Susa. The king and Haman sat down to drink, but the city of Susa was confused.

Mordecai Persuades Esther to Help

4 Mordecai heard about all that had been done. When he heard about the king's commands against the Jews, he tore his clothes. Then he put on clothes of sadness and put ashes on his head. Then he went out into the city crying loudly. ²But Mordecai went only as far as the king's gate. No one was allowed to enter that gate dressed in clothes of sadness. ³In every province where the king's command had come, there was much crying and sadness among the Jews. They were fasting* and crying loudly. Many Jews were lying on the ground dressed in clothes of sadness with ashes on their heads.

⁴Esther's women servants and eunuchs* came to her and told her about Mordecai. That made Queen Esther very sad and upset. She sent clothes for Mordecai to put on instead of the clothes of sadness. But he would not accept those clothes. ⁵Then Esther called Hathach. Hathach was one of the king's eunuchs that had been chosen to serve her. Esther commanded him to find out what was bothering Mordecai, and why. ⁶So Hathach went out to where Mordecai was in the open place of the city in front of the king's gate. ⁷Then Mordecai told Hathach everything that had happened to him. Mordecai told him about the exact amount of money Haman had promised to put into the king's treasury for killing Jews. ⁸Mordecai also gave Hathach a copy of the king's command to kill the Jews. That command had been sent out all over the city of Susa. He wanted Hathach to show it to Esther and tell her everything. And he told him to encourage Esther to go to the king and beg him for mercy for Mordecai and her people. ⁹Hathach went back and told Esther everything Mordecai had said.

¹⁰Then Esther told Hathach to say this to Mordecai: ¹¹"Mordecai, all the king's leaders and all the people of the king's provinces know this: The king has one law for any man or woman that goes to the king without being called. He must be put to death. The only way this law is not carried out is if the king puts out his gold scepter* to the person. If the king does that, then that person's life will be saved. And I have not been called to go see the king for 30 days."

¹²⁻¹³Then Esther's message was given to Mordecai. When Mordecai got her message, he sent his answer back: "Esther, don't think that just because you live in the king's house you will be the only Jew to escape. ¹⁴If you keep quiet now, help and freedom for the Jews will come from another place. But you and your father's family will all die. And who knows, maybe you have been chosen to be the queen for such a time as this?"

¹⁵⁻¹⁶Then Esther sent this answer to Mordecai: "Mordecai, go and get all the Jews in Susa together, and fast* for me. Don't eat or drink for three days and nights. I will fast like you, and my girl servants will fast, too. After we fast, I will go to the king. I know it is against the law to go to the king if he didn't call me, but I will do it anyway. If I die, I die."

¹⁷So Mordecai went away. He did everything Esther told him to do.

Esther Speaks to the King

5 On the third day, Esther put on her special robes. Then she stood in the inside area of the king's palace.* That area was in front of the king's hall. The king was sitting on his throne* in the hall. He was sitting facing the place where people enter the throne room. ²Then the king saw Queen Esther standing in the court. When he saw her, he was very pleased. He held out to her the gold scepter* that was in his hand. So Esther went in to the room and went near the king. Then she touched the end of the king's gold scepter.

³Then the king asked, "What is bothering you Queen Esther? What do you want to ask me? I will give you anything you ask for, even half my kingdom."

---

fast(ing) To live without food for a special time of prayer and worship to God.
eunuchs Men whose testicles have been removed. Rulers often gave such men important positions.

scepter A special stick that a king holds in his hand.
fast To live without food for a special time of prayer and worship to God.
palace A large house for the king and his family.
throne The chair of a king or queen.

⁴Esther said, "I have prepared a party for you and Haman. Will you and Haman please come to the party today?"
⁵Then the king said, "Bring Haman quickly so that we may do what Esther asks."
So the king and Haman went to the party Esther had prepared for them. ⁶While they were drinking wine, the king asked Esther again, "Now Esther, what do you want to ask for? Ask for anything, I will give it to you. So, what is it you want? I will give you anything you want, up to half my kingdom."
⁷Esther answered, "This is what I want to ask for: ⁸If the king approves of me, and if it pleases the king to give me what I ask for, let the king and Haman come tomorrow. I will prepare another party for the king and Haman tomorrow. Then I will tell what I really want."

Haman's Anger at Mordecai

⁹Haman left the king's house that day very happy and in a good mood. But when he saw Mordecai at the king's gate, he became very angry at Mordecai. Haman was very mad at Mordecai because Mordecai didn't show any respect when Haman walked by. Mordecai was not afraid of Haman, and that made Haman mad. ¹⁰But, Haman controlled his anger and went home. Then Haman called his friends and his wife, Zeresh, together. ¹¹Haman started bragging about how rich he was. He was bragging to his friends about his many sons, and about all the ways the king had honored him. And he was bragging about how the king had promoted him higher than all the other leaders. ¹²"And that's not all," Haman added. "I'm the only person Queen Esther invited to be with the king at the party she gave. And the Queen has also invited me to be with the king again tomorrow. ¹³But all those things don't really make me happy. I'm not really happy as long as I see that Jew Mordecai sitting at the king's gate."
¹⁴Then Haman's wife Zeresh and all his friends had a suggestion. They said, "Tell someone to build a post to hang him on! Make it 75 feet* tall! Then in the morning, ask the king to hang Mordecai on it. Then just go to the party with the king and you can be happy."
Haman liked that suggestion, so he ordered someone to build the hanging post.

Mordecai Is Honored

6 That same night, the king could not sleep. So he told a servant to bring the history book and read it to him. (The Book of History of the Kings lists everything that happens during a king's rule.) ²The servant read the book to the king. He read about the evil plan to kill King Xerxes. That was when Mordecai had learned about Bigthana and Teresh. Those two men were the king's officers that guarded the doorway. They had planned to kill the king, but Mordecai learned about the plan and told someone about it.
³Then the king asked, "What honor and good things have been given to Mordecai for this?"
The servants answered the king, "Nothing has been done for Mordecai."
⁴Haman had just entered the outer area of the king's palace.* He had come to ask the king to hang Mordecai on the hanging post Haman had commanded to be built. ⌐The king heard him.⌐ The king said, "Who just came into the courtyard?"
⁵The king's servants said, "Haman is standing in the courtyard."
So the king said, "Bring him in."
⁶When Haman came in, the king asked him a question. He said, "Haman, what should be done for a man the king wants to honor?"
Haman thought to himself, "Who is there that the king would want to honor more than me? The king is talking about honoring me, I'm sure."
⁷So Haman answered the king, "Do this for the man the king loves to honor: ⁸Have the servants bring a special robe the king himself has worn. And also bring a horse the king himself has ridden. Have the servants put the king's special mark on that horse's head. ⁹Then put one of the king's most important leaders in charge of the robe and the horse. And let that leader put the robe on the man the king wants to honor. And then let him lead him on the horse through the city streets. As he leads him, let him announce, 'This is done for the man the king wants to honor!'"
¹⁰"Go quickly," the king commanded Haman. "Get the robe and the horse and do just as you have suggested for Mordecai the Jew. Mordecai is sitting near the king's gate. Do everything that you suggested."
¹¹So Haman got the robe and the horse. Then he put the robe on Mordecai and led him on horseback through the city streets. Haman

---

75 feet Literally, "50 cubits."

palace A large house for the king and his family.

announced ahead of Mordecai, "This is done for the man the king wants to honor!"

¹²After that, Mordecai went back to the king's gate. But Haman hurried home. He covered his head because he was embarrassed and ashamed. ¹³Then Haman told his wife Zeresh and all his friends everything that had happened to him. Haman's wife and the men that gave him advice said, "If Mordecai is a Jew, then you can't win. You have already started to fall. Surely you will be ruined!" ¹⁴While those people were still talking to Haman, the king's eunuchs* came to Haman's house. They made Haman hurry to the party that Esther had prepared.

Haman Is Hanged

7 So the king and Haman went to eat with Queen Esther. ²Then as they were drinking wine on the second day of the party, the king again asked Esther a question, "Queen Esther, what is it you want to ask for? Ask anything and it will be given to you. What do you want? I will give you anything, even half my kingdom."

³Then Queen Esther answered, "King, if you like me and it pleases you, please let me live! And I ask you to let my people live, too! That is what I ask for. ⁴Why? Because I and my people have been sold to be ruined, killed, and completely destroyed. If we had just been sold as slaves, I would have kept quiet, because that would not be enough of a problem to bother the king."

⁵Then King Xerxes asked Queen Esther, "Who did this to you? Where is the man that dared to do such a thing to your people?"

⁶Esther said, "The man against us, our enemy, is this wicked Haman."

Then Haman was filled with terror before the king and queen. ⁷The king was very angry. He got up, left his wine, and went out into the garden. But Haman stayed inside to beg Queen Esther to save his life. Haman begged for his life because he knew that the king had already decided to kill him. ⁸Just as the king was coming back in from the garden to the party room, he saw Haman falling on the couch where Esther was lying. The king said with anger in his voice, "Will you attack the queen even while I am in the house?"

As soon as the king had said that, servants came in and killed Haman.* ⁹One of the eunuchs* that served the king was named Harbona. Harbona said, "A hanging post 75 feet* tall has been built near Haman's house. Haman had it made so he could hang Mordecai on it. Mordecai is the man that helped you when he told about the evil plans to kill you."

The king said, "Hang Haman on that post!" ¹⁰So they hanged Haman on the hanging post he had built for Mordecai. Then the king stopped being angry.

The King's Order To Help the Jews

8 That same day King Xerxes gave Queen Esther all the things that belonged to Haman, the enemy of the Jews. Esther told the king that Mordecai was her cousin. Then Mordecai came to see the king. ²The king had gotten his ring back from Haman. The king took that ring off his finger and gave it to Mordecai. Then Esther put Mordecai in charge of all of the things that belonged to Haman.

³Then Esther spoke to the king again. She fell at the king's feet and began crying. She begged the king to cancel the evil plan of Haman the Agagite. Haman had thought up that plan to hurt the Jews.

⁴Then the king held out the gold scepter* to Esther. Esther got up and stood in front of the king. ⁵Then Esther said, "King, if you like me and if it pleases you, please do this for me. Please do this if you think it is a good idea. If the king is happy with me, please write a command that would stop the command that Haman sent out. Haman the Agagite thought of a plan to destroy the Jews in all the king's provinces, and he sent out commands for that to happen. ⁶I am begging the king because I could not bear to see those terrible things happen to my people. I could not bear to see my family killed."

⁷King Xerxes answered Queen Esther and Mordecai the Jew. This is what the king said, "Because Haman was against the Jews, I have given his property to Esther. And my soldiers have hanged him on the hanging post. ⁸Now write another command by the authority of the king. Write it to help the Jews in a way that seems best to you. Then seal that order with the king's

---

eunuchs Men whose testicles have been removed. Rulers often gave such men important positions.

killed Haman Literally, "covered Haman's face."
75 feet Literally, "50 cubits."
scepter A special stick that a king holds in his hand.

special ring. No official letter written by the authority of the king and sealed with the king's ring can be cancelled."

⁹Very quickly the king's secretaries were called. This was done on the 23rd day of the third month, the month of Sivan. Those secretaries wrote out all of Mordecai's commands to the Jews, and to the satraps *(leaders)*, the governors, and officials of the 127 provinces. Those provinces reached from India to Ethiopia. Those commands were written in the language of each province. And they were translated into the language of each group of people. And those commands were written to the Jews in their own language and their own alphabet. ¹⁰Mordecai wrote commands by the authority of King Xerxes. Then he sealed the letters with the king's ring. And he sent those letters by messengers on horses. Those messengers rode fast horses which were raised especially for the king.

¹¹The king's commands in those letters said this:

The Jews in every city have the right to gather together to protect themselves. They have the right to ruin, kill, and completely destroy any army from any group of people that might attack them and their women and children. And the Jews have the right to take and destroy the property of their enemies.

¹²The day that was set for the Jews to do this was the 13th day of the twelfth month, the month of Adar. The Jews were permitted to do this in all King Xerxes' provinces. ¹³A copy of the letter with the king's command was to be sent out. It became a law. It became a law in every province. They announced it to all the people of every nation living in the kingdom. They did this so the Jews would be ready for that special day. The Jews would be allowed to pay their enemies back. ¹⁴The messengers hurried out, riding on the king's horses. The king commanded those messengers to hurry. And that command was also put in the capital city of Susa.

¹⁵Mordecai left the king. Mordecai was wearing special clothes from the king. His clothes were blue and white, and he had on a large gold crown. He also had a purple robe made of the best linen.* There was a special celebration in Susa. The people were very happy. ¹⁶It was an especially happy day for the Jews. It was a day of great joy and happiness.

¹⁷Wherever the king's command went in every province and every city, there was joy and gladness among the Jews. The Jews were having parties and celebrating. And many of the common people from other groups became Jews. They did that because they were very afraid of the Jews.

Victory for the Jews

9 On the 13th day of the twelfth month (Adar), the people were supposed to obey the king's command. That was the day the enemies of the Jews hoped to defeat them. But now, things had changed. Now, the Jews were stronger than their enemies who hated them. ²The Jews met together in their cities in all the provinces of King Xerxes. They met together so they would be strong enough to attack the people that wanted to destroy them. So no one was strong enough to stand against them. Those people were afraid of the Jews. ³And all the officials of the provinces, the satraps *(leaders)*, the governors, and the king's administrators helped the Jews. All those leaders helped the Jews because they were afraid of Mordecai. ⁴Mordecai had become a very important man in the king's palace.* Everyone in the provinces knew his name and knew how important he was. And Mordecai became more and more powerful.

⁵The Jews defeated all their enemies. They used swords to kill and destroy their enemies. And the Jews did what they wanted to with those people that hated them. ⁶The Jews killed and destroyed 500 men in the capital city of Susa. ⁷The Jews also killed these men: Parshandatha, Dalphon, Aspatha, ⁸Poratha, Adalia, Aridatha, ⁹Parmashta, Arisai, Aridai, and Vaizatha. ¹⁰These men were the ten sons of Haman. Hanıan son of Hammedatha was the enemy of the Jews. The Jews killed all those men, but they didn't take any of the things that belonged to them.

¹¹That day the king heard how many men had been killed in the capital city of Susa. ¹²So the king said to Queen Esther, "The Jews have killed 500 men in Susa, including Haman's ten sons. Now, what do you want done in the other provinces of the king? Tell me, and I will have it done. Ask, and I will do it."

¹³Esther said, "If it pleases the king, please let the Jews in Susa do the same thing again

---

linen Thread or cloth made from the fibers of the flax plant.   **palace** A large house for the king and his family.

tomorrow. Also, hang the bodies of Haman's ten sons on posts."

¹⁴So the king gave the command. That law continued another day in Susa. And they hanged Haman's ten sons. ¹⁵The Jews in Susa met together on the 14th day of the month of Adar. They killed 300 men in Susa, but they didn't take the things that belonged to those men.

¹⁶At the same time, the Jews living in the other provinces also met together. They met together so they would be strong enough to protect themselves. And so they got rid of their enemies. The Jews killed 75,000 of their enemies. But the Jews didn't take any of the things that belonged to those people. ¹⁷This happened on the 13th day of the month Adar. And on the 14th day the Jews rested. The Jews made that day a happy holiday.

The Festival of Purim

¹⁸The Jews in Susa had met together on the 13th and 14th days of the month of Adar. And then on the 15th day they rested. So they made the 15th day a happy holiday. ¹⁹So, the Jews that live in the country and small villages celebrate Purim on the 14th day Adar. They keep the 14th day as a happy holiday. On that day they have parties and give presents to each other.

²⁰Mordecai wrote everything down that had happened. And then he sent letters to all the Jews in all of King Xerxes' provinces. He sent letters far and near. ²¹Mordecai did that to tell the Jews to celebrate Purim every year on the 14th and 15th days of the month of Adar. ²²The Jews were to celebrate those days because on those days the Jews got rid of their enemies. And they were also to celebrate that month as the month when their sadness was turned into joy. And it was a month when their crying was changed into a day of celebration. Mordecai wrote letters to all the Jews. He told them to celebrate those days as a happy holiday. They should have parties and give gifts to each other and give presents to poor people.

²³So the Jews agreed to do what Mordecai had written to them. And they agreed to continue the celebration they had begun.

²⁴Haman son of Hammedatha the Agagite was the enemy of all the Jews. He had made an evil plan against the Jews to destroy them. And Haman had thrown the lot* to choose a day to ruin and to destroy the Jews. At that time, the lot was called a "pur," so the holiday is called "Purim." ²⁵Haman did those things, but Esther went to talk to the king. So he sent out new commands. These commands not only ruined Haman's plans, but these commands caused those bad things to happen to Haman and his family! So Haman and his sons were hung on the posts.

²⁶⁻²⁷At this time, lots* were called "purim". So this holiday is called "Purim." Mordecai wrote a letter and told the Jews to celebrate this holiday. And so the Jews started the custom of celebrating these two days every year. ²⁸They do this to help them remember what they had seen happen to them. The Jews and all the people that join them celebrate these two days every year at the right time in just the right way. Every generation and every family remembers these two days. They celebrate this holiday in each and every province and in each and every town. And the Jews will never stop celebrating the days of Purim. The descendants* of those Jews will always remember this holiday.

²⁹So Queen Esther the daughter of Abihail and Mordecai the Jew wrote an official letter about Purim. They wrote with full authority of the king to prove that the second letter was true. ³⁰So Mordecai sent letters to all the Jews in the 127 provinces of King Xerxes' kingdom. Mordecai told the people that the holiday should bring peace and make people trust* each other. ³¹Mordecai wrote these letters to tell the people to start celebrating Purim. And he told them when to celebrate this new holiday. Mordecai the Jew and Queen Esther had sent out the command for the Jews. They did this to establish this two-day holiday for themselves and their descendants.* They will remember this holiday just like they remember the other holidays when they fast* and cry about the bad things that had happened. ³²Esther's letter made the rules for Purim official. And these things were written down in a book.

Mordecai Honored

10 King Xerxes made people pay taxes. All the people in the kingdom, even the faraway

---

lot(s) Sticks, stones, or pieces of bone used like dice for making decisions. See Proverbs 16:33.

descendants A person's children and all of their future families.

peace and make people trust

peace ... trust Or "fellowship and truth." Zech. 8:19 teaches that this is how people should celebrate the holidays and why God gave them.

fast To live without food for a special time of prayer and worship to God.

cities on the sea coast, had to pay taxes. ²And all the great things that Xerxes did are written in the Book of History of the Kings of Media and Persia. And also written in those history books are all the things that Mordecai did. The king made Mordecai a great man. ³Mordecai the Jew was second in importance to King Xerxes. Mordecai was the most important man among the Jews. And his fellow Jews respected him very much. They respected Mordecai because he worked hard for the good of his people. And Mordecai brought peace for all of the Jews.

Job

Job the Good Man

1 There was a man named Job that lived in the country of Uz. Job was a good and faithful man. Job worshiped God and refused to do evil things. ²Job had seven sons and three daughters. ³Job owned 7,000 sheep, 3,000 camels, 1,000 bulls, and 500 female donkeys. He had many servants. Job was the richest man in the east.

⁴Job's sons took turns having parties in their homes, and they invited their sisters. ⁵Job got up early in the morning after his children had a party. He offered a burnt offering for each of his children. He thought, "Maybe my children were careless and sinned against God at their party." Job always did this so his children would be forgiven of their sins.

⁶Then the day came for the angels* to meet with the Lord. Even Satan was there with those angels. ⁷The Lord said to Satan, "Where have you been?"

Satan answered the Lord, "I have been wandering around on the earth."

⁸Then the Lord said to Satan, "Have you seen my servant Job? There is no person on earth like Job. Job is a good and faithful man. He worships God and refuses to do evil things."

⁹Satan answered, "Sure! But Job has a good reason for worshiping God! ¹⁰You always protect him, his family, and everything he has. You have made him successful in everything he does. Yes, you have blessed him. He is so wealthy that his herds and flocks are all over the country. ¹¹But if you destroy everything he has, I promise you that he will curse* you to your face."

¹²The Lord said to Satan, "All right. Do anything you want to the things Job has. But don't hurt his body."

Then Satan went away from the Lord.

Job Loses Everything

¹³One day, Job's sons and daughters were eating and drinking wine at the oldest brother's house. ¹⁴Then a messenger came to Job and said, "The bulls were plowing and the donkeys were eating grass near by. ¹⁵The Sabean people* attacked us and took your animals! Those people killed the other servants. I am the only person that escaped. So I came to tell you the news!"

¹⁶While that messenger was still speaking, another messenger came to Job. The second messenger said, "Lightning struck from the sky and burned up your sheep and servants. I am the only person that escaped. So I came to tell you the news!"

¹⁷While that messenger was still speaking, another messenger came. This third messenger said, "The Chaldeans sent three groups of soldiers. They attacked us and took the camels! They killed the servants. I am the only person that escaped. So I came to tell you the news!"

¹⁸While the third messenger was still speaking, another messenger came. The fourth messenger said, "Your sons and daughters were eating and drinking wine at the oldest brother's house. ¹⁹Then a strong wind suddenly blew in from the desert and blew the house down. The house fell on your sons and daughters, and they are dead. I am the only person that escaped. So I came to tell you the news!"

²⁰When Job heard this, he tore his clothes and shaved his head ₍to show he was sad and upset₎. Then Job fell on the ground and worshiped God. ²¹He said:

"When I was born into this world,
    I was naked, and I had nothing.
When I die and leave this world,
    I'll be naked, and I'll have nothing.
The Lord gives,

---

angels Literally, "sons of God."
curse(d) To ask for bad things to happen to someone.

Sabean people A group of people from the desert area. They attacked people and took their things.

and the Lord takes away.
Praise the name of the Lord!"

²²All of those things happened, but Job didn't sin. Job didn't say that God did anything wrong.

Satan Bothers Job Again

2 On another day, the angels* came to meet with the Lord. Even Satan came to meet with the Lord. ²The Lord said to Satan, "Where have you been?"

Satan answered the Lord, "I have been wandering around on the earth." ³Then the Lord said to Satan, "Have you seen my servant Job? There is no person on earth like Job. Job is a good and faithful man. He worships God and refuses to do evil things. He still is faithful, even though you asked me to let you destroy everything he has for no reason."

⁴Satan answered, "Skin for skin!* A person will give everything he has to save his life. ⁵If you use your power to hurt his body, then he will curse* you to your face!"

⁶So the Lord said to Satan, "All right, Job is in your power. But you are not allowed to kill him."

⁷Then Satan went away from the Lord. Satan gave Job painful sores. The painful sores were all over Job's body from the bottom of his feet to the top of his head. ⁸So Job sat near the garbage piles. He used a piece of broken pottery to scrape his sores. ⁹Job's wife said to him, "Are you still faithful to God? Why don't you curse* God and die!"

¹⁰Job answered his wife, "You talk like a foolish woman! God gives us good things, and we accept them. So we should also accept trouble ₍and not complain₎." All these things happened. But Job did not sin. He did not speak against God.

Job's Three Friends Come to See Him

¹¹Three of Job's friends were Eliphaz from Teman, Bildad from Shuah, and Zophar from Naamah. These three friends heard about all the bad things that happened to Job. These three friends left their homes and met together. They agreed to go and show sympathy to Job and to comfort him. ¹²But when the three friends saw Job from far away, they were not sure it was Job—he looked so different! They began to cry loudly. They tore their clothes and threw dirt in the air and on their heads ₍to show they were sad and upset₎. ¹³Then the three friends sat on the ground with Job for seven days and seven nights. No one said a word to Job, because they saw Job was suffering so much.

Job Curses the Day He Was Born

3 Then Job opened his mouth and cursed* the day he was born. ²⁻³He said:

"I wish the day I was born
    would be lost forever.
That night they said,
    'It's a boy!'
I wish that night never happened.
⁴ I wish that day had stayed dark.
I wish God would forget that day.
I wish light had not shined on that day.
⁵ I wish that day had stayed dark—
    as dark as death.
I wish clouds would hide that day.
I wish black clouds could
    scare away the light
      from the day I was born.
⁶ Let the darkness keep that night.
Leave that night off the calendar.
Don't put that night in any of the months.
⁷ Don't let that night produce anything.
Let no happy shout be heard on that night.
⁸ Let the magicians say their curses,
    let them curse the day I was born.
Those men always want to wake Leviathan.*
⁹ Let that day's morning star be dark.
Let that night wait for the morning light,
    but let that light never come.
Don't let it see the first rays of sunlight.
¹⁰ Why? Because that night didn't stop me
    from being born.
That night didn't stop me
    from seeing these troubles.
¹¹ Why didn't I die when I was born?
    Why didn't I die at birth?
¹² Why did my mother hold me on her knees?
    Why did my mother's breasts feed me?
¹³ If I died when I was born,
    I would be at peace now.

---

angels Literally, "sons of God."
Skin for skin This means that a person will do anything he can to avoid pain.
curse(d) To ask for bad things to happen to someone.

Leviathan Some people think this is a crocodile. Other people think this is a giant sea monster. People thought magicians were able to make him cause eclipses of the sun.

14 I wish I were asleep and at rest
   with the kings and wise men
   who lived on earth in the past.
   Those men built places for themselves
   that are now destroyed and gone.
15 I wish I were buried with those rulers.
   They filled their graves* with gold
   and silver!
16 Why wasn't I a child who died at birth
   and was buried in the ground?
   I wish I were like a baby
   that never saw the light of day.
17 Bad people stop making trouble
   when they are in the grave.
   And people who are tired
   find rest in the grave.
18 Even prisoners find relief in the grave.
   They don't hear their guards yelling
   at them.
19 All kinds of people are in the grave—
   important people
   and people who are not so important.
   Even the slave is freed from his master.
20 "Why must a suffering person
   continue to live?
   Why give life to a person
   whose soul is bitter?
21 That person wants to die,
   but death does not come.
   That sad person searches for death
   more than for hidden treasure.
22 Those people would be happy
   to find their grave.
   They would rejoice
   to find their tomb.
23 But God keeps their future a secret,
   and builds a wall around them
   to protect them.
24 When it is time to eat,
   I only sigh with sadness
   not with joy.
   My complaints pour out like water.
25 I was afraid that something terrible
   might happen to me.
   And that is what happened!
   The things I feared most
   happened to me.
26 I can't calm down.
   I can't relax.
   I can't rest.
   I'm too upset!"

Eliphaz Speaks

4 ¹⁻²Eliphaz from Teman answered:
   "I must say something.
   Will it upset you if I try to speak?

3 "Job, you have taught many people.
   You gave strength to weak hands.
4 Your words helped people
   who were ready to fall.
   You gave strength to people
   who couldn't stand by themselves.
5 But now trouble comes to you,
   and you are discouraged.
   Trouble hits you,
   and you are upset!
6 You worship God.
   You trust him.
   You are a good man.
   So let that be your hope.

7 "Job, think about this:
   No innocent person was ever destroyed.
   Good people are never destroyed.
8 I have seen some troublemakers
   and people who make life hard.
   But they are always punished!
9 God's punishment kills those people.
   God's anger destroys them.
10 The bad people roar and growl like lions.
   But God makes the bad people be quiet,
   and God breaks their teeth.
11 Yes, those bad people are like lions
   that can't find animals to kill.
   They die and their children wander away.

12 "A message was brought to me in secret.
   My ears caught a whisper of it.
13 Like a bad dream in the night,
   it ruined my sleep.
14 I was afraid, and shook.
   All my bones shook!
15 A ghost passed by my face.
   The hair on my body stood up!
16 The spirit stood still,
   but I could not see what it was.
   A shape stood before my eyes,
   and there was silence.
   Then I heard a very quiet voice:
17 'A person can't be more right than God.
   Man can't be more pure than his Maker.
18 Look, God can't even trust his heavenly servants.
   God sees problems even in his angels.
19 So surely people are worse!
   People live in houses of clay.*
   The foundations of these houses of clay
   are in the dirt.

---

graves Or, "houses."

They are crushed to death
more easily than a moth!
20 People die from dawn to sunset,
and no one even notices.
They die and are gone forever.
21 The ropes of their tent are pulled up,
and these people die without wisdom.'

5

"Job, call out if you want,
but no one will answer you!
You can't turn to any of the angels!
2 A foolish person's anger will kill him.
A fool's strong emotions will kill him.
3 I saw a foolish person
who thought he was safe.
But suddenly, he died.*
4 No one could help his children.
There was no one to defend them in court.
5 Hungry people ate all his crops.
Those hungry people took even
the grain growing among the thorns.
Greedy people took all they had.
6 Bad times don't come up from the dirt.
Trouble does not grow from the ground.
7 But man is born to have trouble,
as sure as sparks fly up from a fire.

8 "But Job, if I were you,
I would turn to God
and tell him about my problems.
9 People can't understand
the wonderful things God does.
There is no end to the miracles God does.
10 God sends rain on the earth.
He sends water to the fields.
11 God raises up the humble person,
and he makes a sad person very happy.
12 God stops the plans of clever, evil people,
so they have no success.
13 God catches wise people in their own traps.
So those clever plans are not successful.
14 Those smart people stumble around
even in the daytime.
Even at noon, they are like a person
who feels his way in the dark.
15 God saves poor people from death.
He saves the poor people from
the power of the clever people.
16 So poor people have hope.
God destroys bad people who are not fair.

17 "A person is fortunate
when God corrects him!
So don't complain when
God All-Powerful punishes you.
18 God puts bandages
on the wounds he makes.
He might injure someone,
but his hands also heal.
19 He will save you from six troubles.
Yes, in seven troubles you won't be hurt!
20 God will save you from death
when there is famine.
And God will protect you from death
when there is war.
21 People might say bad things about you
with their sharp tongues.
But God will protect you.
You won't need to be afraid
when bad things happen!
22 You will laugh at destruction and famine.
You won't be afraid of wild animals!
23 ⌊Your agreement is with God⌋
so even the rocks in the field
share in your agreement.
Even the wild animals
make peace with you.
24 You will live in peace
because your tent is safe.
You will count your property
and find nothing missing.
25 You will have many children.
They will be as many as
the blades of grass on the earth.
26 You will be like the wheat that grows
until harvest time.
Yes, you will live to a ripe old age.

27 "Job, we have studied these things,
and we know they are true.
So Job, listen to us,
and learn them for yourself."

Job Answers Eliphaz

6

1-2 Then Job answered:
"If my suffering could be weighed,
and all my trouble could be
put on the weighing scales,
3 you would understand my sadness.
My sadness would be heavier
than all the sand of the seas!
That is why my words seem foolish.
4 God All-Powerful's arrows are in me.
My spirit feels the poison
from those arrows!

---

houses of clay This means the human body.
But suddenly ,he died Or, "But suddenly his home was cursed."

God's terrible weapons are lined up
against me.
5 ⌊Your words are easy to say
when nothing bad has happened.⌋
Even a wild donkey doesn't complain
when it has grass to eat.
And a cow doesn't complain
when it has its food.
6 Food without salt
doesn't taste good.
And the white of an egg
doesn't have any taste.
7 I refuse to touch it;
that kind of food makes me sick!
⌊And that is what your words
are like to me now.⌋
8 "I wish I could have what I ask for.
I wish God would give me what I want.
9 I wish God would crush me,
just go ahead and kill me!
10 And if he does kill me,
I will be comforted about one thing,
I will be happy about one thing:
Even through all this pain,
I never refused to obey
the commands of the Holy One.
11 "My strength is gone,
so I have no hope to go on living.
I don't know what will happen to me,
so I have no reason to be patient.
12 I am not strong like a rock.
My body is not made from bronze.
13 I don't have power to help myself now.
Why? Because success has been taken
away from me.
14 "A person's friends should be kind
to him if he has troubles.
A person should be loyal to his friend,
even if that friend turned away from
⌊God⌋ All-Powerful.
15 But you, my brothers, have not been loyal.
I can't depend on you.
You are like streams that flow sometimes
and don't flow at other times.
16 You are like streams that overflow
when they are choked with ice
and melting snow.
17 And when the weather is hot and dry
the water stops flowing,
and the streams are gone.
18 Traders follow the twists and turns
out into the desert
and they disappear.
19 Traders from Tema look for water.

20 Travelers from Sheba look hopefully.
They were sure they would find water
but they were disappointed.
21 Now, you are like those streams.
You see my troubles and are afraid.
22 Did I ask for your help? No!
But you freely gave me your advice!
23 Did I say to you,
'Save me from the enemy!
Save me from cruel people!'

24 "So now, teach me,
and I will be quiet.
Show me what I have done wrong.
25 Honest words are powerful.
But your arguments prove nothing.
26 Do you plan to criticize me?
Will you speak more tiring words?
27 You would even gamble to win things
that belong to children without fathers.
You would sell out your own friend.
28 But now, please study my face.
I would not lie to you
29 So now, change your mind.
Don't be unfair, think again.
I have done nothing wrong.
30 I am not lying.
And I know right from wrong."

7 Job said,
"Man has a hard struggle on earth.
His life is like the life of a hired worker.
2 Man is like a slave who wants the
cool shade after hard work on a hot day.
Man is like a hired worker
waiting for payday.
3 Month after frustrating month has gone by.
I have had night after night of suffering.
4 When I lie down, I think,
'How long before it's time to get up?'
The night drags on.
I toss and turn until the sun comes up.
5 My body is clothed with worms and dirt.
My skin is broken and full of running sores.

6 "My days go by faster
than a weaver's shuttle.*
And my life ends without hope.
7 God, remember, my life is only a breath.
I will never see anything good again.
8 And you won't see me again.

weaver's shuttle The tool a person that makes cloth uses to pass the thread between the other threads.

You will look for me,
   but I will be gone.
9 A cloud disappears and is gone.
   In the same way, a person dies
   and is buried in the grave
   and he won't come back.
10 He will never come back
   to his old house again.
   His home won't know him any more.
11 "So I won't be quiet!
   I will speak out!
   My spirit is suffering!
   I will complain because my soul is bitter.
12 God, why do you guard me?
   Am I the sea or a sea monster?
13 My bed should bring me comfort.
   My couch should give me rest and relief.
14 But God, ⌊when I lie down⌋
   you scare me with dreams
   you frighten with visions.*
15 So I prefer to be choked to death
   than to live.
16 I hate my life—I give up.
   I don't want to live forever.
   Leave me alone!
   My life means nothing!
17 God, why is man so important to you?
   Why should you honor him?
   Why do you even notice him?
18 Why do you visit man every morning
   and test him every moment?
19 God, you never look away from me.
   You won't leave me alone for a second.
20 God, you watch over people.
   If I have sinned, fine,
      what can I do?
   Why did you use me for target practice?
   Did I become a problem for you?
21 Why don't you just pardon me
   for doing wrong?
   Why don't you just forgive me
   for my sins?
   Soon I will die and be in my grave.
   Then you will search for me,
   but I will be gone."

Bildad Speaks to Job

8 ² Then Bildad from Shuah answered,
   "How long will you talk like that?
   Your words blow like a strong wind.

3 God is always fair.
   God All-Powerful never changes
   the things that are right.
4 If your children sinned against God,
   then he has punished them.
   They paid for their sins.
5 But now Job, look to God
   and pray to the All-Powerful.
6 If you are pure and good,
   then he will quickly come to help you.
   He will give your family back to you.
7 Then you will have a lot more
   than you had in the beginning!

8 "Ask the old people.
   Find out what their ancestors* learned.
9 It seems like we were born only yesterday.
   We are too young to know for sure.
   Our days on earth are very short,
   like a shadow.
10 Maybe the old people can teach you.
   Maybe they can teach you
   what they have learned.

11 Bildad said,
   "Can papyrus* grow tall on a dry land?
   Can reeds grow without water?
12 No. If the water dries up,
   then they will also be dry.
   They will be too small to cut and use.
13 People who forget God
   are like those reeds.
   The person who forgets God,
   has no hope.
14 That person has nothing to lean on.
   His security is like a spider's web.
15 If a person leans against a spider's web,
   the web will break.
   He holds on to the spider's web,
   but it won't support him.
16 That man is like a plant that has
   plenty of water and sunshine.
   Its branches spread all through the garden.
17 It wraps its roots around a pile of rocks,
   looking for a place to grow in the rocks.
18 But if the plant is moved from its place,
   ⌊it will die⌋ and no one would know
   that it had ever been there.

ancestors Literally, "fathers," meaning a person's parents, grandparents, and all the people they are descended from.

vision(s) Something like a dream that God used to speak to people.

papyrus A plant used to make a kind of paper to write on. Its bark is also used to make coverings for boats and ships.

ⁱ⁹ But the plant was happy.
  And another plant will grow where it was.
²⁰ God doesn't abandon innocent people.
  He doesn't help evil people.
²¹ God will still fill your mouth with laughter
  and your lips with happy shouts.
²² But shame will be the clothes
  your enemies wear.
  And the homes of wicked people
  will be destroyed."

Job Answers Bildad

9 Then Job answered:
² "Yes, I know what you say is true.
  But how can a man be right with God?
³ A person can't argue with God!
  God can ask 1,000 questions and
  no person could answer even one!
⁴ God is very wise
  and his power is very great.
  No person can fight God and not be hurt.
⁵ God moves mountains when he is angry
  and they don't even know it.
⁶ God sends earthquakes to shake the earth.
  God shakes the earth's foundations.
⁷ God can speak to the sun,
  and make it not rise.
  He can lock up the stars,
  so they don't shine.
⁸ God alone made the skies.
  He walks on the ocean waves.
⁹ "God made the Bear, Orion, and the Pleiades.*
  He made the planets that cross
  the southern sky.*
¹⁰ God does wonderful things
  that people can't understand.
  There is no end to God's great miracles.
¹¹ When God goes past me,
  I can't see him.
  When God goes by,
  I can't understand his greatness.

¹² If God takes away,
  no one can stop him.
  No one can say to him,
  'What are you doing?'
¹³ God won't hold his anger back.
  Even Rahab's* helpers
  are afraid of God."
¹⁴ So I can't argue with God.
  I wouldn't know what to say to him.
¹⁵ I am innocent,
  but I can't give him an answer.
  All I can do is beg my Judge *(God)*
  for mercy.
¹⁶ Even if I called and he answered,
  I still wouldn't believe
  that he really listens to me.
¹⁷ God would just send storms to crush me.
  He would just give me more wounds
  for no reason.
¹⁸ God won't let me catch my breath again.
  He will give me more trouble.
¹⁹ I can't defeat God.
  God is too powerful!
  I can't take God to court
  and make him be fair to me.
  Who could force God to come to court?
²⁰ I am innocent, but the things I say
  make me seem guilty.
  I am innocent, but if I speak
  my mouth proves me guilty.
²¹ I am innocent.
  But I don't know what to think.
  I hate my own life.
²² I say to myself,
  'The same thing happens to everybody.
  Innocent people die just like the guilty.
  God ends all their lives.'
²³ When something terrible happens
  and an innocent person is killed,
  does God just laugh at him?
²⁴ When an evil man takes control of a land
  does God keep the leaders
  from seeing what is happening?
  If that is true
  then who is God anyway?
²⁵ "My days go faster than a runner.
  My days fly away and there is
  no happiness in them.

Bear, Orion, and the Pleiades
Bear, Orion, Pleiades These are names of well-known constellations *(groups of stars)* in the night sky.
planets that cross the southern sky Literally, "Rooms of the South," or "Rooms of Teman." This might be the planets or it might be some star groups, possibly the twelve constellations of the Zodiac. In places north of the equator, these seem to move across the southern sky.

Rahab's A dragon or sea monster. People thought Rahab controlled the sea. Rahab is often a symbol for God's enemies or for anything evil.

26 My days go by quickly
    like the papyrus* boats.
    My days go by as fast as eagles
    swooping down to catch an animal.
27 If I say,
    'I won't complain.
    I will forget my pain,
    I will put a smile on my face.'
28 It doesn't really change anything.
    The suffering still scares me!
29 I am already judged guilty.
    So why should I keep trying?
    I say, 'Forget it!'
30 Even if I wash myself with snow
    and make my hands clean with soap,
31 God will still push me into the slime pit.*
    Then even my clothes will hate me.
32 God is not a man like me.
    That is why I can't answer him.
    We can't meet each other in court.
33 I wish there were someone
    to listen to both sides.*
    I wish there were someone
    to judge both of us in a fair way.
34 I wish there were someone to take God's
    punishing stick away.
    Then God would not scare me any more.
35 Then I could say what I want to say
    without being afraid of God.
    But now I can't do that.

10

I hate my own life.
    So I will complain freely.
    My soul is very bitter,
    so now I will speak.
2 I will say to God:
    'Don't blame me!
    Tell me,
       What have I done wrong?
       What do you have against me?
3 God, does hurting me make you happy?
    It seems that you don't care about
       what you made.
    Or maybe you are happy
       with the plans that bad people make?
4 God, do you have human eyes?
    Do you see things the way people do?

5 Is your life as short as ours?
    Is your life as short as a man's life?
    No! So how do you know what it's like?
6 You look for my wrong
    and search for my sin.
7 You know I am innocent,
    but no one can save me from your power!
8 God, your hands made me
    and shaped my body.
    But now they are closing in on me
    and destroying me!
9 God, remember, you made me like clay.
    Will you make into clay again?
10 You pour me out like milk.
    You spin me and squeeze me
    like someone making cheese.
11 You put me together
    with bones and muscles.
    And then you clothed me
    with skin and flesh.
12 You gave me life
    and were very kind to me.
    You cared for me
    and watched over my spirit.
13 But this is what you hid in your heart,
    I know this is what you secretly
       planned in your heart.
    Yes, I know this is what was in your mind:
14 If I sinned, you would be watching me,
    so you could punish me for doing wrong.
15 When I sin, I am guilty
    and it will be very bad for me.
    But I can't lift up my head
    even when I am innocent!
    I am so ashamed and embarrassed.
16 If I have any success and feel proud
    you hunt me like a person hunts a lion.
    You again show your power against me.
17 You always have someone
    to prove I am wrong.
    Your anger will become worse against me.
    You will bring new armies against me.
18 So, God, why did you let me be born?
    I wish I had died before anyone saw me.
19 I wish I had never lived.
    I wish I had been carried from my mother's
       womb straight to the grave.
20 My life is almost finished.
    So leave me alone!
    Let me enjoy the little time I have left,
21 before I go to the place
    that no person comes back from
    the place of darkness and death.

---

papyrus A plant used to make a kind of paper to write on. Its bark is also used to make coverings for boats and ships.
slime pit The grave, a place where bodies rot.
someone ... sides Literally a "mediator" or an "umpire."

²² ₍Let me enjoy the little time I have left₎
   before I go to the place no one can see
   that place of darkness, shadows,
   and confusion.
   In that place even the light is dark."

Zophar Speaks to Job

11 Then Zophar from Naamah answered Job and said,

² "This flood of words should be answered!
   Does all this talking make Job right? No!
³ Job, do you think we don't have
   an answer for you?
   Do you think no one will warn you
   when you laugh at God?
⁴ Job, you say to God,
   'My arguments are right.
   and you can see I am pure.'
⁵ Job, I wish God would answer you
   and tell you that you are wrong.
⁶ God could tell you the secret of wisdom.
   He would tell you that
   every story has two sides.
   Job, listen to me,
   God is not punishing you
   as much as he should.

⁷ "Job, do you think that
   you really understand God?
   You can't understand God All-Powerful.
⁸ You can't do anything about
   what is up in heaven!
   You don't know anything
   about the place of death.
⁹ God is greater than the earth
   and bigger than the seas.
¹⁰ "If God arrests you,
   and brings you to court,
   no person can stop him.
¹¹ Truly, God knows who is worthless.
   When God sees evil,
   he remembers it.
¹² A wild donkey can't give birth
   to a man.
   And a stupid person will never
   become wise.

¹³ "But Job, you should make your heart
   ready to serve only God,
   and you should lift up your hands to
   ₍worship₎ him.
¹⁴ You should put away the sin
   that is in your home.
   Don't let evil live in your tent.
¹⁵ Then you could look to God without shame.
   You could stand strong and not be afraid.
¹⁶ Then you could forget your trouble.
   Your troubles would be like
   water that has passed on by.
¹⁷ Then your life would be brighter
   than the sunshine at noon.
   Life's darkest hours would shine
   like the morning sun.
¹⁸ Then you would feel safe,
   because there would be hope.
   God would care for you
   and give you rest.
¹⁹ You could lie down to rest,
   and no one would bother you.
   And many people would come to you
   for help.
²⁰ Bad people might look for help,
   but they won't escape their troubles.
   Their hope leads only to death."

Job Answers Zophar

12 Then Job answered Zophar:

² "I'm sure you think you are
   the only wise people.
   You think when you die,
   wisdom will be gone with you.
³ But my mind is as good as yours.
   I am as smart as you are.
   Anyone can see this is true.

⁴ "My friends laugh at me now.
   They say,
   'He prayed to God,
   and he got his answer.
   ₍That is why all these bad things
   happened to him.₎'
   "I am a good man.
   I am innocent.
   But still they laugh at me.
⁵ People that don't have troubles
   make fun of people who do have them.
   Those people hit a man when he is down.
⁶ But robbers' tents are not bothered.
   People who make God angry live in peace.
   And their own strength is their only god.

⁷ "But ask the animals,
   they will teach you.
   Or ask the birds of the air,
   they will tell you.

⁸ Or speak to the earth,
    it will teach you.
  Or let the fish in the sea
    tell you their wisdom.
⁹ Everyone knows the Lord
    made those things.
¹⁰ Every animal that lives,
    and every person that breathes,
      is under God's power.
¹¹ But just like the tongue tastes food,
    the ears test the words they hear.
¹² ⌊We say,⌋
  "Wisdom is to be found in old people.
    Long life brings understanding."

¹³ But wisdom and power belong to God.
    Good advice and understanding are his.
¹⁴ If God tears down anything,
    people can't build it again.
  If God puts a person in prison,
    people can't free the person.
¹⁵ If God holds back the rain,
    the earth will dry up.
  If God lets the rain loose,
    it will flood the earth.
¹⁶ God is strong and always wins.
    Winners and losers all belong to God!
¹⁷ God strips advisors of their wisdom
    and makes leaders act like fools.
¹⁸ Kings might put people in prison,
    but God sets those people free
      and makes them powerful.
¹⁹ God strips priests of their power,
    and makes temple servants not important.
²⁰ God makes the trusted advisers be silent.
    He takes away the wisdom of old people.
²¹ God makes leaders not important.
    He takes power away from rulers.
²² God knows even the darkest secrets.
    He sends light into places that are
      as dark as death.
²³ God makes nations big and powerful,
    and then he destroys them.
  He makes nations grow large,
    then he scatters their people.
²⁴ God makes leaders foolish.
    He makes them wander aimlessly
      through the desert.
²⁵ Those leaders are like a person
    feeling his way in the dark.
  They are like a drunk person
    who doesn't know where he is going.

13 ⌊Job said,⌋ "I have seen all this before. I have already heard everything you say. I understand all of those things. ²I know as much as you do. I am as smart as you are. ³But I don't want to argue with you. I want to speak to God All-Powerful. I want to argue with God about my troubles. ⁴But you three men try to cover up your ignorance with lies. You are like worthless doctors that can't heal anyone. ⁵I wish you would shut up. That would be the wisest thing you could do.

⁶ "Now, listen to my argument.
    Listen to what I have to say.
⁷ Will you speak lies for God?
    Do you really believe your lies are what
      God wants you to say?
⁸ Are you trying to defend God against me?
    You are not being fair—You are choosing
      God's side only because he is God.
⁹ If God checked you very closely,
    would he find anything good?
  Do you really think you can fool God
    the same as you fool people?
¹⁰ You know God would criticize you if you
    secretly chose a person's side in court
      simply because the man was important.
¹¹ God's majesty *(importance)* scares you.
    You are afraid of him.
¹² Your arguments are worth nothing.
    Your answers are worthless.

¹³ "Be quiet and let me talk!
    I accept whatever happens to me.
¹⁴ I will put myself in danger,
    and take my life in my own hands.
¹⁵ I will continue to trust God
    even if God kills me.
  But I will defend myself to his face.
¹⁶ And if God lets me live, it will be
    because I was brave enough to speak.
  No evil person would dare
    meet God face to face.
¹⁷ Listen carefully to what I say.
    Let me explain.
¹⁸ I am ready now to defend myself.
    I will carefully present my arguments.
    I know I will be shown to be right.
¹⁹ If any person can prove I am wrong,
    then I will shut up immediately.

²⁰ "God, just give me two things,
    and then I won't hide from you:
²¹ Stop punishing me,
    and stop scaring me with your terrors.
²² Then call to me and I will answer you.
    Or let me speak, and you answer me.

23 How many sins have I done?
   What have I done wrong?
   Show me my sins and my wrongs.
24 God, why do you avoid me,
   and treat me like your enemy?
25 Are you trying to scare me?
   I am only a leaf blowing in the wind.
   You are attacking a little piece of straw!
26 God, you say bitter things against me.
   Are you making me suffer
   for the sins that I did when I was young.
27 You have put chains on my feet.
   You watch every step I take.
   You watch every move I make.
28 So I am becoming weaker and weaker
   like a piece of wood rotting away,
   like a piece of cloth eaten by moths."

14 Job said, "We are all human beings.* Our life is short and full of trouble. ²Man's life is like a flower. He grows quickly, and then dies away. Man's life is like a shadow that is there a short time, and then is gone. ³That is true, but God, will you look at me, a man? And will you come into court with me and let us both give our arguments?

4 "But what does something clean
   have in common with something dirty?
   Nothing!
5 Man's life is limited.
   God, you decide how long a man lives.
   You set those limits for a man
   and nothing can change them.
6 So God, stop watching us.
   Leave us alone.
   Let us enjoy our hard life
   until our time is finished.
7 "There is hope for a tree.
   If it is cut down, it can grow again.
   It will keep sending out new branches.
8 Its roots might grow old in the ground
   and its stump die in the dirt,
9 but with water it will grow again.
   It will grow branches like a new plant.
10 But when man dies, he is finished!
   When man dies, he is gone.
11 You could take all the water from the sea,
   until the rivers all run dry,
   ₍and the man will still be dead₎!

12 When a person dies, he lies down
   and he doesn't get up.
   The skies will all disappear
   before a dead man will wake up.
   No. People don't wake up from that sleep.
13 "I wish you would hide me in my grave.
   I wish you would hide me there,
   until your anger is gone.
   Then you can pick a time
   to remember me.
14 If a person dies, will he live again?
   I will wait as long as I must
   until I am set free.
15 God, you will call me
   and I will answer you.
   You made me,
   and I am important to you.
16 You will watch every step I take.
   But you won't remember my sins.
17 I wish you would tie up my sins in a bag,
   seal it, ₍and throw it away₎!
18 "Mountains fall and crumble away.
   Large rocks break loose and fall.
19 Water flowing over stones wears them down.
   Floods wash away the soil on the ground.
   In the same way, God,
   you destroy a person's hope.
20 You defeat him completely
   and then you leave.
   You make him sad
   and send him away forever
   ₍to the place of death₎.
21 If his sons are honored,
   he never knows it.
   If his sons do wrong,
   he never sees it.
22 That man only feels the pain in his body,
   and he cries loudly only for himself."

Eliphaz Answers Job

15 Then Eliphaz from Teman answered Job:

2 "Job, if you were really wise,
   you would not answer with empty words.
   A wise man would not be so full of hot air.
3 Do you think a wise man would argue
   with worthless words
   and with speeches that mean nothing?
4 Job, if you had your way,
   no person would respect God
   and pray to him.
5 The things you say

---

human beings Literally, "born of woman."

clearly show your sin.
Job, you are trying to hide your sin
by using clever words.
6 I don't need to prove to you that you
are wrong. Why?
The things you say with your own mouth
show that you are wrong.
Your own lips speak against you.

7 "Job, do you think you were the first
person ever to be born?
Were you born before the hills were made?
8 Did you listen to God's secret plans?
Do you think you are the only wise person?
9 Job, we know more than you know.
We understand things that you don't.
10 The gray-haired men
and the old people agree with us.
Yes, even people older than your father
are on our side.
11 God tries to comfort you,
but that is not enough for you.
We have spoken God's message to you
in a gentle way.
12 Job, why won't you understand?
Why can't you see the truth?
13 You are against God
when you say these angry words.

14 "A man can't really be pure.
A person* can't be more right than God!
15 God doesn't even trust his angels.*
Compared to God
even the heavens are not pure.
16 Man is even worse.
Man is dirty and ruined.
He drinks up evil like water.

17 "Listen to me Job,
and I will explain it to you.
I will tell you what I know.
18 I will tell you the things
wise men have told me.
The wise men's ancestors*
told them these things.
They didn't hide any secrets from me.
19 They alone lived in their country.
There were no foreigners passing
through.

⌊So no person told them strange ideas.⌋
20 ⌊These wise people said,⌋
An evil person suffers all his life.
A cruel person suffers all his
numbered years.
21 Every noise scares him.
His enemy will attack him
when he thinks he is safe.
22 The evil person is very frustrated,
and there is no hope for him to
escape the darkness.
There is a sword somewhere
that is waiting to kill him.
23 He wanders here and there,
but his body will be food for the vultures.
He knows that his death* is very near.
24 Worry and suffering make him afraid.
These things attack him like a king
ready to destroy him.
25 Why? Because the evil person refuses
to obey God—
He shakes his fist at God
and tries to defeat God All-Powerful.
26 That evil person is very stubborn.
He tries to attack God with a thick,
strong shield.
27 "A person might be rich and fat
28 but his town will be ruined,
his home will be destroyed,
his house will be empty.
29 The evil person won't be rich for long.
His wealth won't last.
His crops won't grow large.
30 The evil person won't escape the darkness.
He will be like a tree
whose leaves die from disease
and a wind blows them all away.
31 The evil person should not fool himself
when he trusts worthless things.
Why? He will get nothing.
32 Before his life is over,
the evil person will be old and dried up.
He will be like a dried branch,
never to be green again.
33 The evil person will be like a vine
that loses its grapes that are not yet ripe.
That person will be like an olive tree that
loses its buds.
34 Why? Because people without God
have nothing.
People who love money
will have their homes destroyed with fire.

---

person Literally, "A man born of woman."
angels Literally, "holy ones."
ancestors Literally, "fathers," meaning a person's parents, grandparents, and all the people they are descended from.

death Literally, "day of darkness."

35 Evil people are always planning ways
   to do evil and cause trouble.
   They are always planning ways
   to cheat people."

Job Answers Eliphaz

16 Then Job answered,
"I have heard
2   all these things before.
   You three men give me trouble, not
      comfort.
3 Your long speeches never end!
   Why do you continue arguing?
4 I also could say the same things you say,
      if you had my troubles.
   I could say wise things against you
      and shake my head at you.
5 But I could encourage you
      and give you hope
      with the things I say.

6 "Nothing I say makes my pain go away.
   But keeping quiet doesn't help either!
7 Truly, God, you took away my strength.
   You destroyed my whole family.
8 You tied me up,
      and everyone can see.
   My body is sick, I look terrible,
      and people think that means I am guilty.
9 God attacks me,
   he is angry at me and tears my body apart.
   God grinds his teeth against me.
   My enemy looks at me with hate.
10 People laugh at me.
   They join together and crowd around me.
   They embarrass me and slap my face.
11 God has given me to evil people.
   He let wicked people hurt me.
12 Everything was fine with me,
      but then God crushed me!
   Yes, he took me by the neck
      and broke me into pieces!
   God used me for target practice.
13 God's archers* are all around me.
   He shoots arrows in my kidneys.
   He shows no mercy.
   He spills my gall* on the ground.
14 Again and again God attacks me.
   He runs at me like a soldier in battle.

15 "I am very sad,
      so I wear these clothes of sadness.
   I sit here in the dust and ashes,
      and I feel defeated.
16 My face is red from crying.
   There are dark rings around my eyes.
17 I was never cruel to anyone
      ⌊but these bad things happened to me⌋.
   My prayers are right and pure.
18 "Earth, don't hide the wrong things
      that were done to me.
   Don't let my begging for fairness
      be stopped.
19 Even now there is someone in heaven
      that will speak for me.
   There is someone above
      that will prove I am right.
20 My friend speaks for me
      while my eyes pour out tears to God.
21 He speaks to God for me
      like a person arguing for his friend.

22 "In only a few years I will go to that
      place of no return *(death)*.

17 My spirit is broken;
   I am ready to give up.
   My life is almost gone,
      the grave is waiting for me.
2 People stand around me
      and laugh at me.
   I watch them as they tease
      and insult me.

3 "God, show me that you really support me.
   No other person will support me.
4 You have closed my friends' minds
      and they don't understand.
   Please don't let them win.
5 You know what people say,
   'A man neglects his own children
      to help his friends.'*
   But my friends have turned against me.

6 "God has made my name
      a bad word to everyone.
   People spit in my face.
7 My eyes have become almost blind
      because I am very sad and in great pain.
   My whole body has become very thin,
      like a shadow.
8 Good people are upset about this.

---

archers Soldiers that use bows and arrows in war.
gall The gall bladder is a pouch on the liver where bile or gall is stored. When the gall bladder is torn open, gall or bile comes out. Here this means having to endure something bitter and painful.
You know ... friends Literally, "He promises a share to his friends and his children's eyes go blind."

Innocent people are upset against people
that don't care about God.
9 But good people continue to live right.
Innocent people will become stronger.

10 "But come on, all of you,
try again to show me that it is all my fault.
None of you are wise.
11 My life is passing away.
My plans are destroyed.
My hope is gone.
12 But my friends are all mixed up.
They think night is day.
They think darkness drives away the light.

13 "I might hope for the grave
to be my new home.
I might hope to make my bed
in the dark grave.
14 I might say to the grave,
'You are my father,'
and to the worms,
'My mother,' or 'My sister.'
15 But if that is my only hope
then I have no hope at all.
If that is my only hope
then people have found me
no hope at all.
16 ₍Will my hope die with me?₎
Will it also go down to the place of death?
Will we go down into the dirt together?"

Bildad Answers Job

18 Then Bildad from Shuah answered:

2 "Job, when will you stop talking?
Be quiet and listen.
Let us say something.
3 Why do you think we are stupid like cows?
4 Job, your anger is only hurting yourself.
Should people leave the earth
just for you?
Do you think God will move mountains
just to satisfy you?

5 "Yes, the evil person's light will go out.
His fire will stop burning.
6 The light in his house will become dark.
The lamp next to him will go out.
7 His steps won't be strong and fast again.
But he will walk slowly and be weak.
His own evil plans will make him fall.
8 His own feet will lead him into a trap.
He will walk into a trap and be caught.
9 A trap will catch his heel.
A trap will hold him tight.
10 A rope in the ground will trap him.
A trap is waiting in his path.
11 Terror is waiting for him all around.
Fears will follow every step he takes.
12 Bad troubles are hungry for him.
Ruin and disaster are ready for him
when he falls.
13 Terrible sickness will eat away his skin.
It will rot his arms and legs.
14 The evil person will be taken away
from the safety of his house.
He will be led away to meet
the king of terrors.
15 He will have nothing left in his house.
Why? Burning sulfur will be scattered
all through his home.
16 His roots below will dry up,
and his branches above will die.
17 People on earth won't remember him.
No person remembers him anymore.
18 People will push him away from light
into the darkness.
They will chase him out of this world.
19 He will have no children or grandchildren.
None of his family will be left alive.
20 People in the west will be shocked
when they hear what happened
to the evil person.
People in the east will be numb with terror.
21 That will really happen
to the evil person's home.
This is what will happen to the person
that does not care about God!"

Job Answers

19 Then Job answered:

2 "How long will you hurt me
and break me with words?
3 You have insulted me ten times now.
You show no shame when you attack me!
4 Even if I have sinned,
it is my problem.
It does not hurt you.
5 You just want to make yourselves look
better than me.
You say that my troubles
are my own fault.
6 But it is God who did wrong to me.
He set his trap to catch me.

7 "I shout, 'He hurt me!'
But I get no answer.

Even if I call loudly for help,
no person hears my cry for fairness.
8 God has blocked my way
so I can't go through.
He has hidden my path in darkness.
9 God took away my honor.
He took the crown from my head.
10 God hits me from every side
until I am finished.
He takes away my hope
like a tree pulled up by the roots.
11 God's anger burns against me.
He calls me his enemy.
12 God sends his army to attack me.
They build attack towers around me.
They camp around my tent.
13 "God has made my brothers hate me.
I am a stranger to all my friends.
14 My relatives have left me.
My friends have forgotten me.
15 Visitors in my home
and my girl servants
look at me like I am
a stranger and a foreigner.
16 I call for my servant,
but he does not answer.
Even if I beg for help,
my servant will not answer.
17 My wife hates the smell of my breath.
My own brothers hate me.
18 Even little children make fun of me.
When I come near them,
they say bad things to me.
19 All my close friends hate me.
Even the people I love turned against me.
20 I am so thin,
my skin hangs loose on my bones.
I have little life left in me.
21 "Pity me, my friends, pity me!
Why? Because God is against me.
22 Why do you persecute me like God does?
Don't you get tired of hurting me?
23 "I wish someone would remember
what I say and write it in a book.
I wish my words were written on a scroll.
24 I wish the things I say were carved
with an iron tool on lead
or scratched on a rock
so they would last forever.
25 I know there is someone to defend me.
I know he lives!
And in the end he will stand here on earth

and defend me.
26 After I leave my body
and my skin has been destroyed,
I know I will still see God.
27 I will see God
with my own eyes.
I myself, not someone else,
will see God,
And I can't tell you how excited
that makes me feel!

28 "Maybe you will say,
'We will bother Job.
We will find a reason to blame him!'
29 But you yourselves should be afraid
of the sword!
Why? Because God punishes guilty people.
God will use the sword to punish you.
Then you will know that
there is a time of judgment."

Zophar Answers

20 Then Zophar from Naamah answered:
2 "Job, you have troubled thoughts.
So I must answer you.
I must quickly tell you what I am thinking.
3 You insulted us with your answers!
But I am wise, I know how to answer you.
4-5 "You know an evil person's joy
doesn't last long.
That has been true a long time,
from the time Adam was put on earth,
A person who doesn't care about God
is happy for only a short time.
6 Maybe the evil person's pride will
reach up to the sky,
and his head will touch the clouds.
7 But he will be gone forever,
like his own body waste.
People who know him will say,
'Where is he?'
8 Like a dream, he will fly away
and no one will ever find him.
He will be forced away and forgotten
like a bad dream.*
9 The people that saw him,
won't see him again.
His family will never look at him again.
10 The evil person's children will give back
what he took from poor people.

bad dream Or, "vision of the night."

The evil person's own hands
must give back his wealth.
11 When he was young his bones were strong,
but, like the rest of his body,
they soon will lie in the dirt.
12 "Evil tastes sweet
in the bad person's mouth.
He keeps it under his tongue
to enjoy it fully.
13 A bad person enjoys evil.
He hates to let it go.
It is like a sweet candy
he keeps in his mouth.
14 But that evil will become poison
in his stomach.
It will be like bitter poison inside him,
like a snake's poison.
15 The evil man has swallowed riches.
But he will vomit them out.
God will make the evil person
vomit them out.
16 The evil person's drink will be
like the poison from snakes.
The snake's fangs will kill him.
17 Then the evil person won't enjoy
seeing the rivers that flow
with honey and cream.
18 The evil person will be forced
to give back his profits.
He won't be allowed to enjoy
the things he worked for.
19 Why? Because the evil person
hurt poor people
and treated them wrong.
He didn't care about them,
and he took their things.
He took houses someone else built.

20 "The evil person is never satisfied.
His wealth can't save him.
21 When he eats,
there is nothing left.
His success won't continue.
22 While the evil person has plenty,
he will become pressed down with trouble.
His problems will come down on him!
23 When the evil person has eaten all he wants,
God will throw his burning anger
against that person.
God will rain punishment
down on the evil person.
24 Maybe the evil person will run away
from an iron sword.
But a bronze arrow will shoot him down.
25 The bronze arrow will go
all the way through his body,
and stick out from his back.
Its shining point will pierce his liver,
and he will be shocked with terror.
26 All his treasures will be destroyed.
A fire will destroy him—
A fire that no human started.
The fire will destroy everything
left in his house.
27 Heaven will prove the evil person is guilty.
The earth will witness against him.
28 Everything in his house will be
carried away in the flood of God's anger.
29 That is what God plans to do to evil people.
That is what God plans to give them."

Job Answers

21 Then Job answered:

2 "Listen to what I say.
Let that be your way to comfort me.
3 Be patient while I speak.
Then after I have finished speaking,
you may make fun of me.

4 "I am not complaining against people.
There is a good reason
why I am not patient.
5 Look at me and be shocked.
Put your hand over your mouth,
and stare at me in shock!
6 When I think about what happened to me
I feel afraid, and my body shakes!
7 Why do evil people live long lives?
Why do they grow old and successful?
8 Evil people watch their children
grow with them.
Evil people live to see their grandchildren.
9 Their homes are safe
and they are not afraid.
God doesn't use a stick
to punish evil people.
10 Their bulls never fail to mate.
Their cows have baby calves,
and the baby calves don't die at birth.
11 Evil people send their children out
to play like lambs.
Their children dance around.
12 They sing and dance
to the sound of harps and flutes.
13 Evil people enjoy success
during their lives.

Then they die
and go to their grave without suffering.
14 But evil people say to God,
'Leave us alone!
We don't care what you want us to do!'
15 And the evil people say,
'Who is God All-Powerful?
We don't need to serve him!
It won't help to pray to him!'
16 "It is true, evil people don't make
their own success.
I can't follow their advice.
17 But, how often does God blow out
the light of evil people?
How often does trouble come
to the evil people?
When does God become angry at them
and punish them?
18 Does God blow the evil people away,
like the wind blows straw,
like strong winds blow the grain husks?
19 But you say,
'God punishes a child
for his father's sins.'
No! Let God punish the evil person
himself.
Then that evil person will know
he is being punished for his own sins!
20 Let the sinner see his own punishment.
Let him feel the anger of God All-Powerful.
21 When the evil person's life is finished,
and he is dead,
he won't care about the family
he leaves behind.
22 "No person can teach knowledge to God.
God judges even people in high places.
23 One person dies after a full
and successful life.
He lived a life completely safe
and comfortable.
24 His body was well fed
and his bones were still strong.
25 But another person dies
after a hard life, with a bitter soul.
He never enjoyed anything good.
26 In the end, both of those people
will lie together in the dirt.
The worms will cover them both.
27 "But, I know what you are thinking,
and I know you want to hurt me.
28 You might say:
'Show me a good man's house.
Now, show me where evil people live.
29 Surely you have talked with travelers.
Surely you will accept their stories.
30 Evil people are spared
when disaster comes.
They survive when God shows his anger.
31 Nobody criticizes an evil person
to his face for the bad things he did.
No person punishes him for the evil he did.
32 When that evil person is carried to the grave,
a guard will stand near his grave.
33 So even the soil in the valley
will be pleasant for that evil person.
And thousands of people will join
the march to his grave.
34 "So you can't comfort me
with your empty words.
Your answers don't help at all!"

Eliphaz Answers

22 Then Eliphaz from Teman answered:
2 "Does God need our help? No!
Even a very wise person
isn't really useful to God.
3 Does your living right help God? No!
Does God All-Powerful gain anything
if you follow him? No!
4 "Job, why does God punish and blame you?
Is it because you worship him?
5 No, it is because you have sinned much.
Job, you never stop sinning!
6 Maybe you loaned a brother some money
and forced him to give you something
to prove he would pay it back.
Maybe you took some poor man's clothes
as collateral* for a loan.
Maybe you did that for no reason.
7 Maybe you didn't give water and food
to tired, hungry people.
8 Job, you have a lot of farm land.
And people respect you.
9 But maybe you sent widows* away
without giving them anything.
Job, maybe you cheated orphans.*
10 That is why traps are all around you,

---

collateral Something to prove a person will pay back a loan. If he does not pay, the other person gets to keep the collateral.
widow(s) Women whose husbands have died. Often these women had no one to care for them.

and sudden trouble makes you afraid.
11 That is why it is so dark you can't see,
and why a flood of water covers you.
12 "God lives in the highest part of heaven.
See how high the stars are.
God looks down on the highest stars.
13 But Job, you might say,
'What does God know?
Can God see through the dark clouds
and judge us?
14 Thick clouds hide him from us,
so he can't see us as he walks
beyond the edge of the sky.'

15 "Job, you are walking on the old path
that evil people walked on long ago.
16 Those evil people were destroyed
before it was their time to die.
They were washed away by the flood.
17 Those people told God,
'Leave us alone!
God All-Powerful can't do anything to us!'
18 And it was God who filled their houses
with good things!
No, I can't follow the advice of evil people.
19 Good people will see them destroyed
and those good people will be happy.
Innocent people laugh at the evil people.
20 'Truly our enemies are destroyed!
Fire burns up their wealth!'

21 "Now, Job, give yourself to God
and make peace with him.
Do this, and you will get many good things.
22 Accept his teaching.
Pay attention to what he says.
23 Job, come back to God All-Powerful,
and you will be restored.
But, you must remove the evil
from your house.
24 Think of your gold as nothing but dirt,
your best gold* as pebbles from a stream.
25 And let God All-Powerful be your gold.
Let him be your pile of silver.
26 Then you will enjoy God All-Powerful.
Then you will look up to God.
27 You will pray to him,
and he will hear you.
And you will be able to do the things
you promised to do.
28 If you decide to do something,
it will be successful.
And your future will be bright indeed!
29 God makes proud people ashamed.
But God helps humble people.
30 Then you can help people
who make mistakes.
You will pray to God
and he will forgive those people.
Why? Because you will be so pure."

Job Answers

23 Then Job answered:
2 "I am still complaining today.
Why? Because I am still suffering.
3 I wish I knew where to find God.
I wish I knew how to go to God!
4 I would explain to God my story.
My mouth would be full of arguments
to show I am innocent.
5 I want to know how God would
answer my arguments.
I want to understand God's answers.
6 Would God use his power against me?
No, he would listen to me!
7 I am an honest man.
God would let me tell my story.
Then my Judge would set me free!

8 "But if I go to the east,
God is not there.
If I go to the west,
I still don't see God.
9 When God is working in the north,
I don't see him.
When God turns to the south,
I still don't see him.
10 But God knows me.
He is testing me and he will see
that I am as pure as gold.
11 I have always lived the way God wants.
I have never stopped following God.
12 I always obey God's commands.
I love the words from God's mouth
more than I love my food.

13 "But God never changes.
No person can stand against God.
God does anything he wants.

---

orphans Children without any parents to take care of them.
best gold Literally, "Ophir."

14 God will do what he planned to me.
   And he has many other plans for me.
15 That is why I am afraid of God.
   I understand these things.
   That is why I am afraid of God.
16 God makes my heart weak,
   and I lose my courage.
   God All-Powerful makes me afraid.
17 The bad things that happened to me
   are like a black cloud over my face.
   But that darkness won't keep me quiet.

24 "Why is it that God All-Powerful knows when ₗbadⱼ things are going to happen to people, but his followers can't predict when he is going to do something ₗabout itⱼ?"

2 "People move the property markers
   to get more of their neighbor's land.
   People steal flocks and lead them
   to other grasslands.
3 They steal the donkey
   that belongs to children without parents.
   They take a widow's* cow away from her
   until she pays what she owes them.
9 Evil people take a nursing baby from
   its mother.
   They take a poor person's child
   as security* for a loan.
4 They force the poor people to wander
   from place to place without a home.
   All the poor people are forced to hide
   from these evil people.

5 "Poor people are like wild donkeys
   wandering in the desert searching for food.
   They get up early in the morning
   to search for food.
   They work late into the evening
   getting food for their children.
6 Poor people must work late into the night
   cutting hay and straw in fields.
   They must work for rich people*
   gathering the grapes in their fields.
7 Poor people must sleep all night without
   clothes.

They have no covers to protect them from
   the cold.
8 They are soaked with rain in the mountains.
   They have nothing to protect them
   from the cold.
   So they huddle close to the large rocks.
10 Poor people have no clothes.
   So they work naked.
   They carry piles of grain for evil people,
   but they still go hungry.
11 Poor people press out olive oil.
   They walk on grapes in the winepress.*
   But they have nothing to drink.
12 In the city you can hear
   the sad sounds of the dying people.
   Those hurt people cry out for help.
   But God does not listen.

13 "Some people rebel against the light.
   They don't know what God wants.
   They don't live the wasy God wants them to.
14 A murderer geta up early in the morning,
   and kills poor and helpless people.
   And at night he becomes a thief.
15 The person that does adultery,*
   waits for the night to come.
   He thinks, 'No person will see me.'
   But still, he covers his face.
16 At night when it is dark,
   evil people break into peoples' houses.
   But during the daylight,
   they lock themselves in their own houses.
   They avoid the light.
17 The darkest night is like morning
   for those evil people.
   Yes, they know the terrors of that
   deadly darkness very well!

18 "But the evil people are taken away
   like things carried away in a flood.
   The land they own is cursed,*
   so they won't gather grapes from
   their fields.
19 Hot, dry weather takes away their water
   that came from the winter snows.
   So those sinners will be taken to the grave.
20 That evil person will die

---

widow(s) Women whose husbands have died. Often these women had no one to care for them.
security Anything a person gives to show he will pay his loan. If the person does not pay back his loan, then the lender can keep that thing.
rich people Or, "wicked people."

winepress A place for squeezing the juice from grapes. Sometimes this was only a shallow hole in a large rock in the ground.
adultery Breaking the marriage promise by sexual sin.
curse(d) To ask for bad things to happen to someone or something.

and even his own mother will forget him.
His sweetheart will be the worms
   eating his body.
People will not remember him.
So evil is broken like a piece of wood.
21 Evil people hurt women
   who can't have children.
And they refuse to help women
   whose husbands are dead.
22 Evil people use their power
   to ruin powerful men.
Evil people might become powerful
   but they can't be sure of their own lives.
23 Evil people might feel safe and secure
   for a short time.
They might want to be powerful.
24 Bad people might be successful for awhile.
   But then they are gone.
They are cut down like grain.
Those evil people will be cut down,
   just like everyone else.
25 "I swear *(promise)* these things are true!
Who can prove that I lied?
Who can show that I am wrong?"

Bildad Answers Job

25 Then Bildad from Shuah answered:

2 "God is the ruler.
Every person must fear and respect God.
God keeps his heavenly kingdom in peace.
3 No person can count his stars.*
God's sun rises on all people.
4 Compared to God, no person is good.
   No human being* can really be pure.
5 Even the moon is not pure and bright to God.
The stars are not pure to God's eyes.
6 People are much less pure.
People are like maggots,*
   like worthless worms!"

Job Answers Bildad

26 Then Job answered:
2 "Bildad, Zophar, and Eliphaz,
   you have been a big help
   for this tired, weary man!

Oh yes, you have made my weak arms
   strong again!
3 Yes, you have given wonderful advice
   to the person with no wisdom!
You have really shown how wise you are!*
4 Who helped you say these things?
Whose spirit inspired you?

5 "The spirits of dead people shake with fear
   in the waters under the earth.
6 But God can see clearly into
   that place of death
Death* is not hidden from God.
7 God stretched the northern sky over
   empty space.
God hung the earth on nothing.
8 God fills the thick clouds with water.
But God doesn't let that heavy weight
   break the clouds open.
9 God covers the face of the full moon.
He spreads his clouds over it and hides it.
10 God drew the horizon on the ocean,
   like a circle where light and darkness meet.
11 The foundations that hold up the sky
   shake with fear when God threatens them.
12 God's power makes the sea calm.
God's wisdom destroyed Rahab's* helpers.
13 God's breath makes the skies clear.
God's hand destroyed the snake
   that tried to get away.*
14 These are only a few of the amazing things
   that God does.
We only hear a small whisper from God.
No person can really understand
   how great and powerful God is."

27 Then Job continued telling his story. Job
said,
2 "Truly, God lives.
And just as truly as God lives,
   He has truly been unfair with me.
Yes, God All-Powerful made my life bitter.
3 But as long as life is in me
   and God's breath of life is in my nose,
4 then my lips will not speak evil things,
   and my tongue will never tell a lie.

---

his stars Or, "his troops." This means God's heavenly army. It could be all the angels or all the stars in the sky.
human being Literally, "No one born from woman."
maggot(s) An insect that looks like a small worm and becomes a fly. It is usually found in dead bodies and decaying things.

Verses 2-3 Job doesn't really mean what he is saying here. Job is being sarcastic—He is saying these things in a way that shows he doesn't really mean it.
Death Or, "Abaddon, Destruction." See Rev. 9:11.
Rahab A dragon or sea monster. People thought Rahab controlled the sea. Rahab is often a symbol for God's enemies or for anything evil. **snake ... get away** Or, "the escaping monster." This might be another name for Rahab. See Isa.

⁵ I will never admit that you men are right.
  I will continue saying I am innocent
    until the day I die.
⁶ I will hold tightly
    to the right things I did.
  I will never stop living right.
  My conscience will never bother me
    as long as I live.

⁷ "People have stood against me.
  I hope my enemies are punished
    like bad men should be punished.
⁸ If a person does not care about God,
    then here is no hope for that person
      when he dies.
  That person has no hope
    when God takes his life away.
⁹ That evil person will have troubles,
    and he will cry to God for help.
  But God won't listen to him!
¹⁰ That person should have enjoyed
    ₍talking with₎ God All-Powerful.
  That person should have prayed to God
    all the time.

¹¹ "I will teach you about God's power.
  I will not hide God All-Powerful's plans.
¹² You have seen God's power
    with your own eyes.
  So why do you say such useless things?
¹³ This is what God planned for evil people.
  This is what cruel people will get
    from God All-Powerful:
¹⁴ An evil person might have many children.
  But his children will be killed in war.
  The children of an evil person
    will not have enough to eat.
¹⁵ All of his children will die,
    and his widow* will not be sad.
¹⁶ An evil person might get so much silver
    that it is like dirt to him.
  He might have so many clothes
    that they are like piles of clay.
¹⁷ But a good person will get his clothes
    Innocent people will get his silver.
¹⁸ An evil man might build a house,
    but it will not last a long time.
  It will be like a spider's web
    or a watchman's tent.
¹⁹ An evil person might be rich
    when he goes to bed.
  But when he opens his eyes,
    all his riches will be gone.
²⁰ He will be scared.
  It will be like a flood,
    like a storm came
    and carried everything away.
²¹ The east wind will carry him away,
    and he will be gone.
  The storm will sweep him out of his home.
²² The evil person might try to run away
    from the power of the storm.
  But the storm will hit him without mercy.
²³ Men will clap their hands
    as the evil person runs away.
  They will whistle at that evil person
    as he runs from his home.

28

"There are mines where people get
  silver and places where people
  melt gold to make it pure.
² Men dig iron from the ground.
    Copper is melted from the rocks.
³ Workers carry lights into the caves.
  They search deep into the caves.
  They look for rocks in the deep darkness.
⁴ Workers dig deep into the ground,
    following the veins of ore.
  They go deep down into the ground
    far away from the place where people live,
    down where no person has been before.
  They hang ₍from ropes far below ground₎,
    far away from other men.
⁵ Food grows on the ground above.
  But underground, ₍it is different₎—
    as if everything were melted by fire.
⁶ Underground there are sapphires*
    and grains of pure gold.
⁷ Wild birds know nothing about
    the paths under the ground.
  No falcon* has ever seen those dark paths.
⁸ Wild animals haven't walked those paths.
  Lions haven't traveled that way.
⁹ Workers dig the hardest rocks.
  Those workers dig away at the mountains
    and make them bare.
¹⁰ Workers cut tunnels through the rocks.
  They see all the rock's treasures.
¹¹ The workers make dams to stop the water.
  They bring hidden things out into the light.

---

widow(s) Women whose husbands have died. Often these women had no one to care for them.
sapphire(s) A very rare and expensive stone.
falcon A kind of bird, like a hawk.

12 "But where can a person find wisdom?
    Where can we go to find understanding?
13 We don't know how valuable wisdom is.
    People on earth ₍can't dig in the ground₎
    and find wisdom.
14 The deep ocean says,
        'Wisdom is not here with me.'
    The sea says,
        'Wisdom is not here with me.'
15 You can't buy wisdom
        with even the purest gold.
    There isn't enough silver in the world
        to buy wisdom.
16 You can't buy wisdom with
        gold from Ophir or precious onyx*
        or sapphires.*
17 Wisdom is worth more than gold or crystal.
    Expensive jewels set in gold
        can't buy wisdom.
18 Wisdom is worth more than coral*
        and jasper.*
    Wisdom is more precious than rubies.
19 The topaz* from the country of Ethiopia
        is not as precious as wisdom.
    You can't buy wisdom with pure gold.

20 "So, where does wisdom come from?
        Where can we find understanding?
21 Wisdom is hidden from every living thing
        on earth.
    Even the birds in the sky can't see wisdom.
22 Death and destruction* say,
        'We haven't found wisdom
    We have only heard rumors about it.'

23 "Only God knows the way to wisdom.
    Only God knows where wisdom is.
24 God can see to the very ends of the earth.
    God sees everything under the sky.
25 God gave the wind its power.
    God decided how big to make the oceans.
26 God decided where to send the rain,
    and where the thunderstorms should go.

27 At that time God saw wisdom
        and thought about it.
    God saw how much wisdom was worth.
    And God approved of wisdom.
28 And God said to people,
        "Fear and respect the Lord—
        that is wisdom.
    Don't do evil things—
        that is understanding."

Job Continues His Talk

29 Job continued telling his story.
    Job said:
2 "I wish my life was like it was
        a few months ago.
    At that time God watched over me
        and cared for me.
3 At that time, God's light shined above me
        so I could walk through the darkness—
    ₍God showed me the right way to live₎.
4 I wish for the days when I was successful,
        and God was my close friend.
    In those days God blessed my home.
5 I wish for the time when God All-Powerful
        was still with me,
    and my children were all around me.
6 Life was very good then.
    I washed my feet in cream,
        and I had plenty of the finest oils.*

7 "Those were the days
        when I went to the city gate
        and sat with the elders of the city
        in the public meeting place.
8 All the people there respected me!
    The young men stepped out of my way
        when they saw me coming.
    And the old men got up.
        They stood to show they respected me.
9 The leaders of the people stopped talking
        and they put their hand to their mouth
        ₍to make other people be quiet₎.
10 Even the most important leaders
        lowered their voices when they spoke.
    Yes, it seemed like their tongues
        stuck to the roof of their mouths.
11 People listened to what I said,
        and then they said good things about me.

---

onyx A semiprecious stone with many layers of blue or gray.
sapphires A very rare and expensive stone.
coral A mineral found in the ocean. It is from the skeletons of tiny sea animals. Coral is often pink, red, or black.
jasper A semiprecious stone that is often dark green.
topaz A semiprecious stone that is usually yellow.
Death and destruction Literally, "Abaddon." The Hebrew word for "death and destruction," or "destroyer," or "place of destruction."

I had plenty of the finest oils Literally, "Around the anointed rock near me were streams of oil." This probably means that Job had so much olive oil that there were streams of oil running down the altar from the part that Job gave as a gift to God.

People watched what I did,
and then they praised me.
12 Why? Because when the poor person
cried out for help, I helped.
And I helped the child that had no parents
and no one to care for him.
13 The person that was dying blessed me.
I helped widows* that were in need.
14 Right Living was my clothing.
Fairness was like my robe and my turban.*
15 I was the eyes for blind people.
⌊I led them where they wanted to go.⌋
I was the feet for crippled people.
⌊I carried them where they wanted to go.⌋
16 I was like a father for poor people.
I helped people that I didn't even know!
I helped them win their arguments in court.
17 I destroyed evil people's power.
I saved innocent people from them.
18 "I always thought,
'I will live a very long life,
then I will die in my own home.
19 I am like a healthy plant that has
roots that get plenty of water
and branches that are wet with dew.
20 I will feel like a new man every day.
I will always be strong—strong enough
to shoot a new bow every day.'
21 "In the past, people listened to me.
They were quiet while they waited
for my advice.
22 After I had finished speaking,
the people listening to me
didn't have anything else to say.
My words fell gently into their ears.
23 People waited for me to speak,
like they waited for rain.
People drank in my words, like they were
rain in the spring time.
24 I laughed with those people,
and they couldn't believe it.
My smile made them feel better.
25 I chose to be with those people,
even though I was their leader.
I was like a king in camp with his troops,
comforting the people who were sad.

30
"But now, even the men who are younger
than I am are making fun of me.

---

widow(s) Women whose husbands have died. Often these women had no one to care for them.
turban A head covering made by wrapping a long piece of cloth around the head or around a cap worn on the head.

And their fathers were so worthless
that I wouldn't put them with the dogs
guarding my sheep.
2 The fathers of those young men
are too weak to help me.
They are old and tired—their muscles
are not hard and strong any more.
3 They are like dead men—
They are starving with nothing to eat.
So they eat the dry dirt of the desert.
4 Those men pull up salt plants in the desert.
They eat the roots from the broom tree.
5 They are forced away from other people.
People shout at them like they are thieves.
6 They must live in the dry river beds,
in hillside caves and in holes in the ground.
7 They howl in the bushes.
They huddle together under thorn bushes.
8 They are a group of worthless people
with no names who were forced
to leave their country!
9 "Now those men's sons
sing songs about me to make fun of me.
My name has become a bad word to them.
10 Those young men hate me,
they stand away from me,
they think they are better than me.
They even spit in my face!
11 God has taken the string
from my bow and made me weak.
Those young men don't stop themselves
but turn against me with all their anger.
12 They attack me at my right side.
They knock my feet out from under me.
⌊I feel like a city being attacked:⌋
They build dirt ramps against my walls
to attack and destroy me.
13 They guard the road so I can't escape.
They succeed in destroying me.
They don't need anyone to help them.
14 They break a hole in the wall.
They come rushing through it,
and the crashing rocks fall on me.
15 I am shaking with fear.
Those young men chase away my honor
like the wind blows things away.
My safety disappears like a cloud.
16 "Now my life is almost gone,
and I will soon die.
Days of suffering have grabbed me.
17 All my bones ache at night.
Pain never stops chewing on me.
18 God grabbed the collar of my coat
and twisted my clothes out of shape.

¹⁹ God threw me into the mud,
and I become like dirt and ashes.
²⁰ "God, I cry out to you for help,
but you don't answer.
I stand up and pray,
but you don't pay attention to me.
²¹ God, you are mean to me.
You use your power to hurt me.
²² God, you let the strong wind blow me away.
You throw me around in the storm.
²³ I know you will lead me to my death.
Every living person must die.

²⁴ "But, surely no one will hurt a person
that is already ruined and crying for help.
²⁵ God, you know that I have cried for people
in trouble.
You know that my heart was very sad for
poor people.
²⁶ But when I looked for good things
bad things came instead.
When I looked for light, darkness came.
²⁷ I am torn up inside.
The suffering never stops.
And the suffering has just started.
²⁸ I am always sad and depressed,
without relief.
I stand up in the assembly
and yell for help.
²⁹ I am all alone like the wild dogs
and ostriches ⌊in the desert⌋.
³⁰ My skin is burnt and peeling away.
My body is hot with fever.
³¹ My harp is tuned to play sad songs.
My flute makes sounds like sad crying.

31

"I made an agreement with my eyes
not to look at a girl in a way
that would make me want her.
² What does God All-Powerful do to people?
How does God pay people back from his
home high in heaven?
³ God sends trouble and ruin to wicked people,
and disaster to people that do wrong.
⁴ God knows everything I do,
and he sees every step I take.

⁵ "I have not lied and tried to cheat people!
⁶ If God would use accurate scales,*
then he would know that I am innocent.

⁷ ⌊Then God would know⌋
if I walked off the the right path,
if my eyes led my heart to do evil,
or if my hands are dirty with sin,
⁸ Then ⌊it would be right for other people⌋ to
eat the crops I planted
and to pull up the plants I grew.

⁹ "If I have desired another woman
or waited at my neighbor's door
to sin with his wife,
¹⁰ then let my wife cook another man's food,
and let other men sleep with her.
¹¹ Why? Because sexual sin is shameful.
It is a sin that must be punished.
¹² Sexual sin is like a fire that burns
until it destroys everything!
It could ruin everything I have ever done.

¹³ "If I refuse to be fair to my slaves
when they have a complaint against me,
¹⁴ then what will I do when I must face God?
What will I say when God asks me
to explain what I did?
¹⁵ God made me in my mother's body.
And God also made my slaves.
God shaped us all inside our mothers.

¹⁶ "I have never refused to help poor people.
I always gave widows what they needed.
¹⁷ I have never been selfish with my food.
I always gave food to orphans.
¹⁸ All my life,
I have been like a father
to children that had no father.
All my life,
I have taken care of widows.
¹⁹ When I found people suffering
because they didn't have clothes,
or a poor man with no coat,
²⁰ I always gave them clothes.
I used the wool from my own sheep
to make them warm.
And they blessed me with all their heart.
²¹ I never shook my fist at an orphan
when I saw him at the gate
asking for help.*
²² If I ever did that,
then I hope that my arm
would be pulled from its socket
and fall from my shoulder!

---

accurate scales Literally, "scales of righteousness." As a word play, this could mean either "accurate scales" or "scales that show a person is good."

verse 21 Or, "I never threatened an orphan, even when I saw that I was supported in court."

23 But I didn't do any of those bad things.
   I am afraid of God's punishment.
   His majesty *(importance)* scares me.*
24 "I have never trusted in my riches.
   ⌐I always trusted God to help me.⌐
   I never said to pure gold,
   'You are my hope.'
25 I have been wealthy.
   But that didn't make me proud!
   I earned a lot of money.
   But that is not what made me happy!
26 I have never worshiped the bright sun,
   or the beautiful moon.
27 I was never foolish enough
   to worship the sun and the moon.
28 That is also a sin that must be punished.
   If I worshiped those things, then I would be
   unfaithful to God All-Powerful.

29 "I have never been happy
   when my enemies were destroyed.
   I have never laughed at my enemies
   when bad things happened to them.
30 I have never let my mouth sin
   by cursing* my enemies,
   and wishing for them to die.
31 All the people in my house know
   that I have always given food to strangers.
32 I always invited strangers into my home
   so they would not have to sleep
   in the streets at night.
33 Other people try to hide their sins.
   But I have not hidden my guilt.
34 I have never been afraid
   of what people might say.
   That fear never made me keep quiet.
   It never made me refuse to go outside.
   I am not afraid of people's hate for me.

35 "Oh, I wish someone would listen to me!
   Let me explain my side.
   I wish God All-Powerful would answer me.
   I wish he would write down
   what he thinks I did wrong.
36 Then I would wear that sign
   around my neck.
   I would put it on my head
   like a crown.
37 If God did that, then I could explain
   everything that I have done.
   I could come to God like a leader
   with my head held high.
38 "I didn't steal my land from another person.
   No one can accuse me of stealing my land.
39 I always paid the farmers for the food
   that I got from the land.
   And I never tried to take land away from
   the person who owned it.
40 If I ever did any of those bad things,
   then let thorns and weeds grow in my fields
   instead of wheat and barley*!"

Job's words are finished.

Elihu Adds to the Argument

32 Then Job's three friends gave up trying to answer Job. They gave up because Job was so sure that he himself was truly innocent. ²But there was a young man there named Elihu son of Barakel. Barakel was a descendant* of a man named Buz. Elihu was from the family of Ram. Elihu became very angry with Job. Why? Because Job was saying that he himself was right. Job was saying that he was more fair than God. ³Elihu was also angry with Job's three friends. Why? Because Job's three friends could not answer Job's questions. They could not prove that Job was wrong. ⁴Elihu was the youngest person there, so he had waited until everyone was finished talking. Then he felt like he could begin to talk. ⁵But then Elihu saw that Job's three friends had nothing more to say. So he became angry. ⁶So Elihu began to talk. He said:

   "I am only a young man.
   And you are old men.
   That is why I was afraid
   to tell you what I think.
7 I thought to myself,
   'Older people should speak first.
   Older people have lived many years.
   So they have learned many things.'
8 But God's Spirit makes a person wise.
   That "breath" from God All-Powerful
   makes people understand.
9 Old men are not the only wise people.
   Old people are not the only people
   that understand what is right.

His majesty ... me. Or, "I couldn't stand before his majesty."
cursing Asking for bad things to happen to someone.
barley A kind of grain.
descendant(s) A person's children and their future families.

¹⁰ "So please listen to me!
   And I will tell you what I think.
¹¹ I waited patiently while you men talked.
   I listened to the answers
      that you gave to Job.
¹² I listened carefully to the things you said.
   Not one of you criticized Job.
   Not one of you answered his arguments.
¹³ You three men can't say
      that you have found wisdom.
   God must answer Job's arguments,
      not people.
¹⁴ Job did not present his arguments to me.
   So I won't use the arguments
      you three men have used.

¹⁵ "Job, these men lost the argument.
   They don't have anything more to say.
   They don't have any more answers.
¹⁶ Job, I waited for these men to answer you.
   But now, they are quiet,
   They have stopped arguing with you.
¹⁷ So now, I will give you my answer.
   Yes, I will tell you what I think.

¹⁸ "I have so much to say,
      that I am about to explode.
¹⁹ I am like a bottle of new wine
      that hasn't been opened.
   I am like a new wineskin
      that is ready to break open.
²⁰ So I must speak.
      Then I will feel better.
   I must speak and answer Job's arguments.

²¹ "I must treat Job the same
      as I would treat any other person.
   I will not try to say nice things to him.
      ⌊I will say what I must say.⌋
²² I can't treat one person
      better another person!
   If I did that,
      then God would punish me!

33

"Now, Job, listen to me.
   Listen carefully to the things I say.
² I am ready to speak.
³ My heart is honest,
      so I will speak honest words.
   I will speak the truth
      about the things I know.
⁴ God's Spirit made me.
   My life comes from ⌊God⌋ All-Powerful.
⁵ Job, listen to me,
      and answer me if you can.

Get your answers ready,
   so you can argue with me.
⁶ You and I are the same
      in front of God.
   God used clay to make both of us.
⁷ Job, don't be afraid of me.
   I won't be hard on you.

⁸ "But Job, I heard what you said.
⁹ You said:
   'I am pure.
   I am innocent
   I did nothing wrong.
   I am not guilty!
¹⁰ I did nothing wrong,
      but God is against me!
   God treated me like an enemy.
¹¹ God put chains on my feet.
   God watches everything I do.'

¹² "But Job, you are wrong about this.
   And I will prove you are wrong.
   Why? Because God knows more
      than any person.*
¹³ Job, you are arguing with God!
   You think God should explain
      everything to you.
¹⁴ But maybe God does explain what he does.
   Maybe God speaks in ways that
      people don't understand.
¹⁵⁻¹⁶ Maybe God speaks to people in a dream,
   or in a vision* at night,
      when they are in a deep sleep.
   Then they become very afraid
      when they hear God's warnings.
¹⁷ God warns people to stop them
      from doing wrong things,
      and to stop them from becoming proud.
¹⁸ God warns people so he can save them
      from going to the place of death.*
   God does that to save a person
      from being destroyed.

¹⁹ "Or, a person might hear God's voice
      when that person is in bed
      and suffering from God's punishment.
   God is warning that person with pain.
   That person is in so much pain
      that all his bones hurt.

God ... person. Or, "God is much greater than any person."
vision Something like a dream that God used to speak to people.
place of death Literally, "the Pit," the place where people go when they die.

²⁰ Then that person can't eat.
That person has so much pain
that he hates even the best food.
²¹ His body wastes away until
he becomes very thin
and all his bones stick out.
²² That person is near the place of death.*
And his life is close to death.

²³ "God has thousands of angels.
Maybe one of those angels
is watching over that person.
That angel will speak for that person
and tell about the good things he has done.
²⁴ Maybe that angel will be kind to that
person and say ₍to God₎,
'Save this person from the place of death!
I have found a way to pay for his ₍sin₎.'
²⁵ Then that person's body
will become young and strong again.
That person will be the same
as when he was young.
²⁶ That person will pray to God,
and God will answer his prayer.
That person will shout with joy
and worship God.
Then that person will live a good life again.
²⁷ Then that person will confess to people.
He will say,
'I sinned.
I changed good into bad.
But God didn't give me the
punishment I deserved!
²⁸ God saved my soul from going down
to the place of death.
Now I can enjoy life again.'

²⁹ "God does all these things
again and again for that person.
³⁰ Why? To warn that person and to save
his soul from the place of death*
so that person can enjoy his life.

³¹ "Job, pay attention to me.
Listen to me.
Be quiet and let me talk.
³² But Job, if you want to disagree with me,
then go ahead and talk.

---

place of death Literally, "the Pit," the place where people go when they die.

Tell me your argument,
because I want to correct you.
³³ But Job, if you have nothing to say,
then listen to me.
Be quiet, and I will teach you wisdom."

34

Then Elihu continued talking.
He said:
² "Listen to the things I say,
you wise men.
Pay attention to me,
you smart men.
³ Your tongue tastes the food it touches.
And your ear tests the words it hears.
⁴ So, let us test these arguments
and decide for ourselves what is right.
Together we will learn what is good.
⁵ Job says,
'I, Job, am innocent.
And God is not fair to me.
⁶ I am innocent,
but the judgment against me
says that I am a liar.
I am innocent,
but I have been hurt very badly.'

⁷ "Is there any other person like Job?
Job does not care if you insult him.
⁸ Job is friends with bad people.
Job likes to be with evil people.
⁹ Why do I say that?
Because Job says,
'A person will gain nothing
if he tries to please God.'

¹⁰ "You men can understand,
so listen to me.
God would never do what is evil!
God All-Powerful would never do wrong!
¹¹ God will pay a person back
for the things that person has done.
God gives people what they deserve.
¹² This is the truth,
God won't do wrong.
God All-Powerful will always be fair.
¹³ No person chose God to be
in charge over the earth.
No one gave God responsibility
for the whole world.
₍God created everything
and he has always been in control.₎
¹⁴ If God decided to take his spirit
and his breath of life away from people,
¹⁵ then all the people on earth would die.
All people would become dust again.

16 "If you men are wise,
      then you will listen to what I say.
17 A person that hates to be fair
      can't be a ruler.
   Job, God is strong and good.
      Do you think you can judge him guilty?
18 God is the One who says to kings,
      'You are worthless!'
   God says to leaders,
      'You are evil!' .
19 God does not love leaders
      more than other people.
   And God does not love rich people
      more that poor people.
   Why? Because God made every person.
20 People can suddenly die,
      in the middle of the night.
   People become sick and pass away.
   Even powerful people die
      for no apparent reason.
21 "God watches what people do.
      God knows every step a person takes.
22 There is no place dark enough
      for evil people to hide from God.
23 God does not need to pick a time
      to test people some more.
   God does not need to bring people
      in front of him to be judged.
24 If even powerful people do bad things
      God does not need to ask questions.
   God will just destroy those people,
      and chose other people to be leaders.
25 So God knows what people do.
   That is why God will defeat evil people
      over night and destroy them.
26 God will punish the bad people
      because of the evil things they did.
   And God will punish those people
      where other people can see it happen.
27 Why? Because the bad people
      stopped obeying God.
   And those bad people didn't care
      about doing what God wants.
28 Those bad people hurt the poor people,
      and made them cry to God for help.
   And God hears the poor people cry for help.
29 But if God decides not to help poor people,
      then no person can judge God guilty.
   If God hides himself from people,
      then no person can find him.
   God is the ruler over people and nations.

30 But if a person is bad
      and makes other people sin,
   then God will not let that person be a ruler.
31 "Maybe a person will say to God,
      'I am guilty.
      I won't sin any more.
32 God, even if I can't see ₍you₎,
      please teach me ₍the right way to live₎.
   If I have done wrong,
      I won't do it again.'
33 "Job, you want God to reward you.
      But you refuse to change.
   Job, it is your decision, not mine.
      Tell me what you think.
34 "A wise person would listen to me.
      A wise person would say,
35   'Job talks like an ignorant person.
      The things Job says don't make sense!'
36 I think Job should be punished even more!
   Why? Because Job answers us
      the way an evil person would answer.
37 Job adds rebellion to his other sins.
   Job sits there in front of us and insults us
      and makes fun of God!"

35

Elihu continued talking.
He said:
2 "Job, it is not fair for you to say,
      'I am more right than God.'
3 And Job, you ask God,
      'What will a person gain
         if he tries to please God?
      What good will it do me
         if I don't sin?'
4 "Job, I *(Elihu)* want to answer you
      and your friends here with you.
5 Job, look up to the sky.
   Look up at the clouds
      that are higher that you.
6 Job, if you sin,
      it does not hurt God.
   If you have many sins,
      that does nothing to God.
7 And Job, if you are good,
      that does not help God.
   God gets nothing from you.
8 Job, the good and bad things you do
      affect only other people like yourself.
   ₍They do not help or hurt God.₎
9 "If ₍bad₎ people are being hurt,
      then they will cry out for help.

They go to powerful people
and beg them to help them.
¹⁰ But those bad people
will not ask God for help.
They will not say,
'Where is the God who made me?
God helps people when they are
depressed.
So where is he?
¹¹ God makes us wiser
than the birds and animals.
⌊So where is he?⌋'
¹² Or, if those bad people ask God for help
then God will not answer them.
Why? Because those people are too proud.
They still think they are too important.
¹³ It is true, God won't listen
to their worthless begging.
God All-Powerful won't
pay attention to them.
¹⁴ So Job, God won't listen to you
when you say that you don't see him.
You say you are waiting for your chance
to meet with God and prove
that you are innocent.
¹⁵ Job, you think that God
does not punish bad people,
and that God does not pay attention to sin.
¹⁶ "So Job continues his worthless talking.
Job is acting like he is important.
It is easy to see that Job does not
know what he is talking about."

36

Elihu continued talking.
He said:
² "Be patient with me a little longer.
God has a few more words
⌊that he wants me to say⌋.
³ I will share my knowledge with everyone.
God made me and I will prove
that God is fair.
⁴ Job, I am telling the truth.
I know what I am talking about.
⁵ "God is very powerful,
but he doesn't hate people.
God is very powerful,
but he is also very wise.
⁶ God won't let evil people live.
And God always treats poor people fairly.
⁷ God watches over people who live right.
He lets good people be rulers.
God gives good people honor forever.
⁸ So if people are punished,
if they are tied with chains and ropes
then they did something wrong.
⁹ And God will tell them what they did.
God will tell him that they sinned.
God will tell him that they were proud.
¹⁰ God will force those people
to listen to his warning.
He will command them to stop sinning.
¹¹ If those people listen to God,
and obey him,
then God will make them successful
and they will live a happy life.
¹² But if those people refuse to obey God,
then they will be destroyed.
They will die like fools.
¹³ "People that don't care about God
are always bitter.
Even when God punishes them
they refuse to pray to God for help.
¹⁴ Those people will die
when they are still young,
like the male prostitutes.*
¹⁵ But God will humble people
from their troubles.
God uses those troubles
to make people wake up
and listen to him.
¹⁶ "Job, God wants to help you.
God wants to get you out of trouble.
God wants to make life easy for you.
God wants to put plenty of food
on your table.
¹⁷ But now, Job, you were judged guilty.
So you were punished like an evil man.
¹⁸ Job, don't let riches fool you.
Don't let money change your mind.
¹⁹ Your money can't help you now.
And powerful people can't help you either!
²⁰ Don't wish for the night to come.
People try to disappear into the night.
⌊They think they can hide from God.⌋*
²¹ Job, you have suffered a lot.
But don't choose evil.
Be careful not to do wrong.
²² "God has much power.

male prostitutes Men that sold their bodies for sexual sin, often with other men. This was often part of the Canaanite worship of the false gods.
verses 19-20 This is very hard to understand in Hebrew.

God is the greatest teacher of all.
23 No person can tell God what to do.
No person can say to God,
'God, you have done wrong.'
24 Remember to praise God
for the things he did.
People have written many songs
praising God.
25 Every person can see what God did.
People in faraway countries,
can see those things.
26 Yes, God is great.
But we can't understand his greatness.
And we don't know how long God
has lived

27 "God takes up water from the earth
and changes it into mist and rain.
28 So the clouds pour out the water,
and the rain falls on many people.
29 No person can understand
how God spreads the clouds out
or how the thunder rumbles in the sky.
30 Look, God spread the lightning
over the earth and covered
the deepest part of the ocean.
31 God uses them to control the nations
and to give them plenty of food.
32 God grabs the lightning with his hands,
and commands it to hit where he wants.
33 The thunder warns that a storm is coming.
Even the cattle know it is coming.

37

"When I think about these things,
my heart beats very fast.
2 Listen everyone!
God's voice sounds like thunder.
Listen to the thundering sound
that comes from God's mouth.
3 God sends his lightning
to flash across the whole sky.
It flashed all over the earth.
4 Then after the lightning flashes,
God's roaring voice can be heard.
God thunders with his wonderful voice!
While the lightning flashes,
God's voice thunders.
5 God's thundering voice is wonderful!
He does great things
that we can't understand.
6 God says to the snow,
'Fall on the earth.'
And God says to the rain,
'Pour down on the earth.'
7 God does that so all of the people

that God has made
will know what he can do.
That is his proof.
8 The animals run into their dens
and stay there.
9 Whirlwinds come from the south.
The cold winds come from the north.
10 God's breath makes ice,
and freezes the oceans.
11 God fills the clouds with water,
and scatters those thunderclouds.
12 God orders the clouds
to blow all around the earth.
The clouds do anything God commands.
13 God brings the clouds
to bring floods to punish people
or to bring water to show his love.

14 "Job, stop for a minute and listen.
Stop and think about the wonderful things
that God does.
15 Job, do you know how God
controls the clouds?
Do you know how God
makes his lightning flash?
16 Do you know how the clouds
hang in the sky?
Clouds are just one example
of the wonderful things that God made.
And God knows everything about them.
17 But Job, you don't know these things.
All you know is that you sweat,
and your clothes stick to you,
and everything is still
when the hot winds come from the south.
18 Job, can you help God spread out the sky,
and make it shine like a polished mirror?

19 "Job, tell us what we should say to God!
We can't think of anything to say
because we don't know enough.
20 I wouldn't tell God
that I want to talk to him.
That would be the same as asking
to be destroyed.
21 A person cannot look at the sun.
It is very bright and shiny in the sky
after the wind has blown the clouds away.
22 ⌊And God is like that too!⌋
God's golden glory shines
from the Holy Mountain.*
There is a bright light around God.

Holy Mountain Or, "the north" or "Zaphon".

²³ God All-Powerful is great!
We can't understand God!
God is very powerful,
but he is also good and fair to us.
God doesn't want to hurt us!
²⁴ That is why people respect God.
But God doesn't respect proud people
that think they are wise."

God Speaks to Job

38 Then the Lord spoke to Job
from a whirlwind. God said:
² "Who is this ignorant person
that is saying these foolish things?"*
³ Job, brace yourself* and get ready
to answer the questions that I will ask you.

⁴ "Job, where were you
when I made the earth?
If you are so smart,
then answer me.
⁵ If you are so smart,
Who decided how big the world would be?
Who measured the world with
a measuring line?
⁶ What is the earth's foundation resting on?
Who put the first stone in its place?
⁷ The morning stars sang together
and the angels* shouted with joy
when that was done!

⁸ "Job, who closed the gates to stop the sea
when it flowed from deep in the earth?
⁹ At that time I covered it with clouds,
and wrapped it in darkness.
¹⁰ I set the limits for the sea
and put it behind locked gates.
¹¹ I said to the sea,
'You can come this far, but no farther.
Here is where your proud waves will stop.'

¹² "Job, did you ever in your life
command the morning to start
and the day to begin?
¹³ Job, did you ever tell the morning light
to grab the earth and shake the evil people
out of their hiding places?
¹⁴ The morning light makes the hills
and the valleys easy to see.
When the daylight comes to the earth,
the shapes of those places stand out
like the folds of a coat.
Those places take shape like soft clay
that is pressed with a stamp.
¹⁵ Evil people don't like the daylight.
When it shines bright, it stops them
from doing their bad things.

¹⁶ "Job, have you ever gone
to the deepest parts of the sea
where the sea begins?
Have you ever walked on the ocean
bottom?
¹⁷ Job, have you ever seen the gates
leading to the world of the dead?
Have you ever seen the gates
leading to that dark place of death?
¹⁸ Job, do you really understand
how large the earth is?
Tell me, if you know all this.

¹⁹ "Job, where does light come from?
Where does darkness come from?
²⁰ Job, can you take light and dark
back to the place they came from?
Do you know how to go to that place?
²¹ Surely you know these things, Job.
You are very old and wise.
You were alive when I made those things,
weren't you?*

²² "Job, have you ever gone into
the storerooms where I keep
the snow and the hail?
²³ I save the snow and the hail
for times of trouble,
for the times of war and battle.
²⁴ Job, have you ever gone to the place
where the sun comes up,
where it makes the east wind blow
all over the earth?*
²⁵ Job, who dug ditches in the sky
for the heavy rain?
Who made a path for the thunderstorm?
²⁶ Job, who makes in rain

Who ... things? Or, "Who is this person darkening *(hiding)* advice with ignorant words."
brace yourself Literally, "gird yourself like a man *(soldier)*." This means, "get ready for battle."
angels Literally, "sons of God."

verses 19-21 God doesn't really mean this. This kind of talking is called sarcasm. It is saying something that is not true in a way that everyone knows it is not true.
verse 24 Or, "Where is the place that the fog disperses and the place where the east wind scatters it all over the earth."

even in places where no people live?
27 That rain gives plenty of water
to that empty land
and grass begins to grow.
28 Job, does the rain have a father?
Where do the drops of dew come from?
29 Job, who is the mother of the ice?
Who gives birth to the frost from the sky?
30 Water freezes as hard as a rock.
Even the surface of the ocean freezes over!

31 "Job, can you tie up the Pleiades?*
Can you unfasten the belt of Orion?*
32 Job, can you bring out the constellations*
at the right times?
Or can you lead out the Bear* with its cubs?
33 Job, do you know the laws
that control the sky?
Can you make them rule over the earth?

34 "Job, can you shout at the clouds
and command them to cover you with rain?
35 Can you give a command to the lightning?
Will it come to you and say,
"Here we are. What do you want, sir?"
Will it go wherever you want it to go?

36 "Job, who makes people wise?
Who puts wisdom deep inside of them?
37 Job, who is wise enough to count the clouds
and tip them over to pour out their rain?
38 So the dust becomes mud
and the clods of dirt stick together.

39 "Job, do you find food for the lions?
Do you feed their hungry babies?
40 Those lions lie down in their caves,
they crouch down in the grass
⌊ready to attack their prey⌋.
41 Job, who feeds the ravens
when their babies yell out to God
and wander around without food?

39 "Job, do you know when
the mountain goats are born?
Do you watch when the mother deer
has her baby?
2 Job, do you know how many months
the mountain goat and the deer
must carry their babies?
Do you know when it is the right time
for them to be born?
3 Those animals lie down
they feel their birth pains
and their babies are born.
4 Those baby animals grow strong
in the fields.
Then they leave their mothers
and never come back.

5 "Job, who let the wild donkeys go free?
Who untied their ropes and let them loose?
6 I *(God)* let the wild donkey
have the desert for a home.
I gave the salt lands to them
for a place to live.
7 Wild donkeys laugh at the noisy towns.
And no person can control them.
8 Wild donkeys live in the mountains.
That is their pasture.
That is where they look for food to eat.

9 "Job, will a wild bull
agree to serve you?
Will he stay in your barn at night?
10 Job, will a wild bull
let you put ropes on him
so you can plow your fields?
11 A wild bull is very strong!
But can you trust him to do your work?
12 Can you trust him
to gather your grain and bring it
to your threshing* place?

13 "An ostrich gets excited
and flaps his wings.
⌊But an ostrich can't fly.⌋
Its wings and feathers are not like
the wings of a stork.
14 An ostrich lays her eggs on the ground
and they become warm in the sand.
15 The ostrich forgets
that someone might walk on her eggs

Pleiades A famous constellation *(group of stars)*. It is often called, "The Seven Sisters."
Orion A famous constellation. It looks looks like a hunter or powerful soldier.
constellations Groups in the night sky. Here this probably means the twelve constellations of the Zodiac. They seem to pass through the sky so that a new constellation is in a certain part of the sky each month.
Bear A famous constellation. It looks like a bear. It is often called, "the Big Dipper." Near it is a smaller constellation that looks like a small bear. It is often called, "the Little Dipper."

threshing Beating or walking on grain to remove the hulls from the grain.

or that some wild animal might
    break them.
16 An Ostrich leaves her little babies.
    She treats them like they are not hers.
   If her babies die, she doesn't care
    that all her work was for nothing.
17 Why? Because I *(God)* didn't give wisdom
    to the ostrich.
   The ostrich is foolish,
    and I made her that way.
18 But when the ostrich gets up to run,
    she laughs at the horse and its rider,
    because she can run faster than any horse.

19 "Job, did you give the horse its strength?
    Did you put the mane* on his neck?
20 Job, do you make the horse jump far
    like a locust?
   The horse snorts* loudly,
    and it scares people.
21 A horse is happy that he is so strong.
   He scratches the ground with his foot
    and runs quickly into battle.
22 The horse laughs at fear.
    He is not afraid!
   He won't run away from a battle.
23 The soldier's quiver* shakes
    on the horse's side.
   The spear and weapons his rider carries
    shine in the sun.
24 The horse is very excited!
   He runs fast over the ground.*
   When the horse hears the trumpet blow
    he can't stand still.
25 When the trumpet sounds,
    the horse shouts, 'hurray!'
   He smells the battle from far away.
   He hears the commanders shouting orders
    and all the other sounds of the battle.

26 "Job, did you teach the hawk
    how to spread his wings and fly south.*
27 Job, are you the one who told the eagle*
    to fly high into the sky.
   Did you tell him to build his nest
    high in the mountains?
28 The eagle lives on a cliff.

   The cliff is the eagle's fortress.*
29 An eagle watches for his food
    from high in his fortress.
   An eagle can see food that is far away.
30 Eagles will gather where the dead bodies are.
   And the babies will drink the blood."

40

The Lord said to Job:

2 "Job, you argued with God All-Powerful.
   You judged me guilty of doing wrong.
   Now, will you admit that you are wrong?
    Will you answer me!"

3 Then Job answered God. Job said:
4 "I am too insignificant* to speak!
   What can I say to you?
   I can't answer you!
   I will put my hand over my mouth.
5 I spoke once,
   but I won't speak again.
   I spoke twice,
   but I won't say anything more."

6 Then the Lord spoke to Job again from the
    storm. The Lord said:

7 "Job, brace yourself* and get ready
    to answer the questions that I will ask you.
8 "Job, do you think that I am not fair?
   You say that I am guilty of doing wrong
    so that you will appear innocent!
9 Job, are your arms as strong as God's arm?
   Do you have a voice like God's voice
    that can sound loud like thunder?
10 If you are like God,
    then you can be proud.
   If you are like God
    then you can wear glory and honor
    like clothes.
11 If you are like God,
    then you can show your anger
    and punish proud people.
   Make those proud people humble.
12 Yes, Job! Look at those proud people
    and make them humble.
   Crush evil people where they stand.
13 Bury all the proud people in the dirt.
   Wrap their bodies up
    and put them in their graves.

---

mane The hair on a horse's neck.
snorts The sound a horse makes.
quiver A container in which arrows are kept.
runs fast over the ground Literally, "swallows up the ground."
south Or "to Teman."
eagle Or "vulture."

fortress A building or city with tall, strong walls for protection.
insignificant Or, "not important.
brace yourself Literally, "gird yourself like a man *(soldier)*." This means, "get ready for battle."

14 Job, if you can do all these things,
  then even I will praise you.
  And I will admit that you are able
  to save yourself with your own power.
15 "Job, look at the behemoth.*
  I *(God)* made the behemoth
  and I made you.
  The behemoth eats grass like a cow.
16 The behemoth has much strength
  in his body.
  The muscles in his stomach are very powerful.
17 The behemoth's tail stands strong
  like a cedar tree.
  His leg muscles are very strong.
18 The behemoth's bones are strong
  like bronze.
  His legs are like iron bars.
19 The behemoth is the most amazing animal
  that I *(God)* made.
  But I can defeat him.
20 The behemoth eats the grass
  that grows on the hills
  where the wild animals play.
21 The behemoth lies under the lotus plants.*
  The behemoth hides in the reeds
  in the swamp.
22 The lotus plants hide the behemoth
  in their shade.
  He lives under the willow trees
  that grow near the river.
23 If the river floods,
  the behemoth will not run away.
  He is not afraid
  if the Jordan River splashes on his face.
24 No person can blind the behemoth's eyes
  and catch him in a trap.

41

"Job, can you catch Leviathan* with a
  fishhook?
  Can you tie his tongue with a rope?
2 Job, can you put a rope through
  the leviathan's nose,
  or put a hook through his jaw?
3 Job, will the leviathan beg you
  to let him go free?
  Will he speak to you with gentle words?

4 Job, will the leviathan
  make an agreement with you
  and promise to serve you forever?
5 Job, will you play with the leviathan
  like you would play with a bird?
  Will you put a rope on him
  so your servant girls can play with him?
6 Job, will fishermen try to buy
  the leviathan from you?
  Will they cut him in pieces
  and sell him to the merchants?*
7 Job, can you throw spears
  into the leviathan's skin or head?
8 Job, if you ever lay a hand on leviathan,
  you will never do it again!
  Just think about the battle that would be!
9 If you think you can defeat the leviathan,
  forget it!
  There is no hope!
  Just looking at him will scare you!
10 No person is brave enough
  to wake him up and make him angry.
  And no person can stand against me either!*
11 I *(God)* owe no person anything.
  Everything under heaven belongs to me.*
12 Job, I will tell you about leviathan's legs,
  his strength and graceful shape.
13 No person can pierce his skin.
  His skin is like armor!*
14 No person can force the leviathan
  to open his jaws.
  The teeth in his mouth scare people.
15 The leviathan's back has
  rows of shields tightly sealed together.
16 The shields are so close to each other
  that no air can pass between them.
17 The shields are joined to each other.
  They hold together so tightly
  that they can't be pulled apart.
18 When the leviathan sneezes,
  it is like lightning flashing out.
  His eyes shine like the light of dawn.
19 Burning torches come out from his mouth.

---

merchant(s) A person who earns his living by buying and selling things.
And no person can stand against me either Or "No person can stand and fight him."
I ... me Or, "No person has come near to leviathan and survived—no one under heaven!"
His skin is like armor Or, "No one can approach him with a bridle."

---

behemoth We are not sure what this animal is. It might be a hippopotamus or an elephant.
lotus plants A kind of tree. Its leaves give much shade.
Leviathan We are not sure what this animal is. It might be a crocodile or a giant sea monster.

19 Burning torches come out from his mouth.
   Sparks of fire shoot out.
20 Smoke pours from the leviathan's nose
   like burning weeds under a boiling pot.
21 The leviathan's breath
   makes coals burn,
   and flames shoot from his mouth.
22 The leviathan's neck is very powerful,
   People are afraid and run away from him.
23 There is no soft spot in his skin.
   It is hard like iron.
24 The leviathan's heart is like a rock,
   he has no fear.
   It is hard like a lower millstone.*
25 When the leviathan gets up,
   strong people are afraid.
   They run away
   when the leviathan swings his tail.
26 Swords, spears, and darts hit the leviathan,
   but they only bounce off.
   Those weapons don't hurt him at all!
27 Leviathan breaks iron as easily as straw.
   He breaks bronze like rotten wood.
28 Arrows don't make the leviathan run away.
   Rocks bounce off of him like straw.
29 When a wood club hits the leviathan,
   it feels like a piece of straw to him.
   He laughs when men throw spears at him.
30 The skin under the leviathan's body
   is like hard, sharp pieces of
   broken pottery.
   He leaves tracks in the mud
   like a threshing board.*
31 The leviathan stirs up the water
   like a boiling pot.
   He makes it bubble like
   a pot of boiling oil.
32 When the leviathan swims,
   he leaves a path behind himself.
   He stirs up the water,
   and leaves white foam behind him.
33 No animal on earth is like the leviathan.
   He is an animal made without fear.
34 The leviathan looks down
   on the proudest animals.
   He is king over all the wild animals."
   ⌊And I, the Lord, made the leviathan!⌋

Job Answers the Lord

42 Then Job answered the Lord.
Job said,
² "Lord, I know you can do everything.
   You make plans, and nothing
   can change or stop your plans
³ Lord, you asked this question:
   'Who is this ignorant person
   that is saying these foolish things?'*
   "Lord, I talked about things
   that I didn't understand.
   I talked about things that were too amazing
   for me to understand.
⁴ "Lord, you said to me,
   'Listen Job, and I will speak.
   I will ask you questions,
   and you will answer me.'
⁵ Lord, in the past, I heard about you,
   but now I have seen you
   with my own eyes.
⁶ And Lord, I am ashamed of myself.
   Lord, I am so sorry.
   As I sit in the dust and ashes,*
   I promise to change my heart and my life."

The Lord Gives Job's Wealth Back

⁷After the Lord finished talking to Job, he spoke to Eliphaz from Teman. The Lord said to Eliphaz, "I am angry at you and your two friends. Why? Because you didn't say right things about me. But Job is my servant. Job said right things about me. ⁸So now Eliphaz, get seven bulls and seven rams. Take them to my servant Job. Kill them and offer them as a burnt offering for yourselves. My servant Job will pray for you, and I will answer his prayer. Then I won't give you the punishment that you deserve. You should be punished because you were very foolish. You didn't say right things about me. But my servant Job said right things about me."

⁹So Eliphaz from Teman, and Bildad from Shuah, and Zophar from Naamah obeyed the Lord. Then the Lord answered Job's prayer.

¹⁰Job prayed for his friends. And the Lord made Job successful again. God gave Job twice as much as he had before. ¹¹Then all of Job's brothers and sisters and all of the people that knew Job before came to his house. They all ate a

---

lower millstone A flat rock for grinding grain. Another stone was put on top of this flat rock. Then the grain was ground into flour between the stones.
threshing board A board with many pieces of sharp stones or pieces of metal. Farmers pulled these boards over grain to break the hulls away from the grain.

Who ... things? Or, "Who is this person darkening *(hiding)* advice with ignorant words."
dust and ashes People sat in dust and ashes to show that they were very sad about something.

big meal with Job. They comforted Job. They were sorry that the Lord had brought so much trouble to Job. Each person gave Job a piece of silver* and a gold ring. ¹²The Lord blessed the Job with even more things than he had in the beginning. Job got 14,000 sheep, 6,000 camels, 2,000 cows, and 1,000 female donkeys. ¹³Job also got seven sons and three daughters. ¹⁴Job named the first daughter Jemimah. Job named the second daughter Keziah. And Job named the third daughter Keren Happuch. ¹⁵Job's daughters were among the most beautiful women in all the country. And Job even gave part of his property to his daughters—they each got a share of the property, just like their brothers.*

¹⁶So, Job lived for 140 years more. He lived to see his children, his grandchildren, his great-grandchildren, and his great-great-grandchildren. ¹⁷Job lived to be a very old man who had lived a good long life.

---

piece of silver Literally, "a Keshitah." This was a measure that was used in the time of the Patriarchs. See Gen. 33:19 and Josh. 24:32.

Job ... property Usually a person's property was divided only among the sons, but here even Job's daughters also got part of his property.

PSALMS

BOOK 1

Psalm 1

1 A person will be truly happy
    if he doesn't follow the advice of bad people,
    and if he doesn't live like sinners,
    and if he doesn't feel at home
        with people who don't believe God.*
2 A good person loves the Lord's teachings.
    He thinks about them day and night.
3 So that person becomes strong
    like a tree planted by streams of water.
    He is like a tree that makes fruit
        at the right time.
    He is like a tree with leaves that don't die.
    Everything he does is successful.

4 But bad people are not like that.
    Bad people are like chaff*
        that the wind blows away.
5 If good people gather together
    to decide a court case,
    then bad people will be proved guilty.
    Those sinners will not be judged innocent.*
6 Why? Because the Lord
    protects good people,
    but destroys bad people.

Psalm 2

1 Why are the people from other nations
    so angry?
    Why are they making foolish plans?

2 Their kings and leaders joined together
    to fight against the Lord
    and against the king he chose.
3 ⌊Those leaders said,⌋
    "Let's rebel against God
    and against the king he chose.
    "Let's break free from them!"

4 But my Master, the King in heaven,
    laughs at those people.
5-6 God is angry and he tells those people,
    "I chose this man to be king!
    And he will rule on Mount Zion.
    Zion is my special mountain."
And that makes those other leaders afraid.

7 Now I will tell you about the Lord's
    agreement.
The Lord said to me,
    "Today I become your father!*
    And you are my son.
8 If you ask me,
    I will give the nations to you.
    All the people on earth will be yours!
9 You could destroy those nations
    like an iron rod can shatter a clay pot.*"

10 So, you kings, be wise.
    All you rulers, learn this lesson.
11 Obey the Lord with much fear.
12 Show that you are loyal to God's son.*
If you don't do this,
    he will be angry and destroy you.

People who trust the Lord are happy.
    ⌊But other people should be careful.⌋
The Lord is almost ready to show his anger.

A person ... God Or, "The person who doesn't follow the advice of bad people or turn on to Sinners Road or stay at Scoffers' House is fortunate (blessed)."

chaff Seed coverings and stems separated from the seeds of plants like wheat or barley. Farmers did not keep this useless chaff.

If good ... innocent Or, "Bad people will not rise in the place of judgment nor the sinners in the meeting of good people." It is not clear if this verse means that bad people will not become judges, or that bad people will be judged guilty.

I become your father Literally, "I fathered you." This probably shows that God was adopting the king as his son.

You ... pot Or, "You will shepherd them with an iron rod. You will shatter them like a clay pot."

Show that you are loyal to God's son Literally, "Kiss the son!"

Psalm 3

This is David's song from the time he ran away from his son Absalom.

1 "Lord, I have many, many enemies.
   Many people have turned against me.
2 Many people are talking about me.
   ₍Those people say,₎
   "God, won't rescue him!"
                                    SELAH*
3 But, Lord, you are my shield.
   You are my Glory.
   Lord, you make me important!*
4 I will pray to the Lord.
   And he will answer me from his holy mountain!
                                    SELAH*
5 I can lie down and rest,
   and I know I will wake up.
   ₍How do I know this?₎
   Because the Lord covers and protects me!
6 Thousands of soldiers might surround me.
   But I won't be afraid of those enemies!
7 Lord, get up!*
   My God, come rescue me!
   ₍You are very strong!₎
   If you hit my bad enemies on the cheek,
   you will break all their teeth.
8 The Lord can rescue his people.
   Lord, please be good to your people.
                                    SELAH*

Psalm 4

To the director. With stringed instruments. A song of David.*

1 My good God, answer me
   when I pray to you!
   Hear my prayer
   and be kind to me!
   Give me some relief from all my troubles!
2 People, how long will you say bad things about me?
   You people keep looking for new lies ₍to tell about me₎.
   You people love telling those lies.
                                    SELAH*
3 You know that the Lord listens
   to his good people.
   So the Lord hears me when I pray to him.
4 ₍If something is bothering you,₎
   you can be angry,*
   but don't sin.
   Think about those things
   when you go to bed,
   and then relax.*
                                    SELAH*
5 Give good sacrifices* to God,
   and trust the Lord!
6 Many people say,
   "Who will show us ₍God's₎ goodness?
   Lord, let us see your shining face!"
7 Lord, you have made me very happy!
   I am happier now than at harvest time—
   when we celebrate because we have much grain and wine.
8 I go to bed and sleep in peace.
   Why? Because, Lord, you lay me down to sleep in safety.

Psalm 5

To the director. For the flutes.* A song of David.*

1 Lord, hear my words.
   Understand what I am trying to say.
2 My God and King,
   listen to my prayer.
3 Every morning, Lord,
   I lay my gifts before you
   and look to you ₍for help₎.
   And every morning,
   you hear my prayers.
4 God, you don't like evil ₍people near you₎.
   Evil people can't worship you.*
5 Fools* can't come near you.

Selah This word is for the musicians. It probably means the singers should pause here or the music should be louder here.

You ... make me important Literally, "You are my Glory, the One who lifts my head."

Lord, get up The people said this when they lifted the Box of the Agreement and took it into battle with them. This showed that God was with them. See Num. 10:35-36.

director Or, "performer."

A song of David Or, "A song dedicated to David."

be angry Or, "be upset" or "be excited."

relax Or, "be calm" or "be silent."

sacrifice(s) A sacrifice was a gift to God. Usually, it was a special animal that was killed and burned on an altar.

For the flutes This might be the name of a tune instead of a type of instrument.

God ... you. Or, "You are not a God who likes evil {people}, and evil {people} don't respect you."

Fools Usually this means people who don't believe and obey God. This shows they are very foolish.

You hate* people who do evil.
6 You destroy people who tell lies.
The Lord hates people who make secret plans
to hurt other people.
7 But, Lord, by your great mercy,
I will come to your temple.*
I will bow toward your holy temple
with fear and respect for you, Lord.
8 Lord, show me your right way of living.
People are looking for my weaknesses,
so show me how you want me to live.
9 Those people don't tell the truth.
They are liars that twist the truth.
Their mouths are like empty* graves.
They say nice things to other people,
but they are only trying to trap them.
10 Punish them, God!
Let them be caught in their own traps.
Those people have turned against you,
so punish them for their many crimes.
11 But let the people who trust God be happy.
Let them be happy forever!
God, protect and give strength to the people
who love your name.
12 Lord, if you do good things to good people,
then you are like a large shield
protecting them.

Psalm 6

To the director,* with stringed instruments,
⌊accompanied⌋ by the Sheminith.*
A song of David.*

1 Lord, don't correct me in anger.
Don't be angry and punish* me.
2 Lord, be kind to me.
I am sick and weak.
Heal me!
My bones are shaking.
3 My whole body is shaking.
Lord, how long ⌊until you heal me⌋?*

4 Lord, make me strong again!
You are very kind, so save me.
5 Dead people in their graves
don't remember you.
People in the place of death
don't praise you.
⌊So heal me!⌋
6 Lord, all night I prayed to you.
My bed is wet from my tears.
Tears are dripping from my bed.
I am weak from crying to you.
7 My enemies have given me many troubles.
This made me very sad with grief.
Now my eyes are weak from crying.
8 Go away you bad people!
Why? Because the Lord heard me crying.
9 The Lord heard my prayer.
And the Lord accepted and answered
my prayer.
10 All my enemies will be upset and
disappointed.
Something will suddenly happen,
and they will all leave in shame.

Psalm 7

A song* of David that he sang to the Lord.
This song is about ⌊Saul, the son of⌋ Kish,*
from the family group of Benjamin.

1 Lord my God, I trust you.
Save me from the people who are chasing me.
Rescue me!
2 If you don't help me,
I will be like an animal caught by a lion.
I will be carried away,
and no person will be able to save me!
3 Lord my God, I did nothing wrong.
I promise, I did nothing wrong!
4 I did not do bad things to my friend.*
And I did not help my friend's enemies.
5 But an enemy is chasing me.
He wants to kill me.
He wants to trample my life into the ground
and push my soul into the dirt.
SELAH*

---

hate Or, "reject, send away".
temple The special building in Jerusalem for Jewish worship.
empty Literally, "open."
director Or, "performer."
by the Sheminith This might be a special instrument, a special way of tuning an instrument, or one of the groups that played harps in the temple orchestra. See 1 Chron.15:21.
A song of David Or, "A song dedicated to David."
punish Literally, "teach" or "correct."

Lord ... heal me Literally, "As for you, Lord, how long?"
song Literally, "shiggayon." This probably means a song full of emotion.
Kish Or, "Cush."
friend Or, "ally;" a person or country that has agreed to help another person or country.

⁶ Lord, get up* and show your anger!
   My enemy is angry,
      so stand and fight against him.
   Lord, get up and demand fairness!
⁷ Lord, judge the people.
      Gather the nations around you,
⁸   and judge the people.
   Lord, judge me.
      Prove that I am right.
      Prove that I am innocent.
⁹ Punish the bad people,
      and help the good people.
   God, you are good.
      And you can look into peoples' hearts.
¹⁰ God helps people with honest hearts.
      So God will protect me.
¹¹ God is a good judge.
      And God will show his anger at any time.
¹² If God makes a decision,
      he does not change his mind.
¹³ God has the power to punish people.*
¹⁴ Some people are always planning bad things.
      They make secret plans and tell lies.
¹⁵ They try to trap and hurt other people.
      But they will be hurt in their own traps.
¹⁶ They will receive the punishment
      they should get.
   They were cruel to other people.
      But they will get what they deserve.

¹⁷ I praise the Lord because he is good.
   I praise the name of the Lord Most-High.

Psalm 8

To the director, ⌊*accompanied*⌋ *by the Gittith.* * *A song of David.* *

¹ Lord our Master,
      your name is the most wonderful name
      in all the earth!
   Your name brings you praise
      everywhere in heaven.
² From the mouths of children and babies
      come songs of praise to you.
   You gave them ⌊these powerful songs⌋
      to silence all your enemies.
³ Lord, I look at the heavens
      you made with your hands.
   I see the moon and stars you created,
      ⌊and I wonder:⌋
⁴ Why are people so important to you?
      Why do you even remember them?
   Why are people* so important to you?
      Why do you even notice them?
⁵ ⌊But people are important to you!⌋
      You made people* almost like gods.
   And you crowned them
      with glory and honor.
⁶ You put people in charge of
      everything you made.
   You put everything under their* control.
⁷ People rule over the sheep and cattle
      and all the wild animals.
⁸ They rule over the birds in the sky,
      and the fish that swim in the ocean.
⁹ Lord our Master,
      your name is the most wonderful name
      in all the earth!

Psalm 9

To the director. * *Alamoth of Ben.* *
A song of David. *

I praise the Lord with all my heart.
   Lord, I will tell about all the wonderful
      things you did.
² You make me so very happy.
      God Most-High, I praise your name.
³ My enemies turned to run from you.
      But they fell and were destroyed.

Selah This word is for the musicians. It probably means the singers should pause here or the music should be louder here.
Lord, get up The people said this when they lifted the Box of the Agreement and took it into battle with them. This showed that God was with them. See Num. 10:35-36.
If God ... punish people Literally, "He will not turn back. He will sharpen his sword. He will draw and aim his bow. He has prepared the weapon of death. He has made his flaming arrows."
director Or, "performer."
by the Gittith Or, "on the Gittith." This might be a type of instrument, a tune, or a performer in the temple orchestra such as Obed Edom from Gath (the Gittite). See I Chron.15:21, 16:4-7.
A song of David Or, "A song dedicated to David."

people ... people Literally, "man ... son of man" or "Enosh ... son of Adam." This is a Hebrew way of saying people—descendants of Adam and Enosh.
people Literally, "him." This is still talking about "man" and "son of man" and can be understood as one person or as all people.
their Literally, "his".
Alamoth of Ben This might be the name of a tune, "On the Death of the Son." Or, it might refer to one of the two main orchestral groups in the temple. Ben might be Benaiah, one of the musicians. See 1 Chron.15:20.

4 You are the good judge.
  You sat on your throne* as judge.
  Lord, you listened to my case.
  And you made the decision about me.
5 You criticized those other people.
  Lord, you destroyed those bad people.
  You erased their names forever and ever
    ₎from the list of people who are alive₎.
6 The enemy is finished!
  Lord, you destroyed their cities!
  Now, only ruined buildings are left.
  Nothing is left to remind us
    of those bad people.
7 But the Lord rules forever.
  The Lord made his kingdom strong.
  He did this to bring fairness to the world.
8 The Lord judges everyone on earth fairly.
  The Lord judges all the nations the same.
9 Many people are trapped and hurting
    because they have many troubles.
  Those people are crushed by the weight of
    their problems.
  Lord, be a safe place for them to run to.
10 People who know your name should trust you.
   Lord, if people come to you,
     you will not leave them without help.
11 You people living on Zion,
     sing praises to the Lord.*
   Tell other nations about the great things
     the Lord did.
12 The Lord remembered the people who
     went to him for help.*
   Those poor people cried for help.
   And the Lord didn't forget them.
13 ₎I said this prayer to God:₎
   "Lord, be kind to me.
   Look, my enemies are hurting me.
   Save me from the 'gates of death.'
14 Then, at the gates of Jerusalem,
     I can sing praises to you, Lord.
   I will be very happy
     because you saved me."
15 Those people from other nations
     dug holes to trap other people.

But they fell into their own traps.
Those people hid nets to trap other people.
But they were caught in those nets.
16 The Lord caught those bad people.
   So people learned that the Lord punishes
     people who do bad things.
                                          HIGGAYON*
                                          SELAH*
17 People who forget God are bad.
   Those people will go to the place of death.
18 Sometimes it seems that God forgets about
     people with troubles.
   It seems those poor people have no hope.
   But God doesn't really forget them forever.
19 Lord, get up* and judge the nations.
   Don't let people think they are powerful.
20 Teach people a lesson.
   Let them know that they are only people.
                                          SELAH*

Psalm 10

1 Lord, why do you stay so far away?
    People with troubles can't see you.
2 Proud and wicked people make evil plans.
    And they hurt poor people.
3 Evil people brag about the things they want.
    And those greedy people curse God.
  In this way, the evil people show that
    they hate the Lord.
4 Bad people are too proud to follow God.
  They make all their evil plans.
    And they act like there is no God.
5 Bad people are always doing crooked things.
  They don't even notice God's laws
    and wise teachings.*
  God's enemies ignore ₎his teachings₎.
6 Those people think bad things will never
    happen to them.
  ₎They say,₎
  "We will have fun and never be punished."
7 Those people are always cursing.
  They are always saying bad things about
    other people.

---

throne The chair a king or queen sits on.
You people living on Zion,
  sing praises to the Lord Or, "Sing praises to the Lord who sits as King in Zion."
went to him for help Literally, "sought blood." The family of a person who was killed could go to court to ask that the killer be punished. Here, God is like the judge who listens to people who have been hurt by other people.

Higgayon Or, "Meditation." This may mean a time to think quietly during the song.
Selah This word is for the musicians. It probably means the singers should pause here or the music should be louder here.
Lord ,get up The people said this when they lifted the Box of the Agreement and took it into battle with them. This showed that God was with them. See Numbers 10:35-36.
They ... wise teachings Literally, "Your justice is far above him."

They are always planning evil things to do.
8 Those people hide in secret places
     and wait to catch people.
  They hide, looking for people to hurt.
     They kill innocent people.
9 Those bad people are like lions trying to catch
     the animals they will eat.
  They attack poor people.
  The poor people are caught in the traps
     that the evil people make.
10 Again and again, those bad people hurt poor,
     hurting people.
11 So those poor people begin thinking,
  "God has forgotten us!
  He has turned away from us forever!
  God doesn't see what is happening to us!"

12 Lord, get up and do something!
  God, punish those bad people!
  Don't forget the poor people!

13 Why do bad people turn against God?
  Because they think he won't punish them.

14 ₍Lord,₎ surely you see the cruel and evil things
     that bad people do.
  Look at those things,
     and do something!
  People with many troubles
     come to you for help.
  Lord, you are the One who helps orphans.*
     ₍So help them!₎
15 ₍Lord,₎ destroy the evil people.
16 Remove those people from your land!
17 Lord, you heard what poor people want.
  Listen to their prayers
     and do what they ask!
18 Lord, protect the children without parents.
  Don't let sad people suffer more troubles.
  Make bad people too afraid to stay here.

Psalm 11

To the director.* David's ₍song₎*

1 I trust the Lord.
  So why did you tell me ₍to run and hide₎?
  ₍You told me,₎
     "Fly like a bird to your mountain!"

2 ₍Bad people are like a hunter₎
  They hide in the dark.
  They pull back on the bowstring.

  They aim their arrows.
  And they shoot straight into the hearts
     of good, honest people.
3 What would happen if they destroyed
     all that is good?*
  What would good people do then?

4 The Lord is in his holy palace.*
  The Lord sits on his throne* in heaven.
  And the Lord sees everything that happens.
  The Lord's eyes look closely at people to
     see if they are good or bad.
5 The Lord searches for good people,
     but he rejects* cruel, evil people.
6 He will make hot coals and burning
     sulphur fall like rain on those bad people.
  Those bad people will get nothing but
     a hot, burning wind.*
7 But the Lord is good.
  And he loves people doing good things.
  Good people will ₍be with him₎
     and see his face.

Psalm 12

To the director,* ₍accompanied₎ by the Sheminith.* A song of David.*

1 Save ₍me₎ Lord!
  The good people are all gone.
  There are no true believers left among
     all the people on earth.*
2 People tell lies to their neighbors.
  Each and every person flatters* his
     neighbors with lies.
3 The Lord should cut off those lips
     that tell lies.
  The Lord should cut out those tongues
     that tell their big stories.
4 Those people say,
  "We will say the right lies
     and become very important.

What would happen ... good Or, "What if the foundations {of society} were really destroyed?
palace A large house built for a king. Here, it is the temple.
throne The chair a king or queen sits on.
hates Or, "hates" or "refuses to accept."
hot, burning wind This is like the hot fire a worker uses to melt silver. The silver separates from all the worthless things in it. These things are thrown away and only the pure silver is left.
by the Sheminith This might be a special instrument, a special way of tuning an instrument, or one of the groups that played harps in the temple orchestra. See 1 Chron.15:21.
A song of David
all the people on earth Literally, "the sons of man."

---

orphans Children without parents to take care of them.
director Or, "performer."
David's {song Or "{Dedicated} to David"

We know what to say,
so that no one will be our master."
5 But the Lord says:
"Bad people stole from the poor people.
They took things from helpless people.
But now I will stand and defend those
weary (tired) people."
6 The Lord's words are true and pure
like silver melted in a hot fire.
They are pure like silver that was melted and
made pure seven times.
7 Lord, take care of helpless people.
Protect them now and forever!
8 Those bad people act important.
But really, they are like costume jewelry.
It looks expensive,
but it is really very cheap.*

Psalm 13

To the director. A song of David.*
1 How long will you forget me, Lord?
Will you forget me forever?
How long will you refuse to accept me?*
2 How long must I wonder if you have
forgotten me?
How long must I feel this sadness
in my heart?
How long will my enemy win against me?
3 Lord my God, look at me!
Answer my question!
Let me know the answer or I will die!
4 If that happens, my enemy will say
"I beat him!"
My enemy would be happy if he defeated me.
5 Lord, I trusted in your love to help me.
You saved me and made me happy!
6 I sing a happy song to the Lord
because he has done good things for me.

Psalm 14

To the director. David's ₁song₁*
1 A foolish person* says in his heart,
"There is no God."

Foolish people do terrible and rotten things.
Not even one of them does good things.
2 The Lord looked down from heaven
to see if there were any wise people.
Wise people turn to God for help.
3 But every person had turned away from God.
All people had become bad.
Not even one person was doing good things!
4 Bad people have destroyed my people.
And those bad people don't know God.
Bad people have plenty of food to eat.*
And those people don't worship the Lord.
5-6 Those bad people didn't want to listen to
advice from a poor man.
Why? Because that poor man
depended on God.
But God is with his good people.
So bad people have plenty to fear.
7 Who on Zion* saves Israel?
₁It is the Lord who saves Israel!₁
The Lord's people were taken away
and forced to be prisoners.
But the Lord will bring his people back.
Then Jacob (Israel) will be very happy.

Psalm 15

A song of David.
1 Lord, who can live in your Holy Tent?*
Who can live on your holy mountain?*
2 Only a person who lives a pure life,
and does good things,
and speaks truth from the heart
₁can live on your mountain₁.
3 That kind of person does not say bad things
about other people.
That person does not do bad things
to his neighbors.
That person does not tell shameful things
about his own family.
4 That person does not respect the people
that hate God.
But that person shows honor to
all the people who serve the Lord.
If he makes a promise to his neighbor,
then he does what he promised to do.*
5 If that person gives money to someone,
he will not charge interest on that loan.

Those bad people ... really very cheap Literally, "Bad people strut around like expensive cheap things belonging to sons of man."
director Or, "performer."
A song of David
refuse to accept me Literally, "hide your face from me."

eat In Hebrew the word "eat" is like the word "destroyed." This word play shows that the bad people hurt God's followers and still received good things. This confused the writer.
holy mountain Zion, the mountain Jerusalem is built on.

And that person will not take money
to do bad things to innocent people.
If a person lives like that good man,
then he will always be near God.*

Psalm 16

A miktam of David. *

1 Protect me, God, because I depend on you.
2 I said to the Lord,
"Lord, you are my Master.
Every good thing I have comes from you."*
3 The Lord does wonderful things for his
followers on earth.
The Lord shows he truly loves those people.
4 But people who run to worship other gods
will have much pain.
I will not share in their gifts of blood that they
offer to those idols.
I will not even say the names of those idols.
5 No, my share and my cup come only from
the Lord.
Lord, you support me.
You give me my share.
6 My share* is very wonderful.
My inheritance* is very beautiful.
7 I praise the Lord because he taught me well.
At night, instructions came from
deep inside of me.
8 I keep the Lord before me always.
And I will never leave his right side.
9 So my heart and soul will be very happy.
Even my body will live in safety.
10 Why? Because, Lord, you will not leave
my soul in the place of death.
You will not let your faithful one rot
in the grave.*
11 You will teach me the right way to live.
Just being with you, Lord, will bring
complete happiness.
Being at your right side will bring
happiness forever.

If he ... promised to do Or, "That person promised not to do bad things. And he does not do bad things."
he ... near God Literally, "that person will never be moved."
A miktam of David The exact meaning of "miktam" is not clear. It might mean "a well-arranged song." This song was either written by David or dedicated to him.
I said ... from you Or, "I said to the Lord my Master, 'You are my goodness. There is none but you.'"
share Or, "section of land."
inheritance Here, this probably means the land that each Jew received as his part of the country that God gave his family.
rot ... grave Literally, "see decay."

Psalm 17

A prayer of David. *

1 Lord, hear my prayer for fairness.
I am calling loudly to you.
And I am being honest in the things I say.
So, please listen to my prayer.
2 You will make the right decision about me.
You can see the truth.
3 You have looked deep into my heart.
You were with me all night.
You questioned me and found nothing wrong.
I didn't plan any bad thing.
4 I have tried as hard as humanly possible
to obey your commands.
5 I have followed your paths.
My feet never left your way of living.
6 Every time I called to you, God, you
answered me.
So listen to me now.
7 God, you help people who trust you—
those people stand by your right side.
So listen to this prayer
from one of your followers.
8 Protect me like the pupil* of your eye.
Hide me in the shadow under your wings.
9 Lord, save me from the bad people
who are trying to ruin me.
Protect me from the people around me
who are trying to hurt me.
10 Those bad people have become too proud [to
listen to God].
And they brag about themselves.
11 Those people chased me.
Now they are all around me.
And they are ready to attack.*
12 Those bad people are like lions
waiting to kill and eat another animal.
They hide like lions, ready to attack.
13 Lord, get up* and go to the enemy.
Make them surrender.
Use your sword and save me
from the bad people.
14 Lord, use your power and remove
bad people from the [land of] the living.

A prayer of David Or, "A prayer dedicated to David."
pupil The center of the eye, which everyone wants to protect.
And they are ready to attack Or, "They decided to lie on the ground."
Lord, get up The people said this when they lifted the Box of the Agreement and took it into battle with them. This showed that God was with them. See Num. 10:35,36.

Lord, many people come to you for help.
  Those people don't have much in this life.
Give those people plenty of food.
  Give their children all they want.
Give the children so much
  that they will have food left over
    for their children.
¹⁵ ₗI prayed forج fairness.
  So I will see your face, Lord.
And seeing you, Lord,*
  I will be fully satisfied.

Psalm 18*

To the director. The song of the Lord's
servant, David. David wrote* this song at
the time the Lord saved him from Saul and
all his other enemies.*

¹ He said,
  "Lord my strength,
    I love you!"
² The Lord is my Rock,*
  my Fortress,*
    my Place of Safety."
  My God is my Rock.
  I run to him for protection.
  God is my shield.
    His power saves me.*
  The Lord is my hiding place
    high in the hills.
³ They made fun of me.
  But I called to the Lord for help,
  and I was saved from my enemies!
⁴ ₗMy enemies were trying to kill me!ج
  The ropes of death were all around me.
    I was caught in a flood carrying me to that
      place of death.*
⁵ Ropes of the grave were all around me.
  Traps of death lay before me.
⁶ Trapped, I called to the Lord for help.
  Yes, I called to my God.

---

you, Lord Literally, "your likeness."
Psalm 18 This song is also found in II Sam. 22.
director Or, "performer."
wrote Or, "spoke."
Rock A name for God to show he is a strong place of safety.
Fortress A building or city with tall, strong walls for protection.
His power saves me Or, "He is the horn of my salvation."
place of death Or, "the place of no return, the grave."

God was in his temple.
  He heard my voice.
  He heard my cry for help.
⁷ The earth shook and trembled;
  the foundations of heaven shook.
  Why? Because the Lord was angry!
⁸ Smoke came from God's nose.
  Burning flames came from God's mouth,
  Burning sparks flew from him.
⁹ The Lord tore open the sky,
    and he came down!
  He stood on a thick, dark cloud.
¹⁰ The Lord was flying ₗacross the skyج,
    riding on the flying Cherub angels.
  He was soaring high on the wind.
¹¹ The Lord was hidden in the dark clouds
    that surround him like a tent.
  He was hidden in the thick thunder clouds.
¹² Then, God's shining brightness
    broke through the clouds.
  There was hail and flashes of lightning.
¹³ The Lord thundered from the sky!
    God Most-High let his voice be heard.
  There was hail and flashes of lightning.
¹⁴ The Lord shot his arrows*
    and scattered the enemy.
  The Lord sent many bolts of lightning
    and the people scattered in confusion.
¹⁵ Lord, you spoke strongly;
    the powerful wind blew from your mouth.*
  ₗThe water was pushed back,ج
    and we could see the bottom of the sea.
  We could see the earth's foundations.
¹⁶ The Lord reached down from above
    and saved me.
  The Lord caught me and pulled me out of
    deep water *(trouble)*.
¹⁷ My enemies were stronger than me.
  Those people hated me.
  My enemies were too strong for me,
    so God saved me.
¹⁸ I was in trouble,
    and my enemies attacked me.
  But the Lord was there to support me!
¹⁹ The Lord loves me,
    so he rescued me.
  He took me to a safe place.
²⁰ I am innocent,
    so the Lord will give me my reward.
  I did nothing wrong,
    so he will do good things for me.

---

arrows That is, "lightning."
mouth Or, "nostrils."

21 Why? Because I obeyed the Lord!
   I did not sin against my God.
22 I always remember the Lord's decisions.
   I obey his laws!
23 I keep myself pure and innocent before him.
24 So the Lord will give me my reward!
   Why? Because I am innocent!
   The way God sees it,
      I did nothing wrong,
         so he will do good things for me.
25 Lord, if a person really loves you,
      then you will show your true love to him.
   If a person is true to you,
      then you will be true to him.
26 Lord, you are good and pure
      to people that are good and pure.
   But, you can outsmart
      the meanest and sneakiest people.
27 Lord, you help humble people.
   But you humiliate proud people.
28 Lord, you light my lamp.
   My God lights up the darkness around me!
29 With your help, Lord,
      I can run with the soldiers.
   With God's help,
      I can climb over enemy walls.
30 God's power is complete.*
   The Lord's word has been tested.
      He protects people who trust him.
31 There is no God except the Lord.
   There is no Rock,* except our God.
32 God gives me strength.
   He helps me live a pure life.
33 God helps me run fast like a deer.
   He keeps me steady in high places.
34 God trains me for war,
      so my arms can shoot a powerful bow.
35 God, you protected me
      and helped me win.
   You supported me with your right arm.
   You helped me defeat my enemy.
36 Make my legs and ankles strong
      so I can walk fast without stumbling.
37 Then I can chase my enemies
      and catch them.
   I won't come back
      until they are destroyed!
38 I will defeat my enemies.
   They won't get up again.
   All my enemies will be under my feet.

39 God, you made me strong in battle.
   You made my enemies fall before me.
40 You gave me a chance at my enemy's neck,
      and I cut my opponent down!
41 My enemies called for help,
      but there was no one to save them.
   They even called to the Lord,
      but he did not answer them.
42 I beat my enemies to pieces.
   They were like dust blowing in the wind.
   I crushed them into small pieces.
43 Save me from the people
      that fight against me.
   Make me the leader of those nations.
   People I don't even know
      will serve me.
44 Those people will hear about me
      and quickly obey me.
   Those foreigners will be afraid of me.
45 Those foreigners will wilt with fear.
   They will come out of their hiding places
      shaking with fear.
46 The Lord is alive!
   I praise my Rock,*
   God saves me.
   He is great!
47 God punished my enemies for me.
   He put people under my control.
48 Lord, you rescued me from my enemies.
   You helped me defeat the people
      who stood against me.
   You saved me from cruel men.
49 Lord, that is why I praise you
      among the nations.
   That is why I sing songs about your name.
50 The Lord helps his king win many battles!
   He shows his true love for his chosen king.
   He will be loyal to David and his descendants
      forever!

Psalm 19

To the director. A song of David.*

1 The heavens speak about God's glory.
   The skies tell about the good things
      his hands have made.
2 Each new day tells more of the story.
   And each night reveals more and more
      about God's power.

God's power ... complete Or, "God's way is perfect."
Rock A name for God to show he is a strong place of safety.

director Or, "performer."
A song of David Or, "A song dedicated to David."

³ You can't really hear any speech or words.
   They don't make any sound we can hear.
⁴ But their "voice" goes all through the world.
   Their "words" go to the ends of the earth.

⁵ The sky is like a home for the sun.
   The sun comes out like a happy
       bridegroom from his bedroom.
   The sun begins its path across the sky
   like an athlete eager to run his race.
⁶ The sun starts at one end of the sky,
   and it runs all the way to the other end.
   Nothing can hide from its heat.

⁷ ₍The Lord's teachings are like that.₎
   The Lord's teachings are perfect.
   They give strength to God's people.
   The Lord's Agreement* can be trusted.
   It helps foolish people become wise.
⁸ The Lord's laws are right.
   They make people happy.
   The Lord's commands are good.
   They show people the right way to live.

⁹ Worshiping the Lord is like a light
   that will shine bright forever.
   The Lord's judgments are good and fair.
   They are completely right.
¹⁰ The Lord's teachings are worth more than the
       best gold.
   They are sweeter than the best honey
   that comes straight from the honeycomb.
¹¹ The Lord's teachings warned his servant.

Good things come from obeying them.
¹² ₍Lord,₎ no person can see all his own mistakes.
   So don't let me do secret sins.
¹³ Don't let me do the sins I want to do.
   Don't let those sins rule me.
   If you help me, then I can be pure
   and free from my sins.
¹⁴ I hope my words and thoughts please you.
   Lord, you are my Rock,*
       You are the One who saves me.

Psalm 20

To the director. A song of David.*

¹ May the Lord answer your call for help
   when you have troubles.

Agreement This probably means the Law of Moses, the commands and agreement God made with the people of Israel.
Rock A name for God to show he is a strong place of safety.

May the God of Jacob make your name
   important.
² May God send you help from his Holy Place.
   May he support you from Zion.*
³ May God remember all the gifts you offered.
   May he accept all your sacrifices.*
                                          SELAH*
⁴ I hope God gives you what you really want.
   I hope he makes all your plans happen.
⁵ We will be happy when God helps you.
   Let's praise God's name.
   I hope the Lord gives you everything that you
       ask for!

⁶ Now I know the Lord helps the king he chose!
   God was in his holy heaven,
   and he answered his chosen king.
   God used his great power to save the king.
⁷ Some people trust their chariots.*
   Other people trust their soldiers.
   But we remember the Lord our God.
⁸ Those other people were defeated—
   they died in battle.
   But we won! We are the winners!
⁹ The Lord saved his chosen king!
   God's chosen king called for help.
   And God answered!

Psalm 21

To the director. A song of David.*

Lord, your strength makes the king happy.
   He is so very happy when you save him.
² You gave the king the things he wanted.
   Lord, the king asked for some things,
   and you gave him what he asked for.
                                          SELAH*
³ Lord, you really blessed the king.
   You put the gold crown on his head.
⁴ God, the king asked you for life.
   And you gave it to him!
   You gave him a long life that continues
       forever and ever.
⁵ You led the king to victory
   and gave him great glory.
   You gave him honor and praise.

A song of David Or, "A song dedicated to David."
Zion The southeast part of the mountain Jerusalem is built on. Sometimes it means the people of God living in Jerusalem.
sacrifice(s) A sacrifice was a gift to God. Usually, it was a special animal that was killed and burned on an altar.
Selah This word is for the musicians. It probably means the singers should pause here or the music should be louder here.
chariot(s) A small wagon used in war.

⁶ God, you really blessed the king forever.
 When the king sees your face,
  it makes him very happy.
⁷ The king trusts the Lord.
 God Most-High will not disappoint him.
⁸ God, you will show all your enemies that you are strong.
 Your power will defeat the people who hate you.
⁹ Lord, when you are with the king,
 he is like a hot oven ₁that burns up everything in it₁.
 His anger burns like a hot fire,
 and he destroys his enemies.
¹⁰ The families of his enemies will be destroyed.
 They will be gone from the earth.
¹¹ Why? Because those people planned bad things against you, Lord.
 They planned to do bad things,
 but they didn't succeed.
¹² Lord, you made those people your slaves.
 You tied them together with ropes.
 You put ropes around their necks.
 You made them bow down like slaves.
¹³ Lord, let the songs of your power exalt you!
 We will sing and play songs about your greatness!

Psalm 22

To the director.* ₁To the tune₁ "The Deer of Dawn"* A song of David.*

¹ My God, my God!
 Why did you leave me?
 You are too far away to save me!
 You are too far away to hear my cries for help!

² My God, I called to you during the day.
 But you did not answer me.
 And I continued calling you in the night.

³ God, you are the Holy One.
 You sit as King.
 The praises of Israel are your throne.

⁴ Our ancestors* trusted you.
 Yes, they trusted you, God,
 and you saved them.

⁵ God, our ancestors* called to you for help,
 and they escaped ₁their enemies₁.
 They trusted you,
 and they were not disappointed!

⁶ So, am I a worm and not a man?
 The people are ashamed of me.
 The people despise me.

⁷ Everyone who looks at me makes fun of me.
 They shake their heads
 and stick out their tongues at me.

⁸ They tell me:
 "You should ask the Lord to help you.
 Maybe he will save you.
 If he likes you so much,
 then surely he will rescue you!"

⁹ God, ₁the truth is₁ that you really are the One I depend on.
 You have taken care of me
 since the day I was born.
 You assured and comforted me
 while I was still at my mother's breasts.

¹⁰ You have been my God
 since the day I was born.
 I was put in your care as soon as
 I came out of my mother's body.

¹¹ So, God, don't leave me!
 Trouble is near.
 And there is no person to help me.

¹² People are all around me.
 They are like powerful bulls that surrounded me.

¹³ Their mouths are wide open
 like a lion roaring and tearing at an animal.

¹⁴ My strength is gone,
 like water poured out on the ground.
 My bones have separated.
 My courage is gone!*

¹⁵ My mouth* is as dry as a piece of broken pottery.
 My tongue is sticking to the top of my mouth.
 You have put me in the "dust of death."

¹⁶ The "dogs" are all around me.
 That pack* of evil people has trapped me.

---

director Or, "performer."
The Deer of Dawn This is probably the name of the tune for this song. But it might refer to a type of instrument.
A song of David Or, "A song dedicated to David."
ancestors Literally, "fathers," meaning a person's parents, grandparents, and all the people they are descended from.

My courage is gone! Literally, "My heart is melted in me like wax."
mouth Or, "strength."
pack A group of dogs. Dogs travel together in packs to hunt and kill other animals for food.

Like a lion, ₍they have pierced₎
  my hands and my feet."*
17 I can see my bones.
  And the people are staring at me!
  They keep looking at me!*
18 Those people are dividing my clothes
    among themselves.
  They are throwing lots* for my robe.
19 Lord, don't leave me!
  You are my strength.
  Hurry and help me!
20 Lord, save my life from the sword.
  Save my precious life from those dogs.
21 Rescue me from the lion's mouth.
  Protect me from the bulls' horns.*
22 ₍Lord,₎ I will tell my brothers about you.
  I will praise you in the great assembly.
23 Praise the Lord, all you people who worship
    him!
  Show honor to the Lord, you descendants* of
    Israel!
  Fear and respect the Lord, all you people of
    Israel.
24 Why? Because the Lord helps poor people
    who have troubles.
  The Lord is not ashamed of them.
  He doesn't hate them.
  If people call to the Lord for help,
    he will not hide from them.
25 ₍Lord,₎ my praise in the great assembly comes
    from you.
  In front of all these worshipers,
    I will do the things I promised to do.
26 Poor people will eat and be satisfied.
  You people who come looking for the
    Lord, praise him!
  May your hearts be happy* forever!
27 May the people in all the faraway countries
    remember the Lord and come back to him!
  May the people in all the foreign countries
    worship the Lord.
28 Why? Because the Lord is the King.
  He rules all nations.
29 People are like the many blades of grass
    covering the earth.
  We will all eat our food,
    and we will all lie down ₍in the grave₎.
  We can't stop ourselves from dying.
  We will all be buried in the ground.
  Every one of us will bow down to the Lord.
30 And in the future, our descendants will serve
    the Lord.
  People will tell about him forever.
31 They will tell about God's goodness
    to people who are not yet born.
  They will tell about the good things
    that God really did.*

Psalm 23

A song of David.

1 The Lord is my shepherd.
  I will always have everything I need.*
2 He lets me lie down in green pastures.
  He leads me by calm pools of water.
3 He gives new strength to my soul
    for the good of his name.
  He leads me on paths of goodness,*
    to show he is truly good.
4 Even if I walk through a valley as dark as
    the grave,*
  I will not be afraid of any danger."
  Why? Because you are with me, Lord.
  Your rod and staff* comfort me.
5 Lord, you prepared my table
    in front of my enemies.

Like a lion ... feet The Greek version has, "They pierced my hands and my feet." In Hebrew the word for "like a lion" is like the word meaning, "they pierced."

They keep looking at me! This phrase often means "to look at someone with plans to hurt him."

lot(s) Sticks, stones, or pieces of bone used like dice for making decisions. See Proverbs 16:33.

Protect me ... horns Or, "You hurt me more than the bulls' horns." Or, "You have answered me from the bulls' horns." This might mean that this person learned God's answer when he looked at the people around him.

descendants A person's children and their future families.

be happy Literally, "live."

Psalm 22:29-31 The meaning of the Hebrew is not clear.

A song of David Or, "A song dedicated to David."

I will always have everything I need Literally, "I will lack nothing."

paths of goodness This means both "good paths" and "paths where there is goodness."

valley ... grave Or "death's dark valley," or "a very dark valley."

rod and staff The walking sticks a shepherd uses to guide and protect his sheep.

You poured oil on my head.*
My cup is full and spilling over.
6 Goodness and mercy will be with me the rest
of my life.
And I will sit in the Lord's temple for a long,
long time.*

Psalm 24

A song of David.

1 The earth and everything on it
belong to the Lord.
The world and all its people belong to him.
2 The Lord built the earth on the water.
He built it over the rivers.

3 Who can go up the Lord's mountain?*
Who can stand ⌊and worship⌋ in the Lord's
holy ⌊temple⌋?
4 People who have not done evil things,
people who have pure hearts,
people who have not used my name* to
make lies sound like the truth,
and people who have not lied and made
false promises.
⌊Only those people can worship there.⌋

5 Good people ask the Lord to do good things
for other people.
Those good people ask for goodness from
God their Savior.
6 Those good people try to follow God.
They go to the God of Jacob for help.
SELAH*

7 Gates, lift your heads!
Open, ancient doors,
and the glorious King will come in.
8 Who is the glorious King?
The Lord is that King.
He is the powerful soldier.
The Lord is that King.
He is the war hero.

9 Gates, lift your heads!
Open, ancient doors,
and the glorious King will come in.

10 Who is that glorious King?
The Lord All-powerful is that King.
He is the glorious King!

Psalm 25*

David's ⌊song⌋

1 Lord, I give myself to you.*
2 My God, I trust you,
and I will not be disappointed.
My enemies will not laugh at me.
3 If a person trusts you,
he will not be disappointed.
But traitors* will be disappointed.
They will get nothing.

4 Lord, help me learn your ways.
Teach me your ways.
5 Guide me and teach me your truths.
You are my God, my Savior.
I trust you every day.
6 Remember to be kind to me, Lord.
Show me the tender love you always have.
7 Don't remember the sins and bad things I did
when I was young.
For your good name, Lord,
remember me with love.

8 The Lord is truly good.
He teaches sinners the right way to live.
9 He teaches humble people his ways.
He leads them with fairness.
10 The Lord is kind and true to people
who follow his Agreement and promises.*

11 Lord, I have done many wrong things.
But, to show your goodness,
you forgave me for everything I did.
12 If a person chooses to follow the Lord,
then God will show that person the best
way to live.
13 That person will enjoy good things,
and his children will keep the land ⌊God
promised to give him⌋.

---

poured oil on my head This can mean that God gave much wealth to this person, or that God chose him to be someone special, like a king, a priest, or a prophet.
sit ... long time Or, "I will go again and again to the Lord's temple for a long, long time."
A song of David Or, "A song dedicated to David."
Lord's mountain Mountain Zion, where the temple was.
my name Literally, "my soul."
Selah This word is for the musicians. It probably means the singers should pause here or the music should be louder here.

Psalm 25 In Hebrew, each verse in this psalm begins with the next letter of the alphabet.
David's song Or "{Dedicated} to David"
I give myself to you Literally, "I lift my soul to you."
traitors People who turn against their country, friends, or family and do bad things to them.
Agreement and promises This is probably the Law of Moses, the Agreement that God made with the people of Israel.

14 The Lord tells his secrets to his followers.
   He teaches his Agreement* to them.
15 I am always looking to the Lord for help.
   He always frees me from my troubles.*
16 Lord, I am hurt and lonely.
   Turn to me and show me mercy.
17 Free me from my troubles.
   Help me solve my problems.
18 Lord, look at my trials and troubles.
   Forgive me for all the sins I have done.
19 Look at all the enemies I have.
   They hate me and want to hurt me.
20 God, protect me and save me.
   I trust you,
       so don't disappoint me.
21 God, you are truly good.
   I trust you,
       so protect me.
22 God, save the people of Israel from all of their enemies.

Psalm 26

*David's ₍song₎**

1 Lord, judge me.
   Prove that I have lived a pure life.
   I never stopped trusting the Lord.
2 Lord, try me and test me.
   Look closely into my heart and mind.
3 I always see your tender love.
   I live by your truths.
4 I am not one of those worthless people.
5 I hate those evil gangs.
   I won't join those gangs of crooks.
6 Lord, I wash my hands.*
   I come to your altar.*
7 Lord, I sing songs of praise to you.
   I sing about the wonderful things
       you have done.
8 Lord, I love your temple.*
   I love your glorious tent*

Agreement Literally, "Proof." The flat stones with the Ten Commandments written on them were proof of the Agreement between God and Israel.
He ... troubles Literally, "He removes my feet from the net."
David's {song Or "{Dedicated} to David"
I wash my hands People washed their hands as a way to prepare themselves to worship God. This showed they were pure.
altar(s) A stone table or raised area used for offering sacrifices.
temple The special building in Jerusalem for Jewish worship.
tent The temple in Jerusalem or the Holy Tent where the people worshiped God before the temple was built.

9 Lord, don't group me with those sinners.
   Don't kill me with those murderers.
10 Those people might cheat other people.
    They might take money to do bad things.
11 But I am innocent.
    So, God, be kind to me and save me.
12 I have continued living right.
    Lord, I praise you when your followers
        meet together.

Psalm 27

*David's ₍song₎**

1 Lord, you are my Light and my Savior.
   I should not be afraid of anyone!
   The Lord is the place of safety for my life.
   So I will not be afraid of any person.
2 Evil people might attack me.
   They might try to destroy my body.
   My enemies might try to attack
       and destroy me.
3 But even if an army is all around me,
       I will not be afraid.
   Even if people attack me in war,
       ₍I will not be afraid₎.
   Why? Because I trust the Lord.
4 I ask only one thing from the Lord:
   "Let me sit in his temple* all my life,
       so I can see the Lord's beauty
       and visit his palace.*"
5 The Lord will protect me
       when I am in danger.
   He will hide me in his tent.*
   He will take me up to his place of safety.
6 My enemies have surrounded me.
   But the Lord will help me defeat them!
   Then I will offer sacrifices* in his tent.*
   I will give the sacrifices with shouts of joy.
   I will sing and play songs to honor the Lord.
7 Lord, hear my voice.
   Answer me.
   Be kind to me.
8 Lord, I want to talk with you.
   I want to speak to you from my heart.
   I come before you to speak with you.
9 Lord, don't turn away from me, your servant.
   Help me! Don't push me away!
   Don't leave me!

David's song Or "{Dedicated} to David"
palace A large house built for a king. Here, it is the temple.
sacrifice(s) A sacrifice was a gift to God. Usually, it was a special animal that was killed and burned on an altar.

My God, you are my Savior.
10 My mother and my father left me.
But the Lord took me and made me his.
11 I have enemies, Lord.
So teach me your ways.
Teach me to do the right things.
12 My enemies have attacked me.
They have told lies about me.
They have told lies to hurt me.
13 I truly believe that I will see
the Lord's goodness before I die.*
14 Wait for the Lord's help!
Be strong and brave,
and wait for the Lord's help!

Psalm 28

*A song of David.**

1 Lord, you are my Rock,*
I am calling to you for help.
Don't close your ears to my prayers.
If you don't answer my calls for help,
then people will think I am no better
than the dead people in the grave.
2 ₗLord,₎ I raise my arms and pray toward your
Most Holy Place.*
Hear me when I call to you.
Show mercy to me.
3 Lord, don't think that I am a bad person
like those evil people who do bad things.
Those people greet their neighbors with the
word "Shalom."*
But in their hearts they are thinking bad
things about their neighbors.
4 Lord, those people do bad things
to other people.
So make bad things happen to them.
Give them the punishment they deserve.
5 Bad people don't understand the good things
the Lord does.
They don't see the good things God does.
No, they don't understand;
they only try to destroy.

6 Praise the Lord!
He heard my prayer for mercy.
7 The Lord is my strength.
He is my shield.
I trusted him.
And he helped me.
I am very happy!
And I sing songs of praise to him.
8 The Lord protects his chosen one.*
The Lord saves him.
The Lord is his strength.
9 God, save your people.
Bless the people who belong to you.
Lead them and honor them* forever!

Psalm 29

*A song of David.**

1 Sons of God,* praise the Lord!
Praise his glory and power.
2 Praise the Lord and honor his name!
Worship him in your special clothes.*
3 The Lord raises his voice at the sea.
The voice of the glorious God is like
thunder over the great ocean.
4 The Lord's voice shows his power.
His voice shows his glory.
5 The Lord's voice breaks great cedar trees
into little pieces.
The Lord breaks the great cedar trees
of Lebanon.
6 The Lord shakes Lebanon.
It looks like a young calf dancing.
Sirion* shakes.
It looks like a young goat jumping.
7 The Lord's voice strikes with flashes of
lightning.
8 The Lord's voice shakes the desert.
Kadesh desert* shakes at the Lord's voice.
9 The Lord's voice makes the deer* afraid.
The Lord destroys the forests.
But in his palace,* people sing of his glory.

before I die Literally, "in the land of the living."
A song of David Or, "A song dedicated to David."
Rock A name for God to show he is a strong place of safety.
Most Holy Place The most important room in the Holy Tent or the temple, where the Box of the Agreement was kept. It was like a throne where God sat as king of Israel.
Shalom This word means "peace." It was used as a greeting like "hello" and "goodbye."

chosen one Or, "anointed one." This might be any person that God has chosen in a special way, but it is usually his king.
honor them Or, "forgive them." Literally, "lift them up."
Sons of God Or, "Sons of gods." This might mean the priests, or it might mean God's angels.
special clothes The special clothes that people wore when they went to the temple to worship God.
Sirion Or, "Mount Hermon."
Kadesh desert A desert in Syria. This might also mean "the holy desert."
deer Or, "oak trees."
palace A large house built for a king. Here, it is the temple.

¹⁰ The Lord was the king during the flood.
 And the Lord will be the king forever.
¹¹ May the Lord protect his people.
 May the Lord bless his people with peace.

Psalm 30

One of David's songs. This song was for the dedication of the temple.*

¹ Lord, you lifted me up out of my troubles.
 You did not let my enemies ⌊defeat me and⌋
 laugh at me.
 So I will show honor to you.
² Lord my God, I prayed to you.
 And you healed me.
³ You lifted me out of the grave.
 You let me live.
 I did not have to stay with the dead people
 lying in the pit.*

⁴ God's followers, sing praises to the Lord!
 Praise his holy name!*
⁵ God was angry,
 so the decision was "death."
 But he showed his love,
 and gave me "life."
 At night, I lay crying.
 The next morning, I was happy and singing!
⁶ Now I can say this,
 and I know for sure it is true:
 "I will never be defeated!"

⁷ Lord, you were kind to me and let me stand
 on your holy mountain* again.
 For a time, you turned away from me.
 And I was very scared.
⁸ God, I turned and prayed to you.
 I asked you to show mercy to me.
⁹ I said, "God, what good is it if I die
 and go down into the grave?
 Dead people just lie in the dirt!
 They don't praise you.
 They don't tell about your goodness that
 continues forever.
¹⁰ Lord, hear my prayer and be kind to me!
 Lord, help me!"

¹¹ ⌊I prayed and you helped me!⌋
 You changed my crying into dancing.
 You took away my clothes of sadness.
 And you wrapped me in happiness.
¹² Lord, I will praise you forever.
 I will do this so there will never be silence.
 There will always be someone to praise you.

Psalm 31

To the director.* A song of David.*

¹ Lord, I depend on you.
 Don't disappoint me.
 Be kind to me and save me.
² God, listen to me.
 Come quickly and save me.
 Be my Rock,*
 Be my place of safety.
 Be my fortress.*
 Protect me!
³ God, you are my Rock,*
 So, for the good of your name,
 lead me and guide me.
⁴ ⌊My enemies have put a trap in front of me.⌋
 Save me from their trap.
 You are my place of safety.
⁵ Lord, you are the God we can trust.
 I put my life* in your hands.
 Save me!
⁶ I hate people who worship false gods.
 I trust only in the Lord.
⁷ God, your kindness makes me very happy.
 You have seen my suffering.
 You know about the troubles I have.
⁸ You will not let my enemies take me.
 You will free me from their traps.
⁹ Lord, I have many troubles.
 So be kind to me.
 I am so upset that my eyes are hurting.
 My throat and stomach are aching.
¹⁰ My life is ending in sadness.
 My years are passing away in sighing.*
 My troubles are taking away my strength.
 My strength is leaving me.*
¹¹ My enemies hate me.
 And all my neighbors hate me, too.
 All my relatives see me in the street.
 They are afraid of me and avoid me.
¹² People have completely forgotten me,
 like some lost tool.

One of David's songs ... temple Or, "A psalm. The song for the dedication of the house. Dedicated to David."
pit Or, "world of the dead people."
name Literally, "memory" or "memorial."
holy mountain Mount Zion, where the temple was.

director Or, "performer."
A song of David
life Literally, "spirit."
sighing Breathing hard from sadness.
My strength is leaving me. Literally, "My bones are wasting away."

¹³ I hear the terrible things people say about me.
　　Those people turned against me.
　　　They plan to kill me.
¹⁴ Lord, I trust you.
　　You are my God.
¹⁵ My life is in your hands.
　　Save me from my enemies.
　　Some people are chasing me.*
　　　Save me from them.
¹⁶ Please welcome and accept your servant.*
　　Be kind to me and save me!
¹⁷ Lord, I prayed to you.
　　So I will not be disappointed.
　　Bad people will be disappointed.
　　　They will go to the grave in silence.
¹⁸ Those bad people brag
　　and tell lies about good people.
　　Those bad people are very proud.
　　But their lying lips will be silent.
¹⁹ God, you have hidden away many wonderful
　　　things for your followers.
　　You do good things in front of everyone
　　　for the people who trust you.
²⁰ Bad people join together to hurt good people.
　　Those bad people try to start fights.
　　But you hide those good people
　　　and protect them.
　　You protect them in your shelter.
²¹ Bless the Lord!
　　He showed his true love for me
　　　in a wonderful way
　　when the city was surrounded
　　　by enemies.
²² I was afraid, and I said,
　　"I am in a place where God can't see me."
　　But I prayed to you, God,
　　　and you heard my loud prayers for help.
²³ God's followers, you should love the Lord!
　　The Lord protects people that are loyal to
　　　him.
　　But the Lord punishes people that brag about
　　　their own power.
　　He gives them the punishment they deserve.
²⁴ Be strong and brave, all of you people that are
　　waiting for the Lord's help!

---

chasing me Or, "persecuting me," "hurting me."
welcome ... servant Literally, "let your face shine on your servant."

Psalm 32

A maskil* of David.

¹ A person is very happy.*
　　when his sins are forgiven.
　　ₗThat person is very fortunateⱼ
　　　when his sins are erased.*
² A person is very happy*
　　when the Lord says he is not guilty.
　　ₗThat person is very fortunateⱼ
　　　he didn't hide his secret sins.*
³ God, I prayed to you again and again,
　　but I did not talk ₗabout my secret sinsⱼ.
　　I only became weaker every time I prayed.
⁴ God, you made life harder and harder on me,
　　day and night.
　　I became like a dry, dry land in the hot
　　　summertime.
　　　　　　　　　　　　　　　SELAH*
⁵ But then I decided to confess all my sins to
　　the Lord.
　　Lord, I told you about my sins.
　　I did not hide any of my guilt.
　　And you forgave me for all my sins!
　　　　　　　　　　　　　　　SELAH*
⁶ For this reason, God, all your followers
　　should pray to you.
　　Your followers should pray even when
　　　troubles come like a great flood.
⁷ God, you are a hiding place for me.
　　You protect me from my troubles.
　　You surround me and protect me.
　　So I sing about the way you saved me.
　　　　　　　　　　　　　　　SELAH*
⁸ ₗThe Lord says,ⱼ "I will teach you and guide
　　you on the way you should live.
　　I will protect you and be your guide.
⁹ So don't be stupid like a horse or a donkey.
　　People must use bits and reins* to lead
　　　those animals.

---

maskil The exact meaning of "maskil" is not clear. It might mean "a poem of meditation," "a poem of instruction," or "a skillfully-written poem."
happy Or, "fortunate, blessed."
erased Or, "covered over, atoned."
happy Or, "fortunate, blessed."
he didn't hide his secret sins Literally, "There was no deceit in his spirit."
Selah This word is for the musicians. It probably means the singers should pause here or the music should be louder here.
bits and reins A "bit" is a metal bar that fits in the mouth of an animal and helps the rider control it. "Reins" are the ropes tied to the bit and held by the rider.

Without those things, those animals will
not come near* you."

10 Many pains will come to bad people.
But God's true love will surround the
people that trust the Lord.
11 Good people, rejoice and be very happy in the
Lord.
All you people with pure hearts, rejoice!

Psalm 33

1 Rejoice in the Lord, good people!
Good honest people, praise him!
2 Play the lyre* and praise the Lord!
Play to the Lord on the ten-stringed harp.
3 Sing a new song* to him.
Play the happy tune beautifully!
4 God's word is true.
You can depend on everything he does.
5 God loves goodness and fairness.
The Lord has filled the earth with his love.
6 The Lord spoke the command,
and the world was made.
The breath from God's mouth created
everything on earth.
7 God gathered the water in the sea
into one place.
He keeps the ocean in its place.
8 Every person on earth should fear and respect
the Lord.
All the people in the world should fear him.
9 Why? Because God just gives a command,
and that thing happens.
And if he says, "Stop!"
then that thing will stop.*
10 The Lord can make everyone's advice useless.
He can ruin all their plans.
11 But the Lord's advice is good forever.
His plans are good for generation
after generation.
12 Blessed *(happy)* are the people whose God is
the Lord.
God chose them to be his own people.
13 The Lord looked down from heaven.
He saw all the people.

14 From his high throne* he looked down at all
the people living on earth.
15 God created every person's mind.
God knows what every person is thinking.
16 A king is not saved by his own great power.
A strong soldier is not saved by his own
great strength.
17 Horses don't really bring victory in war.
Their strength can't really help you escape.
18 The Lord watches and cares for the people
that follow him.
His great love protects the people that
worship him.
19 God saves those people from death.
He gives them strength when they are
hungry.
20 So we will wait for the Lord.
He is our help and shield.
21 God makes me happy.
I truly trust his holy name.
22 Lord, we truly worship you!
So show your great love for us.

Psalm 34*

*David's ₍song₎ from the time David acted
crazy so Abimelech would send him away.
In this way, David left him.*

1 I will always bless the Lord.
His praise is always on my lips.
2 Humble people, listen and be happy.
My soul brags about the Lord.
3 Tell about the Lord's greatness with me.
Let's honor his name.
4 I went to God for help.
And he listened.
He saved me from all the things I fear.
5 Look to God for help.
You will be accepted.
Don't be ashamed.*
6 This poor man called to the Lord for help.
And the Lord heard me.
He saved me from all my troubles.
7 The Lord's angel builds a camp around the
people that follow him.
The Lord's angel protects those people.
8 Taste the Lord and learn how good he is.

---

come near This can also mean, "to come and worship at the altar." So God may be talking about the people coming to worship him.
lyre(s) An instrument with several strings, like a harp.
new song Whenever God did a new and wonderful thing for his people, they would write a new song about it.
And if ... stop Or, "He gives the command, and it stands!" The word "stand" can mean "stand forever" or "stop."

throne The chair a king or queen sits on.
Psalm 34 In Hebrew, each verse in this psalm begins with the next letter of the alphabet.
You will be accepted ... be ashamed Literally, "Look at him and shine. Don't let your face be pale."

The person that depends on the Lord will
be truly happy.
9 The Lord's holy people should worship him.
There is no other place of safety for the
Lord's followers.
10 Powerful people will become weak
and hungry.
But the people that go to God for help will
have every good thing.
11 Children, listen to me,
and I will teach you how to serve the Lord.
12 If a person loves life and wants to live a good,
long life,
13 then that person must not say bad things;
that person must not tell lies.
14 Stop doing bad things.
Do good things.
Work for peace.
Run after peace until you catch it.
15 The Lord protects good people.
He hears their prayers.
16 But the Lord is against people that
do bad things.
He destroys them completely!
17 Pray to the Lord and he will hear you.
He will save you from all your troubles.
18 Some people have many troubles,
and they stop being proud.
The Lord is close to those people.
He will save those humble people.*
19 Good people might have many problems.
But the Lord will save those good people
from every one of their problems.
20 The Lord will protect all their bones.
Not one bone will be broken.
21 But troubles will kill evil people.
The enemies of good people will all
be destroyed.
22 The Lord saves the souls of his servants.
Those people depend on him.
He won't let them be destroyed.

Psalm 35

David's [song]*

1 Lord, fight my battles.
Fight my wars!
2 Lord, pick up the shield and buckler.*
Get up and help me.

3 Take a spear and javelin*
and fight the people that are chasing me.
Lord, tell my soul,
"I will save you."
4 Some people are trying to kill me.
Disappoint them and make them ashamed.
Make them turn and run away.
Those people are planning to hurt me.
Embarrass them.
5 Make those people be like chaff* blown
by the wind.*
Let them be chased by the Lord's angel.
6 Lord, let their road be dark and slippery.
Let the Lord's angel chase them.
7 I did nothing wrong,
but those people tried to trap me.
For no reason at all,
they tried to trap me.
8 So, Lord, let them fall into their own traps.
Let them stumble into their own nets.
Let some unknown danger catch them.
9 Then I will rejoice in the Lord.
I will be happy when he saves me.
10 With my whole self I will say,
"Lord, there is no one like you.
You save a poor person from people that
are stronger.
You take things from strong people,
and you give those things to the poor,
helpless person."
11 A group of witnesses* are planning to hurt me.
Those people will ask me questions.
And I don't know what they are talking
about.
12 I have done only good things.
But those people will do bad things to me.
13 [Lord,] give me the good things I deserve.
When those people were sick,
I was sad for them.
I showed my sadness by not eating.
Is this what I get for praying for them?
14 I wore clothes of sadness for those people.
I treated those people like my friends or even
like brothers.
I was sad, like a man crying because his
mother had died.

javelin A weapon like a spear.
chaff Seed coverings and stems separated from the seeds of plants like wheat or barley. Farmers did not keep this useless chaff.
wind This may be a word play, because the Hebrew word also means "Spirit."
witnesses People who tell about things they have seen or heard. Here, these people were probably telling lies.

Some ... people. Literally, "The Lord is close to the brokenhearted. He saves people with crushed spirits."
David's song Or "{Dedicated} to David"
buckler A shield large enough to protect the whole body.

I wore black clothes to show my sadness for
those people.
I walked with my head bowed in sadness.
15 But when I made a mistake,*
those people laughed at me.
Those people were not really friends.
I didn't even know those people.
But they surrounded me and attacked me.
16 They used bad language
and made fun of me.
Those people showed they were angry at me
by grinding their teeth.
17 My Master, how long will you watch these
bad things happen?
Those people are trying to destroy me.
Lord, save my life.
Save my dear life from those bad people.
They are like lions.
18 Lord, I will praise you in the great assembly.
I will praise you when I am with
the powerful people.
19 My lying enemies will not keep laughing.
Surely my enemies will be punished for
their secret plans.*
20 My enemies are not really making plans
for peace.
They are secretly making plans
to do bad things to the peaceful people
in this country.
21 My enemies are saying bad things about me.
They tell lies and say,
"Aha! We know what you are doing!"
22 Lord, surely you can see what is happening.
So don't keep quiet.
Don't leave me.
23 Lord, wake up! Get up!
My God and my Lord, fight for me,
and bring me justice.
24 Lord my God, judge me with your fairness.
Don't let those people laugh at me.
25 Don't let those people say,
"Aha! We got what we wanted!"
Lord, don't let them say,
"We destroyed him!"
26 I hope that all my enemies will be ashamed
and embarrassed.
Those people were happy when bad things
happened to me.

They thought they were better than me!
So let those people be covered with shame
and humiliation.
27 Some people want good things to happen
to me.
I hope those people will be very happy!
Those people always say,
"The Lord is great!
He wants what is best for his servant."
28 So Lord, I will tell people how good you are.
I will praise you every day.

Psalm 36

To the director. To the servant of the Lord.
To David.*

1 A bad person does a very bad thing when he
says to himself,
"I will not fear and respect God."
2 That person lies to himself.
That person does not see his own faults.
So he does not ask for forgiveness.
3 His words are only worthless lies.
He does not become wise
or learn to do good.
4 At night, he plans worthless things.
He gets up and does nothing good.
But he doesn't refuse to do evil.

5 Lord, your true love is higher than the sky.
Your loyalty is higher than the clouds.
6 Lord, your goodness is higher than the highest
mountain.*
Your fairness is deeper than the
deepest ocean.
Lord, you protect man and animals.
7 Nothing is more precious than your
loving kindness.
People and angels* come to you for
protection.
8 They get new strength from the good things in
your house, Lord.
You let them drink from your
wonderful river.
9 Lord, the fountain of life flows from you!
Your light lets us see light.
10 Lord, continue to love those people that truly
know you.

---

made a mistake Literally, "stumbled."
Surely ... plans Literally, "Will the people who hate me freely wink their eyes?"

director Or, "performer."
the highest mountain Literally, "El's Mountain." This might be a special mountain in Syria or "God's Mountain," the place where God meets with his angels.
angels Or, "gods" or "powerful people."

Let your goodness be for those people that are
true to you.*
11 Lord, don't let proud people trap me.
Don't let me be caught by evil people.
12 ₍Put this on their grave markers:₎
"Here fell the wicked people.
They were crushed.
They will never stand up again."

Psalm 37*

*David's ₍song₎**

1 Don't get upset at evil people.
Don't be jealous of people
who do bad things.
2 Evil people are like grass and green plants
that quickly turn brown and die.
3 If you trust the Lord and do good things,
you will live and enjoy the many things the
land gives.
4 Enjoy serving the Lord,
and he will give you what you want.
5 Depend on the Lord.
Trust him, and he will do what must
be done.
6 Let your goodness and fairness shine like the
sun at noon.
7 Trust the Lord and wait for his help.
Don't be upset when bad people succeed.
Don't be upset when bad people make evil
plans and their plans succeed.
8 Don't be angry! Don't get mad!
Don't become so upset that you too want to
do bad things.
9 Why? Because evil people will be destroyed.
But people that call to the Lord for help
will get the land ₍God promised₎.
10 In a short time there will be no more
evil people.
You can look for those people,
but they will all be gone!
11 Humble people will get the land ₍God
promised₎.
And they will enjoy peace.
12 Evil people plan bad things against
good people.
Those evil people show they are angry by
grinding their teeth at good people.

13 But our Master laughs at those evil people.
He sees what will happen to them.
14 Bad people get their swords
and aim their bows.
They want to kill poor, helpless people.
They want to kill good, honest people.
15 But their bows will break.
Their swords will go into their own hearts.
16 A few good people are better than a large
crowd of evil people.
17 Why? Because evil people will be destroyed.
But the Lord cares for good people.
18 The Lord protects pure people all their life.
Their reward will continue forever.
19 When trouble comes,
good people will not be destroyed.
When times of hunger come,
good people will have plenty to eat.
20 But evil people are the Lord's enemies,
and those evil people will be destroyed.
Their valleys will become dry and burn.
They will be completely destroyed.
21 An evil man quickly borrows money
and never pays it back.
But a good man gives freely to other people.
22 If a good person blesses people,
then they will get the land ₍God promised₎.
But if he asks for bad things to happen,
then those people will be destroyed.
23 The Lord helps a soldier walk carefully.
The Lord keeps the soldier from falling.
24 If the soldier runs and attacks his enemy,
then the Lord holds the soldier's hand,
and keeps him from falling.
25 I was young, and now I am old.
And I have never seen God abandon
good people.
I have never seen good people's children
begging for food.
26 A good man gives freely to other people.
And a good man's children are a blessing.
27 If you refuse to do bad things,
and if you do good things,
then you will live forever.
28 The Lord loves fairness.
He will not leave his followers
without help.
The Lord will always protect his followers,
but he will destroy wicked people.
29 Good people will get the land ₍God promised₎.
They will live on it forever.
30 A good person gives good advice.
His decisions are fair to every person.
31 The Lord's teachings are in his heart *(mind)*.
He does not quit living the right way.

---

true to you Or, "honest hearted."
Psalm 37 In Hebrew, each verse in this psalm begins with the
next letter of the alphabet.
David's song Or "₍Dedicated₎ to David"

32 But bad people always look for ways to hurt
good people.
Bad people try to kill good people.
33 The Lord will not let them do that.
He will not let good people be
judged guilty.
34 Wait for the Lord's help.
Follow the Lord.
Wicked people will be destroyed.
But the Lord will make you important,
and you will get the land [God
promised].
35 I saw a wicked person that was powerful.
He was like a strong, healthy tree.
36 But then he was gone.
I looked for him,
but I couldn't find him.
37 Be pure and honest,
because that brings peace.
38 But people who break the law will be
destroyed.
39 The Lord saves good people.
When good people have troubles,
the Lord is their strength.
40 The Lord helps good people and saves them.
Good people depend on the Lord,
and he saves them from bad people.

Psalm 38

A song of David for the [day of]
remembrance.**

1 Lord, don't criticize me in anger.
Don't be angry when you discipline me.
2 Lord, you have hurt me.
Your arrows went deep into me.
3 You punished me.
Now my whole body is sore.
I sinned, [and you punished me].
So all my bones hurt.
4 I am guilty of doing bad things.
And that guilt is like a heavy weight on my
shoulders.
5 I did a foolish thing.
Now I have infected sores that stink.
6 I am bent and bowed.
I am depressed all day long.
7 I have a fever,
and my whole body hurts.

8 I am completely weak.
I moan and groan with pain.
9 Lord, you heard my groaning.
My sighs are not hidden from you.
10 I have a fever.
My strength is gone,
and my sight is almost gone.
11 Because of my sickness, my friends and
neighbors will not visit me.
My family will not come near me.
12 My enemies say bad things about me.
They are spreading lies and rumors.*
They talk about me all the time.
13 But I am like a deaf person that cannot hear.
I am like a mute person that cannot speak.
14 I am like a person that cannot hear the things
people are saying about him.
I cannot argue and prove that my enemies
are wrong.
15 So, Lord, you must defend me.
God my Master, you must speak for me.
16 If I say anything,
then my enemies will laugh at me.
They will see I am sick,
and they will say that I am being punished
for doing wrong.
17 I know I am guilty of doing wrong things.
I cannot forget my pain.
18 Lord, I told you about the bad things I did.
I am sad about my sins.
19 My enemies are alive and healthy.
And they have told many, many lies.
20 My enemies do bad things to me,
and I did only good things to them.
I tried to do only good things,
but those people turned against me.
21 Lord, don't leave me!
My God, stay close to me!
22 Quickly come and help me!
My God, save me!

Psalm 39

To the director. To Jeduthun.*
A song of David.**

1 I said,
"I will be careful about the things I say.
I will not let my tongue cause me to sin.

---

rumors Hurtful stories about people that other people tell
without knowing if the stories are true.
To the director Or, "performer."
To Jeduthun Or, "To the director, Jeduthun." This is probably
one of the temple musicians. See 1 Chron. 9:16; 16:38-41.

A song of David Or, "A song dedicated to David."
for ... remembrance The ancient Greek version has "for the
Sabbath."

I will keep my mouth closed* when I am
    around wicked people."
2 So I didn't say anything.
    I didn't even say anything good!
    But I became even more upset.
3 I was very angry.
    And the more I thought about it,
        the angrier I became.
    So I said something.
4 Lord, tell me, what will happen to me now?
    Tell me, how long will I live?
    Let me know how short my life really is.
5 Lord, you gave me only a short life.*
    My life is nothing to you.
    Every person's life is only like a cloud.
    No person lives forever!*
                                    SELAH*
6 The life we live is like an image ₍in a mirror₎.
    All our troubles are for nothing.
    We are always collecting things,
        but we don't know who will get them.
7 So, Master, what hope do I have?
    You are my hope!
8 Lord, save me from the bad things I did.
    Don't let me be treated like a fool.
9 I will not open my mouth.
    I will not say anything.
    Lord, you did what should be done.
10 But God, stop punishing me.
    You will destroy me if you don't stop!
11 Lord, you punish people for doing wrong
        to teach them the right way to live.
    Like a moth destroys cloth,
        you destroy the things people love.
    Yes, our lives are like a small cloud ₍that
        quickly disappears₎.
                                    SELAH*
12 Lord, hear my prayer!
    Listen to the words I cry to you.
        Look at my tears.
    I am only a traveler passing through this life
        with you.

Like all my ancestors, I live here only
    a short time.*
13 Lord, leave me alone* and let me be happy
    before I am dead and gone.

Psalm 40

To the director.* A song of David.*

1 I called* to the Lord,
    and he heard me.
    He heard my cries.
2 The Lord lifted me out of the pit
        of destruction.*
    He lifted me from that muddy place.*
    He picked me up and put me on a rock.
    He made my feet steady.
3 The Lord put a new song* in my mouth,
        a song of praise to my God.
    Many people will see what happened to me,
        and they will worship God.
    They will trust the Lord.
4 If a person trusts the Lord,
        that person will be truly happy.
    A person will be truly happy
        if he doesn't turn to demons and false
            gods* for help.
5 Lord, our God, you have done many
        wonderful things!
    You have wonderful plans for us.
    No person could list them all!
    I will tell again and again about those things
        that are too many to count.
6 Lord, you made me understand this:*
    You don't really want
        sacrifices* and grain offerings.
    You don't really want
        burnt offerings and sin offerings.

I live ... time Literally, "I am a settler."
leave me alone Or, "stop looking at me."
director Or, "performer."
A song of David Or, "A song dedicated to David."
called Or, "waited patiently."
pit of destruction A name for "Sheol," the place of death.
muddy place In many ancient stories, Sheol, the place of death, is a dark place with mud all around, like a grave.
new song Whenever God did a new and wonderful thing for his people, they would write a new song about it.
demons and false gods Or, "proud and deceptive people."
you made me understand this Literally, "you have dug my ears." The ancient Greek version has, "You prepared a body for me."
sacrifice(s) A sacrifice was a gift to God. Usually, it was a special animal that was killed and burned on an altar.

---

keep ... closed Literally, "guard my mouth with a muzzle."
you gave me only a short life Literally, "you made my days only a handbreadth."
No person lives forever Literally, "No one stands."
Selah This word is for the musicians. It probably means the singers should pause here or the music should be louder here.

⁷ So I said,
"Here ⌊I am! Take me.⌋
I am coming.
This was written about me in the book.
⁸ My God, I want to do what you want.
I know your teachings.
⁹ I will tell the good news about goodness to
the great assembly.
I will not keep my mouth shut.
Lord, you know that!
¹⁰ Lord, I will tell about your goodness.
I will not hide those things in my heart.
Lord, I will tell people that they can depend
on you to save them.
I will not hide your kindness and loyalty from
the people in the assembly.
¹¹ So Lord, don't hide your mercy from me!
Let your kindness and loyalty protect me."

¹² Evil people have gathered around me.
They are too many to count!
My sins have caught me,
and I can't escape them.
I have more sins than hair on my head.
I have lost my courage.
¹³ Run to me, Lord, and save me!
Lord, come quickly and help me!
¹⁴ Those evil people are trying to kill me.
Lord, make those people ashamed and
disappointed.
Those people want to hurt me.
Let them run away in shame!
¹⁵ Those bad people make fun of me.
Let them be too embarrassed to speak!
¹⁶ But let those people that come to you
be happy and rejoice.
They love being saved by you.
So let them always say,
"Praise the Lord!"
¹⁷ Master, I am only a poor, helpless man.
Help me. Save me.
My God, don't be too late!

Psalm 41

To the director.* A song of David.*

¹ A person who helps poor people succeed
will get many blessings.*

When trouble comes,
the Lord will save that person.
² The Lord will protect that person
and save his life.
That person will be blessed on earth.
God will not let that person's enemies
destroy him.
³ When that person is sick and in bed,
the Lord will give him strength.
That person may be sick in bed,
but the Lord will make him well!
⁴ I said, "Lord, be kind to me.
I sinned against you,
but forgive me and make me well."
⁵ My enemies say bad things about me.
They are saying,
"When will he die and be forgotten?"
⁶ Some people come to visit me.
But they don't say what they are
really thinking.
Those people come just to get some news
about me,
Then they go and spread their rumors.*
⁷ My enemies whisper bad things about me.
They are planning bad things against me.
⁸ They say, "He did something wrong.
That is why he is sick.
I hope he never gets well."
⁹ My best friend ate with me.
I trusted him.
But now even he has turned against me.
¹⁰ So, Lord, please be kind to me.
Let me get up, and I will pay them back.
¹¹ Lord, don't let my enemy hurt me.
Then I will know that you accept me.
¹² I was innocent and you supported me.
You let me stand and serve you forever.
¹³ Bless the Lord, God of Israel!
He always was,
and he always will be.

Amen and Amen!*

---

director Or, "performer."
A song of David Or, "A song dedicated to David."
get many blessings Or, "be truly fortunate (happy)."

rumors Hurtful stories about people that other people tell
without knowing if the stories are true.
Amen A Hebrew word meaning "truly," "That's right." It
shows that a person agrees with what has been said.

BOOK 2

Psalm 42

To the director. A maskil* from
the Korah family.*

1 A deer gets thirsty for water from a stream.
   In the same way, my soul is thirsty for
       you, God.
2 My soul is thirsty for the Living God.
   When can I go to meet with him?
3 Day and night my tears have been my food!
   The whole time, my enemy said,
       "Where is your God?"
4 So let me remember all these things.
   Let me pour out my soul.
   ⌊I remember⌋ walking and leading the crowd to
       God's temple.
   ⌊I remember⌋ singing happy songs of praise
       with many people celebrating the holiday.
5 Why am I so sad?
   Why am I so upset?
   I should wait for God's help.
   I will get the chance to praise him yet.
   He will save me!
6 My God, I am so very sad.
   That is why I have called for you.
   I have gone from the Jordan Valley,
       to the Hermon mountains,
       and on to Mount Mizar.*
7 From sea to sea I have heard
       the crashing of your waves.
   ⌊Troubles have come to me again and again,
       like waves coming in from the sea.⌋
   Lord, your waves are crashing all around me.
   Your waves have covered me!

8 If the Lord would show his true love
       every day, then each night
       I could sing his songs.
   I could pray to my Living God.
9 I speak to God, my Rock,* I say,
       "Lord, why did you forget me?
   Why didn't you show me
       how to escape my enemies?"

10 My enemies tried to kill me.
    They show they hate me when they say,
        "Where is your God?"
11 Why am I so sad?
    Why am I so upset?
    I should wait for God's help.
    I will get the chance to praise him yet.
    He will save me!

Psalm 43

1 God, there is a man who doesn't follow you.
   That man is crooked and tells lies.
   God, defend me and prove that I am right.
   Save me from that man.
2 God, you are my place of safety!
   Why did you leave me?
   Why didn't you show me
       how to escape from my enemies?
3 God, let your light and truth shine on me.
   Your light and truth will guide me.
   They will lead me to your holy mountain.
   They will lead me to your home.
4 I will come to God's altar.
   I will come to the God who makes me
       so very happy.
   God, my God, I will praise you with a harp.

5 Why am I so sad?
   Why am I so upset?
   I should wait for God's help.
   I will get the chance to praise God yet.
   He will save me!

Psalm 44

To the director. A maskil* from
the Korah family.*

1 God, we have heard about you.
   Our fathers told us what you did
       in their lifetime.
   They told us what you did long ago.
2 God, with your great power
       you took this land from other people,
       and you gave it to us.
   You crushed those foreign people.
   You forced them to leave this land.
3 It was not our father's swords
       that took the land.
   It was not their strong arms
       that made them winners.
   It was because you were with our fathers.
   God, your great power saved our fathers.
   Why? Because you loved them!

---

director Or, "performer."
maskil The exact meaning of "maskil" is not clear. It might
   mean "a poem of meditation," "a poem of instruction," or "a
   skillfully-written poem."
Mount Mizar Or, "the smallest hill."
Rock A name for God to show he is a strong place of safety.

4 My God, you are my king.
　　Give the command
　　　　and lead Jacob's people to victory.
5 My God, with your help,
　　we will push back our enemies.
　　With your name,
　　　we will walk on our enemies.
6 I don't trust my bow ₍and arrows₎.
　　My sword can't save me.
7 God, you saved us from Egypt.
　　You made our enemies ashamed.
8 We will praise God every day!
　　We will praise your name forever!
　　　　　　　　　　　　SELAH*
9 But, God, you left us.
　　You embarrassed us.
　　You did not come with us into battle.
10 You let our enemies push us back.
　　Our enemies took our wealth.
11 You gave us away like sheep
　　　to be eaten as food.
　　You scattered us among the nations.
12 God, you sold your people for nothing.
　　You didn't even argue over the price.
13 You made us a joke to our neighbors.
　　They laugh at us and make fun of us.
14 We are one of the funny stories people tell.
　　Even people without a nation of their own
　　　laugh at us and shake their heads.
15 I am covered with shame.
　　All day long I see my shame.
16 My enemy embarrassed me.
　　My enemy is trying to get even
　　　by making fun of me.
17 God, we have not forgotten you.
　　Yet you do all those things to us.
　　We did not lie when we signed
　　　our Agreement* with you!
18 God, we have not turned away from you.
　　We have not stopped following you.
19 But, God, you crushed us in this place
　　where jackals* live.
　　You covered us in this place
　　　as dark as death.
20 Did we forget the name of our God?
　　Did we pray to foreign gods?
　　　₍No!₎

21 Surely, God knows these things.
　　He knows even our deepest secrets.
22 God, we are being killed for you every day!
　　We are like sheep being led away
　　　to be killed.
23 Get up, my Master!
　　Why are you sleeping?
　　Get up! Don't leave us forever!
24 God, why are you hiding from us?
　　Have you forgotten our pain and troubles?
25 We have been pushed down into the dirt.
　　We are lying with our belly in the dust.*
26 God, get up and help us!
　　For goodness' sake, save us!

Psalm 45

To the director. To the tune of
"Shoshanim."* A maskil* from
the Korah family. A love song.*

1 Beautiful words fill my mind as I write these
　　things for the king.
　　Words come from my tongue like words
　　　coming from a skilled writer's pen.
2 You are more handsome than anyone!
　　You are a very good speaker.
　　　So God will bless you forever!
3 Put your sword on.
　　Put on your glorious uniform.
4 You look wonderful!
　　Go and win the fight
　　　for goodness and fairness.
　　Use your powerful right arm
　　　to do amazing things.
5 Your arrows are ready.
　　You will defeat many people.
　　You will be the king over your enemies.
6 God,* your throne continues forever!
　　Goodness is your royal scepter.*
7 You love goodness and you hate evil.

We ... dust This shows the people were being treated like slaves that must bow down to their masters.
director Or, "performer."
To the tune of Shoshanim Or, "On the Shoshanim."
maskil The exact meaning of "maskil" is not clear. It might mean "a poem of meditation," "a poem of instruction," or "a skillfully-written poem."
God This might be a song to God, as king. Or here the writer might be using the word "God" as a title for the king.
scepter A special stick that kings carried to show they were rulers.

Selah This word is for the musicians. It probably means the singers should pause here or the music should be louder here.
Agreement Literally, "Proof." The flat stones with the Ten Commandments written on them were proof of the Agreement between God and Israel.
jackal(s) A wild animal, like a dog. Jackals live only where no people are.

So God, your God, chose you to be king over
your friends.*
8 Your clothes smell like the sweet spices
myrrh, aloes, and cassia.
From palaces covered with ivory,
comes music to make you happy.
9 The bridesmaids are the daughters of kings.
Your bride* stands at your right side,
wearing a crown of pure gold.
10 Listen to me, daughter.
Listen carefully and you will understand.
Forget your people and your father's family.
11 The king loves your beauty.
He will be your new husband.*
You will honor him.
12 People from Tyre will bring gifts to you.
Wealthy people want to meet with you.
13 The princess is like a beautiful jewel
in an expensive and beautiful gold setting.
14 The bride in her beautiful clothes,
is led to the king,
her bridesmaids following behind her.
15 They come filled with happiness.
Filled with happiness,
they enter the king's palace.
16 ⌊King,⌋ your sons will rule after you.
You will make them rulers throughout
the land.
17 I will make your name famous forever.
People will praise you forever and ever!

Psalm 46

To the director.* ⌊A song⌋ from the Korah family. By the Alamoth.* A song.

1 God is our storehouse of strength.
In him, we can always find help
in times of trouble.
2 So we are not afraid when the earth quakes
and the mountains fall into the sea.
3 We are not afraid when the seas
become rough and dark,
and the mountains shake.

SELAH*

4 There is a river, and its streams
bring happiness to God's city,
to the holy city of God Most High.
5 God is in that city,
so it will never be destroyed.
God will help before sunrise.
6 The nations will shake with fear,
those kingdoms will fall
when the Lord shouts,
and the earth crumbles.
7 The Lord All-Powerful is with us.
The God of Jacob is our place of safety.

SELAH*

8 Look at the powerful things the Lord does.
They made the Lord famous on earth.
9 The Lord can stop wars anywhere on earth.
He can break the soldiers' bows and shatter
their spears.
He can burn the chariots with fire.
10 God says,
"Be calm and learn that I am God!
I will be praised among the nations,
glorified on earth!"
11 The Lord All-Powerful is with us.
The God of Jacob is our place of safety.

SELAH*

Psalm 47

To the director. A song from
the Korah family.*

1 Clap your hands, all you people.
Shout with joy to God!
2 The Lord Most High is awesome.
He is the Great King over all the earth.
3 He helped us defeat other people.
He put those nations under our control.
4 God chose our land for us.
He chose that wonderful land for Jacob,
the man he loved.

SELAH*

5 The Lord goes up ⌊to his throne⌋
at the sound of the trumpet and horn.
6 Sing praises to God.
Sing praises.
Sing praises to our King.
Sing praises.

---

chose you to be king over your friends Literally, "poured the sweet oil on you over your friends." This was the special oil kept in the temple and used to anoint kings, priests, and prophets.
bride Or, "queen."
husband Or, "master."
director Or, "performer."
By the Alamoth This might be a special instrument, a special way of tuning an instrument, or one of the groups that played harps in the temple orchestra. See 1 Chron.15:21.

Selah This word is for the musicians. It probably means the singers should pause here or the music should be louder here.

7 God is the king of the whole world.
    Sing songs of praise.*
8 God sits on his holy throne.
    God rules all the nations.
9 The leaders of the nations meet together
        with the people of the God of Abraham.
    All of the leaders of all the nations
        belong to God.
    God is over them all!*

Psalm 48

A song of praise from the Korah family.

1 The Lord is great.
    He is worthy of praise
        in the city of our God,
        his holy city.
2 God's holy city is beautiful.
    It is the happiest city on earth.
    Mount Zion is the highest and holiest
        mountain.
    It is the city of the Great King.
3 Here in the palaces in that city,
    God is called the Fortress.
4 One time, some kings met together
    ⌊They planned to attack this city⌋.
    They all marched forward together.
5 Those kings looked,
        they were amazed,
        they panicked,
        and they all ran away!
6 Fear grabbed those kings.
    They shook with fear!
7 ⌊God, you used⌋ a strong east wind
    and wrecked their big ships.
8 Yes, we heard the story.
    But we also saw it happen,
        in the city of the Lord All-Powerful,
        in the city of our God.
    God makes that city strong forever!
                                    SELAH*
9 God, in your temple we think carefully
    about your loving kindness.
10 God, you are famous.
    People praise you everywhere on earth.
    Everyone knows how good you are.

11 ⌊God,⌋ Mount Zion is happy.
    the towns of Judah rejoice
        because of your good decisions.
12 Walk around Zion.
    Look at the city.
    Count the towers.
13 See the tall walls.
    Admire Zion's palaces.
    Then you can tell the next generation
        about it.
14 God really will be our God
        forever and ever!
    He will lead us forever
        and he will never die!

Psalm 49

To the director. A song from
the Korah family.*

1 Listen to this all you nations.
    Listen to this all you people on earth.
2 Every person, poor and rich alike,
        should listen.
3 I will tell you some very wise
        and intelligent things.
4 I listened to the stories.
    And now, with my harp,
        I will sing those stories to you.
5 Why should I be afraid
        if trouble comes.
    Why should I be afraid
        if evil people surround me
        and try to trap me.
6 Some people think their strength and wealth
        will protect them.
    But those people are fools.
7 No human friend can save you.
    And you can't bribe* God.
8 No person will ever get enough money
        to buy his own life.
9 No person will ever get enough money
        to buy the right to live forever,
        and to save his own body
        from rotting in the grave.
10 Look, wise people die
        the same as fools and stupid people.
    And other people get all their wealth.
11 The grave will be everyone's new home
        forever and ever,
    And how much land they own
        doesn't make any difference!

songs of praise Literally, "maskil." The exact meaning of "maskil" is not clear. It might mean "a poem of meditation," "a poem of instruction," or "a skillfully-written poem."
God is over them all Or, "God has been very exalted." The Hebrew is the same as the first part of verse 5.
Selah This word is for the musicians. It probably means the singers should pause here or the music should be louder here.

director Or, "performer."
bribe Here this means offering a gift or sacrifice so that God will not punish a guilty person.

12 Wealthy people are no different than
foolish people,
All people ₍die₎ just like animals.
13 But the really foolish thing about people
is that they let their appetites
decide what they should do.
SELAH*
14 All people are just like sheep.
The grave will be their pen.
Death will be their shepherd.
Their bodies will decay
and rot away in the grave.
15 But God will pay the price
and save my life.
He will save me
from the power of the grave!
SELAH*
16 Don't be afraid of people
just because they are rich.
Don't be afraid of people
just because they have big fancy houses.
17 Those people won't take a thing with them
when they die.
They will not take any of those
beautiful things with them.
18 People should praise God
while they live.
People should praise God
while he does good things for them.
19 The time will come for those people
to go to their ancestors.
And they will never again
see the light of day.
20 People will not keep their wealth.
Every person ₍will die₎
just like the animals.

Psalm 50

One of Asaph's songs.

1 The Lord, the God of gods has spoken.
He calls to all the people on earth,
from the rising to the setting sun.
2 God is beautiful shining from Zion!
3 Our God is coming,
and he will not keep quiet.
Fire burns in front of him.
There is a great storm around him.
4 Our God calls to the earth and sky
to judge his people.
5 "My followers, gather around me.
Come my worshipers,
we made an agreement with each other."
6 God is the judge,
and the skies tell about his goodness.
SELAH*
7 God says,
"My people, listen to me!
People of Israel, I will show my evidence
against you.
I am God, your God.
8 I am not complaining about your sacrifices.*
You people of Israel bring me your
burnt offerings all the time.
You give them to me every day.
9 I will not take bulls from your house.
I will not take goats from your stalls.
10 I don't need those animals.
I already own all the animals in the forest.
I already own all the animals on
thousands of mountains.
11 I know every bird on the highest mountain.
Every moving thing in the hills are mine.
12 I am not hungry!
If I were hungry,
I would not have to ask you for food.
I own the world and everything in it.
13 I don't eat meat from bulls.
I don't drink blood from goats."
14 So bring your thank offerings*
and come to be with God.
You made promises to God Most High,
so give him the things you promised.
15 "People of Israel, pray to me
when you have troubles!
I will help you.
And then you can honor me."
16 God says to wicked people,
"You people talk about my laws.
You talk about my Agreement.
17 So why do you hate it when I correct you?
Why do you ignore the things I say?
18 You see a thief,
and you run to join him.
You jump into bed with people
doing the sin of adultery.

---

sacrifice(s) A sacrifice was a gift to God. Usually, it was a special animal that was killed and burned on an altar.

thank offering(s) Special fellowship offerings people gave to praise God and thank him for doing good things for them. A part of the animal was burned on the altar, but the people ate most of it in a fellowship meal at the temple. See Lev. 7:11-26.

Selah This word is for the musicians. It probably means the singers should pause here or the music should be louder here.

19 You people say bad things and tell lies.
20 You constantly say bad things
about other people,
even your own brothers.
21 You do these bad things,
and you think I should be quiet.
You don't say anything,
and you think I should be quiet too.
Well, I won't be quiet!
I will make it very clear to you
and I will criticize you to your face!
22 You people have forgotten God.
So you had better understand
before I tear you apart!
If that happens,
no person can save you!
23 So if a person gives a thank offering*
then he shows me honor.
But if a person lives right,
then I will show him God's power to save."

Psalm 51

To the director.* One of David's songs.
This song is about the time that Nathan the
prophet went to David after David's sin
with Bathsheba.

1 God, be merciful to me,
because of your great loving kindness,
because of your great mercy,
erase all my sins.
2 God, scrub away my guilt.
Wash away my sins,
Make me clean again!
3 I know I sinned.
I always see those sins.
4 I did the things you say are wrong.
God, you are the One I sinned against.
I confess these things so people will know
I am wrong, and you are right.
Your decisions are fair.
5 I was born in sin,
and in sin my mother conceived me.
6 God, you want me to be truly loyal,
so put true wisdom deep inside of me.
7 Use the hyssop plant and do the ceremony
to make me pure.
Wash me until I am whiter than snow!
8 Make me happy!
Tell me how to be happy again.
Let the bones you crushed be happy again!
9 Don't look at my sins!
Erase them all!
10 God, create a pure heart in me!
Make my spirit strong again!
11 Don't push me away!
And don't take your Holy Spirit
away from me!
12 Your help made me so happy!
Give me that joy again.
Make my spirit strong
and ready to obey you.
13 I will teach sinners your way of living,
and they will come back to you.
14 God, don't let me be guilty of murder.
My God, you are my Savior.
Let me sing about how good you are!
15 My Master, I will open my mouth
and sing your praises!
16 You don't really want sacrifices.*
So why should I give sacrifices that you
don't even want!
17 The sacrifices that God wants
is a spirit that is not filled with pride.*
God, you will not turn away a person who is
humble and oppressed.*
18 God, be good and kind to Zion.*
Build the walls of Jerusalem.
19 Then you can enjoy the good sacrifices*
and whole burnt offerings.
And people will again offer bulls on your altar.

Psalm 52

To the director.* A maskil* of David when
Doeg the Edomite went to Saul and told
him, "David is in Ahimelech's house."

1 Big man, why do you brag about
the bad things you do?
You are a disgrace to God.
All day you plan crooked things to do.

---

sacrifice(s) A sacrifice was a gift to God. Usually, it was a special animal that was killed and burned on an altar.
a spirit ... pride Literally, "a broken spirit."
a person ... oppressed Literally, "a broken and crushed heart."
Zion The southeast part of the mountain Jerusalem is built on. Sometimes it means the people of God living in Jerusalem.
maskils The exact meaning of "maskil" is not clear. It might mean "a poem of meditation," "a poem of instruction," or "a skillfully-written poem."
thank offering(s) Special fellowship offerings people gave to praise God and thank him for doing good things for them. A part of the animal was burned on the altar, but the people ate most of it in a fellowship meal at the temple. See Lev. 7:11–26.
director Or, "performer."

2 You make foolish plans and your tongue
   is as dangerous as a sharp razor.
   You are always lying and trying to cheat
   someone!
3 You love evil more than goodness.
   You love lying more than telling the truth.
                              SELAH*
4 You and your lying tongue
   love to hurt people.
5 So God will ruin you forever!
   He will grab you
     and pull you from your home.*
   He will kill you,
     and you will have no descendants.*
6 Good people will see this
     and will learn to fear and respect God.
   They will laugh at you and say,
7 "Look what happened to the man
     who did not depend on God.
   That man thought his wealth and lies
     would protect him."

8 But I am like a green olive tree in God's
     temple ₍that will live a long time₎.
   I will trust God's love forever and ever.
9 God, I praise you forever for the things
     you have done.
   I will speak your name* before your followers
     because it is so good!

Psalm 53

To the director. On the mahalath.*
A maskil* of David.*

1 Only a fool* thinks there is no God.
   People like that are corrupt, evil, malicious,
     and they don't do anything good.
2 There really is a God in heaven
     watching over us.
   God is looking for wise people
     who are looking for God!

3 But everyone has turned away from God.
   Every person is bad.
   No person does anything good.
   No, not one person!
4 God says,
   "Surely those evil people know the truth!
   But they don't pray to me.
   Evil people are as ready to destroy
     my people as they are to eat their food."
5 But those evil people will be scared,
     like they have never been scared before!
   Those evil people are Israel's enemies.
   God has rejected those evil people.
   So God's people will defeat them,
     and God will scatter the bones
     of those evil people.
6 Who in Zion will give victory to Israel?
   ₍God will help them win.₎
   God will bring his people back from exile.*
   Jacob will rejoice.
   Israel will be very happy.

Psalm 54

To the director. With instruments.
A maskil* of David when the Ziphites went
to Saul and told him, "We think David is
hiding among our people."*

1 God, use your authority and save me.
   Use your power to set me free.
2 God, listen to my prayer.
   Listen to the things I say.
3 Strangers have turned against me.
   Powerful men are trying to kill me.
   God, those men don't even think about you.
                              SELAH*
4 Look, my God will help me.
   My Master will support me.
5 My God will punish the people who
     turned against me.
   God will be true to me,
     and he will destroy those people.
6 God, I will give freewill offerings to you.
   Lord, I will praise your good name.
7 But I ask you to save me
     from all my troubles.
   Let me see my enemies defeated.

Selah This word is for the musicians. It probably means the singers should pause here or the music should be louder here.
home This means the body. This is a poetic way of saying God will kill this person.
descendants A person's children and their future families.
speak your name Or, "I will trust your name."
director Or, "performer."
mahalath This is probably a musical word. It might be the name of a tune, or it might mean to dance and shout.
maskils The exact meaning of "maskil" is not clear. It might mean "a poem of meditation," "a poem of instruction," or "a skillfully-written poem."
fool Here this means a person who does not follow God and his teachings.

exile Being forced to leave one's home country.

Psalm 55

To the director.* With instruments.
A maskil* of David.

1 God, hear my prayer.
   Please don't turn away from me.
2 God, please listen to me and answer me.
   Let me tell you my complaints.
3 My enemy said bad things to me.
   That wicked man yelled at me.
   My enemies were angry and attacked me.
   They brought troubles crashing down on
     top of me.
4 My heart is pounding inside me.
   I am scared to death.
5 I am scared and shaking.
   I am terrified.
6 Oh, I wish I had wings like a dove.
   I would fly away and find a place to rest.
7 I would go far, far away into the desert.
                                        SELAH*
8 I will run away. I will escape.
   I will run away from this storm of trouble.
9 My Master, stop their lies.
   I see the violence and fighting in this city.
10 Troubles are all around me, day and night, in
     every part of town.
   There are terrible things happening
     in this town.
11 There is too much crime in the streets.
    People are lying and cheating everywhere.
12 If it were an enemy insulting me,
     I could bear it.
   If it were my enemies attacking me,
     I could hide.
13 But it is you, my companion,
     my colleague, my friend.
   ⌊You are giving me troubles.⌋
14 We shared our secrets together.
    We worshiped together in God's temple.*
15 I hope my enemies die before their time.
    I hope they are buried alive!
    Why? Because they plan such terrible things
      in their homes.
16 I will call to God for help.
    And the Lord will answer me.
17 I talk with God evening, morning, and noon.
    I tell God my complaints.
    And he listens to me!
18 I have fought in many battles.
    But God is with me
      and brings me back safely.
19 God listens to me.
    The Eternal King will help me.
                                        SELAH*
20 My enemies will not change their lives.
    They don't fear and respect God.
21 My enemies attack their own friends.
    They don't do the things they agree to do.
22 My enemies are really smooth talkers;
      they talk about peace,
      but they are really planning wars.
    Their words are as slick as oil,
      but those words cut like a knife.
23 Give your worries to the Lord,
      and he will care for you.
    The Lord will never let good people
      be defeated.
24 God, send those liars and murderers to their
      grave before their life is half finished!
    As for me, I will trust in you.

Psalm 56

To the director.* To the tune "The Dove in
the Distant Oak." A miktam* of David from
the time the Philistines captured him
in Gath.

1 God, people have attacked me
    so be merciful to me.
   They have been chasing me
    and fighting me day and night.
2 My enemies have attacked me all day.
    There are too many fighters to count.
3 When I am afraid,
    I put my trust in you.
4 I trust God,
    so I am not afraid.
   People can't hurt me!
   I praise God for his promise to me.
5 My enemies are always twisting my words.
    They are always making plans against me.
6 They hide together and watch my every move,
    hoping for some way to kill me.
7 God, don't let them escape.
    Punish them for the bad things they do.
8 You know I am very upset.
    You know how much I have cried.

---

director Or, "performer."
Selah This word is for the musicians. It probably means the singers should pause here or the music should be louder here.
temple The special building in Jerusalem for Jewish worship.
miktam(s) The exact meaning of "miktam" is not clear. It might mean "a well-arranged song."

Surely you have kept an account
of all my tears.
9 So, defeat my enemies
when I call to you for help.
I know you can do it.
You are God!
10 I praise God for his promise.
I praise the Lord for his promise to me.
11 I trust God, so I am not afraid.
People can't hurt me!

12 God, I made special promises to you.
And I will do what I promised.
I will give you my thank offering.
13 Why? Because you saved me from death.
You kept me from being defeated.
So I will worship God in the light
that only living people can see.

Psalm 57

To the director. To the tune "Don't
Destroy." A miktam* of David. At the time
he escaped from Saul in the cave.*

1 God, be merciful to me.
Be kind because my soul trusts you.
I have come to you for protection,
while the trouble passes.
2 I pray to God Most High for help.
And God takes care of me completely!
3 From heaven he helps me and saves me.
He defeats the people who bother me.
SELAH*
God shows his true love to me.

4 My life is in danger.
My enemies are all around me
They are like man-eating lions,
with teeth as sharp as spears and arrows,
and tongues as sharp as a sword.

5 God, you are high above the heavens.
Your glory covers the earth.

6 My enemies set a trap for me.
They are trying to trap me.
They dug a deep pit for me to fall into.
SELAH*
7 But God will keep me safe.
He will keep me brave.
I will sing praises to him.

8 Wake up, my soul!
Harps and lyres,* begin your music!
Let's wake the Dawn.
9 My Master, I praise you to everyone.
I sing songs of praise about you
to every nation.
10 Your true love is higher than the highest
clouds in the sky!
11 God is more exalted than the heavens.
His glory covers the earth.

Psalm 58

To the director. To the tune "Don't
Destroy." A miktam* of David.*

1 You judges are not being fair
in your decisions.
You are not judging people fairly.
2 No, you only think of evil things to do.
You do violent crimes in this country.
3 Those evil men started doing wrong
as soon as they were born.
They have been liars from birth.
4 They are as dangerous as snakes.
And, like cobras that can't hear,
they refuse to listen to the truth.
5 Cobras can't hear the music or songs
of snake charmers.
And those evil people are like that.
6 Lord, those people are like lions.
So Lord, break their teeth.
7 May those people disappear like water
draining away.
May they be crushed like weeds on a path.
8 May they be like snails melting away as they
move.
May they be like a baby that was born dead
and never saw the light of day.
9 May they be destroyed quickly like thorns
that burn too fast to heat the pot on the fire.
10 A good man will be happy
when he sees people punished
for the bad things they did to him.
He will wash his feet in the blood of those
wicked men.
11 When that happens, people will say,
"Good people really are rewarded.
There really is a God judging the world!"

director Or, "performer."
Selah This word is for the musicians. It probably means the
singers should pause here or the music should be louder here.

lyre(s) An instrument with several strings, like a harp.

Psalm 59

To the director.* To the tune "Don't Destroy." A miktam* of David from the time Saul sent people to watch David's house to try to kill him.

1 God, save me from my enemies.
   Help me be the winner against the people
      who have come to fight me.
2 Save me from those people who do bad things.
   Save me from those murderers.
3 Look, strong men are waiting for me.
   They are waiting to kill me.
   But I did not sin or commit some crime.
4 They are chasing me,
      but I did nothing wrong.
   Lord, come and see for yourself!
5 You are the Lord God All-Powerful,
      the God of Israel!
   Get up and punish those people.
   Don't show any mercy to those evil traitors.
                                          SELAH*
6 Those evil men are like dogs
      that come into town in the evening,
      growling and roaming through town.
7 Listen to their threats and insults.
   They say such cruel things,
      and they don't care who hears them.
8 Lord, laugh at them.
   Make fun of all those people.
9 God, you are my strength,
   I am waiting for you.
   God, you are my place of safety
      high in the mountains.
10 God loves me, and he will help me win.
   He will help me defeat my enemies.
11 Don't just kill them, God,
      or my people might forget.
   My Master and Protector, scatter them
      and defeat them with your strength.
12 Those evil people curse and tell lies.
   Punish them for the things they said.
   Let their pride trap them.
13 Destroy them in your anger.
   Destroy them completely!
   Then people will know that God rules
      Jacob's people and the whole world!
                                          SELAH*

14 Those evil men come into town at night
      like growling dogs roaming through town.
15 They will look for something to eat,
      but they will find no food
      and no place to sleep.
16 But I will sing songs of praise to you.
   Each morning I will rejoice in your love.
   Why? Because you are my place of safety,
      high in the mountains.
   And I can run to you when troubles come.
17 I will sing my songs of praise to you.
   Why? Because you are my place of safety
      high in the mountains.
   You are the God who loves me!

Psalm 60

To the director.* To the tune "Lily of the Agreement." A miktam* of David. For teaching. This was from the time that David fought Aram Naharaim* and Aram Zobah,* and when Joab came back and defeated 12,000 Edomite soldiers at Salt Valley.

1 God, you were angry at us.
   So you rejected us
      and destroyed us.
   Please come back to us.
2 You shook the earth and split it open.
   Our world is falling apart.
   Please fix it.
3 You have given your people many troubles.
   We are like drunk people
      staggering and falling down.
4 You warned the people who worship you.
   Now they can escape the enemy.
                                          SELAH*
5 Use your great power and save us!
   Answer my prayer
      and save the people you love!
6 God spoke in his temple:*
   "I will win the war
      and be happy about the victory!
   ⌊I will share this land with my people.⌋
   I will give them Shechem.
   I will give them Succoth Valley.

---

director Or, "performer."
Selah This word is for the musicians. It probably means the singers should pause here or the music should be louder here.
miktam(s) The exact meaning of "miktam" is not clear. It might mean "a well-arranged song."
Aram Naharaim Or, "the Arameans of Mesopotamia."
Aram Zobah Or, "the Arameans of central Syria."
in his temple Or, "in his holiness."

7 Gilead and Manasseh will be mine.
　Ephraim will be my helmet.
　Judah will be my royal scepter.*
8 Moab will be the bowl
　　for washing my feet.
　Edom will be the slave
　　who carries my sandals.
　I ⌊will defeat⌋ the Philistine people
　　and shout about the victory!"
9 Who will lead me into the strong,
　　protected city?
　Who will lead me to fight against Edom?
10 God, ⌊only you can help me do this⌋.
　But you left us!
　You did not go with our army!
11 God, help us defeat our enemy!
　People can't help us!
12 Only God can make us strong.
　God can defeat our enemies!

Psalm 61

To the director.* With stringed instruments.
One of David's songs.

1 God, hear my prayer song.
　Listen to my prayer.
2 Wherever I am, however weak,
　　I will call to you for help!
　Carry me to the place of safety far above.
3 You are my place of safety!
　You are the strong tower
　　protecting me from my enemies.
4 I will live in your Tent* forever.
　I will hide where you can protect me.
　　　　　　　　　　　　SELAH*
5 God, you heard what I promised to give you.
　But everything your worshipers have comes
　　from you.
6 Give the king a long life.
　Let him live forever!
7 Let him live with God forever!
　Protect him with your true love.
8 And I will praise your name forever.
　Every day, I will do the things I promised.

---

scepter A special stick. Kings and leaders carried scepters to show they were rulers.
director Or, "performer."
Tent The temple in Jerusalem, or the Holy Tent where the people worshiped God before the temple was built.
Selah This word is for the musicians. It probably means the singers should pause here or the music should be louder here.

Psalm 62

To the director.* To Jeduthun.
One of David's songs.

1 I wait patiently for God to save me.
2 God is my fortress.*
　God saves me.
　God is my place of safety
　　high on the mountain.
　Not even great armies can defeat me.
3 How long will you attack me?
　I am like a leaning wall,
　　a fence ready to fall.
4 Those people are planning to destroy me.
　They tell lies about me.
　In public, they say good things about me,
　　but they secretly curse me.
　　　　　　　　　　　　SELAH*
5 I wait patiently for God to save me.
　God is my only hope.
6 God is my fortress.*
　God saves me.
　God is my place of safety
　　high on the mountain.
7 My glory and victory comes from God.
　He is my strong fortress.
　God is my place of safety.
8 People, trust God all the time!
　Tell God about all your problems.
　God is our place of safety.
　　　　　　　　　　　　SELAH*
9 People can't really help.
　You can't trust them to really help.
　Compared to God,
　　they are like nothing,
　　　like a gentle puff of air!
10 Don't trust the power to take things by force.
　Don't think you will gain anything by
　　stealing.
　And if you become rich,
　　don't trust your riches to help you.
11 God says there is one thing
　　you can really depend on:
　Strength comes from God!
12 My Master, your love is real.
　You reward or punish a person
　　for the things he does.

---

fortress A building or city with tall, strong walls for protection.

Psalm 63

One of David's songs. From the time he was in the desert of Judah.

1 God, you are my God.
   And I want you so much.
   My soul and my body thirst for you,
   like a dry, weary land with no water.
2 Yes, I have seen you in your temple.
   I have seen your strength and glory.
3 Your love is better than life.
   My lips praise you.
4 Yes, I will praise you in my life.
   In your name, I lift my arms in prayer.
5 I will be satisfied
   as if I had eaten the best foods.
   And my mouth will praise you.
6 I will remember you while lying on my bed.
   I will remember you in the middle of the night.
7 You really have helped me!
   I am happy that you protected me!
8 My soul clings to you.
   And you hold my hand.
9 Some people are trying to kill me.
   But they will be destroyed.
   They will go down to their graves.
10 They will be killed with swords.
   Wild dogs will eat their dead bodies.
11 But the king will be happy with his God.
   And the people who promised to obey him
   will praise him.
   Why? Because he defeated all those liars.

Psalm 64

To the director.* One of David's songs.

1 God, listen to me.
   I am afraid of my enemies.
   I am afraid for my life.
2 Protect me from the secret plans of my
   enemies.
   Hide me from those wicked people.
3 They have told many bad lies about me.
   Their tongues are like sharp swords,
   their bitter words like arrows.
4 They hide, and then shoot their arrows
   at a simple, honest man.
   And before he knows it,
   he is wounded.
5 They do bad things to defeat him.
   They tell lies and set their traps.
   They are sure no person will catch them.
6 People can be very tricky.
   It is hard to know what people are thinking.
7 But God can shoot his "arrows" too!
   And before they know it,
   the evil people are wounded.
8 Evil people plan to do bad things to
   other people.
   But God can ⌊ruin their plans,⌋
   and make those bad things happen to them.
   Then everyone that sees them
   will shake their heads in amazement.
9 People will see what God has done.
   They will tell other people about him.
   Then everyone will learn more about God.
   They will learn to fear and respect him.
10 Good people should be happy in the Lord.
   They should trust him.
   Praise the Lord, all of you good people.

Psalm 65

To the director.* One of David's songs of praise.

1 God on Zion,* I praise you.
   I give you the things I promised.
2 We tell about the things you have done.
   And you hear our prayers.
   You hear the prayers of every person who
   comes to you.
3 When our sins become too heavy for us,
   you take away those sins.
4 God, you chose your people.
   You chose us to come to your temple
   and worship you.
   And we are very happy!
   We have all the wonderful things
   in your temple, your holy palace.
5 God, you save us.
   Good people pray to you,
   and you answer their prayers.
   You do amazing things for them.
   People all around the world trust you.
6 God made the mountains with his power.
   We see his power all around us.
7 God made the rough seas calm.
   And God made the "oceans" of people on
   the earth.
8 People all around the world
   are amazed at the wonderful things you do.
   The sunrise and sunset makes us so happy!

---

director Or, "performer."

Zion The southeast part of the mountain Jerusalem is built on. Sometimes it means the people of God living in Jerusalem.

9 You take care of the land.
    You water it and make it grow things.
    God, you fill the streams with water
       and make the crops grow.
10 You pour the rain on the plowed fields.
    You soak the fields with water.
    You make the ground soft with rain,
       and you make the young plants grow.
11 You start the new year with a good harvest.
    You load the wagons with many crops.*
12 The desert and hills are covered with grass.
13 The pastures are covered with sheep.
    The valleys are filled with grain.
    Everyone is singing and shouting with
       happiness.

Psalm 66

To the director.* A song of praise.

1 Everything on earth,
    shout with joy to God!
2 Praise his glorious name!
    Honor him with songs of praise!
3 Tell God how wonderful his works are!
    God, your power is very great!
    Your enemies bow down.
    They are afraid of you!
4 Let the whole world worship you.
    Let everyone sing praises to your name.
                    SELAH*
5 Look at the things God did!
    Those things amaze us.
6 God made the sea become dry land.*
    His happy people walked across the river.*
7 God rules the world with his great power.
    God watches people everywhere.
    No person can rebel against him.
                    SELAH*
8 People, praise our God.
    Sing loud songs of praise to him.
9 God gave us life.
    And God protects us.

10 God tested us,
    like people test silver with fire.
11 God, you let us be trapped.
    You put heavy burdens on us.
12 You let our enemies walk on us.
    You dragged us through fire and water.
    But you brought us to a safe place.
13-14 So I will bring sacrifices* to your temple.
    When I was in trouble,
       I asked you for help.
    I made many promises to you.
    Now, I am giving you the things I promised.
15 I am giving you sin offerings.
    I am giving you incense* with the rams.
    I am giving you bulls and goats.
                    SELAH*
16 All of you people worshiping God,
    come and I will tell you
       what God did for me.
17 I prayed to him.
    I praised him.
18 My heart was pure,
    so my Master listened to me.
19 God listened to me.
    God heard my prayer.
20 Praise God!
    God did not turn away from me—
       he listened to my prayer.
    God showed his love to me!

Psalm 67

To the director. With instruments.
A song of praise.*

1 God, show mercy to me and bless me.
    Please accept us!
                    SELAH*
2 I hope every person on earth
    learns about you, God.
    Let every nation see how you save people.
3 May people praise you, God!
    May all people praise you.
4 May all nations rejoice and be happy!
    Why? Because you judge people fairly.
    And you rule over every nation.
5 May people praise you, God!
    May all people praise you.
6 God, our God, bless us.
    Let our land give us a great harvest.

---

harvest .. crops In ancient Israel there were two calenders. The calendar for religious holidays began in the spring, at barley harvest. The other calendar started in the fall, when they gathered other crops.
director Or, "performer."
Selah This word is for the musicians. It probably means the singers should pause here or the music should be louder here.
sea become dry land This was with Moses at the Red Sea. See Ex. 14.
walked across the river This was with Joshua at the Jordan River. See Joshua 3:14-17.
sacrifice(s) A sacrifice was a gift to God. Usually, it was a special animal that was killed and burned on an altar.
incense Special dried tree sap. Burned to make a sweet-smelling smoke, it was offered as a gift to God.

⁷ May God bless us.
And may all the people on earth
fear and respect God.

Psalm 68

To the director. One of David's
songs of praise.*

¹ God, get up and scatter your enemies.
May all of his enemies run from him.
² May your enemies be scattered,
like smoke blown away by the wind.
May your enemies be destroyed,
like wax melting in a fire.
³ But good people are happy.
Good people have a happy time
together with God.
Good people enjoy themselves
and are very happy!
⁴ Sing to God.
Sing praises to his name.
Prepare the way for God.
He rides his chariot* over the desert.
His name is Yah.*
Praise his name!
⁵ In his holy temple,
God is like a father to orphans.*
God takes care of widows.*
⁶ God gives lonely people a home.
God takes his people out of prison.
They are very happy.
But people who turn against God,
will stay in their hot prison.

⁷ God, you led your people out ⌊of Egypt⌋.
You marched across the desert.
                                                    SELAH*
⁸ And the ground shook.
God, the God of Israel came to Mount Sinai,
and the sky melted.
⁹ God, you sent the rain,
to make tired, old land strong again.
¹⁰ Your animals came back to that land.
God, you gave many good things
to the poor people there.

¹¹ God gave the command and many people
went to tell the good news:
¹² "The armies of powerful kings ran away!
The women at home will divide the things
that the soldiers bring home from the war.
The people who stayed at home
will share in the wealth.
¹³ They will get the dove wings
covered with silver.
They will get the wings
sparkling with gold."
¹⁴ On Mount Zalmon, God scattered
the enemy kings.
They were like falling snow.
¹⁵ Mount Bashan is a great mountain
with many peaks.
¹⁶ Mount Bashan, why do you look down
on Mount Zion?
God loves that mountain *(Zion)*.
The Lord chose to live there forever.
¹⁷ The Lord comes to Holy Mount Zion.
Behind him are millions of his chariots.*
¹⁸ He went up to the high ⌊mountain⌋.
He led a parade of captives;
He took the gifts from men*
even the people who turned against him.
The Lord* God ⌊went up there⌋ to live.
¹⁹ Praise the Lord!
Every day he helps us
with the loads we must carry.
God saves us!
                                                    SELAH*
²⁰ He is our God.
He is the God that saves us.
The Lord our God saves us from death.
²¹ God will show that he defeated his enemies.
God will punish the people
who fought against him.*
²² My Master said,
"I'll bring the enemy back from Bashan,
I'll bring the enemy from the west,
²³ so you can walk in their blood,
so your dogs can lick up their blood."
²⁴ People see God leading the victory parade.
People see my Holy God, my King,
leading the victory parade.

---

director Or, "performer."
chariot(s) A small wagon used in war.
Yah This is a Hebrew name for God. It is like the Hebrew name usually translated, "Lord."
orphan(s) Children whose parents have died.
widow(s) Women whose husbands have died. Often these women had no one to care for them.
Selah This word is for the musicians. It probably means the singers should pause here or the music should be louder here.

He took the gifts from men Or, "He took men as gifts." Or, "He gave gifts to men," as in the ancient Syriac and Aramaic versions and Eph. 4:8.
The Lord Or, "Yah," a Hebrew name for God.
God will show ... him Literally, "God will smash the heads of his enemies. He will smash the hairy skull walking in guilt."

25 Singers come marching in front.
  Then come young girls playing tambourines.
  And the musicians come marching behind.
26 Praise God in the great assembly!
  Praise the Lord, people of Israel!
27 There is little Benjamin, leading them.
  And there is the great family of Judah.
  And there are the leaders of Zebulun and Naphtali.
28 God, show us your power!
  Show us the power you used for us in the past.
29 Kings will bring their wealth to you,
  to your palace in Jerusalem.
30 Use your stick to make those "animals" do what you want.
  Make the "bulls" and "cows" in those nations obey you.
  You defeated those nations in war.
  Now make them bring silver to you.
31 Make them bring wealth from Egypt.
  God, make the Ethiopians bring their wealth to you.
32 Kings on earth, sing to God!
  Sing songs of praise to our Master!
                                        SELAH*
33 Sing to God!
  He rides his chariot through the ancient skies.
  Listen to his powerful voice!
34 God is more powerful than any of your gods.
  The God of Israel makes his people strong.
35 God is wonderful in his temple.
  The God of Israel gives strength and power to his people.
  Praise God!

Psalm 69

To the director.* To the tune "The Lilies."
One of David's songs.

1 God, save me from all my troubles!
  The water has risen to my mouth.
2 There is nothing to stand on.
  I am sinking down, down into the mud.
  I am in deep water.
  And the waves are crashing around me.
  I am about to drown.
3 I am getting weak from calling for help.
  My throat is hurting.
  I have waited and looked for help from you
  until my eyes are hurting.
4 I have more enemies than the hairs on my head.
  They hate me for no reason.
  They try hard to destroy me.
  My enemies tell lies about me.
  They lied and said I stole things.
  And then they forced me to pay for things I did not steal.
5 God, you know I did nothing wrong.
  I can't hide my sins from you.
6 My Master, Lord All-Powerful, don't let your followers be ashamed of me.
  God of Israel, don't let your worshipers be embarrassed because of me.
7 My face is covered with shame.
  I carry this shame for you.
8 My brothers treat me like a stranger.
  My mother's sons treat me like a foreigner.
9 My strong feelings* for your temple are destroying me.
  I get the insults from people who make fun of you.
10 I cry and fast,*
  and they make fun of me for it.
11 I wear rough cloth to show my sadness,
  and people tell jokes about me.
12 They talk about me in public places.
  The beer drinkers make up songs about me.
13 As for me, this is my prayer to you Lord:
  I want you to accept me!
  God, I want you to answer me with love.
  I know I can trust you to save me.
14 Pull me from the mud.
  Don't let me sink down into the mud.
  Save me from the people who hate me.
  Save me from this deep water.
15 Don't let the waves drown me.
  Don't let the deep hole swallow me.
  Don't let the grave close its mouth on me.
16 Lord, your love is good.
  Answer me with all your love.
  With all your kindness,
  turn to me and help me!
17 Don't turn away from your servant.
  I am in trouble!
  Hurry, help me!

Selah This word is for the musicians. It probably means the singers should pause here or the music should be louder here.
director Or, "performer."

strong feelings The Hebrew word means any strong feelings like love, hate, anger, zeal, or jealousy.
fast To live without food for a special time of prayer and worship.

18 Come save my soul.
    Rescue me from my enemies.
19 You know my shame.
    You know my enemies humiliated me.
    You saw them do those things to me.
20 The shame has crushed me!
    I am about to die from shame.
    I waited for sympathy,
    but none could be found.
    I waited for some person to comfort me,
    but no person came.
21 They gave me poison, not food.
    They gave me vinegar, not wine.
22 Their tables are covered with food.
    They have such big fellowship meals.
    I hope those meals destroy them.
23 I hope they become blind
    and their backs become weak.
24 Let them feel all of your anger.
25 Make their homes empty.
    Don't let anyone live there.
26 Punish them, and they will run away.
    Then they really will have pains
    and wounds to talk about.
27 Punish them for the bad things they did.
    Don't show them how good you can be.
28 Erase their names from the Book of Life.
    Don't write their names in the book
    with the names of the good people.
29 I am sad and hurting.
    God, lift me up. Save me!
30 I will praise God's name in song.
    I will praise him with a song of thanks.
31 This will make God happy!
    This will be better than killing a bull and
    offering the whole animal as a sacrifice.*
32 Poor people, you came to worship God.
    You will be happy to know these things.
33 The Lord listens to poor, helpless people.
    The Lord still likes people in prison.
34 Praise God, heaven and earth
    Sea and everything in it, praise the Lord!
35 The Lord will save Zion*!
    The Lord will rebuild the cities of Judah.
    The people who own the land
    will live there again!
36 The descendants* of his servants
    will get that land.
    The people who love his name will live there.

sacrifice(s) A sacrifice was a gift to God. Usually, it was a special animal that was killed and burned on an altar.
Zion The southeast part of the mountain Jerusalem is built on. Sometimes it means the people of God living in Jerusalem.
descendants A person's children and their future families.

Psalm 70

To the director.* One of David's songs to help people remember.

1 God, save me!
    God, hurry and help me!
2 People are trying to kill me.
    Disappoint them!
    Humiliate them!
    People want to do bad things to me.
    I hope they fall and feel the shame.
3 People made fun of me.
    I hope they get what they deserve
    and feel the shame.
4 I hope that the people who worship you
    will be very, very happy.
    I hope that the people who want your help
    will always be able to praise you.
5 I am a poor, helpless man.
    God, hurry! Come and save me!
    God, only you can rescue me.
    Don't be too late!

Psalm 71

1 Lord, I trust you,
    so I will never be disappointed.
2 In your goodness, you will save me.
    You will rescue me.
    Listen to me. Save me.
3 Be my fortress,*
    the home I can run to for safety.
    You are my Rock,*
    my place of safety.
    So give the command to save me.
4 My God, save me from wicked people.
    Save me from cruel, evil people.
5 My Master, you are my hope.
    I have trusted you since I was a young boy.
6 I depended on you even before I was born.
    I relied on you even in my mother's body.
    I have always prayed to you.
7 You are my source of strength.
    So I have been an example to other people.
8 I am always singing about
    the wonderful things you do.
9 Don't throw me away just because I am old.
    Don't leave me as I lose my strength.
10 My enemies have made plans against me.
    Those people really did meet together,
    and they made plans to kill me.

director Or, "performer."
fortress A building or city with tall, strong walls for protection.
Rock A name for God to show he is a strong place of safety.

¹¹ My enemies said,
   "Go get him!
   God left him.
   And no person will help him."
¹² God, don't leave me!
   God, hurry! Come save me!
¹³ Defeat my enemies!
   Destroy them completely!
   They are trying to hurt me.
   I hope they feel the shame and disgrace.
¹⁴ Then I will always trust you.
   And I will praise you more and more.
¹⁵ I will tell people how good you are.
   I will tell about the times you saved me.
   There have been too many times to count.
¹⁶ I will tell about your greatness,
   Lord my Master.
   I will talk only about you and your goodness.
¹⁷ God, you have taught me
   since I was a young boy.
   And to this day I have told people
   about the wonderful things you do!
¹⁸ Now I am old and my hair is gray.
   But I know that you won't leave me, God.
   I will tell each new generation
   about your power and greatness.
¹⁹ God, your goodness reaches
   far above the skies.
   God, there is no god like you.
   You have done wonderful things.
²⁰ You let me see troubles and bad times.
   But you saved me from every one of them
   and kept me alive.
   No matter how deep I sank,
   you lifted me out of my troubles.
²¹ Help me do greater things than before.
   Continue to comfort me.
²² And I will play the harp and praise you.
   My God, I will sing that you can be trusted.
   I will play songs on my lyre*
   for the Holy One of Israel.
²³ You saved my soul.
   My soul will be happy.
   I will sing songs of praise with my lips.
²⁴ My tongue will sing about your goodness all
   the time.
   And the people who want to kill me,
   will be defeated and disgraced.

lyre(s) An instrument with several strings, like a harp.

Psalm 72
*To Solomon.**

¹ God, help the king make wise decisions like you.
  And help the king's son learn about
  your goodness.
² Help the king judge your people fairly.
  Help him make wise decisions for your
  poor people.
³ Let there be peace and justice throughout
  the land.
⁴ Let the king be fair to the poor people.
  Let him help the helpless.
  Let him punish the people who hurt them.
⁵ I hope people fear and respect the king
  as long as the sun shines
  and the moon is in the sky.
  I hope people fear and respect him forever.
⁶ Help the king be like rain falling on the fields.
  Help him be like showers falling on the land.
⁷ Let goodness blossom while he is king.
  Let peace continue as long as the moon.
⁸ Let his kingdom grow from sea to sea,
  from the ₍Euphrates₎ River
  to the faraway places on earth.*
⁹ May all the people living in the desert
  bow down to him.
  May all his enemies bow before him
  with their faces in the dirt.
¹⁰ May the kings of Tarshish*
   and all the faraway lands
   bring gifts to him.
   May the kings of Sheba and Seba
   bring their tribute* to him.
¹¹ May all kings bow down to our king.
   May all nations serve him.
¹² Our king helps the helpless.
   Our king helps poor, helpless people.
¹³ Poor, helpless people depend on him.
   The king keeps them alive.
¹⁴ The king saves them from cruel people
   who try to hurt them.
   The lives of those poor people are
   very important to the king.

To Solomon This might mean this song was written by Solomon or dedicated to him or that it is from some special collection of songs.
faraway places on earth This usually means the countries around the Mediterranean Sea.
Tarshish A city far away from Israel, probably in Spain. Tarshish was famous for its large ships that sailed the Mediterranean Sea.
tribute The money and gifts a country paid to the country that defeated it.

15 Long live the king!
　　And let him receive gold from Sheba.
　　Always pray for the king.
　　Bless him every day.
16 May the fields grow plenty of grain.
　　May the hills be covered with crops.
　　May the fields be as fertile as Lebanon.
　　And may the cities be filled with people
　　　like fields covered with grass.
17 May the king be famous forever.
　　May people remember his name
　　　as long as the sun shines.
　　May the people be blessed by him.
　　And may they all bless him.

18 Praise the Lord God, the God of Israel!
　　Only God can do such amazing things.
19 Praise his glorious name forever!
　　Let his glory fill the whole world!
　　Amen and Amen!*

20 This ends the prayers of David son of Jesse.

BOOK 3

Psalm 73

Asaph's song of praise.

1 God is truly good to Israel.
　　God is good to people whose hearts are pure.
2 I almost slipped and began to sin.
3 I saw that wicked people were successful
　　I became jealous of those proud people.
4 Those people are healthy.
　　They don't have to struggle to survive.*
5 Those proud people don't suffer like we do.
　　They don't have troubles like other people.
6 So they are very proud and hateful people.
　　This is as easy to see as the jewels
　　　and fancy clothes they wear.
7 If those people like something they see,
　　they go and take it.
　　They do whatever they want to do.
8 They say cruel, evil things
　　about other people.
　　They are proud and stubborn.
　　And they are always planning ways
　　　to take advantage of other people.
9 Those proud people think they are gods!
　　They think they are the rulers of earth.

10 *So even God's people turn to them
　　　and do the things they tell them.
11 Those evil people say,
　　"God doesn't know what we are doing!
　　God Most-High does not know!"

12 Those proud people are wicked,
　　　but they are rich and getting richer.
13 So why should I make my heart pure?
　　Why should I make my hands clean?
14 God, I suffer all day long.
　　And you punish me every morning.

15 God, I wanted to talk to other people
　　　about these things.
　　But I knew I would be betraying
　　　your people.
16 I tried hard to understand these things.
　　But it was all too hard for me
17 until I went to your temple.*
　　I went to God's temple,
　　　and then I understood.
18 God, you really have put those people
　　　in a dangerous situation.
　　It is so easy for them to fall and be destroyed.
19 Trouble can come suddenly,
　　　and then those proud people are ruined.
　　Terrible things can happen to them,
　　　and then they are finished.
20 Lord, those people will be like a dream that
　　we forget when we wake up.
　　You will make those people disappear
　　　like the monsters in our dreams.

21-22 I was very stupid.
　　I thought about rich and wicked people,
　　　and I became upset.
　　God, I was upset and angry at you!
　　I acted like a stupid, ignorant animal.
23 ⌊I have everything I need!⌋
　　I am with you always.
　　God, you hold my hand.
24 God, you lead me and give me good advice.
　　And later you will lead me to glory.*
25 God, I have you in heaven.
　　And when I am with you,
　　　what on earth can I want?
26 Maybe my mind* and body will be destroyed,
　　　but I have the Rock,* I love.
　　I have God forever!

Amen A Hebrew word meaning "truly," "indeed." It shows that a person agrees with what has been said.
They don't have to struggle to survive Literally, "They have no bonds to their death."

Verse 10 This verse is hard to understand in Hebrew.
temple The special building in Jerusalem for Jewish worship.
Later ... glory Or, "You take (lead) me after honor."
mind Literally, "heart."

27 God, people who leave you will be lost.
　　You will destroy the people
　　　who are not faithful to you.
28 As for me, I have come to God.
　　And that is good for me.
　　I have made the Lord my Master
　　　my place of safety.
　　God, I have come to tell about
　　　all the things you have done.

Psalm 74

A maskil* of Asaph.

1 God, did you leave us forever?
　　Are you still angry at your people?
2 Remember the people you bought long ago.
　　You saved us.
　　We belong to you.
　　Remember Mount Zion,*
　　　the place that you lived.
3 God, come walk through these ancient ruins.
　　Come back to the Holy Place
　　　that the enemy destroyed.
4 The enemy shouted their war cries
　　　in the temple.
　　They put their flags in the temple to show
　　　they won the war.
5 The enemy soldiers were like people
　　　cutting weeds with a hoe.
6 God, they used their axes and hatchets,
　　and cut the carved, wooden panels
　　　in your temple.
7 Those soldiers burned your Holy Place.
　　That temple was built to honor your name,
　　　and they pulled it down to the ground.
8 The enemy decided to crush us completely.
　　They burned every holy place*
　　　in the country.
9 We could not see any of our own signs.*
　　There are no more prophets.
　　No person knows what to do.

10 God, how much longer will the enemy
　　　make fun of us?
　　Will you let them insult your name forever?
11 God, why did you punish us so hard?
　　You used your great power
　　　and destroyed us completely!
12 God, you have been our King
　　　for a long time.
　　You helped us win many battles
　　　in this country.
13 God, you used your great power,
　　　to split open the Red Sea.
14 You defeated the great sea monsters!
　　You smashed the heads of Leviathan,*
　　　and left his body for the animals to eat.
15 You make the springs and rivers flow.
　　And you make the rivers become dry.
16 God, you control the day,
　　　and you control the night.
　　You made the moon and the sun.
17 You set the limits for everything on earth.
　　And you created summer and winter.
18 God, remember these things.
　　Remember, the enemy insulted you!
　　Those foolish people hate your name!
19 Don't let those wild animals take your dove!
　　Don't forget your poor people forever.
20 Remember our Agreement!*
　　There is violence in every dark place
　　　in this land.
21 God, your people were treated badly.
　　Don't let them be hurt any more.
　　Your poor, helpless people praise you.
22 God, get up and fight!
　　Remember, those fools challenged you!
23 Don't forget the shouts of your enemies.
　　They insulted you again and again.

Psalm 75

To the director.* To the tune "Don't Destroy." One of Asaph's songs of praise.

1 We praise you, God!
　　We praise you.

Rock A name for God to show he is a strong place of safety.
maskil(s) The exact meaning of "maskil" is not clear. It might mean "a poem of meditation," "a poem of instruction," or "a skillfully-written poem."
Zion The southeast part of the mountain Jerusalem is built on. Sometimes it means the people of God living in Jerusalem.
holy place Or, "El meeting place." This means every place where people went to meet with God.
signs These were probably signal fires that people burned as a way of passing messages from one town to the next. In war, this was a way people showed other towns that the enemy had not yet destroyed their own town.
great sea monsters ... Leviathan These were creatures from ancient stories. People believed that these creatures kept the world from being a safe, orderly place. When it says that God destroyed these creatures, it means God showed he really controlled every part of the world, even the animals in the deepest ocean.
Agreement Literally, "Proof." The flat stones with the Ten Commandments written on them were proof of the Agreement between God and Israel.
director Or, "performer."

You* are near and people tell about
the amazing things you do.
2 God says,
"I choose the time for judgment.
I will judge fairly.
3 The earth and everything on it
may be shaking and ready to fall,
but I make it steady."
SELAH*
4-5 "Some people are very proud.
They think they are powerful
and important.
But I tell those people,
'Don't brag!'
'Don't be so proud!'"
6 There is no power on earth
that can make a person important.*
7 God is the judge.
And God decides who will be important.
God lifts up one person
and makes him important,
God brings down another person
and makes him not important.
8 ⌊God is ready to punish evil people.⌋
The Lord has a cup in his hand.
That cup is filled with poisoned wine.
He will pour this wine *(punishment)*,
and wicked people will drink it
to the last drop.
9 I will always tell people about these things.
I will sing praise to the God of Israel.
10 I will take power away from wicked people,
and I will give power to good people.

Psalm 76

To the director. With instruments. One of
Asaph's songs of praise.*

1 People in Judah know God.
People in Israel respect God's name.
2 God's temple is in Salem.*
God's house is on Mount Zion.
3 In that place, God shattered the bows
and arrows, shields, swords, and
other weapons of war.
SELAH*

4 God, you are glorious coming back
from the hills where you defeated
your enemies.
5 Those soldiers thought they were strong.
But now they lie dead in the fields.
Their bodies are stripped of all they owned.
None of those strong soldiers could defend
themselves.
6 The God of Jacob yelled at those soldiers,
and that army with chariots and horses
fell dead.
7 God, you are awesome!
No person can stand against you
when you are angry.
8-9 The Lord stood as judge
and announced his decision.
God saved the humble people of the land.
From heaven he gave the decision.
The whole earth was silent and afraid.
10 God, people respect you
when you punish evil people.
You show your anger,
and the survivors* become stronger.
11 People, you made promises
to the Lord your God.
Now, give him what you promised.
People in every place fear and respect God.
And they will bring gifts to him.
12 God defeats great leaders.
All the kings on earth fear him.

Psalm 77

To the director. To Jeduthun.
One of Asaph's songs.*

1 I lift my voice to God and cry ⌊for help⌋.
I lift my voice to you God, listen to me!
2 My Master, I come to you
when I have trouble.
I reached out for you all night long.
My soul refused to be comforted.
3 I think about God,
and I try to tell him how I feel.
But I can't.
4 You would not let me sleep.
I tried to say something,
but I was too upset.

You Literally, "Your name."
Selah This word is for the musicians. It probably means the singers should pause here or the music should be louder here.
There ... important Literally, "Not from the east or the west and not from the desert mountains."
director Or, "performer."
Salem Another name for Jerusalem. This name means, "Peace."

survivor(s) People who escaped some disaster. Here this means the Jewish people who survived the destruction of Judah and Israel by its enemy armies.

⁵ I kept thinking about the past.
  I kept thinking about things
    that happened long ago.
⁶ At night, I try to think about my songs.
  I talk with myself and try to understand.
⁷ I wonder,
  "Has our Master left us forever?
  Will he ever want us again?
⁸ Is God's love gone forever?
  Will he ever speak to us again?
⁹ Has God forgotten what mercy is?
  Has his compassion changed to anger?"
                                    SELAH*
¹⁰ Then I thought,
  "The thing that really bothers me is this:
    'Has God Most-High lost his power?'"
¹¹ I remember what the Lord did.
  God, I remember the amazing things
    that you did long ago.
¹² I thought about what you have done.
  I thought about those things.
¹³ God, your ways are holy.
  God, no one is great like you are.
¹⁴ You are the God that did amazing things.
  You showed people your great power.
¹⁵ With your power you saved your people.
  You saved the descendants* of
    Jacob and Joseph.
                                    SELAH*
¹⁶ God, the water saw you,
    and became afraid.
  The deep water shook with fear.
¹⁷ The thick clouds dropped their water.
  People heard loud thunder
    in the high clouds.
  Then your arrows of lightning
    flashed through the clouds.
¹⁸ There were loud claps of thunder.
  Lightning lit up the world.
  The earth shook and trembled.
¹⁹ God, you walked through the deep water,
    you crossed the deep sea,
    but you left no footprints.
²⁰ You used Moses and Aaron
    to lead your people like sheep.

Selah This word is for the musicians. It probably means the singers should pause here or the music should be louder here.
descendants A person's children and their future families.

Psalm 78

*One of Asaph's maskils.**

¹ My people, listen to my teachings.
  Listen to the things I say.
² I will tell you this story.
  I will tell you this old story.
³ We heard the story, and we know it well.
  Our fathers told this story.
⁴ And we will not forget the story.
  Our people will be telling the story to the
    last generation.
  We will all praise the Lord,
    and tell about the amazing things he did.
⁵ The Lord made an Agreement with Jacob.*
  God gave the Law to Israel.
  God gave the commands to our ancestors.*
  He told our ancestors to teach the Law
    to their descendants.*
⁶ New children will be born.
  They will grow to become adults.
  And they will tell the stories
    to their children.
  In this is the way, people will know
    the Law, even to the last generation.
⁷ So all those people will trust God.
  They will not forget what God did.
  They will carefully obey his commands.
⁸ If the people teach their God's commands
    to their children,
  then the children will not be like
    their ancestors.
  Their ancestors turned against God.
  They refused to obey him.
  Those people were stubborn.
  They were not loyal to God's Spirit.
⁹ The men from Ephraim had their weapons,
    but they ran away from the battle.
¹⁰ They didn't keep their Agreement with God.
  They refused to obey his teachings.
¹¹ Those men from Ephraim
    forgot the great things God did.
  They forgot the amazing things
    he showed them.
¹² God showed their fathers
    his great power at Zoan in Egypt.

maskil(s) The exact meaning of "maskil" is not clear. It might mean "a poem of meditation," "a poem of instruction," or "a skillfully-written poem."
Jacob Another name for Israel. See Gen. 32:22-28.
ancestors Literally, "fathers," meaning a person's parents, grandparents, and all the people they are descended from.
descendants A person's children and their future families.

¹³ God split the Red Sea
and led the people across.
The water stood like a solid wall
on both sides of them.
¹⁴ Each day God led them with the tall cloud.
And each night God led them
with the light from the column of fire.
¹⁵ God split the rock in the desert.
He gave those people water from
deep in the ground.
¹⁶ God brought the water streaming
from the rock like a river!
¹⁷ But the people continued to sin against God.
They turned against God Most-High even
in the desert.
¹⁸ Then those people decided to test God.
They asked God for food, just to satisfy
their appetites.
¹⁹ They complained about God and said,
"Can God give us food in the desert?
²⁰ He hit the rock
and a flood of water came out.
Surely he can give us some bread and meat!"
²¹ The Lord heard what those people said.
God was very angry at Jacob.*
God was very angry at Israel.
²² Why? Because the people did not trust him.
They did not believe God could save them.
²³⁻²⁴ But then God opened the clouds above,
and manna* rained down on them for food.
It was like doors in the sky opened,
and grain poured down from
a storehouse in the sky.
²⁵ People ate the food of angels.
God sent plenty of food to satisfy them.
²⁶⁻²⁷ God made a strong wind blow from the east,
and quail* fell on them like rain.
God made the wind blow from Teman,
and the blue sky became dark
because there were so many birds.
²⁸ The birds fell right in the middle of camp,
all around those people's tents.
²⁹ They had plenty to eat,
but they let their appetites make them sin.
³⁰ They did not control their appetites,
so they ate the quail before draining
the blood from the birds.
³¹ God became very angry at those people,
and he killed many of them.

God caused many healthy young people to die.
³² But the people still sinned again!
They did not depend on the amazing things
that God could do.
³³ So God ended their worthless lives
with some disaster.
³⁴ Whenever God killed some of them,
the others would turn back to him.
They would come running back to God.
³⁵ Those people would remember
that God was their Rock,*
They would remember that God Most-High
saved them.
³⁶ ⌊They said they loved him,⌋ but they lied.
Those people were not serious.
³⁷ Their hearts were not really with God.
They were not faithful to the Agreement.*
³⁸ But God was merciful.
He forgave them for their sins.
And he did not destroy them.
Many times God controlled his anger.
God did not let himself become too angry.
³⁹ God remembered they were only people.
People are like a wind that blows,
and then it is gone.
⁴⁰ Oh, those people caused God
so many troubles in the desert!
They made him so sad!
⁴¹ Again and again those people
tested God's patience.
They really hurt the Holy One of Israel.
⁴² Those people forgot about God's power.
They forgot the many times that God
saved them from the enemy.
⁴³ They forgot the miracles in Egypt,
the miracles in the fields of Zoan.
⁴⁴ God turned the rivers to blood!
The Egyptians could not drink the water.
⁴⁵ God sent swarms of flies
that bit the people of Egypt.
God sent the frogs
that ruined the Egyptians' lives.
⁴⁶ God gave their crops to the grasshoppers,
and their other plants to the locusts.
⁴⁷ God used hail to destroy their vines.
And he used sleet to destroy their trees.
⁴⁸ God killed their animals with hail,
and their cattle with lightning.
⁴⁹ God showed the Egyptian people his anger.

Jacob Another name for Israel. See Gen. 32:22-28.
manna The special food God sent to the people of Israel while they wandered through the desert for 40 years.
quail A kind of bird.

Rock A name for God to show he is a strong place of safety.
Agreement Literally, "Proof." The flat stones with the Ten Commandments written on them were proof of the Agreement between God and Israel.

50 He sent his destroying angels against them.
God found a way to show his anger.
He did not let any of those people live.
He let them die with a deadly disease.
51 God killed all the firstborn* sons in Egypt.
He killed every firstborn in Ham's* family.
52 Then God led Israel like a shepherd.
He led his people like sheep into the desert.
53 He guided his people safely.
God's people had nothing to be afraid of.
God drowned their enemies in the Red Sea.
54 God led his people to his holy land,
to the mountain he took with his power.
55 God forced the other nations
to leave that land.
God gave each family its share of the land.
God gave each family group of Israel
its home to live in.
56 But they tested God Most-High
and made him very sad.
Those people did not obey God's commands.
57 The people of Israel turned away from God.
They turned against him
just like their fathers did.
They were as bad as a twisted bow.*
58 The people of Israel built high places*
and made God angry.
They built statues of false gods
and made God very jealous.
59 God heard this and became very angry.
And God rejected Israel completely!
60 God abandoned the Holy Tent at Shiloh.*
God lived in that tent among the people.
61 God let other nations capture his people.
Enemies took God's "beautiful jewel."
62 God showed his anger against his people.
He let them be killed in war.
63 The young men were burned to death,
and the girls they were supposed to marry
sang no wedding songs.
64 The priests were killed,
but the widows did not cry for them.
65 Finally, our Master got up
like a man waking from his sleep,
like a soldier after drinking too much wine.

66 God forced his enemy back
and defeated them.
God defeated his enemies
and disgraced them forever.
67 But God rejected Joseph's family.
God did not accept Ephraim's family.
68 No, God chose Judah's family group.
God chose Zion, the mountain he loves.
69 God built his holy temple
high on that mountain.
God built his holy temple to last forever,
just like the earth.
70 God chose David to be his special servant.
David was guarding the sheep pens,
But God took him away from that job.
71 David was caring for sheep
But God took him away from that job.
God gave David the job of caring for
his people,
the people of Jacob,
the people of Israel,
God's property.
72 And David led them with a pure heart.
He led them very wisely.

Psalm 79

One of Asaph's songs of praise.

1 God, some people came to fight your people.
Those people ruined your holy temple.
They left Jerusalem in ruins.
2 The enemy left the bodies of your servants
for the wild birds to eat.
They left the bodies of your followers
for wild animals to eat.
3 God, the enemy killed your people
until the blood flowed like water.
No person is left to bury the dead bodies.
4 The countries around us insulted us.
The people around us laughed at us
and make fun of us.
5 God, will you be angry at us forever?
Will your strong feelings*
continue to burn like a fire?
6 God, turn your anger against the nations that
don't know you.
Turn your anger against nations
that don't worship your name.
7 Those nations destroyed Jacob.*
They destroyed Jacob's country.

firstborn The first child born into a family. The firstborn son was very important in ancient times.
Ham The Egyptians were Ham's descendants. See Gen. 10:6–10.
twisted bow It is very hard to shoot arrows accurately with a bow that is twisted wrong.
high places Places for worshiping God or false gods. These places were often on the hills and mountains.
Holy Tent at Shiloh See 1 Sam. 4:10-11; Jer. 7:17.

strong feelings The Hebrew word can mean any strong feeling such as zeal, jealousy, or love.
Jacob Another name for Israel. See Gen. 32:22-28.

⁸ God, please don't punish us for the sins
    of our ancestors.*
  Hurry, show us your mercy!
  We need you so much!
⁹ Our God and Savior, help us!
  Help us! Save us!
  That will bring glory to your name.
  Erase our sins for the good of your name.
¹⁰ Don't let other nations say to us,
  "Where is your God?
  Can't he help you?"
  God, punish those people so we can see it.
  Punish them for killing your servants.
¹¹ Please listen to the prisoners' groan!
  God, use your great power and save
    the people who were chosen to die.
¹² God, punish the people around us
    seven times for what they did to us.
  Punish those people for insulting you.
¹³ We are your people.
  We are the sheep in your flock.
  We will praise you forever.
  Forever and ever, we will praise you, God.

Psalm 80

To the director. To the tune "Lilies of the
Agreement." One of Asaph's
songs of praise.*

¹ Shepherd of Israel, please listen to me.
  You lead Joseph's sheep *(people)*.
  You sit as king on the Cherub angels.*
  Let us see you.
² Shepherd of Israel, show your greatness
    to Ephraim, Benjamin, and Manasseh.
  Come and save us.
³ God, accept us again.
  Accept us. Save us!
⁴ Lord God All-Powerful,
    when will you listen to our prayers?
  Will you be angry at us forever?
⁵ You have given tears as food to your people.
  You have given your people bowls
    filled with their tears.
  That was their water to drink.
⁶ You let us become something for our
    neighbors to fight about.
  Our enemies laugh at us.

⁷ God All-Powerful, accept us again.
  Accept us. Save us.
⁸ ⌊In the past, you treated us like
    a very important plant.⌋
  You brought your "vine" out of Egypt.
  You forced other people to leave this land,
    and you planted your "vine" here.
⁹ You prepared the ground for the "vine."
  You helped its roots to grow strong.
  Soon the "vine" spread throughout the land.
¹⁰ It covered the mountains.
  Its leaves shaded even the giant cedar trees.
¹¹ Its vines spread to the Mediterranean Sea.
  Its shoots spread to the Euphrates River.
¹² God, why did you pull down the walls
    that protect your "vine"?
  Now every person who passes by
    picks its grapes.
¹³ Wild pigs come and walk on your "vine."
  Wild animals come and eat the leaves.
¹⁴ God All-Powerful, come back.
  Look down from heaven at your "vine"
    and protect it.
¹⁵ God, look at the "vine" you planted
    with your own hands.
  Look at the young plant* you raised.
¹⁶ Your "vine" was burned in the fire
    like dry dung.
  You were angry at it and destroyed it.
¹⁷ God, reach out to the son
    who stood by your right side.
  Reach out to the son you raised.
¹⁸ He will not leave you again.
  Let him live,
    and he will worship your name.
¹⁹ Lord God All-Powerful, come back to us.
  Accept us. Save us.

Psalm 81

To the director, ⌊accompanied⌋ by the
Gittith.* One of Asaph's songs.*

¹ Be happy and sing to God our strength.
  Shout with joy to the God of Israel.
² Begin the music.
  Play the tambourines.

---

ancestors Literally, "fathers," meaning a person's parents, grandparents, and all the people they are descended from.
director Or, "performer."
Cherub angels Special angels from God. Statues of these angels were on top of the Box of the Agreement.
young plant Literally, "son."
by the Gittith Or, "on the Gittith." This might be a type of instrument, or it might be a performer in the temple orchestra, possibly Obed Edom from Gath (the Gittite).

Play the pleasant harps and lyres.*
3 Blow the ram's horn
    at the time of the new moon,*
  Blow the ram's horn
    at the time of the full moon.*
    when our holiday begins.
4 That is a law for the people of Israel.
    God gave that command to Jacob.*
5 God made this Agreement with Joseph*
    at the time God took him away from Egypt.
  In Egypt we heard that language
    we did not understand.
6 God says,
    "I took the load from your shoulder.
    I let you drop the worker's basket.
7 You people were in trouble.
    You called for help
    and I set you free.
  I was hidden in the storm clouds,
    and I answered you.
  I tested you by the water at Meribah."*
                                    SELAH*
8 "My people, listen to me,
    and I will give you my Agreement*
    Israel, please listen to me!
9 Don't worship any of the false gods
    that the foreigners worship.
10 I, the Lord, am your God.
    I brought you out of Egypt.
    Israel, open your mouth,
    and I will feed you.
11 "But my people did not listen to me.
    Israel did not obey me.
12 So I let them do what they wanted to do.
    Israel did anything they wanted to do.
13 If my people would listen to me
    and live the way I want,
14   then I would defeat their enemies.
  I would punish the people
    who bring troubles to Israel.
15 The Lord's enemies would shake with fear.
    They would be punished forever.
16 God would give the best wheat to his people.
    The Rock,* would give honey to his people
    until they were satisfied.

Psalm 82

One of Asaph's songs of praise.

1 God stands in the assembly of the gods.*
    He is the judge in that meeting of the gods.
2 God says,
    "How long will you judge people unfairly?
    How long will you let wicked people go
    free without punishment?"
                                    SELAH*
3 "Defend the poor people and orphans.*
    Protect the rights of those poor people.
4 Help those poor, helpless people.
    Save them from evil people.
5 "They* don't know what is happening.
    They don't understand!
    They don't know what they are doing,
    Their world is falling down around them!"
6 I *(God)* say,
    "You are gods.
    You are sons of God Most-High.
7 But you will die
    the same as all people must die.
  You will die
    the same as all the other leaders."
8 Get up, God!
    You be the judge!
  God, you be the leader
    over all the nations!

---

lyre(s) An instrument with several strings, like a harp.
new moon The first day of the Hebrew month. There were special meetings on these days to worship God.
full moon The middle of the Hebrew month. Many of the special meetings and holidays started at the time of a full moon.
Jacob Another name for Israel. See Gen. 32:22-28.
Joseph Here this means Joseph's family, the people of Israel.
Meribah See Ex. 17:1-7.
Selah This word is for the musicians. It probably means the singers should pause here or the music should be louder here.
Agreement Literally, "Testimony, Proof." The flat stones with the Ten Commandments written on them were proof of the Agreement between God and Israel.

Rock A name for God to show he is a strong place of safety.
assembly of the gods Other nations taught that El (God) and the other gods met together to decide what to do with the people on earth. But many times kings and leaders were also called "gods." So this psalm may be God's warning to the leaders of Israel.
orphan(s) Children whose parents are dead. Often these children have no one to care for them.
They This might mean the poor people don't understand what is happening. Or it might mean that the "gods" don't understand that they are ruining the world by not being fair and by not doing what is right.

Psalm 83

One of Asaph's songs of praise.

1 God, don't keep quiet!
  Don't close your ears!
  Please say something, God.
2 God, your enemies make plans against you.
  Your enemies will soon attack.
3 They make secret plans against your people.
  Your enemies are discussing plans against
    the people you love.
4 The enemies are saying,
  "Come, let us destroy them completely.
  Then no person will ever again
    remember the name 'Israel'."
5 God, all those people joined together to fight
    against you and the Agreement*
    you made with us.
6-7 Those enemies joined together to fight us:
  Edom, the Ishmaelite people,
  Moab and Hagar's descendants,*
  Byblos, Ammon, the Amalekite people,
  the Philistine people, and the people
    living in Tyre.
  All those people joined together to fight us.
8 Even the Assyrians joined those people.
  They made Lot's descendants,*
    very powerful.
                                           SELAH*
9 God, defeat the enemy
  like you defeated Midian,
  like you defeated Sisera and Jabin
    near the Kishon River.
10 You defeated them at En-Dor.
  And their bodies rotted on the ground.
11 God, defeat the enemy's leaders.
  Do what you did to Oreb and Zeeb.
  Do what you did to Zebah and Zalmunna.
12 God, those people wanted to force us
    to leave your land!
13 Make those people like a tumbleweed*
    blown by the wind.
  Scatter those people
    like the wind scatters straw.
14 Destroy the enemy
  like a fire destroys a forest,
  like a wild fire that burns the hills.
15 God, chase those people away
  like ⌊dust blown⌋ by a storm.
  Shake them ⌊and blow them away⌋
    like a tornado.
16 God, teach those people
  so they may learn
    that they are really weak.
  Then they will want to worship your name!
17 God, scare those people
  and make them ashamed forever.
  Disgrace them and destroy them.
18 Then they will know that you are God.
  They will know your name is Yahweh.
  They will know that you, God Most-High,
    are the God of the whole world!

Psalm 84

To the director, ⌊accompanied⌋ by the
Gittith.* A song of praise from
the Korah family.*

1 Lord All-Powerful, your temple*
    is really lovely.
2 Lord, I can't wait to enter your temple.
  I'm so excited!
  Every part of me wants to be with
    the Living God.
3 Lord All-Powerful, my King, my God,
  even the birds have found a home
    in your temple.
  Those birds make their nests near your altar.
  And there they have their babies.
4 People living at your temple are very happy.
  They always praise you.
                                           SELAH*
5 People with songs in their heart who have
    decided to come to your temple are
    very happy!
6 They travel through Baca Valley which God
    has made like a spring.
  Autumn rains form pools of water.*

Agreement Literally, "Proof." The flat stones with the Ten Commandments written on them were proof of the Agreement between God and Israel.
descendants A person's children and their future families.
Selah This word is for the musicians. It probably means the singers should pause here or the music should be louder here.
tumbleweed A large weed with short roots. When a strong wind blows, the dry weed is pulled loose and blown away.

director Or, "performer."
by the Gittith Or, "on the Gittith." This might be a type of instrument, or it might be a performer in the temple orchestra, possibly Obed Edom from Gath (the Gittite).
temple Or, "dwellings."
the Autumn rains forming pools of water Or "The Teacher gives blessings." This might be a different way to say that God is our teacher and that he gives us many blessings.

7 The people travel from town to town,*
    on their way to Zion,
    where they will meet with God.
8 Lord God All-Powerful, listen to my prayer.
    God of Jacob,* listen to me.
                                    SELAH*
9 God, protect our protector.*
    Be kind to your chosen king.*
10 One day in your temple is better
    than a thousand days in any other place.
    Standing at the gate of my God's house
    is better than living in the house
    of a wicked man.
11 The Lord is our protector and glorious king.*
    God blesses us with kindness and glory.
    The Lord gives every good thing
    to people who follow and obey him.
12 Lord All-Powerful,
    people who trust you are truly happy!

Psalm 85

To the director.* A song of praise from the Korah family.

1 Lord, be kind to your country.
    Jacob's ₁people are exiles*
    in a foreign country.₁
    Bring the exiles back to their country.
2 Lord, forgive your people!
    Erase their sins!
                                    SELAH*
3 Lord, stop being angry.
    Don't be mad.
4 Our God and Savior, stop being angry at us,
    and accept us again.
5 Will you be angry at us forever?
6 Please, make us live again!
    Make your people happy.
7 Lord, save us
    and show us that you love us.
8 I heard what God said. The Lord said
    that there would be peace for his people.

His followers will have peace,
    if they don't go back to their foolish
    way of living.
9 God will soon save his followers.
    We will soon live with honor on our land.
10 God's true love will meet his followers.
    Goodness and peace will greet them
    with a kiss.
11 People on earth will be loyal to God,
    And God in heaven will be good to them.*
12 The Lord will give us many good things.
    The ground will grow many good crops.
13 Goodness will go in front of God,
    and prepare the way for him.

Psalm 86

David's prayer.

1 I am a poor, helpless man.
    Lord, please listen to me
    and answer my prayer.
2 Lord, I am your follower,
    please protect me!
    I am your servant.
    You are my God.
    I trust you.
    So save me.
3 My Master, be kind to me.
    I have been praying to you all day.
4 Master, I put my life in your hands.
    Make me happy, I am your servant.
5 Master, you are good and merciful.
    Your people call to you for help.
    You really love those people.
6 Lord, hear my prayer.
    Listen to my prayer for mercy.
7 Lord, I am praying to you
    in my time of trouble.
    I know you will answer me!
8 There is none like you, God.
    No person can do what you have done.
9 Master, you made every person.
    I hope they will all come worship you.
    I hope they all honor your name.
10 God, you are great!
    You do amazing things!
    You, and you only, are God!
11 Lord, teach me your ways,
    and I will live and obey your truths.
    Help me make worshiping your name
    the most important thing in my life.

---

town to town, Or, "wall to wall."
Jacob Another name for Israel. See Gen. 32:22-28.
Selah This word is for the musicians. It probably means the singers should pause here or the music should be louder here.
protector Literally, "shield." This probably means the king. This might also be "God, our Shield, look!"
chosen king Literally, "anointed person."
protector and glorious king Literally, "sun and shield."
director Or, "performer."
exiles People who have been forced to leave their country and live in some other country.

People on earth ... to them Literally, "Loyalty will sprout from the ground. Goodness will look down from the sky."

12 God my Master, I praise you
   with all my whole heart.
   I will honor your name forever!
13 God, you have such great love for me.
   You save me from the place of death below.
14 Proud men are attacking me, God.
   A gang of cruel men are trying to kill me.
   And those men don't respect you.
15 Master, you are a kind and merciful God.
   You are patient, loyal, and full of love.
16 God, show that you hear me
   and be kind to me.
   I am your servant.
   Give me strength.
   I am your servant.
   Save me,
17 God, give me a sign to show
   that you will help me.
   My enemies will see that sign
   and they will be disappointed.
   That will show that you heard my prayer
   and that you will help me.

Psalm 87

A song of praise from the Korah family.

1 God built his temple
   on the holy hills ⌊of Jerusalem⌋.
2 The Lord loves Zion's gates
   more than any other place in Israel.
3 City of God, people say wonderful things
   about you.
                                    SELAH*
4 ⌊God keeps a list of all of his people.⌋
   Some of them live in Egypt* and Babylon.
   Some of them were born in Philistia, Tyre,
   and even Ethiopia.
5 God knows every person born on Zion.
   God Most-High built that city.
6 God keeps a list about all his people.
   God knows where each person was born.
                                    SELAH*
7 ⌊God's people go to Jerusalem
   to celebrate the special holidays.⌋
   They are very happy.
   They are singing and dancing.
   They say,
   "All good things come from Jerusalem."

Psalm 88

A song of praise from the Korah family. To the director.* About a painful sickness. A maskil* from Heman the Ezrahite.

1 Lord God, you are my Savior.
   I have been praying to you day and night.
2 Please pay attention to my prayers.
   Listen to my prayers for mercy.
3 My soul has had enough of this pain!
   I will soon die.
4 People already treat me like a dead man,
   like a man too weak to live.
5 Look for me among the dead people.
   I am like a dead body lying in the grave,
   one of the dead people you forgot,
   cut off from you and your care.
6 You put me in that hole in the ground.
   Yes, you put me in that dark place.
7 God, you were angry at me,
   and you punished me.
                                    SELAH*
8 My friends have left me.
   They all avoid me like a person
   no one wants to touch.
   I am locked in the house
   and I can't go out.
9 My eyes hurt from ⌊crying about⌋
   all my suffering.
   Lord, I pray to you constantly!
   I lift my arms in prayer to you.
10 Lord, do you do miracles for dead people?
   Do ghosts rise up and praise you?
   No!
                                    SELAH*
11 Dead people in their graves
   can't talk about your love.
   Dead people in the world of the dead
   can't talk about your loyalty.
12 Dead people lying in darkness
   can't see the amazing things you do.
   Dead people in the World of the Forgotten
   can't talk about your goodness.
13 Lord, I am asking you to help me!
   Early each morning I pray to you.
14 Lord, why have you abandoned me?
   Why do you refuse to listen to me?
15 Since I was young, I was weak and sick.
   I have suffered your anger, I am helpless.

Selah This word is for the musicians. It probably means the singers should pause here or the music should be louder here.
Egypt Literally, "Rahab." This names means the "Dragon." It became a popular name for Egypt.
director Or, "performer."
maskil The exact meaning of "maskil" is not clear. It might mean "a poem of meditation," "a poem of instruction," or "a skillfully-written poem."

16 Lord, you were angry at me,
 and the punishment is killing me.
17 The aches and pains are always with me.
 I feel like I am drowning
 in my aches and pains.
18 And Lord, you forced all my friends
 and loved ones to leave me.
 Only darkness stayed to be with me.

Psalm 89

A maskil* from Ethan the Ezrahite.

1 I will sing forever about the Lord's love.
 I will sing about his loyalty
 forever and ever!
2 Lord, I truly believe your love lasts forever.
 Your loyalty continues like the skies!
3 God said,
 "I made an agreement with my chosen king.
 I made a promise to my servant, David:
4 David, I will make your family
 continue forever.
 I will make your kingdom continue
 forever and ever."
 SELAH*
5 Lord, you do amazing things.
 The heavens praise you for this.
 People can depend on you.
 The assembly of holy ones sing about this.
6 No one in heaven is equal to the Lord.
 None of the "gods" can compare to the Lord.
7 God meets together with the holy ones.
 Those angels are all around him.
 They fear and respect God.
 They stand in awe of him.
8 Lord God All-Powerful,
 there is no one like you.
 We can trust you completely.
9 You proudly rule the sea.
 You can calm its angry waves.
10 God, you defeated Rahab.*
 You scattered your enemies
 with your own powerful arm.
11 Everything in heaven and earth
 belong to you, God.
 You made the world and everything in it.

12 You created everything north and south.
 Mount Tabor and Mount Hermon
 sing praises to your name.
13 God, you have the power!
 Your power is great!
 The victory is yours!
14 Your kingdom is built on truth and justice.
 Love and faithfulness are servants
 before your throne.
15 God, your loyal followers are truly happy.
 They live in the light of your kindness.
16 Your name always makes them happy.
 They praise your goodness.
17 You are their amazing strength.
 Their power comes from you.
18 Lord, you are our Protector.
 The Holy One of Israel is our King.
19 You spoke to your followers in a vision
 and said,
 "I chose a young man from the crowd.
 And I made that young man important.
 I made that young soldier strong.
20 I found my servant David.
 And I anointed* him with my special oil.
21 I supported David with my right arm.
 And with my power, I made him strong.
22 The enemy could not defeat the chosen king.
 Wicked people could not defeat him.
23 I finished his enemies.
 I defeated the people who hated
 my chosen king.
24 I will always love and support
 my chosen king.
 I will always make him strong.
25 I put my chosen king in charge of the sea.
 He will control the rivers.
26 He will say to me,
 'You are my father.
 You are my God, my Rock,* my Savior.'
27 And I will make him my firstborn* son.
 He will be the great king on earth.
28 My love will protect the chosen king forever.
 My agreement with him will never end.
29 His family will continue forever,
 his kingdom as long as the heavens.
30 If his descendants* quit following my law,
 and if they quit obeying my commands,
 then I will punish them.

maskil The exact meaning of "maskil" is not clear. It might mean "a poem of meditation," "a poem of instruction," or "a skillfully-written poem."
Selah This word is for the musicians. It probably means the singers should pause here or the music should be louder here.
Rahab A sea monster. Some ancient stories say the sea monster was an enemy of God.

anoint(ed) To pour olive oil on things or people to show that they were chosen by God for a special work or purpose.
Rock A name for God to show he is a strong place of safety.
firstborn The first child born into a family. The firstborn son was very important in ancient times.
descendants A person's children and their future families.

31 If the chosen king's descendants* break my
laws and ignore my commands,
32 then I will punish them very hard.
33 But I will never take my love away
from those people.
I will always be loyal to them.
34 I will not break my agreement with David.
I will not change our agreement.
35 By my holiness, I made a promise to him.
And I would not lie to David!
36 David's family will continue forever.
His kingdom will last as long as the sun.
37 It will continue forever, like the moon.
The skies are the proof of the agreement.
That agreement can be trusted."
SELAH*

38 But God, you became angry
at your chosen king,*
and you left him all alone.
39 You rejected your agreement.
You threw the king's crown into the dirt.
40 You pulled down the walls of the king's city.
You destroyed all his fortresses.
41 People passing by steal things from him.
His neighbors laugh at him.
42 You made all the king's enemies happy.
You let his enemies win the war.
43 God, you helped them defend themselves.
You did not help your king win the battle.
44 You didn't let him win.
You threw his throne to the ground.
45 You cut his life short.
You shamed him.
SELAH*

46 Lord, how long will this continue?
Will you ignore us forever?
Will your anger burn like a fire forever?
47 Remember how short my life is:
You created us to live a short life,
and then die.
48 No person will live and never die.
No person will escape the grave.
SELAH*

49 God, where is the love you showed
in the past?
You promised David that you would be loyal
to his family.
50-51 Master, please remember how people
insulted your servant.
Lord, I had to listen to all those insults
from your enemies.

Those people insulted your chosen king!
52 Bless the Lord forever!

Amen and Amen!*

BOOK 4

Psalm 90

The prayer of Moses, the man of God.

1 Master, you have been our home
forever and ever.
2 God, you were God
before the mountains were born
and the earth and the world were made.
God, you have always been,
and you will always be, God!
3 You bring people into this world.
And you change them into dust again.
4 To you, a thousand years is like yesterday,
like last night.
5 You sweep us away.
Our life is like a dream,
and in the morning,
we are gone.
We are like grass.
6 In the morning the grass grows,
and in the evening it is dry and dying.
7 God, we are destroyed when you are angry.
Your anger scares us!
8 You know about all our sins.
God, you see every one of our secret sins.
9 Your anger can end our life.
Our lives fade away like a whisper.
10 We live, maybe 70 years.
And if we are strong, maybe 80 years.
Our lives are filled with hard work and pain.
Then suddenly, our lives are finished!
And we fly away.
11 No person really knows the full power
of your anger, God.
But God, our fear and respect for you
is as great as your anger.
12 Teach us how short our lives really are
so we can become really wise.
13 Lord, always come back to us.
Be kind to your servants.
14 Fill us with your love every morning.
Let us be happy and enjoy our lives.

Selah This word is for the musicians. It probably means the singers should pause here or the music should be louder here.
chosen king Literally, "anointed person."

Amen A Hebrew word meaning "truly," "indeed." It shows that a person agrees with what has been said.
man of God Another name for a prophet.

15 You gave us much sadness and troubles
    in our lives.
    Now make us happy.
16 Let your servants see the wonderful things
    you can do for them.
    And let their children see your glory.
17 May our God and Master be kind to us.
    May the things we do provide for us,
    and may God provide everything we do.*

Psalm 91

1 You can go to God Most-High to hide.
   You can go to the God All-Powerful
       for protection.
2 I say to the Lord,
   "You are my place of safety, my fortress.
   My God, I trust you."
3 God will save you from hidden dangers
       and dangerous diseases.
4 You can go to God for protection.
   He will protect you
       like a bird spreading its wings
           over its babies.
   God will be like a shield and a wall protecting
       you.
5 You will have nothing to fear at night.
   And you won't be afraid
       of enemy arrows during the day.
6 You will not be afraid of diseases
       that come in the dark,
       or terrible sicknesses that come at noon.
7 You will defeat 1,000 enemies.
   Your own right hand will defeat
       10,000 enemy soldiers.
   Your enemies will not even touch you!
8 Just look, and you will see that those
       wicked people are punished!
9 Why? Because you trust the Lord.
   You made God Most-High your safe place.
10 Nothing bad will happen to you.
   There will be no diseases in your home.
11 God will command his angels for you,
   and they will protect you wherever you go.
12 Their hands will catch you,
   so that you will not hit your foot on a rock.
13 You will have power to walk on lions
       and poisonous snakes.
14 The Lord says,
   "If a person trusts me, I will save him.
   I will protect my followers
       who worship my name.
15 My followers will call to me for help,
       and I will answer them.
   I will be with them when they have trouble.
   I will rescue them and honor them.
16 I will give my followers a long life.
   And I will save them."

Psalm 92

A song of praise for the Sabbath. *

1 It is good to praise the Lord. God Most-High,
       it is good to praise your name.
2 It is good to sing
       about your love in the morning,
       and about your faithfulness at night.
3 God, it is good to play music for you
       on ten-stringed instruments,
           harps, and lyres.*
4 Lord, you make us truly happy
       with the things you did.
   We gladly sing about those things.
5 Lord, you did such great things.
   Your thoughts are too hard for us to
       understand.
6 Compared to you,
       people are like stupid animals.
   We are like fools
       who can't understand anything.
7 Wicked people live and die like weeds.
   And the worthless things they do
       will be destroyed forever.
8 But Lord, you will be honored forever.
9 Lord, all your enemies will be destroyed.
   All those people who do bad things
       will be destroyed.
10 But you will make me strong.
   I will be like a ram with strong horns.
   ⌊You chose me for my special work;⌋
       you poured your refreshing oil over me.
11 I see my enemies around me.
   They are like huge bulls ready to
       attack me.
   I hear what they are saying about me.
12-13 Good people are like cedar trees of Lebanon
       planted in the Lord's temple.
   Good people are like budding palm trees
       blossoming in the courtyard
           of the temple of our God.

May our God ... do Or, "May the things we make with our hands establish us, and may He establish the things we make with our hands."

Sabbath Saturday, a special day of rest and worship for Jews.
lyre(s) An instrument with several strings, like a harp.

14 Even when they are old,
they will continue producing fruit
like young, healthy trees.
15 They are there to show everyone
that the Lord is good.*
He is my Rock,*
and he does nothing wrong.*

Psalm 93

1 The Lord is King.
He wears majesty and strength like clothes.
He is ready,
so the whole world is safe.
It will not be shaken *(destroyed)*.
2 God, your kingdom has continued forever.
God, you have lived forever!
3 Lord, the sound of the rivers is very loud.
The crashing waves are very loud.
4 The crashing waves of the sea
are loud and powerful.
But the Lord above is even more powerful.
5 Lord, your laws will continue forever.*
Your holy temple will stand for a long time.

Psalm 94

1 Lord, you are a God that punishes people.
You are a God who comes
and brings punishment to people.
2 You are the judge of the whole earth.
Give proud people the punishment they
deserve.
3 Lord, how long will wicked people
have their fun?
How much longer, Lord?
4 How much longer will those criminals
brag about the bad things they did?
5 Lord, they hurt your people.
They made your people suffer.
6 Those bad people kill widows
and visitors living in our country.
They murder children that have no parents.
7 And they say the Lord does not see them
doing those bad things!
They say the God of Israel doesn't know
what is happening.

8 You bad people are foolish.
When will you learn your lesson?
You evil people are so stupid!
You must try to understand.
9 God made our ears,
so surely he ₁has ears too,
and₁ can hear what is happening!
God made our eyes,
so surely he ₁has eyes too,
and₁ can see what is happening!
10 God will discipline those people.
God will teach people what they should do.
11 God knows what people are thinking.
God knows people are like a puff of wind.
12 The man that the Lord disciplines
will be very happy.
God will teach that person
the right way of living.
13 God, you will help that person stay calm
when trouble comes.
You will help him stay calm
until the evil people are put in their grave.
14 The Lord will not leave his people.
He will not leave his people without help.
15 Justice will return,
and it will bring fairness.
And then there will be good, honest people.
16 No person helped me fight
against the evil people.
No person stood with me to fight
against the people who do bad things.
17 And if the Lord had not helped me,
I would have been silenced!
18 I know I was ready to fall,
but the Lord supported his follower.
19 I was very worried and upset.
But Lord, you comforted me
and made me happy!
20 God, you don't help crooked judges.
Those bad judges use the law
to make life hard for the people.
21 Those judges attack good people.
They say that innocent people are guilty
and kill them.
22 But the Lord is my place of safety
high on the mountain.
God my Rock,* is my safe place!
23 God will punish those evil judges
for the bad things they did.
God will destroy them because they sinned.
The Lord our God will destroy
those evil judges.

good This is a word play. The Hebrew word means "straight"
(like the trees) and "good, honest."
Rock A name for God to show he is a strong place of safety.
he ... wrong Or, "There is no crookedness in him."
your laws will continue forever Or, "your Agreement can
really be trusted."

Psalm 95

1 Come, let us praise the Lord!
   Let's shout praises to the Rock,*
       who saves us.
2 Let's sing songs of thanks to the Lord.
   Let's sing happy songs of praise to him.
3 Why? Because the Lord is a great God!
   He is the Great King ruling over
       all the other "gods."
4 The deepest caves and the highest mountains
       belong to the Lord.
5 The ocean is his—he created it.
   God made the dry land with his own hands.
6 Come, let's bow down and worship him!
   Let's praise the God who made us!
7 He is our God, and we are his people.
   We are his sheep today—
       if we listen to his voice.
8 God says,
   "Don't be stubborn,
       like you were at Meribah,*
       like you were at Massah* in the desert.
9 Your ancestors* tested me.
   They tested me,
       but then they saw what I could do!
10 I was patient with those people for 40 years.
   And I know that they are not faithful.
   Those people refused to follow my teachings.
11 So I was angry, and I promised that
       they would not enter my land of rest.

Psalm 96

1 Sing a new song about the new things
       that the Lord has done!
   Let the whole world sing to the Lord.
2 Sing to the Lord!
       Bless his name!
   Tell the good news!
   Tell about him saving us every day!
3 Tell people that God is truly wonderful.
   Tell people everywhere about the amazing
       things God does.
4 The Lord is great and worthy of praise.
   He is more awesome than any
       of the "gods."
5 All of the "gods" in other nations
       are only statues.
   But the Lord made the heavens.
6 There is a beautiful glory
       shining in front of him.
   There is strength and beauty
       in God's holy temple.
7 Families and nations, sing songs of praise and
       glory to the Lord.
8 Praise the Lord's name.
   Get your offerings,
       and go to the temple.
9 Worship the Lord in his beautiful temple.
   Worship the Lord, every person on earth.
10 Announce to the nations
       that the Lord is King!
   So the world will not be destroyed.
   The Lord will rule the people fairly.
11 Be happy, heavens!
   Rejoice, earth!
   Sea and everything in it, shout with joy!
12 Fields and everything growing on them,
       be happy!
   Trees in the forest, sing and be happy!
13 Be happy because the Lord is coming.
   The Lord is coming to rule* the world.
   He will rule the world with justice
       and fairness.

Psalm 97

1 The Lord rules, and the earth is happy.
   All the faraway lands are happy.
2 Thick dark clouds surround the Lord.
   Goodness and justice make his kingdom
       strong.
3 A fire goes in front of the Lord
       and destroys his enemies.
4 His lightning flashes in the sky.
   The people see it and are afraid.
5 The mountains melt like wax
       before the Lord.
   They melt in front of the Master of the earth.
6 Skies, tell about his goodness!
   Let every person see God's glory!
7 People worship their idols.
   They brag about their "gods."
   But those people will be embarrassed.

Rock A name for God to show he is a strong place of safety.
Meribah, Massah See Ex. 17:1-7.
ancestors Literally, "fathers," meaning a person's parents, grandparents, and all the people they are descended from.
rule Or "judge."

Their "gods" will bow down
and worship the Lord.
8 Zion,* listen and be happy!
Cities of Judah, be happy!
Why? Because the Lord makes wise
decisions.
9 Lord Most-High, you really are
the ruler of the earth.
You are much better than the other "gods."
10 People who love the Lord hate evil.
So God saves his followers.
God saves his followers from evil people.
11 Light and happiness shine on good people.
12 Good people, be happy in the Lord!
Honor his holy name!

Psalm 98

A song of praise.

1 Sing a new song to the Lord
because he has done new
and amazing things!
2 His holy right arm
brought him victory again.
3 The Lord showed the nations
his power to save.
The Lord showed them his goodness.
4 His followers remembered God's loyalty
to the people of Israel.
The people in faraway lands saw
our God's power to save.
5 Every person on earth,
shout with joy to the Lord.
Quickly, start singing songs of praise!
6 Harps, praise the Lord.
Music from the harps, praise him.
7 Blow the pipes and horns,
and shout for joy to the Lord our King!
8 Let the sea, and the earth,
and everything in them sing loudly.
9 Rivers, clap your hands!
All together now, mountains sing out!
10 Sing before the Lord
because he is coming to rule* the world.
He will rule the world fairly.
He will rule the people with goodness.

Psalm 99

1 The Lord is King.
So let the nations shake with fear.
God sits as King above the Cherub angels.*
So let the world shake with fear.
2 The Lord in Zion* is great!
He is the great leader over all people.
3 Let all the people praise your name.
God's name is awesome.
God is holy.
4 The Powerful King loves justice.
God, you made goodness.
You brought goodness and fairness
to Jacob *(Israel)*.
5 Praise the Lord our God,
and worship his holy footstool.*
6 Moses and Aaron were some of his priests.
And Samuel was one of the men
who called on his name.
They prayed to the Lord,
and he answered them.
7 God spoke from the tall cloud.
They obeyed his commands.
And God gave them the Law.
8 Lord our God, you answered their prayers.
You showed them
that you are a forgiving God and
that you punish people
for the bad things they do.
9 Praise the Lord our God.
Bow down toward his holy mountain
and worship him.
The Lord our God is truly holy!

Psalm 100

A song of thanks.

1 Earth, sing to the Lord!
2 Be happy while you serve the Lord!
Come before the Lord with happy songs!
3 Know that the Lord is God.
He made us.
We are his people,
We are his sheep.
4 Come into his city with songs of thanks.
Come into his temple with songs of praise.
Honor him and bless his name.

Zion The southeast part of the mountain Jerusalem is built on. Sometimes it means the people of God living in Jerusalem.
rule Or, "judge."
Cherub angels Special angels from God. Statues of these angels were on top of the Box of the Agreement.
footstool This probably means the temple.

⁵ The Lord is good!
  His love is forever.
  We can trust him forever and ever!

Psalm 101

A song of David.*

¹ I will sing about love and fairness.
  Lord, I will sing to you.
² I will carefully live a pure life.
  I will live a pure life in my house.
  Lord, when will you come to me?
³ I will not have any idols* in front of me.
  I hate people turning against you like that.
  I will not do that!
⁴ I will be honest.
  I will not do evil things.
⁵ If any person secretly says bad things
      about his neighbor,
  I will stop that person.
  I will not allow people to be proud
      and think they are better than other people.
⁶ I will look throughout the country
      for people who can be trusted.
  And I will let only those people serve me.
  Only people who live pure lives
      can be my servants.
⁷ I will not let liars live in my house.
  I will not let liars stay near me.
⁸ I will always destroy bad people
      living in this country.
  I will force the evil people
      to leave the Lord's city.

Psalm 102

A prayer of a person who is suffering. This is for when he feels weak and wants to tell his complaints to the Lord.

¹ Lord, hear my prayer.
  Listen to my cry for help.
² Lord, don't turn away from me when I have troubles.
  Listen to me.
  When I cry for help, quickly answer me.
³ My life is passing away like smoke.
  My life is like a fire slowly burning out.
⁴ My strength is gone—
  I am like dry, dying grass.
  I even forget to eat my food.
⁵ Because of my sadness, I am losing weight.*
⁶ I am lonely
      like an owl living in the desert.
  I am alone like an owl
      living in old ruined buildings.
⁷ I can't sleep.
  I am like a lonely bird on a roof.
⁸ My enemies always insult me.
  They make fun of me and curse me.
⁹ My great sadness is my only food.
  My tears fall into my drinks.
¹⁰ Why? Because you are angry at me, Lord.
  You lifted me up
      and then you threw me away.
¹¹ My life is almost finished,
      like the long shadows at the end of the day.
  I am like dry and dying grass.
¹² But Lord, you will live forever!
  Your name will continue forever and ever!
¹³ You will rise and comfort Zion.*
  The time is coming
      when you will be kind to Zion.
¹⁴ Your servants love her *(Jerusalem's)* stones.
  They like that city.
¹⁵ People will worship the Lord's name.
  God, all the kings on earth will honor you.
¹⁶ The Lord will build Zion again.
  People will again see her glory.
¹⁷ God will answer the prayers
      of the people he left alive.
  God will listen to their prayers.
¹⁸ Write these things for the future generation.
  And in the future, those people
      will praise the Lord.
¹⁹ The Lord will look down
      from his Holy Place above.
  The Lord will look down at the earth
      from heaven.
²⁰ And he will hear the prisoner's prayers.
  He will free the people
      who were condemned to die.
²¹ Then people in Zion will tell about the Lord.
  They will praise his name in Jerusalem.

A song of David Or, "A song dedicated to David."
idols Or "terrible {things}."

I am losing weight Literally, "my bones stick to my skin."
Zion The southeast part of the mountain Jerusalem is built on. Sometimes it means the people of God living in Jerusalem.

²² Nations will be gathered together.
　　Kingdoms will come to serve the Lord.
²³ My strength failed me.
　　My life is cut short.
²⁴ So I said,
　　"Don't let me die while I am still young.
　　God, you will live forever and ever!
²⁵ Long ago, you made the world.
　　You made the sky with your own hands!
²⁶ The world and sky will end,
　　but you will live forever!
　　They will wear out like clothes.
　　And, like clothes, you will change them.
　　They will all be changed.
²⁷ But you, God, never change.
　　You will live forever!
²⁸ We are your servants ₍today₎.
　　Our children will live here.
　　And even their descendants will be here
　　to worship you.

Psalm 103

A song of David.*

¹ My soul, praise the Lord!
　　Every part of me, praise his holy name!
² My soul, praise the Lord!
　　And don't forget that he is truly kind.
³ God forgives us for all the sins we do.
　　He heals all our sicknesses.
⁴ God saves our life from the grave.
　　And he gives us love and compassion.
⁵ God gives us plenty of good things.
　　He makes us young again,
　　like an eagle.
⁶ The Lord is fair.
　　God brings justice to people
　　that have been hurt by other people.
⁷ God taught his laws to Moses.
　　God let Israel see the powerful things
　　he can do!
⁸ The Lord is compassionate and merciful.
　　God is patient and full of love.
⁹ The Lord does not always criticize.
　　The Lord does not stay angry at us forever.
¹⁰ We sinned against God but he didn't give us
　　the punishment we deserved.

¹¹ God's love for his followers
　　is as high above us
　　as heaven is above the earth.
¹² And God has taken our sins
　　as far away from us
　　as the east is from the west.
¹³ The Lord is as kind to his followers
　　as a father is to his children.
¹⁴ God knows all about us.
　　God knows we are made from dust.
¹⁵ God knows our lives are short.
　　He knows our lives are like grass.
¹⁶ God knows we are like a little wildflower.
　　That flower grows quickly.
　　Then the hot wind blows
　　and the flower dies.
　　Soon, you can't even tell
　　where the flower was growing.
¹⁷ But the Lord has always loved his followers.
　　And he will continue to love his followers
　　forever and ever!
　　God will be good to their children
　　and to their children's children.
¹⁸ God is good to people
　　who obey his Agreement.
　　God is good to people
　　who obey his commands.
¹⁹ God's throne is in heaven.
　　And he rules over everything.
²⁰ Angels, praise the Lord!
　　You angels are the powerful soldiers
　　who obey God's commands.
　　You listen to God and obey his commands.
²¹ Praise the Lord, all his armies.*
　　You are his servants.
　　You do the things that God wants.
²² The Lord made everything in every place.
　　God rules everything in every place.
　　And all those things should praise the Lord!
　　My soul, praise the Lord!

A song of David Or, "A song dedicated to David."

armies This word can mean, "armies," "angels," or the "stars and planets." This word is part of the name translated, "Lord All-Powerful!." It shows God is in control of all the powers in the universe.

Psalm 104

1 My soul, praise the Lord!
   Lord my God, you are very great!
   You are clothed with glory and honor.
2 You wear light like a person wears a robe.
   You spread the skies like a curtain.
3 God, you built your home above them.*
   You use the thick clouds like a chariot,
   and ride across the sky
       on the wings of the wind.
4 God, you made your angels like the wind,*
   and your servants* like fire.

5 God, you built the earth on its foundations,
   so it will never be destroyed.
6 You covered it with water like a blanket.
   The water covered the mountains.
7 But you gave the command,
   and the water rushed away.
   God, you shouted at the water,
   and the water rushed away.
8 The water flowed down from the mountains,
   and into the valleys,
       and then to the places you made for it.
9 You set the limits for the seas.
   And the water will never again
       rise to cover the earth.

10 God, you cause water to flow
    from the springs into the streams.
    It flows down through the mountain streams.
11 The streams water all the wild animals.
    Even the wild donkeys come there to drink.
12 Wild birds come to live by the pools,
    They sing in the branches of nearby trees.
13 God sends rain down onto the mountains.
    The things God made give the earth
        everything it needs.
14 God makes grass grow to feed the animals.
    He gives us the plants
        that we work to grow.
    Those plants give us food from the earth.

15 God gives us
    the wine that makes us happy.
    the oil that makes our skin soft.*
    and the food that makes us strong.
16 The great cedar trees of Lebanon
    belong to the Lord.
    The Lord planted those trees,
    and he gives them the water they need.
17 Birds make their nests in those trees.
    Large storks live in the fir trees.
18 The high mountains are a home
    for wild goats.
    The large rocks are hiding places
    for rock-badgers.

19 God, you gave us the moon
    to show us when the holidays begin.
    And the sun always knows when to set.
20 You made darkness to be the night—
    the time when wild animals come out
        and roam around.
21 Lions roar as they attack,
    as if they are asking God
        for the food he gives them.
22 Then the sun rises, and the animals
    go back to their homes and rest.
23 Then people go out to do their work.
    And they work until evening.

24 Lord, you have done many wonderful things.
    The earth is full of the things you made.
    ⌊We see⌋ your wisdom in everything you do.
25 Look at the ocean. It is so big!
    And so many things live there!
    There are creatures large and small—
        too many to count!
26 Ships travel over the ocean while
    Leviathan,* the sea creature you made,
        plays there in the sea.

27 God, all of these things depend on you.
    You give them food at the right time.
28 God, you give all the living things
    the food they eat.
    You open your hands, filled with good food,
    and they eat until they are full.
29 And when you turn away from them,
    they become frightened.

---

above them Literally, "on the water above." This is like the picture of the world in Genesis 1. There, the sky was like a bowl turned upside down on the earth. There was water below the bowl and water above it.

God, you made your angels like the wind Or "You made your messengers spirits."

angels ... servants This probably is talking about the two kinds of angels, the Cherub angels and the Seraph angels. The name Seraph is like a Hebrew word meaning, "fire."

makes our skin soft Literally, "makes our face shine." This can also mean, "make us happy."

Leviathan This might mean any large sea animal, like a whale. But it probably means "the sea monster," the "dragon," "Rahab." This creature represents the great power of the ocean, the power that God controls.

Their spirits leave them;
    they grow weak and die;
    and their bodies become dust again.
30 But when you send out your Spirit, Lord,
    they become healthy!
    And you make the land like new again!
31 May the Lord's glory continue forever!
    May the Lord enjoy the things he made.
32 The Lord can just look at the earth,
    and it will shake.
    He can touch the mountains
    and smoke will begin to rise from them.
33 All my life I will sing to the Lord.
    I will sing praises to the Lord while I live.
34 I hope the things I said will make him happy.
    I am happy with the Lord.
35 May sin disappear from the earth.
    May wicked people be gone forever.

My soul, praise the Lord!
    Praise the Lord!

Psalm 105

1 Thank the Lord.
    Worship his name.
    Tell the nations about the wonderful things
    he does.
2 Sing to the Lord.
    Sing praises to him.
    Tell about all the amazing things he does.
3 Be proud of the Lord's holy name.
    You people came looking for the Lord.
    Be happy!
4 Go to the Lord for strength.
    Always go to him for help.
5 Remember the amazing things he does.
    Remember his miracles and wise decisions.
6 You are descendants* of his servant Abraham.
    You are descendants of Jacob,
    the man God chose.
7 The Lord is our God.
    The Lord rules the whole world.*
8 Remember God's Agreement* forever.
    Remember his commands for 1,000
    generations!
9 God made an Agreement with Abraham.
    God made a promise to Isaac.
10 Then he made it a law for Jacob.
    God made his Agreement with Israel.
    It will continue forever!
11 God said,
    "I will give you the land of Canaan.
    That land will belong to you."
12 God made that promise
    when Abraham's family was small.
    They were only strangers spending time there.
13 They traveled from nation to nation,
    from one kingdom to another.
14 But God did not let people mistreat them.
    God warned kings not to hurt them.
15 God said,
    "Don't hurt my chosen people.
    Don't do anything bad to my prophets.*"
16 God caused a famine* in that country.
    People did not have enough food to eat.
17 But God sent a man named Joseph
    to go ahead of them.
    Joseph was sold like a slave.
18 They tied a rope around Joseph's feet.
    They put an iron ring around his neck.
19 Joseph was a slave until the things he said
    really happened.
    The Lord's message proved
    that Joseph was right.
20 So the king of Egypt set him free.
    That nation's leader let him out of jail.
21 He put Joseph in charge of his house.
    Joseph took care of everything he owned.
22 Joseph gave instructions to the other leaders.
    Joseph taught the older men.
23 Then Israel came to Egypt.
    Jacob lived in Ham's country.*
24 Jacob's family became very large.
    They became more powerful
    than their enemies.
25 So the Egyptians began to hate
    Jacob's family.
    They made plans against their slaves.
26 So God sent his servant, Moses,
    and Aaron, God's chosen priest.

---

descendants A person's children and their future families.
The Lord rules the whole world Literally, "His commands are in the whole earth."
Agreement Literally, "Proof." The flat stones with the Ten Commandments written on them were proof of the Agreement between God and Israel.

prophets A person called by God to be a special servant. God used dreams and visions to show them things to teach the people.
famine A time when there is not enough rain for crops to grow. People and animals die without enough food or water.
Ham's country Or, "Egypt." The Bible teaches that the Egyptians were descendants of Ham. See Gen. 10:6-20.

27 God used Moses and Aaron
to do many miracles in Ham's country.
28 God sent the very dark darkness,
but the Egyptians did not listen to him.
29 So God changed the water into blood,
and all their fish died.
30 Their country was filled with frogs.
Frogs were even in the king's bedroom.
31 God gave the command,
and the flies and gnats came.
They were everywhere!
32 God made the rain become hail.
Lightning struck throughout their country.
33 God destroyed their vines and fig trees.
God destroyed every tree in their country.
34 God gave the command,
and the locusts and grasshoppers came.
There were too many to count!
35 The locusts and grasshoppers
ate all the plants in the country.
They ate all the crops in the fields.
36 And then God killed every firstborn*
in their country.
God killed their oldest sons.
37 Then God took his people out of Egypt.
They brought gold and silver with them.
None of God's people stumbled and fell.
38 Egypt was happy to see God's people go,
because they were afraid of God's people.
39 God spread out his cloud like a blanket.
God used his column of fire
to give his people light at night.
40 The people asked for food,
and God brought them quail.
God gave them plenty of bread from heaven.
41 God split the rock,
and water came bubbling out.
A river began flowing in the desert!
42 God remembered his holy promise.
God remembered the promise
he had made to his servant Abraham.
43 God brought his people out from Egypt.
The people came out rejoicing
and singing their happy songs!
44 Then God gave his people the country
where other people were living.
God's people got the things
other people had worked for.
45 Why did God do this?
So his people could obey his laws.
So they could carefully obey his teachings.
Praise the Lord!

Psalm 106

1 Praise the Lord!
Thank the Lord because he is good!
God's love is forever!
2 No person can describe
how great the Lord really is.
No person can praise God enough.
3 People who obey God's commands are happy.
Those people do good things all the time.
4 Lord, remember me when you are kind
to your people.
Remember to save me, too!
5 Lord, let me share in the good things
you do for your people.
Let me be happy with your people.
Let me be proud of you with your people.
6 We sinned just like our ancestors* sinned.
We were wrong, we did bad things!
7 Lord, our ancestors in Egypt learned nothing
from the miracles you did.
There by the Red Sea,
our ancestors turned against you.
8 But God saved our ancestors*
for his own name's sake.
God saved them to show his great power.
9 God gave the command,
and the Red Sea became dry.
God led our ancestors through the deep sea,
on land as dry as the desert.
10 God saved our ancestors from their enemies!
God rescued them from their enemies.
11 God covered their enemies with the sea.
Not one of their enemies escaped!
12 Then our ancestors* believed God.
They sang praises to him.
13 But our ancestors quickly forgot about the
things God did.
They did not listen to God's advice.
14 Our ancestors became hungry in the desert.
And they tested God in the wilderness.

---

firstborn The first child born into a family. The firstborn son was very important in ancient times.

ancestors Literally, "fathers," meaning a person's parents, grandparents, and all the people they are descended from.

15 But God gave our ancestors the things they
    asked for.
    But God also gave them a terrible disease.
16 The people became jealous of Moses.
    They became jealous of Aaron,
    the Lord's holy priest.
17 So God punished those jealous people.
    The ground opened up
    and swallowed Dathan.
    Then the ground closed up
    and covered Abiram's group.
18 Then a fire burned that mob of people.
    That fire burned those wicked people.
19 Those people made a golden calf
    at Mount Horeb.
    They worshiped a statue!
20 Those people traded their glorious God,
    for a statue of a grass-eating bull!
21 God saved our ancestors.*
    But they forgot all about him.
    They forgot about the God who did
    the miracles in Egypt.
22 God did amazing things in Ham's country.*
    God did awesome things near the Red Sea!
23 God wanted to destroy those people.
    But Moses stopped him.
    Moses was God's chosen servant.
    God was very angry,
    but Moses blocked the way
    so God did not destroy the people.*
24 But then those people refused to go
    into the wonderful land of Canaan.
    They did not believe God would help them
    defeat the people living in that land.
25 Our ancestors* refused to obey God!
26 So God swore that they would die
    in the desert.
27 God promised that he would let
    other people defeat their descendants.*
    God promised he would scatter our ancestors
    among the nations.

28 Then at Baal Peor,
    God's people joined in worshiping Baal.
    God's people [joined in the wild parties
    and] ate sacrifices to honor dead people.*
29 God became very angry at his people,
    and God made them become very sick.
30 But Phinehas prayed* to God,
    and God stopped the sickness.
31 God knew Phinehas did a very good thing.
    God will remember this forever and ever.
32 At Meribah, the people became angry.
    And they made Moses do something bad.
33 Those people made Moses very upset,
    so Moses spoke without stopping to think.
34 The Lord told the people to destroy
    the other nations living in Canaan.
    But the people of Israel did not obey God.
35 They mixed with the other people,
    and did what those people were doing.
36 Those people became a trap to God's people.
    God's people began worshiping the gods
    those other people worshiped.
37 God's people even killed their own children,
    and offered the children to those devils.
38 God's people killed innocent people.
    They killed their own children
    and offered them to those false gods.
39 So God's people became dirty with the sins of
    those other people.
    God's people were unfaithful to their God
    and did the things those other people did.
40 God became angry at his people.
    God was fed up with them!
41 God gave his people to other nations.
    God let their enemies rule over them.
42 The enemies of God's people controlled them
    and made life hard for them.
43 God saved his people many times.
    But they turned against God
    and did what they wanted to do.
    God's people did many, many bad things.
44 But whenever God's people were in trouble,
    [they always called to God for help].
    And God listened to their prayers every time.

ancestors Literally, "fathers," meaning a person's parents, grandparents, and all the people they are descended from.
Ham's country Or "Egypt." The Bible teaches that the Egyptians were descendants of Ham. See Gen. 10:6-20.
verse 23 Or, "God said he would destroy them. But Moses, his chosen one, stood in the breach and repelled his anger from destroying." This shows Moses was like a soldier who stood at a hole in a city wall defending the city {(Israel)} against enemy soldiers {(God's anger)}.
descendants A person's children and their future families.

dead people Or, "dead statues" or "lifeless gods." People often met together to eat meals at graves as a way to honor false gods and dead people.
prayed Or, "intervened, judged." Phinehas not only prayed to God, but he also did something to stop the people from doing these sins. See Num. 25:1-16.
Agreement Literally, "Proof." The flat stones with the Ten Commandments written on them were proof of the Agreement between God and Israel.

⁴⁵ God always remembered his Agreement*
and comforted them with his great love.
⁴⁶ Other nations took them as prisoners.
But God made them be kind to his people.
⁴⁷ The Lord our God saved us!
God brought us back from those nations
so we could praise his holy name,
so we could sing praises to him.
⁴⁸ Bless the Lord God of Israel.
God has always lived,
and he will live forever.
And all the people said,
"Amen!*
Praise the Lord!"

BOOK 5

Psalm 107

¹ Thank the Lord, because he is good!
His love is forever!
² That is what every person that the Lord has saved should say.
The Lord saved them from their enemy.
³ The Lord gathered his people together
from many different countries.
He brought them from east and west,
north and south.*
⁴ Some of them wandered in the dry desert.
They were looking for a place to live,
but they could not find a city.
⁵ They were hungry and thirsty
and growing weak.
⁶ Then they called to the Lord for help.
And he saved them from their troubles.
⁷ God led those people straight to the city
where they would live.
⁸ Thank the Lord for his love,
and for the amazing things
he does for people.
⁹ God satisfies the thirsty soul.
God fills the hungry soul with good things.
¹⁰ Some of God's people were prisoners,
locked behind bars in dark, dark prisons.
¹¹ Why? Because those people fought against
the things God said.

They refused to listen to the advice
from God Most-High.
¹² God made life hard for those people
because of the things they did.
They stumbled and fell,
and there was no person to help them.
¹³ Those people were in trouble,
so they called to the Lord for help.
And he saved them from their troubles.
¹⁴ God took them out of their dark prisons.
God broke the ropes they were tied with.
¹⁵ Thank the Lord for his love.
and for the amazing things
he does for people.
¹⁶ ⌊God helps us defeat our enemies.⌋
God can break down their bronze gates.
God can shatter the iron bars on their gates.
¹⁷ Some people let their sins and guilt
change them into foolish people.
¹⁸ Those people refused to eat,
and they almost died.
¹⁹ They were in trouble,
so they called to the Lord for help.
And he saved them from their troubles.
²⁰ God gave the command and healed them.
So those people were saved from the grave.
²¹ Thank the Lord for his love
and for the amazing things
he does for people.
²² Offer sacrifices* to the Lord
to thank him for all he did.
Gladly tell what the Lord has done.
²³ Some people sailed in boats across the sea.
Their job carried them across the great sea.
²⁴ Those people saw what the Lord can do.
They saw the amazing things he did at sea.
²⁵ God gave the command,
and a strong wind began to blow.
The waves became higher and higher.
²⁶ The waves lifted them high in the sky
and dropped them into the deep sea.
The storm was so dangerous
the men lost their courage.
²⁷ They were stumbling
and falling like drunk men.
Their skill as sailors was useless.

---

south Or, "the Sea." This is west of Israel and would refer to all the coastal areas around the Mediterranean Sea.

sacrifice(s) A sacrifice was a gift to God. Usually, it was a special animal that was killed and burned on an altar.

28 They were in trouble,
so they called to the Lord for help.
And he saved them from their troubles.
29 God stopped the storm.
He calmed the waves.
30 The sailors were happy
that the sea was calm.
And God led them safely
to the place they wanted to go.
31 Thank the Lord for his love,
and for the amazing things
he does for people.
32 Praise God in the great assembly.
Praise him when the older leaders meet
together.
33 God changed rivers into a desert.
God stopped springs from flowing.
34 God changed the fertile land
and it became worthless salty land.
Why? Because of the bad people
who were living in that place.
35 God changed the desert
and it became a land with pools of water.
God caused springs of water to flow
from dry ground.
36 God led hungry people to that good land.
And they built a city to live in.
37 Those people planted seeds in their fields.
They planted grapes in the field.
And they had a good harvest.
38 God blessed those people.
Their families grew.
They had many, many animals.
39 Because of disaster and troubles,
their families were small and weak.
40 God shamed and embarrassed their leaders.
God let them wander through the desert
where there are no roads.
41 But then God rescued those poor people
from their misery.
And now their families are large,
like flocks of sheep.
42 Good people see this,
and they are happy.
But wicked people see this,
and they don't know what to say.
43 If a person is wise,
he will remember these things.
Then he will begin to understand
what God's love really is.

Psalm 108

One of David's songs of praise.

1 God, I am ready, heart and soul,
to sing and play songs of praise.
2 Harps and lyres,* let's wake up the sun!*
3 Lord, we will praise you among the nations.
We will praise you among other people.
4 Lord, your love is higher than the skies.
Your love is higher than the highest clouds.
5 God, rise above the heavens!
Let all the world see your glory.
6 God, do this to save your friends.
Answer my prayer
and use your great power to save.
7 God spoke in his temple:*
"I will win the war
and be happy about the victory!
⌊I will divide this land among my people.⌋
I will give them Shechem.
I will give them Succoth Valley.
8 Gilead and Manasseh will be mine.
Ephraim will be my helmet.
Judah will be my scepter.*
9 Moab will be a bowl for washing my feet.
Edom will be a slave to carry my sandals.
I ⌊will defeat⌋ the Philistines
and shout about the victory."
10 Who will lead me into the enemy fortress?
Who will lead me to fight against Edom?
11 God, ⌊only you can help me do these things⌋.
But you left us!
You did not go with our army!
12 God, please help us defeat our enemy!
People can't help us!
13 Only God can make us strong.
God can defeat our enemies!

Psalm 109

To the director. One of David's
songs of praise.*

1 God, don't close your ears to my prayer!
2 Wicked people are telling lies about me.
They are saying things that are not true.

lyre(s) An instrument with several strings, like a harp.
let's wake up the sun! This song was probably written to be
sung at the temple when they offered the morning sacrifices.
in his temple Or "in his holiness."
scepter A special stick. Kings and leaders carried scepters to
show they were rulers.
director Or, "performer."

3 People are saying hateful things about me.
   People are attacking me for no reason.
4 I loved them,
   but they hate me.
   So now, I am praying to you, God.
5 I did good things to those people,
   but they are doing bad things to me.
   I loved them,
   but they hated me.
6 Punish my enemy for the bad things he did.
   Find a person to prove he is wrong.
7 Let the judge decide my enemy did wrong
   and that he is guilty.
   Let everything my enemy says
   only make things worse for him.
8 Let my enemy die soon.
   Let another person have his job.
9 Make my enemy's children orphans
   and his wife a widow.
10 Let them lose their home
   and become beggars.
11 Let the people my enemy owes money to
   take everything he owns.
   Let strangers take everything he worked for.
12 I hope no person is kind
   to my enemy.
   I hope no person shows mercy
   to his children.
13 Destroy my enemy completely.
   Let the next generation remove his name
   from everything.
14 I hope the Lord is reminded of the sins
   of my enemy's father.
   And I hope his mother's sins
   are never erased.
15 I hope the Lord remembers
   those sins forever.
   And I hope he forces people to forget
   my enemy completely.
16 Why? Because that evil man
   never did anything good.
   He never loved anyone
   He made life hard for poor, helpless people.
17 That evil man loved to ask for bad things
   to happen to other people.
   So let those bad things happen to him.
   That evil man never asked for good things
   to happen to people.
   So don't let good things happen to him.
18 Let curses be his clothes.
   Let curses be the water he drinks.
   Let curses be the oil on his body.

19 Let curses be the clothes they wrap around
   that evil man.
   And let curses be the belt around his waist.
20 I hope the Lord does all those things
   to my enemy.
   I hope the Lord does those things
   to all the people who are trying to kill me.
21 Lord, you are my Master.
   So treat me in a way that brings honor
   to your name.
   You have such great love,
   so save me.
22 I am only a poor, helpless man.
   I am truly sad, my heart is broken.
23 I feel like my life is over,
   like long shadows at the end of a day.
   I feel like a bug that someone brushed away.
24 My knees are weak because I am hungry.
   I am losing weight and becoming thin.
25 Bad people insult me.
   They look at me and shake their heads.
26 Lord my God, help me!
   Show your true love and save me!
27 Then those people will know
   that you helped me.
   Then they will know
   that it was your power that helped me.
28 Those bad people curse me,
   but you can bless me, Lord.
   They attacked me, so defeat them.
   Then I, your servant, will be happy.
29 Embarrass my enemies!
   Let them wear their shame like a coat.
30 I thank the Lord.
   I praise him in front of many people.
31 Why? Because the Lord stands by
   helpless people.
   God saves them from other people
   who try to condemn them to death.

Psalm 110

One of David's songs of praise.

1 The Lord said to my master,
   "Sit by me at my right side,
   while I put your enemies
   under your control.*"

and I ... control Or, "until I make your enemies a footstool for your feet."

² The Lord will help your kingdom grow.
　Your kingdom will start at Zion,*
　and ⌊it will grow until⌋ you rule
　your enemies in their own countries!
³ Your people will volunteer
　when you gather your army together.
　They will wear their special clothes
　and meet together early in the morning,
　Those young men will be
　⌊all around you⌋ like dew on the ground.*
⁴ The Lord made a promise,
　and he will not change his mind.
　"You are a priest forever—
　the kind of priest Melchizedek was."
⁵ My Master is at your right side.
　He will defeat the other kings when he
　becomes angry.
⁶ God will judge the nations.
　The ground will be covered
　with dead bodies.
　And God will punish the leaders
　of powerful nations.
⁷ The king will drink from a stream
　on the way.
　Then he will lift his head
　and become strong!*

Psalm 111*

¹ Praise the Lord!
　I thank the Lord with all my heart
　in the assembly where good people
　meet together.
² The Lord does wonderful things.
　People want those good things
　that come from God.
³ God does truly glorious
　and wonderful things.
　His goodness continues forever.

⁴ God does amazing things
　so that we will remember
　that the Lord is kind and merciful.
⁵ God gives food to his followers.
　God remembers his Agreement* forever.
⁶ The powerful things God did,
　showed his people that he was giving
　their land to them.
⁷ Everything God does is good and fair.
　All his commands can all be trusted.
⁸ God's commands will continue forever.
　God's reasons for giving those commands
　were honest and pure.
⁹ God saves his people.
　God made his Agreement
　to continue forever.
　God's name is amazing and holy.
¹⁰ Wisdom begins with fear and respect
　for God.
　People who obey God are very wise.
　Praises will be sung to God forever.

Psalm 112*

¹ Praise the Lord!
　A person who fears and respects the Lord
　will be very happy.
　That person loves God's commands.
² His descendants* will be great on earth.
　The descendants of good people
　will be truly blessed.
³ That person's family will be very rich.
　And his goodness will continue forever.
⁴ To good people, God is like a light
　shining in the dark.
　God is good and kind and merciful.
⁵ It is good for a person
　to be kind and generous.
　It is good for a person
　to be fair in his business.
⁶ That person will never fall.
　A good person will be remembered forever.
⁷ He will not be afraid of bad news.
　That person is confident
　because he trusts the Lord.

Zion The southeast part of the mountain Jerusalem is built on. Sometimes it means the people of God living in Jerusalem.
Your people ... ground Literally, "Your people will be freewill offerings on your day of power. In holy splendor from the womb of dawn your dew of youth will be yours."
lift his head and become strong Literally, "lift his head." Here the poet probably means two things: "He will raise his head after drinking the water." and "He will become strong or important."
Psalm 111 In Hebrew, each section of this psalm begins with the next letter in the alphabet.

Agreement Literally, "Proof." The flat stones with the Ten Commandments written on them were proof of the Agreement between God and Israel.
Psalm 112 In Hebrew, each section of this psalm begins with the next letter in the alphabet.
descendants A person's children and their future families.

8 That person is confident.
  He will not be afraid.
  He will defeat his enemies.
9 That person freely gives things
    to poor people.
  And his goodness will continue forever.
10 Wicked people see this and become angry.
   They will grind their teeth in anger,
     but then they disappear.
   Wicked people will not get
     what they want most.

Psalm 113

1 Praise the Lord!
  Servants of the Lord, praise him!
  Praise the Lord's name.
2 I want the Lord's name to be blessed.
    now and forever more.
3 I want the Lord's name to be praised
    from the rising sun in the east
    to the place where the sun goes down.
4 The Lord is higher than all nations.
  His glory rises to the skies.
5 No person is like the Lord our God.
  God sits high in heaven.
6 ₁God is so high above us₁
    that he must look down
    to see the sky and the earth,
7 God lifts poor people out of the dirt.
  God takes beggars from the garbage dump.
8 And God makes those people important.
  God makes those people important leaders.
9 A woman might not have children.
  But God will give children to her
    and make her happy.
  Praise the Lord!

Psalm 114

1 Israel left Egypt.
  Jacob *(Israel)* left that foreign country.
2 Judah became God's special people.
  Israel became his kingdom.
3 The Red Sea saw this and ran away.
  The Jordan River turned and ran.
4 The mountains danced like rams.
  The hills danced like lambs.
5 Red Sea, why did you run away?
  Jordan River, why did you turn and run away?
6 Mountains, why did you dance like rams?
  And hills, why did you dance like lambs?
7 The earth shook in front of the Master,
    the Lord God of Jacob.

8 God is the One who caused water to flow
    from a rock.
  God made a spring of water flow
    from that hard rock.

Psalm 115

1 Lord, we should not receive any honor.
  The honor belongs to you.
  The honor is yours because of your love
    and because we can trust you.
2 Why should the nations wonder
    where our God is?
3 God is in heaven,
    and he does whatever he wants.
4 The "gods" of those nations are only statues
    made from gold and silver.
  They are only statues
    that some person made.
5 Those statues have mouths, but can't talk.
  They have eyes, but can't see.
6 They have ears, but can't hear.
  They have noses, but can't smell.
7 They have hands, but can't feel.
  They have legs, but can't walk.
  And no sounds come from their throats.
8 The people who make and trust those statues
    will become just like them!
9 People of Israel, trust the Lord!
  The Lord is their strength and shield.
10 Aaron's family, trust the Lord!
   The Lord is their strength and shield.
11 Followers of the Lord, trust the Lord!
   The Lord is their strength and shield.
12 The Lord remembers us.
   The Lord will bless us.
   The Lord will bless Israel.
   The Lord will bless Aaron's family.
13 The Lord will bless his followers,
     great and small.
14 I hope the Lord gives more and more
     to you and your children.
15 The Lord made heaven and earth.
   And the Lord welcomes you!*
16 Heaven belongs to the Lord.
   But he gave the earth to people.

the Lord welcomes you Literally, "you are blessed to the Lord." This can mean that people ask God to do good things for these people or that God welcomes the people with a blessing.

17 Dead people don't praise the Lord.
People down in the grave
don't praise the Lord.
18 But we bless the Lord now,
and we will bless him forever more!
Praise the Lord!

Psalm 116

1 I love it when the the Lord hears my prayers.
2 I love it when he listens to me
when I call for help.
3 ₍I almost died!₎
Death's ropes were wrapped around me.
The grave was closing in around me.
I was scared and worried.
4 Then I called on the Lord's name.
I said:
"Lord, save me!"
5 The Lord is good and merciful.
God is kind.
6 The Lord takes care of helpless people.
I was without help, and the Lord saved me.
7 My soul, relax!
The Lord is caring for you.
8 God, you saved my soul from death.
You stopped my tears.
You kept me from falling.
9 I will continue to serve the Lord
in the land of the living.
10 I continued believing even when I said,
"I am ruined!"
11 Yes, even when I was afraid and said,
"All men are liars!"
12 What can I give to the Lord?
The Lord gave me everything I have!
13 He saved me,
so I will give him a drink offering.
And I will call on the Lord's name.
14 I will give the Lord the things I promised.
I will go in front of all his people now.
15 The death of one of the Lord's followers
is very important to the Lord.
Lord, I am one of your servants!
16 I am your servant.
I am a child of one of your servant women.
Lord, you were my first teacher!
17 I will give you a thank offering.
I will call on the Lord's name.
18 I will give the Lord the things I promised.
I will go in front of all his people now.
19 I will go to the temple in Jerusalem.
Praise the Lord!

Psalm 117

1 Praise the Lord, all you nations.
Praise the Lord all you people.
2 God loves us very much!
And God will be true to us forever!
Praise the Lord!

Psalm 118

1 Honor the Lord because he is God
His true love continues forever!
2 Israel, say it.
"His true love continues forever!"
3 Priests, say it.
"His true love continues forever!"
4 You people worshiping the Lord, say it.
"His true love continues forever!"
5 I was in trouble
so I called to the Lord for help.
The Lord answered me
and made me free.
6 The Lord is with me so I will not be afraid.
People can't do anything to hurt me.
7 The Lord is my helper.
I will see my enemies defeated.
8 It is better to trust the Lord
than to trust people.
9 It is better to trust the Lord
than to trust your leaders.
10 Many enemies surrounded me.
But with the Lord's power
I defeated my enemies.
11 Enemies surrounded me again and again.
I defeated them with the Lord's power.
12 Enemies surrounded me
like a swarm of bees.
But, they were quickly finished
like a fast burning bush.
I defeated them with the Lord's power.
13 My enemy attacked me
and almost destroyed me.
But the Lord helped me.
14 The Lord is my strength and victory song!
The Lord saves me!
15 You can hear the victory celebration
in good people's houses.
The Lord showed his great power again.
16 The Lord's arms are raised in victory.
The Lord showed his great power again.
17 I will live and not die.
And I will tell what the Lord has done.

18 The Lord punished me,
   but he did not let me die.
19 Good gates, open for me,
   and I will come in and worship the Lord.
20 Those are the Lord's gates.
   Only good people can go through them.
21 Lord, I thank you for answering my prayer.
   I thank you for saving me.

22 The stone that the builders did not want
   became the cornerstone*
23 The Lord made this happen.
   and we think it is wonderful!
24 Today is the day the Lord has made.
   Let's rejoice and be happy today!

25 ₁The people said₁
   "Praise the Lord!
   The Lord saved us!*
26 Welcome the man coming in the name
   of the Lord."

   ₁The priests answered₁
   "We welcome you to the Lord's house!
27 The Lord is God.
   And he accepts us.
   Tie up the lamb for the sacrifice*
   ₁and carry it₁ to the horns of the altar."*

28 Lord, you are my God and I thank you.
   I praise you!
29 Praise the Lord because he is good.
   His true love is forever.

Psalm 119

Aleph*

1 People living pure lives are happy.
  Those people follow the Lord's teachings.
2 People who obey the Lord's Agreement*
  are happy.
  They obey the Lord with all their heart.
3 Those people don't do bad things.
  They obey the Lord.

---

cornerstone First and most important rock of a building.
Praise ... The Lord saved us Literally, "Lord, please save us. Lord, please make us successful." This was a shout of victory to honor the king that was coming back from winning a war.
sacrifice(s) A sacrifice was a gift to God. Usually, it was a special animal that was killed and burned on an altar.
horns of the altar The corners of the altar.
Aleph First letter of the Hebrew alphabet. In Hebrew, each section of this song begins with the next letter of the alphabet.
Agreement Literally, "Proof." The flat stones with the Ten Commandments written on them were proof of the Agreement between God and Israel.

4 Lord, you gave us your commands.
  And you told us to obey those commands
  completely.
5 If I always obey your laws, Lord,
6 Then I will never be ashamed when I study
  your commands.
7 Then I could truly honor you as I study your
  fairness and goodness.
8 Lord, I will obey your commands.
  So please don't leave me!

Beth

9 How can a young person live a pure life?
  By following your instructions.
10 I try to serve God with all my heart.
   God, help me obey your commands.
11 I study your teachings very carefully.
   Why? So I will not sin against you.
12 Bless you Lord.
   Teach me your laws.
13 I will talk about all your wise decisions.
14 I enjoy studying your Agreement*
   more than anything.
15 I discuss your rules.
   I follow your way of living.
16 I enjoy your laws.
   I will not forget your words.

Gimel

17 Be good to me, your servant, so I might be
   able to live and obey your commands.
18 Lord, open my eyes.
   Let me look into your teachings
   and read about the wonderful things
   you did.
19 I am a stranger in this land.
   Lord, don't hide your teachings from me.
20 I want to study your decisions all the time.
21 Lord, you criticize proud people.
   Bad things will happen to them.
   They refuse to obey your commands.
22 Don't let me be ashamed and embarrassed.
   I have obeyed your Agreement.*
23 Even the leaders said bad things about me.
   But I am your servant, Lord,
   and I study your laws.
24 Your Agreement is my best friend.
   It gives me good advice.

Daleth

25 I will soon die.
   Lord, give the command and let me live.

26 I told you about my life.
   And you answered me.
   Now, teach me your laws.
27 Lord, help me understand your laws.
   Let me study about the wonderful things
      you have done.
28 I am sad and tired.
   Give the command
      and make me strong again.
29 Lord, don't let me live a lie.
   Guide me with your teachings.
30 Lord, I chose to be loyal to you.
   I carefully study your wise decisions.
31 I stick with your Agreement* Lord.
   Don't disappoint me.
32 I will gladly obey your commands.
   Lord, your commands make me happy.

He

33 Lord, teach me your laws,
   and I will follow them.
34 Help me understand,
   and I will obey your teachings.
   I will obey them completely.
35 Lord, lead me along the path
      of your commands.
   I truly love that way of living.
36 Help me think about your Agreement*
      instead of how to get rich.
37 Lord, don't let me look at worthless things.
   Help me live your way.
38 Do what you promised for your servant
      so that people will respect you.
39 Lord, take away the shame I fear.
   Your wise decisions are good.
40 Look, I love your commands.
   Be good to me and let me live.

Waw

41 Lord, show me your true love.
   Save me like you promised.
42 Then I will have an answer
      for people who insult me.
   I really trust the things you say, Lord.
43 Let me always speak your true teachings.
   Lord, I depend on your wise decisions.
44 Lord, I will follow your teachings
      forever and ever.
45 So I will be free. Why?
   Because I try hard to obey your laws.
46 I will discuss your Agreement* with kings,
   and they will not embarrass me.
47 I enjoy studying your commands, Lord.
   I love those commands.
48 Lord, I praise your commands.
   I love them.
   And I will study them.

Zain

49 Lord, remember your promise to me.
   That promise gives me hope.
50 I was suffering, and you comforted me.
   Your words let me live again.
51 People who think they are better than me
      insulted me constantly.
   But I did not stop following your teachings.
52 I always remember your wise decisions.
   Lord, your wise decisions comfort me.
53 I become angry when I see
      the wicked people who quit following
         your teachings.
54 Your laws are my songs at home.*
55 Lord, I remember your name at night.
   And I remember your teachings.
56 This happens because I carefully obey
      your commands.

Heth

57 Lord, I decided my duty is to obey
      your commands.
58 Lord, I depend on you completely.
   Be kind to me like you promised.
59 I thought very carefully about my life.
   And I came back to your Agreement.*
60 I hurried back to obey your commands
      without delay.
61 A group of bad people said bad things
      about me.
   But I did not forget your teachings, Lord.
62 In the middle of the night,
   I get up to thank you for your
      good decisions.
63 I am a friend to every person
      who worships you.
   I am a friend to every person
      who obeys your commands.
64 Lord, your true love fills the earth.
   Teach me your laws.

Agreement Literally, "Proof." The flat stones with the Ten Commandments written on them were proof of the Agreement between God and Israel.

at home Or "at the temple, where I live."

Teth

⁶⁵ Lord, you did good things for me,
   your servant.
   You did exactly what you promised to do.
⁶⁶ Lord, give me the knowledge
   to make wise decisions.
   I trust your commands.
⁶⁷ Before I suffered, I did many wrong things.
   But now, I carefully obey your commands.
⁶⁸ God, you are good, and you do good things.
   Teach me your laws.
⁶⁹ People who think they are better than me
   told bad lies about me.
   But I continued to obey your commands
   with all my heart, Lord.
⁷⁰ Those people are very stupid.*
   But I enjoy studying your teachings.
⁷¹ Suffering was good for me.
   I learned your laws.
⁷² Lord, your teachings are good for me.
   They are better than 1,000 pieces
   of silver and gold.

Yod

⁷³ Lord, you made me
   and you support me with your hands.
   Help me learn and understand
   your commands.
⁷⁴ Lord, your followers see me
   and respect me.
   They are happy because I trust
   what you say.
⁷⁵ Lord, I know that your decisions are fair.
   And it was right for you to punish me.
⁷⁶ Now, comfort me with your true love.
   Comfort me like you promised.
⁷⁷ Lord, comfort me and let me live.
   I truly enjoy your teachings.
⁷⁸ People who think they are better than me
   lied about me.
   I hope those people are ashamed.
   Lord, I study your laws.
⁷⁹ I hope your followers come back to me
   so they can learn your Agreement.*
⁸⁰ Lord, let me obey your commands perfectly
   so I will not be ashamed.

Those people are very stupid Or, "It is as hard for their minds to understand things as it is to grab milk with your hand."

Agreement Literally, "Proof." The flat stones with the Ten Commandments written on them were proof of the Agreement between God and Israel.

Kaph

⁸¹ I am about to die waiting for you to save me.
   But I trust the things you say, Lord.
⁸² I keep looking for the things you promised,
   but my eyes are getting tired.
   Lord, when will you comfort me?
⁸³ Even when I am like a dried wineskin
   on the trash pile,
   I will not forget your laws.
⁸⁴ How long will I live?
   Lord, when will you punish the people
   who persecute me?
⁸⁵ Some proud people stabbed me
   with their lies.
   And that is against your teachings.
⁸⁶ People can trust all of your commands, Lord.
   Those people are wrong to persecute me.
   Help me!
⁸⁷ Those people almost destroyed me.
   But I did not stop obeying your commands.
⁸⁸ Lord, show me your true love
   and let me live.
   I will do the things you say.

Lamedh

⁸⁹ Lord, your word continues forever.
   Your word continues forever in heaven.
⁹⁰ You are loyal forever and ever.
   Lord, you made the earth,
   and it still stands.
⁹¹ It still continues today
   because of your laws,
   because it obeys them like a slave.
⁹² If your teachings were not like friends to me,
   then my suffering would have
   destroyed me.
⁹³ Lord, I will never forget your commands,
   because they let me live.
⁹⁴ Lord, I am yours, so save me!
   Why? Because I try hard to obey
   your commands.
⁹⁵ Wicked people tried to destroy me.
   But your Agreement* made me wise.
⁹⁶ Everything has its limits,
   except your law.

Mem

⁹⁷ Oh, I love your teachings, Lord.
   I talk about them all of the time.
⁹⁸ Lord, your commands make me wiser
   than my enemies.
   Your law is with me always.

⁹⁹ I am wiser than all my teachers
because I study your Agreement.*
¹⁰⁰ I understand more than the older leaders
because I keep your commands.
¹⁰¹ You keep me off of the wrong path
every step of the way.
So I can do what you tell me, Lord.
¹⁰² Lord, you are my teacher
so I will not stop obeying your laws.
¹⁰³ Your words are sweeter than honey
in my mouth.
¹⁰⁴ Your teachings make me wise,
so I hate false teachings.

Nun

¹⁰⁵ Lord, your words are like a lamp
lighting my path.
¹⁰⁶ Your laws are good.
I promise to obey them.
And I will keep my promise.
¹⁰⁷ Lord, I suffered for a long time.
Please give the command,
and let me live again!
¹⁰⁸ Lord, accept my praise.
And teach me your laws.
¹⁰⁹ My life is always in danger.
But I have not forgotten your teachings.
¹¹⁰ Wicked people try to trap me.
But I have not disobeyed your commands.
¹¹¹ Lord, I will follow your Agreement* forever.
It makes me very happy.
¹¹² I will always try very hard
to obey all your laws.

Samekh

¹¹³ Lord, I hate people who are not
completely loyal to you.
But I love your teachings.
¹¹⁴ Hide me and protect me.
Lord, I trust everything you say.
¹¹⁵ Lord, don't let bad people come near me.
And I will obey my God's commands.
¹¹⁶ Lord, support me like you promised,
and I will live.
I trust you, so don't disappoint me.
¹¹⁷ Help me, Lord, and I will be saved.
I will study your commands forever.
¹¹⁸ Lord, you turn away every person
who breaks your laws.
Why? Because those people lied
when they agreed to follow you.
¹¹⁹ Lord, you throw away
the wicked people on earth
like trash.
So I will love your Agreement* forever.
¹²⁰ Lord, I am afraid of you.
I fear and respect your laws.

Ain

¹²¹ I have done what is right and good.
Lord, don't give me to the people
who want to hurt me.
¹²² Promise to be good to me.
I am your servant
Lord, don't let those proud people hurt me.
¹²³ Lord, I have worn out my eyes
looking for help from you,
for a good word from you.
¹²⁴ I am your servant.
Show your true love to me.
Teach me your laws.
¹²⁵ I am your servant.
Help me understand
so I can know your Agreement.*
¹²⁶ Lord, it is time for you to do something.
The people have broken your law.
¹²⁷ Lord, I love your commands more than
purest gold.
¹²⁸ I carefully obey all of your commands.*
I hate false teachings.

Pe

¹²⁹ Lord, your Agreement* is wonderful.
That is why I follow it.
¹³⁰ When people begin to understand your word,
it is like a light showing them
the right way of living.
Your word makes even simple people wise.
¹³¹ Lord, I really want to study your commands.
I am like a person breathing hard
and waiting impatiently.
¹³² God, look at me and be kind to me.
Do the things that are right for the people
who love your name.
¹³³ Lord, guide me like you promised.
Don't let anything bad happen to me.
¹³⁴ Lord, save me from the people who hurt me.
And I will obey your commands.

Agreement Literally, "Proof." The flat stones with the Ten Commandments written on them were proof of the Agreement between God and Israel.

I carefully obey all of your commands The meaning of the Hebrew here is not clear.

135 Lord, accept your servant,
and teach me your laws.
136 I have cried a river of tears
because people don't obey your teachings.

Tsadhe

137 Lord, you are good.
And your laws are fair.
138 You gave us good laws in the Agreement.*
We can really trust them.
139 My strong feelings are destroying me.
I am so upset because my enemies
forgot your commands.
140 We have proof that we can trust
your word, Lord.
And I love it.
141 I am a young person,
and people don't respect me.
But I don't forget your commands.
142 Lord, your goodness is forever.
And your teachings can be trusted.
143 I have had troubles and hard times.
But I enjoy your commands.
144 Your Agreement is good forever.
Help me understand it so I can live.

Qoph

145 I call to you with all my heart, Lord.
Answer me!
I obey your commands.
146 Lord, I call to you.
Save me!
And I will obey your Agreement.*
147 I got up early in the morning to pray to you.
I trust the things you say.
148 I stayed up late at night to study your word.
149 With all your love, listen to me.
Lord, do the things you say are right,
and let me live.
150 People are making evil plans against me.
Those people don't follow your teachings.
151 Lord, you are close to me.
And all your commands can be trusted.
152 Long ago I learned from your Agreement*
that your teachings will continue forever.

Resh

153 Lord, see my suffering and rescue me.
I have not forgotten your teachings.
154 Lord, fight my fight for me and save me.
Let me live, like you promised.
155 Wicked people will not win
because they don't follow your laws.
156 Lord, you are very kind.
Do the things you say are right,
and let me live.
157 I have many enemies trying to hurt me.
But I have not stopped following your
Agreement.*
158 I see those traitors.*
They don't obey your word, Lord.
And I hate that.
159 Look, I try hard to obey your commands.
Lord, with all your love, let me live.
160 From the very beginning,
all your words could be trusted, Lord.
And your good law will last forever.

Shin

161 Powerful leaders attacked me for no reason.
But I fear and respect only your law.
162 Lord, your word makes me happy,
as happy as a person who just found
a great treasure.
163 I hate lies! I despise them!
But I love your teachings, Lord.
164 Seven times a day I praise you
for your good laws.
165 People who love your teachings
will find true peace.
Nothing can make those people fall.
166 Lord, I am waiting for you to save me.
I obeyed your commands.
167 I followed your Agreement.*
Lord, I love your laws very much.
168 I have obeyed your Agreement and
commands.
Lord, you know everything I have done.

Taw

169 Lord, listen to my happy song.
Make me wise like you promised.
170 Lord, listen to my prayer.
Save me, like you promised.
171 I burst into songs of praise,
because you taught me your laws.
172 Help me respond to your words and let me
sing my song.
Lord, all your laws are good.

Agreement Literally, "Proof." The flat stones with the Ten Commandments written on them were proof of the Agreement between God and Israel.

traitors People who turn against their country, friends, or family and do bad things to them.

173 I chose to follow your commands,
   so reach out and help me!
174 Lord, I want you to save me.
   But your teachings make me happy.
175 Let me live and praise you, Lord.
   Let your laws help me.
176 I wandered away like a lost sheep.
   Come looking for me, Lord.
   I am your servant,
   and I have not forgotten your commands.

Psalm 120

A song for going up to the temple.

1 I was in trouble.
   I called to the Lord for help.
   And he saved me!
2 Lord, save me from the people
   who lied about me.
   Those people said things that weren't true.
3 Liars, do you know what you will get?
   Do you know what you will gain?
4 A soldier's sharp arrow
   and hot coals to punish you.
5 You people are liars, and living near you
   is like living in Meshech.
   It is like living in tents in Kedar.*
6 I have lived too long with people
   who hate peace.
7 I said I want peace,
   so they want war.

Psalm 121

A song for going up to the temple.

1 I look up to the hills.
   But where will my help really come from?
2 My help will come from the Lord,
   the Creator of heaven and earth.
3 God will not let you fall.
   Your Protector will not fall asleep.
4 Israel's Protector does not become sleepy.
   God never sleeps.
5 The Lord is your Protector.
   He protects you with his great power.
6 The sun can't hurt you during the day.
   And the moon can't hurt you at night.
7 The Lord will protect you
   from every danger.
   The Lord will protect your soul.

8 The Lord will help as you come and go.*
   The Lord will help you now and forever!

Psalm 122

*A song from David for going up
to the temple.*

1 I was very happy when people said,
   "Let us go to the Lord's temple.*"
2 Here we are,
   standing at the gates of Jerusalem.
3 This is New Jerusalem!
   The city has been built again
   as one united city.
4 That is where the family groups go.
   The people of Israel go there
   to praise the Lord's name.
   They are the family groups
   that belong to the Lord
5 The kings from David's family
   put their thrones in that place.
   They set up their thrones there
   to judge the people.

6 Pray for peace in Jerusalem.
   "I hope the people who love you
   will find peace there.
   I hope there will be peace
   inside your walls.
   I hope there will be safety
   in your great buildings."

7 For the good of my brothers and neighbors,
   I pray there will be peace here.
8 For the good of the temple of the Lord
   our God,
   I pray that good things will happen
   to this city.

Psalm 123

A song for going up to the temple

1 God, I look up and pray to you.
   You sit as king in heaven.
2 Slaves depend on their masters
   for the things they need.
3 In the same way,
   we depend on the Lord our God.
   We wait for God to show mercy to us.

Meshech ... Kedar People from these places were famous fighters.

come and go This probably refers to going to war.
temple The special building in Jerusalem for Jewish worship.

⁴ Lord, be merciful to us.
  Be merciful because we have been insulted
    much too long.
⁵ We have had enough of the insults and slurs
    from from those lazy and arrogant people.

Psalm 124

*A song from David for going up
to the temple.*

¹ What would have happened to us
    if the Lord had not been on our side?
  Tell me the answer, Israel.
² What would have happened to us
    if the Lord had not been on our side
    when people attacked us?
³ Our enemies would have swallowed us alive
    whenever they became angry at us.
⁴ Our enemies' armies would have been
    like a flood washing over us,
    like a river drowning us.
⁵ Those proud people would have been
    like water rising up to our mouth
    and drowning us.
⁶ Praise the Lord!
  The Lord did not let our enemies catch us
    and kill us.
⁷ We are like a bird that was trapped in a net,
    and then escaped.
  The net broke, and we escaped!
⁸ Our help came from the Lord.
  The Lord made heaven and earth!

Psalm 125

A song for going up to the temple.

¹ People who trust in the Lord
    will be like Mount Zion.
  They will never be shaken.
  They will continue forever.
² Mountains are all around Jerusalem.
  And the Lord is around his people.
  He will protect his people forever and ever.
³ Evil people will not control
    good people's land forever.
  If that happened, then even good people
    might start doing bad things.
⁴ Lord, be good to good people.
  Be good to people who have pure hearts.

⁵ Evil people do crooked things.
  The Lord will punish those evil people.

Let there be peace in Israel!

Psalm 126

A song for going up to the temple.

¹ When the Lord makes us free again
    it will be like a dream!
² We will be laughing
    and singing happy songs!
  People in other nations will say,
    "The Lord did a wonderful thing
    for the people of Israel."
³ Yes, we would be so happy
    if the Lord did that wonderful thing for us.
⁴ Lord, make us free again,
    like desert streams filled again
    with flowing water.
⁵ A person might be sad
    when he plants the seeds,
  but he will be happy
    when he gathers the crops!
⁶ He might cry when he carries
    the seeds out to the field,
  but he will be happy
    when he brings the harvest in!

Psalm 127

*A song from Solomon for going up
to the temple.*

¹ If it is not the Lord that builds a house,
    the builder is wasting his time.
  If it is not the Lord that watches over a city,
    the guards are wasting their time.
² It is a waste of time
    to get up early and stay up late,
    trying to make a living.
  God cares for the people he loves,
    even while they are sleeping.
³ Children are a gift* from the Lord.
  They are a reward from a mother's body.

---

gift Literally, "inheritance." Usually, this means the land that God gave to each family in Israel. This land was a gift that never really left the family. A person might sell the land, but at the time of Jubilee, the land was given back to the family.

4 A young man's sons are like the arrows
    in a soldier's arrow bag.
5 A man that fills his arrow bag with sons
    will be very happy.
6 That man will never be defeated.
    His sons will defend him against his
    enemies in public places.*

Psalm 128

A song for going up to the temple.

1 All of the Lord's followers are happy.
    Those people live the way God wants.
2 You will enjoy the things you work for.
    You will be happy,
    and good things will happen to you.
3 At home, your wife will be
    like a fruitful grape vine.
    Around the table, your children will be
    like olive trees you planted.
4 The Lord will truly bless his followers
    this way.
5 I hope the Lord blesses you from Zion.*
    I hope you enjoy the blessings in Jerusalem
    all of your life.
6 And I hope you live to see your
    grandchildren.

Let there be peace in Israel!

Psalm 129

A song for going up to the temple.

1 I have had many enemies all my life.

Tell us about those enemies, Israel.

2 I have had many enemies all my life.
    But they never won.
3 They beat me until I had deep cuts
    in my back.
    I had long and deep wounds.
4 But the good Lord cut the ropes
    and set me free from those evil people.
5 The people who hated Zion were defeated.
    They stopped fighting and ran away.
6 Those people were like grass on the roof.
    That grass dies before it has time to grow.

7 A worker can't get a handful of that grass.
    There is not enough for a pile of grain.
8 People walking by them will not say,
    "May the Lord bless you."
    People will not greet them and say,
    "We bless you in the name of the Lord."

Psalm 130

A song for going up to the temple.

1 Lord, I am in deep trouble,
    so I am calling to you for help.
2 My Master, listen to me.
    Listen to my call for help.
3 Lord, if you really punished people
    for all of their sins,
    no person would be left alive.
4 Lord, forgive your people.
    Then there will be people to worship you.
5 I am waiting for the Lord to help me.
    My soul waits for him.
    I trust what the Lord says.
6 I am waiting for my Master.
    I am like guards waiting and waiting for
    the morning to come.
7 Israel, trust the Lord.
    True love is found only with the Lord.
    The Lord saves us again and again.
    And the Lord will forgive Israel for all
    their sins.

Psalm 131

A song for going up to the temple.

1 Lord, I am not proud.
    I don't try to act important.
    I don't try to do great things.
    I don't worry about things
    that are too hard for me.
2 I am calm.
    My soul is quiet.
3 My soul is calm and quiet
    like a satisfied baby in his mother's arms.
4 Israel, trust the Lord.
    Trust him now, and trust him forever!

Psalm 132

A song for going up to the temple.

1 Lord, remember how David suffered.
2 David made a promise to the Lord.
    David made a special promise
    to the Mighty God of Jacob.

---

public places Literally, "the gate." This might mean that a person's sons will defend him whenever his enemies try to take him to court.
Zion The southeast part of the mountain Jerusalem is built on. Sometimes it means the people of God living in Jerusalem.

³ David said,
"I will not go into my house,
I will not lie down on my bed,
⁴ I will not sleep,
I will not let my eyes rest,
⁵ I will not do any of those things
until I find a house for the Lord,
a home for the Mighty God of Jacob!"
⁶ We heard about it in Ephrathah.*
We found the Box of the Agreement*
at Kiriath Jearim.*
⁷ Let us go to the Holy Tent.
Let us worship at the stool
where God rests his feet.*
⁸ Lord, get up* from your resting place.
Get up Lord, you and your powerful Box.
⁹ Lord, your priests are dressed in goodness.
Your loyal followers are very happy.
¹⁰ For the good of your servant, David,
don't reject your chosen king.
¹¹ The Lord made a promise to David.
The Lord promised to be loyal to David.
The Lord promised that the kings would come
from David's family.
¹² ⌊The Lord said,⌋
"David, if your children obey my Agreement*
and the laws I teach them,
then someone from your family will
always be the king."
¹³ The Lord chose Zion* to be the place for
his temple.
That is the place he wanted for his home.

¹⁴ ⌊The Lord said,⌋
"This will be my place forever and ever.
I choose this to be the place
where I will be.
¹⁵ I will bless this city with plenty of food.
Even poor people will have plenty to eat.
¹⁶ I will clothe the priests with salvation.
And my followers will be very happy here.
¹⁷ In this place, I will make David strong.
I will provide a lamp for my chosen king.
¹⁸ I will cover David's enemies in shame.
But I will make David's kingdom grow."

Psalm 133

One of David's songs for going up to the temple.

¹ Oh how good and pleasant it is when brothers
can sit together, truly united!
² It is like the sweet smelling oil
poured over Aaron's head,
running down into his beard
which flows down over his
special clothes.
³ It is like a gentle rain* from Mount Hermon
falling on Mount Zion.*
⁴ Why, Because it was at Zion
that the Lord gave his blessing,
the blessing of eternal life.

Psalm 134

A song for going up to the temple.

¹ Praise the Lord, all of his servants!
You servants served in the temple all night.
² Servants, lift your arms and bless the Lord.
³ And may the Lord bless you from Zion.*
The Lord made heaven and earth.

Psalm 135

¹ Praise the Lord!
Praise the name of the Lord!
Servants of the Lord, praise him!
² Praise him
you people standing in the Lord's temple,
in the courtyard of the temple of our God.
³ Praise the Lord, because he is good.
Praise his name, because it is pleasant.

Ephrathah Bethlehem, the town where David was born.
Box of the Agreement Or, "ark of the Covenant." The box containing the flat stones with the Ten Commandments written on them and other things that proved God was with the people of Israel during their time in the Sinai desert.
Kiriath Jearim Literally, "fields of the forest." The Hebrew word meaning "forest" is like the name of this city.
stool where God rests his feet This can mean the Box of the Agreement, the Holy Tent, or the temple. It is like God is a king sitting on his throne and resting his feet on the place where people worship him.
Lord, get up The people said this when they lifted the Box of the Agreement and took it into battle with them. This showed that God was with them. See Num. 10:35,36.
Agreement Literally, "Proof." The flat stones with the Ten Commandments written on them were proof of the Agreement between God and Israel.
Zion The southeast part of the mountain Jerusalem is built on. Sometimes it means the people of God living in Jerusalem.

gentle rain Or, "mist, snow." The Hebrew can mean either, "the oil is like the mist...," or "Aaron's beard is like the snow..."
Mount Zion Or, "the mountain range of Zion," or possibly "the dry mountains."

4 The Lord chose Jacob.*
   Israel belongs to God.
5 I know the Lord is great!
   Our Master is greater than all the gods!
6 The Lord does anything he wants,
   in heaven and earth,
   in the seas and deep oceans.
7 God makes the clouds all over the earth.
   God makes the lightning and rain.
   And God makes the wind.*
8 God destroyed all the firstborn men
   and all the firstborn animals in Egypt.
9 God did many wonders and miracles
   in Egypt.
   God made those things happen
   to Pharaoh and his officials.
10 God defeated many nations.
    God killed powerful kings.
11 God defeated Sihon, king of the Amorites.
    God defeated Og, king of Bashan.
    God defeated all the nations in Canaan.
12 And God gave their land to Israel.
    God gave that land to his people.

13 Lord, your name will be famous forever!
    Lord, people will remember you
    forever and ever.
14 The Lord punished the nations.
    But the Lord was kind to his servants.
15 The gods of the other people
    were only gold and silver statues.
    Their gods were only statues
    that people made.
16 The statues had mouths, but couldn't speak.
    The statues had eyes, but couldn't see.
17 The statues had ears, but couldn't hear.
    The statues had noses, but couldn't smell.
18 And the people who made the statues
    will become just like them!
    Why? Because they trusted those statues
    to help them.
19 Family of Israel, bless the Lord!
    Aaron's family, bless the Lord!
20 Levi's family, bless the Lord!
    Followers of the Lord, bless the Lord!
21 The Lord is blessed from Zion,
    from Jerusalem, his home.
    Praise the Lord!

Jacob Another name for Israel. See Gen. 32:22-28.
makes the wind Literally, "brings the wind out of the storehouses."

Psalm 136

1 Praise the Lord because he is good.
   His true love continues forever.
2 Praise the God of gods!
   His true love continues forever.
3 Praise the Lord of lords!
   His true love continues forever.
4 Praise God, who alone does wonderful
   miracles!
   His true love continues forever.
5 Praise God, the One that used wisdom
   to make the skies!
   His true love continues forever.
6 God put the dry land on the sea.
   His true love continues forever.
7 God made the great lights.
   His true love continues forever.
8 God made the sun to rule the day.
   His true love continues forever.
9 God made the moon and stars
   to rule the night.
   His true love continues forever.
10 God killed the firstborn men and animals
    in Egypt.
    His true love continues forever.
11 God took Israel out of Egypt.
    His true love continues forever.
12 God showed his great power and strength.
    His true love continues forever.
13 God split the Red Sea into two parts.
    His true love continues forever.
14 God led Israel through the sea.
    His true love continues forever.
15 God drowned Pharaoh and his army
    in the Red Sea.
    His true love continues forever.
16 God led his people through the desert.
    His true love continues forever.
17 God defeated powerful kings.
    His true love continues forever.
18 God defeated strong kings.
    His true love continues forever.
19 God defeated Sihon, king of the Amorites.
    His true love continues forever.
20 God defeated Og, king of Bashan.
    His true love continues forever.
21 God gave their land to Israel.
    His true love continues forever.
22 God gave that land for a gift to Israel.
    His true love continues forever.
23 God remembered us when we were defeated.
    His true love continues forever.
24 God saved us from our enemies.
    His true love continues forever.

25 God gives food to every person.
   His true love continues forever.
26 Praise the God of heaven!
   His true love continues forever.

Psalm 137

1 We sat by the rivers in Babylon
  and cried as we remembered Zion.*
2 We hung our harps
  on the willow trees nearby.*
3 In Babylon, the people who captured us
  told us to sing.
  They told us to sing happy songs.
  They told us to sing songs about Zion.*
4 But we can't sing the Lord's songs
  in a foreign country!
5 Jerusalem, if I ever forget you,
  then I hope I never play a song again.
6 Jerusalem, if I ever forget you,
  then I hope I never sing again.
  I promise, I will never forget you.
7 I promise, Jerusalem will always be
  my greatest joy!
8 Babylon, you will be destroyed!
  Bless the man who gives you
  the punishment you should get.
  Bless the man who hurts you
  like you hurt us.
9 Bless the man who grabs your babies
  and smashes them against a rock.

Psalm 138

*A song of David.**

1 God, I praise you with all my heart.
  I will sing your songs before all the gods.
2 God, I bow down toward your holy temple.
  I praise your name, your true love,
  and your loyalty.
  You are famous ‚for the power of‚ your word.
  Now you have made it even greater!
3 God, I called to you for help.
  And you answered me!
  You gave me strength.

4 Lord, all the kings on earth will praise you
  when they hear what you say.
5 They will sing about the Lord's way
  because the Glory of the Lord is very great.
6 God is very important,
  but he still cares for humble people.
  God knows what proud people do,
  but he stays far away from them.
7 God, if I am in trouble,
  keep me alive.
  If my enemies are angry at me,
  save me from them.
8 Lord, give me the things you promised.
  Lord, your true love continues forever.
  Lord, you made us,
  so don't leave us!

Psalm 139

To the director. One of David's
songs of praise.*

1 Lord, you tested me.
  You know all about me.
2 You know when I sit down
  and when I get up.
  You know my thoughts from far away.
3 Lord, you know where I am going
  and when I am lying down.
  You know everything I do.
4 Lord, you know what I want to say,
  even before the words leave my mouth.
5 Lord, you are all around me—
  in front and in back of me.
  You gently put your hand on me.
6 I am amazed at what you know.
  It is too much for me to understand.
7 Your Spirit is in every place I go.
  Lord, I can't escape you.
8 Lord, if I go up to heaven,
  you are there.
  If I go down to the place of death,
  you are there.
9 Lord, if I go east where the sun rises,
  you are there.
  If I go west to the sea,
  you are there.
10 Even there your right hand holds me,
   and you lead me by the hand.

Zion The southeast part of the mountain Jerusalem is built on. Sometimes it means the people of God living in Jerusalem.

We hung our harps ... nearby These instruments were used to praise God in the temple in Jerusalem. Since the temple was destroyed, these people had no reason to play the songs.

A song of David Or, "A song dedicated to David."

director Or, "performer."

11 Lord, I might try to hide from you and say,
"The day has changed to night.
Surely the darkness will hide me."
12 But even darkness is not dark to you, Lord,
The night is as bright as day to you.
13 Lord, you made my whole body.*
You knew all about me
while I was still in my mother's body.
14 Lord, I praise you!
You made me in an amazing and
wonderful way.
I know very well that what you did
is wonderful!
15 You know all about me.
You watched my bones grow
while my body took shape,
hidden in my mother's body.*
16 You watched my body parts grow.
You listed them all in your book.
You watched me every day.
Not one of them ᵢis missingⱼ.
17 Your thoughts are important to me.
God, you know so much!
18 If I could count them,
they would be more
than all the grains of sand.
And when I finished,
I would still be with you.
19 God, kill the wicked people.
Take those murderers away from me.
20 Those bad people say bad things about you.
They say bad things about your name.*
21 Lord, I hate the people who hate you.
I hate the people who turn against you.
22 I hate them completely!
Your enemies are also my enemies.
23 Lord, look at me and know my heart.
Test me and know my thoughts.
24 See if I have any evil thoughts.
And guide me on the path
that continues forever.*

Psalm 140

To the director. One of David's songs of praise.*

1 Lord, save me from evil people.
Protect me from cruel people.
2 Those people plan to do evil things.
Those people always start fights.
3 Their tongues are like poisonous snakes.
It is like snake poison is under their tongue.
SELAH*
4 Lord, save me from wicked people.
Protect me from cruel people.
Those people chase me and try to hurt me.
5 Those proud people set a trap for me.
They spread a net to catch me.
They set a trap in my path.
SELAH*
6 Lord, you are my God.
Lord, listen to my prayer.
7 Lord, you are my strong Master.
You are my Savior.
You are like a helmet protecting my head
in battle.
8 Lord, those people are wicked.
Don't let them have what they want.
Don't let their plans succeed.
SELAH*
9 Lord, don't let my enemies win.
Those people are planning bad things.
But make those bad things happen to them.
10 Pour burning coals on their heads.
Throw my enemies into the fire.
Throw them into the pit *(grave)*
that they will never climb out of.
11 Lord, don't let those liars live.
Make bad things happen
to those bad people.
12 I know the Lord will judge poor people fairly.
God will help helpless people.
13 Good people will praise your name, Lord.
Good people will worship you.

---

guide ... forever Or, "Guide on the ancient path."
director Or, "performer."
Selah This word is for the musicians. It probably means the singers should pause here or the music should be louder here.
sacrifice(s) A sacrifice was a gift to God. Usually, it was a special animal that was killed and burned on an altar.

Psalm 141
One of David's songs of praise.

1 Lord, I call to you for help.
   Listen to me while I pray to you.
   Hurry and help me!
2 Lord, accept my prayer.
   Let it be like a gift of burning incense.
   Let it be like the evening sacrifice.*
3 Lord, help me control the things I say.
   Help me watch what I say.
4 Don't let me want to do bad things.
   Stop me from joining bad people
      when they do wrong.
   Don't let me share the things
      those bad people enjoy doing.
5 A good person can correct me.
   That would be kind of him.
   Your followers can criticize me.
   That would be a good thing for them to do.
   I would accept that.
   But I will always pray against
      the bad things those bad people do.
6 Let their rulers be punished.
   Then people will know I spoke the truth.
7 People dig and plow the ground.
   And spread the dirt around.
   In the same way, our bones
      will be spread around in their grave.
8 Lord my Master, I look to you for help.
   I trust you.
   Please don't let me die.
9 Bad people set traps for me.
   Don't let me fall into their traps.
   Don't let them trap me.
10 Let wicked people fall into their own trap,
    while I walk away unharmed.

Psalm 142
A maskil of David. This is a prayer from
the time he was in the cave.*

1 I will call to the Lord for help.
   I will pray to the Lord.
2 I will tell the Lord about my problems.
   I will tell the Lord about my troubles.
3 My enemies have set a trap for me.
   I am ready to give up.
   But the Lord knows what is happening to me.
4 I look around,
   and I don't see any of my friends.
   I have no place to run.
   No person is trying to save me.
5 So I cry to the Lord for help.
   Lord, you are my place of safety.
   Lord, you can let me continue to live.
6 Lord, listen to my prayer.
   I need you very much.
   Save me from the people who chase me.
   Those people are too strong for me.
7 Help me escape this trap*
   so I can praise your name.
   And good people will celebrate with me
      because you took care of me.

Psalm 143
One of David's songs of praise.

1 Lord, hear my prayer.
   Listen to my prayer.
   And then answer my prayer.
   Show me that you are truly good and loyal.
2 Don't judge me, your servant.
   Never, in all my life, could I ever be
      judged innocent.
3 But my enemies are chasing me.
   They have crushed my life into the dirt.
   They are pushing me into the dark grave,
      like people who died long ago.
4 I am ready to give up.
   I am losing my courage.
5 But I remember the things
      that happened long ago.
   I am thinking about
      the many things you did.
   I am talking about the things you did
      with your great power!
6 Lord, I lift my arms and pray to you.
   I am waiting for your help,
      like a dry land waiting for rain.
                                            SELAH*
7 Hurry, answer me Lord!
   I have lost my courage.
   Don't turn away from me.
   Don't let me die
      and be like dead people lying in the grave.
8 Lord, show me your true love this morning.
   I trust you.

---

sacrifice(s) A sacrifice was a gift to God. Usually, it was a special animal that was killed and burned on an altar.

trap Literally, "frame around my soul."

Selah This word is for the musicians. It probably means the singers should pause here or the music should be louder here.

Show me the things I should do.
I put my life in your hands!
9 Lord, I come to you for protection.
Save me from my enemies.
10 Show me what you want me to do.
You are my God.
11 Lord, let me live,
so people will praise your name.
Show me that you are truly good,
and save me from my enemies.
12 Lord, show me your love,
and defeat my enemies
who are trying to kill me.
Why? Because I am your servant.

Psalm 144

[A song] of David.*

1 The Lord is my Rock,*
Bless the Lord.
The Lord trains me for war.
The Lord trains me for battle.
2 The Lord loves me and protects me.
The Lord is my safe place high on the mountain.
The Lord rescues me.
The Lord is my shield.
I trust him.
The Lord helps me rule my people.
3 Lord, why are people important to you?
Why do you even notice us?
4 A person's life is like a puff of air.
A person's life is like a passing shadow.

5 Lord, tear open the skies and come down.
Touch the mountains and smoke will rise from them.
6 Lord, send the lightning
and make my enemies run away.
Shoot your "arrows"
and make them run away.
7 Lord, reach down from heaven and save me!
Don't let me drown in this sea of enemies.
Save me from these foreigners.
8 These enemies are liars.
They say things that are not true.

9 Lord, I will sing a new song
about the wonderful things you do.
I will praise you
and play the harp with ten strings.
10 The Lord helps kings win their wars.
The Lord saved his servant David
from his enemy's swords.
11 Save me from these foreigners.
These enemies are liars.
They say things that are not true.

12 Our young sons are like strong trees.
Our daughters are like the beautiful decorations in the palace.
13 Our barns are filled
with all kinds of crops.
There are thousands and thousands of sheep in our fields.
14 Our soldiers are safe.
No enemy is trying to break in.
We are not going to war.
People are not screaming in our streets.
15 At times like this,
people are very happy.
People are very happy
if the Lord is their God.

Psalm 145

A psalm of David.

1 I praise you my God and King.
I bless your name forever and ever.
2 I praise you every day.
I praise your name forever and ever.
3 The Lord is great.
People praise him very much.
We can't count all the great things he does.
4 Lord, people will praise you
forever and ever for the things you do.
They will tell about the great things you do.
5 Your majesty and glory are wonderful.
I will tell about your miracles.
6 Lord, people will tell about
the amazing things you do.
I will tell about the great things you do.
7 People will tell about
the good things you do.
People will sing about your goodness.
8 The Lord is kind and merciful.
The Lord is patient and full of love.
9 The Lord is good to every person.
God shows his mercy to everything he made.
10 Lord, the things you do bring praise to you.
Your followers bless you.

A song of David Or, "A song dedicated to David."
Rock A name for God to show he is a strong place of safety.

11 They tell how great your kingdom is.
   They tell how great you are.
12 So other people learn about
   the great things you do, Lord.
   Those people learn how great and wonderful
   your kingdom is.
13 Lord, your kingdom will continue forever.
   You will rule forever.
14 The Lord lifts up people who have fallen.
   The Lord helps people who are in trouble.
15 Lord, all living things look to you
   for their food.
   And you give them their food
   at the right time.
16 Lord, you open your hands,
   and you give every living thing
   everything it needs.
17 Everything the Lord does is good.
   Everything he does shows how good he is.
18 The Lord is close to every person
   who calls to him for help.
   The Lord is close to every person
   who truly worships him.
19 The Lord does what his followers want.
   The Lord listens to his followers.
   He answers their prayers and saves them.
20 The Lord protects every person
   who loves him.
   But the Lord destroys bad people.
21 I will praise the Lord!
   I want every person to praise his holy name
   forever and ever!

Psalm 146

1 Praise the Lord!
   My soul, praise the Lord!
2 I will praise the Lord all my life.
   I will sing praises to him all my life.
3 Don't depend on your leaders for help.
   Don't trust people.
   Why? Because people can't save you.
4 People die and are buried.
   And then, all of their plans to help
   are gone.
5 But people who ask God for help
   are very happy.
   Those people depend on the Lord their God.
6 The Lord made heaven and earth.
   The Lord made the sea and everything in it.
   The Lord will protect them forever.
7 The Lord does right things for people
   who have been hurt.
   God gives food to hungry people.
   The Lord frees people locked in prison.
8 The Lord helps blind people see again.
   The Lord helps people who are in trouble.
   The Lord loves good people.
9 The Lord protects strangers in our country.
   The Lord cares for widows and orphans.*
   But the Lord destroys bad people.
10 The Lord will rule forever!
   Zion,* your God will rule forever and ever!
   Praise the Lord!

Psalm 147

1 Praise the Lord because he is good.
   Sing praises to our God.
   It is good and pleasant to praise him.
2 The Lord built Jerusalem.
   God brought back the Israelite people
   who were taken as prisoners.
3 God heals their broken hearts
   and bandages their wounds.
4 God counts the stars
   and knows the name of each and every one.
5 Our Master is very great.
   He is very powerful.
   There is no limit to the things he knows.
6 The Lord supports humble people.
   But he embarrasses bad people.
7 Thank the Lord.
   Praise our God with harps.
8 God fills the sky with clouds.
   God makes rain for the earth.
   God makes the grass grow on the mountains.
9 God gives food to the animals.
   God feeds the young birds.
10 War horses and powerful soldiers
   don't make him happy.
11 The Lord is happy with people
   who worship him.
   The Lord is pleased with people
   who trust in his true love.
12 Jerusalem, praise the Lord!
   Zion, praise your God!
13 Jerusalem, God makes your gates strong.
   And God blesses the people in your city.

---

strangers, widows, orphans These were people who had no one else to help them.

Zion The southeast part of the mountain Jerusalem is built on. Sometimes it means the people of God living in Jerusalem.

14 God brought peace to your country.
So enemies did not take your grain in war.
And you have plenty of grain for food.
15 God gives a command to the earth,
and it quickly obeys.
16 God makes the snow fall
until the ground is white like wool.
God makes sleet blow through the air
like dust.
17 God makes hail fall
like rocks from the sky.
No person can stand the cold he sends.
18 Then, God gives another command,
and the warm air blows again.
The ice melts,
and water begins to flow.
19 God gave his commands to Jacob *(Israel)*.
God gave his laws and rules to Israel.
20 God did not do this for any other nation.
God did not teach his laws to other people.
Praise the Lord!

Psalm 148

1 Praise the Lord!
Angels above, praise the Lord from heaven!
2 Praise the Lord, all you angels!
Praise him, all his army*!
3 Sun and moon, praise the Lord!
Stars and lights in the sky, praise him!
4 Praise the Lord in the highest heaven!
Waters above the sky, praise him!
5 Praise the Lord's name.
Why? Because God gave the command,
and we were all created!
6 God made all these things to continue forever.
God made the laws that will never end.
7 Everything on earth, praise the Lord!
Great sea animals in the oceans,
praise the Lord!
8 God made the fire and hail,
the snow and smoke,
and all the stormy winds.
9 God made the mountains and hills,
the fruit trees and cedar trees.

10 God made all the wild animals and cattle,
the reptiles and birds.
11 God made the kings and nations on earth.
God made the leaders and judges.
12 God made the young men and women.
God made the old and young people.
13 Praise the Lord's name!
Honor his name forever!
Everything in heaven and earth, praise him!
14 God will make his people strong.
People will praise God's followers.
People will praise Israel.
They are the people God fights for.
Praise the Lord!

Psalm 149

1 Praise the Lord.
Sing a new song about the new things
the Lord has done!
Sing his praise in the assembly
where his followers meet together.
2 Let Israel enjoy themselves with their Maker.
Let the people on Zion* rejoice with
their King.
3 Let those people praise God by dancing
and playing their tambourines and harps.
4 The Lord is happy with his people.
God did a wonderful thing for his
humble people.
He saved them!
5 God's followers, rejoice in your victory!
Even after going to bed, be happy.
6 Let the people shout praise to God
and take their swords in their hands,
7 Let them go punish their enemies.
Let them go punish those people.
8 God's people will put chains
on those kings and important people.
9 God's people will punish them
like God commanded.
All of God's followers honor him.
Praise the Lord!

---

his army This can mean, "angels," or "stars and planets," or "soldiers in an army."

Zion The southeast part of the mountain Jerusalem is built on. Sometimes it means the people of God living in Jerusalem.

lyre(s) An instrument with several strings, like a harp.

Psalm 150

1 Praise the Lord!
   Praise God in his temple!
     Praise his power in heaven!
2 Praise God for the great things he does!
     Praise him for all his greatness!
3 Praise God with trumpets and horns!
     Praise him with harps and lyres*!
4 Praise God with tambourines and dancing!
     Praise him with stringed instruments
       and flutes!
5 Praise God with loud cymbals!
     Praise him with crashing cymbals!
6 Every living thing, praise the Lord!
     Praise the Lord!

---

lyre(s) An instrument with several strings, like a harp.

Proverbs

Introduction

1 These words are the wise teachings of Solomon, the son of David. Solomon was the king of Israel. ²These words are written so that people can be wise and know the right things to do. These words will help people understand wise teachings. ³These words will teach people to develop their minds in the right way—people will learn the right way to be honest, fair, and good. ⁴These wise words can teach people who need to learn wisdom. These words can teach young people the things they need to know and how to use that information. ⁵Even wise people should listen to these words. They will learn more and become even wiser. And people who are skilled at solving problems will gain even more understanding. ⁶Then those people will be able to understand wise sayings and stories with hidden meanings. Those people will be able to understand the things wise men say.

⁷The first thing a person must learn is to respect and obey the Lord—that leads to true wisdom. But evil people hate discipline and true wisdom.

Solomon's Advice to His Son

⁸My son,* listen to your father when he corrects you. And don't ignore what your mother teaches you. ⁹The things your parents teach you are like a nice hat or a beautiful necklace that makes a person look even better.

Warning Against Joining with Bad People

¹⁰My son, some people love to do bad things—and those people will try to make you do bad things too. Don't listen to them! ¹¹Those bad people might say, "Come with us! We are going to hide and wait for someone to kill. We are going to attack some innocent person. ¹²We will kill that person. We will send that person to the place of death. We will destroy that person and send him to the grave. ¹³We will steal all kinds of things worth lots of money. We will fill our houses with these things. ¹⁴So come with us and help us do these things. We will all share everything we get!"

¹⁵My son, don't follow those people. Don't even take the first step toward the way they live. ¹⁶Those bad people are always ready to do evil. They always want to kill people. ¹⁷People spread out nets to catch birds. But it is useless to set the trap while the birds are watching. ¹⁸So those bad people hide themselves and wait to kill someone. But really, they will be destroyed by their own trap! ¹⁹Greedy people are always destroyed by the things they take.

The Good Woman—Wisdom

²⁰Listen! Wisdom* is trying to teach people. She *(Wisdom)* is shouting in the streets and in the market place. ²¹She is calling out on the busy street corners. She is near the city gates trying to get people to listen to her. ₍Wisdom says:₎ ²²"You are foolish people. How long will you continue doing foolish things? How long will you make fun of wisdom? How long will you continue to hate knowledge? ²³You should have listened to my advice and teaching. I would have told you everything I knew. I would have given you all of my knowledge.

²⁴"But you refused to listen to me. I tried to help. I offered my hand—but you refused to accept my help. ²⁵You turned away and ignored all of my advice. You refused to accept my words. ²⁶So, I will laugh at your trouble. I will enjoy

---

My son The book of Proverbs was probably written to a teenage boy that was becoming a young man. This book teaches him how to be a responsible young man who loves and respects God.

Wisdom Solomon uses the picture of Wisdom and Foolishness as being two women. Both women are trying to get the attention of the young man Solomon is writing to. Wisdom is like a good woman calling the young man to be wise and obey God. Foolishness is like a bad woman calling the young man to be foolish and do many kinds of sin.

seeing trouble come to you! ²⁷Great trouble will come to you like a bad storm. Problems will hit you like a strong wind. Your troubles and sadness will be a very great burden on you. ²⁸"When all these things happen, you will ask for my help. But I will not help you. You will look for me, but you will not find me. ²⁹I will not help because you never wanted my knowledge. You refused to fear and respect the Lord. ³⁰You people refused to listen to my words of advice. You would not listen to me when I showed you the right way. ³¹You people lived the way you wanted to live. You followed your own advice. So now you must accept the result of your own actions!

³²"Foolish people die because they refuse to follow wisdom. They are happy to continue in their foolish ways, and this will destroy them. ³³But the person who obeys me will live safely. That person will be comfortable. He will not have to be afraid of evil."

Listen to Wisdom

2 My son, accept these things I say. Remember my commands. ²Listen to wisdom, and try your best to understand. ³Cry out for wisdom, and shout for understanding. ⁴Look for wisdom like silver. Look for it like a hidden treasure. ⁵If you do these things, then you will learn to respect the Lord. You will truly learn about God.

⁶The Lord gives wisdom. Knowledge and understanding come from his mouth. ⁷He gives help to good and honest people. ⁸He protects people who are fair to other people. He guards His holy people.

⁹So the Lord will give you his wisdom. Then you will understand the things that are good and fair and right. ¹⁰Wisdom will come into your heart, and your soul will be happy with knowledge.

¹¹Wisdom will protect you, and understanding will guard you. ¹²Wisdom and understanding will stop you from living the wrong way like evil people. Those people are evil even in the things they say. ¹³They have given up goodness and now live in darkness (sin). ¹⁴They are happy in doing wrong and enjoy the bad ways of evil. ¹⁵Those people can't be trusted—they lie and cheat. But your wisdom and understanding will keep you away from all these things.

¹⁶Wisdom will save you from the woman stranger. Wisdom will save you from that foreign woman who says such sweet words when she tempts you to sin with her. ¹⁷She married when she was young—but she left her husband. She forgot the marriage vows she made before God. ¹⁸And now, going with her into her house leads to death! If you follow her, she will lead you to the grave! ¹⁹ₗShe herself is like the graveₚ—men who go into her lose their life and never return.

²⁰Wisdom will help you follow the example of good people. Wisdom will help you live the way good people live. ²¹Good honest people will be able to live on their land. Simple honest people will get to keep their land. ²²But evil people will lose their land. People who lie and cheat will be taken away from the land.

Living Right Will Add to Your Life

3 My son, don't forget my teaching. Remember the things I tell you to do. ²The things I teach you will give you a longer, happier, and more peaceful life.

³Never stop loving. Always be loyal and true. ₗMake these things a part of yourselfₚ—tie them around your neck and write them on your heart. ⁴Then you will be wise and pleasing to God and people!

Trust the Lord

⁵Trust the Lord completely! Don't depend on your own knowledge. ⁶Trust the Lord in everything you do. Then he will help you. ⁷Don't depend on your own wisdom. But respect the Lord and stay away from evil. ⁸If you do this, then it will be like medicine for your body or a refreshing drink that makes you strong again.

Give to the Lord

⁹Honor the Lord with your wealth. Give him the best you have. ¹⁰Then you will have all you need. Your barns will be full of grain and your barrels will be flowing over with wine.

Accept the Lord's Punishment

¹¹My son, sometimes the Lord will show you that you are doing wrong. But don't be angry about this punishment. Try to learn from it. ¹²Why? Because the Lord corrects the people he loves. Yes, God is like a father ₗthat punishesₚ the son he loves.

The Blessings of Wisdom

¹³The person who finds wisdom will be very happy. That person will be blessed when he begins to understand. ¹⁴The profit that comes from wisdom is better than silver. The profit from

wisdom is better than fine gold! ¹⁵Wisdom is worth much more than jewels. Nothing you can want is as valuable as wisdom!

¹⁶Wisdom gives you long life, riches, and honor. ¹⁷People with wisdom live peaceful, happy lives. ¹⁸Wisdom is like the Tree of Life.* It gives full life to people that accept it. People that keep wisdom will be truly happy!

¹⁹The Lord used wisdom to make the earth. The Lord used knowledge to make the skies. ²⁰The Lord used his knowledge to make the water. Through his wisdom, the skies drop rain.

²¹My son, don't ever let wisdom out of your sight! Guard your ability to think and plan wisely. ²²Wisdom and understanding will give you life and make it more beautiful. ²³Then you will live safely and you will not fall. ²⁴When you lie down, you will not be afraid. When you rest, your sleep will be peaceful. ²⁵⁻²⁶Don't be afraid of things that might happen to you. Why? Because the Lord is with you. He will keep you safe. And those bad things will happen to bad people.

The Wisdom of Living Right

²⁷Whenever you can, do good things for people who need help. ²⁸If your neighbor asks you for something and you have it, then give it to him right then! Don't tell him, "Come back tomorrow and get it."

²⁹Don't make plans to hurt your neighbor. You live near each other for your own safety!

³⁰Don't take another person to court without a good reason. Don't do that if he hasn't done anything wrong to you.

³¹Some people are easily angered and quickly do evil. Don't be like that. ³²Why? Because the Lord hates people who are evil. But the Lord God supports people who live right.

³³The Lord is against the families of evil people. But he blesses the homes of people who live right.

³⁴If a person is proud and makes fun of other people, the Lord will punish him and make fun of him. But the Lord is kind to humble people.

³⁵Wise people live a life that brings honor. Foolish people live a life that brings shame.

The Importance of Wisdom and Understanding

4 Sons, listen to your father's teachings. Pay attention so you will understand! ²Why?

Tree of Life The tree whose fruit gives people the power to live forever. See Gen. 3:22 and Rev. 22:1-2.

Because the things I teach you are important and good. So don't ever forget my teachings.

³I was young once too! I was my daddy's little boy and my mother's only son. ⁴And my father taught me these things. He said to me, "Remember the things I say. Obey my commands and you will live. ⁵Get wisdom and understanding! Don't forget my words. Always follow my teachings. ⁶Don't turn away from wisdom. Then wisdom will protect you. Love wisdom, and wisdom will keep you safe."

⁷Wisdom begins when you decide to get wisdom. So use everything you own to get wisdom! ⌊Then you will become wise.⌋ ⁸Love wisdom, and wisdom will make you great. Make wisdom most important, and wisdom will bring you honor. ⁹She *(Wisdom)* is the greatest thing that can happen to you.

¹⁰Son, listen to me. Do the things I say, and you will live long. ¹¹I am teaching you about wisdom. I am leading you along the straight path. ¹²Follow this path, and your feet won't be caught ⌊in any trap⌋. You can run and not stumble. ⌊You will be safe in the things you try to do.⌋ ¹³Always remember these lessons. Don't forget these lessons. They are your life!

¹⁴Don't follow the path evil people walk on. ⌊Don't live like that.⌋ Don't try to be like them. ¹⁵Stay away from evil. Don't go near it. Walk straight past it. ¹⁶Bad people can't sleep until they do something wrong. Those people can't sleep until they hurt some other person. ¹⁷Those people can't live without doing evil and hurting other people.

¹⁸Good people are like the early morning light. The sun rises and the day becomes brighter and happier. ¹⁹But bad people are like a dark night. They are lost in the darkness and they fall over things they can't see.

²⁰My son, pay attention to the things I say. Listen closely to my words. ²¹Don't let my words leave you. Remember the things I say. ²²My teaching will give life to people who listen. My words are like good health to the body.

²³The most important thing is for you to be careful in the things you think. Your thoughts control your life.

²⁴Don't bend the truth and say things that are not right. Don't tell lies. ²⁵Don't let yourself turn away from the good and wise goals that are before you. ²⁶Be very careful what you do. Live a good life. ²⁷Don't leave the straight path—the way that is good and right. But always turn away from evil.

The Wisdom of Avoiding Adultery

5 My son, listen to my wise teaching. Pay attention to my words of understanding. ²Then you will remember to live wisely and watch what you say. ³Another man's wife might be very charming; the words from her lips so sweet and inviting. ⁴But in the end, she will bring only bitterness and pain. It will be like bitter poison and a sharp sword! ⁵She is on a path leading to death. She will lead you straight to the grave! ⁶Don't follow her! She has lost the right way and doesn't know it. Be careful! Follow the way that leads to life!

Adultery Can Ruin You

⁷Now my sons, listen to me. Don't forget the words I say. ⁸Stay away from the woman who does the sin of adultery.* Don't even go near the door of her house. ⁹If you do, then other people will get the honor you should have had. And some stranger will get all the things you worked years to get. ¹⁰People you don't know will take all your wealth. Other people will get the things you worked for. ¹¹And in the end, you will be so sad that you ruined your health and lost everything you had. ¹²⁻¹³Then you will say, "Why didn't I listen to my parents? Why didn't I listen to my teachers? I refused to be disciplined. I refused to be corrected. ¹⁴So now I have suffered through almost every kind of trouble people can have—and everyone knows it!"

Enjoy Your Own Wife

¹⁵⁻¹⁶Drink only the water that flows from your own well. And don't let your water flow out into the streets. ⌊You must have sexual relations only with your own wife. Don't become the father of children outside your own home.⌋ ¹⁷Your children should belong only to you. You should not have to share them with people out of your own home. ¹⁸So, be happy with your own wife. Enjoy the woman you married while you were young. ¹⁹She is like a beautiful deer, a lovely fawn. Let her love satisfy you completely. Let her love intoxicate you always. ²⁰But don't go staggering into the arms of another woman!

²¹The Lord clearly sees everything you do. The Lord watches where you go. ²²The sins of an evil person will trap him. His sins will be like ropes holding him. ²³That evil person will die because he refused to be disciplined. He will be trapped by his own desires.

The Dangers of Helping a Person Get a Loan

6 My son, don't be responsible for another man's debt. Have you promised to pay another person's debt if that person can't pay? Have you made yourself responsible for another person's debt? ²Then you have been caught! Your own words trapped you! ³You are under that person's power. So go to him and free yourself. Beg that person to free you from his debt. ⁴Don't even wait to rest or sleep. ⁵Escape from that trap like a deer running from a hunter. Free yourself like a bird flying out of a trap.

The Dangers of Being Lazy

⁶Lazy person, you should become like the ant. See what the ant does. Learn from the ant. ⁷The ant has no ruler, no boss, no leader. ⁸But during summer, the ant gathers all its food. The ant saves its food. And in the winter, it has plenty of food.

⁹Lazy person, how long will you lie there? When will you get up from your rest? ¹⁰The lazy person says, "I need a short nap. I will lie here for a short rest. ¹¹But he sleeps and sleeps. And he becomes poorer and poorer. Soon he will have nothing! It will be like a robber has come and stolen everything.

The Evil Person

¹²An evil and worthless person tells lies and says bad things. ¹³He winks his eye and makes signs with his hands and feet to trick people. ¹⁴That person is evil. All the time he is planning evil. He makes trouble everywhere. ¹⁵⌊But he will be punished.⌋ All of a sudden, disaster will strike. He will suddenly be destroyed! And there will be no one to help him!

Seven Things That the Lord Hates

¹⁶ The Lord hates these six, no seven, things:
¹⁷ eyes that show a man is proud,
tongues that tells lies,
hands that kill innocent people,
¹⁸ hearts that plan bad things to do,
feet that run to do evil things,
¹⁹ a person who tells lies
and says things in court that are not true,
a person who starts arguments
and causes fights between other people.

---

adultery Breaking the marriage promise by sexual sin.

²⁰My son, remember your father's commands. And don't forget your mother's teachings. ²¹⌊Remember their words always⌋—tie them around your neck and keep them over your heart. ²²Their teachings will lead you wherever you go. They will watch over you while you sleep. And when you wake up, they will talk to you and guide you.

²³The commands and teachings from your parents are like a light that shows you the right way. They correct you and train you to follow the path to life. ²⁴Their teaching stops you from going to an evil woman. Their words protect you from the smooth talk of the wife that left her husband. ²⁵That woman might be beautiful. But don't let that beauty burn inside you and tempt you. Don't let her eyes capture you. ²⁶A prostitute* might cost a loaf of bread. But the wife of another man can cost you your life!

²⁷If a man spills fire on himself, his clothes will also be burned. ²⁸If a man steps on a hot coal, his feet will be burned! ²⁹It is the same with any person who sleeps with another man's wife. That person will suffer.

³⁰⁻³¹A man might be hungry and steal food to eat. If that man is caught, he must pay seven times more than he stole. It might cost him everything he owns! But other people understand—they don't lose all their respect for him.

³²But a man who does the sin of adultery is foolish. He is destroying himself—he himself causes his own destruction! ³³People will lose all their respect for him. And he will never lose that shame. ³⁴The woman's husband will become jealous. That husband will be very angry. He will do anything he can to punish the other man. ³⁵No payment—no amount of money—will be enough to stop his anger!

Wisdom Will Keep You from Adultery

7 My son, remember my words. Don't forget the commands I give you. ²Obey my commands and you will have life. Make my teaching the most important thing in your life. ³⌊Keep my commands and teachings with you always.⌋ Tie them around your fingers. Write them on your heart. ⁴Treat wisdom like a sister. Treat understanding like a part of your family. ⁵Then they will protect you from other women. They will protect you from their nice words that can lead you into sin.

⁶One day I looked out my window, ⁷and I saw many foolish young men. And I saw one young man who was very foolish. ⁸He walked down the street near a bad woman's house. The young man walked by this woman's house. ⁹It was almost dark—the sun was setting. The night was beginning. ¹⁰The woman came out of the house to meet him. She was dressed like a prostitute.* She had plans for the young man. ¹¹She was wild and rebellious. She wasn't going to stay at home! ¹²She walked the streets. She went everywhere looking for trouble. ¹³She grabbed the young man and kissed him. Without any shame she looked him in the eye and said, ¹⁴"I had to offer a fellowship sacrifice today. I gave what I promised to give. ¹⁵⌊Now I have plenty of food.⌋ So I came out to invite you to join me. I looked and looked for you. And now I found you! ¹⁶I put clean sheets on my bed. They are very beautiful sheets from Egypt. ¹⁷I put perfume on my bed. The myrrh, aloes, and cinnamon smell wonderful! ¹⁸Come, we can enjoy ourselves all night. We can make love until dawn. ¹⁹My husband is gone. He is away on a business trip. ²⁰He took enough money with him for a long trip. He won't come home for two weeks.*"

²¹The woman used those words to tempt the young man. Her smooth words tricked him. ²²And the young man followed her to the trap. He was like a bull being led to the slaughter. He was like a deer walking into a trap, ²³with a hunter ready to put an arrow through its heart. The boy was like a bird flying into a net. He didn't know the danger he was in.

²⁴Now sons, listen to me. Pay attention to the words I say. ²⁵Don't let an evil woman take you. Don't follow her ways. ²⁶She has caused many men to fall. She has destroyed many men. ²⁷Her house is the place of death. Her path leads straight to death!

Wisdom, the Good Woman

8 Listen! Wisdom and Understanding are calling for you to listen.
² They stand at the top of the hill
by the road where the paths meet.
³ They are near the gates of the city.
They are calling out from the open doors.

---

prostitute A woman paid by men for sexual sin. Sometimes this also means a person who is not faithful to God and stops following him.

He ... two weeks. Literally, "He won't come home until the full moon." The fellowship meal probably shows that this happened at the new moon, the first day of the Hebrew month.

4 Wisdom says,
 "Men, I call out to you.
  I call out to all people.
5 If you are foolish, learn to be wise.
  Foolish men, learn to understand.
6 Listen! The things I teach are important.
  I tell you things that are right.
7 My words are true.
  I hate evil lies.
8 The things I say are right.
  There is nothing false or wrong
   in my words.
9 All these sayings are clear to the person
   who has understanding.
  The person with knowledge
   understands these things.
10 Accept my discipline.
   It is worth more than silver.
   It is worth more than the best gold.
11 Wisdom is worth more than pearls.
   It is worth more than anything a person
    can want."

What Wisdom Does

12 "I am Wisdom.
   I live with good judgment.
   You can find me with Knowledge
    and Good Planning.
13 If a person respects the Lord,
    then that person will hate evil.
   I (Wisdom) hate pride and people who think
    they are better than other people.
   I hate evil ways, and a lying mouth.
14 But I give people the ability
    to make good decisions
    and have good judgment.
   I give understanding and power!
15 Kings use me to rule.
   Rulers use me to make fair laws.
16 Every good ruler on earth uses me
    to rule the people under them.
17 I love people who love me.
   And if people try hard to find me,
    they will find me.
18 I also have riches
    and honor to give.
   I give true wealth and success.
19 The things I give are better than fine gold.
   And my gifts are better than pure silver.
20 I lead people in the right way.
   I lead them along the paths
    of right judgment.

21 I give wealth to people who love me.
   Yes, I will fill their houses with treasures.
22 I was the first thing made,
    long ago in the beginning.
23 I was made in the beginning.
   I was made before the world began.
24 I was born before the oceans;
   I was made before there was water.
25 I was born before the mountains.
   I was born before the hills.
26 I was born before the Lord made the earth.
   I was born before the fields.
   I was born before God made the first dust
    of the world.
27 I was there when the Lord
    made the skies.
   I was there when the Lord
    drew the circle around the land
    and set the limits for the ocean.
28 I was born before the Lord put the clouds
    in the sky.
   And I was there when the Lord put water
    in the ocean.
29 I was there when the Lord set the limits
    for water in the seas.
   The water can't rise higher
    than the Lord allows.
   I was there when the Lord made
    the foundations of the earth.
30 I was beside him like a skilled worker.
   The Lord was happy every day
    because of me.
   I made him laugh and be happy all the time.
31 The Lord was excited about the world
    he made.
   He was happy about the people he put there.
32 "Now, children, listen to me!
   You can be happy too,
    if you follow my ways!
33 Listen to my teachings and become wise.
   Don't refuse to listen.
34 The person who listens to me will be happy.
   He watches every day at my doors.
   He waits at my doorway.
35 Any person who finds me finds life.
   He will get good things from the Lord!
36 But the person who sins against me hurts
    himself.
   All people who hate me love death!"

Wisdom and Stupidity

9 Wisdom built her house. She put the seven columns* in it. ²She *(Wisdom)* cooked meat and made wine. She put food on her table. ³And then she sent her servants to town to invite people to come up to the hill in the city ⌊and eat with her⌋. She said, ⁴"Come, you people who need to learn." She also invited foolish people. She said, ⁵"Come, eat the food of my wisdom. And drink the wine that I have made. ⁶Leave your old, foolish ways, and you will have life. Follow the way of understanding."

⁷If you try to show a proud man that he is wrong, then he will only criticize you. ⌊That man only makes fun of God's wisdom.⌋ If you tell an evil man that he is wrong, then he will make fun of you. ⁸So, if a man thinks that he is better than other people, don't tell him that he is wrong. He will hate you for it. But if you try to help a wise man then he will respect you. ⁹If you teach a wise man, then he will become wiser. If you teach a good man, then he will learn more.

¹⁰Respect for the Lord is the first step toward getting wisdom. Getting knowledge of the Lord is the first step toward getting understanding. ¹¹If you are wise, then your life will be longer. ¹²If you become wise, then you have become wise for your own good. But if you become proud and make fun of other people, then only you are to blame for your trouble.

¹³A foolish person is like a loud, evil woman. She does not have knowledge. ¹⁴She sits at the door of her house. She sits on her chair on the hill in the city. ¹⁵And when people walk by, she calls out to them. Those people are not interested in her, but she says, ¹⁶"Come you people who need to learn." She also invited foolish people. ¹⁷But she *(Foolishness)* says, "If you steal water, it tastes better than your own. If you steal bread, it tastes better than the bread you cook yourself."

¹⁸And those poor foolish people didn't know that her house was filled only with ghosts. She *(Foolishness)* had invited them into the deepest parts of the place of death!

Solomon's Proverbs

10 These are the proverbs *(wise sayings)* of Solomon:

A wise son makes his father happy. But a foolish son makes his mother very sad.

²If a person gets money by doing bad things, then that money is worthless. But doing good can save you from death.

³The Lord cares for good people. He gives them the food they need. But the Lord takes away the things that evil people want.

⁴A lazy person will be poor. But a person that works hard will be rich.

⁵A smart man gathers the crops at the right time. But if a person sleeps during the time of harvest and does not gather the crops, then he will be shamed.

⁶People ask God to bless a good person. Evil people might say those good things, but their words only hide the bad things they are planning.*

⁷Good people leave good memories. But evil people will soon be forgotten.

⁸A wise person obeys when someone tells him to do something. But a fool argues and brings trouble to himself.

⁹A good, honest person is safe. But a crooked person who cheats will be caught.

¹⁰A person who hides the truth causes trouble. A person who speaks openly makes peace.*

¹¹A good man's words make life better. But the words from an evil man only shows the bad that is inside him.*

¹²Hate causes arguments. But love forgives every wrong thing people do.

¹³Wise people say things that are worth hearing. But foolish people must be punished ⌊before they learn their lesson⌋.

¹⁴Wise people ⌊are quiet⌋ and learn new things. But foolish people talk and bring trouble to themselves.

¹⁵Wealth protects the rich person. And poverty destroys a poor person.

¹⁶If a person does good, then he is rewarded. He is given life. Evil brings only punishment.

¹⁷A person who learns from his punishment can help other people live too. But a person who refuses to learn only leads people the wrong way.

¹⁸A person who hides his hate might be telling a lie. But only a fool tries to find gossip he can spread.

Evil people ... planning Or, "But violence will cover the mouth of evil people."

A person ... peace This is from the ancient Greek translation. The Hebrew repeats the second half of verse 8.

But the words ... inside him In Hebrew, this is like the second half of verse 6.

seven columns In ancient Israel, many houses had four main rooms with seven columns to support the roof. This shows Wisdom had a good solid house.

[sup]19[/sup]A person who talks too much gets himself into trouble. A wise person learns to be quiet.
[sup]20[/sup]The words from a good person are like pure silver. But the thoughts from an evil person are worthless.
[sup]21[/sup]A good person's words will help many people. But a fool's stupidity will kill him.
[sup]22[/sup]A blessing from the Lord will bring you true wealth. And it won't bring troubles with it.
[sup]23[/sup]The foolish person enjoys doing wrong. But a wise man is happy with wisdom.
[sup]24[/sup]An evil person will be defeated by the things he fears. But a good person will get the things that he wants.
[sup]25[/sup]Evil people are destroyed by their trouble. But good people will stand strong forever.
[sup]26[/sup]Never let a lazy man do something for you. He will irritate you—like vinegar in your mouth or smoke in your eyes.
[sup]27[/sup]If you respect the Lord, then you will live long. But evil people will lose years from their life.
[sup]28[/sup]The things good people hope for bring happiness. The things bad people hope for bring ruin.
[sup]29[/sup]The Lord protects good people. But the Lord destroys people that do wrong.
[sup]30[/sup]Good people will always be safe. But evil people will be forced to leave the land.
[sup]31[/sup]Good people say wise things. But people will stop listening to a person that says things that bring trouble.
[sup]32[/sup]Good people know the right things to say. But evil people say things that bring trouble.

11

⌊Some people use scales that don't weigh things properly. They use those scales to cheat people.⌋ The Lord hates those false scales. But accurate scales please the Lord.
[sup]2[/sup]People that are proud and boast will become unimportant. But people who are humble will also become wise.
[sup]3[/sup]Good, honest people are guided by honesty. But evil people destroy themselves when they cheat other people.
[sup]4[/sup]On the day God judges people, money is worth nothing. But goodness will save people from death.
[sup]5[/sup]If a good person is honest, then his life will be easy. But an evil person is destroyed by the bad things he does.
[sup]6[/sup]Goodness saves the honest person. But evil people are trapped by the bad things they want.

[sup]7[/sup]After an evil man dies, there is no hope for him. Everything he hoped for is gone—all of it is worth nothing.
[sup]8[/sup]A good person will escape trouble, and that trouble will happen to some evil person.
[sup]9[/sup]An evil person can hurt other people by the things he says. But good people are protected by their wisdom.
[sup]10[/sup]When good people are successful, all the city is happy. When evil people are destroyed, people shout with joy.
[sup]11[/sup]A city becomes great when the honest people living there give it their blessing. But the things an evil person says can destroy a city.
[sup]12[/sup]A person without good sense says bad things about his neighbors. But a wise man knows when to be quiet.
[sup]13[/sup]Any person who tells secrets about other people can't be trusted. But a person that can be trusted does not spread gossip.
[sup]14[/sup]A nation with weak leaders will fall. But many good advisers will make that nation safe.
[sup]15[/sup]If you promise to pay another person's debt, then you will be sorry. You will be safe if you refuse to make those deals.
[sup]16[/sup]A kind, gentle woman gains respect. Pushy men gain only money.
[sup]17[/sup]A kind man will profit. But a mean man will cause trouble for himself.
[sup]18[/sup]An evil man cheats people and takes their money. But a person that is fair and does right will get the real reward.
[sup]19[/sup]Truly, goodness brings life. But evil people chase after evil and find death.
[sup]20[/sup]The Lord hates people that love to do evil. But he is happy with people that try to do right.
[sup]21[/sup]It is true that evil people will surely be punished. And good people will be made free.
[sup]22[/sup]If a woman is beautiful but foolish, it is the same as a beautiful gold ring in a pig's nose.
[sup]23[/sup]When good people get what they want, it brings more good. But when evil people get what they want, it brings only trouble.
[sup]24[/sup]If a person gives freely, then he will gain even more. But if a person refuses to give, then he will become poor.
[sup]25[/sup]A person who gives freely will profit. If you help others, then you will gain more for yourself.
[sup]26[/sup]People become angry at a greedy man who refuses to sell his grain. But they are happy with a man who sells his grain to feed other people.
[sup]27[/sup]People respect a person who tries to do good. But a person who does evil gets nothing but trouble.

²⁸The person who trusts in his riches will fall like a dead leaf. But the good person will grow like a new green leaf.
²⁹If a person causes trouble for his family, then he will gain nothing. And in the end, the foolish person will be forced to serve the wise person.
³⁰The things a good man does are like the Tree of Life.* A wise man gives new life to people.*
³¹If good people are rewarded on earth, then surely evil people will also get what they deserve.

12 If a person wants to be wise, then he is not angry if someone tells him when he does wrong. The person who hates to be told that he is wrong is stupid.
²The Lord is happy with a good person. But the Lord judges an evil man to be guilty.
³Evil people are never safe. But good people will be safe and secure.
⁴A husband is happy and proud with a good wife. But if a woman makes her husband ashamed, then she is like a sickness in his body.
⁵Good people are fair and honest in the things they plan to do. But don't trust the things an evil person tells you.
⁶Evil people use their words to hurt other people. But the words of a good person can save people from danger.
⁷Evil people are destroyed and there is nothing left. But people remember a good man long after he is gone.
⁸People praise a wise man. But people don't respect a stupid person.
⁹It is better to be a person who is not important but works hard than to be a person who pretends to be important but has no food.
¹⁰A good man cares for his animals. But evil people can't be kind.
¹¹The farmer that works with his land will have enough food. But the person who wastes time on worthless ideas is foolish.
¹²Evil people always want to find wrong things to do. But good people have strength that goes deep like roots.
¹³An evil person says foolish things and is trapped by his words. But a good person escapes from that kind of trouble.
¹⁴A person is rewarded because of the good things that he says. In the same way, the work he does gives him profit.

¹⁵A foolish person always thinks his own way is best. But a wise person listens to the things other people tell him.
¹⁶A foolish person is easily upset. But a smart person quickly forgives other people if they say something wrong.
¹⁷If a person tells the truth, then he is honest in the things he says. But if a person lies, then that leads to trouble.
¹⁸If a person speaks words without thinking, then those words can hurt like a sword. But a wise person is careful with the things he says. His words can heal those hurts.
¹⁹If a person tells a lie, then those words are wasted quickly. But the truth will live forever.
²⁰Evil people always want to cause trouble. But people who work for peace will be happy.
²¹Good people will be kept safe by the Lord. But evil people will have many troubles.
²²The Lord hates people who tell lies. But the Lord is happy with people who tell the truth.
²³A smart* person doesn't tell everything he knows. But a foolish person tells everything and shows he is a fool.
²⁴People who work hard will be put in charge of other workers. But a lazy person will have to work like a slave.
²⁵Worry can take away a person's happiness. But a kind word can make a person happy.
²⁶A good man is very careful about the friends he chooses. But evil people always choose the wrong friends.
²⁷A lazy person won't go after the things he wants. But riches come to the person who works hard.
²⁸If you live right, then you will have true life. That is the way to live forever.

13 A wise son listens carefully when his father tells him what to do. But a proud person does not listen when people try to correct him.
²Good people are rewarded for the good things they say. But evil people always want to do wrong.
³The person who is careful about the things he says will save his life. But the person who speaks without thinking will be destroyed.
⁴The lazy person wants things, but he can never get them. But people who work hard will get the things they want.
⁵Good people hate lies. Evil people will be made ashamed.

Tree of Life See Gen. 2:9; 3:22-24; Rev. 22:1-2.
A wise man gives new life to people Or, "A wise man takes souls."

smart Or "crafty."

⁶Goodness protects a good, honest person. But evil defeats the person that loves to sin.

⁷Some people act like they are rich, but they have nothing. Other people act like they are poor, but they are really rich.

⁸A rich person might have to pay a ransom to save his life. But poor people never receive threats like that.

⁹A good person is like a light that shines brightly. But an evil person is like a light that becomes dark.

¹⁰People who think they are better than other people only cause trouble. But people who listen to the things other people tell them are wise.

¹¹If a person cheats to get money, then that money will soon be gone. But the person who earns his money will make it grow more and more.

¹²If there is no hope, then the heart is sad. If the thing you wish for happens, then you are filled with joy.

¹³If a person refuses to listen when other people try to help him, then he will bring trouble to himself. But the person who respects the things other people tell him, will be rewarded.

¹⁴The teachings of a wise person give life. Those words will help you in times of trouble.

¹⁵People like a person with good sense. But life is hard for a person who can't be trusted.

¹⁶A wise person always thinks before he does something. But a foolish person shows he is stupid by the things he does.

¹⁷If a messenger cannot be trusted, then there will be trouble around him. But if a person can be trusted, then there will be peace.

¹⁸If a person refuses to learn from his mistakes, then he will be poor and ashamed. But if a person listens when he is criticized or punished, then he will profit.

¹⁹If a person wants something and then gets it, he will be very happy. But stupid people only want evil, and they refuse to change.

²⁰Be friends with people who are wise, and you will become wise. But if you choose fools to be your friends, then you will have trouble.

²¹Trouble chases sinners wherever they go. But good things happen to good people.

²²A good person will have wealth to give to his children and grandchildren. And in the end, good people will get all the things that evil people have.

²³A poor man might have good land that can produce plenty of food. But he makes bad decisions and stays hungry.

²⁴If a person truly loves his children, then he will correct them when they are wrong. If you love your son, then you will be careful to teach him the right way.

²⁵Good people will have what they really need. But evil people will always be without the most important thing.

14 The wise woman uses her wisdom to make her home what it should be. But the foolish woman destroys her home by the foolish things she does.

²The person who lives right respects the Lord. But the person who is not honest hates the Lord.

³A foolish person's words cause him trouble. But the words of a wise person protect him.

⁴If there are no cows to do the work, then the barn will be empty. The people can use the strength of a cow to have a great harvest.

⁵A truthful person does not lie—he is a good witness. But a person that can't be trusted never tells the truth—he is a bad witness.

⁶People who make fun of God might look for wisdom, but they will never find it. People who believe God are truly wise. Knowledge comes easy to them.

⁷Don't become friends with a foolish person. There is nothing he can teach you.

⁸Smart people are wise because they think carefully about the things they do. But foolish people are fools because they think they can live by cheating.

⁹A foolish person laughs at the idea of paying for the bad things he did. But good people try very hard to get forgiveness.

¹⁰If a person is sad, he is the only one that can feel that sadness. In the same way, if a person is happy, he is the only one that can feel that joy.

¹¹The house of an evil person will be destroyed. But the home of a good person will live forever.

¹²There is a way that people think is right. But that way leads only to death.

¹³A person might be sad, even if he is laughing. And after the laughter, the sadness will still be there.

¹⁴Evil people will be fully paid *(punished)* for the wrong things they do. And good people will be fully rewarded for the good things they do.

¹⁵A fool will believe anything he hears. But a wise man thinks carefully about everything.

¹⁶A wise man respects the Lord and stays away from evil. But a foolish man does things without thinking—he is not careful.

¹⁷A person who becomes angry easily does foolish things. But a wise person is patient.

¹⁸Foolish people are punished for their foolishness. But wise people are rewarded with knowledge.
¹⁹Good people will win against evil people. Evil people will be forced to bow down to them.
²⁰A poor person has no friends, not even his neighbor. But rich people have many friends.
²¹You should not think bad things about your neighbors. If you want to be happy, be kind to those poor people.
²²Any person who plans to do evil is doing wrong. But the person that tries to do good will have friends that love and trust him.
²³If you work hard, then you will have the things you need. But if you do nothing but talk, then you will be poor.
²⁴Wise people are rewarded by wealth. But foolish people are rewarded by foolishness.
²⁵A person who tells the truth helps other people. The person who tells lies hurts other people.
²⁶The person who respects the Lord is safe and his children also live in safety.
²⁷Respect for the Lord gives true life. It saves a person from death's trap.
²⁸If a king rules over many people, then he is great. But if there are no people, then the king is worth nothing.
²⁹A patient person is very smart. A person who is easily angered shows that he is a fool.
³⁰If a person has peace in his mind, then his body will be healthy. But jealousy causes sickness in his body.
³¹The person that causes trouble for poor people shows that he does not respect God—God made both people. But if a person is kind to poor people, then he shows honor to God.
³²During times of trouble, evil people are defeated. But good people win a victory even during death.
³³A wise person is always thinking wise things. But a foolish person knows nothing about wisdom.
³⁴Goodness makes a nation great. But sin is a shame to any people.
³⁵A king is happy when he has wise leaders. But a king is angry with leaders that are foolish.

15 A peaceful answer causes anger to disappear. But a rough answer causes anger to grow.
²When a wise person speaks, other people want to listen. But a foolish person speaks only foolishness.

³The Lord sees what happens everywhere. The Lord watches every person— good and evil.
⁴Kind words are like a Tree of Life.* But lying words will crush a man's spirit.
⁵A foolish person refuses to listen to his father's advice. But a wise person listens closely when people try to teach him.
⁶Good people are rich in many things. But the things that an evil person has only cause him trouble.
⁷Wise people say things that give you new information. But foolish people say nothing worth hearing.
⁸The Lord hates the offerings that evil people give. But the Lord is happy to hear a good person's prayers.
⁹The Lord hates the way evil people live. The Lord loves people who try to do good.
¹⁰If a person begins to live wrong, then he will be punished. And the person that hates to be corrected will be destroyed.
¹¹The Lord knows everything, even what happens in the place of death. So surely the Lord will know what happens in the hearts and minds of people.
¹²The foolish person hates to be told when he is wrong. And that person refuses to ask wise people for advice.
¹³If a person is happy, then his face will show joy. But if a person is sad in his heart, then his spirit will show that sadness.
¹⁴A wise person tries to gain more knowledge. But a foolish person only wants more foolishness.
¹⁵Some poor people are sad all the time. But for people with happiness in their hearts, life is one big party.
¹⁶It is better to be poor and respect the Lord than to be rich and have many troubles.
¹⁷It is better to eat a little in a place where there is love, than to eat a lot where there is hate.
¹⁸People that are easily angered cause trouble. But a patient person causes peace.
¹⁹A lazy person will have trouble everywhere. But life will be easy for honest people.
²⁰A wise son brings happiness to his father. But a foolish person brings shame to his mother.
²¹Doing foolish things makes a foolish person happy. But a wise person is careful to do the things that are right.

Tree of Life See Gen. 2:9; 3:22-24; Rev. 22:1-2.

²²If a person does not get enough advice, then his plans will fail. But a person will succeed if he listens to the things wise people tell him.
²³A person is happy when he gives a good answer. And the right word at the right time is very good.
²⁴The things a wise person does leads to success. And those things stop him from going down to the place of death.
²⁵The Lord will destroy everything a proud person has. But the Lord protects the things that a widow has.
²⁶The Lord hates evil thoughts. But the Lord is happy with kind words.
²⁷If a person cheats to get things, then he will bring trouble to his family. But if a person is honest, then he will have no trouble.
²⁸Good people think before they answer. But evil people speak before they think, and that causes them trouble.
²⁹The Lord is far away from evil people. But he always hears the prayers of good people.
³⁰A person that smiles makes other people happy. And good news makes people feel better.
³¹A person is very wise if he listens when someone tells him that he has done wrong.
³²If a person refuses to learn, then he is only hurting himself. But the person who listens when someone tells him he is wrong, will understand more and more.
³³The person who respects the Lord is learning to be wise. A person must be humble before he can truly respect the Lord.

16 People make their plans. But it is the Lord who makes those things happen.
²A person thinks everything he does is right. But the Lord judges the real reasons people do things.
³Always turn to the Lord for help in everything you do, and you will be successful.
⁴The Lord has a plan for everything. And in the Lord's plan, evil people will be destroyed.
⁵The Lord hates every person who thinks that he is better than other people. The Lord will surely punish all those proud people.
⁶True love and loyalty will make you pure.* Respect the Lord, and you will stay far away from evil.

⁷If a person is living a good life, pleasing to the Lord, then even that person's enemies will be at peace with him.
⁸It is better to gain only a little the right way than to gain much through cheating.
⁹A person can make plans about the things that he wants to do. But it is the Lord who decides what will happen.
¹⁰When a king speaks, his words are law. His decisions should always be fair.
¹¹The Lord wants all scales and balances to be honest. He wants all business agreements to be fair.
¹²Kings hate people who do evil. Goodness will make his kingdom stronger.
¹³Kings want to hear the truth. Kings like people who don't lie.
¹⁴When a king is angry, he can kill someone. And a wise person will try to keep the king happy.
¹⁵When the king is happy, life will be better for everyone. If the king is pleased with you, then it will be like spring rain falling from a cloud.
¹⁶Wisdom is worth much more than gold. Understanding is worth much more than silver.
¹⁷Good people live their lives trying to stay away from evil. The person who is careful with his life, is guarding his soul.
¹⁸If a person is proud, then he is in danger of destruction. If a person thinks he is better than other people, then he is in danger of defeat.
¹⁹It is better to be humble and live with poor people than to share wealth with people who think they are better than other people.
²⁰The person who listens when people try to teach him will profit. And the person who trusts in the Lord will be blessed.
²¹People will know if a person is wise. And a person that carefully chooses his words can be very persuasive.
²²Wisdom brings true life to people who have it. But fools only learn to be more foolish.
²³A wise man always thinks before he speaks. And the words he says are good and worth hearing.
²⁴Kind words are like honey. They are easy to accept and good for your health.
²⁵There is a way that seems right to people. But that way leads only to death.
²⁶A worker's appetite keeps him working. His hunger makes him work so that he can eat.
²⁷A worthless person plans bad things to do. His advice destroys like fire.

---

make ... pure Or, "make atonement." The Hebrew word means "to cover or erase a person's sins."

²⁸Troublemakers are always causing problems. And the person who spreads gossip causes trouble between close friends.
²⁹A person who becomes angry easily will cause trouble for his friends. He will lead them in a way that is not good.
³⁰The person who winks his eye and smiles is planning something wrong and evil.
³¹Gray hair is the crown of glory on people who have lived good lives.
³²It is better to be patient than to be a strong soldier. It is better to control your anger than to take control over a whole city.
³³People throw lots* to make decisions. But the decisions always come from God.

17 ¹It is better to have only a dry piece of bread to eat in peace than to have a whole house full of food with everyone arguing.
²A smart servant will gain control over a master's lazy son. That wise servant will gain everything the master has.
³Gold and silver are put into fire to make them pure. But the Lord is the One who makes peoples' hearts pure.
⁴An evil person listens to the evil things other people say. People who tell lies also listen to lies.
⁵Some people make fun of poor people. They laugh at people who have problems. This shows that those bad people don't respect God who made them. These bad people will be punished.
⁶Grandchildren make old people happy. And children are proud of their parents.
⁷It is not wise for a fool to speak too much. In the same way, it is not wise for a ruler to tell lies.
⁸Some people think a bribe is like a lucky charm—wherever they go, it seems to work.
⁹If you forgive a person who does wrong to you, then you can be friends. But if you continue to remember the wrong that he did, then it will hurt your friendship.
¹⁰A smart person learns from the things he does wrong. But a fool learns nothing, even after a hundred lessons.
¹¹An evil person only wants to do wrong. In the end, God will send a messenger to punish him.
¹²It is very dangerous to meet a mother bear that is angry because her cubs are stolen. But that is better than to meet a fool that is busy doing his foolishness.

¹³Don't do bad things to people who do good things to you. If you do, then you will have trouble for the rest of your life.
¹⁴If you start an argument, it is like breaking a hole in a dam. So stop the argument before it becomes bigger and bigger.
¹⁵The Lord hates these two things—punishing someone that has done nothing wrong, and forgiving someone that is guilty.
¹⁶If a foolish person has money, it is wasted. Why? Because that foolish person does not use the money to become wise.
¹⁷A friend loves at all times. A true brother always supports you, even in times of trouble.
¹⁸Only a fool will promise to be responsible for another person's debts.
¹⁹The person who enjoys arguing also enjoys sin. If you brag about yourself, then you are inviting trouble.*
²⁰An evil person will not profit. The person who tells lies will have trouble.
²¹A father with a foolish son will be very sad. A fool's father won't be happy.
²²Happiness is like good medicine. But sorrow is like a sickness.
²³An evil person accepts secret payment for cheating other people.
²⁴The wise man is always thinking of the best thing to do. But a foolish person is always dreaming about faraway places.
²⁵A foolish son brings sorrow to his father. And a foolish son brings sadness to the mother that gave birth to him.
²⁶It is wrong to punish a person who has done nothing wrong. It is wrong to punish leaders when they are honest.
²⁷A wise person uses words carefully. A wise person does not become angry easily.
²⁸Even a fool seems wise if he keeps quiet. People think he is wise if he doesn't say anything.

18 ¹Some people don't want to be around other people. They do only what they want to do. And they get upset when people give them good advice.
²A foolish person doesn't want to learn from other people. That person only wants to tell his own ideas.
³People don't like an evil person. People make fun of that foolish person.

---

lot(s) Sticks, stones, or pieces of bone used like dice for making decisions.

If you brag ... inviting trouble Literally, "The person who makes his door fall is looking for trouble."

⁴The words of a wise man are like water bubbling up from a deep well—the well of wisdom!
⁵ₗYou must be fair in judging people.ⱼ If you let guilty people go free then you are not being fair to good people.
⁶A foolish person causes himself trouble with the things he says. His words can start fights.
⁷When a foolish person talks, he ruins himself. His own words trap him.
⁸People always want to hear gossip—it is like good food going down into the stomach.
⁹A person who does bad work is as bad as a person who destroys things.
¹⁰There is much strength in the name of the Lord. It is like a strong tower. Good people can run to him and be safe.
¹¹Rich people think that their wealth will protect them. They think that it is like a strong fort.
¹²A proud person will soon be ruined. But an humble person will be honored.
¹³You should let other people finish speaking before you try to answer them. That way you won't be embarrassed and appear foolish.
¹⁴A person's mind can keep him alive during sickness. But if a person thinks he has lost, then all hope is gone.
¹⁵The wise person always wants to learn more. That person listens closely for more wisdom.
¹⁶If you want to meet an important person, give him a gift. Then you can easily get to meet him.
¹⁷The first person to speak always seems right until someone comes and questions him.
¹⁸If two powerful people are arguing, throwing lots* may be the best way to decide the argument.
¹⁹If you insult your friend, then he will be harder to win back than a city with strong walls. And arguments separate people like palace gates with strong bars across them.
²⁰The things you say affect your life. If you say good things, then good things will happen to you. But if you say bad things, then bad things will happen to you.
²¹The tongue can speak words that bring life or death. And people who love to talk must be ready to accept what it brings.
²²If you find a wife, then you have found a good thing. She shows that the Lord is happy with you.
²³A poor person will beg for help, but a rich person is rude when he answers.
²⁴Some friends are fun to be with.* But a close friend can be even better than a brother.

19 It is better to be poor and honest than to be a fool that tells lies and cheats people.
²Being excited about something is not enough. You must also know what you are doing. You should not rush into something or you will do it wrong.
³A person's own foolishness will ruin his life. But he will blame the Lord.
⁴If a person is rich, then his wealth will bring him many friends. But if a person is poor, all his friends will leave him.
⁵A person who tells a lie against another person will be punished. The person who tells lies will not be safe.
⁶Many people want to be friends with the ruler. And everyone wants to be the friend of a person who gives gifts.
⁷If a person is poor, then even his family is against him. And all of his friends turn away from him. That poor person can beg them for help. But they will not go near him.
⁸If a person really likes himself, then he will work hard to become wise. He will try hard to understand, and he will get his reward.
⁹A lying witness must be punished! The person who tells lies will be destroyed.
¹⁰A foolish person should not be rich. That would be like a slave ruling over princes.
¹¹If a person is wise, that wisdom gives him patience. And it is wonderful when he forgives people who do wrong to him.
¹²Angry words from a king are like the roars of a lion. But compliments from him are like a gentle rain falling softly on the grass.
¹³A foolish son can bring a flood of troubles to his father. And a nagging wife is like water that won't stop dripping.
¹⁴People get houses and money from their parents. But a good wife is a gift from the Lord.
¹⁵A lazy person might get plenty of sleep, but he will also be very hungry.
¹⁶If a person obeys the law, then he protects himself. But if a person thinks it is not important, then he will be killed.

---

lot(s) Sticks, stones, or pieces of bone used like dice for making decisions.

Some friends are fun to be with Or, "Some friends can bring disaster."

¹⁷Giving money to poor people is like loaning it to the Lord. The Lord will pay you back for being kind to them.
¹⁸Teach your son and punish him when he is wrong. That is the only hope. If you refuse to do this, then you are helping him destroy himself.
¹⁹A person with a short temper must pay the price. If you keep getting him out of trouble, then he will do the same things again and again.
²⁰Listen to advice and accept discipline. Then you will become wise.
²¹People get a lot of ideas, but only the Lord's plan will happen.
²²People want a person to be loyal and true. So it is better to be a poor man than a person people can't trust.
²³A person who respects the Lord has a good life. That person is satisfied with his life and doesn't have to worry about troubles.
²⁴Some people are too lazy to take care of themselves—they are too lazy to lift their food from their plate to their mouth!
²⁵Some people show no respect for anything—those people must be punished. A foolish person must be forced to learn his lesson. But a little reprimand is enough to make a wise person learn.
²⁶A person who takes everything from his father and chases his mother away is a disgusting, shameful person.
²⁷If you refuse to learn, then you will soon forget the things you already know.
²⁸A lying witness makes justice nothing but a joke! The things evil people say bring more evil.
²⁹The person who thinks that he is better than other people will be punished. The foolish person will get the punishment that is saved for him.

20 Wine and beer make people lose control of themselves. They get loud and start to brag. They become drunk and do foolish things.
²The anger of a king is like the roar of a lion. If you make the king angry, then you could lose your life.
³Any fool can start an argument. So you should respect a person who refuses to argue.
⁴A lazy person is too lazy to plant seeds. So, at the time of harvest he looks for food and finds nothing.
⁵Good advice is like getting water from a deep well. But a wise person will try hard to learn from another person.
⁶Many people say that they are loyal and full of love. But it is very hard to find someone that really is.

⁷A good person lives a good life. And his children will be blessed.
⁸When the king sits and judges people, he can see evil with his own eyes.
⁹Can any person really say that he has always done his best? Can any person really say that he has no sin? ₁No!₁
¹⁰The Lord hates people that cheat other people using weights and measures that are not fair.
¹¹Even a child shows that he is good or bad by the things he does. You can watch that child and know if he is honest and good.
¹²We have eyes to see with and ears to hear with—and the Lord made them for us!
¹³If you love to sleep, then you will become poor. But use your time working and you will have plenty to eat.
¹⁴The person who buys something from you always says, "It's no good! It costs too much!" Then that person goes away and tells other people that he made a good deal.
¹⁵Gold and jewels can make a man rich. But a person who knows what he is talking about is worth much, much more.
¹⁶You will lose your shirt if you make yourself responsible for another man's debts.
¹⁷If you get something by cheating, it may seem like a good thing. But in the end it will be worth nothing.
¹⁸Get good advice before you make plans. If you are starting a war, find good people to guide you.
¹⁹A person who tells gossip about other people can't be trusted. So don't be friends with a person who talks too much.
²⁰If a person speaks against his father or mother, then that person is like a light that becomes dark.
²¹If your wealth was very easy to get, it will not be worth much to you.
²²If someone does something against you, don't try to punish him yourself. Wait for the Lord! In the end, he will make you the winner.
²³Some people use weights and scales that are not accurate. They use those things so they can cheat people. The Lord hates that. That does not make him happy!
²⁴The Lord decides what happens to every person. So how can any person understand what happens in his life?
²⁵Think carefully before you promise to give something to God. Later you might wish that you had not made that promise.

²⁶A wise king will decide which people are evil. And that king will punish those people.
²⁷The Lord is able to know the things that are inside a person.
²⁸If a king is loyal and true, then he will keep his power. His true love will keep his kingdom strong.
²⁹We admire a young man for his strength. But we respect an old man for his gray hair—⌈it shows he lived a full life⌉.
³⁰If we are punished, we will stop doing wrong. Pain can change a person.

21 ⌈Farmers dig small ditches to water their fields. They change where the water goes by closing different ditches.⌋ The Lord controls a king's mind just like that. The Lord can lead the king wherever he wants him to go.
²A person thinks everything he does is right. But the Lord judges the real reasons people do things.
³Do the things that are right and fair. The Lord loves those things better than sacrifices.
⁴Proud looks and proud thoughts are sins. They show a person is evil.
⁵Careful plans can lead to profit. But if you are not careful, and you do things too quickly, then you will become poor.
⁶If you cheat to become rich, then your wealth will soon be gone. And your riches will lead you to death.
⁷The bad things that evil people do will destroy them. Those people refuse to do what is right.
⁸Bad people always try to cheat other people. But good people are honest and fair.
⁹It is better to live on the roof than to live in a house with a wife that wants to argue.
¹⁰Evil people always want to do more evil. And those people show no mercy to people around them.
¹¹Punish the person who makes fun of God and foolish people will learn a lesson. They will become wise. And then they will gain more and more knowledge.
¹²God is good. God knows what evil people are doing, and he will punish them.
¹³If a person refuses to help poor people, then there will be no help for him when he needs it.
¹⁴If a person is angry with you, give him a gift in secret. A gift that is given in secret can stop great anger.
¹⁵Fair judgment makes good people happy. But it makes evil people very afraid.
¹⁶If a person leaves the way of wisdom, then he is going toward destruction.

¹⁷If having fun is the most important thing to a person, then that person will become poor. If that person loves wine and food, then he will never be rich.
¹⁸Evil people have to pay for all the bad things they do to good people. People who are not honest have to pay for the things they do to honest people.
¹⁹It is better to live in the desert than to live with a wife that has a short temper and loves to argue.
²⁰A wise person saves the things he needs. But a foolish person uses everything as fast as he gets it.
²¹The person that always tries to show love and kindness will have a good life, wealth, and honor.
²²A wise person can do almost anything. He can attack a city defended by strong men. And he can destroy the walls that they trusted to save them.
²³If a person is careful about the things he says, then he saves himself from trouble.
²⁴A proud person thinks he is better than other people. He shows that he is evil by the things he does.
²⁵⁻²⁶A lazy person destroys himself when he wants more and more. He destroys himself because he refuses to work for those things. But a good person can give because he has plenty.
²⁷The Lord is not happy when evil people offer him sacrifices, especially when those evil people are trying to get something from him.
²⁸A person who tells lies will be destroyed. Any person who listens to those lies will be destroyed with him.
²⁹A good person always knows that he is right. But an evil person has to pretend.
³⁰There is no person who is wise enough to make a plan that can succeed if the Lord is against it.
³¹People can prepare everything for a battle, even the horses. But they can't win unless the Lord gives them the victory.

22 It is better to be respected than to be rich. A good name is more important than silver or gold.
²Rich people and poor people are the same. The Lord made them all.
³Wise people see trouble coming and get out of its way. But foolish people go straight to the trouble and suffer because of it.
⁴Respect the Lord and be humble. Then you will have wealth, honor, and true life.

⁵Evil people are trapped by many troubles. But the person who cares for his soul stays away from trouble.

⁶Teach a child the right way to live while he is young. Then when he grows older, he will continue living that way.

⁷Poor people are slaves to rich people. The person who borrows is a servant to the person who lends.

⁸A person who spreads trouble will harvest trouble. And in the end, that person will be destroyed because of the trouble he gave other people.

⁹A person who gives freely will be blessed. He will be blessed because he shares his food with poor people.

¹⁰If a person thinks he is better than other people, force him to leave. When that person leaves, trouble will leave with him. Then arguments and bragging will end.

¹¹The king will be your friend if you love a pure heart and kind words.

¹²The Lord watches over and protects people who know him. But he destroys people who turn against him.

¹³The lazy person says, "I can't go to work now. There is a lion outside. It might kill me."

¹⁴The sin of adultery is like a trap. The Lord will become very angry at the person who falls into that trap.

¹⁵Children do foolish things. But if you punish them, they will learn not to do those things.

¹⁶These two things will make you poor—hurting poor people to make yourself rich, and giving gifts to rich people.

Thirty Wise Sayings

¹⁷Listen to the things that I say. I will teach you the things wise men have said. Learn from these teachings. ¹⁸It will be good for you if you remember these things. It will help you if you can say these words. ¹⁹I will teach you these things now. I want you to trust the Lord. ²⁰I have written 30 sayings for you. These are words of advice and wisdom. ²¹These words will teach you true and important things. Then you can give good answers to the one that sent you.

— 1 —

²²It is easy to steal from poor people. But don't do it. And don't take advantage of those poor people in court. ²³The Lord is on their side. He supports them and he will take things away from any person that takes from them.

— 2 —

²⁴Don't be friends with a person who becomes angry easily. Don't go near a person who becomes mad fast. ²⁵If you do, you may learn to be like him. Then you will have the same troubles he has.

— 3 —

²⁶Don't promise to be responsible for another person's debts. ²⁷If you can't pay his debt, then you will lose everything you have. Why should you lose the bed you sleep on?

— 4 —

²⁸Never move an old property line that was marked long ago by your ancestors.*

— 5 —

²⁹If a person is skilled in his work, then he is good enough to serve kings. He will not have to work for people who are not important.

— 6 —

23 When you sit and eat with an important man, remember who you are with. ²Never eat too much, even if you are very hungry. ³And don't eat too much of the fine food he serves. It might be a trick.

— 7 —

⁴Don't ruin your health trying to become rich. If you are wise, you will be patient. ⁵Money goes very quickly, as if it grows wings and flies away like a bird.

— 8 —

⁶Don't eat with a selfish person. And stay away from the special foods he likes. ⁷He is the kind of man who is always thinking about the cost. He might say to you, "Eat and drink." But that is not really what he wants. ⁸And if you eat his food, then you will become sick. And you will be embarrassed.

— 9 —

⁹Don't try to teach a fool. He will make fun of your wise words.

---

ancestor(s) Literally, "fathers," meaning a person's parents, grandparents, and all the people they are descended from.

— 10 —

¹⁰Never move an old property line. And never take land that belongs to orphans.* ¹¹The Lord will be against you. The Lord is powerful and he defends those orphans.

— 11 —

¹²Listen to your teacher and learn all you can.

— 12 —

¹³Always punish a child if it needs it. It will not hurt him to spank him. ¹⁴If you spank him, you may save his life.

— 13 —

¹⁵My son, if you become wise, then I will be very happy. ¹⁶I will be happy in my heart if I hear you say things that are right.

— 14 —

¹⁷Don't be jealous of evil people. But always try as hard as you can to respect the Lord. ¹⁸There is always hope. And that hope will never be gone.

— 15 —

¹⁹So listen, my son, and be wise. Always be careful to live the right way. ²⁰Don't be friends with people who drink too much wine and eat too much food. ²¹People who drink too much and eat too much become poor. All they do is eat, drink, sleep, and soon they have nothing.

— 16 —

²²Listen to the things your father tells you. Without your father, you would never have been born. And respect your mother, even when she is old. ²³Truth, wisdom, learning, and understanding are worth paying money for. And they are worth far too much to even sell. ²⁴The father of a good person is very happy. If a person has a wise child, then that child brings joy. ²⁵So let your father and mother be happy with you. Let your mother have joy.

— 17 —

²⁶My son, listen closely to what I am saying. Let my life be your example. ²⁷Prostitutes and bad women are a trap. They are like a deep well that you can't get out of. ²⁸A bad woman waits for you like a thief. And she causes many men to become sinners.

— 18 —

²⁹⁻³⁰It will be very bad for people who drink too much wine and strong drinks. Those people have many fights and arguments. Their eyes are red and they stumble and hurt themselves. They could have avoided all those troubles! ³¹So be careful with wine. It is pretty and red. It sparkles in the cup. And it goes down so smooth when you drink it. ³²But in the end it bites like a snake. ³³Wine will cause you to see strange things. Your mind will be confused. ³⁴When you lie down, you will think you are on a rough sea. You feel like you are lying on a ship. ³⁵You will say, "They hit me but I never felt it. They beat me but I don't remember it. Now I can't wake up. I need another drink."

— 19 —

24 Don't be jealous of evil people. Don't waste your time with them. ²In their hearts they plan to do evil. All they talk about is making trouble.

— 20 —

³Good homes are built on wisdom and understanding. ⁴And the rooms are filled using knowledge.

— 21 —

⁵Wisdom makes a man more powerful. Knowledge gives a man strength. ⁶You must make careful plans before you start a war. If you want to win, you must have many good advisers.

— 22 —

⁷Foolish people can't understand wisdom. And when people are discussing important things, the foolish person can say nothing.

— 23 —

⁸If you are always planning trouble, then people will know that you are a person who makes trouble. ₁And they will not listen to you.₁ ⁹The things that a foolish person plans to do are sin. People hate a person who thinks he is better than other people.

---

orphan(s) Children whose parents are dead. Often these children have no one to care for them.

— 24 —

¹⁰If you are weak during times of trouble, then you really are weak.

— 25 —

¹¹If people are planning to kill a person, then you must try to save him. ¹²You can't say, "It's none of my business." The Lord knows everything. And he knows why you do things. The Lord watches you. He knows. And the Lord will reward you for the things you do.

— 26 —

¹³My son, eat honey. It is good. Honey from the honeycomb* is sweet. ¹⁴In the same way, wisdom is good for your soul. If you have wisdom, then you will have hope, and your hope will never end.

— 27 —

¹⁵Don't be like a thief that wants to steal from a good person or take away his home. ¹⁶If a good man falls seven times, he will always stand again. But evil people will always be defeated by trouble.

— 28 —

¹⁷Don't be happy when your enemy has troubles. Don't be happy when he falls. ¹⁸If you do, the Lord will see this, and the Lord will not be happy with you. Then the Lord might help your enemy.

— 29 —

¹⁹Don't let evil people cause you worry. And don't be jealous of evil people. ²⁰Those evil people have no hope. Their light will become dark.

— 30 —

²¹Son, respect the Lord and the king. And don't join with the people that are against them. ²²Why? Because men like that can quickly be destroyed. You don't know how much trouble God and the king can make for their enemies.

More Wise Sayings

²³These are the words of wise men:
A judge must be fair. He must not support a person simply because he knows him.

²⁴People will turn against a judge that tells a guilty person that he can go free. Even people from other nations will say bad things against that judge. ²⁵But if a judge punishes a guilty person, then all the people will be happy with him.

²⁶An honest answer is something that makes all people happy—it is like a kiss on the lips.

²⁷Don't build your house before you plant your fields. Make sure that you are prepared to grow food before you build a place to live.

²⁸Don't speak against someone without a good reason. And don't tell lies.

²⁹Don't say, "He hurt me, so I will do the same to him. I will punish him for the things he did to me."

³⁰I walked past a field that belonged to a lazy man. I walked by a field of grapes that belonged to a person who was not wise. ³¹Weeds were growing everywhere in those fields. Worthless plants were growing on the ground. And the wall around the fields was broken and falling down. ³²I looked at this and I thought about it. Then I learned a lesson from these things: ³³a little sleep, a little rest, folding your arms, and taking a nap. ³⁴These things will make you poor very quickly. You will have nothing, as if a thief broke in and took everything away.

More Wise Sayings from Solomon

25 These are some more wise sayings of Solomon. These words were copied by servants of Hezekiah, king of Judah:

²God has the right to hide things that he does not want us to know about. But a king is honored for the things he says.

³The sky is high above and the ground is under us. It is the same with the minds of kings. We can't understand them.

⁴If you take the worthless things from silver and make it pure, then a worker can make beautiful things. ⁵In the same way, if you take evil advisers away from a king, then goodness will make his kingdom strong.

⁶Don't brag about yourself before a king. Don't say that you are a famous person. ⁷It is much better for the king to invite you himself. But if you invite yourself, then you might be embarrassed in front of other people.

⁸Don't be too quick to tell a judge about something you saw. If another person proves that you are wrong, then you will be embarrassed.

⁹If you and another person can't agree, then decide among yourselves what to do. And don't tell about another person's secret. ¹⁰If you do, then

---

honeycomb The wax nest that bees use for storing honey.

you will be ashamed. And you will never lose that bad name.

¹¹Saying the right thing at the right time is like a golden apple in a silver setting.

¹²If a wise person gives you a warning, it is worth more than gold rings or jewelry made from the finest gold.

¹³A messenger that can be trusted is worth much to the people who send him. He is like cool water during the hot days of harvest.

¹⁴People who promise to give gifts, but never give them, are like clouds and wind that bring no rain.

¹⁵Patient talk can make any person change his thinking, even a ruler. Gentle talk is very powerful.

¹⁶Honey is good, but don't eat too much of it. If you do, then you will be sick. ¹⁷In the same way, don't go into your neighbor's home too often. If you do, then he will begin to hate you.

¹⁸A person who does not tell the truth is dangerous. He is like a club, or a sword, or a sharp arrow. ¹⁹Never depend on a liar during times of trouble. That person is like a hurting tooth or a crippled foot. [He hurts you when you need him most.]

²⁰Singing happy songs to a sad person is like taking away his clothes when he is cold. It is like mixing soda and vinegar.

²¹If your enemy is hungry, give him food to eat. If your enemy is thirsty, give him water to drink. ²²If you do this, then you will make him ashamed. It is like putting burning coals on his head. And the Lord will reward you because you were good to your enemy.

²³The wind that blows from the north brings rain. And in the same way, gossip brings anger.

²⁴It is better to live on the roof than to share a house with a wife that wants to argue.

²⁵Good news from a faraway place is like a cool drink of water when you are hot and thirsty.

²⁶If a good person becomes weak and follows an evil person, it is the same as good water that has become dirty.

²⁷If you eat too much honey it is not good for you. In the same way, don't try to get too much honor for yourself.

²⁸If a person can't control himself, then he is like a city with walls that are broken down.

Wise Sayings About Fools

26 Snow shouldn't fall in the summer. And rain shouldn't fall during harvest time. In the same way, people should not honor a fool.

²Don't worry if a person asks for bad things to happen to you. If you did nothing wrong, nothing bad will happen. That person's words are like birds that fly past you and never stop.

³You have to whip a horse. You have to put a bridle on a mule. And you have to beat a fool.

⁴[Here is a difficult situation:] If a fool asks a stupid question, then don't give him a stupid answer or you, too, will look like a fool; ⁵But if a fool asks a stupid question, then you should give him a stupid answer or he will think he is very smart.

⁶Never let a fool carry your message. If you do, it will be like cutting off your own feet. You are asking for trouble.

⁷When a fool tries to say something wise, it is like a crippled person trying to walk.

⁸Showing honor to a fool is as bad as tying a rock in a sling.*

⁹When a fool tries to say something wise, it is the same as a drunk person trying to pick a thorn out of his hand.

¹⁰Hiring a fool, or hiring whoever passes by, is dangerous. You don't know who might get hurt.

¹¹A dog eats food. Then he gets sick and vomits. Then the dog eats that food again. It is the same with a foolish person. He does the same foolish things again and again.

¹²If a person thinks that he is wise but he is not, he is worse than a fool.

Wise Sayings About Lazy People

¹³A lazy person says, "I can't leave my house. There is a lion in the street."

¹⁴A lazy person is like a door. All he does is turn in his bed like a door turns on its hinges. He never goes anywhere.

¹⁵A lazy person is too lazy to lift his food from his plate to his mouth.

¹⁶A lazy person thinks he is very wise. He thinks he is smarter than seven men that can give good reasons for their ideas.

¹⁷It is dangerous to become part of an argument between two people. It is the same as walking along the street and grabbing a dog by the ears.

¹⁸⁻¹⁹A man who tricks another person and then says that he was only joking, is like a crazy person that shoots flaming arrows into the air and accidentally kills someone.

---

sling A strip of leather for throwing rocks.

²⁰If a fire has no wood, then the fire will become cold. In the same way, an argument without gossip is finished.
²¹Charcoal keeps the coals burning. And wood keeps the fire burning. In the same way, people who make trouble keep arguments alive.
²²People love gossip. It is like eating good food.
²³Good words that hide an evil plan is like silver paint over a cheap, clay pot. ²⁴An evil person makes himself look good by the things he says. But he hides his evil plans in his heart. ²⁵The things he says might seem good. But don't trust him. His heart is full of evil ideas. ²⁶He hides his evil plans with nice words. But he is mean. And in the end all people will see the evil things that he does.
²⁷If a person tries to trap another person, then he will trap himself. If a person tries to roll a stone over another person, he will be crushed himself.
²⁸The person that tells lies hates the people he hurts. And if a person says things he does not mean, he is only hurting himself.

27 Never brag about what will happen in the future. You don't know what will happen tomorrow.
²Never praise yourself. Let other people do it.
³A stone is heavy, and sand is hard to carry. But the trouble caused by a fool is much harder to bear than those two things.
⁴Anger is cruel and mean. It causes destruction. But jealousy is much worse.
⁵Open criticism is better than hidden love.
⁶A friend might hurt you sometimes, but he does not want to do this. An enemy is different. Even when an enemy is kind to you, he wants to hurt you.
⁷If you are not hungry, then you will not eat even honey. But if you are hungry, you will eat anything—even if it tastes bad.
⁸A man away from home is like a bird away from its nest.
⁹Perfume and sweet-smelling things make you feel happy. But trouble destroys your peace of mind.
¹⁰Don't forget your friends and your father's friends. And if you have trouble, don't go far away to your brother's house for help. It is better to ask a neighbor that is near you than to go far away to your brother.
¹¹My son, be wise. This will make me happy. Then I will be able to answer any person that criticizes me.

¹²Wise people see trouble coming and get out of its way. But a fool goes straight to the trouble and suffers because of it.
¹³You will lose your shirt if you make yourself responsible for another man's debts.
¹⁴Don't wake up your neighbor early in the morning with a shout of, "Good morning!" He will treat it like a curse, not a blessing.
¹⁵A wife that always wants to argue is like water that never stops dripping on a rainy day. ¹⁶Trying to stop that woman is like trying to stop the wind. It is like trying to grab oil with your hand.
¹⁷People use pieces of iron to sharpen iron knives. In the same way, people learn from other people, making each other sharp.
¹⁸A person who cares for fig trees will be able to eat their fruit. In the same way, a person who cares for his master will be rewarded. His master will care for him.
¹⁹When a person looks into the water he can see his own face. In the same way, a man's heart shows what the man is really like.
²⁰The things that people want are like the grave. In that place of death and destruction there is always room for more.
²¹People use fire to make gold and silver pure. In the same way, a man is tested by the praise people give him.
²²You can grind a fool to powder, and still you will not force the foolishness out of him.
²³Watch your sheep and cattle carefully. Be sure you care for them the best you can. ²⁴Wealth doesn't last forever. Even nations don't last forever.
²⁵Cut the hay, and new grass will grow. Cut the grass growing on the hills. ²⁶Cut the wool from your lambs and make your clothes. Sell some of your goats and buy some land. ²⁷There will be plenty of goat milk for you and your family. It will make your servant girls healthy.

28 Evil people are afraid of everything. But a good person is as brave as a lion.
²If a country refuses to obey, then it will have many bad leaders who rule only a short time. But if a nation has one good and wise leader, then it will continue for a long time.
³If a ruler makes trouble for poor people, he is like a hard rain that destroys the crops.
⁴You are for evil people if you refuse to obey the law. But if you obey the law, then you are against them.
⁵Evil people don't understand fairness. But people who love the Lord understand it.

⁶It is better to be poor but honest than to be rich and evil.

⁷A person who obeys the law is smart. But the person who becomes friends with worthless people brings shame to his father.

⁸If you get rich by cheating poor people, then you will lose your wealth. It will go to another person who is kind to them.

⁹If a person refuses to listen to ⌊God's⌋ teachings, then ⌊God⌋ will refuse to hear his prayers.

¹⁰A bad person might make plans to hurt a good person. But the bad person will fall into his own trap. And good things will happen to the good person.

¹¹Rich people always think they are wise. But a poor person that is wise can see the truth.

¹²When good people become leaders, everyone is happy. But when an evil person is elected, all people go and hide.

¹³A person will never be successful if he tries to hide his sins. But if a person confesses his sins and tells people that he was wrong, then God and everyone else will show mercy to him.

¹⁴If a person always respects the Lord, then that person will be blessed. But if a person is stubborn and refuses to respect the Lord, then he will have trouble.

¹⁵When an evil person rules over weak people, he is like an angry lion or a bear that is ready to fight.

¹⁶If a ruler is not wise, he will hurt the people under him. But the ruler that is honest and hates cheating will rule for a long time.

¹⁷If a person is guilty of killing another person, then that person will never have peace. Don't support that person.

¹⁸If a person is living right, then he will be safe. But if a person is evil, then he will lose his power.

¹⁹A person that works hard will have plenty to eat. But a person that wastes his time with dreams will always be poor.

²⁰God will bless the person who follows him. But a person who is only trying to get rich will be punished.

²¹A judge must be fair. He must not support a person simply because he knows him. But some judges will change their decisions for only the smallest payment.

²²A selfish person only wants to get rich. That person does not realize that he is very close to being poor.

²³If you help someone by telling him he is doing wrong, then later he will be happy with you. That is much better than always saying only nice things to people.

²⁴Some people steal from their father and mother. They say, "It's not wrong." But that person is as bad as a man who comes in and smashes everything in the house.

²⁵A selfish person causes trouble. But the person who trusts in the Lord will be rewarded.

²⁶If a person trusts in himself, then he is a fool. But if a person is wise, then he will escape disaster.

²⁷If a person gives to poor people, then he will have everything he needs. But if a person refuses to help poor people, then he will have much trouble.

²⁸If an evil person is elected to rule, then all the people hide. But when that evil person is defeated, then good people rule again.

29 If a person is stubborn and becomes more angry every time people tell him that he is doing wrong, then that person will be destroyed. There is no hope.

²When the ruler is a good person, then all the people are happy. But when an evil person rules, then all the people complain.

³If a person loves wisdom, then his father is very happy. But if a person wastes his money on prostitutes,* then he will lose his wealth.

⁴If a king is fair, then the nation will be strong. But if a king is selfish and people must pay him to do things for them, then the nation will be weak.

⁵If a person tries to get what he wants by saying nice things to people, then he is only setting a trap for himself.

⁶Evil people are defeated by their own sin. But a good person can sing and be happy.

⁷Good people want to do the right thing for poor people. But evil people don't care.

⁸People who think they are better than other people can cause much trouble. They can put whole cities into confusion. But people who are wise make peace.

⁹If a wise person tries to settle a problem with a fool, then the fool will argue and say stupid things. And the two people will never agree.

¹⁰Murderers always hate honest people. Those evil people want to kill good, honest people.*

prostitute(s) A woman paid by men for sexual sin. Sometimes this also means a person who is not faithful to God and stops following him.

Those evil people want to kill good, honest people Or "But a good, honest person saves his life."

[11] A foolish person becomes angry easily. But a wise person is patient and controls himself.
[12] If a ruler listens to lies, then all his officials will be evil.
[13] In one way a poor person and the person who steals from the poor are the same: The Lord made them both.
[14] If a king is fair to poor people he will rule for a long time.
[15] Spankings and teachings are good for children. If parents let a child do whatever he wants, then he will bring shame to his mother.
[16] If evil people are ruling the nation, then sin will be everywhere. But good people will win in the end.
[17] Punish your son when he is wrong, then you will always be proud of him. He will never make you ashamed.
[18] If a nation is not guided by God, then that nation will not have peace. But the nation that obeys God's law will be happy.
[19] A servant won't learn a lesson if you only talk to him. That servant may understand your words but he won't obey.
[20] If a person speaks without thinking, there is no hope for him. There is more hope for a fool than for the person who speaks without thinking.
[21] If you always give your servant everything he wants, then in the end he will not be a good servant.
[22] An angry person causes trouble. And the person who becomes angry easily is guilty of many sins.
[23] If a person thinks he is better than other people, then that will destroy him. But if a person is humble, then other people will respect him.
[24] Two thieves that work together are enemies. One thief will threaten the other one, so if he is forced to tell the truth in court, he will be too afraid to speak.
[25] Fear is like a trap. But if you trust in the Lord, you will be safe.
[26] Many people want to be the friends of a ruler. But the Lord is the One that judges people fairly.
[27] Good people hate those people who are not honest. And evil people hate people who are honest.

Wise Sayings of Agur Son of Jakeh

30 These are the wise sayings of Agur son of Jakeh. This is his message to Ithiel and Ucal:*

This is his message to Ithiel and Ucal Or "This man said, 'I am too weak. I am too weak, but I will succeed!'"

[2] I am the worst person on earth. I am not able to understand like I should. [3] I have not learned to be wise. And I know nothing about God.
[4] No person has ever learned about the things from heaven. No person has ever caught the wind in his hand. No person has ever held water in a piece of cloth. No person can ever really know the limits of the earth. If any person can do these things, who is he? Where is his family?
[5] Every word that God says is perfect. God is a safe place for people who go to him. [6] So, don't try to change the things God says. If you do, he will punish you and prove that you tell lies.
[7] Lord, I ask you to do two things for me before I die. [8] Help me to not tell lies. And don't make me too rich or too poor—only give me the things I need each day. [9] If I have more than I need, then I will think I don't need you. But if I am poor then I might steal. Then I will bring shame to the name of God.
[10] Never say bad things against a servant to his master. If you do, the master will not believe you. He will think you are guilty.
[11] Some people speak against their fathers. And they don't show respect for their mothers.
[12] Some people think they are good but they are really very bad.
[13] Some people think they are very good. They think they are much better than other people.
[14] There are people whose teeth are like swords. Their jaws are like knives. They use their time to take everything they can from poor people.
[15] Some people want to take everything they can get. All they say is, "Give me, give me, give me." There are three things that are never satisfied—really four things that never have enough: [16] The place of death, a woman with no children, dry ground that needs rain, and a hot fire that can't be stopped.
[17] Any person who makes fun of his father or refuses to obey his mother will be punished. It will be as bad for him as if his eyes were eaten by vultures and wild birds.
[18] There are three things that are hard for me to understand—really four things that I don't understand: [19] An eagle flying in the sky, a snake moving on a rock, a ship moving across the ocean, and a man in love with a woman.
[20] A woman who is not faithful to her husband acts like she has done nothing wrong. She eats, takes a bath, and says she has done nothing wrong.
[21] There are three things that make trouble on the earth—really four that the earth can't bear:

²²A servant that becomes a king, a foolish person that has everything he needs, ²³a woman who is full of hate but still finds a husband, and a servant girl that becomes ruler over the woman she serves.

²⁴There are four things on the earth that are small but very wise: ²⁵Ants are small and weak but they save their food all summer; ²⁶A badger is a small animal but it is able to make its home in the rocks; ²⁷locusts have no king but they are able to work together; ²⁸lizards are small enough to catch with your hands but you can find them living in kings' homes.

²⁹There are three things that seem important when they walk. Really there are four: ³⁰A lion is the strongest of all animals. He is afraid of nothing. ³¹A rooster that walks very proudly, a goat, and a king among his people.

³²If you are foolish and think that you are better than other people and you plan evil, you should stop and think about what you are doing.

³³If a person churns* milk, he makes butter. If a person hits another person's nose, then blood will come. In the same way, if you make people angry you will cause trouble.

Wise Sayings of King Lemuel

31 These are the wise sayings of King Lemuel. His mother taught him these things.

²You are my son. The son that I love. You are the son that I prayed to have. ³Don't waste your strength on women. It is women that destroy kings. Don't waste yourself on them. ⁴Lemuel, it is not wise for kings to drink wine. It is not wise for rulers to want beer. ⁵They may drink too much and forget what the law says. Then they will take away all the rights of poor people. ⁶Give beer to the poor people. Give wine to those people who are in trouble. ⁷Then they will drink and forget that they are poor. They will drink and forget all their troubles.

⁸If a person can't help himself, then you should help him. You should help all people who are in trouble. ⁹Stand for the things you know are right. And judge all people fairly. Protect the rights of poor people and people that need you.

The Perfect Wife

¹⁰ *It is very hard to find "the perfect woman." But she is worth much more than jewels.

¹¹ Her husband depends on her.
 He will never be poor.
¹² She does good for her husband all her life.
 She never causes him trouble.
¹³ She is always busy, making wool and cloth.
¹⁴ She is like a ship from a faraway place.
 She brings food home from everywhere.
¹⁵ She wakes very early in the morning.
 She cooks food for her family
 and tells the servant girls what to do.
¹⁶ She looks at land and buys it.
 She uses money she has saved
 and plants a vineyard.
¹⁷ She works very hard.
 She is strong and able to do all her work.
¹⁸ When she trades the things she has made,
 she always earns a profit.
 And she works until late at night.
¹⁹ She makes her own thread
 and weaves her own cloth.
²⁰ She always gives to poor people
 and helps people that need it.
²¹ She doesn't worry about her family
 when it snows.
 She has given them all good, warm clothes.
²² She makes sheets and spreads for the beds.
 And she wears clothes made of fine linen.
²³ People respect her husband.
 He is one of the leaders of the land.
²⁴ She is a very good businesswoman.
 She makes clothes and belts,
 and sells these things to businessmen.
²⁵ She is strong and people respect her.
²⁶ She speaks with wisdom.
 She is full of wise teaching.
²⁷ She is never lazy.
 She takes care of the things in her house.
²⁸ Her children say good things about her.
 Her husband brags about her and says,
²⁹ "There are many good women.
 But you are the best."
³⁰ Grace and beauty can fool you.
 But a woman who respects the Lord
 should be praised.
³¹ Give her the reward she deserves.
 Praise her in public
 for the things she has done.

---

churn(s) To stir cream for a long time until it becomes butter.

Verses 10-31 In Hebrew, each verse of this poem starts with the next letter of the alphabet, so this poem shows all the good qualities of a woman, "from A to Z".

Ecclesiastes

1 ¹These are the words from the Teacher. The Teacher was a son of David and king of Jerusalem.
²Everything is so meaningless. The Teacher says that it is all a waste of time!* ³Do people really gain anything from all the hard work they do in this life?* ⌊No!⌋

Things Never Change

⁴People live and people die. But the earth continues forever. ⁵The sun rises and the sun goes down. And then the sun hurries to rise again in the same place.
⁶The wind blows to the south, and the wind blows to the north. The wind blows around and around. Then the wind turns and blows back to the place it began.
⁷All rivers flow again and again to the same place. They all flow to the sea, but the sea doesn't become full.
⁸Words can't fully explain things.* But people continue speaking.* Words come again and again to our ears. But our ears don't become full. And our eyes don't become full of the things we see.

Nothing is New

⁹All things continue the way they have been since the beginning. The same things will be done that have always been done. There is nothing new in this life.*

¹⁰A person might say, "Look, this is new!" But that thing has always been here. It was here before we were!
¹¹People don't remember the things that happened long ago. In the future, people will not remember what is happening now. And later, other people will not remember what those people before them did.

Does Wisdom Bring Happiness?

¹²I, the Teacher, was king over Israel in Jerusalem. ¹³I decided to study and to use my wisdom to learn about all the things that are done in this life. I learned that it is a very hard thing that God gave us to do. ¹⁴I looked at all the things done on earth, and I saw that it is all a waste of time. It is like trying to catch the wind.* ¹⁵⌊You can't change these things.⌋ If something is crooked, you can't say it is straight. And if something is missing, you can't say it is there.
¹⁶I said to myself, "I am very wise. I am wiser than all the kings that ruled Jerusalem before me. I know what wisdom and knowledge really are!"
¹⁷I decided to learn how wisdom and knowledge are better than thinking foolish things. But I learned that trying to become wise is like trying to catch the wind.* ¹⁸With much wisdom comes frustration. The person that gains more wisdom also gains more sorrow.

Does "Having Fun" Bring Happiness?

2 ¹I said to myself, "I should have fun—I should enjoy everything the most I can." But I learned that this is also useless. ²It is foolish to laugh all the time. Having fun doesn't do any good.

---

meaningless ... a waste of time The Hebrew word means "vapor or breath" or "something that is useless, meaningless, empty, wrong, or a waste of time."
in this life Literally, "under the sun."
Words can't fully explain things Literally, "All words (things) are weak."
But people continue speaking The Hebrew could also be translated, "Man can't speak."
in this life Literally, "under the sun."

trying to catch the wind Or, "It is very troubling to the spirit." The word for "troubling" can also mean "craving" and the word for "spirit" can also mean "wind."

³So I decided to fill my body with wine while I filled my mind with wisdom. I tried this foolishness because I wanted to find a way to be happy. I wanted to see what was good for people to do during their few days of life.

Does Hard Work Bring Happiness?

⁴Then I began doing great things. I built houses, and I planted fields of grapes for myself. ⁵I planted gardens, and I made parks. I planted all kinds of fruit trees. ⁶I made pools of water for myself. And I used these pools to water my growing trees. ⁷I bought men slaves and women slaves. And there were slaves born in my house. I owned many great things. I had herds of cattle and flocks of sheep. I owned more things than any other person in Jerusalem.

⁸I also gathered silver and gold for myself. I took treasures from kings and their nations. I had men and women singing for me. I had everything anyone could want.

⁹I became very rich and famous. I was greater than any person that lived in Jerusalem before me. And my wisdom was always there to help me. ¹⁰Anything my eyes saw and wanted, I got for myself. My mind was pleased with all the things I did. And this happiness was the reward for all my hard work.

¹¹But then I looked at all the things I had done. I thought about all the hard work I did. I decided it was all a waste of time! It was like trying to catch the wind.* There is nothing to gain from all the things we do in this life.

Maybe Wisdom Is the Answer

¹²No person can do more than a king can do. Some king has already done anything you might want to do.* ⌊And I learned that even the things a king does are a waste of time.⌋ So I again began to think about being wise, being foolish, and doing crazy things. ¹³I saw that wisdom is better than foolishness in the same way that light is better than darkness. ¹⁴It is like this: A wise man uses his mind like eyes to see where he is going. But a fool is like someone walking in the dark.

But I also saw that the foolish man and the wise man both end the same way. ⌊They both die.⌋ ¹⁵I thought to myself, "The same thing that happens to a foolish person will also happen to me. So why have I tried so hard to become wise?" I said to myself, "Being wise is also useless." ¹⁶The wise man and the foolish person will both die! And people will not remember either the wise man or the foolish person forever. In the future, people will forget everything they did. So both the wise man and the foolish person are really the same.

Is There Real Happiness in Life?

¹⁷This made me hate life. It made me very sad to think that everything in this life* is useless, like trying to catch the wind.*

¹⁸I began to hate all the hard work I had done. I had worked hard, but I saw that the people that live after me will get the things that I worked for. I will not be able to take those things with me. ¹⁹Some other person will control everything I worked and studied for. And I don't know if that person will be wise or foolish. This is also senseless.

²⁰So, I became sad about all the work I had done. ²¹A person can work hard using all his wisdom and knowledge and skill. But that person will die and other people will get the things he worked for. Those people did not do the work, but they will get everything. That makes me very sad. That is also not fair and is senseless.

²²What does a person really have after all his work and struggling in this life?* ²³All his life he has pain, frustrations, and hard work. Even at night, a person's mind does not rest. This is also senseless.

²⁴⁻²⁵Is there any person that tried to enjoy life more than I have? No! And this is what I learned: The best thing a person can do is eat, drink, and enjoy the work he must do. I also saw that this comes from God.* ²⁶If a person does good and pleases God, then God will give that person wisdom, knowledge, and joy. But a person that

---

trying to catch the wind Or, "It is very troubling to the spirit." The word for "troubling" can also mean "craving" and the word for "spirit" can also mean "wind."

No person ... want to do The Hebrew is not clear here.

in this life Literally, "under the sun."

Is there ... from God Or, "24The best a person can do is eat, drink, and enjoy his work. I also saw this comes from God. 25No one can eat or enjoy life without God."

sins will get only the work of gathering and carrying things. God takes from the bad person and gives to the good person. But all this work is useless. It is like trying to catch the wind.*

There Is a Time...

3 There is a right time for everything. And everything on earth will happen at the right time.

2 There is a time to be born,
   and a time to die.
   There is a time to plant,
   and a time to pull up plants.
3 There is a time to kill,
   and a time to heal.
   There is a time to destroy,
   and a time to build.
4 There is a time to cry,
   and a time to laugh.
   There is a time to be sad,
   and a time to dance from joy.
5 There is a time to throw weapons down,
   and a time to pick them up.*
   There is a time to hug someone,
   and a time to stop holding so tightly.
6 There is a time to look for something,
   and a time to consider it lost.
   There is a time to keep things,
   and a time to throw things away.
7 There is a time to tear cloth,
   and there is a time to sew it.
   There is a time to be silent,
   and a time to speak.
8 There is a time to love,
   and a time to hate.
   There is a time for war,
   and a time for peace.

God Controls His World

⁹Does a person really gain anything from his hard work? ₍No!₎ ¹⁰I saw all the hard work God gave us to do. ¹¹God gave us the ability to think about his world.* But we can never completely understand everything God does. And yet, God does everything at just the right time.

¹²I learned that the best thing for people to do is to be happy and enjoy themselves as long as they live. ¹³God wants every person to eat, drink, and enjoy his work. These are gifts from God.

¹⁴I learned that anything God does will continue forever. People can't add anything to the work of God. And people can't take anything away from the work of God. God did this so people would respect him. ¹⁵Things that happened in the past have happened, ₍and we can't change them₎. And things that will happen in the future will happen, ₍and we can't change them₎. But God wants to help people that have been treated badly.*

¹⁶I also saw these things in this life.* I saw that the courts should be filled with goodness and fairness—but there is evil there now. ¹⁷So I said to myself, "God has planned a time for everything. And God has planned a time to judge everything people do. God will judge the good people and the bad people."

Are People Just Like Animals?

¹⁸I thought about the things people do to each other. And I said to myself, "God wants people to see that they are like animals. ¹⁹Is a man better than an animal? ₍No!₎ Why? Because everything is useless. The same thing happens to animals and to people—they die. People and animals have the same "breath."* Is a dead animal different from a dead person? ²⁰The bodies of people and animals end the same way. They came from the earth, and in the end they will go back to the earth. ²¹Who knows what happens to the spirit of a man? Who knows if a man's spirit goes up to God while an animal's spirit goes down into the ground?"

²²So I saw that the best thing a person can do is to enjoy what he does. That is all he has. ₍Also a person should not worry about the future.₎ Why? Because no one can help that person see what will happen in the future.

---

trying to catch the wind Or, "It is very troubling to the spirit." The word for "troubling" can also mean "craving" and the word for "spirit" can also mean "wind."
There is a time to ... pick them up Literally, "There is a time to throw stones away, and a time to gather stones."
the ability to think about his world Or, "a desire to know the future."

Verse 15 Or, "What happens now also happened in the past. The things that happen in the future have also happened before. God makes things happen again and again."
in this life Literally, "under the sun."
breath Or, "spirit."

Is It Better to be Dead?

4 Again I saw that many people are treated badly. I saw their tears. And I saw that there was no one to comfort those sad people. I saw cruel people had all the power. And I saw that there was no one to comfort the people they hurt. ²I decided that things are better for people that have died than for people that are still alive. ³And things are even better ₁for people that die at birth! Why? Because₁ they never saw the evil that is done in this world.*

Why Work So Hard?

⁴Then I thought, "Why do people work so hard?" I saw people try to succeed and be better than other people. Why? Because people are jealous. They don't want other people to have more than they have. This is senseless. It is like trying to catch the wind.*

⁵Some people say, "It is foolish to fold your hands and do nothing. If you don't work, you will starve to death." ⁶Maybe that is true. But I say it is better to be satisfied with the few things you have than to always be struggling to get more.

⁷Again I saw something else that didn't make sense: ⁸A person might not have any family. He might not have a son or even a brother. But that person will continue to work very, very hard. That person is never satisfied with what he has. And he works so hard that he never stops and asks himself, "Why am I working so hard? Why don't I let myself enjoy my life?" This is also a very bad and senseless thing.

Friends and Family Give Strength

⁹Two people are better than one. When two people work together, they get more from the work they do.

¹⁰If one person falls, then the other person can help him. But it is very bad for the person that is alone when he falls—there is no one there to help him.

¹¹If two people sleep together, they will be warm. But a person sleeping alone will not be warm.

¹²An enemy might be able to defeat one person, but that enemy can't defeat two people. ₁And three people are even stronger. They are like₁ a rope that has three parts wrapped together—it is very hard to break.

People, Politics, and Popularity

¹³A young leader that is poor but wise is better than a king that is old but foolish. That old king does not listen to warnings. ¹⁴Maybe that young ruler was born a poor man in the kingdom. And maybe he came from prison to rule the country. ¹⁵But I have watched people in this life, ₁and I know this:₁ People will follow that young man. He will become the new king. ¹⁶Many, many people will follow this young man. But later, those same people will not like him. This is also senseless. It is like trying to catch the wind.*

Be Careful About Making Promises

5 Be very careful when you go to worship God. It is better to listen ₁to God₁ than to give sacrifices* like foolish people. Foolish people often do bad things, and they don't even know it. ²Be careful when you make promises to God. Be careful about the things you say to God. Don't let your feelings cause you to speak too soon. God is in heaven, and you are on the earth. So you need to say only a few things to God. This saying is true:

³   Bad dreams come from too much worrying,
    and too many words from foolish people.

⁴If you make a promise to God, then keep your promise. Don't be slow to do the thing you promised. God is not happy with foolish people. Give God what you promised to give him. ⁵It is better to promise nothing than to promise something and not be able to do it. ⁶So don't let your words cause you to sin. Don't say to the priest,* "I didn't mean what I said!" If you do this, then God might become angry with your words and destroy everything you have worked for. ⁷You should not let your useless dreams and

---

in this world Literally, "under the sun."
trying to catch the wind Or, "It is very troubling to the spirit."
    The word for "troubling" can also mean "craving" and the word for "spirit" can also mean "wind."

sacrifices A gift to God. Sometimes it was a special kind of animal that was killed and burned on an altar.
priest Or, "angel," "messenger." This might be an angel, or it might be a priest or a prophet who speaks for God.

bragging ⌊bring you trouble⌋. You should respect God.

For Every Ruler There Is a Ruler

⁸In some country you might see poor people that are forced to work very hard. You might see that this is not fair to the poor people. It is against the rights of the poor people. But don't be surprised! The ruler that forces those people to work has another ruler that forces him. And there is still another ruler that forces both of these rulers. ⁹Even the king is a slave—his country owns him.*

Wealth Can't Buy Happiness

¹⁰The person that loves money will never be satisfied with the money he has. The person that loves wealth will not be satisfied when he gets more and more. This is also senseless.

¹¹The more wealth a person has, the more "friends" he has to help spend it. So that rich person really gains nothing. He can only look at his wealth.

¹²A man that works hard all day comes home and sleeps in peace. It is not important if he has little or much to eat. But a rich person worries about his wealth and is not able to sleep.

¹³There is a very sad thing that I have seen happen in this life. A person saves his money for the future.* ¹⁴And then something bad happens and he loses everything. So that person has nothing to give to his son.

We Come with Nothing. We Leave with Nothing

¹⁵A person comes into the world from his mother's body with nothing. And when that person dies, he leaves the same way—with nothing. He works hard to get things. But he can take nothing with him when he dies. ¹⁶That is very sad. He will leave the world the same way he came. So, what does a person gain from his "trying to catch the wind"? ¹⁷He only gets days that are filled with sadness and sorrow. In the end, he is frustrated, sick, and angry!

Enjoy Your Life's Work

¹⁸I have seen that this is the best a person can do: A person should eat, drink, and enjoy the work he does during his short life on earth. God has given him these few days, and that is all he has.

¹⁹If God gives a person wealth, property, and the power to enjoy those things, then that person should enjoy them. That person should accept the things he has and enjoy his work—that is a gift from God. ²⁰A person does not have many years to live. So he must remember these things all his life. God will keep him busy with the work that person loves to do.*

Wealth Does Not Bring Happiness

6 I have seen another thing in this life that is not fair. It is very hard to understand: ²God gives a person great wealth, riches, and honor. That person has everything he needs and everything he could ever want. But then God does not let that person enjoy those things. Some stranger comes and takes everything. This is a very bad and senseless thing.

³A person might live a long time. And that person might have 100 children. But if that person is not satisfied with those good things, and if no one remembers him after his death, then I say that a baby that dies at birth is better off than that man. ⁴It is really senseless when a baby is born dead. That baby is quickly buried in a dark grave, without even a name. ⁵That baby never saw the sun. That baby never knew anything. But that baby finds more rest than the man that never enjoyed the things God gave him. ⁶That man might live 2,000 years. But if he does not enjoy life, then the baby that was born dead has found the easiest way to the same end.*

⁷A man works and works. Why? To feed himself. But he is never satisfied. ⁸In this way, a

---

The ruler ... owns him Or, "One ruler is cheated by a higher ruler. And they are cheated by an even higher ruler. 9Even the king gets his share of the profit. The wealth of the country is divided among them."
for the future Or, "to his harm."

God ... to do Or, "God will do whatever he wants to that person."
then the baby ... the same end Or, "Isn't it true that all go to the same place."

wise man is no better than a foolish person. It is better to be a poor man that knows how to accept life as it is. ⁹It is better to be happy with the things you have than to always want more and more. Always wanting more and more is useless. It is like trying to catch the wind.*

¹⁰⁻¹¹A man is only what he was created to be— a man. And it is useless to argue about it. A man can't argue with God about this. Why? Because God is more powerful than man. And a long argument will not change that fact.

¹²Who knows what is best for a person during his short life on earth? His life passes like a shadow. No one can tell him what will happen later.

A Collection Of Wise Teachings

7 It is better to have a good name *(respect)* than good perfume.

The day a person dies is even better than the day he is born.

² It is even better to go to a funeral than to a party.
Why? Because all people must die, and every living person should accept this.

³ Sorrow is even better than laughter.
Why? Because when our face is sad, our heart becomes good.

⁴ A wise person thinks about death, but a foolish person thinks only about having a good time.

⁵ It is better to be criticized by a wise man than to be praised by a foolish person.

⁶ The laughter of foolish people is useless.
It is like trying burning thorns to heat a pot.
⌐The thorns burn too fast, so the pot does not get hot.⌐

⁷ Even a wise man will forget his wisdom if someone pays him enough money.
That money destroys his understanding.

⁸ It is better to finish something than to start it.

It is better to be gentle and patient than to be proud and impatient.

⁹ Don't become angry quickly.
Why? Because being angry is foolish.

¹⁰ Don't say,
"Life was better in the 'good old days.'
What happened?"
Wisdom does not lead us to ask that question.

¹¹Wisdom is better if you also have property. Really, wise people* will get more than enough wealth. ¹²A wise person can become wealthy. Wisdom takes care of its owner.

¹³Look at the things God has made. You can't change a thing, even if you think it is wrong! ¹⁴When life is good, enjoy it. But when life is hard, remember that God gives us good times and hard times. And no one knows what will happen in the future.

People Can't Be Truly Good

¹⁵In my short life, I have seen everything. I have seen good men die young. And I have seen evil men living long lives. ¹⁶⁻¹⁷So why kill yourself? Don't be too good or too bad. And don't be too wise or too foolish. Why should you die before your time?

¹⁸Try to be a little of this and a little of that.* Even God's followers will do some good things and some bad things. ¹⁹⁻²⁰Surely there is not a good man on earth that always does good and never sins.

Wisdom gives a person strength. One wise man is stronger than ten ⌐foolish⌐ leaders in a city.

²¹Don't listen to all the things people say. You might hear your own servant saying bad things about you. ²²And you know that many times you too have said bad things about other people.

²³I used my wisdom and thought about all these things. I wanted to be truly wise. But it was impossible. ²⁴I can't understand why things are

---

It is better ... catch the wind Or, "Having what you can see is better than chasing after the things you want. This is also like trying to catch the wind."

wise people Literally, "People that see the sun." This means wise people can see and plan what they should do.

Try to be a little of this and a little of that Or, "Hold onto this, but don't let go of that."

like they are. It is too hard for anyone to understand. ²⁵I studied and I tried very hard to find true wisdom. I tried to find a reason for everything. ₗWhat did I learn?ⱼ I learned that it is foolish to be evil, and it is crazy to act like a foolish person.

²⁶I also found that ₗsome women are dangerous like trapsⱼ. Their hearts are like nets, and their arms are like chains. It is worse than death to be caught by those women. A person that follows God will run away from those women. But a sinner will be caught by them.

²⁷⁻²⁸The Teacher says, "I added all these things together to see what answer I could find. I am still looking for answers. But I did find this: I found one ₗgoodⱼ man in a thousand. But I did not find even one ₗgoodⱼ woman.

²⁹"There is one other thing I have learned: God made people good. But people found many ways to be bad."

Wisdom and Power

8 No one can understand and explain things the way a wise man can. His wisdom makes him happy. It changes a sad face into a happy one.

²I say you should always obey the king's command. Do this because you made a promise to God. ³Don't be afraid to give suggestions to the king. And don't support something that is wrong. But remember, the king gives the commands that please him. ⁴The king has the authority to give commands. And no one can tell him what to do. ⁵A person will be safe if he obeys the king's command. But a wise man knows the right time to do this, and he also knows when to do the right thing.

⁶There is a right time and a right way for a person to do everything. ₗAnd each person must take a chance and decide what he should do.ⱼ He must do this even when he has many troubles ⁷and he isn't sure what will happen. Why? Because no one can tell him what will happen in the future.

⁸No person has the power to keep his spirit from leaving. No person has the power to stop his death. During war, a soldier does not have the freedom to go any place he wants to go. In the same way, if a person does evil, that evil won't allow him to be free.

⁹I saw all those things. I thought very hard about the things that happen in this world. And I saw that people always struggle for the power to rule other people. And this is bad for them.

¹⁰I also saw great and beautiful funerals for evil people. While the people were going home after the funeral services, they said good things about the evil people that had died. This happened even in the same towns where the evil people had done many, many bad things. That is senseless.

Justice, Rewards, and Punishment

¹¹Sometimes people are not immediately punished for the bad things they do. Their punishment is slow to come. And that makes other people want to do bad things too.

¹²A sinner might do a hundred evil things. And he might have a long life. But I know that it is still better to obey and respect God. ¹³Evil people don't respect God, so those people won't really get good things. Those evil people won't live long lives. Their lives won't be like the shadows that become longer and longer ₗas the sun goes downⱼ.

¹⁴There is something else that happens on earth that does not seem fair. Bad things should happen to bad people and good things should happen to good people. But sometimes bad things happen to good people and good things happen to bad people. That is not fair. ¹⁵So I decided it was more important to enjoy life. Why? Because the best thing people can do in this life* is to eat, drink, and enjoy life. At least that will help people enjoy the hard work God gave them to do during their life on earth.

We Can't Understand All God Does

¹⁶I carefully studied the things people do in this life. I saw how busy people are. They work day and night, and they almost never sleep. ¹⁷I also saw the many things that God does. And I saw that people can't understand all the work that God does on earth. A person might try and try to understand, but he can't. Even if a wise man says he understands the work God does, it is not true. No person can understand all those things.

Is Death Fair?

9 I thought about all these things very carefully. I saw that God controls what happens to the good and wise people and the things they do. People don't know if they will be loved or hated.

---

in this life Literally, "under the sun."
sacrifices A gift to God. Sometimes it was a special kind of animal that was killed and burned on an altar.

And people don't know what will happen in the future. ²But, there is one thing that happens to everyone—we all die! Death comes to good people and bad people. Death comes to people that are pure and to people that are not pure. Death comes to people that give sacrifices* and to people that do not give sacrifices. A good man will die just like a sinner. A person that makes special promises to God will die just like a person that is afraid to make those promises. ³Of all the things that happen in this life, the worst thing is that all people end the same way. But it is also very bad that people always think evil and foolish thoughts. And those thoughts lead to death. ⁴There is hope for any person that is still alive—it does not matter who he is. But this saying is true:

> A living dog is better than a dead lion.

⁵Living people know that they will die. But dead people don't know anything. Dead people have no more reward. People will soon forget them. ⁶After a person is dead, his love, hate, and jealousy are all gone. And dead people will never again share in the things that happen on earth.

Enjoy Life While You Can

⁷So go and eat your food now and enjoy it. Drink your wine and be happy. It is all right with God if you do these things. ⁸Wear nice clothes and make yourself look good. ⁹Enjoy life with the wife you love. Enjoy every day of your short life. God has given you this short life on earth—and it is all you have. So, enjoy the work you have to do in this life. ¹⁰Every time you find work to do, do it the best you can. In the grave there is no work. There is no thinking, no knowledge, and there is no wisdom. And we are all going to that ₁place of death₁.

Good Luck? Bad Luck? What Can We Do?

¹¹I also saw other things in this life* that were not fair: The fastest runner does not always win the race; the strongest army does not always win the battle; the wisest man does not always get the food he earns; the smartest man does not always get the wealth; and an educated person does not always get the praise he deserves. When the time comes, bad things happen to everyone! ¹²A person never knows what will happen to him next. He is like a fish caught in a net—the fish does not know what will happen. He is like a bird caught in a trap—the bird does not know what will happen. In the same way, a person is trapped by the bad things that suddenly happen to him.

The Power of Wisdom

¹³I also saw a person doing a wise thing in this life. And it seemed very important to me. ¹⁴There was a small town with a few people in it. A great king fought against that town and put his armies all around it. ¹⁵But there was a wise man in that town. That wise man was poor, but he used his wisdom to save his town. After everything was finished, the people forgot about that poor man. ¹⁶But I still say that wisdom is better than strength. Those people forgot about the poor man's wisdom, and the people stopped listening to what he said. ₁But I still believe that wisdom is better.₁

¹⁷ A few words quietly spoken by a wise man
   are much better than words shouted
      by a foolish ruler.*

¹⁸ Wisdom is better than swords and spears
      in war.
   But one foolish person* can destroy
      much good.

10 A few dead flies will make even the best perfume smell bad. In the same way, a little foolishness can ruin much wisdom and honor. ²A wise man's thoughts lead him in the right way. But the thoughts of a foolish person leads him the wrong way. ³A fool shows his foolishness, even when he is just walking down the road. So everyone sees that he is a foolish person.

A few words ... foolish ruler Or, "Words of a wise man quietly heard are better than the shouts of a ruler among foolish people."
foolish person Literally, "sinner."
If you ... great mistakes Literally, "A healer can put to rest great sins." The word "healer" means a person that is forgiving and that tries to help other people.

in this life Literally, "under the sun."

⁴Don't quit your job just because the boss is angry at you. If you remain calm and helpful, you can correct even great mistakes.*

⁵Here is something else that I have seen in this life. And it is not fair. It is the kind of mistake that rulers make: ⁶Foolish people are given important positions, while rich people get jobs that are not important. ⁷I have seen people that should be servants riding on horses, while people that should be rulers were walking ₍beside them like slaves₎.

Every Job Has Its Dangers

⁸A person that digs a hole might fall into it. A person that knocks down a wall might be bitten by a snake. ⁹A person that moves large stones might be hurt by them. And a person that cuts trees is in danger—₍the trees might fall on him₎.

¹⁰But wisdom will make any job easier. It is very hard to cut with a dull knife. But if a person sharpens the knife, then the job is easier. ₍Wisdom is like that₎.

¹¹A person might know how to control snakes. But that skill is useless if a snake bites someone when he is not around. ₍Wisdom is like that₎.

¹² A wise man's words bring praise.
But a foolish person's words bring destruction.

¹³A foolish person begins by saying foolish things. In the end, he is saying crazy things. ¹⁴A foolish person is always talking ₍about what he will do₎. But no one knows what will happen in the future. No one can tell what will happen later.

¹⁵ A foolish person isn't smart enough to find his way home,
so he must work hard all his life.

The Value of Work

¹⁶It is very bad for a country if the king is like a child. And it is very bad for a country if its rulers use all their time eating. ¹⁷But it is very good for a country if the king comes from a good family.* And it is very good for a country if the rulers control their eating and drinking. Those rulers eat and drink to become strong, not to become drunk.

¹⁸ If a person is too lazy to work,
his house will begin to leak,
and the roof will fall in.

¹⁹People enjoy eating, and wine makes life happier. But money solves a lot of problems.

Gossip

²⁰Don't say bad things about the king. Don't even think bad things about him. And don't say bad things about rich people, even if you are alone in your home. Why? Because a little bird might fly and tell them everything you said.

Boldly Face the Future

11 Do good things every place you go.* After a while, the good things you do will come back to you. ²Invest what you have in several different things.* You don't know what bad things might happen on earth.

³₍There are some things you can be sure of₎. If clouds are full of rain, then they will pour water on the earth. If a tree falls—to the south or to the north—then it will stay where it falls.

⁴₍But there are some things that you can't be sure of. You must take a chance₎. If a person waits for perfect weather, then he will never plant his seeds. And if a person is afraid that every cloud will bring rain, then he will never harvest his crops.

⁵You don't know where the wind blows. And you don't know how a baby grows in its mother's body. In the same way, you don't know what God will do—and he makes everything happen.

⁶So begin planting early in the morning, and don't stop working until evening. Why? Because you don't know which things will make you rich. Maybe everything you do will be successful.

⁷It is good to be alive! It is nice to see the light from the sun. ⁸You should enjoy every day of your life, no matter how long you live! But remember that you will die. And you will be dead much longer than you were alive! And after you are dead, you can't do anything!

---

comes from a good family Literally, "is a son of freedmen." This is a person that was never a slave and whose parents were not slaves.

Do good ... go Or, "Throw your bread on the water."
Invest what you have in several different things Or, "Give a part to seven, or even eight."

Serve God While You are Young

⁹So young people, enjoy yourselves while you are young. Be happy! Do whatever your heart leads you to do. Do whatever you want. But remember that God will judge you for everything you do. ¹⁰Don't let your anger control you. And don't let your body lead you to sin.* People do foolish things in the dawn of life while they are young.

The Problems of Old Age

12¹Remember your Creator while you are young, before the bad times ⌊of old age⌋ come—before the years come when you say, "I have wasted my life."*

²⌊Remember your Creator while you are young,⌋ before the time comes when the sun and the moon and the stars become dark to you. ⌊And troubles come again and again⌋ like one storm after another.

³At that time, your arms will lose their strength. Your legs will become weak and bent. Your teeth will fall out and you will not be able to chew your food. Your eyes will not see clearly. ⁴You will become hard of hearing. You will not hear the noise in the streets. Even the stone grinding your grain will seem quiet to you. You won't be able to hear the women singing. But even the sound of a bird singing will wake you early in the morning ⌊because you won't be able to sleep⌋.

⁵You will be afraid of high places. You will be afraid of tripping over every small thing in your path. Your hair will become white like the flowers on an almond tree. You will drag yourself along like a grasshopper when you walk. You will lose your desire ⌊to live⌋.* And then you will go to your eternal home *(the grave)*. The mourners* will gather in the streets ⌊as they carry your body to the grave⌋.

Death

⁶ ⌊Remember your Creator
while you are young,⌋
before the silver rope snaps
and the golden bowl is crushed.
⌊before your life becomes useless⌋
like a jar broken at the well.
⌊before your life becomes wasted⌋
like a stone cover on a well
that breaks and falls in.

⁷ Your body came from the earth.
And when you die,
your body will go back to the earth.
But your spirit came from God.
And when you die,
your spirit will go back to God.

⁸Everything is so meaningless. The Teacher says that it is all a waste of time!*

CONCLUSION

⁹The Teacher was very wise. He used his wisdom to teach the people. The Teacher very carefully studied and arranged* many wise teachings. ¹⁰The Teacher tried very hard to find the right words. And he wrote the teachings that are true and dependable.

¹¹Words from wise men are like sharp sticks that people use to make their animals go the right way. Those teachings are like strong pegs that won't break. ⌊You can trust those teachings to show you the right way to live.⌋ Those wise teachings all come from the same Shepherd *(God)*. ¹²So son, ⌊study those teachings,⌋ but be careful about other books. People are always writing books, and too much study will make you very tired.

¹³⁻¹⁴Now, what should we learn from all the things that are written in this book?* The most

---

Don't let ... sin Or, "Don't worry about things. Protect yourself from troubles."

I have wasted my life Literally, "I take no pleasure in them." This might mean, "I don't like the things I did when I was young" or "I don't enjoy life now that I am old."

desire {to live Or, "appetite" or "sexual desire." The Hebrew is hard to understand here.

mourners People that cry at a funeral. In Bible times, there were professional mourners that people hired to show great sadness at a person's funeral.

meaningless ... a waste of time The Hebrew word means "vapor or breath" or "something that is useless, meaningless, empty, wrong, or a waste of time."

arranged This Hebrew word means, "to make straight, arrange, correct, edit."

Now... book Literally, "The sum of the matter, when all is heard, is: ... "

important thing a person can do is to respect God and obey his commands. Why? Because God knows about all the things people do—even the secret things. He knows about all the good things and all the bad things. He will judge everything people do.

Song of Solomon

1 Solomon's Most Wonderful Song

The Woman to the Man She Loves

2 Cover me with kisses.
   For your love is better than wine.
3 Your perfume smells wonderful,
   but your name* is sweeter
      than the best perfume.
   That is why the young women love you.
4 Take me with you!
   Let's run away!

The king took me into his room.

The Women of Jerusalem to the Man

We will rejoice
   and be happy for you.
Remember, your love is better than wine.
With good reason the young women
   love you.

She Speaks to the Women

5 Daughters of Jerusalem,
   I am dark and beautiful,
      as black as the tents of
         Teman and Salma.*
6 Don't look at how dark I am,
   at how dark the sun has made me.
   My brothers were angry at me.
      They forced me to take care
         of their vineyards.
   So I could not take care of myself.*

She Speaks to Him

7 I love you with all my soul!
   Tell me;
      Where do you feed ₁your sheep₁?
      Where do you lay ₁them₁ down at noon?
   ₁I should come to be with you₁
      or I will be like a hired woman*
         caring for the sheep of your friends!

He Speaks to Her

8 You are such a beautiful woman!
   Surely you know what to do.
   Go, follow the sheep.
      Feed your young goats
         near the shepherds' tents.
9 My darling, you are more exciting to me
      than any mare among the stallions*
         pulling Pharaoh's chariots.*
   ₁Those horses have beautiful decorations
      at the side of their faces
         and around their necks.₁
10-11 Here are the decorations made for you,
   a golden headband*
      and a silver necklace.
   Your cheeks are so beautiful
      decorated with gold.
   Your neck is so beautiful
      laced with silver.

---

hired woman Or, "a woman wearing a veil." This might mean a prostitute.
mare ... stallions Female and male horses. Only male horses were used to pull chariots.
My darling ... chariots Literally, "To a mare among Pharaoh's chariots I compare you, my darling."
headband We don't know the exact meaning of this Hebrew word. It might be a headband with decorations dangling at the cheeks.

name In Hebrew this word sounds like the word "perfume."
Teman and Salma Arabian tribes. For "Salma" the Hebrew has "Solomon," but compare "Salma, Salmon" in Ruth 4:20-21.
myself Literally, "my own vineyard."

She Speaks

12 The smell of my perfume reaches out
   to the king lying on his couch.
13 My lover is like
   a small bag of myrrh* [around my neck],
   lying all night between my breasts.
14 My lover is like
   a cluster of henna* flowers
   near the vineyards of En-gedi.

He Speaks

15 My darling, you are so beautiful!
   Oh, you are beautiful!
   Your eyes are like doves.

She Speaks

16 You are so handsome, my lover!
   Yes, and so charming!
   Our bed is so fresh and pleasant!*
17 The beams of our house are cedar.
   The rafters are fir.

2 I am a crocus on the plain,*
   a lily in the valleys.

He Speaks

2 My darling, among other women,
   you are like a lily among thorns!

She Speaks

3 My lover, among other men,
   you are an apple tree among the wild
   trees in the forest!

She Speaks to the Women

I enjoy sitting in my lover's shadow;
his fruit is so sweet to my taste.
4 My lover took me to the wine house;
His intent toward me was love.

5 Strengthen me with raisins;*
   refresh me with apples,
   because I am weak with love.*
6 My lover's left arm is under my head,
   and his right arm holds me.
7 Women of Jerusalem, promise me,
   by the gazelles and wild deer,
   don't wake love,
   don't arouse love,
   until I am ready.*

She Speaks Again

8 I hear my lover's voice.
   Here it comes,
   jumping over the mountains,
   skipping over the hills.
9 My lover is like a gazelle
   or a young deer.

Look at him standing behind our wall,
staring out the window,
looking through the lattice.*
10 My lover speaks to me,
   "Get up, my darling, my beautiful one,
   Let's go away!
11 Look, winter is past,
   the rains have come and gone.
12 The flowers are blooming in the fields.
   It's time to sing!*
   Listen, the doves have returned.
13 Young figs are growing on the fig trees.
   Smell the vines in bloom.
   Get up, my darling, my beautiful one,
   Let's go away!"
14 My dove,
   hiding in the caves high on the cliff,
   hidden here on the mountain,
   let me see you,
   let me hear your voice.
   Your voice is so pleasant,
   and you are so beautiful!"

She Speaks to the Women

15 Catch the foxes for us—
   the little foxes that spoil the vineyard!
   Our vineyard is now in bloom.

---

myrrh A perfume made from the gum of certain plants.
henna A plant with sweet smelling, blue-yellow flowers that grow in clusters (*groups*) like grapes.
fresh and pleasant Or, "lush and green" like a fresh field of grass.
crocus on the plain Or, "a rose of Sharon."
raisins Or, "raisin cakes."

I am weak with love Or, "I am lovesick."
until I am ready Literally, "until it desires."
lattice A wooden screen over a window.
sing Or, "prune."

16 My lover is mine,
    and I am his!
17 My lover feeds among the lilies,
    while the day breathes its last breath
    and the shadows run away.
  Turn, my lover,
    be like a gazelle or a young deer
    on the cleft mountains!*

She Speaks

3 At night on my bed,
    I look for the man I love.
  I looked for him,
    but I could not find him!
2 I will get up now!
  I will go around the city.
  In the streets and squares,
    I will look for the man I love.

  I looked for him,
    but I could not find him!
3 The guards patrolling the city found me.
  ⌊I asked them,⌋
    "Have you seen the man I love?"
4 I had just left the guards
    when I found the man I love!
  I held him.
  I would not let him go,
    while I took him to my mother's house,
    to the room of she who bore* me.

She Speaks to the Women

5 Women of Jerusalem, promise me,
    by the gazelles and wild deer,
    don't wake love,
    don't arouse love,
    until I am ready.*

He and His Bride

6 Who is this woman
    coming from the desert*
    ⌊with this large group of people⌋?
  ⌊The dust rises behind them⌋
    like clouds of smoke

  from burning myrrh and frankincense*
    and other spices.*
7 Look, Solomon's traveling chair!*
  There are 60 soldiers guarding it.
  Strong soldiers of Israel!
8 All of them are trained fighting men;
    their swords at their side,
    ready for any danger of the night!
9 King Solomon made a traveling chair*
    for himself.
  The wood came from Lebanon.
10 The poles were made from silver,
    the supports were made from gold.
  The seat was covered with purple cloth.
    It was inlaid with love
    by the women of Jerusalem.
11 Women of Zion, come out
    and see King Solomon
  See the crown* his mother put on him
    the day he was married,
    the day he was so happy!

He Speaks to Her

4 My darling, you are so beautiful!
    Oh, you are beautiful!
  Your eyes are like doves
    under your veil.
  Your hair ⌊is long and flowing⌋,
    like little goats dancing
    down the slopes of Mount Gilead.
2 Your teeth are white like ewes*
    just coming from their bath.
  They all give birth to twins;
    Not one of them has lost a baby.
3 Your lips are like a red silk thread.
    Your mouth is beautiful.
  Your temples* under your veil
    are like two slices of pomegranate.*

---

myrrh and frankincense Expensive spices that smell sweet when burned.
spices Literally, "powders of the trader." These were imported spices and incense.
traveling chair A kind of chair that rich people traveled in. These chairs were covered and had poles that slaves used to carry them.
crown This might be a wreath of flowers he wore on his head at his wedding.
ewes Female goats.
temples The sides of the head.
pomegranate A red fruit with many tiny seeds inside it. Each seed is covered with a soft, tasty part of the fruit.

the cleft mountains Or, "the mountains of Bether" or "the mountains of spice."
bore Or, "taught." See 8:2.
until I am ready Literally, "until it desires."
woman coming from the desert See 8:5.

SONG OF SOLOMON 4:4-5:1

4 Your neck is long and thin
  like David's tower.
  That tower was built to be decorated*
    with a thousand shields on its walls,
    with the shields of powerful soldiers.
5 Your breasts are
  like twin fawns,*
  like twins of a gazelle,*
    feeding among the lilies.
6 I will go to that mountain of myrrh*
  and to that hill of frankincense*
    while the day breathes its last breath,
    and the shadows run away.
7 My darling, you are beautiful all over.
    You have no blemishes* anywhere!
8 Come with me, my bride, from Lebanon.
  Come with me from Lebanon.
  Come from the peak of Amana,*
    from the top of Senir* and Hermon,
    from the lion's caves,
    from the mountain of the leopards!
9 My darling,* my bride, you excite me!
  You have stolen my heart
    with just one of your eyes,
    with just one of the jewels from
      your necklace.
10 Your love is so beautiful, my darling,*
    my bride!
  Your love is better than wine;
  The smell of your perfume
    is better than any kind of spice!
11 My bride, your lips drip honey.
    Honey and milk are under your tongue.
    Your clothes smell as sweet as perfume.*

12 My darling,* my bride, ⌊you are pure⌋
    like a locked garden,
  You are like a locked pool,
    a closed fountain.
13 Your limbs are like a garden
    filled with pomegranates*
    and other pleasant fruit;
    with all the best spices:
      henna* ¹⁴nard,* saffron,* calamus,*
      and cinnamon.*
  ⌊Your limbs are like a garden⌋
    filled with trees of frankincense,* myrrh,*
    and aloes.*
15 You are like a garden fountain,
    a well of fresh water,
    flowing down from the mountains
    of Lebanon.

She Speaks

16 Wake up, north wind!
  Come, south wind!
  Blow on my garden.
    Spread its sweet smell.
  Let my lover enter his garden,
    and eat its pleasant fruit.

He Speaks

5 My darling* my bride,
  I have entered my garden.
  I have gathered my myrrh* and spice.
  I have eaten my honey and honeycomb.
  I have drunk my wine and milk.

The Women Speak to the Lovers

  Dearest friends, eat, drink!
  Be drunk with love!

Your neck ... decorated Or "Your neck is like David's tower, built with rows of stone." This would mean she wore many necklaces, one above the other, which looked like rows of stone in a tower.
fawns Baby deer.
gazelle An animal like a deer or antelope.
myrrh A kind of perfume made from the sap of plants.
frankincense An expensive perfume from Arabia.
blemishes Ugly marks.
Amana The name of a mountain in Lebanon.
Senir The Amorite word for "Snow Mountain." This means Mount Hermon.
darling Literally, "sister."
darling Literally, "sister."
perfume Or, "Lebanon."

darling Literally, "sister."
pomegranate A red fruit containing many tiny seeds covered with a soft, juicy part of the fruit.
henna A plant with sweet smelling, blue-yellow flowers that grow in clusters (*groups*) like grapes.
nard A very expensive oil from the root from the nard plant. It was used as a perfume.
saffron A kind of yellow flower used in making perfume.
calamus A kind of reed plant used in making perfume.
cinnamon A kind of plant used as a spice and in making perfume.
aloes Perfume made from a special kind of tree.
darling Literally, "sister."

She Speaks

2 I am asleep,
   but my heart is awake.
   I hear my lover knocking.
   "Open to me, my darling,* my love,
      my dove, my perfect one!
   My head is soaked with dew.
   My hair is wet with the mist
      of the night."

3 "I have taken off my robe.
      I don't want to put it on again.
   I have washed my feet,
      I don't want to get them dirty again."

4 But my lover put his hand
      through the opening,*
   and I felt sorry for him.*

5 I got up to open for my lover,
   myrrh dripping from my hands,
   myrrh* scented lotion dripped from my
      fingers onto the handles of the lock.

6 I opened for my lover,
   but my lover had turned away
      and was gone!
   I nearly died
      when he left.*
   I looked for him,
      but I couldn't find him;
   I called for him,
      but he didn't answer me.

7 The guards patrolling the city found me.
   They hit me.
      They hurt me.
   The guards on the wall
      took my robe* from me.

8 I tell you, women of Jerusalem,
   if you find my lover,
      tell him I am weak with love.*

The Women of Jerusalem Answer Her

9 Beautiful woman, how is your lover different
      from other lovers?
   Is your lover better than other lovers?
   Is that why you ask us
      to make this promise?

She Answers the Women of Jerusalem

10 My lover is tanned and radiant *(shining)*.
      He would stand out among 10,000 men.
11 His head is like the purest gold.
      His hair is curly
      and as black as a raven.
12 His eyes are like doves by a stream,
      like doves in a pool of milk,
      ⌊like a jewel⌋ in its setting.
13 His cheeks are like a garden of spices,
      like flowers used for perfume.
   His lips ⌊are like⌋ lilies,*
      dripping with liquid myrrh*
14 His arms are like gold rods,
      filled with jewels.
   His body is like smooth ivory
      with sapphires* set in it.
15 His legs are like marble pillars,
      on bases of fine gold.
   He stands tall
      like the finest cedar tree in Lebanon!
16 Yes, women of Jerusalem,
      my lover is the most desirable.
      His mouth is the sweetest of all.
   That is my lover,
      that is my darling.

The Women of Jerusalem Speak to Her

6 Beautiful woman,
   Where has your lover gone?
   Which way did your lover go?
   Tell us so we can help you look for him.

She Answers the Women of Jerusalem

2 My lover has gone down to his garden,
   to the flower beds of spices.

---

darling Literally, "sister."
put his hand through the opening Or "pulled his hand from the opening." In one sense, this might refer to a lock and key. Some ancient keys were shaped like a hand. The key was inserted through a hole in the door, and the "fingers" fit into special holes that allowed the bolt to slide, locking and unlocking the door.
I felt sorry for him Literally, "My insides stirred for him."
myrrh A kind of perfume made from the sap of plants. Here this is probably a reminder the lover left to show he had come by her house.
I nearly died
when he left Or, "My soul sank when he spoke."
robe Or, "veil, a piece of cloth used to cover a person's face."

I am weak with love Literally, "I am lovesick."
lily kind of flower. Here it is probably a red flower.
sapphires Blue stones.

He went to feed in the gardens,
and gather the lilies.
3 I belong to my lover,
and my lover belongs to me.
He is the one feeding among the lilies.

He Speaks to Her

4 My darling,
you are as beautiful as Tirzah,*
as pleasant as Jerusalem;
as awesome as those fortified cities.*
5 Don't look at me!
Your eyes excite me too much!
And your hair ₍is long and flowing₎,
like little goats dancing
down the slopes of Mount Gilead.
6 Your teeth are white like ewes*
just coming from their bath.
They all give birth to twins;
Not one of them has lost a baby.
7 Your temples* under your veil*
are like slices of pomegranate.*
8 There might be 60 queens
and 80 women servants,*
and young women too many to count,
9 but there is only one ₍woman for me₎,
my dove,
my perfect one.
She is the favorite of her mother
Her mother's favorite child!
The young women see her and praise her.
Even the queens and women servants*
praise her.

The Women Praise Her

10 Who is that young woman?
She shines out like the dawn.
She is as pretty as the moon,
She is as radiant as the sun,
She is as awesome as those
armies in the sky.*

Tirzah One of the capitals of northern Israel.
fortified cities We are not sure of the exact meaning of the Hebrew word here and in verse 10.
ewes Female goats.
temples The sides of the head.
veil A piece of cloth used to cover a person's face.
pomegranate A red fruit with many tiny seeds inside it. Each seed is covered with a soft, tasty part of the fruit.
women servants Or, "concubines," slave women who were like wives to a man.

She Speaks

11 I went down to the grove of walnut trees,
to see the fruit of the valley,
to see if the vines were in bloom,
to see if the pomegranates* had budded.
12 Before I realized it,*
my soul had placed me in the chariots*
of the king's people.*

The Women of Jerusalem Call to Her

13 Come back, come back, Shulamith!*
Come back, come back,
so we may look at you.

Why are you staring at Shulamith,
as she dances the Mahanaim dance?*

He Praises Her Beauty

7 Princess,* your feet are beautiful
in those sandals.
The curves of your thighs are like jewelry
made by an artist.
2 Your navel is like a round cup;*
may it never be without wine.
Your belly is like a pile of wheat
bordered with lilies.
3 Your breasts are like twin fawns*
of a young gazelle.*
4 Your neck is like an ivory tower.
Your eyes are like the pools in Heshbon
near the gate of Bath Rabbim.

those armies in the sky We are not sure of the exact meaning of the Hebrew word here and in verse 4.
Before I realized it In Hebrew this verse is very hard to understand.
chariot(s) A small wagon used in war. But here this might mean one of the traveling chairs, as in 3:7.
the king's people Or, "Amminadib," or "my kingly people."
Shulamith Or, "Shulamite." The word might be the feminine form of the name "Solomon." This could mean she was or would become the bride of Solomon. This name might also mean, "perfect, at peace" or "woman from Shunem."
Mahanaim dance Or, "the victory dance," or "the dance of the two camps."
Princess Literally, "Bath Nadib: Daughter of a prince." This is like the word "Amminadib" in 6:12.
round cup Or "turned bowl," a stone bowl made on a lathe and used for mixing wine before it is poured into cups. This might also mean a bowl shaped like a crescent or half-moon.

Your nose is like the tower of Lebanon
which looks toward Damascus.
5 Your head is like Carmel,
and the hair on your head is like silk.
Your long flowing hair
captures even a king!
6 You are so beautiful!
And so pleasant!
A lovely, delightful young woman!
7 You are tall,
as tall as a palm tree.
And your breasts are like
the clusters of fruit on that tree.
8 I would love to climb that tree,
and take hold of its branches.

May your breasts be like
clusters of grapes
and your fragrance* like apples.
9 May your mouth be like the best wine,
flowing straight to my love,
flowing gently to the sleepers' lips.

She Speaks to Him

10 I belong to my lover,
and he wants me!
11 Come, my lover,
let's go out into the field,
let's spend the night in the villages.
12 Let's get up early and go to the vineyards.
Let's see if the vines are in bloom.
Let's see if the blossoms have opened
and if the pomegranates* are in bloom.
There I will give you my love.
13 Smell the mandrakes*
and all the pleasant flowers
by our door!
Yes, I have saved many pleasant things
for you, my lover.
Pleasant things, new and old!

8 ₁I wish₁ you were like my baby brother nursing
at my mother's breasts! If I found you outside,
I could kiss you, and no one would say it was
wrong! ²I would lead you into my mother's house,
to the room of she who taught me. I would give
you spiced wine squeezed from my
pomegranate.*

She Speaks to the Women

3 His left arm is under my head,
and his right hand holds me.
4 Women of Jerusalem, promise me,
don't wake love,
don't arouse love,
until I am ready.*

The Women of Jerusalem Speak

5 Who is this woman
coming from the desert,
leaning on her lover?

She Speaks to Him

I woke you under the apple tree,
where your mother bore you,
where you were born.
6 Keep me ₁near you₁ like a seal
you wear over your heart,
like a signet ring*
you wear on your hand.
Love is as strong as death.
Passion is as strong as the grave.*
Its sparks become a flame
and it grows to become a great fire!*
7 A flood cannot put out love.
Rivers cannot drown love.
No one would blame a man for giving
everything he owns for love!

Her Brothers Speak

8 We have a little sister,
and her breasts are not yet grown.

---

fawns Baby deer.
gazelle An animal like a deer or antelope.
fragrance Literally, "breath of your nose."
pomegranates A red fruit with many tiny seeds inside it. Each seed is covered with a soft, tasty part of the fruit.
mandrakes Plants with roots that look like people. People thought these plants had the power to make people fall in love.

pomegranate A red fruit with many tiny seeds inside it. Each seed is covered with a soft, tasty part of the fruit.
until I am ready Literally, "until it desires."
seal ... signet ring Things that were pressed into clay or hot wax to leave a special mark. This mark was like a person's signature, so it was very important not to lose these things.
the grave Or, "Sheol," the place where dead people go.
great fire Or, "the flame of the Lord."

What should we do for our sister
when a man comes asking to marry her.

9 If she were a wall,
we would put silver trim* around her.
If she were a door,
we would put a cedar board around her.

She Answers Her Brothers

10 I am a wall,
and my breasts are my towers.
And he is satisfied with me!*

He Speaks

11 Solomon had a vineyard at Baal Hamon.
He put men in charge of that
field of grapes.
And each man brought in grapes
worth 1,000 shekels* of silver.

12 Solomon, you can keep your 1,000 shekels.
Give 200 shekels to each man
for the grapes he brought.
But I will keep my own field of grapes!

He Speaks to Her

13 There you sit, in the garden,
friends are listening to your voice.
Let me hear it too!

She Speaks to Him

14 Hurry, my lover.
Be like a gazelle* or a young deer
on the mountains of spice!

---

trim Or "supports." Often horizontal beams and towers were built into walls to strengthen and support them. But here this seems to be a decoration.

he is satisfied with me Literally, "In his eyes I find peace." In Hebrew this is also like the names "Solomon" and "Shulamith."

1,000 shekels About 25 pounds.

gazelle An animal like a deer or antelope.

Isaiah

¹ This is the vision* of Isaiah son of Amoz. God showed Isaiah things that would happen to Judah and Jerusalem. Isaiah saw these things during the time Uzziah,* Jotham,* Ahaz,* and Hezekiah* were kings of Judah.

God's Case Against His People

²Heaven and Earth, listen to the Lord! The Lord says,

"I raised my children.
I helped my children grow.
But my children turned against me.
³ A cow knows its master.
And a donkey knows the place where its owner feeds it.
But the people of Israel don't know me.
My people don't understand."

⁴The nation of Israel is full of guilt. This guilt is like a heavy weight the people have to carry. Those people are like bad children from evil families. They left the Lord. They insulted the Holy One *(God)* of Israel. They left him and treated him like a stranger.

⁵⌊God says,⌋ "Why should I continue to punish you people? ⌊I punished you, but you did not change.⌋ You continue to rebel against me. Now every head and every heart is sick. ⁶From the bottom of your feet to the top of your head, every part of your body has wounds, hurts, and open sores. You have not cared for your sores. Your wounds are not cleaned and covered.

⁷"Your land is ruined. Your cities have been burned with fire. Your enemies have taken your land. Your land is ruined like a country destroyed by armies. ⁸The Daughter of Zion *(Jerusalem)* is now like an empty tent left in a field of grapes. It is like an old house left in a field of cucumbers. It is like a city that has been defeated by enemies." ⁹⌊This is true,⌋ but the Lord All-Powerful did allow a few people to continue living. We were not completely destroyed like the cities of Sodom and Gomorrah.*

God Wants True Service

¹⁰You leaders of Sodom, listen to the Lord's message! You people of Gomorrah, listen to God's teachings! ¹¹⌊God says,⌋ "Why do you continue giving me all these sacrifices?* I have had enough of your sacrifices of goats and fat from bulls, sheep, and goats.

¹²"When you people come to meet with me, you trample *(walk on)* everything in my yard. Who told you to do this?

¹³"Don't continue bringing worthless sacrifices to me. I hate the incense* you give me. I can't bear your feasts for the New Moon,* the Sabbath,* and your holidays. I hate the evil you do during your holy meetings. ¹⁴With my whole self I hate your monthly meetings and councils. These meetings have become like heavy weights to me. And I am tired of carrying those weights.

¹⁵"You people will raise your arms to pray to me—but I will refuse to look at you. You people will say more and more prayers—but I will refuse to listen to you. Why? Because your hands are covered with blood.

Sodom, Gomorrah Two cities that God destroyed because the people were so evil.
sacrifices Gifts to God. Sometimes these were special kinds of animals that were killed and burned on an altar.
incense A kind of spice that smells good when it is burned. It was burned as a gift to God.
New Moon The first day of the Jewish month. This was a special day of worship.
Sabbath Saturday, a special day of rest and worship for Jews.

vision Like a dream. God gave messages to his special people by letting them see and hear things in visions.
Uzziah A king of Judah. He ruled about 767-740 B.C.
Jotham A king of Judah. He ruled about 740-735 B.C.
Ahaz A king of Judah. He ruled about 735-727 B.C.
Hezekiah A king of Judah. He ruled about 727-687 B.C.

ISAIAH 1:16–2:6

¹⁶"Wash yourselves. Make yourselves clean. Stop doing the bad things you do. I don't want to see those bad things. Stop doing wrong! ¹⁷Learn to do good things. Be fair with other people. Punish the people that hurt others. Help the children that have no parents. Help the women whose husbands are dead."

¹⁸The Lord says, "Come, let's discuss these things. Your sins are red like scarlet,* but they can be ⌊washed away and you will be⌋ white like snow. Your sins are bright red, but you can become white like wool.

¹⁹"If you listen to the things I say, then you will have the good things from this land. ²⁰But if you refuse to listen, you are against me. And your enemies will destroy you."

The Lord himself said those things.

Jerusalem Is Not Loyal to God

²¹⌊God says,⌋ "Look at Jerusalem. She was a city that trusted and followed me. What caused her to become like a prostitute?* She does not follow me now. Jerusalem should be filled with fairness. People living in Jerusalem should live the way God wants. But now, murderers live there.

²²"Goodness is like silver. But your silver has become worthless. Your wine *(goodness)* has been mixed with water—it is now weak. ²³Your rulers are rebels and friends of thieves. All of your rulers demand bribes—they accept money for doing wrong things. All of your rulers take pay for cheating people. Your rulers don't try to help the children that have no parents. And your rulers don't listen to the needs of the women whose husbands are dead."

²⁴Because of all these things, the Master, the Lord All-Powerful, the Mighty One of Israel, says, "I will punish you, my enemies. You will not cause me any more trouble. ²⁵People use lye* to clean silver. ⌊In the same way,⌋ I will clean all your wrongs away. I will take all the worthless things out from you. ²⁶I will bring back the kind of judges you had in the beginning. Your counselors will be like the counselors you had long ago. Then you will be called 'The Good and Faithful City.'"

²⁷⌊God is⌋ good and does the things that are right. So he will rescue Zion* and the people that come back to him. ²⁸But all criminals and sinners will be destroyed. (They are the people that don't follow the Lord.)

²⁹⌊In the future,⌋ people will be ashamed of the oak trees* and special gardens* you choose to worship. ³⁰This will happen because you people will be like oak trees with leaves that are dying. You people will be like a garden dying without water. ³¹Powerful people will be like small dry pieces of wood. And the things those people do will be like sparks ⌊that start a fire⌋—the powerful people and the things they do will begin to burn. And no person will be able to stop that fire.

2 Isaiah son of Amoz saw this message about Judah and Jerusalem.

²In the last days, the mountain of the Lord's temple* will be on the highest of the mountains. It will be raised higher than all the hills. There will be a steady stream of people from all nations going there. ³Many people will go there. They will say, "Come! Let's go up to the Lord's mountain. Let's go up to the temple of the God of Jacob. Then God will teach us his way of living. And we will follow him."

The teachings from God—the Lord's message—will begin in Jerusalem on the mountain of Zion* and go out to all the world. ⁴Then God will be a judge for the people of all nations. God will end the arguments for many people. Those people will stop using their weapons for fighting. They will make plows from their swords. And they will use their spears as tools for cutting plants. People will stop fighting against other people. People will never again train for war.

⁵Family of Jacob, you should follow the Lord. ⁶⌊I say this to you⌋ because you have left your people. Your people have become filled with the wrong ideas of the people in the east. Your people try to tell the future like the Philistines.* Your

---

scarlet An expensive, bright red dye or piece cloth.
prostitute A woman that sells her body for sex. Sometimes this also means a person that stops following God.
lye A chemical used like soap.

Zion The southeast part of the mountain Jerusalem is built on. Sometimes it means the people of God living in Jerusalem.
oak trees These were like idols that people worshiped.
special gardens Places where people worshiped false gods.
temple A special building for worshiping God. God commanded the Jews to worship him at the temple in Jerusalem.
Philistines People living on the coast of Palestine. They were one of Israel's enemies.

people have completely accepted those strange ideas. ⁷Your land has been filled with silver and gold from other places. There are many, many treasures there. Your land has been filled with horses. There are many, many chariots* there. ⁸Your land is full of statues that people worship. The people made those idols* and the people worship them. ⁹People have become worse and worse. People have become very low. God, surely you will not forgive them, will you?*

God's Enemies Will Be Afraid

¹⁰Go hide in the dirt and behind the rocks! You should be afraid of the Lord and you should hide from his great power!

¹¹Proud people will stop being proud. Those proud people will bow down to the ground with shame. At that time, only the Lord will still stand high.

¹²The Lord has a special day planned. On that day, the Lord will punish the proud and boastful people. Then those proud people will be made not important. ¹³⌊Those proud people are like⌋ tall cedar trees from Lebanon.* ⌊They are like⌋ great oak trees from Bashan.* ⌊But God will punish those people⌋. ¹⁴⌊Those proud people are like⌋ tall mountains and high hills. ¹⁵⌊Those proud people are like⌋ tall towers and high, very strong walls. ⌊But God will punish those people⌋. ¹⁶Those proud people are like great ships from Tarshish.* (These ships are full of important things.) ⌊But God will punish those proud people.⌋

¹⁷At that time, people will stop being proud. The people that are now proud will bow low to the ground. And at that time, only the Lord will stand high. ¹⁸All the idols *(false gods)* will be gone. ¹⁹People will hide behind rocks and in cracks in the ground. People will be afraid of the Lord and his great power. This will happen when the Lord stands to make the earth shake.

²⁰At that time, people will throw away their gold and silver idols. (The people made those statues so the people could worship them.) The people will throw those statues into holes in the ground where bats and moles* live. ²¹Then the people will hide in cracks in the rocks. They will do this because they will be afraid of the Lord and his great power. This will happen when the Lord stands to make the earth shake.

Israel Should Trust God

²²You should stop trusting other people to save you. They are only people—and people die. ⌊So, you should not think they are strong like God.⌋

3 Understand these things I am telling you. The Master, the Lord All-Powerful, will take away all the things Judah and Jerusalem depend on. God will take away all the food and all the water. ²God will take away all the heroes and great soldiers. God will take away all the judges,* the prophets,* the people that do magic, and the elders.* ³God will take away the military leaders and the government leaders. God will take away the skilled counselors and the wise men that do magic and try to tell the future.

⁴⌊God says,⌋ "I will cause young boys to be your leaders. ⁵Every person will be against every other person. Young people will not respect older people. Common people will not respect the important people."

⁶At that time, a person will grab one of his brothers from his own family. That person will tell the brother, "You have a coat,* so you will be our leader. You will be the leader over all these ruins."

⁷But that brother will stand and say, "I can't help you. I don't have enough food or clothes in my house. You will not make me your leader."

⁸This will happen because Jerusalem has stumbled ⌊and has done wrong⌋. Judah has fallen ⌊and has stopped following God⌋. The things they say and do are against the Lord. The Lord's glorious eyes clearly see all these things.

---

chariots Small wagons used for war.
idols Statues of false gods that people worshiped.
God ... will you Or, "Surely you will not raise them up."
Lebanon A country north of Israel. It was famous for its great cedar and pine trees.
Bashan An area northeast of Israel.
ships from Tarshish This is probably a special type of cargo ship.

bats and moles Small animals that live in caves and holes in the ground.
judges In Israel, judges were people that judged, led, and protected the people.
prophets A true prophet was a person called by God to be a special servant. God used dreams and visions to show them things to teach the people.
elders Older men that were city leaders; they helped make decisions for the people.
coat Or, "robe." This showed a person was a leader of the people.

⁹The faces of the people show that they are guilty of doing wrong. And they are proud of their sin. They are like the people of Sodom*—they don't care who sees their sin. It will be very bad for them. They have brought much trouble to themselves. ¹⁰Tell the good people that good things will happen to them. They will receive a reward for the good things they do. ¹¹But it will be very bad for the evil people. Much trouble will come to them. They will be punished for all the wrong things they have done. ¹²Children will defeat my people. Women will rule over my people. My people, your guides lead you in the wrong way. They turn you away from the right way.

God's Decision About His People

¹³The Lord will stand to judge the people. ¹⁴The Lord will give his judgment against the elders* and leaders for the things they have done.

The Lord says, "You people have burned the field of grapes *(Judah)*. You took things from poor people, and those things are still in your houses. ¹⁵What gives you the right to hurt my people? What gives you the right to push the faces of the poor people into the dirt?" My Master, the Lord All-Powerful said these things.

¹⁶The Lord says, "The women in Zion* have become very proud. They walk around with their heads in the air, acting like they are better than other people. Those women flirt with their eyes. And they dance around making noise with their ankle bracelets."

¹⁷My Master will make sores on the heads of those women in Zion.* The Lord will make the women lose all their hair. ¹⁸At that time, the Lord will take away all the things they are proud of: the beautiful ankle bracelets, the necklaces that look like the sun and the moon, ¹⁹the earrings, bracelets, and veils *(face coverings)*, ²⁰the scarves, the ankle chains, the sashes worn around their waists, the bottles of perfume, and the charms,* ²¹the signet rings,* and the nose-rings, ²²the fine robes, capes, shawls, and purses, ²³the mirrors, linen dresses, turbans, and long shawls.

²⁴⌊Those women now have⌋ sweet smelling perfume, but ⌊at that time, their perfume will become⌋ moldy and rotten. ⌊Now they wear⌋ belts. But ⌊at that time, they will have only⌋ ropes to wear. Now they have their hair fixed fancy ways. But ⌊at that time⌋, their heads will be shaved— they will have no hair.* ⌊Now they have⌋ party dresses. ⌊But at that time, they will have⌋ only clothes to show sadness. They have beauty marks on their faces now. ⌊But at that time, they will have another mark.⌋ It will be a mark burned into their skin.

²⁵At that time, your men will be killed with swords. Your heroes will die in war. ²⁶There will be crying and sadness in the meeting places near the city gates. Jerusalem will sit there empty like a woman that has lost everything to thieves and robbers. She will sit on the ground ⌊and cry⌋.

4 At that time, seven women will grab one man. The women will say, "We will make our own bread to eat. And we will make our own clothes to wear. We will do all these things for ourselves if you will only ⌊marry us⌋. Let us have your name. Please, take away our shame."

²At that time, the Lord's plant *(Judah)* will be very beautiful and great. The people still living in Israel will be very proud of the things the land grows. ³At that time, all the people that are still living in Zion* and Jerusalem will be called holy *(special)* people. This will happen to all the people that have their names on a special list; the list of people that will be allowed to continue living.

⁴The Lord will wash away the blood* from the women of Zion.* The Lord will wash all the blood out of Jerusalem. God will use the spirit of justice ⌊and judge fairly⌋. And he will use the spirit of burning, ⌊and make everything pure (good)⌋.

⁵⌊At that time, God will prove that he is with his people.⌋ During the day, God will make a cloud of smoke. And during the night, God will make a bright flaming fire.* These proofs will be

---

Sodom A city that God destroyed because its people were so evil.
elders Older men that were city leaders; they helped make decisions for the people.
Zion The southeast part of the mountain Jerusalem is built on. Sometimes it means the people of God living in Jerusalem.
charms Things people wore on bracelets and necklaces. People thought these things would protect them from evil or danger.
they will have no hair This shows that those people will become slaves.
wash away the blood This is like a special ceremony for washing the blood after a menstrual period. After this a man and wife could be together and show their love for each other.
cloud of smoke .... fire These were signs that God used to show he was with his people.

in the sky over every building and over every meeting of the people on the mountain of Zion.* There will be a covering over every person* for protection. ⁶This covering will be a place of safety. The covering will protect the people from the heat of the sun. The covering will be a safe place to hide from all kinds of floods and rain.

Israel, God's Special Garden

5 Now, I will sing a song for my friend *(God)*. This song is about the love my friend has for his field of grapes *(Israel)*.

> My friend had a vineyard*
>   in a very rich field.
> ² My friend dug and cleared the field.
>   He planted the best grapevines there.
>   He built a tower in the middle of the field.
>   He hoped for good grapes to grow there.
>   But there were only bad grapes.
>
> ³ ₍So God said₎:
> "You people living in Jerusalem,*
>   and you, man of Judah,*
>   think about me and my vineyard.*
> ⁴ What more could I do for my field of grapes?
>   I did everything I could.
>   I hoped for good grapes to grow.
>   But there were only bad grapes.
>   Why did that happen?"

⁵Now, I will tell you what I will do to my field of grapes:

> I will pull up the thorn bushes
>   ₍that are protecting the field₎,
>   and I will burn them.
> I will break down the stone wall,
>   and the stones will be walked on.
> ⁶ I will make my vineyard* an empty field.
>   No person will care for the plants.
>   No person will work in the field.
>   Weeds and thorns will grow there.
>   I will command the clouds
>   not to rain on the field."

⁷The field of grapes that belongs to the Lord All-Powerful is the nation of Israel. The grapevine—the plant the Lord loves—is the man of Judah.*

> The Lord hoped for justice,
>   but there was only killing.
> The Lord hoped for fairness,
>   but there were only cries
>   ₍from people being treated badly₎.

⁸You people live very close together. You build houses until there is no place for anything else. But ₍the Lord will punish you, and₎ you will be made to live alone. You will be the only people in the whole land!* ⁹The Lord All-Powerful said this to me, and I heard him, "There are many houses now. But I promise that all the houses will be destroyed. There are nice, big houses now. But those houses will be empty. ¹⁰At that time, a ten-acre field of grapes will make only a little wine.* And many sacks of seed will grow only a little grain.*

¹¹You people rise early in the morning and go looking for beer to drink. You stay awake late at night, becoming drunk with wine. ¹²You party with your wine, harps,* drums, flutes, and other musical instruments. And you don't see the things the Lord has done. The Lord's hands have made many, many things—but you don't notice those things. So, it will be very bad for you people.

¹³₍The Lord says₎, "My people will be captured and taken away. Why? Because they don't really know ₍me₎. Some of the people living in Israel are important now. They are happy with their easy lives. But all those great people will become very thirsty and very hungry. ¹⁴Then ₍they will die and₎ Sheol,* ₍the place of death₎, will get more and more people. That ₍place of death₎ will open her mouth with no limit. And all those people will go down into Sheol."

¹⁵Those people will be humbled. Those great people will bow their heads and look at the ground. ¹⁶The Lord All-Powerful will judge fairly,

---

Zion The southeast part of the mountain Jerusalem is built on. Sometimes it means the people of God living in Jerusalem.
person Literally, "glory," but this also means "soul," "person" (see Psalm 16:9).
vineyard A garden for growing grapes.
You people living in Jerusalem Or, "You leaders in Jerusalem."
man of Judah This probably means the king of Judah.

You people ... in the whole land Or, "You join houses to houses and fields to fields until there is no room (for other people), until you are left living alone in the land."
only a little wine Literally, "one bath." A bath is a measure that equals about 6 gallons.
only a little grain Literally, "A homer of seed will grow only an ephah of grain." A homer equals about 6 bushels. An ephah equals about one-half bushel.
harps Musical instruments with several strings.

and people will know he is great. The Holy God will do the things that are right, and the people will respect him. ¹⁷₍God will make the people of Israel leave their country; the land will be empty.₎ Sheep will go any place they want. Lambs will walk on the land that rich people once owned.

¹⁸Look at those people! They pull their guilt and sins behind them like people pull wagons with ropes.* ¹⁹Those people say, "We wish God would hurry and do the things he plans to do. Then we would know what will happen. We wish the Lord's plan would happen soon. Then we would know what his plan is."

²⁰Those people say that good things are bad, and bad things are good. Those people think light is darkness, and darkness is light. Those people think sour is sweet, and sweet is sour. ²¹Those people think they are very smart. They think they are very intelligent. ²²Those people are famous for drinking wine. They are champions at mixing drinks. ²³And if you pay those people money, they will forgive a criminal. But they don't allow good people to be judged fairly. ²⁴₍Bad things will happen to those people₎. Their descendants* will be completely destroyed—like straw and leaves are burned by fire. Their descendants will be destroyed like a root ₍that dies and₎ becomes dust. Their descendants will be destroyed like a fire destroys a flower—the ashes blow away in the wind.

Those people have refused to obey the teachings* of the Lord All-Powerful. Those people hated the message from the Holy One *(God)* of Israel. ²⁵So the Lord has become very angry with his people. And the Lord will raise his hand and punish them. Even the mountains will be frightened. Dead bodies will lie in the streets like garbage. But God will still be angry. His hand will still be raised ₍to punish the people₎.

God Will Bring Armies to Punish Israel

²⁶₍Look!₎ God is giving a sign to the nations in a faraway land. God is raising a flag, and he is whistling to call those people. The enemy is coming from a faraway land. The enemy will soon enter the country. They are moving very quickly. ²⁷The enemy never becomes tired or falls down. They never become sleepy and fall asleep. Their weapon belts are always ready. Their shoestrings never break. ²⁸The enemy's arrows are sharp. All of their bows are ready to shoot. The horses' feet are hard like rock. Clouds of dust rise from behind their chariots.*

²⁹The enemy shouts, and their shout is like a lion's roar. It is loud like a young lion. The enemy growls and grabs the people it is fighting against. The people struggle and try to escape. But there is no person to save them. ³⁰So, the "lion" roars loud like the waves of the sea. And the captured people look at the ground, and then there is only darkness. All light becomes dark in this thick cloud.

God Calls Isaiah to Be a Prophet

6 In the year that King Uzziah* died,* I saw my Master. He was sitting on a very high and wonderful throne.* His long robe filled the temple.* ²Seraph angels* stood around the Lord. Each Seraph angel had six wings. The angels used two of their wings to cover their faces. The angels used two of their wings to cover their feet. And the angels used two of their wings for flying. ³Each angel was calling to the other angels. The angels said, "Holy, holy, holy, the Lord All-Powerful ₍is very holy₎. His Glory* fills the whole earth." The angels' voices were very loud. ⁴Their voices caused the frame around the door to shake. Then the temple* began filling with smoke.*

⁵I became very scared. I said, "Oh, no! I will be destroyed. I am not pure *(good)* enough to speak to God. And I live among people that are not pure enough to speak to God.* Yet I have seen the King, the Lord All-Powerful."

Sheol This is the place where all people go when they die. Usually this means the grave, but it can mean the place where our spirits go.

ropes Literally, "useless ropes." The Hebrew words for useless ropes are like the words meaning "useless things—idols."

descendants A person's children, and all the people born from those children.

teachings This can also mean "laws." Sometimes this means the laws God gave Moses to teach to the people of Israel.

chariots Small wagons used for war.

Uzziah A king of Judah who ruled from 767-740 B.C.

year ... died This was probably 740 B.C.

throne A special chair a king or queen sits on.

temple A special building for worshiping God. God commanded the Jews to worship him at the temple in Jerusalem.

Seraph angels Special angels God used as messengers. The name might mean they were bright like fire.

people ... God Or, "people that do not have pure lips."

⁶[There was a fire on the altar.*] One of the Seraph angels* used a pair of tongs* to take a hot coal from the fire. The angel flew to me with the hot coal in his hand. ⁷The Seraph angel touched my mouth with the hot coal. Then the angel said, "Look! Because this hot coal touched your lips the wrong things you have done are gone from you. Your sins are now erased."

⁸Then I heard my Lord's voice. The Lord said, "Who can I send? Who will go for us?"

So I said, "Here I am. Send me!"

⁹Then the Lord said, "Go and tell this to the people: 'Listen closely, but don't understand! Look closely, but don't learn!' ¹⁰Confuse the people. Make the people not able to understand the things they hear and see. If you don't do this, then people might really understand the things they hear with their ears. The people might really understand in their minds. If they did this, then the people might come back to me and be healed (forgiven)!"

¹¹Then I asked, "Master, how long should I do this?"

The Lord answered, "Do this until the cities are destroyed, and the people are gone. Do this until there are no people left living in the houses. Do this until the land is destroyed and left empty."

¹²The Lord will make the people go far away. There will be large areas of empty land in the country. ¹³But a tenth of the people will be allowed to stay in the land. These people will not be destroyed because they will return to the Lord. These people are like an oak tree. When the tree is chopped down, a stump is left. This stump (the people remaining) is a very special seed.

Trouble with Aram

7 Ahaz* was the son of Jotham.* Jotham was the son of Uzziah.* Rezin* was the king of Aram,* Pekah son of Remaliah* was the king of Israel. During the time Ahaz was king of Judah, Rezin and Pekah went up to Jerusalem to fight against it. But they were not able to defeat the city.

²A message was told to the family of David.* The message said, "The army of Aram and the army of Ephraim (Israel) have joined together. The two armies are camped together."

When King Ahaz heard this message, he and the people became very scared. They were shaking with fear like trees of the forest blowing in the wind. ³Then the Lord told Isaiah, "You and your son Shear Jashub* should go out and talk to Ahaz. Go to the place where the water flows into the upper pool. This is on the street going to Laundryman's Field.

⁴"Tell Ahaz, 'Be careful, but be calm. Don't be afraid. Don't let those two men, Rezin and Remaliah's son,* scare you! Those men are like two burnt sticks. In the past they were burning hot. But now they are only smoke. Rezin, Aram, and Remaliah's son are angry. ⁵They have made plans against you. They said: ⁶We should go and fight against Judah. We will divide Judah for ourselves. We will make Tabeel's son the new king of Judah.'"

⁷The Lord my Master says, "Their plan will not succeed. It will not happen. ⁸It will not happen while Rezin* is the ruler of Damascus.* Ephraim (Israel) is now a nation, but 65 years in the future Ephraim (Israel) will not be a nation. ⁹Their plan will not succeed while Samaria is the capital of Ephraim (Israel) and while the ruler of Samaria is Remaliah's son.* If you don't believe this message then people should not believe you."

His Glory The "Glory of the Lord," one of the forms God used when he appeared to people. It was like a bright shining light.

temple A special building for worshiping God. God commanded the Jews to worship him at the temple in Jerusalem.

smoke This showed that God was in the temple. See Ex. 40:34-35.

altar A stone table used for burning sacrifices as gifts to God.

Seraph angels Special angels God used as messengers. The name might mean they were bright like fire.

tongs A "U-shaped" tool for holding hot things.

Ahaz A king of Judah. He ruled about 735-727 B.C.

Jotham A king of Judah. He ruled about 740-735 B.C.

Uzziah A king of Judah. He ruled about 767-740 B.C.

Rezin A king of Aram. He ruled about 740-731 B.C.

Aram A country north of Israel.

Pekah son of Remaliah A king of north Israel. He ruled about 740-731 B.C.

family of David The royal family of Judah. God promised that men from David's family would be kings in Judah.

Shear Jashub This is a name that means "a few people will come back."

Remaliah's son This is Pekah, the king of north Israel. He ruled about 740-731 B.C.

Immanuel—God Is with Us

¹⁰Then the Lord continued to speak to Ahaz.* ¹¹The Lord said, "Ask for a sign to prove to yourself that these things are true. You can ask for any sign you want. The sign can come from a place as deep as Sheol,* or the sign can come from a place as high as the skies.* ¹²But Ahaz said, "I will not ask for a sign as proof. I will not test the Lord." ¹³Then Isaiah said, "Family of David,* listen very carefully! You test the people's patience—and this is not important to you. So, now you test my God's patience. ¹⁴But ⌊God,⌋ my Master, will show you a sign:

> Look at the young woman.*
> She is pregnant
> and she will give birth to a son.
> She will name him Immanuel.*
> ¹⁵ Immanuel will eat butter and honey.*
> ⌊He will live this way⌋ to learn how
> to choose to do good and
> to refuse to do evil.
> ¹⁶ But before the child ⌊is old enough⌋
> to learn about good and evil,
> the land of Ephraim *(Israel)* and Aram
> will be empty.

"You are afraid of those two kings now. ¹⁷But ⌊you should be afraid of the Lord. Why? Because⌋ the Lord will bring some troubled times to you. Those troubles will come to your people and to the people of your father's family. ⌊What will God do?⌋ God will bring the king of Assyria* to fight against you.

¹⁸"At that time, the Lord will call for the 'Fly.' (The 'Fly' is now near the streams of Egypt.) And the Lord will call for the 'Bee.' (The 'Bee' is now in the country of Assyria.*) These enemies will come to your country. ¹⁹These enemies will camp in the rocky canyons near the desert streams and near the bushes and watering holes. ²⁰The Lord will use Assyria to punish Judah. Assyria will be hired and used like a razor. It will be like the Lord is shaving the hair from Judah's head and legs. It will be like the Lord is shaving off Judah's beard.*

²¹"At that time, a person will be able to keep only one young cow and two sheep alive. ²²There will be only enough milk for that person to eat butter. Every person in the country will eat butter and honey.* ²³In this land, there are now fields that have 1,000 grapevines. Each grapevine is worth 1,000 pieces of silver. But these fields will become full of weeds and thorns. ²⁴The land will become wild and useful only as a hunting ground. ²⁵People once worked and grew food on these hills. But at that time, people will not go there. The land will be filled with weeds and thorns. Only sheep and cattle will go to those places."

Assyria Will Come Soon

8 The Lord told me, "Get a large scroll* and use a pen* to write these words: 'To Maher Shalal Hash Baz.' *(This means 'There will soon be looting and stealing.')*"

²I gathered some people that could be trusted to be witnesses. (These people were Uriah the priest, and Zechariah son of Jeberekiah.) These men watched me write those words. ³Then I went to the woman prophet. She became pregnant and had a son. Then the Lord told me, "Name the boy Maher Shalal Hash Baz. ⁴⌊Why?⌋ Because before the boy learns to say, 'Mama' and 'Daddy,' God will take all the wealth and riches from Damascus* and Samaria,* and God will give those things to the king of Assyria.*"

Rezin A king of Aram. He ruled about 740-731 B.C.
Damascus A city in the country of Aram (Syria).
Remaliah's son This is Pekah, the king of north Israel. He ruled about 740-731 B.C.
Ahaz A king of Judah. He ruled about 735-727 B.C.
The sign ... Sheol Or, "make your question deep." The Hebrew word for "question" is like the word for Sheol.
the sign ... skies Or, "make your question very high."
Family of David The royal family of Judah. God promised that men from David's family would be kings in Judah.
young woman Or, "Look at the virgin. She will become pregnant and give birth to a son." This is possibly the meaning of the ancient Greek version that was translated about 150 B.C. See Gen. 16:11,12 and Lk. 1:30-35 for similar announcements.
Immanuel This name means "God is with us."
butter and honey This probably means the food that poor people can also find and eat.
Assyria This was a powerful nation northeast of Israel.

shaving off Judah's beard This showed that the people of Judah would be made slaves.
butter and honey This probably means the food that poor people also can find and eat.
scroll This Hebrew word might also mean "a clay or stone tablet."
pen Literally, "stylus of a man." This might be a special pen for writing on clay.
Damascus A city in the country of Aram (Syria).
Samaria The capital city of north Israel.
Assyria This was a powerful nation northeast of Israel.

⁵Again the Lord spoke to me. ⁶My Master said, "These people refuse to accept the slow-moving waters of the pool of Shiloah.* These people are happy with Rezin* and Remaliah's son *(Pekah)*. ⁷But I, the Lord, will bring the king of Assyria and all his power against you. They will come like a powerful flood of water from the Euphrates River. It will be like water rising up and over the river banks. ⁸That water will spill out of that river and flow into Judah. The water will rise to Judah's throat—₍it will almost drown Judah₎.

"Immanuel, this flood will spread until it covers your whole country.*"

The Lord Protects His Servants

9   All you nations, prepare for war!
    You will be defeated.
    Listen, all you faraway countries!
    Prepare for battle!
    You will be defeated.
10 Make your plans for the fight!
    Your plans will be defeated.
    Give orders to your armies!
    Your orders will be useless.
    Why? Because God is with us!*

Warnings to Isaiah

¹¹The Lord spoke to me with his great power. The Lord warned me not to be like these other people.* The Lord said, ¹²"Every person is saying that other people are making plans against him. You should not believe those things. Don't be afraid of the things those people fear. Don't be afraid of those things!"

¹³The Lord All-Powerful is the One you should be afraid of. He is the One you should respect. He is the One you should fear. ¹⁴If you will respect the Lord and consider him holy, then he will be a safe place for you. But you don't respect him. So God is like a rock that you people fall over. He is a rock that makes the two families of Israel stumble. The Lord is a trap to catch all the people of Jerusalem. ¹⁵(Many people will fall over this rock. Those people will fall and be broken. They will be trapped and caught.)

¹⁶Isaiah said, "Make an agreement and seal* it. Save my teachings for the future. Do this while my followers are watching. ¹⁷This is the agreement:

I will wait for the Lord to help us.
The Lord is ashamed of the family of Jacob.
    He refuses to look at them.
But I will wait for the Lord.
    He will save us.

¹⁸"My children and I are signs and proofs for the people of Israel. We have been sent by the Lord All-Powerful—the Lord who lives on the Mount Zion.*"

¹⁹Some people say, "Ask the fortune tellers and wizards what to do." (These fortune tellers and wizards whisper and make sounds like birds ₍to make people think that they know secret things₎.) ₍But I tell you that₎ people should ask their God ₍for help₎! Those fortune tellers and wizards ask dead people what to do. Why should living people ask something from the dead?

²⁰You should follow the teachings and the agreement.* If you don't follow these commands, then you might follow the wrong commands. (The wrong commands are those commands that come from the wizards and fortune tellers. Those commands are worth nothing; you will gain nothing by following those commands.)

²¹₍If you follow those wrong commands,₎ then there will be troubles and hunger in the land. People will become hungry. Then they will become angry and say things against their king and his gods.* Then they will look up ₍to God for help₎. ²²If they look around them at their land, then they will see only trouble and depressing darkness—the dark sadness of people forced to leave their country. And the people that are trapped in that darkness will not be able to free themselves.

Shiloah Or, "Siloam," a pool of water in Jerusalem supplied by an underground spring.
Rezin A king of Aram. He ruled about 740-731 B.C.
Immanuel ... country Literally, "Then the edge of his garment will fill your whole land. God is with us." The name "Immanuel" means "God is with us."
God is with us! In Hebrew, this is like the name Immanuel.
The Lord spoke ... people Or, "The Lord spoke to me. With his great power he prevented me from living like these other people."

seal This showed that the agreement should not be changed.
Zion The southeast part of the mountain Jerusalem is built on. Sometimes it means the people of God living in Jerusalem.
agreement Usually this means the agreement God made with Israel through Moses. Here it probably means the agreement in verse 17.
his gods Or possibly, "his God."

A New Day Is Coming

9 In the past, people thought the land of Zebulun and the land of Naphtali were not important. But in a later time, God will make that land great: the land near the sea, the land across the Jordan River, and Galilee where the non-Jews live. ²Now those people live in darkness. But they will see a great light. Those people live in a place that is dark like the place of death. But the "Great Light" will shine on them. ³God, you will cause the nation to grow. You will make the people happy. And the people will show their happiness to you. It will be like the joy during harvest time. It will be like the joy when people take their share of things they have won in war. ⁴Why? Because you will take away the heavy burden. You will take away the heavy pole on the people's backs. You will take away the rod that the enemy uses to punish your people. This will be like the time you defeated Midian.* ⁵Every boot that marched in battle will be destroyed. Every uniform stained with blood will be destroyed. Those things will be thrown into the fire. ⁶This will happen when the special child is born. God will give a son to us. This son will be responsible for leading the people. His name will be "Wonderful Counselor, Powerful God, Father Who Lives Forever, Prince of Peace." ⁷Power and peace will be in his kingdom. It will continue to grow for this king from David's family. This king will use goodness and fair judgment to rule the kingdom forever and ever.

The Lord All-Powerful has a strong love* ₍for his people₎. And this strong love will cause him to do these things.

God Will Punish Israel

⁸My Lord gave a command against the people of Jacob *(Israel)*. That command against Israel will be obeyed. ⁹Then every person in Ephraim *(Israel)*, even the leaders in Samaria, will know that God ₍punished them₎.

Those people are very proud and boastful now. Those people say, ¹⁰"These bricks might fall, but we will build again. And we will build with ₍strong₎ stone. These small trees might be chopped down. But we will put new trees there. And the new trees will be large, strong trees."

¹¹So the Lord will find people to fight against Israel. The Lord will bring Rezin's* enemies against them. ¹²The Lord will bring the Arameans from the east and the Philistines from the west. Those enemies will defeat Israel with their armies. But the Lord will still be angry with Israel. The Lord will still be ready to punish the people.

¹³God will punish the people, but they will not stop sinning. They will not return to him. They will not follow the Lord All-Powerful. ¹⁴So the Lord will cut off Israel's head and tail. The Lord will take away the branch and the stalk in one day. ¹⁵(The head means the elders* and important leaders. The tail means the prophets that speak lies.)

¹⁶The men that lead the people are leading them the wrong way. And the people that follow them will be destroyed. ¹⁷All the people are evil. So the Lord is not happy with the young men. And the Lord will not show mercy to their widows and orphans.* Why? Because all the people are evil. The people do things that are against God. The people speak lies. So God will continue to be angry with the people. God will continue to punish the people.

¹⁸Evil is like a small fire. First, the fire burns weeds and thorns. Next, the fire burns the larger bushes in the forest. And finally, it becomes a great fire—and everything goes up in smoke. ¹⁹The Lord All-Powerful is angry, so the land will be burned. All the people will be burned in that fire. No person will try to save his brother. ²⁰People will grab something on the right, but they will still be hungry. They will eat something on the left, but they will not be filled. Then each person will turn and eat his own body. ²¹(₍This means₎ Manasseh will fight against Ephraim, and Ephraim will fight against Manasseh. And then both of them will turn against Judah.)

The Lord is still angry against Israel. The Lord is still ready to punish his people.

10 Look at the lawmakers that write evil laws. Those lawmakers write laws that make life hard for people. ²Those lawmakers are not fair to

---

Rezin A king of Aram. He ruled about 740-731 B.C.
elders Older men that were city leaders; they helped make decisions for the people.
widows and orphans Widows are women whose husbands have died, and orphans are children whose parents have died. Often these people have no one to care for them.

This ... Midian See Numbers 22:1ff.
strong love This Hebrew word means strong feelings like love, hate, anger, zeal, or jealousy.

the poor people. They take away the poor people's rights. They allow people to steal from widows and orphans.*

³Lawmakers, you will have to explain the things you have done. What will you do at that time? Your destruction is coming from a faraway country. Where will you run for help? Your money and your riches will not help you. ⁴You will have to bow down like a prisoner. You will fall down like a dead person. But that will not help you! God will still be angry. God will still be ready to punish you.

⁵₍God will say,₎ "I will use Assyria* like a stick. In anger, I will use Assyria to punish Israel. ⁶I will send Assyria to fight against the people that do evil things. I am angry at those people, and I will command Assyria to fight against them. Assyria will defeat them and Assyria will take their wealth from them. Israel will become like dirt for Assyria to trample *(walk on)* in the streets. ⁷"But Assyria* does not understand that I will use him. Assyria does not think that he is a tool for me. Assyria only wants to destroy other people. Assyria only plans to destroy many nations. ⁸Assyria says to himself, 'All of my leaders are like kings! ⁹The city Calno is like the city Carchemish. And the city Arpad is like the city Hamath. The city Samaria is like the city Damascus. ¹⁰I defeated those evil kingdoms and now I control them. The idols* those people worship are better than the idols of Jerusalem and Samaria. ¹¹I defeated Samaria and her idols. I will also defeat Jerusalem and the idols her people have made.'"

¹²My Master will finish doing the things he planned to Jerusalem and Mount Zion.* Then the Lord will punish Assyria.* The king of Assyria is very proud. His pride made him do many bad things. So God will punish him.

¹³The king of Assyria says, "I am very wise. By my own wisdom and power I have done many great things. I have defeated many nations. I have taken their wealth. And I have taken their people to be slaves. I am a very powerful man. ¹⁴With my own hands I have taken the riches of all these people—like a person taking eggs from a bird's nest. A bird often leaves its nest and eggs. And there is nothing to protect the nest. There is no bird to chirp and fight with its wings and beak. So people take the eggs. ₍In the same way,₎ there was no person to stop me from taking all the people on earth."

God Controls Assyria's Power

¹⁵An axe is not better than the person that cuts with it. A saw is not better than the person that saws with it. ₍But Assyria thinks he is more important and powerful than God.₎ And this is like a stick being more powerful and important than the person that picks it up and uses it to punish someone.

¹⁶₍Assyria thinks he is great.₎ But the Lord All-Powerful will send a terrible disease against Assyria. Assyria will lose his wealth and power like a sick man loses weight. Then Assyria's glory will be destroyed. It will be like a fire burning until everything is gone. ¹⁷Israel's Light *(God)* will be like a fire. The Holy One will be like a flame. He will be like a fire that first burns the weeds and thorns. ¹⁸Then the fire grows and burns away the great trees and vineyards.* Finally, everything is destroyed—even the people. ₍It will be like that when God destroys Assyria₎. Assyria will be like a rotting log. ¹⁹There might be a few trees left standing in the forest. But even a child will be able to count them.

²⁰At that time, the people that are left living in Israel, the people from Jacob's family, will not continue to depend on the person that beats them. They will learn to truly depend on the Lord, the Holy One of Israel. ²¹The people that are left in Jacob's family will again follow the powerful God.

²²Your people are very many. They are like the sands of the sea. But only a few of the people will be left to come back to the Lord. Those people will return to God, but first, your country will be destroyed. God has announced that he will destroy the land. And then goodness will come into the land; it will be like a river flowing full. ²³My Master, the Lord All-Powerful, will surely destroy this land.

²⁴My Master, the Lord All-Powerful, says, "My people living in Zion,* don't be afraid of Assyria!* He will beat you like Egypt beat you in

---

widows and orphans Widows are women whose husbands have died, and orphans are children whose parents have died. Often these people have no one to care for them.

Assyria This was a powerful nation northeast of Israel.

idols Statues of false gods that people worshiped.

Zion The southeast part of the mountain Jerusalem is built on. Sometimes it means the people of God living in Jerusalem.

vineyards Gardens for growing grapes.

the past. It will be like Assyria is using a stick to hurt you. ²⁵But after a short time my anger will stop. I will be satisfied that Assyria has punished you enough."

²⁶Then the Lord All-Powerful will beat Assyria with a whip. In the past, the Lord defeated Midian at Raven Rock.* It will be the same when the Lord attacks Assyria. ₍In the past, the Lord punished Egypt—₎he lifted the stick over the sea,* and led his people from Egypt. It will be the same when the Lord saves his people from Assyria.

²⁷₍Assyria* will bring troubles to you—those troubles will be like weights you have to carry on₎ a pole across your shoulder. But, that pole will be taken off your neck. That pole will be broken by your strength *(God)*.

The Army of Assyria Invades Israel

²⁸* The army will enter near the "Ruins" (Aiath). The army will walk on the "Threshing Floor" (Migron). The army will keep its food in the "Storehouse" (Micmash). ²⁹The army will cross the river at the "Crossing" (Maabarah). The army will sleep at Geba.* Ramah* will be afraid. The people at Gibeah of Saul* will run away. ³⁰Cry out, Bath Gallim!* Laishah, listen! Anathoth, answer me! ³¹The people of Madmenah are running away. The people of Gebim* are hiding. ³²This day, the army will stop at Nob. And the army will prepare to fight against Mount Zion, the hill of Jerusalem.

³³Watch! Our Master, the Lord All-Powerful, will chop down the great tree *(Assyria)*. The Lord will do this with his great power. The great and important people will be cut down—they will become not important. ³⁴The Lord will cut down the forest with his axe. And the great trees in Lebanon* *(important people)* will fall.

Midian at Raven Rock See Num. 22:1ff.
he lifted the stick ... sea See Ex. 14:1-15:21.
Assyria This was a powerful nation northeast of Israel.
Verses 28-32 Isaiah uses word games to show how the Assyrian army would come and fight against Judah.
Geba, Ramah, Gibeah of Saul Towns north of Jerusalem.
Bath Gallim Gallim, a city south of Jerusalem. This name means "daughter of the waves," and might also mean "seagull." These birds make very loud noises.
Gebim An unknown city. This name is like the Hebrew word for "pit" or "cistern," a hole in the ground for storing water.
Lebanon A country north of Israel. It was famous for its great cedar and pine trees.

The King of Peace Is Coming

11 A small tree *(child)* will begin to grow from the stump *(family)* of Jesse.* That branch will grow from Jesse's roots. ²The Lord's Spirit will be in that child. The Spirit gives wisdom, understanding, guidance, and power. And the Spirit ₍will help this child₎ know and respect the Lord. ³This child will respect the Lord, and this will make the child happy.

This child will not judge people by the way things look. He will not judge by the things he hears. ⁴⁻⁵He will judge the poor people fairly and honestly. He will be fair when he decides the things to do to the poor people of the land. ₍If he decides people should be beaten,₎ then he will give the command, and those people will be beaten. ₍If he decides people must die,₎ then he will give the command, and those evil people will be killed. Goodness and fairness will ₍give this child strength₎. They will be like a belt he wears around his waist.

⁶At that time, wolves will live in peace with lambs. And tigers will lie down in peace with young goats. Calves, lions, and bulls will live together in peace. A little child will lead them. ⁷Cows and bears will live together in peace. All of their children will lie down together and will not hurt each other. Lions will eat hay like cows. Even snakes will not hurt people. ⁸A baby will be able to play near a cobra's* home. A baby will be able to put his hand into the home of a poisonous snake.

⁹₍All these things show that there will be peace₎—no person will hurt any other person. People on my holy mountain will not want to destroy things. Why? Because people will truly know the Lord. They will be full of knowledge ₍about him₎ like the sea is full of water.

¹⁰At that time, there will be a special person from Jesse's* family. This person will be like a flag. This "flag" will show all the nations that they should come together around him. The nations will ask him the things they should do. And the place where he is will be filled with glory.

¹¹At that time, my Master *(God)* will again reach out and take his people that are left. This will be the second time God has done this. (These are God's people that are left in countries like Assyria, North Egypt, South Egypt, Ethiopia,

---

Jesse King David's father.
cobra A very poisonous snake.
Jesse King David's father.

Elam, Babylonia, Hamath, and all the faraway countries around the world.) ¹²God will raise this "flag" as a sign for all people. The people of Israel and Judah were forced to leave their country. The people were scattered to all the faraway places on earth. But God will gather them together.

¹³At that time, Ephraim *(Israel)* will not be jealous of Judah. Judah will have no enemies left. And Judah will not cause trouble for Ephraim. ¹⁴But Ephraim and Judah will attack the Philistines.* These two nations will be like birds flying down to catch a small animal. Together, they will take the riches from the people in the east. Ephraim and Judah will control Edom, Moab,* and the people in Ammon.*

¹⁵The Lord became angry and divided the sea of Egypt. ⌊In the same way,⌋ the Lord will wave his arm over the Euphrates River. He will hit the river, and the river will divide into seven small rivers. The small rivers will not be deep—people will be able to walk across those rivers with their shoes on. ¹⁶God's people that are left will have a way to leave Assyria. It will be like the time God took the people out of Egypt.

A Song of Praise to God

12 At that time, you will say:
"I praise you Lord!
You have been angry at me.
But don't be angry with me now!
Show your love to me."

² God saves me.
I trust him.
I am not afraid.
He saves me.
The Lord Yah is my strength.
He saves me.
And I sing songs of praise about him.*
³ Get your water from the spring of salvation.
Then you will be happy.
⁴ Then you will say,
"Praise the Lord!
Worship his name!

Tell all people about the things he has done!"
⁵ Sing songs of praise about the Lord!
Why? Because he has done great things!
Spread this news about God
through the whole world.
Let all people know these things.
⁶ People of Zion,* shout about these things!
The Holy One of Israel is with you
in a powerful way.
So, be happy!

God's Message to Babylon

13 God showed Isaiah son of Amoz this sad message about Babylon. ²⌊God said:⌋

"Raise a flag on that mountain* where nothing grows.
Call out to the men .
Wave your arms.
Tell them to enter through the gates
for important people!"

³⌊God said:⌋

"I have separated those men from the people.
And I myself will command them.
I am angry.
I gathered my best men to punish
the people.
I am proud of these happy men!
⁴ There is a loud noise in the mountains.
Listen to the noise!
It sounds like many, many people.
People from many kingdoms
are gathering together.
The Lord All-Powerful is calling
his army together.
⁵ The Lord and this army
are coming from a faraway land.
They are coming from beyond the horizon.
The Lord will use this army like a weapon
to show his anger.
This army will destroy the whole country.

⁶The Lord's special day is near. So cry and be sad for yourselves. A time is coming when the enemy will steal your wealth. God All-Powerful

---

Philistines People living on the coast of Palestine. They were one of Israel's enemies.
Edom, Moab Two countries east of Israel. They were Israel's enemies for many, many years.
Ammon A country east of Israel.
The Lord Yah ... him Literally, "Yah, Yahweh is my strength and praise. And he becomes my salvation." This comes from the victory song of Moses. (Exodus 15:2.)
Zion The southeast part of the mountain Jerusalem is built on. Sometimes it means the people of God living in Jerusalem.
mountain This probably means Babylon.

will make that happen.* ⁷People will lose their courage. Fear will make the people weak. ⁸Every person will be afraid. Their fear will cause their stomachs to hurt like a woman giving birth to a baby. Their faces will become red like fire. The people will be amazed because this look of fear will be on all their neighbors' faces.

God's Judgment Against Babylon

⁹Look, the Lord's special day is coming! It will be a terrible day. God will become very angry, and he will destroy the country. God will force all people that sin to leave the country. ¹⁰The skies will be dark. The sun, the moon, and the stars will not shine.

¹¹ₗGod says,₎ "I will cause bad things to happen to the world. I will punish the evil people for their sin. I will cause the proud people to lose their pride. I will stop the bragging of the people that are mean to others. ¹²There will be only a few people left. There will not be many, the same as gold is hard to find. And these people will be worth much more than pure gold. ¹³With my anger, I will make the sky shake. And the earth will be moved from its place."

That will happen on the day the Lord All-Powerful shows his anger. ¹⁴Then the people from Babylon will run away, like wounded deer. They will run like sheep that have no shepherd. Every person will turn and run back to his own country and people. ¹⁵ₗBut the enemy will chase the people of Babylon. And when the enemy₎ catches a person, the enemy will kill that person with a sword. ¹⁶Everything in their houses will be stolen. Their wives will be raped. And their little children will be beaten to death while the people are watching.

¹⁷ₗGod says,₎ "Look, I will cause the armies of Media to attack Babylon. ₗThe armies of Media will not stop attacking,₎ even if they are paid silver and gold. ¹⁸The soldiers will attack and kill the young men of Babylon. The soldiers will not show mercy to the babies. The soldiers will not be kind to the children. Babylon will be destroyed— it will be like the destruction of Sodom and Gomorrah.* God will cause this destruction, and there will be nothing left.

¹⁹"Babylon is the most beautiful of all kingdoms. The Babylonian* people are very proud of their city. ²⁰But Babylon will not continue to be beautiful. People will not continue to live there in the future. Arabs will not put their tents there. Shepherds will not bring their sheep to let them eat there. ²¹The only animals living there will be wild animals from the desert. People will not be living in their houses in Babylon. The houses will be full of owls and large birds. Wild goats* will play in the houses. ²²Wild dogs and wolves will howl in the great and beautiful buildings of Babylon. Babylon will be finished. The end of Babylon is near. I will not let Babylon's destruction wait until later."

Israel Will Return Home

14 ₗIn the future,₎ the Lord will again show his love to Jacob. The Lord will again choose the people of Israel. ₗAt that time,₎ the Lord will give those people their land. Then non-Jewish people* will join themselves to the Jewish people. Both people will join and become one family— Jacob's family. ²Those nations will take the people of Israel back to Israel's land. Those men and women from the other nations will become slaves to Israel. ₗIn the past,₎ those people forced the people of Israel to become their slaves. But ₗat this time,₎ the people of Israel will defeat those nations and Israel will then rule over them. ³The Lord will take away your hard work, and he will comfort you. ₗIn the past,₎ you were slaves. Men forced you to do very hard work. But the Lord will end this hard work for you.

A Song About the King of Babylon

⁴At that time, you will begin to sing this song about the king of Babylon:

> The king was mean when he ruled us.
> But now his rule is finished.
> ⁵ The Lord breaks the scepter* of evil rulers.
> The Lord takes away their power.
> ⁶ In anger, the king of Babylon beat people.
> He never stopped beating people.

A time ... happen This is a word play in Hebrew. The word meaning "stealing things in war" is like the word meaning "God All-Powerful."

Sodom and Gomorrah Two cities that God destroyed because the people were so evil.

Babylonian Literally, "Chaldean."

Wild goats The Hebrew word means "hairy," "goat," or "goat-demon."

non-Jewish people Usually this means "People that live in a country, but are not yet citizens of that country." Here it is the non-Jewish people that decided to follow God.

That evil ruler ruled the people in anger.
  He never stopped hurting people.
7 But now, the whole country rests.
  The country is quiet.
  Now the people begin to celebrate.
8 You were an evil king,
  and now you are finished.
  Even the pine trees are happy.
  The cedar trees of Lebanon are happy.
  The trees say,
  "The king chopped us down.
  But now the king has fallen,
    and he will never stand again."
9 Sheol,* ₍the place of death₎ is excited
    because you are coming.
  Sheol is waking the spirits of all
    the leaders of the earth for you.
  Sheol is making the kings stand
    from their thrones.
  They will be ready for your coming.
10 All these leaders will make fun of you.
  They will say,
  "Now you are a dead body like us.
  Now you are just like us."
11 Your pride has been sent down to Sheol.*
  The music from your harps announces
    the coming of your proud spirit.
  Maggots *(flies)* will eat your body.
  You will lie on them like a bed.
  Worms will cover your body like a blanket.
12 You were like the morning star,
    but you have fallen from the sky.
  In the past, all the nations on earth
    bowed down before you.
  But now you have been cut down.
13 You always told yourself,
  "₍I will be like God Most-High₎.
  I will go to the skies above.
  I will put my throne above God's stars.
  I will sit on holy mountain, Zaphon.*
  I will meet ₍with the gods₎
    on that mountain.
14 I will go up to the altar in the clouds.
  I will be like God Most-High."
15 But that did not happen.
  You did not go to the sky with God.
  You were brought down to the deep pit—
    Sheol, the place of death.

16 The people look at you and think about you.
    ₍They see that you are only a dead body₎
    and the people say;
  "Is this the same man that caused great fear
    in all the kingdoms on earth?
17 Is this the same man that destroyed cities
    and changed the land into a desert?
  Is this the same man that captured people
    in war and would not let them go home?"

18 Every king on earth has died with glory.
  Every king has his own grave.
19 But you, evil king, have been thrown
    from your grave.
  You are like a branch cut from a tree.
  That branch is cut and thrown away.
  You are like a dead man that fell in battle,
    and other soldiers walked on him.
  Now, you look like any other dead person.
  You are wrapped in burial clothes.
20 Many other kings have died.
  And they all have their own graves.
  But you will not join them.
  Why? Because you ruined your own country.
  You killed your own people.
  Your children will not continue
    to destroy like you did.
  Your children will be stopped.
21 Prepare to kill his children.
  Kill them because their father is guilty.
  His children will never again
    take control of the land.
  They will never again
    fill the world with their cities.

²²The Lord All-Powerful said, "I will stand and fight against those people. I will destroy the famous city, Babylon. I will destroy all the people of Babylon. I will destroy their children, their grandchildren, and their great-grandchildren." The Lord himself said those things.

²³The Lord said, "I will change Babylon. That place will be for animals,* ₍not people₎. That place will be a swamp. I will use the 'broom of destruction' to sweep Babylon away." The Lord All-Powerful said those things.

---

scepter A special stick. Kings and leaders carried scepters to show they were rulers.

Sheol This is the place where all people go when they die. Usually this means the grave, but it can mean the place where our spirits go.

holy mountain ,Zaphon Literally, "Zaphon." This Hebrew word means "north, hidden" or "the heavenly mountain where the Canaanite people believed their gods met together."

God Will also Punish Assyria

²⁴The Lord All-Powerful has made a promise. The Lord said, "I promise, these things will happen exactly like I thought. These things will happen exactly the way I planned. ²⁵I will destroy the king of Assyria in my country. I will trample *(walk on)* that king on my mountains. That king made my people be his slaves; he put a yoke* on their necks. That pole will be taken off Judah's neck. That burden will be removed. ²⁶That is the thing I plan to do for my people. And I will use my arm *(power)* to punish all nations."

²⁷When the Lord makes a plan, no person can stop that plan. When the Lord raises his arm to punish people, no person can stop him.

God's Message to Philistia

²⁸This sad message was given the year King Ahaz died.*

²⁹Country of Philistia, you are very happy because the king that beat you is now dead. But you should not be really happy. It is true that his rule has ended. But the king's son will come and rule. And it will be like one snake giving birth to a more dangerous snake. This new king will be like a very quick and dangerous snake to you. ³⁰But my poor people will be able to eat safely. Their children will be safe. My poor people will be able to lie down and feel safe. But I will kill your family with hunger. And all your people that are left will die.

³¹ You people near the city gates, cry!
   You people in the city, cry out!
   All of you people in Philistia
      will be frightened.
   Your courage will melt like hot wax.

   Look to the north!
   There is a cloud of dust!
   ⌊An army from Assyria* is coming!⌋
      All the men in that army are strong!*
³² ⌊That army will send messengers
      to their country.⌋

What will those messengers tell their people?
They will announce:
   ⌊Philistia was defeated,⌋
      but the Lord made Zion* strong.
   And his poor people went there for safety.

God's Message to Moab

15 This is a sad message about Moab:*
One night, armies took the wealth
   from Ar, Moab.
That night, the city was destroyed.
One night, armies took the wealth
   from Kir, Moab.
That night, the city was destroyed.

² The king's family and the people of Dibon*
   are going to the places of worship* to cry.
The people of Moab are crying
   for Nebo* and Medeba.*
The people shaved their heads and beards
   ⌊to show they are sad⌋.
³ Everywhere in Moab,
   on the housetops and in the streets,
   people are wearing black clothes,
   people are crying.
⁴ People in the cities Heshbon and Elealeh
   are crying very loudly.
You can hear their voices far away
   in the city Jahaz.
Even the soldiers are scared.
   The soldiers are shaking from fear.

⁵ My heart cries with sorrow for Moab.
People are running for safety.
   They run far away to Zoar.
   They run to Eglath Shelishiyah.
The people are crying as they go up
   the mountain road to Luhith.
The people are crying very loudly
   as they walk on the road to Horonaim.
⁶ But Nimrim Brook is dry like a desert.
   All the plants are dead.

---

animals Literally, "porcupines."
yoke A pole that was put on the shoulders of men or animals to help them carry or pull things. This often showed that a person was a slave.
year King Ahaz died About 727 B.C.
Assyria This was a powerful nation northeast of Israel.
All the men in that army are strong Or, "There are no stragglers in that group."

Zion The southeast part of the mountain Jerusalem is built on. Sometimes it means the people of God living in Jerusalem.
Moab A country east of Israel.
Dibon A city in the country Moab. This name is like a Hebrew word meaning "to be very sad."
places of worship Or "high places," places for worshiping God or false gods. These places were usually on the hills and mountains.
Nebo A city in the country Moab and the name of a false god.
Medeba A city in the country Moab. This name is like a Hebrew word meaning "to be very sad."

Nothing is green.
⁷ So the people gather the things they own,
  ₍and they leave Moab₎.
They carry those things,
  and cross ₍the border₎ at Poplar Creek.*

⁸ Crying can be heard everywhere in Moab.
The people are crying
  far away in the city Eglaim.
And the people are crying
  in the city Beer Elim.*
⁹ The water of Dimon* is full of blood.
And I *(the Lord)* will bring
  even more troubles to Dimon.
A few people living in Moab
  have escaped the enemy.
But I will send lions to eat those people.

16 You people should send a gift to the king of the land. You should send a lamb from Sela, through the desert, to the mountain of the Daughter of Zion.*

² The women of Moab* try to cross
  the river Arnon.
They run from one place to another
  looking for help.
They are like little birds lost on the ground
  after their nest has fallen from a tree.
³ They say,
"Help us! Tell us what to do!
Protect us ₍from our enemies₎
  like shade protects us from the noon sun.
We are running from our enemies.
Hide us! Don't give us to our enemies."

⁴ Those people from Moab were forced
  to leave their homes.
So let them live in your land.
Hide them ₍from their enemies₎.
The looting will stop.
The enemy will be defeated.
The men that hurt other people
  will be gone from the land.
⁵ Then a new king will come.
This king will be from David's family.*
He will be loyal.
He will be loving and kind.

This king will judge fairly.
He will do things that are right and good.

⁶We have heard that the people of Moab* are very proud and conceited. These people are violent and they boast. But the boasts are only empty words. ⁷₍The whole country of Moab will suffer because of that pride.₎ All the people of Moab will cry. The people will be sad—they will want the things they had in the past. They will want the figcakes made in Kir Hareseth.* ⁸₍The people will be sad₎ because the fields of Heshbon and the vines of Sibmah are not able to grow grapes. Foreign rulers have cut down the grapevines. The ₍enemy armies have₎ spread far to the city of Jazer and into the desert. And they have spread down to the sea.*

A Sad Song about Moab

⁹ "I will cry with the people
  of Jazer and Sibmah
    because the grapes have been destroyed.
I will cry with the people
  of Heshbon and Elealeh
    because there will be no harvest.
There will be no summer fruit.
  And there will be no shouts of joy.
¹⁰ There will be no joy and singing in Carmel.*
I will stop all the happiness at harvest time.
The grapes are ready to become wine.
  But they will all be wasted.
¹¹ So, I am very sad for Moab.
I am very sad for Kir Heres.*
  I am very, very sad for these cities.
¹² The people of Moab will go to their
  places of worship.*
The people will try to pray.
But they will see what happened,
  and they will be too weak to pray."

Poplar Creek A small stream in the country Moab, also called "Arabah Stream."
Beer Elim A city in the country Moab.
Dimon This is probably the city Dibon. Dimon is like the Hebrew word meaning "blood."
Daughter of Zion Another name for Jerusalem.
Moab A country east of Israel.
David's family The royal family of Judah. God promised that men from David's family would be kings in Judah.
Kir Hareseth A city in the country Moab.
Foreign rulers ... the sea Or, "These grapes made many foreign rulers drunk. The vines spread far to the city Jazer and into the desert. The vines have spread down to the sea."
Carmel A name that means, "God's vineyard." There are several cities and hill in north Israel with this name.
Kir Heres This is Kir Hareseth, a city in the country of Moab. Kir Heres means "a city chosen to be destroyed."
places of worship Places for worshiping God or false gods. These places were usually on the hills and mountains.

¹³The Lord said these things about Moab many times. ¹⁴And now the Lord says, "In three years (the way a hired helper counts time) all those people and the things they are proud of will be gone. There will be a few people left, but there will not be many."

God's Message to Aram

17 This is the sad message for Damascus.* The Lord says these things will happen to Damascus:

> Damascus is now a city.
> But Damascus will be destroyed.
> Only destroyed buildings will be left
>   in Damascus.
> ² People will leave the cities of Aroer.*
> Flocks of sheep will wander freely in those
>   empty towns;
> There will be no person to bother them.
> ³ The fort cities of Ephraim *(Israel)*
>   will be destroyed.
> The government in Damascus
>   will be finished.
> The same thing that happens to Israel,
>   will happen to Aram.*
> All the important people
>   will be taken away."
>
> The Lord All-Powerful said those things
>   would happen.
>
> ⁴ At that time, Jacob's *(Israel's)* wealth
>   will all be gone.
> Jacob will be like a man who was sick
>   and became weak and thin.

⁵That time will be like grain harvest in Rephaim Valley.* The workers gather plants that grow in the field. Then they cut the heads of grain from the plants. And they collect the grain. ⁶That time will also be like the time people harvest olives. People knock olives from olive trees. But a few olives are usually left at the top of the tree. Four or five olives are left on some of the top branches. It will be the same for those cities. The Lord All-Powerful said those things.

⁷At that time, people will look up to ⌊God⌋, the One who made them. Their eyes will see the Holy One of Israel. ⁸The people will not trust the great things they have made. They will not go to the special gardens* and altars* ⌊they made for false gods⌋.

⁹At that time, all the fort cities will be empty. Those cities will be like the mountains and the forests* in the land before the people of Israel came. ⌊In the past,⌋ all the people ran away because the people of Israel were coming. ⌊In the future,⌋ the country will be empty again. ¹⁰This will happen because you have forgotten the God who saves you. You have not remembered that God is your place of safety.

You brought some very good grapevines from faraway places. You can plant those grapevines, but those plants will not grow. ¹¹You will plant your grapevines one day and try to make them grow. The next day the plants will begin to grow. But at harvest time, you will go to gather the fruit from the plants, and you will see that everything is dead. A sickness will kill all the plants.

> ¹² Listen to the many, many people!
> They are crying loud like the noise
>   from the sea.
> Listen to the noise.
> It is like the crashing
>   and crashing of waves in the sea.
> ¹³ ⌊And the people will be like those waves—⌋
> God will speak harshly to the people,
>   and they will run away.
> The people will be like chaff*
>   being chased by the wind.
> The people will be like a tumbleweeds*
>   being chased by a storm.
> The wind blows and the weeds go far away.
> ¹⁴ That night, the people will be frightened.
> Before morning, nothing will be left.
> So our enemies will get nothing.
> They will come to our land,
>   but nothing will be there.

---

special gardens Gardens where people worshiped false gods.
altars These might be altars for burning incense or they might be altars for worshiping a special false god.
mountains and the forests This might mean "The Horite and Amorite people."
chaff The seed coverings and stems separated from the seeds of plants like wheat or barley. Farmers saved the seeds and let the wind blow the useless chaff away.
tumbleweeds A small plant with short roots. When a strong wind blows, the plant is pulled loose and blown away.

Damascus A city in the country of Aram (Syria).
Aroer A place in the country of Aram (Syria).
Aram A country north of Israel.
Rephaim Valley A valley southwest of Jerusalem.

God's Message to Ethiopia

18 Look at the land along the rivers of Ethiopia.* ₍The land is filled with insects; you can hear₎ their buzzing wings. ²That land sends people across the sea in reed boats.*
Fast messengers, go to the people that are tall and strong! (People in all places are afraid of these tall and strong people. They are a powerful nation. Their nation defeats other nations. They are in a country divided by rivers.) ³₍Warn those people that something bad will happen to them.₎ All the people in the world will see this thing happen to that nation. People will see this thing clearly like a flag raised on a mountain. All the people living on earth will hear about the thing that happens to these tall people. They will hear it clearly like the noise from a horn before a battle.
⁴The Lord said, "I will be in the place prepared for me.* I will quietly watch these things happen: ⁵On a beautiful summer day, at noon, people will be resting. (It will be during the hot harvest time when there is no rain, but only early morning dew.) Then something terrible will happen. The time will be after the flowers have bloomed. The new grapes will be budding and growing. But before harvest, the enemy will come and cut the plants. The enemy will break the vines and throw them away. ⁶The vines will be left for the birds from the mountains and the wild animals to eat. Birds will live on the vines during the summer. And that winter, wild animals will eat the vines."
⁷At that time, a special offering will be brought to the Lord All-Powerful. The offering will come from the people that are tall and strong. (People in all places are afraid of these tall and strong people. They are a powerful nation. Their nation defeats other nations. They are in a country divided by rivers.) This offering will be brought to the Lord's place, Mount Zion.*

God's Message to Egypt

19 The sad message about Egypt:
Look! The Lord is coming on a fast cloud. The Lord will enter Egypt, and all the false gods of Egypt will shake ₍with fear. Egypt was brave₎, but that courage will melt away like hot wax.
²₍God says,₎ "I will cause the people of Egypt to fight against themselves. Men will fight their brothers. Neighbors will be against neighbors. Cities will be against cities. States will be against states.* ³The people of Egypt will be confused. The people will ask their false gods and wise men what they should do. The people will ask their wizards and magicians. But their advice will be worthless."
⁴The Master, the Lord All-Powerful, says, "I *(God)* will give Egypt to a hard master. A powerful king will rule over the people. ⁵The Nile River will become dry. The water will be gone from the sea. ⁶All the rivers will smell very bad.* The canals in Egypt will become dry and the water will be gone. All the water plants will rot. ⁷All the plants along the river banks will die and blow away. Even the plants at the widest part of the river will be dead.
⁸"The fishermen, all the people that catch fish from the Nile River, will become sad and they will cry. They depend on the Nile River for their food, but it will be dry. ⁹All the people that make cloth will be very, very sad. These people need flax* to make linen.* ₍But the river will be dry, and these plants will not grow.₎ ¹⁰The people that make dams to save water will have no work, so they will be sad.
¹¹"The leaders of the city Zoan are fools. Pharaoh's 'wise advisers' give wrong advice. Those leaders say they are wise. They say they are from the old family of the kings. But they are not wise like they think."
¹²Egypt, where are your wise men? Those wise men should learn what the Lord All-Powerful has planned for Egypt. They should be the people to tell you what will happen.
¹³The leaders of Zoan have been fooled. The leaders of Noph have believed false things. So the leaders lead Egypt the wrong way. ¹⁴The Lord made the leaders confused. They wander and lead Egypt in the wrong ways. Everything the leaders do is wrong. They are like drunk people rolling with sickness on the ground. ¹⁵There is nothing

---

Ethiopia Also called Cush, a country in Africa, by the Red Sea.
reed boats These boats were made by tying many, many reeds (a type of water plant) together.
the place prepared for me Probably the temple in Jerusalem.
Zion The southeast part of the mountain Jerusalem is built on. Sometimes it means the people of God living in Jerusalem.

States will be against states Literally, kingdom will be against kingdom. This means Egyptians will fight other Egyptians.
smell very bad In Hebrew this is like a name for the Nile River.
flax A plant used to make linen.
linen A type of cloth.

the leaders can do. (These leaders are "the heads and the tails." They are "the tops and the stalks of plants.")*

¹⁶At that time, the Egyptians will be like scared women. They will be afraid of the Lord All-Powerful. The Lord will raise his arm to punish the people, and they will be afraid. ¹⁷The land of Judah will be a place for all the people in Egypt to fear. Any person in Egypt that hears the name Judah will be scared. This will happen because the Lord All-Powerful has planned terrible things to happen to Egypt. ¹⁸At that time, there will be five cities in Egypt where people speak the language of Canaan *(the Jewish language)*. One of these cities will be named "Destruction City."*

The people will promise to follow the Lord All-Powerful. ¹⁹At that time, there will be an altar* for the Lord in the middle of Egypt. At the border of Egypt there will be a monument to show honor to the Lord. ²⁰This will be a sign to show that the Lord All-Powerful does powerful things. Any time the people cry for help from the Lord, the Lord will send help. The Lord will send a person to save and defend the people. That person will rescue the people from other people that do wrong things to them.

²¹At that time, the people in Egypt will truly know the Lord. The people of Egypt will love God. The people will serve God and give many sacrifices.* They will make promises* to the Lord. And they will keep those promises.

²²The Lord will punish the people of Egypt. And then the Lord will heal *(forgive)* them, and they will come back to the Lord. The Lord will listen to their prayers and heal *(forgive)* them.

²³At that time, there will be a highway from Egypt to Assyria.* Then people from Assyria will go to Egypt, and people from Egypt will go to Assyria. Egypt will work with Assyria.*

²⁴At that time, Israel, Assyria, and Egypt will join together and control the land. This will be a blessing for the land. ²⁵The Lord All-Powerful will bless these countries. He will say, "Egypt, you are my people. Assyria, I made you. Israel, I own you. You are all blessed!"

Assyria Will Defeat Egypt and Ethiopia

20 Sargon* was the king of Assyria.* Sargon sent Tarton* to Ashdod to fight against that city. Tarton went there and captured the city. ²At that time, the Lord spoke through Isaiah son of Amoz. The Lord said, "Go, take the cloth of sadness off your waist. Take your shoes off your feet." Isaiah obeyed the Lord. And Isaiah walked around without clothes and without shoes.

³Then the Lord said, "Isaiah has walked around without clothes and without shoes for three years. This is a sign for Egypt and Ethiopia. ⁴The king of Assyria will defeat Egypt and Ethiopia. Assyria will take prisoners and lead them away from their countries. The old people and young people will be led without clothes and without shoes. They will be completely naked. The people from Egypt will be shamed. ⁵People looked to Ethiopia for help. Those people will be broken. People were amazed by Egypt's glory. Those people will be shamed."

⁶Those people living near the sea will say, "We trusted those countries to help us. We ran to them so they would rescue us from the king of Assyria. But look at them. Those countries have been captured, so how will we be able to escape?"

God's Message to Babylon

21 The sad message about the Desert of the Sea:*

> Something is coming from the desert.
>   It is coming like wind blowing
>   from the Negev.*
>   It is coming from a terrible country.
> ² I have seen something very terrible
>   that will happen.
>   I see traitors* turning against you.
>   I see people taking your wealth.

---

the heads and ... stalks of plants See Isa. 9:14-15.
Destruction City This name is like a name meaning "Sun City." This is probably the city On (Heliopolis).
altar A stone table used for burning sacrifices as gifts to God.
sacrifices Gifts to God. Sometimes these were special kinds of animals that were killed and burned on an altar.
promises A special kind of promise to God. See Lev. 22:18ff.
Assyria This was a powerful nation northeast of Israel.
Egypt will work with Assyria Or, Egypt will worship with Assyria.

Sargon A king of Assyria at about 721-705 B.C.
Tarton An Assyrian military commander.
Desert of the Sea Probably Babylon.
Negev The desert area south of Judah.
traitors People that turn against their country, friends, or family and do bad things to them.

Elam, go and fight against the people!
Media, put your armies around the city
   and defeat it!
I will end all the evil things in that city.

³I saw those terrible things, and now I am scared. My stomach hurts because of my fear. That pain is like the pain of giving birth. The things I hear make me very afraid. The things I see make me shake with fear. ⁴I am worried and I am shaking from fear. My pleasant evening has become a night of fear.

⁵ ⌊The people think everything is fine..
   The people are saying,⌋
      "Prepare the table!
      Eat and Drink!"
   ⌊At the same time
      the soldiers are saying,⌋
         "Post the guard!
         Officers, get up
            and polish your shields!"

⁶My Master said to me, "Go find a man to guard this city. He must report whatever he sees. ⁷If the guard sees rows of horse soldiers, donkeys, or camels, the guard should listen carefully—very carefully."

⁸⌊Then one day, the guard called out the warning,⌋ 'Lion!'" ⌊The guard was saying,⌋ "My Master, every day I have been in the watchtower* watching. Every night I have been standing and guarding, but ... ⁹Look! They are coming! I see rows of men and horse soldiers."

⌊Then a messenger⌋ said,

   "Babylon ⌊has been defeated.⌋
   Babylon has fallen to the ground.
   All the statues of her false gods
      have been thrown to the ground
         and have broken to pieces."

¹⁰⌊Isaiah said,⌋ "My people, I have told you everything that I heard from the Lord All-Powerful, the God of Israel. You will be crushed like grain on a threshing floor.*

God's Message to Edom

¹¹The sad message about Dumah.*

   Someone called me from Seir *(Edom).*
   He said,
      "Guard, how much of the night is left?
      How much longer will it be night!"

¹² The guard answered,
   "Morning is coming,
      But then night will come again.
   If you have something to ask,
      then come back* and ask."

God' Message to Arabia

¹³The sad message about Arabia.

   A caravan* from Dedan spent the night
      near some trees in Arabian desert.
¹⁴ They gave water to some thirsty travelers.
   The people of Tema gave food
      to some people that were traveling.
¹⁵ Those people were running from swords
      that were ready to kill.
   They were running from bows
      that were ready to shoot.
   They were running from a hard battle.

¹⁶The Lord, my Master, told me those things would happen. The Lord said, "In one year, (the way a hired helper counts time) all Kedar's* glory will be gone. ¹⁷At that time, only a few of the archers,* the great soldiers of Kedar, will be left living." The Lord, the God of Israel, told me those things.

God's Message to Jerusalem

22 The sad message about the Valley of Vision:*

   What is wrong with you people?
   Why are you hiding on your housetops?

² ⌊In the past,⌋ this city was a very busy city.
   This city was very noisy—and very happy.

---

come back This can also mean "change your heart, repent."
caravan A group of traders and their animals that carry wealth from one place to another.
Kedar's A country east of Israel.
archers Soldiers that use bows and arrows in war.
Valley of Vision This probably means one of the valleys near Jerusalem.

---

watchtower A tall building where guards stood and watched to see if anyone was coming near their city.
threshing floor A place where grain is walked on to remove the hulls from the grain.

⌊But now, things have changed.⌋
Your people have been killed—
    but not with swords.
The people died—
    but not while fighting.
³ All of your leaders ran away together.
But they have all been captured—
    and without bows.
All the leaders ran far away together.
But they have been captured.
⁴ So I say,
"Don't look at me!
Let me cry!
Don't rush to comfort me about
    the destruction of Jerusalem."

⁵The Lord has chosen a special day. On that day there will be riots and confusion. People will trample *(walk on)* each other in the Valley of Vision.* The city walls will be pulled down. The people in the valley will be shouting at the people in the city on the mountain. ⁶The horse soldiers from Elam will take their bags of arrows and ride to battle. The people from Kir will make noise with their shields. ⁷The armies will meet in your special valley. The valley will be filled with chariots.* Horse soldiers will be put in front of the city gates. ⁸At that time, the people of Judah will want to use the weapons they keep at the Forest Palace.*

The enemy will pull down the walls protecting Judah. ⁹⁻¹¹The walls of the City of David will begin to crack, and you will see those cracks. So, you will count the houses, and you will use stones from the houses to fix the walls. You will make a place between the double walls for saving water from the old stream, and you will save the water. You will do all this to protect yourselves. But you will not trust the God who made all these things. You will not see the One *(God)* who made all these things long ago.

¹²So, my Master, the Lord All-Powerful, will tell the people to cry and be sad ⌊for their dead friends⌋. People will shave their heads and wear clothes of sadness.

¹³But look! The people are happy now. The people are rejoicing. ⌊The people are saying⌋:

Kill the cattle and the sheep.
We will celebrate.
Eat your food and drink the wine.
Eat and drink because tomorrow we die.

¹⁴The Lord All-Powerful said these things to me and I heard it with my ears: "You are guilty of doing wrong things. And I promise, you will die before this guilt is forgiven." My Master, the Lord All-Powerful said those things.

God's Message to Shebna

¹⁵My Master, the Lord All-Powerful, told me these things: "Go to that servant Shebna. That servant is the palace manager. ¹⁶⌊Ask that servant,⌋ 'What are you doing here? Is any person from your family buried here? Why are you making a grave here?'"

⌊Isaiah said,⌋ "Look at this man! He is making his grave in a high place. This man is cutting into rock to make his grave.

¹⁷⁻¹⁸"Man, the Lord will crush you. The Lord will roll you into ⌊a small⌋ ball and throw you far away into the open arms of another country. And there you will die."

⌊The Lord said,⌋ "You are very proud of your chariots.* But in that faraway land your new ruler will have better chariots. And your chariots will not look important in his palace. ¹⁹I will force you out of your important job here. Your new leader will take you away from your important job. ²⁰At that time, I will call for my servant, Eliakim son of Hilkiah. ²¹I will take your robe and put it on that servant. I will give him your scepter.* I will give him the important job you have. That servant will be like a father to the people of Jerusalem and Judah's family.

²²"I will put the key to David's house around that man's neck. If he opens a door, that door will stay opened. No person will be able to close it. If he closes a door, that door will stay closed. No person will be able to open it. That servant will be like a very honored chair in his father's house. ²³I will make him strong like a nail that is hammered into a very strong board. ²⁴All the honored and important things of his father's house will hang on him. All the adults and little children will depend on him. Those people will be like small dishes and large water bottles hanging on him.

Valley of Vision   This probably means the valley near Jerusalem.
chariots   Small wagons used for war.
Forest Palace   Or, Beth HaYaar, a city built by Solomon for storing his weapons and wealth.
scepter   A special stick. Kings and leaders carried scepters to show they were rulers.

²⁵"At that time, the nail *(Shebna)* that is now hammered into a very strong board will become weak and it will break. That nail will fall to the ground and all the things hanging on that nail will be destroyed. Then everything I said in this message will happen." (Those things will happen because the Lord said them.)

God's Message To Lebanon

23 The sad message about Tyre:
You ships from Tarshish,* be sad! Your harbor has been destroyed. (The people on these ships were told this news while on their way from the land of Kittim.)*

²You people living near the sea should stop and be sad. Tyre was the "Merchant* of Sidon." That city by the sea sent businessmen across the seas, and those men filled you with riches. ³Those men traveled the seas looking for grain. Those men from Tyre bought the grain that grows near the Nile River, and they sold the grain to other nations.

⁴Sidon, you should be very sad. Why? Because now the Sea, and the Fort of the Sea* say:

I have no children.
  I have not felt the pain of birth.
I have not given birth to children.
  I have not raised young men and women.

⁵ Egypt will hear the news about Tyre.
    This news will make Egypt hurt
      with sorrow.
⁶ You ships should return to Tarshish.*
    You people living near the sea
      should be sad.
⁷ In the past, you enjoyed the city of Tyre.
    That city has been growing
      since the beginning.
  People from that city have traveled
      far away to live.
⁸ The city of Tyre has produced many leaders.
  Businessmen from that city are like princes.
  The people that buy and sell things
      are honored everywhere.

  So who made plans against Tyre?
⁹   It was the Lord All-Powerful.
  He decided to make them not important.
¹⁰ You ships from Tarshish should go back
      to your country.
  Cross the sea like it is a small river.
  No person will stop you now.
¹¹ The Lord has stretched his arm over the sea.
  The Lord is gathering kingdoms
      to fight against Tyre.
  The Lord commands Canaan*
      to destroy ₗTyre₎,
      her place of safety.

¹² The Lord says,
    Virgin Daughter of Sidon,*
    you will be destroyed.
    You will not rejoice any more."

  ₗBut the people of Tyre say,₎
    "Cyprus* will help us!"

  But if you cross the sea to Cyprus,
    you will not find a place to rest.

¹³ ₗSo the people of Tyre say,₎
    "The people of Babylon will help us!"

  But look at the land of the Chaldeans!*
    Babylon is not a country now.
  Assyria* attacked Babylon and built war
      towers around it.
  The soldiers took everything from the
      beautiful houses.
  Assyria made Babylon
      a place for wild animals.
  They changed Babylon
      into a place of ruins.
¹⁴ So, be sad, you ships from Tarshish.*
    Your place of safety *(Tyre)*
      will be destroyed.

¹⁵People will forget about Tyre for 70 years. (That is, about the length of a certain king's rule.)

---

ships from Tarshish A special type of cargo ship.
Kittim This could be the island of Cyprus or Crete.
Merchant A businessman who buys and sells things for a living.
Fort of the Sea Another name for the city Tyre.
Tarshish A city far away from Israel, probably in Spain. Tarshish was famous for its large ships that sailed the Mediterranean Sea.
Canaan The land where the Canaanite people lived. This includes part of Israel, Lebanon, and Syria.
Virgin Daughter of Sidon The city Sidon.
Cyprus Literally, "Kittim." This could also mean "Crete."
Chaldeans The people of the land of Babylon.
Assyria This was a powerful nation northeast of Israel.

After 70 years, Tyre will be like the prostitute* in this song:

> ¹⁶ Oh woman that men forgot,
> take your harp and walk through the city.
> Play your song well.
> Sing your song often.
> Then maybe people will remember you.

¹⁷After 70 years, the Lord will review Tyre's case, and he will give her a decision. Tyre will again have trade. Tyre will be like a prostitute* for all the nations on earth. ¹⁸But Tyre will not keep the money she earns. Tyre's profit from her trade will be saved for the Lord. Tyre will give that profit to the people that serve the Lord. So the Lord's servants will eat until they are full, and they will wear nice clothes.

God Will Punish Israel

24 Look! The Lord will destroy this land. The Lord will completely clean everything from the land. The Lord will force the people to go far away.

²At that time, the common people and the priests will be the same. Slaves and masters will be the same. Women slaves and their women masters will be the same. The buyers and sellers will be the same. The people that borrow and the people that lend will be the same. The bankers and the people that owe the bank will be the same. ³All the people will be forced out of the land. The wealth will all be taken. This will happen because the Lord commanded it. ⁴The country will be empty and sad. The world will be empty and weak. The great leaders of the people in this land will become weak.

⁵The people on the land have made the land dirty. ⌊How did this happen⌋? The people did wrong things against God's teaching. The people did not obey God's laws. The people made an agreement with God a long time ago, but those people broke their agreement with God. ⁶The people living in this land are guilty of doing wrong. So God promised to destroy the land. The people will be punished. Only a few people will survive.

⁷The grapevines are dying. The new wine is bad. In the past, people were happy. But now those people are sad. ⁸People have stopped showing their joy. All the happy sounds have stopped. The happy music from the drums and harps has ended. ⁹People don't sing happy songs while they drink their wine. The beer now tastes bitter to the person drinking it.

¹⁰"Total Confusion" is a good name for this city. The city has been destroyed. People can't enter the houses. The doors are blocked. ¹¹People still ask for wine in the market places. But all the happiness is gone. Joy has been carried far away. ¹²Only destruction is left for the city. Even the gates are crushed.

> ¹³ At harvest time, people knock olives
> from olive trees.
> But, a few olives are left in the trees.
> It will be like that in this land
> among the nations.
>
> ¹⁴ The people that are left will begin shouting.
> They will be louder than the noise
> from the ocean.
> They will be happy because of
> the Lord's greatness.
> ¹⁵ Those people will say,
> "People in the east, praise the Lord!
> People in faraway lands, praise the name
> of the Lord God of Israel."
>
> ¹⁶ We will hear songs of praise for God from
> every place on earth.
> These songs will praise the Good God.
>
> But I say;
> "Enough! I have had enough!
> The things I see are terrible.
> Traitors* are turning against people
> and hurting them.
> ¹⁷ ⌊I see danger for the people living in the land.
> I see⌋ fear, holes, and traps for them.
> ¹⁸ People will hear about danger
> and they will be scared.
> Some of the people will run away.
> But they will fall into holes and be trapped.
> Some of those people
> will climb out of the holes,
> but they will be caught in another trap."
>
> The flood gates in the sky above will open,
> ⌊and the floods will begin⌋.
> The foundations of the earth will shake.

---

prostitute A woman that sells her body for sex. Sometimes this also means a person that stops following God.

Traitors People that turn against their country, friends, or family and do bad things to them.

¹⁹ There will be earthquakes.
And the earth will split open.
²⁰ The sins of the world are very heavy.
So the earth will fall under that weight.
The earth will shake like an old house.
The earth will fall like a drunk person.
The earth will not be able to continue.

²¹ At that time, the Lord will judge
the heavenly armies in heaven
and the earthly kings on earth.
²² Many people will be gathered together.
Some of them have been locked in the Pit.
Some of them have been in prison.*
But finally, after much time,
they will be judged.
²³ The Lord will rule as king
on Mount Zion* in Jerusalem.
His Glory* will be before the elders.*
ᴸHis Glory will be so bright thatᴶ
the moon will be embarrassed,
the sun will be ashamed.

A Song of Praise to God

25 Lord, you are my God.
I honor you and praise your name.
You have done amazing things.
The words you said long ago
are completely true.
Everything has happened
exactly as you said it would.
² You have destroyed the city.
It was a city protected by strong walls.
But now it is only a pile of rocks.
The foreign palace has been destroyed.
It will never be built again.

³ People from powerful nations
will honor you.
Powerful people from strong cities
will fear you.
⁴ ᴸLordᴶ you are a safe place
for poor people that have needs.
Many problems begin to defeat these people,
but you protect them.
ᴸLordᴶ you are like a house protecting people
from floods and heat.
Troubles are like terrible winds and rain.
The rain hits the wall and runs down,
but the people in the house are not hurt.
⁵ The enemy shouts and makes noise.
The terrible enemy shouts challenges.
But you, ᴸGodᴶ will stop them.
In the desert during the summer
ᴸplants wilt and fall to the groundᴶ.
In the same way, you will defeat the enemy
and force them to their knees.
Thick clouds stop the summer heat.
In the same way, you will stop the shouts
of the terrible enemy.

God's Banquet for His Servants

⁶At that time, the Lord All-Powerful will give a feast for all the people on this mountain. At the feast, there will be the best foods and wines. The meat will be tender and good.

⁷But now, there is a veil* covering all nations and people. This veil is called, "death." ⁸But death will be destroyed forever.* And the Lord my Master will wipe away every tear from every face. ᴸIn the past,ᴶ all of his people were sad. But God will take away that sadness from the earth. All of this will happen because the Lord said it would.

⁹ At that time, people will say,
"Here is our God!
He is the One we have been waiting for.
He has come to save us.
We have been waiting for our Lord.
So we will rejoice and be happy
when the Lord saves us."
¹⁰ The Lord's power is on this mountain.
And Moab* will be defeated.
The Lord will trample *(walk on)* the enemy.
It will be like walking on straw
in a pile of waste.
¹¹ The Lord will spread his arms
like a person that is swimming.
Then the Lord will gather
all the things the people are proud of.
The Lord will gather
all the beautiful things they made.

Pit ... prison This is probably "Sheol," the grave.
Zion The southeast part of the mountain Jerusalem is built on. Sometimes it means the people of God living in Jerusalem.
His Glory The "Glory of the Lord," one of the forms God used when he appeared to people. It was like a bright shining light. See Ex. 40:34-36.
elders Older men that were city leaders; they helped make decisions for the people.

veil A piece of cloth used to cover a person's face.
death will be destroyed forever Or, "death will be swallowed in victory."
Moab Or "the enemy." This name is like a Hebrew word meaning, "enemy."

And he will throw those things away.
12 The Lord will destroy the people's
high walls and safe places.
The Lord will throw them down
into the dust on the ground.

A Song of Praise to God

26 At that time, people will sing this song in Judah:

ₗThe Lordⱼ gives us our salvation.
We have a strong city.
Our city has strong walls and defenses.
2 Open the gates
and the good people will enter.
Those people obey God's good teachings.

3 Lord, you give true peace
to people who depend on you,
to people who trust you.
4 So, trust the Lord always.
Why? Because in the Lord Yah,* you have
a place of safety forever!
5 But the Lord will destroy the proud city.
And he will punish the people living there.
The Lord will throw that high city down to
the ground.
It will fall into the dust.
6 Then poor and humble people will walk
on those ruins.

7 Honesty is the way of living for good people.
Good people follow the way
that is straight and true.
And God, you make that way smooth
and easy to follow.
8 But Lord, we are waiting for your
way of justice.
Our souls want to remember
you and your name.
9 My soul wants to be with you at night.
And the spirit in me wants to be with you
at the dawning of every new day.
When your way of justice comes to the land,
people will learn the right way of living.
10 An evil person will not learn to do good
if you show him only kindness.
An evil person will do bad things,
even if he lives in a good world.
That evil person might never see
the Lord's greatness.

11 But Lord, if you punish those people,
they will see it.
Lord, show the evil people the strong love*
that you have for your people.
Then evil people will become ashamed.
Your enemies will be burned
in their own fire *(evil)*.
12 Lord, you have succeeded in doing
all the things that we tried to do.
So give us peace.

God Will Give New Life to His People

13 Lord, you are our God.
But in the past, we followed other lords.*
We belonged to other masters.
But now we want people to remember only
one name, your name!
14 Those false gods are not alive.
Those ghosts will not rise from death.
You decided to destroy them.
And you destroyed everything that makes
us think about them.
15 You have helped the nation you love.
You stopped other people
from defeating that nation.
16 Lord, people remember you
when they are in trouble.
People say quiet prayers to you
when you punish them.
17 Lord, when we are not with you,
we are like a woman giving birth to a baby.
She cries with birth pains.
18 In the same way, we have pain.
We give birth, but only to wind.
We don't make new people for the world.
We don't bring salvation to the land.
19 Your people have died,
but they will live again.
The bodies of my people
will rise from death.

Dead people in the ground,
stand and be happy!
The dew covering you is like
the dew sparkling in the light of a new day.
It shows a new time is coming when the earth
will give up the dead people that are in it.

Lord Yah Or, "Yah Yahweh," a Hebrew name for God.

strong love This Hebrew word means strong feelings like love, hate, anger, zeal, or jealousy.
lords The Hebrew word means "husbands, lords," or "Baals (false gods that the Canaanite people worshiped)."

Judgment: Reward or Punishment

²⁰ My people, go into your rooms.
Lock your doors.
Hide in your rooms for a short time.
Hide until God's anger is finished.
²¹ The Lord will leave his place*
to judge the people of the world
for the bad things they have done.
The earth will show the blood
of the people that have been killed.
The earth will not cover the dead people
any more.

27 At that time, the Lord will judge
Leviathan,* the crooked snake.
The Lord will use his great sword,
his hard and powerful sword, to punish
Leviathan, the coiled snake.
The Lord will kill
the large creature in the sea.*
² At that time, people will sing
about the pleasant vineyard.*

³ "I, the Lord, will care for that garden.
I will water the garden at the right time.
I will guard that garden day and night.
No one will hurt that garden.
⁴ I am not angry.
But if there is war and someone builds
a wall of thorn bushes,*
then I will march to it and burn it.
⁵ But if any person comes to me for safety
and wants to make peace with me,
then let him come,
and make peace with me.
⁶ People will come ⌊to me⌋.
Those people will help Jacob ⌊to be strong⌋
like a plant with good roots.
Those people will cause Israel to grow
like a plant beginning to bloom.
Then the land will be filled
with ⌊the children of Israel⌋
like fruit from plants."

God Will Send Israel Away

⁷⌊How will the Lord punish his people? In the past⌋ enemies hurt the people. Will the Lord hurt them that same way? ⌊In the past⌋ many people were killed. Will the Lord do the same thing and kill many people?*

⁸The Lord will settle his argument with Israel by sending her far away. The Lord will speak harshly to Israel. His words will burn like the hot desert wind.

⁹How will Jacob's guilt be forgiven? What will happen so his sins can be taken away? ⌊These things will happen⌋: The rocks of the altar will be crushed to dust; the statues* and altars* for worshiping false gods will all be destroyed.

¹⁰At that time, the great city will be empty—it will be like a desert. All the people will be gone—they will run away. That city will be like an open pasture. Young cattle will eat grass there. The cattle will eat leaves from the branches of the vines. ¹¹The vines will become dry. And the branches will break off. Women will use those branches for firewood.

The people refuse to understand. So God, their Maker, will not comfort them. Their Maker will not be kind to them.

¹²At that time, the Lord will begin separating his people from others. He will begin at the Euphrates River.* The Lord will gather all his people from the Euphrates River to the River of Egypt.*

You people of Israel will be gathered together one by one. ¹³Many of my people are now lost in Assyria.* Some of my people have run away to Egypt. But at that time, a great trumpet will be blown. And all those people will come back to Jerusalem. Those people will bow down before the Lord on that holy mountain.

---

his place Probably the temple in Jerusalem.
Leviathan The Dragon, or giant snake. Some ancient stories say the Dragon was an enemy of God.
large creature in the sea This is probably Rahab. Some ancient stories tell of Rahab fighting with God.
vineyard A garden for growing grapes.
a wall of thorn bushes Literally, "thorns and thistles." Farmers planted walls of thorn bushes around vineyards to protect them from animals. See Isa. 5:5.

How ... people Or, "Israel was not hurt as badly as the enemy who tried to hurt it. Not as many of its people were killed as were those who tried to kill them."
statues Idols, statues of false gods that people worshiped.
altar(s) A stone table used for burning sacrifices as gifts to God.
separating his people ... Euphrates River Literally, "He will begin threshing at the stream of the river." This Hebrew word for stream is like the word meaning "head of grain."
Euphrates River to the River of Egypt These are the borders of the land God promised to give to Israel.
Assyria This was a powerful nation northeast of Israel.

Warnings to North Israel

28 Look at Samaria!
The drunk people of Ephraim
are proud of that city.
That city sits on a hill
with a rich valley around it.
The people of Samaria think their city
is a beautiful crown of flowers.
But they are drunk with wine.
And this "Beautiful Crown"
is just a dying plant.

² Look, my Master has a person
that is strong and brave.
That person will come into the country
like a storm of hail and rain.
He will come like a storm into the country.
He will be like a powerful river of water
flooding the country.
He will throw that crown *(Samaria)*
down to the ground.

³ The drunk people of Ephraim are proud of
their "Beautiful Crown."
But that city will be walked on.

⁴ That city sits on a hill
with a rich valley around it.
And that "Beautiful Crown of Flowers"
is just a dying plant.
That city will be like the first figs of summer.
When a person sees one of those figs,
he quickly picks it and eats it.

⁵At that time, the Lord All-Powerful will become the "Beautiful Crown." He will be the "Wonderful Crown of Flowers" for his people that are left. ⁶Then the Lord will give wisdom to the judges that rule his people. The Lord will give strength to the people in battles at the city gates. ⁷But now those leaders are drunk. The priests and prophets are all drunk with wine and beer. They stumble and fall down. The prophets are drunk when they see their dreams. The judges are drunk when they make their decisions. ⁸Every table is covered with vomit. There is not a clean place anywhere.

God Wants to Help His People

⁹The Lord is trying to teach a lesson to the people. The Lord is trying to make the people understand his teachings. But the people are like little babies. They are like babies that were at their mother's breast only a very short time ago. ¹⁰So the Lord speaks to them like they are babies ⌊:

Saw lasaw saw lasaw
Qaw laqaw qaw laqaw
Ze'er sham ze'er sham.*

¹¹The Lord will use this strange way of talking and he will use other languages to speak to these people. ¹²In the past God spoke to those people, and he said, "Here is a resting place. This is the peaceful place. Let the tired people come and rest. This is the place of peace."

But the people did not want to listen to God. ¹³So the words from God were like a foreign language:*

Saw lasaw saw lasaw.
Qaw laqaw qaw laqaw.
Ze'er sham ze'er sham."*

The people did like they wanted to do. So the people fell back and were defeated. The people were trapped and captured.

No One Escapes God's Judgment

¹⁴You leaders in Jerusalem should listen to the Lord's message. But now you refuse to listen to him. ¹⁵You people say, "We have made an agreement with death. We have a contract with Sheol—⌊the place of death⌋. So we will not be punished. Punishment will pass us without hurting us. We will hide behind our tricks and lies."

¹⁶Because of those things, the Lord my Master says, "I will put a rock—a cornerstone—in the ground in Zion.* This will be a very precious stone.* Everything will be built on this very important rock. Any person that trusts in that rock will not be disappointed.

¹⁷"⌊People use⌋ a measuring line with a weight ⌊to show a wall is straight. In the same way⌋, I will use justice and goodness ⌊to show what is right⌋.

"You evil people are trying to hide behind your lies and tricks. But ⌊you will be punished. It will

---

Saw lasaw ... ze'er sham This is probably a Hebrew song to teach little children how to write. It sounds like baby talk or a foreign language, but it can also be translated, "A command here, a command there. A rule here, a rule there. A lesson here, a lesson there."
foreign language Or, "gibberish" or "baby talk."
Zion The southeast part of the mountain Jerusalem is built on. Sometimes it means the people of God living in Jerusalem.
very precious stone This also means a stone has been tested and shown that it has no cracks.

be like₁ a storm or a flood is coming to destroy your hiding places. ¹⁸Your agreement with death will be erased. Your contract with Sheol* will not help you.

"Some person will come and punish you. He will make you like the dirt he walks on. ¹⁹That person will come and take you away. Your punishment will be terrible. Your punishment will come early in the morning, and it will continue late into the night.

²⁰"Then you will understand this story: A man tried to sleep on a bed that was too short for him. And he had a blanket that was not wide enough to cover him. ₁The bed and blanket were useless, and so were your agreements₁."

²¹The Lord will fight like he did at Mount Perazim. The Lord will be angry like he was in Gibeon Valley.* Then the Lord will do the things he must do. The Lord will do some strange things. But he will finish his work. His work is a stranger's job. ²²Now, you must not fight against those things. If you do, the ropes around you will become tighter.

The words I heard will not change. Those words came from the Lord All-Powerful, the ruler of all the earth. And those things will be done.

The Lord Punishes Fairly

²³Listen closely to the message I am telling you. ²⁴Does a farmer plow his field all the time? No! Does he work the soil all the time? No! ²⁵A farmer prepares the ground, and then he plants the seed. A farmer plants different kinds of seeds different ways. A farmer scatters dill seeds. A farmer throws cummin seeds on the ground. And a farmer plants wheat in rows. A farmer plants barley in its special place, and he plants spelt* seeds at the edge of his field.

²⁶Our God is using this to teach you a lesson. ₁This example₁ shows us that God is fair when he punishes his people. ²⁷Does a farmer use large boards with sharp teeth to crush dill seeds? No! Does a farmer use a wagon to crush cummin seeds? No! A farmer uses a small stick to break the hulls from these seeds of grain.

²⁸When a woman makes bread, she works and presses the dough with her hands, but she does not do this forever. The Lord punishes his people in the same way. He will scare them with the wagon wheel, but he will not crush them completely. He will not allow many horses* to trample *(walk on)* them. ²⁹This lesson comes from the Lord All-Powerful. The Lord gives wonderful advice. God is truly wise.

God's Love for Jerusalem

29 ₁God says,₁ "Look at Ariel!* Ariel, the city where David camped. Her holidays have continued year after year. ²I have punished Ariel. That city has been filled with sadness and crying. But she has always been my Ariel. ³"I have put armies all around you, Ariel.* I raised war towers against you. ⁴You were ₁defeated and₁ pulled to the ground. Now, I hear your voice rising from the ground like the voice of a ghost. Your words come like a quiet voice from the dirt." ⁵There are many strangers there— like very small pieces of dust. There are many cruel people— like chaff* blowing in the wind. ⁶The Lord All-Powerful punished you with earthquakes, thunder, and loud noises. There were storms, strong winds, and fire that burned and destroyed. ⁷Many, many nations fought against Ariel.* It has been like a terrible dream in the night. Armies have surrounded Ariel and punished her. ⁸But it will also be like a dream to those armies. They will not get what they want. It will be like a hungry man dreaming about food. When the man wakes up, he is still hungry. It will be like a thirsty man dreaming about water. When the man wakes up, he is still thirsty.

> The same thing is true about all the nations fighting against Zion.*
> Those nations will not get the things that they want.

⁹ Be surprised and amazed!
You will become drunk—
but not from wine.
Look and be amazed!
You will stumble and fall—
but not from beer.

Sheol This is the place where all people go when they die. Usually this means the grave, but it can mean the place where our spirits go.

Mount Perazim ...Gibeon Valley See 1 Chron. 14:8-17.

spelt A type of grain.

horses This word also means "horse soldiers."

Ariel A name for the altar at the temple in Jerusalem. This name means "hearth" or "fireplace."

chaff The seed coverings and stems separated from the seeds of plants like wheat or barley. Farmers saved the seeds and let the wind blow the useless chaff away.

Zion The southeast part of the mountain Jerusalem is built on. Sometimes it means the people of God living in Jerusalem.

¹⁰ The Lord will make you sleepy.
The Lord will close your eyes.
(The prophets are your eyes.)
The Lord will cover your heads.
(The prophets are your heads.)

¹¹₍I tell you these things will happen, but you don't understand me. My words₎ are like the words in a book that is closed and sealed.* ¹²You can give the book to a person that can read, and tell that person to read the book. But that person will say, "I can't read the book. It is closed and I can't open it." Or you can give the book to a person that can't read, and tell that person to read the book. That person will say, "I can't read the book because I don't know how to read."

¹³My Master says, "These people say they love me. They show honor to me with words from their mouths. But their hearts are far from me. The honor they show me is nothing but human rules they have memorized. ¹⁴So I will continue to amaze these people by doing powerful and amazing things. Their wise men will lose their wisdom. Their wise men will not be able to understand."

¹⁵Those people try to hide things from the Lord. They think the Lord will not understand. Those people do their evil things in darkness. Those people tell themselves. "No person can see us. No person will know who we are."

¹⁶You are confused. You think the clay is equal to the potter.* You think that something made can tell the person that made it, "You did not make me!" This is like a pot telling its maker, "You don't understand."

A Better Time Is Coming

¹⁷This is the truth: After a short time, Lebanon will have rich soil like Mount Carmel.* And Mount Carmel will be like a thick forest. ¹⁸The deaf will hear the words in the book. The blind will see through the darkness and fog. ¹⁹The Lord will make the poor people happy. The poor people will rejoice in the Holy One of Israel.

²⁰This will happen when the mean and cruel people are finished. It will happen when those people that enjoy doing bad things are gone.

²¹(Those people lie about good people. They try to trap people in court. They try to destroy innocent people.)

²²So the Lord speaks to Jacob's family. (This is the Lord that made Abraham free.) The Lord says, "Now Jacob *(the people of Israel)* will not be embarrassed and ashamed. ²³He will see all his children, and he will say my name is holy. I made these children with my hands. And these children will say that the Holy One *(God)* of Jacob is very special. These children will respect the God of Israel. ²⁴Many of these people did not understand, so they did wrong things. These people did not understand, but they will learn their lesson."

Israel Should Trust God, Not Egypt

30 The Lord said, "Look at these children. They don't obey me. They make plans, but they don't ask me to help them. They make agreements with other nations, but my Spirit does not want those agreements. These people are adding more and more sins to themselves. ²These children are going down to Egypt for help, but they did not ask me if that was the right thing to do. They hope they will be saved by the Pharaoh.* They want Egypt to protect them.

³"But I tell you, hiding in Egypt will not help you. Egypt will not be able to protect you. ⁴Your leaders have gone to Zoan* and your ambassadors have gone to Hanes.* ⁵But they will be disappointed. They are depending on a nation that can't help them. Egypt is useless—Egypt will give no help. Egypt will cause only shame and embarrassment."

God's Message to Judah

⁶The sad message about the animals in the Negev:*

The Negev is a dangerous place. This land is full of lions, and adders,* and fast snakes.* ₍But some people are traveling through the Negev— they are going to Egypt₎. Those people have put their wealth on the backs of donkeys. Those people have put their treasure on the backs of camels. ₍This means that₎ the people are depending on a nation that cannot help. ⁷That

---

sealed A piece of clay or wax was put on the closed book to show the book should not be opened.
potter A worker that makes things from clay.
Mount Carmel A hill in north Israel very good for growing plants. This name means "God's vineyard."
Pharaoh A title for the kings of Egypt.
Zoan A city in the country Egypt.
Hanes A city in the country Egypt.
Negev The desert area south of Judah.
adders Very poisonous snakes.
fast snakes Literally, "flying snakes."

useless nation is Egypt. Egypt's help will be worth nothing. So I call Egypt the "Do-Nothing Dragon." ⁸Now write this on a sign so all people can see it. And write this in a book. Write these things for the last days. This will be far, far in the future:

⁹These people are like children that refuse to obey [their parents]. They lie and refuse to listen to the Lord's teachings. ¹⁰They tell the prophets, "Don't see dreams* about things we should do! Don't tell us the truth! Say nice things to us and make us feel good! See only good things for us! ¹¹Stop seeing things that will really happen! Get out of our way! Stop telling us about the Holy One of Israel."

Judah's Help Comes Only from God

¹²The Holy One *(God)* of Israel says, "You people have refused to accept this message from the Lord. You people want to depend on fighting and lies to help you. ¹³You are guilty of these things so you are like a tall wall with cracks in it. That wall will fall and break into small pieces. ¹⁴You will be like a large clay jar that breaks and becomes many, many small pieces. Those pieces are useless. You can't use those pieces to get a hot coal from the fire or to get water from a pool in the ground."

¹⁵The Lord my Master, the Holy One of Israel, says, "If you come back to me you will be saved. The only strength you have will come if you trust me. But you must be calm."

But you don't want to do that! ¹⁶You say, "No, we need horses to run away on!" That is true—you will run away on horses. But the enemy will chase you. And the enemy will be faster than your horses. ¹⁷One enemy will make threats and a thousand of your men will run away. Five enemies will make threats and all of you will run from them. The only thing that will be left of your army will be a flagpole on a hill.

¹⁸The Lord wants to show his mercy to you. The Lord is waiting. The Lord wants to rise and comfort you. The Lord God is fair, and every person that waits for the Lord's help will be blessed *(happy)*.

¹⁹The Lord's people will live in Jerusalem on Mount Zion.* You people will not continue crying. The Lord will hear your crying and he will comfort you. The Lord will hear you, and he will help you.

God Will Help His People

²⁰[In the past,] my Master *(God)* gave you sorrow and hurt—it was like the bread and water you ate every day. But God is your teacher, and he will not continue to hide from you. You will see your teacher with your own eyes. ²¹Then, if you do wrong and go *(live)* the wrong way (to the right or to the left), you will hear a voice behind you saying, "This is the right way. You should go this way!"

²²You have statues covered with silver and gold. Those false gods have made you dirty *(sinful)*. But you will stop serving those false gods. You will throw away those gods like waste and dirty rags.*

²³At that time, the Lord will send rain for you. You will plant seeds in the ground, and the ground will grow food for you. You will have a very large harvest. You will have plenty of food in the fields for your animals. There will be large fields for your sheep. ²⁴Your cattle and donkeys will have all the food they need. There will be very much food. You will have to use shovels and pitchforks* to spread all the food* for your animals to eat. ²⁵Every mountain and hill will have streams filled with water. These things will happen after many people are killed and the towers are pulled down.

²⁶At that time, the light from the moon will be bright like the sun. The light from the sun will be seven times brighter than now. The light from the sun in one day will be like a full week. These things will happen when the Lord bandages his broken people and heals the hurts from their beatings.

²⁷Look! The Lord's Name is coming from far away. His anger is like a fire with thick clouds of smoke. The Lord's mouth is filled with anger, and his tongue is like a burning fire. ²⁸The Lord's

---

You will throw ... dirty rags This also means "You will throw away those gods like menstrual clothes. You will say, 'Go away!'"

pitchforks Tools for throwing or spreading hay.

food This was was special food that was fermented so the meat of the animal would be tender and good.

dreams Or "visions." Special kinds of dreams God used to speak to his prophets.

breath *(Spirit)* is like a great river—rising until it reaches the throat. The Lord will judge the nations. It will be like he shakes them through the 'Strainer of Destruction.' The Lord will control them. It will be like a bit* that controls an animal is in the mouths of the people.

²⁹⌊At that time, you will sing happy songs. That time⌋ will be like the nights when you begin a holiday. You are very happy while walking to the Lord's mountain. You are happy while listening to the flute on the way to worship ⌊the Lord,⌋ the Rock* of Israel.

³⁰The Lord will cause all people to hear his great voice. The Lord will cause all people to see his powerful arm come down with anger. That arm will be like a great fire that burns everything. The Lord's power will be like a great storm with much rain and hail. ³¹Assyria* will be afraid when he hears the Lord's voice. The Lord will beat Assyria with a stick. ³²The Lord will beat Assyria, and it will be like playing music on drums and harps.* The Lord will defeat Assyria with his great arm *(power)*.

³³Topheth* has been made ready for a long time. It is ready for the king.* It was made very deep and wide. There is a very big pile of wood and fire there. And the Lord's breath *(Spirit)* will come like a stream of burning sulfur and burn it.

Israel Should Depend on God's Power

31 Look at the people going down to Egypt for help. The people ask for horses. They think horses will save them. The people hope the chariots* and horse soldiers from Egypt will protect them. The people think they are safe because that army is very big. The people don't trust the Holy One of Israel *(God)*. The people don't ask the Lord for help.

²But, it is the Lord who is wise. And it is the Lord who will bring trouble against them. The people will not be able to change the Lord's command. The Lord will rise and fight against the evil people *(Judah)*. And the Lord will fight against the people *(Egypt)* that try to help them.

³The people of Egypt are only human—not God. The horses from Egypt are only animals—not spirit. The Lord will stretch out his arm and the helper *(Egypt)* will be defeated. And the people that wanted help *(Judah)* will fall. All those people will be destroyed together.

⁴The Lord told me: "When a lion or a lion's cub catches an animal to eat, the lion stands over the dead animal and roars. At that time nothing can scare that great lion. If men come and yell at the lion, the lion will not be afraid. The men can make much noise, but the lion will not run away."

In the same way, the Lord All-Powerful will come down to Mount Zion.* The Lord will fight on that hill. ⁵The Lord All-Powerful will defend* Jerusalem—like birds flying over their nests. The Lord will save her. The Lord will "pass over" and save Jerusalem.

⁶You children of Israel turned against God. You should come back to God. ⁷Then people would stop worshiping the gold and silver idols you made. You truly sinned when you made those idols.

⁸It is true that Assyria* will be defeated with a sword. But that sword will not be a man's sword. Assyria will be destroyed. But that destruction will not come from a man's sword. Assyria will run away from God's sword. But the young men will be caught and made slaves. ⁹Their place of safety will be destroyed. Their leaders will be defeated and leave their flag.

The Lord said all those things. The Lord's fireplace *(altar)* is on Zion*. The Lord's oven *(altar)* is in Jerusalem.

Leaders Should Be Good and Fair

32 Listen to the things I say! A king should rule in a way that brings goodness. Leaders should make fair decisions when they lead the people. ²⌊If this would happen⌋, then the king* would be like a place to hide from the wind and rain. It would be like having streams of water in a dry land. It would be like a cool shadow from a large rock in a hot land. ³People would turn to the king for help, and people would truly listen to the things he says. ⁴People that are now confused

---

bit A piece of metal in a horse's mouth used to make the horse go the right way.
Rock A name for God. It shows he is like a strong place of safety.
Assyria This was a powerful nation northeast of Israel.
harps Musical instruments with several strings.
Topheth Gehenna; the Valley of Hinnom. In this valley people killed their children to honor the false god, "Molech."
king This is like the name of the false god, "Molech."
chariots Small wagons used for war.

Zion The southeast part of the mountain Jerusalem is built on. Sometimes it means the people of God living in Jerusalem.
defend Literally, "fight on" or "fight against."
king Literally, "man."

would be able to understand. People that can't speak clearly now would be able to speak clearly and quickly. ⁵Foolish people would not be called great men. People would not respect men that make secret plans.

⁶A foolish person* says foolish things, and in his heart (mind), plans evil things to do. A foolish person wants to do things that are wrong. A foolish person says bad things about the Lord. A foolish person does not let hungry people eat food. A foolish person does not let thirsty people drink water. ⁷That foolish person uses evil like a tool. He plans ways to take everything from poor people. That foolish person tells lies about the poor people. And his lies keep the poor people from being judged fairly.

⁸But a good leader plans good things to do. And those good things make him a good leader.

Hard Times Are Coming

⁹Some of you women are calm now. You feel safe. But you should stand and listen to the words I say. ¹⁰You women feel safe now, but after one year you will be troubled. ⌊Why?⌋ Because you will not gather grapes next year—there will be no grapes to gather.

¹¹Women, you are calm now, but you should be afraid! Women, you feel safe now, but you should be worried! Take off your nice clothes and put on your clothes of sadness. Wrap those clothes around your waist. ¹²Put those clothes of sadness over your sorrow-filled breasts.

Cry because your fields are empty. Your vineyards* once gave grapes—but now they are empty. ¹³Cry for the land of my people. Cry because only thorns and weeds will grow there. Cry for the city and for all the houses that were once filled with joy.

¹⁴People will leave the capital city. The palace and towers will be left empty. People will not live in houses—they will live in caves. Wild donkeys and sheep will live in the city—animals will go there to eat grass.

¹⁵⁻¹⁶This will continue until God gives us his Spirit from above. Now there is no goodness in the land—it is like a desert. ⌊But in the future,⌋ that desert will be like the land of Carmel*—fair judgment will live there. And Carmel will be like a green forest—goodness will live there. ¹⁷That goodness will bring peace and safety forever. ¹⁸My people will live in the beautiful field of peace. My people will live in tents of safety. They will live in calm and peaceful places.

¹⁹But before these things happen, the forest must fall. That city must be defeated. ²⁰Some of you people plant seeds near every stream of water. You let your cattle and donkeys walk around and eat freely. You people will be very happy.

Evil Causes Only More Evil

33 Look, you people make war and steal things from people, and those people never stole anything from you. You turn against people, and those people never turned against you. So when you stop stealing, other people will begin stealing from you. When you stop turning against people, other people will start turning against you. ⌊Then you will say,⌋

2   Lord, be kind to us.
      We have waited for your help.
      Lord, give us strength every morning.
      Save us when we are in trouble.
3   Your powerful voice scares people,
      and they run away from you.
      Your greatness causes the nations to run away.

⁴You people stole things in war. Those things will be taken from you. Many, many people will come and take your wealth. It will be like the times when locusts* come and eat all your crops.

⁵The Lord is very great. He lives in a very high place. The Lord fills Zion* with fairness and goodness.

⁶Jerusalem, you are rich—you are rich with wisdom and knowledge of God. You are rich with salvation. You respect the Lord and that makes you rich. So you can know that you will continue. ⁷But listen! The angels are crying outside. The messengers* that bring peace are crying very hard. ⁸The roads are destroyed. No one is walking in the streets. People have broken the agreements they made. People refuse to believe the proof from witnesses.* No one respects other people.

---

foolish person   A person that does not follow God and his wise teachings.
vineyards   Gardens for growing grapes.
locusts   Insects like grasshoppers. Locusts can destroy a large crop very quickly.
Zion   The southeast part of the mountain Jerusalem is built on. Sometimes it means the people of God living in Jerusalem.
messengers   This word also means "angels."

⁹The land is sick and dying. Lebanon* is dying and Sharon Valley* is dry and empty. Bashan* and Carmel* once grew beautiful plants—but now those plants have stopped growing.
¹⁰The Lord says, "Now, I will stand and show my greatness. Now, I will become important to the people. ¹¹You people have done useless things. Those things are like hay and straw. They are worth nothing! Your spirit* will be like a fire and burn you. ¹²People will be burned until their bones are like lime.* The people will burn quickly like thorns and dry bushes.
¹³"You people in faraway lands, hear about the things I have done. You people that are near me, learn about my power."
¹⁴The sinners in Zion* are afraid. The people that do wrong things shake with fear. They say, "Can any of us live through this fire that destroys? Who can live near this fire that burns forever?"*
¹⁵Good, honest people that refuse to hurt others for money—₁they will live through that fire₁. Those people refuse to take bribes. They refuse to listen to plans to murder other people. They refuse to look at plans for doing bad things. ¹⁶Those people will live safely in high places. They will be protected in high rock fortresses. Those people will always have food and water.
¹⁷Your eyes will see the King (God) in his beauty. You will see the great land. ¹⁸⁻¹⁹You will think about the troubles you had in the past. You will think, "Where are those people from other countries? Those people spoke languages we could not understand. Where are those officials and tax collectors from other lands? Where are the spies that counted our defense towers? ₍They are all gone!₎"

God Will Protect Jerusalem

²⁰Look at Zion*, the city of our religious holidays. Look at Jerusalem—that beautiful place of rest. Jerusalem is like a tent that will never be moved. The pegs that hold her in place will never be pulled up. Her ropes will never be broken. ²¹⁻²³Why? Because the Powerful Lord is there. That land is a place with streams and wide rivers. But there will be no enemy boats or powerful ships on those rivers. You men that work on those boats can quit your work with the ropes. You can't make the mast* strong enough. You will not be able to open your sails. ₍Why?₎ Because the Lord is our judge.* The Lord makes our laws. The Lord is our king. He saves us. So the Lord will give us much wealth. Even crippled people will win great wealth in war. ²⁴No person living there will say, "I am sick." The people living there are people whose sins are forgiven.

God Will Punish His Enemies

34 All you nations, come near and listen! All you people should listen closely. The earth and all the people on the earth should listen to these things. ²The Lord is angry at all the nations and their armies. The Lord will destroy them all. He will cause them all to be killed. ³Their bodies will be thrown outside. The stink will rise from the bodies, and the blood will flow down the mountains. ⁴The skies will be rolled shut like a scroll.* And the stars will die and fall like leaves from a vine or a fig tree. All the stars* in the sky will melt away. ⁵The Lord says, "This will happen when my sword in the sky is covered with blood."

Look! The Lord's sword will cut through Edom.* The Lord judged those people guilty, and they must die.* ⁶Why? Because the Lord decided there should be a time for killing in Bozrah* and in Edom. ⁷So the rams, the cattle, and the strong bulls will be killed. The land will be filled with their blood. The dirt will be covered with their fat.

---

witnesses Literally, "cities." The Hebrew word is like the word meaning "witnesses."
Lebanon A country north of Israel. It was famous for its great cedar and pine trees.
Sharon Valley The low land along the coast of Palestine.
Bashan An area northeast of Israel.
Carmel A hill in north Israel very good for growing plants. This name means "God's vineyard."
spirit Or, "Spirit."
lime A white powder that is often used to make mortar or cement. It can be made by burning bones, shells, or limestone.
Zion The southeast part of the mountain Jerusalem is built on. Sometimes it means the people of God living in Jerusalem.
fire that ... burns forever This might mean God, the Fire (Light) of Israel.

mast The pole that holds the sail on a sailboat.
judge In Israel judges were leaders that judged, led, and protected the people.
rolled shut like a scroll This is like a person closing a book when he has finished reading it.
stars Literally, "the armies of the skies."
Edom A country east of Judah.
guilty, and they must die The Hebrew means the people belonged completely to God, and if he does not get them, they must die.
Bozrah A city in Edom.

⁸[Those things will happen] because the Lord has chosen a time for punishment. The Lord has chosen a year when people must pay for the wrong things they did to Zion.* ⁹Edom's rivers will be like hot tar.* Edom's ground will be like burning sulfur.* ¹⁰The fires will burn day and night—no person will stop the fire. The smoke will rise from Edom forever. That land will be destroyed forever and ever. No people will ever travel through that land again. ¹¹Birds and small animals will own that land. Owls and ravens will live there. That land will be called "Empty Desert."* ¹²The freemen* and leaders will all be gone. And there will be nothing left for them to rule.

¹³Thorns and wild bushes will grow in all the beautiful homes there. Wild dogs and owls will live in those homes. Wild animals will make their homes there. Big birds will live in the grasses that grow there. ¹⁴Wild cats will live there with hyenas.* And wild goats* will call to their friends. Night animals* will look there and find a place to rest. ¹⁵Snakes will make their homes there. Snakes will lay their eggs there. The eggs will open, and small snakes will crawl from those dark places. Birds that eat dead things will gather like women visiting their friends.

¹⁶Look at the Lord's scroll.* Read what is written there. Nothing is missing. It is written in that scroll that those animals will be together. God said he will gather them together. So God's Spirit will gather them together. ¹⁷God decided what he should do with them. Then God chose a place for them. God drew a line and showed them their land. So the animals will own that land forever. They will live there year after year.

God Will Comfort His People

35 The dry desert will become very happy. The desert will be glad and will grow like a flower. ²The desert will be full of growing flowers and will begin to show its happiness. It will seem like the desert is dancing with joy. The desert will be beautiful like the forest of Lebanon,* the hill of Carmel,* and Sharon Valley.* This will happen because all people will see the Glory of the Lord.* People will see the beauty of our God.

³Make the weak arms strong again. Make the weak knees strong. ⁴People are afraid and confused. Say to those people, "Be strong! Don't be afraid!" Look, your God will come and punish your enemies. He will come and give you your reward. The Lord will save you. ⁵Then the blind people will be able to see again. Their eyes will be opened. Then the deaf people will be able to hear. Their ears will be opened. ⁶Crippled people will dance like deer. And the people that can't talk now will use their voices to sing happy songs. This will happen when springs of water begin flowing in the desert. Springs will flow in the dry land. ⁷Now people see mirages* [that look like water]. But at that time there will be real pools of water. There will be wells in the dry land. Water will flow from the ground. Tall water plants will grow where wild animals once ruled.

⁸At that time, there will be a road there. This highway will be called "The Holy Road." Evil people will not be allowed to walk on that road. No fools* will go to that road. Only good people will walk on that road. ⁹There will be no dangers on that road. There will be no lions on that road to hurt people. There will be no dangerous animals

---

Zion The southeast part of the mountain Jerusalem is built on. Sometimes it means the people of God living in Jerusalem.

tar A very thick oil that must be heated to become liquid.

sulfur A yellow chemical that looks like rock or dirt. Sulfur burns with a hot flame, and it gives a bad odor when it burns.

Empty Desert Literally, "They will measure this city with the measuring string called 'emptiness' and stone weights called 'nothingness.'" These words described the empty earth in Gen. 1:2.

freemen Important citizens of a town or country. These people came from 'good families' and had never been slaves.

hyenas A kind of wild dog that often eats the meat of dead animals that other animals killed.

wild goats This Hebrew word means "goat, or goat-demon."

Night animals Or, "Lilith, the night demon." This name is like the Hebrew word for night.

scroll A long roll of leather or papyrus (paper) used for writing books, letters, and legal documents.

Lebanon A country north of Israel. It was famous for its great cedar and pine trees.

Carmel A hill in north Israel very good for growing plants. This name means "God's vineyard."

Sharon Valley The low land along the coast of Palestine.

Glory of the Lord One of the forms God used when he appeared to people. It was like a bright shining light. See Ex. 40:34-36.

mirages In the desert, heat rising from the ground looks like water from far away. This is a mirage.

fools Here this means people that do not follow God and his wise teachings.

on that road. That road will be for the people God saves.

¹⁰God will make his people free! And those people will come back to him. The people will be happy when they come into Zion.* The people will be happy forever. Their happiness will be like a crown on their heads. Their gladness and joy will fill them completely. Sorrow and sadness will be gone far, far away.

The Assyrians Invade Judah

36 During Hezekiah's* 14th year as king, Sennacherib* king of Assyria went to fight against all the strong cities of Judah. Sennacherib defeated those cities. ²Sennacherib sent his commander with a large army to King Hezekiah in Jerusalem. The commander and his army left Lachish and went to Jerusalem. They stopped near the aqueduct* by the Upper Pool. (The Upper Pool is on the road to Laundryman's Field.

³Three men from Jerusalem went out to talk with the commander. These men were Eliakim son of Hilkiah, Joah son of Asaph, and Shebna. Eliakim was the palace manager. Joah was the record keeper. And Shebna was the royal secretary.

⁴The commander told them, "Tell Hezekiah this is what the great king, the king of Assyria says:

What are you trusting in to help you? ⁵I tell you if you are trusting in power and smart plans for battle—then that is useless. Those are nothing but empty words. Now I ask you, who do you trust so much that you are willing to rebel against me? ⁶Are you depending on Egypt to help you? Egypt is like a broken stick. If you lean on it for support, it will only hurt you and make a hole in your hand. Pharaoh, the king of Egypt, can't be trusted by any of the people that depend on him for help.

⁷But maybe you will say, "We are trusting in the Lord our God to help us." But I know that Hezekiah destroyed the altars* and high places* where people worshiped the Lord. And Hezekiah told the people of Judah and Jerusalem, "You must worship only at this one altar here in Jerusalem."

⁸If you still want to fight, my master, the king of Assyria will make this agreement with you. I promise that I will give you 2,000 horses if you can find enough men to ride those horses into battle. ⁹But even then you will not be able to defeat even one of my master's lowest ranking officers! So why do you continue to depend on Egypt's chariots* and horse soldiers!

¹⁰Now, do you think I came to this country to destroy it without the Lord's help! No! The Lord said to me, "Go up against this country and destroy it!"

¹¹Then Eliakim, Shebna, and Joah, said to the commander, "Please, speak to us in the Aramaic. We understand language. Don't speak to us in the language of Judah. If you use our language, the people on the city walls will understand you."

¹²But the commander said, "My master did not send me to speak only to you and your master. My master sent me to also speak to the people that are sitting on the wall! Those people will not have enough food or water either; they too will eat their own waste and drink their own urine just like you.*"

¹³Then the commander shouted loudly in the Jewish language, ¹⁴"Hear this message from the great king, the king of Assyria:

Don't let Hezekiah fool you! He can't save you from my power! ¹⁵Don't believe Hezekiah when he says, 'Trust in the Lord! The Lord will save us. The Lord will not let the king of Assyria defeat the city.'

¹⁶Don't listen to those words from Hezekiah. Listen to the king of Assyria. The king of Assyria says, "We should make an agreement. You people should come out of the city to me. Then every person will be free to go home. Every person will be free to eat grapes from his own vine. And every

---

Zion The southeast part of the mountain Jerusalem is built on. Sometimes it means the people of God living in Jerusalem.
Hezekiah A king of Judah. He ruled about 727-687 B.C.
Sennacherib A king of Assyria. He was king about 706-681 B.C.
aqueduct A ditch or pipe that carries water from one place to another.

high places Places for worshiping God or false gods. These places were usually on the hills and mountains.
chariot(s) A small wagon used in war.
Those people ... like you The Assyrian army planned to surround Jerusalem and not let people bring any food or water into the city. He thought the people would become hungry enough to eat their own waste.

person will be free to eat the figs from his own fig tree. Every person will be free to drink water from his own well. ¹⁷You can do this until I come and take each of you to a country like your own. In that new country you will have good grain and new wine, bread and fields of grapes."

¹⁸Don't let Hezekiah make trouble for you. He says, "The Lord will save us." But I ask you, did any of the gods of other nations save their country from the king of Assyria? No! ¹⁹Where are the gods of Hamath* and Arpad?* ₍They are defeated!₎ Where are the gods of Sepharvaim?* ₍They are defeated!₎ Did they save Samaria* from my power? No! ²⁰Did any of the gods in the other countries save their land from me? No! Can the Lord save Jerusalem from me? No!"

²¹But the people in Jerusalem were very quiet. They did not say a word to the commander because King Hezekiah had given them a command. He said, "Don't say anything to him." ²²Then the palace manager (Eliakim son of Hilkiah), the royal secretary (Shebna), and the record keeper* (Joah son of Asaph) went to Hezekiah. Their clothes were torn ₍to show they were upset₎. They told Hezekiah all the things that the Assyrian commander had said.

Hezekiah Asks God to Help

37 King Hezekiah listened to those things. Then Hezekiah tore his clothes ₍to show he was upset₎. Then Hezekiah put on the special clothes of sadness and went to the Lord's temple.* ²Hezekiah sent Eliakim the palace manager, Shebna the royal secretary, and the elders *(leaders)* of the priests* to the prophet, Isaiah son of Amoz. They wore the special clothes ₍that showed they were sad and upset₎.

³These men said to Isaiah, "King Hezekiah has commanded that today will be a special day for sorrow and sadness. It will be a very sad day. It will be like a day when a child should be born, but is not strong enough to come from its mother body. ⁴The commander's master, the king of Assyria, has sent him to say bad things about the living God. Maybe the Lord your God will hear all those things. Maybe the Lord will prove the enemy is wrong! So pray for the people that are still left alive."

⁵⁻⁶King Hezekiah's officers went to Isaiah. Isaiah said to them, "Give this message to your master, Hezekiah: The Lord says, 'Don't be afraid of the things you heard from the commanders! Don't believe the evil things those "boys" from the king of Assyria said about me. ⁷Look, I will send a spirit against Assyria. ₍The king of₎ Assyria will get a report warning him about a danger to his country. So, he will go back to his country. At that time, I will kill him with a sword in his own country.'"

The Assyrian Army Leaves Jerusalem

⁸⁻⁹The king of Assyria got a report. The report said, "Tirhakah,* the king of Ethiopia,* is coming to fight you." So, the king of Assyria left Lachish and went to Libnah. The commander heard this, and he went to the city Libnah, where the king of Assyria was fighting. He sent messengers to Hezekiah. He said, ¹⁰"You should tell these things to Hezekiah, the king of Judah:

Don't be fooled by the god you trust. Don't say, "God will not let Jerusalem be defeated by the king of Assyria."

¹¹You have heard what the kings of Assyria did to all the other countries! They destroyed them completely! Will you be saved? No! ¹²Did the gods of those people save them? No! My ancestors* destroyed them all. They destroyed Gozan, Haran, Rezeph, and the people of Eden* living in Tel Assar. ¹³Where is the king of Hamath? The king of Arpad? The king of the city of Sepharvaim? The kings of Hena and Ivvah? ₍They are all finished! They were all destroyed!₎"

Hamath A city in the country of Aram (Syria).
Arpad A city in the country of Aram (Syria).
Sepharvaim A city in the country of Aram (Syria).
Samaria The capital city of north Israel.
record keeper A person that wrote about the things the king did.
temple A special building for worshiping God. God commanded the Jews to worship him at the temple in Jerusalem.
priests Special religious leaders that made sacrifices for the people.

Tirhakah This is probably Taharqa, the pharaoh of Egypt about 690-664 B.C.
Ethiopia Literally, "Cush," a country in Africa by the Red Sea.
ancestors Literally, "fathers." This means a person's parents, grandparents, and all the people they are descended from.
Eden Beth Eden, an area in the country of Aram (Syria).

Hezekiah Prays to God

¹⁴Hezekiah took the letters from the messengers and read them. Then Hezekiah went to the Lord's temple.* Hezekiah opened the letters and laid them out in front of the Lord. ¹⁵Hezekiah began praying to the Lord and said:

¹⁶Lord All-Powerful, God of Israel, you sit as King on the Cherub angels.* You, and only you, are the God that rules all the kingdoms on earth. You made the heavens and the earth! ¹⁷Lord, please listen to me. Lord, open your eyes and look at this message. Hear the words that Sennacherib sent to insult you, the living God!

¹⁸It is true, Lord. The kings of Assyria did destroy all those nations! ¹⁹The kings of Assyria have burned the gods of those nations. But those were not real gods. They were only wood and stone—statues that men made. That is why the kings of Assyria could destroy them. ²⁰But you are the Lord our God. So please save us from the king of Assyria. Then all the other nations will know that you are the Lord, and you are the only ⌊God⌋.

God's Answer to Hezekiah

²¹Then Isaiah son of Amoz sent this message to Hezekiah. Isaiah said, "The Lord, the God of Israel says, 'You prayed to me about the message that came from Sennacherib king of Assyria. I have heard you.'

²²"This is the Lord's message about Sennacherib:

⌊King of Assyria⌋,
The Virgin Daughter of Zion *(Jerusalem)*
    doesn't think you are important.
She laughs at you.
The Daughter of Jerusalem
    makes fun of you.
²³ But who did you insult and make fun of?
    Who did you speak against?
You were against the Holy One of Israel!
    You acted like you were better than him!
²⁴ You sent your officers
    to insult the Lord my Master.
You said,
"⌊I am very powerful!⌋
    I have many, many chariots.*
⌊With my power I defeated Lebanon.⌋
    I climbed the highest mountains
        of Lebanon.*
    I cut down all the great trees *(armies)*
        of Lebanon.
    I have been to the highest mountain
        and into the deepest part of that forest.
²⁵ I dug wells, and drank water
        ⌊from new places⌋.
    I dried up the rivers of Egypt
        and walked on that country."

²⁶ ⌊That is what you said.⌋
    But haven't you heard ⌊what God said⌋?
    "I *(God)* planned it long ago,
        from ancient times I planned it.
    And now, I made it happen.
    I let you tear down the strong cities
        and change them into piles of rocks.
²⁷ The people in the cities had no power.
    Those people were scared and confused.
    They were about to be cut down
        like grass and plants in the field.
    They were like grass growing
        on the housetops,
    dying before it grows tall.
²⁸ ⌊I know all about your battles.⌋
    I know when you rested.
    I know when you went out to war.
    I know when you came home from war.
    I also know when you were upset at me.
²⁹ Yes, you were upset at me.
    I heard your proud insults.
    So I will put my hook in your nose.
    And I will put my bit* in your mouth.
    Then I will turn you around
        and lead you back the way you came."

The Lord's Message for Hezekiah

³⁰⌊Then the Lord said to Hezekiah,⌋ "I will give you a sign to show you that these words are true. ⌊You were not able to plant seeds.⌋ So this year you will eat grain that grew wild from last year's crop. But in three years, you will eat grain that

---

temple A special building for worshiping God. God commanded the Jews to worship him at the temple in Jerusalem.

Cherub angels Special angels God used as messengers. Statues of these angels were on the top of the Box of the Agreement.

chariot(s) Small wagons used in war.

Lebanon A country north of Israel. It was famous for its great cedar and pine trees.

bit A piece of metal people put in a horse's mouth to control the horse.

you planted. You will harvest those crops and you will have plenty to eat. You will plant grapevines and eat their fruit. ³¹The people from the family of Judah that have escaped and are left ₍alive₎ will again begin to grow. ₍These people will be like plants that₎ send their roots deep into the ground and produce fruit above the ground. ³²Why? Because a few people will remain alive. They will go out from Jerusalem. There will be survivors coming from Mount Zion.*" The strong love* of the Lord All-Powerful will do this.

³³So the Lord says this about the king of Assyria:

> He will not come into this city.
> He will not shoot an arrow at this city.
> He will not bring his shields to this city.
> He will not build up a hill of dirt
>   to attack the walls of this city.
> ³⁴ He will go back the same way he came.
> He will not come into this city.
> The Lord says this!
> ³⁵ I will protect this city and save it.
> I will do this for myself
>   and for my servant David.

³⁶₍That night,₎ the angel of the Lord went out and killed 185,000 people in the Assyrian camp. When the people got up in the morning, they saw the dead bodies all around them. ³⁷So Sennacherib, the king of Assyria, went back to Nineveh and stayed there. ³⁸One day, Sennacherib was in the temple of his god, Nisroch, worshiping him. At that time his two sons, Adrammelech and Sharezer, killed him with a sword. Then the sons ran away to Ararat.* So Sennacherib's son Esarhaddon became the new king of Assyria.

Hezekiah's Illness

38 At that time, Hezekiah became sick and almost died. The prophet Isaiah son of Amoz went to see him.

Isaiah told the king, "The Lord told me to tell you these things: 'You will die soon. So you should tell your family what they should do when you die. You will not become well again.'"

²Hezekiah turned toward the wall ₍that faced the temple₎ and began praying. He said: ³"Lord, remember that I have truly served you with all my heart. I have done the things that you say are good." Then Hezekiah cried very hard.

⁴Isaiah received this message from the Lord: ⁵"Go to Hezekiah and tell him that the Lord, the God of your ancestor* David says, 'I heard your prayer, and I saw your tears. I will add 15 years to your life. ⁶I will save you and this city from the king of Assyria. I will protect this city.'"

²²* But Hezekiah asked Isaiah, "What is the sign from the Lord that proves ₍I will become well? What is the sign that proves₎ I will be able to go to the Lord's temple?*"

⁷This is the sign from the Lord to show you that he will do the things he says: ⁸"Look, I am causing the shadow that is on the steps of Ahaz* to move back ten steps. The sun's shadow will go back up the ten steps that it has already been on."

²¹* Then Isaiah told Hezekiah, "You should crush figs together and put them on your sore, then you will become well."

⁹This is the letter from Hezekiah when he became well from the sickness:

> ¹⁰ I told myself I would live to be old.
>   But then it was my time to go through
>   the gates of Sheol.*
>   Now I will spend all of my time there.
> ¹¹ So I said,
>   "I will not see the Lord Yah* in
>   the land of the living again.
>   I will not see the people living on earth.
> ¹² My home, my shepherd's tent,
>   is being pulled down
>   and taken from me.

Zion The southeast part of the mountain Jerusalem is built on. Sometimes it means the people of God living in Jerusalem.

strong love This Hebrew word means strong feelings like love, hate, anger, zeal, or jealousy.

Ararat The ancient country of Urartu, an area in Eastern Turkey.

ancestor Literally, "father." This means a person that people are descended from.

Verse 22 This verse is at the end of the chapter in the printed Hebrew text.

temple A special building for worshiping God. God commanded the Jews to worship him at the temple in Jerusalem.

steps of Ahaz The steps of a special building that Hezekiah used like a clock. When the sun shone on the steps, the shadows showed what time of the day it was.

Verse 21 This verse is at the end of the chapter in the printed Hebrew text.

Sheol This is the place where all people go when they die. Usually this means the grave, but it can mean the place where our spirits go.

I am finished
    like the cloth a man rolls up
    and cuts from the loom.*
You finished my life in such a short time!
¹³ All night I cried loud like a lion.
    But my hopes were crushed
    like a lion eating bones.
You finished my life in such a short time!
¹⁴ I cried like a dove.
    I cried like a bird.
My eyes became tired,
    but I continued looking to the heavens.
My Master, I am so depressed.
    Promise to help me."
¹⁵ What can I say?
My Master told me what will happen.
And my Master will cause that to happen.
I have had these troubles in my soul.
So now I will be humble all my life.
¹⁶ My Master, use this hard time to make
    my spirit live again.
Help my spirit become strong and healthy.
Help me become well!
Help me live again!

¹⁷ Look! My troubles are gone!
I now have peace.
You love me very much.
You did not let me rot in the grave.
⌊You forgave all my sins.⌋
    You threw my sins far away.
¹⁸ Dead people don't sing praises to you.
People in Sheol* don't praise you.
Dead people don't trust you to help them.
    They go into a hole in the ground,
    ⌊and never speak again⌋.
¹⁹ People that are alive—
    like me today—
    are the people that praise you.
A father should tell his children
    that you can be trusted.
²⁰ ⌊So I say:⌋
"The Lord saved me.
So we will sing and play songs
    in the Lord's temple all our lives."

Messengers from Babylon

39 At that time, Merodach Baladan son of Baladan was king of Babylon. Merodach sent letters and a gift to Hezekiah. Merodach did this because he heard that Hezekiah had been sick. ²These things made Hezekiah very happy. So Hezekiah showed the men all the valuable things in his storehouses. Hezekiah showed them the silver, the gold, the spices, and the expensive perfumes. Hezekiah showed them the swords and shields used for war. Hezekiah showed them everything he had saved. Hezekiah showed them everything in his house and in his kingdom.

³Then Isaiah the prophet went to King Hezekiah and asked him, "What did these men say? Where did they come from?"

Hezekiah said, "These men came from a faraway country to see me! They came from Babylon."

⁴So Isaiah asked him, "What did they see in your house?"

Hezekiah said, "They saw everything in my palace.* I showed them all my wealth."

⁵Then Isaiah said this to Hezekiah: "Listen to the words from the Lord All-Powerful. ⁶'The time is coming when all the things in your house and all the things your ancestors* have saved until today will be carried away to Babylon. Nothing will be left!' The Lord All-Powerful said this. ⁷The Babylonians will take your sons—the sons that will come from you. Your sons will become officers* in the palace* of the king of Babylon."

⁸Hezekiah told Isaiah, "This message from the Lord is good." (Hezekiah said this because he thought, "There will be real peace and while I am king.")

Israel's Punishment Will End

40 Your God says,

"Comfort, comfort my people!
² Speak kindly to Jerusalem!
    Tell Jerusalem,
    'Your time of service is finished.
    You have paid the price for your sins.'"
The Lord punished Jerusalem—
    twice for every sin she did.

Lord Yah Or, "Yah Yahweh," a Hebrew name for God.
loom A machine used for making cloth.
Sheol This is the place where all people go when they die. Usually this means the grave, but it can mean the place where our spirits go.

palace A large house for the king and his family.
ancestors Literally, "fathers." This means a person's parents, grandparents, and all the people they are descended from.
officers Literally, "eunuchs." Sometimes their male sex organs were removed so they could not have children.

³ Listen, there is a person shouting!
"Prepare a way in the desert for the Lord!
Make the road in the desert level for our God!
⁴ Fill every valley.
   Make every mountain and hill flat.
Make the crooked roads straight.
   Make the rough ground smooth.
⁵ Then, the Glory of the Lord*
   will be revealed *(shown)*.
And together, all people
   will see the Lord's Glory.
Yes, the Lord himself said these things!"

⁶ A voice said,
   "Speak!"
So the man said,
   "What should I say?"
The voice said,
   "People ₍don't live forever;
   they₎ are all like grass.
      Their goodness is like a wildflower.
⁷ A powerful wind from the Lord
   blows on the grass,
   and the grass dies
      and the wildflower falls.

Yes, all people are like grass.
⁸ Grass dies and wildflowers fall.
But the word of our God continues forever."

Salvation: God's Good News

⁹ Zion,* you have good news to tell.
   Go up on a high mountain
      and shout the good news!
Jerusalem, you have good news to tell.
   Don't be afraid, speak loudly!

Tell this news to all of the cities of Judah:
   "Look, here is your God!
¹⁰ The Lord my Master
   is coming with power.
He will use his power to rule all the people.
The Lord will bring rewards for his people.
   He will have their payment with him.
¹¹ The Lord will lead his people
   like a shepherd leads sheep.

Glory of the Lord One of the forms God used when he appeared to people. It was like a bright shining light. See Ex. 40:34-36.
Zion The southeast part of the mountain Jerusalem is built on. Sometimes it means the people of God living in Jerusalem.

The Lord will use his arm *(power)*
   and gather his sheep together.
The Lord will pick up the little sheep
   and hold them in his arms.
Their mothers will walk beside him.

God Made the World; He Rules It

¹² Who measured the oceans
   in the palm of his hand?
Who used his hand to measure the sky?
Who used a bowl to measure all the dust
   of the earth?
Who used measuring scales to measure
   the mountains and hills?
   ₍It was the Lord₎!
¹³ No person told the Lord's Spirit
   what he should do.
No person told the Lord
   how to do the things he did.
¹⁴ Did the Lord ask for any person's help?
Did any person teach the Lord to be fair?
Did any person teach the Lord knowledge?
Did any person teach the Lord to be wise?
   ₍No! The Lord already knew these things₎.
¹⁵ Look, all the nations in the world are like
   one small drop in the bucket.
If the Lord took all the faraway nations,
   and put them on his weighing scales,
   they would be like small pieces of dust.
¹⁶ ₍All the trees in₎ Lebanon are not enough
   to burn for the Lord.
And all the animals in Lebanon
   are not enough to kill ₍for a sacrifice₎.
¹⁷ Compared to God,
   all the nations of the world are nothing.
Compared to God,
   all the nations are worth nothing at all.

People Can't Imagine What God Is Like

¹⁸ Can you compare God to anything? No!
   Can you make a picture of God? No!
¹⁹ But some people make statues
   from rock or wood,
   and they call them gods.
One worker makes a statue.
Then another worker covers it with gold
   and makes silver chains for it.
²⁰ And for the base,
   he chooses a special kind of wood,
   a kind of wood that will not rot.
Then he finds a good wood worker.
   And the worker makes a "god"
   that won't fall over.

²¹ Surely you know the truth, don't you?
Surely you have heard!
Surely someone told you long ago!
Surely you understand who made the earth!
²² ₓThe Lord is the true God!₎
He sits above the circle of the earth,
ₓand compared to him₎
people are like grasshoppers.
He rolled open the skies
like a piece of cloth.
He stretched the skies
like a tent to sit under.
²³ He makes rulers not important.
He makes the judges of this world
completely worthless.
²⁴ ₓThose rulers are like plants₎;
they are planted in the ground,
but before they can send their roots
into the ground,
God blows on the "plants,"
and they become dead and dry,
And the wind blows them away like straw.
²⁵ The Holy One *(God)* says:
"Can you compare me to anyone? No!
No one is equal to me.
²⁶ Look up to the skies.
Who created all those stars?
Who created all those 'armies' ₓin the sky₎?
Who knows every star by name?
ₓThe true God₎ is very strong and powerful,
so none of these stars is lost."
²⁷ Jacob, this is true!
Israel, you should believe this!
So why do you say:
"The Lord can't see the way I live.
God will not find me and punish me."
²⁸ Surely you have heard and know
that the Lord God is very wise,
People can't learn everything he knows.
The Lord does not become tired
and need to rest.
The Lord made all the faraway places
on earth.
The Lord lives forever.
²⁹ The Lord helps weak people to be strong.
He causes the people without power to
become powerful.
³⁰ Young men become tired and need to rest.
Even young boys stumble and fall.
³¹ But people that trust the Lord
become strong again
like eagles that grow new feathers.
These people run without becoming weak.
These people walk without becoming tired.

The Lord Is the Creator Who Lives Forever

41 The Lord says,
"Faraway countries, be quiet and come to me!
Nations be brave.
Come to me and speak.
We will meet together,
and we will decide who is right.
² ₓTell me the answers to these questions₎:
Who woke the man ₓthat is coming₎
from the east?
Goodness walks with him.
He uses his sword ₓand defeats nations₎—
they become like dust.
He uses his bow and conquers kings—
they run away like straw blown
by the wind.
³ He chases armies and is never hurt.
He goes places he has never been before.
⁴ Who caused ₓthese things to happen₎?
Who did this?
Who called all people from the beginning?
ₓI, the Lord, did these things₎!
I, the Lord, am the first.
I was here before the beginning.
And I will be here when all things
are finished.
⁵ All you faraway places,
look, and be afraid!
All you places far away on the earth,
shake with fear!
Come here ₓand listen to me₎!"
And they came.

⁶"Workers help each other. They encourage each other to be strong. ⁷One worker cuts ₓwood to make a statue₎. That person encourages the man that works with gold. Another worker uses a hammer and makes the metal smooth. Then that worker encourages the man at the anvil.* This last worker says, 'This work is good; the metal will not come off.' So he nails the statue to a base. The statue can't fall over. And it never moves!"

Only The Lord Can Save Us

⁸ₓThe Lord says₎:

"You, Israel, are my servant.
Jacob, I chose you.
You are from Abraham's family.
And I loved Abraham.
⁹ You were in a far away country,
but I reached out to you.
I called you from that faraway place.
I said, 'You are my servant.'
I chose you.
And I have not rejected you.

¹⁰ Don't worry, I am with you.
  Don't be afraid, I am your God.
  I will make you strong.
  I will help you.
  I will support you with my good right hand
¹¹ Look, some people are angry with you.
  But they will be shamed.
  Your enemies will be lost and disappear.
¹² You will look for the people
    that were against you,
    but you will not be able to find them.
  The people that fought against you
    will disappear completely.
¹³ I am the Lord your God.
  I am holding your right hand.
  And I tell you:
    Don't be afraid!
    I will help you.
¹⁴ Precious Judah, don't be afraid!
  My dear* people of Israel, don't be scared!
  I really will help you."

  The Lord himself said those things.

  The Holy One *(God)* of Israel,
    the One who saves you,
    said these things:
¹⁵ "Look, I have made you like
    a new threshing board.
  That tool has many sharp teeth,
  Farmers use it to crush the hulls
    so they will separate from the grain.
  You will trample *(walk on)* mountains
    and crush them.
  You will make the hills like those hulls.
¹⁶ You will throw them into the air,
    and the wind will blow them away
    and scatter them.
  Then you will be happy in the Lord.
  You will be very proud of the Holy One
    (God) of Israel."

¹⁷ "The poor and needy people look for water,
    but they can't find any.
  They are thirsty.
    Their tongues are very dry.
  I will answer their prayers.
  I will not leave them and let them die.
¹⁸ I will make rivers flow on dry hills.
  I will make springs of water flow
    through the valleys.

  I will change the desert into a lake
    filled with water.
  There will be springs of water
    in that dry land.
¹⁹ Trees will grow in the desert.
  There will be cedar trees, acacia trees,
    olive trees, cypress trees, fir trees,
    and pine trees.
²⁰ People will see these things,
    and they will know
    that the Lord's power did this.
  The people will see these things,
    and they will begin to understand.
    that the Holy One *(God)* of Israel
    did these things."

The Lord Challenges the False Gods

²¹The Lord, the king of Jacob, says, "Come, tell me your arguments. Show me your proof, ₍and we will decide the things that are right₎. ²²₍Your statues (false gods)₎ should come and tell us what is happening.

"What happened in the beginning? What will happen in the future? Tell us! We will listen closely. Then we will know what will happen next. ²³Tell us the things we should look for to know what will happen. Then we will believe that you really are gods. Do something! Do anything, good or bad! Then we will see that you are alive. And we will follow you.

²⁴"Look, you false gods are less than nothing! You can't do anything! Only a worthless person would want to worship you!"

The Lord Proves He Is the Only God

²⁵ "I woke a person in the north.*
  He is coming from the east
    where the sun rises.
  He worships my name.
  A man that makes pots walks on wet clay.
    In the same way, this special man will
    trample *(walk on)* kings."

²⁶ Who told us about this before it happened?
  We should call him God.*
  ₍Did one of your statues
    tell us these things₎?
  No! None of those statues
    told us anything.

Precious Judah ... dear Literally, "worm ... men." These are like Aramaic words meaning "scarlet ... silk: very expensive pieces of cloth."

person in the north This probably means Cyrus, a king of Persia. He ruled about 550-530 B.C.
God Literally, "the Good One."

Those statues did not say a word—
and those false gods can't hear the words
that you say.
²⁷ I, the Lord, was the first person to tell Zion*
about these things.
I sent a messenger to Jerusalem
with this message:
"Look, your people are coming back!"

²⁸ I looked at those false gods.
None of them were wise enough
to say anything.
I asked them questions,
and they did not say a word!
²⁹ All of those gods are less than nothing!
They can't do anything!
Those statues are absolutely worthless!

The Lord's Special Servant

42 "Look at my Servant!
I support him.
He is the one I chose.
And I am very pleased with him.
I put my Spirit in him.
He will judge the nations fairly.
² He will not speak loudly in the streets.
He will not cry out or yell.
³ ⌞He will be gentle.⌟
He will not break even a crushed reed.*
He will not put out even a weak flame.
He will judge fairly and find the truth.
⁴ He will not become weak or be crushed
until he brings justice to the world.
And people in faraway places
will trust his teachings."

The Lord Is Ruler and Maker of the World

⁵The Lord, the ⌞true⌟ God, said these things. (The Lord made the skies. The Lord spread the skies over the earth. He also made everything on the earth. The Lord breathes life into all people on earth. The Lord gives a spirit to every person that walks on the earth):

⁶ "I, the Lord, called you to do right.
I will hold your hand.
And I will protect you.
You will be the sign that shows
⌞I have⌟ an Agreement with the people.

You will be a light to shine for all people.
⁷ You will open the eyes of the blind people,
and they will be able to see.
Many people are in prison;
you will free those people.
Many people live in darkness;
you will lead them out of that prison."

⁸ "I am the Lord.
My name is Yahweh.
I will not give my glory to another.
I will not let statues *(false gods)*
take the praise that should be mine.
⁹ In the beginning,
I said some things would happen,
and those things happened!
And now, before it happens,
I am telling you about some things
that will happen in the future."

A Song of Praise to God

¹⁰ Sing a new song to the Lord.
all you people that are in faraway
countries,
all you people that sail on the seas,
all you animals in the oceans,
all you people in faraway places,
praise the Lord!
¹¹ Deserts and cities,
Fields of Kedar,* praise the Lord!
People living in Sela, sing for joy!
Sing from the top of your mountain.
¹² Give glory to the Lord.
Praise him all you people in faraway lands!
¹³ The Lord will go out like a strong soldier.
He will be like a man ready to fight a war.
He will become very excited.
He will cry out and shout loudly,
and he will defeat his enemies.

God Is Very Patient

¹⁴ "For a long time I have said nothing.
I controlled myself
and didn't say anything.
But now I will cry out
like a woman giving birth to a child.
I will breath very hard and loud.
¹⁵ I will destroy the hills and mountains.
I will dry up all the plants that grow there.
I will change rivers to dry land.
I will dry up pools of water.

Zion The southeast part of the mountain Jerusalem is built on. Sometimes it means the people of God living in Jerusalem.
reed A plant that grows near water.
Kedar A country east of Israel.

¹⁶ Then I will lead the blind people
in a way they never knew.
I will lead the blind people
to places they have never been before.
I will change darkness into light for them.
And I will make the rough ground smooth.
I will do the things I promised!
And I will not leave my people.
¹⁷ But some of the people
stopped following me.
Those people have statues
that are covered with gold.
They tell those statues,
'You are my gods.'
Those people trust their false gods.
But those people will be disappointed!"

Israel Refused to Listen to God

¹⁸ "You deaf people should hear me!
You blind people should look and see me!
¹⁹ In all the world, my servant*
is the most blind!
The messenger I send ₍to the world₎
is the most deaf.
The person I own
—the servant of the Lord—
is the most blind.
²⁰ My servant sees what he should do,
but he does not obey me.
He can hear with his ears,
but he refuses to listen to me."
²¹ The Lord wants his servant to be good.
The Lord wants him to honor
his wonderful teachings.*
²² But look at the people.
Other people have defeated them
and have stolen things from them.
All the young men are afraid.
They are locked in the prisons.
People have taken their money from them.
And there is no person to save them.
Other people took their money.
And there was no person to say,
"Give it back!"

²³Did any of you people listen to ₍God's₎ words? No! But you should listen very closely to his words ₍and think about what happened₎. ²⁴Who let people take the wealth from Jacob and Israel?

my servant Here this probably means the people of Israel.
verse 21 Or, "The Lord will make his teachings very wonderful. He will do this because he is good."

The Lord allowed them to do this! We sinned against the Lord. So the Lord allowed people to take away our wealth. The people of Israel did not want to live the way the Lord wanted. The people of Israel did not listen to his teaching. ²⁵So the Lord became angry at them. The Lord caused powerful wars against them. It was like the people of Israel had fire all around them. But they did not know what was happening. It was like they were burning. But they did not try to understand the things that were happening.

God Is Always with His People

43 Jacob, the Lord made you! Israel, the Lord made you! And now the Lord says, "Don't be afraid! I saved you. I named you. You are mine. ²When you have troubles, I am with you. When you cross rivers, you will not be hurt. When you walk through fire, you will not be burned; the flames will not hurt you. ³Why? Because I, the Lord, am your God. I, the Holy One of Israel, am your Savior. I gave Egypt to pay for you. I gave Ethiopia and Seba to make you mine. ⁴You are very important to me, so I will honor you. I love you, and I will give all people and nations so you can live."

God Will Bring His Children Home

⁵"So don't be afraid! I am with you. I will gather your children and bring them to you. I will gather them from the east and from the west. ⁶I will tell the north: Give my people to me! I will tell the south: Don't keep my people in prison! Bring my sons and daughters to me from the faraway places! ⁷Bring to me all the people that are mine—the people that have my name. I made those people for myself. I made those people, and they are mine."

Israel Is God's Witness to the World

⁸"Bring out the people that have eyes but are blind. Bring out the people that have ears but are deaf.* ⁹All people and all nations should also be gathered together. Maybe ₍one of their false gods₎ wants to tell about what happened in the beginning. They should bring their witnesses. The witnesses should speak the truth. This will show they are right."

¹⁰The Lord says, "You people are my witnesses. You are the servant that I chose. I chose you so you would help people to believe me. I chose you so you would understand that 'I Am He'—₍I am the true God₎. There was no God

before me, and there will be no God after me. ¹¹"I myself am the Lord. And there is no other Savior—I am the only One. ¹²I am the One who spoke to you. I saved you. I told you those things. It was not some stranger that was with you. You are my witnesses, and I am God." (The Lord himself said these things.) ¹³"I have always been God. When I do something, no person can change what I have done. And no person can save people from my power."

¹⁴The Lord, the Holy One of Israel, saves you. And the Lord says, "I will send armies to Babylon for you. Many people will be captured. Those people, the Chaldeans, will be taken away in their own boats. (The Chaldeans are very proud of those boats.) ¹⁵I am the Lord your Holy One. I made Israel. I am your king."

God Will Save His People Again

¹⁶The Lord will make roads through the sea. Even through rough waters he will make a path for his people. And the Lord says, ¹⁷"The people that fight against me with their chariots,* horses, and armies will be defeated. They will never rise again. They will be destroyed. They will be stopped like the flame of a candle* is stopped. ¹⁸So don't remember the things that happened in the beginning. Don't think about the things that happened a long time ago. ¹⁹Why? Because I will do new things! Now you will grow like a new plant. Surely you know this is true. I really will make a road in the desert. I really will make rivers in the dry land. ²⁰Even the wild animals will be thankful to me. The large animals and birds will honor me. They will honor me when I put water in the desert. They will honor me when I make rivers in the dry land. I will do this to give water to my people—the people I chose. ²¹These are the people I made. And these people will sing songs to praise me.

²²"Jacob, you did not pray to me. Why? Because you, Israel, have become tired of me. ²³You have not brought your sheep as sacrifices* to me. You have not honored me. You have not given sacrifices to me. I did not force you to give sacrifices to me. I did not force you to burn incense* until you became tired. ²⁴So you did not use your money to buy things to honor me. But you did force me to be like your slave. You sinned until the bad things you did made me very tired.

²⁵"I, I am the One who wipes away all your sins. I do this to please myself. I will not remember your sins. ²⁶But you should remember me. We should meet together and decide what is right. You should tell the things you have done and show you are right. ²⁷Your first father sinned. And your lawyers have done things against me. ²⁸I will make your holy rulers not holy. I will cause Jacob to be completely mine.* Bad things will happen to Israel."

The Lord Is the Only God

44 "Jacob, you are my servant. Listen to me! Israel, I chose you. Hear the things I say! ²I am the Lord, and I made you. I am the One who made you to be what you are. I have helped you since the time you were in your mother's body. Jacob, my servant, don't be afraid. Jeshurun,* I chose you.

³"I will pour water for thirsty people. I will make streams flow on dry land. I will pour my Spirit on your children—it will be like a stream of water flowing over your family. ⁴They will grow among the people in the world. They will be like trees growing beside streams of water.

⁵"One person will say, 'I belong to the Lord.' Another person will use the name 'Jacob.' Another person will sign his name 'I am the Lord's.' And another person will use the name 'Israel.'"

⁶The Lord is the king of Israel. The Lord All-Powerful saves Israel. The Lord says, "I am the only God. There are no other gods. I am the Beginning and the End. ⁷There is no other God like me. If there is, then that god should speak now. That god should come and show proof that he is like me. That god should tell me what has happened since the time I made these people that continue forever. That god should give signs to show that he knows what will happen in the future. ⁸Don't be afraid! Don't worry! I have always told you what will happen. You are my

---

chariots Small wagons used for war.
candle Literally, "lamp." These were small clay bowls filled with oil. A string or strip of cloth was placed in the bowl and lit to produce light.
sacrifices Gifts to God. Sometimes these were special kinds of animals that were killed and burned on an altar.
incense A kind of spice that smells good when it is burned. It was burned as a gift to God.
cause Jacob to be completely mine This means that only God can have this special thing. He gets it, or it must die so no one else will.
Jeshurun Another name for Israel. It means "good" or "honest."

witnesses. There is no other God—I am the only One. There is no other 'Rock*'—I know I am the only One."

False Gods Are Useless

⁹Some people make statues *(false gods)*—but they are worthless. People love those statues—but the statues are useless. Those people are the witnesses of the statues—but they can't see. They know nothing—they don't know enough to be ashamed ₍of the things they do₎.

¹⁰Who made these false gods? Who made these useless statues? ¹¹Workers made those gods! And all those workers are people—₍not gods₎. If all of those people would come together ₍and discuss these things₎, then they would all be ashamed and afraid.

¹²One worker uses his tools to heat iron over hot coals. This man uses his hammer to beat the metal, and the metal becomes a statue. This man uses his own powerful arms. But when the man becomes hungry, he loses his power. If the man does not drink water, he becomes weak.

¹³Another worker uses his stringline* and compass* to draw lines on the wood. ₍This shows where he should cut₎. Then the man uses his chisels* and cuts a statue from the wood. He uses his calipers* to measure the statue. This way, the worker makes the wood look exactly like a man. And this statue of a man does nothing but sit in the house.

¹⁴A man cuts down cedar, cypress, or maybe oak trees. (That man did not make the trees grow—those trees grew by their own power in the forest. If a man plants a pine tree, the rain makes the tree grow.) ¹⁵Then that man uses the tree to burn in his fire. The man cuts the tree into small pieces of wood. And he uses the wood to cook and keep him warm. The man starts a fire with some of the wood and bakes his bread. But the man still uses part of that wood to make a god— and the man worships that god! That god is a statue that the man made—but the man bows down before the statue! ¹⁶The man burns half of the wood in the fire. The man uses the fire to cook his meat and eats the meat until he is full. The man burns the wood to keep himself warm. The man says, "Good! Now I am warm, and I can see because there is light from the fire." ¹⁷But a little wood is left, so the man makes a statue from that wood and calls it his god. He bows down before this god and worships it. The man prays to the god and says, "You are my god, save me!"

¹⁸Those people don't know what they are doing. They don't understand. It is like their eyes are covered so they can't see. Their hearts *(minds)* don't try to understand. ¹⁹Those people have not thought about these things. The people don't understand, so they have never thought to themselves, "I burned half of the wood in the fire. I used the hot coals to bake my bread and cook my meat. Then I ate the meat. And I used the wood that was left to make this terrible thing. I am worshiping a block of wood!"

²⁰That man does not know what he is doing. He is confused, so his heart leads him the wrong way. That man can't save himself. And he can't see that he is doing wrong. That man will not say, "This statue I am holding is a false god."

The Lord, the True God, Helps Israel

²¹ "Jacob, remember these things!
    Israel, remember that you are my servant.
I made you.
    You are my servant.
    So Israel, don't forget me.
²² Your sins were like a big cloud.
    But I wiped away those sins.
Your sins are gone,
    like a cloud that disappeared into the air.
I rescued and protected you,
    so come back to me!"

²³ The skies are happy because the Lord did
    great things.
    The earth is happy, even deep down under
      the earth!
The mountains sing with thanks to God.
    All the trees in the forest are happy!
Why? Because the Lord saved Jacob.
    The Lord did great things for Israel.
²⁴ The Lord made you what you are.
    The Lord did this while you
      were still in your mother's body.
The Lord says,
"I, the Lord, made everything!
    I put the skies there myself!
    I spread the earth before me."

Rock A name for God. It shows he is a strong place of safety.
stringline In ancient times, this was a piece of string with wet paint on it. This was used to make straight lines on wood or stone.
compass A tool used to draw circles and copy measurements.
chisels Sharp tools used to carve wood or stone.
calipers A special measuring tool, like a compass.

²⁵False prophets* tell lies, but the Lord shows their lies are false. The Lord makes foolish people of the men that do magic. The Lord confuses even wise men. They think they know much, but the Lord makes them look foolish. ²⁶The Lord sends his servants to tell messages to the people. And the Lord makes those messages true. The Lord sends messengers to tell the people the things they should do. And the Lord shows their advice is good.

God Chooses Cyrus to Rebuild Judah

The Lord says to Jerusalem,
"People will live in you again!"
The Lord says to the cities of Judah,
"You will be built again!"
The Lord says to the cities
that were destroyed,
"I will make you cities again!"
²⁷ The Lord tells the deep waters,
"Become dry!
I will make your streams become dry!"
²⁸ The Lord says to Cyrus,*
"You are my shepherd.
You will do the things I want.
You will say to Jerusalem,
'You will be built again!'
You will tell the temple,*
'Your foundations will be built again!'"

God Chooses Cyrus to Make Israel Free

45 These are the things the Lord says to Cyrus,* his chosen king:*

"I will hold Cyrus's right hand.
I will help him take power away from kings.
City gates will not stop Cyrus.
I will open the city gates,
and Cyrus will go in."

² "⌊Cyrus, your armies will march,⌋
and I will go in front of you.
I will make the mountains flat.
I will break the city gates of bronze.
I will cut the iron bars on the gates.

³ I will give you the wealth
that is saved in darkness.
I will give you those hidden riches.
I will do this so that you will know
that I am the Lord.
I am the God of Israel,
And I am calling you by name!
⁴ I do these things for my servant, Jacob.
I do these things for my chosen people, Israel.
⌊Cyrus,⌋ I am calling you by name.
You don't know me,
but I am calling you by name.
⁵ I am the Lord!
I am the only God.
There is no other God.
I put your clothes on you,*
but still you don't know me.
⁶ I do these things so all people will know
that I am the only God.
From the east to the west
people will know that I am the Lord,
and there is no other God.
⁷ I made the light,
and I made darkness.
I make peace,
and I make troubles.
I am the Lord—
and I do all these things.

⁸ "May the clouds in the skies above
drop goodness on the earth like rain!
May the earth open
and let salvation grow!
And may goodness grow with it!
I, the Lord, made him.*

God Controls His Creation

⁹"Look at these people! They are arguing with the One who made them. Look at them argue with me! They are like pieces of clay from a broken pot. A man uses soft, wet clay to make a pot. And the clay does not ask, 'Man, what are you doing?' Things that are made don't have the power to question the one who makes them. ⌊People are like this clay.⌋ ¹⁰A father gives life to his children. And the children can't ask, 'Why are you giving me life?' The children can't question their mother and ask, 'Why are you giving birth to me?'"

¹¹The Lord God is the Holy One of Israel. He made Israel. And the Lord says,

---

false prophets People that lie, saying they received a special message from God.
Cyrus A king of Persia. He ruled about 550-530 B.C.
temple A special building for worshiping God. God commanded the Jews to worship him at the temple in Jerusalem.

chosen king Literally, "messiah, the anointed one."
I put ... you This also means "I made you strong."

"You asked me to show you a sign, my sons.
You commanded me to show you
the things I have done.
¹² ⌊So, look⌋!
I made the earth.
And I made all the people living on it.
I used my own hands
and made the skies.
And I command all the armies in the sky.*
¹³ I gave Cyrus his power
so he would do good things.*
And I will make his work easy.
Cyrus will build my city again.
And he will make my people free.
Cyrus will not sell my people to me.
I will not have to pay him
to do these things.
The people will be freed,
and the cost to me will be nothing."
The Lord, All-Powerful, said these things.
¹⁴ The Lord says,
"Egypt and Ethiopia are rich,
but Israel, you will get those riches.
The tall people from Seba will be yours.
They will walk behind you
with chains around their necks.
They will bow down before you.
And they will pray to you."

⌊Israel⌋, God is with you.
And there is no other God.
¹⁵ God, you are the God people can't see.
You are the Savior of Israel.
¹⁶ Many people make false gods.
But those people will be disappointed.
All of those people will go away ashamed.
¹⁷ But Israel will be saved by the Lord.
That salvation will continue forever.
Never, never again will Israel be shamed.
¹⁸ The Lord is God.
He made the skies and the earth.
The Lord put the earth in its place.
The Lord did not want the earth
to be empty when he made it.
He created it to be lived on!

"I am the Lord.
There is no other God.
¹⁹ I did not speak in secret.
I have spoken freely.
I did not hide my words
in a dark place of the world.
I did not tell the people of Jacob
to look for me in empty places.
I am the Lord, and I speak the truth.
I say things that are true."

The Lord Proves He Is the Only God

²⁰"You people have escaped from other nations. So gather together and come before me. (These people carry statues of false gods. These people pray to those useless gods. But the people don't know what they are doing. ²¹Tell these people to come to me. Let them talk about these things together.)

"Who told you about the things that happened a long time ago? Who has continued to tell you these things since long, long ago? I, the Lord, am the One who said these things. I am the only God. Is there another God like me? Is there another good God? Is there another God who saves his people? No! There is no other God! ²²All you people in faraway places should ⌊stop following those false gods⌋. You should follow me and be saved. I am God. There is no other God. I am the only God.

²³"I will make a promise by my own power. And if I promise to do something, then that promise is a command. And if I command something to happen, that thing happens. And I promise that every person will bow before me *(God)*. Every person will promise ⌊to follow me⌋. ²⁴People will say, 'Goodness and power come only from the Lord.'"

Some people are angry at the Lord. But the Lord's witnesses will come ⌊and tell about the things the Lord has done⌋. So those angry people will be ashamed. ²⁵The Lord will help the people of Israel do good, and the people will be very proud of their God.

False Gods Are Useless

46 Bel* and Nebo,* will bow down before me. Those false gods are only statues. Men put those statues on the backs of animals—those statues are only heavy burdens that must be

---

him This probably means Cyrus. Cyrus was a king of Persia. Cyrus lived about 150 years after Isaiah died.
armies in the sky Sometimes this means the angels, and sometimes it means the stars.
I gave ... things This might also mean "I did what was right when I woke him."

Bel A false god.
Nebo A false god.

carried. The false gods do nothing but make people tired. ²Those false gods will all bow down—they will all fall. Those false gods can't escape—they will all be carried away like prisoners.

³"Family of Jacob, listen to me! All you people from Israel that are still alive, listen! I have been carrying you. I have carried you since the time you were in your mother's body. ⁴I carried you when you were born, and I will carry you when you become old. Your hair will become gray, and I will still carry you, because I made you. I will continue to carry you and I will save you.

⁵"Can you compare me to anyone? No! No person is equal to me. You can't understand everything about me. There is nothing like me. ⁶Some people are rich with gold and silver. Gold falls from their purses, and they weigh their silver on scales. Those people pay an artist to make a false god from wood. Then those people bow down and worship that false god. ⁷Those people put their false god on their shoulders and carry it. That false god is useless—people have to carry it! People set the statue on the ground; and that false god can't move. That false god never walks away from its place. People can yell at it, but it will not answer. That false god is only a statue—it can't save people from their troubles.

⁸"You people have sinned. You should think about these things again. Remember these things and be strong. ⁹Remember the things that happened long ago. Remember that I am God. There is no other God. Those false gods are not like me.

¹⁰"In the beginning, I told you about the things that will happen in the end. A long time ago, I told you things that had not yet happened. When I plan something—that thing happens. I do the things I want to do. ¹¹And I am calling a man from the east. That man will be like an eagle. He will come from a faraway country, and he will do the things I decide to do. I am telling you that I will do this, and I will do it. I made him, and I will bring him!

¹²"Some of you think that you have great power—but you don't do good things. Listen to me! ¹³I will do good things! Soon, I will save ⌊my people⌋. I will bring salvation to Zion* and to my wonderful Israel."

God's Message to Babylon

47 "Fall down in the dirt and sit there!
Virgin daughter of the Chaldeans,*
sit on the ground!
You are not the ruler now!
People will not think that you are
a tender, delicate young lady anymore.
² ⌊Now you must work very hard.⌋
Take off your nice skirts.
You must get the mill stones
and grind the grain to make flour.
Raise your skirts until men can see your legs,
and cross the rivers.*
Leave your country!
³ Men will see your body,
and men will use you for sex.
I will make you pay
for the bad things you did.
And no man will come to help you."

⁴ "⌊My people say,⌋
'God saves us.
His name is:
The Lord All-Powerful,
The Holy One of Israel.'"

⁵ "So Babylon, sit there and be quiet.
Daughter of the Chaldeans,*
go into the darkness.
Why? Because you will no longer be
'The Queen of the Kingdoms.'"

⁶ "I was angry at my people.
Those people belong to me,
but I was angry,
so I made them not important.
I gave them to you,
and you punished them.
You showed no mercy to them.
You made even the old people work hard.
⁷ You said,
'I will live forever.
I will always be The Queen.'
You didn't even notice the bad things
you did to those people.
You didn't think about what would happen.

Zion The southeast part of the mountain Jerusalem is built on. Sometimes it means the people of God living in Jerusalem.

daughter of the Chaldeans This is another name for the city Babylon.

rivers The Tigris and Euphrates Rivers. Babylon was between these two rivers.

daughter of the Chaldeans This is another name for the city Babylon.

⁸ So now, 'nice lady' listen to me!
   You feel safe and you tell yourself,
     'I am the only important person.
   No one else is important like me.
   I will never be a widow.
   I will always have children.'
⁹ These two things will happen to you:
   First, you will lose your children.
   And then you will lose your husband.
   Yes, these things will really happen to you.
   And all of your magic
     and all of your powerful tricks
     will not save you.
¹⁰ You do bad things, but still you feel safe.
   You think to yourself,
     'No one sees the wrong things I do.'
   You think that your wisdom and knowledge
     will save you.
   You think to yourself,
     'I am the only one.
     No one is important like me.'"
¹¹ "But troubles will come to you.
     You don't know when it will happen,
       but disaster is coming.
   You will not be able to do anything
     to stop those troubles.
   You will be destroyed so quickly
     that you won't know what happened!
¹² You worked hard all your life
     learning tricks and magic.
   So, start using your tricks and magic!
   Maybe those tricks will help you.
   Maybe you will be able to scare someone.
¹³ You have many, many advisers.
   Are you tired of the advice they give you?
   Then send out your men that read the stars.
   They are able to tell when the month starts.
   So maybe they can tell you
     when your troubles will come.
¹⁴ "But those men will not even be able
     to save themselves.
   They will burn like straw.
   They will burn so fast that
     there will be no coals left
     to cook bread with.
   There will be no fire left to sit by.
¹⁵ That will happen to everything
     that you worked so hard for.
   The people you did business with
     all your life will leave you.
   Every person will go his own way.
   And there will be no one left to save you."

God Rules His World

48 The Lord says,
   "Family of Jacob, listen to me!
   You people call yourself 'Israel.'
   You are from Judah's family.
   You use the Lord's name to make promises.
   You praise the God of Israel.
   But you are not honest and sincere
     when you do these things.
² Yes, they are citizens of the Holy City.
   They depend on the God of Israel.
   The Lord All-Powerful is his Name.
³ "Long ago I told you about the things
     that would happen.
   I told you about those things.
   And then suddenly, I made them happen.
⁴ I did that because I knew you were stubborn.
     ⌊You refused to believe anything I said⌋.
   You were very stubborn—
     like iron ⌊that does not bend⌋
     and as hard as bronze.
⁵ So, a long time ago I told you
     what would happen.
   I told you about those things
     a long time before they happened.
   I did this so that you could not say,
     'We did this with our own power.'
   I did this so that you could not say,
     'Our idols, our statues,
       made these things happen.'"

God Punishes Israel to Make Them Pure

⁶ "You saw and heard what happened.
   So you should tell the news to
     other people.
   Now I will tell you about new things—
     things that you don't know yet.
⁷ These are not things that happened long ago.
   These are things that are happening now.
   You haven't heard about these things
     before today.
   So you can't say,
     'We already knew that.'
⁸ But even if I tell you
     what will happen in the future,
     you will still refuse to listen to me.
   You will learn nothing.
   You never listened to anything I told you.
   I have known since the beginning
     that you would be against me.
   You have rebelled against me
     from the time you were born.

⁹ But, I will be patient.
   I will do this for myself.
   People will praise me for not getting angry
   and destroying you.
   You will praise me for waiting.
¹⁰ Look, I will make you pure.
   People use a hot fire to make silver pure.
   But I will make you pure
   by giving you troubles.
¹¹ I will do this for myself—for me!
   You will not treat me
   like I am not important!
   I will not let some false god
   take my glory and praise!
¹² Jacob, listen to me!
   Israel, I called you to be my people.
   So listen to me!
   I am the Beginning!
   And I am the End!
¹³ I made the earth with my own hands.
   My right hand made the sky.
   And if I call them,
   they will come together before me.
¹⁴ "All of you, come here
   and listen to me!
   Did any of the false gods
   say these things would happen?
   No!"

   The Lord loves Israel.
   And the Lord will do anything he wants
   to Babylon and to the Chaldeans.
¹⁵ ⌊The Lord says,⌋
   "I, I told you I would call him.*
   And I will bring him!
   I will make him succeed!
¹⁶ Come here and listen to me!
   I was there when Babylon began as a nation.
   And from the beginning, I spoke clearly,
   so that people could know what I said."

⌊Then Isaiah said,⌋ "Now, the Lord my Master sends me and his Spirit ⌊to tell you these things⌋. ¹⁷The Lord, the Savior, the Holy One of Israel, says,

   I am the Lord your God.
   I teach you to do good things.
   I lead you in the way you should go.
¹⁸ If you had obeyed me,
   then peace would have come to you
   like a full flowing river.

   Good things would have come to you
   again and again, like the waves of the sea.
¹⁹ If you had obeyed me,
   then you would have had many children.
   They would have been
   like the many grains of sand.
   If you had obeyed me,
   then you would not have been destroyed.
   You would have continued with me."

²⁰ My people, leave Babylon!
   My people, run from the Chaldeans!
   Tell this news with joy to the people!
   Spread this news to the faraway places
   on earth!
   Tell the people,
   "The Lord rescued his servant Jacob!
²¹ The Lord led his people through the desert,
   and they never became thirsty!
   Why? Because he made water
   flow from a rock for his people!
   He split the rock,
   and water flowed out!"
²² But the Lord says,
   "There is no peace for evil people!"

God Calls His Special Servant

49 All you people in faraway places,
   listen to me!
   Listen all of you people living on earth!
   The Lord called me to serve him
   before I was born, .
   The Lord called my name
   while I was still in my mother's body.
² ⌊The Lord uses me to speak for him.⌋
   He uses me like a sharp sword,
   ⌊But he also protects me,⌋
   hiding me in his hand.
   The Lord uses me like a sharp arrow,
   but he also hides me in his arrow bag.

³ ⌊The Lord⌋ told me,
   "Israel, you are my servant.
   I will do wonderful things with you."

⁴ I said,
   "I worked hard for nothing.
   I wore myself out,
   but I did nothing useful.
   I used all my power,
   but I did not really do anything.

---

him This is probably talking about Cyrus, a king of Persia that lived about 150 years after Isaiah died.

him This is probably talking about Cyrus, a king of Persia that lived about 150 years after Isaiah died.

So, the Lord must decide
what to do with me.
God must decide my reward.
5 The Lord made me in my mother's body
so I could be his servant,
and lead Jacob and Israel back to him.
The Lord will honor me.
I will get my strength from my God."

The Lord told me,
6 "You are a very important servant to me.
The people of Israel are prisoners,
but they will be brought back to me.
Jacob's family groups will come back to me.
But, you have another job;
it is even more important than this!
I will make you a light for all nations.
You will be my way to save all the people
on earth."

7 The Lord, the Holy One of Israel,
protects Israel.
And the Lord says,
"My Servant is humble.
He serves rulers.
But people hate him.
But, kings will see him,
and stand ₍to honor him₎.
Great leaders will bow down to him."

This will happen because the Lord,
the Holy One of Israel, wants it.
And the Lord can be trusted.
He is the One who chose you.

The Day of Salvation

8 The Lord says,
"There will be a special time
when I show my kindness.
At that time I will answer your prayers.
There will be a special day
when I save you.
At that time I will help you.
I will protect you.
And you will be the proof that I have
an Agreement with the people.
The country is destroyed now,
but you will give that land back
to the people who own it.
9 You will tell the prisoners,
'Come out of your prison!'
You will tell the people that are in darkness,
'Come out of the dark!'
The people will eat while traveling.
They will have food even on empty hills.

10 The people will not be hungry.
They will not be thirsty.
The hot sun and wind will not hurt them.
Why? Because God comforts them
and God will lead them.
He will lead them near springs of water.

11 "I will make a road for my people.
The mountains will be made flat,
and the low roads will be raised.

12 "Look! People are coming to me
from faraway places.
People are coming to me
from the north and from the west.
People are coming to me
from Aswan in Egypt."

13 Heavens and Earth, be happy!
Mountains, shout with joy!
Why? Because the Lord comforts his people.
The Lord is good to his poor people.

Zion, The Abandoned Woman

14 But now Zion* says,
"The Lord left me.
My Master forgot me."
15 ₍But I say₎,
"Can a woman forget her baby? No!
Can a woman forget the child
that came from her body?
No! A woman can't forget her children.
And I *(the Lord)* can't forget you.
16 Look, I have written your name on my hand.
I always think about you!
17 Your children will come back to you.
People defeated you,
but those people will leave you alone."

Israel's People Return

18 Look up! Look all around you!
All of your children are gathering together
and coming to you.

The Lord says,
"On my life, I promise you this:
Your children will be like jewels
that you tie around your neck.
Your children will be like the necklace
that a bride wears.

Zion The southeast part of the mountain Jerusalem is built on. Sometimes it means the people of God living in Jerusalem.

¹⁹ You are destroyed and defeated now.
   Your land is useless.
   But after a short time, you will have many,
      many people in your land.
   And the people that destroyed you
      will be far, far away.
²⁰ You were sad for the children you lost,
   but those children will tell you,
      'This place is too small!
      Give us a bigger place to live!'
²¹ Then you will say to yourself,
   'Who gave me all these children?
      This is very good!
   I was sad and lonely.
   I was defeated and away from my people.
   So who gave me these children?
   Look, I was left alone.
   Where did all these children come from?'"

²² The Lord my Master says,
   "Look, I will wave my hand to the nations.
   I will raise my flag for all people to see.
   Then they will bring your children to you.
   Those people will carry your children
      on their shoulders,
      and they will hold them in their arms.
²³ Kings will be teachers to your children.
   Kings' daughters will care for them.
   Those kings and their daughters
      will bow down to you.
   They will kiss the dirt at your feet.
   Then you will know
      that I am the Lord.
   Then you will know
      that any person who trusts in me
      will not be disappointed."

²⁴ When a strong soldier wins wealth in war,
      you can't take that wealth from him.
   When a powerful soldier guards a prisoner,
      that prisoner can't escape.

²⁵ But the Lord says,
   "The prisoners will escape.
   Someone will take those prisoners
      away from the strong soldier.
   ⌊How will this happen?⌋
   I will fight your fights.
   I will save your children.
²⁶ Those people hurt you.
   But I will force those people
      to eat their own bodies.
   Their own blood will be
      the wine that makes them drunk.
   Then every person will know that
      the Lord saved you.

   All people will know that
      the Powerful One of Jacob saved you."

Israel Was Punished Because the People Sinned

50 The Lord says,
   "⌊People of Israel, you say that I divorced
      your mother, Jerusalem.⌋
   But where is the legal paper
      that proves I divorced her?
   My children, did I owe money to someone?
      Did I sell you to pay a debt?
   No! I gave you away
      because of the bad things you did.
   I sent your mother *(Jerusalem)* away
      because of the bad things she did.
² I came home and found no one there.
   I called and called,
      but no one answered.
   Do you think I am not able to save you?
   I have the power to save you
      from all of your troubles.
   Look, if I command the sea to become dry,
      then it will become dry!
   The fish will die without water,
      and their bodies will rot.
³ I can make the skies dark.
   I can cover the skies in darkness
      as black as the clothes of sadness."

God's Servant Truly Depends on God

⁴The Lord my Master gave me the ability to teach. So now I teach these sad people. Every morning he wakes me and teaches me like a student. ⁵The Lord my Master helps me learn, and I have not turned against him. I will not stop following him. ⁶I will let those people beat me. I will let them pull the hair from my beard. I will not hide my face when they say bad things to me and spit at me. ⁷The Lord my Master will help me. So the bad things they say will not hurt me. I will be strong. I know I will not be disappointed.

⁸The Lord is with me. He shows I am innocent. So no person will be able to show I am guilty. If someone wants to try to prove I am wrong, that person should come to me, and we will have a trial. ⁹But look, the Lord my Master helps me. So no person can show me to be evil. All those people will become like worthless old clothes. Moths will eat them.

¹⁰The people that respect the Lord also listen to his servant. That servant lives completely trusting in God without knowing what will happen. He truly trusts in the Lord's name, and that servant depends on his God.

¹¹"Look, ₗyou people want to live your own waysⱼ. You light your own fires and torches *(lights)*. So, ₗlive your own wayⱼ. But, you will be punished! You will fall into your fires and torches and you will be burned. I will make that happen."

Israel Should Be Like Abraham

51 "Some of you people try hard to live good lives. You go to the Lord for help. Listen to me. You should look at Abraham your father. He is the rock you were cut from. ²Abraham is your father, and you should look at him. You should look at Sarah—the woman that gave birth to you. Abraham was alone when I called him. Then I blessed him, and he began a great family. Many, many people came from him."

³ₗIn the same way,ⱼ the Lord will bless Zion.* The Lord will feel sorry for her and her people, and he will do a great thing for her. The Lord will change the desert. The desert will become a garden like the garden of Eden. That land was empty, but it will become like the Lord's Garden. People there will be very, very happy. People there will show their joy. They will sing songs about thanks and victory.

⁴ "My people, listen to me!
My decisions will be like lights
showing people how to live.
⁵ I will soon show I am fair.
I will soon save you.
I will use my power and judge all nations.
All the faraway places are waiting for me.
They wait for my power to help them.
⁶ Look up to the heavens!
Look around you at the earth below!
The skies will disappear
like clouds of smoke.
The earth will become
like worthless old clothes.
The people on earth will die,
but my Salvation will continue forever.
My goodness will never end.
⁷ You people that understand goodness
should listen to me.
You people that follow my teachings
should hear the things I say.
Don't be afraid of evil people.
Don't be afraid of the bad things
that they say to you.
⁸ Why? Because they will be like old clothes.
Moths will eat them.
They will be like wood.
Worms will eat them.
But my goodness will continue forever.
My salvation will continue
forever and ever."

God's Own Power Will Save His People

⁹ Arm *(power)* of the Lord, wake up!
Wake up! Be strong!
Use your strength
like you did a long time ago,
like you have from ancient times.
You are the power that defeated Rahab.*
You defeated the Dragon.
¹⁰ You caused the sea to become dry!
You dried the waters of the great deep!
You made the deepest parts of the sea
into a road.
Your people crossed over that road
and were saved.
¹¹ The Lord will save his people.
They will return to Zion* with joy.
They will be very, very happy.
Their happiness will be like
a crown on their heads forever.
They will be singing with joy.
All sadness will be gone far away.

¹² The Lord says,
"I am the One who comforts you.
So why should you be afraid of people?
They are only people that live and die.
They are only humans—
they die the same as grass."
¹³ The Lord made you.
With his power he made the earth!
And with his power he spread the skies
over the earth!
But you forget him and his power.
So you are always afraid of angry men
that hurt you.
Those men planned to destroy you.
But where are they now?
ₗThey are all goneⱼ!

Zion The southeast part of the mountain Jerusalem is built on. Sometimes it means the people of God living in Jerusalem.

Rahab ... Dragon. This is Rahab the great sea monster. Some ancient stories tell about Rahab fighting with God.

¹⁴ People in prison will soon be made free.
Those people will not die and rot in prison.
Those people will have enough food.
¹⁵ "I, the Lord, am your God.
I stir up the sea and make the waves."
(The Lord All-Powerful is his name.)

¹⁶"My servant, I will give you the words I want you to say. And I will cover you with my hands and protect you. I will use you to make the new heaven and earth. I will use you to tell Israel, 'You are my people.'"

God Punished Israel

¹⁷ Wake up! Wake up!
Jerusalem, get up!
The Lord was very angry at you.
So you were punished.
[This punishment was like] a cup of poison
you had to drink.
And you drank it.

¹⁸Jerusalem had many people, but none of those people became leaders for her. None of the children she raised became guides to lead her. ¹⁹Troubles came to Jerusalem in groups of two; stealing and breaking, great hunger and fighting. No person helped you when you were suffering. No person was kind to you. ²⁰Your people became weak. They fell on the ground and lay there. Those people were lying on every street corner. They were like animals caught in a net. They were punished from the Lord's anger until they could not accept any more punishment. When God said he would give them more punishment, they became very weak.

²¹Listen to me, poor Jerusalem. You are [weak like] a drunk person, but you are not drunk from wine. [You are weak from that "cup of poison."]

²²Your God and Master, the Lord, will fight for his people. He says to you, "Look, I am taking this 'cup of poison' *(punishment)* away from you. I am taking my anger away from you. You will not be punished by my anger any more. ²³I will now use my anger to punish the people that hurt you. Those people tried to kill you. They told you, 'Bow down before us, and we will walk on you!' They forced you to bow down before them. And then they walked on your back like dirt. You were like a road for them to walk on."

Israel Will Be Saved

52 Wake up! Wake up Zion!*
Dress yourself!
Put on your strength!
Holy Jerusalem, stand up!
People that have not agreed to follow God*
will not enter you again.
² Those people are not pure and clean.
Shake off the dust!
Put on your wonderful clothes!
Jerusalem, Daughter of Zion,*
you were a prisoner.
But now, free yourself from the chains
that are around your neck!
³ The Lord says,
"You were not sold for money.
So I will not use money
to make you free."

⁴The Lord my Master says, "My people first went down to Egypt to stay—[and then they became slaves]. Later, Assyria made them slaves. ⁵Now look what has happened! Another nation has taken my people. Who is this country that has taken my people like slaves? This country did not pay to take my people. This nation rules my people and laughs at them. Those people always say bad things about me."

⁶The Lord says, "[This has happened] so my people will learn about me. My people will know who I am. My people will know my name, and they will know that I Am He* is speaking to them."

⁷It is a wonderful thing to see a messenger come over the hills with good news. It is wonderful to hear a messenger announce, "There is peace! We have been saved! Your God is king!"

⁸ The city guards* begin shouting.
They are all rejoicing together!
Why? Because every one of them
sees the Lord returning to Zion.*

Zion The southeast part of the mountain Jerusalem is built on. Sometimes it means the people of God living in Jerusalem.
have not agreed to follow God Literally, "People that are not circumcised and that are not pure."
Daughter of Zion This means Jerusalem, the city built on Mount Zion.
I Am He This is like the Hebrew name for God. It shows God lives forever, and that he is always with his people. See Exodus 3:13-17.

⁹ Jerusalem, your destroyed buildings
will be happy again.
You will all rejoice together.
Why? Because the Lord will be kind
to Jerusalem.
The Lord will rescue his people.
¹⁰ The Lord will show his holy strength
to all the nations.
All the faraway countries will see
how God saves his people.
¹¹ You people should leave Babylon!
Leave that place!
₍Priests,₎ you carry the things
that are used in worship.
So make yourselves pure.
Don't touch anything that is not pure.
¹² You will leave Babylon.
But they will not force you to leave
in a hurry.
You will not be forced to run away.
You will walk out,
₍and the Lord will walk with you₎.
The Lord will be in front of you,
and the God of Israel will be behind you.*

God's Suffering Servant

¹³"Look at my Servant. He will be very successful.* He will be very important. ₍In the future₎ people will honor and respect him. ¹⁴"But many people were shocked when they saw my Servant. He was hurt so badly that they could hardly recognize him as a man. ¹⁵But even more people will be amazed. Kings will look at him amazed and not say a word. Those people did not hear the story about my Servant—they saw what happened. They did not hear that story, but they understood."

53 Who really believed the things we announced? Who really accepted the Lord's punishment?

²He grew up like a small plant before the Lord. He was like a root growing in dry ground. He did not look special. He had no special glory. If we looked at him, we would see nothing special that would cause us to like him. ³People made fun of him, and his friends left him. He was a man that had much pain. He knew sickness very well. People did not even give him the honor of looking at him. We did not even notice him.

⁴But he took our troubles and made them his. He bore our pain, and we thought God was punishing him. We thought God beat him ₍for something he did₎. ⁵But he was given pain to suffer for the wrong things we did. He was crushed for our guilt. A debt we owed—our punishment—was given to him. We were healed *(forgiven)* because of his pain. ⁶But ₍even after he did this,₎ all of us wandered away like sheep. We all went out our own way. ₍We did this after₎ the Lord ₍freed us from our guilt and₎ put all our guilt on him.

⁷He was hurt and punished. But he never protested. He said nothing—like a sheep being taken to be killed. He was like a lamb that makes no sound when someone cuts off its wool. He never opened his mouth ₍to defend himself₎. ⁸Men used force and took him—and they did not judge him fairly. No person can tell about his future family, because he was taken from the land of living people. He was punished to pay for the sins of my people.

⁹He died and was buried with the rich. He was buried with evil men. He did nothing wrong—he never spoke lies—but still these things happened to him.

¹⁰The Lord decided to crush him. The Lord decided that he must suffer, so the Servant gave himself to be the one to die. But he will live a new life for a long, long time. He will see his people. He will complete the things the Lord wants him to do.

¹¹He will suffer many things in his soul, but he will see the good things that happen. He will be satisfied with the things he learns. My Good Servant will make many people free from guilt; he will carry away their sins. ¹²For this reason, I will make him a great man among people. He will have a share of all things with the people that are strong. ₍I will do this for him₎ because he gave his life for the people and died.

People said he was a criminal. But ₍the truth is that₎ he carried away the sins of many, many people. And now he speaks for people that have sinned."

---

guards Men that stand on the city walls and watch for messengers or trouble coming to the city. Here this probably means the prophets.

Zion The southeast part of the mountain Jerusalem is built on. Sometimes it means the people of God living in Jerusalem.

The Lord ... behind you This shows God will protect the people. Compare Ex. 14:19,20.

He will be very successful Or, "He is very wise." Or "He will teach people—making them wise."

God Brings His People Home

54 Woman, be happy!
You have not had any children.
But you should be very happy!

The Lord says,
"The woman that is alone*
will have more children
than the woman with a husband."

2 Make your tent bigger.
Open your doors wide.
Don't stop adding to your home.
Make your tent large and strong.
3 Why? Because you will grow very much.
Your children will get people
from many nations,
Your children will again live in the cities
that were destroyed.
4 Don't be afraid!
You will not be disappointed.
People will not say bad things against you.
You will not be embarrassed.
When you were young, you felt shame.
But you will forget that shame now.
You will not remember the shame that
you felt when you lost your husband.
5 Why? Because your husband*
is the One (God) who made you.
His name is the Lord All-Powerful.
He is the One who saves Israel.
He is the Holy One of Israel.
And he will be called
the God of all the earth!

6 You were like a woman
whose husband had left her.
You were very sad in your spirit,
but the Lord called you to be his.
You were like a woman that married young,
and her husband left her.
But God called you to be his.

7 God says,
"I left you,
but only for a short time.
I will gather you to me again.
And I will show you great kindness.
8 I became very angry
and hid from you for a short time.
But I will comfort you with kindness forever."
The Lord your Savior said this.

God Always Loves His People

9 God says,
"Remember, in Noah's time
I punished the world with the flood.
But I made a promise to Noah
that I would never again
destroy the world with a flood.
[In the same way,] I promise you
that I will never again
become angry and say bad things
to you."

10 The Lord says,
"The mountains may disappear,
and the hills may become dust.
But my kindness will never leave you.
I will make peace with you,
and it will never end."
The Lord shows mercy to you.
And he is the One that said these things.

11 "You poor city!
Enemies came against you like storms.
And no one comforted you.
But I will build you again.
I will use a beautiful mortar
to lay the stones of your walls.
I will use sapphire stones
when I lay the foundation.
12 The stones on top of the wall
will be made from rubies.
I will use shiny jewels for the gates.
I will use precious stones
to build the walls around you.
13 Your children will follow God,
and he will teach them.
Your children will have real peace.
14 You will be built on goodness.
So, you will be safe from cruelty and fear.
You will have nothing to fear.
Nothing will come to hurt you.
15 None of my armies will fight against you.
And if any army tries to attack you,
you will defeat that army."

16"Look, I made the blacksmith.* He blows on fire to make it hotter. Then he takes the hot iron and makes the kind of tool he wants to make. In

---

The woman ... alone This Hebrew word is like the word, "destroyed." This probably means "Jerusalem, the city that is destroyed."

husband In Hebrew this word is like the name Baal. This shows that the Lord, not Baal, is the true God.

blacksmith A man that makes things from iron.

the same way, I made the 'Destroyer' that destroys things. ¹⁷"People will make weapons to fight against you, but those weapons will not defeat you. Some people will say things against you. But every person that speaks against you will be shown to be wrong."

The Lord says, "What do the Lord's servants get? They get the good things that come from me!"

God Gives the "Food" That Really Satisfies

55 "All you thirsty people,
Come drink water!
Don't worry if you do not have money.
Come, eat and drink until you are full!
You do not need money;
eat and drink until you are full.
The food and wine cost nothing!
² Why waste your money on something that is not real food?
Why should you work for something that does not really satisfy you?
Listen very closely to me,
and you will eat the good food.
You will enjoy the food
that satisfies your soul.
³ Listen closely to the things I say.
Listen to me so your souls will live.
Come to me and I will make an agreement
with you that will continue forever.
It will be like the agreement
that I made with David.
I promised David that I would love him
and be loyal to him forever.
And you can trust that agreement.
⁴ I made David a witness of my power
for all nations.
I promised David that he would become
a ruler and a commander of many nations."

⁵ There are nations in places you don't know,
but you will call for those nations.
Those nations don't know you,
but they will run to you.
This will happen because the Lord,
your God, wants it.
This will happen because the Holy One
of Israel honors you.
⁶ So you should look for the Lord
before it is too late.
You should call to him now,
while he is near.

⁷ Evil people should stop living their evil way.
They should stop thinking bad thoughts.
They should come to the Lord again.
Then the Lord will comfort them.
Those people should come to the Lord
because our God forgives.

People Cannot Understand God

⁸ The Lord says,
"Your thoughts are not like my thoughts.
Your ways are not like my ways.
⁹ The heavens are higher than the earth.
In the same way, my ways are higher than your ways.
And my thoughts are higher than your thoughts."
The Lord himself said these things.

¹⁰ "Rain and snow fall from the sky.
And they don't go back to the sky
until they touch the ground
and make the ground wet.
Then the ground makes plants sprout
and grow.
These plants make seeds for the farmer.
And people use these seeds to make
bread to eat.
¹¹ In the same way, my words leave my mouth,
and they don't come back until they make
things happen.
My words make the things happen that I want
to happen.
My words succeed in doing the things I send
them to do.
¹² My words will go out with happiness,
and they will bring peace.
Mountains and hills will begin dancing with
happiness.
All the trees in the fields will clap their
hands.
¹³ Large cypress trees will grow
where there were bushes.
Myrtle trees will grow
where there were weeds.
These things will make the Lord famous.
These things will be proof
ₗthat the Lord is powerfulₗ.
This proof will never be destroyed."

All Nations Will Follow the Lord

56 The Lord said these things, "Be fair to all people. Do things that are right! Why?

Because soon my salvation will come to you. My goodness will soon be shown to the whole world." ²The person that obeys God's law about the Sabbath* will be blessed. And the person that does no evil will be happy. ³Some people that are not Jews will join themselves to the Lord. Those people should not say, "The Lord will not accept me with his people." A eunuch* should not say, "I am a dry piece of wood—ᴸI can't make any childrenⱼ."

⁴⁻⁵ᴸThese eunuchs should not say those thingsⱼ because the Lord says, "Some of those eunuchs obey the laws about the Sabbath. And they choose to do the things I want. And they truly follow my Agreement.* So I will put a memorial stone in my temple for them. Their name will be remembered in my city! Yes, I will give those eunuchs something better than sons and daughters. I will give them a name that continues forever. They will not be cut off* from my people."

⁶Some people that are not Jews will join themselves to the Lord. They will do this so they can serve him and love the Lord's name. They will join themselves to the Lord to become his servants. They will keep the Sabbath* ᴸas a special day of worshipⱼ and they will continue to closely follow my Agreement *(Law).*

⁷The Lord says, "I will bring those people to my holy mountain. I will make them happy in my house of prayer. The offerings and sacrifices they give me will please me. Why? Because my temple* will be called a house of prayer for all nations." ⁸The Lord my Master said these things. The people of Israel were forced to leave their country. But the Lord will gather them together again. The Lord says, "I will again gather these people together."

Sabbath Saturday, a special day of rest and worship for Jews.
eunuch(s) Special servants. Sometimes their male sex organs were removed so they could not have children.
Agreement Usually, this means the agreement God made with Israel through Moses. Here it might mean the agreement of Isaiah 55:3.
cut off If a person was "cut off" from Israel, it meant that he died without children or that he was forced to leave his family and the people of Israel. This meant that another family would get his land and his family name would be removed from the list of the people of Israel.
temple A special building for worshiping God. God commanded the Jews to worship him at the temple in Jerusalem.

God Invites All People to Serve Him

⁹ Wild animals in the forest, come and eat!
¹⁰ The guards *(prophets)* are all blind.
They don't know what they are doing.
They are like dogs that won't bark.
They lie on the ground and sleep.
Oh, they love to sleep.
¹¹ They are like hungry dogs.
They are never satisfied.
The shepherds don't know what they are doing.
ᴸThey are like their sheepⱼ
that have all wandered away.
They are greedy.
All they want to do is satisfy themselves.
¹² They come and say,
"I will drink some wine.
I will drink some beer.
I will do the same thing tomorrow.
Only, I will drink even more."

Israel Does Not Follow God

57 The good people are all gone,
and no one even noticed.
The good people have gathered together.
But they don't understand why.
They don't know that trouble is coming.
and that they have been gathered together
ᴸfor protectionⱼ.
² But peace will come,
and the people will rest in their own beds,
They will live the way God wants them to.

³ "Come here you children of witches.
Your father is guilty of sexual sins,
and your mother sells her body for sex.
Come here!
⁴ You are evil and lying children.
You make fun of me.
You make faces at me.
You stick your tongues out at me.
⁵ All you want is to worship false gods
under every green tree.
You kill children by every stream,
and sacrifice them in the rocky places.
⁶ You love to worship the smooth rocks
in the rivers.
You pour wine on them to worship them.
You give sacrifices* to them,

---

sacrifices Gifts to God. Sometimes these were special kinds of animals that were killed and burned on an altar.

but those rocks are all you get.
Do you think this makes me happy?
ͺNo! It does not make me happy.ͺ
You make your bed on every hill
and high mountain.*
⁷ You go up to those places
and offer sacrifices.*
⁸ Then you get in those beds
and sin against me by loving those gods.
You love those gods,
You enjoy looking at their naked bodies.
You were with me,
but you left me to be with them.
You hide the things that help you
remember me.
You hide those things
behind the doors and door posts.*
And then you go and make agreements
with those false gods.
⁹ You use your oils and perfumes
to look nice for Molech.*
You sent your messengers to faraway lands.
And this will bring you down to Sheol,
ͺthe place of deathͺ.

Israel Should Trust God, Not Statues

¹⁰ "You have worked hard to do these things,
but you never became tired.
You found new strength,
because you enjoyed these things.
¹¹ You did not remember me.
You did not even notice me!
So, who were you worrying about?
Who were you afraid of?
Why did you lie?
Look, I have been quiet for a long time—
and you did not honor me.
¹² I could tell about your 'goodness'
and all the 'religious' things you do;
but those things are useless!
¹³ When you need help,
you cry to those false gods
that you have gathered around you.

every hill and high mountain The people worship false gods in these places. The people thought these false gods would give them good crops and more children.
sacrifices Gifts to God. Sometimes these were special kinds of animals that were killed and burned on an altar.
door posts The people of Israel were supposed to put special things on their door frames to help them remember God. See Deut. 6:9.
Molech A false god. This name is like the Hebrew word meaning "king."

But I tell you, the wind will blow them
all away.
A puff of wind will take them
all away from you,
But the person that depends on me
will get the earth.
That person will have my holy mountain.*

The Lord Will Save His People

¹⁴ Clear the road! Clear the road!
Make the way clear for my people!
¹⁵ God is high and lifted up.
God lives forever.
God's name is holy.
God says:
I live in a high and holy place,
but also with people that are sad and
humble.
I will give new life to the people
that are humble in spirit.
I will give new life to the people
that are sad in their hearts.
¹⁶ I will not continue fighting forever.
I will not always be angry.
If I continued to be angry,
then man's spirit
—the life I gave them—
would die in front of me.
¹⁷ These people did evil things,
and it made me angry.
So, I punished Israel.
I turned away from him because I was angry.
And Israel left me.
Israel went any place he wanted.
¹⁸ I saw where Israel went.
So, I will heal *(forgive)* him.
I will comfort him
and say words to make him feel better.
Then he and his people will not feel sad.
¹⁹ I will teach them a new word: 'Peace.'
I will give peace to the people near me
and to the people that are far away.
I will heal *(forgive)* those people!"
The Lord himself said these things.

²⁰But evil people are like the angry ocean. They can't be quiet and peaceful. They are angry, and like the ocean, they stir up mud. My God says, ²¹"There is no peace for evil people."

holy mountain This is the mountain the temple in Jerusalem is built on."

People Must Be Told to Follow God

58 Shout as loud as you can!
  Don't stop yourself!
  Shout loud like a trumpet!
  Tell the people about the wrong things
    they have done!
  Tell Jacob's family about their sins!
² Then they will come every day
    to worship me.
  And the people will want to learn my ways.
  They will become a nation that lives right.
  They will not quit following
    God's good commands.
  They will ask me to judge them fairly.
  They will want to go to God
    ₍for his fair decisions₎.

³Now those people say, "We stop eating food to show honor to you. Why don't you see us? We hurt our bodies to show honor to you. Why don't you notice us?"

But the Lord says, "You do things to please yourselves on those special days for not eating food. And you punish your servants—not your own bodies. ⁴You are hungry; but not for food. You are hungry for arguing and fighting, not bread. You are hungry to hit people with your evil hands. When you stop eating food, it is not for me. You don't want to use your voice to praise me. ⁵Do you think on those special days for not eating food that all I want is to see people punish their bodies? Do you think I want people to look sad? Do you think I want people to bow their heads like dead plants and wear clothes of sadness? Do you think I want people to sit in ashes to show their sadness? That is what you do on your special days for not eating food. Do you think that is what the Lord wants?

⁶"I will tell you the kind of special day I want—a day to make people free. I want a day that you take the burdens off people. I want a day when you make the troubled people free. I want a day when you take the burdens from their shoulders. ⁷I want you to share your food with the hungry people. I want you to find poor people that don't have homes, and I want you to bring them into your own homes. When you see a man that has no clothes—give him your clothes! Don't hide ₍from helping those people₎; they are just like you."

⁸If you do these things, your light will begin shining like the light of dawn. Then your wounds will heal. Your "Goodness" *(God)* will walk in front of you, and the Glory of the Lord* will come following behind you. ⁹Then you will call to the Lord, and the Lord will answer you. You will shout to the Lord, and he will say, "Here I am."

God's People Must Do Right

You should stop making troubles and burdens for people. You should stop using bitter words and blaming people for things. ¹⁰You should feel sorry for hungry people and give them food. You should help the people that are troubled—satisfy their needs. Then your light will shine in the darkness. And you will have no sadness. You will be bright like sunshine at noon.

¹¹The Lord will always lead you. He will satisfy your soul in dry lands. The Lord will give strength to your bones. You will be like a garden that has much water. You will be like a spring that always has water.

¹²Your cities have been destroyed for many, many years. But new cities will be built, and the foundations of these cities will continue for many, many years. You will be called "The One Who Fixes Fences." And you will be called, "The One Who Builds Roads and Houses."

¹³That will happen when you stop sinning against God's law about the Sabbath.* And that will happen when you stop doing things to please yourself on that special day. You should call the Sabbath a happy day. You should honor the Lord's special day. You should honor that special day by not doing and saying those things you do every other day.

¹⁴ Then you can ask the Lord
    to be kind to you.
  And he will carry you to the High Places
    above the earth.
  And he will give you all the things
    that belonged to Jacob your father."

The Lord himself said these things!

Evil People Should Change Their Lives

59 Look, the Lord's power is enough to save you. He can hear you when you ask him for help. ²But your sins separate you from your God.

Glory of the Lord One of the forms God used when he appeared to people. It was like a bright shining light. See Ex. 40:34-36.

Sabbath Saturday, a special day of rest and worship for Jews.

The Lord sees your sins, and he turns away from you. ³Your hands are dirty; they are covered with blood. Your fingers are covered with guilt. You tell lies with your mouth. Your tongue says evil things. ⁴No person tells the truth about other people. People sue each other in court, and they depend on false arguments to win their cases. They tell lies about each other. They are full of trouble, and they give birth to evil. ⁵They hatch ⌊evil, like⌋ eggs from poisonous snakes. If you eat one of those eggs you will die. And if you break one of those eggs, a poison snake will come out.

The lies people tell are like spider webs. ⁶These webs can't be used for clothes. You can't cover yourself with those webs.

Some people do evil things and use their hands to hurt other people. ⁷Those people use their feet to run to evil. They hurry to kill people that have done nothing wrong. They think evil thoughts. Rioting and stealing is their way of living.

⁸Those people don't know the way of peace. There is no goodness in their lives. Their ways are not honest. Any people that live like they live, will never have peace in their lives.

Israel's Sin Brings Trouble

9 All fairness and goodness is gone.
  There is only darkness near us,
    so we must wait for the light.
  We hope for a bright light,
    but all we have is darkness.
10 We are like people without eyes.
  We walk into walls like blind people.
  We stumble and fall like it is night.
    Even in the daylight we can't see.
    At noontime we fail like dead men.
11 We are all ⌊very sad⌋.
  We make sad sounds like doves and bears.
  We are waiting for a time
    when people are fair.
  But there is no fairness yet.
  We are waiting to be saved,
    but salvation is still far away.
12 Why? Because we have done many, many
    wrong things against our God.
  Our sins show we are wrong.
  We know we are guilty of doing these things.
13 We sinned and turned against the Lord.
  We turned away from him and left him.
  We planned evil things.
  We planned things that are against God.
  We have thought of these things
    and planned them in our hearts.

14 Justice has turned away from us.
  Fairness stands far away.
  Truth has fallen in the streets.
  Goodness is not allowed to enter the city.
15 Truth is gone.
  And people that try to do good are robbed.

  The Lord looked,
    and he could not find any goodness.
  The Lord did not like this.
16 The Lord looked,
    and could find no person to stand
    and help the people.
  So the Lord used his own power
    and his own goodness,
    and the Lord saved the people.
17 ⌊The Lord prepared for battle⌋.
  The Lord put on
    the armor of goodness,
    the helmet of salvation,
    the clothes of punishment,
    the coat of strong love.*
18 The Lord is angry at his enemies.
  So the Lord will give them
    the punishment they deserve.
  The Lord is angry with his enemies.
  So the Lord will punish the people
    in all the faraway places.
  The Lord will give them
    the punishment they deserve.
19 Then people in the west
    will fear and respect the Lord's name.
  People in the east
    will fear and respect His Glory.*
  The Lord will come quickly like
    a fast flowing river blown by
    a powerful wind from the Lord.

²⁰Then a Savior will come to Zion.* He will come to the people of Jacob that sinned but came back to God.

²¹The Lord says, "I will make an Agreement with those people. I promise, my Spirit and my words that I put in your mouth will never leave you. They will be with your children and your

strong love This Hebrew word means strong feelings like love, hate, anger, zeal, or jealousy.
His Glory The "Glory of the Lord," one of the forms God used when he appeared to people. It was like a bright shining light. See Ex. 40:34-36.
Zion The southeast part of the mountain Jerusalem is built on. Sometimes it means the people of God living in Jerusalem.

ISAIAH 60:1–16

children's children. They will be with you for now and forever."

God Is Coming!

60 "Jerusalem, my light, get up!
Your Light *(God)* is coming!
The Glory of the Lord* will shine on you.
2 Darkness now covers the earth
and the people are in darkness.
But the Lord will shine on you,
and his Glory will appear on you.
3 The nations will come to your Light *(God)*.
Kings will come to your bright Light.
4 Look around you!
See, people are gathering around
and coming to you.
They are your sons coming from far away.
And your daughters are coming with them.
5 ₍This will happen in the future.₎
And at that time, you will see your people,
and your faces will shine ₍with happiness₎.
₍First,₎ you will be afraid,
but then, you will be excited!
All the riches from across the seas
will be set before you.
The riches of the nations
will come to you.
6 Herds of camels from Midian and Ephah
will cross your land.
Long lines of camels will come from Sheba.
They will bring gold and incense.
People will sing praises to the Lord.
7 People will collect all the sheep from Kedar
and give them to you.
They will bring you rams from Nebaioth.
You will offer those animals on my altar.
And I will accept them.
I will make my wonderful temple*
even more beautiful.
8 Look at the people!
They are hurrying to you
like clouds quickly crossing the sky.
They are like doves flying to their nests.
9 The faraway lands are waiting for me.
The great cargo ships are ready to sail.
Those ships are ready to bring your children
from faraway lands.

They will bring silver and gold with them
to honor the Lord your God,
the Holy One of Israel.
The Lord does wonderful things for you.
10 Children from other lands
will build your walls again.
Their kings will serve you.
"When I was angry, I hurt you.
But now, I want to be kind to you.
So I will comfort you.
11 Your gates will always be open.
They will not be closed night or day.
Nations and kings will bring
their wealth to you.
12 Any nation or kingdom
that does not serve you
will be destroyed.
13 All the great things of Lebanon*
will be given to you.
People will bring pine trees, fir trees,
and cypress trees to you.
These trees will be used for lumber
to make my holy place* more beautiful.
This place is like a stool
in front of my throne,
And I will give it much honor.
14 In the past, people hurt you.
Those people will bow down before you.
In the past, people hated you.
Those people will bow down at your feet.
Those people will call you
'The Lord's City.'
'The Zion* of the Holy One of Israel.'"

The New Israel: Land of Peace

15 "You will never again be left alone.
You will never again be hated.
You will never again be empty.
I will make you great forever.
You will be happy forever and ever.
16 Nations ₍will give you everything you need₎.
It will be like a child
drinking milk from its mother.
But you will 'drink' riches from kings.
Then you will know that it is I, the Lord,
who saves you.
You will know that the Great God of Jacob
protects you.

Zion The southeast part of the mountain Jerusalem is built on. Sometimes it means the people of God living in Jerusalem.
Glory of the Lord One of the forms God used when he appeared to people. It was like a bright shining light. See Ex. 40:34-36.

Lebanon A country north of Israel. It was famous for its great cedar and pine trees.
my holy place This probably means the temple in Jerusalem.

17 You now have copper,
   I will bring you gold.
   You now have iron,
   I will bring you silver.
   I will change your wood into copper.
   I will change your rocks into iron.
   I will change your punishment into peace.
   People now hurt you,
   but people will do good things for you.
18 There will never again be news of violence
   in your country.
   People will never again attack your country
   and steal from you.
   You will name your walls,
   'Salvation.'
   You will name your gates,
   'Praise.'
19 The sun will no longer be your light
   during the day.
   The light from the moon will no longer
   be your light ₍at night₎.
   Because the Lord will be your light forever.
   Your God will be your glory.
20 Your 'sun' will never go down again.
   Your 'moon' will never be dark again.
   Because the Lord will be your light forever.
   And your time of sadness will end.
21 All of your people will be good.
   Those people will get the earth forever.
   I made those people.
   They are the wonderful plant
   that I made with my own hands.
22 The smallest family will become
   a large family group.
   The smallest family will become
   a powerful nation.
   When the time is right,
   I, the Lord, will come quickly.
   I will make these things happen."

The Lord's Message of Freedom

61 ₍The Lord's servant says,₎ "The Lord my Master put his Spirit in me. God chose me to tell good news to poor people and to comfort sad people. God sent me to tell the captives that they are free and to tell the prisoners that they have been set free. ²God sent me to announce the time when the Lord will show his kindness. God sent me to announce the time when our God will punish evil people. God sent me to comfort sad people. ³God sent me to the sad people of Zion. ₍I will get them ready for the celebration.₎ I will take away the ashes on their head, and I will give them a crown. I will take away their sadness, and I will give them the oil of happiness. I will take away their sorrow, and I will give them celebration clothes. God sent me to name those people 'Good Trees' and 'The Lord's Wonderful Plant.'"

⁴"At that time, the old cities that were destroyed will be built again. Those cities will be made new like they were in the beginning. The cities that were destroyed for many, many years will be made like new.

⁵"Then your enemies will come to you and care for your sheep. The children of your enemies will work in your fields and in your gardens. ⁶You will be called, 'The Lord's Priests,' 'The Servants of our God.' You will have the riches that come from all the nations on earth. And you will be proud you have it.

⁷"In the past other people shamed you and said bad things to you. You were shamed much more than any other people. So in your land you will get two times more than other people. You will get happiness that continues forever. ⁸₍Why will this happen?₎ Because I am the Lord and I love fairness. I hate stealing and everything that is wrong. So I will give the people the payment they should have.

"I have made an Agreement with my people forever. ⁹Everyone in all nations will know my people. Everyone will know the children from my nation. Any person that sees them will know that the Lord blesses them."

God's Servant Brings Salvation and Goodness

10 "The Lord makes me very, very happy.
   My whole self is happy in my God.
   The Lord put the clothes of salvation on me.
   These clothes are like the nice clothes
   a man wears at his wedding.
   The Lord put the coat of goodness on me.
   This coat is like the beautiful clothes
   a woman wears at her wedding.
11 The earth causes plants to grow.
   People plant seeds in the garden,
   and the garden makes those seeds grow.
   In the same way, the Lord
   will make goodness grow.
   The Lord will make praise grow
   in all the nations."

New Jerusalem: A City Full of Goodness

62 I love Zion,
   so I will continue to speak for her.

I love Jerusalem,
so I will not stop speaking.
I will speak until goodness shines
like a bright light.
I will speak until salvation burns bright
like a flame.
2 Then all nations will see your goodness.
All kings will see your honor.
Then you will have a new name.
The Lord himself will give you
that new name.
3 The Lord will be very proud of you.
You will be like a beautiful crown
in the Lord's hand.
4 You will never again be called
'The People that God had Left.'
Your land will never again be called
'The Land that God Destroyed.'
You will be called
'The People God Loves.'
Your land will be called
'God's Bride.'
Why? Because the Lord loves you.
And your land will belong to him.
5 When a young man loves a woman,
he marries her,
and she becomes his wife.
In the same way, your land will belong
to your children.
A man is very happy with his new wife.
In the same way, your God
will be very happy with you."

God Will Keep His Promises

6 "Jerusalem, I put guards *(prophets)*
on your walls.
Those guards will not be silent.
They will keep praying day and night."

Guards, you must keep praying to the Lord.
You must make him remember his
promise.
Don't ever stop praying.
7 You must pray to the Lord
until he makes Jerusalem a city
that people on earth will praise.

8 The Lord made a promise.
The Lord used his own power as proof.
And the Lord will use his power
to keep that promise.

The Lord said,

"I promise that I will never again
give your food to your enemies.
I promise that your enemies
will never again take the wine
that you make.
9 The person that gathers food will eat it,
and that person will praise the Lord.
The person that gathers the grapes,
will drink the wine ₍from those grapes₎.
All these things will happen
in my holy land."

10 Come through the gates!
Make the way clear for the people!
Prepare the road!
Move all the stones off the road!
Raise the flag as a sign for the people!

11 Listen, the Lord is speaking to all the
faraway lands:
"Tell the people of Zion:*
Look, your Savior is coming.
He is bringing your reward to you.
He is bringing that reward with him."

12 His people will be called:
"The Holy People,"
"The Saved People of the Lord."
And Jerusalem will be called:
"The City God Wants,"
"The City God Is With."

The Lord Judges His People

63 Who is this coming from Edom?*
He comes from Bozrah.*
And his clothes are bright red.
He is glorious in his clothes.
He is walking tall with his great power.
He says,
"I have the power to save you.
And I speak the truth."

2 "Why are your clothes bright red?
They are like the clothes of a person
that walks on grapes to make wine!"

3 ₍He answers₎,
"I walked in the winepress* by myself.
No one helped me.

Zion The southeast part of the mountain Jerusalem is built on. Sometimes it means the people of God living in Jerusalem.
Edom A country east of Judah.
Bozrah A city in Edom.
winepress A place where people walk on grapes to squeeze the juice from them. This juice then becomes wine.

I was angry and I walked on the grapes.
The juice* splashed on my clothes.
So now my clothes are dirty.
⁴ I chose a time to punish people.
Now the time has come for me
to save and protect my people.
⁵ I looked around, but I saw no person
to help me.
I was surprised that no one supported me.
So I used my own power to save my people.
My own anger supported me.
⁶ While I was angry, I walked on people.
I punished them while I was mad.
I poured their blood* on the ground."

The Lord Has Been Kind to His People

⁷ I will remember that the Lord is kind.
And I will remember to praise the Lord.
The Lord gave many good things to the
family of Israel.
The Lord has been very kind to us.
The Lord showed mercy to us.
⁸ The Lord said,
"These are my people.
These children don't lie."
So the Lord saved those people.
⁹ The people had many troubles,
but the Lord was not against them.
The Lord loved the people
and felt sorry for them.
So the Lord saved them.
He sent his special angel to save them.
And the Lord will care for them forever.
The Lord did not want to stop caring
for those people.
¹⁰ But the people turned against the Lord.
The people made his Holy Spirit very sad.
So the Lord became their enemy.
The Lord fought against those people.
¹¹ But the Lord still remembers
what happened a long time ago.
He remembers Moses and his people.
The Lord is the One who brought the people
through the sea.
The Lord used his shepherds *(prophets)*
to lead his flock *(people).*
But where is the Lord now—
the One who put his Spirit in Moses?
¹² The Lord led Moses by the right hand.

The Lord used his wonderful power
to lead Moses.
The Lord divided the water
so that the people could walk
through the sea.
The Lord made his name famous
by doing those great things.
¹³ The Lord led the people
through the deep seas.
The people walked without falling,
like a horse walking through the desert.
¹⁴ A cow does not fall just walking in the field.
⌊In the same way, the people did not fall
while going through the sea⌋.
The Lord's Spirit led the people
to a resting place.
The people were safe the whole time.
Lord, that is the way you led your people.
You led the people
and you made your name wonderful.

A Prayer for God to Help His People

¹⁵ Lord, look down from the heavens.
See the things that are happening now!
Look down at us from your great and holy
home in heaven.
Where is your strong love* for us?
Where are your powerful works
that come from deep inside you?
Where is your mercy for me?
Why are you hiding your kind love
from me?
¹⁶ Look! You are our father!
Abraham doesn't know us.
Israel *(Jacob)* does not recognize us.
Lord, you are our father!
You are the One who has always saved us!
¹⁷ Lord, why are you pushing us
away from you?
Why are you making it hard
for us to follow you?
Come back to us Lord!
We are your servants.
Come to us and help us!
Our families belong to you.
¹⁸ Your holy people lived in their land
only a short time.

---

juice Or, "strong drink" or "blood."
blood Or, "strong drink" or "strength."

strong love This Hebrew word means strong feelings like love, hate, anger, zeal, or jealousy.

Then our enemies trampled *(walk on)*
your holy temple.*
19 Some people don't follow you.
Those people don't wear your name.
And we were like those people.

64

¹⁻²If you would tear open the skies
and come down to earth,
⌊then everything would change⌋.
The mountains would melt before you.

2 ⌊The mountains⌋ would burn in flames
like burning bushes.
⌊The mountains would boil like⌋
water on the fire.
Then your enemies would learn about you.
Then all nations would shake with fear
when they see you.
3 But we don't really want
you to do these things.
The mountains would melt before you.
4 Your people never really listened to you.
Your people never really heard
the things you said.
No person has ever seen a God like you.
There is no other God—only you.
If people are patient
and wait for you to help them,
then you will do great things for them.
5 You are with people that enjoy doing good.
Those people remember your ways of
living.
But look, in the past we sinned against you.
So you became angry with us.
Now, how will we be saved?
6 We are all dirty with sin.
All our "goodness" is like old dirty clothes.
We are all like dead leaves.
Our sins have carried us away like wind.
7 We don't worship you.
We don't trust in your name.
We aren't excited about following you.
So you have turned away from us.
We are helpless before you,
because we are full of sin.
8 But Lord, you are our father.
We are like clay.
And you are the potter.*

Your hands made us all.
9 Lord, don't continue to be angry with us!
Don't remember our sins forever!
Please, look at us!
We are your people.
10 Your holy cities are empty.
Those cities are like deserts now.
Zion* is a desert!
Jerusalem is destroyed!
11 Our holy temple has been burned by fire.
That temple was great to us.
Our fathers worshiped you there.
All the good things we owned
are now destroyed.
12 Will these things always keep you from
⌊showing your love to us⌋?
Will you continue to say nothing?
Will you punish us forever?

All People Will Learn About God

65

The Lord says, "I helped people that had not come to me for advice. The people that found me were not looking for me. I spoke to a nation that does not wear my name. I said, 'Here I am! Here I am!'

²"I stood ready to accept people that turned against me. I was waiting for those people to come to me. But they continued living a way that is not good. They did anything their hearts wanted to do. ³Those people are in front of me always making me angry. Those people offer sacrifices* and burn incense* in their special gardens.* ⁴Those people sit among the graves. They wait to get messages from dead people. They even live among dead bodies. They eat pig meat. Their forks and knives are dirty with rotten meat.

⁵"But those people tell other people, 'Don't come near me! Don't touch me until I make you clean.' Those people are like smoke in my eyes. And their fire burns all the time."

---

temple A special building for worshiping God. God commanded the Jews to worship him at the temple in Jerusalem.
potter A person that makes pots and other things from clay.

Zion The southeast part of the mountain Jerusalem is built on. Sometimes it means the people of God living in Jerusalem.
sacrifices Gifts to God. Sometimes these were special kinds of animals that were killed and burned on an altar.
incense A kind of spice that smells good when it is burned. It was burned as a gift to God.
special gardens Gardens where people worshiped false gods.

Israel Must Be Punished

⁶"Look, here is a bill that must be paid. ₍This bill shows you are guilty for your sins.₎ I will not be quiet until I pay this bill, and I will pay the bill by punishing you.
⁷"Your sins and your fathers' sins are all the same." The Lord said this, "Your fathers did these sins when they burned incense* in the mountains. They shamed me on those hills. And I punished them first. I gave them the punishment they should have."

God Will Not Completely Destroy Israel

⁸The Lord says, "When there is new wine in the grapes, people squeeze out the wine. But they don't completely destroy the grapes. They do this because the grapes can still be used. I will do the same thing to my servants. I will not completely destroy them. ⁹I will keep some of the people of Jacob *(Israel)*. Some of the people of Judah will get my mountain. My servants will live there. I will choose the people that will live there. ¹⁰Then Sharon Valley* will be a field for sheep. The Valley of Achor* will be a place for cattle to rest. All these things will be for my people—the people that look for me.
¹¹"But you people left the Lord, so you will be punished. You people forgot about my holy mountain.* You began to worship Luck. You depend on the false god Fate.* ¹²₍But I decide your future.₎ And I decided that you will be killed with a sword. You will all be killed. Why? Because I called to you, and you refused to answer me! I spoke to you, and you would not listen. You did the things that I say are evil. You decided to do the things that I don't like."

¹³ So the Lord my Master said these things.
"My servants will eat,
  but you evil people will be hungry.
My servants will drink,
  but you evil people will be thirsty.
My servants will be happy,
  but you evil people will be shamed.

---

incense A kind of spice that smells good when it is burned. It was burned as a gift to God.
Sharon Valley The low land along the coast of Palestine.
Valley of Achor A valley about ten miles north of Jerusalem.
my holy mountain Mount Zion, the mountain Jerusalem is built on.
Luck ... Fate Two false gods. The people thought these gods controlled their futures.'

¹⁴ My servants have goodness in their hearts,
  so they will be happy.
But you evil people will cry,
  because you will have pain in your hearts.
Your spirits will be broken,
  and you will be very sad.
¹⁵ Your names will be like bad words
  to my servants."

The Lord my Master will kill you.
  And he will call his servants
    by a new name.
¹⁶ People now ask blessings from the earth.
  ₍But in the future,₎ they will ask blessings
    from the faithful God.
People now trust in the power of the earth
  when they make a promise.
₍But in the future,₎ they will trust
  in the faithful God.
Why? Because the troubles in the past
  will all be forgotten.
My people will never again
  remember those troubles.

A New Time Is Coming

¹⁷ "I will make a new heaven and a new earth.
  People will not remember the past.
  They won't remember any of those things.
¹⁸ My people will be happy.
  They will rejoice forever and ever.
Why? Because of what I will make.
I will make a Jerusalem that is full of joy,
  and I will make them a happy people.
¹⁹ Then I will be happy with Jerusalem.
  I will be happy with my people.
There will never again be crying
  and sadness in that city.
²⁰ There will never be a child from that city,
  that is born and lives only a few days.
No person from that city will die
  after only a short life.
Every child will live a long life,
  and every older person will live
    for a long, long time.
A person that lives 100 years
  will be called young.
But the person that sins
  will be full of trouble,
    even if he lives 100 years.
²¹ In that city, if a person builds a house,
  that person will live there.
If a person plants a garden of grapes,
  that person will eat the grapes
    from that garden.

²² Never again will
one person build a house
and another person live there.
Never again will
one person plant a garden
and another person eat the fruit from it.
My people will live as long as the trees.
The people I choose will enjoy
the things they make.
²³ People will never again work for nothing.
People will never again give birth
to children that die young.
All my people and their children
will be blessed by the Lord.
²⁴ I will know what they need
before they ask.
And I will help them—
even before they finish asking.
²⁵ Wolves and little lambs will eat together.
Lions will eat with cattle.
A snake on the ground will not scare or hurt
any person on my holy mountain."
The Lord said all those things.

God Will Judge All Nations

66 This is what the Lord says,
"The skies are my throne.
The earth is my footstool.
So do you think you can build
a house for me?
No! You can't!
Can you give me a place to rest?
No! You can't!
² I myself made all things.
All things are here because I made them."
The Lord himself said these things.

"Tell me, what people do I care for?
I care for the poor people.
I care for the people that are very sad.
I care for people that obey my words.
³ Some people kill bulls ₍as a sacrifice₎,
but they also beat people.
Those people kill sheep as a sacrifice,
but they also break the necks of dogs!
And they offer me the blood of pigs!*
Those people remember to burn incense,*
but they also love their worthless idols.*

Those people choose their own ways—
not mine.
They love their terrible idols.
⁴ So I decided to use their own tricks!
₍I mean that₎ I will punish them
using the things they are most afraid of.
I called to those people,
but they did not listen.
I spoke to them,
but they did not hear me.
So I will do the same thing to them.
Those people did things I said are evil.
They chose to do things I did not like."

⁵ You people that obey the Lord's commands
should listen to the things the Lord says,
"Your brothers hated you.
They turned against you
because you followed me.
Your brothers said,
'We will come back to you
when the Lord is honored.
Then we will be happy with you.'
Those bad people will be punished.

Punishment And A New Nation

⁶Listen! There is a loud noise coming from the city and the temple.* That noise is the Lord punishing his enemies. The Lord is giving them the punishment they should have.

⁷⁻⁸"A woman does not give birth before she feels the pain. A woman must feel the pain of childbirth before she can see the boy she gives birth to. ₍In the same way,₎ no person ever saw a new world begin in one day. No person has ever heard of a new nation that began in one day. The land must first have pain like the pain of birth. After the birth pain then the land will give birth to her children—a new nation. ⁹₍In the same way,₎ I will not cause pain without allowing something new to be born."

The Lord says this. "I promise, if I cause you the pain of birth then I will not stop you from having your new nation." Your God said this.

¹⁰ Jerusalem, be happy!
All you people who love Jerusalem be happy!
Sad things happened to Jerusalem,
so some of you people are sad.

---

dogs ... pigs God did not want his people to offer dogs and pigs as sacrifices.
incense A kind of spice that smells good when it is burned. It was burned as a gift to God.
idols Statues of false gods that people worshiped.

temple A special building for worshiping God. God commanded the Jews to worship him at the temple in Jerusalem.

But now you people should be happy.
11 Why? Because you will receive mercy
like milk coming from her breast.
That "milk" will truly satisfy you!
You people will drink the milk,
and you will truly enjoy
the glory of Jerusalem.
12 The Lord says,
"Look, I will give you peace.
This peace will come flowing to you
like a great river.
Wealth from all the nations on earth
will come flowing to you.
That wealth will come like a flood.
⌊You will be like little children⌋.
You will drink the 'milk.'
I will pick you up
and hold you in my arms.
And I will bounce you on my knees.
13 You will be comforted in Jerusalem.
I will comfort you like a mother
comforts her child.
14 You will see the things that you truly enjoy.
You will be free and grow like grass.
The Lord's servants will see his power,
but the Lord's enemies will see his anger.

¹⁵Look, the Lord is coming with fire. The Lord's armies are coming with clouds of dust. The Lord will punish those people with his anger. The Lord will use flames of fire to punish those people while he is angry. ¹⁶The Lord will judge the people. Then the Lord will destroy the people with fire and with his sword. The Lord will destroy many people.

¹⁷Those people wash themselves to make themselves pure for worshiping in their special gardens.* These people follow each other into their special gardens. Then they worship their idols. But, the Lord will destroy all those people.

"Those people eat the meat from pigs, rats, and other dirty things. But, all of those people will be destroyed together." (The Lord himself said these things.)

¹⁸"Those people have evil thoughts and do evil things. So I am coming to punish them. I will gather all nations and all people. All people will come together and see my power. ¹⁹I will put a mark on some of the people—⌐I will save them⌐. I will send some of these saved people to the nations Tarshish,* Libya,* Lud* (the land of archers*), Tubal,* Greece, and all the faraway lands. Those people have never heard my teachings. Those people have never seen my Glory.* So the saved people will tell the nations about my glory. ²⁰And they will bring all your brothers and sisters from all nations. They will bring your brothers and sisters to my holy mountain,* Jerusalem. Your brothers and sisters will come on horses, donkeys, camels, and in chariots and wagons. Your brothers and sisters will be like the gifts that the people of Israel bring on clean plates to the Lord's temple.* ²¹I will also choose some of these people to be priests and Levites.*" The Lord himself said these things.

The New Heavens and the New Earth

²²"I will make a new world—and the new heavens and the new earth ⌊will last forever⌋. In the same way, your names and your children will always be with me. ²³All people will come to worship me on every worship day; they will come every Sabbath* and every first day of the month.*

²⁴"⌊These people will be in my holy city⌋. And if they go out ⌊of the city⌋ they will see the dead bodies of the people that sinned against me. ⌊There will be worms in those bodies⌋—and the worms will never die. ⌊Fires will burn those bodies⌋—and the fires will never stop.

Tarshish A city far away from Israel, probably in Spain. Tarshish was famous for its large ships that sailed the Mediterranean Sea.
Libya A country in North Africa, west of Egypt.
Lud This country was probably in the country that is now western Turkey.
archers Soldiers that use bows and arrows in war.
Tubal This country was probably in the country that is now eastern Turkey.
my Glory The "Glory of the Lord," one of the forms God used when he appeared to people. It was like a bright shining light. See Ex. 40:34-36.
my holy mountain This is probably Mount Zion, the mountain Jerusalem is built on.
temple A special building for worshiping God. God commanded the Jews to worship him at the temple in Jerusalem.
Levites People from the family group of Levi. Only Levites could help the priests in the temple.
Sabbath Saturday, a special day of rest and worship for Jews.
first day of the month Literally, "new moon," the first day of the Jewish month and a special day of worship.

special gardens Gardens where people worshiped false gods.

Jeremiah

1 These are the messages of Jeremiah. Jeremiah was the son of a man named Hilkiah. Jeremiah belonged to the family of priests that lived in the city of Anathoth.* That city is in the land that belongs to the family group of Benjamin. ²The Lord began to speak to Jeremiah during the days when Josiah was king of the nation of Judah. Josiah was the son of a man named Amon. The Lord began to speak to Jeremiah in the 13th year that Josiah was king.* ³The Lord continued to speak to Jeremiah while Jehoiakim was king of Judah. Jehoiakim was the son of Josiah. The Lord continued to speak to Jeremiah during the eleven years and five months that Zedekiah was king of Judah. Zedekiah was also a son of Josiah. In the fifth month of Zedekiah's eleventh year as king, the people that lived in Jerusalem were taken away into exile.

God Calls Jeremiah

⁴The Lord's message came to Jeremiah. This message was from the Lord:

⁵ "Before I made you in your mother's body,
I knew you.
Before you were born,
I chose you for a special work.
I chose you to be a prophet to the nations."

⁶Then Jeremiah said, "But Lord All-Powerful, I don't know how to speak. I am only a boy."

⁷But the Lord said to me,

"Don't say, 'I am only a boy.'
You must go everywhere that I send you.
You must say everything I tell you to say.

⁸ Don't be afraid of anyone.
I am with you,
and I will protect you."
This message is from the Lord.

⁹Then the Lord reached out with his hand and touched my mouth. The Lord said to me,

"Jeremiah, I am putting my words
in your mouth.
¹⁰ Today I have put you in charge
of nations and kingdoms.
You will pull up and tear down.
You will destroy and overthrow.
You will build up and plant."

Two Visions

¹¹The Lord's message came to me. This message was from the Lord: "Jeremiah, what do you see?"

I answered the Lord and said, "I see a stick made from almond wood."

¹²The Lord said to me, "You have seen very well. And I am watching* to make sure that my message to you comes true."

¹³The Lord's message came to me again. This was the Lord's message: "Jeremiah, what do you see?"

I answered the Lord and said, "I see a pot of boiling water. That pot is tipping over from the north."

¹⁴ The Lord said to me,
"Something terrible will come
from the north.
It will happen to all the people
that live in this country.
¹⁵ In a short time I will call all of the people
in the northern kingdoms."
The Lord said those things.

---

priests that lived in the city of Anathoth These priests probably belonged to the family of the priest Abiathar. Abiathar was a high priest in Jerusalem during the time David was king. He was sent away to Anathoth by King Solomon. See 1 Kings 2:26.

13th year that Josiah was king That is 627 B.C.

watching This is a word play. "Shaqed" is the Hebrew word for "almond wood," and "shoqed" means "watching."

"The kings of those countries will come
and set up their thrones
near the gates of Jerusalem.
They will attack the city walls of Jerusalem.
They will attack all the cities in Judah.
¹⁶ And I will announce my judgment
against my people.
I will do this because they are bad people
and they have turned against me.
My people left me.
They offered sacrifices to other gods.
They worshiped idols that they had made
with their own hands.

¹⁷ "As for you, Jeremiah, get ready.
Stand up and speak to the people.
Tell them everything that I tell you to say.
Don't be afraid of the people.
If you are afraid of the people,
then I will give you good reason
to be afraid of them.
¹⁸ As for me, today I will make you
like a strong city,
an iron column,
a bronze wall.
You will be able to stand
against everyone in the land,
against the kings of the land of Judah,
against the leaders of Judah,
against the priests of Judah,
and against the people of the land of Judah.
¹⁹ All those people will fight against you,
but they will not defeat you.
Why? Because I am with you,
and I will save you."
This message is from the Lord.

Judah Was Not Faithful

2 The Lord's message came to Jeremiah. This message was from the Lord: ²"Jeremiah, go and speak to the people of Jerusalem. Say to them:

"'At the time you were a young nation,
you were faithful to me.
You followed me like a young bride.
You followed me through the desert,
through a land that had never been used
for farm land.
³ The people of Israel were a holy gift
to the Lord.
They were the first fruit to be gathered
by the Lord.
Any people that tried to hurt them
were judged guilty.

Bad things happened to those
wicked people.'"
This message was from the Lord.

⁴ Family of Jacob, hear the Lord's message.
Family groups of Israel, hear the message.
⁵ This is what the Lord says:
"Do you think that I was not fair
to your ancestors?*
Is that why they turned away from me?
Your ancestors worshiped worthless idols,
and they became worthless themselves.
⁶ Your ancestors did not say,
'The Lord brought us from Egypt.
The Lord led us through the desert.
The Lord led us through a dry
and rocky land.
The Lord led us through a dark
and dangerous land.
No people live there.
People don't even travel through
that land.
But the Lord led us through that land.
So where is the Lord now?'

⁷ ⌊The Lord says,⌋
"I brought you into a good land,
a land filled with many good things.
I did this so you could eat the fruit and crops
that grow there.
But you only made my land 'dirty.'
I gave that land to you,
but you made it a bad place.

⁸ "The priests did not ask,
'Where is the Lord?'
The people that know the law
did not want to know me.
The leaders of the people of Israel
turned against me.
The prophets prophesied* in the name
of the false god Baal.*
They worshiped worthless idols."

⁹ The Lord says,
"So now I will accuse you again,
And I will also accuse your grandchildren.

---

ancestors Literally, "fathers," meaning a person's parents, grandparents, and all the people they are descended from.
prophesied Or, "spoke."
Baal The Canaanite people believed that this false god brought the rain and storms. They also thought that he made the land produce good crops.

JEREMIAH 2:10–25

¹⁰ Go across the sea to the Islands of Kittim.*
 Send someone to the land of Kedar.* Look
   very carefully.
 See if any person has ever done something
   like this.
¹¹ Has any nation ever stopped worshiping their
   old gods so they could worship new gods?
 No! And their gods are not really gods at all!
 But my people
   stopped worshiping their glorious God
   and started worshiping idols
     that are worth nothing.
¹² "Skies, be shocked at the things
   that have happened!
 Shake with great fear!"
 This message was from the Lord.
¹³ "My people have done two evil things.
 They turned away from me
   (I am the spring of living water),
   and they dug their own water cisterns.
     ₍They turned to other gods.₎₎
 But their cisterns are broken.
 Those cisterns can't hold water.
¹⁴ "Have the people of Israel become slaves?
 Have they become like a person
   that was born a slave?
 Why did people take the wealth
   from the people of Israel?
¹⁵ Young lions' *(enemies)* roar at Israel.
 The lions growl.
 Lions have destroyed the land of Israel.
 The cities of Israel have been burned.
 There are no people left in them.
¹⁶ People from Memphis and Tahpanhes*
   have smashed the top of your head.
¹⁷ This trouble is your own fault!
 The Lord your God
   was leading you the right way,*
   but you turned away from him.
¹⁸ People of Judah, think about this:
 Did it help to go to Egypt?
 Did it help to drink
   from the Nile River? No!
 Did it help to go to Assyria?

 Did it help to drink from
   the Euphrates River? No!
¹⁹ You did bad things,
   and those bad things will only
     bring punishment to you.
 Trouble will come to you.
 And that trouble will teach you a lesson.
 Think about it!
 Then you will understand how bad it is
   to turn away from your God.
 It is wrong not to fear and respect me!"
 This message was from my Master,
   the Lord All-Powerful.
²⁰ "Judah, a long time ago you threw off
   your yoke.
 You broke the ropes
   ₍that I used to control you₎.
 You said to me,
   'I will not serve you!'
 You were like a prostitute
   on every high hill
   and under every green tree.*
²¹ Judah, I planted you like a special vine.
 All of you were like good seed.
 How did you turn into a different vine that
   grows bad fruit?
²² Even if you wash yourself with lye,*
   even if you use much soap,
 I can still see your guilt."
 This message was from the Lord God.
²³ "Judah, how can you say to me,
   'I am not guilty;
   I have not worshiped the Baal* idols'?
 Think about the things you did in the valley.
 Think about what you have done.
 You are like a fast she-camel
   that runs from place to place.
²⁴ You are like a wild donkey
   that lives in the desert.
 At mating time, she sniffs *(smells)*
   the wind.
 No person can bring her back
   at the time she is in heat.
 At mating time, every male that wants her
   will get her.
 It is easy to find her.
²⁵ Judah, stop chasing after idols!
 Stop being thirsty for those other gods.

Islands of Kittim The name means the Island of Cyprus. But the name was often used for the other islands and coastlands of the Mediterranean Sea.
Kedar This was the name of an Arabian family group that lived in the desert to the east of Palestine.
Memphis and Tahpanhes Two cities in Egypt.
was leading ... way This line is not in the Greek translation.

prostitute ... green tree. This means the people worshiped their false gods in these places.
lye A chemical that is used like soap.
Baal The Canaanite people believed that this false god brought the rain and storms. They also thought that he made the land produce good crops.

But you say, 'It is no use! I can't quit!
    I love those other gods.
    I want to worship them.'
26 "A thief is ashamed when people catch him.
    In the same way,
        the people of Israel are ashamed,
        the kings and leaders are ashamed,
        and the priests and prophets are ashamed.
27 Those people talk to pieces of wood!
    They say, 'You are my father.'
    Those people speak to a rock.
    They say, 'You gave birth to me.'
    All those people will be ashamed.
    Those people don't look at me.
    They have turned their backs to me.
    But when the people of Judah
        get into trouble, they say to me,
        'Come and save us!'
28 Let those idols come and save you!
    Where are the idols
        that you have made for yourselves?
    Let's see if those idols come
        and save you when you are in trouble.
    Judah, you have as many idols as cities!

29 "Why do you argue with me?
    All of you have turned against me."
    This message was from the Lord.
30 "I punished you people of Judah,
        but it did not help.
    You did not come back when you were
        punished.
    You killed with your swords the prophets that
        came to you.
    You were like a dangerous lion and you killed
        the prophets."
31 People of this generation, pay attention
        to the Lord's message!

"Have I been like a desert
    to the people of Israel?
Have I been like a dark and dangerous land
    to them?
My people say,
    'We are free to go our own way.
    We will not come back to you, Lord!'
Why do they say those things?
32 A young woman doesn't forget her jewelry.
    A bride doesn't forget the sash for her dress.
    But my people have forgotten me
        too many times to count.

33 "Judah, you really know how
    to chase after lovers (false gods).

You have really learned to do evil things.
34 You have blood on your hands!
    It is the blood of the poor, innocent people.
    You did not catch those people
        breaking into your house!
    You killed them for no reason!
35 But still, you say,
    'I am innocent.
    God is not angry with me.'
    So I will also judge you guilty ⌊of lying⌋.
    Why? Because you say,
    'I have done nothing wrong.'
36 It is so easy for you to change your mind.
    Assyria disappointed you,
        ⌊so you left Assyria
        and went to Egypt for help.⌋
    But Egypt will also disappoint you.
37 So you will eventually leave Egypt, too.
    And you will hide your face in shame.
    You trusted those countries.
    But the Lord rejected those countries,
        so they can't help you win.

3 "If a man divorces his wife,
    and she leaves him
    and marries another man,
    can that man come back to his wife again?
    No! If that man went back to that woman,*
        then that land would become 'dirty.'
    Judah, you acted like a prostitute
        with many lovers (false gods).
    And now you want to come back to me!"
    This message was from the Lord.
2 "Look up to the bare hilltops, Judah.
    Is there any place where you have not
        had sex with your lovers (false gods)?
    You have sat by the road waiting for lovers,
        like an Arab waiting in the desert.
    You made the land 'dirty'!
    How? You did many bad things
        and you were unfaithful to me.
3 You sinned, so the rain has not come.
    There have not been any springtime rains.
    But still you refuse to be ashamed.
    The look on your face is like the look
        that a prostitute has when she
        refuses to be ashamed.
    You refuse to be ashamed of what you did.

If that man went back to that woman It was against the law of Moses for a man to marry a woman he had divorced if that woman had become another man's wife. It was against the law for that man to marry her again even if her second husband divorced her or died. See Deut. 24:1-4.

⁴ But now you are calling me, 'Father.'
You said,
'You have been my friend
since I was a child.'
⁵ You also said,
'God will not always be angry at me.
God's anger will not continue forever.'

"Judah, you say those things,
but you do as much evil as you can."

The Two Bad Sisters: Israel and Judah

⁶The Lord spoke to me during the time King Josiah was ruling the nation of Judah. The Lord said: "Jeremiah, you saw the bad things that Israel* did? You saw how she was unfaithful to me. She did the sin of adultery with idols on every hill and under every green tree. ⁷I said to myself, 'Israel will come back to me after she has finished doing these evil things.' But she did not come back to me. And Israel's unfaithful sister, Judah, saw what she did. ⁸Israel was unfaithful and Israel knew why I sent her away. Israel knew that I divorced her because she did the sin of adultery. But that did not make her unfaithful sister afraid. Judah, was not afraid. Judah also went out and acted like a prostitute. ⁹Judah did not care that she was acting like a prostitute. So she made her country 'dirty.' She did the sin of adultery by worshiping idols made out of stone and wood. ¹⁰Israel's unfaithful sister (Judah) did not come back to me with her whole heart. She only pretended that she came back to me." This message was from the Lord.

¹¹The Lord said to me, "Israel was not faithful to me. But she had a better excuse than unfaithful Judah. ¹²Jeremiah, look toward the north and speak this message:

'Come back, you faithless people of Israel.'
This message was from the Lord.
'I will stop frowning at you.
I am full of mercy.'
This message was from the Lord.
'I will not be angry with you forever.
¹³ But you must recognize your sin.
You turned against the Lord your God.
That is your sin.
You worshiped the idols of people
from other nations.

You worshiped those idols
under every green tree.
You did not obey me.'"
This message was from the Lord.

¹⁴"You people are unfaithful. But Come back to me!" This message was from the Lord. "I am your Master. I will take one person from every city and two people from every family and bring you to Zion.* ¹⁵Then I will give you new rulers. Those rulers will be faithful to me. They will lead you with knowledge and understanding. ¹⁶In those days, there will be many of you in the land." This message is from the Lord.

"At that time, people will never again say, 'I remember the days when we had the Box of the Lord's Agreement.'* They won't even think about the Holy Box anymore. They won't even remember or miss it. They will never make another Holy Box. ¹⁷At that time, the city of Jerusalem will be called the 'Lord's Throne.' All nations will come together in the city of Jerusalem to give honor to the name of the Lord. They won't follow their stubborn, evil hearts anymore. ¹⁸In those days, the family of Judah will join the family of Israel. They will come together from a land in the north. They will come to the land I gave to their ancestors.*

¹⁹ "I, the Lord, said to myself,
'I want to treat you like my own children.
I want to give you a pleasant land,
a land more beautiful
than any other nation.'
I thought that you would call me 'Father.'
I thought that you would always follow me.
²⁰ But you have been like a woman
that is unfaithful to her husband.
Family of Israel, you have been unfaithful
to me!"
This message was from the Lord.
²¹ You can hear crying on the bare hills.
The people of Israel are crying

Zion The southeast part of the mountain Jerusalem is built on. Sometimes it means the people of God living in Jerusalem.
Box of the Agreement The box containing the stone tablets with the Ten Commandments written on them and the other things that proved God was with the people of Israel during their time in the Sinai Desert. Also called "The Ark of the Covenant."
ancestors Literally, "fathers," meaning a person's parents, grandparents, and all the people they are descended from.

Israel Here the name Israel means the northern kingdom of Israel. Israel was destroyed by the Assyrians about 100 years before Jeremiah's time.

and praying for mercy.
They became very evil.
They forgot the Lord their God.

²² ⌊The Lord also said,⌋
"People of Israel, you are unfaithful to me.
But come back to me!
Come back and I will forgive* you
for being unfaithful to me."

⌊The people should say,⌋
"Yes, we will come to you.
You are the Lord our God.
²³ It was foolish to worship idols on the hills.
All the loud parties on the mountains
were wrong.
Surely the salvation of Israel
comes from the Lord our God.
²⁴ That terrible false god Baal has eaten
everything our fathers owned.
This has happened since we were children.
That terrible false god took
our fathers' sheep and cattle,
and their sons and daughters.
²⁵ Let us lie down in our shame.
Let our shame cover us like a blanket.
We have sinned against the Lord our God.
We and our fathers have sinned.
We have not obeyed the Lord our God
from the time we were children."

4 This message is from the Lord.
"Israel, if you want to come back,
then come back to me.
Throw away your idols.
Don't wander away from me.
² If you do those things,
then you will be able to use my name
to make a promise:
You will be able to say,
'As the Lord lives.'
And you will be able to use those words
in a truthful, honest, and right way.
If you do these things, then the nations
will be blessed by the Lord.
They will brag about the things
that the Lord has done."

³This is what the Lord says to the man of Judah and to Jerusalem:

forgive Literally, "heal."

"Your fields have not been plowed.
Plow those fields!
Don't plant seeds among the thorns.
⁴ Become the Lord's people.
Change your hearts!*
Men of Judah and people of Jerusalem,
if you don't change,
then I will become very angry.
My anger will spread fast like a fire,
and my anger will burn you up.
And no person will be able to put out that fire.
Why will this happen?
Because of the evil things you have done."

Disaster from the North

⁵"Give this message to the people of Judah:

Tell every person in the city of Jerusalem,
'blow the trumpet all over the country.'
Shout out loud and say,
'Come together!
Let us all escape to the strong cities for
protection.'
⁶ Raise the signal flag toward Zion.*
Run for your lives!
Don't wait!
Do this because I am bringing disaster from
the north.*
I am bringing terrible destruction."
⁷ A lion has come out of his cave.
A destroyer of nations has begun to march.
He has left his home
to destroy your land.
Your towns will be destroyed.
There will be no people left to live in them.
⁸ So put on sackcloth* and cry out loud!
Why? Because the Lord is angry at us."
⁹ The Lord says,
"At the time this happens,
the king and his officers
will lose their courage,
the priests will be scared,
the prophets will be shocked."

Become the Lord's people ...Change your hearts Literally, "Be circumcised to the Lord. Cut away the foreskin of your hearts." A man cut away the foreskin from his sex organ to show he was becoming one of God's people. Jeremiah is saying that the real circumcision must be from inside a person's heart (mind).

Zion The southeast part of the mountain Jerusalem is built on. Sometimes it means the people of God living in Jerusalem.

north The Babylonian army came from this direction to attack Judah. Armies from countries north and east of Israel often came this way to attack Judah and Israel.

JEREMIAH 4:10–27

¹⁰Then I, Jeremiah, said, "Lord my Master, you have really tricked the people of Judah and Jerusalem. You said to them, 'You will have peace.' But now the sword is pointing at their throats!"

¹¹ At that time a message will be given
   to the people of Judah and Jerusalem:
"A hot wind blows from the bare hills.
   It comes from the desert to my people.
It is not like the gentle wind that farmers use
   to separate the grain from the chaff.*
¹² It is a stronger wind than that,
   and it comes from me.
Now, I will announce my judgment against
   the people of Judah."
¹³ Look! The enemy rises up like a cloud.
   His chariots* look like a wind storm.
   His horses are faster than eagles.
It will be very bad for us!
   We are ruined!

¹⁴ People of Jerusalem, wash the evil
   from your hearts.
Make your hearts pure so you can be saved.
   Don't continue making evil plans.
¹⁵ Listen! The voice of a messenger
   from the land of Dan* is speaking.
A person is bringing bad news
   from the hill country of Ephraim.*
¹⁶ "Report it to this nation.*
   Spread the news to the people in
      Jerusalem.
Enemies are coming from a faraway country.
Those enemies are shouting words of war
   against the cities of Judah.
¹⁷ The enemy has surrounded Jerusalem
   like men guarding a field.
Judah, you turned against me!
   So the enemy is coming against you!"
This message is from the Lord.

¹⁸ "The way you lived and the things you did
      brought this trouble to you.
   It is your evil that made your life so hard.
   Your evil life brought the pain
      that hurts deep in your heart."

Jeremiah's Cry

¹⁹ Oh, my sadness and worry is making
      my stomach hurt.
   I am bent over in pain.
   Oh, I am so scared.
      My heart is pounding inside me.
   I can't keep quiet. Why?
      Because I have heard the trumpet blow.
      The trumpet is calling the army to war!
²⁰ Disaster follows disaster!
      The whole country is destroyed!
   Suddenly my tents are destroyed!
      My curtains are torn down!
²¹ Lord, how long must I see the war flags?
      How long must I hear the war trumpets?

²² ⌊God said,⌋ "My people are foolish.
      They don't know me.
   They are stupid children.
      They don't understand.
   They are skillful at doing evil,
      but they don't know how to do good."

Disaster Is Coming

²³ I looked at the earth.
      The earth was empty;
   nothing was on the earth.
   I looked at the sky.
      and its light was gone.*
²⁴ I looked at the mountains,
      and they were shaking.
   All of the hills were trembling.
²⁵ I looked, but there were no people.
      All the birds of the sky had flown away.
²⁶ I looked, and the good land
      had become a desert.
   All the cities in that land were destroyed.
   The Lord caused this.
      The Lord and his great anger caused this.

²⁷ The Lord says these things:
   "The whole country will be ruined.
   (But I will not completely destroy the land.)

---

sackcloth A kind of cloth that people wore to show they were sad or crying for dead people.
chaff The seed coverings and stems separated from the seeds of plants like wheat or barley. Farmers saved the seeds but let the wind blow the useless chaff away.
chariot(s) A small wagon used in war.
land of Dan The people from the family group of Dan lived near the border in the northern part of Israel. They would be the first to be attacked by an enemy from the north.
hill country of Ephraim This was the central part of the land that had been the northern kingdom of Israel.

The earth ... gone Jeremiah is comparing his country to the time before people were put on the earth. See Gen. 1:1.

²⁸ So the people in the land will cry
for the dead people.
The sky will grow dark.
I have spoken and will not change.
I have made a decision
and I will not change my mind."

²⁹ The people of Judah will hear the sound
of the horse soldiers and the archers,*
and the people will run away!
Some of the people will hide in caves,*
some people will hide in the bushes,
some people will climb up into the rocks.
All of the cities of Judah will be empty.
No person will live in them.

³⁰ Judah, you have been destroyed.
So what are you doing now?
Why are you putting on your best red dress?
Why are you putting on your gold jewelry?
Why are you putting on your eye makeup?
You make yourself beautiful,
but it is a waste of time.
Your lovers hate you.
They are trying to kill you.

³¹ I hear a cry like a woman having a baby.
It is a scream like a woman
that is having her first baby.
It is the cry of the Daughter of Zion.*
She is lifting her hands in prayer, saying,
"Oh! I am about to faint!
Murderers are all around me!"

The Evil of the People of Judah

5 ⌊The Lord says,⌋ "Walk the streets of Jerusalem.
Look around and think about these things.
Search the public squares of the city. See if you can
find one good person, one person that does honest
things, one that searches for the truth. If you find
one good person, I will forgive Jerusalem! ²The
people make promises and say, 'As the Lord lives.'
But they don't really mean it."

³ Lord, I know that you want people
to be loyal to you.
You hit the people of Judah,
but they did not feel any pain.
You destroyed them,
but they refused to learn their lesson.
They became very stubborn.
They refused to be sorry
for the bad things they did.

⁴ But I *(Jeremiah)* said to myself,
"It must be only the poor people
that are so foolish.
Poor people have not learned
the way of the Lord.
Poor people don't know
the teachings of their God.
⁵ So I will go to the leaders of Judah.
I will talk to them.
Surely the leaders know the way of the Lord.
I am sure they know the law of their God."
But the leaders had all joined together
to break away from serving the Lord.
⁶ They turned against God,
so a lion from the forest will attack them.
A wolf from the desert will kill them.
A leopard is hiding near their cities.
The leopard will tear to pieces
any person that comes out of the city.
This will happen because the people
of Judah have sinned again and again.
They have wandered away from the Lord
many times.

⁷ ⌊God said,⌋
"Judah, give me one good reason
why I should forgive you.
Your children have abandoned me.
They made promises to idols
And those idols are not really gods!
I gave your children everything they needed.
But they still were unfaithful to me!
They spent much time with prostitutes.
⁸ They are like horses
that have had plenty to eat
and are ready to mate.
They are like a horse that is
calling its neighbor's wife.
⁹ Should I punish the people of Judah
for doing these things?"
This message is from the Lord.
"Yes! You know I should punish a nation
that lives like that.
I will give them the punishment
that they deserve.

¹⁰ "Go along the rows of Judah's grapevines.
Cut down the vines.
(But don't completely destroy them.)
Cut off all their branches.
Why? Because these branches don't belong to
the Lord.

Daughter of Zion A name for the city of Jerusalem.

¹¹ The family of Israel and the family of Judah
   have been unfaithful to me in every way."
   This message is from the Lord.
¹² "Those people have lied about the Lord.
   They have said,
     'The Lord will not do anything to us.
     Nothing bad will happen to us.
     We will never see an army attack us.
     We will never starve.'
¹³ "The ⌊false⌋ prophets are only empty wind.*
   The word of God is not in them.*
   Bad things will happen to them."
¹⁴ The Lord God All-Powerful said
     these things:
   "Those people said I would not punish them.
   So Jeremiah, the words I give you
     will be like fire.
   And those people will be like wood.
   That fire will burn them up completely!
¹⁵ Family of Israel, this message
     is from the Lord,
   "I will soon bring a nation from far away
     to attack you.
   It is an old nation.
   It is an ancient nation.
   The people of that nation speak a language
     that you don't know.
   You can't understand what they say.
¹⁶ Their arrow bags are like open graves.
   All of their men are strong soldiers.
¹⁷ Those soldiers will eat all the crops
     that you gathered.
   They will eat all of your food.
   They will eat (destroy) your sons
     and daughters.
   They will eat your flocks and your herds.
   They will eat your grapes and your figs.
   They will destroy your strong cities
     with their swords.
   They will destroy the strong cities
     that you trust in!
¹⁸ This message is from the Lord,
   "But Judah, when those terrible days come,
     I will not fully destroy you.
¹⁹ The people of Judah will ask you,
     'Jeremiah, why has the Lord our God
     done this bad thing to us?'

Give them this answer:
   'You people of Judah have left the Lord,
   and you have served foreign idols
     in your own land.
   You did those things, so now
     you will serve foreigners in a land
     that doesn't belong to you.'"
²⁰ ⌊The Lord said,⌋
   "Tell this message to the family of Jacob.
   Tell this message in the nation of Judah:
²¹ Hear this message.
   You foolish people have no sense:
   'You have eyes, but you don't see!
   You have ears, but you don't listen!'
²² Surely you are afraid of me.'"
   This message is from the Lord.
   "You should shake with fear in front of me.
   I am the One who made the beaches
     to be a boundary for the sea.
   I made it that way to keep the water
     in its place forever.
   The waves may pound the beach,
     but they will not destroy it.
   The waves may roar as they come in,
     but they can't go beyond the beach.
²³ But the people of Judah are stubborn.
   They are always planning ways
     to turn against me.
   They turned away from me
     and left me.
²⁴ The people of Judah never say to themselves,
     'Let's fear and respect the Lord our God.
   He gives us autumn and spring rains
     at just the right time.
   He makes sure that we have the harvest
     at just the right time.'
²⁵ People of Judah, you have done wrong.
   So the rains and the harvest have not come.
   Your sins have kept you from enjoying
     those good things from the Lord.
²⁶ There are evil men among my people.
   Those evil men are like men
     that make nets for catching birds.*
   These men set their traps,
     But they catch men instead of birds.
²⁷ The houses of these evil men are full of lies,
     like a cage full of birds.
   Their lies made them rich and powerful.
²⁸ They have grown big and fat
     ⌊from the evil things they have done⌋.
   There is no end to the evil things they do.

---

wind This is a word play. The Hebrew word for wind is like the word for Spirit.
The word of God ... them Literally, "and the 'He said' is not in them."
men ... birds The Hebrew is hard to understand here.

They will not plead the case
  of children that have no parents.
They will not help those orphans.
They will not let poor people
  be judged fairly.
²⁹ Should I punish the people of Judah
  for doing these things?"
This message is from the Lord.
"You know that I should punish a nation
  such as this.
I should give them the punishment
  that they deserve."

³⁰ ⌊The Lord says,⌋
"A terrible and shocking thing
  has happened in the land of Judah.
³¹ The prophets tell lies.
The priests will not do
  what they were chosen to do.*
And my people love it this way!
But what will you people do
  when your punishment comes?"

The Enemy Surrounds Jerusalem

6 Run for your lives, people of Benjamin!
Run away from the city of Jerusalem!
Blow the war trumpet in the city of Tekoa!
Put up the warning flag
  in the city of Beth Hakkerem!
Do these things because disaster is coming
  from the north.*
Terrible destruction is coming to you.
² Daughter of Zion,* you are like
  a beautiful meadow.*
³ Shepherds come to Jerusalem,
  and they bring their flocks.
They set up their tents all around her.
Each shepherd takes care of his own flock.

⁴ "Get ready to fight against Jerusalem.
Get up! We will attack the city at noon.
But it is already getting late.
The evening shadows are growing long.
⁵ So get up! We will attack the city at night!
Let's destroy the strong walls
  that are around Jerusalem."

⁶ This is what the Lord All-Powerful says:
"Cut down the trees around Jerusalem.
And build a siege mound* against it.
This city should be punished.
Inside this city is nothing but oppression.
⁷ A well keeps its water fresh.
In the same way,
  Jerusalem keeps its wickedness fresh.
I hear about the looting and violence
  in this city all the time.
I see the pain and sickness in Jerusalem
  all the time.
⁸ Listen to this warning, Jerusalem.
If you don't listen
  then I will turn my back on you.
I will make your land an empty desert.
  No person will be able to live there."

⁹ This is what the Lord All-Powerful says:
"Gather* the people of Israel
  that were left on their land.
Gather them the way you would gather
  the last grapes on a grapevine.
Check each vine, like a worker checks
  each vine when he picks the grapes."

¹⁰ Who can I speak to?
Who can I warn?
Who will listen to me?
The people of Israel have closed their ears,
  so they can't hear my warnings.
The people don't like the Lord's teachings.
They don't want to hear his message.
¹¹ But I (Jeremiah) am full of the Lord's anger!
I am tired of holding it in!
"Pour out the Lord's anger on the children
  that play in the street.
Pour out the Lord's anger on the young men
  that gather together.
A man and his wife will both be captured.
All the old people will be captured.
¹² Their houses will be given to other people.
Their fields and their wives
  will be given to other people.

---

priests ... were chosen to do The Hebrew is hard to understand here.
north This refers to the army of Babylon coming from the north to attack the nation of Judah.
Daughter of Zion A name for the city of Jerusalem.
you are like a beautiful meadow The Hebrew is hard to understand here.

siege mound A large pile of dirt and rock that an army put against the wall of a city they were attacking. This made it easier for the enemy soldiers to climb over the wall into the city.
Gather Or "Glean." Farmers were supposed to leave a little of their grain and other crops in the field. In this way, poor people and travelers could always find something to eat. Gathering this leftover grain is called gleaning.

I will raise my hand and punish
  the people of Judah."
This message was from the Lord.

¹³ "All the people of Israel want
    more and more money.
  All the people,
    from the least important
      to the most important people,
    are like that.
  All the people,
    from prophets to priests
    tell lies.
¹⁴ My people have been hurt very badly.
  The prophets and priests
    should bandage those wounds.
  But they treat those wounds
    like they are only a small scratch.
  They say,
    'It is all right, everything is fine!'
  But it is not all right!
¹⁵ The priests and prophets should be ashamed
    of the bad things they do.
  But they are not ashamed at all.
  They don't know enough
    to be embarrassed of their sins.
  So they will be punished with everyone else.
  They will be thrown to the ground
    when I punish the people."
  The Lord said those things.

¹⁶ The Lord says these things:
    "Stand at the crossroads and look.
      Ask where the old road is.
      Ask where the good road is,
      and walk on that road.
    If you do, you will find rest for yourselves.
    But you people have said,
      'We will not walk on the good road!'
¹⁷ I chose watchmen to watch over you.
    I told them,
      'Listen for the sound of the war trumpet.'
    But they said,
      'We will not listen!'
¹⁸ So, listen, all you nations!
    Pay attention, you people in those countries!*

¹⁹ Hear this, people of the earth.
    I am going to bring disaster
      to the people of Judah.
    Why? Because of all the bad things
      that those people planned.
    And because they ignored my messages.
    Those people refused to obey my law."

²⁰ ₍The Lord says,₎
    "Why do you bring me incense*
      from the country of Sheba?*
    Why do you bring me sweet-smelling cane
      from a faraway country?
    Your burnt offerings don't make me happy.
    Your sacrifices don't please me."
²¹ So, this is what the Lord says:
    "I will give the people of Judah problems.
    They will be like stones
      that make people fall.
    Fathers and sons will stumble over them.
    Friends and neighbors will die."

²² This is what the Lord says:
    "An army is coming from the north.*
    A great nation is coming from
      faraway places on earth.
²³ The soldiers carry bows and spears.
    They are cruel.
    They have no mercy.
    They are so powerful.
    They sound like the roaring ocean
      as they ride their horses.
    That army is coming ready for battle.
    That army is coming to attack you,
      Daughter of Zion."*
²⁴ We have heard the news about that army.
    We are helpless from fear.
    We feel trapped by our troubles.
    We are like a woman that is having a baby.
²⁵ Don't go out into the fields.
    Don't go on the roads.
    Why? Because the enemy has swords
      and there is danger everywhere.
²⁶ My people, put on sackcloth*,
    and roll in the ashes.*
  Cry loud for the dead people.
  Cry like you lost an only son.

Pay attention ... countries The Hebrew is hard to understand here.
incense Special dried tree sap. Burned to make a sweet-smelling smoke, it was offered as a gift to God.
Sheba A land south of Israel, located where part of Saudi Arabia is today. Sheba controlled the spice trade in the time of Jeremiah.
north This refers to the army of Babylon coming from the north to attack the nation of Judah.
Daughter of Zion A name for the city of Jerusalem.
sackcloth A kind of cloth that people wore to show they were sad or crying for dead people.
roll in the ashes This is one way people showed that they were sad or crying for a dead person.

Do these things because the destroyer
will come against us very quickly.

27 "Jeremiah, I *(the Lord)* made you
like a worker that tests metals.
You will test my people
and watch how they live.
28 My people have turned against me,
and they are very stubborn.
They say bad things about people.
They are like bronze and iron,
that are covered with rust and tarnish.
29 ⌊They are like a worker
that tried to make silver pure.⌋
The bellows* blew strongly
⌊and the fire became hotter⌋.
But only lead came from the fire!*
The worker wasted his time
trying to make that silver pure.
In the same way, the evil was not removed
⌊from my people⌋.
30 My people will be called, 'Rejected Silver.'
They will be given that name
because the Lord did not accept them."

Jeremiah's Temple Sermon

7 This is the Lord's message to Jeremiah:
²Jeremiah, stand at the gate of the Lord's
house. Preach this message at the gate:

"Hear the message from the Lord, all you
people of the nation of Judah. All you people that
come through these gates to worship the Lord,
hear this message. ³The Lord is the God of the
people of Israel. This is what the Lord All-
Powerful says: 'Change your lives and do good
things. If you do this, I will let you live in this
place.* ⁴Don't trust the lies that some people say.
They say, "This is the temple* of the Lord, the
temple of the Lord, the temple of the Lord!"* ⁵If
you change your lives and do good things, I will
let you live in this place. You must be fair to each
other. ⁶You must be fair to strangers. You must do
the right things for widows and orphans.* Don't
kill innocent people! Don't follow other gods!
Why? Because they will ruin your lives. ⁷If you
obey me, I will let you live in this place. I gave
this land to your ancestors* for them to keep
forever.

⁸"'But you are trusting lies. And those lies are
worthless. ⁹Will you steal and murder? Will you
do the sin of adultery?* Will you falsely accuse
other people? Will you worship the false god
Baal* and follow other gods that you have not
known? ¹⁰If you do those sins, do you think that
you can stand before me in this house that is
called by my name? Do you think you can stand
before me and say, "We are safe," just so you can
do all these terrible things? ¹¹This temple is called
by my name! Is this temple nothing more to you
than a hideout for robbers? I have been watching
you.'" This message is from the Lord.

¹²"You people of Judah, go now to the town of
Shiloh. Go to the place where I first made a house
for my name. The people of Israel also did evil
things. Go and see what I did to that place because
of the evil things they did.* ¹³You people of Israel
were doing all these evil things"—This message is
from the Lord!—"I spoke to you again and again,
but you refused to listen to me. I called to you, but
you did not answer. ¹⁴So I will destroy the house
called by my name in Jerusalem. I will destroy
that temple* like I destroyed Shiloh. And that
house in Jerusalem that is called by my name is
the temple that you trust in. I gave that place to
you and to your ancestors.* ¹⁵I will throw you
away from me just like I threw away all your
brothers from Ephraim.*

¹⁶"As for you, Jeremiah, don't pray for these
people of Judah. Don't beg for them or pray for
them. Don't beg for me to help them. I will not
listen to your prayer for them. ¹⁷I know you see
what those people are doing in the towns of

---

bellows A tool for blowing air on a fire to make the fire hotter.
lead came from the fire Workers melted metals like silver to make the metals pure. Lead was the first metal to melt, so the workers poured the lead out, leaving the other metal pure. Here Jeremiah is saying the people are all bad—they are all lead and no silver!
I will ... place This can also mean, "I will live with you."
temple The special building in Jerusalem for Jewish worship.
temple of the Lord Many people in Jerusalem thought that the Lord would always protect Jerusalem because his temple was there. They thought God would protect Jerusalem, no matter how evil the people were.
widows and orphans Widows are women whose husbands have died, and orphans are children whose parents have died. Often these people have no one to care for them.

adultery Breaking the marriage promise by sexual sin.
Baal The Canaanite people believed that this false god brought the rain and storms. They also thought that he made the land produce good crops.
Go ... they did Shiloh was probably destroyed by the Philistines in the time of Eli and Samuel. See 1 Sam. 4.
Ephraim This is the northern kingdom of Israel.

Judah. You can see what they are doing in the streets of the city of Jerusalem. ¹⁸This is what the people of Judah are doing: The children gather wood. The fathers use the wood to make a fire. The women make the dough and make cakes of bread to offer to the Queen of Heaven.* Those people of Judah pour out drink offerings to worship other gods. They do this to make me angry. ¹⁹But I am not the one the people of Judah are really hurting." This message is from the Lord. "They are only hurting themselves. They are bringing shame on themselves."

²⁰So the Lord says this: "I will show my anger against this place. I will punish people and animals. I will punish the trees in the field and the crops that grow in the ground. My anger will be like a hot fire—and no person will be able to stop it."

The Lord Wants Obedience More than Sacrifice

²¹The Lord All-Powerful, the God of Israel, says these things: "Go and offer as many burnt offerings and sacrifices as you want. Eat the meat of those sacrifices yourselves. ²²I brought your ancestors* out of Egypt. I spoke to them, but I did not give them any commands about burnt offerings and sacrifices. ²³I only gave them this command: 'Obey me and I will be your God, and you will be my people. Do all that I command, and good things will happen to you.'

²⁴"But your ancestors* did not listen to me. They did not pay attention to me. They were stubborn and did the things they wanted to do. They did not become good. They became even more evil—they went backward, not forward. ²⁵From the day that your ancestors left Egypt to this day, I have sent my servants to you. My servants are the prophets. I sent them to you again and again. ²⁶But your ancestors did not listen to me. They did not pay attention to me. They were very stubborn and did evil worse than their fathers.

²⁷"Jeremiah, you will tell these things to the people of Judah. But they won't listen to you! You call to them, but they won't answer you. ²⁸So you must tell them these things: This is the nation that did not obey the Lord its God. These people did not listen to God's teachings. These people don't know the true teachings.

The Valley of Slaughter

²⁹"Jeremiah, cut off your hair and throw it away.* Go up to the bare hilltop and cry. Why? Because the Lord has rejected this generation of people. The Lord has turned his back on these people. And in anger, he will punish them. ³⁰Do this because I have seen the people of Judah doing evil things." This message is from the Lord. "They have set up their idols. And I hate those idols! They have set up idols in the temple that is called by my name. They have made my house 'dirty'! ³¹The people of Judah have built the high places* of Topheth in the Valley of Ben Hinnom. In those places the people killed their own sons and daughters—they burned them as sacrifices. This is something I never commanded. Something like this never even entered my mind! ³²So, I warn you. The days are coming," this message is from the Lord, "when people won't call this place Topheth or the Valley of Ben Hinnom anymore. No, they will call it the Valley of Slaughter.* They will give it this name because they will bury the dead people in Topheth until there is no more room to bury anyone else. ³³Then the bodies of the dead people will ₁lie on top of the ground and₁ become food for the birds of the sky. Wild animals will eat the bodies of those people. There will be no person left alive to chase the birds or animals away. ³⁴I will bring an end to the sounds of joy and happiness in the towns of Judah and in the streets of Jerusalem. There will be no more sounds of the bride and bridegroom in Judah or Jerusalem. The land will become an empty desert."

8 This message is from the Lord: "At that time, men will take the bones of the kings and important rulers of Judah from their tombs.* They will take the bones of the priests and prophets from their tombs. They will take the bones of all the people of Jerusalem from their tombs. ²Those

---

cut ... away This showed Jeremiah was sad.
high places Special places where the people worshiped false gods. These places were often on hilltops, but not always. Some high places were in valleys.
Slaughter Usually, this word means to kill an animal and cut it into pieces of meat. But it often means to kill people like they are animals.
tomb(s) A grave dug in a wall of rock.

Queen of Heaven Probably the false god Astarte. She was the goddess of sex and war. People in Mesopotamia worshiped her. They thought she was the planet Venus, which looks like a star in the sky.
ancestors Literally, "fathers," meaning a person's parents, grandparents, and all the people they are descended from.

men will spread those bones on the ground under the sun, the moon, and the stars. The people of Jerusalem love to worship the sun, the moon, and the stars. No person will gather those bones and bury them again. So, the bones of those people will be like dung thrown on the ground.

³"I will force the people of Judah to leave their homes and their land. The people will be taken away to foreign lands. Some of the people of Judah that were not killed in the war will wish that they had been killed." This message is from the Lord.

Sin and Punishment

⁴ Jeremiah, say this to the people of Judah:

The Lord says these things:
"You know if a man falls down,
   he gets up again.
And if a man goes the wrong way,
   he turns around and comes back.
⁵ The people of Judah went *(lived)*
   the wrong way.
But why do those people of Jerusalem
   continue going the wrong way?
They believe their own lies.
   They refuse to turn around and come back.
⁶ I have listened to them very carefully.
   But they don't say what is right.
The people are not sorry for their sins.
   The people don't think about the bad things
      they have done.
The people do things without thinking.
   They are like horses running into a battle.
⁷ Even the birds in the sky
   know the right time to do things.
The storks, doves, swifts, and thrushes
   know when it is time to fly to a new home.
But my people don't know what the Lord
   wants them to do.

⁸ "You keep saying,
   'We have the Lord's teachings!
      So we are wise!'
But that is not true.
   Why? Because the scribes*
      have lied with their pens.

⁹ Those 'wise people' refused to listen
   to the Lord's teachings.
So they are not really wise people at all.
Those 'wise people' were trapped.
   They became shocked and ashamed.
¹⁰ So I will give their wives to other men.
   I will give their fields to new owners.
All the people of Israel want
   more and more money.
All the people,
   from the least important
      to most important people,
         are like that.
All the people,
   from prophets to priests
      tell lies.
¹¹ My people have been hurt very badly.
The prophets and priests
   should bandage those wounds.
But they treat those wounds
   like they are only a small scratch.
They say,
   'It is all right, everything is fine!'
But it is not all right!
¹² They should be ashamed
   of the bad things they do.
But they are not ashamed at all.
They don't know enough
   to be embarrassed of their sins.
So they will be punished with everyone else.
   They will be thrown to the ground
      when I punish the people."
The Lord said those things.

¹³ "I will take away their fruit and crops,
   so that there will be no harvest."
This message is from the Lord.
"There will not be any grapes on the vine.
There will not be any figs on the fig tree.
   Even the leaves will become dry and die.
I will take away the things I gave them.*

¹⁴ "Why are we just sitting here?
   Come, let's run to the strong cities.
If the Lord our God is going to make us die,
   then let's die there.
We have sinned against the Lord,
   so God gave us poisoned water to drink.
¹⁵ We hoped to have peace,
   but nothing good has come.

---

scribes Men that wrote down and copied different writings. Some of those writings included the books that later became the Old Testament. Those men spent so much time with those writings, that they often became experts at knowing what those scriptures (writings) meant.

I will take away ... gave them The Hebrew of this line is hard to understand.

We hoped that he would forgive us,
    but only disaster has come.
16 From the land of the family group of Dan,
    we hear the snorting*
        of the enemy's horses.
    The ground shakes from the pounding
        of their hooves.*
    They have come to destroy the land
        and everything in it.
    They have come to destroy the city
        and all the people that live there.

17 "People of Judah,
    I am sending poisonous snakes*
        to attack you.
    Those snakes can't be controlled.
    Those snakes will bite you."
This message is from the Lord.

18 God, I am very sad and afraid.
19 Listen to my people.
    Everywhere in this country
        people are crying for help.
    They say,
    "Is the Lord still at Zion?*
    Is Zion's King still there?"

[But God says,]
    "The people of Judah worshiped
        their worthless foreign idols.
    That made me very angry!
    Why did they do that?
20 [And the people say,]
    "Harvest time is over. Summer is gone.
    And still we have not been saved."

21 My people are hurt,
    so I am hurt.
    I am too sad to speak.
22 Surely there is some medicine in Gilead.
    Surely there is a doctor in Gilead.
    So why are the hurts of my people
        not healed?

9 If my head was filled with water,
    and if my eyes were a fountain of tears,
    I would cry day and night
        for my people that have been destroyed.

2 If only I had a place in the desert,
    a house where travelers spend the night,
    I could leave my people.
    I could go away from those people.
Why? Because they are all unfaithful to God.
    They have all turned against him.

3 "Those people use their tongues like a bow;
    lies fly from their mouths like arrows.
Lies, not truth, have grown strong in this land.
Those people go from one sin to another.
    They don't know me."
The Lord said these things.

4 "Watch your neighbors!
    Don't trust your own brothers!
Why? Because every brother is a cheat.
    Every neighbor talks behind your back.
5 Every person lies to his neighbor.
    No person speaks the truth.
The people of Judah have taught
    their tongues to lie.
They sinned until they were too tired
    to come back.
6 One bad thing followed another.
    And lies followed lies.
The people refused to know me."
The Lord said those things.

7 So, the Lord All-Powerful says:
"A worker heats metal in a fire
    to test if it is pure.
I will test the people of Judah like that.
I have no other choice.
    My people have sinned.
8 The people of Judah have tongues
    that are like sharp arrows.
Their mouths speak lies.
Each person speaks nice to his neighbor.
But he is secretly planning ways
    to attack his neighbor.
9 I should punish the people of Judah."
This message is from the Lord.
"You know that I should punish
    that kind of people.
I should give them the punishment
    that they deserve."

10 I *(Jeremiah)* will cry loud for the mountains.
    I will sing a funeral song
        for the empty fields.
Why? Because the living things
    were taken away.
No person travels there now.
The sounds of cattle can't be heard there.

---

snorting The sound that comes from breathing very hard through the nose.
hooves The hard part of the feet of certain animals.
poisonous snakes This probably means one of Judah's enemies.
Zion The southeast part of the mountain Jerusalem is built on. Sometimes it means the people of God living in Jerusalem.

The birds have flown away
and the animals are gone.

11 "I *(the Lord)* will make the city of Jerusalem
a pile of garbage.
It will be a home for jackals.*
I will destroy the cities in the land of Judah,
so no one will live there."

12 Is there a man that is wise enough to
understand these things?
Is there some person that has been taught
by the Lord?
Can anyone explain the Lord's message?
Why was the land ruined?
Why was it made like an empty desert
where no people go?

13 The Lord answered these questions. He said,
"It is because the people of Judah quit
following my teachings.
I gave them my teachings,
but they refused to listen to me.
They did not follow my teachings.

14 The people of Judah lived their own way.
They were stubborn.
They followed the false god Baal.*
Their fathers taught them to follow
those false gods."

15 So the Lord All-Powerful,
the God of Israel, says,
"I will soon make the people of Judah
eat bitter food.
I will make them drink poisoned water.

16 I will scatter the people of Judah
through other nations.
They will live in strange nations.
They and their fathers never knew
about those countries.
I will send men with swords.
Those men will kill the people of Judah.
They will kill them until the people
are finished."

17 This is what the Lord All-Powerful says:
"Now, think about these things!
Call for the women that get paid
to cry at funerals.
Send for the people that are good
at that job.

18 ⌊The people say,⌋
'Let those women come quickly
and cry for us.
Then our eyes will fill with tears,
and streams of water will come
out of our eyes.'

19 "The sound of loud crying
is heard from Zion*:
'We are truly ruined!
We are truly ashamed!
We must leave our land,
because our houses have been
destroyed.
Now our houses are only piles of rock.'"

20 Now, women of Judah,
listen to the message from the Lord.
Listen to the words from the Lord's mouth.
⌊The Lord says,⌋
"Teach your daughters how to cry loud.
Each woman must learn to sing
this funeral song:

21 'Death has come.
Death climbed in through our windows.
Death came into our palaces.*
Death has come to our children
that play in the streets.
Death has come to the young men
that meet in the public places.'

22 "Jeremiah, say these things:
'The Lord says,
Dead bodies will lie in the fields
like dung.
Their bodies will lie on the ground
like grain a farmer has cut.
But there will be no one to gather them.'"

23 The Lord says:
"Wise men must not brag
about their wisdom.
Strong men must not brag
about their strength.
Rich men must not brag
about their money.

24 But if someone wants to brag,
then let him brag about these things:
Let him brag that he learned to know me.

---

jackals A wild animal, like a dog. Those animals only live where there are no people.

Baal The Canaanite people believed that this false god brought the rain and storms. They also thought that he made the land produce good crops.

Zion The southeast part of the mountain Jerusalem is built on. Sometimes it means the people of God living in Jerusalem.

palace(s) A large house for the king and his family.

Let him brag that he understands
    that I am the Lord
    that I am kind and fair
    and that I do good things on earth.
I love those things."
This message is from the Lord.

²⁵This message is from the Lord. "The time is coming when I will punish all the people that are circumcised* only in the body. ²⁶I am talking about the people of the nations of Egypt, Judah, Edom, Ammon, Moab, and all the people that live in the desert. The men in all those countries really were not circumcised in their bodies. But the people from the family of Israel were not circumcised in their hearts."

The Lord and the Idols

10 Family of Israel, listen to the Lord! ²This is what the Lord says:

"Don't live like people from other nations.
    Don't be afraid of special signs in the sky.*
The other nations are afraid of the things
    that they see in the sky.
But you must not be afraid of those things.
³ The customs of other people
    are worth nothing.
Their idols are nothing but wood
    from the forest.
Their idols are made by a worker
    with his chisel.
⁴ They make their idols beautiful
    with silver and gold.
They use hammers and nails
    to fasten their idols down,
    so they will not fall over.
⁵ The idols of the other nations are like
    a scarecrow in a cucumber field.
Those idols can't walk.
    They can't talk.
    And the people must carry them.
So don't be afraid of those idols.
    They can't hurt you.

And they can't help you either!"

⁶ Lord, there is no one like you!
    You are great!
    Your name is great and powerful!
⁷ Every person should respect you, God.
    You are the King of all the nations.
    You deserve their respect.
There are many wise men among the nations.
    But none of those people are as wise as
    you.
⁸ All the people of the other nations are stupid
    and foolish.
Their teachings come from worthless wooden
    statues.
⁹ They use silver from the city of Tarshish
    and gold from the city of Uphaz
    and make their statues.
Carpenters and metal-workers make
    those idols.
They put blue and purple clothes on
    those idols.
    "Wise men" make those "gods."
¹⁰ But the Lord is the only true God.
    He is the only God who is truly alive.
    He is the King that rules forever.
The earth shakes when God is angry.
    The people of the nations can't stop his
    anger.

¹¹ ⌊The Lord says⌋
"Tell this message to those people:
    'Those false gods did not make
        heaven and earth.
    And those false gods will be destroyed
        and disappear from heaven and earth.'"*
¹² God is the One who used his power
    and made the earth.
God used his wisdom and built the world.
    With his understanding,
    God stretched out the sky ⌊over the earth⌋.
¹³ God causes the loud thunder,
    and he causes great floods of water to fall
        from the sky.
He makes clouds rise in the sky every place
    on earth.
He sends lightning with the rain.
    He brings out the wind from his
    storehouses.

---

circumcised To have the foreskin cut off. This was done to every Jewish male to show he shared in the Agreement God made with Israel. See Gen. 17:9-14.

special signs in the sky People believed that such things as comets, meteors, or eclipses of the sun and moon could be used to learn what was going to happen in the future.

Tell this message ... earth This part was written in Aramaic, not Hebrew. This was the language people used often when writing to people in other countries. It was also the language spoken in Babylon.

¹⁴ People are so stupid!
    Metal workers are fooled by the idols
        that they themselves made.
    Those statues are nothing but lies.
        They are stupid.*
¹⁵ Those idols are worth nothing.
    They are something to make fun of.
    In the time of judgment,
        those idols will be destroyed.
¹⁶ But Jacob's God* is not like those idols.
    God made everything.
    And Israel is the family that God chose to
        be his own people.
    God's name is "Lord All-Powerful."

Destruction Is Coming

¹⁷ Get everything you own and prepare to leave.
    You people of Judah are caught in the city,
        and the enemy is all around it.
¹⁸ The Lord says:
    "This time, I will throw the people of Judah out
        of this country.
    I will bring pain and trouble to them.
    I will do this so they will learn their
        lesson."*
¹⁹ Oh, I (Jeremiah) am hurt badly.
    I am injured and I can't be healed.
    Yet I told myself,
    "This is my sickness,
        I must suffer through it."
²⁰ My tent is ruined.
    All the tent's ropes are broken.
    My children left me.
        They are gone.
    No person is left to put up my tent.
    No person is left to fix a shelter for me.
²¹ The shepherds (leaders) are stupid.
    They don't try to find the Lord.
    They are not wise, so their flocks (people) are
        scattered and lost.
²² Listen! A loud noise!
    The loud noise is coming from the north.*

It will destroy the cities of Judah.
    Judah will become an empty desert.
    It will be a home for jackals.*
²³ Lord, I know that a person does not really
        own his life.
    People don't really know the right way to
        live.
²⁴ Lord, correct us!
    But be fair!
    Don't punish us in anger!
²⁵ If you are angry, then punish the other
        nations.
    They don't know or respect you.
    Those people don't worship you.
    Those nations destroyed Jacob's family.
    They destroyed Israel completely.
    They destroyed Israel's homeland.

The Agreement Is Broken

11 This is the message that came to Jeremiah. This message came from the Lord: ²"Jeremiah, listen to the words of this Agreement.* Tell the people of Judah about these things. Tell these things to the people living in Jerusalem. ³This is what the Lord, the God of Israel, says: 'Bad things will happen to any person that does not obey this Agreement.' ⁴I am talking about the Agreement I made with your ancestors.* I made that Agreement with them at the time I brought them out of Egypt. ₍Egypt was a place of many troubles—₎it was like an oven hot enough to melt iron. I told those people: Obey me and do everything I command you. If you do this, you will be my people, and I will be your God.

⁵"I did this to keep the promise that I had made to your ancestors.* I promised to give them a very fertile land—a land flowing with milk and honey. And you are living in that country today."

I (Jeremiah) answered, "Amen,* Lord."

⁶The Lord said to me, "Jeremiah, preach this message in the towns of Judah and in the streets of Jerusalem. This is the message: Listen to the

---

They are stupid Literally, "they have no spirit." The Bible teaches that it is the Spirit of God that makes people wise. This might also mean "they are not alive."

Jacob's God Literally, "Jacob's share." This shows that God and Israel had a special relationship—God belonged to Israel, and Israel belonged to God.

they will learn their lesson The Hebrew here is hard to understand.

north This refers to the army of Babylon coming from the north to attack the nation of Judah.

jackals A wild animal, like a dog. Those animals only live where no people are.

Agreement Literally, "Proof." The flat stones with the Ten Commandments written on them were proof of the Agreement between God and Israel.

ancestors Literally, "fathers," meaning a person's parents, grandparents, and all the people they are descended from.

Amen The Hebrew word "amen" means, "truly," or "indeed." It is used to show that the person agrees with what has been said.

words of this Agreement.* And then obey those laws. ⁷I gave a warning to your ancestors* at the time I brought them out of the land of Egypt. I warned them again and again to this very day. I told them to obey me. ⁸But your ancestors did not listen to me. They were stubborn and did what their own evil hearts wanted. The Agreement says that bad things will happen to them if they don't obey. So I made all those bad things happen to them! I commanded them to obey the Agreement, but they did not."

⁹The Lord said to me, "Jeremiah, I know that the people of Judah and the people living in Jerusalem have made secret plans. ¹⁰Those people are doing the same sins that their ancestors did. Their ancestors refused to listen to my message. They followed and worshiped other gods. The family of Israel and the family of Judah have broken the Agreement I made with their ancestors."

¹¹So the Lord says: "I will soon make something terrible happen to the people of Judah. They will not be able to escape! They will be sorry. And they will cry to me for help. But I will not listen to them. ¹²The people in the towns of Judah and in the city of Jerusalem will go and pray to their idols for help. Those people burn incense* to those idols. But those idols will not be able to help the people of Judah when that terrible time comes.

¹³"People of Judah, you have many idols—there are as many idols as there are towns in Judah. You have built many altars for worshiping that disgusting god Baal*—there are as many altars as there are streets in Jerusalem.

¹⁴"As for you, Jeremiah, don't pray for these people of Judah. Don't beg for them. Don't say prayers for them. I will not listen. Those people will begin to suffer. And then they will call to me for help. But I will not listen."

¹⁵ "Why* is my lover *(Judah)*
in my house *(temple)*?
She has no right to be there.
She had done many evil things.
Judah, do you think that special promises
and animal sacrifices will stop you
from being destroyed?
Do you think you can escape punishment
by offering sacrifices to me?"

¹⁶ The Lord gave you a name.
He called you,
' A green olive tree,
beautiful to look at.'
But with a strong storm,
the Lord will set that tree on fire,
and its branches will be burned up.
¹⁷ The Lord All-Powerful planted you.
And he said that disaster will come to you.
Why? Because the family of Israel
and the family of Judah
have done evil things.
They offered sacrifices to Baal."*
And that made me angry!

Evil Plans Against Jeremiah

¹⁸The Lord showed me that the men of Anathoth* were making plots against me. The Lord showed me the things they were doing, so I knew they were against me. ¹⁹Before the Lord showed me that the people were against me, I was like a gentle lamb waiting to be butchered. I did not understand that they were against me. They were saying these things about me: "Let us destroy the tree and its fruit! Let us kill him! Then people will forget him." ²⁰But Lord, you are a fair judge. You know how to test peoples' hearts and minds. I will tell you my arguments. And I will let you give them the punishment they deserve.

²¹The men from Anathoth were planning to kill Jeremiah. Those men said to Jeremiah, "Don't prophesy* in the name of the Lord, or we will kill you." The Lord made a decision about those men from Anathoth. ²²The Lord All-Powerful said, "I will soon punish those men from Anathoth. Their young men will die in war. Their sons and daughters will die from hunger. ²³No person from

---

Agreement Literally, "Proof." The flat stones with the Ten Commandments written on them were proof of the Agreement between God and Israel.

ancestors Literally, "fathers," meaning a person's parents, grandparents, and all the people they are descended from.

incense Special dried tree sap. Burned to make a sweet-smelling smoke, it was offered as a gift to God.

Baal The Canaanite people believed that this false god brought the rain and storms. They also thought that he made the land produce good crops.

Verse 15,16 We are not sure of the exact meaning of verses 15 and 16.

men of Anathoth Anathoth was Jeremiah's home town. The people that were plotting against him there included his own relatives. See Jer. 12:6.

prophesy To speak for God.

the city of Anathoth will be left. No person will survive. I will punish them. I will cause something bad to happen to them."

Jeremiah Complains to God

12 Lord, if I argue with you,

you are always right!
But I want to ask you about some things that
   don't seem right.
Why are wicked people successful?
Why do people you can't trust have such
   easy lives?
2 You have put those wicked people here.
They are like plants with strong roots,
   they grow and produce fruit.
With their mouths, they say that you are near
   and dear to them.
But in their hearts, they are really far away
   from you.
3 But you know my heart, Lord.
You see me and test my mind.
Drag those evil people away
   like sheep to be butchered.
Choose them for the day of slaughter.
4 How much longer will the land be dry?
How long will the grass be dry and dead?
The animals and birds in the land have died,
And it is the fault of the wicked people.
Yet those wicked people are saying,
   "Jeremiah will not live long enough
   to see what happens to us."

God's Answer to Jeremiah

5 "Jeremiah, if you get tired running
   in a footrace with men,
how will you race against horses?
If you get tired in a safe place,
   what will you do in a dangerous place?
What will you do in the thorn bushes
   that grow along the Jordan River?
6 These men are your own brothers.
Members of your own family
   are making plans against you.
People from your own family
   are yelling at you.
Don't trust them,
   even when they speak to you like friends."

The Lord Rejects His People, Judah

7 "I *(the Lord)* have abandoned my house.
I have left my own property.*
I have given the one I love *(Judah)*
   to her enemies.
8 My own people turned against me
   like a wild lion.
They roared at me,
   so I turned away from them.
9 My own people have become like
   a dying animal surrounded by vultures.
Those birds fly around her.
Come on, wild animals.
Come get something to eat.
10 Many shepherds *(leaders)* have ruined
   my field of grapes.
Those shepherds have walked
   on the plants in my field.
Those shepherds have made my beautiful field
   into an empty desert.
11 They changed my field to a desert.
It is dry and dead.
No people live there.
The whole country is an empty desert.
There is no person left to care for that field.
12 Soldiers came to take things
   from every place in that empty land.
The Lord used those armies
   to punish that land.
People from one end of the land
   to the other were punished.
No person was safe.
13 The people will plant wheat,
   but they will harvest only thorns.
They will work hard until they are very tired,
   but they will get nothing for all their work.
They will be ashamed of their crop.
The Lord's anger caused those things."

The Lord's Promise to Israel's Neighbors

14 This is what the Lord says: "I will tell you what I will do for all the people that live around the land of Israel. Those people are very wicked. They have destroyed the land I gave to the people of Israel. I will pull those evil people up and throw them out of their land. And I will pull the people of Judah up with them. 15 But after I pull

---

house... my own property That is, the people of Judah.

those people out of their land, I will feel sorry for them. I will bring each family back to its own property and to its own land. ¹⁶I want those people to learn their lessons well. In the past, those people taught my people to use Baal's* name to make promises. Now, I want those people to learn their lessons just as well. I want those people to learn to use my name. I want those people to say, 'As the Lord lives ... ' If those people do that, then I will allow them to be successful and I will let them live among my people. ¹⁷But if any nation does not listen to my message, then I will completely destroy it. I will pull it up like a dead plant." This message is from the Lord.

The Sign of the Loincloth

13 This is what the Lord said to me: "Jeremiah, go and buy a linen loincloth.* Then put it around your waist. Don't let the loincloth get wet."

²So I bought a linen loincloth,* just as the Lord told me to do. And I put it around my waist. ³Then the message of the Lord came to me a second time. ⁴This was the message: "Jeremiah, take the loincloth you bought and are wearing, and go to Perath.* Hide the loincloth there in a crack in the rocks."

⁵So I went to Perath* and hid the loincloth* there, just like the Lord told me to do. ⁶Many days later, the Lord said to me, "Now, Jeremiah, go to Perath. Get the loincloth that I told you to hide there."

⁷So I went to Perath and dug up the loincloth. I took it out of the crack in the rocks where I had hidden it. But now I could not wear the loincloth, because it was ruined. It was not good for anything.

⁸Then the message of the Lord came to me. ⁹This is what the Lord said: "The loincloth* is ruined and not good for anything. In the same way, I will ruin the proud people of Judah and Jerusalem. ¹⁰I will ruin those proud and evil people of Judah. They refuse to listen to my messages. They are stubborn and do only the things they want to do. They follow and worship other gods. Those people of Judah will become like this linen loincloth. They will be ruined and not good for anything. ¹¹A loincloth is wrapped tightly around a man's waist. In the same way, I wrapped all the family of Israel and all the family of Judah around me." This message is from the Lord." I did that so those people would be my people. Then my people would bring fame, praise, and honor to me. But my people would not listen to me."

Warnings to Judah

¹²"Jeremiah, say to the people of Judah: 'This is what the Lord, the God of Israel, says: Every wineskin* should be filled with wine.' Those people will laugh and say to you, 'Of course, we know that every wineskin should be filled with wine.' ¹³Then you will say to them, 'This is what the Lord says: I will make everyone that lives in this land helpless, like a drunken man. I am talking about the kings that sit on David's throne. I am also talking about the priests, the prophets, and all the people that live in Jerusalem. ¹⁴I will make the people of Judah stumble and fall into one another. Fathers and sons will fall into one another.'" This message is from the Lord. "'I will not feel sorry or have pity for them. I will not allow compassion to stop me from destroying the people of Judah.'"

¹⁵ Listen and pay attention.
   The Lord has spoken to you.
   Don't be proud.
¹⁶ Honor the Lord your God.
   Praise him or he will bring darkness.
     Praise him before you fall on the dark hills.
   You people of Judah are hoping for light.
     But the Lord will turn the light into thick
       darkness.
     The Lord will change the light into a
       very thick darkness.
¹⁷ If you people of Judah don't listen to the
       Lord,
   I will hide and cry.
   Your pride will cause me to cry.
   I will cry very hard.
   My eyes will overflow with tears.

Baal The Canaanite people believed that this false god brought the rain and storms. They also thought that he made the land produce good crops.

loincloth A common undergarment in ancient Judah. It was a short skirt that was wrapped around the hips. It reached about halfway down the thighs.

Perath Probably a village near Jerusalem. It is probably the town that is called Parah in the list of the cities of the land of Benjamin in Joshua 18:23. But the name "Perath" also means the Euphrates River.

wineskin A bottle made from the skin of an animal and used for storing wine.

Why? Because the Lord's flock*
will be captured.
18 Tell these things to the king and his wife,
"Come down from your thrones.
Your beautiful crowns have fallen from
your heads."
19 The cities in the Negev desert* are locked.
No person can open them.
All the people of Judah are taken into exile.*
They were carried away as prisoners.
20 Jerusalem, look!
The enemy is coming from the north!*
Where is your flock?*
God gave that beautiful flock to you.
⌐You were supposed to care for that flock.⌐
21 What will you say when the Lord asks you
to account for that flock?
You were supposed to teach the people
⌐about God⌐.
Your leaders were supposed to lead
the people.
⌐But they did not do their job!⌐
So you will have much pain and troubles.
You will be like a woman having a baby.
22 You might ask yourself,
"Why has this bad thing happened to me?"
Those things happened because of your
many sins.
Because of your sins,
your skirt was torn off
and your shoes were taken away.
They did this to embarrass you.
23 A black man can't change
the color of his skin.
And a leopard can't change his spots.
In the same way, Jerusalem, you can't change
and do good.
You always do bad things.
24 "I will force you to leave your homes.
You will run in all directions.

You will be like chaff* blown away
by the desert wind.
25 These are the things that will happen to you.
This is your part in my plans."

This message is from the Lord.
"Why will this happen?
Because you forgot me.
You trusted false gods.
26 Jerusalem, I will pull your skirt up over
your face.
Everyone will see you,
and you will be ashamed.
27 I saw the terrible things you did.*
I saw you laughing
and having sex with your lovers.
I know about your plans
to be like a prostitute.*
I have seen you on the hills
and in the fields.
It will be very bad for you, Jerusalem.
I wonder how long you will continue doing
your dirty sins."

Drought and False Prophets

14 This is the Lord's message to Jeremiah
about the drought:*

2 "The nation of Judah cries for people
that have died.
The people in the cities of Judah
grow weaker and weaker.
Those people lie on the ground.
People in Jerusalem cry to God for help.
3 The leaders of the people send their servants
to get water.
The servants go to the water storage places,
but they don't find any water.
The servants come back with empty jars.
So they are ashamed and embarrassed.
They cover their heads from shame.

Lord's flock This is a figurative name for the people of Judah. The Lord is thought of as a shepherd, while his people are seen as his flock of sheep.
Negev desert The desert area in the southern part of the kingdom of Judah.
exile Being forced to leave one's home country and being moved to a foreign country.
north This refers to the army of Babylon coming from the north to attack the nation of Judah.
flock Here, the word "flock" refers to all the towns around Jerusalem, as if Jerusalem were the shepherd and the towns of Judah were her flock.

chaff The seed coverings and stems separated from the seeds of plants like wheat or barley. Farmers saved the seeds but let the wind blow the useless chaff away.
I saw ... you did This is probably talking about worshiping false gods. But part of that worship was having sex with temple prostitutes.
prostitute A woman paid by men for sexual sin. Sometimes this also means a person that is not faithful to God and stops following him.
drought A time when no rain falls and the crops become dry and die.

⁴ No person prepares the ground for crops.*
    No rain falls on the land.
    The farmers are depressed.
        So they cover their heads from shame.
⁵ Even the mother deer in the field
        leaves her newborn baby alone.
            She does this because there is no grass.
⁶ Wild donkeys stand on the bare hills.
    They sniff the wind like jackals.*
    But their eyes can't find any food,
        because there are no plants to eat.

⁷ "We know that those things are our fault.
        We are now suffering because of our sins.
    Lord, do something to help us for the good of
        your name.
    We admit that we left you many times.
        We have sinned against you.
⁸ God, you are the Hope of Israel!
        You save Israel in times of trouble.
    But now it seems like you are
        a stranger in the land.
    It seems like you are a traveler that only stays
        one night.
⁹ You seem like a man that has been attacked
        by surprise.
    You seem like a soldier that does not have
        the power to save anyone.
    But Lord, you are with us.
    We are called by your name,
        So don't leave us without help!"

¹⁰This is what the Lord says about the people of Judah: "The people of Judah really love to leave me. Those people don't stop themselves from leaving me. So now, the Lord will not accept them. Now the Lord will remember the bad things they do. The Lord will punish them for their sins."

¹¹Then the Lord said to me, "Jeremiah, don't pray for good things to happen to the people of Judah. ¹²The people of Judah might begin to fast* ₍and pray to me₎. But I will not listen to their prayers. Even if they offer burnt offerings and grain offerings to me, I will not accept those people. I will destroy the people of Judah with war. I will take away their food, and the people of Judah will starve. And I will destroy them with terrible diseases."

¹³But I said to the Lord, "Lord, my Master, the prophets were telling the people something different. They were telling the people of Judah, 'You people will not suffer from an enemy's sword. You will never suffer from hunger. The Lord will give you peace in this land.'"

¹⁴Then the Lord said to me, "Jeremiah, those prophets are preaching lies in my name. I did not send those prophets. I did not command them or speak to them. Those prophets have been preaching false visions, worthless magic, and their own wishful thinking. ¹⁵So this is what I say about the prophets that are preaching in my name. I did not send those prophets. Those prophets said, 'No enemy with swords will ever attack this country. There will never be hunger in this land.' Those prophets will die from hunger and an enemy's sword will kill them. ¹⁶And the people those prophets spoke to will be thrown into the streets. Those people will die from hunger and from an enemy's sword. No person will be there to bury those people, or their wives or their sons or daughters. I will punish them.

¹⁷ "Jeremiah, speak this message
        to the people of Judah:
    'My eyes are filled with tears.
        I will cry night and day without stopping.
        I will cry for my virgin daughter.*
        I will cry for my people.
    Why? Because someone hit them
        and crushed them.
    They have been hurt very badly.
¹⁸ If I go into the country,
        I see the people that were killed
            with swords.
    If I go into the city,
        I see much sickness,
            because the people have no food.
    The priests and the prophets
        have been taken away to a foreign land.'"

¹⁹ "Lord, have you completely rejected
        the nation of Judah?
    Lord, do you hate Zion*?
    You hurt us so badly
        that we can't be made well again.

No person prepares the ground for crops Following the ancient Greek translation. The Hebrew is hard to understand.
jackals A wild animal, like a dog. Those animals only live where no people are.
fast Going without food for a special time of prayer and worship.

virgin daughter This is another name for Jerusalem.
Zion The southeast part of the mountain Jerusalem is built on. Sometimes it means the people of God living in Jerusalem.

Why did you do that?
We were hoping for peace,
but nothing good has come.
We were hoping for a time of healing,
but only terror came.
20 Lord, we know that we are evil people.
We know that our ancestors* did bad
things.
Yes, we sinned against you.
21 Lord, for the good of your name,
don't push us away.
Don't take away the honor
from your glorious throne.
Remember your Agreement* with us.
Don't break that Agreement.
22 Foreign idols don't have the power
to bring rain.
The sky does not have the power
to send showers of rain down.
You are our only hope.
You are the One who made all these
things."

15 The Lord said to me, "Jeremiah, even if Moses and Samuel were here to pray for the people of Judah, I would not feel sorry for these people. Send the people of Judah away from me. Tell them to go. ²Those people might ask you, 'Where will we go?' You tell them this: This is what the Lord says:

'I have chosen some people to die.
Those people will die.
I have chosen some people
to be killed with swords.
Those people will be killed with swords.
I have chosen some people
to die from hunger.
Those people will die from hunger.
I have chosen some people
to be captured and carried to a foreign
country.
Those people will be prisoners in that foreign
country.
³ I will send four kinds of destroyers
against them.'
This message is from the Lord.

'I will send the enemy with a sword to kill.
I will send the dogs to drag their bodies away.
I will send birds of the air and wild animals
to eat and destroy their bodies.
4 I will make the people of Judah
an example of some terrible thing
for all the people on earth.
I will do this to the people of Judah
because of what Manasseh* did in
Jerusalem.
Manasseh was the son of King Hezekiah.
Manasseh was a king of Judah.'
5 "No person will feel sorry for you,
city of Jerusalem.
No person will be sad and cry for you.
No person will go out of his way
to even ask how you are!
6 Jerusalem, you left me."
This message is from the Lord.
"Again and again you left me!
So I will punish and destroy you.
I am tired of holding back your
punishment.
7 I will separate the people of Judah
with my pitchfork.*
I will scatter them at the city gates of the land.
My people have not changed.
So I will destroy them.
I will take away their children.
8 Many women will lose their husbands.
There will be more widows
than there is sand in the sea.
I will bring a destroyer at noontime.
The destroyer will attack the mothers
of the young men of Judah.
I will bring pain and fear
on the people of Judah.
I will make this happen very quickly.
9 The enemy will attack with swords
and kill the people.
They will kill the survivors* from Judah.
A woman might have seven sons,
⌊but they will all die.⌋
She will cry and cry
until she becomes weak
and not able to breathe.

---

ancestors Literally, "fathers," meaning a person's parents, grandparents, and all the people they are descended from.

Agreement Literally, "Proof." The flat stones with the Ten Commandments written on them were proof of the Agreement between God and Israel.

Manasseh Manasseh was the most evil king of Judah, according to 2 Kings 21:1-16. He worshiped many gods.

pitchfork A tool with sharp points for throwing hay from one place to another.

survivor(s) People that escaped some disaster. Here this means the Jewish people that survived the destruction of Judah and Israel by its enemy armies.

She will be upset and confused.
Her bright day will become dark
from sadness."

Jeremiah Again Complains to God

¹⁰ Mother, I *(Jeremiah)* am sorry
that you gave birth to me.
I am the person that must accuse
and criticize the whole land.
I have not loaned or borrowed anything.
But every person curses me.
¹¹ Truly, Lord, I have served you well.
In time of troubles, I prayed to you
about my enemies.

God Answers Jeremiah

¹² "Jeremiah, you know that no person
can shatter a piece of iron.
I mean the kind of iron
that is from the north.*
And no person can shatter a piece of
bronze either.
¹³ The people of Judah have many treasures.
I will give those riches to other people.
Those other people will not have to buy them.
⌊I will give those riches to them.⌋
Why? Because Judah has many sins.
People sinned in every part of Judah
¹⁴ People of Judah, I will make you slaves
of your enemies.
You will be slaves in a land
that you never knew.
I am very angry.
My anger is like a hot fire,
and you will be burned."

¹⁵ Lord, you understand me.
Remember me and take care of me.
People are hurting me.
Give those people the punishment
that they deserve.
You are being patient with those people.
But don't destroy me
while you remain patient with them.
Think about me.
Think about the pain I suffer for you, Lord.
¹⁶ Your message came to me
and I ate your words.
Your message made me very happy.

---

north This refers to the army of Babylon coming from the north to attack the nation of Judah.

I was happy to be called by your name.
Your name is Lord All-Powerful.
¹⁷ I never sat with the crowd
as they laughed and had fun.
I sat by myself because of your
influence on me.
You filled me with anger
at the evil around me.
¹⁸ I don't understand why I still hurt.
I don't understand why my wound
is not cured and cannot be healed.
Lord, I think you have changed.
You are like a spring of water
that became dry.
You are like a spring
whose water has stopped flowing.

¹⁹ Then, the Lord said,
"Jeremiah, if you change
and come back to me,
then I will not punish you.
If you change and come back to me,
then you can serve me.
If you speak important things,
and not those worthless words,
then you can speak for me.
The people of Judah should change
and come back to you ⌊Jeremiah⌋.
But don't you change
and be like them.
²⁰ I will make you strong.
Those people will think you are strong
like a wall made of bronze.
The people of Judah will fight against you.
But they will not defeat you.
They will not defeat you.
Why? Because I am with you.
I will help you and I will save you."

This message is from the Lord.
²¹ "I will save you from those evil people.
Those people scare you.
But I will save you from those people."

The Day of Disaster

16 The Lord's message came to me:
²"Jeremiah, you must not get married. You must not have sons or daughters in this place." ³The Lord says these things about the sons and daughters that are born in the land of Judah. And this is what the Lord says about the mothers and fathers of those children: ⁴"Those people will die a terrible death. No person will cry for those people. No person will bury them. Their bodies

will lie on the ground like dung. Those people will die by an enemy's sword, or they will starve to death. Their dead bodies will be food for the birds of the sky and the wild animals of the earth."

⁵So the Lord says: "Jeremiah, don't go into a house where people are eating a funeral meal. Don't go there to cry for the dead or show your sorrow. Don't do those things. Why? Because I have taken back my blessing. I will not be kind to these people of Judah. I will not feel sorry for them." This message is from the Lord.

⁶"Important people and common people will die in the land of Judah. No person will bury those people or cry for them. No person will cut himself or shave his head to show sorrow for those people. ⁷No person will bring food to the people that are crying for the dead. No person will comfort those people whose mother or father has died. No person will offer a drink to comfort the people that are crying for the dead.

⁸"Jeremiah, don't go into a house where the people are having a party. Don't go into that house and sit down to eat and drink. ⁹The Lord All-Powerful, the God of Israel says these things: 'I will soon stop the sounds of people having fun. I will stop the happy sounds people make during a wedding party. This will happen during your lifetime. I will do these things quickly.'

¹⁰"Jeremiah, you will tell the people of Judah these things. And the people will ask you, 'Why has the Lord said these terrible things to us? What have we done wrong? What sin have we done against the Lord our God?' ¹¹You must say these things to those people: 'Terrible things will happen to you because your ancestors* quit following me.' This message is from the Lord. 'They quit following me and began to follow and serve other gods. They worshiped those other gods. Your ancestors left me and `quit obeying my law. ¹²But you people have sinned more than your ancestors. You are very stubborn. And you are doing only the things that you want to do. You are not obeying me. You do only what you want to do. ¹³So I will throw you out of this country. I will force you to go to a foreign country. You will go to a land that you and your ancestors never knew. In that land you can serve false gods all you want to. I will not help you or show you any favors.'

¹⁴"People make promises and say, 'As surely as the Lord lives. He is the One who brought the people of Israel out of the land of Egypt.' But the time is coming," this message is from the Lord, "when people will not say those things. ¹⁵The people will say something new. They will say, 'As surely as the Lord lives. He is the One who brought the people of Israel out of the northern land. He brought them out of all the countries where he had sent them.' Why will the people say these things? Because I will bring the people of Israel back to the land that I gave to their ancestors.

¹⁶"I will soon send for many fishermen to come to this land." This message is from the Lord. "Those fishermen will catch the people of Judah. After that happens, I will send for many hunters to come to this land. Those hunters* will hunt the people of Judah on every mountain and hill and in the cracks of the rocks. ¹⁷I see everything they do. The people of Judah can't hide from me the things they do. Their sin is not hidden from me. ¹⁸I will pay the people of Judah back for the bad things they did—I will punish them two times for every sin. I will do this because they have made my land 'dirty.' They made my land 'dirty' with their terrible idols. I hate those idols. But they have filled my country with their idols."

¹⁹ Lord, you are my strength
and my protection.
You are a safe place to run to
in time of trouble.
The nations will come to you
from all around the world.
They will say,
"Our fathers had false gods.
They worshiped those worthless idols,
but those idols did not help them at all."
²⁰ Can people make real gods for themselves?
No! They can make statues,
but those statues are not really gods.
²¹ So I will teach those people that make idols.
Right now I will teach them
about my power and my strength.
Then they will know that I am God.
They will know that I am the Lord."

---

ancestors Literally, "fathers," meaning a person's parents, grandparents, and all the people they are descended from.

fishermen ... hunters This means the enemy soldiers from Babylon.

JEREMIAH 17:1-13

Guilt Written on the Heart

17 "The sins of the people of Judah
are written down in a place
where they can't be erased.
Those sins were cut into stone
with an iron pen.
Their sins were cut into stone
with a diamond tipped pen.*
And that stone is their heart.
Those sins were cut
into the horns of their altars.*
2 Their children remember the altars
that were dedicated to false gods.
They remember the wooden poles
that were dedicated to Asherah.*
They remember those things
under the green trees and on the hills.
3 They remember those things
on the mountains in the open country.
The people of Judah have many treasures.
I will give those things to other people.
People will destroy all the high places*
in your country.
You worshiped at those places.
And that was a sin.
4 You will lose the land I gave you.
I will let your enemies take you
to be their slaves.
Why? Because I am very angry.
My anger is like a hot fire,
and you will be burned forever."

Trusting in People, and Trusting in God

5 The Lord says these things:
"Bad things will happen to people
that trust only other people.
Bad things will happen to people
that depend on other people for strength.
Why? Because those people have stopped
trusting the Lord.

6 Those people are like a bush in a desert.
That bush is in a land where no people live.
That bush is in a hot and dry land.
That bush is in a bad soil.
That bush does not know
about the good things that God can give.
7 But the person that trusts in the Lord
will be blessed.
Why? Because the Lord will show him
that the Lord can be trusted.
8 That person will be strong
like a tree planted near water.
That tree has large roots that find the water.
That tree is not afraid
when the days are hot.
Its leaves are always green.
It does not worry in a year
when no rain comes.
That tree always produces fruit.

9 "A person's mind is very tricky!
The mind can be very sick,
and no person truly understands it.
10 But I am the Lord,
and I can look into a person's heart.
I can test a person's mind.
I can decide what each person should have.
I can give each person the right payment
for the things he does.
11 Sometimes a bird will hatch an egg
that it did not lay.
A person that cheats to get money
is like that bird.
When that man's life is half finished,
he will lose the money.
At the end of his life, it will be clear
that he was a foolish person."

12 From the very beginning, our temple*
has been a glorious throne for God.
It is a very important place.
13 Lord, you are the hope of Israel.
Lord, you are like a spring of living water.
If a person quits following the Lord,
then his life will be very short.*

---

diamond tipped pen Or, "flint-tipped pen."
horns of their altars The corners of altars were shaped like horns. This was like a place of safety for the people. If a person did something wrong, he could run to the altar. People could punish them only if they proved the person was guilty. Here Jeremiah is saying that there is no safe place for the people of Judah.
Asherah An important Canaanite goddess. At this time, the people thought she was the wife of Baal.
high places Special places where the people worshiped false gods. These places were often on hilltops, but not always. Some 'high places' were in valleys.

temple The special building in Jerusalem for Jewish worship.
his life will be very short Literally, "He will be written in the dirt." This might mean a person's name was written on a list of people that would soon die. Or that a person's life will soon be gone—like a name written in the sand.

Jeremiah's Third Complaint

¹⁴ Lord, if you heal me,
    I truly will be healed.
    Save me,
    and I truly will be saved.
    Lord, I praise you!
¹⁵ The people of Judah continue to ask me
        questions.
    They say,
    "Jeremiah, what about the message from the
        Lord?
    Let's see that message come true."
¹⁶ Lord, I did not run away from you.
    I followed you.
    I became the shepherd* you wanted.
    I did not want the terrible day to come.
    Lord, you know the things I said.
    You see all that is happening.
¹⁷ Lord, don't ruin me.
    I depend on you in times of trouble.
¹⁸ People are hurting me.
    Make those people ashamed.
        But don't disappoint me.
    Let those people be scared.
    But don't scare me.
    Bring the terrible day of disaster
        to my enemies.
    Break them.
        And break them again.

Keeping the Sabbath Day Holy

¹⁹The Lord said these things to me: "Jeremiah, go and stand at the People's Gate,* where the kings of Judah go in and out. Tell the people my message, and then go to all the other gates of Jerusalem and do the same things."

²⁰Say to those people: "Listen to the message of the Lord. Listen, kings of Judah. Listen, all you people of Judah. All you people that come through these gates into Jerusalem, listen to me! ²¹The Lord says these things: Be careful that you don't carry a load on the Sabbath* day. And don't bring a load through the gates of Jerusalem on the Sabbath day. ²²Don't bring a load out of your houses on the Sabbath day. Don't do any work on that day. You must make the Sabbath day a holy day. I gave this same command to your ancestors.* ²³But your ancestors did not obey me. They did not pay attention to me. Your ancestors were very stubborn. I punished them, but it did not do any good. They did not listen to me. ²⁴But you must be careful to obey me." This message is from the Lord. "You must not bring a load through the gates of Jerusalem on the Sabbath. You must make the Sabbath day a holy day. You will do this by not doing any work on that day.

²⁵"If you obey this command, then kings that sit on David's throne will come through the gates of Jerusalem. Those kings will come riding on chariots* and on horses. The leaders of the people of Judah and Jerusalem will be with those kings. And Jerusalem will have people living in it forever! ²⁶People will come to Jerusalem from the towns of Judah. People will come to Jerusalem from the little villages that are around it. People will come from the land where the family group of Benjamin lives.* People will come from the western foothills and from the hill country. And people will come from the Negev.* All those people will bring burnt offerings, sacrifices, grains offerings, incense,* and thank offerings. They will bring those offerings and sacrifices to the temple of the Lord.

²⁷"But if you don't listen to me and obey me, then bad things will happen. If you carry loads into Jerusalem on the Sabbath* day, then you are not keeping it a holy day. So I will start a fire that can't be put out. That fire will start at the gates of Jerusalem, and it will burn until it burns even the palaces.*"

The Potter and the Clay

18 This is the message that came to Jeremiah from the Lord: ²"Jeremiah, go down to the

---

ancestors Literally, "fathers," meaning a person's parents, grandparents, and all the people they are descended from.
chariot(s) A small wagon used in war.
the land where ... Benjamin lives The land of Benjamin was just north of the land of Judah.
Negev The desert area south of Judah.
incense Special dried tree sap. Burned to make a sweet-smelling smoke, it was offered as a gift to God.
palaces A large house for the king and his family.

---

shepherd God's people are sometimes called his "sheep," and the person that takes care of them is called the "shepherd."
People's Gate This might be one of the gates into Jerusalem or perhaps one of the southern gates the non-priests used to go up into the temple.
Sabbath Saturday, a special day of rest and worship for Jews.

potter's* house. I will give you my message at the potter's house."

³So I went down to the potter's house. I saw the potter working with clay at the wheel. ⁴He was making a pot from clay. But there was something wrong with the pot. So the potter used that clay again, and he made another pot. He used his hands to shape the pot the way that he wanted it to be.

⁵Then the message from the Lord came to me: ⁶"Family of Israel, you know that I *(God)* can do the same thing with you. You are like the clay in the potter's* hands. And I am like the potter! ⁷There may come a time that I will speak about a nation or a kingdom. I may say that I will pull that nation up. Or maybe I will say that I will pull that nation down and destroy that nation or kingdom. ⁸But the people of that nation might change their hearts and lives. The people in that nation might stop doing evil things. Then I would change my mind. I would not follow my plans to bring disaster to that nation. ⁹There might come another time when I speak about a nation. I might say that I will build up and plant that nation. ¹⁰But I might see that nation doing evil things and not obeying me. Then I would think again about the good I had planned to do for that nation.

¹¹"So, Jeremiah, say to the people of Judah and the people that live in Jerusalem, 'This is what the Lord says: I am preparing troubles for you right now. I am making plans against you. So stop doing the evil things that you are doing. Each person must change and start doing good things!' ¹²But the people of Judah will answer, 'It will not do any good to try. We will continue to do what we want. Each of us is going to do the things his stubborn, evil heart wants.'"

¹³ Listen to the things the Lord says:
"Ask the other nations this question:
'Have you ever heard of anyone
doing the evil things Israel has done?'
And Israel is special to God.
Israel is like God's bride!
¹⁴ You know that rocks never leave the fields
by themselves.*

potter's Someone that makes pottery (jars, bowls, etc.) from clay. The Hebrew word also means, "Creator, or "a person that makes new things."
You know ... themselves This is probably a word play. In Hebrew this sounds like, "Would anyone leave the Rock, Shaddai?" These are two names for God. But this could also be translated, "Does Lebanon's snow ever melt from Shaddai's mountain?" This would probably mean Mount Hermon.

You know that the snow on the mountains
of Lebanon never melts.
You know that cool, flowing streams
do not become dry.
¹⁵ But my people have forgotten about me.
They make offerings to worthless idols.
My people stumble in the things they do.
They stumble about in the old paths
of their ancestors.*
My people would rather walk
along back roads and poor highways,
than to follow me on the good roads.
¹⁶ So Judah's country will become
an empty desert.
People will whistle and shake their heads
every time they pass by.
They will be shocked
at how the country was destroyed.
¹⁷ I will scatter the people of Judah.
They will run from their enemies.
I will scatter the people of Judah like
an east wind that blows things away.
I will destroy those people.
They won't see me coming to help them.
No! They will see me leaving!"

Jeremiah's Fourth Complaint

¹⁸Then the enemies of Jeremiah said, "Come, let us make plans against Jeremiah. Surely the teaching of the law by the priest will not be lost. And the advice from the wise men will still be with us. We will still have the words of the prophets. So let us tell lies about him. That will ruin him. We will not pay attention to anything he says."

¹⁹ Lord, listen to me!
Listen to my arguments
and decide who is right.
²⁰ I have been good to the people of Judah.
But now they are paying me back with evil.
They are trying to trap me and kill me.
²¹ So make their children starve in a famine.*
Let their enemies defeat them with swords.
Let their wives be without children.
Let the men from Judah be put to death.
Make their wives into widows.

ancestors Literally, "fathers," meaning a person's parents, grandparents, and all the people they are descended from.
famine A time when there is not enough rain for crops to grow. People and animals die without enough food or water.

Let the men from Judah be put to death.
Let the young men be killed in battle.
²² Let there be crying in their houses.
Make them cry when you suddenly
bring an enemy against them.
Let all this happen because my enemies
tried to trap me.
They hid traps for me to step in.
²³ Lord, you know about their plans to kill me.
Don't forgive their crimes.
Don't erase their sins.
Destroy my enemies!
Punish those people while you are angry!

The Broken Jar

19 The Lord said to me: "Jeremiah, go and buy a clay jar from a potter.* ²Go out to the Valley of Ben Hinnom, near the front of the Potsherd Gate.* Take some of the elders *(leaders)* of the people and some priests with you. At that place, tell them the things that I tell you. ³Say to those people with you, 'King of Judah and people of Jerusalem, listen to this message from the Lord! This is what the Lord All-Powerful, the God of the people of Israel, says: I will soon make a terrible thing happen to this place! Every person that hears about it will be amazed and full of fear. ⁴I will do these things because the people of Judah quit following me. They have made this a place for foreign gods. The people of Judah have burned sacrifices in this place to other gods. The people did not worship those gods long ago. Their ancestors* did not worship those gods. These are new gods from other countries. The kings of Judah filled this place with the blood of the innocent children. ⁵The kings of Judah built high places* for the god Baal.* They use those places to burn their sons in the fire. They burned their sons as burnt offerings to the god Baal. I did not tell them to do that. I did not ask you to offer your sons as sacrifices. I never even thought of such a thing. ⁶Now people call this place Topheth and the Valley of Hinnom. But, I give you this warning. This message is from the Lord: The days are coming, when people will call this place the Valley of Slaughter.* ⁷At this place, I will ruin the plans of the people of Judah and Jerusalem. The enemy will chase these people. And I will let the people of Judah be killed with swords in this place. And I will make their dead bodies food for the birds and wild animals. ⁸I will completely destroy this city. People will whistle and shake their heads when they pass by Jerusalem. They will be shocked when they see how the city was destroyed. ⁹The enemy will bring its army around the city. That army will not let people go out to get food. So the people in the city will begin to starve. They will become so hungry that they will eat the bodies of their own sons and daughters. And then they will begin to eat each other.'

¹⁰"Jeremiah, you will tell those things to the people. And while they are watching, you will break that jar. ¹¹At that time, say these things: 'The Lord All-Powerful says, I will break the nation of Judah and the city of Jerusalem just like someone breaking a clay jar! This jar can't be put back together again. It will be the same for the nation of Judah. The dead people will be buried here in Topheth until there is no more room. ¹²I will do this to these people and to this place. I will make this city like Topheth.' This message is from the Lord. ¹³"The houses in Jerusalem will become as "dirty" as this place, Topheth. The kings' palaces* will be ruined like this place, Topheth. Why? Because the people worshiped false gods on the roofs of those houses.* They worshiped the stars and burned sacrifices to honor them. They gave drink offerings to false gods.'"

¹⁴Then Jeremiah left Topheth where the Lord had told him to preach. Jeremiah went to the Lord's temple* and stood in the courtyard* of the temple. Jeremiah said to all the people: ¹⁵"This is

---

potter A worker that makes things from clay. The Hebrew word also means "creator."
Potsherd Gate The exact location of this gate is not known, though it was probably at the southwestern part of the city.
ancestors Literally, "fathers," meaning a person's parents, grandparents, and all the people they are descended from.
high places Special places where the people worshiped false gods. These places were often on hilltops, but not always. Some 'high places' were in valleys.
Baal The Canaanite people believed that this false god brought the rain and storms. They also thought that he made the land produce good crops.

Slaughter Usually, this word means to kill an animal and cut it into pieces of meat. But it often means to kill people like they are animals.
palace(s) A large house for the king and his family.
roofs of those houses People built their house with a flat roof, and they used the roof like an extra room.
temple The special building in Jerusalem for Jewish worship.
courtyard The large area around the temple sanctuary.

what the Lord All-Powerful, the God of Israel says: 'I said I would bring many disasters to Jerusalem and the villages around it. I will soon make those things happen. Why? Because the people are very stubborn—they refused to listen and obey me.'"

Jeremiah and Pashhur

20 A man named Pashhur was a priest. He was the highest officer in the temple* of the Lord. Pashhur was the son of a man named Immer. Pashhur heard Jeremiah preach those things in the temple yard. ²So he had Jeremiah the prophet beaten. And he had Jeremiah's hands and feet locked between large blocks of wood. This was at the Upper Gate of Benjamin at the temple. ³The next day Pashhur took Jeremiah out from between the blocks of wood. Then Jeremiah said to Pashhur, "The Lord's name for you is not Pashhur. Now the Lord's name for you is Terror on Every Side. ⁴That is your name, because the Lord says: 'I will soon make you a terror to yourself! I will soon make you a terror to all your friends. You will watch enemies killing your friends with swords. I will give all the people of Judah to the king of Babylon. He will take the people of Judah away to the country of Babylon. And his army will kill the people of Judah with their swords. ⁵The people of Jerusalem worked hard to build things and become wealthy. But I will give all those things to their enemies. The king in Jerusalem has many treasures. But I will give all those treasures to the enemy. The enemy will take those things and carry them away to the country of Babylon. ⁶And Pashhur, you and all the people living in your house will be taken away. You will be forced to go and live in the country of Babylon. You will die in Babylon. And you will be buried in that foreign country. You preached lies to your friends. ⌊You said these things would not happen.⌋ But all of your friends will also die and be buried in Babylon.'"

Jeremiah's Fifth Complaint

⁷ Lord, you tricked me,
    and I certainly was fooled.
You are stronger than I am,
    so you won.

I have become a joke.
People laugh at me
    and make fun of me all day long.
⁸ Every time I speak, I shout.
I am always shouting about
    violence and destruction.
I tell the people about the message
    that I received from the Lord.
But people only insult me
    and make fun of me.
⁹ Sometimes I say to myself,
"I will forget about the Lord.
I will not speak any more
    in the name of the Lord!"
But when I say that,
    then the Lord's message is like a fire
    burning inside of me!
It feels like it is burning
    deep in my bones!
I get tired of trying to hold
    the Lord's message inside of me.
And finally, I am not able to hold it in.
¹⁰ I hear people whispering against me.
Everywhere, I hear things that scare me.
Even my friends are saying things
    against me.
People are just waiting for me
    to make some mistake.
They are saying,
"Let us lie and say he did some bad thing.
Maybe we can trick Jeremiah.
Then we will have him.
We will finally be rid of him.
Then we will grab him
    and take our revenge on him."
¹¹ But the Lord is with me.
The Lord is like a strong soldier.
So the people that are chasing me will fall.
Those people will not defeat me.
Those people will fail.
They will be disappointed.
Those people will be ashamed.
And people will never forget that shame.

¹² Lord All-Powerful, you test good people.
You look deeply into a person's mind.
I told you my arguments
    against those people.
So let me see you give them
    the punishment that they deserve.
¹³ Sing to the Lord! Praise the Lord!
The Lord saves the lives of poor people!
He saves them from wicked people!

---

temple The special building in Jerusalem for Jewish worship.
courtyard The large area around the temple sanctuary.

Jeremiah's Sixth Complaint

14 Curse the day that I was born!
Don't bless the day my mother had me.
15 Curse the man that told my father
the news that I was born.
"You have a son," he said.
"It is a boy!"
He made my father very happy
when he told him that news.
16 Let that man be the same as
the cities that the Lord destroyed.*
The Lord did not have any pity
on those cities.
Let that man hear shouts of war
in the morning.
And let him hear battle cries
at noontime.
17 Why? Because that man did not kill me
while I was in my mother's body.
If he had killed me at that time,
my mother would have been my grave,
and I would never have been born.
18 Why did I have to come out of the body?
All I have seen is trouble and sorrow.
And my life will end in shame.

God Rejects King Zedekiah's Request

21 This is the message that came to Jeremiah from the Lord. This message came when Zedekiah, the king of Judah, sent a man named Pashhur and a priest named Zephaniah to Jeremiah. Pashhur* was the son of a man named Malkijah. Zephaniah was the son of a man named Maaseiah. Pashhur and Zephaniah brought a message for Jeremiah. ²Pashhur and Zephaniah said to Jeremiah, "Pray to the Lord for us. Ask the Lord what will happen. We want to know, because Nebuchadnezzar, the king of Babylon, is attacking us. Maybe the Lord will do great things for us, like he did in the past. Maybe the Lord will make Nebuchadnezzar stop attacking us and leave."

³Then Jeremiah answered Pashhur and Zephaniah. He said, "Tell King Zedekiah: ⁴This is what the Lord, the God of Israel, says: 'You have weapons of war in your hands. You are using those weapons to defend yourselves against the king of Babylon and the Babylonians.* But I will make those weapons worthless.

"'The army from Babylon is outside the wall around the city. That army is all around the city. Soon I will bring that army into Jerusalem. ⁵I myself will fight against you people of Judah. I will fight against you with my own powerful hand. I am very angry with you, so I will fight against you with my own powerful arm. I will fight very hard against you and show how angry I am. ⁶I will kill the people living in Jerusalem. I will kill people and animals. They will die from terrible sicknesses that will spread all through the city. ⁷After that happens,'" this message is from the Lord, "'I will give Zedekiah king of Judah to Nebuchadnezzar king of Babylon. I will also give Zedekiah's officials to Nebuchadnezzar. Some of the people in Jerusalem will not die from the terrible sicknesses. Some of the people will not be killed with swords. Some of them will not die from hunger. But I will give those people to Nebuchadnezzar. I will let Judah's enemy win. Nebuchadnezzar's army wants to kill the people of Judah. So the people of Judah and Jerusalem will be killed with swords. Nebuchadnezzar will not show any mercy. He will not feel sorry for those people.'

⁸"Also tell these things to the people of Jerusalem. The Lord says these things: 'Understand that I will let you choose to live or die. ⁹Any person that stays in Jerusalem will die. That person will die by a sword, or from hunger, or from a terrible sickness. But any person that goes out of Jerusalem and surrenders to the Babylonian army will live! That army has surrounded the city. So no person can bring food into the city. But any person that leaves the city will save his life. ¹⁰I have decided to make trouble for the city of Jerusalem. I will not help the city.'" This message is from the Lord. "'I will give the city of Jerusalem to the king of Babylon. He will burn it with fire.'

11 "Tell these things to Judah's royal family:
Listen to the message from the Lord.
12 Family of David,*
the Lord says these things:
'You must judge people fairly every day.
Protect the victims* from the criminals.
If you don't do that,
then I will become very angry.

---

cities that the Lord destroyed Sodom and Gomorrah. See Gen. 19.
Pashhur This is not the same Pashhur as in Jer. 20:1.

Babylonians The Babylonians were the family group to which King Nebuchadnezzar belonged. They were the group that controlled the land of Babylon at this time.

My anger will be like a fire
   that no person will be able to put out.
This will happen because you
   have done evil things.'
¹³ "Jerusalem, I am against you.
   You sit on top of the mountain.
   You sit like a queen over this valley.
You people of Jerusalem say,
   'No person can attack us.
   No person can come into our strong city.'
But listen to this message from the Lord.
¹⁴ 'You will get the punishment you deserve.
   I will start a fire in your forests.
   That fire will completely burn everything
      around you.'"

Judgment Against Evil Kings

22 The Lord said: "Jeremiah, go down to the king's palace. Go to the king of Judah and preach this message there: ²'Listen to the message from the Lord, King of Judah. You rule from David's throne, so listen. King, you and your officials must listen well. All of your people that come through the gates of Jerusalem must listen to the message from the Lord. ³The Lord says: Do the things that are fair and right. Protect the person that has been robbed from the person that robbed him. Don't hurt or do anything wrong to orphans* or widows.* Don't kill innocent people. ⁴If you obey these commands, then this is what will happen: kings that sit on David's throne will continue to come through the gates into the city of Jerusalem. Those kings will come through the gates with their officials. Those kings, their officials, and their people will come riding in chariots* and on horses. ⁵But if you don't obey these commands, this is what the Lord says: I, the Lord, promise that this king's palace* will be destroyed—it will become a pile of rocks.'"

⁶This is what the Lord says about the palace where the king of Judah lives:

"The palace* is tall,
   like the forests of Gilead.
The palace is tall
   like the mountains of Lebanon.
But I will make it like a desert.
This palace will be empty
   like a city where no person lives.
⁷ I will send men to destroy the palace.
Each man will have weapons
   that he will use to destroy that house.
Those men will cut up your strong,
   beautiful cedar beams.
Those men will throw those beams
   into the fire."

⁸"People from many nations will pass by this city. They will ask one another, 'Why has the Lord done such a terrible thing to Jerusalem? Jerusalem was such a great city.' ⁹This will be the answer to that question: 'God destroyed Jerusalem because the people of Judah quit following the Agreement* of the Lord their God. Those people worshiped and served other gods.'"

Judgment Against King Jehoahaz

¹⁰ Don't cry for the king that has died.*
      Don't cry for him.
   But cry very hard for the king
      that must leave this place.*
   Cry for him
      because he will never come back again.
   Jehoahaz will never see his homeland again.

¹¹This is what the Lord says about Shallum (Jehoahaz) son of Josiah. (Shallum became king of Judah after his father Josiah died.) "Jehoahaz has gone away from Jerusalem. He will never come back to Jerusalem again. ¹²Jehoahaz will die in the place where the Egyptians have taken him. He will not see this land again."

Family of David The royal family of Judah. God promised that men from David's family would be kings in Judah.
victims People that have suffered some kind of hurt or trouble. Often this means people that were hurt or lost something during a crime.
orphan(s) Children whose parents are dead. Often these children have no one to care for them.
widow(s) Women whose husbands have died. Often these women had no one to care for them.
chariot(s) A small wagon used in war.

palace A large house for the king and his family.
Agreement Literally, "Proof." The flat stones with the Ten Commandments written on them were proof of the Agreement between God and Israel.
king that has died This means King Josiah that was killed in battle against the Egyptians in 609B.C.
king ... place This means Josiah's son, Jehoahaz. He became king after Josiah died. He is also called Shallum. Neco, the king of Egypt, defeated Josiah. And Neco took Jehoahaz off the throne of Judah and made him a prisoner in Egypt.

Judgment Against King Jehoiakim

13 It will be very bad for King Jehoiakim.
  He is doing bad things
    so he can build his palace.
  He is cheating people
    so he can build rooms upstairs.
  He is making his own people
    work for nothing.
  He is not paying them for their work.
14 Jehoiakim says,
  'I will build a great palace for myself.
  I will have large upper rooms.'
  So he builds the house with large windows.
  He uses cedar word for paneling,
    and he paints it red.
15 Jehoiakim,
  having a lot of cedar in your house
    does not make you a great king.
  Your father Josiah was satisfied
    to have food and drink.
  He did what was right and fair.
  Josiah did that,
    so everything went well for him.
16 Josiah helped the poor and needy people.
  Josiah did that,
    so everything went well for him.
  Jehoiakim, what does it mean
    "to know God?"
  It means living right and being fair.
  That is what it means to know me.
  This message is from the Lord.
17 "Jehoiakim, your eyes look
    only for what benefits yourself.
  You are always thinking about
    getting more for yourself.
  You are willing to kill innocent people.
  You are willing to steal things
    from other people."
18 So this is what the Lord says
    to King Jehoiakim son of Josiah:
  "The people of Judah will not cry
    for Jehoiakim.
  They will not say to each other,
  'Oh, my brother,
    ⌊I am so sad about Jehoiakim⌋!
  Oh, my sister,
    ⌊I am so sad about Jehoiakim⌋!'
  The people of Judah will not cry
    for Jehoiakim.
  They will not say about him,
  'Oh, master, ⌊I am so sad⌋!
  Oh, King, ⌊I am so sad⌋!'

19 The people of Jerusalem will bury Jehoiakim
    like they were burying a donkey.
  They will just drag his body away.
  And they will throw his body
    outside the gates of Jerusalem.
20 "Judah, go up to the mountains of Lebanon
    and cry out.
  Let your voice be heard
    in the mountains of Bashan.
  Cry out in the mountains of Abarim.
  Why? Because your 'lovers'
    will all be destroyed.
21 Judah, you felt safe.
    But I warned you!
  I warned you,
    but you refused to listen.
  You have lived like this
    from the time you were young.
  And from the time you were young,
    you have not obeyed me, Judah.
22 Judah, the punishment I give
    will come like a storm.
  And it will blow all your shepherds away.
  You thought some of the other nations
    would help you.
  But those nations will also be defeated.
  Then you will really be disappointed.
  You will be ashamed of all the bad things
    that you did.
23 King, you live high on the mountain
    in your house made from cedar wood.
  It is almost like you live in Lebanon
    where that wood came from.
  ⌊You think you are safe,
    high on the mountain in your big house.⌋
  But you will really groan
    when your punishment comes.
  You will hurt like a woman
    giving birth to a baby."

Judgment Against King Jehoiachin

24 "As surely as I live," this message is from the Lord, "I will do this to you, Jehoiachin son of Jehoiakim, king of Judah: Even if you were a signet ring* on my right hand, I would still pull you off. 25 Jehoiachin, I will give you to Nebuchadnezzar, the king of Babylon, and the Babylonians. Those are the people you are afraid of. Those people want to kill you. 26 I will throw you and your mother into another country where neither of you was born. You and your mother will die in that country. 27 Jehoiachin, you will

want to come back to your land—but you will never be allowed to come back."

²⁸ Coniah *(Jehoiachin)* is like a broken pot
    that some person threw away.
He is like a pot that no person wants.
Why will Jehoiachin and his children
    be thrown out?
Why will they be thrown away
    into a foreign land?
²⁹ Land, land, land of Judah!
    Listen to the message of the Lord!
³⁰ The Lord says,
"Write this down about Jehoiachin:
    'He is a man that has no children anymore!
Jehoiachin will not be successful
    in his lifetime.
And none of his children
    will sit on the throne of David.
None of his children
    will rule in Judah.'"

23 "It will be very bad for the shepherds *(leaders)* of the people of Judah. Those shepherds are destroying the sheep. They are making the sheep run from my pasture in all directions." This message is from the Lord. ²Those shepherds *(leaders)* are responsible for my people. And the Lord, the God of Israel, says these things to those shepherds: "You shepherds *(leaders)* have made my sheep run away in all directions. You have forced them to go away. And you have not taken care of them. But I will take care of you—I will punish you for the bad things you did." This message is from the Lord: ³"I sent my sheep *(people)* to other countries. But I will gather together my sheep that are left. And I will bring them back to their pasture *(country)*. When my sheep are back in their pasture, they will have many children and grow in number. ⁴I will place new shepherds *(leaders)* over my sheep. Those shepherds will take care of my sheep. And my sheep will not be scared or afraid. None of my sheep will be lost." This message is from the Lord.

The Righteous "Sprout"

⁵ This message is from the Lord,
"The time is coming,"
    "when I will raise up a good 'sprout.'*

sprout This means a new king from the family of David.

He will be a king
    who will rule in a wise way.
He will do what is fair and right
    in the land.
⁶ In the time of that good 'sprout,'
    the people of Judah will be saved.
And Israel will live in safety.
This will be his name:
    The Lord is our Goodness.*

⁷"So the time is coming," this message is from the Lord, "when people won't say the old promise by the Lord any more. The old promise is: 'As surely as the Lord lives, the Lord is the One who brought the people of Israel out of the land of Egypt.' ⁸But people will say something new. They will say, 'As surely as the Lord lives, the Lord is the One who brought the people of Israel out of the land of the north. He brought them out of all the countries where he had sent them.' Then the people of Israel will live in their own land."

Judgments Against False Prophets

⁹ A message to the prophets:

I am very sad—my heart is broken.
    All my bones are shaking.
I *(Jeremiah)* am like a man that is drunk.
    Why? Because of the Lord
    and his holy words.
¹⁰ The land of Judah is full of people that do the
    sin of adultery.*
They are unfaithful in many ways.
The Lord cursed the land,
    and it became very dry.
The plants are dried and dying in the pastures.
    The fields have become like the desert.
The prophets are evil.
Those prophets use their influence
    and power in the wrong way.
¹¹ "The prophets and even the priests are evil.
    I have seen them doing evil things
    in my own temple."
This message is from the Lord.
¹²"I will stop giving my messages to them.
    It will be like they must walk in darkness.
    It will be like the road is slippery
        for those prophets and priests.

The Lord is our Goodness This is a word play. In Hebrew, this is like the name Zedekiah, the king of Judah at the time that this prophecy was probably given. But Jeremiah is talking about another king.

adultery Breaking the marriage promise by sexual sin.

And they will fall in that darkness.
   I will bring disaster on them.
   I will punish those prophets and priests."
   This message is from the Lord.
13 "I saw the prophets of Samaria*
      doing wrong things.
   I saw those prophets prophesy*
      in the name of the false god Baal.*
   Those prophets led the people of Israel
      away from the Lord.
14 Now I have seen the prophets of Judah
      do those terrible things in Jerusalem.
   These prophets do the sin of adultery.*
   They listened to lies—and they obeyed
      those false teachings.
   They encourage wicked people
      to continue doing evil things.
   So the people did not stop sinning.
   They are like the people of Sodom.
   Now Jerusalem is like Gomorrah* to me."
15 So, this is what the Lord All-Powerful says
      about the prophets:
   "I will punish those prophets.
      The punishment will be
         like eating poisoned food and water.
   The prophets started a spiritual sickness.
      And that sickness spread through
         the whole country.
   So I will punish those prophets.
      That sickness came from the prophets
         in Jerusalem."

16 The Lord All-Powerful says these things:
   "Don't pay attention to the things
      that those prophets are saying to you.
   They are trying to fool you.
   Those prophets talk about visions.*
      But they did not get their visions from me.
   Their visions come from their own minds.
17 Some of the people hate
      the real messages from the Lord.

Samaria The capital of the northern kingdom of Israel. This kingdom was destroyed by God because its people did many bad things.
prophesy To speak for God or for a false god.
Baal The Canaanite people believed that this false god brought the rain and storms. They also thought that he made the land produce good crops.
adultery Breaking the marriage promise by sexual sin.
Sodom, Gomorrah Two cities that God destroyed because the people were so evil. See Gen. 19.
vision(s) Something like a dream that God used to speak to people.

So those prophets give a different message
   to those people.
They say,
   'You will have peace.'
Some of the people are very stubborn.
   They do only the things they want to do.
So those prophets say,
   'Nothing bad will happen to you!'
18 But none of those prophets
      has stood in the heavenly council.*
   None of them has seen or heard
      the message of the Lord.
   None of them has paid close attention
      to the Lord's message.
19 Now the punishment from the Lord
      will come like a storm.
   The Lord's anger will be like a tornado.
      It will come crashing down
         on the heads of those wicked people.
20 The Lord's anger will not stop
      until he finishes what he plans to do.
   When that day is over,
      you will understand this clearly.
21 I did not send those prophets.
      But they ran to tell their messages.
   I did not speak to them.
      But they preached in my name.
22 If they had stood in my heavenly council,
      then they would have told my messages
         to the people of Judah.
   They would have stopped the people
      from doing bad things.
   They would have stopped them
      from doing evil."

23 "I am God, and I am always near!"
   This message is from the Lord.
      "I am not far away!
24 A person might try to hide from me
      in some hiding place.
   But it is easy for me to see him.
   Why? Because I am everywhere
      in heaven and earth!"
The Lord said these things.

25"There are prophets that preach lies in my name. They say, 'I have had a dream! I have had a dream!' I heard them say those things. 26How long will this continue? Those prophets think up lies.

---

heavenly council The people in the Old Testament often talk about God like he was the leader of a council of heavenly beings (angels). Compare 1 Kings 22:19-23; Isa. 6:1-8; and Job chapters 1 and 2.

And then they teach those lies to the people. ²⁷These prophets are trying to make the people of Judah forget my name. They are doing this by telling each other these false dreams. They are trying to make my people forget me in the same way that their ancestors* forgot me. Their ancestors forgot me and worshiped the false god Baal.* ²⁸Straw is not the same thing as wheat! In the same way, those prophets' dreams are not messages from me. If a person wants to tell about his dreams, then let him. But let the man that hears my message speak my message truthfully. ²⁹My message is like a fire." This message is from the Lord. "It is like a hammer that smashes a rock. ³⁰"So I am against the false prophets." This message is from the Lord. "These prophets keep stealing my words from one another. ³¹I am against the false prophets." This message is from the Lord. "They use their own words and pretend that it is a message from me. ³²I am against the false prophets that preach fake dreams." This message is from the Lord. "They mislead my people with their lies and false teachings. I did not send those prophets to teach the people. I never commanded them to do anything for me. They can't help the people of Judah at all." This message is from the Lord.

The Sad Message from the Lord

³³"The people of Judah, or a prophet, or a priest may ask you, 'Jeremiah, what is the announcement of the Lord?' You will answer them and say, 'You are a heavy load* to the Lord. And I will throw down this heavy load.' This message is from the Lord.

³⁴"A prophet, or a priest, or maybe one of the people might say, 'This is an announcement from the Lord ... ' ⌐That person lied,⌐ so I will punish that person and his whole family. ³⁵This is what you will say to one another: 'What did the Lord answer?' or 'What did the Lord say?' ³⁶But you will never again use the expression, 'The announcement (heavy load) of the Lord.' This is because the Lord's message should not be a heavy load for anyone. But you changed the words of our God. He is the living God, the Lord All-Powerful!

³⁷"If you want to learn about God's message, then ask a prophet, 'What answer did the Lord give you?' or 'What did the Lord say?' ³⁸But don't say, 'What was the announcement (heavy load) from the Lord?' If you use these words, then the Lord will say these things to you: 'You should not have called my message an 'announcement (heavy load) from the Lord.' I told you not to use those words. ³⁹But you called my message a heavy load, so I will pick you up like a heavy load and throw you away from me. I gave the city of Jerusalem to your ancestors.* But I will throw you and that city away from me. ⁴⁰And I will make you a disgrace forever. You will never forget your embarrassment.'"

The Good Figs and the Bad Figs

24 The Lord showed me these things: I saw two baskets of figs arranged in front of the temple* of the Lord. (I saw this vision after Nebuchadnezzar, the king of Babylon, took Jeconiah* as a prisoner. Jeconiah was the son of King Jehoiakim. Jeconiah and his important officials were taken away from Jerusalem. They were taken to Babylon. Nebuchadnezzar also took away all the carpenters and metal-workers of Judah.) ²One basket had very good figs in it. Those figs were like figs that ripen early in the season. But the other basket had rotten figs. They were too rotten to eat.

³The Lord said to me, "What do you see, Jeremiah?" I answered, "I see figs. The good figs are very good. And the rotten figs are very rotten. They are too rotten to eat."

⁴Then the message of the Lord came to me. ⁵The Lord, the God of Israel, said: "The people of Judah were taken from their country. Their enemy brought them to Babylon. Those people will be like these good figs. I will be kind to those people. ⁶I will protect them. I will bring them back to the land of Judah. I will not tear them down—I will build them up. I will not pull them up—I will plant them so they can grow. ⁷I will make them want to know me. They will know that I am the Lord. They will be my people, and I will be their

---

ancestors Literally, "fathers," meaning a person's parents, grandparents, and all the people they are descended from.
Baal The Canaanite people believed that this false god brought the rain and storms. They also thought that he made the land produce good crops.
heavy load This is a word play. The Hebrew word for "announcement" is like the word translated "heavy load."

temple The special building in Jerusalem for Jewish worship.
Jeconiah This is another name for King Jehoiachin. Jehoiachin was taken prisoner in the year 597 B.C.

God. I will do this because those prisoners in Babylon will turn to me with their whole hearts.

⁸"But Zedekiah king of Judah will be like those figs that are too rotten to eat. Zedekiah, his high officials, all the people that are left in Jerusalem, and those people of Judah that are living in Egypt will be like those rotten figs.

⁹"I will punish those people. The punishment will shock all the people on earth. People will make fun of those people from Judah. People will tell jokes about them. People will curse them in all the places where I scatter them. ¹⁰I will send a sword, starvation, and disease against them. I will attack them until they have all been killed. Then they will no longer be on the land which I gave to them and to their ancestors.*

A Summary of Jeremiah's Preaching

25 This is the message that came to Jeremiah concerning all of the people of Judah. This message came in the fourth year* that Jehoiakim was king of Judah. Jehoiakim was the son of Josiah. The fourth year of his time as king was the first year that Nebuchadnezzar was king of Babylon. ²This is the message that Jeremiah the prophet spoke to all the people of Judah and all the people of Jerusalem:

³I have given you messages from the Lord again and again for these past 23 years. I have been a prophet since the 13th year that Josiah son of Amon was the king of Judah. I have spoken messages from the Lord to you from that time until today. But you have not listened. ⁴The Lord has sent his servants, the prophets, to you over and over again. But you have not listened to them. You have not paid any attention to them.

⁵Those prophets said, "Change your lives! Stop doing those bad things! If you change, then you can return to the land which the Lord gave you and your ancestors* long ago. He gave you this land to live in forever. ⁶Don't follow other gods. Don't serve or worship them. Don't worship idols that some person has made. That only makes me angry at you. Doing this only hurts yourselves."*

⁷"But you did not listen to me." This message is from the Lord. "You worshiped idols that some person made. And that made me angry. And that only hurt you."

⁸So, this is what the Lord All-Powerful says, "You have not listened to my messages. ⁹So I will soon send for all the family groups of the north.*" This message is from the Lord. "I will soon send for Nebuchadnezzar king of Babylon. He is my servant. I will bring those people against the land of Judah and against the people of Judah. I will bring them against all the nations around you too. I will destroy all of those countries. I will make those lands like an empty desert forever. People will see those countries, and whistle at how badly they were destroyed. ¹⁰I will bring an end to the sounds of joy and happiness in those places. There will be no more happy sounds of the brides and bridegrooms. I will take away the sound of people grinding meal. I will take away the light of the lamp. ¹¹That whole area will be an empty desert. All of those people will be slaves of the king of Babylon for 70 years.

¹²"But when the 70 years have passed, I will punish the king of Babylon. I will punish the nation of Babylon." This message is from the Lord. "I will punish the land of the Babylonians for their sins. I will make that land a desert forever. ¹³I have said many bad things will happen to Babylon. All of those things will happen. Jeremiah preached about those foreign nations. And all of those warnings are written in this book. ¹⁴Yes, the people of Babylon will have to serve many nations and many great kings. I will give them the punishment they deserve for all the things they will do."

Judgment on the Nations of the World

¹⁵The Lord, the God of Israel, said these things to me: "Jeremiah, take this cup of wine from my hand. It is the wine of my anger. I am sending you to different nations. Make all those nations drink from this cup. ¹⁶They will drink this wine. Then they will vomit and act like crazy people. They will do this because of the sword that I will soon send against them."

¹⁷So I took the cup of wine from the Lord's hand. I went to those nations and I made those people drink from the cup. ¹⁸I poured this wine for the people of Jerusalem and Judah. I made the kings and leaders of Judah drink from the cup. I

---

ancestors Literally, "fathers," meaning a person's parents, grandparents, and all the people they are descended from.
fourth year This was the year 605 B.C.

Doing this only hurts yourselves Following the ancient Greek translation. The Hebrew reads, "Then I will not hurt you."
north This refers to the army of Babylon coming from the north to attack the nation of Judah.

did this so that they would become an empty desert. I did this so that place would be destroyed so badly that people would whistle about it and say curses about that place. And it happened—Judah is like that now!

¹⁹I also made Pharaoh king of Egypt drink from the cup. I made his officials, his important leaders, and all his people drink from the cup of the Lord's anger.

²⁰I also made all the Arabs and all of the kings of the land of Uz drink from the cup.

I also made all the kings of the land of the Philistines drink from the cup. These were the kings of the cities of Ashkelon, Gaza, Ekron, and what remains of the city Ashdod. ²¹Then I made the people of Edom, Moab, and Ammon drink from the cup. ²²I made all the kings of Tyre and Sidon drink from the cup.

I also made all the kings of the faraway countries drink from that cup. ²³I made the people of Dedan, Tema, and Buz drink from the cup. I made all those that cut their hair at their temples drink from the cup. ²⁴I made all the kings of Arabia drink from the cup. These kings live in the desert. ²⁵I made all the kings from Zimri, Elam, and Media drink from the cup. ²⁶I made all the kings of the north, those that were near and far, drink from the cup. I made them drink one after the other. I made all the kingdoms that are on earth drink from the cup of the anger of the Lord. But the king of Babylon will drink from this cup after all of these other nations.

²⁷"Jeremiah, say to those nations, this is what the Lord All-Powerful, the God of the people of Israel, says, 'Drink this cup of my anger. Get drunk from it and vomit! Fall down and don't get up. Don't get up because I am sending a sword to kill you.'

²⁸"Those people will refuse to take the cup from your hand. They will refuse to drink it. But you will say to them, 'The Lord All-Powerful says these things: You will indeed drink from this cup! ²⁹I am already making these bad things happen to Jerusalem, the city that is called by my name. Maybe you people think that you will not be punished. But you are wrong. You will be punished. I am calling out a sword to attack all the people of the earth.'" This message is from the Lord.

³⁰ "Jeremiah, you will give them this message:
'The Lord shouts from above.
He shouts from his holy temple!

The Lord shouts at his pasture *(people)*!
His shouts are loud like the songs
of people walking on grapes to make wine.

³¹ The noise spreads to all the people on earth.
What is all the noise about?
The Lord is punishing the people
from all the nations.
The Lord told his arguments
against the people.
He judged the people.
And now he is killing the evil people
with a sword.'"
This message is from the Lord.

³² This is what the Lord All-Powerful says:
"Disasters will soon spread
from country to country.
They will come like a powerful storm
to all the faraway places on earth!"

³³The dead bodies of those people will reach from one end of the country to the other. No person will cry for those dead people. No person will gather up their bodies and bury them. They will be left lying on the ground like dung.

³⁴ Shepherds *(leaders)*, you should be leading
the sheep *(people)*.
Start crying you great leaders!
Roll around on the ground in pain,
you leaders of the sheep *(people)*.
Why? Because it is now time
for your slaughter.*
⌊I will scatter your sheep.⌋
They will scatter everywhere,
like pieces flying from a broken jar.

³⁵ There will be no place for the shepherds
to hide.
Those leaders will not escape.

³⁶ I hear the shepherds *(leaders)* shouting.
I hear the leaders of the sheep *(people)* crying.
The Lord is destroying
their pastures *(country)*.

³⁷ Those peaceful pastures are like
an empty desert.
This happened because the Lord is angry.

³⁸ The Lord is like a dangerous lion
leaving his cave.
The Lord is angry!
And that anger will hurt those people.
Their country will be an empty desert.

slaughter Usually, this means to kill an animal and cut it into pieces of meat. But it often means to kill people like they are animals.

Jeremiah's Lesson at the Temple

26 This message came from the Lord during the first year that Jehoiakim was king* of Judah. Jehoiakim was the son of King Josiah. ²The Lord said: "Jeremiah, stand in the temple* yard of the Lord. Give this message to all the people of Judah that are coming to worship at the temple of the Lord. Tell them everything that I tell you to speak. Don't leave out any part of my message. ³Maybe they will listen and obey my message. Maybe they will stop living such evil lives. If they change, then I might change my mind about my plans to punish them. I am planning this punishment because of many bad things those people have done. ⁴You will say to them, 'This is what the Lord says: I gave my teachings to you. You must obey me and follow my teachings. ⁵You must listen to the things my servants say to you. (The prophets are my servants.) I have sent prophets to you again and again, but you did not listen to them. ⁶If you don't obey me, then I will make my temple in Jerusalem just like my Holy Tent at Shiloh.* People all over the world will think of Jerusalem when they ask for bad things to happen to other cities.'"

⁷The priests, the prophets, and all the people heard Jeremiah say all of these words at the Lord's temple.* ⁸Jeremiah finished speaking everything the Lord had commanded him to say to the people. Then the priests, the prophets, and all the people grabbed Jeremiah. They said, "You will die for saying such terrible things! ⁹How dare you preach such a thing in the name of the Lord! How dare you say that this temple will be destroyed like the one at Shiloh! How dare you say that Jerusalem will become a desert with no people living in it!" All the people gathered around Jeremiah in the temple of the Lord.

¹⁰Now the rulers of Judah heard about all of the things that were happening. So they came out of the king's palace. They went up to the Lord's temple. There, they took their places at the entrance of the New Gate. The New Gate is a gate leading to the Lord's temple. ¹¹Then the priests and the prophets spoke to the rulers and all the other people. They said, "Jeremiah should be killed. He said bad things about Jerusalem. You heard him say those things."

¹²Then Jeremiah spoke to all the rulers of Judah and all the other people. He said, "The Lord sent me to say these things about this temple and this city. Everything that you have heard is from the Lord. ¹³You people change your lives! You must start doing good things! You must obey the Lord your God. If you do that, then the Lord will change his mind. The Lord will not do the bad things he told you about. ¹⁴As for me, I am in your power. Do to me what you think is good and right. ¹⁵But if you kill me, be sure of one thing. You will be guilty of killing an innocent person. You will make this city and everyone that lives in it guilty, too. The Lord really did send me to you. The message you heard really is from the Lord."

¹⁶Then the rulers and all the people spoke. Those people said to the priests and the prophets, "Jeremiah must not be killed. The things Jeremiah told us come from the Lord our God."

¹⁷Then some of the elders *(leaders)* stood up and spoke to all the people. ¹⁸They said, "Micah the prophet was from the city of Moresheth. Micah was a prophet during the time that Hezekiah was king of Judah. Micah said these things to all the people of Judah:

> The Lord All-Powerful says:
> "Zion* will be destroyed.
> It will become a plowed field.
> Jerusalem will become a pile of rocks.
> Temple Mount will be an empty hill*
>   overgrown with bushes."
> *Micah 3:12*

¹⁹"Hezekiah was the king of Judah. And Hezekiah didn't kill Micah. None of the people of Judah killed Micah. You know that Hezekiah respected the Lord. He wanted to please the Lord. The Lord had said he would do bad things to Judah. But Hezekiah prayed to the Lord, and the Lord changed his mind. The Lord didn't do those bad things. If we hurt Jeremiah, then we will bring many troubles on ourselves. And those troubles will be our own fault."

---

first year that Jehoiakim was king This was 609 B.C.
temple The special building in Jerusalem for Jewish worship.
my Holy Tent at Shiloh The holy place at Shiloh was probably destroyed during the time of Samuel. See Jer. 7 and 1 Sam. 4.

Zion The southeast part of the mountain Jerusalem is built on. Sometimes it means the people of God living in Jerusalem.
empty hill Or, "high place," a term usually used for local shrines *(places for worship)* where people often worshiped idols.

²⁰In the past, there was another man that preached the Lord's message. His name was Uriah. He was the son of a man named Shemaiah. Uriah was from the city of Kiriath Jearim. Uriah preached the same things against this city and this land as Jeremiah did. ²¹King Jehoiakim and his army officers and the leaders of Judah heard Uriah preach. They became angry. King Jehoiakim wanted to kill Uriah. But Uriah heard that Jehoiakim wanted to kill him. Uriah was afraid, so he escaped to the land of Egypt. ²²But King Jehoiakim sent a man named Elnathan and some other men to Egypt. Elnathan was the son of a man named Acbor. ²³Those men brought Uriah from Egypt. Then those men took Uriah to King Jehoiakim. Jehoiakim ordered Uriah to be killed with a sword. Uriah's body was thrown into the burial place where poor people are buried.

²⁴There was an important man named Ahikam son of Shaphan. Ahikam supported Jeremiah. So Ahikam kept Jeremiah from being killed by the priests and prophets.

The Lord Made Nebuchadnezzar Ruler

27 A message from the Lord came to Jeremiah. It came during the fourth year that Zedekiah was king of Judah.* Zedekiah was the son of King Josiah. ²This is what the Lord said to me: "Jeremiah, make a yoke* out of straps and poles. Put that yoke on the back of your neck. ³Then send messages to the kings of Edom, Moab, Ammon, Tyre, and Sidon. Send the messages with the messengers of these kings that have come to Jerusalem to see Zedekiah king of Judah. ⁴Tell those messengers to give this message to their masters. Tell them, 'The Lord All-Powerful, the God of Israel, says: Tell your masters that ⁵I made the earth and all the people on it. I made all the animals on the earth. I did this with my great power and my strong arm. I can give the earth to anyone I want. ⁶Now I have given all your countries to Nebuchadnezzar king of Babylon. He is my servant. I will make even the wild animals obey him. ⁷All nations will serve Nebuchadnezzar and his son and his grandson. Then the time will come for Babylon to be defeated. Many nations and great kings will make Babylon their servant.

⁸"'But now, some nations or kingdoms might refuse to serve Nebuchadnezzar king of Babylon. They might refuse to put his yoke* on their necks. If that happens, this is what I will do: I will punish that nation with sword, hunger, and terrible sickness.'" This message is from the Lord. "I will do that until I destroy that nation. I will use Nebuchadnezzar to destroy the nation that fights against him. ⁹So don't listen to your prophets. Don't listen to the people that use magic to tell what will happen in the future. Don't listen to people that say they can interpret dreams. Don't listen to people that talk to the dead or to people that practice magic. All those people tell you, "You will not be slaves to the king of Babylon." ¹⁰But those people are telling you lies. They will only cause you to be taken far from your homeland. I will force you to leave your homes. And you will die in another land.

¹¹"'But the nations that put their necks under the yoke* of the king of Babylon and obey him will live. I will let those nations stay in their own country and serve the king of Babylon.'" This message is from the Lord. "'The people from those nations will live in their own land and farm it.'"

¹²"I gave the same message to Zedekiah king of Judah. I said, "Zedekiah, you must place your neck under the yoke* of the king of Babylon and obey him. If you serve the king of Babylon and his people, then you will live. ¹³If you don't agree to serve the king of Babylon, then you and your people will die from the enemy's sword, from hunger, and from terrible sicknesses. The Lord said those things will happen. ¹⁴But the false prophets are saying: You will never be slaves to the king of Babylon.

"'Don't listen to those prophets, because they are preaching lies to you. ¹⁵I didn't send those prophets.'" This message is from the Lord. "They are preaching lies and saying that the message is from me. So, I will send you people of Judah away. You will die. And those prophets that preach to you will die also."

¹⁶Then I *(Jeremiah)* said to the priests and all those people, "The Lord says: Those false prophets are saying, 'The Babylonians took many things from the Lord's temple.* Those things will

---

the fourth year that Zedekiah was king of Judah The Hebrew has, "At the beginning of the kingship of Jehoiakim." This is probably a scribal error. Vs. 3 talks about Zedekiah. Jer. 28:1 mentions the fourth year: 594-593 B.C.

yoke A pole that was put on the shoulders of men or animals to help them carry or pull things. This often showed that a person was a slave.

temple The special building in Jerusalem for Jewish worship.

be brought back soon.' Don't listen to those prophets because they are preaching lies to you. ¹⁷Don't listen to those prophets. Serve the king of Babylon. Accept your punishment, and you will live. There is no reason for you to cause this city of Jerusalem to be destroyed. ¹⁸If those men are prophets and have the message from the Lord, let them pray. Let them pray about the things that are still in the Lord's temple. Let them pray about the things that are still in the king's palace. And let them pray about the things that are still in Jerusalem. Let those prophets pray that all those things will not be taken away to Babylon."

¹⁹The Lord All-Powerful says this about those things that are still left in Jerusalem. In the temple,* there are the pillars, the bronze sea, the moveable stands, and other things.* Nebuchadnezzar king of Babylon, left those things in Jerusalem. ²⁰Nebuchadnezzar didn't take those things away at the time he took Jehoiachin king of Judah away as a prisoner. Jehoiachin was the son of King Jehoiakim. Nebuchadnezzar also took other important people away from Judah and Jerusalem. ²¹The Lord All-Powerful, the God of the people of Israel, says this about the things still left in the Lord's temple, and in the king's palace and in Jerusalem: "All of those things will also be taken to Babylon. ²²Those things will be brought to Babylon until the day comes when I go to get them." This message is from the Lord. "Then I will bring those things back. I will put those things back in this place."

The False Prophet Hananiah

28 In the fifth month of the fourth year* that Zedekiah was king of Judah, Hananiah the prophet spoke to me. Hananiah was the son of a man named Azzur. Hananiah was from the town of Gibeon. Hananiah was in the Lord's temple when he spoke to me. The priests and all the people were there also. This is what Hananiah said: ²"The Lord All-Powerful, the God of the people of Israel, says: 'I will break the yoke* that the king of Babylon has put on the people of Judah. ³Before two years are over, I will bring back all the things that Nebuchadnezzar king of Babylon took from the Lord's temple. Nebuchadnezzar has carried those things to Babylon. But I will bring those things back here to Jerusalem. ⁴I will also bring Jehoiachin king of Judah back to this place. Jehoiachin is the son of Jehoiakim. And I will bring back all those people of Judah that Nebuchadnezzar forced to leave their homes and go to Babylon.' This message is from the Lord. 'So I will break the yoke that the king of Babylon put on the people of Judah!'"

⁵Then the prophet Jeremiah answered the prophet Hananiah. They were standing in the temple of the Lord. The priests and all the people there could hear Jeremiah's answer. ⁶Jeremiah said to Hananiah, "Amen!* I hope the Lord will really do that! I hope the Lord will make the message you preach come true. I hope the Lord will bring the things of the Lord's temple back to this place from Babylon. And I hope the Lord will bring all the people that were forced to leave their homes back to this place.

⁷"But listen to what I must say, Hananiah. Listen to what I say to all you people. ⁸There were prophets long before you and I became prophets, Hananiah. They preached that war, hunger, and terrible sicknesses would come to many countries and great kingdoms. ⁹But the prophet that preaches that we will have peace must be tested to see if he truly was sent by the Lord. If the message of that prophet comes true, then people can know that he truly was sent by the Lord."

¹⁰Jeremiah was wearing a yoke* around his neck. Then the prophet Hananiah took that yoke from Jeremiah's neck. Hananiah broke that yoke. ¹¹Then Hananiah spoke loudly, so all the people could hear him. He said, "The Lord says: 'In the same way I will break the yoke of Nebuchadnezzar king of Babylon. He put that yoke on all the nations of the world. But I will break that yoke before two years are over.'"

After Hananiah said that, Jeremiah left the temple.

¹²Then the message of the Lord came to Jeremiah. This happened after Hananiah had taken the yoke* off of Jeremiah's neck and had broken it. ¹³The Lord said to Jeremiah, "Go and tell Hananiah, 'This is what the Lord says: You have

---

temple The special building in Jerusalem for Jewish worship.
pillars ... other things For a description of these things, see 1 Kings 7:23-37.
fourth year This was about 593 B.C.
yoke A pole that was put on the shoulders of men or animals to help them carry or pull things. This often showed that a person was a slave.

Amen A Hebrew word meaning "truly, indeed." It is used to show that a person agrees with what has been said.

broken a wooden yoke. But I will make a yoke of iron in the place of the wooden yoke.' ¹⁴The Lord All-Powerful, the God of Israel, says: 'I will put a yoke of iron on the necks of all these nations. I will do that to make them serve Nebuchadnezzar king of Babylon. And they will be slaves to him. I will even give Nebuchadnezzar control over the wild animals.'"

¹⁵Then the prophet Jeremiah said to the prophet Hananiah, "Listen, Hananiah! The Lord did not send you. But you have made the people of Judah trust in lies. ¹⁶So this is what the Lord says, 'Soon I will take you from this world, Hananiah. You will die this year. Why? Because you taught the people to turn against the Lord.'"

¹⁷Hananiah died in the seventh month of that same year.

A Letter to the Jewish Captives in Babylon

29 Jeremiah sent a letter to the Jewish captives* in Babylon. He sent it to the elders (leaders), the priests, the prophets, and all the other people that were living in Babylon. These were the people that Nebuchadnezzar took from Jerusalem and brought to Babylon. ²(This letter was sent after King Jehoiachin, the queen mother, the officials and the leaders of Judah and Jerusalem, the carpenters, and the metal workers had been taken from Jerusalem.) ³Zedekiah sent Elasah and Gemariah to King Nebuchadnezzar. Zedekiah was the king of Judah. Elasah was the son of Shaphan. And Gemariah was the son of Hilkiah. Jeremiah gave the letter to those men to take to Babylon. This is what the letter said:

⁴The Lord All-Powerful, the God of the people of Israel, says these things to all those people he sent into captivity from Jerusalem to Babylon: ⁵"Build houses and live in them. Settle in the land. Plant gardens and eat the food you grow. ⁶Get married and have sons and daughters. Find wives for your sons. And let your daughters be married. Do that so they also may have sons and daughters. Have many children and grow in number in Babylon. Don't become fewer in number. ⁷Also, do good things for the city I sent you to. Pray to the Lord for the city you are living in. Why? Because if there is peace in that city, then you will have peace also." ⁸The Lord All-Powerful, the God of the people of Israel, says: "Don't let your prophets and the people that practice magic fool you. Don't listen to the dreams they have. ⁹They are preaching lies. And they are saying that their message is from me. But I didn't send it." This message is from the Lord.

¹⁰This is what the Lord says: "Babylon will be powerful for 70 years. After that time, I will come to you people that are living in Babylon. I will keep my good promise to bring you back to Jerusalem. ¹¹I say this because I know the plans that I have for you." This message is from the Lord. "I have good plans for you. I don't plan to hurt you. I plan to give you hope and a good future. ¹²Then you people will call my name. You will come to me and pray to me. And I will listen to you. ¹³You people will search for me. And when you search for me with all your heart, you will find me. ¹⁴I will let you find me." This message is from the Lord. "And I will bring you back from your captivity. I forced you to leave this place. But I will gather you from all the nations and places where I have sent you," — this message is from the Lord — "and I will bring you back to this place."

¹⁵You people might say, "But the Lord has given us prophets here in Babylon." ¹⁶But the Lord says these things about your relatives that were not carried away to Babylon. I am talking about the king that is sitting on David's throne now and all the other people that are still in the city of Jerusalem. ¹⁷The Lord All-Powerful says: "I will soon send the sword, hunger, and terrible sicknesses against those people that are still in Jerusalem. And I will make them the same as bad figs, which are too rotten to eat. ¹⁸I will chase those people that are still in Jerusalem with the sword, with hunger, and terrible sicknesses. And I will make it so that all the kingdoms of the earth will be frightened at what has happened to those people. Those people will be destroyed. People will whistle with amazement when they hear about the things that happened. And people use them as an example when they ask for bad things to happen to people. People will insult them wherever I force those people to go. ¹⁹I will make all those

---

captives People that were taken away like prisoners. Here this means the Jewish people that were taken to Babylon.

things happen because those people of Jerusalem have not listened to my message." This message is from the Lord. "I sent my message to them again and again. I used my servants, the prophets, to give my messages to those people. But the people didn't listen." This message is from the Lord. ²⁰"You people are captives.* I forced you to leave Jerusalem and go to Babylon. So, listen to the message from the Lord."

²¹The Lord All-Powerful says this about Ahab son of Kolaiah and Zedekiah son of Maaseiah: "These two men have been preaching lies to you. They have said that their message is from me. ₁But they were lying.₁ I will give those two prophets to Nebuchadnezzar king of Babylon. And Nebuchadnezzar will kill those prophets in front of all you people that are captives in Babylon. ²²All of the Jewish captives will use those men as examples when they ask for bad things to happen to other people. Those captives will say: 'May the Lord treat you like Zedekiah and Ahab. The king of Babylon burned those two in the fire!' ²³Those two prophets did very bad things among the people of Israel. They did the sin of adultery* with their neighbors' wives. They also spoke lies and said those lies were a message from me, the Lord. I did not tell them to do those things. I know what they have done. I am a witness." This message is from the Lord.

God's Message to Shemaiah

²⁴Also give a message to Shemaiah. Shemaiah is from the Nehelam family. ²⁵The Lord All-Powerful, the God of Israel, says: "Shemaiah, you sent letters to all the people in Jerusalem. And you sent letters to the priest Zephaniah son of Maaseiah. You also sent letters to all the priests. You sent those letters in your own name and not by the authority of the Lord. ²⁶Shemaiah, this is what you said in your letter to Zephaniah: 'Zephaniah, the Lord has made you priest in place of Jehoiada. You are to be in charge of the Lord's temple. You should arrest anyone that acts like a crazy person* and acts like a prophet. You should put that person's feet between large blocks of wood and put neck-irons* on him. ²⁷Now, Jeremiah is acting like a prophet. So why have you not arrested him? ²⁸Jeremiah has sent this message to us in Babylon: "You people in Babylon will be there for a long time. So build houses and settle down. Plant gardens and eat what you grow."'

²⁹Zephaniah the priest read the letter to Jeremiah the prophet. ³⁰Then the message from the Lord came to Jeremiah: ³¹"Jeremiah, send this message to all the captives* in Babylon: 'This is what the Lord says about Shemaiah, the man from the Nehelam family: Shemaiah has preached to you, but I didn't send him. Shemaiah has made you believe a lie. ³²Because Shemaiah has done that, this is what the Lord says: I will soon punish Shemaiah, the man from the Nehelam family. I will completely destroy his family. And he will not share in the good things I will do for my people.'" This message is from the Lord. "'I will punish Shemaiah because he has taught the people to turn against the Lord.'"

Promises of Hope

30 This is the message that came to Jeremiah from the Lord. ²The Lord, the God of the people of Israel, said: "Jeremiah, write in a book the words I have spoken to you. Write this book for yourself. ³Do this because the days will come" — this message is from the Lord — "when I will bring my people, Israel and Judah, back from exile."* This message is from the Lord. "I will put those people back in the land that I gave to their ancestors.* Then my people will own that land again."

⁴The Lord spoke this message about the people of Israel and Judah. ⁵This is what the Lord said:

"We hear people crying from fear!
People are scared!
There is no peace!

⁶ "Ask this question, and consider it:
Can a man have a baby? Of course not!

---

captives People taken away like prisoners. Here this means the Jewish people that were taken to Babylon.
adultery Breaking the marriage promise by sexual sin.
crazy person Shemaiah is referring to Jeremiah here. See verses 27-28.

exile Being forced to leave one's home country.
ancestors Literally, "fathers," meaning a person's parents, grandparents, and all the people they are descended from.

JEREMIAH 30:7–18

Then why do I see every strong man
  holding his stomach
  like a woman having labor pains?
Why is every person's face turning white
  like a dead man?
  ₍Why? Because the men are very scared.₎

⁷ "This is a very important time for Jacob.*
  This is a time of great trouble.
  There will never be another time like this.
  But Jacob* will be saved.

⁸"At that time," this message is from the Lord All-Powerful, "I will break the yoke* from the necks of the people of Israel and Judah. And I will break the ropes holding you. People from foreign countries will never again force my people to be slaves. ⁹The people of Israel and Judah will not serve foreign countries. No! They will serve the Lord their God. And they will serve David their king,* I will send that king to them.

¹⁰ "So, Jacob* my servant, don't be afraid!"
  This message is from the Lord.
"Israel, don't be afraid.
  I will save you from that faraway place.
  You are captives* in that faraway land,
  But I will save your descendants.*
    ₍I will bring them back₎ from that land.
  Jacob will have peace again.
  People will not bother Jacob.
  There will be no enemy to scare my people.
¹¹ People of Israel and Judah, I am with you."
  This message is from the Lord.
"And I will save you.
  I sent you to those nations.
  But I will completely destroy
    all those nations.
  It is true, I will destroy those nations,
    but I will not destroy you.
  You must be punished
    for the bad things you did.
  But I will discipline you fairly."

¹² The Lord says:
"You people of Israel and Judah
  have a wound that can't be cured.
  You have an injury that will not heal.
¹³ There is no person to care for your sores.
  So you will not be healed.
¹⁴ You became friends with many nations.
  But those nations don't care about you.
  Your 'friends' have forgotten you.
  I hurt you like an enemy.
  I punished you very hard.
  I did this because of your great guilt.
  I did this because of your many sins.
¹⁵ Israel and Judah, why are you yelling
    about your wound?
  Your wound is painful,
    and there is no cure for it.
  I, the Lord, did these things to you
    because of your great guilt.
  I did these things
    because of your many sins.
¹⁶ Those nations destroyed you,
    but now they have been destroyed.
  Israel and Judah,
    your enemies will become captives.*
  Those people stole things from you.
    But other people will steal from them.
  Those people took things from you in war.
    But other people will take things
      from them in war.
¹⁷ And I will bring your health back.
  And I will heal your wounds."
  This message is from the Lord.
"Why? Because other people
    said you were outcasts.*
  Those people said,
    'No one cares about Zion.*'"

¹⁸ The Lord says:
"Jacob's* people are now in captivity.
  But they will come back.
  And I will have pity on Jacob's houses.
  The city* is now only an empty hill
    covered with ruined buildings.
  But the city will be built again on its hill.
  And the king's house will be built again
    where it should be.

Jacob Another name for Israel. See Gen. 32:22-28.
yoke A pole that was put on the shoulders of men or animals to help them carry or pull things. This often showed that a person was a slave.
David their king This means another king of Israel, that will be great like King David.
captives People that were taken away like prisoners. Here this means the Jewish people that were taken to Babylon.
descendants A person's children and their future families.

outcasts People that were thrown out of some special group of people. Often people don't like or respect outcasts.
Zion The southeast part of the mountain Jerusalem is built on. Sometimes it means the people of God living in Jerusalem.
city This probably refers to Jerusalem. But it might also mean all of the cities of Israel and Judah.

19 People in those places
   will sing songs of praise.
   And there will be the sound of laughter.
   I will give them many children.
   Israel and Judah will not be small.
   I will bring honor to them.
   No person will look down on them.
20 Jacob's family will be
   like the family of Israel long ago.
   I will make Israel and Judah strong,
   and I will punish the people that hurt them.
21 One of their own people will lead them.
   That ruler will come from my people.
   People can come close to me
   only if I ask them to.
   So I will ask that leader to come to me,
   and he will be close to me.
22 You will be my people.
   And I will be your God."
23 The Lord was very angry!
   He punished the people.
   The punishment came like a storm.
   The punishment came like a tornado
   against those wicked people.
24 The Lord will be angry
   until he finishes punishing the people.
   He will be angry until he finishes
   the punishment he planned.
   When that day comes,
   you people of Judah will understand.

The New Israel

31 The Lord said these things, "At that time, I will be the God of all the family groups of Israel. And they will be my people."

2 The Lord says:
   "The people who escaped the enemy's sword
   will find comfort in the desert.
   Israel will go there looking for rest."
3 From far away, the Lord
   will appear to his people.

⌊The Lord says,⌋
"I love you people with a love
   that continues forever.
   That is why I have continued
   showing you kindness.
4 Israel, my bride, I will build you again.
   You will be a country again.
   You will pick up your tambourines again.
   You will dance with all the other people
   that are having fun.

5 You farmers of Israel will plant
   fields of grapes again.
   You will plant those vineyards on the hills
   around the city of Samaria.
   And those farmers will enjoy the fruit
   from those vineyards.
6 There will be a time when watchmen*
   shout this message:
   'Come, let's go up to Zion*
   to worship the Lord our God!'
   Even the watchmen in the hill country of
   Ephraim* will shout that message."

7 The Lord says:
   "Be happy and sing for Jacob*!
   Shout for Israel,
   the greatest of the nations!
   Sing your praises and shout:
   'The Lord saved his people!*
   He has saved the people that are left alive
   from the nation of Israel.'
8 Remember, I will bring Israel
   from that country in the north.
   I will gather the people of Israel
   from the faraway places on earth.
   Some of the people will be blind and crippled.
   Some of the women will be pregnant
   and ready to give birth.
   But many, many people will come back.
9 Those people will come back crying.
   But I will lead them and comfort them.
   I will lead those people by streams of water.
   I will lead them on an easy road,
   so that they will not stumble.
   I will lead them in that way
   because I am Israel's father.
   And Ephraim* is my firstborn son.

10 "Nations, listen to this message
    from the Lord!
    Tell this message in the faraway lands
    by the sea:
    'God scattered the people of Israel
    But God will bring them back together.

---

watchmen Usually this means a guard that stands on the city walls watching for people coming to the city. But here it probably means the prophets.
Zion The southeast part of the mountain Jerusalem is built on. Sometimes it means the people of God living in Jerusalem.
Ephraim This means the northern kingdom of Israel.
Jacob Another name for Israel. See Gen. 32:22-28.
' **The Lord saved his people** Or, "Lord, save your people!" This is often a shout of victory.

And he will watch over his flock *(people)*
   like a shepherd.'
11 The Lord will bring Jacob* back.
   The Lord will save his people from people
      that were stronger than them.
12 The people of Israel will come
      to the top of Zion,*
      and they will shout with joy.
   Their faces will shine with happiness
      about the good things the Lord gives them.
   The Lord will give them grain, new wine,
      olive oil, young sheep, and cows.
   They will be like a garden
      that has plenty of water.
   And the people of Israel will not
      be troubled anymore.
13 Then the young women of Israel
      will be happy and dance.
   And the young men and old men
      will join in the dancing.
   I will change their sadness into happiness.
   I will comfort the people of Israel.
   I will change their sadness to happiness.
14 I will give the priests plenty of food.
   And my people will be filled and satisfied
      with the good things I give them."
   This message is from the Lord.

15 The Lord says:
   "A sound will be heard in Ramah.
      It will be bitter crying and much sadness.
   Rachel* will be crying for her children.
      Rachel will refuse to be comforted,
      because her children are dead."

16 But the Lord says:
   "Stop crying!
      Don't fill your eyes with tears!
   You will be rewarded for your work!"
   This message is from the Lord.
   "The people of Israel will come back from
      their enemy's land.
17 Israel, there is hope for you."
   This message is from the Lord.
   "Your children will come back
      to their own land.

18 I have heard Ephraim* crying.
   I heard Ephraim say these things:
   'Lord, you really punished me!
      And I learned my lesson.
   I was like a calf that was never trained.
   Please stop punishing me,
      and I will come back to you.
   You truly are the Lord my God.
19 Lord, I wandered away from you.
      But I learned about the bad things I did.
      So I changed my heart and life.
   I am ashamed and embarrassed about the
      foolish things I did when I was young.'

20 ⌊God says⌋
   "You know that Ephraim* is my dear son.
      I love that child.
   Yes, I often criticized Ephraim,
      but I still think about him.
   I love him very much.
      And I really do want to comfort him."
   This message is from the Lord.

21 "People of Israel, fix the road signs.
      Put up the signs that show the way home.
   Watch the road.
      Remember the road you are leaving on.
   Israel, my bride, come home.
      Come back to your towns.
22 Unfaithful daughter,
      how long will you wander around?
   ⌊When will you come home?⌋"

   When the Lord creates something new in
      the land: A woman surrounding a man.*

²³The Lord All-Powerful, the God of Israel, says: "I will again do good things for the people of Judah. I will bring back the people who were taken away as prisoners. At that time, the people in the land of Judah and in its towns will once again use these words: 'May the Lord bless you, good home and holy mountain!'*

²⁴"People in all the towns of Judah will live together in peace. Farmers and those that move around with their flocks will live peacefully together in Judah. ²⁵I will give rest and strength to the people that are weak and tired."

Jacob Another name for Israel. See Gen. 32:22-28.
Zion The southeast part of the mountain Jerusalem is built on. Sometimes it means the people of God living in Jerusalem.
Rachel Jacob's wife. Here this means all the women that are crying for their husbands and children that have died in the war with Babylon.

Ephraim This means the norther kingdom of Israel.
A woman surrounding a man This is a word play, but it is hard to understand. It was probably some saying that was familiar to the people in Jeremiah's time.
good home and holy mountain This was a blessing for the temple and for Zion, the mountain the temple was built on.

²⁶After hearing that, I *(Jeremiah)* woke up and looked around. That was a very pleasant sleep.
²⁷"The days are coming," this message is from the Lord, "when I will help the family of Israel and Judah to grow. I will help their children and animals to grow too. It will be like planting and caring for a plant. ²⁸In the past, I watched over Israel and Judah, but I watched for the time to pull them up. I tore them down. I destroyed them. I gave many troubles to them. But now, I will watch over them to build them up and make them strong." This message is from the Lord.
²⁹"People won't use this saying anymore:

The parents ate the sour grapes,
but the children got the sour taste.*

³⁰No, each person will die for his own sin. The person that eats sour grapes will get the sour taste."

The New Agreement

³¹The Lord said these things, "The time is coming when I will make a new Agreement* with the family of Israel, and with the family of Judah. ³²It will not be like the Agreement I made with their ancestors.* I made that Agreement when I took them by the hand and brought them out of Egypt. I was their Master, but they broke that Agreement." This message is from the Lord.
³³"In the future, I will make this Agreement with the people of Israel." This message is from the Lord. "I will put my teachings in their minds, and I will write them on their hearts. I will be their God, and they will be my people. ³⁴People will not have to teach their neighbors and relatives to know the Lord. Why? Because all people, from the least important to the greatest, will know me." This message is from the Lord. "I will forgive them for the bad things they did. I won't remember their sins."

The Lord Will Never Leave Israel

³⁵ The Lord says:

"The Lord makes the sun shine in the day.
And the Lord makes the moon and the stars shine at night.
The Lord stirs up the sea so that its waves crash on the shore.
The Lord All-Powerful is his name."

³⁶ The Lord says these things:
"The descendants* of Israel will never stop being a nation.
That would happen only if I lost control of the sun, moon, stars, and sea."

³⁷ The Lord says:
"I'll never reject the descendants of Israel.
That would happen only if people could measure the sky above,
and learn all the secrets of the earth below.
Only then would I reject the descendants of Israel.
Only then would I reject them for the bad things they have done."
This message is from the Lord.

The New Jerusalem

³⁸This message is from the Lord, "The days are coming when the city of Jerusalem will be built again for the Lord. The whole city will be built again—from the Tower of Hananel to the Corner Gate. ³⁹The measuring line* will stretch from the Corner Gate straight to the hill of Gareb and then turn to the place named Gorah. ⁴⁰The whole valley where dead bodies and ashes are thrown will be holy to the Lord. And all the terraces down to the bottom of Kidron Valley all the way to the corner of Horse Gate will be included. All that area will be holy to the Lord. The city of Jerusalem will never again be torn down or destroyed."

Jeremiah Buys a Field

32 ¹This is the message from the Lord that came to Jeremiah during the tenth year that Zedekiah was king of Judah.* The tenth year of Zedekiah was the 18th year of Nebuchadnezzar. ²At that time, the army of the king of Babylon was surrounding the city of Jerusalem. And Jeremiah

---

parents ... sour taste This means that children were suffering for the things their parents did.
Agreement Literally, "Proof." The flat stones with the Ten Commandments written on them were proof of the Agreement between God and Israel.
ancestors Literally, "fathers," meaning a person's parents, grandparents, and all the people they are descended from.

descendants A person's children and their future families.
measuring line A rope or chain for measuring property lines.
tenth year ... Judah This was 588-587B.C. This was the year Jerusalem was destroyed by Nebuchadnezzar.

JEREMIAH 32:3-24

was under arrest in the courtyard of the guard. This courtyard was at the palace of the king of Judah. ³(Zedekiah king of Judah had put Jeremiah in prison in that place. Zedekiah didn't like the things Jeremiah prophesied.* Jeremiah had said, "The Lord says: 'I will soon give the city of Jerusalem to the king of Babylon. Nebuchadnezzar will capture this city. ⁴Zedekiah king of Judah will not escape from the army of the Babylonians. But he will surely be given to the king of Babylon. And Zedekiah will speak to the king of Babylon face to face. Zedekiah will see him with his own eyes. ⁵The king of Babylon will take Zedekiah to Babylon. Zedekiah will stay there until I have punished him.' This message is from the Lord. 'If you fight against the army of the Babylonians, you will not succeed.'")

⁶While Jeremiah was prisoner, he said, "The message from the Lord came to me. This was the message: ⁷Jeremiah, your cousin, Hanamel, will come to you soon. He is the son of your uncle Shallum. Hanamel will say to you, 'Jeremiah, buy my field near the town of Anathoth. Buy it because you are my nearest relative. It is your right and your responsibility to buy that field.'

⁸"Then it happened just as the Lord said. My cousin Hanamel came to me in the courtyard of the guard. Hanamel said to me, 'Jeremiah, buy my field near the town of Anathoth, in the land of the family group of Benjamin. Buy that land for yourself because it is your right to buy it and own it.'"

So I knew that this was a message from the Lord. ⁹I bought the field at Anathoth from my cousin Hanamel. I weighed out 17 shekels* of silver for him. ¹⁰I signed the deed.* And I had a copy of the deed sealed up.* And I got some men to witness the things I had done. And I weighed out the silver on the scales. ¹¹Then I took the sealed copy of the deed and the copy that was not sealed, ¹²and I gave them to Baruch. Baruch was the son of Neriah. Neriah was the son of Mahseiah. The sealed copy of the deed had all the terms and conditions of my purchase. I gave this deed to Baruch while my cousin Hanamel and the other witnesses were there. Those witnesses also signed the deed. There were also many people of Judah sitting in the courtyard that saw me give the deed to Baruch.

¹³With all the people watching, I said to Baruch: ¹⁴"The Lord All-Powerful, the God of Israel, says: 'Take both copies of the deed—the sealed copy and the copy that was not sealed—and put them in a clay jar. Do this so that these deeds will last a long time.' ¹⁵The Lord All-Powerful, the God of Israel, says: 'In the future, my people will once again buy houses, fields, and vineyards in the land of Israel.'"

¹⁶After I gave the deed to Baruch son of Neriah I prayed to the Lord. I said:

¹⁷"Lord God, you made the skies and the earth. You made them with your great power. There is nothing too wonderful for you to do. ¹⁸Lord, you are loyal and kind to thousands of people. But you also bring punishment to children for their fathers' sins. Great and powerful God, your name is the Lord All-Powerful. ¹⁹You plan and do great things, Lord. You see everything that people do. You give reward to people that do good things and you punish people that do bad things—you give them what they deserve. ²⁰Lord, you did powerful miracles in the land of Egypt. You have done powerful miracles even until today. You did those things in Israel and you did those things wherever there are people. You have become famous because of these things. ²¹Lord, you used powerful miracles and brought your people Israel out of Egypt. You used your own powerful hand to do those things. Your power was amazing!

²²"Lord, you gave this land to the people of Israel. This is the land you promised to give to their ancestors* long ago. It is a very good land. It is a good land with many good things. ²³The people of Israel came into this land and took it for their own. But those people didn't obey you. They didn't follow your teachings. They didn't do the things you commanded. So you made all these terrible things happen to the people of Israel. ²⁴"And now, the enemy has surrounded the city. They are building ramps, so that

---

prophesied Spoke for God.
shekel Or, "2/5 of an ounce."
deed A piece of paper that proves a person owns a certain piece of property.
sealed up Important documents were rolled up and tied with a string. Then a piece of clay or wax was put on the string. Then a person's mark was put in that clay or wax. This way, people could prove nothing in the document was changed.

ancestors Literally, "fathers," meaning a person's parents, grandparents, and all the people they are descended from.

they can get over the walls of Jerusalem and capture it. By using their swords, and hunger, and terrible sicknesses, the Babylonian army will defeat the city of Jerusalem. The Babylonian army is attacking the city now. Lord, you said this would happen—and now you see it is happening. ²⁵"Lord my Master, all of those bad things are happening. But now you are telling me, 'Jeremiah, buy the field with silver and choose some men to witness the purchase.' You are telling me this while the Babylonian army is ready to capture the city. Why should I waste my money like that?"

²⁶Then the message from the Lord came to Jeremiah: ²⁷"Jeremiah, I am the Lord. I am the God of every person on the earth. Jeremiah, you know that nothing is impossible for me." ²⁸The Lord also said, "I will soon give the city of Jerusalem to the Babylonian army and to Nebuchadnezzar king of Babylon. That army will capture the city. ²⁹The Babylonian army is already attacking the city of Jerusalem. They will soon enter the city and start a fire. They will burn this city down. There are houses in this city where the people of Jerusalem made me angry by offering sacrifices to the false god Baal* on the housetops. And the people poured out drink offerings to other idol gods. The Babylonian army will burn down those houses. ³⁰I have watched the people of Israel and the people of Judah. Everything they do is evil. They have done evil things since they were young. The people of Israel have made me very angry. They have made me angry because they worship idols that they made with their own hands." This message is from the Lord. ³¹"From the time that Jerusalem was built until now, the people of this city have made me angry. This city has made me so angry, I must remove it from my sight. ³²I will destroy Jerusalem because of all the evil things the people of Israel and Judah have done. The people, their kings, leaders, their priests and prophets, the men of Judah, and the people of Jerusalem have all made me angry.

³³"Those people should have come to me for help. But they turned their backs to me. I tried to teach those people again and again. But they would not listen to me. I tried to correct them, but they would not listen. ³⁴Those people have made their idols—and I hate those idols. They put their idols in the temple* that is called by my name. In this way, they made my temple 'dirty.'

³⁵"In the Valley of Ben Hinnom,* those people built high places* to the false god Baal.* They built those worship places so that they could burn their sons and daughters as child sacrifices. I never commanded them to do such a terrible thing. I never even thought the people of Judah would do such a terrible thing.

³⁶"You people are saying, 'The king of Babylon will capture Jerusalem. He will use swords, hunger, and terrible sicknesses to defeat this city.' But the Lord, the God of the people of Israel, says: ³⁷'I have forced the people of Israel and Judah to leave their land. I was very angry with those people. But I will bring them back to this place. I will gather those people from the land where I forced them to go. I will bring them back to this place. I will let them live in peace and safety. ³⁸The people of Israel and Judah will be my people. And I will be their God. ³⁹I will give those people the desire to be truly one people. They will have one goal—they will truly want to worship me all their lives. They will truly want to do this, and so will their children.

⁴⁰"'I will make an Agreement with the people of Israel and Judah. This Agreement will last forever. In this Agreement, I will never turn away from those people. I will always be good to them. I will make them want to respect me. Then they will never turn away from me. ⁴¹They will make me happy. I will enjoy doing good to them. And I will surely plant them in this land and make them grow. I will do this with all my heart and soul.'"

⁴²This is what the Lord says: "I have brought this great disaster to the people of Israel and Judah. In the same way, I will bring good things to them. I promise to do good things for them. ⁴³You people are saying: 'This land is an empty desert. There are no people or animals here. The Babylonian army defeated this country.' But in the future, people will once again buy fields in this land. ⁴⁴People will use their money and buy

---

Baal The Canaanite people believed that this false god brought the rain and storms. They also thought that he made the land produce good crops.

temple The special building in Jerusalem for Jewish worship.

Valley of Ben Hinnom This valley is also called, "Gehenna." This name comes from the Hebrew name "Ge Hinnom—Hinnom's Valley." This place became an example of how God punishes wicked people.

high places Special places where the people worshiped false gods. These places were often on hilltops, but not always. Some 'high places' were in valleys.

fields. They will sign and seal their agreements. People will witness the people signing their deeds.* People will again buy fields in the land where the family group of Benjamin lives. They will buy fields in the area around Jerusalem. They will buy fields in the towns of the land of Judah, in the hill country, in the western foothills, and in the area of the southern desert. That will happen because I will bring your people back home." This message is from the Lord.

The Promise of God

33 The message from the Lord came to Jeremiah a second time. Jeremiah was still locked up in the courtyard* of the guards. ²The Lord made the earth, and he keeps it safe. The Lord is his name. The Lord says, ³"Judah, pray to me, and I will answer you. I will tell you important secrets. You have never heard these things before. ⁴The Lord is the God of Israel. The Lord says these things about the houses in Jerusalem and about the palaces* of the kings of Judah. The enemy will pull those houses down. The enemy will build ramps up to the top of the city walls. The enemy will use swords and fight the people in these cities.

⁵"The people in Jerusalem have done many bad things. I am angry at those people. I have turned against them. So I will kill many, many people there. The Babylonian army will come to fight against Jerusalem. There will be many, many dead bodies in the houses in Jerusalem.

⁶"But then I will heal the people in that city. I will let those people enjoy peace and safety. ⁷I will make good things happen to Judah and Israel again. I will make those people strong like in the past. ⁸They sinned against me—but I will wash away that sin. They fought against me—but I will forgive them. ⁹Then Jerusalem will be a wonderful place. People will be happy. And people from other nations will praise it. This will happen at the time those people hear about the good things happening there. They will hear about the good things I am doing for Jerusalem.

¹⁰"You people are saying, 'Our country is an empty desert. There are no people or animals living there.' It is now quiet in the streets of Jerusalem and in the towns of Judah. But it will be noisy there soon. ¹¹There will be sounds of joy and happiness. There will be the happy sounds of a bride and groom. There will be the sounds of people bringing their gifts to the Lord's temple.* Those people will say, 'Praise the Lord All-Powerful! The Lord is good! The Lord's kindness continues forever!' The people will say these things because I will again do good things to Judah. It will be like in the beginning." The Lord said these things.

¹²The Lord All-Powerful says, "This place is empty now. There are no people or animals living here. But there will be people in all the towns of Judah. There will be shepherds, and there will be pastures where they will let their flocks rest. ¹³Shepherds count their sheep as the sheep walk in front of them. People will be counting their sheep all around the country—in the hill-country, in the western foothills, in the Negev,* and in all the other towns of Judah."

The Good Branch

¹⁴This message is from the Lord: "I made a special promise to the people of Israel and Judah. The time is coming when I will do the things I promised. ¹⁵At that time, I will make a good 'branch' grow from David's family. That good 'branch' will do the things that are good and right for the country. ¹⁶At the time of this 'branch,' the people of Judah will be saved. The people will live safely in Jerusalem. The branch's name is: 'The Lord is Good.'"

¹⁷The Lord says, "A person from David's family will always sit on the throne and rule the family of Israel. ¹⁸And there will always be priests from the family of Levi. Those priests will always stand before me and offer burnt offerings and sacrifice grain offerings and give sacrifices to me."

¹⁹This message from the Lord came to Jeremiah. ²⁰The Lord says, "I have an agreement with day and night. I agreed that they will continue forever. You can't change that agreement. Day and night will always come at the right time. If you could change that agreement, ²¹then you could change my Agreement with David and Levi. Then descendants* from David

---

deed(s) A piece of paper that proves a person owns a certain piece of property.
courtyard An area around the king's house.
palace(s) A large house for the king and his family.

temple The special building in Jerusalem for Jewish worship.
Negev The desert area south of Judah.
descendants A person's children and their future families.

would not be the kings and the family of Levi would not be priests. ²²But I will give many descendants to my servant David and to the family group of Levi. They will be as many as the stars in the sky—no person can count all those stars. And they will be as many as the pieces of sand on the seashore—no person can count those pieces of sand."

²³Jeremiah received this message from the Lord: ²⁴"Jeremiah, have you heard what the people are saying? Those people are saying, 'The Lord turned away from the two families of Israel and Judah. The Lord chose those people, but now he does not even accept them as a nation.'"

²⁵The Lord says, "If my agreement with day and night does not continue, and if I didn't make the laws for the sky and earth, then maybe I would leave those people. ²⁶Then maybe I would turn away from Jacob's* descendants.* And then maybe I would not let David's descendants rule over the descendants of Abraham, Isaac, and Jacob. But David is my servant. And I will be kind to those people. And I will again cause good things to happen to those people."

A Warning to Zedekiah King of Judah

34 The message from the Lord came to Jeremiah. The message came at the time when Nebuchadnezzar king of Babylon, was fighting against Jerusalem and all the towns around it. Nebuchadnezzar had with him all his army and the armies of all the kingdoms and peoples in the empire he ruled.

²This was the message: "This is what the Lord, the God of the people of Israel, says: Jeremiah, go to Zedekiah king of Judah and give him this message: 'Zedekiah, this is what the Lord says: I will give the city of Jerusalem to the king of Babylon very soon, and he will burn it down. ³Zedekiah, you will not escape from the king of Babylon. You will surely be caught and given to him. You will see the king of Babylon with your own eyes. He will talk to you face to face, and you will go to Babylon. ⁴But listen to the promise of the Lord, Zedekiah king of Judah. This is what the Lord says about you: You will not be killed with a sword. ⁵You will die in a peaceful way. People made funeral fires to honor your ancestors,* the kings that ruled before you became king. In the same way, people will make a funeral fire to honor you. They will cry for you. They will sadly say, "Oh, master!" I myself make this promise to you.'" This message is from the Lord.

⁶So Jeremiah gave the message from the Lord to Zedekiah in Jerusalem. ⁷This was while the army of the king of Babylon was fighting against Jerusalem. The army of Babylon was also fighting against the cities of Judah that had not been captured. Those cities were Lachish and Azekah. These were the only fortified cities left in the land of Judah.

The People Break One of their Agreements

⁸King Zedekiah had made an agreement with all the people in Jerusalem to give freedom to all the Hebrew slaves. A message from the Lord came to Jeremiah after Zedekiah had made that agreement. ⁹Every person was supposed to free his Hebrew slaves. All male and female Hebrew slaves were to be set free. No one was supposed to keep another person from the family group of Judah in slavery. ¹⁰So all the leaders of Judah and all the people accepted this agreement. Every person would free their male and female slaves and no longer keep them as slaves. Every person agreed, and so all the slaves were set free. ¹¹But after that,* the people that had slaves changed their minds. So they took the people they had set free and made them slaves again.

¹²Then the message from the Lord came to Jeremiah: ¹³Jeremiah, this is what the Lord, the God of the people of Israel, says: "I brought your ancestors* out of the land of Egypt, where they were slaves. When I did that, I made an Agreement with them. ¹⁴I said to your ancestors: 'At the end of every seven years, each person must set his Hebrew slaves free. If you have a fellow Hebrew that has sold himself to you, you must let him go free after he has served you for six years.' But your ancestors didn't listen to me or pay attention to me. ¹⁵A short time ago, you changed your hearts to do what is right. Each of

---

Jacob's Another name for Israel. See Gen. 32:22-28.
descendants A person's children and their future families.

after that In the summer of 588 B.C., the Egyptian army came to help the people of Jerusalem, and the Babylonian army had to leave Jerusalem briefly to fight the Egyptians. The people of Jerusalem thought that God had helped them, and that things were back to normal, so they didn't keep their promise. They took the slaves that they had set free back into slavery.

you gave freedom to his fellow Hebrews that were slaves. And you even made an agreement before me in the temple* that is called by my name. ¹⁶But now, you have changed your minds. You have shown you don't honor my name. How did you do this? Each of you has taken back the male and female slaves that you had set free. You have forced them to become slaves again.

¹⁷"So this is what the Lord says: 'You people have not obeyed me. You have not given freedom to your fellow Hebrews. Because you have not kept the agreement, I will give "freedom."' This is the message of the Lord. '(I will give) "freedom" to be killed by swords, by terrible sicknesses, and by hunger! I will make you become something that terrifies all the kingdoms of the earth, when they hear about you. ¹⁸I will hand over the men that broke my Agreement, and have not kept the promises they made before me. These men cut a calf into two pieces before me and walked between the two pieces.* ¹⁹These are the people that walked between the two pieces of the calf when they made the Agreement before me: the leaders of Judah and Jerusalem, the important officials of the court, the priests, and the people of the land. ²⁰So I will give those people to their enemies and to every person that wants to kill them. The bodies of those people will become food for the birds of the air and for the wild animals of the earth. ²¹I will give Zedekiah king of Judah, and his leaders to their enemies and to every person that wants to kill them. I will give Zedekiah and his people to the army of the king of Babylon, even though that army has left Jerusalem.* ²²But I will give the order,' this message is from the Lord, 'to bring the Babylonian army back to Jerusalem. That army will fight against Jerusalem. They will capture it and set it on fire and burn it down. And I will destroy the cities in the land of Judah. Those cities will become empty deserts. No people will live there.'"

The Good Example of the Recabite Family

35 During the time when Jehoiakim was king of Judah, the message from the Lord came to Jeremiah. Jehoiakim was the son of King Josiah. This was the message from the Lord: ²"Jeremiah, go to the Recabite family.* Invite them to come to one of the side rooms of the temple* of the Lord. Offer them wine to drink."

³So I (Jeremiah) went to get Jaazaniah.* Jaazaniah was the son of a man named Jeremiah,* that was the son of a man named Habazziniah. And I got all of Jaazaniah's brothers and sons. I got the whole family of the Recabites together. ⁴Then I brought the Recabite family into the temple of the Lord. We went into the room called the room of the sons of Hanan. Hanan was the son of a man named Igdaliah. Hanan was a man of God.* The room was next to the room where the princes of Judah stay. It was over the room of Maaseiah son of Shallum. Maaseiah was the doorkeeper in the temple. ⁵Then I (Jeremiah) put some bowls full of wine with some cups in front of the Recabite family. And I said to them, "Drink some wine."

⁶But the Recabite people answered, "We never drink wine. We never drink it because our ancestor* Jonadab son of Recab, gave us this command: 'You and your descendants* must never drink wine. ⁷Also, you must never build houses, plant seeds, or plant vineyards. You must never do any of those things. You must live only in tents. If you do that, then you will live a long time in the land where you move from place to place.' ⁸So, we Recabite people have obeyed everything our ancestor Jonadab commanded us. We never drink wine. And our wives, sons, and daughters never drink wine. ⁹We never build

---

temple The special building in Jerusalem for Jewish worship.
These men ... two pieces This is part of a ceremony people used when they made an important agreement. An animal was cut into two pieces and the people that were making the agreement would walk between the pieces. Then they would say something like, "I hope this same thing happens to me if I don't keep the agreement." See Gen.15
left Jerusalem An army from Egypt came to help the people of Jerusalem in the summer of 588B.C. So the Babylonian army left Jerusalem for a short time to fight them. See Jer. 37:5. See also the footnote to Jer. 34:11.

Recabite family A group of people descended from Jonadab son of Recab. The family was very loyal to the Lord. See 2 Kings 10:15-28 for the story of Jonadab.
Jaazaniah He was the head of the Recabite family at that time.
Jeremiah Not the prophet Jeremiah, but a different man of the same name.
man of God This is usually an honorable title for a prophet. We know nothing else about Hanan.
ancestor Literally, "father," meaning a person that people are descended from.
descendants A person's children and their future families.

houses to live in. And we never own vineyards or fields. And we never plant crops. ¹⁰We have lived in tents and have obeyed everything our ancestor Jonadab commanded us. ¹¹But when Nebuchadnezzar king of Babylon attacked the country of Judah, we did go into Jerusalem. We said to each other, 'Come, we must enter the city of Jerusalem, so that we can escape the Babylonian army and the Aramean army.' So we have stayed in Jerusalem."

¹²Then the message from the Lord came to Jeremiah: ¹³The Lord All-Powerful, the God of Israel, says: "Jeremiah, go and tell this message to the men of Judah and to the people of Jerusalem: You people should learn a lesson and obey my message." This message is from the Lord. ¹⁴"Jonadab son of Recab ordered his sons not to drink wine, and that command has been obeyed. Until today, the descendants of Jonadab obeyed their ancestor's command. They don't drink wine. But I am the Lord. And I have given you people of Judah messages again and again, but you didn't obey me. ¹⁵I sent my servants the prophets to you people of Israel and Judah. I sent them to you again and again. Those prophets said to you, 'Each of you people of Israel and Judah must stop doing evil things. You must be good. Don't follow other gods. Don't worship or serve them. If you obey me, then you will live in the land I have given to you and your ancestors.' But you people have not paid attention to my message. ¹⁶The descendants of Jonadab obeyed the commands that their ancestor gave them. But the people of Judah have not obeyed me."

¹⁷So the Lord God All-Powerful, the God of Israel, says: "I said many bad things would happen to Judah and Jerusalem. I will soon make all those bad things happen. I spoke to those people, but they refused to listen. I called out to them, but they didn't answer me."

¹⁸Then Jeremiah said to the family of the Recabite people, "The Lord All-Powerful, the God of Israel, says, 'You people have obeyed the commands of your ancestor* Jonadab. You have followed all of Jonadab's teachings. You have done everything he commanded. ¹⁹So the Lord All-Powerful, the God of Israel, says: There will always be a descendant of Jonadab son of Recab to serve me.'"

---

ancestor Literally, "father," meaning a person that people are descended from.

King Jehoiakim Burns Jeremiah's Scroll

36 The message from the Lord came to Jeremiah. This was during the fourth year that Jehoiakim son of Josiah was king of Judah. This was the message from the Lord: ²"Jeremiah, get a scroll* and write on it all the messages I have spoken to you. I have spoken to you about the nations of Israel and Judah and all the nations. Write all the words that I have spoken to you from the time that Josiah was king, until now. ³Maybe the family of Judah will hear what I am planning to do to them. And maybe they will stop doing bad things. If they will do that, I will forgive them for the bad sins they have done."

⁴So Jeremiah called a man named Baruch. Baruch was the son of Neriah. Jeremiah spoke the messages the Lord had given him. While Jeremiah spoke, Baruch wrote those messages on the scroll.* ⁵Then Jeremiah said to Baruch, "I can't go to the Lord's temple. I am not allowed to go there. ⁶So I want you to go to the temple of the Lord. Go there on a day of fasting* and read to the people from the scroll. Read to the people the messages from the Lord that you wrote on the scroll as I spoke them to you. Read those messages to all the people of Judah that come into Jerusalem from the towns where they live. ⁷Perhaps those people will ask the Lord to help them. Perhaps each person will stop doing bad things. The Lord has announced that he is very angry with those people." ⁸So Baruch son of Neriah did everything Jeremiah the prophet told him to do. Baruch read aloud the scroll that had the Lord's messages written on it. He read it in the Lord's temple.

⁹In the ninth month of the fifth year that Jehoiakim was king, a fast* was announced. All the people that lived in the city of Jerusalem, and everyone that had come into Jerusalem from the towns of Judah were supposed to fast before the Lord. ¹⁰At that time, Baruch read the scroll* that contained Jeremiah's words. He read the scroll in the temple of the Lord. Baruch read the scroll to all the people that were in the Lord's temple. Baruch was in the room of Gemariah in the upper courtyard when he read from the scroll. That room was located at the entrance of the New Gate of the

---

Scroll(s) A long roll of leather or papyrus (*paper*) used for writing books, letters, and legal documents.

fast(ing) To live without food for a special time of prayer and worship to God.

fast Going without food for a special time of prayer and worship.

temple. Gemariah was the son of Shaphan. Gemariah was a scribe* in the temple.

¹¹A man named Micaiah heard all the messages from the Lord that Baruch read from the scroll.* Micaiah was the son of Gemariah, the son of Shaphan. ¹²When Micaiah heard the messages from the scroll, he went down to the secretary's room in the king's palace. All of the royal officials were sitting there in the king's palace. These are the names of those officials: Elishama the secretary, Delaiah son of Shemaiah, Elnathan son of Acbor, Gemariah son of Shaphan, Zedekiah son of Hananiah; and all the other royal officials were there too. ¹³Micaiah told those officials everything he had heard Baruch read from the scroll.

¹⁴Then all those officials sent a man named Jehudi to Baruch. Jehudi was the son of Nethaniah, son of Shelemiah. Shelemiah was the son of Cushi. Jehudi said to Baruch, "Bring the scroll* that you read from and come with me." Baruch son of Neriah took the scroll and went with Jehudi to the officials.

¹⁵Then those officials said to Baruch, "Sit down and read the scroll to us."

So Baruch read the scroll to them.

¹⁶Those royal officials heard all the messages from the scroll. Then they became afraid, and they looked at one another. They said to Baruch, "We must tell King Jehoiakim about these messages on the scroll." ¹⁷Then the officials asked Baruch a question. They said, "Tell us, Baruch, where did you get these messages that you wrote on the scroll? Did you write down the things Jeremiah spoke to you?"

¹⁸"Yes," Baruch answered. "Jeremiah spoke, and I wrote down all the messages with ink on this scroll."

¹⁹Then the royal officials said to Baruch, "You and Jeremiah must go and hide. Don't tell anyone where you are hiding."

²⁰Then the royal officials put the scroll in the room of Elishama the scribe. They went to King Jehoiakim and told him all about the scroll.

²¹So King Jehoiakim sent Jehudi to get the scroll. Jehudi brought the scroll from the room of Elishama the scribe. Then Jehudi read the scroll to the king and all of the servants that stood around the king. ²²The time this happened was in the ninth month,* so King Jehoiakim was sitting in the winter apartment. There was a fire burning in a small fireplace in front of the king. ²³Jehudi began to read from the scroll. But whenever he would read two or three columns, King Jehoiakim would grab the scroll. Then he would cut those columns off of the scroll with a small knife and throw them into the fireplace. Finally, the whole scroll was burned in the fire. ²⁴And, when King Jehoiakim and his servants heard the message from the scroll, they were not afraid. They didn't tear their clothes to show sorrow for doing wrong.

²⁵Elnathan, Delaiah, and Gemariah tried to talk King Jehoiakim into not burning the scroll.* But the king would not listen to them. ²⁶And King Jehoiakim commanded some men to arrest Baruch the scribe* and Jeremiah the prophet. Those men were Jerahmeel, a son of the king, Seraiah son of Azriel, and Shelemiah son of Abdeel. But those men could not find Baruch and Jeremiah, because the Lord had hidden them.

²⁷The message from the Lord came to Jeremiah. This happened after King Jehoiakim burned the scroll* that had contained all the messages from the Lord. Jeremiah had spoken to Baruch, and Baruch had written the messages on the scroll. This was the message from the Lord that came to Jeremiah:

²⁸"Jeremiah, get another scroll.* Write all the messages on it that were on the first scroll. That is the scroll that Jehoiakim king of Judah burned. ²⁹Jeremiah, also say this to Jehoiakim king of Judah, 'This is what the Lord says: Jehoiakim, you burned that scroll. You said, "Why did Jeremiah write that the king of Babylon will surely come and destroy this land? Why did he say that the king of Babylon will destroy both men and animals in this land?" ³⁰So, this is what the Lord says about Jehoiakim king of Judah: Jehoiakim's descendants* will not sit on David's throne. When Jehoiakim dies, he will not get a king's funeral, but his body will be thrown out on the ground. His body will be left out in the heat of the day and the cold frost of the night. ³¹I, the Lord, will punish Jehoiakim and his children. And I will punish his officials. I will do this because they are wicked. I have promised to bring terrible disasters on them and on all the people that live in

---

scribe A man that wrote down and copied books and letters. He often become an expert at the meaning of those writings (*scriptures*).

Scroll(s) A long roll of leather or papyrus (*paper*) used for writing books, letters, and legal documents.

ninth month This was in November or December.
descendants A person's children and their future families.

Jerusalem and on the people from Judah. I will bring all the bad things on them, just as I promised, because they have not listened to me.'"

³²Then Jeremiah took another scroll* and gave it to Baruch son of Neriah, the scribe.* As Jeremiah spoke, Baruch wrote on the scroll the same messages that were on the scroll that King Jehoiakim had burned in the fire. And many other words like those messages were added to the second scroll.

Jeremiah Is Put in Prison

37 Nebuchadnezzar was the king of Babylon. Nebuchadnezzar appointed Zedekiah as king of Judah in the place of Jehoiachin son of Jehoiakim. Zedekiah was a son of King Josiah. ²But Zedekiah did not pay attention to the messages the Lord had given to Jeremiah the prophet to preach. And Zedekiah's servants and the people of Judah did not pay attention to the Lord's messages.

³King Zedekiah sent a man named Jehucal and the priest Zephaniah to Jeremiah the prophet with a message. Jehucal was the son of Shelemiah. The priest Zephaniah was the son of Maaseiah. This was the message they brought to Jeremiah: "Jeremiah, pray to the Lord our God for us."

⁴(At that time, Jeremiah had not yet been put into prison, so he was free to go anywhere he wanted. ⁵Also at that time, Pharaoh's army had marched from Egypt toward Judah. The Babylonian army had surrounded the city of Jerusalem, in order to defeat it. Then they had heard about the army from Egypt marching toward them. So the army from Babylon had left Jerusalem to fight with the army from Egypt.)

⁶The message from the Lord came to Jeremiah the prophet: ⁷"This is what the Lord, the God of the people of Israel, says: 'Jehucal and Zephaniah, I know that Zedekiah king of Judah, sent you to me to ask questions. Tell this to King Zedekiah: Pharaoh's army marched out of Egypt to come here to help you against the army of Babylon. But Pharaoh's army will go back to Egypt. ⁸After that, the army from Babylon will come back here. They will attack Jerusalem. Then that army from Babylon will capture and burn Jerusalem.' ⁹This is what the Lord says: 'People of Jerusalem, don't fool yourselves. Don't say to yourselves, "The army of Babylon will surely leave us alone." They will not. ¹⁰People of Jerusalem, even if you could defeat all of the Babylonian army that is attacking you, there would still be a few wounded men left in their tents. Even those few wounded men would come out of their tents and burn Jerusalem down.'"

¹¹When the Babylonian army left Jerusalem to fight the army of the Pharaoh of Egypt, ¹²Jeremiah wanted to travel from Jerusalem to the land of Benjamin.* He was going there to attend a division of some property that belonged to his family. ¹³But when Jeremiah got to the Benjamin Gate of Jerusalem,* the captain in charge of the guards arrested him. The captain's name was Irijah. Irijah was the son of Shelemiah. Shelemiah was the son of Hananiah. So Irijah the captain arrested Jeremiah and said, "Jeremiah, you are leaving us to join the Babylonian side."

¹⁴Jeremiah said to Irijah, "That is not true. I am not leaving to join the Babylonians." But Irijah refused to listen to Jeremiah. And Irijah arrested Jeremiah and took him to the royal officials of Jerusalem. ¹⁵Those officials were very angry with Jeremiah. They gave an order for Jeremiah to be beaten. Then they put Jeremiah in a prison. The prison was in the house of a man named Jonathan. Jonathan was a scribe* for the king of Judah. Jonathan's house had been made into a prison. ¹⁶Those people put Jeremiah into a cell under the house of Jonathan. That cell was in a dungeon* under the ground. Jeremiah was there for a long time.

¹⁷Then King Zedekiah sent for Jeremiah and had him brought to the king's house. Zedekiah talked to Jeremiah in private. He asked Jeremiah, "Is there any message from the Lord?"

Jeremiah answered, "Yes, there is a message from the Lord. Zedekiah, you will be given to the king of Babylon." ¹⁸Then Jeremiah said to King Zedekiah, "What have I done wrong? What crime have I done against you or your officials or the people of Jerusalem? Why have you thrown me into prison? ¹⁹King Zedekiah, where are your prophets now? Those prophets preached a false

---

Scroll(s) A long roll of leather or papyrus *(paper)* used for writing books, letters, and legal documents.

scribe A man that wrote down and copied books and letters. He often become an expert at the meaning of those writings *(scriptures).*

the land of Benjamin Jeremiah was going to his home town, Anathoth, which was in the land of Benjamin.

Benjamin Gate of Jerusalem This gate led out of Jerusalem to the road which went north to the land of Benjamin.

dungeon A deep pit in the ground, like a cave, used as a prison.

message to you. They said, 'The king of Babylon will not attack you or this land of Judah.' ²⁰But now, my lord, king of Judah, please listen to me. Please let me bring my request to you. This is what I ask: Don't send me back to the house of Jonathan the scribe. If you send me back, I will die there."

²¹So King Zedekiah gave orders for Jeremiah to be put under guard in the courtyard. And he ordered that Jeremiah should be given bread from the street bakers. Jeremiah was given bread until there was no more bread in the city. So Jeremiah stayed under guard in the courtyard.

Jeremiah Is Thrown into a Cistern

38 Some of the royal officials heard what Jeremiah was preaching. They were: Shephatiah son of Mattan, Gedaliah son of Pashhur, Jehucal son of Shelemiah, and Pashhur son of Malkijah. Jeremiah was telling all the people this message: ²"This is what the Lord says: 'Everyone that stays in Jerusalem will die by a sword, or hunger, or terrible sickness. But everyone that surrenders to the army of Babylon will live. Those people will escape with their lives.' ³And this is what the Lord says: 'This city of Jerusalem will surely be given to the army of the king of Babylon. He will capture this city.'"

⁴Then those royal officials that heard the things Jeremiah was telling the people went to King Zedekiah. They said to the king, "Jeremiah must be put to death. He is making the soldiers that are still in the city become discouraged. Jeremiah is discouraging everyone by the things he is saying. Jeremiah does not want good to happen to us. He wants to ruin the people of Jerusalem."

⁵So King Zedekiah said to those officials, "Jeremiah is in your control. I can't do anything to stop you."

⁶So those officials took Jeremiah and put him into Malkijah's cistern.* (Malkijah was the king's son.) That cistern was in the temple yard where the king's guard stayed. Those officials used ropes to lower Jeremiah into the cistern. The cistern didn't have any water in it, but only mud. And Jeremiah sank down into the mud.

⁷But a man named Ebed Melech heard that those officials had put Jeremiah into the cistern.* Ebed Melech was a man from Ethiopia, and he was a eunuch* in the king's house. King Zedekiah was sitting at the Benjamin Gate. So Ebed Melech left the king's house and went to talk to the king at that gate. ⁸⁻⁹Ebed Melech said, "My lord and king, those officials have acted in a wicked way. They have treated Jeremiah the prophet wickedly. They have thrown him into a cistern. They have left him there to die."*

¹⁰Then King Zedekiah gave a command to Ebed Melech, the Ethiopian. This was the command: "Ebed Melech, take three* men from the king's house with you. Go and lift Jeremiah out of the cistern before he dies."

¹¹So Ebed Melech took the men with him. But first he went to a room under the storeroom in the king's house. He took some old rags and worn-out clothes from that room. Then he let those rags down with some ropes to Jeremiah in the cistern. ¹²Ebed Melech, the Ethiopian, said to Jeremiah, "Put these old rags and worn-out clothes under your arms. When we pull you out, these rags will pad your underarms. Then the ropes will not hurt you." So Jeremiah did as Ebed Melech said. ¹³Those men pulled Jeremiah up with the ropes and lifted him out of the cistern. And Jeremiah stayed under guard in the temple yard.

Zedekiah Asks Jeremiah Some Questions Again

¹⁴Then King Zedekiah sent someone to get Jeremiah the prophet. He had Jeremiah brought to the third entrance to the temple of the Lord. Then the king said, "Jeremiah, I am going to ask you something. Don't hide anything from me, but tell me everything honestly."

¹⁵Jeremiah said to Zedekiah, "If I give you an answer, you will probably kill me. And even if I did give you advice, you would not listen to me."

¹⁶But King Zedekiah secretly swore an oath to Jeremiah. Zedekiah said, "The Lord gives us breath and life. As surely as the Lord lives I will not kill you, Jeremiah. And I promise not to give you to those officials that want to kill you."

¹⁷Then Jeremiah said to King Zedekiah, "The Lord God All-Powerful is the God of Israel. The Lord says, 'If you surrender to the officials of the king of Babylon, your life will be saved and Jerusalem will not be burned down. And you and

---

cistern A deep hole in the ground used to store water.

They have left him there to die Literally, "He will starve to death because there is no more bread in the city."

three Some Hebrew copies have, "30."

your family will live. ¹⁸But if you refuse to surrender then Jerusalem will be given to the Babylonian army. They will burn Jerusalem down, and you will not escape from them.'"

¹⁹But King Zedekiah said to Jeremiah, "But I am afraid of the men of Judah that have already gone over to the side of the Babylonian army. I am afraid that the soldiers will give me to those men of Judah and they will treat me badly and hurt me."

²⁰But Jeremiah answered, "The soldiers will not give you to those men of Judah. King Zedekiah, obey the Lord by doing what I tell you. Then things will go well for you, and your life will be saved. ²¹But if you refuse to surrender to the army of Babylon, the Lord has shown me what will happen. This is what the Lord has told me: ²²All the women that are left in the house of the king of Judah will be brought out. They will be brought to the important officials of the king of Babylon. Your women will make fun of you with a song. This is what the women will say:

'Your good friends led you the wrong way and
were stronger than you.
Those were friends that you trusted.
Your feet are stuck in the mud.
Your friends have left you.'

²³All your wives and children will be brought out. They will be given to the Babylonian army. You yourself will not escape from the army of Babylon. You will be captured by the king of Babylon, and Jerusalem will be burned down."

²⁴Then Zedekiah said to Jeremiah, "Don't tell any person that I have been talking to you. If you do, you might die. ²⁵Those officials might find out that I talked to you. Then they will come to you and say, 'Jeremiah, tell us what you said to King Zedekiah. And tell us what King Zedekiah said to you. Be honest with us and tell us everything, or we will kill you.' ²⁶If they say this to you, then tell them, 'I was begging the king not to send me back to the cell in the dungeon* under Jonathan's house. If I were to go back there, I would die.'"

²⁷It happened that those royal officials of the king did come to Jeremiah to question him. So Jeremiah told them everything the king had ordered him to say. Then those officials left Jeremiah alone. No person had heard what Jeremiah and the king had talked about.

²⁸So Jeremiah stayed under guard in the temple yard until the day Jerusalem was captured.

The Fall of Jerusalem

39 This is how Jerusalem was captured: During the tenth month of the ninth year that Zedekiah was king of Judah, Nebuchadnezzar king of Babylon marched against Jerusalem with his whole army. He surrounded the city to defeat it. ²And on the ninth day of the fourth month in Zedekiah's eleventh year, the wall of Jerusalem was broken through. ³Then all the royal officials of the king of Babylon came into the city of Jerusalem. They came in and sat down at the Middle Gate. These are the names of those officials: Nergal-Sharezer, the governor of the district of Samgar, a very high official; Nebo Sarsekim, another very high official; and various other important officials were there also.

⁴Zedekiah king of Judah saw those officials from Babylon, so he and the soldiers with him ran away. They left Jerusalem at night. They went out through the king's garden and out through the gate that was between the two walls. Then they went toward the desert. ⁵The Babylonian army chased Zedekiah and the soldiers with him. Those soldiers caught up with Zedekiah in the plains of Jericho. They captured Zedekiah and took him to Nebuchadnezzar, the king of Babylon. Nebuchadnezzar was at the town of Riblah, in the land of Hamath. At that place, Nebuchadnezzar decided what to do to Zedekiah. ⁶There at the town of Riblah, the king of Babylon killed Zedekiah's sons, while Zedekiah watched. And Nebuchadnezzar killed all the royal officials of Judah while Zedekiah watched. ⁷Then Nebuchadnezzar tore out Zedekiah's eyes. He put bronze chains on Zedekiah and took him to Babylon.

⁸The army of Babylon set fire to the king's house and the houses of the people of Jerusalem. And they broke down the walls of Jerusalem. ⁹A man named Nebuzaradan was the commander of the king of Babylon's special guards. He took the people that were left in Jerusalem and made them captives. He carried them away to Babylon. Nebuzaradan also made those people of Jerusalem captives that had surrendered to him earlier. He made all the others of the people of Jerusalem captives and carried them away to Babylon. ¹⁰But Nebuzaradan, the commander of the special guards, left some of the poor people of Judah behind. Those were the people that owned

---
dungeon A deep pit in the ground, like a cave, used as a prison.

nothing. So on that day, Nebuzaradan gave those poor people of Judah vineyards and fields.

¹¹But Nebuchadnezzar gave some orders to Nebuzaradan about Jeremiah. Nebuzaradan was the commander of Nebuchadnezzar's special guards. These were the orders: ¹²"Find Jeremiah and take care of him. Don't hurt him. Give him whatever he asks for."

¹³So Nebuzaradan, the commander of the king's special guards, Nebushazban, a chief officer in the army of Babylon, Nergal-Sharezer, a high official, and all the other officers of the army of Babylon sent for Jeremiah. ¹⁴Those men had Jeremiah taken out of the temple yard where he had been under the guard of the king of Judah. Those officers of the army of Babylon turned Jeremiah over to Gedaliah.* Gedaliah was the son of Ahikam. Ahikam was the son of Shaphan. Gedaliah had orders to take Jeremiah back home. So Jeremiah was taken home, and he stayed among his own people.

A Message from the Lord to Ebed-Melech

¹⁵While the guards were watching Jeremiah in the temple yard, a message from the Lord came to him. This was the message: ¹⁶"Jeremiah, go and tell Ebed-Melech,* the man from Ethiopia, this message: 'This is what the Lord Almighty, the God of the people of Israel, says: Very soon I will make my messages about this city of Jerusalem come true. My messages will come true through disaster and not good things. You will see everything come true with your own eyes. ¹⁷But I will save you on that day, Ebed-Melech.' This is the message of the Lord. 'You won't be given to the people you are afraid of. ¹⁸I will save you, Ebed-Melech. You won't die from a sword, but you will escape and live. That will happen because you have trusted in me.'" This message is from the Lord.

Jeremiah Is Set Free

40 The message from the Lord came to Jeremiah after he was set free at the city of Ramah. Nebuzaradan, the commander of the king of Babylon's special guards, found Jeremiah in Ramah. Jeremiah was bound with chains. He was with all the captives from Jerusalem and Judah. Those captives were being taken away in captivity to Babylon. ²When commander Nebuzaradan found Jeremiah, he spoke to him. He said, "Jeremiah, the Lord, your God, announced that this disaster would come to this place. ³And now the Lord has done everything just as he said he would do. This disaster happened because you people of Judah sinned against the Lord. You people didn't obey the Lord. ⁴But now, Jeremiah, I will set you free. I am taking the chains off your wrists. If you want to, come with me to Babylon, and I will take good care of you. But if you don't want to come with me, then don't come. Look, the whole country is open to you. Go anywhere you want. ⁵Or go back to Gedaliah* son of Ahikam, the son of Shaphan. The king of Babylon has chosen Gedaliah to be governor over the towns of Judah. Go and live with Gedaliah among the people. Or you can go anywhere you want."

Then Nebuzaradan gave Jeremiah some food and a present and let him go. ⁶So Jeremiah went to Gedaliah son of Ahikam at Mizpah. Jeremiah stayed with Gedaliah among the people that were left behind in the land of Judah.

The Short Rule of Gedaliah

⁷There were some soldiers from the army of Judah, officers and their men, still out in the open country when Jerusalem was destroyed. Those soldiers heard that the king of Babylon had put Gedaliah son of Ahikam in charge of the people that were left in the land. The people that were left were men, women, and children that were very poor and were not carried off to Babylon as captives. ⁸So those soldiers came to Gedaliah at Mizpah. Those soldiers were: Ishmael son of Nethaniah, Johanan, and his brother Jonathan, sons of Kareah, Seraiah son of Tanhumeth, sons of Ephai from Netophah, and Jaazaniah son of the Maacathite, and the men that were with them.

⁹Gedaliah son of Ahikam, son of Shaphan, made an oath to make those soldiers and their men feel more secure. This is what Gedaliah said: "You soldiers, don't be afraid to serve the Babylonian people. Settle down in the land and serve the king of Babylon. If you do this, things will go well for you. ¹⁰I, myself, will live in Mizpah. I will speak for you before the Chaldean people that come here. You people leave that work to me. You should harvest the wine, the summer fruit, and the oil. Put what you harvest in

---

Gedaliah Gedaliah was the man that Nebuchadnezzar appointed as his governor for the land of Judah.
Ebed-Melech See Jeremiah 38:7-13.

Or ... Gedaliah Or, "Go to Gedaliah before he goes back..."

your storage jars. Live in the towns that you have taken control of."

¹¹All the people of Judah that were in the countries of Moab, Ammon, Edom, and all the other countries heard that the king of Babylon had left some people of Judah in the land. And they heard that the king of Babylon had chosen Gedaliah son of Ahikam, son of Shaphan, to be governor over them. ¹²When those people of Judah heard that news, they came back to the land of Judah. They came back to Gedaliah at Mizpah from all the countries where they had been scattered. So they came back and gathered a large harvest of wine and summer fruit.

¹³Johanan son of Kareah and all the officers of the army of Judah that were still in the open country came to Gedaliah. Gedaliah was at the town of Mizpah. ¹⁴Johanan and those officers with him said to Gedaliah, "Do you know that Baalis, the king of the Ammonite people, wants to kill you? He has sent Ishmael son of Nethaniah to kill you." But Gedaliah son of Ahikam didn't believe them.

¹⁵Then Johanan son of Kareah spoke to Gedaliah in private at Mizpah. Johanan said to Gedaliah, "Let me go and kill Ishmael son of Nethaniah. No person will know anything about it. We should not let Ishmael kill you. That would cause all the people of Judah that are gathered around you to be scattered to different countries again. And that would mean that the few survivors of Judah would be lost."

¹⁶But Gedaliah son of Ahikam said to Johanan son of Kareah, "Don't kill Ishmael. The things you are saying about Ishmael are not true."

41 In the seventh month, Ishmael son of Nethaniah (the son of Elishama) came to Gedaliah son of Ahikam. Ishmael came with ten of his men. Those men came to the town of Mizpah. Ishmael was a member of the king's family. He had been one of the officers of the king of Judah. Ishmael and his men ate a meal with Gedaliah. ²While they were eating together, Ishmael and his ten men got up and killed Gedaliah son of Ahikam with a sword. Gedaliah was the man that the king of Babylon had chosen to be governor of Judah. ³Ishmael also killed all the men of Judah that were with Gedaliah at the town of Mizpah. Ishmael also killed the Babylonian soldiers that were there with Gedaliah.

⁴⁻⁵The day after Gedaliah was murdered, 80 men came to Mizpah. They were bringing grain offerings and incense* to the Lord's temple.* Those 80 men had shaved off their beards, torn their clothes, and cut themselves.* They came from Shechem, Shiloh, and Samaria. None of these men knew that Gedaliah had been murdered. ⁶Ishmael left Mizpah and went to meet those 80 men. He cried* while he walked out to meet them. Ishmael met those 80 men and said, "Come with me to meet with Gedaliah son of Ahikam." ⁷⁻⁸As soon as they were in the city, Ishmael and the men with him began to kill the 80 men and throw them into a deep cistern!* But ten of the men said to Ishmael, "Don't kill us! We have hidden some things in a field. We have wheat and barley, and oil and honey. ₍We will give those things to you!₎" So Ishmael stopped and didn't kill them with the others. ⁹(Ishmael threw the dead bodies into the cistern until it was full—and that cistern was very big! It had been built by a king of Judah named Asa. King Asa had made the cistern so that during war there would be water in the city.* Asa did this to protect his city from Baasha, the king of Israel.)

¹⁰Ishmael captured all the other people in the town of Mizpah and started to cross over to the country of the Ammonite people. (Those people included the king's daughters, and all the other people that were left there. Nebuzaradan, the commander of the king of Babylon's special guards, had chosen Gedaliah to watch over those people.)

¹¹Johanan son of Kareah and all the army officers that were with him, heard about all the evil things Ishmael had done. ¹²So Johanan and the army officers with him took their men and went to fight Ishmael son of Nethaniah. They caught Ishmael near the big pool of water that is at the town of Gibeon. ¹³The captives* that Ishmael had taken captive saw Johanan and the army officers. Those people became very happy. ¹⁴Then

---

incense Special dried tree sap. Burned to make a sweet-smelling smoke, it was offered as a gift to God.

temple The special building in Jerusalem for Jewish worship.

shaved ... cut themselves The men did this to show that they were sad about the destruction of the Lord's temple in Jerusalem.

He cried Ishmael was acting like he was sad about the destruction of the temple.

cistern A deep hole in the ground used to store water.

King Asa ... city King Asa lived about 300 years before the time of Gedaliah. See 1 Kings 15:22 for the story about Asa building defenses for Mizpah.

captives People that were taken away like prisoners.

all those people that Ishmael had taken captive at the town of Mizpah ran to Johanan son of Kareah. [15]But Ishmael and eight of his men escaped from Johanan. They ran away to the Ammonite people.

[16]So Johanan son of Kareah and all his army officers rescued the captives.* Ishmael had murdered Gedaliah and then he had taken those people from Mizpah. Among the survivors* were soldiers, women, children, and court officials. Johanan brought them back from the town of Gibeon.

The Escape to Egypt

[17-18]Johanan and the other army officers were afraid of the Chaldeans.* The king of Babylon had chosen Gedaliah to be governor of Judah. But Ishmael murdered Gedaliah, and Johanan was afraid that the Chaldeans would be angry. So they decided to run away to Egypt. On the way to Egypt, they stayed at Geruth Kimham. Geruth Kimham is near the town of Bethlehem.

42 While they were at Geruth Kimham, Johanan and a man named Jezaniah son of Hoshaiah went to Jeremiah the prophet. All the army officers went with Johanan and Jezaniah. All the people, from the least important to the most important person, went to Jeremiah. [2]All those people said to him, "Jeremiah, please listen to what we ask. Pray to the Lord your God for all these people that are survivors* from the family of Judah. Jeremiah, you can see that there are not many of us left. At one time there were many of us. [3]Jeremiah, pray that the Lord your God will tell us where we should go and what we should do."

[4]Then Jeremiah the prophet answered, "I understand the things you want me to do. I will pray to the Lord your God, like you asked me to do. I will tell you everything the Lord says. I will not hide anything from you."

[5]Then those people said to Jeremiah, "If we don't do everything the Lord your God tells us, then we hope the Lord will be a true and faithful witness against us. We know the Lord your God will send you to tell us what to do. [6]It does not matter if we like the message or if we don't like the message. We will obey the Lord our God. We are sending you to the Lord for a message from him. We will obey what he says. Then good things will happen to us. Yes, we will obey the Lord our God."

[7]At the end of ten days, the message from the Lord came to Jeremiah. [8]Then Jeremiah called together Johanan son of Kareah and the army officers that were with him. Jeremiah also called all the other people together, from the least important to the most important person. [9]Then Jeremiah said to them, "This is what the Lord, the God of the people of Israel, says. You sent me to him. I asked the Lord what you wanted me to ask. This is what the Lord says: [10]'If you people will stay in Judah, I will make you strong—I will not destroy you. I will plant you, and I will not pull you up. I will do this because I am sad about the terrible things that I made happen to you. [11]Now you are afraid of the king of Babylon. But don't be afraid of him. Don't be afraid of the king of Babylon,' this is the message of the Lord, 'because I am with you. I will save you. I will rescue you. He will not get his hands on you. [12]I will be kind to you. And the king of Babylon will also treat you with mercy. And he will bring you back to your land.' [13]But you might say, 'We will not stay in Judah.' If you say that, you will disobey the Lord your God. [14]And you might say, 'No, we will go and live in Egypt. We will not be bothered with war in that place. We will not hear the trumpets of war. And in Egypt we will not be hungry.' [15]If you say those things, then listen to the message of the Lord, you survivors* from Judah. This is what the Lord All-Powerful, the God of the people of Israel, says: 'If you decide to go to live in Egypt, then these things will happen: [16]You are afraid of the sword of war, but it will defeat you there. And you are worried about hunger, but you will be hungry in Egypt. You will die there. [17]Every person that decides to go live in Egypt will die by a sword, or hunger, or terrible sickness. Not one person that goes to Egypt will survive. Not one of them will escape the terrible things that I will bring to them.'

[18]"The Lord All-Powerful, the God of the people of Israel, says: 'I showed my anger against Jerusalem. I punished the people that lived in Jerusalem. In the same way, I will show my anger against every person that goes to Egypt. People will use you as an example when they ask for bad things to happen to other people. You will become like a curse word. People will be ashamed of you.

---

captives People that were taken away like prisoners.
survivor(s) People that escaped some disaster.
Chaldeans The Chaldeans were a powerful family group in Babylon at this time. King Nebuchadnezzar was from this family group.

survivor(s) People that escaped some disaster.

People will insult you. And you will never see Judah again.'

¹⁹"Survivors* of Judah, the Lord told you: 'Don't go to Egypt.' I warn you right now, ²⁰you people are making a mistake that will cause your deaths. You people sent me to the Lord your God. You said to me, 'Pray to the Lord our God for us. Tell us everything the Lord says to do. We will obey the Lord.' ²¹So today, I have told you the message from the Lord. But you have not obeyed the Lord your God. You have not done all that he sent me to tell you to do. ²²So now, be sure you understand this: You people want to go live in Egypt. But these things will happen to you in Egypt: You will die by a sword, or hunger, or terrible sickness."

43 So Jeremiah finished telling the people the message from the Lord their God. Jeremiah told them everything that the Lord had sent him to tell the people.

²Azariah son of Hoshaiah, Johanan son of Kareah, and some other men were proud and stubborn. Those people became angry at Jeremiah. Those men said to Jeremiah, "Jeremiah, you are lying! The Lord our God didn't send you to say to us, 'You people must not go to Egypt to live there.' ³Jeremiah, we think that Baruch son of Neriah is encouraging you to be against us. He wants you to give us to the Babylonian people. He wants you to do this so they can kill us. Or he wants you to do this so that they can make us captives* and carry us to Babylon."

⁴So Johanan, the army officers, and all the people disobeyed the Lord's command. The Lord had commanded them to stay in Judah. ⁵But instead of obeying the Lord, Johanan and the army officers took those survivors* from Judah to Egypt. In the past, the enemy had taken those survivors to other countries. But they had come back to Judah. ⁶Now, Johanan and all the army officers took all the men, women, and children and led them to Egypt. Among those people were the king's daughters. (Nebuzaradan had put Gedaliah in charge of those people. Nebuzaradan was the commander of the king of Babylon's special guards.) Johanan also took Jeremiah the prophet and Baruch son of Neriah. ⁷Those people didn't listen to the Lord. So all those people went to Egypt. They went to the town of Tahpanhes.*

⁸In the town of Tahpanhes, Jeremiah received this message from the Lord: ⁹"Jeremiah, get some large stones. Take them and bury them in the clay and brick sidewalk in front of Pharaoh's official building in Tahpanhes. Do this while the men of Judah are watching you. ¹⁰Then say to those men of Judah that are watching you: 'This is what the Lord All-Powerful, the God of Israel, says: I will send for Nebuchadnezzar, the king of Babylon, to come here. He is my servant. And I will set his throne over these stones I have buried here. Nebuchadnezzar will spread his canopy* above these stones. ¹¹Nebuchadnezzar will come here and attack Egypt. He will bring death to those that are to die. He will bring captivity to those that are to be taken captive. And he will bring the sword to those that are to be killed with a sword. ¹²Nebuchadnezzar will start a fire in the temples of the false gods of Egypt. He will burn those temples and he will take those idols away. A shepherd picks the bugs and stickers off of his clothes to make them clean. In the same way, Nebuchadnezzar will pick Egypt clean. Then he will safely leave Egypt. ¹³Nebuchadnezzar will destroy the memorial stones* that are in the temple of the Sun God* in Egypt. And he will burn down the temples of the false gods of Egypt.'"

The Lord's Messages to the People of Judah in Egypt

44 Jeremiah received a message from the Lord. This message was for all the people of Judah living in Egypt. The message was for the people of Judah living in the towns of Migdol, Tahpanhes, Memphis, and southern Egypt. This was the message: ²The Lord All-Powerful, the God of Israel, says, "You people saw the terrible happenings that I brought on the city of Jerusalem and on all the towns of Judah. Those towns are empty piles of stones today. ³Those places were destroyed because the people living in them did evil things. Those people gave sacrifices to other

---

captives People that were taken away like prisoners.
survivor(s) People that escaped some disaster.
Tahpanhes A town in northeastern Egypt.

canopy A temporary covering used for shade. It is like a tent without sides.
memorial stones Stones that were set up to help people remember something special. In ancient Israel, people often set up stones as special places to worship false gods.
Sun God This was the most important god in Egypt.
ancestors Literally, "fathers," meaning a person's parents, grandparents, and all the people they are descended from.

gods — and that made me angry! Your people and your ancestors* did not worship those gods in the past. ⁴I sent my prophets to those people again and again. Those prophets were my servants. Those prophets spoke my message and said to the people, 'Don't do this terrible thing. I hate for you to worship idols.' ⁵But those people didn't listen to the prophets. They didn't pay attention to those prophets. Those people didn't stop doing wicked things. They didn't stop making sacrifices to other gods. ⁶So, I showed my anger against those people. I punished the towns of Judah and the streets of Jerusalem. My anger made Jerusalem and the towns of Judah the empty piles of stone they are today."

⁷So, the Lord God All-Powerful, the God of Israel, says: "Why are you hurting yourselves by continuing to worship idols? You are separating the men and women, the children and babies from the family of Judah. And so you leave yourselves without any survivors* from the family of Judah. ⁸Why do you people want to make me angry by making idols? Now you are living in Egypt. And now you are making me angry by offering sacrifices to the false gods of Egypt. You people will destroy yourselves. It will be your own fault. You will make yourselves something that people of other nations will speak evil of. And all the other nations on the earth will make fun of you. ⁹Have you forgotten about the wicked things your ancestors* did? And have you forgotten about the wicked things the kings and queens of Judah did? Have you forgotten about the wicked things you and your wives did in Judah and in the streets of Jerusalem? ¹⁰Even to this day, the people of Judah have not made themselves humble. They have not shown any respect for me. And those people have not followed my teachings. They have not obeyed the laws I gave you and your ancestors.*"

¹¹So, this is what the Lord All-Powerful, the God of Israel, says: "I have decided to make terrible things happen to you. I will destroy the whole family of Judah. ¹²There were a few survivors from Judah. Those people came here to Egypt. But I will destroy those few survivors from the family of Judah. They will be killed with swords or die from hunger. They will be something that people of other nations will speak evil about. Other nations will be afraid at what happened to those people. Those people will become a curse word. Other nations will insult those people of Judah. ¹³I will punish those people that have gone to live in Egypt. I will use swords, hunger, and terrible sicknesses to punish them. I will punish those people just like I punished the city of Jerusalem. ¹⁴Not one of the few survivors of Judah that have gone to live in Egypt will escape my punishment. None of them will survive to come back to Judah. Those people want to come back to Judah and live there. But not one of those people will go back to Judah, except maybe a few people that escape."

¹⁵Many of the women of Judah that lived in Egypt were making sacrifices to other gods. Their husbands knew it, but didn't stop them. There was a large group of people of Judah meeting together. They were the people of Judah that were living in southern Egypt. The husbands of those women that were making sacrifices to other gods said to Jeremiah, ¹⁶"We will not listen to the message from the Lord that you spoke to us. ¹⁷We promised to make sacrifices to the Queen of Heaven.* And we will do everything we promised. We will offer sacrifices and pour out drink offerings in worship to her. We did that in the past. And our ancestors, our kings, and our officials did that in the past. All of us did those things in the towns of Judah and in the streets of Jerusalem. At the time we worshiped the Queen of Heaven, we had plenty of food. We were successful. Nothing bad happened to us. ¹⁸But then we stopped making sacrifices to the Queen of Heaven. And we stopped pouring out drink offerings to her. Since we have stopped doing those things in worship to her, we have had problems. Our people have been killed by swords and hunger."

¹⁹Then the women spoke up.* They said to Jeremiah, "Our husbands knew what we were doing. We had their permission to make sacrifices to the Queen of Heaven. We had their permission to pour out drink offerings to her. Our husbands also knew that we were making cakes that looked like her."

---

survivor(s) People that escaped some disaster.
ancestors Literally, "fathers," meaning a person's parents, grandparents, and all the people they are descended from.
Queen of Heaven Probably the false god Astarte. She was the goddess of sex and war. People in Mesopotamia worshiped her. They thought she was the planet Venus, which looks like a star in the sky.
Then the women spoke up This is from the ancient Greek translation. The Hebrew does not have this sentence.

20Then Jeremiah spoke to all those men and women. He spoke to the people that had just said those things. 21Jeremiah said to those people, "The Lord remembered that you made sacrifices in the towns of Judah and in the streets of Jerusalem. You and your ancestors,* your kings, your officials, and the people of the land did that. The Lord remembered what you had done, and thought about that. 22Then the Lord could not be patient with you any longer. The Lord hated the terrible things you did. So the Lord made your country an empty desert. No person lives there now. Other people say bad things about that country. 23All of those bad things happened to you because you made sacrifices to other gods. You sinned against the Lord. You didn't obey the Lord. You didn't follow his teachings or the laws he gave you. You didn't keep your part of the Agreement."*

24Then Jeremiah spoke to all those men and women. Jeremiah said, "All you people of Judah that are now in Egypt, listen to the message from the Lord: 25The Lord All-Powerful, the God of the people of Israel, says: 'You women did what you said you would do. You said, "We will keep the promises we made. We promised to make sacrifices and pour out drink offerings to the Queen of Heaven." So, go ahead. Do the things you promised you would do. Keep your promises. 26But, listen to the message from the Lord, all you people of Judah that are living in Egypt: 'I use my great name and make this promise: I promise none of the people of Judah that are now living in Egypt will ever again use my name to make promises. They will never again say, "As surely as the Lord lives, " 27I am watching over those people of Judah. But I am not watching over them to take care of them. I am watching over them to hurt them. The people of Judah that live in Egypt will die from hunger and be killed by swords. They will continue to die until they are finished. 28Some people of Judah will escape being killed by the sword. They will come back to Judah from Egypt. But there will be very few people of Judah that escape. Then those survivors* of Judah that came to live in Egypt will know whose word will come true. They will know whether my word or their word came true. 29I will give you people proof' — this is the message of the Lord — 'that I will punish you here in Egypt. Then you will know for sure that my promises to hurt you will really happen. 30This will be your proof that I will do what I say.' This is what the Lord says: 'Pharaoh Hophra is the king of Egypt. His enemies want to kill him. I will give Pharaoh Hophra to his enemies. Zedekiah was the king of Judah. Nebuchadnezzar was Zedekiah's enemy. And I gave Zedekiah to his enemy. In the same way, I will give Pharaoh Hophra to his enemy.'"

A Message to Baruch

45 Jehoiakim was the son of Josiah. In the fourth year Jehoiakim was king of Judah,* Jeremiah the prophet told these things to Baruch son of Neriah. Baruch wrote these things on a scroll.* This is what Jeremiah said to Baruch: 2"This is what the Lord, the God of Israel, says to you: 3'Baruch, you have said: It is very bad for me. The Lord has given me sorrow along with my pain. I am very tired. I am worn out because of my suffering. I can't find rest.' 4Jeremiah, say this to Baruch: 'This is what the Lord says: I will tear down what I have built. And I will pull up what I have planted. I will do that everywhere in Judah. 5Baruch, you are looking for great things for yourself. But don't look for those things. Don't look for them, because I will make terrible things happen to all the people.' The Lord said these things. 'You will have to go many places. But I will let you escape alive wherever you go.'"

Messages from the Lord About the Nations

46 These messages came to Jeremiah the prophet. These messages are about different nations.

Messages About Egypt

2This message is about the nation of Egypt. This message is about the army of Pharaoh Neco. Neco was the king of Egypt. His army was defeated at the town of Carchemish. Carchemish

---

ancestors Literally, "fathers," meaning a person's parents, grandparents, and all the people they are descended from.
Agreement This is probably the Law of Moses, the Agreement between God and the people of Israel.
survivor(s) People that escaped some disaster. Here this means the Jewish people that survived the destruction of Judah and Israel by its enemy armies.

fourth year ... was king of Judah This was 605 B.C.
Scroll(s) A long roll of leather or papyrus (paper) used for writing books, letters, and legal documents.
fourth year ... Judah This was about 605 B.C.

is on the Euphrates River. Nebuchadnezzar king of Babylon defeated the army of Pharaoh Neco at Carchemish in the fourth year that Jehoiakim was king of Judah.* Jehoiakim was the son of King Josiah. This is the Lord's message to Egypt:

3 "Get your large and small shields ready.
    March out for battle.
4 Get the horses ready.
    Soldiers, get on your horses.
        Go to your places for battle.
    Put your helmets on.
    Sharpen your spears.
        Put your armor on.
5 What do I see?
    That army is scared.
    The soldiers are running away.
    Their brave soldiers are defeated.
    They run away in a hurry.
    They don't look back.
    There is danger all around."
    The Lord said these things.

6 "Fast men can't run away.
    Strong soldiers can't escape.
    They will all stumble and fall.
    This will happen in the north,
        by the Euphrates River.
7 Who is coming like the Nile River?
    Who is coming like that strong, fast river?
8 It is Egypt that comes
        like the rising Nile River.
    It is Egypt that comes
        like that strong, fast river.
    Egypt says,
        'I will come and cover the earth.
    I will destroy the cities
        and the people in them.'
9 Horse soldiers, charge into battle.
    Chariot drivers, drive fast.
    March on, brave soldiers.
    Soldiers from Cush and Put,
        carry your shields.
    Soldiers from Lydia,
        use your bows.
10 "But at that time, our Master,
        the Lord All-Powerful, will win.
    At that time, he will give the punishment
        that they deserve.
    The Lord's enemies will get the punishment
        that they should have.

The sword will kill until it is finished.
The sword will kill until it satisfies
    its thirst for blood.
This will happen because there is a sacrifice
    for our Master, the Lord All-Powerful.
That sacrifice is ⌊Egypt's army⌋
    in the land of the north,
    by the Euphrates River.

11 "Egypt, go to Gilead and get some medicine.
    You will make up many medicines,
        but they will not help.
    You will not be healed.
12 The nations will hear you crying.
    Your cries will be heard all over the earth.
    One 'brave soldier' will run into another
        'brave soldier.'
    And both 'brave soldiers'
        will fall down together."

¹³This is the message the Lord spoke to Jeremiah the prophet. This message is about Nebuchadnezzar coming to attack Egypt.

14 "Announce this message in Egypt.
    Tell it in the city of Migdol.
    Tell it in Memphis and Tahpanhes.
        'Get ready for war.
    Why? Because people all around you
        are being killed with swords.'
15 Egypt, your strong soldiers will be killed.
    They won't be able to stand
        because the Lord will push them down.
16 Those soldiers will stumble again and again.
    They will fall over each other.
    They will say,
        'Get up, let us go back to our own people.
    Let us go back to our homeland.
    Our enemy is defeating us.
    We must get away.'
17 In their homelands, those soldiers will say,
    'Pharaoh king of Egypt is only
        a lot of noise.
    His time of glory is over.'"
18 This message is from the King.
    The King is the Lord All-Powerful.
    "I promise, as surely as I live,
        a powerful leader⌋ will come.
    He will be great like Mount Tabor
        and Mount Carmel near the sea.
19 People of Egypt, pack your things.
    Get ready for captivity.
    Why? Because Memphis will be
        a ruined, empty land.
    Those cities will be destroyed,
        and no person will live there.

---

fourth year ... Judah This was about 605 B.C.

²⁰ "Egypt is like a beautiful cow.
  But a horsefly* is coming from the north*
    to bother her.
²¹ The hired soldiers in Egypt's army
    are like fat calves.
  They will all turn and run away.
  They will not stand strong
    against the attack.
  Their time of destruction is coming.
  They will soon be punished.
²² Egypt is like a snake hissing
    and trying to escape.
  The enemy comes closer and closer,
    and the Egyptian army is trying
      to slither away *(escape)*.
  The enemy will attack Egypt with axes.
  They are like men that cut down trees."
²³ The Lord says these things.
  "They will chop down Egypt's forest *(army)*.
  There are many trees *(soldiers)*
    in that forest *(army)*
  but they will all be cut down.
  There are more enemy soldiers than locusts.*
  There are so many soldiers,
    that no person can count them.
²⁴ Egypt will be ashamed.
  The enemy from the north will defeat her.

²⁵The Lord All-Powerful, the God of Israel, says: "Very soon I will punish Amon,* the god of Thebes. And I will punish Pharaoh, Egypt, and her gods. I will punish the kings of Egypt. And I will punish the people that depend on Pharaoh. ²⁶I will let all those people be defeated by their enemies—and those enemies want to kill them. I will give those people to Nebuchadnezzar, the king of Babylon, and his servants."

Long ago, Egypt lived in peace. And after all these times of trouble, Egypt will live in peace again." The Lord said these things.

A Message for North Israel

²⁷ "Jacob,* my servant, don't be afraid.
  Don't be scared, Israel.

---

locusts Insects like grasshoppers that could destroy a large crop very quickly.
Amon For many centuries Amon was the most important god of Egypt. At the time of this prophecy he was not worshiped as much in northern Egypt. But he was still the most important god in southern Egypt, especially around the old Egyptian capital city of Thebes.
Jacob Another name for Israel. See Gen. 32:22-28.

  I will save you from those faraway places.
  I will save your children
    from the countries where they are
      captives.*
  Jacob will have peace and safety again.
  And no person will make him afraid."
²⁸ The Lord says these things.
  "Jacob, my servant, don't be afraid.
  I am with you.
  I sent you away to many different places.
  But I will not destroy you completely.
  But I will destroy all those nations.
  You must be punished
    for the bad things you did.
  So I won't let you escape your punishment.
  I will discipline you, but I will be fair."

A Message About the Philistine People

47 This is the message from the Lord that came to Jeremiah the prophet. This message is about the Philistine people. This message came before Pharaoh attacked the city of Gaza.

² The Lord says:
  "Look, ₍the enemy soldiers
    are meeting together₎ in the north.*
  They will come like a fast river
    spilling over its banks.
  They will cover the whole country
    like a flood.
  They will cover the towns
    and the people living in them.
  Everyone living in that country
    will cry for help.

³ "They will hear the sound of running horses.
  They will hear the noisy chariots.
    They will hear the rumbling wheels.
  Fathers won't be able to protect their children.
  They will be too weak to help.

⁴ "The time has come to destroy
    all the Philistine people.
  The time has come to destroy
  Tyre and Sidon's remaining helpers.
  The Lord will destroy the Philistine people
    very soon.
  He will destroy the survivors
    from the Island of Crete.*

---

captives People that were taken away like prisoners.
north This refers to the army of Babylon coming from the north to attack the nation of Judah.

⁵ The people from Gaza will be sad
and shave their heads.
The people from Ashkelon will be silenced.
Survivors from the valley,
how long will you cut yourselves?*

⁶ "Sword of the Lord, you have not quit.
How long will you keep fighting?
Go back into your scabbard!*
Stop! Be still!
⁷ But how can the sword of the Lord rest?
The Lord gave it a command.
The Lord commanded it to attack
the city of Ashkelon and the seacoast."

A Message About Moab

48 This message is about the country of Moab. This is what the Lord All-Powerful, the God of the people of Israel, says:*

"It will be bad for Mount Nebo.*
Mount Nebo will be ruined.
The town of Kiriathaim will be humbled.
It will be captured.
The strong place will be humbled.
It will be shattered.
² Moab will not be praised again.
Men in Heshbon will plan Moab's defeat.
They will say,
'Come, let us put an end to that nation.'
Madmenah, you will also be silenced.
The sword will chase you.
³ Listen to the cries from Horonaim.
They are cries of much confusion
and destruction.
⁴ Moab will be destroyed.
Her little children will cry for help.
⁵ Moab's people go up the path to Luhith.
They are crying bitterly as they go.
On the road down to the town of Horonaim,
Cries of pain and suffering can be heard.
⁶ Run away! Run for your lives!
Run away like a tumbleweed*
⌊blowing⌋ through the desert.

⁷ You trust in the things you made
and in your wealth.
So you will be captured.
The god Chemosh*
will be taken into captivity.
And his priests and officials
will be taken with him.
⁸ The Destroyer will come against every town.
Not one town will escape.
The valley will be ruined.
The high plain will be destroyed.
The Lord said this would happen,
so it will happen.
⁹ Spread salt* over the fields in Moab.
The country will be an empty desert.
Moab's towns will become empty.
No people will live in them.
¹⁰ If a person does not do what the Lord says,
if he does not use his sword
to kill those people,
then bad things will happen
to that person.

¹¹ "Moab has never known trouble.
Moab is like wine left to settle.
Moab has never been poured
from one jar to another.
He has not been taken into captivity.
So he tastes like he did before.
And his smell has not changed."
¹² The Lord says these things.
"But I will soon send men
to pour you from your jars.*
Then they will empty the jars
and smash them to pieces."

¹³Then the people of Moab will be ashamed of their false god, Chemosh.* The people of Israel trusted that ⌊false god⌋ in Bethel.* And the people of Israel were embarrassed ⌊when that false god did not help them⌋. Moab will be like that.

Island of Crete Literally, "Island of Caphtor." Sometimes this means Crete, and sometimes it means Cyprus. The Bible says the Philistines originally came from Caphtor.
sad ... cut yourselves The people did these things to show their sadness.
scabbard A holder for a sword.
This message ... says: See Isa. 15 for a similar message.
Mount Nebo A mountain in Moab, a country east of Israel.

brush A small bush short roots that is easily blown away by the wind. In Hebrew this word is like the name "Aroer," an important city in Moab.
Chemosh The god of the people of Moab.
salt This is a word play, and we are not sure of the exact meaning of this Hebrew word.
jars This probably means the cities in Moab.

JEREMIAH 48:14–33

14 "You can't say,
  'We are good soldiers.
  We are brave men in battle.'
15 The enemy will attack Moab.
  The enemy will enter those towns
    and destroy them.
  Her best young men will be killed
    in the slaughter."
  This message is from the King.
  The King's name is the Lord All-Powerful.
16 "The end of Moab is near.
  Moab will soon be destroyed.
17 All of you people living around Moab should
    cry for that country.
  You people know how famous Moab is.
    So cry for him.
  Say,
  'The ruler's power is broken.
  Moab's power and glory is gone.'

18 "You people living in Dibon,*
    come down from your place of honor.
  Sit on the ground in the dust.
  Why? Because the Destroyer is coming.
  And he will destroy your strong cities.

19 "You people living in Aroer,
    stand next to the road and watch.
  See the man running away.
  See that woman running away.
  Ask them what happened.

20 "Moab will be ruined and filled with shame.
  Moab will cry and cry.
  Announce at the Arnon River,*
    that Moab is destroyed.
21 People on the high plain have been punished.
  Judgment has come to the towns of
    Holon, Jahzah, and Mephaath,
22 Judgment has come to the towns of
    Dibon, Nebo, and Beth Diblathaim,
23 Judgment has come to the towns of
    Kiriathaim, Beth Gamul, and Beth Meon,
24 Judgment has come to the towns of
    Kerioth and Bozrah.
  Judgment has come to all the towns of
    Moab, far and near.

25 Moab's strength has been cut off.
  Moab's arm has been broken."
  The Lord said these things.

26 "Moab thought he was more important
    than the Lord.
  So punish Moab until he staggers
    like a drunk person.
  Moab will fall and roll around in his vomit.
  People will make fun of Moab.
27 "Moab, you made fun of Israel.
  Israel was caught by a gang of thieves.
  Every time you spoke about Israel,
    you shook your head and acted like you
    were better than Israel.
28 People in Moab, leave your towns.
  Go live among the rocks;
  be like a dove that makes its nest
    at the opening of a cave."

29 "We have heard about Moab's pride.
  He was very proud.
  He thought he was important.
  He was always bragging.
  He was very, very proud."
30 The Lord says,
  "I know that Moab becomes angry quickly
    and brags about himself.
  But his boasts are lies.
  He can't do the things he says.
31 So, I cry for Moab.
  I cry for everyone in Moab.
  I cry for the men from Kir Hareseth.
32 I cry with the people of Jazer for Jazer.
  Sibmah, in the past your vines
    spread all the way to the sea.
  They reached as far as the town of Jazer.
  But the Destroyer has taken your fruit
    and grapes.
33 Joy and happiness are gone
    from the large vineyards* of Moab.
  I stopped the flow of wine
    from the winepresses.*
  There is no singing and dancing
    from people walking on the grapes
    to make wine.
  There are no shouts of joy.

Chemosh The god of the people of Moab.
in Bethel This means the temple that King Jeroboam built in the town of Bethel. See 1 Kings 12:28-33. It is not clear whether the people still worshiped the Lord there, but in a wrong way, or whether they worshiped a false god, perhaps the Canaanite god El or Baal.
Dibon A town in the country of Moab.
Arnon River An important river in Moab.

vineyard(s) A garden for growing grapes.

³⁴"The people of the towns of Heshbon and Elealeh are crying. Their cry is heard even as far away as the town of Jahaz. Their cry is heard from the town of Zoar, as far away as the towns of Horonaim and Eglath Shelishiyah. Even the waters of Nimrim are dried. ³⁵I will stop Moab from making burnt offerings on the high places.* I will stop them from making sacrifices to their gods." The Lord said those things.
³⁶"I am very sad for Moab. My hearts cries like the sad sound of a flute playing a funeral song. I am sad for the people from Kir Hareseth. Their money and riches have all been taken away. ³⁷Everyone has a shaved head. Everyone's beard is cut off. Everyone's hands are cut and bleeding.* Everyone is wearing their clothes of sadness around their waists. ³⁸People are crying for the dead everywhere in Moab—on every housetop and in every public square. There is sadness because I have broken Moab like an empty jar." The Lord said these things.
³⁹"Moab is shattered. The people are crying. Moab surrendered. Now Moab is ashamed. People make fun of Moab—but the things that happened fill them with fear."

⁴⁰ The Lord says, "Look!
An eagle is diving down from the sky.
It is spreading its wings over Moab.
⁴¹ The towns of Moab will be captured.
The strong hiding places will be defeated.
At that time, Moab's soldiers will be scared,
like a woman that is having a baby.
⁴² The nation of Moab will be destroyed.
Why? Because they thought
that they were more important
than the Lord."

⁴³ The Lord says these things:
"People of Moab,
fear, deep holes, and traps* wait for you.
⁴⁴ People will be afraid and run away,
and they will fall into the deep holes.
If anyone climbs out of the deep holes,
he will be caught in the traps.

I will bring the year of punishment
to Moab."
The Lord said these things.
⁴⁵ "People have run from the powerful enemy.
They ran to safety in the town Heshbon.
ᴌBut there was no safety.ᴊ
A fire started in Heshbon.
That fire started in Sihon's town*
And it is destroying the leaders of Moab.
It is destroying those proud people.
⁴⁶ It will be bad for you, Moab.
Chemosh's* people are being destroyed.
Your sons and daughters
are being taken away
as prisoners and captives.*

⁴⁷"Moab's people will be taken away as captives. But in days to come, I will bring Moab's people back." This message is from the Lord.
This ends the judgment on Moab.

A Message About Ammon

49 This message is about the Ammonite people. The Lord says:
"Ammonite people, do you think that
the people of Israel don't have children?
Do you think there are no children
to take the land when the parents die?
Maybe that is why Milcom*
took Gad's* land?"

² The Lord says,
"The time will come in Rabbah of Ammon*
when people hear the sounds of battle.
Rabbah of Ammon will be destroyed.
It will be an empty hill
covered with destroyed buildings.
And the towns around it will be burned.

---

winepresses A place for squeezing the juice from grapes. Sometimes this was only a shallow hole in a large rock in the ground.
high places Special places where the people worshiped false gods. These places were often on hilltops, but not always. Some 'high places' were in valleys.
Everyone ... cut and bleeding The people did these things to show their sadness for people that had died.

fear ,deep holes ,and traps This is a word play in Hebrew. The Hebrew words are: "Pahad, Pahat, and Pah."
Sihon's town This was Heshbon. See Num. 21:25-30.
Chemosh The national god of the land of Moab, even though Milcom was the god of the Ammonite people.
captives People that were taken away like prisoners. Here this means the Moabite people.
Milcom The god of the Ammonite people.
Gad's One of the family groups of Israel. Their land was on the east side of the Jordan River, near the country of Ammon.

Those people forced the people of Israel
to leave their own land.
But later, Israel will force them to leave."
The Lord said these things.

3 "People in Heshbon, cry!
Why? Because the town of Ai is destroyed.
Women in Rabbah of Ammon, cry!
Put on your clothes of sadness and cry.
Run to the city for safety.
Why? ⌊Because the enemy is coming.⌋
They take away the god, Milcom.*
And they will take away Milcom's
priests and officials.
4 You brag about your strength.
But you are losing your strength.
You trust your money will save you.
You think no one would even think of
attacking you."
5 But the Lord All-Powerful says this:
"I will bring troubles to you
from every side.
You will all run away.
And no one will be able
to bring you together again."

6"The Ammonite people will be taken away as captives. But the time will come that I will bring the Ammonite people back." This message is from the Lord.

A Message About Edom

7This message is about Edom.

The Lord All-Powerful says:
"Is there no more wisdom in Teman*?
Are the wise men of Edom
not able to give good advice?
Have they lost their wisdom?
8 You people living in Dedan, run away!
Hide! Why? Because I will punish Esau*
for the bad things he did.

9 "Workers pick grapes from grapevines.
But they leave a few grapes on the plants.
If thieves come at night,
they don't take everything.

10 But I will take everything from Esau*.
I will find all of his hiding places.
He will not be able to hide from me.
His children, relatives, and neighbors
will all die.
11 No person will be left
to care for his children.
His wives will have no one to depend on."

12This is what the Lord says, "Some people don't deserve to be punished—but they suffer. But Edom, you deserve to be punished—so you will really be punished. You will not escape the punishment you deserve. You will be punished." 13The Lord says, "By my own power, I make this promise: I promise that the city of Bozrah will be destroyed. That city will become a ruined pile of rocks. People will use that city as an example when they ask for bad things to happen to other cities. People will insult that city. And all the towns around Bozrah will become ruins forever."

14 I heard a message from the Lord:
The Lord sent a messenger to the nations.
This is the message:
"Gather your armies together!
Get ready for battle!
March against the nation of Edom!
15 Edom, I will make you become not important.
Every person will hate you.
16 Edom, you scared other nations.
So you thought you were important.
But you were fooled.
Your pride has tricked you.
Edom, you live high in the hills.
You live in places protected by big rocks
and hills.
But even if you build your home
as high as an eagle's nest,
I will get you,
and I will bring you down from there."
The Lord said these things.

17 "Edom will be destroyed.
People will be shocked
to see the destroyed cities.
People will whistle from amazement
at the destroyed cities.
18 Edom will be destroyed
like Sodom and Gomorrah* and the
towns around them.

Rabbah of Ammon The capital city of the Ammonite people.
Milcom The god of the Ammonite people.
Teman This town was in the northern part of Edom.

Esau Jacob's twin brother. But here this means Edom whose people were descendants of Esau.

No people will live there."
The Lord said these things.

¹⁹"Sometimes a lion will come from the thick bushes near the Jordan River. And that lion will go into the fields where people put their sheep and cattle. I am like that lion. I will go to Edom. And I will scare those people. I will make them run away. None of their young men will stop me. No one is like me. No one will challenge me. None of their shepherds *(leaders)* will stand up against me."

20 So listen to what the Lord has planned
    to do to the people of Edom.
Listen to what the Lord has decided
    to do to the people in Teman.*
The enemy will drag away the young kids
    of Edom's flock *(people)*.
Edom's pastures will be empty because of
    what they did.
21 At the sound of Edom's fall,
    the earth will shake.
Their cry will be heard
    all the way to the Red Sea.

22 The Lord will be like an eagle
    flying over the animal that it will attack.
The Lord will be like an eagle
    spreading its wings over Bozrah.
At that time, Edom's soldiers
    will become very scared.
They will be crying from fear
    like a woman having a baby.

A Message About Damascus

²³This message is about the city of Damascus:

"The towns of Hamath and Arpad are afraid.
    They are afraid
        because they heard the bad news.
    They are discouraged.
        They are worried and scared.
24 The city of Damascus has become weak.
    The people want to run away.
    The people are ready to panic.
    The people feel pain and suffering
        like a woman having a baby.

25 "Damascus, is a happy city.
    The people have not left that 'fun city' yet.

26 So the young men will die
    in the public squares of that city.
All of her soldiers will be killed at that time."
    The Lord All-Powerful said these things.
27 "I will set the walls of Damascus on fire.
    The fire will completely burn up
        the strong forts of Ben-Hadad."*

A Message About Kedar and Hazor

²⁸This message is about the family group of Kedar and the rulers of Hazor.* Nebuchadnezzar, the king of Babylon, defeated them.

The Lord says:
    "Go and attack the family group of Kedar.
        Destroy the people of the East.
29 Their tents and flocks will be taken away.
        Their tent and all their riches
            will be carried off.
    Their enemy will take away the camels.
    Men will shout this to them:
        'Terrible things are happening all around us.'
30 Run away quickly!
        People in Hazor,
            find a good place to hide."
    This message is from the Lord.
    "Nebuchadnezzar made plans against you.
        He thought of a smart plan to defeat you.
31 "There is a nation that feels safe.
        That nation feels secure.
        That nation does not have gates
            or fences to protect it.
    No people live near them.

The Lord says,
    'Attack that nation!'
32 The enemy will steal their camels
        and take their large herds of cattle.
    The enemy will steal their large herds.
    Those people cut the corners of their beards.*
        Well, I will make them run away
            to the far corners of the earth.
    And I will bring terrible troubles to them
        from everywhere."
    This message is from the Lord.

Ben-Hadad This was the name of several of the kings of Aram-Damascus.

family group of Kedar and the rulers of Hazor Kedar was the name of an Arab family group that lived in the desert southeast of the land of Judah.

corners of their beards The Jewish men did not cut their beards like the Arabs did.

Sodom and Gomorrah Two cities that God destroyed because the people were so evil.

Teman This town was in the northern part of Edom.

³³ "The land of Hazor will become a place
where only wild dogs live.
No person will live there.
No person will live in that place.
It will become an empty desert forever."

A Message About Elam

³⁴Early in the time when Zedekiah was king of Judah, Jeremiah the prophet received a message from the Lord. This message is about the nation of Elam.*

³⁵ The Lord All-Powerful says,
"I will break Elam's bow very soon.
The bow is Elam's strongest weapon.
³⁶ I will bring the four winds against Elam.
I will bring them from
the four corners of the skies.
I will send the people of Elam
to every place on the earth
where the four winds blow.
Elam's captives will be carried away
to every nation.
³⁷ I will break Elam to pieces
while their enemies are watching.
I will break Elam in front of those people
that want to kill them.
I will bring terrible troubles to them.
I will show them how angry I am."
This message is from the Lord.
"I will send a sword to chase Elam.
The sword will chase them
until I have killed them all.
³⁸ I will show Elam that I am in control.
And I will destroy her king and his
officials."
This message is from the Lord.
³⁹ "But in the future, I will make good things
happen to Elam."
This message is from the Lord.

A Message About Babylon

50 This is the message the Lord spoke about the nation of Babylon and the Babylonian people. The Lord spoke this message through Jeremiah.

² "Announce this to all nations!
Lift up a flag and announce the message!
Speak the whole message and say,

'The nation of Babylon will be captured.
The god Bel* will be put to shame.
The god Marduk* will be very afraid.
Babylon's idols will be put to shame.
Her idol gods will be filled with terror.'
³ A nation from the north will attack Babylon.
That nation will make Babylon
like an empty desert.
No people will live there.
Both men and animals
will run away from there."
⁴ The Lord says,
"At that time, the people of Israel
and the people of Judah will be together.
They will cry and cry together.
And together, they will go to look
for the Lord their God.
⁵ Those people will ask how to go to Zion.*
They will start to go in that direction.
The people will say,
'Come, let us join ourselves to the Lord.
Let's make an agreement
that will last forever.
Let's make an agreement
that we will never forget.'
⁶ "My people have been like lost sheep.
Their shepherds *(leaders)*
led them the wrong way,
Their leaders made them wander around
in the mountains and hills.
They forgot where their resting place is.
⁷ Whoever found my people hurt them.
And those enemies said,
'We did nothing wrong.'
Those people sinned against the Lord.
The Lord was their true resting place.
The Lord was the God
that their fathers trusted in.
⁸ "Run away from Babylon.
Leave the land of the Babylonian people.
Be like the goats that lead the flock.
⁹ I will bring many nations together
from the north.
This group of nations will get ready for war
against Babylon.

Bel This is one of the names of the god Marduk, the most important god of the Babylonians.
Marduk Marduk was the most important god of the Babylonians.
Zion The southeast part of the mountain Jerusalem is built on. Sometimes it means the people of God living in Jerusalem.

Elam A nation east of Babylon.

Babylon will be captured by people
    from the north.
Those nations will shoot many arrows
    at Babylon.
Those arrows will be like soldiers
    that don't come back from war with
    their hands empty.
¹⁰ The enemy will take all the wealth
    from the Chaldean people.
Those soldiers will take all they want."
The Lord said these things.

¹¹ "Babylon, you are excited and happy.
    You took my land.
You dance around like a young cow
    that got into the grain.
Your laughter is like the happy sounds
    that horses make.
¹² Now your mother will be very ashamed.
The woman that gave you birth
    will be embarrassed.
Babylon will be the least important
    of all the nations.
She will be an empty, dry desert.
¹³ The Lord will show his anger,
    so no people will live there.
Babylon will be completely empty.
Everyone that passes by Babylon
    will be afraid.
They will shake their heads when they see
    how badly it has been destroyed.

¹⁴ "Prepare for war against Babylon.
All you soldiers with bows,
    shoot your arrows at Babylon.
Don't save any of your arrows.
Babylon has sinned against the Lord.
¹⁵ Soldiers around Babylon,
    shout the cry of victory!
Babylon has surrendered!
Her walls and towers
    have been pulled down!
The Lord is giving those people
    the punishment they should have.
You nations should give Babylon
    the punishment she deserves.
Do to her what she has done
    to other nations.
¹⁶ Don't let the people from Babylon
    plant their crops.
Don't let them gather the harvest.
The soldiers of Babylon
    brought many prisoners to their city.
Now the enemy soldiers have come,
So those prisoners are going back home.
Those prisoners are running back
    to their own countries.

¹⁷ "Israel is like a flock of sheep
    that were scattered all over the country.
Israel is like sheep that were chased away
    by lions.
The first lion to attack
    was the king of Assyria.
The last lion to crush his bones
    was Nebuchadnezzar king of Babylon.
¹⁸ So the Lord All-Powerful,
    the God of Israel, says:
'I will soon punish the king of Babylon
    and his country.
I will punish him
    like I punished the king of Assyria.
¹⁹ "I will bring Israel back to his own fields.
He will eat food that grows
    on Mount Carmel
    and in the land of Bashan.
He will eat and be full.
He will eat on the hills
    in the lands of Ephraim and Gilead."
²⁰ The Lord says,
"At that time, people will try hard
    to find Israel's guilt.
But there will be no guilt.
People will try to find Judah's sins,
    but no sins will be found.
Why? Because I am saving a few
    survivors* from Israel and Judah.
And I am forgiving them
    for all of their sins."

²¹ The Lord says,
"Attack the country of Merathaim!
Attack the people living in Pekod!
Attack them!
Kill them and completely destroy them!
Do everything I commanded you!

²² "The noise of battle can be heard
    all over the country.
It is the noise of much destruction.
²³ Babylon was called
    'The Hammer of the Whole Earth.'
But now the 'Hammer' is shattered.
Babylon is the most ruined of the nations.
²⁴ Babylon, I set a trap for you.

survivor(s) People that escaped some disaster. Here this means the Jewish people that survived the destruction of Judah and Israel by its enemy armies.

And you were caught before you knew it.
You fought against the Lord,
so you were found and captured.
25 The Lord has opened up his storeroom.
The Lord brought out the weapons of his
anger.
The Lord God All-Powerful
brought out those weapons
because he has work to do.
He has work to do
in the land of the Chaldean people.

26 "Come against Babylon from far away.
Break open the storehouses
where she keeps her grain.
Completely destroy Babylon.
Don't leave anyone alive.
Pile her dead bodies like big piles of grain.
27 Kill all the young bulls *(men)* in Babylon.
Let them be slaughtered.*
The time has come for them to be defeated,
so it will be very bad for them.
It is time for them to be punished.
28 People are running out of Babylon.
They are escaping from that country.
Those people are coming to Zion.*.
And those people are telling everyone
about the things the Lord is doing.
They are telling people that the Lord
is giving Babylon the punishment it
deserves.
Babylon destroyed the Lord's temple,
so now the Lord is destroying Babylon.

29 "Call for the men that shoot arrows.
Tell them to attack Babylon.
Tell those men to surround the city.
Don't let anyone escape.
Pay her back for the bad things she has done.
Do to her what she has done
to other nations.
Babylon did not respect the Lord.
Babylon was very rude
to the Holy One of Israel.
So punish Babylon.
30 Babylon's young men
will be killed in the streets.
All her soldiers will die on that day."

The Lord says these things.
31 "Babylon, you are too proud.
And I am against you."
Our Master, the Lord All-Powerful,
says these things.
"I am against you,
and the time has come
for you to be punished.
32 Proud Babylon will stumble and fall.
And no person will help her get up.
I will start a fire in her towns.
That fire will completely burn
everyone around her."

33 The Lord All-Powerful says:
"The people of Israel and Judah are slaves.
The enemy took them,
and the enemy will not let Israel go.
34 But God will get those people back.
His name is the Lord God All-Powerful.
He will defend those people very strongly.
He will defend them so that he can let that
land rest.
But there will be no rest
for the people living in Babylon."

35 The Lord says,
"Sword, kill the people living in Babylon.
Sword, kill the king's officials
and the wise men of Babylon.
36 Sword, kill the priests of Babylon.
Those priests will be like foolish people.
Sword, kill the soldiers of Babylon.
Those soldiers will be full of terror.
37 Sword, kill the horses and chariots of Babylon.
Sword, kill all the soldiers hired
from other countries.
Those soldiers will be
like frightened women.
Sword, destroy the treasures of Babylon.
Those treasures will be taken away.
38 Sword, strike the waters of Babylon.
Those waters will be dried up.
Babylon has many, many idols.
Those idols show
that the people of Babylon are foolish.
So bad things will happen to those people.

39 "Babylon will never again
be filled with people.
Wild dogs, ostriches,* and other desert
animals will live there.
But no people will live there ever again.
40 God completely destroyed

---

slaughter(ed) Usually, this word means to kill an animal and cut it into pieces of meat. But it often means to kill people like they are animals.
Zion The southeast part of the mountain Jerusalem is built on. Sometimes it means the people of God living in Jerusalem.

Sodom and Gomorrah*
and the towns around them.
⌊And no person lives in those towns now.⌋
In the same way, no people
will live in Babylon.
And no people will ever go to live there.

⁴¹ "Look!
There are people coming from the north.
They come from a powerful nation.
Many kings are coming together
from all around the world.
⁴² Their armies have bows and spears.
The soldiers are cruel.
They have no mercy.
The soldiers come riding on their horses,
and the sound is loud like the roaring sea.
They stand in their places, ready for battle.
They are ready to attack you,
city of Babylon.
⁴³ The king of Babylon
heard about those armies.
And he became very scared.
He is so afraid,
his hands will not move.
His fear makes his stomach hurt
like a woman having a baby."

⁴⁴ ⌊The Lord says,⌋
"Sometimes a lion will come from
the thick bushes near the Jordan River.
That lion will walk into the fields
where people have their animals.
⌊and the animals will all run away.⌋
I will be like that lion,
I will chase Babylon from its land.
Who should I choose to do this?
There is no person like me.
There is no person that can challenge me.
⌊So I will do it.⌋
No shepherd will come to chase me away.
I will chase away the people of Babylon."

⁴⁵ Listen to what the Lord has planned
to do to Babylon.
Listen to what the Lord has decided
to do to the Babylonian people.
The enemy will drag away the young kids
of Babylon's flock *(people)*.
Babylon's pastures will be empty because of
what they did.

⁴⁶ Babylon will fall,
and that fall will shake the earth.
People in all nations will hear about
the destruction of Babylon.

51

The Lord says, "I will cause
a powerful wind to blow.
I will cause it to blow against Babylon
and the Babylonian people.*
² I will send people to winnow* Babylon.
They will winnow* Babylon.
Those people will take everything from
Babylon.
Armies will surround the city,
and terrible destruction will happen.
³ The Babylonian soldiers
will not use their bows and arrows.
Those soldiers will not even put on
their armor.
Don't feel sorry
for the young men of Babylon.
Completely destroy her army.
⁴ Babylon's soldiers will be killed
in the land of the Chaldeans.
They will be badly wounded
in the streets of Babylon."

⁵ The Lord All-Powerful
did not leave Israel and Judah alone,
like a woman whose husband has died.
God did not leave those people.
No! Those people are guilty
of leaving the Holy One of Israel.
They left him,
but he has not left them.

⁶ Run away from Babylon.
Run to save your lives!
Don't stay and be killed
because of Babylon's sins!
It is time for the Lord to punish
the people of Babylon
for the bad things they did.
Babylon will get the punishment
that she should have.
⁷ Babylon was like a golden cup

---

ostriches Large birds that live in the desert. These birds can't fly.
Sodom and Gomorrah Two cities that God destroyed because the people were so evil.

Babylonian people Literally, "Leb Kammai." In Hebrew this was a secret way of writing "Chaldeans."
winnow To separate grain, which is good to eat, from the shell that the grain is in. Farmers winnowed the grain by throwing the grain and the hulls in the air. The air blew the hulls away. And the good grain fell back to the ground.

in the Lord's hand.
Babylon made the whole world drunk.
The nations drank Babylon's wine.
So they went crazy.

⁸ But Babylon will suddenly fall
and be broken.
Cry for her!
Get medicine for her pain!
Maybe she can be healed!

⁹ We tried to heal Babylon,
but she can't be healed.
So let us leave her,
and let each of us
go to our own country.
God in heaven will decide
Babylon's punishment.
He will decide what will happen to Babylon.

¹⁰ The Lord got even for us.
Come, let's tell about that in Zion.*
Let us tell about the things
that the Lord our God has done.

¹¹ Sharpen the arrows!
Get your shields!
The Lord stirred up the kings
of the Medes.*
He has stirred them up
because he wants to destroy Babylon.
The Lord will give the people of Babylon
the punishment that they deserve.
The army from Babylon destroyed
the Lord's temple* in Jerusalem.
So the Lord will give them
the punishment they should have.

¹² Lift up a flag against the walls of Babylon.
Bring more guards.
Put the watchmen in their places.
Get ready for a secret attack.
The Lord will do what he has planned.
He will do what he said he would do
against the people of Babylon.

¹³ Babylon, you live near much water.
You are rich with treasures.
But your end as a nation has come.
It is time for you to be destroyed.

¹⁴ The Lord All-Powerful used his name
to make this promise:
"Babylon, I will fill you
with many enemy soldiers.
They will be like a swarm of locusts.*
They will win their war against you.
And they will stand over you
and shout the cry of victory."

¹⁵ The Lord used his great power
and made the earth.
He used his wisdom to build the world.
He used his understanding
to stretch out the skies.

¹⁶ When he thunders,
the water in the skies roar.
He sends clouds all over the earth.
He sends lightning with the rain.
He brings out the wind
from his storehouses.

¹⁷ But people are so stupid.
They don't understand what God has done.
Skilled workers make statues of false gods.
Those statues are only false gods.
They show how foolish that worker is.
Those statues are not alive.

¹⁸ Those idols are worthless.
People made those idols,
and they are nothing but a joke.
Their time of judgment will come,
and those idols will be destroyed.

¹⁹ But Jacob's Portion *(God)* is not like those
worthless statues.
People didn't make God,
God made his people.
God made everything.
His name is the Lord All-Powerful.

²⁰ ⌊The Lord says,⌋
"⌊Babylon,⌋ you are my club.
I used you to smash nations.
I used you to destroy kingdoms.

²¹ I used you to smash horse and rider.
I used you to smash chariot and driver.

²² I used you to smash men and women.
I used you to smash men, old and young.
I used you to smash young men
and young women.

²³ I used you to smash shepherds and flocks.

Zion   The southeast part of the mountain Jerusalem is built on. Sometimes it means the people of God living in Jerusalem.
Medes   People from the Medo-Persian Empire. This empire defeated the country Babylon.
temple   The special building in Jerusalem for Jewish worship.

locusts   Insects like grasshoppers that could destroy a large crop very quickly.

I used you to smash farmers and cows.
I used you to smash governors
and important officials.
24 But I will pay Babylon back.
I will pay all the Babylonian people back.
I will pay them back for all the bad things
that they did to Zion.*
I will pay them back so that you can see it,
Judah."
The Lord said those things.

25 The Lord says,
"Babylon, you are a destroying mountain,
and I am against you.
Babylon, you destroyed the whole country,
and I am against you.
I will put my hand out against you.
I will roll you off the cliffs.
I will make you into a burned-up mountain.
26 People will not take any rocks from Babylon
to use for the foundation of a building.
People will not find any rocks
big enough for cornerstones.
Why? Because your city will be
a pile of broken rocks forever."
The Lord said these things.

27 "Lift up the war flag in the land!
Blow the trumpet in all the nations!
Prepare the nations for war against Babylon!
Call these kingdoms to come fight
against Babylon:
Ararat, Minni, and Ashkenaz.
Choose a commander to lead the army
against her.
Send so many horses
that they are like a swarm of locusts.*
28 Get the nations ready for battle against her.
Get the kings of the Medes* ready.
Get their governors and all their important
officials ready.
Get all the countries they rule ready for
battle against Babylon.
29 The land shakes and moves like it is in pain.
It will shake when the Lord does what he
planned to Babylon.

The Lord's plan is to make the land of
Babylon into an empty desert.
No person will live there.
30 Babylon's soldiers have stopped fighting.
They stay in their forts.
Their strength is gone.
They have become like scared women.
Babylon's houses are burning.
The bars of her gates are broken.
31 One messenger follows another.
Messenger follows messenger.
They announce to the king of Babylon,
that his whole city has been captured.
32 The places where people cross the rivers
have been captured.
The swamplands are burning.
All of Babylon's soldiers are afraid."

33 The Lord All-Powerful,
the God of the people of Israel, says:
"Babylon is like a threshing floor.*
At harvest time, people beat grain
to separate the good parts from the chaff.*
And the time to beat Babylon
is coming soon.

34 "Nebuchadnezzar king of Babylon, destroyed
us in the past.
In the past, Nebuchadnezzar hurt us.
In the past, he took our people away,
and we became like an empty jar.
He took the best we had.
He was like a giant monster
that ate everything until it was full.
He took the best we had
and threw us away.
35 Babylon did terrible things to hurt us.
Now I want those things
to happen to Babylon."

The people living in Zion* said these things:
"The people of Babylon are guilty
of killing our people.
Now they are being punished
for the bad things they did."
The city of Jerusalem said those things.
36 So the Lord says:

Zion The southeast part of the mountain Jerusalem is built on. Sometimes it means the people of God living in Jerusalem.
locusts Insects like grasshoppers that could destroy a large crop very quickly.
Medes People from the Medo-Persian Empire. This empire defeated the country Babylon.
threshing floor A place where grain is beaten or walked on to remove the hulls from the grain.
chaff The seed coverings and stems separated from the seeds of plants like wheat or barley. Farmers saved the seeds but let the wind blow the useless chaff away.

"I will defend you, Judah.
I will make sure
that Babylon is punished.
I will dry up Babylon's sea.
And I will make her water springs
become dry.
37 Babylon will become
a pile of ruined buildings.
Babylon will be a place for wild dogs
to live.
People will look at that pile of rocks
and be amazed.
People will shake their heads
when they think about Babylon.
Babylon will be a place
where no people live.

38 "The people of Babylon
are like roaring young lions.
They growl like baby lions.
39 Those people are acting like powerful lions.
I will give a party for them.
I will make them drunk.
They will laugh and have a good time.
And then they will sleep forever.
They will never wake up."

The Lord said these things.
40 "Babylon will be like sheep, rams, and goats
waiting to be killed.
I will lead them to the slaughter.
41 "Sheshach* will be defeated.
The best and proudest country
of the whole earth
will be taken captive.
People from other nations
will look at Babylon,
and the things they see
will make them afraid.
42 The sea will rise over Babylon.
Its roaring waves will cover her.
43 Babylon's towns will be ruined and empty.
Babylon will become a dry, desert land.
It will become a land where no people live.
People will not even travel through Babylon.
44 I will punish the false god Bel* in Babylon.

Zion The southeast part of the mountain Jerusalem is built on. Sometimes it means the people of God living in Jerusalem.
Sheshach Jeremiah used a special code to create this name. It is like the code an army might use. It is a secret word for Babylon.
Bel This is one of the names of the god Marduk, the most important god of the Babylonians.

I will make him vomit out the people
that he swallowed.
The wall around Babylon will fall.
And other nations will stop coming
to Babylon.
45 Come out of the city of Babylon, my people.
Run to save your lives.
Run from the Lord's great anger.
46 "Don't be sad, my people.
Rumors will spread, but don't be afraid.
One rumor comes this year.
Another rumor will come next year.
There will be rumors about terrible fighting
in the country.
There will be rumors about rulers fighting
against other rulers.
47 The time will surely come—
I will punish the false gods of Babylon.
And the whole land of Babylon
will be put to shame.
There will be many, many dead people,
lying in the streets of that city.
48 Then heaven and earth and all that is in them
will shout with joy about Babylon.
They will shout because
an army came from the north
and fought against Babylon."

The Lord said these things.
49 "Babylon killed people from Israel.
Babylon killed people
from every place on earth.
So Babylon must fall!
50 You people escaped the swords.
You must hurry and leave Babylon.
Don't wait!
You are in a faraway land.
But remember the Lord where you are.
And remember Jerusalem.
51 "We people of Judah are ashamed.
We have been insulted.
Why? Because strangers have gone into
the Holy Places of the Lord's temple."
52 The Lord says,
"The time is coming, when I will punish
the idols of Babylon.
At that time, wounded people will cry
with pain everywhere in that country.
53 Babylon might grow
until she touches the sky.

Bel This is one of the names of the god Marduk, the most important god of the Babylonians.

Babylon might make her forts strong.
But I will send people
to fight against that city.
And those people will destroy her."
The Lord said these things.

⁵⁴ "We can hear people crying in Babylon.
We hear the sound of people destroying
things in the land of Babylon.
⁵⁵ The Lord will destroy Babylon very soon.
He will stop the loud noises in that city.
Enemies will come roaring in
like ocean waves.
People all around will hear that roar.
⁵⁶ The army will come and destroy Babylon.
Babylon's soldiers will be captured.
Their bows will be broken.
Why? Because the Lord punishes people
for the bad things they do.
The Lord gives them the full punishment
that they deserve.
⁵⁷ I will make Babylon's wise men
and important officials drunk.
I will make the governors, officers,
and soldiers drunk too.
Then they will sleep forever.
They will never wake up."
The King said these things.
His name is the Lord All-Powerful.

⁵⁸ The Lord All-Powerful says:
"Babylon's thick, strong wall
will be pulled down.
Her high gates will be burned.
The people of Babylon will work hard,
but it will not help.
They will become very tired
trying to save the city.
But they will only become fuel
for the flames."

Jeremiah Sends a Message to Babylon

⁵⁹This is the message that Jeremiah gave to the officer Seraiah.* Seraiah was the son of Neriah. Neriah was the son of Mahseiah. Seraiah went to Babylon with Zedekiah king of Judah. This happened in the fourth year that Zedekiah was king of Judah.* At that time, Jeremiah gave this message to Seraiah, the officer. ⁶⁰Jeremiah had written on a scroll* all the terrible things that would happen to Babylon. He had written all these things about Babylon.
⁶¹Jeremiah said to Seraiah, "Seraiah, go to Babylon. Be sure to read this message so all the people can hear you. ⁶²Then say, 'Lord, you have said that you will destroy this place, Babylon. You will destroy it so that no people or animals will live in it. This place will be an empty ruin forever.' ⁶³After you finish reading this scroll, tie a stone to it. Then throw this scroll* into the Euphrates River. ⁶⁴Then say, 'In the same way, Babylon will sink. Babylon will rise no more. Babylon will sink because of the terrible things that I will make happen here.'"
The words of Jeremiah end here.

The Fall of Jerusalem

52 Zedekiah was 21 years old when he became king of Judah. Zedekiah ruled in Jerusalem for eleven years. His mother's name was Hamutal daughter of Jeremiah.* Hamutal's family was from the town of Libnah. ²Zedekiah did evil things, just like King Jehoiakim had done. The Lord did not like Zedekiah doing those evil things. ³Terrible things happened to Jerusalem and Judah because the Lord was angry with them. Finally, the Lord threw the people of Jerusalem and Judah away from his presence.
Zedekiah rebelled against the king of Babylon. ⁴So, in the ninth year of Zedekiah's rule, on the tenth day of the tenth month* Nebuchadnezzar king of Babylon, marched against Jerusalem. Nebuchadnezzar had his whole army with him. The army of Babylon set up their camp outside of Jerusalem. Then they built ramps all around the city walls ₍so they could get over those walls₎. ⁵The city of Jerusalem was surrounded by the army of Babylon until the eleventh year that Zedekiah was king.* ⁶By the ninth day of the fourth month of that year, the hunger in the city was very bad. There was no food left for the people in the city to eat. ⁷On that day, the army of Babylon broke into Jerusalem. The soldiers of

---

Seraiah Seraiah was a brother of Baruch, Jeremiah's secretary.
fourth year that Zedekiah was king of Judah That is, 594B.C.

Scroll(s) A long roll of leather or papyrus *(paper)* used for writing books, letters, and legal documents.
Jeremiah This is not Jeremiah the prophet, but a different man with the same name.
ninth year ... tenth month That is, January of 588B.C.
eleventh year ... king That is, 587B.C.

Jerusalem ran away. They left the city at night. They went through the gate between the two walls. That gate was near the king's garden. Even though the army of Babylon had surrounded the city, the soldiers of Jerusalem still ran away. They ran away toward the desert. ⁸But the Babylonian army chased King Zedekiah. They caught him on the plains of Jericho. All of Zedekiah's soldiers ran away. ⁹The army of Babylon captured King Zedekiah. They took him to the king of Babylon at the city of Riblah. Riblah is in the land of Hamath. At Riblah the king of Babylon announced his judgment on King Zedekiah. ¹⁰There at the city of Riblah, the king of Babylon killed Zedekiah's sons. Zedekiah was forced to watch his sons being killed. The king of Babylon also killed all the king's officials of Judah. ¹¹Then the king of Babylon tore out Zedekiah's eyes. He put bronze chains on him. Then he carried Zedekiah away to Babylon. In Babylon he put Zedekiah into prison. Zedekiah stayed in prison until the day he died.

¹²Nebuzaradan, the commander of the king of Babylon's special guard, came to Jerusalem. This was on the tenth day of the fifth month, in the 19th year that Nebuchadnezzar was king.* Nebuzaradan was an important leader in Babylon. ¹³Nebuzaradan burned the Lord's temple. He also burned down the king's house and all the houses of Jerusalem. He burned down every important building in Jerusalem. ¹⁴The whole Babylonian army broke down the walls around Jerusalem. That army was under the commander of the king's special guard. ¹⁵Nebuzaradan, the commander, took the rest of the people that were still in Jerusalem* into captivity. He also carried away those that had surrendered to the king of Babylon earlier. He also carried away the skilled craftsmen that were left in Jerusalem. ¹⁶But Nebuzaradan left some of the poorest people behind in the land. He left those people to work in the vineyards and the fields.

¹⁷The Babylonian army broke up the bronze columns of the temple. They also broke up the stands and the Bronze Tank* that were in the Lord's temple. They carried all that bronze away to Babylon. ¹⁸The army of Babylon also took these things from the temple: pots, shovels, wick trimmers, large bowls, pans, and all the bronze things that were used in the temple service. ¹⁹The commander of the king's special guards took these things away: basins, firepans, large bowls, pots, lampstands, pans, and bowls used for drink offerings. He took everything that was made of gold or silver. ²⁰The two pillars, the Sea and the twelve bronze bulls under it, and the moveable stands were very heavy. King Solomon had made those things for the Lord's temple. The bronze that those things were made of was so heavy it could not be weighed.

²¹Each of the bronze pillars was 27 feet* high. Each pillar was 18 feet* around. Each pillar was hollow. The walls of each pillar was 4 inches* thick. ²²The bronze capital on top of the first pillar was 7 1/2 feet* high. It was decorated with a net design and bronze pomegranates* all around it. The other pillar had pomegranates too. It was like the first pillar. ²³There were 96 pomegranates on the sides of the pillars. All together, there were 100 pomegranates above the net design that went around the pillars.

²⁴The commander of the king's special guards took Seraiah and Zephaniah as prisoners. Seraiah was the high priest, and Zephaniah was the next highest priest. The three doorkeepers were also taken as prisoners. ²⁵The commander of the king's special guards also took the officer in charge of the fighting men. He also took seven of the king's advisers as prisoners. Those men were still there in Jerusalem. He also took the scribe* that was in charge of putting people in the army. And he took 60 of the ordinary people that were there in the city. ²⁶⁻²⁷Nebuzaradan, the commander, took all those officials. He brought them to the king of

---

bronze columns ... Bronze Tank These verses list the things that the Babylonian army took away from the Lord's temple. For a description of the temple furniture, see 1 Kings 7:13-26.
27 feet Literally, "18 cubits."
18 feet Literally, "12 cubits."
4 inches Literally, "4 fingers."
7 1/2 feet Literally, "7 cubits."
pomegranate A red fruit containing many tiny seeds covered with a soft, juicy part of the fruit.
scribe A man that wrote down and copied books and letters. He often become an expert at the meaning of those writings (scriptures).

19th year ... king That is, 587 B.C.
the rest ... Jerusalem This is from the ancient Greek translation. The Hebrew adds, "some of the poorest people" before this line. This seems to have been accidentally copied from the next verse.

Babylon. The king of Babylon was at the city of Riblah. Riblah is in the country of Hamath. There at the city of Riblah, the king ordered all those officials to be killed.

So the people of Judah were taken from their country. ²⁸This is how many people Nebuchadnezzar carried into captivity:

In Nebuchadnezzar's 7th year* as king of Babylon, 3,023 men were taken from Judah.

²⁹In Nebuchadnezzar's 18th year* as king of Babylon, 832 people were taken from Jerusalem.

³⁰In Nebuchadnezzar's 23rd year* as king, Nebuzaradan took 745 men of Judah into captivity. Nebuzaradan was the commander of the king's special guards.

In all, 4,600 people were taken captive.

Jehoiachin Is Set Free

³¹Jehoiachin, the king of Judah, was in prison in Babylon for 37 years. In the 37th year of his imprisonment,* Evil-Merodach, the king of Babylon, was very kind to Jehoiachin. He let Jehoiachin out of prison in that year. This was the same year that Evil-Merodach became king of Babylon. Evil-Merodach set Jehoiachin free from prison on the 25th day of the 12th month. ³²Evil-Merodach spoke in a kind way to Jehoiachin. He gave Jehoiachin a place of honor higher than the other kings that were with him in Babylon. ³³So Jehoiachin took his prison clothes off. For the rest of his life, he ate regularly at the king's table. ³⁴Every day the king of Babylon gave Jehoiachin an allowance. This continued until Jehoiachin died.

Nebuchadnezzar's 7th year That is from the middle of 598 B.C. to the middle of 597 B.C.
Nebuchadnezzar's 18th year That is from the middle of 588 B.C. to the middle of 587 B.C.
Nebuchadnezzar's 23rd year That is from the middle of 582 B.C. to the middle of 581 B.C.

37th year of his imprisonment That is 561 B.C.

Lamentations

Jerusalem Cries Over Her Destruction

1 Jerusalem once was a city full of people.
  But now the city is so deserted!
  Jerusalem was one of the greatest cities
      in the world.
  But now she* has become like a widow.
  She was once a princess among cities.
  But now she has been made a slave.
² She cries bitterly in the night.
  Her tears are on her cheeks.
  She has no one to comfort her.
  Many nations were friendly to her.
  But none of them comforts her now.
  All of her friends turned their backs on her.
  Her friends became her enemies.
³ Judah suffered very much.
  And then Judah was taken into captivity.
  Judah lives among other nations.
  But she has found no rest.
  The people that chased her caught her.
  They caught her in the narrow valleys.
⁴ The roads to Zion* are very sad.
  They are sad because no person comes to
      Zion for the holidays anymore.
  All of Zion's gates have been destroyed.
  All of Zion's priests groan.
  Zion's young women
      have been taken away.*
  And all of this is a bitter sadness to Zion.
⁵ Jerusalem's enemies have won.
  Her enemies have been successful.
  This happened because the Lord
      punished her.
  He punished Jerusalem for her many sins.
  Her children have gone away.

⁶ Their enemies captured them
      and took them away.
  The beauty of the Daughter of Zion*
      has gone away.
  Her princes became like deer.
  They were like deer
      that can't find a meadow to feed in.
  They ran away without strength.
  They ran away from those people
      that chased them.
⁷ Jerusalem thinks back.
  Jerusalem remembers the time
      when she was hurt
      and when she lost her home.
  She remembers all the nice things
      that she had in the past.
  She remembers those nice things
      that she had in the old days.
  She remembers when her people
      were captured by the enemy.
  She remembers when there was no person
      to help her.
  When her enemies saw her, they laughed.
  They laughed because she was destroyed.
⁸ Jerusalem sinned very badly.
  Because Jerusalem sinned,
      she became a ruined city
      that people shake their heads about.
  In the past people respected her.
  Now those people hate her.
  They hate her because they abused her.
  Jerusalem groans.
  She turns away.
⁹ Jerusalem's skirts became dirty.
  She didn't think about the things
      that would happen to her.
  Her fall was amazing.
  She had no person to comfort her.
  She says,
  "Lord, see how I am hurt!
  See how my enemy thinks he is so great!"

---

she In this poem, the poet speaks of the city of Jerusalem as if it was a woman.
Zion The southeast part of the mountain Jerusalem is built on. Sometimes it means the people of God living in Jerusalem.
have been taken away Following the ancient Greek translation. The Hebrew has "are upset."
Daughter of Zion Another name for Jerusalem.

10 The enemy stretched out his hand.
   He took all of her nice things.
   In fact, she saw the foreign nations
     go inside her temple.
   And Lord, you said those people
     could not join in our assembly!
11 All the people of Jerusalem are groaning.
   All of her people are looking for food.
   They are giving away all their nice things for
     food.
   They are doing this to keep alive.
   Jerusalem says,
   "Look, Lord. Look at me!
   See how people hate me.
12 All you people that pass by on the road,
     you don't seem to care.
   But look at me and see.
   Is there any pain like my pain?
   Is there any pain like the pain
     that has come to me?
   Is there any pain like the pain
     that the Lord has punished me with?
   He has punished me on the day
     of his great anger.
13 The Lord sent fire from above.
   That fire went down into my bones.
   He stretched out a net for my feet.
   He turned me all the way around.
   He made me into a wasteland.
   I am sick all day.
14 "My sins were tied up like a yoke.*
   My sins were tied up in the Lord's hands.
   The Lord's yoke is on my neck.
   The Lord has made me weak.
   The Lord has given me to people
     that I can't stand up against.
15 "The Lord rejected all my strong soldiers.
   Those soldiers were inside the city.
   Then the Lord brought a group of people
     against me.
   He brought those people to kill my young
     soldiers.
   The Lord has stepped on the grapes in the
     winepress.
   That winepress belongs to the virgin daughter
     of Jerusalem.*

16 "I cry about all these things.
   My eyes, my eyes run down with water.
   There is no comforter near me.
   There is no person that can make me
     feel better.
   My children are like a wasteland.
   They are like that because the enemy won."
17 Zion* spread out her hands.
   There was no person to comfort her.
   The Lord had given orders to Jacob's*
     enemies.
   The Lord ordered Jacob's enemies
     to surround the city.
   Jerusalem has become something dirty.
   She is something dirty among
     those enemies.
18 Now Jerusalem says,
   "I refused to listen to the Lord.
   So the Lord is right for doing these things.
   So listen, all you people!
   Look at my pain!
   My young women and men
     have gone into captivity.
19 I called out to my lovers.
   But they tricked me.
   My priests and my elders
     have died in the city.
   They were looking for food for themselves.
   They wanted to keep themselves alive.
20 "Look at me, Lord. I am in distress!
   My insides are upset!
   My heart feels like it has turned upside down
     inside me!
   My heart feels this way
     because I have been so stubborn!
   In the streets, the sword killed my children.
   Inside the houses, death was there.
21 "Listen to me, because I am groaning!
   I have no person to comfort me.
   All my enemies have heard of my trouble.
   They are happy.
   They are happy that you did this to me.
   You said there would be a time of
     punishment.
   You said you would punish my enemies.
   Now do what you said.
   Let my enemies be like I am now.

---

yoke A pole that was put on the shoulders of men or animals to help them carry or pull things. This often showed that a person was a slave.

virgin daughter of Jerusalem Another name for the city of Jerusalem.

Zion The southeast part of the mountain Jerusalem is built on. Sometimes it means the people of God living in Jerusalem.

Jacob Another name for Israel. See Gen. 32:22-28.

²² "Look at how evil my enemies are.
    Then you can treat them
    the same way you treated me
    because of all my sins.
Do this because I am groaning
    again and again.
Do this because my heart is sick."

The Lord Destroyed Jerusalem

2 Look how the Lord has set
    the Daughter of Zion* under a cloud.
He has thrown the glory of Israel
    from the sky to the ground.
The Lord didn't keep in mind that Israel was
    his footstool,
    on the day of his anger.
² The Lord destroyed the houses of Jacob.*
    He destroyed them without mercy.
He destroyed in his anger
    the fortresses of the Daughter of Judah.*
The Lord threw the kingdom of Judah
    and its rulers to the ground.
He ruined the kingdom of Judah.
³ The Lord was angry and he destroyed
    all the strength of Israel.
He took away his right hand from Israel.
    He did this when the enemy came.
He burned like a flaming fire in Jacob.*
He was like a fire that burns all around.
⁴ The Lord bent his bow like an enemy.
    He held his sword in his right hand.
He killed all the good looking men of Judah.
    The Lord killed them
    as if he were the enemy.
The Lord poured out his anger.
    He poured it out on the tents of Zion.
⁵ The Lord has become like an enemy.
    He has swallowed up Israel.
He has swallowed up all her palaces.
    He has swallowed up all her fortresses.
He has made much sadness
    and crying for the dead
    in the Daughter of Judah.*
⁶ The Lord pulled up his own tent*
    as if it were a garden.

He has ruined the place where the people
    went to meet to worship him.
The Lord has made people forget
    the special assemblies
    and special days of rest* in Zion.
The Lord rejected the king and the priests.
    He was angry and rejected them.
⁷ The Lord rejected his altar.
    He rejected his Holy Place of worship.
He let the enemy pull down the walls
    of the palaces of Jerusalem.
The enemy shouted with joy
    in the Lord's temple.
They made noise, as if it were a holiday.
⁸ The Lord planned to destroy
    the wall of the Daughter of Zion.
He marked the wall with a measuring line
    ₗto show where the wall
    should be torn downﺍ.
He didn't stop himself from destroying.
So he made all the walls
    cry out in sadness.
    Together they wasted away.
⁹ Jerusalem's gates have sunk into the ground.
    He destroyed and smashed the bars
    of the gates.
Her king and princes are in other nations.
    There is no more teaching for them.
Also Jerusalem's prophets have not found
    any visions from the Lord.
¹⁰ The elders of Zion* sit on the ground.
    They sit on the ground and are quiet.
They pour dust on their heads.
    They put on sackcloth.*
The young women of Jerusalem
    bow their heads to the ground in sorrow.
¹¹ My eyes are worn out with tears!
    My insides are upset!
My heart feels like it has been poured
    on the ground!
I feel this way because of the destruction
    of my people.

(Virgin) Daughter of Zion Another name for the city of Jerusalem.
Jacob Another name for Israel. See Gen. 32:22-28.
Daughter of Judah Another name for Jerusalem or the nation of Judah.
his own tent The Lord's temple in Jerusalem.
special days of rest Or, "Sabbaths." This might mean Saturday, or it might mean all of the special days when the people were not supposed to work.
Zion The southeast part of the mountain Jerusalem is built on. Sometimes it means the people of God living in Jerusalem.
sackcloth A kind of cloth that people wore to show they were sad or crying for dead people.

Children and babies are fainting.
    They are fainting in the public squares
        of the city.
12 Those children say to their mothers,
    "Where is bread and wine?"
    They ask this question as they die.
    They die on their mother's laps.
13 Daughter of Zion,*
    what can I compare you to?
    What can I compare you to,
        Virgin Daughter of Zion*?
    How can I comfort you?
    Your destruction is as big as the sea!
    I don't think anyone can heal you.

14 Your prophets saw visions for you.
    But their visions were only worthless lies.
    They didn't preach against your sins.
    They didn't try to make things better.
    They preached messages for you,
        but they were false messages
        that fooled you.

15 The people that pass by on the road
    clap their hands at you in shock.
    They whistle and shake their heads
        at the Daughter of Jerusalem.
    They ask,
    "Is this the city that people called,
        'The Perfectly Beautiful City' and
        'The Joy of all the Earth'?"

16 All your enemies laugh at you.
    They whistle and grind their teeth at you.
    They say,
    "We have swallowed them up!
    This is truly the day we were hoping for.
    We have finally seen this happen."

17 The Lord did what he planned to do.
    He has done what he said he would do.
    He has done what he commanded
        from times of long ago.
    He destroyed, and he had no pity.
    He made your enemies happy
        because of what happened to you.
    He made your enemies strong.

18 Cry out* with your hearts to the Lord!
    Wall of the Daughter of Zion,
        let tears roll down like a stream!
        let your tears roll down day and night.

(Virgin) Daughter of Zion Another name for the city of Jerusalem.
Cry out The Hebrew says, "Their hearts cried out."

Don't stop!
    Don't let your eyes be still!
19 Get up! Cry out in the night!
    Cry out at the beginning of each of the
        parts of the night!
    Pour out your heart as if it were water!
    Pour out your heart before the Lord!
    Lift up your hands in prayer to the Lord.
    Ask him to let your children live.
    Ask him to let your children live that are
        fainting with starvation.
    They are fainting with starvation
        in all the streets of the city.

20 Look at me, Lord!
    See who it is
        that you have treated this way!
    Let me ask this question:
    Should women eat the children
        they have given birth to?
    Should women eat the children
        that they have cared for?
    Should priest and prophet
        be killed in the temple of the Lord?
21 Young men and old men
    lie on the ground in the streets of the city.
    My young women and young men
        have been killed by the sword.
    You, Lord, killed them on the day
        of your anger!
    You killed them without mercy!

22 You invited terror to come to me
        from all around.
    You invited terror like you were inviting it
        to a holiday.
    No person escaped
        on the day of the Lord's anger.
    My enemy has killed
        those that I raised and brought up.

A Man Considers the Meaning of His Suffering

3 I am a man that has seen much trouble.
    The Lord beat us with a stick.
        And I saw it happen!
2 The Lord led and brought me
    into darkness, not light.
3 The Lord turned his hand against me.
    He did this again and again, all day.
4 He wore out my flesh and skin.
    He broke my bones.
5 The Lord built up bitterness
    and trouble against me.

He made bitterness and trouble
  come all around me.
6 He made me sit in the dark.
  He made me like some person
    that has been dead a long time.
7 The Lord shut me in, so I could not get out.
  He put heavy chains on me.
8 Even when I cry out and ask for help,
    the Lord does not listen to my prayer.
9 He has blocked up my path with stones.
  He has made my path crooked.
10 The Lord is like a bear about to attack me.
  He is like a lion that is in a hiding place.
11 The Lord led me off my path.
  He tore me to pieces.
  He ruined me.
12 He made his bow ready.
  He made me the target for his arrows.
13 He shot me in the stomach.
  He shot me with his arrows.
14 I have become a joke to all of my people.
  All day long they sing songs about me
    and make fun of me.
15 The Lord gave me this poison *(punishment)*
    to drink.
  He filled me with this bitter drink.
16 The Lord pushed my teeth
    into rocky ground.
  He pushed me into the dirt.
17 I thought I would never have peace again.
  I forgot about good things.
18 I said to myself,
  "I no longer have any hope
    that the Lord will help me."
19 Lord, remember,
  I am very sad.
  And I have no home.
  Remember the bitter poison *(punishment)*
    that you gave me.
20 I remember well all my troubles.
  And I am very sad.
21 But then I think of something else,
    then I have hope. What I think of is this:
22 The Lord's love and kindness never ends.*
  His compassion never ends.
23 Every morning he shows it in new ways!
  Lord, you are so very true and loyal!
24 I say to myself,
  "The Lord is my God,
    and I trust him."*

25 The Lord is good to people
    that wait for him.
  The Lord is good to people
    that look for him.
26 It is good for a person to wait quietly
    for the Lord to save him.
27 It is good for a person to wear the yoke*
    of the Lord.
  It is good for a person to wear that yoke
    from the time he is young.
28 That person should sit alone and be quiet
    when the Lord puts his yoke on him.
29 That person should bow to the Lord
    with his face to the ground.
  Maybe there is still hope.
30 That person should turn his cheek
    to the one that hits him.
  That person should let people insult him.
31 That person should remember that
    the Lord does not reject people forever.
32 When the Lord punishes,
    he also has mercy.
  He has mercy because of his great love
    and kindness.
33 The Lord does not want to punish people.
  He does not like to make people unhappy.
34 The Lord does not like these things:
  He does not like for someone to crush
    all the prisoners of the earth under his feet.
35 He does not like for someone
    to be unfair to another person.
  But some people do those bad things
    right in front of God Most High.
36 The Lord does not like for a person
    to cheat another person.
  The Lord does not like any of these things.
37 Nobody can say something
    and have it happen,
    unless the Lord orders it to happen.
38 God Most High commands
    both good and bad things to happen.
39 No person alive can complain
    when the Lord punishes him for his sins.
40 Let us check and see what we have done.
  Then let us turn back to the Lord.
41 Let us lift up our hearts and our hands
    to the God of heaven.

---

never ends Literally, "we don't come to an end."
I belong ... him. Or, "The Lord is my portion and I trust him."

yoke A pole that was put on the shoulders of men or animals to help them carry or pull things. This often showed that a person was a slave.

⁴² Let us say to him,
"We have sinned and have been stubborn.
Because of this, you have not forgiven us.
⁴³ You wrapped yourself with anger.
You chased us.
You killed us without mercy!
⁴⁴ You wrapped yourself in a cloud.
You did that so that no prayer
could get through.
⁴⁵ You made us like garbage and dirt
to the other nations.
⁴⁶ All of our enemies
speak angrily to us.
⁴⁷ We have been frightened.
We have fallen into a pit.
We have been hurt bad!
We have been broken!"
⁴⁸ My eyes flow with streams of tears!
I cry because of the destruction
of my people!
⁴⁹ My eyes will flow without stopping!
I will keep on crying!
⁵⁰ I will continue to cry
until you look down and see us, Lord!
I will continue to cry
until you see us from heaven!
⁵¹ My eyes make me sad,
when I see what happened
to the girls in my city.
⁵² Those people were my enemies
for no good reason,
but they hunted me like a bird.
⁵³ They threw me into a pit
while I was still alive.
They threw stones at me.
⁵⁴ Water came up over my head.
I said to myself,
"I am finished."
⁵⁵ Lord, I called your name.
I called out your name
from the bottom of the pit.
⁵⁶ You heard my voice.
You didn't close your ears.
You didn't refuse to rescue me.
⁵⁷ You came to me
on the day that I called out to you.
You said to me,
"Don't be afraid."
⁵⁸ Lord, you defended me.
You bought back my life for me.
⁵⁹ Lord, you have seen my trouble.
Now judge my case for me.
⁶⁰ You have seen how my enemies
have hurt me.

You have seen all the evil plans
that they made against me.
⁶¹ You heard them insult me, Lord.
You have heard all the evil plans
that they made against me.
⁶² The words and the thoughts of my enemies
are against me all the time.
⁶³ When they sit down and when they stand up.
Lord, look how they make fun of me!
⁶⁴ Give them back what they deserve, Lord!
Pay them back for what they have done!
⁶⁵ Give them stubbornness of heart!
Then put your curse on them!
⁶⁶ Chase them in anger!
Destroy them!
Destroy them from under the sky, Lord!

The Horrors of the Attack on Jerusalem

4 See how the gold has grown dark.
See how the good gold is changed.
There are jewels* scattered all around.
They are scattered at every street corner.
² The people of Zion* were worth a lot.
They were worth their weight in gold.
But now the enemy treats those people
like old clay jars.
The enemy treats them
like clay jars made by a potter.
³ Even a wild dog feeds her babies.
Even the jackal lets her pups suck
at her breast.
But the daughter of my people* is cruel.
She is like the ostrich
that lives in the desert.
⁴ The little baby's tongue
sticks to the roof of its mouth from thirst.
Young children ask for bread.
But no one gives any bread to them.
⁵ The people that at one time ate rich food
now are dying in the streets.
The people that grew up
wearing nice red clothes
now pick through garbage piles.
⁶ The sin of the daughter of my people*
was very great.

jewels The meaning of the Hebrew word here is uncertain.
Zion The southeast part of the mountain Jerusalem is built on.
Sometimes it means the people of God living in Jerusalem.
daughter of my people This means the women of Jerusalem or
the city itself.

Their sin was greater than the sins
of Sodom and Gomorrah.*
Sodom and Gomorrah
were destroyed suddenly.
No human hand caused that destruction.*
7 Some of the men of Judah
were dedicated to God in a special way.
Those men were very pure.
They were whiter than snow.
They were whiter than milk.
Their bodies were red like coral.
Their beards were sapphire stones.
8 But now their faces are blacker than soot.
No one even recognizes them in the streets.
Their skin is wrinkled over their bones.
Their skin is like wood.
9 The people that were killed by the sword
had it better than
the people that were killed by famine.
The starving people were very sad.
They were hurt.
They died because they got no food
from the field.
10 At that time, even very nice women
cooked their own children.
Those children became food
for their mothers.
This happened when my people
were destroyed.
11 The Lord used all of his anger.
He poured out all his anger.
He made a fire in Zion.*
That fire burned down Zion
to its foundations.
12 The kings of the earth could not believe
what had happened.
The people of the world could not believe
what had happened.
They could not believe
that enemies would be able to come
through the city gates of Jerusalem.
13 This happened because the prophets
of Jerusalem sinned.
This happened because the priests
of Jerusalem did evil things.
Those people were shedding blood
in the city of Jerusalem.

They were shedding the blood
of good people.
14 The prophets and priests walked around
like blind men in the streets.
They had become dirty with blood.
No one could even touch their clothes
because they were dirty.
15 People shouted,
"Go away!
Go away!
Don't touch us."
Those people wandered around
and had no home.
People in other nations said,
"We don't want them to live with us."
16 The Lord himself destroyed those people.
He didn't look after them anymore.
He didn't respect the priests.
He was not friendly to the elders of Judah.
17 We have worn out our eyes
looking for help.
But no help comes.
We kept on looking for a nation to save us.
We kept watch from our watch tower,
But no nation came to us.
18 Our enemies hunted us all the time.
We could not even go out into the streets.
Our end came near. Our time was up.
Our end came!
19 The men that chased us
were faster than eagles in the sky.
Those men chased us into the mountains.
They hid in the desert to catch us.
20 The king was very important to us.
He was like the breath we breath.
But the king was trapped by them.
The king was chosen by the Lord himself.
We had said about the king,
"We will live in his shadow.
He protects us from the nations."
21 Be happy, people of Edom.
Be happy, you people that live
in the land of Uz.
But remember, the cup of the Lord's anger
will come around to you, too.
When you drink from that cup *(punishment)*,
you will get drunk
and will make yourselves naked.
22 Your punishment is complete, Zion.*
You will not go into captivity again.

dom and Gomorrah Two cities that God destroyed because
the people were so evil.
human hand caused that destruction The Hebrew of this
line is unclear.
on The southeast part of the mountain Jerusalem is built on.
Sometimes it means the people of God living in Jerusalem.

Zion The southeast part of the mountain Jerusalem is built on.
Sometimes it means the people of God living in Jerusalem.

But the Lord will punish your sins,
people of Edom.
He will uncover your sins.

A Prayer to the Lord

5 Remember, Lord, what happened to us.
Look and see our disgrace.
2 Our land has been turned over to strangers.
Our houses have been given to foreigners.
3 We have become orphans.
We have no father.
Our mothers have become like widows.
4 We have to buy the water that we drink.
We have to pay for the wood that we use.
5 We are forced to wear a yoke* on our necks.
We get tired, and we have no rest.
6 We made an agreement with Egypt.
We also made an agreement with Assyria
to get enough bread.
7 Our ancestors sinned against you.
Now they are dead.
Now we are suffering because of their sins.
8 Slaves have become our rulers.
No person can save us from them.
9 We risk our lives to get food.
There are men in the desert with swords.
10 Our skin is hot like an oven.
We have a high fever
because of our hunger.
11 The enemy raped the women of Zion.
They raped the women
in the cities of Judah.
12 The enemy hanged our princes.
They didn't honor our elders.
13 The enemy made our young men
grind grain at the mill.
Our young men stumbled
under loads of wood.
14 The elders no longer sit at the gates
of the city.
The young men no longer make music.
15 We have no more joy in our hearts.
Our dancing was changed into
crying for the dead.
16 The crown has fallen from our head.
Things have gone bad for us
because we sinned.
17 Because of these things,
our hearts have become sick,
our eyes cannot see clearly.
18 Mount Zion is a wasteland.
Foxes run around on Mount Zion.
19 But you rule forever, Lord.
Your kingly chair lasts forever and ever.
20 You seem to have forgotten us forever, Lord.
You seem to have left us alone
for such a long time.
21 Bring us back to you, Lord.
We will gladly come back to you.
Make our lives like they were before.
22 You were very angry at us.
Have you completely rejected us?

---

yoke A pole that was put on the shoulders of men or animals to help them carry or pull things. This often showed that a person was a slave.

Ezekiel

INTRODUCTION

1 ¹⁻³I am the priest, Ezekiel son of Buzzi. I was in exile* by the Kebar Canal in Babylonia when the skies opened up and I saw visions* of God. This was on the fifth day of the fourth month *(July)* of the thirtieth year.*

During King Jehoiachin's fifth year in exile,* on the fifth day of the month, the word of the Lord came to Ezekiel. The Lord's power came on him at that place.

The Chariot of the Lord—God's Throne

⁴I *(Ezekiel)* saw a big storm coming from the north. It was a big cloud with a strong wind, and there was fire flashing from it. Light was shining out all around it. It looked like hot metal* glowing in a fire. ⁵Inside the cloud, there were four animals that looked like people. ⁶But each animal had four faces and four wings. ⁷Their legs were straight. Their feet looked like cow's feet. And they sparkled like polished brass. ⁸Under their wings were human arms. There were four animals. And each animal had four faces and four wings. The wings touched each other. The animals did not turn when they moved. They went in the direction they were looking.

¹⁰Each animal had four faces. ⌊In the front⌋ they each had a man's face. On the right side there was a lion's face. On the left side there was a bull's face. And on the back there was an eagle's face. ¹¹The wings of the animals were spread out over them. With two of the wings each animal reached out to touch the animals near it and with the other two wings it covered its body. ¹²Each animal went in the direction it was looking. They went wherever the wind* caused them to go. But they did not turn when they moved. ¹³That is what the animals looked like.

Inside the area between the animals, there was something that looked like burning coals of fire. This fire was like small torches that kept moving around among the animals. The fire glowed brightly and lightning flashed from it! ¹⁴The animals ran back and forth—fast like lightning!*

¹⁵⁻¹⁶I was looking at the animals when I noticed four wheels that touched the ground. There was one wheel at each animal. All of the wheels looked the same. The wheels looked like they were made from a clear, yellow jewel. They looked like there was a wheel inside a wheel. ¹⁷⌊The wheels⌋ could ⌊turn to⌋ move in any direction. ⌊But the animals⌋ did not turn when they moved.* ¹⁸The rims of the wheels were tall and frightening! There were eyes all over the rims of all four wheels.

¹⁹The wheels always moved with the animals. If the animals went up into the air, the wheels went with them. ²⁰They went wherever the wind wanted them to go, and the wheels went with them. Why? Because the wind *(power)* of the animal was in the wheels. ²¹So if the animals moved, the wheels moved. If the animals stopped, the wheels stopped. If the wheels went into the air, the animals went with them. Why? Because the wind* was in the wheels.

²²There was an amazing thing over the heads of animals. It was like a bowl* turned upside down.

---

exile Being forced to live in a foreign country. King Nebuchadnezzar forced many Jewish people to leave Judah and live in foreign countries.

vision(s) Like a dream that God used to speak to people.

thirtieth year We are not sure what this year refers to. It might be Ezekiel's age and it is probably the same as the fifth year of the exile, that is, the summer of 593B.C. It might be that Ezekiel is beginning his book with the last vision he saw of God, and it was the same as the first vision he saw.

hot metal We are not sure of the meaning of this Hebrew word. It might mean, "melted copper" or "amber."

wind Or, "Spirit."

The animals ... lightning! Or, "And there was something like lighting shooting back and forth among the animals."

The wheels ... moved. Or, "The wheels could move in any four directions, but they did not turn when they moved."

bowl This Hebrew word is the same word used in Gen. 1:6-7 to describe the dome of the sky.

And the bowl was clear like crystal! ²³Under this bowl each animal had wings reaching out it to the animals next to it. Two wings spread out one way and two wings spread out in the other way, covering its body.

²⁴Then I heard the wings. Every time the animals moved, their wings made a very loud noise. They were loud like a lot of water rushing by. They were loud like ₍God₎ All-Powerful. They were loud like an army or a crowd of people. And when the animals stopped moving, they put their wings down ₍by their side₎.

²⁵The animals stopped moving and lowered their wings. And there was another loud sound. That sound came from above the bowl over their heads. ²⁶There was something that looked like a throne on top of that bowl. It was blue like sapphire. And there was something that looked like a man sitting on that throne! ²⁷I looked at him from his waist up. He looked like hot metal.* It looked like fire all around him! And I looked at him from his waist down. It looked like fire with a glow that was shining all around him. ²⁸The light shining around him was like a rainbow in a cloud. It was the Glory of the Lord. As soon as I saw that, I fell to the ground. I bowed with my face to the ground. And then I heard a voice speaking to me.

2 The voice said, "Son of man,* stand up and I will speak with you."

²Then a wind came and lifted me up on my feet. And I listened to the person *(God)* that spoke to me. ³He said to me, "Son of man, I am sending you to speak to the family of Israel. Those people turned against me many times. And their ancestors turned against me. They have sinned against me many times—and they are still sinning against me today. ⁴I am sending you to speak to those people. But they are very stubborn. They are very hard headed. But you must speak to those people. You must say, 'The Lord our Master says these things.' ⁵But those people won't listen to you. They won't stop sinning against me. Why? Because they are a very rebellious people—they always turn against me! But you must say those things so they will know that there is a prophet* living among them.

⁶"Son of man,* don't be afraid of those people. Don't be afraid of the things they say. It is true, they will turn against you and try to hurt you. They will be like thorns. You will think you are living with scorpions.* But don't be afraid of the things they say. They are a rebellious people. But don't be afraid of them. ⁷You must tell them the things I say. I know they won't listen to you. And they won't stop sinning against me! Why? Because they are a rebellious people.

⁸"Son of man,* you must listen to the things I say to you. Don't turn against me like those rebellious people. Open your mouth and ₍accept the words I give you and then speak those words to the people₎. Eat these words."

⁹Then I *(Ezekiel)* saw an arm reach out towards me. It was holding a scroll* with words written on it. ¹⁰I rolled the scroll open and there were words written on the front and on the back. There were all kinds of sad songs, sad stories, and warnings.

3 ₍God₎ said to me, "Son of man,* eat what you see. Eat this scroll,* and then go tell these things to the family of Israel."

²So I opened my mouth and he put the scroll into my mouth. ³Then ₍God₎ said, "Son of man, I am giving you this scroll. Swallow it! Let that scroll fill your body."

So I ate the scroll.* It was as sweet as honey in my mouth.

⁴Then ₍God₎ said to me, "Son of man,* go to the family of Israel. Speak my words to them. ⁵I am not sending you to some foreigners you can't understand. You don't have to learn another language. I am sending you to the family of Israel! ⁶I am not sending you to many different countries where people speak languages you can't understand. If you went to those people and spoke to them, they would listen to you. But you won't have to learn those hard languages. ⁷No! I am sending you to the family of Israel. Only, these people have hard heads—they are very stubborn! And the people of Israel will refuse to listen to you. They don't want to listen to me! ⁸But I will make you just as stubborn as they are. Your head will be just as hard as theirs! ⁹A diamond is harder than flint rock. In the same way, your head will be harder than theirs. You will be more stubborn, so you won't be afraid of those people. You won't be

---

hot metal We are not sure of the meaning of this Hebrew word. It might mean, "melted copper" or "amber."

Son of man This was usually just a way of saying "a person," or "a human being." But here this is a title for the man, Ezekiel.

prophet A person called by God to be a special servant. God used dreams and visions to show them things to teach to the people.

scorpion(s) Insects with stingers in their tails that cause pain.

Scroll(s) A long roll of leather or papyrus *(paper)* used for writing books, letters, and legal documents.

afraid of those people that always turn against me."

¹⁰Then ⌊God⌋ said to me, "Son of man,* you must listen to every word I say to you. And you must remember those words. ¹¹Then go to all of your people that are in exile.* Go to them and say, 'The Lord our Master says these things.' They won't listen and they won't stop sinning, ⌊but you must tell them these things⌋."

¹²Then the wind* lifted me up and I heard a voice behind me. It was very loud, like thunder. ⌊It said,⌋ "Blessed is the Glory of the Lord!" ¹³Then the wings of the animals began moving. The wings made a very loud noise as they touched each other. And the wheels in front of them began making a loud noise—it was loud like thunder. ¹⁴The wind* lifted me and took me away. I left that place. I was very sad and upset in my spirit.* But I felt Lord's power in me! ¹⁵I went to the people of Israel that were forced to live in Tel Aviv* by the Kebar Canal. I sat there among them for seven days, shocked and silent.

¹⁶After seven days, the word of the Lord came to me. He said, ¹⁷"Son of man,* I am making you a watchman* for Israel. I will tell you about bad things that will happen to them. And you must warn Israel about those things. ¹⁸If I say, 'This bad man will die!' Then you must warn him! You must tell him to change his life and stop doing bad things. If you don't warn that person, then he will die. He will die because he sinned. But I will also make you responsible for his death! Why? Because you did not go to him and save his life.

¹⁹"Maybe you will warn a person and tell him to change his life and stop doing bad things. If that person refuses to listen to you, then that person will die. He will die because he sinned. But you warned him, so you saved your own life.

²⁰"Or maybe a good man will stop being good. I might put something in front of him that causes him to fall *(sin)*. He will start to do bad things, so he will die. He will die because he is sinning and you did not warn him. I will make you responsible

for his death. And people won't remember all the good things he did.

²¹"But if you warn the good person and tell him to stop sinning, and if he stops sinning, then he won't die. Why? Because you warned him and he listened. In this way, you saved your own life."

²²The Lord's power came to me. He said to me, "Get up and go to the valley.* I will speak to you in that place."

²³So I got up and went out to the valley. The Glory of the Lord* was there—just like I had seen it by the Kebar Canal. So I bowed with my face to the ground. ²⁴But a wind* came and lifted me up on my feet. He said to me, "Go home and lock yourself in your house. ²⁵Son of man,* people will come with ropes and tie you up. They won't let you go out among the people. ²⁶I will make your tongue stick to the roof of your mouth—you won't be able to talk. So those people won't have any person to teach them that they are doing wrong. Why? Because those people are always turning against me. ²⁷But I will talk to you. And then I will allow you to speak. But you must say to them, 'The Lord our Master says these things.' If a person wants to listen, then fine. If a person doesn't want to listen, then fine. But those people always turn against me.

4 Son of man,* take a brick. Scratch a picture on it. Draw a picture of a city—the city Jerusalem. ²And then act like you are an army surrounding the city. Build a dirt wall around the city ⌊to help you attack it⌋. Build a dirt road leading up to the city wall. Bring battering rams* and set up army camps around the city. ³And then take an iron pan and put it between you and the city. It will be like an iron wall separating you and the city. In this way, you will show that you are against that city. You will surround and attack that city. Why? Because this is an example for the family of Israel. ⌊It will show that I *(God)* will destroy Jerusalem.⌋

⁴"Then you must lie down on your left side. You ⌊must do the thing that shows that you⌋ are taking the sins of the people of Israel on yourself. You will carry that guilt for as many days as you lie on your left side. ⁵You must bear the guilt of Israel for 390 days.* In this way, I am telling you

---

Son of man This was usually just a way of saying "a person," or "a human being." Here this is a title for the man, Ezekiel.

exile Being forced to live in a foreign country. King Nebuchadnezzar forced many Jewish people to leave Judah and live in foreign countries.

wind Or, "Spirit."

spirit Or, "wind."

Tel Aviv This was a place outside of Israel. We are not sure where it is exactly. The name means "Spring Hill."

watchman A guard that stood on the city wall and looked for enemy soldiers. If he saw trouble coming, he would warn the people in the city.

the valley Possibly Jezreel Valley which is often called simply, "The Valley." This is a fertile area in Israel where many battles were fought.

Glory of the Lord One of the forms God used when he appeared to people. This was like a bright shining light.

battering rams Heavy logs that soldiers used to break holes into the gates or walls around a city.

how long Israel will be punished, one day equals one year. ⁶"After that time, you will lie on your right side for 40 days. This time you will bear the guilt of Judah for 40 days. One day equals one year. I am telling you ˪how long Judah must be punished˩."

⁷˪God again spoke. He said,˩ "Now, roll up your sleeve and raise your arm over the brick. Act like you are attacking the city Jerusalem. Do this to show that you are speaking as my messenger to the people. ⁸Now look, I am tying ropes on you. You won't be able to roll over from one side to another until your attack against the city* is finished."

⁹˪God also said,˩ "You must get some grain to make bread. Get some wheat, barley, beans, lentils, millet, and spelt. Mix all those things together in one bowl and grind them to make flour. You will use this flour to make bread. You will eat only this bread during the 390 days that you lie on your side. ¹⁰You will be allowed to use only 1 cup* of that flour each day to make bread. You will eat that bread from time to time throughout the day. ¹¹And you can drink only 3 cups* of water each day. You can drink it from time to time throughout the day. ¹²You must make your bread each day. You must get dry human dung and burn it. Then you must cook the bread over this burning dung. You must eat this bread in front of the people." ¹³Then the Lord said, "This will show that the family of Israel will eat unclean bread* in foreign countries. And I forced them to leave Israel and go to those countries!"

¹⁴Then I (Ezekiel) said, "Oh, but Lord my Master, I have never eaten any unclean food. I have never eaten meat from an animal that died from a disease or from an animal that was killed by a wild animal. I have never eaten unclean meat—not from the time I was a little baby until today. None of that bad meat ever entered my mouth."

¹⁵Then God said to me, "Ok! I will let you use dry cow dung to cook your bread. You don't have to use dry human dung."

¹⁶Then God said to me, "Son of man,* I am destroying Jerusalem's supply of bread. People will have only a little bread to eat. They will be very worried ˪about their food supply˩. And they will have only a little water to drink. They will be very scared when they drink that water. ¹⁷Why? Because there won't be enough food and water for the people. People will be terrified of each other— they will see each other wasting away because of their sins."

5 ¹⁻²Son of man,* after your time of hunger* you must do these things. You must get a sharp sword. Use that sword like a barber's razor. Shave off your hair and beard. Put the hair on a scale and weigh it. Separate your hair into three equal parts. Put one third of your hair on the brick that has the picture of the city on it. Burn that hair in that 'city.' ˪This shows that some of the people will die inside the city.˩ Then use a sword and cut one third of your hair into small pieces all around the city (brick). ˪This will show that some of the people will die outside the city.˩ Then throw one third of your hair into the air—let the wind blow it far away. ˪This will show that˩ I will pull out my sword and chase some of the people into faraway countries. ³But then you must get a few of those hairs and wrap them up in your robe. ˪This will show that I will save a few of my people.˩ ⁴You must also get some more of those hairs and throw them into the fire. ˪This will show that˩ a fire will start there and destroy the whole house of Israel.*

⁵Then the Lord my Master said to me, "That ˪brick˩ is a picture of Jerusalem. I put Jerusalem in the middle of other nations. And there are countries all around her. ⁶The people ˪of Jerusalem˩ rebelled against my commands. They were worse than any of the other nations! They broke more of my laws than any of the people in the countries around them. They refused to listen to my commands! They did not obey my laws!"

⁷So, the Lord my Master says, "˪I will do terrible things to you! Why?˩ Because you did not obey my laws. You did not obey my commands. You broke more of my laws than the people that live around you! And you even did things those

---

your attack against the city This is a word play. The Hebrew word can mean, "time of hunger", "time of trouble," or "attack against a city."
1 cup Literally, "20 shekels."
3 cups Literally, "1/6 hin."
unclean bread Bread that touched something unclean. If a person ate this bread, then that person could not join in worshiping God. See Lev. 11-15 for rules about clean and unclean things.

your time of hunger Or, "your attack on the city." See Ez. 4:8.
house of Israel This probably means the people of the northern ten family groups of Israel.

people say are wrong!" ⁸So the Lord my Master says, "So now, even I am against you! And I will punish you while those other people watch. ⁹I will do things to you that I have never done before. And I will never do those terrible things again! Why? Because you did so many terrible things. ¹⁰People in Jerusalem will be so hungry that parents will eat their own children. and children will eat their own parents. I will punish you in many ways. And the people that are left alive, I will scatter them to the winds.

¹¹The Lord my Master says, "⌊Jerusalem,⌋ I promise by my life ⌊that I will punish you⌋! I promise that I will punish you! Why? Because you did terrible things to my Holy Place. You did horrible things that made it dirty! I will punish you! I won't show any mercy. I will not feel sorry for you! ¹²One third of your people will die inside the city from diseases and hunger. One third of your people will die in battle outside the city. And then I will pull out my sword and chase one third of your people into faraway countries. ¹³Only then will I stop being angry at your people. I will know that they have been punished for the bad things they did to me. And they will know that I am the Lord, and that I spoke to them because of my strong love* for them!"

¹⁴⌊God said,⌋ "⌊Jerusalem,⌋ I will destroy you—you will be nothing but a pile of rocks. The people around you will make fun of you. Every person that walks by will make fun of you. ¹⁵People around you will make fun of you, but you will also be a lesson for them. They will see that I was angry and punished you. I was very angry. I warned you. I, the Lord, told you what I would do! ¹⁶I told you I would send you terrible times of hunger. I told you I would send you things that would destroy you. I told you that I would take away your supply of food and that those times of hunger would come again and again. ¹⁷I told you I would send hunger and wild animals against you that would kill your children. I told you there would be disease and death everywhere in the city. I told you I would bring those enemy soldiers to fight against you. I, the Lord, told you all these things would happen—⌊and they will happen⌋!"

6 Then the word of the Lord came to me again. ²He said, "Son of man,* turn towards the mountains of Israel. Speak against them for me. ³Tell those mountains these things:

'Mountains of Israel, listen to this message from the Lord my Master! The Lord my Master says these things to the hills and mountains, and to the ravines and valleys. Look! I (God) am bringing the enemy to fight against you. I will destroy your high places.* ⁴Your altars* will be broken into pieces! Your incense* altars will be smashed! And I will throw down your dead bodies in front of your filthy idols. ⁵I will put the dead bodies of the people of Israel in front of their filthy idols. I will scatter your bones around your altars. ⁶Bad things will happen wherever your people live. Their cities will become piles of rock. Their high places will be destroyed. Why? So that those places of worship will never be used again. Those altars will all be destroyed. People will never worship those filthy idols again. Those incense altars will be smashed. All the things you made will be completely destroyed! ⁷Your people will be killed. And then you will know that I am the Lord!"

⁸⌊God said,⌋ "But I will let a few of your people escape. They will live in other countries for a short time. I will scatter them and force them to live in other countries. ⁹Then those survivors* will be taken prisoners. They will be forced to live in other countries. But those survivors will remember me. I broke their spirit.* They will hate themselves for the bad things they did. In the past, they turned away from me and left me. They chased after their filthy idols. They were like a woman leaving her husband and running after some other man. They did many terrible things. ¹⁰But they will know that I am the Lord. And they will know that if I say that I will do something, then I will do it! They will know that I caused all of the bad things that happened to them."

¹¹Then the Lord my Master said to me, "Clap your hands and stamp your feet. Speak against all

---

strong love   The Hebrew word means strong feelings like love, hate, anger, zeal, or jealousy.

high places   Places for worshiping God or false gods. These places were often on the hills and mountains.

altar(s)   A stone table used for burning sacrifices offered as gifts to God.

incense   Special dried tree sap. Burned to make a sweet-smelling smoke, it was offered as a gift to God.

survivor(s)   People that escaped some disaster. Here this means the Jewish people that survived the destruction of Judah and Israel by its enemy armies.

spirit   Literally, "heart."

the terrible things that the people of Israel have done. Warn them that they will be killed by disease and hunger. Tell them they will be killed in war. ¹²People far away will die from disease. People near this place will be killed with swords. And the people that are left in the city will starve to death. Only then will I stop being angry. ¹³And only then will you know that I am the Lord. You will know this when you see your dead bodies in front of your filthy idols and around their altars. Those bodies will be near every one of your places of worship—on every high hill and mountain, under every green tree and every oak tree with leaves. In all those places you offered your sacrifices. They were a sweet smell for your filthy idols. ¹⁴But I will raise my arm over you people and punish you and your people, wherever they live! I will destroy your country! It will be emptier than Diblah Desert.* Then they will know that I am the Lord!"

7 Then the word of the Lord came to me. ²He said, "Now, Son of man,* here is a message from the Lord my Master. This message is for the land of Israel.

    The end.
    The end is coming.
    The whole country will be destroyed.
³ Your end is coming now!
    I will show how angry I am at you.
    I will punish you for the bad things you did.
    I will make you pay for all the terrible
        things you did.
⁴ I won't show you any mercy.
    I won't feel sorry for you.
    I am punishing you for the bad things
        you did.
    You have done such terrible things.
    Now, you will know that I am the Lord."

⁵The Lord my Master said these things. "There will be one disaster after another! ⁶The end is coming, and it will come quickly! ⁷You people living in Israel, do you hear the whistle? The enemy is coming. That time of punishment is coming very soon! The noise of the enemy is getting louder and louder on the mountains. ⁸Very soon now, I will show you how angry I am. I will show all of my anger against you. I will punish you for the bad things you did. I will make you pay for all the terrible things you did. ⁹I won't show you any mercy. I won't feel sorry for you. I am punishing you for the bad things you did. You have done such terrible things. Now, you will know that I am the Lord.

¹⁰"That time of punishment has come. Do you hear the whistle? ⌊God gave the signal. The punishment is starting.⌋ The stick has started sprouting.* The proud ⌊king⌋ *(Nebuchadnezzar)* has already begun to grow more powerful. ¹¹That violent man is ready to punish those evil people. There are very many people ⌊in Israel⌋—but he is not one of them. He is not a person in that crowd. He is not some important leader from those people.

¹²"That time of punishment has come. That day is here. People that buy things won't be happy. And people that sell things won't feel bad about selling them. Why? Because that terrible punishment will happen to every person. ¹³The people that sold their property* will never go back to it. Even if a person escapes alive, he will never go back to his property. Why? Because this vision* is for the whole crowd of people. So even if a person escapes alive, it won't make people feel better.

¹⁴"They will blow the trumpet to warn the people. The people will get ready for battle. But they won't go out to fight. Why? Because I will show the whole crowd how angry I am. ¹⁵The enemy with his sword is outside the city. Disease and hunger is inside the city. If a person goes out into the fields, then an enemy soldier will kill him. If he stays in the city, hunger and disease will destroy him. ¹⁶But some of the people will escape. Those survivors will run to the mountains. But those people won't be happy. They will be sad for all their sins. They will cry and make sad noises like doves. ¹⁷People will be too tired and sad to raise

---

Diblah Desert This is probably "Riblah Desert."
Son of man This was usually just a way of saying "a person," or "a human being." But here this is a title for the man, Ezekiel.

The stick ... sprouting. This is a picture of God using the enemy like a stick to punish Israel.
sold their property In ancient Israel property did not belong to a person, it belonged to a family. A person might sell his property, but at the time of Jubilees his family would get the land back. Here, Ezekiel says the people will never get their property again.
vision Something like a dream that God used to speak to people.

their arms. Their legs will be like water. ¹⁸They will wear clothes of sadness and be covered with fear. You will see the shame on every face. They will shave their heads ⌊to show their sadness⌋. ¹⁹They will throw their silver ⌊idols⌋ into the streets. They will treat their gold ⌊statues⌋ like dirty rags! Why? Because those things will not be able to save them when the Lord shows his anger. Those things were nothing but a trap that caused the people to fall *(sin)*. Those things will not give food to the people and they won't put food in their bellies. ²⁰"Those people used their beautiful jewelry and made an idol. They were proud of that statue. They made their terrible statues. They made those filthy things. So I *(God)* will throw them away like a dirty rag. ²¹I will let strangers take them. Those strangers will make fun of them. Those strangers will kill some of the people and take others away as prisoners. ²²I will turn my head away from them—I won't look at them. Those strangers will ruin my temple—they will go into the secret parts of that holy building and make it not holy.

²³"Make chains ⌊for the prisoners⌋! Why? Because many people will be punished for killing other people. There will be violence every place in the city. ²⁴I will bring evil people from other nations. And those evil people will get all the houses of the people of Israel. I will stop all of you powerful people from being so proud. Those people from other nations will get all your places of worship.*

²⁵"You people will shake with fear. You will look for peace, but there will be none. ²⁶You will hear one sad story after another. You will hear nothing but bad news. You will look for a prophet and ask him for a vision.* ⌊But there won't be one.⌋ The priests will have nothing to teach you. And the elders *(leaders)* won't have any good advice to give you. ²⁷Your king will be crying for the people that died. The leaders will wear clothes of sadness. The common people will be very scared. Why? Because I will pay them back for the things they did. I will decide their punishment. And I will punish them. Then those people will know that I am the Lord."

8 One day I *(Ezekiel)* was sitting in my house, and the elders *(leaders)* of Judah were sitting there in front of me. This was on the fifth day of the sixth month *(September)* of the sixth year ⌊of exile⌋.* Suddenly, the power of the Lord my Master came on me. ²I saw something that looked like fire. ⌊It looked like a man's body.⌋ From the waist down, he was like fire. From the waist up, he was bright and shining like hot metal* in a fire. ³Then I saw something that looked like an arm. The arm reached out and grabbed me by the hair on my head. Then the wind* lifted me into the air. And in God's vision,* he took me to Jerusalem. He took me to the inner gate—the gate that is on the north side. The statue that makes God jealous is by that gate. ⁴But the Glory of the God of Israel was there. The Glory looked just like the vision I saw in the valley ⌊by the Kebar Canal⌋.

⁵⌊God⌋ spoke to me. He said, "Son of man,* look towards the north!" So I looked towards the north. And there, north of the Altar Gate by the entrance, was that statue that made God jealous.

⁶Then ⌊God⌋ said to me, "Son of man,* do you see what terrible things the people of Israel are doing? They built that thing here, right next to my temple! And if you come with me, you will see even more terrible things!"

⁷So I went to the entrance to the courtyard, and I saw a hole in the wall. ⁸⌊God⌋ said to me, "Son of man,* make a hole in the wall." So I made a hole in the wall. And there I saw a door.

⁹Then ⌊God⌋ said to me, "Go in and look at the terrible, evil things that the people are doing here." ¹⁰So I went in and looked. I saw statues of all kinds of reptiles* and animals that you hate to think about. Those statues were the filthy idols that the people of Israel worshiped. There were pictures of those animals carved all around on every wall!

¹¹Then I noticed that Jaazaniah son of Shapham and the 70 elders *(leaders)* of Israel were there with the people worshiping in that place. There they were, right at the front of the people! And each leader had his own incense* dish in his hand. The smoke from the burning incense was rising into the air. ¹²Then ⌊God⌋ said to me, "Son of

---

Those people ... places of worship. Or, "Those people will make your places of worship dirty and not holy."
vision Like a dream that God used to speak to people.
sixth year of exile This is the fall of 592 B.C.
hot metal We are not sure of the meaning of this Hebrew word. It might mean, "melted copper" or "amber."
wind Or, "Spirit."
Son of man This was usually just a way of saying "a person," or "a human being." But here this is a title for the man, Ezekiel.
reptiles The Hebrew word can mean, "lizards," "snakes," and "all kinds of bugs and insects."
incense Special dried tree sap. Burned to make a sweet-smelling smoke, it was offered as a gift to God.

man,* do you see what the elders of Israel do in the dark? Each man has a special room for his own false god! Those men say to themselves, 'The Lord can't see us. The Lord left this country.'" ¹³Then ˻God˼ said to me, "If you come with me, you will see those men doing even more terrible things!"

¹⁴Then ˻God˼ led me to the entrance to the Lord's temple. This gate was on the north side. And there I saw women sitting and crying. They were sad about the false god Tammuz!*

¹⁵˻God˼ said to me, "Son of man,* do you see these terrible things? Come with me and you will see things that are even worse than this!" ¹⁶Then he led me to the inner courtyard of the Lord's temple. At that place, I saw 25 men bowing down and worshiping. They were between the porch and the altar—but they were facing the wrong way! Their backs were to the Holy Place. They were bowing down to worship the sun!

¹⁷Then ˻God˼ said, "Son of man,* do you see this? The people of Judah think my temple is so unimportant that they will do these terrible things here in my temple! This country is filled with violence. And they constantly do things to make me mad. Look, they are wearing rings in their noses to honor the moon like a false god!* ¹⁸I will show them my anger! I won't show them any mercy! I will not feel sorry for them! They will shout to me—but I refuse to listen to them!"

9 Then ˻God˼ shouted to the leaders ˻in charge of punishing˼ the city. Each leader had his own destructive weapon in his hand.* ²Then I saw six men walking on the road from the upper gate. This gate is on the north side. Each man had his own deadly weapon in his hand. One of the men wore linen clothes.* He wore a scribe's pen and ink set* at his waist. Those men went to the bronze altar ˻in the temple˼ and stood there. ³Then the Glory of the God of Israel rose from above the Cherub angels* where he had been. Then the Glory went to the door of the temple. He stopped when he was over the threshold. Then the Glory called to the man wearing the linen clothes and the scribe's pen and ink set.

⁴Then the Lord *(Glory)* said to him, "Go through the city of Jerusalem. Put a mark on the forehead of every person that feels sad and upset about all the terrible things people are doing in this city."

⁵⁻⁶Then I heard ˻God˼ say to the other men, "I want you to follow the first man. You must kill every person that does not have the mark on his forehead. It does not matter if they are elders *(leaders)*, young men or young women, children or mothers—you must use your weapon and kill every person that does not have the mark on his forehead. Don't show any mercy. Don't feel sorry for any person! Start here at my temple." So they started with the elders *(leaders)* in front of the temple.

⁷God said to them, "Make this temple unclean*—fill this courtyard with dead bodies! Now go!" So they went and killed the people in the city.

⁸I stayed there while those men went to kill the people. I bowed with my face to the ground and said, "Oh Lord my Master, in showing your anger against Jerusalem, are you killing all the survivors in Israel?"

⁹˻God˼ said, "The family of Israel and Judah have done many, many very bad sins! People are being murdered everywhere in this country. And this city is filled with crime. Why? Because the people say to themselves, 'The Lord left this country. He can't see the things we are doing.' ¹⁰And I won't show any mercy. I won't feel sorry for these people. They brought it on themselves—I am only giving these people the punishment they deserve!"

¹¹Then the man wearing linen clothes and a scribe's pen and ink set* spoke up. He said, "I have done what you commanded."

Son of man This was usually just a way of saying "a person," or "a human being." But here this is a title for the man, Ezekiel.

Tammuz People thought this false god died and his wife Ishtar asked everyone to be sad and cry with her. Ishtar hoped this would bring him back to life. This ceremony was on the 2nd day of the fourth month *(June/July)*. This month was named Tammuz because of this holiday.

Look ... god Or, "Look at them putting that cut branch in their noses."

Each ... hand In Hebrew, this is like Ez. 8:11.

linen clothes Priests usually wore these clothes.

Cherub angels Special angels from God. Statues of these angels were on top of the Box of the Agreement.

unclean Not pure or not acceptable to God for worship.

10 Then I looked up at the bowl* over the heads of the Cherub angels.* The bowl looked clear blue like sapphire. And there was something that looked like a throne over the bowl. ²Then ₗthe person sitting on the throneⱼ said to the man dressed in linen clothes, "Step into the area between the wheels* under the Cherub angels. Take a handful of the burning coals from between the Cherub angels and go throw them over the city of Jerusalem."

The man walked past me. ³The Cherub angels* were standing in the area south* of the temple as the man walked to them. The cloud filled the inner courtyard. ⁴Then the Glory of the Lord rose up off of the Cherub angels near the threshold of the door of the temple. Then the cloud filled the temple. And the bright light from the Glory of the Lord filled the whole courtyard. ⁵The noise from the wings of the Cherub angels could be heard all the way out in the outer courtyard. The sound was very loud—like the thundering voice when God All-Powerful speaks.

⁶ₗGodⱼ had given the man dressed in linen clothes a command. ₗGodⱼ had told him to go into the area between the wheels* among the Cherub angels* and get some hot coals. So the man went there and stood by the wheel. ⁷One of the Cherub angels reached out his hand and took some of the hot coals from the area between the Cherub angels. He poured the coals into the man's hands. And the man left. (⁸The Cherub angels had what looked like human arms under their wings.)

⁹Then I noticed that there were four wheels. There was one wheel by each Cherub angel.* And the wheels looked like a clear yellow jewel. ¹⁰There were four wheels and they all looked the same. They looked like there was a wheel in a wheel. ¹¹They could go in any direction when they moved. But ₗthe Cherub angelsⱼ did not turn around when they moved. They went in the direction that the head was looking. They did not turn around when they moved. ¹²There were eyes all over their bodies. There were eyes on their backs, on their arms, on their wings, and on their wheels. ₗYes, there were eyes onⱼ all four wheels! ¹³These wheels were what I heard called the "area between the wheels".

¹⁴⁻¹⁵Each Cherub angel* had four faces. The first face was a Cherub's face.* The second face was a man's face. The third face was a lion's face. And the fourth face was an eagle's face. Then ₗI realized thatⱼ the animals I saw in the vision by the Kebar Canal* were Cherub angels!

Then the Cherub angels* rose into the air. ¹⁶And the wheels rose with them. When the Cherub angels raised their wings and flew into the air, not even the wheels turned around. ¹⁷If the Cherub angels flew into the air, the wheels went with them. If the Cherub angels stood still, so did the wheels. Why? Because the wind* *(power)* of the animal was in them.

¹⁸Then the Glory of the Lord rose from the threshold of the temple, moved to the place over the Cherub angels* and stopped there. ¹⁹Then the Cherub angels raised their wings and flew into the air. I saw them leave ₗthe templeⱼ! The wheels went with them. Then they stopped at the East Gate of the Lord's temple. The Glory of the God of Israel was in the air above them.

²⁰Then I remembered the animals under the Glory of the God of Israel in the vision at the Kebar Canal. And I realized those animals were Cherub angels. ²¹ₗI mean,ⱼ each animal had four faces, four wings, and something that looked like human arms under their wings. ²²The faces of the Cherub angels were the same as the four faces on the animals in the vision by the Kebar Canal. And they all looked straight ahead in the direction they were going.

11 Then the wind* carried me to the East Gate of the Lord's temple. This gate faces the east, ₗwhere the sun comes upⱼ. I saw 25 men there at the entrance of this gate. Jaazaniah son of Azzur was with those men. And Pelatiah son of Benaiah was there. Pelatiah was the leader of the people.

---

bowl This Hebrew word is the same word used in Gen. 1:6-7 to describe the dome over the sky.
Cherub angels Special angels from God. Statues of these angels were on top of the Box of the Agreement.
area between the wheels The Hebrew word can mean, "chariot wheel," "whirling (spinning) wheel," or "tumbleweed" See chapter 1 for Ezekiel's full description.
Cherub angel Special angels from God. Statues of these angels were on top of the Box of the Agreement.
Cherub's face This is the bull's face mentioned in Ez. 1:10. See Ez. 10:22.
vision by Kebar Canal See Ez. 1.
wind Or, "Spirit."
Son of man This was usually just a way of saying "a person," or "a human being." But here this is a title for the man, Ezekiel.

²Then ₍God₎ spoke to me. He said, "Son of man,* these are the men who make evil plans for this city. These men always tell the people to do bad things. ³These men say, 'We will be building our houses again very soon. ₍We are as safe in this city as₎ meat in a pot!' ⁴₍They are telling these lies.₎ So you must speak to the people for me. Son of man, go prophesy to the people."

⁵Then the Spirit of the Lord came on me. He said to me, "Tell them that the Lord said these things: House of Israel, you are planning big things. But I know what you are thinking! ⁶You have killed many people in this city. You have filled the streets with dead bodies. ⁷Now, the Lord our Master says these things, 'Those dead bodies are the meat. And the city is the pot. But he (Nebuchadnezzar) will come and take you out of this safe pot! ⁸You are afraid of the sword. But I am bringing the sword against you!'" The Lord our Master said these things. ₍So they will happen!₎

⁹₍God also said,₎ "I will take you people out of this city. And I will give you to strangers. I will punish you! ¹⁰You will die by the sword. I will punish you here in Israel, so you will know that ₍I am the One punishing you₎. I am the Lord. ¹¹Yes, this place will be the cooking pot. And you will be the meat cooking in it! I will punish you here in Israel. ¹²Then you will know that I am the Lord. It was my law that you broke! You did not obey my commands. You decided to live like the nations around you."

¹³As soon as I finished speaking for God, Pelatiah son of Benaiah died! I fell to the ground. I bowed with my face touching the ground and said, "Oh, Lord my Master, you are going to completely destroy all the survivors of Israel!"

¹⁴But then the word of the Lord came to me. He said, ¹⁵"Son of man,* remember your brothers, the family of Israel. They were forced to leave their country, but I will bring them back!* But now, the people living in Jerusalem are saying, "Stay far away from the Lord. This land was given to us—it is ours!"

¹⁶So tell those people these things: The Lord our Master says, "It is true, I forced my people to go far away to other nations. I did scatter them among many countries. And they will be sad about my temple for a short time in those other countries. ¹⁷But you must tell those people that the Lord their Master will bring them back. I have scattered you among many nations. But I will gather you together and bring you back from those nations. I will give the land of Israel back to you! ¹⁸And when my people come back, they will destroy all the terrible, filthy idols that are here now. ¹⁹I will bring them together and make them like one person. I will put a new spirit* in them. I will take away that heart of stone, and I will put a real heart in its place. ²⁰Then they will obey my laws. They will obey my commands. They will do the things I tell them. They will truly be my people, and I will be their God."

²¹₍Then God said,₎ "But now, their hearts belong to those terrible, filthy idols. And I must punish those people for the bad things they did." The Lord my Master said those things. ²²And then the Cherub angels* raised their wings ₍and flew into the air₎. The wheels went with them. And the Glory of the God of Israel was above them. ²³The Glory of the Lord rose into the air and left Jerusalem. He stopped on the hill east of Jerusalem.* ²⁴Then the wind* lifted me into the air and brought me back to Babylonia. It brought me back to the people that were forced to leave Israel. I saw all of those things in the vision of God. Then ₍the One I saw₎ in the vision rose into the air and left me. ²⁵Then I spoke to the people in exile. I told them about all the things the Lord showed me.

12 Then the word of the Lord came to me. He said, ²"Son of man,* you live among rebellious people—they always turn against me. They have eyes to see ₍the things I have done for them₎. But they don't see those things. They have ears to hear ₍the things I told them to do₎. But they don't hear my commands. Why? Because they are a rebellious people. ³So, Son of man,* pack your bags. Act like you are going to a faraway country. Do this so the people can see you. Maybe they will see you—but they are a very rebellious people.

⁴"During the day, take your bags outside so the people can see you. Then in the evening, act like you are going away like a prisoner to a faraway

---

Son of man This was usually just a way of saying "a person," or "a human being." But here this is a title for the man, Ezekiel.
They were forced ... bring them back! This is a word play. The word meaning, "redeemed" sounds like the word

Cherub angels Special angels from God. Statues of these angels were on top of the Box of the Agreement.
hill east of Jerusalem This is the Mount of Olives.
wind Or, "Spirit."
Spirit Or, "wind."
spirit Or, "Spirit."

country. ⁵While the people are watching, make a hole in the wall and go out through that hole in the wall. ⁶At night, put your bag on your shoulder and leave. Cover your face so you can't see where you are going. You must do these things so the people can see you. Why? Because I am using you as an example to the family of Israel."

⁷So I *(Ezekiel)* did as I was commanded. During the day, I took my bags and acted like I was going to a faraway country. That evening I used my hands and made a hole in the wall. During the night I put my bag on my shoulder and left. I did this so all the people could see me.

⁸The next morning, the word of the Lord came to me. He said, ⁹"Son of man,* did those rebellious people of Israel ask you what you were doing? ¹⁰Tell them that the Lord their Master said these things. This sad message is about the leader of Jerusalem and all the people of Israel living there. ¹¹Tell them, 'I *(Ezekiel)* am an example for all you people. The things I have done will really happen to you.' You really will be forced to go to a faraway country as prisoners. ¹²And your leader will make a hole in the wall and sneak out at night. He will cover his face [so people won't recognize him]. His eyes won't be able to see where he is going. ¹³[He will try to escape.] But I *(God)* will catch him! He will be caught in my trap. And I will bring him to Babylonia—the land of the Chaldean people. But he will not be able to see where he is going. [The enemy will poke out his eyes and make him blind.] ¹⁴I will force the king's people to live in the foreign countries around Israel. And I will scatter his army to the winds. And the enemy soldiers will chase after them. ¹⁵Then those people will know that I am the Lord. They will know that I scattered them among the nations. They will know that I forced them to go to other countries.

¹⁶"But I will let a few of the people live. They won't die from the disease, hunger, and war. I will let those people live so they can tell other people about the terrible things they did against me. And then they will know that I am the Lord."

¹⁷Then the word of the Lord came to me. He said, ¹⁸"Son of man,* you must act like you are very scared. You must shake when you eat your food. You must act worried and afraid when you drink your water. ¹⁹You must tell these things to the common people. You must say, 'The Lord our Master says these things to the people living in Jerusalem and in the other parts of Israel. You people will be very worried while you eat your food. You will be terrified while you drink your water. Why? Because all the things in your country will be destroyed! The enemy will be very cruel to all the people living there. ²⁰Many people live in your cities now—but those cities will be ruined. Your whole country will be destroyed! Then you will know that I am the Lord."

²¹Then the word of the Lord came to me. He said, ²²"Son of man,* why do people say this poem about the land of Israel:

> Trouble won't come soon,
> the visions won't happen.

²³"Tell those people that the Lord their Master will stop that poem. They won't say those things about Israel any more. Now they will say this poem:

> Trouble will come soon,
> the visions will happen.

²⁴It is true, there won't be any more false visions in Israel. There won't be any more magicians telling things that don't come true. ²⁵Why? Because I am the Lord. And I will say what I want to say, and that thing will happen! And I won't let the time stretch out. Those troubles are coming soon—in your own lifetime. You rebellious people, when I say something, I make it happen." The Lord my Master said those things.

²⁶Then the word of the Lord came to me. He said, ²⁷"Son of man,* the people of Israel think that the visions I give you are for a time far in the future. They think you are talking about things that will happen many, many years from now. ²⁸So you must tell them these things, 'The Lord my Master says: I won't delay any longer. If I say something will happen, then it will happen!'" The Lord my Master said those things.

13 Then the word of the Lord came to me. He said, ²"Son of man,* you must speak to the prophets of Israel for me. [Those prophets are not really speaking for me.] Those prophets are saying things they want to say. So you must speak to

---

Son of man This was usually just a way of saying "a person," or "a human being." But here this is a title for the man, Ezekiel.

them. Tell them these things, 'Listen to this message from the Lord! ³The Lord my Master says these things. Bad things will happen to you foolish prophets. You are following your own spirits. You are not telling people what you really see ˻in visions˼.

⁴"'Israel, your prophets will be like foxes running through empty, destroyed buildings. ⁵You have not put soldiers near the broken walls of the city. You have not built walls to protect the family of Israel. So when the day comes for the Lord to punish you, you will lose the war!

⁶"'False prophets said they saw visions. They did their magic and said things would happen—but they lied. They said the Lord sent them—but they lied. They are still waiting for their lies to come true.

⁷"'False prophets, the visions you saw were not true. You did your magic and said things would happen. But you lied! You said that the Lord said those things. But I did not speak to you!'"

⁸So now, the Lord my Master really will speak! He says, "You told lies. You saw visions that were not true. So now I *(God)* am against you!" The Lord my Master said these things. ⁹The Lord says, "I will punish the prophets that saw false visions and told lies. I will remove them from my people. Their names won't be in the list of the family of Israel. They will never again come to the land of Israel. Then you will know that I am the Lord and Master!

¹⁰"Again and again those false prophets lied to my people. The prophets said there would be peace. And there is no peace. The people need to fix the walls and prepare for war. But they only slap a thin coat of plaster* over the broken walls. ¹¹Tell those men that I will send hail and a strong rain *(enemy army)*. The wind will blow hard and a tornado will come. Then the wall will fall down. ¹²The wall will fall down. And the people will ask the prophets, 'What happened to the plaster you put on the wall?'" ¹³The Lord my Master says, "I am angry and I will send a storm against you. I am angry and I will send a strong rain. I am angry and I will make hail fall from the sky and completely destroy you! ¹⁴You put plaster* on the wall. But I will destroy the whole wall. I will pull it to the ground. The wall will fall on you. And then you will know that I am the Lord. ¹⁵I will finish showing my anger against the wall and the people that put plaster on it. Then I will say, 'There is no wall. And there are no workers to put plaster on it.'

¹⁶"All those things will happen to the false prophets of Israel. Those prophets speak to the people of Jerusalem. Those prophets say there will be peace, but there is no peace." The Lord my Master said those things.

¹⁷˻God said,˼ "Son of man,* look at the women prophets in Israel. Those women prophets ˻don't speak for me˼. They say the things they want to say. So you must speak against them for me. You must say these things to them. ¹⁸'The Lord my Master says these things: Bad things will happen to you women. You sew cloth bracelets for people to wear on their arms. You make special scarves for people to wear on their heads. ˻You say those things have magic powers˼ to control people's lives. You trap those people only to keep yourselves alive! ¹⁹You make the people think I am not important. You turn them against me for a few handfuls of barley and a few scraps of bread. You tell lies to my people. Those people love to listen to lies. You kill people that should live. And you let people live that should die. ²⁰So the Lord and Master says these things to you: You make those cloth bracelets to trap people—but I will set those people free. I will tear those bracelets off your arms, and the people will be free from you. They will be like birds flying from a trap! ²¹And I will tear up those scarves, and save my people from your power. Those people will escape from your trap. And you will know that I am the Lord.

²²"'You prophets tell lies. Your lies hurt good people—I did not want to hurt those good people! You support bad people and encourage them. You don't tell them to change their lives. You don't try to save their lives! ²³So you won't see any more useless visions. You won't do any more magic. I will save my people from your power. And you will know that I am the Lord.'"

14 Some of the elders of Israel came to me. They sat down to talk with me. ²The word of the Lord came to me. He said, ³"Son of man,* these men came to talk to you. ˻They wanted you to ask me for advice.˼ But these men still have their filthy idols. They kept the things that made them sin. They still worship those statues. So why do they come to me for advice? Should I answer

---

plaster A type of cement people put on stone walls to make them smooth and waterproof. This is also a word play. The Hebrew word is like the word meaning, "It will fall."

Son of man This was usually just a way of saying "a person," or "a human being." But here this is a title for the man, Ezekiel.

their questions? No! ⁴But I will give them an answer. ₍I will punish them!₎ You must tell those people these things. 'The Lord my Master says: If any Israelite comes to a prophet and asks me for advice, then ₍the prophet won't give that person an answer₎. I myself will answer that person's question. I will answer him even if he still has his filthy idols, even if he kept the things that made him sin, and even if he still worships those statues. I will speak to him in spite of all his filthy idols. ⁵Why? Because I want to touch their heart. I want to show them I love them, even though they left me for their filthy idols.'

⁶"So tell the family of Israel these things. Tell them, 'The Lord my Master says: Come back ₍to me₎ and leave your filthy idols. Turn away from those terrible false gods. ⁷If any Israelite or foreigner living in Israel comes to me for advice, I will give him an answer. I will answer him even if he still has his filthy idols and even if he kept the things that made him sin and even if he worships those statues. And this is the answer I will give him: ⁸I will turn against that person. I will destroy him. He will be an example to other people. People will laugh at him. I will remove him from my people. Then you will know that I am the Lord! ⁹And if a prophet is foolish enough to give his own answer, then I will show him how foolish he is! I will use my power against him. I will destroy him and remove him from among my people, Israel. ¹⁰So, both the person that came for advice and the prophet that gave an answer will get the same punishment. ¹¹Why? So those prophets will stop leading my people away from me. And so my people will stop becoming filthy with their sins. Then they will be my special people. And I will be their God.'" The Lord my Master said those things.

¹²Then the word of the Lord came to me. He said, ¹³"Son of man,* I will punish any nation that leaves me and sins against me. I will stop their food supply. I might cause a time of hunger and remove the people and animals from that country. ¹⁴₍I would punish that country₎ even if Noah, Danel, and Job* lived there. Those men could save their own lives by their goodness, ₍but they could not save the whole country₎." The Lord my Master said these things.

¹⁵₍God said,₎ "Or, I might send wild animals through that country. And those animals might kill all the people. No person would travel through that country because of the wild animals. ¹⁶If Noah, Danel, and Job lived there, ₍then I would save those three good men₎. Those three men could save their own lives. But by my life I promise, they could not save the lives of other people—not even their own sons and daughters! That evil country would be destroyed!" The Lord my Master said these things.

¹⁷₍God said,₎ "Or, I might send an enemy army to fight against that country. Those soldiers would destroy that country—I would remove all the people and animals from that country. ¹⁸If Noah, Danel, and Job lived there, ₍then I would save those three good men₎. Those three men could save their own lives. But by my life I promise, they could not save the lives of other people—not even their own sons and daughters! That evil country would be destroyed!" The Lord my Master said these things.

¹⁹₍God said,₎ "Or, I might send a disease against that country. I will pour my anger down on those people. I will remove all the people and animals from that country. ²⁰If Noah, Danel, and Job lived there, ₍then I would save those three men₎ because they are good men. Those three men could save their own lives. But by my life I promise, they could not save the lives of other people—not even their own sons and daughters!" The Lord my Master said these things.

²¹Then the Lord my Master said, "So think how bad it will be for Jerusalem: I will send all four of those punishments against that city! I will send enemy soldiers, hunger, disease, and wild animals against that city. I will remove all the people and animals from that country! ²²Some of the people will escape from that country. They will bring their sons and daughters and come to you for help. Then you will see how bad those people really are. And you will feel better about all the troubles that I will bring to Jerusalem. ²³You will see the way they live and the bad things they do. And then you will know that I had a good reason for punishing those people." The Lord my Master said these things.

Son of man This was usually just a way of saying "a person," or "a human being." But here this is a title for the man, Ezekiel.

Noah, Danel, and Job Three men from ancient times. They were famous for being very good and wise men. Stories about Noah and Job are in the Bible. Stories about Danel are in writings from Ras Shamra.

grapevine Many times the prophets said Israel was God's vineyard or grapevine.

15 Then the word of the Lord came to me. He said, ²"Son of man,* are the pieces of wood from a grapevine* any better than the little branches cut from trees in the forest? No! ³Can you use that wood from a grapevine to make anything? No! Can you use that wood to make pegs to hang dishes on? No! ⁴People only throw that wood into the fire. Some sticks begin to burn on the ends, the middles turn black from the fire, ⌊but the sticks don't burn completely⌋. Can you make anything from that burnt stick? ⁵If you can't make anything from that wood before it is burned, then you surely can't make anything from that wood after it is burned! ⁶So the pieces of wood from a grapevine are just like pieces of wood from trees in the forest. People throw those pieces of wood into the fire. And the fire burns them. In the same way, I will throw the people living in Jerusalem into the fire!" The Lord my Master said these things. ⁷"I will punish those people. But some of those people will be like the sticks that don't burn completely—they will be punished, but they won't be destroyed completely. You will see that I punished these people, and you will know that I am the Lord! ⁸I will destroy that country because the people left me ⌊to worship false gods⌋." The Lord my Master said those things.

16 Then the word of the Lord came to me. He said, ²"Son of man,* tell the people of Jerusalem about the terrible things they have done. ³You must say, 'The Lord my Master says these things to Jerusalem: Look at your history. You were born in Canaan. Your father was an Amorite. Your mother was a Hittite. ⁴⌊Jerusalem,⌋ on the day you were born, there was no one to cut your naval cord. No one put salt on you and washed you to make you clean. No one wrapped you in cloth. ⁵⌊Jerusalem, you were all alone.⌋ No one felt sorry for you or took care of you. ⌊Jerusalem,⌋ on the day you were born, your parents threw you out in the field. You were still covered with the blood and afterbirth.

⁶"'Then I (God) passed by. I saw you lying there, kicking in the blood. You were covered with blood but I said, "Please live!" Yes, you were covered with blood but I said, "Please live!" ⁷I helped you grow like a plant in the field. You grew and grew. You became a young woman: your periods began, your breasts grew, your hair began to grow. But you were still bare and naked. ⁸I looked you over. I saw you were ready for love. So I spread my clothes over you* and covered your nakedness. I promised to marry you. I made the agreement* with you. And you became mine.'" The Lord my Master said these things. ⁹"'I washed you in water. I washed away your blood. And I rubbed oil on your skin. ¹⁰* I gave you a nice dress and soft leather shoes. I gave you a linen headband and a silk scarf. ¹¹Then I gave you some jewelry. I put bracelets on your arms and a necklace around your neck. ¹²I gave you a nose ring, some earrings, and a beautiful crown to wear. ¹³You were beautiful in your silver and gold jewelry, and your linen, silk, and embroidered material. You ate the best foods. You were very, very beautiful. And you became the queen! ¹⁴You became famous for your beauty. And all because I made you so lovely!'" The Lord my Master said these things.

¹⁵⌊God said,⌋ "But you began to trust in your beauty. You used the good name you had and became unfaithful to me. You acted like a prostitute* with every man that passed by. You gave yourself to them all! ¹⁶You took your beautiful clothes and used them to decorate your places of worship. And you acted like a prostitute* in those places. You gave yourself to every man that came by! ¹⁷Then you took your beautiful jewelry that I gave you. And you used that gold and silver to make statues of men. And you had sex with them too! ¹⁸Then you took the beautiful cloth and made clothes for those statues. You took the perfume and incense I gave you, and you put it in front of those idols. ¹⁹I gave you bread, honey, and oil. But you gave that food to your idols. You offered them as a sweet smell to please your false gods. You acted like a prostitute with those false gods!" The Lord my Master said these things.

Son of man   This was usually just a way of saying "a person," or "a human being." But here this is a title for the man, Ezekiel.

spread my clothes over you   This showed that he was agreeing to protect her and care for her. See Ruth 3:1-15.

agreement   Here this means the marriage agreement. But it also refers to the Agreement God made with the people of Israel.

Verses 10-13   All the materials in this list are the things used in building the Holy Tent. See Ex. 25-40.

prostitute   A woman paid by men for sexual sin. Sometimes this also means a person that is not faithful to God and stops following him.

²⁰ₗGod said,ⱼ "You and I had children together. But you took our children. You killed them and gave them to those false gods! But that is only some of the bad things you did when you cheated on me and went to those false gods. ²¹You slaughtered* my sons and then passed them ₗthrough the fireⱼ to those false gods. ²²You left me and did all those terrible things. And you never remembered the time when you were young. You did not remember that you were naked and kicking in blood ₗwhen I found youⱼ.
²³"After all those bad things, ... Oh Jerusalem, it will be very bad for you!" The Lord my Master said all these things. ²⁴"After all those things you made that mound ₗfor worshiping that false godⱼ. You built those places for worshiping false gods on every street corner. ²⁵You built your mounds at the head of every road. Then you degraded your beauty. You used it to catch every man that walked by. You raised your skirt so they could see your legs, and then you were like a prostitute* with those men. ²⁶Then you went to Egypt, your neighbor with the big sex organ. You had sex with him many times to make me angry. ²⁷So I punished you! I took away part of your allowance *(land)*. I let your enemies, the daughters *(cities)* of the Philistines do what they wanted to you. Even they were shocked at the bad things you did. ²⁸Then you went to have sex with Assyria. You could not get enough. You were never satisfied. ²⁹So you turned to Canaan, and then to Babylonia. And still you were not satisfied. ³⁰You are so weak. You let all those men *(countries)* cause you to sin. You acted just like a prostitute.*" The Lord my Master said those things.
³¹ₗGod said,ⱼ "But you were not exactly like a prostitute.* You built your mounds at the head of every road and you built your places of worship at every street corner. You had sex with all those men. But you did not ask them to pay you like a prostitute does. ³²You adulterous woman. You prefer having sex with strangers rather than your own husband. ³³Most prostitutes force men to pay them for sex. But you gave money to your many lovers. You paid all the men around to come in to have sex with you. ³⁴You are just the opposite of most prostitutes. Most prostitutes force men to pay them. But you pay the men to have sex with you."

³⁵Prostitute, listen to the message from the Lord. ³⁶The Lord my Master says these things: "You have spent your money* and let your lovers and filthy gods see your naked body and have sex with you. You have killed your children and poured out their blood. This was your gift to those false gods. ³⁷So I am bringing all of your lovers together. I will bring all the men you loved and all the men you hated. I will bring them all together and let them see you naked.* They will see you completely naked. ³⁸Then I will punish you. I will punish you as a murderer and a woman that did the sin of adultery. You will be punished as if by an angry and jealous husband. ³⁹I will let those lovers have you. They will destroy your mounds. They will burn your places of worship. They will tear off your clothes and take your beautiful jewelry. They will leave you bare and naked ₗlike you were when I found youⱼ. ⁴⁰They will bring a crowd of people and throw rocks at you to kill you. Then they will cut you in pieces with their swords. ⁴¹They will burn your house *(temple)*. They will punish you so all the other women can see. I will stop you from living like a prostitute. I will stop you from paying money to your lovers. ⁴²Then I will stop being angry and jealous. I will calm down. I won't be angry any more. ⁴³Why will all these things happen? Because you did not remember what happened when you were young. You did all those bad things and made me angry. So I had to punish you for doing those bad things. But you planned even more terrible things." The Lord my Master said those things.

⁴⁴"All the people that talk about you will now have one more thing to say. They will say, 'Like mother, like daughter.' ⁴⁵You are your mother's daughter. You don't care about your husband or your children. You are just like your sister. Both of you hated your husband and your children. ₗYou are just like your parents.ⱼ Your mother was a Hittite and your father was an Amorite. ⁴⁶Your

---

slaughtered Usually, this word means to kill an animal and cut it into pieces for meat. But it often means to kill people like they are animals.

prostitute A woman paid by men for sexual sin. Sometimes this also means a person that is not faithful to God and stops following him.

spent your money Literally, "poured out your copper." This might also mean, "you have done the things that stain you with sin."

let them see you naked The Hebrew words are like the words meaning, "to be carried away as a prisoner to a foreign country."

older sister was Samaria. She lived to the north of you with her daughters *(towns)*. And your younger sister was Sodom.* She lived to the south of you with her daughters *(towns)*. ⁴⁷You did all the terrible things they did. But you also did things that were even worse! ⁴⁸I am the Lord and Master. I am alive. And by my life I promise, your sister Sodom and her daughters never did as many bad things as you and your daughters."

⁴⁹ˌGod said,ⱼ "Your sister Sodom and her daughters were proud, they had too much to eat, and too much time on their hands. And they did not help poor, helpless people. ⁵⁰Sodom and her daughters became too proud and began to do terrible things in front of me. And when I saw them doing those things, I punished them."

⁵¹ˌGod said,ⱼ "And Samaria did only half as many bad things as you did. You did many more terrible things than Samaria! You have done so many more terrible things than your sisters. Sodom and Samaria seem good compared to you. ⁵²So you must bear your shame. You have made your sisters look good compared to you. You have done terrible things, so you should be ashamed."

⁵³ˌGod said,ⱼ "I destroyed Sodom and the towns around it. And I destroyed Samaria around it. And ˌJerusalem,ⱼ I will destroy you. But I will build those cities again. And ˌJerusalem,ⱼ I will build you again too. ⁵⁴I will comfort you. Then you will remember the terrible things you did, and you will be ashamed. ⁵⁵So you and your sisters will be built again. Sodom and the towns around her, Samaria and the towns around her, and you and the towns around you will all be built again."

⁵⁶ˌGod said,ⱼ "In the past, you were proud and made fun of your sister Sodom. But you won't do that again. ⁵⁷You did that before you were punished, before your neighbors started making fun of you. The daughters *(towns)* of Edom* and Philistia are making fun of you now. ⁵⁸Now you must suffer for the terrible things you did." The Lord said these things.

⁵⁹The Lord my Master said these things. "I will treat you like you treated me! You broke your marriage promise. You did not respect our Agreement. ⁶⁰But I will remember the agreement we made when you were young. I made an agreement with you that will continue forever! ⁶¹I will bring your sisters to you, and I will make them your daughters. That was not in our agreement, but I will do that for you. Then you will remember the terrible things you did, and you will be ashamed. ⁶²So I will make my agreement with you. And you will know that I am the Lord. ⁶³ˌI will be good to you,ⱼ so you will remember me and be ashamed of the bad things you did. I will make you pure, and you will never be ashamed again!" The Lord my Master said those things.

17 Then the word of the Lord came to me. He said, ²"Son of man,* tell this story to the family of Israel. Ask them what it means. ³Say to them:

A large eagle *(Nebuchadnezzar)* with big
  wings came to Lebanon.
The eagle had feathers covered with spots.
⁴ The eagle broke the top out of the big cedar
  tree *(Lebanon)* and brought it to Canaan.
The eagle set down the branch in the town of
  businessmen.
⁵ Then the eagle took some of the seeds
  (people) from Canaan
He planted them in good soil.
He planted them by a good river.
⁶ The seeds grew and became a grapevine.
It was a good vine.
The vine was not tall,
  but it spread to cover a large area.
The vine grew stems,
  and smaller vines grew very long.
⁷ Then another eagle with big wings
  saw the grapevine.
The eagle had many feathers.
The grapevine wanted this new eagle
  to care for it.
So it made its roots grow toward this eagle.
Its branches stretched toward this eagle.
The branches grew away from the field
  that it was planted in.
The grapevine wanted the new eagle
  to water it.
⁸ The grapevine was planted in a good field.
It was planted near plenty of water.
It could have grown branches and fruit.
It could have become a very good
  grapevine."

Samaria ... Sodom Ezekiel is saying that the people in Judah are just as evil as the people that lived in Samaria and Sodom—And those people were so evil that God completely destroyed those cities.
Edom Or, "Aram."

Son of man This was usually just a way of saying "a person," or "a human being." But here this is a title for the man, Ezekiel.

⁹ The Lord my Master said these things.
"Do you think that plant will succeed?
No! The new eagle will pull the plant
from the ground.
And the bird will break the plant's roots.
It will eat up all the grapes.
Then the new leaves will become dry
and die.
That plant will be very weak.
It won't take strong arms or a powerful nation
to pull that plant up by the roots.
¹⁰ Will the plant grow where it is planted?
No! The hot east wind will blow
and the plant will become dry and die.
It will die there where it was planted."

¹¹The word of the Lord came to me. He said, ¹²"Explain this story to the people ₍of Israel₎—they always turn against me. Tell them these things: The first eagle is ₍Nebuchadnezzar₎, the king of Babylonia. He came to Jerusalem and took away the king and other leaders. He brought them to Babylonia. ¹³Then Nebuchadnezzar made an agreement with a man from the king's family. Nebuchadnezzar forced that man to make a promise. So this man promised to be loyal to Nebuchadnezzar. Nebuchadnezzar made this man the new king of Judah. Then he took all the powerful men away from Judah. ¹⁴So Judah became a weak kingdom that could not turn against King Nebuchadnezzar. The people were forced to keep the agreement Nebuchadnezzar made with the new king of Judah. ¹⁵But this new king tried to rebel against Nebuchadnezzar anyway! He sent messengers to Egypt to ask for help. The new king asked for many horses and soldiers. Now, do you think the new king of Judah will succeed? Do you think the new king will have enough power to break the agreement and escape punishment?"

¹⁶The Lord my Master says, "By my life, I promise this new king will die in Babylonia! Nebuchadnezzar made this man the new king of Judah. But this man broke his promise with Nebuchadnezzar. This new king ignored that agreement. ¹⁷And the king of Egypt won't be able to save the king of Judah. He might send many soldiers, but Egypt's great power won't save Judah. Nebuchadnezzar's army will build dirt roads and dirt walls to capture the city. Many people will die. ¹⁸But the king of Judah won't escape. Why? Because he ignored his agreement. He broke his promise to Nebuchadnezzar. ¹⁹The Lord my Master makes this promise: "By my life, I swear that I will punish the king of Judah. Why? Because he ignored my warnings. He broke our agreement. ²⁰I will set my trap, and he will be caught in it. And I will bring him to Babylonia and I will punish him in that place. I will punish him because he turned against me. ²¹And I will destroy his army. I will destroy his best soldiers. And I will scatter the survivors to the winds. Then you will know that I am the Lord and that I told you these things."

²²The Lord my Master said these things:

"I will take a branch from
    a tall cedar tree.
I will take a small branch from
    the top of the tree.
And I myself will plant it
    on a very high mountain.
²³ I myself will plant it
    on a high mountain in Israel.
That branch will grow into a tree.
It will grow branches and make fruit.
It will become a beautiful cedar tree.
Many birds will sit on its branches.
Many birds will live in the shadows
    under its branches.
²⁴ "Then the other trees will know that
    I make tall trees fall to the ground,
    and I make small trees grow tall.
I make green trees become dry,
    and I make dry trees become green.
I am the Lord.
If I say that I will do something,
    then I will do it!"

18 The word of the Lord came to me. He said, ²"You people keep repeating this proverb. Why? You say:

The parents ate the sour grapes,
    but the children got the sour taste.

₍You think you can sin, and some person in the future will be punished for it.₎ ³But the Lord my Master says, "By my life, I promise that people in Israel won't think this proverb is true anymore! ⁴I will treat each person just the same. It won't matter if that person is the parent or the child. The person that sins is the person that will die!

⁵"If a person is good, then he will live! That good person treats people fairly. ⁶That good person does not go to the mountains and share in foods offered to false gods. He does not pray to those filthy idols in Israel. He does not do the sin of adultery with his neighbor's wife. He does not

have sex with his wife during her period. ⁷That good person does not take advantage of people. If a person borrows money from him, the good man takes the collateral* and gives the other person the money. And when that person pays him back, then the good man gives the collateral back. The good person gives food to hungry people. And he gives clothes to people that need them. ⁸If a person wants to borrow money, the good man lends him the money. And he does not charge interest on that loan. The good man refuses to be crooked. He is always fair with every person. People can trust him. ⁹He obeys my laws. He thinks about my decisions and learns to be fair and dependable. He is a good person, so he will live.

¹⁰"But that good person might have a son that does not do any of those good things. The son might steal things and kill people. ¹¹The son might do any of these bad things. He might go to the mountains and share in foods offered to false gods. That evil son might do the sin of adultery with his neighbor's wife. ¹²He might mistreat poor, helpless people. He might take advantage of people. He might not give back the collateral* when a person pays his debt. That evil son might pray to those filthy idols and do other terrible things. ¹³A person might need to borrow money from that evil son. The son might lend him the money, but he will force that person to pay interest on that loan. So that evil son won't live. He did terrible things, so he will be put to death. And he is responsible for his own death.

¹⁴"Now, that evil son might also have a son. But this son might see the bad things his father did, and he might refuse to live like his father. That good son treats people fairly. ¹⁵That good son does not go to the mountains and share in foods offered to false gods. He does not pray to those filthy idols in Israel. He does not do the sin of adultery with his neighbor's wife. ¹⁶That good son does not take advantage of people. If a person borrows money from him, the good son takes the collateral* and gives the other person the money. And when that person pays him back, then the good son gives the collateral back. The good son gives food to hungry people. And he gives clothes to people that need them. ¹⁷He helps poor people. If a person wants to borrow money, the good son lends him the money. And he does not charge interest on that loan! The good son obeys my laws and follows my laws. That good son will not be put to death for his father's sins! That good son will live. ¹⁸The father might hurt people and steal things. He might never do anything good for my people! That father will die because of his own sins. ⌊But the son won't be punished for his father's sins.⌋

¹⁹"You might ask, 'Why won't the son be punished for his father's sins?' The reason is that the son was fair and did good things! He very carefully obeyed my laws! So he will live. ²⁰The person that sins is the person that will be put to death! A son won't be punished for his father's sins. And a father won't be punished for his son's sins. A good man's goodness belongs to him alone. And a bad man's evil belongs to him alone.

²¹"Now, if a bad person changes his life then he will live and not die. That person might stop doing all the bad things he did. He might begin to carefully obey all my laws. He might become fair and good. ²²God won't remember all the bad things he did. God will remember only his goodness! So that man will live!"

²³The Lord my Master says, "I don't want bad people to die. I want them to change their lives so they can live!

²⁴"Now, maybe a good man might stop being good. He might change his life and begin to do all the terrible things that bad person had done in the past. (That bad person changed, so he can live!) So if that good person changes and becomes bad, then God won't remember all the good things that person did. God will remember that that man turned against him and began to sin. So that man will die because of his sin."

²⁵⌊God said,⌋ "You people might say, '⌊God⌋ my Master isn't fair!' But listen, family of Israel. I am fair. You are the ones who are not fair! ²⁶If a good person changes and becomes evil, then he must die for the bad things he does. ²⁷And if a bad man changes and become good and fair, then he will save his life. He will live! ²⁸That person saw how bad he was and came back to me. He stopped doing the bad things he did in the past. So he will live! He won't die!"

²⁹The people of Israel said, "That's not fair! ⌊The Lord⌋ my Master isn't fair!"

⌊God said,⌋ "I am fair. You are the ones who are not fair! ³⁰Why? Because family of Israel, I

---

collateral Things that a person uses to borrow money. If that person does not pay his debt, then the person he borrowed from can keep those things. It was against Moses' law to take a person's clothes as collateral. See Deut. 24:12-13.

will judge each person only for the things that person does!" The Lord my Master said these things. "So come back to me! Stop doing bad things! Don't let those terrible things *(idols)* cause you to sin! ³¹Throw away all the terrible things *(idols)* you made—they only cause you to sin! Change your heart and spirit! Why should you bring death to yourselves, people of Israel? ³²I don't want to kill you! Please come back and live!" The Lord my Master said those things.

19 God said to me, "You must sing this sad song about the leaders of Israel.

²"'Your mother is like female lion
  lying there with the male lions.
The mother lion lies down with
  the young lions.
She has many babies.
³ One of those cubs gets up.
  He has grown to be a strong young lion.
  He has learned to catch his food.
  He killed and ate a man.
⁴ The people heard him roar.
  And they caught him in their trap!
  They put hooks in his mouth,
  and carried the young lion to Egypt.
⁵"'The mother lion had hoped that cub would
    become the leader.
  But now she lost all hope.
  So she took another of her cubs.
  She trained him to be a lion.
⁶ He went on hunts with the adult lions.
  He became a strong young lion.
  He learned to catch his food.
  He killed and ate a man.
⁷ He attacked the palaces.
  He destroyed the cities.
  Every person in that country was too
    scared to speak when they heard his
    growl.
⁸ Then the people living around him
    set a trap for him.
  And they caught him in their trap.
⁹ They put hooks on him and locked him up.
  They had him in their trap.
  So they took him to the king of Babylon.
  And now, you can't hear his roar
  on the mountains of Israel.

¹⁰"'Your mother is like a grapevine
  planted near the water.

  She had plenty of water,
  so she grew many strong vines.
¹¹ Then she grew large branches.
  They were like a strong walking stick.
  They were like a king's scepter.*
  The vine grew taller and taller.
  It had many branches
  and reached to the clouds.
¹² But the vine was pulled up by the roots,
  and thrown down to the ground.
  The hot east wind blew and dried its fruit.
  The strong branches broke.
  And they were thrown into the fire.
¹³ Now that grapevine is planted in the desert.
  It is a very dry and thirsty land.
¹⁴ A fire started in the large branch and spread.
  The fire destroyed all its twigs and fruit.
  So there was no strong walking stick.
  There was no king's scepter.'*

This was a sad song about death, and it was sung as a sad song about death."

20 One day, some of the elders *(leaders)* of Israel came to me to ask the Lord for advice. This was on the tenth day of the fifth month *(August)*, of the seventh year ₁of exile₁.* The elders *(leaders)* sat down in front of me.

²Then the word of the Lord came to me. He said, ³"Son of man,* speak to the elders *(leaders)* of Israel. Tell them 'The Lord my Master says these things: Have you men come to ask me advice? If you have, then I won't give it to you. The Lord my Master said these things.' ⁴"Should you judge them? Will you judge them, Son of man?* You must tell them about the terrible things their fathers have done. ⁵You must tell them, 'The Lord my Master says these things: On the day I chose Israel, I raised my hand to Jacob's family and made a promise to them in Egypt. I raised my hand and said: "I am the Lord your God. ⁶On that day, I promised to take you out of Egypt and lead you to the land I was giving to you. That was a good land filled with many good things.* It was the most beautiful of all countries!

---

scepter A special stick. Kings and leaders carried scepters to show they were rulers.
seventh year of exile This was the summer of 591 B.C.
Son of man This was usually just a way of saying "a person," or "a human being." But here this is a title for the man, Ezekiel.
a good land ... good things Literally, "a land flowing with milk and honey."

7"I told the family of Israel to throw away their horrible idols. I told them not to become filthy with those filthy statues from Egypt. I am the Lord your God." 8But they turned against me and refused to listen to me. They did not throw away their horrible idols. They did not leave their filthy statues in Egypt. So I *(God)* decided to destroy them in Egypt—to let them feel the full force of my anger. 9But I did not destroy them. I had already told the people where they were living that I would bring my people out of Egypt. I did not want to ruin my good name, so I did not destroy Israel in front of those other people. 10I brought the family of Israel out of Egypt. I led them into the desert. 11Then I gave them my laws. I told them all my rules. If a person obeys those rules, then he will live. 12I also told them about all the special days of rest. Those holidays were a special sign between me and them. They showed that I am the Lord and that I was making them special to me.

13"'But the family of Israel turned against me in the desert. They did not follow my laws. They refused to obey my rules. ⌊And they are good rules⌋—if a person obeys those rules, then he will live. They treated my special days of rest as if they were not important. They worked on those days many, many times. I decided to destroy them in the desert—to let them feel the full force of my anger. 14But I did not destroy them. The other nations saw me bring Israel out of Egypt. I did not want to ruin my good name, so I did not destroy Israel in front of those other people. 15I made another promise to those people in the desert. I promised that I would not bring them into the land I was giving them. That was a good land filled with many good things.* It was the most beautiful of all countries!

16"'The people of Israel refused to obey my rules. They did not follow my laws. They treated my days of rest as if they were not important. They did all these things because their hearts belonged to their filthy idols. 17But I felt sorry for them, so I did not destroy them. I did not completely destroy them in the desert. 18I spoke to their children. I told them, 'Don't be like your parents. Don't make yourself filthy with their filthy idols. Don't follow their laws. Don't obey their commands. 19I am the Lord. I am your God. Obey my laws. Keep my commands. Do the things I tell you. 20Show that my days of rest are important to you. Remember, they are a special sign between me and you. I am the Lord. And those holidays show you that I am your God.

21"'But those children turned against me. They did not obey my laws. They did not keep my commands. They did not do the things I told them. ⌊And those are good laws.⌋ If a person obeys them, then he will live. They treated my special days of rest like they were not important. So I decided to destroy them completely in the desert, to let them feel the full force of my anger. 22But I stopped myself. The other nations saw me bring Israel out of Egypt. I did not want to ruin my good name, so I did not destroy Israel in front of those other people. 23So I made another promise to those people in the desert. I promised to scatter them among the nations, to send them to many different countries.

24"'The people of Israel did not obey my commands. They refused to obey my laws. They treated my special days of rest like they were not important. And they worshiped the filthy idols of their fathers. 25So I gave them laws that were not good. I gave them commands that would not bring life. 26I let them make themselves filthy with their gifts. They even began to sacrifice their own firstborn children. In this way, I would destroy those people. Then they would know that I am the Lord.' 27So now, Son of man,* speak to the family of Israel. Tell them, 'The Lord my Master says these things: The people of Israel said bad things about me and made evil plans against me. 28But I still brought them to the land I promised to give to them. They saw all the hills and green trees, so they went to all those places to worship. They took their sacrifices and anger offerings* to all those places. They offered their sacrifices that made a sweet smell and they offered their drink offerings at those places. 29I asked the people of Israel why they were going to those high places.*

---

a good land ... good things Literally, "a land flowing with milk and honey."

Son of man This was usually just a way of saying "a person," or "a human being." But here this is a title for the man, Ezekiel.

anger offerings The people called these meals "fellowship offerings," but Ezekiel is making fun and saying that those meals only made God angry.

high places Places for worshiping God or false gods. These places were often on the hills and mountains.

And those places of worship are still called "high places" today.'"

³⁰₍God said,₎ "₍The people of Israel did all those bad things.₎ So speak to the family of Israel. Tell them, 'The Lord my Master says these things: You people have made yourselves filthy by doing the things your ancestors* did. You have acted like a prostitute.* You have left me to be with the horrible gods your ancestors worshiped. ³¹You are giving the same kind of gifts. You are putting your children in the fire ₍as a gift to your false gods₎. You are still making yourself filthy with those filthy idols today! Do you really think that I should let you come to me and ask me for advice? I am the Lord and Master. By my life I promise, I won't answer your questions and give you advice! ³²You keep saying you want to be like the other nations. You live like the people in other nations. You serve pieces of wood and stone *(idols)*!'"

³³The Lord my Master says, "By my life, I promise that I will rule over you as king. But I will raise my powerful arm and punish you. I will show my anger against you! ³⁴I will bring you out of these other nations. I scattered you among these nations. But I will gather you together and bring you back from these countries. But I will raise my powerful arm and punish you. I will show my anger against you! ³⁵I will lead you into a desert ₍like I did before₎. But this will be a place where other nations live. We will stand face to face and I will judge you. ³⁶I will judge you just like I judged your ancestors* in the desert near Egypt." The Lord my Master said these things.

³⁷"I will judge you guilty and punish you according to the Agreement.* ³⁸I will remove all the people that turned against me and sinned against me. I will remove those people from your homeland. They will never again come to the Land of Israel. Then you will know that I am the Lord."

³⁹Now, family of Israel, the Lord my Master says these things, "If any person wants to worship his filthy idols, then let him go and worship them. But later, don't think you will get any advice from me! You will not ruin my name any more! Not when you continue to give your gifts to your filthy idols."

⁴⁰The Lord my Master says, "People must come to my holy mountain—the high mountain in Israel—to serve me! The whole family of Israel will be on their land—they will be there in their country. That is the place you can come to ask me for advice. And you must come to that place to bring me your offerings. You must bring the first part of your crops to me there in that place. You must bring all your holy gifts to me in that place. ⁴¹Then I will be pleased with the sweet smell of your sacrifices. That will happen when I bring you back. I scattered you among many nations. But I will gather you together and make you my special people again. And all those nations will see it. ⁴²Then you will know that I am the Lord. You will know this when I bring you back to the Land of Israel. That is the land I promised to give to your ancestors.* ⁴³In that country you will remember all the bad things you did that made you filthy. And you will be ashamed. ⁴⁴Family of Israel, you did many bad things. And you should be destroyed because of those bad things. But to protect my good name, I won't give you the punishment you really deserve. Then you will know that I am the Lord. The Lord my Master said these things."

⁴⁵Then the word of the Lord came to me. He said, ⁴⁶"Son of man,* look toward the Negev, the southern part of Judah. Speak against the Negev Forest.* ⁴⁷Say to the Negev Forest, 'Listen to the word of the Lord. The Lord my Master said these things: Look, I am ready to start a fire in your forest. The fire will destroy every green tree and every dry tree. The flame that burns won't be put out. All the land from south to north will be burned by the fire. ⁴⁸Then all people will see that I, the Lord, have started the fire. The fire won't be put out!'"

⁴⁹Then I *(Ezekiel)* said, "Oh, Lord my Master! ₍If I say those things₎, then the people will say that I am only telling them stories. ₍They won't think that it will really happen!₎"

---

ancestors Literally, "fathers," meaning a person's parents, grandparents, and all the people they are descended from.

prostitute A woman paid by men for sexual sin. Sometimes this also means a person that is not faithful to God and stops following him.

Agreement Literally, "Proof." The flat stones with the Ten Commandments written on them were proof of the Agreement between God and Israel.

ancestors Literally, "fathers," meaning a person's parents, grandparents, and all the people they are descended from.

Son of man This was usually just a way of saying "a person," or "a human being." But here this is a title for the man, Ezekiel.

Negev Forest God is probably making fun. The Negev is a desert area, there are no forests in the Negev.

EZEKIEL 21:1–22

21 So the word of the Lord came to me again. He said, ²"Son of man,* look toward Jerusalem and speak against their holy places. Speak against the land of Israel for me. ³Say to the land of Israel, 'The Lord said these things: I am against you! I will pull my sword from its sheath!* I will remove all people from you—the good people and the evil people! ⁴I will cut both good people and evil people from you. I will pull my sword from its sheath and use it against all people from south to north. ⁵Then all people will know that I am the Lord. And they will know that I have pulled my sword from its sheath. My sword won't go back into its sheath again ₍until it is finished₎.'"

⁶₍God said to me,₎ "Son of man,* make sad sounds like a sad person with a broken heart. Make these sad sounds in front of the people. ⁷Then they will ask you, 'Why are you making these sad sounds?' Then you must say, 'Because of the sad news that is coming. Every heart will melt with fear. All hands will become weak. Every spirit will become weak. All knees will be like water.' Look, that bad news is coming. These things will happen! The Lord my Master said these things."

The Sword Is Ready

⁸The word of the God came to me. He said, ⁹"Son of man,* speak to the people for me. Say these things, 'The Lord my Master says these things:

"'Look, a sword, a sharp sword.
    And the sword has been polished.
10 The sword was made sharp for killing.
    It was polished to flash like lightning.
"'My son, you ran away from the stick I used to punish you.
    You refused to be punished with that wooden stick.
11 So the sword has been polished.
    Now it can be used.
    The sword was sharpened and polished.
    Now it can be put in the hand of the killer.

¹²"'Shout out and scream, Son of man!* Why? Because the sword will be used against my people and all the rulers of Israel! Those rulers wanted war—so they will be with my people when the sword comes! So slap your thigh ₍and make loud noises to show your sadness₎! ¹³Why? Because it is not just a test! You refused to be punished with the wooden stick, so what ₍else should I use to punish you₎? ₍Yes, the sword.₎' The Lord my Master said those things.

¹⁴₍God said,₎ "Son of man,* clap your hands and speak to the people for me.

"Let the sword come down twice,
    Yes, three times!
This sword is for killing the people.
    This is the sword for the great killing!
15 This sword will cut into them.
    Their hearts will melt with fear.
    And many people will fall.
The sword will kill many people
    by the city gates.
Yes, the sword will flash like lightning.
    It was polished to kill the people!
16 Sword, be sharp!
    Cut on the right side.
    Cut straight ahead.
    Cut on the left side.
Go every place your edge was chosen to go!
17 "Then I too will clap my hands.
    And I will stop showing my anger.
    I, the Lord, have spoken!"

Choosing the Way to Jerusalem

¹⁸The word of the Lord came to me. He said, ¹⁹"Son of man,* draw two roads that the sword of the king of Babylon can use to come ₍to Israel₎. Both roads will come from the same country (Babylon). Then draw a sign at the head of the road to the city. ²⁰₍Use the sign₎ to show which road the sword will use. One road leads to the Ammonite city of Rabbah. The other road leads to Judah, to the protected city, Jerusalem! ²¹This shows that the king of Babylon ₍is planning the way he wants to attack that area₎. The king of Babylon has come to the place where the two roads separate. The king of Babylon has used ₍magic₎ signs to find the future. He shook some arrows. He asked questions from family idols. He looked at the liver* ₍from an animal he killed₎. ²²"The signs tell him to take the road on his right, the road leading to Jerusalem! He plans to

---

Son of man This was usually just a way of saying "a person," or "a human being." But here this is a title for the man, Ezekiel.

sheath A place for the sword to be kept in when not in use. It was worn around the waist.

arrows, idols, liver People who believed in false gods used these things to try to learn the future.

bring the battering rams.* He will give the command, and his soldiers will begin the killing. They will shout the battle cry. Then they will build a wall of dirt around the city. They will build a dirt road leading up to the walls. They will build wooden towers to attack the city. ²³Those ₍magic₎ signs mean nothing to the people of Israel. They have the promises they made. But ₍the Lord₎ will remember their sin! Then the Israelites will be captured."

²⁴The Lord my Master says this, "You have done many bad things. Your sins are very clear. You forced me to remember that you are guilty. So the enemy will catch you in his hand. ²⁵And you, evil leader of Israel, you will be killed. Your time of punishment has come! The end is here!" ²⁶The Lord my Master says these things, "Take off the turban!* Take off the crown! The time has come to change. The important leaders will be brought low. And people that are not important now will become important leaders. ²⁷I will completely destroy that city! But this won't happen until the right man becomes the new king. Then I will let him *(the king of Babylon)* have this city."

Prophecy Against Ammon

²⁸₍God said₎ "Son of man,* speak to the people for me. Say these things, 'The Lord my Master says these things to the people of Ammon and their shameful ₍god₎:

"'Look, a sword!
The sword is out of its sheath.*
The sword has been polished!
The sword is ready to kill.
It was polished to flash like lightning!

²⁹ Your visions* are useless.
Your magic won't help you.
It is only a bunch of lies.
The sword is now at the throats of evil men.
They will soon be only dead bodies.

battering rams Heavy logs that soldiers used to break holes into the gates or walls around a city.
turban(s) A head covering made by wrapping a long piece of cloth around the head or around a cap worn on the head.
Son of man This was usually just a way of saying "a person," or "a human being." But here this is a title for the man, Ezekiel.
sheath A place for the sword to be kept in when not in use. It was worn around the waist.
vision(s) Something like a dream that God used to speak to people.

Their time has come.
The time has come for their evil to end.

Prophecy Against Babylon

³⁰"'Put the sword *(Babylon)* back in its sheath.* ₍Babylon,₎ I will judge you in the place where you were created, in the land where you were born. ³¹I will pour out my anger against you. My anger will burn you like a hot wind. I will hand you over to cruel men.* Those men are skilled at killing people. ³²You will be like fuel for the fire. Your blood will flow deep into the earth—people will never remember you again. I, the Lord, have spoken!'"

Ezekiel Speaks Against Jerusalem

22 The word of the Lord came to me. He said, ²"Son of man,* will you judge? Will you judge the city of murderers *(Jerusalem)*? Will you tell her about all the terrible things she has done? ³You must say, 'The Lord my Master says this: The city is full of murderers. So her time of punishment will come! She made filthy idols for herself. And those idols made her filthy!

⁴"'People of Jerusalem, you killed many people. You made filthy idols. You are guilty, and the time has come to punish you. Your end has come. Other nations will make fun of you. Those countries will laugh at you. ⁵People far and near will make fun of you. You have ruined your name. You can hear the loud laughter.

⁶"'Look! In Jerusalem, every ruler of Israel made himself strong so he could kill other people. ⁷People in Jerusalem don't respect their parents. They hurt foreigners in that city. They cheat orphans and widows* in that place. ⁸You people hate my holy things. You treat my special days of rest like they are not important. ⁹People in Jerusalem tell lies about other people. They do this to kill those innocent people. People go to the mountains ₍to worship false gods₎ and then come to Jerusalem to eat ₍their fellowship meals₎.

¹⁰"'In Jerusalem, people do many sexual sins. ¹⁰In Jerusalem, people do sexual sins with their father's wife. In Jerusalem, men rape women—even during their monthly time of bleeding. ¹¹One

cruel men This is a word play. The Hebrew word is like the word meaning "to burn."
orphans and widows Widows are women whose husbands have died, and orphans are children whose parents have died. Often these people have no one to care for them.

man does that terrible sin against his own neighbor's wife. Another man has sex with his own daughter-in-law and makes her unclean.* And another man rapes his father's daughter—his very own sister. ¹²"'In Jerusalem, you men take money to kill people. You people lend money and charge interest on those loans. You people cheat their neighbors just to make a little money. And you people have forgotten me.'" The Lord my Master said these things.

¹³₍God said,₎ "Now look! I will slam my hand down and stop you! I will punish you for cheating and killing people. ¹⁴Will you be brave then? Will you be strong at the time I come to punish you? No! I am the Lord. I have spoken. And I will do the things I said! ¹⁵I will scatter you among the nations. I will force you to go to many countries. I will completely destroy the filthy things in this city. ¹⁶But Jerusalem, you will become unclean.* And the other nations will see all these things happen. Then you will know that I am the Lord.'"

Israel Is Like Worthless Waste

¹⁷The word of the Lord came to me. He said, ¹⁸"Son of man,* bronze, iron, lead, and tin are worthless compared to silver. ₍Workers put silver into fire to make it pure. The silver melts and the workers separate it from the waste.₎ The nation of Israel has become like that worthless waste. ¹⁹So the Lord and Master says these things, 'All of you people have become like worthless waste. So I will gather you into Jerusalem. ²⁰Workers put silver, bronze, iron, lead, and tin into a fire. They blow on the fire to make it hotter. Then the metals begin to melt. In the same way, I will put you in my fire and melt you. That fire is my hot anger. ²¹I will put you in that fire. I will blow on the fire of my anger. And you will begin to melt. ²²Silver melts in the fire ₍and workers pour off the silver and save it₎. In the same way, you will melt in the city. Then you will know that I am the Lord. And you will know that I have poured out my anger against you.'"

Ezekiel Speaks Against Jerusalem

²³The word of the Lord came to me. He said, ²⁴"Son of man,* speak to Israel. Tell her that she is not pure.* I am angry at that country, so that country has not received its rain. ²⁵The prophets in Jerusalem are making evil plans. They are like a lion—it roars when it begins to eat the animal it caught. Those prophets have destroyed many lives. They have taken many valuable things. They caused many women to become widows* in Jerusalem.

²⁶"The priests have really hurt my teachings. They don't treat my holy things right—they don't show they are important. They treat holy things just like things that are not holy. They treat clean* things just like things that are unclean. They don't teach the people about these things. They refuse to respect my special days of rest. They treat me like I am not important.

²⁷"The leaders in Jerusalem are like a wolf eating the animal it has caught. Those leaders attack and kill people just to get rich.

²⁸"The prophets ₍don't warn the people—they cover up the truth. They are like workers that don't really fix a wall₎—they only put plaster over the holes. They only see lies. They do their magic to learn the future, but they only tell lies. They say, 'The Lord my Master said these things.' But they are only lying—the Lord did not speak to them!

²⁹"The common people take advantage of each other. They cheat and steal from each other. They treat poor, helpless people like they are not important. They cheat foreigners and they act like there are no laws against it.

³⁰"I asked the people to ₍change their lives and₎ protect their country. I asked people to fix the walls. I wanted them to stand by those holes in the wall and fight to protect their city. But no person came to help! ³¹So I will show them my anger—I will completely destroy them! I will punish them for the bad things they have done. It is all their fault!" The Lord my Master said these things.

23 The word of the Lord came to me. He said, ²"Son of man,* ₍listen to this story about Samaria and Jerusalem₎. There were two sisters. They were daughters of the same mother. ³They

---

unclean Not pure or not acceptable to God for worship.
Son of man This was usually just a way of saying "a person," or "a human being." But here this is a title for the man, Ezekiel.

not pure This is a word play. The Hebrew word also means "not rained on."
widow(s) Women whose husbands have died. Often these women had no one to care for them.
clean Pure or acceptable to God for worship.

became prostitutes* in Egypt while they were still young girls. In Egypt, they first made love and let men touch their nipples and hold their young breasts. ⁴The older daughter was named Oholah.* And her sister was named Oholibah.* Those sisters became my wives. And we had children. (Oholah is really Samaria. And Oholibah is really Jerusalem.)

⁵"Then Oholah became unfaithful to me—she began to live like a prostitute. She began to want her lovers. She saw the Assyrian soldiers ⁶in their blue uniforms. They were all desirable young men riding horses. They were leaders and officers. ⁷And Oholah gave herself to all those men. All of them were hand-picked soldiers in the Assyrian army. And she wanted them all! She became filthy with their filthy idols. ⁸Besides that, she never stopped her love affair with Egypt. Egypt made love to her when she was a young girl. Egypt was the first lover to touch her young breasts. Egypt poured his untrue love on her. ⁹So I let her lovers have her. She wanted Assyria, so I gave her to them! ¹⁰They raped* her. They took her children. And they used a sword and killed her. They punished her. And women still talk about her.

¹¹"Her younger sister, Oholibah, saw all these things happen. But Oholibah did more sins than her sister! She was more unfaithful than Oholah. ¹²She wanted the Assyrian leaders and officers. She wanted those soldiers in blue uniforms riding their horses. They were all desirable young men. ¹³I saw that both women were going to ruin their lives with the same mistakes.

¹⁴"Oholibah continued to be unfaithful to me. In Babylon, she saw pictures of men carved on the walls. These were pictures of Chaldean* men wearing their red uniforms. ¹⁵They wore belts around their waists and long turbans on their heads. All of those men looked like chariot* officers. They all looked like native born Babylonian men. ¹⁶And Oholibah wanted them. ¹⁷So those Babylonian men came to her love bed to have sex with her. They used her and made her so filthy that she became disgusted with them!

¹⁸"Oholibah let everyone see that she was unfaithful. She let so many men enjoy her naked body, that I became disgusted with her—just like I had become disgusted with her sister. ¹⁹Again and again Oholibah was unfaithful to me. And then she remembered the love affair she had as a young girl in Egypt. ²⁰She remembered her lover with the penis like a donkey and a flood of semen like a horse.

²¹"Oholibah, you dreamed of those times when you were young; when your lover touched your nipples and held your young breasts. ²²So Oholibah, the Lord my Master says these things, "You became disgusted with your lovers. But I will bring your lovers here. They will surround you. ²³I will bring all those men from Babylon, especially the Chaldeans. I will bring the men from Pekod, Shoa, and Koa. And I will bring all those men from Assyria. So I will bring all those leaders and officers. They were all desirable young men, chariot* officers and hand-picked soldiers riding their horses. ²⁴Those crowd of men will come to you. They will come riding on their horses and in their chariots.* There will be many, many people. They will have their spears, shields, and helmets. They will gather together around you. I will tell them what you have done to me. And they will punish you their own way. ²⁵I will show you how jealous I am. They will be very angry and hurt you. They will cut off your nose and ears. They will use a sword and kill you. Then they will take your children, and burn whatever is left of you. ²⁶They will take your nice clothes and jewelry. ²⁷And I will stop your dreams about your love affair with Egypt. You will never again look for them. You will never remember Egypt again!"

²⁸The Lord my Master says these things, "I am giving you to the men you hate. I am giving you to the men you became disgusted with. ²⁹And they will show how much they hate you! They will take everything you worked for. And they will leave you bare and naked! People will clearly see your sins. They will see that you acted like a prostitute and dreamed wicked dreams. ³⁰You did those bad things when you left me to chase after those other nations. You did those bad things when you began to worship their filthy idols. ³¹You followed your sister and lived like her. You, yourself, took the cup of poison and held it

---

prostitute(s) A woman paid by men for sexual sin. Sometimes this also means a person that is not faithful to God and stops following him.
Oholah This name means "Tent." It probably refers to the Holy Tent where the people of Israel went to worship God.
Oholibah This name means "My Tent is in her ₁country₁."
raped Literally, "revealed her nakedness." The Hebrew word meaning "revealed" is like the word meaning "carried away as a prisoner to a faraway country."
Chaldean An important family group in Babylonia. Sometimes this name means simply, "people from Babylonia."
chariot(s) A small wagon used in war.

in your hands. ₍You caused your own punishment₎." ³²The Lord my Master says these things:

"You will drink your sister's cup of poison.
It is a tall, wide cup of poison.
That cup holds much poison *(punishment)*.
People will laugh at you
and make fun of you.
³³ You will stagger like a drunk person.
You will become very dizzy.
That is the cup of destruction
and devastation.
It is like the cup *(punishment)*
that your sister drank.
³⁴ You will drink the poison in that cup.
You will drink it to the last drop.
You will throw down the glass
and break it to pieces.
And you will tear at your breasts
from the pain.
This will happen because
I am the Lord and Master.
And I said these things.

³⁵"So, the Lord my Master said these things, '₍Jerusalem,₎ you forgot me. You threw me away and left me behind. So now you must suffer for leaving me and living like a prostitute. You must suffer for your wicked dreams.'"

Judgment Against Oholah and Oholibah

³⁶The Lord my Master said to me, "Son of man,* will you judge Oholah and Oholibah? Then tell them about the terrible things they have done. ³⁷They have done the sin of adultery.* They are guilty of murder. They acted like prostitutes—they left me to be with their filthy idols. They had my children. But they forced them to pass through fire. They did this to give food to their filthy idols. ³⁸They also treated my special days of rest and my holy place like they were not important. ³⁹They killed their children for their idols,* and then they went into my holy place and made it filthy too! They did this inside my temple!*

⁴⁰"They have sent for men from faraway places. You sent a messenger to these men. And those men came to see you. You bathed for them, painted your eyes, and put on your jewelry. ⁴¹You sat on a fine bed with a table set before it. You put my incense* and my oil* on this table.

⁴²"The noise in Jerusalem sounded like a crowd of people having a party.* Many people came to the party. People were already drinking as they came in from the desert. They gave bracelets and beautiful crowns to the women. ⁴³Then I spoke to one of the women who was worn out from her sexual sins. I told her, 'Will they continue to do sexual sins with her, and she with them?' ⁴⁴But they kept going to her like they would go to a prostitute.* Yes, they went again and again to Oholah and Oholibah, those wicked women.

⁴⁵"But good men will judge them guilty. They will judge those women guilty of the sin of adultery* and murder. Why? Because Oholah and Oholibah have done the sin of adultery* and the blood from people they killed is still on their hands!"

⁴⁶The Lord my Master said these things, "Gather the people together. Then let those people punish Oholah and Oholibah. This group of people will punish and make fun of these two women. ⁴⁷Then the group will throw stones at them and kill them. Then the group will cut the women to pieces with their swords. They will kill the women's children and burn their houses. ⁴⁸In this way, I remove that shame from this country. And all the other women will be warned not to do the shameful things you have done. ⁴⁹They will punish you for the wicked things you did. And you will be punished for worshiping your filthy idols. Then you will know that I am the Lord and Master."

---

my incense A special blend of spices that were burned as a gift to God. This special incense was to be burned only in the temple. See Ex. 30:34-38.

my oil The special oil that was used for anointing priests and things in the temple to make them holy *(special)*. See Ex. 30:22-33.

party The Hebrew word is like the word for a fellowship offering, a time when people came to share a meal and enjoy themselves together with the Lord. Here it seems this time of worship turned into a wild party. See Deut 14:22-29,26:1-15.

prostitute A woman paid by men for sexual sin. Sometimes this also means a person that is not faithful to God and stops following him.

Son of man This was usually just a way of saying "a person," or "a human being." But here this is a title for the man, Ezekiel.

adultery Breaking the marriage promise by sexual sin.

idols Statues of false gods that people worshiped.

temple The special building in Jerusalem for Jewish worship.

The Pot and the Meat

24 The word of the Lord my Master came to me. This was on the tenth day of the tenth month, in the ninth year ⌊of exile⌋.* He said, ²"Son of man,* write today's date and this note: 'On this date the army of the king of Babylon surrounded Jerusalem.' ³Tell this story to the family that refuses to obey *(Israel)*. Tell them these things, 'The Lord my Master says this:

"'Put the pot on the fire.
   Put on the pot and pour in the water.
⁴ Put in the pieces of meat.
   Put in every good piece,
      the thighs and the shoulders.
   Fill the pot with the best bones.
⁵ Use the best animals in the flock.
   Pile the wood under the pot.
   And boil the pieces of meat.
   Boil the soup until even the bones
      are cooked!

⁶ So the Lord my Master says these things:
"'It will be bad for ⌊Jerusalem⌋.
   It will be bad for that city of murderers.
   Jerusalem is like a pot with rust on it.
      And those spots of rust can't be removed!
   ⌊That pot is not clean, so you must⌋
      take every piece of meat out of the pot!
   ⌊Don't eat that meat!⌋
   And don't let ⌊the priests⌋ choose any
      ⌊of that ruined meat⌋.
⁷ Jerusalem is like a pot with rust on it.
   Why? Because the blood from those murders
      is still there!
   She put the blood on the bare rock!
   She did not pour the blood on the ground
      and cover it with dirt.*
⁸ I put her blood on the bare rock,
      so it would not be covered.
   I did this so people would get angry and
      punish her for killing innocent people.'"

⁹ So the Lord my Master says these things: "It
   will be bad for the city full of murderers!
   I will pile up plenty of wood for the fire.
¹⁰ Put plenty of wood ⌊under the pot⌋.
   Light the fire.
   Cook the meat well done!
   Mix in the spices.*
      And let the bones be burned up.
¹¹ Then let the pot stand empty on the coals.
   Let it become so hot that its stains*
      begin to glow.
   Those stains will be melted away.
   The rust will be destroyed.

¹² ⌊Jerusalem⌋ might work hard
      to scrub away her stains.
   But that 'rust' won't go away!
   Only fire *(punishment)* will remove that rust!

¹³ You sinned against me
      and became stained with sin.
   I wanted to wash you and make you clean.
   But the stains would not come out.
   I won't try washing you again
      until my hot anger is finished with you!

¹⁴"I am the Lord. I said your punishment would come, and I will make it happen. I won't hold back the punishment. I won't feel sorry for you. I will punish you for the bad things you did." The Lord my Master said those things.

The Death of Ezekiel's Wife

¹⁵Then the word of the Lord came to me. He said, ¹⁶, "Son of man,* you love your wife very much, but I am going to take her away from you. Your wife will die suddenly. But you must not show your sadness. You must not cry loudly. You will cry and your tears will fall, ¹⁷but you must make your sad sounds quietly. Don't cry out loud for your dead wife. ⌊You must wear the clothes you normally wear.⌋ Wear your turban* and your shoes. Don't cover your mustache ⌊to show your sadness⌋. And don't eat the food people normally eat when a person dies."

¹⁸The next morning I told the people what God had said. That evening, my wife died. The next

---

ninth year of exile This was 15 Jan 588B.C., the date that king Nebuchadnezzar began his attack on Jerusalem.

Son of man This was usually just a way of saying "a person," or "a human being." Here this is a title for the man, Ezekiel.

blood ... dirt The Law of Moses teaches that if a person killed an animal for food, he must pour the blood on the ground and cover it with dirt. This showed that he was giving the life of that animal back to God. See Lev. 17:1-16 and Deut. 12:1-25. If the blood was not covered with dirt, then it was a witness against the killer. See Gen. 4:10, Job 15:18, and Isa. 26:21.

Mix in the spices We are not sure of the meaning of this sentence.

stains Or, "bronze."

turban(s) A head covering made by wrapping a long piece of cloth around the head or around a cap worn on the head.

morning I did the things God commanded. ¹⁹Then the people said to me, "Why are you doing these things? What does it mean?"

²⁰Then I said to them, "The word of the Lord came to me. He told me ²¹to speak to the family of Israel. The Lord my Master said, 'Look, I will destroy my holy place. You are proud of that place and sings songs of praise about it. You love to see that place. You really love that place. ₍But I will destroy that place₎ and your children that you left behind will be killed in battle. ²²But you will do the same things that I have done ₍about my dead wife₎. You won't cover your mustache ₍to show your sadness₎. You won't eat the food people normally eat when a person dies. ²³You will wear your turbans* and your shoes. You won't show your sadness. You won't cry. But you will be wasting away because of your sins. You will make your sad sounds quietly to each other. ²⁴So Ezekiel is an example for you. You will do all the same things he did. That time of punishment will come. And then you will know that I am the Lord.'"

²⁵⁻²⁶"Son of man,* I will take away that safe place *(Jerusalem)* from the people. That beautiful place makes them happy. They love to see that place. They really love that place. But at that time, I will take that city and their children away from these people. One of the survivors will come to you with the bad news about Jerusalem. ²⁷At that time, you will be able to speak to that person. You won't be silent any more. In this way, you will be an example for them. Then they will know that I am the Lord."

Prophecy Against Ammon

25 The word of the Lord came to me. He said, ²"Son of man,* look toward the people of Ammon and speak against them for me. ³Say to the people of Ammon: 'Listen to the word of the Lord my Master! The Lord my Master says this: You were happy when my holy place was destroyed. You were against the land of Israel when it was polluted. You were against the family of Judah when the people were carried away as prisoners. ⁴So I will give you to the people from the east. They will get your land. Their armies will set up their camps in your country. They will live among you. They will eat your fruit and drink your milk.

⁵"'I will make the city Rabbah a pasture for camels and the country of Ammon a sheep pen. Then you will know that I am the Lord. ⁶The Lord says these things: You were happy that Jerusalem was destroyed. You clapped your hands and stamped your feet. You had fun insulting the land of Israel. ⁷So I will punish you. You will be like the valuable things soldiers take in war. You will lose your inheritance. You will die in faraway lands. I will destroy your country! Then you will know that I am the Lord.'"

Prophecy Against Moab and Seir

⁸The Lord my Master says these things, "Moab and Seir *(Edom)* say, 'The family of Judah is just like any other nation.' ⁹I will cut into Moab's shoulder—I will take away its cities which are on its borders, the glory of the land, Beth Jeshimoth, Baal Meon, and Kiriathaim. ¹⁰Then I will give these cities to the people of the east. They will get your land. And I will let those people from the east destroy the people of Ammon. Then everyone will forget that the people of Ammon were a nation. ¹¹So, I will punish Moab. Then they will know that I am the Lord."

Prophecy Against Edom

¹²The Lord my Master says these things, "The people of Edom turned against the family of Judah and tried to get even. The people of Edom are guilty." ¹³So the Lord my Master says: "I will punish Edom. I will destroy the people and the animals in Edom. I will destroy the whole country of Edom, all the way from Teman to Dedan. The Edomites will be killed in battle. ¹⁴I will use my people Israel and get even against Edom. In this way, the people of Israel will show my anger against Edom. Then those people of Edom will know that I punished them." The Lord my Master said these things.

Prophecy Against the Philistines

¹⁵The Lord my Master says these things, "The Philistines tried to get even. They were very cruel. They let their anger burn inside them too long!" ¹⁶So the Lord my Master said, "I will punish the Philistines. Yes, I will destroy those people from Crete. I will completely destroy those people living on the sea coast. ¹⁷I will punish those people—I will get even. I will let my anger teach

---

turban(s) A head covering made by wrapping a long piece of cloth around the head or around a cap worn on the head.

Son of man This was usually just a way of saying "a person," or "a human being." But here this is a title for the man, Ezekiel.

them a lesson. Then they will know that I am the Lord!"

The Sad Message About Tyre

26 In the eleventh year ₁of exile₁,* on the first day of the month, the word of the Lord came to me. He said, ²"Son of man,* Tyre said bad things about Jerusalem: 'Hurray! The city gate protecting the people is destroyed! The city gate is open for me. The city *(Jerusalem)* is ruined, so I can get plenty of valuable things out of it!'"

³So the Lord my Master says: "I am against you, Tyre! I will bring many nations to fight against you. They will come again and again, like waves on the beach."

⁴₁God said,₁ "Those enemy soldiers will destroy the walls of Tyre and pull down her towers. I will also scrape the topsoil from her land. I will make Tyre a bare rock. ⁵Tyre will become a place by the sea for spreading fishing nets. I have spoken!" The Lord my Master says, "Tyre will be like the valuable things soldiers take in war. ⁶Her daughters *(small towns)* on the mainland will be killed in battle. Then they will know that I am the Lord."

Nebuchadnezzar Will Attack Tyre

⁷The Lord my Master says these things, "I will bring an enemy from the north against Tyre. That enemy is Nebuchadnezzar, the great king of Babylon! He will bring a very large army. There will be horses, chariots,* horse soldiers and many, many other soldiers! Those soldiers will be from many different nations. ⁸Nebuchadnezzar will kill your daughters *(small towns)* on the mainland. He will build towers to attack your city. He will build a dirt road around your city. He will build a dirt road leading up to the walls. ⁹He will bring the logs to break down your walls. He will use picks and break down your towers. ¹⁰There will be so many of his horses that the dust from them will cover you. Your walls will shake at the noise of horse soldiers, wagons, and chariots* when the king of Babylon enters the city through your city gates. Yes, they will come into your city because its walls will be pulled down. ¹¹The king of Babylon will come riding through your city. His horses' hoofs* will come pounding over your streets. He will kill your people with swords. The strong columns in your city will fall to the ground. ¹²Nebuchadnezzar's men will take away your riches. They will take the things you wanted to sell. They will break down your walls and destroy your pleasant houses. They will throw your stones and wood ₁houses₁ into the sea like garbage. ¹³So I will stop the sound of your happy songs. People won't hear your harps any more. ¹⁴I will make you a bare rock. You will be a place by the sea for spreading fishing nets! You won't be built again. Why? Because I, the Lord, have spoken!" The Lord my Master said those things.

Other Nations Will Cry for Tyre

¹⁵The Lord my Master says this to Tyre: "The countries along the Mediterranean coast will shake at the sound of your fall. That will happen when your people are hurt and killed. ¹⁶Then all the leaders of the countries by the sea will step down from their thrones ₁and show their sadness₁. They will take off their special robes. They will take off their beautiful clothes. Then they will put on their 'clothes of shaking' *(fear)*. They will sit on the ground and shake with fear. They will be shocked at how quickly you were destroyed. ¹⁷They will sing this sad song about you:

"'Tyre, you were a famous city.*
   People came from across the sea
      to live in you.*
   You were famous,
      but now you are gone!
   You were strong on the sea,
      and so were the people living in you.
   You made all the people living
      on the mainland afraid of you.
¹⁸ Now, on the day you fall,
      the countries along the coast
         will shake with fear.
   You started many colonies along the coast.
      Now those people will be scared
         when you are gone!'"

¹⁹The Lord my Master says these things, "₁Tyre, I will destroy you₁ and you will become an old, empty city. No one will live there. I will cause the sea to flow over you. The great sea will

---

eleventh year of exile This was probably the summer of 587B.C. See 2 Kings 25:3.
Son of man This was usually just a way of saying "a person," or "a human being." Here this is a title for the man, Ezekiel.
chariot(s) A small wagon used in war.
hoof(s) The hard part of a horse's foot.
you were a famous city This can also mean, "People have cried for you."
People ... you This can also mean, "People have lived in you for a long time."

cover you. ²⁰I will send you down into that deep hole—to the place where dead people are. You will join the people that died long ago. I will send you to the world below, like all the other old, empty cities. You will be with all the others that go down to the grave. No one will live in you then. You will never again be in the land of the living! ²¹Other people will be afraid about what happened to you. You will be finished! People will look for you, but they will never find you again!" That is what the Lord my Master says.

Tyre the Great Center of Trade on the Seas

27 The word of the Lord came to me again. He said, ²"Son of man,* sing this sad song about Tyre. ³Say these things about Tyre:

"'⌊Tyre,⌋ you are the door to the seas.
　　You are the merchant* for many nations.
　　You travel to many countries
　　　along the coast.'
　The Lord my Master says these things:
"'Tyre, you think that you are so beautiful.
　　You think you are perfectly beautiful!
⁴　The Mediterranean Sea is the border
　　　around your city.
　　Your builders made you perfectly beautiful,
　　　⌊like the ships that sail from you.⌋
⁵　Your builders used cypress trees from
　　　the Senir mountains to make your planks.
　　They used cedar trees from Lebanon
　　　to make your mast.
⁶　They used oak trees from Bashan
　　　to make your oars.
　　They used pine trees from Cyprus
　　　to make the cabin on your deck.*
　　They decorated that shelter with ivory.
⁷　For your sail,
　　　they used colorful linen made in Egypt.
　　That sail was your flag.
　　The coverings over your cabin
　　　were blue and purple.
　　They came from the coast of Cyprus.*
⁸　Men from Sidon and Arvad
　　　rowed your boats for you.

Tyre, your wise men were the pilots
　　on your ships.
⁹　The elders and wise men from Byblos*
　　were on board to help put caulking*
　　　between the boards on your ship.
　All the ships of the sea and their sailors
　　came to trade and do business with you.'

¹⁰"Men from Persia, Lud, and Put were in your army. They were your men of war. They hung their shields and helmets on your walls. They brought honor and glory to your city. ¹¹Men from Arvad and Cilicia were guards standing on the wall around your city. Men from Gammad were in your towers. They hung their shields on the walls around your city. They made your beauty complete.

¹²"Tarshish* was one of your best customers. They traded silver, iron, tin, and lead for all the wonderful things you sold. ¹³People in Greece, Turkey, and the area around the Black Sea traded with you. They traded slaves and bronze for the things you sold. ¹⁴People from the nation* of Togarmah traded horses, war horses, and mules for the things you sold. ¹⁵The people of Rhodes* traded with you. You sold your things in many places. People brought ivory tusks and ebony wood to pay you. ¹⁶Edom traded with you because you had so many good things. ⌊The people of Edom⌋ traded emeralds, purple cloth, fine needlework, fine linen, coral* and rubies for the things you sold.

¹⁷"The people in Judah and Israel traded with you. They paid for the things you sold with the wheat, olives, early figs, honey, oil, and balm.* ¹⁸Damascus was a good customer. They traded with you for the many wonderful things you had. They traded wine from Helbon and white wool for those things. ¹⁹Damascus traded wine from Uzal for the things you sold. They paid wrought iron,

---

Byblos Literally, "Gebal."
caulking Often a mixture of tar and rope that was put between the boards to make a ship watertight so it would not leak.
Tarshish This is probably a city in Spain.
nation Literally, "house." This might mean the royal family of that country.
Rhodes Or, "Dedan." See verse 20.
coral Sea animals that leave skeletons after they die. The skeletons are hard like rocks and are used for jewelry.
balm An ointment from some kinds of trees and plants. It is used as medicine.

Son of man This was usually just a way of saying "a person," or "a human being." But here this is a title for the man, Ezekiel.
merchant A person who buys and sells things for a living.
deck The floor of a ship.
Cyprus Literally, "Elishah." This might be the area near Enkomi, Cyprus or it might be the Greek islands.

cassia* and sugar cane for those things. ²⁰Dedan provided good business. They traded with you for saddlecloths and for riding horses. ²¹Arabia and all the leaders of Kedar traded lambs, rams, and goats for your goods. ²²The merchants* of Sheba and Raamah traded with you. They traded all the best spices and every kind of precious stone and gold for your goods. ²³Haran, Canneh, Eden, the merchants of Sheba, Asshur and Kilmad traded with you. ²⁴They paid with the best clothes, clothes from blue and fine needlework, carpets of many colors, tightly wound ropes and ₗthings made fromⱼ cedar wood. These were the things they traded with you. ²⁵The ships of Tarshish carried the things you sold.

ₗTyre, you are like one of those cargo ships.ⱼ
You are on the sea, loaded with many riches.
²⁶ Your oarsmen rowed you far out to sea.
But a powerful east wind
will destroy your ship at sea.
²⁷ And all your wealth will spill into the sea.
Your wealth, the things you buy and sell,
will spill into the sea.
Your whole crew—sailors, pilots, and the men
who put caulking* between the boards
on your ship will spill into the sea.
The merchants and soldiers in your city,
will all sink into the sea.
That will happen on the day
that you are destroyed!

²⁸ "You send your businessmen
to faraway places.
Those places will shake with fear
when they hear your pilot's cry!
²⁹ Your whole crew will jump ship.
The sailors and pilots will jump ship
and swim to the shore.
³⁰ They will be very sad about you.
They will cry.
They will throw dust on their heads,
They will roll in ashes.
³¹ They will shave their heads for you.
They will put on clothes of sadness.
They will cry for you like someone crying
for a person that died.

³²"And in their heavy crying they will sing this sad song about you, and cry about you.

"'No one is like Tyre!
Tyre is destroyed,
in the middle of the sea!
³³ Your businessmen sailed across the seas.
You satisfied many people
with your great wealth
and the things you sold.
You made the kings of the earth rich!
³⁴ But now you are broken by the seas,
and by the deep waters.
All the things you sell
and all your people have fallen!
³⁵ All the people living on the coast
are shocked about you.
Their kings are terribly afraid.
Their faces show their shock.
³⁶ The merchants* in other nations
whistle about you.
The things that happened to you
will scare people.
Why? Because you are finished.
You will be no more.'"

Tyre Thinks It Is like a God

28 The word of the Lord came to me. He said, ²"Son of man,* say to the ruler of Tyre, 'The Lord my Master says these things:

"'You are very proud!
And you say,
"I am a god!
I sit on the seat of gods
in the middle of the seas."
"'But you are a man and not God!
You only think you are a god.
³ You think you are wiser than Danel!*
You think you can find out all secrets!
⁴ Through your wisdom and understanding
you have gotten riches for yourself.
And you put gold and silver
in your treasuries.
⁵ Through your great wisdom and trade,
you have made your riches grow.

---

cassia A spice or perfume.
merchant(s) A person who buys and sells things for a living.
caulking Often, a mixture of tar and rope that was put between the boards to make a ship watertight so it would not leak.

Son of man This was usually just a way of saying "a person," or "a human being." But here this is a title for the man, Ezekiel.
Danel An ancient wise man.

And now you are proud because of
those riches.

⁶"'So the Lord my Master says these things: Tyre,
you thought you were like a god.
⁷ I will bring strangers to fight against you.
They are most terrible among the nations!
They will pull out their swords
and use them against the beautiful things
that your wisdom brought you.
They will ruin your glory.
⁸ They will bring you down to the grave.
You will be like a sailor that died at sea.
⁹ That person will kill you.
Will you still say, "I am a god"?
No! He will have you in his power.
You will see that you are a man, not God!
¹⁰ Strangers will treat you like a foreigner*
and kill you.
⌊Those things will happen because⌋
I gave the command!'"
The Lord my Master said those things.

¹¹The word of the Lord came to me. He said, ¹²"Son of man,* sing this sad song about the king of Tyre. Say to him, 'The Lord my Master says these things:

"'You were the ideal man.
You were full of wisdom.
You were perfectly handsome.
¹³ You were in Eden,
the Garden of God.
You had every precious stone—
rubies, topaz, and diamonds;
beryls, onyx, and jasper;
sapphires, turquoise, and emeralds.
And each of these stones was set in gold.
You were given this beauty
on the day you were created.
⌊God⌋ made you strong.
¹⁴ You were one of the chosen Cherubs.*
⌊Your wings⌋ spread over ⌊my throne⌋.

And I put you on the holy mountain of God.
You walked among the jewels
that sparkled like fire.
¹⁵ You were good and honest
when I created you.
But then you became evil.
¹⁶ Your business brought you ⌊many riches⌋.
But they also put cruelty inside you.
And you sinned.
So I treated you like you were some
unclean thing—
I threw you off the mountain of God.
You were one of the special Cherub angels—
⌊Your wings⌋ spread over ⌊my throne⌋.
But I forced you to leave the jewels
that sparkled like fire.
¹⁷ Your beauty made you proud.
Your glory ruined your wisdom.
So I threw you down to the ground.
And now other kings stare at you.
¹⁸ You did many wrong things.
You were a very crooked businessman.
In this way, you made the holy places
unclean.
So I brought fire from inside you.
It burned you!
You burned to ashes on the ground.
Now everyone can see your shame.
¹⁹ All the people in other nations
were shocked about what happened to you.
What happened to you will make people very
afraid.
You are finished!'"

The Message Against Sidon

²⁰The word of the Lord came to me. He said, ²¹"Son of man,* look toward Sidon and speak for me against that place. ²²Say, 'The Lord my Master says these things:

"'I am against you, Sidon!
Your people will learn to respect me!
I will punish Sidon.
Then people will know that I am the Lord.
Then they will learn that I am holy
and they will treat me that way.
²³ I will send disease and death to Sidon,
and many people inside the city will die.
The sword (enemy soldiers) outside the city
will kill many people.
Then they will know that I am the Lord!'

---

foreigner Literally, "uncircumcised." To have the foreskin cut off. This was done to every Jewish male to show he shared in the Agreement God made with Israel. See Gen. 17:9-14.

Son of man This was usually just a way of saying "a person," or "a human being." But here this is a title for the man, Ezekiel.

Cherubs Angels that were often used like guards to be around the king (God) or to protect things (the Garden of Eden). The Cherub angels on the Box of the Agreement were like guards by the king's throne.

The Nations Will Stop Making Fun of Israel

24"'The countries around Israel hated her. ⌊But bad things will happen to those countries.⌋ Then there won't be any sharp stickers or thorn bushes to hurt the family of Israel. And they will know that I am the Lord their Master.'"

25The Lord my Master said these things, "I scattered the people of Israel among other nations. But I will gather the family of Israel together again. Then those nations will know that I am holy and they will treat me that way. At that time, the people of Israel will live in their land—I gave that land to my servant Jacob. 26They will live safely in the land. They will build houses and plant vineyards. I will punish the nations around them that hated them. Then the people of Israel will live in safety. And they will know that I am the Lord their God."

The Message Against Egypt

29 On the twelfth day of the tenth month *(January)* of the tenth year ⌊of exile⌋,* the word of the Lord my Master came to me. He said, 2"Son of man,* look toward Pharaoh, king of Egypt. Speak for me against him and Egypt. 3Say, 'The Lord my Master says these things:

"'I am against you, Pharaoh, king of Egypt.
You are the great monster*
  lying beside the Nile River.
You say,
  "This is my river!
  I made this river!"

4-5"'But I will put hooks in your jaws.
The fish in the Nile River
  will stick to your scales.
I will pull you and your fish up
  out of your rivers
  and onto the dry land.
You will fall on the ground,
  And no one will pick you up or bury you.
I will give you to the wild animals and birds.
  You will be their food.
6 Then all the people living in Egypt
  will know that I am the Lord!

"'⌊Why will I do these things?⌋
Because the people of Israel leaned
  on Egypt for support.
But Egypt was only a weak blade of grass.
7 The people of Israel leaned on Egypt
  for support.
But Egypt only pierced their hands
  and shoulder.
They leaned on you for support,
  but you broke and twisted their back.'"

8 So the Lord my Master says these things:
  "I will bring a sword against you.
  I will destroy all your people and animals.
9 Egypt will be empty and destroyed.
  Then they will know that I am the Lord."

⌊God said,⌋ "Why will I do those things? Because you said, 'This is my river. I made this river.' 10So, I *(God)* am against you. I am against the many branches of your Nile River. I will destroy Egypt completely. The cities will be empty from Migdol to Aswan, and as far as the border of Ethiopia. 11No person or animal will pass through Egypt. Nothing will pass through or settle there for 40 years. 12I will destroy Egypt. The cities will be in ruins for 40 years! I will scatter the Egyptians among the nations. I will make them strangers* in foreign lands."

13The Lord my Master says these things, "I will scatter the people of Egypt among many nations. But at the end of 40 years, I will gather those people together again. 14I will bring back the Egyptian captives. I will bring back the Egyptians to the land of Pathros, to the land where they were born. But their kingdom won't be important. 15It will be the least important kingdom. It will never again lift itself above the other nations. I will make them so small that they won't rule over the nations. 16And the family of Israel will never again depend on Egypt. The Israelites will remember their sin—they will remember that they turned to Egypt ⌊for help and not to God⌋. And they will know that I am the Lord and Master."

Babylon Will Get Egypt

17On the first day of the first month *(April)* in the twenty-seventh year ⌊of exile⌋,* the word of the Lord came to me. He said, 18"Son of man,*

Son of man This was usually just a way of saying "a person," or "a human being." But here this is a title for the man, Ezekiel.
tenth year of exile This was the winter of 587 B.C.
great monster There were ancient stories about a sea monster that fought against God. The prophets called Egypt that sea monster many times. But here this might mean the crocodiles that rest on the banks of the Nile River.

I will ... strangers Or, "I will scatter them..."
Son of man This was usually just a way of saying "a person," or "a human being." Here it is a title for the man Ezekiel.
twenty-seventh year of exile This was in the spring of 571 B.C.

Nebuchadnezzar, king of Babylon, made his army fight hard against Tyre. They shaved every soldiers' hair. Every shoulder was rubbed bare [from carrying heavy loads]. Nebuchadnezzar and his army worked hard to defeat Tyre. But they got nothing from all that hard work. [19]So the Lord my Master says these things, "I will give the land of Egypt to Nebuchadnezzar, king of Babylon. And Nebuchadnezzar will carry away Egypt's people. Nebuchadnezzar will take the many valuable things in Egypt. This will be the pay for Nebuchadnezzar's army. [20]I have given Nebuchadnezzar the land of Egypt as a reward for the hard work he did. Why? Because they worked for me!" The Lord my Master said these things!

[21]"On that day I will make the family of Israel strong. Your people will laugh at the Egyptians. And they will know that I am the Lord."

The Army of Babylon Will Attack Egypt

30 The word of the Lord came to me again. He said, [2]"Son of man,* speak for me. Say, 'The Lord my Master says these things:

"'Cry and say,
"That terrible day is coming."
[3] That day is near!
Yes, the Lord's day for judging is near.
It will be a cloudy day,
It will be the time for judging the nations!
[4] A sword will come against Egypt!
People in Ethiopia will shake with fear,
at the time that Egypt falls.
The army of Babylon will take Egypt's people
away as prisoners.
Egypt's foundations will be torn down!

[5]"'Many people made peace agreements with Egypt. But all those people from Ethiopia, Put, Lud, all Arabia, Libya and the people of Israel* will be destroyed!

[6] The Lord my Master says these things:
"The people who support Egypt will fall!
The pride in her power will end.
The people in Egypt will be killed in battle,
all the way from Migdol to Aswan."'

The Lord my Master said those things!
[7] Egypt will join the other countries
that were destroyed.
Egypt will be one of those empty lands.
[8] I will start a fire in Egypt,
and all her helpers will be destroyed.
Then they will know that I am the Lord!

[9]"'At that time, I will send out messengers. They will go in ships to carry the bad news to Ethiopia. Ethiopia now feels safe. But the people of Ethiopia will shake with fear at the time Egypt is punished. That time is coming!

[10] The Lord my Master says these things:
"I will use the king of Babylon.
I will use Nebuchadnezzar to destroy
the people of Egypt.
[11] Nebuchadnezzar and his people
are the most terrible of the nations.
And I will bring them to destroy Egypt.
They will pull out their swords against Egypt.
They will fill the land with dead bodies.
[12] I will make the Nile River become dry land.
Then I will sell the dry land to evil people.
I will use strangers to make that land empty.
I, the Lord, have spoken!"

The Idols of Egypt Will Be Destroyed

[13] The Lord my Master says these things:
"I will also destroy the idols* in Egypt.
I will take the statues away from Memphis.
There won't be a leader anymore
in the land of Egypt,
And I will put fear in the land of Egypt.
[14] I will make Pathros empty.
I will start a fire in Zoan.
I will punish No,
[15] And I will pour out my anger against Sin,
the fortress* of Egypt!
I will destroy the people of No.
[16] I will start a fire in Egypt;
The place named Sin will be in great pain.
The soldiers will break into the city No,
and Memphis will have new troubles
every day.
[17] The young men of On and Pi Beseth*
will die in battle.
And the women will be captured
and taken away.

Son of man This was usually just a way of saying "a person," or "a human being." But here this is a title for the man, Ezekiel.

people of Israel Literally, "sons of the Agreement." This might mean "all the people that made peace agreements with Egypt" or it might mean "Israel, the people that made the Agreement with God."

idols Statues of false gods that people worshiped.
fortress A building or city with tall, strong walls for protection.
On, Pi Beseth Heliopolis and Bubastis, cities in Egypt.
control Literally, "yoke."

¹⁸ It will be a dark day in Tahpanhes
when I break Egypt's control.*
Egypt's proud power will be finished!
A cloud will cover Egypt,
and her daughters will be captured
and taken away.
¹⁹ So I will punish Egypt.
Then they will know I am the Lord!

Egypt Will Become Weak Forever

²⁰On the seventh day of the first month *(April)* of the eleventh year ₍of exile₎,* the word of the Lord came to me. He said, ²¹"Son of man,* I have broken the arm *(power)* of Pharaoh, king of Egypt. No one will wrap his arm with a bandage. It won't heal. So his arm won't be strong enough to hold a sword."

²²The Lord my Master says these things, "I am against Pharaoh, king of Egypt. I will break both his arms, the strong arm and the arm that is already broken. I will make the sword fall from his hand. ²³I will scatter the Egyptians among the nations. ²⁴I will make the arms of the king of Babylon strong. I will put my sword in his hand. But I will break the arms of Pharaoh. Then Pharaoh will cry out in pain, the kind of cry that a dying man makes. ²⁵So I will make the arms of the king of Babylon strong, but the arms of Pharaoh will fall. Then they will know that I am the Lord.

"I will put my sword in the hand of the king of Babylon. Then he will stretch the sword out against the land of Egypt. ²⁶I will scatter the Egyptians among the nations. Then they will know that I am the Lord!"

Assyria Is Like A Cedar Tree

31 On the first day of the third month *(June)* in the eleventh year ₍of exile₎,* the word of the Lord came to me. He said, ²"Son of man,* say these things to Pharaoh, king of Egypt, and to his people:

"'You are so great!
Who can I compare you to?
³   Assyria was a cedar tree in Lebanon
With beautiful branches,
With forest shade,
And very tall.
Its top was among the clouds!

---
eleventh year of exile This was the spring-summer of 587B.C.
Son of man This was usually just a way of saying "a person," or "a human being." Here it is a title for the man Ezekiel.

⁴   The water made the tree grow.
The deep river made the tree tall.
Rivers flowed around the place
where the tree was planted.
Only small streams flowed from that tree
to all the other trees of the field.
⁵ So that tree was taller
than all the other trees of the field.
And it grew many branches.
There was plenty of water,
so the tree branches spread out.
⁶ All the birds of the sky made their nests
in the branches of that tree.
And all the animals of the field gave birth
under the branches of that tree.
All the great nations lived
under the shade of that tree.
⁷ The tree was very beautiful.
It was so large!
It had such long branches.
Its roots had plenty of water!
⁸ Even the cedar trees in God's garden
were not as big as this tree.
Cypress trees did not have as many branches.
Plane-trees did not have such branches.
No tree in God's garden
was as beautiful as this tree.
⁹ I gave it many branches
and made it beautiful.
And all the trees in Eden, God's garden,
were jealous!'"

¹⁰So the Lord my Master says these things: "That tree grew tall. Its top reached up to the clouds. It grew so big that it became proud! ¹¹So I let a powerful king have that tree. That ruler punished the tree for the bad things it did. I took that tree out of my garden. ¹²Strangers—the most terrible people in the world—cut it down and scattered its branches on the mountains and in the valleys. Its broken limbs drifted down the rivers flowing through that land. There was no more shadow under that tree, so all the people left. ¹³Now birds live in that fallen tree. Wild animals walk over its fallen branches.

¹⁴"Now, none of the trees by that water will be proud. They won't try to reach the clouds. None of the strong trees that drink that water will brag about being tall. Why? Because all of them have been appointed to die. They will all go down into the world below—to Sheol, the place of death. They will join the other people who died and went down into that deep hole."

¹⁵The Lord my Master says these things, "I made the people cry on the day that tree went down to Sheol.* I covered him with the deep ocean. I stopped its rivers and all the water stopped flowing. I made Lebanon mourn* for it. All the trees of the field became sick with sadness for that big tree. ¹⁶I made the tree fall—and the nations shook with fear at the sound of the falling tree. I sent the tree down to the place of death, to join the other people that had gone down into that deep hole. In the past, all the trees of Eden, the best of Lebanon, drank that water. Those trees were comforted in the world below. ¹⁷Yes, those trees also went down with the big tree to the place of death. They joined the people that were killed in battle. That big tree made the other trees strong. Those trees had lived under the big tree's shadow among the nations.

¹⁸"Egypt, there were many big and powerful trees in Eden. Which of those trees should I compare you to! They all went down into the world below! And You too will join those foreigners* in that place of death. You will lie there among the people killed in battle.

"Yes, that will happen to Pharaoh and to the crowds of people with him!" The Lord my Master said those things.

Pharaoh: a Lion Or a Dragon?

32 On the first day of the twelfth month (March) in the twelfth year ₍of exile₎,* the word of the Lord came to me. He said, ²"Son of man,* sing this sad song about Pharaoh, king of Egypt. Say to him:

"'You thought you were like
   a powerful young lion
      walking proud among the nations.
But really, you are like
   a dragon* in the lakes.
You push your way through the streams.
You make the water muddy with your feet.
You stir up the rivers of Egypt.'"

Sheol The place where people go when they die. Usually this means the grave, but it can mean the place where spirits go.
mourn Crying and showing sadness for a person that died.
foreigners Literally, "uncircumcised."
Son of man This was usually just a way of saying "a person," or "a human being." But here this is a title for the man, Ezekiel.
twelfth year of exile This was early spring, 585B.C.
dragon This might be a crocodile or a giant sea creature. The giant sea creature represented the power of the sea, and the Nile River made Egypt a powerful nation.

³The Lord my Master says these things:

"I have gathered many people together.
   Now I will throw my net over you.
      Then those people will pull you in.
⁴ Then I will drop you on the dry ground.
   I will throw you down in the field.
I will let all the birds come and eat you.
   I will let wild animals from every place
      come and eat you until they are full.
⁵ I will scatter your body on the mountains.
   I will fill the valleys with your dead body.
⁶ I will pour your blood on the mountains,
   and it will soak down into the ground.
The rivers will be full of you.
⁷ I will make you disappear.
   I will cover the sky
      and make the stars dark.
I will cover the sun with a cloud,
   and the moon will shine.
⁸ I will make all the shining lights in the sky
      become dark over you.
   I will cause your whole country to be dark.

⁹"I will make many people sad and upset when I bring an enemy to destroy you. Nations you don't even know will be upset. ¹⁰I will make many people shocked about you. Their kings will be terribly afraid about you, when I swing my sword before them. The kings will shake with fear every moment on the day you fall. Each king will be afraid for his own life."

¹¹Why? Because the Lord my Master says these things: "The sword of the king of Babylon will come to fight against you. ¹²I will use those soldiers to kill your people in battle. Those soldiers come from the most terrible of the nations. They will destroy the things Egypt is proud of. The people of Egypt will be destroyed. ¹³There are many animals by the rivers in Egypt. I will also destroy all those animals! People won't make the waters muddy with their feet any more. The hoofs of cows won't make the water muddy any more. ¹⁴So I will make the water in Egypt calm. I will cause their rivers to run slowly—they will be slick like oil." The Lord my Master said those things. ¹⁵"I will make the land of Egypt empty. That land will lose everything. I will punish all the people living in Egypt. Then they will know that I am the Lord and Master!

¹⁶"This is a sad song that people will sing for Egypt. The daughters (cities) in other nations will sing this sad song about Egypt. They will sing it

as a sad song about Egypt and all its people." The Lord my Master said those things!

Egypt to Be Destroyed

¹⁷On the fifteenth day of that month, in the twelfth year ⌊of exile⌋,* the word of the Lord came to me. He said, ¹⁸"Son of man,* cry for the people of Egypt. Lead Egypt and those daughters from powerful nations to the grave. Lead them to the world below where they will be with the other people that went down into that deep hole. ¹⁹"Egypt, you are no better than anyone else! Go down to the place of death. Go lie down with those foreigners.*

²⁰"Egypt will go to be with all the other men that were killed in battle. The enemy has pulled her and all her people away.

²¹"Strong and powerful men were killed in battle. Those foreigners went down to the place of death. And from that place, those men that were killed will speak to Egypt and his helpers.

²²⁻²³"Assyria and all its army are there in the place of death. Their graves are deep down in that deep hole. All those Assyrian soldiers were killed in battle. Their graves are all around his grave. When they were alive, they made people afraid. But now all of them ⌊are quiet⌋—they were all killed in battle.

²⁴"Elam is there and all its army is around her grave. All of them were killed in battle. Those foreigners went deep down into the ground. When they were alive, they made people afraid. But they carried their shame with them down to that deep hole. ²⁵They have made a bed for Elam and all its soldiers that were killed in battle. Elam's army is all around its grave. All those foreigners were killed in battle. When they were alive, they scared people. But they carried their shame with them down into that deep hole. They were put with all the other people that were killed.

²⁶"Meshech, Tubal, and all their armies are there. Their graves are around it. All of those foreigners were killed in battle. When they were alive, they made people afraid. ²⁷But now they are lying down by the powerful men that died long, long ago! They were buried with their weapons of war. Their swords will be laid under their heads. But their sins are on their bones. Why? Because when they were alive, they scared people.

²⁸"Egypt, you too will be destroyed. And you will lie down by those foreigners. You will lie with those other soldiers that were killed in battle.

²⁹"Edom is there also. His kings and other leaders are there with him. They were powerful soldiers too. But now they lie with the other men that were killed in battle. They are lying there with those foreigners. They are there with the other people that went down into that deep hole.

³⁰"The rulers from the north are there, all of them! And there are all the soldiers from Sidon. Their strength scared people. But they are embarrassed. Those foreigners lie there with the other men that were killed in battle. They carried their shame with them down into that deep hole.

³¹"Pharaoh will see the people that went down to the place of death. He and all his people with him will be comforted. Yes, Pharaoh and all his army will be killed in battle." The Lord my Master said these things.

³²"When Pharaoh was alive, I made people afraid of him. But now, he will lie down with those foreigners. Pharaoh and his army will lie down with the other soldiers that were killed in battle." The Lord my Master said those things.

God Chooses Ezekiel To Be a Watchman for Israel

33 The word of the Lord came to me. He said, ²"Son of man,* speak to your people. Say to them, 'I might bring enemy soldiers to fight against this country. When that happens people choose a man to be the watchman. ³If this guard sees the enemy soldiers coming, then he blows the trumpet and warns the people. ⁴If people hear the warning but ignore it, then the enemy will capture them and take them away as prisoners. That person will be responsible for his own death. ⁵He heard the trumpet, but he ignored the warning. So he is to blame for his death. If he had paid attention to the warning, then he could have saved his own life.

⁶"'But maybe that guard sees the enemy soldiers coming, but does not blow the trumpet. That guard did not warn the people. The enemy will capture them and take them away as

---

twelfth year of exile This was early spring, 585 B.C.
Son of man This was usually just a way of saying "a person," or "a human being." But here this is a title for the man, Ezekiel.
foreigners Literally, "uncircumcised." This showed that those people did not share in the Agreement that God made with Israel.

Son of man This was usually just a way of saying "a person," or "a human being." But here this is a title for the man, Ezekiel.

prisoners. That person will be taken away because he sinned. But the guard will also be responsible for that man's death.

⁷"Now, Son of man,* I am choosing you to be a watchman for the family of Israel. If you hear a message from my mouth, you must warn the people for me. ⁸I might say to you, 'This evil person will die.' Then you must go warn that person for me. If you don't warn that evil person and tell him to change his life, then that evil person will die because he sinned. But I will make you responsible for his death. ⁹But if you do warn the evil person to change his life and stop sinning, and if he refuses to stop sinning, then he will die because he sinned. But you have saved your life.

God Does Not Want to Destroy People

¹⁰"So, Son of man,* speak to the family of Israel for me. Those people might say, 'We have sinned and broken the law. Our sins are too heavy to bear. We rot away because of those sins. What can we do to live?'

¹¹"You must say to them, 'The Lord my Master says: On my life, I promise, I don't enjoy seeing people die—not even evil people! I don't want them to die. I want those evil people to come back to me. I want them to change their lives so they can really live! So come back to me! Stop doing bad things! Why must you die, family of Israel?'"

¹²"And Son of man,* say to your people: 'The good things a person did in the past won't save him if he becomes bad and begins to sin. And the bad things a person did in the past won't destroy him if he turns from his evil. So remember, the good things a person did in the past won't save him if he begins to sin.

¹³"Maybe I will tell a good person that he will live. But maybe that good person will begin to think that the good things he did in the past will save him. So he might begin to do bad things. But I won't remember the good things he did in the past! No, he will die because of the bad things he begins to do.

¹⁴Or maybe I will tell a bad person that he will die. But he might change his life. He might stop sinning and begin to live right. He might become good and fair. ¹⁵He might give back the things he took when he loaned money. He might pay for the things he stole. He might begin to follow the laws that give life. He stops doing bad things. Then that person will surely live. He won't die. ¹⁶I won't remember the bad things he did in the past. Why? Because now he lives right and is fair. So he will live!

¹⁷"But your people say, 'That's not fair! ₍The Lord₎ my Master can't be like that!'

"But they are the people that are not fair! They are the people who must change! ¹⁸If a good person stops doing good things and begins to sin, then he will die because of his sins. ¹⁹And if an evil person stops doing bad things and begins to live right and be fair, then he will live! ²⁰But you people still say that I am not fair. But I am telling you the truth. Family of Israel, each person will be judged for the things he does!"

Jerusalem Has Been Taken

²¹On the fifth day of the tenth month *(January)* in the twelfth year ₍of exile₎,* a person came to me from Jerusalem. He had escaped from the battle there. He said, "The city *(Jerusalem)* has been taken!"

²²Now the power of the Lord my Master had come on me the evening before that person came to me. ₍God made me not able to speak.₎ At the time that person came to me, the Lord had opened my mouth and let me speak again. ²³Then the word of the Lord came to me. He said, ²⁴"Son of man,* there are Israelite people living in the ruined cities in Israel. Those people are saying, 'Abraham was only one man, and God gave him all this land. Now, we are many people, so surely this land belongs to us! It is our land!'

²⁵"You must tell them that the Lord and Master says these things, 'You eat meat with the blood still in it. You look to your idols* for help. You murder people. So why should I give you this land? ²⁶You depend on your own sword. Each of you does terrible things. Each of you does sexual sins with his neighbor's wife. So you cannot have the land!'"

²⁷"You must tell them that the Lord and Master says these things, "On my life I promise, those people living in those ruined cities will be killed with a sword! If anyone is out in the country, I will let animals kill him and eat him. If people are hiding in the fortresses* and the caves, they will die from disease. ²⁸I will make the land empty and

---

Son of man This was usually just a way of saying "a person," or "a human being." But here this is a title for the man, Ezekiel.

twelfth year of exile This was the winter of 586B.C.

idols Statues of false gods that people worshiped.

fortress(es) A building or city with tall, strong walls for protection.

a waste. That country will lose all the things it was proud of. The mountains of Israel will become empty. No one will pass through that place. ²⁹Those people have done many terrible things. So I will make that land an empty wasteland. Then these people will know that I am the Lord.'"

³⁰"And now, about you, Son of man.* Your people lean against the walls and stand in their doorways, and they talk about you. They tell each other, 'Come on, let's go hear what the Lord says.' ³¹So they come to you like they are my people. They sit in front of you like they are my people. They hear your words. But they won't do the things you say. They only want to do what feels good. They only want to cheat people and make more money."

³²"You are nothing to these people but a singer singing love songs. You have a good voice. You play your instrument well. They hear your words, but they won't do the things you say. ³³But the things you sing about really will happen. And then the people will know that there really was a prophet living among them!"

Israel Is Like a Flock of Sheep

34 The word of the Lord came to me. He said, ²"Son of man,* speak against the shepherds *(leaders)* of Israel for me. Speak to them for me. Tell them that the Lord and Master says these things, "You shepherds of Israel have only been feeding yourselves. It will be very bad for you! Why don't you shepherds feed the flock? ³You eat the fat sheep and use their wool to make clothes for yourselves. You kill the fat sheep, but you don't feed the flock. ⁴You have not made the weak strong. You have not cared for the sick sheep. You have not put bandages on the sheep that were hurt. Some of the sheep wandered away, and you did not go get them and bring them back. You did not go to look for those lost sheep. No, you were cruel and severe—that's the way you tried to lead the sheep!

⁵"And now the sheep are scattered because there was no shepherd. They became food for every wild animal. So they were scattered. ⁶My flock wandered over all the mountains and on every high hill. My flock was scattered over all the face of the earth. There was no one to search or to look for them.

⁷So, you shepherds, listen to the word of the Lord. The Lord my Master says, ⁸"By my life, I promise this to you. Wild animals caught my sheep. Yes, my flock has become food for all the wild animals. Why? Because they did not have a real shepherd. My shepherds did not look out for my flock. No, those shepherds only killed the sheep and fed themselves. They did not feed my flock."

⁹So, you shepherds, listen to the word of the Lord! ¹⁰The Lord says, "I am against those shepherds! I will demand my sheep from them. I will fire them! They won't be my shepherds any more! Then the shepherds won't be able to feed themselves. And I will save my flock from their mouths. Then my sheep won't be food for them."

¹¹The Lord my Master says, "I, myself, will be their Shepherd. I will search for my sheep. I will look out for them. ¹²If a shepherd is with his sheep when they begin to wander away, then he will go searching for them. In the same way I will search for my sheep. I will save my sheep. I will bring them back from all the places where they were scattered on that dark and cloudy day. ¹³I will bring them back from those nations. I will gather them from those countries. I will bring them to their own land. And I will feed them on the mountains of Israel, by the streams, in all the places where people live. ¹⁴I will lead them to grassy fields. They will go to the place high on the mountains of Israel. There they will lie down on good ground and eat the grass. They will eat in rich grassland on the mountains of Israel. ¹⁵Yes, I will feed my flock and I will lead them to a place of rest." The Lord my Master said those things.

¹⁶"I will search for the lost sheep. I will bring back the sheep that were scattered. I will put bandages on the sheep that were hurt. I will make the weak sheep strong. But I will destroy those fat and powerful ₁shepherds₁. I will feed them the punishment they deserve.

¹⁷The Lord my Master says these things, "And you, my flock, I will judge between one sheep and another. I will judge between the rams* and the male goats. ¹⁸You can eat the grass growing on the good land. So why do you also crush the grass that other sheep want to eat? You can drink plenty of clear water. So why do you also stir the water that other sheep want to drink? ¹⁹My flock must

---

Son of man This was usually just a way of saying "a person," or "a human being." But here this is a title for the man, Ezekiel.

ram(s) A male sheep.

eat the grass you crushed with your feet, and they must drink the water you stir with your feet!" ²⁰So the Lord my Master says to them: "I, myself, will judge between the fat sheep and the thin sheep! ²¹You push with your side and shoulder. You knock down all the weak sheep with your horns. You push until you have forced them away. ²²So I will save my flock. They won't be caught by wild animals any more. I will judge between one sheep and another. ²³Then I will put one shepherd over them, my servant David. He will feed them and be their shepherd. ²⁴Then I, the Lord and Master, will be their God. And my servant David will be the ruler living among them. I, the Lord, have spoken."

²⁵"And I will make a peace agreement with my sheep. I will take harmful animals away from the land. Then the sheep can be safe in the desert and sleep in the woods. ²⁶I will bless the sheep and the places around my hill *(Jerusalem)*. I will cause the rains to fall at the right time. They will shower them with blessings. ²⁷And the trees growing in the field will produce their fruit. The earth will give its harvest. So the sheep will be safe on their land. I will break the yokes* on them. I will save them from the power of the people that made them slaves. Then they will know that I am the Lord. ²⁸They won't be caught like an animal by the nations any more. Those animals won't eat them any more. But they will live safely. No one will make them afraid. ²⁹I will give them some land that will make a good garden. Then they won't suffer from hunger in that land. They won't suffer the insults from the nations any more. ³⁰Then they will know that I am the Lord their God. And they will know that I am with them. And the family of Israel will know that they are my people!" The Lord my Master said those things!

³¹"You are my sheep, the sheep of my grassland. You are only human beings. And I am your God." The Lord my Master said those things.

The Message Against Edom

35 The word of the Lord came to me. He said, ²"Son of man,* look toward Mount Seir,

---

yokes A pole that was put on the shoulders of men or animals to help them carry or pull things. This often showed that a person was a slave.

Son of man This was usually just a way of saying "a person," or "a human being." But here this is a title for the man, Ezekiel.

---

and speak against it for me. ³Say to it, 'The Lord my Master says these things:

"'I am against you, Mount Seir!
    I will punish you.
    I will make you an empty wasteland.
⁴ I will destroy your cities.
    And you will become empty.
    Then you will know that I am the Lord.
⁵ Why? Because you have always been
        against my people.
    You used your sword against Israel
        at the time of their trouble,
        at the time of their final punishment.'"

⁶So the Lord my Master says, "By my life I promise that I will let death have you. Death will chase you. You did not hate killing people. So death will chase you. ⁷And I will make Mount Seir an empty ruin. I will kill every person that comes from that city. And I will kill every person that tries to go into that city. ⁸I will cover its mountains with dead bodies. Those dead bodies will be all over your hills, in your valleys, and in all your ravines. ⁹I will make you empty forever. No one will live in your cities. Then you will know that I am the Lord."

¹⁰You said, "These two nations and countries *(Israel and Judah)* will be mine. We will take them for our own.'

But the Lord is there! ¹¹And the Lord my Master says, "You were jealous of my people. You were angry at them and you were hateful to me. So by my life, I promise that I will punish you the same way you hurt them! I will punish you and let my people know that I am with them. ¹²And then you too will know that I have heard all your insults. You said many bad things against the mountain of Israel. You said, 'Israel has been destroyed! We will chew them up like food!' ¹³And you were proud and said things against me. You spoke too many times and I have heard every word you said! Yes, I heard you."

¹⁴The Lord my Master says these things, "All the earth will be happy when I destroy you ¹⁵You were happy when the country of Israel was destroyed. I will treat you the same way. Mount Seir and the whole country of Edom will be destroyed. Then you will know that I am the Lord."

The Land of Israel Will Be Built again

36 "Son of man,* speak to the mountains of Israel for me. Tell the mountains of Israel to

listen to the word of the Lord! ²Tell them that the Lord and Master says these things, 'The enemy said bad things against you. They said: Hurrah! Now the ancient mountains* will be ours!'"

³"So speak to the mountains of Israel for me. Tell them that the Lord and Master says these things, 'The enemy destroyed your cities and attacked you from every direction. They did this so you would belong to the other nations. Then people talked and whispered about you. ⁴So, mountains of Israel, listen to the word of the Lord my Master! The Lord my Master says this to the mountains, hills, streams, valleys, empty ruins, and abandoned cities that have been looted and laughed at by the other nations around them. ⁵The Lord my Master says: I swear *(promise)*, I will let my strong feelings speak for me! I will let Edom and the other nations feel my anger. Those nations took my land for themselves. They really had a good time when they showed how much they hated this land. They took the land for themselves just so they could destroy it!"

⁶"So, Say these things about the land of Israel. Speak to the mountains and to the hills, to the streams and to the valleys. Tell them that the Lord and Master says these things, 'I will let my strong feelings and anger speak for me. Why? Because you had to suffer the insults from those nations.'"

⁷So the Lord my Master says these things, "I am the One making this promise! I swear that the nations around you will have to suffer for those insults.

⁸"But mountains of Israel, you will grow new trees and produce fruit for my people Israel. My people will soon come back. ⁹I am with you. I will help you. People will till your soil. People will plant seeds in you. ¹⁰There will be many, many people living on you. The whole family of Israel—all of them—will live there. The cities will have people living in them. The destroyed places will be built like new. ¹¹I will give you many people and animals. And they will grow and have many children. I will bring people to live on you like in the past. I will make it better for you than before. Then you will know that I am the Lord. ¹²Yes, I will lead many people—my people, Israel—to your land. You will be their property. And you won't take away their children again."

¹³The Lord my Master says these things, "Land of Israel, people say bad things to you. They say you destroyed your people. They say you took the children away from your people. ¹⁴But you won't destroy people any more. You won't take away their children again." The Lord my Master said those things. ¹⁵"I won't let those other nations insult you any more. You won't be hurt by those people any more. You won't take the children away from your people again." The Lord my Master said those things.

The Lord Will Protect His Own Good Name

¹⁶Then the word of the Lord came to me. He said, ¹⁷"Son of man,* the family of Israel lived in their own country. But they made that land filthy by the bad things they did. To me, they were like a woman that becomes unclean* because of her monthly time of bleeding. ¹⁸They spilled blood on the ground when they murdered people in that land. They made the land filthy with their idols.* So I showed them how angry I was. ¹⁹I scattered them among the nations and spread them through all the lands. I gave them the punishment they should have for the bad things they did. ²⁰But even in those other nations they ruined my good name. How? Those nations said, 'These are the Lord's people, but they left his land. ₍So there must be something wrong with the Lord!₎'

²¹"The people of Israel ruined my holy name in the places where the went. And I felt sorry for my name. ²²So tell the family of Israel that the Lord and Master says these things, 'Family of Israel, you ruined my holy name in the places where you went. I am going to do something to stop this. I won't do it for your sake, Israel. I will do those things for my holy name. ²³I will show those nations that my great name is truly holy. You ruined my good name in those nations! But I will show you that I am holy. I will make you respect my name. And then those nations will know that I am the Lord." The Lord my Master said those things.

²⁴₍God said,₎ "I will take you out of those nations, gather you together, and bring you back to your own land. ²⁵Then I will sprinkle pure water on you and make you pure. I will wash away all your filth. I will wash away the filth from those nasty idols and make you pure."

²⁶₍God said,₎ "I will also put a new spirit in you ₍and change your way of thinking₎. I will take out

---

Son of man This was usually just a way of saying "a person," or "a human being." But here this is a title for the man, Ezekiel.

unclean Not pure or not acceptable to God for worship.

idols Statues of false gods that people worshiped.

---

mountains Literally, "high places"—usually a reference to places of worship.

the heart of stone from your body and give you a tender, human heart. ²⁷And I will put my Spirit inside you.* I will change you so you will obey my laws. You will carefully obey my commands. ²⁸Then you will live in the land that I gave to your ancestors.* You will be my people, and I will be your God."

²⁹⌊God said,⌋ "Also, I will save you and keep you from becoming unclean.* I will command the grain to grow. I won't bring a time of hunger against you. ³⁰I will give you large crops of fruit from your trees and the harvest from your fields so you will never again feel the shame of being hungry in a foreign country. ³¹You will remember the bad things you did. You will remember that those things were not good. Then you will hate yourselves because of your sins and the terrible things you did."

³²The Lord my Master says, "I want you to remember this: I am not doing these things for your good! ⌊I am doing them for my good name!⌋ Family of Israel, you should be ashamed and embarrassed about the way you lived!"

³³The Lord my Master says these things, "On the day that I wash away your sins, I will bring people back to your cities. Those ruined cities will be built again. ³⁴People will again begin to work the land so when other people pass by they won't see ruins any more. ³⁵They will say, 'In the past, this land was ruined. But now it is like the garden of Eden. The cities were destroyed. They were ruined and empty. But now they are protected, and there are people living in them.'

³⁶⌊God said,⌋ "Then those nations that are still around you will know I am the Lord and that I built those ruined places again. I planted things in this land that was empty. I am the Lord. I said these things, and I will make them happen!"

³⁷The Lord my Master says these things, "I will also let the family of Israel come to me and ask me to do these things for them. I will make them grow and become many, many people. They will be like flocks of sheep. ³⁸During the special festivals, Jerusalem is filled with flocks of sheep and goats that have been made holy. In the same way, the cities and ruined places will be filled with flocks of people. Then they will know that I am the Lord."

The Vision of the Dry Bones

37 The Lord's power came on me. The Spirit* of the Lord carried me ⌊out of the city⌋ and put me down in the middle of the valley.* The valley was full of dead men's bones. ²There were many, many bones lying on the ground in the valley. The Lord made me walk all around among the bones. I saw the bones were very dry.

³Then the Lord my Master said to me, "Son of man,* can these bones come to life?"

I answered, "Lord my Master, only you know the answer to that question."

⁴The Lord my Master said to me. "Speak to those bones for me. Tell those bones, 'Dry bones, listen to the word of the Lord! ⁵The Lord my Master says these things to you: I will cause breath* to come into you, and you will come to life! ⁶I will put sinews and muscles on you. And I will cover you with skin. Then I will put breath in you, and you will come back to life! Then you will know that I am the Lord and Master."

⁷So I spoke to the bones for the Lord, like he said. I was still speaking, when I heard the loud noise. The bones began to rattle, and bone joined together with bone! ⁸There before my eyes, I saw sinew and muscles begin to cover the bones. And skin began to cover them. But ⌊the bodies didn't move⌋—there was no breath in them.

⁹Then the Lord my Master said to me, "Speak to the wind* for me. Son of man,* speak to the wind for me. Tell the wind that the Lord and Master says these things: 'Wind, come from every direction and breathe air into these dead bodies! Breathe into them and they will come to life again!'"

¹⁰So I spoke to the wind for the Lord, like he said. And the breath came into the dead bodies. They came to life and stood up. There were many, many men—they were a very large army!

¹¹Then the Lord my Master said to me, "Son of man,* these bones are like the whole family of Israel. The people of Israel say, 'Our bones have dried up,* our hope is gone. We have been completely destroyed!' ¹²So, speak to them for

---

Spirit Or "wind."
the valley Possibly Jezreel Valley, a fertile area where many battles were fought. It is often called simply, "The Valley."
Son of man This was usually just a way of saying "a person," or "a human being." Here this is a title for the man, Ezekiel.
breath Or "wind," or "a spirit."
wind This could also be translated "breath" or "spirit."
bones ... dried up This is a way of saying, "We have lost our strength."

I will put my Spirit inside you. Or, "I will make my Spirit live among you."
ancestors Literally, "fathers," meaning a person's parents, grandparents, and all the people they are descended from.
unclean Not pure or not acceptable to God for worship.

me. Tell them the Lord and Master says these things, "My people, I will open your graves and bring you up out of your graves! Then I will bring you to the land of Israel. ¹³My people, I will open your graves and bring you up out of your graves. And then you will then know that I am the Lord. ¹⁴I will put my Spirit* in you and you will come to life again. Then I will lead you back to your own land. Then you will know that I am the Lord. You will know that I said these things and that I made them happen." The Lord said those things.

Judah and Israel to Become One Again

¹⁵The word of the Lord came to me again. He said, ¹⁶"Son of man,* get one stick and write this message on it: 'This stick belongs to Judah and his friends,* the people of Israel. Then take another stick and write on it, 'This stick of Ephraim belongs to Joseph and his friends, the people of Israel.' ¹⁷Then join those two sticks together. In your hand, they will be one stick.

¹⁸"Your people will ask you to explain what that means. ¹⁹Tell them that the Lord and Master says these things, 'I will take the stick of Joseph, which is in the hand of Ephraim and his friends, the people of Israel. Then I will put that stick with the stick of Judah, and make them one stick. In my hand, they will become one stick!

²⁰"Hold those sticks in your hands in front of you. You wrote those names on those sticks. ²¹Tell the people that the Lord and Master says these things: 'I will take the people of Israel from among the nations where they have gone. I will gather them from all around, and I will bring them into their own land. ²²I will make them one nation in the land on the mountains of Israel. One king will be king for all of them. They won't continue to be two nations. They won't be divided into two kingdoms any more. ²³And they won't continue to make themselves filthy with their idols* and horrible statues or with any of their other crimes. But I will save them from all the places where they have sinned. And I will wash them and make them pure. And they will be my people, and I will be their God.

²⁴"'And my servant David will be the king over them. There will be only one shepherd over all of them. They will live by my rules and obey my laws. They will do the things I tell them. ²⁵They will live on the land that I gave to my servant Jacob. Your ancestors* lived in that place. And my people will live there. They and their children, and their grandchildren will live there forever. And David my servant will be their leader forever. ²⁶And I will make a peace agreement with them. This agreement will continue forever. I agree to give them their land. I agree to make them become many, many people. And I agree to put my holy place among them forever. ²⁷My Holy Tent will be with them. Yes, I will be their God and they will be my people. ²⁸And the other nations will know that I am the Lord. And they will know that I make Israel my special people by putting my holy place there among them forever.'"

The Message Against Gog

38 The word of the Lord came to me. He said, ²Son of man,* look toward Gog in the land of Magog. He is the most important leader of the nations of Meshech and Tubal. Speak for me against Gog. ³Tell him that the Lord and Master says these things, 'Gog, you are the most important leader of the nations of Meshech and Tubal! But I am against you. ⁴I will capture you and bring you back. I will bring back all the men in your army. I will bring back all the horses and horse soldiers. I will put hooks in your mouths, and I will bring all of you back. All of the soldiers will be wearing their uniforms with all their shields and swords. ⁵Soldiers from Persia, Ethiopia, and Put will be with them. They will all be wearing their shields and helmets. ⁶There will also be Gomer with all his groups of soldiers. And there will be the nation of Togarmah* from the far north with all its groups of soldiers. There will be many, many people in that parade of prisoners.

⁷"Be prepared. Yes, prepare yourself and the armies that have joined with you. You must watch and be ready. ⁸After a long time you will be called for duty. In the later years you will come into the land that has been healed from war. The people in that land were gathered from many nations and brought back to the mountains of Israel. In the

---

Spirit Or "spirit," or "wind."
Son of man This was usually just a way of saying "a person," or "a human being." But here this is a title for the man, Ezekiel.
friends This is a word play. The Hebrew word is like the word meaning "joined together."
idols Statues of false gods that people worshiped.
nation of Togarmah Or, "Beth Togarmah."
ancestors Literally, "fathers," meaning a person's parents, grandparents, and all the people they are descended from.

past, the mountains of Israel had been destroyed again and again. But these people will have come back from those other nations. They all will have lived in safety. ⁹But you will come to attack them. You will come like a storm. You will come like a thundercloud covering the land. You and all your groups of soldiers from many nations will come to attack these people."

¹⁰The Lord my Master says these things: "At that time, an idea will come into your mind. You will begin to make an evil plan. ¹¹You will say, 'I will go attack that country that has towns without walls *(Israel)*. Those people live in peace. They think they are safe. There are not any walls around the cities to protect them. They don't have any locks on their gates—they don't even have gates! ¹²I will defeat those people and take all their valuable things away from them. I will fight against the places that were destroyed but now have people living in them. I will fight against those people *(Israel)* that were gathered from the nations. Now those people have cattle and property. They live at the crossroads of the world—ˌThe powerful countries must travel through that place to get to all the other powerful countriesˌ.'

¹³"Sheba, Dedan, and the businessmen of Tarshish, and all the cities they trade with will ask you, 'Did you come to capture valuable things? Did you bring your groups of soldiers together to grab those good things and to carry away silver, gold, cattle, and property. Did you come to take all those valuable things?'"

¹⁴ˌGod said,ˌ "Son of man,* speak to Gog for me. Tell him that the Lord and Master says these things: 'You will come to attack my people while they are living in peace and safety. ¹⁵You will come from your place out of the far north. And you will bring many people with you. All of them will ride on horses. You will be a large and a powerful army. ¹⁶You will come to fight against my people Israel. You will be like a thundercloud covering the land. When that time comes, I will bring you to fight against my land. Then, Gog, the nations will learn how powerful I am! They will learn to respect me and know that I am holy. They will see what I will do to you!'"

¹⁷The Lord my Master says these things, "ˌAt that time, people will rememberˌ that I spoke about you in the past. They will remember that I used my servants the prophets of Israel. They will remember that the prophets of Israel spoke for me in the past and said that I would bring you to fight against them."

¹⁸The Lord my Master said, "At that time, Gog will come to fight against the land of Israel. I will show my anger. ¹⁹In my anger and strong emotions I make this promise: I promise that there will be a strong earthquake in the land of Israel. ²⁰At that time, all living things will quake *(shake)* with fear. The fish in the sea, the birds in the air, the wild animals in the fields, and all the little creatures crawling on the ground will shake with fear. The mountains will fall down and the cliffs will collapse. Every wall will fall to the ground!"

²¹The Lord my Master says, "And on the mountains of Israel, I will call for every kind of terror against* Gog. His soldiers will be so scared that they will attack each other and kill each other with their swords. ²²I will punish Gog with diseases and death. I will cause hailstones, fire, and sulfur to rain down on Gog and his groups of soldiers from many nations. ²³Then I will show how great I am. I will prove that I am holy. Many nations will see me do these things and they will learn who I am. Then they will know that I am the Lord."

The Death of Gog and His Army

39 "Son of man,* speak against Gog for me. Tell him that the Lord and Master says these things, 'Gog, you are the most important leader of the countries Meshech and Tubal! But I am against you. ²I will capture you and bring you back. I will bring you from the far north. I will bring you to fight against the mountains of Israel. ³But I will knock your bow from your left hand. I will knock your arrows from your right hand. ⁴You will be killed on the mountains of Israel. You, your groups of soldiers, and all the other nations with you will be killed in the battle. I will give you as food to every kind of bird that eats meat and to all the wild animals. ⁵ˌYou will not enter the city.ˌ You will be killed out in the open fields. I have spoken!'" The Lord my Master said those things.

⁶ˌGod said,ˌ "I will send fire against Magog and those people living along the coast. They think they are safe, but they will know that I am the Lord. ⁷And I will make my holy name known among my people Israel. I will not let people ruin

---

Son of man This was usually just a way of saying "a person," or "a human being." But here this is a title for the man, Ezekiel.

every kind of terror against This is from the ancient Greek translation. The Hebrews has, "a sword against."

my holy name any more. The nations will know that I am the Lord. They will know that I am the Holy One in Israel. ⁸That time is coming! It will happen!" The Lord said these things. "That is the day I am talking about.

⁹"At that time, the people living in the cities of Israel will go out to the fields. They will collect the enemy's weapons and burn them. They will burn all the shields, bows and arrows, clubs and spears. They will use those weapons as firewood for seven years. ¹⁰They won't have to gather wood from the fields or chop firewood from the forests because they will use the weapons as firewood. They will take the valuable things from the soldiers that wanted to steal from them. They will take the good things from the soldiers that took good things from them." The Lord my Master said these things.

¹¹₍God said,₎ "At that time, I will choose a place in Israel to bury Gog. He will be buried in the Valley of the Travelers,* east of the Dead Sea. It will block the road for travelers. Why? Because Gog and all his army will be buried in that place. People will call it "The Valley of Gog's Army." ¹²It will take seven months for the family of Israel to bury them. They must do this to make the land pure. ¹³The common people will bury those enemy soldiers. And those people will become famous on the day that I bring honor to myself." The Lord my Master said those things.

¹⁴₍God said,₎ "Workers will given a fulltime job burying those dead soldiers to make the land pure. Those workers will work for seven months. They will go around looking for dead bodies. ¹⁵Those workers will go around looking. If one of them sees a bone, then he will put up a marker by it. The sign will stay there until the grave diggers come and bury the bone in the Valley of Gog's Army. ¹⁶That city of dead people *(graveyard)* will be named Hamonah.* In this way, they will make the country pure."

¹⁷The Lord my Master said these things, "Son of man,* speak to all the birds and wild animals for me. Tell them, 'Come here! Come here! Gather around. Come eat this sacrifice I am preparing for you. There will be a very big sacrifice on the mountains of Israel. Come, eat the meat and drink the blood. ¹⁸You will eat the meat from the bodies of powerful soldiers. You will drink the blood from world leaders. They will be like rams, lambs, goats and fat bulls from Bashan. ¹⁹You can eat all the fat you want. You can drink blood until you are full. You will eat and drink from my sacrifice which I will kill for you. ²⁰You will have plenty of meat to eat at my table. There will be horses and chariot ₍drivers₎, powerful soldiers, and all the other fighting men.'" The Lord my Master said those things.

²¹₍God said,₎ "I will let the other nations see what I have done. And those nations will begin to respect me! They will see my power that I used against that enemy. ²²Then from that day on, the family of Israel will know that I am the Lord their God. ²³And the nations will know why the family of Israel was carried away as prisoners to other countries. They will learn that my people turned against me. So I turned away from them. I let their enemies defeat them. So my people were killed in battle. ²⁴They sinned and made themselves filthy. So I punished them for the things they did. I turned away from them ₍and refused to help them₎."

²⁵So the Lord my Master says these things: "Now I will bring the family of Jacob back from captivity. I will have mercy on the whole family of Israel. I will show my strong feelings for my holy name. ²⁶The people will forget their shame and all the times they turned against me. They will live in safety on their own land. No one will make them afraid. ²⁷I will bring my people back from other countries. I will gather them from the lands of their enemies. Then many nations will see how holy I am. ²⁸They will know that I am the Lord their God. Why? Because I made them to leave their homes and go as prisoners to other countries. And then I gathered them together and brought them back to their own land. ²⁹I will pour my Spirit onto the family of Israel. And after that time, I will never turn away from my people again." The Lord my Master said those things.

The New Temple

40 In the twenty-fifth year after we were taken away into captivity, at the beginning of the year *(October)*, on the tenth day of the month* the Lord's power came on me. This was fourteen years after the Babylonians took Jerusalem. On that day, the Lord took me there ₍in a vision₎.

²In a vision,* God carried me to the land of Israel. He put me down near a very high

---

Valley of the Travelers This is a word play on the name Arabah Valley.

Hamonah This Hebrew word means "crowd."

Son of man This was usually just a way of saying "a person," or "a human being." Here it is a title for the man, Ezekiel.

tenth day of the month This was the Day of Atonement, 573B.C. See Lev. 25:9 and Lev. 36:24

vision(s) Like a dream that God used to speak to people.

mountain. On that mountain in front of me was a building that looked like a city.* ³The Lord brought me there. There was a man there that looked ˻shiny˼ like ˻polished˼ bronze. That man had a cloth tape measure and a measuring rod in his hand. He was standing by the gate. ⁴The man said to me, "Son of man,* use your eyes and ears. Look at these things and listen to me. Pay attention to everything that I show you. Why? Because you have been brought here so I can show you these things. You must tell the family of Israel all that you see."

⁵I saw a wall that went all the way around the outside of the temple.* In the man's hand there was a ruler for measuring things. It was 6 cubits* long using the long measurement.* So the man measured the thickness of the wall. It was one ruler* thick. The man measured the height of the wall. It was one ruler* tall.

⁶Then the man went to the east gate. The man walked up its steps and measured the opening for the gate. It was one ruler* wide. ⁷The rooms for the guards were one ruler* long and one ruler* wide. The walls between the rooms were 5 cubits* thick. The opening by the porch at the end of the gateway that faced the temple was also one ruler* wide. ⁸Then the man measured the porch. ⁹It was 8 cubits* long. The man measured the walls on either side of the gate. Each side wall was 2 cubits* wide. The porch was at the end of the gateway that faced the temple. ¹⁰There were three little rooms on each side of the gateway. All of these rooms measured the same. And all of their side walls measured the same. ¹¹The man measured the entrance to the gateway. It was 10 cubits* wide and 13 cubits* long. ¹²There was a low wall in front of each room. That wall was 1 cubit* tall and 1 cubit* thick. The rooms were square. Each wall was 6 cubits* long.

¹³The man measured the gateway from ˻outside edge of˼ the roof of one room to the ˻outside edge of˼ roof of the opposite room. It was 25 cubits.* Each door was directly opposite the other door. ¹⁴* The man measured the faces of all the side walls, including the side walls on either side of the porch at the courtyard. The total was 60 cubits.* ¹⁵From the inside edge of the outer gate to the far end of the porch was 50 cubits.* ¹⁶There were small windows* above all the guard rooms, the side walls, and the porch. The wide part of the windows faced into the gateway. There were carvings of palm trees on the walls that were on either side of the gateway.

The Outside Courtyard

¹⁷Then the man led me into the outer courtyard. I saw thirty rooms and a pavement that went all the way around the courtyard. The rooms were along the wall and faced in toward the pavement. ¹⁸The pavement was as wide as the gates were long. The pavement reached to the inside end of the gateway. This was the lower pavement. ¹⁹The man measured the distance from the inside of the lower gateway to the outside of the ˻inner˼ courtyard. It was 100 cubits* on the east side as well as on the north side.

²⁰Then the man measured the length and width of the north gate that was in the wall surrounding the outer courtyard. ²¹This gateway, its three rooms on each side, and its porch all measured the same as the first gate. The gateway was 50 cubits* long and 25 cubits* wide. ²²Its windows, its porch, and its carvings of palm trees measured the same as the east gate. ˻On the outside,˼ there were seven steps leading up to the gate. And its porch was at the inside end of the gateway. ²³Across ˻the courtyard˼ from the north gate, there was a gate to the inner courtyard. It was like the gate on the east. The man measured from the gate ˻on the inner wall˼ to the gate ˻on the outer wall˼. It was 100 cubits* from gate to gate.

²⁴Then the man led me to the south wall. I saw a gate in the south ˻wall˼. The man measured its side walls and its porch. They measured the same

---

On the mountain ... city. Or, "On the mountain, there was a building that looked like a city with a city south of it."
Son of man This was usually just a way of saying "a person," or "a human being." But here this is a title for the man, Ezekiel.
temple The special building in Jerusalem for Jewish worship.
6 cubits 10'4" or 3.15m.
long measurement Literally, "a cubit and a handbreadth." This cubit equals 20.67 inches (52.5cm).
one ruler That is, 6 cubits (10'4" or 3.15m).
5 cubits 8' 7 5/16" or 26.25m.
8 cubits 13'9 5/16" or 4.2m.
2 cubits 3'5 5/16" or 105cm.
10 cubits 17'2 11/16" or 5.25m.
13 cubits 22'4 11/16" or 6.825m.
1 cubit 1' 8 5/8" or 52.5cm.
25 cubits 43' 3/4" or 13.125m.
40:14 The meaning of this verse is very uncertain.
60 cubits 103' 4 3/16" or 31.5m.
50 cubits 86'1 1/2" or 26.25m.
small windows These let the soldiers defending the city shoot arrows out at the enemy. The narrow part of the window was on the enemy's side of the wall to give the smalles target.
100 cubits 172'3" or 52.5m.

as the other gates. ²⁵The gateway and its porch had windows all around like the other gates. The gateway was 50 cubits* long and 25 cubits* wide. ²⁶There were seven steps going up to this gate. And its porch was at the inside end of the gateway. It had carvings of palm trees on the walls that were on either side of the gateway. ²⁷A gate was on the south side of the inner courtyard. The man measured from the gate ⌊on the inner wall⌋ to the gate ⌊on the outer wall⌋. It was 100 cubits* from gate to gate.

The Inner Courtyard

²⁸Then the man led me through the south gate into the inner courtyard. He measured this gate. This gateway measured the same as the other gates to the inner courtyard. ²⁹Its rooms, side walls, and porch also measured the same as the other gates. There were windows all around gateway and its porch. The gateway was 50 cubits* long and 25 cubits* wide. ³⁰The porch was 25 cubits* wide and 5 cubits* long. ³¹And its porch was at the end of the gateway next to the outer courtyard. Carvings of palm trees were on the walls ⌊on either side of the gateway⌋. There were eight steps leading up to the gate.

³²Then the man led me into the inner courtyard on the east side. He measured the gate. It measured the same as the other gates. ³³Its rooms, side walls, and porch also measured the same as the other gates. There were windows all around gateway and its porch. The gateway was 50 cubits* long and 25 cubits* wide. ³⁴And its porch was at the end of the gateway next to the outer courtyard. Carvings of palm trees were on the walls on either side of the gateway. There were eight steps leading up to the gate.

³⁵Then the man led me to the north gate. He measured it. It measured the same as the other gates. ³⁶Its rooms, side walls, and porch also measured the same as the other gates. There were windows all around gateway and its porch. The gateway was 50 cubits* long and 25 cubits* wide. ³⁷And its porch* was at the end of the gateway next to the outer courtyard. Carvings of palm trees were on the walls on either side of the gateway. There were eight steps leading up to the gate.

50 cubits 86'1 1/2" or 26.25m.
25 cubits 43' 3/4" or 13.125m.
100 cubits 172'3" or 52.5m.
5 cubits 8' 7 5/16" or 26.25m.
porch Hebrew has "side walls."

The Rooms For Preparing Sacrifices

³⁸There was a room with a door that opened onto the porch of this gate. This is where the priests wash the animals for the burnt offerings. ³⁹There were two tables on each side ⌊of the door⌋ of this porch. The animals for the burnt offerings, the sin offerings, and the guilt offerings were killed on these tables. ⁴⁰There were also two tables on each side of the door on the outside ⌊wall⌋ of this porch. ⁴¹So there were four tables on the inside ⌊wall⌋ and four tables on the outside ⌊wall⌋—eight tables that the priests used when they killed the animals for sacrifices. ⁴²There were also four tables made from cut stone for the burnt offerings. These tables were 1 1/2 cubits* long, 1 1/2 cubits* wide, and 1 cubit* high. On these tables, the priests put their tools that they used to kill the animals for the burnt offerings and other sacrifices. ⁴³There were meat hooks three inches long* on all the walls in this area. The meat of the offerings was put on the tables.

The Priests' Rooms

⁴⁴There were two rooms in the inner courtyard. One was by the north gate facing south. The other room was by the south* gate facing north. ⁴⁵The man said to me, "The room that looks to the south is for the priests who are on duty and serving in the temple area. ⁴⁶But the room that looks to the north is for the priests who are on duty and serving at the altar.* The priests are from the family group of Levi. But this second group of priests are the descendants* of Zadok. They are the only people who can carry the sacrifices to the altar to serve the Lord."*

⁴⁷The man measured the ⌊inner⌋ courtyard. The courtyard was a perfect square. It was 100 cubits* long and 100 cubits* wide. The altar* was in front of the temple.

The Porch of the Temple

⁴⁸Then the man led me to the porch of the temple and measured the walls on either side of the porch. Each side wall was 5 cubits* thick and 3 cubits* wide. And the opening ⌊between them⌋

1 1/2 cubits 2'7" or 78.75cm.
1 cubit 1' 8 5/8" or 52.5cm.
Meat hooks ... long Or, "Double shelves three inches wide...".
south This is from the ancient Greek translation. The Hebrew has "east."
altar(s) A stone table or raised area used for offering sacrifices.
descendants A person's children and their future families.
carry the sacrifices ... to serve the Lord Literally, "approach the Lord to serve him."

was 14 cubits.* ⁴⁹The porch was 20 cubits* wide and 12 cubits* long.* Ten steps went up to the porch. There were two columns for the walls on either side of the porch—one at each wall.

The Holy Place of the Temple

41 Then the man led me into the Holy Place. He measured the walls on either side of the room. Those side walls were 6 cubits* thick on each side. ²The door was 10 cubits* wide. The sides of the doorway were 5 cubits* on each side. The man measured that room. It was 40 cubits* long, and 20 cubits* wide.

The Most Holy Place in the Temple

³Then the man went into the last room. He measured the walls on either side of the doorway. Each side wall was 2 cubits* thick and 7 cubits* wide. The doorway was 6 cubits* wide. ⁴Then the man measured the length of the room. It was 20 cubits* long and 20 cubits* wide. The man said to me, "This is the Most Holy Place."

Other Rooms around the Temple

⁵Then the man measured the wall of the temple. It was 6 cubits* thick. There were side rooms all around the temple. They were 4 cubits* wide. ⁶The side rooms were on three different floors, one above the other. There were 30 rooms on each floor. The wall of the temple was built with ledges. The side rooms rested on these ledges but were not attached to the temple wall itself. ⁷Each floor of the side rooms around the temple was wider than the floor below. The ₍walls of₎ the rooms around the temple ₍became narrower₎ the higher they went so the rooms on the top floors were wider. A stairway went up from the lowest floor to the highest floor through the middle floor. ⁸I also saw that the temple had a raised base all the way around it. It was the foundation for the side rooms, and it was a full ruler* high. ⁹The outer wall of the side rooms was 5 cubits* thick. There was an open area between the side rooms of the temple ¹⁰and ₍the priests'₎ rooms. It was 20 cubits* wide and went all the way around the temple. ¹¹The doors of the side rooms opened onto the raised base. There was one entrance on the north side and one entrance on the south side. The raised base was 5 cubits* wide all around.

¹²There was a building in this restricted area west of the temple. The building was 70 cubits* wide and 90 cubits* long. The wall of the building was 5 cubits* thick all around. ¹³Then the man measured the temple. The temple was 100 cubits* long. The restricted area, including the building and its walls, was also 100 cubits* long. ¹⁴The restricted area on the east side, in front of the temple, was 100 cubits* long.

¹⁵The man measured the length of the building in the restricted area at the rear of the temple. It was 100 cubits* from one wall to the other wall.

The Most Holy Place, the Holy Place, and the Porch ₍that looked out onto the inner₎ courtyard ¹⁶had wood paneling on all the walls. All the windows and doors had wood trim around them. By the doorway, the Temple had wood paneling from the floor up to the windows, up to the part of the wall ¹⁷over the doorway.

On all the walls in the inner room and the outer room of the temple were carvings ¹⁸of Cherub angels and palm trees. A palm tree was between Cherub angels. Every Cherub angel had two faces. ¹⁹One face was a man's face looking toward the palm tree on one side. The other face was a lion's face looking toward the palm tree on the other side. They were carved all around on the temple. ²⁰From the floor to the area above the door, Cherub angels and palm trees were carved on all walls of the Holy Place.

²¹The walls on either side of the Holy Place were square. In front of the Most Holy Place, there was something that looked like ²²an altar* made from wood. It was 3 cubits* high and 2 cubits* long. Its corners, its base, and its sides were wood. The man said to me, "This is the table that is before the Lord."

²³Both the Holy Place and the Most Holy Place had a double door. ²⁴Each of the doors was made from two smaller doors. Each door was really two swinging doors. ²⁵Also Cherub angels and palm

3 cubits 5'2" or 157.5cm.
14 cubits 24'1 3/8" or 7.35m.
20 cubits 34'5 3/8" or 10.5m.
12 cubits 20'8" or 6.3m.
20 ... long Literally, "20 cubits long ... 12 cubits wide."
6 cubits 10' 4" or 3.15m.
10 cubits 17'2 11/16" or 5.25m.
5 cubits 8' 7 5/16" or 26.25m.
40 cubits 68'10 3/4" or 21m.
2 cubits 3'5 5/16" or 105cm.
7 cubits 12' 11/16" or 3.675m.
4 cubits 6'10 5/8" or 2.1m.
one ruler That is, 6 cubits (10'4" or 3.15m).

one ruler That is, 6 cubits (10'4" or 3.15m).
70 cubits 120'6 7/8" or 36.75m.
90 cubits 155' 1/4" or 47.25m.
100 cubits 172'3" or 52.5m.
altar* A stone table or raised area used for offering sacrifices.

trees were carved on the doors of the Holy Place. They were like those carved on the walls. There was a wood roof over the front of the porch. ²⁶There were windows with frames around them and palm trees on the walls on both sides of the porch, on the roof over the porch, and on the rooms around the temple.

The Priests' Room

42 Then the man led me through the north gate out into the outer courtyard. He led me ₍west₎ to a building with many rooms that was west of the restricted area and the building on the north side. ²This building was 100 cubits* long and 50 cubits* wide. People entered it from ₍the courtyard on₎ the north side. ³The building was three stories tall and had balconies. The 20-cubit* inner courtyard was between the building and the Temple. On the other side, the rooms faced the pavement of the outer courtyard. ⁴There was a path 10 cubits* wide and 100 cubits* long running along the south side of the building, even though the entrance was on the north side. ⁵⁻⁶Since this building was three stories tall and did not have columns like the columns of the outer courtyards, the top rooms were farther back than the rooms on the middle and bottom floors. The top floor was narrower than the middle floor which was narrower than the bottom floor because the balconies used this space. ⁷There was a wall outside that was parallel to the rooms and ran along the outer courtyard. It ran in front of the rooms for 50 cubits.* ⁸The row of rooms that ran along the outer courtyard was 50 cubits* long, although the total length of the building, as on the Temple side, was 100 cubits* long. ⁹The entrance was below these rooms at the east end of the building so people could enter from the outer courtyard. ¹⁰The entrance was at the start of the wall beside the courtyard.

There were rooms on the south side, by the restricted area and the other building. These rooms had a ¹¹path in front of them. They were like the rooms on the north side. They had the same length and width and the same kind of doors. ¹²The entrance to the lower rooms was at the east end of the building so people could enter from the open end of the path by the wall.

¹³The man said to me, "The north rooms and south rooms across from the restricted area are holy. These rooms are for the priests that offer the sacrifices to the Lord. That is where the priests will eat the most holy offerings. And that is where they will put the most holy offerings. Why? Because this place is holy. The most holy offerings are: the grain offerings, the sin offerings, and the guilt offerings. ¹⁴The priests who enter the holy area must leave their serving clothes in that holy place before they go out into the outer courtyard. Why? Because these clothes are holy. If a priest wants to go to the part of the temple where the other people are, then he must go to those rooms and put on other clothes.

The Outer Courtyard

¹⁵The man had finished measuring inside the Temple area. Then he brought me out through the east gate and measured all around that area. ¹⁶The man measured the east side with the ruler. It was 500 cubits* long. ¹⁷He measured the north side. It was 500 cubits* long. ¹⁸He measured the south side. It was 500 cubits* long. ¹⁹He went around to the west side and measured it. It was 500 cubits* long. ²⁰He measured the four walls that went all the way around ₍the temple₎. The wall was 500 cubits* long and 500 cubits* wide. It separated the holy area from the area that is not holy.

The Lord Will Live Among His People

43 The man led me to the east gate. ²There the Glory of the God of Israel came from the east. God's voice was loud like the sound of the sea. The ground was bright with the light from the Glory of God. ³The vision* that I saw was like the vision I saw by the Kebar Canal. I bowed with my face to the ground. ⁴The Glory of the Lord came into the temple through the east gate.

⁵Then the Spirit* picked me up and brought me into the inner courtyard. The Glory of the Lord filled the temple. ⁶I heard someone speaking to me from inside the temple. The man was still standing beside me. ⁷The voice from the temple said to me, "Son of man,* this is the place with my throne and footstool. I will live in this place among the

---

100 cubits 172'3" or 52.5m.
50 cubits 86'1 1/2" or 26.25m.
20 cubits 34'5 3/8" or 10.5m.
10 cubits 17'2 11/16" or 5.25m.

500 cubits 861'3" or 262.5m.
vision Something like a dream that God used to speak to people.
Spirit Or "spirit," or "wind."
Son of man This was usually just a way of saying "a person," or "a human being." But here this is a title for the man, Ezekiel.

people of Israel forever. The family of Israel won't ruin my holy name again. The kings and their people won't bring shame to my name by doing sexual sins* or by burying the dead bodies of their kings in this place. ⁸They won't bring shame to my name by putting their threshold next to my threshold, and their door post next to my door post. In the past, only a wall separated them from me. So they brought shame to my name every time they sinned and did those terrible things. That is why I became angry and destroyed them. ⁹Now let them take their sexual sins and the dead bodies of their kings far away from me. Then I will live among them forever.

¹⁰"Now, Son of man,* tell the family of Israel about the temple. Then, when they learn about the plans for the temple, they will be ashamed of their sins. ¹¹And they will be ashamed of all the bad things they have done. Let them know the design of the temple. Let them know how it should be built, where the entrances and exits are, and all the designs on it. Teach them about all its rules and all its laws. And write down these things for everyone to see so they can obey all the laws and rules for the temple. ¹²This is the law of the temple: The whole area on the top of the mountain within these boundaries is most holy. This is the law of the temple.

The Altar

¹³"And these are the measurements of the altar* in cubits using the long measurement.* There was a gutter all the way around the base of the altar. It was 1 cubit* deep, and ₍each side₎ was 1 cubit* wide. There was a rim around the edge 1 span* high. And this was how tall the altar was: ¹⁴From the ground to the lower ledge, the base measures 2 cubits.* It was 1 cubit* wide. It measures 4 cubits* from the smaller ledge to the larger ledge. It was 2 cubits* wide. ¹⁵The place for the fire on the altar was 4 cubits* high. The four corners were shaped like horns. ¹⁶The place for the fire on the altar was 12 cubits* long by 12 cubits* wide. It was perfectly square. ¹⁷The ledge was also square, 14 cubits* long by 14 cubits* wide. The border around it was 1/2 cubit* wide. (The gutter around the base was 2 cubits* wide.) The steps going up to the altar were on the east side."

¹⁸Then the man said to me, "Son of man,* the Lord and Master says these things: 'These are the rules for the altar:* At the time you build the altar, use these rules to offer burnt offerings and to sprinkle blood on it. ¹⁹You will give a young bull as a sin offering to the men from Zadok's family. These men are the priests from the family group of Levi. They are the men who serve me by bringing the offerings to me.'" The Lord my Master said these things. ²⁰"You will take some of the bull's blood and put it on the altar's four horns, on the four corners of the ledge, and on the rim around it. In this way, you will make the altar pure. ²¹Then take the bull for the sin offering and burn it in the proper place in the temple area, outside the Temple building.

²²On the second day you will offer a male goat that has nothing wrong with it. It will be for a sin offering. The priests will make the altar* pure the same way they made it pure with the bull. ²³When you have finished making the altar pure you will offer a young bull that has nothing wrong with it and a ram* from the flock that has nothing wrong in it. ²⁴Then you will offer them before the Lord. The priests will sprinkle salt on them. Then the priests will offer the bull and ram up as a burnt offering to the Lord. ²⁵You will prepare a goat every day for seven days for a sin offering. Also, you will prepare a young bull and a ram from the flock. These animals must have nothing wrong with them. ²⁶For seven days the priests will make the altar pure and ready for use in worshiping God. ²⁷After seven days, on the eighth day, the priests must offer your burnt offerings and fellowship offerings on the altar. Then I will accept you." The Lord my Master said these things.

The Outer Gate

44 Then the man brought me back to the east gate of the temple area. We were outside the gate and the gate was shut. ²The Lord said to me, "This gate will stay shut. It won't be opened.

---

sexual sins This might also mean "turning away from God and being unfaithful to him."
Son of man This was usually just a way of saying "a person," or "a human being." But here this is a title for the man, Ezekiel.
altar(s) A stone table or raised area used for offering sacrifices.
long measurement Literally, "a cubit and a handbreadth."
1 cubit 1' 8 5/8" or 52.5cm.
1 span The distance from the tip of the thumb to the tip of the little finger, about 9" or 22cm.
2 cubits 3' 5 5/16" or 105cm.
4 cubits 6'10 5/8" or 2.1m.
12 cubits 20'8" or 6.3m.
14 cubits 24'1 3/8" or 7.35m.
1/2 cubit 10 5/16" or 26.25cm.
ram(s) A male sheep.

No one will enter through it. Why? Because the Lord of Israel has entered through it. So it must stay shut. ³Only the ruler of the people may sit at this gate when he eats a meal with the Lord. He must enter through the porch of the gateway and go out the same way."

The Holiness of the Temple

⁴Then the man led me through the north gate to the front of the temple. I looked and saw the Glory of the Lord filling the Lord's temple. I bowed with my face touching the ground. ⁵The Lord said to me, "Son of man,* look very carefully! Use your eyes and ears. Look at these things. And listen very carefully to everything that I tell you about all the rules and laws about the Lord's temple. Look carefully at the entrances to the temple and at all the exits from the holy place. ⁶Then give this message to all the people of Israel that refused to obey me. Tell them, "The Lord my Master says these things: 'Family of Israel, I have had enough of the terrible things you have done! ⁷You brought foreigners into my temple—and those people were not truly circumcised*—they did not give themselves completely to me. In this way you made my temple unclean. You broke our agreement and did terrible things, and then you gave me the offerings of bread, the fat, and the blood. But this only made my temple unclean. ⁸You did not take care of my holy things. No, you let foreigners have responsibility of my holy place!'"

⁹The Lord my Master says these things, "A foreigner that is not truly circumcised* must not come into my temple—not even a foreigner living permanently among the people of Israel. He must be circumcised and he must give himself completely to me ₍before he can come into my temple₎. ¹⁰In the past, the Levites left me when Israel turned away from me. Israel left me to follow their idols.* The Levites will be punished for their sin. ¹¹The Levites were chosen to serve in my holy place. They guarded the gates of the temple. They served in the temple. They killed the animals for the sacrifices and burnt offerings for the people. They were chosen to help the people and to serve them. ¹²But those Levites helped the people sin against me! They helped the people worship their idols!* So I am making this promise against them: 'They will be punished for their sin.'" The Lord my Master said this.

¹³"So the Levites will not bring offerings to me like the priests. They won't come near any of my holy things or the things that are most holy. They must carry their shame because of the terrible things that they did. ¹⁴But I will let them take care of the temple. They will work in the temple and do the things that must be done in it.

¹⁵"The priests are all from the family group of Levi. But only priests from Zadok's family took care of my holy place when the people of Israel turned away from me. So only Zadok's descendants will bring offerings to me. They will stand before me to offer me the fat and the blood from the animals they sacrifice." The Lord my Master said those things! ¹⁶"They will enter my holy place. They will come near my table to serve me. They will take care of the things I gave them. ¹⁷When they enter the gates of the inner courtyard, they will wear linen clothes. They won't wear wool while they serve at the gates of the inner courtyard and in the temple. ¹⁸They will wear linen turbans* on their heads. And they will wear linen underwear. They won't wear anything that makes them sweat. ¹⁹Before they go out into the outer courtyard to the people, they will take off the clothes they wear while serving me. They will put these clothes away in the holy rooms. Then they will put on other clothes. In this way, they will not let people touch those holy clothes.

²⁰"These priests won't shave their heads or let their hair grow long. ₍This would show they are sad, and the priests must be happy about serving the Lord.₎ The priests may only trim the hair of their heads. ²¹None of the priests may drink wine when they go into the inner courtyard. ²²The priests must not marry a widow* or a divorced woman. No, they must marry only a virgin* from the family of Israel or a woman whose dead husband was a priest.

²³"Also, the priests must teach my people the difference between the holy things and the things that are not holy. They must help my people know what is clean and what is unclean. ²⁴The priests

Son of man This was usually just a way of saying "a person," or "a human being." But here this is a title for the man, Ezekiel.

truly circumcised Literally, "they were not circumcised in their heart or in their body." This was done to every male to show he shared in the Agreement God made with Israel. See Gen. 17:9-14.

idols Statues of false gods that people worshiped.

turban(s) A head covering made by wrapping a long piece of cloth around the head or around a cap worn on the head.

widow A woman whose husband has died.

virgin A pure young woman that has not had sexual relations with anyone.

will be the judges in court. They will follow my laws when they judge people. They will obey my laws and my rules at all my special feasts. They will respect my special days of rest and keep them holy. ²⁵They won't go near a dead person to make themselves unclean. But they may make themselves unclean if the dead person is their father, mother, son, daughter, brother, or a sister that is not married. ²⁶ₗThis will make the priest unclean.ⱼ After the priest has been made clean, he must wait seven days. ²⁷Then he can go back into the holy place. But on the day he goes into the inner courtyard to serve in the holy place, he must offer a sin offering for himself." The Lord my Master said these things.

²⁸"About the land that will belong to the Levites: I am their property. You won't give the Levites any property *(land)* in Israel. I am their share in Israel. ²⁹They will get to eat the grain offerings, the sin offerings, and the guilt offerings. Everything the people in Israel give to the Lord will be theirs. ³⁰And the first part of the harvest from every kind of crop will be for the priests. You will also give the priests the first of your dough. This will bring blessings to your house. ³¹The priests must not eat any bird or animal that died a natural death or was been torn to pieces ₗby a wild animalⱼ.

The Division of the Land for Holy Use

45 "You will divide the land for the Israelite family groups by throwing lots.* At that time, you will separate a part of the land. It will be a holy part for the Lord. The land will be 25,000 cubits* long and 20,000 cubits* wide. All of this land will be holy. ²A square area that is 500 cubits* long on each side will be for the temple. There will be an open space around the temple that is 50 cubits* wide. ³In the holy area you will measure 25,000 cubits* long and 10,000 cubits* wide. The temple will be in this area. The temple area will be the Most Holy Place.

⁴This holy part of the land will be for the priests, the servants of the temple, where they come near to serve the Lord. It will be a place for the priests' houses and a place for the temple. ⁵Another area, 25,000 cubits* long and 10,000 cubits* wide, will be for the Levites who serve in the temple. This land will also belong to the Levites for their cities to live in.

⁶"And you will give the city an area that is 5,000 cubits* wide and 25,000 cubits* long. It will be along the side of the holy area. It will be for all the family of Israel. ⁷The ruler will have land on both sides of the holy area and of the land belonging to the city. It will be in the area between the holy area and the area belonging to the city. It will be the same width as the land that belongs to a family group. It will go all the way from the west border to the east border. ⁸This land will be the ruler's property in Israel. So the ruler won't need to make life hard for my people any more. But they will give the land to the Israelites for their family groups."

⁹The Lord my Master said these things, "Enough, you rulers of Israel! Stop being cruel and stealing things from people! Be fair and do good things! Stop forcing my people out from their homes!" The Lord my Master said these things.

¹⁰"Stop cheating people. Use accurate scales and measures! ¹¹The ephah *(a dry measure)* and the bath *(a liquid measure)* must be the same size: A bath and an ephah must both equal 1/10 homer.* Those measures will be based on the homer. ¹²A shekel* must equal 20 gerahs. A mina must equal 60 shekels. It must be equal to 20 shekels plus 25 shekels plus 15 shekels.

¹³"This is a special offering that you must give:

14   1/6 ephah* of wheat for every homer* of wheat;
     1/6 ephah* of barley for every homer* of barley;
     1/10 bath* of olive oil for every cor* of olive oil;
     Remember:
         Ten baths make a homer.
         Ten baths make a cor.
15   And one sheep for every 200 sheep
     from every watering hole in Israel.

---

lot(s) Sticks, stones, or pieces of bone used like dice for making decisions. See Proverbs 16:33.
25,000 cubits 8.12 miles or 13.125km.
20,000 cubits 6.52 miles or 10.5km. This is from the Greek translation. The Hebrew has 10,000 cubits (3.26 miles or 5.25km).
500 cubits 861'3" or 262.5m.
50 cubits 86'1 1/2" or 26.25m.
10,000 cubits 3.26 miles or 5.25km.

5,000 cubits 1.63 miles or 2.625km.
homer A measure that equals about 6 bushels or 48.4 gallons or 220 liters.
shekel A weight equal to 2/5 of an ounce or 11.5 grams. This also this became an amount of money too.
1/6 ephah 14 cups or 3.67 liters.
1/10 bath 1/2 gallon or 2.2 liters.
cor 55 gallons or 220 liters.

"Those special offerings are for the grain offerings, for the burnt offerings, and for the fellowship offerings. These offerings are to make the people pure." The Lord my Master said these things.

¹⁶"Every person in the country will give to this offering for the ruler of Israel. ¹⁷But the ruler must give the things needed for the special holy days. The ruler must provide the burnt offerings, the grain offerings, and the drink offerings for the feast days, for the New Moons, for the sabbaths, and for all the special feasts of the family of Israel. The ruler must give all the sin offerings, grain offerings, burnt offerings, and fellowship offerings that are used to make the family of Israel pure."

¹⁸The Lord my Master says these things, "In the first month, on the first day of the month, you will take a young bull that has nothing wrong with it. You must use that bull to make the temple pure. ¹⁹The priest will take some of the blood from the sin offering and put it on the doorposts of the temple and on the four corners of the ledge of the altar,* and on the posts of the gate to the inner courtyard. ²⁰You will do the same thing on the seventh day of the month for any person who has sinned by mistake or by not knowing it. So you will make the temple pure.

Offerings During the Passover Feast

²¹"On the 14th day of the first month you must celebrate the Passover. The festival of unleavened bread* begins at this time. That festival continues for seven days. ²²At that time, the ruler will offer a bull for himself and for all the people of Israel. The bull will be for a sin offering. ²³During the seven days of the feast the ruler will offer seven bulls and seven rams* that have nothing wrong with them. They will be burnt offerings to the Lord. The ruler will offer one bull on every day of the seven days of the festival. And he will offer a male goat every day for a sin offering. ²⁴The ruler will give an ephah* ₍of barley₎ as a grain offering with each bull, and an ephah* ₍of barley₎ with each ram. And the ruler must give a hin* of oil for each ephah* ₍of grain₎. ²⁵The ruler must do the same thing for the seven days of the Festival ₍of Shelters₎. This festival begins on the 15th day of the seventh month. These offerings will be the sin offering, the burnt offering, the grain offering and the oil offering."

The Ruler and the Festivals

46 The Lord my Master says these things, "The east gate of the inner courtyard will be closed on the six working days. But it will be opened on the sabbath* day and on the day of the New Moon. ²The ruler will go into the porch of that gate and stand by the gatepost. Then the priests will offer the ruler's burnt offering and fellowship offerings. The ruler will worship at the opening of that gate. Then he will go out. But the gate will not be shut until evening. ³On the sabbath* day and on the day of the New Moon, the common people will also worship the Lord at that gate.

⁴"The ruler will offer burnt offerings to the Lord on the sabbath.* He must provide six lambs that have nothing wrong with them, and a ram* that has nothing wrong with it. ⁵He must give an ephah* of grain offering with the ram. As for the grain offering with the lambs, the ruler can give as much as he wants. But he must give 1 hin* of olive oil for each ephah* of grain.

⁶On the day of the New Moon he must offer a young bull that has nothing wrong it. He will also offer six lambs and a ram that have nothing wrong with them. ⁷The ruler must give an ephah* of grain offering with the bull, and an ephah* of grain offering with the ram. As for the grain offering with the lambs, the ruler can give as much as he wants. But he must give 1 hin* of olive oil for each ephah* of grain.

⁸When the ruler goes in, he must enter at the porch of the east gate—and he must leave that same way.

⁹When the common people come to meet with the Lord at the special feasts, the person who enters through the north gate to worship will go out through the south gate. The person who enters through the south gate will go out through the north gate. No one will return the same way he entered. Each person must go out straight ahead. ¹⁰The ruler should be there among the people. When the people go in, the ruler will go in with them. When they go out, the ruler will go out.

¹¹"At the feasts and other special meetings, an ephah* of grain offering must be offered with each young bull. And an ephah* of grain offering

---

altar(s) A stone table or raised area used for offering sacrifices.
unleavened bread Bread made without yeast.
ram(s) A male sheep.
ephah A dry measure (3/5 bushel or 22 liters).
hin A liquid measure (1 gallon or 2.2 liters).

ephah A dry measure (3/5 bushel or 22 liters).
sabbath Saturday, a special day of rest and worship for Jews.

must be offered with each ram. As for the grain offering with the lambs, the ruler can give as much as he wants. But he must give 1 hin* of olive oil for each ephah* of grain.

[12] "When the ruler gives a freewill offering to the Lord—it might be a burnt offering, a fellowship offering, or a freewill offering—the east gate will be opened for him. Then he will offer his burnt offering and his fellowship offerings like he does on the sabbath* day. After he leaves, the gate will be shut.

The Daily Offering

[13] "Every day you will provide a year-old lamb that has nothing wrong with it. It will be for a burnt offering to the Lord. You will provide it every morning. [14] Also, you will offer a grain offering with the lamb every morning. You will give 1/6 ephah* of flour and 1/3 hin* of oil to make the fine flour moist. It will be the daily grain offering to the Lord. [15] So they will give the lamb, the grain offering and the oil every morning, for a burnt offering forever."

Laws of Inheritance for the Ruler

[16] The Lord my Master says these things, "If the ruler gives a gift from part of his land to any of his sons, it will belong to his sons. It is their property. [17] But if the ruler gives a gift from part of his land to one of his slaves, the gift will belong to the slave only until the year of freedom.* Then the gift will go back to the ruler. Only the ruler's sons will keep a gift of land from the ruler. [18] And the ruler will not take any of the people's land or force them to leave their land. He must give some of his own land to his sons. In that way, my people will not be forced to lose their land."

The Special Kitchens

[19] The man led me through the entrance at the side of the gate. He led me to the holy rooms for the priests on the north side. There I saw a place at the west end of the path. [20] The man said to me, "This is the place where the priests will boil the guilt offering and the sin offering. It is where the priests will bake the grain offering. Why? So they will not need to bring these offerings out into the outer courtyard. So they will not bring those holy things out where the common people are."

[21] Then the man led me out to the outer courtyard. He led me to the four corners of the courtyard. I saw smaller courtyards in each corner of the large courtyard. [22] There was a small, enclosed area in each of the four corners of the courtyard. Each small courtyard was 40 cubits* long and 30 cubits* wide. The four areas measured the same. [23] There was a brick wall around each of the four small courtyards. And there were places built into the brick walls for cooking. [24] The man said to me, "These are the kitchens where the people that serve at the temple cook the sacrifices for the people."

The Water Flowing From the Temple

47 The man led me back to the entrance of the temple. I saw water coming out from under the east gate of the temple. (The front of the temple is on the east side.) The water flowed down from under the south end of the temple and ran south of the altar.* [2] The man led me out through the north gate and then around the outside to the outer gate on the east side. The water was flowing out on the south side of the gate.

[3] The man walked east with a tape measure in his hand. He measured 1,000 cubits.* Then he told me to walk through the water at that place. The water was only ankle deep. [4] The man measured another 1,000 cubits.* Then he told me to walk through the water at that place. There, the water came up to my knees. Then he measured another 1,000 cubits* and told me to walk through the water at that place. There, the water was waist deep. [5] The man measured another 1,000 cubits.* But there the water was too deep to cross. It had become a river. The water was deep enough to swim in. It was a river that was too deep to cross. [6] Then the man said to me, "Son of Man,* did you pay close attention to the things you saw?"

Then the man led me back along the side of the river. [7] As I walked back along the side of the river, I saw very many trees on both sides of the

---

hin A liquid measure (1 gallon or 2.2 liters).
ephah A dry measure (3/5 bushel or 22 liters).
sabbath Saturday, a special day of rest and worship for the Jews.
1/6 ephah 14 cups or 3.67 liters.
year of freedom Also called "Jubilee." Every 50 years the Israelites were to set their slaves free if they were Israelites. Also the people gave all the land back to the Israelite family that originally owned the land.

Son of Man This was usually just a way of saying "a person," or "a human being." But here this is a title for the man, Ezekiel.
40 cubits 68'10 3/4" or 21m.
30 cubits 51'8 1/16" or 15.75m.
altar(s) A stone table or raised area used for offering sacrifices.
1,000 cubits 1/3 mile or .525km.

water. ⁸The man said to me, "This water flows east, down to the Arabah Valley. The water enters the Dead Sea and the water in that sea becomes fresh. ⁹This water flows into the Dead Sea so the water in that sea becomes fresh and clean. There are many fish in this water. And all kinds of animals live where this river goes. ¹⁰You can see fishermen standing by the river all the way from En Gedi to En Eglaim. You can see them throwing their fishing nets and catching many kinds of fish. There are as many kinds of fish in the Dead Sea as there are in the Mediterranean Sea. ¹¹But the swamps and small areas of wet land will not become fresh. They will be left for salt. ¹²All kinds of fruit trees will grow on both sides of the river. Their leaves never will become dry and fall. The fruit will never stop growing on those trees. The trees will produce fruit every month. Why? Because the water for the trees comes from the temple. The fruit from the trees will be for food, and their leaves will be for healing."

Division of the Land for the Family Groups

¹³The Lord my Master says these things, "These are the borders for dividing the land among the twelve family groups of Israel. Joseph will have two parts. ¹⁴You will divide the land equally. I promised to give this land to your ancestors.* So I am giving this land to you.

¹⁵Here are the borders of the land: On the north side, it goes from the Mediterranean Sea by the way of Hethlon where the road turns toward Hamath, and on to Zedad, ¹⁶Berothah, Sibraim (which is on the border between Damascus and Hamath) and Hazer Hatticon, which is on the border of Hauran. ¹⁷So the border will go from the sea to Hazar Enan on the northern border of Damascus, and Hamath. This will be on the north side.

¹⁸"On the east side, the border will go from Hazar Enan between Hauran and Damascus and continue along the Jordan River between Gilead and the land of Israel, to the eastern sea and all the way to Tamar. This will be the eastern border.

¹⁹"On the south side, the border will go from Tamar all the way to the oasis at Meribah-kadesh. Then it will go along the Brook of Egypt to the Mediterranean Sea. This will be the southern border.

²⁰"On the west side, the Mediterranean Sea will be the border all the way to the area in front of Lebo Hamath. This will be your western border.

²¹"So you will divide this land among you for the family groups of Israel. ²²You will divide it as a property for yourselves and for the foreigners who live among you and who have had children among you. These foreigners will be residents—they will be like natural born Israelites. You will divide some land for them among the family groups of Israel. ²³The family group where that resident lives must give him some land." The Lord my Master said these things!

The Land for the Family Groups of Israel

48 ¹⁻⁷The northern border goes east from the Mediterranean Sea, to Hethlon to Hamath Pass, and then all the way to Hazar Enan. This is on the border between Damascus and Hamath. The land for the family groups in this group will go from the east of these borders to the west. From north to south, the family groups in this area are: Dan, Asher, Naphtali, Manasseh, Ephraim, Reuben, Judah.

The Special Section of Land

⁸The next area of land will be for a special use. This land is south of Judah's land. This area is 25,000 cubits* long from north to south. And from east to west, it will be as wide as the land that belongs to the other family groups. The temple will be in the middle of this section of land. ⁹You will dedicate this land to the Lord. It will be 25,000 cubits* long and 20,000 cubits* wide. ¹⁰This special area of land will be divided among the priest and Levites.

The priests will get one part of this area. The land will be 25,000 cubits* long on the north side, 10,000 cubits* wide on the west side, 10,000 cubits* wide on the east side, and 25,000 cubits* long on the south side. The Lord's temple will be in the middle of this area of land. ¹¹This land is for Zadok's descendants. These men were chosen to be my holy priests. Why? Because they continued to serve me when the other people of Israel left me. Zadok's family did not leave me like the other people from the family group of Levi. ¹²This special share from this holy part of the land will

---

ancestors Literally, "fathers," meaning a person's parents, grandparents, and all the people they are descended from.

25,000 cubits 8.12 miles or 13.125km.
20,000 cubits 6.52 miles or 10.5 km. Most Greek copies have 25,000 cubits and Hebrew has 10,000 cubits. But see Ez.45:1.
10,000 cubits 3.26 miles or 5.25km.

EZEKIEL 48:13-20

be especially for these priests. It will be next to the land of the Levites.

¹³"Next to the land for the priests, the Levites will have a share of the land. It will be 25,000 cubits* long and 10,000 cubits* wide. They will get the full length and width of this land—25,000 cubits* long and 20,000 cubits* wide. ¹⁴The Levites will not sell or trade any of this land. They will not be able to sell any of this land. They must not cut up this part of the country! Why? Because this land belongs to the Lord—it is very special. It is the best part of the land.

The Shares for the City Property

¹⁵"There will be an area of land 5,000 cubits* wide by 25,000 cubits* long that is left over from the land given to the priests and Levites. This land can be for the city, for grasslands for animals and for building houses. The common people may use this land. The city will be in the middle of it. ¹⁶These are the city's measurements: The north side will be 4,500 cubits.* The south side will be 4,500 cubits.* The east side will be 4,500 cubits.* The west side will be 4,500 cubits.* ¹⁷The city will have grasslands. These grasslands will be 250 cubits* on the north and 250 cubits* on the south. They will be 250 cubits* on the east and 250 cubits* on the west. ¹⁸What is left of the length along the side of the holy area will be 10,000 cubits* on the east and 10,000 cubits* on the west. This land will be along the side of the holy area. This land will grow food for the city workers. ¹⁹The city workers will till this land. The workers will be from all the family groups of Israel.

²⁰"This special area of land will be square. It will be 25,000 cubits* long by 25,000 cubits* wide. You must set apart this area for its special purposes. One part is for the priests. One part is for the Levites. And one part is for the city.

²¹⁻²²"Part of that special land will be for the ruler of the country. That special area of land is square. It is 25,000 cubits* long by 25,000 cubits* wide. Part of this special land is for the priests and part of it is for the Levites, and part of it is for the temple. The temple is in the middle of this area of land. The rest of the land belongs to the ruler of the country. The ruler will get the area between the land of Benjamin and the land of Judah.

²³⁻²⁷South of this special area will be the land for the family groups that lived east of the Jordan River. Each family group will get a section of land that goes from the eastern border to the Mediterranean Sea. From north to south, these family groups are: Benjamin, Simeon, Issachar, Zebulun, and Gad.

²⁸"The south border of Gad's land will go from Tamar to the Oasis of Meribah-kadesh, then along the Brook of Egypt to the Mediterranean Sea. ²⁹And that is the land that you will divide among the family groups of Israel. That is what each group will get." The Lord my Master said these things!

The Gates of the City

³⁰"These are the gates of the city. The gates will be named for the family groups of Israel.

"The north side of the city will be 4,500 cubits* long. ³¹There will be three gates: Reuben's Gate, Judah's Gate, and Levi's Gate.

³²"The east side of the city will be 4,500 cubits* long. There will be three gates: Joseph's Gate, Benjamin's Gate, and Dan's Gate.

³³"The south side of the city will be 4,500 cubits* long. There will be three gates: Simeon's Gate, Issachar's Gate, and Zebulun's Gate.

³⁴"The west side of the city will be 4,500 cubits* long. There will be three gates: Gad's Gate, Asher's Gate, and Naphtali's Gate.

³⁵"The distance around the city will be 18,000 cubits.* From now on, the name of the city will be: THE LORD IS THERE.*

25,000 cubits 8.12 miles or 13.125km.
10,000 cubits 3.26 miles or 5.25km.
20,000 cubits 6.52 miles or 10.5 km. Most Greek copies have 25,000 cubits and Hebrew has 10,000 cubits. But see Ez.45:1.
5,000 cubits 1.63 miles or 2.625km.
4,500 cubits 1.47 miles or 2.36km.
250 cubits 430'7 1/2" or 131.25m.
18,000 cubits 5.87 miles or 9.45km.
The Lord is There In Hebrew this sounds like the name Jerusalem.

A Reconstruction of the Temple Described by Ezekiel

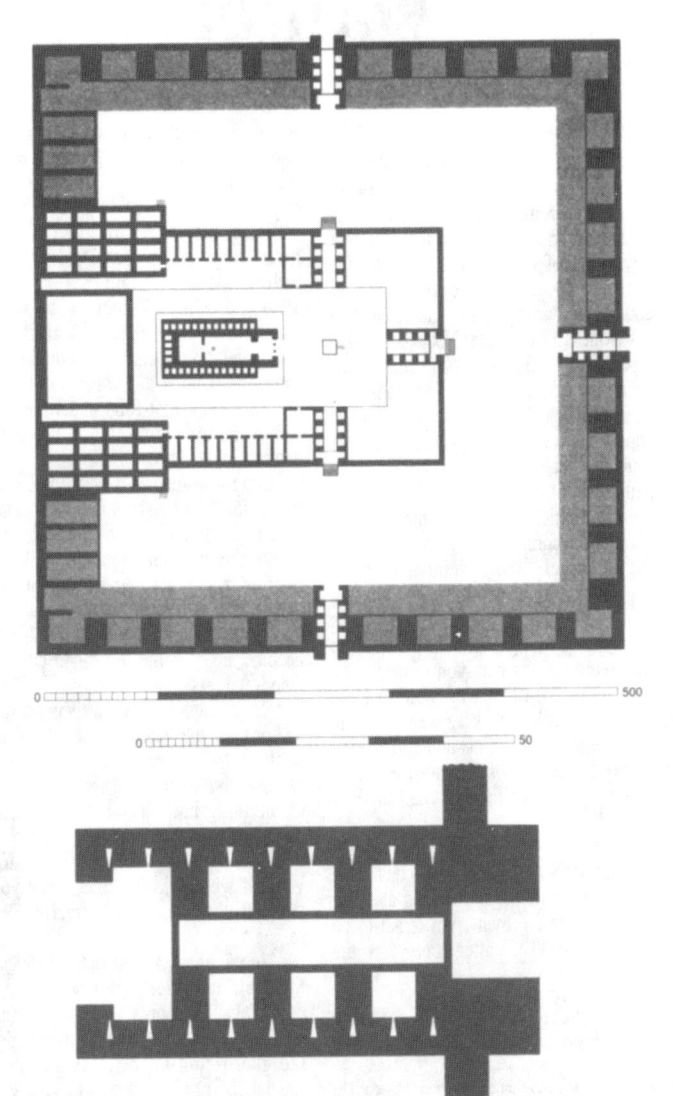

The Eastern Gate in the Outer Courtyard

Daniel

Daniel Taken to Babylon

1 Nebuchadnezzar was the king of Babylon. Nebuchadnezzar came to Jerusalem. Nebuchadnezzar surrounded Jerusalem with his army. This happened during the third year that Jehoiakim was king of Judah.* ²The Lord allowed Nebuchadnezzar to defeat Jehoiakim king of Judah. Nebuchadnezzar took all of the dishes and other things from God's temple. Nebuchadnezzar carried those things to Babylon. Nebuchadnezzar put those things in the temple of his idol gods.

³Then King Nebuchadnezzar gave Ashpenaz an order. (Ashpenaz was the most important leader of all the eunuchs* that served the king.) The king told Ashpenaz to bring some of the Jewish men into his house. Nebuchadnezzar wanted Jewish men from important families and from the family of the king of Israel. ⁴King Nebuchadnezzar wanted only healthy young Jewish men. The king wanted young men that did not have any bruises or scars, or anything wrong with their bodies. The king wanted handsome, smart young men. The king wanted young men that were able to learn things quickly and easily. The king wanted young men that were able to serve in his house. The king told Ashpenaz to teach those young men from Israel the language and writings of the Chaldean people.*

⁵King Nebuchadnezzar gave those young men a certain amount of food and wine every day. That was the same kind of food that the king ate. The king wanted those young men from Israel to be trained for three years. Then after three years, the young men would become servants of the king of Babylon. ⁶Among those young men were Daniel, Hananiah, Mishael, and Azariah. These young men were from the family group of Judah.

⁷Then Ashpenaz gave those young men from Judah Babylonian names. Daniel's new name was Belteshazzar. Hananiah's new name was Shadrach. Mishael's new name was Meshach. And Azariah's new name was Abednego.

⁸Daniel did not want to eat the king's rich food and wine. Daniel did not want to make himself unclean* with that food and wine. So he asked Ashpenaz for permission not to make himself unclean in this way.

⁹God made Ashpenaz want to be good and kind to Daniel. ¹⁰But Ashpenaz said to Daniel, "I am afraid of my master, the king. The king ordered me to give you this food and drink. If you don't eat this food, then you will begin to look weak and sick. You will look worse than other young men your age. The king will see this, and he will become angry at me. He might cut off my head! And it would be your fault."

¹¹Then Daniel talked to their guard. Ashpenaz had ordered the guard to watch Daniel, Hananiah, Mishael, and Azariah. ¹²Daniel said to the guard, "Please give us this test for ten days: Don't give us anything but vegetables to eat and water to drink. ¹³Then after ten days, compare us with the other young men who eat the king's food. See for yourself who looks healthier. Then you judge for yourself how you want to treat us. We are your servants."

¹⁴So the guard agreed to test Daniel, Hananiah, Mishael, and Azariah for ten days. ¹⁵After ten days, Daniel and his friends looked healthier than all of the young men that ate the king's food. ¹⁶So the guard continued to take away the king's special food and wine and to give vegetables to Daniel, Hananiah, Mishael, and Azariah.

---

third year ... Judah This is probably 605b.c.

eunuchs Men whose testicles have been removed. Rulers often gave such men important positions.

Chaldean people An important family group in Babylon. The king of Babylon was from this family group. The Chaldeans were educated people—they studied science, history, languages, and astronomy. But they also believed they could do magic and look at the stars to learn what would happen in the future.

unclean See Lev. 11-15 for the rules about clean and unclean things.

[17] God gave Daniel, Hananiah, Mishael, and Azariah the wisdom and ability to learn many different kinds of writing and science. Daniel could also understand all kinds of visions* and dreams. [18] The king wanted all the young men to be trained for three years. At the end of that time, Ashpenaz brought all of the young men to King Nebuchadnezzar. [19] The king talked to them. The king found that none of the young men were as good as Daniel, Hananiah, Mishael, and Azariah. So those four young men became the king's servants. [20] Every time the king asked them about something important, they showed much wisdom and understanding. The king found they were ten times better than all the magic men and wise men in his kingdom. [21] So Daniel continued to be the king's servant until the first year that Cyrus was king.*

Nebuchadnezzar's Dream

2 During Nebuchadnezzar's second year as king, he had some dreams. Those dreams bothered him and he could not sleep. [2] So the king called his wise men to come to him. Those men used magic tricks and they watched the stars. They did this to try to interpret dreams and to learn what will happen in the future. The king wanted those men to tell him what he had dreamed. So they came in and stood in front of the king.

[3] Then the king said to those men, "I had a dream that bothers me. I want to know what the dream means."

[4] Then the Chaldeans* answered the king. They spoke in the Aramaic language.* They said, "King, live forever! We are your servants. Please tell us your dream, then we will tell you what it means."

[5] Then King Nebuchadnezzar said to those men, "No! You must tell me the dream. And then you must tell me what it means. If you don't do these things, then I will give an order for you to be cut into pieces. And I will order your houses to be destroyed until they become piles of dust and ashes. [6] But if you tell me my dream and explain the meaning, then I will give you gifts, rewards, and great honor. So tell me about my dream and tell me what it means."

[7] Again the wise men said to the king, "Please, sir, tell us about the dream, and we will tell you what the dream means."

[8] Then King Nebuchadnezzar answered, "I know that you are trying to get more time. You know that I meant what I said. [9] You know that you will be punished if you don't tell me about my dream. So you have all agreed to lie to me. You are hoping for more time. You are hoping that I will forget what I want you to do. Now, tell me the dream. If you can tell me the dream, then I will know that you can tell me what it really means!"

[10] The Chaldeans* answered the king. They said, "There is not a man on earth that can do what the king is asking! No king has ever asked the wise men or the men that do magic or the Chaldeans to do something like this. Not even the greatest and most powerful king ever asked his wise men to do something like this. [11] The king is asking something that is too hard to do. Only the gods could tell the king his dream and what it means. But the gods don't live with people."

[12] When the king heard that, he became very angry. So he gave an order for all the wise men of Babylon to be killed. [13] King Nebuchadnezzar's order was announced. All the wise men were to be killed. The king's men were sent to look for Daniel and his friends to kill them.

[14] Arioch was the commander of the king's guards. He was going to kill the wise men of Babylon. But Daniel talked to him. Daniel spoke to Arioch in a wise and polite way. [15] Daniel said to Arioch, "Why did the king order such a severe punishment?"

Then Arioch explained the whole story about the king's dreams, and Daniel understood. [16] When Daniel heard the story, he went to King Nebuchadnezzar. Daniel asked the king to give him some more time. Then he would tell the king about the dream and what it meant.

[17] So Daniel went to his house. He explained the whole story to his friends Hananiah, Mishael, and Azariah. [18] Daniel asked his friends to pray to the God of heaven. Daniel asked them to pray that God would be kind to them and help them understand this secret. Then Daniel and his friends

---

vision Something like a dream that God used to speak to people.
first year that Cyrus was king This is probably 539-538 B.C.
Chaldean(s) An important family group in Babylonia. Sometimes this name means simply "People from Babylonia."
Aramaic language This was the official language of the Babylonian Empire. People from many countries also used this language when they wrote official letters to people in other countries. The text of Daniel from here to Daniel 7:28 is written in Aramaic.

would not be killed with the other wise men of Babylon.

¹⁹During the night, God explained the secret to Daniel in a vision.* Then Daniel praised the God of heaven. ²⁰Daniel said:

> "Praise God's name for ever and ever!
> Power and wisdom belong to him!
> ²¹ He changes the times and seasons.
> And he changes the kings.
> He gives power to kings,
> and he takes their power away!
> He gives wisdom to people
> so they become wise,
> He lets people learn things
> and become wise.
> ²² He knows hidden secrets
> that are hard to understand.
> Light lives with him,
> so he knows what is in the dark
> and secret places!
> ²³ God of my ancestors,*
> I thank you and praise you!
> You gave me wisdom and power.
> You told us the things we asked for!
> You told us about the king's dream."

Daniel Tells What the Dream Means

²⁴Then Daniel went to Arioch. King Nebuchadnezzar had chosen Arioch to kill the wise men of Babylon. Daniel said to Arioch, "Don't kill the wise men of Babylon. Take me to the king. I will tell him about his dream and what it means."

²⁵So very quickly, Arioch took Daniel to the king. Arioch said to the king, "I have found a man among the captives* from Judah. He can tell the king what his dream means."

²⁶The king asked Daniel (Belteshazzar) a question. He said to Daniel, "Are you able to tell me about my dream, and what it means?"

²⁷Daniel answered, "King Nebuchadnezzar, no wise man, no man that does magic tricks, and no Chaldean could tell the king the secret things he has asked about. ²⁸But there is a God in heaven who tells secret things. God gave King Nebuchadnezzar dreams to show him what will happen at a later time. This was your dream, and these are the things you saw while lying on your bed: ²⁹King, you were lying there on your bed. And you began thinking about things that will happen in the future. God can tell people about secret things—and he showed you what will happen in the future. ³⁰God also told this secret to me! Why? It is not because I have greater wisdom than other men. No, God told me about this secret so that you, king, may know what it means. In that way, you will understand what went through your mind.

³¹"King, in your dream you saw a large statue* in front of you. The statue was very large and it was shiny and very impressive. It would make a person's eyes wide from amazement. ³²The head of the statue was made from pure gold. The chest and the arms of the statue were made from silver. The belly and upper part of the legs of the statue were made from bronze. ³³The lower part of the legs of the statue were made from iron. The feet of the statue were made partly of iron and partly of clay. ³⁴While you were looking at the statue, you saw a rock. The rock was cut loose—but a person did not cut the rock. Then the rock ₜwent through the air andⱼ hit the statue on its feet of iron and clay. The rock smashed the feet of the statue. ³⁵Then the iron, the clay, the bronze, the silver, and gold broke to pieces all at the same time. And all those pieces became like chaff* on a threshing floor* in the summertime. The wind blew those pieces away, and there was nothing left. No one could tell that a statue had ever been there. Then the rock that hit the statue became a very large mountain and filled up the whole earth.

³⁶"That was your dream. Now we will tell the king what it means. ³⁷King, you are the most important king. The God of heaven has given you a kingdom, power, strength, and glory. ³⁸God has given you control and you rule over people and over the wild animals and over the birds. Wherever they live, God has made you ruler over them all. King Nebuchadnezzar, you are that head of gold on the statue.*

---

vision Something like a dream that God used to speak to people.
ancestors Literally, "fathers, " meaning a person's parents, grandparents, and all the people they are descended from.
captives People taken away like prisoners. Here this means the Jewish people that were taken to Babylon.
statue An image, made to look like a person or an animal. Statues are made from stone, metal, or wood.
chaff The seed coverings and stems separated from the seeds of plants like wheat or barley. Farmers saved the seeds but let the wind blow the useless chaff away.
threshing floor A place where grain is beaten or walked on to remove the hulls from the grain.

⁃³⁹"Another kingdom will come after you—that is the silver part₁. But that kingdom will not be as great as your kingdom. Next, a third kingdom will rule over the earth—that is the bronze part. ⁴⁰Then there will be a fourth kingdom. That kingdom will be strong like iron. Iron breaks and smashes things to pieces. In the same way, that fourth kingdom will smash and break all the other kingdoms. ⁴¹"You saw that the feet and toes of the statue* were partly clay and partly iron. That means the fourth kingdom will be a divided kingdom. It will have some of the strength of iron in it because you saw the iron mixed with clay. ⁴²The toes of the statue were partly iron and partly clay. So the fourth kingdom will be partly strong like iron, and partly weak like clay. ⁴³You saw the iron mixed with clay. But iron and clay don't mix completely together. In the same way, the people of the fourth kingdom will be a mixture. Those people will not be united as one people.

⁴⁴"During the time of the kings ₁of the fourth kingdom₁, the God of heaven will set up another kingdom. This kingdom will continue forever! It will never be destroyed! And it will be the kind of kingdom that can't be passed on to another group of people. This kingdom will crush all those other kingdoms. It will bring those kingdoms to an end. But that kingdom itself will continue forever.

⁴⁵"King Nebuchadnezzar, you saw a rock cut from a mountain—but no person cut that rock! The rock broke the iron, the bronze, the clay, the silver, and the gold to pieces. In this way, God showed you what will happen in the future. The dream is true and you can trust this interpretation."

⁴⁶Then King Nebuchadnezzar bowed down in front of Daniel. The king praised Daniel. The king gave an order that an offering and incense be given to honor Daniel. ⁴⁷Then the king said to Daniel, "I know for sure your God is the most important and powerful God. And he is the Lord of all the kings. He tells people about things they can't know. I know this is true because you were able to tell these secret things to me."

⁴⁸Then the king gave Daniel a very important job in his kingdom. And the king gave many expensive gifts to Daniel. Nebuchadnezzar made Daniel ruler over the whole province of Babylon. And he put Daniel in charge of all the wise men of Babylon. ⁴⁹Daniel asked the king to make Shadrach, Meshach, and Abednego important officials over the province of Babylon. And the king did as Daniel asked. And Daniel himself became one of the important people that stayed near the king.

The Idol of Gold and the Hot Furnace

3 King Nebuchadnezzar had a gold idol made. That idol was 60 cubits* high and 6 cubits* wide. Then he set the idol up on the plain of Dura in the province of Babylon. ²Then the king called the satraps,* the prefects,* governors, advisers, treasurers, judges, rulers, and all the other officials in his kingdom to come together. The king wanted all those men to come to the dedication ceremony for the idol.

³So all those men came and stood in front of the idol that King Nebuchadnezzar had set up. ⁴Then the man that makes the announcements for the king spoke in a loud voice. He said, "All you people from many nations and language groups, ₁listen to me₁. This is what you are commanded to do: ⁵You must bow down as soon as you hear the sound of all the musical instruments. When you hear the horns, flutes, lyres,* sambucas,* harps, bagpipes,* and all of the other musical instruments, you must worship the gold idol. King Nebuchadnezzar has set this idol up. ⁶If any person does not bow down and worship this gold idol, then that person will be quickly thrown into a very hot furnace."

⁷So, as soon as they heard the sound of the horns, flutes, lyres,* sambucas,* bagpipes,* and all of the other musical instruments, they bowed down and worshiped the gold idol. All the peoples, nations, and men of every kind of

---

60 cubits 88' 6 15/16" (27m) using the short cubit.
6 cubits 8' 10 1/4" (2.7m) using the short cubit.
satraps Persian officials that were governors of a province.
prefects Important officials.
lyres A musical instrument like a harp. The name in Hebrew comes from some other language, possibly the Greek word "kithara."
sambuca(s) A musical instrument. It might be a seven stringed instrument like a harp. The name in Hebrew comes from some other language, possibly Greek.
bagpipes A musical instrument with a bag and several horns or pipes. The name in Hebrew comes from some other language, possibly the Greek word "symphony."

statue An image, made to look like a person or an animal. Statues are made from stone, metal, or wood.

language there worshiped the gold idol that King Nebuchadnezzar had set up. ⁸Then, some of the Chaldean* men came up to the king. Those men began speaking against the Jews. ⁹They said to King Nebuchadnezzar, "King, may you live forever! ¹⁰King, you gave a command. You said that everyone that hears the sound of the horns, flutes, lyres,* sambucas,* harps, bagpipes,* and all the other musical instruments must bow down and worship the gold idol. ¹¹And you also said that if any person does not bow down and worship the gold idol, then that person will be thrown into a very hot furnace. ¹²There are some Jews that did not pay attention to your order, king. You made those Jews important officials in the province of Babylon. Their names are Shadrach, Meshach, and Abednego. They don't worship your gods. And they didn't bow down and worship the gold idol you set up."

¹³Nebuchadnezzar became very angry. He called Shadrach, Meshach, and Abednego. So those men were brought to the king. ¹⁴And Nebuchadnezzar said to those men, "Shadrach, Meshach, and Abednego, is it true that you don't worship my gods? And is it true that you didn't bow down and worship the gold idol I have set up? ¹⁵Now, when you hear the sound of the horns, flutes, lyres,* sambucas,* harps, bagpipes,* and all the other musical instruments, you must bow down and worship the gold idol. If you are ready to worship the idol I have made, that will be good. But if you don't worship it, you will be thrown very quickly into the hot furnace. Then no god will be able to save you from my power!"

Chaldean(s) An important family group in Babylonia. Sometimes this name means simply "People from Babylonia."
lyres A musical instrument like a harp. The name in Hebrew comes from some other language, possibly the Greek word "kitharis."
sambuca(s) A musical instrument. It might be a seven stringed instrument like a harp. The name in Hebrew comes from some other language, possibly Greek.
bagpipes A musical instrument with a bag and several horns or pipes. The name in Hebrew comes from some other language, possibly the Greek word "symphony."
lyre(s) A musical instrument like a harp. The name in Hebrew comes from some other language, possibly the Greek word "kitharis."
bagpipe(s) A musical instrument with a bag and several horns or pipes. The name in Hebrew comes from some other language, possibly the Greek word "symphony."

¹⁶Shadrach, Meshach, and Abednego answered the king, "Nebuchadnezzar, we don't need to explain these things to you! ¹⁷If you throw us into the hot furnace, then the God we serve can save us. And if he wants to, he can save us from your power. ¹⁸But even if God does not save us, we want you to know, king, that we refuse to serve your gods. We won't worship the gold idol you have set up."

¹⁹Then Nebuchadnezzar was very angry! He looked very mean at Shadrach, Meshach, and Abednego. He gave an order for the oven to be heated seven times hotter that it usually was. ²⁰Then Nebuchadnezzar commanded some of the strongest soldiers in his army to tie up Shadrach, Meshach, and Abednego. The king told the soldiers to throw Shadrach, Meshach, and Abednego into the hot furnace. ²¹So Shadrach, Meshach, and Abednego were tied up and thrown into the hot furnace. They were wearing their robes, pants, hats, and other clothes. ²²The king was very angry when he gave the command, so they quickly made the furnace very hot! The fire was so hot that the flames killed the strong soldiers! They were killed when they went close to the fire and threw in Shadrach, Meshach, and Abednego. ²³Shadrach, Meshach, and Abednego fell into the fire. They were tied up very tightly.

²⁴Then King Nebuchadnezzar jumped to his feet. He was very surprised and he asked his advisers, "We tied only three men and we threw only three men into the fire! Is that right?"

His advisers said, "Yes, king."

²⁵The king said, "Look! I see four men walking around in the fire. They are not tied up and they are not burned. The fourth man looks like an angel!*

²⁶Then Nebuchadnezzar went to the opening of the hot furnace. He shouted, "Shadrach, Meshach, and Abednego, come out! Servants of the Most High God, come here!"

So Shadrach, Meshach, and Abednego came out of the fire. ²⁷When they came out, the satraps* , prefects*, governors, and royal advisers crowded around them. They could see that the fire had not burned Shadrach, Meshach, and Abednego. Their bodies were not burned at all. Their hair was not burned, their robes were not burned, and they didn't even smell like they had been near fire.

angel Literally, "son of the god."
satraps Persian officials that were governors of a province.
prefects Important officials.

²⁸Then Nebuchadnezzar said, "Praise the God of Shadrach, Meshach, and Abednego. Their God has sent his angel and saved his servants from the fire! These three men trusted their God. They refused to obey my command and were willing to die instead of serving or worshiping any other God. ²⁹So, I now make this law: The people of any nation or of any language that says anything against the God of Shadrach, Meshach, and Abednego will be cut to pieces. And that person's house will be destroyed until it is a pile of dirt and ashes. No other god can save his people like this." ³⁰Then the king gave Shadrach, Meshach, and Abednego more important jobs in the province of Babylon.

Nebuchadnezzar's Dream about a Tree

4 King Nebuchadnezzar sent this letter to the many nations and people that speak other languages and live all around the world.

Greetings:
²I am very happy to tell you about the miracles and wonderful things that the Most High God did for me.

3   God has done amazing miracles!
     God has done powerful miracles!
     God's kingdom continues forever;
     God's rule will continue for all
        generations.

⁴I, Nebuchadnezzar, was at my palace.* I was happy and successful. ⁵I had a dream that made me afraid. I was lying on my bed, and I saw pictures and visions* in my mind. Those things made me very afraid. ⁶So I gave an order that all the wise men of Babylon be brought to me. Why? So they could tell me what my dream meant. ⁷When the men of magic, and the Chaldeans* came, I told them about the dream. But those men could not tell me what it meant. ⁸Finally, Daniel came to me. (I gave Daniel the name, Belteshazzar, to honor my god. The spirit of the holy gods is in him.) I told Daniel about my dream. ⁹I said,

"Belteshazzar, you are the most important of all the men of magic. I know that the spirit of the holy gods is in you. I know there is no secret that is too hard for you to understand. This was what I dreamed. Tell me what it means. ¹⁰These are the visions* I saw while I was lying in my bed: I looked, and there in front of me was a tree standing in the middle of the earth. The tree was very tall. ¹¹The tree grew large and strong. The top of the tree touched the sky.* It could be seen from anywhere on earth. ¹²The leaves of the tree were beautiful. It had much good fruit on it. And on the tree was plenty of food for everyone. The wild animals found shelter under the tree. And the birds lived in its branches. Every animal ate from the tree. ¹³"I was looking at those things in the vision* while lying on my bed. And then I saw a holy angel coming down from heaven. ¹⁴He spoke very loud. He said, 'Cut down the tree, and cut off its branches. Strip off its leaves. Scatter its fruit around. The animals that are under the tree will run away. The birds that were in its branches will fly away. ¹⁵But let the stump and roots stay in the ground. Put a band of iron and bronze around it. The stump and roots will stay in the field with the grass all around it. It will live among the wild animals and plants in the fields. It will become wet with dew.* ¹⁶He will not think like a man any longer. He will have the mind of an animal. Seven seasons *(years)* will pass while he is like this.'
¹⁷"A holy angel announced this punishment. Why? So all the people on earth may know that God Most High rules over the kingdoms of men. God gives those kingdoms to anyone he wants to. And God chooses humble people to rule those kingdoms!
¹⁸"That is what I, King Nebuchadnezzar, dreamed. Now, Belteshazzar *(Daniel),* tell me what it means. None of the wise men in my kingdom can interpret that dream for me. But Belteshazzar, you can interpret the

---

palace A large house for the king and his family.
vision Something like a dream that God used to speak to people.
Chaldean(s) An important family group in Babylonia. Sometimes this name means simply "People from Babylonia."

middle of the earth... the sky The Babylonian people thought the earth was flat and round like a plate or a wheel. And they thought the sky was like a glass bowl turned upside down on the earth.
dew Drops of water that collect on the ground during the night.

dream because the spirit of the holy gods is in you.

¹⁹Then Daniel (also named Belteshazzar) became very quiet for about an hour. The things he was thinking bothered him. So the king said, "Belteshazzar *(Daniel)*, don't let the dream or its meaning make you afraid." Then Belteshazzar *(Daniel)* answered the king, "My lord, I wish the dream were about your enemies. And I wish the meaning of the dream were about those against you. ²⁰⁻²¹You saw a tree in your dream. The tree grew large and strong. Its top touched the sky. It could be seen from all over the earth. Its leaves were beautiful, and it had plenty of fruit. The fruit gave plenty of food for everyone. It was a home for the wild animals, and its branches were nesting places for the birds. That is the tree you saw. ²²King, you are that tree! You have become great and powerful. You are like the tall tree that touched the sky—and your power reaches to the far parts of the earth.

²³"King, you saw a holy angel coming down from heaven. He said, 'Cut the tree down and destroy it. Put a band of iron and bronze around the stump and leave the stump and its roots in the ground. Leave it in the grass in the field. It will become wet with dew.* He will live like a wild animal. Seven seasons *(years)* will pass while he is like this.'

²⁴"King, this is the meaning of the dream. God Most High has commanded these things to happen to my lord the king: ²⁵King Nebuchadnezzar, you will be forced to go away from people. You will live among the wild animals. You will eat grass like cattle. And you will become wet with dew.* Seven seasons *(years)* will pass, and then you will learn this lesson. You will learn God Most High rules over the kingdoms of men. And God Most High gives kingdoms to anyone he wants.

²⁶"The command to leave the stump of the tree and its roots in the ground means this: Your kingdom will be given back to you. This will happen when you learn that Most High *(God)* rules your kingdom. ²⁷So, king, please accept my advice. I advise you to stop sinning and do what is right. Stop doing bad things. And be kind to poor people. Then you might continue to be successful."

²⁸All those things happened to King Nebuchadnezzar. ²⁹⁻³⁰Twelve months after the dream, King Nebuchadnezzar was walking on the roof* of his palace* in Babylon. While on the roof, the king said, "Look at Babylon! I built this great city. It is my palace! I built this great place by my power. I built this place to show how great I am!"

³¹The words were still in his mouth when a voice came from heaven. The voice said, "King Nebuchadnezzar, these things will happen to you: Your power as king has been taken away from you. ³²You will be forced to go away from people. You will live with the wild animals. You will eat grass like a cow. Seven seasons *(years)* will pass before you learn your lesson. Then you will learn that God Most High rules over the kingdoms of men. And that God Most High gives kingdoms to anyone he wants."

³³Those things happened immediately. Nebuchadnezzar was forced to go away from people. He began eating grass like a cow. He became wet from dew.* His hair grew long like the feathers of an eagle. And his nails grew long like the claws of a bird. ³⁴Then at the end of that time, I Nebuchadnezzar, looked up toward heaven. And I was in my right mind again. Then I gave praise to God Most High. I gave honor and glory to him who lives forever.

> God rules forever!
>   His kingdom continues for all generations.
> ³⁵ People on earth are not truly important.
>   God does what he wants
>   with the powers of heaven
>   and the people on earth.
>   No one can stop his powerful hand!
>   No one can question the things he does!

³⁶So, at that time, God gave me my right mind again. And he gave back my great honor and power as king. My advisers and the royal people began to ask my advice again. I became the king again. And I became even greater and more powerful than before. ³⁷Now I, Nebuchadnezzar, give

---

dew Drops of water that collect on the ground during the night.

roof In ancient Israel, houses had flat roofs that were used like an extra room.

palace A large house for the king and his family.

praise, honor, and glory to the King of Heaven. Everything he does is right. He is always fair. And he is able to make proud people humble!

The Writing on the Wall

5 King Belshazzar gave a big party for 1,000 of his officials. The king was drinking wine with them. ²As Belshazzar was drinking his wine, he ordered his servants to bring the gold and silver cups. These were the cups that his grandfather* Nebuchadnezzar had taken from the temple* in Jerusalem. King Belshazzar wanted his royal people, his wives and his women slaves* to drink from those cups. ³So they brought the gold cups that had been taken from the temple of God in Jerusalem. And the king and his officials, his wives, and his women slaves drank from them. ⁴As they were drinking they were giving praise to their idol gods. They gave praise to those gods—and those gods were only statues made from gold, silver, bronze, iron, wood, and stone.

⁵Then all of a sudden, a man's hand appeared and began writing on the wall. The fingers scratched words into the plaster on the wall. The hand wrote on the wall there in the king's house near the lampstand. The king was watching the hand as it wrote.

⁶King Belshazzar was very afraid. His face became white from fear and his knees were shaking and knocking together. He could not stand up because his legs were too weak. ⁷The king called for the men of magic and Chaldeans* to be brought to him. He said to these wise men, "I will give a reward to any man that can read this writing and explain to me what it means. I will give purple clothes* to that man. I will put a gold chain around his neck, and I will make him the third highest ruler in the kingdom."

⁸So all the king's wise men came in. But they could not read the writing. They could not understand what it meant. ⁹King Belshazzar's officials were confused. And the king became even more afraid and worried. His face was white from fear.

¹⁰Then the king's mother came into the place where the party was. She had heard the voices of the king and his royal officials. She said, "King, may you live forever! Don't be afraid! Don't let your face be so white with fear! ¹¹There is a man in your kingdom that has the spirit of the holy gods in him. In the days of your father this man showed that he could understand secrets. He showed that he was very smart and very wise. He showed that he was like the gods in these things. Your grandfather,* King Nebuchadnezzar, put this man in charge of all the wise men. He ruled over all the men of magic, and the Chaldeans.* ¹²The man I am talking about is named Daniel. The king gave him the name Belteshazzar. Belteshazzar (Daniel) is very smart and he knows many things. He could interpret dreams, explain secrets, and answer very hard problems. Call for Daniel. He will tell you what the writing on the wall means."

¹³So they brought Daniel to the king. The king said to Daniel, "Is your name Daniel, one of the captives my father the king brought here from Judah? ¹⁴I have heard that the spirit of the gods is in you. And I have heard that you understand secrets, and are very smart and very wise. ¹⁵The wise men and the men of magic were brought to me to read this writing on the wall. I wanted those men to explain to me what this writing means. But they could not explain this writing on the wall to me. ¹⁶I have heard about you. I have heard that you are able to explain what things mean, and that you can find the answer to very hard problems. If you can read this writing on the wall and explain to me what it means, this is what I will do for you: I will give you purple clothes* and I will put a gold chain around your neck. Then you will become the third highest ruler in the kingdom."

¹⁷Then Daniel answered the king. Daniel said, "King Belshazzar, you can keep your gifts for yourself. Or you can give those rewards to someone else. But I will still read the writing on the wall for you. And I will explain to you what it means.

¹⁸"King, God Most High made your grandfather* Nebuchadnezzar a very great and powerful king. God made him very important. ¹⁹People from many nations and people that spoke many languages were very afraid of Nebuchadnezzar. Why? Because the God Most High made him a very important king. If

---

grandfather Or, "father." We are not sure if Belshazzar was really Nebuchadnezzar's grandson. Here the word "father" might only mean, "the previous king."

temple The special building in Jerusalem for Jewish worship.

women slaves Or, "concubine, " a slave woman like a wife to her master.

Chaldean(s) An important family group in Babylonia. Sometimes this name means simply "People from Babylonia."

purple clothes These clothes showed that a person was rich and powerful, like a king.

Nebuchadnezzar wanted a person to die, then he killed that person. And if he wanted a person to live, then that person was allowed to live. If he wanted to make people important, then he made those people important. And if he wanted to make people not important, then he made them not important. ²⁰But Nebuchadnezzar became proud and stubborn. So his power was taken away from him. He was taken off his royal throne and stripped of his glory. ²¹Then Nebuchadnezzar was forced to go away from people. His mind became like the mind of an animal. He lived with the wild donkeys and ate grass like a cow. He became wet with dew.* These things happened to him until he learned his lesson. Then he learned that God Most High rules over the kingdoms of men. And God Most High sets anyone he wants over kingdoms.

²²"But Belshazzar, you already knew these things! You are Nebuchadnezzar's grandson.* But still you have not made yourself humble. ²³No, you did not become humble. Instead, you have turned against the Lord of heaven. You ordered the drinking cups from the Lord's temple to be brought to you. Then you and your royal officials, your wives, and your women servants* drank wine from those cups. You gave praise to the gods of silver and gold, of bronze, iron, wood, and stone. Those are not really gods, they can't see, or hear, or understand anything. But you did not give honor to the God who has the power over your life and everything you do. ²⁴So, because of that, God sent the hand that wrote on the wall. ²⁵These are the words that were written on the wall:

MENE, MENE, TEKEL, UPARSIN.

²⁶"This is what these words mean:

MENE:*
    God has counted the days
        until your kingdom will end.
²⁷ TEKEL:*

dew Drops of water that collect on the ground during the night.
grandson Or, "son." This does not necessarily mean they were from the same family. It might only mean that Belshazzar was one of the kings of Babylon after Nebuchadnezzar was king.
woman servant Or, "concubine," "a slave woman who was like a wife to a man.
Mene A weight, like the Hebrew word "mina." This is like the word "to count."
Tekel A weight, like the Hebrew word "shekel." This word is like the word meaning "to weigh."

    You have been weighed on the scales,
        and found not good enough.
²⁸ UPARSIN:*
    Your kingdom is being taken from you
    It will be divided among
        the Medes and Persians."

²⁹Then Belshazzar gave an order for Daniel to be dressed in purple clothes.* A gold chain was put around his neck, and he was announced to be the third highest ruler in the kingdom. ³⁰That very same night, Belshazzar king of the Babylonian people, was killed. ³¹A man named Darius the Mede became the new king. Darius was about 62 years old.

Daniel and the Lions

6 Darius thought it would be a good idea to choose 120 satraps* to rule throughout all of his kingdom. ²And he chose three men to rule over those 120 satraps. Daniel was one of these three supervisors. The king set up these men so that no one would cheat him and he would not lose anything in his kingdom. ³Daniel showed himself to be better than the other supervisors. Daniel did this by his good character and great abilities. The king was so impressed with Daniel that he planned to make Daniel ruler over the whole kingdom. ⁴But when the other supervisors and the satraps heard about this, they were very jealous. They tried to find reasons to accuse Daniel. So they watched the things Daniel did as he went about doing the business of the government. But they could not find anything wrong with Daniel. So they could not accuse him of doing anything wrong. Daniel was a man people could trust. He did not cheat the king and he worked very hard.

⁵Finally those men said, "We will never find any reason to accuse Daniel of doing something wrong. So we must find something to complain about that is connected to the law of his God."

⁶So those two supervisors and the satraps* went as a group to the king. They said: "King Darius, live forever! ⁷The supervisors, prefects,* satraps*, advisers, and governors have all agreed

Uparsin Literally, "peres." A weight. This word is like the word meaning "to divide," "to split." It is also like the name of the country Persia.
purple clothes These clothes showed that a person was rich and powerful, like a king.
satraps Persian officials that were governors of a province.
prefects Important officials.

on something. We think that the king should make this law. Everyone must obey this law. This is the law: If anyone prays to any god or man, except to you, king, for the next 30 days, then that person will be thrown into the lions' den *(cage)*. ⁸Now, king, make the law and sign the paper it is written on. In this way, the law can't be changed. Why? Because the laws of the Medes and Persians can't be canceled or changed." ⁹So King Darius made the law and signed it.

¹⁰Daniel always prayed to God three times every day. Three times every day, Daniel got down on his knees and prayed and praised God. When Daniel heard about the new law he went to his house. Daniel went up to his room on the roof of his house. Daniel went to the windows that opened toward Jerusalem. Then Daniel got down on his knees and prayed, like he always did.

¹¹Then those men went as a group and found Daniel. They saw Daniel praying and asking God for help. ¹²So those men went to the king. They talked to him about the law he had made. They said, "King Darius, you signed a law that says, for the next 30 days anyone that prays to any god or man except you, the king, would be thrown into the lions' den *(cage)*. You did sign that law, didn't you?"

The king answered, "Yes, I signed that law. And the laws of the Medes and Persians can't be canceled or changed."

¹³Then those men said to the king, "That man named Daniel is not paying any attention to you. Daniel is one of the captives* from Judah. And Daniel is not paying attention to the law you signed. Daniel still prays to his God three times every day."

¹⁴The king became very sad and upset when he heard this. The king decided to save Daniel. He worked until sunset trying to think of a way to save Daniel. ¹⁵Then those men went as a group to the king. They said to him, "Remember, king, that the law of the Medes and Persians says that no law or command signed by the king can ever be canceled or changed."

¹⁶So King Darius gave the order. They brought Daniel and threw him into the lions' den *(cage)*. The king said to Daniel, "I hope the God you worship saves you!" ¹⁷A big rock was brought and put over the opening of the lions' den. Then the king used his ring and put his seal* on the rock. And he used the rings of his officials and put their seals on the rock also. This showed that no one could move that rock and bring Daniel out of the lion's den *(cage)*. ¹⁸Then King Darius went back to his house. The king did not eat that night. He did not want anyone to come and entertain him. The king could not sleep all night.

¹⁹The next morning, King Darius got up just as it was getting light. He ran to the lions' den *(cage)*. ²⁰The king was very worried. When the king went to the lions' den, he called to Daniel. The king said, "Daniel, servant of the living God, has your God been able to save you from the lions? You always serve your God."

²¹Daniel answered, "King, live forever! ²²My God sent his angel to save me. The angel closed the lions' mouths. The lions have not hurt me because my God knows I am innocent. I never did anything wrong to you, king."

²³King Darius was very happy. He told his servants to lift Daniel out of the lions' den *(cage)*. And when Daniel was lifted out of the den they did not find any injury on his body. Daniel was not hurt by the lions because he trusted in his God.

²⁴Then the king gave a command to bring the men that had accused Daniel to the lions' den *(cage)*. Those men and their wives and children were thrown into the lion's den. The lions grabbed them before they hit the floor of the lions' den. The lions ate their bodies and then chewed on their bones.

²⁵Then King Darius wrote this letter to all the people from other nations that spoke many different languages all around the world:

Greetings.
²⁶I am making a new law. This law is for people in every part of my kingdom. All of you people must fear and respect the God of Daniel.

> Daniel's God is the living God.
> God lives forever!
> His kingdom will never be destroyed.
> His rule will never end.
> ²⁷ God helps and saves people.
> God does amazing miracles
> in heaven and on earth.
> God saved Daniel from the lions."

---

captives People taken away like prisoners. Here this means the Jewish people that were taken to Babylon.

seal(s) Small stones or rings with special shapes that could be used like a rubber stamp. When pressed into wet clay or hot wax, they left a special mark that was like a signature.

²⁸So Daniel was successful during the time that Darius was king and during the time that Cyrus the Persian was king.

Daniel's Dream about Four Animals

7 During the first year that Belshazzar was king of Babylon,* Daniel had a dream. Daniel saw these visions* while he was lying on his bed. Daniel wrote what he had dreamed about. ²Daniel said: "I saw my vision at night. In the vision, the wind was blowing from all four directions. Those winds made the sea rough. ³I saw four big animals and each one was different from the others. Those four animals came up out of the sea.

⁴"The first animal looked like a lion, and it had wings like an eagle. I watched this animal. Then its wings were torn off. It was lifted from the ground so that it stood up on two feet like a man. And it was given the heart (mind) of a man.

⁵"And then I saw a second animal there in front of me. This animal looked like a bear. It was raised up on one of its sides, and it had three ribs in its mouth between its teeth. It was told, 'Get up and eat all the meat you want!'

⁶"After that, I looked, and there in front of me was another animal. This animal looked like a leopard.* And the leopard had four wings on its back. The wings looked like a bird's wings. This animal had four heads. It was given authority to rule.

⁷"After that, in my vision* at night I looked, and there in front of me was a fourth animal. This animal looked very mean and terrible. It looked very strong. It had large iron teeth. This animal crushed and ate up its victims.* And this animal walked on whatever was left of its victims. This fourth animal was different from all the animals I saw before it. This animal had ten horns.

⁸"I was thinking about those horns, and then another horn grew up among those horns. This horn was a little horn. There were eyes on this little horn—the eyes looked like a person's eyes. And there was a mouth on this little horn. And the mouth was bragging. The little horn pulled out three of the other horns.

first year that Belshazzar was king of Babylon This is probably 553b.c.
vision Something like a dream that God used to speak to people.
leopard An animal like a tiger, but with black spots.
victims People that have suffered some kind of hurt or trouble. Often this means people that were hurt or lost something during a crime.

Judgment of the Fourth Animal

⁹ "As I was looking,
    thrones were put in their places.
And the Ancient King*
    sat on his throne.
His clothes were very white;
    They were white like snow.
The hair on his head was white;
    it was white like wool.
His throne was made from fire.
    And the wheels of his throne were made from flames.
¹⁰ A river of fire was flowing
    in front of the Ancient King.*
Millions of people were serving him.
    Hundreds of millions of people stood in front of him.
ʟThis was likeʜ court was ready to begin,
    and the books were opened.

¹¹"I kept on looking because the little horn was bragging. I kept watching until finally the fourth animal was killed. Its body was destroyed and it was thrown into the burning fire. ¹²The authority and rule of the other animals had been taken from them. But they were permitted to live for a certain period of time.

¹³"In my vision at night I looked, and there in front of me was a person that looked like a human being.* He was coming on the clouds in the sky. He came to the Ancient King,* and they brought him before him.

¹⁴"The person that looked like a human being was given authority, glory, and complete ruling power. All peoples, nations, and men of every language will worship him. His rule will last forever. His kingdom will continue forever. It will never be destroyed.

The Interpretation of the Dream about the Fourth Animal

¹⁵"I, Daniel, was confused and worried. The visions* that went through my mind bothered me. ¹⁶I came near one of those that was standing there. I asked him what all this meant. So he told me. He explained to me what these things meant. ¹⁷He said, 'The four great animals are four kingdoms. Those four kingdoms will come from the earth.

Ancient King Literally, "Ancient of Days." This name for God shows that God has been the great king for a long, long time.
human being Literally, "son of man." This means he looked like a normal person, and not an angel or an animal.

¹⁸But God's special people will receive the kingdom. And they will have the kingdom forever and ever.'

¹⁹"Then I wanted to know what the fourth animal was and what it meant. The fourth animal was different from all the other animals. It was very terrible. It had iron teeth and bronze claws. It was the animal that crushed and completely ate up its victims. And it walked on whatever was left of its victims. ²⁰And I wanted to know about the ten horns that were on the fourth animal's head. And I wanted to know about the little horn that grew there. That little horn pulled out three of the other ten horns. That little horn looked meaner than the other horns. And that little horn continued bragging. ²¹As I was watching, this little horn began attacking and making war against God's special people. And the horn was killing them. ²²The little horn kept killing God's special people until the Ancient King* came and judged him. The Ancient King announced a judgment on the little horn. This judgment helped God's special people. And they received the kingdom.

²³"And he explained this to me: 'The fourth animal is a fourth kingdom that will come on the earth. It will be different from all the other kingdoms. That fourth kingdom will destroy people all around the world. It will walk on and crush nations all around the world. ²⁴The ten horns are ten kings that will come from this fourth kingdom. After those ten kings are gone, another king will come. He will be different from the kings that ruled before him. He will defeat three of the other kings. ²⁵This special king will say things against God Most High. And that king will hurt and kill God's special people. That king will try to change the times and laws that have already been set. God's special people will be in that king's power for three and one-half years.*

²⁶"'But the court will decide what should happen. And that king's power will be taken away. His kingdom will end completely. ²⁷Then God's special people will rule the kingdom. And they will rule over all the people from all the kingdoms of earth.* This kingdom will last forever. And people from all the other kingdoms will respect and serve them.'

²⁸"And that was the end of the dream. I, Daniel, was very afraid. My face became very white from fear. And I did not tell the other people about the things I saw and heard."

Daniel's Vision of a Ram and a Goat

8 During* the third year that Belshazzar was king,* I saw this vision.* This was after the other vision. ²In the vision, I saw that I was in the city of Susa.* Susa was the capital city in the province of Elam. I was standing by the Ulai River. ³I looked up, and I saw a ram* standing at the side of the Ulai River. The ram had two long horns. The horns were both long, but one horn was longer than the other horn. The long horn was farther back than the other horn. ⁴I watched the ram run into things with its horns. I watched the ram run to the west and to the north and to the south. No animal could stop the ram. And no one could save the other animals. That ram could do whatever it wanted to do. So the ram became very powerful.

⁵I thought about the ram.* While I was thinking, I saw a male goat come from the west. This goat ran over the whole earth. This goat's feet did not even touch the ground. This goat had one large horn that was easy to see. That horn was right between the goat's eyes.

⁶That goat came to the ram* with the two horns. This was the ram I had seen standing by the Ulai River. The goat was very angry. And it ran toward the ram. ⁷I watched the goat run toward the ram. The goat was very angry. It broke the ram's two horns. The ram could not stop the goat. The goat knocked the ram to the ground. Then the goat stepped all over the ram. There was no one to save the ram from the goat.

⁸So the goat became very powerful. But when he was strong, his big horn broke. Then four horns grew in place of the one big horn. Those four horns were easy to see. Those four horns pointed in four different directions.

Ancient King Literally, "Ancient of Days." This name for God shows that God has been the great king for a long, long time.
three and one-half years Literally, "a time, times, and half a time."
God's special people ... all the kingdoms of earth Literally, "The rule and kingdom and greatness of the kingdoms under heaven will be given to the saints."
During At this point, the book of Daniel is written in the Hebrew language again. Daniel 2:7–7:28 was written in Aramaic, the official language of the Babylonian Empire.
third year that Belshazzar was king This is probably 551 b.c.
vision Something like a dream that God used to speak to people.
Susa The capital city of Persia.
ram(s) A male sheep.

⁹Then a little horn grew from one of those four horns. That little horn grew and became very big. It grew toward the southeast. It grew toward the Beautiful Land. ¹⁰That little horn became very big. It grew until it reached the sky. The little horn even threw some of the stars to the ground. And it stepped all over those stars. ¹¹That little horn became very strong. And then it turned against the Ruler of the Stars *(God)*. The little horn stopped the daily sacrifices that were offered to the Ruler *(God)*. The place where people worshiped the Ruler was pulled down. ¹²The little horn sinned and stopped the daily sacrifices. It threw goodness down to the ground. The little horn did these things and was very successful.

¹³Then I heard one of the holy ones* speaking. Then I heard another holy one answer the first one. The first holy one said, "This vision shows what will happen to the daily sacrifice. It is about that terrible sin that destroys. It shows what will happen when people destroy the place where the Ruler is worshiped. It shows what will happen when those people step all over that place. It shows what will happen when the people step all over those stars. But how long will these things happen?"

¹⁴The other holy one* said, "This will happen for 2,300 days. Then the holy place will be fixed."

The Vision Is Explained to Daniel

¹⁵I, Daniel, saw this vision. And I tried to understand what it meant. While I was thinking about the vision, someone that looked like a man suddenly stood in front of me. ¹⁶Then I heard a man's voice. This voice came from above the Ulai River. The voice called out, "Gabriel, explain the vision to this man."

¹⁷So Gabriel, the angel that looked like a man, came to me. I was very afraid. I fell down to the ground. But Gabriel said to me, "Man,* understand that this vision is for the time of the end."

¹⁸While Gabriel was speaking, I fell to the ground and went to sleep. It was a very deep sleep. Then Gabriel touched me and lifted me to my feet. ¹⁹Gabriel said, "Now, I will explain the vision to you. I will tell you what will happen in the future. Your vision was about the end times.

²⁰"You saw a ram with two horns. Those horns are the countries of Media and Persia. ²¹The goat is the king of Greece. The big horn between its eyes is the first king. ²²That horn broke. And four horns grew in its place. Those four horns are four kingdoms. Those four kingdoms will come from the nation of the first king. But those four nations will not be as strong as the first king.

²³"When the end is near for those kingdoms, there will be a very bold and cruel king. This king will be very tricky. This will happen when there have become many, many sinful people. ²⁴This king will be very powerful—but his power does not come from himself.* This king will cause terrible destruction. He will be successful in everything he does. He will destroy powerful people—even God's special people.

²⁵"This king will be very smart and tricky. He will use his wisdom and lies to be successful. He will think that he is very important. He will destroy many people, when they least expect it. He will try to fight even the Prince of Princes *(God)*. But that cruel king's power will be destroyed. And it will not be a human hand that destroys him.

²⁶"The vision about those times, and the things I said, are true. But seal* the vision. Those things won't happen for a long, long time."

²⁷I, Daniel, became very weak. I was sick for several days after that vision. Then I got up and went back to work for the king. But I was very upset about the vision. I did not understand what the vision meant.

Daniel's Prayer

9 These things happened during the first year that Darius was king. Darius was the son of a man named Ahasuerus.* Darius belonged to the Median people. He became king over Babylon. ²During the first year that Darius was king, I, Daniel, was reading some books. In the books, I saw that the Lord told Jeremiah how many years would pass before Jerusalem would be built again. The Lord said 70 years would pass.

³Then I turned to God, my Master. I prayed to him and asked him for help. I did not eat any

---

holy one(s) Here this probably means an angel.
Man Literally, "son of man." This was a Hebrew way of saying, "human being."

but his power ... himself Some ancient translations don't have this verse, so this may have been accidentally copied from verse 22.
seal Small stones or rings with special shapes that could be used like a rubber stamp. When pressed into wet clay or hot wax, they left a special mark that was like a signature.
Ahasuerus Or, "Xerxes."

food, and I put on the clothes that showed I was sad. And I put dirt on my head. ⁴I prayed to the Lord my God. I told him about all of my sins. I said: "Lord, you are a great and awesome God. You keep your agreement of love and kindness with people that love you. You keep your agreement with the people who obey your commands.

⁵"But Lord, we have sinned! We have done wrong. We have done bad things. We turned against you. We turned away from your commands and fair decisions. ⁶We did not listen to the prophets. They were your servants. The prophets spoke for you. They spoke to our kings, our leaders, and our fathers. They spoke to all of the people from Israel. ₍But we did not listen to those prophets!₎

⁷"Lord, you are good, and goodness belongs to you! But shame belongs to us today. Shame belongs to the people from Judah and Jerusalem. Shame belongs to all the people of Israel—to the people that are near, and to the people that are far away. Lord, you scattered those people among many nations. And the people of Israel in all those nations should be ashamed. They should be ashamed of all the bad things they did against you, Lord. ⁸"Lord, we should all be ashamed. All of our kings and leaders should be ashamed. Our ancestors* should be ashamed. Why? Because we sinned against you, Lord.

⁹"But Lord, you are kind. You forgive people for the bad things they do. And we really turned against you. ¹⁰We have not obeyed the Lord our God. The Lord used his servants, the prophets, and gave us laws—but we have not obeyed his laws. ¹¹None of the people of Israel obeyed your teachings. They all have turned away. They did not obey you. There are curses* and promises written in the Law of Moses. (Moses was God's servant.) Those curses and promises tell about the punishment for not obeying the law—and all those things have happened to us. Those things happened to us because we sinned against the Lord.

¹²"God said those things would happen to us and our leaders—and he made them happen. He made terrible things happen to us. No other city suffered the way Jerusalem suffered. ¹³All of those terrible things happened to us. This happened just like it is written in the Law of Moses. But we still have not asked the Lord for help! We still have not stopped sinning. We still do not pay attention to your truth, Lord. ¹⁴The Lord kept the terrible things ready for us—and he made those things happen to us. The Lord did this because he is fair in everything he does. But we still have not listened to him.

¹⁵"Lord, our God, you used your power and brought us out of Egypt. We are your people. You are famous because of that even today. Lord, we have sinned. We have done terrible things. ¹⁶Lord, stop being angry at Jerusalem. Jerusalem is on your holy mountain. You do the right things, so stop being angry at Jerusalem. People all around us insult us and make fun of your people. This happens because we and our ancestors* sinned against you.

¹⁷"Now, Lord, listen to my prayer. I am your servant. Listen to my prayer for help. Do good things for your holy place.* That building was destroyed. But Master, do these good things for your own good. ¹⁸My God, listen to me! Open your eyes and see all the terrible things that have happened to us! See what has happened to the city that is called by your name! I am not saying we are good people. That is not why I am asking these things. I am asking these things because I know you are kind. ¹⁹Lord, listen to me! Lord, forgive us! Lord, pay attention, and then do something! Don't wait! Do something now! Do it for your own good! My God, do something now, for your city and your people that are called by your name."

The Vision about the 70 Weeks

²⁰I was saying those things in my prayer to God. I was telling about my sins and the sins of the people of Israel. I was praying for God's holy mountain. ²¹While I was praying, the man Gabriel came to me. Gabriel was the person I saw in the vision. Gabriel came flying quickly to me. He came at the time of the evening sacrifice. ²²Gabriel helped me understand the things I wanted to know. Gabriel said, "Daniel, I have come to give you wisdom and to help you understand. ²³When you first started praying, the command was given. And I came to tell you. God

---

ancestors Literally, "fathers, " meaning a person's parents, grandparents, and all the people they are descended from.

curses Warnings about bad things that will happen to a person that does not obey God.

Do good things for your holy place Literally, "Let your face shine on your holy place."

loves you very much! You will understand this command, and you will understand the vision. ²⁴"God has allowed 70 weeks* for your people and your holy city, Daniel. The 70 weeks* are ordered for these reasons: to stop doing bad things, to stop sinning, to make people pure, to bring the goodness that continues forever, to put a seal* on visions and prophets, and to dedicate a very holy place. ²⁵"Learn these things, Daniel. Understand these things! From the time that the message went out to go back and build Jerusalem again until the time for the chosen king* to come will be seven weeks.* Then Jerusalem will be built again. There will again be places for people to meet together in Jerusalem. And there will be a ditch around the city to protect it. Jerusalem will be built for 62 weeks.* But there will be many troubles during that time. ²⁶After the 62 weeks,* the chosen person will be killed.* He will be gone.* Then the people of the future leader will destroy the city and the holy place. That end will come like a flood. War will continue until the end. God has ordered that place to be completely destroyed. ²⁷"Then the future ruler will make an agreement with many people. That agreement will continue for one week.* The offerings and sacrifices will stop for a half of a week.* And a destroyer will come. He will do terrible, destructive things!* But God has ordered that destroyer to be completely destroyed."

Daniel's Vision by the Tigris River

10 Cyrus was the king of Persia. During Cyrus' third year as king, Daniel learned about these things. (Daniel's other name is Belteshazzar.) These things are true, but very hard to understand. But Daniel understood these things. They were explained to him in a vision.
²₍Daniel says,₎ "At that time, I, Daniel, was very sad for three weeks. ³During those three weeks, I didn't eat any fancy food. I didn't eat any meat. I didn't drink any wine. I didn't put any oil on my head. I didn't do any of these things for three weeks.
⁴"On the 28th day of the first month of the year, I was standing beside the great Tigris River. ⁵While I was standing there, I looked up. And I saw a man standing in front of me. He was wearing linen* clothes. He wore a belt made of pure gold* around his waist. ⁶His body was like a smooth, shiny stone. His face was bright like lightning! His eyes were like flames of fire. His arms and feet were shiny like polished brass! His voice was loud like a crowd of people!
⁷"I, Daniel, was the only person that saw the vision.* The men with me didn't see the vision, but they were still afraid. They were so afraid that they ran away and hid. ⁸So I was left alone. I was watching this vision—and it made me afraid. I lost my strength. My face turned white like a dead person's face, and I was helpless. ⁹Then I heard the man in the vision talking. As I listened to his voice, I fell into a deep sleep. My face was flat on the ground.
¹⁰"Then a hand touched me. When that happened I got on my hands and knees. I was so afraid that I was shaking. ¹¹The man in the vision* said to me, 'Daniel, God loves you very much. Think very carefully about the words I will speak to you. Stand up, I have been sent to you.' And when he said this, I stood up. I was still shaking because I was afraid. ¹²Then the man in the vision started talking again. He said, 'Daniel, don't be afraid. From the very first day you decided to have wisdom and to be humble in front of God. He has been listening to your prayers. I came to you because you have been praying. ¹³But the prince *(angel)* of Persia has been fighting against me and bothering me for 21 days. Then Michael, one of the most important princes *(angels)*, came to help me because I was stuck there with the king of Persia. ¹⁴Now I have come to you Daniel, to explain to you what will happen to your people in the future. The vision is about a time in the future.'
¹⁵"While the man was talking to me, I bowed low with my face toward the ground. I could not speak. ¹⁶Then the one that looked like a man touched my lips. I opened my mouth and started to speak. I said to the one standing in front of me, 'sir, I am upset and afraid because of what I saw

---

week(s) Or, "units of seven." The Hebrew word could mean "week, " or it could mean "period of seven years."
seal(s) Small stones or rings with special shapes that could be used like a rubber stamp. When pressed into wet clay or hot wax, they left a special mark that was like a signature.
chosen king Literally, "anointed person."
killed Literally, "cut off."
He will be gone Or, "he will have nothing."
He will do ... things Or, "He will come on the wings of terrible destruction."

linen Thread or cloth made from the fibers of the flax plant.
pure gold Literally, "gold from Uphaz."
vision Something like a dream that God used to speak to people.

in the vision.* I feel helpless. ¹⁷Sir, I am Daniel your servant. How can I talk with you? My strength is gone and it is hard for me to breathe.'

¹⁸"The one that looked like a man touched me again. When he touched me I felt better. ¹⁹Then he said, 'Daniel, don't be afraid. God loves you very much. Peace be with you. Be strong now, be strong.'

"When he spoke to me, I became stronger. Then I said, 'sir, you have given me strength. Now you can speak.'

²⁰"So then he said, 'Daniel, do you know why I have come to you? Soon I must go back to fight against the prince *(angel)* of Persia. When I go, the prince *(angel)* of Greece will come. ²¹But Daniel, before I go, I must first tell you what is written in the Book of Truth. No one stands with me against those evil angels except Michael. Michael is the prince *(angel)* ruling over your people.

11 During the first year that Darius the Mede was king,* I stood up to support Michael* in his fight against the prince *(angel)* of Persia.

²"'Now then, Daniel, I tell you the truth: three more kings will rule in Persia. Then a fourth king will come. That fourth king will be much richer than all the other kings of Persia before him. That fourth king will use his riches to get power. And he will cause everyone to be against the kingdom of Greece. ³Then a very strong and powerful king will come. He will rule with much power. He will do anything he wants. ⁴After that king has come, his kingdom will be broken up. His kingdom will be divided out toward the four parts of the world. His kingdom will not be divided among his children or grandchildren. And his kingdom will not have the power that he had. Why? Because his kingdom will be pulled up and given to other people.

⁵"'The southern king will become strong. But then one of his commanders will defeat the southern king. The commander will begin to rule. And he will be very powerful.

⁶"'Then after a few years, the southern king and that commander will make an agreement. The daughter of the southern king will marry the northern king. She will do this to bring peace. But she and the southern king will not be strong enough. People will turn against her and against the person that brought her to that country. And those people will turn against her child and against the person that helped her.

⁷"'But a person from her family will come to take the southern king's place. He will attack the armies of the northern king. He will go into that king's strong fort. He will fight and win. ⁸He will take their idol gods. He will take their metal idols and their expensive things made from silver and gold. He will take those things away to Egypt. Then he will not bother the northern king for a few years. ⁹The northern king will attack the southern kingdom. But he will lose, and then he will go back to his own country.

¹⁰"'The northern king's sons will prepare for war. They will get a large army together. That army will move through the land very quickly, like a powerful flood. That army will fight all the way to the strong fort of the southern king. ¹¹Then the southern king will become very angry. He will march out to fight against the northern king. The northern king will have a large army, but he will lose the war. ¹²The northern army will be defeated, and those soldiers will be carried away. The southern king will be very proud, and he will kill thousands of soldiers from the northern army. But he will not continue to be successful. ¹³The northern king will get another army. That army will be larger than the first army. After several years he will attack. That army will be very large and it will have many weapons. That army will be ready for war.

¹⁴"'In those times, many people will be against the southern king. Some of your own people that love to fight will rebel against the southern king. They will not win, but they will make the vision* come true when they do this. ¹⁵Then the northern king will come and build ramps against the walls and capture a strong city. The southern army will not have the power to fight back. Even the best soldiers from the southern army will not be strong enough to stop the northern army.

¹⁶"'The northern king will do whatever he wants. No one will be able to stop him. He will gain power and control in the Beautiful land. And he will have the power to destroy it. ¹⁷The northern king will decide to use all of his power to fight against the southern king. He will make an agreement with the southern king. The king of the north will let one of his daughters marry the southern king. The northern king will do that so he can defeat the southern king, but those plans will not succeed. His plans will not help him.

---

vision Something like a dream that God used to speak to people.

first year that Darius ... king This is probably 521b.c.

Michael See Dan. 10:13.

¹⁸"'Then the northern king will turn his attention to the countries along the coast of the Mediterranean Sea. He will defeat many of those cities, but then a commander will put an end to the pride and rebellion of that northern king. That commander will make that northern king ashamed.

¹⁹"'After that happens, that northern king will go back to the strong forts of his own country. But he will be weak, and he will fall. He will be finished.

²⁰"'A new ruler will come after that northern king. That ruler will send out a tax collector. That ruler will do this so he will have enough money to live in a very rich way. But, in a few years, that ruler will be destroyed. But he will not die in a battle.

²¹"'That ruler will be followed by a very cruel and hated man. That man will not have the honor of being from a king's family.* He will become a ruler by being tricky. He will attack the kingdom when the people feel safe. ²²He will defeat large and powerful armies. He will even defeat the Leader with the Agreement. ²³Many nations will make agreements with that cruel and hated ruler. But he will lie and trick them. He will gain much power. But only a few people will support him.

²⁴"'When the richest countries feel safe, that cruel and hated ruler will attack them. He will attack at just the right time and will be successful where his fathers were not successful. He will take things from the countries he defeated, and he will give those things to his followers. He will plan to defeat and destroy strong cities. He will be successful, but only for a short time.

²⁵"'That very cruel and hated ruler will have a very large army. He will use that army to show his strength and courage and attack the southern king. The southern king will get a very large and powerful army and go to war. But the people that are against him will make secret plans. And the southern king will be defeated. ²⁶People that were supposed to be good friends of the southern king will try to destroy him. His army will be defeated. Many of his soldiers will be killed in battle. ²⁷Those two kings will have their hearts set on hurting each other. They will sit at the same table and lie to each other, but it will not do either one any good. Why? Because God has set a time for their end to come.

²⁸"'The northern king will go back to his own country with much wealth. Then he will decide to do bad things against the holy agreement.* He will do the things he planned, and then he will go back to his own country.

²⁹"'At the right time, the northern king will attack the southern king again. But this time he will not be successful like he was before. ³⁰Ships from Cyprus will come and fight against the northern king. He will see those ships coming and be afraid. Then he will turn back and take his anger out on the holy agreement. He will turn back and help the people that quit following the holy agreement. ³¹The northern king will send his army to do terrible things to the temple in Jerusalem. They will stop the people from offering the daily sacrifice.* Then they will do something really terrible. They will set up that terrible thing that causes destruction.

³²"'The northern king will use lies and smooth talking to trick the Jews that quit following the holy agreement. Those Jews will sin even worse. But the Jews that know God and obey him will be strong. They will fight back!

³³"'Those Jews that are wise will help the other people understand what is happening. But even those that are wise will have to suffer persecution. Some of those wise Jews will be killed with swords. Some of them will be burned, or taken prisoner. Some of those Jews will have their homes and things taken away. ³⁴When those wise Jews are punished they will get a little help. But many Jews that join those wise Jews will be hypocrites.* ³⁵Some of the wise Jews will make mistakes and fall. But the persecution must come. Why? So that they can be made stronger, purer, and without faults until the time of the end comes. Then, at the right time, that time of the end will come.'"

The King Who Praises Himself

³⁶"'The northern king will do whatever he wants. He will brag about himself. He will praise himself and think that he is even better than a god. He will say things that no one has ever heard of. He will say those things against the God of gods. He will be successful until all the bad things have happened. What God has planned to happen will happen.

holy agreement This probably means the Jewish people.
sacrifice(s) A gift to God. Usually, it was a special animal that was killed and burned on an altar.
hypocrites Bad people that act like they are good.

That man ... king's family Or, "That person will not have the good qualities a king should have."

37 "That northern king will not care about the gods his fathers worshiped. He will not care about the idol gods women worship. He will not care about any god. Instead, he will praise himself, and make himself more important than any god. 38The northern king will not worship any god, but he will worship power. Power and strength will be his god. His fathers didn't love power like he does. He honors the god of power with gold and silver, expensive jewels, and gifts.

39 "That northern king will attack strong fortresses* with the help of this foreign god. He will give much honor to those foreign rulers that join him. He will put many people under those rulers. He will make those rulers pay him for the land they rule over.

40 "At the time of the end, the southern king will fight a battle against the northern king. The northern king will attack him. He will attack with chariots and soldiers on horses and many large ships. The northern king will rush through the land like a flood. 41The northern king will attack the Beautiful Land. Many countries will be defeated by the northern king. But Edom, Moab, and the leaders of Ammon will be saved from him. 42The northern king will show his power in many countries. Egypt will also learn how powerful he is. 43He will get treasures of gold and silver and all the riches of Egypt. The Libyan and Nubian people will obey him. 44But that northern king will hear news from the east and the north that will make him afraid and angry. He will go to completely destroy many nations. 45He will set up his king's tents between the seas at the beautiful holy mountain.* But finally, that bad king will die. There will not be anyone to help him when his end comes.'"

12 ⌊The man in the vision said,⌋ 'Daniel, at that time, the great prince *(angel)* Michael will stand up. Michael is in charge of your people, the Jews. There will be a time of much trouble. A time like that has not happened since there was a nation on earth. But Daniel, at that time, every one of your people whose name is found written in the book ⌊of life⌋ will be saved. 2Many, many people of the earth that are dead and buried* will wake up. Some of them will wake up to have life forever. But some will wake up to have shame and hate that continues forever. 3The wise people will shine as the bright as the sky. The wise people that taught others to live right will shine like stars forever and ever.

4 "But you, Daniel, keep this message a secret. You must close the book. You must keep this secret until the time of the end. Many people will go here and there looking for true knowledge. And the true knowledge will increase.'

5 "Then I, Daniel, looked and I saw two other people. One person was standing on my side of the river. And the other person was standing on the other side of the river. 6The man who was dressed in linen* was standing over the water in the river. One of the two people said to him, 'How long will it be before these amazing things come true?'

7 "The man dressed in linen* and standing over the water lifted his right and left hands toward heaven. And I heard him make a promise using the name of God who lives forever. He said, 'It will be for three and one-half years.* The power of the holy people will be broken, and then all these things will finally come true.'

8 "I heard the answer, but I really didn't understand. So I asked, 'Sir, what will happen after all these things come true?'

9 "He answered, 'Go on about your life Daniel. The message is hidden. It will be a secret until the time of the end. 10Many people will be made pure—they will make themselves clean.* But evil people will continue to be evil. And those wicked people will not understand these things. But the wise people will understand these things.

11 "The daily sacrifice will be stopped. There will be 1,290 days from that time until the time that the terrible thing that destroys is set up. 12The person that waits for, and comes to, the end of the 1,335 days will be very happy.

13 "As for you Daniel, go and live your life till the end. You will get your rest. At the end, you will rise ⌊from death⌋ to get your share.'"

---

fortress(es) A building or city with tall, strong walls for protection.

holy mountain The mountain Jerusalem is built on.

are dead and buried Literally, "sleep in the dust."

linen Thread or cloth made from the fibers of the flax plant.

three and one-half years Literally, "a time, times, and half a time."

clean Or, "acceptable." Pure or able to be used in worshiping God. See Lev. 11-15 for the Old Testament rules about clean and unclean things.

Hosea

The Lord God's Message Through Hosea

1 This is the Lord's message that came to Hosea son of Beeri. This message came during the time that Uzziah, Jotham, Ahaz, and Hezekiah were kings of Judah. This was during the time of Jeroboam son of Joash, king of Israel. ²This was the Lord's first message to Hosea. The Lord said, "Go, and marry a prostitute.* Have children from that prostitute. Why? Because the people in this country have acted like prostitutes—they have been unfaithful to the Lord."

The Birth of Jezreel

³So Hosea married Gomer daughter of Diblaim. Gomer became pregnant and gave birth to a son for Hosea. ⁴The Lord said to Hosea, "Name him Jezreel.* Why? Because in a little while I will punish the family of Jehu for the blood ˌhe spilledˌ at Jezreel Valley.* Then I will put an end to the kingdom of the nation* of Israel. ⁵And at that time, I will break Israel's bow at Jezreel Valley."

The Birth of Lo-Ruhamah

⁶Then Gomer became pregnant again and gave birth to a daughter. ˌThe Lordˌ said to Hosea, "Name her Lo-Ruhamah.* Why? Because I will not show mercy to the nation* of Israel any more. I will not forgive them. ⁷But I will show mercy to the nation of Judah. ˌI will save the nation of Judah.ˌ I will not use the bow or the sword to save them. I will not use war horses and soldiers to save them. I will save them by my own power."*

The Birth of Lo-Ammi

⁸After Gomer had finished nursing Lo-Ruhamah, she became pregnant again. She gave birth to a son. ⁹Then ˌthe Lordˌ said, "Name him Lo-Ammi.* Why? Because you are not my people. I am not your God."

The Lord God Promises There Will Be Many Israelites

¹⁰"ˌIn the future,ˌ the number of the people of Israel will be like the sand of the sea. You can't measure the sand or count it. Then it will happen that in the place where it was said to them, 'You are not my people,' it will be said to them, 'You are the children of the living God.'

¹¹"Then the people of Judah and the people of Israel will be gathered together. They will choose one ruler for themselves. And their nation will be too large for the land!* Jezreel's day will be truly great."

2 "Then you will tell your brothers, 'You are my people.' And you will tell your sisters, 'He has shown mercy to you.'"*

The Lord Speaks to the Nation of Israel

²"Argue with your mother.* Argue! Because she is not my wife! I am not her husband! Tell her

---

prostitute A woman paid by men for sexual sin. Sometimes this also means a person that is not faithful to God and stops following him.
Jezreel This name in Hebrew means "God will plant seeds."
blood ... at Jezreel Valley See 2 Kings 9-10 for the story of Jehu's revolt at Jezreel Valley.
nation Literally, "house." This might mean the royal family of that country.
Lo-Ruhamah This name in Hebrew means "She receives no mercy."
by my own power Literally, "by the Lord their God."
Lo-Ammi This name in Hebrew means "not my people."
their nation ... land Literally, "they will go up from the land."
you will tell your brothers ... mercy to you Or, "Say to your brothers, 'My people,' and to your sisters, 'You have been shown mercy.'"
mother This means the nation of Israel.

to stop being like a prostitute.* Tell her to take away her lovers* from between her breasts. ³If she refuses to stop her adultery, I will strip her naked. I will leave her like the day she was born. I will take away her people and she will be like an empty, dry desert. I will kill her with thirst. ⁴I will have no pity on her children because they are the children of prostitution. ⁵Their mother has acted like a prostitute. Their mother should be ashamed of the things she did. She said, 'I will go to my lovers.* My lovers give me food and water. They give me wool and linen. They give me wine and olive oil.'

⁶"So, I *(the Lord)* will block your *(Israel's)* road with thorns. I will build a wall. Then she will not be able to find her paths. ⁷She will run after her lovers, but she will not be able to catch up with them. She will look for her lovers, but she will not be able to find them. Then she will say, 'I will go back to my first husband *(God)*. Life was better for me when I was with him. Life was better then than it is now.'

⁸"She *(Israel)* didn't know that I *(the Lord)* was the One who gave her grain, wine, and oil. I kept giving her more and more silver and gold. But the Israelites used this silver and gold to make statues of Baal.* ⁹So I will come back. I will take back my grain at the time it is ready to be harvested. I will take back my wine at the time the grapes are ready. I will take back my wool and linen. I gave those things to her so she could cover her naked body. ¹⁰Now I will strip her. She will be naked, so all her lovers can see her. No person will be able to save her from my power.* ¹¹I *(God)* will take away all her fun. I will stop her holidays, her new moon feasts, her days of rest. I will stop all of her special feasts. ¹²I will destroy her vines and fig trees. She said, 'My lovers gave these things to me.' But I will change her gardens— they will become like a wild forest. Wild animals will come and eat from those plants.

¹³"She served the Baals.* So I will punish her. She burned incense* to the Baals. She dressed up—she put on her jewelry and nose ring. Then she went to her lovers and forgot me." The Lord has said this.

¹⁴"So, I *(the Lord)* will say romantic words to her. I will lead her into the desert and speak tender words. ¹⁵There I will give her fields of grapes. I will give her Achor Valley as a doorway of hope. Then she will answer like the time she came out of the land of Egypt. ¹⁶The Lord says this.

"At that time you will call me 'My husband.' You will not call me 'My Baal.'* ¹⁷I will take away the names of the Baals out of her mouth. Then people will not use the Baals' names again. ¹⁸"At that time, I will make an agreement for the Israelites with the animals of the field, with the birds of the sky, and with the crawling things on the ground. I will break the bow, the sword, and weapons of war. No weapons will be left in that land. I will make the land safe, so the people of Israel can lie down in peace. ¹⁹And I *(the Lord)* will make you my bride* forever. I will make you my bride with goodness and fairness and with love and mercy. ²⁰I will make you my faithful bride. Then you will truly know the Lord. ²¹And at that time, I will respond." The Lord says this.

"I will speak to the skies,
    and they will give rain to the earth.
²² The earth will produce grain, wine, and oil.
    And they will meet Jezreel's needs.
²³ I will sow her many seeds* on her land.
    To Lo-Ruhamah,*
    I will show mercy.
    To Lo-Ammi,*
    I will say, 'You are my people.'

---

prostitute A woman paid by men for sexual sin. Sometimes this also means a person that is not faithful to God and stops following him.

her lovers Or "adulteries." Adultery means not being faithful in marriage. God was like a husband to Israel. But Israel was worshiping false gods—this was like a spiritual adultery against God.

lovers This means Israel's false gods.

Baal The Canaanite people believed that this false god brought the rain and storms. They also thought that he made the land produce good crops.

power Literally, "hand."

Baals False gods worshiped by the Canaanites in the land where the Israelites lived.

incense Special dried tree sap. Burned to make a sweet-smelling smoke, it was offered as a gift to God.

My Baal This is a word play. The name Baal also means, "lord, or husband."

make you my bride Literally, "I will betroth you to me."

I will sow her many seeds Jezreel, Lo-Ruhamah, and Lo-Ammi are Hosea's children. But the names also have special meanings. The name Jezreel means, "God will plant seeds." But Jezreel is also the name of a large valley in Israel. This probably shows that God will bring his people back to Israel. Lo-Ruhamah means "She was not shown mercy," and Lo-Ammi means "Not my people."

Lo-Ruhamah This name in Hebrew means "She receives no mercy."

Lo-Ammi This name in Hebrew means "not my people."

And they will say to me,
'You are my God.'"

Hosea Buys Gomer Back from Slavery

3 Then the Lord said to me again, "Gomer* has many lovers. But you must continue loving her. Why? Because that is like the Lord. The Lord continues loving the people of Israel. But they continue to worship other gods. And they love to eat raisin cakes."* ²So I bought Gomer for 6 ounces* of silver and 9 bushels* of barley. ³Then I told her, "You must stay at home with me for many days. You must not be like a prostitute.* You will not be with another man. And I will be your husband."

⁴In the same way, the people of Israel will continue many days without a king or a leader. They will be without a sacrifice or a memorial stone.* They will be without an ephod* or a household god. ⁵After this the people of Israel will come back. Then they will look for the Lord their God, and for David their king. In the last days, they will come to honor the Lord and his goodness.

The Lord Is Angry Against Israel

4 People of Israel, listen to the Lord's message! The Lord will tell his argument against the people that live in this country. People in this country don't really know God. The people are not true and loyal to God. ²The people swear, lie, kill, and steal. They do the sin of adultery,* and they have their babies. The people murder again and again.* ³So the country is like a person crying for the dead, and all of its people are weak. Even the animals of the field, the birds of the sky, and the fish in the sea are dying.* ⁴No person should argue or blame another person. Priest, my argument is with you!* ⁵You (priests) will fall in the daytime. And at night, the prophet will also fall with you. And I will destroy your mother.

⁶"My people are destroyed because they have no knowledge. You have refused to learn. So I will refuse to let you be a priest for me. You have forgotten the law of your God, so I will forget your children. ⁷They became proud! They sinned more and more against me. So I will change their glory to shame.

⁸"The priests joined in the people's sins. They wanted more and more of those sins.* ⁹So the priests are no different than the people. I will punish them for the things they did. I will pay them back for the wrong things they did. ¹⁰They will eat, but they will not be satisfied! They will do sexual sins, but they will not have babies.* Why? Because they left the Lord and became like prostitutes.

¹¹"Sexual sins, strong drink, and new wine will ruin a person's ability to think straight. ¹²My people are asking pieces of wood for advice. They think those sticks will answer them. Why? Because they have chased after those false gods like prostitutes. They left their God and became like prostitutes. ¹³They make sacrifices on the tops of the mountains and burn incense* on the hills under oak trees, poplar trees, and elm trees.* The shade under those trees looks nice. So your daughters lie under those trees like prostitutes. And your daughters-in-law do their sexual sins.

Gomer Literally, "a woman."
raisin cakes This kind of food was apparently used in the feasts that honored false gods.
6 ounces Literally, "15 pieces₁."
9 bushels Literally, "1 homer and 1 letek."
prostitute A woman paid by men for sexual sin. Sometimes this also means a person that is not faithful to God and stops following him.
memorial stone(s) Stones that were set up to help people remember something special. In ancient Israel, people often set up stones as special places to worship false gods.
ephod A special coat worn by the priests.
adultery Breaking the marriage promise by sexual sin.
and they have ... again Literally, "they break out, and blood touches blood."
dying Literally, "being taken away."

No person ... you Or, "The people can't complain or blame someone else. The people are helpless, like arguing with a priest." Many times the priests and Levites served as judges, and their decisions were final.
The priests ... those sins This is a word play. The word "sins" also means "sin offerings." So instead of eating sacrifices, the priests became hungry for sin itself.
They will do sexual sins, but they will not have babies A part of worshiping the false gods was having sexual relations with temple prostitutes. The people thought that this would make the gods happy. And then the gods would give the people large families and good crops.
incense Special dried tree sap. Burned to make a sweet-smelling smoke, it was offered as a gift to God.
under oak trees, poplar trees, and elm trees Trees and groves were an important part of the worshiping false gods.

¹⁴"I can't blame* your daughters for being prostitutes, or your daughters-in-law for doing sexual sins. The men go and sleep with prostitutes. They go and offer sacrifices with the temple prostitutes.* So, those foolish people are destroying themselves.

The Shameful Sins of Israel

¹⁵"Israel, you act like a prostitute.* But don't let Judah be guilty. Don't go to Gilgal* or go up to Beth-aven.* Don't use the Lord's name to make promises. Don't say, 'As the Lord lives ... !' ¹⁶The Lord has given many things to Israel. He is like a shepherd that takes his sheep to a large field with much grass. But Israel is stubborn. Israel is like a young cow that runs away again and again. ¹⁷Ephraim* has joined his idols.* So leave him alone.

¹⁸"Ephraim has joined their drunkenness. Let them continue to be prostitutes. Let them be with their lovers. ¹⁹They went to those gods for safety, and they have lost their ability to think.* Their sacrifices bring them shame."

The Leaders Cause Israel and Judah to Sin

5 "Priests, nation of Israel, and people in the king's family, listen to me.

"You were like a trap at Mizpah.* You were like a net spread on the ground at Tabor.* ²You have done many, many bad things.* So I will punish you all! ³I know Ephraim.* I know the things that Israel has done. Ephraim, right now you act like a prostitute. Israel is dirty with sins. ⁴The people of Israel have done many bad things. And those bad things keep them from coming back to their God. They are always thinking of ways to chase after other gods. They don't know the Lord. ⁵Israel's pride is a witness against them.* So Israel and Ephraim will stumble in their sin. But Judah will also stumble with them.

⁶"The leaders of the people will go to look for the Lord. They will take their 'sheep' and 'cows' with them. But they will not find the Lord. Why? Because he left them. ⁷They have not been faithful to the Lord. Their children are from some stranger. And now, he will destroy them and their land again."*

A Prophecy of Israel's Destruction

⁸ Blow the horn in Gibeah.
 Blow the trumpet in Ramah.*
 Give the warning at Beth-Aven.*
 The enemy is behind you, Benjamin.
⁹ Ephraim* will become empty
 at the time of punishment.
 I *(God)* warn the families of Israel
 that those things really will happen.
¹⁰ The leaders of Judah are like thieves
 trying to steal another man's property.
 So I *(God)* will pour out my anger
 on them like water.
¹¹ Ephraim* will be punished.
 He will be crushed and pressed like grapes.
 Why? Because he decided to follow filth.
¹² I will destroy Ephraim,
 like a moth destroys a piece of cloth.

---

blame This word can mean, "visit," "put in charge of," "take account of," or "to hold responsible for."
temple prostitutes Women that were prostitutes at the temples of the false gods. Their sexual sins were part of worshiping those false gods.
prostitute A woman paid by men for sexual sin. Sometimes this also means a person that is not faithful to God and stops following him.
Gilgal A city in Israel. The people worship false gods there.
Beth-aven In Hebrew the meaning is "House of Evil." It is a word play on the name "Bethel," a town in Israel. There was a temple in this town.
Ephraim Joseph's younger son (Gen. 41:50-52). Ephraim's family became a family group in Israel. Here the name is used to mean the northern kingdom of Israel.
idols Statues of false gods that people worshiped.
They ... think Or, "The wind has carried them away on its wings," or "The spirit held them tight in its wings." This verse is very hard to understand in Hebrew.

Mizpah A mountain in Israel. The people worshiped the false gods on many of the hills and mountains.
Tabor A mountain in Israel.
You have done ... bad things This sentence is hard to understand in Hebrew, probably because there is a word play and a reference to things we are not sure of.
Ephraim Joseph's younger son (Gen. 41:50-52). Ephraim's family became a family group in Israel. Here the name is used to mean the northern kingdom of Israel.
them Literally, "his face."
And now ... again This is hard to understand in Hebrew.
Gibeah, Ramah Hills on Judah's border with Israel.

I ₍will destroy₎ Judah,
   like rot ₍destroys a piece of wood₎.
¹³ Ephraim saw his sickness,
   and Judah saw his wound.
   So they went to Assyria for help.
   They told their problems to the great king.
   But that king can't heal you.
   He can't cure your wound.
¹⁴ Why? Because I will be like a lion
      to Ephraim.
   I will be like a young lion
      to the nation* of Judah.
   I—yes, I *(the Lord)*—will rip them into
      pieces.
   I will carry them away,
      And no person can save ₍them from me₎.
¹⁵ I will go back to my place,
   until the people admit they are guilty,
   until they come looking for me.
   Yes, in their trouble they will try hard
      to find me."

The Rewards of Coming Back to the Lord

6 "Come, let's go back to the Lord.
   He hurt us, but he will heal us.
   He wounded us,
      but he will put bandages on us.
² After two days he will bring us back to life.
   He will raise us up on the third day.
   Then we can live near him.
³ Let's learn about the Lord.
   Let's try very hard to know the Lord.
   We know he is coming,
      like we know the dawn is coming.
   The Lord will come to us like the rain,
      like the spring rain that waters the ground."

The People Are Not Faithful

⁴ "Ephraim,* what should I do with you?
   Judah, what should I do with you?
   Your faithfulness is like a morning mist,
   Your faithfulness is like the dew
      that goes away early in the morning.
⁵ I used the prophets,
      and made laws for the people.
   The people were killed at my command.

But good things will come
   from those decisions.*
⁶ Why? Because I want faithful love,
      not sacrifice,
   ₍I want people₎ to know God,
      not ₍to bring₎ burnt offerings.
⁷ But the people broke the Agreement
      just like Adam did.*
   They were unfaithful to me
      in their country.
⁸ Gilead* is a city of people that do evil.
   People have tricked and killed other people.
⁹ Robbers hide and wait to attack someone.
   In the same way,
   priests wait on the road to Shechem
      and attack the people that pass by.
   They have done evil things.
¹⁰ I have seen a terrible thing
      in the nation* of Israel.
   Ephraim* was unfaithful to God.
   Israel is dirty with sin.
¹¹ Judah, there is also a time of harvest for you.
   It will happen at the time that I bring
      my people back from captivity."

7 "I will heal Israel!
   Then people will know
      that Ephraim* sinned.
   People will know about Samaria's* lies.
   People will know about the thieves
      that come and go in that town.
² Those people don't believe
      that I will remember their crimes.
   The bad things they did are all around.
   I can see their sins clearly.
³ Their evil makes their king happy.
   Their false gods please their leaders.
⁴ A baker presses dough ₍to make bread₎.
   ₍He puts the bread in the oven.₎
   The baker does not make the fire hotter
      while the bread is rising.
   ₍But the people of Israel are not like that.₎
   The people of Israel are always making
      their fire hotter.

But good things ... decisions Or, "I cut them with the prophets. I killed them with the words from my mouth. Light will come from your decisions."
like Adam did See Gen. 3.
Gilead An area where some of the people from the family group of Manasseh lived. See Numbers 26:29.
Samaria The capital of the northern ten-family group kingdom of Israel. Here it is often used to mean the northern kingdom itself.

Ephraim Joseph's younger son (Gen. 41:50-52). Ephraim's family became a family group in Israel. Here the name is used to mean the northern kingdom of Israel.
nation Literally, "house." This might mean the royal family of that country.

⁵ On Our King's Day,
  ₗthey make the fire hotter」
  ₗthey give their drinking parties.」
  The leaders become sick from the heat
    of wine.
  So the kings join hands with people
    that laugh at God.
⁶ The people make their secret plans.
  Their hearts burn with excitement
    like an oven.
  Their excitement burns all night.
  And in the morning it is like a hot, hot fire.
⁷ They are all like hot ovens.
  They destroyed their rulers.
  All of their kings fell.
  Not one of them called to me for help."

Israel Does Not Know It Will Be Destroyed

⁸ Ephraim* mixes with the nations.
  Ephraim is like a cake
    that was not cooked on both sides.
⁹ Strangers destroy Ephraim's strength.
  But Ephraim does not know it.
  Gray hairs* are also sprinkled on Ephraim.
  But Ephraim does not know it.
¹⁰ ₗEphraim's」 pride speaks against him.
  The people had many, many troubles,
    but they still didn't go back
    to the Lord their God.
  The people didn't look to him for help.
¹¹ So Ephraim has become like a silly dove
    without understanding.
  The people called to Egypt for help.
  The people went to Assyria for help.
¹² They go to those countries for help,
    but I will trap them.
  I will throw my net over them,
    and I will bring them down like
      the birds of the sky.
  I will punish them for their agreements.*
¹³ It will be bad for them.
  They left me.
  They refused to obey me.
  So they will be destroyed.
  I saved those people.
  But they speak lies against me.
¹⁴ They never call to me from their hearts.
  Yes, they cry on their beds.
  And they cut themselves
    when they ask for grain and new wine.
  But ₗin their hearts,」 they have turned away
    from me.
¹⁵ I trained them and made their arms strong.
  But they have made evil plans against me.
¹⁶ They turned to the "no-god."*
  They are like a cracked bow.*
  Their leaders bragged ₗabout their strength」.
  But they will be killed with swords.
  Then the people in Egypt will laugh at them.

Idol Worship Leads to the Destruction of Israel

8 Put the trumpet to your lips ₗand give the warning」. Be like an eagle over the Lord's house.* The Israelites have broken my Agreement. They have not obeyed my law. ²They yell to me, "My God, we in Israel know you!" ³But Israel refused the good things. So the enemy chases him. ⁴The Israelites chose their kings, but they didn't come to me for advice. The Israelites chose leaders. But they didn't choose men that I knew. The Israelites used their silver and gold to make idols* for themselves. So they will be destroyed. ⁵⁻⁶The Lord has refused your calf, Samaria.* God says, "I am very angry against the Israelites. The people of Israel will be punished for their sin. Some worker made those statues. They are not God. Samaria's calf will be broken into pieces. ⁷The Israelites ₗdid a foolish thing」—it was like trying to plant the wind. But ₗthey will get only troubles」—they will harvest a whirlwind. The grain in the fields will grow. It will give no food. Even if it grew something, strangers would eat it.

no-god This means the false gods that the people began worshiping.
cracked bow Literally, "a bow of treachery."
Be like an eagle over the Lord's house Or, "Like a guard over the Lord's house."
idols Statues of false gods that people worshiped.
calf, Samaria Samaria was the capital of Israel. The people of Israel made statues of calves and put them in the temples at Dan and Bethel. It is not clear if these statues represented the Lord or some false god. But God didn't want them to use these statues. See 1 Kings 12:26-30.

Ephraim Joseph's younger son (Gen. 41:50-52). Ephraim's family became a family group in Israel. Here the name is used to mean the northern kingdom of Israel.
Gray hairs This word might describe something that was put on the food when people cooked, something that looked like gray hairs.
for their agreements Or, "for the report of their treaties."

⁸ Israel was destroyed.
⌊Its people are scattered among the⌋ nations
like some dish that was thrown away
because no one wanted it.
⁹ Ephraim* went to his 'lovers.'
Like a wild donkey,
he wandered off to Assyria.
¹⁰ Israel went to his 'lovers' among the nations.
But I will gather the Israelites together.
But they must suffer a little from the burden
of that mighty king.

Israel Forgets God and Worships Idols

¹¹ Ephraim* built more and more altars,*
and that was a sin.
They have been altars of sin for Ephraim.
¹² Even if I wrote 10,000 laws for Ephraim,
he would treat them like they were
for some stranger.
¹³ The Israelites love sacrifices.*
They offer the meat and eat it.
The Lord does not accept their sacrifices.
He remembers their sins.
And he will punish them.
They will be carried as prisoners to Egypt.
¹⁴ Israel built kings' houses.
But it forgot its Maker!
Now Judah builds fortresses.*
But I will send a fire on Judah's cities.
And the fire will destroy its fortresses!

The Sadness of Exile

9 Israel, don't celebrate like the nations do!
Don't be happy! You acted like a prostitute*
and left your God. You did your sexual sin* on
every threshing floor.* ²But ⌊the grain from those⌋
threshing floors will not give enough food for
Israel. There will not be enough wine for Israel.

³The Israelites will not stay in the Lord's land.
Ephraim will return to Egypt. In Assyria they will
eat food that they should not eat. ⁴The Israelites
will not give offerings of wine to the Lord. They
will not offer sacrifices to him. Their sacrifices
will be like food eaten at a funeral*—whoever
eats it will become unclean. Their bread will not
go into the Lord's temple—they will have to eat
that bread themselves. ⁵They will not be able to
celebrate the Lord's holidays or festivals.*

⁶The people of Israel left because the enemy
took everything from them. But Egypt will take
the people themselves. Memphis* will bury them.
Weeds will grow over their silver treasures.
Thorns will grow where the Israelites lived.

Israel Rejected the True Prophets

⁷The prophet says, "Israel, learn these things:
The time of punishment has come. The time has
come for you to pay ⌊for the evil things you did⌋."
But the people of Israel say, "The prophet is a
fool. This man with ⌊God's⌋ Spirit is crazy." The
prophet says, "You will be punished for your bad
sins. You will be punished for your hate." ⁸God
and the prophet are like guards watching over
Ephraim.* But there are many traps along the
way. And people hate the prophet, even in the
house of his God.
⁹The Israelites have gone deep into ruin like in
the time of Gibeah.* The Lord will remember the
Israelites' sins. He will punish their sins.

Israel Is Ruined by Its Worship of Idols

¹⁰To me, Israel was like finding grapes in the
desert. Your ancestors were like finding the first
figs on the tree at the beginning of the season. But
then they came to Baal-Peor.* And they were

Ephraim Joseph's younger son (Gen. 41:50-52). Ephraim's family became a family group in Israel. Here the name is used to mean the northern kingdom of Israel.
altar(s) A stone table used for burning sacrifices offered as gifts to God.
The Israelites love sacrifices This line is uncertain.
fortress(es) A building or city with tall, strong walls for protection.
prostitute A woman paid by men for sexual sin. Sometimes this also means a person that is not faithful to God and stops following him.
You did your sexual sin This means that the people were not faithful to God. But it also means the people had sexual relations with temple prostitutes. They believed their false gods would give them many children and good crops.

threshing floor A place where grain is beaten or walked on to remove the hulls from the grain.
sacrifices ... funeral Literally, "bread of mourners." See Num. 19:11-22.
They ... the Lord's holidays or festivals Literally, "What will you do for a day of solemn assembly, for the Lord's festival day?"
Memphis An important city in Egypt.
Ephraim Joseph's younger son (Gen. 41:50-52). Ephraim's family became a family group in Israel. Here the name is used to mean the northern kingdom of Israel.
Gibeah At this place, men of the Benjamin family group did a very terrible sin. See Judges 19- 20.
Baal-Peor This happened when Moses was still leading the Israelites in the desert. Read Num. 25:1-5.

changed—they were like something rotten.* They became like the terrible things *(the false gods)* that they loved.

The Israelites Will Have No Children

¹¹Like a bird, Ephraim's* glory will fly away. There will be no more pregnancies, no more births, no more babies. ¹²But even if the Israelites do raise their children, ₍it will not help₎. I will take the children away from them. I will leave them, and they will have nothing but troubles. ¹³I can see that Ephraim is leading his children into a trap.* Ephraim brings out his children to the killer. ¹⁴Lord, give them what you will. Give them a womb that loses babies, give them breasts that can't give milk.

15 All their evil is in Gilgal;*
    I began hating them there.
    I will force them to leave my house,
    because of the evil things they do.
    I will not love them any more.
    Their leaders are rebels—
       ₍they have turned against me₎.
16 Ephraim* will be punished.
    Their root is dying.
    They will not have any more babies.
    They might give birth to babies,
    but I will kill the precious babies that come
       from their bodies.
17 Those people will not listen to my God.
    So he will refuse to listen to them.
    And they will wander among the nations
       without a home.

Israel's Riches Led to Its Worship of Idols

10 Israel is like a vine that grows plenty of fruit. But as Israel got more and more ₍things₎ he built more and more altars* ₍to honor false gods₎. His land became better and better, so he put up better and better stones ₍to honor false gods₎.

² The people of Israel tried to trick God. But now they must accept their guilt. The Lord will break down their altars.* He will destroy their memorial stones.*

The Evil Decisions of the Israelites

³Now the Israelites say, "We have no king. We don't honor the Lord! And his king can't do anything to us!" ⁴They make promises—but they are only telling lies. They don't keep their promises! They make agreements ₍with other countries₎. God does not like those agreements₎. The judges are like poisonous weeds growing in a plowed field. ⁵The people from Samaria* worship the calves at Beth-Aven.* Those people will really cry. Those priests will really cry. Why? Because their beautiful ₍idol₎ is gone. It was carried away. ⁶It was carried away as a gift to the great king of Assyria. He will keep Ephraim's shameful ₍idol₎. Israel will be ashamed of its idol.* ⁷Samaria's false god* will be destroyed. It will be like a piece of wood floating away on the water's surface. ⁸Israel sinned and built many high places.* The high places of Aven* will be destroyed. Thorns and weeds will grow on their altars.* Then they will say to the mountains, "Cover us!" and to the hills, "Fall on us!"

Israel Will Pay For Sin

⁹Israel, you have sinned since the time of Gibeah.* (And those people have continued sinning there. War truly will catch those evil people at Gibeah. ¹⁰I will come to punish them. Armies will come together against them. They will punish the Israelites for both of their sins.

---

altar(s) A stone table used for burning sacrifices offered as gifts to God.
memorial stones Stones that were set up to help people remember something special. In ancient Israel, people often set up stones as special places to worship false gods.
Samaria The capital city of north Israel.
Beth-Aven In Hebrew the meaning is "House of Evil." It is a word play on the name "Bethel," a town in Israel. There was a temple in this town.
idol Or, "advice."
false god Or, "king."
high places Places for worshiping God or false gods. These places were often on the hills and mountains.
high places of Aven Aven means "evil," "wickedness." This probably means the temple and other places of worship at Bethel.
Gibeah At this place, men of the Benjamin family group did a very terrible sin. See Judges 19 and 20.

---

changed ... rotten Or "the were pruned awaylike some rotten fruit," or "they dedicated themselves to a shameful idol."
Ephraim Joseph's younger son (Gen. 41:50-52). Ephraim's family became a family group in Israel. Here the name is used to mean the northern kingdom of Israel.
I can see ... trap The Hebrew is not clear here.
Gilgal A city in Israel. The people worship false gods there.
altar(s) A stone table used for burning sacrifices offered as gifts to God.

¹¹Ephraim* is like a trained young cow that loves to walk on grain on the threshing floor.* I will put a good yoke* on her neck. I will put the ropes on Ephraim. Then Judah will begin plowing. Jacob* will break the ground himself. ¹²If you plant goodness, you will harvest true love. Plow your ground, and you will harvest with the Lord. He will come, and he will make goodness fall on you like rain! ¹³But you planted evil, and you harvested trouble. You ate the fruit of your lies. Why? Because you have trusted in your power and your soldiers. ¹⁴So your armies will hear the noise of battle. And all your fortresses* will be destroyed. It will be like the time Shalman* destroyed Beth Arbel. At that time of war, mothers were killed with their children. ¹⁵And that will happen to you at Bethel. Why? Because you did so many evil things. ₗWhen that day₁ begins, the king of Israel will be fully destroyed.

Israel Has Forgotten the Lord

11 "I *(the Lord)* loved Israel when he was a child,
  and I called my son out of Egypt.
² But the more I* called the Israelites,
  the more the Israelites left me.
 The Israelites gave sacrifices to the Baals.*
  They burned incense* to the idols.*

³ "But it was I who taught Ephraim* to walk!
  I took the Israelites in my arms!
 I healed them!
  But they don't know that.
⁴ I led them with ropes.*
  But they were ropes of love.

Ephraim Joseph's younger son (Gen. 41:50-52). Ephraim's family became a family group in Israel. Here the name is used to mean the northern kingdom of Israel.
threshing floor A place where grain is beaten or walked on to remove the hulls from the grain.
yoke A pole that was put on the shoulders of men or animals to help them carry or pull things. This often showed that a person was a slave.
Jacob Another name for Israel. See Gen. 32:22-28.
fortress(es) A building or city with tall, strong walls for protection.
Shalman This is probably Shalmaneser, king of Assyria.
I This is what the ancient Greek says. The Hebrew says, "they."
Baals False gods worshiped by the Canaanites in the land where the Israelites lived.
incense Special dried tree sap. Burned to make a sweet-smelling smoke, it was offered as a gift to God.
idols Statues of false gods that people worshiped.
ropes The Hebrew says, "ropes of a man."

 I was like a person who set them free.*
  I bent down and fed them.

⁵"The Israelites refuse to turn back ₗto God₁. So they will go to Egypt! ₗThe king of₁ Assyria will become their king. ⁶The sword will swing against their cities. It will kill their strong men. It will destroy their leaders.
⁷"My people expect me to come back. They will call to God above. But God will not help them."

The Lord Does Not Want to Destroy Israel

⁸ "Ephraim,* I don't want to give you up.
  Israel, I want to protect you.
 I don't want to make you like Admah!
  I don't want to make you like Zeboiim!*
 I am changing my mind.
  My love for you is too strong.
⁹ I will not let my terrible anger win.
  I will not destroy Ephraim again.
 I am God, and not man.
  I am the Holy One, I am with you.
  I will not show my anger.
¹⁰ I will roar like a lion.
 I will roar, and my children will come
  and follow me.
 My children will come from the west,
  shaking with fear.
¹¹ They will come from Egypt
  shaking like birds.
 They will come shaking like doves
  from the land of Assyria.
 And I will take them back home."
  The Lord said that.
¹² Ephraim surrounded me with false gods.
  The people of Israel turned against me.*
  ₗAnd they were destroyed!₁
 But Judah still walks with El.*
  Judah is true to the holy ones.*"

set them free Literally, "lifted the yoke from their jaws."
Admah, Zeboiim Two cities that were destroyed when God destroyed Sodom and Gomorrah. See Gen. 19; Deut. 29:23.
Ephraim ... me Or, "Ephraim surrounded me with lies. The house of Israel surrounded me with deception."
El This might be one of the names of God, or it might be El, the most important god of the Canaanite people. It is not clear if this means that Judah was being faithful to God, or if Judah was worshiping the false gods.
holy ones These might be angels or Canaanite false gods.

The Lord Is Against Israel

12 Ephraim* is wasting its time—Israel "chases the wind" all day long. The people tell more and more lies. They steal more and more. They have made agreements with Assyria, and they are carrying their olive oil to Egypt. ²⌊The Lord says,⌋ "I have an argument against Israel.* Jacob* must be punished for the things he did. He must be punished for the bad things he did. ³Jacob was still in his mother's body, and he had already started tricking his brother.* Jacob was a strong young man. And at that time, he fought with God. ⁴Jacob wrestled with God's angel and won.* He cried and asked for a favor. That happened at Bethel. At that place, he spoke with us. ⁵Yes, Yahweh is the God of the armies.* His name is Yahweh (the Lord). ⁶So come back to your God. Be loyal to him. Do the right thing! Always trust your God!

⁷"Jacob* is a real businessman. He even cheats his friend! Even his scales* lie. ⁸Ephraim* said, 'I am rich! I have found true riches! No person will learn about my crimes. No person will learn about my sins.'

⁹"But I have been the Lord your God since ⌊the time you were in⌋ the land of Egypt. I will make you live in tents—like during the time of the Tent of Meeting.* ¹⁰I spoke to the prophets. I gave them many visions.* I gave the prophets many ways to teach my lessons to you. ¹¹But the people in Gilead* have sinned. There are many terrible idols in that place. The people offer sacrifices to bulls at Gilgal. Those people have many altars.* There are rows and rows of altars—like the rows of dirt in a plowed field.

¹²"Jacob ran away to the land of Aram. In that place, Israel* worked for a wife. He kept sheep to get another wife. ¹³But the Lord used a prophet and brought Israel out of Egypt. The Lord used a prophet and kept Israel safe. ¹⁴But Ephraim caused the Lord to be very angry. Ephraim killed many people. So he will be punished for his crimes. His master (the Lord) will make him bear his shame."

Israel Has Ruined Itself

13 "Ephraim* made himself very important in Israel. Ephraim spoke and people shook with fear. But Ephraim sinned—he began worshiping Baal.* ²Now the Israelites sin more and more. They make idols* for themselves. Workers make those fancy statues from silver. And then those people talk to their statues! They offer sacrifices to those statues. They kiss those ⌊golden⌋ calves. ³That is why those people will soon disappear. They will be like the fog that comes early in the morning—that fog comes and then soon disappears. The Israelites will be like chaff* that is blown from the threshing floor.* The Israelites will be like smoke that rises from a chimney and disappears.

⁴"I have been the Lord your God since the time you were in the land of Egypt. You did not know any other god except me. I am the One who saved you. ⁵I knew you in the desert—I knew you in that dry land. ⁶⌊I gave food to the Israelites.⌋ They ate that food. They became full and satisfied. They became proud. And they forgot me!

⁷"That is why I will be like a lion to them. I will be like a leopard waiting by the road. ⁸I will attack them like a bear whose cubs were robbed from her. I will attack them. I will rip open their

---

Ephraim Joseph's younger son (Gen. 41:50-52). Ephraim's family became a family group in Israel. Here the name is used to mean the northern kingdom of Israel.

Israel Hebrew has, "Judah."

Jacob Another name for Israel. See Gen. 32:22-28.

he had already started tricking his brother Or "he grabbed his brother's heel." This is a word play. The Hebrew word is like the name "Jacob." See Gen. 25:26.

Jacob wrestled with God's angel and won See Gen. 32:22-28.

Yahweh is the God of the armies This is like one of the names for God. It is usually translated "Lord All-Powerful."

scales Or, "balances." A tool for weighing things.

during the time of the Tent of Meeting The special tent where the people worshiped God. This might also mean, "like during the holiday of Succoth." The Jewish people live in tents or temporary buildings during this holiday.

vision(s) Something like a dream that God used to speak to people.

Israel Another name for Jacob. See Gen. 32:22-28.

Baal The Canaanite people believed that this false god brought the rain and storms. They also thought that he made the land produce good crops.

idols Statues of false gods that people worshiped.

chaff The seed coverings and stems separated from the seeds of plants like wheat or barley. Farmers saved the seeds but let the wind blow the useless chaff away.

threshing floor A place where grain is beaten or walked on to remove the hulls from the grain.

chests. I will be like a lion or other wild animal tearing and eating its prey."

No One Can Save Israel from God's Anger

⁹"Israel, I helped you. But you turned against me. So now I will destroy you! ¹⁰Where is your king? He can't save you in all your cities! Where are your judges? You asked for them, saying, "Give me a king and leaders."* ¹¹I was angry, and I gave you a king. And when I became very angry, I took him away.

¹² "Ephraim tried to hide his guilt.
　　He thought his sins were a secret.
　　　⌊But he will be punished.⌋
¹³　⌊His punishment⌋ will be like the pain a
　　　woman feels giving birth.
　　He will not be a wise son.
　　The time will come for his birth,
　　　and he will not survive.

¹⁴ "I will save them from the grave!
　　I will rescue them from death!
　　Death, where are your diseases?
　　Grave, where is your power?
　　I am not looking for revenge!
¹⁵　⌊Israel⌋ grows among his brothers.
　　But a powerful east wind will come—
　　　the Lord's wind will blow from the desert.
　　Then ⌊Israel's⌋ well will become dry.
　　His spring of water will become dry.
　　The wind will take every valuable thing
　　　from ⌊Israel's⌋ treasure.
¹⁶　Samaria must be punished.
　　Why? Because she turned against her God.
　　The Israelites will be killed with swords.
　　Their children will be torn to pieces.
　　Their pregnant women will be ripped open."

Return to the Lord

14 Israel, you fell and sinned against God. So come back to the Lord your God. ²Think about the things you will say. And come back to the Lord. Say to him, "Take away our sin. Accept the good ⌊things that we are doing⌋. We will offer praise from our lips.*

³Assyria will not save us. We will not ride on horses. We will not say again, "Our god," to the things our hands made. Why? Because you are the One who shows mercy to orphans.*"

The Lord Will Forgive Israel

⁴　The Lord says,
　　"I will forgive them for leaving me.
　　I will love them freely.
　　I am not angry at them now.
⁵　I will be like the dew to Israel.
　　Israel will blossom like the lily.*
　　He will grow like the cedar trees of Lebanon.
⁶　His branches will grow,
　　　and he will be like a beautiful olive tree.
　　He will be like the sweet smell
　　　from the cedar trees of Lebanon.
⁷　The people of Israel will again
　　　live under my protection.
　　They will grow like grain.
　　They will bloom like a vine.
　　They will be like the wine of Lebanon."

The Lord Warns Israel About Idols

⁸ "Ephraim,* I will have nothing more
　　to do with idols.*
　　I am the One who answers your prayers.
　　I am the One who watches over you.*
　　I am like a fir tree that is always green.
　　　Your fruit comes from me."

Final Advice

⁹　A wise person understands these things.
　　A smart person should learn these things.
　　　The Lord's ways are right.
　　　Good people will live by them.
　　　Sinners will die by them.*

---

orphans children with no parents.
lily A kind of flower.
Ephraim Joseph's younger son (Gen. 41:50-52). Ephraim's family became a family group in Israel. Here the name is used to mean the northern kingdom of Israel.
idols Statues of false gods that people worshiped.
I am the One who watches over you This is a word play. The Hebrew word is like the name "Assyria." God is saying that he, not some foreign country, protects Israel.
Good people ... die by them Literally, "Good people will walk on them. Sinners will stumble on them."

You asked for ... leaders See 1 Sam. 8:4-9.
praise from our lips Literally, "the fruit of our lips."

Joel

Locusts Will Destroy the Crops

1 Joel son of Pethuel received this message from the Lord:

² Leaders, listen to this message!
Listen to me, all you people
that live in the land.
Has anything like this happened before
during your lifetime? No!
Did anything like this happen
during your fathers' lifetime? No!
³ You will tell these things to your children.
And your children will tell their children.
And your grandchildren will tell
the people of the next generation.
⁴ What the cutting locust* has left,
the swarming locust has eaten.
And what the swarming locust has left,
the hopping locust has eaten.
And what the hopping locust has left,
the destroying locust* has eaten!

The Locusts Arrive

⁵ Drunks, wake up and cry!
All of you people that drink wine, cry.
Why? Because your sweet wine is finished.
You will not get another taste of that wine.
⁶ A large and powerful country is coming
to fight against my nation.
There are too many soldiers to count.
⌊Those "locusts" (enemy soldiers) will be able
to tear you apart!⌋
It is like they have teeth like a lion.

---

locust Insects, like grasshoppers. Locusts can quickly destroy all trees and plants in a farmer's fields. So locusts made the people very scared. Here, Joel might be talking about an enemy's army.
cutting ... destroying locusts These are the different names for the locusts. These may be different names for the same kind of locusts—only at different times of the locust's growth period.

⁷ The "locusts" will eat all of the grapes from
my grapevines!
They will destroy my fig tree.
The locusts will eat the bark off my trees.
The branches will become white.
The trees will be destroyed.

The People Cry

⁸ Cry like the young woman that was ready to
be married,
and her husband-to-be was killed.
⁹ Priests! Servants of the Lord, cry!
Why? Because there will be no more
grain and drink offerings
in the Lord's temple.*
¹⁰ The fields are ruined.
Even the ground is crying.
Why? Because the grain is destroyed;
the new wine is dried up,
and the olive oil is gone.
¹¹ Be sad, farmers!
Cry loud, grape farmers!
⌊Cry⌋ for the wheat and for the barley!*
Why? Because the harvest in the field is lost.
¹² The vines have become dry.
And the fig tree is dying.
The pomegranate tree the palm tree,
and the apple tree—
all the trees in the field have become dry.
And happiness among the people is dead.
¹³ Priests, put on your clothes of sadness
and cry loudly.
Servants of the altar,* cry loudly.
Servants of my God, you will sleep
in your clothes of sadness.
Why? Because there will be no more
grain and drink offerings in God's temple.*

---

temple The special building in Jerusalem for Jewish worship.
barley A kind of grain.
altar(s) A stone table or raised area used for offering sacrifices.

The Terrible Destruction of the Locusts

¹⁴Tell the people that there will be a special time for not eating food. Call the people together for a special meeting. Bring the leaders and all the people that live in the land together. Bring them to the temple* of the Lord your God, and pray to the Lord. ¹⁵Be sad! Why? Because the Lord's special day is near. At that time, punishment will come like an attack from God All-Powerful. ¹⁶Our food is gone. Joy and happiness are gone from the temple* of our God. ¹⁷⌊We planted seeds,⌋ but the seeds became dry and dead lying in the soil. Our plants are dry and dead. Our barns are empty and falling down. ¹⁸The animals ⌊are hungry and⌋ groaning. The herds of cattle wander around, confused. They have no grass to eat. The sheep are dying.* ¹⁹Lord, I am calling to you ⌊for help⌋. Fire has changed our green fields into a desert. Flames have burned all the trees in the field. ²⁰Wild animals also need your help. The streams are dry—there is no water! Fire has changed our green fields into a desert.

The Coming Day of the Lord

2 Blow the trumpet at Zion.*
　　Shout a warning on my holy mountain.
Let all the people that live in the land
　　shake with fear.
The Lord's special day is coming.
　　The Lord's special day is near.
² It will be a dark, gloomy day.
　　It will be a dark and cloudy day.
At sunrise, you will see the army
　　spread over the mountains.
It will be a great and powerful army.
There has never been anything like it before.
And there will never be anything like it again.
³ The army destroys the land like a burning fire.
In front of them, the land is like
　　the Garden of Eden.
Behind them, the land is like
　　an empty desert.
Nothing will escape them.
⁴ They look like horses.
　　They run like war horses.
⁵ Listen to them.
　　It is like the noise of chariots*
　　　　riding over the mountains.
　　It is like the noise of flames
　　　　burning the chaff.*
They are a powerful people.
　　They are ready for war.
⁶ Before this army, people shake with fear.
　　Their faces become pale from fear.
⁷ The soldiers run fast.
　　The soldiers climb over the walls.
Each soldier marches straight ahead.
　　They don't move from their path.
⁸ They don't trip each other.
　　Each soldier walks in his ⌊own⌋ path.
If one of the soldiers is hit and falls down,
　　the others keep right on marching.
⁹ They run to the city.
　　They quickly climb over the wall.
They climb into the houses.
　　They climb through the windows
　　　　like thieves.
¹⁰ Before them, earth and sky shake.
　　The sun and the moon become dark.
　　And the stars stop shining.
¹¹ The Lord calls loudly to his army.
　　His camp is very large.
That army obeys his commands.
　　That army is very powerful.
The Lord's special day
　　is a great and terrible day.
No person can stop it.

The Lord Tells the People to Change

¹² This is the Lord's message:
"Now come back to me with all your heart,
　⌊You did bad things,⌋
　　cry, cry and don't eat any food!
¹³ Tear your hearts, not your clothes."*
Come back to the Lord your God.
He is kind and merciful.
He does not become angry quickly.
He has great love.
Maybe he will change his mind
　about the bad ⌊punishment he planned⌋.
¹⁴ Who knows, maybe the Lord
　　will change his mind.

---

chariot(s) A small wagon used in war.
chaff The seed coverings and stems separated from the seeds of plants like wheat or barley. Farmers saved the seeds but let the wind blow the useless chaff away.
Tear your hearts, not your clothes People tore their clothes to show their sadness. Here God wants the people to truly be sad for the bad things they did.

dying Literally, "being punished."
Zion The southeast part of the mountain Jerusalem is built on. Sometimes it means the people of God living in Jerusalem.

And maybe he will leave behind
a blessing for you.
Then you can give grain and drink offerings
to the Lord your God.

Pray to the Lord

15 Blow the trumpet at Zion.*
Call for a special meeting.
Call for a special time for not eating.
16 Bring together the people.
Call for a special meeting.
Bring together the older men.
Bring together the children.
Bring the small babies
that still suck their mother's breasts.
Let the bride and her new husband
come from their bedroom.
17 Let the priests, the Lord's servants,
cry between the porch* and the altar.*
All of those people should say these things:
"Lord, have mercy on your people.
Don't let your people be put to shame.
Don't let other people tell jokes
about your people.
Don't let people in other nations
ₗlaugh at us andⱼ say,
'Where is their God'?"

The Lord Will Restore the Land

18 Then the Lord became excited about his land.
He felt sorry for his people.
19 The Lord spoke to his people.
He said,
"I will send you grain, wine, and oil.
You will have plenty.
I won't shame you among the nations any
more.
20 No, I will force those people from the north*
to leave your land.
I will make them go into a dry, empty land.
Some of them will go to the eastern sea.l
Some of them will go to the western sea.
Those people did such terrible things.
But they will be like a dead
and rotting thing.
There will be such a terrible smell!"

The Land Will Be Made New Again

21 Land, don't be afraid.
Be happy and full of joy.
The Lord will do great things.
22 Animals of the field, don't be afraid.
The desert pastures will grow grass.
The trees will grow fruit.
The fig trees and the vines will grow
plenty of fruit.
23 So be happy, people of Zion.*
Be joyful in the Lord your God.
He will be good and give you rain.
He will send you the early rains
and the late rains like before.
24 The threshing floors* will be filled
with wheat.
And the barrels will overflow
with wine and olive oil.
25 I, the Lord, sent my army against you.
The swarming locusts and the hopping
locusts and the destroying locusts and
the cutting locusts* ate everything you had.
But I, the Lord, will pay you back
for those years ₍of troubleⱼ.
26 Then you will have plenty to eat.
You will be full.
You will praise the name
of the Lord your God.
He has done wonderful things for you.
My people will never ₍again₎ be ashamed.
27 You will know that I am with Israel.
You will know that I am the Lord your God.
There is no other God.
My people will never be ashamed again.

God Will Give His Spirit to All People

28 After this I will pour *(give)* my Spirit on all
kinds of people.
Your sons and daughters will prophesy.*
Your old men will dream dreams.
Your young men will see visions.*
29 At that time I will pour *(give)* give my Spirit
even on servants, both men and women.

Zion The southeast part of the mountain Jerusalem is built on. Sometimes it means the people of God living in Jerusalem.
porch An open area in front of the temple.
altar(s) A stone table or raised area used for offering sacrifices.
north The Babylonian army came from this direction to attack Judah. Armies from countries north and east of Israel often came this way to attack Judah and Israel.

threshing floor(s) A place where grain is beaten or walked on to remove the hulls from the grain.
swarming locusts ... cutting locusts See Joel 1:4.
prophesy To receive special messages from God, and then teach those things to people.
vision(s) Something like a dream that God used to speak to people.

⁣
³⁰ I will show amazing things
   in the sky and on the earth—
   There will be blood, fire, and thick smoke.
³¹ The sun will be changed into darkness,
   The moon will be changed into blood.
   And then the great and wonderful
   Day of the Lord will come!
³² And then, any person
   that calls on the name of the Lord
   will be saved.
   On Mount Zion* and in Jerusalem
   there will be people that were saved.
   This will happen just like the Lord said.
   Among those survivors*
   will be the people
   that the Lord has called.

The Lord Promises Punishment for Judah's Enemies

3 "At that time, I will bring back Judah and Jerusalem from captivity. ²I will also gather all the nations together. I will bring all these nations down into Jehoshaphat Valley.* There I will judge them. Those nations scattered my people, Israel. They forced them to live in other nations. So I will punish those nations. Those nations divided up my land. ³They threw lots* for my people. They sold a boy to buy a prostitute.* And they sold a girl to buy wine to drink.
⁴"Tyre! Sidon! All of you areas of Philistia! You are not important to me!* Are you punishing me for something I did? You might think that you are punishing me, but I will soon punish you. ⁵You took my silver and gold. You took my precious treasures and put it in your temples.*
⁶"You sold the people of Judah and Jerusalem to the Greeks. That way, you could take them far from their land. ⁷You sent my people to that faraway place. But I will bring them back. And I will punish you for what you did. ⁸I will sell your sons and daughters to the people of Judah. Then they will sell them to the faraway Sabean people." The Lord said those things.

Prepare for War

⁹ Announce this among the nations:
   Prepare for war!
   Wake up the strong men!
   Let all the men of war come near.
   Let them come up!
¹⁰ Beat your plows into swords.
   Make spears from your pruning hooks.*
   Let the weak man say,
   "I am a strong soldier."
¹¹ All of you nations, hurry!
   Come together in that place!
   Lord, bring your strong soldiers!
¹² Wake up, nations!
   Come to Jehoshaphat Valley!
   There I will sit to judge
   all the surrounding nations.
¹³ Bring the sickle,*
   because the harvest is ripe.*
   Come, walk on ⌊the grapes,⌋
   because the winepress is full.
   The barrels will be full and spilling over,
   because their evil is great.
¹⁴ There are many, many people
   in the Valley of Decision.*
   The Lord's special day is near
   in the Valley of Decision.
¹⁵ The sun and the moon will become dark.
   The stars will stop shining.
¹⁶ The Lord God will shout from Zion,*
   He will shout from Jerusalem,
   and the sky and the earth will shake.
   But the Lord God will be a safe place
   for his people.

Zion The southeast part of the mountain Jerusalem is built on. Sometimes it means the people of God living in Jerusalem.
survivor(s) People that escaped some disaster. Here this means the Jewish people that survived the destruction of Judah and Israel by its enemy armies.
Jehoshaphat Valley This name means, "The Lord judged."
lot(s) Sticks, stones, or pieces of bone used like dice for making decisions. See Proverbs 16:33.
You are not important to me Literally, "What are you to me?"
temples Buildings used for worship. Here, the temples were used to worship idols.

pruning hooks These tools were used to prune (cut) branches of trees. Read Isa. 2:4.
sickle A tool with a curved blade for cutting grain.
harvest is ripe This time of judgment is compared to harvest time.
Valley of Decision This is like the name, "Jehoshaphat Valley."

He will be a place of safety
for the people of Israel.
17 Then you will know
that I am the Lord your God,
I live on Zion,* my holy mountain.
Jerusalem will become holy.
Strangers will never pass through
that city again.

A New Life for Judah Promised

18 On that day, the mountains will drip
with sweet wine.
The hills will flow with milk.
And water will flow through all
the empty rivers of Judah.
A fountain will come from
the Lord's temple.*
It will give water to Acacia Valley.
19 Egypt will be empty.
Edom* will be an empty wilderness.
Why? Because they were cruel
to the people of Judah.
They killed innocent people*
in their country.
20 But there will always be people
living in Judah,
People will live in Jerusalem
through many generations.
21 Those people killed my people.
So I really will punish those people!

Zion The southeast part of the mountain Jerusalem is built on. Sometimes it means the people of God living in Jerusalem.
temple The special building in Jerusalem for Jewish worship.
Edom A country southeast of Judah.
killed innocent people Literally, "shed innocent blood."

Amos

Introduction

1 The message of Amos. Amos was one of the shepherds from the city Tekoa. Amos saw visions* about Israel during the time that Uzziah was king of Judah and during the time that Jeroboam son of Joash was king of Israel. This was two years before the earthquake.

Punishment for Aram

² Amos said:
The Lord will shout like a lion in Zion.*
His loud voice will roar from Jerusalem.
And the green pastures of the shepherds will turn brown and die.
Even Mount Carmel* will become dry.

³The Lord says these things: "I will definitely punish ₍the people of₎ Damascus for the many crimes they did. Why? Because they crushed ₍the people of₎ Gilead* with iron threshing tools.* ⁴So I will start a fire at Hazael's* house *(Aram)*. And that fire will destroy the great palaces of Ben Hadad.*

⁵"I will also break open the gates of Damascus.* I will remove the person sitting ₍on the throne₎ in the the Valley of Aven.* I will remove the symbol of power from Beth-Eden.* And the Aramean people will be ₍defeated and₎ taken ₍back₎ to Kir.* The Lord said those things.

Punishment for the Philistines

⁶The Lord says this: "I will definitely punish ₍the people of₎ Gaza* for the many crimes they did.* Why? Because they took an entire nation of people and sent them as slaves to Edom.* ⁷So I will send a fire on the wall of Gaza.* This fire will destroy the high towers in Gaza. ⁸And I will destroy the one that sits ₍on the throne₎ in Ashdod.* I will destroy the king that holds the scepter in Ashkelon.* I will punish the people of Ekron.* Then the Philistines that are still left alive, will die." The Lord God said those things.

Punishment for Phoenicia

⁹The Lord says these things: "I will definitely punish ₍the people of₎ Tyre* for the many crimes they did.* Why? Because they took an entire

---

vision(s) Something like a dream that God used to speak to people.
Zion The southeast part of the mountain Jerusalem is built on. Sometimes it means the people of God living in Jerusalem.
Mount Carmel A mountain in north Israel. This name means, "God's vineyard." This shows it was a very fertile hill.
Gilead An area where some of the people from the family group of Manasseh lived. See Num. 26:29.
threshing tools Boards with pieces of sharp stone or iron that were dragged over grain to remove the hulls.
Hazael Hazael was the king of Aram (Syria). He murdered Ben Hadad I so he could become king. See 2 Kings 8:7.
Ben Hadad Ben Hadad II, the son of Hazael, king of Aram (Syria). See 2 Kings 13:3.

Damascus The capital of Aram (Syria).
the Valley of Aven A name that can mean, "Leisure Valley" or "Empty Valley of Misfortune".
Beth-Eden The royal city of Aram (Syria) on Mount Lebanon. This name means, "House of Pleasure" or "Paradise".
Kir Or, "Kur," an area controlled by the Assyrians. See Amos 9:7.
Gaza An important city of the Philistines.
for the many crimes they did Literally, "For three crimes ... and for four ... " This shows that these people had done plenty of sins—and it was time to punish those people.
Edom A nation southeast of Israel.
Ashdod Another important city of the Philistines.
Ashkelon Another important city of the Philistines.
Ekron Another important city of the Philistines.
Tyre The capital of Phoenicia.

nation and sent them as slaves to Edom.* They did not remember the agreement they had made with their brothers (Israel). ¹⁰So I will start a fire at the walls of Tyre. That fire will destroy the high towers in Tyre."

Punishment for the Edomites

¹¹The Lord says these things: "I will definitely punish ₍the people of ₎ Edom* for the many crimes they did.* Why? Because Edom chased his brother (Israel) with the sword. Edom showed no mercy. Edom's anger continued forever—he kept tearing and tearing ₍at Israel like a wild animal₎. ¹²So I will start a fire at Teman.* That fire will destroy the high towers of Bozrah."*

Punishment for the Ammonites

¹³The Lord says these things: "I will definitely punish ₍the people of₎ Ammon* for the many crimes they did.* Why? Because they killed the pregnant women in Gilead.* The Ammonite people did this so they could ₍take that land₎ and make their country larger. ¹⁴So I will start a fire at the wall of Rabbah.* That fire will destroy the high towers of Rabbah. Troubles will come to them like a whirlwind* into their country. ¹⁵Then their kings and leaders will be captured. They will all be taken together." The Lord said those things.

Punishment for Moab

2 The Lord says these things: "I will definitely punish the people of Moab* for the many crimes they did.* Why? Because Moab burned the bones of the king of Edom* into lime. ²So I will start a fire in Moab. And that fire will destroy the high towers of Kerioth.* There will be terrible shouting and the sounds of a trumpet, and Moab will die. ³So, I will bring an end to the kings* of Moab. And I will kill all the leaders of Moab." The Lord said those things.

Punishment for Judah

⁴The Lord says this: "I will definitely punish Judah for the many crimes they did.* Why? Because they refused to obey the Lord's commands. They didn't keep his commands. Their ancestors* believed ₍lies₎. And those same lies caused the people of Judah to quit following God. ⁵So I will start a fire in Judah. And that fire will destroy the high towers of Jerusalem."

Punishment for Israel

⁶The Lord says this: "I will definitely punish Israel for the many crimes they did.* Why? Because they sold good, ₍innocent₎ people for a little silver. They sold poor people for the price of a pair of shoes. ⁷They pushed those poor peoples' faces into the ground and walked on them. They stopped listening to suffering people. Fathers and sons have sexual relations with the same woman. They have ruined my holy name. ⁸They take clothes from poor people, and then they sit on those clothes while they worship at their altars.* They loaned money to poor people, and then took their clothes as collateral.* They make people pay fines, and then they use that money to buy wine for themselves to drink in the temple of their God.

⁹"But it was I who destroyed the Amorites* before them. The Amorites* were tall like cedar trees. They were as strong as oak trees. But I destroyed their fruit above and their roots below.*

¹⁰"I was the One who brought you from the land of Egypt. For 40 years I led you through the

---

Edom A nation southeast of Israel.
for the many crimes they did Literally, "For three crimes ... and for four ... " This shows that these people had done plenty of sins—and it was time to punish those people.
Teman A city at the north part of the country of Edom.
Bozrah A city at the south part of the country of Edom.
Ammon The Ammonites were the descendants of Ben-Ammi, son of Lot. Read Genesis 19:38.
Gilead An area where some of the people from the family group of Manasseh lived. See Num. 26:29.
Rabbah The capital of the Ammonites.
whirlwind A strong wind that blows in a circle.
Moab A country east of Israel. The Moabite people were descendants of Lot's son, Moab. See Genesis 19:37.
Kerioth A city in Moab. This might be Ar, the capital of Moab.

kings Literally, "judge."
ancestors Literally, "fathers," meaning a person's parents, grandparents, and all the people they are descended from.
altar(s) A stone table used for offering sacrifices to God.
collateral Things that a person uses to borrow money. If that person does not pay his debt, then the person he borrowed from can keep those things. It was against Moses' law to take a person's clothes as collateral. See Deut. 24:12-13.
Amorites One of the nations who lived in Canaan before the Israelites came. They were the people that scared the Israelites while Moses was leading them in the desert. See Num. 13:33.
fruit above and their roots below This means the parents and their children.

desert. I helped you take the Amorites' land. ¹¹I made some of your sons to be prophets. I made some of your young men to be Nazirites.* People of Israel, it is true." The Lord said these things. ¹²"But you made the Nazirites drink wine. You told the prophets not to prophesy. ¹³You are like a heavy weight to me. I am bent low like a wagon loaded with too much straw. ¹⁴No person will escape—not even the fastest runner. Strong men will not be strong enough. Soldiers will not be able to save themselves. ¹⁵People with bows ₍and arrows₎ will not survive. Fast runners will not escape. People on horses will not escape alive. At that time, even very brave soldiers will run away. They will not take the time to put their clothes on." The Lord said these things!

Warning to Israel

3 People of Israel, listen to this message! The Lord said these things about you, Israel. This message is about all the families *(Israel)* that I brought from the land of Egypt. ²"There are many families on earth. But you are the only family I chose to know in a special way. ₍And you turned against me.₎ So I will punish you for all your sins."

The Cause of Israel's Punishment

³Two people will not walk together unless they agree! ⁴A lion in the forest will roar only after catching an animal. If a young lion is roaring in his cave, then it means he caught something. ⁵A bird will not fly into a trap on the ground if there is no food in the trap. And if the trap closes, then it will catch the bird. ⁶If a trumpet blows a warning, then the people will surely shake with fear. If trouble comes to a city, then the Lord caused it. ⁷The Lord my Master might decide to do something. But before he does anything, he will tell his plans to his servants, the prophets. ⁸If a lion roars, people will be scared. If the Lord speaks, prophets will prophesy.*

⁹⁻¹⁰Go to the high towers in Ashdod* and Egypt and announce this message: "Come to the mountains of Samaria. There you will see great confusion. Why? Because the people don't know how to live right. Those people were cruel to other people. They took things from other people and hid those things in their high towers. Their treasuries are filled with things they took in war."

¹¹So the Lord says, "An enemy will come to that land. That enemy will take away your strength. He will take the things you hid in your high towers."

¹²The Lord says,

"A lion might attack a lamb,
  and a shepherd might try to save the lamb.
But the shepherd will save
  only a part of that lamb.
He might pull two legs
  or a part of an ear
  from the lion's mouth.
In the same way,
  most of the people of Israel
  will not be saved.
The people living in Samaria
  will save only a corner from a bed,
  or a piece of cloth from a couch."

¹³My Master, the Lord God All-Powerful, says these things: "Warn Jacob's family (Israel) about these things. ¹⁴Israel sinned, and I will punish them for their sins. I will also destroy the altars* at Bethel.* The horns of the altar* will be cut off and fall to the ground. ¹⁵I will destroy the winter house with the summer house. The houses of ivory will be destroyed. Many houses will be destroyed." The Lord said those things.

The Women That Love Pleasure

4 Listen to me, you cows of Bashan* on Samaria's mountain. You hurt poor people. You crush those poor people. You tell your husbands,* "Bring us something to drink!"

²The Lord my Master made a promise. He promised by his holiness, that troubles will come to you. People will use hooks and take you away as prisoners. They will use fishhooks to take away your children. ³₍Your city will be destroyed.₎ The

---

altar(s) A stone table used for offering sacrifices to God.
Bethel A town in Israel. This name means "God's house."
horns of the altar The corners of the altars were made in the shape of horns. These were important parts of the altar.
cows of Bashan This means the wealthy women in Samaria. Bashan was a place east of the Jordan River. It was famous for its big bulls and cows.
your husbands Literally, "their masters."

Nazirite(s) A person that has made a special promise to God. This name is from the Hebrew word meaning "to separate from."
prophesy To speak for God.
Ashdod Another important city of the Philistines.

women will rush out through cracks in the wall and throw themselves onto the pile {of dead bodies}.*

The Lord says this. ⁴"Go to Bethel and sin! Go to Gilgal* and sin even more. Offer your sacrifices in the morning. Bring a tenth of your crops for the three-day holiday. ⁵And offer a thank offering made with yeast. Tell everyone about the freewill offerings.* Israel, you love to do those things. So go and do them." The Lord said ₍this.₎

⁶"₍I did many things to try to make you come to me.₎ I didn't give you any food to eat.* There was no food in any of your cities. But you didn't come back to me." The Lord said those things.

⁷"I also stopped the rain—and it was three months before harvest time. So no crops grew. Then I let it rain on one city, but not on another city. Rain fell on one part of the country. But on the other part of the country, the land became very dry. ⁸So the people from two or three cities staggered to another city to get water—but there was not enough water for every person. Still you didn't come to me for help." The Lord said those things.

⁹"I made your crops die from heat and disease. I destroyed your gardens and your fields of grapes. Locusts* ate your fig trees and olive trees. But you still didn't come to me ₍for help₎." The Lord said those things.

¹⁰"I sent diseases against you, like I did to Egypt. I killed your young men with swords. I took away your horses. I made your camp smell very bad ₍from all the dead bodies₎. But still you didn't come back to me ₍for help₎." The Lord said those things.

¹¹"I destroyed you like I destroyed Sodom and Gomorrah.* And those cities were completely destroyed. You were like a burnt stick pulled from a fire. But still you didn't come back to me ₍for help₎." The Lord said those things.

¹²"So I will do these things to you, Israel. I will do this to you. Israel, prepare to meet your God! ¹³₍Who am I?₎ I am the One who made the mountains. I created your minds.* I taught people how to speak and I changed the darkness into dawn. I walk over the mountains of the earth. ₍Who am I?₎ My name is Yahweh, God of the armies."*

A Sad Song for Israel

5 People of Israel, listen to this song. This funeral song is about you.

² The virgin* of Israel has fallen.
   She will not get up any more.
   She was left alone, lying in the dirt.
   There is no person to lift her up.

³The Lord my Master says these things:

   "Officers leaving the city with 1,000 men,
      will return with only 100 men.
   Officers leaving the city with 100 men,
      will return with only ten men.

The Lord Encourages Israel to Come Back

⁴ The Lord says this to the nation* of Israel:
   "Come looking for me and live.
⁵ But don't look in Bethel.
   Don't go to Gilgal.
   Don't cross the border
      and go down to Beersheba.*

---

throw ... dead bodies Or, "You will be thrown away. People will take you to Mount Hermon." The Hebrew is hard to understand. It is not clear if the women will be "thrown away" or if the women will be "throwing something away."

Bethel ... Gilgal Places of worship for the people of Israel. God wanted the people of Israel and the people of Judah to worship him only in the temple at Jerusalem.

Offer your sacrifices ... freewill offerings All of these things were against the Law of Moses. The leaders and false priests started these new holidays and different ways of worshiping God.

I didn't give you any food to eat Literally, "I gave you clean teeth."

Locusts Insects like grasshoppers that could destroy a large crop very quickly.

Sodom and Gomorrah Two cities that God destroyed because the people were very evil.

your minds Or, "the wind."

Yahweh, God of the armies This is like the name that is usually translated, "Lord All-Powerful."

virgin The Hebrew word can mean "a woman that has not had sexual relations with anyone," "bride," or "fiancee." Here it means the city Samaria.

nation Literally, "house." This might mean the royal family of that country.

Bethel, Gilgal, Beersheba These were ancient places of worship. Abraham and Jacob built altars in these places. But God had told the people of Israel that they should go to the temple in Jerusalem to worship him.

The people of Gilgal will be taken away
as prisoners.*
And Bethel will be destroyed.*
6 Go to the Lord, and live.
If you don't go to the Lord,
then a fire will start at Joseph's house.*
That fire will destroy Joseph's house,
and no person will be able to stop
that fire at Bethel.
7-9 ₎You should go to the Lord for help.₎
God made the Pleiades and Orion.*
He changes darkness into the morning light.
He changes the day into the dark night.
He calls for the waters of the sea,
and pours them out on the earth.
His name is Yahweh!*
He keeps one strong city safe,
and he lets another strong city
be destroyed."

The Evil Things That the Israelites Did

You change goodness to poison.*
You killed justice,
and let it fall to the ground.
10 ₎Prophets₎ go to the public places
and speak against ₎the bad things people
are doing₎.
And the people hate ₎those prophets₎.
₎The prophets₎ teach good, simple truths.
And the people hate those ₎prophets₎.
11 You take unfair taxes* from poor people.
You take loads of wheat from them.
You build fancy houses with cut stone.
But you will not live in those houses.
You plant beautiful fields of grapes.
But you will not drink the wine from them.

taken away as prisoners In Hebrew this sounds like the name "Gilgal."
destroyed The Hebrew word is like the name "Beth Aven." This name means "House of Wickedness." The prophets often used this name for Bethel.
Joseph's house Here this means the ten-family-group nation of Israel. Joseph was the ancestor of the family groups of Ephraim and Manasseh in Israel.
Pleiades and Orion Two well-known groups of stars {(constellations)}.
Yahweh This name is usually translated, "Lord."
poison Literally, "wormwood," a type of plant with bitter leaves. It could be used as a medicine, or if strong enough, as a poison.
take unfair taxes We are not sure of the exact meaning of this Hebrew word.

12 Why? Because I know about your many sins.
You have done some really bad things.
You hurt people that do right.
You accept money to do wrong.
You keep justice from the poor people
in court.
13 At that time, wise teachers will be quiet.
Why? Because it is a bad time.
14 You say ₎that God is with you₎.
So you should do good things, not evil.
Then you will live.
And the Lord God All-Powerful
really will be with you.
15 Hate evil and love goodness.
Bring fairness back into the courts.
Maybe then the Lord God All-Powerful
will be kind to the survivors*
from Joseph's family.

A Time of Great Sadness Is Coming

16 My Master, God All-Powerful, says,
"People will be crying in the public places.
People will be crying in the streets.
People will hire the professional criers.*
17 People will be crying in the fields of grapes.
Why? Because I will pass through
₎and punish₎ you."
The Lord said those things.
18 Some of you want ₎to see₎
the Lord's special day ₎of judgment₎.
Why do you want ₎to see₎ that day?
The Lord's special day will bring darkness
not light!
19 You will be like a man
that escapes a lion
only to be attacked by a bear!
You will be like a man
that goes into the safety of his house,
leans against the wall,
and is bitten by a snake!
20 The Lord's special day will be
₎a day of sadness, not joy₎
a day of darkness, not light,
a day of gloom, without a glimmer of light.

survivor(s) People that escaped some disaster. Here this means the Jewish people that survived the destruction of Judah and Israel by its enemy armies.
professional criers People that went to funerals and cried loudly for the dead people. Families and friends of the dead person often gave food or money to these people.

The Lord Rejects Israel's Worship

21 "I hate your holidays!
  I will not accept them!
  I don't enjoy your religious meetings!
22 Even if you offer me burnt offerings
    and grain offerings,
  I will not accept them!
  I will not even look at the fat animals
    you give as fellowship offerings.
23 Take your noisy songs away from here.
  I will not listen to the music
    from your harps.
24 You should let fairness flow like water
    ⌊through your country⌋.
  Let goodness flow like a stream
    that never becomes dry.
25 Israel, you offered me sacrifices
    and offerings in the desert for 40 years.*
26 But you also carried statues
    of Sakkuth, your king, and Kaiwan.*
  And you made yourselves
    that star for your god!*
27 So I will cause you to be taken captive
    beyond Damascus."
  The Lord says those things.
  His name is God All-Powerful.

Good Times Will Be Taken Away from Israel

6 Oh, it will be very bad
    for you people taking it easy in Zion.*
  and for you people who feel so safe on
    Mount Samaria.
  You are "important" leaders
    of the most important nation!
  The "House of Israel"
    comes to you ⌊for advice⌋!

2 Go look at Calneh.*
  From there, go to the large city Hamath.*
  Go to the Philistine city Gath.
  Are you better than these kingdoms? No.
  Their countries are larger than yours.
3 You people are rushing towards
    that day of punishment.
  You bring that rule of violence
    nearer and nearer.
4 ⌊But now, you enjoy all the comforts.⌋
  You lie on ivory beds,
    and stretch out on your couches.
  You eat tender young lambs from the flock,
    and young calves from the stable.
5 You play your harps.
  And like David, you practice on*
    your musical instruments.
6 You drink wine in fancy cups.*
  You use the best perfumes.
  And you are not even upset that Joseph's
    family is being destroyed."

⁷Those people are stretched out on their couches now. But their good times will end. They will be taken away like prisoners to a foreign country. And they will be some of the first people taken. ⁸The Lord my Master used his own name and made a promise. The Lord God All-Powerful made this promise:

  "I hate the things that Jacob* is proud of.
  I hate his strong towers.
  So I will let ⌊the enemy⌋ take the city
    and everything in it."

There Will Be Few Israelites Left Alive

⁹At that time, even if ten people in one house survive, they will die. ¹⁰And when a person dies, a relative will come to get the body so he can take it out and burn it.* The relative will come to take away the bones. He will call to any person who might be hiding way back in the house, "Are there any other ⌊dead bodies⌋ in there with you?"

Israel ... 40 years Or, "Israel, did you offer me sacrifices and offerings in the desert for 40 years? No!"
Sakkuth ... Kaiwan These were names of Assyrian gods.
star for your god This might be to honor a special god or all the stars in the sky. Many people thought the sun, moon, stars, and planets were gods or angels. This verse might also be translated, "You carried the shelter for your king and the footstool for your idols—the star of your gods which you made for yourselves." The ancient Greek translation gives the names Moloch and Raphan.
Zion The southeast part of the mountain Jerusalem is built on. Sometimes it means the people of God living in Jerusalem.

Calneh A powerful city in northern Syria.
Hamath A powerful city in Syria.
practice on Or, "invent." The Hebrew word means to "think," "become skilled," or "design."
fancy cups Very large bowls used in worship rituals.
Jacob Another name for Israel. See Gen. 32:22-28.
And when a person dies ... burn it The exact meaning of the Hebrew is not clear here.

That person will answer, "No, ... "*
But the relative will ⌊interrupt him and⌋ say, "Hush! We must not mention the name of the Lord."

11 Look, the Lord God will give the command,
and the large houses
will be broken to pieces,
and the small houses
will be broken to small pieces.
12 Do horses run oover rocks? No!
and people don;t use cows for plowing.
But you people turn everything upside down.
You changed goodness to poison.
You changed fairness to bitter poison.
13 You are happy in Lo-Debar;*
You say,
"We have taken Karnaim*
by our own strength."

14 "But Israel, I will bring a nation against you. That nation will bring troubles to your whole country—all the way from Lebo-Hamath to Arabah Brook." The Lord God All-Powerful said those things.

The Vision of the Locusts

7 The Lord showed this to me: He was making locusts* at the time the second crop began growing. It was the second crop after the king's cutting ⌊of the first crop⌋. ²The locusts ate all the grass in the country. After that I said, "Lord my Master, I beg you, forgive us! Jacob* can't survive! He is ⌊too⌋ small!" ³Then the Lord changed his mind about this. The Lord said, "That thing will not happen."

The Vision of the Fire

⁴The Lord my Master showed these things to me: ⌊I⌋ saw the Lord God calling for judgment by fire. The fire destroyed the Great Deep. The fire was beginning to eat up the land. ⁵But I said, "Lord God, stop, I beg you! Jacob* can't survive! He is ⌊too⌋ small!"

No, ... This answer might have been, "No, bless the Lord." But the person was stopped before he finished speaking.
Lo-Debar A place name, meaning "nothing."
Karnaim Another place name, meaning "horns." Horns are often a symbol *(picture)* for strength.
locusts Insects like grasshoppers that could destroy a large crop very quickly.
Jacob Another name for Israel. See Gen. 32:22-28.

⁶Then the Lord changed his mind about this. The Lord God said, "That thing will not happen either."

The Vision of the Plumbline

⁷The Lord showed me this: The Lord stood by a wall with a plumbline* in his hand. (The wall had been marked with a plumbline.) ⁸The Lord said to me, "Amos, what do you see?"
I said, "A plumbline."
Then my Master said, "See, I will put a plumbline among my people Israel. I will not let their 'crookedness' pass inspection any more. ⌊I will remove those bad spots.⌋ ⁹Isaac's high places* will be destroyed. Israel's holy places will be made into a pile of rocks. I will attack and kill Jeroboam's* family with swords."

Amaziah Tries to Stop Amos

¹⁰Amaziah, a priest at Bethel,* sent this message to Jeroboam, the king of Israel: "Amos is making plans against you. He is trying to make the people of Israel fight against you. ⌊He has been speaking so much that⌋ this country can't hold all his words. ¹¹Amos has said, 'Jeroboam will die by the sword, and the people of Israel will be taken as prisoners out of their country.'"
¹²Amaziah also said to Amos, "You seer,* go down to Judah and eat there.* Do your preaching there. ¹³But don't prophesy* any more here at Bethel! This is Jeroboam's holy place. This is Israel's temple!"
¹⁴Then Amos answered Amaziah, "I am not a professional prophet. And I am not from a prophet's family. I keep cattle and take care of sycamore trees. ¹⁵⌊I was a shepherd⌋ and the Lord

---

plumbline A string with a weight on one end. Workers used plumblines to make sure the walls they were building were straight. The workers often put paint on the string and popped the string. This left a straight line of paint on the wall. Then the workers chipped away the crooked part of the wall.
high places Places for worshiping God or false gods. These places were often on the hills and mountains.
Jeroboam's The king of Israel. See verse 10.
Bethel A town in Israel. This name means "God's house."
seer This is another name for a prophet. See 1 Samuel 9:9-11.
eat there This shows that Amaziah thought that Amos was a professional prophet. He thought he preached to receive food or money.
prophesy To speak for God.

took me from following the sheep. The Lord said to me, 'Go, prophesy to my people Israel.' ¹⁶So listen to the Lord's message. You tell me, 'Don't prophesy* against Israel. Don't preach against Isaac's family.' ¹⁷But the Lord says: 'Your wife will become a prostitute* in the city. Your sons and daughters will be killed with swords. Other people will take your land and divide it among themselves. And you will die in a foreign* country. The people of Israel will definitely be taken from this country as prisoners.'"

The Vision of the Ripe Fruit

8 The Lord showed me this: ⌊I⌋ saw a basket of summer fruit. ²The Lord said to me, "Amos, what do you see?"

I said, "A basket of summer fruit."

Then the Lord said to me, "The end* has come to my people Israel. I will not overlook their sins any more. ³The temple* songs will become sad funeral songs. The Lord my Master said those things. There will be dead bodies everywhere. In silence, people will take out the dead bodies and throw them {onto the pile}."*

Israel's Businessmen Are Interested Only in Making Money

⁴ Listen to me!
You people walk on helpless people.
You are trying to destroy the poor people
of this country.
⁵ You businessmen say,
"When will the New Moon* be over
so we can sell grain?
When will the Sabbath be over
so we can bring our wheat ⌊to sell⌋?
We can raise the price
and make the measure smaller.*
We can adjust the scales
and cheat the people.*
⁶ ⌊The poor people can't pay their loans,⌋
so we will buy them as slaves.
We will buy those helpless people
for the price of a pair of shoes.
Oh, and we can sell the wheat
that was spilled on the floor."

⁷The Lord made a promise. He used his name, Pride of Jacob, and made this promise:

"I will never forget the things
that those people did.
⁸ The whole land will shake
because of those things.
Every person that lives in the land
will cry for people that died.
The whole land will rise and fall
like the Nile River in Egypt.
The land will be tossed around."

⁹ The Lord also said these things:
"At that time I will cause the sun
to go down at noon.
I will make the earth dark on a clear day.
¹⁰ I will change your holidays
into days of crying for the dead.
All your songs will be songs of sadness
for dead people.
I will put clothes of sadness on everyone.
I will make every head bald.*
I will make it like heavy crying
for an only son that has died.
It will be a very bitter end."

A Terrible Time of Hunger for God's Word Is Coming

¹¹The Lord says:

"Look, the days are coming when I will cause a
time of hunger in the land.
The people will not be hungry for bread.
The people will not be thirsty for water.
No, the people will be hungry
for words from the Lord.

---

prostitute A woman paid by men for sexual sin. Sometimes this also means a person that is not faithful to God and stops following him.
foreign Literally, "unclean."
end This Hebrew word sounds like the word for "summer fruit."
temple The special building in Jerusalem for Jewish worship.
In silence ... the pile Or, "People will be saying, 'Hush!'" See Amos 6:10.
New Moon This was the first day of the Hebrew month. There were special meetings on these days to worship God.

We ... smaller Literally "We will make the ephah small and the shekel large."
We ... people Literally, "Cheat with lying balances."
head bald People often cut their hair to show they were very sad or upset.

¹² The people will wander around the country,
    from the Dead Sea
      to the Mediterranean Sea,
    and from the north part of the country,
      to the east.
  The people will go back and forth
    looking for a message from the Lord.
  But they will not find it.
¹³ At that time,
    the beautiful young men and women
      will become weak from thirst.
  Those people made promises
    by the sin of Samaria,*
  They said,
    'Dan,* as surely as your god lives,
      ⌊we promise⌋ ... '
  And they said,
    'As surely as the god of Beersheba* lives,
      ⌊we promise⌋ ... '
  But those people will fall,
    and they will never get up again."

Vision of the Lord Standing by the Altar

9 I saw my Master standing by the altar.* He said,

  "Hit the top of the columns,
    and the building will shake
      all the way down to the thresholds*
  Make the columns fall on the peoples' heads.
    If any people are left alive,
      then I will kill them with a sword.
  A person might run away,
    but he will not escape.
  Not one of the people will escape.
² If they dig deep into the ground,*
    I will pull them from there.
  If they go up into the skies,*
    I will bring them down from there.
³ If they hide at the top of Mount Carmel,*
    I will find them there,
      and I will take them from that place.

  If they try to hide from me
    at the bottom of the sea,
  I will command the snake,
    and it will bite them.
⁴ If they are captured
    and taken away by their enemies,
  I will command the sword,
    and it will kill them there.
  Yes, I will watch over them,
    but I will watch for ways
      to give them troubles,
    not for ways to do good things."

Punishment Will Destroy the People

⁵ My Master, the Lord All-Powerful,
    will touch the land,
      and the land will melt.
  Then all the people that live in the land
    will cry for the dead people.
  The land will rise and fall
    like the Nile River in Egypt.
⁶ The Lord built his upper rooms
    above the skies.
  He put his skies* over the earth.
  He calls for the waters of the sea,
    and pours them out ⌊as rain⌋ on the land.
  Yahweh* is his name.

The Lord Promises Destruction for Israel

⁷The Lord says this:

  "Israel, you are like the Ethiopians to me.
  I brought Israel out of the land of Egypt.
  I brought the Philistines from Caphtor,*
    and the Aramean people from Kir.*"

⁸ The Lord my Master is watching
    the sinful kingdom *(Israel)*.
  The Lord said,
    "I will wipe Israel off the face of the earth.
  But I will not completely destroy
    Jacob's family.
⁹ I am giving the command
    ⌊to destroy the nation Israel⌋.
  I will scatter the people of Israel
    among all nations.

---

sin of Samaria The calf god in Samaria.
Dan One of Israel's holy places was in this city.
Beersheba A town in Judah. This name means "well of the oath (promise)."
altar(s) A stone table used for offering sacrifices to God.
thresholds The wood or stone under the door.
ground Literally, "Sheol, the place of the dead."
skies Or "heaven."
Mount Carmel A hill in north Israel very good for growing plants. This name means "God's vineyard."

skies Literally, "dome, vault."
Yahweh This Hebrew name for God is usually translated "Lord." This name is like the Hebrew word meaning "He is" or "He makes things exist."
Caphtor This might be Crete or Cyprus.
Kir A place of exile for the Aramean people. We are not sure where Kir was.

But it will be like a person ₍sifting flour₎.
A person shakes flour through a sifter.*
  ₍The good flour falls through₎
    but the bad lumps are caught.
  ₍It will be that way with Jacob's family.₎
¹⁰ Sinners among my people say,
    'Nothing bad will happen to us!'
  But all those people will be killed with
    swords!"

God Promises to Restore the Kingdom

¹¹ "David's tent* has fallen,
    but at that time, I will set his tent up again.
  I will fix the holes in the walls.
  I will build the ruined buildings again.
  I will build it like it was before.
¹²* Then the people left alive in Edom,
    and all the people called by my name,
    will look to the Lord ₍for help₎."
  The Lord said those things,
    and he will make them happen.
¹³ The Lord says,
  "The time is coming when
    the person plowing the field,
    will catch up with the person
    harvesting the crops.
  The person that walks on the grapes,
    will catch up with the person
    that pulls the grapes from the plants.
  The sweet wine will pour
    from the hills and mountains.
¹⁴ I will bring my people, Israel,
    back from captivity.
  They will build the ruined cities again.
    And they will live in those cities.
  They will plant fields of grapes,
    and they will drink the wine
    that comes from them.
  They will plant gardens,
    and they will eat the crops
    that come from them.
¹⁵ I will plant my people on their land,
    and they will not be pulled out again
    from the land that I have given them."
  The Lord your God said these things.

---

sifter Something like a cup with a screen on its bottom. A sifter is used for removing large lumps from the good flour.
David's tent This probably means the city Jerusalem or the country Judah.
Verse 12 This is from the ancient Greek translation. The Hebrew has, "Then they will take the people that are left in Edom and the other nations that are called by my name."

Obadiah

Edom Will Be Punished

This is the vision* of Obadiah. The Lord my Master says this about Edom:*

We heard a report from the Lord God.
A messenger was sent to the nations.
He said,
"Let's go fight against Edom."

The Lord Speaks to Edom

2 "Edom, I will make you the smallest nation.
  Everyone will hate you very much.
3 Your pride has fooled you.
  You live in those caves high on the cliff.
  Your home is high in the hills.
So you say to yourself,
  'No one can bring me to the ground.'"

Edom Will Be Brought Low

4 The Lord God says this:
"Even though you fly high like the eagle
  and put your nest among the stars,
  I will bring you down from there."
5 You really will be ruined!
  Thieves will come to you!
  Robbers will come in the night!
  And those thieves will take all they want!
  When workers gather grapes in your fields,
    they leave a few grapes behind.
6 But the enemy will search hard
    for Esau's hidden treasures.
  And they will find them all!
7 All the people that are your friends
    will force you out of the land.
  The people at peace with you
    will trick you and defeat you.

Your war buddies,
  are planning a trap for you.
₍They say₎
  'He doesn't expect a thing!'

8 The Lord says,
"On that day,
  I will destroy the wise people
    from Edom.*
  I will destroy the intelligent people
    from Esau's Mountain.*
9 Teman,* your mighty men will be scared.
  Every person will be destroyed
    from the mountain of Esau.*
10 Many, many people will be killed.
  You will be covered with shame,
    and you will be destroyed forever.
  Why? Because you were very cruel
    to your brother Jacob.*
11 You joined the enemies of Israel.
  Strangers carried Israel's treasures away.
  Foreigners entered Israel's ₍city₎ gate.
    Those foreigners threw lots* ₍to decide
    what part of₎ Jerusalem ₍they would get₎.
  And you were right there with them
    ₍waiting to get your share₎.
12 You laughed at* your brother's trouble.
  You should not have done that.
  You were happy when they destroyed Judah.
  You should not have done that.
  You bragged* at the time of their trouble.
  You should not have done that.

Esau's Mountain That is, Mount Seir.
Teman One of Edom's important cities in the south, maybe its capital.
mountain of Esau That is, Mount Seir.
Jacob Israel was Jacob's other name. (See Genesis 32:28.) Jacob is often used to mean Israel, the nation that descended from him.
lot(s) Sticks, stones, or pieces of bone used like dice for making decisions. See Prov. 16:33.
laughed at Literally, "looked at."
bragged Literally, "made your mouth big."

vision Something like a dream that God used to speak to people.
Edom A country southeast of Judah. The people of Edom are descendants of Esau, Jacob's twin brother. They were enemies of the Israelites.

¹³ You entered the city gate of my people,
and laughed at* their problems.
You should not have done that.
At the time of their trouble,
you took their treasures.
You should not have done that.
¹⁴ You stood where the roads cross,
and destroyed the people
that were trying to escape.
You should not have done that.
You captured the people that escaped alive.
You should not have done that.
¹⁵ The Day of the Lord is soon coming
to all the nations.
And the bad things you did to other people
will happen to you.
Those same bad things
will come falling onto your own head.
¹⁶ Why? Because you spilled* blood
on my holy mountain.*
So other nations will spill your blood.*
You will be finished.
It will be like you never existed.
¹⁷ But there will be survivors* on Mount Zion.*
They will be my special people.
The nation of Jacob* will take back
the things that belong to it.

¹⁸ The family of Jacob will be like a fire.
The nation of Joseph will be like a flame.
But the nation of Esau* ₗwill be likeⱼ ashes.
The people of Judah will burn Edom.
The people of Judah will destroy Edom.
Then there will be no survivors
in the nation of Esau.
Why? Because the Lord God has said it.
¹⁹ Then people from the Negev*
will live on the mountain of Esau.
And people from the foothills
will take the Philistine ₗlandsⱼ.
Those people will live
in the land of Ephraim and Samaria.
Gilead will belong to Benjamin.
²⁰ People from Israel were forced
to leave ₗtheir homesⱼ.
But those people will take the land Canaan
ₗall the way toⱼ Zarephath.
People from Judah were forced
to leave Jerusalem
and go to live in Sepharad.
But they will take the cities of the Negev.*
²¹ The Winners* will go up onto Mount Zion*
to rule the people living on
Esau's mountain.
And the kingdom will belong to the Lord.

---

laughed at Literally, "looked at."
spilled Literally, "drank."
holy mountain, Mount Zion One of the mountains Jerusalem was built on. Sometimes Zion is used to mean Jerusalem itself.
spill your blood Literally, "drink and swallow."
holy mountain, Mount Zion One of the mountains Jerusalem was built on. Sometimes Zion is used to mean Jerusalem itself.
survivors People who escape and live through an accident or a war.
nation of Jacob Literally, "the house of Jacob." This could mean the people of Israel, or the leaders.

nation of Esau Literally, "the house of Esau."
Negev The desert area south of Judah.
Winners Or "Saviors." People that led their people to victory in war.

Jonah

God Calls and Jonah Runs

1 The Lord spoke to Jonah* son of Amittai. The Lord said, ²"Nineveh* is a big city. I have heard about the many evil things people are doing there. So go to that city and tell the people to stop doing those bad things."

³Jonah did not want to obey God, so Jonah tried to run away from the Lord. Jonah went to Joppa.* Jonah found a boat that was going to the faraway city of Tarshish.* Jonah paid money for the trip and went on the boat. Jonah wanted to travel with the people on this boat to Tarshish and run away from the Lord.

The Great Storm

⁴But the Lord brought a great storm on the sea. The wind made the sea very rough. The storm was very strong and the boat was ready to break apart. ⁵The men wanted to make the boat lighter to stop it from sinking. So they began throwing the cargo* into the sea. The sailors were very scared. Each man began praying to his god.

Jonah had gone down into the boat to lie down. Jonah was sleeping. ⁶The captain of the boat saw Jonah and said, "Wake up! Why are you sleeping? Pray to your god! Maybe your god will hear your prayer and save us!"

What Caused This Storm?

⁷Then the men said to each other, "We should throw lots* to learn why these troubles are happening to us."

So the men threw lots. The lots showed that the trouble happened because of Jonah. ⁸Then the men said to Jonah, "It is your fault that this terrible thing is happening to us! So tell us what you have done? What is your job? Where are you coming from? What is your country? Who are your people?"

⁹Jonah said to the men, "I am a Hebrew *(Jew)*. And I worship the Lord, the God of heaven. He is the God who made the sea and the land."

¹⁰Jonah told the men he was running away from the Lord. The men became very scared when they learned this. The men asked Jonah, "What terrible thing did you do against your God?"

¹¹The wind and the waves of the sea were becoming stronger and stronger. So the men said to Jonah, "What should we do to save ourselves? What should we do to you to make the sea calm?"

¹²Jonah said to the men, "I know I did wrong—that is why the storm came on the sea. So throw me into the sea, and the sea will become calm."

¹³But the men did not want to throw Jonah into the sea. The men tried to row the ship back to the shore, but they were not able to. The wind and the waves of the sea were too strong—and they were becoming stronger and stronger!

Jonah's Punishment

¹⁴So the men cried to the Lord, "Lord, we are throwing this man into the sea because of the bad things he did. Please don't say we are guilty of killing an innocent man. Please don't make us die for killing him. We know you are the Lord, and

---

Jonah This is probably the same prophet mentioned in 2 Kings 14:25.
Nineveh The capital of Assyria. The Assyrian army destroyed north Israel in 723—721 B.C.
Joppa A town on the coast of Israel by the Mediterranean Sea.
Tarshish This is probably a city in Spain. This was as far west as Jonah could travel. Nineveh was east of Israel.
cargo The Hebrew word can mean "dishes, jars, or tools." Here this could mean all the jars and boxes the boat carried on its way to Tarshish or the rigging and other heavy tools on the boat.

lots Small rocks, sticks, or pieces of bone used like dice. Lots were used for making a choice or decision. See Proverbs 16:33.

you will do whatever you want. ₍But please be kind to us.₎"
¹⁵So the men threw Jonah into the sea. The storm stopped—the sea became calm! ¹⁶When the men saw this, they began to fear and respect the Lord. The men offered a sacrifice* and made special promises to the Lord.
¹⁷When Jonah fell into the sea, the Lord chose a very big fish to go and swallow Jonah. Jonah was in the fish's stomach for three days and three nights.

2 While Jonah was in the fish's stomach, he prayed to the Lord his God. Jonah said,

² "I was in very bad trouble.
   I called to the Lord for help,
       and he answered me!
   I was deep in the grave.*
   I cried to you, Lord,
       and you heard my voice!
³ "You threw me into the sea.
   Your powerful waves splashed over me.
   I went down, down into the deep sea.
   The water was all around me.
⁴ Then I thought,
   'Now I must go where you cannot see me.'
   But I continued looking to your holy
       temple* for help.
⁵ "The seawater closed over me.
   The water covered my mouth,
       and I could not breathe.*
   I went down, down into the deep sea.
   Seaweed wrapped around my head.
⁶ I was at the bottom of the sea,
       the place where mountains begin.
   I thought I was locked in this prison forever.
   But the Lord my God took me out of
       my grave!
   God, you gave me life again!
⁷ "My soul gave up all hope.
   But then I remembered the Lord.
   Lord, I prayed to you.
   And you heard my prayers in your
       holy temple.*

---
sacrifice(s) Offerings or gifts to God. Usually these were animals that were killed and burned on an altar.
grave Or, "Sheol," the place where dead people go.
temple The special building in Jerusalem where God wanted Jews to go to worship him.
mouth, and I could not breathe Or, "The water surrounded me to my soul." The Hebrew word for soul also means "life, self, appetite," and "throat or mouth."

⁸ "Some people worship useless idols.
   But those statues never help them.*
⁹ Salvation comes only from the Lord!
   "Lord, I will give sacrifices to you,
       and I will praise and thank you.
   I will make special promises to you,
       and I will do the things I promise."

¹⁰Then the Lord spoke to the fish. And the fish vomited Jonah out of its stomach onto the dry land.

God Calls and Jonah Obeys

3 Then the Lord spoke to Jonah again. The Lord said, ²"Go to that big city Nineveh, and preach the things that I tell you."
³So Jonah obeyed the Lord and went to Nineveh. Nineveh was a very big city. A person had to walk for three days to travel through the city.
⁴Jonah went to the center of the city and began preaching to the people. Jonah said, "After 40 days, Nineveh will be destroyed!"
⁵The people of Nineveh believed ₍the message from₎ God. The people decided to stop eating for a time ₍to think about their sins₎. The people put on special clothes ₍to show that they were sorry₎. All the people in the city did this—the most important people and the least important people.
⁶The king of Nineveh heard about these things. And the king was also sorry for the bad things he did. So the king left his throne.* The king removed his robe and put on special clothes ₍to show he was sorry₎. Then the king sat in ashes.* ⁷The king wrote a special message. The king sent this message through the city:

A command from the king and his great rulers:
   For a short time no man or animal should eat anything. No herd or flock will be allowed in the fields. Nothing living in Nineveh will eat or drink water. ⁸But every person and every animal must be covered with a special cloth ₍to show he is sad₎. People must cry loudly to God. Every

---
Some people ... them Or, "People that worship useless things have left the One who is kind to them."
throne The special chair a king or queen sits on.
sat in ashes People did this to show they were sad.

person must change his life and stop doing bad things. ⁹Then maybe God will change and not do the things he had planned. Maybe God will change and not be angry. Then maybe we will not be punished.

¹⁰God saw the things the people did. God saw that the people stopped doing evil things. So God changed and did not do what he planned. God did not punish the people.

God's Mercy Makes Jonah Angry

4 Jonah was not happy that God saved the city. Jonah became angry. ²Jonah complained to the Lord and said, "I knew this would happen! I was in my own country, and you told me to come here. At that time, I knew that you would forgive the people of this evil city. So I decided to run away to Tarshish. I knew that you are a kind God! I knew that you show mercy and don't want to punish people! I knew that you are full of kindness! I knew that if these people stopped sinning, you would change your plans to destroy them. ³So now I ask you, Lord, please kill me. It is better for me to die than to live!"

⁴Then the Lord said, "Do you think it is right for you to be angry just because I did not destroy those people?"

⁵ⱼJonah was still angry about all these things.ⱼ So he went out of the city. Jonah went to a place near the city on the east side. Jonah made a shelter for himself. Then he sat there in the shade, waiting to see what would happen to the city.

The Gourd Plant and the Worm

⁶The Lord made a gourd plant grow quickly over Jonah. This made a cool place for Jonah to sit. This helped Jonah to be more comfortable. Jonah was very happy because of this plant.

⁷The next morning, God sent a worm to eat part of the plant. The worm began eating the plant and the plant died.

⁸After the sun was high in the sky, God caused a hot east wind to blow. The sun became very hot on Jonah's head and Jonah became very, very weak. Jonah asked God to let him die. Jonah said, "It is better for me to die than to live."

⁹But God said to Jonah, "Do you think it is right for you to be angry just because this plant died?"

Jonah answered, "Yes, it is right for me to be angry! I am angry enough to die!"

¹⁰And the Lord said, "You did nothing for that plant! You did not make it grow. It grew up in the night, and the next day it died. And now you are sad about that plant. ¹¹ⱼIf you can be upset about a plant,ⱼ then surely I can feel sorry for a big city like Nineveh. There are many people and animals in that city. There are more than 120,000 people in that city that did not know they were doing wrong!*"

---

people ... wrong Literally, "People that do not know their right from their left." This might mean "innocent children."

Micah

Samaria and Israel to Be Punished

1 The word of the Lord came to Micah. This was during the time of kings Jotham, Ahaz, and Hezekiah. These men were kings of Judah. Micah was from Moresheth. Micah saw ⌊these visions⌋ about Samaria and Jerusalem.

2 Listen, all of you people!
  Earth and everyone on it,* listen!
 My Master, the Lord will come
  from his holy temple.*
 My Master will come as a witness*
  against you.
3 See, the Lord is coming out of his place.
 He is coming down to walk on
  the high places* of the earth.
4 The mountains will melt under him
  like wax before a fire.
 The valleys will split open
  and flow like water down a steep hill.
5 Why? Because of Jacob's* sin.
  Because of the sins of the nation* of Israel.

Samaria, the Cause of Sin

What caused Jacob to sin?
 It was Samaria!
Where is the high place* in Judah?
 It is Jerusalem!
6 So I will change Samaria into
  a pile of rocks in the field,
  a place ready for planting grapes.
 I will push Samaria's stones down
  into the valley, leaving nothing
   but the foundations!
7 All her idols*
  will be broken into pieces.
 Her prostitute's wages *(idols)*
  will be burned in fire.
 I will destroy all her statues
  ⌊of false gods⌋.
 Why? Because Samaria got her riches
  by being unfaithful to me.*
 So those things will be taken by people
  that are not faithful to me.*

Micah's Great Sadness

8 I will be very sad about what will happen.
 I will go without shoes and clothes.
 I will cry like a dog.*
 I will mourn like a bird.*
9 Samaria's* wound can't be healed.
 Her disease *(sin)* has spread to Judah.
 It has reached the city gate of my people.
 It has spread all the way to Jerusalem.
10 Don't tell it in Gath.*
 Don't cry in Acco.*
 Roll yourself in the dust at Beth Ophrah.*

---

everyone on it Literally, "its fullness."
temple The special building in Jerusalem for Jewish worship.
witness A person that tells in court what he has seen or heard.
high places Here this might simply mean "hills" or it might be the places for worshiping God or false gods. These places were often on the hills and mountains.
Jacob Israel was Jacob's other name. (See Gen. 32:28.) Jacob is often used to mean Israel, the nation that descended from him.
nation Literally, "house." This might mean the royal family of that country.
high place(s) This might simply mean "hill" or it might be a place for worshiping God or false gods. These places were often on the hills and mountains.
idols Statues of false gods that people worshiped.
her riches ... me Literally, "her wages were a prostitute's wages."
will be ... me Literally, "will return to prostitute's wages."
dog Literally, "jackal", a kind of wild dog.
bird Literally, "ostrich", a large bird.
Samaria The capital of the northern ten-family group kingdom of Israel. Here it is often used to mean the northern kingdom itself.
Gath This is a word play. This name means, "tell."
Acco This name means, "cry."
Beth Ophrah This name means, "House of Dust."

¹¹ You people living in Shaphir,*
    pass on your way, naked and ashamed.
  People living in Zaanan* will not come out.
  The people in Beth Ezel* will cry,
    and take its support from you.
¹² People living in Maroth* become weak
    waiting for good ⌊news to come⌋.
  Why? Because trouble has come down
    from the Lord to the city gate of Jerusalem.
¹³ Lady of Lachish,* hitch *(tie)* a fast horse
    to the wagon.*
  Zion's sins started in Lachish.
  Why? Because you follow in Israel's sins.*
¹⁴ So you must give goodbye gifts
    to Moresheth* in Gath.
  The houses in Aczib* will trick
    the kings of Israel.
¹⁵ You people living in Mareshah,*
    I will bring a person against you.
  That person will take the things you own.
  The Glory of Israel *(God)*
    will come into Adullam.*
  So cut off your hair,
    make yourself bald.*
  Why? Because ⌊you will cry for⌋
    the children you love.
  Make yourself bald like an eagle*
    ⌊and show your sadness⌋.
  Why? Because your children
    will be taken away from you.

Shaphir This name means, "beautiful."
Zaanan This name means, "come out."
Beth Ezel This name means, "House of Support."
Maroth This name means, "bitter," "angry," or "sad."
Lachish In Hebrew this word sounds like the word meaning, "horse."
wagon Or, "chariot," a small wagon used in war.
Israel's sins That is, building places of worship other than the temple in Jerusalem. Archaeologists have discovered this "temple" and the memorial stones at Tel Lachish.
Moresheth Micah's home town.
Aczib This name means, "lie," or "trick."
Mareshah The name means, "a person that takes things."
Adullam A cave in which David hid when he ran away from Saul. (1 Samuel 22:1).
cut off your hair,
 make yourself bald This showed a person made a special agreement with God, or that a person was very sad.
eagle Or, "vulture."

The Evil Plans of People

2 Trouble will come to people
    that make plans to sin.
  Those people lie on their beds
    making their evil plans
  Then when the morning light comes,
    they do the bad things they planned.
  Why? Simply because they have the power
    to do what they want.
² They want fields,
    so they take them.
  They want houses,
    so they take them.
  They cheat a man
    and take his house.
  They cheat a man
    and take his land from him.

The Lord's Plans to Punish the People

³ That is why the Lord says these things.
  "Look, I am planning trouble
    against this family.
  You will not be able to save yourselves.*
  You will stop being proud.
  Why? Because bad times are coming.
⁴ Then people will sing songs about you.
  People will sing this sad song:
  "We are ruined!
  The Lord took away our land.
    And gave it to other people.
  Yes, he took my land away from me.
  The Lord has divided our fields
    ⌊among our enemies⌋."
⁵ So we will not be able
    to measure the land
    and divide it among the Lord's people.

Micah Is Asked Not to Preach

⁶ People say, "Don't preach to us.
    Don't say those bad things about us.
    Nothing bad will happen to us."

⁷ But people of Jacob,*
    I must say these things.
  The Lord is losing his patience
    because of the bad things you did.
  If you people lived right,
    then I could say nice words to you.
⁸ But to my people,
    they are like an enemy.

save yourselves Literally, "take your necks off it."
Jacob Another name for Israel. See Gen. 32:22-28.

You steal the clothes right off the backs
of people walking by.
Those people think they are safe.
But you ₎take things from them₎
like they are prisoners of war.*

9 You have taken nice houses
away from the women of my people.
You have taken my wealth
away from their small children forever
10 Get up and leave!
This will not be your place of rest.
Why? Because you ruined this place!
You made it unclean,
So it will be destroyed!
It will be a terrible destruction!

11 ₎These people don't want to listen to me.₎
But if a man came telling lies
then they would accept him.
They would accept a false prophet
if he comes and says,
"There will be good times in the future,
with plenty of wine and beer."

The Lord Will Bring His People Together

12 Yes, people of Jacob,*
I will bring all of you together.
I will bring together all the survivors*
of Israel.
I will put them together
like sheep in the sheep pen,
like a flock in its pasture.
Then the place will be filled
with the noise of many people.
13 Then the "Crasher" will push through
and walk to the front of his people
They will break through the gates.
and leave ₎that city₎.
They will leave
with their King marching before them.
with the Lord at the front of his people.

The Leaders of Israel Are Guilty of Evil

3 Then I said,
"Hear now, leaders of Jacob,*
and officers of the nation* of Israel.
You should know what justice is!

2 But you hate good and love evil!
You tear the skin off the people.
You tear the flesh off their bones!
3 You are destroying my people!*
You take their skin off them,
and break their bones.
You chop their bones up like ₎meat₎
to put in the pot!
4 So, you might pray to the Lord,
but he will not answer you.
No, the Lord will hide his face from you.
Why? Because you do evil things!"

False Prophets

⁵Some false prophets are telling lies to the Lord's people. The Lord says this about those prophets:

"These prophets are led by their stomachs!
The prophets promise peace
to people who give them food.
But they promise war
to people who won't give them food.

6 That is why it is like night for you.
That is why you don't have visions.*
You can't see what will happen
in the future,
so it is like darkness to you.
The sun has gone down on the prophets.
They can't see what will happen
in the future,
so it is like darkness to them.
7 The seers* are ashamed.
The fortune tellers* are embarrassed.
They won't say anything.
Why? Because God will not speak to them!

Micah Is an Honest Prophet of God

8 But the Lord's Spirit has filled me
with power, goodness, and strength.
Why? So I can tell Jacob* about his crimes,
and so I can tell Israel* about his sins!"

Those people ... war. Or, "Those people think they are safe, returning from war."
Jacob Another name for Israel. See Gen. 32:22-28.
survivors People that escape some accident or war.
nation Literally, "house." This might mean the royal family of that country.

You are destroying my people Literally, "They eat the flesh of my people."
vision(s) Like a dream. God used visions to teach prophets what they should say to the people.
seers Another name for prophets.
fortune tellers People that try to use magic to learn what will happen in the future.
Israel Another name for Jacob. Here it means the people of Israel.

The Leaders of Israel Are to Blame

9 Leaders of Jacob and rulers of Israel,
    listen to me!
  You hate the right way of living!
  If something is straight,
    then you make it crooked!
10 You build Zion* by murdering people.*
    You build Jerusalem by cheating people!
11 The judges in Jerusalem accept bribes
    to help them decide who wins in court.
  The priests in Jerusalem must be paid
    before they will teach the people.
  People must pay the prophets
    before they will look into the future.
  And then those leaders say,
    "The Lord lives here with us.
    So nothing bad will happen to us."

12 ⌊Leaders,⌋ because of you,
    Zion* will be destroyed.
  It will become a plowed field.
  Jerusalem will become a pile of rocks.
  Temple Mount will be an empty hill*
    overgrown with bushes.'"

The Law Will Come from Jerusalem

4 In the last days, the mountain of the Lord's
    temple* will be on the highest of all mountains.
  It will be raised higher than the hills.
  There will be a steady stream of people
    going there.
2 People from many nations will go there.
  They will say,
    "Come! Let's go up to the Lord's mountain.
    Let's go to the temple of the God of Jacob.
    Then God will teach us his way of living.
    And we will follow him."
  The teachings from God
    —the Lord's message—
  will begin in Jerusalem on Mount Zion*
    and go out ⌊to all the world⌋.
3 Then God will be a judge
    for the people of many nations.
  God will end the arguments
    for many* people in faraway countries.
  Those people will stop using their weapons
    for fighting.
  They will make plows from their swords.
  And they will use their spears
    as tools for cutting plants.
  People will stop fighting other people.
  People will never again train for war.
4 Each person will sit under his own grapevine
    and fig tree.
  No person will make ⌊them⌋ afraid!
  Why? Because the Lord All-Powerful
    said it would happen like that!

5 All the people ⌊from other nations⌋
    follow their own gods.
  But we will remember the name
    of the Lord our God forever and ever!

The Kingdom to Be Brought Back

6 The Lord says,
  "⌊Jerusalem⌋ was hurt and crippled.
  ⌊Jerusalem⌋ was thrown away.
  ⌊Jerusalem⌋ was hurt and punished.
  But I will bring her back ⌊to me⌋.

7 The people of that 'crippled' city
    will become the survivors.*
  The people of that city
    were forced to leave.
  But I will make them into a strong nation."
  The Lord will be their king.
  He will rule from Mount Zion* forever.
8 And you, Tower of Flocks,*
    your time will come.
  Ophel, hill of Zion,
    you will again be the seat of government.
  Yes, the kingdom will be in Jerusalem
    like it was in the past."

Why Must the Israelites Go to Babylon?

9 Now, why are you crying so loud?
  Is your king gone?
  Have you lost your leader?
  You are suffering like a woman
    that is giving birth.
10 Daughter of Zion,* feel the pain.
  Give birth to your "baby".

Zion The southeast part of the mountain Jerusalem is built on. Sometimes it means the people of God living in Jerusalem.
murdering people Literally, "bloodshed."
empty hill Or, "high place," a term usually used for local shrines (places for worship) where people often worshiped idols.
temple A special building for worshiping God. God commanded the Jews to worship him at the temple in Jerusalem.
many Or, "powerful."
survivors People that escape some accident or war.
Tower of Flocks Or, "Migdal Eder." This probably means a part of Jerusalem. The leaders would be like shepherds in a tower watching their sheep.

You must go out of this city *(Jerusalem)*.
You will live in the field.
I mean, you will go to Babylon.
But you will be saved from that place.
The Lord will go there and rescue you.
He will take you away from your enemies.

The Lord Will Destroy the Other Nations

11 Many nations have come
to fight against you.
They say,
"Look, there is Zion!*
Let's attack her!"

12 ⌊Those people have their plans⌋.
But they don't know what the Lord
is planning.
The Lord brought those people here
⌊for a special purpose⌋.
Those people will be ⌊crushed⌋
like grain on a threshing floor.*

Israel Will Win Defeat Its Enemies

13 Daughter of Zion,*
get up and crush those people!
⌊I will make you very strong⌋.
It will be like you have horns of iron,
and hooves* of bronze.
You will beat many people into small pieces.
You will give their wealth to the Lord.
You will give their treasure
to the Lord of all the earth."

5 Now, strong city,* gather your soldiers.
They are surrounding us for the attack!
They will hit the Judge of Israel
on the cheek with their stick.

The Messiah to be Born in Bethlehem

2 But you, Bethlehem Ephrathah,
are the smallest town in Judah.
Your family is almost too small to count.
But the "Ruler of Israel"
will come from you for me.
His beginnings are from ancient times,
from long, long ago.
3 So the Lord* will give up his people until
the woman gives birth to her child.
Then the rest of his brothers
will come back to the people of Israel.
4 Then ⌊the Ruler of Israel⌋ will stand
in the power of the Lord and
in the wonderful name of the Lord his God
and feed ⌊the flock⌋.
They will live ⌊in peace⌋
because at that time, his greatness
will reach to the ends of the earth.*
5 There will be peace.
Yes, the Assyrian army
will come into our country
and trample our large buildings.
But the Ruler of Israel* will choose
seven shepherds and eight leaders.*
6 They will use their swords
and rule the Assyrians.
They will rule the land of Nimrod*
with swords in hand.
They will use their swords
to rule those people.
But then ⌊the Ruler of Israel⌋
will save us from the Assyrians
who will come into our land
and trample our territory.
7 But the survivors* from Jacob
scattered among the nations
will be like dew from the Lord
that doesn't wait for any man.
They will be like rain on the grass
that doesn't wait for anyone.
8 But the survivors* from Jacob in the nations
scattered among those people
will be like a lion
among the animals in the forest.
They will be like a young lion
among flocks of sheep.
If the lion passes through,
he goes where he wants to go.
If he attacks an animal,
then no one can save that animal.
⌊The survivors will be like that⌋.

---

threshing floor A place where grain is beaten or walked on to remove the hulls from the grain.
Daughter of Zion Another name for Jerusalem.
hooves The hard part of a horse's foot.
strong city Literally, "Daughter of troops."
the Lord Or, "the Ruler of Israel."
They ... earth Or, "They will settle here because at that time his kingdom will extend to the ends of the earth.
the Ruler of Israel Or, "We."
seven shepherds and eight leaders Or, "seven shepherds, no eight leaders."
land of Nimrod Another name for Assyria.
survivors People that escape some accident or war.

⁹ You will lift your hand against your enemies,
 and you will destroy them.

People Will Depend on God

¹⁰ The Lord says,
 "At that time, I will take away your horses,
 and I will destroy your chariots.*
¹¹ I will destroy the cities in your country.
 I will pull down all your fortresses.*
¹² You will no longer try to do magic.
 You will not have any more people that try
 to tell the future.
¹³ I will destroy your statues ⌊of false gods⌋.
 I will pull down your stones for
 remembering those false gods.
 You will not worship the things
 that your hands have made.
¹⁴ I will destroy the Asherah poles.*
 And I will destroy your false gods.*
¹⁵ Some people will not listen to me.
 But I will show my anger.
 And I will get even with those people.

The Lord's Complaint

6 Now hear what the Lord says:
 Tell your side of the story
 to the mountains.
 Let the hills* hear your story.
² The Lord has a complaint against his people.
 Mountains, listen to the Lord's complaint.
 Foundations of the earth, hear the Lord.
 He will prove that Israel is wrong!
³ ⌊The Lord says⌋,
 "My people, tell me what I did!
 Did I do something wrong against you?
 Did I make life too hard for you?
⁴ ⌊I will tell you the things I did!⌋
 I sent Moses, Aaron, and Miriam to you.
 I brought you from the land of Egypt.
 I freed you from slavery.
⁵ My people, remember the ⌊evil⌋ plans
 of Balak king of Moab.
 Remember what Balaam son of Beor
 said to Balak.
 Remember the things that happened
 from Acacia to Gilgal*.
 Remember those things and
 you will know the Lord is right!"

What Does God Want from Us?

⁶ What must I bring when I come
 to meet with the Lord
 What must I do when I bow down
 to God above?
 Should I come to the Lord
 with burnt-offerings and a year-old calf?
⁷ Will the Lord be pleased
 with 1,000 rams or 10,000 rivers of oil?
 Should I give my first child
 as payment for my crimes?
 Should I give the child
 that came from my body
 as payment for my sins?
⁸ Man, the Lord told you what goodness is.
 This is what the Lord wants from you:
 Be fair to other people.
 Love kindness and loyalty.
 Live humbly with your God.
 ⌊Don't try to impress him with gifts.⌋

What Were the Israelites Doing?

⁹ The voice of the Lord shouts to the city.
 The wise person honors the Lord's name.*
 So pay attention to the rod ⌊of punishment⌋,
 and to the One who holds that rod!*
¹⁰ Do the bad people still hide treasures
 that they have stolen?
 Do bad people still cheat people
 with]baskets that are too small?[s
 Literally, "short ephahs." An ephah is
 about 1/2 bushel.
 ⌊Yes! All of those things are still happening!⌋
¹¹ Should I pardon the bad people who still
 use weights and scales to cheat people?
 Should I pardon the people who still
 have bags with weights that give the wrong
 measure?
¹² The rich men in that city still do cruel things!
 The people in that city still tell lies.
 Yes, those people tell their lies!

---

chariot(s) A small wagon used in war.
fortress(es) A building or city with tall, strong walls for protection.
Asherah poles Poles that helped people remember the Canaanite goddess, Asherah. At this time, the people thought she was the wife of Baal.
false gods Or, "cities."
Let the hills This is like a case in court. The mountains and hills are like the judge and jury.

Acacia to Gilgal This story is found in Num. 22-25.
the Lord's name. Literally, "your name."
So pay attention ... rod The Hebrew is not clear here.

¹³ So I have started to punish you.
   I will destroy you because of your sins.
¹⁴ You will eat,
   but you will not become full.
   You will still be hungry and empty.*
   You will try to bring people in to safety.
   But people with swords
   will kill the people you rescued!
   People catch you.
¹⁵ You will plant your seeds,
   but you will not gather food.
   You will try to squeeze oil from your olives,
   but you will not get any oil.
   You will walk on your grapes,
   but you will not get enough juice
   to have wine to drink.
¹⁶ Why? Because you obey the laws of Omri.*
   You do all the ₍bad₎ things
   that Ahab's family does.
   You follow their teachings.
   So I will let you be destroyed.
   People will whistle in amazement
   when they see your destroyed city.
   Then you will bear the shame
   that the other nations bring to you.*

Micah Is Upset at the Evil People Do

7 I am upset because I am
   like fruit that has been gathered,
   like grapes that have already been picked.
   There are no grapes left to eat.
   There are none of the early figs that I love.
² I mean, all of the faithful people are gone.
   There are no good people left
   in this country.
   Every person is waiting to kill someone.
   Every person is trying to trap his brother.
³ People are good at doing bad things
   with both hands.
   Official asks for bribes.
   Judges take money
   to change their decisions in court.
   "Important leaders" ₍don't make
   good and fair decisions₎.
   They do whatever they want to do.
⁴ ₍Even₎ the best of them is like a thorn bush.
   Even the best of them is more crooked
   than a tangled thorn bush.

The Day of Punishment Is Coming

   ₍Your prophets said this day would come₎.
   And the day of your watchmen* has come.
   Now you will be punished!
   Now you will be confused!
⁵ Don't trust your neighbor!
   Don't trust a friend!
   Don't even speak freely with your wife!
⁶ A person's enemies will be
   the people in his own house.
   A son will not honor his father.
   A daughter will turn against her mother.
   A daughter-in-law will turn against
   her mother-in-law.

The Lord Is the Savior

⁷ So I will look to the Lord ₍for help₎!
   I will wait for God to save me.
   My God will hear me.
⁸ I have fallen.
   But enemy, don't laugh at me!
   I will get up again.
   I sit in darkness now.
   But the Lord will be a light for me.

The Lord Forgives

⁹ I sinned against the Lord.
   So he was angry at me.
   But he will argue my case for me in court.
   He will do the things that are right for me.
   Then he will bring me out into the light.
   And I will see that he is right.
¹⁰ My enemy said to me,
   "Where is the Lord your God?"
   But my enemy will see this,
   and she will be ashamed.
   At that time, I will laugh at her.*
   People will walk over her,
   like mud in the streets.

The Jews to Return

¹¹ The time ₍will come₎ when your walls
   will be built again.
   At that time, the country will grow.
¹² Your people will come back to your land.
   They will come back from Assyria
   and from the cities of Egypt.

You ... empty The Hebrew is not clear here.
Omri A king of Israel that led his nation to worship false gods. See 1 Kings 16:21-26.
Then... you Or, "My people's shame will taken away."

watchmen Another name for prophets. This shows that the prophets were like guards that stood on a city's wall and watched for trouble coming from far away.
laugh at her Literally, "my eyes will gawk (*stare, look*) at her."

Your people will come from Egypt and from
the other side of the Euphrates River.
They will come from the the sea ⌊in the west⌋
and from the mountains ⌊in the east⌋.

13 The land was ruined by the people
that lived there and by the things they did.
14 So rule your people with your rod.
Rule the flock of people that belong to you.
That flock lives alone in the woods,
and up on Mount Carmel.
That flock lives in Bashan and Gilead
like they did in time past.

Israel Will Defeat Its Enemies

15 I did many miracles
when I took you out of Egypt.
I will let you see more miracles like that.
16 The nations will see those miracles,
and they will be ashamed.
They will see that their "power"
⌊is nothing compared to mine⌋.
They will ⌊be amazed⌋
and put their hands over their mouths!

They will cover their ears
⌊and refuse to listen⌋.
17 They will crawl in the dust like a snake.
They will shake with fear.
They will be like insects crawling
from their holes in the ground
and coming to the Lord our God.
God, they will fear and respect you!

Praise for the Lord

18 There is no God like you.
You forgive people that are guilty of sin.
You will forgive your people that survived.
You do not stay angry forever.
Why? Because you enjoy being kind.
19 Lord, comfort us again.
Take away our sins.
Throw away all our sins
into the deep sea.
20 You will be true to Jacob,*
you will be kind and loyal to Abraham,*
like you promised to our ancestors*
a long time ago.

---

laugh at her Literally, "my eyes will gawk (stare, look) at her."

Jacob Another name for Israel. See Gen. 32:22-28.
Abraham The father of the Israelites. Here Abraham is used to mean all the people of Israel.
ancestors Literally, "fathers," meaning a person's parents, grandparents, and all the people they are descended from.

Nahum

¹ This book is the vision of Nahum from Elkosh. This is the sad message about the city of Nineveh.*

The Lord Is Angry at Nineveh

² The Lord is a jealous God.
The Lord punishes guilty people.
The Lord punishes guilty people,
and the Lord is very angry!
The Lord punishes his enemies.
He stays angry at his enemies.
³ The Lord is patient.
But he is also very powerful!
And the Lord will punish guilty people.
He will not let them go free.
The Lord ⌊is coming to punish bad people⌋.
He will use whirlwinds and storms
to show his power.
⌊A man walks⌋ on the dust ⌊on the ground⌋.
But the Lord walks on the clouds!
⁴ The Lord will speak harshly to the sea,
and it will become dry.
He will make all the rivers become dry!
The rich lands of Bashan and Carmel
become dry and dead.
The flowers in Lebanon fade away.
⁵ The Lord will come,
and the mountains will shake ⌊with fear⌋,
and the hills will melt away.
The Lord will come,
and the earth will shake with fear,
The world and every person on it
will shake with fear.
⁶ No person can stand against
the Lord's great anger.
No one can endure his terrible anger.
His anger will burn like fire.
The rocks will shatter when he comes.

⁷ The Lord is good.
He is a safe place to go in times of trouble.
He takes care of the people who trust him.
⁸ But he will destroy completely his enemies.
He will wash them away like a flood.
He will chase his enemies
into the darkness.
⁹ Why are you making plans against the Lord?
He will bring complete destruction,
so ⌊you⌋ will not cause trouble again!
¹⁰ You will be completely destroyed
like thorn bushes burning under a pot.
You will be destroyed quickly
like dry weeds that burn fast.
¹¹ ⌊Assyria,⌋ a man came from you.
He made evil plans against the Lord.
He gave evil advice.
¹² The Lord said these things ⌊to Judah⌋:
"The people of Assyria are at full strength.
They have many soldiers.
But they will all be cut down.
They will all be finished.
My people, I made you suffer.
But I will make you suffer no more.
¹³ Now I will set you free
from the power of Assyria.
I will take that yoke* off your neck.
I will tear away the chains holding you.
¹⁴ ⌊King of Assyria,⌋
the Lord gave this command about you:
"You will not have any descendants
to wear your name.
I will destroy your carved idols
and metal statues that are in the temple
of your gods.
I am preparing your grave for you
because your end is coming soon!*

Nineveh The capital city of the country of Assyria. Assyria destroyed Israel in 722-721 B.C.

yoke A pole people used for carrying things on their shoulder. This often showed that a person was a slave.

because your end is coming soon Or, "You are not important" or "You are so hated."

¹⁵ Judah, look!
　　Look there, coming over the mountains.
　Here comes a messenger
　　bringing good news!
　He says there is peace!
　Judah, celebrate your special holidays.
　Judah, do the things you promised.
　Those worthless people will not come through
　　and attack you again!
　Why? Because all those bad people
　　have been destroyed!

Nineveh Will Be Destroyed

2 　An enemy is coming to attack you
　　So guard the strong places of your city.
　Watch the road.
　　Get ready for war.
　　　Prepare for battle!
² 　Yes, the Lord changed Jacob's* pride.
　　He made it like Israel's pride.
　ₗThe enemyⱼ destroyed them
　　and ruined their grape vines.

³ 　The shields of those soldiers are red.
　　Their uniforms are bright red.
　Their chariots* are lined up for battle,
　　and shining like flames of fire.
　And their horses are ready to go.
⁴ 　The chariots race wildly through the streets.
　　They rush back and forth through the square.
　They look like burning torches,
　　like lightning flashing from place to place!

⁵ 　ₗThe enemyⱼ calls for his best soldiers.
　　They stumble as they rush ahead.
　They run to the wall and set up their shield
　　ₗover the battering ramⱼ.
⁶ 　But the gates by the rivers are open,
　　and the enemy comes flooding in
　　and destroys the king's house.
⁷ 　The enemy takes away the queen.
　　And her slave girls moan sadly like doves.
　They beat their breasts
　　ₗto show their sadnessⱼ.
⁸ 　Nineveh is like a pool whose water
　　is draining away.
　People yell,
　　"Stop! Stop running away!"
　But it doesn't do any good!

⁹ 　ₗYou soldiers that are destroying Ninevehⱼ,
　　take the silver!
　Take the gold!
　There are many things to take.
　　There are many treasures!
¹⁰ 　Now ₗNinevehⱼ is empty
　　Everything is stolen.
　　　The city is ruined!
　People have lost their courage,
　　their hearts are melting with fear,
　　their knees are knocking together,
　　their bodies are shaking,
　　their faces become pale from fear.

¹¹ 　Where is the lion's cave *(Nineveh)* now?
　　The male and female lions lived there.
　　Their babies were not afraid.
¹² 　The lion *(king of Nineveh)* killed people
　　to feed his cubs and lionnesses.
　He filled his cave *(Nineveh)*
　　with men's bodies.
　He filled his cave
　　with women he had killed.
¹³ 　The Lord All-Powerful says,
　　"I am against you, ₗNinevehⱼ!
　I will burn your chariots.
　I will kill your 'young lions' in battle.
　You will not hunt anyone on earth again.
　People will never again hear bad news
　　from your messengers."

Bad News for Nineveh

3 　It will be very bad
　　for that city of murderers.
　ₗNineveh,ⱼ is a city full of lies.
　It is filled with things taken
　　from other countries.
　It is filled with plenty of people
　　that it hunted and killed!
² 　You can hear the sounds
　　of whips cracking,
　　the noise of wheels,
　　horses galloping,
　　and chariots bouncing along!
³ 　Soldiers on horses are attacking,
　　their swords are shining,
　　their spears are gleaming!
　There are many dead people,
　　dead bodies piled up,
　　too many bodies to count!
　People are tripping over all the dead bodies.
⁴ 　All this happened because of ₗNinevehⱼ.
　Nineveh is like a prostitute
　　that could never get enough.

Jacob's Another name for Israel. See Gen. 32:22-28.
chariot(s) A small wagon used in war.

She wanted more and more.
She sold herself to many nations,
and she used her magic
to make them her slaves.
⁵ The Lord All-Powerful says,
"I am against you Nineveh.
I will pull your dress* up over your face.
I will let the nations see your naked body.
Those kingdoms will see your shame.
⁶ I will throw dirty things on you.
I will treat you in a hateful way.
People will look at you and laugh.
⁷ Everyone who sees you will be shocked.
They will say,
'Nineveh is destroyed.
Who will cry for her?'
I know I cannot find anyone
to comfort you, Nineveh."

⁸Nineveh, are you better than Thebes* on the Nile River? No! Thebes also had water all around her. Thebes used the water to protect herself from enemies. She used that water like a wall too! ⁹Ethiopia and Egypt gave Thebes much strength. The Sudan and Libya supported her. ¹⁰But Thebes was defeated. Her people were taken away as prisoners to a foreign country. Soldiers beat her small children to death at every street corner. They threw lots* to see who got to keep the important people as slaves. They put chains on all the important men of Thebes.

¹¹So Nineveh, you will also fall like a drunk person! You will try to hide. You will look for a safe place away from the enemy. ¹²But ⌊Nineveh⌋, all your strong places will be like fig trees. New figs become ripe. A person comes and shakes the tree. The figs fall into the mouth of that person. He eats them, and they are gone!

¹³⌊Nineveh⌋, your people are all like women—and the enemy soldiers are ready to take them. The gates of your land are open wide for your enemies to come in. Fire has destroyed the wooden bars across the gates. ¹⁴Get water and store it inside your city. Why? Because the enemy soldiers will surround your city. ⌊They will not let any person bring food or water into the city.⌋ Make your defenses strong! Get clay to make more bricks! Mix the mortar! Get the molds for making bricks! ¹⁵You can do all those things, but the fire will still destroy you completely! And the sword will kill you. Your land will look like a swarm of grasshoppers came and ate everything.

Nineveh, you grew and grew. You became like a swarm of grasshoppers. You were like a swarm of locusts. ¹⁶You have many, many businessmen that go places and buy things. They are as many as the stars in the sky! And they are like locusts that come, eat everything until it is finished, and then leave. ¹⁷And your government officials are also like locusts. They are like locusts that settle on a stone wall on a cold day. But when the sun comes up, the rocks become warm, and the locusts all fly away. And no one knows where! ⌊Your officials will be like that.⌋

¹⁸King of Assyria, your shepherds *(leaders)* fell asleep. Those powerful men are sleeping. And now your sheep *(people)* have wandered away on the mountains. And there is no person to bring them back. ¹⁹Nineveh, you have been hurt badly, and nothing can heal your wound. Everyone who hears the news of your destruction claps his hands. They are all happy! Why? Because they all felt the pain you always caused!

---

pull your dress This is a word play in Hebrew. The Hebrew word also means "to destroy a country and take its people away as prisoners to other nations."

Thebes A great city in Egypt. It was destroyed in 663 B.C. by the Assyrian army.

lot(s) Sticks, stones, or pieces of bone used like dice for making decisions. See Proverbs 16:33.

Habakkuk

Habakkuk Complains to God

1 This is the message that was given to Habakkuk the prophet.*

² Lord, I continue to ask for help. When will you listen to me? I cried to you about the violence. But you did nothing! ³People are stealing things and hurting other people. People are arguing and fighting. Why do you make me look at these terrible things? ⁴The law is weak and not fair to people. Evil people win their fights against good people. So, the law is no longer fair. Justice doesn't win anymore!

God Answers Habakkuk

⁵ ⌊The Lord answered,⌋ "Look at the other nations! Watch them, and you will be amazed. I will do something in your lifetime that will amaze you. ⌊You will have to see it to believe it.⌋ You would not believe it if you were told about it. ⁶I will make the Babylonian people a strong nation. Those people are mean and powerful fighters. They will march across the earth. They will take houses and cities that don't belong to them. ⁷The Babylonian people will scare the other people. The Babylonian people will do what they want to do and go where they want to go. ⁸Their horses will be faster than leopards* and meaner than wolves* at sunset. Their horse soldiers will come from faraway places. They will attack their enemies quickly, like a hungry eagle swooping down from the sky. ⁹The one thing they all want to do is fight. Their armies will march fast like the wind in the desert. And the Babylonian soldiers will take many, many prisoners—as many as the grains of sand.

¹⁰"The Babylonian soldiers will laugh at the kings of other nations. Foreign rulers will be like jokes to them. The Babylonian soldiers will laugh at the cities with tall, strong walls. The soldiers will simply build dirt roads up to the top of the walls and easily defeat the cities. ¹¹Then they will leave like the wind and go on to fight against other places. The only thing those Babylonians will worship is their own strength."

Habakkuk's Second Complaint

¹² ⌊Then Habakkuk said,⌋

"Lord, you are the Lord who lives forever!
You are my holy God who never dies!*
Lord, you created the Babylonian people
  to do what must be done.
Our Rock,* you created them
  to punish ⌊the people of Judah⌋.
¹³ Your eyes are too good to look at evil.
  You can't watch people doing wrong.
So how can you watch
  those evil people win?
How can you watch bad people
  defeating good people?

¹⁴ "You have made the people
  like fish in the sea.
They are like little sea-animals
  without a leader.
¹⁵ The enemy catches all of them
  with hooks and nets.
The enemy catches them in his net
  and drags them in.
And the enemy is very happy
  with what he caught.
¹⁶ His net helps him live like a rich man
  and enjoy the best food.

---

prophet A person called by God to be a special servant. God used dreams and visions to show them things to teach to the people.
leopard A large animal, like a lion.
wolves A wolf is a type of wild dog.

Lord, you are ... never dies Or, "Lord, you have been my holy God forever! Surely we will not die."
Rock A name for God. It shows he is like a fortress or a strong place of safety.

So the enemy worships his net.
He makes sacrifices* and burns incense*
to honor his net.
17 Will he continue to take riches with his net?
Will he continue destroying people
without showing mercy?

2 "I will stand like a guard and watch.
I will wait to see what the Lord
will say to me.
I will wait and learn how he answers
my questions."

God Answers Habakkuk

²The Lord answered me, "Write down what I show you. Write clearly on a sign so people can read it easily.* ³This message is about a special time in the future. This message is about the end, and it will come true! ₍It may seem like that time will never come.₎ But be patient and wait for it. That time will come. It will not be late. ⁴This message can't help people that refuse to listen to it. ₍But a good person will believe this message.₎ And the good person will live because of his faith.

⁵₍God said,₎ "Wine can trick a person. In the same way, a strong man's pride can fool him. But he will not find peace. He is like death—he always wants more and more. And, like death, he will never be satisfied. He will continue defeating other nations. He will continue to make those people his prisoners. ⁶But soon enough, all of those people will laugh at him. They will tell stories about his defeat. They will laugh and say, 'It's too bad that the man who took so many things will not get to keep them! He made himself rich collecting debts.'

⁷₍Strong man,₎ you have taken money from people. One day those people will wake up and realize what is happening. And they will stand against you. Then they will take things from you. And you will be very afraid. ⁸You have stolen things from many nations. So those people will take much from you. You have killed many people. You have destroyed lands and cities. You have killed all the people there. ⁹Yes, it will be very bad for the person that becomes rich by doing wrong. That person does those things to live in a safe place. He thinks that he can stop other people from stealing from him. ₍But bad things will happen to him.₎

¹⁰"You have made plans to destroy many people. But those plans will bring shame to your house. You have done bad things, and you will lose your life. ¹¹The stones of the walls will cry out against you. Even the wooden rafters* in your own house will agree that you are wrong.

¹²"It will be very bad for the leader that does wrong and kills people to build a city. ¹³The Lord All-Powerful has decided that a fire will destroy everything that those people worked to build. All their work will be for nothing. ¹⁴Then people everywhere will know about the Glory of the Lord.* This news will spread like water spreads out into the sea. ¹⁵It will be very bad for that person that becomes angry and then makes other people suffer. In anger, that person knocks other people to the ground. And he treats those people like they are naked and drunk.

¹⁶"But that person will know the Lord's anger. That anger will be like a cup of poison in the Lord's right hand. That person will taste that anger and then he will fall to the ground like a drunk person.

"Evil ruler, you will drink from that cup. You will get shame, not honor. ¹⁷You hurt many people in Lebanon. You stole many animals there. So you will be afraid because of the people that died and because of the bad things you did to that country. You will be afraid because of the things you did to those cities and to the people that lived in those cities."

The Message About Idols

¹⁸That person's false god will not help him. Why? Because it is only a statue that some man covered with metal. It is only a statue. So the person that made it can't expect it to help. That statue can't even speak! ¹⁹It will be very bad for the person that says to a wooden statue, "Get up!" It will be very bad for the person that says to a stone that can't speak, "Wake up!" Those things can't help him. That statue may be covered with gold and silver, but there is no life in that statue.

---

sacrifice(s) A gift to God. Usually, it was a special animal that was killed and burned on an altar.

incense Special dried tree sap. Burned to make a sweet-smelling smoke, it was offered as a gift to God.

Write clearly on a sign so people can read it easily Or, "Write clearly on tablets so the person that reads it can run and tell other people the message."

rafters Boards that support the roof.

Glory of the Lord One of the forms God used when he appeared to people. It was like a bright shining light. See Ex. 16:6, 40:34-38.

²⁰ ₍But the Lord is different₎! The Lord is in his holy temple. So all the earth should be silent and show respect in front of the Lord.

Habakkuk's Prayer

3 The Shiggayon prayer of Habakkuk the prophet.*

2 Lord, I have heard the news about you.
  Lord, I am amazed at the powerful things
    that you did in the past.
  Now I pray that you will do great things
    in our time.
  Please make those things happen
    in our own days.
  But in your excitement, remember to show
    mercy to us.
                              SELAH*
3 God is coming from Teman.*
  The Holy One is coming from Mount Paran.*
                              SELAH*
  The glory of the Lord covers the heavens!
    His praise fills the earth!
4 Rays of light shine from his hand,
    a bright, shining light.
  There is such power hiding ₍in that hand₎.
5 The sickness went before him.
  And the destroyer followed behind him.*
6 The Lord stood and judged the earth.
    He looked at the people of all the nations.
    And they shook with fear.
  For many years the mountains stood strong.
    But those mountains fell to pieces.
    The old, old hills fell down.
  God has always been like that!
7 I saw the cities of Cushan were in trouble.
    The houses of Midian trembled with fear.
8 Lord, were you angry at the rivers?
    Were you angry at the streams?
    Were you angry at the sea?
  Were you angry when you rode
    your horses and chariots to victory?
9 Even then you showed your rainbow.
    It was proof of your Agreement
    with the families of the earth.
                              SELAH*
  And the dry land split the rivers.
10 The mountains saw you and shook.
    The water flowed off the land.
    The water from the sea made a loud noise
    as it lost its power over the land.
11 The sun and the moon lost their brightness.
    They stopped shining when they saw
      your bright flashes of lightning.
    That lightning was like spears and arrows
      shooting through the air.
12 In anger you walked on the earth
    and punished the nations.
13 You came to save your people.
    You came to lead your chosen king*
      to victory.
    You killed the leader in every evil family,
      from the least important person
      to the most important in the land.*
                              SELAH*
14 You used Moses' walking stick
    to stop the enemy soldiers.
  Those soldiers came like a powerful storm
    to fight against us.
  They thought they could defeat us easily,
    like robbing a poor man in secret.
15 But you marched your horses
    through the sea.
  They stirred up that great sea.
16 My whole body shook
    when I heard the story.
  I whistled out loud!
  I felt weak down to my bones.
  I just stood there shaking.
  So I will wait patiently
    for the day of destruction when they come
    to attack the people.

Always Rejoice in the Lord

17 Figs might not grow on the fig trees.
    Grapes might not grow on the vines.
    Olives might not grow on the olive trees.

Shiggayon ... prophet Or, "The prayer of Habakkuk on the Shiggayon." The exact meaning of "Shiggayon" is not clear.
Selah This word is for the singers or the musicians. It probably means that the singers should pause or that the music should be louder here.
Teman One of Edom's important cities in the south, maybe its capital.
Mount Paran This is probably an important mountain west of the Gulf of Aqaba and north of Mount Sinai.
The sickness ... behind him This probably refers to the diseases and the Angel of Death God sent against the Egyptians when God freed Israel from slavery.

chosen king Literally, "anointed one."
You killed ... in the land Literally, "You struck the head from the evil house. From the foundation to the neck they were laid bare."

Food might not grow in the fields.
There might not be any sheep in the pens.
There might not be any cattle in the barns.
¹⁸ But I will still be glad in the Lord.
I will rejoice in God my savior.

¹⁹ The Lord, my Master,
gives me my strength.
He helps me run fast like a deer.
He leads me safely on the mountains.

To the music director.
On my stringed instruments.

Zephaniah

1 This is the message that the Lord gave to Zephaniah. Zephaniah received this message during the time that Josiah son of Amon was king of Judah. Zephaniah was the son of Cush. Cush was the son of Gedaliah. Gedaliah was the son of Amariah. Amariah was the son of Hezekiah.

The Lord's Day for Judging the People

²The Lord says, "I will destroy everything on earth!* ³I will destroy all the people and all the animals. I will destroy the birds in the air and the fish in the sea. I will destroy the evil people and all the things that make them sin. I will remove all people from the earth." The Lord said those things!

⁴⌊The Lord said,⌋ "I will punish Judah and the people living in Jerusalem. I will remove these things from that place: I will remove the last signs of Baal worship. I will remove the priests and all the people that ⁵go on their roofs* to worship the stars.* People will forget about those false priests. Some people say they worship me. Those people promised to worship me, but now they worship the false god Milcom.* So I will remove those people from that place. ⁶Some people turned away from the Lord. They quit following me. Those people stopped asking the Lord for help. So I will remove those people from that place."

⁷Be silent before the Lord my Master! Why? Because the Lord's day for judging the people is coming soon! The Lord has prepared his sacrifice and he has told his invited guests to get ready.*

⁸⌊The Lord said,⌋ "On the Lord's day of sacrifice, I will punish the king's sons and other leaders. I will punish all the people wearing clothes from other countries. ⁹At that time, I will punish all the people that jump over the threshold.* I will punish the people that fill their master's house* with lies and violence."

¹⁰The Lord also said, "At that time, people will be calling for help at Fish Gate in Jerusalem. People will be crying in the other parts of town. And the people will hear loud noises of things being destroyed in the hills around the city. ¹¹You people living in the lower part of town will cry. Why? Because all the businessmen and rich merchants will be destroyed.

¹²"At that time, I will take a lamp and search through Jerusalem. I will find all the people that are satisfied to live their own way. Those people say, 'The Lord does nothing. He does not help and he does not hurt!' I will find those people and I will punish them! ¹³Then other people will take their wealth and destroy their houses. At that time, people that built houses will not live in them and people that planted fields of grapes will not drink the wine from those grapes—⌊other people will get those things⌋."

¹⁴The Lord's special day for judging is coming soon! That day is near and coming fast. People will hear very sad sounds on the Lord's special day of judgment. Even strong soldiers will cry! ¹⁵God will show his anger at that time. It will be a time of terrible troubles. It will be a time of destruction. It will be a time of darkness—a black, cloudy, and stormy day. ¹⁶It will be ⌊like a time of war when⌋ people hear horns and trumpets in the defense towers and protected cities.

---

earth Or, "the land," or "the country."
roof(s) In ancient Israel, houses had flat roofs that were used like an extra room.
stars Literally, "army of heaven." This might mean the stars and planets or the angels.
Milcom The god of the Ammonite people.
prepared ... get ready Literally, "prepared his sacrifice. He has made holy his called ones." Here this time of judgment is compared to a fellowship meal when priests offered a sacrifice to God and had the guests get ready for this special meal with God.

people wearing ... threshold This probably means the priests and people that worshiped foreign gods, such as Dagon, or people that copied their ways of worshiping. See I Samuel 5:5.
master's house This means the temple where the people worshiped God or their false gods.

¹⁷₍The Lord said,₎ "I will make life very hard on the people. People will walk around like blind men that don't know where they are going. Why? Because those people sinned against the Lord. ₍Many people will be killed.₎ Their blood will be spilled on the ground. Their dead bodies will lie like dung on the ground. ¹⁸Their gold and silver won't help them! At that time, the Lord will become very upset and angry. The Lord will destroy the whole world!* The Lord will completely destroy everyone on earth!*"

God Asks People to Change Their Lives

2 Shameless people, change your lives ²before you become like a dry and dying flower. In the heat of day, a flower will wilt and die. You will be like that when the Lord shows his terrible anger. So change your lives before the Lord shows his anger against you! ³All you humble people, come to the Lord! Obey his laws. Learn to do good things. Learn to be humble. Maybe then you will be safe when the Lord shows his anger.

The Lord Will Punish Israel's Neighbors

⁴No one will be left in Gaza. Ashkelon will be destroyed. By noon, the people will be forced to leave Ashdod. Ekron will be empty!* ⁵You Philistine people, you people living by the sea, this message from the Lord is about you. Land of Canaan, land of Palestine,* you will be destroyed—no one will live there! ⁶Your land by the sea will become empty* fields for shepherds and their sheep. ⁷Then that land will belong to the survivors* from Judah. The Lord will remember those people from Judah. Those people are prisoners in a foreign country. But the Lord will bring them back. Then the people from Judah will let their sheep eat the grass in those fields. In the evenings, they will lie down in the empty houses of Ashkelon.

⁸The Lord says, "I know what the people of Moab and Ammon did! Those people embarrassed my people. Those people took their land to make their own countries bigger. ⁹So, as sure as I am live, Moab and the people of Ammon will be destroyed like Sodom and Gomorrah.* I am the Lord All-Powerful, the God of Israel. And I promise those countries will be completely destroyed forever. Their land will be overgrown with weeds. Their land will be like the land covered with salt by the Dead Sea. The survivors of my people will take that land and all the things left in it."

¹⁰Those things will happen to the people of Moab and Ammon because they were so proud and because they were cruel to the people of the Lord All-Powerful and they humiliated them. ¹¹Those people will be afraid of the Lord! Why? Because the Lord will destroy their gods. Then all the people in all the faraway lands will worship the Lord. ¹²People of Ethiopia, this means even you! The Lord's sword will kill your people. ¹³And the Lord will turn north and punish Assyria. He will destroy Nineveh—that city will be like an empty, dry desert. ¹⁴Then only sheep and wild animals will live in that ruined city. Owls and crows will sit on the columns that are left standing. Their calls will be heard coming through the windows. Crows will sit on the doorsteps. Black birds* will sit in those empty houses. ¹⁵Nineveh is so proud now. It is such a happy city. The people think they are safe. They think Nineveh is the greatest place in the world. But that city will be destroyed! It will be an empty place where only wild animals go to rest. People that pass that place will whistle and shake their heads ₍when they see how badly the city was destroyed₎.

The Future of Jerusalem

3 Jerusalem, your people fought against God! Your people hurt other people, and you have been stained with sin! ²Your people didn't listen to me! They didn't accept my teachings. Jerusalem didn't trust the Lord. Jerusalem didn't go to her God. ³Jerusalem's leaders are like roaring lions. Her judges* are like hungry wolves that come in the evening ₍to attack the sheep₎—

---

world Or, "land" or "country."
earth Or, "the land" or "the country."
Gaza, Ashkelon, Ashdod, Ekron Philistine cities. In Hebrew, Zephaniah is making word plays on the names of these cities
Palestine Or, "the Philistines."
empty In Hebrew, this word is like the word meaning "Philistine people."
survivor(s) People that escaped some disaster. Here this means the Jewish people that survived the destruction of Judah and Israel by its enemy armies.

Sodom and Gomorrah Two cities that God destroyed because the people were so evil.
Black birds Or, "cedar beams."
judge(s) A man that decides matters in court.

and in the morning nothing is left. ⁴Her prophets* are always making their secret plans to get more and more. Her priests have treated holy things like they are not holy. They have done bad things to God's teachings. ⁵But God is still in that city. And he continues to be good. God does not do anything wrong. He continues to help his people. Morning after morning he helps his people make good decisions. But those bad people are not ashamed of the bad things they do.

⁶God says, "I have destroyed whole nations. I destroyed their defense towers. I destroyed their streets and now no one goes there any more. Their cities are empty— no one lives there any more. ⁷I tell you these things so you will learn a lesson. I want you to fear and respect me. If you do this, then your home won't be destroyed. If you do this, then I won't have to punish you the way I planned." But those bad people only wanted to do more of the same bad things they had already done!

⁸The Lord said, "So just wait! Wait for me to stand and judge you. I have the right to bring people from many nations and use them to punish you. I will use those people to show my anger against you. I will use them to show how upset I am—and the whole country will be destroyed! ⁹Then I will change people from other nations so they can speak the language clearly and call out the name of the Lord. They will all worship me together, shoulder to shoulder, as one people. ¹⁰People will come all the way from the other side of the river in Ethiopia. My scattered people will come to me. My worshipers will come and bring their gifts to me.

¹¹Then, Jerusalem, you will no longer be ashamed of the bad things your people do against me. Why? Because I will remove all of those bad people from Jerusalem. I will take away all of those proud people. There won't be any of those proud people on my holy mountain.* ¹²I will let only meek and humble people stay in my city (*Jerusalem*). And they will trust the Lord's name. ¹³The survivors* of Israel won't do bad things.

They won't tell lies. They won't try to trick people with lies. They will be like sheep that eat and lie down in peace—and no one will bother them.

A Happy Song

14 Jerusalem, sing and be happy!
Israel, shout for joy!
Jerusalem, be happy and have fun!
15 Why? Because the Lord stopped
your punishment!
He destroyed your enemies' strong towers!
King of Israel, the Lord is with you.
You don't need to worry
about anything bad happening.
16 At that time, Jerusalem will be told,
"Be strong, don't be afraid!
17 The Lord your God is with you.
He is like a powerful soldier.
He will save you.
He will show how much he loves you.
He will show you how happy he is
with you.
He will laugh and be happy about you,
18 like people at a party."
The Lord said,
"I will take away your shame.
I will make those people stop hurting you.*
19 At that time, I will punish the people
that hurt you.
I will save my hurt people.
I will bring back the people
that were forced to run away.
And I will make them famous.
People everywhere will praise them.
20 At that time, I will bring you back.
I will bring you back together.
I will make you famous.
People everywhere will praise you.
That will happen when I bring back the
prisoners before your very own eyes!"
The Lord said those things.

---

prophet(s) A person called by God to be a special servant. God used dreams and visions to show them things to teach the people.

holy mountain Mount Zion, one of the mountains Jerusalem was built on.

survivor(s) People that escaped some disaster. Here this means the Jewish people that survived the destruction of Judah and Israel by its enemy armies.

I will make ... stop hurting you This verse in hard to understand in the Hebrew.

Haggai

It Is Time to Build the Temple!

1 On the first day of the sixth month of Darius' second year as king ⌊of Persia⌋, Haggai received a message from the Lord. This message was for Zerubbabel son of Shealtiel and Joshua son of Jehozadak. Zerubbabel was the governor of Judah and Joshua was the high priest. This is the message: ²The Lord All-Powerful says this: "The people say it is not the right time yet to build the Lord's temple.*"

³Again Haggai received a message from the Lord. Haggai spoke this message: ⁴"You people think the right time has come for you to live in nice houses. You live in houses with beautiful wooden panelling on the walls. But the Lord's house is still in ruins! ⁵Now, the Lord All-Powerful says, 'Think about what is happening! ⁶You have planted many seeds, but you have gathered only a few crops. You have food to eat, but not enough to get full. You have something to drink, but not enough to get drunk. You have some clothes to wear, but not enough to keep warm. You earn a little money, but ⌊you don't know where it all goes⌋. It's like there is a hole in your pocket!'*

⁷"The Lord All-Powerful says, 'Think about what you are doing! ⁸Go up to the mountains to get the wood. And build the temple.* Then I will be pleased with the temple, and I will be honored.' The Lord said these things.

⁹The Lord All-Powerful says, "You people look for a big harvest. But when you go to gather the crop, there is only a little grain. So you bring that grain home. And then I ⌊send a wind that⌋ blows it all away! Why are these things happening? Why? Because my house is still in ruins while each of you runs home to take care of his own house. ¹⁰That is why the sky holds back its dew. And that is why the earth holds back its crops."

¹¹⌊The Lord says,⌋ "I gave the command for the land and the mountains to be dry. The grain, the new wine, the olive oil, and everything the earth produces will all be ruined!* And all the people and all the animals will become weak.'"

Work Begins on the New Temple

¹²The Lord God had sent Haggai to speak to Zerubbabel son of Shealtiel and to the high priest, Joshua son of Jehozadak. So these men and all the people listened to the voice of the Lord their God and to the words of Haggai the prophet. And the people showed their fear and respect for the Lord their God.

¹³Haggai was a messenger that the Lord God had sent to deliver this message to the people: The Lord says, "I am with you!"

¹⁴⌊Then the Lord God made the people excited about building the temple⌋. Zerubbabel son of Shealtiel was the governor of Judah. The Lord made him excited! Joshua son of Jehozadak was the high priest. The Lord made him excited! And the Lord made all the people excited ⌊about building the temple⌋. So they began working on the temple* of their God, the Lord All-Powerful. ¹⁵They began this work on the 24th day of the sixth month of Darius' second year as the king ⌊of Persia⌋.

The Lord Encourages the People

2 On the 21st day of the seventh month, this message from the Lord came to Haggai: ²Speak to Zerubbabel son of Shealtiel, the governor of Judah, and to Joshua son of Jehozadak, the high priest, and to all the people. Say these things: ³"How many of you people look at this temple and try to compare it to the

---

temple The special building in Jerusalem for Jewish worship.
You ... pocket Or, "The person who saves money is putting it into a purse full of holes."

dry ... ruined The Hebrew word "dry" is like the Hebrew word "ruined."

beautiful temple that was destroyed? What do you think? Does this temple seem like nothing when you compare it with the first temple? ⁴But now, Zerubbabel, the Lord says, 'Don't be discouraged!' High Priest Joshua son of Jehozadak, 'Don't be discouraged!' All you people of this country, the Lord says, 'Don't be discouraged! Continue this work, because I am with you!' The Lord All-Powerful said these things!"

⁵₍The Lord says,₎ "I made an agreement with you when you left Egypt. ₍And I have kept my promise!₎ My Spirit is among you. So don't be afraid!! ⁶Why? Because the Lord All-Powerful is saying these things! In just a little while, I will once again shake things up! I will shake heaven and earth. And I will shake the sea and the dry land! ⁷I will shake up the nations, and they will come to you with wealth from every nation. And then I will fill this temple* with glory. The Lord All-Powerful is saying these things! ⁸All of their silver really belongs to me! And all of the gold is mine! The Lord All-Powerful is saying these things. ⁹And the Lord All-Powerful says that this last temple will be more beautiful than the first temple! And I will bring peace to this place! Remember, the Lord All- Powerful is saying these things!"

The Work Has Begun—
The Blessings Will Come

¹⁰On the 24th day of the ninth month of Darius' second year as king ₍of Persia₎, this message from the Lord came to Haggai the prophet: ¹¹The Lord All-Powerful commands you to ask the priests what the law says about these things: ¹²"Suppose a man carries some meat in the fold of his clothes. This meat ₍is part of a sacrifice, so it₎ is holy. What if those clothes touch some bread, or cooked food, wine, oil or some other food. Will the thing the clothes touch become holy?'"

The priests answered, "No."

¹³Then Haggai said, "If a person touches a dead body, then he will become unclean.* Now, if he touches anything else, will that thing also become unclean?"

The priests answered, "Yes, that thing will become unclean."

¹⁴Then Haggai said, "The Lord God says these things, 'That is also true about the people of this nation! They were not pure and holy before me. So anything they touched with their hands became unclean! * ¹⁵Think about the things that happened before today. Think about the time before you began working on the Lord's temple. ¹⁶People wanted 20 measures of grain, but there were only 10 measures of grain in the pile. People wanted to get 50 jars of wine from the wine vat, but there were only 20! ¹⁷Why? Because I punished you. I sent the diseases that killed your plants. I sent the hail that destroyed the things you made with your hands. I did these things, but still you did not come to me.' The Lord said these things."

¹⁸₍The Lord said,₎ "Today is the 24th day of the ninth month. You have finished laying the foundation of the Lord's temple. So notice what happens from this day forward! ¹⁹Is there is any grain still in the barn? ₍No!₎ Look at the vines, the fig trees, the pomegranates, and the olive trees. Are they producing fruit? ₍No!₎ But, starting today, I will bless you!'"

²⁰Another message from the Lord came to Haggai on the 24th day of the month. This is the message: ²¹"Go to Zerubbabel, the governor of Judah. Tell him that I will shake heaven and earth. ²²And I will overthrow many kings and kingdoms. I will destroy the power of the kingdoms of those other people. I will destroy their chariots* and their riders. I will defeat their war horses and riders. Those armies are friends now, but they will turn against each other and kill each other with swords. ²³The Lord All- Powerful is saying these things. Zerubbabel son of Shealtiel, you are my servant. I have chosen you. And at that time, I will make you like a signet ring.* ₍You will be the proof that I have done these things!₎"

The Lord All-Powerful said these things.

---

chariot(s) A small wagon used in war.
signet ring This ring had the owner's name or design on it. The ring was pressed on clay or wax, and this proved that belonged to the person with the ring.

temple The special building in Jerusalem for Jewish worship.
unclean Not pure or not acceptable to God for worship.

Zechariah

The Lord Wants His People to Come Back

1 Zechariah son of Berekiah received a message from the Lord. This was in the eighth month of the second year that Darius was king* in Persia. (Zechariah was the son of Berekiah. Berekiah was the son of Iddo the prophet.) This is that message: ²The Lord became very angry at your ancestors. ³So you must tell the people these things. The Lord says, "Come back to me and I will come back to you." The Lord All-Powerful said these things.

⁴The Lord said, "Don't be like your ancestors. In the past, the prophets spoke to them. They said, 'The Lord All-Powerful wants you to change your bad way of living. Stop doing bad things!' But your ancestors did not listen to me." The Lord said those things.

⁵God said, "Your ancestors are gone. And those prophets did not live forever. ⁶The prophets were my servants. I used them to tell your ancestors about my laws and teachings. And your ancestors finally learned their lesson. They said, 'The Lord All-Powerful did the things he said he would do. He punished us for the way we lived and for all the bad things we did.' So they came back to God."

The Four Horses

⁷On the 24th day of the eleventh month (Shebat) of the second year that Darius was king* of Persia, Zechariah received another message from the Lord. (This was Zechariah son of Berekiah, son of Iddo, the prophet.) This is the message:

⁸At night, I saw a man riding a red horse. He was standing among some myrtle bushes in the valley. Behind him, there were red, brown, and white horses. ⁹I said, "Sir, what are these horses for?"

Then the angel speaking to me said, "I will show you what these horses are for."

¹⁰Then the man standing among the myrtle bushes said, "The Lord sent these horses to go here and there on earth."

¹¹Then the horses spoke to the Lord's angel standing among the myrtle bushes. They said, "We have walked here and there on the earth, and everything is calm and quiet."

¹²Then the Lord's angel said, "Lord, how long before you comfort Jerusalem and the cities of Judah? You have shown your anger at these cities for 70 years now."

¹³Then the Lord answered the angel that was talking with me. The Lord spoke good, comforting words. ¹⁴Then the angel told me to tell the people these things:

The Lord All-Powerful says:
"I have a strong love for Jerusalem
  and Zion.*

15 And I am very angry at the nations
  that feel so safe.
I was a little angry,
  and I used those nations
    to punish my people.
But those nations caused too much damage."

16 So the Lord says,
"I will come back to Jerusalem
  and comfort her."
The Lord All-Powerful says,
"Jerusalem will be built again.
  And my house will be built there."

17 The angel said,
"Also, tell the people these things:
"The Lord All-Powerful says,
'My towns will again be rich.
  I will comfort Zion.
  I will choose Jerusalem
    to be my special city.'"

---

second year that Darius was king About 520 B.C.

Zion The southeast part of the mountain Jerusalem is built on. Sometimes it means the people of God living in Jerusalem.

The Four Horns and Four Workers

¹⁸Then I looked up and I saw four horns. ¹⁹Then I asked the angel that was talking with me, "What do these horns mean?"

He said, "These are the horns (*Powerful nations*) that forced the people of Israel, Judah, and Jerusalem to go to foreign countries."

²⁰The Lord showed me four workers. ²¹I asked him, "What are these four workers coming to do?"

He said, "The horns represent the nations that attacked the people of Judah and forced them to go to foreign countries. The horns 'threw' the people of Judah to the foreign countries. Those horns didn't show mercy to anyone. But these four workers have come to frighten the horns and throw them away!"

Measuring Jerusalem

2 Then I looked up, and I saw a man holding a rope for measuring things. ²I asked him, "Where are you going?"

He said to me, "I am going to measure Jerusalem, to see how wide and how long it is."

³Then the angel that was speaking to me left. And another angel went out to talk to him. ⁴He said to him, "Run and tell that young man that ⌊Jerusalem will be too big to measure⌋. Tell him these things:

"Jerusalem will be a city without walls.
Why? Because there will be
too many people and animals living there.
⁵ The Lord says,
'I will be a wall of fire around her,
protecting her.
And to bring glory to that city,
I will live there.'"

God Calls His People Home

The Lord says,
⁶ "Hurry! Leave the land in the North in a hurry!
Yes, it is true that I scattered your people
in every direction.
⁷ You people from Zion now live Babylon.
Escape! Run away from that city!"
The Lord All-Powerful said ⌊these things⌋.
He sent me to the nations that stole thing
from you.
He sent me to bring ⌊you⌋ honor!
⁸ Why? Because hurting you
is like hurting the pupil of God's eye.
⁹ ⌊The people of Babylon took my people
and made them slaves.

But I will beat them, and they will become
the slaves of my people.
And then you will know
that the Lord All-Powerful sent me.
¹⁰ The Lord says,
"Zion, be happy!
Why? Because I am coming.
And I will live in your city.
¹¹ At that time, people from many nations
will come to me.
They will become my people.
And I will live in your city.
And then you will know
that the Lord All-Powerful sent me.
¹² The Lord will again choose Jerusalem
to be his special city.
Judah will be his share of the holy land.
¹³ Everyone, be quiet!
The Lord is coming out of his holy house.

The High Priest

3 The angel showed me Joshua the High Priest. Joshua was standing in front of the angel of the Lord and Satan was standing by Joshua's right side. Satan was there to accuse Joshua of doing bad things. ²Then ⌊the angel of⌋ the Lord said, "The Lord rebukes you and he will continue to criticize you! The Lord has chosen Jerusalem to be his special city. He saved that city—it was like a burning stick pulled from the fire."

³Joshua was standing in front of the angel. And Joshua was wearing a dirty robe. ⁴Then the angel said to the other angels standing near him, "Take those dirty clothes off of Joshua." Then the angel spoke to Joshua. He said, "Now, I have taken away your guilt, and I am giving you a new change of clothes."

⁵Then I said, "Put a clean turban* on his head." So they put the clean turban on him. They also put clean clothes on him while the Lord's angel stood there. ⁶Then the Lord's angel said these things to Joshua:

⁷ The Lord All-Powerful said these things.
"Live the way I tell you,
and do all the things I say.
And you will be in charge of my temple.
You will care of its courtyard.
You will be free to go anywhere in my temple
just like these angels standing here.

---

turban(s) A head covering made by wrapping a long piece of cloth around the head or around a cap worn on the head.

⁸ Listen to me High Priest Joshua
and your fellow priests seated before you.
These men are examples
that show what will happen
when I bring my special servant.
He is called, THE BRANCH.
⁹ Look, I put a special stone in front of Joshua.
There are seven sides* on that stone.
And I will carve a special message on
on that special stone.
That will show that in one day,
I will remove the guilt from this land."
¹⁰ The Lord All-Powerful says,
"At that time, people will sit and talk
with their friends and neighbors.
They will invite each other to come sit under
the fig trees and grape vines."

The Lampstand and the Two Olive Trees

4 Then the angel that was talking to me came to me and woke me up. I was like a person waking up from sleep. ²Then the angel asked me, "What do you see?"

I said, "I see a solid gold lampstand. There are seven lamps* on the lampstand. And there is a bowl on top of the lampstand. There are seven tubes coming from the bowl. One tube goes to each lamp. ₍The tubes bring the oil in the bowl to each of the lamps.₎ ³There are two olive trees by the bowl, one on the right side and one on the left side. ₍These trees produce the oil for the lamps.₎"

⁴Then I asked the angel that was speaking with me, "Sir, what do these things mean?"

⁵The angel speaking with me said, "Don't you know what these things are?"

"No sir," I said.

⁶He said, "This is the message from the Lord to Zerubbabel: 'Your help will not come from your strength and power. No, your help will come from my Spirit.' The Lord All-Powerful said those things! ⁷That tall mountain will be like a flat place for Zerubbabel. He will build the temple, and when the most important stone is put in place, the people will shout, 'Beautiful! Beautiful!'"

⁸The Lord's message to me also said, ⁹"Zerubbabel will lay the foundations for my temple. And Zerubbabel will finish building the temple. Then you will know that the Lord All-Powerful sent me to you people. ¹⁰People will not be ashamed of the small beginnings, and they will be very happy when they see Zerubbabel with the plumbline,* measuring and checking the finished building. Now, the seven sides* of the stone you saw represent the eyes of the Lord looking in every direction. They see everything on earth."

¹¹Then I *(Zechariah)* said to him, "I saw one olive tree on the right side of the lampstand and one on the left side. What do those two olive trees mean?" ¹²I also said to him, "I saw two olive branches by the gold tubes with gold colored oil flowing from them. What do these things mean?"

¹³Then the angel said to me, "Don't you know what these things mean?"

I said, "No, sir."

¹⁴So he said, "They represent the two men chosen* to serve the Lord of the whole world."

The Flying Scroll

5 I looked up again, and I saw a flying scroll.* ²The angel asked me, "What do you see?"

I said, "I see a flying scroll. The scroll is 30 feet* long and 15 feet* wide."

³Then the angel told me, "There is a curse written on that scroll. On one side of the scroll, there is a curse about people that steal. On the other side of the scroll is a curse about people that lie when they make promises. ⁴The Lord All-Powerful says: I will send that scroll to the houses of thieves and to houses of people that lie when they use my name to make promises. That scroll will stay there and destroy those houses. Even the stones and wooden posts will be destroyed."

The Woman and the Bucket

⁵The angel that was talking to me went outside. He said, "Look! What do you see coming?"

⁶I said, "I don't know—what is it?"

He said, "That is a measuring bucket." He also said, "That bucket is for measuring the sins* of the people in this country."

plumbline A string with a weight on one end. Workers used plumblines to make sure the walls they were building were straight. The workers often put paint on the string and popped the string. This left a straight line of paint on the wall. Then the workers chipped away the crooked part of the wall.
sides The Hebrew word also means, "eyes."
men that were chosen Literally, "sons of extra pure olive oil." Often a special oil was poured over new kings, priests, and prophets. This showed that these people were chosen by God.
Scroll(s) A long roll of leather or papyrus *(paper)* used for writing books, letters, and legal documents.
30 feet Literally, "20 cubits."
15 feet Literally, "10 cubits."
sins Hebrew has "their eye," but with a minor change of one character, "their guilt."

---

sides Literally, "eyes."
lamps These lamps made light by burning olive oil.

⁷A lid made of lead was lifted off the bucket, and there was a woman in the bucket. ⁸The angel said, "The woman represents evil." Then the angel pushed the woman down into the bucket and put the lead lid on it. ⁹Then I looked up and saw two women with wings like a stork. They flew out, and with the wind in their wings, they picked up the bucket. They flew through the air carrying the bucket. ¹⁰Then I asked the angel that was speaking with me, "Where are they carrying the bucket?"

¹¹The angel told me, "They are going to build a house for it in Shinar.* After they build that house, they will put the bucket there."

The Four Chariots

6 Then I turned around. I looked up and saw four chariots* going between four bronze mountains. ²Red horses were pulling the first chariot. Black horses were pulling the second chariot. ³White horses were pulling the third chariot. And horses with red spots were pulling the fourth chariot. ⁴I asked the angel that was talking with me, "Sir, what does this mean?"

⁵The angel said, "These are the four winds.* They have just come from the Master of the whole world. ⁶The black horses will go north, ⌊the red horses will go east,⌋ the white horses will go west, and the horses with red spots will go south."

⁷The red spotted horses were anxious to go look at their part of the earth, so the angel told them, "Go walk through the earth." So they went walking through their part of the earth.

⁸Then ⌊the Lord⌋ yelled at me. He said, "Look, those horses that were going north finished their job ⌊in Babylon⌋. They have calmed my spirit—I am not angry now!"

Joshua the Priest Gets a Crown

⁹Then I received another message from the Lord. He said, ¹⁰"Heldai, Tobijah, and Jedaiah have come from the captives* in Babylon. Get silver and gold from those men and then go to the house of Josiah son of Zephaniah. ¹¹Use that silver and gold to make a crown. Put that crown on Joshua's head. (Joshua was the high priest.

Joshua was the son of Jehozadak.) Then tell Joshua these things:

¹² The Lord All-Powerful says these things: "There is a man called THE BRANCH.
He will grow strong.
He will build the Lord's temple.
¹³ He will build the Lord's temple,
and he will receive the honor.
He will sit on his throne
and be the ruler.
And a priest will stand by his throne.
These two men will work together in peace.

¹⁴"They will put the crown in the temple to help people remember. It will bring honor to Heldai, Tobijah, Jedaiah, and Zephaniah's son, Josiah. ¹⁵People living far away will come and build the temple. Then you will know for sure that the Lord sent me to you people. All these things will happen if you do what the Lord says."

The Lord Wants Kindness and Mercy

7 Zechariah received a message from the Lord in the fourth year that Darius was the king* of Persia. This was on the fourth day of the ninth month (Kislev). ²The people of Bethel sent Sharezer, Regem-Melech, and his men to ask the Lord a question. ³They went to the prophets and to the priests at the temple of the Lord All-Powerful. Those men asked them this question: "For many years we have shown our sadness for the destruction of the temple. In the fifth month of each year we have had a special time of crying and fasting. Should we continue to do this?"

⁴I received this message from the Lord All-Powerful: ⁵"Tell the priests and the other people in this country these things: You fasted and showed your sadness in the fifth month and in the seventh month. But was that fasting really for me? No! ⁶And when you ate and drank, was that for me? No! It was for your own good. ⁷God used the earlier prophets to say these same things long ago. He said these things while Jerusalem was still a prosperous city filled with people. God said these things while there were still people living in the towns around Jerusalem, and in the Negev, and in the western foothills."

⁸ This is the Lord's message to Zechariah:
⁹ The Lord All-Powerful said these things.
"You must do what is right and fair.
You must be kind and merciful to each other.

Shinar The flat land that the tower of Babel (Gen. 11:2) and the city of Babylon were built on.
chariot(s) A small wagon used in war.
four winds Or, "four spirits." Four winds often means winds that blow from every direction: north, south, east, and west.
captives People taken away like prisoners. Here this means the Jewish people that were taken to Babylon.
fourth year that Darius was the king About 518 b.c.

¹⁰ Don't hurt widows and orphans,*
strangers, or poor people.
Don't even think of doing bad things
to each other!"
¹¹ But those people refused to listen.
They refused to do what he wanted.
They closed their ears so they
could not hear what God said.
¹² They were very stubborn.
They would not obey the law.
The Lord All-Powerful used his Spirit
and sent messages to his people
through the prophets.
But the people would not listen.
So the Lord All-Powerful
became very angry.
¹³ So the Lord All-Powerful said,
"I called to them,
and they did not answer.
So now, if they call to me,
I will not answer.
I will bring the other nations against them
like a storm.
They didn't know those nations,
but the country will be destroyed
after those nations pass through.
This pleasant country will be destroyed."

The Lord Promises to Bless Jerusalem

8 This is a message from the Lord All-Powerful. ²The Lord All-Powerful says, "I truly love ₍Mount₎ Zion. I love her so much that I became angry when she was not faithful to me." ³The Lord says, "I have come back to Zion. I am living in Jerusalem. Jerusalem will be called FAITHFUL CITY. The Lord All-Powerful's mountain will be called HOLY MOUNTAIN."

⁴The Lord All-Powerful says, "Old men and women will again be seen in the public places in Jerusalem. People will live so long that they will need their walking sticks. ⁵And the city will be filled with children playing in the streets. ⁶The survivors* will think it is wonderful. And I will think it is wonderful too!"

⁷The Lord All-Powerful says, "Look, I am rescuing my people from countries in the east and west. ⁸I will bring them back here, and they will live in Jerusalem. They will be my people, and I will be their good and faithful God."

⁹The Lord All-Powerful says, "Be strong! You people are hearing the same message today that the prophets gave when the Lord All-Powerful first laid the foundations to build his temple again. ¹⁰Before that time, men didn't have the money to hire workers or to rent animals. And it was not safe for people to come and go. There was no relief from all the troubles. I had turned every man against his neighbor. ¹¹But it is not like that now. It will not be like that for the survivors.*" The Lord All-Powerful said these things.

¹²"These people will plant in peace. Their grapevines will produce grapes. The land will give good crops, and the skies will give rain. I will give all these things to these, my people. ¹³People began using the names Israel and Judah in their curses. But I will save Israel and Judah, and their names will become a blessing. So don't be afraid. Be strong!"

¹⁴The Lord All-Powerful says, "Your ancestors made me angry. So I decided to destroy them. I decided not to change my mind." The Lord All-Powerful said these things. ¹⁵"But now I have changed ₍my mind₎. And in the same way, I have decided to be good to Jerusalem and to the people of Judah. So don't be afraid! ¹⁶But you must do these things: Tell the truth to your neighbors. When you make decisions in your cities, do the things that are true and right and that bring peace. ¹⁷Don't make secret plans to hurt your neighbors! Don't make false promises! You must not enjoy doing those things. Why? Because I hate those things!" The Lord said these things.

¹⁸I received this message from the Lord All-Powerful. ¹⁹The Lord All-Powerful says, "You have special days of sadness and fasting in the fourth month, the fifth month, the seventh month, and the tenth month.* Those days of sadness must be changed into days of happiness. Those will be good and happy holidays. And you must love truth and peace!"

²⁰ The Lord All-Powerful says,
"In the future, people from many cities
will come to Jerusalem.
²¹ People from different cities
will greet each other.
Some of them will say,
'We are going to worship
the Lord All-Powerful.'
₍And the other person will say,₎
'I would like to go with you!'

---

widows and orphans Widows are women whose husbands have died, and orphans are children whose parents have died. Often these people have no one to care for them.

survivor(s) Jewish people that escaped the destruction of Judah and Israel by its enemy armies.

days of sadness and fasting ... month These were days when the people remembered the destruction of Jerusalem and the temple. See 2 Kings 25:1-25 and Jer. 41:1-17, 52:1-12.

²²Many people and many powerful nations will come to Jerusalem to find the Lord All-Powerful and to worship him. ²³The Lord All-Powerful says, "At that time, people that speak many different languages will come to a Jewish person and say, 'We heard that God is with you. Can we come with you to worship him?'"

Judgment Against Other Nations

9 A message from God. This is the Lord's message against Hadrach's country and his capital city, Damascus. "The family groups of Israel are not the only people that know about God. Everyone looks to him for help.* ²⌊And this message is against⌋ Hamath which borders Hadrach's country. ⌊And this message is against⌋ Tyre and Sidon, even though those people have been so wise and skillful. ³Tyre is built like a fort. The people there have collected so much silver that it is like dust, and gold is as common as clay. ⁴But the Lord our Master will take it all. He will destroy her powerful navy and that city will be destroyed by fire!

⁵"The people in Ashkelon will see those things and they will be afraid. The people of Gaza will shake with fear. And the people of Ekron will lose all hope when they see those things happen. There will be no king left in Gaza. No person will live in Ashkelon any more. ⁶The people in Ashdod will not even know who their real fathers are. I will completely destroy the proud Philistine people. ⁷They will no longer eat meat with the blood still in it or any other forbidden food. Any Philistine left living will become a part of my people—they will be just one more family group in Judah. The people of Ekron will become a part of my people, just like the Jebusite people did. I will protect my country. ⁸I will not let enemy armies pass through it. I will not let them hurt my people any more. With my own eyes I saw how much my people suffered ⌊in the past⌋."

The Future King

9 City of Zion, rejoice!
  People of Jerusalem, shout with joy!
  Look, your king is coming to you!
  He is the good king that won the victory.
    But he is humble.
    He is riding on a donkey,
      on a young donkey
        born from a work animal.

¹⁰ The king says,
  "I destroyed the chariots in Ephraim
    and the horse soldiers in Jerusalem.
  I destroyed the bows used in war."
  ⌊That king⌋ will bring news of peace
    to the nations.
  He will rule from sea to sea,
    from the ⌊Euphrates⌋ River
    to all the faraway places on earth.

The Lord Will Save His People

¹¹ Jerusalem, we used blood
    to seal your Agreement.
  So I am setting your people free
    from that empty hole in the ground.*
¹² Prisoners, go home!
  Now you have something to hope for.
  I am telling you now,
    I am coming back to you!
¹³ Judah, I will use you like a bow.
  Ephraim I will use you like arrows.
  Israel, I will use you like a sword
    to fight against the people of Greece.
¹⁴ The Lord will appear to them,
    and he will shoot his arrows like lightning.
  The Lord my Master will blow the trumpet,
    and the army will rush forward
      like a desert dust storm.
¹⁵ The Lord All-Powerful will protect them.
  The soldiers will use rocks and slings*
    to defeat the enemy.
  They will spill the blood of their enemies.
    It will flow like wine.
    It will be like the blood that is thrown
      on the corners of the altar!
¹⁶ At that time, the Lord their God
    will save his people
    like a shepherd saves his sheep.
  They will be very precious to him.
  They will be like sparkling jewels
    on his land.
¹⁷ Everything will be good and beautiful!
  There will be a wonderful crop,
    but it will not be just the food and wine.
  It will be all the young men and women!

The Lord's Promises

10 Pray to the Lord for rain in the springtime.
The Lord will send the lightning and the rain

This ... help This verse is very hard to understand in the Hebrew.
empty hole in the ground People stored water in large holes in the ground. People sometimes used those holes as prisons.
sling(s) A strip of leather for throwing rocks.

will fall. And God will make the plants grow in each person's field.

²People use their little statues and magic to learn the things that will happen in the future—but that is all useless. Those people see visions and tell about their dreams, but it is nothing but worthless lies. So the people are like sheep wandering here and there crying for help—but there is no shepherd to lead them.

³The Lord says, "I am very angry at the shepherds *(leaders)*. I made those leaders responsible for what happens to my sheep *(people)*." (The people of Judah are God's flock. And the Lord All-Powerful really does take care of his flock. He cares for them like a soldier cares for his beautiful war horse.)

⁴"The cornerstone, the tent peg, the war bow, and the advancing soldiers will all come ⌊from Judah⌋ together. ⁵⌊They will defeat their enemy⌋—it will be like soldiers marching through mud in the streets. They will fight, and since the Lord is with them, they will defeat even the enemy soldiers riding horses. ⁶I will make Judah's family strong. I will help Joseph's family win the war. I will bring them back safe and sound. I will comfort them. It will be like I never left them. I am the Lord their God, and I will help them. ⁷The people of Ephraim* will be as happy as soldiers that have too much to drink. Their children will be rejoicing and they, too, will be happy. They will all have a happy time together with the Lord.

⁸"I will whistle for them and call them all together. I really will save them. There will be many, many people. ⁹Yes, I have been scattering my people throughout the nations. But in those faraway places they will remember me. They and their children will survive. And they will come back. ¹⁰I will bring them back from Egypt and Assyria. I will bring them to the area of Gilead. And since there will not be enough room, I will also let them live in nearby Lebanon." (¹¹⌊It will be like it was before, when God brought them out of Egypt.⌋ He hit the sea waves, ⌊the sea split,⌋ and the people walked across that sea of troubles. The Lord will make the river streams become dry. He will destroy Assyria's pride and Egypt's power.)

¹²The Lord will make his people strong. And they will live for him and his name. The Lord said these things.

Ephraim Another name for the northern kingdom of Israel.

God Will Punish the Other Nations

11 Lebanon, open your gates so the fire
will come and burn your cedar trees.*
² The cypress trees will cry
because the cedar trees have fallen.
Those powerful trees will be taken away.
Oak trees in Bashan will cry
for the forest that was cut down.
³ Listen to the crying shepherds.
Their powerful leaders were taken away.
Listen to the roaring of the young lions.
Their thick bushes near the Jordan River
have all been taken away.

⁴The Lord my God says, "Care for the sheep that have been raised to be killed. ⁵⌊Their leaders are like owners and businessmen.⌋ Owners kill their sheep and are not punished. Businessmen sell the sheep and say, 'Praise the Lord, I am rich!' The shepherds don't feel sorry for their sheep. ⁶And I don't feel sorry for the people living in this country." The Lord said these things, "Look, I will let everyone be abused by his neighbor and king. I will let them destroy their country—I will not stop them!"

⁷So I took care of the sheep that had been raised to be killed—those poor sheep. I found two sticks. I called one stick Favor, and I called the other stick Union. Then I began caring for the sheep. ⁸I fired the three shepherds all in one month. I became angry at the sheep, and they began to hate me. ⁹Then I said, "I quit! I will not take care of you! I will let those that want to die, die. I will let those that want to be destroyed, be destroyed. And those that are left will destroy each other." ¹⁰Then I took the stick named Favor, and I broke it. I did this to show that God's Agreement* with his people was broken. ¹¹So that day, the Agreement was finished. And those poor sheep watching me knew that this message was from the Lord.

¹²Then I said, "If you want to pay me, then pay me. If not, then don't!" So they paid me 30 pieces of silver. ¹³Then the Lord told me, "So that's how much they think I'm worth. Throw that large amount of money* into the temple treasury." So I

cedar trees In this poem, the trees, bushes, and animals are symbols for the leaders of the countries around Judah.
Agreement Literally, "Proof." The flat stones with the Ten Commandments written on them were proof of the Agreement between God and Israel.
large amount of money The Lord was making fun. This was only the amount of money a person paid for a slave.

took the 30 pieces of silver and threw them into the treasury at the Lord's temple. ¹⁴Then I cut the stick named Union into two pieces. I did this to show that the union between Judah and Israel had been broken.

¹⁵Then the Lord said to me, "Now, get the things a foolish shepherd might use. ¹⁶This will show that I will get a new shepherd for this country. But this young man will not be able to take care of the sheep that are being destroyed. He will not be able to heal the hurt sheep. He will not be able to feed those that are left alive. And the healthy ones will be eaten completely—only their hoofs will be left."

¹⁷ Oh my worthless shepherd.
You abandoned my sheep.
Punish him!
Hit his right arm and right eye
with a sword.
His right arm will be useless.
His right eye will be blind.

Visions About the Nations Around Judah

12 The sad message from the Lord about Israel. The Lord made the sky and the earth. He put man's spirit in him. And the Lord said these things. ²"Look, I will make Jerusalem like a cup of poison to the nations around her. The nations will come and attack that city. And all of Judah will be caught in the trap. ³But I will make Jerusalem like a heavy rock—anyone that tries to take it will hurt himself. Those people will really be cut and scratched. But all the nations on earth will come together to fight against Jerusalem. ⁴But at that time, I will scare the horse, and the soldier riding it will panic. I will make all the enemy horses blind, but my eyes will be open—and I will be watching over Judah's family. ⁵The family leaders of Judah will encourage the people. They will say, 'The Lord All-Powerful is your God. He makes us strong.' ⁶At that time, I will make the family leaders of Judah like a fire burning in a forest. They will destroy their enemies like fire burning straw. They will destroy the enemy all around them. And the people in Jerusalem will again be able to sit back and relax."

⁷The Lord will save the people of Judah first, so the people in Jerusalem will not be able to brag too much. David's family and the other people living in Jerusalem will not be able to brag that they are better than the other people in Judah. ⁸But the Lord will protect the people in Jerusalem. Even the clumsiest person will be a great soldier like David. And the men from David's family will be like gods—like the Lord's own angel leading the people.

⁹The Lord says, "At that time, I will destroy the nations that came to fight against Jerusalem. ¹⁰I will fill David's family and the people living in Jerusalem with a spirit of kindness and mercy. They will look to me, the One they pierced. And they will be very sad. They will be as sad as a person crying over the death of his only son; as sad as someone crying over the death of his firstborn* son. ¹¹There will be a time of great sadness and crying in Jerusalem. It will be like the time people cried over the death of Hadad Rimmon in Megiddo Valley. ¹²Each and every family will cry by itself. The men in David's family will cry by themselves. And their wives will cry by themselves. The men in Nathan's family will cry by themselves. And their wives will cry by themselves. ¹³The men in Levi's family will cry by themselves. And their wives will cry by themselves. The men in Simeon's family will cry by themselves. And their wives will cry by themselves. ¹⁴And the same thing will happen in all the other family groups. The men and women will cry by themselves."

13 But at that time, a new spring of water will be opened for David's family and for the other people living in Jerusalem. That fountain will be to wash away their sins and to make the people pure.

No More False Prophets

²The Lord All-Powerful says, "At that time, I will remove all the idols from the earth. People will not even remember their names. And I will remove the ₁false₁ prophets and unclean* spirits from the earth. ³If a person continues to prophesy, then he will be punished. Even his parents, his own mother and father, will say to him, 'You have spoken lies in the name of the Lord, so you must die!' His own mother and father will stab him for prophesying. ⁴At that time, the prophets will be ashamed of their visions and prophecies. They will not wear the rough cloth that shows a person is a prophet. They will not wear those clothes to trick people with the lies they call prophecies. ⁵Those people will say, 'I am not a prophet. I am a farmer. I have worked as a farmer since I was a little child.' ⁶But other people will say, 'But what

---

firstborn The first child born into a family. The firstborn son was very important in ancient times.
unclean Not pure or not acceptable to God.

are these wounds in your hands?' He will say, 'I was beaten in the house of my friends.'"

⁷The Lord All-Powerful says, "Sword, hit the shepherd! Hit my friend! Hit the shepherd and the sheep will run away. And I will punish those little ones. ⁸Two-thirds of the people in the land will be hurt and die. But one-third of them will survive. ⁹Then I will test those survivors. I will give them many troubles. The troubles will be like the fire a man uses to prove silver is pure. I will test them the way a person tests gold. Then they will call to me for help, and I will answer them. I will say, 'You are my people.' And they will say, 'The Lord is my God.'"

The Day of Judgment

14 Look, the Lord has a special day for judging. And the wealth you have taken will be divided in your city. ²I will bring all the nations together to fight against Jerusalem. They will capture the city and destroy the houses. The women will be raped, and half of the people will be taken away as prisoners. But the rest of the people will not be taken from the city. ³Then the Lord will go to war with those nations. It will be a real battle. ⁴At that time, he will stand on the Mount of Olives, the hill east of Jerusalem. The Mount of Olives will split. Part of the mountain will move to the north, and part to the south. A deep valley will open up, from the east to the west. ⁵You will try to run away as that mountain valley comes closer and closer to you. You will run away like the time you ran from the earthquake during the time of Uzziah, king of Judah. But the Lord my God will come, and all his holy ones will be with him.

⁶⁻⁷That will be a very special day. There will not be any light, cold, or frost. Only the Lord knows how, but there will not be any day or night. Then, when darkness usually comes, there will still be light. ⁸At that time, water will flow continually from Jerusalem.* That stream will split and part of it will flow east, and part of it will flow west to the Mediterranean Sea. And it will flow all year long, in the summer as well as in the winter. ⁹And the Lord will be the King of the whole world at that time. The Lord is One. His name is One. ¹⁰At that time, the whole area around Jerusalem will become ₍empty₎ like the Arabah desert. The country will be like a desert from Geba to Rimmon in the Negev. But the whole city of Jerusalem will be built again—from Benjamin Gate to the First Gate (that is, the Corner Gate) and from the Tower of Hananel to the king's winepresses. ¹¹People will move there to live. No enemy will come to destroy them any more. Jerusalem will be safe.

¹²But the Lord will punish the nations that fought against Jerusalem. He will send a terrible disease against them. Their skin will begin to rot while the people are still alive. Their eyes will rot in their sockets and their tongues will rot in their mouths. ¹³⁻¹⁵That terrible disease will be in the enemy camp. And their horses, mules, camels, and donkeys will all catch that terrible disease.

At that time, those people will really be afraid of the Lord. They will try to encourage each other. They will join hands and lift hands together to show they are united.* The people of Judah will fight in Jerusalem. But they will get the wealth from all the nations around the city. They will get much gold, silver, and clothing. ¹⁶Some of the people that came to fight Jerusalem will survive. And every year they will come to worship the king, the Lord All-Powerful. And they will come to celebrate the Festival of Shelters.* ¹⁷And if people from any of the families on earth don't go to Jerusalem to worship the king, the Lord All-Powerful, then the Lord will not let them have any rain. ¹⁸If any of the families in Egypt don't come to celebrate the Festival of Shelters, then they will get that terrible disease that the Lord caused the enemy nations to get. ¹⁹That will be the punishment for Egypt, and for any other nation that does not come to celebrate the Festival of Shelters.

²⁰At that time, everything will belong to God. Even the harnesses on the horses will have the label, HOLY TO THE LORD.* And all the pots used in the Lord's temple will be just as important as the bowls used at the altar. ²¹In fact, every dish in Jerusalem and Judah will have the label, HOLY TO THE LORD ALL-POWERFUL. All the people offering sacrifices will come and take those dishes and cook ₍their special meals₎ in them.

At that time, there will not be any businessmen buying and selling things* in the temple of the Lord All-Powerful.

---

water will flow continually from Jerusalem Literally, "Living water will flow from Jerusalem." Jerusalem's main water supply, the Gihon spring, did not flow continuously.

They ... united The Hebrew is hard to understand here.

Festival of Shelters At this fall holiday, the people traveled to Jerusalem, built temporary shelters, camped out in them for a week, and enjoyed themselves together with the Lord.

businessmen ... selling things Literally, "Canaanites."

Malachi

1 A message from God. This message is from the Lord to Israel. God used Malachi to give this message.

God Loves Israel

²The Lord said, "I love you people."
But you said, "What shows you love us?"
The Lord said, "Esau was Jacob's brother. Right? But I chose* Jacob. ³And I did not accept* Esau. I destroyed Esau's hill-country.* Esau's country was destroyed, and now only wild dogs* live there."

⁴Maybe the people of Edom will say, "We were destroyed. But we will go back and build our cities again."

But the Lord All-Powerful says, "If they build those cities again, then I will destroy them again!" That is why people say Edom is an evil country—a nation the Lord hates forever.

⁵You people saw these things and you said, "The Lord is great, even outside of Israel!"

The People Don't Respect God

⁶The Lord All-Powerful said, "Children honor their father. Servants honor their masters. I am your Father, so why don't you honor me? I am your Master, so why don't you respect me? You priests don't respect my name."

But you say, "What have we done that shows we don't respect your name?"

⁷⌊The Lord said,⌋ "You bring unclean* bread to my altar!"

But you say, "What makes that bread unclean?"

⌊The Lord said,⌋ "You don't show respect for my table (altar). ⁸You bring blind animals as sacrifices.* And that is wrong! You bring sick and crippled animals for sacrifices. And that is wrong! Try giving those sick animals as a gift to your governor. Would he accept those sick animals? No! He would not accept those gifts!" The Lord All-Powerful said these things!

⁹"Priests, you should ask the Lord to be good to us. But he does not listen to you. And it is all your fault." The Lord All-Powerful said these things.

¹⁰"Surely, some of you priests could close the temple doors and light the fires correctly. I am not pleased with you. I will not accept your gifts." The Lord All-Powerful said these things.

¹¹"People all around the world respect my name. All around the world people bring good gifts to me. They burn good incense* as a gift to me. Why? Because my name is important to all those people." The Lord All-Powerful said these things.

¹²"But you people show that you don't respect my name. You say that the Lord's table (altar) is unclean.* ¹³And you don't like the food from that table. You smell the food and refuse to eat it. You say it is bad. ⌊But that is not true⌋. Then you bring sick, crippled, and hurt animals to me. You try to give sick animals to me as sacrifices. But I will not accept those sick animals from you. ¹⁴Some people have good, male animals that they could give as sacrifices. ⌊But they don't give those good animals to me.⌋ Some people bring good animals to me. They promise to give those healthy animals to me. But then they secretly exchange those good animals and they give me sick animals. Bad things will happen to those people! I am the Great King. ⌊You should respect me!⌋ People all around the world respect me!" The Lord All-Powerful said those things.

---

chose Or, "loved."
did not accept Or, "hated."
Esau's hill-country This means the country Edom. Edom was another name for Esau.
wild dogs Literally, "jackals."
unclean Not pure or not acceptable to God for worship.
sacrifice(s) A gift to God. Usually, it was a special animal that was killed and burned on an altar.
incense Special dried tree sap. Burned to make a sweet-smelling smoke, it was offered as a gift to God.

Rules for Priests

2 "Priests, this rule is for you! Listen to me! Pay attention to the things I say! Show honor to my name! ²If you don't respect my name, then bad things will happen to you. You will say blessings,* but they will become curses.* I will make bad things happen because you don't show respect for my name!" The Lord All-Powerful said these things.

³"Look, I will punish your descendants. During the holidays, you priests offer sacrifices to me. You take the dung and inside parts from the dead animals, and throw those parts away. But I will smear that dung on your faces, and you will be thrown away with it! ⁴Then you will learn why I am giving you this command. I am telling you these things so my Agreement* with Levi* will continue." The Lord All-Powerful said these things.

⁵ₗThe Lord said,ⱼ "I made that Agreement with Levi. I promised to give him life and peace—and I gave those things to him! Levi respected me! He showed honor to my name! ⁶Levi taught the true teachings. Levi didn't teach lies! Levi was honest and he loved peace. Levi followed me and saved many people from being punished for the bad things they did. ⁷A priest should know God's teachings. People should be able to go to a priest and learn God's teachings. A priest should be God's messenger to the people.

⁸ₗThe Lord said,ⱼ "But you priests stopped following me! You used the teachings to make people do wrong. You ruined the Agreement with Levi!" The Lord All-Powerful said these things! ⁹"You don't live the way I told you! You have not accepted my teachings! So I will make you become not important—people will not respect you!"

Judah Was Not True to God

¹⁰We all have the same father (God). The same God made every one of us! So why do people cheat their brothers? Those people show that they don't respect the Agreement. They don't respect the Agreement that our ancestors made with God. ¹¹The people of Judah cheated other people. People in Jerusalem and Israel did terrible things! God loves the temple.* But the people in Judah didn't respect the Lord's holy temple.* The people of Judah began to worship that foreign goddess. ¹²The Lord will remove those people from Judah's family. Those people might bring gifts to the Lord—but it will not help. ¹³You can cry and cover the Lord's altar with tears, but the Lord will not accept your gifts. The Lord will not be pleased with the things you bring to him.

¹⁴You ask, "Why are our gifts not accepted by the Lord?" Why? Because the Lord saw the bad things you did—he is a witness* against you. He saw you cheat on your wife. You have been married to that woman since you were young. She was your girlfriend. Then you made your vows* to each other—and she became your wife. ₗBut you cheated on herⱼ. ¹⁵God wants husbands and wives to become one body and one spirit. Why? So they would have holy children. So protect that spiritual unity. Don't cheat on your wife. She has been your wife from the time you were young.

¹⁶The Lord God of Israel says, "I hate divorce. And I hate the cruel things that men do. So protect your spiritual unity. Don't cheat on your wife."

The Special Time of Judgment

¹⁷You have taught wrong things. And those wrong teachings made the Lord very sad. You taught that God likes people that do bad things. You said God thinks those people are good. And you taught that God does not punish people for doing bad things.

3 The Lord All-Powerful says, "I am sending my messenger to prepare the way for me. Then suddenly, the Master you are looking for will come to his temple.* Yes, the messenger of the New Agreement that you want really is coming!"

²"No person can prepare for that time. No person can stand against him when he comes. He will be like a burning fire. He will be like the strong soap people use to make things clean. ³He will make the Levites* clean.* He will make them

---

blessings Words asking for good things to happen to a person that tries to obey God's law.
curses Warnings about bad things that will happen to a person that does not obey God.
Agreement Literally, "Proof." The flat stones with the Ten Commandments written on them were proof of the Agreement between God and Israel.
Levi The family group of Israel that did the work of priests.
temple The special building in Jerusalem for Jewish worship.
witness A person that tells what he has seen or heard.
vow(s) A special promise. Here it means the promise a man and woman make to each other when they are married.
temple Or, "palace."
Levite(s) A person from the family group of Levi. The Levites helped the priests in the temple and also worked for the civil government.
clean Pure or acceptable to God for worship.

pure, like silver is made pure—with fire! He will make them pure like gold and silver. Then they will bring gifts to the Lord—and they will do those things the right way. ⁴Then the Lord will accept the gifts from Judah and Jerusalem. It will be like in the past. It will be like the time long ago. ⁵Then I will come to you—and I will do the right thing. I will be like a person that is ready to tell the judge about the bad things people did. Some people do evil magic. Some people do the sin of adultery.* Some people make false promises. Some people cheat their workers—they don't pay them the money they promised. People don't help widows and orphans.* People don't help strangers. People don't respect me!" The Lord All-Powerful said these things.

Stealing from God

⁶"I am the Lord, and I don't change. You are Jacob's children, and you have not been completely destroyed. ⁷But you never obeyed my laws. Even your ancestors stopped following me. Come back to me, and I will come back to you." The Lord All-Powerful said these things.

You say, "How can we come back?"

⁸⌊Stop stealing things from God!⌋ People should not steal things from God, but you stole things from me!"

You say, "What did we steal from you?"

"You should have given me one-tenth of your things. You should have given me special gifts. ⌊But you did not give those things to me.⌋ ⁹In this way, your whole nation has stolen things from me. So bad things are happening to you." The Lord All-Powerful said these things.

¹⁰The Lord All-Powerful says, "Try this test. Bring one-tenth of your things to me. Put those things in the treasury. Bring food to my house. Test me! If you do those things, then I will truly bless you. Good things will come to you like rain falling from the sky. You will have more than enough of everything. ¹¹I will not let pests destroy your crops. Your grapevines will all produce grapes." The Lord All-Powerful said these things.

¹²"People from other nations will be good to you. You will truly have a wonderful country." The Lord All-Powerful said these things.

The Special Time of Judgment

¹³The Lord says, "You said mean things to me."

But you ask, "What did we say about you?"

¹⁴You said, "It is useless to worship the Lord. We did the things the Lord told us— but we didn't gain anything. We were sad ⌊for our sins⌋ like people crying at a funeral. But it didn't help. ¹⁵We think proud people are happy. Evil people succeed. They do bad things to test God's patience—and God does not punish them."

¹⁶God's followers spoke with each other, and the Lord listened to them. There is a book in front of him. In that book are the names of God's followers. Those are the people that honor the Lord's name.

¹⁷The Lord said, "Those people belong to me. I will be kind to them. A man is very kind to his children that obey him. In the same way, I will be kind to my followers. ¹⁸You people will come back to me. And you will learn the difference between good and evil. You will learn the difference between a person that follows God and a person that does not.

4 "That time of judgment is coming. It will be like a hot furnace. All those proud people will be punished. All those evil people will burn like straw. At that time, they will be like a bush burning in the fire—and there will not be a branch or root left." The Lord All-Powerful said these things.

²"But, for my followers, goodness will shine on you like the rising sun. And it will bring healing power like the sun's rays. You will be free and happy, like calves freed from their stalls.* ³Then you will walk on those evil people—they will be like ashes under your feet. I will make those things happen at that time of judgment." The Lord All-Powerful said these things!

⁴"Remember and obey the law of Moses. Moses was my servant. I gave those laws and rules to him at Mount Horeb *(Sinai)*. Those laws are for all the people of Israel.

⁵⌊The Lord said,⌋ "Look, I will send Elijah the prophet to you. He will come before that great and terrible time of judgment from the Lord. ⁶Elijah will help the parents become close to their children. And he *(Elijah)* will help the children become close to their parents. This must happen, or I *(God)* will come and completely destroy your country!"

---

adultery Breaking the marriage promise by sexual sin.
widows and orphans Widows are women whose husbands have died, and orphans are children whose parents have died. Often these people have no one to care for them.

stalls Small rooms or areas surrounded by a fence where people keep their animals.

The
New Testament

Matthew

The Family History of Jesus

1 This is the family history of Jesus Christ. He came from the family of David. David came from the family of Abraham.

2 Abraham was the father of Isaac.
Isaac was the father of Jacob.
Jacob was the father of Judah and his brothers.
3 Judah was the father of Perez and Zerah. (Their mother was Tamar.)
Perez was the father of Hezron.
Hezron was the father of Ram.
4 Ram was the father of Amminadab.
Amminadab was the father of Nahshon.
Nahshon was the father of Salmon.
5 Salmon was the father of Boaz. (Boaz' mother was Rahab.)
Boaz was the father of Obed. (Obed's mother was Ruth.)
Obed was the father of Jesse.
6 Jesse was the father of King David.
David was the father of Solomon. (Solomon's mother had been Uriah's wife.)
7 Solomon was the father of Rehoboam.
Rehoboam was the father of Abijah.
Abijah was the father of Asa.
8 Asa was the father of Jehoshaphat.
Jehoshaphat was the father of Joram.
Joram was the father of Uzziah.
9 Uzziah was the father of Jotham.
Jotham was the father of Ahaz.
Ahaz was the father of Hezekiah.
10 Hezekiah was the father of Manasseh.
Manasseh was the father of Amon.
Amon was the father of Josiah.
11 Josiah was the grandfather of Jehoiachin* and his brothers. (This was during the time that the ⌊Jewish⌋ people were taken to Babylon ⌊to be slaves⌋.)
12 After they were taken to Babylon:
Jehoiachin was the father of Shealtiel.
Shealtiel was the grandfather of Zerubbabel.
13 Zerubbabel was the father of Abiud.
Abiud was the father of Eliakim.
Eliakim was the father of Azor.
14 Azor was the father of Zadok.
Zadok was the father of Achim.
Achim was the father of Eliud.
15 Eliud was the father of Eleazar.
Eleazar was the father of Matthan.
Matthan was the father of Jacob.
16 Jacob was the father of Joseph.
Joseph was the husband of Mary, and Mary was the mother of Jesus.
Jesus is called the Christ.*

17 So there were fourteen generations from Abraham to David. And there were fourteen generations from David until the time when the people were taken to Babylon. And there were fourteen generations from the time when the people were taken to Babylon until Christ was born.

The Birth of Jesus Christ

18 The mother of Jesus Christ was Mary. And this is how the birth of Jesus happened. Mary was engaged to marry Joseph. But before they married, Mary learned that she was pregnant with a child. Mary was pregnant by ⌊the power of⌋ the Holy Spirit. 19 Mary's husband, Joseph, was a good man. He did not want to bring shame to Mary before the people. So he planned to divorce her secretly.

20 But after Joseph thought about this, an angel of the Lord came to Joseph in a dream. The angel said, "Joseph, son of David,* don't be afraid to

---

Jehoiachin Literally, "Jechoniah," another name for Jehoiachin.

Christ The "anointed one" (Messiah) or chosen of God.

son of David Person from the family of David, second king of Israel, about 1000 years before Christ.

accept Mary to be your wife. The baby that is in her is from the Holy Spirit.* ²¹She will give birth to a son. You will name the son Jesus.* Give him that name because he will save his people from their sins."

²²All this happened to make clear the full meaning of the things the Lord said through the prophet*: ²³"The virgin* will be pregnant and will give birth to a son. They will name him Immanuel."* (Immanuel means, "God with us.")

²⁴When Joseph woke up, he did the thing that the Lord's angel told him to do. Joseph married Mary. ²⁵But Joseph had no sexual union with Mary until she gave birth to the son. And Joseph named the son Jesus.

Wise Men Come to Visit Jesus

2 Jesus was born in the town of Bethlehem in Judea. He was born during the time when Herod* was king. After Jesus was born, some wise men from the east came to Jerusalem. ²The wise men asked people, "Where is the new baby that is the king of the Jews? We saw the star that shows he was born. We saw the star rise in the sky in the east. We came to worship him."

³King Herod* heard about this new king of the Jews. Herod was troubled about this. And all the people in Jerusalem were worried too. ⁴Herod called a meeting of all the leading Jewish priests and teachers of the law. Herod asked them where the Christ* would be born. ⁵They answered, "In the town of Bethlehem in Judea. The prophet* wrote about this ⌊in the Scriptures⌋*:

⁶ 'Bethlehem, in the land of Judah,
    you are important among
        the rulers of Judah.
  Yes, a ruler will come from you,
    and that ruler will lead Israel,
        my people.'"

Micah 5:2

Holy Spirit Called the Spirit of God, the Spirit of Christ, and the Comforter. Joined with God and Christ, he does God's work among people in the world.
Jesus The name Jesus means "salvation."
prophet Person that spoke for God. He often told things that would happen in the future.
virgin A pure girl that is not married.
"The virgin ... Immanuel" Quote from Isa. 7:14.
Herod Herod I (the Great), ruler of Judea, 40 B.C. to 4 B.C.
Christ The "anointed one" (Messiah) or chosen of God.
Scriptures Holy Writings—the Old Testament.

⁷Then Herod* had a secret meeting with the wise men from the east. Herod learned from the wise men the exact time they first saw the star. ⁸Then Herod sent the wise men to Bethlehem. Herod said to the wise men, "Go and look carefully to find the new baby. When you find the baby, come tell me. Then I can go worship him too."

⁹The wise men heard the king and then left. They saw the same star they had seen in the east. The wise men followed the star. The star went before them until it stopped above the place where the baby was. ¹⁰The wise men were happy to see the star. They were filled with joy. ¹¹The wise men came to the house where the baby was. They saw the baby with his mother Mary. The wise men bowed down and worshiped the baby. The wise men opened the gifts they brought for the baby. They gave the baby treasures of gold, frankincense, and myrrh.* ¹²But God warned the wise men in a dream. God warned them not to go back to Herod. So the wise men went home to their own country a different way.

Jesus' Parents Take Him to Egypt

¹³After the wise men left, an angel of the Lord came to Joseph in a dream. The angel said, "Get up! Take the baby and his mother and escape to Egypt. Herod* will start looking for the baby. Herod wants to kill him. So stay in Egypt until I tell you ⌊it is safe⌋."

¹⁴So Joseph got up and left for Egypt with the baby and the baby's mother. They left during the night. ¹⁵Joseph stayed in Egypt until Herod* died. This happened to make clear the full meaning of what the Lord said through the prophet.* The Lord said, "I called my son to come out of Egypt."*

Herod Kills the Baby Boys in Bethlehem

¹⁶Herod* saw that the wise men had fooled him. Herod was very, very angry. So Herod gave an order to kill all the boys in Bethlehem and in all the area around Bethlehem. Herod had learned from the wise men the time ⌊the baby was born⌋. It was now two years from that time. So Herod said to kill all the boys that were two years old and younger. ¹⁷So the thing God said through the prophet* Jeremiah happened:

frankincense and myrrh Expensive perfumes.
"I called ... Egypt" Quote from Hos. 11:1.

[18] "A sound was heard in Ramah.
It was bitter crying
and much sadness.
Rachel cries for her children;
and she cannot be comforted,
because her children are dead."
Jeremiah 31:15

Joseph and Mary Return from Egypt

[19] After Herod* died, an angel of the Lord came to Joseph in a dream. This happened while Joseph was in Egypt. [20] The angel said, "Get up! Take the baby and his mother and go to Israel. The people that were trying to kill the baby are now dead." [21] So Joseph took the baby and the baby's mother and went to Israel. [22] But Joseph heard that Archelaus was now king in Judea. Archelaus became king when his father Herod died. So Joseph was afraid to go there. Joseph was warned in a dream. So Joseph left there and went to the area of Galilee. [23] Joseph went to a town called Nazareth and lived there. And so the thing happened that God said through the prophets.* God said that ⌊the Christ⌋ would be called a Nazarene.*

The Work of John the Baptizer

3 At that time John the Baptizer came and began preaching. He preached in the desert area of Judea. [2] John said, "Change your hearts and lives because the kingdom of heaven is coming soon." [3] John the Baptizer is the one that Isaiah the prophet* was talking about. Isaiah said:

"There is a person shouting
in the desert:
'Prepare the way for the Lord;
make his paths straight.'"
Isaiah 40:3

[4] John's clothes were made from camel's hair. John had a leather belt around his waist. For food, John ate locusts* and wild honey. [5] People went to hear John preach. The people came from Jerusalem and all Judea and all the area around the Jordan River. [6] People told the sins they had done, and John baptized* them in the Jordan River.

[7] Many Pharisees* and Sadducees* came to the place where John was baptizing people. When John saw them he said to them: "You are all snakes! Who warned you to run away from God's anger that is coming? [8] You must do the things that show that you have really changed your hearts and lives. [9] And don't think that you can boast and say to yourselves, 'Abraham is our father.' I tell you that God could make children for Abraham from these rocks here. [10] The ax is now ready to cut down the trees.* Every tree that does not make good fruit will be cut down and thrown into the fire.

[11] "I baptize you with water to show that you changed your hearts and lives. But there is a person coming later that is greater than I am. I am not good enough to take off his shoes for him. He will baptize you with the Holy Spirit* and with fire. [12] He will come ready to clean the grain.* He will separate the good grain from the straw. He will put the good part of the grain into his barn. And he will burn the part that is not good. He will burn it with a fire that cannot be stopped."

Jesus Is Baptized by John

[13] At that time Jesus came from Galilee to the Jordan River. Jesus came to John and wanted John to baptize* him. [14] But John tried to say that he was not good enough to baptize Jesus. John said, "Why do you come to me to be baptized? I should be baptized by you!"

[15] Jesus answered, "Let it be this way for now. We should do all things that are right." So John agreed to baptize Jesus.

[16] Jesus was baptized and he came up out of the water. The sky opened, and he saw God's Spirit coming down on him like a dove. [17] And a voice

---

baptize(d) A Greek word meaning to immerse, dip, or bury a person or thing briefly under water.

Pharisees The Pharisees were a Jewish religious group that claimed to follow carefully all Jewish laws and customs.

Sadducees A leading Jewish religious group. They accepted only the first five books of the Old Testament. They believed that people don't live again after death.

trees The people that don't accept Jesus. They are like "trees" that will be cut down.

Holy Spirit Called the Spirit of God, the Spirit of Christ, and the Comforter. Joined with God and Christ, he does God's work among people in the world.

clean the grain John means that Jesus will separate the good people from the bad people.

Herod Herod I (the Great), ruler of Judea, 40 B.C. to 4 B.C.

prophet(s) Prophets were people who spoke for God. Their writings are part of the Old Testament.

Nazarene A person from the city of Nazareth, a name probably meaning "branch" (See Isa. 11:1).

locusts Insects like grasshoppers. The law of Moses said that locusts could be eaten (See Lev. 11:21-22).

spoke from heaven. The voice said, "This *(Jesus)* is my Son and I love him. I am very pleased with him."

The Temptation of Jesus

4 Then the Spirit* led Jesus into the desert. Jesus was taken there to be tempted by the devil. ²Jesus ate nothing for 40 days and nights. After this, he was very hungry. ³The devil came to Jesus to tempt him. The devil said, "If you are the Son of God, tell these rocks to become bread." ⁴Jesus answered him, "It is written ⌊in the Scriptures⌋,*

> 'It is not just bread that keeps people alive.
> People's lives depend on what God says.'"
> *Deuteronomy 8:3*

⁵Then the devil led Jesus to the holy city *(Jerusalem)*. The devil put Jesus on a very high place on the temple.* ⁶The devil said, "If you are the Son of God, jump off. Why? Because it is written ⌊in the Scriptures⌋,

> 'God will command his angels for you,
> and their hands will catch you,
> so that you will not hit your foot
> on a rock.'"
> *Psalm 91:11-12*

⁷Jesus answered him, "It also says ⌊in the Scriptures⌋,

> 'You must not test *(doubt)* the
> Lord your God.'"
> *Deuteronomy 6:16*

⁸Then the devil led Jesus to the top of a very high mountain. The devil showed Jesus all the kingdoms of the world, and all the great things that are in those kingdoms. ⁹The devil said, "If you will bow down and worship me, I will give you all these things." ¹⁰Jesus said to the devil, "Go away from me, Satan! It is written ⌊in the Scriptures⌋,*

> 'You must worship the Lord your God.
> Serve only him!'"
> *Deuteronomy 6:13*

¹¹So the devil left Jesus. And then some angels came to Jesus and helped him.

Jesus Begins His Work in Galilee

¹²Jesus heard that John was put in prison. So Jesus went back to Galilee. ¹³Jesus did not stay in Nazareth. He went and lived in Capernaum, a town near the lake *(Lake Galilee)*. Capernaum is in the area near Zebulun and Naphtali. ¹⁴Jesus did this to make happen what the prophet* Isaiah said:

> ¹⁵ "The land of Zebulun
> and the land of Naphtali,
> the way to the sea,
> past the Jordan River,
> Galilee, the land of non-Jewish people—
> ¹⁶ those people live in darkness *(sin)*,
> but they have seen a great light;
> the light has come for those people
> that live in the land that is dark
> like a grave."
> *Isaiah 9:1-2*

Jesus Chooses Some Followers

¹⁷From that time Jesus began to preach. This is what he said: "Change your hearts and lives, because the kingdom of heaven is coming soon." ¹⁸Jesus was walking by Lake Galilee. He saw two brothers, Simon (called Peter) and Simon's brother Andrew. The two brothers were fishermen and they were fishing in the lake with a net. ¹⁹Jesus said, "Come follow me. I will make you ⌊a different kind of⌋ fishermen. You will work to gather people, ⌊not fish⌋." ²⁰Simon and Andrew left their nets and followed Jesus. ²¹Jesus continued walking by Lake Galilee. He saw two other brothers, James and John, the sons of Zebedee. They were in a boat with their father Zebedee. They were preparing their nets to catch fish. Jesus told the brothers to come with him. ²²So the brothers left the boat and their father, and they followed Jesus.

Jesus Teaches and Heals People

²³Jesus went everywhere in the country of Galilee. Jesus taught in the synagogues* and preached the Good News about the kingdom of heaven. And Jesus healed all the people's diseases and sicknesses. ²⁴The news about Jesus spread all over Syria. And people brought all the sick people to Jesus. These sick people were suffering from

---

Spirit The Holy Spirit. Also called the Spirit of God, Spirit of Christ, and the Comforter. Joined with God and Christ, he does God's work among people in the world.
Scriptures Holy Writings—the Old Testament.
temple The special building in Jerusalem for Jewish worship.

prophet Person who spoke for God. He often told things that would happen in the future.
synagogues Synagogues were places where Jews gathered for prayer, study of the Scriptures, and other public meetings.

different kinds of diseases and pain. Some people were suffering with very bad pain, some people had demons* inside them, some people were epileptics,* and some people were paralyzed (crippled). Jesus healed all these people. ²⁵Many, many people followed Jesus. These people were from Galilee, the Ten Towns,* Jerusalem, Judea, and the area across the Jordan River.

Jesus Teaches the People

5 Jesus saw the many people that were there. So Jesus went up on a hill and sat down. His followers came to him. ²Jesus taught the people. He said:

³ "People that ₍know they₎ have
great spiritual needs are blessed.
The kingdom of heaven belongs
to those people.
⁴ People that are sad now are blessed.
God will comfort those people.
⁵ People that are humble are blessed.
They will have the land ₍God promised₎.*
⁶ People that want to do right
more than anything else are blessed.
God will fully satisfy them.
⁷ People that give mercy to other people are
blessed.
Mercy will be given to them.
⁸ People that are pure in their thinking
are blessed.
Those people will be with God.
⁹ People that work to bring peace are blessed.
God will call those people his sons.
¹⁰ People that are treated badly
for doing good are blessed.
The kingdom of heaven belongs
to those people.

¹¹"People will say bad things against you and hurt you. They will lie and say all kinds of evil things against you because you follow me. But when people do those things to you, you are blessed. ¹²Be happy and glad. You have a great reward waiting for you in heaven. People did those same bad things to the prophets* that lived before you.

---

demons Demons are evil spirits from the devil.
epileptics People with a sickness that causes them sometimes to lose control of their bodies.
Ten Towns Greek, "Decapolis," an area on the east side of Lake Galilee. It once had ten main towns.
land God promised See Ps. 37:11.
prophets People who spoke for God. Their writings are part of the Old Testament.

You Are like Salt and You Are like Light

¹³"You are the salt of the earth. But if the salt loses its taste, then it cannot be made salty again. Salt is good for nothing if it loses its salty taste. It must be thrown out and people walk on it.

¹⁴"You are the light that gives light to the world. A city that is built on a hill cannot be hidden. ¹⁵And people don't hide a light under a bowl. No. People put the light on a lamp table. Then the light shines for all the people in the house. ¹⁶In the same way, you should be a light for other people. Live so that people will see the good things you do. Live so that people will praise your Father in heaven.

Jesus and the Old Testament Writings

¹⁷"Don't think that I have come to destroy the law ₍of Moses₎ or the ₍teaching of the₎ prophets.* I have not come to destroy their teachings. I came to give full meaning to their teachings. ¹⁸I tell you the truth. Nothing will disappear from the law until heaven and earth are gone. The law will not lose even the smallest letter or the smallest part of a letter until all has happened. ¹⁹A person should obey every command, even a command that does not seem important. If a person refuses to obey any command and teaches other people not to obey that command, then that person will be the least important in the kingdom of heaven. But the person that obeys the law and teaches other people to obey the law will be great in the kingdom of heaven. ²⁰I tell you that you must do better than the teachers of the law and the Pharisees.* If you are not better people, then you will not enter the kingdom of heaven.

Jesus Teaches About Anger

²¹"You have heard that it was said to our people long ago, 'Don't kill any person.* And any person that kills will be judged.' ²²But I tell you, don't be angry with another person. Every person is your brother. If you are angry with other people, you will be judged. And if you say bad things to another person, you will be judged by the Jewish council. And if you call another person a fool, you will be in danger of the fire of hell.

²³"So when you offer your gift to God, think about other people. If you are offering your gift

---

Pharisees The Pharisees were a Jewish religious group that claimed to follow carefully all Jewish laws and customs.
'Don't kill any person' Quote from Ex. 20:13; Deut. 5:17.

before the altar,* and you remember that your brother has something against you, ²⁴then leave your gift there at the altar. Go and make peace with that person. Then come and offer your gift.

²⁵"If your enemy is taking you to court, then become friends with him quickly. You should do that before you go to court. If you don't become his friend, then he might give you to the judge. And the judge might give you to a guard to put you in jail. ²⁶And I tell you that you will not leave that jail until you have paid everything you owe.

Jesus Teaches About Sexual Sin

²⁷"You have heard that it was said, 'Don't do the sin of adultery.'* ²⁸But I tell you that if a person looks at a woman and wants to sin sexually with her, then that person has already done that sin with the woman in his mind. ²⁹If your right eye makes you sin, then take it out and throw it away. It is better to lose one part of your body than to have your whole body thrown into hell. ³⁰If your right hand makes you sin, cut it off and throw it away. It is better to lose one part of your body than for your whole body to go into hell.

Jesus Teaches About Divorce

³¹"It was also said, 'Any person that divorces his wife must give her a written notice of divorce.'* ³²But I tell you that any person that divorces his wife is causing his wife to be guilty of the sin of adultery.* The only reason for a person to divorce his wife is if his wife had sexual relations with another man. And any person that marries that divorced woman is guilty of the sin of adultery.

Jesus Teaches About Making Promises

³³"You have heard that it was said to our people long ago, 'When you make a vow* (promise), don't break that promise. Keep the vows (promises) that you make to the Lord.'* ³⁴But I tell you, never make a vow. Don't make a vow using the name of heaven, because heaven is God's throne. ³⁵Don't make a vow using the name of the earth, because the earth belongs to God. Don't make a vow using the name of Jerusalem, because that is the city of the great King (God). ³⁶And don't even say that your own head is proof that you will keep your vow. You cannot make one hair on your head become white or black. ³⁷Say only 'yes' if you mean yes, and say only 'no' if you mean no. If you must say more than 'yes' or 'no,' it is from the Evil One (the devil).

Jesus Teaches About Fighting Back

³⁸"You have heard that it was said, 'An eye for an eye, and a tooth for a tooth.'* ³⁹But I tell you, don't stand against an evil person. If someone hits you on the right cheek, then turn and let him hit the other cheek too. ⁴⁰If a person wants to sue you in court and take your shirt, then let him have your coat too. ⁴¹If a soldier forces you to walk with him one mile, then go with him two miles. ⁴²If a person asks you for something, then give it to him. Don't refuse to give to a person that wants to borrow from you.

Love All People

⁴³"You have heard that it was said, 'Love your neighbor* and hate your enemy.' ⁴⁴But I tell you, love your enemies. Pray for those people that do bad things to you. ⁴⁵If you do this, then you will be true sons of your Father in heaven. Your Father lets the sun rise for the good people and the bad people. Your Father sends rain to people that do good and to people that do wrong. ⁴⁶If you love only the people that love you, then you will get no reward. Even the tax collectors* do that. ⁴⁷And if you are nice only to your friends, then you are no better than other people. Even the people without God are nice to their friends. ⁴⁸So you must be perfect, the same as your Father in heaven is perfect.

Jesus Teaches About Giving

6"Be careful! When you do good things, don't do those things in front of people. Don't do those things for people to see you. If you do that, then you will have no reward from your Father in heaven.

²"When you give to poor people, don't announce that you are giving. Don't do like the hypocrites* do. They blow trumpets before they

---

altar Place where sacrifices or gifts are offered to God.
'Don't ... adultery' Quote from Ex. 20:14; Deut. 5:18.
'Any person ... divorce' Quote from Deut. 24:1.
adultery Breaking a marriage promise by sexual sin.
vow A very strong promise that a person makes, often using the name of something important.
'When ... Lord.' See Lev. 19:12; Num. 30:2; Deut. 23:21.

'An eye ... tooth' Quote from Ex. 21:24; Lev. 24:20.
'Love your neighbor' Quote from Lev. 19:18.
tax collectors Jews hired by the Romans to collect taxes. They often cheated, and the other Jews hated them.
hypocrites Bad people that act like they are good.

give so that people will see them. They do that in the synagogues* and on the streets. They want other people to give honor to them. ³So when you give to poor people, give very secretly. Don't let any person know what you are doing. ⁴Your giving should be done in secret. Your Father can see the things that are done in secret. And he will reward you.

Jesus Teaches About Prayer

⁵"When you pray, don't be like the hypocrites.* The hypocrites love to stand in the synagogues* and on the street corners and pray loudly. They want people to see them pray. I tell you the truth. They already have their full reward. ⁶When you pray, you should go into your room and close the door. Then pray to your Father that cannot be seen. Your Father can see the things that are done in secret. And he will reward you.

⁷"And when you pray, don't be like those people that don't know God. They continue saying things that mean nothing. Don't pray like that. They think that God will hear them because of the many things they say. ⁸Don't be like those people. Your Father knows the things you need before you ask him. ⁹So when you pray, you should pray like this:

'Our Father in heaven,
we pray that your name will always
be kept holy.
¹⁰ We pray that your kingdom will come,
and that the things you want
will be done here on earth,
the same as in heaven.
¹¹ Give us the food we need for each day.
¹² Forgive the sins we have done,
the same as we have forgiven the people
that did wrong to us.
¹³ Don't cause us to be tempted *(tested)*;
but save us from the Evil One *(the devil)*.'*

¹⁴Yes, if you forgive other people for the things they do wrong, then your Father in heaven will also forgive you for the things you do wrong. ¹⁵But if you don't forgive the wrong things people do to you, then your Father in heaven will not forgive the wrong things you do.

---

synagogues Synagogues were places where Jews gathered for prayer, study of the Scriptures, and other public meetings.
hypocrites Bad people that act like they are good.
Verse 13 Some Greek copies add: "For the kingdom and the power and the glory belong to you forever and ever. Amen."

Jesus Teaches About Fasting

¹⁶"When you fast,* don't make yourselves look sad. The hypocrites* do that. Don't be like the hypocrites. They make their faces look strange to show people that they are fasting. I tell you the truth, those hypocrites already have their full reward. ¹⁷So when you fast, make yourself look nice. Wash your face. ¹⁸Then people will not know that you are fasting. But your Father that you cannot see will see you. Your Father sees the things that are done in secret. And he will reward you.

God Is More Important than Money

¹⁹"Don't save treasures for yourselves here on earth. Moths and rust will destroy treasures here on earth. And thieves can break into your house and steal the things you have. ²⁰So save your treasure in heaven. The treasures in heaven cannot be destroyed by moths or rust. And thieves cannot break in and steal that treasure. ²¹Your heart will be where your treasure is.

²²"The eye is a light for the body. If your eyes are good, then your whole body will be full of light. ²³But if your eyes are bad, then your whole body will be full of darkness *(sin)*. And if the only light you have is really darkness, then you have the worst darkness.

²⁴"No person can serve two masters at the same time. He will hate one master and love the other master. Or he will follow one master and refuse to follow the other master. So you cannot serve God and money at the same time.

Put God's Kingdom First

²⁵"So I tell you, don't worry about the food you need to live. And don't worry about the clothes you need for your body. Life is more important than food. And the body is more important than clothes. ²⁶Look at the birds. They don't plant or harvest or save food in barns. But your heavenly Father feeds those birds. And you know that you are worth much more than the birds. ²⁷You cannot add any time to your life by worrying about it.

²⁸"And why do you worry about clothes? Look at the flowers in the field. See how they grow. They don't work or make clothes for themselves. ²⁹But I tell you that even Solomon, the great and rich king, was not dressed as beautifully as one of these flowers. ³⁰God clothes the grass in the field like that. That grass is living today, but tomorrow

---

fast To live without food for a special time of prayer.

it is thrown into the fire to be burned. So you know that God will clothe you much more. Don't have so little faith! ³¹Don't worry and say, 'What will we eat?' or 'What will we drink?' or 'What will we wear?' ³²All the people that don't know God try to get these things. Don't worry, because your Father in heaven knows that you need these things. ³³The thing you should want most is God's kingdom and doing the good things God wants you to do. Then all these other things you need will be given to you. ³⁴So don't worry about tomorrow. Each day has enough trouble of its own. Tomorrow will have its own worries.

Jesus Teaches About Judging People

7 "Don't judge other people, and God will not judge you. ²If you judge other people, you will be judged in the same way you judge them. And the forgiveness you give to other people will be given to you. ³"Why do you notice the small piece of dust that is in your brother's eye, but you don't notice the big piece of wood that is in your own eye? ⁴Why do you say to your brother, 'Let me take that little piece of dust out of your eye'? Look at yourself first! You still have that big piece of wood in your own eye. ⁵You are a hypocrite.* First, take the wood out of your own eye. Then you will see clearly to take the dust out of your brother's eye.

⁶"Don't give holy things to dogs. They will only turn and hurt you. And don't throw your pearls to pigs. They will only step on them.

Continue to Ask God for All You Need

⁷"Continue to ask, and God will give to you. Continue to search, and you will find. Continue to knock, and the door will open for you. ⁸Yes, if a person continues asking, that person will receive. If a person continues looking, that person will find. And if a person continues knocking, the door will open for that person.

⁹"Do any of you have a son? If your son asked for bread, would you give him a rock? No! ¹⁰Or if your son asked for a fish, would you give him a snake? No! ¹¹ ⌊You are not like God⌋—you are evil. But you know how to give good things to your children. So surely your heavenly Father will give good things to those people that ask him.

hypocrite A bad person that acts like he is good.

The Most Important Rule

¹²"Do to other people the same things you want them to do to you. This is the meaning of the law ⌊of Moses⌋ and the ⌊teaching of the⌋ prophets.*

The Way to Heaven and the Way to Hell

¹³"Enter through the narrow gate ⌊that opens the way to heaven⌋. The road that leads to hell is a very easy road. And the gate to hell is very wide. Many people enter that gate. ¹⁴But the gate that opens the way to ⌊true⌋ life is very small. And the road to ⌊true⌋ life is very difficult *(hard)*. Only a few people find that road.

Watch the Things People Do

¹⁵"Be careful of false prophets.* They come to you and look ⌊gentle⌋ like sheep. But they are really dangerous ⌊like⌋ wolves. ¹⁶You will know these people because of the things they do. Good things don't come from bad people, the same as grapes don't come from thorn bushes. And figs don't come from thorny weeds. ¹⁷In the same way, every good tree makes good fruit. And bad trees make bad fruit. ¹⁸A good tree cannot make bad fruit. And a bad tree cannot make good fruit. ¹⁹Every tree that does not make good fruit is cut down and thrown into the fire. ²⁰You will know these false people by the fruit they make *(things they do)*.

²¹"Not every person that says that I am his Lord will enter the kingdom of heaven. The only people that will enter the kingdom of heaven are those people that do the things that my Father in heaven wants. ²²On the last day many people will say to me, 'You are our Lord! We spoke for you. And for you we forced out demons* and did many miracles.*' ²³Then I will tell those people clearly, 'Go away from me, you people that do wrong. I never knew you.'

A Wise Person and a Foolish Person

²⁴"Every person that hears these things I say and obeys these things is like a wise man. The wise man built his house on rock. ²⁵It rained hard and the water rose. The winds blew and hit that house. But the house did not fall, because the

prophets People who spoke for God. Their writings are part of the Old Testament.
false prophets People who say they speak for God but do not really speak God's truth.
demons Demons are evil spirits from the devil.
miracles Amazing works done by God's power.

house was built on rock. ²⁶But the person that hears the things I teach and does not obey those things is like a foolish man. The foolish man built his house on sand. ²⁷It rained hard, the water rose, and the winds blew and hit that house. And the house fell with a loud noise."

²⁸When Jesus finished saying these things, the people were amazed at his teaching. ²⁹Jesus did not teach like their teachers of the law. Jesus taught like a person that had authority *(power)*.

Jesus Heals a Sick Man

8 Jesus came down from the hill. Many, many people followed him. ²Then a man sick with leprosy* came to Jesus. The man bowed down before Jesus and said, "Lord, you have the power to heal me if you want."

³Jesus touched the man. Jesus said, "I want to heal you. Be healed!" And immediately the man was healed from his leprosy.* ⁴Then Jesus said to him, "Don't tell any person about what happened. But go and show yourself to the priest.* And offer the gift that Moses commanded ⌊for people that are made well⌋. This will show people that you are healed."

Jesus Heals an Officer's Servant

⁵Jesus went to the city of Capernaum. When Jesus entered the city, an army officer* came to him and begged for help. ⁶The officer said, "Lord, my servant is very sick at home in bed. He can't move his body and has much pain."

⁷Jesus said to the officer, "I will go and heal him."

⁸The officer answered, "Lord, I am not good enough for you to come into my house. All you need to do is command that my servant be healed, and he will be healed. ⁹I myself am a man under the authority *(power)* of other men. And I have soldiers under my authority. I tell one soldier, 'Go,' and he goes. I tell another soldier, 'Come,' and he comes. I say to my servant, 'Do this,' and my servant obeys me. ⌊I know that you also have power like this⌋."

¹⁰When Jesus heard this, he was amazed. Jesus said to those people that were with him, "I tell you the truth. This man has more faith than any person I have found, even in Israel.* ¹¹Many people will come from the east and from the west. Those people will sit and eat with Abraham, Isaac, and Jacob* in the kingdom of heaven. ¹²And those people *(the Jews)* that should have the kingdom will be thrown out. They will be thrown outside into the darkness. In that place people will cry and grind their teeth ⌊with pain⌋."

¹³Then Jesus said to the officer,* "Go home. Your servant will be healed the way you believed he would." And at that same time his servant was healed.

Jesus Heals Many People

¹⁴Jesus went to Peter's house. There Jesus saw that Peter's mother-in-law was in bed with a high fever. ¹⁵Jesus touched her hand and the fever left her. Then she stood up and began to serve Jesus.

¹⁶That evening people brought to Jesus many people that had demons* inside them. Jesus spoke and the demons left the people. Jesus healed all the people that were sick. ¹⁷Jesus did these things to make happen what Isaiah the prophet* said:

> "He took away our diseases
> and carried away our sicknesses."
> *Isaiah 53:4*

Following Jesus

¹⁸Jesus saw that all the people were around him. So Jesus told his followers to go to the other side of the lake. ¹⁹Then a teacher of the law came to Jesus and said, "Teacher, I will follow you any place you go."

²⁰Jesus said to him, "The foxes have holes to live in. The birds have nests to live in. But the Son of Man* has no place where he can rest his head."

²¹Another man, one of Jesus' followers, said to Jesus, "Lord, let me go and bury my father first. ⌊Then I will follow you⌋."

²²But Jesus said to him, "Follow me, and let the people that are dead bury their own dead."

Jesus Stops a Storm

²³Jesus got into a boat and his followers went with him. ²⁴After the boat left the shore, a very

---

leprosy A very bad skin disease.
show yourself to the priest The law of Moses said a priest must say when a Jew with leprosy was well.
officer A centurion, a Roman army officer who had authority over 100 soldiers.
Israel The Jewish nation (people).
Abraham, Isaac, Jacob Three of the most important Jewish leaders during the time of the Old Testament.
demons Demons are evil spirits from the devil.
prophet Person who spoke for God. He often told things that would happen in the future.
Son of Man Jesus. In Dan. 7:13-14 this is the name for the Messiah, the one God chose to save his people.

bad storm began on the lake. The waves covered the boat. But Jesus was sleeping. ²⁵The followers went to Jesus and woke him. They said, "Lord, save us! We will drown!"

²⁶Jesus answered, "Why are you afraid? You don't have enough faith." Then Jesus stood and gave a command to the wind and the waves. The wind stopped, and the lake became very calm.

²⁷The men were amazed. They said, "What kind of man is this? Even the wind and the water obey him!"

Jesus Sends Demons Out from Two Men

²⁸Jesus arrived at the other side of the lake in the country of the Gadarene* people. There, two men came to Jesus. They had demons* inside them. These men lived in the burial caves. They were very dangerous. So people could not use the road by those caves. ²⁹The two men came to Jesus and shouted, "What do you want with us, Son of God? Did you come here to punish us before the right time?"

³⁰Near that place there was a large herd of pigs feeding. ³¹The demons begged Jesus, "If you make us leave these men, please send us into that herd of pigs."

³²Jesus said to them, "Go!" So the demons left those men and went into the pigs. Then the whole herd of pigs ran down the hill and into the lake. All the pigs drowned in the water. ³³The men that had the work of caring for the pigs ran away. They went into town and told the people what happened. They told about all that happened with the pigs and with the men that had demons. ³⁴Then the whole town went out to see Jesus. When the people saw Jesus, they begged him to leave their area.

Jesus Heals a Crippled Man

9 Jesus got into a boat and went back across the lake to his own town. ²Some people brought to Jesus a man that was paralyzed *(crippled)*. The man was lying on his bed. Jesus saw that these people had much faith. So Jesus said to the paralyzed man, "Be happy, young man. Your sins are forgiven."

³Some of the teachers of the law heard this. They said to themselves, "This man *(Jesus)* speaks like he is God—that is blasphemy.*"

⁴Jesus knew they were thinking this. So Jesus said, "Why are you thinking evil thoughts? ⁵Which is easier: to tell this paralyzed man, 'Your sins are forgiven,' or to tell him, 'Stand up and walk'? ⁶But I will prove to you that the Son of Man* has power on earth to forgive sins." Then Jesus said to the paralyzed man, "Stand up. Take your bed and go home." ⁷And the man stood up and went home. ⁸The people saw this and they were amazed. The people praised God for giving power like this to men.

Jesus Chooses Matthew

⁹When Jesus was leaving, he saw a man named Matthew. Matthew was sitting in the tax office. Jesus said to him, "Follow me." Then Matthew stood up and followed Jesus.

¹⁰Jesus ate dinner at Matthew's house. Many tax collectors* and other bad people came and ate with Jesus and his followers. ¹¹The Pharisees* saw that Jesus was eating with these people. The Pharisees asked Jesus' followers, "Why does your teacher eat with tax collectors and other bad people?"

¹²Jesus heard the Pharisees* say this. So Jesus said to the Pharisees, "Healthy people don't need a doctor. It is the sick people that need a doctor. ¹³I will tell you something. Go and learn what it means: 'I don't want animal sacrifices. I want kindness ⌊among people⌋.'* I did not come to invite good people. I came to invite sinners."

Jesus Is Not Like Other Religious Jews

¹⁴Then the followers of John* came to Jesus. They said to Jesus, "We and the Pharisees* fast* often. But your followers don't fast. Why?"

¹⁵Jesus answered, "⌊When there is a wedding⌋, the friends of the bridegroom* are not sad while he is with them. But the time will come when the bridegroom will leave them. The friends are sad when the bridegroom leaves. Then they will fast.*

¹⁶"When a person sews a patch over a hole on an old coat, he never uses a piece of cloth that is not yet shrunk. If he does, the patch will ⌊shrink

---

tax collectors Jews hired by the Romans to collect taxes. They often cheated, and the other Jews hated them.
Pharisees The Pharisees were a Jewish religious group that claimed to follow carefully all Jewish laws and customs.
'I don't want ... people' Quote from Hos. 6:6.
John John the Baptizer. He preached to people about Christ's coming (Mt. 3; Lk. 3).
fast To live without food for a time of prayer or mourning.
bridegroom A man ready to be married.

Gadarene From Gadara, an area southeast of Lake Galilee.
demons Demons are evil spirits from the devil.
blasphemy Saying things against God.

and₁ pull away from the coat. Then the hole will be worse. ¹⁷Also, people never pour new wine into old wine bags.* Why? Because the old bags will break. The wine will spill, and the wine bags will be ruined. But people always pour new wine into new wine bags. Then the wine and the wine bags will continue to be good."

Jesus Gives Life to a Dead Girl and Heals a Sick Woman

¹⁸While Jesus was saying these things, a ruler of the synagogue* came to him. The ruler bowed down before Jesus and said, "My daughter has just died. But come and touch her with your hand, and she will live again." ¹⁹So Jesus stood up and went with the ruler. Jesus' followers went too.

²⁰There was a woman that had been bleeding for twelve years. The woman came behind Jesus and touched the bottom of his coat. ²¹The woman was thinking, "If I can touch his coat, then I will be healed."

²²Jesus turned and saw the woman. Jesus said, "Be happy, dear woman. You are made well because you believed." Then the woman was healed.

²³Jesus continued going with the ruler, and went into the ruler's house. Jesus saw people there that make music for funerals. And he saw many people there crying ₁because the girl died₁. ²⁴Jesus said, "Go away. The girl is not dead. She is only asleep." But the people laughed at Jesus. ²⁵After the people were put out of the house, Jesus went into the girl's room. Jesus held the girl's hand, and the girl stood up. ²⁶The news about this spread all around the area.

Jesus Heals More People

²⁷When Jesus was leaving there, two blind men followed him. The blind men said loudly, "Show kindness to us, Son of David.*"

²⁸Jesus went inside, and the blind men went with him. Jesus asked the men, "Do you believe that I am able to make you see again?" The blind men answered, "Yes, Lord, we believe."

²⁹Then Jesus touched their eyes and said, "You believe that I can make you see again, so this will happen." ³⁰Then the men were able to see again. Jesus warned them very strongly. Jesus said, "Don't tell any person about this." ³¹But the blind men left and spread the news about Jesus all around that area.

³²When the two men were leaving, some people brought another man to Jesus. This man could not talk because he had a demon* inside him. ³³Jesus forced the demon to leave the man. Then the man that couldn't talk was able to speak. The people were amazed and said, "We have never seen anything like this in Israel."

³⁴But the Pharisees* said, "The leader of demons *(the devil)* is the one that gives him *(Jesus)* power to force demons out."

Jesus Feels Sorry for the People

³⁵Jesus traveled through all the towns and villages. Jesus taught in their synagogues* and told people the Good News about the kingdom. And Jesus healed all kinds of diseases and sicknesses. ³⁶Jesus saw the many people and felt sorry for them. Jesus felt sorry for the people because the people were worried and helpless. The people were like sheep without a shepherd to lead them. ³⁷Jesus said to his followers, "There are many, many people to harvest *(save)*. But there are only a few workers to help harvest them. ³⁸God owns the harvest *(people)*. Pray to him that he will send more workers to help gather his harvest."

Jesus Sends His Apostles to Preach

10 Jesus called his twelve followers together. Jesus gave them power over evil spirits. Jesus gave them power to heal every kind of disease and sickness. ²These are the names of the twelve apostles*: Simon (also called Peter) and his brother Andrew; James, son of Zebedee, and his brother John; ³Philip and Bartholomew; Thomas and Matthew, the tax collector; James, son of Alphaeus, and Thaddaeus; ⁴Simon the Zealot* and Judas Iscariot. Judas is the one that gave Jesus to his enemies.

⁵Jesus gave these twelve apostles* some orders. Then he sent them ₁to tell people about the kingdom₁. Jesus said, "Don't go to the non-Jewish people. And don't go into any town where the

---

wine bags Bags made from the skin of an animal and used for holding wine.

synagogue(s) Synagogues were places where Jews gathered for prayer, study of the Scriptures, and other public meetings.

Son of David Name for the Christ. He was from the family of David, king of Israel.

demon A demon is an evil spirit from the devil.

Pharisees The Pharisees were a Jewish religious group that claimed to follow carefully all Jewish laws and customs.

apostles The men Jesus chose to be his special helpers.

Zealot The Zealots were a Jewish political group.

Samaritans* live. ⁶But go to the people of Israel *(the Jews)*. They are like sheep that are lost. ⁷When you go, preach this: 'The kingdom of heaven is coming soon.' ⁸Heal sick people. Give dead people life again. Heal those people that have leprosy.* Force demons* to leave people. I give you these powers freely. So help other people freely. ⁹Don't carry any money with you—gold or silver or copper. ¹⁰Don't carry a bag. Take for your trip only the clothes and shoes you are wearing. Don't take a walking stick. A worker should be given the things he needs.

¹¹"When you enter a city or town, find some worthy person there and stay in his home until you leave. ¹²When you enter that home say, 'Peace be with you.' ¹³If the people in that home welcome you, then they are worthy of your peace. May they have the peace you wished them. But if the people don't welcome you, then they are not worthy of your peace. Take back the peace you wished for them. ¹⁴And if a home or town refuses to welcome you or listen to you, then leave that place. Shake their dust off your feet.* ¹⁵I tell you the truth. On the judgment day it will be worse for that town than for the towns of Sodom and Gomorrah.*

Jesus Warns About Troubles

¹⁶"Listen! I am sending you, and you will be like sheep among wolves. So be smart like snakes. But also be like doves and do nothing wrong. ¹⁷Be careful of people. They will arrest you and take you to be judged. They will whip you in their synagogues.* ¹⁸You will be taken to stand before governors and kings. People will do this to you because of me. You will tell about me to those kings and governors and to the non-Jewish people. ¹⁹When you are arrested, don't worry about what to say or how you should say it. At that time you will be given the things to say. ²⁰It will not really be you speaking. The Spirit of your Father will be speaking through you.

²¹"Brothers will turn against their own brothers and give them to be killed. Fathers will turn against their own children and give them to be killed. Children will fight against their own parents and will send their parents to be killed. ²²All people will hate you because you follow me. But the person that continues strong until the end will be saved. ²³When you are treated badly in one city, go to another city. I tell you the truth. You will not finish going through all the cities of Israel before the Son of Man* comes again.

²⁴"A student is not better than his teacher. A servant is not better than his master. ²⁵A student should be satisfied to become like his teacher. A servant should be satisfied to become like his master. If the head of the family is called Beelzebul *(the devil)*, then the other members of the family will be called worse names!"

Fear God, Not People

²⁶"So don't be afraid of those people. Everything that is hidden will be shown. Everything that is secret will be made known. ²⁷I tell you these things in the dark *(secretly)*. But I want you to tell these things in the light. I speak these things quietly and only to you. But you should tell these things freely to all people. ²⁸Don't be afraid of people. They can only kill the body. They cannot kill the soul. The only one you should fear is the One *(God)* that can destroy the body and the soul. He can send the body and the soul to hell. ²⁹When birds are sold, two small birds cost only a penny. But not even one of those little birds can die without your Father allowing it. ³⁰God even knows how many hairs are on your head. ³¹So don't be afraid. You are worth much more than many birds.

Telling People About Your Faith

³²"When a person stands before other people and says he believes in me, then I will say that person belongs to me. I will say this before my Father in heaven. ³³But when a person stands before people and says he does not believe in me, then I will say that person does not belong to me. I will say this before my Father in heaven.

³⁴"Don't think that I have come to bring peace to the earth. I did not come to bring peace. I came to bring a sword. ³⁵⁻³⁶I have come to make this happen:

Samaritans People from Samaria. They were part Jewish, but the Jews did not accept them as pure Jews.
leprosy A very bad skin disease.
demons Demons are evil spirits from the devil.
Shake their dust off your feet A warning. It would show that they were finished talking to these people.
Sodom and Gomorrah Cities that God destroyed to punish the evil people that lived there.
synagogues Synagogues were places where Jews gathered for prayer, study of the Scriptures, and other public meetings.
Son of Man Jesus. In Dan. 7:13-14 this is the name for the Messiah, the one God chose to save his people.

'The people in a person's own family will be his enemies.
A son will be against his father.
A daughter will be against her mother.
A daughter-in-law will be against her mother-in-law.
Micah 7:6

³⁷"Any person that loves his father or mother more than he loves me is not good enough to follow me. Any person who loves his son or daughter more than he loves me is not good enough to follow me. ³⁸If a person will not accept the cross *(suffering)* that will be given to him when he follows me, then that person is not good enough for me. ³⁹Any person that loves his life ⌊more than he loves me⌋ will lose true life. Any person that gives up his life for me will find true life. ⁴⁰The person that accepts you also accepts me. And the person that accepts me also accepts the One *(God)* that sent me. ⁴¹Any person that meets a prophet* and accepts him will get the reward of a prophet. And any person that accepts a good man because that man is good will get the reward of a good man. ⁴²If any person helps one of these little ones because they are my followers, then that person will truly get his reward. That person will get his reward even if he only gave my follower a cup of cold water."

Jesus and John the Baptizer

11 Jesus finished telling these things to his twelve followers. Then Jesus left there and went to the towns in Galilee to teach and preach.

²John the Baptizer was in prison. He heard about the things Christ was doing. So John sent some of his followers to Jesus. ³John's followers asked Jesus, "Are you the man that ⌊John said⌋ was coming, or should we wait for another man?" ⁴Jesus answered, "Go back to John and tell him about the things that you hear and see: ⁵Blind people are able to see again; crippled people are able to walk again; people that have leprosy* are healed; deaf people can hear again; dead people are raised from death; and the Good News* is told to the poor people. ⁶The person that can accept* me is blessed."

⁷While John's followers were leaving, Jesus began talking to the people about John. Jesus said, "What did you people go out to the desert to see? A weed* blown by the wind? No! ⁸Really, what did you go out to see? A man dressed in fine clothes? No! Those people that wear fine clothes live in king's palaces. ⁹So what did you go out to see? A prophet*? Yes, and I tell you, John is more than a prophet. ¹⁰This Scripture* was written about John:

'Listen! I *(God)* will send my helper* ahead of you.
He will prepare the way for you.'
Malachi 3:1

¹¹I tell you the truth: John the Baptizer is greater than any man that has ever lived. But even the least important person in the kingdom of heaven is greater than John. ¹²Since the time John the Baptizer came until now, the kingdom of heaven has been going forward strongly.* People using force have been trying to get the kingdom. ¹³All the prophets* and the law ⌊of Moses⌋ spoke until the time John came. They told about the things that would happen. ¹⁴And if you will believe the things the law and the prophets said, then you will believe that John is Elijah.* The law and the prophets said he would come. ¹⁵You people that hear me, listen!

¹⁶"What can I say about the people that live today? What are they like? The people today are like children sitting in the market place. One group of children calls to the other group,

¹⁷ 'We played music for you,
but you did not dance;
we sang a sad song,
but you were not sad.'

¹⁸⌊Why do I say people are like that⌋? Because John* came and he did not eat ⌊like other people⌋ or drink wine. And people say, 'He has a demon* inside him.' ¹⁹The Son of Man* came eating ⌊like

---

weed Literally, "reed." Jesus means that John was not weak like a reed blown by the wind.
Scripture Part of the Holy Writings—Old Testament.
helper Literally, "messenger."
has been ... strongly Or, "has suffered violence."
prophets People who spoke for God. Their writings are part of the Old Testament.
Elijah See Mal. 4:5-6.
John John the Baptizer. He preached to people about Christ's coming (Mt. 3; Lk. 3).
demon Demons are evil spirits from the devil.
Son of Man Jesus. In Dan. 7:13-14 this is the name for the Messiah, the one God chose to save his people.

---

prophet Person that spoke for God.
leprosy A very bad skin disease.
Good News The news that God has made a way for people to have their sins forgiven and live with God.
can accept Literally, "is not offended by."

other people, and drinking wine, and people say, 'Look at him! He eats too much and drinks too much wine. He is a friend of tax collectors* and other bad people.' But wisdom is shown to be right by the things it does."

Jesus Warns People That Don't Believe

²⁰Then Jesus criticized the cities where he did most of his miracles.* Jesus criticized those cities because the people there did not change their lives and stop sinning. ²¹Jesus said, "It will be bad for you Chorazin.* It will be bad for you Bethsaida.* I did many miracles in you. If those same miracles had happened in Tyre and Sidon,* then those people in Tyre and Sidon would have changed their lives a long time ago. Those people would have worn sackcloth* and put ashes on themselves to show that they were sorry for their sins. ²²But I tell you, on the day of judgment it will be worse for you than for Tyre and Sidon. ²³And you, Capernaum,* will you be lifted up to heaven? No! You will be thrown down to the place of death. I did many miracles in you. If those same miracles had happened in Sodom, ₍the people of₎ Sodom ₍would have stopped sinning and it₎ would still be a city today. ²⁴But I tell you it will be worse for you in the day of judgment than for Sodom."

Jesus Offers Rest to His People

²⁵Then Jesus said, "I thank you, Father, Lord of heaven and earth. I praise you because you have hidden these things from the wise and smart people. But you have shown these things to people that are like little children. ²⁶Yes, Father, you did this because this is what you really wanted to do.

²⁷"My Father has given me all things. No person knows the Son—only the Father knows the Son. And no person knows the Father—only the Son knows the Father. And the only people that will know about the Father are those people the Son chooses to tell.

²⁸"Come to me all you people that are tired and have heavy burdens. I will give you rest. ²⁹Accept my work and learn from me. I am gentle and humble in spirit. And you will find rest for your souls. ³⁰Yes, the work that I ask you to accept is easy. The burden I give you to carry is not heavy."

Some Jews Criticize Jesus

12 About that same time, Jesus was walking through the fields of grain on a Sabbath day.* Jesus' followers were with him, and they were hungry. So the followers began to pick the grain and eat it. ²The Pharisees* saw this. They said to Jesus, "Look! Your followers are doing something that is against the ₍Jewish₎ law to do on the Sabbath day."

³Jesus said to them, "You have read what David* did when he and the people with him were hungry. ⁴David went into God's house. David and the people with him ate the bread that was offered to God. It was against the law for David or the people with him to eat that bread. Only the priests were allowed to eat it. ⁵And you have read in the law ₍of Moses₎ that on every Sabbath day* the priests in the temple* break the law about the Sabbath day. But the priests are not wrong for doing that. ⁶I tell you that there is something here that is greater than the temple. ⁷The Scripture* says, 'I don't want animal sacrifices; I want kindness ₍among people₎.'* You don't really know what those words mean. If you understood those words, then you would not judge those people that have done nothing wrong.

⁸"The Son of Man* is Lord *(ruler)* over the Sabbath day.*

Jesus Heals a Man's Crippled Hand

⁹Jesus left that place and went into their synagogue.* ¹⁰In the synagogue there was a man with a crippled hand. Some Jews there were

---

tax collectors Jews hired by the Romans to collect taxes. They often cheated, and the other Jews hated them.
miracles Amazing works done by the power of God.
Chorazin, Bethsaida, Capernaum Towns by Lake Galilee where Jesus preached to the people.
Tyre and Sidon Towns in Lebanon where very bad people lived.
sackcloth A rough cloth made from animal hair. People sometimes wore it to show sadness.
Sabbath day The seventh day of the Jewish week. It was a special religious day for the Jews.
Pharisees The Pharisees were a Jewish religious group that claimed to follow carefully all Jewish laws and customs.
David King of Israel about 1000 years before Christ.
temple The special building in Jerusalem for Jewish worship.
Scripture Part of the Holy Writings—Old Testament.
'I don't ... people' Quote from Hos. 6:6.
Son of Man Jesus. In Dan. 7:13-14 this is the name for the Messiah, the one God chose to save his people.
synagogue Synagogues were places where Jews gathered for prayer, study of the Scriptures, and other public meetings.

looking for a reason to accuse Jesus of doing wrong. So they asked Jesus, "Is it right to heal on the Sabbath day?"*

¹¹Jesus answered, "If any of you has a sheep, and the sheep falls into a ditch on the Sabbath day, then you will take the sheep and help it out of the ditch. ¹²Surely a man is more important than a sheep. So the law ₍of Moses₎ allows people to do good things on the Sabbath day."

¹³Then Jesus said to the man with the crippled hand, "Let me see your hand." The man put his hand out for Jesus, and the hand became well again, the same as the other hand. ¹⁴But the Pharisees* left and made plans to kill Jesus.

Jesus Is God's Chosen Servant

¹⁵Jesus knew what the Pharisees* were doing. So Jesus left that place. Many people followed Jesus, and he healed all the sick people. ¹⁶But Jesus warned the people not to tell other people who he was. ¹⁷Jesus did these things to make happen what Isaiah the prophet* said. Isaiah said,

¹⁸ "Here is my servant;
I *(God)* have chosen him.
I love him and I am pleased with him;
I will put my Spirit on him,
and he will judge the nations fairly.
¹⁹ He will not argue or shout;
People will not hear his voice in the streets.
²⁰ He will not break the reed
that is already bent;
He will not stop the light
that has almost stopped burning.
He will continue until he makes fair judgment win the victory.
²¹ All people will hope in him."
Isaiah 42:1-4

Jesus' Power Is from God

²²Then some people brought a man to Jesus. This man was blind and could not talk, because he had a demon* inside him. Jesus healed the man, and the man could talk and see. ²³All the people were amazed. The people said, "Maybe this man *(Jesus)* is the Son of David* ₍that God promised to send to us₎!"

²⁴The Pharisees* heard the people saying this. The Pharisees said, "Jesus uses the power of Beelzebul *(the devil)* to force demons out of people. Beelzebul is the ruler of demons."

²⁵Jesus knew the things that the Pharisees* were thinking. So Jesus said to them, "Every kingdom that is fighting against itself will be destroyed. And every city that is divided cannot continue. And every family that is divided cannot succeed. ²⁶So if Satan *(the devil)* forces out his own demons,* then Satan is divided. And his kingdom will not be able to continue. ²⁷You say that I use the power of Satan when I force out demons. If that is true, then what power do your people use when they force out demons? So your own people prove that you are wrong. ²⁸But I use the power of God's Spirit to force out demons. This shows that the kingdom of God has come to you.

²⁹"If a person wants to enter a strong man's house and steal his things, first the person must tie the strong man. Then the person can steal the things from the strong man's house.

³⁰"If a person is not with me, then he is against me. The person that does not work with me is working against me. ³¹So I tell you, people can be forgiven of every sin they do. And people can be forgiven for every bad thing they say. But if a person speaks against *(refuses to accept)* the Holy Spirit,* then that person will not be forgiven. ³²Any person that says things against the Son of Man* can be forgiven. But any person that says things against the Holy Spirit will not be forgiven. That person will not be forgiven now or in the future.

The Things You Do Show What You Are

³³"If you want good fruit, you must make the tree good. If your tree is not good then it will have bad fruit. A tree is known by the kind of fruit it makes. ³⁴You snakes! You are evil people! How can you say anything good? The mouth speaks the things that are in the heart. ³⁵A good person has

---

"Is it right ... day" It was against Jewish law to work on the Sabbath day.
Pharisees The Pharisees were a Jewish religious group that claimed to follow carefully all Jewish laws and customs.
prophet Person who spoke for God. He often told things that would happen in the future.
demon(s) Demons are evil spirits from the devil.
Son of David Name for the Christ. He was from the family of David, king of Israel.
if Satan ... demons Literally, "if Satan forces out Satan."
Holy Spirit Called the Spirit of God, the Spirit of Christ, and the Comforter. Joined with God and Christ, he does God's work among people in the world.
Son of Man Jesus. In Dan. 7:13-14 this is the name for the Messiah, the one God chose to save his people.

good things saved in his heart. And so he speaks the good things that come from his heart. But an evil person has evil saved in his heart. So he speaks the evil things that come from his heart. ³⁶And I tell you that people will have to explain about every careless thing they have said. This will happen on the day of judgment. ³⁷The words you have said will be used to judge you. Some of your words will make you right, but some of your words will make you guilty."

The Jews Ask Jesus for Proof

³⁸Then some of the Pharisees* and teachers of the law answered Jesus. They said, "Teacher, we want to see you do a miracle* as a sign (proof)."
³⁹Jesus answered, "Evil and sinful people are the ones that want to see a miracle for a sign (proof). But no miracle will be given as a sign to those people. The only sign will be the miracle that happened to the prophet* Jonah. ⁴⁰Jonah was in the stomach of the big fish for three days and three nights. In the same way, the Son of Man* will be in the grave three days and three nights. ⁴¹And on the judgment day the men from Nineveh* will stand up with you people that live today, and they will show that you are wrong (guilty). Why? Because when Jonah preached to those people, they changed their lives. And I tell you that I am greater than Jonah! ⁴²On the judgment day, the Queen of the South* will stand up with you people that live today, and she will show that you are wrong (guilty). Why? Because that queen traveled from far, far away to listen to Solomon's wise teaching. And I tell you that I am greater than Solomon!

People Today Are Full of Evil

⁴³"When an evil spirit ⌊from the devil⌋ comes out of a person, that spirit travels through dry places looking for a place to rest. But that spirit finds no place to rest. ⁴⁴So the spirit says, 'I will go back to the home (person) I left.' When the spirit comes back to that person, the spirit finds that home (person) still empty. That home is swept clean and made neat. ⁴⁵Then the evil spirit goes out and brings seven other spirits more evil than itself. Then all the spirits go into that person and live there. And that person has even more trouble than he had before. It is the same way with the evil people that live today."

Jesus' Followers Are His Family

⁴⁶While Jesus was talking to the people his mother and brothers stood outside. They wanted to talk to Jesus. ⁴⁷A person told Jesus, "Your mother and brothers are waiting for you outside. They want to talk to you."
⁴⁸Jesus answered, "Who is my mother? Who are my brothers?" ⁴⁹Then Jesus pointed to his followers and said, "See! These people are my mother and my brothers. ⁵⁰My true brother and sister and mother is any person that does the things my Father in heaven wants."

Jesus Uses a Story About Planting Seed

13 That same day Jesus went out of the house and sat by the lake. ²Many, many people gathered around Jesus. So Jesus got into a boat and sat down. All the people stayed on the shore. ³Then Jesus used stories to teach the people many things. Jesus said: "A farmer went out to plant his seed. ⁴While the farmer was planting, some seed fell by the road. The birds came and ate all that seed. ⁵Some seed fell on rocky ground. The ground there did not have enough dirt. The seed grew very fast there, because the ground was not deep. ⁶But when the sun rose, it burned the plants. The plants died because they did not have deep roots. ⁷Some other seed fell among thorny weeds. The weeds grew and stopped the good plants from growing. ⁸Some other seed fell on good ground. In the good ground, the seed grew and made grain. Some plants made 100 times more grain. Some plants made 60 times more, and some made 30 times more grain. ⁹You people that hear me, listen!"

Why Jesus Used Stories to Teach

¹⁰The followers came to Jesus and asked, "Why do you use these stories to teach the people?"
¹¹Jesus answered, "Only you can know the secret truths about the kingdom of heaven. Those other people cannot know these secret truths. ¹²The person that has ⌊some understanding⌋ will be given more. And he will have even more than he needs. But the person that does not have ⌊much

---

Pharisees The Pharisees were a Jewish religious group that claimed to follow carefully all Jewish laws and customs.
miracle Amazing work done by the power of God.
prophet Person who spoke for God. The story of Jonah is in the Old Testament book of Jonah.
Son of Man Jesus. In Dan. 7:13-14 this is the name for the Messiah, the one God chose to save his people.
Nineveh City where Jonah preached. Read Jonah 3.
Queen of the South Queen of Sheba. She went 1000 miles to learn God's wisdom from Solomon. Read 1 Kings 10:1-13.

understanding⌋ will lose even the little ⌊understanding⌋ that he has. ¹³This is why I use these stories to teach the people: The people see, but they don't really see. The people hear, but they don't really understand. ¹⁴So these people show that the things Isaiah said about them are true:

> 'You people will listen
> and you will hear,
> but you will not understand.
> You people will look
> and you will see,
> but you will not understand
> what you see.
> ¹⁵ Yes, the hearts *(minds)* of these people *(the Jews)* are now hard.
> These people have ears,
> but they don't listen,
> and they refuse to see ⌊the truth⌋.
> This has happened so that they will not
> see with their eyes,
> hear with their ears,
> understand with their minds.
> This has happened so that they will not turn to
> me to heal them.'
> *Isaiah 6:9-10*

¹⁶But you are blessed. You understand the things you see with your eyes. And you understand the things you hear with your ears. ¹⁷I tell you the truth. Many prophets* and good people wanted to see the things that you now see. But they did not see these things. And many prophets and good people wanted to hear the things that you now hear. But they did not hear these things.

Jesus Explains the Seeds

¹⁸"So listen to the meaning of that story about the farmer. ¹⁹What is the seed that fell by the path? That seed is like the person that hears the teaching about the kingdom but does not understand it. The Evil One *(the devil)* comes and takes away the things that were planted in that person's heart. ²⁰And what is the seed that fell on rocky ground? That seed is like the person that hears the teaching and quickly accepts that teaching with joy. ²¹But that person does not let the teaching go deep into his life. He keeps that teaching only a short time. When trouble or persecution* comes because of the teaching he accepted, then he quickly quits. ²²And what is the seed that fell among the thorny weeds? That seed is like the person that hears the teaching but lets worries about this life and love for money stop that teaching from growing. So the teaching does not make fruit* ⌊in that person's life⌋. ²³But what is the seed that fell on the good ground? That seed is like the person that hears the teaching and understands it. That person grows and makes fruit, sometimes 100 times more, sometimes 60 times more, and sometimes 30 times more."

A Story About Wheat and Weeds

²⁴Then Jesus used another story to teach them. Jesus said, "The kingdom of heaven is like a man that planted good seed in his field. ²⁵That night, all the people were asleep. The man's enemy came and planted weeds among the wheat. Then the enemy went away. ²⁶Later, the wheat grew and heads of grain grew on the wheat plants. But at the same time the weeds also grew. ²⁷Then the man's servants came to him and said, 'You planted good seed in your field. Where did the weeds come from?'

²⁸"The man answered, 'An enemy planted weeds.'

"The servants asked, 'Do you want us to go pull the weeds?'

²⁹"The man answered, 'No, because when you pull up the weeds, you might also pull up the wheat. ³⁰Let the weeds and the wheat grow together until the harvest time. At the harvest time I will tell the workers this: First gather the weeds and tie them together to be burned. Then gather the wheat and bring it to my barn.'"

Jesus Teaches with More Stories

³¹Then Jesus told the people another story: "The kingdom of heaven is like a mustard seed. A person plants that seed in his field. ³²That seed is one of the smallest of all seeds. But when the seed grows, it is one of the largest garden plants. It becomes a tree, big enough for the birds to come and make nests in its branches."

³³Then Jesus told the people another story: "The kingdom of heaven is like yeast that a woman mixes into a big bowl of flour to make bread. The yeast makes all the dough *(bread)* rise."

³⁴Jesus used stories to tell all these things to the people. Jesus always used stories to teach the

---

prophets People that spoke for God in Old Testament times.
persecution Being hurt or bothered by God's enemies.

fruit The good things God wants his people to do.

people. ³⁵This is the same as what the prophet* said:

> "I will speak using stories;
> I will tell things that have been secrets since the world was made."
>
> *Psalm 78:2*

Jesus Explains a Hard Story

³⁶Then Jesus left the people and went into the house. His followers came to him and said, "Explain to us the meaning of the story about the weeds in the field."

³⁷Jesus answered, "The person that planted the good seed in the field is the Son of Man.* ³⁸The field is the world. And the good seed are all of God's children in the kingdom. The weeds are those people that belong to the Evil One *(the devil)*. ³⁹And the enemy that planted the bad seed is the devil. The harvest time is the end of the world.* And the workers that gather are God's angels.

⁴⁰"The weeds are pulled up and burned in the fire. It will be the same at the end of this world.* ⁴¹The Son of Man* will send his angels, and his angels will find the people that cause sin and all people that do evil. The angels will take those people out of his kingdom. ⁴²The angels will throw those people into the place of fire. In that place the people will be crying and grinding their teeth ⌊with pain⌋. ⁴³Then the good people will shine like the sun. They will be in the kingdom of their Father. You people that hear me, listen!

Stories About a Treasure and a Pearl

⁴⁴"The kingdom of heaven is like a treasure hidden in a field. One day a man found the treasure. The man was very happy to find the treasure. He hid the treasure in the field again. The man went and sold everything that he owned to buy that field.

⁴⁵"Also, the kingdom of heaven is like a salesman looking for fine pearls. ⁴⁶One day the salesman found a very fine pearl. The salesman went and sold everything he had to buy that pearl.

A Story About a Fishing Net

⁴⁷"Also, the kingdom of heaven is like a net that was put into the lake. The net caught many different kinds of fish. ⁴⁸The net became full, so the fishermen pulled the net to the shore. The fishermen sat down and put all the good fish in baskets. Then they threw away the bad fish. ⁴⁹It will be the same at the end of this world.* The angels will come and separate the evil people from the good people. ⁵⁰The angels will throw the evil people into the place of fire. In that place the people will cry and grind their teeth ⌊with pain⌋."

⁵¹⌊Then Jesus asked his followers,⌋ "Do you understand all these things?"

The followers said, "Yes, we understand."

⁵²Then Jesus said to the followers, "So every teacher of the law who has been taught about the kingdom of heaven is like the owner of a house. That person has new things and old things saved in that house. And that person brings out those new things and old things."

Jesus Goes to His Home Town

⁵³When Jesus finished teaching with these stories, he left there. ⁵⁴Jesus went to the town where he grew up. Jesus taught the people in the synagogue,* and the people were amazed. The people said, "Where did this man get this wisdom and this power to do miracles*? ⁵⁵This is only the son of the carpenter. And his mother is Mary. His brothers are James, Joseph, Simon and Judas. ⁵⁶And all his sisters are here with us. So where does this man get this wisdom and the power to do these things?" ⁵⁷And the people refused to accept Jesus.

But Jesus said to the people, "Other people give honor to a prophet.* But people in that prophet's own town or own home don't give honor to him."

⁵⁸The people there did not believe in Jesus. So Jesus did not do many miracles there.

Herod Hears About Jesus

14 At that time Herod,* the ruler ⌊of Galilee⌋, heard the things people said about Jesus. ²So Herod said to his servants, "This man *(Jesus)* is really John the Baptizer. He must have risen from death. That is why he is able to do these miracles.*"

---

prophet Person that spoke for God. He often told things that would happen in the future.
Son of Man Jesus. In Dan. 7:13-14 this is the name for the Messiah, the one God chose to save his people.
world Literally, "this age," or "this time."
synagogue Synagogues were places where Jews gathered for prayer, study of the Scriptures, and other public meetings.
miracles Amazing works done by the power of God.
prophet Person that spoke for God.
Herod Herod Antipas, the son of Herod the Great.

How John the Baptizer Was Killed

³Before this time, Herod* had arrested John. Herod had tied John with chains and put him into prison. Herod arrested John because of Herodias. Herodias was the wife of Philip, Herod's brother. ⁴Herod arrested John because John told Herod: "It is not right for you to have Herodias." ⁵Herod wanted to kill John, but he was afraid of the people. The people believed that John was a prophet.*

⁶On Herod's birthday, the daughter of Herodias danced for Herod and his group. Herod was very pleased with her. ⁷So Herod promised that he would give her anything she wanted. ⁸Herodias told her daughter what to ask for. So she said to Herod, "Give me the head of John the Baptizer here on this plate." ⁹King Herod was very sad. But he had promised to give the daughter anything she wanted. And the people eating with Herod had heard his promise. So Herod ordered that the thing she asked be done. ¹⁰He sent men to cut off John's head in the prison. ¹¹And the men brought John's head on a plate and gave it to the girl. Then the girl took the head to her mother, Herodias. ¹²John's followers came and got his body and buried it. Then they went and told Jesus what happened.

Jesus Feeds More than 5,000 People

¹³When Jesus heard what happened to John, Jesus left in a boat. Jesus went alone to a place where there were no people. But the people heard that Jesus left. So the people left their towns and followed Jesus. They went by land to the same place Jesus went. ¹⁴When Jesus came there, he saw many, many people there. Jesus felt sorry for them, and he healed the people that were sick.

¹⁵Late that afternoon, the followers came to Jesus and said, "No people live in this place. And it is already late. Send the people away so they can go to the towns and buy food for themselves."

¹⁶Jesus answered, "The people don't need to go away. You give them some food to eat."

¹⁷The followers answered, "But we have only five loaves of bread and two fish."

¹⁸Jesus said, "Bring the bread and the fish to me." ¹⁹Then Jesus told the people to sit down on the grass. Jesus took the five loaves of bread and the two fish. Jesus looked into the sky and thanked God for the food. Then Jesus divided the loaves of bread. Jesus gave the bread to the followers, and the followers gave the bread to the people. ²⁰All the people ate and were filled. After the people finished eating, the followers filled twelve baskets with the pieces of food that were not eaten. ²¹There were about 5,000 men there that ate. There were also women and children that ate.

Jesus Walks on the Lake

²²Then Jesus made the followers get into the boat. Jesus told them to go to the other side of the lake. Jesus said that he would come later. Jesus stayed there to tell the people they could go home. ²³After Jesus said good-bye to the people, he went up into the hills. Jesus went there alone to pray. It was late, and Jesus was there alone. ²⁴At this time, the boat was already far away on the lake. The boat was having trouble because of the waves. The wind was blowing against it.

²⁵Between three and six o'clock in the morning, Jesus' followers were still in the boat. Jesus came to them. He was walking on the water. ²⁶The followers saw Jesus walking on the water and they were afraid. They said, "It's a ghost!" The followers shouted with fear.

²⁷But Jesus quickly spoke to them. Jesus said, "Don't worry! It's me! Don't be afraid."

²⁸Peter said, "Lord, if that is really you, then tell me to come to you on the water."

²⁹Jesus said, "Come, Peter."

Then Peter left the boat and walked on the water to Jesus. ³⁰But while Peter was walking on the water, he saw the wind and the waves. Peter became afraid and began sinking down into the water. Peter shouted, "Lord, save me!"

³¹Then Jesus caught Peter with his hand. Jesus said, "Your faith is small. Why did you doubt?" ³²After Peter and Jesus were in the boat, the wind became calm. ³³Then those followers in the boat worshiped Jesus and said, "Truly you are the Son of God."

³⁴After they crossed the lake, they came to shore at Gennesaret. ³⁵The people in that place saw Jesus. They knew who he was. So they told the other people all around there that Jesus had come. The people brought all their sick people to Jesus. ³⁶The people begged Jesus to let them only touch his coat to be healed. And all the sick people that touched Jesus' coat were healed.

Herod Herod Antipas, the son of Herod the Great.
prophet Person that spoke for God.

God's Law and Rules That People Make

15 Then some Pharisees* and teachers of the law came to Jesus. They came from Jerusalem and asked Jesus, ²"Why do your followers not obey the rules given to us by our great people that lived before us? Your followers don't wash their hands before they eat!"

³Jesus answered, "And why do you refuse to obey God's command so that you can follow those rules you have? ⁴God said, 'You must honor (respect) your father and mother.'* And God also said, 'Any person that says bad things to his father or mother must be killed.'* ⁵But you teach that a person can say to his father or mother, 'I have something I could use to help you. But I will not use it to help you. I will give it to God.' ⁶You teach that person to not honor his father. So you teach that it is not important to do what God said. You think that it is more important to follow those rules you have. ⁷You are hypocrites*! Isaiah was right when he spoke about you. Isaiah said:

⁸ 'These people say they honor me,
but they don't really make me
an important part of their lives.
⁹ Their worship of me is for nothing.
The things they teach are only rules
that people have made.'"
Isaiah 29:13

¹⁰Jesus called the people to him. Jesus said, "Listen and understand what I am saying. ¹¹It is not the things a person puts in his mouth that make him wrong.* It is the things a person says with his mouth that make him wrong."

¹²Then the followers came to Jesus and asked, "Do you know that the Pharisees* are angry because of what you said?"

¹³Jesus answered, "Every plant that my Father in heaven has not planted himself will be pulled up by the roots. ¹⁴Stay away from the Pharisees.* They lead the people, but they are like blind men leading other blind men. And if a blind man leads another blind man, then both men will fall into a hole."

¹⁵Peter said, "Explain to us what you said earlier to the people."

¹⁶Jesus said, "You still have trouble understanding? ¹⁷Surely you know that all the food that enters a person's mouth goes into the stomach. Then that food goes out of the body. ¹⁸But the bad things a person says with his mouth come from the way a person thinks. And these are the things that make a person wrong.* ¹⁹All these bad things begin in a person's mind: evil thoughts, murder, adultery,* sexual sins, stealing, lying, saying bad things against other people. ²⁰These things make a person wrong. But not washing his hands before he eats does not make a person wrong."

Jesus Helps a Non-Jewish Woman

²¹Jesus left that place and went to the area of Tyre and Sidon. ²²A Canaanite woman from that area came to Jesus. The woman shouted, "Lord, Son of David,* please help me! My daughter has a demon* inside her, and she is suffering very much."

²³But Jesus did not answer the woman. So the followers came to Jesus and begged him, "Tell the woman to go away. She is following us and shouting."

²⁴Jesus said, "God sent me only to the lost people* of Israel *(the Jews)*."

²⁵Then the woman came to Jesus again. She bowed before Jesus and said, "Lord, help me!"

²⁶Jesus answered, "It is not right to take the children's bread and give it to the dogs."

²⁷The woman said, "Yes, Lord, but even the dogs eat the pieces of food that fall from their master's table."

²⁸Then Jesus answered, "Woman, you have great faith! I will do the thing you wanted me to do." And at that time the woman's daughter was healed.

Jesus Heals Many People

²⁹Then Jesus left that place and went to the shore of Lake Galilee. Jesus went up on a hill and sat down.

³⁰Many, many people came to Jesus. These people brought many other sick people and put the sick people before Jesus. There were people that could not walk, blind people, crippled people,

---

Pharisees The Pharisees were a Jewish religious group that claimed to follow carefully all Jewish laws and customs.
'You must ... mother' Quote from Ex. 20:12; Deut. 5:16.
'Any person ... killed' Quote from Ex. 21:17.
hypocrites Bad people who act like they are good.
wrong Literally, "unclean" or "not pure."

adultery Breaking a marriage promise by sexual sin.
Son of David Name for Christ. He was from the family of David, king of Israel.
demon A demon is an evil spirit from the devil.
people Literally, "sheep."

deaf people, and many others. Jesus healed all these people. ³¹People were amazed when they saw that people that could not speak were able to speak again. Crippled people were made strong again. People that could not walk were able to walk again. The blind were able to see again. All the people thanked the God of Israel *(the Jews)* for this.

Jesus Feeds More than 4,000 People

³²Jesus called his followers to him and said, "I feel sorry for these people. They have been with me three days, and now they have nothing to eat. I don't want to send them away hungry. They might faint while going home."

³³The followers asked Jesus, "Where can we get enough bread to feed all these people? We are far away from any town."

³⁴Jesus asked, "How many loaves of bread do you have?"

The followers answered, "We have seven loaves of bread and a few small fish."

³⁵Jesus told the people to sit on the ground. ³⁶Jesus took the seven loaves of bread and the fish. Then Jesus gave thanks to God for the food. Jesus divided the food and gave it to the followers. The followers gave the food to the people. ³⁷All the people ate and were full. After this, the followers filled seven baskets with the pieces of food that were not eaten. ³⁸There were about 4,000 men there that ate. There were also women and children that ate. ³⁹After they ate, Jesus told the people they could go home. Jesus got into the boat and went to the area of Magadan.

The Jewish Leaders Test Jesus

16 The Pharisees* and Sadducees* came to Jesus. They wanted to test Jesus. So they asked Jesus to show them a miracle* to prove that he was from God.

²Jesus answered, "When you people see the sunset, you know what the weather will be. If the sky is red, then you say we will have good weather. ³And in the morning you watch the sunrise. If the sky is dark and red, then you say that it will be a rainy day. These things are signs of the weather. You see these signs in the sky and you know what they mean. In the same way, you see the things that are happening now. These things are also signs. But you don't know the meaning of these signs. ⁴Evil and sinful people are the kind of people that want a miracle* for a sign *(proof)*. But those people will have no sign—only the sign of Jonah.*" Then Jesus left that place and went away.

Jesus Warns Against the Jewish Leaders

⁵Jesus and his followers went across the lake *(Lake Galilee)*. But the followers forgot to bring bread. ⁶Jesus said to the followers, "Be careful! Guard against the yeast *(bad influence)* of the Pharisees* and the Sadducees.*"

⁷The followers discussed the meaning of this. They said, "Did Jesus say this because we forgot to bring bread?"

⁸Jesus knew that the followers were talking about this. So Jesus asked them, "Why are you talking about not having bread? Your faith is small. ⁹You still don't understand? Remember the five loaves of bread that fed the 5,000 people? And remember that you filled many baskets ₍with bread after the people finished eating₎? ¹⁰And remember the seven loaves of bread that fed the 4,000 people? Remember that you filled many baskets ₍with bread after the people finished eating₎? ¹¹So I was not talking to you about bread. Why don't you understand that? I am telling you to be careful and guard against the yeast *(bad influence)* of the Pharisees* and the Sadducees.*"

¹²Then the followers understood what Jesus meant. Jesus was not telling them to guard against the yeast used in bread. Jesus was telling them to guard against the teaching of the Pharisees and the Sadducees.

Peter Says That Jesus Is the Christ

¹³Jesus went to the area of Caesarea Philippi. Jesus said to his followers, "I am the Son of Man.* Who do the people say I am?"

¹⁴The followers answered, "Some people say you are John, the Baptizer. Other people say you

---

Pharisees The Pharisees were a Jewish religious group that claimed to follow carefully all Jewish laws and customs.

Sadducees A leading Jewish religious group. They accepted only the first five books of the Old Testament. They believed that people don't live again after death.

miracle An amazing work done by the power of God.

sign of Jonah Jonah's three days in a big fish are like Jesus' three days in the grave. Read the book of Jonah.

Son of Man Jesus. In Dan. 7:13-14 this is the name for the Messiah, the one God chose to save his people.

are Elijah.* And some people say that you are Jeremiah* or one of the prophets.*"
¹⁵Then Jesus said to his followers, "And who do you say I am?"
¹⁶Simon Peter answered, "You are the Christ,* the Son of the living God."
¹⁷Jesus answered, "You are blessed, Simon son of Jonah. No person taught you that. My Father in heaven showed you who I am. ¹⁸So I tell you, you are Peter.* And I will build my church on this rock. The power of death* will not be able to defeat my church. ¹⁹I will give you the keys of the kingdom of heaven. When you speak judgment here on earth, that judgment will be God's judgment. When you promise forgiveness here on earth, that forgiveness will be God's forgiveness."* ²⁰Then Jesus warned his followers not to tell anyone that he was the Christ.*

Jesus Says He Must Die

²¹From that time Jesus began telling his followers that he must go to Jerusalem. Jesus explained that the older Jewish leaders, the leading priests, and the teachers of the law would make him suffer many things. And Jesus told his followers that he must be killed. Then, on the third day, he would be raised from death.
²²Peter spoke to Jesus alone. Peter began to criticize Jesus. Peter said, "God save you from those things, Lord! Those things will never happen to you!"
²³Then Jesus said to Peter, "Go away from me, Satan*! You are not helping me! You don't care about the things of God. You only care about things that people think are important."
²⁴Then Jesus said to his followers, "If any person wants to follow me, he must say 'No' to the things he wants. That person must accept the cross (suffering) that is given to him, and he must follow me. ²⁵The person that wants to save his life will lose it. And every person that gives his life for me will save it. ²⁶It is worth nothing for a person to have the whole world, if he loses his soul. A person could never pay enough to buy back his soul. ²⁷The Son of Man* will come again with his Father's glory and with his angels. At that time, the Son of Man will reward each person for the things he has done. ²⁸I tell you the truth. There are some people standing here that will see the Son of Man coming with his kingdom before they die."

Jesus Seen with Moses and Elijah

17 Six days later, Jesus took Peter, James, and John the brother of James and went up on a high mountain. They were all alone there. ²While these followers watched him, Jesus was changed. His face became bright like the sun. And his clothes became white as light. ³Then two men were there, talking with Jesus. The men were Moses and Elijah.*
⁴Peter said to Jesus, "Lord, it is good that we are here. If you want, I will put three tents here—one for you, one for Moses, and one for Elijah."
⁵While Peter was talking, a bright cloud came over them. A voice came from the cloud. The voice said, "This (Jesus) is my Son and I love him. I am very pleased with him. Obey him!"
⁶The followers with Jesus heard this voice. They were very afraid, so they fell to the ground. ⁷But Jesus came to the followers and touched them. Jesus said, "Stand up. Don't be afraid." ⁸The followers looked up, and they saw Jesus was now alone.
⁹Jesus and the followers were walking down the mountain. Jesus commanded the followers, "Don't tell any person about the things you saw on the mountain. Wait until the Son of Man* has been raised from death. Then you can tell people about what you saw."
¹⁰The followers asked Jesus, "Why do the teachers of the law say that Elijah must come* first ₁before the Christ* comes₁?"
¹¹Jesus answered, "They are right to say that Elijah is coming. And it is true that Elijah will make all things the way they should be. ¹²But I tell you, Elijah has already come. People did not know who he was. People did to him all the ₁bad₁ things they wanted to do. It is the same with the

---

Elijah Man who spoke for God about 850 B.C.
Jeremiah Man who spoke for God about 600 B.C.
prophets People who spoke for God. Their writings are part of the Old Testament.
Christ The "anointed one" (Messiah) or chosen of God.
Peter The Greek name "Peter," like the Aramaic name "Cephas," means "rock."
power of death Literally, the "gates of Hades."
When you speak ... forgiveness Literally, "Whatever you bind on earth will be bound in heaven, and whatever you loose on earth will be loosed in heaven."
Satan Name for the devil meaning "the enemy." Jesus means that Peter was talking like Satan.

Son of Man Jesus. In Dan. 7:13-14 this is the name for the Messiah, the one God chose to save his people.
Moses and Elijah Two important Jewish leaders in the past.
Elijah must come See Mal. 4:5-6.

Son of Man.* Those same people will make the Son of Man suffer." ¹³Then the followers understood that Jesus meant that John the Baptizer was really Elijah.

Jesus Heals a Sick Boy

¹⁴Jesus and the followers went back to the people. A man came to Jesus and bowed before him. ¹⁵The man said, "Lord, be kind to my son. He has epilepsy* and is suffering very much. My son often falls into the fire or into the water. ¹⁶I brought my son to your followers, but they could not heal him."

¹⁷Jesus answered, "You people have no faith. Your lives are all wrong. How long must I stay with you? How long must I continue to be patient with you? Bring the boy here." ¹⁸Jesus gave a strong command to the demon* inside the boy. Then the demon came out of the boy, and the boy was healed.

¹⁹Then the followers came to Jesus alone. They said, "We tried to force the demon out of the boy, but we could not. Why were we not able to make the demon go out?"

²⁰Jesus answered, "You were not able to make the demon go out, because your faith is too small. I tell you the truth. If your faith is as big as a mustard seed,* then you can say to this mountain, 'Move from here to there.' And it will move. All things will be possible for you." ²¹*

Jesus Talks About His Death

²²Later, the followers met together in Galilee. Jesus said to the followers, "The Son of Man* will be given into the control of men. ²³Those men will kill the Son of Man. But on the third day the Son of Man will be raised from death." The followers were very sad ⌊to hear that Jesus would be killed⌋.

Jesus Teaches About Paying Taxes

²⁴Jesus and his followers went to Capernaum. In Capernaum some men came to Peter. They were the men that collected the two-drachma tax.* They asked, "Does your teacher pay the two-drachma tax?"

²⁵Peter answered, "Yes, Jesus pays the tax."

Peter went into the house where Jesus was. Before Peter could speak, Jesus said to him, "The kings on the earth get different kinds of taxes from people. But who are the people that pay the taxes? Are these people the king's children? Or is it other people that pay the taxes? What do you think?"

²⁶Peter answered, "The other people pay the taxes."

Jesus said, "Then the children of the king don't have to pay taxes. ²⁷But we don't want to make these tax collectors angry. So ⌊pay the tax in this way⌋: Go to the lake and fish. After you catch the first fish, open the fish's mouth. Inside its mouth you will find a four-drachma coin. Take that coin and give it to the tax collectors. That will pay the tax for you and me."

Jesus Tells Who Is the Greatest

18 At that time the followers came to Jesus and asked, "Who is the greatest in the kingdom of heaven?"

²Jesus called a little child to come to him. Jesus stood the child before the followers. ³Then Jesus said, "I tell you the truth. You must change and become like little children ⌊in your hearts⌋. If you don't do this, you will never enter the kingdom of heaven. ⁴The greatest *(most important)* person in the kingdom of heaven is the person that makes himself humble like this child.

⁵"If a person accepts a little child like this in my name, then that person accepts me. ⁶If one of these little children believes in me, and another person causes that child to sin, then it will be very bad for that person. It would be better for that person to have a millstone* tied around his neck and be drowned in the deep sea. ⁷I feel sorry for the people in the world because of the things that make people sin. Those things must happen. But it will be very bad for the person that causes those things to happen. ⁸If your hand or your foot makes you sin, cut it off and throw it away. It is better for you to lose part of your body but have life forever. That is much better than to have two hands and two feet but be thrown into the fire *(hell)* that burns forever. ⁹If your eye makes you

---

Son of Man Jesus. In Dan. 7:13-14 this is the name for the Messiah, the one God chose to save his people.

epilepsy A sickness that causes a person sometimes to lose control of his body.

demon A demon is an evil spirit from the devil.

mustard seed This seed is very, very small, but the plant grows taller than a man.

Verse 21 Some Greek copies add verse 21: "That kind of spirit comes out only if you use prayer and fasting."

two-drachma tax A tax that every Jew had to pay once each year for the temple.

millstone A large, round stone used for grinding grain.

sin, take it out and throw it away. It is better for you to have only one eye but have life forever. That is much better than to have two eyes but be thrown into the fire of hell.

Jesus Uses a Story About a Lost Sheep

¹⁰"Be careful. Don't think these little children are worth nothing. I tell you that these children have angels in heaven. And those angels are always with my Father in heaven. ¹¹*

¹²"If a man has 100 sheep, but one of the sheep becomes lost, then the man will leave the other 99 sheep on the hill. He will go to look for the lost sheep. Right? ¹³And if the man finds the lost sheep, the man is happier about that one sheep than about the 99 sheep that were never lost. I tell you the truth. ¹⁴In the same way, your Father in heaven does not want any of these little children to be lost.

When a Person Does Something Wrong

¹⁵"If your brother ₍or sister₎ does something wrong to you, go and tell that person what he did wrong. Do this alone with that person. If that person listens to you, then you have helped that person to be your brother again. ¹⁶But if that person refuses to listen, then go to him again and bring one or two people with you. Then there will be two or three other people that will be able to tell all that happened. ¹⁷If that person refuses to listen to them, then tell the church *(group of believers)*. If that person refuses to listen to the church, then treat him like he is a person that does not believe in God. Treat him like he is a tax collector.*

¹⁸"I tell you the truth. When you speak judgment here on earth, that judgment will be God's judgment. When you promise forgiveness here on earth, that forgiveness will be God's forgiveness.*

¹⁹"Also, I tell you that if two of you on earth agree about something, then you can pray for it. And the thing you ask for will be done for you by my Father in heaven. ²⁰This is true, because if two or three people are together believing in me, I am there with them."

Verse 11 Some Greek copies add verse 11: "The Son of Man came to save lost people."

tax collector A Jew hired by the Romans to collect taxes. Tax collectors often cheated, and the other Jews hated them.

When you speak ... God's forgiveness Literally, "Whatever you bind on earth will be bound in heaven, and whatever you loose on earth will be loosed in heaven."

Story About Forgiveness

²¹Then Peter came to Jesus and asked, "Lord, when my brother continues to do something wrong to me, how many times must I forgive him? Should I forgive him as many as seven times?"

²²Jesus answered, "I tell you, you must forgive him more than seven times. You must continue to forgive him even if he does wrong to you seventy-seven times.*

²³"So the kingdom of heaven is like a king that decided to collect the money that his servants owed him. ²⁴The king began to collect his money. One servant owed the king several thousand pounds of silver. ²⁵The servant was not able to pay the money to his master, the king. So the master ordered that everything the servant owned should be sold, even the servant's wife and children. The money would be used to pay the king what the servant owed.

²⁶"But the servant fell on his knees and begged, 'Be patient with me. I will pay you everything I owe.' ²⁷The master felt sorry for his servant. So the master told the servant he did not have to pay. The master let the servant go free.

²⁸"Later, that same servant found another servant that owed him a few dollars' worth of silver. The servant grabbed the other servant around the neck and said, 'Pay me the money you owe me!'

²⁹"The other servant fell on his knees and begged him, 'Be patient with me. I will pay you everything I owe.'

³⁰"But the first servant refused to be patient. The servant told the judge that the other servant owed him money, and the other servant was thrown into prison. The servant had to stay in prison until he could pay everything he owed. ³¹All the other servants saw what happened. They were very sorry. So they went and told their master everything that happened.

³²"Then the master called his servant in and said, 'You evil servant. You owed me much money, but you begged me to forgive your debt. So I told you that you did not have to pay anything. ³³So you should have given the same mercy to that other man that is a servant with you. You should have given him the same mercy that I gave you.' ³⁴The master was very angry, so he put the servant in prison to be punished. And the

---

seventy-seven times Or, "seventy times seven." See Gen. 4:24.

servant had to stay in prison until he could pay everything he owed. ³⁵"This king did the same as my heavenly Father will do to you. You must truly forgive your brother ⌊or sister⌋, or my heavenly Father will not forgive you."

Jesus Teaches About Divorce

19 After Jesus said all these things, he left Galilee. Jesus went into the area of Judea on the other side of the Jordan River. ²Many people followed Jesus. Jesus healed the sick people there.

³Some Pharisees* came to Jesus. They tried to make Jesus say something wrong. They asked Jesus, "Is it right for a man to divorce his wife for any reason he chooses?"

⁴Jesus answered, "Surely you have read this ⌊in the Scriptures⌋*: When God made the world, 'he made people male and female.'* ⁵And God said, 'So a man will leave his father and mother and be joined to his wife. And the two people will become one.'* ⁶So the two people are not two, but one. God joined those two people together. So no person should separate them."

⁷The Pharisees* asked, "So why did Moses give a command allowing a man to divorce his wife by writing a certificate of divorce?"

⁸Jesus answered, "Moses allowed you to divorce your wives because you refused to accept God's teaching. But divorce was not allowed in the beginning. ⁹I tell you that any person that divorces his wife and marries another woman is guilty of the sin of adultery.* The only reason for a person to divorce and marry again is if his first wife had sexual relations with another man."

¹⁰The followers said to Jesus, "If that is the only reason a man can divorce his wife, then it is better not to marry."

¹¹Jesus answered, "Not every person can accept this truth ⌊about marriage⌋. But God has made some people able to accept it. ¹²There are different reasons why some men cannot marry.* Some men were born without the ability to make children. Other men were made that way later in life by other people. And other men have given up marriage because of the kingdom of heaven. But the person that can ⌊marry⌋ should accept this teaching ⌊about marriage.⌋*"

Jesus Welcomes Children

¹³Then the people brought their little children to Jesus so that Jesus could put his hands on them* and pray for them. When the followers saw this, they told the people to stop bringing their children to Jesus. ¹⁴But Jesus said, "Let the little children come to me. Don't stop them, because the kingdom of heaven belongs to people that are like these children." ¹⁵After Jesus put his hands on the children he left there.

A Rich Man Refuses to Follow Jesus

¹⁶A man came to Jesus and asked, "Teacher, what good thing must I do to have life forever?"

¹⁷Jesus answered, "Why do you ask me about what is good? Only God is good. But if you want to have life forever, obey the commands."

¹⁸The man asked, "Which commands?"

Jesus answered, "'You must not murder anyone, you must not do the sin of adultery,* you must not steal anything, you must not tell lies about other people, ¹⁹you must honor *(respect)* your father and mother,'* and 'you must love other people the same as you love yourself.'*"

²⁰The young man said, "I have obeyed all these things. What else do I need?"

²¹Jesus answered, "If you want to be perfect, then go and sell all the things you own. Give the money to the poor people. If you do this, you will have a rich treasure in heaven. Then come and follow me!"

²²But when the man heard this, he was very sad. The man was very rich ⌊and wanted to keep his money⌋. So he left Jesus.

²³Then Jesus said to his followers, "I tell you the truth. It will be very hard for a rich person to enter the kingdom of heaven. ²⁴Yes, I tell you that it is easier for a camel to go through the eye of a needle than for a rich person to enter the kingdom of God."

Pharisees The Pharisees were a Jewish religious group that claimed to follow carefully all Jewish laws and customs.
Scriptures Holy Writings—the Old Testament.
'he made ... female' Quote from Gen. 1:27 or 5:2.
'So a man ... one' Quote from Gen. 2:24.
adultery Breaking a marriage promise by sexual sin.
some men cannot marry Literally, "there are eunuchs."
But ... marriage Or, "The person that can accept this teaching about not marrying should accept it."
put his hands on them This showed that Jesus was giving special blessings to these children.
'You must not ... mother' Quote from Ex. 20:12-16.
'you must love ... yourself' Quote from Lev. 19:18.

[25] When the followers heard this, they were very surprised. They asked, "Then who can be saved?"

[26] Jesus looked at his followers and said, "This is something that people cannot do themselves. But God can do all things."

[27] Peter said to Jesus, "We left everything we had and followed you. So what will we have?"

[28] Jesus said to the followers, "I tell you the truth. When the new world is made, the Son of Man* will sit on his great throne. And all of you that followed me will also sit on thrones. You will sit on twelve thrones and you will judge the twelve family groups of Israel.* [29] And every person that has left houses, brothers, sisters, father, mother, children, or farms to follow me will get much more than he left. And that person will have life forever. [30] Many people that have the highest place in life now will have the lowest place in the future. And many people that have the lowest place now will have the highest place in the future.

Jesus Uses a Story About Farm Workers

20 "The kingdom of heaven is like a man that owned some land. The man grew grapes on his land. One morning, the man went out very early to hire some other people to work in his field. [2] The man agreed to pay the workers one silver coin* for working that day. Then the man sent the people into the field to work.

[3] "At about nine o'clock the man went to the market place and saw some other people standing there. These people were doing nothing. [4] So the man said to them, 'If you go and work in my field, I will pay you what your work is worth.' [5] So the people went to work in the field.

[6] "The man went out again about twelve o'clock and again at three o'clock. Both times the man hired some other people to work in his field. [6] At about five o'clock the man went to the market place again. He saw some other people standing there. The man asked them, 'Why did you stand here all day doing nothing?'

[7] "The people said, 'No person gave us a job.'

"The man said to them, 'Then you can go and work in my field.'

[8] "At the end of the day, the owner of the field said to the boss of all the workers, 'Call the workers and pay all of them. Start by paying the last people I hired. Then pay all of them, ending with the workers I hired first.'

[9] "The workers that were hired at five o'clock came to get their pay. Each worker got one silver coin.* [10] Then those workers that were hired first came to get their pay. Those workers thought they would be paid more than the other workers. But each one of those workers also received one silver coin. [11] When they got their silver coin, these workers complained to the man that owned the land. [12] The workers said, 'Those people were hired last and worked only one hour. But you paid them the same as us. And we worked hard all day in the hot sun.'

[13] "But the man that owned the field said to one of those workers, 'Friend, I am being fair with you. You agreed to work for one silver coin. Right? [14] So take your pay and go. I want to give the man that was hired last the same pay that I gave you. [15] I can do what I want with my own money. Are you jealous because I am good to those people?'

[16] "So the people that have the last place now will have the first place in the future. And the people that have the first place now will have the last place in the future."

Jesus Talks About His Own Death

[17] Jesus was going to Jerusalem. His twelve followers were with him. While they were walking, Jesus gathered the followers together and spoke to them privately. Jesus said to them, [18] "We are going to Jerusalem. The Son of Man* will be given to the leading priests and the teachers of the law. The priests and teachers of the law will say that the Son of Man must die. [19] They will give the Son of Man to the non-Jewish people. Those people will laugh at him and beat him with whips, and then they will kill him on a cross. But on the third day after his death, he will be raised to life again."

A Mother Asks a Special Favor

[20] Then Zebedee's wife came to Jesus. Her sons were with her. The mother bowed before Jesus and asked him to do something for her.

Son of Man Jesus. In Dan. 7:13-14 this is the name for the Messiah, the one God chose to save his people.

Israel First, Israel was the Jewish nation, but the name is also used to mean all of God's people.

silver coin A Roman denarius. One coin was the average pay for one day's work.

²¹Jesus said, "What do you want?"

She said, "Promise that one of my sons will sit at your right side in your kingdom. And promise that the other son will sit at your left side in your kingdom."

²²So Jesus said to the sons, "You don't understand what you are asking. Can you accept the kind of suffering that I must have?*

The sons answered, "Yes, we can!"

²³Jesus said to them, "Truly you will suffer the same things that I will suffer. But I cannot choose the person that will sit at my right side or my left side. My Father has decided who will have those places. He has prepared those places for those people. Those places belong to them."

²⁴The other ten followers heard this. They became angry with the two brothers. ²⁵Jesus called all the followers together. Jesus said, "You know that the rulers of the non-Jewish people love to show their power over the people. And their important leaders love to use all their authority over the people. ²⁶But it should not be that way with you. If one of you wants to become great, then he must serve you like a servant. ²⁷If one of you wants to become first, then he must serve you like a slave. ²⁸It is the same with the Son of Man.* The Son of Man did not come for other people to serve him. The Son of Man came to serve other people. The Son of Man came to give his life to save many people."

Jesus Heals Two Blind Men

²⁹When Jesus and his followers were leaving Jericho, many, many people followed Jesus. ³⁰There were two blind men sitting by the road. The blind men heard that Jesus was coming by. So the blind men shouted, "Lord, Son of David,* please help us!"

³¹All the people criticized the blind men. They told the blind men not to speak. But the blind men shouted more and more, "Lord, Son of David, please help us!"

³²Jesus stopped and said to the blind men, "What do you want me to do for you?"

³³The blind men answered, "Lord, we want to be able to see."

³⁴Jesus felt sorry for the blind men. Jesus touched their eyes and they were able to see. Then the men followed Jesus.

Jesus Enters Jerusalem like a King

21 Jesus and his followers were coming closer to Jerusalem. But first they stopped at Bethphage at the hill called the Mount of Olives.* There Jesus sent two of his followers into the town. ²Jesus said to the followers, "Go to the town you can see there. When you enter it you will find a donkey tied there. With the donkey you will find a young donkey. Untie the two donkeys and bring them to me. ³If any person asks you why you are taking the donkeys, tell that person, 'The Master needs these donkeys. He will send them back soon.'"

⁴This happened to make clear the full meaning of what the prophet* said:

⁵ "Tell the city of Zion,
'Now your king is coming to you.
He is humble and he is riding on a donkey.
He is riding on a young donkey,
born from a work animal.'"
Zechariah 9:9

⁶The followers went and did what Jesus told them to do. ⁷The followers brought the mother donkey and the young donkey to Jesus. They put their coats on the donkeys, and Jesus sat on the coats. ⁸ₗJesus rode along the road to Jerusalemⱼ. Many people spread their coats on the road for Jesus. Other people cut branches from the trees and spread the branches on the road. ⁹Some of the people were walking ahead of Jesus. Other people were walking behind Jesus. The people shouted,

"Praise* to the Son of David*!
Welcome! God bless the One that comes
in the name of the Lord!
Praise* to God in heaven!"
Psalm 118:26

¹⁰Then Jesus went into Jerusalem. All the people in the city were confused. They asked, "Who is this man?"

---

accept the kind of suffering that I must have Literally, "drink the cup that I must drink." Jesus used the idea of drinking from a cup to mean accepting the terrible things that would happen to him.
Son of Man Jesus. In Dan. 7:13-14 this is the name for the Messiah, the one God chose to save his people.
Son of David Name for the Christ. He was from the family of David, king of Israel.

Mount of Olives A hill near the city of Jerusalem.
prophet Person who spoke for God.
Praise Literally, "Hosanna," a Hebrew word used in praying to God for help. At this time it was probably a shout of joy used in praising God or His Messiah.

MATTHEW 21:11–21:31

¹¹The many people following Jesus answered, "This man is Jesus. He is the prophet* from the town of Nazareth in Galilee."

Jesus Goes to the Temple

¹²Jesus went into the temple.* He threw out all the people that were selling and buying things there. Jesus turned over the tables that belonged to the men that were exchanging different kinds of money. And Jesus turned over the benches of those men that were selling doves. ¹³Jesus said to all the people there, "It is written ⌊in the Scriptures⌋, 'My house will be called a house for prayer.'* But you are changing God's house into a 'hiding place for thieves.'*"

¹⁴Some blind people and some crippled people came to Jesus in the temple.* Jesus healed these people. ¹⁵The leading priests and the teachers of the law saw what Jesus did. They saw that Jesus was doing great things and saw the children praising Jesus in the temple. The children were saying, "Praise* to the Son of David.*" All these things made the priests and the teachers of the law angry.

¹⁶The leading priests and the teachers of the law asked Jesus, "Do you hear the things these children are saying?"

Jesus answered, "Yes. The Scripture* says, 'You *(God)* have taught children and babies to give praise.'* Have you not read that Scripture?"

¹⁷Then Jesus left that place and went out of the city to Bethany. Jesus stayed there that night.

Jesus Shows the Power of Faith

¹⁸Early the next morning, Jesus was going back to the city. Jesus was very hungry. ¹⁹Jesus saw a fig tree beside the road. Jesus went to the fig tree ⌊to get a fig to eat⌋. But there were no figs on the tree. There were only leaves. So Jesus said to the tree, "You will never again have fruit!" And then the tree dried up and died.

²⁰The followers saw this. They were very surprised. They asked, "How did the fig tree dry up and die so quickly?"

²¹Jesus answered, "I tell you the truth. If you have faith and no doubts, you will be able to do the same as I did to this tree. And you will be able to do more. You will be able to say to this mountain, 'Go, mountain, fall into the sea.' And if you have faith, it will happen. ²²If you believe, you will get anything you ask for in prayer."

Jewish Leaders Doubt Jesus' Authority

²³Jesus went to the temple.* While Jesus was teaching there, the leading priests and the older leaders of the people came to Jesus. They said to Jesus, "Tell us! What authority *(power)* do you have to do these things? Who gave you this authority?"

²⁴Jesus answered, "I will ask you a question too. If you answer me, then I will tell you what authority I have to do these things. ²⁵Tell me: When John baptized* people, did that come from God or from man?"

The priests and the Jewish leaders talked about Jesus' question. They said to each other, "If we answer, 'John's baptism was from God,' then Jesus will say, 'Then why didn't you believe John?' ²⁶But if we say, 'It was from man,' then ⌊all the people will be angry with us⌋. We are afraid of the people, because they all believe that John was a prophet.*"

²⁷So they answered Jesus, "We don't know ⌊where John's authority came from⌋."

Then Jesus said, "Then I won't tell you what authority I have to do these things!

Jesus Uses a Story About Two Sons

²⁸"Tell me what you think about this: There was a man that had two sons. The man went to the first son and said, 'Son, go and work today in my field of grapes.'

²⁹"The son answered, 'I will not go.' But later the son decided he should go, and the son went.

³⁰"Then the father went to the other son and said, 'Son, go and work today in my field of grapes.' The son answered, 'Yes, sir, I will go and work.' But the son did not go.

³¹"Which of the two sons obeyed his father?"

The Jewish leaders answered, "The first son."

---

prophet Person that spoke for God.
temple The special building in Jerusalem for Jewish worship.
'My house ... prayer' Quote from Isa. 56:7.
'hiding place for thieves' Quote from Jer. 7:11.
Praise Literally, "Hosanna," a Hebrew word used in praying to God for help. At this time it was probably a shout of joy used in praising God or His Messiah.
Son of David Name for the Christ. He was from the family of David, king of Israel.
Scripture Part of the Holy Writings—Old Testament.
'You ... praise' Quote from Ps. 8:3 (Greek version).

baptized A Greek word meaning to immerse, dip, or bury person or thing briefly under water.

Jesus said to them, "I tell you the truth. ₍You think₎ the tax collectors* and the prostitutes* ₍are bad people. But they₎ will enter the kingdom of God before you enter. ³²John came showing you the right way to live. And you did not believe John. But the tax collectors and prostitutes believed John. And you saw that the tax collectors and prostitutes believed him. But you still refused to change and believe him.

God Sends His Son

³³"Listen to this story: There was a man that owned a field. He planted the field with grapes. He put a wall around the field and dug a hole for a wine press.* Then the man built a tower. He leased the land to some farmers. Then he left for a trip. ³⁴Later, it was time for the grapes to be picked. So the man sent his servants to the farmers to get his share of the grapes.

³⁵"But the farmers grabbed the servants and beat one. They killed another one and then killed a third servant with rocks. ³⁶So the man sent some other servants to the farmers. The man sent more servants than he sent the first time. But the farmers did the same thing to the servants that they did the first time. ³⁷So the man decided to send his son to the farmers. The man said, 'The farmers will respect my son.'

³⁸"But when the farmers saw the son, they said to each other, 'This is the owner's son. This field will be his. If we kill him, then his field will be ours!' ³⁹So the farmers took the son, threw him out of the field, and killed him.

⁴⁰"So what will the owner of the field do to these farmers when he comes?"

⁴¹The Jewish priests and leaders said, "He will surely kill those evil men. Then he will lease the field to some other farmers. He will lease it to farmers that will give him his share of the crop at harvest time."

⁴²Jesus said to them, "Surely you have read this in the Scriptures*:

> 'The stone that the builders did not want
> became the cornerstone.*
> The Lord did this,
> and it is wonderful to us.'
> *Psalm 118:22-23*

⁴³"So I tell you that the kingdom of God will be taken away from you. God's kingdom will be given to people that do the things God wants in his kingdom. ⁴⁴The person that falls on this stone will be broken. And if the stone falls on a person, then it will crush that person."

⁴⁵The leading priests and the Pharisees* heard these stories that Jesus told. They knew that Jesus was talking about them. ⁴⁶They wanted to find a way to arrest Jesus. But they were afraid of the people, because the people believed that Jesus was a prophet.*

Story About People Invited to a Dinner

22 Jesus used stories to say some other things to the people. Jesus said, ²"The kingdom of heaven is like a king that prepared a wedding dinner for his son. ³The king invited some people to the feast. When the feast was ready, the king sent his servants to tell those people to come. But the people refused to come to the king's feast.

⁴"Then the king sent some more servants. The king said to the servants, 'I have already invited those people. So tell them that my feast is ready. I have killed my best bulls and calves to be eaten. Everything is ready. Come to the wedding feast.'

⁵"₍The servants went and told the people to come₎. But the people refused to listen to the servants. Those people went to do other things. One person went to work in his field, and another person went to his business. ⁶Some of the other people grabbed the servants, beat them, and killed them. ⁷The king was very angry. The king sent his army to kill those people that killed his servants. And the army burned their city.

⁸"After that, the king said to his servants, 'The wedding feast is ready. I invited those people, but they were not good enough to come to my feast. ⁹So go to the street corners and invite all the people you see. Tell them to come to my feast.' ¹⁰So the servants went into the streets. They gathered all the people they could find. The servants brought good people and bad people to the place where the wedding feast was ready. And that place was filled with people.

¹¹"Then the king came in to see all the people. The king saw a man there that was not dressed in the right clothes for a wedding. ¹²The king said, 'Friend, how were you allowed to come in here? You are not wearing the right clothes for a

---

tax collectors Jews hired by the Romans to collect taxes. They often cheated, and the other Jews hated them.
prostitutes Women paid by men for sexual sin.
wine press A place dug in rock used to mash grapes and collect the juice for making wine.
Scriptures Holy Writings—the Old Testament.
cornerstone First and most important rock of a building.

Pharisees The Pharisees were a Jewish religious group that claimed to follow carefully all Jewish laws and customs.
prophet Person that spoke for God.

wedding.' But the man said nothing. ¹³So the king told some servants, 'Tie this man's hands and feet. Throw the man out into the darkness. In that place, people will cry and grind their teeth ₍with pain₎.'
¹⁴"Yes, many people are invited. But only a few are chosen."

Some Jewish Leaders Try to Trick Jesus

¹⁵Then the Pharisees* left the place where Jesus was teaching. They made plans to catch Jesus saying something wrong. ¹⁶The Pharisees sent some men to Jesus ₍to trick him₎. They sent some of their own followers and some men from the group called Herodians.* These men said, "Teacher, we know that you are an honest man. We know that you teach the truth about God's way. You are not afraid of what other people think about you. All men are the same to you. ¹⁷So tell us what you think. Is it right to pay taxes to Caesar*? Yes or no?"
¹⁸But Jesus knew that these men were trying to trick him. So he said, "You hypocrites*! Why are you trying to catch me saying something wrong? ¹⁹Show me a coin used for paying the tax." The men showed Jesus a silver coin.* ²⁰Then Jesus asked, "Whose picture is on the coin? And whose name is written on the coin?"
²¹The men answered, "It is Caesar's picture and Caesar's name."
Then Jesus said to them, "Give to Caesar the things that are Caesar's. And give to God the things that are God's."
²²Those men heard what Jesus said, and they were amazed. They left him and went away.

Some Sadducees Try to Trick Jesus

²³That same day some Sadducees* came to Jesus. (Sadducees believe that no person will rise from death.) The Sadducees asked Jesus a question. ²⁴They said, "Teacher, Moses told us that if a married man dies and he had no children, then his brother must marry the woman. Then they will have children for the dead brother. ²⁵There were seven brothers among us. The first one married but died. He had no children. So his brother married the woman. ²⁶Then the second brother also died. The same thing happened to the third brother and all the other brothers. ²⁷The woman was last to die. ²⁸But all seven men had married her. So when people rise from death, whose wife will she be?"
²⁹Jesus answered, "You don't understand because you don't know what the Scriptures* say. And you don't know about the power of God. ³⁰At the time when people rise from death, there will be no marriage. People will not be married to each other. All people will be like the angels in heaven. ³¹Surely you have read what God said to you about the rising from death? ³²God said, 'I am the God of Abraham, the God of Isaac, and the God of Jacob.'* ₍If God said he is their God, then₎ these men are not really dead. He is the God only of living people."
³³All the people heard this. They were amazed at Jesus' teaching.

Which Command Is the Most Important?

³⁴The Pharisees* learned that Jesus told the Sadducees* things they could not argue with. So the Pharisees met together. ³⁵One Pharisee was an expert in the law ₍of Moses₎. That Pharisee asked Jesus a question to test him. ³⁶The Pharisee said, "Teacher, which command in the law is the most important?"
³⁷Jesus answered, "'You must love the Lord your God. You must love him with all your heart, all your soul, and all your mind.'* ³⁸This is the first and most important command. ³⁹And the second command is like the first: 'You must love other people the same as you love yourself.'* ⁴⁰All of the law and the writings of the prophets* take their meaning from these two commands."

Pharisees The Pharisees were a Jewish religious group that claimed to follow carefully all Jewish laws and customs.
Herodians A Jewish political group.
Caesar The name given to the emperor (ruler) of Rome.
hypocrites Bad people who act like they are good.
silver coin A Roman denarius. One coin was the average pay for one day's work.
Sadducees A leading Jewish religious group. They accepted only the first five books of the Old Testament. They believed that people don't have another life after death.

Scriptures Holy Writings—the Old Testament.
Abraham, Isaac, Jacob Three of the most important Jewish leaders during the time of the Old Testament.
'I am ... Jacob' Quote from Ex. 3:6.
'You must love ... mind' Quote from Deut. 6:5.
'You must ... yourself' Quote from Lev. 19:18.
prophets People who spoke for God. Their writings are part of the Old Testament.

Jesus Asks the Pharisees a Question

⁴¹So while the Pharisees* were together, Jesus asked them a question. ⁴²Jesus said, "What do you think about the Christ*? Whose son is he?"

The Pharisees answered, "The Christ is the Son of David.*

⁴³Then Jesus said to the Pharisees, "Then why did David call him 'Lord'? David was speaking by the power of the ₍Holy₎ Spirit.* David said,

⁴⁴ 'The Lord *(God)* said to my Lord *(Christ)*:
Sit by me at my right side,
and I will put your enemies
under your control.*'
Psalm 110:1

⁴⁵David calls the Christ 'Lord.' So how can he be David's son?" ⁴⁶None of the Pharisees could answer Jesus' question. And after that day no person was brave enough to ask Jesus any more questions ₍to try to trick him₎.

Jesus Criticizes the Religious Leaders

23 Then Jesus spoke to the people and to his followers. Jesus said, ²"The teachers of the law and the Pharisees* have the authority *(power)* to tell you what the law of Moses says. ³So you should obey the things they say. You should do all the things they tell you to do. But their lives are not good examples for you to follow. They tell you to do things, but they don't do those things themselves. ⁴They make strict rules that are hard for people to obey. They try to force other people to obey all those rules. But they themselves will not try to follow any of those rules.

⁵"The only reason they do good things is for other people to see them. They wear special boxes* full of Scriptures.* They make these boxes bigger and bigger. And they make their special prayer clothes very long ₍so that people will see them₎. ⁶Those Pharisees* and teachers of the law love to get the most important seats at the feasts. And they love to get the most important seats in the synagogues.* ⁷They love for people to show respect to them in the market places. And they love to have people call them 'Teacher.'

⁸"But you must not be called 'Teacher.' You are all brothers ₍and sisters₎ together. You have only one Teacher. ⁹And don't call any person on earth 'Father.' You have one Father. He is in heaven. ¹⁰And you should not be called 'Master.' You have only one Master, the Christ.* ¹¹The person that serves you like a servant is the greatest person among you. ¹²Every person that makes himself better than other people will be made humble. Every person that makes himself humble will be made great.

¹³"It will be bad for you teachers of the law and Pharisees.* You are hypocrites.* You close the way for people to enter the kingdom of heaven. You yourselves don't enter, and you stop the people that are trying to enter. ¹⁴*

¹⁵"It will be bad for you teachers of the law and Pharisees.* You are hypocrites.* You travel across the seas and across different countries to find one person that will follow your ways. When you find that person, you make him worse than you are. And you are so bad that you belong in hell!

¹⁶"It will be bad for you teachers of the law and Pharisees.* You guide the people, but you are blind. You say, 'If any person uses the name of the temple* to make a promise, that means nothing. But if any person uses the gold that is in the temple to make a promise, then he must keep that promise.' ¹⁷You are blind fools! Which is greater: the gold, or the temple? The temple makes that gold holy. ₍So the temple is greater₎. ¹⁸And you say, 'If any person uses the altar* to make a promise, that means nothing. But if any person uses the gift on the altar to make a promise, then he must keep his promise.' ¹⁹You are blind. ₍You understand nothing!₎ Which is greater: the gift, or the altar? The altar makes the

---

Pharisees The Pharisees were a Jewish religious group that claimed to follow carefully all Jewish laws and customs.
Christ The "anointed one" (Messiah) or chosen of God.
Son of David Name for the Christ. He was from the family of David, king of Israel.
Holy Spirit Called the Spirit of God, the Spirit of Christ, and the Comforter. Joined with God and Christ, he does God's work among people in the world.
control Literally, "feet."
special boxes Small leather boxes containing four important Scriptures. Some Jews tied these to the forehead and left arm to show they were very religious.
Scriptures Holy Writings—the Old Testament.

synagogues Synagogues were places where Jews gathered for prayer, study of the Scriptures, and other public meetings.
hypocrites Bad people who act like they are good.
Verse 14 Some Greek copies add verse 14: "It will be bad for you, teachers of the law and Pharisees. You are hypocrites. You take away widows' houses, and you make long prayers so that people can see you. So you will have a worse punishment."
temple The special building in Jerusalem for Jewish worship.
altar Place where sacrifices or gifts are offered to God.

gift holy. [So the altar is greater]. ²⁰The person that uses the altar* to make a promise is really using the altar and also everything on the altar. ²¹And the person that uses the temple* to make a promise is really using the temple and also the One that lives in the temple. ²²The person that uses heaven to make a promise is also using God's throne and the One that sits on that throne.

²³"It will be bad for you teachers of the law and Pharisees.* You are hypocrites.* You give God one tenth of everything you own—even your mint, dill, and cummin.* But you don't obey the really important teachings of the law—being fair, showing mercy, and being honest. These are the things you should do. And you should also continue to do those other things. ²⁴You guide the people, but you are blind! Think about a person picking a little fly out of his drink and then swallowing a camel! You are like that.*

²⁵"It will be bad for you teachers of the law and Pharisees.* You are hypocrites.* You wash clean the outside of your cups and dishes. But inside they are full of things that you got by cheating other people and pleasing yourselves. ²⁶Pharisees, you are blind! First make the inside of the cup clean and good. Then the outside of the cup can be truly clean.

²⁷"It will be bad for you teachers of the law and Pharisees.* You are hypocrites.* You are like tombs* that are painted white. The outside of those tombs looks fine. But inside, the tombs are full of the bones of dead people. And all kinds of unclean things are inside there. ²⁸It is the same with you. People look at you and think that you are good. But on the inside you are full of hypocrisy* and evil.

²⁹"It will be bad for you teachers of the law and Pharisees.* You are hypocrites.* You build tombs for the prophets.* And you show honor to the graves of people that lived good lives. ³⁰And you say, 'If we had lived during the time of our fathers *(ancestors)*, we would not have helped them kill these prophets.' ³¹You give proof that you are children *(descendants)* of those people that killed the prophets. ³²And you will finish the sin that your fathers started!

³³"You are snakes! You are from a family of poisonous snakes! You will not escape God. You will all be judged guilty and go to hell! ³⁴So I tell you this: I send to you prophets* and wise men and teachers. You will kill some of these people. You will hang some of them on crosses. You will beat some of these people in your synagogues.* You will chase them from town to town. ³⁵So you will be guilty for the death of all the good people that have been killed on earth. You will be guilty for the killing of that good man Abel. And you will be guilty for the killing of Zechariah* son of Berachiah. He was killed between the temple* and the altar.* You will be guilty for the killing of all the good people that lived between the time of Abel and the time of Zechariah. ³⁶I tell you the truth. All of these things will happen to you people that are living now.

Jesus Warns the People of Jerusalem

³⁷"O Jerusalem, Jerusalem! You kill the prophets.* You kill with rocks those men that God sent to you. Many, many times I wanted to help your people. I wanted to gather your people together like a hen gathers her chicks under her wings. But you did not let me. ³⁸Now your house will be left completely empty. ³⁹I tell you, you will not see me again until that time when you will say, 'Welcome! God bless the one that comes in the name of the Lord *(God)*.'*

Future Destruction of the Temple

24 Jesus left the temple* and was walking away. But his followers came to him to show him the temple's buildings. ²Jesus asked the followers, "See all these buildings? I tell you the

---

altar An altar is a place where sacrifices are offered to God. An altar stood in front of the temple in Jerusalem.
temple The special building in Jerusalem for Jewish worship.
Pharisees The Pharisees were a Jewish religious group that claimed to follow carefully all Jewish laws and customs.
hypocrites Bad people who act like they are good.
mint, dill, cummin Small plants grown in gardens and used for spices. Only very religious people would be careful enough to give a tenth of these plants.
You are like that Meaning, "You worry about the smallest mistakes, but do the biggest sin."
tombs Small buildings made to show respect for important persons that had died.
hypocrisy Acting like you are good when you are not.

prophets People that spoke for God. Their writings are part of the Old Testament.
synagogues Synagogues were places where Jews gathered for prayer, study of the Scriptures, and other public meetings.
Abel, Zechariah In the Hebrew Old Testament, the first and last men to be murdered.
'Welcome! ... Lord' Quote from Ps. 118:26.

truth. ₍All these buildings will be destroyed₎. Every stone will be thrown down to the ground. Not one stone will be left on another."

³Later, Jesus was sitting at a place on the Mount of Olives.* The followers came to be alone with Jesus. They said, "Tell us when these things will happen. And what will happen to show us that it is time for you to come again and time for the world* to end?"

⁴Jesus answered: "Be careful! Don't let any person fool you. ⁵Many people will come and use my name. They will say, 'I am the Christ.*' And they will fool many people. ⁶You will hear about wars and stories about wars that are being fought. But don't be afraid. These things must happen before the end comes. ⁷Nations will fight against other nations. Kingdoms will fight against other kingdoms. There will be times when there is no food for people to eat. And there will be earthquakes in different places. ⁸These things are like the first pains when something new is born.

⁹"Then people will treat you badly. People will give you ₍to the rulers₎ to be persecuted *(hurt)* and killed. All people will hate you. All these things will happen to you because you believe in me. ¹⁰At that time, many believers will lose their faith. They will turn against each other and hate each other. ¹¹Many false prophets* will come. They will cause many people to believe wrong things. ¹²There will be more and more evil in the world. So most believers will stop showing love. ¹³But the person that continues strong to the end will be saved. ¹⁴The Good News about ₍God's₎ kingdom will be preached in the whole world. It will be told to every nation. Then the end will come.

¹⁵"Daniel the prophet* spoke about 'the terrible thing that causes destruction.'* You will see this terrible thing standing in the holy place *(the temple).*" (You that read this should understand what it means.) ¹⁶"At that time, the people in Judea should run away to the mountains. ¹⁷People should run away without wasting the time to stop for anything. If a person is on the roof of his house, he must not go down to get things out of his house. ¹⁸If a person is in the field, he must not go back to get his coat. ¹⁹At that time, it will be bad for women that are pregnant or have small babies! ²⁰Pray that it will not be winter or a Sabbath day* when these things happen and you have to run away. ²¹Why? Because at that time there will be much trouble. There will be more trouble than has ever happened since the beginning of the world. And nothing as bad as that will ever happen again. ²²God has decided to make that terrible time short. If that time were not made short, then no person would continue living. But God will make that time short to help the people he has chosen. ²³At that time, some person might say to you, 'Look, there is the Christ!*' Or another person might say, 'There he is!' But don't believe them. ²⁴False Christs and false prophets* will come and do great things and miracles.* They will do these things to the people God has chosen. They will do these things to try to fool his people, if that is possible. ²⁵Now I have warned you about this before it happens.

²⁶"Some person might tell you, 'The Christ* is there in the desert!' But don't go into the desert to look for the Christ. Another person might say, 'There is the Christ in that room!' But don't believe that. ²⁷When the Son of Man* comes, he will be seen by all people. It will be like lightning flashing in the sky that can be seen everywhere. ²⁸₍My coming will be clear, the same as₎ any time you see vultures* gathering, you know there is a dead body.

²⁹"Soon after the trouble of those days, this will happen:

> 'The sun will become dark,
> and the moon will not give light.
> The stars will fall from the sky,
> and everything in the sky will be changed.'
> *Isaiah 13:10; 34:4 5*

³⁰"At that time, there will be something in the sky that shows the Son of Man* coming. All the people of the world will cry. All the people will see the Son of Man coming on the clouds in the sky. The Son of Man will come with power and great glory. ³¹The Son of Man will use a loud

---

Mount of Olives A hill east of the city of Jerusalem where a person could look down into the temple area.
world Literally, "this age," or "this time."
Christ The "anointed one" (Messiah) or chosen of God.
false prophets People who say they speak for God but do not really speak God's truth.
prophet Person who spoke for God. He often told things that would happen in the future.
'the terrible thing ... destruction' See Dan. 9:27; 12:11 (cf. Dan. 11:31).

Sabbath day The seventh day of the Jewish week. It was a special religious day for the Jews.
miracles Here, powerful acts done by the power of Satan.
Son of Man Jesus. In Dan. 7:13-14 this is the name for the Messiah, the one God chose to save his people.
vultures Or, "eagles"—birds that eat dead animals.

trumpet to send his angels all around the earth. The angels will gather his chosen people from every part of the earth.

³²"The fig tree teaches us a lesson: When the fig tree's branches become green and soft, and new leaves begin to grow, then you know that summer is near. ³³It is the same with these things that I told you would happen. When you see all these things happening, you will know that the time* is near, ready to come. ³⁴I tell you the truth. All these things will happen while the people of this time* are still living! ³⁵The whole world, earth and sky, will be destroyed, but the words I have said will never be destroyed!

Only God Knows When the Time Will Be

³⁶"No person knows when that day or time will be. The Son and the angels in heaven don't know when that day or time will be. Only the Father knows. ³⁷When the Son of Man* comes, it will be the same as the thing that happened during Noah's time. ³⁸In those days before the flood, people were eating and drinking. People were marrying and giving their children to be married. The people were still doing those things until the day Noah entered the boat. ³⁹Those people knew nothing about what was happening. But then the flood came and all those people were destroyed. It will be the same when the Son of Man comes. ⁴⁰Two men will be working together in the field. One man will be taken and the other left. ⁴¹Two women will be grinding grain with a mill.* One woman will be taken and the other woman will be left.

⁴²"So always be ready. You don't know the day your Lord will come. ⁴³Remember this: If the owner of the house knew what time the thief was coming, then the owner would be ready for him. The owner would watch and not let the thief enter his house. ⁴⁴So you also must be ready. The Son of Man* will come at a time when you don't expect him.

⁴⁵"Who is the wise and trusted servant? The master trusts one servant to give the other servants their food at the right time. Who is the servant that the master trusts to do that work? ⁴⁶When the master comes and finds that servant doing the work he gave him, the servant will be very happy. ⁴⁷I tell you the truth. The master will choose that servant to take care of everything the master owns. ⁴⁸But what will happen if the servant is evil and thinks his master will not come back soon? ⁴⁹Then that servant will begin to beat the other servants. That servant will eat the food and get drunk with other people like him. ⁵⁰Then the master of that servant will come when the servant is not ready. It will be a time when the servant is not expecting the master. ⁵¹Then the master will punish that servant. The master will send him away to be with the hypocrites.* And in that place people will cry and grind their teeth ⌊with pain⌋.

Story About Ten Girls

25 "At that time the kingdom of heaven will be like ten girls that went to wait for the bridegroom.* They brought their lamps with them. ²Five of the girls were foolish. And five of the girls were wise. ³The five foolish girls brought their lamps, but they did not bring more oil for the lamps to burn. ⁴The wise girls brought their lamps and more oil in jars. ⁵The bridegroom was very late. All the girls became tired and began sleeping.

⁶"At midnight someone announced, 'The bridegroom is coming! Come and meet him!'

⁷"Then all the girls woke up. The girls made their lamps ready. ⁸But the foolish girls said to the wise girls, 'Give us some of your oil. The oil in our lamps is all gone.'

⁹"The wise girls answered, 'No! The oil we have might not be enough for all of us. But go to the people that sell oil and buy some for yourselves.'

¹⁰"So the five foolish girls went to buy oil. While they were gone, the bridegroom came. The girls that were ready went in with the bridegroom to the wedding feast. Then the door was closed and locked.

¹¹"Later the other girls came. The girls said, 'Sir, sir, open the door to let us in.'

¹²"But the bridegroom answered, 'I tell you the truth. I don't know you.'

¹³"So always be ready. You don't know the day or the time ⌊when the Son of Man* will come⌋.

---

time The time Jesus has been talking about when a very important thing will happen. In Luke Jesus says that it is the time for God's kingdom to come (Lk. 21:31).
the people of this time Or, "the people of this nation."
Son of Man Jesus. In Dan. 7:13-14 this is the name for the Messiah, the one God sent to save his people.
mill Two large, flat rocks used for grinding grain to make flour.

hypocrites Bad people who act like they are good.
bridegroom A man ready to be married.

Story About Three Servants

¹⁴"₍The kingdom of heaven is₎ like a man leaving home to travel to another place for a visit. Before the man left, he talked with his servants. The man told his servants to take care of the things he owned while he was gone. ¹⁵He decided how much each servant would be able to care for. The man gave one servant five bags of money.* He gave another servant two bags of money. And he gave a third servant one bag of money. Then that man left. ¹⁶The servant that got five bags of money went quickly to invest the money. Those five bags of money earned five more. ¹⁷It was the same with the servant that had two bags of money. That servant invested the money and earned two more. ¹⁸But the servant that got one bag of money went away and dug a hole in the ground. Then the servant hid his master's money in that hole. ¹⁹"After a long time the master came home. The master asked the servants what they did with his money. ²⁰The servant that got five bags of money brought five more bags of money to the master. The servant said, 'Master, you trusted me to care for five bags of money. So I used your five bags of money to earn five more.'

²¹"The master answered, 'You did right. You are a good servant that can be trusted. You did well with that small amount of money. So I will let you care for much greater things. Come and share my happiness with me.'

²²"Then the servant that got two bags of money came to the master. The servant said, 'Master, you gave me two bags of money to care for. So I used your two bags of money to earn two more.'

²³"The master answered, 'You did right. You are a good servant that can be trusted. You did well with a small amount of money. So I will let you care for much greater things. Come and share my happiness with me.'

²⁴"Then the servant that got one bag of money came to the master. The servant said, 'Master, I knew that you were a very hard man. You harvest things you did not plant. You gather crops where you did not put any seed. ²⁵So I was afraid. I went and hid your money in the ground. Here is the one bag of money you gave me.'

²⁶"The master answered, 'You are a bad and lazy servant! You say you knew that I harvest things I did not plant, and that I gather crops where I did not put any seed. ²⁷So you should have put my money in the bank. Then, when I came home, I would get my money back. And I would also get the interest that my money earned.'

²⁸"₍So the master told his other servants,₎ 'Take the one bag of money from that servant and give it to the servant that has ten bags of money. ²⁹Every person that uses what he has will get more. That person will have much more than he needs. But the person that does not use what he has will have everything taken away from him.' ³⁰Then the master said, 'Throw that useless servant outside, into the darkness! In that place people will cry and grind their teeth ₍with pain₎.'

The Son of Man Will Judge All People

³¹"The Son of Man* will come again. He will come with great glory. All his angels will come with him. He will be king and sit on his great throne. ³²All the people of the world will be gathered before the Son of Man. Then the Son of Man will separate all people into two groups. This is like a shepherd separates the sheep from the goats. ³³The Son of Man will put the sheep *(good people)* on his right and the goats *(bad people)* on his left.

³⁴"Then the king will say to those good people on his right, 'Come. My Father has given you great blessings. Come and get the kingdom God promised you. That kingdom has been prepared for you since the world was made. ³⁵You can have this kingdom, because I was hungry and you gave me food to eat. I was thirsty, and you gave me something to drink. I was alone and away from home, and you invited me into your home. ³⁶I was without clothes, and you gave me something to wear. I was sick, and you cared for me. I was in prison, and you came to visit me.'

³⁷"Then the good people will answer, 'Lord, when did we see you hungry and give you food? When did we see you thirsty and give you something to drink? ³⁸When did we see you alone and away from home and invite you into our home? When did we see you without clothes and give you something to wear? ³⁹When did we see you sick or in prison and care for you?'

---

bags of money Literally, "talents." A talent was about 60 to 80 pounds of gold, silver or copper coins.

Son of Man Jesus. In Dan. 7:13-14 this is the name for the Messiah, the one God chose to save his people.

⁴⁰"Then the king will answer, 'I tell you the truth. Anything you did for any of my people here,* you also did for me.'

⁴¹"Then the king will say to those bad people on his left, 'Go away from me. God has already decided that you will be punished. Go into the fire that burns forever. That fire was prepared for the devil and his angels. ⁴²You must go away, because I was hungry, and you gave me nothing to eat. I was thirsty, and you gave me nothing to drink. ⁴³I was alone and away from home, and you did not invite me into your home. I was without clothes, and you gave me nothing to wear. I was sick and in prison, and you did not care for me.'

⁴⁴"Then those people will answer, 'Lord, when did we see you hungry or thirsty? When did we see you alone and away from home? Or when did we see you without clothes or sick or in prison? When did we see these things and not help you?'

⁴⁵"Then the king will answer, 'I tell you the truth. Anything you refused to do for any of my people here,* you refused to do for me.'

⁴⁶"Then those bad people will go away. They will have punishment forever. But the good people will go and have life forever."

The Jewish Leaders Plan to Kill Jesus

26 After Jesus finished saying all these things, he said to his followers, ²"You know that the day after tomorrow is Passover.* On that day the Son of Man* will be given ⌊to his enemies⌋ to be killed on a cross."

³Then the leading priests and the older Jewish leaders had a meeting at the palace where the high priest* lived. The high priest's name was Caiaphas. ⁴In the meeting, they tried to find a way to arrest Jesus. They planned to lie so that they could arrest Jesus and kill him. ⁵The men in the meeting said, "We cannot arrest Jesus during Passover. We don't want the people to become angry and cause a riot."

A Woman Does Something Special

⁶Jesus was in Bethany. He was at the house of Simon the leper.* ⁷While Jesus was there, a woman came to him. She had an alabaster* jar filled with very expensive perfume. The woman poured this perfume on Jesus' head while Jesus was eating.

⁸The followers saw the woman do this and became upset at the woman. The followers asked, "Why waste that perfume? ⁹That perfume could be sold for much money and the money could be given to poor people."

¹⁰But Jesus knew what happened. Jesus said, "Why are you troubling this woman? She did a very good thing for me. ¹¹You will always have poor people with you.* But you will not always have me. ¹²This woman poured perfume on my body. She did this to prepare me for burial after I die. ¹³I tell you the truth. The Good News* will be told to people in all the world. And in every place where the Good News is told, the story of what this woman did will also be told. And people will remember her."

Judas Becomes an Enemy of Jesus

¹⁴Then one of the twelve followers went to talk to the leading priests. This was the follower named Judas Iscariot. ¹⁵Judas said, "I will give you Jesus. What will you pay me for doing this?" The priests gave Judas 30 silver coins. ¹⁶After that time Judas waited for the best time to give Jesus to the priests.

Jesus Eats the Passover Meal

¹⁷On the first day of the Festival of Unleavened Bread,* the followers came to Jesus. The followers said, "We will prepare everything for you to eat the Passover* meal. Where do you want us to have the meal?"

¹⁸Jesus answered, "Go into the city. Go to a man I know. Tell him that the teacher says, 'The chosen time is near. I will have the Passover* meal with my followers at your house.'" ¹⁹The

---

any of my people here Literally, "one of the least of these brothers of mine."
Passover Important Jewish holy day. They ate a special meal on this day every year to remember that God freed them from slavery in Egypt in the time of Moses.
Son of Man Jesus. In Dan. 7:13-14, this is the name for the Messiah, the one God chose to save his people.
high priest Most important Jewish priest and leader.

leper A person that had leprosy, a very bad skin disease.
alabaster A beautiful kind of stone that can be carved.
You will ... with you See Deut. 15:11.
Good News The news that God has made a way for people to have their sins forgiven and live with God.
Festival of Unleavened Bread An important Jewish holiday week. In the Old Testament it began the day after Passover, but by this time the two holidays had become one.

followers obeyed and did the thing Jesus told them to do. They prepared the Passover meal. ²⁰In the evening Jesus was sitting at the table with the twelve followers. ²¹They were all eating. Then Jesus said, "I tell you the truth. One of you twelve here will soon give me to my enemies." ²²The followers were very sad to hear this. Each follower said to Jesus, "Lord, surely I am not the one!" ²³Jesus answered, "The man that has dipped his hand into the same bowl with me is the person that will be against me. ²⁴The Son of Man* will go ⌊and die⌋. The Scriptures* say this will happen. But it will be very bad for the person that gives the Son of Man ⌊to be killed⌋. It would be better for that person if he were never born." ²⁵Then Judas said to Jesus, "Teacher, surely I will not be against you!" (Judas is the one that would give Jesus to his enemies.)

Jesus answered, "Yes, it is you."

The Lord's Supper

²⁶While they were eating, Jesus took some bread. Jesus thanked God for the bread and divided it. He gave the bread to his followers. Jesus said, "Take this bread and eat it. This bread is my body." ²⁷Then Jesus took a cup of wine. Jesus thanked God for it and gave it to the followers. Jesus said, "Every one of you drink this. ²⁸This wine is my blood. My blood *(death)* begins the new agreement ⌊from God to his people⌋. This blood is given for many people to forgive their sins. ²⁹I tell you this: I will not drink this wine again until that day when we are together in my Father's kingdom and the wine is new. Then I will drink it again with you." ³⁰All the followers sang a song. Then they went out to the Mount of Olives.*

Jesus Says His Followers Will Leave Him

³¹Jesus told the followers, "Tonight you will lose your faith because of me. It is written ⌊in the Scriptures⌋*

'I will kill the shepherd,
  and the sheep will run away.'
                            Zechariah 13:7

³²But ⌊after I die⌋, I will rise from death. Then I will go into Galilee. I will be there before you go there."

³³Peter answered, "All the other followers may lose their faith because of you. But I will never lose my faith."

³⁴Jesus answered, "I tell you the truth. Tonight you will say you don't know me. You will say this three times before the rooster crows."

³⁵But Peter answered, "I will never say that I don't know you! I will even die with you!" And all the other followers said the same thing.

Jesus Prays Alone

³⁶Then Jesus went with his followers to a place called Gethsemane. Jesus said to his followers, "Sit here while I go there and pray." ³⁷Jesus told Peter and the two sons of Zebedee to come with him. Then Jesus began to be very sad and troubled. ³⁸Jesus said to Peter and the two sons of Zebedee, "My soul is full of sorrow. My heart is breaking with sadness. Stay awake here with me and wait."

³⁹Then Jesus walked a little farther away from them. Jesus fell on the ground and prayed, "My Father, if it is possible, don't give me this cup* ⌊of suffering⌋. But do what you want, not what I want." ⁴⁰Then Jesus went back to his followers. Jesus found his followers sleeping. Jesus said to Peter, "You men could not stay awake with me for one hour? ⁴¹Stay awake and pray that you will not be tempted. Your spirit wants to do what is right. But your body is weak."

⁴²Then Jesus went away a second time and prayed, "My Father, if it is not possible for this ⌊painful⌋ thing to be taken from me, and if I must do it, then I pray that what you want will be done."

⁴³Then Jesus went back to the followers. Again Jesus found them sleeping. Their eyes were very tired. ⁴⁴So Jesus left them and went away one more time and prayed. This third time he prayed, he said the same thing.

⁴⁵Then Jesus went back to the followers and said, "You are still sleeping and resting? The time has come for the Son of Man* to be given to sinful people. ⁴⁶Stand up! We must go. Here comes the man that is giving me ⌊to my enemies⌋."

Son of Man Jesus. In Dan. 7:13-14, this is the name for the Messiah, the one God chose to save his people.
Scriptures Holy Writings—the Old Testament.
Mount of Olives A hill near the city of Jerusalem.

cup Jesus is talking about the bad things that will happen to him. Accepting these things will be very hard, like drinking a cup of something that tastes very bad.

Jesus Is Arrested

⁴⁷While Jesus was still speaking, Judas came there. Judas was one of the twelve followers. Judas had many people with him. These people were sent from the leading priests and the older leaders of the people. These people with Judas had swords and clubs. ⁴⁸Judas* planned to do something to show the people which man was Jesus. Judas said, "The man I kiss is Jesus. Arrest him." ⁴⁹So Judas went to Jesus and said, "Hello, teacher!" Then Judas kissed Jesus.

⁵⁰Jesus answered, "Friend, do the thing you came to do."

Then the men came and grabbed Jesus and arrested him. ⁵¹When that happened, one of the followers with Jesus grabbed his sword and pulled it out. This follower hit the servant of the high priest* with the sword and cut off his ear.

⁵²Jesus said to the man, "Put your sword back in its place. People that use swords will be killed with swords. ⁵³Surely you know I could ask my Father and he would give me more than twelve armies of angels. ⁵⁴But this thing must happen this way so that it will be like the Scriptures* said."

⁵⁵Then Jesus said to all the people, "You came to get me with swords and clubs like I am a criminal. Every day I sat in the temple* teaching. You did not arrest me there. ⁵⁶But all these things have happened so that it will be like the prophets* wrote." Then all of Jesus' followers left him and ran away.

Jesus Before the Jewish Leaders

⁵⁷The men that arrested Jesus led him to the house of Caiaphas the high priest.* The teachers of the law and the older Jewish leaders were gathered there. ⁵⁸Peter followed Jesus, but he did not come near Jesus. Peter followed Jesus to the yard of the high priest's house. He went in and sat with the guards. Peter wanted to see what would happen to Jesus.

⁵⁹The leading priests and the Jewish council tried to find something against Jesus so that they could kill him. They tried to find people to lie and say that Jesus had done wrong. ⁶⁰Many people came and told false things about Jesus. But the council could find no real reason to kill Jesus. Then two people came and said, ⁶¹"This man *(Jesus)* said, 'I can destroy the temple* of God and build it again in three days.'"

⁶²Then the high priest* stood and said to Jesus, "These people have said things against you. Do you have something to say about these charges against you? Are these people telling the truth?" ⁶³But Jesus said nothing.

Again the high priest* said to Jesus, "You are now under oath. I command you by the power of the living God to tell us the truth. Tell us, are you the Christ,* the Son of God?"

⁶⁴Jesus answered, "Yes, I am. But I tell you, in the future you will see the Son of Man* sitting at the right side of God. And you will see the Son of Man coming on the clouds of heaven."

⁶⁵When the high priest* heard this, [he was very angry]. He tore his clothes and said, "This man has said things that are against God! We don't need any more witnesses. You all heard him say these things against God. ⁶⁶What do you think?"

The Jews answered, "He is guilty, and he must die."

⁶⁷Then the people there spit in Jesus' face. And they hit him with their fists. Other people slapped Jesus. ⁶⁸They said, "Show us that you are a prophet,* Christ! Tell us who hit you!"

Peter Is Afraid to Say He Knows Jesus

⁶⁹At that time, Peter was sitting in the yard. A servant girl came to Peter. The girl said, "You were with Jesus, that man from Galilee."

⁷⁰But Peter said that he was never with Jesus. He said this to all the people there. Peter said, "I don't know what you are talking about."

⁷¹Then Peter left the yard. At the gate, another girl saw him. The girl said to the people there, "This man was with Jesus of Nazareth."

⁷²Again, Peter said that he was never with Jesus. Peter said, "I promise to God that I don't know this man Jesus!"

Judas Literally, "the one that betrayed him."
high priest Most important Jewish priest and leader.
Scriptures Holy Writings—the Old Testament.
temple The special building in Jerusalem for Jewish worship.
prophets People who spoke for God. Their writings are part of the Old Testament.

Christ The "anointed one" (Messiah) or chosen of God.
Son of Man Jesus. In Dan. 7:13-14 this is the name for the Messiah, the one God chose to save his people.
prophet Person who spoke for God. Prophets could say things that most people could not know.

[73] A short time later, some people standing there went to Peter and said, "We know you are one of those men that followed Jesus. We know this because of the way you talk." [74] Then Peter began to curse. He said strongly, "I promise to God that I don't know this man Jesus!" After Peter said this, a rooster crowed. [75] Then Peter remembered what Jesus had told him: "Before the rooster crows, you will say three times that you don't know me." Then Peter went outside and cried bitterly.

Jesus Is Taken to Governor Pilate

27 Early the next morning, all the leading priests and older leaders of the people decided to kill Jesus. [2] They tied Jesus with chains. Then they led him to Pilate the governor. They gave Jesus to Pilate.

Judas Kills Himself

[3] Judas saw that they had decided to kill Jesus. Judas was the one that gave Jesus ₍to his enemies₎. When Judas saw what happened, he was very sorry for what he did. So he took the 30 silver coins back to the priests and the leaders. [4] Judas said, "I sinned. I gave you an innocent man to be killed."

The Jewish leaders answered, "We don't care! That's a problem for you, not us."

[5] So Judas threw the money into the temple. Then Judas left that place and hanged himself.

[6] The leading priests picked up the silver coins in the temple. They said, "Our law does not allow us to keep this money with the temple money, because this money has paid for a man's death." [7] So they decided to use the money to buy a field called Potter's Field. This field would be a place to bury people that died while visiting ₍in Jerusalem₎. [8] That is why that field is still called the Field of Blood. [9] So the thing happened that Jeremiah the prophet* said:

> "They took 30 silver coins. That was how much the Jewish people decided to pay for his life. [10] They used those 30 silver coins to buy the potter's field, like the Lord commanded me."*

Governor Pilate Questions Jesus

[11] Jesus stood before Pilate the governor. Pilate asked him questions. He said, "Are you the king of the Jews?"

Jesus answered, "Yes, I am."

[12] When the leading priests and the older Jewish leaders accused Jesus, he said nothing.

[13] So Pilate said to Jesus, "You hear these people accusing you of all these things. Why don't you answer?"

[14] But Jesus said nothing to answer Pilate. Pilate was very surprised at this.

Pilate Tries but Fails to Free Jesus

[15] Every year at the Passover* time the governor would free one person from the prison. This was always a person that the people wanted to be made free. [16] At that time there was a man in prison who was known to be very bad. His name was Barabbas.* [17] All the people gathered at Pilate's house. Pilate asked the people, "I will free one man for you. Which man do you want me to free: Barabbas, or Jesus who is called the Christ*?" [18] Pilate knew that the people gave Jesus to him because the people were jealous.

[19] Pilate said these things while he was sitting in the place for judging. While he was sitting there, his wife sent a message to him. The message said, "Don't do anything with that man *(Jesus)*. He is not guilty. And today I had a dream about him, and it troubled me very much."

[20] But the leading priests and older Jewish leaders told the people to ask for Barabbas to be made free and for Jesus to be killed.

[21] Pilate said, "I have Barabbas and Jesus. Which do you want me to make free for you?"

The people answered, "Barabbas!"

[22] Pilate asked, "So what should I do with Jesus, the one called the Christ?"

All the people answered, "Kill him on a cross!"

[23] Pilate asked, "Why do you want me to kill him? What wrong has he done?"

But all the people shouted louder, "Kill him on a cross!"

[24] Pilate saw that he could do nothing to make the people change. And he saw that the people

---

prophet Person who spoke for God. He often told things that would happen in the future.
"They took ... me" See Zech. 11:12-13; Jer. 32:6-9.

Passover Important Jewish holy day. They ate a special meal on this day every year to remember that God freed them from slavery in Egypt in the time of Moses.
Barabbas In some Greek copies the name is Jesus Barabbas.
Christ The "anointed one" (Messiah) or chosen of God.

MATTHEW 27:25-53

were becoming upset. So Pilate took some water and washed his hands* so that all the people could see. Then Pilate said, "I am not guilty of this man's death. You are the ones that are doing it!" ²⁵All the people answered, "We will be responsible for his death. We accept for ourselves and for our children any punishment for his death." ²⁶Then Pilate freed Barabbas. Pilate told some soldiers to beat Jesus with whips. Then Pilate gave Jesus to the soldiers to be killed on a cross.

Pilate's Soldiers Tease Jesus

²⁷Then Pilate's soldiers brought Jesus into the governor's palace. All the soldiers gathered around Jesus. ²⁸The soldiers took off Jesus' clothes and put a red robe on him. ²⁹Then the soldiers used thorny branches to make a crown. They put this crown of thorns on Jesus' head, and they put a stick in his right hand. Then the soldiers bowed before Jesus and teased him. They said, "Hello, king of the Jews!" ³⁰The soldiers spit on Jesus. Then they took his stick and hit him on the head many times. ³¹After they finished teasing Jesus, the soldiers took off the robe and put his own clothes on him again. Then they led Jesus away to be killed on a cross.

Jesus Is Killed on a Cross

³²The soldiers were going out of the city with Jesus. The soldiers forced another man there to carry the cross for Jesus. This man's name was Simon from Cyrene. ³³They came to the place called Golgotha. (Golgotha means "The Place of the Skull.") ³⁴At Golgotha, the soldiers gave Jesus wine to drink. This wine was mixed with gall.* Jesus tasted the wine but refused to drink it. ³⁵The soldiers nailed Jesus to a cross. Then the soldiers gambled with dice to decide who would get Jesus' clothes. ³⁶The soldiers sat there and continued watching Jesus. ³⁷The soldiers put a sign above Jesus' head with the charge against him written on it. The sign said: "THIS IS JESUS, THE KING OF THE JEWS." ³⁸Two robbers were nailed to crosses beside Jesus. One robber was put beside Jesus on the right and the other was put on the left. ³⁹People walked by and said bad things to Jesus. People shook their heads ⁴⁰and said, "You said you could destroy the temple and build it again in three days. So save yourself! Come down from that cross, if you are really the Son of God!" ⁴¹The leading priests, the teachers of the law, and the older Jewish leaders were also there. These men teased Jesus the same as the other people. ⁴²They said, "He saved other people. But he can't save himself! People say he is the king of Israel (the Jews). If he is the king, then he should come down now from the cross. Then we will believe in him. ⁴³He trusted God. So let God save him now, if God really wants him. He himself said, 'I am the Son of God.'" ⁴⁴And in the same way, the robbers that were being killed on crosses beside Jesus also said bad things to him.

Jesus Dies

⁴⁵At noon the whole country became dark. This darkness continued for three hours. ⁴⁶At about three o'clock Jesus cried with a loud voice, "Eli, Eli, lema sabachthani?" This means, "My God, my God, why have you left me alone?"* ⁴⁷Some of the people standing there heard this. The people said, "He is calling Elijah."* ⁴⁸Quickly one of the people ran and got a sponge. That person filled the sponge with vinegar and tied the sponge to a stick. Then he used the stick to give the sponge to Jesus to drink from it. ⁴⁹But the other people said, "Don't bother him (Jesus). We want to see if Elijah will come to save him."
⁵⁰Again Jesus cried with a loud voice. Then he died.*
⁵¹When Jesus died, the curtain in the temple* was torn into two pieces. The tear started at the top and tore all the way to the bottom. Also, the earth shook and rocks were broken. ⁵²All the graves opened, and many of God's people that had died were raised from death. ⁵³Those people came out of the graves. After Jesus was raised from death, those people went into the holy city (Jerusalem), and many people saw them.

---

washed his hands Pilate did this as a sign to show that he wanted no part in what the people did.
gall Probably a drink of wine mixed with drugs to help a person feel less pain.
"**My God ... alone**" Quote from Ps. 22:1.
"**He is calling Elijah**" The word for "My God" ("Eli") sounded to the people like the name of Elijah, a famous man who spoke for God about 850 B.C.
died Literally, "he let his spirit leave."
curtain in the temple A curtain divided the "most holy place" from the other part of the temple, the special building in Jerusalem for Jewish worship.

⁵⁴The army officer* and the soldiers guarding Jesus saw this earthquake and everything that happened. They were very afraid and said, "He really was the Son of God!" ⁵⁵Many women were standing away from the cross, watching. These were the women that followed Jesus from Galilee to care for him. ⁵⁶Mary Magdalene, Mary the mother of James and Joseph, and the mother of James and John* were there.

Jesus Is Buried

⁵⁷That evening a rich man named Joseph came to Jerusalem. Joseph was a follower of Jesus from the town of Arimathea. ⁵⁸Joseph went to Pilate and asked to have Jesus' body. Pilate gave orders for the soldiers to give Jesus' body to Joseph. ⁵⁹Then Joseph took the body and wrapped it in a new linen cloth. ⁶⁰Joseph put Jesus' body in a new tomb *(grave)* that Joseph had dug in a wall of rock. Then he closed the tomb by rolling a very large stone to cover the entrance. After he did these things, Joseph went away. ⁶¹Mary Magdalene and the other woman named Mary were sitting near the tomb.

The Tomb of Jesus Is Guarded

⁶²That day was the day called Preparation day.* The next day, the leading priests and the Pharisees* went to Pilate. ⁶³They said, "Sir, we remember that while that liar was still alive he said, 'After three days I will rise from death.' ⁶⁴So give the order for the tomb to be guarded well until after three days. His followers might come and try to steal the body. Then they could tell the people that he has risen from death. That lie will be even worse than what they said about him before."

⁶⁵Pilate said, "Take some soldiers and go guard the tomb the best way you know." ⁶⁶So they all went to the tomb and made it safe from thieves. They did this by sealing the stone in the entrance and putting soldiers there to guard it.

News That Jesus Has Risen from Death

28 The day after the Sabbath day* was the first day of the week. At dawn on the first day, Mary Magdalene and the other woman named Mary went to look at the tomb.* ²At that time there was a very strong earthquake. An angel of the Lord came from the sky. The angel went to the tomb and rolled the stone away from the entrance. Then the angel sat on the stone. ³The angel was shining very bright like lightning. His clothes were white like snow. ⁴The soldiers guarding the tomb were very afraid of the angel. They shook with fear and became like dead men.

⁵The angel said to the women, "Don't be afraid. I know that you are looking for Jesus, the one that was killed on the cross. ⁶But Jesus is not here. He has risen from death, like he said he would. Come and see the place where his body was. ⁷And go quickly and tell his followers. Tell them: 'Jesus has risen from death. He is going into Galilee. He will be there before you. You will see him there.'" Then the angel said, "Now I have told you."

⁸So the women left the tomb quickly. They were afraid, but they were also very happy. They ran to tell his followers what happened. ⁹While the women were running to tell the followers, Jesus was standing there before them. Jesus said, "Hello!" The women went to Jesus. They held him at his feet and worshiped him. ¹⁰Then Jesus said to the women, "Don't be afraid. Go and tell my brothers *(followers)* to go to Galilee. They will see me there."

Report to the Jewish Leaders

¹¹The women went to tell the followers. At the same time, some of the soldiers that were guarding the tomb* went into the city. They went to tell the leading priests everything that happened. ¹²Then the priests met with the older Jewish leaders and made a plan. They paid the soldiers much money ₍to tell a lie₎. ¹³They said to the soldiers, "Tell the people that Jesus' followers came during the night and stole the body while you were sleeping. ¹⁴If the governor hears about this, we will satisfy him and save you from trouble." ¹⁵So the soldiers kept the money and

---

army officer A centurion, a Roman army officer that had authority over 100 soldiers.
James and John Literally, "the sons of Zebedee."
Preparation day Friday, day before the Sabbath day.
Pharisees The Pharisees were a Jewish religious group that claimed to follow carefully all Jewish laws and customs.

Sabbath day The seventh day of the Jewish week. It was a special religious day for the Jews.
tomb A grave dug in a wall of rock.

obeyed the priests. And that story is still spread among the Jews even today.

Jesus Talks to His Followers

[16] The eleven followers went to Galilee. They went to the mountain where Jesus told them to go. [17] On the mountain the followers saw Jesus. They worshiped him. But some of the followers did not believe that it was really Jesus. [18] So Jesus came to them and said, "All authority *(power)* in heaven and on earth is given to me. [19] So go and make followers of all people in the world. Baptize* them in the name of the Father and the Son and the Holy Spirit.* [20] Teach those people to obey everything that I have told you. You can be sure that I will be with you always. I will continue with you until the end of the world."

Baptize A Greek word meaning to immerse, dip, or bury a person or thing briefly under water.
Holy Spirit Called the Spirit of God, the Spirit of Christ, and the Comforter. Joined with God and Christ, he does God's work among people in the world.

Mark

The Coming of Jesus

1 The Good News* about Jesus Christ, the Son of God,* begins ²with what the prophet* Isaiah said would happen. Isaiah wrote:

"Listen! I *(God)* will send my helper*
ahead of you.
He will prepare the way for you."
Malachi 3:1

³ "There is a person shouting in the desert:
'Prepare the way for the Lord.
Make his paths straight.'"
Isaiah 40:3

⁴So John the Baptizer came and was baptizing people in the desert area. He told the people to be baptized* to show they wanted to change their lives. Then their sins would be forgiven. ⁵All the people from Judea and Jerusalem went out to John. These people told the sins they had done, and then they were baptized by John in the Jordan River. ⁶John wore clothes made from camel's hair. John had a leather belt around his waist. He ate locusts* and wild honey. ⁷This is what John preached to the people: "There is a person coming later who is greater than I am. I am not good enough to kneel down and untie his shoes. ⁸I baptize you with water. But that person who is coming will baptize you with the Holy Spirit.*"

Good News The news that God has made a way for people to have their sins forgiven and live with God.
the Son of God Some Greek copies omit these words.
prophet Person who spoke for God. He often told things that would happen in the future.
helper Literally, "messenger."
baptized A Greek word meaning to be immersed, dipped, or buried briefly under water.
locusts Insects like grasshoppers. The law of Moses said that locusts could be eaten (See Lev. 11:21-22).
Holy Spirit Called the Spirit of God, the Spirit of Christ, and the Comforter. Joined with God and Christ, he does the God's work among people in the world.

Jesus Is Baptized

⁹At that time Jesus came from the town of Nazareth in Galilee to the place where John was. John baptized* Jesus in the Jordan River. ¹⁰While Jesus was coming up out of the water, he saw the sky open. The Holy Spirit* came down to Jesus like a dove. ¹¹A voice came from heaven and said: "You are my Son and I love you. I am very pleased with you."

Jesus Goes Away to Be Tempted

¹²Then the Spirit sent Jesus into the desert alone. ¹³Jesus was in the desert 40 days. He was there with the wild animals. While Jesus was in the desert, he was tempted by Satan *(the devil)*. Then angels came and helped Jesus.

Jesus Chooses Some Followers

¹⁴After this, John was put into prison. Jesus went into Galilee and preached the Good News from God. ¹⁵Jesus said, "The right time is now here. The kingdom of God is near. Change your hearts and lives and believe the Good News!" ¹⁶Jesus was walking by Lake Galilee. Jesus saw Simon* and Simon's brother, Andrew. These two men were fishermen, and they were throwing a net into the lake to catch fish. ¹⁷Jesus said to them, "Come and follow me. I will make you ₍a different kind of₎ fishermen. You will work to gather people, ₍not fish₎." ¹⁸So Simon and Andrew left their nets and followed Jesus.

¹⁹Jesus continued walking by Lake Galilee. He saw two more brothers, James and John, the sons of Zebedee. They were in their boat, preparing their nets to catch fish. ²⁰Their father Zebedee and the men that worked for him were in the boat with the brothers. When Jesus saw the brothers he told them to come. They left their father and followed Jesus.

Simon Simon's other name was Peter.

Jesus Heals a Man That Had an Evil Spirit

²¹Jesus and his followers went to Capernaum. On the Sabbath day* Jesus went into the synagogue* and taught the people. ²²The people there were amazed at Jesus' teaching. Jesus did not teach like their teachers of the law. Jesus taught like a person that had authority *(power)*. ²³While Jesus was in the synagogue, a man was there that had an evil spirit ₁from the devil₁ inside him. The man shouted, ²⁴"Jesus of Nazareth! What do you want with us? Did you come to destroy us? I know who you are—God's Holy One!" ²⁵Jesus said strongly, "Be quiet! Come out of the man!" ²⁶The evil spirit made the man shake. Then the spirit made a loud noise and came out of the man.

²⁷The people were amazed. They asked each other, "What is happening here? This man is teaching something new. And he teaches with authority *(power)*! He even gives commands to evil spirits, and the spirits obey him." ²⁸So the news about Jesus spread quickly everywhere in the area of Galilee.

Jesus Heals Many People

²⁹Jesus and the followers left the synagogue.* They all went with James and John to the home of Simon* and Andrew. ³⁰Simon's mother-in-law was very sick. She was in bed and had fever. The people there told Jesus about her. ³¹So Jesus went to her bed. Jesus held her hand and helped her stand up. The fever left her, and she was healed. Then she began serving them.

³²That night, after the sun went down, the people brought many sick people to Jesus. They also brought people that had demons* inside them. ³³All the people in the town gathered at the door of that house. ³⁴Jesus healed many people that had different kinds of sicknesses. Jesus also forced many demons to leave people. But Jesus would not allow the demons to speak, because the demons knew who he was.*

Jesus Prepares to Preach the Good News

³⁵The next morning, Jesus woke up very early. Jesus left the house while it was still dark. He went to a place to be alone and pray. ³⁶Later, Simon* and his friends went to look for Jesus. ³⁷They found Jesus and said, "All the people are looking for you!" ³⁸Jesus answered, "We should go to another place. We can go to other towns around here. Then I can preach in those places also. That is why I came." ³⁹So Jesus traveled everywhere in Galilee. He preached in the synagogues.* And he forced demons* to leave people.

Jesus Heals a Sick Man

⁴⁰A man that had leprosy* came to Jesus. The man bowed on his knees and begged Jesus, "You have the power to heal me if you want." ⁴¹Jesus felt sorry for the man. So Jesus touched the man and said, "I want to heal you. Be healed!" ⁴²Then the sickness left the man, and he was healed.

⁴³Jesus told the man to go. But Jesus warned him strongly. Jesus said, ⁴⁴"Don't tell any person about what I did for you. But go and show yourself to the priest. And offer a gift to God because you have been healed. Offer the gift that Moses commanded.* This will show the people that you are healed." ⁴⁵The man left there and told all the people he saw that Jesus had healed him. So the news about Jesus spread. And that is why Jesus could not enter a town if people saw him. Jesus stayed in places where people did not live. But people came from all the towns to the places where Jesus was.

Jesus Heals a Crippled Man

2 A few days later, Jesus came back to Capernaum. The news spread that Jesus was back home. ²Many, many people gathered to hear Jesus preach. The house was full. There was no place to stand, not even outside the door. Jesus was teaching these people. ³Some people brought a paralyzed *(crippled)* man to Jesus. Four men were carrying the paralyzed man. ⁴But they could not bring the man to Jesus because the house was full of people. So the men went to the roof above

---

Sabbath day The seventh day of the Jewish week. It was a special religious day for the Jews.
synagogue(s) Synagogues were places where Jews gathered for prayer, study of the Scriptures, and other public meetings.
Simon Simon's other name was Peter.
demons Demons are evil spirits from the devil.
who he was The demons knew that Jesus was the Christ, the Son of God.

leprosy A very bad skin disease.
Moses commanded See Lev. 14:1-32.

Jesus and made a hole in the roof. Then they lowered the bed with the paralyzed man on it. ⁵Jesus saw that these men had much faith. So Jesus said to the paralyzed man, "Young man, your sins are forgiven." ⁶Some of the teachers of the law were sitting there. They saw what Jesus did, and they said to themselves, ⁷"Why does this man say things like that? He is saying things that are against God. Only God can forgive sins." ⁸Jesus knew that these teachers of the law were thinking those things about him. So Jesus said to them, "Why are you thinking these things? ⁹Which is easier: to tell this crippled man, 'Your sins are forgiven,' or to tell him, 'Stand up. Take your bed and walk'? ¹⁰But I will prove to you that the Son of Man has power on earth to forgive sins." So Jesus said to the paralyzed man, ¹¹"I tell you, stand up. Take your bed and go home." ¹²The paralyzed man stood up. He took his bed and walked out of the room. All the people could see him. The people were amazed and praised God. They said, "This is the most amazing thing we have ever seen!"

¹³Jesus went to the lake again. Many people followed him there. So Jesus taught them. ¹⁴Jesus was walking beside the lake, and he saw a tax collector* named Levi, son of Alphaeus. Levi was sitting in the tax office. Jesus said to him, "Follow me." Then Levi stood up and followed Jesus.

¹⁵Later that day, Jesus ate at Levi's house. There were many tax collectors* and other bad people eating there with Jesus and his followers. There were many of these people that followed Jesus. ¹⁶The teachers of the law (they were Pharisees*) saw Jesus eating with these tax collectors and other bad people. They asked Jesus' followers, "Why does he *(Jesus)* eat with tax collectors and sinners?"

¹⁷Jesus heard this, and he said to them, "Healthy people don't need a doctor. It is the sick people that need a doctor. I did not come to invite good people. I came to invite sinners."

Jesus Not Like Other Religious Leaders

¹⁸The followers of John* and the Pharisees* were fasting.* Some people came to Jesus and said, "John's followers fast,* and the followers of the Pharisees fast. But your followers don't fast. Why?"

¹⁹Jesus answered, "⌊When there is a wedding⌋, the friends of the bridegroom* are not sad while he is with them. They cannot fast* *(be sad)* while the bridegroom is still there. ²⁰But the time will come when the bridegroom will leave them. The friends are sad when the bridegroom leaves. Then they will fast.

²¹"When a person sews a patch over a hole on an old coat, that person never uses a piece of cloth that is not yet shrunk. If he does, the patch will ⌊shrink and⌋ pull away from the coat. Then the hole will be worse. ²²Also, people never pour new wine into old wine bags.* Why? Because the new wine will break the bags, and the wine will be ruined with the wine bags. People always put new wine into new wine bags."

Some Jews Criticize Jesus

²³On the Sabbath day,* Jesus was walking through some grain fields. Jesus' followers were walking with him. The followers picked some grain ⌊to eat⌋. ²⁴The Pharisees* saw this and said to Jesus, "Why are your followers doing that? It is against the ⌊Jewish⌋ law to do that on the Sabbath day."

²⁵Jesus answered, "You have read what David* did when he and the people with him were hungry and needed food. ²⁶It was during the time of Abiathar the high priest. David went into God's house and ate the bread that was offered to God. And the law ⌊of Moses⌋ says that only priests can eat that bread. David also gave some of the bread to those people with him."

²⁷Then Jesus said to the Pharisees,* "The Sabbath day* was made to help people. People

---

John John the Baptizer, who preached to the Jews about Christ's coming (See Mk. 1:4-8).
fasting, fast To fast is to live without food for a special time of prayer and worship or for a time of mourning.
bridegroom A man ready to be married.
wine bags Animal skins used for holding wine.
Sabbath day The seventh day of the Jewish week. It was a special religious day for the Jews.
David King of Israel about 1000 years before Christ.

---

tax collector(s) Jews hired by the Romans to collect taxes. They often cheated, and the other Jews hated them.
Pharisees The Pharisees were a Jewish religious group that claimed to follow carefully all Jewish laws and customs.

were not made to be ruled by the Sabbath day. ²⁸So the Son of Man* is Lord *(master)* of every day, even the Sabbath."

Jesus Heals a Man's Crippled Hand

3 Another time Jesus went into the synagogue.* In the synagogue there was a man with a crippled hand. ²Some Jews there wanted to see Jesus do something wrong so that they could accuse him. So those people watched him closely. They wanted to see if Jesus would heal the man on a Sabbath day.* ³Jesus said to the man with the crippled hand, "Stand up here so that all the people can see you."

⁴Then Jesus asked the people, "Which thing is right to do on the Sabbath day: to do good, or to do evil? Is it right to save a life or to destroy one?" The people said nothing to answer Jesus.

⁵Jesus looked at the people. He was angry. But he felt very sad because they were stubborn. Jesus said to the man, "Let me see your hand." The man put his hand out for Jesus, and it was healed. ⁶Then the Pharisees* left and made plans with the Herodians* about a way to kill Jesus.

Many People Follow Jesus

⁷Jesus went away with his followers to the lake. Many people from Galilee followed him. ⁸Many, many people also came from Judea, from Jerusalem, from Idumea, from the area across the Jordan River, and from the area around Tyre and Sidon. These people came because they heard about all the things Jesus was doing. ⁹Jesus saw the many people. So he told his followers to get a small boat and make it ready for him. Jesus wanted the boat so that the many, many people would not push against him. ¹⁰Jesus had healed many people. So all the sick people were pushing toward him to touch him. ¹¹Some people had evil spirits ⌊from the devil⌋ inside them. When the evil spirits saw Jesus, they bowed before him and shouted, "You are the Son of God!" ¹²But Jesus commanded the spirits strongly not to tell people who he was.

Jesus Chooses His Twelve Apostles

¹³Then Jesus went up on a hill. Jesus told some men to come to him. These were the men Jesus wanted. These men went up to Jesus. ¹⁴Jesus chose twelve men and called them apostles.* Jesus wanted these twelve men to be with him, and he wanted to send them to other places to preach. ¹⁵And Jesus wanted these men to have the power to force demons* out of people. ¹⁶These are the names of the twelve men Jesus chose: Simon (Jesus gave him the name Peter); ¹⁷James and John, the sons of Zebedee (Jesus gave them the name Boanerges. This name means "Sons of Thunder"); ¹⁸Andrew, Philip, Bartholomew, Matthew, Thomas, James the son of Alphaeus, Thaddaeus, Simon the Zealot,* ¹⁹and Judas Iscariot. Judas is the one that gave Jesus ⌊to his enemies⌋.

Some Say Jesus Has a Devil in Him

²⁰Then Jesus went home. But again many people gathered there. There were so many people that Jesus and his followers could not eat. ²¹Jesus' family heard about all these things. They went to get him because people said that Jesus was crazy.

²²And the teachers of the law from Jerusalem said, "Beelzebul *(the devil)* is living inside him *(Jesus)*! He uses power from the ruler of demons* to force demons out of people."

²³So Jesus called the people together and used stories to teach the people. Jesus said, "Satan will not force his own demons* out of people. ²⁴A kingdom that fights against itself cannot continue. ²⁵And a family that is divided cannot succeed. ²⁶And if Satan is against himself and fights against his own people, then he cannot continue. That would be the end of Satan. ²⁷If a person wants to enter a strong man's house and steal his things, first the person must tie the strong man. Then the person can steal the things from the strong man's house. ²⁸I tell you the truth. All sins that people do can be forgiven. And all the bad things people say against God can be forgiven. ²⁹But any person that says bad things against *(refuses to accept)* the Holy Spirit* will never be forgiven. He will always be guilty of that sin."

Son of Man Jesus. In Dan. 7:13-14 this is the name for the Messiah, the one God chose to save his people.

synagogue Synagogues were places where Jews gathered for prayer, study of the Scriptures, and other public meetings.

Sabbath day The seventh day of the Jewish week. It was a special religious day for the Jews.

Pharisees The Pharisees were a Jewish religious group that claimed to follow carefully all Jewish laws and customs.

Herodians A Jewish political group.

apostles The men Jesus chose to be his special helpers.

demons Demons are evil spirits from the devil.

Zealot Zealots were a Jewish Political group.

Holy Spirit Called the Spirit of God, the Spirit of Christ, and the Comforter. Joined with God and Christ, he does God's work among people in the world.

30 Jesus said this because the teachers of the law said that Jesus had an evil spirit *(devil)* inside him.

Jesus' Followers Are His True Family

31 Then Jesus' mother and brothers came. They stood outside and sent a person in to tell Jesus to come out. 32 Many people were sitting around Jesus. They said to him, "Your mother and brothers are waiting for you outside." 33 Jesus asked, "Who is my mother? Who are my brothers?" 34 Then Jesus looked at those people sitting around him. He said, "These people are my mother and my brothers! 35 My true brother and sister and mother are those people that do the things God wants."

Story About a Farmer Planting Seed

4 Another time Jesus began teaching by the lake. Many, many people gathered around Jesus. So Jesus got into a boat and went out on the lake. All the people stayed on the shore next to the water. 2 Jesus taught the people from the boat. Jesus used many stories to teach them. He said, 3 "Listen! A farmer went out to plant his seed. 4 While the farmer was planting, some seed fell by the road. The birds came and ate all that seed. 5 Some seed fell on rocky ground. The ground there did not have enough dirt. The seed grew very fast there because the ground was not deep. 6 But the sun rose and the plants were burned. The plants died because they did not have deep roots. 7 Some other seed fell among thorny weeds. The weeds grew and stopped the good plants from growing. So those plants did not make grain. 8 Some other seed fell on good ground. In the good ground, the seed began to grow. It grew and made grain. Some plants had 30 grains, other plants had 60 grains, and some had 100 grains."

9 Then Jesus said, "You people that hear me, listen!"

Jesus Tells Why He Used Stories

10 Later, Jesus was away from the people. The twelve apostles* and Jesus' other followers asked him about the stories. 11 Jesus said, "Only you can know the secret truth about the kingdom of God. But to those other people I tell everything by using stories. 12 I do this so that:

'They will look and look,
 but never really see;
they will listen and listen,
 but never understand.
If they saw and understood,
 they might change and be forgiven.'"
Isaiah 6:9-10

Jesus Explains the Story About the Seed

13 Then Jesus said to the followers, "Do you understand this story? If you don't, then how will you understand any story? 14 The farmer is like a person that plants God's teaching in people. 15 Sometimes the teaching falls on the path. This is like some people. Those people hear the teaching of God. But Satan *(the devil)* comes and takes away the teaching that was planted in them. 16 Other people are like the seed planted on rocky ground. They hear the teaching and quickly accept it with joy. 17 But those people don't allow the teaching to go deep into their lives. They keep that teaching only a short time. When trouble or persecution* comes because of the teaching they accepted, they quickly quit. 18 Other people are like the seed planted among the thorny weeds. These people hear the teaching. 19 But then these things come into their lives: the worries of this life, the love of money, and wanting all kinds of other things. These things stop the teaching from growing. So that teaching does not make fruit* in the lives of those people. 20 Other people are like the seed planted on the good ground. They hear the teaching and accept it. Then they grow and make fruit—sometimes 30 times more, sometimes 60 times more, and sometimes 100 times more."

You Must Use What You Have

21 Then Jesus said to them, "Do you take a lamp and hide it under a bowl or under a bed? No! You put the lamp on a lamp table. 22 Everything that is hidden will be made clear. Every secret thing will be made known. 23 You people that hear me, listen!

24 "Think carefully about the things you hear. The way you give is the way God will give to you. But God will give you more than you give.

---

apostles The men Jesus chose to be his special helpers.
persecution Being hurt or bothered by Christ's enemies.
fruit The good things God wants his people to do.

MARK 4:25–5:17

[25] The person that has ₍something₎ will receive more. But the person that does not have ₍much₎ will lose even the little amount he has."

Jesus Uses a Story About Seed

[26] Then Jesus said, "The kingdom of God is like a man that plants seed in the ground. [27] The seed begins to grow. It grows night and day. It is not important if the man is sleeping or awake; the seed still grows. The man does not know how the seed grows. [28] Without any help, the ground grows grain. First the plant grows, then the head, and then all the grain in the head. [29] When the grain is ready, the man cuts it. This is the harvest time."

The Kingdom Is Like a Mustard Seed

[30] Then Jesus said, "What can I use to show you what the kingdom of God is like? What story can I use to explain it? [31] The kingdom of God is like a mustard seed. The mustard seed is the smallest seed that you plant in the ground. [32] But when you plant this seed, it grows and becomes the largest of all the plants in your garden. It has branches that are very big. The wild birds can come and make nests there and be protected from the sun."

[33] Jesus used many stories like these to teach them. He taught them all that they could understand. [34] Jesus always used stories to teach the people. But when Jesus and his followers were alone together, Jesus explained everything to them.

Jesus Stops a Storm

[35] That day, at evening, Jesus said to his followers, "Come with me across the lake." [36] Jesus and the followers left the people there. They went in the same boat that Jesus was already sitting in. There were also other boats with them. [37] A very bad wind came on the lake. The waves were coming over the sides and into the boat. The boat was almost full of water. [38] Jesus was inside the boat, sleeping with his head on a pillow. The followers went to him and woke him. They said, "Teacher, do you care about us? We will drown!"

[39] Jesus stood up and commanded the wind and the waves to stop. Jesus said, "Quiet! Be still!" Then the wind stopped and the lake became calm.

[40] Jesus said to his followers, "Why are you afraid? You still have no faith?"

[41] The followers were very afraid and asked each other, "What kind of man is this? Even the wind and the water obey him!"

Jesus Frees a Man from Evil Spirits

5 Jesus and his followers went across the lake to the area where the Gerasene people lived. [2] When Jesus got out of the boat, a man came to him from the caves where dead people are buried. This man had an evil spirit ₍from the devil₎ living inside of him. [3] This man lived in the burial caves. No person could tie him. Even chains could not keep this man tied. [4] Many times people had used chains to tie the man's hands and feet. But the man broke the chains on his hands and feet. No person was strong enough to control him. [5] Day and night the man walked around the burial caves and on the hills. The man would scream and cut himself with rocks.

[6] While Jesus was far away, the man saw him. The man ran to Jesus and bowed down before him. [7-8] Jesus said to the man, "You evil spirit, come out of that man." So the man shouted with a loud voice, "What do you want with me, Jesus, Son of the Most High God? I beg you to promise to God that you will not punish me!"

[9] Then Jesus asked the man, "What is your name?"

The man answered, "My name is Legion,* because there are many spirits inside me." [10] The spirits inside the man begged Jesus again and again not to send them out of that area.

[11] A large herd of pigs was eating on a hill near there. [12] The evil spirits begged Jesus, "Send us to the pigs. Let us go into them." [13] So Jesus allowed them to do this. The evil spirits left the man and went into the pigs. Then the herd of pigs ran down the hill and into the lake. All the pigs were drowned. There were about 2,000 pigs in that herd.

[14] The men that had the work of caring for the pigs ran away. The men ran to the town and to the farms. They told all the people what happened. The people went out to see what happened. [15] The people came to Jesus. They saw the man that had the many evil spirits. The man was sitting and was wearing clothes. His mind was right again. The people were afraid. [16] Some people were there and saw what Jesus did. These people told the other people what happened to the man that had the demons* living in him. And they also told about the pigs. [17] Then the people began to beg Jesus to leave their area.

Legion Means very many. A legion was about 5,000 men in the Roman army.

demons Demons are evil spirits from the devil.

[18] Jesus was preparing to leave in the boat. The man that was freed from the demons begged to go with Jesus. [19] But Jesus did not allow the man to go. Jesus said, "Go home to your family and friends. Tell them about all the things the Lord did for you. Tell them that the Lord was good to you." [20] So the man left and told the people in the Ten Towns* about the great things Jesus did for him. All the people were amazed.

Jesus Gives Life to a Dead Girl and Heals a Sick Woman

[21] Jesus went in the boat back across to the other side of the lake. There, many people gathered around him by the lake. [22] A leader of the synagogue* came to that place. His name was Jairus. Jairus saw Jesus and bowed down before him. [23] Jairus begged and begged Jesus. He said, "My little daughter is dying. Please come and put your hands on her. Then she will be healed and will live."

[24] So Jesus went with Jairus. Many people followed Jesus. They were pushing very close around him.

[25] A woman was there among the people. This woman had been bleeding for the past twelve years. [26] The woman suffered very much. Many doctors tried to help her. All the money she had was spent. But she was not improving. Her sickness was becoming worse. [27] The woman heard about Jesus. So she followed Jesus with the people and touched his coat. [28] The woman thought, "If I can touch his clothes, that will be enough to heal me." [29] When the woman touched his coat, her bleeding stopped. The woman felt that her body was healed from the suffering. [30] And Jesus felt power go out from him. So he stopped and turned around. Then he asked, "Who touched my clothes?"

[31] The followers said to Jesus, "There are many people pushing against you. But you ask, 'Who touched me?'"

[32] But Jesus continued looking for the person that touched him. [33] The woman knew that she was healed. So she came and bowed at Jesus' feet. The woman was shaking with fear. She told Jesus the whole story. [34] Jesus said to the woman, "Dear woman, you are made well because you believed. Go in peace. You will have no more suffering."

[35] Jesus was still there speaking. Some men came from the house of Jairus, the synagogue* leader. The men said, "Your daughter is dead. There is now no need to bother the teacher (Jesus)."

[36] But Jesus did not care what the men said. Jesus said to the synagogue leader, "Don't be afraid; only believe."

[37] Jesus let only Peter, James, and John the brother of James go with him. [38] Jesus and these followers went to the house of Jairus, the synagogue* leader. Jesus saw many people there crying loudly. There was much confusion. [39] Jesus entered the house and said to the people, "Why are you people crying and making so much noise? This child is not dead. She is only sleeping." [40] But all the people laughed at Jesus. Jesus told the people to leave the house. Then Jesus went into the room where the child was. He brought the child's father and mother and his three followers into the room with him. [41] Then Jesus held the girl's hand and said to her, "*Talitha, koum!*" (This means, "Little girl, I tell you to stand up!") [42] The girl stood up and began walking. (The girl was twelve years old.) The father and mother and the followers were amazed. [43] Jesus gave the father and mother very strict orders not to tell people about this. Then Jesus told them to give the girl some food to eat.

Jesus Goes to His Home Town

6 Jesus left there and went back to his home town. His followers went with him. [2] On the Sabbath day* Jesus taught in the synagogue.* Many people heard him teach and were amazed. These people said, "Where did this man get this teaching? How did he get this wisdom? Who gave it to him? And where did he get the power to do miracles*? [3] He is only the carpenter. And his mother is Mary. He is the brother of James, Joses, Judas, and Simon. And his sisters are here with us." The people did not accept Jesus.

[4] Jesus said to the people, "Other people give honor to a prophet.* But in his own town with his own people and in his own home, a prophet does not get honor." [5] Jesus was not able to do many

---

Ten Towns Greek, "Decapolis," an area on the east side of Lake Galilee. It once had ten main towns.

synagogue Synagogues were places where Jews gathered for prayer, study of the Scriptures, and other public meetings.

Sabbath day The seventh day of the Jewish week. It was a special religious day for the Jews.

miracles Amazing works done by God's power.

prophet Person who spoke for God. He often told things that would happen in the future.

miracles* in that town. The only miracles he did were to heal some sick people by putting his hands on them. ⁶Jesus was very surprised because those people did not have faith.

Then Jesus went to other villages in that area and taught. ⁷Jesus called the twelve followers together. Jesus sent them out in groups of two. Jesus gave them power over evil spirits. ⁸This is what Jesus told his followers: "Take nothing for your trip. Take only a stick for walking. Take no bread, no bag, and no money in your pockets. ⁹Wear shoes, and take only the clothes you are wearing. ¹⁰When you enter a house, stay in that house until you leave that town. ¹¹If any town refuses to accept you or refuses to listen to you, then leave that town. Shake their dust off your feet.* This will be a warning to them."

¹²The followers left there and went to other places. They preached to the people and told them to change their hearts and lives. ¹³The followers forced many demons* out of people. And the followers put olive oil on* sick people and healed them.

Herod Thinks Jesus Is John the Baptizer

¹⁴King Herod* heard about Jesus, because Jesus was now famous. Some people said, "₍He (Jesus) is₎ John the Baptizer. He is risen from death. That is why he can do these miracles.*"

¹⁵Other people said, "He is Elijah.*"

Other people said, "Jesus is a prophet.* He is like the prophets that lived long ago."

¹⁶Herod heard these things about Jesus. He said, "I killed John by cutting off his head. Now John has been raised from death!"

How John the Baptizer Was Killed

¹⁷Herod* himself had ordered his soldiers to arrest John. So John was put into prison. Herod did this to please his wife, Herodias. Herodias was the wife of Philip, Herod's brother. But then Herod married Herodias. ¹⁸John told Herod that it was not right for him to be married to his brother's wife. ¹⁹So Herodias hated John. She wanted to kill him. But Herodias was not able to persuade Herod to kill John. ²⁰Herod was afraid to kill John. Herod knew that all the people thought John was a good and holy man. So Herod protected John. Herod enjoyed listening to John preach. But John's preaching always bothered Herod.

²¹Then the right time came for Herodias to cause John's death. It happened on Herod's birthday. Herod gave a dinner party for the most important government leaders, the commanders of his army, and the most important people in Galilee. ²²The daughter of Herodias came to the party and danced. When she danced, Herod and the people eating with him were very pleased.

So King Herod said to the girl, "I will give you anything you want." ²³Herod promised her, "Anything you ask for I will give to you. I will even give you half of my kingdom."

²⁴The girl went to her mother and asked, "What should I ask King Herod to give me?"

Her mother answered, "Ask for the head of John the Baptizer."

²⁵Quickly the girl went back in to the king. The girl said to the king, "Please give me the head of John the Baptizer. Bring it to me now on a plate."

²⁶King Herod was very sad. But he had promised to give the girl anything she wanted. And the people eating there with Herod heard his promise. So Herod did not want to refuse the thing she asked for. ²⁷So the king sent a soldier to cut off John's head and bring it. So the soldier went and cut off John's head in the prison. ²⁸Then the soldier brought John's head back on a plate. He gave the head to the girl. Then the girl gave the head to her mother. ²⁹John's followers heard about what happened. So they came and got John's body. They put it in a tomb *(grave)*.

Jesus Feeds More than 5,000 People

³⁰The apostles* ₍that Jesus sent to preach₎ came back to Jesus. They gathered around Jesus and told him about all the things they did and taught. ³¹Jesus and his followers were in a very busy place. There were many, many people. Jesus and his followers did not even have time to eat. Jesus said to his followers, "Come with me. We will go to a quiet place to be alone. There we will get some rest."

---

miracles Amazing works done by the power of God.
Shake their dust off your feet A warning. It would show that they were finished talking to these people.
demons Demons are evil spirits from the devil.
put olive oil on Oil was used like a medicine, so that is probably how the followers used it.
Herod Herod Antipas, tetrarch (ruler) of Galilee and Perea, son of Herod the Great.
Elijah A man who spoke for God about 850 B.C.
prophet A person who spoke for God.

apostles The men Jesus chose to be his special helpers.

³²So Jesus and his followers went away alone. They went in a boat to a place where there were no people. ³³But many people saw them leave. The people knew it was Jesus. So people from all the towns ran to the place where Jesus was going. The people were there before Jesus arrived. ³⁴When Jesus arrived there, he saw many people waiting. Jesus felt sorry for them, because they were like sheep without a shepherd ₍to care for them₎. So Jesus taught the people many things. ³⁵It was now late in the day. So Jesus' followers came to him. They said, "No people live in this place. And it is already very late. ³⁶So send the people away. They need to go to the farms and towns around here to buy some food to eat."

³⁷But Jesus answered, "You give them some food to eat."

The followers said to Jesus, "We can't buy enough bread to feed all these people! We would all have to work a month to earn enough money to buy that much bread!"

³⁸Jesus asked the followers, "How many loaves of bread do you have now? Go and see."

The followers counted their loaves of bread. They came to Jesus and said, "We have five loaves of bread and two fish."

³⁹Then Jesus said to the followers, "Tell all the people to sit in groups on the green grass." ⁴⁰So all the people sat in groups. There were about 50 or 100 people in each group. ⁴¹Jesus took the five loaves and two fish. He looked up to the sky and thanked God for the bread. Then Jesus divided the bread and gave it to his followers. Jesus told his followers to give the bread to the people. Then Jesus divided the two fish and gave the fish to the people. ⁴²All the people ate and were full. ⁴³After the people finished eating, the followers filled twelve baskets with the pieces of bread and fish that were not eaten. ⁴⁴There were about 5,000 men there that ate.

Jesus Walks on the Water

⁴⁵Then Jesus told the followers to get into the boat. Jesus told them to go to the other side of the lake to Bethsaida. Jesus said that he would come later. Jesus stayed there to tell the people they could go home. ⁴⁶After Jesus said good-bye to the people, he went into the hills to pray.

⁴⁷That night, the boat was still in the middle of the lake. Jesus was alone on the land. ⁴⁸Jesus saw the boat far away on the lake. He saw the followers working hard to row the boat. The wind was blowing against them. Sometime between three and six o'clock in the morning, Jesus went to the boat. Jesus was walking on the water. Jesus continued walking until he was almost past the boat. ⁴⁹But the followers saw Jesus walking on the water. They thought he was a ghost. The followers shouted with fear. ⁵⁰All the followers saw Jesus and were very afraid. But Jesus spoke to the followers and said, "Don't worry! It's me! Don't be afraid." ⁵¹Then Jesus got into the boat with the followers. And the wind became calm. The followers were completely amazed. ⁵²They had seen Jesus make more bread from the five loaves. But they did not understand what it meant. They were not able to understand it.

⁵³The followers of Jesus crossed the lake. They came to shore at Gennesaret. They tied the boat there. ⁵⁴When they were out of the boat, the people saw Jesus. They knew who he was. ⁵⁵The people ran ₍to tell other people₎ everywhere in that area ₍that Jesus was there₎. The people brought sick people on beds to every place Jesus went. ⁵⁶Jesus went into towns and cities and farms around that area. And every place Jesus went, the people brought sick people to the market places. They begged Jesus to let them touch any part of his coat. And all the people that touched him were healed.

God's Law and Rules that People Make

7 Some Pharisees* and some teachers of the law came from Jerusalem. They gathered around Jesus. ²The Pharisees and teachers of the law saw that some of Jesus' followers ate food with hands that were not clean. ("Not clean" means that they did not wash their hands ₍in the way the Pharisees* said people must₎.) ³The Pharisees and all the Jews never eat before washing their hands in this special way. They do this to follow the teaching given to them by their great people that lived before them. ⁴And when the Jews buy something in the market, they never eat it until they wash it in a special way. They also follow other rules from their people that lived before them. They follow rules like the washing of cups, pitchers, and pots.

⁵The Pharisees* and teachers of the law said to Jesus, "Your followers don't follow the rules given to us by our great people that lived before us. Your followers eat their food with hands that are not clean. Why do they do this?"

Pharisees The Pharisees were a Jewish religious group that claimed to follow carefully all Jewish laws and customs.

⁶Jesus answered, "You are all hypocrites.* Isaiah was right when he spoke about you. Isaiah wrote,

> 'These people say they honor me,
> but they don't really make me an
> important part of their lives.
> ⁷ Their worship of me is for nothing.
> The things they teach are only rules
> that people have made.'
> Isaiah 29:13

⁸You have stopped following the commands of God. Now you follow the teachings of men."

⁹Then Jesus said to them: "You think you are smart! You ignore the commands of God so that you can follow your own teachings! ¹⁰Moses said, 'You must honor *(respect)* your father and mother.'* Then Moses also said, 'Any person that says bad things to his father or mother must be killed.'* ¹¹But you teach that a person can say to his father or mother, 'I have something I could use to help you. But I will not use it to help you. I will give it to God.' ¹²You are telling that person that he does not have to do anything for his father or mother. ¹³So you are teaching that it is not important to do what God said. You think that it is more important to follow those rules you teach people. And you do many things like that."

¹⁴Jesus called the people to him again. He said, "Every person should listen to me and understand what I am saying. ¹⁵There is nothing a person puts into his body that makes him wrong. A person is made wrong by the things that come from him." ¹⁶*

¹⁷Then Jesus left the people and went into the house. The followers asked Jesus about this story. ¹⁸Jesus said, "You still have trouble understanding? Surely you know that nothing that enters a person from the outside can make him wrong. ¹⁹Food does not go into a person's mind. Food goes into the stomach. Then that food goes out of the body." (When Jesus said this, he meant that there is no food that is wrong for people to eat.)

²⁰And Jesus said, "The things that come from a person are the things that make that person wrong. ²¹All these bad things begin inside a person, in the mind: bad thoughts, sexual sins, stealing, murder, ²²adultery,* selfishness, doing bad things to people, lying, doing sinful things, jealousy, saying bad things about people, proud boasting, and foolish living. ²³All these evil things come from inside a person. These things make a person wrong."

Jesus Helps a Non-Jewish Woman

²⁴Jesus left that place and went to the area around Tyre. Jesus went into a house there. Jesus did not want the people in that area to know he was there. But Jesus could not stay hidden. ²⁵A woman heard that Jesus was there. Her little daughter had an evil spirit ⌊from the devil⌋ inside her. So the woman came to Jesus and bowed down near his feet. ²⁶The woman was not a Jew. She was Greek, born in Phoenicia, an area in Syria. The woman begged Jesus to force the demon* out of her daughter.

²⁷Jesus told the woman: "It is not right to take the children's bread and give it to the dogs. First let the children eat all they want."

²⁸The woman answered, "That is true, Lord. But the dogs under the table can eat the pieces of food that the children don't eat."

²⁹Then Jesus told the woman, "That is a very good answer. You may go. The demon* has left your daughter."

³⁰The woman went home and found her daughter lying on the bed. The demon was gone.

Jesus Heals a Deaf Man

³¹Then Jesus left the area around Tyre and went through Sidon. Jesus went to Lake Galilee. Jesus went through the area of the Ten Towns.* ³²While he was there, some people brought a man to him. This man was deaf and could not talk. The people begged Jesus to put his hand on the man ⌊to heal him⌋.

³³Jesus led the man away from the people to be alone with him. Jesus put his fingers in the man's ears. Then Jesus spit and touched the man's tongue. ³⁴Jesus looked up to the sky and made a breathing sound. Jesus said to the man, "*Ephphatha!*" (This means, "Open!") ³⁵When Jesus did this, the man was able to hear. The man was able to use his tongue and spoke clearly.

---

hypocrites Bad people that act like they are good.
'You must ... mother' Quote from Ex. 20:12; Deut. 5:16.
'Any person ... killed' Quote from Ex. 21:17.
Verse 16 Some Greek copies add verse 16: "You people that hear me, listen!"

adultery Breaking a marriage promise by sexual sin.
demon A demon is an evil spirit from the devil.
Ten Towns Greek, "Decapolis," an area on the east side of Lake Galilee. It once had ten main towns.

³⁶Jesus commanded the people not to tell any person about what happened. Jesus always commanded people not to tell other people about him. But this only caused the people to tell about him more and more. ³⁷The people were really amazed. The people said, "Jesus does everything in a good way. Jesus makes deaf people able to hear. And people that can't talk—Jesus makes them able to talk."

Jesus Feeds More than 4,000 People

8 Another time there were many people [with Jesus]. The people had nothing to eat. So Jesus called his followers to him. Jesus said, ²"I feel sorry for these people. They have been with me for three days. And now they have nothing to eat. ³I should not send them home hungry. If they leave without eating, they will faint while going home. Some of these people live a long way from here."

⁴Jesus' followers answered, "But we are far away from any towns. Where can we get enough bread to feed all these people?"

⁵Then Jesus asked them, "How many loaves of bread do you have?"

The followers answered, "We have seven loaves of bread."

⁶Jesus told the people to sit on the ground. Then Jesus took the seven loaves and gave thanks to God. Jesus divided the bread and gave the pieces to his followers. Jesus told the followers to give the bread to the people. The followers obeyed him. ⁷The followers also had a few small fish. Jesus gave thanks for the fish and told the followers to give the fish to the people. ⁸All the people ate and were full. Then the followers filled seven baskets with the pieces of food that were not eaten. ⁹There were about 4,000 men that ate. After they ate, Jesus told them to go home. ¹⁰Then Jesus went in a boat with his followers to the area of Dalmanutha.

The Pharisees Try to Test Jesus

¹¹The Pharisees* came to Jesus and asked him questions. They wanted to test Jesus. So they asked Jesus to do a miracle* to show that he was from God. ¹²Jesus made a sad sound like he was troubled. He said, "Why do you people ask to see a miracle as proof? I tell you the truth. No proof like that will be given to you." ¹³Then Jesus left the Pharisees. Jesus went in the boat to the other side of the lake.

Jesus Warns Against the Jewish Leaders

¹⁴The followers had only one loaf of bread with them in the boat. They forgot to bring more bread. ¹⁵Jesus warned them, "Be careful! Guard against the yeast* of the Pharisees* and the yeast of Herod."

¹⁶The followers discussed the meaning of this. They said, "He said this because we have no bread."

¹⁷Jesus knew that the followers were talking about this. So Jesus asked them, "Why are you talking about having no bread? You still don't see or understand? Are you not able to understand? ¹⁸Do you have eyes that can't see? Do you have ears that can't hear? Remember what I did before, when we did not have enough bread? ¹⁹I divided five loaves of bread for 5,000 people. Remember how many baskets you filled with pieces of food that were not eaten?"

The followers answered, "We filled twelve baskets."

²⁰"And remember that I divided seven loaves of bread for 4,000 people. Remember how many baskets you filled with pieces of food that were not eaten?"

The followers answered, "We filled seven baskets."

²¹Then Jesus said to them, "[You remember these things I did], but you still don't understand?"

Jesus Heals a Blind Man In Bethsaida

²²Jesus and his followers came to Bethsaida. Some people brought a blind man to Jesus. They begged Jesus to touch the man. ²³So Jesus held the blind man's hand and led him out of the village. Then Jesus spit on the man's eyes. Jesus put his hands on the blind man and asked him, "Can you see now?"

²⁴The blind man looked up and said, "Yes, I see people. They look like trees walking around."

²⁵Again Jesus put his hands on the blind man's eyes. Then the man opened his eyes wide. His eyes were healed, and he was able to see everything clearly. ²⁶Jesus told him to go home. Jesus said, "Don't go into the town."

Pharisees The Pharisees were a Jewish religious group that claimed to follow carefully all Jewish laws and customs.
miracle Amazing work done by God's power.
yeast Used here as a symbol of bad influence.

Peter Says that Jesus Is the Christ

²⁷Jesus and his followers went to the towns in the area of Caesarea Philippi. While they were traveling, Jesus asked the followers, "Who do people say I am?" ²⁸The followers answered, "Some people say you are John the Baptizer. Other people say you are Elijah.* And other people say that you are one of the prophets.*" ²⁹Then Jesus asked, "Who do you say I am?" Peter answered, "You are the Christ.*" ³⁰Jesus told the followers, "Don't tell any person who I am."

³¹Then Jesus began to teach his followers that the Son of Man* must suffer many things. Jesus taught that the Son of Man would not be accepted by the older Jewish leaders, the leading priests, and the teachers of the law. Jesus taught that the Son of Man must be killed and then rise from death after three days. ³²Jesus told them everything that would happen. He did not keep anything secret. Peter spoke to Jesus alone. Peter criticized Jesus for saying ˻those things˼. ³³But Jesus turned and looked at his followers. Then he criticized Peter. Jesus said to Peter, "Go away from me, Satan*! You don't care about the things of God. You care only about things that people think are important."

³⁴Then Jesus called the people to him. His followers were also there. Then Jesus said, "If any person wants to follow me, he must say 'No' to the things he wants. That person must accept the cross *(suffering)* that is given to him, and he must follow me. ³⁵The person that wants to save his life will lose it. And every person that gives his life for me and for the Good News* will save his life forever. ³⁶It is worth nothing for a person to have the whole world, if he loses his soul ˻in hell˼. ³⁷A person could never pay enough to buy back his soul. ³⁸The people that live now are living in a sinful and evil time. If any person is ashamed of me and my teaching, then I* will be ashamed of that person. I will be ashamed of that person at the time I come with the glory of my Father and the holy angels."

9 Then Jesus said, "I tell you the truth. Some of you people standing here will see the kingdom of God come before you die. The kingdom of God will come with power."

Jesus with Moses and Elijah

²Six days later Jesus took Peter, James, and John and went up on a high mountain. They were all alone there. While these followers watched him, Jesus was changed. ³Jesus' clothes became shining white. The clothes were whiter than any person could make them. ⁴Then two men were there, talking with Jesus. The men were Moses and Elijah.*

⁵Peter said to Jesus, "Teacher, it is good that we are here. We will put three tents here—one for you, one for Moses, and one for Elijah." ⁶Peter did not know what to say, because he and the other two followers were very afraid.

⁷Then a cloud came and covered them. A voice came from the cloud and said, "This *(Jesus)* is my Son and I love him. Obey him!"

⁸Then Peter, James, and John looked, but they saw only Jesus there alone with them.

⁹Jesus and the followers were walking back down the mountain. Jesus commanded the followers, "Don't tell any person about the things you saw on the mountain. Wait until after the Son of Man* rises from death. Then you can tell people what you saw."

¹⁰So the followers obeyed Jesus and said nothing about what they saw. But they discussed what Jesus meant about rising from death. ¹¹The followers asked Jesus, "Why do the teachers of the law say that Elijah must come* first?"

¹²Jesus answered, "They are right to say that Elijah must come first. Elijah makes all things the way they should be. But why does the Scripture* say that the Son of Man* will suffer much and that people will think he is worth nothing? ¹³I tell you that Elijah has already come. And people did to him all the ˻bad˼ things they wanted to do. The Scriptures said this would happen to him."

Elijah Man who spoke for God about 850 B.C.
prophets People who spoke for God. Their writings are part of the Old Testament.
Christ The "anointed one" (Messiah) or chosen of God.
Son of Man Jesus. In Dan. 7:13-14 this is the name for the Messiah, the one God chose to save his people.
Satan Name for the devil meaning "the enemy." Jesus means that Peter was talking like Satan.
Good News The news that God has made a way for people to have their sins forgiven and live with God.
I Literally, "the Son of Man."

Moses and Elijah Two important Jewish leaders during the time of the Old Testament.
Elijah must come See Mal. 4:5-6.
Scripture Part of the Holy Writings—Old Testament.

Jesus Heals a Sick Boy

¹⁴Then Jesus, Peter, James, and John went to the other followers. They saw many people around them. The teachers of the law were arguing with the followers. ¹⁵When the people saw Jesus, they were very surprised. They ran to him to welcome him.

¹⁶Jesus asked, "What are you arguing with the teachers of the law about?"

¹⁷A man answered, "Teacher, I brought my son to you. My son has a spirit ₍from the devil₎ inside him. This spirit stops my son from talking. ¹⁸The spirit attacks my son and throws him on the ground. My son foams from his mouth, grinds his teeth, and becomes very stiff. I asked your followers to force the evil spirit out, but they could not."

¹⁹Jesus answered, "You people don't believe! How long must I stay with you? How long must I continue to be patient with you? Bring the boy to me!"

²⁰So the followers brought the boy to Jesus. When the ₍evil₎ spirit saw Jesus, the spirit attacked the boy. The boy fell down and rolled on the ground. He was foaming from his mouth.

²¹Jesus asked the boy's father, "How long has this been happening to the boy?"

The father answered, "Since he was very young. ²²The spirit often throws him into a fire or into water to kill him. If you can do anything for him, please have pity on us and help us."

²³Jesus said to the father, "You said, 'Help him if you can.' All things are possible for the person that believes."

²⁴The father became very excited. He said, "I do believe. Help me to believe more!"

²⁵Jesus saw that all the people were running there to see what was happening. So Jesus spoke to the evil spirit. Jesus said, "You evil spirit that makes this boy deaf and stops him from talking—I command you to come out of this boy and never enter him again!"

²⁶The ₍evil₎ spirit screamed. The spirit caused the boy to fall on the ground again, and then the spirit came out. The boy looked like he was dead. Many people said, "He is dead!" ²⁷But Jesus held the boy's hand and helped him stand.

²⁸Jesus went into the house. His followers were alone with him there. They said, "We could not force that evil spirit out. Why?"

²⁹Jesus answered, "That kind of spirit can only be forced out by using prayer."

Jesus Talks About His Death

³⁰Then Jesus and his followers left that place. They went through Galilee. Jesus did not want the people to know where they were. ³¹Jesus wanted to teach his followers alone. Jesus said to them, "The Son of Man* will be given to people that will kill him. After three days, he will rise from death." ³²But the followers did not understand what Jesus meant. And they were afraid to ask him what he meant.

Jesus Tells Who Is the Greatest

³³Jesus and his followers went to Capernaum. They went into a house. Then Jesus said to his followers, "I heard you arguing on the road today. What were you arguing about?" ³⁴But the followers did not answer, because their argument on the road was about which one of them was the greatest.

³⁵Jesus sat down and called the twelve apostles* to him. Jesus said, "If any person wants to be the most important, then he must make all other people more important than himself. That person must serve all other people."

³⁶Then Jesus took a small child. Jesus stood the child before the followers. Jesus held the child in his arms and said, ³⁷"If a person accepts children like these in my name, then that person is also accepting me. And if a person accepts me, then that person is also accepting the One *(God)* that sent me."

Any Person Not Against Us Is for Us

³⁸Then John said, "Teacher, we saw a man using your name to force demons* out of a person. He is not one of us. So we told him to stop, because he does not belong to our group."

³⁹Jesus said, "Don't stop him. Any person that uses my name to do powerful things will not say bad things about me. ⁴⁰The person that is not against us is with us. ⁴¹I tell you the truth. If a person helps you by giving you a drink of water because you belong to the Christ,* then that person will truly get his reward.

⁴²"If one of these little children believes in me, and another person causes that child to sin, then it will be very bad for that person. It would be better

---

Son of Man Jesus. In Dan. 7:13-14 this is the name for the Messiah, the one God chose to save his people.
apostles The men Jesus chose to be his special helpers.
demons Demons are evil spirits from the devil.
Christ The "anointed one" (Messiah) or chosen of God.

for that person to have a millstone* tied around his neck and be drowned in the sea. ⁴³If your hand makes you sin, cut it off. It is better for you to lose part of your body but have life forever. That is much better than to have two hands and go to hell. In that place the fire never stops. ⁴⁴* ⁴⁵If your foot makes you sin, cut it off. It is better for you to lose part of your body but have life forever. That is much better than to have two feet and be thrown into hell. ⁴⁶* ⁴⁷If your eye makes you sin, take it out. It is better for you to have only one eye but have life forever. That is much better than to have two eyes and be thrown into hell. ⁴⁸The worms that eat the people in hell never die. In hell the fire is never stopped. ⁴⁹Every person will be punished* with fire.

⁵⁰"Salt is good. But if the salt loses its salty taste, then you can't make it salty again. So, be full of goodness. And have peace with each other."

Jesus Teaches About Divorce

10 Then Jesus left that place. He went into the area of Judea and across the Jordan River. Again, many people came to him. And Jesus taught the people like he always did.

²Some Pharisees* came to Jesus. They tried to make Jesus say something wrong. They asked Jesus, "Is it right for a man to divorce his wife?"

³Jesus answered, "What did Moses command you to do?"

⁴The Pharisees said, "Moses allowed a man to divorce his wife by writing a certificate of divorce."

⁵Jesus said, "Moses wrote that command for you because you refused to accept God's teaching. ⁶But when God made the world, 'he made people male and female.'* ⁷'That is why a man will leave his father and mother and be joined to his wife. ⁸And the two people will become one.'* So the people are not two, but one. ⁹God has joined those two people together. So no person should separate them."

¹⁰Later, the followers and Jesus were in the house. The followers asked Jesus again about the question of divorce. ¹¹Jesus answered, "Any person that divorces his wife and marries another woman is guilty of sin against his wife. He is guilty of the sin of adultery.* ¹²And the woman that divorces her husband and marries another man is also guilty of adultery."

Jesus Accepts Children

¹³People brought their small children to Jesus, so that Jesus could touch them. But the followers told the people to stop bringing their children to Jesus. ¹⁴Jesus saw what happened. He did not like his followers telling the children not to come. Jesus said to them, "Let the little children come to me. Don't stop them, because the kingdom of God belongs to people that are like these little children. ¹⁵I tell you the truth. You must accept the kingdom of God like a little child accepts things, or you will never enter it." ¹⁶Then Jesus held the children in his arms. Jesus put his hands on them and blessed them.

A Rich Man Refuses to Follow Jesus

¹⁷Jesus started to leave, but a man ran to him and bowed on his knees before Jesus. The man asked, "Good teacher, what must I do to get the life that never ends?"

¹⁸Jesus answered, "Why do you call me good? No person is good. Only God is good. ¹⁹ₗBut I will answer your questionⱼ. You know the commands: 'You must not murder anyone, you must not do the sin of adultery,* you must not steal, you must not lie, you must not cheat, you must honor (respect) your father and mother....'*"

²⁰The man said, "Teacher, I have obeyed all these commands since I was a boy."

²¹Jesus looked at the man. Jesus felt love for him. Jesus said, "There is still one more thing you need to do. Go and sell everything you have. Give the money to the poor people. You will have a reward in heaven. Then come and follow me."

²²The man was very sorry to hear Jesus say this, and he left. The man was sad because he was very rich ₗand wanted to keep his moneyⱼ.

²³Then Jesus looked at his followers and said to them, "It will be very hard for a rich person to enter the kingdom of God!"

---

millstone A large, round stone used for grinding grain.
Verse 44 Some Greek copies of Mark add verse 44, which is the same as verse 48.
Verse 46 Some Greek copies of Mark add verse 46, which is the same as verse 48.
punished Literally, "salted."
Pharisees The Pharisees were a Jewish religious group that claimed to follow carefully all Jewish laws and customs.
'he made ... female' Quote from Gen. 1:27.
'That is why ... one' Quote from Gen. 2:24.

adultery Breaking a marriage promise by sexual sin.
'You must not ... mother' Quote from Ex. 20:12-16; Deut. 5:16-20.

²⁴The followers were amazed at what Jesus said. But Jesus said again, "My children, it is very hard to enter the kingdom of God! ²⁵And it will be very hard for rich people to enter the kingdom of God! It would be easier for a camel to go through the eye of a needle!" ²⁶The followers were more amazed and said to each other, "Then who can be saved?" ²⁷Jesus looked at the followers and said, "This is something that people cannot do themselves. It must come from God. God can do all things." ²⁸Peter said to Jesus, "We left everything to follow you!" ²⁹Jesus said, "I tell you the truth. Every person that has left his home, brothers, sisters, mother, father, children, or farm for me and for the Good News* ³⁰will get a hundred times more than he left. Here in this world that person will get more homes, brothers, sisters, mothers, children, and farms. And with those things, that person will have persecutions.* But he will also have a reward in the world that is coming. That reward is life forever. ³¹Many people that have the highest place now will have the lowest place in the future. And the people that have the lowest place now will have the highest place in the future."

Jesus Talks Again About His Death

³²Jesus and the people with him were going to Jerusalem. Jesus was leading the people. Jesus' followers were amazed. But those people that followed behind them were afraid. Jesus gathered the twelve apostles* again and talked with them alone. Jesus told them what would happen in Jerusalem. ³³Jesus said, "We are going to Jerusalem. The Son of Man* will be given to the leading priests and teachers of the law. The priests and the teachers of the law will say that the Son of Man must die. They will give the Son of Man to the non-Jewish people. ³⁴Those people will laugh at him and spit on him. They will beat him with whips and kill him. But on the third day after his death, he will rise to life again."

James and John Ask a Favor

³⁵Then James and John, sons of Zebedee, came to Jesus. They said, "Teacher, we want to ask you to do something for us." ³⁶Jesus asked, "What do you want me to do for you?" ³⁷The sons answered, "You will have glory ₍in your kingdom₎. Let one of us sit at your right, and let one of us sit at your left." ³⁸Jesus said, "You don't understand what you are asking. Can you accept the kind of suffering that I must have*? And can you be baptized with the same kind of baptism* that I must have?" ³⁹The sons answered, "Yes, we can!" Jesus said to the sons, "You will suffer the same things that I will suffer. And you will be baptized with the same baptism that I must have. ⁴⁰But I cannot choose the person that will sit at my right or my left. There are some people that will have those places. Those places are prepared for them." ⁴¹The other ten followers heard this. They became angry with James and John. ⁴²Jesus called all the followers together. Jesus said, "The non-Jewish people have men they call rulers. You know that those rulers love to show their power over the people. And their important leaders love to use all their authority over the people. ⁴³But it should not be that way with you. If one of you wants to become great, then he must serve you like a servant. ⁴⁴If one of you wants to become the most important, then he must serve all of you like a slave. ⁴⁵In the same way, the Son of Man* did not come for other people to serve him. But the Son of Man came to serve other people. The Son of Man came to give his life to save many people."

Jesus Heals a Blind Man

⁴⁶Then they came to the town of Jericho. Jesus was leaving that town with his followers and many other people. A blind man named Bartimaeus (son of Timaeus) was sitting by the road. This man was always begging for money. ⁴⁷The blind man heard that Jesus from Nazareth was walking by. The blind man shouted, "Jesus, Son of David,* please help me!"

Good News The news that God has made a way for people to have their sins forgiven and live with God.
persecutions Being hurt or bothered by Christ's enemies.
apostles The men Jesus chose to be his special helpers.
Son of Man Jesus. In Dan. 7:13-14 this is the name for the Messiah, the one God chose to save his people.

accept the kind of suffering that I must have Literally, "drink the cup that I must drink."
baptized with the same kind of baptism Has a special meaning here—being "baptized" or "buried" in troubles.
Son of David Name for the Christ, who was from the family of David, king of Israel.

MARK 10:48–11:23

⁴⁸Many people criticized the blind man. They told him not to speak. But the blind man shouted more and more, "Son of David, please help me!" ⁴⁹Jesus stopped and said, "Tell the man to come here." So they called the blind man. They said, "Be happy! Stand up! Jesus is calling you." ⁵⁰The blind man stood quickly. He left his coat there and went to Jesus. ⁵¹Jesus asked the man, "What do you want me to do for you?"

The blind man answered, "Teacher, I want to see again."

⁵²Jesus said, "Go. You are healed because you believed." Then the man was able to see again. He followed Jesus on the road.

Jesus Enters Jerusalem like a King

11 Jesus and his followers were coming closer to Jerusalem. They came to the towns of Bethphage and Bethany at the Mount of Olives.* There Jesus sent two of his followers to do something. ²Jesus said to the followers, "Go to the town you can see there. When you enter it, you will find a young donkey tied there. No person has ever ridden this donkey. Untie the donkey and bring it here to me. ³If any person asks you why you are taking the donkey, tell that person, 'The Master needs this donkey. He will send it back soon.'"

⁴The followers went into the town. They found a young donkey tied in the street near the door of a house. The followers untied the donkey. ⁵Some people were standing there and saw this. The people asked, "What are you doing? Why are you untying that donkey?" ⁶The followers answered the way Jesus told them to answer. The people let the followers take the donkey. ⁷The followers brought the donkey to Jesus. The followers put their coats on the donkey, and Jesus sat on it. ⁸Many people spread their coats on the road for Jesus. Other people cut branches in the fields and spread the branches on the road. ⁹Some of the people were walking ahead of Jesus. Other people were walking behind him. All the people shouted,

"'Praise* Him!'
'Welcome! God bless the One that comes
in the name of the Lord!'
Psalm 118:25, 26

¹⁰ God bless the kingdom of our father David.*
That kingdom is coming!
Praise* to God in heaven!"

¹¹Jesus went into Jerusalem and went to the temple.* Jesus looked at everything in the temple. But it was already late. So Jesus went to Bethany with the twelve apostles.*

¹²The next day, Jesus was leaving Bethany. He was hungry. ¹³Jesus saw a fig tree with leaves. So Jesus went to the tree to see if it had any figs growing on it. But Jesus found no figs on the tree. There were only leaves. It was not the right time for figs to grow. ¹⁴So Jesus said to the tree, "People will never eat fruit from you again." Jesus' followers heard him say this.

Jesus Goes to the Temple

¹⁵Jesus went to Jerusalem. He went into the temple.* Jesus began to throw out the people that were selling and buying things there. Jesus turned over the tables that belonged to the people that were exchanging different kinds of money. And Jesus turned over the benches of those people that were selling doves. ¹⁶Jesus refused to allow any person to carry things through the temple. ¹⁷Then Jesus taught the people. He said, "It is written in the Scriptures,* 'My house will be called a house for prayer for all people.'* But you are changing God's house into a 'hiding place for thieves.'*"

¹⁸The leading priests and the teachers of the law heard these things. They began trying to find a way to kill Jesus. They were afraid of Jesus because all the people were amazed at his teaching. ¹⁹That night, Jesus and his followers left the city.

Jesus Shows the Power of Faith

²⁰The next morning, Jesus was walking with his followers. They saw the fig tree ₍that Jesus spoke to the day before₎. The fig tree was dry and dead, even the roots. ²¹Peter remembered the tree and said to Jesus, "Teacher, look! Yesterday, you told that fig tree to die. Now it is dry and dead!"

²²Jesus answered, "Have faith in God. ²³I tell you the truth. You can say to this mountain, 'Go, mountain, fall into the sea.' And if you have no

---

Mount of Olives A hill near the city of Jerusalem.
Praise Literally, "Hosanna," a Hebrew word used in praying to God for help. At this time it was probably a shout of joy used in praising God or His Messiah.
David King of Israel about 1000 years before Christ.
temple The special building in Jerusalem for Jewish worship.
apostles Men that Jesus chose to be his special helpers.
Scriptures Holy Writings—the Old Testament.
'My house ... people' Quote from Isa. 56:7.
'hiding place for thieves' Quote from Jer. 7:11.

doubts in your mind and believe that the thing you say will happen, then God will do it for you. ²⁴So I tell you to ask for things in prayer. And if you believe that you have received those things, then they will be yours. ²⁵When you are praying, and you remember that you are angry with another person about something, then forgive that person. If you do this, then your Father in heaven will also forgive your sins." ²⁶*

Jewish Leaders Doubt Jesus' Authority

²⁷Jesus and his followers went again to Jerusalem. Jesus was walking in the temple.* The leading priests, the teachers of the law, and the older Jewish leaders came to Jesus. ²⁸They said to Jesus, "Tell us! What authority *(power)* do you have to do these things? Who gave you this authority?" ²⁹Jesus answered, "I will ask you a question. You answer my question. Then I will tell you whose authority I use to do these things. ³⁰Tell me: When John baptized* people, did that come from God or from man? Answer me!"

³¹These Jewish leaders talked about Jesus' question. They said to each other, "If we answer, 'John's baptism was from God,' then Jesus will say, 'Then why didn't you believe John?' ³²But if we say, 'John's baptism was from man,' then the people will be angry with us]." (These leaders were afraid of the people. All the people believed that John was a prophet.*)

³³So the leaders answered Jesus, "We don't know the answer."

Jesus said, "Then I will not tell you what authority I use to do these things."

God Sends His Son

12 Jesus used stories to teach the people. Jesus said, "A man planted a field with grapes. The man put a wall around the field and dug a hole for a wine press.* Then the man built a tower. The man leased the field to some farmers. Then the man left for a trip. ²Later, it was time for the grapes to be picked. So the man sent a servant to the farmers to get his share of the grapes. ³But the farmers grabbed the servant and beat him. They sent the servant away with nothing. ⁴Then the man sent another servant to the farmers. The farmers hit this servant on the head. They showed no respect for him. ⁵So the man sent another servant. The farmers killed this servant. The man sent many other servants to the farmers. The farmers beat some of the servants and killed the others.

⁶"The man had one person left to send to the farmers. This person was the man's son. The man loved his son. But the man decided to send the son to the farmers. The son was the last person he could send. The man said, 'The farmers will respect my son.'

⁷"But the farmers said to each other, 'This is the owner's son. This field will be his. If we kill him, then his field will be ours.' ⁸So the farmers took the son, killed him, and threw him out of the field.

⁹"So what will the man that owns the field do? He will go to the field and kill those farmers. Then he will give the field to other farmers. ¹⁰Surely you have read this Scripture*:

> 'The stone that the builders did not want
> became the cornerstone.*
> ¹¹ The Lord did this,
> and it is wonderful to us.'"
> *Psalm 118:22-23*

¹²These Jewish leaders heard this story that Jesus told. They knew that this story was about them. So they wanted to find a way to arrest Jesus. But they were afraid of the people. So the Jewish leaders left Jesus and went away.

The Jewish Leaders Try to Trick Jesus

¹³Later, the Jewish leaders sent some Pharisees* and some men from the group called Herodians* to Jesus. They wanted to catch Jesus saying something wrong. ¹⁴The Pharisees and Herodians went to Jesus and said, "Teacher, we know that you are an honest man. You are not afraid of what other people think about you. All men are the same to you. And you teach the truth about God's way. Tell us: Is it right to pay taxes

---

Verse 26 Some early Greek copies add verse 26: "But if you don't forgive other people, then your Father in heaven will not forgive your sins."
temple The special building in Jerusalem for Jewish worship.
baptized A Greek word meaning to immerse, dip, or bury a person or thing briefly under water.
prophet A person who spoke for God.
wine press Place dug in rock used to mash grapes and collect the juice for making wine.

Scripture Part of the Holy Writings—Old Testament.
cornerstone First and most important rock of a building.
Pharisees The Pharisees were a Jewish religious group that claimed to follow carefully all Jewish laws and customs.
Herodians A Jewish political group.

to Caesar*? Yes or no? Should we pay taxes, or should we not pay taxes?"

¹⁵But Jesus knew that these men were really trying to trick him. Jesus said, "Why are you trying to catch me saying something wrong? Bring me a silver coin. Let me see it." ¹⁶They gave Jesus a coin and Jesus asked, "Whose picture is on the coin? And whose name is written on it?" They answered, "It is Caesar's picture and Caesar's name." ¹⁷Then Jesus said to them, "Give to Caesar the things that are Caesar's. And give to God the things that are God's." The men were amazed at what Jesus said.

Some Sadducees Try to Trick Jesus

¹⁸Then some Sadducees* came to Jesus. (Sadducees believe that no person will rise from death.) The Sadducees asked Jesus a question. ¹⁹They said, "Teacher, Moses wrote that if a married man dies and he had no children, then his brother must marry the woman. Then they will have children for the dead brother. ²⁰There were seven brothers. The first brother married but died. He had no children. ²¹So the second brother married the woman. But he also died and had no children. The same thing happened with the third brother. ²²All seven brothers married the woman and died. None of the brothers had any children with the woman. The woman was last to die. ²³But all seven brothers had married her. So at the time when people rise from death, whose wife will the woman be?"

²⁴Jesus answered, "Why did you make this mistake? Is it because you don't know what the Scriptures* say? Or because you don't know about God's power? ²⁵When people rise from death, there will be no marriage. People will not be married to each other. All people will be like angels in heaven. ²⁶Surely you have read what God said about people rising from death. In the book where Moses wrote about the ⌊burning⌋ bush,* it says that God told Moses this: 'I am the God of Abraham, the God of Isaac, and the God of Jacob.'* ²⁷If God said he is their God, then⌋ these men are not really dead. He is the God only of living people. You Sadducees* are wrong!"

Which Command Is Most Important?

²⁸One of the teachers of the law came to Jesus. He heard Jesus arguing with the Sadducees* and the Pharisees.* He saw that Jesus gave good answers to their questions. So he asked Jesus, "Which of the commands is most important?"

²⁹Jesus answered, "The most important command is this: 'People of Israel, listen! The Lord our God is the only Lord. ³⁰You must love the Lord your God. You must love him with all your heart, all your soul, all your mind, and all your strength.'* ³¹The second most important command is this: 'You must love other people the same as you love yourself.'* These two commands are the most important."

³²The man answered, "That was a good answer, Teacher. You were right when you said these things. God is the only Lord, and there is no other God. ³³And a person must love God with all his heart, all his mind, and all his strength. And a person must love other people the same as he loves himself. These commands are more important than all the animals and sacrifices we offer to God."

³⁴Jesus saw that the man answered him wisely. So Jesus said to the man, "You are close to the kingdom of God." And after that time, no person was brave enough to ask Jesus any more questions.

³⁵Jesus was teaching in the temple.* Jesus asked, "Why do the teachers of the law say that the Christ* is the son of David*? ³⁶With the help of the Holy Spirit,* David himself says:

'The Lord *(God)* said to my Lord *(Christ)*:
Sit by me at my right side,
and I will put your enemies
under your control.*'

Psalm 110:1

Caesar The name given to the emperor (ruler) of Rome.
Sadducees A leading Jewish religious group. They accepted only the first five books of the Old Testament. They believed that people don't live again after death.
Scriptures Holy Writings—the Old Testament.
burning bush Read Ex. 3:1-12.
Abraham, Isaac, Jacob Three of the most important Jewish leaders during the time of the Old Testament.
'I am ... Jacob' Quote from Ex. 3:6.
Pharisees The Pharisees were a Jewish religious group that claimed to follow carefully all Jewish laws and customs.
'People ... strength' Quote from Deut. 6:4-5.
'You must ... yourself' Quote from Lev. 19:18.
temple The special building in Jerusalem for Jewish worship.
Christ The "anointed one" (Messiah) or chosen of God.
David King of Israel about 1000 years before Christ.
Holy Spirit Called the Spirit of God, the Spirit of Christ, and the Comforter. Joined with God and Christ, he does God's work among people in the world.
control Literally, "feet."

³⁷David himself calls the Christ 'Lord.' So how can the Christ be David's son?" Many people listened to Jesus and were very pleased.
³⁸Jesus continued teaching. Jesus said, "Be careful of the teachers of the law. They like to walk around wearing clothes that look important. And they love for people to show respect to them in the market places. ³⁹They love to get the most important seats in the synagogues.* And they love to get the most important seats at the feasts. ⁴⁰They are mean to widows* and steal their homes. Then they try to make themselves look good by saying long prayers. God will punish them very much."

A Widow Shows the Meaning of Giving

⁴¹Jesus sat near the temple money box* where people put their gifts. He watched the people put money in the box. Many rich people gave much money. ⁴²Then a poor widow* came and gave two very small copper coins. These coins were not even worth a penny.
⁴³Jesus called his followers to him. Jesus said, "I tell you the truth. This poor widow gave only two small coins. But she really gave more than all the rich people. ⁴⁴Those people have plenty; they gave only what they did not need. This woman is very poor. But she gave all she had. And she needed that money to help her live."

Future Destruction of the Temple

13 Jesus was leaving the temple.* One of his followers said to him, "Look, Teacher! This temple has very beautiful buildings with very big stones."
²Jesus said, "You see these great buildings? All these buildings will be destroyed. Every stone will be thrown down to the ground. Not one stone will be left on another."
³Later, Jesus was sitting at a place on the Mount of Olives.* He was alone with Peter, James, John, and Andrew. They could all see the temple. Those followers asked Jesus, ⁴"Tell us, when will these things happen? And what will show us it is time for these things to happen?"

⁵Jesus said to the followers: "Be careful! Don't let any person fool you. ⁶Many people will come and use my name. They will say, 'I am the One.' And they will fool many people. ⁷You will hear about wars and stories about wars that are being fought. But don't be afraid. These things must happen before the end comes. ⁸Nations will fight against other nations. Kingdoms will fight against other kingdoms. There will be times when there is no food for people to eat. And there will be earthquakes in different places. These things are like the first pains when something new is born.
⁹"You must be careful. People will arrest you and take you to be judged. They will beat you in their synagogues.* You will be forced to stand before kings and governors. You will tell them about me. This will happen to you because you follow me. ¹⁰Before these things happen, the Good News* must be told to all people. ¹¹You will be arrested and judged. But don't worry about what you should say. Say the things God gives you to say at that time. It will not really be you speaking. It will be the Holy Spirit* speaking.
¹²"Brothers will turn against their own brothers and give them to be killed. Fathers will turn against their own children and give them to be killed. Children will fight against their own parents and find ways for their parents to be killed. ¹³All people will hate you because you follow me. But the person that continues strong until the end will be saved.
¹⁴"You will see 'the terrible thing that causes destruction.'* You will see this thing standing in the place where it should not be." (You that read this should understand what it means.) "At that time, the people in Judea should run away to the mountains. ¹⁵People should run away without wasting time to stop for anything. If a person is on the roof of his house, he must not go down to take things out of his house. ¹⁶If a person is in the field, he must not go back to get his coat. ¹⁷At that time, it will be bad for women that are pregnant or have small babies. ¹⁸Pray that these things will not happen in winter. ¹⁹Why? Because those days will be full of much trouble. There will be more

---

synagogues Synagogues were places where Jews gathered for prayer, study of the Scriptures, and other public meetings.
widow(s) A widow is a woman whose husband has died.
money box Special box in the Jewish place for worship where people put their gifts to God.
temple The special building in Jerusalem for Jewish worship.
Mount of Olives A hill east of the city of Jerusalem where a person could look down into the temple area.

Good News The news that God has made a way for people to have their sins forgiven and live with God.
Holy Spirit Called the Spirit of God, the Spirit of Christ, and the Comforter. Joined with God and Christ, he does God's work among people in the world.
'the terrible thing ... destruction' See Dan. 9:27; 12:11 (Compare Dan. 11:31).

MARK 13:20–14:9

trouble than has ever happened since the beginning, when God made the world. And nothing as bad as that will ever happen again. [20]God has decided to make that terrible time short. If that time were not made short, then no person could continue living. But God will make that time short to help his special people that he has chosen. [21]At that time, some person might say to you, 'Look, there is the Christ*!' Or another person might say, 'There he is!' But don't believe them. [22]False Christs and false prophets will come and do great things and miracles. They will do these things to the people God has chosen. They will do these things to try to fool his people, if that is possible. [23]So be careful. Now I have warned you about all this before it happens.

[24]"During the days after this trouble happens,

'The sun will become dark,
and the moon will not give light.
[25] The stars will fall from the sky,
and everything in the sky will be changed.'
Isaiah 13:10; 34:4

[26]"Then people will see the Son of Man* coming in the clouds with power and great glory. [27]The Son of Man will send his angels all around the earth. The angels will gather his chosen people from every part of the earth.

[28]"The fig tree teaches us a lesson: When the fig tree's branches become green and soft, and new leaves begin to grow, then you know that summer is near. [29]It is the same with these things that I told you would happen. When you see all these things happening, then you will know that the time* is near, ready to come. [30]I tell you the truth. All these things will happen while the people of this time are still living. [31]The whole world, earth and sky, will be destroyed. But the words I have said will never be destroyed.

[32]"No person knows when that day or time will be. The Son and the angels in heaven don't know when that day or time will be. Only the Father knows. [33]Be careful! Always be ready! You don't know when that time will be. [34]This is like a man that goes on a trip and leaves his house. The man lets his servants take care of the house. He gives each servant a special job to do. One servant has the work of guarding the door. The man tells this servant to always be ready. This is the same as I am now telling you. [35]So you must always be ready. You don't know when the owner of the house will come back. He might come in the afternoon, or at midnight, or in the early morning, or when the sun rises. [36]The owner might come back quickly. If you are always ready, then he will not find you sleeping. [37]I tell you this, and I say this to every person: 'Be ready!'"

The Jewish Leaders Plan to Kill Jesus

14 It was now only two days before the Passover* and the Festival of Unleavened Bread.* The leading priests and teachers of the law were trying to find a way to use some lie to arrest Jesus. Then they could kill him. [2]They said, "But we cannot arrest Jesus during the festival. We don't want the people to become angry and cause a riot."

A Woman Does Something Special

[3]Jesus was in Bethany. He was eating in the house of Simon the leper.* While Jesus was there a woman came to him. The woman had an alabaster* jar filled with very expensive perfume. This perfume was made of pure nard.* The woman opened the jar and poured the perfume on Jesus' head.

[4]Some of the followers there saw this. They became upset and complained to each other. They said, "Why waste that perfume? [5]That perfume was worth a full year's work. It could be sold and the money could be given to poor people." And they criticized the woman strongly.

[6]Jesus said, "Don't bother the woman. Why are you troubling her? She did a very good thing for me. [7]You will always have poor people with you. You can help them any time you want. But you will not always have me. [8]This woman did the only thing she could do for me. She poured perfume on my body. She did this before I die to prepare me for burial. [9]I tell you the truth. The

---

Passover Important Jewish holy day. Jews eat a special meal on this day every year to remember that God freed them from slavery in Egypt in the time of Moses.
Festival of Unleavened Bread An important Jewish holiday week. In the Old Testament it began the day after Passover, but by this time the two holidays had become one.
leper A person who had leprosy, a very bad skin disease.
alabaster A beautiful kind of stone that can be carved.
nard Very expensive oil from the root of the nard plant.

Christ The "anointed one" (Messiah) or chosen of God.
Son of Man Jesus. In Dan. 7:13-14 this is the name for the Messiah, the one God chose to save his people.
time The time that Jesus has been talking about when something important will happen. See Lk. 21:31, where Jesus says that this is the time for God's kingdom to come.

Good News* will be told to people in all the world. And in every place where the Good News is told, the story of what this woman did will also be told. The thing she has done will be told and people will remember her."

¹⁰Then one of the twelve apostles* went to talk to the leading priests. This was the follower named Judas Iscariot. Judas wanted to give Jesus to them. ¹¹The leading priests were very happy about this. They promised to pay Judas for doing this. So Judas waited for the best time to give Jesus to them.

¹²It was now the first day of the Festival of Unleavened Bread.* This was a time when the Jews always sacrificed *(killed)* the Passover* lambs.* Jesus' followers came to him. They said, "We will go and prepare everything for you to eat the Passover meal. Where do you want us to have the meal?"

¹³Jesus sent two of his followers into the city. Jesus said to them, "Go into the city. You will see a man carrying a jar of water. The man will come to you. Follow that man. ¹⁴That man will walk into a house. Tell the person who owns the house, 'The Teacher asks that you show us the room where he and his followers can eat the Passover* meal.' ¹⁵The owner will show you a large room upstairs. This room is ready for you. Prepare the food for us there."

¹⁶So the followers left and went into the city. Everything happened the way Jesus said. So the followers prepared the Passover* meal.

¹⁷In the evening, Jesus went to that house with the twelve apostles.* ¹⁸While they were all eating, Jesus said, "I tell you the truth. One of you twelve will be against me—one of you eating with me now."

¹⁹The followers were very sad to hear this. Each follower said to Jesus, "Surely I will not be against you!"

²⁰Jesus answered, "The man who is against me is one of you twelve. He is the one who dips his bread into the same bowl with me. ²¹The Son of Man* will go ₍and die₎. The Scriptures* say this will happen. But it will be very bad for the person who gives the Son of Man ₍to be killed₎. It would be better for that person if he were never born."

The Lord's Supper

²²While they were eating, Jesus took some bread. Jesus thanked God for the bread and divided it. He gave the bread to his followers. Jesus said, "Take this bread ₍and eat it₎. This bread is my body."

²³Then Jesus took a cup of wine. He thanked God for it and gave it to the followers. All the followers drank from the cup.

²⁴Then Jesus said, "This wine is my blood. My blood *(death)* begins the new agreement ₍from God to his people₎. This blood is given for many people. ²⁵I tell you the truth. I will not drink this wine again until that day when I drink it in the kingdom of God and the wine is new."

²⁶All the followers sang a song. Then they went out to the Mount of Olives.*

Jesus' Followers Will All Leave Him

²⁷Then Jesus told the followers, "You will all lose your faith. It is written ₍in the Scriptures₎*:

> 'I will kill the shepherd,
> and the sheep will run away.'
>
> *Zechariah 13:7*

²⁸But ₍after I die₎, I will rise from death. Then I will go to Galilee. I will be there before you go there."

²⁹Peter said, "All the other followers may lose their faith. But I will never lose my faith."

³⁰Jesus answered, "I tell you the truth. Tonight you will say you don't know me. You will say this three times before the rooster crows twice."

³¹But Peter answered strongly, "I will never say I don't know you! I will even die with you!" And all the other followers said the same thing.

Jesus Prays Alone

³²Jesus and his followers went to a place named Gethsemane. Jesus said to the followers, "Sit here while I pray." ³³Jesus told Peter, James, and John to come with him. Then Jesus began to be very troubled and full of sorrow. ³⁴Jesus said to Peter, James, and John, "My soul is full of sorrow. My

---

Good News The news that God has made a way for people to have their sins forgiven and live with God.

apostles The men Jesus chose to be his special helpers.

Festival of Unleavened Bread An important Jewish holiday week. In the Old Testament it began the day after Passover, but by this time the two holidays had become one.

Passover Important Jewish holy day. Jews eat a special meal on this day every year to remember that God freed them from slavery in Egypt in the time of Moses.

Passover lambs Part of the celebration of Passover was the sacrifice of a lamb. See Ex. 12:3-9.

Son of Man Jesus. In Dan. 7:13-14 this is the name for the Messiah, the one God chose to save his people.

Scriptures Holy Writings—the Old Testament.

Mount of Olives A hill near the city of Jerusalem.

heart is breaking with sadness. Wait here and stay awake." ³⁵Jesus walked a little more away from them. Then Jesus fell on the ground and prayed. Jesus prayed that, if possible, he would not have this time of suffering. ³⁶Jesus prayed, "Abba,* Father! You can do all things. Let me not have this cup* ₍of suffering₎. But do what you want, not what I want." ³⁷Then Jesus went back to his followers. He found them sleeping. He said to Peter, "Simon, why are you sleeping? You could not stay awake with me for one hour? ³⁸Stay awake and pray that you will not be tempted. Your spirit wants to do what is right. But your body is weak." ³⁹Again Jesus went away and prayed the same thing. ⁴⁰Then Jesus went back to the followers. Again Jesus found them sleeping. Their eyes were very tired. The followers did not know what they should say to Jesus. ⁴¹After Jesus prayed a third time, he went back to his followers. Jesus said to them, "You are still sleeping and resting? That's enough! The time has come for the Son of Man* to be given to sinful people. ⁴²Stand up! We must go. Here comes the man who is giving me to those people."

Jesus Is Arrested

⁴³While Jesus was still speaking, Judas came there. Judas was one of the twelve apostles.* Judas had many people with him. These people were sent from the leading priests, the teachers of the law, and the older Jewish leaders. These people with Judas had swords and clubs. ⁴⁴Judas* planned to do something to show the people which man was Jesus. Judas said, "The man I kiss is Jesus. Arrest him and guard him while you lead him away." ⁴⁵So Judas went to Jesus and said, "Teacher!" Then Judas kissed Jesus. ⁴⁶Then the men grabbed Jesus and arrested him. ⁴⁷One of the followers standing near Jesus grabbed his sword and pulled it out. This follower hit the servant of the high priest* with the sword and cut off his ear. ⁴⁸Then Jesus said, "You came to get me with swords and clubs like I am a criminal. ⁴⁹Every day I was with you teaching in the temple.* You did not arrest me there. But all these things have happened so that it will be like the Scriptures* said." ⁵⁰Then all of Jesus' followers left him and ran away. ⁵¹There was a young man following Jesus. He was wearing only a linen cloth. The people also grabbed this man. ⁵²The cloth he was wearing came off, and he ran away wearing nothing.

Jesus Before the Jewish Leaders

⁵³The people who arrested Jesus led him to the house of the high priest.* All the leading priests, the older Jewish leaders, and the teachers of the law were gathered there. ⁵⁴Peter followed Jesus, but he did not come near Jesus. Peter followed Jesus to the yard of the high priest's house. Peter went into the yard. Peter was sitting there with the guards. He was warming himself by their fire. ⁵⁵The leading priests and all the Jewish council tried to find something that Jesus had done wrong so they could kill him. But the council could find no proof that would allow them to kill Jesus. ⁵⁶Many people came and told false things against Jesus. But the people all said different things—none of them agreed. ⁵⁷Then some people stood and said something false against Jesus. They said, ⁵⁸"We heard this man *(Jesus)* say, 'I will destroy this temple* that men made. And three days later, I will build another temple—a temple not made by men.'" ⁵⁹But also the things these people said did not agree.

⁶⁰Then the high priest* stood before all the people and said to Jesus, "These people said things against you. Do you have something to say about these charges against you? Are these people telling the truth?" ⁶¹But Jesus said nothing. He did not answer.

The high priest* asked Jesus another question: "Are you the Christ,* the Son of the blessed ₍God₎?"

⁶²Jesus answered, "Yes, I am the Son of God. And in the future you will see the Son of Man* sitting at the right side of the Great One *(God)*.

Abba Name that a child called his father. It was used like the English word "daddy."
cup Jesus is talking about the bad things that will happen to him. Accepting these things will be very hard, like drinking a cup full of something that tastes very bad.
Son of Man Jesus. In Dan. 7:13-14 this is the name for the Messiah, the one God chose to save his people.
apostles The men Jesus chose to be his special helpers.
Judas Literally, "the one who betrayed him."

high priest Most important Jewish priest and leader.
temple The special building in Jerusalem for Jewish worship.
Scriptures Holy Writings—the Old Testament.
Christ The "anointed one" (Messiah) or chosen of God.

And you will see the Son of Man coming on the clouds of heaven."

⁶³When the high priest* heard this, he was very angry. He tore his clothes and said, "We don't need any more witnesses! ⁶⁴You all heard him say these things against God. What do you think?"

All the people said that Jesus was wrong. They said he was guilty and must be killed. ⁶⁵Some of the people there spit at Jesus. They covered Jesus' eyes and hit him with their fists. They said, "Show us that you are a prophet*!" Then the guards led Jesus away and beat him.

Peter Is Afraid to Say He Knows Jesus

⁶⁶At that time, Peter was still in the yard. A servant girl of the high priest* came to Peter. ⁶⁷The girl saw Peter warming himself at the fire. She looked closely at Peter.

Then the girl said, "You were with Jesus, that man from Nazareth."

⁶⁸But Peter said that he was never with Jesus. He said, "I don't know or understand what you are talking about." Then Peter left and went to the entrance of the yard.*

⁶⁹The servant girl saw Peter there. Again the girl said to the people who were standing there, "This man is one of those people ₗthat followed Jesus⌋." ⁷⁰Again Peter said that it was not true.

A short time later, some people were standing near Peter. The people said, "We know you are one of those people ₗthat followed Jesus⌋. You are from Galilee, ₗthe same as Jesus⌋."

⁷¹Then Peter began to curse. He said strongly, "I promise to God that I don't know this man you are talking about!"

⁷²After Peter said this, the rooster crowed the second time. Then Peter remembered what Jesus told him: "Before the rooster crows twice, you will say three times that you don't know me." Then Peter was very sad and began to cry.

Governor Pilate Questions Jesus

15 Very early in the morning, the leading priests, the older Jewish leaders, the teachers of the law, and all the Jewish council decided what to do with Jesus. They tied Jesus and led him to Pilate, ₗthe governor⌋. They gave Jesus to Pilate.

²Pilate asked Jesus, "Are you the king of the Jews?"

Jesus answered, "Yes, that is right."

³The leading priests accused Jesus of many things. ⁴So Pilate asked Jesus another question. Pilate said, "You can see that these people are accusing you of many things. Why don't you answer?"

⁵But Jesus still did not answer. Pilate was very surprised at this.

Pilate Tries but Fails to Free Jesus

⁶Every year at the Passover* time the governor would free one person from the prison. He would free any person the people wanted him to free. ⁷At that time, there was a man named Barabbas in prison. He was in prison with the rebels. These rebels were guilty of murder during a riot. ⁸The people came to Pilate and asked him to free a prisoner like he always did.

⁹Pilate asked the people, "Do you want me to free the king of the Jews?" ¹⁰Pilate knew that the leading priests had given Jesus to him because they were jealous of Jesus. ¹¹But the leading priests persuaded the people to ask Pilate to free Barabbas, not Jesus.

¹²Pilate asked the people again, "So what should I do with this man you call the king of the Jews?"

¹³The people shouted, "Kill him on a cross!"

¹⁴Pilate asked, "Why? What wrong has he done?"

But the people shouted louder and louder, "Kill him on a cross!"

¹⁵Pilate wanted to please the people. So Pilate freed Barabbas for them. And Pilate told the soldiers to beat Jesus with whips. Then Pilate gave Jesus to the soldiers to be killed on a cross.

¹⁶Pilate's soldiers brought Jesus into the governor's palace (called the Praetorium). They called all the other soldiers together. ¹⁷The soldiers put a purple robe on Jesus. Then they used thorny weeds to make a crown. They put the crown of thorns on Jesus' head. ¹⁸Then they called to Jesus. They said, "Hello, king of the Jews!" ¹⁹The soldiers hit Jesus on the head many times with a stick. They also spit on him. Then ₗthey teased Jesus by⌋ bowing on their knees and worshiping him. ²⁰After they finished teasing Jesus, the soldiers took off the purple robe and put his own clothes on him again. Then they led Jesus out of the palace to be killed on a cross.

---

high priest Most important Jewish priest and leader.
prophet A person who spoke for God. He often said things that most people could not know.
Verse 68 Many Greek copies add: "and the rooster crowed."

Passover Important Jewish holy day. They ate a special meal on this day every year to remember that God freed them from slavery in Egypt in the time of Moses.

Jesus Is Killed on a Cross

²¹There was a man from Cyrene walking into the city. The man was Simon, the father of Alexander and Rufus. Simon was walking into the city from the fields. The soldiers forced Simon to carry the cross for Jesus. ²²They led Jesus to the place called Golgotha. (Golgotha means "The Place of the Skull.") ²³At Golgotha the soldiers tried to give Jesus wine to drink. This wine was mixed with myrrh.* But Jesus refused to drink it. ²⁴The soldiers nailed Jesus to a cross. Then the soldiers divided Jesus' clothes among themselves. They gambled with dice to decide which clothes each soldier would get.

²⁵It was nine o'clock in the morning when they nailed Jesus to the cross. ²⁶There was a sign with the charge against Jesus written on it. The sign said: "THE KING OF THE JEWS." ²⁷They also put two robbers on crosses beside Jesus. They put one robber beside Jesus on the right, and they put the other robber beside Jesus on the left. ²⁸* ²⁹People walked by and said bad things to Jesus. They shook their heads and said, "You said you could destroy the temple* and build it again in three days. ³⁰So save yourself! Come down from that cross!"

³¹The leading priests and the teachers of the law were also there. They teased Jesus the same as the other people did. They said to themselves, "He saved other people. But he can't save himself. ³²If he is really the Christ,* the king of Israel (the Jews), then he should [save himself by] coming down from the cross now. We will see this, and then we will believe in him." The robbers that were being killed on the crosses beside Jesus also said bad things to him.

Jesus Dies

³³At noon the whole country became dark. This darkness continued until three o'clock. ³⁴At three o'clock Jesus cried with a loud voice, "*Eloi, Eloi, lama sabachthani.*" This means, "My God, my God, why have you left me alone?"*

³⁵Some of the people standing there heard this. The people said, "Listen! He is calling Elijah."*
³⁶One man there ran and got a sponge. The man filled the sponge with vinegar and tied the sponge to a stick. Then he used the stick to give the sponge to Jesus to drink from it. The man said, "We should wait now and see if Elijah will come to take him down from the cross."
³⁷Then Jesus cried with a loud voice and died. ³⁸When Jesus died, the curtain* in the temple* was torn into two pieces. The tear started at the top and tore all the way to the bottom. ³⁹The army officer* that was standing there before the cross saw what happened when Jesus died. The officer said, "This man really was the Son of God!"
⁴⁰Some women were standing away from the cross, watching. Some of these women were Mary from the town of Magdala, Salome, and Mary the mother of James and Joses. (James was her youngest son.) ⁴¹These were the women that followed Jesus in Galilee and cared for him. Many other women were also there. These women had come with Jesus to Jerusalem.

Jesus Is Buried

⁴²This day was called Preparation day. (That means the day before the Sabbath day.*) It was becoming dark. ⁴³A man named Joseph from Arimathea was brave enough to go to Pilate and ask for Jesus' body. Joseph was an important member of the Jewish council. He was one of the people that wanted the kingdom of God to come. ⁴⁴Pilate was surprised to hear that Jesus was already dead. Pilate called the army officer* that guarded Jesus. Pilate asked the officer if Jesus was already dead. ⁴⁵The officer told Pilate that Jesus was dead. So Pilate told Joseph he could have the body. ⁴⁶Joseph bought some linen cloth. Joseph took the body [from the cross] and wrapped the body in the linen. Then Joseph put the body in a tomb (*grave*) that was dug in a wall of rock. Then Joseph closed the tomb by rolling a very large stone to cover the entrance. ⁴⁷Mary from Magdala

---

myrrh Myrrh was mixed with wine, and this was used as a drug to help a person feel less pain.
Verse 28 Some Greek copies add verse 28: "And the Scripture happened that says, 'They put him with criminals.'"
temple The special building in Jerusalem for Jewish worship.
Christ The "anointed one" (Messiah) or chosen of God.
"My God ... alone" Quote from Ps. 22:1.
"He is calling Elijah" The word for "My God" ("*Eloi*" or "*Eli*") sounded to the people like the name of Elijah, a famous man who spoke for God about 850 B.C.
curtain A curtain divided the "most holy place" from the other part of the temple.
army officer A centurion, a Roman army officer who had authority over 100 soldiers.
Sabbath day The seventh day of the Jewish week. It was a special religious day for the Jews.

and Mary the mother of Joses saw the place where Jesus was put.

News that Jesus Has Risen from Death

16 The next day after the Sabbath day,* Mary from Magdala, Salome, and Mary the mother of James bought some sweet-smelling spices. They wanted to put the spices on Jesus' body. ²Very early on that day, the first day of the week, the women were going to the tomb. It was very early after sunrise. ³The women said to each other, "There is a large stone covering the entrance of the tomb. Who will move the stone for us?" ⁴Then the women looked and saw that the stone was moved. The stone was very large, but it was moved away from the entrance. ⁵The women walked into the tomb. They saw a young man there wearing a white robe. The man was sitting on the right side of the tomb. The women were afraid. ⁶But the man said, "Don't be afraid. You are looking for Jesus from Nazareth, the one that was killed on a cross. He has risen from death! He is not here. Look, here is the place they put him when he was dead. ⁷Now go and tell his followers. And ₍be sure to₎ tell Peter. Tell them, 'Jesus is going into Galilee. He will be there before you. You will see him there like he told you before.'"

⁸The women were very afraid and confused. They left the tomb and ran away. The women did not tell about what happened, because they were afraid.

[Some of the oldest Greek copies of Mark end the book here.]

Some Followers See Jesus

⁹Jesus rose from death early on the first day of the week. Jesus showed himself first to Mary from Magdala. One time in the past, Jesus had forced seven demons* to leave Mary. ¹⁰After Mary saw Jesus, she went and told his followers. His followers were very sad and were crying. ¹¹But Mary told them that Jesus was alive. Mary said that she had seen Jesus. But the followers did not believe her.

¹²Later, Jesus showed himself to two followers while they were walking in the country. But Jesus did not look the same as before he was killed. ¹³These followers went back to the other followers and told them what happened. Again, the followers did not believe them.

Jesus Talks to the Apostles

¹⁴Later Jesus showed himself to the eleven followers while they were eating. Jesus criticized the followers because they had little faith. They were stubborn and refused to believe the people that said Jesus had risen from death.

¹⁵Jesus said to the followers, "Go everywhere in the world. Tell the Good News* to every person. ¹⁶Any person that believes and is baptized* will be saved. But the person that does not believe will be judged guilty. ¹⁷And the people that believe will be able to do these things as proof: They will use my name to force demons* out of people. They will speak in languages they never learned. ¹⁸Those people will hold snakes without being hurt. And those people will drink poison without being hurt. Those people will touch sick people, and the sick people will be healed."

¹⁹After the Lord Jesus said these things to the followers, he was carried up into heaven. There, Jesus sat at the right side of God. ²⁰The followers went everywhere in the world and told the Good News* to people. And the Lord helped them. The Lord proved that the Good News they told people was true. He proved this by giving the followers power to do miracles.*

Sabbath day The seventh day of the Jewish week. It was a special religious day for the Jews.

demons Demons are evil spirits from the devil.
Good News The news that God has made a way for people to have their sins forgiven and live with God.
baptized A Greek word meaning to be immersed, dipped, or buried briefly under water.
miracles Amazing works done by the power of God.

Luke

Luke Writes About the Life of Jesus

1 Dear Theophilus,
Many people have tried to give a history of the things that happened among us. ²They have written the same things that we learned from some other people—the people that saw those things from the beginning and served God by telling people his message. ³I myself studied everything carefully from the beginning, your Excellency.* Then I thought I should write it for you. So I put it in order in a book. ⁴I write these things so that you can know that what you have been taught is true.

Zechariah and Elizabeth

⁵During the time when Herod* ruled Judea, there was a priest named Zechariah. Zechariah belonged to Abijah's group.* Zechariah's wife came from the family of Aaron. Her name was Elizabeth. ⁶Zechariah and Elizabeth were truly good people before God. They did everything the Lord *(God)* commanded and told people to do. They were without fault. ⁷But Zechariah and Elizabeth had no children. Elizabeth could not have a baby; and both of them were very old.
⁸Zechariah was serving as a priest before God for his group. It was his group's time to serve. ⁹The priests always chose one priest to offer the incense.* Zechariah was chosen to do this. So Zechariah went into the temple* of the Lord *(God)* to offer the incense. ¹⁰There were many, many people outside. They were praying at the time the incense was offered. ¹¹Then, on the right side of the incense table, an angel of the Lord *(God)* came and stood before Zechariah. ¹²When he saw the angel, Zechariah was confused and very afraid. ¹³But the angel said to him, "Zechariah, don't be afraid. Your prayer has been heard by God. Your wife, Elizabeth, will give birth to a baby boy. You will name him John. ¹⁴You will be very, very happy. Many people will be happy because of his birth. ¹⁵John will be a great man for the Lord *(God)*. He will never drink wine or liquor. Even at the time when John is being born, he will be filled with the Holy Spirit.* ¹⁶John will help many Jews return to the Lord their God. ¹⁷John himself will go first before the Lord. John will be powerful like Elijah.* He will have the same spirit Elijah had. He will make peace between fathers and their children. Many people are not obeying God. John will bring those people back to the right way that people should think. He will make people ready for the [coming of] the Lord."
¹⁸Zechariah said to the angel, "How can I know that what you say is true? I am an old man, and my wife is also old."
¹⁹The angel answered him, "I am Gabriel. I stand before God. God sent me to talk to you and to tell you this good news. ²⁰Now, listen! You will not be able to talk until the day when these things happen. You will lose your speech. Why? Because you did not believe what I told you. But these things will really happen."
²¹Outside, the people were still waiting for Zechariah. They were surprised that he was staying so long in the temple.* ²²Then Zechariah came outside, but he could not speak to them. So the people knew that Zechariah had seen a vision* inside the temple. Zechariah could not speak. He could only make signs to the people. ²³When

---

Excellency This word was used in speaking or writing to an important person like a king or ruler to show respect.
Herod Herod I (the Great), of Judea, 40 B.C. to 4 B.C.
Abijah's group Jewish priests were divided into 24 groups. See 1 Chron. 24.
incense Special dried tree sap used for a sacrifice. It was burned to make a sweet-smelling smoke.
temple The special building in Jerusalem for Jewish worship.

Holy Spirit Called the Spirit of God, the Spirit of Christ, and the Comforter. Joined with God and Christ, he does God's work among people in the world.
Elijah A prophet who lived about 850 B.C.
vision A vision is something like a dream that God used to speak to people.

Zechariah's time of service was finished, he went home. ²⁴Later, Zechariah's wife, Elizabeth, became pregnant. So she did not go out of her house for five months. Elizabeth said, ²⁵"Look what the Lord *(God)* has done for me! My people were ashamed* of me, but now the Lord has taken away that shame."

The Virgin Mary

²⁶⁻²⁷During Elizabeth's sixth month of pregnancy, God sent the angel Gabriel to a virgin* girl that lived in Nazareth, a town in Galilee. The girl was engaged to marry a man named Joseph from the family of David.* Her name was Mary. ²⁸The angel came to her and said, "Greetings! The Lord *(God)* is with you. He wants to bless you."
²⁹But Mary was very confused about what the angel said. Mary wondered, "What does this mean?"
³⁰The angel said to her, "Don't be afraid, Mary, because God is very pleased with you. ³¹Listen! You will become pregnant. You will give birth to a baby boy. And you will name him Jesus. ³²He will be great *(important)*. People will call him the Son of the Most High *(God)*. The Lord God will give him the authority of David,* his ancestor. ³³Jesus will rule over the people of Jacob forever. Jesus' kingdom will never end."
³⁴Mary said to the angel, "How will this happen? I am not married!"
³⁵The angel said to Mary, "The Holy Spirit* will come to you and the power of the Most High *(God)* will cover you. The baby will be holy. He will be called the Son of God. ³⁶Also, your relative Elizabeth is pregnant. She is very old, but she is going to have a son. Everyone thought she could not have a baby, but she has been pregnant now for six months! ³⁷God can do anything!"
³⁸Mary said, "I am the servant girl of the Lord *(God)*. Let this thing you have said happen to me!" Then the angel went away.

Mary Visits Zechariah and Elizabeth

³⁹Mary got up and went quickly to a town in the hill country of Judea. ⁴⁰She went into Zechariah's house and greeted Elizabeth. ⁴¹When Elizabeth heard Mary's greeting, the unborn baby inside Elizabeth jumped. Then Elizabeth was filled with the Holy Spirit.* ⁴²Elizabeth said with a loud voice, "God has blessed you *(Mary)* more than any other woman. And God has blessed the baby which you will give birth to. ⁴³You are the mother of my Lord, and you have come to me! Why has something so good happened to me? ⁴⁴When I heard your voice, the baby inside me jumped with joy. ⁴⁵You are blessed because you believed what the Lord *(God)* said to you. You believed this would happen."

Mary Praises God

⁴⁶Then Mary said,

⁴⁷ "My soul praises the Lord *(God)*;
   my heart is happy because God
      is my Savior.
⁴⁸ I am not important.
   But God has shown his care for me,
      his servant girl.
   From now on, all people will say
      that I am blessed,
⁴⁹ because the Powerful One *(God)*
      has done great things for me.
   His name is very holy.
⁵⁰ God always gives mercy to those people
      that worship him.
⁵¹ God reached out his arm and
      showed his power:
   He scattered those people that are proud
      and think great things about themselves.
⁵² God brought down rulers from their thrones,
      and he raised up the humble people.
⁵³ God filled the hungry people
      with good things,
   but he sent the rich, selfish people
      away with nothing.
⁵⁴ God has helped Israel—the people he chose
      to serve him.
   He gave us his mercy.
⁵⁵ God has done what he promised
      to our ancestors,
   to Abraham and to his children forever."

⁵⁶Mary stayed with Elizabeth for about three months. Then Mary went home.

The Birth of John

⁵⁷When it was time for Elizabeth to give birth, she had a boy. ⁵⁸Her neighbors and relatives heard

---

ashamed The Jews thought it was a shame for women not to have children.
virgin A pure girl who is not married.
David King of Israel about 1000 years before Christ.
Holy Spirit Called the Spirit of God, the Spirit of Christ, and the Comforter. Joined with God and Christ, he does God's work among people in the world.

that the Lord *(God)* was very good to her. They were happy for her.

⁵⁹When the baby was eight days old, they came to circumcise* him. They wanted to name him Zechariah because this was his father's name. ⁶⁰But his mother said, "No! He will be named John."

⁶¹The people said to Elizabeth, "But no one in your family has this name *(John)*!" ⁶²Then they made signs to his father, "What would you like to name him?"

⁶³Zechariah asked for something to write on. Then Zechariah wrote, "His name is John." All the people were surprised. ⁶⁴Then Zechariah could talk again. He began to praise God. ⁶⁵And all their neighbors became afraid. In all the hill country of Judea people continued talking about all these things. ⁶⁶All the people that heard about these things wondered about them. They thought, "What will this child *(John)* be?" They said this because the Lord *(God)* was with this child.

Zechariah Praises God

⁶⁷Then Zechariah, John's father, was filled with the Holy Spirit.* He told the people what would happen:

⁶⁸ "Praise to the Lord God of Israel *(the Jews)*.
God has come to help his people
and has given them freedom.
⁶⁹ God has given us a powerful Savior
from the family of God's servant,
David.
⁷⁰ God said that he would do this.
He said it through his holy prophets*
that lived long ago.
⁷¹ God will save us from our enemies
and from the power of all those
that hate us.
⁷² God said he would give mercy to our fathers.
And he remembered his holy promise.
⁷³ God promised Abraham,
our father *(ancestor)*,
that he would free us from the
power of our enemies,
⁷⁴ so that we could serve him without fear.

---

circumcise To cut off the foreskin. This was done to every Jewish baby boy. It was a mark of the agreement that God made with Abraham (Gen. 17:9-14).
Holy Spirit Called the Spirit of God, the Spirit of Christ, and the Comforter. Joined with God and Christ, he does God's work among people in the world.
prophet(s) Person who spoke for God. He often told things that would happen in the future.

⁷⁵ We will be righteous and holy before God
as long as we live.
⁷⁶ "Now you, little boy, will be called a prophet*
of the Most High *(God)*.
You will go first before the Lord
to make the people ready for the
Lord's coming.
⁷⁷ You will make his people know
that they will be saved.
They will be saved by having
their sins forgiven.
⁷⁸ With the loving mercy of our God,
a new Day from heaven will shine upon us.
⁷⁹ God will help the people that live in darkness,
in the fear of death.
He will lead us in the way
that goes toward peace."

⁸⁰And so the little boy *(John)* was growing up and becoming stronger in spirit. John lived in a place away from other people, until the time when he came out ⌊to preach⌋ to Israel *(the Jews)*.

The Birth of Jesus

2 At that time, Augustus Caesar* sent out an order to all people in the countries that were under Roman rule. The order said that all people must write their name in a book *(register)*. ²This was the first registration.* It happened while Quirinius was governor of Syria. ³All people traveled to their own towns to be registered.

⁴So Joseph left Nazareth, a town in Galilee. He went to the town of Bethlehem in Judea. This town was known as the town of David. Joseph went there because he was from the family of David. ⁵Joseph registered with Mary because she was engaged to marry him. (Mary was now pregnant.) ⁶While Joseph and Mary were in Bethlehem, the time came for Mary to have the baby. ⁷She gave birth to her first son *(Jesus)*. There were no rooms left in the hotel. So Mary wrapped the baby with cloths and laid the baby in a box where cattle are fed.

Some Shepherds Hear About Jesus

⁸That night, some shepherds were in the fields there watching their sheep. ⁹An angel of the Lord

---

Caesar The name given to the emperor (ruler) of Rome.
registration Census. A counting of all the people and the things they own.

(God) stood before the shepherds. The glory of the Lord was shining around them. The shepherds became very afraid. ¹⁰The angel said to them, "Don't be afraid, because I am telling you some good news. It will make all the people very happy. ¹¹Today your Savior was born in David's town. He is Christ,* the Lord. ¹²This is how you will know him: You will find a baby wrapped in cloths and lying in a feeding box."

¹³Then a very large group of angels from heaven joined the first angel. All the angels were praising God, saying:

> ¹⁴ "Give glory to God in heaven,
> and on earth let there be peace
> to the people that please God."

¹⁵The angels left the shepherds and went back to heaven. The shepherds said to each other, "We will go to Bethlehem and see this thing that has happened. We will see this thing the Lord *(God)* told us about."

¹⁶So the shepherds went quickly and found Mary and Joseph. The baby was lying in the feeding box. ¹⁷The shepherds saw the baby. Then they told what the angels said about this child. ¹⁸Everyone was surprised when they heard what the shepherds told them. ¹⁹Mary hid these things in her heart; she continued to think about them. ²⁰The shepherds went back to their sheep, praising God and thanking him for everything that they had seen and heard. It was just as the angel had told them.

²¹When the baby was eight days old, he was circumcised,* and he was named Jesus. This name was given by the angel before the baby began to grow inside Mary.

Jesus Is Presented in the Temple

²²The time came for Mary and Joseph to do the things the law of Moses taught about being made pure.* Joseph and Mary brought Jesus to Jerusalem so they could present him to the Lord *(God)*. ²³It is written in the law of the Lord *(God)*: "When the first boy in every family is born, he shall be called 'special for the Lord.'"* ²⁴The law of the Lord also says that the people must give a sacrifice*: "You must sacrifice two doves or two young pigeons."* So Joseph and Mary went to Jerusalem to do this.

Simeon Sees Jesus

²⁵A man named Simeon lived in Jerusalem. He was a good man and very religious. Simeon was waiting for the time when God would help Israel *(the Jews)*. The Holy Spirit* was in him. ²⁶The Holy Spirit told Simeon that he would not die before he saw the Christ* from the Lord *(God)*. ²⁷The Spirit led Simeon to the temple.* Mary and Joseph went to the temple to do what the Jewish law said they must do. They brought the baby Jesus to the temple. ²⁸Simeon held the baby in his arms and thanked God:

> ²⁹ "Now, Lord *(God)*, you can let me, your
> servant, die in peace like you said.
> ³⁰ I have seen your Salvation*
> with my own eyes.
> ³¹ You prepared him *(Jesus)* before
> all people.
> ³² He *(Jesus)* is a light to show your way to the
> non-Jewish people.
> He will bring honor to your people,
> Israel *(the Jews)*."

³³Jesus' father and mother were amazed at what Simeon said about him. ³⁴Then Simeon blessed them and said to Mary, "Many Jews will fall and many will rise because of this boy. He will be a sign *(proof)* from God that some people will not accept. ³⁵The things that people think in secret will be made known. The things that will happen will make your heart very sad."

Anna Sees Jesus

³⁶Anna, a prophetess,* was there at the temple.* She was from the family of Phanuel in the Asher family group. Anna was very old. She had been married for seven years. ³⁷Then her husband died and she lived alone. She was now

---

Christ The "anointed one" (Messiah) or chosen of God.
circumcised To have the foreskin cut off. This was done to every Jewish baby boy. It was a mark of the agreement that God made with Abraham (Gen. 17:9-14).
pure The law of Moses said that 40 days after a Jewish woman gave birth to a baby, she must be cleansed by a ceremony at the temple. Read Lev. 12:2-8.
"When ... the Lord'" Quote from Ex. 13:2.

sacrifice An offering or gift to God.
"You must ... pigeons" Quote from Lev. 12:8.
Holy Spirit Called the Spirit of God, the Spirit of Christ, and the Comforter. Joined with God and Christ, he does God's work among people in the world.
temple The special building in Jerusalem for Jewish worship.
Salvation The name Jesus means "salvation."
prophetess A woman who spoke for God.

84 years old. Anna was always at the temple; she never left. She worshiped God by fasting* and praying day and night. ³⁸Anna was standing there at that same time, thanking God. She talked about Jesus to all people who were waiting for God to free Jerusalem.

Joseph and Mary Return Home

³⁹Joseph and Mary finished doing all the things that the law of the Lord commanded. Then they went home to Nazareth, their own town in Galilee. ⁴⁰The little boy *(Jesus)* was growing. He became stronger and wiser. God's blessings were with him.

Jesus As a Boy

⁴¹Every year Jesus' parents went to Jerusalem for the Passover* festival. ⁴²When Jesus was twelve years old, they went to the feast like they always did. ⁴³When the feast days were finished, they went home. But the boy Jesus stayed in Jerusalem. His parents did not know about it. ⁴⁴Joseph and Mary traveled for a whole day. They thought that Jesus was with them in the group. They began to look for him among their family and close friends. ⁴⁵But Joseph and Mary did not find Jesus in the group. So they went back to Jerusalem to look for him there. ⁴⁶After three days they found him. Jesus was sitting in the temple* with the religious teachers, listening and asking them questions. ⁴⁷Everyone heard him. They were amazed at his understanding and wise answers. ⁴⁸When Jesus' parents saw him, they were amazed. His mother said to him, "Son, why did you do this to us? Your father and I were very worried about you. We have been looking for you."

⁴⁹Jesus said to them, "Why did you have to look for me? You should have known that I must be where my Father's *(God's)* work is!" ⁵⁰But they did not understand the meaning of what he said to them.

⁵¹Jesus went with them to Nazareth. He obeyed everything his parents said. His mother was still thinking about all these things. ⁵²Jesus continued to learn more and more. He grew taller. People liked Jesus, and he pleased God.

---

fasting Living without food for a special time of prayer.
Passover Important Jewish holy day. They ate a special meal on this day every year to remember that God freed them from slavery in Egypt in the time of Moses.
temple The special building in Jerusalem for Jewish worship.

The Preaching of John

3 It was the 15th year of the rule of Tiberius Caesar.* These men were under Caesar:
Pontius Pilate, the ruler of Judea;
Herod,* the ruler of Galilee;
Philip, Herod's brother, the ruler of Iturea and Trachonitis;
Lysanias, the ruler of Abilene.
²Annas and Caiaphas were the high priests.* At that time, a command from God came to John, the son of Zechariah. John was living in the desert. ³John went through the whole area around the Jordan River. He preached to the people. John told the people to change their hearts and lives and to be baptized* so that their sins would be forgiven. ⁴This is like the words written in the book of Isaiah the prophet*:

> "There is a person shouting in the desert:
> 'Prepare the way for the Lord.
> Make his paths straight.
> ⁵ Every valley will be filled.
> And every mountain and hill
> will be made flat.
> Roads with turns will be made straight.
> And rough roads will be made smooth.
> ⁶ Every person will know about the
> salvation of God!'"
>
> *Isaiah 40:3-5*

⁷People came to be baptized* by John. John said to them, "You are like poisonous snakes! Who warned you to run away from God's anger that is coming? ⁸You must do the things that will show that you have really changed your hearts. Don't ⌊boast and⌋ say, 'Abraham is our father.' I tell you that God can make children for Abraham from these rocks here. ⁹The ax is now ready to cut down the trees.* Every tree that does not make good fruit will be cut down and thrown into the fire."

Caesar The name given to the emperor (ruler) of Rome.
Herod Herod Antipas, tetrarch (ruler) of Galilee and Perea, son of Herod the Great.
high priests Most important Jewish priests.
baptize(d) A Greek word meaning to immerse, dip, or bury a person or thing briefly under water.
prophet Person who spoke for God. He often told things that would happen in the future.
trees The people who do not accept Jesus. They are like "trees" that will be cut down.

¹⁰The people asked John, "What should we do?"

¹¹John answered, "If you have two coats, share with the person who does not have one. If you have food, share that too."

¹²Even the tax collectors* came to John. They wanted to be baptized.* They said to John, "Teacher, what should we do?"

¹³John said to them, "Don't take more taxes from people than you have been ordered to take."

¹⁴The soldiers asked John, "What about us? What should we do?"

John said to them, "Don't make people give you money. Don't tell lies about anyone. Be happy with the pay you get."

¹⁵All the people were hoping ⌊for the Christ* to come⌋, and they wondered about John. They thought, "Maybe he is the Christ."

¹⁶John answered everyone, "I baptize* you in water, but there is a person coming later who can do more than I can. I am not good enough to untie his shoes for him. He will baptize you with the Holy Spirit* and with fire. ¹⁷He will come ready to clean the grain.* He will separate the good grain from the straw. He will put the good part of the grain into his barn. Then he will burn the part that is not good. He will burn it with a fire that cannot be stopped." ¹⁸And John continued to preach the Good News,* saying many other things to help the people.

How John's Work Later Ended

¹⁹(John criticized Governor Herod.* John criticized Herod for the bad thing he did with Herodias, the wife of Herod's brother. John also criticized Herod for the many other bad things Herod did. ²⁰So Herod did another bad thing: He put John in jail. This was added to all the other bad things Herod did.)

Jesus Is Baptized by John

²¹⌊Before John was put into prison⌋, all the people were being baptized* by him. Then Jesus came and was baptized too. While Jesus was praying, the sky opened. ²²The Holy Spirit* came down on him. The Spirit looked like a real dove. Then a voice came from heaven and said, "You are my Son and I love you. I am very pleased with you."

The Family History of Joseph

²³When Jesus began to teach, he was about 30 years old. People thought that Jesus was Joseph's son.

Joseph was the son of Eli.
24 Eli was the son of Matthat.
Matthat was the son of Levi.
Levi was the son of Melchi.
Melchi was the son of Jannai.
Jannai was the son of Joseph.
25 Joseph was the son of Mattathias.
Mattathias was the son of Amos.
Amos was the son of Nahum.
Nahum was the son of Esli.
Esli was the son of Naggai.
26 Naggai was the son of Maath.
Maath was the son of Mattathias.
Mattathias was the son of Semein.
Semein was the son of Josech.
Josech was the son of Joda.
27 Joda was the son of Joanan.
Joanan was the son of Rhesa.
Rhesa was the son of Zerubbabel.
Zerubbabel was the son of Shealtiel.
Shealtiel was the son of Neri.
28 Neri was the son of Melchi.
Melchi was the son of Addi.
Addi was the son of Cosam.
Cosam was the son of Elmadam.
Elmadam was the son of Er.
29 Er was the son of Joshua.
Joshua was the son of Eliezer.
Eliezer was the son of Jorim.
Jorim was the son of Matthat.
Matthat was the son of Levi.
30 Levi was the son of Simeon.
Simeon was the son of Judah.
Judah was the son of Joseph.
Joseph was the son of Jonam.
Jonam was the son of Eliakim.

---

tax collectors Jews hired by the Romans to collect taxes. They often cheated, and the other Jews hated them.

baptize(d) A Greek word meaning to immerse, dip, or bury a person or thing briefly under water.

Christ The "anointed one" (Messiah) or chosen of God.

Holy Spirit Called the Spirit of God, the Spirit of Christ, and the Comforter. Joined with God and Christ, he does God's work among people in the world.

clean the grain John means that Jesus will separate the good people from the bad people.

Good News The news that God has made a way for people to have their sins forgiven and live with God.

Herod Herod Antipas, tetrarch (ruler) of Galilee and Perea, son of Herod the Great.

³¹ Eliakim was the son of Melea.
Melea was the son of Menna.
Menna was the son of Mattatha.
Mattatha was the son of Nathan.
Nathan was the son of David.
³² David was the son of Jesse.
Jesse was the son of Obed.
Obed was the son of Boaz.
Boaz was the son of Salmon.
Salmon was the son of Nahshon.
³³ Nahshon was the son of Amminadab.
Amminadab was the son of Admin.
Admin was the son of Arni.
Arni was the son of Hezron.
Hezron was the son of Perez.
Perez was the son of Judah.
³⁴ Judah was the son of Jacob.
Jacob was the son of Isaac.
Isaac was the son of Abraham.
Abraham was the son of Terah.
Terah was the son of Nahor.
³⁵ Nahor was the son of Serug.
Serug was the son of Reu.
Reu was the son of Peleg.
Peleg was the son of Eber.
Eber was the son of Shelah.
³⁶ Shelah was the son of Cainan.
Cainan was the son of Arphaxad.
Arphaxad was the son of Shem.
Shem was the son of Noah.
Noah was the son of Lamech.
³⁷ Lamech was the son of Methuselah.
Methuselah was the son of Enoch.
Enoch was the son of Jared.
Jared was the son of Mahalaleel.
Mahalaleel was the son of Cainan.
³⁸ Cainan was the son of Enos.
Enos was the son of Seth.
Seth was the son of Adam.
Adam was the son of God.

Jesus Is Tempted by the Devil

4 Jesus returned from the Jordan River. He was full of the Holy Spirit.* The Spirit led Jesus into the desert. ²There the devil tempted Jesus for 40 days. Jesus ate nothing during that time. When those days were finished, Jesus was very hungry.

³The devil said to Jesus, "If you are the Son of God, tell this rock to become bread."

⁴Jesus answered, "It is written ⌊in the Scriptures⌋*:

'It is not just bread that keeps people alive.'"
Deuteronomy 8:3

⁵Then the devil took Jesus and showed him all the kingdoms of the world in a moment of time. ⁶The devil said to Jesus, "I will give you all these kingdoms and all the power and glory that is in them. It has all been given to me. I can give it to any person I want. ⁷I will give it all to you, if you will only worship me."

⁸Jesus answered, "It is written ⌊in the Scriptures⌋*:

'You must worship the Lord your God.
Serve only him!'"
Deuteronomy 6:13

⁹Then the devil led Jesus to Jerusalem. The devil put Jesus on a very high place of the temple.* He said to Jesus, "If you are the Son of God, jump off! ¹⁰It is written ⌊in the Scriptures⌋:

'God will command his angels
to take care of you.'
Psalm 91:11

¹¹It is also written:

'Their hands will catch you
so that you will not hit your foot
on a rock.'"
Psalm 91:12

¹²Jesus answered, "But it also says ⌊in the Scriptures⌋:

'You must not test *(doubt)* the Lord
your God.'"
Deuteronomy 6:16

¹³The devil finished tempting Jesus in every way and went away to wait until a better time.

Jesus Teaches the People

¹⁴Jesus went back to Galilee with the power of the Holy Spirit.* Stories about Jesus spread all over the area around Galilee. ¹⁵Jesus began to teach in the synagogues.* All the people praised him.

Holy Spirit Called the Spirit of God, the Spirit of Christ, and the Comforter. Joined with God and Christ, he does God's work among people in the world.

Scriptures Holy Writings—the Old Testament.
temple The special building in Jerusalem for Jewish worship.
synagogue(s) Synagogues were places where Jews gathered for prayer, study of the Scriptures, and other public meetings.

¹⁶Jesus traveled to Nazareth, the town where he grew up. On the Sabbath day* he went to the synagogue* like he always did. Jesus stood up to read. ¹⁷The book of Isaiah the prophet* was given to him. Jesus opened the book and found the place where this is written:

> 18 "The Spirit of the Lord *(God)* is in me.
> God chose me to tell good news to people
>   that have nothing.
> God sent me to tell people who are prisoners
>   that they are free,
> and to tell the blind people
>   that they can see again.
> God sent me to free the weak people
>   from their suffering,
> 19 and to announce that the time has come
>   for the Lord to show his kindness."
>
> *Isaiah 61:1-2*

²⁰Jesus closed the book. He gave the book back to the helper and sat down. Every person in the synagogue watched Jesus closely. ²¹Jesus began to speak to them. He said, "While you heard me reading these words just now, the words were coming true!" ²²All the people said good things about Jesus. They were amazed at the beautiful words Jesus spoke. The people said, ⌊"How can he speak like this?⌋ He is only Joseph's son, isn't he?" ²³Jesus said to them, "I know that you will tell me the old saying: 'Doctor, heal yourself.' You want to say, 'We heard about some things that you did in Capernaum. Do those same things here in your own home town!'" ²⁴Then Jesus said, "I tell you the truth. A prophet* is not accepted in his own home town. ²⁵What I say is true. During the time of Elijah* it did not rain in Israel for three and a half years. There was no food anywhere in the whole country. There were many widows* in Israel during that time. ²⁶But Elijah was sent to none of those widows ⌊in Israel⌋. Elijah was sent only to a widow in Zarephath, a town in Sidon. ²⁷And there were many people with leprosy* living in Israel during the time of the prophet Elisha.* But none of those people were healed; the only one was Naaman. And Naaman was from the country of Syria, ⌊not from Israel⌋."

²⁸All the people in the synagogue* heard these things. They became very, very angry. ²⁹The people got up and forced Jesus to go out of town. Their town was built on a hill. They brought Jesus to the edge of the hill. The people wanted to throw him off. ³⁰But Jesus walked through the middle of them and went away.

Jesus Heals a Man That Has an Evil Spirit

³¹Jesus went to Capernaum, a city in Galilee. On the Sabbath day* Jesus taught the people. ³²They were amazed at Jesus' teaching, because he spoke with authority *(power)*. ³³In the synagogue* there was a man that had an evil spirit from the devil inside him. The man shouted with a loud voice, ³⁴"Jesus of Nazareth! What do you want with us? Did you come here to destroy us? I know who you are—God's Holy One!" ³⁵But Jesus warned the evil spirit to stop. Jesus said, "Be quiet! Come out of the man!" The evil spirit threw the man down on the ground before all the people. Then the evil spirit left the man and did not hurt him.

³⁶The people were amazed. They said to each other, "What does this mean? With authority and power he *(Jesus)* commands evil spirits and they come out." ³⁷And so the news about Jesus spread to every place in the whole area.

Jesus Heals a Woman

³⁸Jesus left the synagogue.* He went to Simon's* house. Simon's mother-in-law was very sick. She had a high fever. They asked Jesus to do something to help her. ³⁹Jesus stood very close to her and commanded the sickness to leave her. The sickness left her. Then she got up and began serving them.

Jesus Heals Many Other People

⁴⁰When the sun went down, the people brought their sick friends to Jesus. They had many different kinds of sickness. Jesus put his hands on each sick person and healed them. ⁴¹Demons* came out of many people. The demons shouted, "You are the Son of God." But Jesus gave a strong command for the demons not to speak. The demons knew Jesus was the Christ.*

Sabbath day The seventh day of the Jewish week. It was a special religious day for the Jews.
synagogue(s) Synagogues were places where Jews gathered for prayer, study of the Scriptures, and other public meetings.
prophet Person who spoke for God. He often told things that would happen in the future.
Elijah A prophet who lived about 850 B.C.
widows A widow is a woman whose husband has died.
leprosy A very bad skin disease.

Elisha A prophet who lived after Elijah's time.
Simon Simon's other name was Peter.
Demons Demons are evil spirits from the devil.
Christ The "anointed one" (Messiah) or chosen of God.

Jesus Goes to Other Towns

⁴²The next day Jesus went to a place to be alone. The people looked for Jesus. When the people found Jesus, they tried to stop him from leaving. ⁴³But Jesus said to them, "I must tell the Good News about God's kingdom to other towns, too. This is why I was sent." ⁴⁴Then Jesus preached in the synagogues* in Judea.

Peter, James, and John Follow Jesus

5 Jesus stood beside Lake Gennesaret *(Galilee)*. Many people pushed to get all around him. They wanted to hear the teachings of God. ²Jesus saw two boats at the shore of the lake. The fishermen were washing their nets. ³Jesus got into the boat that belonged to Simon.* Jesus asked Simon to push off a little from the shore.

⁴Jesus finished speaking. He said to Simon, "Take the boat into the deep water. If all of you will put your nets into the water, you will catch some fish."

⁵Simon answered, "Master, we worked hard all night trying to catch fish, but we caught nothing. But you say I should put the nets into the water; so I will." ⁶The fishermen put their nets into the water. Their nets became so full of fish that the nets began to break. ⁷They called to their friends in the other boat to come and help them. The friends came, and both boats were filled so full of fish that they were almost sinking.

⁸⁻⁹The fishermen were all amazed at the many fish they caught. When Simon Peter saw this, he bowed down before Jesus and said, "Go away from me, Lord. I am a sinful man!" ¹⁰James and John, the sons of Zebedee, were amazed too. (James and John worked together with Simon.)

Jesus said to Simon, "Don't be afraid. From now on you will work to gather people, ⌊not fish⌋!" ¹¹The men brought their boats to the shore. They left everything and followed Jesus.

Jesus Heals a Sick Man

¹²One time Jesus was in a town where a very sick man lived. This man was covered with leprosy.* When the man saw Jesus, he bowed before Jesus and begged him, "Lord, heal me. I know you can if you want to."

¹³Jesus said, "I want to heal you. Be healed!" Then Jesus touched the man. Immediately the leprosy* disappeared. ¹⁴Then Jesus said, "Don't tell anyone about what happened. But go show yourself to the priest.* And offer a gift ⌊to God⌋ for your healing like Moses commanded. This will show people that you are healed."

¹⁵But the news about Jesus spread more and more. Many people came to hear Jesus and to be healed of their sicknesses. ¹⁶Jesus often went away to other places to be alone so that he could pray.

Jesus Heals a Crippled Man

¹⁷One day Jesus was teaching the people. The Pharisees* and teachers of the law were sitting there too. They had come from every town in Galilee and from Judea and Jerusalem. The Lord *(God)* was giving Jesus the power to heal people. ¹⁸There was a man that was paralyzed *(crippled)*. Some men carried him on a small bed. The men tried to bring him and put him down before Jesus. ¹⁹But there were so many people that the men could not find a way to Jesus. So the men went up on the roof and lowered the crippled man down through a hole in the ceiling. They lowered the bed ⌊into the room⌋ so that the crippled man was lying before Jesus. ²⁰Jesus saw that these men believed. Jesus said to the sick man, "Friend, your sins are forgiven."

²¹The Jewish teachers of the law and the Pharisees* thought to themselves, "Who is this man *(Jesus)*? He is saying things that are against God! Only God can forgive sins."

²²But Jesus knew what they were thinking. He said, "Why do you have thoughts like that in your hearts? ²³Which is easier: to tell this crippled man, 'Your sins are forgiven,' or to tell him, 'Stand up and walk'? ²⁴But I will prove to you that the Son of Man* has power on earth to forgive sins." So Jesus said to the paralyzed man, "I tell you, stand up! Take your bed and go home!"

²⁵Then the man stood up before the people there. He picked up his bed and walked home, praising God. ²⁶All the people were fully amazed.

---

show yourself to the priest The law of Moses said a priest must say when a Jew with leprosy was well.
Pharisees The Pharisees were a Jewish religious group that claimed to follow carefully all Jewish laws and customs.
Son of Man Jesus. In Dan. 7:13-14 this is the name for the Messiah, the one God chose to save his people.

synagogue(s) Synagogues were places where Jews gathered for prayer, study of the Scriptures, and other public meetings.
Simon Simon's other name was Peter.
leprosy A very bad skin disease.

They began to praise God. The people were filled with much respect ₍for God's power₎. They said, "Today we saw amazing things!"

Levi Follows Jesus

²⁷After this Jesus went out and saw a tax collector* sitting in the tax office. His name was Levi. Jesus said to him, "Follow me!" ²⁸Levi got up, left everything, and followed Jesus.

²⁹Then Levi gave a big dinner for Jesus. The dinner was at Levi's house. At the table there were many tax collectors* and some other people too. ³⁰But the Pharisees* and those men that taught the law for the Pharisees began to complain to the followers of Jesus, "Why do you eat and drink with tax collectors and other bad people?"

³¹Jesus answered them, "Healthy people don't need a doctor. It is the sick people that need a doctor. ³²I have not come to ask good people to change. I have come to ask bad people to change their hearts and lives!"

Jesus Answers a Question About Fasting

³³They said to Jesus, "John's followers often fast* and pray, the same as the Pharisees.* But your followers eat and drink all the time."

³⁴Jesus said to them, ₍"When there is a wedding₎, you cannot make the friends of the bridegroom* fast *(be sad)* while the bridegroom is still with them. ³⁵But the time will come when the groom will be taken away from them. Then his friends will fast.*"

³⁶Jesus told them this story: "No person takes cloth off a new coat to cover a hole on an old coat. Why? Because he ruins the new coat, and the cloth from the new coat will not be the same as the old cloth. ³⁷People never pour new wine into old wine bags.* Why? Because the new wine will break the bags, and the wine will spill out and the wine bags will be ruined. ³⁸People always put new wine into new wine bags. ³⁹No person that drinks old wine wants new wine. Why? Because he says, 'The old wine is fine.'"

Jesus Is Lord over the Sabbath Day

6 One time on a Sabbath day,* Jesus was walking through some grain fields. His followers picked the grain, rubbed it in their hands, and ate it. ²Some Pharisees* said, "Why are you doing that? It is against the law ₍of Moses₎ to do that on the Sabbath day."

³Jesus answered, "You have read about what David did when he and the people with him were hungry. ⁴David went into God's house. David took the bread that was offered to God and ate it. And David gave some of the bread to the people with him. This was against the law ₍of Moses₎. The law says that only the priests can eat that bread." ⁵Then Jesus said to the Pharisees,* "The Son of Man* is Lord *(Master)* over the Sabbath day."

Jesus Heals a Man on the Sabbath Day

⁶On another Sabbath day* Jesus went into the synagogue.* Jesus taught the people. A man with a crippled right hand was there. ⁷The teachers of the law and the Pharisees* were waiting to see if Jesus would heal on the Sabbath day. They wanted to see Jesus do something wrong so that they could accuse him. ⁸But Jesus knew what they were thinking. He said to the man with the crippled hand, "Get up and stand before these people." The man got up and stood there. ⁹Then Jesus said to them, "I ask you, which thing is right to do on the Sabbath day: to do good, or to do evil? Is it right to save a life or to destroy one?" ¹⁰Jesus looked around at all of them. Jesus said to the man, "Let me see your hand." The man put his hand out. His hand was healed. ¹¹The Pharisees and the teachers of the law became very, very angry. They said to each other, "What can we do to Jesus?"

Jesus Chooses His Twelve Apostles

¹²At that time Jesus went out to a mountain to pray. He stayed there all night praying to God. ¹³The next morning, Jesus called his followers. He chose twelve of them. He named these men

---

tax collector(s) Jews hired by the Romans to collect taxes. They often cheated, and the other Jews hated them.
Pharisees The Pharisees were a Jewish religious group that claimed to follow carefully all Jewish laws and customs.
fast To live without food for a time of prayer or mourning.
bridegroom A man ready to be married.
wine bags Animal skins used for holding wine.

Sabbath day The seventh day of the Jewish week. It was a special religious day for the Jews.
Son of Man Jesus. In Dan. 7:13-14 this is the name for the Messiah, the one God chose to save his people.
synagogue(s) Synagogues were places where Jews gathered for prayer, study of the Scriptures, and other public meetings.

"apostles."* They were: ¹⁴Simon (Jesus named him Peter) and Andrew, Peter's brother; James and John, Philip and Bartholomew; ¹⁵Matthew, Thomas, James (the son of Alphaeus), and Simon (called the Zealot*), ¹⁶Judas (the son of James) and Judas Iscariot. This Judas was the one that gave Jesus to his enemies.

Jesus Teaches and Heals the People

¹⁷Jesus and the apostles* came down from the mountain. Jesus stood on a flat place. A large group of his followers were there. Also, there were many people from all around Judea, Jerusalem, and the seacoast cities of Tyre and Sidon. ¹⁸They all came to hear Jesus teach and to be healed of their sicknesses. Jesus healed those people that were troubled by evil spirits ⌊from the devil⌋. ¹⁹All the people were trying to touch Jesus, because power was coming out from him. Jesus healed them all!

²⁰Jesus looked at his followers and said,

"Poor people, you are blessed *(happy)*,
because God's kingdom belongs to you.
²¹ You people that are hungry now,
you are blessed,
because you will be filled.
You people that are crying now,
you are blessed,
because you will laugh ⌊with joy⌋."

²²"You are blessed when people hate you and make you leave their group. You are blessed when they say that you are bad and send you away. They will do these things because you belong to the Son of Man.* When this happens, you are blessed. ²³At that time be full of joy, because you have a great reward in heaven. Their fathers *(ancestors)* were mean to the prophets* in the same way that these people are mean to you.

²⁴ "But it will be bad for you, you rich people,
because you had your easy life.
²⁵ It will be bad for you people that are full now,
because you will be hungry.
It will be bad for you people that are
laughing now,
because you will be sad and cry.

²⁶"It is bad when all people say good things about you. Their fathers *(ancestors)* always said good things about the false prophets.*

Love Your Enemies

²⁷"I say to you people that are listening to me, love your enemies. Do good to those people that hate you. ²⁸Ask God to bless those people that say bad things to you. Pray for those people that are mean to you. ²⁹If a person hits you on the side of your face, let him hit the other side too. ³⁰Give to every person that asks you. When a person takes something that is yours, don't ask for it back. ³¹Do for other people what you want them to do for you. ³²If you love only those people that love you, should you get some special praise for doing that? No! Even sinners love the people that love them! ³³If you do good only to those people that do good to you, should you get some special praise for doing that? No! Even sinners do that! ³⁴If you loan things to people, always hoping to get something back, should you get some special praise for that? No! Even sinners lend to other sinners so that they can get back the same amount! ³⁵So love your enemies. Do good to them, and lend to them without hoping to get anything back. If you do these things, you will have a great reward. You will be children of the Most High *(God)*. Yes, because God is good even to the people that are full of sin and not thankful. ³⁶Give love and mercy the same as your Father gives love and mercy.

Look at Yourselves

³⁷"Don't judge other people, and you will not be judged. Don't condemn *(find guilty)* other people, and you will not be condemned. Forgive other people, and you will be forgiven. ³⁸Give to other people, and you will receive. You will be given much. It will be poured into your hands—more than you can hold. You will be given so much that it will spill into your lap. The way you give to other people is the way God will give to you."

³⁹Jesus told them this story: "Can a blind man lead another blind man? No! Both of them will fall into a hole. ⁴⁰A student is not better than his teacher. But when the student has fully learned, then he will be like his teacher.

---

apostles The men Jesus chose to be his special helpers.
Zealot The Zealots were a Jewish political group.
Son of Man Jesus. In Dan. 7:13-14 this is the name for the Messiah, the one God chose to save his people.
prophets People who spoke for God. They often told things that would happen in the future.

false prophets People who say they speak for God but do not really speak God's truth.

⁴¹"Why do you notice the small piece of dust that is in your brother's eye, but you don't see the big piece of wood that is in your own eye? ⁴²You say to your brother, 'Brother, let me take that little piece of dust out of your eye.' Why do you say this? You can't see that big piece of wood in your own eye! You are a hypocrite.* First, take the piece of wood out of your own eye. Then you will see clearly to take the dust out of your brother's eye.

Two Kinds of Fruit

⁴³"A good tree does not give bad fruit. Also, a bad tree does not give good fruit. ⁴⁴Each tree is known by the fruit it gives. People don't gather figs from thorny weeds. And they don't get grapes from bushes! ⁴⁵A good person has good things saved in his heart. And so he brings good things out of his heart. But an evil person has evil things saved in his heart. So he brings out bad things. A person speaks the things that are in his heart.

Two Kinds of People

⁴⁶"Why do you call me, 'Lord, Lord,' but you are not doing what I say? ⁴⁷Every person that comes to me and listens to my words and obeys ⁴⁸is like a man building a house. He digs deep and builds his house on strong rock. The floods come, and the water tries to wash the house away. But the flood cannot move the house, because the house was built well *(strong)*. ⁴⁹But the person that hears my words and does not obey is like a man that does not build his house on strong rock. When the floods come, the house falls down easily. And the house is completely destroyed."

Jesus Heals a Servant

7 Jesus finished saying all these things to the people. Then Jesus went into Capernaum. ²In Capernaum there was an army officer.* The officer had a servant that was very sick; he was near death. The officer loved the servant very much. ³When the officer heard about Jesus, he sent some older Jewish leaders to him. The officer wanted the men to ask Jesus to come and save the life of his servant. ⁴The men went to Jesus. They begged Jesus ⌊to help the officer⌋. They said, "This officer is worthy to have your help. ⁵He loves our people and he built the synagogue* for us."

⁶So Jesus went with the men. Jesus was coming near the officer's house when the officer sent friends to say, "Lord, you don't need to come into my house. I am not good enough to be with you. ⁷That is why I did not come to you myself. You only need to give the order and my servant boy will be healed. ⁸⌊I understand your authority⌋. I am a man under the authority *(power)* of other men. And I have soldiers under my authority. I tell one soldier, 'Go,' and he goes. And I tell another soldier, 'Come,' and he comes. And I say to my servant, 'Do this,' and my servant obeys me."

⁹When Jesus heard this, he was amazed. Jesus turned to the people that were following him. Jesus said, "I tell you, this is the most faith I have seen anywhere, even in Israel.*"

¹⁰The group that was sent to Jesus went back to the house. There they found that the servant was healed.

Jesus Brings a Man Back to Life

¹¹The next day Jesus went to a town called Nain. Jesus' followers and a large group of people were traveling with him. ¹²When Jesus came near the town gates, he saw a funeral. A mother, who was a widow,* had lost her only son. Many people from the town were there with the mother while her son was being carried out. ¹³When the Lord *(Jesus)* saw her, he felt very sorry for her in his heart. Jesus said to her, "Don't cry." ¹⁴Jesus walked to the coffin* and touched it. The men that were carrying the coffin stopped. Jesus said to the dead son, "Young man, I tell you, get up!" ¹⁵Then the son sat up and began to talk. Jesus gave him to his mother.

¹⁶All the people were amazed. They were praising God. They said, "A great prophet has come to us!" And they said, "God is taking care of his people."

¹⁷This news about Jesus spread into all Judea and into all the places around there.

John Asks a Question

¹⁸John's followers told John about all these things. John called for two of his followers. ¹⁹John sent them to the Lord *(Jesus)* to ask, "Are you the

---

hypocrite A bad person that acts like he is good.
army officer A centurion, a Roman army officer who had authority over 100 soldiers.
synagogue(s) Synagogues were places where Jews gathered for prayer, study of the Scriptures, and other public meetings.
Israel The Jewish nation (people).
widow A widow is a woman whose husband has died.
coffin A wooden box used for burying dead bodies.

One that is coming, or should we wait for another person?"

²⁰So the men came to Jesus. They said, "John the Baptizer sent us to you with this question: 'Are you the One that is coming, or should we wait for another person?'"

²¹At that time, Jesus healed many people of their sicknesses, diseases, and evil spirits [from the devil]. Jesus healed many blind people so that they could see again. ²²Then Jesus said to John's followers, "Go tell John the things that you saw and heard here. Blind people are healed and can see. Crippled people are healed and can walk. People with leprosy* are healed. Deaf people are healed and can hear. Dead people are given life. And the Good News [about God's kingdom] is given to the poor people. ²³The person that can accept* me is blessed!"

²⁴When John's followers left, Jesus began to tell the people about John: "What did you people go out into the desert to see? A weed* blown by the wind? ²⁵What did you go out to see? A man dressed in fine clothes? No. Those people that have fine, nice clothes live in kings' houses. ²⁶Really, what did you go out to see? A prophet*? Yes, and I tell you, John is more than a prophet. ²⁷This was written about John:

> 'Listen! I *(God)* will send my helper*
> ahead of you.
> He will prepare the way for you.'
> *Malachi 3:1*

²⁸I tell you, John is greater than any man ever born. But even the least important person in the kingdom of God is greater than John."

²⁹(When the people heard this, they all agreed that God's teaching was good. Even the tax collectors* agreed. These were the people that were baptized* by John. ³⁰But the Pharisees* and teachers of the law refused to accept God's plan for themselves; they did not let John baptize them.)

³¹"What shall I say about the people of this time? What can I compare them to? What are they like? ³²The people of this time are like children sitting in the market place. One group of children calls to the other children and says,

> 'We played music for you,
> but you did not dance;
> we sang a sad song,
> but you were not sad.'

³³John the Baptizer came and did not eat [like other people] or drink wine. And you say, 'He has a demon* inside him.' ³⁴The Son of Man* came eating [like other people] and drinking wine. And you say, 'Look at him! He eats too much and drinks too much wine! He is a friend of the tax collectors* and other bad people!' ³⁵But wisdom is shown to be right by the things it does."

Simon the Pharisee

³⁶One of the Pharisees* asked Jesus to eat with him. Jesus went into the Pharisee's house and sat at the table. ³⁷At that time there was a sinful woman in the town. She knew that Jesus was eating at the Pharisee's* house. So the woman brought some perfume in an alabaster jar. ³⁸She stood at Jesus' feet, crying. Then she began to wash his feet with her tears. She dried Jesus' feet with her hair. She kissed his feet many times and rubbed them with perfume. ³⁹The Pharisee that asked Jesus to come to his house saw this. He thought to himself, "If Jesus were a prophet,* he would know that the woman who is touching him is a sinner!"

⁴⁰Jesus said to the Pharisee,* "Simon, I have something to say to you."

Simon said, "Teacher, you can speak. [I am listening]."

⁴¹Jesus said, "There were two men. Both men owed money to the same banker. One man owed the banker 500 silver coins.* The other man owed the banker 50 silver coins. ⁴²The men had no money, so they could not pay their debt. But the

---

leprosy A very bad skin disease.
can accept Literally, "is not offended by."
weed Literally, "reed." Jesus means that John was not weak like a reed blown by the wind.
prophet A person who spoke for God.
helper Literally, "messenger."
tax collectors Jews hired by the Romans to collect taxes. They often cheated, and the other Jews hated them.
baptized A Greek word meaning to be immersed, dipped, or buried briefly under water.
Pharisee(s) The Pharisees were a Jewish religious group that claimed to follow all Jewish laws and customs very carefully.

demon A demon is an evil spirit from the devil.
Son of Man Jesus. In Dan. 7:13-14, this is the name for the Messiah (Christ), the person God chose to save his people.
silver coins One coin, a Roman denarius, was the average pay for one day's work.

banker told the men that they did not have to pay him. Which one of those two men will love the banker more?"

⁴³Simon answered, "I think it would be the one that owed him the most money."

Jesus said to Simon, "You are right." ⁴⁴Then Jesus turned to the woman and said to Simon, "Do you see this woman? When I came into your house, you gave me no water for my feet. But she washed my feet with her tears and dried my feet with her hair. ⁴⁵You did not kiss me, but she has been kissing my feet since I came in! ⁴⁶You did not rub my head with oil, but she rubbed my feet with perfume. ⁴⁷I tell you that her many sins are forgiven. This is clear, because she showed great love. But the person that feels only a little need to be forgiven will feel only a little love when he is forgiven."

⁴⁸Then Jesus said to her, "Your sins are forgiven."

⁴⁹The people sitting at the table began to think to themselves, "Who does this man *(Jesus)* think he is? How can he forgive sins?"

⁵⁰Jesus said to the woman, "Because you believed, you are saved ₍from your sins₎. Go in peace."

The Group with Jesus

8 The next day, Jesus traveled through some cities and small towns. Jesus preached and told the Good News about God's kingdom. The twelve apostles* were with him. ²There were also some women with him. Jesus had healed these women of sicknesses and evil spirits ₍from the devil₎. One of the women was named Mary. She was from a town called Magdala. Seven demons had come out of her. ³Also with these women were: Joanna, the wife of Chuza (Herod's* helper), Suzanna, and many other women. These women used their own money to help Jesus and his apostles.

Jesus Uses a Story About Planting Seed

⁴Many people came together. People came to Jesus from every town. Jesus told the people this story:

⁵"A farmer went out to plant his seed. While the farmer was planting, some seed fell beside the road. People walked on the seed, and the birds ate all this seed. ⁶Some seed fell on rock. This seed began to grow, but then died because the seed had no water. ⁷Some seed fell among thorny weeds. This seed grew, but later the weeds stopped the good plants from growing. ⁸And some seed fell on good ground. This seed grew and made 100 times more grain."

Jesus finished the story. Then Jesus said, "You people that hear me, listen!"

⁹Jesus' followers asked him, "What does this story mean?"

¹⁰Jesus said, "You have been chosen to know the secrets of the kingdom of God. But I use stories to speak to other people. I do this so that:

> 'They will look, but they will not see;
> and they will listen, but they will not understand.'
>
> *Isaiah 6:9*

Jesus Explains the Story About the Seeds

¹¹"This is what the story means: The seed is God's teaching. ¹²What is the seed that fell beside the path? That is like the people that hear God's teaching, but then the devil comes and takes the teaching away from their hearts. So those people cannot believe the teaching and be saved. ¹³What is the seed that fell on rock? That is like the people that hear God's teaching and accept it gladly. But these people don't have deep roots. They believe for a while. But then trouble comes. They stop believing and turn away from God. ¹⁴What is the seed that fell among the thorny weeds? That is like the people that hear God's teaching, but they let the worries, riches, and pleasures of this life stop them from growing. So they never make good fruit.* ¹⁵And what is the seed that fell on the good ground? That is like the people that hear God's teaching with a good, honest heart. They obey God's teaching and patiently make good fruit.

Use the Understanding You Have

¹⁶"No person lights a lamp and then covers it with a bowl or hides it under a bed. Instead, that person puts the lamp on a lamp table so that the people that come in will have enough light to see. ¹⁷Everything that is hidden will become clear. Every secret thing will be made known. ¹⁸So be careful how you listen. The person that has ₍some understanding₎ will receive more. But the person

---

apostles The men Jesus chose to be his special helpers.
Herod Herod Antipas, Tetrarch (ruler) of Galilee and Perea, son of Herod the Great.

make good fruit Do the things God wants his people to do.

that does not have ₁understanding₁ will lose even ₁the understanding₁ that he thinks he has."

Jesus' Followers Are His True Family

¹⁹Jesus' mother and brothers came to visit him. There were so many people that Jesus' mother and brothers could not get close to him. ²⁰Someone said to Jesus, "Your mother and your brothers are standing outside. They want to see you."

²¹Jesus answered them, "My mother and my brothers are those people that listen to God's teaching and obey it!"

The Followers See Jesus' Power

²²One day Jesus and his followers got into a boat. Jesus said to them, "Come with me across the lake." And so they started across. ²³While they were sailing, Jesus slept. A big storm blew down on the lake. The boat began to fill with water. They were in danger. ²⁴The followers went to Jesus and woke him. They said, "Master! Master! We will drown!"

Jesus got up. He gave a command to the wind and the waves. The wind stopped, and the lake became calm. ²⁵Jesus said to his followers, "Where is your faith?"

The followers were afraid and amazed. They said to each other, "What kind of man is this? He commands the wind and the water, and they obey him!"

A Man with Demons Inside Him

²⁶Jesus and his followers sailed across the lake from Galilee. They sailed to the area where the Gerasene people live. ²⁷When Jesus got out of the boat, a man from that town came to Jesus. This man had demons* inside him. For a long time he had worn no clothes. He lived in the caves where dead people are buried, not in a house. ²⁸⁻²⁹The demon had often seized him. The man had been put in jail, and his hands and feet had been tied with chains. But the man would always break the chains, and the demon inside him would force him to go out to the places where no people lived. Then Jesus commanded the evil spirit *(the demon)* to come out of this man. The man fell down before Jesus and shouted with a loud voice, "What do you want with me, Jesus, Son of the Most High God? Please, don't punish me!"

³⁰Jesus asked him, "What is your name?"

The man answered, "Legion."* (He said his name was "Legion" because many demons* had gone into him.) ³¹The demons begged Jesus not to send them into eternal darkness.* ³²On that hill there was a big herd of pigs eating. The demons begged Jesus to allow them to go into the pigs. So Jesus allowed the demons to do this. ³³Then the demons came out of the man and went into the pigs. The herd of pigs ran down the hill and into the lake. All the pigs drowned.

³⁴The men that were caring for the pigs ran away. The men told the story in the fields and in the town. ³⁵People went out to see what happened. The people came to Jesus and found the man sitting there at the feet of Jesus. The man had clothes on and his mind was right again; the demons* were gone. The people became afraid. ³⁶The men that saw these things happen told the other people all about how Jesus made the man well. ³⁷All the people asked Jesus to go away. The people were all very afraid. So Jesus got into the boat and went back to Galilee. ³⁸The man that Jesus healed begged to go with Jesus.

But Jesus sent the man away, saying, ³⁹"Go back home and tell people what God did for you."

So the man went all over town telling what Jesus had done for him.

Jesus Gives Life to a Dead Girl and Heals a Sick Woman

⁴⁰When Jesus went back to Galilee, the people welcomed him. Everyone was waiting for him. ⁴¹A man named Jairus came to Jesus. Jairus was a leader of the synagogue.* Jairus bowed down at the feet of Jesus and begged him to come to his house. ⁴²Jairus had only one daughter. She was twelve years old, and she was dying.

While Jesus was going ₁to Jairus' house₁, the people came all around him. ⁴³A woman was there who had been bleeding for twelve years. She had spent all her money on doctors, but no doctor was able to heal her. ⁴⁴The woman came behind Jesus and touched the bottom of his coat. At that moment, her bleeding stopped. ⁴⁵Then Jesus said, "Who touched me?"

Legion   The name Legion means very many. A legion was about 5,000 men in the Roman army.

eternal darkness   Literally, "the abyss," something like a pit or a hole that has no end.

synagogue(s)   Synagogues were places where Jews gathered for prayer, study of the Scriptures, and other public meetings.

demons   Demons are evil spirits from the devil.

All the people said they had not touched Jesus. Peter said, "Master, the people are all around you and are pushing against you."
⁴⁶But Jesus said, "Someone touched me! I felt power go out from me." ⁴⁷When the woman saw that she could not hide, she came forward, shaking. She bowed down before Jesus. While all the people listened, she told why she touched Jesus. Then she said that she was healed immediately when she touched him. ⁴⁸Jesus said to her, "My daughter, you are made well because you believed. Go in peace."

⁴⁹While Jesus was still speaking, a person came from the house of the synagogue* leader *(Jairus)* and said, "Your daughter has died! Don't bother the teacher *(Jesus)* now."
⁵⁰Jesus heard this. He said to Jairus, "Don't be afraid! Just believe and your daughter will be well."
⁵¹Jesus went to the house. Jesus let only Peter, John, James, and the girl's father and mother go inside with him. Jesus did not let any other person go inside. ⁵²All the people were crying and feeling sad because the girl was dead. But Jesus said, "Don't cry. She is not dead; she is only sleeping."
⁵³The people laughed at Jesus, because they knew that the girl was dead. ⁵⁴But Jesus held her hand and called to her, "Little girl, stand up!" ⁵⁵Her spirit came back into her and she stood up immediately. Jesus said, "Give her something to eat." ⁵⁶The girl's parents were amazed. Jesus told them not to tell any person about what happened.

Jesus Sends the Twelve Apostles

9 Jesus called the twelve apostles* together. He gave the apostles power to heal sicknesses and power over all demons.* ²Jesus sent the apostles to tell about God's kingdom and to heal the sick. ³He said to the apostles, "When you travel, don't take a walking stick. Also, don't carry a bag, food, or money. Take for your trip only the clothes you are wearing. ⁴When you go into a house, stay there until it is time to leave. ⁵If the people in the town will not welcome you, go outside the town and shake their dust off of your feet.* This will be a warning to them."

⁶So the apostles went out. They traveled through all the towns. They told the Good News* and healed people everywhere.

Herod Is Confused About Jesus

⁷Governor Herod* heard about all these things that were happening. He was confused because some people said, "John the Baptizer is risen from death." ⁸Other people said, "Elijah* has come to us." And some other people said, "One of the prophets* from long ago has risen from death." ⁹Herod said, "I cut off John's head. So who is this man I hear these things about?" Herod continued trying to see Jesus.

Jesus Feeds More than 5,000 People

¹⁰When the apostles* came back, they told Jesus the things they had done on their trip. Then Jesus took them away to a town called Bethsaida. There, Jesus and his apostles could be alone together. ¹¹But the people learned where Jesus went. They followed him. Jesus welcomed them and talked with them about God's kingdom. He healed the people that were sick.
¹²Late in the afternoon, the twelve apostles* came to Jesus and said, "No people live in this place. Send the people away. They need to find food and places to sleep in the farms and towns around here."
¹³But Jesus said to the apostles,* "You give them something to eat."
The apostles said, "We have only five loaves of bread and two fish. Do you want us to go buy food for all these people?" ⌊There are too many!⌋ ¹⁴(There were about 5,000 men there.)
Jesus said to his followers, "Tell the people to sit in groups of about 50 people."
¹⁵So the followers did this and all the people sat down. ¹⁶Then Jesus took the five loaves of bread and two fish. Jesus looked up into the sky and thanked God for the food. Then Jesus divided the food and gave it to the followers. Jesus told the followers to give the food to the people. ¹⁷All the people ate and were filled. And there was much food left. Twelve baskets were filled with the pieces of food that were not eaten.

---

synagogue(s) Synagogues were places where Jews gathered for prayer, study of the Scriptures, and other public meetings.
apostles The men Jesus chose to be his special helpers.
demons Demons are evil spirits from the devil.
shake their dust off of your feet A warning. It would show that they were finished talking to these people.

Good News The news that God has made a way for people to have their sins forgiven and live with God.
Herod Herod Antipas, tetrarch (ruler) of Galilee and Perea, son of Herod the Great.
Elijah A prophet that lived about 850 B.C.
prophets People who spoke for God. They often told things that would happen in the future.

Jesus Is the Christ

¹⁸One time Jesus was praying alone. His followers came together there. Jesus asked them, "Who do the people say I am?" ¹⁹The followers answered, "Some people say you are John, the Baptizer. Other people say you are Elijah.* And some people say you are one of the prophets* from long ago that has come back to life."

²⁰Then Jesus said to his followers, "And who do you say I am?"

Peter answered, "You are the Christ* from God."

²¹Jesus warned them not to tell anyone. Then Jesus said, ²²"The Son of Man* must suffer many things. He will be rejected by the older Jewish leaders, the leading priests, and teachers of the law. The Son of Man will be killed. But after three days he will be raised from death."

²³Jesus continued to say to all of them, "If any person wants to follow me, he must say 'No' to the things he wants. That person must accept the cross *(suffering)* that is given to him every day, and he must follow me. ²⁴The person that wants to save his life will lose it. And every person that gives his life for me will save it. ²⁵It is worth nothing for a person to have the whole world, if he himself is destroyed or lost. ²⁶If any person is ashamed of me and my teaching, then I* will be ashamed of that person. I will be ashamed of that person at the time I come with my glory and with the glory of the Father and the holy angels. ²⁷I tell you the truth. Some of you people standing here will see the kingdom of God before you die."

Moses, Elijah, and Jesus

²⁸About eight days after Jesus said these things, he took Peter, James, and John and went up on a mountain to pray. ²⁹While Jesus was praying, his face began to change. His clothes became shining white. ³⁰Then two men were talking with Jesus. The men were Moses and Elijah.* ³¹Moses and Elijah were shining bright too. They were talking with Jesus about his death that would happen in Jerusalem. ³²Peter and the others were asleep. But they woke up and saw the glory of Jesus. They also saw the two men that were standing with Jesus. ³³When Moses and Elijah were leaving, Peter said, "Master, it is good that we are here. We will put three tents here—one for you, one for Moses, and one for Elijah." (Peter did not know what he was saying.)

³⁴While Peter was saying these things, a cloud came all around them. Peter, James, and John became afraid when the cloud covered them. ³⁵A voice came from the cloud. The voice said, "This is my Son. He is the One I have chosen. Obey him."

³⁶When the voice finished, only Jesus was there. Peter, James, and John said nothing. At that time they told no person about what they had seen.

Jesus Heals a Boy That Has an Evil Spirit

³⁷The next day, Jesus, Peter, James, and John came down from the mountain. A large group of people met Jesus. ³⁸A man in the group shouted to Jesus, "Teacher, please come and look at my son. He is the only child I have. ³⁹An evil spirit ₍from the devil₎ comes into my son, and then he shouts. He loses control of himself and he foams from the mouth. The evil spirit continues to hurt him and almost never leaves him. ⁴⁰I begged your followers to make the evil spirit leave my son, but they could not do it."

⁴¹Jesus answered, "You people that live now have no faith. Your lives are all wrong. How long must I be with you and be patient with you?" Then Jesus said to the man, "Bring your son here."

⁴²While the boy was coming, the demon* threw the boy to the ground. The boy lost control of himself. But Jesus gave a strong command to the evil spirit. Then the boy was healed. And Jesus gave the boy back to his father. ⁴³All the people were amazed at the great power of God.

Jesus Talks About His Death

The people were still amazed about all the things Jesus did. Jesus said to his followers, ⁴⁴"Don't forget the things I will tell you now: The Son of Man* will be given into the control of some men." ⁴⁵But the followers did not

---

Elijah A prophet that lived about 850 B.C.
prophets People who spoke for God. They often told things that would happen in the future.
Christ The "anointed one" (Messiah) or chosen of God.
Son of Man Jesus. In Dan. 7:13-14 this is the name for the Messiah, the one God chose to save his people.
I Literally, "the Son of Man" (Jesus).
Moses and Elijah Two very important Jewish leaders during the time of the Old Testament.

demon(s) Demons are evil spirits from the devil.

understand what Jesus meant. The meaning was hidden from them so that they could not understand it. But the followers were afraid to ask Jesus about what he said.

The Most Important Person

⁴⁶Jesus' followers began to have an argument about which one of them was the greatest *(most important)*. ⁴⁷Jesus knew what they were thinking. So Jesus took a little child and stood the child beside him. ⁴⁸Then Jesus said to the followers, "If a person accepts a little child like this in my name, then that person accepts me. And when a person accepts me, that person accepts the One *(God)* that sent me. The person among you that is the most humble—that person is a great *(important)* person."

Any Person Not Against You Is for You

⁴⁹John answered, "Master, we saw a person using your name to force demons* out of people. We told him to stop because he does not belong to our group."

⁵⁰Jesus said to John, "Don't stop him. If a person is not against you, then he is for you."

A Samaritan Town

⁵¹The time was coming near when Jesus would leave and go back to heaven. He decided to go to Jerusalem. ⁵²Jesus sent some men ahead of him. The men went into a town in Samaria to make everything ready for Jesus. ⁵³But the people there would not welcome Jesus because he was going toward Jerusalem. ⁵⁴James and John, the followers of Jesus, saw this. They said, "Lord, do you want us to call fire down from heaven and destroy those people?"* ⁵⁵But Jesus turned and scolded them.* ⁵⁶Then Jesus and his followers went to another town.

Following Jesus

⁵⁷They were all traveling along the road. Someone said to Jesus, "I will follow you any place you go."

⁵⁸Jesus answered, "The foxes have holes to live in. The birds have nests to live in. But the Son of Man* has no place where he can rest his head."

⁵⁹Jesus said to another man, "Follow me!"

But the man said, "Lord, let me go and bury my father first."

⁶⁰But Jesus said to him, "Let the people that are dead bury their own dead! You must go and tell about the kingdom of God."

⁶¹Another man said, "I will follow you, Lord, but first let me go and say good-bye to my family."

⁶²Jesus said, "If any person begins to plow a field, but looks back, he is not prepared for the kingdom of God."

Jesus Sends the 72 Men

10 After this, the Lord *(Jesus)* chose 72* more men. Jesus sent the men out in groups of two. He sent them ahead of him into every town and place where he planned to go. ²Jesus said to them, "There are many, many people to harvest *(save)*. But there are only a few workers to help harvest them. God owns the harvest *(people)*. Pray to God that he will send more workers to help gather his harvest. ³You can go now. But listen! I am sending you, and you will be like sheep among wolves. ⁴Don't carry any money, a bag, or shoes. Don't stop to talk with people on the road. ⁵Before you go into a house, say, 'Peace be with this home.' ⁶If a peaceful man lives there, your blessing of peace will stay with him. If the man is not peaceful, then your blessing of peace will come back to you. ⁷Stay in the peaceful house. Eat and drink what the people there give you. A worker should be given his pay. Don't leave that house to stay in another house. ⁸If you go into a town and the people welcome you, eat the food they give you. ⁹Heal the sick people that live there. Then tell them, 'The kingdom of God is soon coming to you!' ¹⁰But if you go into a town, and the people don't welcome you, then go out into the streets of that town and say, ¹¹'Even the dirt *(dust)* from your town that sticks to our feet we wipe off against you. But remember that the kingdom of God is coming soon.' ¹²I tell you, on the judgment day it will be worse for the people of that town than for the people of Sodom.*"

---

demon(s) Demons are evil spirits from the devil.
Verse 54 Some Greek copies add: "... like Elijah did?"
Verse 55 Some Greek copies add: "And Jesus said, 'You don't know what kind of spirit you belong to. ⁵⁶The Son of Man did not come to destroy the souls of men but to save them.'"

Son of Man Jesus. In Dan. 7:13-14 this is the name for the Messiah, the one God chose to save his people.
72 Some Greek copies of Luke say 70.
Sodom A town where very bad people lived. God punished them by destroying their city.

Jesus Warns People That Don't Believe

¹³"It will be bad for you, Chorazin*! It will be bad for you, Bethsaida*! I did many miracles* in you. If those same miracles had happened in Tyre and Sidon,* then the people in those cities would have changed their lives and stopped sinning a long time ago. They would have worn sackcloth* and put ashes on themselves to show that they were sorry for their sins. ¹⁴But on the judgment day it will be worse for you than for Tyre and Sidon. ¹⁵And you, Capernaum,* will you be lifted up to heaven? No! You will be thrown down to the place of death!

¹⁶"When a person listens to you, that person is really listening to me. But when a person refuses to accept you, that person is really refusing to accept me. And when a person refuses to accept me, he is refusing to accept the One *(God)* that sent me."

Satan Falls

¹⁷When the 72* men came back from their trip, they were very happy. They said, "Lord, even the demons* obeyed us when we used your name!" ¹⁸Jesus said to the men, "I saw Satan *(the devil)* falling like lightning from the sky. ¹⁹Listen! I gave you power to walk on snakes and scorpions.* I gave you more power than the Enemy *(the devil)* has. Nothing will hurt you. ²⁰Yes, the spirits obey you. And be happy. Why? Not because you have this power, but be happy because your names are written in heaven."

Jesus Prays to the Father

²¹Then the Holy Spirit* made Jesus feel very happy. Jesus said, "I thank you, Father, Lord of heaven and earth. I praise you because you have hidden these things from the wise and smart people. But you have shown these things to people that are like little children. Yes, Father, you did this because this is what you really wanted to do. ²²My Father has given me all things. No person knows who the Son is—only the Father knows. And only the Son knows who the Father is. The only people that will know about the Father are those people the Son chooses to tell."

²³Then Jesus turned to his followers. They were there alone with him. Jesus said, "You are blessed to see the things you now see! ²⁴I tell you, many prophets* and kings wanted to see the things that you now see. But they did not see these things. And many prophets and kings wanted to hear the things that you now hear. But they did not hear these things."

Story About the Good Samaritan

²⁵Then a teacher of the law stood up. He was trying to test Jesus. He said, "Teacher, what must I do to get life forever?"

²⁶Jesus said to him, "What is written in the law? What do you read there?"

²⁷The man answered, "'You must love the Lord your God. You must love him with all your heart, all your soul, all your strength, and all your mind.'* Also, 'You must love other people the same as you love yourself.'*"

²⁸Jesus said to him, "Your answer is right. Do this and you will have life forever."

²⁹But the man wanted to show that the way he was living was right. So he said to Jesus, "But who are these other people I must love?"

³⁰To answer this question, Jesus said, "A man was going down the road from Jerusalem to Jericho. Some robbers surrounded him. They tore off his clothes and beat him. Then the robbers left the man lying there on the ground. He was almost dead. ³¹It happened that a Jewish priest was going down that road. When the priest saw the man, he did not stop to help him; he walked away. ³²Next, a Levite* came near. The Levite saw the hurt man, but he went around him. He would not stop to help him either; he just walked away. ³³Then a Samaritan* man traveled down that road. He came

---

Chorazin, Bethsaida Towns by Lake Galilee where Jesus preached to the people.
miracles Amazing works done by the power of God.
Tyre and Sidon Towns where very bad people lived.
sackcloth A rough cloth made from animal hair. People sometimes wore it to show sadness.
Capernaum Town in Galilee where Jesus preached.
72 Many Greek copies of Luke say 70.
demons Demons are evil spirits from the devil.
scorpions A scorpion is an insect with a poison sting.
Holy Spirit Called the Spirit of God, the Spirit of Christ, and the Comforter. Joined with God and Christ, he does God's work among people in the world.

prophets People who spoke for God. They often told things that would happen in the future.
'You must ... mind' Quote from Deut. 6:5.
'You must ... yourself' Quote from Lev. 19:18.
Levite Levites were men from the family group of Levi who helped the Jewish priests in the temple.
Samaritan From Samaria. Samaritans were part Jewish, but the Jews did not accept them. Jews hated Samaritans.

to the place where the hurt man was lying. The Samaritan saw the man. He felt very sorry for the hurt man. ³⁴The Samaritan went to him and poured olive oil and wine* on his wounds. Then he covered the man's wounds with cloth. The Samaritan had a donkey. He put the hurt man on his donkey, and he took him to an inn. At the inn, the Samaritan cared for him. ³⁵The next day, the Samaritan brought out two silver coins* and gave them to the man that worked at the inn. The Samaritan said, 'Take care of this hurt man. If you spend more money on him, I will pay it back to you when I come again.'"

³⁶Then Jesus said, "Which one of these three men *(the priest, the Levite, or the Samaritan)* do you think showed love to the man that was hurt by the robbers?"

³⁷The teacher of the law answered, "The one that helped him."

Jesus said to him, "Then you go and do the same [for other people]!"

Mary and Martha

³⁸While Jesus and his followers were traveling, Jesus went into a town. A woman named Martha let Jesus stay at her house. ³⁹Martha had a sister named Mary. Mary was sitting at Jesus' feet and listening to him teach. But her sister Martha was doing the housework. ⁴⁰Martha became angry because she had so much work to do. Martha went in and said, "Lord, don't you care that my sister has left me alone to do all the housework? Tell her to help me!"

⁴¹But the Lord answered her, "Martha, Martha, you are getting worried and upset about too many things. ⁴²Only one thing is important. Mary has made the right choice; and it will never be taken away from her."

Jesus Teaches About Prayer

11 One time Jesus was praying in a place. When Jesus finished praying, one of his followers said to him, "John taught his followers how to pray. Lord, teach us how to pray too."

²Jesus said to the followers, "When you pray, pray like this:

'Father, we pray that your name
  will always be kept holy.
We pray that your kingdom will come.
³ Give us the food we need for each day.
⁴ Forgive us the sins we have done,
  because we forgive every person
  that has done wrong to us.
And don't cause us to be tempted *(tested).*'"

Continue to Ask

⁵⁻⁶Then Jesus said to them, "Suppose one of you went to your friend's house very late at night and said to him, 'A friend of mine has come into town to visit me. But I have nothing for him to eat. Please give me three loaves of bread.' ⁷Your friend inside the house answers, 'Go away! Don't bother me! The door is already locked. My children and I are in bed. I cannot get up and give you the bread now.' ⁸I tell you, maybe friendship is not enough to make him get up to give you the bread. But he will surely get up to give you what you need if you continue to ask. ⁹So I tell you, continue to ask, and God will give to you. Continue to search, and you will find. Continue to knock, and the door will open for you. ¹⁰Yes, if a person continues asking, that person will receive. If a person continues looking, that person will find. And if a person continues knocking, the door will open for that person. ¹¹Does any of you have a son? What would you do if your son asked you for a fish? Would any father give his son a snake? No! You would give him a fish. ¹²Or, if your son asks for an egg, would you give him a scorpion*? No! ¹³[You are like all other people]—you are evil. But you know how to give good gifts to your children. So surely your heavenly Father knows how to give the Holy Spirit* to those people that ask him."

Jesus' Power Is from God

¹⁴One time Jesus was sending a demon* out of a man that could not talk. When the demon came out, the man was able to speak. The people were amazed. ¹⁵But some of the people said, "Jesus uses the power of Beelzebul *(the devil)* to force demons* out of people. Beelzebul is the ruler of demons."

---

olive oil and wine Oil and wine were used like medicine to soften and clean wounds.
silver coins One coin, a denarius, was the average pay for one day's work.
scorpion A scorpion is an insect that has a poison sting.
Holy Spirit Called the Spirit of God, the Spirit of Christ, and the Comforter. Joined with God and Christ, he does God's work among people in the world.
demon(s) Demons are evil spirits from the devil.

¹⁶Other people wanted to test Jesus. They asked Jesus to show them a sign *(proof)* from heaven. ¹⁷But Jesus knew the things they were thinking. So Jesus said to the people, "Every kingdom that is divided and fights against itself will be destroyed. And a family that fights against itself will break apart. ¹⁸So if Satan *(the devil)* is fighting against himself, then how will his kingdom continue? You say that I use the power of Beelzebul *(the devil)* to force out demons.* ¹⁹But if I use the power of Beelzebul to force out demons, then what power do your people use when they force out demons? So your own people prove that you are wrong. ²⁰But I use the power of God to force out demons. This shows that the kingdom of God has come to you! ²¹"When a strong man with many weapons guards his own house, then the things in his house are safe. ²²But suppose a stronger man comes and defeats him. The stronger man will take away the weapons that the first man trusted to keep his house safe. Then the stronger man will do what he wants with the other man's things.

²³"If a person is not with me, he is against me. The person that does not work with me is working against me.

The Empty Man

²⁴"When an evil spirit ⌊from the devil⌋ comes out of a person, that spirit travels through dry places, looking for a place to rest. But that spirit finds no place to rest. So the spirit says, 'I will go back to the home *(person)* I left.' ²⁵When the spirit comes back to that person, the spirit finds that home *(person)* swept clean and made neat. ²⁶Then the evil spirit goes out and brings seven other spirits more evil than itself. Then all the evil spirits go into that person and live there. And that person has even more trouble than he had before."

The People That Are Truly Happy

²⁷When Jesus said these things, a woman with the people there began to speak. She said to Jesus, "Your mother is blessed *(happy)*, because she gave birth to you and fed you."

²⁸But Jesus said, "The people that hear the teaching of God and obey it—they are the people that are truly happy!"

Give Us Proof!

²⁹The group of people grew larger and larger. Jesus said, "The people that live today are evil. They ask for a miracle* as a sign *(proof)* from God. But no miracle will be given as a sign to them. The only sign will be the miracle that happened to Jonah.* ³⁰Jonah was a sign for those people that lived in Nineveh. It is the same with the Son of Man.* The Son of Man will be a sign for the people of this time. ³¹On the judgment day the Queen of the South* will stand up with the men that live now, and she will show that they are wrong *(guilty)*. Why? Because that queen came from far, far away to listen to Solomon's wise teaching. And I tell you that I am greater than Solomon! ³²On the judgment day the men of Nineveh will stand up with the people that live now, and they will show that you are wrong *(guilty)*. Why? Because when Jonah preached to those people, they changed their hearts and lives. And I tell you that I am greater than Jonah!

Be a Light for the World

³³"No person takes a light and puts it under a bowl or hides it. Instead, a person puts the light on a lamp table so that the people that come in can see. ³⁴Your eye is a light for the body. If your eyes are good, then your whole body will be full of light. But if your eyes are bad, then your whole body will be full of darkness *(sin)*. ³⁵So be careful! Don't let the light in you become dark. ³⁶If your whole body is full of light, and none of it is dark, then it will be all bright. It will be like you have the light of a lamp shining on you."

Jesus Criticizes the Pharisees

³⁷After Jesus had finished speaking, a Pharisee* asked Jesus to eat with him. So Jesus came and sat at the table. ³⁸But the Pharisee was surprised when he saw that Jesus did not wash ⌊his hands⌋* first

---

demon(s) Demons are evil spirits from the devil.
miracle An amazing work done by the power of God.
Jonah A prophet in the Old Testament. After 3 days in a big fish he came out alive, like Jesus would come out from the tomb on the third day.
Son of Man Jesus. In Dan. 7:13-14 this is the name for the Messiah, the one God chose to save his people.
Queen of the South Queen of Sheba. She traveled 1000 miles to learn God's wisdom. Read 1 Kings 10:1-3.
Pharisee(s) The Pharisees were a Jewish religious group that claimed to follow carefully all Jewish laws and customs.
wash his hands Washing the hands was Jewish religious custom that the Pharisees thought was very important.

before the meal. ³⁹The Lord *(Jesus)* said to him, "You Pharisees* clean the outside of the cup and the dish. But inside you are full of things you got by cheating other people and being evil. ⁴⁰You are foolish! The same One *(God)* that made what is outside also made what is inside. ⁴¹So give the things in your cups and dishes to the people that need it. Then you will be fully clean. ⁴²But it will be bad for you Pharisees! You give God one-tenth of ₍everything you own₎—even your mint, your rue, and every other little plant in your garden. But you forget to be fair to other people and to love God. These are the things you should do. And you should also continue to do those other things—₍like giving₎ one-tenth. ⁴³It will be bad for you Pharisees, because you love to get the most important seats in the synagogues.* And you love for people to show respect to you in the market places. ⁴⁴It will be bad for you, because you are like hidden graves. People walk on them without knowing it."

Jesus Talks to the Jewish Teachers

⁴⁵One of the teachers of the law said to Jesus, "Teacher, when you say these things ₍about the Pharisees₎,* you are criticizing our group too."

⁴⁶Jesus answered, "It will be bad for you, teachers of the law! You make strict rules that are very hard for people to obey.* You try to force other people to obey those rules. But you yourselves don't even try to follow any of those rules. ⁴⁷It will be bad for you, because you build tombs* for the prophets.* But these are the same prophets that your fathers *(ancestors)* killed! ⁴⁸And now you show all people that you agree with what your fathers did. They killed the prophets, and you build tombs for the prophets! ⁴⁹This is why the Wisdom of God said, 'I will send prophets and apostles* to them. Some of my prophets and apostles will be killed by evil men. Others will be treated badly.' ⁵⁰So you people that live now will be punished for the deaths of all the prophets that were killed since the beginning of the world. ⁵¹You will be punished for the killing of Abel.* And you will be punished for the killing of Zechariah.* Zechariah was killed between the altar* and the temple.* Yes, I tell you that you people that live now will be punished for them all.

⁵²"It will be bad for you, you teachers of the law. You have hidden the key to learning about God. You yourselves would not learn, and you stopped others from learning, too."

⁵³When Jesus was leaving, the teachers of the law and the Pharisees* began to give him much trouble. They tried to make Jesus answer questions about many things. ⁵⁴They were trying to find a way to catch Jesus saying something wrong.

Don't Be Like the Pharisees

12 Many thousands of people came together. There were so many people that they were stepping on each other. Before Jesus spoke to the people, he said to his followers, "Be careful of the yeast *(bad influence)* of the Pharisees.* I mean that they are hypocrites.* ²Everything that is hidden will be shown. Everything that is secret will be made known. ³The things you say in the dark *(secretly)* will be told in the light *(openly)*. The things you whisper in a secret room will be shouted from the top of the house."

Fear Only God

⁴Then Jesus said to the people, "I tell you, my friends, don't be afraid of people. People can kill the body, but after that they can do nothing more to hurt you. ⁵I will show you the One to fear. You should fear him *(God)* who has the power to kill you and also to throw you into hell. Yes, he is the One you should fear.

⁶"When birds are sold, five small birds cost only two pennies. But God does not forget any of them. ⁷Yes, God even knows how many hairs you have on your head. Don't be afraid. You are worth much more than many birds.

Pharisee(s) The Pharisees were a Jewish religious group that claimed to follow carefully all Jewish laws and customs.

synagogue(s) Synagogues were places where Jews gathered for prayer, study of the Scriptures, and other public meetings.

You make ... obey Literally, "You put heavy burdens on people that are hard for them to carry."

tombs Small buildings made to show respect for important persons that had died.

prophets People who spoke for God. They often told things that would happen in the future.

prophets, apostles People chosen by God to tell his Good News to the world.

Abel, Zechariah In the Hebrew Old Testament, the first and last men to be murdered.

altar ... temple This altar was the place where sacrifices were offered to God outside the temple, the building in Jerusalem for Jewish worship.

hypocrites Bad people that act like they are good.

Don't Be Ashamed of Jesus

⁸"I tell you, if any person stands before other people and says that he believes in me, then I* will say that person belongs to me. I will say this before the angels of God. ⁹But if any person stands before people and says he does not believe in me, then I will say that person does not belong to me. I will say this before the angels of God. ¹⁰"If a person says something against the Son of Man,* he can be forgiven. But a person that says bad things against *(refuses to accept)* the Holy Spirit* will not be forgiven.

¹¹"When men bring you into the synagogues* before the leaders and other important men, don't worry about what you will say. ¹²At that time the Holy Spirit* will teach you what you must say."

Jesus Warns Against Selfishness

¹³One of the men in the crowd said to Jesus, "Teacher, ₍our father just died₎. Tell my brother to share with me the things our father owned."

¹⁴But Jesus said to him, "Who said that I should be your judge or decide how to divide your father's things between you two?" ¹⁵Then Jesus said to them, "Be careful and guard against all kinds of selfishness. A person does not get life from the many things he owns."

¹⁶Then Jesus used this story: "There was a rich man that had some land. His land grew a very good crop of food. ¹⁷The rich man thought to himself, 'What will I do? I have no place to keep all my crops.' ¹⁸Then the rich man said, 'I know what I will do. I will tear down my barns and build bigger barns! I will put all my wheat and good things together in my new barns. ¹⁹Then I can say to myself, I have many good things stored. I have saved enough for many years. Rest, eat, drink, and enjoy life!' ²⁰But God said to that man, 'Foolish man! Tonight you will die. So what about the things you prepared for yourself? Who will get those things now?'

²¹"This is how it will be for the person that saves things only for himself. To God that person is not rich."

I Literally, "the Son of Man" (Jesus).

Son of Man Jesus. In Dan. 7:13-14 this is the name for the Messiah, the one God chose to save his people.

Holy Spirit Called the Spirit of God, the Spirit of Christ, and the Comforter. Joined with God and Christ, he does God's work among people in the world.

synagogue(s) Synagogues were places where Jews gathered for prayer, study of the Scriptures, and other public meetings.

Putting God's Kingdom First

²²Jesus said to his followers, "So I tell you, don't worry about the food you need to live. Don't worry about the clothes you need for your body. ²³Life is more important than food. And the body is more important than clothes. ²⁴Look at the birds. They don't plant or harvest. Birds don't save food in houses or barns. But God takes care of them. And you are worth much more than birds. ²⁵None of you can add any time to your life by worrying about it. ²⁶If you cannot do the little things, then why worry about the big things? ²⁷Look at the wild flowers. See how they grow. They don't work or make clothes for themselves. But I tell you that even Solomon, the great and rich king, was not dressed as beautifully as one of these flowers. ²⁸God clothes the grass in the field like that. That grass is living today, but tomorrow it will be thrown into the fire to be burned. So you know that God will clothe you much more. Don't have so little faith! ²⁹So don't always think about what you will eat or what you will drink. Don't worry about it. ³⁰All the people in the world try to get those things. Your Father *(God)* knows that you need those things. ³¹The thing you should want is God's kingdom. Then all these other things you need will be given to you.

Don't Trust in Money

³²"Don't fear, little flock *(group)*. Your Father *(God)* wants to give you the kingdom. ³³Sell the things you have and give that money to people that need it. The riches of this world don't continue. So get the kind of riches that continue. Get the treasure of heaven. That treasure continues forever. Thieves can't steal your treasure in heaven, and moths can't destroy it. ³⁴Your heart will be where your treasure is.

Always Be Ready

³⁵"Be ready! Be fully dressed and have your lights shining. ³⁶Be like servants that are waiting for their master to come home from a wedding party. The master comes and knocks. The servants open the door for the master. ³⁷Those servants will be blessed when their master comes home, because he sees that his servants are ready and waiting for him. I tell you the truth. The master will dress himself for work and tell the servants to sit at the table. Then the master will serve them. ³⁸Those servants might have to wait until midnight or later for their master. But they will be happy when their master comes in and finds them

still waiting. ³⁹Remember this: If the owner of the house knew what time a thief was coming, then the owner would not allow the thief to enter his house. ⁴⁰So you also must be ready! The Son of Man* will come at a time when you don't expect him!"

Who Is the Trusted Servant?

⁴¹Peter said, "Lord, did you tell this story for us or for all people?"

⁴²The Lord said, "Who is the wise and trusted servant? The master trusts one servant to give the other servants their food at the right time. Who is the servant that the master trusts to do that work? ⁴³When the master comes and finds that servant doing the work he gave him, that servant will be very happy. ⁴⁴I tell you the truth. The master will choose that servant to take care of everything the master owns. ⁴⁵But what will happen if that servant is evil and thinks that his master will not come back soon? That servant will begin to beat the other servants, men and women. He will eat and drink and get drunk. ⁴⁶Then the master of that servant will come when that servant is not ready. It will be a time when that servant is not expecting the master. Then the master will punish that servant. The master will send him away to be with the other people that don't obey.

⁴⁷"That servant knew what his master wanted him to do. But that servant did not make himself ready or try to do what his master wanted. So that servant will be punished very much! ⁴⁸But what about the servant that does not know what his master wants? The servant does things that deserve punishment. But he will get less punishment than the servant that knew what he should do. Any person that has been given much will be responsible for much. Much more will be expected from the person that has been given more."

People Will Not Agree About Jesus

⁴⁹Jesus continued speaking: "I came to bring fire to the world. I wish it were already burning! ⁵⁰I must be baptized with a ₁different kind of₁ baptism.* I feel very troubled until it is finished. ⁵¹Do you think that I came to give peace to the world? No! I came to divide the world! ⁵²From now on, a family with five people will be divided, three against two, and two against three.

⁵³ A father and son will be divided:
The son will be against his father.
The father will be against his son.
A mother and her daughter will be divided:
The daughter will be against her mother.
The mother will be against her daughter.
A mother-in-law and her daughter-in-law will be divided:
The daughter-in-law will be against her mother-in-law.
The mother-in-law will be against her daughter-in-law."

Understanding the Times

⁵⁴Then Jesus said to the people, "When you see clouds growing bigger in the west, you say, 'A rainstorm is coming.' And soon it begins to rain. ⁵⁵When you feel the wind begin to blow from the south, you say, 'It will be a hot day.' And you are right. ⁵⁶Hypocrites*! You can understand the weather. Why don't you understand what is happening now?

Settle Your Problems

⁵⁷"Why can't you decide for yourselves what is right? ⁵⁸When a person is suing you, and you are going with him to court, try hard to settle it on the way. If you don't settle it, he may take you to the judge. The judge will throw you into jail. ⁵⁹You will not get out of there until you have paid every cent of what you owe."

Change Your Hearts

13 At that time some people were there with Jesus. These people told Jesus about what happened to some people from Galilee. Pilate* killed those people while they were worshiping. Pilate mixed their blood with the blood of the animals they were sacrificing* ₁to God₁. ²Jesus answered, "Do you think this happened to those people because they were more sinful than all other people from Galilee? ³No, they were not! But if all of you don't change your hearts and lives, then you will be destroyed like those people

---

Son of Man Jesus. In Dan. 7:13-14 this is the name for the Messiah, the one God chose to save his people.
baptized ... baptism These words have a special meaning here—being "baptized" or "buried" in troubles.

Hypocrites Bad people that act like they are good.
Pilate Pontius Pilate was the Roman governor of Judea from 26 A.D. to 36 A.D.
sacrificing Killing an animal as an offering to God.

were! ⁴What about those 18 people that died when the tower of Siloam fell on them? Do you think those people were more sinful than all the people that live in Jerusalem? ⁵They were not! But I tell you if you don't change your hearts and lives, then you will all be destroyed too!"

The Useless Tree

⁶Jesus told this story: "A man had a fig tree. He planted the tree in his garden. The man came looking for some fruit on the tree, but he found none. ⁷The man had a servant that took care of his garden. So the man said to his servant, 'I have been looking for fruit on this tree for three years, but I never find any. Cut it down! Why should it waste the ground?' ⁸But the servant answered, 'Master, let the tree have one more year to make fruit. Let me dig up the dirt around it and put on some plant food. ⁹Maybe the tree will make fruit next year. If the tree still does not make fruit, then you can cut it down.'"

Jesus Heals a Woman on the Sabbath Day

¹⁰Jesus taught in one of the synagogues* on the Sabbath day.* ¹¹In that synagogue there was a woman that had a spirit [from the devil] inside her. This spirit had made the woman crippled for 18 years. Her back was always bent; she could not stand up straight. ¹²When Jesus saw her, he called to her, "Woman, your sickness has gone away from you!" ¹³Jesus put his hands on her. Then she was able to stand up straight. She praised God.

¹⁴The synagogue* leader was angry because Jesus healed on the Sabbath day.* The leader said to the people, "There are six days for work. So come to be healed on one of those days. Don't come for healing on the Sabbath day."

¹⁵The Lord (Jesus) answered, "You people are hypocrites*! All of you untie your work animals and lead them to drink water every day—even on the Sabbath day*! ¹⁶This woman that I healed is our Jewish sister.* But Satan (the devil) has held her for 18 years. Surely it is not wrong for her to be made free from her sickness on a Sabbath day!" ¹⁷When Jesus said this, all the men that were criticizing him felt ashamed of themselves. And all the people were happy for the wonderful things Jesus was doing.

What Is God's Kingdom Like?

¹⁸Then Jesus said, "What is God's kingdom like? What can I compare it with? ¹⁹God's kingdom is like the seed of the mustard plant.* A person plants this seed in his garden. The seed grows and becomes a tree. The birds build nests on its branches."

²⁰Jesus said again, "What can I compare God's kingdom with? ²¹It is like yeast* that a woman mixes into a big bowl of flour to make bread. The yeast makes all the dough (bread) rise."

The Narrow Door

²²Jesus was teaching in every town and village. He continued to travel toward Jerusalem. ²³Someone said to Jesus, "Lord, how many people will be saved? Only a few?"

Jesus said, ²⁴"Try hard to enter through the narrow door [that opens the way to heaven]! Many people will try to enter there, but they will not be able to enter. ²⁵If a man locks the door of his house, then you can stand outside and knock on the door, but he won't open it. You can say, 'Sir, open the door for us!' But the man will answer, 'I don't know you! Where did you come from?' ²⁶Then you will say, 'We ate and drank with you. You taught in the streets of our town.' ²⁷Then he will say to you, 'I don't know you! Where did you come from? Go away from me! You are all people that do wrong!' ²⁸You will see Abraham, Isaac, Jacob,* and all the prophets* in God's kingdom. But you will be left outside. Then you will scream with fear and anger. ²⁹People will come from the east, west, north, and south. They will sit down at the table in the kingdom of God. ³⁰People that have the lowest place in life now will have the highest place in God's kingdom. And people that have the highest place now will have the lowest place in God's kingdom."

---

synagogue(s) Synagogues were places where Jews gathered for prayer, study of the Scriptures, and other public meetings.
Sabbath day The seventh day of the Jewish week. It was a special religious day for the Jews.
hypocrites Bad people that act like they are good.
Jewish sister Literally, "daughter of Abraham."

mustard plant A plant that grows taller than a man, but has a very, very small seed.
yeast Used here as a symbol of good influence.
Abraham, Isaac, Jacob Three of the most important Jewish leaders during the time of the Old Testament.
prophets People who spoke for God.

Jesus Will Die in Jerusalem

³¹At that time some Pharisees* came to Jesus and said, "Go away from here and hide! Herod* wants to kill you!"

³²Jesus said to them, "Go tell that fox* (Herod), 'Today and tomorrow I am forcing demons* out of people and finishing my work of healing. Then, the next day, the work will be finished.' ³³After that, I must go, because all prophets* should die in Jerusalem.

³⁴"O Jerusalem, Jerusalem! You kill the prophets.* You kill with rocks those men that God has sent you. Many, many times I wanted to help your people. I wanted to gather your people together like a hen gathers her chicks under her wings. But you did not let me. ³⁵Now your home will be left completely empty. I tell you, you will not see me again until that time when you will say, 'Welcome! God bless the One that comes in the name of the Lord *(God).*'*"

Is It Right to Heal on the Sabbath Day?

14 On a Sabbath day,* Jesus went to the home of a leading Pharisee* to eat with him. The people there were all watching Jesus very closely. ²A man with a bad disease* was put before Jesus. ³Jesus said to the Pharisees and teachers of the law, "Is it right or wrong to heal on the Sabbath day?" ⁴But they would not answer his question. So Jesus took the man and healed him. Then Jesus sent the man away. ⁵Jesus said to the Pharisees* and teachers of the law, "If your son or work animal falls into a well on the Sabbath day, you know you would pull him out quickly." ⁶The Pharisees and teachers of the law could say nothing against what Jesus said.

Pharisee(s) The Pharisees were a Jewish religious group that claimed to follow carefully all Jewish laws and customs.
Herod Herod Antipas, Tetrarch (ruler) of Galilee and Perea, son of Herod the Great.
fox Jesus means Herod is clever and sly like a fox.
demons Demons are evil spirits from the devil.
prophets People who spoke for God.
'Welcome! ... Lord' Quote from Ps. 118:26.
Sabbath day The seventh day of the Jewish week. It was a special religious day for the Jews.
disease The man had dropsy, a sickness that causes the body to swell larger and larger.

Don't Make Yourself Important

⁷Then Jesus noticed that some of the guests were choosing the best places to sit. So Jesus told this story: ⁸"When a person invites you to a wedding, don't sit in the most important seat. The person may have invited someone more important than you. ⁹And if you are sitting in the most important seat, then the person that invited you will come to you and say, 'Give this man your seat!' Then you will begin to move down to the last place. And you will be very embarrassed. ¹⁰So when a person invites you, go sit in the seat that is not important. Then the person that invited you will come to you and say, 'Friend, move up here to a more important seat!' Then all the other guests will respect you. ¹¹Every person that makes himself important will be made humble. But the person that makes himself humble will be made important."

You Will Be Rewarded

¹²Then Jesus said to the Pharisee* that had invited him, "When you give a lunch or a dinner, don't invite only your friends, brothers, relatives, and rich neighbors. At another time they will invite you to eat with them. Then you will have your reward. ¹³Instead, when you give a feast, invite the poor people, the crippled, and the blind. ¹⁴Then you will be blessed, because these people cannot pay you back. They have nothing. But you will be rewarded at the time when good people rise from death."

Story About a Big Dinner Party

¹⁵One of the men sitting at the table with Jesus heard these things. The man said to Jesus, "The people that eat a meal in God's kingdom will be very happy!"

¹⁶Jesus said to him, "A man gave a big dinner. The man invited many people. ¹⁷When it was time to eat, the man sent his servant to tell the guests, 'Come! The food is ready!' ¹⁸But all the guests said they could not come. Each man made an excuse. The first man said, 'I have just bought a field, so I must go look at it. Please excuse me.' ¹⁹Another man said, 'I have just bought five pairs of work animals; I must go and try them. Please excuse me.' ²⁰A third man said, 'I just got married; I can't come.' ²¹So the servant returned. He told his master what had happened. Then the master became angry and said, 'Hurry! Go into the streets and alleys of the town. Bring me the poor people, the crippled, the blind, and the lame.'

²²Later the servant said to him, 'Master, I did what you told me to do, but we still have places for more people.' ²³The master said to the servant, 'Go out to the highways and country roads. Tell the people there to come. I want my house to be full! ²⁴None of those people that I invited first will ever eat with me!'"

You Must First Plan

²⁵Many people were traveling with Jesus. Jesus said to the people, ²⁶"If a person comes to me, but loves his father, mother, wife, children, brothers, or sisters more than he loves me, then that person cannot be my follower. A person must love me more than he loves himself! ²⁷If a person will not carry the cross *(suffering)* that is given to him when he follows me, then that person cannot be my follower. ²⁸If you wanted to build a building, you would first sit down and decide how much it would cost. You must see if you have enough money to finish the job. ²⁹If you don't do that, you might begin the work, but you would not be able to finish. And if you could not finish it, then all the people watching would laugh at you. ³⁰They would say, 'This man began to build, but was not able to finish!'

³¹"If a king is going to fight against another king, first he will sit down and plan. If the king has only 10,000 men, he will plan to see if he is able to defeat the other king that has 20,000 men. ³²If he cannot defeat the other king, then he will send some men to speak to the other king and ask for peace. ³³In the same way, all of you ⌊must first plan⌋. You must leave everything you have to follow me. If you don't, you cannot be my follower!

Don't Lose Your Influence

³⁴"Salt is a good thing. But if the salt loses its salty taste, then it is worth nothing. You cannot make it salty again. ³⁵You can't even use it for soil or for plant food. People throw it away.

"You people that hear me, listen!"

Joy in Heaven

15 Many tax collectors* and bad people came to listen to Jesus. ²Then the Pharisees* and the teachers of the law began to complain, "Look! This man *(Jesus)* welcomes bad people and even eats with them!"

³Then Jesus told them this story: ⁴"Suppose one of you has 100 sheep, but he loses one of them. Then he will leave the other 99 sheep alone and go out and look for the lost sheep. The man will continue to search for the lost sheep until he finds it. ⁵And when he finds the sheep, the man is very happy. The man carries the sheep ⁶to his home. He goes to his friends and neighbors and says to them, 'Be happy with me because I found my lost sheep!' ⁷In the same way, I tell you, there is much joy in heaven when one sinner changes his heart. There is more joy for that one sinner than there is for 99 good people that don't need to change their hearts.

⁸"Suppose a woman has ten silver coins,* but she loses one of them. The woman will take a light and clean the house. She will look carefully for the coin until she finds it. ⁹And when she finds the lost coin, she will call her friends and neighbors and say to them, 'Be happy with me because I have found the coin that I lost!' ¹⁰In the same way, there is joy before the angels of God when one sinner changes his heart."

The Son That Left Home

¹¹Then Jesus said, "A man had two sons. ¹²The younger son said to his father, 'Give me my part of all the things we own!' So the father divided the wealth with his two sons. ¹³Then the younger son gathered up all that he had and left. He traveled far away to another country. There the son wasted his money like a fool. ¹⁴He spent everything that he had. Soon after that, the land became very dry, and there was no rain. There was not enough food to eat anywhere in that country. The son was hungry and needed money. ¹⁵So he went and got a job with one of the people of that country. The man sent the son into the fields to feed pigs. ¹⁶The son was so hungry that he wanted to eat the food that the pigs were eating. But no person gave him anything. ¹⁷The boy realized that he had been very foolish. He thought, 'All of my father's servants have plenty of food. But I am here, almost dead because I have nothing to eat. ¹⁸I will leave and go to my father. I will say to him: Father, I sinned against God and have done wrong to you. ¹⁹I am not good enough to be called your son. But let me be like

---

tax collectors Jews hired by the Romans to collect taxes. They often cheated, and the other Jews hated them.

Pharisee(s) The Pharisees were a Jewish religious group that claimed to follow carefully all Jewish laws and customs.

silver coins One coin, a denarius, was the average pay for one day's work.

one of your servants.' ²⁰So the son left and went to his father.

The Son Returns

"While the son was still a long way off, his father saw him coming. The father felt sorry for his son. So the father ran to him. He hugged and kissed his son. ²¹The son said, 'Father, I sinned against God and have done wrong to you. I am not good enough to be called your son.' ²²But the father said to his servants, 'Hurry! Bring the best clothes and dress him. Also, put a ring on his finger and good shoes on his feet. ²³Bring our fat calf. We will kill it and have plenty to eat. Then we can have a party! ²⁴My son was dead, but now he is alive again! He was lost, but now he is found!' So they began to have a party.

The Older Son Comes

²⁵"The older son was in the field. He came closer to the house. He heard the sound of music and dancing. ²⁶So the older son called to one of the servant boys and asked, 'What does all this mean?' ²⁷The servant said, 'Your brother has come back. Your father killed the fat calf to eat. Your father is happy because your brother came home safely!' ²⁸The older son was angry and would not go in to the party. So his father went out to ask him to come in. ²⁹The son said to his father, 'I have served you like a slave for many years! I have always obeyed your commands. But you never even killed a goat for me. You never gave a party for me and my friends. ³⁰But your other son has wasted all your money on prostitutes.* Then he comes home, and you kill the fat calf for him!' ³¹But the father said to him, 'Son, you are always with me. All that I have is yours too. ³²We must be happy and have a party; because your brother was dead, but now he is alive. He was lost, but now he is found.'"

True Wealth

16 Jesus said to his followers, "Once there was a rich man. This rich man hired a manager to take care of his business. Later, the rich man learned that his manager was cheating him. ²So he called the manager in and said to him, 'I have heard bad things about you. Give me a report of what you have done with my money. You can't be my manager now!' ³Later, the manager thought to himself, 'What will I do? My master is taking my job away from me! I am not strong enough to dig ditches. I am too proud to beg. ⁴I know what I will do! I will do something so that when I lose my job, other people will welcome me into their homes.' ⁵So the manager called in each person that owed the master some money. He said to the first man, 'How much do you owe my master?' ⁶The man answered, 'I owe him 8,000 pounds of olive oil.' The manager said to him, 'Here is your bill; sit down quickly and make the bill less. Write 4,000 pounds.' ⁷Then the manager said to another man, 'How much do you owe my master?' The man answered, 'I owe him 60,000 pounds of wheat.' Then the manager said to him, 'Here is your bill; you can make it less. Write 50,000 pounds.' ⁸Later, the master told the dishonest manager that he had done a smart thing. Yes, worldly people are smarter ₍in their business₎ with the people of their time than spiritual people are.

⁹"I tell you, use the things you have here in this world to make friends ₍with God₎. Then, when those things are gone, you will be welcomed in that home that continues forever. ¹⁰If a person can be trusted with small things, then he can also be trusted with big things. If a person is dishonest in little things, then he will be dishonest in big things too. ¹¹If you cannot be trusted with worldly riches, then you will not be trusted with the true *(heavenly)* riches. ¹²And if you cannot be trusted with the things that belong to someone else, then you will not be given things of your own.

¹³"No servant can serve two masters at the same time. The servant will hate one master and love the other. Or he will be loyal to one and not care about the other. You cannot serve God and money at the same time."

God's Law Cannot Be Changed

¹⁴The Pharisees* were listening to all these things. The Pharisees criticized Jesus because they all loved money. ¹⁵Jesus said to the Pharisees, "You make yourselves look good in front of people. But God knows what is really in your hearts. The things that people think are important are worth nothing to God.

¹⁶"God wanted the people to live by the law ₍of Moses₎ and the writings of the prophets.* But since the time John ₍the Baptizer₎ came, the Good News about the kingdom of God is being told.

---

prostitutes Women that are paid by men for sexual sin.

Pharisee(s) The Pharisees were a Jewish religious group that claimed to follow carefully all Jewish laws and customs.
prophets People who spoke for God. Their writings are part of the Old Testament.

Many people are trying hard to get into the kingdom of God. ¹⁷Even the smallest part of a letter in the law cannot be changed. It would be easier for heaven and earth to pass away.

Divorce and Remarriage

¹⁸"If a man divorces his wife and marries another woman, he is guilty of the sin of adultery.* And the man that marries a divorced woman is also guilty of adultery."

The Rich Man and Lazarus

¹⁹Jesus said, "There was a rich man that always dressed in the finest clothes. He was so rich that he was able to feast and have a party every day. ²⁰There was also a very poor man named Lazarus. Lazarus' body was covered with sores. Lazarus was often put at the rich man's gate. ²¹Lazarus wanted only to eat the small pieces of food left from the rich man's table. And the dogs came and licked his sores! ²²Later, Lazarus died. The angels took Lazarus and placed him in the arms of Abraham.* The rich man also died and was buried. ²³He was sent to the place of death* and had much pain. The rich man saw Abraham far away with Lazarus in his arms. ²⁴He called, 'Father Abraham, have mercy on me! Send Lazarus to me so that he can dip his finger in water and cool my tongue. I am suffering in this fire!' ²⁵But Abraham said, 'My child, remember when you lived? You had all the good things in life. But all the bad things happened to Lazarus. Now he is comforted here, and you are suffering. ²⁶Also, there is a big pit *(hole)* between you and us. No person can cross over to help you. And no person can leave there and come here.' ²⁷The rich man said, 'Then please send Lazarus to my father's house on earth! ²⁸I have five brothers. Lazarus could warn my brothers so that they will not come to this place of pain.' ²⁹But Abraham said, 'They have the law of Moses and the writings of the prophets* to read; let them learn from that!' ³⁰But the rich man said, 'No, father Abraham! If someone came to them from the dead, they would believe and change their hearts and lives.' ³¹But Abraham said to him, 'No! If your brothers won't listen to Moses and the prophets, then they won't listen to someone that comes back from death.'"

17 Jesus said to his followers, "Things will surely happen that will make people sin. But it will be very bad for the person that makes this happen. ²It will be very bad for a person if he makes one of these weak persons sin. It would be better for him to have a millstone* tied around his neck and be drowned in the sea. ³So be careful!

"If your brother sins, tell him he is wrong. But if he is sorry ₍and stops sinning₎, forgive him. ⁴If your brother does something wrong to you seven times in one day, but he says that he is sorry each time, then you should forgive him."

How Big Is Your Faith?

⁵The apostles* said to the Lord *(Jesus)*, "Give us more faith!"

⁶The Lord said, "If your faith is as big as a mustard seed,* then you can say to this mulberry tree, 'Dig yourself up and plant yourself in the ocean!' And the tree will obey you.

Be Good Servants

⁷"Suppose one of you has a servant that has been working in the field. The servant has been plowing the ground or caring for the sheep. When he comes in from work, what would you say to him? Would you say, 'Come in and sit down to eat'? ⁸No! You would say to your servant, 'Prepare something for me to eat. Then get dressed and serve me. When I finish eating and drinking, then you can eat.' ⁹The servant should not get any special thanks for doing his job. He is only doing what his master told him to do. ¹⁰It is the same with you. When you do all the things you are told to do, you should say, 'We are not worthy of any special thanks. We have only done the work we should do.'"

Be Thankful

¹¹Jesus was traveling to Jerusalem. He went from Galilee to Samaria. ¹²He came into a small town. Ten men met him there. These men did not come close to Jesus, because they all had leprosy.* ¹³But the men yelled to Jesus, "Jesus! Master! Please help us!"

---

adultery Breaking a marriage promise by sexual sin.
Abraham Most respected ancestor of the Jews.
place of death Literally, "Hades."
prophets People who spoke for God. Their writings are part of the Old Testament.

millstone A large, round stone used for grinding grain.
apostles The men Jesus chose to be his special helpers.
mustard seed The very small seed of the mustard plant.
leprosy A very bad skin disease.

¹⁴When Jesus saw the men, he said, "Go and show yourselves to the priests.*"

While the ten men were going to the priests, they were healed. ¹⁵When one of the men saw that he was healed, he went back to Jesus. He thanked God with a loud voice. ¹⁶He bowed down at Jesus' feet. The man thanked Jesus. (This man was a Samaritan,* ₍not a Jew₎.) ¹⁷Jesus answered, "Ten men were healed; where are the other nine? ¹⁸Is this Samaritan man the only one that came back to thank God?" ¹⁹Then Jesus said to him, "Stand up! You can go. You were healed because you believed."

God's Kingdom Is Inside You

²⁰Some of the Pharisees* asked Jesus, "When will the kingdom of God come?"

Jesus answered, "God's kingdom is coming, but not in a way that you will be able to see with your eyes. ²¹People will not say, 'Look, God's kingdom is here!' Or, 'There it is!' No, God's kingdom is inside you."

²²Then Jesus said to his followers, "The time will come when you will want very much to see one of the days of the Son of Man,* but you will not be able. ²³People will say to you, 'Look, there it is!' or, 'Look, here it is!' Stay where you are; don't go away and search.

When Jesus Comes Again

²⁴"₍You will know it₎ when the Son of Man* comes again. On the day when he comes he will shine like lightning flashes across the sky. ²⁵But first, the Son of Man must suffer many things and be killed by the people of this time. ²⁶It will be the same when the Son of Man comes again as it was when Noah lived. ²⁷In the time of Noah, people were eating, drinking, and getting married even on the day when Noah entered the boat. Then the flood came and killed all the people. ²⁸It will be the same as during the time of Lot when God destroyed Sodom.* Those people were eating, drinking, buying, selling, planting, and building houses for themselves. ²⁹The people were doing these things even on the day when Lot left town. Then fire rained down from the sky and killed them all. ³⁰This is exactly how it will be when the Son of Man* comes again.

³¹"On that day, if a man is on his roof, he will not have time to go inside and get his things. If a man is in the field, he cannot go back home. ³²Remember what happened to Lot's wife*? ³³The person that tries to save his life will lose it. But the person that gives his life away will save it. ³⁴At the time when I come again, there may be two people sleeping in one room. One person will be taken and the other person will be left. ³⁵There may be two women working together. One woman will be taken and the other woman will be left." ³⁶*

³⁷The followers asked Jesus, "Where will this be, Lord?"

Jesus answered, "People can always find a dead body by looking for the vultures.*"

God Will Answer His People

18 Then Jesus taught the followers that they should always pray and never lose hope. Jesus used this story to teach them: ²"Once there was a judge in a town. He did not care about God. The judge also did not care what people thought about him. ³In that same town there was a woman. Her husband was dead. The woman came many times to this judge and said, 'There is a man that is doing bad things to me. Give me my rights!' ⁴But the judge did not want to help the woman. After a long time, the judge thought to himself, 'I don't care about God. And I don't care about what people think. ⁵But this woman is bothering me. If I give her what she wants, then she will leave me alone. But if I don't give her what she wants, she will bother me until I am sick!'"

⁶The Lord *(Jesus)* said, "Listen! ₍There is meaning₎ in what the bad judge said. ⁷God's people shout to him night and day. God will always give his people what is right. God will not be slow to answer his people. ⁸I tell you, God will help his people quickly! But when the Son of Man* comes again, will he find people on earth who believe in him?"

---

show yourselves to the priests The law of Moses said a priest must decide when a Jew with leprosy was well.

Samaritan A person from Samaria. Samaritans were part Jewish, but the Jews did not accept them as pure Jews.

Pharisees The Pharisees were a Jewish religious group that claimed to follow carefully all Jewish laws and customs.

Son of Man Jesus. In Dan. 7:13-14 this is the name for the Messiah, the one God chose to save his people.

Sodom A town where very bad people lived. God punished the people by destroying their city.

Lot's wife The story about what happened to Lot's wife is found in Gen. 19:15-17, 26.

Verse 36 A few Greek copies of Luke add verse 36: "Two men will be in the same field. One man will be taken, but the other man will be left behind."

vultures Or, "eagles"—birds that eat dead animals.

Being Right with God

⁹There were some people that thought that they were very good. These people acted like they were better than other people. Jesus used this story to teach them: ¹⁰"One time there was a Pharisee* and a tax collector.* One day they both went to the temple* to pray. ¹¹The Pharisee stood alone, away from the tax collector. When the Pharisee prayed, he said, 'O God, I thank you that I am not as bad as other people. I am not like men that steal, cheat, or do the sin of adultery.* I thank you that I am better than this tax collector. ¹²⌐I am good⌐; I fast* twice a week, and I give one-tenth of everything I earn!'

¹³"The tax collector* stood alone too. But when he prayed, he would not even look up to heaven. The tax collector felt very humble before God. He said, 'O God, have mercy on me. I am a sinner!' ¹⁴I tell you, when this man finished his prayer and went home, he was right with God. But the Pharisee,* who felt that he was better than other people, was not right with God. Every person that makes himself important will be made humble. But the person that makes himself humble will be made important."

Who Will Enter God's Kingdom?

¹⁵Some people brought their small children to Jesus so that Jesus could touch them. But when the followers saw this, they told the people not to do this. ¹⁶But Jesus called the little children to him and said to his followers, "Let the little children come to me. Don't stop them, because the kingdom of God belongs to people that are like these little children. ¹⁷I tell you the truth. You must accept God's kingdom like a little child accepts things, or you will never enter it!"

A Rich Man Asks Jesus a Question

¹⁸A ⌐Jewish⌐ leader asked Jesus, "Good teacher, what must I do to get the life that continues forever?"

¹⁹Jesus said to him, "Why do you call me good? Only God is good. ²⁰⌐But I will answer your question⌐. You know ⌐God's⌐ commands: 'You must not do the sin of adultery,* you must not murder anyone, you must not steal anything, you must not tell lies about other people, you must honor *(respect)* your father and mother....'*"

²¹But the leader said, "I have obeyed all these commands since I was a boy!"

²²When Jesus heard this, he said to the leader, "But there is still one more thing you need to do. Sell everything you have and give the money to the poor people. You will have a reward in heaven. Then come and follow me!" ²³But when the man heard this, he was very sad. The man was very rich ⌐and wanted to keep his money.⌐

²⁴When Jesus saw that the man was sad, he said, "It will be very hard for rich people to enter the kingdom of God! ²⁵It would be easier for a camel to go through the eye of a needle than for a rich person to enter the kingdom of God!"

Who Can Be Saved?

²⁶When the people heard this, they said, "Then who can be saved?"

²⁷Jesus answered, "God can do things that are not possible for people to do!"

²⁸Peter said, "Look, we left everything we had and followed you!"

²⁹Jesus said, "I tell you the truth. Every person that has left his home, wife, brothers, parents, or children for God's kingdom ³⁰will get much more than he left. That person will get many times more in this life. And after that person dies, he will live with God forever."

Jesus Will Rise from Death

³¹Then Jesus talked to the twelve apostles* alone. Jesus said to them, "Listen! We are going to Jerusalem. Everything that God told the prophets* to write about the Son of Man* will happen! ³²His people will turn against him and give him to the non-Jewish people.* They will laugh at him and spit on him. He will be insulted and embarrassed. ³³They will beat him with whips and then kill him! But on the third day after his death, he will rise to life again." ³⁴The apostles tried to understand this, but they could not; the meaning was hidden from them.

'You must not ... mother' Quote from Ex. 20:12-16; Deut. 5:16-20.
apostles The men Jesus chose to be his special helpers.
prophets People who spoke for God. They often told things that would happen in the future.
Son of Man Jesus. In Dan. 7:13-14 this is the name for the Messiah, the one God chose to save his people.
non-Jewish people Literally, "nations" (Gentiles).

Pharisee(s) The Pharisees were a Jewish religious group that claimed to follow carefully all Jewish laws and customs.
tax collector A Jew hired by the Romans to collect taxes. Tax collectors often cheated, and the other Jews hated them.
temple The special building in Jerusalem for Jewish worship.
adultery Breaking a marriage promise by sexual sin.
fast To live without food for a special time of prayer.

Jesus Heals a Blind Man

³⁵Jesus came near the city of Jericho. There was a blind man sitting beside the road. The blind man was begging people for money. ³⁶When this man heard the people coming down the road, he asked, "What is happening?" ³⁷The people told him, "Jesus, the one from Nazareth, is coming here." ³⁸The blind man was excited and said, "Jesus, Son of David*! Please help me!" ³⁹The people that were in front, leading the group, criticized the blind man. They told him not to speak. But the blind man shouted more and more, "Son of David, please help me!" ⁴⁰Jesus stopped there and said, "Bring that blind man to me!" When the blind man came near, Jesus asked him, ⁴¹"What do you want me to do for you?"

The blind man said, "Lord, I want to see again."

⁴²Jesus said to him, "See! You are healed because you believed."

⁴³Then the man was able to see. The man followed Jesus, thanking God. All the people that saw this praised God for what happened.

Zacchaeus

19 Jesus was going through the city of Jericho. ²In Jericho there was a man named Zacchaeus. He was a wealthy, very important tax collector.* ³He wanted to see who Jesus was. There were many other people that wanted to see Jesus too. Zacchaeus was too short to see above the people. ⁴So he ran to a place where he knew Jesus would come. Then Zacchaeus climbed a sycamore tree so he could see Jesus. ⁵When Jesus came to that place, Jesus looked up and saw Zacchaeus in the tree. Jesus said to him, "Zacchaeus, hurry! Come down! I must stay at your house today."

⁶Then Zacchaeus came down quickly. He was happy to have Jesus in his house. ⁷All the people saw this. They began to complain, "Look at the kind of man Jesus stays with. Zacchaeus is a sinner!"

⁸Zacchaeus said to the Lord (Jesus), "I want to do good. I will give half of my money to the poor. If I have cheated any person, I will pay that person back four times more!"

⁹Jesus said, "This man ⌊is a good man—he⌋ truly belongs to the family of Abraham. So today, Zacchaeus has been saved ⌊from his sins⌋! ¹⁰The Son of Man* came to find lost people and save them."

Use the Things God Gives You

¹¹Jesus traveled closer to Jerusalem. Some of the people thought that God's kingdom would come soon. ¹²Jesus knew the people thought this, so he told them this story: "A very important man was preparing to go to a country far away to be made a king. Then the man planned to return home and rule his people. ¹³So he called ten of his servants together. He gave a bag of money* to each servant. The man said, 'Do business with this money until I come back.' ¹⁴But the people in the kingdom hated the man. So the people sent a group to follow the man to the other country. In the other country, this group said, 'We don't want that man to be our king!'

¹⁵"But the man became king. When he came home, he said, 'Call those servants that have my money. I want to know how much more money they earned with it.' ¹⁶The first servant came and said, 'Sir, I earned ten bags of money* with the one bag you gave me!' ¹⁷The king said to the servant, 'Fine! You are a good servant. I see that I can trust you with small things. So now I will let you rule over ten of my cities!' ¹⁸The second servant said, 'Sir, with your one bag of money I earned five bags!' ¹⁹The king said to this servant, 'You can rule over five cities!' ²⁰Then another servant came in. The servant said to the king, 'Sir, here is your bag of money. I wrapped it in a piece of cloth and hid it. ²¹I was afraid of you because you are powerful. I know you are a hard man. You even take money that you didn't earn and gather food that you didn't grow!' ²²Then the king said to the servant, 'You bad servant! I will use your own words to condemn you. You said that I am a hard man. You said that I even take money that I didn't earn and gather food that I didn't grow. ²³If that is true, you should have put my money in the bank. Then, when I came back, my money would have earned some interest.' ²⁴Then the king said to the men that were watching, 'Take the bag of

---

Son of David Name for the Christ, who was from the family of David, king of Israel.

tax collector A Jew hired by the Romans to collect taxes. Tax collectors often cheated, and the other Jews hated them.

Son of Man Jesus. In Dan. 7:13-14 this is the name for the Messiah, the one God chose to save his people.

bag(s) of money One bag of money was a Greek "mina," enough to pay a person for working three months.

money away from this servant and give it to the servant that earned ten bags of money.' ²⁵The men said to the king, 'But sir, that servant already has ten bags of money!' ²⁶The king said, 'The person that uses what he has will get more. But the person that does not use what he has will have everything taken away from him. ²⁷Now where are my enemies? Where are the people that did not want me to be king? Bring my enemies here and kill them. I will watch them die!'"

Jesus Enters Jerusalem

²⁸After Jesus said these things, he continued traveling toward Jerusalem. ²⁹Jesus came near Bethphage and Bethany, towns near the hill called the Mount of Olives.* Jesus sent out two of his followers. ³⁰He said, "Go into the town you can see there. When you enter the town, you will find a young donkey tied there. No person has ever ridden this donkey. Untie the donkey, and bring it here to me. ³¹If any person asks you why you are taking the donkey, you should say, 'The Master needs this donkey.'"

³²The two followers went into town. They found the donkey exactly like Jesus told them. ³³The followers untied the donkey. But the owners of the donkey came out. They said to the followers, "Why are you untying our donkey?"

³⁴The followers answered, "The Master needs it." ³⁵So the followers brought the donkey to Jesus. The followers put their coats on the donkey's back. Then they put Jesus on the donkey. ³⁶Jesus rode along the road toward Jerusalem. The followers spread their coats on the road before Jesus.

³⁷Jesus was coming close to Jerusalem. He was already near the bottom of the Mount of Olives.* The whole group of followers were happy. They were very excited and praised God. They thanked God for all the powerful things they had seen. They said,

> ³⁸"'Welcome! God bless the king that comes
> in the name of the Lord *(God)*!'
> *Psalm 118:26*
>
> Peace in heaven and glory to God!"

³⁹Some of the Pharisees* said to Jesus, "Teacher, tell your followers not to say these things!"

⁴⁰But Jesus answered, "I tell you, these things must be said. If my followers don't say these things, then these rocks will say them."

Jesus Cries for Jerusalem

⁴¹Jesus came near Jerusalem. He saw the city and began to cry for it. ⁴²Jesus spoke to Jerusalem. He said, "I wish you knew today what would bring you peace! But you can't know it, because it is hidden from you. ⁴³A time is coming when your enemies will build a wall around you. Your enemies will hold you on all sides. ⁴⁴They will destroy you and all your people. Not one stone of your buildings will stay on top of another. All this will happen because you did not know the time when God came to save you."

Jesus Goes to the Temple

⁴⁵Jesus went into the temple.* He began to throw out the people that were selling things there. ⁴⁶Jesus said, "It is written ⌊in the Scriptures⌋,* 'My house will be a house of prayer.'* But you have changed it into a 'hiding place for thieves'*"

⁴⁷Jesus taught the people in the temple* every day. The leading priests, the teachers of the law, and some of the leaders of the people wanted to kill Jesus. ⁴⁸But all the people were listening closely to Jesus. They were very interested in the things Jesus said. So the leading priests, the teachers of the law, and the leaders did not know how they could kill Jesus.

The Jewish Leaders Ask Jesus a Question

20 One day Jesus was in the temple.* He was teaching the people. Jesus told the people the Good News ⌊about the kingdom of God⌋. The leading priests, teachers of the law, and older Jewish leaders came to talk to Jesus. ²They said, "Tell us! What authority do you have to do these things? Who gave you this authority?"

³Jesus answered, "I will ask you a question too. Tell me: ⁴When John baptized* people, did that come from God or from man?"

⁵The priests, the teachers of the law, and the Jewish leaders all talked about this. They said to

---

Mount of Olives A hill near the city of Jerusalem.
Pharisee(s) The Pharisees were a Jewish religious group that claimed to follow carefully all Jewish laws and customs.
temple The special building in Jerusalem for Jewish worship.
Scriptures Holy Writings—the Old Testament.
'My house ... prayer' Quote from Isa. 56:7.
'hiding place for thieves' Quote from Jer. 7:11.
baptized A Greek word meaning to immerse, dip, or bury a person or thing briefly under water.

each other, "If we answer, 'John's baptism was from God,' then he will say, 'Then why did you not believe John?' ⁶But if we say, 'John's baptism was from man,' then all the people will kill us with rocks. They will kill us because they believe that John was a prophet.*" ⁷So they answered, "We don't know the answer."
⁸So Jesus said to them, "Then I will not tell you what authority I use to do these things!"

God Sends His Son

⁹Then Jesus told the people this story: "A man planted a field with grapes. The man leased the land to some farmers. Then he went away for a long time. ¹⁰Later, it was time for the grapes to be picked. So the man sent a servant to those farmers so that they would give him his share of the grapes. But the farmers beat the servant and sent him away with nothing. ¹¹So the man sent another servant. The farmers beat this servant too. They showed no respect for him. The farmers sent the servant away with nothing. ¹²So the man sent a third servant to the farmers. The farmers hurt this servant badly and threw him out. ¹³The owner of the field said, 'What will I do now? I will send my son. I love my son very much. Maybe the farmers will respect my son!' ¹⁴When the farmers saw the son, they said to each other, 'This is the owner's son. This field will be his. If we kill him, then his field will be ours!' ¹⁵So the farmers threw the son out of the field and killed him.

"What will the owner of this field do? ¹⁶He will come and kill those farmers! Then he will give the field to some other farmers."

The people heard this story. They said, "No! Let this never happen!" ¹⁷But Jesus looked into their eyes and said, "Then what does this verse mean:

'The stone that the builders did not want
became the cornerstone*'?
Psalm 118:22

¹⁸Every person that falls on that stone will be broken. If that stone falls on you, it will crush you!"

¹⁹The Jewish leaders heard this story that Jesus told. They knew this story was about them. So they wanted to arrest Jesus at that time. But they were afraid of what the people would do.

The Jewish Leaders Try to Trick Jesus

²⁰So the teachers of the law and the priests waited for the right time to get Jesus. They sent some men to Jesus. They told these men to act like they were good men. They wanted to find something wrong with the things Jesus said. (If they found something wrong, then they could give Jesus to the governor, who had power and authority ₍over him₎.) ²¹So the men asked Jesus, "Teacher, we know that what you say and teach is true. It doesn't matter who is listening—you teach the same to all people. You always teach the truth about God's way. ²²Tell us, is it right that we should pay taxes to Caesar*? Yes or No?"

²³But Jesus knew that these men were trying to trick him. Jesus said to them, ²⁴"Show me a coin. Whose name is on the coin? And whose picture is on it?"

They said, "Caesar's."

²⁵Jesus said to them, "Then give to Caesar the things that are Caesar's. And give to God the things that are God's."

²⁶The men were amazed at his wise answer. They could say nothing. The men were not able to trick Jesus before the people. Jesus said nothing they could use against him.

Some Sadducees Try to Trick Jesus

²⁷Some Sadducees* came to Jesus. (Sadducees believe that people will not rise from death.) They asked Jesus, ²⁸"Teacher, Moses wrote that if a married man dies and had no children, then his brother must marry the woman. Then they will have children for the dead brother. ²⁹One time there were seven brothers. The first brother married a woman, but died. He had no children. ³⁰Then the second brother married the woman, and he died. ³¹And the third brother married the woman, and he died. The same thing happened with all the other brothers. They all died and had no children. ³²The woman was the last to die. ³³But all seven brothers married her. So when people rise from death, whose wife will this woman be?"

³⁴Jesus said to the Sadducees,* "On earth, people marry each other. ³⁵Some people will be worthy to be raised from death and live again after this life. In that life they will not marry. ³⁶In that life people are like angels and cannot die. They

---

prophet A person who spoke for God.
cornerstone First and most important rock of a building.

Caesar The name given to the emperor (ruler) of Rome.
Sadducees A leading Jewish religious group. They accepted only the first five books of the Old Testament.

are children of God, because they have been raised from death. ³⁷Moses clearly showed that people are raised from death. When Moses wrote about the ₍burning₎ bush,* he said that the Lord ₍God₎ is 'the God of Abraham, the God of Isaac, and the God of Jacob.*'* ³⁸₍If God said he is their God, then₎ these men are not really dead. He is God only of living people. All people that belong to God are alive."

³⁹Some of the teachers of the law said, "Teacher, your answer was very good." ⁴⁰No person was brave enough to ask him another question.

Is the Christ the Son of David?

⁴¹Then Jesus said, "Why do people say that the Christ* is the Son of David*? ⁴²In the book of Psalms, David himself says:

> 'The Lord *(God)* said to my Lord *(Christ)*:
> Sit by me at my right side,
⁴³   and I will put your enemies
> under your power.*'
> *Psalm 110:1*

⁴⁴David calls the Christ 'Lord.' But the Christ is also the son of David. How can both these things be true?"

Warning Against the Teachers of the Law

⁴⁵All the people listened to Jesus. Jesus said to his followers, ⁴⁶"Be careful of the teachers of the law. They like to walk around wearing clothes that look important. And they love for people to show respect to them in the market places. They love to get the most important seats in the synagogues.* And they love to get the most important seats at the feasts. ⁴⁷But they are mean to widows* and steal their homes. Then they try to make themselves look good by saying long prayers. God will punish these people very much."

burning bush Read Exodus 3:1-12.
Abraham, Isaac, Jacob Three of the most important Jewish leaders during the time of the Old Testament.
'the God of ... Jacob' Words taken from Ex. 3:6.
Christ The "anointed one" (Messiah) or chosen of God.
Son of David Name for the Christ, who was from the family of David, king of Israel.
and I ... power Literally, "until I make your enemies a footstool for your feet."
synagogue(s) Synagogues were places where Jews gathered for prayer, study of the Scriptures, and other public meetings.
widow(s) Women whose husbands have died.

True Giving

21 Jesus saw some rich people putting their gifts for God into the temple money box.* ²Then Jesus saw a poor widow.* She put two small copper coins into the box. ³Jesus said, "I tell you the truth. This poor widow gave only two small coins. But she really gave more than all those rich people. ⁴The rich people have plenty; they gave only what they did not need. This woman is very poor. But she gave all she had. And she needed that money to help her live."

The Destruction of the Temple

⁵Some of the followers were talking about the temple.* They said, "This is a beautiful temple, built with the best stones. Look at the many good gifts that have been offered to God!"

⁶But Jesus said, "The time will come when all that you see here will be destroyed. Every stone ₍of these buildings₎ will be thrown down to the ground. Not one stone will be left on another!"

⁷Some followers asked Jesus, "Teacher, when will these things happen? What will show us that it is time for these things to happen?"

⁸Jesus said, "Be careful! Don't be fooled. Many people will come using my name. They will say, 'I am ₍the Christ₎' and, 'The right time has come!' But don't follow them. ⁹When you hear about wars and riots, don't be afraid. These things must happen first. Then the end will come later."

¹⁰Then Jesus said to them, "Nations will fight against other nations. Kingdoms will fight against other kingdoms. ¹¹There will be great earthquakes, sicknesses, and other bad things in many places. In some places there will be no food for the people to eat. Terrible things will happen, and amazing things will come from heaven to warn people.

¹²"But before all these things happen, people will arrest you and do bad things to you. People will judge you in their synagogues* and put you in jail. You will be forced to stand before kings and governors. People will do all these things to you because you follow me. ¹³But this will give you an opportunity to tell about me. ¹⁴Don't worry about what you will say. ¹⁵I will give you the wisdom to say things that none of your enemies can answer. ¹⁶Even your parents, brothers,

money box A special box in the Jewish place for worship where people put their gifts to God.
temple The special building in Jerusalem for Jewish worship.

relatives, and friends will turn against you. They will kill some of you. ¹⁷All people will hate you because you follow me. ¹⁸But none of these things can really harm you. ¹⁹You will save yourselves by continuing strong in your faith through all these things.

The Destruction of Jerusalem

²⁰"You will see armies all around Jerusalem. Then you will know that the time for the destruction of Jerusalem has come. ²¹At that time, the people in Judea should run away to the mountains. The people in Jerusalem must leave quickly. If you are near the city, don't go in! ²²The prophets* wrote many things about the time when God will punish his people. The time I am telling you about is the time when all these things must happen. ²³At that time, it will be bad for women that are pregnant or have small babies. Why? Because very bad times will come to this land. God will be angry with these people *(the Jews)*. ²⁴Some of the people will be killed by soldiers. Other people will be made prisoners and taken to every country. The holy city of Jerusalem will be walked on by non-Jewish people until their time is finished.

Don't Fear

²⁵"Amazing things will happen with the sun, moon, and stars. The people on earth will feel trapped. The oceans will be upset, and the people will not know why. ²⁶People will become afraid. They will be very worried about what will happen to the world. Everything in the sky will be changed. ²⁷Then people will see the Son of Man* coming on a cloud with power and great glory. ²⁸When these things begin to happen, don't fear. Look up and be happy! Don't worry. Be happy, because you know that the time when God will free you is near!"

My Words Will Live Forever

²⁹Then Jesus told this story: "Look at all the trees. The fig tree is a good example. ³⁰When it becomes green *(grows buds)*, you know that summer is near. ³¹It is the same with these things I told you would happen. When you see all these things happening, then you will know that God's kingdom is coming very soon.

prophets People who spoke for God. They often told things that would happen in the future.
Son of Man Jesus. In Dan. 7:13-14 this is the name for the Messiah, the one God chose to save his people.

³²"I tell you the truth. All these things will happen while the people of this time are still living! ³³The whole world, earth and sky, will be destroyed; but the words I have said will never be destroyed!

Be Ready All the Time

³⁴"Be careful! Don't spend your time drinking and getting drunk. Or don't be too busy with worldly things. If you do that, you will not be able to think right. And then the end might come when you are not ready. ³⁵It will come like a surprise to all people on earth. ³⁶So be ready all the time. Pray that you will be strong enough to continue safely through all these things that will happen. And pray that you will be able to stand before the Son of Man.*"

³⁷During the day, Jesus taught the people in the temple.* At night he went out of the city and stayed all night on the Mount of Olives.* ³⁸Every morning all the people got up early to go listen to Jesus in the temple.

The Jewish Leaders Want to Kill Jesus

22 It was almost time for the Jewish Festival of Unleavened Bread,* called the Passover.* ²The leading priests and teachers of the law were trying to find a way to kill Jesus. But they were afraid of the people.

Judas Makes Plans Against Jesus

³One of Jesus' twelve apostles* was named Judas Iscariot. Satan *(the devil)* went into Judas and made him do a bad thing. ⁴Judas went and talked with the leading priests and some of the soldiers who guarded the temple.* Judas talked to them about a way to give Jesus to them. ⁵The priests were very happy about this. They promised to give Judas money ⌊if he would give Jesus to them⌋. ⁶Judas agreed. Then Judas waited for the best time to give Jesus to them. Judas wanted to do it when there were no people around to see him do it.

temple The special building in Jerusalem for Jewish worship.
Mount of Olives A hill near the city of Jerusalem.
Festival of Unleavened Bread An important Jewish holiday week. In the Old Testament it began the day after Passover, but by this time the two holidays had become one.
Passover Important Jewish holy day. They ate a special meal on this day every year to remember that God freed them from slavery in Egypt in the time of Moses.
apostles The men Jesus chose to be his special helpers.

Preparation of the Passover Meal

⁷The Day of Unleavened Bread* came. This was the day when the Jews sacrificed* the Passover* lambs. ⁸Jesus said to Peter and John, "Go and prepare the Passover meal for us to eat." ⁹Peter and John said to Jesus, "Where do you want us to prepare the meal?"

Jesus said to them, ¹⁰"Listen! After you go into the city *(Jerusalem)*, you will see a man carrying a jar of water. Follow him. He will go into a house. You go with him. ¹¹Tell the person who owns that house, 'The Teacher asks that you please show us the room where he and his followers can eat the Passover* meal.' ¹²Then the man who owns the house will show you a large room upstairs. This room is ready for you. Prepare the Passover meal there."

¹³So Peter and John left. Everything happened the way Jesus said. So they prepared the Passover* meal.

The Lord's Supper

¹⁴The time came for them to eat the Passover* meal. Jesus and the apostles* were sitting at the table. ¹⁵Jesus said to them, "I wanted very much to eat this Passover meal with you before I die. ¹⁶I will never eat another Passover meal until it is given its true meaning in the kingdom of God."

¹⁷Then Jesus took a cup of wine. He gave thanks to God for it. Then he said, "Take this cup and give it to everyone here. ¹⁸I will never drink wine again until God's kingdom comes."

¹⁹Then Jesus took some bread. He thanked God for the bread and divided it. He gave it to the apostles.* Then Jesus said, "This bread is my body that I am giving for you. Do this to remember me." ²⁰In the same way, after supper, Jesus took the cup of wine and said, "This wine shows the new agreement ₁from God to his people₁. This new agreement begins with my blood *(death)* that I am giving for you."*

Who Will Turn Against Jesus?

²¹Jesus said, "One of you will soon be against me. His hand is by my hand on the table. ²²The Son of Man* will do what God has planned. But it will be very bad for that person who gives the Son of Man ₁to be killed₁."

²³Then the apostles* asked each other, "Which one of us would do that to Jesus?"

Be Like a Servant

²⁴Later the apostles* began to argue about which one of them was the most important. ²⁵But Jesus said to them, "The kings of the world rule over their people. Men who have authority over other people make the people call them 'great helpers ₁of the people₁.' ²⁶But you must not be like that. The greatest person should become like the youngest person! Leaders should be like servants. ²⁷Who is more important: the person sitting at the table or the person serving him? You think the person sitting at the table is more important. But I am like a servant among you!

²⁸"You men have stayed with me through many struggles. ²⁹My Father has given me a kingdom. I also give you authority to rule with me. ³⁰You will eat and drink at my table in my kingdom. You will sit on thrones and judge the twelve tribes *(family groups)* of Israel.*

Don't Lose Your Faith!

³¹"Satan *(the devil)* has asked to test you like a farmer tests his wheat. O Simon, Simon *(Peter)*, ³²I have prayed that you will not lose your faith! Help your brothers be stronger when you come back to me."

³³But Peter said to Jesus, "Lord, I am ready to go to jail with you. I will even die with you!"

³⁴But Jesus said, "Peter, before the rooster crows tomorrow morning, you will say you don't know me. You will say this three times!"

Be Ready for Trouble

³⁵Then Jesus said to the apostles,* "I sent you ₁to preach to the people₁. I sent you without money, a bag, or shoes. But did you need anything?"

The apostles said, "No."

³⁶Jesus said to them, "But now if you have money or a bag, carry that with you. If you don't have a sword, sell your coat and buy one. ³⁷The Scripture* says:

Day of Unleavened Bread Same as Passover.
sacrificed To kill something as a gift to God.
Passover Important Jewish holy day. They ate a special meal on this day every year to remember that God freed them from slavery in Egypt in the time of Moses.
apostles The men Jesus chose to be his special helpers.
Verse 20 A few Greek copies do not have the last part of verse 19 and all of verse 20.

Son of Man Jesus. In Dan. 7:13-14 this is the name for the Messiah, the one God chose to save his people.
Israel First, Israel was the Jewish nation, but the name is also used to mean all of God's people.
Scripture Part of the Holy Writings—Old Testament.

'People said he was a criminal.'
Isaiah 53:12

This Scripture must happen. It was written about me, and it is happening now."
[38] The followers said, "Look, Lord, here are two swords!"
Jesus said to them, "Two will be enough."

Jesus Tells the Apostles to Pray

[39-40] Jesus left the city *(Jerusalem)* and went to the Mount of Olives.* His followers went with him. (Jesus went there often.) Jesus said to his followers, "Pray that you will not be tempted." [41] Then Jesus went about 50 yards away from them. He kneeled down and prayed, [42] "Father, if it is what you want, then let me not have this cup* ₍of suffering₎. But do what you want, not what I want." [43] Then an angel from heaven appeared. The angel was sent to help Jesus. [44] Jesus was full of pain; he struggled hard in prayer. Sweat dripped from his face like he was bleeding. [45] When Jesus finished praying, he went to his followers. They were asleep. (Their sadness had made them very tired.) [46] Jesus said to them, "Why are you sleeping? Get up and pray for strength against temptation."

Jesus Is Arrested

[47] While Jesus was speaking, a group of people came. One of the twelve apostles* was leading the group. He was Judas. Judas came close to Jesus so that he could kiss Jesus. [48] But Jesus said to him, "Judas, are you using the kiss ₍of friendship₎ to give the Son of Man* ₍to his enemies₎?" [49] The followers of Jesus were standing there too. They saw what was happening. The followers said to Jesus, "Lord, should we use our swords?" [50] And one of the followers did use his sword. He cut off the right ear of the servant of the high priest.* [51] Jesus said, "Stop!" Then Jesus touched the servant's ear and healed him. [52] The group that came to arrest Jesus were the leading priests, the older Jewish leaders, and the Jewish soldiers. Jesus said to them, "Why did you come out here with swords and sticks? Do you think I am a criminal? [53] I was with you every day in the temple.* Why didn't you try to arrest me there? But this is your time—the time when darkness *(sin)* rules."

Peter Is Afraid to Say He Knows Jesus

[54] They arrested Jesus and took him away. They brought Jesus into the house of the high priest.* Peter followed them, but he did not come near Jesus. [55] The soldiers started a fire in the middle of the yard and sat together. Peter sat with them. [56] A servant girl saw Peter sitting there. She could see because of the light from the fire. The girl looked closely at Peter's face. Then she said, "This man was also with him *(Jesus)!*"
[57] But Peter said this was not true. He said, "Lady, I don't know him." [58] A short time later, another person saw Peter and said, "You are also one of those people ₍that follow Jesus₎."
But Peter said, "Man, I am not one of his followers!"
[59] About an hour later, another man said, "It is true! This man was with him *(Jesus).* He is from Galilee!" The man said he was sure about this.
[60] But Peter said, "Man, I don't know what you are talking about!"
Immediately, while Peter was still speaking, a rooster crowed. [61] Then the Lord *(Jesus)* turned and looked into Peter's eyes. And Peter remembered what the Lord had said: "Before the rooster crows in the morning, you will say three times that you don't know me." [62] Then Peter went outside and cried bitterly.

The People Laugh at Jesus

[63-64] Some men were holding *(guarding)* Jesus. They made fun of Jesus like this: They covered his eyes so that he could not see them. Then they hit him and said, "Be a prophet* and tell us who hit you!" [65] The men said many very bad things to Jesus.

Jesus Before the Jewish Leaders

[66] The next morning, the older leaders of the people, the leading priests, and the teachers of the law came together. They led Jesus away to their

---

Mount of Olives A hill near the city of Jerusalem.
cup Jesus is talking about the bad things that will happen to him. Accepting these things will be hard, like drinking a cup full of something that tastes very bad.
apostles The men Jesus chose to be his special helpers.
Son of Man Jesus. In Dan. 7:13-14 this is the name for the Messiah, the one God chose to save his people.
high priest Most important Jewish priest and leader.
temple The special building in Jerusalem for Jewish worship.
prophet A person who spoke for God. He could tell things that most people could not know.

highest court. ⁶⁷They said, "If you are the Christ,* then tell us that you are!"

Jesus said to them, "If I tell you I am the Christ, you will not believe me. ⁶⁸And if I ask you, you will not answer. ⁶⁹But beginning now, the Son of Man* will sit at the right side of God's throne."

⁷⁰They all said, "Then are you the Son of God?" Jesus said to them, "Yes, you are right when you say that I am."

⁷¹They said, "Why do we need witnesses now? We ourselves heard him say this!"

Governor Pilate Questions Jesus

23 Then the whole group stood up and led Jesus to Pilate.* ²They began to accuse Jesus. They told Pilate, "We caught this man trying to change the thinking of our people. He says we should not pay taxes to Caesar.* He calls himself the Christ,* a king."

³Pilate asked Jesus, "Are you the king of the Jews?"

Jesus answered, "Yes, that is right."

⁴Pilate said to the leading priests and the people, "I find nothing wrong with this man."

⁵They said again and again, "But Jesus is making trouble with the people! He teaches all around Judea. He began in Galilee, and now he is here!"

Pilate Sends Jesus to Herod

⁶Pilate heard this and asked if Jesus was from Galilee. ⁷Pilate learned that Jesus was under Herod's* authority. Herod was in Jerusalem at that time, so Pilate sent Jesus to him. ⁸When Herod saw Jesus, he was very happy. Herod had heard all about Jesus. So he had wanted to meet Jesus for a long time. Herod wanted to see a miracle.* So he hoped that Jesus would do a miracle. ⁹Herod asked Jesus many questions, but Jesus said nothing. ¹⁰The leading priests and teachers of the law were standing there. They were shouting things against Jesus. ¹¹Then Herod and his soldiers laughed at Jesus. They made fun of Jesus by dressing him in clothes like kings wear. Then Herod sent Jesus back to Pilate. ¹²In the past, Pilate and Herod had always been enemies. But on that day Herod and Pilate became friends.

Jesus Must Die

¹³Pilate called all the people together with the leading priests and the ₍Jewish₎ leaders. ¹⁴Pilate said to them, "You brought this man *(Jesus)* to me. You said that he was trying to change the people. But I judged him before you all. I found no wrong that he had done. Jesus is not guilty of the things you say. ¹⁵Also, Herod* found nothing wrong with him; Herod sent Jesus back to us. Look, Jesus has done nothing wrong. He should not be killed. ¹⁶So, after I punish him a little, I will let him go free." ¹⁷*

¹⁸But all the people shouted, "Kill him! Let Barabbas go free!" ¹⁹(Barabbas was a man that was in jail because he started a riot in the city. He had also killed some people.)

²⁰Pilate wanted to let Jesus go free. So again Pilate told them that he would let Jesus go. ²¹But they shouted again, "Kill him! Kill him on a cross!"

²²A third time Pilate said to the people, "Why? What wrong has he done? He is not guilty. I can find no reason to kill him. So I will let him go free after I punish him a little."

²³But the people continued to shout. They demanded that Jesus be killed on the cross. Their shouting became so loud that ²⁴Pilate decided to give them what they wanted. ²⁵The people wanted Barabbas to go free. Barabbas was in jail for starting a riot and for killing people. Pilate let Barabbas go free. And Pilate gave Jesus to the people to be killed. This is what the people wanted.

Jesus Is Killed on a Cross

²⁶The soldiers led Jesus away ₍to be killed₎. At that same time, there was a man coming into the city from the fields. His name was Simon. Simon was from the city of Cyrene. The soldiers forced Simon to carry Jesus' cross and walk behind Jesus.

Christ The "anointed one" (Messiah) or chosen of God.
Son of Man Jesus. In Dan. 7:13-14 this is the name for the Messiah, the one God chose to save his people.
Pilate Pontius Pilate was the Roman governor of Judea from 26 A.D. to 36 A.D.
Caesar The name given to the emperor (ruler) of Rome.
Herod Herod Antipas, tetrarch (ruler) of Galilee and Perea, son of Herod the Great.
miracle An amazing work done by the power of God.

Verse 17 A few Greek copies of Luke add verse 17: "Every year at the Passover festival, Pilate had to release one prisoner to the people."

27 Many, many people followed Jesus. Some of the women were sad and crying. They felt sorry for Jesus. 28 But Jesus turned and said to the women, "Women of Jerusalem, don't cry for me. Cry for yourselves and for your children too! 29 The time is coming when people will say, 'Happy are the women that cannot have babies! Happy are the women that have no children to care for.' 30 Then the people will say to the mountain, 'Fall on us!' The people will say to the hills, 'Cover us!'* 31 If people act like this now when life is good, what will happen when bad times come?*"

32 There were also two criminals led out with Jesus to be killed. 33 Jesus and the two criminals were led to a place called "The Skull." There the soldiers nailed Jesus to his cross. They also nailed the criminals to their crosses. They put one criminal beside Jesus on the right, and they put the other criminal beside Jesus on the left. 34 Jesus said, "Father, forgive these people [that are killing me]. They don't know what they are doing.*"

The soldiers gambled with dice to decide who would get Jesus' clothes. 35 The people stood there watching [Jesus]. The Jewish leaders laughed at Jesus. They said, "If he is God's Chosen One, the Christ,* then let him save himself. He saved other people, didn't he?" 36 Even the soldiers laughed at Jesus and teased him. They came to Jesus and offered him some wine. 37 The soldiers said, "If you are the king of the Jews, save yourself!" 38 (At the top of the cross these words were written: "THIS IS THE KING OF THE JEWS.")

39 One of the criminals began to shout very bad things at Jesus: "Aren't you the Christ*? Then save yourself! And save us too!" 40 But the other criminal stopped him. He said, "You should fear God! All of us will die soon! 41 You and I are guilty; we should be killed because we did wrong. But this man *(Jesus)* has done nothing wrong!" 42 Then this criminal said to Jesus, "Jesus, remember me when you begin ruling as king!"

43 Then Jesus said to him, "Listen! What I say is true: Today you will be with me in Paradise*!"

Jesus Dies

44 It was about noon, but the whole area became dark until three o'clock in the afternoon. 45 There was no sun! The curtain in the temple* was torn into two pieces. 46 Jesus shouted, "Father, I give you my spirit." After Jesus said this, he died. 47 The army officer* there saw what happened. He praised God, saying, "I know this man was a good man!" 48 Many people had come out of the city to see this thing. When the people saw it, they felt very sorry and left. 49 The people who were close friends of Jesus were there. Also, there were some women that had followed Jesus from Galilee. They all stood far away from the cross and watched these things.

Joseph of Arimathea

50-51 A man was there from the Jewish town of Arimathea. His name was Joseph. He was a good, religious man. He wanted the kingdom of God to come. Joseph was a member of the Jewish council. But he did not agree when the other Jewish leaders decided to kill Jesus. 52 Joseph went to Pilate to ask for the body of Jesus. [Pilate let Joseph have the body]. 53 So Joseph took the body down from the cross and wrapped it in cloth. Then he put Jesus' body in a tomb *(grave)* that was dug in a wall of rock. This tomb had never been used before. 54 This was late on Preparation day.* When the sun went down, the Sabbath day* would begin.

55 The women that had come from Galilee with Jesus followed Joseph. They saw the tomb. Inside they saw where the body of Jesus was put. 56 Then the women left to prepare some sweet-smelling spices [to put on Jesus' body].

On the Sabbath day* they rested. The law of Moses commanded all people to do this.

News That Jesus Has Risen from Death

24 Very early Sunday morning, the women came to the tomb *(grave)* where Jesus' body was laid. They brought the sweet-smelling spices they had prepared. ² [A heavy stone had been put

---

the people ... 'Cover us!' Quote from Hos. 10:8
If people act ... come? Literally, "If they do these things in the green tree, what will happen in the dry?"
Jesus said, "Father ... doing" Some early copies of Luke do not have these words.
Christ The "anointed one" (Messiah) or chosen of God.
Paradise Place where good people go when they die.

curtain in the temple A curtain divided the "most holy place" from the other part of the temple, the special building in Jerusalem for Jewish worship.
army officer A centurion, a Roman army officer who had authority over 100 soldiers.
Preparation day Friday, the day before the Sabbath.
Sabbath day The seventh day of the Jewish week. It was a special religious day for the Jews.

in the doorway to close the tomb]. But the women found that the stone was rolled away. ³They went in, but they did not find the Lord Jesus' body. ⁴The women did not understand this. While they were wondering about it, two men *(angels)* in shining clothes stood beside them. ⁵The women were very afraid; they bowed their heads down. The two men said to the women, "Why are you looking for a living person here? This is a place for dead people! ⁶Jesus is not here. He has risen from death! Do you remember what he said in Galilee? ⁷Jesus said that the Son of Man* must be given to evil men, be killed on a cross, and rise from death on the third day." ⁸Then the women remembered the things that Jesus said.

⁹The women left the tomb *(grave)* and went to the eleven apostles* and the other followers. The women told them everything that happened at the tomb. ¹⁰These women were Mary Magdalene, Joanna, Mary, the mother of James, and some other women. These women told the apostles everything that happened. ¹¹But the apostles did not believe what the women said. It sounded like crazy talk. ¹²But Peter got up and ran to the tomb to see if this was true. He looked in, but he saw only the cloth that Jesus' body had been wrapped in. The cloth was lying there alone. ⌊Jesus was gone⌋. Peter went away to be alone, wondering what had happened.

On The Road to Emmaus

¹³That same day two of Jesus' followers were going to a town named Emmaus. It is about seven miles from Jerusalem. ¹⁴They were talking about everything that had happened. ¹⁵While they were discussing these things, Jesus himself came near and walked with them. ¹⁶(But the two men were not allowed to recognize Jesus.) ¹⁷Then Jesus said, "What are these things you are talking about while you walk?"

The two men stopped. Their faces looked very sad. ¹⁸The one named Cleopas answered, "You must be the only man in Jerusalem who does not know what has just happened there."

¹⁹Jesus said to them, "What are you talking about?"

The men said to him, "It's about Jesus, the one from Nazareth. To God and to all the people he was a great prophet.* He said and did many powerful things. ²⁰But our leaders and the leading priests gave him away to be judged and killed. They nailed Jesus to a cross. ²¹We were hoping that Jesus would be the one to free Israel *(the Jews)*. But then all this happened. And now something else: It has been three days since ⌊Jesus was killed⌋, ²²but today some of our women told us an amazing thing. Early this morning the women went to the tomb *(grave)* where the body of Jesus was laid. ²³But they did not find his body there. They came and told us that they had seen two angels in a vision.* The angels said that Jesus was alive! ²⁴So some of our group went to the tomb too. It was just like the women said—⌊the tomb was empty⌋. We looked, but none of us saw him *(Jesus)*."

²⁵Then Jesus said to the two men, "You are foolish and slow to realize what is true. You should believe everything the prophets* said. ²⁶The prophets said that the Christ* must suffer these things before he enters his glory." ²⁷Then Jesus began to explain everything that had been written about himself in the Scriptures.* Jesus started with the books of Moses and then he talked about what the prophets had said about him.

²⁸They came near the town of Emmaus and Jesus acted like he did not plan to stop there. ²⁹But they wanted him to stay. They begged him, "Stay with us. It is late; it is almost night." So he went in to stay with them.

³⁰Jesus sat down with them and took some bread. He gave thanks for the food and divided it. Then he gave it to them. ³¹At that time, the men were allowed to recognize Jesus. But when they saw who he was, he disappeared. ³²The two men said to each other, "When Jesus talked to us on the road, it felt like a fire burning in us. It was exciting when he explained the true meaning of the Scriptures."*

³³So the two men got up then and went back to Jerusalem. In Jerusalem they found the followers of Jesus meeting together. The eleven apostles* and those people that were with them ³⁴said, "The

---

Son of Man Jesus. In Dan. 7:13-14, this is the name for the Messiah (Christ), the person God chose to save his people.

apostles Men that Jesus chose to be his special helpers for telling his Good News to the world.

prophet A person who spoke for God.

vision A vision is something like a dream that God used to speak to people.

prophets Men who spoke for God. Some of them wrote books that are in the Old Testament.

Christ The "anointed one" (Messiah) or chosen of God.

Scriptures Holy Writings—the Old Testament.

Lord *(Jesus)* really has risen from death! He showed himself to Simon *(Peter)*."

³⁵Then the two men told the things that had happened on the road. They talked about how they recognized Jesus when he divided the bread.

Jesus Appears to His Followers

³⁶While the two men were saying these things, Jesus himself stood among the group of followers. Jesus said to them, "Peace be with you." ³⁷This surprised the followers. They became afraid. They thought they were seeing a ghost. ³⁸But Jesus said, "Why are you troubled? Why do you doubt what you see? ³⁹Look at my hands and my feet. It is really me! Touch me. You can see that I have a living body; a ghost does not have a body like this."

⁴⁰After Jesus told them this, he showed them ₍the holes in₎ his hands and feet. ⁴¹The followers were amazed and very, very happy to see that Jesus was alive. They still could not believe what they saw. Jesus said to them, "Do you have any food here?" ⁴²They gave him a piece of cooked fish. ⁴³While the followers watched, Jesus took the fish and ate it.

⁴⁴Jesus said to them, "Remember when I was with you before? I said that everything written about me must happen—everything written in the law of Moses, the books of the prophets,* and the Psalms."

⁴⁵Then Jesus explained all the Scriptures* to the followers. Jesus helped them understand the things written ₍about him₎. ⁴⁶Then Jesus said to them, "It is written that the Christ* would be killed and rise from death on the third day. ⁴⁷⁻⁴⁸You saw these things happen—you are witnesses. You must go and tell people that their sins can be forgiven. Tell them that they must change their hearts and be sorry for their sins. If they will do this, then God will forgive them. You must start from Jerusalem and preach these things in my name. This Good News must be told to all people in the world. ⁴⁹Listen! My Father has promised you something; I will send it to you. But you must stay in Jerusalem until you have received that power from heaven."

Jesus Goes Back to Heaven

⁵⁰Jesus led his followers out of Jerusalem almost to Bethany. Jesus raised his hands and blessed his followers. ⁵¹While Jesus was blessing them, he was separated from them and carried into heaven. ⁵²The followers worshiped him there. Then they went back to the city. They were very happy. ⁵³They stayed at the temple* all the time, praising God.

---

prophets Men who spoke for God. Some of them wrote books that are in the Old Testament.
Scriptures Holy Writings—the Old Testament.
Christ The "anointed one" (Messiah) or chosen of God.
temple The special building in Jerusalem for Jewish worship.

John

Christ Comes to the World

1 Before the world began, the Word* was there. The Word was there with God. The Word was God. ²He was there with God in the beginning. ³All things were made through him *(the Word)*. Nothing was made without him. ⁴In him there was life. That life was light *(understanding, goodness)* for the people of the world. ⁵The Light shines in the darkness. The darkness did not defeat* the Light.

⁶There was a man named John.* He was sent by God. ⁷John came to tell people about the Light *(Christ)*. Through John all people ⌊could hear about the Light⌋ and believe. ⁸John was not the Light. But John came to tell people about the Light. ⁹The true Light was coming into the world. This is the true Light that gives light to all people.

¹⁰The Word* was already in the world. The world was made through him. But the world *(people)* did not know him. ¹¹He came to the world that was his own. But his own people did not accept him. ¹²Some people did accept him. They believed in him. He gave something to those people who believed. He gave them the right to become children of God. ¹³These children were not born like little babies are born. They were not born from the wish or plan of a ⌊mother and⌋ father. These children were born from God.

¹⁴The Word* became a man and lived among us. We saw his glory—the glory that belongs to the only Son of the Father. The Word was full of grace *(kindness)* and truth. ¹⁵John told people about him. John said, "This is the One I was talking about. I said, 'The One who comes after me is greater than I am. He was living before me.'"

¹⁶The Word* *(Christ)* was full of grace and truth. From him we all received more and more blessings. ¹⁷The law was given through Moses. But grace and ⌊the way of⌋ truth came through Jesus Christ. ¹⁸No man has ever seen God. But the only Son *(Jesus)* is God. He is very close to the Father* *(God)*. And the Son has shown us what God is like.

John Tells People About Jesus

¹⁹The Jews in Jerusalem sent some priests and Levites* to John.* The Jews sent them to ask, "Who are you?"

²⁰John spoke freely. John did not refuse to answer. John said clearly, "I am not the Christ.*" That is what John told people.

²¹The Jews asked John, "Then who are you? Are you Elijah*?"

John answered, "No, I am not Elijah."

The Jews asked, "Are you the Prophet*?"

John answered, "No, I am not the Prophet."

²²Then the Jews said, "Who are you? Tell us about yourself. Give us an answer to tell the people who sent us. What do you say about yourself?"

²³John told them the words of the prophet Isaiah:

"I am the voice of a person shouting
   in the desert:
'Make a straight road ready for the Lord.'"
                                    Isaiah 40:3

But the only Son ... Father Or, "But the only God is very close to the Father." Some Greek copies say, "But the only Son is very close to the Father."

Levites Levites were men from the family group of Levi who helped the Jewish priests in the temple.

Christ The "anointed one" (Messiah) or chosen of God.

Elijah Man who spoke for God about 850 B.C. Jews thought Elijah would come before the Messiah. See Mal. 4:5-6.

Prophet This probably meant the prophet that God told Moses he would send (Deut. 18:15-19).

Word The Greek word is *"logos,"* meaning any kind of communication. It could be translated "message." Here, it means Christ—the way God told people about himself.

defeat Or, "understand."

John John the Baptizer, who preached to people about Christ's coming (Read Mt. 3; Lk. 3).

²⁴These Jews were sent from the Pharisees.*
²⁵These men said to John: "You say you are not the Christ.* You say you are not Elijah* or the Prophet.* Then why do you baptize* people?"
²⁶John answered, "I baptize people with water. But there is a person here with you that you don't know. ²⁷That person is the One who comes after me. I am not good enough to untie the strings on his shoes."
²⁸These things all happened at Bethany on the other side of the Jordan River. This is where John was baptizing people.
²⁹The next day John saw Jesus coming toward him. John said, "Look, the Lamb of God.* He takes away the sins of the world! ³⁰This is the One I was talking about. I said, 'A man will come after me, but he is greater than I am, because he was living before me—he has always lived.' ³¹Even I did not know who he was. But I came baptizing* people with water so that Israel (the Jews) could know that Jesus is the Christ.*"
³²⁻³³Then John said, "I also did not know who the Christ was. But God sent me to baptize* people with water. And God told me, 'You will see the Spirit come down and rest on a man. That man is the One who will baptize with the Holy Spirit.*'" John said, "I have seen this happen. I saw the Spirit come down from heaven. The Spirit looked like a dove and sat on him (Jesus). ³⁴So this is what I tell people: 'He (Jesus) is the Son of God.'"

The First Followers of Jesus

³⁵The next day John was there again. John had two of his followers with him. ³⁶John saw Jesus walking by. John said, "Look, the Lamb of God*!"

³⁷The two followers heard John say this, so they followed Jesus. ³⁸Jesus turned and saw the two men following him. Jesus asked, "What do you want?"
The two men said, "Rabbi, where are you staying?" ("Rabbi" means "Teacher.")
³⁹Jesus answered, "Come with me and you will see." So the two men went with Jesus. They saw the place where Jesus stayed. They stayed there with Jesus that day. It was about four o'clock.
⁴⁰These two men followed Jesus after they heard about Jesus from John. One of these two men was named Andrew. Andrew was Simon Peter's brother. ⁴¹The first thing Andrew did was to go find his brother, Simon. Andrew said to Simon, "We have found the Messiah." ("Messiah" means "Christ."*)
⁴²Then Andrew brought Simon to Jesus. Jesus looked at Simon and said, "You are Simon, the son of John. You will be called Cephas." ("Cephas" means "Peter."*)
⁴³The next day Jesus decided to go to Galilee. Jesus found Philip and said to him, "Follow me." ⁴⁴Philip was from the town of Bethsaida, the same as Andrew and Peter. ⁴⁵Philip found Nathaniel and told him, "Remember what Moses wrote in the law. Moses wrote about a man that was coming. The prophets* wrote about him too. We have found him. His name is Jesus, the son of Joseph. He is from Nazareth."
⁴⁶But Nathaniel said to Philip, "Nazareth! Can anything good come from Nazareth?"
Philip answered, "Come and see."
⁴⁷Jesus saw Nathaniel coming toward him. Jesus said, "This man coming is truly one of God's people.* There is nothing false in him."
⁴⁸Nathaniel asked, "How do you know me?"
Jesus answered, "I saw you when you were under the fig tree. That was before Philip told you about me."
⁴⁹Then Nathaniel said to Jesus, "Rabbi (Teacher), you are the Son of God. You are the King of Israel (the Jews)."
⁵⁰Jesus said to Nathaniel, "I told you that I saw you under the fig tree. That is why you believe in me. But you will see much greater things than

---

Pharisees The Pharisees were a Jewish religious group that claimed to follow carefully all Jewish laws and customs.
Christ The "anointed one" (Messiah) or chosen of God.
Elijah Man who spoke for God about 850 B.C. Jews thought Elijah would come before the Messiah. See Mal. 4:5-6.
Prophet They probably meant the prophet that God told Moses he would send (Deut. 18:15-19).
baptize, baptizing Greek word meaning to immerse, dip, or bury a person or thing briefly under water.
Lamb of God Name for Jesus. It means that Jesus is like the lambs that were offered for a sacrifice to God.
Holy Spirit Called the Spirit of God, the Spirit of Christ, and the Comforter. Joined with God and Christ, he does God's work among people in the world.

Peter The Greek name "Peter," like the Aramaic name "Cephas," means "rock."
prophets Men who spoke for God. Their writings are part of the Old Testament.
one of God's people Literally, "an Israelite."

that!" ⁵¹Jesus also said, "I tell you the truth. You will all see heaven open. You will see 'angels of God going up and coming down'* on the Son of Man.*"

The Wedding at Cana

2 Two days later there was a wedding in the town of Cana in Galilee. Jesus' mother was there. ²Jesus and his followers were also invited to the wedding. ³At the wedding there was not enough wine. After the wine was all gone, Jesus' mother said to him, "They have no more wine."
⁴Jesus answered, "Dear woman, you should not tell me what to do. My time has not yet come."
⁵Jesus' mother said to the servants, "Do what Jesus tells you to do."
⁶In that place there were six large waterpots made of stone. The Jews used waterpots like these in their washing ceremonies.* Each waterpot held about 20 or 30 gallons.
⁷Jesus said to the servants, "Fill those waterpots with water." So the servants filled the pots to the top.
⁸Then Jesus said to the servants, "Now take out some water. Carry the water to the master of the feast."
So the servants brought the water to the master. ⁹Then the man in charge of the wedding feast tasted it, but the water had become wine. The man did not know where the wine came from. But the servants that brought the water knew where it came from. The master of the wedding called the bridegroom.* ¹⁰He said to the bridegroom, "People always serve the best wine first. Later, after the guests have become drunk, people serve the cheaper wine. But you have saved the best wine until now."
¹¹This was the first miracle* that Jesus did. Jesus did this miracle in the town of Cana in Galilee. So Jesus showed his greatness. And his followers believed in him.

Jesus in the Temple

¹²Then Jesus went to the town of Capernaum. Jesus' mother and brothers and his followers went with him. They all stayed in Capernaum a few days. ¹³It was almost time for the Jewish Passover.* So Jesus went to Jerusalem. ¹⁴In Jerusalem Jesus went to the temple.* In the temple Jesus found men selling cattle, sheep, and doves. Jesus saw other men sitting at tables. These men were exchanging and trading people's money. ¹⁵Jesus made a whip with some pieces of rope. Then Jesus forced all these men and the sheep and cattle to leave the temple. Jesus turned over the tables and scattered the money of the men that exchange money. ¹⁶Then Jesus said to the men that were selling pigeons, "Take these things out of here! Don't make my Father's house a place for buying and selling!"
¹⁷When this happened the followers of Jesus remembered what was written ⌊in the Scriptures⌋*:

> "My excitement for your house
> will destroy me."
>
> *Psalm 69:9*

¹⁸The Jews said to Jesus, "Show us a miracle* for a sign. Prove that you have the right to do these things."
¹⁹Jesus answered, "Destroy this temple and I will build it again in three days."
²⁰The Jews answered, "People worked 46 years to build this temple! Do you really believe you can build it again in three days?"
²¹(But the temple Jesus meant was his own body. ²²After Jesus was raised from death, his followers remembered that Jesus had said this. So his followers believed the Scripture* ⌊about him⌋, and they believed the words Jesus said.)
²³Jesus was in Jerusalem for the Passover* festival. Many people believed in Jesus because they saw the miracles* he did. ²⁴But Jesus did not trust them. Why? Because Jesus knew the things people were thinking. ²⁵Jesus did not need any person to tell him about people. Jesus knew what was in a person's mind.

Jesus and Nicodemus

3 There was a man named Nicodemus. Nicodemus was one of the Pharisees.* He was an important Jewish leader. ²One night

---

'angels ... coming down' Quote from Gen. 28:12.
Son of Man Jesus. In Dan. 7:13-14 this is the name for the Messiah, the one God chose to save his people.
washing ceremonies The Jews had religious rules about washing in special ways before eating, before worshiping in the temple, and at other special times.
bridegroom A man ready to be married.
miracle(s) Miracles are amazing works done by God's power.

Passover Important Jewish holy day. They ate a special meal on this day every year to remember that God freed them from slavery in Egypt in the time of Moses.
temple The special building in Jerusalem for Jewish worship.
Scriptures Holy Writings—the Old Testament.
Pharisees The Pharisees were a Jewish religious group that claimed to follow carefully all Jewish laws and customs.

Nicodemus came to Jesus. Nicodemus said, "Rabbi *(Teacher)*, we know that you are a teacher sent from God. No person can do these miracles* that you do without God's help." ³Jesus answered, "I tell you the truth. A person must be born again. If a person is not born again, then that person cannot be in God's kingdom." ⁴Nicodemus said, "But if a man is already old, how can he be born again? A person cannot enter his mother's body again! So a person cannot be born a second time!" ⁵But Jesus answered, "I tell you the truth. A person must be born from water and the Spirit.* If a person is not born from water and the Spirit, then he cannot enter God's kingdom. ⁶A person's body is born from his human parents. But a person's spiritual life is born from the Spirit. ⁷Don't be surprised that I told you, 'You must be born again.' ⁸The wind blows where it wants to go. You hear the wind blow. But you don't know where the wind comes from or where the wind is going. It is the same with every person that is born from the Spirit."

⁹Nicodemus asked, "How can all this be possible?"

¹⁰Jesus said, "You are an important teacher of Israel *(the Jews)*. But you still don't understand these things? ¹¹I tell you the truth. We talk about what we know. We tell about what we have seen. But you people don't accept what we tell you. ¹²I have told you about things here on earth. But you do not believe me. So surely you will not believe me if I tell you about the things of heaven! ¹³The only one that has ever gone up to heaven is the One that came down from heaven—the Son of Man.*

¹⁴"Moses lifted up the snake in the desert.* It is the same with the Son of Man. The Son of Man must be lifted up too. ¹⁵Then every person that believes in the Son of Man can have life forever."

¹⁶Yes, God loved the world so much that he gave his only Son. God gave his Son so that every person that believes in him would not be lost, but have life forever. ¹⁷God sent his Son into the world. God did not send his Son to judge the world guilty. God sent his Son so that the world could be saved through his Son. ¹⁸The person that believes in God's Son is not judged *(condemned)*. But the person that does not believe is already judged. Why? Because that person has not believed in God's only Son. ¹⁹People are judged by this fact: The Light *(goodness)* has come into the world. But men did not want light. They wanted darkness *(sin)*. Why? Because they were doing evil things. ²⁰Every person that does evil hates the light. That person will not come to the light. Why? Because then the light will show all the bad things he has done. ²¹But the person that follows the true way comes to the light. Then the light will show that the things that person has done were done through God.*

Jesus and John the Baptizer

²²After this, Jesus and his followers went into the area of Judea. There Jesus stayed with his followers and baptized* people. ²³John was also baptizing people in Aenon. Aenon is near Salim. John was baptizing there because there was plenty of water. People were going there to be baptized. ²⁴(This happened before John was put into prison.) ²⁵Some of John's followers had an argument with another Jew. They were arguing about religious washing.* ²⁶So the followers came to John. They said, "Rabbi *(Teacher)*, remember the man that was with you on the other side of the Jordan River? He is the man you were telling people about. That man is baptizing* people, and many people are going to him."

²⁷John answered, "A man can get only what God gives him. ²⁸You yourselves heard me say, 'I am not the Christ.* I am only the one that God sent to prepare the way for him.' ²⁹The bride belongs only to the bridegroom.* The friend that helps the bridegroom waits and listens ₁for the bridegroom to come₁. This friend is very happy when he hears the bridegroom's voice. That is the same pleasure I have. And my time of joy is now

---

Verses 16-21 Some scholars think verses 16-21 are Jesus' words. Others think John wrote them.

baptize(d) Greek word meaning to immerse, dip, or bury a person or thing briefly under water.

religious washing The Jews had religious rules about washing in special ways before eating, before worshiping in the temple, and at other special times.

baptize, baptizing Greek word meaning to immerse, dip, or bury a person or thing briefly under water.

Christ The "anointed one" (Messiah) or chosen of God.

bridegroom A man ready to be married.

---

miracle(s) Miracles are amazing works done by God's power.

Spirit The Holy Spirit. Also called the Spirit of God, Spirit of Christ, and the Comforter. Joined with God and Christ, he does God's work among people in the world.

Son of Man Jesus. In Dan. 7:13-14 this is the name for the Messiah, the one God chose to save his people.

Moses lifted ... desert When God's people were dying from snake bites, God told Moses to put a brass snake on a pole for them to look at and be healed. Read Num. 21:4-9.

here. ³⁰He *(Jesus)* must become greater. And I must become less important.

The One That Comes from Heaven

³¹"The One *(Jesus)* that comes from above is greater than all other people. The person that is from the earth belongs to the earth. That person talks about things that are on the earth. But the One *(Jesus)* that comes from heaven is greater than all other people. ³²He *(Jesus)* tells what he has seen and heard. But people don't accept what he says. ³³The person that accepts what he *(Jesus)* says has given proof that God is true. ³⁴God sent him *(Jesus)*. And he tells the things that God says. God gives ₗhimⱼ the Spirit* fully. ³⁵The Father loves the Son. The Father has given the Son power over everything. ³⁶The person that believes in the Son has life forever. But the person that does not obey the Son will never have that life. God's anger stays with that person."

Jesus Talks to a Woman in Samaria

4 The Pharisees* heard that Jesus was making and baptizing* more followers than John. ²(But really Jesus himself did not baptize people. His followers baptized people for him.) Jesus knew that the Pharisees had heard about him. ³So Jesus left Judea and went back to Galilee. ⁴On the way to Galilee Jesus had to go through the country of Samaria.

⁵In Samaria Jesus came to the town called Sychar. This town is near the field that Jacob gave to his son Joseph. ⁶Jacob's well was there. Jesus was tired from his long trip. So Jesus sat down beside the well. It was about noon. ⁷A Samaritan* woman came to that well to get some water. Jesus said to her, "Please give me a drink of water." ⁸(This happened while Jesus' followers were in town buying some food.)

⁹The Samaritan woman answered, "I am surprised that you ask me for a drink! You are a Jew and I am a Samaritan woman!" (Jews are not friends with Samaritans.*)

¹⁰Jesus answered, "You don't know about the thing God gives. And you don't know who I am that asked you for a drink. If you knew these things, you would have asked me and I would have given you living water."

¹¹The woman said, "Sir, where will you get that living water? The well is very deep, and you have nothing to get water with. ¹²Are you greater than Jacob our father *(ancestor)*? Jacob is the one that gave us this well. He drank from it himself. Also, his sons and all his animals drank water from this well."

¹³Jesus answered, "Every person that drinks this water will be thirsty again. ¹⁴But the person that drinks the water I give will never be thirsty again. That water I give will become like a spring of water flowing inside that person. That water will bring that person life forever."

¹⁵The woman said to Jesus, "Sir, give me this water. Then I will never be thirsty again. And I will not have to come back here to get more water."

¹⁶Jesus told her, "Go get your husband and come back here."

¹⁷The woman answered, "But I have no husband."

Jesus said to her, "You are right to say you have no husband. ¹⁸Really you have had five husbands. But the man you live with now is not your husband. You told me the truth."

¹⁹The woman said, "Sir, I can see that you are a prophet.* ²⁰Our fathers worshiped on this mountain. But you Jews say that Jerusalem is the place where people must worship."

²¹Jesus said, "Believe me, woman! The time is coming when you will not have to be in Jerusalem or on that mountain to worship the Father *(God)*. ²²You Samaritans worship something that you don't understand. We Jews understand what we worship. Salvation comes from the Jews. ²³The time is coming when the true worshipers will worship the Father in spirit and truth. That time is now here. And those are the kind of people the Father wants to be his worshipers. ²⁴God is spirit. So the people that worship God must worship in spirit and truth."

Spirit The Holy Spirit. Also called the Spirit of God, Spirit of Christ, and the Comforter. Joined with God and Christ, he does God's work among people in the world.

Pharisees The Pharisees were a Jewish religious group that claimed to follow carefully all Jewish laws and customs.

baptize, baptizing Greek word meaning to immerse, dip, or bury a person or thing briefly under water.

Samaritan From Samaria. Samaritans were part Jewish, but the Jews did not accept them as pure Jews.

Jews are not friends with Samaritans Or, "Jews don't use things that Samaritans have used."

prophet A person who spoke for God. He could tell things that most people could not know.

²⁵The woman said, "I know that the Messiah is coming." (Messiah is the One called Christ.*) "When the Messiah comes, he will explain everything to us."
²⁶Then Jesus said, "That person is talking to you now. I am ₍the Messiah₎."
²⁷At that time Jesus' followers came back from town. They were surprised because they saw Jesus talking with a woman. But none of them asked, "What do you want?" or "Why are you talking with her?"
²⁸Then the woman left her water and went back to town. She told the people in town, ²⁹"A man told me everything I have ever done. Come see him. Maybe he is the Christ.*" ³⁰So the people left the town and went to see Jesus.
³¹While the woman was in town, Jesus' followers were begging him, "Teacher, eat something!"
³²But Jesus answered, "I have food to eat that you know nothing about."
³³So the followers asked themselves, "Did somebody already bring Jesus some food?"
³⁴Jesus said, "My food is to do what the One *(God)* who sent me wants me to do. My food is to finish the work that he gave me to do. ³⁵₍When you plant₎ you always say, 'Four more months to wait before we gather the grain.' But I tell you, open your eyes. Look at the ₍people₎. They are like₍ fields ready for harvesting now. ³⁶Even now, the person that harvests the crop is being paid. He is gathering crops for eternal life. So now the person that plants can be happy together with the person that harvests. ³⁷It is true when we say, 'One person plants, but another person harvests the crop.' ³⁸I sent you to harvest a crop that you did not work for. Other people did the work, and you get the profit from their work."
³⁹Many of the Samaritan people in that town believed in Jesus. They believed because of what the woman had told them about Jesus. She had told them, "He *(Jesus)* told me everything I have ever done." ⁴⁰The Samaritans went to Jesus. They begged Jesus to stay with them. So Jesus stayed there two days. ⁴¹Many more people believed because of the things Jesus said.
⁴²The people said to the woman, "First we believed in Jesus because of what you told us. But now we believe because we heard him ourselves. We know now that he really is the one that will save the world."

Jesus Heals an Official's Son

⁴³Two days later Jesus left and went to Galilee. ⁴⁴(Jesus had said before that a prophet* is not respected in his own country.) ⁴⁵When Jesus arrived in Galilee, the people there welcomed him. These people had seen all the things Jesus did at the ₍Passover₎* festival in Jerusalem. These people had been at the festival too.
⁴⁶Jesus went to visit Cana in Galilee again. Cana is where Jesus had changed the water into wine. One of the king's important officials lived in the city of Capernaum. This man's son was sick. ⁴⁷The man heard that Jesus had come from Judea and was now in Galilee. So the man went to Jesus ₍in Cana₎. He begged Jesus to come to Capernaum and heal his son. His son was almost dead. ⁴⁸Jesus said to him, "You people must see miracles* and wonderful works before you will believe in me."
⁴⁹The king's official said, "Sir, come ₍to my house₎ before my little son dies."
⁵⁰Jesus answered, "Go. Your son will live."
The man believed what Jesus told him and went home. ⁵¹On the way home the man's servants came and met him. They told him, "Your son is well."
⁵²The man asked, "What time did my son begin to get well?"
The servants answered, "It was about one o'clock yesterday when the fever left him."
⁵³The father knew that one o'clock was the same time that Jesus had said, "Your son will live." So the man and all the people in his home believed in Jesus.
⁵⁴That was the second miracle* that Jesus did after coming from Judea to Galilee.

Jesus Heals a Man at a Pool

5 Later Jesus went to Jerusalem for a special Jewish festival. ²In Jerusalem there is a pool with five covered porches. In the Jewish language* it is called Bethzatha.* This pool is near the Sheep Gate. ³Many sick people were

---

Christ The "anointed one" (Messiah) or chosen of God.

prophet A person who spoke for God.
Passover Important Jewish holy day. They ate a special meal on this day every year to remember that God freed them from slavery in Egypt in the time of Moses.
miracle(s) Miracles are amazing works done by God's power.
Jewish language Aramaic, a language like Hebrew that was spoken by the Jews in the first century.
Bethzatha Also called Bethsaida or Bethesda, a pool of water north of the temple in Jerusalem.

lying on the porches ₍beside the pool₎. Some of the people were blind, some were crippled, and some were paralyzed.* ⁵There was a man lying there who had been sick for 38 years. ⁶Jesus saw the man lying there. Jesus knew that the man had been sick for a very long time. So Jesus asked the man, "Do you want to be well?"

⁷The sick man answered, "Sir, there is no person to help me get into the water when the water starts moving. I try to be the first person into the water. But when I try, another person always goes in before I can."

⁸Then Jesus said, "Stand up! Pick up your bed and walk." ⁹Then immediately the man was well. The man picked up his bed and started walking.

The day all this happened was a Sabbath day.* ¹⁰So the Jews said to the man that had been healed, "Today is the Sabbath. It is against our law for you to carry your bed on the Sabbath day."

¹¹But the man answered, "The person *(Jesus)* that made me well told me, 'Pick up your bed and walk.'"

¹²The Jews asked the man, "Who is the person that told you to pick up your bed and walk?"

¹³But the man that had been healed did not know who the person was. There were many people in that place, and Jesus had left.

¹⁴Later Jesus found the man at the temple.* Jesus said to him, "See, you are well now. But stop sinning or something worse may happen to you!"

¹⁵Then the man left and went back to those Jews. The man told them that Jesus was the one that made him well.

¹⁶Jesus was doing these things *(healing)* on the Sabbath day.* So the Jews began to do bad things to Jesus. ¹⁷But Jesus said to the Jews, "My Father never stops working. And so I work too."

¹⁸This made the Jews try harder to kill him. ₍The Jews said₎, "First Jesus was breaking the law about the Sabbath day. Then he said that God is his Father! He is making himself equal with God!"

Verse 3   Some Greek copies add "and they waited for the water to move." A few later copies add verse 4: "Sometimes an angel of the Lord came down to the pool and shook the water. After the angel did this, the first person to go into the pool was healed from any sickness he had."
Sabbath day   The seventh day of the Jewish week. It was a special religious day for the Jews.
temple   The special building in Jerusalem for Jewish worship.

Jesus Has God's Authority

¹⁹But Jesus answered, "I tell you the truth. The Son can do nothing alone. The Son does only what he sees his Father doing. The Son does the same things that the Father does. ²⁰The Father loves the Son, and the Father shows the Son all the things he does. ₍This man was healed₎. But the Father will show the Son greater things than this to do. Then you will all be amazed. ²¹The Father raises dead people and gives them life. In the same way, the Son gives life to the people he wants to. ²²Also, the Father judges no one. But the Father has given the Son power to do all the judging. ²³God did this so that all people will respect the Son the same as they respect the Father. If a person does not respect the Son, then that person does not respect the Father. The Father is the One who sent the Son.

²⁴"I tell you the truth. If a person hears what I say and believes in the One who sent me, that person has life forever. That person will not be judged guilty. He has already left death and has entered into life. ²⁵I tell you the truth. An ₍important₎ time is coming. That time is already here. People that are dead ₍in sin₎ will hear the voice of the Son of God. And the people that ₍accept the things they₎ hear ₍from the Son₎ will have life ₍forever₎. ²⁶Life comes from the Father *(God)* himself. So the Father has also allowed the Son *(Jesus)* to give life. ²⁷And the Father has given the Son the power to judge ₍all people₎. Why? Because that Son is the Son of Man.* ²⁸Don't be surprised at this. A time is coming when all people that are dead and in their graves will hear his voice. ²⁹Then they will come out of their graves. The people that did good ₍in life₎ will rise and have life forever. But the people that did evil will rise to be judged guilty.

Jesus Continues Talking to the Jews

³⁰"I can do nothing alone. I judge only the way I am told. So my judgment is right. Why? Because I don't try to please myself. But I want to please the One *(God)* who sent me.

³¹"If I tell people about myself, then people cannot accept those things I say about myself. ³²But there is another person that tells people about me. And I know that the things he says about me are true.

Son of Man   Jesus. In Dan. 7:13-14 this is the name for the Messiah, the one God chose to save his people.

³³"You have sent men to John. And he has told you about the truth. ³⁴I don't need a man to tell people about me. But I tell you these things so that you can be saved. ³⁵John was like a lamp that burned and gave light. And you were happy to enjoy his light for a while.

³⁶"But I have a proof about myself that is greater than John. The things I do are my proof. These are the things my Father gave me to do. These things show that the Father sent me. ³⁷And the Father that sent me has given proof about me himself. But you have never heard his voice. You have never seen what he looks like. ³⁸The Father's teaching does not live in you. Why? Because you don't believe in the One the Father sent. ³⁹You carefully study the Scriptures.* You think that those Scriptures give you life forever. Those same Scriptures tell about me! ⁴⁰But you refuse to come to me to have that life ⌊you want⌋.

⁴¹"I don't want praise from men. ⁴²But I know you—I know that you don't have God's love in you. ⁴³I have come from my Father—I speak for him. But you don't accept me. But when another person comes speaking only for himself, you will accept him. ⁴⁴You like to have praise from each other. But you never try to get the praise that comes from the only God. So how can you believe? ⁴⁵Don't think that I will stand before the Father and say that you are wrong. Moses is the person that says that you are wrong. And Moses is the one that you hoped would save you. ⁴⁶If you really believed Moses, you would believe me. Why? Because Moses wrote about me. ⁴⁷But you don't believe what Moses wrote. So you cannot believe the things I say."

Jesus Feeds More than 5,000 People

6 Later, Jesus went across Lake Galilee (or, Lake Tiberias). ²Many people followed Jesus. They followed him because they saw the ways Jesus showed his power by healing the sick people. ³Jesus went up on the side of the hill. He sat there with his followers. ⁴It was almost the time for the Jewish Passover* festival.

⁵Jesus looked up and saw many people coming toward him. Jesus said to Philip, "Where can we buy ⌊enough⌋ bread for all these people to eat?" ⁶(Jesus asked Philip this question to test him. Jesus already knew what he planned to do.)

⁷Philip answered, "We would all have to work a month to buy enough bread for each person here to have only a little piece."

⁸Another follower there was Andrew. Andrew was Simon Peter's brother. Andrew said, ⁹"Here is a boy with five loaves of barley bread and two little fish. But that is not enough for so many people."

¹⁰Jesus said, "Tell the people to sit down." This was a very grassy place. There were about 5,000 men that sat down there. ¹¹Then Jesus held the loaves of bread. Jesus thanked God for the bread and gave it to the people that were sitting down. He did the same with the fish. Jesus gave the people as much as they wanted.

¹²All the people had enough to eat. When they finished Jesus said to his followers, "Gather the pieces of fish and bread that were not eaten. Don't waste anything." ¹³So the followers gathered up the pieces that were left. The people had started eating with only five loaves of barley bread. But the followers filled twelve large baskets with the pieces of food that were left.

¹⁴The people saw this miracle* that Jesus did. The people said, "He must truly be the Prophet* that is coming into the world."

¹⁵Jesus knew that the people wanted him to become king. The people planned to come get Jesus and make him their king. So Jesus left and went into the hills alone.

Jesus Walks on the Water

¹⁶That evening Jesus' followers went down to the lake *(Lake Galilee)*. ¹⁷It was dark now and Jesus had not yet come back to them. The followers got into a boat and started going across the lake to Capernaum. ¹⁸The wind was blowing very hard. The waves on the lake were becoming bigger. ¹⁹They rowed the boat about three or four miles. Then they saw Jesus. He was walking on the water. He was coming to the boat. The followers were afraid. ²⁰But Jesus said to them, "Don't be afraid. It's me." ²¹After Jesus said this, the followers were happy to take Jesus into the boat. Then the boat came to land at the place where they wanted to go.

Scriptures Holy Writings—the Old Testament.
Passover Important Jewish holy day. They ate a special meal on this day every year to remember that God freed them from slavery in Egypt in the time of Moses.

miracle(s) Miracles are amazing works done by God's power.
Prophet They probably meant the prophet that God told Moses he would send (Deut. 18:15-19).

The People Seek Jesus

²²The next day came. Some people had stayed on the other side of the lake. These people knew that Jesus did not go with his followers in the boat. The people knew that Jesus' followers had left in the boat alone. And they knew that it was the only boat that was there. ²³But then some boats from Tiberias came. The boats landed near the place where the people had eaten ₍the day before₎. This was where they had eaten the bread after the Lord *(Jesus)* gave thanks. ²⁴The people saw that Jesus and his followers were not there now. So the people got into the boats and went to Capernaum. They wanted to find Jesus.

Jesus, the Bread of Life

²⁵The people found Jesus on the other side of the lake. They asked Jesus, "Teacher, when did you come here?"

²⁶Jesus answered, "Why are you looking for me? Are you looking for me because you saw me do miracles* that prove my power? No! I tell you the truth. You are looking for me because you ate the bread and you were satisfied *(full)*. ²⁷Earthly food spoils and ruins. So don't work to get that kind of food. But work to get the food that stays good always and gives you life forever. The Son of Man* will give you that food. God the Father showed that he is with the Son of Man."

²⁸The people asked Jesus, "What are the things God wants us to do?"

²⁹Jesus answered, "The work God wants you to do is this: to believe in the One that God sent."

³⁰So the people asked, "What miracle* will you do to prove ₍that you are the One God sent₎? If we can see you do a miracle, then we will believe you. What will you do? ³¹Our fathers *(ancestors)* ate the manna *(food)* God gave them in the desert. This is written in the Scriptures*: 'God gave them bread from heaven to eat.'*"

³²Jesus said, "I tell you the truth. Moses was not the one that gave your people bread from heaven. But my Father gives you the true bread from heaven. ³³What is the bread of God? God's bread is the One that comes down from heaven and gives life to the world."

³⁴The people said, "Sir, give us this bread always."

³⁵Then Jesus said, "I am the bread that gives life. The person that comes to me will never be hungry. The person that believes in me will never be thirsty. ³⁶I told you before that you have seen me, and still you don't believe. ³⁷The Father gives me my people. Every one of those people will come to me. I will always accept every person that comes to me. ³⁸I came down from heaven to do what God wants me to do. I did not come to do what I want to do. ³⁹I must not lose any person that God has given me. But I must raise up those people on the last day. This is what the One who sent me wants me to do. ⁴⁰Every person that sees the Son and believes in him has life forever. I will raise up that person on the last day. This is what my Father wants."

⁴¹The Jews began to complain about Jesus. They complained because Jesus said, "I am the bread that comes down from heaven." ⁴²The Jews said, "This is Jesus. We know his father and mother. Jesus is only Joseph's son. How can he say, 'I came down from heaven'?"

⁴³But Jesus said, "Stop complaining to each other. ⁴⁴The Father is the One who sent me. And the Father is the One who brings people to me. I will raise up those people on the last day. If the Father does not bring a person to me, then that person cannot come to me. ⁴⁵It is written in the prophets*: 'God will teach all the people.'* People listen to the Father and learn from him. Those people come to me. ⁴⁶I don't mean that anyone has seen the Father. The only person that has ever seen the Father is the One that came from God. That person has seen the Father. ⁴⁷I tell you the truth. If a person believes, then that person has life forever. ⁴⁸I am the bread that gives life. ⁴⁹Your ancestors ate the manna *(food)* God gave them in the desert. But ₍like all people₎, they died. ⁵⁰₍I am₎ that bread that comes down from heaven. If a person eats this bread, he will never die. ⁵¹I am the living bread that came down from heaven. If a person eats this bread, then that person will live forever. This bread is my body. I will give my body so that the people in the world can have life."

⁵²Then the Jews began to argue among themselves. They said, "How can this man give us his body to eat?"

---

miracle(s) Miracles are amazing works done by God's power.
Son of Man Jesus. In Dan. 7:13-14 this is the name for the Messiah, the one God chose to save his people.
Scriptures Holy Writings—the Old Testament.
'God gave ... eat' Quote from Ps. 78:24.

prophets People who spoke for God. Their writings are part of the Old Testament.
'God will teach ... people' Quote from Isa. 54:13.

⁵³Jesus said, "I tell you the truth. You must eat the body of the Son of Man.* And you must drink his blood. If you don't do this, then you don't have real life in you. ⁵⁴The person that eats my body and drinks my blood has eternal life. I will raise up that person on the last day. ⁵⁵My body is true food. My blood is true drink. ⁵⁶If a person eats my body and drinks my blood, then that person lives in me, and I live in that person. ⁵⁷The Father sent me. The Father lives, and I live because of the Father. So the person that eats me will live because of me. ⁵⁸I am not like the bread that our ancestors ate ⌊in the desert⌋. They ate that bread. But, ⌊like all people⌋, they died. I am the bread that came down from heaven. The person that eats this bread will live forever." ⁵⁹Jesus said all these things while he was teaching in the synagogue* in the city of Capernaum.

The Words of Eternal Life

⁶⁰The followers of Jesus heard this. Many of the followers said, "This teaching is hard ⌊to accept⌋. Who can accept this teaching?"

⁶¹Jesus knew that his followers were complaining about this. So Jesus said, "Does this teaching bother you? ⁶²Then will it also bother you to see the Son of Man* going back to the place where he came from? ⁶³It is not the body that gives a person life. It is the spirit that gives life. The things I told you are spirit. And so these things give life. ⁶⁴But some of you don't believe." (Jesus knew the people that did not believe. Jesus knew this from the beginning. And Jesus knew the person that would turn against him.) ⁶⁵Jesus said, "That is why I said, 'If the Father does not let a person come to me, then that person cannot come.'"

⁶⁶After Jesus said these things, many of his followers left him. They stopped following Jesus.

⁶⁷Jesus asked the twelve apostles,* "Do you want to leave too?"

⁶⁸Simon Peter answered Jesus, "Lord, where would we go? You have the things that give life forever. ⁶⁹We believe in you. We know that you are the Holy One from God."

⁷⁰Then Jesus answered, "I chose all twelve of you. But one of you is a devil."

⁷¹Jesus was talking about Judas, the son of Simon Iscariot. Judas was one of the twelve ⌊apostles⌋.* But later Judas would turn against Jesus.

Jesus and His Brothers

7 After this, Jesus traveled around the country of Galilee. Jesus did not want to travel in Judea, because the Jews there wanted to kill him. ²It was time for the Jewish Festival of Shelters.* ³So Jesus' brothers said to him, "You should leave here and go to ⌊the festival in⌋ Judea. Then your followers there can see the miracles* you do. ⁴If a person wants the people to know him, then that person must not hide the things he does. Show yourself to the world. ⌊Let them see⌋ these things (miracles) you do." ⁵(Even Jesus' brothers did not believe in him.) ⁶Jesus said to his brothers, "The right time for me has not yet come. But any time is right for you ⌊to go⌋. ⁷The world cannot hate you. But the world hates me. Why? Because I tell the people in the world that they do evil things. ⁸So you go to the festival. I will not go to the festival now. The right time for me has not yet come." ⁹After Jesus said this, he stayed in Galilee.

¹⁰So Jesus' brothers left to go to the festival. After they left, Jesus went too. But Jesus did not let people see him. ¹¹At the festival the Jews were looking for Jesus. The Jews said, "Where is that man?"

¹²There was a large group of people there. Many of these people were talking secretly to each other about Jesus. Some people said, "He is a good man." But other people said, "No, he fools the people." ¹³But none of the people were brave enough to talk about Jesus openly. The people were afraid of the Jewish leaders.

Jesus Teaches in Jerusalem

¹⁴The festival* was about half finished. Then Jesus went to the temple* and began to teach. ¹⁵The Jews were amazed. They said, "This man has never studied in school. How did he learn so much?"

¹⁶Jesus answered, "The things I teach are not my own. My teaching comes from him (God) who sent me. ¹⁷If a person wants to do what God

---

Son of Man Jesus. In Dan. 7:13-14 this is the name for the Messiah, the one God chose to save his people.
synagogue Synagogues were places where Jews gathered for prayer, study of the Scriptures, and other public meetings.
apostles The men Jesus chose to be his special helpers.

Festival of Shelters Special week each year when the Jews lived in tents to remember that their people wandered in the desert 40 years during the time of Moses.
miracle(s) Miracles are amazing works done by God's power.
festival The Festival of Shelters. See footnote on verse 2.
temple The special building in Jerusalem for Jewish worship.

wants, then that person will know that my teaching comes from God. That person will know that this teaching is not my own. ¹⁸Any person that teaches his own ideas is trying to get honor for himself. But a person that tries to bring honor to the one that sent him—that person speaks the truth. There is nothing false in him. ¹⁹Moses gave you the law.* Right? But none of you obey that law. Why are you trying to kill me?"

²⁰The people answered, "A demon* has come into you ₍and made you crazy₎! We are not trying to kill you."

²¹Jesus said to them, "I did one miracle* and you are all amazed. ²²Moses gave you the law about circumcision.* (But really Moses did not give you circumcision. Circumcision came from our people ₍that lived before Moses₎.) So sometimes you circumcise a baby on a Sabbath day.* ²³This shows that a person can be circumcised on a Sabbath day to obey the law of Moses. So why are you angry at me for healing a person's whole body on the Sabbath day? ²⁴Stop judging by the way things look. Be fair and judge by what is really right."

The People Wonder If Jesus Is the Christ

²⁵Then some of the people that lived in Jerusalem said, "This is the man they are trying to kill. ²⁶But he is teaching where everyone can see and hear him. And no person is trying to stop him from teaching. Maybe the leaders have decided that he really is the Christ.* ²⁷But we know where this man's home is. And when the real Christ comes, no person will know where he comes from."

²⁸Jesus was still teaching in the temple.* Jesus said, "Yes, you know me and you know where I am from. But I have not come by my own authority. I was sent by the One *(God)* who is true. You don't know him. ²⁹But I know him and I am from him. He sent me."

³⁰When Jesus said this, the people tried to get him. But no person was able to touch Jesus. It was not yet the right time ₍for Jesus to be killed₎. ³¹But many of the people believed in Jesus. The people said, "We are waiting for the Christ* to come. When the Christ comes, will he do more miracles* than this man *(Jesus)* has done? No! ₍So this man must be the Christ₎."

The Jews Try to Arrest Jesus

³²The Pharisees* heard these things the people were saying about Jesus. So the leading priests and the Pharisees sent some temple police to arrest Jesus. ³³Then Jesus said, "I will be with you people a little while longer. Then I will go back to the One *(God)* who sent me. ³⁴You will look for me, but you will not find me. And you cannot come where I am."

³⁵The Jews said to each other, "Where will this man go that we cannot find him? Will he go to the Greek cities where our people live? Will he teach the Greek people there? ³⁶This man *(Jesus)* says, 'You will look for me but you will not find me.' He also says, 'You cannot come where I am.' What does this mean?"

Jesus Talks About the Holy Spirit

³⁷The last day of the festival came. It was the most important day. On that day Jesus stood and said with a loud voice, "If a person is thirsty, let him come to me and drink. ³⁸If a person believes in me, rivers of living water will flow out from his heart. That is what the Scripture* says." ³⁹Jesus was talking about the ₍Holy₎ Spirit.* The Spirit had not yet been given to people, because Jesus had not yet ₍died and₎ been raised to glory. But later, those people that believed in Jesus would receive the Spirit.

The People Argue About Jesus

⁴⁰The people heard these things that Jesus said. Some of the people said, "This man really is the Prophet.*"

⁴¹Other people said, "He is the Christ.*"

---

law Moses gave God's people the law that God gave him on Mount Sinai (Ex. 34:29-32).
demon A demon is an evil spirit from the devil.
miracle(s) Miracles are amazing works done by God's power.
circumcision Cutting off the foreskin. This was done to every Jewish baby boy. It was a mark of the agreement God made with Abraham (Gen. 17:9-14).
Sabbath day The seventh day of the Jewish week. It was a special religious day for the Jews.
Christ The "anointed one" (Messiah) or chosen of God.
temple The special building in Jerusalem for Jewish worship.
Pharisees The Pharisees were a Jewish religious group that claimed to follow carefully all Jewish laws and customs.
Scripture Part of the Holy Writings—Old Testament.
Holy Spirit Also called the Spirit of God, the Spirit of Christ, and the Comforter. Joined with God and Christ, he does God's work among people in the world.
Prophet They probably meant the prophet God told Moses he would send. See Deut. 18:15-19.

Other people said, "The Christ will not come from Galilee. ⁴²The Scripture* says that the Christ will come from the family of David.* And the Scripture says that the Christ will come from Bethlehem, the town where David lived." ⁴³So the people did not agree with each other about Jesus. ⁴⁴Some of the people wanted to arrest Jesus. But no person tried to do this.

The Jewish Leaders Refuse to Believe

⁴⁵The temple* police went back to the leading priests and the Pharisees.* The priests and the Pharisees asked, "Why did you not bring Jesus?" ⁴⁶The temple police answered, "The things he says are greater than the words of any man!" ⁴⁷The Pharisees* answered, "So Jesus has fooled you too! ⁴⁸Have any of the leaders believed in Jesus? No! Have any of us Pharisees believed in him? No! ⁴⁹But those people ₍out there₎ know nothing about the law.* They are under God's curse!"

⁵⁰But Nicodemus was there in that group. Nicodemus was the one that had gone to see Jesus before.* Nicodemus said, ⁵¹"Our law will not let us judge a man without hearing him. We cannot judge him until we know what he has done."

⁵²The Jewish leaders answered, "Are you from Galilee too? Study the Scriptures.* You will learn that no prophet* comes from Galilee."

[The oldest and best Greek copies of John do not have verses 7:53–8:11]

The Woman Caught in Adultery

⁵³All the Jewish leaders left and went home. 8Jesus went to the Mount of Olives.* ²Early in the morning Jesus went back to the temple.* All the people came to Jesus. Jesus sat and taught the people. ³The teachers of the law and the Pharisees* brought a woman there. The woman had been caught doing the sin of adultery.* These Jews forced the woman to stand before the people. ⁴They said to Jesus, "Teacher, this woman was caught having sex with a man that is not her husband. ⁵The law of Moses commands that we kill with rocks every woman that does this. What do you say we should do?" ⁶The Jews were using this question to trick Jesus. They wanted to catch Jesus saying something wrong. Then they could have a charge against him. But Jesus kneeled down and started writing on the ground with his finger. ⁷The Jewish leaders continued to ask Jesus their question. So Jesus stood up and said, "Is there any person here that has never sinned? That person without sin can throw the first rock at this woman." ⁸Then Jesus knelt down again and wrote on the ground.

⁹The people that heard Jesus began to leave one by one. The older men left first, and then the others. Jesus was left there alone with the woman. She was standing before him. ¹⁰Jesus looked up again and asked her, "Woman, all of those people are gone. None of them judged you guilty?"

¹¹The woman answered, "None of them judged me, sir."

Then Jesus said, "So I also don't judge you. You can go now, but don't sin again."

Jesus Is the Light of the World

¹²Later, Jesus talked to the people again. Jesus said, "I am the light of the world. The person that follows me will never live in darkness. That person will have the light that gives life."

¹³But the Pharisees* said to Jesus, "When you talk about yourself, you are the only one to say that these things are true. So we cannot accept these things you say."

¹⁴Jesus answered, "Yes, I am saying these things about myself. But people can believe these things I say. Why? Because I know where I came from. And I know where I am going. ₍I am not like you people₎. You don't know where I came from or where I am going. ¹⁵You judge me the way you would judge any man. I don't judge any person. ¹⁶But if I judge, my judging is true. Why? Because when I judge I am not alone. The Father who sent me is with me. ¹⁷Your own law says that when two witnesses say the same thing, then you must accept what they say. ¹⁸I am one of the witnesses that speaks about myself. And the Father who sent me is my other witness."

Scripture   Part of the Holy Writings—Old Testament.
David   King of Israel about 1000 years before Christ.
temple   The special building in Jerusalem for Jewish worship.
Pharisees   The Pharisees were a Jewish religious group that claimed to follow carefully all Jewish laws and customs.
law   The law of Moses.
Nicodemus was the one ... before   The story about Nicodemus going and talking to Jesus is in Jn. 3:1-21.
Scriptures   Holy Writings—the Old Testament.
prophet   A person who spoke for God.
Mount of Olives   A hill near the city of Jerusalem.

adultery   Breaking a marriage promise by sexual sin.

[19] The people asked, "Where is your father?"

Jesus answered, "You don't know me or my Father. But if you knew me, then you would know my Father too." [20] Jesus said these things while he was teaching in the temple.* He was near the place where all the people came to give money. But no person arrested him. The right time for Jesus had not yet come.

The Jews Don't Understand About Jesus

[21] Again, Jesus said to the people, "I will leave you. You will look for me, but you will die with your sin. You cannot come where I am going."

[22] So the Jews asked themselves, "Will Jesus kill himself? Is that why he said, 'You cannot come where I am going'?"

[23] But Jesus said to those Jews, "You people are from here below. But I am from above. You belong to this world, but I don't belong to this world. [24] I told you that you would die with your sins. Yes, you will die with your sins, if you don't believe that I AM.*"

[25] The Jews asked, "Then who are you?"

Jesus answered, "I am what I have told you from the beginning. [26] I have many things to say about you. I could judge you. But I tell people only the things I have heard from the One that sent me. And he speaks the truth."

[27] The people did not understand who Jesus was talking about. Jesus was telling them about the Father *(God)*. [28] So Jesus said to the people, "You will lift up *(kill)* the Son of Man.* Then you will know that I AM.* You will know that these things I do are not by my own authority *(power)*. You will know that I say only the things that the Father has taught me. [29] The One *(God)* who sent me is with me. I always do what pleases him. So he has not left me alone." [30] While Jesus was saying these things, many people believed in him.

Jesus Talks About Freedom from Sin

[31] So Jesus said to the Jews that believed in him, "If you continue to obey my teaching, then you are truly my followers. [32] Then you will know the truth. And the truth will make you free."

[33] The Jews answered, "We are Abraham's people. And we have never been slaves. So why do you say that we will be free?"

[34] Jesus answered, "I tell you the truth. Every person that sins is a slave. Sin is his master. [35] A slave does not stay with a family forever. But a son belongs to the family forever. [36] So if the Son makes you free, then you will be truly free. [37] I know you are Abraham's people. But you want to kill me. Why? Because you don't want to accept my teaching. [38] I am telling you what my Father has shown me. But you do the things that your father has told you."

[39] The Jews said, "Our father is Abraham."

Jesus said, "If you were really Abraham's children, then you would do the things Abraham did. [40] I am a man who has told you the truth I heard from God. But you are trying to kill me. Abraham did nothing like that. [41] So you are doing the things your own father did."

But the Jews said, "We are not like children that never knew who their father was. God is our Father. He is the only Father we have."

[42] Jesus said to those Jews, "If God were really your Father, then you would love me. I came from God, and now I am here. I did not come by my own authority. God sent me. [43] You don't understand these things I say. Why? Because you cannot accept my teaching. [44] Your father is the devil. You belong to him. You want to do what he wants. The devil was a murderer from the beginning. The devil was against the truth. And there is no truth in him. He is like the lies he tells. The devil is a liar, and he is the father of lies. [45] I speak the truth. That is why you don't believe me. [46] Can any of you prove that I am guilty of sin? If I tell the truth, then why don't you believe me? [47] The person that belongs to God accepts what God says. But you don't accept what God says, because you don't belong to God."

Jesus Talks About Himself and Abraham

[48] The Jews answered, "We say you are a Samaritan.* We say a demon* has come into you ₗand made you crazyⱼ! Are we not right when we say these things?"

[49] Jesus answered, "I have no demon in me. I give honor to my Father. But you give no honor to me. [50] I am not trying to get honor for myself.

---

temple The special building in Jerusalem for Jewish worship.
I AM This is like the name of God used in Ex. 3:14, but it can also mean "I am he (the Christ)."
Son of Man Jesus. In Dan. 7:13-14 this is the name for the Messiah, the one God chose to save his people.

Samaritan A person from Samaria. Samaritans were part Jewish, but the Jews did not accept them as pure Jews.
demon A demon is an evil spirit from the devil.

There is One who wants this honor for me. He is the judge. ⁵¹I tell you the truth. If a person obeys my teaching, then that person will never die."

⁵²The Jews said to Jesus, "Now we know that you have a demon* in you! Even Abraham and the prophets* died. But you say, 'The person that obeys my teaching will never die.' ⁵³Do you think you are greater than our father Abraham? Abraham died. And the prophets died too. Who do you think you are?"

⁵⁴Jesus answered, "If I give honor to myself, then that honor is worth nothing. The One that gives me honor is my Father. And you say that he is your God. ⁵⁵But you don't really know him. I know him. If I said I did not know him, then I would be a liar like you are liars. But I do know him. And I obey what he says. ⁵⁶Your father Abraham was very happy that he would see the day when I came. He saw that day and was happy."

⁵⁷The Jews said to Jesus, "What? You have never seen Abraham! You are not even 50 years old!"

⁵⁸Jesus answered, "I tell you the truth. Before Abraham was born, I AM.*" ⁵⁹When Jesus said this, the people picked up rocks to throw at him. But Jesus hid, and then he left the temple.*

Jesus Heals a Man Born Blind

9 While Jesus was walking, he saw a blind man. This man had been blind since the time he was born. ²Jesus' followers asked him, "Teacher, this man was born blind. But whose sin made him be born blind? His own sin, or his parents' sin?"

³Jesus answered, "It is not this man's sin or his parents' sin that made him be blind. This man was born blind so that God's power could be shown to people ⌊when I heal him⌋. ⁴While it is daytime, we must continue doing the work of the One that sent me. The night is coming. And no person can work at night. ⁵While I am in the world, I am the light of the world."

⁶After Jesus said this, Jesus spit on the dirt and made some mud with it. Jesus put the mud on the man's eyes. ⁷Jesus told the man, "Go and wash in the pool Siloam." (Siloam means "Sent.") So the man went to the pool. He washed and came back. Now he was able to see.

⁸Some people had seen this man begging before. These people and the man's neighbors said, "Look! Is this the same man that always sits and begs?"

⁹Some people said, "Yes! He is the one." But other people said, "No, he is not the same man. He only looks like him."

So the man himself said, "I am the man ⌊that was blind before⌋."

¹⁰The people asked, "What happened? How did you get your sight?"

¹¹The man answered, "The man that people call Jesus made some mud. He put the mud on my eyes. Then Jesus told me to go to Siloam and wash. So I went to Siloam and washed. And then I could see."

¹²The people asked the man, "Where is this man *(Jesus)*?"

The man answered, "I don't know."

The Jews Question the Man Jesus Healed

¹³Then the people brought the man to the Pharisees.* This was the man that had been blind. ¹⁴Jesus had made mud and healed the man's eyes. The day Jesus did this was a Sabbath day.* ¹⁵So now the Pharisees asked the man, "How did you get your sight?"

The man answered, "He put mud on my eyes. I washed, and now I can see."

¹⁶Some of the Pharisees said, "This man *(Jesus)* does not obey the law about the Sabbath day. So he is not from God."

Other men said, "But a person that is a sinner cannot do miracles* like these." These Jews could not agree with each other.

¹⁷The Jewish leaders asked the man again, "This man *(Jesus)* healed you, and you can see. What do you say about him?"

The man answered, "He is a prophet.*"

¹⁸The Jews still did not believe that this really happened to the man. They did not believe that this man was blind and was now healed. But later they sent for the man's parents. ¹⁹The Jews asked his parents, "Is this your son? You say that he was born blind. So why can he see now?"

---

demon A demon is an evil spirit from the devil.
prophets People who spoke for God. Their writings are part of the Old Testament.
I AM This is like the name of God used in Ex. 3:14, but it can also mean "I am he (the Christ)."
temple The special building in Jerusalem for Jewish worship.

Pharisees The Pharisees were a Jewish religious group that claimed to follow carefully all Jewish laws and customs.
Sabbath day The seventh day of the Jewish week. It was a special religious day for the Jews.
miracle(s) Miracles are amazing works done by God's power.
prophet A person who spoke for God.

²⁰The parents answered, "We know that this man is our son. And we know that he was born blind. ²¹But we don't know why he can see now. We don't know who healed his eyes. Ask him. He is old enough to answer for himself." ²²His parents said this because they were afraid of the Jewish leaders. The Jewish leaders had already decided that they would punish any person that said Jesus was the Christ.* The Jewish leaders would put those people out of the synagogue.* ²³That is why his parents said, "He is old enough. Ask him."

²⁴So the Jewish leaders called the man that had been blind. They told the man to come in again. The Jewish leaders said, "You should give God the glory ⌊by telling the truth⌋. We know that this man *(Jesus)* is a sinner."

²⁵The man answered, "I don't know if he is a sinner. But I do know this: I was blind, and now I can see."

²⁶The Jewish leaders asked, "What did he *(Jesus)* do to you? How did he heal your eyes?"

²⁷The man answered, "I have already told you that. But you would not listen to me. Why do you want to hear it again? Do you want to become his followers too?"

²⁸The Jewish leaders ⌊became angry and⌋ said some very bad things to the man. Then they said, "You are a follower of that man *(Jesus)*. We are followers of Moses. ²⁹We know that God spoke to Moses. But we don't even know where this man *(Jesus)* comes from!"

³⁰The man answered, "This is a very strange thing. You don't know where Jesus comes from. But he healed my eyes. ³¹We all know that God does not listen to sinners. But God will listen to a person that worships and obeys him. ³²This is the first time that any person ever healed a man that was born blind. ³³This man *(Jesus)* must be from God. If he were not from God, he could not do anything ⌊like this⌋."

³⁴The Jewish leaders answered, "You were born full of sin! Are you trying to teach us?" And the Jewish leaders forced the man to leave.

Spiritual Blindness

³⁵Jesus heard that the Jewish leaders had forced the man to leave. Jesus found the man and said, "Do you believe in the Son of Man*?"

³⁶The man asked, "Who is the Son of Man, sir? Tell me, so I can believe in him!"

³⁷Jesus said to him, "You have already seen him. The Son of Man is the one talking with you now."

³⁸The man answered, "Yes, I believe, Lord!" Then the man bowed and worshiped Jesus.

³⁹Jesus said, "I came into this world so that the world could be judged. I came so that blind people* could see. And I came so that people that ⌊think they can⌋ see will become blind."

⁴⁰Some of the Pharisees* were near Jesus. They heard Jesus say this. They asked, "What? Are you saying that we are blind too?"

⁴¹Jesus said, "If you were really blind *(without understanding)*, you would not be guilty of sin. But you say that you see *(know what you are doing)*. So you are guilty."

The Shepherd and His Sheep

10 Jesus said, "I tell you the truth. When a man enters the sheep pen, he should use the gate. If he climbs in some other way, then he is a robber. He is trying to steal the sheep. ²But the man that takes care of the sheep enters through the gate. He is the shepherd. ³The man that guards the gate opens the gate for the shepherd. And the sheep listen to the voice of the shepherd. The shepherd calls his own sheep, using their names, and he leads them out. ⁴The shepherd brings all of his sheep out. Then he goes ahead of them and leads them. The sheep follow him because they know his voice. ⁵But sheep will never follow a person they don't know. They will run away from that person, because they don't know his voice." ⁶Jesus told the people this story. But the people did not understand what the story meant.

Jesus Is the Good Shepherd

⁷So Jesus said again, "I tell you the truth. I am the gate for the sheep. ⁸All the people that came before I came were thieves and robbers. The sheep did not listen to them. ⁹I am the gate. The person that enters through me will be saved. That person will be able to come in and go out. He will

---

Son of Man Jesus. In Dan. 7:13-14 this is the name for the Messiah, the one God chose to save his people.
blind people Now Jesus is talking about people that are spiritually blind, not physically blind.
Pharisees The Pharisees were a Jewish religious group that claimed to follow carefully all Jewish laws and customs.

Christ The "anointed one" (Messiah) or chosen of God.
synagogue Synagogues were places where Jews gathered for prayer, study of the Scriptures, and other public meetings.

find everything he needs. ¹⁰A thief comes to steal and kill and destroy. But I came to give life—life that is full and good.

¹¹"I am the good shepherd. The good shepherd gives his life for the sheep. ¹²The worker that is paid to keep the sheep is different from the shepherd. The paid worker does not own the sheep. So when the worker sees a wolf coming, he runs away and leaves the sheep alone. Then the wolf attacks the sheep and scatters them. ¹³The man runs away because he is only a paid worker. He does not really care for the sheep.

¹⁴⁻¹⁵"I am the shepherd that cares for the sheep *(people)*. I know my sheep like the Father knows me. And my sheep know me like I know the Father. I give my life for these sheep. ¹⁶I have other sheep too. They are not in this flock here. I must lead them also. They will listen to my voice. In the future there will be one flock and one shepherd. ¹⁷The Father loves me because I give my life. I give my life so that I can get it back again. ¹⁸No person takes my life away from me. I give my own life freely. I have the right to give my life. And I have the right to get it back again. This is what the Father told me."

¹⁹Again the Jews did not agree with each other because of these things Jesus said. ²⁰Many of these Jews said, "A demon* has come into him and made him crazy. Why listen to him?"

²¹But other Jews said, "A man that is crazy with a demon does not say things like this. Can a demon heal the eyes of blind people? No!"

The Jews Against Jesus

²²It was winter, and the time came for the Festival of Dedication* at Jerusalem. ²³Jesus was in the temple* at Solomon's Porch.* ²⁴The Jews gathered around Jesus. They said, "How long will you make us wonder about you? If you are the Christ,* then tell us clearly."

²⁵Jesus answered, "I told you already, but you did not believe. I do miracles* in my Father's name. Those miracles show who I am. ²⁶But you don't believe. Why? Because you are not my sheep *(people)*. ²⁷My sheep listen to my voice. I know them, and they follow me. ²⁸I give my sheep eternal life. They will never die. And no person can take them out of my hand. ²⁹My Father gave my sheep to me. He is greater than all. No person can steal my sheep out of my Father's hand. ³⁰The Father and I are one."

³¹Again the Jews picked up rocks to kill Jesus. ³²But Jesus said to them, "I have done many good things from the Father. You have seen those things. Which of those good things are you killing me for?"

³³The Jews answered, "We are not killing you for any good thing you did. But you say things that are against God. You are only a man, but you say you are the same as God! That is why we are trying to kill you with rocks!"

³⁴Jesus answered, "It is written in your law, 'I *(God)* said you are gods.'* ³⁵This Scripture* called those people gods—the people that received God's message. And Scripture is always true. ³⁶So why do you say that I am saying things that are against God because I said, 'I am God's Son'? I am the one God chose and sent into the world. ³⁷If I don't do what my Father does, then don't believe what I say. ³⁸But if I do the same things my Father does, then you should believe in the things I do. You might not believe in me, but you should believe in the things I do. Then you will know and understand that the Father is in me and I am in the Father."

³⁹The Jews tried to get Jesus again. But Jesus escaped from them.

⁴⁰Then Jesus went back across the Jordan River. Jesus went to the place where John* was baptizing* before. Jesus stayed there, ⁴¹and many people came to him. The people said, "John never did a miracle.* But everything John said about this man *(Jesus)* is true." ⁴²And many people there believed in Jesus.

The Death of Lazarus

11 There was a man named Lazarus who was sick. He lived in the town of Bethany. This is the town where Mary and her sister Martha lived. ²(Mary is the same woman that later put perfume on the Lord *(Jesus)* and wiped his feet with her hair.) Mary's brother was Lazarus, the

---

demon A demon is an evil spirit from the devil.
Festival of Dedication Hanukkah, a special week celebrated by the Jews in December.
temple The special building in Jerusalem for Jewish worship.
Solomon's Porch An area on the east side of the temple. It was covered by a roof.
Christ The "anointed one" (Messiah) or chosen of God.
miracle(s) Miracles are amazing works done by God's power.

'I ... gods' Quote from Ps. 82:6.
Scripture Part of the Holy Writings—Old Testament.
John John the Baptizer, who preached to people about Christ's coming (Mt. 3; Lk. 3).
baptize, baptizing Greek word meaning to immerse, dip, or bury a person or thing briefly under water.

man that was now sick. ³So Mary and Martha sent a person to tell Jesus, "Lord, your dear friend Lazarus is sick."

⁴When Jesus heard this he said, "The end of this sickness will not be death. But this sickness is for the glory of God. This has happened to bring glory to the Son of God." ⁵(Jesus loved Martha and her sister and Lazarus.) ⁶When Jesus heard that Lazarus was sick, he stayed where he was for two more days. ⁷Then Jesus said to his followers, "We should go back to Judea."

⁸The followers answered, "But teacher, the Jews in Judea tried to kill you with stones. That was only a short time ago. Now you want to go back there?"

⁹Jesus answered, "There are twelve hours of light in the day. Right? If a person walks in the day, then he will not stumble and fall. Why? Because he can see with the light of this world. ¹⁰But when a person walks at night he stumbles. Why? Because there is no light to help him see."

¹¹After Jesus said these things, he said, "Our friend Lazarus is now sleeping. But I am going there to wake him."

¹²The followers answered, "But Lord, if he can sleep, he will be well."

¹³Jesus meant that Lazarus was dead. But Jesus' followers thought Jesus meant that Lazarus was really sleeping. ¹⁴So then Jesus said clearly, "Lazarus is dead. ¹⁵And I am glad that I was not there. I am happy for you, because now you will believe ₍in me₎. We will go to him now."

¹⁶Then Thomas (the one called Didymus) said to the other followers, "We will go too. We will die with Jesus ₍in Judea₎."

Jesus in Bethany

¹⁷Jesus arrived in Bethany. Jesus found that Lazarus had already been dead and in the tomb* for four days. ¹⁸Bethany was about two miles from Jerusalem. ¹⁹Many Jews had come to Martha and Mary. The Jews came to comfort Martha and Mary about their brother ₍Lazarus₎.

²⁰Martha heard that Jesus was coming. She went out to greet Jesus. But Mary stayed at home. ²¹Martha said to Jesus, "Lord, if you had been here, my brother would not have died. ²²But I know that even now God will give you anything you ask."

²³Jesus said, "Your brother will rise and be alive again."

²⁴Martha answered, "I know that he will rise and live again when people are resurrected *(raised from death)* on the last day."

²⁵Jesus said to her, "I am the resurrection.* I am life. The person that believes in me will have life ₍again₎ after he dies. ²⁶And the person that lives and believes in me will never really die. Martha, do you believe this?"

²⁷Martha answered, "Yes, Lord. I believe that you are the Christ,* the Son of God. You are the One that was coming to the world."

Jesus Cries

²⁸After Martha said these things, she went back to her sister Mary. Martha talked to Mary alone. Martha said, "The Teacher *(Jesus)* is here. He is asking for you." ²⁹When Mary heard this, she stood up and went quickly to Jesus. ³⁰Jesus had not yet come into the village. He was still at the place where Martha met him. ³¹The Jews were with Mary in the house. They were comforting her. They saw Mary stand and leave quickly. They thought that she was going to the tomb* ₍of Lazarus₎. They thought she was going there to cry. So they followed her. ³²Mary went to the place where Jesus was. When she saw Jesus, she bowed at his feet. Mary said, "Lord, if you had been here, my brother would not have died."

³³Jesus saw that Mary was crying. Jesus saw the Jews that came with her. They were crying too. Jesus felt very sad in his heart and was deeply troubled. ³⁴Jesus asked, "Where did you put him *(Lazarus)*?"

³⁵Jesus cried.

³⁶And the Jews said, "Look! Jesus loved Lazarus very much!"

³⁷But some of the Jews said, "Jesus healed the eyes of the blind man. Why didn't Jesus help Lazarus and stop him from dying?"

Jesus Makes Lazarus Alive Again

³⁸Again Jesus felt very sad in his heart. Jesus came to the tomb* ₍where Lazarus was₎. The tomb was a cave with a large stone covering the entrance. ³⁹Jesus said, "Move the stone away."

Martha said, "But Lord, it has been four days since Lazarus died. There will be a bad smell." Martha was the sister of the dead man *(Lazarus)*.

---

tomb A grave dug in a wall of rock.

resurrection Being raised from death to live again.
Christ The "anointed one" (Messiah) or chosen of God.

⁴⁰Then Jesus said to Martha, "Remember what I told you? I said that if you believed then you would see the glory of God." ⁴¹So they moved the stone away from the entrance. Then Jesus looked up and said, "Father, I thank you that you heard me. ⁴²I know that you always hear me. But I said these things because of the people here around me. I want them to believe that you sent me." ⁴³After Jesus said this he called in a loud voice, "Lazarus, come out!" ⁴⁴The dead man *(Lazarus)* came out. His hands and feet were wrapped with pieces of cloth. He had a handkerchief covering his face.

Jesus said to the people, "Take the cloth off of him and let him go."

The Jewish Leaders Plan to Kill Jesus

⁴⁵There were many Jews that came to visit Mary. These Jews saw what Jesus did. And many of these Jews believed in Jesus. ⁴⁶But some of the Jews went to the Pharisees.* They told the Pharisees what Jesus did. ⁴⁷Then the leading priests and Pharisees called a meeting of the Jewish council. They asked, "What should we do? This man *(Jesus)* is doing many miracles.* ⁴⁸If we let him continue doing these things, all the people will believe in him. Then the Romans will come and take away our temple* and our nation."

⁴⁹One of the men there was Caiaphas. He was the high priest that year. Caiaphas said, "You people know nothing! ⁵⁰It is better for one man to die for the people than for the whole nation to be destroyed. But you don't realize this."

⁵¹Caiaphas did not think of this himself. He was high priest that year. So he was really prophesying* that Jesus would die for the Jewish people. ⁵²Yes, Jesus would die for the Jewish people. But Jesus would also die for God's other children that were scattered ₍in all the world₎. He would die to bring them all together and make them one people.

⁵³That day the Jewish leaders began planning to kill Jesus. ⁵⁴So Jesus stopped traveling around openly among the Jews. Jesus left ₍Jerusalem₎ and went to a place near the desert. Jesus went to the town called Ephraim. Jesus stayed there with his followers.

⁵⁵It was almost time for the Jewish Passover* festival. Many people from the country went to Jerusalem before the Passover. They went to do the special things to make themselves pure ₍for the Passover₎. ⁵⁶The people looked for Jesus. They stood in the temple* and asked each other, "Is he *(Jesus)* coming to the festival? What do you think?" ⁵⁷But the leading priests and the Pharisees* had given a special order about Jesus. They said that if any person knew where Jesus was, the person must tell them. Then the leading priests and the Pharisees could arrest Jesus.

Jesus in Bethany with His Friends

12 Six days before the Passover* festival, Jesus went to Bethany. Bethany is the town where Lazarus lived. (Lazarus is the man Jesus raised from death.) ²In Bethany they had a dinner for Jesus. Martha served the food. Lazarus was one of the people eating with Jesus. ³Mary brought in a pint of very expensive perfume made from pure nard.* Mary poured the perfume on Jesus' feet. Then she wiped his feet with her hair. And the sweet smell from the perfume filled the whole house.

⁴Judas Iscariot was there. Judas was one of Jesus' followers. (He was the one that would later be against Jesus.) ₍Judas did not like what Mary did₎. Judas said, ⁵"That perfume was worth 300 silver coins.* It should have been sold, and the money should have been given to the poor people." ⁶But Judas did not really care about poor people. Judas said this because he was a thief. Judas was the one that kept the money box ₍for the group of followers₎. And Judas often stole money from the box.

⁷Jesus answered, "Don't stop her. It was right for her to save this perfume for today—the day for me to be prepared for burial. ⁸The poor people will always be with you. But you will not always have me."

The Plot Against Lazarus

⁹Many of the Jews heard that Jesus was in Bethany. So they went there to see Jesus. They also went there to see Lazarus. Lazarus was the one Jesus raised from death. ¹⁰So the leading

---

Pharisees The Pharisees were a Jewish religious group that claimed to follow carefully all Jewish laws and customs.
miracle(s) Miracles are amazing works done by God's power.
temple The special building in Jerusalem for Jewish worship.
prophesying Here, to prophesy means to tell something that will happen in the future.

Passover Important Jewish holy day. They ate a special meal on this day every year to remember that God freed them from slavery in Egypt in the time of Moses.
nard An expensive oil from the root of the nard plant.
silver coins One coin, a denarius, was the average pay for one day's work.

priests made plans to kill Lazarus too. ¹¹Because of Lazarus, many Jews were leaving [their leaders] and believing in Jesus. That is why the Jewish leaders wanted to kill Lazarus too.

Jesus Enters Jerusalem

¹²The next day the people in Jerusalem heard that Jesus was coming there. These were the many people that had come to the Passover* festival. ¹³The people took branches of palm trees and went out to meet Jesus. The people shouted,

> "Praise* Him!
> Welcome! God bless the One that comes
>   in the name of the Lord!
> God bless the King of Israel!"
>
> *Psalm 118:25-26*

¹⁴Jesus found a donkey and rode on it. This was like the Scripture* says:

> ¹⁵ "Do not be afraid, city of Zion*!
> Look! Your king is coming.
> He is riding on a young donkey."
>
> *Zechariah 9:9*

¹⁶The followers of Jesus did not understand at that time what was happening. But after Jesus was raised to glory, they understood that these things were written about him. Then the followers remembered that they had done these things for him.

People Tell About Jesus

¹⁷There were many people with Jesus when he raised Lazarus from death and told him to come out of the tomb.* Now those people were telling other people about what Jesus did. ¹⁸Many people went out to meet Jesus, because they heard that Jesus did this miracle.* ¹⁹So the Pharisees* said to each other, "Look! Our plan is not working. All the people are following him!"

Passover Important Jewish holy day. They ate a special meal on this day every year to remember that God freed them from slavery in Egypt in the time of Moses.
Praise Literally, "Hosanna," a Hebrew word used in praying to God for help. At this time it was probably a shout of joy used in praising God or his Messiah.
Scripture Part of the Holy Writings—Old Testament.
Zion Literally, "daughter of Zion," meaning Jerusalem.
tomb A grave dug in a wall of rock.
miracle(s) Miracles are amazing works done by God's power.
Pharisees A Jewish religious group that claimed to follow carefully all Jewish laws and customs.

Jesus Talks About Life and Death

²⁰There were some Greek people there too. These were some of the people that went to Jerusalem to worship at the Passover* festival. ²¹These Greek people went to Philip. (Philip was from Bethsaida, in Galilee.) The Greek people said, "Sir, we want to meet Jesus." ²²Philip went and told Andrew. Then Andrew and Philip went and told Jesus.

²³Jesus said to them, "Now is the time for the Son of Man* to receive his glory. ²⁴I tell you the truth. A grain of wheat must fall to the ground and die. Then it grows and makes many seeds. But if it never dies, then it will always be only a single seed. ²⁵The person that loves his own life will lose it. But the person that hates his life in this world will keep it. He will have life forever. ²⁶The person that serves me must follow me. Then my servant will be with me everywhere I am. My Father will give honor to people that serve me.

Jesus Talks About His Death

²⁷"Now I am very troubled. What should I say? Should I say, 'Father save me from this time [of suffering,]'? No, I came to this time so that I could suffer. ²⁸Father, bring glory to your name!"

Then a voice came from heaven, "I have brought glory to that name. I will do it again."

²⁹The people standing there heard the voice. Those people said it was thunder.

But other people said, "An angel spoke to Jesus!"

³⁰Jesus said to the people, "That voice was for you and not for me. ³¹Now is the time for the world to be judged. Now the ruler of this world *(the devil)* will be thrown out. ³²I will be lifted up from the earth. And when this happens, I will bring all people to me." ³³Jesus said this to show how he would die.

³⁴The people said, "But our law says that the Christ* will live forever. So why do you say, 'The Son of Man* must be lifted up'? Who is this 'Son of Man'?"

³⁵Then Jesus said, "The light will be with you for only a short time more. So walk while you have the light. Then the darkness *(sin)* will not catch you. The person that walks in the darkness does not know where he is going. ³⁶So put your trust in the light while you still have it. Then you

---

Son of Man Jesus. In Dan. 7:13-14 this is the name for the Messiah, the one God chose to save his people.
Christ The "anointed one" (Messiah) or chosen of God.

will become sons of light." When Jesus finished saying these things, he left. Jesus went to a place where the people could not find him.

The Jews Refuse to Believe in Jesus

³⁷Jesus did all these many miracles.* The people saw these things, but they still did not believe in him. ³⁸This was to make clear the full meaning of what Isaiah the prophet* said:

"Lord, who believed the things we told them?
Who has seen the Lord's power?"
Isaiah 53:1

³⁹This is why the people could not believe. Because Isaiah also said,

⁴⁰ "God made the people blind.
God closed their minds.
God did this so that they will not
see with their eyes
and understand with their minds.
Then I would heal them."
Isaiah 6:10

⁴¹Isaiah said this because he saw his *(Jesus')* glory. So Isaiah spoke about him *(Jesus)*.
⁴²But many people believed in Jesus. Even many of the Jewish leaders believed in Jesus. But they were afraid of the Pharisees.* So they did not say openly that they believed. They were afraid that they would be put out of the synagogue.* ⁴³These men loved praise from people more than praise from God.

Jesus' Teaching Will Judge People

⁴⁴Then Jesus said loudly, "The person that believes in me is really believing in the One *(God)* who sent me. ⁴⁵The person that sees me is really seeing the One who sent me. ⁴⁶I am light, and I came into this world. I came so that every person that believes in me would not stay in darkness.

⁴⁷"I did not come into the world to judge people. I came to save the people in the world. So I am not the one that judges the people who hear my teaching but don't obey. ⁴⁸There is a judge for the person that refuses to believe in me and does not accept what I say. The message I have taught will judge that person on the last day. ⁴⁹Why?

Because the things I taught were not from myself. The Father *(God)* who sent me told me what to say and what to teach. ⁵⁰And I know that eternal life comes from what the Father commands. So the things I say are what the Father told me to say."

Jesus Washes His Followers' Feet

13 It was almost time for the Jewish Passover* festival. Jesus knew that it was time for him to leave this world. It was now time for Jesus to go back to the Father. Jesus had always loved those people in the world who were his. Now was the time Jesus showed them his love the most.

²Jesus and his followers were at the evening meal. The devil had already persuaded Judas Iscariot to turn against Jesus. (Judas was the son of Simon.) ³The Father had given Jesus power over everything. Jesus knew this. Jesus also knew that he had come from God. And he knew that he was going back to God. ⁴While they were eating, Jesus stood up and took off his robe. Jesus got a towel and wrapped the towel around his waist. ⁵Then Jesus poured water into a pitcher. He began to wash the followers' feet. He dried their feet with the towel that was wrapped around his waist.

⁶Jesus came to Simon Peter. But Peter said to Jesus, "Lord, you should not wash my feet."
⁷Jesus answered, "You don't know what I am doing now. But later you will understand."
⁸Peter said, "No! You will never wash my feet."

Jesus answered, "If I don't wash your feet, then you cannot be one of my people."
⁹Simon Peter answered, "Lord, after you wash my feet, wash my hands and my head too!"
¹⁰Jesus said, "After a person has a bath, his whole body is clean. He needs only to wash his feet. And you men are clean, but not every one of you." ¹¹Jesus knew who would turn against him. That is why Jesus said, "Not every one of you is clean."

¹²Jesus finished washing their feet. Then he put on his clothes and sat down again. Jesus asked, "Do you understand what I did for you? ¹³You call me 'Teacher.' And you call me 'Lord.' And this is right, because that is what I am. ¹⁴I am your Lord and Teacher. But I washed your feet like a servant. So you also should wash each other's feet. ¹⁵I did this as an example for you. So you

---

miracle(s) Miracles are amazing works done by God's power.
prophet A person who spoke for God to his people.
Pharisees A Jewish religious group that claimed to follow carefully all Jewish laws and customs.
synagogue Synagogues were places where Jews gathered for prayer, study of the Scriptures, and other public meetings.

Passover Important Jewish holy day. They ate a special meal on this day every year to remember that God freed them from slavery in Egypt in the time of Moses.

should do ₍for each other₎ like I did for you. ¹⁶I tell you the truth. A servant is not greater than his master. The person that is sent to do something is not greater than the one that sent him. ¹⁷If you know these things, you will be happy if you do them.

¹⁸"I am not talking about all of you. I know the people I have chosen. But what the Scripture* said must happen: 'The man that shared my food has turned against me.'* ¹⁹I am telling you this now before it happens. Then when it happens you will believe that I AM.* ²⁰I tell you the truth. The person that accepts anyone I send also accepts me. And the person that accepts me also accepts the One who sent me."

Jesus Tells Who Will Be Against Him

²¹After Jesus said these things, he felt very troubled. Jesus said openly, "I tell you the truth. One of you will be against me."

²²Jesus' followers all looked at each other. They did not understand who the person was that Jesus was talking about. ²³One of the followers was sitting* next to Jesus. This was the follower that Jesus loved. ²⁴Simon Peter made signs to this follower to ask Jesus who the person was that he was talking about.

²⁵That follower leaned closer to Jesus and asked, "Lord, who is it that will be against you?"

²⁶Jesus answered, "I will dip this bread into the dish. The man I give it to is the man that will turn against me." So Jesus took a piece of bread. He dipped it and gave it to Judas Iscariot, the son of Simon. ²⁷When Judas took the bread, Satan *(the devil)* entered him. Jesus said to Judas. "The thing that you will do—do it quickly!" ²⁸None of the men at the table understood why Jesus said this to Judas. ²⁹Judas was the one that kept the money box ₍for the group₎. So some of the followers thought that Jesus meant for Judas to go and buy some things they needed for the feast. Or they thought that Jesus wanted Judas to go give something to the poor people.

³⁰Judas accepted the bread Jesus gave him. Then Judas went out. It was night.

Scripture Part of the Holy Writings—Old Testament.
'has turned against me' Literally, 'has lifted up his heel against me' (Ps. 41:9).
I AM This is like the name of God used in Ex. 3:14, but it can also mean "I am he (the Christ)."
sitting Literally, "lying." At Passover, people eat lying down and leaning on one arm to show they are free and not slaves.

Jesus Talks About His Death

³¹When Judas was gone, Jesus said, "Now the Son of Man* receives his glory. And God receives glory through the Son of Man. ³²If God receives glory through him, then God will give glory to the Son through himself. God will give him glory quickly."

³³Jesus said, "My children, I will be with you only a short time more. You will look for me. And what I told the Jews, I tell you now: Where I am going you cannot come.

³⁴"I give you a new command: Love each other. You must love each other like I loved you. ³⁵All people will know that you are my followers if you love each other."

Jesus Says that Peter Will Deny Him

³⁶Simon Peter asked Jesus, "Lord, where are you going?"

Jesus answered, "Where I am going you cannot follow now. But you will follow later."

³⁷Peter asked, "Lord, why can't I follow you now? I am ready to die for you!"

³⁸Jesus answered, "Will you really give your life for me? I tell you the truth. Before the rooster crows, you will say three times that you don't know me."

Jesus Comforts His Followers

14 Jesus said, "Don't let your hearts be troubled. Trust in God. And trust in me. ²There are many rooms in my Father's house. I would not tell you this if it were not true. I am going there to prepare a place for you. ³After I go and prepare a place for you, I will come back. Then I will take you with me, so that you can be where I am. ⁴You know the way to the place where I am going."

⁵Thomas said, "Lord, we don't know where you are going. So how can we know the way?"

⁶Jesus answered, "I am the way. I am the truth and the life. The only way to the Father is through me. ⁷If you really knew me, then you would know my Father too. But now you know the Father. You have seen him."

⁸Philip said to Jesus, "Lord, show us the Father. That is all we need."

⁹Jesus answered, "Philip, I have been with you for a long time. So you should know me. The person that has seen me has seen the Father too.

Son of Man Jesus. In Dan. 7:13-14 this is the name for the Messiah, the one God chose to save his people.

So why do you say, 'Show us the Father'? [10]Do you truly believe that I am in the Father and the Father is in me? The things I have told you don't come from me. The Father lives in me, and he is doing his own work. [11]Believe me when I say that I am in the Father and the Father is in me. Or believe because of the miracles* I have done. [12]I tell you the truth. The person that believes in me will do the same things I have done. Yes! He will do even greater things than I have done. Why? Because I am going to the Father. [13]And if you ask for anything in my name, I will do it for you. Then the Father's glory will be shown through the Son. [14]If you ask me for anything in my name, I will do it.

The Promise of the Holy Spirit

[15]"If you love me, then you will do the things I command. [16]I will ask the Father, and he will give you another Helper.* He will give you this Helper to be with you forever. [17]The Helper is the Spirit of truth.* The world cannot accept him. Why? Because the world does not see him or know him. But you know him. He lives with you and he will live in you.

[18]"I will not leave you all alone like children without parents. I will come back to you. [19]In a very short time the people in the world will not see me any more. But you will see me. You will live because I live. [20]On that day you will know that I am in the Father. You will know that you are in me and I am in you. [21]If a person knows my commands and obeys those commands, that person truly loves me. And my Father will love the person that loves me. And I will love that person. I will show myself to him."

[22]Then Judas (not Judas Iscariot) said, "But Lord, why do you plan to show yourself to us, but not to the world?"

[23]Jesus answered, "If any person loves me, then he will obey my teaching. My Father will love that person. My Father and I will come to that person and live with him. [24]But the person that does not love me does not obey my teaching. This teaching that you hear is not really mine. It is from my Father who sent me.

[25]"I have told you all these things while I am with you. [26]But the Helper* will teach you everything. The Helper will cause you to remember all the things I told you. This Helper is the Holy Spirit* that the Father will send in my name.

[27]"I leave you peace. It is my own peace I give you. I give you peace in a different way than the world does. So don't let your hearts be troubled. Don't be afraid. [28]You heard me say to you, 'I am leaving, but I will come back to you.' If you loved me, then you would be happy that I am going back to the Father. Why? Because the Father is greater than I am. [29]I have told you this now, before it happens. Then when it happens, you will believe. [30]I will not talk with you much longer. The ruler of this world (the devil) is coming. He has no power over me. [31]But the world must know that I love the Father. So I do exactly what the Father told me to do.

"Come now. We will leave this place."

Jesus Is Like a Vine

15 Jesus said, "I am the true vine; my Father is the gardener. [2]He cuts off every branch* of mine that does not make fruit.* And he trims and cleans every branch that makes fruit, so that it will make even more fruit. [3]You are already clean because of the teaching I have told you. [4]Continue in me and I will continue in you. No branch can make fruit alone. It must continue in the vine. It is the same with you. You cannot make fruit alone. You must continue in me.

[5]"I am the vine and you are the branches. If a person continues in me and I continue in that person, then that person will make much fruit. But without me that person can do nothing. [6]If a person does not continue in me, then he is like a branch that is thrown away. That branch dies. People pick up dead branches, throw them into the fire, and burn them.

[7]"Continue in me and follow my teachings. If you do this, then you can ask for anything you want, and it will be given to you. [8]You should make much fruit and show that you are my followers. This brings glory to my Father. [9]I loved you like the Father loved me. Now continue in my love. [10]I have obeyed my Father's commands, and I continue in his love. In the same way, if you obey my commands, you will continue in my

---

miracle(s) Miracles are amazing works done by God's power.
Helper Or, "Comforter," the Holy Spirit.
Spirit of truth The Holy Spirit. It was his work to help Jesus' followers understand God's truth. See Jn. 16:13.

Holy Spirit Called the Spirit of God, the Spirit of Christ, and the Comforter. Joined with God and Christ, he does God's work among people in the world.
branch The "branches" are Jesus' followers. See verse 5.
fruit This means the way Jesus' followers live that shows they belong to him. See verses 7-10.

love. ¹¹I have told you these things so that you can have the same joy I have. I want your joy to be the fullest joy. ¹²This is what I command you: Love each other like I have loved you. ¹³The greatest love a person can show is to die for his friends. ¹⁴You are my friends if you do the things I tell you to do. ¹⁵I don't call you servants now. A servant does not know what his master is doing. But now I call you friends because I have told you everything I heard from my Father. ¹⁶You did not choose me; I chose you. And I gave you this work: to go and make fruit. I want this fruit to continue ⌊in your life⌋. Then the Father will give you anything you ask for in my name. ¹⁷This is my command: Love each other.

Jesus Warns His Followers

¹⁸"If the world hates you, remember that the world hated me first. ¹⁹If you belonged to the world, then the world would love you like it loves its own people. But I have chosen you out of the world. So you don't belong to the world. That is why the world hates you. ²⁰Remember the lesson I told you: A servant is not greater than his master. If people did wrong to me, then they will do wrong to you too. And if people obeyed my teaching, then they will obey yours too. ²¹People will do all this to you because of me. They don't know the One who sent me. ²²If I had not come and spoken to the people of the world, then they would not be guilty of sin. But now I have spoken to them. So they have no excuse for their sin. ²³Any person that hates me also hates my Father. ²⁴I did things among those people that no other person has ever done. If I had not done those things, they would not be guilty of sin. But they have seen those things I did. And still they hate me and my Father. ²⁵But this happened so that what is written in their law would be true: 'They hated me for no reason.'*

²⁶"I will send you the Helper* from the Father. The Helper is the Spirit of truth* who comes from the Father. When he comes, he will tell about me. ²⁷And you will tell people about me too, because you have been with me from the beginning.

16 ¹"I have told you these things so that people will not be able to destroy your faith.

'They hated me ... reason' These words could be from Ps. 35:19 or Ps. 69:4.
Helper Or, "Comforter," the Holy Spirit.
Spirit of truth The Holy Spirit. It was his work to help Jesus' followers understand God's truth. See Jn. 16:13.

²People will make you leave their synagogues.* Yes, a time is coming when people will think that killing you would be doing service for God. ³People will do these things because they have not known the Father, and they have not known me. ⁴I have told you these things now. So when the time comes for these things to happen, you will remember that I warned you.

The Work of the Holy Spirit

"I did not tell you these things at the beginning, because I was with you then. ⁵Now I am going back to the One who sent me. But none of you asks me, 'Where are you going?' ⁶Your hearts are filled with sadness because I have told you these things. ⁷But I tell you the truth. It is better for you that I go away. Why? Because when I go away I will send the Helper* to you. But if I did not go away, then the Helper would not come. ⁸When the Helper comes, he will prove to the people of the world the truth about these things: about sin, about being right with God, and about judgment. ⁹The Helper will prove that people have sin, because they don't believe in me. ¹⁰He will prove to them about ⌊my⌋ being right with God, because I am going to the Father. You will not see me then. ¹¹And the Helper will prove to the world the truth about judgment, because the ruler of this world *(the devil)* is already judged.

¹²"I have many more things to say to you. But those things are too much for you to accept now. ¹³But when the Spirit of truth* comes, he will lead you into all truth. The Spirit of truth will not speak his own words. He will speak only what he hears. He will tell you the things that will happen. ¹⁴The Spirit of truth will bring glory to me. How? He will get things from me and tell them to you. ¹⁵All the things that the Father has are mine. That is why I said that the Spirit will get things from me and tell them to you.

Sadness Will Change to Happiness

¹⁶"After a short time you won't see me. Then after another short time you will see me again."

¹⁷Some of the followers said to each other, "What does Jesus mean when he says, 'After a short time you will not see me. And then after another short time you will see me again'? And what does he mean when he says, 'Because I am going to the Father'?" ¹⁸The followers asked,

---

synagogues Synagogues were places where Jews gathered for prayer, study of the Scriptures, and other public meetings.

"What does he mean by 'a short time'? We don't understand what he is saying."

¹⁹Jesus saw that the followers wanted to ask him about this. So Jesus said to the followers, "Are you asking each other what I meant when I said, 'After a short time you will not see me. And then after another short time you will see me again'? ²⁰I tell you the truth. You will cry and be sad, but the world will be happy. You will be sad, but your sadness will become joy. ²¹When a woman gives birth to a baby, she has pain, because her time has come. But when her baby is born, she forgets the pain. She forgets because she is so happy that a child has been born into the world. ²²It is the same with you. Now you are sad. But I will see you again and you will be happy. And no one will take away your joy. ²³In that day you will not ask me for anything. I tell you the truth. My Father will give you anything you ask for in my name. ²⁴You have never asked for anything in my name. Ask and you will receive. And your joy will be the fullest joy.

Victory over the World

²⁵"I have told you these things, using words that hide the meaning. But the time will come when I will not use words like that to tell you things. I will speak to you in plain words about the Father. ²⁶In that day you will ask the Father for things in my name. I am saying that I will not need to ask the Father for you. ²⁷No! The Father himself loves you. He loves you because you have loved me. And he loves you because you have believed that I came from God. ²⁸I came from the Father into the world. Now I am leaving the world and going back to the Father."

²⁹Then the followers of Jesus said, "You are speaking clearly to us now. You are not using words that are hard to understand. ³⁰We can see now that you know all things. You can answer a person's question even before he asks it. This makes us believe that you came from God."

³¹Jesus said, "So now you believe? ³²Listen to me. A time is coming when you will be scattered. Each of you will be scattered to his own home. That time is now here. You will leave me. I will be alone. But I am never really alone. Why? Because the Father is with me.

³³"I told you these things so that you can have peace in me. In this world you will have trouble. But be brave! I have defeated the world!"

Jesus Prays for His Followers

17 After Jesus said these things he looked toward heaven. Jesus prayed, "Father, the time has come. Give glory to your Son so that the Son can give glory to you. ²You gave the Son power over all people so that the Son could give eternal life to all those people you have given to him. ³And this is eternal life: that men can know you, the only true God, and that men can know Jesus Christ, the One you sent. ⁴I finished the work you gave me to do. I brought you glory on earth. ⁵And now, Father, give me glory with you. Give me the glory I had with you before the world was made.

⁶"You gave me some men from the world. I have shown them what you are like. Those men belonged to you, and you gave them to me. They have obeyed your teaching. ⁷Now they know that everything you gave me comes from you. ⁸I gave these men the teachings that you gave me. They accepted those teachings. They know that I truly came from you. And they believed that you sent me. ⁹I pray for them now. I am not praying for the people in the world. But I am praying for those men you gave me, because they are yours. ¹⁰All I have is yours, and all you have is mine. And these men bring glory to me. ¹¹Now I am coming to you. I will not stay in the world now. But these men are still in the world. Holy Father, keep them safe. Keep them safe by the power of your name (the name you gave me), so that they will be one, the same as you and I are one. ¹²While I was with them, I kept them safe. I kept them safe by the power of your name—the name you gave me. I protected them. And only one of them was lost—the man *(Judas)* that chose to be lost. He was lost so that what was said in the Scripture* would happen.

¹³"I am coming to you now. But I pray these things while I am still in the world. I say these things so that these men can have my joy. I want them to have all of my joy. ¹⁴I have given them your teaching. And the world has hated them. The world hated these men, because they don't belong to the world, the same as I don't belong to the world. ¹⁵I am not asking you to take them out of the world. But I am asking that you keep them safe from the Evil One *(the devil)*. ¹⁶They don't belong to the world, the same as I don't belong to the world. ¹⁷Make them ready for your service through your truth. Your teaching is truth. ¹⁸I have

Scripture Part of the Holy Writings—Old Testament.

sent them into the world, the same as you sent me into the world. ¹⁹I am making myself ready to serve. I do this for them, so that they can truly be ready for your service.

²⁰"I pray for these men. But I am also praying for all people that will believe in me because of the teaching of these men. ²¹Father, I pray that all people that believe in me can be one. You are in me and I am in you. I pray that these people can also be one in us, so that the world will believe that you sent me. ²²I have given these people the glory that you gave me. I gave them this glory so that they can be one, the same as you and I are one. ²³I will be in them, and you will be in me. So they will be completely one. Then the world will know that you sent me. And the world will know that you loved these people the same as you loved me.

²⁴"Father, I want these people that you have given me to be with me in every place I am. I want them to see my glory. This is the glory you gave me because you loved me before the world was made. ²⁵Father, you are the One who is good. The world does not know you, but I know you. And these people know that you sent me. ²⁶I showed them what you are like. And again I will show them what you are like. Then they will have the same love that you have for me. And I will live in them."

Jesus Is Arrested

18 When Jesus finished praying, he left with his followers. They went across the Kidron Valley. On the other side there was a garden ⌊of olive trees⌋. Jesus and his followers went there.

²Judas knew where this place was, because Jesus met there often with his followers. Judas was the one that turned against Jesus. ³So Judas led a group of soldiers to the garden. Judas also brought some guards from the leading priests and the Pharisees.* They were carrying torches, lanterns, and weapons.

⁴Jesus knew everything that would happen to him. Jesus went out and asked, "Who are you looking for?"

⁵The men answered, "Jesus from Nazareth."

Jesus said, "I am Jesus." (Judas, the one that turned against Jesus, was standing there with them.) ⁶When Jesus said, "I am Jesus," the men moved back and fell to the ground.

⁷Jesus asked them again, "Who are you looking for?"

The men said, "Jesus from Nazareth."

⁸Jesus said, "I told you that I am Jesus. So if you are looking for me, then let these other men go free." ⁹This happened so that the words Jesus said before would be true: "I have not lost any of the men you gave me."

¹⁰Simon Peter had a sword. He took out the sword and struck the servant of the high priest.* Peter cut off the servant's right ear. (The servant's name was Malchus.) ¹¹Jesus said to Peter, "Put your sword back in its place! I must accept the cup* ⌊of suffering⌋ the Father has given me."

Jesus Is Brought Before Annas

¹²Then the soldiers with their commander and the Jewish guards arrested Jesus. They tied Jesus ¹³and brought him to Annas. Annas was the father-in-law of Caiaphas. Caiaphas was the high priest* that year. ¹⁴Caiaphas was the one that had told the Jews that it would be better if one man died for all the people.

Peter Lies About Knowing Jesus

¹⁵Simon Peter and another one of Jesus' followers went with Jesus. This follower knew the high priest.* So he went with Jesus into the yard of the high priest's house. ¹⁶But Peter waited outside near the door. The follower that knew the high priest came back outside. He spoke to the girl that opened the gate for people. Then he brought Peter inside. ¹⁷The girl at the gate said to Peter, "Are you also one of the followers of that man *(Jesus)*?"

Peter answered, "No, I am not!"

¹⁸It was cold, so the servants and guards had built a fire. They were standing around it and warming themselves. Peter was standing with these men.

The High Priest Questions Jesus

¹⁹The high priest* asked Jesus questions about his followers. He asked Jesus questions about the things Jesus taught. ²⁰Jesus answered, "I have always spoken openly to all people. I always

---

Pharisees The Pharisees were a Jewish religious group that claimed to follow carefully all Jewish laws and customs.

high priest Most important Jewish priest and leader.

cup Jesus is talking about the bad things that will happen to him. Accepting these things will be very hard, like drinking a cup of something that tastes very bad.

taught in the synagogues* and in the temple.* All the Jews come together there. I never said anything in secret. ²¹So why do you question me? Ask the people that heard my teaching. They know what I said."

²²When Jesus said this, one of the guards standing there hit him. The guard said, "You should not talk to the high priest* like that!"

²³Jesus answered, "If I said something wrong, then tell everyone here what was wrong. But if the things I said are right, then why do you hit me?"

²⁴So Annas sent Jesus to Caiaphas the high priest. Jesus was still tied.

Peter Lies Again

²⁵Simon Peter was standing ₍at the fire₎, keeping himself warm. The other men said to Peter, "Are you one of the followers of that man (Jesus)?"

But Peter denied it. He said, "No, I am not."

²⁶One of the servants of the high priest* was there. This servant was a relative to the man whose ear Peter had cut off. The servant said, "I think I saw you with him (Jesus) in the garden!"

²⁷But again Peter said, "No, I was not with him!" And at that same time a rooster crowed.

Jesus Is Brought Before Pilate

²⁸Then the Jews took Jesus from Caiaphas' house to the ₍Roman governor's₎ palace. It was early in the morning. The Jews would not go inside the palace. They did not want to make themselves unclean,* because they wanted to eat the Passover* meal. ²⁹So Pilate went outside to the Jews. He asked, "What do you say this man has done wrong?"

³⁰The Jews answered, "He is a bad man. That is why we brought him to you."

³¹Pilate said to the Jews, "You Jews take him yourselves and judge him by your own law."

The Jews answered, "But your law does not allow us to punish a person by killing him." ³²(This happened so that what Jesus said about how he would die would be true.)

³³Then Pilate went back inside the palace. Pilate called Jesus to him. He asked Jesus, "Are you the king of the Jews?"

³⁴Jesus said, "Is that your own question, or did other people tell you about me?"

³⁵Pilate said, "I am not a Jew! It was your own people and their leading priests that brought you before me. What have you done wrong?"

³⁶Jesus said, "My kingdom does not belong to this world. If it belonged to this world, then my servants would fight so that I would not be given to the Jews. But my kingdom is from another place."

³⁷Pilate said, "So you are a king!"

Jesus answered, "You say that I am a king. That is true. I was born for this: to tell people about the truth. That is why I came into the world. And every person that belongs to the truth listens to me."

³⁸Pilate said, "What is truth?" When Pilate said this, he went out to the Jews again. Pilate said to the Jews, "I can find nothing to charge against this man. ³⁹But it is one of your customs for me to free one prisoner to you at the time of the Passover.* Do you want me to free this 'king of the Jews'?"

⁴⁰The Jews yelled back, "No, not him! Let Barabbas go free!" (Barabbas was a robber.)

19 Then Pilate ordered that Jesus be taken away and be whipped. ²The soldiers used some thorny branches to make a crown. They put this crown of thorns on Jesus' head. Then the soldiers put a purple robe around Jesus. ³The soldiers came to Jesus many times and said, "Hello, O king of the Jews!" They hit Jesus in the face.

⁴Again Pilate came out and said to the Jews, "Look! I am bringing Jesus out to you. I want you to know that I find nothing I can charge against him." ⁵Then Jesus came out. He was wearing the crown of thorns and the purple robe. Pilate said to the Jews, "Here is the man!"

⁶When the leading priests and the Jewish guards saw Jesus they yelled, "Kill him on a cross! Kill him on a cross!"

But Pilate answered, "You take him and nail him to a cross yourselves. I find nothing I can charge against him."

⁷The Jews answered, "We have a law that says he must die, because he said that he is the Son of God."

⁸When Pilate heard this, he was more afraid. ⁹Pilate went back inside the palace. He asked Jesus, "Where are you from?" But Jesus did not answer him. ¹⁰Pilate said, "You refuse to speak to

---

synagogues Synagogues were places where Jews gathered for prayer, study of the Scriptures, and other public meetings.

temple The special building in Jerusalem for Jewish worship.

high priest Most important Jewish priest and leader.

unclean Going into a non-Jewish place would ruin the special cleansing the Jews had done (See Jn. 11:55).

Passover Important Jewish holy day. They ate a special meal on this day every year to remember that God freed them from slavery in Egypt in the time of Moses.

me? Remember, I have the power to make you free. I also have the power to kill you on a cross." ¹¹Jesus answered, "The only power you have over me is the power given to you by God. So the man who gave me to you is guilty of a greater sin."

¹²After this, Pilate tried to let Jesus go free. But the Jews yelled, "Any person who makes himself a king is against Caesar. So if you let this man *(Jesus)* go free, that means you are not Caesar's friend."

¹³Pilate heard what the Jews said. So he brought Jesus out to the place called "The Stone Pavement." (In the Jewish language* the name is "Gabbatha.") Pilate sat down on the judge's seat there. ¹⁴It was now almost noon on Preparation day* of Passover* week. Pilate said to the Jews, "Here is your king!"

¹⁵The Jews yelled, "Take him away! Take him away! Kill him on a cross!"

Pilate asked the Jews, "Do you want me to kill your king on a cross?"

The leading priests answered, "The only king we have is Caesar!"

¹⁶So Pilate gave Jesus to them to be killed on a cross.

Jesus Is Killed on a Cross

The soldiers took Jesus. ¹⁷Jesus carried his own cross. He went out to a place called "The Place of the Skull." (In the Jewish language* the name of this place is "Golgotha.") ¹⁸At Golgotha they nailed Jesus to the cross. They also put two other men on crosses. They put the men on each side of Jesus with Jesus in the middle. ¹⁹Pilate wrote a sign and put it on the cross. The sign said, "JESUS OF NAZARETH, THE KING OF THE JEWS." ²⁰The sign was written in the Jewish language, in Latin, and in Greek. Many of the Jews read the sign, because this place where they killed Jesus on the cross was near the city. ²¹The leading Jewish priests said to Pilate, "Don't write, 'The King of the Jews.' But write, 'This man said, I am the King of the Jews.'"

²²Pilate answered, "I will not change what I have written."

²³After the soldiers nailed Jesus to the cross, they took his clothes. They divided his clothes into four parts. Each soldier got one part. They also took his tunic.* It was all one piece of cloth woven from top to bottom. ²⁴So the soldiers said to each other, "We should not tear this into parts ₍to divide it₎, We should choose lots* to see who will get it." This happened so that it would be like the Scripture* said:

"They divided my clothes among them.
And they threw lots* for my clothing."
Psalm 22:18

So the soldiers did this.

²⁵Jesus' mother stood near his cross. His mother's sister was also standing there with Mary the wife of Clopas, and Mary of Magdala. ²⁶Jesus saw his mother. He also saw the follower that he loved standing there. He said to his mother, "Dear woman, here is your son." ²⁷Then Jesus said to the follower, "Here is your mother." So after that, this follower took Jesus' mother to live in his home.

Jesus Dies

²⁸Later, Jesus knew that everything had been done. To make the Scripture* happen he said, "I am thirsty."* ²⁹There was a jar full of vinegar there. So the soldiers soaked a sponge in it. They put the sponge on a branch of a hyssop plant. Then they lifted it to Jesus' mouth. ³⁰Jesus tasted the vinegar. Then he said, "It is finished." Jesus bowed his head and died.

³¹This day was Preparation day.* The next day was a special Sabbath day.* The Jews did not want the bodies to stay on the cross on the Sabbath day. So they asked Pilate to order that the legs of the men be broken ₍to make them die sooner₎. And they asked that the bodies of the men be taken down from the crosses. ³²So the soldiers came and broke the legs of the first man on the cross beside Jesus. Then they broke the legs of the other man on the cross beside Jesus. ³³But when the soldiers came close to Jesus, they saw that he was already dead. So they did not break his legs. ³⁴But one of the soldiers stuck his spear into Jesus' side. Blood and water came out. ³⁵(The one

---

Jewish language Aramaic, a language like Hebrew that was spoken by the Jews in the first century.
Preparation day Friday, the day before the Sabbath day.
Passover Important Jewish holy day. They ate a special meal on this day every year to remember that God freed them from slavery in Egypt in the time of Moses.
tunic A piece of clothing like a long undershirt.
lots Rocks or sticks used like dice for making a choice.
Scripture Part of the Holy Writings—Old Testament.
"I am thirsty" See Ps. 22:15; 69:21.
Sabbath day The seventh day of the Jewish week. It was a special religious day for the Jews.

who saw this happen has told about it. He told about it so that you also can believe. The things he says are true. He knows that he tells the truth.) ³⁶These things happened so that it would be like the Scripture* said: "None of his bones will be broken."* ³⁷And another Scripture said, "People will look at the one they stuck ₍with the spear₎."*

Jesus Is Buried

³⁸Later, a man named Joseph from Arimathea asked Pilate for the body of Jesus. (Joseph was a follower of Jesus. But he did not tell people, because he was afraid of the Jews.) Pilate said that Joseph could take the body of Jesus. So Joseph came and took Jesus' body away. ³⁹Nicodemus went with Joseph. Nicodemus was the man who had come to Jesus before and talked to him at night. Nicodemus brought about 100 pounds* of spices. This was a mixture of myrrh and aloes.* ⁴⁰These two men took Jesus' body. They wrapped it in pieces of linen cloth with the spices. (This is how the Jews bury people.) ⁴¹In the place where Jesus was killed on the cross, there was a garden. In the garden there was a new tomb.* No person had ever been buried there before. ⁴²The men put Jesus in that tomb because it was near, and the Jews were preparing to start their Sabbath day.*

Some Followers Find Jesus' Tomb Empty

20 Early on Sunday morning Mary Magdalene went to the tomb* ₍where Jesus' body was₎. It was still dark. Mary saw that the large stone ₍that covered the entrance₎ was moved away. ²So Mary ran to Simon Peter and the other follower (the one Jesus loved). Mary said, "They have taken the Lord out of the tomb. We don't know where they put him."

³So Peter and the other follower started going to the tomb.* ⁴They were both running, but the other follower ran faster than Peter. So the other follower reached the tomb first. ⁵The follower bent down and looked in. He saw the pieces of linen cloth lying there, but he did not go in. ⁶Then Simon Peter came from behind him. Peter went into the tomb. He saw the pieces of linen lying there. ⁷He also saw the cloth that had been around Jesus' head. The cloth was folded up and laid in a different place from the pieces of linen. ⁸Then the other follower went in. This was the follower that had reached the tomb first. He saw what had happened and believed. ⁹(These followers did not yet understand from the Scriptures* that Jesus must rise from death.)

Jesus Appears to Mary Magdalene

¹⁰Then the followers went back home. ¹¹But Mary stood outside the tomb,* crying. While she was crying, she bent down and looked inside the tomb. ¹²Mary saw two angels dressed in white. They were sitting where Jesus' body had been. One angel was sitting where Jesus' head had been, and the other angel was sitting where Jesus' feet had been.

¹³The angels asked Mary, "Woman, why are you crying?"

Mary answered, "Some people have taken away ₍the body of₎ my Lord. I don't know where they put him." ¹⁴When Mary said this she turned around and saw Jesus standing there. But she did not know that it was Jesus.

¹⁵Jesus asked her, "Woman, why are you crying? Who are you looking for?"

Mary thought that this was the man that takes care of the garden. So Mary said to him, "Did you take Jesus away, sir? Tell me where you put him. I will go and get him."

¹⁶Jesus said to her, "Mary."

Mary turned toward Jesus and said in the Jewish language,* *"Rabboni."* (This means "Teacher.")

¹⁷Jesus said to her, "Don't hold me. I have not yet gone back up to the Father. But go to my brothers *(followers)* and tell them this: 'I am going back to my Father and your Father. I am going back to my God and your God.'"

¹⁸Mary Magdalene went to the followers and told them, "I saw the Lord!" And she told them the things Jesus said to her.

Scripture Part of the Holy Writings—Old Testament.
"None ... broken" Quote from Ps. 34:20. The idea is from Ex. 12:46; Num. 9:12.
"People ... spear" Quote from Zech. 12:10.
100 pounds Roman pounds, equal to about 75 pounds today.
myrrh and aloes Sweet-smelling spices used for perfume and also to prepare a body to be buried.
tomb A grave dug in a wall of rock.
Sabbath day The seventh day of the Jewish week. It was a special religious day for the Jews.

Scriptures Holy Writings—the Old Testament.
Jewish language Aramaic, a language like Hebrew that was spoken by the Jews in the first century.

Jesus Appears to His Followers

¹⁹The day was Sunday. That same evening the followers were together. The doors were locked, because they were afraid of the Jews. Then Jesus came and stood among them. Jesus said, "Peace be with you!" ²⁰After Jesus said this, he showed the followers his hands and his side. The followers were very happy when they saw the Lord.

²¹Then Jesus said again, "Peace be with you! The Father sent me. In the same way, I now send you." ²²After Jesus said that, he breathed ₍on the followers₎. Jesus said, "Receive the Holy Spirit.* ²³If you forgive people's sins, then their sins are forgiven. If you don't forgive people's sins, then their sins are not forgiven."

Jesus Appears to Thomas

²⁴Thomas (called Didymus) was not with the followers when Jesus came. Thomas was one of the twelve. ²⁵The other followers told Thomas, "We saw the Lord." Thomas said, "I will not believe it until I see the nail holes in his hands. And I will not believe until I put my finger where the nails were and put my hand into his side."

²⁶A week later the followers were in the house again. Thomas was with them. The doors were locked, but Jesus came and stood among them. Jesus said, "Peace be with you!" ²⁷Then Jesus said to Thomas, "Put your finger here. Look at my hands. Put your hand here in my side. Stop doubting and start believing."

²⁸Thomas said to Jesus, "My Lord and my God!"

²⁹Jesus said to Thomas, "You believe because you see me. Those people that believe without seeing me will be truly blessed."

Why John Wrote This Book

³⁰Jesus did many other miracles* that his followers saw. Those miracles are not written in this book. ³¹But these things are written so that you can believe that Jesus is the Christ,* the Son of God. Then, by believing, you can have life through his name.

Holy Spirit Called the Spirit of God, the Spirit of Christ, and the Comforter. Joined with God and Christ, he does God's work among people in the world.
miracle(s) Miracles are amazing works done by God's power.
Christ The "anointed one" (Messiah) or chosen of God.

Jesus Appears to Seven Followers

21 Later, Jesus showed himself to his followers. This was by Lake Tiberias *(Galilee)*. This is how it happened: ²Some of the followers were together. They were Simon Peter, Thomas (called Didymus), Nathanael from Cana in Galilee, the two sons of Zebedee, and two other followers. ³Simon Peter said, "I am going out to fish."

The other followers said, "We will go with you." So all the followers went out and got into the boat. They fished that night but caught nothing.

⁴Early the next morning Jesus stood on the shore. But the followers did not know it was Jesus. ⁵Then Jesus said to the followers, "Friends, have you caught any fish?"

The followers answered, "No."

⁶Jesus said, "Throw your net into the water on the right side of your boat. You will find some fish there." So the followers did this. They caught so many fish that they could not pull the net back into the boat.

⁷The follower that Jesus loved said to Peter, "That man is the Lord *(Jesus)*!" Peter heard him say, "That man is the Lord." Peter put his coat around himself. (Peter had taken his clothes off ₍to work₎.) Then he jumped into the water. ⁸The other followers went to shore in the boat. They pulled the net full of fish. They were not very far from shore, only about 100 yards. ⁹When the followers stepped out of the boat and onto the shore, they saw a fire of hot coals. There were fish on the fire and some bread there too. ¹⁰Then Jesus said, "Bring some of the fish that you caught."

¹¹Simon Peter went into the boat and pulled the net to the shore. It was full of big fish. There were 153. The fish ₍were very heavy₎, but the net did not tear. ¹²Jesus said to them, "Come and eat." None of the followers would ask him, "Who are you?" They knew he was the Lord. ¹³Jesus walked to the food. He took the bread and gave it to them. Jesus also got the fish and gave it to them.

¹⁴This was now the third time Jesus showed himself to his followers after he was raised from death.

Jesus Talks to Peter

¹⁵When they finished eating, Jesus said to Simon Peter, "Simon, son of John, do you love me more than these ₍other men love me₎?"

Peter answered, "Yes, Lord, you know that I love you."

Then Jesus said to Peter, "Take care of my lambs.*"
¹⁶Again Jesus said to Peter, "Simon, son of John, do you love me?" Peter answered, "Yes, Lord, you know that I love you." Then Jesus said to Peter, "Take care of my sheep.*"
¹⁷A third time Jesus said, "Simon, son of John, do you love me?" Peter was sad because Jesus asked him three times, "Do you love me?" Peter said, "Lord, you know everything. You know that I love you!" Jesus said to Peter, "Take care of my sheep. ¹⁸I tell you the truth. When you were young, you tied your own belt and went where you wanted. But when you are old, you will put out your hands and another person will tie you. That person will lead you where you don't want to go." ¹⁹(Jesus said this to show how Peter would die to give glory to God.) Then Jesus said to Peter, "Follow me!"

²⁰Peter turned and saw the follower that Jesus loved walking behind them. (This was the follower that had leaned against Jesus at the supper and said, "Lord, who will turn against you?") ²¹When Peter saw this follower behind them he asked Jesus, "Lord, what about him?"
²²Jesus answered, "Maybe I want him to live until I come. That should not be important to you. You follow me!"
²³So a story spread among the brothers *(followers)*. They were saying that this follower ₍that Jesus loved₎ would not die. But Jesus did not say that he would not die. He only said, "Maybe I want him to live until I come. That should not be important to you."
²⁴That follower is the one that is telling these things. He is the one that has now written these things. We know that what he says is true.
²⁵There are many other things that Jesus did. If every one of these things were written down, I think the whole world would not be big enough for all the books that would be written.

lambs, sheep Jesus uses these words to mean his followers, as in John 10.

Acts

Luke Writes Another Book

1 Dear Theophilus, The first book I wrote was about everything that Jesus did and taught. ²I wrote about the whole life of Jesus, from the beginning until the day he was carried up into heaven. Before this happened, Jesus talked to the apostles* he had chosen. With the help of the Holy Spirit,* Jesus told the apostles what they should do. ³This was after Jesus' death, but he showed the apostles that he was alive. Jesus proved this by doing many powerful things. The apostles saw Jesus many times during the 40 days after he was raised from death. Jesus spoke to the apostles about the kingdom of God. ⁴One time when Jesus was eating with them, he told them not to leave Jerusalem. Jesus said, "The Father has promised you something; I told you about it before. Wait here ⌊in Jerusalem⌋ to receive this promise. ⁵John baptized* people with water, but in a few days you will be baptized with the Holy Spirit.*"

Jesus Is Carried Up into Heaven

⁶The apostles* were all together. They asked Jesus, "Lord, is this the time for you to give the Jews their kingdom again?"

⁷Jesus said to them, "The Father is the only One who has the authority to decide dates and times. You cannot know these things. ⁸But the Holy Spirit* will come to you. Then you will receive power. You will be my witnesses—⌊you will tell people about me⌋. First, you will tell people in Jerusalem. Then you will tell people in all of Judea, in Samaria, and in every part of the world."

⁹After Jesus told the apostles these things, he was lifted up into the sky. While the apostles were watching, Jesus went into a cloud, and they could not see him. ¹⁰Jesus was going away, and the apostles were looking into the sky. Suddenly, two men *(angels)* wearing white clothes stood beside them. ¹¹The two men said to the apostles, "Men from Galilee, why are you standing here looking into the sky? You saw Jesus carried away from you into heaven. He will come back in the same way you saw him go."

A New Apostle Is Chosen

¹²Then the apostles* went back to Jerusalem from the Mount of Olives. (This mountain is about one-half mile from Jerusalem.) ¹³The apostles entered the city. They went to the place where they were staying; this was in a room upstairs. The apostles were: Peter, John, James, Andrew, Philip, Thomas, Bartholomew, Matthew, James (the son of Alphaeus), Simon (known as the Zealot*), and Judas (the son of James).

¹⁴The apostles* were all together. They were constantly praying with the same purpose. Some women, Mary, the mother of Jesus, and his brothers were there with the apostles.

¹⁵After a few days there was a meeting of the believers. (There were about 120 of them.) Peter stood up and said, ¹⁶⁻¹⁷"Brothers, in the Scriptures* the Holy Spirit* said through David that something must happen. He was talking about Judas, one of our own group. Judas served together with us. The Spirit said that Judas would lead men to arrest Jesus."

¹⁸(Judas was paid money for doing this. His money was used to buy him a field. But Judas fell on his head, and his body broke open. All his intestines poured out. ¹⁹And all the people of Jerusalem learned about this. That is why they

---

apostles   The men Jesus chose to be his special helpers.
Holy Spirit   Called the Spirit of God, the Spirit of Christ, and the Comforter. Joined with God and Christ, he does God's work among people in the world.
baptized   A Greek word meaning to immerse, dip, or bury a person or thing briefly under water.

Zealot   The Zealots were a Jewish political group.
Scriptures   Holy Writings—the Old Testament.

named that field Akeldama. In their language Akeldama means "field of blood.")

²⁰Peter said, "In the book of Psalms, this is written about Judas:

'People should not go
near his land *(property)*;
No one should live there!'
Psalm 69:25

And it is also written:

'Let another man have his work.'
Psalm 109:8

²¹⁻²²So now another man must join us and become a witness of Jesus' resurrection *(rising from death)*. This man must be one of those men who were part of our group during all the time when the Lord Jesus was with us. This man must have been with us from the time John began to baptize* people until the day when Jesus was carried up from us into heaven."

²³The apostles* put two men before the group. One was Joseph Barsabbas. He was also called Justus. The other man was Matthias. ²⁴⁻²⁵The apostles prayed, "Lord, you know the minds of all men. Show us which one of these two men you choose to do this work. Judas turned away from it and went where he belongs. Lord, show us which man should take his place as an apostle!" ²⁶Then the apostles used lots* to choose one of the two men. The lots showed that Matthias was the one that the Lord wanted. So he became an apostle with the other eleven.

The Coming of the Holy Spirit

2 When the day of Pentecost* came, the apostles* were all together in one place. ²Suddenly a noise came from the sky. It sounded like a strong wind blowing. This noise filled the whole house where they were sitting. ³They saw something that looked like flames of fire. The flames were separated and stood over each person there. ⁴They were all filled with the Holy Spirit,* and they began to speak different languages. The Holy Spirit was giving them the power to do this.

⁵There were some very religious Jewish men in Jerusalem at this time. These men were from every country in the world. ⁶A large group of these men came together because they heard the noise. They were surprised because the apostles* were speaking, and every man heard in his own language. ⁷The Jews were all amazed at this. They did not understand how the apostles could do this. They said, "Look! These men *(the apostles)* that we hear speaking are all from Galilee*! ⁸But we hear them in our own languages. How is this possible? We are from different places: ⁹Parthia, Media, Elam, Mesopotamia, Judea, Cappadocia, Pontus, Asia,* ¹⁰Phrygia, Pamphylia, Egypt, the areas of Libya near the city of Cyrene, Rome, ¹¹Crete and Arabia. Some of us were born Jews. Others are converts.* We are from these different countries. But we can hear these men in our own languages! We can all understand the great things they are saying about God." ¹²The people were all amazed and confused. They asked each other, "What is happening?" ¹³Other people were laughing at the apostles. These people thought the apostles were drunk from too much wine.

Peter Speaks to the People

¹⁴Then Peter stood up with the other eleven apostles.* He spoke loudly so that all the people could hear. He said, "My Jewish brothers and all of you who live in Jerusalem, listen to me. I will tell you something you need to know. Listen carefully. ¹⁵These men are not drunk like you think; it is only nine o'clock in the morning! ¹⁶But Joel the prophet* wrote about the things you see happening here today. This is what Joel wrote:

¹⁷ 'God says: In the last days,
I will pour out *(give)* my Spirit*
to all people.
Your sons and daughters will prophesy.*
Your young men will see visions.*
Your old men will have special dreams.

---

baptize A Greek word meaning to immerse, dip, or bury a person or thing briefly under water.
apostles The men Jesus chose to be his special helpers.
lots Rocks or sticks used like dice for making a choice.
Pentecost Jewish festival celebrating the wheat harvest. It was fifty days after Passover.
Holy Spirit, Spirit Also called the Spirit of God, the Spirit of Christ, and the Comforter. Joined with God and Christ, he does God's work among people in the world.

from Galilee The people thought men from Galilee could speak only their own language.
Asia The western part of Asia Minor.
converts People that changed their religion to become Jews.
prophet A prophet was a person who spoke for God.
prophesy Speak for God.
visions Something like dreams used by God to speak to people.

¹⁸ At that time I will pour out *(give)* my Spirit*
to my servants, men and women,
and they will prophesy.*
¹⁹ I will show amazing things in the sky above.
I will give proofs on the earth below.
There will be blood, fire, and thick smoke.
²⁰ The sun will be changed into darkness,
and the moon will become red like blood.
Then the great and glorious day of the Lord
will come.
²¹ And every person who trusts in the Lord
will be saved.'

Joel 2:28-32

²²"My Jewish brothers, listen to these words: Jesus from Nazareth was a very special man. God clearly showed this to you. God proved this by the powerful and amazing things he did through Jesus. You all saw these things. So you know this is true. ²³Jesus was given to you, and you killed him. With the help of bad men you nailed Jesus to a cross. But God knew all this would happen. This was God's plan. God made this plan long ago. ²⁴Jesus suffered the pain of death, but God made him free. God raised Jesus from death. Death could not hold Jesus. ²⁵David said this about Jesus:

'I saw the Lord before me always;
he is at my right side to keep me safe.
²⁶ So my heart is glad,
and my mouth speaks with joy.
²⁷ Yes, even my body will live with hope;
because you will not leave my soul
in the place of death.*
You will not let the body of your Holy One
rot in the grave.
²⁸ You taught me how to live.
You will come close to me
and give me great joy.'

Psalm 16:8-11

²⁹"My brothers, I can tell you truly about David, our ancestor. He died and was buried. His grave is still here with us today. ³⁰David was a prophet* and knew something God said. God promised David that he would make a person from David's family to be a king like David. ³¹David knew this before it happened. That is why David said this about that person:

'He was not left in the place of death.*
His body did not rot in the grave.'

David was talking about the Christ* rising from death. ³²So Jesus is the One God raised from death, ₍not David₎! We are all witnesses of this. We saw him! ³³Jesus was lifted up to heaven. Now Jesus is with God, at God's right side. The Father *(God)* has now given the Holy Spirit* to Jesus. The Holy Spirit is what God promised to give. So now Jesus is pouring out *(giving)* that Spirit. This is what you see and hear. ³⁴David was not the one who was lifted up to heaven. ₍It was Jesus who was lifted up to heaven₎. David himself said:

'The Lord *(God)* said to my Lord:
Sit at my right side,
³⁵ until I put your enemies
under your power.*'

Psalm 110:1

³⁶"So, all the Jewish people should know this truly: God has made Jesus to be Lord and Christ.* He is the man you nailed to the cross!"

³⁷When the people heard this, they felt very, very sorry. They asked Peter and the other apostles,* "What should we do?"

³⁸Peter said to them, "Change your hearts and lives and be baptized,* each one of you, in the name of Jesus Christ. Then God will forgive your sins, and you will receive the gift of the Holy Spirit.* ³⁹This promise is for you. It is also for your children and for the people who are far away. It is for every person that the Lord our God calls to himself."

⁴⁰Peter warned them with many other words; he begged them, "Save yourselves from the evil of the people that live now!" ⁴¹Then those people who accepted *(believed)* what Peter said were baptized.* On that day about 3,000 people were added to the group of believers. ⁴²₍The believers continued to meet together.₎ They used their time to learn the teaching of the apostles.* The

---

Spirit, Holy Spirit Also called the Spirit of God, the Spirit of Christ, and the Comforter. Joined with God and Christ, he does God's work among people in the world.
prophesy Speak for God.
place of death Literally, "Hades."
prophet Person who spoke for God. He often told things that would happen in the future.

Christ The "anointed one" (Messiah) or chosen of God.
until I put ... power Literally, "until I make your enemies a footstool for your feet."
apostles The men Jesus chose to be his special helpers.
baptized A Greek word meaning to be immersed, dipped, or buried briefly under water.

believers shared with each other. They ate* together and prayed together.

The Believers Share

⁴³The apostles* were doing many powerful and amazing things; and every person felt great respect for God. ⁴⁴All the believers stayed together. They shared everything. ⁴⁵The believers sold their land and the things they owned. Then they divided the money and gave it to those people who needed it. ⁴⁶The believers met together in the temple* yard every day. They all had the same purpose. They ate* together in their homes. They were happy to share their food and ate with joyful hearts. ⁴⁷The believers praised God, and all the people liked them. More and more people were being saved every day; the Lord was adding those people to the group ₍of believers₎.

Peter Heals a Crippled Man

3 One day Peter and John went to the temple.* It was three o'clock in the afternoon. This was the time for the daily temple prayer service. ²When they were going into the temple yard, a man was there. This man had been crippled all his life. He could not walk, so some friends carried him. His friends brought him to the temple every day. They put the crippled man by one of the gates outside the temple. It was called Beautiful Gate. There the man begged for money from the people going to the temple. ³₍That day₎ the man saw Peter and John going into the temple yard. He asked them for money. ⁴Peter and John looked at the crippled man and said, "Look at us!" ⁵The man looked at them; he thought they would give him some money. ⁶But Peter said, "I don't have any silver or gold, but I do have something else I can give you: By the power of Jesus Christ from Nazareth—stand up and walk!" ⁷Then Peter held the man's right hand and lifted him up. Immediately the man's feet and legs became strong. ⁸The man jumped up, stood on his feet, and began to walk. He went into the temple with them. The man was walking and jumping, and he was praising God. ⁹⁻¹⁰All the people recognized him. The people knew he was the crippled man who always sat by Beautiful Gate to beg for money. Now they saw this same man walking and praising God. The people were amazed. They could not understand how this could happen.

Peter Speaks to the People

¹¹The man was holding on to Peter and John. All the people were amazed ₍because the man was healed₎. They ran to Peter and John at Solomon's Porch.* ¹²When Peter saw this, he said to the people, "My Jewish brothers, why are you surprised at this? You are looking at us like it was our power that made this man walk. Do you think this was done because we are good? ¹³No! God did it! He is the God of Abraham, the God of Isaac, and the God of Jacob. * He is the God of all our fathers *(ancestors)*. He gave glory to Jesus, his special servant. But you gave Jesus to be killed. Pilate decided to let Jesus go free. But you told Pilate you did not want Jesus. ¹⁴Jesus was pure and good *(innocent)*, but you said you did not want him. You told Pilate to give you a murderer* instead of Jesus. ¹⁵And so you killed the One that gives life! But God raised him from death. We are witnesses of this—we saw this with our own eyes. ¹⁶It was the power of Jesus that made this crippled man well. This happened because we trusted in the power of Jesus. You can see this man, and you know him. He was made completely well because of trust in Jesus. You all saw it happen!

¹⁷"My brothers, I know you did those things to Jesus because you did not understand what you were doing. Your leaders also did not understand. ¹⁸God said that these things would happen. God said through the prophets* that his Christ* would suffer and die. I have told you how God made this happen. ¹⁹So you must change your hearts and lives! Come back to God and he will forgive your sins. ²⁰Then the Lord *(God)* will give you times of spiritual rest. He will give you Jesus, the One he chose to be the Christ. ²¹But Jesus must stay in heaven until the time when all things will be made

---

ate Literally, "broke bread." This may mean a meal or the Lord's Supper, the special meal Jesus told his followers to eat to remember him (Lk. 22:14-20).

apostles The men Jesus chose to be his special helpers.

temple The special building in Jerusalem for Jewish worship.

ate (verse 46) Literally, "broke bread," the same as in verse 42.

Solomon's Porch An area on the east side of the temple. It was covered by a roof.

Abraham, Isaac, Jacob Three of the most important Jewish leaders during the time of the Old Testament.

murderer Barabbas, the man the Jews asked Pilate to let go free instead of Jesus (Lk. 23:18).

prophets People who spoke for God. Their writings are part of the Old Testament.

Christ The "anointed one" (Messiah) or chosen one of God.

right again. God told about this time long ago when he spoke through his holy prophets. ²²Moses said, 'The Lord your God will give you a prophet. That prophet will come from among your own people *(the Jews)*. He will be like me. You must obey everything that prophet tells you. ²³And if any person refuses to obey that prophet, then that person will die, separated from God's people.'* ²⁴Samuel, and all the other prophets who spoke for God after Samuel, talked about this time now. ²⁵You have received the things the prophets talked about. You have received the agreement that God made with your fathers *(ancestors)*. God said to your father Abraham, 'Every nation on earth will be blessed through your descendants.*'* ²⁶God has sent his special servant *(Jesus)*. God sent him to you first. God sent Jesus to bless you. He does this by making each of you turn away from doing bad things."

Peter and John Before the Jewish Council

4 While Peter and John were speaking to the people, some men came to them. There were some Jewish priests, the captain of the soldiers that guarded the temple,* and some Sadducees.* ²They were upset because of what Peter and John were teaching the people. By telling people about Jesus, the two apostles* were teaching that people will rise from death. ³The Jewish leaders grabbed Peter and John and put them in jail. It was already night, so they kept Peter and John in jail until the next day. ⁴But many of the people that heard Peter and John preach believed the things they said. There were now about 5,000 men in the group of believers.

⁵The next day the Jewish leaders, the older Jewish leaders, and the teachers of the law met in Jerusalem. ⁶Annas (the high priest*), Caiaphas, John, and Alexander were there. Everyone from the high priest's family was there. ⁷They made Peter and John stand before all the people there. The Jewish leaders asked them many times, "How did you make this crippled man well? What power did you use? With whose authority did you do this?"

⁸Then Peter was filled with the Holy Spirit.* He said to them, "Leaders of the people and you older leaders: ⁹Are you questioning us about the good thing that was done to this crippled man? Are you asking us who made him well? ¹⁰We want all of you and all the Jewish people to know that this man was made well by the power of Jesus Christ from Nazareth! You nailed Jesus to a cross. God raised him from death. This man was crippled, but he is now well and able to stand here before you because of the power of Jesus! ¹¹Jesus is

> 'the stone* that you builders
>   thought was not important.
> But this stone has become
>   the cornerstone.*'
>
> *Psalm 118:22*

¹²Jesus is the only One who can save people. His name is the only power in the world that has been given to save people. We must be saved through Jesus!"

¹³The Jewish leaders understood that Peter and John had no special training or education. But the leaders also saw that Peter and John were not afraid to speak. So the leaders were amazed. Then they realized that Peter and John had been with Jesus. ¹⁴They saw the crippled man standing there beside the two apostles.* They saw that the man was healed. So they could say nothing against the apostles. ¹⁵The Jewish leaders told them to leave the meeting. Then the leaders talked to each other about what they should do. ¹⁶They said, "What shall we do with these men *(the apostles)*? Every person in Jerusalem knows that they have done a great miracle.* This is clear. We cannot say it is not true. ¹⁷But we must make them afraid to talk to people about this man *(Jesus)*. Then this problem will not spread among the people."

¹⁸So the Jewish leaders called Peter and John in again. They told the apostles* not to say anything or to teach anything in the name of Jesus. ¹⁹But Peter and John answered them, "What do you think is right? What would God want? Should we obey you or God? ²⁰We cannot be quiet. We must

---

'The Lord ... people'   Quote from Deut. 18:15, 19.
descendants   All the people born in a person's family after that person dies.
'Every ... descendants'   Quote from Gen. 22:18; 26:24.
temple   A building in Jerusalem for Jewish worship.
Sadducees   A leading Jewish religious group. They accepted only the first five books of the Old Testament. They believed that people don't live again after death.
apostles   Men Jesus chose to be his special helpers.
high priest   Most important Jewish priest and leader.

Holy Spirit   Called the Spirit of God, the Spirit of Christ, and the Comforter. Joined with God and Christ, he does God's work among people in the world.
stone   A picture or symbol meaning Jesus.
cornerstone   First and most important rock of a building.
miracle(s)   Miracles are amazing works done by God's power.

tell people about the things we saw and heard."
²¹⁻²²The Jewish leaders could not find a way to punish the apostles, because all the people were praising God for what had been done. (This miracle* was a proof from God. The man that was healed was more than 40 years old!) So the Jewish leaders warned the apostles again and let them go free.

Peter and John Return to the Believers

²³Peter and John left the meeting of Jewish leaders and went to their own group. They told the group everything that the leading priests and the older Jewish leaders had said to them. ²⁴When the believers heard this, they all prayed to God. They all wanted the same thing. They prayed, "Master, you are the One who made the sky, the earth, the sea, and everything in the world. ²⁵Our father (ancestor) David was your servant. With the help of the Holy Spirit* he wrote these words:

> 'Why are the nations shouting?
> Why are the people of the world
>   planning things ₍against God₎?
> It is hopeless!
>
> ²⁶ The kings of the earth prepare
>   themselves to fight,
>   and the rulers all come together
>   against the Lord (God)
>   and against his Christ.*'
>
> *Psalm 2:1-2*

²⁷These things really happened when Herod,* Pontius Pilate, the nations, and the Jewish people all 'came together' against Jesus here in Jerusalem. Jesus is your holy Servant. He is the One you (God) made to be the Christ.* ²⁸These people that 'came together' against Jesus made your plan happen; it happened because of your power and your will. ²⁹And now, Lord, listen to what they are saying. They are trying to make us afraid! Lord, we are your servants. Help us to speak the things you want us to say without fear. ³⁰Help us to be brave by showing us your power; make sick people well, give proofs, and make miracles* happen by the power of Jesus, your holy servant."

---

miracle(s) Miracles are amazing works done by God's power.

Holy Spirit Called the Spirit of God, the Spirit of Christ, and the Comforter. Joined with God and Christ, he does God's work among people in the world.

Christ The "anointed one" (Messiah) or chosen of God.

Herod Herod Antipas, tetrarch (ruler) of Galilee and Perea, son of Herod the Great.

³¹After the believers prayed, the place where they were meeting shook. They were all filled with the Holy Spirit,* and they continued to speak God's message* without fear.

The Believers Share

³²The group of believers were joined in their hearts, and they had the same spirit. No person in the group said that the things he had were his own. Instead, they shared everything. ³³With great power the apostles* told the people that the Lord Jesus was truly raised from death. And God blessed all the believers very much. ³⁴They all received the things they needed. Everyone that owned fields (land) or houses sold them for money. They brought the money ³⁵and gave it to the apostles. Then each person was given the things he needed.
³⁶One of the believers was named Joseph. The apostles* called him Barnabas. (This name means "a person who helps others.") He was a Levite* born in Cyprus. ³⁷Joseph owned a field. He sold the field, brought the money, and gave it to the apostles.

Ananias and Sapphira

5 There was a man named Ananias. His wife's name was Sapphira. Ananias sold some land that he had. ²But he gave only part of the money to the apostles.* He secretly kept some of the money for himself. His wife knew this, and she agreed with it. ³Peter said, "Ananias, why did you let Satan (the devil) rule your heart? You lied and tried to deceive (fool) the Holy Spirit.* You sold your field, but why did you keep part of the money for yourself? ⁴Before you sold the field, it belonged to you. And even after you sold it, you could have used the money any way you wanted. Why did you think of doing this bad thing? You lied to God, not to men!" ⁵⁻⁶When Ananias heard this, he fell down and died. Some young men came and wrapped his body. They carried it out and buried it. And every person that heard about this was filled with fear.
⁷About three hours later his wife (Sapphira) came in. Sapphira did not know about this thing that had happened to her husband. ⁸Peter said to

---

God's message The news that God has made a way for people to have their sins forgiven and live with God.

apostles The men Jesus chose to be his special helpers.

Levite Levites were men from the family group of Levi who helped the Jewish priests in the temple.

her, "Tell me how much money you got for your field. Was it this much *(the amount Ananias had said)*?"

Sapphira answered, "Yes, that was all we got for the field."

⁹Peter said to her, "Why did you and your husband agree to test the Spirit of the Lord? Listen! Do you hear those footsteps? The men that buried your husband are at the door! They will carry you out in the same way." ¹⁰At that moment Sapphira fell down by his feet and died. The young men came in and saw that she was dead. The men carried her out and buried her beside her husband. ¹¹All the believers and all the other people who heard about these things were filled with fear.

Proofs from God

¹²The apostles* did many miracles* and powerful things. All the people saw these things. The apostles were together in Solomon's Porch*; they all had the same purpose. ¹³None of the other people felt worthy to stand with them. All the people were saying good things about the apostles. ¹⁴And more and more people believed in the Lord *(Jesus)*—many men and women were added to the group of believers. ¹⁵So the people brought their sick people into the streets. ₍The people heard that₎ Peter was coming by. So the people put their sick on little beds and mattresses. They thought that if the sick people could be close enough for Peter's shadow to touch them, it would be enough to heal them. ¹⁶People came from all the towns around Jerusalem. They brought their sick people and those that were bothered by evil spirits ₍from the devil₎. All of these people were healed.

The Jews Try to Stop the Apostles

¹⁷The high priest* and all his friends (a group called the Sadducees*) became very jealous. ¹⁸They grabbed the apostles* and put them in jail. ¹⁹But during the night, an angel of the Lord opened the doors of the jail. The angel led the apostles outside and said, ²⁰"Go and stand in the temple* yard. Tell the people everything about this new life ₍in Jesus₎." ²¹When the apostles heard this, they obeyed and went to the temple. It was early in the morning. The apostles began to teach the people.

The high priest* and his friends came ₍to the temple*₎. They called a meeting of the Jewish leaders and all the important older men of the Jews. They sent some men to the jail to bring the apostles* to them. ²²When the men went to the jail, they could not find the apostles there. So they went back and told the Jewish leaders about this. ²³The men said, "The jail was closed and locked. The guards were standing at the doors. But when we opened the doors, the jail was empty!" ²⁴The captain of the temple guards and the leading priests heard this. They were confused. They wondered, "What will happen because of this?" ²⁵Then another man came and told them, "Listen! The men you put in jail are standing in the temple yard. They are teaching the people!" ²⁶Then the captain and his men went out and brought the apostles back. But the soldiers did not use force, because they were afraid of the people. The soldiers were afraid that the people would ₍become angry and₎ kill them *(the soldiers)* with rocks.

²⁷The soldiers brought the apostles* to the meeting and made them stand before the Jewish leaders. The high priest* questioned the apostles. ²⁸He said, "We told you never to teach about this man *(Jesus)*! But look what you have done! You have filled Jerusalem with your teaching. You are trying to make us responsible *(guilty)* for the death of this man *(Jesus)*."

²⁹Peter and the other apostles* answered, "We must obey God, not you! ³⁰You killed Jesus. You hung him on a cross. But God, the same God our fathers *(ancestors)* had, raised Jesus up from death! ³¹Jesus is the One that God raised to his right side. God made Jesus our Leader and Savior. God did this so that all Jews can change their hearts and lives. Then God can forgive their sins. ³²We saw all these things happen, and we can say these things are true. The Holy Spirit* also shows that these things are true. God has given the Spirit to all people who obey him."

³³The Jewish leaders heard these words. They became very angry. They began to plan a way to

---

apostles The men Jesus chose to be his special helpers.

miracle(s) Miracles are amazing works done by God's power.

Solomon's Porch An area on the east side of the temple. It was covered by a roof.

high priest Most important Jewish priest and leader.

Sadducees A leading Jewish religious group. They accepted only the first five books of the Old Testament. They believed that people don't live again after death.

temple A building in Jerusalem for Jewish worship.

Holy Spirit Called the Spirit of God, the Spirit of Christ, and the Comforter. Joined with God and Christ, he does God's work among people in the world.

kill the apostles.* ³⁴One of the Pharisees* in the meeting stood up. His name was Gamaliel. He was a teacher of the law, and all the people respected him. He told the men to make the apostles leave the meeting for a few minutes. ³⁵Then he said to them, "Men of Israel, be careful of what you are planning to do to these men! ³⁶Remember when Theudas appeared? He said that he was an important man. About 400 men joined him. But he was killed. And all who followed him were scattered and ran away. They were able to do nothing. ³⁷Later, a man named Judas came from Galilee. It was at the time of the registration.* He led a group of followers, too. He was also killed. And all his followers were scattered and ran away. ³⁸And so now I tell you: Stay away from these men. Leave them alone. If their plan comes from men, it will fail. ³⁹But if this is from God, then you will not be able to stop them. You might even be fighting against God himself!"

The Jewish leaders agreed with the thing that Gamaliel said. ⁴⁰They called the apostles* in again. They beat the apostles and told them not to talk to people about Jesus again. Then they let the apostles go free. ⁴¹The apostles left the meeting. The apostles were happy because they were given the honor of suffering dishonor *(shame)* for the name ₍of Jesus₎. ⁴²The apostles did not stop teaching people. The apostles continued to tell the people the Good News—that Jesus is the Christ.* They did this every day in the temple* yard and in people's homes.

Seven Men Chosen for a Special Work

6 More and more people were becoming followers of Jesus. But during this same time, the Greek-speaking followers had an argument with the other Jewish followers. They said that their widows* were not getting their share of the things that the followers received every day. ²The twelve apostles* called the whole group of followers together. The apostles said to them, "Our work of teaching God's word has stopped. That's not good! It is better for us to continue teaching God's word than to help people have something to eat. ³So, brothers, choose seven of your own men. They must be men that people say are good. They must be full of wisdom and full of the Spirit.* We will give them this work to do. ⁴Then we can use all our time to pray and to teach the word ₍of God₎."

⁵The whole group liked the idea. So they chose these seven men: Stephen (a man with great faith and full of the Holy Spirit*) Philip,* Prochorus, Nicanor, Timon, Parmenas, and Nicolaus (a man from Antioch, who had become a Jew). ⁶Then they put these men before the apostles.* The apostles prayed and put their hands on* the men.

⁷The word of God was reaching more and more people. The group of followers in Jerusalem became larger and larger. Even a big group of Jewish priests believed and obeyed.

The Jews Against Stephen

⁸Stephen *(one of the seven men)* received a great blessing. God gave Stephen power to do miracles* and to show proofs from God to the people. ⁹But some Jews came and argued with Stephen. These Jews were from a synagogue.* It was called a synagogue for Libertines.* (This synagogue was also for Jews from Cyrene, and for Jews from Alexandria.) Jews from Cilicia and Asia were with them. They all came and argued with Stephen. ¹⁰But the Spirit* was helping Stephen speak with wisdom. His words were so strong that the Jews could not argue with him. ¹¹So the Jews paid some men to say, "We heard Stephen say bad things against Moses and against God!" ¹²By doing this, these Jews upset the people, the older Jewish leaders, and the teachers of the law. They became so angry that they came and grabbed Stephen. They took him to a meeting of the Jewish leaders. ¹³The Jews brought some men into the meeting. They told those men to tell lies about Stephen. The men said, "This man *(Stephen)* always says bad things about this holy

---

apostles The men Jesus chose to be his special helpers.
Pharisees The Pharisees were a Jewish religious group that claimed to follow carefully all Jewish laws and customs.
registration A census or counting of all the people and the things they own.
Christ The "anointed one" (Messiah) or chosen of God.
temple A building in Jerusalem for Jewish worship.
widows A widow is a woman whose husband has died.

Spirit, Holy Spirit Also called the Spirit of God, the Spirit of Christ, and the Comforter. Joined with God and Christ, he does God's work among people in the world.
Philip Not the apostle named Philip.
put their hands on Here, doing this showed that these men were given a special work of God.
miracles Amazing works done by the power of God.
synagogue Synagogues were places where Jews gathered for prayer, study of the Scriptures, and other public meetings.
Libertines Jews who had been slaves or whose fathers had been slaves, but were now free.

place *(the temple)*. And he always says bad things against the law ₍of Moses₎. ¹⁴We heard him say that Jesus from Nazareth will destroy this place. He also said that Jesus will change the things that Moses told us to do." ¹⁵All the people sitting in the meeting watched Stephen closely. His face looked like the face of an angel, and they saw it.

Stephen's Speech

7 The high priest* said to Stephen, "Are these things true?" ²Stephen answered, "My Jewish fathers and brothers, listen to me. Our glorious God appeared to Abraham, our father *(ancestor)*. Abraham was in Mesopotamia. This was before he lived in Haran. ³God said to Abraham, 'Leave your country and your people, and go to the country I will show you.'* ⁴So Abraham left the country of Chaldea.* He went to live in Haran. After Abraham's father died, God sent him to this place here, where you live now. ⁵But God did not give Abraham any of this land. God did not give him even a foot of it. But God promised that in the future he would give Abraham this land for himself and for his children. (This was before Abraham had any children.) ⁶This is what God said to him: 'Your descendants* will live in another country. They will be strangers. The people there will make them slaves and do bad things to them for 400 years. ⁷But I will punish the nation that made them slaves.'* And God also said, 'After those things happen, your people will come out of that country. Then your people will worship me here in this place.'* ⁸God made an agreement with Abraham; the sign for this agreement was circumcision.* And so when Abraham had a son, he circumcised his son when he was eight days old. His son's name was Isaac. Isaac also circumcised his son Jacob. And Jacob did the same for ₍his sons. These sons later became₎ the twelve fathers.*

⁹"These fathers became jealous of Joseph *(their younger brother)*. They sold Joseph to be a slave in Egypt. But God was with Joseph. ¹⁰Joseph had many troubles there, but God saved him from all those troubles. Pharaoh was the king of Egypt. He liked Joseph and respected him because of the wisdom that God gave Joseph. Pharaoh gave Joseph the job of being a governor of Egypt. He even let Joseph rule over all the people in Pharaoh's house. ¹¹But all the land of Egypt and of Canaan became dry. It became so dry that food could not grow there. This made the people suffer very much. Our fathers* could not find anything to eat. ¹²But Jacob heard that there was food ₍stored₎ in Egypt. So he sent our fathers *(Jacob's sons)* there. (This was their first trip to Egypt.) ¹³Then they went there a second time. This time, Joseph told his brothers who he was. And Pharaoh learned about Joseph's family. ¹⁴Then Joseph sent some men to invite Jacob, his father, to come to Egypt. He also invited all his relatives (75 persons altogether). ¹⁵So Jacob went down to Egypt. Jacob and our fathers *(ancestors)* ₍lived there until they₎ died. ¹⁶Later their bodies were moved to Shechem. They were put in a grave there. (It was the same grave that Abraham had bought in Shechem from the sons of Hamor. He paid them with silver.)

¹⁷"The number of Jewish people in Egypt grew. There were more and more of our people there. (The promise that God made to Abraham was soon to come true.) ¹⁸Then a different king began to rule Egypt. He knew nothing about Joseph. ¹⁹This king tricked *(deceived)* our people. He was bad to our fathers *(ancestors)*. The king made them put their children outside to die. ²⁰This was the time when Moses was born. He was a very fine child. For three months they took care of Moses in his father's house. ²¹When they put Moses outside, Pharaoh's daughter took him. She raised him like he was her own son. ²²The Egyptians taught Moses about all the things they knew. He was powerful in the things he said and did.

²³"When Moses was about 40 years old, he thought it would be good to visit his brothers, the Jewish people. ²⁴Moses saw an Egyptian man doing wrong to a Jew. So he defended the Jew. Moses punished the Egyptian for hurting the Jew; Moses hit him so hard that he died. ²⁵Moses thought that his Jewish brothers would understand that God was using him to save them. But they did not understand. ²⁶The next day, Moses saw two Jewish men fighting. He tried to make peace

---

high priest Most important Jewish priest and leader.
'Leave ... show you' Quote from Gen. 12:1.
Chaldea Or Babylonia, a land in the southern part of Mesopotamia. See verse 2.
descendants A person's children and all their future families.
'Your ... slaves' Quote from Gen. 15:13-14.
'After those ... place' Quote from Gen. 15:14; Ex. 3:12.
circumcision Cutting off the foreskin. This was done to every Jewish baby boy. It was a mark of the agreement God made with Abraham (Gen. 17:9-14).
fathers Important ancestors of the Jews; the leaders of the twelve Jewish family groups.

between them. He said, 'Men, you are brothers! Why are you doing wrong to each other?' ²⁷The man who was doing wrong to the other man pushed Moses away. He said to Moses, 'Did anyone say you could be our ruler and judge? No! ²⁸Will you kill me like you killed the Egyptian man yesterday?'* ²⁹When Moses heard him say this, he left Egypt. He went to live in the land of Midian. He was a stranger there. While Moses lived in Midian, he had two sons.

³⁰"After 40 years Moses was in the desert near Mount Sinai. An angel appeared to him in the flame of a burning bush. ³¹When Moses saw this, he was amazed. He went near to look closer at it. Moses heard a voice; it was the Lord's *(God's)*. ³²The Lord said, 'I am the same God your fathers *(ancestors)* had—the God of Abraham, the God of Isaac, and the God of Jacob*.'* Moses began to shake with fear. He was afraid to look at the bush. ³³The Lord said to him, 'Take off your shoes, because the place where you are now standing is holy ground. ³⁴I have seen my people suffer much in Egypt. I have heard my people crying. I have come down to save them. Come now, ₍Moses,₎ I am sending you back to Egypt.'*

³⁵"This Moses was the same man the Jews said they did not want. They had said to him, 'Did anyone say you could be our ruler and judge? No!' Moses is the same man that God sent to be a ruler and savior. God sent Moses with the help of an angel. This was the angel Moses saw in the ₍burning₎ bush. ³⁶So Moses led the people out. He did powerful things and miracles.* Moses did these things in Egypt, at the Red Sea, and then in the desert for 40 years. ³⁷This is the same Moses that said these words to the Jewish people: 'God will give you a prophet.* That prophet will come from among your own people. He will be like me.'* ³⁸This is the same Moses who was with the gathering ₍of the Jews₎ in the desert. He was with the angel that spoke to him at Mount Sinai, and he was with our fathers *(ancestors)*. Moses received commands ₍from God₎ that give life. Moses gave us those commands.

³⁹"But our fathers *(ancestors)* did not want to obey Moses. They rejected him. They wanted to go back to Egypt again. ⁴⁰Our fathers said to Aaron, 'Moses led us out of the country of Egypt. But we don't know what has happened to him. So make some gods to go before us and lead us.'* ⁴¹So the people made an idol that looked like a calf. Then they brought sacrifices *(gifts)* to it. The people were very happy with what they had made with their own hands! ⁴²But God turned against them. God finished trying to stop them from worshiping the army ₍of false gods₎ in the sky. This is what is written in the book of the prophets*: God says,

> 'You Jewish people did not bring me blood
>   offerings and sacrifices*
>   in the desert for 40 years;
> 43 You carried with you the tent *(place of
>   worship)* for Moloch *(a false god)*
>   and the image of the star of your god
>   Rephan.
> These were the idols you made to worship.
> So I will send you away beyond Babylon.'
>   *Amos 5:25-27*

⁴⁴"The Holy Tent* was with our fathers *(ancestors)* in the desert. God told Moses how to make this tent. He made it like the plan that God showed him. ⁴⁵Later, Joshua led our fathers to capture the lands of the other nations. Our people went in and God made the other people go out. When our people went into this new land, they took with them this same tent. Our people received this tent from their fathers, and our people kept it until the time of David. ⁴⁶God was very pleased with David. David asked God to let him build a house *(temple*)* for him, the God of Jacob. ⁴⁷But Solomon *(David's son)* was the person who built the temple.

'Did anyone ... yesterday?' Quote from Ex. 2:14.
  Abraham, Isaac, Jacob Three of the most important Jewish leaders during the time of the Old Testament.
'I am ... Jacob' Quote from Ex. 3:6.
'Take off ... Egypt' Quote from Ex. 3:5-10.
  miracle(s) Miracles are amazing works done by God's power.
  prophet Person who spoke for God.
'God will give ... me' Quote from Deut. 18:15.

'Moses led us out ... lead us' Quote from Ex. 32:1.
  prophets People who spoke for God. Their writings are part of the Old Testament.
  sacrifices Offerings or gifts to God.
  Holy Tent Literally, "Tent of the Testimony," the movable tent where the Ten Commandments were kept and where God lived among his people in the time of Moses.
  temple A building in Jerusalem for Jewish worship.

48"But the Most High *(God)* does not live in houses that men build with their hands. This is what the prophet* writes:

'The Lord says,
  Heaven is my throne.
49   The earth is a place to rest my feet.
  What kind of house can you build for me?
  There is no place where I need to rest!
50   Remember, I made all these things!'"
                                    Isaiah 66:1-2

51 ⌊Then Stephen said,⌋ "You stubborn Jewish leaders! You have not given your hearts to God! You won't listen to him! You are always against what the Holy Spirit* is trying to tell you. Your fathers *(ancestors)* did this, and you are just like them! 52Your fathers persecuted* every prophet* that ever lived. Those prophets said long ago that the Righteous One *(Christ)* would come. But your fathers killed those prophets. And now you have turned against the Righteous One and killed him. 53You are the people that received the law ⌊of Moses⌋. God gave you this law through his angels. But you don't obey this law!"

Stephen Is Killed

54The Jewish leaders heard Stephen say these things. They became very angry. The Jewish leaders were so mad that they were grinding their teeth at Stephen. 55But Stephen was full of the Holy Spirit.* Stephen looked up into the sky. He saw the Glory of God. He saw Jesus standing at God's right side. 56Stephen said, "Look! I see heaven open. And I see the Son of Man *(Jesus)* standing at God's right side!"

57Then the Jewish leaders all shouted with a loud voice. They closed *(covered)* their ears with their hands. They all ran at Stephen together. 58They took him out of the city and threw rocks at him until he was dead. The men who told lies against Stephen gave their coats to a young man named Saul. 59Then they threw rocks at Stephen. But Stephen was praying. He said, "Lord Jesus, receive my spirit!" 60He fell on his knees and shouted, "Lord, don't blame them for this sin!" After Stephen said this, he died.

8 Saul agreed that the killing of Stephen was a good thing.

Trouble for the Believers

2-3Some good *(religious)* men buried Stephen. They cried very loudly for him. On that day the Jews began to persecute* the group of believers in Jerusalem. The Jews made them suffer very much. Saul was also trying to destroy the group. Saul went into their houses. He dragged out men and women and put them in jail. All the believers left Jerusalem. Only the apostles* stayed. The believers went to different places in Judea and Samaria. 4The believers were scattered everywhere. Every place the believers went they told people the Good News.*

Philip Preaches in Samaria

5Philip* went to the city of Samaria. He preached about the Christ.* 6The people there heard Philip and saw the miracles* he was doing. They all listened carefully to the things Philip said. 7Many of these people had evil spirits ⌊from the devil⌋ inside them. But Philip made the evil spirits leave them. The spirits made a loud noise when they came out. There were also many weak and crippled people there. Philip made these people well, too. 8The people in that city were very happy because of this.

9But there was a man named Simon in that city. Before Philip came there, Simon did magic tricks. He amazed all the people of Samaria with his tricks. Simon boasted and called himself a great man. 10All the people—the least important and the most important—believed the things Simon said. The people said, "This man has the power of God that is called 'the Great Power'!" 11Simon amazed the people with his magic tricks so long that the people became his followers. 12But Philip told the people the Good News* about the kingdom of God and the power of Jesus Christ. Men and women believed Philip. They were baptized.*

---

prophet Isaiah, who spoke for God about 740-700 B.C.
Holy Spirit Called the Spirit of God, the Spirit of Christ, and the Comforter. Joined with God and Christ, he does God's work among people in the world.
persecute(d) To persecute is to hurt or do bad things to.
prophet Person who spoke for God.

apostles The men Jesus chose to be his special helpers.
Good News The news that God has made a way for people to have their sins forgiven and live with God.
Philip Not the apostle named Philip.
Christ The "anointed one" (Messiah) or chosen of God.
miracle(s) Miracles are amazing works done by God's power.
baptized A Greek word meaning to be immersed, dipped, or buried briefly under water.

¹³Simon himself also believed and was baptized. Simon stayed very close to Philip. He saw the miracles* and the very powerful things that Philip did. Simon was amazed. ¹⁴The apostles* were still in Jerusalem. They heard that the people of Samaria had accepted the word of God. So the apostles sent Peter and John to the people in Samaria. ¹⁵When Peter and John arrived, they prayed for the Samaritan believers to receive the Holy Spirit.* ¹⁶These people had been baptized* in the name of the Lord Jesus. But the Holy Spirit had not yet come down on any of them. This is why Peter and John prayed. ¹⁷The two apostles put their hands on* the people. Then the people received the Holy Spirit.

¹⁸Simon saw that the Spirit* was given to people when the apostles* put their hands on them. So Simon offered the apostles money. ¹⁹Simon said, "Give me this power so that when I put my hands on a person, he will receive the Holy Spirit.*

²⁰Peter said to Simon, "You and your money should both be destroyed! You thought you could buy God's gift with money. ²¹You cannot share with us in this work. Your heart is not right before God. ²²Change your heart! Turn away from this bad thing you have done. Pray to the Lord *(God)*. Maybe he will forgive you for thinking this. ²³I see that you are full of bitter jealousy and ruled by sin."

²⁴Simon answered, "Both of you pray for me to the Lord *(God)*. Pray that the things you have said will not happen to me!"

²⁵Then the two apostles* told the people the things they had seen ¡Jesus do¡. The apostles told the people the message* of the Lord. Then they went back to Jerusalem. On the way they went through many Samaritan towns and preached the Good News* to the people.

Philip Teaches a Man from Ethiopia

²⁶An angel of the Lord spoke to Philip.* The angel said, "Get ready and go south. Go to the road that leads down to Gaza from Jerusalem—the road that goes through the desert." ²⁷So Philip got ready and went. On the road he saw a man from Ethiopia. This man was a eunuch.* He was an important officer in the service of Candace, the queen of the Ethiopians. He was responsible for taking care of all her money. This man had gone to Jerusalem to worship. ²⁸Now he was on his way home. He was sitting in his chariot* and reading from the book of Isaiah, the prophet.* ²⁹The Spirit* said to Philip, "Go to that chariot and stay near it." ³⁰So Philip went toward the chariot, and he heard the man reading. He was reading from Isaiah, the prophet. Philip said to him, "Do you understand what you are reading?"

³¹The man said, "How can I understand? I need some person to explain it to me!" Then he invited Philip to climb in and sit with him. ³²The part of Scripture* that he was reading was this:

> "He was like a sheep when it is taken
>   to be killed.
> He was like a lamb that makes no sound
>   when someone cuts off its wool.
> He says nothing.
> ³³ He was shamed, and all his rights
>   were taken away.
> His life on earth was ended;
> There will be no story
>   about his family *(descendants)*."
>   *Isaiah 53:7-8*

³⁴The officer said to Philip, "Please, tell me, who is the prophet* talking about? Is he talking about himself or about someone else?" ³⁵Philip began to speak. He started with this same Scripture and told the man the Good News* about Jesus.

³⁶While they were traveling down the road, they came to some water. The officer said, "Look! Here is water! What is stopping me from being

---

miracle(s) Miracles are amazing works done by God's power.
apostles The men Jesus chose to be his special helpers.
Holy Spirit, Spirit Called the Spirit of God, the Spirit of Christ, and the Comforter. Joined with God and Christ, he does God's work among people in the world.
baptized A Greek word meaning to be immersed, dipped, or buried briefly under water.
put their hands on Here, doing this showed that the apostles had God's authority or power to give people the special powers of the Holy Spirit.
message, Good News The news that God has made a way for people to have their sins forgiven and live with God.

Philip Not the apostle named Philip.
eunuch Man whose testicles have been removed. Rulers often gave such men important positions.
chariot Something like a wagon pulled by horses.
prophet Person who spoke for God. He often told things that would happen in the future.
Scripture A part of the Holy Writings—the Old Testament.

baptized*?" ³⁷* ³⁸Then the officer commanded the chariot to stop. Both Philip and the officer went down into the water, and Philip baptized him. ³⁹When they came up out of the water, the Spirit* of the Lord took Philip away; the officer never saw him again. The officer continued on his way home. He was very happy. ⁴⁰But Philip appeared in a city called Azotus. He was going to the city of Caesarea. He preached the Good News* in all the towns on the way from Azotus to Caesarea.

Saul Is Converted

9 In Jerusalem ⌊Saul was still trying to scare and kill the followers of the Lord *(Jesus)* all the time. So he went to the high priest.* ²Saul asked him to write letters to the Jews of the synagogues* in the city of Damascus. Saul wanted the high priest to give him the authority to find people in Damascus who were followers of ⌊Christ's⌋ Way. If he found any believers there, men or women, he would arrest them and bring them back to Jerusalem.

³So Saul went to Damascus. When he came near the city, a very bright light from the sky suddenly shined around him. ⁴Saul fell to the ground. He heard a voice saying to him: "Saul, Saul! Why are you doing these bad things to me?"

⁵Saul said, "Who are you, Lord?"

The voice answered, "I am Jesus. I am the One you are trying to hurt. ⁶Get up now and go into the city. Someone there will tell you what you must do."

⁷The men traveling with Saul stood there. They said nothing. The men heard the voice, but they saw no one. ⁸Saul got up from the ground. He opened his eyes, but he could not see. So the men with Saul held his hand and led him into Damascus. ⁹For three days Saul could not see; he did not eat or drink.

¹⁰There was a follower ⌊of Jesus⌋ in Damascus. His name was Ananias. The Lord *(Jesus)* spoke to Ananias in a vision.* The Lord said, "Ananias!"

Ananias answered, "Here I am, Lord."

¹¹The Lord said to Ananias, "Get up and go to the street called Straight Street. Find the house of Judas.* Ask for a man named Saul from the city of Tarsus. He is there now, praying. ¹²Saul has seen a vision.* In this vision a man named Ananias came to him and put his hands on him. Then Saul could see again."

¹³But Ananias answered, "Lord *(Jesus)*, many people have told me about this man *(Saul)*. They told me about the many bad things this man did to your holy people in Jerusalem. ¹⁴Now he *(Saul)* has come here to Damascus. The leading priests have given him the power to arrest all people who believe in you.*"

¹⁵But the Lord *(Jesus)* said to Ananias, "Go! I have chosen Saul for an important work. He must tell about me to kings, to the Jewish people, and to other nations. ¹⁶I will show Saul the things he must suffer for my name."

¹⁷So Ananias left and went to the house of Judas. He put his hands on Saul and said, "Saul, my brother, the Lord Jesus sent me. He is the One you saw on the road when you came here. Jesus sent me so that you can see again and so that you can be filled with the Holy Spirit.* ¹⁸Immediately, something that looked like fish scales fell off Saul's eyes. Saul was able to see again! Saul got up and was baptized.* ¹⁹Then he ate some food and began to feel strong again.

Saul Preaches in Damascus

Saul stayed with the followers ⌊of Jesus⌋ in Damascus for a few days. ²⁰Soon he began to preach about Jesus in the synagogues.* He told the people, "Jesus is the Son of God!"

²¹All the people who heard Saul were amazed. They said, "This is the same man that was in Jerusalem. He was trying to destroy the people that trust in this name *(Jesus)*! He *(Saul)* has come

---

baptized A Greek word meaning to be immersed, dipped, or buried briefly under water.

Verse 37 Some late copies of Acts add verse 37: "Philip answered, 'If you believe with all your heart, you can.' The officer said, 'I believe that Jesus Christ is the Son of God.'"

Spirit, Holy Spirit Also called the Spirit of God, the Spirit of Christ, and the Comforter. Joined with God and Christ, he does God's work among people in the world.

Good News The news that God has made a way for people to have their sins forgiven and live with God.

high priest Most important Jewish priest and leader.

synagogues Synagogues were places where Jews gathered for prayer, study of the Scriptures, and other public meetings.

vision Something like a dream used by God to speak to people.

Judas This is not either of the apostles named Judas.

believe in you Literally, "call on your name," meaning to show faith in Jesus by worshiping him.

here to do the same thing. He came here to arrest the followers ₍of Jesus₎ and take them back ₍to Jerusalem₎ to the leading priests."
²²But Saul became more and more powerful. He proved that Jesus is the Christ.* His proofs were so strong that the Jews who lived in Damascus could not argue with him.

Saul Escapes from the Jews

²³After many days, the Jews made plans to kill Saul. ²⁴The Jews were watching the city gates day and night, ₍waiting for Saul₎. They wanted to kill him. But Saul learned about their plan. ²⁵One night some followers that Saul had taught helped him leave the city. The followers put Saul in a basket. They put the basket through a hole in the city wall and lowered him down.

Saul in Jerusalem

²⁶Then Saul went to Jerusalem. He tried to join the group of followers *(believers)*, but they were all afraid of him. They did not believe that Saul was really a follower ₍of Jesus₎. ²⁷But Barnabas accepted Saul and brought him to the apostles.* Barnabas told the apostles that Saul had seen the Lord *(Jesus)* on the road ₍to Damascus₎. Barnabas explained to the apostles how the Lord had spoken to Saul. Then he told the apostles that Saul preached for the Lord *(Jesus)* without fear to the people in Damascus.
²⁸And so Saul stayed with the followers. He went everywhere in Jerusalem, preaching for the Lord *(Jesus)* without fear. ²⁹Saul often talked with the Jews that spoke Greek. He had arguments with them. But they were trying to kill him. ³⁰When the brothers *(believers)* learned about this, they took Saul to the city of Caesarea. From Caesarea they sent Saul to the city of Tarsus.
³¹The church *(believers)* everywhere in Judea, Galilee, and Samaria had a time of peace. With the help of the Holy Spirit,* the group became stronger. The believers showed that they respected the Lord by the way they lived. Because of this, the group of believers grew larger and larger.
³²Peter traveled through all the towns ₍around Jerusalem₎. He visited the believers* who lived in Lydda. ³³In Lydda he met a paralyzed *(crippled)* man named Aeneas. Aeneas had not been able to leave his bed for the past eight years. ³⁴Peter said to him, "Aeneas, Jesus Christ heals you. Stand up and make your bed! You can do this for yourself now!" Aeneas stood up immediately. ³⁵All the people living in Lydda and on the plain of Sharon saw him. These people turned to *(believed in)* the Lord ₍Jesus₎.

Peter in Joppa

³⁶In the city of Joppa there was a follower ₍of Jesus₎ named Tabitha. (Her Greek name, Dorcas, means "a deer.") She always did good things for people. She always gave money to people who needed it. ³⁷While Peter was in Lydda, Tabitha became sick and died. They washed her body and put it in a room upstairs. ³⁸The followers in Joppa heard that Peter was in Lydda. (Lydda is near Joppa.) So they sent two men to Peter. They begged him, "Hurry, please come quickly!" ³⁹Peter got ready and went with them. When he arrived, they took him to the room upstairs. All the widows* stood around Peter. They were crying. They showed Peter the coats and other clothes that Dorcas *(Tabitha)* had made when she was still alive. ⁴⁰Peter sent all the people out of the room. He kneeled and prayed. Then he turned to Tabitha's body and said, "Tabitha, stand up!" She opened her eyes. When she saw Peter, she sat up. ⁴¹He gave her his hand and helped her up. Then he called the believers* and the widows into the room. He showed them Tabitha; she was alive! ⁴²People everywhere in Joppa learned about this. Many of these people believed in the Lord *(Jesus)*. ⁴³Peter stayed in Joppa for many days. He stayed with a man named Simon who was a leatherworker.*

Peter and Cornelius

10 In the city of Caesarea there was a man named Cornelius. He was an army officer* in the "Italian" group ₍of the Roman army₎. ²Cornelius was a good *(religious)* man. He and all the other people who lived in his home worshiped

---

Christ The "anointed one" (Messiah) or chosen of God.
apostles The men Jesus chose to be his special helpers.
Holy Spirit Called the Spirit of God, the Spirit of Christ, and the Comforter. Joined with God and Christ, he does God's work among people in the world.

believers Literally, "holy ones," a name for people that believe in Jesus.
widows A widow is a woman whose husband has died.
leatherworker Man who made leather from animal skins.
army officer A centurion, a Roman army officer who had authority over 100 soldiers.

the true God. He gave much of his money to the poor people. Cornelius prayed to God always. ³One afternoon about three o'clock, Cornelius saw a vision.* He saw it clearly. In the vision an angel from God came to him and said, "Cornelius!" ⁴Cornelius looked at the angel. He became afraid and said, "What do you want, sir?"

The angel said to Cornelius, "God has heard your prayers. He has seen the things you give to the poor people. God remembers you. ⁵Send some men now to the city of Joppa. Send your men to bring back a man named Simon. Simon is also called Peter. ⁶Simon is staying with a man, also named Simon, who is a leatherworker.* He has a house beside the sea." ⁷The angel who spoke to Cornelius left. Then Cornelius called two of his servants and a soldier. This soldier was a good *(religious)* man. The soldier was one of Cornelius' close helpers. ⁸Cornelius explained everything to these three men. Then he sent them to Joppa.

⁹The next day these men came near Joppa. At that time, Peter was going up to the roof to pray. It was about noon. ¹⁰Peter was hungry. He wanted to eat. But while they were preparing the food for Peter to eat, a vision* came to him. ¹¹He saw something coming down through the open sky. It looked like a big sheet coming down to the ground. It was being lowered to the ground by its four corners. ¹²Every kind of animal was in it— animals that walk, animals that crawl on the ground, and birds that fly in the air. ¹³Then a voice said to Peter, "Get up, Peter; kill any of these animals and eat it."

¹⁴But Peter said, "I would never do that, Lord! I have never eaten food that is unholy or not pure."

¹⁵But the voice said to him again, "God has made these things clean *(pure)*. Don't call them 'unholy'!" ¹⁶This happened three times. Then the whole thing was taken back up into the sky.

¹⁷Peter wondered what this vision* meant. The men that Cornelius sent had found Simon's house. They were standing at the door. ¹⁸They asked, "Is Simon Peter staying here?"

¹⁹Peter was still thinking about the vision.* But the Spirit* said to him, "Listen! Three men are looking for you. ²⁰Get up and go downstairs. Go with these men and don't ask questions. I have sent them to you." ²¹So Peter went downstairs to the men. He said, "I am the man you are looking for. Why did you come here?"

²²The men said, "A holy angel told Cornelius to invite you to his house. Cornelius is an army officer.* He is a good *(righteous)* man; he worships God. All the Jewish people respect him. The angel told Cornelius to invite you to his house so that he can listen to the things you have to say." ²³Peter asked the men to come in and stay for the night.

The next day Peter got ready and went away with the three men. Some of the brothers *(believers)* from Joppa went with Peter. ²⁴The next day they came into the city of Caesarea. Cornelius was waiting for them. He had already gathered his relatives and close friends ₍at his house₎. ²⁵When Peter entered the house, Cornelius met him. Cornelius fell down at Peter's feet and worshiped him. ²⁶But Peter told him to get up. Peter said, "Stand up! I am only a man like you." ²⁷Peter continued talking with Cornelius. Then Peter went inside and saw a large group of people together there. ²⁸Peter said to the people, "You people understand that it is against our Jewish law for a Jew to associate with or visit any person who is not a Jew. But God has shown me that I should not call any person 'unholy' or 'not clean.' ²⁹That is why I did not argue when the men asked me to come here. Now, please tell me why you sent for me."

³⁰Cornelius said, "Four days ago, I was praying in my house. It was at this same time—three o'clock in the afternoon. Suddenly, there was a man *(angel)* standing before me. He was wearing bright, shiny clothes. ³¹The man said, 'Cornelius! God has heard your prayer. God has seen the things you give to the poor people. God remembers you. ³²So send some men to the city of Joppa. Ask Simon Peter to come. Peter is staying in the house of a man, also named Simon, who is a leatherworker.* His house is beside the sea.' ³³So I sent for you immediately. It was very good of you to come here. Now we are all here before God to hear everything the Lord has commanded you to tell us."

---

vision Something like a dream used by God to speak to people.
leatherworker Man who made leather from animal skins.
Spirit Also called the Spirit of God, the Spirit of Christ, and the Comforter. Joined with God and Christ, he does God's work among people in the world.

army officer A centurion, a Roman army officer who had authority over 100 soldiers.

Peter Speaks in the House of Cornelius

³⁴Peter began to speak: "I really understand now that to God every person is the same. ³⁵And God accepts any person who worships him and does what is right. It is not important what country a person comes from. ³⁶God has spoken to the Jewish people. God sent them the Good News* that peace has come through Jesus Christ. Jesus is the Lord *(Ruler)* of all people! ³⁷You know what has happened all over Judea. It began in Galilee after John* preached to the people about baptism.* ³⁸You know about Jesus from Nazareth. God made him the Christ* by giving him the Holy Spirit* and power. Jesus went everywhere doing good things for people. Jesus healed the people who were ruled by the devil. This showed that God was with Jesus. ³⁹We saw all the things that Jesus did in Judea and in Jerusalem. We are witnesses. But Jesus was killed. They put him on a cross made of wood. ⁴⁰But, on the third day [after his death], God raised Jesus to life! God let people see Jesus clearly. ⁴¹But Jesus was not seen by all the people. Only the witnesses that God had already chosen saw him. We are those witnesses! We ate and drank with Jesus after he was raised from death. ⁴²Jesus told us to preach to the people. He told us to tell people that he is the One that God chose to be the Judge of all people who are living and all people who are dead. ⁴³Every person who believes *(trusts)* in Jesus will be forgiven. God will forgive the sins of that person through the name of Jesus. All the prophets* say this is true."

The Holy Spirit Comes to Non-Jews

⁴⁴While Peter was still speaking these words, the Holy Spirit* came down on all those people who were listening to his speech. ⁴⁵The Jewish believers who came with Peter were amazed. They were amazed that the Holy Spirit was poured out *(given)* to the non-Jewish people too. ⁴⁶These Jewish believers heard them speaking different languages and praising God. Then Peter said, ⁴⁷"We cannot refuse to allow these people to be baptized* in water. They have received the Holy Spirit the same as we did!" ⁴⁸So Peter commanded that Cornelius and his relatives and friends be baptized in the name of Jesus Christ. Then the people asked Peter to stay with them for a few days.

Peter Returns to Jerusalem

11 The apostles* and the brothers in Judea heard that non-Jewish people had accepted God's teaching too. ²But when Peter came to Jerusalem, some Jewish believers* argued with him. ³They said, "You went into the homes of people that are not Jews and are not circumcised*! You even ate with them!"

⁴So Peter explained the whole story to them. ⁵Peter said, "I was in the city of Joppa. While I was praying, a vision* came to me. In the vision I saw something coming down from the sky. It looked like a big sheet. It was being lowered to the ground by its four corners. It came down and stopped very close to me. ⁶I looked inside it. I saw animals, both tame and wild. I saw animals that crawl and birds that fly in the air. ⁷I heard a voice say to me, 'Get up, Peter. Kill any of these animals and eat it!' ⁸But I said, 'I would never do that, Lord! I have never eaten anything that is unholy or not pure.' ⁹But the voice from the sky answered again, 'God has made these things clean *(pure)*. Don't call them unholy!' ¹⁰This happened three times. Then the whole thing was taken back into the sky. ¹¹Then three men came to the house where I was staying. These three men were sent to me from the city of Caesarea. ¹²The Spirit* told me to go with them without doubting. These six brothers *(believers)* here also went with me. We went to the house of Cornelius. ¹³Cornelius told us about the angel he saw standing in his house. The

---

Good News The news that God has made a way for people to have their sins forgiven and live with God.
John John the Baptizer, who preached to people about Christ's coming (Mt. 3; Lk. 3).
baptism A Greek word meaning to be immersed, dipped, or buried briefly under water.
Christ The "anointed one" (Messiah) or chosen of God.
Spirit, Holy Spirit Also called the Spirit of God, the Spirit of Christ, and the Comforter. Joined with God and Christ, he does God's work among people in the world.
prophets People who spoke for God. Their writings are part of the Old Testament.

baptized A Greek word meaning to be immersed, dipped, or buried briefly under water.
apostles The men Jesus chose to be his special helpers.
Jewish believers Literally, "those of circumcision." This may mean Jews who thought that all Christians must be circumcised and obey the law of Moses (See Gal. 2:12).
circumcised To have the foreskin cut off. This was done to every Jewish baby boy. It was a mark of the agreement God made with Abraham (Gen. 17:9-14).
vision Something like a dream used by God to speak to people.

angel said to Cornelius, 'Send some men to Joppa. Invite Simon Peter to come. ¹⁴He will speak to you. The things he will say will save you and all your family.' ¹⁵After I began my speech, the Holy Spirit* came on them the same as he *(the Spirit)* came on us at the beginning.* ¹⁶Then I remembered the words of the Lord *(Jesus)*. The Lord said, 'John baptized* people in water, but you will be baptized in the Holy Spirit!' ¹⁷God gave to these people the same gift that he gave to us who believed in the Lord Jesus Christ. So could I stop the work of God? No!"

¹⁸When the Jewish believers heard these things, they stopped arguing. They praised God and said, "So God is allowing the non-Jewish people to change their hearts and have life the same as us!"

The Good News Comes to Antioch

¹⁹The believers were scattered by the persecution* that happened after Stephen was killed. Some of the believers went to places far away like Phoenicia, Cyprus, and Antioch. The believers told the Good News* in these places; but they told it only to Jews. ²⁰Some of these believers were men from Cyprus and Cyrene. When these men came to Antioch, they also spoke to Greeks *(non-Jews)*. They told these Greek people the Good News about the Lord Jesus. ²¹The Lord was helping the believers. And a large group of people believed and started following the Lord *(Jesus)*. ²²The church *(group of believers)* in Jerusalem heard about these new believers ⌊in Antioch⌋. So the believers in Jerusalem sent Barnabas to Antioch. ²³⁻²⁴Barnabas was a good man. He was full of the Holy Spirit* and full of faith. When Barnabas went to Antioch, he saw that God had blessed those people very much. This made Barnabas very happy. He encouraged all the believers in Antioch. He told them, "Never lose your faith. Always obey the Lord with all your hearts." Many, many people became followers of the Lord ⌊Jesus⌋.

²⁵Then Barnabas went to the city of Tarsus. He was looking for Saul. ²⁶When he found Saul, Barnabas brought him to Antioch. Saul and Barnabas stayed there a whole year. Every time the group of believers came together, Saul and Barnabas met with them and taught many people. In Antioch the followers ⌊of Jesus⌋ were called "Christians" for the first time.

²⁷About that same time some prophets* went from Jerusalem to Antioch. ²⁸One of these prophets was named Agabus. In Antioch, Agabus stood up and spoke. With the help of the Holy Spirit* he said, "A very bad time is coming to the whole world. There will be no food for people to eat." (This time without food happened when Claudius was emperor.*) ²⁹The believers decided that they would all try to help their brothers ⌊and sisters⌋ who lived in Judea. Each believer planned to send them as much as he could. ³⁰They gathered the money and gave it to Barnabas and Saul. Then Barnabas and Saul brought it to the elders* in Judea.

Herod Agrippa Hurts the Church

12 During that same time King Herod* began to persecute* some of the people who belonged to the church *(group of believers)*. ²Herod ordered James to be killed with a sword. James was the brother of John. ³Herod saw that the Jews liked this. So he decided to arrest Peter, too. (This happened during the time of the Jewish holiday called the Passover.*) ⁴Herod arrested Peter and put him in jail. A group of 16 soldiers guarded Peter. Herod wanted to wait until after the Passover festival. Then he planned to bring Peter before the people. ⁵So Peter was kept in jail. But the church was constantly praying to God for Peter.

Spirit, Holy Spirit Also called the Spirit of God, the Spirit of Christ, and the Comforter. Joined with God and Christ, he does God's work among people in the world.

beginning The beginning of the church on the day of Pentecost. (Read Acts 2).

baptize(d) A Greek word meaning to immerse, dip, or bury a person or thing briefly under water.

persecution A time when the Jews were punishing people who believed in Christ (Acts 8:1-4).

Good News The news that God has made a way for people to have their sins forgiven and live with God.

prophets People who spoke for God.

emperor The ruler (leader) of the Roman empire.

elders Men chosen to lead a church. Also called "overseers" and "pastors" ("shepherds"), they have the work of caring for God's people (Acts 20:28; Eph. 4:11).

Herod Herod Agrippa I, grandson of Herod the Great.

persecute To persecute is to hurt or do bad things to.

Passover Important Jewish holy day. They ate a special meal on this day every year to remember that God freed them from slavery in Egypt in the time of Moses.

Peter Leaves the Jail

⁶Peter was sleeping between two of the soldiers. He was bound with two chains. More soldiers were guarding the door of the jail. It was at night, and Herod planned to bring Peter out before the people the next day. ⁷Suddenly, an angel of the Lord stood there. A light shined in the room. The angel touched Peter on the side and woke him up. The angel said, "Hurry, get up!" The chains fell off Peter's hands. ⁸The angel said to Peter, "Get dressed and put on your shoes." And so Peter did this. Then the angel said, "Put on your coat and follow me." ⁹So the angel went out and Peter followed. Peter did not know if the angel was really doing this. He thought he might be seeing a vision.* ¹⁰Peter and the angel went past the first guard and the second guard. Then they came to the iron gate that separated them from the city. The gate opened itself for them. Peter and the angel went through the gate and walked about a block. Then the angel suddenly left.

¹¹Peter realized then what had happened. He thought, "Now I know that the Lord really sent his angel to me. He rescued *(saved)* me from Herod. The Jewish people thought that bad things would happen to me. But the Lord saved me from all these things."

¹²When Peter realized this, he went to the home of Mary. She was the mother of John. (John was also called Mark.) Many people were gathered there. They were all praying. ¹³Peter knocked on the outside door. A servant girl named Rhoda came to answer it. ¹⁴Rhoda recognized Peter's voice, and she was very happy. She even forgot to open the door. She ran inside and told the group, "Peter is at the door!" ¹⁵The believers said to Rhoda, "You are crazy!" But she continued to say that it was true. So they said, "It must be Peter's angel."

¹⁶But Peter continued to knock. When the believers opened the door, they saw Peter. They were amazed. ¹⁷Peter made a sign with his hand to tell them to be quiet. He explained to them how the Lord led him out of the jail. He said, "Tell James and the other brothers what happened." Then Peter left to go to another place.

¹⁸The next day the soldiers were very upset. They wondered what happened to Peter. ¹⁹Herod looked everywhere for Peter but could not find him. So Herod questioned the guards. Then he ordered that the guards be killed.

The Death of Herod Agrippa

Later Herod* moved from Judea. He went to the city of Caesarea and stayed there a while. ²⁰Herod was very angry with the people from the cities of Tyre and Sidon. Those people all came in a group to Herod. They were able to get Blastus on their side. Blastus was the king's personal servant. The people asked Herod for peace because their country needed food from Herod's country.

²¹Herod decided a day to meet with them. On that day Herod was wearing a beautiful royal robe. He sat on his throne and made a speech to the people. ²²The people shouted, "This is the voice of a god, not a man!" ²³Herod ₁accepted this praise and₁ did not give the glory to God. So an angel of the Lord caused him to become sick. He was eaten by worms inside him, and he died.

²⁴The message* of God was spreading and influencing more and more people. The group of believers became larger and larger.

²⁵After Barnabas and Saul finished their work in Jerusalem, they returned to Antioch. John Mark was with them.

Barnabas and Saul Given a Special Work

13 In the church *(group of believers)* at Antioch there were some prophets* and teachers. They were: Barnabas, Simeon (also called Niger), Lucius (from the city of Cyrene), Manaen (who had grown up with Herod,* the ruler) and Saul. ²These men were all serving the Lord and fasting.* The Holy Spirit* said to them, "Give Barnabas and Saul to me to do a special work. I have chosen them to do this work."

³So the church fasted* and prayed. They put their hands on* Barnabas and Saul and sent them out.

Herod Herod Agrippa I, grandson of Herod the Great.
message The news that God has made a way for people to have their sins forgiven and live with God.
prophets People who spoke for God.
fasting, fasted To fast is to live without food for a special time of prayer and worship to God.
Holy Spirit Called the Spirit of God, the Spirit of Christ, and the Comforter. Joined with God and Christ, he does God's work among people in the world.
put their hands on Here, this was a sign to show that these men were given a special work of God.

---

vision Something like a dream used by God to speak to people.

Barnabas and Saul in Cyprus

⁴Barnabas and Saul were sent out by the Holy Spirit.* They went to the city of Seleucia. Then they sailed from Seleucia to the island of Cyprus. ⁵When Barnabas and Saul came to the city of Salamis, they preached the message* of God in the Jewish synagogues.* (John ⌊Mark⌋ was with them to help.) ⁶They went across the whole island to the city of Paphos. In Paphos they met a Jewish man who did magic tricks. His name was Barjesus. He was a false prophet.* ⁷Barjesus always stayed close to Sergius Paulus, the governor. Sergius Paulus was a wise man. He asked Barnabas and Saul to come to him. He wanted to hear the message* of God. ⁸But Elymas, the magician, was against Barnabas and Saul. (Elymas is the name for Barjesus in the Greek language.) Elymas tried to stop the governor from believing ⌊in Jesus⌋. ⁹But Saul was filled with the Holy Spirit.* Paul (Saul's other name) looked at Elymas *(Barjesus)* ¹⁰and said, "You son of the devil! You are an enemy of everything that is right! You are full of evil tricks and lies. You always try to change the Lord's truths into lies! ¹¹Now the Lord will touch you and you will be blind. For a time you will not be able to see anything—not even the light from the sun."

Then everything became dark for Elymas. He walked around lost. He was trying to find someone to lead him by the hand. ¹²When the governor *(Sergius Paulus)* saw this, he believed. He was amazed at the teaching about the Lord.

Paul and Barnabas Leave Cyprus

¹³Paul and those people with him sailed away from Paphos. They came to Perga, a city in Pamphylia. But John ⌊Mark⌋ left them; he returned to Jerusalem. ¹⁴They continued their trip from Perga and went to Antioch, a city near Pisidia. In Antioch on the Sabbath day* they went into the Jewish synagogue* and sat down. ¹⁵The law of Moses and the writings of the prophets* were read. Then the leaders of the synagogue sent a message to Paul and Barnabas: "Brothers, if you have something to say that will help the people here, please speak!"

¹⁶Paul stood up. He raised his hand* and said, "My Jewish brothers and you other people who also worship the true God, please listen to me! ¹⁷The God of Israel *(the Jews)* chose our fathers *(ancestors)*. God helped his people to have success during the time they lived in Egypt as strangers. God brought them out of that country with great power. ¹⁸And God was patient with them for 40 years in the desert. ¹⁹God destroyed seven nations in the land of Canaan. He gave their land to his people. ²⁰All this happened in about 450 years.

"After this, God gave ⌊our people⌋ judges *(leaders)* until the time of Samuel* the prophet. ²¹Then the people asked for a king. God gave them Saul, the son of Kish. Saul was from the family group of Benjamin. He was king for 40 years. ²²After God took Saul away, God made David their king. This is what God said about David: 'David, the son of Jesse, is a man who is like me in his thinking. He will do all the things I want him to do.' ²³God has brought one of David's descendants to Israel *(the Jews)* to be their Savior.* That descendant is Jesus. God promised to do this. ²⁴Before Jesus came, John* preached to all the Jewish people. John told the people to be baptized* to show they wanted to change their lives. ²⁵When John was finishing his work, he said, 'Who do you think I am? I am not the Christ.* He is coming later. I am not worthy to untie his shoes.'

²⁶"My brothers, sons in the family of Abraham, and you non-Jews who also worship the true God, listen! The news about this salvation has been sent to us. ²⁷The ⌊Jews⌋ living in Jerusalem and the Jewish leaders did not realize that ⌊Jesus⌋ was the

---

Holy Spirit Called the Spirit of God, the Spirit of Christ, and the Comforter. Joined with God and Christ, he does God's work among people in the world.
message The news that God has made a way for people to have their sins forgiven and live with God.
synagogue(s) Synagogues were places where Jews gathered for prayer, study of the Scriptures, and other public meetings.
false prophet A person who says he speaks for God but does not really speak God's truth.
Sabbath day The seventh day of the Jewish week. It was a special religious day for the Jews.

prophets People who spoke for God. Their writings are part of the Old Testament.
raised his hand A sign to make the people listen.
Samuel Last judge and first prophet of Israel.
Savior The One that God promised to send to save his people from punishment for their sins.
John John the Baptizer, who preached to people about Christ's coming (Mt. 3; Lk 3).
baptized A Greek word meaning to be immersed, dipped, or buried briefly under water.
Christ The "anointed one" (Messiah) or chosen of God.

Savior. The words that the prophets* wrote ⌊about Jesus⌋ were read to the Jews every Sabbath day,* but they did not understand. The Jews condemned Jesus. When they did this, they made the words of the prophets come true! ²⁸They could not find any real reason why Jesus should die, but they asked Pilate to kill him. ²⁹These Jews did all the bad things that the Scriptures* said would happen to Jesus. Then they took Jesus down from the cross and put him in a grave. ³⁰But God raised him up from death! ³¹After this, for many days, the people who had gone with Jesus from Galilee to Jerusalem saw Jesus. These people are now his witnesses to the people. ³²We tell you the Good News* about the promise God made to our fathers *(ancestors)*. ³³We are their children *(descendants)*, and God has made this promise come true for us. God did this by raising Jesus from death. We also read about this in Psalm 2:

> 'You are my Son.
> Today I have become your Father.'
> *Psalm 2:7*

³⁴God raised Jesus from death. Jesus will never go back to the grave and become dust. So God said:

> 'I will give you the true and holy promises that I made to David.'
> *Isaiah 55:3*

³⁵But in another place God says:

> 'You will not let ⌊the body of⌋ your Holy One rot in the grave.'
> *Psalm 16:10*

³⁶David did God's will during the time when he lived. Then he died. David was buried with his fathers. And his body did rot in the grave! ³⁷But the One *(Jesus)* that God raised from death did not rot in the grave. ³⁸⁻³⁹Brothers, you must understand what we are telling you: You can have forgiveness of your sins through this One *(Jesus)*. The law of Moses could not free you from your sins. But every person who believes ⌊in Jesus⌋ is free from all his sins through him *(Jesus)*. ⁴⁰The prophets* said some things would happen. Be careful! Don't let these things happen to you. The prophets said:

⁴¹ 'Listen, you people who doubt!
> You can wonder, but then go away and die; because during your time,
> I *(God)* will do something
> that you will not believe.
> You will not believe it,
> even if someone explains it to you!'"
> *Habakkuk 1:5*

⁴²While Paul and Barnabas were leaving ⌊the synagogue,⌋* the people asked Paul and Barnabas to ⌊come again⌋ on the next Sabbath day* and tell them more about these things. ⁴³After the meeting, many of the Jews followed Paul and Barnabas from that place. With the Jews there were many converts* to the Jewish religion. These converts also worshiped the true God. Paul and Barnabas were persuading them to continue trusting in God's grace *(kindness)*.

⁴⁴On the next Sabbath day,* almost all the people in the city came together to hear the word of the Lord. ⁴⁵The Jews saw all these people there. So the Jews became very jealous. They said some very bad things and argued against the words that Paul said. ⁴⁶But Paul and Barnabas spoke very boldly. They said, "We must speak the message* of God to you Jews first. But you refuse to listen. You are making yourselves lost—not worthy of having eternal life! So we will now go to the people of other nations! ⁴⁷This is what the Lord *(God)* told us to do. The Lord said:

> 'I have made you to be a light
> for other nations,
> so that you can show the way of salvation
> to people all over the world.'"
> *Isaiah 49:6*

⁴⁸When the non-Jewish people heard Paul say this, they were happy. They gave honor to the message* of the Lord. And many of the people believed the message. These were the people chosen to have life forever.

⁴⁹And so the message* of the Lord was being told through the whole country. ⁵⁰But the Jews

---

prophets People who spoke for God. Their writings are part of the Old Testament.
Sabbath day The seventh day of the Jewish week. It was a special religious day for the Jews.
Scriptures Holy Writings—the Old Testament.
Good News The news that God has made a way for people to have their sins forgiven and live with God.

synagogue Synagogues were places where Jews gathered for prayer, study of the Scriptures, and other public meetings.
converts People that changed their religion to become Jews.
message The news that God has made a way for people to have their sins forgiven and live with God.

caused some of the important religious women and the leaders of the city to become angry and to be against Paul and Barnabas. These people did things against Paul and Barnabas and threw them out of town. ⁵¹So Paul and Barnabas shook the dust off their feet.* Then they went to the city of Iconium. ⁵²But the followers ⌊of Jesus in Antioch⌋ were happy and full of the Holy Spirit.*

Paul and Barnabas in Iconium

14 Paul and Barnabas went to the city of Iconium. They entered the Jewish synagogue.* (This is what they did in every city.) They spoke to the people there. Paul and Barnabas spoke so well that many Jews and Greeks *(non-Jews)* believed what they said. ²But some of the Jews did not believe. These Jews excited the non-Jewish people and made them think bad things about the brothers *(believers)*. ³So Paul and Barnabas stayed in Iconium a long time, and they spoke bravely for the Lord. Paul and Barnabas preached about God's grace *(kindness)*. The Lord proved that what they said was true by helping the apostles* *(Paul and Barnabas)* do miracles and wonders.* ⁴But some of the people in the city agreed with the Jews. Other people in the city believed Paul and Barnabas. So the city was divided.

⁵Some non-Jewish people, some Jews, and their Jewish leaders tried to hurt Paul and Barnabas. These people wanted to kill them with rocks. ⁶When Paul and Barnabas learned about this, they left that city. They went to Lystra and Derbe, cities in Lycaonia, and to the areas around those cities. ⁷They told the Good News* there too.

Paul in Lystra and Derbe

⁸In Lystra there was a man who had something wrong with his feet. He had been born crippled; he had never walked. ⁹This man was sitting and listening to Paul speak. Paul looked at him. Paul saw that the man believed that God could heal him. ¹⁰So Paul shouted, "Stand up on your feet!" The man jumped up and began walking around. ¹¹When the people saw what Paul did, they shouted in their own Lycaonian language. They said, "The gods have become like men! They have come down to us!" ¹²The people began to call Barnabas "Zeus."* They called Paul "Hermes,"* because he was the main speaker. ¹³The temple of Zeus was near the city. The priest of this temple brought some bulls and flowers to the city gates. The priest and the people wanted to give an offering to ⌊worship⌋ Paul and Barnabas.

¹⁴But when the apostles,* Barnabas and Paul, understood what the people were doing, they tore their own clothes.* Then they ran in among the people and shouted to them: ¹⁵"Men, why are you doing these things? We are not gods! We have the same feelings as you have! We came to tell you the Good News.* We are telling you to turn away from these worthless things. Turn to the true living God. He is the One who made the sky, the earth, the sea, and everything that is in them. ¹⁶In the past, God let all the nations do what they wanted. ¹⁷But God did things that prove he is real: He does good things for you. He gives you rain from the sky. He gives you good harvests at the right times. He gives you plenty of food, and he fills your hearts with joy." ¹⁸Paul and Barnabas told the people these things. But still Paul and Barnabas almost could not stop the people from offering sacrifices to ⌊worship⌋ them.

¹⁹Then some Jews came from Antioch and Iconium. They persuaded the people to be against Paul. And so the people threw rocks at Paul and dragged him out of the town. The people thought that they had killed Paul. ²⁰The followers ⌊of Jesus⌋ gathered around Paul and he got up and went back into the town. The next day, he and Barnabas left and went to the city of Derbe.

The Return to Antioch in Syria

²¹Paul and Barnabas told the Good News* in the city of Derbe too. Many people became followers ⌊of Jesus⌋. Paul and Barnabas returned to

---

shook the dust off their feet A warning. It showed that they were finished talking to these people.
Holy Spirit Called the Spirit of God, the Spirit of Christ, and the Comforter. Joined with God and Christ, he does God's work among people in the world.
synagogue Synagogues were places where Jews gathered for prayer, study of the Scriptures, and other public meetings.
apostles The men Jesus chose to be his special helpers.
miracles and wonders Amazing works or great things done by the power of God.
Good News The news that God has made a way for people to have their sins forgiven and live with God.

Zeus The most important of the many Greek gods.
Hermes Another Greek god. The Greeks believed he was a messenger for the other gods.
tore ... clothes This showed they were very angry.

the cities of Lystra, Iconium, and Antioch. ²²In those cities Paul and Barnabas made the followers ₍of Jesus₎ stronger. They helped them to stay in the faith. Paul and Barnabas said, "We must suffer many things on our way into God's kingdom." ²³Paul and Barnabas chose elders* for each church *(group of believers)*. They fasted* and prayed for these elders. These elders were men who had trusted the Lord ₍Jesus.₎ So Paul and Barnabas put them in the Lord's care. ²⁴Paul and Barnabas went through the country of Pisidia. Then they came to the country of Pamphylia. ²⁵They preached the message* ₍of God₎ in the city of Perga, and then they went down to the city of Attalia. ²⁶And from there Paul and Barnabas sailed away to Antioch ₍in Syria₎. This is the city where the believers had put them into God's care and sent them to do this work. Now they had finished the work.

²⁷When Paul and Barnabas arrived, they gathered the church *(group of believers)* together. Paul and Barnabas told them about all the things God had done with them. They said, "God opened a door so that the people of other nations *(non-Jews)* could also believe!" ²⁸Paul and Barnabas stayed there a long time with the followers ₍of Christ₎.

The Meeting at Jerusalem

15 Then some men came ₍to Antioch₎ from Judea. They began teaching the non-Jewish brothers: "You cannot be saved if you are not circumcised.* Moses taught us to do this." ²Paul and Barnabas were against this teaching. They argued with these men about it. So the group decided to send Paul, Barnabas, and some other men to Jerusalem. These men were going there to talk more about this with the apostles* and elders.*

³The church helped the men leave on the trip. These men went through the countries of Phoenicia and Samaria. In these countries they told all about how the non-Jewish people had turned to the true God. This made all the brothers very happy. ⁴Paul, Barnabas, and the others arrived in Jerusalem. The apostles,* the elders,* and the whole group of believers welcomed them. Paul, Barnabas, and the others told about all the things that God had done with them. ⁵Some of the believers ₍in Jerusalem₎ had belonged to the Pharisees.* They stood up and said, "The non-Jewish believers must be circumcised.* We must tell them to obey the law of Moses!"

⁶Then the apostles* and the elders* gathered to study this problem. ⁷There was a long debate. Then Peter stood up and said to them, "My brothers, I know that you remember what happened in the early days. God chose me then from among you to preach the Good News* to the non-Jewish people. They heard the Good News from me and they believed. ⁸God knows the thoughts of all men, and he accepted these non-Jewish people. God showed this to us by giving them the Holy Spirit* the same as he did to us. ⁹To God, those people are not different from us. When they believed, God made their hearts pure. ¹⁰So now, why are you putting a heavy burden* around the necks of the non-Jewish brothers? Are you trying to make God angry? We and our fathers *(ancestors)* were not strong enough to carry that burden! ¹¹No, we believe that we and these people will be saved by the grace *(mercy)* of the Lord Jesus!"

¹²Then the whole group became quiet. They listened to Paul and Barnabas speak. Paul and Barnabas told about all the miracles and wonders* that God did through them among the non-Jewish people. ¹³Paul and Barnabas finished speaking. Then James spoke. He said, "My brothers, listen to me. ¹⁴Simon *(Peter)* has told us how God showed his love for the non-Jewish people. For the first time, God accepted the non-Jewish people and made them his people. ¹⁵The words of the prophets* agree with this too:

---

elders A group of men chosen to lead a church. Also called "overseers" and "pastors" (shepherds), they have the work of caring for God's people (Acts 20:28; Eph. 4:11).
fasted To live without food for a special time of prayer.
message, Good News The news that God has made a way for people to have their sins forgiven and live with God.
circumcised To have the foreskin cut off. This was done to every Jewish baby boy. It was a mark of the agreement that God made with Abraham (Gen. 17:9-14).
apostles The men Jesus chose to be his special helpers.

Pharisees A Jewish religious group that claimed to follow carefully all Jewish laws and customs.
Holy Spirit Called the Spirit of God, the Spirit of Christ, and the Comforter. Joined with God and Christ, he does God's work among people in the world.
burden The Jewish law. Some of the Jews tried to make the non-Jewish believers follow this law.
miracles and wonders Amazing works or great things done by the power of God.
prophets People who spoke for God. Their writings are part of the Old Testament.

¹⁶ 'I *(God)* will return after this.
   I will build David's house again.
   It has fallen down.
   I will build again the parts of his house that
   have been pulled down.
   I will make his house new.
¹⁷ Then all other people will look for
   the Lord *(God)*—
   all the non-Jewish people that are
   my people too.
   The Lord *(God)* said this.
   And he is the One who does
   all these things.
¹⁸ These things have been known
   from the beginning of time.'
                                     Amos 9:11-12

¹⁹"So I think we should not bother the non-Jewish brothers who have turned to God. ²⁰Instead, we should write a letter to them. We should tell them these things:

   Don't eat food that has been given to idols.*
   (This makes the food unclean.)
   Don't do any kind of sexual sin.
   Don't taste *(eat)* blood.
   Don't eat animals that have been
   strangled *(choked)*.

²¹They should not do these things, because there are still men *(Jews)* in every city who teach the law of Moses. The words of Moses have been read in the synagogue* every Sabbath day* for many years."

The Letter to the Non-Jewish Believers

²²The apostles,* the elders,* and the whole church *(group of believers)* wanted to send some men with Paul and Barnabas to Antioch. The group decided to choose some of their own men. They chose Judas (also called Barsabbas) and Silas. These men were respected by the brothers ₍in Jerusalem₎. ²³The group sent the letter with these men. The letter said:

From the apostles and elders, your brothers.
To all the non-Jewish brothers
   in the city of Antioch and in the
   countries of Syria and Cilicia:

Dear Brothers,

²⁴We have heard that some men have come to you from our group. The things they said troubled and upset you. But we did not tell them to do this! ²⁵We have all agreed to choose some men and send them to you. They will be with our dear friends, Barnabas and Paul. ²⁶Barnabas and Paul have given their lives to serve our Lord Jesus Christ. ²⁷So we have sent Judas and Silas with them. They will tell you the same things. ²⁸The Holy Spirit* thinks that you should have no more burdens, and we agree. You need to do only these things:

²⁹ Don't eat food that has been given
    to idols.*
    Don't taste *(eat)* blood.
    Don't eat animals that have been
    strangled *(choked)*.
    Don't do any kind of sexual sin.

If you stay away from these things, you will do well.

We say good-bye now.

³⁰So Paul, Barnabas, Judas, and Silas left Jerusalem. They went to Antioch. In Antioch they gathered the group of believers and gave them the letter. ³¹When the believers read it, they were happy. The letter comforted them. ³²Judas and Silas were also prophets.* They said many things to help the brothers *(believers)* and make them stronger. ³³After Judas and Silas stayed there for a while, they left. They received a blessing of peace from the brothers. Judas and Silas went back to the brothers ₍in Jerusalem₎ who had sent them. ³⁴*

---

idols The false gods that the non-Jewish people worshiped.
synagogue Synagogues were places where Jews gathered for prayer, study of the Scriptures, and other public meetings.
Sabbath day The seventh day of the Jewish week. It was a special religious day for the Jews.
apostles The men Jesus chose to be his special helpers.
elders Men chosen to lead a church. Also called "overseers" and "pastors" (shepherds), they have the work of caring for God's people (Acts 20:28; Eph. 4:11).

Holy Spirit Called the Spirit of God, the Spirit of Christ, and the Comforter. Joined with God and Christ, he does God's work among people in the world.
prophets Men who spoke for God.
Verse 34 Some Greek copies of Acts add verse 34: "... but Silas decided to remain there."

³⁵But Paul and Barnabas stayed in Antioch. They and many others told the Good News* and taught the people the message* of the Lord.

Paul and Barnabas Separate

³⁶A few days later, Paul said to Barnabas, "We told the message* of the Lord in many towns. We should go back to all those towns to visit the brothers ₍and sisters₎ and see how they are doing." ³⁷Barnabas wanted to bring John Mark with them too. ³⁸But ₍on their first trip₎ John Mark had left them at Pamphylia; he did not continue with them in the work. So Paul did not think it was a good idea to take him. ³⁹Paul and Barnabas had a big argument about this. They separated and went different ways. Barnabas sailed to Cyprus and took Mark with him. ⁴⁰Paul chose Silas to go with him. The brothers ₍in Antioch₎ put Paul into the Lord's care and sent him out. ⁴¹Paul and Silas went through the countries of Syria and Cilicia, helping the churches* grow stronger.

Timothy Goes with Paul and Silas

16 Paul went to the cities of Derbe and Lystra. A follower ₍of Christ₎ named Timothy was there. Timothy's mother was a Jewish believer. His father was a Greek *(not a Jew)*. ²The believers in the cities of Lystra and Iconium respected Timothy. They said good things about him. ³Paul wanted Timothy to travel with him. But all the Jews living in that area knew that Timothy's father was Greek *(not Jewish)*. So Paul circumcised* Timothy to please the Jews. ⁴Then Paul and the men with him traveled through other cities.* They gave the believers the rules and decisions from the apostles* and elders* in Jerusalem. They told the believers to obey these rules. ⁵So the churches *(groups of believers)* were becoming stronger in the faith and were growing bigger every day.

Paul Is Called out of Asia

⁶Paul and the men with him went through the countries of Phrygia and Galatia. The Holy Spirit* did not allow them to preach the Good News* in the country of Asia.* ⁷Paul and Timothy went near the country of Mysia. They wanted to go into the country of Bithynia. But the Spirit of Jesus did not let them go in. ⁸So they passed by Mysia and went to the city of Troas. ⁹That night Paul saw a vision.* In this vision, a man from the country of Macedonia came to Paul. The man stood there and begged, "Come across to Macedonia. Help us!" ¹⁰After Paul had seen the vision, we immediately prepared to leave for Macedonia. We understood that God had called us to tell the Good News to those people.

The Conversion of Lydia

¹¹We left Troas in a ship, and we sailed to the island of Samothrace. The next day we sailed to the city of Neapolis. ¹²Then we went to Philippi. Philippi is an important city in that part of Macedonia. It is a city for Romans. We stayed in that city for a few days. ¹³On the Sabbath day* we went out the city gate to the river. At the river we thought we might find a special place for prayer. Some women had gathered there. So we sat down and talked with them. ¹⁴There was a woman named Lydia from the city of Thyatira. Her job was selling purple cloth. She worshiped the true God. Lydia listened to Paul. The Lord opened her heart. She believed the things Paul said. ¹⁵She and all the people living in her home were baptized.* Then Lydia invited us into her home. She said, "If you think I am truly a believer in the Lord Jesus, then come stay in my house." She persuaded us to stay with her.

Good News, message The news that God has made a way for people to have their sins forgiven.
churches Groups of believers in the towns where Paul and Barnabas went before.
circumcised To have the foreskin cut off. This was done to every Jewish baby boy. It was a mark of the agreement God made with Abraham (Gen. 17:9-14).
cities The cities where there were groups of believers.
apostles The men Jesus chose to be his special helpers.
elders Men chosen to lead a church. Also called "overseers" and "pastors" (shepherds), they have the work of caring for God's people (Acts 20:28; Eph. 4:11).

Holy Spirit Called the Spirit of God, the Spirit of Christ, and the Comforter. Joined with God and Christ, he does God's work among people in the world.
Asia The western part of Asia Minor.
vision Something like a dream used by God to speak to people.
Sabbath day The seventh day of the Jewish week. It was a special religious day for the Jews.
baptized A Greek word meaning to be immersed, dipped, or buried briefly under water.

Paul and Silas in Jail

[16] One time something happened to us while we were going to the place for prayer. A servant girl met us. She had a special spirit* in her. This spirit gave her the power to tell what would happen in the future. By doing this she earned a lot of money for the men who owned her. [17] This girl followed Paul and us. She said loudly, "These men are servants of the Most High God! They are telling you how you can be saved!" [18] She continued doing this for many days. This bothered Paul, so he turned and said to the spirit, "By the power of Jesus Christ, I command you to come out of her!" Immediately, the spirit came out.

[19] The men that owned the servant girl saw this. These men knew that now they could not use her to make money. So they grabbed Paul and Silas and dragged them into the meeting place of the city. The city officials were there. [20] The men brought Paul and Silas to the leaders and said, "These men are Jews. They are making trouble in our city. [21] They are telling the people to do things that are not right for us. We are Roman citizens and cannot do these things." [22] The people were against Paul and Silas. Then the leaders tore the clothes of Paul and Silas and told some men to beat Paul and Silas with rods. [23] The men beat Paul and Silas many times. Then the leaders put Paul and Silas in jail. The leaders told the jailer, "Guard them very carefully!" [24] The jailer heard this special order. So he put Paul and Silas far inside the jail. He tied their feet between large blocks of wood.

[25] About midnight Paul and Silas were praying and singing songs to God. The other prisoners were listening to them. [26] Suddenly, there was a big earthquake. It was so strong that it shook the foundation of the jail. Then all the doors of the jail opened. All the prisoners were freed from their chains. [27] The jailer woke up. He saw that the jail doors were open. He thought that the prisoners had already escaped. So the jailer got his sword and was ready to kill himself.* [28] But Paul shouted, "Don't hurt yourself! We are all here!"

[29] The jailer told someone to bring a light. Then he ran inside. He was shaking. He fell down in front of Paul and Silas. [30] Then he brought them outside and said, "Men, what must I do to be saved?"

[31] They said to him, "Believe in the Lord Jesus and you will be saved—you and all the people living in your house." [32] So Paul and Silas told the message* of the Lord to the jailer and all the people in his house. [33] It was late at night, but the jailer took Paul and Silas and washed their wounds. Then the jailer and all his people were baptized.* [34] After this the jailer took Paul and Silas home and gave them some food. All the people were very happy because they now believed in God.

[35] The next morning, the leaders sent some soldiers to tell the jailer, "Let these men (Paul and Silas) go free!"

[36] The jailer said to Paul, "The leaders have sent these soldiers to let you go free. You can leave now. Go in peace."

[37] But Paul said to the soldiers, "Your leaders did not prove that we did wrong. But they beat us in front of the people and put us in jail. We are Roman citizens,* ⌊so we have rights⌋. Now the leaders want to make us go quietly. No! The leaders must come and bring us out!"

[38] The soldiers told the leaders what Paul said. When the leaders heard that Paul and Silas were Roman citizens,* they were afraid. [39] So they came and told Paul and Silas they were sorry. They took Paul and Silas out of jail and asked them to leave the city. [40] But when Paul and Silas came out of the jail, they went to Lydia's house. They saw some of the believers there and comforted them. Then Paul and Silas left.

Paul and Silas in Thessalonica

17 Paul and Silas traveled through the cities of Amphipolis and Apollonia. They came to the city of Thessalonica. In that city there was a Jewish synagogue.* [2] Paul went into this synagogue to see the Jews. This is what he always did. Every Sabbath day* for three weeks Paul talked with the Jews about the Scriptures.* [3] Paul

---

spirit A spirit from the devil that gave special knowledge.
kill himself He thought the leaders would kill him for letting the prisoners escape.
message The news that God has made a way for people to have their sins forgiven and live with God.
baptized A Greek word meaning to be immersed, dipped, or buried briefly under water.
Roman citizens Roman law said that Roman citizens must not be beaten before they had a trial.
synagogue Synagogues were places where Jews gathered for prayer, study of the Scriptures, and other public meetings.
Sabbath day The seventh day of the Jewish week. It was a special religious day for the Jews.
Scriptures Holy Writings—the Old Testament.

explained these Scriptures to the Jews. He showed that the Christ* must die and then rise from death. Paul said "This man Jesus that I am telling you about is the Christ." ⁴In the synagogue there were some Greek men who worshiped the true God. There were also some important women. Many of these people also joined Paul and Silas.

⁵But the Jews ₁that did not believe₎ became jealous. They hired some bad men from the city. These bad men gathered many people and made trouble in the city. The people went to Jason's house, looking for Paul and Silas. The men wanted to bring Paul and Silas out before the people. ⁶But they did not find Paul and Silas. So the people dragged Jason and some of the other believers to the leaders of the city. The people all yelled, "These men *(Paul and Silas)* have made trouble everywhere in the world. And now they have come here too! ⁷Jason is keeping them in his house. All of them do things against the laws of Caesar.* They say that there is another king called Jesus."

⁸The leaders of the city and the other people heard these things. They became very upset. ⁹They made Jason and the other believers pay a fine. Then they let the believers go free.

Paul and Silas Go to Berea

¹⁰That same night the believers sent Paul and Silas to another city named Berea. In Berea, Paul and Silas went to the Jewish synagogue.* ¹¹These Jews were better people than the Jews in Thessalonica. These Jews were very happy to listen to the things Paul and Silas said. These Jews in Berea studied the Scriptures* every day. They wanted to know if these things were true. ¹²Many of these Jews believed. Many important Greek men and Greek women also believed. ¹³But when the Jews in Thessalonica learned that Paul was telling the word of God in Berea, they came to Berea too. The Jews from Thessalonica upset the people in Berea and made trouble. ¹⁴So the believers sent Paul away quickly to the sea. But Silas and Timothy stayed in Berea. ¹⁵The believers that went with Paul took him to the city of Athens. These brothers carried a message from Paul back to Silas and Timothy. The message said, "Come to me as soon as you can."

Paul in Athens

¹⁶Paul was waiting for Silas and Timothy in Athens. Paul was troubled because he saw that the city was full of idols.* ¹⁷In the synagogue,* Paul talked with the Jews and the Greeks who worshiped the true God. Paul also talked with some people in the business area of the city. Paul did this every day. ¹⁸Some of the Epicurean and Stoic philosophers* argued with him.

Some of them said, "This man doesn't really know what he is talking about. What is he trying to say?" Paul was telling them the Good News about Jesus' rising from death. So they said, "He seems to be telling us about some other gods." ¹⁹They got Paul and took him to a meeting of the Areopagus council.* They said, "Please explain to us this new idea that you have been teaching. ²⁰The things that you are saying are new to us. We have never heard these things before. We want to know what this teaching means." ²¹(All the people of Athens and the people from other countries who lived there always used their time talking about all the newest ideas.)

²²Then Paul stood before the meeting of the Areopagus council.* Paul said, "Men of Athens, I can see that you are very religious in all things. ²³I was going through your city and I saw the things you worship. I found an altar that had these words written on it: 'TO THE GOD WHO IS NOT KNOWN.' You worship a god that you don't know. This is the God I am telling you about! ²⁴He is the God who made the whole world and everything in it. He is the Lord *(Ruler)* of the land and the sky. He does not live in temples* that men build! ²⁵This God is the One who gives life, breath, and everything else to people. He does not need any help from people. God has everything he needs. ²⁶God began by making one man *(Adam)*. From him God made all the different people. God made them to live everywhere in the world. God decided exactly when and where they must live. ²⁷God wanted the people to look for him. Maybe

---

Christ The "anointed one" (Messiah) or chosen of God.
Caesar The name given to the emperor (ruler) of Rome.
synagogue Synagogues were places where Jews gathered for prayer, study of the Scriptures, and other public meetings.
Scriptures Holy Writings—the Old Testament.

idols The false gods that the non-Jewish people worshiped.
philosophers People who study and talk about their own ideas and the ideas and teachings of other people.
Areopagus council A group of important leaders in Athens. They were like judges.
temples Buildings where people go to worship.

they could search all around for him and find him. But he is not far from any of us:

> 28 'We live with him.
> We walk with him.
> We are with him.'

Some of your own writers have said:

> 'For we are his children.'

²⁹We are God's children. So, you must not think that God is like something that people imagine or make. He is not like gold, silver, or rock. ³⁰In the past, people did not understand God, but God ignored this. But now, God tells every person in the world to change his heart and life. ³¹God has decided a day when he will judge all the people in the world. He will be fair. He will use a man *(Jesus)* to do this. God chose this man long ago. And God has proved this to every person; God proved it by raising that man from death!"

³²When the people heard about ⌊Jesus⌋ being raised from death, some of them laughed. The people said, "We will hear more about this from you later." ³³Paul went away from them. ³⁴But some of the people believed Paul and joined him. One of the people who believed was Dionysius. He was a member of the Areopagus council.* Another person who believed was a woman named Damaris. There were also some other people who believed.

Paul in Corinth

18 Later, Paul left Athens and went to the city of Corinth. ²In Corinth Paul met a Jewish man named Aquila. Aquila was born in the country of Pontus. But Aquila and his wife, Priscilla, had recently moved ⌊to Corinth⌋ from Italy. They left Italy because Claudius* commanded that all Jews must leave Rome. Paul went to visit Aquila and Priscilla. ³They were tentmakers, the same as Paul. Paul stayed with them and worked with them. ⁴Every Sabbath day* Paul talked with the Jews and Greeks in the synagogue.* Paul tried to persuade these people ⌊to believe in Jesus⌋.

⁵Silas and Timothy came from Macedonia to Paul in Corinth. After this, Paul used all his time telling people the Good News.* He showed the Jews that Jesus is the Christ.* ⁶But the Jews would not accept Paul's teaching. The Jews said some very bad things. So Paul shook off the dust from his clothes.* He said to the Jews, "If you are not saved, it will be your own fault! I have done all I can do! After this, I will go only to non-Jewish people!" ⁷Paul left the synagogue* and moved into the home of Titius Justus. This man worshiped the true God. His house was next to the synagogue. ⁸Crispus was the leader of that synagogue. Crispus and all the people living in his house believed in the Lord *(Jesus)*. Many other people in Corinth also listened to Paul. They too believed and were baptized.*

⁹During the night, Paul had a vision.* The Lord said to him, "Don't be afraid! Continue talking to people and don't stop! ¹⁰I am with you. No one will be able to hurt you. Many of my people are in this city." ¹¹Paul stayed there for a year and a half, teaching God's truth to the people.

Paul Is Brought Before Gallio

¹²Gallio became the governor of the country of Achaia. At that time, some of the Jews came together against Paul. They took Paul to the court. ¹³The Jews said to Gallio, "This man is teaching people to worship God in a way that is against our ⌊Jewish⌋ law!"

¹⁴Paul was ready to say something, but Gallio spoke to the Jews. Gallio said, "I would listen to you Jews if you were complaining about a bad crime or some wrong. ¹⁵But the things you Jews are saying are only questions about words and names—arguments about your own ⌊Jewish⌋ law. So you must solve this problem yourselves. I don't want to be a judge of these things!" ¹⁶Then Gallio made them leave the court.

¹⁷Then they all grabbed Sosthenes. (Sosthenes was ⌊now⌋ the leader of the synagogue.*) They beat Sosthenes before the court. But this did not bother Gallio.

Areopagus council A group of important leaders in Athens. They were like judges.
Claudius The emperor (ruler) of Rome, 41-54 A.D.
Sabbath day The seventh day of the Jewish week. It was a special religious day for the Jews.
synagogue Synagogues were places where Jews gathered for prayer, study of the Scriptures, and other public meetings.
Good News The news that God has made a way for people to have their sins forgiven and live with God.
Christ The "anointed one" (Messiah) or chosen of God.
shook off the dust from his clothes This was a warning. It showed that Paul was finished talking to the Jews.
baptized A Greek word meaning to be immersed, dipped, or buried briefly under water.
vision Something like a dream used by God to speak to people.

Paul Returns to Antioch

¹⁸Paul stayed with the brothers for many days. Then he left and sailed for Syria. Priscilla and Aquila were also with him. At Cenchrea, Paul cut off his hair.* ₍This showed that₎ he had made a promise *(vow)* to God. ¹⁹Then they went to the city of Ephesus. This is where Paul left Priscilla and Aquila. While Paul was in Ephesus, he went into the synagogue* and talked with the Jews. ²⁰The Jews asked Paul to stay longer, but he refused. ²¹Paul left them and said, "I will come back to you again if God wants me to." And so Paul sailed away from Ephesus. ²²Paul went to the city of Caesarea. Then he went and said hello to the church *(group of believers)* ₍in Jerusalem₎. After that, Paul went to the city of Antioch. ²³Paul stayed in Antioch for a while. Then he left Antioch and went through the countries of Galatia and Phrygia. Paul traveled from town to town in these countries. He made all the followers ₍of Jesus₎ stronger.

Apollos in Ephesus and Achaia (Corinth)

²⁴A Jew named Apollos came to Ephesus. Apollos was born in the city of Alexandria. He was an educated man. He knew very much about the Scriptures.* ²⁵Apollos had been taught about the Lord *(Jesus)*. Apollos was always very excited when he talked to people about Jesus. The things Apollos taught about Jesus were right. But the only baptism* that Apollos knew about was the baptism that John* taught. ²⁶Apollos began to speak very boldly in the synagogue.* Priscilla and Aquila heard him speak. They took him to their home and helped him understand the way of God better. ²⁷Apollos wanted to go to the country of Achaia. So the brothers ₍in Ephesus₎ helped him. They wrote a letter to the followers ₍of Jesus in Achaia₎. In the letter they asked these followers to accept Apollos. These followers ₍in Achaia₎ had believed in Jesus because of God's grace *(kindness)*. When Apollos went there, he helped them very much. ²⁸He argued very strongly against the Jews before all the people. Apollos clearly proved that the Jews were wrong. He used the Scriptures* and showed that Jesus is the Christ.*

Paul in Ephesus

19 While Apollos was in the city of Corinth, Paul was visiting some places on the way to the city of Ephesus. In Ephesus Paul found some followers ₍of John₎.* ²Paul asked them, "Did you receive the Holy Spirit* when you believed?"

These followers said to him, "We have never even heard of a Holy Spirit!"

³So Paul asked them, "What kind of baptism* did you have?"

They said, "It was the baptism that John* taught."

⁴Paul said, "John told people to be baptized to show they wanted to change their lives. John told people to believe in the One who would come after him. That person is Jesus."

⁵When these followers ₍of John₎ heard this, they were baptized in the name of the Lord Jesus. ⁶Then Paul put his hands on them* and the Holy Spirit* came into them. They began speaking different languages and prophesying.* ⁷There were about twelve men in this group.

⁸Paul went into the synagogue* and spoke very boldly. Paul continued doing this for three months. He talked with the Jews and persuaded them to accept the things he said about the kingdom of God. ⁹But some of the Jews became stubborn. They refused to believe. These Jews said some very bad things about the Way ₍of God₎. All the people heard these things. So Paul left those Jews and took the followers ₍of Jesus₎ with him. Paul went to a place where a man named Tyrannus had a school. There Paul talked with people every day. ¹⁰Paul did this for two years. Because of this work, every Jew and Greek *(non-Jew)* in the country of Asia* heard the word of the Lord.

---

cut off his hair Jews did this to show that the time of a special promise to God was finished.
synagogue Synagogues were places where Jews gathered for prayer, study of the Scriptures, and other public meetings.
Scriptures Holy Writings—the Old Testament.
baptism A Greek word meaning to be immersed, dipped, or buried briefly under water.
John John the Baptizer, who preached to people about Christ's coming (Mt. 3; Lk. 3).
Christ The "anointed one" (Messiah) or chosen of God.
Holy Spirit Called the Spirit of God, the Spirit of Christ, and the Comforter. Joined with God and Christ, he does God's work among people in the world.
put his hands on them Here, doing this was a sign to show that Paul had God's authority or power to give these people special powers of the Holy Spirit.
prophesying Speaking or teaching things from God.
Asia The western part of Asia Minor.

The Sons of Sceva

[11] God used Paul to do some very special miracles.* [12] Some people carried away handkerchiefs and clothes that Paul had used. The people put these things on sick people. When they did this, the sick people were healed, and evil spirits ₍from the devil₎ left them.

[13-14] Some Jews also were traveling around and making evil spirits go out of people. The seven sons of Sceva were doing this. (Sceva was a high priest.*) These Jews tried to use the name of the Lord Jesus to make the evil spirits go out of people. They all said, "By the same Jesus that Paul talks about, I order you to come out!"

[15] But one time an evil spirit said to these Jews, "I know Jesus, and I know about Paul, but who are you?"

[16] Then the man, who had the evil spirit ₍from the devil₎ inside him, jumped on these Jews. He was much stronger than all of them. He beat them up and tore their clothes off. These Jews ran away from that house. [17] All the people in Ephesus, Jews and Greeks *(non-Jews)*, learned about this. They all began to have great respect ₍for God₎. And the people gave great honor to the name of the Lord Jesus. [18] Many of the believers began to confess and tell all the bad things they had done. [19] Some of the believers had used magic. These believers brought their magic books and burned them before everyone. Those books were worth about 50,000 silver coins.* [20] This is how the word of the Lord was influencing more and more people in a powerful way. And more and more people believed.

Paul Plans a Trip

[21] After these things, Paul made plans to go to Jerusalem. Paul planned to go through the countries of Macedonia and Achaia, and then go to Jerusalem. Paul thought, "After I visit Jerusalem, I must also visit Rome." [22] Timothy and Erastus were two of Paul's helpers. Paul sent them ahead to the country of Macedonia. Paul stayed in Asia* for a while.

Trouble in Ephesus

[23] But during that time, there was some bad trouble in Ephesus. This trouble was about the Way ₍of God₎. This is how it all happened: [24] There was a man named Demetrius. He worked with silver. He made little silver models that looked like the temple* of the goddess Artemis.* The men that did this work made much money. [25] Demetrius had a meeting with these men and some other men who did the same kind of work. Demetrius told them, "Men, you know that we make much money from our business. [26] But look at what this man Paul is doing! Listen to what he is saying! Paul has influenced and changed many people. He has done this in Ephesus and all over the country of Asia.* Paul says the gods that men make are not real. [27] These things that Paul says might turn the people against our work. But there is also another problem: People will begin to think that the temple of the great goddess Artemis is not important! Her greatness will be destroyed. Artemis is the goddess that everyone in Asia and the whole world worships."

[28] When the men heard this, they became very angry. They shouted, "Artemis,* the goddess of the city of Ephesus, is great!" [29] All the people in the city became upset. The people grabbed Gaius and Aristarchus. (These two men were from Macedonia and were traveling with Paul.) Then all the people ran to the stadium. [30] Paul wanted to go in and talk to the people, but the followers ₍of Jesus₎ did not let him go. [31] Also, some leaders of the country were friends of Paul. These leaders sent him a message. They told Paul not to go into the stadium. [32] Some people were yelling one thing and other people were yelling other things. The meeting was very confused. Most of the people did not know why they had come there. [33] The Jews made a man named Alexander stand before the people. The people told him what to do. Alexander waved his hand because he wanted to explain things to the people. [34] But when the people saw that Alexander was a Jew, they all began shouting the same thing. They continued shouting for two hours. The people said, "Great is Artemis* of Ephesus! Great is Artemis of Ephesus! Great is Artemis...!"

[35] Then the city clerk persuaded the people to be quiet. He said, "Men of Ephesus, all people know that Ephesus is the city that keeps the temple* of the great goddess Artemis.* All people know that

---

miracle(s) Miracles are amazing works done by God's power.
high priest Most important Jewish priest and leader.
50,000 silver coins Probably drachmas. One coin was enough to pay a man for working one day.
Asia The western part of Asia Minor.

temple The special building in Ephesus where the people worshiped the false goddess Artemis.
Artemis Greek goddess worshiped by the people of Asia Minor.

we also keep her holy rock.* ³⁶No person can say that this is not true. So you should be quiet. You must stop and think before you do anything. ³⁷You brought these men,* but they have not said anything bad against our goddess. They have not stolen anything from her temple. ³⁸We have courts of law and there are judges. Do Demetrius and those men that work with him have a charge against anyone? They should go to the courts! That is where they can argue with each other! ³⁹Is there something else you want to talk about? Then come to the regular town meeting of the people. It can be decided there. ⁴⁰I say this because some person might see this trouble today and say that we are rioting *(making trouble)*. We could not explain all this trouble, because there is no real reason for this meeting." ⁴¹After the city clerk said these things, he told the people to go home. And all the people left.

Paul Goes to Macedonia and Greece

20 When the trouble stopped, Paul invited the followers ˻of Jesus˼ to come visit him. He said things to comfort them and then told them good-bye. Paul left and went to the country of Macedonia. ²He said many things to strengthen the followers ˻of Jesus˼ in the different places on his way through Macedonia. Then Paul went to Greece *(Achaia)*. ³He stayed there three months. He was ready to sail for Syria, but some Jews were planning something against him. So Paul decided to go back through Macedonia to Syria. ⁴Some men were with him. They were: Sopater, the son of Pyrrhus, from the city of Berea, Aristarchus and Secundus, from the city of Thessalonica, Gaius, from the city of Derbe, Timothy, and Tychicus and Trophimus, two men from Asia.* ⁵These men went first, ahead of Paul. They waited for us in the city of Troas. ⁶We sailed from the city of Philippi after the ˻Jewish˼ Festival of Unleavened Bread.* We met these men in Troas five days later. We stayed there seven days.

Paul's Last Visit to Troas

⁷On Sunday,* we all met together to eat the Lord's Supper.* Paul talked to the group. He was planning to leave the next day. Paul continued talking until midnight. ⁸We were all together in a room upstairs, and there were many lights in the room. ⁹There was a young man named Eutychus sitting in the window. Paul continued talking, and Eutychus became very, very sleepy. Finally, Eutychus went to sleep and fell out of the window. He fell to the ground from the third floor. When the people ˻went and˼ lifted him up, he was dead. ¹⁰Paul went down to Eutychus. He kneeled down and hugged Eutychus. Paul said to the other believers, "Don't worry. He is alive now." ¹¹Paul went upstairs again. He divided the bread and ate. Paul spoke to them a long time. When he finished talking, it was early morning. Then Paul left. ¹²The people took the young man *(Eutychus)* home. He was alive, and the people were very much comforted.

The Trip from Troas to Miletus

¹³We sailed for the city of Assos. We went first, ahead of Paul. He planned to meet us in Assos and join us on the ship there. Paul told us to do this because he wanted to go to Assos by land. ¹⁴Later, we met Paul at Assos, and then he came on the ship with us. We all went to the city of Mitylene. ¹⁵The next day, we sailed away from Mitylene. We came to a place near the island of Chios. Then the next day, we sailed to the island of Samos. A day later, we came to the city of Miletus. ¹⁶Paul had already decided not to stop at Ephesus. He did not want to stay too long in Asia.* He was hurrying because he wanted to be in Jerusalem on the day of Pentecost* if possible.

Paul Speaks to the Elders from Ephesus

¹⁷In Miletus Paul sent a message back to Ephesus. Paul invited the elders* *(leaders)* of the church in Ephesus to come to him. ¹⁸When the elders came, Paul said to them, "You know about

---

holy rock Probably a meteorite or rock that the people worshiped because they thought it looked like Artemis.
men Gaius and Aristarchus, the men traveling with Paul.
Asia The western part of Asia Minor.
Festival of Unleavened Bread An important Jewish holiday week. In the Old Testament it began the day after Passover, but by this time the two holidays had become one.

Sunday Literally, "first day of the week," which for the Jews began at sunset on Saturday. But if Luke is using Greek time here, then the meeting was Sunday night.
Lord's Supper The meal Jesus told his followers to eat to remember him (Lk. 22:14-20).
Pentecost Jewish festival celebrating the wheat harvest.
elders Men chosen to lead a church. Also called "overseers" and "pastors" (shepherds), they have the work of caring for God's people (Acts 20:28; Eph. 4:11).

my life from the first day I came to Asia.* You know the way I lived all the time I was with you. ¹⁹The Jews planned things against me. This gave me much trouble, and I often cried. But you know that I always served the Lord. I never thought about myself first. ²⁰I always did what was best for you. I told you the Good News* about Jesus in public before the people and also taught in your homes. ²¹I told all people—Jewish people and Greek (non-Jewish) people—to change their hearts and turn to God. I told them all to believe in our Lord Jesus. ²²But now I must obey the Holy Spirit* and go to Jerusalem. I don't know what will happen to me there. ²³I know only that in every city the Holy Spirit tells me that troubles and even jail wait for me [in Jerusalem]. ²⁴I don't care about my own life. The most important thing is that I finish my work. I want to finish the work that the Lord Jesus gave me to do—to tell people the Good News about God's grace (kindness).

²⁵"And now listen to me. I know that none of you will ever see me again. All the time I was with you, I told you the Good News* about the kingdom of God. ²⁶So today I can tell you one thing that I am sure of: God will not blame me if some of you are not saved! ²⁷I can say this because I know that I told you everything that God wants you to know. ²⁸Be careful for yourselves and for all the people that God has given you. The Holy Spirit* gave you the work of caring for this flock (God's people). You must be like shepherds to the church (people) of God.* This is the church that God bought with his own blood.* ²⁹I know that after I leave, some men will come into your group. They will be like wild wolves. They will try to destroy the flock (group). ³⁰Also, men from your own group will become bad leaders. They will begin to teach things that are wrong. They will lead some followers [of Jesus] away from the truth. ³¹So be careful! Always remember this: I was with you for three years. During this time, I never stopped warning you. I taught you night and day. I often cried for you.

³²"Now I am giving you to God. I am depending on the message* about God's grace

---

Asia The western part of Asia Minor.
Good News, message The news that God has made a way for people to have their sins forgiven.
Holy Spirit Called the Spirit of God, the Spirit of Christ, and the Comforter. Joined with God and Christ, he does God's work among people in the world.
of God Some Greek copies say, "of the Lord."
his own blood Or, "the blood of his own son."

(kindness) to make you strong. That message is able to give you the blessings that God gives to all his holy people. ³³When I was with you, I never wanted anyone's money or fine clothes. ³⁴You know that I always worked to take care of my own needs and the needs of the people that were with me. ³⁵I always showed you that you should work like I did and help people that are weak. I taught you to remember the words of the Lord Jesus. Jesus said, 'You will be happier when you give than when you receive.'"

³⁶When Paul finished saying these things, he kneeled down and they all prayed together. ³⁷⁻³⁸They all cried and cried. The men were very sad because Paul had said that they would never see him again. They hugged Paul and kissed him. They went with him to the ship to say good-bye.

Paul Goes to Jerusalem

21 We all said good-bye to the elders.* Then we sailed away. We sailed straight to Cos island. The next day, we went to the island of Rhodes. From Rhodes we went to Patara. ²At Patara we found a ship that was going to the area of Phoenicia. We went on the ship and sailed away. ³We sailed near the island of Cyprus. We could see it on the north side, but we did not stop. We sailed to the country of Syria. We stopped at the city of Tyre because the ship needed to unload its cargo there. ⁴We found some followers [of Jesus] in Tyre, and we stayed with them for seven days. They warned Paul not to go to Jerusalem because of what the Holy Spirit* had told them. ⁵But when we finished our visit, we left. We continued our trip. All the followers [of Jesus], even the women and children, came outside the city with us to say good-bye. We all kneeled down on the beach and prayed. ⁶Then we said good-bye and got on the ship. The followers went home.

⁷We continued our trip from Tyre and went to the city of Ptolemais. We greeted the brothers (believers) there and stayed with them one day. ⁸The next day we left Ptolemais and went to the city of Caesarea. We went into the home of Philip and stayed with him. Philip had the work of telling the Good News.* He was one of the seven helpers.* ⁹He had four daughters who were not married. These daughters had the gift of

---

elders Men chosen to lead a church. Also called "overseers" and "pastors" (shepherds), they have the work of caring for God's people (Acts 20:28; Eph. 4:11).
helpers Men chosen for a special work. Read Acts 6:1-6.

prophesying.* ¹⁰After we had been there for many days, a prophet* named Agabus came from Judea. ¹¹He came to us and borrowed Paul's belt. Then Agabus used the belt to tie his own hands and feet. Agabus said, "The Holy Spirit* tells me, 'This is how the Jews in Jerusalem will tie the man who wears this belt.* Then they will give him to the non-Jewish people.'"
¹²We all heard these words. So we and the other followers ₍of Jesus₎ there begged *(asked)* Paul not to go to Jerusalem. ¹³But Paul said, "Why are you crying? Why are you making me so sad? I am ready to be tied in Jerusalem. I am also ready to die for the name of the Lord Jesus!"
¹⁴We could not persuade him to stay away from Jerusalem. So we stopped begging him and said, "We pray that what the Lord wants will be done."
¹⁵After this, we got ready and left for Jerusalem. ¹⁶Some of the followers ₍of Jesus₎ from Caesarea went with us. These followers took us to the home of Mnason, a man from Cyprus. Mnason was one of the first people to be a follower ₍of Jesus₎. They took us to his home so that we could stay with him.

Paul Visits James

¹⁷In Jerusalem the believers were very happy to see us. ¹⁸The next day, Paul went with us to visit James. All the elders *(church leaders)* were there too. ¹⁹Paul greeted all of them. Then he told them about how God used him to do many things among the non-Jewish people. He told them all the things that God did through him. ²⁰When the leaders heard these things, they praised God. Then they said to Paul, "Brother, you can see that thousands of Jews have become believers. But they think it is very important to obey the law of Moses. ²¹These Jews have heard about your teaching. They heard that you tell the Jews who live in other countries among non-Jews to leave the law of Moses. They heard that you tell those Jews not to circumcise* their children and not to obey Jewish customs. ²²What should we do? The Jewish believers here will learn that you have come. ²³So we will tell you what to do: Four of our men have made a vow* *(promise)* to God. ²⁴Take these men with you and share in their cleansing *(washing)* ceremony.* Pay their expenses. Then they can shave their heads.* Do this and it will prove to everyone that the things they have heard about you are not true. They will see that you obey the law of Moses in your own life. ²⁵We have already sent a letter to the non-Jewish believers. The letter said:

> 'Don't eat food that has been given to idols.*
> Don't taste *(eat)* blood.
> Don't eat animals that have been strangled *(choked)*.
> Don't do any kind of sexual sin.'"

²⁶Then Paul took the four men with him. The next day, Paul shared in the cleansing *(washing)* ceremony.* Then he went to the temple.* Paul announced the time when the days of the cleansing ceremony would be finished. On the last day an offering would be given for each of the men.

²⁷The seven days were almost finished. But some Jews from Asia* saw Paul at the temple.* They caused all the people to be upset, and they grabbed Paul. ²⁸They shouted, "You Jewish men, help us! This is the man who is teaching things that are against the law of Moses, against our people, and against this place *(the temple)*. This man is teaching these things to all people everywhere. And now he has brought some Greek *(non-Jewish)* men into the temple yard! He has made this holy place unclean!" ²⁹(The Jews said this because they had seen Trophimus with Paul in Jerusalem. Trophimus was a ₍Greek₎ man from Ephesus. The Jews thought that Paul had taken him into the holy area of the temple.)

³⁰All the people in Jerusalem became very upset. They all ran and grabbed Paul. They dragged him out of the holy area of the temple.* The temple gates were closed immediately. ³¹The

---

prophesying Speaking or teaching things from God.
prophet Person who spoke for God. He often told things that would happen in the future.
Holy Spirit Called the Spirit of God, the Spirit of Christ, and the Comforter. Joined with God and Christ, he does God's work among people in the world.
belt Paul's belt; so Agabus means that the Jews in Jerusalem will tie (arrest) Paul.
circumcise To cut off the foreskin. This was done to every Jewish baby boy. It was a mark of the agreement God made with Abraham (Gen. 17:9-14).

vow Probably a Nazirite vow, a time of special service that Jews promised to give to God.
cleansing ceremony The special things the Jews did to end the Nazirite vow.
shave their heads To show their vow was finished.
idols The false gods that the non-Jewish people worship.
temple The special building in Jerusalem for Jewish worship.
Asia The western part of Asia Minor.

people were trying to kill Paul. The commander of the Roman army in Jerusalem learned that there was trouble in the whole city. ³²Immediately the commander went to the place where the people were. He brought some army officers* and soldiers with him. The people saw the commander and his soldiers. So they stopped beating Paul. ³³The commander went to Paul and arrested him. The commander told his soldiers to tie Paul with two chains. Then the commander asked, "Who is this man? What has he done wrong?" ³⁴Some people there were yelling one thing and other people were yelling other things. Because of all this confusion and shouting, the commander could not learn the truth about what had happened. So the commander told the soldiers to take Paul to the army building. ³⁵⁻³⁶All the people were following them. When the soldiers came to the steps, they had to carry Paul. They did this ₍to protect Paul₎, because the people were ready to hurt him. The people shouted, "Kill him!"

³⁷The soldiers were ready to take Paul into the army building. But Paul spoke to the commander. Paul asked, "Do I have the right to say something to you?"

The commander said, "Oh, you speak Greek? ³⁸Then you are not the man I thought you were? I thought you were the Egyptian man who started some trouble against the government not long ago. That Egyptian man led 4,000 killers out to the desert."

³⁹Paul said, "No, I am a Jewish man from Tarsus. Tarsus is in the country of Cilicia. I am a citizen of that important city. Please, let me speak to the people."

⁴⁰The commander let Paul speak to the people. So Paul stood on the steps. He made signs with his hands so that the people would be quiet. The people became quiet and Paul spoke to them. He used the Jewish language.*

Paul Speaks to the People

22 Paul said, "My brothers and my fathers, listen to me! I will make my defense to you." ²The Jews heard Paul speaking the Jewish language.* So they became very quiet. Paul said, ³"I am a Jew. I was born in Tarsus in the country of Cilicia. I grew up in this city *(Jerusalem)*. I was a student of Gamaliel.* He carefully taught me everything about the law of our fathers *(ancestors)*. I was very serious about serving God, the same as all of you here today. ⁴I persecuted* the people who followed the Way ₍of Jesus₎. Some of them were killed because of me. I arrested men and women. I put them in jail. ⁵The high priest* and the whole council of older Jewish leaders can tell you that this is true! One time these leaders gave me some letters. The letters were to the Jewish brothers in the city of Damascus. I was going there to arrest the followers of Jesus and bring them back to Jerusalem for punishment.

Paul Tells About His Conversion

⁶"But something happened to me on my way to Damascus. It was about noon when I came close to Damascus. Suddenly a bright light from the sky shined all around me. ⁷I fell to the ground. I heard a voice saying to me: 'Saul, Saul, why are you doing these bad things to me?' ⁸I asked, 'Who are you, Lord?' The voice said, 'I am Jesus from Nazareth. I am the One you are persecuting.' ⁹The men who were with me did not understand the voice. But the men saw the light. ¹⁰I said, 'What shall I do, Lord?' The Lord *(Jesus)* answered, 'Get up and go into Damascus. There you will be told all the things I have planned for you to do.' ¹¹I could not see, because the bright light had made me blind. So the men led me into Damascus.

¹²"In Damascus a man named Ananias* came to me. Ananias was a religious man; he obeyed the law ₍of Moses₎. All the Jews who lived there respected him. ¹³Ananias came to me and said, 'Brother Saul, see again!' Immediately I was able to see him. ¹⁴Ananias told me, 'The God of our fathers *(ancestors)* chose you long ago. God chose you to know his plan. He chose you to see the Righteous One *(Jesus)* and to hear words from him. ¹⁵You will be his witness to all people. You will tell men about the things you have seen and heard. ¹⁶Now, don't wait any longer. Get up, be baptized* and wash your sins away. Do this, trusting in him *(Jesus)* ₍to save you.'₎

Gamaliel A very important teacher of the Pharisees, a Jewish religious group (See Acts 5:34).
persecuted To persecute is to hurt or do bad things to.
high priest Most important Jewish priest and leader.
Ananias In Acts there are three men with this name. See Acts 5:1; 23:2 for the other two.
baptized A Greek word meaning to be immersed, dipped, or buried briefly under water

---

army officers Centurions, Roman army officers who had authority over 100 soldiers.
Jewish language Probably Aramaic, a language like Hebrew that was spoken by the Jews in the first century.

17"Later, I came back to Jerusalem. I was praying in the temple* yard, and I saw a vision.* 18I saw Jesus, and Jesus said to me: 'Hurry! Leave Jerusalem now! The people here will not accept the truth about me.' 19I said, 'But Lord, the people know that I was the one who put the believers in jail and beat them. I went through all the synagogues* to find and arrest the people who believe in you. 20The people also know that I was there when Stephen, your witness, was killed. I stood there and agreed that they should kill Stephen. I even held the coats of the men who were killing him!' 21But Jesus said to me, 'Leave now. I will send you far away to the non-Jewish people.'"

22The people stopped listening when Paul said this last thing ∣about going to the non-Jewish people∣. They all shouted, "Kill him! Get him out of the world! A man like this should not be allowed to live!" 23They yelled and threw off their coats.* They threw dust into the air.* 24Then the commander told the soldiers to take Paul into the army building. He told the soldiers to beat Paul. He wanted to make Paul tell why the people were shouting against him like this. 25So the soldiers were tying Paul, preparing to beat him. But Paul said to an army officer* there, "Do you have the right to beat a Roman citizen* who has not been proven guilty?"

26When the officer heard this, he went to the commander and told him about it. The officer said, "Do you know what you are doing? This man *(Paul)* is a Roman citizen!"

27The commander came to Paul and said, "Tell me, are you really a Roman citizen?"

Paul answered, "Yes."

28The commander said, "I paid much money to become a Roman citizen."

But Paul said, "I was born a citizen."

29The men who were preparing to question Paul moved away from him immediately. The commander was afraid because he had already tied Paul, and Paul was a Roman citizen.*

Paul Speaks to the Jewish Leaders

30The next day the commander decided to learn why the Jews were speaking against Paul. So he commanded the leading priests and the Jewish council to meet together. The commander took Paul's chains off. Then he brought Paul out and stood Paul before their meeting.

23 Paul looked at the Jewish council meeting and said, "Brothers, I have lived my life in a good way before God. I have always done what I thought was right." 2Ananias,* the high priest,* was there. Ananias heard Paul and told the men who were standing near Paul to hit him on his mouth. 3Paul said to Ananias, "God will hit you too! You are like a ∣dirty∣ wall that has been painted white! You sit there and judge me, using the law ∣of Moses∣. But you are telling them to hit me, and that is against the law ∣of Moses∣."

4The men standing near Paul said to him, "You cannot talk like that to God's high priest.* You are insulting him!"

5Paul said, "Brothers, I did not know this man was the high priest. It is written in the Scriptures,* 'You must not say bad things about a leader of your people.'*"

6Some of the men in the meeting were Sadducees* and some others were Pharisees.* So Paul had an idea: He shouted to them, "My brothers, I am a Pharisee and my father was a Pharisee! I am on trial here because I hope *(believe)* that people will rise from death!"

7When Paul said this, there was a big argument between the Pharisees* and the Sadducees.* The group was divided. 8(The Sadducees believe that after people die, they cannot live again. The Sadducees also teach that there are no angels or spirits. But the Pharisees believe in all these things.) 9All these Jews began shouting louder and louder. Some of the teachers of the law, who were Pharisees, stood up and argued, "We find nothing

---

temple The special building in Jerusalem for Jewish worship.
vision Something like a dream used by God to speak to people.
synagogues Synagogues were places where Jews gathered for prayer, study of the Scriptures, and other public meetings.
threw off their coats This showed that the Jews were very angry at Paul.
threw dust into the air In this way they showed that they were very, very angry.
army officer A centurion, a Roman army officer who had authority over 100 soldiers.
Roman citizen: Roman law said that Roman citizens must not be beaten before their trial.

Ananias Not the same man named Ananias in Acts 22:12.
high priest Most important Jewish priest and leader.
Scriptures Holy Writings—the Old Testament.
'You must not say ... people' Quote from Ex. 22:28.
Sadducees A leading Jewish religious group. They accepted only the first five books of the Old Testament.
Pharisees The Pharisees were a Jewish religious group that claimed to follow carefully all Jewish laws and customs.

wrong with this man! Maybe an angel or a spirit did speak to him [on the road to Damascus]!"

¹⁰The argument became a fight. The commander was afraid that the Jews would tear Paul to pieces. So the commander told the soldiers to go down and take Paul away from these Jews and to put him in the army building.

¹¹The next night the Lord [Jesus] came and stood by Paul. He said, "Be brave! You have told people in Jerusalem about me. You must also go to Rome to tell people there about me!"

¹²The next morning some of the Jews made a plan. They wanted to kill Paul. The Jews made a promise *(vow)* to themselves that they would not eat or drink anything until they had killed Paul. ¹³There were more than 40 Jews who made this plan. ¹⁴These Jews went and talked to the leading priests and the older Jewish leaders. The Jews said, "We have made a serious promise to ourselves. We promised that we will not eat or drink until we have killed Paul! ¹⁵So this is what we want you to do: Send a message to the commander from you and all the Jewish leaders. Tell the commander you want him to bring Paul out to you. Tell the commander that you want to ask Paul more questions. We will be waiting to kill Paul while he is on the way here."

¹⁶But Paul's nephew heard about this plan. He went to the army building and told Paul about the plan. ¹⁷Then Paul called one of the army officers* and said to him, "Take this young man to the commander. He has a message for him." ¹⁸So the army officer brought Paul's nephew to the commander. The officer said, "The prisoner, Paul, asked me to bring this young man to you. He wants to tell you something."

¹⁹The commander led the young man to a place where they could be alone. The commander asked, "What do you want to tell me?"

²⁰The young man said, "The Jews have decided to ask you to bring Paul down to their council meeting tomorrow. The Jews want you to think that they plan to ask Paul more questions. ²¹But don't believe them! There are more than 40 Jews who are hiding and waiting to kill Paul. They have all promised *(vowed)* not to eat or drink until they have killed him! Now they are waiting for you to say yes."

²²The commander sent the young man away. The commander told him, "Don't tell anyone that you have told me about their plan."

Paul Is Sent to Caesarea

²³Then the commander called two army officers.* He said to them, "I need some men to go to Caesarea. Get 200 soldiers ready. Also, get 70 soldiers on horses and 200 men to carry spears. Be ready to leave at nine o'clock tonight. ²⁴Get some horses for Paul to ride. He must be taken to Governor Felix safely." ²⁵The commander wrote a letter. This is what the letter said:

²⁶From Claudius Lysias
To the Most Excellent Governor Felix:
Greetings.

²⁷The Jews had taken this man *(Paul)*, and they planned to kill him. But I learned that he is a Roman citizen, so I went with my soldiers and saved him. ²⁸I wanted to know why they were accusing him. So I brought him before their council meeting. ²⁹This is what I learned: The Jews said Paul did some things that were wrong. But these charges were about their own Jewish laws. And none of these things were worthy of jail or death. ³⁰I was told that some of the Jews were making a plan to kill Paul. So I send him to you. I also told those Jews to tell you the things they have against him.

³¹The soldiers did the things they were told. The soldiers got Paul and took him to the city of Antipatris that night. ³²The next day the soldiers on horses went with Paul to Caesarea. But the other soldiers and the spearmen went back to the army building [in Jerusalem]. ³³The soldiers on horses entered Caesarea and gave the letter to the governor *(Felix)*. Then they gave Paul to him. ³⁴The governor read the letter. Then he asked Paul, "What country are you from?" The governor learned that Paul was from Cilicia. ³⁵The governor said, "I will hear your case when the Jews who are against you come here too." Then the governor gave orders for Paul to be kept in the palace. (This building had been built by Herod.*)

The Jews Accuse Paul

24 Five days later Ananias went to the city of Caesarea. Ananias was the high priest.* Ananias also brought some of the older Jewish leaders and a lawyer named Tertullus. They went to Caesarea to make charges against Paul before

---

army officer(s) A centurion, a Roman army officer who had authority over 100 soldiers.

Herod Herod I (the Great), ruler of Judea, 40 B.C. to 4 B.C.
high priest Most important Jewish priest and leader.

the governor. ²Paul was called into the meeting, and Tertullus began to make his charges.

Tertullus said, "Most Excellent Felix! Our people enjoy much peace because of you, and many wrong things in our country are being made right through your wise help. ³We are very thankful to accept these things from you. We accept these things always and in every place. ⁴But I don't want to take any more of your time. So I will say only a few words. Please be patient. ⁵This man *(Paul)* is a troublemaker. He makes trouble with the Jews everywhere in the world. He is a leader of the Nazarene group. ⁶Also, he was trying to make the temple* unclean, but we stopped him. ⁸* You can decide if all these things are true. Ask him some questions yourself." ⁹The other Jews agreed. They said, "These things are really true!"

¹⁰The governor made a sign for Paul to speak. So Paul answered, "Governor Felix, I know that you have been a judge over this nation *(Israel)* for a long time. So I am happy to defend myself before you. ¹¹I went to worship in Jerusalem only twelve days ago. You can learn for yourself that this is true. ¹²These Jews who are accusing me did not find me arguing with anyone at the temple.* I was not making trouble with the people. And I was not making trouble or arguing in the synagogues* or any other place in the city. ¹³These Jews cannot prove the things they are saying against me now. ¹⁴But I will tell you this: I worship the God of our fathers *(ancestors)* as a follower of the Way ₍of Jesus₎. The Jews say that the Way ₍of Jesus₎ is not the right way. But I believe everything that is taught in the law of Moses. And I believe everything that is written in the books of the prophets.* ¹⁵I have the same hope in God that these Jews have—the hope that all people, good and bad, will be raised from death. ¹⁶This is why I always try to do what I believe is right before God and men.

¹⁷"I was away ₍from Jerusalem₎ for many years. I went back there to bring money to my people and to give some offerings *(gifts)*. ¹⁸I was doing this when some Jews saw me at the temple.* I had finished the cleansing *(washing)* ceremony.* I had not made any trouble; no people were gathering around me. ¹⁹But some Jews from Asia* were there. They should be here, standing before you. If I have really done anything wrong, those Jews from Asia are the ones who should accuse me. They were there! ²⁰Ask these Jews here if they found any wrong in me when I stood before the Jewish council meeting in Jerusalem. ²¹I did say one thing when I stood before them: I said, 'You are judging me today because I believe that people will rise from death!'"

²²Felix already understood a lot about the Way ₍of Jesus₎. He stopped the trial and said, "When commander Lysias comes here, I will decide about these things." ²³Felix told the army officer* to keep Paul guarded. But he told the officer to give Paul some freedom and to let Paul's friends bring the things that Paul needed.

Paul Speaks to Felix and His Wife

²⁴After a few days Felix came with his wife, Drusilla. She was a Jew. Felix asked for Paul to be brought to him. Felix listened to Paul talk about believing in Christ Jesus. ²⁵But Felix became afraid when Paul spoke about things like living right, self-control, and the judgment that will come in the future. Felix said, "Go away now! When I have more time, I will call you." ²⁶But Felix had another reason for talking with Paul. Felix hoped that Paul would pay him a bribe.* So Felix sent for Paul often and talked with him.

²⁷But after two years, Porcius Festus became governor. So Felix was no longer governor. But Felix left Paul in prison, because Felix wanted to do something to please the Jews.

Paul Asks to See Caesar

25 Festus became governor, and three days later he went from Caesarea to Jerusalem. ²The leading priests and the important Jewish leaders made charges against Paul before Festus. ³They asked Festus to do something for them; the Jews wanted Festus to send Paul back to Jerusalem. They had a plan to kill Paul on the

---

temple The special building in Jerusalem for Jewish worship.
Verses 6-8 Some Greek copies add 6b-8a: "And we wanted to judge him by our own law. ⁷But the officer Lysias came and used much force to take him from us. ⁸And Lysias commanded his people to come to you to accuse us."
synagogues Synagogues were places where Jews gathered for prayer, study of the Scriptures, and other public meetings.
prophets People who spoke for God. Their writings are part of the Old Testament.

cleansing ceremony The special things Jews did to end the Nazirite vow.
Asia The western part of Asia Minor.
army officer A centurion, a Roman army officer who had authority over 100 soldiers.
bribe Money to pay for Paul's freedom.

way. ⁴But Festus answered, "No! Paul will be kept in Caesarea. I myself will go to Caesarea soon. ⁵Some of your leaders should go with me. They can accuse the man *(Paul)* there in Caesarea, if he has really done something wrong."
⁶Festus stayed in Jerusalem another eight or ten days. Then he went back to Caesarea. The next day Festus told the soldiers to bring Paul before him. Festus was seated on the judgment seat. ⁷Paul came into the room. The Jews who had come from Jerusalem stood around him. The Jews said that Paul had done many wrong things. But they could not prove any of these things. ⁸This is what Paul said to defend himself: "I have done nothing wrong against the Jewish law, against the temple,* or against Caesar.*"
⁹But Festus wanted to please the Jews. So he asked Paul, "Do you want to go to Jerusalem? Do you want me to judge you there on these charges?"
¹⁰Paul said, "I am standing at Caesar's* judgment seat now. This is where I should be judged! I have done nothing wrong to the Jews; you know this is true. ¹¹If I have done something wrong, and the law says I must die, then I agree that I should die. I don't ask to be saved from death. But if these charges are not true, then no person can give me to these Jews. No! I want Caesar* to hear my case!"
¹²Festus talked about this with his advisers. Then he said, "You have asked to see Caesar,* so you will go to Caesar!"

Paul Before Herod Agrippa

¹³A few days later King Agrippa* and Bernice* came to Caesarea to visit Festus. ¹⁴They stayed there many days. Festus told the king about Paul's case. Festus said, "There is a man that Felix left in prison. ¹⁵When I went to Jerusalem, the leading priests and the older Jewish leaders there made charges against him. These Jews wanted me to order his death. ¹⁶But I answered, 'When a man is accused of doing something wrong, Romans don't give the man to other people to judge. First, the man must face the people who are accusing him. And he must be allowed to defend himself against their charges.' ¹⁷So these Jews came here ⌊to Caesarea⌋ for the trial. And I did not waste time. The next day I sat on the judgment seat and commanded that the man *(Paul)* be brought in. ¹⁸The Jews stood up and accused him. But the Jews did not accuse him of any bad crimes. I thought they would. ¹⁹The things they said were about their own religion and about a man named Jesus. Jesus died, but Paul said that he is still alive. ²⁰I did not know much about these things, so I did not ask questions. But I asked Paul, 'Do you want to go to Jerusalem and be judged there?' ²¹But Paul asked to be kept in Caesarea. He wants a decision from the Emperor *(Caesar*)*. So I commanded that Paul be held until I could send him to Caesar ⌊in Rome⌋."
²²Agrippa* said to Festus, "I would like to hear this man, too."
Festus said, "Tomorrow you can hear him!"
²³The next day Agrippa* and Bernice* appeared. They dressed and acted like very important people. Agrippa and Bernice, the army leaders, and the important men of Caesarea went into the judgment room. Festus commanded the soldiers to bring Paul in. ²⁴Festus said, "King Agrippa and all of you men gathered here with us, you see this man *(Paul)*. All the Jewish people, here and in Jerusalem, have complained to me about him. When they complain about him, they shout that he should be killed. ²⁵When I judged him, I could find nothing wrong. I found no reason to order his death. But he asked to be judged by Caesar.* So I decided to send him ⌊to Rome⌋. ²⁶But I don't really know what to tell Caesar that this man has done wrong. So I have brought him before all of you—especially you, King Agrippa. I hope that you can question him and give me something to write to Caesar. ²⁷I think it is foolish to send a prisoner ⌊to Caesar⌋ without making some charges against him."

Paul Before King Agrippa

26 Agrippa* said to Paul, "You may now speak to defend yourself."
Then Paul raised his hand* and began to speak. ²He said, "King Agrippa, I will answer all the charges that the Jews say against me. I think it is a blessing that I can stand here before you today and do this. ³I am very happy to talk to you, because you know much about all the Jewish customs and the things that the Jews argue about. Please listen to me patiently.

---

temple The special building in Jerusalem for Jewish worship.
Caesar The name given to the emperor (ruler) of Rome.
Agrippa Herod Agrippa II, great-grandson of Herod the Great.
Bernice Agrippa's sister. She was the oldest daughter of Herod Agrippa I.

raised his hand A sign to make the people listen

⁴"All the Jews know about my whole life. They know the way I lived from the beginning in my own country and later in Jerusalem. ⁵These Jews have known me for a long time. If they want to, they can tell you that I was a good Pharisee.* And the Pharisees obey the laws of the Jewish religion more carefully than any other group of Jewish people. ⁶Now I am on trial because I hope for the promise that God made to our fathers *(ancestors)*. ⁷This is the promise that all the twelve tribes *(family groups)* of our people hope to receive. For this hope the Jews serve God day and night. My king, the Jews have accused me because I hope for this same promise! ⁸Why do you people think it is impossible for God to raise people from death?

⁹⌊When I was a Pharisee⌋, even I thought I should do many things against the name of Jesus from Nazareth. ¹⁰And in Jerusalem I did many things against the believers.* The leading priests gave me the power to put many of these people *(believers)* in jail. When the followers of Jesus were being killed, I agreed that it was a good thing. ¹¹In every synagogue,* I punished them. I tried to make them say bad things against* ⌊Jesus⌋. I was so angry against these people *(believers)* that I went to other cities to find them and hurt them.

Paul Tells About Seeing Jesus

¹²"One time the leading priests gave me permission and the power to go to the city of Damascus. ¹³I was on the way to Damascus. It was noon. I saw a light from the sky. The light was brighter than the sun. The light shined all around me and the men who were traveling with me. ¹⁴We all fell to the ground. Then I heard a voice talking to me in the Jewish language.* The voice said, 'Saul, Saul, why are you doing these bad things to me? You are only hurting yourself by fighting me.' ¹⁵I said, 'Who are you, Lord?' The Lord said, 'I am Jesus. I am the One you are persecuting. ¹⁶Stand up! I have chosen you to be my servant. You will be my witness—you will tell people the things that you have seen about me today and the things that I will show you. This is why I have come to you today. ¹⁷I will not let ⌊your own⌋ people *(the Jews)* hurt you. And I will keep you safe from the non-Jewish people too. I am sending you to these people. ¹⁸You will show the people the Truth. The people will turn away from darkness *(sin)* to the light *(good)*. They will turn away from the power of Satan, and they will turn to God. Then their sins can be forgiven. They can have a share with those people who have been made holy* by believing in me.'"

Paul Tells About His Work

¹⁹Paul continued speaking: "King Agrippa,* after I had this vision* from heaven, I obeyed it. ²⁰I began telling people that they should change their hearts and lives and turn back to God. I told the people to do things that show that they really changed their hearts. I told these things first to people in Damascus. Then I went to Jerusalem and to every part of Judea and told these things to the people there. I also went to the non-Jewish people. ²¹This is why the Jews grabbed me and were trying to kill me at the temple.* ²²But God helped me, and he is still helping me today. With God's help I am standing here today and telling all people the things I have seen. But I am saying nothing new. I am saying the same things that Moses and the prophets* said would happen. ²³They said that the Christ* would die and be the first to rise from death. Moses and the prophets said that the Christ would bring light to the Jewish people and to the non-Jewish people."

Paul Tries to Persuade Agrippa

²⁴While Paul was saying these things to defend himself, Festus shouted, "Paul, you are crazy! Too much study has made you crazy!"

²⁵Paul said, "Most Excellent Festus, I am not crazy. The things I say are true. My words are not the words of a foolish man; I am serious. ²⁶King Agrippa* knows about these things. I can speak freely to him. I know that he has heard about all of these things. Why? Because these things

---

Pharisee The Pharisees were a Jewish religious group that claimed to follow carefully all Jewish laws and customs.

believers Literally, "holy ones," a name for people that believe in Jesus.

synagogue Synagogues were places where Jews gathered for prayer, study of the Scriptures, and other public meetings.

say bad things against Literally, "blaspheme," the same as saying they did not believe in Jesus.

Jewish language Probably Aramaic, a language like Hebrew that was spoken by the Jews in the first century.

holy A holy person is pure and belongs only to God.

Agrippa Herod Agrippa II, great-grandson of Herod the Great.

vision Something like a dream used by God to speak to people.

temple The special building in Jerusalem for Jewish worship.

prophets People who spoke for God. Their writings are part of the Old Testament.

Christ The "anointed one" (Messiah) or chosen of God.

happened where all people could see. ²⁷King Agrippa,* do you believe the things the prophets* wrote? I know you believe!"

²⁸King Agrippa said to Paul, "Do you think you can persuade me to become a Christian so easily?"

²⁹Paul said, "It is not important if it is easy or if it is hard; I pray to God that not only you but every person listening to me today could be saved and be like me—except for these chains I have!"

³⁰King Agrippa,* Governor Festus, Bernice,* and all the people sitting with them stood up ³¹and left the room. They were talking to each other. They said, "This man should not be killed or put in jail; he has done nothing really bad!" ³²And Agrippa said to Festus, "We could let this man go free, but he has asked to see Caesar.*"

Paul Sails for Rome

27 It was decided that we would sail for Italy. An army officer* named Julius guarded Paul and some other prisoners. Julius served in the emperor's* army. ²We got on a ship and left. The ship was from the city of Adramyttium and was ready to sail to different places in Asia.* Aristarchus went with us. He was a man from the city of Thessalonica in Macedonia. ³The next day we came to the city of Sidon. Julius was very good to Paul. He gave Paul freedom to go visit his friends. These friends took care of Paul's needs. ⁴We left the city of Sidon. We sailed close to the island of Cyprus because the wind was blowing against us. ⁵We went across the sea by Cilicia and Pamphylia. Then we came to the city of Myra in Lycia. ⁶In Myra the army officer* found a ship from the city of Alexandria. This ship was going to Italy. So he put us on it.

⁷We sailed slowly for many days. It was hard for us to reach the city of Cnidus because the wind was blowing against us. We could not go any farther that way. So we sailed by the south side of the island of Crete near Salmone. ⁸We sailed along the coast, but the sailing was hard. Then we came to a place called Safe Harbors. The city of Lasea was near there.

⁹But we had lost much time. It was now dangerous to sail, because it was already after the Jewish day of fasting.* So Paul warned them, ¹⁰"Men, I can see that there will be much trouble on this trip. The ship and the things in the ship will be lost. Our lives may even be lost!" ¹¹But the captain and the owner of the ship did not agree with Paul. So the army officer* did not believe Paul. Instead, the officer believed what the captain and owner of the ship said. ¹²And that harbor *(Safe Harbors)* was not a good place for the ship to stay for the winter. So most of the men decided that the ship should leave there. The men hoped we could go to Phoenix. The ship could stay there for the winter. (Phoenix was a city on the island of Crete. It had a harbor which faced southwest and northwest.)

The Storm

¹³Then a good wind began to blow from the south. The men on the ship thought, "This is the wind we wanted, and now we have it!" So they pulled up the anchor. We sailed very close to the island of Crete. ¹⁴But then a very strong wind named the "Northeaster" came from across the island. ¹⁵This wind took the ship and carried it away. The ship could not sail against the wind. So we stopped trying and let the wind blow us. ¹⁶We went below a small island named Cauda. Then* we were able to bring in the lifeboat, but it was very hard to do. ¹⁷After the men took the lifeboat in, they tied ropes around the ship to hold the ship together. The men were afraid that the ship would hit the sandbanks of Syrtis.* So they lowered the sail and let the wind carry the ship. ¹⁸The next day the storm was blowing us so hard that the men threw some things out of the ship.* ¹⁹A day later they threw out the ship's equipment. ²⁰For many days we could not see the sun or the stars. The storm was very bad. We lost all hope of staying alive—we thought we would die.

²¹The men did not eat for a long time. Then one day Paul stood up before them and said, "Men, I told you not to leave Crete. You should have listened to me. Then you would not have all this trouble and loss. ²²But now I tell you to be happy.

Agrippa Herod Agrippa II, great-grandson of Herod the Great.
prophets People who spoke for God. Their writings are part of the Old Testament.
Bernice King Agrippa's sister. She was the oldest daughter of Herod Agrippa I.
Caesar The name given to the emperor (ruler) of Rome.
army officer A centurion, a Roman army officer who had authority over 100 soldiers.
emperor The ruler (leader) of the Roman empire.
Asia The western part of Asia Minor.

day of fasting The day of Atonement, an important Jewish holy day in the fall of the year. This was the time of year that bad storms happened on the sea.
Then While the island protected them from the wind.
Syrtis Shallow area in the sea near the Libyan coast.
threw some things ... ship The men did this to make the ship lighter so that it would not sink easily.

None of you will die! But the ship will be lost. ²³Last night an angel came to me from God. This is the God I worship. I am his. ²⁴God's angel said, 'Paul, don't be afraid! You must stand before Caesar.* And God has given you this ₁promise₁: He will save the lives of all those men sailing with you.' ²⁵So men, be happy! I trust in God. Everything will happen like his angel told me. ²⁶But we will crash on an island."

²⁷On the 14th night we were floating around in the Adriatic Sea.* The sailors thought we were close to land. ²⁸They threw a rope into the water with a weight on the end of it. They found that the water was 120 feet deep. They went a little farther and threw the rope in again. It was 90 feet deep. ²⁹The sailors were afraid that we would hit the rocks. So they threw four anchors into the water. Then they prayed for daylight to come. ³⁰Some of the sailors wanted to leave the ship. They lowered the lifeboat to the water. The sailors wanted the other men to think that they were throwing more anchors from the front of the ship. ³¹But Paul told the army officer* and the other soldiers, "If these men do not stay in the ship, then your lives cannot be saved!" ³²So the soldiers cut the ropes and let the lifeboat fall into the water.

³³Just before dawn Paul began persuading all the people to eat something. He said, "For the past two weeks you have been waiting and watching. You have not eaten for 14 days. ³⁴Now I beg *(ask)* you to eat something. You need it to stay alive. None of you will lose even one hair off your heads." ³⁵After he said this, Paul took some bread and thanked God for it before all of them. He broke off a piece and began eating. ³⁶All the men felt better. They all started eating too. ³⁷(There were 276 people on the ship.) ³⁸We ate all we wanted. Then we began making the ship lighter by throwing the grain into the sea.

The Ship Is Destroyed

³⁹When daylight came the sailors saw land. But they did not know what land it was. They saw a bay with a beach. The sailors wanted to sail the ship to the beach if they could. ⁴⁰So they cut the ropes that were holding the rudders. Then they raised the front sail into the wind and sailed toward the beach. ⁴¹But the ship hit a sandbank. The front of the ship stuck there. The ship could not move. Then the big waves began to break the back of the ship to pieces.

⁴²The soldiers decided to kill the prisoners so that none of the prisoners could swim away and escape. ⁴³But the army officer* *(Julius)* wanted to let Paul live. So he did not allow the soldiers to kill the prisoners. Julius told the people who could swim to jump into the water and swim to land. ⁴⁴The other people used wooden boards or pieces of the ship. And this is how all the people went to land. None of the people died.

Paul on the Island of Malta

28 When we were safe on land, we learned that the island was called Malta. ²It was raining and very cold. But the people who lived there were very good to us. They made a fire for us and welcomed all of us. ³Paul gathered a pile of sticks for the fire. Paul was putting the sticks on the fire. A poisonous snake came out because of the heat and bit Paul on the hand. ⁴The people living on the island saw the snake hanging from Paul's hand. They said, "This man must be a murderer! He did not die in the sea, but Justice* does not want him to live." ⁵But Paul shook the snake off into the fire. Paul was not hurt. ⁶The people thought that Paul would swell up or fall down dead. The people waited and watched Paul for a long time, but nothing bad happened to him. So the people changed their opinion of Paul. They said, "He is a god!"

⁷There were some fields around that same area. A very important man on the island owned these fields. His name was Publius. He welcomed us into his home. Publius was very good to us. We stayed in his house for three days. ⁸Publius' father was very sick. He had a fever and dysentery.* But Paul went to him and prayed for him. Paul put his hands on the man and healed him. ⁹After this happened, all the other sick people on the island came to Paul. Paul healed them too. ¹⁰⁻¹¹The people on the island gave us many honors. We stayed there three months. When we were ready to leave, the people gave us the things we needed.

Paul Goes to Rome

We got on a ship from the city of Alexandria. The ship had stayed on the island of Malta during

---

Caesar The name given to the emperor (ruler) of Rome.
Adriatic Sea The sea between Greece and Italy, including the central part of the Mediterranean Sea.
army officer A centurion, a Roman army officer who had authority over 100 soldiers.

Justice The people thought there was a god named Justice who would punish bad people.
dysentery A very bad sickness like diarrhea.

the winter. On the front of the ship was the sign for the twin gods.* ¹²We stopped at the city of Syracuse. We stayed in Syracuse three days and then left. ¹³We came to the city of Rhegium. The next day a wind began to blow from the southwest, so we were able to leave. A day later we came to the city of Puteoli. ¹⁴We found some brothers *(believers)* there. They asked us to stay with them a week. Finally, we came to Rome. ¹⁵The believers in Rome heard that we were there. They came out to meet us at the Market of Appius* and at the Three Inns.* When Paul saw these believers, he felt better. Paul thanked God.

Paul in Rome

¹⁶Then we went to Rome. In Rome Paul was allowed to live alone. But a soldier stayed with Paul to guard him.

¹⁷Three days later Paul sent for some of the most important Jews. When they came together, Paul said, "My Jewish brothers, I have done nothing against our people *(the Jews)*. I have done nothing against the customs of our fathers *(ancestors)*. But I was arrested in Jerusalem and given to the Romans. ¹⁸The Romans asked me many questions. But they could not find any reason why I should be killed. So they wanted to let me go free. ¹⁹But the Jews there did not want that. So I had to ask ⌊to come to Rome⌋ to have my trial before Caesar.* But I am not saying that my people *(the Jews)* have done anything wrong. ²⁰That is why I wanted to see you and talk with you. I am bound with this chain because I believe in the hope of Israel.*

²¹The Jews answered Paul, "We have received no letters from Judea about you. None of our Jewish brothers who have traveled from there *(Judea)* brought news about you or told us anything bad about you. ²²We want to hear your ideas. We know that people everywhere are speaking against this group *(Christians)*."

²³Paul and the Jews chose a day for a meeting. On that day many more of these Jews met with Paul at his house. Paul spoke to them all day long. Paul explained the kingdom of God to them. Paul tried to persuade them to believe the things about Jesus. He used the law of Moses and the writings of the prophets* to do this. ²⁴Some of the Jews believed the things Paul said, but others did not believe. ²⁵They had an argument. The Jews were ready to leave, but Paul said one more thing to them: "The Holy Spirit* spoke the truth to your fathers *(ancestors)* through Isaiah the prophet.* He said,

26 'Go to this people *(the Jews)* and tell them:
You will listen and you will hear,
but you will not understand!
You will look and you will see,
but you will not understand
what you see!
27 Yes, the hearts *(minds)* of these
people *(the Jews)* are now hard.
These people have ears,
but they don't listen.
And these people refuse to see ⌊the truth⌋.
This has happened so that
these people will not
see with their eyes,
hear with their ears,
understand with their minds.
This has happened so that they will not
turn to me to heal them.'

Isaiah 6:9-10

²⁸"I want you Jews to know that God has sent his salvation to the non-Jewish people. They will listen!" ²⁹*

³⁰Paul stayed two full years in his own rented house. He welcomed all people who came and visited him. ³¹Paul preached about the kingdom of God. He taught about the Lord Jesus Christ. He was very bold *(brave)*, and no one tried to stop him from speaking.

---

twin gods Statues of Castor and Pollux, Greek gods.
Market of Appius Town about 27 miles from Rome.
Three Inns Town about 30 miles from Rome.
Caesar The name given to the emperor (ruler) of Rome.
Israel The Jewish nation (people).

prophet(s) People who spoke for God. Their writings are part of the Old Testament.
Holy Spirit Called the Spirit of God, the Spirit of Christ, and the Comforter. Joined with God and Christ, he does God's work among people in the world.
Verse 29 Some late copies of Acts add verse 29: "After Paul said this, the Jews left. They were arguing very much with each other."

Romans

1 From Paul, a servant of Christ Jesus. God called me to be an apostle.* I was chosen to tell God's Good News* to all people.

²God promised long ago to give this Good News to his people. God used his prophets* to promise this. That promise is written in the Holy Scriptures.* ³⁻⁴The Good News is about God's Son, Jesus Christ our Lord. As a person, he was born from the family of David.* But through the Spirit* of holiness Jesus was shown to be God's Son. He was shown to be God's Son with great power by rising from death. ⁵Through Christ, God gave me the special work of an apostle.* God gave me this work to lead people of all nations to believe and obey God. And I do this work for Christ. ⁶And you people in Rome were also called to belong to Jesus Christ.

⁷This letter is to all of you in Rome that God has called to be his holy people.* You are people that God loves.

Grace *(kindness)* and peace to you from God our Father and from the Lord Jesus Christ.

A Prayer of Thanks

⁸First I want to say that I thank my God through Jesus Christ for all of you. I thank God because people everywhere in the world are talking about your great faith. ⁹⁻¹⁰Every time I pray I always remember you. God knows this is true. God is the One I worship *(serve)* in my spirit by telling people the Good News* about his Son. I pray that I will be allowed to come to you. It will happen if God wants it. ¹¹I want very much to see you. I want to give you some spiritual gift to make you strong. ¹²I mean that I want us to help each other with the faith that we have. Your faith will help me, and my faith will help you. ¹³Brothers ₍and sisters₎, I want you to know that I planned many times to come to you. But I have not been allowed to come to you. I wanted to come so that I could help you grow spiritually. I want to help you like I have helped the other non-Jewish people.

¹⁴I must serve all people—Greeks and non-Greeks, wise people and foolish people. ¹⁵That is why I want so much to preach the Good News* to you there in Rome.

¹⁶I am proud of the Good News. The Good News is the power God uses to save every person that believes—to save the Jews first, and also to save the non-Jews. ¹⁷The Good News shows how God makes people right with himself. God's way of making people right begins and ends with faith. Like the Scripture* says, "The person that is right with God by faith will live forever."*

All People Have Done Wrong

¹⁸God's anger is shown from heaven. God is angry with all the evil and wrong things that people do against God. They have the truth, but by their evil lives they hide the truth. ¹⁹God shows his anger, because everything that is known about God has been made clear to them. Yes, God has clearly shown people everything that is known about him. ²⁰There are things about God that people cannot see—his eternal power and all the things that make him God. But since the beginning of the world those things have been easy for people to understand. Those things are made clear in the things that God has made. So people have no excuse for the bad things they do. ²¹People knew God. But they did not give glory to God and they did not thank him. People's thinking

---

apostle Person Jesus chose to be a special helper.
Good News The news that God has made a way for people to have their sins forgiven and live with God.
prophets People who spoke for God.
Scripture(s) Holy Writings—the Old Testament.
David King of Israel about 1000 years before Christ.
Spirit "Spirit of holiness" is probably the Holy Spirit.
holy people God's people are called holy because they are made pure through Christ and belong only to God.

"The person ... forever" Quote from Hab. 2:4.

became useless. Their foolish minds were filled with darkness *(sin)*. ²²People said they were wise, and they became fools. ²³They gave up the glory of God who lives forever. People traded that glory for the worship of idols* made to look like earthly people. People traded God's glory for things that look like birds, animals, and snakes.

²⁴People were full of sin, wanting only to do evil things. So God left them and let them go their sinful way. And so they became full of sexual sins, using their bodies wrongly with each other. ²⁵Those people traded the truth of God for a lie. Those people worshiped and served things that were made. But people did not worship and serve the God who made those things. God should be praised forever. Amen.

²⁶Because people did those things, God left them and let them do the shameful things they wanted to do. Women stopped having natural sex with men. They started having sex with other women. ²⁷In the same way, men stopped having natural sex with women. The men began wanting each other all the time. Men did shameful things with other men. And in their bodies they received the punishment for those wrong things they did.

²⁸People did not think it was important to have a true knowledge of God. So God left them and allowed those people to have their own worthless thinking. And so those people do the things that they should not do. ²⁹Those people are filled with every kind of sin, evil, selfishness, and hatred. Those people are full of jealousy, murder, fighting, lying, and thinking the worst things about each other. Those people gossip ³⁰and say evil things about each other. Those people hate God. They are rude and conceited and boast about themselves. Those people invent ways of doing evil. They don't obey their parents, ³¹they are foolish, they don't keep their promises, and they show no kindness or mercy to other people. ³²Those people know God's law. They know that God's law says that people that live like this should die. But they continue to do these wrong things. And they also feel that people who do these things are doing right.

You Jews Also Are Sinful

2 If you think that you can judge those other people, then you are wrong. You too are guilty of sin. You judge those people, but you do the same bad things they do. So when you judge them, you are really judging yourself guilty. ²God judges the people that do those wrong things. And we know that God's judgment is right. ³You also judge the people that do those wrong things. But you do those wrong things too. So surely you understand that God will judge you. You will not be able to escape. ⁴God has been very kind to you. And he has been patient with you. God has been waiting for you to change. But you think nothing of his kindness. Maybe you don't understand that God is kind to you so that you will change your hearts and lives. ⁵But you people are hard and stubborn. You refuse to change. So you are making your own punishment greater and greater. You will get that punishment on the day when God will show his anger. On that day people will see God's right judgments. ⁶God will reward or punish every person for the things that person has done. ⁷Some people live for God's glory, for honor, and for life that cannot be destroyed. Those people live for those things by always continuing to do good. God will give life forever to those people. ⁸But other people are selfish and refuse to follow truth. Those people follow evil. God will give those people his punishment and anger. ⁹God will give trouble and suffering to every person that does evil—to the Jews first and also to the non-Jews. ¹⁰But God will give glory, honor, and peace to every person that does good—to the Jews first and also to the non-Jews. ¹¹God judges all people the same.

¹²People that have the law* and people that have never heard of the law are all the same when they sin. People that don't have the law and are sinners will be lost. And, in the same way, people that have the law and are sinners will be judged by the law. ¹³Hearing the law does not make people right with God. The law makes people right with God only if those people always obey everything the law says. ¹⁴(The non-Jews don't have the law. But when they freely do things that the law commands without even knowing the law, then they are the law for themselves. This is true even though they don't have the law. ¹⁵They show that in their hearts they know what is right and wrong the same as the law commands. And those people also show this by the way they feel about right and wrong. Sometimes their thoughts tell them that they did wrong, and this makes them guilty. And sometimes their thoughts tell them that did right, and this makes them not guilty.) ¹⁶All

---

idols Statues made from wood, stone, or metal that people worshiped like gods.

law God's law. It is represented in the law of Moses.

these things will happen on the day when God will judge the secret things inside of people. The Good News* that I tell people says that God will judge people through Christ Jesus.

The Jews and the Law

¹⁷What about you? You say you are a Jew. You trust in the law and boast that you are close to God. ¹⁸You know what God wants you to do. And you know the things that are important, because you have learned the law. ¹⁹You think you are a guide for people that don't know the right way. You think you are a light for people that are in darkness *(sin)*. ²⁰You think you can show foolish people what is right. And you think you are a teacher for people that still need to learn. You have the law and so you think that you know everything and have all truth. ²¹You teach other people. So why don't you teach yourself? You tell people not to steal. But you yourselves steal. ²²You say that people must not do the sin of adultery.* But you yourselves are guilty of that sin. You hate idols.* But you steal from temples.* ²³You boast about God's law. But you bring shame to God by breaking his law. ²⁴It is written in the Scriptures*: "The non-Jews say bad things about God because of you ˌJewsˌ."*

²⁵If you follow the law,* then your circumcision* has meaning. But if you break the law, then it is like you were never circumcised. ²⁶The non-Jews are not circumcised. But if they do what the law says, then it is like they were circumcised. ²⁷You Jews have the written law and circumcision, but you break the law. So the people that are not circumcised in their bodies, but still obey the law, will show that you people are guilty.

²⁸A person is not a true Jew if he is only a Jew in his physical body. True circumcision* is not only on the outside of the body. ²⁹A person is a true Jew only if he is a Jew inside. True circumcision is done in the heart. It is done by the Spirit,* not by the written law. And a person that is circumcised in the heart by the Spirit gets praise from God, not from people.

3 So, do Jews have anything that other people don't have? Is there anything special about being circumcised*? ²Yes, the Jews have many special things. The most important thing is this: God trusted the Jews with his teachings. ³It is true that some Jews were not faithful to God. But will that stop God from doing what he promised? ⁴No! God will continue to be true even when every person is false. Like the Scriptures* say:

> "You will be proved right in your words,
> and you will win when you are
> being judged."
>
> *Psalm 51:4*

⁵When we do wrong, that shows more clearly that God is right. So can we say that God does wrong when he punishes us? (I am using an idea that some people might have.) ⁶No! If God could not punish us, then God could not judge the world.

⁷A person might say, "When I lie it really gives God glory, because my lie shows God's truth. So why am I judged a sinner?" ⁸It would be the same to say, "We should do evil so that good will come." Many people criticize us and say that we teach those things. People that say those things are wrong, and they should be condemned.

All People Are Guilty

⁹So are we Jews better than other people? No! We have already said that Jews and non-Jews are the same. They are all guilty of sin. ¹⁰Like the Scriptures* say:

> "There is no person without sin. None!
> 11   There is no person that understands.
>   There is no person that really wants to
>   be with God.
> 12   All people have turned away,
>   and all people have become worthless.
> There is no person that does good. None!"
>
> *Psalm 14:1-3*

> 13   "People's mouths are like open graves;
>   they use their tongues for telling lies."
>
> *Psalm 5:9*

Good News The news that God has made a way for people to have their sins forgiven and live with God.
adultery Breaking a marriage promise by sexual sin.
idols The false gods that the non-Jewish people worship.
temples Places where people worship.
Scripture(s) Holy Writings—the Old Testament.
"The non-Jews ... Jews" Quote from Isa. 52:5.
law God's law. It is represented in the law of Moses.
circumcision, circumcised To have the foreskin cut off. This was done to every Jewish baby boy. It was a mark of the agreement God made with Abraham (Gen. 17:9-14).
Spirit The Holy Spirit. Called the Spirit of God, the Spirit of Christ, and the Comforter. Joined with God and Christ, he does God's work among people in the world.

"The things they say are like the poison
of snakes";
Psalm 140:3

14 "their mouths are full of cursing and
bitterness."
Psalm 10:7

15 "People are always ready to hurt and kill;
16 everywhere they go they cause ruin
and sadness.
17 People don't know the way of peace."
Isaiah 59:7-8

18 "They have no fear or respect for God."
Psalm 36:1

19 These things the law* says are for the people that are under the law. This stops all ⌊Jewish⌋ people from making excuses and brings the whole world *(Jews and non-Jews)* under God's judgment. 20 Why? Because no person can be made right with God by following the law. The law only shows us our sin.

How God Makes People Right

21 But God has a way to make people right without the law. And God has now shown us that new way. The law and the prophets* told us about this new way. 22 God makes people right through their faith in Jesus Christ. God does this for all people that believe in Christ. All people are the same. 23 All people have sinned and are not good enough for God's glory. 24 People are made right with God by his grace *(kindness)*. This is a free gift. People are made right with God by being made free from sin through Jesus Christ. 25 God gave Jesus as a way to forgive people's sins through faith. God does this by the blood *(death)* of Jesus. This showed that God always does what is right and fair. God was right in the past when he was patient and did not punish people for their sins. 26 And God gave Jesus to show today that God does what is right. God did this so that he could judge rightly and also make right any person that has faith in Jesus.

27 So do we have a reason to boast about ourselves? No! And why not? It is the way of faith that stops all boasting, not the way of following the law. 28 Why? Because a person is made right with God through faith, not through the things he has done to follow the law. This is what we believe. 29 God is not only the God of the Jews. He is also the God of the non-Jews. 30 There is only one God. He will make Jews* right with him by their faith. And he will also make non-Jews* right with him through their faith. 31 So do we destroy the law by following the way of faith? No! Faith causes us to be what the law truly wants.

The Example of Abraham

4 So what can we say about Abraham,* the father of our people? What did he learn about faith? 2 If Abraham was made right by the things he did, then he had a reason to boast. But Abraham could not boast before God. 3 The Scripture* says, "Abraham believed God. And God accepted Abraham's faith. That made Abraham right with God."*

4 When a person works, his pay is not given to him as a gift. He earns the pay he gets. 5 But a person cannot do any work that will make him right with God. So that person must trust in God. Then God accepts that person's faith *(trust)*, and that makes him right with God. God is the One who makes even evil people right. 6 David said the same thing. David said that a person is truly happy when God does not look at the things that person has done but accepts him like a good person:

7 "People are truly blessed *(happy)*
when their wrongs are forgiven,
and when their sins are covered!
8 And when the Lord accepts a person
like he was without sin,
that person is truly blessed!"
Psalm 32:1-2

9 Is this happiness only for those people that are circumcised* *(the Jews)*? Or is this happiness also for people that are not circumcised *(non-Jews)*? We have already said that God accepted Abraham's faith, and that faith made him right with God. 10 So how did this happen? Did God accept Abraham* before or after he was circumcised? God accepted him before his

---

law God's law. It is represented in the Old Testament.
prophets People who spoke for God. Their writings are part of the Old Testament.

Jews Literally, "circumcision."
non-Jews Literally, "uncircumcision."
Abraham Most respected ancestor of the Jews.
Scripture(s) Holy Writings—the Old Testament.
"Abraham ... God" Quote from Gen. 15:6.
circumcised, circumcision To have the foreskin cut off. This was done to every Jewish baby boy as a mark of the agreement God made with Abraham (Gen. 17:9-14).

circumcision.* ¹¹Abraham was circumcised later to show that God accepted him. His circumcision was proof that he was right with God through faith before he was circumcised. So Abraham is the father of all people that believe but are not circumcised. Those people believe and are accepted like people that are right with God. ¹²And Abraham is also the father of people that have been circumcised. But it is not their circumcision that makes Abraham their father. He is their father only if they live following the faith that our father Abraham* had before he was circumcised.

God's Promise Received Through Faith

¹³Abraham* and his descendants* received the promise that they would get the whole world. But Abraham did not receive that promise because he followed the law.* Abraham received that promise because he was right with God through his faith. ¹⁴If people could get the things that God promised by following the law, then faith is worthless. And God's promise to Abraham is worthless. ¹⁵Why? Because the law can only bring God's anger ₍when the law is not obeyed₎. But if there is no law, then there is nothing to disobey.

¹⁶So people get God's promise by having faith. This happens so that the promise can be a free gift. And if the promise is a free gift, then all of Abraham's people can have that promise. The promise is not only for those people that live under the law ₍of Moses₎. The promise is for any person that lives with faith like Abraham. Abraham is the father of us all. ¹⁷Like it is written ₍in the Scriptures₎* "I have made you (Abraham) a father of many nations."* This is true before God. Abraham believed in God—the God who gives life to dead people and decides that things will happen that have not yet happened.

¹⁸There was no hope ₍that Abraham would have children₎. But Abraham believed God and continued hoping. And that is why he became the father of many nations. Like God told him, "You will have many descendants (children)."* ¹⁹Abraham was almost 100 years old, so his body was much past the age for having children. Also, Sarah could not have children. Abraham thought about this. But his faith in God did not become weak. ²⁰Abraham never doubted that God would do the thing that God promised. Abraham never stopped believing. He grew stronger in his faith and gave praise to God. ²¹Abraham felt sure that God was able to do the thing that God promised. ²²So, "God accepted Abraham's faith. That made him right with God."* ²³Those words ("God accepted Abraham's faith") were written not only for Abraham. ²⁴Those words were also written for us. God will also accept us because we believe. We believe in the One (God) that raised Jesus our Lord from death. ²⁵Jesus was given to die for our sins. And he was raised from death to make us right with God.

Right With God

5 We have been made right with God because of our faith. So we have peace with God through our Lord Jesus Christ. ²Through our faith, Christ has brought us into that blessing of God's grace (kindness) that we now enjoy. And we are very happy because of the hope we have of sharing God's glory. ³And we are also happy with the troubles we have. Why are we happy with troubles? Because we know that these troubles make us more patient. ⁴And this patience is proof that we are strong. And this proof gives us hope. ⁵And this hope will never disappoint us—₍it will never fail₎. Why? Because God has poured out his love to fill our hearts. God gave us his love through the Holy Spirit.* That Holy Spirit was a gift to us from God.

⁶Christ died for us while we were still weak people. We were living against God, but at the right time, Christ died for us. ⁷Very few people will die to save the life of another person, even if that other person is a good person. If the person is a very good person, then someone might be willing to die for that person. ⁸But Christ died for us while we were still sinners. In that way God showed us that he loves us very much.

⁹We have been made right with God by Christ's blood (death). So through Christ we will

---

circumcision To have the foreskin cut off. Done to every Jewish baby boy as a mark of the agreement God made with Abraham (Gen. 17:9-14).
Abraham Most respected ancestor of the Jews.
descendants A person's children and all their future families.
law God's law. It is represented in the law of Moses.
Scripture(s) Holy Writings—the Old Testament.
"I ... nations" Quote from Gen. 17:5.

"You ... descendants" Quote from Gen. 15:5.
"God accepted ... God" Quote from Gen. 15:6.
Holy Spirit Called the Spirit of God, the Spirit of Christ, and the Comforter. Joined with God and Christ, he does God's work among people in the world.

surely be saved from God's anger. ¹⁰I mean that while we were God's enemies, God made friends with us through the death of his Son. So surely, now that we are God's friends, God will save us through his Son's life. ¹¹And not only will we be saved, but we are also very happy now. We are happy in God through our Lord Jesus Christ. It is because of Jesus that we are now God's friends.

Adam and Christ

¹²Sin came into the world because of what one man *(Adam)* did. And with sin came death. So this is why all people must die—because all people sinned. ¹³Sin was in the world before the law ₍of Moses₎. But God does not make people guilty for sin if there is no law. ¹⁴But from the time of Adam to the time of Moses, all people had to die. Adam died because he sinned by not obeying God's command. But even those people that did not sin the way Adam sinned had to die.

Adam was like the One *(Christ)* who was coming in the future. ¹⁵But God's free gift is not like Adam's sin. Many people died because of the sin of that one man *(Adam)*. But the grace *(kindness)* that people received from God was much greater. Many people received God's gift ₍of life₎ by the grace of the one man, Jesus Christ. ¹⁶After Adam sinned once, he was judged guilty. But the gift of God is different. God's free gift came after many sins. And the gift makes people right with God. ¹⁷One man sinned, and so death ruled all people because of that one man. But now some people accept God's full grace *(kindness)* and his great gift of being made right. Surely those people will have true life and rule through the one man, Jesus Christ.

¹⁸So one sin ₍of Adam₎ brought the punishment ₍of death₎ to all people. But in the same way, one good thing ₍that Christ did₎ makes all people right with God. And that brings true life for those people. ¹⁹One man *(Adam)* disobeyed God and many people became sinners. But in the same way, one man *(Christ)* obeyed God and many people will be made right. ²⁰The law came to make people have more sin. But when people had more sin, God gave them more of his grace *(kindness)*. ²¹Sin once used death to rule us. But God gave people more of his grace so that grace could rule by making people right with him. This brings life forever through Jesus Christ our Lord.

Dead to Sin but Alive in Christ

6 So do you think that we should continue sinning so that God will give us more and more grace *(kindness)*? ²No! We died to *(quit living)* our old sinful lives. So how can we continue living with sin? ³Did you forget that all of us became part of Christ Jesus when we were baptized*? We shared his death in our baptism.* ⁴So when we were baptized, we were buried with Christ and shared his death. We were buried with Christ so that we could ₍be raised up and₎ live a new life. This happened the same as Christ was raised from death by the wonderful power of the Father.

⁵Christ died, and we have been joined with Christ by dying too. So we will also be joined with him by rising from death like Christ rose from death. ⁶We know that our old life died with Christ on the cross. This happened so that our sinful selves would have no power over us. And then we would not be slaves to sin. ⁷Any person that has died is made free from sin's control *(power)*.

⁸If we died with Christ, we know that we will also live with him. ⁹Christ was raised from death. And we know that he cannot die again. Death has no power over him now. ¹⁰Yes, when Christ died, he died to ₍defeat the power of₎ sin one time—enough for all time. He now has a new life, and his new life is with God. ¹¹In the same way, you should see yourselves as being dead to the power of sin. And see yourselves as being alive for God through Christ Jesus.

¹²But don't let sin control you in your life here on earth. You must not be ruled by the things your sinful self makes you want to do. ¹³Don't offer the parts of your body to serve sin. Don't use your bodies as things to do evil with. But you should offer yourselves to God. Be like people that have died and now live. Offer the parts of your body to God to be used for doing good. ¹⁴Sin will not be your master. Why? Because you are not under law. You now live under God's grace *(kindness)*.

Slaves of Righteousness

¹⁵So what should we do? Should we sin because we are under grace *(kindness)* and not under law? No! ¹⁶Surely you know that when you give yourselves like slaves to obey someone, then you are really slaves of that person. The person

---

baptized, baptism Greek words meaning to be immersed, dipped, or buried briefly under water.

you obey is your master. You can follow sin, or obey God. Sin brings spiritual death. But obeying God makes you right with him. [17]In the past you were slaves to sin—sin controlled you. But thank God, you fully obeyed the things that were taught to you. [18]You were made free from sin. And now you are slaves to goodness *(right living)*. [19]I explain this by using an example that people know. I explain it this way because it is hard for you to understand. In the past you offered the parts of your body to be slaves to sin and evil. You lived only for evil. In the same way now you must give yourselves to be slaves of goodness. Then you will live only for God.

[20]In the past you were slaves to sin, and goodness *(right living)* did not control you. [21]You did evil things. Now you are ashamed of those things. Did those things help you? No. Those things only bring ⌊spiritual⌋ death. [22]But now you are free from sin. You are now slaves of God. And this brings you a life that is only for God. And from that you will get life forever. [23]When people sin, they earn what sin pays—death. But God gives his people a free gift—life forever in Christ Jesus our Lord.

An Example from Marriage

7 Brothers ⌊and sisters⌋, you all understand the law ⌊of Moses⌋. So surely you know that the law rules over a person only while he is alive. [2]⌊I will give you an example⌋: A woman must stay married to her husband as long as he is alive. But if her husband dies, then she is made free from the law of marriage. [3]But if that woman marries another man while her husband is still alive, the law says she is guilty of adultery.* But if the woman's husband dies, then that woman is made free from the law of marriage. So if that woman marries another man after her husband dies, she is not guilty of adultery.

[4]In the same way, my brothers ⌊and sisters⌋, your old selves died and you became free from the law* through the body of Christ. Now you belong to someone else. You belong to the One *(Christ)* that was raised from death. We belong to Christ so that we can be used in service to God. [5]In the past, we were ruled by our sinful selves. The law made us want to do sinful things. And those sinful things we wanted to do controlled our bodies, so that the things we did were only bringing us spiritual death. [6]In the past, the law held us like prisoners. But our old selves died and we were made free from the law. So now we serve God in a new way, not in the old way with the written rules. Now we serve God in the new way with the Spirit.*

Our Fight Against Sin

[7]You might think that I am saying that sin and the law* are the same thing. That is not true. But the law was the only way I could learn what sin means. I would never have known what it means to want something wrong. But the law said, "You must not want ⌊things that belong to other people⌋."* [8]And sin found a way to use that command and make me want every kind of wrong thing. So sin came to me because of that command. But without the law, sin has no power. [9]I was alive without the law before I knew the law. But when the law's command came to me, then sin began to live. [10]And I died ⌊spiritually⌋ because of sin. The command was meant to bring life, but for me that command brought death. [11]Sin found a way to fool me by using the command. Sin used the command to make me die ⌊spiritually⌋.

[12]So the law is holy, and the command is holy and right and good. [13]Does this mean that something that is good brought death to me? No! But sin used something that is good to bring death to me. This happened so that I could see what sin is really like. It happened to show that sin is something very, very bad. And the command was used to show this.

The Conflict in Man

[14]We know that the law* is spiritual. But I am not spiritual. Sin rules me like I am its slave. [15]I don't understand the things I do. I don't do the ⌊good⌋ things I want to do. And I do the ⌊bad⌋ things I hate to do. [16]And if I don't want to do the ⌊bad⌋ things I do, then that means that I agree that the law is good. [17]But I am not really the one doing these ⌊bad⌋ things. It is sin living in me that does these things. [18]Yes, I know that nothing good lives in me—I mean nothing good lives in the part of me that is not spiritual. I want to do the things that are good. But I don't do those things. [19]I don't do the good things that I want to do. I do the bad things that I don't want to do. [20]So if I do things I

---

adultery Breaking a marriage promise by sexual sin.
law God's law. It is represented in the law of Moses.

Spirit The Holy Spirit. Called the Spirit of God, the Spirit of Christ, and the Comforter. Joined with God and Christ, he does God's work among people in the world.
"You ... people" Quote from Ex. 20:17; Deut. 5:21.

don't want to do, then it is not really me doing those things. It is sin living in me that does those bad things. ²¹So I have learned this rule: When I want to do good, evil is there with me. ²²In my mind, I am happy with God's law. ²³But I see another law working in my body. That law makes war against the law that my mind accepts. That other law working in my body is the law of sin, and that law makes me its prisoner. ²⁴This is terrible! Who will save me from this body that brings me death? ²⁵God ₗwill save meₗ! I thank him ₗfor his salvationₗ through Jesus Christ our Lord! So in my mind I am a slave to God's law. But in my sinful self I am a slave to the law of sin.

Life in the Spirit

8 So now people that are in Christ Jesus are not judged guilty. ²Why am I not judged guilty? Because in Christ Jesus the law of the Spirit* that brings life made me free. It made me free from the law that brings sin and death. ³The law* was without power because the law was made weak by our sinful selves. But God did what the law could not do. God sent his own Son to earth with the same human life that other people use for sin. God sent his Son to be an offering to pay for sin. So God used a human life to condemn *(destroy)* sin. ⁴God did this so that we could be right like the law said we must be. Now we don't live following our sinful selves. We live following the Spirit.

⁵People that live following their sinful selves think only about things that their sinful selves want. But those people that live following the Spirit* are thinking about the things that the Spirit wants them to do. ⁶If a person's thinking is controlled by his sinful self, then there is spiritual death. But if a person's thinking is controlled by the Spirit, then there is life and peace. ⁷Why is this true? Because if a person's thinking is controlled by his sinful self, then that person is against God. That person refuses to obey God's law. And really that person is not able to obey God's law. ⁸Those people that are ruled by their sinful selves cannot please God.

⁹But you are not ruled by your sinful selves. You are ruled by the Spirit,* if that Spirit of God really lives in you. But if any person does not have the Spirit of Christ, then that person does not belong to Christ. ¹⁰Your body will always be dead because of sin. But if Christ is in you, then the Spirit gives you life, because Christ made you right with God. ¹¹God raised Jesus from death. And if God's Spirit is living in you, then he will also give life to your bodies that die. God is the One who raised Christ from death. And he will give life to your bodies through his Spirit that lives in you.

¹²So, my brothers ₗand sistersₗ, we must not be ruled by our sinful selves. We must not live the way our sinful selves want. ¹³If you use your lives to do the wrong things your sinful selves want, then you will die spiritually. But if you use the Spirit's* help to stop doing the wrong things you do with your body, then you will have ₗtrueₗ life.

¹⁴The true children of God are those people that let God's Spirit* lead them. ¹⁵The Spirit that we received is not a spirit that makes us slaves again and causes us to fear. The Spirit that we have makes us children of God. And with that Spirit we say, "Father, dear Father."* ¹⁶And the Spirit himself joins with our spirits to say we are God's children. ¹⁷If we are God's children, then we will get the blessings God has for his people. We will get these things from God. We will receive those blessings together with Christ. But we must suffer like Christ suffered. Then we will have glory like Christ has glory.

We Will Have Glory in the Future

¹⁸We have sufferings now. But the sufferings we have now are nothing compared to the great glory that will be given to us. ¹⁹Everything that God made is waiting with excitement for the time when God will show the world who his children are. The whole world wants very much for that to happen. ²⁰Everything that God made was changed to be like it was worth nothing. It did not want to change, but God decided to change it. But there was this hope: ²¹That everything God made would be made free from ruin *(decay)*. There was hope that everything God made would have the freedom and glory that belong to God's children. ²²We know that everything God made has been waiting until now in pain like a woman ready to give birth to a child. ²³Not only the world, but we

---

Spirit The Holy Spirit. Called the Spirit of God, the Spirit of Christ, and the Comforter. Joined with God and Christ, he does God's work among people in the world.

law God's law. It is represented in the law of Moses.

Father, dear Father Literally, "Abba, Father." Jewish children called their fathers "Abba," a name that was used like the English word "Daddy."

also have been waiting with pain inside us. We have the Spirit* as the first part of God's promise. So we are waiting for God to finish making us his own children. I mean we are waiting for our bodies to be made free. ²⁴We were saved, and we have this hope. If we can see what we are waiting for, then that is not really hope. People don't hope for something they already have. ²⁵But we are hoping for something that we don't have yet. We are waiting for it patiently. ²⁶Also, the Spirit* helps us. We are very weak, but the Spirit helps us with our weakness. We don't know how to pray like we should. But the Spirit himself speaks to God for us. The Spirit begs God for us. The Spirit speaks to God with deep feelings that words cannot explain. ²⁷God can see what is in people's hearts. And God knows what is in the mind of the Spirit, because the Spirit speaks to God for his people in the way that God wants.

²⁸We know that in everything God works for the good of those people that love him. These are the people God called *(chose)*, because that was his plan. ²⁹God knew those people before he made the world. And God decided that those people would be like his Son *(Jesus)*. Then Jesus would be the firstborn* of many brothers ⌊and sisters⌋. ³⁰God planned for those people to be like his Son. And he called *(chose)* those people. God called those people and made them right with him. And God gave his glory to those people that he made right.

God's Love in Christ Jesus

³¹So what should we say about this? If God is with us, then no person can defeat us. ³²⌊God will do anything for us⌋. God even let his own Son suffer for us. God gave his Son for us all. So with Jesus now, God will surely give us all things. ³³Who can accuse the people that God has chosen? No one! God is the One who makes his people right. ³⁴Who can say that God's people are guilty? No one! Christ Jesus died ⌊for us⌋, but that is not all. He was also raised from death. And now he is at God's right side and is begging God for us. ³⁵Can anything separate us from Christ's love?

No! Can trouble separate us from Christ's love? No! Can problems or persecution* separate us from Christ's love? No! If we have no food or clothes, will that separate us from Christ's love? No! Will danger or even death separate us from Christ's love? No! ³⁶Like it is written in the Scriptures*:

"For you *(Christ)* we are in danger of death
all the time.
People think we are worth no more
than sheep to be killed."
Psalm 44:22

³⁷But in all these things we have full victory through God who showed his love for us. ³⁸⁻³⁹Yes, I am sure that nothing can separate us from God's love. Not death, not life, not angels, not ruling spirits, nothing now or nothing in the future, no powers, nothing above us, nothing below us, or anything else in the whole world will ever be able to separate us from God's love that is in Christ Jesus our Lord.

God and the Jewish People

9 I am in Christ and I am telling you the truth. I don't lie. My feelings are ruled by the Holy Spirit.* And those feelings tell me that I am not lying: ²I have great sorrow and always feel much sadness ⌊for the Jewish people⌋. ³They are my brothers ⌊and sisters⌋, my earthly family. I wish I could help them. I would even have a curse on me and cut myself off from Christ if that would help them. ⁴They are the people of Israel.* Those people *(the Jews)* are God's chosen children. Those people have the glory of God and the agreements that God made between himself and his people. God gave them the law ⌊of Moses⌋ and the right way of worship. And God gave his promises to those people *(the Jews)*. ⁵Those people are the descendants* of our great fathers *(ancestors)*. And they are the earthly family of Christ. Christ is God over all things. Praise him forever!* Amen.

⁶⌊Yes, I feel sorry for the Jewish people⌋. I don't mean that God failed to keep his promise to them. But only some of the people of Israel *(the*

Spirit, Holy Spirit Also called the Spirit of God, the Spirit of Christ, and the Comforter. Joined with God and Christ, He does God's work among people in the world.
firstborn This probably means that Christ was the first in God's family to share God's glory.

persecution Being hurt or bothered by Christ's enemies.
Scripture(s) Holy Writings—the Old Testament.
Israel The Jewish nation (people).
descendants A person's children and all their future families.
Christ ... forever This can also mean, "May God, who rules over all things, be praised forever!"

Jews) are truly God's people.* ⁷And only some of Abraham's* descendants* are true children of Abraham *(God's people)*. ₍This is what God said to Abraham₎: "Isaac will be your only legal son."* ⁸This means that not all of Abraham's descendants are God's true children. Abraham's true children are those people that become God's children because of the promise God made to Abraham. ⁹God's promise to Abraham was like this: "At the right time I will come back, and Sarah will have a son."*

¹⁰And that is not all. Rebecca also had sons. And those sons had the same father. He is our father *(ancestor)* Isaac. ¹¹⁻¹²But before the two sons were born, God told Rebecca, "The older son will serve the younger."* This was before the boys had done anything good or bad. God said this before they were born so that the boy God chose would be chosen because of God's own plan. He was chosen because he was the one God wanted to call, not because of anything the boys did. ¹³Like the Scripture* says, "I loved Jacob, but I hated Esau."*

¹⁴So what should we say about this? Is God not fair? We cannot say that. ¹⁵God said to Moses, "I will show mercy to the person that I want to show mercy to. I will show pity to the person that I want to show pity to."* ¹⁶So God will choose the person he decides to show mercy to. And his choice does not depend on what people want or try to do. ¹⁷₍In₎ the Scripture* ₍God₎ says to Pharaoh*: "I made you king so you could do this for me. I wanted to show my power in you. I wanted my name to be announced in all the world."* ¹⁸So God shows mercy to the people he wants to show mercy to. And God makes the people stubborn that he wants to make stubborn.

¹⁹So one of you will ask me: "If God controls the things we do, then why does God blame us ₍for our sins₎?" ²⁰₍Don't ask that₎. You are only people. And people have no right to question God. A clay jar does not question the man that made it. The jar does not say, "Why did you make me like this?" ²¹The man that makes the jar can make anything he wants to make. He can use the same clay to make different things. He can make one thing for special purposes and another thing for daily use.

²²It is the same way with what God has done. God wanted to show his anger and to let people see his power. But God endured patiently those people he was angry with—people that were ready to be destroyed. ²³God waited with patience so that he could make known his rich glory. God wanted to give that glory to the people that receive his mercy. God has prepared these people to have his glory. ²⁴We are those people. We are the people God called *(chose)*. God called us from the Jews and from the non-Jews. ²⁵Like the Scripture* says in ₍the book of₎ Hosea:

> "The people that are not mine—
> I will say that they are my people.
> And the people that I did not love—
> I will say that they are the people I love."
> *Hosea 2:23*

²⁶ "And in the same place that God said,
  'You are not my people'—
in that place they will be called
  sons of the living God."
Hosea 1:10

²⁷And Isaiah cries out about Israel*:

"There are so many people of Israel that they are like the grains of sand by the sea. But only a few of those people will be saved. ²⁸Yes, the Lord will quickly finish judging the people on the earth."*

²⁹It is like Isaiah said:

"The Lord has all power. The Lord saved some of his people for us. If he had not done that, then we would now be like Sodom,* and we would now be like Gomorrah.*"*

³⁰So what does all this mean? It means this: That the non-Jews were not trying to make themselves right with God. But they were made right with God. They became right because of

---

God's people Literally, "Israel," the people God chose to bring his blessings to the world.
Abraham Most respected ancestor of the Jews.
descendants A person's children and all their future families.
"Isaac ... son" Quote from Gen. 21:12.
"At ... son" Quote from Gen. 18:10,14.
"The older ... younger" Quote from Gen. 25:23.
Scripture(s) Holy Writings—the Old Testament.
"I ... Esau" Quote from Mal. 1:2-3.
"I will ... to" Quote from Ex. 33:19.
Pharaoh The title of the king of Egypt.
"I made ... world" Quote from Ex. 9:16.

Israel The Jewish nation (people).
"There are ... earth" Quote from Isa. 10:22-23.
Sodom, Gomorrah Cities where evil people lived. God punished them by destroying their cities.
"The Lord ... Gomorrah" Quote from Isa. 1:9.

their faith. ³¹And the people of Israel* tried to follow a law to make themselves right with God. But they did not succeed. ³²Why not? Because they tried to make themselves right by the things they did. They did not trust in God to make them right. They fell over the stone that makes people fall. ³³The Scripture* talks about that stone:

"Look, I put in Zion* a stone
that will make people fall.
It is a rock that will make people sin.
But any person that trusts in that rock
will not be disappointed."
Isaiah 8:14; 28:16

10 Brothers ₍and sisters₎, the thing I want most is for all the Jews to be saved. That is my prayer to God. ²I can say this about the Jews: They really try to follow God. But they don't know the right way. ³They did not know the way that God makes people right with him. And they tried to make themselves right in their own way. So they did not accept God's way of making people right. ⁴Christ ended the law so that every person that believes in him is made right with God.

⁵Moses writes about being made right by following the law. Moses says, "A person that wants to find life by following these things *(the law)* must do the things the law says."* ⁶But this is what the Scripture* says about being made right through faith: "Don't say to yourself, 'Who will go up into heaven?'"* (That means, "Who will go up to heaven to get Christ and bring him down to earth?") ⁷"And don't say, 'Who will go down into the world below?'"* (That means, "Who will go down to get Christ and bring him up from death?") ⁸This is what the Scripture says: "God's teaching is near you; it is in your mouth and in your heart."* That teaching is the teaching of faith that we tell people. ⁹If you use your mouth to say, "Jesus is Lord," and if you believe in your mind that God raised Jesus from death, then you will be saved. ¹⁰Yes, we believe with our hearts, and so we are made right with God. And we use our mouths to say that we believe, and so we are saved. ¹¹Yes, the Scripture* says, "Any person who believes in him *(Christ)* will not be ashamed."* ¹²That Scripture* says "any person" because there is no difference between Jew and non-Jew. The same Lord is the Lord of all people. The Lord gives many blessings to all people that trust in him. ¹³Yes, ₍the Scripture says₎, "Every person that trusts in the Lord will be saved."*

¹⁴But before people can trust in the Lord for help, they must believe in him. And before people can believe in the Lord, they must hear about him. And for people to hear about the Lord, another person must tell them. ¹⁵And before a person can go and tell them, that person must be sent. It is written, "Beautiful are the feet of those people that come to tell good news."*

¹⁶But not all ₍the Jews₎ accepted that good news. Isaiah said, "Lord, who believed the things we told them?"* ¹⁷So faith comes from hearing ₍the Good News₎.* And people hear ₍the Good News₎ when a person tells them about Christ.

¹⁸But I ask, "Did people not hear ₍the Good News₎*?" Yes, they heard—₍like the Scripture* says₎:

"Their voices went out all around the world.
Their words went everywhere
in the world."
Psalm 19:4

¹⁹Again I ask, "Did the people of Israel* not understand?" Yes, they did understand. First, Moses says this ₍for God₎:

"I will use a people that is not really a nation
to make you jealous.
I will use a nation that does not understand
to make you angry."
Deuteronomy 32:21

²⁰Then Isaiah is bold enough to say this ₍for God₎:

"The people that were not looking for me—
those people found me.
I showed myself to people that did not
ask for me."
Isaiah 65:1

²¹₍God said this through Isaiah about the non-Jewish people₎. But about the Jewish people God

---

Israel The Jewish nation (people).
Scripture(s) Holy Writings—the Old Testament.
Zion Another name for Jerusalem, city of God's people.
"A person ... says" Quote from Lev. 18:5.
Verses 6-8 Quotes from Deut. 30:12-14.

"Any person ... ashamed" Quote from Isa. 28:16.
"Every person ... saved" Quote from Joel 2:32.
"Beautiful ... news" Quote from Isa. 52:7.
"Lord ... them" Quote from Isa. 53:1.
Good News The news that God has made a way for people to have their sins forgiven and live with God.

says, "All day long I have waited for those people, but they refuse to obey and refuse to follow me."*

God Has Not Forgotten His People

11 So I ask, "Did God throw out his people?" No! I myself am an Israelite *(Jew)*. I am from the family of Abraham,* from the family group of Benjamin. ²God chose the Israelites to be his people before ₍they were born₎. And God did not throw out those people. Surely you know what the Scripture* says about Elijah.* The Scripture tells about Elijah praying to God against the people of Israel. Elijah said, ³"Lord, the people have killed your prophets* and destroyed your altars.* I am the only prophet still living. And the people are trying to kill me now."* ⁴But what answer did God give Elijah? God said, "I have kept for myself 7,000 men that still worship me. These 7,000 men have not given worship to Baal.*"* ⁵It is the same now. There are a few people that God has chosen by his grace *(kindness)*. ⁶And if God chose his people by grace, then it is not the things they have done that made them God's people. If they could be made God's people by the things they did, then God's gift of grace would not really be a gift.

⁷So this is what has happened: The people of Israel *(the Jews)* tried ₍to be right with God₎. But they did not succeed. But the people God chose did ₍become right with him₎. The other people became hard and refused to listen to God. ⁸Like it is written ₍in the Scriptures₎*:

> "God caused the people to fall asleep."
>
> *Isaiah 29:10*

> "God closed their eyes so that
> they could not see ₍the truth₎,
> and God closed their ears so that
> they could not hear ₍the truth₎.
> This continues until now."
>
> *Deuteronomy 29:4*

⁹And David says:

> "Let those people be caught and trapped
> at their own feasts.
> Let those people fall and be punished.
> ¹⁰ Let their eyes be closed so they
> cannot see ₍the truth₎.
> And let them be troubled forever."
>
> *Psalm 69:22-23*

¹¹So I ask: When the Jews fell, did that fall destroy them? No! But their mistake brought salvation to the non-Jews. This happened to make Jews jealous. ¹²The Jews' mistake brought rich blessings for the world. And what the Jews lost brought rich blessings for the non-Jewish people. So surely the world will get much richer blessings when enough Jews become the kind of people God wants.

¹³Now I am speaking to you people that are not Jews. I am an apostle* to the non-Jews. So while I have that work, I will do the best I can. ¹⁴I hope I can make my own people *(the Jews)* jealous. That way, maybe I can help some of them to be saved. ¹⁵God turned away from the Jews. When that happened, God became friends with the other people in the world. So when God accepts the Jews, then surely that will bring to people life after death.

¹⁶If the first piece of bread is offered to God, then the whole loaf is made holy. If the roots of a tree are holy, then the tree's branches are holy too.

¹⁷₍It is like₎ some of the branches from an olive tree have been broken off, and the branch of a wild olive tree has been joined to that first tree. You non-Jews are the same as that wild branch, and you now share the strength and life of the first tree *(the Jews)*. ¹⁸So don't boast about those branches that were broken off. You have no reason to boast. Why? You don't give life to the root. The root gives life to you. ¹⁹You will say, "Branches were broken off so that I could be joined to their tree." ²⁰That is true. But those branches were broken off because they did not believe. And you continue to be part of the tree only because you believe. Don't be proud, but be afraid. ²¹If God did not let the natural branches of that tree stay, then he will not let you stay ₍if you don't believe₎.

²²So you see that God is kind, but he can also be very strict. God punishes those people that stop following him. But God is kind to you, if you continue following in his kindness. If you don't continue following him, you will be cut off ₍from

---

"All day ... me" Quote from Isa. 65:2.
Abraham Most respected ancestor of the Jews.
Scripture(s) Holy Writings—the Old Testament.
Elijah A prophet who lived about 850 B.C.
prophets People who spoke for God.
altars An altar is a place where sacrifices are offered.
"Lord ... now" Quote from 1 Kings 19:10, 14.
Baal The name of a false god.
"I have ... Baal" Quote from 1 Kings 19:18.

apostle Man Jesus chose to represent him in a special way.

the tree₁. ²³And if the Jews will believe in God again, then God will accept the Jews back again. God is able to put them back where they were. ²⁴It is not natural for a wild branch to become part of a good tree. But you non-Jews are like a branch cut from a wild olive tree. And you were joined to a good olive tree. But those Jews are like a branch that grew from the good tree. So surely they can be joined to their own tree again.
²⁵I want you to understand this secret truth, brothers ₍and sisters₎. This truth will help you understand that you don't know everything. The truth is this: Part of Israel* has been made stubborn. But that will change when enough non-Jews have come to God. ²⁶And that is how all Israel will be saved. It is written ₍in the Scriptures₎*:

"The Savior will come from Zion*;
He will take away all evil from the family of Jacob.*
27 And I will make this agreement with those people
when I take away their sins."
Isaiah 59:20-21; 27:9

²⁸The Jews refuse to accept the Good News,* so they are God's enemies. This has happened to help you non-Jews. But the Jews are still God's chosen people. So God loves them very much. God loves them because of ₍the promises he made to₎ their fathers. ²⁹God never changes his mind about the people he calls and the things he gives them. And God never takes back his call to the people. ³⁰At one time you refused to obey God. But now you have received mercy, because those people *(the Jews)* refused to obey. ³¹And now the Jews refuse to obey, because God showed mercy to you. But this happened so that they can also receive mercy from God. ³²All people have refused to obey God. God has put all people together as people that don't obey him, so that God can show mercy to all people.

Praise to God

³³Yes, God's riches are very great! God's wisdom and knowledge have no end! No person can explain the things God decides. No person can understand God's ways. ³⁴Like the Scripture* says,

"Who knows the mind of the Lord?
Who is able to give God advice?"
Isaiah 40:13

35 "Who has ever given God anything?
God owes nothing to any person."
Job 41:11

³⁶Yes, God made all things. And everything continues through God and for God. To God be the glory forever! Amen.

Give Your Lives to God

12 So brothers ₍and sisters₎, I beg you to do something. God has shown us great mercy. So offer your lives as a living sacrifice* to God. Your offering must be only for God and will be pleasing to him. This offering of yourselves is the spiritual way for you to worship *(serve)* God. ²Don't change yourselves to be like the people of this world. But be changed inside yourselves with a new way of thinking. Then you will be able to decide and accept what God wants for you. You will be able to know what things are good and pleasing to God and what things are perfect.

³God has given me a special gift. That is why I have something to say to every person among you. Don't think that you are better than you really are. You must see yourself like you really are. Decide what you are by the kind of faith God has given you. ⁴Each one of us has one body, and that body has many parts. These parts don't all do the same thing. ⁵In the same way, we are many people, but in Christ we are all one body. We are the parts of that body. And each part of that body belongs to all the other parts. ⁶We all have different gifts. Each gift came because of the grace *(kindness)* that God gave us. If a person has the gift of prophecy,* then that person should use that gift with the faith he has. ⁷If a person has the gift of serving, then that person should serve. If a person has the gift of teaching, then that person should teach. ⁸If a person has the gift of comforting other people, then that person should comfort. If a person has the gift of giving to help other people, then that person should give freely. If a person has the gift of being a leader, then that person should work hard when he leads. If a

---

Israel The Jewish nation (people).
Scripture(s) Part of the Holy Writings—the Old Testament.
Zion Another name for Jerusalem, city of God's people.
Jacob Father of the twelve family groups of Israel.
Good News The news that God has made a way for people to have their sins forgiven and live with God.

sacrifice An offering or gift to God.
gift of prophecy The ability that God gives a person to speak for him.

person has the gift of showing kindness to other people, then that person should do that with joy. ⁹Your love must be real. Hate the things that are evil. Do only the things that are good. ¹⁰Love each other in a way that you feel close to each other like brothers and sisters. You should want to give your brothers and sisters more honor than you want for yourself. ¹¹Don't be lazy when you need to be working for the Lord. Be spiritually excited about serving him. ¹²Be happy because you have hope. Be patient when you have troubles. Pray all the time. ¹³Share with God's people that need help. Look for people that need help, and welcome those people into your homes. ¹⁴Say only good things to those people that do bad things to you. Say good things to them and don't curse them. ¹⁵When other people are happy, you should be happy with them. And when other people are sad, you should be sad with them. ¹⁶Live together in peace with each other. Don't be proud. Be willing to be friends with people who are not important to other people. Don't be conceited. ¹⁷If someone does wrong to you, don't pay him back by doing wrong to him. Try to do the things that all people think are good. ¹⁸Do the best you can to live in peace with all people. ¹⁹My friends, don't try to punish people when they do wrong to you. Wait for God to punish them with his anger. It is written: "I am the One who punishes; I will pay people back,"* says the Lord. ²⁰But you should do this: "If your enemy is hungry, feed him; if your enemy is thirsty, give him something to drink. In this way you will make that person ashamed."* ²¹Don't let evil defeat you. You should defeat evil by doing good.

13 All of you must obey the government rulers. Every person who rules was given the power to rule by God. And all the people that rule now were given that power by God. ²So the person that is against the government is really against something God has commanded. People that are against the government cause themselves to be punished. ³People that do right don't have to fear the rulers. But those people that do wrong must fear the rulers. Do you want to be free from fearing the rulers? Then you should do right. If you do right, then the rulers will praise you. ⁴A ruler is God's servant to help you. But if you do wrong, then be afraid. The ruler has the power to punish, and he will use that power. He is God's servant to punish people that do wrong. ⁵So you must obey the government. You should obey because you might be punished if you don't obey. And you should also obey because you know that is the right thing to do. ⁶And this is why you pay taxes too. Those rulers are working for God and give all their time to the work of ruling. ⁷Give all people what you owe them. If you owe them any kind of tax, then pay it. Show respect to the people you should respect. And show honor to the people you should honor.

Loving Other People Is the Only Law

⁸Don't owe people anything. But you will always owe love to each other. The person that loves other people has obeyed all the law.* ⁹ןWhy do I say this?ן Because the law says, "You must not do the sin of adultery*, you must not murder anyone, you must not steal anything, you must not want things that belong to other people."* All these commandments and all other commandments are really only one rule: "Love other people the same as you love yourself."* ¹⁰Love doesn't hurt other people. So loving is the same as obeying all the law.*

¹¹I say these things because you know that we live in an important time. Yes, it is now time for you to wake up from your sleep. Our salvation is nearer now than when we first believed. ¹²The "night"* is almost finished. The "day"* is almost here. So we should stop doing things that belong to darkness *(sin)*. We should prepare ourselves with the things that belong to light *(good)*. ¹³Let us live in a right way, like people that belong to the day. We should not have wild and wasteful parties. We should not be drunk. We should not do sexual sins or sin in any way with our bodies. We should not cause arguments and trouble or be jealous. ¹⁴But clothe yourselves with the Lord Jesus Christ. Don't think about how to satisfy your sinful self and the bad things you want to do.

"I am ... back" Quote from Deut. 32:35.
you will make that person ashamed Literally, "you will pour burning coals on his head." People in Old Testament times often put ashes on their heads to show they were sad or sorry.
"If your ... ashamed" Quote from Prov. 25:21-22.

law God's law. It is represented in the law of Moses.
adultery Breaking a marriage promise by sexual sin.
"You ... people" Quote from Ex. 20:13-15, 17.
"Love other ... yourself" Quote from Lev. 19:18.
night Used as a symbol of the sinful world we live in.
day Used as a symbol of the good time that is coming.

Don't Criticize Other People

14 Don't refuse to accept into your group a person that is weak in faith. And don't argue with that person about his different ideas. ²One person believes that he can eat any kind of food* he wants. But if another person's faith is weak, then that person believes he can eat only vegetables. ³The person that knows that he can eat any kind of food must not feel that he is better than the person that eats only vegetables. And the person that eats only vegetables must not decide that the person that eats all foods is wrong. God has accepted that person. ⁴You cannot judge another person's servant. His own master decides if he is doing right or wrong. And the Lord's servant will be right, because the Lord is able to make him right.

⁵One person might believe that one day is more important than another. And another person might believe that every day is the same. Each person should be sure about his own beliefs in his own mind. ⁶The person that thinks one day is more important than other days is doing that for the Lord. And the person that eats all kinds of food is doing that for the Lord. Yes, he gives thanks to God ₗfor that foodⱼ. And the person that refuses to eat some foods does that for the Lord. And he gives thanks to God. ⁷Yes, ₗwe all live for the Lordⱼ. We don't live or die for ourselves. ⁸If we live, we are living for the Lord. And if we die, we are dying for the Lord. So living or dying, we belong to the Lord.

⁹That is why Christ died and rose from death to live again. Christ did this so that he could be Lord *(ruler)* over people that have died and people that are living. ¹⁰So why do you judge your brother ₗin Christⱼ? Or why do you think that you are better than your brother? We will all stand before God, and he will judge us all. ¹¹Yes, it is written in the Scriptures*:

"Every person will bow before me;
every person will say that I am God.
As surely as I live, these things will happen,
says the Lord *(God)*."
Isaiah 45:23

¹²So each of us will have to explain to God about his life.

Don't Cause Other People to Sin

¹³So we should stop judging each other. We must decide not to do anything that will make a brother ₗor sisterⱼ weak or fall into sin. ¹⁴I am in the Lord Jesus. And I know that there is no food that is wrong to eat. But if a person believes that something is wrong, then that thing is wrong for him. ¹⁵If you hurt your brother's faith because of something you eat, then you are not really following the way of love. Don't destroy a person's faith by eating something ₗthat he thinks is wrongⱼ. Christ died for that person. ¹⁶Don't allow something that you think is good to become something that other people say is evil. ¹⁷In the kingdom of God, eating and drinking are not important. In the kingdom of God, the important things are these: living right with God, peace, and joy in the Holy Spirit.* ¹⁸Any person who serves Christ by living this way is pleasing God. And that person will be accepted by other people.

¹⁹So let us try as hard as we can to do the things that make peace. And let us try to do the things that will help each other. ²⁰Don't let the eating of food destroy the work of God. All food is right to eat. But it is wrong for a person to eat something that makes another person fall into sin. ²¹It is better not to eat meat or drink wine if that makes your brother ₗor sisterⱼ fall into sin. It is better not to do anything that will make your brother ₗor sisterⱼ sin.

²²Your beliefs about these things should be kept secret between yourself and God. A person is blessed *(happy)* if he can do the things he thinks are right without feeling guilty. ²³But if a person eats something without being sure that it is right, then that person makes himself wrong. Why? Because that person did not believe that it was right. And if a person does anything without believing that it is right, then it is sin.

15 We are strong with faith. So we should help the people who are weak. We should help those people with their weaknesses. We should not try to please ourselves. ²Each of us should please other people. We should do this to help them. We should try to help them be stronger in faith. ³Even Christ did not live trying to please himself. It was like the Scriptures* said ₗabout himⱼ: "Those people that insulted you have also

---

any kind of food The Jewish law said there were some foods Jews should not eat. When Jews became Christians, some of them did not understand they could now eat all foods.
Scriptures Holy Writings—the Old Testament.

Holy Spirit Called the Spirit of God, the Spirit of Christ, and the Comforter. Joined with God and Christ, he does God's work among people in the world.

insulted me."* ⁴Everything that was written in the past was written to teach us. Those things were written so that we could have hope. That hope comes from the patience and strength that the Scriptures give us. ⁵Patience and strength come from God. And I pray that God will help you all agree together the way Christ Jesus wants. ⁶Then you will all be joined together. And all together you will give glory *(praise)* to God the Father of our Lord Jesus Christ. ⁷Christ accepted you. So you should accept each other. This will bring glory to God. ⁸I tell you that Christ became a servant of the Jews to show that what God promises is true. Christ did this to prove that God will do the things he promised the Jewish fathers. ⁹Christ also did this so that the non-Jews could give glory to God for the mercy he gives to them. It is written ⌊in the Scriptures⌋*:

"So I will give thanks to you among the
non-Jewish people;
I will sing praise to your name."

Psalm 18:49

¹⁰The Scripture* also says,

"You non-Jews should be happy
together with God's people."

Deuteronomy 32:43

¹¹The Scripture* also says,

"Praise the Lord all you non-Jews;
all people should praise the Lord."

Psalm 117:1

¹²And Isaiah says,

"A person will come from Jesse's family.*
That person will come to rule over
the non-Jews;
and the non-Jews will have hope
because of that person."

Isaiah 11:10

¹³I pray that the God who gives hope will fill you with much joy and peace while you trust in him. Then you will have more and more hope, and it will flow out of you by the power of the Holy Spirit.*

"Those people ... me"   Quote from Ps. 69:9.
Scripture(s)   Holy Writings—the Old Testament.
Jesse's family   Jesse was the father of David, king of Israel. Jesus was from their family.
Holy Spirit   Called the Spirit of God, the Spirit of Christ, and the Comforter. Joined with God and Christ, he does God's work among people in the world.

Paul Talks About His Work

¹⁴My brothers ⌊and sisters⌋, I am sure that you are full of good. I know that you have all the knowledge you need and that you are able to teach each other. ¹⁵But I have written to you very openly about some things that I wanted you to remember. I did this because God gave me this special gift: ¹⁶to be a minister of Christ Jesus. God made me a minister to help the non-Jewish people. I serve God by teaching his Good News.* I do this so that the non-Jewish people may be an offering that God will accept. Those people are made holy* for God by the Holy Spirit.*

¹⁷So I am proud of the things I have done for God in Christ Jesus. ¹⁸I will not talk about anything I did myself. I will talk only about the things that Christ has done with me in leading the non-Jewish people to obey God. They have obeyed God because of the things I have said and done. ¹⁹And they obeyed God because of the power of the miracles* and the great things they saw, and because of the power of the Holy Spirit.* I preached the Good News* from Jerusalem all the way around to Illyricum. And so I have finished that part of my work. ²⁰I always want to preach the Good News in places where people have never heard of Christ. I do this because I don't want to build on the work that another person has already started. ²¹But it is written ⌊in the Scriptures⌋*:

"Those people that were not told
about him *(the Christ)* will see,
and those people that have not heard about
him will understand."

Isaiah 52:15

Paul's Plan to Visit Rome

²²That is why many times I was stopped from coming to you. ²³Now I have finished my work in these areas here. And for many years I have wanted to visit you. ²⁴So I will visit you when I go to Spain. Yes, I hope to visit you while I am traveling to Spain, and I will stay and enjoy being with you. Then you can help me on my trip. ²⁵Now I am going to Jerusalem to help God's people. ²⁶Some of God's people in Jerusalem are poor. ⌊The believers in⌋

Good News   The news that God has made a way for people to have their sins forgiven and live with God.
holy   A holy person is pure, belongs only to God, and does only the things that God wants.
miracles   Amazing things done by the power of God.

Macedonia and Achaia were happy to give. They gave to help those people in Jerusalem. ²⁷The believers in Macedonia and Achaia were happy to do this. And really they should help those believers in Jerusalem. They should help because they are non-Jews and have shared in the Jews' spiritual blessings. So they should use the things they have to help the Jews. They owe this to the Jews. ²⁸I must be sure that the poor people in Jerusalem get all this money that has been given for them. After I finish this work, then I will leave for Spain. While I am traveling to Spain, I will stop and visit you. ²⁹I know that when I visit you, I will bring you Christ's full blessing.

³⁰Brothers ₍and sisters₎, I beg you to help me in my work by praying to God for me. Do this because of our Lord Jesus and the love that the Holy Spirit* gives us. ³¹Pray that I will be saved from the non-believers in Judea. And pray that this help I bring to Jerusalem will please God's people there. ³²Then, if God wants me to, I will come to you. I will come with joy, and together you and I will have a time of rest. ³³The God that gives peace be with you all. Amen.

Paul Has Some Final Things to Say

16 I want you to know that you can trust our sister ₍in Christ₎, Phoebe. She is a special helper* in the church in Cenchrea. ²I ask you to accept her in the Lord. Accept her the way God's people should. Help her with anything she needs from you. She has helped me very much, and she has helped many other people too.

³Say hello to Priscilla and Aquila. They work together with me in Christ Jesus. ⁴They risked their own lives to save my life. I am thankful to them, and all the non-Jewish churches are thankful to them. ⁵Also, say hello to the church that meets at their house.

Say hello to my dear friend Epaenetus. He was the first person to follow Christ in Asia.* ⁶Say hello to Mary. She worked very hard for you. ⁷Say hello to Andronicus and Junias. They are my relatives, and they were in prison with me. They are some of God's most important workers.* They were believers in Christ before I was. ⁸Say hello to Ampliatus, my dear friend in the Lord. ⁹Say hello to Urbanus. He is a worker together with me for Christ. And say hello to my dear friend Stachys. ¹⁰Say hello to Apelles. He was tested and proved that he truly loves Christ. Say hello to all those people that are in the family of Aristobulus. ¹¹Say hello to Herodion, my relative. Say hello to all the people in the family of Narcissus that belong to the Lord. ¹²Say hello to Tryphaena and Tryphosa. Those women work very hard for the Lord. Say hello to my dear friend Persis. She has also worked very hard for the Lord. ¹³Say hello to Rufus. He is a special person in the Lord. Say hello to his mother. She has been a mother to me also. ¹⁴Say hello to Asyncritus, Phlegon, Hermes, Patrobas, Hermas, and all the brothers ₍in Christ₎ that are with them. ¹⁵Say hello to Philologus and Julia, Nereus and his sister, and Olympas. And say hello to all the saints *(believers)* with them. ¹⁶When you see each other, say hello with a holy kiss. All of Christ's churches *(groups of believers)* say hello to you.

¹⁷Brothers ₍and sisters₎, I ask you to be very careful of those people that cause people to be against each other. Be very careful of those people that upset other people's faith. Those people are against the true teaching you learned. Stay away from those people. ¹⁸People like that are not serving our Lord Christ. They are only doing things to please themselves. They use fancy talk and say nice things to fool the minds of people that don't know about evil. ¹⁹All the believers have heard that you obey. So I am very happy because of you. But I want you to be wise about the things that are good. And I want you to know nothing about things that are evil.

²⁰The God that brings peace will soon defeat Satan *(the devil)* and give you power over him.

The grace *(kindness)* of our Lord Jesus be with you.

²¹Timothy, a worker together with me, says hello to you. Also Lucius, Jason, and Sosipater (these are my relatives) say hello to you.

²²I am Tertius, and I am writing these things that Paul says. I say hello to you in the Lord.

²³Gaius is letting me and the whole church here use his home. He also says hello to you. Erastus and our brother Quartus say hello to you. Erastus is the city treasurer here. ²⁴*

Holy Spirit Called the Spirit of God, the Spirit of Christ, and the Comforter. Joined with God and Christ, he does God's work among people in the world.
special helper Literally, "deacon," a Greek word meaning "servant." See 1 Tim. 3:11.
Asia The western part of Asia Minor.
most important workers Literally, "important among (or to) the apostles."

Verse 24 Some Greek copies add verse 24: "The grace *(kindness)* of our Lord Jesus Christ be with all of you. Amen."

ROMANS 16:25–27

²⁵Glory to God. God is the One who can make you strong in faith. God can use the Good News* that I teach to make you strong. That is the Good News about Jesus Christ that I tell people. That Good News is the secret truth that God has made known. That secret truth was hidden since the beginning. ²⁶But that secret truth has now been shown to us. And that truth has been made known to all people. It has been made known by the things the prophets* wrote. This is what God commanded. And that secret truth has been made known to all people, so that they can believe and obey God. God lives forever. ²⁷Glory forever to the only wise God through Jesus Christ. Amen.

Good News The news that God has made a way for people to have their sins forgiven and live with God.

prophets People who spoke for God. Their writings are part of the Old Testament.

1 Corinthians

1 From Paul. I was called *(chosen)* to be an apostle* of Christ Jesus. I was called because that is what God wanted.

Also from Sosthenes, our brother ⌊in Christ⌋.

²To the church of God in Corinth, to those people that have been made holy* in Christ Jesus. You were called to be God's holy people. You were called with all the people everywhere that trust in the name of the Lord Jesus Christ—their Lord and ours: ³Grace *(kindness)* and peace to you from God our Father and the Lord Jesus Christ.

Paul Gives Thanks to God

⁴I always thank my God for you because of the grace *(kindness)* that God has given you through Christ Jesus. ⁵In Jesus you have been blessed in every way. You have been blessed in all your speaking and all your knowledge. ⁶The truth about Christ has been proved in you. ⁷So you have every gift from God while you wait for our Lord Jesus Christ to come again. ⁸Jesus will keep you strong always until the end. He will keep you strong, so that there will be no wrong in you on the day when our Lord Jesus Christ comes again. ⁹God is faithful. He is the One who has called you to share life with his Son, Jesus Christ our Lord.

Problems in the Church at Corinth

¹⁰I beg you brothers ⌊and sisters⌋ in the name of our Lord Jesus Christ. I beg that all of you agree with each other, so that there will be no divisions among you. I beg that you be completely joined together by having the same kind of thinking and the same purpose. ¹¹My brothers ⌊and sisters⌋, some people from Chloe's family told me about you. I heard that there are arguments among you. ¹²This is what I mean: One of you says, "I follow Paul"; another person says, "I follow Apollos"; another person says, "I follow Cephas *(Peter)*"; and another person says, "I follow Christ." ¹³Christ cannot be divided ⌊into different groups⌋! Did Paul die on the cross for you? No! Were you baptized* in the name of Paul? No! ¹⁴I am thankful that I did not baptize any of you except Crispus and Gaius. ¹⁵I am thankful, because now no one can say that you people were baptized in my name. ¹⁶(I also baptized the family of Stephanas. But I don't remember that I myself baptized any others.) ¹⁷Christ did not give me the work of baptizing people. Christ gave me the work of telling the Good News.* But Christ sent me to tell the Good News without using words of worldly wisdom. If I used worldly wisdom to tell the Good News, then the cross* of Christ would lose its power.

God's Power and Wisdom in Christ

¹⁸The teaching about the cross seems foolish to those people that are lost. But to us who are being saved it is the power of God. ¹⁹It is written ⌊in the Scriptures⌋*:

"I will destroy the wisdom of the wise people.
I will make the intelligence of the intelligent people worth nothing."

Isaiah 29:14

²⁰Where is the wise person? Where is the educated person? Where is the philosopher* of this time? God has made the wisdom of the world foolish. ²¹This is what God with his wisdom wanted: The world did not know God through the

---

baptized A Greek word meaning to be immersed, dipped, or buried briefly under water.
Good News The news that God has made a way for people to have their sins forgiven and live with God.
cross Paul uses the cross as a picture of the gospel, the story of Christ's death to pay for people's sins. The cross (Christ's death) was God's way to save people.
Scripture(s) Holy Writings—the Old Testament.
philosopher A person who studies and talks about his own ideas and the ideas of other people.

---

apostle Person Jesus chose to be a special helper for telling the Good News of God's love to the world.
holy A holy person is pure and belongs only to God.

world's own wisdom. So God used the message* that sounds foolish to save the people that believe it. ²²The Jews ask for miracles* as proofs. The Greeks want wisdom. ²³But we preach this: Christ was killed on a cross. This is a big problem to the Jews. And it seems foolish to the non-Jews. ²⁴But Christ is the power of God and the wisdom of God to those people that God has called *(chosen)*—Jews and Greeks *(non-Jews)*. ²⁵Even the foolishness of God is wiser than men. Even the weakness of God is stronger than men.

²⁶Brothers ₍and sisters₎, God called *(chose)* you. Think about that! And not many of you were wise in the way the world judges wisdom. Not many of you had great influence. Not many of you came from important families. ²⁷But God chose the foolish things of the world to give shame to the wise people. God chose the weak things of the world to give shame to the strong people. ²⁸And God chose what the world thinks is not important. He chose what the world hates and thinks is nothing. God chose these to destroy what the world thinks is important. ²⁹God did this so that no man can boast before him. ³⁰It is God that has made you part of Christ Jesus. Christ has become wisdom for us from God. Christ is the reason we are right with God and have freedom from sin; Christ is the reason we are holy.* ³¹So, like the Scripture*: says, "If a person boasts, that person should boast only in the Lord."*

The Message About Christ on the Cross

2 Dear brothers ₍and sisters₎, when I came to you, I told you the truth of God. But I did not use fancy words or great wisdom. ²I decided that while I was with you I would forget about everything except Jesus Christ and his death on the cross. ³When I came to you, I was weak and shook with fear. ⁴My teaching and my speaking were not with wise words that persuade people. But the proof of my teaching was the power that the Spirit* gives. ⁵I did this so that your faith would be in God's power, not in the wisdom of a man.

---

message The news that God has made a way for people to have their sins forgiven and live with God.
miracles Amazing things done by the power of God.
holy A holy person is pure and belongs only to God.
Scripture(s) Holy Writings—the Old Testament.
"If a person ... Lord" Quote from Jer. 9:24.
Spirit The Holy Spirit. Called the Spirit of God, the Spirit of Christ, and the Comforter. Joined with God and Christ, he does God's work among people in the world.

God's Wisdom

⁶We teach wisdom to people that are mature. But this wisdom we teach is not from this world. It is not the wisdom of the rulers of this world. Those rulers are losing their power. ⁷But we speak God's secret wisdom. This wisdom has been hidden ₍from people₎. God planned this wisdom for our glory. He planned it before the world began. ⁸None of the rulers of this world understood this wisdom. If they had understood it, then they would not have killed the Lord of glory on a cross. ⁹But like it is written ₍in the Scriptures₎*

> "No eye has seen,
> no ear has heard,
> no person has imagined
> what God has prepared for those people
> that love him."
> *Isaiah 64:4*

¹⁰But God has shown us these things through the Spirit.*

The Spirit knows all things. The Spirit even knows the deep secrets of God. ¹¹It is like this: No person knows the thoughts that another person has. Only that person's spirit that lives inside him knows those thoughts. It is the same with God. No one knows the thoughts of God. Only the Spirit of God knows those thoughts. ¹²We did not receive the spirit of the world. But we received the Spirit that is from God. We received this Spirit so that we can know the things that God has given us. ¹³When we speak these things, we don't use words taught to us by the wisdom that men have. We use words taught to us by the Spirit. We use spiritual words to explain spiritual things. ¹⁴A person that is not spiritual does not accept the things that come from the Spirit of God. That person thinks that those things are foolish. That person cannot understand the things of the Spirit, because those things can only be judged spiritually. ¹⁵But the spiritual person is able to make judgments about all things. Other people cannot judge that person. ₍The Scripture* says₎:

¹⁶ "Who knows the mind of the Lord?
Who can tell the Lord what to do?"
Isaiah 40:13

But we have the mind of Christ.

Following Men Is Wrong

3 Brothers ₍and sisters₎, in the past I could not talk to you like I talk to spiritual people. I had

to talk to you like worldly people—like babies in Christ. ²The teaching I gave you was like milk, not solid food. I did this because you were not ready for solid food. And even now you are not ready for solid food. ³You are still not spiritual people. You have jealousy and arguing among you. This shows that you are not spiritual. You are acting the same as people of the world. ⁴One of you says, "I follow Paul," and another person says, "I follow Apollos." When you say things like that, you are acting like ₍worldly₎ people.

⁵Is Apollos important? No! Is Paul important? No! We are only servants of God who helped you believe. Each one of us did the work God gave us to do. ⁶I planted the seed *(teaching)* and Apollos watered it. But God is the One who made the seed grow. ⁷So the person that plants is not important, and the person that waters is not important. Only God is important, because he is the One who makes things grow. ⁸The person that plants and the person that waters have the same purpose. And each person will be rewarded for his own work. ⁹We are workers together for God. And you are like a farm that belongs to God.

And you are a house that belongs to God. ¹⁰Like an expert builder I built the foundation* of that house. I used the gift that God gave me to do this. Other people are building on that foundation. But each person should be careful how he builds. ¹¹The foundation has already been built. No person can build any other foundation. The foundation that has already been built is Jesus Christ. ¹²A person can build on that foundation, using gold, silver, jewels, wood, grass, or straw. ¹³But the work that each person does will be clearly seen, because the Day* will make it plain. That Day will appear with fire, and the fire will test every man's work. ¹⁴If the building that a person puts on the foundation still stands, then that person will get his reward. ¹⁵But if that person's building is burned up, then he will suffer loss. The person will be saved, but it will be like he escaped from a fire.

¹⁶You should know that you yourselves are God's temple *(house)*. God's Spirit* lives in you. ¹⁷If any person destroys God's temple, then God will destroy that person. Why? Because God's temple is holy.* You yourselves are God's temple.

¹⁸Don't fool yourselves. If any person among you thinks that he is wise in this world, then he should become a fool. Then that person can become truly wise. ¹⁹Why? Because the wisdom of this world is foolishness to God. It is written ₍in the Scriptures₎,* "He *(God)* catches the wise *(smart)* people when they use their sneaky ways."* ²⁰It is also written ₍in the Scriptures₎, "The Lord knows the thoughts of the wise people. He knows that their thoughts are worth nothing."* ²¹So you should not boast about men. All things are yours: ²²Paul, Apollos, and Cephas *(Peter)*; the world, life, death, the present, and the future— all these things are yours. ²³And you belong to Christ, and Christ belongs to God.

Apostles of Christ

4 This is what people should think about us: We are servants of Christ. We are the people that God has trusted with his secret truths. ²A person that is trusted with something must show that he is worthy of that trust. ³I don't care if I am judged by you. And I don't care if I am judged by any human court. I don't even judge myself. ⁴I don't know of any wrong that I have done. But that does not make me innocent *(without guilt)*. The Lord is the One who judges me. ⁵So don't judge before the right time; wait until the Lord comes. He will shine light on the things that are hidden in darkness. He will make known the secret purposes of people's hearts. Then God will give every person the praise he should get.

⁶Brothers ₍and sisters₎, I have used Apollos and myself as examples for you in these things. I did this so that you could learn from us the meaning of the words, "Follow only what is written ₍in the Scriptures₎.* Then you will not be proud of one man and hate another. ⁷Who says that you are better than other people? Everything you have was given to you. So, if everything you have was given to you, then why do you boast like you got those things by your own power?

⁸₍You think₎ you have everything you need. ₍You think₎ you are rich. ₍You think₎ you have become kings without us. I wish you really were kings! Then we could be kings together with you.

---

foundation The bottom part or first part of a house that the rest of the house is built on.
Day The day Christ will come to judge all people.
Spirit The Holy Spirit. Called the Spirit of God, the Spirit of Christ, and the Comforter. Joined with God and Christ, he does God's work among people in the world.

holy Something holy belongs only to God and should be used only for the things God wants.
Scriptures Holy Writings—the Old Testament.
"He ... ways" Quote from Job 5:13.
"The Lord ... nothing" Quote from Ps. 94:11.

⁹But it seems to me that God has given me and the other apostles* the last place. We are like men condemned to die ⌊with all the people watching⌋. We are like a show for the whole world to see—angels and people. ¹⁰We are fools for Christ. But ⌊you think⌋ you are very wise in Christ. We are weak, but ⌊you think⌋ you are strong. People give you honor, but they don't honor us. ¹¹Even now we still don't have ⌊enough⌋ to eat or drink, and we don't have ⌊enough⌋ clothes. We often get beatings. We have no homes. ¹²We work hard with our own hands ⌊to feed ourselves⌋. People curse us, but we speak a blessing for them. People persecute* us, and we accept it. ¹³People say bad things about us, but we say good things to them. At this time people still treat us like we are the world's garbage—the dirt of the earth.

¹⁴I am not trying to make you feel ashamed. But I am writing these things to give you a warning like you were my own dear children. ¹⁵You may have 10,000 teachers in Christ, but you don't have many fathers. Through the Good News* I became your father in Christ Jesus. ¹⁶So I beg you to please be like me. ¹⁷That is why I am sending Timothy to you. He is my son in the Lord. I love Timothy, and he is faithful. He will help you remember the way I live in Christ Jesus. That way of life is what I teach in all the churches everywhere.

¹⁸Some of you have become boasters. You boast, thinking that I will not come to you again. ¹⁹But I will come to you very soon. I will come, if the Lord wants me to. Then I will see what these boasters can do, not what they can say. ²⁰I will want to see this because the kingdom of God is not talk but power. ²¹Which do you want:

> That I come to you with punishment, or
> that I come with love and gentleness?

A Moral Problem in the Church

5 People are really saying that there is sexual sin among you. And it is such a bad kind of sexual sin that it does not happen even among those people that don't know God. People say that a man there has his father's wife. ²And still you are proud of yourselves! You should have been filled with sadness. And the man that did that sin should be put out of your group. ³My body is not there with you, but I am with you in spirit. And I have already judged the man who did that sin. I judged him the same as I would if I were really there. ⁴Come together in the name of our Lord Jesus. I will be with you in spirit, and you will have the power of our Lord Jesus with you. ⁵Then give this man to Satan *(the Devil)*, so that his sinful self* will be destroyed. Then his spirit can be saved on the day of the Lord.

⁶Your proud boasting is not good. You know the saying, "Just a little yeast* makes the whole batch of dough rise." ⁷Take out all the old yeast *(sin)*, so that you will be a new batch of dough. You really are ⌊Passover⌋ bread* without yeast. Yes, Christ, our Passover lamb,* has ⌊already⌋ been killed. ⁸So let us eat our Passover meal, but not with ⌊the bread that has⌋ the old yeast. That old yeast is the yeast of sin and wrong doing. But let us eat the bread that has no yeast. This is the bread of goodness and truth.

⁹I wrote to you in my letter that you should not associate with people that sin sexually. ¹⁰But I did not mean that you should not associate with the sinful people of this world. Those people of the world do sin sexually, or they are selfish and cheat each other, or they worship idols *(false gods)*. To get away from those people you would have to leave this world. ¹¹I am writing to tell you that the person you must not associate with is this: any person that calls himself a brother in Christ but sins sexually, or is selfish, or worships idols, or talks bad to people, or gets drunk, or cheats people. Don't even eat with a person like that.

¹²⁻¹³It is not my business to judge those people that are not part of the church *(group of believers)*. God will judge those people. But you must judge the people that are part of the church. The Scripture* says, "Take the evil person out of your group."*

---

sinful self Or, "body." Literally, "flesh."
yeast Used here as a symbol of evil or bad influence.
Passover bread The special bread without yeast that the Jews ate at their Passover meal every year. Paul means that Christians are free from sin like the Passover bread was free from yeast.
Passover lamb Jesus was a sacrifice for his people, like a lamb killed for the Jewish Passover Feast.
Scripture Part of the Holy Writings—Old Testament.
"Take ... group" Quote from Deut. 22:21, 24.

---

apostles The men Jesus chose to be his special helpers.
persecute To hurt, bother, or do bad things to.
Good News The news that God has made a way for people to have their sins forgiven and live with God.

Judging Problems Between Christians

6 When one of you has something against another person, why do you go to ₍the judges in the law courts₎? Those people are not right with God. So why do you let those people decide who is right? You should be ashamed! Why don't you let God's people decide who is right? ²Surely you know that God's people will judge the world. So if you will judge the world, then surely you are able to judge small things ₍like this₎. ³You know that in the future we will judge angels. So surely we can judge things in this life. ⁴So if you have those disagreements that must be judged, why do you take those things to people who are not part of the church? Those people mean nothing to the church. ⁵I say this to shame you. Surely there is some person in your group wise enough to judge a complaint between two brothers *(believers)*! ⁶But now one brother goes to court against another brother. You let men that are not believers judge their case!

⁷The lawsuits that you have against each other show that you are already defeated. It would be better for you to let someone do wrong against you! It would be better for you to let someone cheat you! ⁸But you yourselves do wrong and cheat! And you do this to your own brothers ₍in Christ₎!

⁹⁻¹⁰Surely you know that the people that do wrong will not get God's kingdom. Don't be fooled. These people will not get God's kingdom: people that sin sexually, people that worship idols,* people that do the sin of adultery,* men that let other men use them for sex or that have sex with other men, people that steal, people that are selfish, people that get drunk, people that say bad things to other people, and people that cheat. ¹¹In the past, some of you were like that. But you were washed clean, you were made holy,* and you were made right with God in the name of the Lord Jesus Christ and by the Spirit of our God.

Use Your Bodies for God's Glory

¹²"All things are allowed for me." But not all things are good. "All things are allowed for me." But I will not let anything be my master. ¹³"Food is for the stomach, and the stomach for food." Yes. But God will destroy them both. The body is not for sexual sin. The body is for the Lord, and the Lord is for the body. ¹⁴By God's power God raised the Lord ₍Jesus₎ from death. God will also raise us from death. ¹⁵Surely you know that your bodies are parts of Christ himself. So I must never take the parts of Christ and join those parts to a prostitute*! ¹⁶It is written ₍in the Scriptures₎*: "The two people will become one."* So you should know that a person that ₍sexually₎ joins himself with a prostitute becomes one with her in body. ¹⁷But the person who joins himself with the Lord is one with the Lord in spirit.

¹⁸So run away from sexual sin. Every other sin that a person does is outside his body. But the person that sins sexually sins against his own body. ¹⁹You should know that your body is a temple *(house)* for the Holy Spirit.* The Holy Spirit is in you. You have received the Holy Spirit from God. You don't own yourselves. ²⁰You were bought ₍by God₎ at a price. So honor God with your bodies.

About Marriage

7 Now ₍I will discuss₎ the things you wrote to me about. It is good for a man not to marry. ²But sexual sin is a danger. So each man should have his own wife. And each woman should have her own husband. ³The husband should give his wife all that she should have as his wife. And the wife should give her husband all that he should have as her husband. ⁴The wife does not have power over her own body. Her husband has the power over her body. And the husband does not have power over his own body. His wife has the power over his body. ⁵Don't refuse to give your bodies to each other. But you might both agree to stay away ₍from sex₎ for a time. You might do this so that you can give your time to prayer. Then come together again. This is so that Satan *(the Devil)* cannot tempt you in your weakness. ⁶I say this to give you permission ₍to be separated for a time₎. It is not a command. ⁷I wish all people were like me. But each person has his own gift from God. One person has one gift, another person has another gift.

⁸Now for the people who are not married and for the widows* I say this: It is good for them to

---

prostitute A woman paid by men for sexual sin.
Scriptures Holy Writings—the Old Testament.
"The two ... one" Quote from Gen. 2:24.
Holy Spirit Called the Spirit of God, the Spirit of Christ, and the Comforter. Joined with God and Christ, he does God's work among people in the world.
widows A widow is a woman whose husband has died.

---

idols False gods that the non-Jewish people worshiped.
adultery Breaking a marriage promise by sexual sin.
holy A holy person is pure and belongs only to God.

stay single like me. ⁹But if they cannot control their bodies, then they should marry. It is better to marry than to burn ₍with sexual desire₎.

¹⁰Now I give this command for the married people. (The command is not from me; it is from the Lord.) A wife must not leave her husband. ¹¹But if a wife leaves her husband she must not marry again. Or she should go back together with her husband. Also the husband must not divorce his wife.

¹²For all the other people I say this (I am saying these things, not the Lord): A brother ₍in Christ₎ might have a wife who is not a believer. If she will live with him, then he must not divorce her. ¹³And a woman might have a husband who is not a believer. If he will live with her, then she must not divorce him. ¹⁴The husband who is not a believer is made holy through his ₍believing₎ wife. And the wife who is not a believer is made holy through her ₍believing₎ husband. If this were not true, then your children would not be clean. But now your children are holy.

¹⁵But if the person who is not a believer decides to leave, let that person leave. When this happens, the brother or sister ₍in Christ₎ is free. God called us to a life of peace. ¹⁶Wives, maybe you will save your husband; and husbands, maybe you will save your wife. You don't know now what will happen later.

Live as God Called You

¹⁷But each person should continue to live the way God has given him to live—the way you were when God called you. This is a rule I make in all the churches. ¹⁸If a man was already circumcised* when he was called, then he should not change his circumcision.* If a man was without circumcision when he was called, then he should not be circumcised. ¹⁹It is not important if a person is circumcised or not circumcised. The important thing is obeying God's commands. ²⁰Each person should stay the way he was when God called him. ²¹If you were a slave when God called you, don't let that bother you. But if you can be free, then become free. ²²The person who was a slave when the Lord called him is free in the Lord. That person belongs to the Lord. In the same way, the person who was free when he was called is now Christ's slave. ²³You people were bought at a price. So don't become slaves of men. ²⁴Brothers ₍and sisters₎, in your new life with God each one of you should continue the way you were when you were called.

Questions About Getting Married

²⁵Now I write about people who are not married.* I have no command from the Lord about this. But I give my opinion. And I can be trusted, because the Lord has given me mercy. ²⁶This is a time of trouble. So I think that it is good for you to stay the way you are *(not married)*. ²⁷If you have a wife, then don't try to become free from her. If you are not married, then don't try to find a wife. ²⁸But if you decide to marry, that is not a sin. And it is not a sin for a girl that has never married to get married. But those people who marry will have trouble in this life. I want you to be free from this trouble.

²⁹Brothers ₍and sisters₎, this is what I mean: We don't have much time left. So starting now, people who have wives should use their time ₍to serve the Lord₎ like they don't have wives. ³⁰People who are sad should live like they are not sad. People who are happy should live like they are not happy. People who buy things should live like they own nothing. ³¹People who use the things of the world should live like those things are not important to them. You should live like this, because this world, the way it is now, will soon be gone.

³²I want you to be free from worry. A man who is not married is busy with the Lord's work. He is trying to please the Lord. ³³But a man who is married is busy with things of the world. He is trying to please his wife. ³⁴He must think about two things—₍pleasing₎ his wife and pleasing the Lord₎. A woman who is not married or a girl who has never married is busy with the Lord's work. She wants to give herself fully—body and soul—to the Lord. But a married woman is busy with things of the world. She is trying to please her husband. ³⁵I am saying these things to help you. I am not trying to limit you. But I want you to live in the right way. And I want you to give yourselves fully to the Lord without giving your time to other things.

³⁶A man might think that he is not doing the right thing with his virgin* ₍daughter₎ if she is almost past the best age to marry. So he might

---

circumcised, circumcision To have the foreskin cut off. This was done to every Jewish baby boy. It was a mark of the agreement God made with Abraham (Gen. 17:9-14).

people who are not married Literally, "virgins."
virgin A pure girl who is not married.

think that marriage is necessary. He should do what he wants. He should let them marry. It is no sin. ³⁷But another man might be more sure in his mind. There may be no need for marriage, so that he is free to do what he wants. If this person has decided in his own heart to keep his virgin ₍unmarried₎, then he is doing the right thing. ³⁸So the person who gives his virgin ₍daughter₎ in marriage does right. And the person who does not give his virgin ₍daughter₎ in marriage does better.*

³⁹A woman must stay with her husband as long as he lives. But if the husband dies, the woman is free to marry any man she wants. But she must marry in the Lord. ⁴⁰The woman is happier if she does not marry again. This is my opinion, and I believe that I have God's Spirit.*

About Food Offered to Idols

8 Now ₍I will write₎ about meat that is sacrificed* to idols.* We know that "we all have knowledge." "Knowledge" puffs you up full of pride. But love makes ₍you help₎ others grow stronger. ²The person who thinks he knows something does not yet know anything like he should. ³But the person who loves God is known by God.

⁴So ₍this is what I say₎ about eating meat: We know that an idol* is really nothing in the world. And we know that there is only one God. ⁵It's really not important if there are things called gods, in heaven or on earth. (And there are many ₍things that people call₎ "gods" and "lords.") ⁶But for us there is only one God. He is our Father. All things came from him and we live for him. And there is only one Lord. He is Jesus Christ. All things were made through Jesus, and we also have life through him.

⁷But not all people know this. Some people have had the habit of worshiping idols* until now. So now when those people eat meat, they still feel like it belongs to an idol. They are not sure that it is right to eat this meat. So when they eat it, they feel guilty. ⁸But food will not make us closer to God. Refusing to eat does not make us less ₍pleasing to God₎. And eating does not make us better.

⁹But be careful with your freedom. Your freedom may make those people who are weak in faith fall into sin. ¹⁰You have understanding *(knowledge)*, so you might ₍feel free to₎ eat in an idol's temple.* A person who is weak in faith might see you eating there. This will encourage him to eat meat sacrificed* to idols too. But he really thinks it is wrong. ¹¹So this weak brother is ruined *(destroyed)* because of your knowledge. And Christ died for this brother. ¹²When you sin against your brothers ₍and sisters in Christ₎ like this and you hurt them by causing them do things they feel are wrong, then you are also sinning against Christ. ¹³So if the food I eat makes my brother fall into sin, then I will never eat meat again. I will stop eating meat, so that I will not make my brother sin.

9 I am a free man! I am an apostle*! I have seen Jesus our Lord! You people are ₍an example of₎ my work in the Lord. ²Other people may not accept me as an apostle. But surely you accept me as an apostle. You people are proof that I am an apostle in the Lord.

³Some people want to judge me. So this is the answer I give them: ⁴We have the right to eat and drink, don't we? ⁵We have the right to bring a believing wife with us when we travel, don't we? The other apostles* and the Lord's brothers and Cephas all do this. ⁶And are Barnabas and I the only ones that must work to earn our living? ⁷No soldier ever serves in the army and pays his own salary. No person ever plants a garden of grapes without eating some of the grapes himself. No person takes care of a flock of sheep without drinking some of the milk himself.

⁸These things are not only what men think. God's law says the same things. ⁹Yes, it is written in the law of Moses: "When a work animal is being used to separate grain, don't cover its mouth ₍and stop it from eating the grain₎."* When God

---

Verses 36-38 Another possible translation is: "³⁶A person might think that he is not doing the right thing with his virgin *(the girl he is engaged to)*. The girl might be almost past the best age to marry. So the man might feel that he should marry her. He should do what he wants. They should get married. It is no sin. ³⁷But another person might be more sure in his mind. There may be no need for marriage, so he is free to do what he wants. If this person has decided in his own heart to keep his virgin ₍unmarried₎, then he is doing the right thing. ³⁸So the person who marries his virgin does right. And the person who does not marry does better."

Spirit The Holy Spirit. Called the Spirit of God, the Spirit of Christ, and the Comforter. Joined with God and Christ, he does God's work among people in the world.

sacrificed Killed and offered as a gift to show worship.

idol(s) The false gods made from wood or stone and worshiped by the non-Jewish people.

idol's temple Place for worship of a false god.

sacrificed Killed and offered as a gift to show worship.

apostle(s) The men Jesus chose to be his special helpers.

"When ... eating the grain" Quote from Deut. 25:4.

said this, was he thinking only about work animals? No. ¹⁰He was really talking about us. Yes, that Scripture* was written for us. The person that plows and the person that separates the grain should hope *(expect)* to get some of the grain for their work. ¹¹We planted spiritual seed among you. So we should be able to harvest *(get)* from you some things for this life. Surely that is not asking too much. ¹²Other men have this right to get things from you. So surely we have this right too. But we don't use this right. No, we endure everything ourselves so that we will not stop ⌊anyone from obeying⌋ the Good News* of Christ. ¹³Surely you know that people that work at the temple* get their food from the temple. And people that serve at the altar* get part of what is offered at the altar. ¹⁴It is the same with people that preach the Good News. The Lord has commanded that those people that preach the Good News should get their living from this work.

¹⁵But I have not used any of these rights. And I am not trying to get these things. That is not my purpose for writing this to you. I would rather die than to have my reason for boasting taken away. ¹⁶Preaching the Good News* is not my reason for boasting. Preaching the Good News is my duty—something I must do. It will be bad for me if I don't preach the Good News. ¹⁷If I preach the Good News because it is my own choice, then I deserve a reward. But I have no choice. I must preach the Good News. I am only doing the duty that was given to me. ¹⁸So what reward do I get? This is my reward: that when I preach the Good News I can offer it freely. In this way I don't use the right ⌊to be paid⌋ that I have in ⌊preaching⌋ the Good News.

¹⁹I am free. I belong to no man. But I make myself a slave to all people. I do this to help save as many people as I can. ²⁰To the Jews I became like a Jew. I did this to help save the Jews. I myself am not ruled by the law.* But to people that are ruled by the law I became like a person who is ruled by the law. I did this to help save those people that are ruled by the law. ²¹To those that are without the law I became like a person that is without the law. I did this to help save those people that are without the law. (But really, I am not without God's law—I am ruled by Christ's law.) ²²To the people that are weak, I became weak so that I could help save them. I have become all things to all people. I did this so that I could save people in any way possible. ²³I do all these things because of the Good News.* I do these things so that I can share in ⌊the blessings of⌋ the Good News.

²⁴You know that in a race all the runners run. But only one runner gets the prize. So run like that. Run to win! ²⁵All people that compete in the games use strict training. They do this so that they can win a crown *(reward)*. That crown is an earthly thing that lasts only a short time. But our crown *(reward)* will continue forever. ²⁶So I run like a person that has a goal. I fight like a boxer that is hitting something—not just the air. ²⁷It is my own body that I hit. I make it my slave. I do this so that I myself will not be rejected *(thrown out by God)* after I preached to other people.

Don't Be like the Jews

10 Brothers ⌊and sisters⌋, I want you to know what happened to our ancestors ⌊that followed Moses⌋. They were all under the cloud, and they all walked through the sea. ²Those people were all baptized* into Moses in the cloud and in the sea. ³They all ate the same spiritual food. ⁴And they all drank the same spiritual drink. They drank from that spiritual rock that was with them. That rock was Christ. ⁵But God was not pleased with most of those people. They were killed in the desert.

⁶And these things that happened are examples for us. These examples should stop us from wanting evil things like those people did. ⁷Don't worship idols* like some of those people did. It is written ⌊in the Scriptures⌋*: "The people sat down to eat and drink. The people stood up to dance."* ⁸We should not do sexual sins like some of those people did. In one day 23,000 of them died ⌊because of their sin⌋. ⁹We should not test the Lord like some of those people did. They were killed by snakes ⌊because they tested the Lord⌋. ¹⁰And

---

Scripture Part of the Holy Writings—Old Testament.
Good News The news that God has made a way for people to have their sins forgiven and live with God.
temple Special building in Jerusalem for Jewish worship.
altar A stone table at the temple used for offering sacrifices.
law Probably the Jewish law—the law of Moses.

baptized A Greek word meaning to be immersed, dipped, or buried briefly under water. Here, the "water" was the cloud and sea which covered and surrounded the people of Israel.
idol(s) False gods made from wood or stone and worshiped by the non-Jewish people.
Scriptures Holy Writings—the Old Testament.
"The people ... dance" Quote from Ex. 32:6.

don't complain like some of those people did. Those people were killed by the angel that destroys. [11]The things that happened to those people are examples. And those things were written to be warnings for us. We live in a time when all those past histories have come to their end. [12]So the person that thinks he is standing strong should be careful that he doesn't fall. [13]The only temptations that you have are the same temptations that all people have. But you can trust God. He will not let you be tempted more than you can bear. But when you are tempted, God will also give you a way to escape that temptation. Then you will be able to endure it.

[14]So, my dear friends, stay away from worshiping idols.* [15]I am speaking to you like you are intelligent people; judge for yourselves what I say. [16]The cup of blessing* that we give thanks for is a sharing in the blood *(death)* of Christ, isn't it? And the bread that we break is a sharing in the body of Christ, isn't it? [17]There is one loaf of bread. And we are many people. But we all share from that one loaf. So we are really one body.

[18]Think about the people of Israel *(the Jews)*. Those people that eat the sacrifices* share in the altar,* don't they? [19]I don't mean that the food sacrificed to an idol* is something important. And I don't mean that an idol is anything at all. No! [20]But I say that the things people sacrifice ⌊to idols⌋ are offered to demons,* not to God. And I don't want you to share anything with demons. [21]You cannot drink the cup of the Lord and the cup of demons too. You cannot share in the Lord's table and the table of demons too. [22]Do we want to make the Lord jealous? Are we stronger than he is? No!

Use Your Freedom for God's Glory

[23]"All things are allowed." Yes. But not all things are good. "All things are allowed." Yes. But some things don't help ⌊others⌋ grow stronger. [24]No person should try to do the things that will help ⌊only⌋ himself. He should try to do what is good for other people.

---

idol(s) False gods made from wood or stone and worshiped by the non-Jewish people.
cup of blessing The cup of wine that Christians thank God for and drink at the Lord's Supper.
sacrifices Animals killed and offered as gifts to God.
altar A stone table at the temple used for offering sacrifices.
demons Demons are evil spirits from the devil.

[25]Eat any meat that is sold in the meat market. Don't ask questions ⌊about the meat⌋ to see if it is something you think is wrong to eat. [26]⌊You can eat it⌋, "because the earth and everything in it belong to the Lord."*
[27]A person that is not a believer might invite you to eat with him. If you want to go, then eat anything that is put before you. Don't ask questions to see if it is something you think is wrong to eat. [28]But if a person tells you, "That food was offered to idols,*" then don't eat that food. Don't eat it. Why? Because ⌊you don't want to hurt the faith⌋ of the person that told you and because eating that meat is something that people think is wrong. [29]I don't mean that you think it is wrong. But the other person might think it is wrong. ⌊That is the only reason I would not eat the meat⌋. My own freedom should not be judged by what another person thinks. [30]I eat the meal with thankfulness. So I don't want to be criticized because of something I thank God for.

[31]So if you eat or if you drink or if you do anything, do it for the glory of God. [32]Never do anything that might make other people do wrong—Jews, Greeks *(non-Jews)*, or God's church. [33]I do the same thing. I try to please everybody in every way. I am not trying to do what is good for me. I try to do what is good for the most people, so that they can be saved.

11
Follow my example, like I follow the example of Christ.

Being Under Authority

[2]I praise you because you remember me in all things. You follow closely the teachings that I gave you. [3]But I want you to understand this: The head *(authority)* of every man is Christ. And the head of a woman is the man.* And the head of Christ is God. [4]Every man that prophesies* or prays with his head covered brings shame to his head. [5]But every woman that prays or prophesies should have her head covered. If her head is not covered, then she brings shame to her head. Then she is the same as a woman that has her head shaved. [6]If a woman does not cover her head, then it is the same as cutting off all her hair. But it is shameful for a woman to cut off her hair or to shave her head. So she should cover her head. [7]But a man should not cover his head. Why?

"because ... Lord" Quote from Ps. 24:1; 50:12; 89:11.
the man This could also mean "her husband."
prophesies Speaks or teaches things from God.

Because he is made like God and is God's glory. But woman is man's glory. ⁸Man did not come from woman. Woman came from man. ⁹And man was not made for woman. Woman was made for man. ¹⁰So that is why a woman should have her head covered with ₍something to show that she is under₎ authority. And also she should do this because of the angels. ¹¹But in the Lord the woman is important to the man, and the man is important to the woman. ¹²This is true because woman came from man, but also man is born from woman. Really, everything comes from God. ¹³Decide this for yourselves: Is it right for a woman to pray to God without something on her head? ¹⁴Even nature itself teaches you that wearing long hair is shameful for a man. ¹⁵But wearing long hair is a woman's honor. Long hair is given to the woman to cover her head. ¹⁶Some people may still want to argue ₍about this₎. But we and the churches of God don't accept what those people are doing.

The Lord's Supper

¹⁷In the things I tell you now I don't praise you. Your meetings hurt you more than they help you. ¹⁸First, I hear that when you meet together as a church you are divided. And I believe some of this. ¹⁹(It is necessary for there to be differences among you. That is the way to make it clear which ones of you are really doing right.) ²⁰When you all come together, you are not really eating the Lord's Supper.* ²¹Why? Because when you eat, each person eats without waiting for the others. Some people don't get enough to eat ₍or drink₎, while other people ₍have so much that they₎ become drunk. ²²You can eat and drink in your own homes! It seems that you think God's church *(people)* is not important. You embarrass those people that are poor. What should I tell you? Should I praise you for doing this? I don't praise you.

²³The teaching that I gave you is the same teaching that I received from the Lord: On the night when Jesus was given to be killed, he took bread ²⁴and gave thanks for it. Then he divided the bread and said, "This is my body; it is for you. Do this to remember me." ²⁵In the same way, after they ate, Jesus took the cup of wine. Jesus said, "This wine shows the new agreement ₍from God to his people₎. This new agreement begins with my blood *(death)*. When you drink this, do it to remember me." ²⁶Every time you eat this bread and drink this cup, you make known the Lord's death until he comes.

²⁷So if a person eats the bread or drinks the cup of the Lord in a way that is not worthy of it, then that person is sinning against the body and the blood of the Lord. ²⁸Every person should look into his own heart before he eats the bread and drinks the cup. ²⁹If a person eats ₍the bread₎ and drinks ₍the cup₎ without recognizing the body, then that person is judged guilty by eating and drinking. ³⁰That is why many in your group are sick and weak. And many have died. ³¹But if we judged ourselves in the right way, then God would not judge us. ³²But when the Lord judges us, he punishes us to show us the right way. He does this so that we will not be condemned with ₍the other people in₎ the world.

³³So, my brothers ₍and sisters₎, when you come together to eat, wait for each other. ³⁴If a person is ₍too₎ hungry, then he should eat at home. Do this so that your meeting together will not bring God's judgment on you. I will tell you what to do about the other things when I come.

Gifts from the Holy Spirit

12 Now, brothers ₍and sisters₎, I want you to understand about spiritual ₍gifts₎. ²You remember the lives you lived before you were believers. You let yourselves be influenced and led away ₍to worship₎ idols*—things that have no life. ³So I tell you that no person that is speaking with the help of God's Spirit says, "Jesus be cursed." And no person can say, "Jesus is Lord," without the help of the Holy Spirit.*

⁴There are different kinds of ₍spiritual₎ gifts; but ₍they are all from₎ the same Spirit.* ⁵There are different ways to serve; but ₍all these ways are from₎ the same Lord. ⁶And there are different ways that God works in people; but ₍all these ways are from₎ the same God. God works in us all to do everything. ⁷Something from the Spirit can be seen in each person. The Spirit gives this to each person to help other people. ⁸The Spirit gives one person the ability to speak with wisdom. And

---

idols False gods made from wood or stone and worshiped by the non-Jewish people.
Holy Spirit, Spirit Called the Spirit of God, the Spirit of Christ, and the Comforter. Joined with God and Christ, he does God's work among people in the world.

Lord's Supper The meal Jesus told his followers to eat to remember him. See Lk. 22:14-20.

the same Spirit gives another person the ability to speak with knowledge. ⁹The same Spirit gives faith to one person. And that one Spirit gives another person gifts of healing. ¹⁰The Spirit gives to another person the power to do miracles,* to another person the ability to prophesy,* to another person the ability to know the difference between good and evil spirits. The Spirit* gives one person the ability to speak in different kinds of languages, and to another person the ability to interpret those languages. ¹¹One Spirit, the same Spirit, does all these things. The Spirit decides what to give each person.

The Body of Christ

¹²A person's body is only one thing, but it has many parts. Yes, there are many parts to a body, but all those parts make only one body. Christ is like that too: ¹³Some of us are Jews and some of us are Greeks *(non-Jews)*; some of us are slaves and some of us are free. But we were all baptized* into one body through one Spirit.* And we were all given* the one Spirit.

¹⁴And a person's body has more than one part. It has many parts. ¹⁵The foot might say, "I am not a hand. So I don't belong to the body." But saying this would not stop the foot from being a part of the body. ¹⁶The ear might say, "I am not an eye. So I don't belong to the body." But saying this would not make the ear stop being a part of the body. ¹⁷If the whole body were an eye, then the body would not be able to hear. If the whole body were an ear, then the body would not be able to smell anything. ¹⁸⁻¹⁹If each part of the body were the same part, then there would be no body. But truly God put the parts in the body like he wanted them. He made a place for each one of them. ²⁰And so there are many parts, but only one body.

²¹The eye cannot say to the hand, "I don't need you!" And the head cannot say to the foot, "I don't need you!" ²²No! Those parts of the body that seem to be weaker are really very important. ²³And the parts of the body that we think are not worth very much are the parts that we give the most care to. And we give special care to the parts of the body that we don't want to show. ²⁴The more beautiful parts of our body don't need this special care. But God put the body together and gave more honor to the parts that need it. ²⁵God did this so that our body would not be divided. God wanted the different parts to care the same for each other. ²⁶If one part of the body suffers, then all the other parts suffer with it. Or if one part of our body is honored, then all the other parts share its honor too.

²⁷All of you together are the body of Christ. Each one of you is a part of that body. ²⁸And in the church God has given a place first to apostles,* second to prophets,* and third to teachers. Then God has given a place to those people that do miracles,* those people that have gifts of healing, those people that can help others, those people that are able to lead, and those people that can speak in different kinds of languages. ²⁹Not all people are apostles. Not all people are prophets. Not all people are teachers. Not all people do miracles. ³⁰Not all people have gifts of healing. Not all people speak in ⌊different kinds of⌋ languages. Not all people interpret those languages. ³¹But you should truly want to have the greater gifts ⌊of the Spirit⌋.*

Love Is the Best Gift

And now I will show you the best way of all.

13 I may speak in different languages of men or even angels. But if I don't have love, then I am only a noisy bell or a ringing cymbal. ²I may have the gift of prophecy*; I may understand all the secret things ⌊of God⌋ and know everything; and I may have faith so great that I can move mountains. But even with all these things, if I don't have love, then I am nothing. ³I may give everything I have to feed people. And I may even give my body ⌊as an offering⌋ to be burned. But I gain nothing by doing these things if I don't have love.

⁴Love is patient, and love is kind. Love is not jealous, it does not boast, and it is not proud. ⁵Love is not rude, love is not selfish, and love does not become angry easily. Love does not remember wrongs done against it. ⁶Love is not

---

miracles Amazing works done by the power of God.
prophesy To speak or teach things from God.
Spirit Called the Spirit of God, the Spirit of Christ, and the Comforter. Joined with God and Christ, he does God's work among people in the world.
baptized A Greek word meaning to be immersed, dipped, or buried briefly under water.
given Literally, "given to drink."

apostles Men that Jesus chose to be his special helpers.
prophets People who speak for God.
prophecy Speaking or teaching things from God.

happy with evil, but love is happy with the truth. ⁷Love patiently accepts all things. Love always trusts, always hopes, and always continues strong. ⁸Love never ends. There are ⌊gifts of⌋ prophecy,* but they will be ended. There are ⌊gifts of speaking in different kinds of⌋ languages, but those gifts will end. There is ⌊the gift of⌋ knowledge, but it will be ended. ⁹These things will end, because this knowledge and these prophecies we have are not complete *(not perfect)*. ¹⁰But when perfection comes, the things that are not complete will end. ¹¹When I was a child, I talked like a child; I thought like a child; I made plans like a child. When I became a man, I stopped those childish ways. ¹²It is the same with us. Now we see like we are looking into a dark mirror. But at that time, in the future, we shall see clearly. Now I know only a part. But at that time I will know fully, like God has known me. ¹³So these three things continue: faith, hope, and love. And the greatest of these is love.

Use Spiritual Gifts to Help the Church

14 Love is the thing you should try for. And you should truly want to have the spiritual gifts. And the gift you should want most is to be able to prophesy.* ²I will explain why: A person ⌊that has the gift of⌋ speaking in a ⌊different⌋ language is not speaking to people. He is speaking to God. No one understands that person—he is speaking secret things through the Spirit.* ³But a person that prophesies is speaking to people. He gives people strength, encouragement, and comfort. ⁴The person that speaks in a ⌊different⌋ language is helping only himself. But the person that prophesies is helping the whole church. ⁵I would like all of you ⌊to have the gift of⌋ speaking in ⌊different⌋ languages. But more, I want you to prophesy. The person that prophesies is greater than the person that can only speak in ⌊different⌋ languages. But the person speaking in ⌊different⌋ languages is the same as the person that prophesies if he can also interpret those languages. Then the church can be helped ⌊by what he says⌋.

⁶Brothers ⌊and sisters⌋, will it help you if I come to you speaking in ⌊different⌋ languages? No! It will help you only if I bring you a new truth or some knowledge, or some prophecy,* or some teaching. ⁷It is the same as with non-living things that make sounds—like a flute or a harp. If the different musical notes are not made clear, then you can't understand what song is being played. Each note must be played clearly for you to be able to understand the tune. ⁸And ⌊in a war⌋, if the trumpet does not sound clearly, then the soldiers will not know it is time to prepare for fighting. ⁹It is the same with you. The words you speak with your tongue must be clear. If you don't speak clearly, then no person can understand what you are saying. You will be talking to the air! ¹⁰It is true that there are many kinds of speech in the world. And they all have meaning. ¹¹So if I don't understand the meaning of what a person says to me, then I think that he talks strange, and he thinks that I talk strange. ¹²It is the same with you. You want spiritual gifts very much. So try most to have those things that help the church grow stronger. ¹³So the person that has the gift of speaking in a ⌊different⌋ language should pray that he can also interpret the things he says. ¹⁴If I pray in a ⌊different⌋ language, then my spirit is praying, but my mind does nothing. ¹⁵So what should I do? I will pray with my spirit, but I will also pray with my mind. I will sing with my spirit, but I will also sing with my mind. ¹⁶You might be praising God with your spirit. But a person there without understanding cannot say "Amen*" to your prayer of thanks. Why? Because he does not know what you are saying. ¹⁷You may be thanking God in a good way, but the other person is not helped.

¹⁸I thank God that my gift of speaking in ⌊different kinds of⌋ languages is greater than any of yours. ¹⁹But in the church meetings I would rather speak five words that I understand than thousands of words in a ⌊different⌋ language. I would rather speak with my understanding, so that I can teach other people.

²⁰Brothers ⌊and sisters⌋, don't think like children. In evil things be like babies. But in your thinking you should be like full grown people. ²¹It is written in the Scriptures*:

---

prophecy Speaking or teaching things from God.
prophesy To speak or teach things from God.
Spirit The Holy Spirit. Called the Spirit of God, the Spirit of Christ, and the Comforter. Joined with God and Christ, he does God's work among people in the world.

prophecy A message from God.
Amen When a person says, "Amen," it means he agrees with the things that were said.
Scriptures Holy Writings—the Old Testament.

"Using people that speak different kinds of languages and using the lips of foreigners, I will speak to these people; but even then these people will not obey me."

Isaiah 28:11-12

That is what the Lord says.

²²So ⌊the gift of speaking in different⌋ languages is a proof for people that don't believe, not for people that believe. And prophecy* is for people that believe, not for people that don't believe. ²³Suppose the whole church meets together and you all speak in ⌊different⌋ languages. If some people come in that are without understanding or don't believe, then those people will say you are crazy. ²⁴But suppose you are all prophesying* and a person comes in that does not believe or a person without understanding comes in. If you are all prophesying,* then that person's sin will be shown to him, and he will be judged by all the things you say. ²⁵The secret things in that person's heart will be made known. So that person will bow down and worship God. He will say, "Truly, God is with you."

Your Meetings Should Help the Church

²⁶So, brothers ⌊and sisters⌋, what should you do? When you meet together, one person has a song, another person has a teaching, another person has a new truth from God, another person speaks in a ⌊different⌋ language, and another person interprets that language. The purpose of all these things should be to help ⌊the church⌋ grow strong. ²⁷When you meet together, if any person speaks to the group in a ⌊different⌋ language, then it should be only two or not more than three people that do this. And they should speak one after the other. And another person should interpret ⌊what they say⌋. ²⁸But if there is no interpreter, then any person that speaks in a ⌊different⌋ language should be quiet in the church meeting. That person should speak only to himself and to God.

²⁹And only two or three prophets* should speak. The others should judge what they say. ³⁰And if a message from God comes to another person that is sitting, then the first speaker should stop. ³¹You can all prophesy* one after the other. In that way all the people can be taught and encouraged. ³²The spirits of prophets are under the control of the prophets themselves. ³³God is not a God of confusion but a God of peace.

³⁴Women should keep quiet in the church meetings. This is the same as in all the churches of God's people. Women are not allowed to speak. They must be under control, like the law ⌊of Moses⌋ says. ³⁵If there is something the women want to know, then they should ask their own husbands at home. It is shameful for a woman to speak in the church meeting. ³⁶Did God's teaching come from you? No! Or are you the only ones that have received that teaching? No!

³⁷If any person thinks that he is a prophet* or that he has a spiritual gift, then that person should understand that what I am writing to you is the Lord's command. ³⁸If that person does not know this, then he is not known ⌊by God⌋.

³⁹So my brothers ⌊and sisters⌋, you should truly want to prophesy.* And don't stop people from ⌊using the gift of⌋ speaking in ⌊different⌋ languages. ⁴⁰But everything should be done in a way that is right and orderly.

The Good News About Christ

15 Now, brothers ⌊and sisters⌋, I want you to remember the Good News* I told you about. You received this message, and you continue strong in it. ²You are saved by this message. But you must continue believing the things I told you. If you don't do that, then you believed for nothing.

³I gave you the message that I received. I told you the most important things: that Christ died for our sins, like the Scriptures* say; ⁴that Christ was buried and was raised to life on the third day, like the Scriptures say; ⁵and that Christ showed himself to Peter and then to the twelve ⌊apostles* together⌋. ⁶After that, Christ showed himself to more than 500 of the brothers at the same time. Most of these brothers are still living today. But some have died. ⁷Then Christ showed himself to James and later to all the apostles ⌊again⌋. ⁸Last of all, Christ showed himself to me. ⌊I was different⌋, like a baby that is born before the normal time.

---

prophecy Speaking or teaching things from God.
prophesy(ing) To speak or teach things from God.
prophet(s) Person who speaks or teaches things from God.

Good News The news that God has made a way for people to have their sins forgiven and live with God.
Scripture(s) Holy Writings—the Old Testament.
apostles The men Jesus chose to be his special helpers.

⁹All the other apostles are greater than I am. This is because I persecuted* the church of God. That is why I am not even good enough to be called an apostle. ¹⁰But, because of God's grace *(gift)*, that is what I am. And his grace that he gave me was not wasted. I worked harder than all the other apostles. (But I was not really the one working. It was God's grace that was with me.) ¹¹So then ⌊it is not important⌋ if I ⌊preached to you⌋ or if the other apostles ⌊preached to you⌋—we all preach the same thing, and this is what you believed.

We Will Be Raised from Death

¹²It is preached that Christ was raised from death. So why do some of you say that people will not be raised from death? ¹³If people will never be raised from death, then Christ has never been raised from death. ¹⁴And if Christ has never been raised, then our preaching is worth nothing. And your faith is worth nothing. ¹⁵And also we will be guilty of lying about God. Why? Because we have preached about God by saying that he raised Christ from death. And if people are not raised from death, then God never raised Christ from death. ¹⁶If dead people are not raised, then Christ has not been raised either. ¹⁷And if Christ has not been raised from death, then your faith is for nothing; you are still guilty of your sins. ¹⁸And those people in Christ who have already died are lost. ¹⁹If our hope in Christ is only for this life ⌊here on earth⌋, then people should feel more sorry for us than for anyone else.

²⁰But Christ has truly been raised from death—the first one of all those ⌊believers⌋ who are asleep in death. ²¹Death happens to people because of what one man *(Adam)* did. But the rising from death also happens because of one man *(Christ)*. ²²In Adam all of us die. In the same way, in Christ all of us will be made alive again. ²³But every man will be raised to life in the right order. Christ was first to be raised. Then when Christ comes again, the people who belong to Christ will be raised to life. ²⁴Then the end will come. Christ will destroy all rulers, authorities, and powers. Then Christ will give the kingdom to God the Father. ²⁵Christ must rule until God puts all enemies under Christ's control.* ²⁶The last enemy to be destroyed will be death. ²⁷⌊The Scripture* says⌋, "God put all things under his control."* When it says that "all things" are put under him *(Christ)*, it is clear that this does not include God himself. God is the one putting everything under Christ's control. ²⁸After everything has been put under Christ, then the Son *(Christ)* himself will be put under God. God is the One who put all things under Christ. Christ will be put under God, so that God will be the complete ruler over everything.

²⁹If people will never be raised from death, then what will people do who are baptized* for those who have died? If dead people are never raised, then why are people baptized for them? ³⁰And what about us? Why do we put ourselves in danger every hour? ³¹I die every day. That is true, brothers, the same as it is true that I boast about you in Christ Jesus our Lord. ³²If I fought wild animals in Ephesus only for human reasons, to satisfy my own pride, then I have gained nothing. If people are not raised from death then, "Let us eat and drink, because tomorrow we die."*

³³Don't be fooled: "Bad friends will ruin good habits." ³⁴Come back to your right way of thinking and stop sinning. Some of you don't know God. I say this to shame you.

What Kind of Body Will We Have?

³⁵But some person may ask, "How are dead people raised? What kind of body will they have?" ³⁶Those are stupid questions. When you plant something, it must die ⌊in the ground⌋ before it can live and grow. ³⁷And when you plant something, the thing you plant does not have the same "body" that it will have later. The thing you plant is only a seed, maybe wheat or something else. ³⁸But God gives it a body that he has planned for it. And God gives each kind of seed its own body. ³⁹All things made of flesh *(bodies)* are not the same kind of flesh: People have one kind of flesh *(body)*, animals have another kind, birds have another kind, and fish have another kind. ⁴⁰Also there are heavenly bodies and earthly bodies. But the beauty of the heavenly bodies is one kind. The beauty of the earthly bodies is another kind. ⁴¹The sun has one kind of beauty, the moon has another kind of beauty, and the stars

---

persecuted To hurt, bother, or do bad things to.
control Literally, "feet."
Scripture(s) Holy Writings—the Old Testament.

"God put ... control" Quote from Ps. 8:6.
baptized A Greek word meaning to be immersed, dipped, or buried briefly under water.
"Let us ... die" Quote from Isa. 22:13; 56:12.

have another. And each star is different in its beauty. ⁴²It is the same with the dead people who are raised to life. The body that is "planted" will ruin and decay. But that body is raised to a life that cannot be destroyed. ⁴³When the body is "planted," it is without honor. But it is raised in glory. When the body is "planted," it is weak. But when it is raised, it has power. ⁴⁴The body that is "planted" is a physical body. When it is raised, it is a spiritual body.

There is a physical body. So there is also a spiritual body. ⁴⁵It is written ₍in the Scriptures₎* "The first man (Adam) became a living thing.*"* But the last Adam *(Christ)* became a spirit that gives life. ⁴⁶The spiritual ₍man₎ did not come first. It was the physical ₍man₎ that came first; then came the spiritual. ⁴⁷The first man came from the dust of the earth. The second man *(Christ)* came from heaven. ⁴⁸People belong to the earth. They are like that first man of earth. But those people who belong to heaven are like that man of heaven. ⁴⁹We were made like that man of earth. So we will also be made like that man of heaven.

⁵⁰I tell you this, brothers ₍and sisters₎: Flesh and blood *(a physical body)* cannot have a part in the kingdom of God. A thing that will ruin cannot have a part in something that never ruins. ⁵¹But listen, I tell you this secret: We will not all die, but we will all be changed. ⁵²It will only take the time of a second. We will be changed as quickly as an eye blinks. This will happen when the last trumpet blows. The trumpet will blow and those ₍believers₎ who have died will be raised to live forever. And we ₍also₎ will all be changed. ⁵³This ₍body₎ that will ruin must clothe itself with something that will never ruin. And this ₍body₎ that dies must clothe itself with something that will never die. ⁵⁴So this ₍body₎ that ruins will clothe itself with that which never ruins. And this body that dies will clothe itself with that which never dies. When this happens, then this Scripture* will be made true:

"Death is swallowed *(defeated)* in victory."
Isaiah 25:8

⁵⁵ "Death, where is your victory?
Grave, where is your power to hurt?"
Hosea 13:14

⁵⁶Death's power to hurt is sin. And the power of sin is the law. ⁵⁷But we thank God! He gives us the victory through our Lord Jesus Christ.

⁵⁸So my dear brothers ₍and sisters₎, stand strong. Don't let anything change you. Always give yourselves fully to the work of the Lord. You know that your work in the Lord is never wasted.

The Collection for Other Believers

16 Now ₍I will write₎ about the collection ₍of money₎ for God's people. Do the same thing that I told the Galatian churches to do: ²On the first day of every week each one of you should save as much money as you can from what you are blessed with. You should put this money in a special place and keep it there. Then you will not have to gather your money after I come. ³When I come I will send some men to take your gift to Jerusalem. These men will be the men that you all agree should go. I will send them with letters of introduction. ⁴If it seems good for me to go also, then those men will go with me.

Paul's Plans

⁵I plan to go through Macedonia. So I will come to you after I go through Macedonia. ⁶Maybe I will stay with you for a time. I might even stay all winter. Then you can help me on my trip, wherever I go. ⁷I don't want to come see you now, because I would have to leave to go to other places. I hope to stay a longer time with you if the Lord allows it. ⁸But I will stay at Ephesus until Pentecost.* ⁹I will stay here, because a good opportunity for a great and growing work has been given to me now. And there are many people working against it.

¹⁰Timothy might come to you. Try to make him feel comfortable with you. He is working for the Lord the same as I am. ¹¹So none of you should refuse to accept Timothy. Help him on his trip in peace, so that he can come back to me. I am expecting him to come back with the brothers.

¹²Now about our brother Apollos: I strongly encouraged him to visit you with the other brothers. But he was sure that he did not want to go now. But when he has the opportunity, he will go to you.

Scripture(s) Holy Writings—the Old Testament.
thing Literally, "soul."
"The first man ... thing" Quote from Gen. 2:7.

Pentecost Jewish festival celebrating the harvest of wheat. It was always 50 days after Passover.

1 CORINTHIANS 16:13–24

Paul Ends his Letter

[13] Be careful. Continue strong in the faith. Have courage, and be strong. [14] Do everything in love.

[15] You know that Stephanas and his family were the first believers in Achaia. They have given themselves to the service of God's people. I ask you, brothers ⌊and sisters⌋, [16] to follow the leading of people like these, and any other person that works and serves with them.

[17] I am happy that Stephanas, Fortunatus, and Achaicus have come. You are not here, but they have filled your place. [18] They have given rest to my spirit and to yours. You should recognize the value of men like these.

[19] The churches in Asia* say hello to you. Aquila and Priscilla say hello to you in the Lord. Also the church that meets in their house says hello to you. [20] All the brothers ⌊and sisters⌋ here say hello to you. Give each other a holy kiss when you meet.

[21] I am Paul, and I am writing this greeting with my own hand.

[22] If any person does not love the Lord, then let that person be separated from God—lost forever! Come, O Lord!*

[23] The grace of the Lord Jesus be with you.

[24] My love be with all of you in Christ Jesus.

Asia The western part of Asia Minor.
Come, O Lord! This translates the Aramaic "*marana tha.*"

2 Corinthians

1 From Paul, an apostle* of Christ Jesus. I am an apostle because that is what God wanted.
Also from Timothy our brother ⌊in Christ⌋.
To the church of God that lives in Corinth and to all of God's people in the whole country of Achaia: ²Grace *(kindness)* and peace to you from God our Father and the Lord Jesus Christ.

Paul Gives Thanks to God

³Praise be to the God and Father of our Lord Jesus Christ. God is the Father who is full of mercy. He is the God of all comfort. ⁴He comforts us every time we have trouble, so that we can comfort other people any time they have trouble. We can comfort them with the same comfort that God gives us. ⁵We share in the many sufferings of Christ. In the same way, much comfort comes to us through Christ. ⁶If we have troubles, those troubles are for your comfort and salvation. If we have comfort, it is for your comfort. This helps you to patiently accept the same sufferings that we have. ⁷Our hope for you is strong. We know that you share in our sufferings. So we know that you also share in our comfort.

⁸Brothers ⌊and sisters⌋, we want you to know about the trouble we suffered in the country of Asia.* We had great burdens there. The burdens were greater than our own strength. We even gave up hope for life. ⁹Truly in our own hearts we believed that we would die. But this happened so that we would not trust in ourselves. It happened so that we would trust in God, who raises people from death. ¹⁰God saved us from these great dangers of death. And God will continue to save us. We have put our hope in him, and he will continue to save us. ¹¹And you can help us with your prayers. Then many people will give thanks for us—that God blessed us because of their many prayers.

The Change in Paul's Plans

¹²This is what we are proud of, and I can say with all my heart that it is true: In all the things we have done in the world, we have done everything with an honest and pure heart from God. And this is even more true in the things we have done with you. We did this by God's grace *(kindness)*, not by the kind of wisdom the world has. ¹³The only things we write to you are things that you can read and understand. And I hope that you will always understand, ¹⁴like you have already understood some things about us. I hope that you will understand that you can be proud of us, like we will be proud of you on the day our Lord Jesus Christ comes again.

¹⁵I was very sure of all this. That is why I made plans to visit you first. Then you could be blessed twice. ¹⁶I planned to visit you on my way to Macedonia. Then I planned to visit you again on my way back. I wanted to get help from you for my trip to Judea. ¹⁷Do you think that I made those plans without really thinking? Or maybe you think I make plans like the world makes plans, so that I say, "Yes, yes," and at the same time I say, "No, no."

¹⁸But if you can believe God, then you can believe that what we tell you is never both "Yes" and "No." ¹⁹The Son of God, Jesus Christ, that Silas and Timothy and I preached to you was not "Yes" and "No." In Christ it has always been "Yes." ²⁰The "Yes" to all of God's promises is in Christ. And that is why we say "Amen"* through Christ to the glory of God. ²¹And God is the One who makes you and us strong in Christ. God gave us his special blessing.* ²²He put his mark on us to show that we are his. And he put his Spirit* in our hearts to be a guarantee—⌊a proof that he will give us what he promised⌋.

---

apostle Person Jesus chose to be a special helper for telling the Good News to the world.
Asia The western part of Asia Minor.
Amen To say "Amen" means to agree strongly.
gave us his special blessing Literally, "anointed us."
Spirit The Holy Spirit. Called the Spirit of God, the Spirit of Christ, and the Comforter. Joined with God and Christ, he does God's work among people in the world.

[23] I tell you this, and I ask God to be my witness that this is true: The reason I did not come back to Corinth was that I did not want to punish or hurt you. [24] I don't mean that we are trying to control your faith. You are strong in faith. But we are workers with you for your own happiness.

[2] So I decided that my next visit to you would not be another visit to make you sad. [2] If I make you sad, then who will make me happy? Only you can make me happy—you that I made sad. [3] I wrote you a letter for this reason: so that when I came to you I would not be made sad by those people who should make me happy. I felt sure of all of you. I felt sure that all of you would share my joy. [4] When I wrote to you before, I was very troubled and unhappy in my heart. I wrote with many tears. I did not write to make you sad. I wrote so that you could know how much I love you.

Forgive the Person Who Did Wrong

[5] A person ⌊in your group⌋ has caused sadness. He caused this sadness not to me, but to all of you—I mean he caused sadness to all in some way. (I don't want to make it sound worse than it really is.) [6] The punishment that most of your group gave him is enough for him. [7] But now you should forgive him and comfort him. This will keep him from having too much sadness and giving up completely. [8] So I beg you to show him that you love him. [9] This is why I wrote to you. I wanted to test you and see if you obey in everything. [10] If you forgive a person, then I also forgive that person. And what I have forgiven—if I had anything to forgive—I forgave it for you, and Christ was with me. [11] I did this so that Satan *(the Devil)* would not win anything from us. We know very well what Satan's plans are.

Paul's Anxiety in Troas

[12] I went to Troas to preach the Good News* of Christ. The Lord gave me a good opportunity there. [13] But I had no peace because I did not find my brother Titus there. So I said good-bye and went to Macedonia.

Victory Through Christ

[14] But thanks be to God. God always leads us in victory through Christ. God uses us to spread his knowledge everywhere like a sweet-smelling perfume. [15] Our offering to God is this: We are the sweet smell of Christ among people who are being saved and among people who are being lost. [16] To the people who are being lost, we are the smell of death that brings death. But to the people who are being saved, we are the smell of life that brings life. So who is good enough to do this work? [17] We don't sell the word of God for a profit like many other people do. No! But in Christ we speak in truth before God. We speak like men sent from God.

Servants of God's New Agreement

[3] Are we starting to boast about ourselves again? Do we need letters of introduction to you or from you, like some other people? [2] You yourselves are our letter. That letter is written on our hearts. It is known and read by all people. [3] You show that you are a letter from Christ that he sent through us. This letter is not written with ink but with the Spirit* of the living God. It is not written on stone tablets.* It is written on human hearts.

[4] We can say these things, because through Christ we feel sure before God. [5] I don't mean that we are able to say that we can do anything ⌊good⌋ ourselves. It is God who makes us able to do all that we do. [6] God made us able to be servants of a new agreement ⌊from God to his people⌋. This new agreement is not a written law. It is of the Spirit.* The written law brings death, but the Spirit gives life.

The New Agreement Brings Greater Glory

[7] The service that brought death *(the law)* was written with words on stone.* It came with ⌊God's⌋ glory. Moses' face was so bright with glory that the people of Israel *(the Jews)* could not continue looking at his face. And that glory later disappeared. [8] So surely the service that brings the Spirit* has even more glory. [9] This is what I mean: That service *(the law)* judged people guilty of sin, but it had glory. So surely the service that makes people right ⌊with God⌋ has much greater glory. [10] That ⌊old service⌋ had glory. But it really loses its glory when it is compared to the much greater glory ⌊of this new service⌋. [11] If that ⌊service⌋ that disappeared came with glory, then this ⌊service⌋ that continues forever has much greater glory.

[12] We have this hope, so we are very brave. [13] We are not like Moses. He put a covering over his face. Moses covered his face so that the people

---

Good News The news that God has made a way for people to have their sins forgiven and live with God.

Spirit The Holy Spirit. Called the Spirit of God, the Spirit of Christ, and the Comforter. Joined with God and Christ, he does God's work among people in the world.

stone tablets, stone Meaning the law that God gave to Moses, which was written on stone tablets (Ex. 24:12; 25:16).

of Israel *(the Jews)* would not see it. The glory *(brightness)* was disappearing, and Moses did not want them to see it end. ¹⁴But their minds were closed—they could not understand. Even today that same covering hides the meaning when they *(the Jews)* read the old testament. That covering has not been removed. It is taken away only through Christ. ¹⁵But even today, when these people read the law of Moses, there is a covering over their minds. ¹⁶But when a person changes and follows the Lord, that covering is taken away. ¹⁷The Lord is the Spirit. And where the Spirit of the Lord is, there is freedom. ¹⁸And our faces are not covered. We all show the Lord's glory. We are being changed to be like him. This change in us brings more and more glory. This glory comes from the Lord, who is the Spirit.

Spiritual Treasure in Clay Jars

4 God, with his mercy, gave us this work to do. So we don't give up. ²But we have turned away from secret and shameful ways. We don't use trickery, and we don't change the teaching of God. No! We teach the truth plainly. This is how we show people who we are. And this is how they can know in their hearts what kind of people we are before God. ³The Good News* that we preach may be hidden. But it is hidden only to those people who are lost. ⁴The ruler* of this world *(the devil)* has blinded the minds of people who don't believe. They cannot see the light *(truth)* of the Good News—the Good News about the glory of Christ. Christ is the One who is exactly like God. ⁵We don't preach about ourselves. But we preach that Jesus Christ is Lord; and we preach that we are your servants for Jesus. ⁶God once said, "The light will shine out of the darkness!" And this is the same God who made his light shine in our hearts. He gave us light by letting us know the glory of God that is in the face of Christ.

⁷We have this treasure from God. But we are only like clay jars that hold the treasure. This shows that this great power is from God, not from us. ⁸We have troubles all around us, but we are not defeated. We often don't know what to do, but we don't give up. ⁹We are persecuted, but God does not leave us. We are hurt sometimes, but we are not destroyed. ¹⁰We have the death of Jesus in our own bodies. We carry this death so that the life of Jesus can also be seen in our bodies *(lives)*. ¹¹We are alive, but for Jesus we are always in danger of death. This happens to us so that the life of Jesus can be seen in our bodies that die. ¹²So death is working in us, but life is working in you. ¹³It is written in the Scriptures,* "I believed, so I spoke."* Our faith is like that too. We believe, and so we speak. ¹⁴God raised the Lord Jesus from death. And we know that God will also raise us with Jesus. God will bring us together with you, and we will stand before him. ¹⁵All these things are for you. And so the grace *(kindness)* of God is being given to more and more people. This will bring more and more thanks to God for his glory.

Living by Faith

¹⁶That is why we never become weak. Our physical body is becoming older and weaker, but our spirit inside us is made new every day. ¹⁷We have small troubles for a while now, but those troubles are helping us gain an eternal glory. That eternal glory is much greater than the troubles. ¹⁸So we think about the things we cannot see, not what we see. The things we see continue only a short time. And the things we cannot see will continue forever.

5 We know that our body—the tent we live in here on earth—will be destroyed. But when that happens, God will have a home for us to live in. It will not be a home made by men. It will be a home in heaven that will continue forever. ²But now we are tired of this body. We want God to give us our heavenly home. ³It will clothe us and we will not be naked. ⁴While we live in this tent *(body)*, we have burdens and we complain. I don't mean that we want to remove this tent *(body)*. But we want to be clothed with our heavenly home. Then this body that dies will be fully covered with life. ⁵This is what God made us for. And he has given us the Spirit* to be a guarantee—a proof that he will give us this new life.

⁶So we always have courage *(confidence)*. We know that while we live in this body, we are away from the Lord. ⁷We live by what we believe, not by what we can see. ⁸So I say that we have confidence. And we really want to be away from this body and be at home with the Lord. ⁹Our only goal is to please God. We want to please him when we are living here in our body or there

---

Good News The news that God has made a way for people to have their sins forgiven and live with God.

The ruler Literally, "The god."

Scriptures Holy Writings—the Old Testament.

"I believed ... spoke" Quote from Ps. 116:10.

Spirit The Holy Spirit. Called the Spirit of God, the Spirit of Christ, and the Comforter. Joined with God and Christ, he does God's work among people in the world.

₍with the Lord₎. ¹⁰We must all stand before Christ to be judged. Each person will get what he should. Each person will be paid for the things he did—good or bad—when he lived in the earthly body.

Helping People Become God's Friends

¹¹We know what it means to fear the Lord. So we try to help people accept the truth. God knows what we really are. And I hope that in your hearts you know us too. ¹²We are not trying to prove ourselves to you again. But we are telling you about ourselves. We are giving you reasons to be proud of us. Then you will have an answer for those people who are proud about things that can be seen. Those people don't care about what is in a person's heart. ¹³If we are crazy, then it is for God. If we have our right mind, then it is for you. ¹⁴The love of Christ controls us. Why? Because we know that One *(Christ)* has died for all people. So all have died. ¹⁵Christ died for all people so that the people who live would not continue to live for themselves. He died for them and was raised from death so that those people would live for him.

¹⁶From this time on we don't think of any person like the world thinks of people. It is true that in the past we thought of Christ like the world thinks. But we don't think that way now. ¹⁷If any person is in Christ, then that person is made new. The old things have gone; everything is made new! ¹⁸All this is from God. Through Christ, God made peace between us and himself. And God gave us the work of bringing people into peace with him. ¹⁹I mean that God was in Christ, making peace between the world and himself. In Christ, God did not hold people guilty for their sins. And he gave us this message of peace ₍to tell people₎. ²⁰So we have been sent to speak for Christ. It is like God is calling to people through us. We speak for Christ when we beg you to be at peace with God. ²¹Christ had no sin. But God made him become sin. God did this for us, so that in Christ we could become right with God.

6 We are workers together with God. So we beg you: Don't let the grace *(kindness)* that you received from God be for nothing. ²God says,

"I heard you at the right time,
  and I gave you help on the
    day of salvation."
Isaiah 49:8

I tell you that the "right time" is now. The "day of salvation" is now.

³We don't want people to find anything wrong with our work. So we do nothing that will be a problem to other people. ⁴But in every way we show that we are servants of God: in accepting many hard things, in troubles, in difficulties, and in great problems. ⁵We are beaten and thrown into prison. People become upset and fight us. We work hard, and sometimes we get no sleep or food. ⁶₍We show that we are servants of God₎ by our understanding, by our patience, by our kindness, and by living pure. ₍We show this₎ by the Holy Spirit,* by true love, ⁷by speaking the truth, and by God's power. We use our right living to defend ourselves against everything. ⁸Some people honor us, but other people shame us. Some people say good things about us, but other people say bad things. Some people say we are liars, but we speak the truth. ⁹To some people we are not known *(not important)*, but we are well known. We seem to be dying, but look! We continue to live. We are punished, but we are not killed. ¹⁰We have much sadness, but we are always rejoicing. We are poor, but we are making many people rich ₍in faith₎. We have nothing, but really we have everything.

¹¹We have spoken freely to you people in Corinth. We have opened our hearts to you. ¹²Our feelings of love for you have not stopped. It is you that have stopped your feelings of love for us. ¹³I speak to you like you are my children. Do the same as we have done—open your hearts also.

Warning About Living with Non-Christians

¹⁴You are not the same as those people who don't believe. So don't join yourselves to them. Good and bad don't belong together. Light and darkness cannot have fellowship *(sharing)*. ¹⁵How can Christ and Belial *(the devil)* have any agreement? What can a believer have together with a non-believer? ¹⁶God's temple* cannot have any agreement with idols.* And we are the temple of the living God. Like God said:

"I will live with them
  and walk with them,
I will be their God,
  and they will be my people."
Leviticus 26:11-12

Holy Spirit Also called the Spirit of God, the Spirit of Christ, and the Comforter. Joined with God and Christ, he does God's work among people in the world.
God's temple The place where people worship and serve God. Here it means a Christian's body.
idols False gods made from wood or stone and worshiped by the non-Jewish people.

¹⁷ "So come away from those people
and separate yourselves from them,
says the Lord.
Touch nothing that is not clean,
and I will accept you."
Isaiah 52:11

¹⁸ "I will be your father,
and you will be my sons and daughters,
says the Lord All-Powerful."
2 Samuel 7:14; 7:8

7 Dear friends, we have these promises ⌊from God⌋. So we should make ourselves pure—free from anything that makes our body or our soul unclean. We should try to become perfect in the way we live, because we respect God.

Paul's Joy

²Open your hearts to us. We have not done wrong to any person. We have not ruined ⌊the faith of⌋ any person, and we have not cheated any person. ³I do not say this to blame you. I told you before that we love you so much that we would live or die with you. ⁴I feel very sure of you. I am very proud of you. You give me much courage. And in all of our troubles I have great joy.

⁵When we came into Macedonia, we had no rest. We found trouble all around us. We had fighting on the outside and fear on the inside. ⁶But God comforts people who are troubled. And God comforted us when Titus came. ⁷We were comforted by his coming and also by the comfort that you gave him. Titus told us about your wish to see me. He told us that you are very sorry for the things you did. And Titus told me about your great care for me. When I heard this, I was much happier.

⁸Even if the letter I wrote you made you sad, I am not sorry I wrote it. I know that letter made you sad, and I was sorry for that. But it made you sad only for a short time. ⁹Now I am happy. My happiness is not because you were made sad. I am happy because your sorrow made you change your hearts. You became sad like God wanted. So you were not hurt by us in any way. ¹⁰Being sorry like God wants makes a person change his heart and life. This leads a person to salvation, and we cannot be sorry for that. But the kind of sorrow the world has will bring death. ¹¹You had the kind of sorrow God wanted you to have. Now see what that sorrow has brought you: That sorrow has made you very serious. It made you want to prove that you were not wrong. It made you angry and afraid. It made you want ⌊to see me⌋. It made you care. It made you want the right thing to be done.

You proved that you were not guilty in any part of that problem. ¹²I wrote that letter, but not because of the one who did the wrong. And it was not written because of the person who was hurt. But I wrote that letter so that you could see, before God, the great care that you have for us. ¹³That is why we were comforted.

We were very comforted. And we were even happier to see that Titus was so happy. All of you made him feel good. ¹⁴I boasted to Titus about you. And you showed that I was right. Everything that we said to you was true. And you have proved that the things that we boasted about to Titus are true. ¹⁵And his love for you is stronger when he remembers that you were all ready to obey. You welcomed him with respect and fear. ¹⁶I am very happy that I can trust you fully.

Christian Giving

8 And now, brothers ⌊and sisters⌋, we want you to know about the grace *(kindness)* that God gave the churches *(groups of believers)* in Macedonia. ²Those believers have been tested by great troubles. And they are very poor people. But they gave much because of their great joy. ³I can tell you that they gave as much as they were able. Those believers gave even more than they could afford. They did this freely. No person told them to do this. ⁴But they asked us again and again—they begged us to let them share in this service for God's people. ⁵And they gave in a way that we did not expect: They gave themselves to the Lord and to us before ⌊they gave their money⌋. This is what God wants. ⁶So we asked Titus to help you finish this special work of grace *(kindness)*. Titus is the one who started this work. ⁷You are rich in everything—in faith, in speaking, in knowledge, in truly wanting to help, and in the love you learned from us. And so we want you to also be rich in this gift of giving.

⁸I am not commanding you to give. But I want to see if your love is true love. I do this by showing you that other people really want to help. ⁹You know the grace *(kindness)* of our Lord Jesus Christ. You know that Christ was rich ⌊with God⌋, but for you he became poor. Christ did this so that you could become rich by his becoming poor.

¹⁰This is what I think you should do: Last year you were the first to want to give. And you were the first that gave. ¹¹So now finish the work ⌊you started⌋. Then your "doing" will be equal to your "wanting to do." Give from what you have. ¹²If you want to give, then your gift will be accepted. Your gift will be judged by what you have, not by

what you don't have. ¹³We don't want you to have troubles while other people are comforted. We want everything to be equal. ¹⁴At this time you have plenty. These things you have can help other people to have the things they need. Then later, when they have plenty, they can help you to have the things you need. Then all will be equal. ¹⁵Like it is written ⌊in the Scriptures⌋,*

"The person that gathered much
did not have too much,
and the person that gathered little
did not have too little."

Exodus 16:18

Titus and His Companions

¹⁶I thank God because he gave Titus the same love for you that I have. ¹⁷Titus accepted the things we asked him to do. He wanted very much to go to you. This was his own idea. ¹⁸We are sending with Titus the brother who is praised by all the churches *(groups of believers)*. This brother is praised because of his service in the gospel.* ¹⁹Also, this brother was chosen by the churches to go with us when we carry this gift *(the money)*. We are doing this service to bring glory to the Lord and to show that we really want to help. ²⁰We are being careful so that no person will criticize us about the way we are caring for this large gift. ²¹We are trying to do what is right. We want to do what the Lord accepts as right and also what people think is right. ²²Also, we are sending with them our brother who is always ready to help. He has proved this to us in many ways. And he wants to help even more now because he has much faith in you.

²³Now about Titus—he is my partner. He is working together with me to help you. And about the other brothers—they are sent from the churches *(groups of believers)*, and they bring glory to Christ. ²⁴So show these men that you really have love. Show them why we are proud of you. Then all the churches can see it.

Help for Fellow Christians

9 I really don't need to write to you about this help for God's people. ²I know that you want to help. I have been boasting about this to the people in Macedonia. I have told them that you people in Achaia were ready to give since last year. And your wanting to give has made most of the people here ready to give also. ³But I am sending the brothers to you. I don't want our boasting about you in this to be for nothing. I want you to be ready like I said you would be. ⁴If any of the people from Macedonia come with me, and they find that you are not ready, then we will be ashamed. We will be ashamed that we were so sure of you. (And you will be ashamed too!) ⁵So I thought that I should ask these brothers to go to you before we come. They will finish making ready the gift you promised. Then the gift will be ready when we come, and it will be a gift you wanted to give—not a gift that you hated to give.

⁶Remember this: The person who plants little will harvest only a little. But the person who plants much will harvest much. ⁷Each person should give what he has decided in his heart to give. A person should not give if it makes him sad. And a person should not give if he thinks he is forced to give. God loves the person who gives happily. ⁸And God can give you more blessings than you need. Then you will always have plenty of everything. You will have enough to give to every good work. ⁹It is written ⌊in the Scriptures⌋*:

"He gives generously to the poor;
his kindness will continue forever."

Psalm 112:9

¹⁰God is the One who gives seed to the person who plants. And he gives bread for food. And God will give you ⌊spiritual⌋ seed and make your seed grow. He will make a great harvest from your goodness *(giving)*. ¹¹God will make you rich in every way so that you can always give freely. And your giving through us will make people give thanks to God. ¹²This service that you do helps the needs of God's people. But that is not all your service does. It is also bringing more and more thanks to God. ¹³This service you do is a proof ⌊of your faith⌋. People will praise God because of this. They will praise God because you follow the gospel* of Christ—the gospel you say you believe. People will praise God because you freely share with them and with all people. ¹⁴And when those people pray, they will wish they could be with you. They will feel this because of the great grace *(kindness)* that God gave you. ¹⁵Thanks be to God for his gift that is too wonderful to explain.

Paul Defends His Ministry

10 I am Paul, and I am begging you. I beg you with the gentleness and the kindness of Christ. ⌊Some people say that⌋ I am humble when I am with you, and brave when I am away. ²Some people think that we live in a worldly way. I plan

---

Scriptures Holy Writings—the Old Testament.
gospel The Good News that God has made a way for people to have their sins forgiven and live with God.

to be very bold against those people when I come. I beg you that when I come I will not need to use that same boldness ₍with you₎. ³We do live in the world. But we don't fight in the same way that the world fights. ⁴We fight with weapons that are different from the weapons the world uses. Our weapons have power from God. These weapons can destroy ₍the enemy's₎ strong places. We destroy ₍people's₎ arguments. ⁵And we destroy every proud thing that raises itself against the knowledge of God. And we capture *(catch)* every thought and make it give up and obey Christ. ⁶We are ready to punish any person there who does not obey. But first we want you to obey fully.

⁷You must look at the facts before you. If a person feels sure that he belongs to Christ, then he must remember that we belong to Christ the same as that person. ⁸It is true that we boast freely about the authority *(power)* the Lord gave us. But he gave us this power to strengthen you, not to hurt you. So I will not be ashamed of that boasting we do. ⁹I don't want you to think that I am trying to scare you with my letters. ¹⁰Some people say, "Paul's letters are powerful and sound important. But when he is with us, he is weak. And his speaking is nothing." ¹¹Those people should know this: We are not there with you now, so we say these things in letters. But when we are there with you, we will show the same power that we show in our letters.

¹²We don't dare to put ourselves in the same group with those people who think that they are very important. We don't compare ourselves to them. They use themselves to measure themselves, and they judge themselves by what they themselves are. This shows that they know nothing. ¹³But we will not boast about things outside the work that was given us to do. We will limit our boasting to the work that God gave us. But this work includes our work with you. ¹⁴We are not boasting too much. We would be boasting too much if we had not already come to you. But we have come to you. We came to you with the Good News* of Christ. ¹⁵We limit our boasting to the work that is ours. We don't boast in the work other people have done. We hope that your faith will continue to grow. We hope that you will help our work to grow much larger. ¹⁶We want to tell the Good News in the areas beyond your city. We don't want to boast about work that has already been done in another man's area. ¹⁷But, "The person who boasts should boast in the Lord."* ¹⁸It is not the person who says that he is good who is accepted. It is the person that the Lord thinks is good who is accepted.

Paul and the False Apostles

11 I wish you would be patient with me even when I am a little foolish. But you are already patient with me. ²I feel jealousy for you. And this jealousy is a jealousy that comes from God. I promised to give you to Christ. Christ must be your only husband. I want to give you to Christ to be his pure bride.* ³But I am afraid that your minds will be led away from your true and pure following of Christ. This might happen the same as Eve was tricked *(fooled)* by the snake *(the devil)* with his evil ways. ⁴You are very patient with any person who comes to you and preaches things about Jesus that are different from the things we told you. You are very willing to accept a spirit or a gospel that is different from the Spirit* and gospel* that you received from us. ₍So you should be patient with me.₎

⁵I don't think that those "great apostles" are any better than I am. ⁶It is true that I am not a trained speaker. But I do have knowledge. We have shown this to you clearly in every way.

⁷I preached God's Good News* to you without pay. I humbled myself to make you important. Do you think that was wrong? ⁸I accepted pay from other churches. I took their money so that I could serve you. ⁹If I needed something when I was with you, I did not trouble any of you. The brothers who came from Macedonia gave me all that I needed. I did not allow myself to be a burden to you in any way. And I will never be a burden to you. ¹⁰No person in Achaia* will stop me from boasting about that. I say this with the truth of Christ in me. ¹¹And why ₍do I not burden you₎? Do you think it is because I don't love you? No. God knows that I love you.

¹²And I will continue doing what I am doing now. I will continue this because I want to stop those people from having a reason to boast. They would like to say that the work they boast about is the same as ours. ¹³These people are not true apostles.* They are workers who lie. And they

---

Good News, gospel The news that God has made a way for people to have their sins forgiven and live with God.

"The person ... Lord" Quote from Jer. 9:24.
bride Literally, "virgin."
Spirit The Holy Spirit. Called the Spirit of God, the Spirit of Christ, and the Comforter. Joined with God and Christ, he does God's work among people in the world.
Achaia The southern part of Greece where Corinth was.
apostles The men Jesus chose to be his special helpers.

change themselves to ₍make people think they are₎ apostles of Christ. ¹⁴That does not surprise us. Why? Even Satan *(the devil)* changes himself to ₍make people think he is₎ an angel of light.* ¹⁵So it does not surprise us if Satan's servants make themselves look like servants who work for what is right. But in the end those people will be paid *(punished)* for the things they do.

Paul Tells About His Sufferings

¹⁶I tell you again: No person should think that I am a fool. But if you think that I am a fool, then accept me like you accept a fool. Then I can boast a little too. ¹⁷I boast because I feel sure of myself. But I am not talking like the Lord would talk. I am boasting like a fool. ¹⁸Many people are boasting about their lives in the world. So I will boast too. ¹⁹You are wise, so you will gladly be patient with fools! ²⁰₍I know you will be patient,₎ because you are even patient with a person who forces you to do things and uses you! You are patient with people that trick you, or think they are better than you, or hit you in the face! ²¹It is shameful to me to say this, but we were too "weak" ₍to do those things to you₎!

But if any person is brave enough ₍to boast₎, then I also will be brave and boast. (I am talking like a fool.) ²²Are those people Hebrews*? I am too. Are they Israelites*? I am too. Are they from Abraham's* family? I am too. ²³Are those people serving Christ? I am serving him more. (I am crazy to talk like this.) I have worked much harder than those people. I have been in prison more often. I have been hurt more in beatings. I have been near death many times. ²⁴Five times the Jews have given me their punishment of 39 hits with a whip. ²⁵Three different times I was beaten with rods. One time I was almost killed with rocks. Three times I was in ships that were wrecked, and one of those times I spent the night and the next day in the sea. ²⁶I have traveled many, many times. And I have been in danger from rivers, from thieves, from my own people *(the Jews)*, and from people who are not Jews. I have been in danger in cities, in places where no people live, and on the sea. And I have been in danger with people who say they are brothers, but are really not brothers. ²⁷I have done hard and tiring work, and many times I did not sleep. I have been hungry and thirsty. Many times I have been without food. I have been cold and without clothes. ²⁸And there are many other problems. One of these is the care I have for all the churches. I worry about them every day. ²⁹I feel weak every time another person is weak. I feel upset inside myself every time another person is led into sin.

³⁰If I must boast, then I will boast about the things that show that I am weak. ³¹God knows that I am not lying. He is the God and Father of the Lord Jesus Christ, and he is to be praised forever. ³²When I was in Damascus, the governor under King Aretas wanted to arrest me. So he put guards around the city. ³³But ₍some friends₎ put me in a basket. Then they put the basket through a hole in the wall and lowered me down. So I escaped from the governor.

A Special Blessing in Paul's Life

12¹I must continue to boast. It won't help, but I will talk now about visions* and revelations* from the Lord. ²I know a man in Christ who was taken up to the third heaven. This happened 14 years ago. I don't know if the man was in his body or out of his body. But God knows. ³⁻⁴And I know that this man was taken up to paradise.* I don't know if he was in his body or away from his body. But he heard things which he is not able to explain. He heard things that no man is allowed to tell. ⁵I will boast about a man like that. But I will not boast about myself. I will boast only about my weaknesses. ⁶But if I wanted to boast about myself, I would not be a fool. I would not be a fool, because I would be telling the truth. But I won't boast about myself. Why? Because I don't want people to think more of me than what they see me do or hear me say.

⁷But I must not become too proud of the wonderful things that were shown to me. So a painful problem* was given to me. That problem is an angel from Satan *(the devil)*. It is sent to beat me and keep me from being too proud. ⁸I begged the Lord three times to take this problem away from me. ⁹But the Lord said to me, "My grace *(kindness)* is enough for you. When you are weak, then my power is made perfect in you." So I am very happy to boast about my weaknesses. Then Christ's power can live in me. ¹⁰So I am happy when I have weaknesses. I am happy when people

---

angel of light Messenger from God. The devil fools people so that they don't see who he really is and think he is from God.
Hebrews, Israelites Other names for the Jewish people.
Abraham Most respected ancestor of the Jews.
visions Something like a dream God used to speak to people.
revelation(s) A revelation is an opening up (making known) of truth that was hidden.
paradise A place where good people go when they die.
painful problem Literally, "thorn in the flesh."

say bad things to me. I am happy when I have hard times. I am happy when people treat me badly. And I am happy when I have problems. All these things are for Christ. And I am happy with these things, because when I am weak, then I am truly strong.

Paul's Love for the Christians in Corinth

[11] I have been ₁talking like₁ a fool. But you made me do it. You people are the ones who should say good things about me. I am worth nothing, but those "great apostles" are not worth any more than I am! [12] When I was with you, I did the things that prove that I am an apostle*—I did signs, wonders, and miracles.* I did these things with much patience. [13] So you received everything that the other churches have received. Only one thing was different: I was not a burden to you. Forgive me for this!

[14] I am now ready to visit you the third time. And I will not be a burden to you. I don't want any of the things you own. I only want you. Children should not have to save things to give to their parents. Parents should save to give to their children. [15] So I am happy to give everything I have for you. I will even give myself for you. If I love you more, will you love me less?

[16] It is clear that I was not a burden to you. But ₁you think that₁ I was tricky and used lies to catch you. [17] Did I cheat you by using any of the men I sent to you? No! You know I didn't. [18] I asked Titus to go to you. And I sent our brother with him. Titus did not cheat you, did he? No! You know that Titus and I did the same things and with the same spirit.

[19] Do you think that we have been defending ourselves to you all this time? No. We say these things in Christ. And we say these things before God. You are our dear friends. And everything that we do is to make you stronger. [20] I do this because I am afraid that when I come you will not be what I want you to be. And I am afraid that I will not be what you want me to be. I am afraid that ₁in your group₁ there may be arguing, jealousy, anger, selfish fighting, evil talk, gossip, pride, and confusion. [21] I am afraid that when I come to you again, my God will make me humble before you. I may be saddened by many of you who have sinned. I may be saddened because those people have not changed their hearts to be sorry for their evil lives, for their sexual sins, and for the shameful things they have done.

Final Warnings and Greetings

13 [1] I will come to you again. This will be the third time. And remember, "For every complaint there must be two or three people to say that they know it is true."* [2] When I was with you the second time, I gave a warning to those people who had sinned. Now I am away from you, and I give a warning to all the other people ₁who have sinned₁: When I come to you again, I will punish you ₁for your sin₁. [3] You want proof that Christ is speaking through me. ₁My proof is that₁ Christ is not weak in ₁punishing₁ you. But Christ is powerful among you. [4] It is true that Christ was weak when he was killed on the cross. But he lives now by God's power. And it is true that we are weak in Christ. But for you we will be alive in Christ by God's power.

[5] Look closely at yourselves. Test yourselves to see if you are ₁living₁ in the faith. You know that Christ Jesus is in you. But if you fail the test *(are not living in the faith)*, then Christ is not living in you. [6] But I hope you will see that we have not failed the test. [7] We pray to God that you will not do anything wrong. It is not important that people see that we have passed the test. But it is important that you do what is right, even if ₁people think₁ that we have failed the test. [8] We cannot do things that are against the truth. We can only do things that are for the truth. [9] We are happy to be weak, if you are strong. And we pray that you will grow stronger and stronger. [10] I'm writing these things while I'm not with you. I'm writing so that when I come I will not have to use my power to punish you. The Lord gave me that power to make you stronger, not to destroy you.

[11] Now, brothers ₁and sisters₁, I say good-bye. Try to be perfect. Do the things I have asked you to do. Agree in your minds with each other, and live in peace. Then the God of love and peace will be with you.

[12] Give each other a holy kiss when you greet each other. [13] All God's holy people say hello to you.

[14] The grace *(kindness)* of the Lord Jesus Christ, the love of God, and the fellowship *(sharing)* of the Holy Spirit* be with you all.

---

apostle Person Jesus chose to be a special helper for telling the Good News to the world.

signs, wonders, miracles Powerful works from God that men cannot do without God's help.

"For every complaint ... true" Quote from Deut. 19:15.

Holy Spirit Called the Spirit of God, the Spirit of Christ, and the Comforter. Joined with God and Christ, he does God's work among people in the world.

Galatians

1 From Paul, an apostle.* I was not chosen to be an apostle by men. I was not sent from men. No! It was Jesus Christ and God the Father who made me an apostle. God is the One who raised Jesus from death. ²This letter is also from all the brothers [in Christ] who are with me.
To the churches *(groups of believers)* in Galatia.* ³I pray that God our Father and the Lord Jesus Christ will be good to you and give you peace. ⁴Jesus gave himself for our sins. Jesus did this to free us from this evil world we live in. This is what God the Father wanted. ⁵The glory belongs to God forever and ever. Amen.

There Is Only One True Gospel

⁶A short time ago God called you to follow him. He called you through his grace *(kindness)* that came through Christ. But now I am amazed at you people! You are already turning away and believing a different gospel. ⁷Really, there is no other true gospel.* But some people are confusing you. They want to change the gospel of Christ. ⁸We told you the true gospel. So if we ourselves or even an angel from heaven tells you a different gospel, he should be condemned! ⁹I said this before. Now I say it again: You have already accepted the true gospel. If any person tells you another way to be saved, he should be condemned!
¹⁰Now do you think I am trying to make people accept me? No! God is the One I am trying to please. Am I trying to please men? If I wanted to please men, I would not be a servant of Jesus Christ.

Paul's Authority Is from God

¹¹Brothers, I want you to know that the gospel* I preached to you was not made by men. ¹²I did not get the gospel from men. No man taught me the gospel. Jesus Christ gave it to me. He showed me the gospel that I should tell people.
¹³You have heard about my past life. I was in the Jewish religion. I persecuted the church of God very much. I tried to destroy the church *(believers)*. ¹⁴I was becoming a leader in the Jewish religion. I did better than most other Jews my own age. I tried harder than anyone else to follow the old rules. These rules were the customs we got from our ancestors.
¹⁵But God had special plans for me even before I was born. So God called me with his grace *(kindness)*. God wanted me ¹⁶to tell the Good News* about his Son *(Jesus)* to the non-Jewish people. So God showed *(taught)* me about his Son. When God called me, I did not get advice or help from any man. ¹⁷I did not go to see the apostles* in Jerusalem. These men were apostles before I was. But, without waiting, I went away to Arabia. Later I went back to the city of Damascus.
¹⁸Three years later I went to Jerusalem; I wanted to meet Peter.* I stayed with Peter 15 days. ¹⁹I met no other apostles*— only James, the brother of the Lord *(Jesus)*. ²⁰God knows that these things I write are not lies. ²¹Later I went to the areas of Syria and Cilicia.
²²In Judea the churches *(groups of believers)* in Christ had never met me before. ²³They had only heard this about me: "This man was persecuting us. But now he is telling people about the same faith that he once tried to destroy." ²⁴These believers praised God because of me.

---

apostle(s) The men Jesus chose to be his special helpers.
Galatia Probably the area where Paul began churches on his first missionary trip. See Acts 13 and 14.
gospel, Good News The news that God has made a way for people to have their sins forgiven and live with God.

Peter The text says "Cephas," the Jewish name for Peter. He was one of Jesus' twelve apostles.

GALATIANS 2:1–3:2

The Other Apostles Accepted Paul

2 After 14 years, I went to Jerusalem again. I went with Barnabas, and I took Titus with me. ²I went because God showed me that I should go. I went to those men who were the leaders [of the believers]. When we were alone, I told these men the gospel* I preach to the non-Jewish people. [I wanted these men to understand my work], so that my past work and the work I do now would not be wasted. ³⁻⁴Titus was with me. Titus is a Greek *(non-Jew)*. But these leaders did not force even Titus to be circumcised.* [We needed to talk about these problems], because some false brothers had come into our group secretly. They came in like spies to find out about the freedom we have in Christ Jesus. ⁵But we did not agree with anything those false brothers wanted! We wanted the truth of the gospel to continue for you.

⁶Those men who seemed to be important did not change the gospel* I preach. (It doesn't matter to me if they were "important" or not. To God all men are the same.) ⁷But these leaders saw that God had given me a special work, the same as Peter.* God gave Peter the work of telling the Good News* to the Jews. But God gave me the work of telling the Good News to the non-Jewish people. ⁸God gave Peter the power to work as an apostle.* Peter is an apostle for the Jewish people. God gave me the power to work as an apostle too. But I am an apostle for the people who are not Jews. ⁹James, Peter, and John seemed to be the leaders. They saw that God had given me this special grace *(gift)*. So they accepted Barnabas and me. Peter, James, and John said, "Paul and Barnabas, we agree that you should go to the people who are not Jews. We will go to the Jews." ¹⁰They asked us to do only one thing—to remember to help the poor people. And this was something that I really wanted to do.

Paul Shows that Peter Was Wrong

¹¹Peter came to Antioch. He did something that was not right. I was against Peter, because he was wrong. ¹²This is what happened: When Peter first came to Antioch, he ate and associated with the non-Jewish people. But then some Jewish men were sent from James. When these Jewish men came, Peter stopped eating with the non-Jewish people. Peter separated himself from the non-Jews. He was afraid of the Jews who believe that all non-Jewish people must be circumcised.* ¹³So Peter was a hypocrite.* The other Jewish believers joined with Peter. So they were hypocrites too. Even Barnabas was influenced by the things these Jewish believers did. ¹⁴I saw what these Jews did. They were not following the truth of the gospel.* So I spoke to Peter in a way that all the other Jews could hear what I said. This is what I said: "Peter, you are a Jew. But you don't live like a Jew. You live like the non-Jewish people. So why do you now force the non-Jewish people to live like Jews?"

¹⁵We Jews were not born as non-Jews and sinners. We were born as Jews. ¹⁶We know that a person is not made right with God by following the law.* No! It is trusting in Jesus Christ that makes a person right with God. So we have put our faith in Christ Jesus, because we wanted to be made right with God. And we are right with God because we trusted in Christ—not because we followed the law. [This is true] because no person can be made right with God by following the law.

¹⁷We Jews came to Christ to be made right with God. So it is clear that we were sinners too. Does this mean that Christ makes us sinners? No! ¹⁸But I would really be wrong to begin teaching again those things *(the law)* that I gave up. ¹⁹I stopped living for the law. It was the law that killed me. I died to the law so that I can now live for God. I *(my old life)* was killed on the cross with Christ. ²⁰So the life that I live now is not really me—it is Christ living in me. I still live in my body, but I live by faith in the Son of God *(Jesus)*. Jesus is the One who loved me. He gave himself to save me. ²¹This gift is from God, and it is very important to me. Why? Because if the law could make us right with God, then Christ did not have to die.

God's Blessing Comes Through Faith

3 You people in Galatia were told very clearly about the death of Jesus Christ on the cross. But you were very foolish. You let someone trick you. ²Tell me this one thing: How did you receive the [Holy] Spirit*? Did you receive the Spirit by

---

gospel, Good News The news that God has made a way for people to have their sins forgiven and live with God.
circumcised To have the foreskin cut off. This was done to every Jewish baby boy. It was a mark of the agreement God made with Abraham (Gen. 17:9-14).
Peter The text says, "Cephas," the Jewish name for Peter. He was one of Jesus' twelve apostles.
apostle(s) The men Jesus chose to be his special helpers.

hypocrite(s) Bad people that act like they are good.
law God's law. It is represented in the law of Moses.
Holy Spirit Called the Spirit of God, the Spirit of Christ, and the Comforter. Joined with God and Christ, he does God's work among people in the world.

following the law*? No! You received the Spirit because you heard ₗthe Good News₎* and believed it. ³You began ₗyour life in Christ₎ with the Spirit. Now do you try to continue it by your own power? That is foolish. ⁴You have experienced many things. Were all those experiences wasted? I hope they were not wasted! ⁵Does God give you the Spirit because you follow the law? No! Does God work miracles* among you because you follow the law? No! God gives you his Spirit and works miracles among you because you heard ₗthe Good News₎ and believed it.

⁶ₗThe Scriptures* say₎ the same thing about Abraham.* "Abraham believed God. And God accepted Abraham's faith. That made Abraham right with God."* ⁷So you should know that the true children of Abraham are the people who have faith. ⁸The Scriptures told what would happen in the future. These writings said that God would make the non-Jewish people right through their faith. This Good News* was told to Abraham before, like the Scripture says: "God will use you, ₗAbraham₎, to bless all the people on earth."* ⁹Abraham believed this. Because Abraham believed, he was blessed. ₗIt is the same today₎. All people who believe are blessed the same as Abraham was blessed. ¹⁰But people who depend on following the law ₗto make them right₎ are under a curse. Why? Because the Scriptures* say, "A person must do all the things that are written in the law.* If he does not always obey, then that person is under a curse!"* ¹¹So it is clear that no person can be made right with God by the law. ₗThe Scriptures say₎, "The person who is right with God by faith will live ₗforever₎."* ¹²The law does not use faith; ₗit uses a different way₎. The law says, "A person who wants to find life by following these things *(the law)* must do the things the law says."* ¹³The law put a curse on us. But Christ took away that curse. He changed places with us. Christ put himself under that curse. It is written in the Scriptures, "When a person's body is put *(hung)* on a tree,* that person is under a curse."* ¹⁴Christ did this so that God's blessing could be given to all people. God promised this blessing to Abraham. The blessing comes through Jesus Christ. ₗJesus died₎ so that we could have the ₗHoly₎ Spirit* that God promised. We receive this promise by believing.

The Law and the Promise

¹⁵Brothers ₗand sisters₎, let me give you an example: Think about an agreement that one person makes with another person. After that agreement is made official, no person can stop that agreement or add anything to it. And no person can ignore that agreement. ¹⁶God made promises to Abraham* and his Descendant.* God did not say, "and to your descendants." (That would mean many people. But God said, "and to your Descendant." That means only one person; that person is Christ.) ¹⁷This is what I mean: The agreement ₗthat God gave to Abraham₎ was made official long before the law* came. The law came 430 years later. So the law could not take away the agreement and change God's promise ₗto Abraham₎. ¹⁸Can following the law give us the things God promised? No! If we could receive those things by following the law, then it is not God's promise that brings us those things. But God freely gave ₗhis blessings₎ to Abraham through the promise God made.

¹⁹So what was the law* for? The law was given to show the wrong things people do. The law continued until the special Descendant of Abraham came. God's promise was about this Descendant *(Christ)*. The law was given through angels. The angels used ₗMoses₎ for a mediator* to give the law to men. ²⁰But a mediator is not needed when there is only one side, and God is only one.

The Purpose of the Law of Moses

²¹Does this mean that the law* is against God's promises? No! If there was a law that could give life to people, then we could be made right by following the law. ²²But this is not true, because

---

law God's law. It is represented in the law of Moses.
Good News, gospel The news that God has made a way for people to have their sins forgiven and live with God.
miracles Powerful works or great things done by God's power.
Scriptures Holy Writings—the Old Testament.
Abraham Most respected ancestor of the Jews.
"Abraham believed ... God" Quote from Gen. 15:6.
"God will use ... earth" Quote from Gen. 12:3.
law The law of Moses.
"A person ... curse!" Quote from Deut. 27:26.
"The person ... forever" Quote from Hab. 2:4.
"A person ... law says" Quote from Lev. 18:5.

put ... on a tree Deut. 21:22-23 says that when a person was killed for doing wrong, his body was hung on a tree to show shame. Paul means that the cross of Jesus was like that.
"When ... curse" Quote from Deut. 21:23.
Holy Spirit Called the Spirit of God, the Spirit of Christ, and the Comforter. Joined with God and Christ, he does God's work among people in the world.
Descendant Literally, "seed."
mediator A person who helps one person talk to or give something to another person.

the Scriptures* showed that all people are bound by sin. Why did the Scriptures do this? So that the promise would be given to people through faith. The promise is given to people who believe in Jesus Christ. ²³Before this faith came, we were all held prisoners by the law. We had no freedom until God showed us the way of faith that was coming. ²⁴So the law was our master until Christ came. After Christ came, we could be made right with God through faith. ²⁵Now the way of faith has come. So we don't live under the law now.

²⁶⁻²⁷You were all baptized* into Christ. So you were all clothed with Christ. This shows that you are all children of God through faith in Christ Jesus. ²⁸Now, in Christ, there is no difference between Jew and Greek *(non-Jew)*. There is no difference between slaves and free men. There is no difference between male and female. You are all the same in Christ Jesus. ²⁹You belong to Christ. So you are Abraham's* descendants. You get all of God's blessings because of the promise ₍that God made to Abraham₎.

4 I want to tell you this: While the heir* is still a child, he is no different from a slave. It doesn't matter that the heir owns everything. Why? ²Because while he is a child, he must obey the people who are chosen to care for him. But when the child reaches the age his father set, he is free. ³It is the same for us. We were once like children. We were slaves to the useless rules of this world. ⁴But when the right time came, God sent his Son. God's Son was born from a woman. God's Son lived under the law.* ⁵God did this so that he could buy the freedom of the people who were under the law. God's purpose was to make us his children.

⁶You are God's children. That is why God sent the Spirit of his Son into your hearts. The Spirit* cries out, "Father, dear Father."* ⁷So now you are not a slave like before. You are God's child. God will give you the things he promised, because you are his child.

Paul's Love for the Galatian Christians

⁸In the past you did not know God. You were slaves to gods that were not real. ⁹But now you know the true God. Really, it is God who knows you. So why do you turn back to those weak and useless rules you followed before? Do you want to be slaves to those things again? ¹⁰You still follow ₍the teaching of the law about₎ special days, months, seasons, and years. ¹¹I am afraid for you. I fear that my work for you has been wasted.

¹²Brothers ₍and sisters₎, I was like you; so please become like me. You were very good to me before. ¹³You remember why I came to you the first time. It was because I was sick. That was when I preached the Good News* to you. ¹⁴My sickness was a burden to you. But you did not show hate for me. You did not make me leave. You welcomed me like I was an angel from God. You accepted me like I was Jesus Christ himself! ¹⁵You were very happy then. Where is that joy now? I remember that ₍you wanted to do anything possible to help me₎. You would have taken out your own eyes and given them to me if that were possible. ¹⁶Now am I your enemy because I tell you the truth?

¹⁷Those people* are working hard to persuade you. But this is not good for you. Those people want to persuade you to turn against us. They want you to follow only them and no other people. ¹⁸It is good for people to show interest in you, but only if their purpose is good. This is always true. It is true when I am with you and when I am away. ¹⁹My little children, again I feel pain for you like a mother feels when she gives birth. I will feel this until you truly become like Christ. ²⁰I wish I could be with you now. Then maybe I could change the way I am talking to you. Now I don't know what to do about you.

The Example of Hagar and Sarah

²¹Some of you people still want to be under the law ₍of Moses₎. Tell me, do you know what the law says? ²²The Scriptures* say that Abraham* had two sons. The mother of one son was a slave woman. The mother of the other son was a free woman. ²³Abraham's son from the slave woman was born in the normal human way. But the son from the free woman was born because of the promise ₍God made to Abraham₎.

Scriptures Holy Writings—the Old Testament.
baptized A Greek word meaning to be immersed, dipped, or buried briefly under water.
Abraham Most respected ancestor of the Jews.
heir A person who will be given all that his father owned.
law The law of Moses.
Spirit The Holy Spirit. Called the Spirit of God, the Spirit of Christ, and the Comforter. Joined with God and Christ, he does God's work among people in the world.
Father, dear Father Literally, "Abba, Father." Jewish children called their fathers "Abba," meaning "Daddy."
Good News The news that God has made a way for people to have their sins forgiven and live with God.
Those people The false teachers who were bothering the believers in Galatia (Gal. 1:7).

²⁴This true story makes a picture for us. The two women are like the two agreements *(covenants)* between God and men. One agreement is ⌊the law that God made⌋ on Mount Sinai.* The people who are under this agreement are like slaves. The mother named Hagar is like that agreement. ²⁵So Hagar is like Mount Sinai in Arabia. She is a picture of the earthly ⌊Jewish⌋ city of Jerusalem. This city is a slave, and all its people *(the Jews)* are slaves ⌊to the law⌋. ²⁶But the heavenly Jerusalem that is above is like the free woman. This is our mother. ²⁷It is written in the Scriptures*:

"Be happy, woman who cannot have children!
You never gave birth.
Shout and cry with joy!
You never felt the pain of giving birth.
The woman who is alone* will have
    more children
than the woman who has a husband."

Isaiah 54:1

²⁸⁻²⁹One son ⌊of Abraham⌋* was born in the normal way. ⌊Abraham's⌋ other son *(Isaac)* was born by the power of the Spirit,* ⌊because of God's promise⌋. My brothers ⌊and sisters⌋, you are also children of promise like Isaac was then. The son who was born in the normal way treated the other son *(Isaac)* badly. It is the same today. ³⁰But what does the Scripture* say? "Throw out the slave woman and her son! The son of the free woman will receive everything his father has. But the son of the slave woman will receive nothing."* ³¹So, my brothers ⌊and sisters⌋, we are not children of the slave woman. We are children of the free woman.

Keep Your Freedom

5 We have freedom now. Christ made us free. So stand strong. Don't change and go back into the slavery ⌊of the law⌋. ²Listen! I am Paul. I tell you that if you ⌊go back to the law⌋ by being circumcised,* then Christ is no good for you. ³Again, I warn every man: If you allow yourselves to be circumcised, then you must follow all the law. ⁴If you try to be made right with God through the law, then your life with Christ is finished—you have left God's grace *(kindness)*. ⁵But we hope to be made right with God through faith. We are waiting for this with the Spirit's help. ⁶When a person is in Christ Jesus, it is not important if he is circumcised or not. The important thing is faith—the kind of faith that works through love.

⁷You were running a good race. You were obeying the truth. Who persuaded you to stop following the true way? ⁸That persuasion does not come from the One *(God)* who chose you. ⁹⌊Be careful!⌋ "Just a little yeast* makes the whole batch of dough rise."* ¹⁰I trust in the Lord that you will not believe those different ideas. Some person is confusing you with those ideas. That person will be punished, whoever he is.

¹¹My brothers ⌊and sisters⌋, I don't teach that people must be circumcised.* If I do teach circumcision,* then why am I still being persecuted? If I still taught that people must be circumcised, then my preaching about the cross would not be a problem. ¹²I wish those people who are bothering you would add castration* ⌊to their circumcision⌋.

¹³My brothers ⌊and sisters⌋, God called you to be free. But don't use your freedom as an excuse to do the things that please your sinful selves. But serve each other with love. ¹⁴The whole law* is made complete in this one command: "Love other people the same as you love yourself."* ¹⁵If you continue hurting each other and tearing each other apart, be careful! You will completely destroy each other.

The Spirit and Human Nature

¹⁶So I tell you: Live by following the Spirit.* Then you will not do the evil things your sinful selves want. ¹⁷Our sinful selves want things that are against the Spirit. The Spirit wants things that are against our sinful selves. These two different

---

Mount Sinai Mountain in Arabia where God gave his laws to Moses (Ex. 19 and 20).
Scripture(s) Holy Writings—the Old Testament.
woman ... alone This means her husband has left her.
Abraham Most respected ancestor of the Jews.
Spirit The Holy Spirit. Called the Spirit of God, the Spirit of Christ, and the Comforter. Joined with God and Christ, he does God's work among people in the world.
"Throw out ... nothing" Quote from Gen. 21:10.
circumcised To receive the mark of circumcision.
yeast Used here as a symbol of evil or bad influence.
"Just ... rise" A proverb meaning that a small thing (like a little wrong teaching) can make a big problem or that just one person can have a bad influence on the whole group.
circumcised, circumcision Cutting off the foreskin. This was done to every Jewish baby boy. It was a mark of the agreement God made with Abraham (Gen. 17:9-14).
castration To cut off part of the male sex organs. Paul uses this word because it is like "circumcision." Paul shows that he is very upset with the false teachers.
law God's law. It is represented in the law of Moses.
"Love other people ... yourself" Quote from Lev. 19:18.

things are against each other. So you don't do the things you really want to do. ¹⁸But if you let the Spirit lead you, then you are not under the law.*

¹⁹The wrong things our sinful self does are clear: being sexually unfaithful, not being pure, doing sexual sins, ²⁰worshiping false gods, doing witchcraft,* hating, making trouble, having jealousy, being very angry, being selfish, making people mad at each other, making divisions, ²¹having envy, being drunk, having wild and wasteful parties, and doing other things like this. I warn you now like I warned you before: The people who do these things will not be in God's kingdom. ²²But the Spirit* gives love, joy, peace, patience, kindness, goodness, faithfulness, ²³gentleness, self-control. There is no law that can say these things are wrong. ²⁴Those people who belong to Christ Jesus have crucified *(killed)* their own sinful selves. They have given up their old selfish feelings and the evil things they wanted to do. ²⁵We get our new life from the Spirit.* So we should follow the Spirit. ²⁶We must not be vain *(conceited)*. We must not make trouble with each other. And we must not be jealous of each other.

Help Each Other

6 Brothers ⌊and sisters⌋, a person in your group might do something wrong. You people who are spiritual should go to the person who is sinning. You should help to make him right again. You should do this in a gentle way. But be careful! You might be tempted to sin, too. ²Help each other with your troubles. When you do this, you truly obey the law of Christ. ³If a person thinks that he is important when he is really not important, he is only fooling himself. ⁴A person should not compare himself with other people. Each person should judge his own actions. Then he can be proud for what he himself has done. ⁵Each person must accept his own responsibility.

⁶The person who is learning the teaching of God should share all the good things he has with the person who is teaching him.

Life Is Like Planting a Field

⁷Don't be fooled: You cannot cheat God. A person harvests only the things he plants.* ⁸If a person plants *(lives)* to satisfy his sinful self, then his sinful self will bring him eternal death. But if a person plants to please the Spirit,* he will get eternal life from the Spirit. ⁹We must not become tired of doing good. We will receive our harvest ⌊of eternal life⌋ at the right time. We must not give up! ¹⁰When we have the opportunity to do good to any person, we should do it. But we should give special attention to the people that are in the family of believers *(the church)*.

Paul Ends His Letter

¹¹I am writing this myself. See what big letters I use. ¹²Some men are trying to force you to be circumcised.* They do these things so that other people *(the Jews)* will accept them. Those men fear that they will be persecuted if they follow only the cross of Christ* *(the gospel)*. ¹³Those men who are circumcised don't obey the law* themselves. But they want you to be circumcised. Then they can boast about what they forced you to do. ¹⁴I hope I will never boast about things like that. The cross *(death)* of our Lord Jesus Christ is my only reason for boasting. Through Jesus' death on the cross the world is dead* to me; and I am dead to the world. ¹⁵It is not important if a person is circumcised or not circumcised. The important thing is being the new people God has made. ¹⁶Peace and mercy to the people who follow this rule—to all of God's people.

¹⁷So don't give me any more trouble. I have scars on my body. These scars show* that I belong to Christ Jesus.

¹⁸My brothers ⌊and sisters⌋, I pray that the grace *(kindness)* of our Lord Jesus Christ will be with your spirits. Amen.

---

harvests only the things he plants Paul uses these words about farming to show that life is like a farmer planting a field. A farmer will get from the field only what he plants.
circumcised To have the foreskin cut off. This was done to every Jewish baby boy. It was a mark of the agreement God made with Abraham (Gen. 17:9-14).
cross of Christ Paul uses the cross as a picture of the gospel, the story of Christ's death to pay for men's sins.
law The law of Moses.
is dead Literally, "has been crucified."
These scars show Many times Paul was beaten by people who were against him because he was teaching about Christ. The scars were from these beatings.

---

law A law system, like the law of Moses.
witchcraft Using magic or the power of Satan.
Spirit The Holy Spirit. Called the Spirit of God, the Spirit of Christ, and the Comforter. Joined with God and Christ, he does God's work among people in the world.

Ephesians

1 From Paul, an apostle* of Christ Jesus. I am an apostle because that is what God wanted.

To God's holy people* living in Ephesus, believers in Christ Jesus.

²Grace *(kindness)* and peace to you from God our Father and the Lord Jesus Christ.

Spiritual Blessings in Christ

³Praise be to the God and Father of our Lord Jesus Christ. In Christ, God has given us every spiritual blessing in heaven. ⁴In Christ, God chose us before the world was made. God chose us in love to be his holy people*—people without blame before him. ⁵And before the world was made, God decided to make us his own children through Jesus Christ. That was what God wanted to do. That pleased him. ⁶And this brings praise to God because of his wonderful grace *(kindness)*. God gave that grace to us freely. He gave us that grace in [Christ], the One he loves. ⁷In Christ we are made free by Christ's blood *(death)*. We have forgiveness of sins because of God's rich grace. ⁸God gave us that grace fully and freely. God, with full wisdom and understanding, ⁹let us know his secret plan. This was what God wanted. And he planned to do it through Christ. ¹⁰God's goal was to finish his plan when the right time came. God planned that all things in heaven and on earth be joined together with Christ as the head.

¹¹In Christ we were chosen [to be God's people]. God had already planned for us to be his people, because that is what God wanted. And God is the One who makes everything agree with what he decides and wants. ¹²We are the first people who hoped in Christ. And we were chosen so that we would bring praise to God's glory. ¹³It is the same with you people. You heard the true teaching—the Good News* about your salvation. When you heard that Good News, you believed in Christ. And in Christ, God put his special mark on you by giving you the Holy Spirit* that he promised. ¹⁴That Holy Spirit is the guarantee that we will get the things God promised for his people. This will bring full freedom to those people who belong to God. The goal of all this is to bring praise to God's glory.

Paul's Prayer

¹⁵⁻¹⁶That is why I always remember you in my prayers and always thank God for you. I have always done this since the time I heard about your faith in the Lord Jesus and your love for all God's people. ¹⁷I always pray to the God of our Lord Jesus Christ—to the glorious Father. I pray that he will give you a spirit that will make you wise with the knowledge of God—the knowledge that he has shown you. ¹⁸I pray that you will have greater understanding in your heart. Then you will know the hope that God has chosen us to have. You will know that the blessings God has promised his holy people* are rich and glorious. ¹⁹And you will know that God's power is very great for us who believe. That power is the same as the great strength ²⁰that God used to raise Christ from death. God put Christ at his right side in the heavenly places. ²¹God made Christ more important than all rulers, authorities, powers, and kings. Christ is more important than anything that has power in this world or in the next world. ²²God put everything under Christ's power. And God gave him to be the head *(ruler)* over everything for the church. ²³The church is Christ's body. The church is filled with Christ. He makes everything complete in every way.

---

apostle Person Jesus chose to be a special helper for telling the Good News to the world.

holy people God's people are called holy because they are made pure through Christ, and they belong only to God.

Good News The news that God has made a way for people to have their sins forgiven and live with God.

Holy Spirit Called the Spirit of God, the Spirit of Christ, and the Comforter. Joined with God and Christ, he does God's work among people in the world.

From Death to Life

2 In the past your spiritual lives were dead because of your sins and the things you did wrong against God. ²Yes, in the past you lived doing those sins. You lived the way the world lives. You followed the ruler of the evil powers over the earth. That same spirit is now working in those people who refuse to obey God. ³In the past all of us lived like those people. We lived trying to please our sinful selves. We did all the things our bodies and minds wanted. We were ⌊evil⌋ people. We should have suffered God's anger because of the way we were. We were the same as all other people.

⁴But God's mercy is very great, and God loved us very much. ⁵We were ⌊spiritually⌋ dead. We were dead because of the things we did wrong against God. But God gave us new life with Christ. You have been saved by God's grace *(kindness)*. ⁶And God raised us up with Christ and gave us a seat with him in the heavenly places. God did this for us who are in Christ Jesus. ⁷God did this so that for all future time he could show the very great riches of his grace. God shows that grace by being kind to us in Christ Jesus. ⁸I mean that you are saved by grace. And you got that grace by believing. You did not save yourselves. It was a gift from God. ⁹No! You are not saved by the things you have done. So no person can boast ⌊that he saved himself⌋. ¹⁰God has made us what we are. In Christ Jesus, God made us new people so that we would do good things. God had already planned those good things for us. God had planned for us to live our lives doing those good things.

One in Christ

¹¹You were born non-Jews. You are the people the Jews call "uncircumcised.*" Those Jews who call you "uncircumcised" call themselves "circumcised.*" (Their circumcision* is only something they themselves do on their bodies.) ¹²Remember that in the past you were without Christ. You were not citizens of Israel.* And you did not have the agreements* with the promise ⌊that God made to his people⌋. You had no hope, and you did not know God. ¹³Yes, at one time you were far away ⌊from God⌋. But now in Christ Jesus you are brought near to him. You are brought near ⌊to God⌋ through the blood *(death)* of Christ. ¹⁴Because of Christ we now have peace. Christ made us both *(Jews and non-Jews)* one people. The Jews and the non-Jews were separated like there was a wall between them. They hated each other. But Christ broke down that wall of hate by ⌊giving⌋ his own body. ¹⁵The Jewish law had many commandments and rules. But Christ ended that law. Christ's purpose was to make the two groups of people *(Jew and non-Jew)* become one new people in him. By doing this Christ would make peace. ¹⁶Through the cross Christ ended the hate between the two groups. And after the two groups became one body, Christ wanted to bring them both back to God. Christ did this with his death on the cross. ¹⁷Christ came and preached peace to you people *(non-Jews)* who were far away ⌊from God⌋. And he preached peace to the people *(Jews)* who were near ⌊to God⌋. ¹⁸Yes, through Christ we all have the right to come to the Father in one Spirit.*

¹⁹So now you ⌊non-Jews⌋ are not visitors or strangers. Now you are citizens together with God's holy people.* You belong to God's family. ²⁰You believers are like a building that God owns. That building was built on the foundation that the apostles* and prophets* prepared. Christ himself is the most important stone* in that building. ²¹That whole building is joined together in Christ. And Christ makes it grow and become a holy temple* in the Lord. ²²And in Christ you people are being built together with the other people *(the Jews)*. You are being made into a place where God lives through the Spirit.*

---

agreements The agreements that God gave to his people, in the Old Testament.
Spirit The Holy Spirit. Called the Spirit of God, the Spirit of Christ, and the Comforter. Joined with God and Christ, he does God's work among people in the world.
holy people God's people are called holy because they are made pure through Christ, and they belong only to God.
apostles The men Jesus chose to be his special helpers.
prophets People who spoke for God.
most important stone Literally, "cornerstone." The first and most important rock in a building.
temple God's house—the place where God's people worship him. Here it means that God lives is his people.

---

uncircumcised People not having the mark of circumcision like the Jews have.
circumcised People having the mark of circumcision.
circumcision Cutting off the foreskin. This was done to every Jewish baby boy. It was a mark of the agreement God made with Abraham (Gen. 17:9-14).
Israel The Jewish nation (people).

Paul's Work for the Gentiles

3 So I *(Paul)* am a prisoner of Christ Jesus. I am a prisoner for you people who are not Jews. ²Surely you know that God gave me this work through his grace *(kindness)*. God gave me this work to help you. ³God let me know his secret plan. He showed it to me. I have already written a little about this. ⁴And if you read these things I wrote, then you can see that I truly understand the secret truth about the Christ. ⁵People who lived in other times were not told that secret truth. But now, through the Spirit,* God has shown that secret truth to his holy apostles* and prophets.* ⁶This is that secret truth: that the non-Jews will get the things God has for his people, the same as the Jews. The non-Jews are together with the Jews in the same body. And they share together in the promise that God made in Christ Jesus. The non-Jews have all these things because of the Good News.*

⁷By God's special gift of grace *(kindness)*, I became a servant to tell that Good News.* God gave me that grace by using his power. ⁸I am the least important of all of God's people. But God gave me this gift—to tell the non-Jewish people the Good News about the riches Christ has. Those riches are too great to understand fully. ⁹And God gave me the work of telling all people about the plan for God's secret truth. That secret truth has been hidden in God since the beginning of time. God is the One who created everything. ¹⁰God's purpose was that all the rulers and powers in the heavenly places will now know the many different ways God shows his wisdom. They will know this because of the church.* ¹¹This agrees with the plan God had since the beginning of time. God did what he planned. He did it through Christ Jesus our Lord. ¹²In Christ we can come before God with freedom and without fear. We can do this through faith in Christ. ¹³So I ask you not to become discouraged ₍and lose hope₎ because of the sufferings I am having for you. My sufferings bring honor to you.

The Love of Christ

¹⁴So I bow in prayer before the Father. ¹⁵Every family in heaven and on earth gets its true name from him. ¹⁶I ask the Father with his great glory to give you the power to be strong in your spirits. He will give you that strength through his Spirit.* ¹⁷I pray that Christ will live in your hearts because of your faith. I pray that your life will be strong in love and be built on love. ¹⁸And I pray that you and all God's holy people* will have the power to understand the greatness of Christ's love. I pray that you can understand how wide and how long and how high and how deep that love is. ¹⁹Christ's love is greater than any person can ever know. But I pray that you will be able to know that love. Then you can be filled with the fullness of God.

²⁰With God's power working in us, God can do much, much more than anything we can ask or think of. ²¹To him be glory in the church and in Christ Jesus for all time, forever and ever. Amen.

The Unity of the Body

4 I am in prison because I belong to the Lord. And God chose you to be his people. I tell you now to live the way God's people should live. ²Always be humble and gentle. Be patient and accept each other with love. ³You are joined together with peace through the Spirit.* Do all you can to continue together in this way. Let peace hold you together. ⁴There is one body and one Spirit. And God called you to have one hope. ⁵There is one Lord, one faith, and one baptism.* ⁶There is one God and Father of everything. He rules everything. He is everywhere and in everything.

⁷Christ gave each one of us a special gift. Each person received what Christ wanted to give that person. ⁸That is why it says ₍in the Scriptures₎,*

> "He went up high into the sky;
> he took prisoners with him,
> and he gave gifts to people."
>
> *Psalm 68:18*

⁹When it says, "He went up," what does it mean? It means that he first came down low to earth. ¹⁰So Jesus came down, and he is the same One who went up. He went up above all the sky. Christ did that to fill everything with himself.

Spirit The Holy Spirit. Called the Spirit of God, the Spirit of Christ, and the Comforter. Joined with God and Christ, he does God's work among people in the world.
apostles The men Jesus chose to be his special helpers for telling his Good News to the world.
prophets People who spoke for God.
Good News The news that God has made a way for people to have their sins forgiven and live with God.
church God's church—his people in Christ.

holy people God's people are called holy because they are made pure through Christ, and they belong only to God.
baptism A Greek word meaning to be immersed, dipped, or buried briefly under water.
Scriptures Holy Writings—the Old Testament.

11And that same Christ gave gifts to people—he made some people to be apostles,* some people to be prophets,* some people to go and tell the Good News,* and some people to have the work of caring for and teaching God's people. 12Christ gave those gifts to prepare God's holy people* for the work of serving. He gave those gifts to make the body of Christ stronger. 13₁This work must continue₁ until we are all joined together in the same faith and in the same knowledge about the Son of God. We must become like a mature *(perfect)* person—we must grow until we become like Christ and have all his perfection.

14Then we will not still be babies. We will not be people who change like a ship that the waves carry one way and then another. We will not be influenced *(changed)* by every new teaching we hear from men who try to fool us. Those men make plans and try any kind of trick to fool people into following the wrong way. 15No! We will speak the truth with love. We will grow to be like Christ in every way. Christ is the head ₁and we are the body₁. 16The whole body depends on Christ. And all the parts of the body are joined and held together. Each part of the body does its own work. And this makes the whole body grow and be strong with love.

The Way You Should Live

17For the Lord I tell you this. I warn you: Don't continue living like those people who don't believe. Their thoughts are worth nothing. 18Those people don't understand. They know nothing, because they refuse to listen. So they cannot have the life that God gives. 19They have lost their feeling of shame. And they use their lives for doing evil. More and more they want to do all kinds of bad things. 20But the things you learned in Christ were not like those bad things. 21I know that you heard about him. And you are in him, so you were taught the truth. Yes, the truth is in Jesus. 22You were taught to leave your old self— to stop living the evil way you lived before. That old self becomes worse and worse, because people are fooled by the evil things they want to do. 23But you were taught to be made new in your hearts. 24You were taught to become a new person. That new person is made to be like God—made to be truly good and holy.*

25So you must stop telling lies. You must always speak the truth to each other, because we all belong to each other in the same body. 26When you become angry, don't let that anger make you sin. And don't continue to be angry all day. 27Don't give the devil a way to defeat you. 28If a person is stealing, he must stop stealing. That person must start working. He must use his hands for doing something good. Then he will have something to share with those people who are poor.

29When you talk, don't say any bad things. But say things that people need—things that will help other people become stronger. Then the things you say will help the people who listen to you. 30And don't make the Holy Spirit* sad. The Spirit is God's proof that you belong to God. God gave you that Spirit to show that God will make you free at the right time. 31Never be bitter or angry or mad. Never shout angrily or say things to hurt other people. Never do anything evil. 32Be kind and loving to each other. Forgive each other the same as God forgave you in Christ.

5 You are God's children that he loves. So try to be like God. 2Live a life of love. Love other people the same as Christ loved us. Christ gave himself for us—he was a sweet-smelling offering and sacrifice* to God.

3But there must be no sexual sin among you. There must not be any kind of evil or selfishly wanting more and more. Why? Because those things are not right for God's holy people.* 4Also, there must be no evil talk among you. You must not speak foolishly or tell evil jokes. These things are not right for you. But you should be giving thanks to God. 5You can be sure of this: No person will have a place in the kingdom of Christ and of God if that person does sexual sins, or does evil things, or is a person who always wants more and more for himself. A person who always wants more and more for himself is serving a false god.

6Don't let any person fool you by telling you things that are not true. Those evil things make God angry with the people who don't obey. 7So don't do those things with them. 8In the past you were ₁full of₁ darkness *(sin)*, but now you are ₁full

---

apostles The men Jesus chose to be his special helpers.
prophets People who spoke for God to God's people.
Good News The news that God has made a way for people to have their sins forgiven and live with God.
holy people God's people are called holy because they are made pure through Christ, and they belong only to God.

holy A holy person is pure and belongs only to God.
Holy Spirit Called the Spirit of God, the Spirit of Christ, and the Comforter. Joined with God and Christ, he does God's work among people in the world.
sacrifice An offering or gift to God.

of₁ light *(goodness)* in the Lord. So live like children who belong to the light. ⁹Light brings every kind of goodness, right living, and truth. ¹⁰Try to learn what pleases the Lord. ¹¹Don't do the things that people in darkness do. Doing those things brings nothing good. But ₁do the good things to₁ show that those things in darkness are wrong. ¹²It is really very shameful to even talk about the things those people in darkness do in secret. ¹³But when we show that those things are wrong, the light makes all those things easy to see. ¹⁴And everything that is made easy to see can become light. This is why we say:

"Wake up, you sleeping person!
Rise from death,
and Christ will shine on you."

¹⁵So be very careful how you live. Don't live like people who are not wise. But live wisely. ¹⁶I mean that you should use every chance you have for doing good, because these are evil times. ¹⁷So don't be foolish with your lives. But learn what the Lord wants you to do. ¹⁸Don't be drunk with wine. That will ruin *(destroy)* you spiritually. But be filled with the Spirit.* ¹⁹Communicate to each other with psalms, hymns, and spiritual songs. Sing and make music in your hearts to the Lord. ²⁰Always give thanks to God the Father for everything. Give him thanks in the name of our Lord Jesus Christ.

Wives and Husbands

²¹Be willing to obey each other. Do this because you respect Christ.

²²Wives, be under the authority of *(obey)* your husbands, the same as the Lord. ²³The husband is the head of the wife, the same as Christ is the head of the church. The church is Christ's body— Christ is the Savior of the body. ²⁴The church is under the authority of Christ. So it is the same with you wives. You should be under the authority of your husbands in everything.

²⁵Husbands, love your wives the same as Christ loved the church. Christ died for the church. ²⁶He died to make the church holy.* Christ used the telling of the Good News* to make the church clean by washing it with water. ²⁷Christ died so that he could give the church to himself ₁like a bride₁ full of glory *(beauty)*. He died so that the church could be pure and without fault, with no evil or sin or any other thing wrong in the church. ²⁸And husbands should love their wives like that. They should love their wives like they love their own bodies. The man who loves his wife loves himself. ²⁹Why? Because no person ever hates his own body. Every person feeds and takes care of his body. And that is what Christ does for the church, ³⁰because we are parts of his body. ³¹₁The Scripture* says₁, "So a man will leave his father and mother and join his wife. And the two people will become one."* ³²That secret truth is very important—I am talking about Christ and the church. ³³But each one of you must love his wife like he loves himself. And a wife must respect her husband.

Children and Parents

6 Children, obey your parents the way the Lord wants. That is the right thing to do. ²The commandment says, "You must honor *(respect)* your father and mother."* That is the first commandment that has a promise with it. ³That promise is: "Then everything will be fine with you. And you will have a long life on the earth."*

⁴Fathers, don't make your children angry. But raise your children with the training and teaching of the Lord.

Slaves and Masters

⁵Slaves, obey your masters here on earth. Obey with fear and respect. And do that with a heart that is true, the same as you obey Christ. ⁶You must do more than just obey your masters to please them while they are watching you. You must obey them like you are obeying Christ. With all your heart you must do what God wants. ⁷Do your work, and be happy to do it. Work like you are serving the Lord, not like you are serving only men. ⁸Remember that the Lord will give every person a reward for doing good. Every person, slave or free, will get a reward for the good things he does.

⁹Masters, in the same way, be good to your slaves. Don't say things to scare them. You know

---

Spirit The Holy Spirit. Called the Spirit of God, the Spirit of Christ, and the Comforter. Joined with God and Christ, he does God's work among people in the world.

holy God's people are holy because they are made pure through Christ, and they belong only to God.

Good News The news that God has made a way for people to have their sins forgiven and live with God.

Scripture Part of the Holy Writings—Old Testament.

"So a man ... one" Quote from Gen. 2:24.

"You must ... mother" Quote from Ex. 20:12; Deut. 5:16.

"Then everything ... earth" Quote from Ex. 20:12; Deut. 5:16.

that the One who is your Master and their Master is in heaven. And that Master *(God)* judges every person the same.

Wear the Full Armor of God

[10] To end my letter I tell you, be strong in the Lord and in his great power. [11] Wear the full armor *(protection)* of God. Wear God's armor so that you can fight against the devil's evil tricks. [12] Our fight is not against people on earth. We are fighting against the rulers and authorities and the powers of this world's darkness. We are fighting against the spiritual powers of evil in the heavenly places. [13] That is why you need to get God's full armor. Then on the day of evil you will be able to stand strong. And when you have finished the whole fight, you will still be standing. [14] So stand strong, with the belt of truth tied around your waist. And on your chest wear the protection of right living. [15] And on your feet wear the Good News* of peace to help you stand strong. [16] And also use the shield of faith. With that you can stop all the burning arrows of the Evil One *(the devil)*. [17] Accept God's salvation to be your helmet. And take the sword of the Spirit*—that sword is the teaching of God. [18] Pray in the Spirit at all times. Pray with all kinds of prayers, and ask for everything you need. To do this you must always be ready. Never give up. Always pray for all God's people. [19] Also pray for me. Pray that when I speak, God will give me words so that I can tell the secret truth of the gospel* without fear. [20] I have the work of speaking for that gospel. I am doing that now, here in prison. Pray that when I preach that gospel I will speak without fear like I should.

Final Greetings

[21] I am sending to you Tychicus, our brother that we love. He is a faithful servant of the Lord's work. He will tell you everything that is happening with me. Then you will know how I am and what I am doing. [22] That is why I am sending him. I want you to know how we are. I am sending him to encourage you.

[23] Peace and love with faith to you from God the Father and the Lord Jesus Christ. [24] God's grace *(kindness)* to all of you who love our Lord Jesus Christ with love that never ends.

Good News, gospel The news that God has made a way for people to have their sins forgiven and live with God.

Spirit The Holy Spirit. Called the Spirit of God, the Spirit of Christ, and the Comforter. Joined with God and Christ, he does God's work among people in the world.

Philippians

1 From Paul and Timothy, servants of Jesus Christ.
To all of God's holy people* in Christ Jesus that live in Philippi. And to all your elders* and special helpers.*
²Grace *(kindness)* and peace to you from God our Father and the Lord Jesus Christ.

Paul's Prayer

³I thank God every time I remember you. ⁴And I always pray for all of you with joy. ⁵I thank God for the help you gave me while I told people the Good News.* You helped from the first day you believed until now. ⁶God began doing good things with you. And God is continuing that work in you. God will finish that work in you when Jesus Christ comes again. I am sure of that.
⁷And I know that I am right to think like this about all of you. I am sure because I have you in my heart—I feel very close to you. I feel close to you because all of you share in God's grace *(kindness)* with me. You share in God's grace with me while I am in prison, while I am defending the Good News,* and while I am proving the truth of the Good News. ⁸God knows that I want to see you very much. I love all of you with the love of Christ Jesus.
⁹This is my prayer for you:

> that your love will grow more and more;
> that you will have knowledge and understanding with your love;
> ¹⁰ that you will see the difference between good and bad and choose the good;
> that you will be pure and without wrong for the coming of Christ;
> ¹¹ that you will do many good things with the help of Christ to bring glory and praise to God.

Paul's Troubles Help the Lord's Work

¹²Brothers ₍and sisters₎, I want you to know that those bad things that happened to me have helped to spread the Good News.* ¹³It is clear why I am in prison. I am in prison because I am a believer in Christ. All the guards know this, and so do all the other people. ¹⁴I am still in prison, but most of the believers feel better about it now. And so they are much braver about telling people the message* ₍about Christ₎.
¹⁵Some people preach about Christ because they are jealous and bitter. Other people preach about Christ because they want to help. ¹⁶These people preach because they have love. They know that God gave me the work of defending the Good News.* ¹⁷But those other people preach about Christ because they are selfish. Their reason for preaching is wrong. They want to make trouble for me in prison.
¹⁸I don't care if they make trouble for me. The important thing is that they are telling people about Christ. I want them to tell people about Christ. They should do it for the right reasons. But I am happy even if they do it for false and wrong reasons. I am happy because they tell people about Christ, and I will continue to be happy. ¹⁹You are praying for me, and the Spirit* of Jesus Christ helps me. So I know that this trouble will bring my freedom. ²⁰The thing I want and hope for is that I will not fail Christ in anything. I hope

---

holy people God's people are called holy because they are made pure through Christ, and they belong only to God.
elders Men chosen to lead a church. Also called "overseers" and "pastors" (shepherds), they have the work of caring for God's people (Acts 20:28; Eph. 4:11).
special helpers Literally, "deacons," a Greek word meaning "servants." These people, it seems, were chosen to serve the church in special ways.
Good News, message The news that God has made a way for people to have their sins forgiven and live with God.

Spirit The Holy Spirit. Called the Spirit of God, the Spirit of Christ, and the Comforter. Joined with God and Christ, he does God's work among people in the world.

that I will have the courage now, like always, to show the greatness of Christ in my life here on earth. I want to do that if I die or if I live. ²¹I mean that to me the only important thing about living is Christ. And even death would be profit for me.* ²²If I continue living in the body, then I will be able to work for the Lord. But what would I choose—living or dying? I don't know. ²³It is hard to choose between living or dying. I want to leave this life and be with Christ. That is much better. ²⁴But you people need me here in my body. ²⁵I know that you need me. And so I know that I will stay with you. I will help you grow and have joy in your faith. ²⁶You will be very happy in Christ Jesus when I am with you again.

²⁷Be sure that you live in a way that fits the Good News* of Christ. Then if I come and visit you or if I am away from you, I will hear good things about you. I will hear that you continue strong with the same purpose and work together like a team for the faith (truth) that comes from the Good News. ²⁸And you will not be afraid of those people who are against you. All of these things are proof from God that you are being saved and that your enemies will be lost. ²⁹God gave you the honor of believing in Christ. But that is not all. God also gave you the honor of suffering for Christ. Both these things bring glory to Christ. ³⁰When I was with you, you saw the struggles I had ⌊with people who were against the gospel⌋. And now you hear about the struggles I am having. You yourselves are having the same kind of struggles.

Be United and Care for Each Other

2 Is there any way in Christ that I can ask you to do something? Does your love make you want to comfort me? Do we share together in the Spirit*? Do you have mercy and kindness? ²If you have these things, then I ask you to do something for me. This will make me very happy. I ask that all your minds be joined together by believing the same things. Be joined together in your love for each other. Live together by agreeing with each other and having the same goals. ³When you do things, don't let selfishness or pride be your guide. Be humble and give more honor to other people than to yourselves. ⁴Don't be interested only in your own life, but be interested in the lives of other people, too.

Learn from Christ to be Unselfish

⁵In your lives you must think and act like Christ Jesus.

⁶Christ himself was like God in everything. Christ was equal with God. But Christ did not think that being equal with God was something that he must keep.

⁷He gave up his place with God and agreed to be like a servant. He was born to be a man and became like a servant. ⁸And when he was living as a man, he humbled himself by being fully obedient to God. He obeyed even when that caused him to die. And he died on a cross.

⁹Christ obeyed God, so God raised Christ to the most important place. God made the name of Christ greater than every other name. ¹⁰God did this because he wants every person to bow for the name of Jesus. Every person in heaven, on the earth, and under the earth will bow. ¹¹Every person will confess (say), "Jesus Christ is Lord (Master)." When they say this, it will bring glory to God the Father.

Be the People God Wants You to Be

¹²My dear friends, you have always obeyed. You obeyed God when I was with you. It is even more important that you obey now while I am not with you. Without my help you must make sure that you get your salvation. Do this with respect and fear for God. ¹³Yes, God is working in you. God helps you want to do the things that please him. And he gives you the power to do these things.

¹⁴Do everything without complaining or arguing. ¹⁵Then you will be innocent and without anything wrong in you. You will be God's children without fault. But you are living with evil people all around you who have become very bad. Among those people you shine like lights in the dark world. ¹⁶You offer those people the teaching that gives life. So I can be happy when Christ comes again. I can be happy because my work was not wasted. I ran in the race and won.

¹⁷Your faith makes you give your lives as a sacrifice* in serving God. Maybe I will have to

---

death ... profit for me Paul says that death would be better, because death would bring him nearer to Christ.
Good News The news that God has made a way for people to have their sins forgiven and live with God.
Spirit The Holy Spirit. Called the Spirit of God, the Spirit of Christ, and the Comforter. Joined with God and Christ, he does God's work among people in the world.

sacrifice An offering or gift to God.

offer my own blood *(death)* with your sacrifice. But if that happens, I will be happy and full of joy with all of you. ¹⁸You also should be happy and full of joy with me.

News About Timothy and Epaphroditus

¹⁹I hope in the Lord Jesus to send Timothy to you soon. I will be happy to learn how you are. ²⁰I have no other person like Timothy. He truly cares for you. ²¹Other people are interested only in their own lives. They are not interested in the work of Christ Jesus. ²²You know the kind of person Timothy is. You know that he has served with me in telling the Good News* like a son serves his father. ²³I plan to send him to you quickly. I will send him when I know what will happen to me. ²⁴I am sure that the Lord will help me to come to you soon.

²⁵Epaphroditus is my brother in Christ. He works and serves with me in the army of Christ. When I needed help, you sent him to me. I think now that I must send him back to you. ²⁶I send him because he wants very much to see all of you He is worried because you heard that he was sick. ²⁷He was sick and was near death. But God helped him and me too, so that I would not have more sadness. ²⁸So I want very much to send him to you. When you see him, you can be happy. And I can stop worrying about you. ²⁹Welcome him in the Lord with much joy. Give honor to people like Epaphroditus. ³⁰He should be honored because he almost died for the work of Christ. He put his life in danger so that he could help me. This was help that you could not give me.

Christ Is More Important Than Anything

3 And now, my brothers ₍and sisters₎, be happy in the Lord. It is no trouble for me to write the same things to you again, and it will help you to be more ready. ²Be careful of those people who do evil. They are like dogs. They demand to cut* the body. ³But we are the people who are truly circumcised.* We worship *(serve)* God through his Spirit.* We are proud to be in Christ Jesus. And we don't trust in ourselves or anything we can do. ⁴Even if I am able to trust in myself, still I don't trust in myself. If any other person thinks that he has a reason to trust in himself, then he should know that I have a greater reason for trusting in myself. ⁵I was circumcised eight days after my birth. I am from the people of Israel* and the family group of Benjamin. I am a Hebrew *(Jew)*, and my parents were Hebrews. The law ₍of Moses₎ was very important to me. That is why I became a Pharisee.* ⁶I was so excited ₍about my Jewish religion₎ that I persecuted* the church *(the believers)*. No person could find fault with the way I always obeyed the law ₍of Moses₎. ⁷At one time all these things were important to me. But I decided that those things are worth nothing because of Christ. ⁸Not only those things, but now I think that all things are worth nothing compared with the greatness of knowing Christ Jesus my Lord. Because of Christ, I lost all those things ₍I thought were important₎. And now I know that all those things are worthless trash. This allows me to have Christ. ⁹It allows me to be in Christ. In Christ I am right with God, and this being right does not come from my following the law. It comes from God through faith. God uses my faith in Christ to make me right with him. ¹⁰All I want is to know Christ and the power of his rising from death. I want to share in Christ's sufferings and become like him in his death. ¹¹If I have those things, then I have hope that I myself will be raised from death.

Trying to Reach the Goal

¹²I don't mean that I am already exactly like God wants me to be. I have not yet reached that goal. But I continue trying to reach that goal and to make it mine. Christ wants me to do that. That is the reason Christ made me his. ¹³Brothers ₍and sisters₎, I know that I have not yet reached that goal. But there is one thing I always do: I forget the things that are past. I try as hard as I can to reach the goal that is before me. ¹⁴I keep trying to reach the goal and get the prize. That prize is mine

---

Good News The news that God has made a way for people to have their sins forgiven and live with God.

cut The word in Greek is like the word "circumcise," but it means "to cut completely off."

circumcised To have the foreskin cut off. This was a mark of the agreement God made with Abraham (Gen. 17:9-14). Paul uses the idea here in a spiritual sense of Christians who share in a new agreement God gave his people through Jesus.

Spirit The Holy Spirit. Called the Spirit of God, the Spirit of Christ, and the Comforter. Joined with God and Christ, he does God's work among people in the world.

Israel The Jewish nation (people).

Pharisee Pharisees were a Jewish religious group that claimed to follow carefully all Jewish laws and customs.

persecuted To hurt, bother, or do bad things to.

because God called me through Christ to the life above. ¹⁵All of us who have grown spiritually to be mature *(perfect)* should think this way too. And if there is any of these things you don't agree with, God will make it clear to you. ¹⁶But we should continue following the ₍truth₎ we already have.

¹⁷Brothers ₍and sisters₎, all of you should try to live like me. And copy those people who live the way we showed you. ¹⁸Many people live like enemies of the cross of Christ. I have often told you about these people. And it makes me cry to tell you about them now. ¹⁹The way these people live is leading them to destruction. They don't serve God. Those people live only to please themselves. They do shameful things, and they are proud of those things. They think only about earthly things. ²⁰But our homeland is in heaven. We are waiting for our Savior to come from heaven. Our Savior is the Lord Jesus Christ. ²¹He will change our humble bodies and make them like his own glorious body. Christ can do this by his power. With that power Christ is able to rule all things.

Some Things to Do

4 My dear brothers ₍and sisters₎, I love you and want to see you. You bring me joy and make me proud of you. Continue following the Lord like I have told you.

²I ask Euodia and Syntyche to agree in the Lord. ³And because you serve faithfully with me, my friend, I ask you to help these women do this. These women served with me in telling people the Good News.* They served together with Clement and the other people who worked with me. Their names are written in the book of life.*

⁴Be full of joy in the Lord always. I will say again, be full of joy.

⁵Let all people see that you are gentle and kind. The Lord is coming soon. ⁶Don't worry about anything. But pray and ask God for everything you need. And when you pray, always give thanks. ⁷And God's peace will keep your hearts and minds in Christ Jesus. That peace which God gives is so great that we cannot understand it.

⁸Brothers ₍and sisters₎, continue to think about the things that are good and worthy of praise. Think about the things that are true and honorable and right and pure and beautiful and respected. ⁹And do the things that you learned and received from me. Do the things I told you and the things you saw me do. And the God who gives peace will be with you.

Paul Thanks the Philippian Christians

¹⁰I am very happy in the Lord that you have shown your care for me again. You continued to care about me, but there was no way for you to show it. ¹¹I am telling you these things, but it is not because I need something. I have learned to be satisfied with the things I have and with everything that happens. ¹²I know how to live when I am poor. And I know how to live when I have plenty. I have learned the secret of being happy at any time in everything that happens. I have learned to be happy when I have enough to eat and when I don't have enough to eat. I have learned to be happy when I have all the things I need and when I don't have the things I need. ¹³I can do all things through Christ, because he gives me strength.

¹⁴But it was good that you helped me when I needed help. ¹⁵You people in Philippi remember when I first preached the Good News* there. When I left Macedonia, you were the only church that gave me help. ¹⁶Several times you sent me things I needed when I was in Thessalonica. ¹⁷Really, it is not that I want to get gifts from you. But I want you to have the good that comes ₍from giving₎. ¹⁸I have all the things I need. I have even more than I need. I have all I need because Epaphroditus brought your gift to me. Your gift is like a sweet-smelling sacrifice* offered to God. God accepts that sacrifice and it pleases him. ¹⁹My God is very rich with the glory of Christ Jesus. God will use his riches in Christ Jesus to give you everything you need. ²⁰Glory to our God and Father forever and ever. Amen.

²¹Say hello to each of God's people in Christ. God's people who are with me say hello to you. ²²All of God's people say hello to you. And those believers from Caesar's* palace say hello, too.

²³The grace *(kindness)* of the Lord Jesus Christ be with you all.

Good News The news that God has made a way for people to have their sins forgiven and live with God.

book of life God's book that has the names of all God's chosen people (Rev. 3:5; 21:27).

sacrifice An offering or gift to God.

Caesar The name or title given to the emperor (ruler) of Rome.

Colossians

1 From Paul, an apostle* of Christ Jesus. I am an apostle because that is what God wanted.
Also from Timothy, our brother ⌊in Christ⌋.

²To the holy* and faithful brothers ⌊and sisters⌋ in Christ that live in Colossae. Grace *(kindness)* and peace from God our Father.

³In our prayers we always thank God for you. God is the Father of our Lord Jesus Christ. ⁴We thank God because we have heard about the faith you have in Christ Jesus and the love you have for all of God's people. ⁵You have faith in Christ and love God's people because of the hope you have. You know that the things you hope for are saved for you in heaven. You learned about this hope when you heard the true teaching, the Good News* ⁶that was told to you. Everywhere in the world that Good News is bringing blessings and growing. This same thing has happened with you since the time you heard that Good News and understood the truth about the grace *(kindness)* of God. ⁷You learned about the grace of God from Epaphras. Epaphras works together with us, and we love him. He is a faithful servant of Christ for us. ⁸Epaphras also told us about the love you have from the ⌊Holy⌋ Spirit.*

⁹Since the day we heard these things about you, we have continued praying for you. We pray these things for you:

> that you will know fully the things
>   that God wants;
> that with your knowledge you will also have
>   great wisdom and understanding
>   in spiritual things;
> ¹⁰ that you will use these things to live in a way
>   that brings honor to the Lord
>   and pleases him in every way;
> that you will do all kinds of good things
>   and grow in the knowledge of God;
> ¹¹ that God will strengthen you with his
>   own great power;
> that God will strengthen you,
>   so that you will be patient
>   and not quit when troubles come.

Then you will be happy ¹²and give thanks to the Father. He has made you able to have the things he prepared for you. He has prepared these things for all his people who live in the light *(good)*. ¹³God made us free from the power of darkness *(evil)*. And he brought us into the kingdom of his dear Son *(Jesus)*. ¹⁴The Son paid for our sins. In him we have forgiveness of our sins.

When We Look at Christ, We See God

¹⁵No person can see God. But Jesus is exactly like God. Jesus is ruler over all the things that have been made. ¹⁶Through his power all things were made—things in heaven and on earth, things seen and not seen, all ⌊spiritual⌋ powers, authorities, lords, and rulers. All things were made through Christ and for Christ. ¹⁷Christ was there before anything was made. And all things continue because of him. ¹⁸Christ is the head of the body. (The body is the church.) Everything comes from him. And he is the Lord* who was raised from death. So in all things Jesus is most important. ¹⁹God was pleased for all of himself to live in Christ. ²⁰And through Christ, God was happy to bring all things back to himself again—things on earth and things in heaven. God made peace by using Christ's blood *(death)* on the cross.

---

apostle Person Jesus chose to be a special helper for telling the Good News to the world.
holy A holy person is pure and belongs only to God.
Good News The news that God has made a way for people to have their sins forgiven and live with God.
Holy Spirit Called the Spirit of God, the Spirit of Christ, and the Comforter. Joined with God and Christ, he does God's work among people in the world.

Lord Literally, "firstborn."

²¹At one time you were separated from God. You were God's enemies in your minds, because the evil things you did were against God. ²²But now Christ has made you God's friends again. Christ did this by his death while he was in his body. Christ did this so that he could bring you before God. He brings you before God as people who are holy,* with no wrong in you, and with nothing that God can judge you guilty of. ²³Christ will do this if you continue to believe in the Good News* you heard. You must continue strong and sure in your faith. You must not be moved away from the hope that Good News gave you. That same Good News has been told to all people in the world. I, Paul, help in telling that Good News.

Paul's Work for the Church

²⁴I am happy in my sufferings for you. There are many things that Christ must still suffer through his body, the church. I am accepting my part of these things that must be suffered. I accept these sufferings in my body. I suffer for his body, the church. ²⁵I became a servant of the church because God gave me a special work to do. This work helps you. My work is to tell fully the teaching of God. ²⁶This teaching is the secret truth that was hidden since the beginning of time. This truth was hidden from all people. But now that secret truth is made known to God's holy people.* ²⁷God decided to let his people know that rich and glorious truth. That great truth is for all people. That truth is Christ himself, who is in you. He is our only hope for glory. ²⁸So we continue to tell people about Christ. We use all wisdom to strengthen every person and teach every person. We are trying to bring all people before God as people who have grown to be spiritually mature *(perfect)* in Christ. ²⁹To do this, I work and struggle using the great strength that Christ gives me. That strength is working in my life.

2 I want you to know that I am trying very hard to help you. And I am trying to help the people in Laodicea and other people who have never seen me. ²I want them to be strengthened and joined together with love. I want them to be rich in the strong belief that comes from understanding. I mean I want you to know fully the secret truth that God has made known. That truth is Christ himself. ³In Christ all the treasures of wisdom and knowledge are safely kept.

⁴I tell you these things so that no person can fool you by telling you ideas that seem good, but are false. ⁵I am not there with you, but my heart is with you. I am happy to see your good lives and your strong faith in Christ.

Continue to Live in Christ

⁶You received Christ Jesus the Lord. So continue to live following him without changing anything. ⁷You must depend on Christ only. Life and strength come from him. You were taught the truth. You must continue to be sure of that true teaching. And always be thankful.

⁸Be sure that no person leads you away with false ideas and words that mean nothing. Those ideas come from people, not Christ. Those ideas are the worthless ideas of people in the world. ⁹All of God lives in Christ fully (even in Christ's life on earth). ¹⁰And in Christ you are full. You need nothing else. Christ is ruler over all rulers and powers.

¹¹In Christ you had a different kind of circumcision.* That circumcision was not done by the hands of any person. I mean you were made free from the power of your sinful self. That is the kind of circumcision Christ does. ¹²When you were baptized,* ₗyour old self died andⱼ you were buried with Christ. And in that baptism* you were raised up with Christ because of your faith in God's power. God's power was shown when he raised Christ from death. ¹³You were spiritually dead because of your sins and because you were not free from the power of your sinful self. But God made you alive with Christ. And God forgave all our sins. ¹⁴We owed a debt because we broke God's laws. That debt listed all the rules we failed to follow. But God forgave us of that debt. God took away that debt and nailed it to the cross. ¹⁵God defeated the spiritual rulers and powers. With the cross God won the victory and defeated those rulers and powers. God showed the world that they were powerless.

Don't Follow Rules That Men Make

¹⁶So don't let any person make rules for you about eating and drinking or about Jewish

---

holy A holy person is pure and belongs only to God.
Good News The news that God has made a way for people to have their sins forgiven and live with God.
holy people God's people are called holy because they are made pure through Christ, and they belong only to God.

circumcision Cutting off the foreskin. This was done to every Jewish baby boy. It was a mark of the agreement God made with Abraham (Gen. 17:9-14).
baptized, baptism A Greek word meaning to be immersed, dipped, or buried briefly under water.

customs (festivals, new moon celebrations,* or Sabbath days*). ¹⁷In the past, these things were like a shadow that showed what was coming. But the new things that were coming are found in Christ. ¹⁸Some people enjoy acting like they are humble and love to worship angels. Those people always talk about the visions* they have seen. Don't let those people say, "You don't do these things, so you are wrong." Those people are full of foolish pride because they think only the thoughts of people, ⌊not the thoughts of God⌋. ¹⁹Those people don't keep themselves under the control of the head *(Christ)*. The whole body depends on Christ. Because of Christ all the parts of the body care for each other and help each other. This strengthens the body and holds it together. And so the body grows in the way God wants.

²⁰You died with Christ and were made free from the worthless rules of the world. So why do you act like you still belong to this world? I mean, why do you follow rules like these: ²¹"Don't eat this," "Don't taste that," "Don't touch that thing"? ²²These rules are talking about earthly things that are gone after they are used. These rules are only commands and teachings from people, ⌊not God⌋. ²³These rules seem to be wise. But these rules are only part of a man-made religion that makes people pretend to be humble and makes them punish their bodies. But these rules don't help people to stop doing the evil things their sinful selves want to do.

Your New Life in Christ

3 You were raised from death with Christ. So try to get the things in heaven. I mean the things where Christ is, sitting at the right hand of God. ²Think only about the things in heaven, not the things on earth. ³Your old sinful self has died, and your new life is kept with Christ in God. ⁴Christ is your life. When he comes again, you will share in his glory.

⁵So put all evil things out of your life: sexual sinning, doing evil, letting evil thoughts control you, wanting things that are evil, and always selfishly wanting more and more. This wanting really means to live serving a false god. ⁶These things make God angry.* ⁷In your evil life in the past, you also did these things.

⁸But now put these things out of your life: anger, being very mad, doing or saying things to hurt other people, and using evil words when you talk. ⁹Don't lie to each other. Why? Because you have left your old sinful life and the things you did before. ¹⁰You have begun to live the new life. In your new life you are being made new. You are becoming like the One who made you. This new life brings you the true knowledge of God. ¹¹In the new life there is no difference between Greeks and Jews. There is no difference between people that are circumcised* and people that are not circumcised, or people that are from some foreign country, or Scythians.* There is no difference between slaves and free people. But Christ is in all those believers. And Christ is all that is important.

¹²God has chosen you and made you his holy people.* He loves you. So always do these things: Show mercy to people; be kind, humble, gentle, and patient. ¹³Don't be angry with each other, but forgive each other. If another person does something wrong against you, then forgive that person. Forgive other people because the Lord forgave you. ¹⁴Do all these things; but most important, love each other. Love is the thing that holds you all together in perfect unity. ¹⁵Let the peace that Christ gives control your thinking. You were all called together in one body* to have peace. Always be thankful. ¹⁶Let the teaching of Christ live inside you richly. Use all wisdom to teach and strengthen each other. Sing psalms, hymns, and spiritual songs with thankfulness in your hearts to God. ¹⁷Everything you say and everything you do should all be done for Jesus your Lord *(Master)*. And in all you do, give thanks to God the Father through Jesus.

Your New Life with Other People

¹⁸Wives, be under the authority of *(obey)* your husbands. This is the right thing to do in the Lord.

Verse 6 Some Greek copies add: "against the people who don't obey God."
circumcised To have the foreskin cut off. This was done to every Jewish baby boy. It was a mark of the agreement God made with Abraham (Gen. 17:9-14).
Scythians Known as wild and uncivilized people.
holy people God's people are called holy because they are made pure through Christ, and they belong only to God.
body Christ's spiritual body, meaning the church or his people.

---

new moon celebrations The first day of the Jewish month. This was a holy day for the Jewish people.
Sabbath days The Sabbath day (seventh day of the week) was a special religious day for the Jews.
visions A vision is something like a dream that God used to speak to people.

¹⁹Husbands, love your wives, and be gentle to them.
²⁰Children, obey your parents in all things. This pleases the Lord.
²¹Fathers, don't frustrate your children. If you are too hard to please, they might want to quit trying.
²²Servants, obey your masters in all things. Obey all the time, even when your masters can't see you. But it is not people you are really trying to please—you are trying to please the Lord⌋. So obey honestly because you respect the Lord. ²³In all the work you are doing, work the best you can. Work like you are working for the Lord, not for people. ²⁴Remember that you will receive your reward from the Lord. He will give you what he promised his people. You are serving the Lord Christ. ²⁵Remember that any person who does wrong will be punished for that wrong. And the Lord treats every person the same.

4 Masters, give the things that are good and fair to your servants. Remember that you have a Master in heaven.

Paul Tells Christians Some Things to Do

²Continue praying. And when you pray, always thank God. ³Also pray for us. Pray that God will give us an opportunity to tell people his message.* Pray that we can preach the secret truth that God has made known about Christ. I am in prison because I preach this truth. ⁴Pray that I can make this truth clear to people. That is what I should do.
⁵Be wise in the way you act with those people who are not believers. Use your time in the best way you can. ⁶When you talk, you should always be kind and wise. Then you will be able to answer every person in the way you should.

News About the People with Paul

⁷Tychicus is my dear brother in Christ. He is a faithful minister and servant with me in the Lord. He will tell you all the things that are happening to me. ⁸That is why I am sending him. I want you to know how we are. And I am sending him to encourage you. ⁹I am sending him with Onesimus. Onesimus is a faithful and dear brother in Christ. He is from your group. Tychicus and Onesimus will tell you all that has happened here.
¹⁰Aristarchus says hello. He is a prisoner with me. And Mark, the cousin of Barnabas, also says hello. (I have already told you what to do about Mark. If he comes, welcome him.) ¹¹Jesus (he is also called Justus) also says hello. These are the only Jewish believers who work with me for the kingdom of God. They have been a comfort to me.
¹²Epaphras also says hello. He is a servant of Jesus Christ. And he is from your group. He always prays for you. He prays that you will grow to be spiritually mature *(perfect)* and have everything that God wants for you. ¹³I know that he has worked hard for you and the people in Laodicea and in Hierapolis. ¹⁴Demas and our dear friend Luke, the doctor, say hello.
¹⁵Say hello to the brothers ⌊and sisters⌋ in Laodicea. And say hello to Nympha and to the church that meets in her house. ¹⁶After this letter is read to you, be sure that it is also read to the church in Laodicea. And you read the letter that I wrote to Laodicea. ¹⁷Tell Archippus, "Be sure to do the work the Lord gave you."
¹⁸I say hello and write this with my own hand—Paul. Remember me in prison. God's grace *(kindness)* be with you.

---

message The news that God has made a way for people to have their sins forgiven and live with God.

1 Thessalonians

1 From Paul, Silvanus, and Timothy.
To the church *(group of believers)* that lives in Thessalonica. That church is in God the Father and the Lord Jesus Christ. ⌊God's⌋ grace *(kindness)* and peace be yours.

The Life and Faith of the Thessalonians

²We always remember you when we pray and we thank God for all of you. ³When we pray to God our Father we always thank him for the things you have done because of your faith. And we thank him for the work you have done because of your love. And we thank him that you continue to be strong because of your hope in our Lord Jesus Christ. ⁴Brothers ⌊and sisters⌋, God loves you. And we know that he has chosen you to be his. ⁵We brought the Good News* to you. But we did not use only words. We brought that Good News with power. We brought it with the Holy Spirit* and with sure knowledge that it was true. Also you know how we lived when we were with you. We lived that way to help you. ⁶And you became like us and like the Lord. You suffered much, but still you accepted the teaching with joy. The Holy Spirit gave you that joy. ⁷You became an example to all the believers in Macedonia and Achaia. ⁸The Lord's teaching spread from you in Macedonia and Achaia. And also your faith in God has become known everywhere. So we don't need to say anything about your faith. ⁹People everywhere tell about the good way you accepted us when we were there with you. Those people tell about how you stopped worshiping idols* and changed to serve the living and true God. ¹⁰And you stopped worshiping idols to wait for God's Son to come from heaven. God raised that Son from death. He is Jesus, who saves us from God's angry judgment that is coming.

Paul's Work in Thessalonica

2 Brothers ⌊and sisters⌋, you know that our visit to you was not a failure. ²Before we came to you, we suffered in Philippi. People there said bad things against us. You know all about that. And when we came to you, many people were against us. But our God helped us to be brave. He helped us to tell you his Good News.* ³We encourage *(teach)* people. No person has fooled us. We are not evil. We are not trying to trick people. Those are not our reasons for doing what we do. ⁴No. We speak the Good News because God tested us and trusted us to tell the Good News. So when we speak, we are not trying to please men. We are trying to please God. God is the One who tests *(looks closely at)* our hearts. ⁵You know that we never tried to influence you by saying nice things about you. We were not trying to get your money. We had no selfishness to hide from you. God knows that this is true. ⁶We were not looking for praise from people. We were not looking for praise from you or any other people.

⁷We are apostles* of Christ. And so when we were with you, we could have used our authority to make you do things. But we were very gentle with you. We were like a mother caring for her little children. ⁸We loved you very much. So we were happy to share God's Good News* with you; but not only that—we were also happy to share even our own lives with you. ⁹Brothers ⌊and sisters⌋, I know that you remember how hard we worked. We worked night and day. We did not want to burden you ⌊by making you pay us⌋ while we preached God's Good News to you.

¹⁰When we were with you believers, we lived in a holy and right way, without fault. You know that this is true, and God knows that this is true. ¹¹You know that we treated each one of you like a father treats his own children. ¹²We strengthened

---

Good News The news that God has made a way for people to have their sins forgiven and live with God.
Holy Spirit Called the Spirit of God, the Spirit of Christ, and the Comforter. Joined with God and Christ, he does God's work among people in the world.
idols False gods made of wood or stone and worshiped by the non-Jewish people.

apostles The men Jesus chose to be his special helpers.

you, we comforted you, and we told you to live good lives for God. God calls you to his kingdom and glory. ¹³Also, we always thank God because of the way you accepted God's message *(teaching)*. You heard that message from us, and you accepted it like it was God's words, not the words of men. And it really is God's message *(teaching)*. And that message works in you people who believe. ¹⁴Brothers ₍and sisters₎, you are like God's churches *(people)* in Christ that are in Judea.* God's people in Judea suffered bad things from the other Jews there. And you suffered the same bad things from the people of your own country. ¹⁵Those Jews killed the Lord Jesus. And they killed the prophets.* And those Jews forced us to leave that country *(Judea)*. God is not pleased with them. They are against all people. ¹⁶Yes. They try to stop us from teaching the non-Jews. We teach the non-Jews so that the non-Jews can be saved. But those Jews are adding more and more sins to the sins they already have. The anger of God has fully come to them now.

Paul's Desire to Visit Them Again

¹⁷Brothers ₍and sisters₎, we were separated from you for a short time. (We were not there with you, but our thoughts were still with you.) We wanted very much to see you, and we tried very hard to do this. ¹⁸Yes, we wanted to come to you. Truly I, Paul, tried to come many times, but Satan *(the devil)* stopped us. ¹⁹You are our hope, our joy, and the crown we will be proud of when our Lord Jesus Christ comes. ²⁰Truly you are our joy and our glory.

3 We couldn't come to you, but it was very hard to wait any longer. ²So we decided to send Timothy to you and stay in Athens alone. Timothy is our brother. He works with us for God. He helps us tell people the Good News* about Christ. We sent Timothy to strengthen and comfort you in your faith. ³We sent Timothy so that none of you would be upset by these troubles we have now. You yourselves know that we must have these troubles. ⁴Even when we were with you, we told you that we all would have to suffer. And you know that it happened the way we said. ⁵This is why I sent ₍Timothy₎ to you, so that I could know about your faith. I sent him when I could not wait any more. I was afraid that the one *(the devil)* who tempts people might have defeated you with temptations. Then our hard work would have been wasted. ⁶But Timothy came back to us from you. He told us good news about your faith and love. Timothy told us that you always remember us in a good way. He told us that you want very much to see us again. And it is the same with us—we want very much to see you. ⁷So, brothers ₍and sisters₎, we are comforted about you, because of your faith. We have much trouble and suffering, but still we are comforted. ⁸Our life is really full if you stand strong in the Lord. ⁹We have so much joy before our God because of you! So we thank God for you. But we cannot thank him enough for all the joy we feel. ¹⁰We continue praying very strongly for you night and day. We pray that we can be there and see you again and give you all the things you need to make your faith strong.

¹¹We pray that our God and Father and our Lord Jesus will prepare the way for us to come to you. ¹²We pray that the Lord will make your love grow. We pray that he will give you more and more love for each other and for all people. We pray that you will love all people like we love you. ¹³We pray this so that your hearts will be made strong. Then you will be holy* and without fault before our God and Father when our Lord Jesus comes with all his holy people.

A Life That Pleases God

4 Brothers ₍and sisters₎, now I have some other things to tell you. We taught you how to live in a way that will please God. And you are living that way. Now we ask you and encourage you in the Lord Jesus to live that way more and more. ²You know the things we told you to do. We told you those things by the authority *(power)* of the Lord Jesus. ³God wants you to be holy.* He wants you to stay away from sexual sins. ⁴God wants each one of you to learn to control your own body. Use your body in a way that is holy and that gives honor to God.* ⁵Don't use your body for sexual sin. The people who don't know God use their bodies for that. ⁶None of you should do wrong to your brother ₍in Christ₎ or cheat him in this way. The Lord will punish people that do those things. We have already told you and warned you about that. ⁷God called us to be holy. He does not want us to live in sin. ⁸So the person

---

Judea The Jewish land where Jesus lived and taught and where the church first began.
prophets People who spoke for God.
Good News The news that God has made a way for people to have their sins forgiven and live with God.

holy A holy person is pure and belongs only to God.
God wants ... honor to God Or, "God wants each of you to learn to live with your wife in a way that is holy and that gives honor to God."

who refuses to obey this teaching is refusing to obey God, not man. And God is the One who gives us his Holy Spirit.*

⁹We don't need to write to you about having love for your brothers and sisters in Christ. God has already taught you to love each other. ¹⁰And truly you do love the brothers ₍and sisters₎ in all of Macedonia. Brothers ₍and sisters₎, now we encourage you to love them more and more.

¹¹Do all you can to live a peaceful life. Take care of your own business. Do your own work. We have already told you to do these things. ¹²If you do these things, then people who are not believers will respect the way you live. And you will not have to depend on other people for what you need.

The Lord's Coming

¹³Brothers ₍and sisters₎, we want you to know about those people who have died. We don't want you to be sad like other people—people who have no hope. ¹⁴We believe that Jesus died. But we believe that Jesus rose again. So, because of Jesus, God will bring together with Jesus those people who have died. ¹⁵What we tell you now is the Lord's own message. We who are living now might still be living when the Lord comes again. We who are living at that time will be with the Lord, but not before those people who have already died. ¹⁶The Lord himself will come down from heaven. There will be a loud command. That command will be given with the voice of the archangel* and with the trumpet call of God. And the people who have died and were in Christ will rise first. ¹⁷After that, we people who are still alive at that time will be gathered up with those people who have died. We will be taken up in the clouds and meet the Lord in the air. And we will be with the Lord forever. ¹⁸So comfort each other with these words.

Be Ready for the Lord's Coming

5 Now, brothers ₍and sisters₎, we don't need to write to you about times and dates. ²You know very well that the day the Lord comes again will be ₍a surprise₎ like a thief who comes at night. ³People will say, "We have peace and we are safe." At that time destruction will come to them quickly. Destruction will come like the pains of a woman who is having a baby. And those people will not escape. ⁴But you, brothers ₍and sisters₎, are not living in darkness *(sin)*. And so that day will not surprise you like a thief. ⁵You are all people who belong to the light *(goodness)*. You belong to the day. We don't belong to the night or to darkness *(evil)*. ⁶So we should not be like other people. We should not be sleeping. We should be awake and have self-control. ⁷People who sleep, sleep at night. People who get drunk, get drunk at night. ⁸But we belong to the day *(goodness)*, so we should control ourselves. We should wear faith and love to protect us. And the hope of salvation should be our helmet. ⁹God did not choose us to suffer his anger. God chose us to have salvation through our Lord Jesus Christ. ¹⁰Jesus died for us so that we can live together with him. It is not important if we are alive or dead ₍when Jesus comes₎. ¹¹So comfort each other and give each other strength. And you are doing that now.

Final Instructions and Greetings

¹²Now brothers ₍and sisters₎, we ask you to respect those people who work hard with you—those who lead you in the Lord and teach you. ¹³Respect those people with a very special love because of the work they do ₍with you₎.

Live in peace with each other. ¹⁴We ask you, brothers ₍and sisters₎, to warn those people who don't work. Encourage the people who are afraid. Help the people who are weak. Be patient with every person. ¹⁵Be sure that no person pays back wrong for wrong. But always try to do what is good for each other and for all people.

¹⁶Always be full of joy. ¹⁷Never stop praying. ¹⁸Give thanks ₍to God₎ at all times. That is what God wants for you in Christ Jesus.

¹⁹Don't stop the work of the ₍Holy₎ Spirit.* ²⁰Don't treat prophecy* like it is not important. ²¹But test everything. Keep what is good. ²²And stay away from everything that is evil.

²³We pray that God himself, the God of peace, will make you pure—belonging only to him. We pray that your whole self—spirit, soul, and body—will be kept safe and be without wrong when our Lord Jesus Christ comes. ²⁴The One *(God)* who calls you will do that for you. You can trust him.

²⁵Brothers ₍and sisters₎, please pray for us. ²⁶Give all the brothers ₍and sisters₎ a holy kiss when you meet. ²⁷I tell you by the authority *(power)* of the Lord to read this letter to all the brothers ₍and sisters₎. ²⁸The grace *(kindness)* of our Lord Jesus Christ be with you.

Holy Spirit Called the Spirit of God, the Spirit of Christ, and the Comforter. Joined with God and Christ, he does God's work among people in the world.

archangel The leader among God's angels.

prophecy Teaching by a person who speaks for God.

2 Thessalonians

1 From Paul, Silvanus, and Timothy.
To the church *(group of believers)* that lives in Thessalonica. You people are in God our Father and the Lord Jesus Christ.
²Grace *(kindness)* and peace to you from God the Father and the Lord Jesus Christ.
³We thank God for you always. And we should do that because that is right for us to do. It is right because your faith is growing more and more. And the love that every one of you has for each other is also growing. ⁴So we boast about you to the other churches of God. We tell the other churches the way you continue to be strong and have faith. You are being persecuted and are suffering many troubles, but you continue with strength and faith.

Paul Tells About God's Judgment

⁵That is proof that God is right in his judgment. God wants you to be worthy of his kingdom. Your suffering is for that kingdom. ⁶God will do what is right. He will give trouble to those people who trouble you. ⁷And God will give peace to you people who are troubled. And he will give peace to us. God will give us this help when the Lord Jesus is shown to us. Jesus will come from heaven with his powerful angels. ⁸He will come from heaven with burning fire to punish those people who don't know God. He will punish those people who don't obey the gospel* of our Lord Jesus Christ. ⁹Those people will be punished with a destruction that continues forever. They will not be allowed to be with the Lord. Those people will be kept away from his great power. ¹⁰This will happen on the day when the Lord ⌊Jesus⌋ comes. Jesus will come to receive glory with his holy people.* And all the people who have believed will be amazed at Jesus. You will be in that group of believers, because you believed the things we told you.

¹¹That is why we always pray for you. We ask our God to help you live the good way that he called you to live. The goodness you have makes you want to do good. And the faith you have makes you work. We pray that with his power God will help you do these things more and more. ¹²We pray all this so that the name of our Lord Jesus Christ can have glory in you. And you can have glory in him. That glory comes from the grace *(kindness)* of our God and the Lord Jesus Christ.

Evil Things Will Happen

2 Brothers ⌊and sisters⌋, we have something to say about the coming of our Lord Jesus Christ. We want to talk to you about that time when we will meet together with him. ²Don't become easily upset in your thinking or afraid if you hear that the day of the Lord has already come. Some person may say this in a prophecy* or in some message. Or you may read it in a letter that some person tells you came from us. ³Don't let any person fool you in any way. ⌊That day of the Lord will not come⌋ until the turning away ⌊from God⌋ happens. And ⌊that day will not come⌋ until the Man of Evil appears *(comes)*. That Man of Evil belongs to hell.* ⁴That Man of Evil is against anything called God or anything that people worship. And that Man of Evil puts himself above anything called God or anything that people worship. And that Man of Evil even goes into God's temple* and sits there. Then he says that he is God.

⁵I told you before that all these things would happen. Remember? ⁶And you know what is stopping that Man of Evil now. He is being stopped now so that he will appear *(come)* at the right time. ⁷The secret power of evil is already working in the world now. But there is one who is stopping that secret power of evil. And he will

---

gospel The Good News that God has made a way for people to have their sins forgiven and live with God.
holy people God's people are called holy because they are made pure through Christ, and they belong only to God.
prophecy Teaching by a person who speaks for God.
belongs to hell Literally, "{He is} the son of destruction."
temple Probably the special building in Jerusalem where God commanded the Jews to worship.

continue to stop it until he is removed *(taken out of the way).* ⁸Then that Man of Evil will appear *(come).* And the Lord Jesus will kill that Man of Evil with the breath that comes from his mouth. The Lord Jesus will destroy that Man of Evil with the glory of his coming. ⁹The Man of Evil will come by the power of Satan *(the devil).* He will have great power, and he will do many different false miracles, signs, and wonders.* ¹⁰The Man of Evil will use every kind of evil to trick those people who are lost. Those people are lost because they refused to love the truth. (If they loved the truth, they would be saved.) ¹¹But those people refused to love the truth, so God sends them something powerful that leads them away from the truth. God sends them that power so that they will believe something that is not true. ¹²So all those people who don't believe the truth will be condemned *(judged guilty).* They did not believe the truth, and they enjoyed doing evil things.

You Are Chosen for Salvation

¹³Brothers ⌊and sisters⌋, the Lord loves you. God chose you from the beginning to be saved. So we should always thank God for you. You are saved by the Spirit* making you holy* and by your faith *(believing)* in the truth. ¹⁴God called you to have that salvation. He called you by using the Good News* that we preached. God called you so that you can share in the glory of our Lord Jesus Christ. ¹⁵So, brothers ⌊and sisters⌋, stand strong and continue to believe the teachings we gave you. We taught you those things in our speaking and in our letter to you.

¹⁶⁻¹⁷We pray that the Lord Jesus Christ himself and God our Father will comfort you and strengthen you in every good thing you do and say. God loved us. Through his grace *(kindness)* he gave us a good hope and comfort that continues forever.

Pray for Us

3 And now, brothers ⌊and sisters⌋, pray for us. Pray that the Lord's teaching will continue to spread quickly. And pray that people will give honor to that teaching, the same as happened with you. ²And pray that we will be protected from bad and evil people. (Not all people believe ⌊in the Lord⌋.)

³But the Lord is faithful. He will give you strength and protect you from the Evil One *(the devil).* ⁴The Lord makes us feel sure that you are doing the things we told you. And we know that you will continue to do those things. ⁵We pray that the Lord will lead your hearts into God's love and Christ's patience.

The Obligation to Work

⁶Brothers ⌊and sisters⌋, by the authority *(power)* of our Lord Jesus Christ we command you to stay away from any believer who refuses to work. People who refuse to work are not following the teaching that we gave them. ⁷You yourselves know that you should live like we live. We were not lazy when we were with you. ⁸And when we ate another person's food, we always paid for it. We worked and worked so that we would not be trouble to any of you. We worked night and day. ⁹We had the right ⌊to ask you to help us⌋. But ⌊we worked to take care of ourselves⌋ so that we would be an example for you to follow. ¹⁰When we were with you, we gave you this rule: "If a person will not work, then he will not eat."

¹¹We hear that some people in your group refuse to work. They do nothing. And they make themselves busy in other people's lives. ¹²We command those people to stop bothering other people. We command them to work and earn their own food. In the Lord Jesus Christ we beg them to do this. ¹³Brothers ⌊and sisters⌋, never become tired of doing good.

¹⁴If any person does not obey what we tell you in this letter, then remember who that person is. Don't associate with that person. Then maybe that person will feel ashamed. ¹⁵But don't treat him like an enemy—warn him like a brother.

Final Words

¹⁶We pray that the Lord of peace will give you peace. We pray that he will give you peace at all times and in every way. The Lord be with all of you.

¹⁷I am Paul, and I end this letter now with my own writing. All my letters have this to show they are from me. This is the way I write.

¹⁸The grace *(kindness)* of our Lord Jesus Christ be with you all.

---

false miracles, signs, and wonders Here, this means amazing acts done by the devil's power.

Spirit The Holy Spirit. Called the Spirit of God, the Spirit of Christ, and the Comforter. Joined with God and Christ, he does God's work among people in the world.

holy God's people are called holy because they are made pure through Christ, and they belong only to God.

Good News The news that God has made a way for people to have their sins forgiven and live with God.

1 Timothy

1 From Paul, an apostle* of Christ Jesus. I am an apostle by the command of God our Savior and Christ Jesus our hope.

²To Timothy. You are ₁like₁ a true son to me because you believe.

Grace *(kindness)*, mercy, and peace from God the Father and Christ Jesus our Lord.

Warnings Against False Teachings

³I want you to stay in Ephesus. I asked you to do that when I went into Macedonia. Some people there in Ephesus are teaching false things. Stay there so that you can command those people not to teach those false things. ⁴Tell those people not to give their time to stories that are not true and to long lists of names in family histories. Those things only bring arguments. Those things don't help God's work. God's work is done by faith. ⁵The goal of this command is for people to have love. To have this love people must have a pure heart, they must do what they know is right, and they must have true faith. ⁶Some people have not done these things. They have wandered away, and now they talk about things that are worth nothing. ⁷Those people want to be teachers of the law.* But they don't know what they are talking about. They don't even understand the things that they say they are sure about.

⁸We know that the law* is good if a man uses it right. ⁹We also know that the law is not made for good men. The law is made for people who are against the law and for people who refuse to follow the law. The law is for people who are against God and are sinful, people who are not holy and have no religion, people who kill their fathers and mothers, murderers, ¹⁰people who do sexual sins, homosexuals, people who sell slaves, people who tell lies, people who speak falsely, and people who do anything that is against the true teaching ₁of God₁. ¹¹That teaching is part of the Good News* that God gave me to tell. That glorious Good News is from the blessed God.

Thanks for God's Mercy

¹²I thank Christ Jesus our Lord because he trusted me and gave me this work of serving him. He gives me strength. ¹³In the past I spoke against Christ and persecuted him and did things to hurt him. But God gave me mercy because I did not know what I was doing. I did those things when I did not believe. ¹⁴But the grace *(kindness)* of our Lord was fully given to me. And with that grace came the faith and love that are in Christ Jesus.

¹⁵What I say is true, and you should fully accept it: Christ Jesus came into the world to save sinners. And I am the worst of those sinners. ¹⁶But I was given mercy. I was given mercy so that in me Christ Jesus could show that he has patience without limit. Christ showed his patience with me, the worst of all sinners. Christ wanted me to be an example for those people who would believe in him and have life forever. ¹⁷Honor and glory to the King that rules forever. He cannot be destroyed and cannot be seen. Honor and glory forever and ever to the only God. Amen.

¹⁸Timothy, you are ₁like₁ a son to me. I am giving you a command. This command agrees with the prophecies* that were told about you in the past. I tell you these things so that you can follow those prophecies and fight the good fight ₁of faith₁. ¹⁹Continue to have faith and do what you know is right. Some people have not done this. Their faith has been destroyed. ²⁰Hymenaeus and Alexander are men who have done that. I have given those men to Satan *(the devil)* so that they will learn not to speak against God.

---

apostle   Person Jesus chose to be a special helper for telling the Good News to the world.

law   Probably the Jewish law that God gave to Moses on Mount Sinai. (Read Ex. 19 and 20.)

Good News   The news that God has made a way for people to have their sins forgiven and live with God.

prophecies   Things that prophets said about Timothy's life before those things happened.

Some Rules for Men and Women

2 First, I tell you to pray for all people. Talk to God about all people. Ask him for the things people need, and be thankful to him. ²You should pray for kings and for all people who have authority *(power)*. Pray for those leaders so that we can have quiet and peaceful lives—lives full of worship and respect for God. ³This is good and it pleases God our Savior. ⁴God wants all people to be saved. And he wants all people to know the truth. ⁵There is only one God. And there is only one way that people can reach God. That way is through Jesus Christ, who is also a man. ⁶Jesus gave himself to pay for ⌊the sins of⌋ all people. Jesus is proof ⌊that God wants all people to be saved⌋. And he came at the right time. ⁷That is why I was chosen to tell the Good News.* That is why I was chosen to be an apostle.* (I am telling the truth. I am not lying.) I was chosen to be a teacher of the non-Jewish people. I teach them to believe and know the truth.

⁸I want men everywhere to pray. These men who lift up their hands in prayer must be holy.* They must not be men who become angry and have arguments.

⁹I also want women to wear clothes that are right for them. Women should dress with respect and right thinking. They should not use fancy braided hair or gold or pearls or expensive clothes to make themselves beautiful. ¹⁰But they should make themselves beautiful by doing good things. Women who say they worship God should make themselves beautiful in that way.

¹¹A woman should learn while listening quietly and while being fully ready to obey. ¹²I don't allow a woman to teach a man. And I don't allow a woman to have authority *(power)* over a man. The woman must continue in quietness. Why? ¹³Because Adam was made first. Eve was made later. ¹⁴Also, Adam was not the one who was tricked ⌊by the devil⌋.* It was the woman who was tricked and became a sinner. ¹⁵But women will be saved in their work of having children. They will be saved if they continue in faith, love, and holiness, and control themselves in the right way.

Leaders in the Church

3 What I say is true: If any person is trying hard to become an elder,* that person is wanting a good work. ²An elder must be good enough that people cannot rightly criticize him. He must have only one wife. An elder must have self-control and be wise. He must be respected by other people. He must be ready to help people by accepting them into his home. He must be a good teacher. ³He must not drink too much wine, and he must not be a person who likes to fight. He must be gentle and peaceful. He must not be a person who loves money. ⁴He must be a good leader of his own family. This means that his children obey him with full respect. ⁵(If a man does not know how to be a leader over his own family, then he will not be able to take care of God's church.) ⁶But an elder* must not be a new believer. It might make a new believer be too proud of himself ⌊if he were made an elder⌋. Then he would be judged *(condemned)* for his pride the same as the devil was. ⁷An elder must also have the respect of people who are not in the church. Then he will not be criticized by other people and be caught in the devil's trap.

Helpers in the Church

⁸In the same way, the men who serve as special helpers* must be men that people can respect. These men must not say things they don't mean, and they must not use their time drinking too much wine. They must not be men who are always trying to get rich by cheating others. ⁹They must follow the faith *(truth)* that God made known to us and always do what they know is right. ¹⁰You should test those men first. If you find nothing wrong in them, then they can serve as special helpers. ¹¹In the same way, the women* must have the respect of other people. They must not be women who talk evil about other people. They must have self-control and be women who can be trusted in everything. ¹²The men who serve as special helpers must have only one wife. They must be good leaders of their children and their

---

Good News The news that God has made a way for people to have their sins forgiven and live with God.

apostle Person Jesus chose to be a special helper for telling the Good News to the world.

holy A holy person is pure and belongs only to God.

Adam was not ... devil The devil tricked Eve, and Eve caused Adam to sin (Gen. 3:1-13).

elder Literally, "overseer," one of the men chosen to lead a church. Also called "pastors" (shepherds), they have the work of caring for God's people (Acts 20:28).

men who serve as special helpers Literally, "deacons," a Greek word meaning "servants." These people, it seems, were chosen to serve the church in special ways.

women This can mean women who serve as special helpers, or it might mean the wives of the special helpers.

own families. ¹³Those persons who serve in a good way are making an honorable place for themselves. And they will feel very sure of their faith in Christ Jesus.

The Secret of Our Life

¹⁴I hope I can come to you soon. But I am writing these things to you now. ¹⁵Then, even if I cannot come soon, you will know about the things that people must do in the family* of God. That family is the church of the living God. And God's church is the support and foundation of the truth. ¹⁶Without any doubt, the secret of our life of worship is great:

> He *(Christ)* was shown to us in a human body;
> the Spirit* proved that he was right;
> he was seen by angels.
> ⌊The Good News* about him⌋ was preached to the nations *(non-Jews)*;
> people in the world believed in him;
> he was taken up to heaven in glory.

A Warning About False Teachers

4 The Holy Spirit* clearly says that in the later times some people will stop believing the ⌊true⌋ faith *(teaching)*. Those people will obey spirits that tell lies. And those people will follow the teachings of demons.* ²Those teachings come through men who tell lies and trick people. Those men cannot see what is right and what is wrong. It is like their understanding was destroyed by a hot iron. ³Those men tell people that it is wrong to marry. And those men tell people that there are some foods that people must not eat. But God made those foods. And those people who believe and who know the truth can eat those foods with thanks. ⁴Everything that God made is good. Nothing that God made should be refused if it is accepted with thanks to God. ⁵Everything God made is made holy by what God has said and by prayer.

Be A Good Servant of Christ Jesus

⁶Tell these things to the brothers ⌊and sisters⌋ there. This will show that you are a good servant of Christ Jesus. You will show that you are made strong by the words of faith and good teaching that you have followed. ⁷People tell silly stories that don't agree with God's truth. Don't follow ⌊what⌋ those stories ⌊teach⌋. But teach yourself to truly serve God. ⁸Training *(teaching)* your body helps you in some ways. But serving God helps you in every way. Serving God brings you blessings in this life and in the future life too. ⁹What I say is true, and you should fully accept it. ¹⁰This is why we work and struggle: We hope in the living God. He is the Savior of all people. And in a special way, he is the Savior of all those people who believe in him.

¹¹Command and teach these things. ¹²You are young, but don't let any person treat you like you are not important. Be an example to show the believers how they should live. Show them with the things you say, with the way you live, with your love, with your faith, and with your pure life. ¹³Continue to read the Scriptures* to the people, strengthen them, and teach them. Do those things until I come. ¹⁴Remember to use the gift that you have. That gift was given to you through a prophecy* when the group of elders* put their hands on* you. ¹⁵Continue to do those things. Give your life to doing those things. Then all the people can see that your work is progressing *(continuing)*. ¹⁶Be careful in your life and in your teaching. Continue to live and teach rightly. Then you will save yourself and those people who listen to your teaching.

Some Rules for Living with Other People

5 Don't speak angrily to an older man. But talk to him like he was your father. Treat the younger men like brothers. ²Treat the older women like mothers. And treat the younger women like sisters. Always treat them in a good way.

---

family Literally, "house." This could mean that God's people are like God's temple.
Spirit, Holy Spirit Called the Spirit of God, the Spirit of Christ, and the Comforter. Joined with God and Christ, he does God's work among people in the world.
Good News The news that God has made a way for people to have their sins forgiven and live with God.
demons Demons are evil spirits from the devil.

Scriptures The Holy Writings—God's message to people through the writers of the Bible.
prophecy Something said about Timothy's life before that thing happened.
elders A group of men chosen to lead a church. Also called "overseers" and "pastors" (shepherds), they have the work of caring for God's people (Acts 20:28).
put their hands on A sign to show that Timothy was being given a special work of God.

³Give honor to *(take care of)* widows* who are really alone. ⁴But if a widow has children or grandchildren, the first thing they need to learn is this: to show respect for their own family ⌊by helping their parents⌋. When they do this, they will be repaying their parents or grandparents. That pleases God. ⁵If a widow is really alone and without help, then she hopes in God ⌊to take care of her⌋. That woman prays all the time, night and day. She asks God for help. ⁶But the widow who uses her life to please herself is really dead while she is still living. ⁷Tell the believers there to do these things *(take care of their family)* so that no other person can say they are doing wrong. ⁸A person should take care of all his own people. Most important, he should take care of his own family. If a person does not do that, then he does not accept the ⌊true⌋ faith *(teaching)*. That person is worse than a person who does not believe.

⁹To be added to your list of widows,* a woman must be 60 years old or older. She must have been faithful to her husband. ¹⁰She must be known as a woman who has done good things. I mean good things like raising her children, accepting visitors in her home, washing the feet of God's people, helping people in trouble, and using her life to do all kinds of good things.

¹¹But don't put younger widows* on that list. When they give themselves to Christ, they are often pulled away from him by their strong physical needs. Then they want to marry again. ¹²And they will be judged for that. They will be judged for not doing what they first promised to do. ¹³Also, those younger widows begin to waste their time going from house to house. They also begin to gossip and be busy with other people's lives. They say things that they should not say. ¹⁴So I want the younger widows to marry, have children, and take care of their homes. If they do this, then our enemy will not have any reason to criticize them. ¹⁵But some of the younger widows have already turned away to follow Satan *(the devil)*.

¹⁶If any woman who is a believer has widows* in her family, then she should care for them herself. The church should not be troubled to care for them. Then the church will be able to care for the widows who have no living family.

¹⁷The elders* who lead the church in a good way should receive great honor. Those elders who work by speaking and teaching are the men who should have that great honor. ¹⁸Why? Because the Scripture* says, "When a work animal is doing the work of separating grain, don't cover its mouth ⌊and stop it from eating the grain⌋."* And the Scripture also says, "A worker should be given his pay."*

¹⁹Don't listen to a person who accuses an elder.* You should listen to that person only if there are two or three other people who can say what the elder did wrong. ²⁰Tell those people who sin that they are wrong. Do this in front of the whole church. In that way the others will have a warning.

²¹Before God and Jesus Christ and the chosen angels I command you to do these things. But don't judge people before you know the truth. And do these things equally to every person.

²²Think carefully before you put your hands on* any person, ⌊making him an elder⌋. Don't share in the sins of other people. Keep yourself pure.

²³Timothy, you have been drinking only water. Stop doing that, and drink a little wine. This will help your stomach, and you will not be sick so often.

²⁴The sins of some people are easy to see. Their sins show that they will be judged. But the sins of some other people are seen only later. ²⁵It is the same with the good things people do. The good things people do are easy to see. But even when those good things are not easy to see, they cannot stay hidden.

6 All people who are slaves should show full respect to their masters. When they do that, then God's name and our teaching will not be criticized. ²Some slaves have masters who are believers. So those slaves and those masters are brothers. But the slaves should not show them any less respect. No! Those slaves should serve those believing masters even better. Why? Because those slaves are helping believers that they love.

---

widows A widow is a woman whose husband has died.
elder(s) An elder is one of a group of men chosen to lead a church. Also called "overseers" and "pastors" (shepherds), they have the work of caring for God's people (Acts 20:28).
Scripture Part of the Holy Writings—God's message to people through the writers of the Bible.
"When a work animal ... grain" Quote from Deut. 25:4.
"A worker should be given his pay" Quote from Lk. 10:7.
put your hands on A sign of giving authority or power to another person.

False Teaching and True Riches

You must teach and tell the people to do these things. ³Some people will teach things that are false. Those people will not agree with the true teaching of our Lord Jesus Christ. And they will not accept the teaching that agrees with the true way to serve God. ⁴That person who teaches falsely is full of pride and understands nothing. That person is sick with a love for arguing and fighting about words. And that brings jealousy, making trouble, insults, and evil mistrust. ⁵And also that brings arguments from men who have evil minds. Those people have lost the truth. They think that serving God is a way to get rich.

⁶It is true that serving God makes a person very rich, if that person is satisfied with what he has. ⁷When we came into the world, we brought nothing. And when we die, we can take nothing out. ⁸So, if we have food and clothes, we will be satisfied with that. ⁹People who want to become rich bring temptations to themselves. They are caught in a trap. They begin to want many foolish things that will hurt them. Those things ruin and destroy people. ¹⁰The love of money causes all kinds of evil. Some people have left the ⌊true⌋ faith *(teaching)* because they want to get more and more money. But they have caused themselves to be very, very sad.

Some Things You Should Remember

¹¹But you are a man of God. So you should stay away from all those things. Try to live in the right way, serve God, have faith, love, patience, and gentleness. ¹²Keeping your faith is like running a race. Try as hard as you can to win that race. Be sure you get that life that continues forever. You were called to have that life. And you confessed the great truth ⌊about Christ⌋ in a way that many people heard you. ¹³Before God and Christ Jesus I give you a command. Christ Jesus is the One that confessed that same great truth when he stood before Pontius Pilate. And God is the One that gives life to everything. Now I tell you: ¹⁴Do the things you were commanded to do. Do those things without wrong or blame until the time when our Lord Jesus Christ comes again. ¹⁵God will make that happen at the right time. God is the blessed and only Ruler. God is the King of all kings and the Lord of all lords *(rulers)*. ¹⁶God is the only One who never dies. God lives in light so bright that men cannot go near it. No person has ever seen God. No person is able to see God. Honor to God and power forever. Amen.

¹⁷Give this command to the people who are rich with the things this world has. Tell them not to be proud. Tell those rich people to hope in God, not their money. Money cannot be trusted. But God takes care of us richly. He gives us everything to enjoy. ¹⁸Tell the rich people to do good. Tell them to be rich in doing good things. And tell them to be happy to give and ready to share. ¹⁹By doing that they will be saving a treasure for themselves ⌊in heaven⌋. That treasure will be a strong foundation*—their future life can be built on that treasure. Then they will be able to have the life that is true life.

²⁰Timothy, God has trusted you with many things. Keep those things safe. Stay away from people who say foolish things that are not from God. Stay away from people who argue against ⌊the truth⌋. Those people use something they call "knowledge"—but it is really not knowledge. ²¹Some people say that they have that "knowledge." Those people have left the ⌊true⌋ faith *(teaching)*.

God's grace *(kindness)* be with you all.

---

foundation The bottom part or first part of a house that the rest of the house is built on.

2 Timothy

1 ¹From Paul, an apostle* of Christ Jesus. I am an apostle because God wanted me to be. God sent me to tell people about the promise of life that is in Christ Jesus. ²To Timothy. You are ⌊like⌋ a dear son to me. Grace *(kindness)*, mercy, and peace to you from God the Father and from Christ Jesus our Lord.

Thanksgiving and Encouragement

³I always remember you in my prayers day and night. I thank God for you in those prayers. He is the God my ancestors served. I have always served him, doing what I know is right. ⁴I remember that you cried for me. I want very much to see you so that I can be filled with joy. ⁵I remember your true faith. That kind of faith first belonged to your grandmother Lois and to your mother Eunice. I know that you now have that same faith. ⁶That is why I want you to remember the gift God gave you. God gave you that gift when I put my hands on* you. Now I want you to use that gift and let it grow more and more, like a small flame grows into a fire. ⁷God did not give us a spirit that makes us afraid. God gave us a spirit of power and love and self control.

⁸So don't be ashamed to tell people about our Lord ⌊Jesus⌋. And don't be ashamed of me—I am in prison for the Lord. But suffer with me for the gospel.* God gives us the strength to do that. ⁹God saved us and made us his holy people.* That happened not because of anything we did ourselves. No! God saved us and made us his people because that was what he wanted and because of his grace *(kindness)*. That grace was given to us through Christ Jesus before time began. ¹⁰That grace was not shown to us until now. It was shown to us when our Savior Christ Jesus came. Jesus destroyed death and showed us the way to have life. Yes! Through the Good News* Jesus showed us the way to have life that cannot be destroyed. ¹¹I was chosen to tell that Good News. I was chosen to be an apostle* and a teacher of that Good News. ¹²And I suffer now because I tell that Good News. But I am not ashamed. I know the One *(Jesus)* that I have believed. I am sure that he is able to protect the things that he has trusted me with until that Day.* ¹³Follow the true teachings you heard from me. Follow those teachings with the faith and love we have in Christ Jesus. Those teachings are an example ⌊that shows you what you should teach⌋. ¹⁴Protect the truth that you were given. Protect those things with the help of the Holy Spirit.* That Holy Spirit lives inside us.

¹⁵You know that every person in the country of Asia* has left me. Even Phygelus and Hermogenes have left me. ¹⁶I pray that the Lord will show mercy to the family of Onesiphorus. Many times Onesiphorus helped me. He was not ashamed that I was in prison. ¹⁷No. He was not ashamed. When he came to Rome, he looked and looked for me until he found me. ¹⁸I pray that the Lord will allow Onesiphorus to have mercy from the Lord on that Day.* You know how many ways Onesiphorus helped me in Ephesus.

A Loyal Soldier of Christ Jesus

2 ¹Timothy, you are ⌊like⌋ a son to me. Be strong in the grace *(kindness)* that we have in Christ Jesus. ²You have heard the things that I have

---

apostle Person Jesus chose to be his special helper for telling the Good News to the world.
put my hands on A sign to show that Paul had power from God to give Timothy a special blessing.
gospel, Good News The news that God has made a way for people to have their sins forgiven and live with God.
holy people God's people are called holy because they are made pure through Christ, and they belong only to God.

Day The day Christ will come to judge all people and take his people to live with him.
Holy Spirit Called the Spirit of God, the Spirit of Christ, and the Comforter. Joined with God and Christ, he does God's work among people in the world.
Asia The western part of Asia Minor.

taught. Many other people heard those things too. You should teach those same things. Give those teachings to some people you can trust. Then they will be able to teach those things to other people. ³Share in the troubles that we have. Accept those troubles like a true soldier of Christ Jesus. ⁴A person that is a soldier wants to please his commanding officer. So that soldier does not use his time doing the things that most people do. ⁵If an athlete is running a race, he must obey all the rules to win. ⁶The farmer who works hard should be the first person to get some of the food that he grew. ⁷Think about these things that I am saying. The Lord will give you the ability to understand all these things.

⁸Remember Jesus Christ. He is from the family of David.* After Jesus died, he was raised from death. This is the Good News* that I tell people. ⁹And I am suffering because I tell that Good News. I am even bound with chains like a person who has really done wrong. But God's teaching is not bound. ¹⁰So I patiently accept all these troubles. I do this to help all the people that God has chosen. I accept these troubles so that those people can have the salvation that is in Christ Jesus. With that salvation comes glory that never ends.

¹¹This teaching is true:

If we died with him *(Jesus)*,
   then we will also live with him.
¹² If we accept suffering,
   then we will also rule with him.
If we refuse to accept him,
   then he will refuse to accept us.
¹³ If we are not faithful,
   he will still be faithful,
      because he cannot be false to himself.

An Approved Worker

¹⁴Continue telling the people these things. And warn those people before God not to argue about words. Arguing about words does not help any person. And it ruins those people who listen. ¹⁵Do the very best you can to be the kind of person that God will accept, and give yourself to him. Be a worker who is not ashamed of his work—a worker who uses the true teaching in the right way. ¹⁶Stay away from people who talk about useless things that are not from God. That kind of talk will lead a person more and more against God. ¹⁷Their ₍evil₎ teaching will spread like a sickness inside the body. Hymenaeus and Philetus are men like that. ¹⁸They have left the true teaching. They say that the rising from death ₍of all people₎ has already happened. And those two men are destroying the faith of some people. ¹⁹But God's strong foundation* continues to be the same. These words are written on that foundation: "The Lord knows those people who belong to him."* Also, these words are written on that foundation: "Every person who says that he believes in the Lord must stop doing wrong."

²⁰In a large house there are things made of gold and silver. But also there are things made of wood and clay. Some things are used for special purposes. Other things are made for dirty jobs. ²¹If any person will make himself clean from all the evil things, then that person will be used for special purposes. That person will be made holy,* and the master can use him. That person will be ready to do any good work.

²²Stay away from the evil things a young person wants to do. Try very hard to live right and to have faith, love, and peace. Do these things together with those people who have pure hearts and trust in the Lord. ²³Stay away from foolish and stupid arguments. You know that those arguments grow into bigger arguments. ²⁴A servant of the Lord must not argue! He must be kind to every person. A servant of the Lord must be a good teacher. He must be patient. ²⁵The Lord's servant must gently teach those people that don't agree with him. Maybe God will let those people change their hearts so that they can accept the truth. ²⁶The devil has trapped those people and makes them do what he wants. But maybe they can wake up ₍and see that the devil is using them₎ and free themselves from the devil's trap.

The Last Days

3 Remember this! There will be many troubles in the last days. ²In those times people will love only themselves and money. They will be boastful and proud. People will say bad things against other people. People will not obey their parents. People will not be thankful. They will not be the kind of people God wants. ³People will not have

---

David King of Israel about 1000 years before Christ.
Good News The news that God has made a way for people to have their sins forgiven and live with God.

foundation The bottom part or first part of a house that the rest of the house is built on.
"The Lord knows ... him" Quote from Num. 16:5.
holy A holy person is pure and belongs only to God.

love for other people. They will refuse to forgive other people, and they will speak bad things. People will not control themselves. They will be angry and mean and will hate things that are good. ⁴In the last days people will turn against their friends. They will do foolish things without thinking. They will be conceited and proud. People will love pleasure—they will not love God. ⁵Those people will continue to act like they serve God. But the way they live shows that they don't really serve God. Timothy, stay away from those people. ⁶Some of those people go into homes and get women who are weak. Those women are full of sin. Those women are led to sin by the many evil things they want to do. ⁷Those women always try to learn ₍new teachings₎, but they are never able to fully understand the truth. ⁸Remember Jannes and Jambres. They were against Moses. It is the same with these people. They are against the truth. They are people whose thinking has been confused. They have failed in trying to follow the faith. ⁹But they will not be successful in the things they do. All the people will see that they are foolish. That is what happened to Jannes and Jambres.

Last Instructions

¹⁰But you know all about me. You know what I teach and the way I live. You know my goal in life. You know my faith, my patience, and my love. You know that I never stop trying. ¹¹You know about my persecutions *(troubles)* and my sufferings. You know all the things that happened to me in Antioch, Iconium, and Lystra. You know the persecutions I suffered in those places. But the Lord saved me from all those troubles. ¹²Every person who wants to live the way God wants, in Christ Jesus, will be persecuted. ¹³People who are evil and cheat other people will become worse and worse. They will fool other people, but they will also be fooling themselves.

¹⁴But you should continue following the teachings you learned. You know that those teachings are true. You know you can trust the people who taught you those things. ¹⁵You have known the Holy Scriptures* since you were a child. Those Scriptures are able to make you wise. And that wisdom leads to salvation through faith in Christ Jesus. ¹⁶All Scripture is given by God. And all Scripture is useful for teaching and for showing people the things that are wrong in their lives. It is useful for correcting faults and teaching how to live right. ¹⁷Using the Scriptures, the person who serves God will be ready and will have everything he needs to do every good work.

4 Before God and Jesus Christ I give you a command. Christ Jesus is the One who will judge the people who are living and the people who have died. Jesus has a kingdom, and he is coming again. So I give you this command: ²Tell people the Good News.* Be ready at all times. Tell people the things they need to do, tell them when they are wrong, and encourage them. Do these things with great patience and careful teaching. ³The time will come when people will not listen to the true teaching. But people will find more and more teachers that please them. People will find teachers that say the things those people want to hear. ⁴People will stop listening to the truth. They will begin to follow the teaching in false stories. ⁵But you should control yourself at all times. When troubles come, accept those troubles. Do the work of telling the Good News. Do all the duties of a servant of God.

⁶My life is being given as an offering for God. The time has come for me to leave this life here. ⁷I have fought the good fight. I have finished the race. I have kept the faith. ⁸Now, a crown *(reward)* is waiting for me. I will get that crown for being right with God. The Lord is the judge who judges rightly. He will give me the crown on that Day.* Yes! He will give that crown to me. He will give that crown to all people who have wanted him to come again and have waited for him.

Personal Words

⁹Do your best to come to me as soon as you can. ¹⁰Demas loved this world too much. That is why he left me. He went to Thessalonica. Crescens went to Galatia. And Titus went to Dalmatia. ¹¹Luke is the only one still with me. Get Mark and bring him with you when you come. He can help me in my work here. ¹²I sent Tychicus to Ephesus.

¹³When I was in Troas, I left my coat there with Carpus. So when you come, bring it to me. Also,

---

Holy Scriptures Holy Writings—the Old Testament.

Good News The news that God has made a way for people to have their sins forgiven and live with God.

Day The day Christ will come to judge all people and take his people to live with him.

bring my books. The books written on parchment* are the ones I need most.

¹⁴Alexander the metalworker did many bad things against me. The Lord will punish Alexander for the things he did. ¹⁵You should be careful that he doesn't hurt you too. He fought strongly against our teaching.

¹⁶The first time I defended myself, no person helped me. Every person left me. I pray that God will forgive them. ¹⁷But the Lord stayed with me. The Lord gave me strength so that I could fully tell the Good News* to the non-Jews. The Lord wanted all the non-Jews to hear that Good News. I was saved from the lion's *(enemy's)* mouth. ¹⁸The Lord will save me when any person tries to hurt me. The Lord will bring me safely to his heavenly kingdom. Glory forever and ever be the Lord's.

Final Greetings

¹⁹Say hello to Priscilla and Aquila and to the family of Onesiphorus. ²⁰Erastus stayed in Corinth. And I left Trophimus in Miletus—he was sick. ²¹Try as hard as you can to come to me before winter.

Eubulus says hello to you. Also Pudens, Linus, Claudia, and all the brothers in Christ say hello to you.

²²The Lord be with your spirit. Grace *(kindness)* be with you.

---

parchment Something like paper made from the skins of sheep and used for writing on.

Good News The news that God has made a way for people to have their sins forgiven and live with God.

Titus

¹ From Paul, a servant of God and an apostle* of Jesus Christ. I was sent to help the faith of God's chosen people. I was sent to help those people to know the truth. And that truth shows people how to serve God. ²That faith and that knowledge come from our hope for life forever. God promised that life to us before time began—and God does not lie. ³At the right time God let the world know about that life. God told the world through preaching. God trusted me with that work. I preached those things because God our Savior commanded me to.

⁴To Titus. You are ⌊like⌋ a true son to me in the faith we share together.

Grace *(kindness)* and peace to you from God the Father and Christ Jesus our Savior.

Titus' Work in Crete

⁵I left you in Crete so that you could finish doing the things that still needed to be done. And I also left you there so that you could choose men to be elders* in every town. ⁶To be an elder, a man must not be guilty of doing anything wrong. He must have only one wife. His children must be believers. They must not be known as children that are wild and don't obey. ⁷An elder* has the job of taking care of God's work. So he must not be guilty of doing anything wrong. He must not be a person who is proud and selfish or who becomes angry quickly. He must not drink too much wine. He must not be a person who likes to fight. And he must not be a person who always tries to get rich by cheating people. ⁸An elder must be ready to help people by accepting them into his home. He must love what is good. He must be wise. He must live right. He must be holy.* And he must be able to control himself. ⁹An elder must faithfully follow the truth the same as we teach it. An elder must be able to help people by using true and right teaching. And he must be able to show the people who are against the true teaching that they are wrong.

¹⁰There are many people who refuse to obey—people who talk about worthless things and lead other people into the wrong way. I am talking mostly about those people who say that all non-Jewish people must be circumcised.* ¹¹An elder* must ⌊be able to show that those people are wrong and⌋ stop them from talking ⌊about those worthless things⌋. Those people are destroying whole families by teaching things that they should not teach. They teach those things only to cheat people and make money. ¹²Even one of their own prophets *(teachers)* ⌊from Crete⌋ said, "Cretan people are always liars. They are evil animals and lazy people who do nothing but eat." ¹³The words that prophet said are true. So tell those people that they are wrong. You must be strict with them. Then they will become strong in the faith. ¹⁴Then those people will stop accepting Jewish stories. And they will stop following the commands of those people who don't accept the truth. ¹⁵To people that are pure, all things are pure. But to people who are full of sin and don't believe, nothing is pure. Really, those people's thinking has become evil and their knowledge of what is right has been ruined. ¹⁶Those people say they know God. But the ⌊evil⌋ things those people do show that they don't accept God. They are terrible people, they refuse to obey, and they are not useful for doing anything good.

---

apostle Person Jesus chose to be a special helper for telling the Good News to the world.
elder(s) Elders are men chosen to lead a church. Also called "overseers" and "pastors" (shepherds), they have the work of caring for God's people (Acts 20:28).
elder Here (verse 7), literally, "overseer."
holy A holy person is pure and belongs only to God.
circumcised To have the foreskin cut off. This was done to every Jewish baby boy. It was a mark of the agreement God made with Abraham (Gen. 17:9-14).

Following the True Teaching

2 You must tell people the things they must do to follow the true teaching. ²Teach the older men to have self-control, to be serious, and to be wise. They should be strong in the faith, strong in love, and strong in patience.

³Also, teach the older women to be holy* in the way they live. Teach them not to speak against other people or have the habit of drinking too much wine. Those women should teach what is good. ⁴In that way they can teach the younger women to love their husbands and children. ⁵They can teach the younger women to be wise and to be pure, to take care of their homes, to be kind, and to obey their husbands. Then no person will be able to criticize the teaching God gave us.

⁶In the same way, tell the young men to be wise. ⁷You should do good things to be an example in every way for the young men. When you teach, be honest and serious. ⁸And when you speak, speak the truth so that you cannot be criticized. Then any person who is against you will be ashamed because he has nothing bad that he can say against us.

⁹And tell these things to the people who are slaves: They should obey their masters at all times; they should try to please their masters; they should not argue with their masters; ¹⁰they should not steal from their masters; and they should show their masters that they can be trusted. The slaves should do these things so that in everything they do, they will show that the teaching of God our Savior is good.

¹¹⌊That is the way we should live⌋, because God's grace (kindness) has come. That grace can save every person. And that grace has been given to us. ¹²That grace teaches us not to live against God and not to do the bad things the world wants to do. That grace teaches us to live on earth now in a wise and right way—a way that shows that we serve God. ¹³We should live like that while we are waiting for the coming of our great God and Savior Jesus Christ. He is our great hope, and he will come with glory. ¹⁴He gave himself for us. He died to free us from all evil. He died to make us pure people that belong only to him—people that are always wanting to do good things.

¹⁵Tell the people these things. You have full authority (power). So use that authority to strengthen the people and tell them what they should do. And don't let any person treat you like you are not important.

The Right Way to Live

3 Tell the people to remember always to do these things: to be under the authority of rulers and government leaders; to obey those leaders and be ready to do good; ²to speak no evil against any person; to live in peace with other people; to be gentle to other people; and to be polite to other people. Tell the believers to do these things to all people.

³In the past we were foolish people too. We did not obey, we were wrong, and we were slaves to the many things our bodies wanted and enjoyed. We lived doing evil and being jealous. People hated us and we hated each other. ⁴But then the kindness and love of God our Savior was made known. ⁵He saved us because of his mercy (love)—not because of the good things we did to be right with God. He saved us through the washing that made us new people. He saved us by making us new through the Holy Spirit.* ⁶God poured out (gave) to us that Holy Spirit fully through Jesus Christ our Savior. ⁷We were made right with God by His grace (kindness). And God gave us the Spirit so that we could receive the life that never ends. That is what we hope for. ⁸This teaching is true.

And I want you to be sure that the people understand these things. Then the people who believe in God will be careful to use their lives for doing good. These things are good and will help all people.

⁹Stay away from people who have foolish arguments, people who talk about useless family histories, people who make trouble and fight about what the law ⌊of Moses⌋ teaches. Those things are worth nothing and will not help people. ¹⁰If a person causes arguments, then give him a warning. If that person continues to cause arguments, then warn him again. If he still continues causing arguments, then don't associate with him. ¹¹You know that a person like that is evil and sinful. His sins prove that he is wrong.

Some Things to Remember

¹²I will send Artemas and Tychicus to you. When I send them, try hard to come to me at Nicopolis. I have decided to stay there this winter.

---

holy Being pure and belonging only to God.

Holy Spirit Called the Spirit of God, the Spirit of Christ, and the Comforter. Joined with God and Christ, he does God's work among people in the world.

¹³Zenas the lawyer and Apollos will be traveling from there. Do all that you can to help them on their trip. Be sure that they have everything they need. ¹⁴Our people must learn to use their lives for doing good things. They should do good for people who need it. Then our people will not have empty lives.

¹⁵All the people with me here say hello to you. Say hello to those people who love us in the faith.

Grace *(kindness)* be with you all.

Philemon

From Paul, a prisoner of Jesus Christ, and from Timothy, our brother.

To Philemon, our dear friend and worker with us. ²Also to Apphia, our sister; to Archippus, a worker with us; and to the church that meets in your home. ³Grace *(kindness)* and peace to you from God our Father and the Lord Jesus Christ.

Philemon's Love and Faith

⁴I remember you in my prayers. And I always thank my God for you. ⁵I hear about the love you have for all God's holy people* and the faith you have in the Lord Jesus. And I thank God for that love and faith you have. ⁶I pray that the faith you share will make you understand every good thing that we have in Christ. ⁷My brother, you have shown love to God's people. You have made them feel happy. This has given me great joy and comfort.

Accept Onesimus Like a Brother

⁸There is something that you should do. And because of your love in Christ, I feel free to command you to do that. ⁹But I am not commanding you; I am asking you to do it. I am Paul. I am an old man now, and I am a prisoner for Christ Jesus. ¹⁰I am asking you for my son Onesimus. He became my son while I was in prison. ¹¹In the past he was useless to you. But now he has become useful for both you and me. ¹²I am sending him back to you. With him I am sending my own heart. ¹³I wanted to keep him with me to help me while I am in prison for the gospel.* By helping me he would be serving you. ¹⁴But I did not want to do anything without asking you first. Then the good thing you do for me will be because you wanted to do it, not because I forced you to do it.

¹⁵Onesimus was separated from you for a short time. Maybe that happened so that you could have him back forever—¹⁶not to be a slave, but better than a slave, to be a brother that is loved. I love him very much. But you will love him even more. You will love him as a man and as a brother in the Lord.

¹⁷If you accept me to be your friend, then accept Onesimus back. Welcome him like you would welcome me. ¹⁸If Onesimus has done anything wrong to you, charge that to me. If he owes you anything, charge that to me. ¹⁹I am Paul, and I am writing this with my own hand. I will pay back anything Onesimus owes. And I will say nothing about what you owe me for your own life. ²⁰So, my brother, I ask that you do something for me in the Lord. Comfort my heart in Christ. ²¹I write this letter knowing that you will do what I ask you. I know that you will do even more than I ask.

²²Also, please prepare a room for me to stay in. I hope that God will answer your prayers and I will be able to come to you.

Final Greetings

²³Epaphras is a prisoner with me for Christ Jesus. He says hello to you. ²⁴And also Mark, Aristarchus, Demas, and Luke say hello to you. They are workers together with me.

²⁵The grace *(kindness)* of our Lord Jesus Christ be with your spirit.

---

holy people God's people are called holy because they are made pure through Christ, and they belong only to God.

gospel The Good News that God has made a way for people to have their sins forgiven and live with God.

Hebrews

God Has Spoken Through His Son

1 In the past God spoke to our people through the prophets.* God spoke to them many times and in many different ways. ²And now in these last days God has spoken to us again. God has spoken to us through his Son. God made the whole world through his Son. And God has chosen his Son to have all things. ³The Son shows the glory of God. He is a perfect copy of God's nature. The Son holds everything together with his powerful command. The Son made people clean from their sins. Then he sat down at the right side of the Great One *(God)* in heaven. ⁴God gave him a name that is a much greater name than any of the angels have. And he became that much greater than the angels.

⁵God never said these things to any of the angels:

"You are my Son;
Today I have become your Father."
Psalm 2:7

God also never said to an angel,

"I will be his Father,
And he will be my son."
2 Samuel 7:14

⁶And when God brings his firstborn* Son into the world, he says,

"Let all God's angels worship the Son."*
Deuteronomy 32:43

⁷This is what God said about the angels:

"God makes his angels become like winds,*

and God makes his servants become
like flames of fire."
Psalm 104:4

⁸But God said this about his Son:

"Your throne, O God, will continue forever
and ever,
You will rule your kingdom with
right judgments.
⁹ You love the right,
and you hate the wrong.
So, God, your God has given you
a greater joy
than he gave the people with you."
Psalm 45:6-7

¹⁰God also says,

"O Lord, in the beginning you made the earth.
And your hands made the sky.
¹¹ These things will disappear, but you will stay.
All things will become old like clothes.
¹² You will fold them like a coat.
And they will be changed like clothes.
But you never change.
And your life will never end."
Psalm 102:25-27

¹³And God never said this to an angel:

"Sit at my right side
until I put your enemies
under your power."*
Psalm 110:1

¹⁴All the angels are spirits who serve God and are sent to help those people who will receive salvation.

Our Salvation Is Greater than the Law

2 So we must be more careful to follow the things that we were taught. We must be careful so that we will not be pulled away ₁from the true

---

prophets People who spoke for God. They often told things that would happen in the future.
firstborn This word means that Christ was the first and most important of all God's children.
"Let ... Son" These words are found in Deuteronomy 32:43 in the Septuagint, the Greek version of the Old Testament, and in a Hebrew copy among the Dead Sea Scrolls.
winds This can also mean "spirits."

until I put ... power Literally, "until I make your enemies a footstool for your feet."

way⌊. ²The teaching *(the law)* that God spoke through angels was shown to be true. And every time the ⌊Jewish⌋ people did something against that teaching they were punished for what they did. They were punished when they did not obey that teaching. ³The salvation ⌊that was given to us⌋ is very great. So surely we also will be punished if we live like this salvation is not important. It was the Lord *(Jesus)* who first told people about this salvation. And the people who heard him proved to us that this salvation is true. ⁴God also proved it by using wonders, great signs, and many kinds of miracles.* And he proved it by giving people gifts through the Holy Spirit.* He gave those gifts the way he wanted.

Christ Became Like Men to Save Them

⁵God did not choose angels to be the rulers over the new world that was coming. That future world is the world we have been talking about. ⁶It is written some place ⌊in the Scriptures⌋,*

"⌊God⌋, why do you care about man *(people)*?
Why do you care about the son of man*?
Is he so important?
⁷ For a short time you made him lower
than the angels.
You gave him glory and honor
to be his crown.
⁸ You put everything under his control.*"
Psalm 8:4-6

If God put everything under his control, then there was nothing left that he did not rule. But we don't yet see him ruling over everything. ⁹For a short time Jesus was made lower than the angels, but now we see him wearing a crown of glory and honor because he suffered and died. Because of God's grace *(kindness)* Jesus died for every person.

¹⁰God is the One who made all things. And all things are for his glory. God wanted to have many sons *(people)* to share his glory. So God did what he needed to do. He made perfect the One *(Jesus)* who leads those people to salvation. God made Jesus ⌊a⌋ perfect ⌊Savior⌋ through Jesus' suffering.

¹¹The One *(Jesus)* who makes people holy* and those people who are made holy are from the same family. So he *(Jesus)* is not ashamed to call those people his brothers ⌊and sisters⌋. ¹²Jesus says,

"God, I will tell my brothers ⌊and sisters⌋
about you.
Before all your people I will sing
your praises."
Psalm 22:22

¹³He also says,

"I will trust in God."
Isaiah 8:17

And he says,

"I am here.
And with me are the children that
God has given me."
Isaiah 8:18

¹⁴Those children are people with physical bodies. So Jesus himself became like those people and had the same experiences people have. Jesus did this so that, by dying, he could destroy the one who has the power of death. That one is the devil. ¹⁵Jesus became like those people and died so that he could free them. They were like slaves all their lives because of their fear of death. ¹⁶Clearly, it is not angels that Jesus helps. Jesus helps the people who are from Abraham.* ¹⁷For this reason Jesus had to be made like his brothers ⌊and sisters⌋ in every way. Jesus became like people so that he could be their merciful and faithful high priest* in service to God. Then Jesus could bring forgiveness for the people's sins. ¹⁸And now Jesus can help those people who are tempted. Jesus is able to help because he himself suffered and was tempted.

Jesus Is Greater Than Moses

3 So all of you should think about Jesus. God sent Jesus to us, and he is the high priest* of our faith. I tell this to you, my holy* brothers ⌊and sisters⌋, you were all called by God. ²God sent Jesus to us and made him our high priest. And

---

miracle(s) Amazing works done by the power of God.
Holy Spirit Called the Spirit of God, the Spirit of Christ, and the Comforter. Joined with God and Christ, he does God's work among people in the world.
Scriptures Holy Writings—the Old Testament.
son of man This can mean any man (person), but the name "Son of Man" is often used to mean Jesus. Jesus showed what God planned for all men (people) to be.
control Literally, "feet."

holy God's people are holy because they are made pure through Christ, and they belong only to God.
Abraham Most respected ancestor of the Jews.
high priest Most important priest for God's people.

Jesus was faithful to God like Moses was. He did everything God wanted him to do in God's house (family). ³When a man builds a house, people will honor the man more than the house. It is the same with Jesus. Jesus should have more honor than Moses. ⁴Every house is built by some person. But God built everything. ⁵Moses was faithful in all God's house (family) like a servant. He told people the things that God would say in the future. ⁶But Christ is faithful in ruling God's house like a Son. We ⌊believers⌋ are God's house (family). We are God's house if we continue to be sure and proud of the great hope we have.

We Must Continue to Follow God

⁷So it is like the Holy Spirit* says:

"If you hear God's voice today,
⁸   don't be stubborn like in the past,
        when you were against God.
    That was the day you tested God in the
        desert.
⁹   For 40 years in the desert your people
        saw the things I did.
    But they tested me and my patience.
¹⁰ So I was angry with those people.
    I said, 'Those people's thoughts are
        always wrong.
    Those people have never understood
        my ways.'
¹¹ So I was angry and made a promise:
    'Those people will never enter
        and have my rest.*'"
                                Psalm 95:7-11

¹²So, brothers ⌊and sisters⌋, be careful that none of you is sinful, and refuses to believe, and stops following the living God. ¹³But comfort each other every day. Do this while it is "today."* Help each other so that none of you will become hardened because of sin and the way sin fools people. ¹⁴We all share together with Christ. This is true if we continue until the end to have the sure faith we had in the beginning. ¹⁵This is what that Scripture* said:

"If you hear God's voice today,
    don't be stubborn like in the past
    when you were against God."
                                Psalm 95:7-8

¹⁶Who were those people who heard God's voice and were against him? It was all those people that Moses led out of Egypt. ¹⁷And who was God angry with for 40 years? God was angry with those people who sinned. Those people died in the desert. ¹⁸And what people was God talking to when he promised that they would never enter and have his rest*? God was talking about those people who did not obey him. ¹⁹So we see that those people were not allowed to enter and have God's rest. Why? Because they did not believe.

4 And we still have that promise God gave those people. That promise is that we can enter and have God's rest. So we should be very careful, so that none of you fail to get that promise. ²The way to be saved* was told to us the same as to those people. But the teaching those people heard did not help them. They heard that teaching but did not accept it with faith. ³We people who believe are able to enter and have God's rest. Like God said,

"I was angry and made a promise:
'Those people will never enter
    and have my rest.*'"
                                Psalm 95:11

God said this. But God's work was finished from the time he made the world. ⁴Some place ⌊in the Scriptures⌋* God talked about the seventh day of the week: "So on the seventh day God rested from all his work."* ⁵And in that other Scripture God also said, "Those people will never enter and have my rest."

⁶It is still true that some people will enter and have God's rest. But those people who first heard the way to be saved* did not enter. They did not enter because they did not obey. ⁷So God planned another special day. It is called "today." God spoke about that day through David a long time later. It is the same Scripture* we used before:

"If you hear God's voice today,
    don't be stubborn like in the past."
                                Psalm 95:7-8

Holy Spirit Called the Spirit of God, the Spirit of Christ, and the Comforter. Joined with God and Christ, he does God's work among people in the world.
rest A place of rest God promised to give his people.
today This word is taken from verse 7. It means that it is important to do these things now.
Scripture(s) Holy Writings—the Old Testament.

way to be saved Literally, "Good News" or "gospel." See Rom. 1:16.
"So ... his work" Quote from Gen. 2:2.

⁸We know that Joshua* did not lead the people into the rest* ₍God promised₎. We know this because God spoke later about another day ₍for rest₎ ("today"). ⁹This shows that the seventh-day rest* for God's people is still coming. ¹⁰God rested after he finished his work. So the person who enters and has God's rest is the person who has finished his work like God did. ¹¹So let us try as hard as we can to enter God's rest. We must try hard so that none of us will be lost by following the example of those people who refused to obey God.

¹²God's word* (message) is alive and working. His word is sharper than the sharpest sword. God's word cuts all the way into us ₍like a sword₎. It cuts deep to the place where the soul and the spirit are joined. God's word cuts to the center of our joints and our bones. It judges the thoughts and feelings in our hearts. ¹³Nothing in all the world can be hidden from God. He can clearly see all things. Everything is open before him. And to him we must explain the way we have lived.

Jesus Helps Us Come Before God

¹⁴We have a great high priest* who has gone to live with God in heaven. He is Jesus the Son of God. So let us continue strongly in the faith we have. ¹⁵Jesus, the high priest that we have, is able to understand our weaknesses. When Jesus lived on earth, he was tempted in every way. He was tempted in the same ways that we are tempted, but he never sinned. ¹⁶With Jesus as our high priest we can feel free to come before God's throne where there is grace (forgiveness). There we receive mercy and kindness to help us when we need it.

5 Every Jewish high priest* is chosen from among men. That priest is given the work of helping people with the things they must do for God. That priest must offer to God gifts and sacrifices* for sins. ²The high priest himself is weak ₍like all people₎. So he is able to be gentle with those people who don't understand and who are doing wrong things. ³The high priest offers sacrifices for the sins of the people. But the high priest has weaknesses himself. So he also must offer sacrifices for his own sins.

⁴To be a high priest* is an honor. But no person chooses himself for this work. That person must be called by God like Aaron* was. ⁵It is the same with Christ. He did not choose himself to have the glory of becoming a high priest. But God chose him. God said to Christ,

> "You are my Son;
> today I have become your Father."
>
> *Psalm 2:7*

⁶And in another Scripture* God says,

> "You will be a priest forever,
> the same as Melchizedek.*"
>
> *Psalm 110:4*

⁷While Christ lived on earth he prayed to God and asked God for help. God is the One who could save him from death, and Jesus prayed to God with loud cries and tears. And God answered Jesus' prayers because Jesus was humble and did everything God wanted. ⁸Jesus was the Son of God. But Jesus suffered and learned to obey by the things that he suffered. ⁹Then Jesus was perfect. And Jesus is the reason that all those people who obey him can have salvation forever. ¹⁰And God made Jesus the high priest,* the same as Melchizedek.

Warning Against Falling Away

¹¹We have many things to tell you about this. But it is hard to explain because you have stopped trying to understand. ¹²You have had enough time that by now you should be teachers. But you need some person to teach you again the first lessons of God's teaching. You still need the teaching that is like milk. You are not ready for solid food. ¹³Any person who lives on milk is still a baby. That person knows nothing about right teaching. ¹⁴But solid food is for people who have stopped being like babies. It is for people who are grown-up in their spirits. Those people have practiced and taught themselves to know the difference between good and evil.

Joshua After Moses died, Joshua became leader of the Jewish people. He led them into the land God promised to give them.
rest A place of rest God promised to give his people.
seventh-day rest Literally, "sabbath rest," meaning a sharing in the rest God began after he created the world.
God's word God's teachings and commands.
high priest Most important priest for God's people.
sacrifices A sacrifice is a gift or offering to God. The Jewish priests killed animals and offered them to God. Jesus Christ gave his own life as a sacrifice to pay for people's sins.

Aaron First Jewish high priest. He was Moses' brother.
Scripture Part of the Holy Writings—Old Testament.
Melchizedek A priest and king who lived in the time of Abraham. (Read Gen. 14:17-24.)

6 So we should be finished with the beginning lessons about Christ. We should not go back to the things we started with. We began ₍our life in Christ₎ by turning away from the evil things we did before and by believing in God. ²At that time we were taught about baptisms,* and about the special act of a person putting his hands on people.* We were taught about people rising from death and about the judgment that will continue forever. But now we need to go forward to more mature *(advanced)* teaching.* ³And we will do this if God allows.

⁴⁻⁶After people have left ₍the way of Christ₎, can you make them change their life again? I am talking about people who have learned the truth. They received God's gift and also shared in the Holy Spirit.* Those people heard the things God said, and they saw the great powers of God's new world. And they saw for themselves that those things are very good. But then those people left ₍the way of Christ₎. It is not possible to make those people change their lives ₍and come to Christ₎ again. Why? Because those people ₍that leave Christ's way₎ are really nailing Christ to the cross again. Those people bring shame to Christ before all people.

⁷₍Those people are like₎ land that gets plenty of rain. A farmer plants and cares for that land so that it will give food for people. If that land grows plants that help people, then that land has the blessing of God. ⁸But if that land grows thorns and weeds, it is worthless. That land is in danger that it will be cursed by God. And that land will be destroyed by fire.

⁹Dear friends, we are saying these things to you. But really we expect better things from you. We feel sure that you will do the things that are a part of salvation. ¹⁰God is fair. God will remember all the work you have done. And God will remember that you showed your love to him by helping his people. And God will remember that you continue to help his people. ¹¹We want each of you to continue with the same hard work all your lives. Then you will surely get that great thing you hope for. ¹²We don't want you to become lazy. We want you to be like those people who get the things that God promised. Those people get God's promises because they have faith and patience.

¹³God made a promise to Abraham. And there is no one greater than God, so God used himself to vow *(promise)* that he would do what he said. ¹⁴God said, "I will truly bless you. I will give you many, many descendants."** ¹⁵Abraham waited patiently for this to happen. And later Abraham received what God promised.

¹⁶People always use the name of someone greater than themselves to make a vow *(promise)*. The vow proves that what they say is true. And this ends all arguing about what they say. ¹⁷God wanted to prove that his promise was true. God wanted to prove this to those people who would get what he promised. God wanted those people to understand clearly that his purposes *(plans)* never change. So God said something would happen, and he proved what he said by also making a vow *(promise)*. ¹⁸Those two things cannot change. God cannot lie when he says something and he cannot lie when he makes a vow. So those things give great comfort to us who came to God for safety. Those two things give us comfort and strength to continue in the hope that God gives us. ¹⁹We have this hope. And it is like an anchor. It is strong and sure and keeps our soul safe. It goes into ₍the most holy place₎ behind the curtain ₍in the heavenly temple₎. ²⁰Jesus has already entered there and opened the way for us. Jesus has become the high priest* forever the same as Melchizedek.*

The Priest Melchizedek

7 Melchizedek* was the king of Salem and a priest for God the Most High. Melchizedek met Abraham when Abraham was coming back after defeating the kings. That day Melchizedek blessed Abraham. ²And Abraham gave Melchizedek one-tenth of everything he had. (The name Melchizedek, king of Salem, has two meanings. First, Melchizedek means "king of goodness." Also, "king of Salem" means "king of peace.") ³No person knows who Melchizedek's father or

---

baptisms The word here may mean Christian baptism (a brief burial in water), or it may mean the Jewish ceremonial washings.
putting his hands on people This showed that they were given a special work or blessing.
now ... teaching The Greek text has these words in verse 1.
Holy Spirit Called the Spirit of God, the Spirit of Christ, and the Comforter. Joined with God and Christ, he does God's work among people in the world.

descendants A person's children and all their future families.
I will ... descendants Quote from Gen. 22:17.
high priest Most important priest for God's people.
Melchizedek A priest and king who lived in the time of Abraham. (Read Gen. 14:17-24.)

mother was or where he came from.* And no person knows when he was born or when he died. Melchizedek is like the Son of God and he continues being a priest forever.

⁴You can see that Melchizedek was very great. Abraham, the great father, gave Melchizedek one-tenth of everything that Abraham won in battle. ⁵Now the law says that people in the family group* of Levi who become priests must get one-tenth from the people. The priests collect it from their own people *(the Jews)*, even though the priests and their people are both from the family of Abraham. ⁶Melchizedek was not from the family group of Levi. But he got one-tenth from Abraham. And he blessed Abraham—the man who had God's promises. ⁷And all people know that the more important person blesses the less important person. ⁸Those priests get one-tenth, but they are only men who live and then die. But Melchizedek, who got one-tenth ₍from Abraham₎, continues living, like the Scripture* says. ⁹It is Levi who gets one-tenth ₍from the people₎. But we can say that when Abraham paid Melchizedek one-tenth, then Levi also paid it. ¹⁰Levi was not yet born. But Levi was in the body of his ancestor Abraham when Melchizedek met Abraham.

¹¹People were given the law* under the system of priests from the Levi family group.* But people could not be made spiritually perfect through that system of priests. So there was a need for another priest to come. I mean a priest that is like Melchizedek, not Aaron. ¹²And when a different kind of priest comes, then the law must be changed too. ¹³We are saying these things about Christ. He belonged to a different family group. No person from that family group ever served ₍as a priest₎ at the altar.* ¹⁴It is clear that our Lord *(Christ)* came from the family group of Judah. And Moses said nothing about priests belonging to that family group.

Jesus Is a Priest like Melchizedek

¹⁵And these things become even more clear. We see that another priest *(Jesus)* comes who is like Melchizedek. ¹⁶He was made a priest not by human rules and laws. He became a priest through the power of his life which continues forever. ¹⁷₍In the Scriptures₎,* this is said about him: "You are a priest forever—the kind of priest Melchizedek was."*

¹⁸The old rule *(law)* is now ended because it was weak and worthless. ¹⁹The law ₍of Moses₎ could not make anything perfect. And now a better hope has been given to us. And with that hope we can come near to God.

²⁰Also, it is important that God made a vow *(promise)* when he made Jesus high priest.* When those other men became priests, there was no vow. ²¹But Christ became a priest with God's vow. God said:

> "The Lord has made a vow *(promise)*
> and will not change his mind:
> 'You are a priest forever.'"
>
> *Psalm 110:4*

²²So this means that Jesus is the guarantee of a better agreement* ₍from God to his people₎.

²³Also, when one of those other priests died, he could not continue being a priest. So there were many of those priests. ²⁴But Jesus lives forever. He will never stop serving as priest. ²⁵So Christ can save those people who come to God through him. Christ can do this forever, because he always lives, ready to help people when they come before God.

²⁶So Jesus is the kind of high priest* that we need. He is holy—he has no sin in him. He is pure and not influenced by sinners. And he is raised above the heavens. ²⁷He is not like those other priests. Those other priests had to offer *(give)* sacrifices* every day. They had to offer sacrifices first for their own sins and then for the sins of the people. But Christ doesn't need to do that. Christ offered only one sacrifice for all time. Christ offered himself. ²⁸The law chooses high priests who are people and have the same weaknesses as people. But God made a promise that came after the law. God spoke those words with a vow *(promise)*, and those words made the Son of God to be the high priest.* And that Son has been made perfect forever.

"You ... Melchizedek was" Quote from Ps. 110:4.
high priest Most important priest for God's people.
agreement God gives a contract or agreement to his people. For the Jews, the agreement was the law of Moses. Now God has given a better agreement to his people through Christ.
sacrifices A sacrifice is a gift or offering to God. The Jewish priests killed animals and offered them to God. Jesus Christ gave his own life as a sacrifice to pay for people's sins.

No person ... came from Literally, "Melchizedek was without father, without mother, without genealogy."
family group One of the twelve "tribes" of the Jewish people, named after Jacob's twelve sons.
Scripture(s) Part of the Holy Writings—Old Testament.
law The law of Moses.
altar A stone table used for burning sacrifices offered to God.

Jesus Our High Priest

8 Here is the point of what we are saying: We have a high priest* like we have been telling you about. That high priest now sits on the right side of God's throne in heaven. ²Our high priest serves in the Most Holy Place.* He serves in the true place of worship* that was made by God, not by people. ³Every high priest has the work of offering gifts and sacrifices* to God. So our high priest must also offer something to God. ⁴If our high priest were now living on earth, then he would not be a priest. I say this because there are already priests here who follow the law by offering gifts to God. ⁵The work that these priests do is really only a copy and a shadow of the things that are in heaven. That is why God warned Moses when Moses was ready to build the Holy Tent*: "Be sure to make everything exactly like the pattern I showed you on the mountain." ⁶But the work that has been given to Jesus is much greater than the work that was given to those priests. In the same way, the new agreement* that Jesus brought from God to his people is much greater than the old one. And the new agreement is based on promises of better things.

⁷If there was nothing wrong with the first agreement, then there would be no need for a second agreement. ⁸But God found something wrong with the people. God said:

> "The time is coming, says the Lord,
> when I will give a new agreement
> to the people of Israel*
> and to the people of Judah.*
> ⁹ It will not be like the agreement
> that I gave to their fathers.
> That is the agreement I gave
> when I took them by the hand
> and led them out of Egypt.
> They did not continue following the
> agreement I gave them,
> and I turned away from them,
> says the Lord.
> ¹⁰ This is the new agreement I will give to the
> people of Israel.*
> I will give this agreement in the future,
> says the Lord:
> I will put my laws in their minds,
> and I will write my laws on their hearts.
> I will be their God,
> and they will be my people.
> ¹¹ Never again will a person have to teach his
> brother or God's other people.
> He will not need to tell them
> to know the Lord.
> Why? Because all people—the greatest
> people and the least important people—
> will know me.
> ¹² And I will forgive the wrong things they do
> against me,
> and I will not remember their sins."
>
> *Jeremiah 31:31-34*

¹³God called this a new agreement, so God has made the first agreement* old. And anything that is old and useless is ready to disappear.

Worship Under the Old Agreement

9 The first agreement* had rules for worship. And it had a man-made place for worship. ²This place was inside a tent. The first area in the tent was called the Holy Place. In the Holy Place were the lamp and the table with the special bread offered to God. ³Behind the second curtain was a room called the Most Holy Place.* ⁴In the Most Holy Place was a golden altar* for burning incense.* And also there was the holy box that held the old agreement.* The box was covered with gold. Inside this box was a golden jar of manna* and Aaron's rod *(stick)*—the rod that

---

high priest Most important priest for God's people.
Most Holy Place Literally, "holies," for "holy of holies," the spiritual place where God lives and is worshiped.
place of worship Literally, "tabernacle" or "tent."
sacrifices Gifts or offerings to God. The Jewish priests killed animals and offered them to God. Jesus Christ gave his own life as a sacrifice to pay for people's sins.
Holy Tent Or, "tabernacle." The special tent where God lived among his people and where the Jewish priests worshiped.
agreement God gives a contract or agreement to his people. For the Jews, the agreement was the law of Moses. Now God has given a better agreement to his people through Christ.
Israel The northern part of the Jewish nation.
Judah The southern part of the Jewish nation.

Israel First, Israel was the Jewish nation (people), but the name is also used to mean all of God's people.
first agreement The contract God gave the Jewish people when he gave them the law of Moses.
Most Holy Place Literally, "holy of holies," the room in the Jewish place of worship where God met with the high priest.
altar A stone table used for burning sacrifices offered to God.
incense Special dried tree sap used for a sacrifice. It was burned to make a sweet-smelling smoke.
holy box ... agreement Wooden box covered with gold that had in it God's law on two flat stones.
manna The food God gave the Jewish people in the desert.

once grew leaves. Also in the box were the flat rocks ⌊with the Ten Commandments⌋ of the old agreement ⌊written on them⌋. ⁵Above the box were the cherub angels* that showed God's glory. These cherub angels were over the mercy seat.* But we cannot say everything about these things now.

⁶Everything in the tent was made ready in the way I have explained. Then the priests went into the first room every day to do their worship. ⁷But only the high priest* could go into the second room. And the high priest went into that room only once a year. And the high priest could never enter that room without taking blood with him. The priest offered that blood to God for himself and for the people's sins. Those sins were the sins the people did without knowing that they were sinning. ⁸The Holy Spirit* uses those two separate rooms to teach us this: that the way into the Most Holy Place* was not open while that first room was still there. ⁹This is an example for us today. This shows that the gifts and sacrifices* that were offered to God were not able to fully cleanse the person who was worshiping God. Those sacrifices could not make that person perfect in his heart. ¹⁰Those gifts and sacrifices were only about food and drink and special washings. Those things were only rules about the body—⌐not about things inside people's hearts⌐. God gave those rules ⌊for his people to follow⌋ until the time of God's new way.

Worship Under the New Agreement

¹¹But Christ has already come to be the high priest.* He is the high priest of the good things we now have. But Christ does not serve in a place like the tent that those other priests served in. Christ serves in a place that is better than that tent. It is more perfect. And that place is not made by men. It does not belong to this world. ¹²Christ entered the Most Holy Place* only one time—enough for all time. Christ entered the Most Holy Place by using his own blood *(death)*, not the blood of goats or young bulls. Christ entered there and got for us freedom forever. ¹³The blood of goats and bulls and the ashes of a cow were sprinkled on those people who were no longer pure ⌊enough to enter that place of worship⌋. That blood and those ashes made those people pure again—but only their bodies. ¹⁴So surely the blood of Christ can do much, much more. Christ offered himself through the eternal Spirit* as a perfect sacrifice* to God. His blood will make us fully clean from the evil things we have done. His blood will make us pure even in our hearts. We are made pure so that we can worship *(serve)* the living God.

¹⁵So Christ brings a new agreement* from God to his people. Christ brings this new agreement so that those people that are called by God can have the things that God promised. God's people can have those things forever. They can have those things because Christ died to pay for the sins that people did under the first agreement.* Christ died to make people free from those sins.

¹⁶When a man dies, he leaves a will* *(agreement)*. But people must prove that the man who wrote that will is dead. ¹⁷A will means nothing while the man who wrote it is still living. The will can be used only after the man dies. ¹⁸It is the same with the first agreement ⌊between God and his people⌋. There had to be blood *(death)* before the agreement could be made good. ¹⁹First, Moses told all the people every commandment in the law. Then Moses took the blood of calves and mixed it with water. Then he used red wool and a branch of hyssop* to sprinkle the blood and water on the book of the law and on all the people. ²⁰Then Moses said, "This is the blood that makes the agreement good—the agreement that God commanded you to follow." ²¹In the same way, Moses sprinkled the blood on the Holy Tent.* He

---

cherub angels Two images or statues of angels.
mercy seat Place on top of "the holy box that held the agreement," where the high priest put the blood of an animal once a year to pay for the sins of the people.
high priest Most important priest for God's people.
Holy Spirit Called the Spirit of God, the Spirit of Christ, and the Comforter. Joined with God and Christ, he does God's work among people in the world.
Most Holy Place Literally, "holies," for "holy of holies," the spiritual place where God lives and is worshiped.
sacrifices Animals the Jewish priests killed and offered to God.

Spirit Probably the Holy Spirit. See note on Holy Spirit.
sacrifice Any gift offered to God. Jesus Christ gave his own life as a payment for people's sins.
new agreement This is the "better agreement" that God has given to his people through Jesus.
first agreement The contract God gave to the Jewish people when he gave them the law of Moses.
will The paper a person signs to show which people he wants to have his things after he dies.
hyssop A special plant.
Holy Tent Or, "tabernacle." The special tent where God lived among his people and where the Jewish priests worshiped.

sprinkled the blood over all the things used in worship. ²²The law says that almost everything must be made clean by blood. And sins cannot be forgiven without blood *(death).*

Christ's Sacrifice Takes Away Sins

²³These things are copies of the real things that are in heaven. These copies had to be made clean by animal sacrifices.* But the real things in heaven must have much better sacrifices. ²⁴Christ went into the Most Holy Place.* But Christ did not go into the Most Holy Place that was made by men. That Most Holy Place is only a copy of the real one. Christ went into heaven. Christ is there now before God to help us. ²⁵The high priest* enters the Most Holy Place once every year. He takes with him blood to offer. But he does not offer his own blood ⌊like Christ did⌋. Christ went into heaven, but not to offer himself many times like the high priest ⌊offers blood again and again⌋. ²⁶If Christ had offered himself many times, then he would have needed to suffer many times since the time the world was made. But Christ came ⌊and offered himself⌋ only once. And that once is enough for all time. Christ came at a time when the world is nearing an end. Christ came to take away all sin by offering himself as a sacrifice.* ²⁷Every person must die once. After a person dies, he is judged. ²⁸So Christ was offered as a sacrifice one time to take away the sins of many people. And Christ will come a second time, but not for people's sin. Christ will come the second time to bring salvation to those people who are waiting for him.

Christ's Sacrifice Makes Us Perfect

10 The law* gave us only an unclear picture of the good things coming in the future. The law is not a perfect picture of the real things. The law tells people to offer the same sacrifices* every year. The people who come to worship God continue to offer those sacrifices. But the law can never make those people perfect. ²If the law could make people perfect, then those sacrifices would have already stopped. Those people would already be clean ⌊from their sins⌋. And they would not still feel guilty for their sins. ⌊But the law cannot do that⌋. ³Those people's sacrifices make them remember their sins every year, ⁴because it is not possible for the blood of bulls and goats to take away sins.

⁵So when Christ came into the world he said:

"You *(God)* don't want sacrifices* and
  offerings,
 but you have prepared a body for me.
⁶ You are not pleased with the sacrifices* of
  animals killed and burned.
 And you are not pleased with sacrifices to
  take away sins.
⁷ Then I said, 'Here I am, God.
 It is written about me in the book of
  the law.
 I have come to do the things you want.'"
           Psalm 40:6-8

⁸⌊In this Scripture⌋* he *(Christ)* first said, "You don't want sacrifices* and offerings. You are not pleased with animals killed and burned or with sacrifices to take away sin." (These are all sacrifices that the law* commands.) ⁹Then he *(Christ)* said, "Here I am, God. I have come to do the things you want." So God ends that first system of sacrifices and starts his new way. ¹⁰Jesus Christ did the things God wanted him to do. And because of that, we are made holy through the sacrifice* of Christ's body. Christ made that sacrifice one time—enough for all time.

¹¹Every day the priests stand and do their religious service. Again and again the priests offer the same sacrifices.* But those sacrifices can never take away sins. ¹²But Christ offered only one sacrifice* for sins, and that sacrifice is enough for all time. Then Christ sat down at the right side of God. ¹³And now Christ waits there for his enemies to be put under his power.* ¹⁴With one sacrifice Christ made his people perfect forever. Those people are the ones who are being made holy.*

---

sacrifices Animals killed and offered to God.
Most Holy Place Literally, "holies," for "holy of holies," the place where God met the high priest.
high priest Most important priest for God's people.
sacrifice A gift or offering to God. Jewish priests killed animals and offered them to God. Jesus Christ gave his own life as a sacrifice to pay for people's sins.
law The law of Moses.

Scripture Part of the Holy Writings—Old Testament.
to be put under his power Literally, "to be made a footstool for his feet."
holy God's people are called holy because they are made pure through Christ, and they belong only to God.

¹⁵The Holy Spirit* also tells us about this. First he says:

¹⁶ "This is the agreement* I will make with my people in the future, says the Lord.
I will put my laws in their hearts.
I will write my laws in their minds."
Jeremiah 31:33

¹⁷Then he says:

"I will forgive their sins
and the evil things they do—
I will never remember those things again."
Jeremiah 31:34

¹⁸And after all these things are forgiven, there is no more need for a sacrifice* ₍to pay₎ for sins.

Come Near to God

¹⁹And so, brothers ₍and sisters₎, we are completely free to enter the Most Holy Place.* We can do this without fear because of the blood *(death)* of Jesus. ²⁰We can enter through a new way that Jesus opened for us. It is a living way. This new way leads through the curtain—Christ's body. ²¹And we have a great priest who rules the house *(people)* of God. ²²We have been cleansed and made free from feelings of guilt. And our bodies have been washed with pure water. So come near to God with a sincere *(true)* heart, feeling sure because of our faith. ²³We should hold strongly to the hope that we have. And we should never fail to tell people about our hope. We can trust God to do what he promised.

Help Each Other Be Strong

²⁴We should think about each other and see how we can help each other to show love and do good things. ²⁵We should not quit meeting together. That's what some people are doing. But we should ₍meet together and₎ strengthen each other. You should do this more and more as you see the Day* coming.

Don't Turn Away from Christ

²⁶If we decide to continue sinning after we have learned the truth, then there is no other sacrifice* that will take away sins. ²⁷If we continue sinning, all we have is fear in waiting for the judgment and the angry fire that will destroy all people who live against God. ²⁸Any person who refused to obey the law of Moses was found guilty from the proof given by two or three witnesses. That person was not forgiven. He was killed. ²⁹So what do you think should be done to a person who shows his hate for the Son of God? Surely that person should have a much worse punishment. Yes, that person should have a worse punishment for not showing respect for the blood *(Jesus' death)* that began the new agreement.* That blood once made that person holy. And that person should have a worse punishment for showing his hate against the Spirit* of God's grace *(kindness)*. ³⁰We know that God said, "I will punish people ₍for the wrong things they do₎; I will repay them."* And God also said, "The Lord will judge his people."* ³¹It is a terrible thing ₍for a sinful person₎ to fall into the hands of the living God.

Don't Lose the Courage and Joy You Had

³²Remember those days when you first learned the truth. You had a hard struggle with many sufferings, but you continued strong. ³³Sometimes people said hateful things to you and persecuted* you before many people. And sometimes you helped other people who were being treated that same way. ³⁴Yes, you helped those people in prison and shared in their suffering. And you still had joy when all the things you owned were taken away from you. You continued with joy because you knew that you had something much better that would continue forever.

Holy Spirit Called the Spirit of God, the Spirit of Christ, and the Comforter. Joined with God and Christ, he does God's work among people in the world.

agreement The new and better agreement that God has given to his people through Jesus.

sacrifice A gift or offering to God. Jewish priests killed animals and offered them to God. Jesus Christ gave his own life as a sacrifice to pay for people's sins.

Most Holy Place Literally, "holies," for "holy of holies," the spiritual place where God lives and is worshiped.

Day Probably the time Christ will come again.

new agreement This is the "better agreement" that God has given to his people through Jesus.

Spirit The Holy Spirit. Called the Spirit of God, the Spirit of Christ, and the Comforter. Joined with God and Christ, he does God's work among people in the world.

"I will repay them" Quote from Deut. 32:35.

"The Lord ... people" Quote from Ps. 135:14.

persecuted To persecute is to hurt, bother, or do bad things to.

[35] So don't lose the courage that you had in the past. Your courage will be rewarded richly. [36] You must be patient. After you have done what God wants, then you will get the things that he promised you. [37] In a very short time,

> "The One who is coming will come.
> He will not be late.
> [38] The person who is right with me *(God)*
> will have life because of his faith.
> But if that person turns back ⌊in fear⌋,
> I will not be pleased with him."*
>
> *Habakkuk 2:3-4*

[39] But we are not those people who turn back and are lost. No. We are the people who have faith and are saved.

Faith

11 Faith means being sure of the things we hope for. And faith means knowing that something is real even if we don't see it. [2] God was pleased with those people who lived a long time ago because they had faith like this.

[3] Faith helps us understand that God created the whole world with his command. This means that the things we see were made by something that cannot be seen.

[4] Cain and Abel both offered sacrifices* to God. But Abel offered a better sacrifice to God because Abel had faith. God said he was pleased with the things Abel offered. And so God called Abel a good man because Abel had faith. Abel died, but through his faith he is still speaking.

[5] Enoch was carried away from this earth. He never died. The Scripture* says that, before Enoch was carried off, he was a man who truly pleased God. Later, people could not find Enoch, because God took Enoch to be with him. This happened to Enoch because he had faith. [6] Without faith, a person cannot please God. Any person who comes to God must believe that God is real. And any person who comes to God must believe that God rewards those people who truly want to find him.

[7] Noah was warned by God about things that Noah could not yet see. But Noah had faith and respect for God. So Noah built a large boat to save his family. With his faith, Noah showed that the world was wrong. And Noah became one of those people who are made right with God through faith.

[8] God called Abraham to travel to another place that God promised to give Abraham. Abraham did not know where that other place was. But Abraham obeyed God and started traveling, because Abraham had faith. [9] Abraham lived in that country that God promised to give him. Abraham lived there like a visitor who did not belong. Abraham did this because he had faith. Abraham lived in tents with Isaac and Jacob. Isaac and Jacob also received that same promise from God. [10] Abraham was waiting for the city* that has real foundations. He was waiting for the city that is planned and built by God.

[11] Abraham was too old to have children. And Sarah was not able to have children. But Abraham had faith in God, and so God made them able to have children. Abraham trusted God to do the things he promised. [12] This man was so old that he was almost dead. But from that one man came as many descendants *(people)* as there are stars in the sky. So many people came from that one man that they are like grains of sand on the seashore.

[13] All those great men continued living with faith until they died. Those men did not get the things that God promised his people. The men only saw those things coming far in the future and were glad. Those men accepted the fact that they were like visitors and strangers on earth. [14] When people accept something like that, then those people show that they are waiting for a country that will be their own country. [15] If those men were thinking about that country they had left, then they could have gone back. [16] But those men were waiting for a better country—a heavenly country. So God is not ashamed to be called their God. And God has prepared a city for those men.

[17-18] God tested Abraham's faith. God told Abraham to offer Isaac as a sacrifice.* Abraham obeyed because he had faith. Abraham already had the promises from God. And God had already said to Abraham, "It is through Isaac that your descendants will come." But Abraham was ready to offer his only son *(Isaac)*. Abraham did this because he had faith. [19] Abraham believed that God could raise people from death. And really, ⌊when God stopped Abraham from killing Isaac⌋, it was like Abraham got Isaac back from death.

"The One ... him" This quote is from the Septuagint, the Greek version of the Old Testament.
sacrifice(s) Gifts or offerings to God.
Scripture Part of the Holy Writings—Old Testament.

city The spiritual "city" where God's people live with him. Also called "the heavenly Jerusalem" (Heb. 12:22).

²⁰Isaac blessed the future of Jacob and Esau. Isaac did that because he had faith. ²¹And Jacob blessed each one of Joseph's sons. Jacob did this while he was dying. He was leaning on his rod and worshiping God. Jacob did those things because he had faith. ²²And when Joseph was almost dead, he spoke about the Israelites* *(the Jews)* leaving Egypt. And Joseph told the people what they should do with his body. Joseph said those things because he had faith.

²³And the mother and father of Moses hid Moses for three months after he was born. They did this because they had faith. They saw that Moses was a beautiful baby. And they were not afraid to disobey the king's *(Pharaoh's)* order. ²⁴Moses grew up and became a man. Moses refused to be called the son of Pharaoh's daughter. ²⁵Moses chose not to enjoy the pleasures of sin. Those pleasures end quickly. Instead, Moses chose to suffer bad things with God's people. Moses did this because he had faith. ²⁶Moses thought that it was better to suffer for the Christ* than to have all the treasures of Egypt. Moses was waiting for the reward ⌊that God would give him⌋. ²⁷Moses left Egypt. He left because he had faith. Moses was not afraid of the king's *(Pharaoh's)* anger. Moses continued strong like he could see the God that no person can see. ²⁸Moses prepared the Passover* and spread the blood ⌊on the doors⌋. This blood was spread ⌊on the doors⌋ so that the Angel of Death* would not kill the firstborn* sons ⌊of the Jewish people⌋. Moses did this because he had faith.

²⁹And the people ⌊that Moses led⌋ all walked through the Red Sea like it was dry land. They were able to do this because they had faith. The Egyptians also tried to walk through the Red Sea, but they were all drowned.

³⁰And the walls of Jericho fell because of the faith of God's people. The people marched around the walls of Jericho for seven days, and then the walls fell.

³¹And Rahab, the prostitute,* welcomed the ⌊Israelite⌋ spies and helped them like friends. And because of her faith she was not killed with those other people who refused to obey.

³²Do I need to give you more examples? I don't have enough time to tell you about Gideon, Barak, Samson, Jephthah, David, Samuel, and the prophets.* ³³All those people had great faith. And with that faith they defeated kingdoms. They did the things that are right, and they got the things that God promised. With their faith some people closed the mouths of lions. ³⁴Some people stopped great fires, and other people were saved from being killed with swords. They did those things because they had faith. Weak people were made strong because of their faith. They became powerful in battle and defeated other armies. ³⁵People that had died were raised from death, and they were given back to the women in their family. Other people were tortured* and refused to accept their freedom. They did this so that they could be raised from death to a better life. ³⁶Some people were laughed at and beaten. Other people were tied and put into prison. ³⁷They were killed with stones and they were cut in half. They were killed with swords. Some of these people wore the skins of sheep and goats. They were poor, persecuted,* and treated badly by other people. ³⁸The world was not good enough for these great people. These people wandered in deserts and mountains, living in caves and holes in the ground.

³⁹All these people are known for their faith. But none of these people got God's great promise. ⁴⁰God planned to give us something better. Then those people could be made perfect, but only together with us.

We Should Also Follow Jesus' Example

12 We have those many people ⌊of faith⌋ around us. Their lives tell us what faith means. So we should be like them. We too should run the race that is before us and never stop trying. We should take away ⌊from our lives⌋ anything that would stop us. And we should take away the sin that so easily catches us. ²We should always follow the example of Jesus. Jesus is the

Israelites The Jewish people were from the twelve sons of Jacob, who is also called "Israel."
Christ The "anointed one" (Messiah) or chosen of God.
Passover Important holy day for Jews. They ate a special meal on this day every year to remember that God freed them from slavery in Egypt in Moses' time.
Angel of Death Literally, "the destroyer." To punish the Egyptian people, God sent an angel to kill the oldest son in each home (Ex. 12:29-32).
firstborn The first child born into a family.

prostitute(s) Women paid by men for sexual sin.
prophets People who spoke for God. Their writings are part of the Old Testament.
tortured To be bound or tied and then hurt or punished.
persecuted To be hurt or bothered by other people.

leader in our faith. And he makes our faith perfect. He suffered death on the cross. But Jesus accepted the shame of the cross like it was nothing. He did this because of the joy that God put before him. And now he is sitting at the right side of God's throne. ³Think about Jesus. He was patient while sinful men were doing bad things against him. Jesus did this so that you also will be patient and not stop trying.

God Is Like a Father

⁴You are struggling against sin, but your struggles have not yet caused you to be killed. ⁵You are sons of God, and he speaks words of comfort to you. You have forgotten those words:

> "My son, don't think it is worth nothing
>   when the Lord punishes you,
> and don't stop trying when the Lord
>   corrects you.
> ⁶ The Lord punishes every person he loves,
>   and he punishes every person
>   he accepts as a son."
>
>   *Proverbs 3:11-12*

⁷So accept sufferings like those sufferings are a father's punishment. God does these things to you like a father punishing his sons. All sons are punished by their fathers. ⁸If you are never punished (and every son must be punished), then you are not true children and not really sons. ⁹We have all had fathers here on earth who punished us. And we respected our fathers. So it is even more important that we accept punishment from the Father of our spirits. If we do this we will have life. ¹⁰Our fathers on earth punished us for a short time. They punished us the way they thought was best. But God punishes us to help us, so that we can become holy* like him. ¹¹We don't enjoy punishment when we get it. Being punished is painful. But later, after we have learned from being punished, we have peace, because we start living right.

Be Careful How You Live

¹²You have become weak. So make yourselves strong again. ¹³Walk *(live)* in the right way so that you will be saved and your weakness will not cause you to be lost.

¹⁴Try to live in peace with all people. And try to live lives free from sin. If a person's life is not holy,* then he will never see the Lord. ¹⁵Be careful that no person fails to get God's grace *(kindness)*. Be careful that no person becomes like a bitter weed growing among you. A person like that can ruin your whole group. ¹⁶Be careful that no person does sexual sin. And be careful that no person is like Esau and never thinks about God. Esau was the oldest son and he would have inherited *(received)* everything from his father. But Esau sold all that for a single meal. ¹⁷You remember that after Esau did this, he wanted to get his father's blessing. Esau wanted that blessing so much that he cried. But his father refused to give him the blessing, because Esau could find no way to change the thing he had done.

¹⁸You have come to a new place. It is not a place like the mountain that the people of Israel* came to. You have not come to a mountain that can be touched and that is burning with fire. You have not come to a place with darkness, sadness, and storms. ¹⁹There is no sound of a trumpet or a voice speaking words *(like those people heard)*. When the people heard the voice, they begged to never hear another word. ²⁰They did not want to hear the command: "If anything, even an animal, touches the mountain, it must be killed with stones."* ²¹The things those people saw were so terrible that Moses said, "I am shaking with fear."*

²²But you have not come to that kind of place. The new place you have come to is Mount Zion.* You have come to the city of the living God, the heavenly Jerusalem.* You have come to thousands of angels gathered together with joy. ²³You have come to the meeting of God's firstborn* children. Their names are written in heaven. You have come to God, the judge of all people. And you have come to the spirits of good people who have been made perfect. ²⁴You have come to Jesus—the One that brought the new agreement* from God to his people. You have

---

Israel The Jewish nation (people).
"If anything ... stones" Quote from Ex. 19:12-13.
"I am shaking with fear" Quote from Deut. 9:19.
Mount Zion Another name for Jerusalem.
Jerusalem Here, the spiritual city of God's people.
firstborn The first son born in a Jewish family had the most important place in the family and received special blessings. All God's children are like that.
new agreement This is the "better agreement" that God has given to his people through Jesus.

---

holy A holy person is pure and belongs only to God.

come to the sprinkled blood* that tells us about better things than the blood of Abel.*

²⁵Be careful and don't refuse to listen when God speaks. Those people *(Israelites)* refused to listen to him when he warned them on earth. And those people did not escape. Now God is speaking from heaven. So now it will be worse for those people who refuse to listen to him. ²⁶When he spoke before, his voice shook the earth. But now he has promised, "Once again I will shake the earth. But I will also shake heaven."* ²⁷The words "once again" clearly show us that everything that was made will be destroyed. Those are the things that can be shaken. And only the things that cannot be shaken will continue.

²⁸So we should be thankful because we have a kingdom that cannot be shaken. We should be thankful and worship God in a way that will please him. We should worship him with respect and fear, ²⁹because our God is like a fire that can destroy.

13 You are brothers ₍and sisters₎ in Christ, so continue loving each other. ²Always remember to help people by accepting them into your home. Some people have done that and have helped angels without knowing it. ³Don't forget those people in prison. Remember them like you are in prison with them. And don't forget those people who are suffering. Remember them like you are suffering with them.

⁴Marriage should be honored by all people. And every marriage should be kept pure between only two people. God will judge guilty those people who do sexual sins and adultery.* ⁵Keep your lives free from the love of money. And be satisfied with the things you have. God has said,

"I will never leave you;
I will never run away from you."
Deuteronomy 31:6

⁶So we can feel sure and say,

"The Lord is my helper;
I will not be afraid.
People can do nothing to me."
Psalm 118:6

⁷Remember your leaders. They taught God's message to you. Remember how they lived and died, and copy their faith. ⁸Jesus Christ is the same yesterday, today, and forever.

⁹Don't let all kinds of strange teachings lead you into the wrong way. Your hearts should be strengthened by God's grace *(kindness)*, not by obeying rules about foods. Obeying those rules doesn't help people.

¹⁰We have a sacrifice.* And those priests who serve in the Holy Tent* cannot eat from our sacrifice. ¹¹The high priest* carries the blood of animals into the Most Holy Place.* He offers that blood for sins. But the bodies of those animals are burned outside the camp. ¹²So Jesus also suffered outside the city. Jesus died to make his people holy* with his own blood *(death)*. ¹³So we should go to Jesus outside the camp. We should accept the same shame that Jesus had. ¹⁴Here on earth we don't have a city that continues forever. But we are waiting for the city that we will have in the future. ¹⁵So through Jesus we should never stop offering our sacrifice to God. That sacrifice is our praise, coming from lips that speak his name. ¹⁶And don't forget to do good for other people. And share with other people. These are the sacrifices that please God.

¹⁷Obey your leaders and be under their authority. Those men are responsible for you. So they are always watching to protect your souls. Obey those men so that they will do this work with joy, not sadness. It will not help you to make their work hard.

¹⁸Continue praying for us. We feel right about the things we do, because we always try to do the best thing. ¹⁹And I beg you to pray that God will send me back to you soon. I want this more than anything else.

²⁰⁻²¹I pray that the God of peace will give you every good thing you need so that you can do the things he wants. God is the One who raised our Lord Jesus from death. He raised Jesus, the Great Shepherd of the sheep. God raised Jesus because of his blood *(death)*. His blood began the new

---

sacrifice Here, the sacrifice (offering) of Jesus. He gave his life to pay for people's sins.
Holy Tent Or, "tabernacle." The special tent where God lived among his people and where the Jewish priests worshiped.
high priest Most important Jewish priest and leader.
Most Holy Place Literally, "holies," for "holy of holies," the place where God met the high priest.
holy God's people are called holy because they are made pure through Christ, and they belong only to God.

---

sprinkled blood The blood (death) of Jesus.
Abel The son of Adam and Eve. He was killed by his brother Cain. See Gen. 4:8.
"Once again ... heaven" Quote from Hag. 2:6.
adultery Breaking a marriage promise by sexual sin.

agreement* that continues forever. I pray that God will do the things in us that please him. I ask that he will do those things through Jesus Christ. To Jesus be glory forever. Amen.

²²My brothers ₍and sisters₎, I beg you to listen patiently to these things I have said. I said these things to strengthen you. And this letter is not very long. ²³I want you to know that our brother Timothy is out of prison. If he comes to me soon, we will both come to see you.

²⁴Say hello to all your leaders and to all God's people. All ₍God's people₎ in Italy say hello to you.

²⁵God's grace *(kindness)* be with you all.

---

new agreement This is the "better agreement" that God has given to his people through Jesus.

James

1 From James, a servant of God and of the Lord Jesus Christ.
To all of God's people that are scattered everywhere in the world: Greetings.

Faith and Wisdom

²My brothers ₍and sisters₎, you will have many kinds of troubles. But when these things happen, you should be very happy. ³Why? Because you know that these things are testing your faith. And this will give you patience. ⁴Let your patience show itself perfectly in what you do. Then you will be perfect and complete. You will have everything you need. ⁵But if any of you needs wisdom, then you should ask God for it. God is generous. He enjoys giving to all people. So God will give you wisdom. ⁶But when you ask God, you must believe. Don't doubt God. The person who doubts is like a wave in the sea. The wind blows the wave up and down. The person who doubts is like that wave. ⁷⁻⁸The person who doubts is thinking two different things at the same time. He cannot decide about anything he does. A person like that should not think that he will receive anything from the Lord.

True Riches

⁹If a believer is poor, he should be proud because God has made him ₍spiritually₎ rich. ¹⁰If a believer is rich, he should be proud because ₍God has shown him that₎ he is ₍spiritually₎ poor. The rich person will die like a wild flower. ¹¹The sun rises and becomes hotter and hotter. The sun's heat makes the plant very dry. The flower falls off. The flower was beautiful, but now it is dead. It is the same with a rich person. While he is still making plans for his business, he will die.

Temptation Does Not Come from God

¹²When a person is tempted and still continues strong, he should be happy. Why? Because after he has proved ₍his faith₎, God will give him the reward of life forever. God promised this to all people who love him. ¹³When a person is being tempted, he should not say, "God is tempting me." Evil cannot tempt God. And God himself does not tempt any person. ¹⁴It is the evil things a person wants that tempt that person. His own evil desire leads him away and holds him. ¹⁵This desire causes sin. Then the sin grows and brings death.

¹⁶My dear brothers ₍and sisters₎, don't be fooled about this. ¹⁷Everything good comes from God. And every perfect gift is from God. These good gifts come down from the Father *(Maker)* of all light *(sun, moon, stars)*. God does not change. He is always the same. ¹⁸God decided to give us life through the word of truth. He wanted us to be the most important of all the things he made.

Listening and Obeying

¹⁹My dear brothers ₍and sisters₎, always be more willing to listen than to speak. Don't become angry easily. ²⁰A person's anger does not help him live right like God wants. ²¹So put out of your life every evil thing and every kind of wrong thing you do. Be humble and accept God's teaching that is planted in your hearts. This teaching can save your souls.

²²Do what God's teaching says; don't just listen and do nothing. Why? Because when you only sit and listen, you are fooling yourselves. ²³If a person hears God's teaching and does nothing, he is like this: He is like a man who looks at his face in the mirror. ²⁴The man sees himself, then goes away and quickly forgets what he looked like. ²⁵But the truly happy person is the person who carefully studies God's perfect law that makes people free. He continues to study it. He listens to God's teaching and does not forget what he heard. Then he obeys what God's teaching says. When that person does this, it makes that person happy.

The True Way to Worship God

²⁶Some person might think he is religious *(good)*. But if that person says things he should

not say, then he is fooling himself. His "religion" is worth nothing. ²⁷The kind of religion *(worship)* that God accepts is this: caring for orphans* or widows* who need help, and keeping yourself free from the world's ₍evil₎ influence. This is the kind of religion *(worship)* that God accepts as pure and good.

Love All People

2My dear brothers ₍and sisters₎, you are believers in our glorious Lord Jesus Christ. So don't think that some people are more important than other people. ²Suppose a person comes into your group. He is wearing very nice clothes and a gold ring. At the same time a poor man comes in wearing old, dirty clothes. ³You show special attention to the man wearing nice clothes. You say, "Sit here in this good seat." But you say to the poor man, "Stand there!" or, "Sit on the floor by our feet!" ⁴What are you doing? You are making some people more important than others. With evil thoughts you are deciding which person is better.

⁵Listen, my dear brothers ₍and sisters₎! God chose the poor people in the world to be rich with faith. He chose them to receive the kingdom God promised to people who love him. ⁶But you show no respect to the poor man. And you know that the rich people are the people who always try to control your lives. And they are the people who take you to court. ⁷And the rich people are the people who say bad things against the good name of the One *(Jesus)* who owns you.

⁸One law rules over all other laws. This royal law is found in the Scriptures*: "Love other people the same as you love yourself."* If you obey this law, then you are doing right. ⁹But if you are treating one person like he is more important than another person, then you are sinning. That ₍royal₎ law proves that you are guilty of breaking ₍God's₎ law. ¹⁰A person might follow all of ₍God's₎ law. But if that person fails to obey only one command, then he is guilty of breaking all the commands in that law. ¹¹God said, "Don't do the sin of adultery."* The same God also said, "Don't kill."* So if you don't do the sin of adultery, but you kill a person, then you are guilty of breaking all of ₍God's₎ law. ¹²You will be judged by the law that makes people free. You should remember this in everything you say and do. ¹³Yes, you must show mercy to other people. If you do not show mercy, then God will not show mercy to you when he judges you. But the person who shows mercy can stand without fear when he is judged.

Faith and Good Works

¹⁴My brothers ₍and sisters₎, if a person says that he has faith, but does nothing, then that faith is worth nothing. Can faith like that save him? No! ¹⁵A brother or sister ₍in Christ₎ might need clothes or might need food to eat. ¹⁶And you say to that person, "God be with you! I hope you stay warm and get plenty to eat." You say these things, but you don't give that person those things he needs. If you don't help that person, your words are worth nothing. ¹⁷It is the same with faith. If faith does nothing, then that faith is dead, because it is alone.

¹⁸A person might say, "You have faith, but I do things. Show me your faith! Your faith does nothing. I will show you my faith by the things I do." ¹⁹You believe there is one God. Good! But the demons* believe, too! And they shake with fear.

²⁰You foolish person! Must you be shown that faith that does nothing is worth nothing? ²¹Abraham is our father *(ancestor)*. Abraham was made right with God by the things he did. He offered *(gave)* his son Isaac to God on the altar.* ²²So you see that Abraham's faith and the things he did worked together. His faith was made perfect by the things he did. ²³This shows the full meaning of the Scripture* that says: "Abraham believed God. And God accepted Abraham's faith. That faith made Abraham right with God."* Abraham was called "God's friend."* ²⁴So you see that a person is made right with God by the things he does. He cannot be made right by faith only.

²⁵Another example is Rahab. Rahab was a prostitute.* But she was made right with God by

---

orphans Children whose mother and father have died.
widows A widow is a woman whose husband has died.
Scriptures Holy Writings—the Old Testament.
"Love other people ... yourself" Quote from Lev. 19:18.
adultery Breaking a marriage promise by sexual sin.
"Don't do ... adultery" Quote from Ex. 20:14; Deut. 5:18.
"Don't kill" Quote from Ex. 20:13; Deut. 5:17.

demons Demons are evil spirits from the devil.
altar Place for offering sacrifices (gifts) to God.
Scripture Part of the Holy Writings—the Old Testament.
"Abraham ... right with God" Quote from Gen. 15:6.
"God's friend" Quote from 2 Chron. 20:7; Is. 41:8.
prostitute(s) Women paid by men for sexual sin.

something she did: She helped the spies ₍for God's people₎. She welcomed them into her home and helped them escape by a different road.*

²⁶A person's body that does not have a spirit is dead. It is the same with faith—faith that does nothing is dead!

Controlling the Things We Say

3 My brothers ₍and sisters₎, not many of you should become teachers. Why? Because you know that we who teach will be judged more strictly than other people. ²We all make many mistakes. If there were a person who never said anything wrong, then that person would be perfect. He would be able to control his whole body, too. ³We put bits into the mouths of horses to make them obey us. With these bits in the horses' mouths, we can control their whole body. ⁴It is the same with ships. A ship is very big, and it is pushed by strong winds. But a very small rudder controls that big ship. The man who controls the rudder decides where the ship will go. The ship goes where the man wants. ⁵It is the same with our tongue. It is a small part of the body, but it boasts about doing great things.

A big forest fire can be started with only a little flame. ⁶The tongue is like a fire. It is a world of evil among the parts of our body. How? The tongue spreads its evil through our whole body. It starts a fire that influences all of life. The tongue gets this fire from hell. ⁷People can tame every kind of wild animal, bird, reptile, and fish. People have already tamed all these things. ⁸But no person can tame *(control)* the tongue. It is wild and evil. It is full of poison that can kill. ⁹We use our tongues to praise our Lord and Father *(God)*, but then we curse *(say bad things to)* people. And God made those people like himself. ¹⁰Praises and curses come from the same mouth! My brothers ₍and sisters₎, this should not happen. ¹¹Do good water and bad water flow from the same spring? No! ¹²My brothers ₍and sisters₎, can a fig tree make olives? No! Can a grapevine make figs? No! And a well full of salty water cannot give good water.

True Wisdom

¹³Is there any person among you who is truly wise and understanding? Then he should show his wisdom by living right. He should do good things with humility. A wise person does not boast. ¹⁴If you are selfish and have bitter jealousy in your hearts, then you have no reason to boast. Your boasting is a lie that hides the truth. ¹⁵That kind of "wisdom" does not come from God. That "wisdom" comes from the world. It is not spiritual. It is from the devil. ¹⁶Where there is jealousy and selfishness, there will be confusion and every kind of evil. ¹⁷But the wisdom that comes from God is like this: First, it is pure. It is also peaceful, gentle, and easy to please. This wisdom is always ready to help people who have trouble and to do good things for other people. This wisdom is always fair and honest. ¹⁸People who work for peace in a peaceful way get the good things that come from right-living.

Give Yourselves to God

4 Do you know where your fights and arguments come from? Your fights and arguments come from the selfish desires that make war inside you. ²You want things, but you don't get them. So you kill and are jealous of other people. But you still cannot get what you want. So you argue and fight. You don't get the things you want because you don't ask ₍God₎. ³Or when you ask, you don't receive. Why? Because the reason you ask is wrong. You only want things so that you can use those things for your own pleasures. ⁴So you people are not faithful to God! You should know that loving the world is the same as hating God. So if a person wants to be a part* of the world, then he makes himself God's enemy. ⁵Do you think the Scripture* means nothing? The Scripture says, "The Spirit* that ₍God₎ made to live in us wants us only for himself."* ⁶But the grace *(kindness)* that God gives is greater. Like the Scripture says, "God is against proud people, but he gives grace *(kindness)* to people who are humble."* ⁷So give yourselves to God. Be against the devil, and the devil will run away from you. ⁸Come near to God and God will come near to you. You are sinners. So clean sin out of your lives.* You are trying to follow God and the world at the same time. Make your thinking pure. ⁹Be sad, be sorry, and cry! Change your laughter

---

part Literally, "friend."
Scripture Part of the Holy Writings—Old Testament.
Spirit The Holy Spirit. Called the Spirit of God, the Spirit of Christ, and the Comforter. Joined with God and Christ, he does God's work among people in the world.
"The Spirit ... himself" See Ex. 20:5.
"God is against ... humble" Quote from Prov. 3:34.
So clean sin out of your lives Literally, "So wash your hands."

She helped ... road The story about Rahab is in Josh. 2:1-21.

into crying. Change your joy into sadness. ¹⁰Be humble before the Lord, and he will make you great.

You Are Not the Judge

¹¹Brothers ₍and sisters₎, don't say things against each other. If you criticize your brother ₍in Christ₎ or judge him, then you are criticizing the law ₍he follows₎. When you judge a brother ₍in Christ₎, you are really judging the law ₍he follows₎. And when you are judging the law, you are not a follower of the law. You have become a judge! ¹²God is the only One who makes laws. He is the only Judge. God is the only One who can save and destroy. So it is not right for you to judge another person.

Let God Plan Your Life

¹³Some of you say, "Today or tomorrow we will go to some city. We will stay there a year, do business, and make money." Listen! Think about this: ¹⁴You don't know what will happen tomorrow! Your life is like a fog. You can see it for a short time, but then it goes away. ¹⁵So you should say, "If the Lord wants, we will live and do this or that." ¹⁶But now you are proud and you boast. All of this boasting is wrong. ¹⁷And when a person knows how to do good, but does not do good, then he is sinning.

Selfish Rich People Will Be Punished

5 You rich people, listen! Cry and be very sad because much trouble will come to you. ²Your riches will rot and be worth nothing. Your clothes will be eaten by moths. ³Your gold and silver will rust, and that rust will be a proof that you were wrong. That rust will eat your bodies like fire. You saved your treasure in the last days. ⁴People worked in your fields, but you did not pay them. Those people are crying out against you. Those people harvested your crops. Now the Lord *(God)* of heaven's armies* has heard the things they are shouting. ⁵Your life on earth was full of rich living. You pleased yourselves with everything you wanted. You made yourselves fat, ₍like an animal ready₎ for the day of slaughter.* ⁶You showed no mercy to good people. They were not against you, but you killed them.

Be Patient

⁷Brothers ₍and sisters₎, be patient; the Lord ₍Jesus₎ will come. So be patient until that time. Farmers are patient. A farmer waits for his valuable crop to grow up from the earth. A farmer waits patiently for his crop to receive the first rain and the last rain.* ⁸You must be patient, too. Don't stop hoping. The Lord ₍Jesus₎ is coming soon. ⁹Brothers, ₍and sisters₎, don't complain against each other. If you don't stop complaining, you will be judged guilty. And the Judge is ready to come! ¹⁰Brothers ₍and sisters₎, follow the example of the prophets* who spoke for the Lord *(God)*. They suffered many bad things, but they were patient. ¹¹We say that those people who accepted their troubles with patience are now happy. You have heard about Job's patience.* You know that after all Job's trouble, the Lord helped him. This shows that the Lord is full of mercy and is kind.

Be Careful What You Say

¹²My brothers ₍and sisters₎, it is very important that you not use an oath when you make a promise. Don't use the name of heaven, earth, or anything else to prove what you say. When you mean yes, say only "yes." When you mean no, say only "no." Do this so that you will not be judged guilty.

The Power of Prayer

¹³If one of you is having troubles, he should pray. If one of you is happy, he should sing. ¹⁴If one of you is sick, he should call the church's elders.* The elders should rub oil on him* in the name of the Lord and pray for him. ¹⁵And the prayer that is said with faith will make the sick person well. The Lord will heal him. And if this person has sinned, then God will forgive him. ¹⁶Always tell each other the wrong things you

---

first rain, last rain The "first rain" came in the Fall, and the "last rain" came in the Spring.
prophets People who spoke for God. They often told things that would happen in the future.
Job's patience Read the book of Job.
elders Men chosen to lead a church. Also called "overseers" and "pastors" (shepherds), they have the work of caring for God's people (Acts 20:28; Eph. 4:11).
rub oil on him Oil was used like medicine.

Lord of heaven's armies Literally, "Lord Sabaoth," meaning ruler of all heavenly powers.
You made yourselves fat ... slaughter Literally, "You fattened your hearts for the day of slaughter."

have done. Then pray for each other. Do this so that God can heal you. When a good person prays hard, great things happen. ¹⁷Elijah* was a person the same as us. He prayed that it would not rain. And it did not rain on the land for three and a half years! ¹⁸Then Elijah prayed that it would rain. And the rain came down from the sky, and the land grew crops again.

Saving a Soul

¹⁹My brothers ⌊and sisters⌋, one of you may wander away from the truth. And another person may help him come back to the truth. ²⁰Remember this: Any person who brings a sinner back from the wrong way will save that sinner's soul from death *(hell)*. By doing this, that person will cause many sins to be forgiven.

Elijah Man who spoke for God about 850 B.C.

1 Peter

1 From Peter, an apostle* of Jesus Christ. To God's chosen people who are away from their homes—people scattered all around the areas of Pontus, Galatia, Cappadocia, Asia, and Bithynia. ²God planned long ago to choose you by making you his holy people.* Making you holy is the Spirit's* work. God wanted you to obey him and to be made clean by the blood *(death)* of Jesus Christ. Grace *(kindness)* and peace be yours more and more.

A Living Hope

³Praise be to the God and Father of our Lord Jesus Christ. God has great mercy, and because of his mercy he gave us a new life. This new life brings us a living hope through Jesus Christ's rising from death. ⁴Now we hope for the blessings God has for his children. Those blessings are kept for you in heaven. Those blessings cannot ruin or be destroyed or lose their beauty. ⁵God's power protects you through your faith, and it keeps you safe until your salvation comes. That salvation is ready to be given to you at the end of time. ⁶This makes you very happy. But now for a short time different kinds of troubles may make you sad. ⁷Why do these troubles happen? To prove that your faith is pure *(true)*. This purity of faith is worth more than gold. Gold can be proved to be pure by fire, but gold will ruin. The purity of your faith will bring you praise and glory and honor when Jesus Christ appears *(comes)*. ⁸You have not seen Christ, but still you love him. You can't see him now, but you believe in him. You are filled with a joy that cannot be explained. And that joy is full of glory. ⁹Your faith has a goal. That goal is to save your souls. And you are receiving that goal—your salvation.

¹⁰The prophets* studied carefully and tried to learn about this salvation. Those prophets spoke about the grace *(kindness)* that was coming to you. ¹¹The Spirit of Christ was in those prophets. And the Spirit was telling about the sufferings that would happen to Christ and about the glory that would come after those sufferings. Those prophets tried to learn about what the Spirit was showing them. They tried to learn when those things would happen and what the world would be like at that time. ¹²It was shown to those prophets that their service was not for themselves. The prophets were serving you. They were serving you when they told about the things that you have heard. The men who preached the gospel* to you told you those things. They told you with the help of the Holy Spirit* that was sent from heaven. The things you were told are things that even the angels want very much to know about.

A Call to Holy Living

¹³So prepare your minds for service, and have self-control. All your hope should be for the gift of grace *(kindness)* that will be yours when Jesus Christ appears *(comes)*. ¹⁴In the past you did not understand about these things, so you did the evil things you wanted. But now you are children ₍of God₎ who obey. So don't live like you lived in the past. ¹⁵But be holy* in all the things you do, the same as God is holy. God is the One who called you. ¹⁶It is written ₍in the Scriptures₎*: "Be holy, because I *(God)* am holy."*

---

apostle Person Jesus chose to be a special helper for telling the Good News to the world.
holy people God's people are called holy because they are made pure through Christ, and they belong only to God.
Spirit, Holy Spirit Also called the Spirit of God, the Spirit of Christ, and the Comforter. Joined with God and Christ, he does God's work among people in the world.
prophets People who spoke for God. They often told things that would happen in the future.
gospel The news that God has made a way for people to have their sins forgiven and live with God forever.
holy A holy person is pure and belongs only to God.
Scripture(s) Holy Writings—the Old Testament.
"Be ... holy" Quote from Lev. 11:44, 45; 19:2; 20:7.

¹⁷You pray to God and call him Father. God judges each man's work equally. So while you are visiting ⌊here on earth⌋, you should live with fear *(respect)* for God. ¹⁸You know that ⌊in the past⌋ you were living in a worthless way. You got that way of living from the people who lived before you. But you were saved from that way of living. You were bought, but not with things that ruin like gold or silver. ¹⁹But you were bought with the precious blood *(death)* of Christ—a pure and perfect lamb. ²⁰Christ was chosen before the world was made. But he was shown ⌊to the world⌋ in these last times for you. ²¹You believe in God through Christ. God raised Christ from death. Then God gave glory to him. So your faith and your hope is in God.

²²Now you have made yourselves pure by obeying the truth. Now you can have true love for your brothers and sisters. So love each other deeply—with all your heart. ²³You have been born again. This new life did not come from something that dies. That life came from something that cannot die. You were born again through God's living message* that continues forever. ²⁴The Scripture* says,

"People ⌊don't live forever;
they⌋ are all like grass,
and all their glory is like a wild flower.
The grass dies,
and the flower falls.
²⁵ But the word of God will live forever."
Isaiah 40:6-8

And this is the word *(teaching)* that was told to you.

The Living Stone and the Holy Nation

2 So don't do anything to hurt ⌊other people⌋, don't lie, don't do things to fool people, don't be jealous, don't say bad things about people. Put all these things out of your life. ²Be like babies that are newly born. Be hungry for the pure milk *(teaching)* that feeds your spirit. By drinking that you can grow up and be saved. ³You have already tasted the goodness of the Lord.

⁴The Lord ⌊Jesus⌋ is the "stone"* that lives. The people ⌊of the world⌋ decided they did not want that stone *(Jesus)*. But he was the stone God chose. To God he was worth much. So come to him. ⁵You also are like living stones. Let yourselves be used to build a spiritual temple*— to be holy priests who give spiritual sacrifices* to God that he will accept. You give those sacrifices through Jesus Christ. ⁶The Scripture* says:

"Look, I have chosen a precious *(valuable)*
cornerstone,*
and I put that stone *(Jesus)* in Zion*;
the person that trusts in him will never
be ashamed."
Isaiah 28:16

⁷That stone *(Jesus)* is worth much to you people who believe. But to the people who don't believe, he is:

"the stone that the builders decided they
did not want.
That stone became the most important stone."
Psalm 118:22

⁸To people who don't believe, he is:

"a stone that makes people stumble,
a stone that makes people fall."
Isaiah 8:14

People stumble because they don't obey what God says. This is what God planned to happen to those people.

⁹But you are chosen people. You are the King's priests. You are a holy* nation of people. You are people who belong to God. God chose you to tell about the wonderful things he has done. He called *(brought)* you out of darkness *(sin)* into his wonderful light. ¹⁰At one time you were not God's people. But now you are God's people. In the past you had never received mercy. But now you have received mercy ⌊from God⌋.

Live for God

¹¹Dear friends, you are like visitors and strangers ⌊in this world⌋. So I beg you to stay away from the evil things your bodies want to do. These things fight against your soul. ¹²People who don't believe are living all around you. Those people

---

message The news that God has made a way through Christ for people to have their sins forgiven and live with God forever.
Scripture Part of the Holy Writings—Old Testament.
stone The most important stone in God's spiritual temple or house (his people).
temple God's house—the place where God's people worship and serve him.
sacrifices A sacrifice is a gift or offering for God.
cornerstone First and most important rock of a building.
Zion A name for Jerusalem, the city of God's chosen people.
holy God's people are called holy because they are made pure through Christ, and they belong only to God.

may say that you are doing wrong. So live good lives. Then they will see the good things you do, and they will give glory to God on that day when he comes.

Obey Every Human Authority

[13] Obey the people who have authority* in this world. Do this for the Lord. Obey the king who is the highest authority. [14] And obey the leaders who are sent by the king. They are sent to punish people who do wrong and to praise those people who do good. [15] So when you do good, you stop foolish people from saying stupid things about you. This is what God wants. [16] Live like free men. But don't use your freedom as an excuse to do evil. Live like you are serving God. [17] Show respect for all people. Love all the brothers and sisters of God's family. Fear *(respect)* God, and honor the king.

The Example of Christ's Suffering

[18] Slaves, accept the authority of your masters. Do this with all respect. You should obey the masters that are good and kind, and you should obey the masters that are bad. [19] A person might have to suffer even when he has done nothing wrong. If that person thinks of God and bears the pain, then this pleases God. [20] But if you are punished for doing wrong, there is no reason to praise you for bearing that punishment. But if you suffer for doing good, and you are patient, then that pleases God. [21] That is what you were called to do. Christ gave you an example to follow. You should do the same as he did. ⌊You should be patient when you suffer⌋, because Christ suffered for you.

[22] "He *(Christ)* did no sin,
and no lies were found in his mouth."
Isaiah 53:9

[23] People said bad things to Christ, but he did not say bad things to them. Christ suffered, but he did not threaten *(speak against)* the people. No! Christ let God take care of him. God is the One who judges rightly. [24] Christ carried our sins in his body on the cross. He did this so that we would stop living for sin and live for what is right. By his *(Christ's)* wounds you were healed. [25] You were like sheep that went the wrong way. But now you have come back to the Shepherd and Protector of your souls.

Wives and Husbands

3 In the same way you wives should accept the authority of your husbands. Then, if some of your husbands have not obeyed ⌊God's⌋ teaching, they will be persuaded to believe. You will not need to say anything. They will be persuaded by the way their wives live. [2] Your husbands will see the pure lives that you live with your respect ⌊for God⌋. [3] It is not fancy hair, gold jewelry, or fine clothes that should make you beautiful. [4] No, your beauty should come from inside you—the beauty of a gentle and quiet spirit. That beauty will never disappear. It is worth very much to God. [5] It was the same with the holy women who lived long ago and followed God. They made themselves beautiful in that same way. They accepted the authority of their husbands. [6] ⌊I am talking about women⌋ like Sarah. She obeyed Abraham, her husband, and called him her master. And you women are true children of Sarah if you always do what is right and are not afraid.

[7] In the same way, you husbands should live with your wives in an understanding way. You should show respect to your wives. They are weaker than you. But God gives your wives the same blessing that he gives you—the grace *(kindness)* that gives true life. Do these things so that nothing will trouble your prayers.

Suffering for Doing Right

[8] So all of you should live together in peace. Try to understand each other. Love each other like brothers. Be kind and humble. [9] Don't do wrong to a person to pay him back for doing wrong to you. Or don't say something bad to a person to pay him back for saying something bad to you. But ⌊ask God to⌋ bless that person. Do this, because you yourselves were called to receive a blessing. [10] ⌊The Scripture* says⌋,

"The person that wants to love life
and wants to enjoy good days
must stop speaking evil,
and he must stop telling lies.
[11] That person must stop doing evil and do good;
that person should look for peace
and try to get it.

---

people ... authority Rulers, governors, presidents, or other government leaders.

Scripture Part of the Holy Writings—Old Testament.

¹² The Lord sees the good people,
and the Lord listens to their prayers;
but the Lord is against those people
that do evil."

Psalm 34:12-16

¹³If you are always trying to do good, then no person can really hurt you. ¹⁴But you may suffer for doing right. If that happens, then you are blessed *(happy)*. "Don't be afraid of those people ₍that make you suffer₎; don't be worried."* ¹⁵But you should keep the Lord Christ holy in your hearts. Always be ready to answer every person who asks you to explain about the hope you have. ¹⁶But answer those people in a gentle way with respect. Always be able to feel that you are doing right. When you do that, the people who say bad things about you will be made ashamed. They say these bad things about the good way you live in Christ. They will be made ashamed for the bad things they said about you. ¹⁷It is better to suffer for doing good than for doing wrong. Yes, it is better if that is what God wants. ¹⁸Christ himself died for you. And that one death paid for your sins. He was not guilty, but he died for people who are guilty. He did this to bring you all to God. His body was killed, but he was made alive in the spirit. ¹⁹And in the spirit he went and preached to the spirits in prison. ²⁰Those were the spirits who refused to obey God long ago in the time of Noah. God was waiting patiently for them while Noah was building the ark *(boat)*. Only a few people—eight in all—were saved in that ark. Those people were saved by water. ²¹That water is like baptism* that now saves you. Baptism is not the washing of dirt from the body. Baptism is asking God for a pure heart. It saves you because Jesus Christ was raised from death. ²²Now Jesus has gone into heaven. He is at God's right side. He rules over angels, authorities, and powers.

Changed Lives

4 Christ suffered while he was in his body. So you should strengthen yourselves with the same kind of thinking Christ had. The person who has suffered in his body is finished with sin. ²₍Strengthen yourselves₎ so that you will live your lives here on earth doing what God wants, not doing the evil things that people want. ³In the past you wasted too much time doing the things that the non-believers like to do. You were doing sexual sins. You were doing the ₍evil₎ things you wanted. You were becoming drunk, having wild and wasteful parties, having drunken parties, and doing wrong by worshiping idols *(false gods)*. ⁴Those non-believers think that it is strange that you don't do the many wild and wasteful things that they do. And so they say bad things about you. ⁵But those people will have to explain about the things they have done. They will have to explain to the One *(Christ)* who is ready to judge the people who are living and the people who are dead. ⁶The gospel* was preached to those people who are now dead, because those people will be judged like all people are judged. They will be judged for the things they did while they were living. But the gospel was preached to them so that they could live in the spirit like God lives.

Be Good Managers of God's Gifts

⁷The time is near when all things will end. So keep your minds clear, and control yourselves. This will help you to pray. ⁸Most important, love each other deeply. Love hides many, many sins. ⁹Share your homes with each other without complaining. ¹⁰Each of you received a spiritual gift ₍from God₎. God has shown you his grace *(kindness)* in many different ways. And you are like servants who are responsible for using God's gifts. So be good servants and use your gifts to serve each other. ¹¹The person who speaks should speak words from God. The person who serves should serve with the strength that God gives. You should do these things so that in everything God will be praised through Jesus Christ. Power and glory belong to him forever and ever. Amen.

Suffering as a Christian

¹²My friends, don't be surprised at the painful things that you are now suffering. Those things are testing your faith. Don't think that something strange is happening to you. ¹³But you should be happy that you are sharing in Christ's sufferings. You will be happy and full of joy when Christ shows his glory. ¹⁴When people say bad things to you because you follow Christ, then you are blessed *(happy)*. You are blessed because the Spirit* of glory is with you. That is the Spirit of

---

"Don't be afraid ... worried" Quote from Isa. 8:12.
baptism A Greek word meaning to be immersed, dipped, or buried briefly under water.

gospel The Good News that God was making a way for people to be saved.
Spirit The Holy Spirit. Called the Spirit of God, the Spirit of Christ, and the Comforter. Joined with God and Christ, he does God's work among people in the world.

God. ¹⁵Don't be like a criminal or a person who kills, steals, or bothers other people. A person will suffer for doing those things. None of you should ever suffer like that. ¹⁶But if you suffer because you are a Christian, then don't be ashamed. You should praise *(thank)* God for that name *(Christian)*. ¹⁷It is time for judging to begin. That judging will begin with God's family. If that judgment begins with us, then what will happen to those people who don't obey the gospel* of God? ¹⁸"It is very hard for a good person to be saved. So what will happen to the person who is against God and is full of sin?"* ¹⁹So those people who suffer like God wants them to should trust their souls to him. God is the One who made them, and they can trust him. So they should continue to do good.

The Flock of God

5 Now I have something to say to the elders* in your group. I am also an elder. I myself have seen Christ's sufferings. And I will share in the glory that will be shown to us. I beg you to ²take care of the group of people that you are responsible for. They are God's flock.* Watch over that flock because you want to, not because you are forced to do it. That is how God wants it. Do it because you are happy to serve, not because you want money. ³Don't be like a hard ruler over those people you are responsible for. But be good examples to those people. ⁴Then when the Ruling Shepherd *(Christ)* comes, you will get a crown. That crown will be very glorious, and it will never lose its beauty.

⁵Young men, I have something to say to you, too. You should accept the authority of the elders.* All of you should be very humble with each other.

"God is against the proud people,
but he gives grace *(kindness)* to
the humble people."

Proverbs 3:34

⁶So be humble under God's powerful hand. Then he will lift you up when the right time comes. ⁷Give all your worries to him, because he cares for you.

⁸Control yourselves and be careful! The devil is your enemy. And he goes around like a roaring lion looking for some person to eat. ⁹Refuse to follow the devil. Stand strong in your faith. You know that your brothers and sisters all over the world are having the same sufferings that you have.

¹⁰Yes, you will suffer for a short time. But after that, God will make everything right. He will make you strong. He will support you and keep you from falling. He is the God that gives all grace *(kindness)*. He called you to share in his glory in Christ. That glory will continue forever. ¹¹All power is his forever and ever. Amen.

Final Greetings

¹²I wrote this short letter with the help of Silas. I know that he is a faithful brother ₍in Christ₎. I wrote to comfort and encourage you. I wanted to tell you that this is the true grace *(kindness)* of God. Stand strong in that grace.

¹³The church in Babylon* says hello to you. Those people were chosen the same as you. Mark, my son ₍in Christ₎, also says hello. ¹⁴Give each other a kiss of love when you meet.

Peace to all of you that are in Christ.

---

gospel The Good News that God has made a way for people to have their sins forgiven and live with God.
"It is ... sin" Quote from Prov. 11:31 in the Greek version of the Old Testament.
elders Men chosen to lead a church. Also called "overseers" and "pastors" (shepherds), they have the work of caring for God's people (Acts 20:28).
God's flock God's people. They are like a flock (group) of sheep that need to be cared for.

church in Babylon Literally, "She in Babylon."

2 Peter

1 From Simon Peter, a servant and apostle* of Jesus Christ.
To all you people who have a faith that is so valuable, like ours. You received that faith because our God and Savior Jesus Christ is fair. He does what is right. ²Grace *(kindness)* and peace be given to you more and more. You will have grace and peace because you truly know God and Jesus our Lord.

God Has Given Us Everything We Need

³Jesus has the power of God. His power has given us everything we need to live and to serve God. We have these things because we know him. Jesus called us by his glory and goodness. ⁴Through his glory and goodness, Jesus gave us the very great and rich gifts that he promised us. With those gifts you can share in being like God. And so the world will not ruin you with the evil things it wants. ⁵Because you have these blessings, you should try as much as you can to add these things ₍to your life₎: to your faith add goodness; and to your goodness add knowledge; ⁶and to your knowledge add self-control; and to your self-control add patience; and to your patience add service for God; ⁷and to your service for God add kindness for your brothers and sisters ₍in Christ₎; and to this kindness for your brothers and sisters add love. ⁸If all these things are in you and they are growing, then these things will help you to never be useless. These things will help you to never be worthless in the knowledge of our Lord Jesus Christ. ⁹But if a person does not have these things, then he cannot see clearly. That person is blind. He has forgotten that he was cleansed *(forgiven)* from his past sins.

¹⁰My brothers ₍and sisters₎, God called you and chose you to be his. Try hard to show that you really are God's called and chosen people. If you do all those things, you will never fall. ¹¹And you will be given a very great welcome into the kingdom of our Lord and Savior Jesus Christ. That kingdom continues forever.

¹²You know these things. You are very strong in the truth you have. But I will always help you to remember these things. ¹³I think it is right for me to help you remember these things while I am still living here on earth. ¹⁴I know that I must soon leave this body. Our Lord Jesus Christ has shown me that. ¹⁵I will try the best I can to help you remember these things always. I want you to be able to remember these things after I am gone.

We Saw Christ's Glory

¹⁶We told you about the power of our Lord Jesus Christ. We told you about his coming. Those things we told you were not just smart stories that people invented. No! We saw the greatness of Jesus with our own eyes. ¹⁷Jesus heard the voice of the Greatest Glory *(God)*. That was when Jesus received honor and glory from God the Father. The voice said, "This is my Son, and I love him. I am very pleased with him." ¹⁸And we heard that voice. It came from heaven while we were with Jesus on the holy mountain.

¹⁹This makes us more sure about the things the prophets* said. And it is good for you to follow closely what the prophets said. The things they said are like a light shining in a dark place. You have that light until the day begins and the morning star brings new light to your minds. ²⁰Most important, you must understand this: No prophecy* in the Scriptures* ever comes from a person's own interpretation. ²¹No! No prophecy

---

apostle Person Jesus chose to be a special helper for telling the Good News to the world.

prophets People who spoke for God. They often told things that would happen in the future.

prophecy Teaching from God, given by a person who speaks for God.

Scriptures Holy Writings—the Old Testament.

ever came from what a man wanted to say. But people were led by the Holy Spirit* and spoke things from God.

False Teachers

2 In the past there were false prophets* among ₍God's₎ people. It is the same now. You will have some false teachers in your group. They will teach things that are wrong—teachings that will make people be lost. And those false teachers will teach in a way that will be hard for you to see that they are wrong. They will even refuse to accept the Master *(Jesus)* who bought their freedom. And so they will quickly destroy themselves. ²Many people will follow them in the evil *(bad)* things they do. And other people will say bad things about the Way of truth because of those people. ³Those false teachers only want your money. So they will use you by telling you things that are not true. But the judgment against those false teachers has been ready for a long time. And they will not escape the One *(God)* who will destroy them.

⁴When angels sinned, God did not let them go free without punishment. No! God sent them to hell. God put those angels in caves of darkness. They are being held there until the judgment. ⁵And God punished the ₍evil₎ people who lived long ago. God brought a flood to the world that was full of people who were against God. But God saved Noah and seven other people with Noah. Noah was a man who told people about living right. ⁶And God also punished the ₍evil₎ cities of Sodom and Gomorrah.* God burned those cities until there was nothing left but ashes. God made those cities be an example to show what will happen to people who are against God. ⁷But God saved Lot ₍from those cities₎. Lot was a very good man. He was troubled because of the dirty lives of evil people. ⁸(Lot was a good man, but he lived with those evil people every day. Lot's good heart was hurt by the evil things that he saw and heard.) ⁹₍Yes, God did all these things₎. So the Lord ₍God₎ will always save the people who serve him. He will save them when troubles come. And the Lord will hold evil people and punish them while waiting for the day of judgment. ¹⁰That punishment is mostly for those people who live by doing the bad things their sinful selves want, and it is for people who hate the Lord's authority *(power)*.

These ₍false teachers₎ will do anything they want, and they boast about themselves. They are not afraid to say bad things against the glorious ₍angels₎.* ¹¹The angels are much stronger and more powerful than these false teachers. But even the angels don't accuse the false teachers and say bad things about them to the Lord. ¹²But these false teachers speak evil against things they don't understand. These false teachers are like animals that do things without really thinking—like wild animals that are born to be caught and killed. And, like wild animals, these false teachers will be destroyed. ¹³These false teachers have made many people suffer. So they themselves will suffer. That is their pay for what they have done. These false teachers think it is fun to do evil things openly ₍where all people can see₎. They enjoy the evil things that please them. So they are like dirty spots and stains among you—₍they bring shame to you₎ in the meals that you eat together. ¹⁴Every time they look at a woman they want her. These false teachers are always sinning this way. They lead weaker people into the trap ₍of sin₎. They have taught their own hearts to be selfish. They are under a curse.* ¹⁵These false teachers left the right way and went the wrong way. They followed the same way that Balaam went. Balaam was the son of Beor. He loved being paid for doing wrong. ¹⁶But a donkey told Balaam that he was doing wrong. And the donkey is an animal that cannot talk. But that donkey spoke with a man's voice and stopped the prophet's *(Balaam's)* crazy thinking.

¹⁷Those false teachers are like rivers that have no water. They are like clouds that are blown by a storm. A place in the deepest darkness has been kept for them. ¹⁸Those false teachers boast with words that mean nothing. They lead people into the trap ₍of sin₎. They lead away people who are just beginning to come away from other people who live wrong. Those false teachers do this by using the evil things people want to do in their sinful selves. ¹⁹These false teachers promise that those people will have freedom. But the false

---

Holy Spirit Called the Spirit of God, the Spirit of Christ, and the Comforter. Joined with God and Christ, he does God's work among people in the world.

false prophets People who say they speak for God but do not really speak God's truth.

Sodom and Gomorrah Cities that God destroyed to punish the evil people who lived there.

the glorious angels Literally, "the glories" or "the glorious ones."

under a curse Literally, "children of a curse," meaning that God will punish them.

teachers themselves are not free. They are slaves of things that will be destroyed. A person is a slave to the thing that controls him. ²⁰Those people were made free from the evil things in the world. They were made free by knowing our Lord and Savior Jesus Christ. But if those people go back into those evil things and those things control them, then it is worse for them than it was before. ²¹Yes, it would be better for those people to have never known the right way. That would be better than to know the right way and then to turn away from the holy teaching that was given to them. ²²What those people did is like this true saying: "When a dog vomits *(throws up)*, he comes back to his vomit."* And, "After a pig is washed, the pig goes back and rolls in the mud again."

Jesus Will Come Again

3 My friends, this is the second letter I have written to you. I wrote both letters to you to help your honest minds remember something. ²I want you to remember the words that the holy prophets* spoke in the past. And remember the command that our Lord and Savior gave us. He gave us that command through your apostles.* ³It is important for you to understand what will happen in the last days. People will laugh ⌊at you⌋. Those people will live following the evil things they want to do. ⁴Those people will say, "He *(Jesus)* promised to come again. Where is he? Our fathers have died. But the world continues the way it has been since it was made." ⁵But those people don't want to remember what happened long ago. The skies were there, and God made the earth from water and with water. All this happened by God's word. ⁶Then that world was flooded and destroyed with water. ⁷And that same word ⌊of God⌋ is keeping the skies and the earth that we have now. The skies and the earth are being kept to be destroyed by fire. The skies and the earth are kept for the day of judgment and the destruction of all people who are against God.

⁸But don't forget this one thing, dear friends: To the Lord a day is like a thousand years, and a thousand years is like a day. ⁹The Lord is not being slow in doing what he promised—the way some people understand slowness. But God is being patient with you. God doesn't want any person to be lost. God wants every person to change his heart and stop sinning.

¹⁰But the Day when the Lord comes again will be a surprise like a thief. The sky will disappear with a loud noise. All the things in the sky will be destroyed with fire. And the earth and everything in it will be burned.* ¹¹In that way everything will be destroyed like I told you. So what kind of people should you be? You should live holy* lives and do things to serve God. ¹²You should wait for the Day of God. You should want very much for that Day to come. When that Day comes, the sky will be destroyed with fire, and everything in the sky will melt with heat. ¹³But God made a promise to us. And we are waiting for what he promised—a new sky and a new earth. That will be the place where goodness lives.

¹⁴Dear friends, we are waiting for this to happen. So try as hard as you can to be without sin and without fault. Try to be at peace with God. ¹⁵Remember that we are saved because our Lord is patient. Our dear brother Paul told you that same thing when he wrote to you with the wisdom that God gave him. ¹⁶Paul writes like this about these things in all his letters. Sometimes there are things in Paul's letters that are hard to understand. Some people explain those things falsely. Those people are ignorant and weak in faith. Those same people also falsely explain the other Scriptures.* But they are destroying themselves by doing that.

¹⁷Dear friends, you already know about this. So be careful. Don't let those evil people lead you away by the wrong things they do. Be careful so that you will not fall from your strong ⌊faith⌋. ¹⁸But grow in the grace *(kindness)* and knowledge of our Lord and Savior Jesus Christ. Glory be to him now and forever! Amen.

"When a dog ... vomit" Quote from Prov. 26:11.
  prophets People who spoke for God. They often told things that would happen in the future.
  apostles The men Jesus chose to be his special helpers.

will be burned Many Greek copies say, "will be found." One copy says, "will disappear."
  holy Being pure and belonging only to God.
  Scriptures Holy Writings—the Old Testament.

1 John

1 We tell you now about something that has existed *(lived)* since before the world began:
> This we heard,
> we saw with our own eyes,
> we watched,
> we touched with our hands.

We write to you about the Word *(Christ)* that gives life. ²That Life was shown to us. We saw it. We can give proof about it. Now we tell you about that Life. It is Life that continues forever. This is the Life that was with God the Father. God showed this Life to us. ³Now we tell you the things that we have seen and heard. Why? Because we want you to have fellowship* together with us. The fellowship we share together is with God the Father and his Son Jesus Christ. ⁴We write these things to you so that you can be full of joy with us.

God Forgives Our Sins

⁵We heard the true teaching from God. Now we tell it to you: God is light* *(goodness)*. In God there is no darkness *(sin)*. ⁶So if we say that we have fellowship* with God, but we continue living in darkness *(sin)*, then we are liars—we don't follow the truth. ⁷God is in the light *(goodness)*. We should live in the light, too. If we live in the light, then we share fellowship with each other. And when we live in the light, the blood *(death)* of Jesus cleanses us from all sin. (Jesus is God's Son.)

⁸If we say that we have no sin, we are fooling ourselves, and the truth is not in us. ⁹But if we confess *(admit)* our sins, then God will forgive our sins. We can trust God. God does what is right. God will make us clean from all the wrong things we have done. ¹⁰If we say that we have not sinned, then we make God a liar—we don't accept God's true teaching.

Jesus Is Our Helper

2 My dear children, I write this letter to you so that you will not sin. But if any person sins, we have Jesus Christ to help us. He is the righteous *(good)* One. Jesus defends us before God the Father. ²Jesus is the way our sins are taken away. And Jesus is the way that all people can have their sins taken away, too.

³If we obey what God has told us to do, then we are sure that we truly know God. ⁴A person says, "I know God!" But if that person does not obey God's commands, then that person is a liar. The truth is not in him. ⁵But when a person obeys God's teaching, then God's love has truly arrived at its goal in that person. This is how we know that we are following God: ⁶If a person says that he lives in God, then he must live like Jesus lived.

God Commanded Us to Love Other People

⁷My dear friends, I am not writing a new command to you. It is the same command you have had since the beginning. This command is the teaching you have already heard. ⁸But also I write this command to you as a new command. This command is true; you can see its truth in Jesus and in yourselves. The darkness *(sin)* is passing away and the true light is already shining.

⁹A person says, "I am in the light.*" But if that person hates his brother, then he is still in the darkness *(sin)*. ¹⁰The person that loves his brother lives in the light, and there is nothing in that person that will make him do wrong. ¹¹But the person who hates his brother is in darkness. He lives in darkness. That person does not know where he is going. Why? Because the darkness has made him blind.

---

fellowship Associating with people and sharing things together with them. Christians share love, joy, sorrow, faith, and other things with each other and with God.

light This word is used to show what God is like. It means goodness or truth.

¹² I write to you, dear children,
because your sins are forgiven
through Christ.
¹³ I write to you, fathers,
because you know the One who existed
(lived) from the beginning.
I write to you, young men,
because you have defeated the
Evil One *(the devil).*
¹⁴ I write to you, children,
because you know the Father.
I write to you, fathers,
because you know the One who existed
(lived) from the beginning.
I write to you, young men,
because you are strong;
the word of God lives in you,
and you have defeated the Evil One.

¹⁵Don't love the world or the things in the world. If a person loves the world, the love of the Father *(God)* is not in that person. ¹⁶These are the ₍evil₎ things in the world:

Wanting things to please our sinful selves,
Wanting the sinful things we see,
Being too proud of the things we have.

But none of those things come from the Father *(God)*. All of those things come from the world. ¹⁷The world is passing away. And all the things that people want in the world are passing away. But the person who does what God wants lives forever.

Don't Follow the Enemies of Christ

¹⁸My dear children, the end is near! You have heard that the Enemy of Christ* is coming. And now many enemies of Christ are already here. So we know that the end is near. ¹⁹Those enemies of Christ were in our group. But they left us. They did not really belong with us. If they were really part of our group, then they would have stayed with us. But they left. This shows that none of them really belonged with us. ²⁰You have the gift* that the Holy One *(God or Christ)* gave you. So you all know ₍the truth₎. ²¹Why do I write to you? Do I write because you don't know the truth? No! I write this letter because you do know the truth. And you know that no lie comes from the truth. ²²So who is the liar? It is the person that says Jesus is not the Christ.* A person that says Jesus is not the Christ is the enemy of Christ. That person does not believe in the Father *(God)* or in his Son *(Christ)*. ²³If a person does not believe in the Son, then he does not have the Father. But the person who accepts the Son has the Father, too.

²⁴Be sure that you continue to follow the teaching that you heard from the beginning. If you continue in that teaching, then you will stay in the Son *(Christ)* and in the Father *(God)*. ²⁵And this is what the Son promised to us—life forever.

²⁶I am writing this letter about those people who are trying to lead you into the wrong way. ²⁷Christ gave you a special gift.* You still have this gift in you. So you don't need any person to teach you. The gift he gave you teaches you about everything. This gift is true. It is not false. So continue to live in Christ, like his gift taught you.

²⁸Yes, my dear children, live in him. If we do this, we can be without fear *(have confidence)* on the day when Christ comes back. We will not need to hide and be ashamed when he comes. ²⁹You know that Christ is righteous *(good)*. So you know that all people who do what is right *(good)* are God's children.

We Are God's Children

3 The Father *(God)* has loved us so much! This shows how much he loved us: We are called children of God. And we really are God's children. But the people in the world *(people who don't believe)* don't understand that we are God's children, because they have not known him *(God)*. ²Dear friends, now we are children of God. We have not yet been shown what we will be in the future. But we know that when Christ comes again, we will be like him. We will see him like he really is. ³Christ is pure. And every person who has this hope in Christ keeps himself pure like Christ.

⁴When a person sins, he breaks ₍God's₎ law. Yes, sinning is the same as living against ₍God's₎ law. ⁵You know that Christ came to take away people's sins. There is no sin in Christ. ⁶So the person who lives in Christ does not continue to sin. If a person continues to sin, he has never really understood Christ and has never known Christ.

⁷Dear children, don't let any person lead you into the wrong way. Christ is righteous *(good)*. To be good like Christ, a person must do what is right

---

Christ The "anointed one" (Messiah) or chosen of God.
gift The word in the Greek text is "anointing." This might mean the Holy Spirit. Or it might mean teaching or truth as in verse 24.

(good). ⁸The devil has been sinning since the beginning. The person who continues to sin belongs to the devil. The Son of God *(Christ)* came for this: to destroy the devil's work.

⁹When God makes a person his child, that person does not continue to sin. Why? Because the new life* God gave that person stays in him. So that person is not able to continue sinning. Why? Because he has become a child of God. ¹⁰So we can see who God's children are. Also, we can know who the children of the devil are. The people who don't do what is right are not children of God. And the person who does not love his brother is not a child of God.

We Must Love One Another

¹¹This is the teaching you have heard from the beginning: We must love each other. ¹²Don't be like Cain.* Cain belonged to the Evil One *(the devil)*. Cain killed his brother ⌊Abel*⌋. But why did Cain kill his brother? Because the things Cain did were evil, and the things his brother ⌊Abel⌋ did were good.

¹³Brothers ⌊and sisters⌋, don't be surprised when the people of this world hate you. ¹⁴We know that we have left death *(sin)* and have come into life. We know this because we love our brothers ⌊and sisters in Christ⌋. The person who does not love is still in death. ¹⁵Every person who hates his brother is a murderer.* And you know that no murderer has eternal life in him. ¹⁶This is how we know what real love is: Jesus gave his life for us. So we should give our lives for our brothers ⌊and sisters in Christ⌋. ¹⁷Suppose a believer is rich enough to have all the things he needs. He sees his brother ⌊in Christ⌋ who is poor and does not have the things he needs. What if the believer who has things does not help the poor brother? Then the believer who has the things he needs does not have God's love in his heart. ¹⁸My children, our love should not be only words and talk. No! Our love must be true love. We should show our love by the things we do.

¹⁹⁻²⁰That is the way we know that we belong to the way of truth. And when our hearts make us feel guilty, we can still have peace before God. Why? Because God is greater than our heart *(conscience)*. God knows everything.

²¹My dear friends, if we don't feel that we are doing wrong, then we can be without fear *(have confidence)* when we come to God. ²²And God gives us the things we ask for. We receive these things because we obey God's commands and we do the things that please God. ²³This is what God commands: that we believe in his Son Jesus Christ and that we love each other. This is what he commanded. ²⁴The person who obeys God's commands lives in God. And God lives in that person. How do we know that God lives in us? We know because of the Spirit* that God gave us.

John Warns Against False Teachers

4 My dear friends, many false prophets* are in the world now. So don't believe every spirit. But test the spirits to see if they are from God. ²This is how you can know God's Spirit.* One spirit says, "I believe that Jesus is the Christ who came to earth and became a man." That Spirit is from God. ³Another spirit refuses to say this about Jesus. That spirit is not from God. This is the spirit of the Enemy of Christ. You have heard that the Enemy of Christ is coming. And now the Enemy of Christ is already in the world.

⁴My dear children, you belong to God. So you have defeated them *(the false teachers)*. Why? Because the One *(God)* who is in you is greater than the one *(the devil)* who is in ⌊the people of⌋ the world. ⁵And those people *(the false teachers)* belong to the world. So the things they say are from the world, too. And the world listens to what they say. ⁶But we are from God. So the people who know God listen to us. But the people who are not from God don't listen to us. That is how we know the Spirit* that is true and the spirit that is false.

Love Comes from God

⁷Dear friends, we should love each other, because love comes from God. The person who loves has become God's child. And so the person who loves knows God. ⁸The person that does not love does not know God, because God is love. ⁹This is how God showed his love to us: God sent his only Son into the world to give us life through

---

new life The Greek text says literally, "his seed."

Cain, Abel Sons of Adam and Eve. Cain was jealous of Abel and killed him (Gen. 4:1-16).

Every person ... murderer If a person hates his brother in Christ, then in his mind he has killed his brother. Jesus taught his followers about this sin (Mt. 5:21-26).

Spirit The Holy Spirit. Called the Spirit of God, the Spirit of Christ, and the Comforter. Joined with God and Christ, he does God's work among people in the world.

false prophets People who say they speak for God but do not really speak God's truth.

him. ¹⁰True love is God's love for us, not our love for God. God sent his Son to be the way that God takes away our sins.
¹¹That is how much God loved us, dear friends! So we also must love each other. ¹²No person has ever seen God. But if we love each other, then God lives in us. If we love each other, then God's love has reached its goal—it is made perfect in us.
¹³We know that we live in God and God lives in us. We know this because God gave us his Spirit.* ¹⁴We have seen that the Father sent his Son to be the Savior of the world. That is what we tell people now. ¹⁵If a person says, "I believe that Jesus is the Son of God," then God lives in that person. And that person lives in God. ¹⁶And so we know the love that God has for us. And we trust that love.
God is love. The person who lives in love lives in God. And God lives in that person. ¹⁷If God's love is made perfect in us, then we can be without fear on the day when God judges us. We will be without fear, because in this world we are like him *(Christ or God)*. ¹⁸Where ⌊God's⌋ love is, there is no fear. Why? Because God's perfect love takes away fear. It is ⌊God's⌋ punishment that makes a person fear. So ⌊God's⌋ love is not made perfect in the person who has fear.
¹⁹We love because God first loved us. ²⁰If a person says, "I love God," but that person hates his brother ⌊or sister in Christ⌋, then that person is a liar. That person can see his brother, but he hates him. So that person cannot love God, because he has never seen God! ²¹And he *(God)* gave us this command: The person who loves God must also love his brother.

God's Children Win Against the World

5The people who believe that Jesus is the Christ* are God's children. The person who loves the Father *(God)* also loves the Father's children. ²How do we know that we love God's children? We know because we love God and we obey his commands. ³Loving God means obeying his commands. And God's commands are not too hard for us. ⁴Why? Because every person that is a child of God ⌊has the power to⌋ win against the world. ⁵It is our faith that has won the victory against the world. So who is the person that wins against the world? Only the person who believes that Jesus is the Son of God.

God Told Us About His Son

⁶Jesus Christ is the One who came. Jesus came with water* and with blood.* Jesus did not come by water only. No, Jesus came by both water and blood. And the Spirit* tells us that this is true. The Spirit is the truth. ⁷So there are three witnesses that tell us ⌊about Jesus⌋: ⁸the Spirit, the water, and the blood. These three witnesses agree. ⁹We believe people when they say something is true. But what God says is more important. And this is what God told us: He told us the truth about his own Son. ¹⁰The person who believes in the Son of God has the truth that God told us. The person who does not believe God makes God a liar. Why? Because that person does not believe what God told us about his Son. ¹¹This is what God told us: God has given us eternal life. And this eternal life is in his Son *(Jesus)*. ¹²The person who has the Son has ⌊true⌋ life. But the person who does not have the Son of God does not have life.

We Have Eternal Life Now

¹³I write this letter to you people who believe in the Son of God. I write so that you will know that you have eternal life now. ¹⁴We can come to God with no doubts. This means that when we ask God for things (and those things agree with what God wants for us), then God cares about what we say. ¹⁵God listens to us every time we ask him. So we know that he gives us the things that we ask from him.
¹⁶Suppose a person sees his brother ⌊or sister in Christ⌋ sinning (sin that does not lead to ⌊eternal⌋ death). That person should pray for his brother ⌊or sister⌋ who is sinning. Then God will give the brother ⌊or sister⌋ life. I am talking about people whose sin does not lead to ⌊eternal⌋ death. There is sin that leads to death. I don't mean that a person should pray about that sin. ¹⁷Doing wrong is always sin. But there is sin that does not lead to ⌊eternal⌋ death.
¹⁸We know that any person who has been made God's child does not continue to sin. The Son of God keeps God's child safe.* The Evil One *(the devil)* cannot hurt that person. ¹⁹We know that we

---

Spirit The Holy Spirit. Called the Spirit of God, the Spirit of Christ, and the Comforter. Joined with God and Christ, he does God's work among people in the world.
Christ The "anointed one" (Messiah) or chosen of God.
water This probably means the water of Jesus' baptism.
blood This probably means the blood of Jesus' death.
The Son ... safe The Greek says literally, "The one who was born from God keeps him safe" or "... keeps himself safe."

belong to God. But the Evil One *(the devil)* controls the whole world. ²⁰And we know that the Son of God has come. The Son of God has given us understanding. Now we can know God. God is the One who is true. And our lives are in that true God and in his Son, Jesus Christ. He is the true God, and he is eternal life. ²¹So, dear children, keep yourselves away from false gods.

2 John

From the Elder.*
To the lady* chosen ₍by God₎, and to her children:
I love all of you in the truth.* Also, all those people who know the truth love you. ²We love you because of the truth—the truth that lives in us. This truth will be with us forever.

³Grace *(kindness)*, mercy, and peace will be with us from God the Father and from his Son, Jesus Christ. We receive these blessings through truth and love.

⁴I was very happy to learn about some of your children. I am happy that they are following the way of truth, like the Father *(God)* commanded us. ⁵And now, dear lady, I tell you: We should all love each other. This is not a new command. It is the same command we had from the beginning. ⁶And loving means living the way he commanded us to live. And God's command is this: that you live a life of love. You heard this command from the beginning.

⁷Many false teachers are in the world now. These false teachers refuse to confess *(say)* that Jesus Christ came ₍to earth₎ and became a man. A person who refuses to confess this fact is a false teacher and an enemy of Christ. ⁸Be careful! Don't lose the reward that you have worked for. Be careful, so that you will receive all of your reward.

⁹A person must continue to follow only the teaching of Christ. If a person changes the teaching of Christ, then that person does not have God. But if a person continues following the teaching of Christ, then that person has both the Father *(God)* and the Son *(Christ)*. ¹⁰If a person comes to you, but does not bring this teaching, then don't accept him into your house. Don't welcome him. ¹¹If you accept him, then you are helping him with his evil work.

¹²I have much to say to you. But I don't want to use paper and ink. Instead, I hope to come visit you. Then we can be together and talk. That will make us very happy. ¹³The children of your sister* who was chosen ₍by God₎ send you their love.

Elder This is probably John the apostle. "Elder" means an older man. It can also mean a special leader in the church (like in Titus 1:5).

lady This might mean a woman. Or, in this letter, it might mean a church. If it is a church, then "her children" would be the people of the church.

truth The truth or "Good News" about Jesus Christ that joins all believers together.

sister Sister of the "lady" in verse 1. This might be another woman or another church.

3 John

From the Elder.*

To my dear friend Gaius that I love in the truth*:

²My dear friend, I know that your soul is doing fine. So I pray that you are doing fine in every way. And I pray that you are feeling well. ³Some brothers ₍in Christ₎ came and told me about the truth* in your life. They told me that you continue to follow the way of truth. This made me very happy. ⁴It always gives me the greatest joy when I hear that my children are following the way of truth.

⁵My dear friend, it is good that you continue to help the brothers ₍in Christ₎. You are helping brothers that you don't even know! ⁶These brothers told the church *(believers)* about the love you have. Please help them to continue their trip. Help them in a way that will please God. ⁷These brothers went on their trip to serve Christ. They did not accept any help from people who are not believers. ⁸So we should help these brothers. When we help them, we share with their work for the truth.*

⁹I wrote a letter to the church. But Diotrephes will not listen to what we say. He always wants to be their leader. ¹⁰When I come, I will talk about what Diotrephes is doing. He lies and says evil things about us. But that is not all he does! He refuses to help those brothers ₍who are working to serve Christ₎. Diotrephes also stops those people who want to help the brothers. He makes those people leave the church *(group of believers)*.

¹¹My dear friend, don't follow what is bad; follow what is good. The person who does what is good is from God. But the person who does evil has never known God.

¹²All the people say good things about Demetrius. And the truth* agrees with what they say. Also, we say good about him. And you know that what we say is true.

¹³I have many things I want to tell you. But I don't want to use pen and ink. ¹⁴I hope to visit you soon. Then we can be together and talk. ¹⁵Peace to you. The friends *(believers)* here with me send their love. Please give our love to each one of the friends there.

Elder This is probably John the apostle. "Elder" means an older man. It can also mean a special leader in the church (like Titus 1:5).

truth The truth or "Good News" about Jesus Christ that joins all believers together.

Jude

From Jude, a servant of Jesus Christ and a brother of James.

To all those people who have been called by God. God the Father loves you, and you have been kept safe in Jesus Christ.

²All mercy, peace, and love be yours.

God Will Punish People Who Do Wrong

³Dear friends, I wanted very much to write to you about the salvation we all share together. But I felt the need to write to you about something else: I want to encourage you to fight hard for the faith that God gave his holy people.* God gave this faith once, and it is good for all time. ⁴Some people have secretly entered your group. These people have already been judged guilty for the things they are doing. Long ago ₍the prophets₎* wrote about these people. These people are against God. They have used the grace *(kindness)* of our God in the wrong way—to do sinful things. These people refuse to accept Jesus Christ, our only Master and Lord.

⁵I want to help you remember some things that you already know: Remember that the Lord saved his people by bringing them out of the land of Egypt. But later the Lord destroyed all those people who did not believe. ⁶And remember the angels who had power but did not keep it. They left their own home. So the Lord has kept these angels in darkness. They are bound with everlasting chains. He has kept them to be judged on the great day. ⁷Also remember the cities of Sodom and Gomorrah* and the other towns around them. They are the same as those angels. Those towns were full of sexual sin and wrong doing. They suffer the punishment of eternal fire. Their punishment is an example ₍for us to see₎.

⁸It is the same way with these people ₍who have entered your group₎. They are guided by dreams. They make themselves dirty with sin. They reject ₍God's₎ authority *(rule)* and say bad things against the glorious ₍angels₎.* ⁹Not even the archangel* Michael did this. Michael argued with the devil about who would have the body of Moses. But Michael did not dare to condemn the devil with criticizing words. But Michael said, "The Lord punish you." ¹⁰But these people criticize things they don't understand. They do understand some things. But they understand these things not by thinking, but by feeling, the way dumb animals understand things. And these are the things that destroy them. ¹¹It will be bad for them. These people have followed the way that Cain* went. To make money, they have given themselves to following the wrong way that Balaam went. These people have fought against ₍God₎ like Korah did. And like Korah, they will be destroyed. ¹²These people are like dirty spots in the special meals you share together. They eat with you and have no fear. They take care of only themselves. They are clouds without rain. The wind blows them around. They are trees that have no fruit when it is time and are pulled out of the ground. So they are dead two times. ¹³They are like wild waves in the sea. The waves make foam. These people do shameful things like the waves make foam. These people are like stars that wander in the sky. ₍A place in₎ the blackest darkness has been kept for those people forever.

¹⁴Enoch, the seventh descendant* from Adam, said this about these people: "Look, the Lord is

---

holy people God's people are called holy because they are made pure through Christ, and they belong only to God.
prophets People who spoke for God. They often told things that would happen in the future.
Sodom and Gomorrah Cities God destroyed to punish the evil people that lived there.
the glorious angels Literally, "the glories" or "the glorious ones."
archangel The leader among God's angels or messengers.
Cain The son of Adam and Eve who killed his brother Abel (Gen. 4:1-16).
descendant Someone born into a person's family after him.

coming with thousands and thousands of his holy angels. ¹⁵The Lord will judge every person. The Lord is coming to judge all people and to punish all people who are against God. He will punish these people for all the evil things they have done against God. And God will punish these sinners who are against God. He will punish them for all the bad things they have said against God."

¹⁶These people always complain and find wrong ₍in other people₎. They always do the ₍evil₎ things they want to do. They boast about themselves. The only reason they say good things about other people is to get what they want.

A Warning and Things to Do

¹⁷Dear friends, remember what the apostles* of our Lord Jesus Christ said before. ¹⁸The apostles said to you, "In the last times there will be people who laugh ₍about God₎." These people do only the things they want to do—things that are against God. ¹⁹These are the people who divide you. These people do only what their sinful selves want. They don't have the Spirit.*

²⁰But dear friends, use your most holy faith to build yourselves up strong. Pray with the Holy Spirit.* ²¹Keep yourselves in God's love. Wait for the Lord Jesus Christ with his mercy to give you life forever.

²²Help the people that have doubts. ²³You need to save some people. You will be pulling them out of the fire. But be careful when you want to help other people ₍that are sinners₎. Hate even their clothes that are dirty from sin.

Praise God

²⁴He *(God)* is strong and can help you not to fall. He can bring you before his glory without any wrong in you and give you great joy. ²⁵He is the only God. He is the One who saves us. To him be glory, greatness, power, and authority through Jesus Christ our Lord for all time past, now, and forever. Amen.

---

apostles Men that Jesus chose to be his special helpers for telling his Good News to the world.

Spirit, Holy Spirit Called the Spirit of God, the Spirit of Christ, and the Comforter. Joined with God and Christ, he does God's work among people in the world.

Revelation

John Tells About This Book

1 This is the revelation* of Jesus Christ. God gave Jesus these things to show his servants what must happen soon. Christ sent his angel to show these things to his servant John. ²John has told everything that he saw. It is the truth that Jesus Christ told him; it is the message from God. ³The person who reads the words of this message from God is blessed *(happy)*. And the people who hear this message and do the things that are written in it are blessed. There is not much time left.

John Writes Jesus' Messages to the Churches

⁴From John,
To the seven churches in the province of Asia*:
Grace *(kindness)* and peace to you from the One *(God)* who is, who ₁always₁ was, and who is coming; and from the seven spirits before his throne; ⁵and from Jesus Christ. Jesus is the faithful witness. He was first among those to be raised from death. Jesus is the ruler of the kings of the earth.
Jesus is the One who loves us. And Jesus is the One who made us free from our sins with his blood *(death)*. ⁶Jesus made us to be a kingdom. He made us to be priests who serve God his Father. To Jesus be glory and power forever and ever! Amen.
⁷Look, Jesus is coming with the clouds! Every person will see him, even the people who pierced* him. All people of the earth will cry loudly because of him. Yes, this will happen! Amen.

⁸The Lord God says, "I am the Alpha and the Omega.* I am the One who is, who ₁always₁ was, and who is coming. I am the All-Powerful."
⁹I am John, and I am your brother ₁in Christ₁. We are together in Jesus, and we share these things: suffering, the kingdom, and patient endurance. I was on the island of Patmos* because I was faithful to God's message* and to the truth of Jesus. ¹⁰On the Lord's day the Spirit* took control of me. I heard a loud voice behind me. It sounded like a trumpet. ¹¹The voice said, "Write in a book all these things you see, and send it to the seven churches: to Ephesus, Smyrna, Pergamum, Thyatira, Sardis, Philadelphia, and Laodicea."
¹²I turned to see who was talking to me. When I turned, I saw seven golden lampstands. ¹³I saw someone among the lampstands who was "like a Son of Man."* He was dressed in a long robe. He had a golden sash *(belt)* tied around his chest. ¹⁴His head and hair were white like wool—wool that is white as snow. His eyes were like flames of fire. ¹⁵His feet were like brass that glows hot in a furnace. His voice was like the noise of flooding water. ¹⁶He held seven stars in his right hand. A sharp two-edged sword came out of his mouth. He looked like the sun shining at its brightest time.
¹⁷When I saw him, I fell down at his feet like a dead man. He put his right hand on me and said, "Don't be afraid! I am the First and the Last. ¹⁸I am the One who lives. I was dead, but look: I am

---

Alpha, Omega First and last letters in the Greek alphabet, meaning the beginning and the end.
Patmos A small island in the Aegean Sea, near the coast of Asia Minor (modern Turkey).
message The news that God has made a way for people to have their sins forgiven and live with God.
Spirit The Holy Spirit. Called the Spirit of God, the Spirit of Christ, and the Comforter. Joined with God and Christ, he does God's work among people in the world.
like a Son of Man These words are from Dan. 7:13. "Son of Man" is a name Jesus called himself.

revelation An opening, uncovering, or making known of truth that has been hidden.
Asia The western part of Asia Minor (modern Turkey).
pierced When Jesus was killed, he was stuck with a spear in the side (John 19:34).

alive forever and ever! And I hold the keys of death and Hades.* ¹⁹So write the things you see. Write the things that happen now and the things that will happen later. ²⁰Here is the hidden meaning of the seven stars that you saw in my right hand and the seven golden lampstands that you saw: The seven lampstands are the seven churches. The seven stars are the angels of the seven churches.

Jesus' Letter to the Church in Ephesus

2"Write this to the angel of the church in Ephesus:

"The One who holds the seven stars in his right hand and walks among the seven golden lampstands is saying these things ⌊to you⌋. ²I know what you do. You work hard, and you never quit. I know that you don't accept evil people. You have tested those people who say that they are apostles* but are really not. You found that they are liars. ³You continue to try without quitting. You endured ⌊troubles⌋ for my name. And you have not become tired of doing this.

⁴"But I have this against you: You have left the love you had in the beginning. ⁵So remember where you were before you fell. Change your hearts and do the things you did at first. If you don't change, I will come to you. I will take away your lampstand from its place. ⁶But there is something you do ⌊that is right⌋: You hate the things that the Nicolaitans* do. I also hate what they do.

⁷"Every person who hears these things should listen to what the Spirit* says to the churches. To the person who wins the victory I will give the right to eat ⌊the fruit⌋ from the tree of life. This tree is in the garden of God.

Jesus' Letter to the Church in Smyrna

⁸"Write this to the angel of the church in Smyrna:

"The One who is the First and the Last is saying these things ⌊to you⌋. He is the One who died and came to life again. ⁹I know your troubles, and I know that you are poor. But really you are rich! I know the bad things that some people say ⌊about you⌋. Those people say they are Jews. But they are not true Jews. They are a synagogue *(group)* that belongs to Satan *(the devil)*. ¹⁰Don't be afraid of the things that will happen to you. I tell you, the devil will put some of you in prison. He will do this to test you. You will suffer for ten days. But be faithful, even if you have to die. If you continue faithful, then I will give you the crown of life.

¹¹"Every person who hears these things should listen to what the Spirit* says to the churches. The person who wins the victory will not be hurt by the second death.

Jesus' Letter to the Church in Pergamum

¹²"Write this to the angel of the church in Pergamum:

"The One who has the sharp two-edged sword is saying these things ⌊to you⌋. ¹³I know where you live. You live where Satan *(the devil)* has his throne. But you are true to me. You did not refuse to tell about your faith in me even during the time of Antipas. Antipas was my faithful witness* who was killed in your city. Your city is where Satan lives.

¹⁴"But I have a few things against you: You have people there ⌊in your group⌋ who follow the teaching of Balaam. Balaam taught Balak how to make the people of Israel* sin. Those people sinned by eating food offered to idols* and by doing sexual sins. ¹⁵It is the same ⌊in your group⌋. You have people who follow the teaching of the Nicolaitans.* ¹⁶So change your hearts! If you don't change, I will come to you quickly and fight against those people with the sword that comes out of my mouth.

¹⁷"Every person who hears these things should listen to what the Spirit* says to the churches!

"I will give the hidden manna* to every person who wins the victory. I will also give that person a white rock. On this rock a new name is written. No person knows this new name. Only the person who gets the rock will know the new name.

Hades Place where people go after death.
apostles Men Jesus chose to be his special helpers.
Nicolaitans Religious group that followed wrong ideas.
Spirit The Holy Spirit. Called Spirit of God, Spirit of Christ, and the Comforter. He does God's work among people in the world. Here, he brings God's message to God's people.

faithful witness A person who speaks God's message truthfully, even in a time of danger.
Israel The Jewish nation (people).
idols Statues that people worshiped as gods.
manna Food from heaven that God gave his people in the desert (Ex. 16:4-36).

Jesus' Letter to the Church in Thyatira

[18] "Write this to the angel of the church in Thyatira:

"The Son of God is saying these things. He is the One who has eyes that blaze like fire and feet like shining brass. This is what he says ₍to you₎: [19] I know the things you do. I know about your love, your faith, your service, and your patience. I know that you are doing more now than you did at first. [20] But I have this against you: You let that woman named Jezebel do what she wants. She says that she is a prophet.* But she is leading my people away with her teaching. Jezebel leads my people to do sexual sins and to eat food that is offered to idols.* [21] I have given her time to change her heart and turn away from her sin. But she does not want to change. [22] And so I will throw her on a bed ₍of suffering₎. And all the people who do the sin of adultery* with her will suffer greatly. I will do this now if they don't turn away from the things she does. [23] I will also kill her followers. Then all the churches will know that I am the One who knows what people feel and think. And I will repay each of you for the things you have done.

[24] "But you other people in Thyatira have not followed her teaching. You have not learned the things that they call Satan's *(the devil's)* deep secrets. This is what I say to you: I will not put any other burden on you. [25] Only continue the way you are until I come.

[26] "I will give power to every person who wins the victory and continues until the end to do the things I want. I will give that person power over the nations:

[27] 'He will rule them with an iron rod.
He will break them to pieces like clay pots.'
Psalm 2:9

[28] This is the same power I received from my Father. I will also give that person the morning star. [29] Every person who hears these things should listen to what the Spirit* says to the churches.

Jesus' Letter to the Church in Sardis

3 "Write this to the angel of the church in Sardis:
"The One who has the seven spirits and the seven stars is saying these things ₍to you₎. I know the things you do. People say that you are alive. But really you are dead. [2] Wake up! Make yourselves stronger while you still have something left. Make yourselves stronger before it dies completely. I find that the things you do are not good enough for my God. [3] So don't forget what you have received and heard. Obey it. Change your hearts and lives! You must wake up, or I will come to you ₍and surprise you₎ like a thief. You will not know when I will come. [4] But you have a few people ₍in your group₎ there in Sardis who have kept themselves clean. Those people will walk with me. They will wear white clothes, because they are worthy. [5] Every person who wins the victory will be dressed in white clothes like these people. I will not take away that person's name from the book of life. I will say that he belongs to me. I will say this before my Father and before his angels. [6] Every person who hears these things should listen to what the Spirit* says to the churches.

Jesus' Letter to the Church in Philadelphia

[7] "Write this to the angel of the church in Philadelphia:

"The One who is holy and true is saying these words to you. He holds the key of David. When he opens something, it cannot be closed. And when he closes something, it cannot be opened. [8] I know the things you do. I have put an open door before you. No person can close it. I know that you are weak. But you have followed my teaching. You were not afraid to speak my name. [9] Listen! There is a synagogue *(group)* that belongs to Satan *(the devil)*. Those people say they are Jews, but they are liars. Those people are not ₍true₎ Jews. I will make those people come before you and bow at your feet. They will know that you are the people I have loved. [10] You followed my command to endure patiently. So I will keep you from the time of trouble that will come to the whole world. This trouble will test the people who live on the earth.

[11] "I am coming soon. Continue the way you are now. Then no person will take away your crown *(reward)*. [12] The person who wins the victory will be a pillar* in the temple* of my God. I will do

---

prophet Jezebel was a false prophet. She claimed to speak for God, but she didn't really speak God's truth.
idols Statues that people worshiped as gods.
adultery Breaking a marriage promise by sexual sin.
Spirit The Holy Spirit. Called Spirit of God, Spirit of Christ, and the Comforter. He does God's work among people in the world. Here, he brings God's message to God's people.

pillar One of the tall, carved stones used to hold up the roof of a building.
temple God's house—the place where God's people worship and serve him.

that for the person who wins the victory. That person will never again have to leave God's temple. I will write the name of my God on that person. And I will write the name of the city of my God on that person. That city is the new Jerusalem.* That city is coming down out of heaven from my God. I will also write my new name on that person. ¹³Every person who hears these things should listen to what the Spirit* says to the churches.

Jesus' Letter to the Church in Laodicea

¹⁴"Write this to the angel of the church in Laodicea:

"The Amen* is the One saying these things ⌊to you⌋. He is the faithful and true witness. He is the ruler of all that God has made. This is what he says: ¹⁵I know what you do. You are not hot or cold. I wish that you were hot or cold! ¹⁶But you are only warm—not hot, not cold. So I am ready to spit you out of my mouth. ¹⁷You say you are rich. You think you have become wealthy and don't need a thing. But you don't know that you are really terrible, pitiful, poor, blind, and naked. ¹⁸I advise you to buy gold from me—gold made pure in fire. Then you can be truly rich. I tell you this: Buy clothes that are white. Then you can cover your shameful nakedness. I also tell you to buy medicine to put on your eyes. Then you can truly see.

¹⁹"I correct and punish those people that I love. So start trying hard! Change your hearts and lives! ²⁰Here I am! I stand at the door and knock. If a person hears my voice and opens the door, I will come in and eat with that person. And that person will eat with me.

²¹"I will let every person who wins the victory sit with me on my throne. It was the same with me. I won the victory and sat down with my Father on his throne. ²²Every person who hears these things should listen to what the Spirit* says to the churches."

John Sees Heaven

4 Then I looked, and there before me was an open door in heaven. And I heard the same voice that spoke to me before. It was the voice that sounded like a trumpet. The voice said, "Come up here, and I will show you what must happen after this." ²Then the Spirit* took control of me. There before me was a throne in heaven. Someone was sitting on the throne. ³The One who sat on the throne looked like precious stones, like jasper and carnelian. All around the throne was a rainbow with clear colors like an emerald. ⁴Around the throne there were 24 other thrones. There were 24 elders* sitting on the 24 thrones. The elders were dressed in white, and they had golden crowns on their heads. ⁵Lightning flashes and noises of thunder came from the throne. Before the throne there were seven lamps burning. These lamps are the seven Spirits of God. ⁶Also before the throne there was something that looked like a sea of glass. It was clear like crystal.

In front of the throne and on each side of it there were four living things. These living things had eyes all over them, in front and in back. ⁷The first living thing was like a lion. The second was like a cow. The third had a face like a man. The fourth was like a flying eagle. ⁸Each of these four living things had six wings. These living things were covered all over with eyes, inside and out. Day and night these four living things never stop saying:

> "Holy, holy, holy is the Lord God All-
> Powerful.
> He ⌊always⌋ was, he is, and he is coming."

⁹These living things give glory and honor and thanks to the One who sits on the throne. He is the One who lives forever and ever. And every time the living things do this, ¹⁰the 24 elders* bow down before the One who sits on the throne. The elders worship him who lives forever and ever. The elders put their crowns down before the throne and say:

> ¹¹ "Our Lord and God!
> You are worthy to receive glory and
> honor and power.
> You made all things.
> Everything existed and was made
> because you wanted it."

5 Then I saw a scroll* in the right hand of the One sitting on the throne. The scroll had

---

Jerusalem The spiritual city God built for his people.
Spirit The Holy Spirit. Called Spirit of God, Spirit of Christ, and the Comforter. He does God's work among people in the world. Here, he brings God's message to God's people.
Amen Used here as a name for Jesus, it means to agree strongly that something is true.

elders These are probably great leaders of God's people. They may be the leaders of the twelve Jewish family groups, plus the twelve apostles of Jesus.
scroll A long roll of paper or leather used for writing.

writing on both sides. The scroll was kept closed with seven seals. ²And I saw a powerful angel. The angel called in a loud voice, "Who is worthy to break the seals and open the scroll?" ³But there was no one in heaven or on earth or under the earth who could open the scroll or look inside it. ⁴I cried and cried because there was no one who was worthy to open the scroll or look inside. ⁵But one of the elders* said to me, "Don't cry! The Lion *(Christ)* from Judah's family group has won the victory. He is David's descendant. He is able to open the scroll and its seven seals."

⁶Then I saw a Lamb standing in the center of the throne with the four living things around it. The elders* were also around the Lamb. The Lamb looked like it had been killed. It had seven horns and seven eyes. These are the seven spirits of God that were sent into all the world. ⁷The Lamb came and took the scroll* from the right hand of the One sitting on the throne. ⁸After the Lamb took the scroll, the four living things and the 24 elders* bowed down before the Lamb. Each one of them had a harp.* Also they were holding golden bowls full of incense.* These bowls of incense are the prayers of God's holy people *(believers)*. ⁹And they all sang a new song ⌊to the Lamb⌋:

"You are worthy to take the scroll
   and to open its seals,
because you were killed;
   and with your blood *(death)* you bought
      people for God
   from every tribe, language, race of
      people, and nation.
¹⁰ You made these people to be a kingdom,
   and you made these people to be priests
      for our God.
   And they will rule on the earth."

¹¹Then I looked, and I heard the voices of many angels. The angels were around the throne, the ⌊four⌋ living things, and the elders.* There were thousands and thousands of angels—there were 10,000 times 10,000. ¹²The angels said with a loud voice,

"The Lamb who was killed is worthy
   to receive power, wealth, wisdom and
      strength, honor, glory, and praise!"

¹³Then I heard every living thing that is in heaven and on earth and under the earth and in the sea. I heard every thing in all these places. I heard them all saying:

"All praise and honor and glory and power
   forever and ever
to the One who sits on the throne
   and to the Lamb!"

¹⁴The four living things said, "Amen!"* And the elders* bowed down and worshiped.

6 Then I watched while the Lamb opened the first of the seven seals. I heard one of the four living things speak with a voice like thunder. It said, "Come!" ²I looked and there before me was a white horse. The rider on the horse held a bow. The rider was given a crown. And he rode out, defeating the enemy. He rode out to win the victory.

³The Lamb opened the second seal. Then I heard the second living thing say, "Come!" ⁴Then another horse came out. This was a red horse. The rider on the horse was given power to take away peace from the earth. He was given power to make people kill each other. This rider was given a big sword.

⁵The Lamb opened the third seal. Then I heard the third living thing say, "Come!" I looked, and there before me was a black horse. The rider on the horse held a pair of scales in his hand. ⁶Then I heard something that sounded like a voice. The voice came from where the four living things were. The voice said, "A quart of wheat for a day's pay. And three quarts of barley for a day's pay. And don't hurt the oil and wine!"

⁷The Lamb opened the fourth seal. Then I heard the voice of the fourth living thing say, "Come!" ⁸I looked and there before me was a pale colored horse. The rider on the horse was death. Hades* was following close behind him. They were given power over a fourth of the earth. They were given power to kill people by using the sword, by starving, by disease, and with the wild animals of the earth.

⁹The Lamb opened the fifth seal. Then I saw some souls under the altar.* They were the souls

---

elders These are probably great leaders of God's people. They may be the leaders of the twelve Jewish family groups, plus the twelve apostles of Jesus.
scroll A long roll of paper or leather used for writing.
harp A musical instrument with strings.
incense Special dried tree sap used for a sacrifice. It was burned to make a sweet-smelling smoke.

Amen When a person says, "Amen," it means that person agrees strongly with something.
Hades Place where people go after they die.
altar Place where sacrifices or gifts are offered to God.

of those people who had been killed because they were faithful to God's message* and to the truth they had received. ¹⁰These souls shouted in a loud voice, "Holy and true Lord, how long until you judge the people of the earth and punish them for killing us?" ¹¹Then each one of those souls was given a white robe. They were told to wait a short time longer. There were still some of their brothers in the service of Christ who must be killed like they were. Those souls were told to wait until all of this killing was finished.

¹²Then I watched while the Lamb opened the sixth seal. There was a great earthquake. The sun became dark like ₗblackⱼ cloth made from hair. The full moon became red like blood. ¹³The stars in the sky fell to the earth like a fig tree drops its figs when the wind blows. ¹⁴The sky was divided. It was rolled up like a scroll.* And every mountain and island was moved from its place.

¹⁵Then all the people hid in caves and behind the rocks on the mountains. There were the kings of the world, the rulers, the generals, the rich people and the powerful people. Every person, slave and free, hid himself. ¹⁶The people said to the mountains and the rocks, "Fall on us. Hide us from the face of the One who sits on the throne. Hide us from the anger of the Lamb! ¹⁷The great day for their anger has come. No person can stand against it."

The 144,000 People of Israel

7 After this happened I saw four angels standing at the four corners of the earth. The angels were holding the four winds of the earth. They were stopping the wind from blowing on the land or on the sea or on any tree. ²Then I saw another angel coming from the east. This angel had the seal of the living God. The angel called out with a loud voice to the four angels. These were the four angels that God had given the power to hurt the earth and the sea. The angel said to the four angels, ³"Don't hurt the land or the sea or the trees before we put the sign on the people who serve our God. We must put the sign on their foreheads." ⁴Then I heard how many people were marked with the sign. There were 144,000. They were from every family group of the people of Israel.*

	From Judah's family group	12,000
	from Reuben's family group	12,000
	from Gad's family group	12,000
⁶	from Asher's family group	12,000
	from Naphtali's family group	12,000
	from Manasseh's family group	12,000
⁷	from Simeon's family group	12,000
	from Levi's family group	12,000
	from Issachar's family group	12,000
⁸	from Zebulun's family group	12,000
	from Joseph's family group	12,000
	from Benjamin's family group	12,000

The Great Crowd

⁹Then I looked, and there were many, many people. There were so many people that a person could not count them all. They were from every nation, tribe, race of people, and language of the earth. These people were standing before the throne and before the Lamb *(Jesus).* They all wore white robes and had palm branches in their hands. ¹⁰They shouted with a loud voice, "Victory belongs to our God, who sits on the throne, and to the Lamb." ¹¹The elders* and the four living things were there. All the angels were standing around them and the throne. The angels bowed down on their faces before the throne and worshiped God. ¹²They said, "Amen*! Praise, glory, wisdom, thanks, honor, power, and strength belong to our God forever and ever. Amen!"

¹³Then one of the elders* asked me, "Who are these people in white robes? Where did they come from?"

¹⁴I answered, "You know who they are, sir."

And the elder* said, "These are the people who have come out of the great suffering. They have washed their robes* with the blood of the Lamb. Now they are clean and white. ¹⁵So now these people are before the throne of God. They worship God day and night in his temple.* And the One *(God)* who sits on the throne will protect them. ¹⁶They will never be hungry again. They will never be thirsty again. The sun will not hurt them. No heat will burn them. ¹⁷The Lamb at the center of the throne will be their shepherd. He will

---

elder(s) These are probably great leaders of God's people. They may be the leaders of the twelve Jewish family groups, plus the twelve apostles of Jesus.

Amen When a person says, "Amen," it means that person agrees strongly with something.

washed their robes Meaning they believed in Jesus so that their sins could be forgiven.

temple God's house—the place where God's people worship and serve him.

message The news that God has made a way for people to have their sins forgiven and live with God.

scroll A long roll of paper or leather used for writing on.

Israel The Jews—God's chosen people in the Old Testament.

lead them to springs of water that give life. And God will wipe away every tear from their eyes."

The Seventh Seal

8 The Lamb opened the seventh seal. Then there was silence in heaven for about half an hour. ²And I saw the seven angels who stand before God. They were given seven trumpets.

³Another angel came and stood at the altar.* This angel had a golden holder for incense.* The angel was given much incense to offer with the prayers of all God's holy people *(believers)*. The angel put this offering on the golden altar before the throne. ⁴The smoke from the incense went up from the angel's hand to God. The smoke went up with the prayers of God's people. ⁵Then the angel filled the incense holder with fire from the altar. The angel threw the incense holder on the earth. Then there were flashes of lightning, thunder and other noises, and an earthquake.

The Seven Angels Blow Their Trumpets

⁶Then the seven angels with the seven trumpets prepared to blow their trumpets.

⁷The first angel blew his trumpet. Then hail and fire mixed with blood was poured down on the earth. And one third of the earth and all the green grass and one third of the trees were burned up.

⁸The second angel blew his trumpet. Then something that looked like a big mountain burning with fire was thrown into the sea. And one third of the sea became blood. ⁹And one third of the living things in the sea died, and one third of the ships were destroyed.

¹⁰The third angel blew his trumpet. Then a large star, burning like a torch, fell from the sky. The star fell on one third of the rivers and on the springs of water. ¹¹The name of the star is Wormwood.* And one third of all the water became bitter. Many people died from drinking the water that was bitter.

¹²The fourth angel blew his trumpet. Then one third of the sun and one third of the moon and one third of the stars were struck. So one third of them became dark. A third of the day and night was without light.

¹³While I watched, I heard an eagle that was flying high in the air. The eagle said with a loud voice, "Trouble! Trouble! Trouble for the people that live on the earth! The trouble will begin after the sounds of the trumpets that the other three angels will blow."

9 The fifth angel blew his trumpet. Then I saw a star fall from the sky to the earth. The star was given the key to the deep hole that leads down to the bottomless pit. ²Then the star opened the hole leading to the bottomless pit. Smoke came up from the hole like smoke from a big furnace. The sun and sky became dark because of the smoke from the hole. ³Then locusts* came down to the earth out of the smoke. They were given the power to sting like scorpions.* ⁴The locusts were told not to hurt the grass on the earth or any plant or tree. They could hurt only the people who did not have the sign of God on their foreheads. ⁵These locusts were given the power to give pain to the people for five months. But the locusts were not given the power to kill the people. And the pain that the people felt was like the pain that a scorpion gives when it stings a person. ⁶During those days people will look for a way to die, but they will not find it. They will want to die, but death will hide from them.

⁷The locusts* looked like horses prepared for battle. On their heads they wore things that looked like crowns of gold. Their faces looked like human faces. ⁸Their hair was like women's hair. Their teeth were like lions' teeth. ⁹Their chests looked like iron breastplates. The sound their wings made was like the noise of many horses and chariots hurrying into battle. ¹⁰The locusts had tails with stingers like scorpions.* The power they had to give people pain for five months was in their tails. ¹¹The locusts had a king. The king was the angel of the bottomless pit. His name in the Hebrew language is Abaddon.* In the Greek language his name is Apollyon *(Destroyer).*

¹²The first great trouble is past. There are still two other great troubles that will come.

¹³The sixth angel blew his trumpet. Then I heard a voice coming from the horns on the golden altar* that is before God. ¹⁴The voice said to the sixth angel who had the trumpet, "Free the four angels who are tied at the great river Euphrates." ¹⁵These four angels had been kept ready for this hour and day and month and year. The angels were freed to kill one third of all the

---

altar Place where sacrifices or gifts are offered to God.
incense Special dried tree sap used for a sacrifice. It was burned to make a sweet-smelling smoke.
Wormwood Name of a very bitter plant, used here to give the idea of bitter sorrow.

locusts Insects like grasshoppers. Sometimes many locusts came and ate all the plants (Ex. 10).
scorpions Insects that sting with a strong poison.
Abaddon In the Old Testament this was a name for the place of death (Job 26:6; Psalm 88:11).

people on the earth. ¹⁶I heard how many troops on horses were in ˻their˼ army. There were 200,000,000.

¹⁷In my vision* I saw the horses and the riders on the horses. They looked like this: They had breastplates that were fiery red, dark blue, and yellow like sulfur. The heads of the horses looked like heads of lions. The horses had fire, smoke, and sulfur coming out of their mouths. ¹⁸One third of all the people on earth were killed by these three bad things coming out of the horses' mouths: the fire, the smoke, and the sulfur. ¹⁹The horses' power was in their mouths and also in their tails. Their tails were like snakes that have heads to bite and hurt people.

²⁰The other people ˻on the earth˼ were not killed by these bad things. But these people still did not change their hearts and lives and turn away from the things they had made with their own hands. They did not stop worshiping demons* and idols* made of gold, silver, bronze, stone, and wood—things that cannot see or hear or walk. ²¹These people did not change their hearts and lives and turn away from killing other people. They did not turn away from their evil magic, their sexual sins, and their stealing.

The Angel and the Little Scroll

10 Then I saw another powerful angel coming down from heaven. The angel was dressed in a cloud. He had a rainbow around his head. The angel's face was like the sun, and his legs were like poles of fire. ²The angel was holding a small scroll. The scroll was open in his hand. The angel put his right foot on the sea and his left foot on the land. ³The angel shouted loudly like the roaring of a lion. After the angel shouted, the voices of seven thunders spoke. ⁴The seven thunders spoke, and I started to write. But then I heard a voice from heaven. The voice said, "Don't write what the seven thunders said. Keep those things secret."

⁵Then the angel I saw standing on the sea and on the land raised his right hand to heaven. ⁶The angel made a promise by ˻the power of˼ the One who lives forever and ever. He *(God)* is the One who made the skies and all that is in them. He made the earth and all that is in it, and he made the sea and all that is in it. The angel said, "There will be no more waiting! ⁷In the days when the seventh angel is ready to blow his trumpet, God's secret plan will be finished. This plan is the Good News* God told to his servants, the prophets.*"

⁸Then I heard the same voice from heaven again. The voice said to me, "Go and take the open scroll that is in the angel's hand. This is the angel that is standing on the sea and on the land." ⁹So I went to the angel and asked him to give me the little scroll. The angel said to me, "Take the scroll and eat it. It will be sour in your stomach. But in your mouth it will be sweet like honey." ¹⁰So I took the little scroll from the angel's hand. I ate the scroll. In my mouth it tasted sweet like honey. But after I ate it, it was sour in my stomach. ¹¹Then I was told, "You must prophesy* again about many races of people, many nations, languages, and kings."

The Two Witnesses

11 Then I was given a measuring rod as long as a walking stick. I was told, "Go and measure the temple* of God and the altar,* and count the people worshiping there. ²But don't measure the yard outside the temple. Leave that alone. That has been given to the people who are not Jews. Those people will walk on the holy city for 42 months. ³And I will give power to my two witnesses. And they will prophesy* for 1,260 days. They will be dressed in sackcloth.*" ⁴These two witnesses are the two olive trees and the two lampstands that stand before the Lord of the earth. ⁵If a person tries to hurt the witnesses, fire comes from the mouths of the witnesses and kills their enemy. Any person who tries to hurt them will die like this. ⁶These witnesses have the power to stop the sky from raining during the time they are prophesying. These witnesses have power to make the water become blood. They have power to send every kind of trouble to the earth. They can do this as many times as they want.

⁷When the two witnesses have finished telling their message, the animal will fight against them. This is the animal that comes up from the bottomless pit. The animal will defeat them and

---

Good News The news that God has made a way for people to have their sins forgiven and live with God.
prophets People who spoke for God.
prophesy To speak or teach things from God.
temple God's house—the place where God's people worship and serve him. Here, John sees it pictured as the special building in Jerusalem for Jewish worship.
altar Place where sacrifices or gifts are offered to God.
sackcloth A rough cloth made from animal hair. People sometimes wore it to show sadness.

vision A vision is something like a dream that God used to speak to people.
demons Demons are evil spirits from the devil.
idols Statues that people worshiped as gods.

kill them. ⁸The bodies of the two witnesses will lie in the street of the great city. This city is named Sodom* and Egypt. These names for the city have a special meaning. This is the city where the Lord was killed. ⁹People from every race of people, tribe, language, and nation will look at the bodies of the two witnesses for three and a half days. The people will refuse to bury them. ¹⁰People who live on the earth will be happy because these two are dead. They will have parties and send each other gifts. They will do these things because these two prophets *(witnesses)* brought much suffering to the people who live on the earth.

¹¹But after three and a half days God let life enter the two prophets again. They stood on their feet. All the people who saw them were filled with fear. ¹²Then the two prophets heard a loud voice from heaven say, "Come up here!" And the two prophets went up into heaven in a cloud. Their enemies watched them go.

¹³At that same time there was a great earthquake. One tenth of the city was destroyed. And 7,000 people were killed in the earthquake. The people that did not die were very afraid. They gave glory to the God of heaven.

¹⁴The second great trouble is finished. The third great trouble is coming soon.

The Seventh Trumpet

¹⁵The seventh angel blew his trumpet. Then there were loud voices in heaven. The voices said:

> "The kingdom of the world has now become
> the kingdom of our Lord ₍God₎ and
> of his Christ.*
> And he will rule forever and ever."

¹⁶Then the 24 elders* bowed down on their faces and worshiped God. These are the elders who sit on their thrones before God. ¹⁷The elders said:

> "We give thanks to you,
> Lord God All-Powerful.
> You are the One who is and
> who ₍always₎ was.
> We thank you because you have used
> your great power
> and have begun to rule!
> ¹⁸ The people of the world were angry;
> but now is the time for your anger.

Sodom A town where very bad people lived. God punished them by destroying their city.
Christ The "anointed one" (Messiah) or chosen of God.
24 elders These are probably great leaders of God's people. They may be the leaders of the twelve Jewish family groups, plus the twelve apostles of Jesus.

> Now is the time for the dead people
> to be judged.
> It is time to reward your servants,
> the prophets,*
> and to reward your holy people,*
> the people, great and small,
> who respect you, .
> It is time to destroy those people
> who destroy the earth!"

¹⁹Then God's temple* in heaven was opened. The holy chest that holds the agreement* ₍that God gave to his people₎ could be seen in his temple. Then there were flashes of lightning, noises, thunder, an earthquake, and a great hailstorm.

The Woman and the Giant Snake

12 And then a great wonder appeared in heaven: There was a woman who was clothed with the sun. The moon was under her feet. She had a crown of twelve stars on her head. ²The woman was pregnant. She cried out with pain because she was about to give birth. ³Then another wonder appeared in heaven: There was a giant red snake there. The giant snake had seven heads with seven crowns on each head. The snake also had ten horns. ⁴The snake's tail swept a third of the stars out of the sky and threw them down to the earth. The giant snake stood in front of the woman who was ready to give birth to the baby. The snake wanted to eat the woman's baby when it was born. ⁵The woman gave birth to a son, a male child. He will rule all the nations with an iron rod. And her child was taken up to God and to his throne. ⁶The woman ran away into the desert to a place that God prepared for her. In the desert she will be taken care of for 1,260 days.

⁷Then there was a war in heaven. Michael* and his angels fought against the giant snake. The snake and his angels fought back. ⁸But the snake was not strong enough. The giant snake and his angels lost their place in heaven. ⁹The snake was thrown down out of heaven. (The giant snake is that old snake called the devil or Satan. He leads

---

prophets People who spoke for God.
holy people God's people are called holy because they are made pure through Christ, and they belong only to God.
temple God's house—the place where God's people worship and serve him. John sees the heavenly temple pictured to be like the Jewish temple in the Old Testament.
holy chest that holds the agreement In the Most Holy Place of the Jewish temple was a box that held the agreement God gave to his people (Ex. 25:10-22; 1 Kings 8:1-9; Heb. 9:4).
Michael The archangel—leader of God's angels (Jude 9).

the whole world into the wrong way.) The snake with his angels were thrown to the earth.

¹⁰Then I heard a loud voice in heaven say: "The victory and the power and the kingdom of our God and the authority *(power)* of his Christ* have now come. These things have come, because the accuser of our brothers has been thrown out. He is the one who accused our brothers day and night before our God. ¹¹Our brothers defeated him by the blood *(death)* of the Lamb and by the truth they preached. They did not love their lives too much. They were not afraid of death. ¹²So be happy you heavens and all who live there! But it will be bad for the earth and sea, because the devil has gone down to you! The devil is filled with anger. He knows he doesn't have much time."

¹³The giant snake saw that he had been thrown down to the earth. So he chased the woman who had given birth to the boy child. ¹⁴But the woman was given the two wings of a great eagle. Then she could fly to the place that was prepared for her in the desert. In that place she would be taken care of for three and one-half years. There she would be away from the snake. ¹⁵Then the snake poured water out of its mouth like a river. The snake poured the water toward the woman so that the flood would carry her away. ¹⁶But the earth helped the woman. The earth opened its mouth and swallowed the river that came from the mouth of the giant snake. ¹⁷Then the snake was very angry at the woman. The snake went away to make war against all her other children. Her children are those people who obey God's commandments and have the truth that Jesus taught.

¹⁸The giant snake stood on the seashore.

The Two Animals

13 Then I saw an animal coming up out of the sea. It had ten horns and seven heads. There was a crown on each of its horns. It had a bad name written on each head. ²This animal looked like a leopard, with feet like a bear's feet. It had a mouth like a lion's mouth. The giant snake ₍on the seashore₎ gave the animal all of his power and his throne and great authority. ³One of the heads of the animal looked like it had been wounded and killed. But this death wound was healed. All the people in the world were amazed, and they all followed the animal. ⁴People worshiped the giant snake because he had given his power to the animal. And the people also worshiped the animal. They asked, "Who is as powerful as the animal? Who can make war against him?"

⁵The animal was allowed to say proud words and very evil things. The animal was allowed to use his power for 42 months. ⁶The animal opened his mouth to say bad things against God. The animal also said bad things against God's name, against the place where God lives, and against all those who live in heaven. ⁷The animal was given power to make war against God's holy people *(believers)* and to defeat them. The animal was given power over every tribe, race of people, language, and nation. ⁸All the people who live on earth will worship the animal. These are all the people since the beginning of the world whose names are not written in the Lamb's book of life. The Lamb is the One who was killed.

⁹If a person hears these things, then he should listen to this:

10   If any person is to be a prisoner,
       then that person will be a prisoner.
    If any person kills with a sword,
       then that person will be killed
          with a sword.

This means that God's holy people *(believers)* must have patience and faith.

¹¹Then I saw another animal coming up out of the earth. He had two horns like a lamb, but he talked like a giant snake. ¹²This animal stands before the first animal and uses the same power that the first animal has. He uses this power to make all the people living on the earth worship the first animal. The first animal was the one that had the death wound that was healed. ¹³This second animal does great miracles.* He even makes fire come down from heaven to earth while people are watching. ¹⁴This second animal fools the people that live on the earth. He fools them by using the miracles that he has been given the power to do. He does these miracles to serve the first animal. The second animal ordered people to make an idol* to honor the first animal. This was the animal that was wounded by the sword but did not die. ¹⁵The second animal was given power to give life to the idol of the first animal. Then the idol could speak and order all the people who did not worship it to be killed. ¹⁶The second animal also forced all people, small and great, rich and poor, free and slave, to have a mark on their right hand or on their forehead. ¹⁷No person could buy

---

Christ   The "anointed one" (Messiah) or chosen of God.
miracles   Here, powerful acts done by the power of the devil.
idol   A statue that people worshiped as a god.

or sell without this mark. This mark is the name of the animal or the number of his name. ¹⁸A person who has understanding can find the meaning of the animal's number. This requires wisdom. This number is the number of a man. It is 666.

The Song of the Redeemed

14 Then I looked, and there before me was the Lamb. He was standing on Mount Zion.* There were 144,000 people with him. They all had his name and his Father's name written on their foreheads. ²And I heard a sound from heaven like the noise of flooding water and like the sound of loud thunder. The sound I heard was like people playing their harps.* ³The people sang a new song before the throne and before the four living things and the elders.* The only people that could learn the new song were the 144,000 who had been redeemed *(saved)* from the earth. No one else could learn the song. ⁴These 144,000 people are the ones who did not do wrong things with women. They kept themselves pure. They follow the Lamb every place he goes. These 144,000 were redeemed *(saved)* from among the people of the earth. They are the first people to be offered to God and the Lamb. ⁵These people were not guilty of telling lies. They are without fault.

The Three Angels

⁶Then I saw another angel flying high in the air. The angel had an eternal gospel* to preach to the people who live on the earth—to every nation, tribe, language, and race of people. ⁷The angel said in a loud voice, "Fear God and give him praise. The time has come for God to judge ₍all people₎. Worship God. He made the heavens, the earth, the sea, and the springs of water."

⁸Then the second angel followed the first angel and said, "She is destroyed! The great city of Babylon is destroyed! She *(Babylon)* made all the nations drink the wine of her adultery* and of God's anger."

⁹A third angel followed the first two angels. This third angel said in a loud voice: "₍It will be bad for₎ the person who worships the animal and the animal's idol* and gets the animal's mark on his forehead or on his hand. ¹⁰That person will drink the wine of God's anger. This wine is prepared with all its strength in the cup of God's anger. That person will be tortured *(hurt)* with burning sulfur before the holy angels and the Lamb. ¹¹And the smoke from their burning pain will rise forever and ever. There will be no rest, day or night, for those people who worship the animal and his idol or who get the mark of his name." ¹²This means that God's holy people *(believers)* must be patient. They must obey God's commandments and keep their faith in Jesus.

¹³Then I heard a voice from heaven. The voice said, "Write this: From now on, the dead people who were in the Lord when they died are blessed *(happy)*."

The Spirit* says, "Yes, that is true. Those people will rest from their hard work. The things they have done will stay with them."

The Earth Is Harvested

¹⁴I looked and there before me was a white cloud. Sitting on the white cloud was One that looked like a Son of Man.* He had a gold crown on his head and a sharp sickle* in his hand. ¹⁵Then another angel came out of the temple.* This angel called to the One who was sitting on the cloud, "Take your sickle and gather ₍from the earth₎. The time to harvest has come. The fruit of the earth is ripe." ¹⁶So the One that was sitting on the cloud swung his sickle over the earth. And the earth was harvested.

¹⁷Then another angel came out of the temple* in heaven. This angel also had a sharp sickle. ¹⁸And then another angel came from the altar.* This angel has power over the fire. This angel called to the angel with the sharp sickle. He said, "Take your sharp sickle and gather the bunches of grapes from the earth's vine. The earth's grapes are ripe." ¹⁹The angel swung his sickle over the earth. The angel gathered the earth's grapes and threw them into the great winepress of God's anger. ²⁰The grapes were squeezed in the

---

Mount Zion Another name for Jerusalem, here meaning the spiritual city where God's people live with him.
harps Musical instruments with strings.
elders These are probably great leaders of God's people. They may be the leaders of the twelve Jewish family groups, plus the twelve apostles of Jesus.
gospel The Good News that God has made a way for people to have their sins forgiven and live with God.
adultery Breaking a marriage promise by sexual sin.
idol A statue that people worshiped as a god.
Spirit The Holy Spirit. Called Spirit of God, Spirit of Christ, and the Comforter. Joined with God and Christ, he does God's work among people in the world.
Son of Man This name is from Dan. 7:13-14. Jesus used this name when talking about himself.
sickle Farming tool with a curved blade used to cut grain.
temple God's house, where God's people worship and serve.
altar Place where sacrifices or gifts are offered to God.

winepress outside the city. Blood flowed out of the winepress. It rose as high as the heads of the horses for a distance of 200 miles.

The Angels with the Last Plagues

15 Then I saw another wonder in heaven. It was great and amazing. There were seven angels bringing seven troubles. These are the last troubles, because after these troubles God's anger is finished.
²I saw what looked like a sea of glass mixed with fire. All the people who had won the victory over the animal and his idol* and over the number of his name were standing by the sea. These people had harps that God had given them. ³They sang the song of Moses, the servant of God, and the song of the Lamb:

"Great and wonderful are the things you do,
Lord God All-Powerful.
Right and true are your ways,
King of the nations.
⁴ All people will fear you, O Lord.
All people will praise your name.
Only you are holy.
All people will come and worship before you,
because it is clear that you do the things that are right."

⁵After this I saw the temple* (the holy place of God's presence*) in heaven. The temple was opened. ⁶And the seven angels bringing the seven troubles came out of the temple. They were dressed in clean shining linen cloth. They wore golden bands tied around their chests. ⁷Then one of the four living things gave seven golden bowls to the seven angels. The bowls were filled with the anger of God, who lives forever and ever. ⁸The temple was filled with smoke from the glory and the power of God. No one could enter the temple until the seven troubles of the seven angels were finished.

The Bowls Filled with God's Anger

16 Then I heard a loud voice from the temple.* The voice said to the seven angels, "Go and pour out the seven bowls of God's anger on the earth."

²The first angel left. He poured out his bowl on the land. Then all the people who had the mark of the animal and who worshiped his idol* got sores that were ugly and painful.
³The second angel poured out his bowl on the sea. Then the sea became blood like the blood of a dead man. Every living thing in the sea died.
⁴The third angel poured out his bowl on the rivers and the springs of water. The rivers and the springs of water became blood. ⁵Then I heard the angel of the waters say ˻to God˼:

"You are the One who is and who
˻always˼ was.
You are the Holy One.
You are right in these judgments
you have made.
⁶ The people have spilled the blood of
your holy people *(believers)*
and your prophets.*
Now you have given those people blood
to drink.
This is what they deserve."

⁷And I heard the altar* say:

"Yes, Lord God All-Powerful,
your judgments are true and right."

⁸The fourth angel poured out his bowl on the sun. The sun was given power to burn the people with fire. ⁹The people were burned by the great heat. Those people cursed the name of God. God is the One who had control over these troubles. But the people refused to change their hearts and lives and give glory to God.
¹⁰The fifth angel poured out his bowl on the throne of the animal. And darkness covered the animal's kingdom. People bit their tongues because of the pain. ¹¹People cursed the God of heaven because of their pain and the sores they had. But the people refused to change their hearts and turn away from the ˻bad˼ things they did.
¹²The sixth angel poured out his bowl on the great river Euphrates. The water in the river was dried up. This prepared the way for the kings from the east to come. ¹³Then I saw three unclean *(evil)* spirits that looked like frogs. They came out of the mouth of the giant snake, out of the mouth of the animal, and out of the mouth of the false prophet.* ¹⁴These evil spirits are the spirits of

---

idol A statue that people worshiped as a god.
temple God's house—the place where God's people worship and serve him.
holy place of God's presence Literally, "tent of the testimony," the room inside the Holy Tent where the Ten Commandments were kept. These were the "testimony" or "proof" of God's Agreement with his people. This room is where God lived among his people. (Read Ex. 25:8-22.)

prophets People who spoke for God.
altar Place where sacrifices or gifts are offered to God.
false prophet A person who says he speaks for God but does not really speak God's truth.

demons.* They ₍have power to₎ do miracles.* These evil spirits go out to the kings of the whole world. They go out to gather the kings for battle on the great day of God the All-Powerful. ¹⁵"Listen! I will come like a thief comes! Happy is the person who stays awake and keeps his clothes with him. Then he will not have to go without clothes, and people will not see the things he is ashamed for them to see."

¹⁶Then the evil spirits gathered the kings together to the place that is called Armageddon in the Hebrew language.

¹⁷The seventh angel poured out his bowl into the air. Then a loud voice came out of the temple* from the throne. The voice said, "It is finished!" ¹⁸Then there were flashes of lightning, noises, thunder, and a big earthquake. This was the worst earthquake that has ever happened since people have been on earth. ¹⁹The great city split into three parts. The cities of the nations were destroyed. And God did not forget ₍to punish₎ Babylon the Great. He gave that city the cup filled with the wine of his terrible anger. ²⁰Every island disappeared and there were no more mountains. ²¹Giant hailstones fell on the people from out of the sky. These hailstones weighed about 100 pounds each. People cursed God because of this trouble of the hail. This trouble was a terrible thing.

The Woman on the Animal

17 One of the seven angels came and spoke to me. This was one of the angels that had the seven bowls. The angel said, "Come, and I will show you the punishment that will be given to the famous prostitute.* She is the one sitting over many waters. ²The kings of the earth sinned sexually with her. The people of the earth became drunk from the wine of her sexual sin."

³Then the angel carried me away by the Spirit* to the desert. There I saw a woman sitting on a red animal. The animal was covered with bad names written on him. The animal had seven heads and ten horns. ⁴The woman was dressed in purple and red. She was shining with the gold, jewels, and pearls she was wearing. She had a golden cup in her hand. This cup was filled with terrible (evil) things and the uncleanness of her sexual sin. ⁵She had a title written on her forehead. This title has a hidden meaning. This is what was written:

THE GREAT BABYLON
MOTHER OF PROSTITUTES
AND THE EVIL THINGS OF THE EARTH

⁶I saw that the woman was drunk. She was drunk with the blood of God's holy people. She was drunk with the blood of those people who told about ₍their faith in₎ Jesus.

When I saw the woman, I was fully amazed. ⁷Then the angel said to me, "Why are you amazed? I will tell you the hidden meaning of this woman and the animal she rides—the animal with seven heads and ten horns. ⁸The animal that you saw was once ₍alive₎. But that animal is not ₍alive₎ now. But that animal will ₍be alive and₎ come up out of the bottomless pit and go away to be destroyed. The people that live on the earth will be amazed when they see the animal. They will be amazed because he was once ₍alive₎, is not ₍alive₎ now, but will come again. These are the people whose names have never been written in the book of life since the beginning of the world.

⁹"You need a wise mind to understand this. The seven heads on the animal are the seven hills where the woman sits. They are also seven kings. ¹⁰Five of the kings have already died. One of the kings lives now. And the last king is coming. When he comes, he will stay only a short time. ¹¹The animal that was once ₍alive₎ but is not ₍alive₎ now is an eighth king. This eighth king also belongs to the first seven kings. And he will go away to be destroyed.

¹²"The ten horns you saw are ten kings. These ten kings have not yet received their kingdom. But they will receive power to rule with the animal for one hour. ¹³All ten of these kings have the same purpose. And they will give their power and authority to the animal. ¹⁴They will make war against the Lamb. But the Lamb will defeat them, because he is Lord of lords and King of kings. He will defeat them with his chosen and faithful followers—the people that he has called."

¹⁵Then the angel said to me, "You saw the water where the prostitute* sits. These waters are the many peoples, the different races, nations, and languages ₍in the world₎. ¹⁶The animal and the ten horns (ten kings) you saw will hate the prostitute. They will take everything she has and leave her naked. They will eat her body and burn her with fire. ¹⁷God made the ten horns want to do his

---

demons Demons are evil spirits from the devil.
miracles False miracles—powerful acts done by the power of the devil.
temple God's house—the place where God's people worship and serve him.
prostitute(s) Women paid by men for sexual sin.
Spirit The Holy Spirit. Called Spirit of God, Spirit of Christ, and the Comforter. Joined with God and Christ, he does God's work among people in the world.

purpose: They agreed to give the animal their power to rule. They will rule until the things God has said are completed. ¹⁸The woman you saw is the great city that rules over the kings of the earth."

Babylon Is Destroyed

18 Then I saw another angel coming down from heaven. This angel had much power. The angel's glory made the earth bright. ²The angel shouted with a powerful voice:

"She is destroyed!
　The great city of Babylon is destroyed!
She *(Babylon)* has become a home
　for demons.*
That city has become a place for every
　unclean spirit to live.
She has become a city filled with all kinds
　of unclean birds.
She has become a city for every unclean
　and hated animal.
³ All the peoples of the earth have drunk
　the wine of her sexual sin and of
　⌊God's⌋ anger.
The kings of the earth sinned sexually
　with her,
and the businessmen of the world grew rich
　from the great wealth of her luxury."

⁴Then I heard another voice from heaven say:

"Come out of that city, my people,
　so that you will not share in her sins.
Then you will not get any of the bad things
　that will happen to her.
⁵ That city's sins are stacked *(piled)* up
　as far as heaven.
God has not forgotten the wrong things
　she has done.
⁶ Give that city the same as she gave to others.
Pay her back twice as much as she did.
Prepare wine for her that is twice as strong as
　the wine she prepared for others.
⁷ She *(Babylon)* gave herself much glory
　and rich living.
Give her that much suffering and sadness.
She says to herself, 'I am a queen sitting
　⌊on my throne⌋.
I am not a widow*
I will never be sad.'
⁸ So these bad things will come to her
　in one day:
　death, sad crying, and great hunger.

demons Demons are evil spirits from the devil.
widow A widow is a woman whose husband has died.

She will be destroyed by fire,
　because the Lord God who judges her
　　is powerful."

⁹The kings of the earth who sinned sexually with her *(Babylon)* and shared her wealth will see the smoke from her burning. Then those kings will cry and be sad because of her ⌊death⌋. ¹⁰The kings will be afraid of her suffering and stand far away. The kings will say:

"Terrible! How terrible, O great city,
　O powerful city of Babylon!
Your punishment came in one hour!"

¹¹And the businessmen of the earth will cry and be sad for her *(Babylon)*. They will be sad because now there is no one to buy the things they sell. ¹²They sell gold, silver, jewels, pearls, fine linen cloth, purple cloth, silk, and scarlet cloth, all kinds of citron wood, and all kinds of things made from ivory, expensive wood, bronze, iron, and marble. ¹³Those businessmen also sell cinnamon, spice, incense, frankincense, myrrh, wine, and olive oil; fine flour, wheat, cattle, sheep, horses, carriages, and the bodies and souls of men. ⌊The businessmen will cry and say:⌋

¹⁴"⌊O Babylon⌋, the good things you wanted are
　gone from you.
All your rich and fancy things have
　disappeared.
You will never have those things again."

¹⁵The businessmen will be afraid of her suffering and stand far away from her *(Babylon)*. These are the men who became rich from selling those things to her. The men will cry and be sad. ¹⁶They will say:

"Terrible! How terrible for the great city!
She was dressed in fine linen, purple,
　and scarlet cloth.
She was shining with gold, jewels,
　and pearls!
¹⁷　All these riches have been destroyed
　　in one hour!"

Every sea captain, all the people who travel on ships, the sailors, and all the people who earn money from the sea stood far away from Babylon. ¹⁸They saw the smoke from her burning. They said loudly, "There was never a city like this great city!" ¹⁹They threw dust on their heads. They cried and were sad. They said loudly:

"Terrible! How terrible for the great city!
All the people who had ships on the sea
　became rich because of her wealth!
But she has been destroyed in one hour!

²⁰ Be happy because of this, O heaven!
Be happy, God's holy people *(believers)* and
apostles* and prophets*!
God has punished her because of the things
she did to you."
²¹Then a powerful angel picked up a large rock. This rock was as big as a large millstone.* The angel threw the rock into the sea and said:
"That is how the great city of Babylon will
be thrown down.
That city will never be found again.
²² The music of people playing harps and other
instruments, flutes and trumpets,
will never be heard in you again.
No workman doing any job will ever be
found in you again.
The sound of a millstone* will never be
heard in you again.
²³ The light of a lamp will never shine
in you again.
The voice of a bridegroom* and bride
will never be heard in you again.
Your businessmen were the world's
great men.
All the nations were tricked by your magic.
²⁴ She *(Babylon)* is guilty of the blood *(death)*
of the prophets* and of God's
holy people *(believers)*,
and of all the people who have been
killed on earth."

People in Heaven Praise God

19 After this I heard what sounded like many, many people in heaven. The people were saying:

"Hallelujah *(Praise God)*!
² Victory, glory, and power belong to our God.
His judgments are true and right.
Our God has punished the prostitute.*
She is the one who made the earth evil
with her sexual sin.
God has punished the prostitute
to pay her for the blood *(death)*
of his servants."
³Those people in heaven also said:
"Hallelujah *(Praise God)*!
⌊She is burning and⌋ her smoke will rise
forever and ever."

⁴Then the 24 elders* and the four living things bowed down. They worshiped God, who sits on the throne. They said:
"Amen, Hallelujah *(Praise God)*!"
⁵Then a voice came from the throne. The voice said:
"Praise our God, all you people that serve him!
Praise our God, all you people small and great
that honor him!"
⁶Then I heard something that sounded like many, many people. It sounded like the noise of flooding water and like loud thunder. The people were saying:
"Hallelujah *(Praise God)*!
Our Lord God rules.
He is the All-Powerful.
⁷ Let us rejoice and be happy
and give God glory!
Give God glory, because the wedding
of the Lamb *(Jesus)* has come.
And the Lamb's bride *(the church)*
has made herself ready.
⁸ Fine linen was given to the bride
for her to wear.
The linen was bright and clean."
(The fine linen means the good things that God's holy people *(believers)* did.)
⁹Then the angel said to me, "Write this: Those people who are invited to the wedding meal of the Lamb are blessed *(happy)*!" Then the angel said, "These are the true words of God."
¹⁰Then I bowed down before the angel's feet to worship him. But the angel said to me, "Don't ⌊worship me⌋! I am a servant like you and your brothers who have the truth of Jesus. So worship God! Because the truth of Jesus is the spirit of prophecy.*"

The Rider on the White Horse

¹¹Then I saw heaven open. There before me was a white horse. The rider on the horse is called Faithful and True. He is right in his judging and in making war. ¹²His eyes are like burning fire. He has many crowns on his head. He has a name written on him, but he is the only one who knows the name. No other person knows the name. ¹³He is dressed in a robe dipped in blood. His name is

---

apostles The men Jesus chose to be his special helpers.
prophets People who spoke for God.
millstone A large, round stone used for grinding grain.
bridegroom A man ready to be married.
prostitute(s) Women paid by men for sexual sin.

24 elders Elder means "older." These are probably great leaders of God's people. They may be the leaders of the twelve Jewish family groups plus Jesus' twelve apostles.
prophecy Teaching from God by a person who speaks for God.

the Word of God. ¹⁴The armies of heaven were following him. They were riding white horses. They were dressed in fine linen, white and clean. ¹⁵A sharp sword comes out of the rider's mouth. He will use this sword to defeat the nations. He will rule the nations with a rod of iron. He will squeeze ⌊the grapes⌋ in the winepress of the terrible anger of God the All-Powerful. ¹⁶On his robe and on his leg was written this name:

KING OF KINGS AND LORD OF LORDS

¹⁷Then I saw an angel standing in the sun. The angel said with a loud voice to all the birds flying in the sky, "Come together for the great supper of God. ¹⁸Come together so that you can eat the bodies of kings and generals and famous men. Come to eat the bodies of the horses and their riders and the bodies of all people, free, slave, small, and great."

¹⁹Then I saw the animal and the kings of the earth. Their armies were gathered together to make war against the rider on the horse and his army. ²⁰But the animal was captured. Also the false prophet* was captured. This false prophet was the one who did the miracles* for the animal. The false prophet had used these miracles to trick the people who had the mark of the animal and worshiped his idol.* The false prophet and the animal were thrown alive into the lake of fire that burns with sulfur. ²¹Their armies were killed with the sword that came out of the mouth of the rider on the horse. All the birds ate these bodies until the birds were full.

The 1000 Years

20 ¹I saw an angel coming down out of heaven. The angel had the key to the bottomless pit. The angel also held a large chain in his hand. ²The angel grabbed the giant snake (that old serpent). The giant snake is the devil (or Satan). The angel tied him ⌊with the chain⌋ for 1,000 years. ³The angel threw the snake into the bottomless pit and closed it. The angel locked it over the snake. The angel did this so that the snake could not trick the people of the earth until the 1,000 years were ended. After 1,000 years the snake must be made free for a short time.

The Defeat of Satan

⁴Then I saw some thrones and people sitting on them. These were the people who had been given the power to judge. And I saw the souls of those people who had been killed because ⌊they were faithful to⌋ the truth of Jesus and the message* from God. Those people did not worship the animal or his idol.* They did not receive the mark of the animal on their foreheads or on their hands. Those people became alive again and ruled with Christ for 1,000 years. ⁵(The other dead people did not live again until the 1,000 years were ended.) This is the first raising of the dead. ⁶Blessed *(happy)* and holy* are those people who share in this first raising of the dead. The second death has no power over those people. Those people will be priests for God and for Christ. They will rule with him for 1,000 years.

The Defeat of Satan

⁷When the 1,000 years are ended, Satan *(the devil)* will be made free from his prison ⌊in the bottomless pit⌋. ⁸Satan will go out to trick the nations in all the earth—Gog and Magog. Satan will gather the people for battle. There will be so many people that they will be like sand on the seashore. ⁹Satan's army marched across the earth and gathered around the camp of God's people and the city that God loves. But fire came down from heaven and destroyed Satan's army. ¹⁰And Satan (the one who tricked those people) was thrown into the lake of burning sulfur with the animal and the false prophet.* There they will be tortured *(punished)* day and night forever and ever.

People of the World Are Judged

¹¹Then I saw a large white throne. I saw the One who was sitting on the throne. Earth and sky ran away from him and disappeared. ¹²And I saw the people that had died, great and small, standing before the throne. And the book of life was opened. There were also other books opened. These dead people were judged by the things they had done. These things are written in the books. ¹³The sea gave up the dead people that were in it. Death and Hades* gave up the dead people that

---

false prophet A person who says he speaks for God but does not really speak God's truth.
miracles Here, powerful acts done by the power of the devil.
idol A statue that people worship as a god.
message The news that God has made a way for people to have their sins forgiven and live with God.
holy God's people are called holy because they are made pure through Christ, and they belong only to God.
Hades Place where people go after they die.

were in them. Each person was judged by the things he had done. ¹⁴And Death and Hades were thrown into the lake of fire. This lake of fire is the second death. ¹⁵And if a person's name was not found written in the book of life, then that person was thrown into the lake of fire.

The New Jerusalem

21 Then I saw a new heaven and a new earth. The first heaven and the first earth had disappeared. Now there was no sea. ²And I saw the holy city coming down out of heaven from God. This holy city is the new Jerusalem.* It was prepared like a bride dressed for her husband. ³I heard a loud voice from the throne. The voice said, "Now God's home is with people. He will live with them. They will be his people. God himself will be with them and will be their God. ⁴God will wipe away every tear from their eyes. There will be no more death, sadness, crying, or pain. All the old ways are gone."

⁵The One that was sitting on the throne said, "Look! I am making everything new!" Then he said, "Write this, because these words are true and can be trusted."

⁶The One on the throne said to me: "It is finished! I am the Alpha and the Omega,* the Beginning and the End. I will give free water from the spring of the water of life to any person who is thirsty. ⁷Any person who wins the victory will receive all this. And I will be his God, and he will be my son. ⁸But the people who are cowards, people who refuse to believe, people who do terrible things, people who kill, people who sin sexually, people who do evil magic, people who worship idols,* and people who tell lies—all those people will have a place in the lake of burning sulfur. This is the second death."

⁹One of the seven angels came to me. This was one of the angels who had the seven bowls full of the seven last troubles. The angel said, "Come with me. I will show you the bride, the wife of the Lamb." ¹⁰The angel carried me away by the Spirit* to a very large and high mountain. The angel showed me the holy city, Jerusalem. The city was coming down out of heaven from God. ¹¹The city was shining with the glory of God. It was shining bright like a very expensive jewel, like a jasper. It was clear as crystal. ¹²The city had a large high wall with twelve gates. There were twelve angels at the gates. On each gate was written the name of one of the twelve family groups of Israel.* ¹³There were three gates on the east, three gates on the north, three gates on the south, and three gates on the west. ¹⁴The walls of the city were built on twelve foundation stones.* On the stones were written the names of the twelve apostles* of the Lamb.

¹⁵The angel who talked with me had a measuring rod made of gold. The angel had this rod to measure the city, its gates, and its wall. ¹⁶The city was built in a square. Its length was equal to its width. The angel measured the city with the rod. The city was 12,000 stadia* long, 12,000 stadia wide, and 12,000 stadia high. ¹⁷The angel also measured the wall. It was 144 cubits* high, by people's measurement. That was the measurement the angel was using. ¹⁸The wall was made of jasper. The city was made of pure gold, as pure as glass. ¹⁹The foundation stones* of the city walls had every kind of expensive jewels in them. The first cornerstone was jasper, the second was sapphire, the third was chalcedony, the fourth was emerald, ²⁰the fifth was onyx, the sixth was carnelian, the seventh was yellow quartz, the eighth was beryl, the ninth was topaz, the tenth was chrysoprase, the eleventh was jacinth, and the twelfth was amethyst. ²¹The twelve gates were twelve pearls. Each gate was made from one pearl. The street of the city was made of pure gold. The gold was clear like glass.

²²I did not see a temple* in the city. The Lord God All-Powerful and the Lamb *(Jesus)* are the city's temple. ²³The city does not need the sun or the moon to shine on it. The glory of God gives the city light. The Lamb *(Jesus)* is the city's lamp. ²⁴The peoples of the world will walk by the light given by the Lamb. The kings of the earth will bring their glory into the city. ²⁵The city's gates will never close on any day, because there is no night there. ²⁶The greatness and the honor of the nations will be brought into the city. ²⁷Nothing

---

new Jerusalem Spiritual city where God's people live with him.
Alpha, Omega The first and last letters in the Greek alphabet, meaning the beginning and the end.
idols Statues that people worship as gods.
Spirit The Holy Spirit. Also called the Spirit of God and the Spirit of Christ.
Israel The Jews—God's chosen people in the Old Testament.
foundation stones The large rocks that are used as the bottom or the first part in a building.
apostles The men Jesus chose to be his special helpers.
stadia One stadion was a distance of about 200 yards. It was one-eighth of a Roman mile.
cubits A cubit is about half a yard, the length from the elbow to the tip of the little finger.
temple A building where people worship God.

REVELATION 22:1–22:21

unclean will ever enter the city. No person who does shameful things or tells lies will ever enter the city. Only the people whose names are written in the Lamb's book of life will enter the city.

22 Then the angel showed me the river of water of life. The river was bright like crystal. The river flows from the throne of God and the Lamb. ²It flows down the middle of the street of the city. The tree of life was on each side of the river. The tree of life makes fruit twelve times a year. It gives fruit every month. The leaves of the tree are for healing all the people. ³Nothing that God judges guilty will be there in that city. The throne of God and the Lamb *(Jesus)* will be in the city. God's servants will worship him. ⁴They will see his face. God's name will be written on their foreheads. ⁵There will never be night again. People will not need the light of a lamp or the light of the sun. The Lord God will give them light. And they will rule like kings forever and ever.

⁶The angel said to me, "These words are true and can be trusted. The Lord is the God of the spirits of the prophets.* God sent his angel to show his servants the things that must happen soon."

⁷"Listen! I am coming soon! The person who obeys the words of prophecy* in this book will be blessed."

⁸I am John. I am the one who heard and saw these things. After I heard and saw these things, I bowed down to worship before the feet of the angel who showed these things to me. ⁹But the angel said to me, "Don't ₍worship me₎! I am a servant like you and your brothers the prophets.* I am a servant like all the people who obey the words in this book. You should worship God!"

¹⁰Then the angel told me, "Don't keep secret the words of prophecy* in this book. The time is near ₍for these things to happen₎. ¹¹Let the person who is doing wrong continue to do wrong. Let the person who is unclean continue to be unclean. Let the person who is doing right continue to do right. Let the person who is holy continue to be holy."

¹²"Listen! I am coming soon! I will bring rewards with me. I will repay each person for the things he has done. ¹³I am the Alpha and the Omega,* the First and the Last, the Beginning and the End.

¹⁴"Those people who washed their robes* will be blessed. They will have the right to ₍eat the food from₎ the tree of life. They can go through the gates into the city. ¹⁵Outside the city are the dogs *(bad people)*, people who do evil magic, people who sin sexually, people who murder, people who worship idols,* and people who love lies and tell lies.

¹⁶"I, Jesus, have sent my angel to tell you these things for the churches *(groups of believers)*. I am the descendant from the family of David. I am the bright morning star."

¹⁷The Spirit* and the bride say, "Come!" Every person who hears this should also say, "Come!" If a person is thirsty, let him come; that person can have the water of life as a free gift if he wants it.

¹⁸I warn every person who hears the words of the prophecy* of this book: If a person adds anything to these words, then God will give that person the troubles written about in this book. ¹⁹And if any person takes away from the words of this book of prophecy, then God will take away that person's share of the tree of life and of the holy city, which are written about in this book.

²⁰₍Jesus is₎ the One who says that these things are true. Now he says, "Yes, I am coming soon."

Amen. Come, Lord Jesus!

²¹The grace *(kindness)* of the Lord Jesus be with all people.

---

prophets People who spoke for God.
prophecy A message or teaching from God by a person who speaks for God.

Alpha, Omega The first and last letters in the Greek alphabet, meaning the beginning and the end.
washed their robes Meaning they believed in Jesus so that their sins could be forgiven.
idols Statues that people worship as gods.
Spirit The Holy Spirit. Called the Spirit of God, the Spirit of Christ, and the Comforter. Joined with God and Christ, he does God's work among people in the world.

The Ancient Near East in Abraham's Time

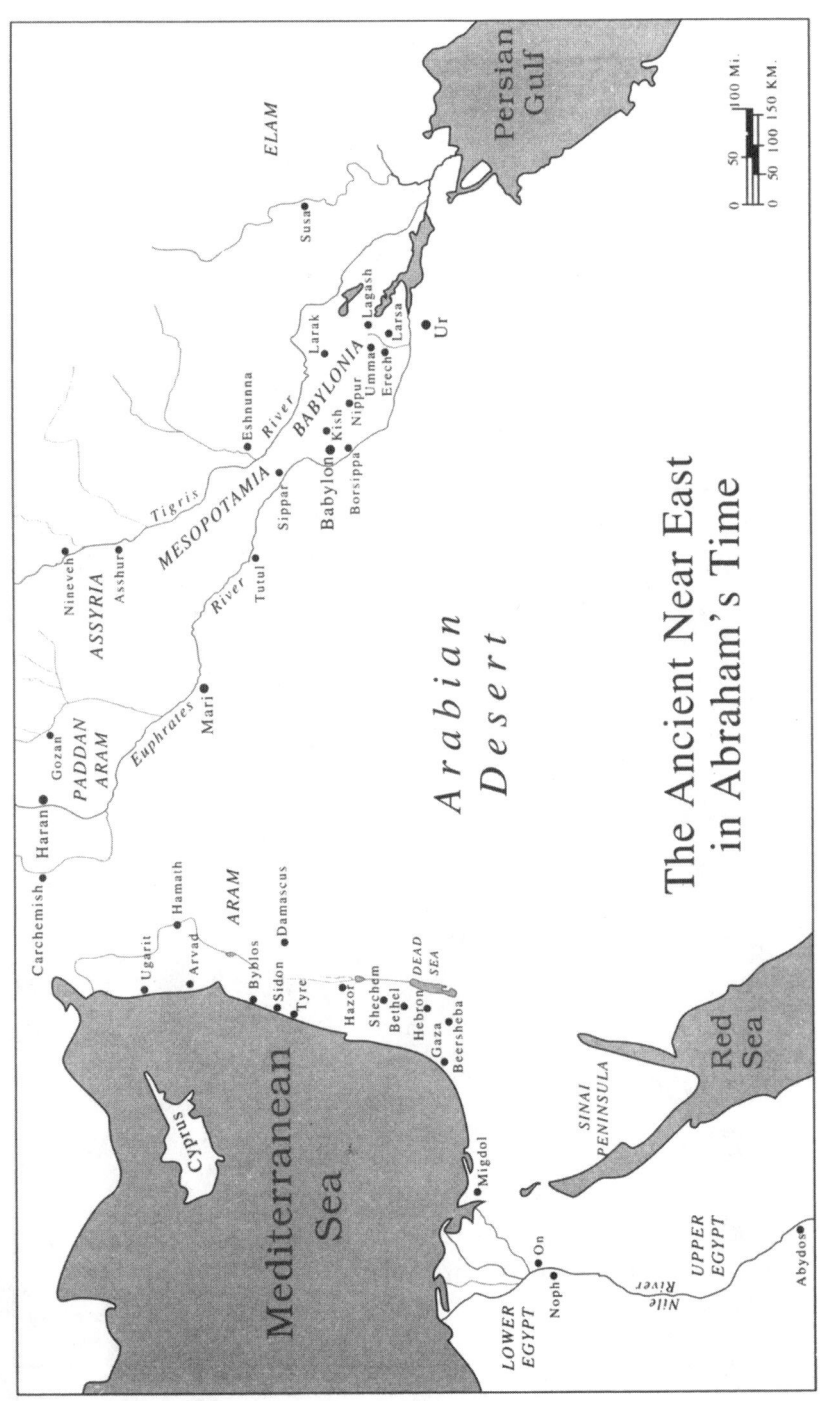

The Exodus and the Desert Wandering

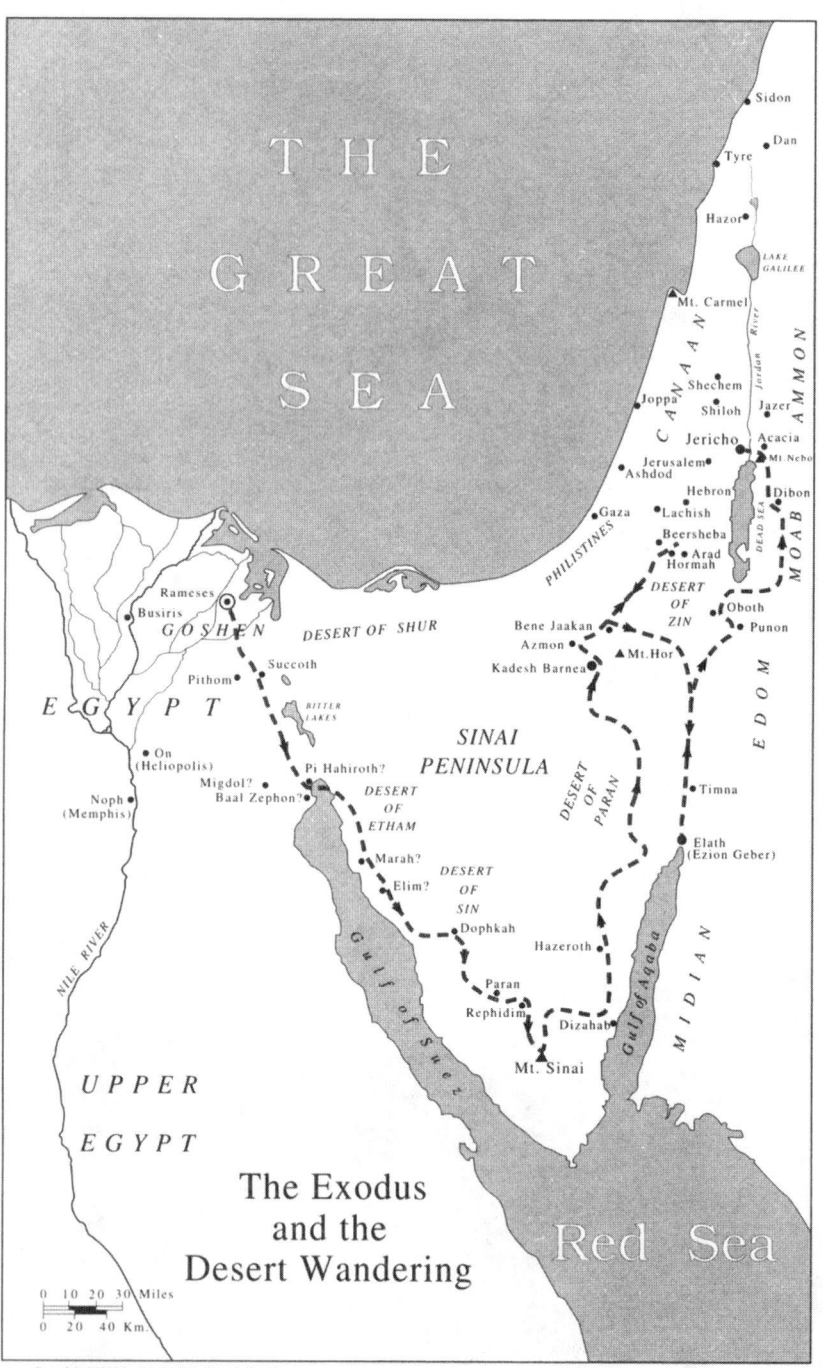

The Land of Canaan during the Judges

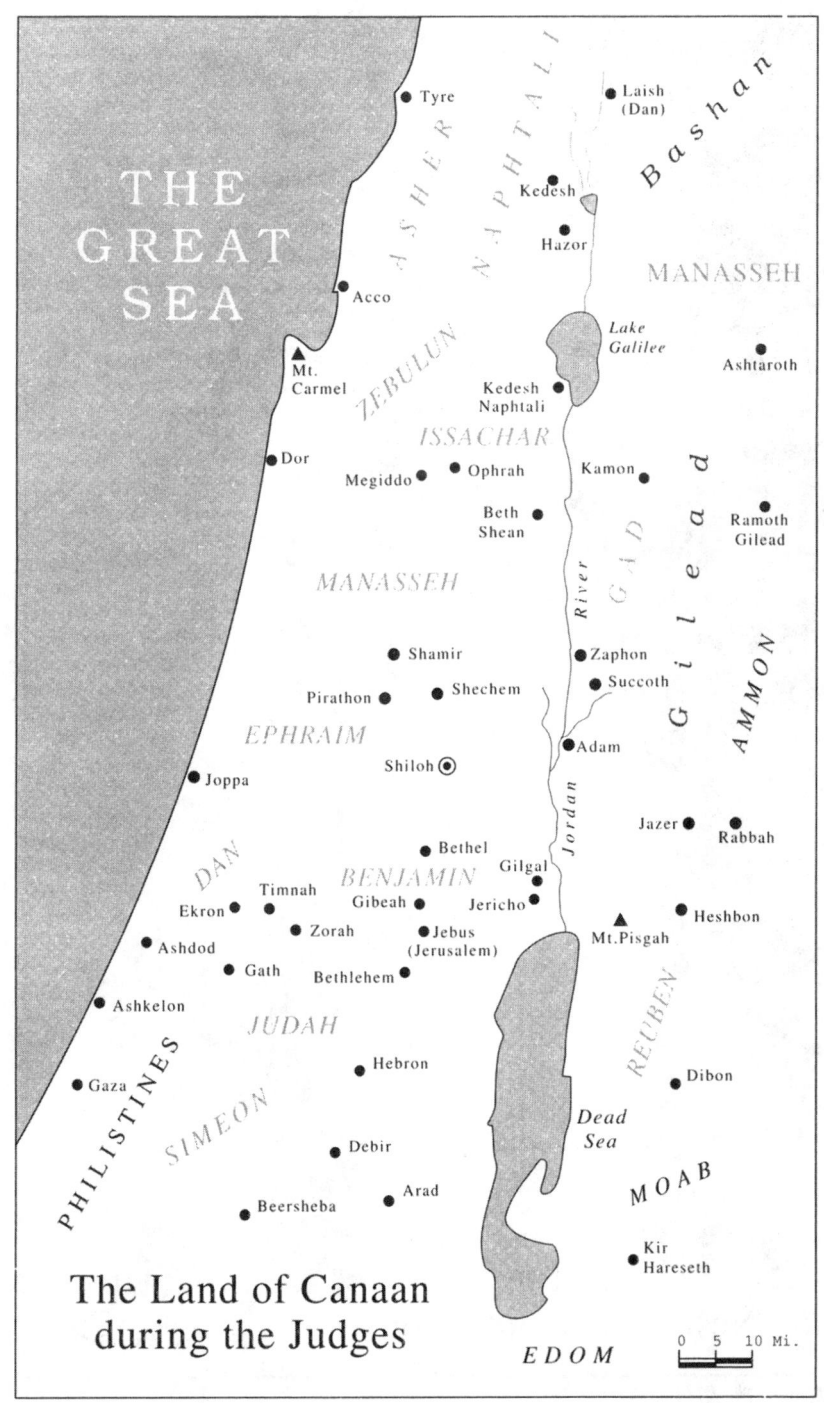

Palestine in New Testament Times

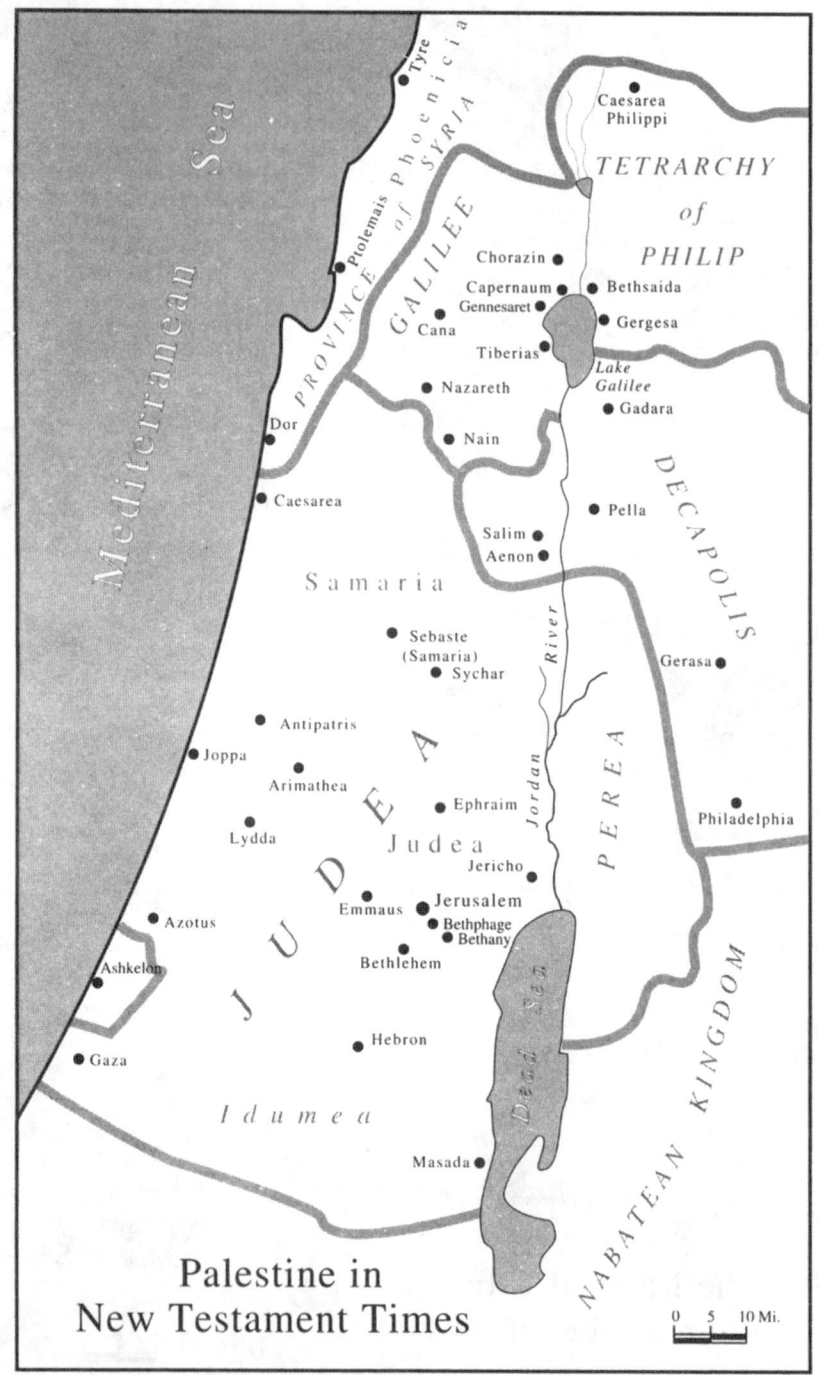

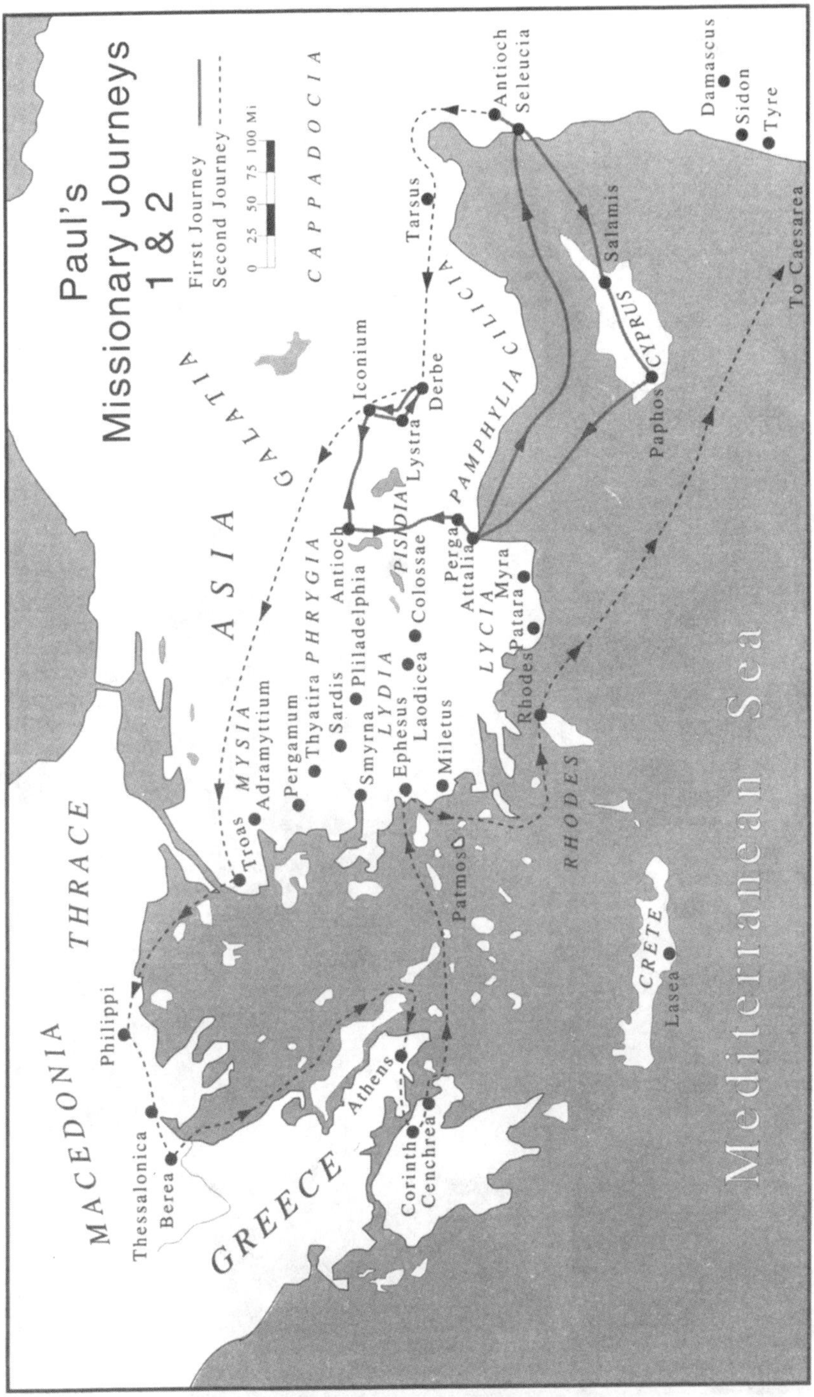

Paul's Missionary Journeys 1 & 2
First Journey
Second Journey
0 25 50 75 100 Mi
MACEDONIA
THRACE
GREECE
ASIA
GALATIA
CAPPADOCIA
MYSIA
LYDIA
PHRYGIA
PISIDIA
PAMPHYLIA
CILICIA
LYCIA
RHODES
CYPRUS
CRETE
Mediterranean Sea
Philippi
Thessalonica
Berea
Athens
Corinth
Cenchrea
Troas
Adramyttium
Pergamum
Thyatira
Sardis
Smyrna
Ephesus
Miletus
Pliladelphia
Laodicea
Colossae
Antioch
Iconium
Lystra
Derbe
Tarsus
Perga
Attalia
Myra
Patara
Rhodes
Patmos
Lasea
Salamis
Paphos
Antioch
Seleucia
Damascus
Sidon
Tyre
To Caesarea

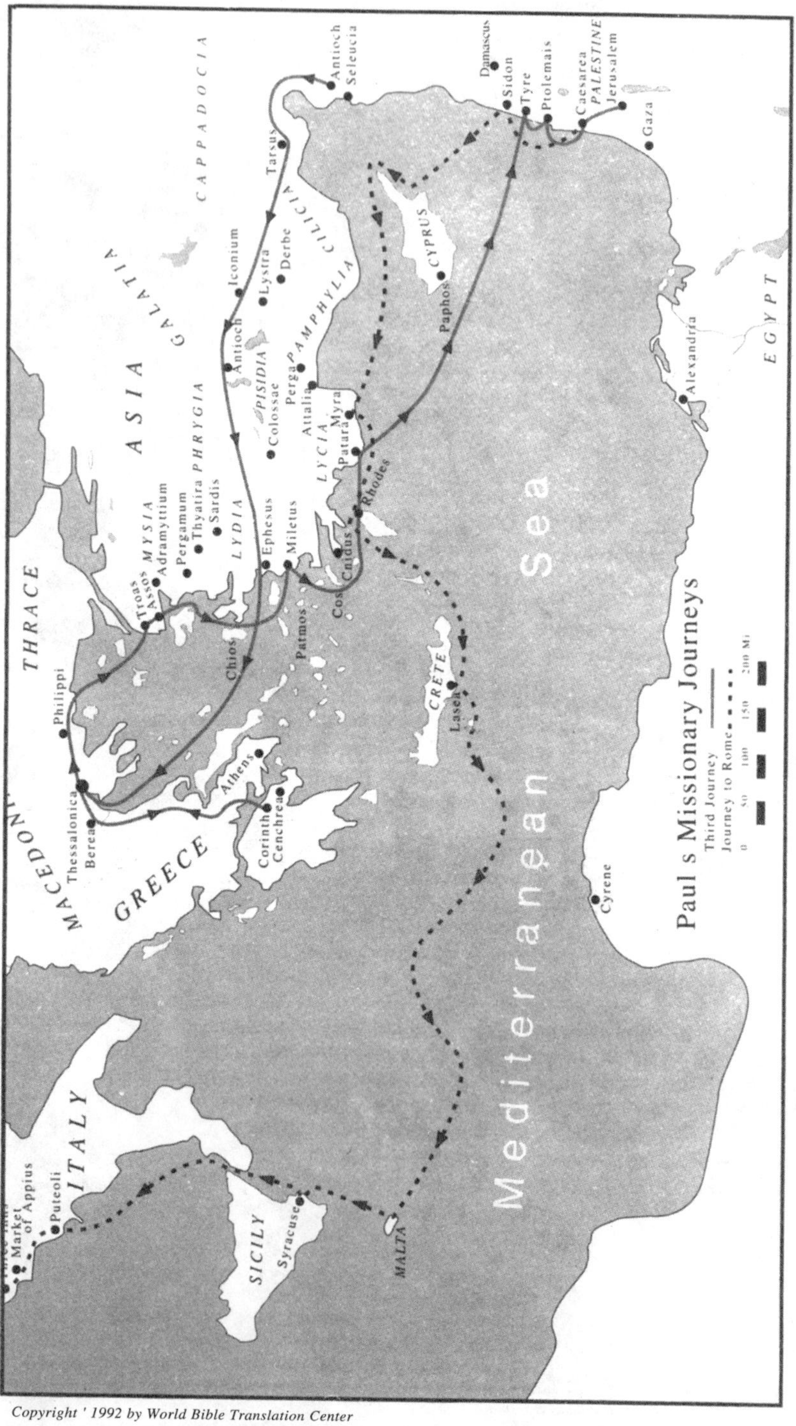
Paul s Missionary Journeys
Third Journey
Journey to Rome
0 50 100 150 200 Mi
Mediterranean Sea
MACEDONIA
THRACE
GREECE
ASIA
GALATIA
CAPPADOCIA
PHRYGIA
MYSIA
LYDIA
PISIDIA
PAMPHYLIA
CILICIA
LYCIA
CYPRUS
CRETE
PALESTINE
EGYPT
ITALY
SICILY
MALTA
Philippi
Thessalonica
Berea
Athens
Corinth
Cenchrea
Troas
Assos
Adramyttium
Pergamum
Thyatira
Sardis
Ephesus
Miletus
Chios
Patmos
Cos
Cnidus
Rhodes
Patara
Myra
Attalia
Perga
Colossae
Antioch
Iconium
Lystra
Derbe
Tarsus
Antioch
Seleucia
Paphos
Damascus
Sidon
Tyre
Ptolemais
Caesarea
Jerusalem
Gaza
Alexandria
Cyrene
Lasea
Syracuse
Puteoli
Market of Appius